HAMMOND

CITATION

WORLD ATLAS

HAMMOND CITATION
WORLD

ATLAS

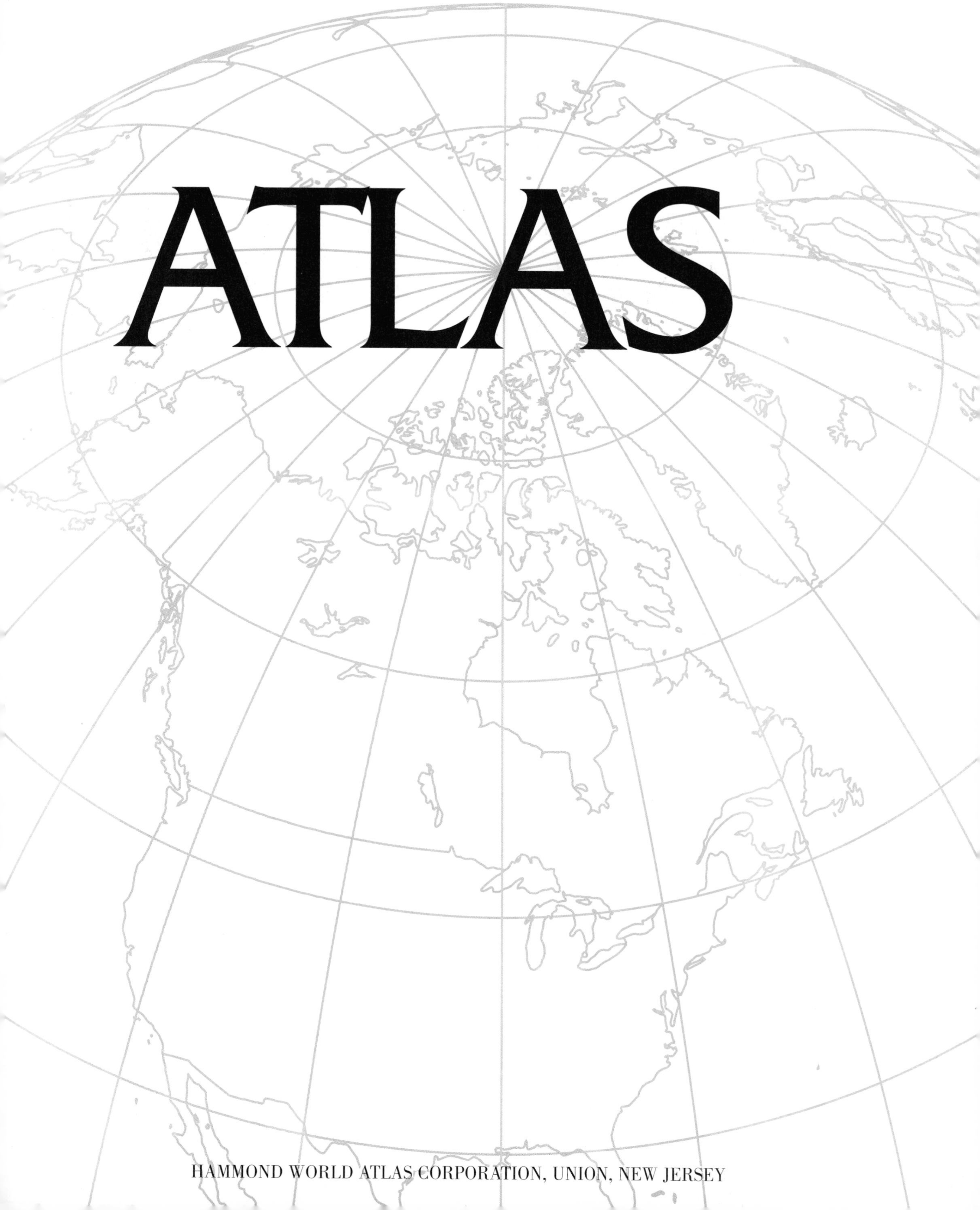

HAMMOND WORLD ATLAS CORPORATION, UNION, NEW JERSEY

Hammond Publications Advisory Board

PRINTED IN THE UNITED STATES OF AMERICA

Library of Congress Cataloging-in-Publication Data
Hammond World Atlas Corporation.
Citation world atlas. -- Rev.
p. cm.
At head of title: Hammond
Includes indexes.
ISBN 0-8437-1295-3 (softcover)
ISBN 0-8437-1382-8 (hardcover)
1. Atlases. I. Title. II. Title: Hammond citiation world atlas.
G1021. H2446 1998 <G&M>
912--DC21 98-12358
CIP
MAP

Contents

Part I—Terrain Maps of Land Forms and Ocean Floors

Part II—Modern Maps and Indexes

Introduction

This unique Hammond World Atlas is organized to make the retrieval of information as pleasant and quick as possible. Our guiding principle is to present individual subjects on separate maps. In this manner, each map topic is shown with the greatest degree of clarity, unencumbered by extraneous information. Equally important is the use of separate atlas units to present all information on a given country or state. Thus, the basic reference map of an area is accompanied on adjacent pages by all supplementary information relating to that area. For example, the detailed index for any map always appears on the same page as, or on the pages immediately following, the reference map. This index provides population data for many cities, towns, and villages shown on the map. Pertinent statistics on the area, i.e. the total population and area, the capital, and the highest point, are found in the summary fact listing accompanying each unit. An adjacent locator map relates the subject area to the larger world, and a "three-dimensional" picture of the area is provided by a full-color topographic map. A separate economic map defines vital agricultural, industrial, and mineral resources. The flag of each independent nation or state also appears on the appropriate page. Finally, certain country units contain special subject maps dealing with the history, climate, demography, and vegetation of the area.

Another section features The Physical World - an outstanding series of terrain maps of land forms and ocean floors. These physical maps were originally produced as sculptured terrain models, thus simulating the earth's surface in a highly realistic manner. The three-dimensional effect is both informative and pleasing to the eye.

Of course, the maps have been thoroughly updated. These revisions reflect the new nations, and shifting international boundaries, and internal divisions of many countries. Even new communities generated by the tapping of resources in developing nations are recorded. Thorough research and worldwide contacts provide the most up-to-date geographical and demographic information available.

Uniquely designed, comprehensive, and easy-to-use, this World Atlas is the ideal reference for families, executives, students, travelers, or anyone who wants to be geographically informed about today's fast-changing world. Enjoy the adventure as you explore the pages of one of the world's finest atlases.

The Publisher

Introduction to the Maps and Indexes

The following notes have been added to aid the reader in making the best use of this atlas. Though the reader may be familiar with maps and map indexes, the publisher believes that a quick review of the material below will add to his enjoyment of this reference work.

Arrangement—The Plan of the Atlas. The atlas has been designed with maximum convenience for the user as its objective. Part I of the atlas is devoted to the physical world—terrain maps of land forms and the sea floor. Part II contains the general political reference maps, area by area. All geographically related information pertaining to a country or region appears on adjacent pages, eliminating the task of searching throughout the entire volume for data on a given area. Thus, the reader will find, conveniently assembled, political, topographic, economic and special maps of a political area or region, accompanied by detailed map indexes, statistical data, and illustrations of the national flags of the area.

The sequence of country units in this American-designed atlas is international in arrangement. Units on the world as a whole are followed by a section on the polar regions which, in turn, is followed by pages devoted to Europe and its countries. Every continent map is accompanied by special population distribution, climatic and vegetation maps of that continent. Following the maps of the European continent and its countries, the geographic sequence plan proceeds as follows: Asia, the Pacific and Australia, Africa, South America, North America, and ends with detailed coverage on the United States.

Political Maps—The Primary Reference Tool. The most detailed maps in each country unit are the *political maps*. It is our feeling that the reader is likely to refer to these maps more often than to any other in the book when confronted by such questions as—Where? How big? What is it near? Answering these common queries is the function of the political maps. Each political map stresses *political* phenomena—countries, internal political divisions, boundaries, cities and towns. The major political unit or units, shown on the map, are banded in distinctive colors for easy identification and delineation. First-order political subdivisions (states, provinces, counties on the state maps) are shown, scale permitting.

The reader is advised to make use of the *legend* appearing under the title on each political map. Map *symbols*, the special "language" of maps, are explained in the legend. Each variety of dot, circle, star or interrupted line has a special meaning which should be clearly understood by the user so that he may interpret the map data correctly.

Each country has been portrayed at a *scale* commensurate with its political, areal, economic or tourist importance. In certain cases, a whole map unit may be devoted to a single nation if that nation is considered to be of prime interest to most atlas users. In other cases, several nations will be shown on a single map if, as separate entities, they are of lesser relative importance. Areas of dense settlement and important significance within a country have been enlarged and portrayed in inset maps inserted on the margins of the main map. The scale of each map is indicated as a fractional representation (1:1,000,000). The reader is advised to refer to the linear or "bar" scale appearing on each map or map inset in order to determine the distance between points.

The *projection* system used for each map is noted near the title of the map. Map projections are the special graphic systems used by cartographers to render the curved three-dimensional surface of the globe on a flat surface. Optimum map projections determined by the attributes of the area have been used by the publishers for each map in the atlas.

A word here as to the choice of place names on the maps. Throughout the atlas names appear, with a few exceptions, in their local official spellings. However, conventional Anglicized spellings are used for major geographical divisions and for towns and topographic features for which English forms exist; i.e., "Spain" instead of "España" or "Munich" instead of "München." Names of this type are normally followed by the local official spelling in parentheses. As an aid to the user the indexes are cross-referenced for all current and most former spellings of such names.

Names of cities and towns in the United States follow the forms listed in the *Post Office Directory* of the United States Postal Service. Domestic physical names follow the decisions of the Board on Geographic Names, U.S. Department of the Interior, and of various state geographic name boards. It is the belief of the publishers that the boundaries shown in a general reference atlas should reflect current geographic and political realities. This policy has been followed consistently in the atlas. The presentation of *de facto* boundaries in cases of territorial dispute between various nations does not imply the political endorsement of such boundaries by the publisher, but simply the honest representation of boundaries as they exist at the time of the printing of the atlas maps.

Indexes—Pinpointing a Location. Each political map is accompanied by a comprehensive index of the place names appearing on the map. If you are unfamiliar with the location of a particular geographical place and wish to find its position within the confines of the subject area of the map, consult the map index as your first step. The name of the feature sought will be found in its proper alphabetical sequence with a key reference letter-number combination corresponding to its location on the map. After noting the key reference letter-number combination for the place name, turn to the map. The place name will be found within the square formed by the two lines of latitude and the two lines of longitude which enclose the coordinates—i.e., the marginal letters and numbers. The diagram below illustrates the system of indexing.

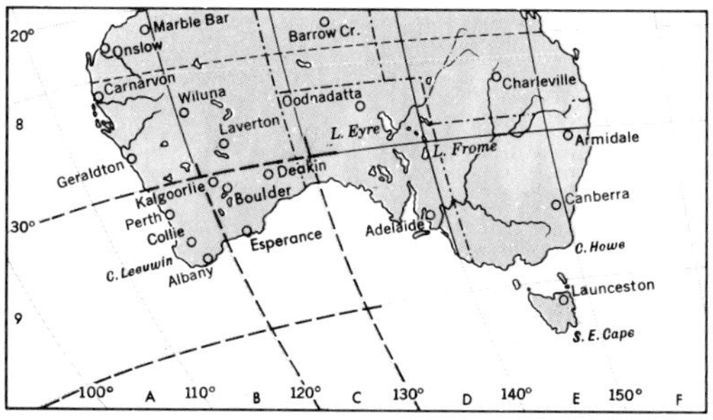

Marble Bar
Onslow
Barrow Cr.
Carnarvon
Wiluna
Oodnadatta
Charleville
Laverton
L. Eyre
L. Frome
Armidale
Geraldton
Kalgoorlie
Deakin
Boulder
Canberra
Perth
Collie
Adelaide
Esperance
C. Howe
C. Leeuwin
Albany
Launceston
S. E. Cape
20°
8
30°
9
100°
A
110°
B
120°
C
130°
D
140°
E
150°
F

In the case of maps consisting entirely of insets, the place name is found near the intersection point of the imaginary lines connecting the coordinates at right angles. See below.

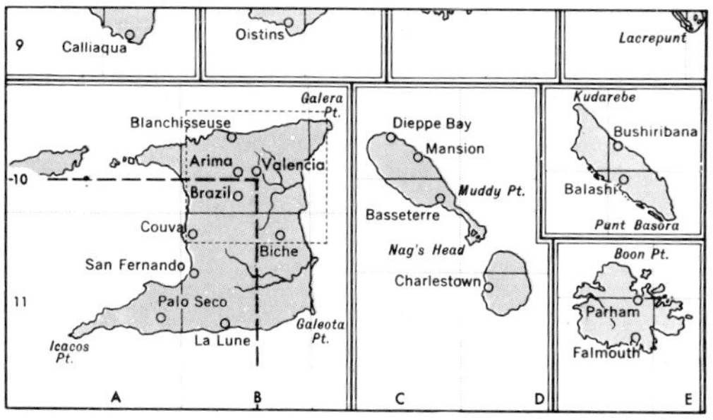

9
Calliaqua
Oistins
Lacrepunt
Galera Pt.
Blanchisseuse
Arima
Valencia
10
Brazil
Couva
Biche
San Fernando
Palo Seco
11
Icacos Pt.
La Lune
Galeota Pt.
Dieppe Bay
Mansion
Muddy Pt.
Basseterre
Nag's Head
Charlestown
Kudarebe
Bushiribana
Balashi
Punt Basora
Boon Pt.
Parham
Falmouth
A
B
C
D
E

Where space on the map has not permitted giving the complete form of the place name, the complete form is shown in the index. Where a place is known by more than one name or by various spellings of the same name, the different forms have been included in the index. Physical features are listed under their proper names and not according to their generic terms; that is to say, Rio Negro will be found under Negro and not under Rio Negro. On the other hand, Rio Grande will be found under Rio Grande. Accompanying most index entries for cities and towns, and for other political units, are *population figures* for the particular entries. The large number of population figures in the atlas makes this work one of the most comprehensive statistical sources available to the public today. The population figures have been taken from the latest official censuses and estimates of the various nations.

Population and area figures for countries and major political units are listed in bold type *fact lists* on the margins of the index. In addition, the capital, largest city, highest point, monetary unit, principal languages and the prevailing religions of the country concerned are also listed, The Gazetteer-Index of the World on the following pages provides a quick reference index for countries and other important areas. Though population and area figures for each major unit are also found in the map section, the Gazetteer-Index provides a conveniently arranged statistical comparison contained in five pages.

Relief Maps. Accompanying each political map is a relief map of the area. The purpose of the relief map is to illustrate the surface configuration (TOPOGRAPHY) of the region. A shading technique in color simulates the relative ruggedness of the terrain — plains, plateaus, valleys, hills and mountains. Graded colors, ranging from greens for lowlands, yellows for intermediate elevations to brown in the highlands, indicate the height above sea level of each part of the land. A vertical scale at the margin of the map shows the approximate height in meters and feet represented by each color.

Economic Maps—Agriculture, Industry and Resources. One of the most interesting features that will be found in each country unit is the economic map. From this map one can determine the basic activities of a nation as expressed through its economy. A perusal of the map yields a full understanding of the area's economic geography and natural resources.

The agricultural economy is manifested in two ways: color bands and commodity names. The color bands express broad categories of dominant land use, such as cereal belts, forest lands, livestock range lands or nonagricultural wastes. The red commodity names, on the other hand, pinpoint the areas of production of *specific* crops, i.e., wheat, cotton, sugar beets, etc.

Major mineral occurrences are denoted by standard letter symbols appearing in blue. The relative size of the letter symbols signifies the relative importance of the deposit.

The manufacturing sector of the economy is presented by means of diagonal line patterns expressing the various *industrial* areas of consequence within a country.

The fishing industry is represented by names of commercial fish species appearing offshore in blue letters. Major waterpower sites are designated by blue symbols.

The publishers have tried to make this work the most comprehensive and useful atlas available, and it is hoped that it will prove a valuable reference work. Any constructive suggestions from the reader will be welcomed.

Sources and Acknowledgements

A multitude of sources goes into the making of a large-scale reference work such as this. To list them all would take many pages and would consume space better devoted to the maps and reference materials themselves. However, certain general sources were very useful in preparing this work and are listed below.

STATISTICAL OFFICE OF THE UNITED NATIONS.
Demographic Yearbook. New York. Issued annually.

STATISTICAL OFFICE OF THE UNITED NATIONS.
Statistical Yearbook. New York. Issued annually.

THE GEOGRAPHER, U.S. DEPARTMENT OF STATE.
International Boundary Study papers. Washington. Various dates.

THE GEOGRAPHER, U.S. DEPARTMENT OF STATE.
Geographic Notes. Washington. Various dates.

UNITED STATES BOARD ON GEOGRAPHIC NAMES.
Decisions on Geographic Names in the United States. Washington. Various dates.

UNITED STATES BOARD ON GEOGRAPHIC NAMES.
Official Standard Names Gazetteers. Washington. Various dates.

CANADIAN PERMANENT COMMITTEE ON GEOGRAPHICAL NAMES.
Gazetteer of Canada series. Ottawa. Various dates.

UNITED STATES POSTAL SERVICE.
National Five Digit ZIP Code and Post Office Directory. Washington. Issued annually.

UNITED STATES POSTAL SERVICE.
Postal Bulletin. Washington. Issued weekly.

UNITED STATES DEPARTMENT OF THE INTERIOR, BUREAU OF MINES.
Minerals Yearbook. 4 vols. Washington. Various dates.

UNITED STATES GEOLOGICAL SURVEY.
Elevations and distances in the United States. Reston, Va. 1990.

CARTACTUAL.
Cartactual — Topical Map Service. Budapest. Issues bi-monthly.

AMERICAN GEOGRAPHICAL SOCIETY.
Focus. New York. Issued ten times a year.

THE AMERICAN UNIVERSITY.
Foreign Area Studies. Washington. Various dates.

CENTRAL INTELLIGENCE AGENCY.
General reference maps. Washington. Various dates.

A sample list of sources used for <u>specific</u> countries follows:

Afghanistan
CENTRAL STATISTICS OFFICE.
Preliminary Results of the First Afghan Population Census 1979. Kabul.

Albania
DREJTORIA E STATISTIKES.
1979 Census. Tiranë.

Argentina
INSTITUTO NACIONAL DE ESTADISTICA Y CENSOS.
Censo Nacional de Población y Vivienda 1980. Buenos Aires.

Australia
AUSTRALIAN BUREAU OF STATISTICS.
Census of Population and Housing 1986. Canberra.

Brazil
FUNDACAO INSTITUTO BRASILEIRO DE GEOGRAFIA E ESTATISTICA.
IX Recenseamento Geral do Brasil 1980. Rio de Janeiro.

Canada
STATISTICS CANADA.
1986 Census of Canada. Ottawa.

Cuba
COMITE ESTATAL DE ESTADISTICAS.
Censo de Población y Viviendas 1981. Havana.

Hungary
HUNGARIAN CENTRAL STATISTICAL OFFICE.
1990 Census. Budapest.

Indonesia
BIRO PUSAT STATISTIK.
Sensus Penduduk 1980. Jakarta.

Kuwait
CENTRAL OFFICE OF STATISTICS.
1985 Census. Al Kuwait.

New Zealand
DEPARTMENT OF STATISTICS.
New Zealand Census of Population and Dwellings 1986. Wellington.

Panama
DIRECCION DE ESTADISTICA Y CENSO.
Censos Nacionales de 1990. Panamá.

Papua New Guinea
BUREAU OF STATISTICS.
National Population Census 1980. Port Moresby.

Philippines
NATIONAL CENSUS AND STATISTICS OFFICE.
1980 Census of Population. Manila.

Saint Lucia
CENSUS OFFICE.
1980 Population Census. Castries.

Singapore
DEPARTMENT OF STATISTICS.
Census of Population 1980. Singapore.

Russia
CENTRAL STATISTICAL ADMINISTRATION.
1989 Census. Moscow.

United States
BUREAU OF THE CENSUS.
1990 Census of Population. Washington.

Vanuatu
CENSUS OFFICE.
1979 Population Census. Port Vila.

Zambia
CENTRAL STATISTICAL OFFICE.
1980 Census of Population and Housing. Lusaka.

Gazetteer-Index of the World

This alphabetical list of continents, countries, states, possessions and other major geographical areas provides a quick reference to their area in square miles and square kilometers, population, capital or chief town, map page number and an alpha-numeric index reference. The index reference indicates the square on the respective page in which the name may be found. The population figures used in each case are the latest reliable figures obtainable. The government listings are based primarily on the nomenclature contained in the World Factbook published by the CIA of the United States Government. Those governments currently unsettled or in transition are indicated with a † symbol.

Country	Area Square Miles	Area Square Kilometers	Population	Capital or Chief Town	Page and Index Ref.	Government or Ownership
*Afghanistan	250,775	649,507	26,668,251	Kabul	68/A 2	authoritarian†
Africa	11,707,000	30,321,130	705,924,000	....	102/....	
Alabama, U.S.	51,705	133,916	4,040,587	Montgomery	195/....	state of the U.S.
Alaska, U.S.	591,004	1,530,700	550,043	Juneau	196/....	state of the U.S.
*Albania	11,100	28,749	3,401,126	Tiranë	45/E 5	emerging democracy†
Alberta, Canada	255,285	661,185	2,696,826	Edmonton	182/....	province of Canada
*Algeria	919,591	2,381,740	31,787,647	Algiers	106/D 3	republic
American Samoa	77	199	65,446	Pago Pago	87/J 7;	
					86/....	unincorporated, unorganized territory of the U.S.
*Andorra	188	487	67,673	Andorra la Vella	33/G 1	parliamentary democracy
*Angola	481,351	1,246,700	11,486,729	Luanda	114/C 6	Marxist people's republic†
Anguilla, U.K.	35	91	11,875	The Valley	156/F 3	dependent territory of the U.K.
Antarctica	5,500,000	14,245,000	....	....	5/....	
*Antigua and Barbuda	171	443	64,461	St. John's	161/E11;	
					156/G 3	parliamentary democracy
*Argentina	1,072,070	2,776,661	37,214,757	Buenos Aires	143/....	republic
Arizona, U.S.	114,000	295,260	3,665,228	Phoenix	198/....	state of the U.S.
Arkansas, U.S.	53,187	137,754	2,350,725	Little Rock	202/....	state of the U.S.
*Armenia	11,506	29,800	3,396,184	Yerevan	52/F 6	republic
Aruba, Netherlands	75	193	69,080	Oranjestad	161/E 9	autonomous member of the Netherlands realm
Ascension Island, St. Helena	34	88	719	Georgetown	102/A 5	part of St. Helena
Ashmore & Cartier Islands, Australia	61	159	....	(Canberra, Austr.)	88/C 2	territory of Australia
Asia	17,128,500	44,362,815	3,407,967,000	....	54/....	
*Australia	2,966,136	7,682,300	18,950,108	Canberra	88/....	federal parliamentary state
Australian Capital Territory	927	2,400	310,800	Canberra	96/E 4	territory of Australia
*Austria	32,375	83,851	8,148,007	Vienna	40/B 3	federal republic
*Azerbaijan	33,436	86,600	7,955,772	Baku	52/G 6	republic
Azores, Portugal	902	2,335	275,900	Ponta Delgada	32/....	autonomous region of Portugal
*Bahamas	5,382	13,939	287,548	Nassau	156/C 1	independent commmonwealth
*Bahrain	240	622	641,539	Manama	58/F 4	traditional monarchy
Baker Island, U.S.	1	2.6	....	....	87/J 5	unincorporated territory of the U.S.
Balearic Islands, Spain	1,936	5,014	655,909	Palma	33/H 3	autonomous community of Spain
*Bangladesh	55,126	142,776	129,146,695	Dhaka	68/G 4	republic
*Barbados	166	430	259,248	Bridgetown	161/B 8	parliamentary democracy
*Belarus	80,154	207,600	10,390,697	Minsk	52/C 4	republic
*Belgium	11,781	30,513	10,185,894	Brussels	27/E 7	constitutional monarchy
*Belize	8,867	22,966	241,546	Belmopan	154/C 2	parliamentary democracy
*Benin	43,483	112,620	6,516,630	Porto-Novo	106/E 6	democratic reform†
Bermuda, U.K.	21	54	62,912	Hamilton	156/H 3	dependent territory of the U.K.
*Bhutan	18,147	47,000	1,996,221	Thimphu	68/G 3	monarchy
*Bolivia	424,163	1,098,582	8,139,180	La Paz; Sucre	136/.....	republic
Bonaire, Neth. Antilles	112	291	8,087	Kralendijk	161/E 9	part of Netherland Antilles
*Bosnia & Herzegovina	19,940	51,129	3,591,618	Sarajevo	45/C 3	emerging democracy†
*Botswana	224,764	582,139	1,479,039	Gaborone	119/C 4	parliamentary republic
Bouvet Island, Norway	22	57	....	....	5/D 1	territory of Norway
*Brazil	3,284,426	8,506,663	173,790,810	Brasília	132/.....	federal republic
British Columbia, Canada	366,253	948,596	3,724,500	Victoria	184/.....	province of Canada
British Indian Ocean Terr., U.K.	29	75	2,000	(London, U.K.)	54/L10	dependent territory of the U.K.
British Virgin Islands	59	153	12,000	Road Town	157/H 1	dependent territory of the U.K.
*Brunei	2,226	5,765	330,689	Bandar Seri Begawan	85/E 4	constitutional sultanate
*Bulgaria	42,823	110,912	8,155,828	Sofia	45/F 4	democratic reform†
*Burkina Faso	105,869	274,200	11,892,029	Ouagadougou	106/D 6	parliamentary
Burma, see Myanmar						
*Burundi	10,747	27,835	5,930,805	Bujumbura	114/E 4	republic
California, U.S.	158,706	411,049	29,760,021	Sacramento	204/.....	state of the U.S.
*Cambodia	69,898	181,036	11,918,865	Phnom Penh	72/E 4	constitutional monarchy†
*Cameroon	183,568	475,441	15,891,531	Yaoundé	114/B 2	one-party republic
*Canada	3,851,787	9,976,139	31,330,255	Ottawa	162/.....	confederation with parliamentary democracy
Canary Islands, Spain	2,808	7,273	1,367,646	Las Palmas;		
				Santa Cruz	32/B 4	autonomous community of Spain
*Cape Verde	1,557	4,033	411,487	Praia	106/B 8	republic
Cayman Islands, U.K.	100	259	41,011	Georgetown	156/B 3	dependent territory of the U.K.
Celebes, Indonesia	72,986	189,034	7,732,383	Ujung Pandang	85/G 6	part of Indonesia
*Central African Republic	242,000	626,780	3,515,657	Bangui	114/C 2	republic
Central America	197,480	511,475	28,296,000	....	154/.....	
*Chad	495,752	1,283,998	7,760,252	N'Djamena	111/C 4	republic
Channel Islands, U.K.	75	194	133,000	St. Helier;		
				St. Peter Port	13/E 8	part of the United Kingdom
*Chile	292,257	756,946	15,155,495	Santiago	138/.....	republic
*China, People's Rep. of	3,705,386	9,596,960	1,256,167,701	Beijing	77/.....	communist party-led state
China, Republic of (Taiwan)	13,971	36,185	22,319,222	T'aipei	77/K 7	multiparty democratic
Christmas Island, Australia	52	135	3,184	Flying Fish Cove	54/M11	territory of Australia
Clipperton Island, France	2	5.2	....	....	146/H 8	possession of France
Cocos (Keeling) Islands,						
Australia	5.4	14	555	West Island	54/N11	territory of Australia

***Member of the United Nations**

Gazetteer-Index of the World

Country	Area Square Miles	Area Square Kilometers	Population	Capital or Chief Town	Page and Index Ref.	Government or Ownership
*Colombia	439,513	1,138,339	40,036,927	Bogotá	126/.....	republic
Colorado, U.S.	104,091	269,596	3,294,394	Denver	208/.....	state of the U.S.
*Comoros	719	1,862	580,509	Moroni	119/G 2	republic
*Congo, Dem. Rep. of the	905,063	2,344,113	51,987,773	Kinshasa	114/D 4	republic
*Congo, Rep. of the	132,046	342,000	2,775,659	Brazzaville	114/B 4	republic
Connecticut, U.S.	5,018	12,997	3,287,116	Hartford	210/.....	state of the U.S.
Cook Islands, New Zealand	91	236	20,407	Avarua	87/K 7	self-governing in free association with New Zealand
Coral Sea Islands, Australia	8.5	22	....	....	88/J 3	territory of Australia
Corsica, France	3,352	8,682	249,737	Ajaccio; Bastia	28/B 6	part of France
*Costa Rica	19,575	50,700	3,743,677	San José	154/E 5	democratic republic
Côte d'Ivoire, see Ivory Coast						
*Croatia	22,050	56,538	4,681,015	Zagreb	45/B 3	parliamentary democracy
*Cuba	44,206	114,494	11,139,412	Havana	158/.....	communist state
Curaçao, Neth. Antilles	178	462	145,430	Willemstad	161/G 7	part of Netherlands Antilles
*Cyprus	3,473	8,995	759,048	Nicosia	62/E 5	republic
*Czech Republic	30,449	78,863	10,283,762	Prague	41/C 2	parliamentary democracy
Delaware, U.S.	2,044	5,294	666,168	Dover	245/R 3	state of the U.S.
*Denmark	16,629	43,069	5,374,554	Copenhagen	21/.....	constitutional monarchy
District of Columbia, U.S.	69	179	606,900	Washington	244/F 5	district of the United States
*Djibouti	8,880	23,000	454,294	Djibouti	111/H 5	republic
*Dominica	290	751	63,944	Roseau	161/E 7	parliamentary democracy
*Dominican Republic	18,704	48,443	8,261,536	Santo Domingo	158/D 6	republic
*Ecuador	109,483	283,561	12,782,161	Quito	128/C 3	republic
*Egypt	386,659	1,001,447	68,494,584	Cairo	110/E 2	republic
*El Salvador	8,260	21,393	5,925,374	San Salvador	154/C 4	republic
England, U.K.	50,516	130,836	49,089,100	London	13/.....	part of the United Kingdom
*Equatorial Guinea	10,831	28,052	477,763	Malabo	114/A 3	republic
*Eritrea	45,410	117,600	4,142,481	Asmara	110/G 4	transitional government†
*Estonia	17,413	45,100	1,398,140	Tallinn	53/.....	republic
*Ethiopia	426,366	1,104,300	60,967,436	Addis Ababa	110/G5.	federal republic
Europe	4,057,000	10,507,630	732,653,000	....	7/......	
Falkland Islands & Dependencies, U.K.	6,198	16,053	1,813	Stanley	120/E 8; 143/D 7	dependent territory of the U.K.
Faroe Islands, Denmark	540	1,399	40,172	Tórshavn	21/B 2	self-governing overseas administrative division of Denmark
*Fiji	7,055	18,272	823,376	Suva	87/H 8; 86/.....	republic
*Finland	130,128	337,032	5,164,825	Helsinki	18/O 6	republic
Florida, U.S.	58,664	151,940	12,937,926	Tallahassee	212/.....	state of the U.S.
*France	210,038	543,998	59,128,187	Paris	28/.....	republic
French Guiana	35,135	91,000	173,246	Cayenne	131/E 3	overseas department of France
French Polynesia	1,544	4,000	246,171	Papeete	87/L 8	overseas territory of France
*Gabon	103,346	267,666	1,244,192	Libreville	114/B 4	republic
*Gambia	4,127	10,689	1,381,496	Banjul	106/A 6	republic
Gaza Strip	139	360	1,162,777	Gaza	65/A 4	occupied by Israel
*Georgia	26,911	69,700	5,034,051	T'bilisi	52/F 6	republic
Georgia, U.S.	58,910	152,577	6,478,216	Atlanta	217/.....	state of the U.S.
*Germany	137,753	356,780	82,081,365	Berlin	22/.....	republic
*Ghana	92,099	238,536	19,271,744	Accra	106/D 7	constitutional democracy
Gibraltar, U.K.	2.28	5.91	29,272	Gibraltar	33/D 4	dependent territory of the U.K.
*Great Britain & Northern Ireland (United Kingdom)	94,399	244,493	57,236,000	London	10/.....	see United Kingdom
*Greece	50,944	131,945	10,750,705	Athens	45/F 6	presidential parliamentary republic
Greenland, Denmark	840,000	2,175,600	60,324	Nuuk (Godthåb)	4/B12	self-governing overseas administrative division of Denmark
*Grenada	133	344	97,913	St. George's	161/D 9; 156/G 4	parliamentary democracy
Guadeloupe & Dependencies, France	687	1,779	425,317	Basse-Terre	161/A 5; 156/F 4	overseas department of France
Guam, U.S.	209	541	154,623	Hagåtña	87/E 4; 86/.....	organized, unincorporated territory of the U.S.
*Guatemala	42,042	108,889	12,669,576	Guatemala	154/B 3	republic
*Guinea	94,925	245,856	7,610,869	Conakry	106/B 6	republic
*Guinea-Bissau	13,948	36,125	1,263,341	Bissau	106/A 6	republic
*Guyana	83,000	214,970	703,399	Georgetown	131/B 3	republic
*Haiti	10,694	27,697	6,991,589	Port-au-Prince	158/C 5	republic
Hawaii, U.S.	6,471	16,760	1,108,229	Honolulu	218/.....	state of the U.S.
Heard & McDonald Islands, Australia	113	293	....	....	2/N 8	territory of Australia
Holland, see Netherlands						
*Honduras	43,277	112,087	6,130,135	Tegucigalpa	154/D 3	republic
Hong Kong	422	1,092	6,966,929	Victoria	77/H 7; 78/.....	special administrative region of China
Howland Island, U.S.	1	2.6	....	....	87/J 5	unincorporated territory of the U.S.
*Hungary	35,919	93,030	10,167,182	Budapest	41/D 3	republic
*Iceland	39,768	103,000	274,141	Reykjavík	21/B 1	republic
Idaho, U.S.	83,564	216,431	1,006,749	Boise	220/.....	state of the U.S.
Illinois, U.S.	56,345	145,934	11,430,602	Springfield	222/.....	state of the U.S.
*India	1,269,339	3,287,588	1,017,645,163	New Delhi	68/D 4	federal republic
Indiana, U.S.	36,185	93,719	5,544,159	Indianapolis	227/.....	state of the U.S.
*Indonesia	788,430	2,042,034	219,266,557	Jakarta	85/D 7	republic
Iowa, U.S.	56,275	145,752	2,776,755	Des Moines	229/.....	state of the U.S.

Gazetteer-Index of the World

Country	Area Square Miles	Area Square Kilometers	Population	Capital or Chief Town	Page and Index Ref.	Government or Ownership
*Iran	636,293	1,648,000	65,865,302	Tehran	66/F 4	theocratic republic
*Iraq	172,476	446,713	23,150,926	Baghdad	66/C 4	republic
*Ireland	27,136	70,282	3,647,348	Dublin	17/.....	republic
Ireland, Northern, U.K.	5,452	14,121	1,543,000	Belfast	17/F 2	part of the United Kingdom
Isle of Man, U.K.	227	588	76,191	Douglas	13/C 3	part of the United Kingdom
*Israel	7,847	20,324	5,851,913	Jerusalem	65/B 4	republic
*Italy	116,303	301,225	56,686,568	Rome	34/.....	republic
*Ivory Coast (Côte d'Ivoire)	124,504	322,465	16,190,105	Yamoussoukro	106/C 7	republic
*Jamaica	4,411	11,424	2,668,740	Kingston	158/.....	parliamentary democracy
Jan Mayen, Norway	144	373	....	....	6/D 1	territory of Norway
*Japan	145,730	377,441	126,434,470	Tokyo	81/.....	constitutional monarchy
Jarvis Island, U.S.	1	2.6	....	....	87/K 6	unincorporated territory of the U.S.
Java, Indonesia	48,842	126,500	73,712,411	Jakarta	85/J 2	part of Indonesia
Johnston Atoll, U.S.	0.91	2.4	327	....	87/K 4	unincorporated territory of the U.S.
*Jordan	35,000	90,650	4,700,843	Amman	65/D 3	constitutional monarchy
Kansas, U.S.	82,277	213,097	2,477,574	Topeka	232/.....	state of the U.S.
*Kazakhstan	1,048,300	2,715,100	16,816,150	Astana	48/G 5	republic
Kentucky, U.S.	40,409	104,659	3,685,296	Frankfort	237/.....	state of the U.S.
*Kenya	224,960	582,646	29,250,541	Nairobi	115/G 3	republic
Kermadec Islands, New Zealand	13	33	5	....	87/J 9	part of New Zealand
Kingman Reef, U.S.	0.1	0.26	....	....	87/K 5	unincorporated territory of the U.S.
Kiribati	277	717	87,025	Tarawa	87/J 6	republic
*Korea, North	46,540	120,539	21,815,000	P'yŏngyang	80/D 3	communist
*Korea, South	38,175	98,873	43,134,000	Seoul	80/D 5	republic
*Kuwait	6,532	16,918	2,067,728	Kuwait	58/E 4	constitutional monarchy
*Kyrgyzstan	76,641	198,500	4,584,341	Bishkek	48/H 5	republic
*Laos	91,428	236,800	5,556,821	Vientiane	72/D 3	communist
*Latvia	24,595	63,700	2,326,689	Riga	53/.....	republic
*Lebanon	4,015	10,399	3,619,971	Beirut	62/F 6	republic
*Lesotho	11,720	30,355	2,166,520	Maseru	119/D 5	constitutional monarchy
*Liberia	43,000	111,370	3,089,980	Monrovia	106/C 7	republic
*Libya	679,358	1,759,537	5,114,032	Tripoli	110/B 2	socialist people's (masses) state
*Liechtenstein	61	158	32,410	Vaduz	39/J 2	hereditary constitutional monarchy
*Lithuania	25,174	65,200	3,571,552	Vilnius	53/.....	republic
Louisiana, U.S.	47,752	123,678	4,219,973	Baton Rouge	238/.....	state of the U.S.
*Luxembourg	999	2,587	432,577	Luxembourg	27/J 9	constitutional monarchy
Macau	8	21	445,427	Macau	77/H 7	special administrative region of China
*Macedonia, Former Yugo. Rep. of	9,889	25,713	2,035,044	Skopje	45/E 5	emerging democracy
*Madagascar	226,657	587,041	15,294,535	Antananarivo	119/H 3	republic
Madeira Islands, Portugal	307	796	262,800	Funchal	32/A 2	autonomous region of Portugal
Maine, U.S.	33,265	86,156	1,227,928	Augusta	243/.....	state of the U.S.
*Malawi	45,747	118,485	10,154,299	Lilongwe	114/F 6	multiparty democracy
Malaya, Malaysia	50,806	131,588	11,138,227	Kuala Lumpur	72/D 6	part of Malaysia
*Malaysia	128,308	332,318	21,820,143	Kuala Lumpur	72/D 6; 85/E 4	constitutional monarchy
*Maldives	115	298	310,425	Male	54/L 9	republic
*Mali	464,873	1,204,021	10,750,686	Bamako	106/C 6	republic
*Malta	122	316	383,285	Valletta	34/E 7	parliamentary democracy
Manitoba, Canada	250,999	650,087	1,113,898	Winnipeg	179/.....	province of Canada
Marquesas Islands, French Polynesia	492	1,274	5,419	Atuona	87/N 6	part of French Polynesia
*Marshall Islands	70	181	68,088	Majuro	87/G 4	constitutional; free association with the U.S.
Martinique, France	425	1,101	415,724	Fort-de-France	161/D 5	overseas department of France
Maryland, U.S.	10,460	27,091	4,781,468	Annapolis	245/.....	state of the U.S.
Massachusetts, U.S.	8,284	21,456	6,016,425	Boston	249/.....	state of the U.S.
*Mauritania	419,229	1,085,803	2,660,155	Nouakchott	106/B 5	republic
*Mauritius	790	2,046	1,196,172	Port Louis	119/G 5	parliamentary democracy
Mayotte, France	144	373	156,852	Mamoutzou	119/G 2	territorial collectivity of France
*Mexico	761,601	1,972,546	102,026,691	Mexico City	150/.....	federal republic
Michigan, U.S.	58,527	151,585	9,295,297	Lansing	250/.....	state of the U.S.
*Micronesia, Federated States of	271	702	133,144	Palikir	87/E 5	constitutional; free association with the U.S.
Midway Islands, U.S.	1.9	4.9	453	....	87/J 3	unincorporated territory of the U.S.
Minnesota, U.S.	84,402	218,601	4,375,099	St. Paul	255/.....	state of the U.S.
Mississippi, U.S.	47,689	123,515	2,573,216	Jackson	256/.....	state of the U.S.
Missouri, U.S.	69,697	180,515	5,117,073	Jefferson City	261/.....	state of the U.S.
*Moldova	13,012	33,700	4,466,758	Chişinău	52/C 5	republic
*Monaco	368 acres	149 hectares	32,231	....	28/G 6	constitutional monarchy
*Mongolia	606,163	1,569,962	2,654,572	Ulaanbaatar	77/E 2	republic
Montana, U.S.	147,046	380,849	799,065	Helena	262/.....	state of the U.S.
Montserrat, U.K.	40	104	12,875	Plymouth	157/G 3	dependent territory of the U.K.
*Morocco	172,414	446,550	30,205,387	Rabat	106/C 2	constitutional monarchy
*Mozambique	303,769	786,762	19,614,345	Maputo	119/E 4	republic
*Myanmar (Burma)	261,789	678,034	48,852,098	Rangoon	72/B 2	military
*Namibia	317,827	823,172	1,674,116	Windhoek	118/B 3	republic
Nauru	7.7	20	10,704	Yaren (district)	87/G 6	republic
Navassa Island, U.S.	2	5	....	....	156/C 3	unincorporated territory of the U.S.
Nebraska, U.S.	77,355	200,349	1,578,385	Lincoln	264/.....	state of the U.S.
*Nepal	54,663	141,577	24,920,211	Kathmandu	68/E 3	parliamentary democracy
*Netherlands	15,892	41,160	15,878,304	The Hague; Amsterdam	27/F 5	constitutional monarchy
Netherlands Antilles	320	817	209,888	Willemstad	156/E 4	autonomous member of the Netherlands realm
Nevada, U.S.	110,561	286,353	1,201,833	Carson City	266/.....	state of the U.S.

Gazetteer-Index of the World

Country	Area Square Miles	Area Square Kilometers	Population	Capital or Chief Town	Page and Index Ref.	Government or Ownership
New Brunswick, Canada	28,354	73,437	738,133	Fredericton	170/.....	province of Canada
New Caledonia & Dependencies, France	7,335	18,998	200,481	Nouméa	87/G 8	overseas territory of France
Newfoundland, Canada	156,184	404,517	551,792	St. John's	166/.....	province of Canada
New Hampshire, U.S.	9,279	24,033	1,109,252	Concord	268/.....	state of the U.S.
New Jersey, U.S.	7,787	20,168	7,730,188	Trenton	273/.....	state of the U.S.
New Mexico, U.S.	121,593	314,926	1,515,069	Santa Fe	274/.....	state of the U.S.
New South Wales, Australia	309,498	801,600	6,428,700	Sydney	96/B 2	state of Australia
New York, U.S.	49,108	127,190	17,990,455	Albany	276/.....	state of the U.S.
*New Zealand	103,736	268,676	3,697,850	Wellington	100/.....	parliamentary democracy
*Nicaragua	45,698	118,358	4,850,976	Managua	154/D 4	republic
*Niger	489,189	1,267,000	10,260,316	Niamey	106/F 5	republic
*Nigeria	357,000	924,630	117,170,948	Abuja	106/F 6	military
Niue, New Zealand	100	259	3,578	Alofi	87/K 7	self-governing territory in free association with New Zealand
Norfolk Island, Australia	13.4	34.6	2,175	Kingston	88/L 5	territory of Australia
North America	9,363,000	24,250,170	443,438,000	....	146/.....	
North Carolina, U.S.	52,669	136,413	6,628,637	Raleigh	281/.....	state of the U.S.
North Dakota, U.S.	70,702	183,118	638,800	Bismarck	282/.....	state of the U.S.
Northern Ireland, U.K.	5,452	14,121	1,663,300	Belfast	17/F 2	part of the United Kingdom
Northern Marianas, U.S.	184	477	71,912	Saipan	87/E 4	commonwealth associated with the U.S.
Northern Territory, Australia	519,768	1,346,200	193,400	Darwin	93/.....	territory of Australia
*North Korea	46,540	120,539	21,687,550	P'yŏngyang	80/D 3	communist state
Northwest Territories, Canada	589,315	1,526,328	39,672	Yellowknife	187/F 3	territory of Canada
*Norway	125,053	323,887	4,455,707	Oslo	18/F 7	constitutional monarchy
Nova Scotia, Canada	21,425	55,491	909,282	Halifax	168/.....	province of Canada
Nunavut, Canada	733,590	1,900,000	24,730	Iqaluit	187/J 3	territory of Canada
Oceania	3,292,000	8,526,280	23,000,000	....	87/.....	
Ohio, U.S.	41,330	107,045	10,847,115	Columbus	284/.....	state of the U.S.
Oklahoma, U.S.	69,956	181,186	3,145,585	Oklahoma City	288/.....	state of the U.S.
*Oman	120,000	310,800	2,532,556	Muscat	58/G 6	absolute monarchy
Ontario, Canada	412,580	1,068,582	10,753,573	Toronto	175,177/	province of Canada
Oregon, U.S.	97,073	251,419	2,842,321	Salem	291/.....	state of the U.S.
Orkney Islands, Scotland	376	974	17,675	Kirkwall	15/E 1	part of the United Kingdom
*Pakistan	310,403	803,944	141,145,344	Islamabad	68/B 3	federal republic
*Palau	188	487	18,827	Koror	86/D 5	constitutional; free association with the U.S.
Palmyra Atoll, U.S.	12	31	....	....	87/K 5	unincorporated territory of the U.S.
*Panama	29,761	77,082	2,821,085	Panamá	154/G 6	constitutional republic
*Papua New Guinea	183,540	475,369	4,811,939	Port Moresby	85/B 7; 87/E 6	parliamentary democracy
Paracel Islands, China	....	....	....	....	85/E 2	occupied by China; claimed by Taiwan and Vietnam
*Paraguay	157,047	406,752	5,579,503	Asunción	144/.....	republic
Pennsylvania, U.S.	45,308	117,348	11,881,643	Harrisburg	294/.....	state of the U.S.
*Peru	496,222	1,285,215	27,135,689	Lima	128/.....	republic
*Philippines	115,707	299,681	80,961,430	Manila	82/.....	republic
Pitcairn Islands, U.K.	18	47	54	Adamstown	87/O 8	dependent territory of the U.K.
*Poland	120,725	312,678	38,644,184	Warsaw	47/.....	democratic
*Portugal	35,549	92,072	9,902,147	Lisbon	32/B 3	parliamentary democracy
Prince Edward Island, Canada	2,184	5,657	134,557	Charlottetown	168/E 2	province of Canada
Puerto Rico, U.S.	3,515	9,104	3,522,037	San Juan	161/.....	commonwealth associated with the U.S.
*Qatar	4,247	11,000	749,542	Doha	58/F 4	traditional monarchy
Québec, Canada	594,857	1,540,680	7,138,795	Québec	172,174/	province of Canada
Queensland, Austraila	666,872	1,727,200	3,525,600	Brisbane	95/.....	state of Australia
Réunion, France	969	2,510	730,201	St-Denis	119/F 5	overseas department of France
Rhode Island, U.S.	1,212	3,139	1,003,464	Providence	249/H 5	state of the U.S.
*Romania	91,699	237,500	22,291,200	Bucharest	45/F 3	republic
*Russia	6,592,812	17,075,400	145,904,542	Moscow	48/D 4	federation
*Rwanda	10,169	26,337	8,336,995	Kigali	114/E 4	republic
Sabah, Malaysia	29,300	75,887	1,002,608	Kota Kinabalu	85/F 4	state of Malaysia
Saint Helena & Dependencies, U.K.	162	420	7,197	Jamestown	102/B 6	dependent territory of the U.K.
*Saint Kitts and Nevis	104	269	43,441	Basseterre	156/F 3; 161/C11	constitutional monarchy
*Saint Lucia	238	616	155,678	Castries	161/G 6	parliamentary democracy
Saint Pierre & Miquelon, France	93.5	242	7,018	Saint-Pierre	166/C 4	territorial collectivity of France
*Saint Vincent & the Grenadines	150	388	121,188	Kingstown	161/A 8; 157/G 4	constitutional monarchy
Sakhalin, Russia	29,500	76,405	655,000	Yuzhno-Sakhalinsk	48/P 4	part of Russia
*Samoa	1,133	2,934	235,302	Apia	87/J 7	constitutional monarchy
*San Marino	23.4	60.6	25,215	San Marino	34/D 3	republic
*São Tomé and Príncipe	372	963	159,832	São Tomé	106/F 8	republic
Sarawak, Malaysia	48,202	124,843	1,294,753	Kuching	85/E 5	state of Malaysia
Sardinia, Italy	9,301	24,090	1,450,483	Cagliari	34/B 4	region of Italy
Saskatchewan, Canada	251,699	651,900	990,237	Regina	181/.....	province of Canada
*Saudi Arabia	829,995	2,149,687	22,245,751	Riyadh	58/D 4	monarchy
Scotland, U.K.	30,414	78,772	5,128,000	Edinburgh	15/.....	part of the United Kingdom
*Senegal	75,954	196,720	10,390,296	Dakar	106/A 5	republic
*Seychelles	145	375	79,672	Victoria	119/H 5	republic
Shetland Islands, Scotland	552	1,430	18,494	Lerwick	15/G 2	part of the United Kingdom
Siam, see Thailand						
Sicily, Italy	9,926	25,708	4,628,918	Palermo	34/D 6	region of Italy
*Sierra Leone	27,925	72,325	5,509,263	Freetown	106/B 7	constitutional democracy
*Singapore	226	585	3,571,710	Singapore	72/F 6	republic
*Slovakia	18,924	49,014	5,401,134	Bratislava	41/E 2	parliamentary democracy

Gazetteer-Index of the World

Country	Area Square Miles	Area Square Kilometers	Population	Capital or Chief Town	Page and Index Ref.	Government or Ownership
*Slovenia	7,898	20,251	1,970,056	Ljubljana	45/A 3	emerging democracy
Society Islands, French Polynesia	677	1,753	117,703	Papeete	87/L 7	part of French Polynesia
*Solomon Islands	11,500	29,785	470,000	Honiara	87/G 6; 86/.....	parliamentary democracy
*Somalia	246,200	637,658	7,433,922	Mogadishu	115/H 3	no functioning government
*South Africa	455,318	1,179,274	43,981,758	Cape Town; Pretoria	118/C 5	republic
South America	6,875,000	17,806,250	314,335,000	....	120/.....	
South Australia, Australia	379,922	984,000	1,494,800	Adelaide	94/.....	state of Australia
South Carolina, U.S.	31,113	80,583	3,486,703	Columbia	296/.....	state of the U.S.
South Dakota, U.S.	77,116	199,730	696,004	Pierre	298/.....	state of the U.S.
*South Korea	38,175	98,873	47,350,529	Seoul	80/D 5	republic
*Spain	194,881	504,742	39,208,236	Madrid	33/.....	parliamentary monarchy
Spratly Islands	....	....	....	....	85/E 4	in dispute; claims by China, Malaysia, Philippines, Taiwan, Vietnam
*Sri Lanka	25,332	65,610	19,355,053	Colombo	68/E 7	republic
*Sudan	967,494	2,505,809	35,530,371	Khartoum	110/E 4	transitional†
Sumatra, Indonesia	164,000	424,760	19,360,400	Medan	84/B 5	see Indonesia
*Suriname	55,144	142,823	434,093	Paramaribo	131/C 3	republic
Svalbard, Norway	23,957	62,049	3,431	Longyearbyen	18/C 2	territory of Norway
*Swaziland	6,705	17,366	1,004,072	Mbabane	119/E 5	monarchy
*Sweden	173,665	449,792	8,938,559	Stockholm	18/J 8	constitutional monarchy
Switzerland	15,943	41,292	7,288,715	Bern	39/.....	federal republic
*Syria	71,498	185,180	17,758,925	Damascus	62/G 5	military republic
Tahiti, French Polynesia	402	1,041	95,604	Papeete	87/L 7	see French Polynesia
Taiwan	13,971	36,185	22,319,222	T'aipei	77/K 7	multiparty democratic
*Tajikistan	55,251	143,100	6,194,373	Dushanbe	48/G 6	republic
*Tanzania	363,708	942,003	31,962,769	Dar es Salaam	114/F 5	republic
Tasmania, Australia	26,178	67,800	470,100	Hobart	99/.....	state of Australia
Tennessee, U.S.	42,144	109,153	4,877,185	Nashville	237/.....	state of the U.S.
Texas, U.S.	266,807	691,030	16,986,510	Austin	303/.....	state of the U.S.
*Thailand	198,455	513,998	61,163,833	Bangkok	72/D 3	constitutional monarchy
Tibet, China	463,320	1,200,000	1,790,000	Lhasa	76/C 5	part of China
*Togo	21,622	56,000	5,262,611	Lomé	106/E 7	republic†
Tokelau, New Zealand	3.9	10	1,575	Fakaofo	87/J 6	territory of New Zealand
Tonga	270	699	109,959	Nuku'alofa	87/J 8	hereditary constitutional monarchy
*Trinidad and Tobago	1,980	5,128	1,086,908	Port-of-Spain	157/G 5; 161/A10	parliamentary democracy
Tristan da Cunha, St. Helena	38	98	251	Edinburgh	2/J 7	see St. Helena
Tuamotu Archipelago, French Polynesia	341	883	9,052	Apataki	87/M 7	see French Polynesia
*Tunisia	63,378	164,149	9,645,499	Tunis	106/F 1	republic
*Turkey	300,946	779,450	66,620,120	Ankara	62/D 3	republican parliamentary democracy
*Turkmenistan	188,455	488,100	4,435,507	Ashgabat	48/F 6	republic
Turks and Caicos Islands, U.K.	166	430	17,480	Cockburn Town, Grand Turk	156/D 2	dependent territory of the U.K.
Tuvalu	9.78	25.33	10,730	Funafuti	87/H 6	democracy
*Uganda	91,076	235,887	23,451,687	Kampala	114/F 3	republic
*Ukraine	233,089	603,700	49,506,779	Kiev	52/D 5	republic
*United Arab Emirates	32,278	83,600	2,386,472	Abu Dhabi	58/F 5	federation of sheikdoms
*United Kingdom	94,399	244,493	59,247,439	London	10/.....	constitutional monarchy
*United States	3,623,420	9,384,658	274,943,496	Washington, D.C.	188/.....	federal republic
*Uruguay	72,172	186,925	3,332,782	Montevideo	145/.....	republic
Utah, U.S.	84,899	219,888	1,722,850	Salt Lake City	304/.....	state of the U.S.
*Uzbekistan	173,591	449,600	24,422,518	Tashkent	48/G 5	republic
*Vanuatu	5,700	14,763	192,848	Port-Vila	87/G 7	republic
Vatican City	108.7 acres	44 hectares	1,000	....	34/B 6	sacerdotal (priest-related) monarchy
*Venezuela	352,143	912,050	23,595,822	Caracas	124/.....	republic
Vermont, U.S.	9,614	24,900	562,758	Montpelier	268/.....	state of the U.S.
Victoria, Australia	87,876	227,600	4,726,600	Melbourne	96/B 5	state of Australia
*Vietnam	128,405	332,569	78,349,503	Hanoi	72/E 3	communist state
Virginia, U.S.	40,767	105,587	6,187,358	Richmond	307/.....	state of the U.S.
Virgin Islands, British	59	153	19,610	Road Town	157/H 1	dependent territory of the U.K.
Virgin Islands, U.S.	132	342	101,809	Charlotte Amalie	161/A 4	organized, unincorporated territory of the U.S.
Wake Island, U.S.	2.5	6.5	302	Wake Islet	87/G 4	unincorporated territory of the U.S.
Wales, U.K.	8,017	20,764	2,921,100	Cardiff	13/D 5	part of the United Kingdom
Wallis and Futuna, France	106	275	15,283	Mata Utu	87/J 7	overseas territory of France
Washington, U.S.	68,139	176,480	4,866,692	Olympia	310/.....	state of the U.S.
West Bank	2,100	5,439	1,661,749	....	65/C 3	occupied by Israel
Western Australia, Australia	975,096	2,525,500	1,868,200	Perth	92/.....	state of Australia
Western Sahara	102,703	266,000	244,943	....	106/B 3	occupied by Morocco
West Virginia, U.S.	24,231	62,758	1,793,477	Charleston	312/.....	state of the U.S.
Wisconsin, U.S.	56,153	145,436	4,891,769	Madison	317/.....	state of the U.S.
World (land)	57,970,000	150,142,300	5,292,000,000	....	1,2/.....	
Wyoming, U.S.	97,809	253,325	453,588	Cheyenne	319/.....	state of the U.S.
*Yemen	188,321	487,752	17,521,085	Sanaa	58/D 7	republic
*Yugoslavia	38,989	102,173	11,210,243	Belgrade	45/C 3	republic
Yukon Territory, Canada	207,075	536,324	30,766	Whitehorse	186/E 3	territory of Canada
*Zambia	290,586	752,618	9,872,007	Lusaka	114/E 7	republic
*Zimbabwe	150,803	390,580	11,272,013	Harare	119/D 3	parliamentary democracy

Glossary of Abbreviations

A

A.A.F. — Army Air Field
Acad. — Academy
A.C.T. — Australian Capital Territory
adm. — administration; administrative
A.F.B. — Air Force Base
Afgh., Afghan. — Afghanistan
Afr. — Africa
Ala. — Alabama
Alb. — Albania
Alg. — Algeria
Alta. — Alberta
Amer. — American
Amer. Samoa — American Samoa
And. — Andorra
Ant., Antarc. — Antarctica
Ant. & Bar. — Antigua and Barbuda
Ar. — Arabia
arch. — archipelago
Arg. — Argentina
Ariz. — Arizona
Ark. — Arkansas
Arm. — Armenia
Aust. — Austria
Aust. Cap. Terr. — Australian Capital Territory
Austr., Austral. — Australian, Australia
aut. — autonomous
Aut. Obl. — Autonomous Oblast
Aut. Rep. — Autonomous Republic
Azer. — Azerbaijan

B

B. — Bay
Bah. — Bahamas
Barb. — Barbados
Battlef. — Battlefield
Bch. — Beach
Bel. — Belarus
Belg. — Belgium
Berm. — Bermuda
Bol. — Bolivia
Bos. — Bosnia & Hercegovina
Bots. — Botswana
Br. — Branch
Br. — British
Braz. — Brazil
Br. Col. — British Columbia
Br. Ind. Oc. Terr. — British Indian Ocean Territory
Bulg. — Bulgaria

C

C. — Cape
Calif. — California
Can. — Canada
can. — canal
cap. — capital
Cent. Afr. Rep. — Central African Republic
Cent. Amer. — Central America
C.G. Sta. — Coast Guard Station
C.H. — Court House
chan. — channel
Chan. Is. — Channel Islands
Chem. Ctr. — Chemical Center
co. — county
Col. — Colombia
Colo. — Colorado
comm. — commlssary
Conn. — Connecticut
cont. — continent
cord. — cordillera (mountain range)
C. Rica — Costa Rica
Cro. — Croatia
C.S. — County Seat
C. Verde — Cape Verde
Czech. — Czech Republic

D

D.C. — District of Columbia
Del. — Delaware
Dem. — Democratic
Den. — Denmark
depr. — depression
dept. — department
des. — desert
dist., dist's — district, districts
div. — division
Dom. Rep. — Dominican Republic

E

E. — East
Ec., Ecua. — Ecuador
elec. div. — electoral division
El Salv. — El Salvador
Eng. — England
Equat. Guinea, Eq. Guin. — Equatorial Guinea
Erit. — Eritrea
escarp. — escarpment
est. — estuary
Est. — Estonia
Eth. — Ethiopia

F

Falk. Is. — Falkland Islands
Fin. — Finland
Fk., Fks. — Fork, Forks
Fla. — Florida
for. — forest
Fr. — France, French
Fr. Gui. — French Guiana
Fr. Poly. — French Polynesia
Ft. — Fort

G

G. — Gulf
Ga. — Georgia (state)
Game Res. — Game Reserve
Geo. — Georgia (nation)
Ger. — Germany
geys. — geyser
Gibr. — Gibraltar
glac. — glacier
gov. — governorate
Gr. — Group
Greenl. — Greenland
Gren. — Grenada
Gt. Brit. — Great Britain
Guad. — Guadeloupe
Guat. — Guatemala
Guinea-Biss. — Guinea-Bissau
Guy. — Guyana

H

har., harb., hbr. — harbor
hd. — head
highl. — highland, highlands
Hist. — Historic, Historical
Hond. — Honduras
Hts. — Heights
Hung. — Hungary

I

I., isl. — island, isle
I.C. — independent city
Ice., Icel. — Iceland
Ida. — Idaho
Ill. — Illinois
Ind. — Indiana
ind. city — independent city
Indon. — Indonesia
Ind. Res. — Indian Reservation
int. div. — internal division
inten. — intendency
Int'l — International
Ire. — Ireland
Is., isls. — islands
Isr. — Israel
isth. — isthmus
Iv. Coast — Ivory Coast

J

Jam. — Jamaica
Jct. — Junction

K

Kans. — Kansas
Kaz., Kazakh. — Kazakhstan
Ky. — Kentucky
Kyr. — Kyrgyzstan

L

L. — Lake, Loch, Lough
La. — Louisiana
Lab. — Laboratory
lag. — lagoon
Lat. — Latvia
ld. — land
Leb. — Lebanon
Les. — Lesotho
Liecht. — Liechtenstein
Lith. — Lithuania
Lux. — Luxembourg

M

Mac. — Macedonia
Mad., Madag. — Madagascar
Man. — Manitoba
Mart. — Martinique
Mass. — Massachusetts
Maur. — Mauritania
Md. — Maryland
met. area — metropolitan area
Mex. — Mexico
Mich. — Michigan
Minn. — Minnesota
Miss. — Mississippi
Mo. — Missouri
Mold. — Moldova
Mon. — Monument
Mong. — Mongolia
Mont. — Montana
Mor. — Morocco
Moz., Mozamb. — Mozambique
mt. — mount
mtn. — mountain

N

N., No. — North
N. Amer. — North America
Nam., Namib. — Namibia
N.A.S. — Naval Air Station
Nat'l — National
Nat'l Cem. — National Cemetery
Nat'l Mem. Park — National Memorial Park
Nat'l Mil. Park — National Military Park
Nat'l Pkwy. — National Parkway
Nav. Base — Naval Base
Nav. Sta. — Naval Station
N.B., N. Br. — New Brunswick
N.C. — North Carolina
N. Dak. — North Dakota
Nebr. — Nebraska
Neth. — Netherlands
Neth. Ant. — Netherlands Antilles
Nev. — Nevada
New Bruns. — New Brunswick
New Cal., New Caled. — New Caledonia
Newf. — Newfoundland
New Hebr. — New Hebrides
N.H. — New Hampshire
Nic. — Nicaragua
N. Ire. — Northern Ireland
N.J. — New Jersey
N. Mex. — New Mexico
Nor. — Norway, Norwegian
North. — Northern
North. Terr., No. Terr. — Northern Territory (Australia)
N.S. — Nova Scotia
N.S.W., N.S. Wales — New South Wales
N.W.T., N.W. Terrs. — Northwest Territories (Canada)
N.Y. — New York
N.Z., N. Zealand — New Zealand

O

Obl. — Oblast
Okla. — Oklahoma
Okr. — Okrug
Ont. — Ontario
Ord. Depot — Ordnance Depot
Oreg. — Oregon

P

Pa. — Pennsylvania
Pak. — Pakistan
Pan. — Panama
Papua N.G. — Papua New Guinea
Par. — Paraguay
par. — parish
passg. — passage
P.E.I. — Prince Edward Island
pen. — peninsula
Phil., Phil. Is. — Philippines
Pk. — Park
pk. — peak
plat. — plateau
P.N.G. — Papua New Guinea
Pol. — Poland
Port. — Portugal, Portuguese
Pr. Edward I. — Prince Edward Island
pref. — prefecture
P. Rico — Puerto Rico
prom. — promontory
prov. — province, provincial
pt. — point

Q

Que. — Québec
Queens. — Queensland

R

R. — River
ra. — range
Rec., Recr. — Recreation, Recreational
reg. — region
Rep. — Republic
res. — reservoir
Res. — Reservation, Reserve
R.I. — Rhode Island
riv. — river
Rom. — Romania

S

S. — South
sa. — sierra, serra
S. Afr., S. Africa — South Africa
salt dep. — salt deposit
salt des. — salt desert
S. Amer. — South America
São T. & Pr. — São Tomé and Príncipe
Sask. — Saskatchewan
Saudi Ar. — Saudi Arabia
S. Aust., S. Austral. — South Australia
S.C. — South Carolina
Scot. — Scotland
Sd. — Sound
S. Dak. — South Dakota
Sen. — Senegal
Seych. — Seychelles
Sing. — Singapore
S. Leone — Sierra Leone
Slvk. — Slovakia
Slvn. — Slovenia
S. Marino — San Marino
Sol. Is. — Solomon Islands
Sp. — Spanish
Spr., Sprs. — Spring, Springs
St., Ste. — Saint, Sainte
Sta. — Station
St. P.& M. — Saint Pierre and Miquelon
St. Vin. & Grens. — St. Vincent & The Grenadines
str., strs. — strait, straits
Sur. — Suriname
Swaz. — Swaziland
Switz. — Swltzerland

T

Taj. — Tajikistan
Tanz. — Tanzania
Tas. — Tasmania
Tenn. — Tennessee
terr., terrs. — territory, territories
Tex. — Texas
Thai. — Thailand
trad. — traditional
Trin. & Tob. — Trinidad and Tobago
Tun. — Tunisia
Turk. — Turkmenistan
twp. — township

U

U.A.E. — United Arab Emirates
U.K. — United Kingdom
Ukr. — Ukraine
urb. area — urban area
Urug. — Uruguay
U.S. — United States
Uzb. — Uzbekistan

V

Va. — Virginia
Ven., Venez. — Venezuela
V.I. (U.K.) — Virgin Islands (U.K.)
V.I. (U.S.) — Virgin Islands (U.S.)
Vic. — Victoria
Viet. — Vietnam
Vill. — Village
vol. — volcano
Vt. — Vermont

W

W. — West, Western
Wash. — Washington
W. Aust., W. Austral. — Western Australia
W. Indies — West Indies
Wis. — Wisconsin
W. Va. — West Virginia
Wyo. — Wyoming

Y

Yugo. — Yugoslavia
Yukon — Yukon Territory

Z

Zim. — Zimbabwe

Index to Terrain Maps

on pages X through XXXII

This index contains only names of land and ocean physical features. Names of towns, internal divisions and countries are not included. The entry name is followed by a letter-number combination which refers to the area on the map in which the name will be found. The number following the map reference for the entry refers, not to the page on which the entry will be found, but to the map plate number.

Index Continued

THE PHYSICAL WORLD
Terrain Maps of Land Forms and Ocean Floors

CONTENTS

RELIEF MODELS BY ERNST G. HOFMANN, ASSISTED BY RAFAEL MARTINEZ

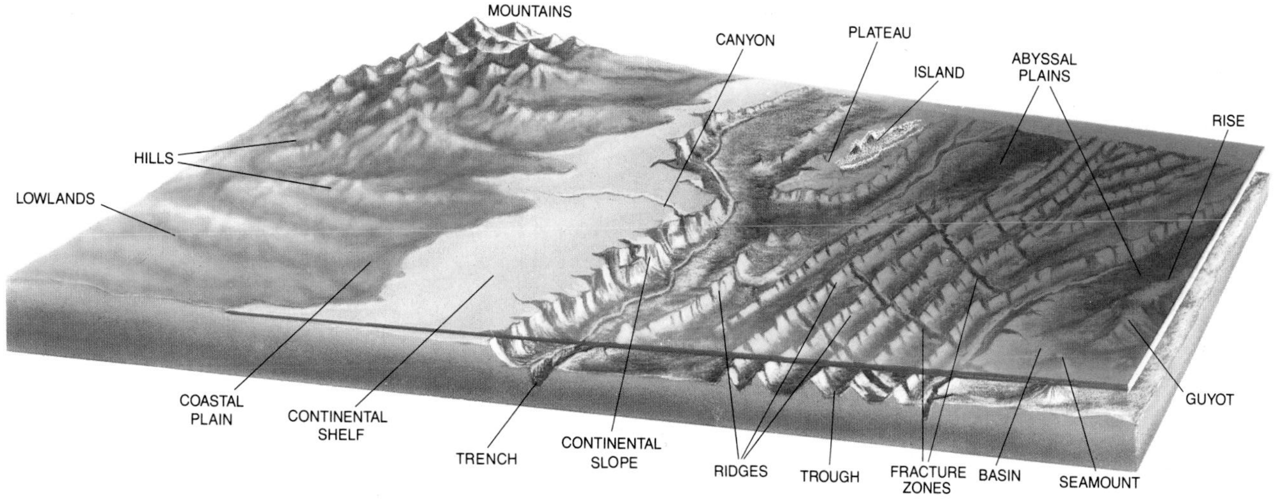

MOUNTAINS
CANYON
PLATEAU
ISLAND
ABYSSAL PLAINS
RISE
HILLS
LOWLANDS
GUYOT
COASTAL PLAIN
CONTINENTAL SHELF
TRENCH
CONTINENTAL SLOPE
RIDGES
TROUGH
FRACTURE ZONES
BASIN
SEAMOUNT

The oblique view diagram above is designed to provide a detailed view of the ocean floor as if seen through the depth of the sea. Graduating blue tones are used to contrast ocean floor depths: from light blue to represent shallow continental shelves to dark blues in the greater depths. Land relief is shown in conventional hypsometric tints.

In this dramatic collection of topographic maps of continents, oceans and major regions of the world, Hammond introduces a revolutionary new technique in cartography.

While most maps depicting terrain are created from painted artwork that is then photographed, Hammond now premiers the use of a remarkable sculptured model mapping technique created by one of our master cartographers.

The process begins with the sculpting of large scale three-dimensional models. Once physical details have been etched on the models and refinements completed, relief work is checked for accurate elevation based on a vertical scale exaggerated for visual effect.

Finished models are airbrushed and painted, then photographed using a single northwesterly light source to achieve a striking three-dimensional effect. The result is the dynamic presentation of mountain ranges and peaks on land, and canyons, trenches and seamounts on the ocean floor. Never before have maps conveyed such rich beauty while providing a realistic representation of the world as we know it.

X
A B C D E F
1 2 3 4 5 6 7
ARCTIC OCEAN
CANADA BASIN
QUEEN ELIZABETH ISLANDS
Ellesmere I.
GREENLAND
Greenland Sea
Wrangel I.
Beaufort Sea
Banks I.
Devon I.
Baffin Bay
Baffin Island
Pt. Barrow
Victoria I.
Chukchi Sea
Arctic Circle
Norwegian Sea
Iceland
Yukon
Mackenzie
Mt. McKinley
Great Bear L.
Great Slave L.
Rocky Mountains
Peace
Hudson Bay
LABRADOR BASIN
Denmark Str.
IRMINGER BASIN
ICELAND BASIN
Great Britain
Bering Sea
Gulf of Alaska
ALEUTIAN BASIN
ALEUTIAN ISLANDS
ALEUTIAN TRENCH
NORTH AMERICA
Great Plains
CHARLIE-GIBBS FRACTURE ZONE
Ireland
Newfoundland
Great Lakes
C. Race
Missouri
Appalachian Mts.
MENDOCINO FRACTURE ZONE
C. Mendocino
Colorado
Ohio
C. Hatteras
Mississippi
Rio Grande
ATLANTIC
Atlas Mts.
HAWAIIAN ISLANDS
HAWAIIAN RIDGE
MOLOKAI FRACTURE ZONE
Tropic of Cancer
Lower California
Gulf of Mexico
Cuba
WEST INDIES
Caribbean Sea
MID-ATLANTIC RIDGE
C. Verde
CENTRAL PACIFIC BASIN
PACIFIC
CLIPPERTON FRACTURE ZONE
GUATEMALA BASIN
Orinoco
Equator
Negro
Amazon
ROMANCHE FRACTURE ZONE
C. de São Roque
Madeira
Andes
SOUTH AMERICA
PERU-CHILE TRENCH
PERU BASIN
BRAZIL BASIN
São Francisco
OCEAN
TONGA TRENCH
Tropic of Capricorn
NAZCA RIDGE
Paraná
CHILE BASIN
Cerro Aconcagua
Mountains
KERMADEC TRENCH
SOUTHWEST PACIFIC BASIN
EAST PACIFIC RISE
ARGENTINE BASIN
Falkland Is.
Tierra del Fuego
C. Horn
SOUTH SANDWICH TRENCH
Drake Passage
PACIFIC-ANTARCTIC RIDGE
AMUNDSEN ABYSSAL PLAIN
Antarctic Peninsula
WEDDELL ABYSSAL PLAIN
Antarctic Circle
Bellingshausen Sea
Weddell Sea
ANTARCTICA
0 500 1000 1500 2000 2500 3000 MILES at Equator
0 500 1000 1500 2000 2500 3000 KILOMETERS at Equator

G H J K L M
1 2 3 4 5 6 7
RCTIC OCEAN
FRANZ JOSEF LAND
SEVERNAYA ZEMLYA
SVALBARD
Novaya Zemlya
NEW SIBERIAN IS.
Laptev Sea
Nordkapp
Barents Sea
Kara Sea
Wrangel I.
Kjølen
Siberia
Ural Mountains
Ob
Yenisey
Lena
Aldan
Angara
L. Ladoga
Baltic Sea
Bering Sea
ALEUTIAN BASIN
ALEUTIAN ISLANDS
ALEUTIAN TRENCH
Kamchatka Pen.
Sea of Okhotsk
EUROPE
Volga
Dnieper
ASIA
Irtysh
L. Balkhash
L. Baykal
Amur
Sakhalin
KURIL-KAMCHATKA TRENCH
Danube
Black Sea
Caspian Sea
Aral Sea
Gobi
Sea of Japan
Honshu
JAPAN TRENCH
NORTHWEST PACIFIC BASIN
Mediterranean Sea
Euphrates
Kunlun
Himalaya
Mt. Everest
Huang
East China Sea
Chang
Indus
Ganges
PACIFIC
Tropic of Cancer
Nile
Red Sea
Arabian Sea
ARABIAN BASIN
Salween
Mekong
Taiwan
South China Sea
PHILIPPINE BASIN
Luzon
MARIANA IS.
MARIANA TRENCH
Challenger Deep
MARSHALL IS.
CENTRAL PACIFIC BASIN
AFRICA
Bay of Bengal
C. Comorin
Ceylon
CARLSBERG RIDGE
Borneo
Mindanao
CAROLINE IS.
MELANESIAN BASIN
Equator
SOMALI BASIN
CEYLON PLAIN
CENTRAL
L. Victoria
Kilimanjaro
Congo
New Guinea
Sumatra
Java
Celebes
OCEAN
JAVA TRENCH
INDIAN RIDGE
NINETYEAST RIDGE
INDIAN
Zambezi
Coral Sea
Great Barrier Reef
Fiji Is.
Madagascar
Tropic of Capricorn
OCEAN
AUSTRALIA
BROKEN PLATEAU
Orange
CAPE BASIN
C. of Good Hope
AGULHAS RIDGE
SOUTHWEST INDIAN RIDGE
SOUTHEAST INDIAN RIDGE
C. Leeuwin
S. AUSTRALIA BASIN
Tasman Sea
North Cape
North I.
South I.
Tasmania
KERGUELEN PLATEAU
ENDERBY ABYSSAL PLAIN
AUSTRALIAN-ANTARCTIC BASIN
SOUTHEAST INDIAN RIDGE
Antarctic Circle
Amery Ice Shelf
ANTARCTICA
C. Adare
Ross Sea
G H J K L M

LEGEND FOR TERRAIN MAPS

International Boundaries		Mountain Peaks	
State and Provincial Boundaries		National Capitals	
Other Boundaries		Other Capitals	
Boundaries Along Rivers		Canals	

BARENTS SEA
WHITE SEA
Kola Pen.
NORWEGIAN SEA
NORWEGIAN BASIN
ICELAND
GREENLAND (Den.)
DENMARK STRAIT
ICELAND-FAEROE RISE
ICELAND BASIN
ROCKALL TROUGH
PORCUPINE ABYSSAL PLAIN
BISCAY ABYSSAL PLAIN
IBERIAN ABYSSAL PLAIN
ATLANTIC
OCEAN
NORTH SEA
BALTIC SEA
Gulf of Bothnia
Gulf of Finland
Skagerrak
Kattegat
English Channel
IRISH SEA
Bay of Biscay
MEDITERRANEAN SEA
TYRRHENIAN SEA
ADRIATIC SEA
IONIAN SEA
AEGEAN SEA
BLACK SEA
SEA OF AZOV
CASPIAN SEA
ARAL SEA
Ural Mountains
NORWAY
SWEDEN
FINLAND
ESTONIA
LATVIA
LITHUANIA
RUSSIA
BELARUS
UKRAINE
MOLDOVA
POLAND
GERMANY
DENMARK
NETHERLANDS
BELGIUM
LUX.
FRANCE
SWITZ.
AUSTRIA
CZECH REP.
SLOVAKIA
HUNGARY
ROMANIA
BULGARIA
YUGOSLAVIA
BOS. & HERZ.
CROATIA
SLOV.
ALBANIA
FYROM
GREECE
ITALY
SPAIN
PORTUGAL
UNITED KINGDOM
Great Britain
IRELAND
TURKEY
CYPRUS
SYRIA
LEBANON
IRAQ
IRAN
GEORGIA
ARMENIA
AZERBAIJAN
KAZAKHSTAN
UZBEK.
TURKMENISTAN
MOROCCO
ALGERIA
TUNISIA
AFRICA
Sardinia
Sicily
Corsica
Crete
Balearic Is.
Moscow
St. Petersburg
London
Paris
Berlin
Rome
Madrid
Kiev
Warsaw
Vienna
Budapest
Bucharest
Athens
Istanbul
Volga
Dnieper
Don
Danube
Elbe
Rhine
Caucasus
Pyrenees
Alps
Carpathian Mts.
Apennines
© Copyright by HAMMOND INCORPORATED, Maplewood, N.J.
0 100 200 300 400 500 MILES
0 100 200 300 400 500 KILOMETERS

A B C D E F
1 2 3 4 5 6 7 8
GREENLAND
DENMARK STRAIT
ICELAND
Reykjavík
ICELANDIC PLATEAU
NORWEGIAN BASIN
Jan Mayen (Nor.)
AEGIR RIDGE
VORING PLATEAU
NORWEGIAN SEA
ICELAND BASIN
ICELAND FAEROE RISE
Faeroe Is.
FAEROE SHELF
FAEROE-SHETLAND CHANNEL
ATLANTIC OCEAN
Rockall
ROCKALL PLATEAU
ROCKALL BANK
ROCKALL TROUGH
FENI RIDGE
HEBRIDEAN SHELF
Hebrides
Shetland Is.
Orkney Is.
NORWEGIAN DEEP
NORTH SEA
Nordkapp
Hammerfest
Vesterålen
Lofoten
Arctic Circle
Murmansk
Kola Peninsula
WHITE SEA
Kiruna
Oulu
NORWAY
Trondheim
Glittertinden
Bergen
Oslo
Lindesnes
Skagerrak
Kattegat
SWEDEN
Sundsvall
Gulf of Bothnia
Åland Is.
Stockholm
Vänern
Vättern
Göteborg
Gotland
Öland
FINLAND
Tampere
Helsinki
Lake Ladoga
Lake Onega
Leningrad
Gulf of Finland
Tallinn
ESTONIA
L. Peipus
Hiiumaa
Saaremaa
G. of Riga
Riga
LATVIA
RUSSIA
LITHUANIA
Vilnius
Minsk
BELARUS
Kaliningrad
BALTIC SEA
DENMARK
Jutland
Fyn
Sjaelland
Copenhagen
Bornholm
Rügen
Ben Nevis
Aberdeen
SCOTLAND
Glasgow
Great Britain
UNITED KINGDOM
Belfast
Isle of Man
IRELAND
Dublin
IRISH SEA
PORCUPINE BANK
C. Clear
St. George's Channel
Liverpool
Birmingham
WALES
ENGLAND
London
Thames
CELTIC SHELF
Land's End
English Channel
Channel Is. (UK)
Frisian Is.
NETHERLANDS
Amsterdam
Rotterdam
BELGIUM
Antwerp
Brussels
Ardennes
Hamburg
Bremen
Elbe
Szczecin
Gdańsk
Berlin
GERMANY
POLAND
Warsaw
Łódź
UKRAINE
L'viv
Dniester
Cologne
Bonn
Leipzig
Dresden
Wrocław
Oder
Vistula
Frankfurt
Main
Prague
CZECH REP.
Brno
Cracow
SLOVAKIA
Carpathian Mts.
Stuttgart
Munich
Danube
Linz
Vienna
Bratislava
AUSTRIA
Budapest
HUNGARY
Cluj-Napoca
ROMANIA
Le Havre
Seine
Paris
Brest
Nantes
Loire
FRANCE
Zürich
Bern
SWITZ.
Geneva
Lyon
Mt. Blanc
Graz
SLOVENIA
Ljubljana
Zagreb
CROATIA
Trieste
Sava
L. Balaton
Belgrade
Bucharest
YUGOSLAVIA
BOS. & HERZ.
Sarajevo
Dinaric Alps
BULGARIA
Sofia
Skopje
F.Y.R.O.M.
Tirane
ALBANIA
Thessaloniki
GREECE
AEGEAN SEA
Athens
Peloponnisos
Évvoia
Crete
BISCAY ABYSSAL PLAIN
PORCUPINE ABYSSAL PLAIN
Bay of Biscay
Bordeaux
Dordogne
Massif Central
Garonne
Toulouse
Pyrenees
ANDORRA
Turin
Milan
Venice
Po
Genoa
Bologna
MONACO
Nice
Marseille
Gulf of Lions
LIGURIAN SEA
SAN MARINO
ITALY
Corsica
Elba
VATICAN CITY
Rome
Apennines
ADRIATIC SEA
ADRIATIC BASIN
Naples
G. of Taranto
C. Finisterre
Bilbao
Cantabrian Mts.
Porto
Douro
Ebro
Saragossa
Barcelona
PORTUGAL
Iberian Peninsula
Madrid
Tagus
SPAIN
Lisbon
Guadiana
Júcar
Valencia
Sierra Morena
Guadalquivir
Córdoba
Seville
C. de São Vicente
Cádiz
Málaga
Mulhacén
Str. of Gibraltar
GIBRALTAR (UK)
Balearic Is.
Minorca
Majorca
Ibiza
Sardinia
TYRRHENIAN SEA
TYRRHENIAN BASIN
ALGERIAN PLAIN
C. Teulada
MEDITERRANEAN SEA
Palermo
Etna
Sicily
C. Passero
IONIAN SEA
IONIAN BASIN
Ionian Is.
MALTA
Valletta
Tangier
Algiers
Oran
Tunis
C. Bon
MOROCCO
ALGERIA
TUNISIA
AFRICA
© Copyright by HAMMOND INCORPORATED, Maplewood, N.J.
0 100 200 300 400 500 MILES
0 100 200 300 400 500 KILOMETERS

A | B | C | D | E | F

GREENLAND (Den.)
ICELAND
ATLANTIC OCEAN
ARCTIC OCEAN
CANADA BASIN
BEAUFORT SEA
LINCOLN SEA
Alaska
UNITED STATES
Pt. Barrow
Kodiak I.
Alaska Pen.
Bering Str.
C. Dezhnev
NORWEGIAN SEA
NORTH SEA
IRELAND
UNITED KINGDOM
London
Paris
Berlin
Rome
SPAIN
PORTUGAL
Bay of Biscay
English Chan.
BALTIC SEA
NORWAY
SWEDEN
FINLAND
POLAND
BELARUS
UKRAINE
MOLDOVA
GREECE
BLACK SEA
MEDITERRANEAN SEA
CYPRUS
LEBANON
ISRAEL
JORDAN
SYRIA
IRAQ
Baghdad
Cairo
EGYPT
Suez Canal
RED SEA
BARENTS SEA
KARA SEA
Novaya Zemlya
Severnaya Zemlya
LAPTEV SEA
EAST SIBERIAN SEA
New Siberian Is.
LOMONOSOV RIDGE
MENDELEYEV RIDGE
MAKAROV BASIN
AMUNDSEN BASIN
NANSEN BASIN
BERING SEA
ALEUTIAN BASIN
BOWERS RIDGE
Aleutian Is.
Kamchatka
SEA OF OKHOTSK
Sakhalin
EUROPE
Moscow
Volga
RUSSIA
Ural Mountains
Ob'
Yekaterinburg
Chelyabinsk
Omsk
Novosibirsk
Krasnoyarsk
Norilsk
Yenisei
Lena
Yakutsk
Angara
Lake Baykal
Irkutsk
Yablonovyy Ra.
Amur
Khabarovsk
Kolyma Ra.
SIBERIA
ASIA
CASPIAN SEA
Caucasus
ARAL SEA
KAZAKHSTAN
Astana
Karaganda
L. Balkhash
Syr Darya
UZBEKISTAN
TURKMENISTAN
Ashgabat
Tashkent
Almaty
KYRGYZSTAN
TAJIKISTAN
Tian Shan
Ürümqi
Altai Mts.
MONGOLIA
Ulaanbaatar
Gobi
Great Khingan Ra.
Harbin
Shenyang
N. KOREA
S. KOREA
Seoul
SEA OF JAPAN
JAPAN
Honshu
Tokyo
Osaka
Nagoya
Kyushu
Tehran
IRAN
Zagros Mountains
Euphrates
KUWAIT
Persian Gulf
BAHRAIN
QATAR
UAE
SAUDI ARABIA
Riyadh
Rub' al Khali
Gulf of Oman
Muscat
OMAN
YEMEN
Aden
Gulf of Aden
ERITREA
ETHIOPIA
SOMALIA
Socotra
AFGHANISTAN
Kabul
Islamabad
Hindu Kush
PAKISTAN
Karachi
Lahore
K2 (Godwin Austen) 28,250 ft. (8611 m)
Taklimakan
Tarim
Kunlun Shan
Tibet
Himalaya
NEPAL
Mt. Everest 29,028 ft. (8848 m)
BHUTAN
Delhi
New Delhi
Kanpur
Ganges
Jumna
Brahmaputra
INDIA
Ahmadabad
Narbada
Mumbai (Bombay)
Godavari
Hyderabad
Kistna
Bangalore
Chennai (Madras)
Western Ghats
BANGLADESH
Dhaka
Calcutta
MYANMAR (BURMA)
Yangon (Rangoon)
Irrawaddy
Salween
Mekong
CHINA
Beijing
Tianjin
Dalian
Huang
Taiyuan
Lanzhou
Xi'an
Nanjing
Shanghai
Chengdu
Wuhan
Chongqing
Chang
Xi
Guangzhou
HONG KONG
Taipei
YELLOW SEA
EAST CHINA SEA
Hainan
Hanoi
THAILAND
Bangkok
CAMBODIA
VIETNAM
Ho Chi Minh City
Gulf of Thailand
SOUTH CHINA SEA
PHILIPPINES
Luzon
Manila
Mindanao
Palawan
SULU SEA
CELEBES SEA
PHILIPPINE SEA
PHILIPPINE BASIN
PARECE VELA BASIN
PALAU RIDGE
PACIFIC OCEAN
Tropic of Cancer
MALAYSIA
Kuala Lumpur
SINGAPORE
BRUNEI
SUNDA SHELF
Sumatra
Borneo
Celebes
Java
Jakarta
Surabaya
JAVA SEA
FLORES SEA
BANDA SEA
TIMOR SEA
Timor
INDONESIA
New Guinea
ANDAMAN SEA
Andaman Is.
Nicobar Is.
SRI LANKA (CEYLON)
Colombo
MALDIVES
ARABIAN SEA
ARABIAN BASIN
OWEN FRACTURE ZONE
BAY OF BENGAL
GANGES CONE
CARLSBERG RIDGE
SOMALI BASIN
CEYLON PLAIN
Equator
MID INDIAN BASIN
COCOS BASIN
INDIAN OCEAN
OCEAN BASIN
NINETY EAST RIDGE
INVESTIGATOR RIDGE
CENTRAL INDIAN RIDGE
CHAGOS TRENCH
BRITISH INDIAN OCEAN TERR.
SEYCHELLES
MASCARENE BASIN
MASCARENE PLAIN
MADAGASCAR
MAURITIUS
Réunion
Tropic of Capricorn
SUNDA TRENCH
JAVA TRENCH
LOMBOK BASIN
NORTH AUSTRALIA BASIN
EXMOUTH PLATEAU
Great Sandy Desert
AUSTRALIA
© Copyright by HAMMOND INCORPORATED, Maplewood, N.J.

A | B | C | D

0 300 600 900 1200 1500 MILES
0 300 600 900 1200 1500 KILOMETERS

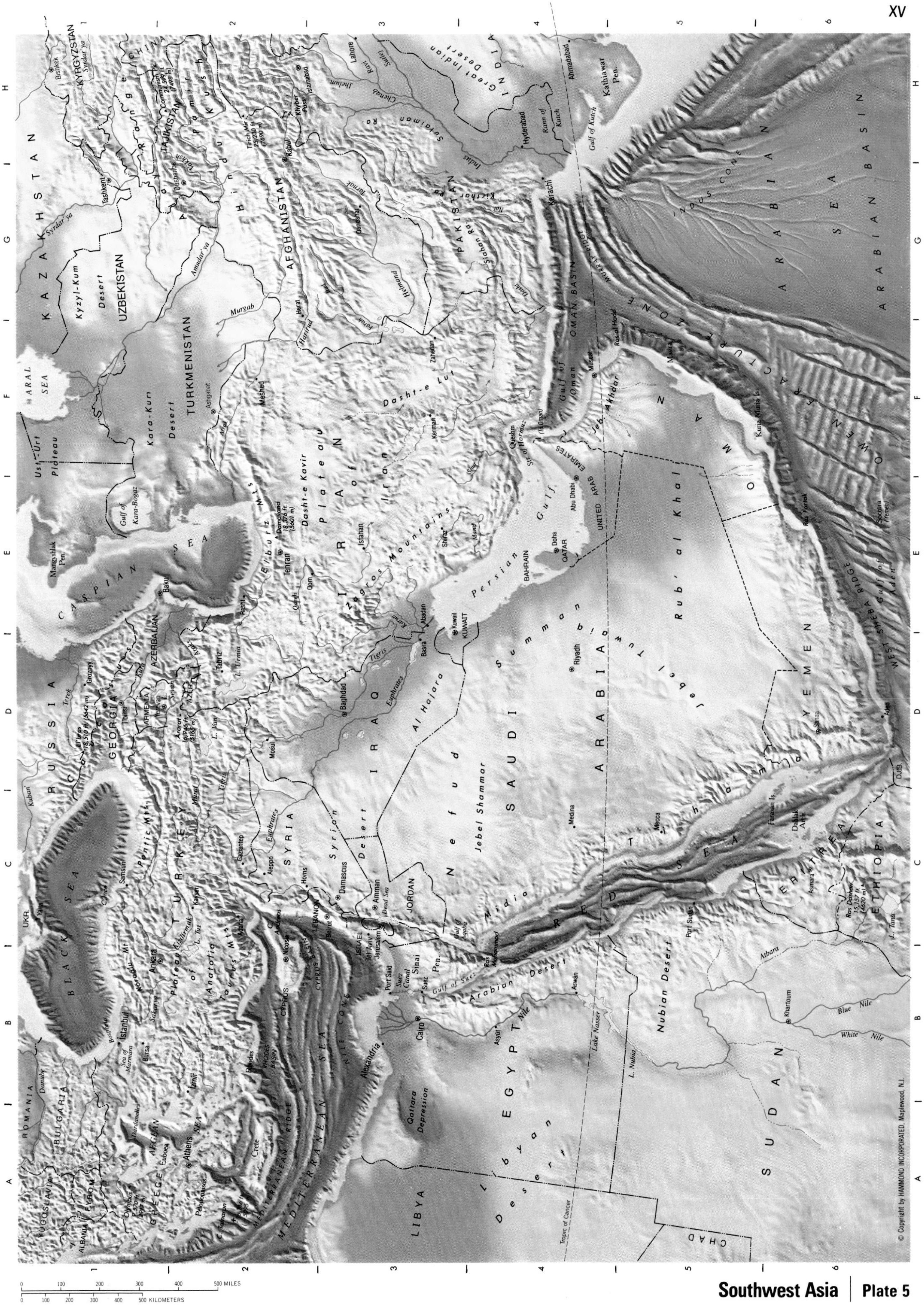
KAZAKHSTAN
UZBEKISTAN
TURKMENISTAN
KYRGYZSTAN
TAJIKISTAN
AFGHANISTAN
PAKISTAN
INDIA
IRAN
IRAQ
SYRIA
JORDAN
SAUDI ARABIA
KUWAIT
QATAR
BAHRAIN
UNITED ARAB EMIRATES
OMAN
YEMEN
ERITREA
ETHIOPIA
DJIB.
SUDAN
EGYPT
LIBYA
CHAD
TURKEY
GEORGIA
ARMENIA
AZERBAIJAN
RUSSIA
UKR.
ROMANIA
BULGARIA
GREECE
ALBANIA
CYPRUS
LEBANON
ISRAEL
CASPIAN SEA
BLACK SEA
ARAL SEA
MEDITERRANEAN SEA
AEGEAN SEA
RED SEA
ARABIAN SEA
Persian Gulf
Gulf of Oman
Gulf of Aden
Kyzyl-Kum Desert
Kara-Kum Desert
Dasht-e Kavir
Dasht-e Lut
Plateau of Iran
Zagros Mountains
Elburz Mts.
Hindu Kush
Rub' al Khali
Syrian Desert
Nefud
Arabian Desert
Nubian Desert
Libyan Desert
Qattara Depression
Great Indian Desert
Tropic of Cancer
Tehran
Baghdad
Riyadh
Mecca
Medina
Cairo
Alexandria
Damascus
Amman
Jerusalem
Beirut
Ankara
Istanbul
Athens
Baku
Tbilisi
Tashkent
Kabul
Karachi
Aden
Khartoum
Muscat
Doha
Abu Dhabi
Kuwait
Basra
Isfahan
Shiraz
Mashhad
Ashgabat
Dushanbe
Bishkek
Islamabad
Lahore
Hyderabad
Ahmadabad
Nicosia
Port Said
Suez
Aswan
Port Sudan
Asmara
San'a
Tigris
Euphrates
Nile
Blue Nile
White Nile
Indus
Amudar'ya
Syrdar'ya
INDUS CONE
OMAN BASIN
ARABIAN BASIN
NILE CONE
MEDITERRANEAN RIDGE
WEST SHEBA RIDGE
0 100 200 300 400 500 MILES
0 100 200 300 400 500 KILOMETERS

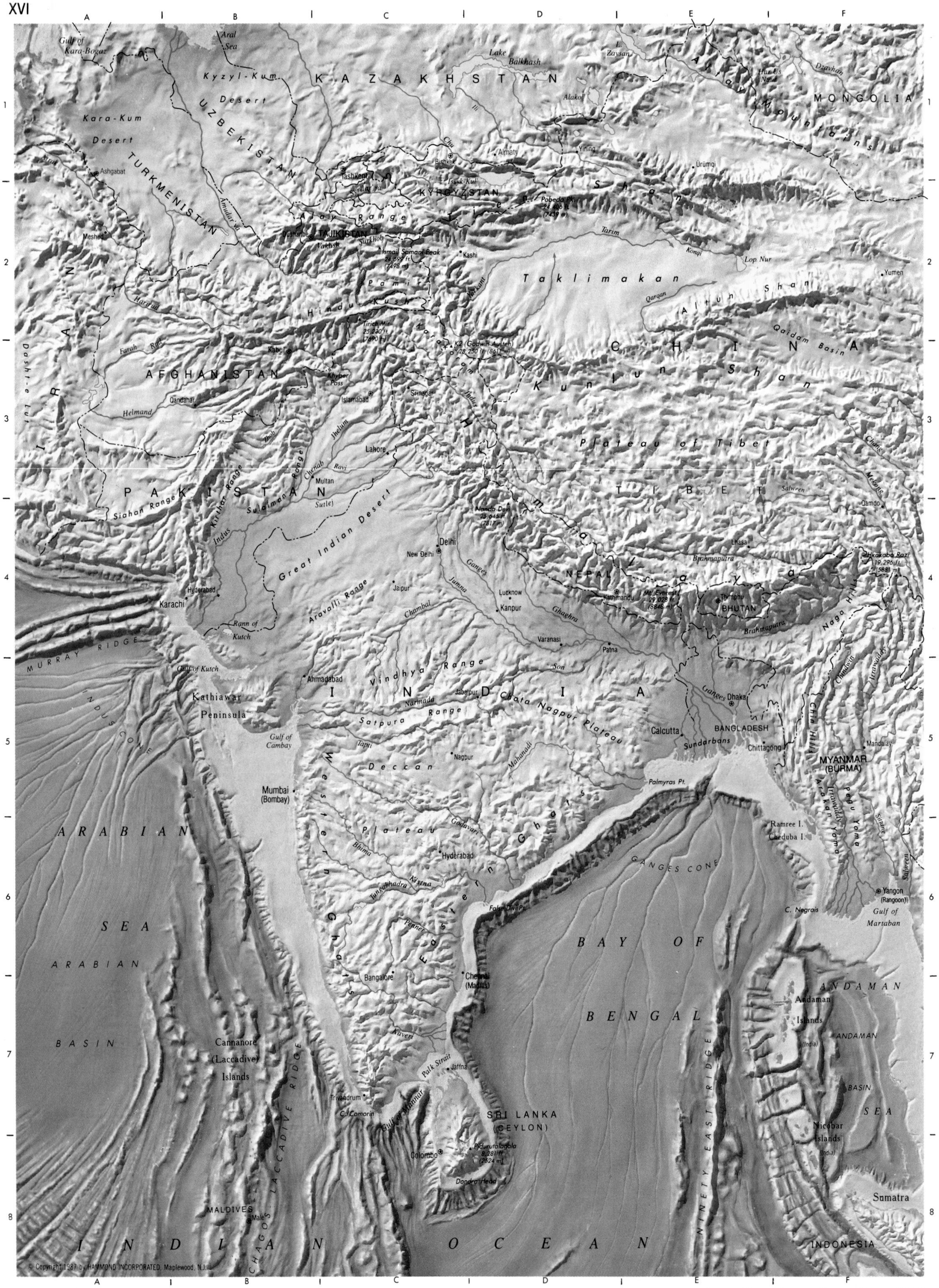

Gulf of Kara-Bogaz
Aral Sea
Kyzyl-Kum Desert
KAZAKHSTAN
Lake Balkhash
Zaysan
Alakol
MONGOLIA
Altay Mountains
Kara-Kum Desert
UZBEKISTAN
TURKMENISTAN
Ashgabat
Tashkent
Bishkek
Almaty
Yining
Ürümqi
KYRGYZSTAN
Issyk-Kul
Pobeda Pk. 24,406 ft. (7439 m)
Tian Shan
Alay Range
TAJIKISTAN
Dushanbe
Ismail Samani Peak 24,590 ft. (7495 m)
Kashi
Tarim
Konqi
Lop Nur
Yumen
Meshed
Taklimakan
Pamirs
Hindu Kush
Tirich Mir 25,230 ft. (7690 m)
Altun Shan
Qaidam Basin
CHINA
Karakoram
K2 (Godwin Austen) 28,250 ft. (8611 m)
Kabul
Khyber Pass
AFGHANISTAN
Kunlun Shan
Farah Rud
Harirud
Srinagar
Islamabad
Qandahar
Helmand
Indus
Jhelum
Plateau of Tibet
Lahore
Chenab
Ravi
Multan
PAKISTAN
Sulaiman Range
Kirthar Range
Siahan Range
Sutlej
TIBET
Salween
Mekong
Qamdo
Nanda Devi 25,645 ft. (7817 m)
Great Indian Desert
Delhi
New Delhi
Lhasa
Brahmaputra
Hkakabo Razi 19,296 ft. (5881 m)
Himalaya
NEPAL
Kathmandu
Mt. Everest 29,028 ft. (8848 m)
Thimphu
BHUTAN
Hyderabad
Karachi
Jaipur
Aravalli Range
Ganges
Jumna
Lucknow
Kanpur
Ghaghra
Chambal
Rann of Kutch
Naga Hills
MURRAY RIDGE
Varanasi
Patna
Gulf of Kutch
Ahmadabad
Vindhya Range
Son
INDIA
Kathiawar Peninsula
Jabalpur
Narmada
Chota Nagpur Plateau
Dhaka
Chindwin
Irrawaddy
INDUS CONE
Satpura Range
Calcutta
BANGLADESH
Sundarbans
Gulf of Cambay
Tapti
Chittagong
Mandalay
Nagpur
Mahanadi
MYANMAR (BURMA)
Deccan
Palmyras Pt.
Mumbai (Bombay)
Western Ghats
Eastern Ghats
Arakan Yoma
Pegu Yoma
ARABIAN
Plateau
Godavari
Ramree I.
Cheduba I.
Bhima
Hyderabad
GANGES CONE
Tungabhadra
Kistna
Yangon (Rangoon)
SEA
False Divi Pt.
C. Negrais
Gulf of Martaban
BAY OF
ARABIAN
Chennai (Madras)
Bangalore
ANDAMAN
Andaman Islands
BENGAL
BASIN
Kaveri
Cannanore (Laccadive) Islands
ANDAMAN
LACCADIVE RIDGE
Palk Strait
Jaffna
NINETY EAST RIDGE
Trivandrum
C. Comorin
Gulf of Mannar
BASIN
SRI LANKA (CEYLON)
SEA
Nicobar Islands
Colombo
Pidurutalagala 8,281 ft. (2524 m)
Dondra Head
Sumatra
MALDIVES
Male
CHAGOS
INDIAN OCEAN
INDONESIA
© Copyright 1987 by HAMMOND INCORPORATED, Maplewood, N.J.

0 100 200 300 400 500 MILES
0 100 200 300 400 500 KILOMETERS

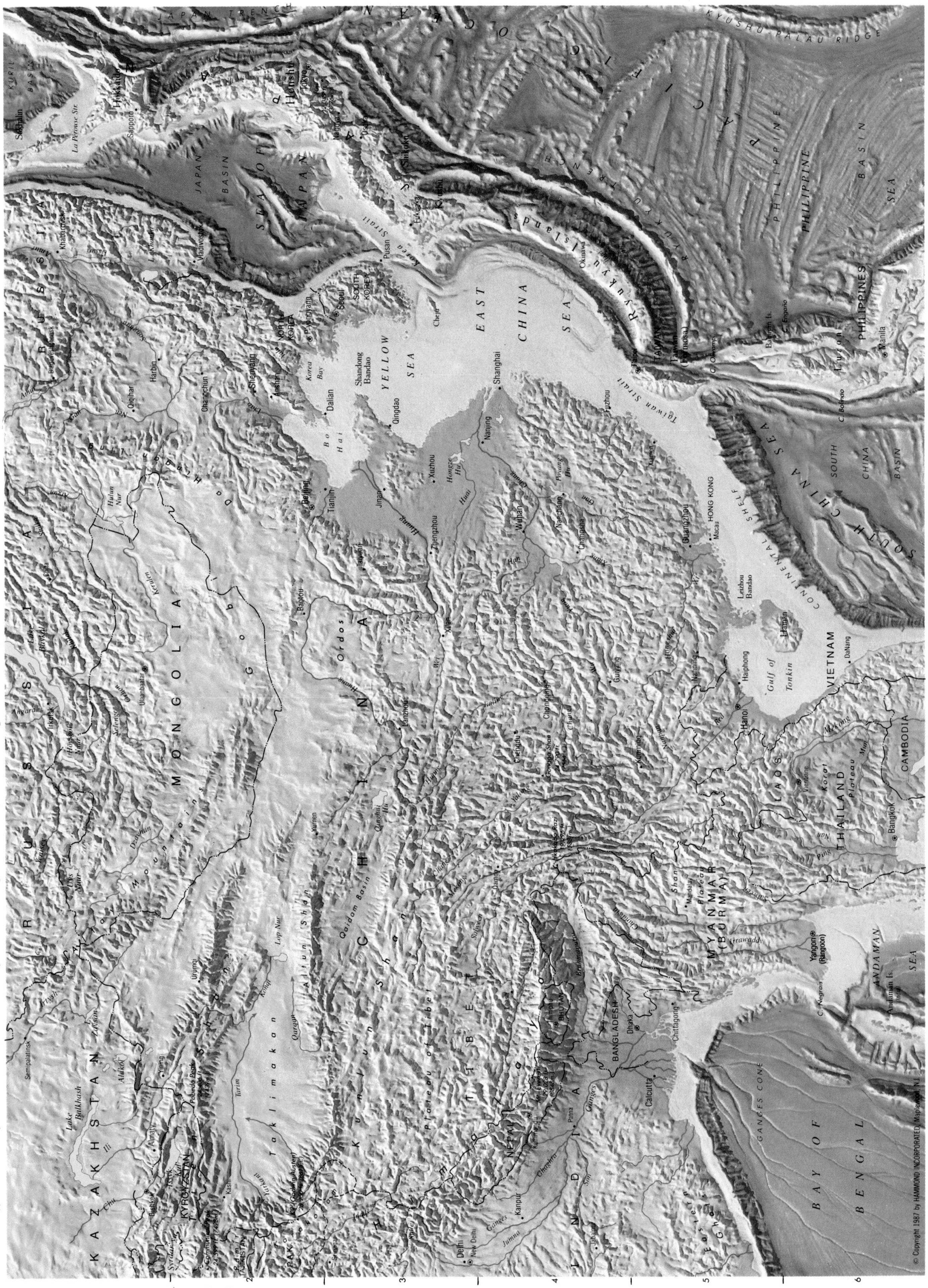

MONGOLIA
KAZAKHSTAN
KYRGYZSTAN
TIBET
NEPAL
BHUTAN
BANGLADESH
MYANMAR (BURMA)
THAILAND
LAOS
CAMBODIA
VIETNAM
PHILIPPINES
NORTH KOREA
SOUTH KOREA
HONG KONG
YELLOW SEA
EAST CHINA SEA
SOUTH CHINA SEA
SEA OF JAPAN
PHILIPPINE SEA
BAY OF BENGAL
ANDAMAN SEA
Gulf of Tonkin
Taiwan Strait
Korea Strait
Ryukyu Islands
Taklimakan
Qaidam Basin
Plateau of Tibet
Ordos
Beijing
Tianjin
Shanghai
Nanjing
Wuhan
Guangzhou
Chongqing
Chengdu
Lanzhou
Hanoi
Bangkok
Yangon (Rangoon)
Dhaka
Calcutta
Delhi
Seoul
Pyongyang
Vladivostok
Manila
© Copyright 1987 by HAMMOND INCORPORATED, Maplewood, N.J.

0 100 200 300 400 500 600 MILES
0 100 200 300 400 500 600 KILOMETERS

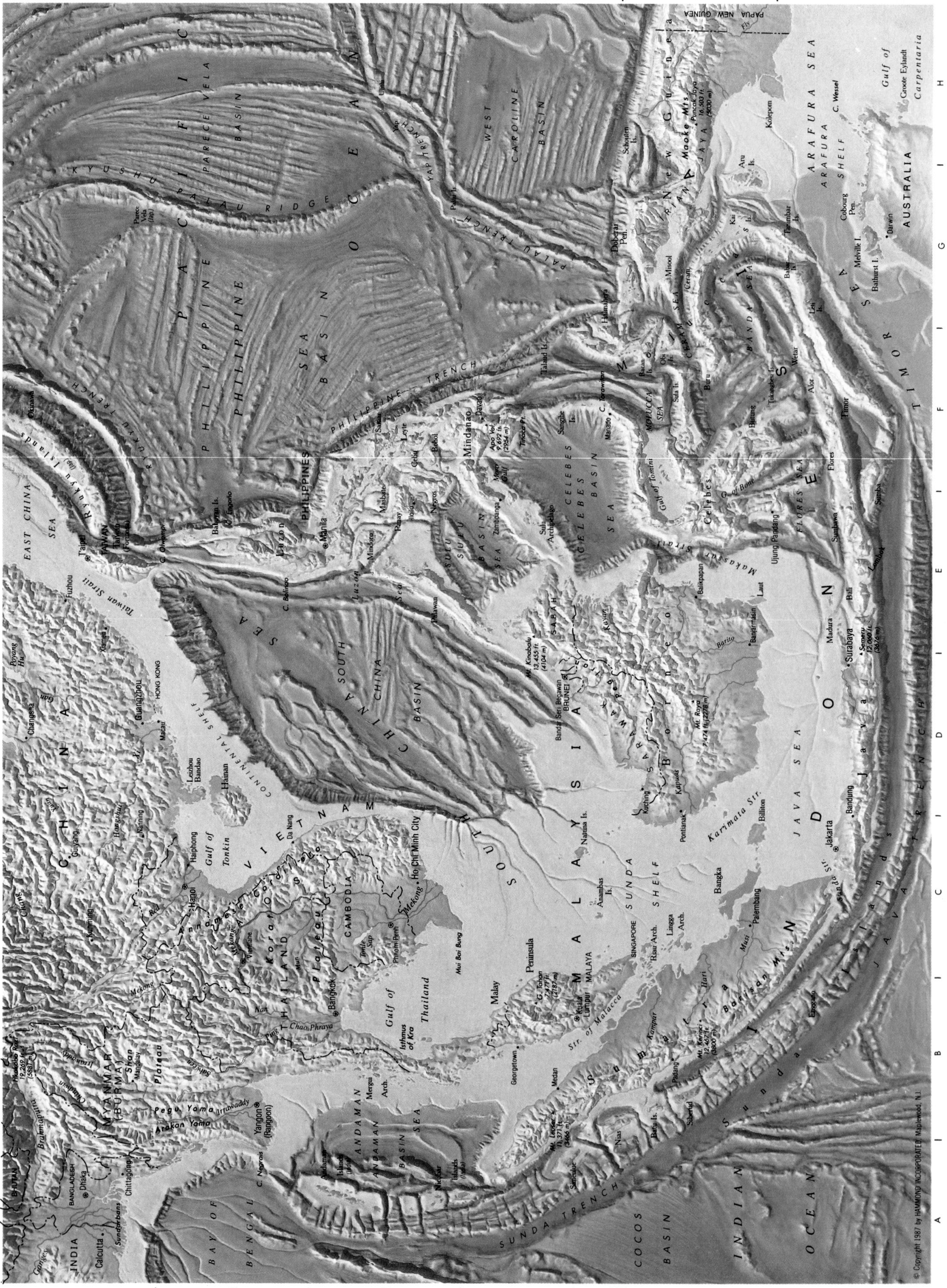
PACIFIC OCEAN
PHILIPPINE SEA
PHILIPPINE BASIN
PARECE VELA BASIN
KYUSHU PALAU RIDGE
WEST CAROLINE BASIN
PALAU TRENCH
YAP TRENCH
PHILIPPINE TRENCH
RYUKYU TRENCH
Ryukyu Islands
EAST CHINA SEA
Taiwan Strait
TAIWAN
PHILIPPINES
Luzon
Manila
Mindanao
SULU SEA
SULU BASIN
CELEBES SEA
CELEBES BASIN
Celebes
MOLUCCA SEA
CERAM SEA
BANDA SEA
FLORES SEA
ARAFURA SEA
ARAFURA SHELF
TIMOR SEA
TIMOR TRENCH
Gulf of Carpentaria
AUSTRALIA
IRIAN JAYA
New Guinea
PAPUA NEW GUINEA
Maoke Mts.
SOUTH CHINA SEA
SOUTH CHINA BASIN
CONTINENTAL SHELF
CHINA
HONG KONG
Guangzhou
Hainan
Gulf of Tonkin
VIETNAM
Hanoi
Ho Chi Minh City
CAMBODIA
Mekong
THAILAND
Bangkok
Gulf of Thailand
Khorat Plateau
Annamese Cordillera
MYANMAR (BURMA)
Shan Plateau
Yangon (Rangoon)
Irrawaddy
BANGLADESH
Dhaka
INDIA
Calcutta
BHUTAN
MALAYSIA
Malay Peninsula
Kuala Lumpur
SINGAPORE
Str. of Malacca
SABAH
SARAWAK
BRUNEI
Borneo
Makassar Strait
SUNDA SHELF
JAVA SEA
Java
Jakarta
Surabaya
Sumatra
Barisan Mts.
Sunda Str.
JAVA TRENCH
SUNDA TRENCH
INDONESIA
BAY OF BENGAL
ANDAMAN SEA
ANDAMAN BASIN
Andaman Islands (India)
Nicobar Islands (India)
COCOS BASIN
INDIAN OCEAN
© Copyright 1987 by HAMMOND INCORPORATED, Maplewood, N.J.

0 100 200 300 400 500 600 MILES
0 100 200 300 400 500 600 KILOMETERS

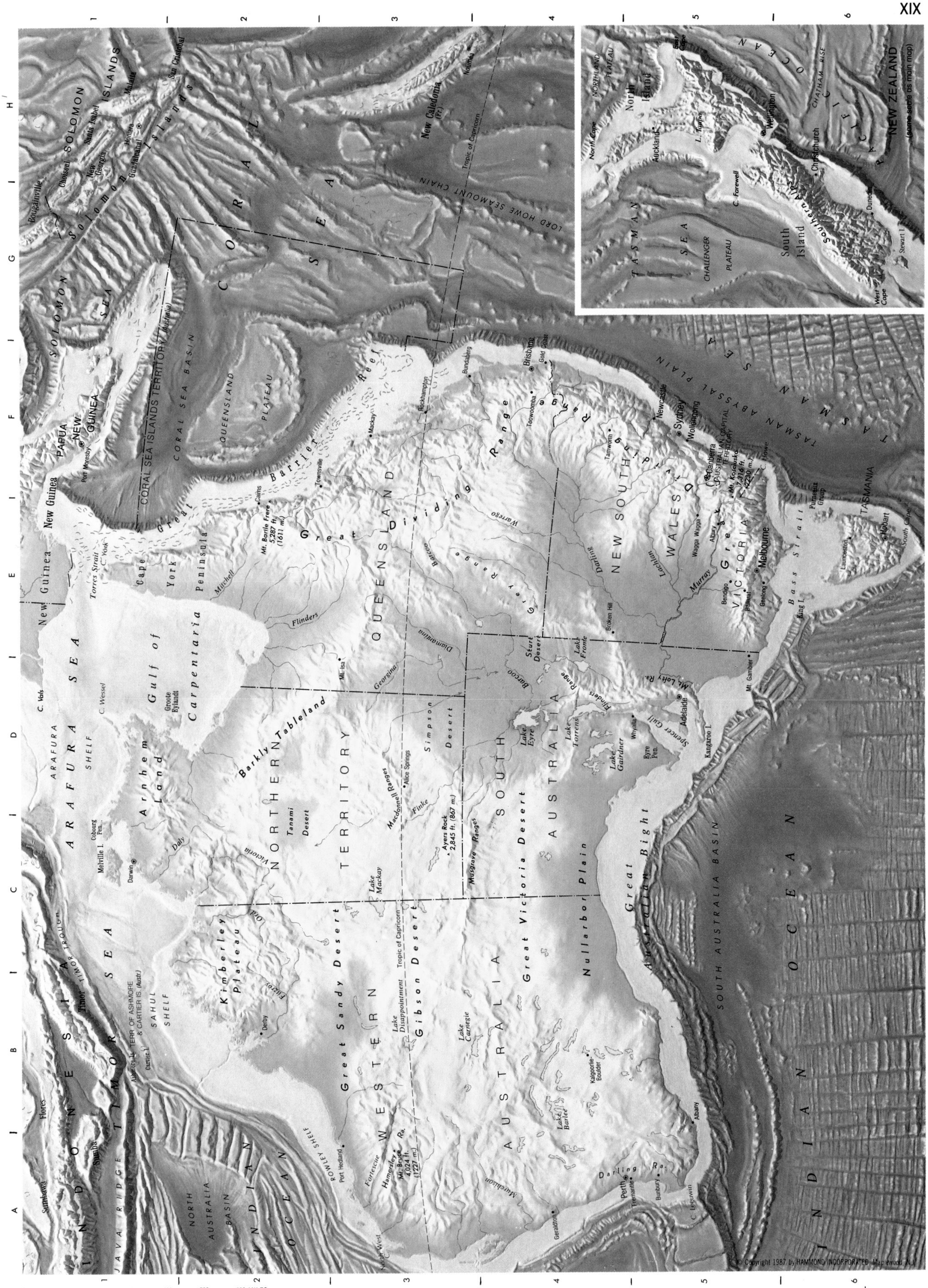

INDONESIA
TIMOR SEA
ARAFURA SEA
INDIAN OCEAN
CORAL SEA
SOLOMON SEA
TASMAN SEA
SOLOMON ISLANDS
Solomon Islands
PAPUA NEW GUINEA
New Guinea
Gulf of Carpentaria
Cape York Peninsula
Torres Strait
Great Barrier Reef
CORAL SEA ISLANDS TERRITORY (Austr.)
CORAL SEA BASIN
QUEENSLAND PLATEAU
New Caledonia (Fr.)
Nouméa
Tropic of Capricorn
LORD HOWE SEAMOUNT CHAIN
TASMAN ABYSSAL PLAIN
NORTHERN TERRITORY
QUEENSLAND
WESTERN AUSTRALIA
SOUTH AUSTRALIA
NEW SOUTH WALES
VICTORIA
TASMANIA
AUSTRALIAN CAPITAL TERRITORY
Great Dividing Range
Arnhem Land
Barkly Tableland
Tanami Desert
Great Sandy Desert
Gibson Desert
Great Victoria Desert
Simpson Desert
Sturt Desert
Nullarbor Plain
Great Australian Bight
Kimberley Plateau
Macdonnell Ranges
Musgrave Ranges
Flinders Ranges
Grey Range
Darling Ra.
Hamersley Ra.
Mt. Bruce 4,024 ft. (1227 m.)
Ayers Rock 2,845 ft. (867 m.)
Mt. Bartle Frere 5,287 ft. (1611 m.)
Mt. Kosciusko 7,316 ft. (2230 m.)
Lake Eyre
Lake Torrens
Lake Gairdner
Lake Frome
Lake Mackay
Lake Disappointment
Lake Carnegie
Lake Barlee
Darwin
Alice Springs
Port Hedland
Perth
Fremantle
Bunbury
Albany
Geraldton
Kalgoorlie-Boulder
Derby
Adelaide
Whyalla
Mt. Gambier
Melbourne
Geelong
Ballarat
Bendigo
Canberra
Sydney
Wollongong
Newcastle
Tamworth
Wagga Wagga
Albury
Broken Hill
Brisbane
Gold Coast
Toowoomba
Bundaberg
Rockhampton
Mackay
Townsville
Cairns
Mt. Isa
Port Moresby
Hobart
Launceston
Bass Strait
Spencer Gulf
Kangaroo I.
King I.
Furneaux Group
Melville I.
Groote Eylandt
SAHUL SHELF
ROWLEY SHELF
NORTH AUSTRALIA BASIN
SOUTH AUSTRALIA BASIN
TIMOR TROUGH
JAVA RIDGE
TERR. OF ASHMORE & CARTIER IS. (Austr.)
Flinders
Georgina
Diamantina
Barcoo
Darling
Murray
Lachlan
Warrego
Mitchell
Victoria
Ord
Fitzroy
Finke
Fortescue
Murchison
NEW ZEALAND (same scale as main map)
North Island
South Island
Stewart I.
Auckland
Wellington
Christchurch
Dunedin
L. Taupo
Southern Alps
NORTHLAND PLATEAU
CHALLENGER PLATEAU
CHATHAM RISE
PACIFIC OCEAN
© Copyright 1987 by HAMMOND INCORPORATED, Maplewood, N.J.

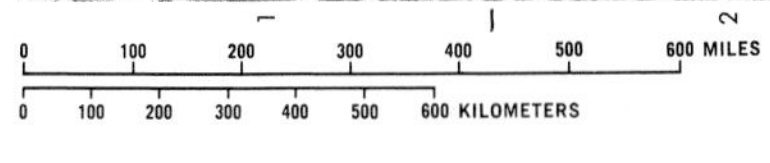

0 100 200 300 400 500 600 MILES
0 100 200 300 400 500 600 KILOMETERS

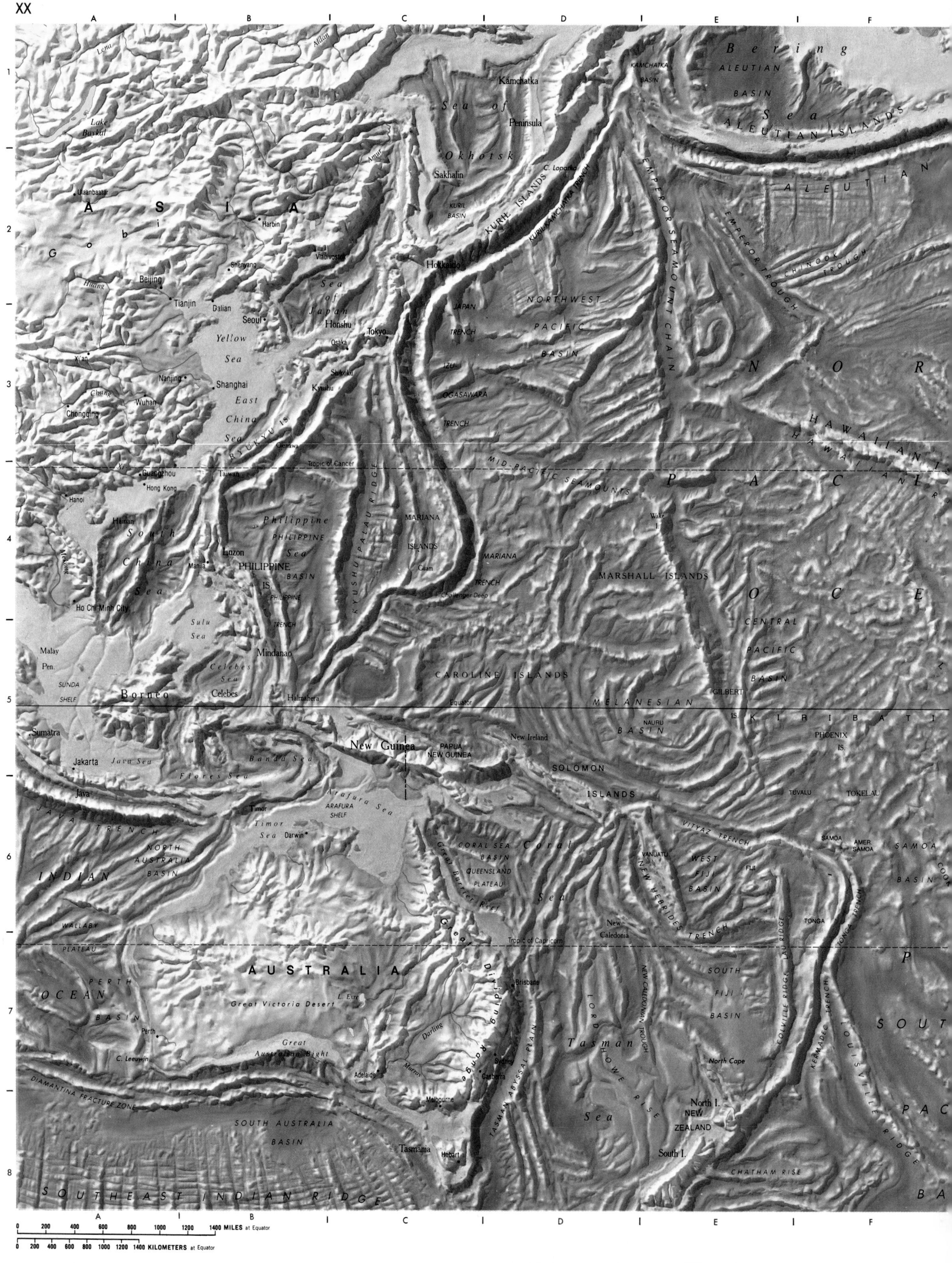
A
B
C
D
E
F
1
2
3
4
5
6
7
8
Lena
Aldan
Lake Baykal
Amur
Bering Sea
ALEUTIAN BASIN
ALEUTIAN ISLANDS
KAMCHATKA BASIN
Kamchatka Peninsula
Sea of Okhotsk
Sakhalin
KURIL BASIN
C. Lopatka
KURIL ISLANDS
KURIL-KAMCHATKA TRENCH
EMPEROR SEAMOUNT CHAIN
EMPEROR TROUGH
ALEUTIAN
CHINOOK TROUGH
Ulaanbaatar
A S I A
Gobi
Harbin
Vladivostok
Shenyang
Beijing
Tianjin
Dalian
Huang
Seoul
Sea of Japan
Hokkaido
Honshu
Tokyo
Osaka
Shikoku
Kyushu
JAPAN TRENCH
NORTHWEST PACIFIC BASIN
IZU-OGASAWARA TRENCH
Xi'an
Yellow Sea
Nanjing
Shanghai
East China Sea
Chang
Wuhan
Chongqing
RYUKYU IS.
Okinawa
Tropic of Cancer
Taiwan
Guangzhou
Hong Kong
Hanoi
Hainan
MID-PACIFIC SEAMOUNTS
N O R
P A C I
HAWAIIAN
Wake I.
South China Sea
Mekong
Philippine Sea
PHILIPPINE BASIN
KYUSHU-PALAU RIDGE
MARIANA ISLANDS
Guam
MARIANA TRENCH
Challenger Deep
Luzon
Manila
PHILIPPINE IS.
PHILIPPINE TRENCH
MARSHALL ISLANDS
O C E
Ho Chi Minh City
Sulu Sea
Mindanao
CENTRAL PACIFIC BASIN
Malay Pen.
SUNDA SHELF
Celebes Sea
Borneo
Celebes
Halmahera
CAROLINE ISLANDS
Equator
MELANESIAN BASIN
GILBERT IS.
K I R I B A T I
NAURU
Sumatra
New Guinea
PAPUA NEW GUINEA
New Ireland
PHOENIX IS.
Jakarta
Java Sea
Banda Sea
Flores Sea
SOLOMON ISLANDS
Java
Timor
Arafura Sea
ARAFURA SHELF
TUVALU
TOKELAU
JAVA TRENCH
Timor Sea
Darwin
VITYAZ TRENCH
SAMOA
AMER. SAMOA
NORTH AUSTRALIA BASIN
CORAL SEA BASIN
QUEENSLAND PLATEAU
Coral Sea
Great Barrier Reef
VANUATU
NEW HEBRIDES TRENCH
WEST FIJI BASIN
FIJI
INDIAN OCEAN
WALLABY PLATEAU
Great Dividing Range
New Caledonia
Tropic of Capricorn
TONGA
TONGA TRENCH
COLVILLE RIDGE
LAU RIDGE
AUSTRALIA
PERTH BASIN
Brisbane
L. Eyre
Great Victoria Desert
NEW CALEDONIAN TROUGH
LORD HOWE RISE
SOUTH FIJI BASIN
KERMADEC TRENCH
LOUISVILLE RIDGE
Perth
Darling
Tasman Sea
TASMAN ABYSSAL PLAIN
Great Australian Bight
C. Leeuwin
Sydney
Canberra
Murray
Adelaide
North Cape
DIAMANTINA FRACTURE ZONE
Melbourne
North I.
NEW ZEALAND
South I.
SOUTH AUSTRALIA BASIN
Tasmania
Hobart
CHATHAM RISE
SOUTHEAST INDIAN RIDGE
P
SOUT
PAC
BA
SAMOA
COOK
BASIN
0 200 400 600 800 1000 1200 1400 MILES at Equator
0 200 400 600 800 1000 1200 1400 KILOMETERS at Equator

Gulf of Alaska
Juneau
Kodiak I.
Alaska Pen.
TRENCH
Coast Mountains
Rocky Mountains
Hudson Bay
Nelson
Churchill
NORTH
AMERICA
Edmonton
Calgary
Fraser
Lake Winnipeg
S. Saskatchewan
Regina
Winnipeg
Thunder Bay
Vancouver
Seattle
Coast Ranges
Columbia
Missouri
Great Lakes
Ottawa
Montreal
St. Lawrence
Minneapolis
Mississippi
Toronto
Detroit
Boston
Chicago
New York
Snake
Salt Lake City
Platte
Appalachian Mts.
C. Mendocino
Denver
St. Louis
Ohio
Washington
MENDOCINO FRACTURE ZONE
San Francisco
Colorado
Arkansas
Tennessee
C. Hatteras
Los Angeles
Phoenix
Dallas
Atlanta
ATLANTIC
OCEAN
San Diego
Rio Grande
Red
MURRAY FRACTURE ZONE
Houston
New Orleans
Lower California
C. Canaveral
MOLOKAI FRACTURE ZONE
Gulf of Mexico
Miami
Monterrey
Tropic of Cancer
C. San Lucas
Havana
Cuba
WEST INDIES
Hawaii
Mexico City
Acapulco
MIDDLE AMERICA TRENCH
Caribbean Sea
CLARION FRACTURE ZONE
CLIPPERTON FRACTURE ZONE
Panama
GUATEMALA BASIN
PANAMA BASIN
Magdalena
Orinoco
Bogotá
COLON RIDGE
Vaupés
Equator
GALÁPAGOS ISLANDS
Guayaquil
GALÁPAGOS FRACTURE ZONE
MARQUESAS FRACTURE ZONE
Amazon
PENRHYN BASIN
SOUTH
Marañón
Pta. Aguja
Purus
MARQUESAS Is.
PERU
Andes
Ucayali
TIKI BASIN
BAUER BASIN
Lima
AMERICA
MENDAÑA FRACTURE ZONE
L. Titicaca
SOCIETY ISLANDS
Tahiti
TUAMOTU ARCH
PERU-CHILE TRENCH
Tropic of Capricorn
NAZCA RIDGE
AUSTRALIS
Pitcairn I.
CHILE BASIN
Easter I.
SALA Y GOMEZ RIDGE
ROGGEVEEN BASIN
CHALLENGER FRACTURE ZONE
Santiago
CHILE RISE
Mountains
Salado
EAST PACIFIC RISE
I. de Chiloé
PACIFIC OCEAN

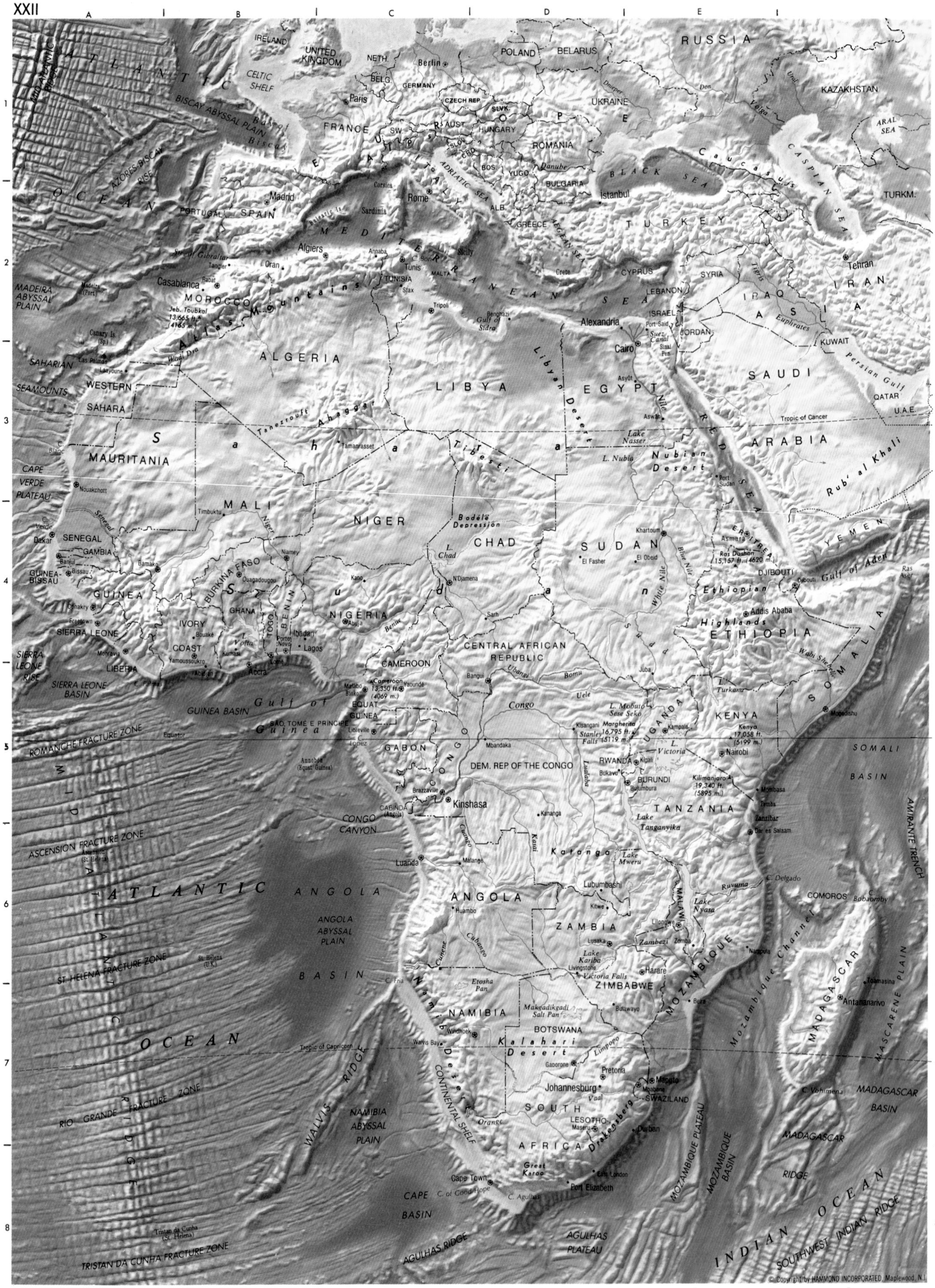
A
B
C
D
E
F
ATLANTIC
OCEAN
IRELAND
UNITED KINGDOM
CELTIC SHELF
NETH.
BELG.
Berlin
POLAND
BELARUS
RUSSIA
GERMANY
Paris
CZECH REP.
SLVK.
UKRAINE
KAZAKHSTAN
FRANCE
AUST.
HUNGARY
ARAL SEA
BISCAY ABYSSAL PLAIN
Bay of Biscay
ROMANIA
Danube
BLACK SEA
Caucasus
CASPIAN SEA
AZORES-BISCAY RISE
BOS.
YUGO.
BULGARIA
Istanbul
TURKM.
Madrid
Rome
ITALY
ADRIATIC SEA
Corsica
Sardinia
PORTUGAL
SPAIN
ALB.
GREECE
TURKEY
AEGEAN SEA
MEDITERRANEAN SEA
Algiers
Sicily
Str. of Gibraltar
Tangier
Oran
Annaba
Tunis
TUNISIA
MALTA
Crete
CYPRUS
SYRIA
IRAQ
Tehran
IRAN
MADEIRA ABYSSAL PLAIN
Madeira (Port.)
Casablanca
Rabat
MOROCCO
Sfax
Tripoli
LEBANON
ISRAEL
JORDAN
ASIA
Atlas Mountains
Jeb. Toubkal 13,665 ft. (4165 m.)
Benghazi
Gulf of Sidra
Alexandria
Port Said
Suez Canal
Sinai Pen.
Euphrates
Tigris
Canary Is. (Sp.)
Las Palmas
Cairo
KUWAIT
Persian Gulf
SAHARIAN SEAMOUNTS
Laayoune
Wadi Dra
WESTERN SAHARA
ALGERIA
LIBYA
Libyan Desert
EGYPT
Asyût
Nile
SAUDI
QATAR
U.A.E.
Tropic of Cancer
Aswân
Lake Nasser
L. Nubia
Ahaggar
Tanezrouft
Tamanrasset
Tibesti
Sahara
MAURITANIA
C. Blanc
ARABIA
RED SEA
Nubian Desert
Port Sudan
Rub' al Khali
CAPE VERDE PLATEAU
Nouakchott
MALI
Timbuktu
NIGER
Niger
Bodélé Depression
Senegal
C. Verde
Dakar
SENEGAL
GAMBIA
Banjul
GUINEA-BISSAU
Bissau
CHAD
L. Chad
SUDAN
Khartoum
El Fasher
El Obeid
Blue Nile
White Nile
ERITREA
Asmara
Ras Dashen 15,157 ft. (4620 m.)
YEMEN
Gulf of Aden
DJIBOUTI
Djibouti
Ras Asir
Bamako
Niamey
BURKINA FASO
Ouagadougou
Kano
N'Djamena
GUINEA
Conakry
Freetown
SIERRA LEONE
GHANA
TOGO
BENIN
NIGERIA
Abuja
Benue
Sarh
Ethiopian Highlands
Addis Ababa
ETHIOPIA
Sudd
IVORY COAST
Bouaké
Volta
Porto Novo
Ibadan
Lagos
Monrovia
LIBERIA
Yamoussoukro
Kumasi
Lomé
Abidjan
Accra
C. Palmas
SIERRA LEONE RISE
SIERRA LEONE BASIN
CENTRAL AFRICAN REPUBLIC
CAMEROON
Bangui
Ubangi
Bomu
Uele
Juba
Wabi Shebeli
SOMALIA
L. Turkana
Cameroon 13,350 ft. (4069 m.)
Malabo
Bioko
Yaoundé
Gulf of Guinea
GUINEA BASIN
EQUAT. GUINEA
SÃO TOMÉ E PRÍNCIPE
Congo
L. Mobutu Sese Seko
Margherita 16,795 ft. (5119 m.)
Stanley Falls
Kisangani
UGANDA
Kampala
KENYA
Kenya 17,058 ft. (5199 m.)
Mogadishu
ROMANCHE FRACTURE ZONE
Equator
Libreville
C. Lopez
GABON
Mbandaka
L. Victoria
Nairobi
SOMALI BASIN
Annobón (Equat. Guinea)
DEM. REP. OF THE CONGO
Lualaba
RWANDA
Kigali
Bukavu
BURUNDI
Bujumbura
Kilimanjaro 19,340 ft. (5895 m.)
Mombasa
Pemba
Brazzaville
Kinshasa
CABINDA (Angola)
CONGO CANYON
TANZANIA
Zanzibar
Dar es Salaam
AMIRANTE TRENCH
Kananga
ASCENSION FRACTURE ZONE
Ascension (St. Helena)
Cuango
Kasai
Lake Tanganyika
Katanga
Lake Mweru
Luanda
Malanje
C. Delgado
MID-ATLANTIC RIDGE
ATLANTIC
ANGOLA
ANGOLA ABYSSAL PLAIN
Lubumbashi
Ruvuma
Lake Nyasa
COMOROS
C. Bobaomby
Kitwe
Huambo
Lilongwe
MALAWI
Lusaka
Zambezi
Zomba
Nampula
Mozambique Channel
Cubango
Cunene
Lake Kariba
Livingstone
Victoria Falls
Harare
ZIMBABWE
Beira
MOZAMBIQUE
MADAGASCAR
Toamasina
Antananarivo
MASCARENE PLAIN
ST. HELENA FRACTURE ZONE
St. Helena (U.K.)
BASIN
C. Fria
Etosha Pan
Makgadikgadi Salt Pan
Bulawayo
NAMIBIA
BOTSWANA
Namib Desert
Windhoek
Walvis Bay
Kalahari Desert
OCEAN
Tropic of Capricorn
Limpopo
Gaborone
Pretoria
Maputo
Mbabane
SWAZILAND
Johannesburg
Vaal
WALVIS RIDGE
CONTINENTAL SHELF
RIO GRANDE FRACTURE ZONE
NAMIBIA ABYSSAL PLAIN
Orange
SOUTH AFRICA
LESOTHO
Maseru
Drakensberg
Durban
MOZAMBIQUE PLATEAU
MOZAMBIQUE BASIN
C. Vohimena
MADAGASCAR BASIN
MADAGASCAR RIDGE
Great Karoo
Cape Town
East London
Port Elizabeth
C. of Good Hope
C. Agulhas
CAPE BASIN
INDIAN OCEAN
Tristan da Cunha (St. Helena)
AGULHAS RIDGE
AGULHAS PLATEAU
SOUTHWEST INDIAN RIDGE
TRISTAN DA CUNHA FRACTURE ZONE
MILES 0 200 400 600 800 1000
KILOMETERS 0 200 400 600 800 1000

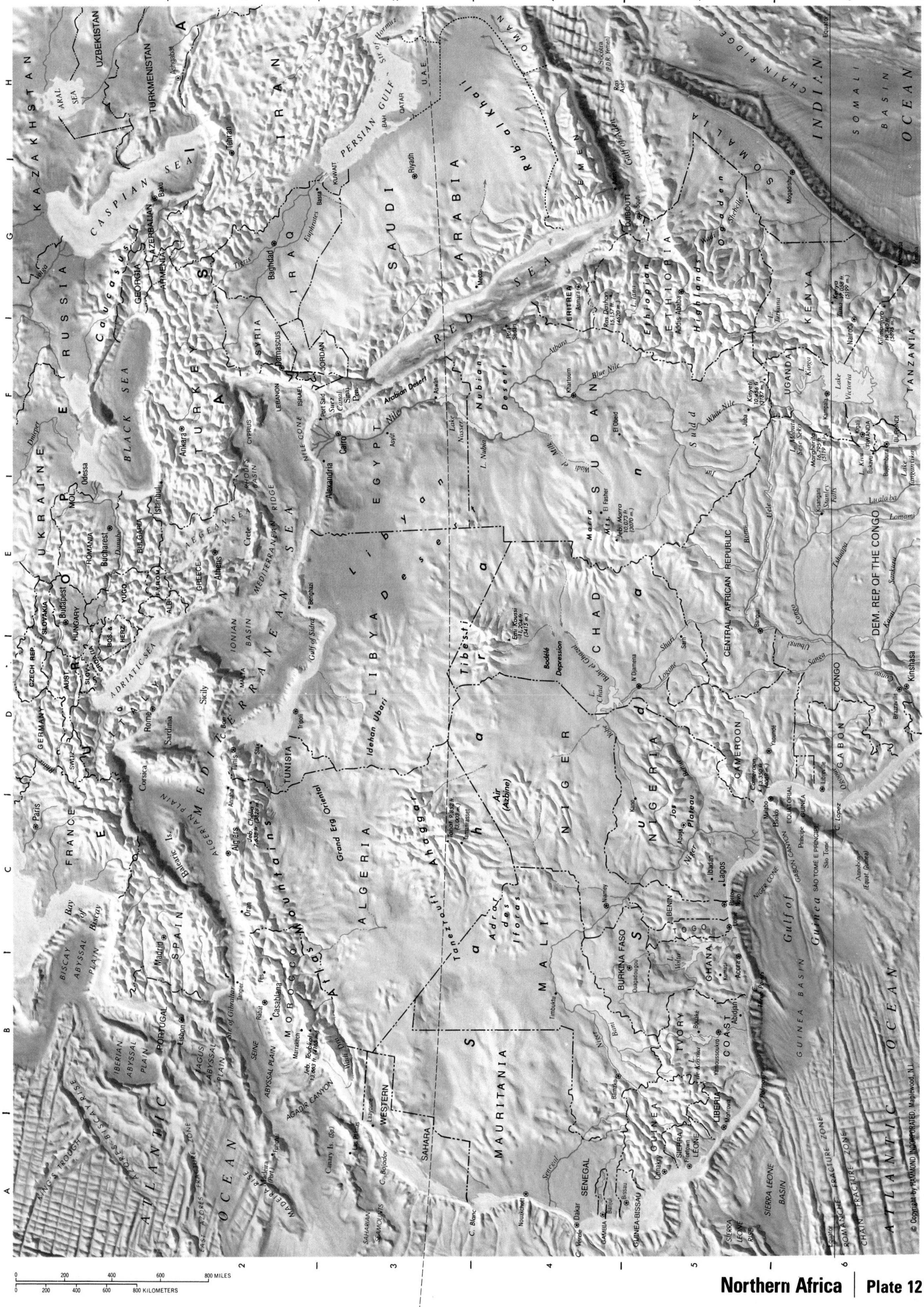

ATLANTIC OCEAN
MEDITERRANEAN SEA
BLACK SEA
CASPIAN SEA
RED SEA
PERSIAN GULF
INDIAN OCEAN
Gulf of Guinea
Gulf of Aden
Gulf of Sidra
ADRIATIC SEA
AEGEAN SEA
ARAL SEA
BISCAY ABYSSAL PLAIN
IBERIAN ABYSSAL PLAIN
SAHARA
Libyan Desert
Nubian Desert
Arabian Desert
Rub al Khali
Ahaggar
Tibesti
Grand Erg Oriental
Atlas Mountains
Ethiopian Highlands
Jos Plateau
Bodélé Depression
MOROCCO
ALGERIA
TUNISIA
LIBYA
EGYPT
SUDAN
CHAD
NIGER
MALI
MAURITANIA
WESTERN SAHARA
SENEGAL
GAMBIA
GUINEA-BISSAU
GUINEA
SIERRA LEONE
LIBERIA
IVORY COAST
GHANA
BURKINA FASO
BENIN
NIGERIA
CAMEROON
CENTRAL AFRICAN REPUBLIC
ETHIOPIA
ERITREA
DJIBOUTI
SOMALIA
KENYA
UGANDA
TANZANIA
CONGO
GABON
EQUATORIAL GUINEA
DEM. REP. OF THE CONGO
SAUDI ARABIA
YEMEN
OMAN
IRAQ
IRAN
SYRIA
JORDAN
ISRAEL
LEBANON
TURKEY
CYPRUS
KUWAIT
QATAR
U.A.E.
SPAIN
PORTUGAL
FRANCE
ITALY
GREECE
RUSSIA
UKRAINE
KAZAKHSTAN
UZBEKISTAN
TURKMENISTAN
Cairo
Alexandria
Tripoli
Tunis
Algiers
Casablanca
Rabat
Dakar
Lagos
Accra
Abidjan
Khartoum
Addis Ababa
Mogadishu
Nairobi
Kinshasa
Riyadh
Baghdad
Damascus
Tehran
Ankara
Athens
Rome
Madrid
Lisbon
Paris
© Copyright by HAMMOND INCORPORATED, Maplewood, N.J.
0 200 400 600 800 MILES
0 200 400 600 800 KILOMETERS

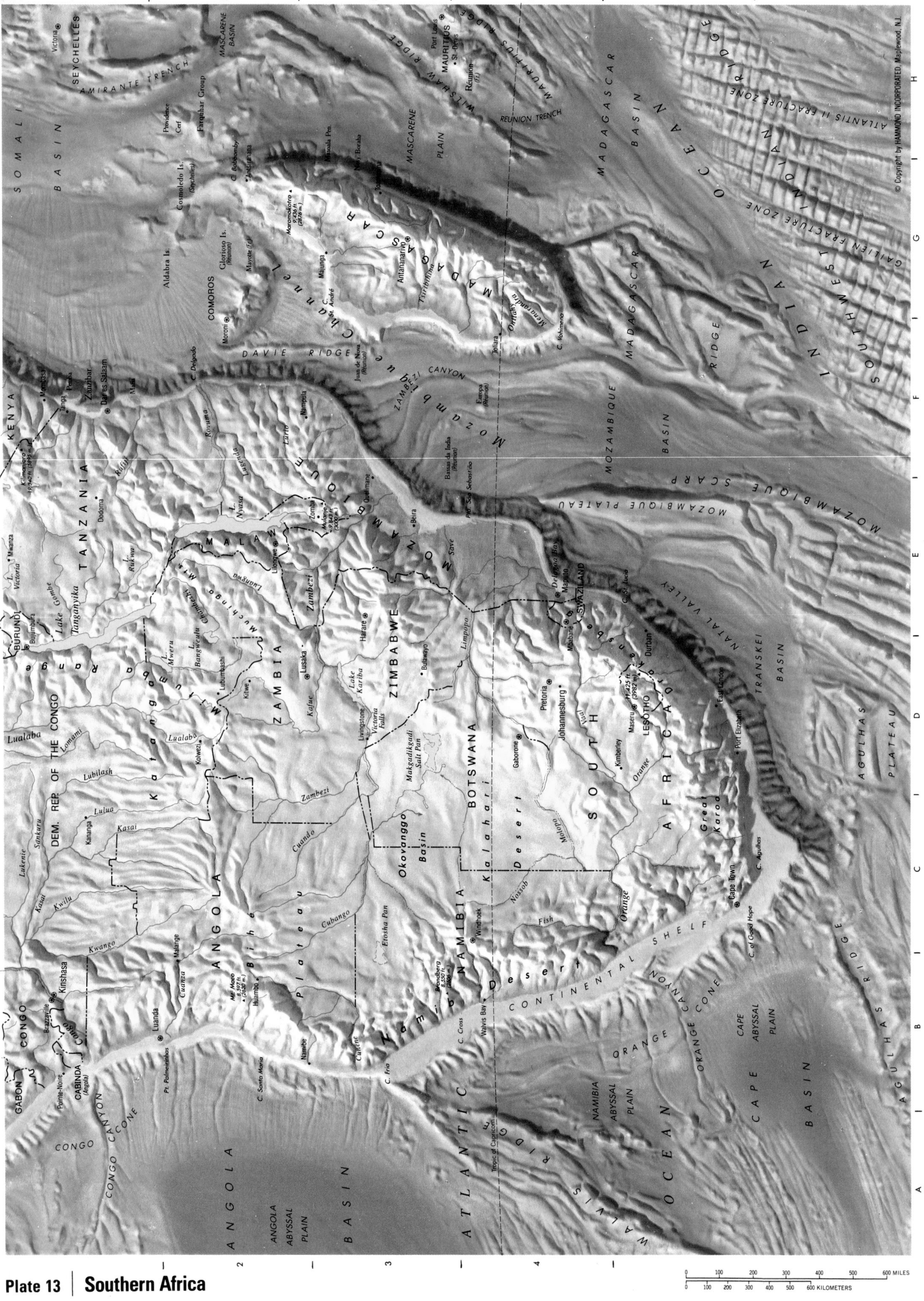
SEYCHELLES
Victoria
AMIRANTE TRENCH
MASCARENE BASIN
SOMALI BASIN
Providence
Cerf
Farquhar Group
Cosmoledo Is. (Seychelles)
Aldabra Is.
COMOROS
Glorioso Is. (Réunion)
Mayotte (Fr.)
Moroni
C. Bobaomby
Antsiranana
Masoala Pen.
Nosy Boraha
Toamasina
Maromokotro 9,436 ft. (2876 m.)
Majunga
C. St. André
Antananarivo
Tsiribihina
MADAGASCAR
Toliara
C. Vohimena
Onilahy
Mangoky
Mozambique Channel
DAVIE RIDGE
Juan de Nova (Réunion)
ZAMBEZI CANYON
Europa (Réunion)
Bassas da India (Réunion)
MASCARENE PLAIN
REUNION TRENCH
Port Louis
MAURITIUS
St-Denis
Réunion (Fr.)
WILSHAW RIDGE
MAURITIUS RIDGE
MADAGASCAR BASIN
MADAGASCAR RIDGE
MOZAMBIQUE BASIN
MOZAMBIQUE PLATEAU
MOZAMBIQUE SCARP
NATAL VALLEY
TRANSKEI BASIN
AGULHAS PLATEAU
AGULHAS RIDGE
ATLANTIS II FRACTURE ZONE
GAILLIEN FRACTURE ZONE
SOUTHWEST INDIAN RIDGE
INDIAN OCEAN
KENYA
Mombasa
Tanga
Pemba
Zanzibar
Dar es Salaam
Mafia
Kilimanjaro 19,340 ft. (5895 m.)
TANZANIA
Dodoma
Mwanza
L. Victoria
L. Rukwa
Lake Tanganyika
Gombe
BURUNDI
Bujumbura
Rufiji
Rovuma
Lugenda
Lurio
Nampula
MOZAMBIQUE
Quelimane
Zomba
Mulanje 9,843 ft. (3000 m.)
L. Nyasa
MALAWI
Lilongwe
Luangwa
Muchinga Mts.
Chambeshi
L. Mweru
L. Bangweulu
Lubumbashi
Mitumba Range
Katanga
ZAMBIA
Lusaka
Kitwe
Kafue
Zambezi
Harare
ZIMBABWE
Bulawayo
Lake Kariba
Victoria Falls
Livingstone
Beira
Save
Limpopo
Delagoa Bay
Maputo
SWAZILAND
Mbabane
C. St. Lucia
Durban
Drakensberg
11,425 ft. (3482 m.)
Maseru
LESOTHO
Pretoria
Johannesburg
Vaal
Kimberley
Orange
East London
Port Elizabeth
C. Agulhas
Cape Town
C. of Good Hope
Great Karoo
SOUTH AFRICA
Gaborone
BOTSWANA
Makgadikgadi Salt Pan
Okavango Basin
Kalahari Desert
Molopo
Nossob
Fish
NAMIBIA
Windhoek
Etosha Pan
Brandberg 8,550 ft. (2606 m.)
Walvis Bay
C. Cross
Namib Desert
Cunene
Cubango
Cuando
ANGOLA
Bihe Plateau
Mt. Moco 8,597 ft. (2620 m.)
Huambo
Malange
Luanda
Cuanza
Namibe
Kwango
Kasai
Kwilu
Lukenie
Sankuru
Lulua
Kananga
Lubilash
Lomami
Lualaba
Kolwezi
DEM. REP. OF THE CONGO
Kinshasa
Brazzaville
CONGO
GABON
Pointe-Noire
CABINDA (Angola)
Congo
CONGO CANYON
CONGO CONE
Pt. Palmeirinhas
C. Santa Maria
C. Fria
Tropic of Capricorn
ANGOLA BASIN
ANGOLA ABYSSAL PLAIN
WALVIS RIDGE
NAMIBIA ABYSSAL PLAIN
ATLANTIC OCEAN
CONTINENTAL SHELF
ORANGE CONE
ORANGE CANYON
CAPE BASIN
CAPE ABYSSAL PLAIN
0 100 200 300 400 500 600 MILES
0 100 200 300 400 500 600 KILOMETERS

CARIBBEAN SEA
COLOMBIA BASIN
VENEZUELA BASIN
NICARAGUA
COSTA RICA
Panama Canal
G. of Venezuela
Pta. Gallinas
ARUBA (Neth.)
NETH. ANTILLES
Curaçao
Bonaire
Willemstad
GRENADA
ST. LUCIA
BARBADOS
West Indies
Tobago
TRINIDAD & TOBAGO
Port of Spain
Trinidad
Barranquilla
Maracaibo
L. Maracaibo
Caracas
Pico Bolívar 16,427 ft. (5007 m.)
Ciudad Guayana
Orinoco
VENEZUELA
Guri Res.
Bucaramanga
Medellín
Bogotá
PANAMA
Gulf of Panamá
Malpelo I. (Col.)
Cali
COLOMBIA
Magdalena
Cauca
Meta
Arauca
Guiana Highlands
Angel Fall
Mt. Roraima 9,094 ft. (2772 m.)
GUYANA
Georgetown
Paramaribo
SURINAME
FRENCH GUIANA
Cayenne
DEMERARA ABYSSAL PLAIN
GUIANA PLATEAU
CONTINENTAL SHELF
AMAZON CANYONS
MID-ATLANTIC RIDGE
ATLANTIC OCEAN
PARA ABYSSAL PLAIN
CEARA ABYSSAL PLAIN
Pico da Neblina 9,889 ft. (3014 m.)
Vaupés
Caquetá
Putumayo
Quito
Chimborazo 20,561 ft. (6267 m.)
ECUADOR
Guayaquil
Gulf of Guayaquil
Equator
Japurá
Negro
Içá
Iquitos
Amazon
Manaus
I. de Marajó
B. de Marajó
Belém
São Luís
Rep. de Tucuruí
Tocantins
Xingu
Tapajós
Selvas
Javari
Juruá
Purus
Madeira
Aripuanã
Teles Pires
Fortaleza
Teresina
Cabo de São Roque
Parnaíba
Caatingas
Recife
Maceió
Rep. de Sobradinho
Araguaia
Juruena
BRAZIL
Planalto de Mato Grosso
Brazilian Highlands
Salvador
Paraguaçu
Brasília
Goiânia
São Francisco
Jequitinhonha
Ucayali
Marañón
Trujillo
Huascarán 22,205 ft. (6768 m.)
PERU
Callao
Lima
Cusco
Andes
Beni
Mamoré
Guaporé
BOLIVIA
Lake Titicaca
Nev. Ancohuma 21,489 ft. (6550 m.)
La Paz
Arequipa
Cochabamba
L. Poopó
Sucre
Arica
Grande
Chaco
Paraguai
Campo Grande
Paraná
Belo Horizonte
Pico da Bandeira 9,482 ft. (2890 m.)
Grande
Tietê
Paraíba
Cabo São Tomé
C. Frio
Rio de Janeiro
São Paulo
Santos
PARAGUAY
Tropic of Capricorn
Antofagasta
Atacama Desert
Pilcomayo
Bermejo
Asunción
Itaipu Res.
Curitiba
Iguaçu
Serra do Mar
Vol. Llullaillaco 22,057 ft. (6723 m.)
San Miguel de Tucumán
Nev. Ojos del Salado 22,572 ft. (6880 m.)
Salado del Norte
Gran Chaco
PERU BASIN
NAZCA RIDGE
PERU-CHILE TRENCH
PACIFIC OCEAN
CHILE BASIN
I. de San Félix (Chile)
I. San Ambrosio (Chile)
CHILE
Uruguay
I. de Santa Catarina
SANTOS PLATEAU
Porto Alegre
Lagoa dos Patos
Lagoa Mirim
RIO GRANDE PLATEAU
Córdoba
Santa Fe
Rosario
Negro
URUGUAY
Cerro Aconcagua 22,831 ft. (6959 m.)
Valparaíso
Mendoza
Santiago
Buenos Aires
La Plata
Montevideo
Río de la Plata
C. San Antonio
Salado
Pampas
ARGENTINA
I. Robinson Crusoe
I. Alejandro Selkirk
Juan Fernández Is. (Chile)
CHALLENGER FRACTURE ZONE
Concepción
Colorado
Bahía Blanca
Negro
Limay
Golfo San Matías
Pen. Valdés
Puerto Montt
Isla de Chiloé
CHILE RISE
Chubut
Archipiélago de los Chonos
Golfo San Jorge
C. Tres Puntas
Pen. Taitao
Deseado
G. de Penas
Patagonia
ARGENTINE BASIN
FALKLAND ESCARPMENT
FALKLAND PLATEAU
FALKLAND RIDGE
Falkland Islands (U.K.)
Stanley
GEORGIA BASIN
Bahía Grande
Archipiélago Reina Adelaida
Str. of Magellan
Tierra del Fuego
Punta Arenas
MORNINGTON ABYSSAL PLAIN
NORTH SCOTIA RIDGE
South Georgia (U.K.)
Cape Horn
DRAKE PASSAGE
SCOTIA SEA
BRAZIL BASIN
A B C D E F
1 2 3 4 5 6 7 8
0 200 400 600 800 MILES
0 200 400 600 800 KILOMETERS

ATLANTIC OCEAN
CARIBBEAN SEA
PACIFIC OCEAN
COLOMBIA
VENEZUELA
GUYANA
SURINAME
FRENCH GUIANA
ECUADOR
PERU
BRAZIL
BOLIVIA
PARAGUAY
CHILE
ARGENTINA
PANAMA
COSTA RICA
NICARAGUA
WEST INDIES
TRINIDAD AND TOBAGO
BARBADOS
GRENADA
ST. VINCENT & GRENS.
ST. LUCIA
DOMINICA
NETH. ANTILLES
ARUBA (Neth.)
Amazon
Negro
Madeira
Tapajós
Xingu
Tocantins
Araguaia
São Francisco
Orinoco
Bogotá
Caracas
Quito
Lima
La Paz
Manaus
Belém
Brasília
Georgetown
Paramaribo
Cayenne
Fortaleza
Recife
Salvador
Belo Horizonte
Goiânia
Campo Grande
Santa Cruz
Sucre
Arica
Guayaquil
Iquitos
Medellín
Cali
Barranquilla
Cartagena
Maracaibo
AMAZON CANYONS
DEMERARA ABYSSAL PLAIN
CEARA ABYSSAL PLAIN
PARA ABYSSAL PLAIN
GUIANA PLATEAU
CONTINENTAL SHELF
PANAMA BASIN
PERU BASIN
NAZCA RIDGE
CARNEGIE RIDGE
Equator
© Copyright 1987 by HAMMOND INCORPORATED, Maplewood, N.J.

0 100 200 300 400 500 600 MILES
0 100 200 300 400 500 600 KILOMETERS

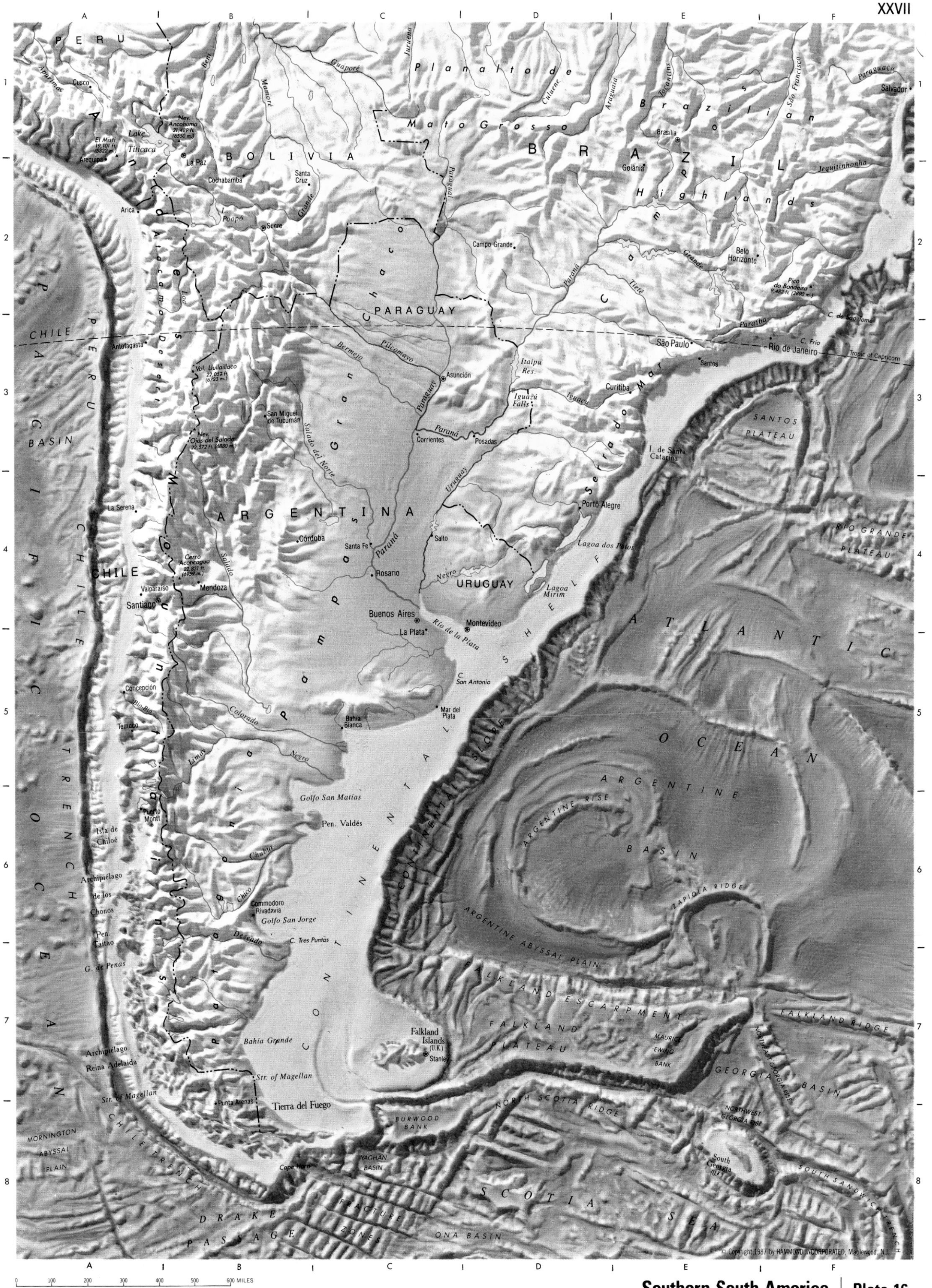
PERU
Apurímac
Cusco
Beni
Arequipa
El Misti 19,101 ft. (5822 m.)
Lake Titicaca
Nev. Ancohuma 21,489 ft. (6550 m.)
La Paz
BOLIVIA
Cochabamba
Santa Cruz
Grande
Sucre
L. Poopó
Arica
Mamoré
Guaporé
Juruena
Planalto de Mato Grosso
Culuene
Araguaia
Tocantins
São Francisco
Paraguaçu
Salvador
Brasília
BRAZIL
Brazilian Highlands
Goiânia
Jequitinhonha
Paraguai
Campo Grande
Belo Horizonte
Pico da Bandeira 9,482 ft. (2890 m.)
Grande
Paraná
Tietê
Paraíba
C. de São Tomé
C. Frio
São Paulo
Rio de Janeiro
Santos
Tropic of Capricorn
Andes
Desierto de Atacama
Loa
Gran Chaco
PARAGUAY
CHILE
Antofagasta
Bermejo
Pilcomayo
Asunción
Itaipu Res.
Iguaçu Falls
Iguaçu
Curitiba
Serra do Mar
Vol. Llullaillaco 22,057 ft. (6723 m.)
San Miguel de Tucumán
Nev. Ojos del Salado 22,572 ft. (6880 m.)
Salado del Norte
Paraná
Corrientes
Posadas
I. de Santa Catarina
Uruguay
Porto Alegre
La Serena
ARGENTINA
Córdoba
Santa Fe
Salto
Lagoa dos Patos
Cerro Aconcagua 22,831 ft. (6959 m.)
Salado
Rosario
Negro
URUGUAY
Lagoa Mirim
Valparaíso
Santiago
Mendoza
Pampas
Buenos Aires
Montevideo
La Plata
Río de la Plata
C. San Antonio
Concepción
Bío-Bío
Temuco
Colorado
Mar del Plata
Bahía Blanca
Limay
Negro
Patagonia
Golfo San Matías
Pen. Valdés
Puerto Montt
Isla de Chiloé
Chubut
Archipiélago de los Chonos
Chico
Commodoro Rivadavia
Golfo San Jorge
Pen. Taitao
Deseado
C. Tres Puntas
G. de Penas
Bahía Grande
Falkland Islands (U.K.)
Stanley
Archipiélago Reina Adelaida
Str. of Magellan
Punta Arenas
Tierra del Fuego
Cape Horn
PERU-CHILE TRENCH
PERU BASIN
PACIFIC OCEAN
CONTINENTAL SHELF
CONTINENTAL SLOPE
SANTOS PLATEAU
RIO GRANDE PLATEAU
ATLANTIC OCEAN
ARGENTINE BASIN
ARGENTINE RISE
ZAPIOLA RIDGE
ARGENTINE ABYSSAL PLAIN
FALKLAND ESCARPMENT
FALKLAND PLATEAU
MAURICE EWING BANK
FALKLAND RIDGE
NORTHEAST GEORGIA RISE
GEORGIA BASIN
NORTH SCOTIA RIDGE
BURWOOD BANK
NORTHWEST GEORGIA RISE
South Georgia (U.K.)
SOUTH SANDWICH TRENCH
MORNINGTON ABYSSAL PLAIN
CHILE TRENCH
YAGHAN BASIN
SCOTIA SEA
FRACTURE ZONES
ONA BASIN
DRAKE PASSAGE

0 100 200 300 400 500 600 MILES
0 100 200 300 400 500 600 KILOMETERS

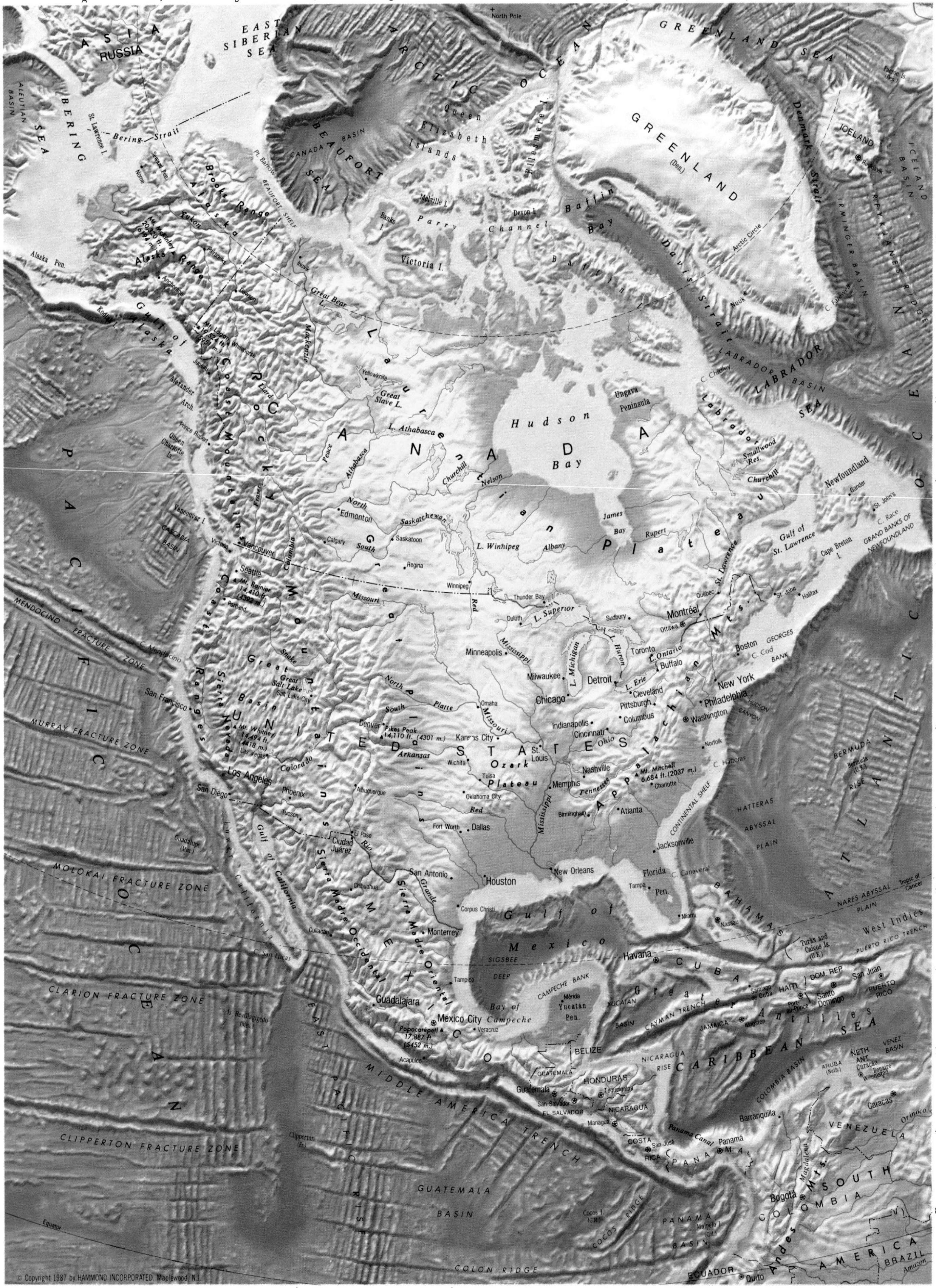
ASIA
RUSSIA
EAST SIBERIAN SEA
ARCTIC OCEAN
GREENLAND SEA
GREENLAND (Den.)
ICELAND
BERING SEA
Bering Strait
BEAUFORT SEA
Queen Elizabeth Islands
Parry Channel
Baffin Bay
Davis Strait
Denmark Strait
Victoria I.
Brooks Range
Alaska Range
Gulf of Alaska
LABRADOR SEA
Hudson Bay
CANADA
Laurentian Plateau
Great Slave L.
L. Athabasca
L. Winnipeg
Newfoundland
Gulf of St. Lawrence
PACIFIC OCEAN
MENDOCINO FRACTURE ZONE
MURRAY FRACTURE ZONE
MOLOKAI FRACTURE ZONE
CLARION FRACTURE ZONE
CLIPPERTON FRACTURE ZONE
Rocky Mountains
Coast Ranges
Sierra Nevada
Great Basin
Great Plains
UNITED STATES
Ozark Plateau
Appalachian Mts.
ATLANTIC OCEAN
HATTERAS ABYSSAL PLAIN
Gulf of Mexico
Sierra Madre Occidental
Sierra Madre Oriental
MEXICO
CUBA
Greater Antilles
CARIBBEAN SEA
West Indies
MIDDLE AMERICA TRENCH
EAST PACIFIC RISE
GUATEMALA BASIN
PANAMA BASIN
COLON RIDGE
SOUTH AMERICA
COLOMBIA
VENEZUELA
BRAZIL
ECUADOR
0 200 400 600 800 1000 MILES
0 200 400 600 800 1000 KILOMETERS

GREENLAND
(Denmark)
ICELAND
Reykjavík
DENMARK STRAIT
IRMINGER BASIN
REYKJANES
C. Farewell
Nuuk
Arctic Circle
BAFFIN BAY
DAVIS STRAIT
LABRADOR SEA
LABRADOR BASIN
OCEAN
ATLANTIC
Baffin Island
Bylot I.
Devon I.
Ellesmere Island
Axel Heiberg I.
C. Columbia
QUEEN ELIZABETH ISLANDS
Ellef Ringnes I.
N. Mag. Pole
Bathurst I.
Melville I.
Prince Patrick I.
Banks Island
Victoria Island
Parry Channel
M'Clintock Chan.
Pr. of Wales I.
Somerset I.
Boothia Pen.
Gulf of Boothia
Brodeur Pen.
Melville Pen.
Southampton I.
Coats I.
Mansel I.
Foxe Basin
Foxe Pen.
Pt. Charles I.
Cumberland Pen.
Cumberland Sd.
Iqaluit
Hudson Strait
Ungava Bay
Ungava Peninsula
C. Chidley
HUDSON BAY
Belcher Is.
James Bay
Akimiski I.
Rankin Inlet
Churchill
Cambridge Bay
Amundsen Gulf
ARCTIC OCEAN
CANADA BASIN
NORTHWIND RIDGE
BEAUFORT SEA
BEAUFORT SHELF
CHUKCHI SEA
Bering Strait
RUSSIA
Nome
Pt. Barrow
Brooks Range
UNITED STATES
ALASKA
Fairbanks
Tanana
Yukon
Alaska Range
Anchorage
Gulf of Alaska
Mt. Logan
Whitehorse
Dawson
Juneau
YUKON TERRITORY
BRITISH COLUMBIA
NORTHWEST TERRITORIES
NUNAVUT
ALBERTA
SASKATCHEWAN
MANITOBA
Inuvik
Mackenzie
Great Bear Lake
Great Slave Lake
Yellowknife
Coppermine
Back
Dubawnt
Kazan
L. Athabasca
Athabasca
Peace
Liard
Ft. Nelson
Reindeer L.
So. Indian L.
Nelson
Churchill
Lake Winnipeg
L. Manitoba
Winnipeg
Brandon
Regina
Saskatoon
Prince Albert
Saskatchewan
N. Sask.
S. Sask.
Swift Current
Edmonton
Calgary
Lethbridge
Bow
Laurentian Plateau
Rocky Mountains
Coast Mts.
Prince George
Prince Rupert
Kamloops
Columbia
Fraser
Vancouver
Vancouver I.
Victoria
Seattle
Portland
C. Flattery
Queen Charlotte Is.
Queen Charlotte Sd.
Alexander Archipelago
CASCADIA BASIN
PACIFIC OCEAN
C. Mendocino
Coast Ranges
Great Salt Lake
Snake
Missouri
Yellowstone
Mississippi
Minneapolis
Red
L. of the Woods
Thunder Bay
L. Nipigon
Lake Superior
Sault Ste. Marie
Lake Michigan
Milwaukee
Chicago
Lake Huron
Georgian Bay
Sudbury
Timmins
Abitibi
Albany
Severn
Detroit
Windsor
L. Erie
Cleveland
Hamilton
Toronto
L. Ontario
Niagara Falls
Pittsburgh
Philadelphia
New York
Boston
C. Cod
Ottawa
Montreal
Quebec
St. Lawrence
Hudson
Rouyn
QUEBEC
ONTARIO
L. Mistassini
L. St. Jean
Rupert
La Grande
Peribonca
Caniapiscau
Smallwood Res.
Churchill
Goose Bay
Labrador
NEWFOUNDLAND
Sept-Îles
Île d'Anticosti
Gulf of St. Lawrence
Gaspé Pen.
NEW BR.
Fredericton
Saint John
Bay of Fundy
P.E.I.
Charlottetown
NOVA SCOTIA
Halifax
C. Sable
Cape Breton I.
Newfoundland
St. John's
C. Race
GRAND BANKS OF NEWFOUNDLAND
SCOTIAN SHELF
CONTINENTAL SHELF
UNITED STATES
© Copyright 1987 by HAMMOND INCORPORATED Maplewood, N.J.
0 100 200 300 400 500 600 MILES
0 100 200 300 400 500 600 KILOMETERS

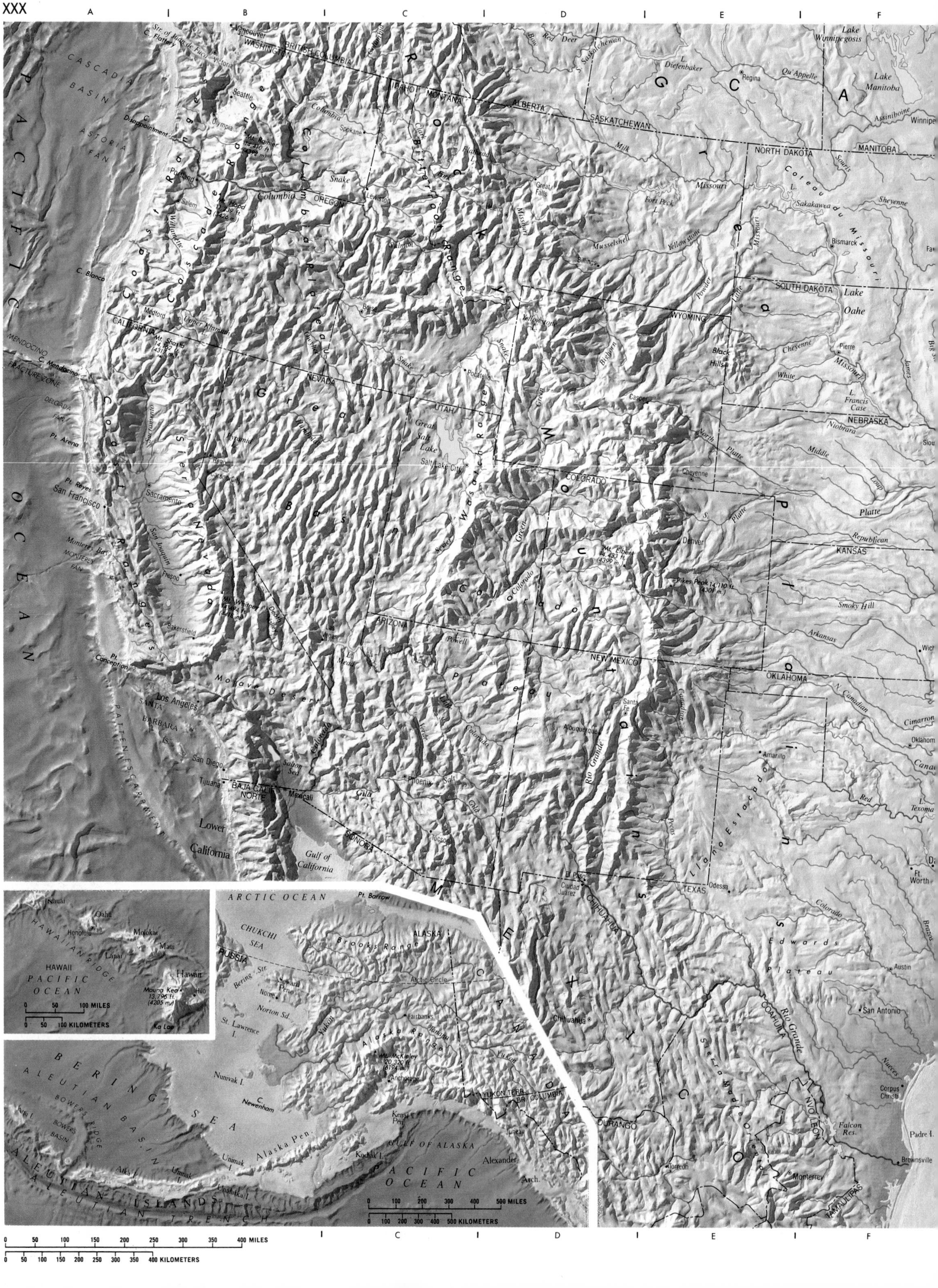

A B C D E F
1 2 3 4 5 6 7 8
PACIFIC OCEAN
CASCADIA BASIN
ASTORIA FAN
Str. of Juan de Fuca
C. Flattery
Vancouver
Victoria
BRITISH COLUMBIA
WASHINGTON
Seattle
Olympia
C. Disappointment
Mt. Rainier 14,410 ft. (4392 m.)
Portland
Salem
Mt. Hood 11,239 ft. (3426 m.)
Willamette
Columbia
Snake
Spokane
Lewiston
OREGON
IDAHO
MONTANA
ALBERTA
SASKATCHEWAN
MANITOBA
NORTH DAKOTA
SOUTH DAKOTA
WYOMING
NEBRASKA
COLORADO
KANSAS
OKLAHOMA
NEW MEXICO
TEXAS
ARIZONA
UTAH
NEVADA
CALIFORNIA
Bow
Red Deer
S. Saskatchewan
L. Diefenbaker
Regina
Qu'Appelle
Lake Winnipegosis
Lake Manitoba
Assiniboine
Winnipeg
Souris
Milk
Missouri
Fort Peck L.
Great Falls
Helena
Musselshell
Yellowstone
Billings
Powder
Little Missouri
Coteau du Missouri
L. Sakakawea
Sheyenne
Bismarck
Lake Oahe
Cheyenne
Pierre
White
Black Hills
L. Francis Case
Niobrara
James
Rocky
Columbia Plateau
Bitterroot Range
Clark Fork
Flathead L.
Salmon
Boise
Snake River Plain
C. Blanco
Medford
Upper Klamath L.
Mt. Shasta 14,162 ft. (4317 m.)
MENDOCINO FRACTURE ZONE
C. Mendocino
DELGADA FAN
Pt. Arena
Pt. Reyes
San Francisco
Sacramento
San Joaquin
Monterey Bay
MONTEREY FAN
Fresno
Bakersfield
Coast Ranges
Sierra Nevada
Cascade Range
Great Basin
Pyramid L.
Reno
Carson City
Humboldt
Great Salt Lake
Salt Lake City
Wasatch Range
Pocatello
Yellowstone L.
Green
Bighorn
Casper
North Platte
Cheyenne
Sevier
Mt. Whitney 14,494 ft. (4418 m.)
Death Valley
Las Vegas
L. Mead
Powell
Colorado Plateau
Mt. Elbert 14,433 ft. (4399 m.)
Denver
Pikes Peak 14,110 ft. (4301 m.)
S. Platte
Platte
Loup
Middle
Republican
Smoky Hill
Arkansas
Wichita
N. Canadian
Cimarron
Oklahoma City
Canadian
Amarillo
Red
L. Texoma
Llano Estacado
Great Plains
Pt. Conception
Los Angeles
SANTA BARBARA IS.
PATTON ESCARPMENT
Mojave Desert
San Diego
Tijuana
BAJA CALIF. NORTE
Mexicali
Salton Sea
Colorado
Little Colorado
Verde
Phoenix
Salt
Gila
Tucson
SONORA
Lower California
Gulf of California
Santa Fe
Albuquerque
Rio Grande
Pecos
El Paso
Ciudad Juárez
CHIHUAHUA
Chihuahua
Odessa
Ft. Worth
Dallas
Brazos
Colorado
Edwards Plateau
Austin
San Antonio
Nueces
Corpus Christi
COAHUILA
NUEVO LEÓN
Falcon Res.
Padre I.
Brownsville
Monterrey
Torreón
DURANGO
TAMAULIPAS
Sierra Madre Oriental
MEXICO
Kauai
Oahu
Honolulu
Molokai
Maui
Lanai
HAWAIIAN RIDGE
HAWAII
PACIFIC OCEAN
Hawaii
Hilo
Mauna Kea 13,796 ft. (4205 m.)
Ka Lae
0 50 100 MILES
0 50 100 KILOMETERS
ARCTIC OCEAN
Pt. Barrow
CHUKCHI SEA
RUSSIA
ALASKA
Brooks Range
Arctic Circle
Bering Str.
Seward Pen.
Nome
Norton Sd.
St. Lawrence I.
Yukon
Fairbanks
Tanana
Alaska Range
Mt. McKinley 20,320 ft. (6194 m.)
Anchorage
Nunivak I.
C. Newenham
CANADA
YUKON TERR.
BR. COLUMBIA
Kenai Pen.
Juneau
BERING SEA
ALEUTIAN BASIN
BOWERS RIDGE
BOWERS BASIN
Attu I.
Adak
Umnak
Unimak
Unalaska I.
Alaska Pen.
Kodiak I.
GULF OF ALASKA
PACIFIC OCEAN
Alexander Arch.
ALEUTIAN ISLANDS
ALEUTIAN TRENCH
0 100 200 300 400 500 MILES
0 100 200 300 400 500 KILOMETERS
0 50 100 150 200 250 300 350 400 MILES
0 50 100 150 200 250 300 350 400 KILOMETERS

Lake Winnipeg
Lac Seul
C A N A D A
L. Nipigon
Lake of the Woods
Rainy
Red Lakes
Ogoki
Albany
Missinaibi
Abitibi
Harricana
Saguenay
St. Lawrence
L. St-Jean
Gaspé Pen.
Gulf of St. Lawrence
NEW BRUNSWICK
P.E.I.
MAINE
Québec
Fredericton
Bay of Fundy
NOVA SCOTIA
C. Sable
Thunder Bay
I. Royale
Lake Superior
Keweenaw Pen.
Marquette
Mississippi
WISCONSIN
St. Croix
Minneapolis
St. Paul
Minnesota
Green Bay
Wisconsin
L. Winnebago
Madison
Milwaukee
Lake Michigan
Muskegon
Grand
Lansing
Detroit
Saginaw Bay
Manitoulin I.
Lake Huron
Georgian Bay
Sudbury
Ottawa
QUÉBEC
ONTARIO
Montreal
Laurentian Mts.
VERMONT
L. Champlain
Montpelier
Augusta
Portland
Concord
N.H.
MASS.
Boston
C. Cod
Providence
R.I.
CONN.
Hartford
Martha's Vineyard
Nantucket I.
GEORGES BANK
Toronto
Lake Ontario
Rochester
Buffalo
London
Albany
Hudson
Connecticut
Penobscot
NEW YORK
PENNSYLVANIA
Lake Erie
Cleveland
Toledo
MICHIGAN
INDIANA
OHIO
Allegheny
Susquehanna
N.J.
New York
Long I.
Trenton
Philadelphia
Harrisburg
Pittsburgh
Akron
HUDSON CANYON
MINNESOTA
IOWA
Iowa
Cedar
ILLINOIS
Des Moines
Davenport
Omaha
Chicago
Fox
Illinois
Ft. Wayne
Wabash
Indianapolis
Columbus
Scioto
Ohio
MD.
Baltimore
Annapolis
Dover
DEL.
Washington
W. VA.
Potomac
C. May
Delaware Bay
MISSOURI
Grand
Des Moines
Mississippi
Springfield
Cincinnati
Kansas
Topeka
Kansas City
Jefferson City
Missouri
St. Louis
Ohio
White
Louisville
Frankfort
Charleston
New
James
Richmond
Chesapeake Bay
Norfolk
Roanoke
VIRGINIA
NORTH CAROLINA
Appalachian Mountains
ATLANTIC OCEAN
CONTINENTAL SHELF
Neosho
Ozark Plateau
Black
Green
Clinch
Cumberland
KENTUCKY
Raleigh
C. Hatteras
Pamlico Sound
Neuse
ARKANSAS
Kentucky Lake
Nashville
Mt. Mitchell 6,684 ft. (2037 m.)
Charlotte
C. Lookout
Fear
Memphis
TENNESSEE
Chattanooga
S. CAROLINA
MISSISSIPPI
ALABAMA
GEORGIA
C. Fear
Columbia
Arkansas
Little Rock
White
Ouachita
Tennessee
Coosa
Atlanta
Savannah
Birmingham
Yazoo
Chattahoochee
Ocmulgee
Oconee
Charleston
LOUISIANA
Shreveport
Sabine
Montgomery
Altamaha
Savannah
Jackson
Tombigbee
Alabama
Pearl
Red
Toledo Bend Res.
BLAKE RIDGE
FLORIDA
Mobile
Tallahassee
Jacksonville
St. Johns
BLAKE PLATEAU
BAHAMA RIDGE
Baton Rouge
New Orleans
SHELF
C. San Blas
Houston
Orlando
C. Canaveral
Galveston Bay
Delta of the Mississippi
Florida
Tampa
CONTINENTAL
MISSISSIPPI FAN
Tampa Bay
Grand Bahama
Great Abaco
L. Okeechobee
Peninsula
BAHAMAS
GULF OF MEXICO
Eleuthera
Nassau
New Providence
Miami
SIGSBEE ESCARPMENT
GREAT BAHAMA BANK
Cat I.
San Salvador
Andros I.
C. Sable
FLORIDA KEYS
Straits of Florida
Great Exuma
Long I.
Acklins I.
G H I J K L M

ATLANTIC OCEAN
BERMUDA RISE
NARES ABYSSAL PLAIN
HATTERAS ABYSSAL PLAIN
BLAKE RIDGE
BAHAMA RIDGE
CONTINENTAL SHELF
BLAKE PLATEAU
Tropic of Cancer
West Indies
BAHAMAS
Gt. Abaco
Eleuthera
Nassau
Andros I.
Gd. Bahama
Gt. Exuma
Crooked I.
Acklins I.
Gt. Inagua
Mayaguana
TURKS AND CAICOS IS. (U.K.)
CUBA
Havana
Santa Clara
Camagüey
Holguín
Santiago
I. de la Juventud
Cabo de San Antonio
GREATER ANTILLES
Hispaniola
HAITI
DOMINICAN REPUBLIC
Santo Domingo
Santiago
PUERTO RICO (U.S.)
San Juan
PUERTO RICO TRENCH
MUERTOS TROUGH
JAMAICA
Kingston
CAYMAN TRENCH
CAYMAN IS. (U.K.)
YUCATAN BASIN
LESSER ANTILLES
ANTIGUA AND BARBUDA
ST. CHRISTOPHER & NEVIS
Basseterre
Guadeloupe (Fr.)
DOMINICA
Roseau
Martinique (Fr.)
Fort-de-France
ST. LUCIA
Castries
BARBADOS
Bridgetown
ST. VINCENT AND THE GRENADINES
Kingstown
GRENADA
St. George's
TRINIDAD AND TOBAGO
Port of Spain
Tobago
Trinidad
AVES RIDGE
I. de Margarita
VENEZUELA BASIN
ARUBA (Neth.)
NETH. ANTILLES
Curaçao
Bonaire
CARIBBEAN SEA
BEATA RIDGE
COLOMBIA BASIN
Guajira Pen.
Barranquilla
Cartagena
Magdalena
Maracaibo
Lake Maracaibo
Barquisimeto
Caracas
Cumaná
VENEZUELA
Orinoco
Ciudad Guayana
Guri Res.
Guiana Highlands
Sierra Pacaraima
GUYANA
BRAZIL
COLOMBIA
Bogotá
Medellín
Bucaramanga
Cali
Buenaventura
Atrato
Arauca
Meta
Guaviare
Pico Bolívar
San Cristóbal
PANAMA
Panama
Panama Canal
Colón
Gulf of Panama
COSTA RICA
San José
NICARAGUA
Lake Nicaragua
Managua
NICARAGUA RISE
C. Gracias a Dios
HONDURAS
Tegucigalpa
San Pedro Sula
EL SALVADOR
San Salvador
GUATEMALA
Guatemala
BELIZE
Belmopan
Usumacinta
Yucatán Pen.
Mérida
Campeche
CAMPECHE BANK
Bay of Campeche
Gulf of Mexico
SIGSBEE DEEP
SIGSBEE ESCARPMENT
MISSISSIPPI FAN
Isthmus of Tehuantepec
Veracruz
Tampico
Puebla
Mexico City
Citlaltépetl
Popocatépetl
MEXICO
Sierra Madre Oriental
Sierra Madre Occidental
Sierra Madre del Sur
Monterrey
Nuevo Laredo
San Luis Potosí
León
Guadalajara
Torreón
Chihuahua
Ciudad Juárez
Culiacán
Mazatlán
Islas Marías
C. Corrientes
Acapulco
Gulf of California
Lower California
C. San Lucas
DELFIN BASIN
UNITED STATES
Washington
Richmond
Norfolk
C. Charles
C. Hatteras
Charleston
Savannah
Jacksonville
C. Canaveral
Miami
Tampa
Lake Okeechobee
Florida Peninsula
C. Sable
Straits of Florida
Appalachian Mountains
Atlanta
Chattahoochee
Nashville
Cincinnati
Louisville
Ohio
Cumberland
Tennessee
Alabama
Tombigbee
Mobile
Memphis
St. Louis
Mississippi
Missouri
New Orleans
Red
Arkansas
White
Sabine
Houston
Dallas
Ft. Worth
Brazos
Colorado
San Antonio
Corpus Christi
Río Grande
Oklahoma City
Tulsa
Wichita
Cimarron
Canadian
Pecos
El Paso
Albuquerque
Rocky Mts.
Phoenix
Tucson
Gila
San Diego
PACIFIC OCEAN
MIDDLE AMERICA TRENCH
GUATEMALA BASIN
PANAMA BASIN
COCOS RIDGE
Cocos I. (C.R.)
Malpelo I. (Col.)
TEHUANTEPEC FRACTURE ZONE
OROZCO FRACTURE ZONE
Clipperton (Fr.)
© Copyright 1987 by HAMMOND INCORPORATED, Maplewood, N.J.
0 100 200 300 400 500 600 MILES
0 100 200 300 400 500 600 KILOMETERS

This map has been prepared with the North Pole as the mathematical center. From it, distances to any part of the world may be measured. On Mercator's map of the world, the polar regions are so scattered that their relatively small area and availability for flight routes are disregarded. Today, with airplanes following great circle courses, often within the Arctic Circle, polar projection maps are indispensable to the people of this air-minded age.

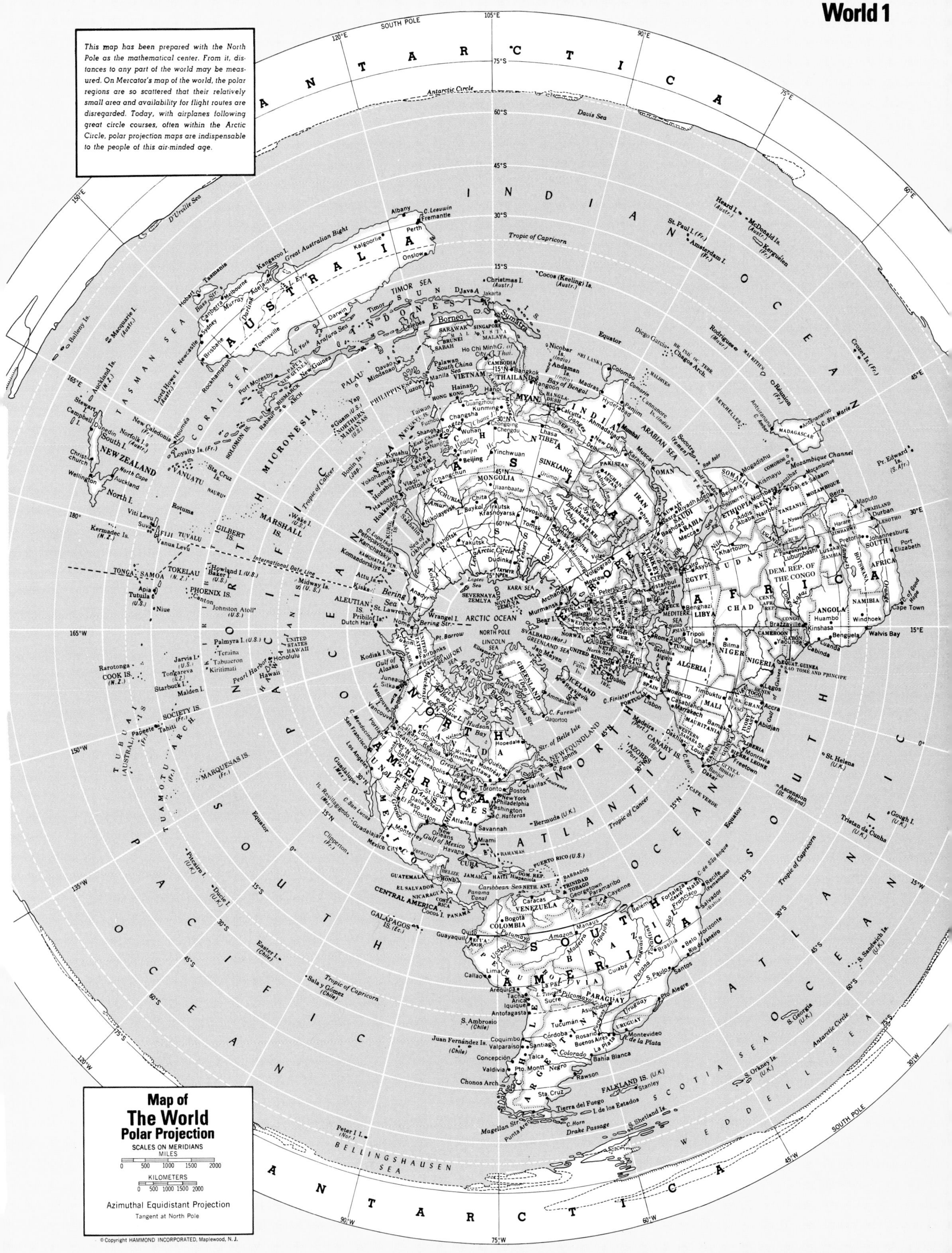
SOUTH POLE
ANTARCTICA
Antarctic Circle
Davis Sea
D'Urville Sea
INDIAN OCEAN
Tropic of Capricorn
Great Australian Bight
AUSTRALIA
Tasmania
TASMAN SEA
CORAL SEA
NEW ZEALAND
TIMOR SEA
SUNDA IS.
INDONESIA
Borneo
PHILIPPINES
MICRONESIA
MARSHALL IS.
GILBERT IS.
FIJI
TUVALU
SAMOA
TONGA
TOKELAU
PHOENIX IS.
COOK IS.
SOCIETY IS.
TUAMOTU ARCH.
MARQUESAS IS.
PACIFIC OCEAN
NORTH PACIFIC OCEAN
SOUTH PACIFIC OCEAN
Equator
Tropic of Cancer
JAPAN
CHINA
MONGOLIA
ASIA
INDIA
ARABIAN SEA
Bay of Bengal
SAUDI ARABIA
IRAN
AFGHAN.
PAKISTAN
TIBET
SINKIANG
EUROPE
ARCTIC OCEAN
NORTH POLE
Arctic Circle
KARA SEA
GREENLAND
ICELAND
NORTH AMERICA
CANADA
UNITED STATES
ALASKA
Hudson Bay
Gulf of Mexico
CENTRAL AMERICA
NORTH ATLANTIC OCEAN
SOUTH ATLANTIC OCEAN
AFRICA
EGYPT
LIBYA
ALGERIA
NIGER
CHAD
SUDAN
MALI
NIGERIA
ETHIOPIA
SOMALIA
KENYA
TANZANIA
ANGOLA
NAMIBIA
SOUTH AFRICA
DEM. REP. OF THE CONGO
MADAGASCAR
Mozambique Channel
SOUTH AMERICA
BRAZIL
COLOMBIA
VENEZUELA
PERU
BOLIVIA
PARAGUAY
ARGENTINA
CHILE
URUGUAY
FALKLAND IS. (U.K.)
Drake Passage
SCOTIA SEA
WEDDELL SEA
BELLINGSHAUSEN SEA
Tropic of Capricorn
International Date Line

Map of
The World
Polar Projection

SCALES ON MERIDIANS
MILES
0 500 1000 1500 2000
KILOMETERS
0 500 1000 1500 2000

Azimuthal Equidistant Projection
Tangent at North Pole

The World

BRIESEMEISTER ELLIPTICAL
EQUAL-AREA PROJECTION

Capitals of Countries ⊛
Other Capitals ◉
International Boundaries – – –

Scale 1:80,000,000

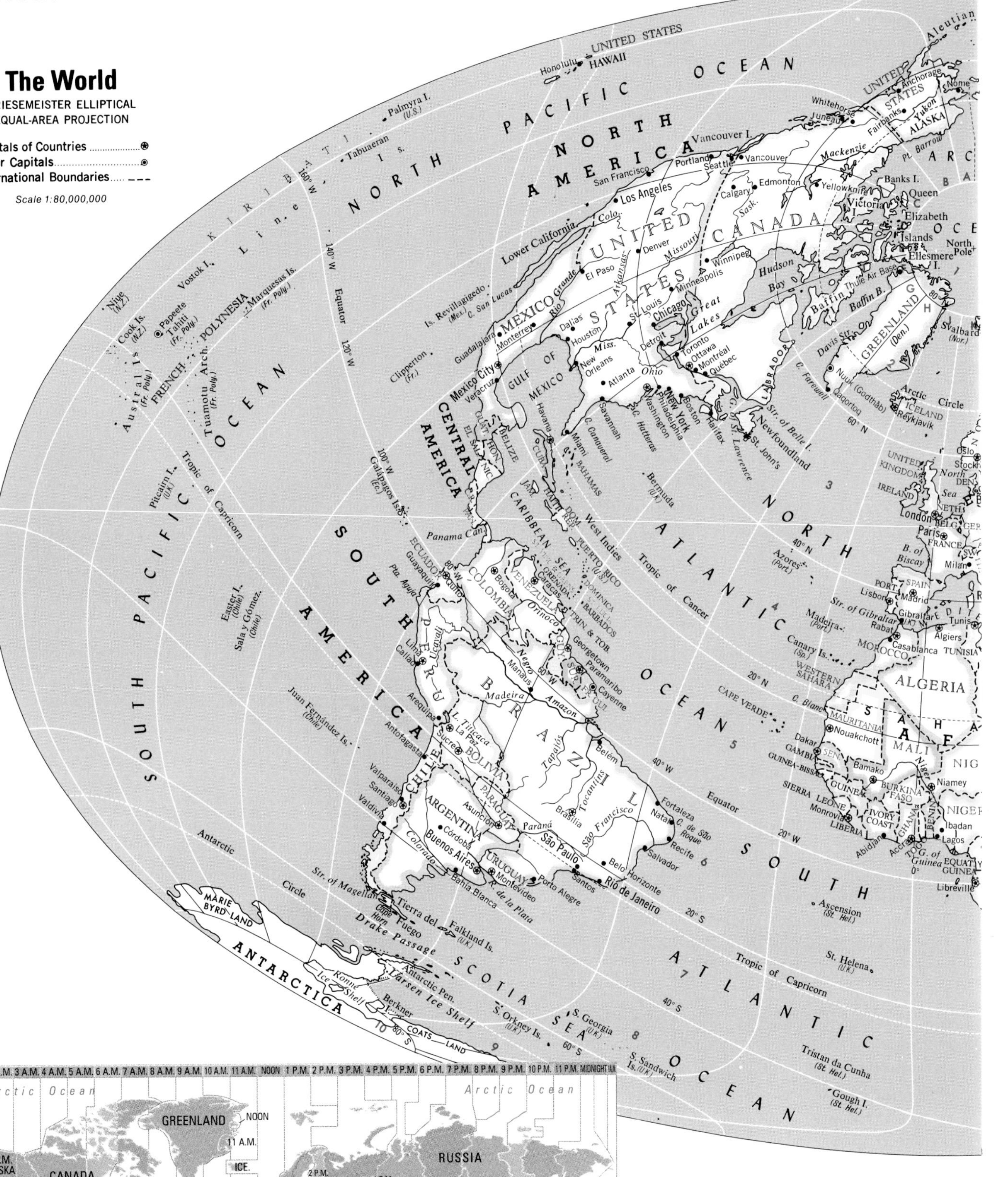
PACIFIC OCEAN
NORTH PACIFIC OCEAN
SOUTH PACIFIC OCEAN
NORTH ATLANTIC OCEAN
SOUTH ATLANTIC OCEAN
NORTH AMERICA
SOUTH AMERICA
CENTRAL AMERICA
ANTARCTICA
UNITED STATES
CANADA
MEXICO
GREENLAND (Den.)
BRAZIL
ARGENTINA
ALGERIA
GULF OF MEXICO
CARIBBEAN SEA
SCOTIA SEA
Drake Passage
Equator
Tropic of Cancer
Tropic of Capricorn
Antarctic Circle
Arctic Circle
Hudson Bay
Baffin B.
Los Angeles
San Francisco
Chicago
New York
Washington
Mexico City
Bogotá
Lima
Santiago
Buenos Aires
Rio de Janeiro
São Paulo
Brasília
London
Paris
Madrid
Dakar

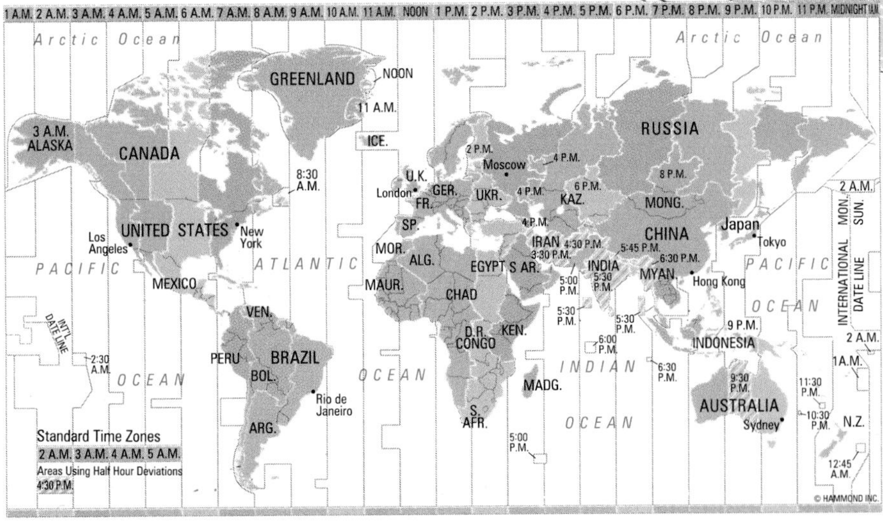
1 A.M. 2 A.M. 3 A.M. 4 A.M. 5 A.M. 6 A.M. 7 A.M. 8 A.M. 9 A.M. 10 A.M. 11 A.M. NOON 1 P.M. 2 P.M. 3 P.M. 4 P.M. 5 P.M. 6 P.M. 7 P.M. 8 P.M. 9 P.M. 10 P.M. 11 P.M. MIDNIGHT
Arctic Ocean
GREENLAND
NOON
11 A.M.
ICE.
3 A.M. ALASKA
CANADA
RUSSIA
8:30 A.M.
UNITED STATES
New York
Los Angeles
MEXICO
PACIFIC
ATLANTIC
OCEAN
INDIAN
VEN.
PERU
BRAZIL
BOL.
ARG.
Rio de Janeiro
U.K.
London
GER.
FR.
SP.
UKR.
Moscow
KAZ.
MONG.
CHINA
Japan
Tokyo
MOR.
ALG.
EGYPT
S. AR.
IRAN
INDIA
MYAN.
Hong Kong
MAUR.
CHAD
D.R. CONGO
KEN.
MADG.
S. AFR.
INDONESIA
AUSTRALIA
Sydney
N.Z.
INTERNATIONAL DATE LINE
INT'L DATE LINE
MON. SUN.
Standard Time Zones
2 A.M. 3 A.M. 4 A.M. 5 A.M.
Areas Using Half Hour Deviations
4:30 P.M.
© HAMMOND INC.

LAND AREA 57,970,000 sq. mi.
(150,142,300 sq. km.)
WATER AREA 139,781,000 sq. mi.
(362,032,790 sq. km.)
TOTAL SURFACE AREA 197,751,000 sq.mi.
(512,175,090 sq. km.)
POPULATION 5,292,000,000

International Date Line
NORTH PACIFIC OCEAN
BERING SEA
Komandorskiye Is.
Kamchatka Pen.
Petropavlovsk-Kamchatskiy
Anadyr'
SEA OF OKHOTSK
Kuril Is.
Magadan
Sakhalin
Hokkaido
Nikolayevsk
Sapporo
JAPAN
SEA OF JAPAN
Tokyo
Yokohama
Honshu
Osaka
Nagoya
Kitakyushu
Shikoku
Kyushu
Ryukyu Is.
Bonin Is.
MARSHALL IS.
Gilbert Is.
KIRIBATI
NAURU
TUVALU
NORTHERN MARIANAS (U.S.)
Guam (U.S.)
FED. STATES OF MICRONESIA
Bismarck Arch.
SOLOMON IS.
SAMOA
AM. SAMOA
FIJI
Suva
TONGA
VANUATU
New Caledonia (Fr.)
Nouméa
Kermadec Is. (N.Z.)
Norfolk I. (Austr.)
Lord Howe I. (Austr.)
Auckland
NEW ZEALAND
Wellington
Christchurch
Dunedin
TASMAN SEA
Tasmania
Hobart
CORAL SEA
C. York
New Guinea
PAPUA NEW GUINEA
IRIAN JAYA
Arafura Sea
Timor
Darwin
Townsville
Rockhampton
Brisbane
Newcastle
Sydney
Canberra
Melbourne
Adelaide
AUSTRALIA
Port Hedland
Kalgoorlie
Perth
Fremantle
C. Leeuwin
Auckland Is. (N.Z.)
Verkhoyansk
Yakutsk
Khabarovsk
Vladivostok
Harbin
Changchun
Shenyang
N. KOR.
Seoul
S. KOR.
Dalian
Beijing
Tianjin
Shanghai
Nanjing
Fuzhou
Taipei
Taiwan
HONG KONG
MACAU
Hainan
Hanoi
SOUTH CHINA SEA
Luzon
Manila
PHILIPPINES
Cebu
Mindanao
Davao
Palawan
SABAH
SARAWAK
BRUNEI
Borneo
Celebes
Flores Sea
Java Sea
Java
Jakarta
Christmas I. (Austr.)
INDONESIA
Sumatra
SING.
MALAYSIA
Kuala Lumpur
Ho Chi Minh City
VIETNAM
CAMB.
THAILAND
G. of Thailand
Bangkok
LAOS
MYANMAR (BURMA)
Rangoon
Andaman Is.
Mekong
Kunming
Guangzhou
Chengdu
Chongqing
Wuhan
Changsha
Lanzhou
Xi'an
Yangtze (Chang J.)
Huang He
CHINA
MONGOLIA
Ulaanbaatar
Ulan-Ude
Baykal
Irkutsk
Lena
Noril'sk
SIBERIA
ASIA
Yenisey
Ob'
Salekhard
Novosibirsk
Krasnoyarsk
Omsk
Urumqi
SINKIANG
TIBET
Lhasa
NEPAL
BHUTAN
BANGLADESH
Calcutta
B. of Bengal
Ganges
Tropic of Cancer
INDIA
Delhi
New Delhi
Indus
PAKISTAN
Karachi
Ahmadabad
Mumbai (Bombay)
Hyderabad
Chennai (Madras)
Bangalore
SRI LANKA
Colombo
C. Comorin
Male
MALDIVES
80° E
Cocos (Keeling) Is. (Austr.)
INDIAN OCEAN
ARABIAN SEA
Equator
Chagos Arch. (Br. Ind. Oc. Terr.)
60° E
SEYCHELLES
Tropic of Capricorn
MAURITIUS
Réunion (Fr.)
Amsterdam I. (Fr.)
St. Paul I. (Fr.)
Kerguelen (Fr.)
Heard I. (Austr.)
McDonald Is. (Austr.)
Crozet Is. (Fr.)
Pr. Edward Is. (S. Afr.)
60° S
Antarctic Circle
Cape Adare
Novaya Zemlya
Barents Sea
Severnaya Zemlya
Franz Josef Ld.
New Siberian Is.
ARCTIC OCEAN
Murmansk
Archangel
FINLAND
SWEDEN
Helsinki
St. Petersburg
Novgorod
EUROPE
RUSSIA
Moscow
Perm
Yekaterinburg
Chelyabinsk
Nizh. Novgorod
Volga
Samara
Ufa
Astana
KAZAKHSTAN
Balkhash L.
Almaty
KYR.
Tashkent
Syrdar'ya
UZBEK.
Aral Sea
Amudar'ya
TAJIK.
TURK.
AFGHANISTAN
Kabul
Islamabad
Caspian Sea
Baltic Sea
LITH.
BEL.
Warsaw
POL.
Berlin
Kiev
UKRAINE
Kharkov
Odessa
Volgograd
Rostov
ROM.
Bucharest
HUN.
AUST.
BULG.
Black Sea
GEO.
ARM.
AZER.
Istanbul
Ankara
TURKEY
Tehran
IRAN
Baghdad
IRAQ
SYRIA
LEB.
CYP.
ISR.
JOR.
Athens
GR.
ALB.
Rome
MAL.
MEDITERRANEAN SEA
Tripoli
Benghazi
Alexandria
Cairo
Suez Can.
LIBYA
EGYPT
SAUDI ARABIA
Riyadh
Mecca
KUWAIT
Basra
QATAR
U.A.E.
Muscat
OMAN
YEMEN
Socotra (Yemen)
Ras Aser
G. of Aden
Red Sea
AFRICA
CHAD
N'Djamena
SUDAN
Khartoum
ERIT.
DJIBOUTI
ETHIOPIA
Addis Ababa
SOMALIA
Mogadishu
Nile
White Nile
CENT. AFR. REP.
Bangui
CAMEROON
Yaoundé
GAB.
CONGO
Brazzaville
Congo
DEM. REP. OF THE CONGO
Kinshasa
UGANDA
Kampala
KENYA
Nairobi
L. Victoria
RWA.
BUR.
TANZANIA
Zanzibar
Dar es Salaam
L. Tanganyika
L. Nyasa
COMOROS
MADAGASCAR
Antananarivo
C. Vohimena
Mozambique Chan.
MAL.
Lilongwe
MOZAMBIQUE
ZAMBIA
Lusaka
Zambezi
Harare
ZIMBABWE
Lubumbashi
ANGOLA
Luanda
Huambo
NAMIBIA
Windhoek
Walvis Bay
BOTSWANA
Gaborone
Pretoria
Maputo
SWAZILAND
Johannesburg
LESOTHO
Durban
SOUTH AFRICA
Orange
Cape Town
Cape of Good Hope
20° E
40° E
100° E
140° E
160° E
180°

0°
20° W
20° E
40° W
40° E
60° W
60° E
80° W
80° E
100° W
100° E
120° W
120° E
140° W
140° E
160° W
160° E
180°
ATLANTIC OCEAN
INDIAN OCEAN
PACIFIC OCEAN
Antarctic Circle
South Orkney Is. (U.K.)
70° S
80° S
Riiser-Larsen Pen.
QUEEN MAUD LAND
ENDERBY LAND
C. Batterbee
WEDDELL SEA
COATS LAND
ANTARCTIC PENINSULA
GRAHAM LAND
Larsen Ice Shelf
Drake Passage
S. Shetland Is.
PALMER LAND
Filchner Ice Shelf
Berkner I.
Ronne Ice Shelf
Amery Ice Shelf
AMERICAN HIGHLAND
Bellingshausen Sea
Peter I I. (Nor.)
ANTARCTICA
SOUTH POLE
Shackleton Ice Shelf
Amundsen Sea
MARIE BYRD LAND
Ross Ice Shelf
Little America
Roosevelt I.
Ross I.
McMurdo Sd.
ROSS SEA
VICTORIA LAND
WILKES LAND
C. Adare
SOUTH MAGNETIC POLE
Scott I.
Balleny Is.

Antarctica
AZIMUTHAL EQUIDISTANT PROJECTION

Arctic Ocean

Arctic Ice
Bering Sea
Nome
UNITED STATES
ALASKA
Ambarchik
CANADA
Barrow
East Siberian Sea
RUSSIA
Beaufort Sea
Approximate Limit of Pack Ice in September
Laptev Sea
Nordvik
ARCTIC OCEAN
NORTH POLE
CANADA
Kara Sea
Thule Air Base
Baffin Bay
Barents Sea
Qeqertarsuaq
GREENLAND
Approximate Limit of Pack Ice in March
Murmansk
Archangel
Norwegian Sea
ICELAND
ATLANTIC OCEAN
RUSSIA
FINLAND
NORWAY
SWEDEN
© C.S. Hammond & Co.

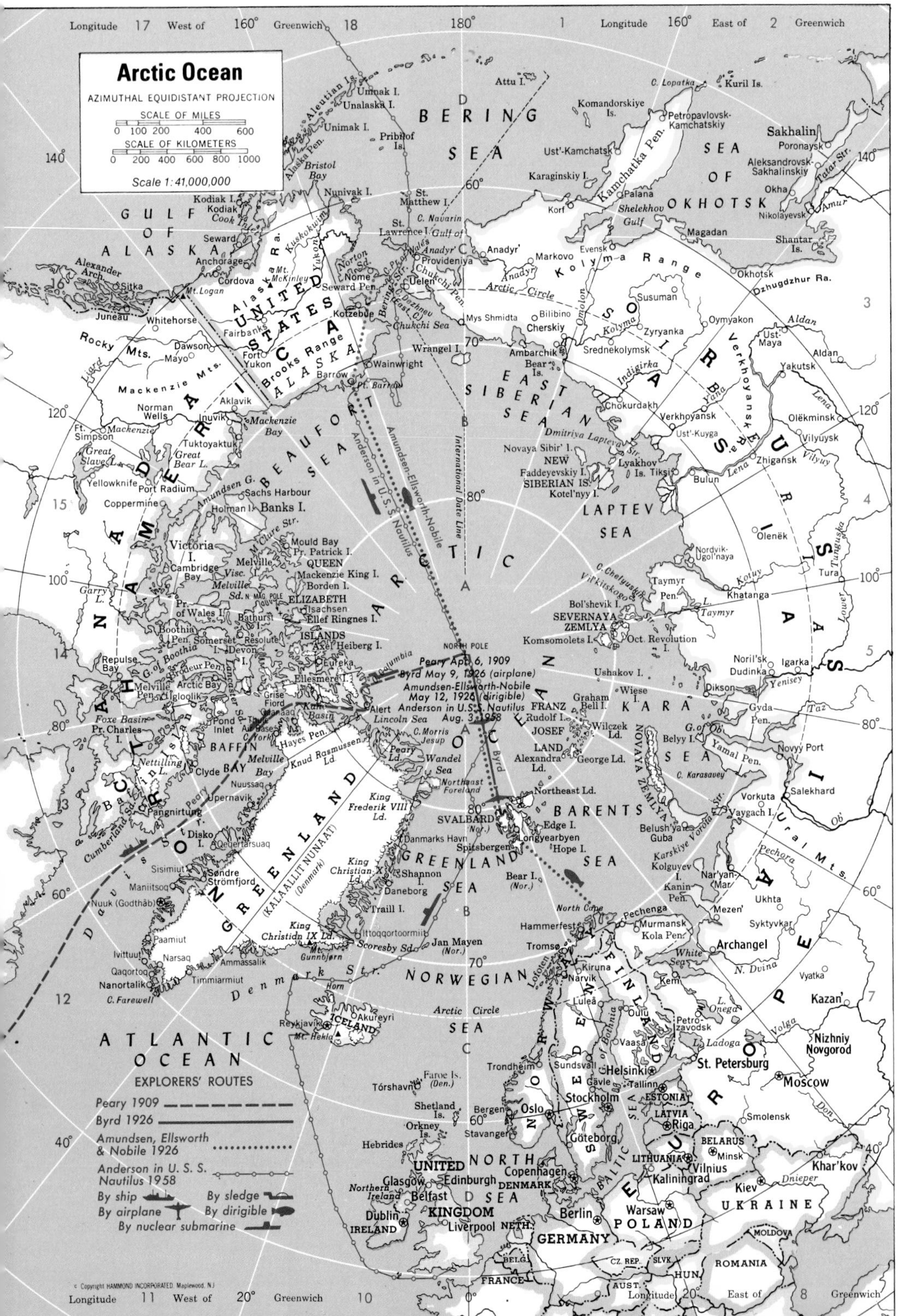

Arctic Ocean
AZIMUTHAL EQUIDISTANT PROJECTION
SCALE OF MILES
0 100 200 400 600
SCALE OF KILOMETERS
0 200 400 600 800 1000
Scale 1: 41,000,000
Longitude 17 West of 160° Greenwich 18
180° 1 Longitude 160° East of 2 Greenwich
BERING SEA
SEA OF OKHOTSK
GULF OF ALASKA
UNITED STATES
ALASKA
BEAUFORT SEA
EAST SIBERIAN SEA
LAPTEV SEA
ARCTIC OCEAN
KARA SEA
BARENTS SEA
GREENLAND SEA
NORWEGIAN SEA
NORTH SEA
CANADA
RUSSIA
GREENLAND (KALAALLIT NUNAAT) (Denmark)
NORTH POLE
Peary Apr. 6, 1909
Byrd May 9, 1926 (airplane)
Amundsen-Ellsworth-Nobile May 12, 1926 (dirigible)
Anderson in U.S.S. Nautilus Aug. 3, 1958
ATLANTIC OCEAN
EXPLORERS' ROUTES
Peary 1909
Byrd 1926
Amundsen, Ellsworth & Nobile 1926
Anderson in U. S. S. Nautilus 1958
By ship
By sledge
By airplane
By dirigible
By nuclear submarine
© Copyright HAMMOND INCORPORATED, Maplewood, N.J.
Longitude 11 West of 20° Greenwich 10
Longitude 20° East of 8 Greenwich

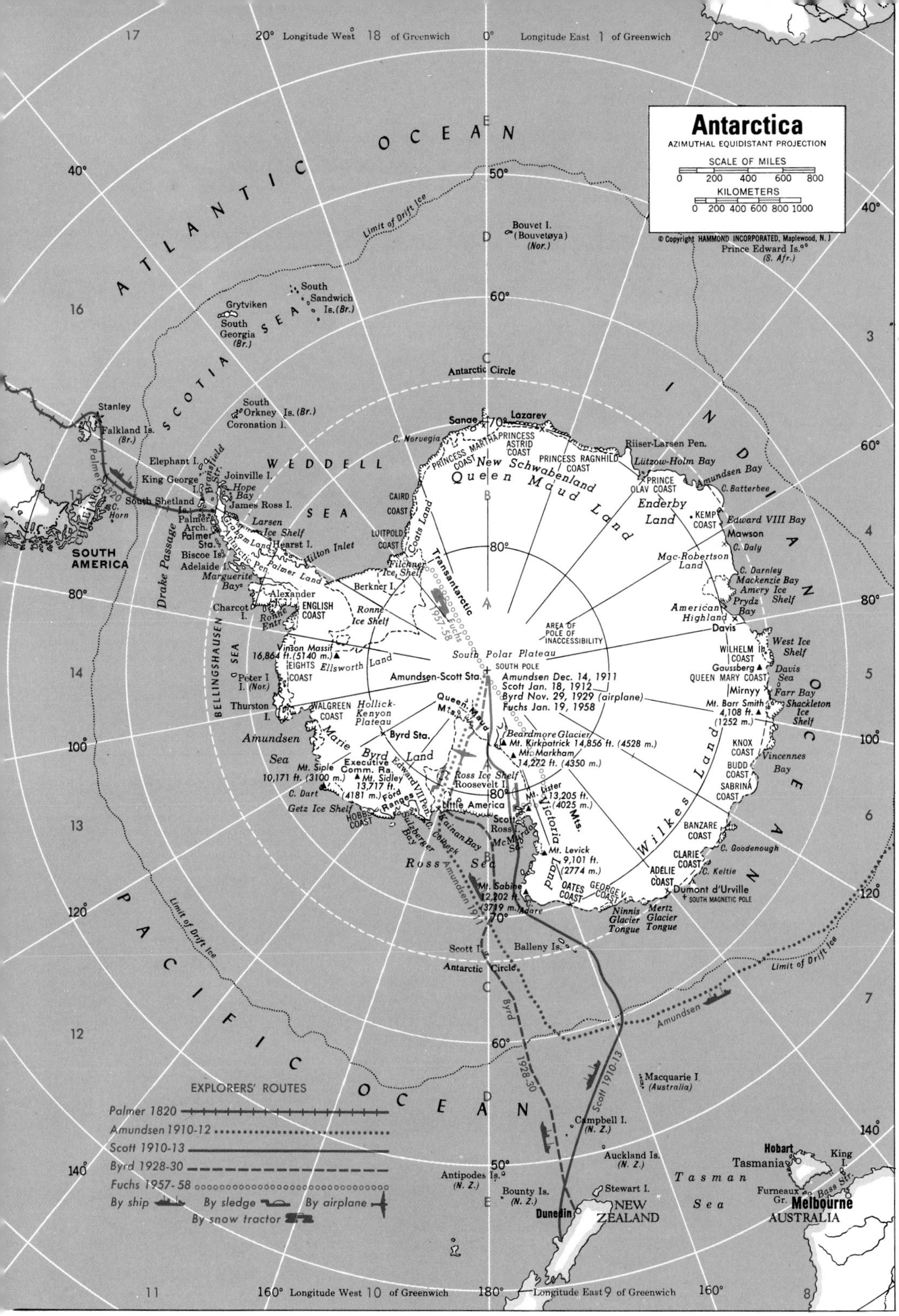
Antarctica
AZIMUTHAL EQUIDISTANT PROJECTION
SCALE OF MILES
0 200 400 600 800
KILOMETERS
0 200 400 600 800 1000
© Copyright HAMMOND INCORPORATED, Maplewood, N. J.
20° Longitude West 18 of Greenwich
0°
Longitude East 1 of Greenwich 20°
160° Longitude West 10 of Greenwich
180° Longitude East 9 of Greenwich 160°
ATLANTIC OCEAN
INDIAN OCEAN
PACIFIC OCEAN
SCOTIA SEA
WEDDELL SEA
Limit of Drift Ice
Bouvet I. (Bouvetøya) (Nor.)
Prince Edward Is. (S. Afr.)
South Sandwich Is. (Br.)
Grytviken
South Georgia (Br.)
Antarctic Circle
South Orkney Is. (Br.)
Coronation I.
Stanley
Falkland Is. (Br.)
SOUTH AMERICA
C. Horn
Drake Passage
Elephant I.
King George I.
South Shetland Is.
Joinville I.
Hope Bay
James Ross I.
Larsen Ice Shelf
Palmer Arch.
Palmer Sta.
Biscoe Is.
Adelaide I.
Marguerite Bay
Hearst I.
Hilton Inlet
Palmer Land
Alexander I.
Charcot I.
ENGLISH COAST
Ronne Entr.
Ronne Ice Shelf
Berkner I.
Filchner Ice Shelf
Coats Land
CAIRD COAST
LUITPOLD COAST
Sanae
Lazarev
C. Norvegia
PRINCESS MARTHA COAST
PRINCESS ASTRID COAST
PRINCESS RAGNHILD COAST
New Schwabenland
Queen Maud Land
Riiser-Larsen Pen.
Lützow-Holm Bay
PRINCE OLAV COAST
Amundsen Bay
C. Batterbee
Enderby Land
KEMP COAST
Edward VIII Bay
Mawson
C. Daly
Mac-Robertson Land
C. Darnley
Mackenzie Bay
Amery Ice Shelf
Prydz Bay
American Highland
Davis
West Ice Shelf
WILHELM II COAST
Gaussberg
QUEEN MARY COAST
Davis Sea
Mirnyy
Farr Bay
Mt. Barr Smith 4,108 ft. (1252 m.)
Shackleton Ice Shelf
KNOX COAST
Vincennes Bay
BUDD COAST
SABRINA COAST
Wilkes Land
BANZARE COAST
C. Goodenough
CLARIE COAST
C. Keltie
ADÉLIE COAST
Dumont d'Urville
SOUTH MAGNETIC POLE
GEORGE V COAST
OATES COAST
Ninnis Glacier Tongue
Mertz Glacier Tongue
AREA OF POLE OF INACCESSIBILITY
South Polar Plateau
SOUTH POLE
Amundsen-Scott Sta.
Amundsen Dec. 14, 1911
Scott Jan. 18, 1912
Byrd Nov. 29, 1929 (airplane)
Fuchs Jan. 19, 1958
Transantarctic
Fuchs 1957-58
Vinson Massif 16,864 ft. (5140 m.)
EIGHTS COAST
Ellsworth Land
BELLINGSHAUSEN SEA
Peter I I. (Nor.)
Thurston I.
WALGREEN COAST
Hollick-Kenyon Plateau
Queen Maud Mts.
Byrd Sta.
Beardmore Glacier
Mt. Kirkpatrick 14,856 ft. (4528 m.)
Mt. Markham 14,272 ft. (4350 m.)
Amundsen Sea
Marie Byrd Land
Executive Comm. Ra.
Mt. Siple 10,171 ft. (3100 m.)
Mt. Sidley 13,717 ft. (4181 m.)
Ford Ranges
Edward VII Pen.
C. Dart
Getz Ice Shelf
HOBBS COAST
Ross Ice Shelf
Roosevelt I.
Little America
Mt. Lister 13,205 ft. (4025 m.)
Victoria Land
Scott
Ross I.
McMurdo Sd.
Kainan Bay
Sulzberger Bay
C. Colbeck
Ross Sea
Mt. Levick 9,101 ft. (2774 m.)
Mt. Sabine 12,202 ft. (3719 m.)
C. Adare
Scott I.
Balleny Is.
Amundsen 1911
Byrd 1928-30
Scott 1910-13
Amundsen
Macquarie I. (Australia)
Campbell I. (N. Z.)
Auckland Is. (N. Z.)
Antipodes Is. (N. Z.)
Bounty Is. (N. Z.)
Stewart I.
Dunedin
NEW ZEALAND
Tasman Sea
Hobart
Tasmania
King I.
Furneaux Gr.
Bass Str.
Melbourne
AUSTRALIA
EXPLORERS' ROUTES
Palmer 1820
Amundsen 1910-12
Scott 1910-13
Byrd 1928-30
Fuchs 1957-58
By ship
By sledge
By airplane
By snow tractor

Adare (cape)	B9
Adelaide (isl.)	C15
Adélie Coast (reg.)	C7
Alexander (isl.)	B15
American Highland	B4
Amery Ice Shelf	C4
Amundsen (bay)	C3
Amundsen (sea)	B13
Amundsen-Scott Station	A14
Antarctic (pen.)	C15
Balleny (isls.)	C9
Banzare Coast (reg.)	C7
Barr Smith (mt.)	C5
Batterbee (cape)	C3
Beardmore (glac.)	A8
Bellingshausen (sea)	C14
Berkner (isl.)	B16
Biscoe (isls.)	C15
Bouvet (isl.)	D1
Bouvetøya (Bouvet) (isl.)	D1
Bransfield (str.)	C16
Budd Coast (reg.)	C6
Byrd Station	A12
Caird Coast (reg.)	B17
Charcot (isl.)	C15
Clarie Coast (reg.)	C7
Coats Land (reg.)	B17
Colbeck (cape)	B10
Coronation (isl.)	C16
Daly (cape)	C4
Darnley (cape)	C4
Dart (cape)	B12
Davis (sea)	C5
Davis Station	C4
Drake (passage)	C15
Dumont d'Urville Station	C7
Edward VII (pen.)	B11
Edward VIII (bay)	C4
Eights Coast (reg.)	B14
Elephant (isl.)	D16
Ellsworth Land (reg.)	B14
Enderby Land (reg.)	B3
English Coast (reg.)	B15
Executive Committee (range)	B12
Farr (bay)	C5
Filchner Ice Shelf	B16
Ford Ranges (mts.)	B11
Gaussberg (mt.)	C5
George V Coast (reg.)	C8
Getz Ice Shelf	B12
Goodenough (cape)	C7
Graham Land (reg.)	C15
Grytviken	D17
Hearst (isl.)	B16
Hilton (inlet)	B16
Hobbs Coast (reg.)	B12
Hollick-Kenyon (plat.)	B13
Hope (bay)	C16
Indian Ocean	C3
James Ross (isl.)	C16
Joinville (isl.)	C16
Kainan (bay)	B10
Keltie (cape)	C7
Kemp Coast (reg.)	C3
King George (isl.)	C16
Kirkpatrick (mt.)	A8
Knox Coast (reg.)	C6
Larsen Ice Shelf	C16
Lazarev Station	C1
Levick (mt.)	B8
Lister (mt.)	B8
Little America	B10
Luitpold Coast (reg.)	B17
Lützow-Holm (bay)	C3
Mackenzie (bay)	C4
Mac-Robertson Land (reg.)	B4
Marguerite (bay)	C15
Marie Byrd Land (reg.)	B13
Markham (mt.)	A8
Mawson	C4
McMurdo (sound)	B9
Mertz Glacier Tongue	C8
Mirnyy	C5
New Schwabenland (reg.)	B1
Ninnis Glacier Tongue	C8
Norvegia (cape)	B18
Oates Coast (reg.)	B8
Palmer (arch.)	C15
Palmer Land (reg.)	B15
Palmer Station	C15
Peter I (isl.)	B14
Prince Edward (isls.)	E2
Prince Olav Coast (reg.)	C3
Princess Astrid Coast (reg.)	B1
Princess Martha Coast (reg.)	B18
Princess Ragnhild Coast (reg.)	B2
Prydz (bay)	C4
Queen Mary Coast (reg.)	C5
Queen Maud (mts.)	A12
Queen Maud Land (reg.)	B1
Riiser-Larsen (pen.)	C2
Ronne Entrance (inlet)	B15
Ronne Ice Shelf	B15
Roosevelt (isl.)	A10
Ross (isl.)	B9
Ross (sea)	B10
Ross Ice Shelf	A10
Sabine (mt.)	B9
Sabrina Coast (reg.)	C6
Sanae Station	B18
Scotia (sea)	D16
Scott (isl.)	C10
Scott Station	B9
Shackleton Ice Shelf	C5
Sidley (mt.)	B12
Siple (mt.)	B12
South Georgia (isl.)	D17
South Magnetic Pole	C8
South Orkney (isls.)	C16
South Polar (plat.)	A1
South Pole	A4
South Sandwich (isls.)	D17
South Shetland (isls.)	C15
Sulzberger (bay)	B11
Thurston (isl.)	C14
Transantarctic (mts.)	B17
Victoria Land (reg.)	B8
Vincennes (bay)	C6
Vinson Massif (mt.)	B14
Walgreen Coast (reg.)	B13
Weddell (sea)	C16
West Ice Shelf	C5
Wilhelm II Coast (reg.)	C5
Wilkes Land (reg.)	B7

Weddell Sea
Traverse of Cross Section Shown Below
SOUTH POLE
ANTARCTICA
Ross Sea

Antarctic Cross Section: Weddell Sea to Ross Sea

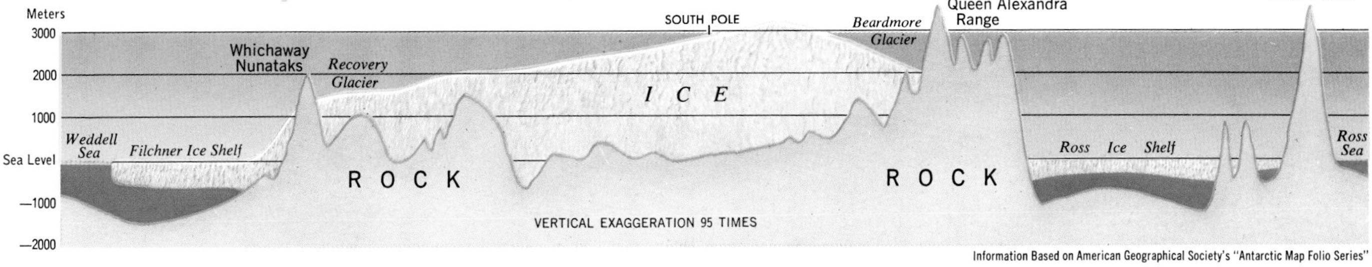
Meters
3000
2000
1000
Sea Level
—1000
—2000
SOUTH POLE
Whichaway Nunataks
Recovery Glacier
Beardmore Glacier
Queen Alexandra Range
Ross Island
Weddell Sea
Filchner Ice Shelf
ICE
ROCK
ROCK
Ross Ice Shelf
Ross Sea
VERTICAL EXAGGERATION 95 TIMES

Information Based on American Geographical Society's "Antarctic Map Folio Series"

Europe
POLYCONIC PROJECTION
SCALE OF MILES
0 100 200 300 400
KILOMETERS
0 100 200 300 400
Capitals of Countries
Other Capitals
International Boundaries
Internal Boundaries
Canals
Longitude West of Greenwich 0° Longitude East of Greenwich
ICELAND
NORWEGIAN SEA
BARENTS SEA
WHITE SEA
NORTH SEA
BALTIC SEA
ATLANTIC OCEAN
BLACK SEA
MEDITERRANEAN SEA
Bay of Biscay
UNITED KINGDOM
IRELAND
NORWAY
SWEDEN
FINLAND
DENMARK
ESTONIA
LATVIA
LITHUANIA
BELARUS
POLAND
GERMANY
NETHERLANDS
BELGIUM
LUX.
FRANCE
SPAIN
PORTUGAL
SWITZERLAND
AUSTRIA
CZECH REP.
SLOVAKIA
HUNGARY
ROMANIA
MOLDOVA
UKRAINE
BULGARIA
YUGOSLAVIA
CROATIA
F.Y.R.O.M.
ALBANIA
GREECE
ITALY
TURKEY
MOROCCO
ALGERIA
TUNISIA
AFRICA
RUSSIA

Aberdeen, Scotland D3
Adriatic (sea) F4
Aegean (sea) G5
Albania G4
Ålborg, Denmark F3
Alps (mts.) E4
Andorra E4
Antwerp, Belgium E3
Araks (riv.) J5
Archangel, Russia J2
Århus, Denmark E3
Armenia J4
Astrakhan', Russia J4
Athens (cap.), Greece G5
Austria F4
Azerbaijan J4
Azov (sea) H4
Baku (cap.), Azerbaijan J4
Balearic (isls.), Spain E5
Balkan (mts.) G4
Baltic (sea) F3
Barcelona, Spain E4
Barents (sea) J1
Basel, Switzerland E4
Belarus (Belorussia) G3
Belfast (cap.), N. Ireland D3
Belgium E3
Belgrade (cap.), Yugoslavia G4
Bergen, Norway E2
Berlin (cap.), Germany F3
Bern (cap.), Switzerland E4
Bilbao, Spain D4
Birmingham, England D3
Biscay (bay) B4
Black (sea) H4
Bologna, Italy F4
Bonn, Germany E3
Bordeaux, France D4
Bornholm (isl.), Denmark F3
Bosnia and Herzegovina F4
Bosporus (str.), Turkey G4
Bothnia (gulf) G2
Bratislava (cap.), Slovakia. F4
Bremen, Germany E3
Bristol, England D3
British Isles D3
Brussels (cap.), Belgium E3
Bucharest (cap.), Romania G4
Budapest (cap.), Hungary F4
Bulgaria G4
Calais, France E3
Cardiff (cap.), Wales D3
Carpathian (mts.) G4
Cartagena, Spain D5
Caspian (sea) J4
Caucasus (mts.) J4
Channel (isls.), U.K. D4
Chişinău (cap.), Moldova G4
Cologne, Germany E3
Copenhagen (cap.), Denmark F3
Córdoba, Spain D5
Cork, Ireland D3
Corsica (isl.), France E4
Cracow, Poland F3
Crete (isl.), Greece G5
Croatia F4
Crimea (pen.), Ukraine H4
Czech Republic F4
Danube (riv.) G4
Dardanelles (str.), Turkey G5
Denmark E3
Dnieper (riv.) H3
Dniester (riv.) G4
Don (riv.), Russia J4
Donets (riv.), Ukraine H4
Douro (riv.), Portugal D4
Dover, England E3
Dresden, Germany F3
Dublin (cap.), Ireland D3
Dvina, Northern (riv.), Russia J2
Ebro (riv.), Spain D4
Edinburgh (cap.), Scotland D3
Elba (isl.), Italy E4
Elbe (riv.) F3
El'brus (mt.), Russia J4
England, U.K. D3
English (chan.) D3
Essen, Germany E3
Estonia G3
Etna (vol.), Italy F5
Faroe (isls.), Denmark D2
Finisterre (cape), Spain C4
Finland G2
Finland (gulf), Finland G3
Florence, Italy F4
France E4
Frankfurt, Germany E3
Gdańsk, Poland F3
Geneva, Switzerland E4
Genoa, Italy E4
Georgia J4
Germany F3
Gibraltar D5
Glasgow, Scotland D3
Göteborg, Sweden F3
Granada, Spain D5
Hague, The (cap.) Netherlands E3
Hamburg, Germany F3
Helsinki (cap.), Finland G2
Hungary F4
Iceland C2
Ionian (sea) F5
Ireland D3
Irish (sea) D3
İstanbul, Turkey G4
Italy F4
Jan Mayen (isl.), Norway D1
Jönköping, Sweden F3
Kaliningrad, Russia G3
Karlsruhe, Germany E4
Katowice, Poland F3
Khar'kov, Ukraine H4
Kiev (cap.), Ukraine H3
Kjölen (mts.) F2
Kola (pen.), Russia H2
Kursk, Russia H3
Ladoga (lake), Russia H2
Land's End (prom.), England D3
Latvia G3
Leeds, England D3
Le Havre, France E4
Leipzig, Germany F3
León, Spain D4
Liechtenstein F4
Liège, Belgium E3
Lille, France E3
Limerick, Ireland D3
Limoges, France E4
Linz, Austria F4
Lisbon (cap.), Portugal D5
Lithuania G3
Liverpool, England D3
Ljubljana, (cap.), Slovenia F4
Łódź, Poland F3
Lofoten (isls.), Norway F2
Loire (riv.), France E4
London (cap.), England D3
Luxembourg E4
Lyon, France E4
Lviv (L'vov), Ukraine G4
Macedonia G4
Madrid (cap.), Spain D4
Majorca (isl.), Spain E5
Málaga, Spain D5
Malmö, Sweden F3
Malta F5
Manchester, England D3
Marmara (sea), Turkey G4
Marseille, France E4
Mediterranean (sea) E5
Milan, Italy E4
Minsk (cap.), Belarus G3
Moldova G4
Monaco E4
Moscow (cap.), Russia H3
Munich, Germany F4
Murmansk, Russia H2
Naples, Italy F4
Nice, France E4
Nizhniy Novgorod (Gor'kiy), Russia J3
North (Nordkapp) (cape), Norway G1
North (sea) E3
Northern Ireland D3
Norway E2
Norwegian (sea) D2
Nürnberg (Nuremberg), Germany F4
Odense, Denmark F3
Oder (riv.) F3
Odessa, Ukraine H4
Onega (lake), Russia H2
Orkney (isls.), Scotland D3
Orléans, France E4
Oslo (cap.), Norway F2
Palermo, Italy F5
Palma, Spain E5
Paris (cap.), France E4
Piraiévs, Greece G5
Plymouth, England D3
Po (riv.), Italy E4
Poland F3
Porto, Portugal D4
Portugal D5
Poznań, Poland F3
Prague (cap.), Czech Rep. F3
Prut (riv.) G4
Pyrenees (mts.) D4
Reykjavík (cap.), Iceland B2
Rhine (riv.) E4
Rhône (riv.), France E4
Riga (cap.), Latvia G3
Romania G4
Rome (cap.), Italy F4
Rostov, Russia J4
Rotterdam, Netherlands E3
Russia. H3
Saarbrücken, Germany E4
St. Petersburg (Leningrad), Russia H3
Salzburg, Austria F4

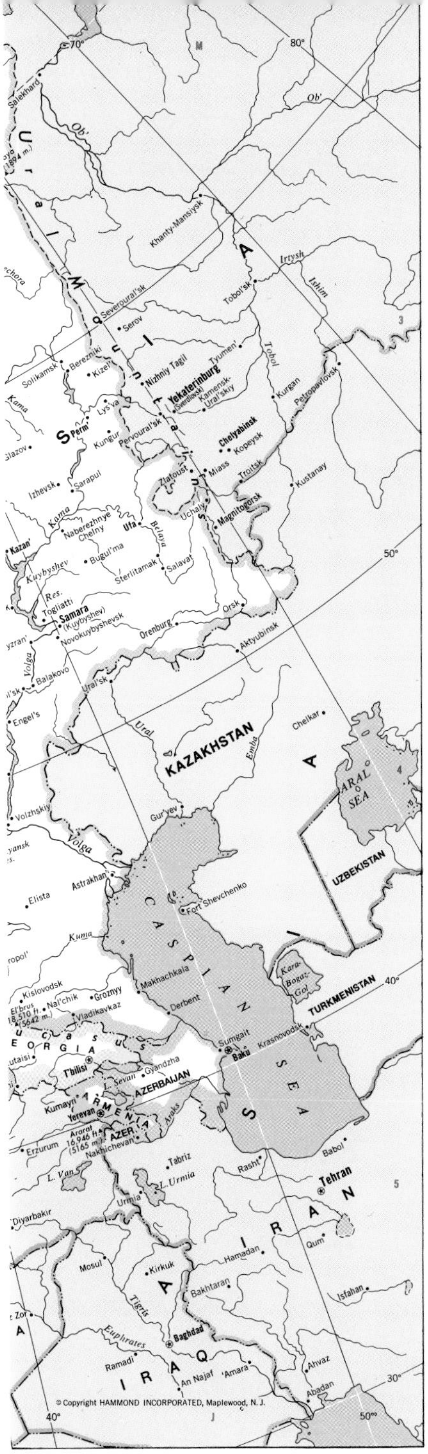
KAZAKHSTAN
ARAL SEA
CASPIAN SEA
UZBEKISTAN
TURKMENISTAN
AZERBAIJAN
IRAN
IRAQ
Tehran
Baghdad
Baku
T'bilisi
Yerevan
Samara (Kuybyshev)
Yekaterinburg
Chelyabinsk
Perm'
Ufa
Orenburg
Astrakhan'
Volga
Ural
Ob'
Irtysh
Tobol
Tigris
Euphrates
© Copyright HAMMOND INCORPORATED, Maplewood, N.J.

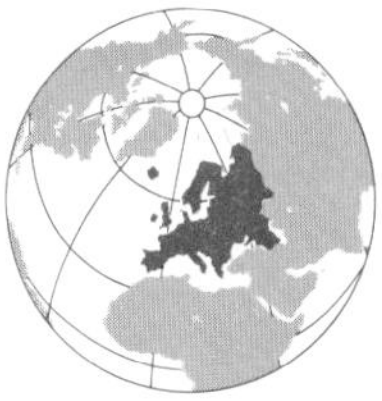

AREA 4,057,000 sq. mi. (10,507,630 sq. km.)
POPULATION 689,000,000
LARGEST CITY Paris
HIGHEST POINT El'brus 18,510 ft. (5,642 m.)
LOWEST POINT Caspian Sea -92 ft. (-28 m.)

Population Distribution

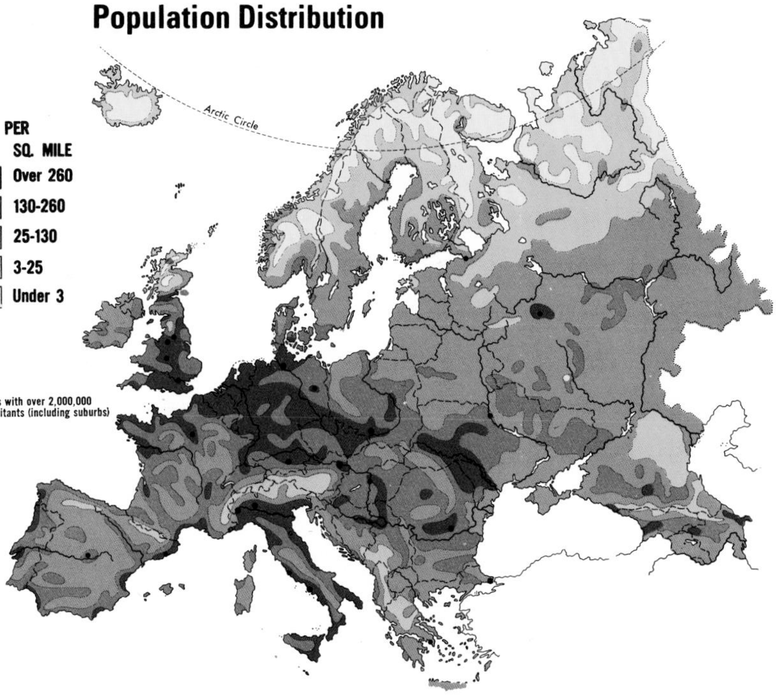
Arctic Circle

DENSITY PER

SQ. KILOMETER	SQ. MILE
Over 100	Over 260
50-100	130-260
10-50	25-130
1-10	3-25
Under 1	Under 3

• LONDON Cities with over 2,000,000 inhabitants (including suburbs)

Vegetation

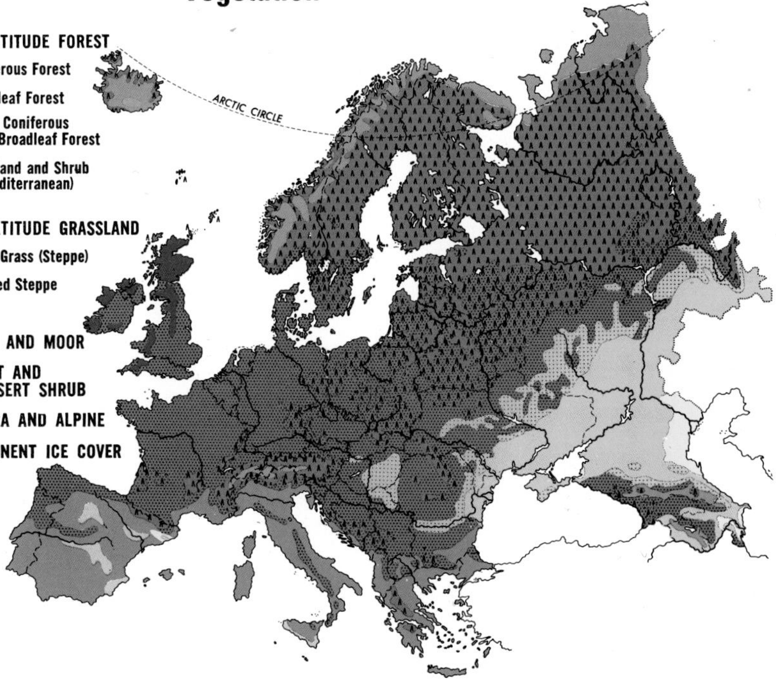
ARCTIC CIRCLE

MID-LATITUDE FOREST
- Coniferous Forest
- Broadleaf Forest
- Mixed Coniferous and Broadleaf Forest
- Woodland and Shrub (Mediterranean)

MID-LATITUDE GRASSLAND
- Short Grass (Steppe)
- Wooded Steppe

HEATH AND MOOR

DESERT AND DESERT SHRUB

TUNDRA AND ALPINE

PERMANENT ICE COVER

NORWEGIAN SEA
Arctic Circle
BARENTS SEA
WHITE SEA
Nordkapp
Kolguyev I.
Cheshskaya Bay
Pechora
Reykjavík
Vesterålen
Lofoten
Vestfjord
Kiruna
Oulu
FINLAND
Gulf of Bothnia
Lake Onega
Lake Ladoga
Archangel
Northern Dvina
Faroe Is. (Den.)
Shetland Is.
Orkney Is.
Hebrides
Moray Firth
Hardangerfjord
Sundsvall
Tampere
Åland Is.
Helsinki
St. Petersburg
Gulf of Finland
Tallinn
ESTONIA
Hiiumaa
Saaremaa
Västerås
Stockholm
Vänern
Lindesnes
Skagerrak
Kattegat
Göteborg
Gotland
Aberdeen
UNITED KINGDOM
NORTH SEA
DENMARK
Copenhagen
Bornholm
Riga
LATVIA
Western Dvina
LITHUANIA
Vilnius
RUSSIA
Minsk
BELARUS
Moscow
Volga
Nizhniy Novgorod
RUSSIA
Dublin
IRELAND
IRISH SEA
Liverpool
Great Britain
Birmingham
C. Clear
St. Georges Chan.
Land's End
London
English Channel
ATLANTIC OCEAN
Frisian Is.
Amsterdam
NETHERLANDS
Hamburg
Elbe
Rügen
Gdańsk
Berlin
GERMANY
POLAND
Vistula
Łódź
Warsaw
BELGIUM
Brussels
Cologne
Bonn
Leipzig
Oder
Bug
Kiev
Khar'kov
Don
Channel Is. (U.K.)
Le Havre
Seine
Paris
Lux.
Prague
CZECH REP.
Cracow
Lvov
Dnieper
UKRAINE
Donetsk
Nantes
Loire
FRANCE
Stuttgart
Danube
Brno
SLOVAKIA
Bratislava
Munich
Vienna
AUSTRIA
Budapest
HUNGARY
Cluj-Napoca
MOLDOVA
Carpathian Mts.
Odessa
SEA OF AZOV
Crimea
Krasnodar
Bay of Biscay
Bordeaux
Dordogne
Garonne
Lyon
Rhône
SWITZ.
Alps
SLOVENIA
Zagreb
CROATIA
ROMANIA
Bucharest
Belgrade
C. Finisterre
Pyrenees
Porto
Douro
SPAIN
Madrid
Saragossa
Tagus
Guadiana
Lisbon
PORTUGAL
Barcelona
Valencia
Gulf of Lions
Genoa
MONACO
Turin
Venice
SAN MARINO
BOSNIA HERZEGOVINA
YUGOSLAVIA
Balkan Mts.
Sofia
BULGARIA
BLACK SEA
Istanbul
Bosporus
Sea of Marmara
Ankara
TURKEY
C. de São Vicente
Balearic Is.
Minorca
Majorca
Ibiza
Corsica
VATICAN CITY
Rome
ADRIATIC SEA
Sardinia
Naples
Tirana
ALBANIA
Skopje
MACEDONIA
Thessaloniki
Cádiz
Str. of Gibraltar
Tangier
GIBRALTAR (U.K.)
MEDITERRANEAN SEA
TYRRHENIAN SEA
C. Teulada
Dardanelles
Lesvos
AEGEAN SEA
Athens
GREECE
Rabat
Casablanca
MOROCCO
Oran
Algiers
Constantine
ALGERIA
C. Bon
Tunis
TUNISIA
AFRICA
Palermo
Sicily
Etna
C. Passero
MALTA
Valletta
IONIAN SEA
C. Tainaron
Crete
Rhodes
CYPRUS
Nicosia
LEBANON
Beirut
Damascus
SYRIA
Longitude West of Greenwich
Longitude East of Greenwich

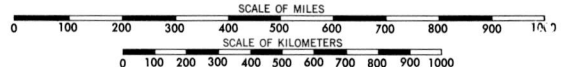

Vegetation/Relief

SCALE OF MILES

0 100 200 300 400 500 600 700 800 900 1000

SCALE OF KILOMETERS

0 100 200 300 400 500 600 700 800 900 1000

Capitals of Countries ⊛

International Boundaries —·-—

Canals ┴┴┴

Depths in Fathoms

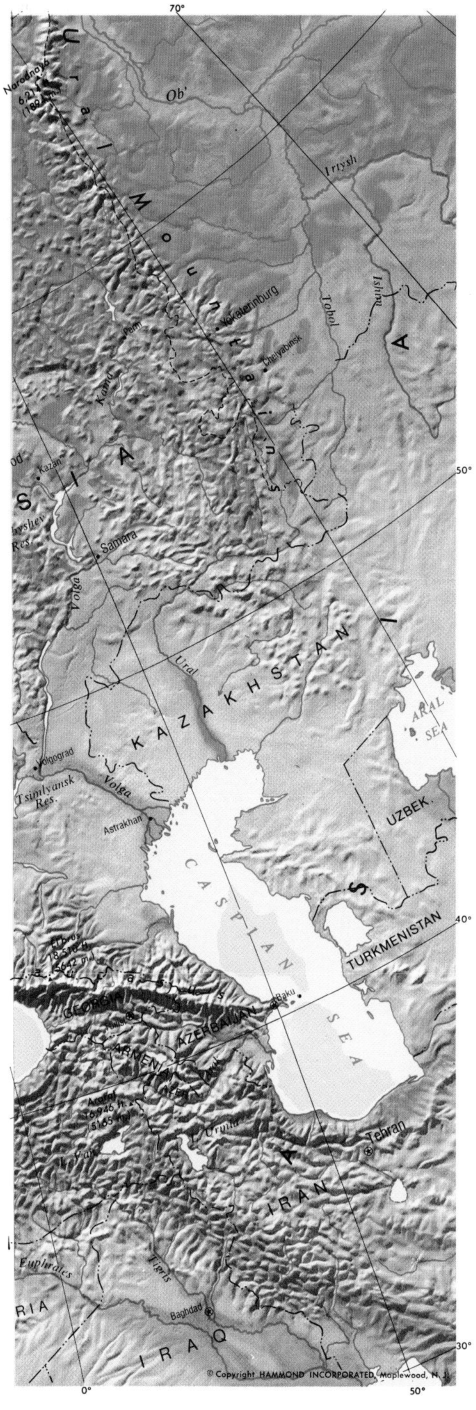
Ural Mountains
Ob'
Irtysh
Tobol
Ishim
Yekaterinburg
Chelyabinsk
Kazan'
Samara
Volga
Ural
KAZAKHSTAN
ARAL SEA
Volgograd
Tsimlyansk Res.
Astrakhan
UZBEK.
CASPIAN SEA
TURKMENISTAN
GEORGIA
AZERBAIJAN
ARMENIA
Baku
Tehran
IRAN
Euphrates
Tigris
Baghdad
IRAQ
70°
50°
40°
30°
0°
© Copyright HAMMOND INCORPORATED, Maplewood, N.J.

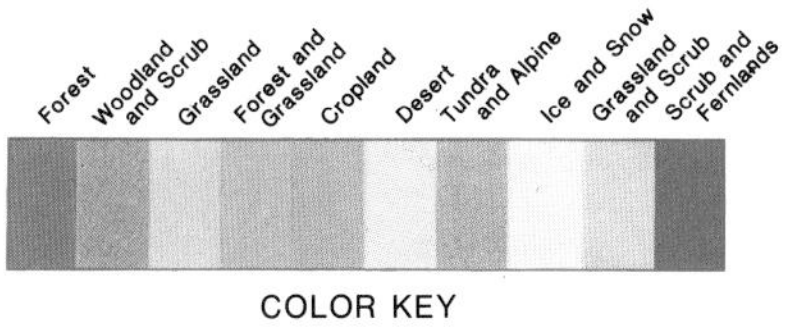
Forest
Woodland and Scrub
Grassland
Forest and Grassland
Cropland
Desert
Tundra and Alpine
Ice and Snow
Grassland and Scrub
Scrub and Fernlands

COLOR KEY

Rainfall

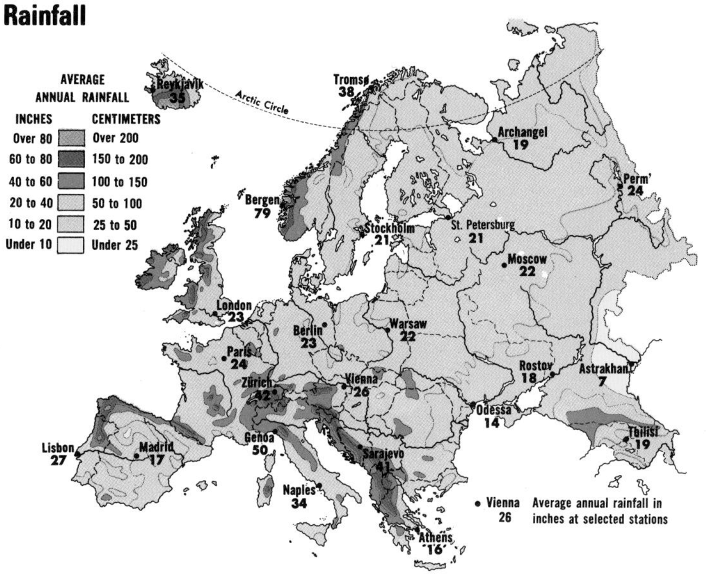
AVERAGE ANNUAL RAINFALL
INCHES | CENTIMETERS
Over 80 | Over 200
60 to 80 | 150 to 200
40 to 60 | 100 to 150
20 to 40 | 50 to 100
10 to 20 | 25 to 50
Under 10 | Under 25
Arctic Circle
Reykjavík 35
Tromsø 38
Archangel 19
Perm' 24
Bergen 79
Stockholm 21
St. Petersburg 21
Moscow 22
London 23
Berlin 23
Warsaw 22
Paris 24
Zürich 42
Vienna 26
Rostov 18
Astrakhan 7
Odessa 14
Tbilisi 19
Lisbon 27
Madrid 17
Genoa 50
Sarajevo 41
Naples 34
Athens 16
Vienna 26 Average annual rainfall in inches at selected stations

Average January Temperature

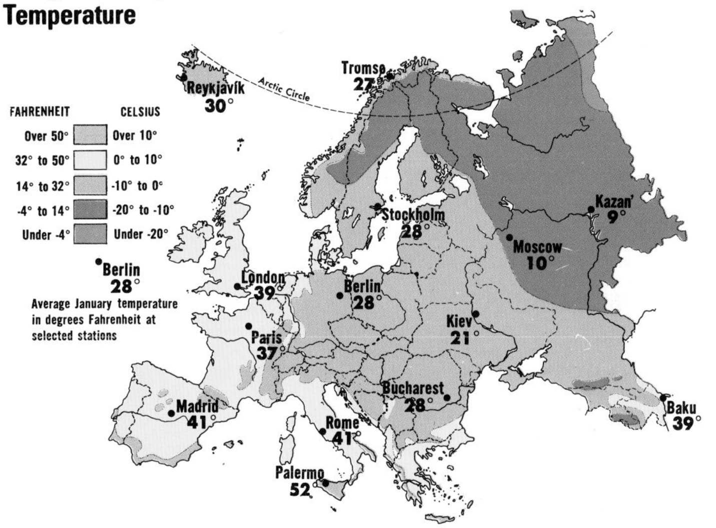
FAHRENHEIT | CELSIUS
Over 50° | Over 10°
32° to 50° | 0° to 10°
14° to 32° | -10° to 0°
-4° to 14° | -20° to -10°
Under -4° | Under -20°
Berlin 28° Average January temperature in degrees Fahrenheit at selected stations
Arctic Circle
Reykjavík 30°
Tromsø 27°
Stockholm 28°
Kazan' 9°
Moscow 10°
London 39°
Berlin 28°
Kiev 21°
Paris 37°
Bucharest 28°
Madrid 41°
Rome 41°
Baku 39°
Palermo 52°

Average July Temperature

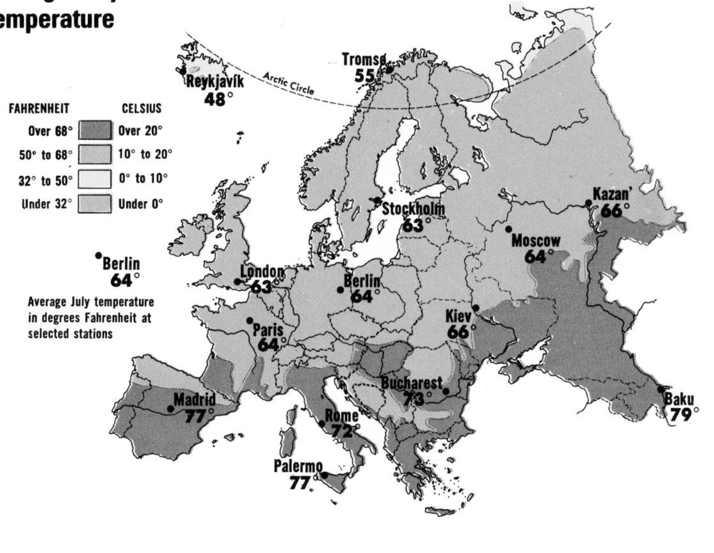
FAHRENHEIT | CELSIUS
Over 68° | Over 20°
50° to 68° | 10° to 20°
32° to 50° | 0° to 10°
Under 32° | Under 0°
Berlin 64° Average July temperature in degrees Fahrenheit at selected stations
Arctic Circle
Reykjavík 48°
Tromsø 55°
Stockholm 63°
Kazan' 66°
Moscow 64°
London 63°
Berlin 64°
Kiev 66°
Paris 64°
Bucharest 73°
Madrid 77°
Rome 72°
Baku 79°
Palermo 77°

United Kingdom and Ireland
BONNE PROJECTION
SCALE OF MILES
SCALE OF KILOMETERS
Capitals of Countries
International Boundaries
Other Boundaries
Canals
Shetland Islands
Same scale as main map.
Unst
Yell
Fetlar
Sullom Voe
Whalsay
St. Magnus B.
Papa Stour
Mainland
Bressay
Scalloway
Lerwick
Foula
SHETLAND ISLANDS
Fair Isle
Papa Westray
N. Ronaldsay
Westray
Sanday
Rousay
Eday
Stronsay
Stromness
Kirkwall
Mainland
ORKNEY ISLANDS
Hoy
S. Ronaldsay
Pentland Firth
Dunnet Hd.
Duncansby Hd.
Strathy Pt.
C. Wrath
Thurso
Halkirk
Wick
Lybster
Butt of Lewis
Barvas
Stornoway
Lewis
Flannan Is.
OUTER HEBRIDES
Harris
North Uist
Benbecula
South Uist
BARRA ISLES
Barra
Barra Hd.
North Minch
Little Minch
Sea of the Hebrides
INNER HEBRIDES
Skye
Portree
Uig
Canna
Rhum
Eigg
Muck
Coll
Tiree
Mull
Tobermory
Iona
Colonsay
Jura
Islay
Bowmore
Mull of Oa
Lochinver
Loch Shin
Lairg
Helmsdale
Dornoch Firth
Ullapool
Dornoch
Tain
Invergordon
Cromarty
Moray Firth
Dingwall
Inverness
Nairn
Forres
Elgin
Banff
Macduff
Fraserburgh
Kinnairds Hd.
Peterhead
Ellon
Huntly
Turriff
Keith
Achnasheen
Loch Maree
Beauly
Lochcarron
Fort Augustus
Loch Ness
Grantown-on-Spey
Spey
Kingussie
Glenelg
Mallaig
Fort William
Ben Nevis 4,406 ft. (1343 m.)
Braemar
Ballater
BALMORAL CASTLE
Banchory
Aberdeen
Stonehaven
Laurencekirk
Inverbervie
Montrose
Brechin
Kirriemuir
Forfar
Arbroath
Carnoustie
Dundee
Perth
Pitlochry
Aberfeldy
Blair Atholl
Loch Tay
Oban
Dalmally
Firth of Lorne
Inveraray
Callander
Crieff
Auchterarder
Dunblane
Stirling
Kinross
Kirkcaldy
Cupar
St. Andrews
Firth of Tay
Firth of Forth
North Berwick
Dunbar
Dunfermline
Edinburgh
Haddington
Falkirk
Greenock
Paisley
Glasgow
Hamilton
Lanark
Peebles
Galashiels
Melrose
Kelso
Duns
Lauder
Eyemouth
Berwick-upon-Tweed
Holy I. (Lindisfarne)
Coldstream
Jedburgh
Hawick
Selkirk
Alnwick
Rothbury
Morpeth
Ashington
Blyth
Tynemouth
Newcastle upon Tyne
South Shields
Sunderland
Seaham
Hexham
Gateshead
Durham
Hartlepool
Middlesbrough
Redcar
Whitby
Scarborough
Filey
Flamborough Hd.
Bridlington
Rothesay
Ardrossan
Saltcoats
Irvine
Troon
Kilmarnock
Ayr
Arran
Brodick
Campbeltown
Firth of Clyde
Girvan
Maybole
Dalmellington
Moffat
Langholm
Lockerbie
Dumfries
Annan
Gretna
Carlisle
Penrith
Newton Stewart
Castle Douglas
Kirkcudbright
Wigtown
Stranraer
Portpatrick
Whithorn
Luce Bay
Mull of Galloway
Solway Firth
Workington
Whitehaven
Keswick
Scafell Pike 3,210 ft. (978 m.)
Windermere
Kendal
Sedbergh
Appleby
Darlington
Richmond
Northallerton
Ripon
Harrogate
Knaresborough
York
Malton
Driffield
Beverley
Hull
Withernsea
Spurn Hd.
Grimsby
Cleethorpes
Isle of Man
Ramsey
Peel
Douglas
Snaefell 2,034 ft. (620 m.)
Pt. of Ayre
Barrow-in-Furness
Lancaster
Skipton
Morecambe Bay
Fleetwood
Blackpool
Preston
Blackburn
Burnley
Bradford
Leeds
Halifax
Huddersfield
Wakefield
Dewsbury
Doncaster
Southport
Wigan
Bolton
Oldham
Manchester
Stockport
St. Helens
Liverpool
Birkenhead
Sheffield
Rotherham
Chesterfield
Mansfield
Lincoln
Gainsborough
Louth
Skegness
Boston
The Wash
Hunstanton
King's Lynn
Cromer
Sheringham
Norwich
Great Yarmouth
Lowestoft
Southwold
Ipswich
Felixstowe
Harwich
Colchester
Chelmsford
Clacton
Southend-on-Sea
Margate
Ramsgate
Canterbury
Deal
Dover
Folkestone
Hythe
Hastings
Eastbourne
Brighton
Worthing
Chichester
Portsmouth
Southampton
Isle of Wight
Newport
Ryde
Ventnor
Bournemouth
Poole
Swanage
Weymouth
Bill of Portland
Dorchester
Exeter
Exmouth
Torquay
Torbay
Plymouth
Salcombe
Prawle Pt.
Bodmin
Padstow
Newquay
Truro
Falmouth
Penzance
Helston
Lizard Pt.
Land's End
Is. of Scilly
St. Ives
Camborne-Redruth
Launceston
Tavistock
Barnstaple
Barnstaple Bay
Bideford
Hartland Pt.
Ilfracombe
Lundy I.
Minehead
Bridgwater
Taunton
Yeovil
Bristol Channel
Weston-super-Mare
Bristol
Bath
Swindon
Oxford
Reading
LONDON
Gravesend
Rochester
Chatham
Maidstone
Guildford
Crawley
Winchester
Salisbury
Gloucester
Cheltenham
Worcester
Hereford
Birmingham
Coventry
Wolverhampton
Walsall
Stafford
Stoke-on-Trent
Derby
Nottingham
Leicester
Northampton
Peterborough
Cambridge
Bedford
Luton
Cardiff
Swansea
Newport
Merthyr Tydfil
Llanelli
Carmarthen
Tenby
Pembroke
Milford Haven
Haverfordwest
Fishguard
St. David's Hd.
St. Brides B.
Cardigan
Cardigan Bay
Aberystwyth
Aberaeron
Barmouth
Dolgellau
Harlech
Porthmadog
Pwllheli
Bardsey I.
Caernarfon
Bangor
Anglesey (Ynys Môn)
Holyhead
Holy I.
Llandudno
Colwyn Bay
Rhyl
Snowdon 3,560 ft. (1085 m.)
Wrexham
Chester
Shrewsbury
Welshpool
Newtown
Llandrindod Wells
Brecon
Abergavenny
Monmouth
Chepstow
WALES
ENGLAND
SCOTLAND
ATLANTIC OCEAN
NORTH SEA
GREAT BRITAIN
IRISH SEA
North Channel
St. George's Channel
Carmarthen Bay
ENGLISH CHANNEL
Strait of Dover
Dungeness
Beachy Hd.
N. Foreland
CHANNEL ISLANDS
Alderney
Guernsey
St. Peter Port
Sark
Jersey
St. Helier
Cap de la Hague
Pte. de Barfleur
Cherbourg
Bay of the Seine
Le Havre
Rouen
Fécamp
Dieppe
Neufchâtel
St-Valery
Étaples
Boulogne-sur-Mer
Calais
FRANCE
Malin Head
Tory I.
Bloody Foreland
Rathlin I.
Portrush
Coleraine
Ballycastle
Ballymoney
Ballymena
Larne
Carrickfergus
Belfast
Belfast L.
Lisburn
Antrim
Lough Neagh
NORTHERN IRELAND
Londonderry
Limavady
Strabane
Omagh
Cookstown
Dungannon
Enniskillen
Lough Erne
Upper L. Erne
Armagh
Craigavon
Newry
Downpatrick
Newcastle
Slieve Donard 2,796 ft. (852 m.)
Monaghan
Castleblayney
Clones
Cavan
Dundalk
Dundalk Bay
Drogheda
Letterkenny
Buncrana
L. Swilly
Burtonport
Aran I.
Donegal
Donegal Bay
Ballyshannon
Sligo
Sligo Bay
Rossan Pt.
Erris Head
Achill Head
Achill I.
Clare I.
Inishturk
Inishbofin
Slyne Head
Ballina
Ballymote
Boyle
Lough Conn
Lough Mask
Lough Corrib
Lough Ree
Lough Derg
Castlebar
Westport
Claremorris
Ballinrobe
Castlerea
Roscommon
Tuam
Clifden
Galway
Galway Bay
Aran Is.
Ballinasloe
Loughrea
Gort
Athlone
Longford
Mullingar
Trim
Navan
Kells
Balbriggan
Skerries
Dublin (Baile Átha Cliath)
Dublin Bay
Dún Laoghaire (Kingstown)
Bray
Greystones-Delgany
Wicklow
Wicklow Hd.
Arklow
Naas
Athy
Carlow
Portlaoise (Maryborough)
Tullamore
Birr
Roscrea
Nenagh
Ennis
Ennistymon
Kilkee
Loop Head
Shannon
Limerick (Luimneach)
Thurles
Templemore
Kilkenny
Tipperary
Cashel
Clonmel
Carrick-on-Suir
Waterford
Wexford
Wexford Har.
Carnsore Pt.
New Ross
Enniscorthy
Gorey
Tralee
Listowel
Abbeyfeale
Castleisland
Dingle
Dingle Bay
Blasket Is.
Valentia I. (Valencia)
Cahirciveen
Killarney
Lakes of Killarney
Carrantuohill 3,415 ft. (1041 m.)
Kenmare
Macroom
Mallow
Fermoy
Lismore
Dungarvan
Youghal
Midleton
Cork
Cobh (Queenstown)
Kinsale
Bandon
Bantry
Bantry B.
Skibbereen
Baltimore
Mizen Head
Cape Clear
IRELAND
Loch Lomond
Dumbarton
Clydebank
Kirkintilloch
Airdrie
Coatbridge
Motherwell & Wishaw
Rutherglen
Johnstone
Renfrew
Largs
Millport
Gourock
Dunoon
Helensburgh
Alloa
Bridge of Allan
Bannockburn
Grangemouth
Linlithgow
Bo'ness
Queensferry
Livingston
Bathgate
Musselburgh
Dalkeith
Penicuik
Burntisland
Firth of Forth
Kirkcaldy
Thornton Cleveleys
Lytham St. Anne's
Poulton le Fylde
Longridge
Clitheroe
Colne
Nelson
Accrington
Rochdale
Bury
Leigh
Warrington
Widnes
Runcorn
Northwich
Winsford
Macclesfield
Sandbach
Crewe & Nantwich
Alsager
Ellesmere Port
Wallasey
Hoylake
Neston
Formby
Crosby
Bootle
Burton upon Trent
Swadlincote
Rugeley
Lichfield
Cannock
Burntwood
Tamworth
Aldridge-Brownhills
Sutton Coldfield
Wolverhampton
W. Bromwich
Dudley
Stourbridge
Halesowen
Solihull
Kidderminster
Stourport-on-Sev.
Bewdley
Redditch
GREATER LONDON
Potters Bar
Cheshunt
Epping
Enfield
Waltham Holy Cross
Chorleywood
Watford
Bushey
Barnet
Chigwell
Brentwood
Rickmansworth
Harrow
Haringey
Waltham Forest
Havering
Hackney
Redbridge
Barking
Brent
Islington
Camden
Newham
Hillingdon
Ealing
Kensington & Chelsea
Westminster
Hammersmith
Greenwich
Thurrock
Hounslow
Richmond upon T.
Wandsworth
Lambeth
Southwark
Lewisham
Bexley
Dartford
Swanscombe
Northfleet
Gravesend
Staines
Sunbury-on-T.
Kingston upon T.
Merton
Bromley
Chertsey
Esher
Croydon
Sutton
Walton & Weybridge
Epsom & Ewell
Banstead
Woking
Leatherhead
Caterham & Warlingham
Sevenoaks
N
Longitude
West of
Greenwich

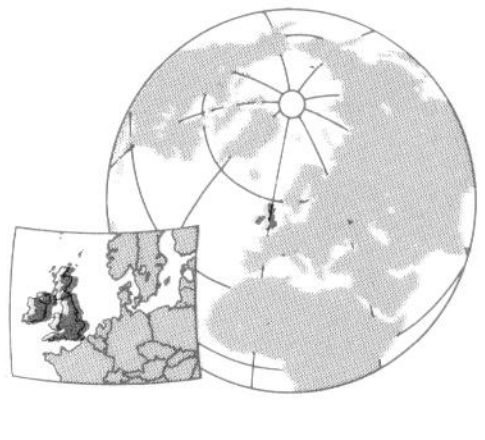

UNITED KINGDOM

AREA 94,399 sq. mi. (244,493 sq. km.)
POPULATION 57,236,000
CAPITAL London
LARGEST CITY London
HIGHEST POINT Ben Nevis 4,406 ft. (1,343 m.)
MONETARY UNIT pound sterling
MAJOR LANGUAGES English, Gaelic, Welsh
MAJOR RELIGIONS Protestantism, Roman Catholicism

IRELAND

AREA 27,136 sq. mi. (70,282 sq. km.)
POPULATION 3,540,643
CAPITAL Dublin
LARGEST CITY Dublin
HIGHEST POINT Carrantuohill 3,415 ft. (1,041 m.)
MONETARY UNIT Irish pound
MAJOR LANGUAGES English, Gaelic (Irish)
MAJOR RELIGION Roman Catholicism

UNITED KINGDOM

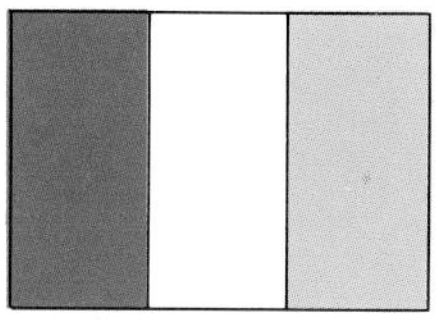

IRELAND

ENGLAND

AREA 50,516 sq. mi. (130,836 sq. km.)
POPULATION 46,220,955
CAPITAL London
LARGEST CITY London
HIGHEST POINT Scafell Pike 3,210 ft. (978 m.)

WALES

AREA 8,017 sq. mi. (20,764 sq. km.)
POPULATION 2,749,640
CAPITAL Cardiff
LARGEST CITY Cardiff
HIGHEST POINT Snowdon 3,560 ft. (1,085 m.)

SCOTLAND

AREA 30,414 sq. mi. (78,772 sq. km.)
POPULATION 5,130,735
CAPITAL Edinburgh
LARGEST CITY Glasgow
HIGHEST POINT Ben Nevis 4,406 ft. (1,343 m.)

NORTHERN IRELAND

AREA 5,452 sq. mi. (14,121 sq. km.)
POPULATION 1,543,000
CAPITAL Belfast
LARGEST CITY Belfast
HIGHEST POINT Slieve Donard 2,796 ft. (852 m.)

ENGLAND
(map on page 13)

COUNTIES

Avon 900,947 ..... E6
Bedfordshire 502,164 ..... G5
Berkshire 670,859 ..... F6
Buckinghamshire 562,221 ..... G6
Cambridgeshire 569,893 ..... G5
Cheshire 921,623 ..... E4
Cleveland 565,845 ..... F3
Cornwall 418,631 ..... C7
Cumbria 471,696 ..... D3
Derbyshire 901,831 ..... F5
Devon 930,112 ..... D7
Dorset 578,993 ..... E7
Durham 598,881 ..... F3
East Sussex 641,016 ..... H7
Essex 1,416,890 ..... H6
Gloucestershire 493,166 ..... E6
Hampshire 1,442,598 ..... F6
Hereford and Worcester 624,393 ..... E5
Hertfordshire 950,760 ..... G6
Humberside 843,282 ..... G4
Isle of Wight 114,879 ..... F7
Isles of Scilly A7
Kent 1,448,393 ..... H6
Lancashire 1,362,801 ..... E4
Leicestershire 835,647 ..... F5
Lincolnshire 542,944 ..... G4
London 6,608,598 ..... H8
Manchester 2,575,407 ..... H2
Merseyside 1,503,120 ..... G2
Norfolk 685,232 ..... H5
North Yorkshire 653,456 ..... F3
Northamptonshire 524,967 ..... G5
Northumberland 295,451 ..... E2
Nottinghamshire 976,748 ..... F4
Oxfordshire 507,230 ..... F6
Shropshire 370,355 ..... E5
Somerset 417,457 ..... E6
South Yorkshire 1,292,029 ..... F4
Staffordshire 1,005,641 ..... E5
Suffolk 590,133 ..... H5
Surrey 992,489 ..... G6
Tyne and Wear 1,135,492 ..... H3
Warwickshire 469,801 ..... F5
West Midlands 2,628,419 ..... F5
West Sussex 650,124 ..... G7
West Yorkshire 2,021,707 ..... J1
Wiltshire 512,635 ..... E6
Yorkshire, North 653,456 ..... F3
Yorkshire, South 1,292,029 ..... F4
Yorkshire, West 2,021,707 ..... J1

CITIES and TOWNS

Abingdon 29,130 ..... F6
Accrington 36,459 ..... H1
Adwickle Street 10,293 ..... K2
Aldershot 53,665 ..... G8
Aldridge 17,549 ..... E5
Alfreton 21,284 ..... F4
Alsager 12,944 ..... E4
Alton 14,163 ..... G6
Altrincham 39,528 ..... H2
Amersham⊙ 21,326 ..... G7
Andover 30,632 ..... F6
Arnold 37,721 ..... F4
Ashford 45,198 ..... H6
Ashington 27,786 ..... F2
Ashton-under-Lyne 43,605 ..... H2
Aylesbury 51,999 ..... G7
Aylesford 21,017 ..... J8
Bacup 14,082 ..... H1
Banbury 37,463 ..... F5
Banstead 35,360 ..... H8
Barking 149,132 ..... H8
Barnet 289,277 ..... H7
Barnoldswick 10,125 ..... H1
Barnsley 76,783 ..... J2
Barnstaple 24,490 ..... D6
Barrow-in-Furness 50,174 ..... D3
Basildon 94,800 ..... J8
Basingstoke 73,027 ..... F6
Bath 84,283 ..... E6
Batley 45,582 ..... J1
Beaconsfield 13,397 ..... G8
Bebington 62,618 ..... G2
Beccles 10,677 ..... J5
Bedford 75,632 ..... G5
Bedlington 15,074 ..... F2
Bedworth 29,192 ..... F5
Beeston and Stapleford 64,785 ..... F5
Benfleet 50,783 ..... J8
Bentley with Arksey 34,273 ..... F4
Berkhamsted 16,874 ..... G7
Berwick-upon-Tweed 12,772 ..... F2
Beverley 19,368 ..... G4
Bexhill 34,625 ..... H7
Bexley 213,215 ..... H8
Bicester 15,946 ..... F6
Biddulph 16,697 ..... H2
Bideford 13,826 ..... C6
Biggleswade 10,905 ..... G5
Birkenhead 99,075 ..... G2
Birmingham 1,013,995 ..... F5
Bishop Auckland 23,560 ..... E3
Bishop's Stortford 22,535 ..... H6
Blackburn 109,564 ..... H1
Blackpool 146,297 ..... G1
Blaydon 16,719 ..... H3
Blyth 35,101 ..... F2
Bodmin 11,992 ..... C7
Bognor Regis 50,323 ..... G7
Boldon 11,639 ..... J3
Bolsover 11,497 ..... J2
Bolton 143,960 ..... H2
Bootle 70,860 ..... G2
Boston 33,908 ..... G5
Bournemouth 142,829 ..... F7
Bracknell 52,257 ..... G8
Bradford 293,336 ..... J1
Braintree 30,975 ..... H6
Brent 251,238 ..... H8
Brentwood 51,212 ..... J8
Bridgnorth 10,332 ..... E5
Bridgwater 30,782 ..... E6
Bridlington 28,426 ..... G3
Bridport 10,615 ..... E7
Brighouse 32,597 ..... J1
Brighton 134,581 ..... G7
Bristol 413,861 ..... E6
Broadstairs 21,551 ..... J6
Bromley 280,525 ..... H8
Bromsgrove 24,576 ..... E5
Brownhills 18,200 ..... E5
Buckingham 6,439 ..... G6
Burgess Hill 23,577 ..... G7
Burnham-on-Sea 17,022 ..... D6
Burnley 76,365 ..... H1
Burntwood 28,938 ..... F5
Burton upon Trent 59,040 ..... F5
Bury 61,785 ..... H2
Bury Saint Edmunds 30,563 ..... H5
Bushey 15,759 ..... H7
Buxton 19,502 ..... J2
Calne 10,235 ..... F6
Camborne-Redruth 34,262 ..... B7
Cambridge 87,111 ..... G5
Camden 161,098 ..... H8
Cannock 54,503 ..... E5
Canterbury 34,546 ..... H6
Canvey Island 35,243 ..... J8
Carlisle 72,206 ..... D3
Carlton 46,053 ..... F5
Carterton 10,876 ..... F6
Caterham and Warlingham 30,331 ..... H8
Charlton Kings 10,786 ..... F6
Chatham 65,835 ..... J8
Cheadle 10,470 ..... E5
Cheadle and Gatley 59,478 ..... H2
Chelmsford 91,109 ..... J7
Cheltenham 87,188 ..... E6
Chertsey 10,195 ..... G8
Chesham 20,883 ..... G7
Cheshunt 49,616 ..... H7
Chester 80,154 ..... G2
Chester-le-Street 34,776 ..... J3
Chesterfield 73,352 ..... J2
Chichester 26,050 ..... G7
Chippenham 21,325 ..... E6
Chorley 33,465 ..... G2
Christchurch 32,854 ..... F7
Cirencester 13,491 ..... E6
Clacton 39,618 ..... J6
Clay Cross 22,635 ..... J2
Cleethorpes 33,238 ..... H4
Clevedon 17,875 ..... D6
Clitheroe 13,671 ..... H1
Coalville 28,831 ..... F5
Colchester 87,476 ..... H6
Colne 19,094 ..... H1
Congleton 23,482 ..... H2
Consett 22,409 ..... H3
Corby 48,704 ..... G5
Corsham 11,259 ..... E6
Coventry 318,718 ..... F5
Cowes 16,134 ..... F7
Cranleigh 10,334 ..... G6
Crawley 80,113 ..... G6
Crewe 59,097 ..... E4
Crosby 54,103 ..... G2
Crowborough 17,008 ..... H6
Croydon 298,794 ..... H8
Darlington 85,519 ..... F3
Dartford 62,032 ..... J8
Darton 13,743 ..... J2
Darwen 30,883 ..... H1
Daventry 16,096 ..... F5
Deal 26,311 ..... J6
Dearne 13,391 ..... K2
Denton 37,784 ..... H2
Derby 218,026 ..... F5
Devizes 12,430 ..... F6
Dewsbury 49,612 ..... J1
Didcot⊙ 15,147 ..... F6
Doncaster 74,727 ..... F4
Dorchester 13,734 ..... E7
Dorking 14,602 ..... G8
Dover 33,461 ..... J6
Droitwich 18,025 ..... E5
Dronfield 22,641 ..... J2
Dudley 186,513 ..... E5
Dunstable 48,436 ..... G6
Durham 38,105 ..... J3
Ealing 278,677 ..... H8
East Dereham 11,798 ..... H5
East Grinstead 23,867 ..... G6
East Retford 19,308 ..... G4
Eastbourne 86,715 ..... H7
Eastleigh 58,585 ..... F7
Egham 21,810 ..... G8
Ellesmere Port 65,829 ..... G2
Enfield 257,154 ..... H7
Epping 10,148 ..... H7
Epsom and Ewell 65,830 ..... G8
Esher 46,688 ..... H8
Eston⊙ 37,694 ..... F3
Eton G8
Evesham 15,069 ..... F5
Exeter 88,235 ..... D7
Exmouth 28,037 ..... D7
Falmouth 17,810 ..... B7
Fareham 55,563 ..... F7
Farnborough 48,063 ..... G8
Farnham 34,541 ..... G8
Farnworth 25,591 ..... H2
Faversham 15,914 ..... H6
Felixstowe 24,207 ..... J6
Felling 36,377 ..... J3
Fleet 27,406 ..... G8
Fleetwood 27,899 ..... D4
Folkestone 42,949 ..... J6
Formby 26,852 ..... G2
Frinton and Walton 12,689 ..... J6
Frome 19,678 ..... E6
Gainsborough 20,326 ..... G4
Gateshead 91,421 ..... J3
Gillingham 92,531 ..... J8
Glastonbury 6,751 ..... E6
Glossop 29,923 ..... J2
Gloucester 106,526 ..... E6
Godalming 18,758 ..... G8
Golborne 20,633 ..... G2
Goole 19,394 ..... G4
Gosport 69,664 ..... F7
Grantham 30,700 ..... G5
Gravesend 53,450 ..... J8
Great Grimsby 91,532 ..... G4
Great Harwood 10,968 ..... H1
Great Malvern (Malvern) 30,153 ..... E5
Great Yarmouth 54,777 ..... J5
Greenwich 211,013 ..... H8
Guildford 61,509 ..... G8
Guisborough 19,242 ..... F3
Hackney 179,529 ..... H8
Hailsham 16,367 ..... H7
Hale 16,362 ..... H2
Halesowen 57,533 ..... E5
Halifax 76,675 ..... J1
Hammersmith 144,616 ..... H8
Haringey 202,650 ..... H8
Harlow 79,150 ..... H7
Harrogate 63,637 ..... J1
Harrow 195,292 ..... G8
Hartlepool 91,749 ..... F3
Harwich 17,245 ..... J6
Haslemere 10,544 ..... G6
Haslingden 14,347 ..... H1
Hastings 74,979 ..... H7
Hatfield 33,174 ..... H7
Havant 50,098 ..... G7
Haverhill 16,970 ..... H5
Havering 238,335 ..... J8
Haxby 11,415 ..... F3
Hazel Grove and Bramhall 40,819 ..... H2
Heanor 21,863 ..... F4
Hebburn 20,098 ..... J3
Hemel Hempstead 80,110 ..... G7
Henley-on-Thames 10,910 ..... G8
Hereford 48,277 ..... E5
Hertford 21,350 ..... H7
Hetton 14,529 ..... J3
Heywood 29,639 ..... H2
High Wycombe 69,575 ..... G8
Hillingdon 226,659 ..... G8
Hinckley 35,510 ..... F5
Hitchin 33,480 ..... G6
Hoddesdon 37,960 ..... H7
Holmfirth 21,138 ..... J2
Horley 17,700 ..... H8
Horsham 38,356 ..... G6
Horwich 16,758 ..... G2
Houghton-le-Spring 35,337 ..... J3
Hounslow 198,938 ..... G8
Hove 65,587 ..... G7
Hoylake 24,815 ..... G2
Hoyland Nether 15,845 ..... J2
Hucknall 27,463 ..... F4

(continued on following page)

Topography

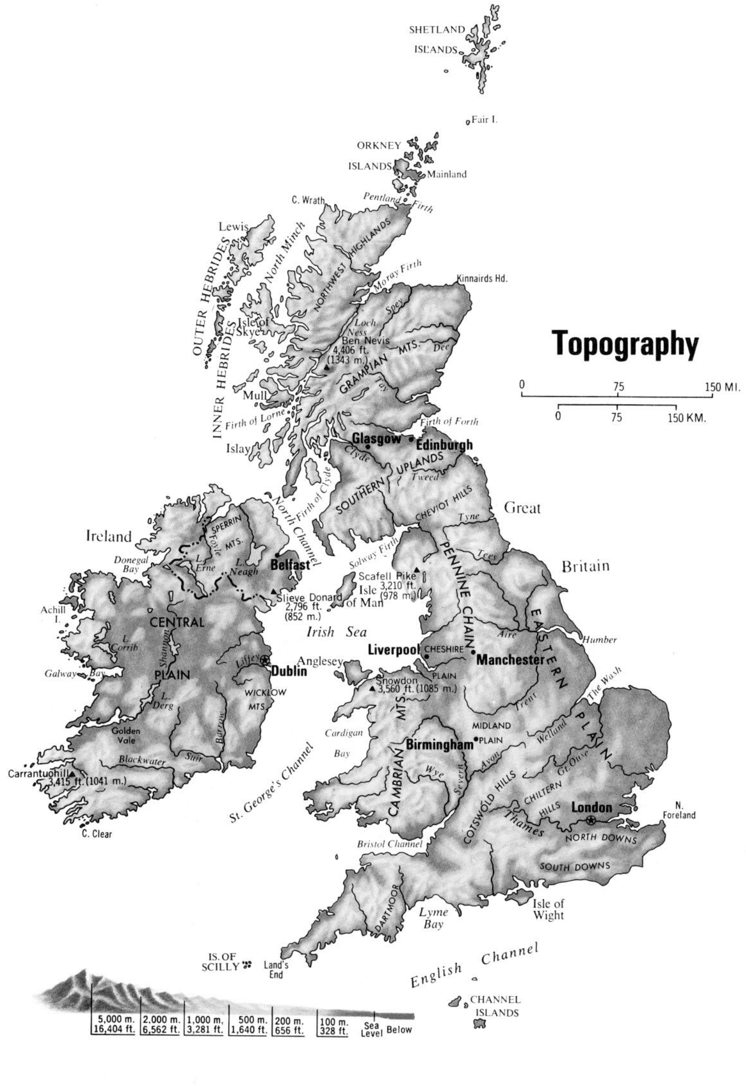

0 75 150 MI.
0 75 150 KM.
SHETLAND ISLANDS
Fair I.
ORKNEY ISLANDS
Mainland
C. Wrath
Pentland Firth
Lewis
North Minch
OUTER HEBRIDES
NORTHWEST HIGHLANDS
Moray Firth
Kinnairds Hd.
Isle of Skye
Loch Ness
Ben Nevis 4,406 ft. (1343 m.)
GRAMPIAN MTS.
Dee
Spey
Mull
INNER HEBRIDES
Firth of Lorne
Firth of Forth
Islay
Glasgow
Edinburgh
SOUTHERN UPLANDS
Tweed
Clyde
Firth of Clyde
North Channel
CHEVIOT HILLS
Tyne
Great
Britain
Ireland
SPERRIN MTS.
Donegal Bay
Lough Erne
Lough Neagh
Belfast
Slieve Donard 2,796 ft. (852 m.)
Solway Firth
Scafell Pike 3,210 ft. (978 m)
Isle of Man
Tees
PENNINE CHAIN
Achill I.
CENTRAL PLAIN
Irish Sea
Liverpool
CHESHIRE PLAIN
Manchester
Aire
EASTERN PLAIN
Humber
Anglesey
Dublin
Liffey
Galway Bay
WICKLOW MTS.
Snowdon 3,560 ft. (1085 m.)
Trent
The Wash
Cardigan Bay
CAMBRIAN MTS.
MIDLAND PLAIN
Birmingham
Welland
Ouse
Golden Vale
Blackwater
Suir
Barrow
Shannon
Avon
Wye
Severn
Carrantuohill 3,415 ft. (1041 m.)
St. George's Channel
COTSWOLD HILLS
CHILTERN HILLS
London
Thames
N. Foreland
C. Clear
NORTH DOWNS
Bristol Channel
SOUTH DOWNS
DARTMOOR
Lyme Bay
Isle of Wight
IS. OF SCILLY
Land's End
English Channel
CHANNEL ISLANDS
5,000 m. 16,404 ft.
2,000 m. 6,562 ft.
1,000 m. 3,281 ft.
500 m. 1,640 ft.
200 m. 656 ft.
100 m. 328 ft.
Sea Level
Below

Huddersfield 147,825 J2
Hugh Town⊙ A8
Hull 322,144 G4
Huntingdon 14,395 G5
Huyton-with-Roby 62,011 G2
Hyde 30,461 H2
Hythe 13,118 H6
Ilkeston 34,683 F5
Immingham⊙ 11,480 G4
Ipswich 129,661 J5
Islington 157,522 H8
Jarrow 31,345 J3
Kempston 15,454 G5
Kendal 23,710 E3
Kenilworth 18,782 F5
Kensington and Chelsea 125,892 G8
Kettering 44,758 G5
Kidderminster 50,385 E5
Kidsgrove 27,999 E4
King's Lynn 37,323 H5
Kingston upon Thames 130,829 H8
Kingswood 54,736 E6
Kirkby 52,825 G2
Knaresborough 12,910 F4
Knutsford 13,628 H2
Lambeth 244,143 H8
Lancaster 43,902 E3
Leamington Spa 56,552 F5
Leatherhead 42,399 G8
Leeds 451,841 J1
Leek 18,495 H2
Leicester 324,394 F5
Leigh 42,627 H2
Letchworth 31,146 G6
Lewes 14,499 H7
Lewisham 230,488 H8
Leyland 36,694 G1
Lichfield 25,408 F5
Lincoln 79,980 G4
Litherland 21,989 G2
Littlehampton 46,028 G7
Liverpool 538,809 G2
London (cap.) 7,566,620 H8
Long Eaton 42,285 F5
Longbenton 36,780 J3
Loughborough 44,895 F5
Louth 13,019 H4
Lowestoft 59,430 J5
Luton 163,209 G6
Lymington 11,614 F7
Lymm 10,036 H2
Lytham Saint Anne's 39,559 G1
Macclesfield 47,525 H2
Maidenhead 59,809 G8
Maidstone 86,067 J8
Maldon 14,638 H6
Malvern 30,153 E5
Manchester 448,604 H2
Mangotsfield 28,664 E6
Mansfield 71,325 K2
Mansfield Woodhouse 17,564 F4
March 14,155 H5
Margate 53,137 J6
Market Harborough 15,852 G5
Marlow 18,584 G8
Matlock 13,706 J2
Melksham 13,248 E6
Melton Mowbray 23,379 G5
Merton 165,102 H8
Middlesbrough 158,516 F3
Middleton 51,373 H2
Milton Keynes 93,305 G5
Morpeth 14,301 F2
Nantwich 11,867 E4
Nelson 30,449 H1
Neston 14,902 G2
New Romney 6,559 J7
Newark 33,143 G4
Newbury 31,488 F6
Newcastle upon Tyne 199,064 H3
Newcastle-under-Lyme 73,208 E4
Newham 209,128 H8
Newhaven 10,697 H7
Newmarket 15,861 H5
Newport, Isle of Wight 19,758 F7
Newport, Shropshire 10,339 E5
Newport Pagnell 10,733 G5
Newquay 13,905 B7
Newton Abbot 20,567 D7
Newton-le-Willows 19,466 H2
Northallerton 13,566 F3
Northampton 154,172 F5
Northfleet 21,400 J8
Northwich 32,664 H2
Norton-Radstock 17,668 E6
Norwich 169,814 J5
Nottingham 273,300 F5
Nuneaton 60,337 F5
Oadby 18,331 F5
Oldham 107,095 H2
Ormskirk 22,308 G2
Oswaldtwistle 11,188 H1
Oswestry 13,200 E5
Oxford 113,847 F6
Padiham 13,856 H1
Penrith 12,086 E3
Penzance 18,501 B7
Peterborough 113,404 G5
Peterlee⊙ 31,405 J3
Petersfield 10,078 F6
Plymouth 238,583 C7
Ponteland 10,215 H3
Poole 122,815 E7
Portishead 13,684 E6
Portslade 17,831 G7
Portsmouth 174,218 F7
Potters Bar 22,610 H7
Poulton-le-Fylde 18,477 G1
Preston 166,675 G1
Prestwich 31,854 H2
Prudhoe 11,140 H3
Radcliffe 27,664 H2
Ramsbottom 16,334 H2
Ramsgate 36,678 J6
Rawtenstall 21,247 H1
Rayleigh 28,574 J8
Reading 194,727 G8
Redbridge 226,977 H8
Redcar⊙ 35,373 F3
Redditch 61,639 E5
Reigate 48,241 H8
Richmond upon Thames 157,304 H8
Rickmansworth 15,960 G8
Ringwood 10,941 F7
Ripley 17,548 F4
Ripon 13,036 F3
Rochdale 97,292 H2
Rochester 23,840 J8
Romney (New Romney) 6,559 J7
Romsey 14,818 F6
Rotherham 122,374 K2
Royal Leamington Spa 56,552 F5
Royal Tunbridge Wells 57,699 H6
Royston 12,904 G5
Rugby 59,039 F5
Rugeley 23,751 E5
Runcorn 63,995 G2
Rushden 22,394 G5
Ryde 19,384 F7
Ryton 15,138 H3
Saffron Walden 11,879 H5
Saint Albans 76,709 H7
Saint Austell 20,267 C7
Saint Helens 114,397 G2
Saint Ives, Cambridgeshire 13,431 G5
Saint Ives, Cornwall 9,439 B7
Saint Neots 12,468 G5
Sale 57,872 H2
Salford 96,525 H2
Salisbury 36,890 F6
Saltash 12,486 C7
Sandbach 13,734 H2
Sandhurst 13,539 G8
Sandown-Shanklin 15,252 F7
Scarborough 36,665 G3
Scunthorpe 79,043 G4
Seaford 16,367 H7
Seaham 21,807 J3
Selby 12,224 F4
Sevenoaks 24,493 J8
Sheffield 470,685 J2
Shepshed 10,479 F5
Shildon 11,583 F3
Shoreham 20,562 G7
Shrewsbury 57,731 E5
Sidmouth 10,808 D7
Sittingbourne 35,893 H6
Skegness 12,645 H4
Skelmersdale 42,611 G2
Skipton 13,009 H1
Slough 106,341 G8
Solihull 93,940 F5
South Shields 86,488 J3
Southampton 211,321 F7
Southend-on-Sea 155,720 H6
Southport 88,596 G1
Southwark 209,735 H8
Southwick 11,364 G7
Sowerby Bridge 11,280 H1
Spalding 18,182 G5
Spennymoor 18,563 F3
Stafford 60,915 E5
Staines 51,949 G8
Stamford 16,127 G5
Standish 11,504 G2
Stanley 20,058 H3
Staveley 24,457 K2
Stevenage 74,757 G6
Stockport 135,489 H2
Stocksbridge 13,394 J2
Stockton-on-Tees 86,699 F3
Stoke-on-Trent 272,446 E4
Stone 12,119 E5
Stourbridge 55,136 E5
Stourport-on-Severn 17,880 E5
Stowmarket 10,913 J5
Stratford-upon-Avon 20,941 F5
Stretford 47,522 H2
Stroud 37,791 E6
Sudbury 17,723 H5
Sunbury 28,240 G8
Sunderland 195,064 J3
Sutton 165,323 H8
Sutton in Ashfield 39,536 K2
Swadlincote 33,667 F5
Swindon 127,348 F6
Tadley 13,668 F6
Tamworth 63,260 F5
Taunton 47,793 D6
Teignmouth 11,995 D7
Telford⊙ 28,645 E5
Tewkesbury 9,454 E6
Thatcham 14,940 F6
Thetford 19,529 H5
Thornaby⊙ 26,319 F3
Thornbury 11,948 E6
Thorne⊙ 16,662 F4
Thornton Cleveleys 26,697 G1
Tiverton 14,745 D7
Todmorden 11,936 H1
Tonbridge 34,407 H8
Torbay 93,995 D7
Tower Hamlets 139,996 H8
Tring 10,610 G7
Trowbridge 27,299 E6
Truro 17,852 B7
Tynemouth 17,877 J3
Uckfield 10,749 H7
Ulverston 11,976 D3
Urmston 43,706 H2
Uttoxeter 10,008 E5
Wakefield 74,764 J2
Wallasey 62,465 G2
Wallsend 44,542 J3
Walsall 177,923 E5
Waltham Forest 214,595 H8
Waltham Holy Cross 16,498 H7
Walton and Weybridge 50,031 G8
Wandsworth 252,240 H8
Ware 15,344 H7
Warminster 14,826 E6
Warrington 81,366 G2
Warsop 10,294 F4
Warwick 21,701 F5
Washington 48,856 J3
Waterloo 57,296 G7
Watford 109,503 H7
Wellingborough 38,598 G5
Wellington 8,980 D7
Welwyn 40,665 H7
West Bridgford 27,463 F5
West Bromwich 153,725 F5
Westminster 163,892 H8
Weston-super-Mare 60,821 D6
Weymouth 38,384 E7
Whickham 17,882 J3
Whitby 12,982 G3
Whitehaven 27,512 D3
Whitley Bay 36,040 J3
Widnes 55,973 G2
Wigan 88,725 G2
Wigston 32,373 F5
Wilmslow 28,827 H2
Wilton 4,002 F6
Wimborne Minster 14,193 E7
Winchester 34,127 F6
Windermere 6,835 E3
Windsor 30,832 G8
Winsford 26,548 G2
Wisbech 22,932 H5
Witham 21,875 H6
Witney 14,215 F6
Woking 92,667 G8
Wokingham 30,344 G8
Wolverhampton 263,501 E5
Wombwell 17,143 K2
Worcester 75,466 E5
Workington 25,978 D3
Worksop 34,551 F4
Worsbrough 10,821 J2
Worthing 90,687 G7
Yateley⊙ 14,121 G8
Yeovil 36,114 E7
York 123,126 F4

OTHER FEATURES

Aire (riv.) F4
Avon (riv.) F5
Barnstaple (bay) C6
Beachy (head) H7
Blackwater (riv.) H6
Bristol (chan.) C6
Cheviot (hills) E2
Chiltern (hills) G6
Cleveland (hills) F3
Colne (riv.) G8
Cotswold (hills) E6
Cross Fell (mt.) E3
Cumbrian (mts.) D3
Dart (riv.) D7
Dartmoor National Park C7
Dee (riv.) D4
Derwent (riv.) G3
Derwent (riv.) H3
Don (riv.) F4
Dove (riv.) J2
Dover (strait) J7
Dungeness (prom.) J7
Eddyston (rocks) C7
Eden (riv.) E3
English (chan.) D8
Esk (riv.) D2
Exe (riv.) D7
Exmoor National Park D6
Fens, The (reg.) G5
Flamborough (head) G3
Foulness Island (pen.) J6
Great Ouse (riv.) H5
Hartland (pt.) C6
Holderness (pen.) G4
Holy (isl.) F2
Humber (riv.) G4
Irish (sea) B4
Kennet (riv.) F6
Lake District National Park D3
Land's End (prom.) B7
Lea (riv.) G6
Lincoln Wolds (hills) G4
Lindisfarne (Holy) (isl.) F2
Lizard (pt.) B8
Lundy (isl.) C6
Lyme (bay) D7
Medway (riv.) H6
Mendip (hills) E6
Mersey (riv.) G2
Morecambe (bay) D3
Mounts (bay) B7
Naze, The (prom.) J6
Nene (riv.) H5
New (for.) F6
North (sea) J4
North Downs (hills) G6
North Foreland (prom.) J6
Northumberland National Park E2
North York Moors National Park G3
Ouse (riv.) G6
Ouse (riv.) G4
Peak District National Park F4
Peak, The (mt.) J2
Pennine Chain (range) E3
Portland, Bill of (pt.) E7
Purbeck, Isle of (pen.) F7
Ribble (riv.) E4
Saint Bees (head) D3
Saint Mary's (isl.) A8
Scafell Pike (mt.) D3
Scilly (isls.) A7
Severn (riv.) E6
Sheppey (isl.) J6
Sherwood (for.) F4
Solent (chan.) F7
Solway (firth) D3
South Downs (hills) G7
South Foreland (prom.) J6
Spithead (chan.) F7
Stonehenge (ruin) F6
Stour (riv.) H6
Stour (riv.) E7
Stour (riv.) J6
Swale (riv.) F3
Tees (riv.) F3
Thames (riv.) H6
Tintagel (head) C7
Trent (riv.) G4
Tweed (riv.) E2
Tyne (riv.) F3
Ure (riv.) F3
Walney, Isle of (isl.) D3
Wash, The (bay) H5
Weald, The (reg.) H6
Wear (riv.) F3
Welland (riv.) G5
Wey (riv.) G6
Wharfe (riv.) E3
Wight (isl.) 114,879 F7
Wirral (pen.) G2
Wolds, The (hills) G4
Wye (riv.) D5
Yare (riv.) J5
Yorkshire Dales National Park E3

CHANNEL ISLANDS

CITIES and TOWNS

Saint Helier (cap.), Jersey⊙ 27,549 E8
Saint Peter Port (cap.), Guernsey⊙ 16,085 E8
Saint Sampson's⊙ 7,475 E8

OTHER FEATURES

Alderney (isl.) 2,130 E8
Guernsey (isl.) 55,421 E8
Herm (isl.) 59 E8
Jersey (isl.) 82,809 E8
Sark (isl.) 560 E8

ISLE of MAN

CITIES and TOWNS

Castletown 2,788 C3
Douglas (cap.) 19,897 C3
Laxey 1,242 C3
Onchan 6,395 C3
Peel 3,295 C3
Port Erin 2,356 C3
Port Saint Mary 1,525 C3
Ramsey 5,372 C3

OTHER FEATURES

Ayre (pt.) C3
Calf of Man (isl.) C3
Langness (prom.) C3
Snaefell (mt.) C3

WALES

COUNTIES

Clwyd 385,581 D4
Dyfed 323,040 C6
Gwent 436,500 D6
Gwynedd 222,291 C4
Mid Glamorgan 533,770 D6
Powys 108,121 D5
South Glamorgan 376,718 A7
West Glamorgan 363,619 D6

CITIES and TOWNS

Abercarn 16,811 B6
Aberdare 31,617 A6
Abergavenny 13,880 B6
Abergele 12,264 D4
Abertillery and Brynmawr 28,239 B6
Aberystwyth 10,290 C5
Ammanford 10,735 C6
Bangor 12,244 C4
Barry 44,443 B7
Bethesda 3,558 D4
Brecknock (Brecon) 7,166 D6
Bridgend 31,008 A7
Brynmawr and Abertillery 28,239 B6
Buckley 16,693 G2
Caernarfon 9,271 C4
Caerphilly 28,681 B6
Caldicot 12,310 E6
Cardiff (cap.) 262,313 B7
Cardigan 3,815 C5
Carmarthen 13,860 C6
Chepstow 9,039 E6
Colwyn Bay 27,002 D4
Connah's Quay 14,785 G2
Cwmbran 44,592 B6
Denbigh 7,710 D4
Ebbw Vale 21,048 B6
Ffestiniog 4,507 D5
Flint 11,411 G2
Gelligaer 16,812 A6
Gwersyllt 13,374 E4
Harlech⊙ 1,292 C5
Haverfordwest 13,572 B6
Hawarden⊙ 22,361 G2
Holyhead 12,569 C4
Holywell 11,101 G2
Llandeilo 1,598 C6
Llandovery 1,676 D5
Llandrindod Wells 4,232 D5
Llandudno 13,202 D4
Llanelli 45,336 C6
Llanfairfechan 3,173 D4
Llangollen 2,546 D5
Llanidloes 2,392 D5
Llantrisant⊙ 8,317 A7
Llantwit Major 13,375 A7
Maesteg 21,821 D6
Menai Bridge 2,942 C4
Merthyr Tydfil 38,893 A6
Milford Haven 13,883 B6
Mold 8,487 G2
Monmouth 7,379 E6
Montgomery D5
Mountain Ash 23,520 A6
Narberth C6
Neath 48,687 D6
Nefyn⊙ 2,086 C5
Newport 115,896 B6
Newtown 8,906 D5
Neyland 3,095 B6
Ogmore 7,092 A6
Pembroke 8,235 C6
Penarth 22,467 B7
Pontypool 36,064 B6
Pontypridd 29,465 A6
Port Talbot 40,078 D6
Porthcawl 15,162 D6
Prestatyn 16,246 D4
Pwllheli 3,978 C5
Rhondda 70,980 A6
Rhosllanerchrugog 11,080 D4
Rhyl 23,130 D4
Risca 16,627 B6
Ruthin 4,417 D4
Saint David's⊙ 1,428 B6
Swansea 172,433 C6
Tenby 5,226 C6
Tredegar 16,188 B6
Welshpool 4,869 D5
Wrexham 39,929 E4
Ystradgynlais 10,406 D6

OTHER FEATURES

Anglesey (isl.) C4
Bardsey (isl.) C5
Brecon Beacons National Park D6
Bristol (chan.) C6
Caldy (isl.) C6
Cambrian (mts.) D5
Cardigan (bay) C5
Carmarthen (bay) C6
Conwy (bay) C4
Dee (riv.) D4
Gower (pen.) C6
Great Ormes (head) C4
Holy (isl.) C4
Irish (sea) B4
Lleyn (pen.) C5
Menai (strait) C4
Milford Haven (inlet) B6
Pembrokeshire Coast National Park C6
Radnor (for.) D5
Saint Brides (bay) B6
Saint George's (chan.) B5
Severn (riv.) E6
Snowdon (mt.) C4
Snowdonia National Park D4
Taff (riv.) B7
Teifi (riv.) C5
Towy (riv.) D6
Tremadoc (prom.) C5
Usk (riv.) B6
Wye (riv.) D5
Ynys Môn (Anglesey) (isl.) C4

⊙ Population of parish.

SCOTLAND

(map on page 15)

REGIONS

Borders 99,784 E5
Central 273,391 D4
Dumfries and Galloway 145,139 E5
Fife 327,362 E4
Grampian 471,942 F3
Highland 200,150 D3
Lothian 738,372 E5
Orkney (islands area) 19,056 E1
Shetland (islands area) 27,277 F2
Strathclyde 2,404,532 C4
Tayside 391,846 E4
Western Isles (islands area) 31,884 A3

CITIES and TOWNS

Aberchirder 1,021 F3
Aberdeen 190,465 F3
Aberfeldy 1,613 E4
Aberfoyle 793 D4
Abernethy 776 E4
Aboyne 1,529 F3
Achiltibuie⊙ 1,564 C3
Achnasheen⊙ 1,078 C3
Airdrie 45,747 C2
Alexandria 26,329 A1
Alford 764 F3
Alloa 26,428 C1
Alness 6,289 D3
Altnaharra⊙ 1,227 D2
Alva 4,874 C1
Alyth 2,289 E4
Annan 8,314 E6
Annbank Station 3,223 D5
Arbroath 24,119 F4
Ardrishaig 1,325 C4
Ardrossan 11,421 D5
Armadale 9,527 C2
Auchinleck 4,463 D5
Auchterarder 2,904 E4
Auchtermuchty 1,646 E4
Aviemore 1,224 E3
Ayr 49,522 D5
Baillieston 7,671 B2
Balerno 3,576 D2
Balfron 1,127 B1
Ballantrae 262 C5
Ballater 1,218 F3
Ballingry 7,021 D1
Balloch 1,484 B1
Banchory 4,890 F3
Banff 3,938 F3
Bankhead 1,492 F3
Bannockburn 5,889 C1
Barrhead 18,418 B2
Bathgate 14,477 C2
Bearsden 27,183 B2
Beauly 1,148 D3
Beith 5,742 D5
Bellsbank 2,482 D5
Bellshill 39,676 C2
Berriedale⊙ 1,927 E2
Bieldside 1,137 F3
Biggar 1,938 E5
Bishopbriggs 23,501 B2
Bishopton 5,283 B2
Blackburn 5,785 C2
Blair Atholl 437 E4
Blairgowrie and Rattray 7,184 E4
Blantyre 19,948 B2
Bo'ness 14,641 C1
Boddam 1,367 G3
Bonhill 4,385 B1
Bonnybridge 5,701 C1
Bonnyrigg and Lasswade 14,399 D2
Brechin 7,692 F4
Bridge of Allan 4,694 C1
Bridge of Don 4,086 F3
Bridge of Weir 4,724 A2
Brightons 3,106 C1
Brora 1,736 E2
Broxburn 12,032 D1
Buckhaven and Methil 18,265 F4
Buckie 7,839 E3
Bucksburn 6,567 F3
Burghead 1,380 E3
Burntisland 5,865 D1
Callander 2,520 D4
Cambuslang 14,607 B2
Campbeltown 6,098 C5
Caol 3,719 C4
Cardenden 5,898 D1
Carluke 11,674 E5
Carnoustie 9,225 F4
Carnwath 1,374 E5
Carron 2,626 C1
Castle Douglas 3,521 E6
Catrine 2,790 D5
Cawdor 111 E3
Chirnside 1,263 F5
Chryston 11,067 C2
Clackmannan 3,258 C1
Clarkston 8,404 B2
Clydebank 51,854 B2
Coalburn 1,241 E5
Coatbridge 50,957 C2
Cockenzie and Port Seton 3,760 D1
Coldstream 1,645 F5
Comrie 1,477 E4
Cononbridge 2 187 D3
Corpach 1,296 C4
Coupar Angus 2,186 E4
Cove and Kilcreggan 1,220 A1
Cove Bay 2,840 F3
Cowdenbeath 12,272 D1
Cowie 2,513 C1
Crail 1,181 F4
Creetown 769 D6
Crieff 5,477 E4
Crimond 1,002 G3
Cromarty 492 E3
Cruden Bay 1,453 G3
Cullen 1,414 F3
Culross 504 C1
Cults 3,336 F3
Cumbernauld 47,901 C1
Cumnock and Holmhead 9,650 D5
Cupar 6,637 E4
Currie 6,764 D2
Dailly 1,098 D5
Dalbeattie 3,917 E6
Dalkeith 11,255 D2
Dalmellington 1,425 D5
Dalry 5,856 D5
Dalrymple 1,237 D5
Darvel 3,461 D5
Denny and Dunipace 23,158 C1
Dervaig⊙ 1,081 B4
Dingwall 4,842 D3
Dollar 2,486 E4
Dornoch 880 D3
Douglas 1,727 E5
Doune 1,046 D4
Drongan 3,129 D5
Dufftown 1,643 E3
Dumbarton 23,430 B1
Dumfries 32,100 E5
Dunbar 6,035 F4
Dunblane 6,855 E4
Dundee 174,345 F4
Dundonald 2,669 D5
Dunfermline 52,227 D1
Dunoon 9,369 A2
Duns 2,253 F5
Duntocher 3,532 B2
Dyce 7,039 F3
Eaglesham 3,166 D5
Earlston 1,610 F5
East Calder 5,112 D2
East Kilbride 70,676 B2
East Linton 1,206 F5
Eastriggs 1,845 E5
East Wemyss 1,782 D1
Edinburgh (cap.) 420,169 D1
Elderslie 5,204 B2
Elgin 18,908 E3
Ellon 6,319 F3
Errol 762 E4
Eyemouth 3,398 F5
Fairlie 1,326 D5
Falkirk 36,880 C1
Falkland 998 E4
Fallin 2,663 C1
Fauldhouse 5,036 C2
Findhorn 664 E3
Findochty 1,019 E3
Fochabers 1,483 E3
Forfar 12,770 F4
Forres 8,354 E3
Forth 2,890 C2
Fortrose 1,332 D3
Fort William 11,061 C4
Fraserburgh 12,512 G3
Gairloch 125 C3
Galashiels 12,244 F5
Galston 5,311 D5
Garelochhead 2,072 A1
Gatehouse-of-Fleet 835 D6
Giffnock 33,634 B2
Girvan 7,795 D5
Glamis 190 F4
Glasgow 765,030 B2
Glenbarr⊙ 691 C5
Glencoe 195 C4
Glenelg⊙ 1,468 C3
Glenrothes 32,971 E4
Golspie 1,491 E3
Gorebridge 6,036 D2
Gourock 11,203 A1
Grangemouth 21,599 C1
Grantown-on-Spey 2,034 E3
Greenock 59,016 A2
Gretna 2,811 E5
Gullane 2,232 F4
Haddington 8,139 F5
Halkirk 679 E2
Hamilton 51,718 C2
Harthill 4,161 C2
Hawick 16,364 F5
Heathhall 1,365 E5
Helensburgh 16,621 A1
Helmsdale 727 E2
Hillside 1,233 F4
Hillswick⊙ 696 G2
Hopeman 1,398 E3
Huntly 3,952 F3
Hurlford 4,294 D5
Inchnadamph⊙ 833 D2
Innerleithen 2,468 E5
Insch 1,256 F3
Inveraray 473 C4
Inverbervie 1,799 F4
Invercassley⊙ 1,067 D3
Invergordon 4,067 D3
Invergowrie 1,389 E4
Inverie⊙ 1,468 C3
Inverkeithing 5,770 D1
Inverness 40,010 D3
Inverurie 7,680 F3
Irvine 32,968 D5
Jedburgh 4,069 F5
John O'Groats 195 E2
Johnstone 42,669 B2
Keith 4,407 F3
Kelso 5,648 F5
Kelty 5,623 D1
Kemnay 3,034 F3
Kilbarchan 2,669 A2
Kilbirnie 8,710 A2
Kilchoan⊙ 764 B4
Kildonan⊙ 1,105 E2
Killearn 1,771 B1
Kilmacolm 3,676 A2
Kilmarnock 52,083 D5
Kilmaurs 2,738 D5
Kilrenny and Anstruther 2,951 F4
Kilsyth 10,538 B1
Kilwinning 16,266 D5
Kinbrace⊙ 1,105 E2
Kincardine 3,166 C1
Kinghorn 2,698 D1
Kingussie 1,229 D3
Kinlochewe⊙ 1,794 C3
Kinlochleven 1,047 D4
Kinloss 2,813 E3
Kinross 3,496 E4
Kintore 1,644 F3
Kirkcaldy 46,522 D1
Kirkconnel 2,656 E5
Kirkcudbright 3,427 E6
Kirkintilloch 33,148 B2
Kirkmuirhill 3,624 E5
Kirkwall 5,995 E2
Kirriemuir 5,326 E4
Kyle of Lochalsh 687 C3
Kylestrome⊙ 745 D2
Ladybank 1,355 E4
Lairg 572 D2
Lanark 9,806 E5
Langholm 2,615 E5
Larbert 4,922 C1
Largs 9,905 A2
Larkhall 16,216 E5
Lauder 639 F5
Laurencekirk 1,329 F4
Lennoxtown 4,829 B1
Lerwick 7,561 G2
Leslie 3,551 E4
Lesmahagow 3,408 E5
Letham 804 F4
Leuchars 2,244 F4
Leven 8,624 F4
Lhanbryde 1,811 E3
Limekilns 1,444 D1
Linlithgow 9,582 C1
Linwood 10,510 B2
Livingston 38,954 C2
Loanhead 6,159 D2
Lochailort⊙ 673 C4
Locharbriggs 4,230 E5
Lochgelly 7,334 D1
Lochgilphead 2,461 C4
Lochinver 283 C2
Lochmaben 1,713 E5
Lochore 2,994 D1
Lochwinnoch 2,273 A2
Lockerbie 3,561 E5

(continued)

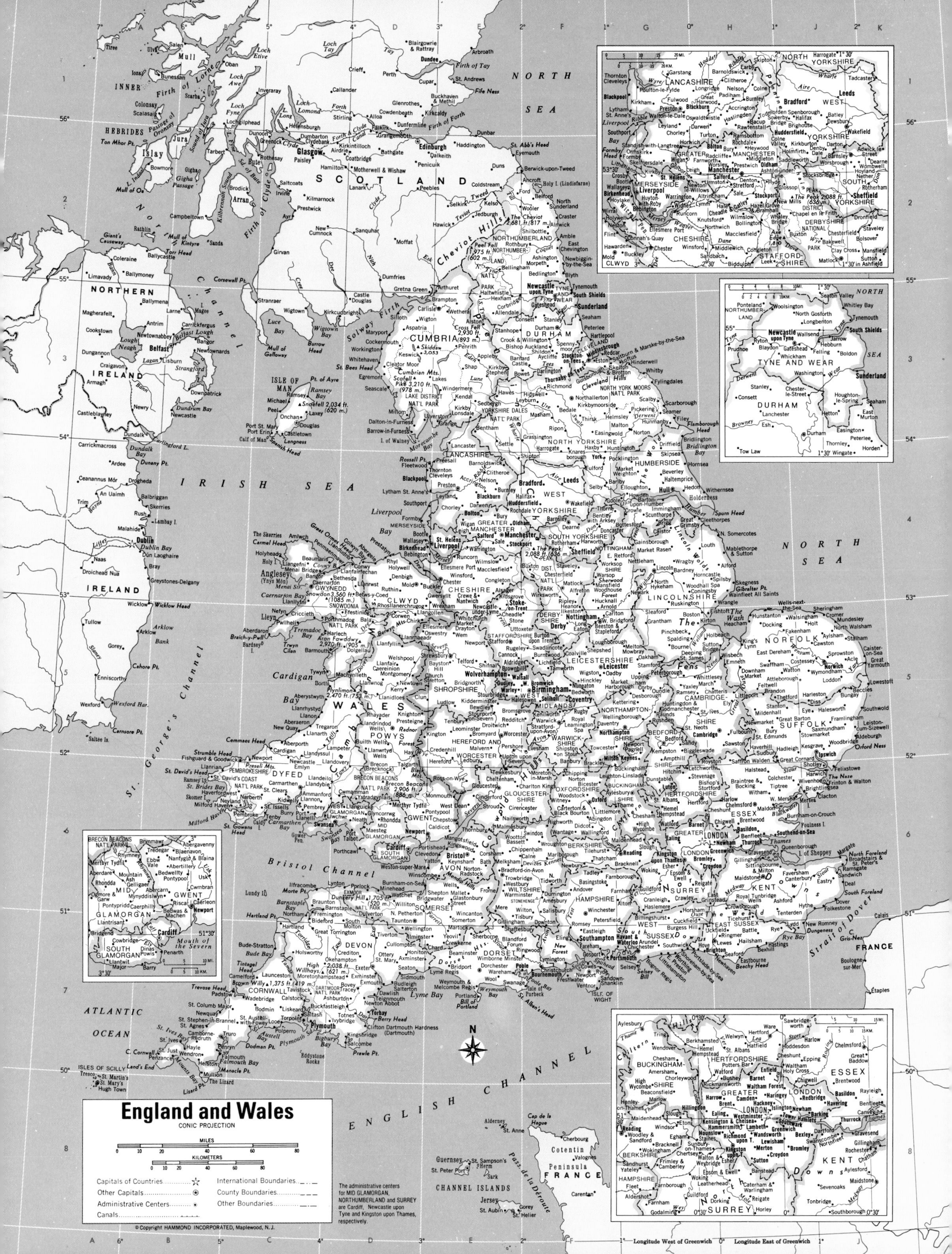

England and Wales
CONIC PROJECTION
MILES
0 10 20 40 60 80
KILOMETERS
0 10 20 40 60 80
Capitals of Countries
Other Capitals
Administrative Centers
Canals
International Boundaries
County Boundaries
Other Boundaries
The administrative centers for MID GLAMORGAN, NORTHUMBERLAND and SURREY are Cardiff, Newcastle upon Tyne and Kingston upon Thames, respectively.
© Copyright HAMMOND INCORPORATED, Maplewood, N. J.
SCOTLAND
WALES
NORTH SEA
IRISH SEA
ENGLISH CHANNEL
ATLANTIC OCEAN
IRELAND
NORTHERN IRELAND
FRANCE
CHANNEL ISLANDS
Longitude West of Greenwich 0° Longitude East of Greenwich

OTHER FEATURES

⊙ Population of parish.

Agriculture, Industry and Resources

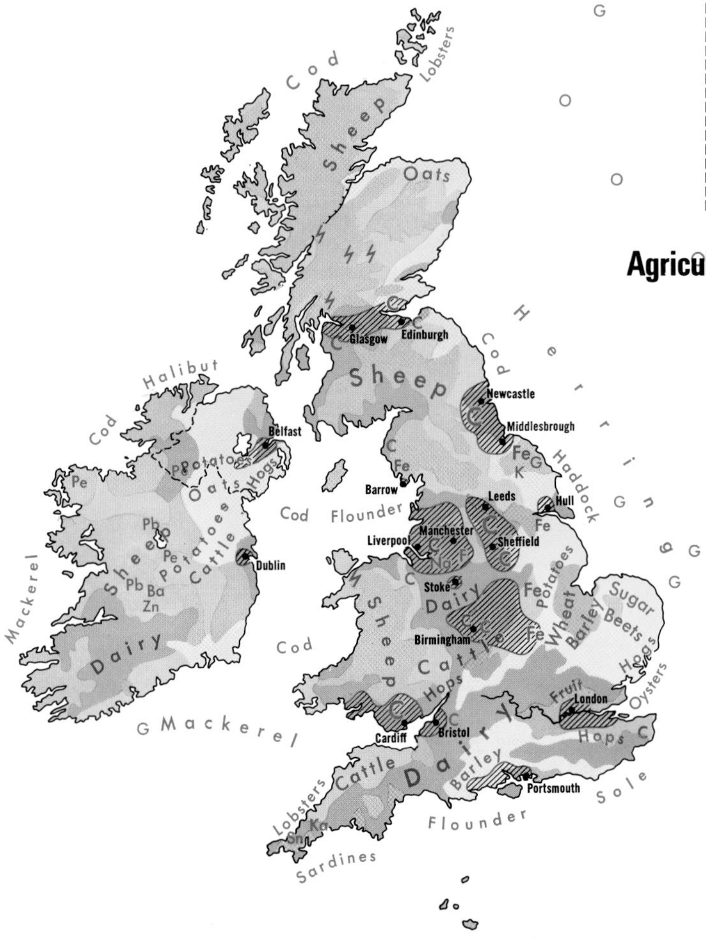
Cod
Lobsters
Sheep
Oats
Glasgow
Edinburgh
Sheep
Herring
Cod
Newcastle
Middlesbrough
Halibut
Cod
Belfast
Potatoes
Oats
Hogs
Pe
Haddock
Barrow
Leeds
Hull
Cod
Flounder
Manchester
Liverpool
Sheffield
Dublin
Cattle
Sheep
Potatoes
Mackerel
Stoke
Dairy
Wheat
Barley
Sugar Beets
Birmingham
Dairy
Cod
Sheep
Cattle
Hops
Fruit
London
Oysters
Hogs
G Mackerel
Cardiff
Bristol
Dairy
Hops
Cattle
Barley
Portsmouth
Sole
Lobsters
Flounder
Sardines

DOMINANT LAND USE

- Cereals (chiefly oats, barley)
- Truck Farming, Horticulture
- Dairy, Mixed Farming
- Livestock, Mixed Farming
- Pasture Livestock

MAJOR MINERAL OCCURRENCES

Ba	Barite	Na	Salt
C	Coal	O	Petroleum
F	Fluorspar	Pb	Lead
Fe	Iron Ore	Pe	Peat
G	Natural Gas	Sn	Tin
K	Potash	Zn	Zinc
Ka	Kaolin (china clay)		

Water Power

Major Industrial Areas

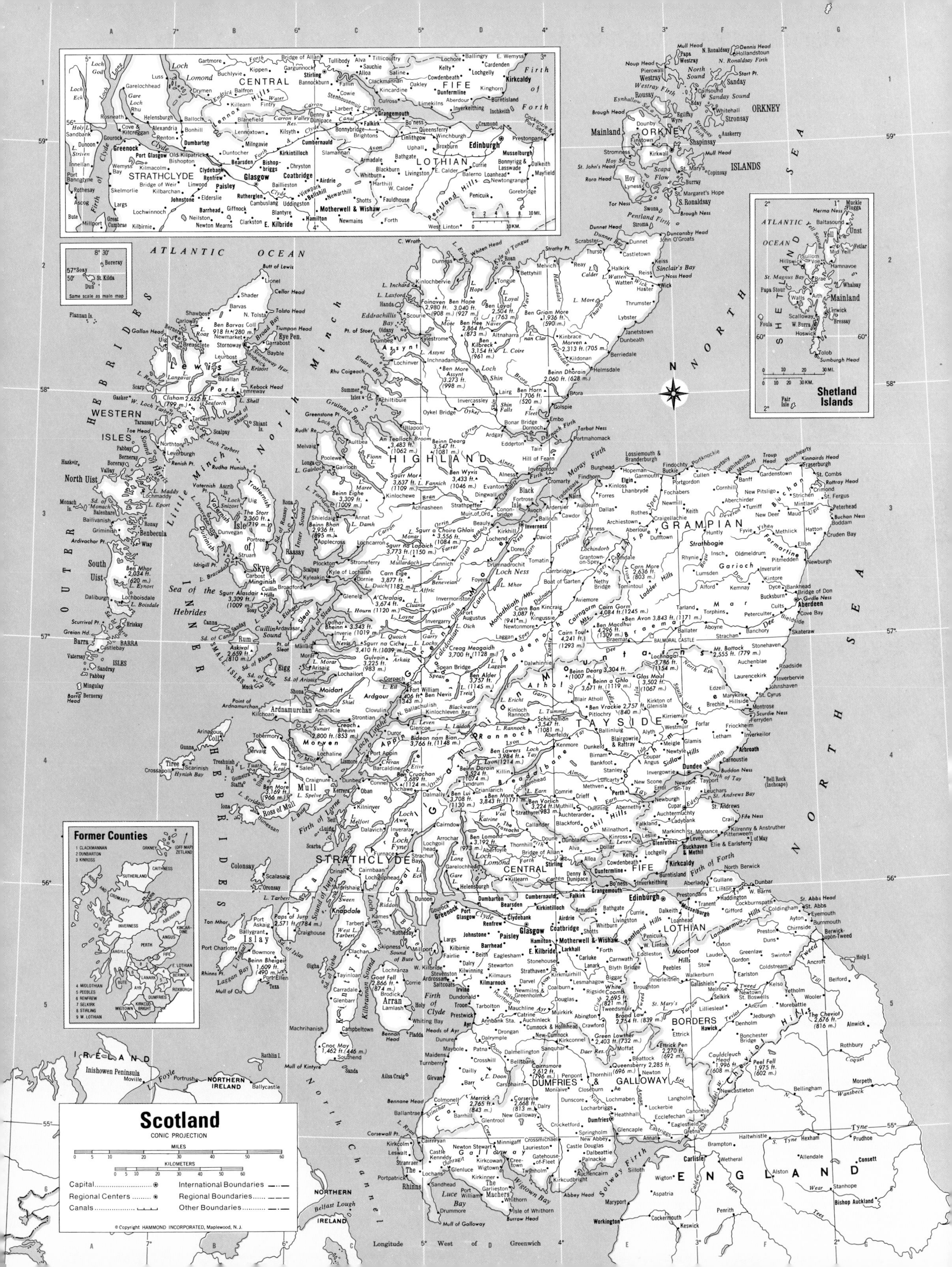
Scotland
CONIC PROJECTION
MILES
0 5 10 20 30 40 50 60
KILOMETERS
0 5 10 20 30 40 50 60
Capital
Regional Centers
Canals
International Boundaries
Regional Boundaries
Other Boundaries
© Copyright HAMMOND INCORPORATED, Maplewood, N. J.
Former Counties
1 CLACKMANNAN
2 DUNBARTON
3 KINROSS
4 MIDLOTHIAN
5 PEEBLES
6 RENFREW
7 SELKIRK
8 STIRLING
9 W. LOTHIAN
ORKNEY
(OFF MAP) ZETLAND
SUTHERLAND
CAITHNESS
ROSS AND CROMARTY
INVERNESS
NAIRN
MORAY
BANFF
ABERDEEN
KINCARDINE
ANGUS
PERTH
ARGYLL
FIFE
E. LOTHIAN
BERWICK
LANARK
AYR
DUMFRIES
ROXBURGH
KIRKCUDBRIGHT
WIGTOWN
Shetland Islands
ATLANTIC OCEAN
SHETLAND
Muckle Flugga
Herma Ness
Baltasound
Unst
Yell
Fetlar
Mid Yell
Hillswick
Sullom Voe
Hamnavoe
Brae
St. Magnus Bay
Whalsay
Papa Stour
Walls
Aith
Mainland
Lerwick
Scalloway
W. Burra
Bressay
Foula
Hoswick
Tolob
Sumburgh Head
Fair Isle
ORKNEY ISLANDS
Mull Head
Papa Westray
N. Ronaldsay
Dennis Head
Hollandstoun
N. Ronaldsay Firth
Noup Head
Pierowall
Westray
North Sound
Start Pt.
Sanday
Sanday Sound
Rousay
Eday
Whitehall
Stronsay
Brough Head
Mainland
Dounby
Finstown
Shapinsay
Auskerry
Stromness
Kirkwall
Mull Head
St. John's Head
Hoy Sd.
Hoy
Scapa Flow
St. Mary's
Copinsay
Rora Head
Lyness
Burray
St. Margaret's Hope
Tor Ness
Swona
S. Ronaldsay
Pentland Firth
Brough Ness
Stroma
ATLANTIC OCEAN
Soay
Boreray
St. Kilda
Dun
Same scale as main map
CENTRAL
FIFE
LOTHIAN
STRATHCLYDE
Firth of Forth
Glasgow
Edinburgh
Stirling
Dunfermline
Kirkcaldy
Falkirk
Grangemouth
Paisley
Greenock
Dumbarton
Motherwell & Wishaw
Hamilton
E. Kilbride
Coatbridge
Airdrie
Cumbernauld
Linlithgow
Musselburgh
Pentland Hills
Loch Lomond
NORTH SEA
HEBRIDES
OUTER HEBRIDES
INNER HEBRIDES
WESTERN ISLES
HIGHLAND
GRAMPIAN
TAYSIDE
CENTRAL
FIFE
LOTHIAN
BORDERS
STRATHCLYDE
DUMFRIES & GALLOWAY
ORKNEY
North Minch
Little Minch
Sea of the Hebrides
Moray Firth
Firth of Forth
Firth of Tay
Firth of Clyde
Firth of Lorne
Solway Firth
North Channel
Pentland Firth
Grampian Mountains
Cairngorm Mts.
Monadhliath Mts.
Lewis
Harris
North Uist
Benbecula
South Uist
Barra
Skye
Rum
Eigg
Mull
Tiree
Coll
Colonsay
Jura
Islay
Arran
Kintyre
Butt of Lewis
Stornoway
C. Wrath
Durness
Thurso
Wick
Dunnet Head
Duncansby Head
John O'Groats
Ullapool
Inverness
Nairn
Elgin
Aberdeen
Peterhead
Fraserburgh
Ben Nevis
Fort William
Oban
Perth
Dundee
Arbroath
Montrose
Stirling
Edinburgh
Glasgow
Ayr
Dumfries
Stranraer
Hawick
Berwick-upon-Tweed
Loch Ness
Caledonian Canal
Ben Macdhui 4,296 ft. (1309 m.)
Ben Nevis 4,406 ft. (1343 m.)
Ben Lomond 3,192 ft. (973 m.)
Ben Lawers 3,984 ft. (1214 m.)
The Cheviot 2,676 ft. (816 m.)
Merrick 2,765 ft. (843 m.)
Goat Fell 2,866 ft. (874 m.)
Mull of Kintyre
Mull of Galloway
Mull of Oa
Rhinns Pt.
Ailsa Craig
Rathlin I.
IRELAND
NORTHERN IRELAND
Inishowen Peninsula
Moville
Portrush
Ballycastle
Belfast Lough
ENGLAND
Carlisle
Newcastleton
Hexham
Consett
Workington
Keswick
Maryport
Penrith
Bishop Auckland
Morpeth
Rothbury
Alnwick
Longitude 5° West of Greenwich
59°
58°
57°
56°
55°

IRELAND

COUNTIES

Carlow 40,988 H6
Cavan 53,965 G4
Clare 91,344 D6
Cork 412,735 D7
Donegal 129,664 F2
Dublin 1,021,449 J5
Galway 178,552 D5
Kerry 124,159 B7
Kildare 116,247 H5
Kilkenny 73,186 G6
Laois 53,284 G6
Leitrim 27,035 E3
Leix (Laois) 53,284 G6
Limerick 164,569 D7
Longford 31,496 F4
Louth 91,810 J4
Mayo 115,184 C4
Meath 103,881 H4
Monaghan 52,379 H3
Offaly 59,835 F5
Roscommon 54,592 E4
Sligo 56,046 D3
Tipperary 136,619 F6
Waterford 91,151 F7
Westmeath 63,379 G5
Wexford 102,552 H7
Wicklow 94,542 J6

CITIES and TOWNS

Abbeyfeale 1,483 C7
Abbeyleix 1,468 G6
Adare 792 D6
Aghada-Farsid-Rostellan 818 E8
An Uaimh 3,660 H4
Ardee 3,253 H4
Ardfinnan 827 F7
Ardmore 343 F8
Arklow 8,388 J6
Ashford 782 J5
Askeaton 951 D6
Athboy 1,055 H4
Athenry 1,642 D5
Athlone 8,815 F5
Athy 4,734 H6
Aughrim 756 J6
Avoca 490 J6
Bagenalstown (Muinebeag) 2,653 H6
Baile Atha Cliath (Dublin) (cap.) 502,749 K5
Bailieborough 1,645 G4
Balbriggan 5,680 J4
Ballaghaderreen 1,366 E4
Ballina, Mayo 6,714 C3
Ballina, Tipperary 507 E6
Ballinamore 810 F3
Ballinasloe 6,125 E5
Ballincollig-Carrigrohane 7,231 D8
Ballineen 592 D8
Ballinrobe 1,270 C4
Ballybofey-Stranorlar 2,964 F2
Ballybunion 1,452 B7
Ballycastle 219 C3
Ballyconnell 466 F3
Ballygar 472 E4
Ballygeary 891 J7
Ballyhaunis 1,338 D4
Ballyheigue 660 B7
Ballyjamesduff 842 G4
Ballylanders 343 E7
Ballylongford 523 B6
Ballymahon 859 F4
Ballymore Eustace 575 J5
Ballymote 1,064 D3
Ballyragget 833 G6
Ballyshannon 2,573 E3
Baltinglass 1,089 H6
Banagher 1,465 F5
Bandon 1,943 D8
Bantry 2,811 C8
Belmullet 1,033 B3
Belturbet 1,228 G3
Bennettsbridge 601 G6
Birr 3,417 F5
Blanchardstown H5
Blarney 1,952 D8
Blessington 1,322 J5
Borrisokane 837 E6
Borrisoleigh 624 E6
Boyle 1,859 E4
Bray 24,686 K5
Bri Chualann (Bray) 24,686 K5
Bruff 819 D7
Bunbeg-Derrybeg 1,469 E1
Bunclody-Carrickduff 1,423 H6
Buncrana 3,106 G1
Bundoran 1,535 E3
Buttevant 1,133 D7
Cahir 2,118 F7
Cahirciveen 1,310 A8
Callan 1,266 G7
Cappamore 765 E6
Cappoquin 920 F7
Carlingford 635 J3
Carlow 11,509 H6
Carndonagh 1,600 G1
Carnew 723 H6
Carrickmacross 1,815 H4
Carrick-on-Shannon 1,984 F4
Carrick-on-Suir 5,353 F7
Carrigaline 5,893 E8
Carrigtwohill 1,272 E8
Cashel 2,458 F7
Castlebar 6,349 C4
Castlebellingham 848 J4
Castleblayney 2,157 H3
Castlebridge 655 J7
Castlecomer-Donaguile 1,490 G6
Castledermot 792 H6
Castlefin 694 F2
Castleisland 2,281 B7
Castlemartyr 585 E8
Castlepollard 803 G4
Castlerea 1,840 D4
Castletown 303 F6
Castletownbere 905 B8
Castletownroche 474 D7
Cavan 3,381 G3
Ceanannus Mór 2,413 G4
Celbridge 7,135 H5
Charlestown-Bellahy 754 D4
Charleville (Rathluirc) 2,814 D7
Clara 2,736 F5
Claremorris 1,992 C4
Clifden 896 B5
Cloghan 496 F5
Clogh-Chatsworth 319 G6
Clogheen 502 F7
Clogherhead 765 J4
Clonakilty 2,567 D8
Clones 2,280 G3
Clonfert E5
Clonmel 11,759 F7
Cloughjordan 499 E6
Cloyne 721 E8
Cóbh 6,369 E8
Coill Dubh 772 H5
Collooney 705 E3
Convoy 891 F2
Coolgreany 352 J6
Cootehill 1,487 G3
Cork 133,271 E8
Corofin 391 C6
Courtown Harbour 317 J6
Creeslough 340 F1
Croom 1,024 D6
Crosshaven 1,362 E8
Crossmolina 1,250 C3
Daingean 659 G5
Delvin 309 G4
Dingle 1,253 A7
Donabate 599 J5
Donegal 2,242 F2
Doneraile 846 D7
Dooagh-Keel 650 A4
Doon 308 E6
Drimoleague 381 C8
Drogheda 24,086 J4
Droichead Nua 5,983 H5
Dromahair 353 E3
Drumconrath 334 H4
Drumshanbo 622 E3
Dublin (cap.) 502,749 K5
Duleek 1,679 J4
Duncannon 388 H7
Dundalk 26,669 H3
Dunfanaghy 314 F1
Dungarvan 6,849 F7
Dungloe 940 E2
Dún Laoghaire 54,715 K5
Dunkineely 442 E2
Dunlavin 734 H5
Dunleer 1,184 J4
Dunmanway 1,382 C8
Dunmore 445 D4
Dunmore East 1,041 G7
Dunshaughlin 878 H5
Durrow 707 G6
Edenderry 3,539 G5
Elphin 513 E4
Emyvale 464 G3
Ennis 5,917 D6
Enniscorthy 4,483 J7
Enniskerry 1,229 J5
Ennistymon 1,039 C6
Eyrecourt 351 E5
Fahan 367 G1
Falcarragh 996 E1
Fenit 401 B7
Ferbane 1,374 F5
Fermoy 2,872 E7
Ferns 811 J6
Fethard 982 F7
Foxford 1,033 C4
Foynes 707 C6
Frankford (Kilcormac) 1,118 F5
Freshford 700 G6
Galbally 248 E7
Galway 47,104 C5
Geashill 339 G5
Glanworth 379 E7
Glenamaddy 369 D4
Glenties 914 E2
Glin 569 C6
Golden 295 F7
Gorey 2,445 J6
Gormanston 870 J4
Gort 1,021 D5
Gowran 517 G6
Graiguenamanagh-Tinnahinch 1,485 H6
Granard 1,338 F4
Greencastle 584 H1
Greystones 8,455 K5
Hacketstown 710 H6
Headford 675 C5
Holycross 274 F6
Hospital 751 E7
Inniscrone 633 C3
Johnstown 408 G6
Kanturk 1,870 D7
Keel-Dooagh 650 A4
Kells (Ceanannus Mór) 2,413 G4
Kenmare 1,130 B8
Kilbeggan 603 G5
Kilcar 345 D2
Kilcock 1,414 H5
Kilcoole 2,335 K5
Kilcormac 1,118 F5
Kilcullen 1,693 H5
Kildare 4,268 H5
Kildysart 347 C6
Kilfinane 788 D7
Kilkee 1,448 B6
Kilkenny 8,969 G6
Killala 674 C3
Killaloe 1,033 D6
Killarney 7,837 C7
Killenaule 717 F6
Killeshandra 455 F3
Killorglin 1,304 B7
Killucan-Rathwire 353 G4
Killybegs 1,632 E2
Kilmacrennan 412 F1
Kilmacthomas 648 G7
Kilmallock 1,424 D7
Kilmihill 338 C6
Kilmore Quay 458 H7
Kilnaleck 321 G4
Kilronan 282 B5
Kilrush 2,961 C6
Kiltimagh 982 C4
Kilworth 411 E7
Kingscourt 1,242 H4
Kingstown (Dún Laoghaire) 54,715 K5
Kinnegad 433 G5
Kinnitty 261 F5
Kinsale 1,811 D8
Kinvara 425 D5
Knightstown 204 A8
Knock 332 D4
Knocklong 273 D7
Lahinch 511 C6
Lanesborough-Ballyleague 1,058 E4
Laytown-Bettystown-Mornington 3,321 J4
Leighlinbridge 540 H6
Leitrim F3
Leixlip 11,938 H5
Letterkenny 6,691 F2
Lifford 1,478 F2
Limerick 56,279 D6
Lisdoonvarna 648 C5
Lismore 703 F7
Listowel 3,494 C7
Littleton 566 F6
Longford 6,457 F4
Loughrea 3,360 E5
Louisburgh 209 B4
Louth 435 J4
Lucan 12,259 J5
Luimneach (Limerick) 56,279 D6
Lusk 1,831 J4
Macroom 2,449 C8
Malahide 9,940 J5
Mallow 6,488 D7
Manorhamilton 1,031 E3
Maryborough (Portlaoise) 3,773 G5
Maynooth 4,768 H5
Meathas Truim 806 G4
Midleton 3,111 E8
Milford 981 F1
Millstreet 1,330 D7
Milltown 347 A7
Miltownmalbay 719 C6
Mitchelstown 3,210 E7
Moate 1,659 F5
Mohill 930 F4
Monaghan 6,075 G3
Monasterevan 2,143 H5
Moneygall 346 F6
Mooncoin 868 G7
Mount Bellew 519 D5
Mountcharles 480 E2
Mountmellick 2,789 G5
Mountrath 1,402 F5
Moville 1,331 G1
Moycullen 366 C5
Muinebeag 2,653 H6
Mullagh 462 H4
Mullinahone 385 F7
Mullinavat 355 G7
Mullingar 8,077 G4
Naas 10,017 H5
Navan (An Uaimh) 3,660 H4
Nenagh 5,483 E6
Newbliss 293 G3
Newbridge (Droichead Nua) 5,983 H5
Newcastle 3,370 C7
Newmarket 1,022 C7
Newmarket-on-Fergus 1,678 D6
Newport, Mayo 492 C4
Newport, Tipperary 857 E6
New Ross 5,343 H7
Newtown Forbes 393 F4
Newtownmountkennedy 2,183 J5
Newtownsandes 357 C6
O'Briensbridge-Montpelier 385 D6
Oldcastle 869 G4
Oola 451 E6
Oranmore 1,064 D5
Oughterard 682 C5
Passage East 563 G7
Passage West 3,511 E8
Patrickswell 905 D6
Piltown 691 G7
Portarlington 3,295 G5
Portlaoise 3,773 G5
Portlaw 1,260 G7
Portmarnock 9,055 J5
Portumna 1,062 E5
Queenstown (Cóbh) 6,369 E8
Ramelton 989 F1
Raphoe 1,027 F2
Rathangan 1,270 G5
Rathcoole 2,991 J5
Rathdowney 1,095 F6
Rathdrum 1,307 J6
Rathkeale 1,815 D7
Rathluirc 2,814 D7
Rathmore 548 C7
Rathmullen 554 F1
Rathnew 1,389 J6
Rathvilly 512 H6
Ratoath 551 J5
Riverstown 1,416 E8
Roscommon 1,363 E4
Roscrea 4,378 F6
Rosscarbery 425 C8
Rosses Point 598 D3
Rosslare 704 J7
Rosslare Harbour (Ballygeary) 891 J7
Roundwood 371 J5
Rush 4,513 J4
Saint Johnston 468 F2
Scarriff 847 E6
Schull 509 B8
Shanagolden 402 C6
Shannon 8,005 D6
Shannon Bridge 310 F5
Shercock 406 G4
Shillelagh 334 J6
Shinrone 479 F5
Sixmilebridge 1,182 D6
Skerries 6,864 J4
Skibbereen 1,999 C8
Slane 689 H4
Sligo 17,259 E3
Sneem 309 B8
Stepaside 748 J5
Stradbally, Laois 1,046 G5
Stradbally, Waterford 255 F7
Strokestown 620 E4
Swinford 1,197 C4
Swords 15,312 J5
Taghmon 607 H7
Tallow 867 E7
Tarbert 683 C6
Templemore 2,258 F6
Templetuohy 242 F6
Termonfeckin 741 J4
Thomastown 1,465 G7
Thurles 7,049 F6
Timoleague 330 D8
Tinahely 594 H6
Tipperary 5,033 E7
Toomevara 428 E6
Tralee 17,109 B7
Tramore 5,999 G7
Trim 1,967 H4
Tuam 4,109 D4
Tubbercurry 1,250 D3
Tulla 403 D6
Tullamore 8,484 G5
Tullow 2,324 H6
Tyrrellspass 328 G5
Urlingford 676 F6
Virginia 699 G4
Waterford 39,529 G7
Waterville-Spunkane 475 A8
Westport 3,456 C4
Wexford 10,336 H7
Wicklow 5,304 K6
Woodford 242 E5
Youghal 5,706 F8

OTHER FEATURES

Achill (head) A4
Achill (isl.) A4
Allen (lake) E3
Allen, Bog of (marsh) H5
Annalee (riv.) G3
Aran (isls.) B5
Aran (isl.) D2
Arrow (lake) E3
Ballinskelligs (bay) A8
Ballyhoura (hills) E7
Ballyteige (bay) H7
Bandon (riv.) D8
Bantry (bay) B8
Barrow (riv.) H7
Baurtregaum (mt.) B7
Bear (isl.) B8
Ben Dash (hill) C6
Bertraghboy (bay) A5
Black (head) C5
Blacksod (bay) A3
Blackstairs (mt.) H6
Blackwater (riv.) H4
Blackwater (riv.) D7
Blasket (isls.) A7
Bloody Foreland (prom.) E1
Blue Stack (mts.) E2
Boderg (lake) E4
Boggeragh (mts.) D7
Bolus (head) A8
Boyne (riv.) J4
Brandon (bay) A7
Brandon (head) A7
Brandon (mt.) A7
Bray (head) A8
Bride (riv.) E7
Broad Haven (harb.) B3
Brosna (riv.) F5
Bull, The (isl.) A8
Caha (mts.) B8
Cahore (pt.) J6
Cark (mt.) F2
Carlingford (inlet) J3
Carnsore (pt.) J7
Carra (lake) C4
Carrantuohill (mt.) B7
Carrowmore (lake) B3
Clare (isls.) A4
Clare (riv.) D5
Clear (cape) B9
Clear (isl.) C9
Clew (bay) B4
Clonakilty (bay) D8
Comeragh (mts.) F7
Conn (lake) C3
Connacht (prov.) 431,409 C4
Connemara (dist.) B5
Cork (harb.) E8
Corrib (lake) C5
Croagh Patrick (mt.) C4
Cuilcagh (mt.) F3
Cullin (lake) C4
Curragh, The (plain) H5
Dash, Ben (hill) C6
Dee (riv.) H4
Deel (riv.) C3
Deel (riv.) C7
Deel (riv.) G4
Deele (riv.) F2
Derg (lake) F2
Derg (lake) E6
Derravaragh (lake) G4
Derryveagh (mts.) E2
Devilsbit (mt.) E6
Dingle (bay) A7
Donegal (bay) D3
Donegal (pt.) B6
Doulus (head) A8
Downpatrick (head) C3
Drum (hills) F7
Dublin (bay) J5
Dunany (pt.) J4
Dundalk (bay) J4
Dungarvan (harb.) G7
Dunkellin (riv.) D5
Dunmanus (bay) B8
Dursey (isl.) A8
Eask (lake) E2
Ennell (lake) G5
Erne (riv.) E3
Errigal (mt.) E1
Erris (head) A3
Fanad (head) F1
Fastnet Rock (isl.) B9
Feale (riv.) C7
Feeagh (lake) B4
Fergus (riv.) D6
Finn (riv.) F2
Finn (riv.) G3
Foul (sound) B5
Foyle (inlet) G1
Foyle (riv.) G2
Galley (head) D9
Galtee (mts.) E7
Galtymore (mt.) E7
Galway (bay) C5
Gara (lake) D4
Garadice (lake) F3
Gill (lake) E3
Gola (isl.) E1
Golden Vale (plain) E7
Gorumna (isl.) B5
Gowna (lake) G4
Grand (canal) G5
Great Blasket (isl.) A7
Gregory's (sound) B5
Gweebarra (bay) D2
Hags (head) B6
Hook (head) H7
Horn (head) E1
Iar Connacht (dist.) C5
Inishbofin (isl.) A4
Inisheer (isl.) B5
Inishmaan (isl.) C5
Inishmore (isl.) B5
Inishmurray (isl.) D3
Inishowen (head) H1
Inishowen (pen.) G1
Inishshark (isl.) A4
Inishtrahull (isl.) G1
Inishtrahull (sound) G1
Inishturk (isls.) A4
Inny (riv.) F4
Ireland's Eye (isl.) K5
Irish (sea) K4
Joyce's Country (dist.) B4
Keeper (hill) E6
Kenmare (riv.) A8
Kerry (head) A7
Key (lake) E3
Kilkieran (bay) B5
Killala (bay) C3
Killary (harb.) A4
Kinsale (harb.) E8
Kinsale, Old Head of (head) E8
Kippure (mt.) J5
Knockanefune (mt.) C7
Knockboy (mt.) B8
Knockmealdown (mts.) F7
Lambay (hill) K4
Laune (riv.) B7
Leane (lake) G4
Lee (riv.) D8
Leinster (mt.) H6
Leinster (prov.) 1,852,649 G5
Lettermullan (isl.) B5
Liffey (riv.) H5
Liscannor (bay) B6
Loop (head) A6
Loughros More (bay) D2
Lugnaquillia (mt.) J5
Lung (riv.) D4
Macgillicuddy's Reeks (mts.) B7
Macnean (lake) F3
Maigue (riv.) D6
Malin (head) F1
Mangerton (mt.) C8
Mask (lake) C4
Maumakeogh (mt.) C3
Maumturk (mts.) B5
Melvin (lake) E3
Mine (head) F8
Mizen (head) B9
Mizen (head) K6
Moher (cliff) B6
Monavullagh (mts.) F7
Moy (riv.) C3
Mullaghareirk (mts.) C7
Mulroy (bay) F1
Munster (prov.) 1,020,577 D7
Mutton (isl.) B6
Mweelrea (mt.) B4
Nagles (mts.) E7
Nephin (mt.) C3
Nephin Beg (mt.) B3
Nore (riv.) G7
North (sound) B5
North Inishkea (isl.) A3
Oughter (lake) G3
Ovoca (riv.) J6
Owenmore (riv.) B3
Owenmore (riv.) D3
Paps, The (mt.) C7
Partry (mts.) C4
Pollaphuca (res.) J5
Puffin (isl.) A8
Punchestown H5
Ramor (lake) G4
Rathlin O'Birne (isl.) C2
Ree (lake) F5
Rinn (lake) F4
Roaringwater (bay) B9
Rosscarbery (bay) D9
Rosskeeragh (pt.) D3
Royal (canal) G4
Saint Finan's (bay) A8
Saint George's (chan.) K7
Saint John's (pt.) D2
Saltee (isls.) H7
Scarriff (isl.) A8
Seven Hogs, The (isls.) A7
Shannon (riv.) E6
Shannon, Mouth of the (delta) B6
Sheeffry (hills) B4
Sheelin (lake) G4
Sheep Haven (harb.) F1
Sheeps (head) B8
Shehy (mts.) C8
Sherkin (isl.) C9
Silvermine (mts.) E6
Slaney (riv.) H7
Slieve Anierin (mt.) F3
Slieve Aughty (mts.) D5
Slieve Bernagh (mt.) D6
Slieve Bloom (mts.) F5
Slieve Callan (mt.) C6
Slieve Car (mt.) B3
Slieve Elva (mt.) C5
Slieve Gamph (Ox) (mts.) D3
Slievefelim (mts.) E6
Slievenaman (mt.) F7
Sligo (bay) D3
Slyne (head) A5
Smerwick (harb.) A7
South (sound) C5
Stacks (mts.) B7
Suck (riv.) E5
Sugarloaf (mt.) B8
Suir (riv.) G7
Swilly (inlet) F1
Tara (hill) H4
Toe (head) C9
Tory (isl.) E1
Tory (sound) E1
Tralee (bay) B7
Tramore (bay) G7
Truskmore (mt.) E3
Twelve Pins (mt.) B4
Ulster (part) (prov.) 236,008 G2
Valencia (Valentia) (isl.) A8
Valentia (isl.) A8
Waterford (harb.) G7
Wexford (harb.) J7
Wexford (bay) J7
Wicklow (mts.) J6
Youghal (bay) F8

NORTHERN IRELAND

DISTRICTS

Antrim 44,384 J2
Ards 57,626 K2
Armagh 47,618 H3
Ballymena 54,426 J2
Ballymoney 22,873 J1
Banbridge 29,885 J3
Belfast 295,223 J2
Carrickfergus 28,458 K2
Castlereagh 60,757 K2
Coleraine 46,272 H1
Cookstown 26,624 H2
Craigavon 71,202 J3
Down 52,869 K3
Dungannon 41,073 H3
Fermanagh 51,008 F3
Larne 28,929 K2
Limavady 26,270 H1
Lisburn 82,091 J2
Londonderry 83,384 G2
Magherafelt 30,825 H2
Mourne (Newry and Mourne) 72,243 J3
Moyle 14,252 J1
Newtownabbey 71,631 J2
North Down 65,849 K2
Omagh 41,159 G2
Strabane 35,028 G2

CITIES and TOWNS

Annalong 1,823 K3
Antrim 22,342 J2
Armagh 12,700 H3
Augher 1,874 G3
Aughnacloy 1,659 H3
Ballycarry 1,652 K2
Ballycastle 3,284 J1
Ballyclare 6,159 J2
Ballygawley 2,099 G3
Ballymena 28,166 J2
Ballymoney 5,679 J1
Ballynahinch 3,721 J3
Banbridge 9,650 J3
Bangor 46,585 K2
Belfast (cap.) 295,223 J2
Bellaghy 1,854 H2
Belleek and Boa 2,469 E3
Beragh 2,028 G2
Bessbrook 2,756 J3
Brookeborough 2,250 G3
Broughshane 1,503 J2
Bushmills 1,381 J1
Caledon 1,633 H3
Carnlough 1,462 K2
Carrickfergus 17,633 K2
Carrowdore 3,019 K2
Carryduff 2,666 K2
Castledawson 1,460 H2
Castlederg 1,730 F2
Castlewellan 2,105 K3
Claudy 2,516 G2
Clogher 1,792 G3
Cloughmills 1,558 J2
Coalisland 3,324 H2
Coleraine 15,967 H1
Comber 7,600 K2
Cookstown 7,649 H2
Craigavon 10,195 J3
Crumlin 1,708 J2
Cullybackey 2,098 J2
Derrygonnelly 2,627 F3
Donaghadee 3,874 K2
Downpatrick 8,245 K3
Dromore, Banbridge 3,089 J3
Dromore, Omagh 2,286 G3
Drumquin 1,865 F2
Dundrum 2,295 K3
Dungannon 8,295 H3
Dungiven 2,249 H2
Dunloy 1,593 J1
Dunnamanagh 2,191 G2
Ederney, Kesh and Lark 2,607 F2
Enniskillen 10,429 F3
Feeny 1,402 H2
Fintona 1,353 G3
Fivemiletown 1,758 G3
Garvagh 2,222 H2
Gilford 1,512 J3
Glenarm 1,533 J2
Glenavy 2,402 J2
Glynn 1,689 K2
Gortin 1,877 G2
Greenisland 5,103 K2
Grey Abbey 2,945 K2
Groomsport 3,870 K2
Holywood 9,462 K2
Irvinestown 1,827 F3
Keady 2,561 H3
Kells 2,564 J2
Kesh, Ederney and Lark 2,607 F3
Kilkeel 6,036 K3
Killough 3,104 K3
Killyclogher 5,557 G2
Killyleagh 2,094 K3
Kilrea 1,320 H2
Lambeg J2
Larne 18,224 K2
Limavady 8,015 H1
Lisbellaw 2,395 K2
Lisburn 40,391 J2
Lisnaskea 1,568 G3
Londonderry (Derry) 62,692 G2
Loughbrickland 2,244 J3
Lurgan 20,991 J3
Macosquin 2,267 H1
Maghera 1,953 H2
Magherafelt 5,044 H2
Millisle 1,373 K2
Moy 2,163 H3
Newcastle 6,246 J3
Newry 19,426 J3
Newtownabbey 56,149 K2
Newtownards 20,531 K2
Newtownbutler 2,632 G3
Newtownhamilton 1,654 H3
Newtownstewart 1,425 G2
Omagh 14,627 G2
Pomeroy 1,638 H2
Portadown 21,333 H3
Portaferry 2,148 K3
Portglenone 2,017 H2
Portrush 5,114 H1
Portstewart 5,312 H1
Randalstown 3,591 J2
Rathfriland 2,243 J3
Richhill 1,728 H3
Rostrevor 1,852 J3
Sion Mills 1,771 G2
Sixmilecross 1,613 G2
Stewartstown 1,554 H2
Strabane 9,413 G2
Strangford 2,062 K3
Strathfoyle 2,050 G1
Tandragee 2,224 J3
Tempo 2,149 G3
Trillick 2,017 G3
Warrenpoint 4,798 J3
Whitehead 3,546 K2

OTHER FEATURES

Arney (riv.) F3
Bann (riv.) H2
Beg (lake) J2
Belfast (inlet) K2
Blackwater (riv.) H3
Bush (riv.) H1
Copeland (isl.) K2
Derg (riv.) F2
Divis (mt.) J2
Dundrum (bay) K3
Erne, Lough (lake) F3
Fair (head) J1
Foyle (riv.) G2
Foyle (inlet) G1
Garron (pt.) K1
Giant's Causeway H1
Lagan (riv.) K2
Larne (inlet) K2
Macnean (lake) F3
Magee, Island (pen.) K2
Main (riv.) J2
Mourne (riv.) G2
Mourne (mts.) J3
Neagh (lake) J2
North (chan.) K1
Owenkillew (riv.) G2
Rathlin (sound) J1
Rathlin (isl.) J1
Red (bay) K1
Roe (riv.) H1
Saint John's (pt.) K3
Slieve Beagh (mt.) G3
Slieve Donard (mt.) K3
Sperrin (mts.) G2
Strangford (inlet) K3
Trostan (mt.) J1
Ulster (part) (prov.) G2
Upper Lough Erne (lake) F3

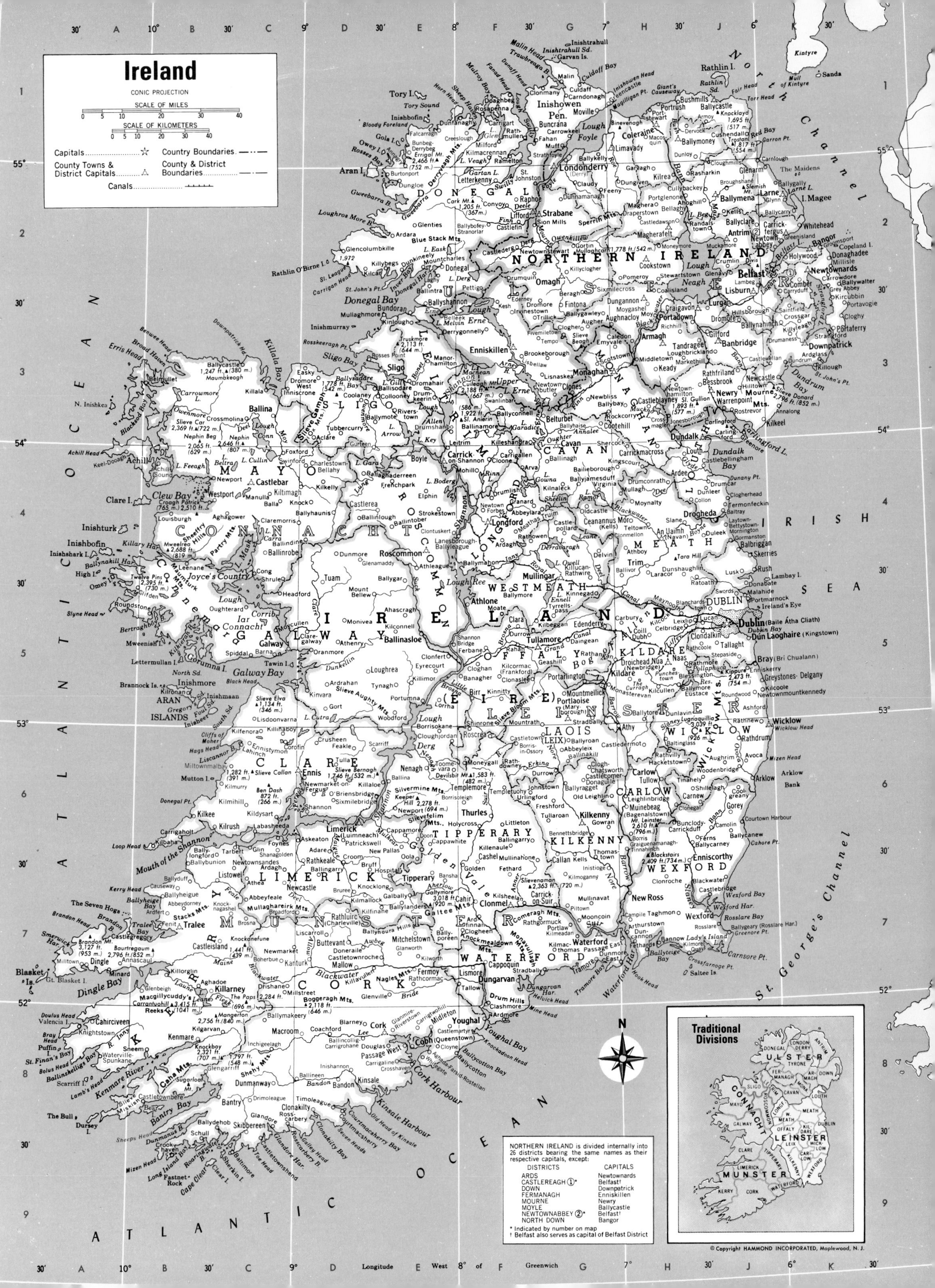
Ireland
CONIC PROJECTION
SCALE OF MILES
0 5 10 20 30 40
SCALE OF KILOMETERS
0 5 10 20 30 40
Capitals
County Towns & District Capitals
Country Boundaries
County & District Boundaries
Canals
NORTHERN IRELAND is divided internally into 26 districts bearing the same names as their respective capitals, except:
DISTRICTS
ARDS
CASTLEREAGH ①*
DOWN
FERMANAGH
MOURNE
MOYLE
NEWTOWNABBEY ②*
NORTH DOWN
CAPITALS
Newtownards
Belfast†
Downpatrick
Enniskillen
Newry
Ballycastle
Belfast†
Bangor
* Indicated by number on map
† Belfast also serves as capital of Belfast District
Traditional Divisions
ULSTER
CONNACHT
LEINSTER
MUNSTER
DONEGAL
LONDON-DERRY
ANTRIM
TYRONE
FERMANAGH
ARMAGH
DOWN
SLIGO
LEITRIM
MONAGHAN
CAVAN
MAYO
ROSCOMMON
LONGFORD
W. MEATH
MEATH
LOUTH
DUBLIN
GALWAY
OFFALY
KILDARE
WICKLOW
LAOIS
CARLOW
CLARE
TIPPERARY
KILKENNY
WEXFORD
LIMERICK
KERRY
CORK
WATERFORD
© Copyright HAMMOND INCORPORATED, Maplewood, N.J.
Longitude West 8° of Greenwich
ATLANTIC OCEAN
NORTH CHANNEL
IRISH SEA
ST. GEORGE'S CHANNEL
NORTHERN IRELAND
ULSTER
CONNACHT
LEINSTER
MUNSTER
IRELAND (EIRE)
DONEGAL
SLIGO
LEITRIM
MAYO
ROSCOMMON
GALWAY
CLARE
LIMERICK
KERRY
CORK
TIPPERARY
WATERFORD
KILKENNY
WEXFORD
CARLOW
WICKLOW
KILDARE
LAOIS (LEIX)
OFFALY
WESTMEATH
LONGFORD
MEATH
LOUTH
MONAGHAN
CAVAN
DUBLIN
Kintyre
Sanda
Mull of Kintyre
Rathlin I.
Malin Head
Inishtrahull
Garvan Is.
Tory I.
Tory Sound
Bloody Foreland
Aran I.
Inishmurray
Achill Head
Achill
Clare I.
Inishturk
Inishbofin
Inishshark I.
High I.
Slyne Head
Mweenish I.
Lettermullan I.
North Sd.
Inishmore
ARAN ISLANDS
Inishmaan
Inisheer
Brannock Is.
Mutton I.
Loop Head
Kerry Head
The Seven Hogs
Brandon Head
Blasket Is.
Dingle Bay
Valencia I.
Bray Head
Puffin I.
Scarriff I.
Bolus Head
The Bull
Dursey I.
Mizen Head
Cape Clear
Clear I.
Fastnet Rock
Sherkin I.
Long Island
Old Head of Kinsale
Seven Heads
Galley Head
Toe Head
Cork Harbour
Youghal Bay
Mine Head
Helvick Head
Hook Head
Saltee Is.
Carnsore Pt.
Greenore Pt.
Rosslare Bay
Wexford Bay
Cahore Pt.
Courtown Harbour
Mizen Head
Arklow Bank
Wicklow Head
Ireland's Eye
Lambay I.
Dublin Bay
Dundalk Bay
Carlingford L.
Dundrum Bay
St. John's Pt.
Strangford Lough
Copeland I.
The Maidens
Belfast Lough
Larne
Fair Head
Torr Head
Giant's Causeway
Lough Foyle
Lough Swilly
Inishowen Pen.
Lough Neagh
Lough Erne
Upper L. Erne
Lough Ree
Lough Derg
Lough Corrib
Lough Mask
Lough Conn
Galway Bay
Clew Bay
Blacksod Bay
Donegal Bay
Sligo Bay
Killala Bay
Mouth of the Shannon
Tralee Bay
Kenmare River
Bantry Bay
Dunmanus B.
Roaringwater B.
Blue Stack Mts.
Derryveagh Mts.
Sperrin Mts.
Mourne Mts.
Wicklow Mts.
Slieve Bloom Mts.
Slieve Aughty Mts.
Silvermine Mts.
Galtee Mts.
Knockmealdown Mts.
Comeragh Mts.
Boggeragh Mts.
Nagles Mts.
Shehy Mts.
Caha Mts.
Macgillycuddy's Reeks
Carrantuohill 3,415 ft. (1041 m.)
Brandon Mt. 3,127 ft. (953 m.)
Lugnaquillia 3,039 ft. (926 m.)
Galtymore 3,018 ft. (920 m.)
Slieve Donard 2,796 ft. (852 m.)
Mweelrea 2,688 ft. (819 m.)
Errigal Mt. 2,466 ft. (752 m.)
Mt. Leinster 2,610 ft. (796 m.)
Shannon
Blackwater
Barrow
Nore
Suir
Boyne
Bann
Foyle
Erne
Dublin (Baile Átha Cliath)
Dún Laoghaire (Kingstown)
Belfast
Londonderry (Derry)
Cork
Limerick (Luimneach)
Galway
Waterford
Wexford
Kilkenny
Sligo
Donegal
Letterkenny
Lifford
Strabane
Omagh
Enniskillen
Armagh
Newry
Downpatrick
Lisburn
Bangor
Newtownards
Ballymena
Coleraine
Ballycastle
Ballymoney
Limavady
Antrim
Cookstown
Dungannon
Craigavon
Portadown
Lurgan
Banbridge
Monaghan
Cavan
Longford
Mullingar
Athlone
Tullamore
Portlaoise
Naas
Kildare
Carlow
Wicklow
Arklow
Gorey
Enniscorthy
New Ross
Clonmel
Tipperary
Thurles
Nenagh
Ennis
Tralee
Killarney
Dingle
Kenmare
Bantry
Skibbereen
Clonakilty
Kinsale
Cobh (Queenstown)
Youghal
Dungarvan
Mallow
Fermoy
Lismore
Mitchelstown
Castlebar
Westport
Ballina
Tuam
Roscommon
Boyle
Carrick-on-Shannon
Ballinasloe
Loughrea
Drogheda
Dundalk
Navan (An Uaimh)
Trim
Kells (Ceanannus Mór)
Bray
Greystones-Delgany

Norway, Sweden, Finland and Denmark
CONIC PROJECTION
SCALE OF MILES
0 50 100 150
SCALE OF KILOMETERS
0 50 100 150 200
Capitals of Countries
Administrative Centers
International Boundaries
Internal Boundaries
Canals
SUBDIVISIONS Indicated by Numbers
Counties in NORWAY
1 Akershus G 6
2 Vestfold G 7
3 Østfold G 7
4 Oslo G 7
Oslo is the administrative center for Akershus and Oslo County.
Counties in SWEDEN
5 Göteborg och Bohus G 7
6 Västmanland K 7
7 Södermanland K 7
8 Östergötland J 7
9 Malmöhus H 9
10 Kristianstad J 8
Svalbard
GREENLAND SEA
Spitsbergen
Nordaustlandet
Longyearbyen
Barentsburg
Bjørnøya
STOCKHOLM
ARCTIC OCEAN
BARENTS SEA
NORWEGIAN SEA
ATLANTIC OCEAN
NORTH SEA
SKAGERRAK
KATTEGAT
BALTIC SEA
GULF OF BOTHNIA
Gulf of Finland
Gulf of Riga
Arctic Circle
DENMARK
RUSSIA
ESTONIA
LATVIA
LITHUANIA
BELARUS
POLAND
GERMANY
NETH.
Oslo
Bergen
Trondheim
Stavanger
Kristiansand
Tromsø
Narvik
Hammerfest
Kiruna
Luleå
Umeå
Sundsvall
Uppsala
Göteborg
Malmö
Helsinki
Turku
Tampere
Oulu
Vaasa
COPENHAGEN
Århus
Odense
Ålborg
ST. PETERSBURG
Murmansk
Tallinn
Riga
Kaliningrad
Gdańsk
HAMBURG
BERLIN
WARSAW
Gotland
Öland
Bornholm
AHVENANMAA (ÅLAND)
Lake Ladoga
Lake Peipus
Lake Imandra
Kebnekaise 6,946 ft. (2117 m.)
Haltiatunturi 4,343 ft. (1324 m.)
Glittertinden 8,110 ft. (2472 m.)
Sulitjelma 6,276 ft. (1913 m.)
16° Longitude East of Greenwich 18°
© Copyright HAMMOND INCORPORATED, Maplewood, N.J.

AREA 125,053 sq. mi. (323,887 sq. km.)
POPULATION 4,242,000
CAPITAL Oslo
LARGEST CITY Oslo
HIGHEST POINT Glittertinden 8,110 ft. (2,472 m.)
MONETARY UNIT krone
MAJOR LANGUAGE Norwegian
MAJOR RELIGION Protestantism

AREA 173,665 sq. mi. (449,792 sq. km.)
POPULATION 8,541,000
CAPITAL Stockholm
LARGEST CITY Stockholm
HIGHEST POINT Kebnekaise 6,946 ft. (2,117 m.)
MONETARY UNIT krona
MAJOR LANGUAGES Swedish
MAJOR RELIGION Protestantism

AREA 130,128 sq. mi. (337,032 sq. km.)
POPULATION 4,973,000
CAPITAL Helsinki
LARGEST CITY Helsinki
HIGHEST POINT Haltiatunturi 4,343 ft. (1,324 m.)
MONETARY UNIT markka
MAJOR LANGUAGES Finnish, Swedish
MAJOR RELIGION Protestantism

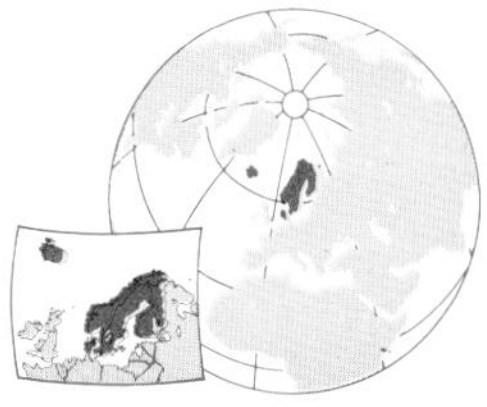

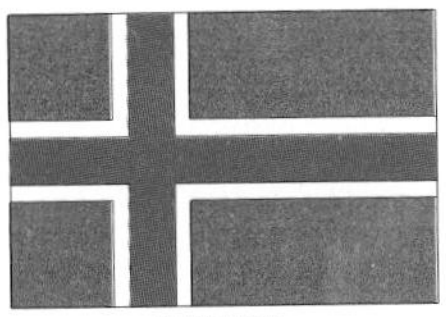
NORWAY

SWEDEN

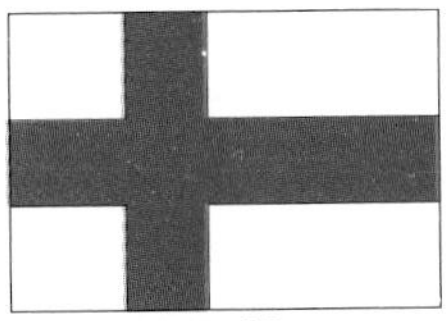
FINLAND

FINLAND

PROVINCES

Ahvenanmaa 23,591 .... L6
Åland (Ahvenanmaa) 23,591 .... L6
Häme 677,750 .... O6
Keski-Suomi 247,693 .... O5
Kuopio 256,036 .... P5
Kymi 340,665 .... Q6
Lappi 200,943 .... P3
Mikkeli 239,029 .... P6
Oulu 432,141 .... P4
Pohjois-Karjala 177,567 .... Q5
Turku ja Pori 713,050 .... N6
Uusimaa 1,187,851 .... O6
Vaasa 444,348 .... N5

CITIES and TOWNS

Abo (Turku) 161,398 .... N6
Alavus 10,701 .... N5
Äänekoski 11,447 .... O5
Anjalamkoski 19,703 .... P6
Borga 19,513 .... O6
Espoo 156,778 .... O6
Forssa 20,074 .... N6
Haapajärvi 8,454 .... O5
Hämeenlinna 42,382 .... O6
Hamina 10,313 .... P6
Hangö 12,071 .... N7
Hanko (Hangö) 12,071 .... N7
Harjavalta 8,955 .... M6
Heinola 16,112 .... P6
Helsinki (cap.) 485,795 .... O6
Hyvinkää 38,742 .... O6
Iisalmi 23,612 .... P5
Ikaalinen 8,184 .... N6
Imatra 35,085 .... Q6
Jakobstad 20,458 .... N5
Jämsä 12,498 .... O6
Järvenpää 27,220 .... O6
Joensuu 46,850 .... R5
Jyväskylä 65,282 .... O5
Kajaani 36,020 .... P4
Kankaanpää 13,652 .... M6
Karis (Karjaa) N6
Karkkila 8,355 .... N6
Kauniainien 7,746 .... O6
Kemi 26,421 .... O4
Kemijärvi 12,762 .... P3
Kerava 26,207 .... O6
Kokemäki 9,741 .... N6
Kokkola 34,489 .... N5
Kotka 58,956 .... P6
Kouvola 31,829 .... P6
Kristiinankaupunki (Kristinestad) 9,081 .... N5
Kristinestad 9,081 .... N5
Kuopio 78,124 .... Q5
Kurikka 11,512 .... M5
Kuusankoski 22,089 .... P6
Lahti 94,447 .... O6
Lappeenranta 54,102 .... P6
Lapua 14,644 .... N5
Lieksa 18,588 .... R5
Loimaa 7,053 .... N6
Lovisa 8,697 .... P6
Maarianhamina (Mariehamn) 9,829 .... M7
Mänttä 8,092 .... O6
Mariehamn 9,829 .... M7
Mikkeli 31,636 .... P6
Naantali 10,246 .... M6
Nokia 24,325 .... N6
Nurmes 11,419 .... Q5
Nykarleby 7,768 .... N5
Oulainen 8,225 .... O4
Oulu 97,297 .... O4
Outokumpu 9,678 .... Q5
Parainen 11,618 .... M6
Parkano 8,692 .... N6
Pieksämäki 14,372 .... P5
Pietarsaari (Jakobstad) 20,458 .... N5
Pori 78,376 .... M6
Pudasjärvi 11,453 .... P4
Raahe 18,932 .... O4
Raisio 19,671 .... M6
Rauma 30,921 .... M6
Riihimäki 24,366 .... O6
Rovaniemi 32,782 .... O3
Salo 20,495 .... N6
Savonlinna 28,667 .... Q6
Seinäjoki 26,257 .... N5
Suonenjoki 8,981 .... P5
Tampere 169,026 .... N6
Toijala 8,046 .... N6
Tornio 22,328 .... O4
Turku 161,398 .... N6
Utsjoki 1,548 .... P2
Uusikaarlepyy (Nykarleby) 7,768 .... N5
Uusikaupunki 14,026 .... M6
Vaasa 54,333 .... M5
Valkeakoski 22,582 .... N6
Vammala 16,024 .... N6
Vantaa 143,844 .... O6
Varkaus 24,856 .... Q5
Vasa (Vaasa) 54,333 .... M5
Virrat 9,391 .... N5
Ylivieska 12,559 .... O4

OTHER FEATURES

Åland (isls.) L6
Baltic (sea) K9
Bothnia (gulf) M5
Finland (gulf) P7
Hailuoto (isl.) O4
Haltiatunturi (mt.) M2
Haukivesi (lake) Q5
Iijoki (riv.) O4
Inari (lake) P2
Ivalojoki (riv.) P2
Kallavesi (lake) P5
Karlö (Hailuoto) (isl.) O4
Keitele (lake) O5
Kemijärvi (lake) Q3
Kemijoki (riv.) O3
Lapland (reg.) O2
Lappajärvi (lake) O5
Lapuanjoki (riv.) N5
Lokka (reg.) Q3
Muojärvi (lake) R4
Muonio (riv.) M2
Näsijärvi (lake) O6
Orihvesi (lake) Q5
Oulujärvi (lake) P4
Oulujoki (riv.) O4
Ounasjoki (riv.) O3
Päijänne (lake) O6
Pielinen (lake) Q5
Porkkala (pen.) O7
Puruvesi (lake) Q6
Saimaa (lake) Q6
Tana (riv.) P2
Tornionjoki (riv.) O3
Ylikitka (lake) Q3

NORWAY

COUNTIES

Akershus 399,797 .... G6
Aust-Agder 95,475 .... E7
Buskerud 221,384 .... F6
Finnmark 74,690 .... O2
Hedmark 186,305 .... G6
Hordaland 402,343 .... E6
Møre og Romsdal 237,489 .... E5
Nordland 241,048 .... J3
Nord-Trøndelag 126,648 .... H4
Oppland 181,620 .... F6
Oslo (city) 449,220 .... D3
Østfold 235,813 .... G7
Rogaland 326,611 .... E7
Sogn og Fjordane 105,466 .... E6
Sør-Trøndelag 247,354 .... G5
Telemark 162,595 .... F7
Troms 146,595 .... L2
Vest-Agder 141,284 .... E7
Vestfold 192,934 .... G7

CITIES and TOWNS

Ålesund 40,868 .... D5
Ålgård 2,322 .... D7
Alta 5,582 .... N2
Åndalsnes 2,574 .... F5
Årdalstangen 2,360 .... F6
Arendal 11,701 .... F7
Årnes 2,267 .... G6
Askim 8,413 .... E4
Bamble† 7,031 .... F7
Bergen 213,434 .... D6
Bodø 31,077 .... J3
Borge† 3,294 .... H2
Brate 2,107 .... G7
Brønnøysund 3,130 .... G4
Drammen 50,777 .... C4
Drøbak 4,538 .... D4
Eidsvoll 2,906 .... G6
Eigersund 11,379 .... D7
Elverum 7,391 .... G6
Farsund 8,908 .... E7
Flekkefjord 8,750 .... E7
Flora 8,822 .... D6
Fredrikstad 29,024 .... D4
Gjøvik 25,963 .... G6
Grimstad 13,091 .... F7
Halden 27,087 .... G7
Hamar 16,418 .... G6
Hammerfest 7,610 .... N1
Harstad 21,125 .... K2
Hauge 2,079 .... E7
Haugesund 27,386 .... D7
Holmestrand 8,246 .... C4
Honningsvag 3,780 .... O1
Horten 13,746 .... D4
Kirkenes 4,466 .... Q2
Kongsberg 19,854 .... F7
Kongsvinger 16,146 .... H6
Kopervik 4,221 .... D7
Kornsjø† 6,079 .... G7
Kragerø 5,249 .... F7
Kristiansand 59,488 .... F8
Kristiansund 18,847 .... E5
Kvinnherad† 2,898 .... E6
Larvik 9,097 .... C4
Lenvik† 11,098 .... L2
Levanger 5,066 .... G5
Lillehammer 21,248 .... F6
Lillesand 3,028 .... F7
Lillestrøm† 11,550 .... E3
Lodingen 1,840 .... J2
Longyearbyen D2
Lysaker† 81,612 .... D3
Mandal 11,579 .... E7
Meråker† 2,907 .... G5
Mo 21,033 .... J3
Molde 20,334 .... E5
Mosjøen 9,341 .... H4
Moss 25,786 .... D4
Mysen 3,760 .... G7
Namsos 11,452 .... G4
Narvik 19,582 .... K2
Nesttun† 11,519 .... D6
Nittedal† 8,889 .... D3
Notodden 12,970 .... F7
Nøtterøy 11,944 .... D4
Odda 7,401 .... E6
Oppdal 2,173 .... F5
Orkanger 3,685 .... F5
Oslo (cap.) 462,732 .... D3
Oslo* 645,413 .... D3
Porsgrunn 31,709 .... G7
Rakkestad 2,392 .... G7
Ringerike 30,156 .... C3
Risør 6,560 .... F7
Rjukan 5,334 .... F7
Røros 3,041 .... G5
Saetermoen 2,114 .... L2
Sandefjord 33,350 .... C4
Sandnes 33,934 .... D7
Sandvika† 34,337 .... C3
Sarpsborg 12,889 .... D4
Selje† 3,386 .... D5
Ski 9,081 .... D4
Skien 47,105 .... F7
Skudeneshavn 2,206 .... D7
Stavanger 86,639 .... D7
Stavern 2,604 .... D4
Steinkjer 20,553 .... G4
Stor-Elvdal† 2,993 .... G6
Sunndalsøra 5,114 .... F5
Svelvik 2,256 .... D4
Svolvaer 3,942 .... J2
Tana 1,893 .... Q1
Tønsberg 9,964 .... D4
Tromsø 43,830 .... L2
Trondheim 134,910 .... F5
Tvedestrand 1,689 .... F7
Ullensvang† 2,326 .... E6
Vadsø 6,019 .... Q1
Vanylven 1,966 .... E5
Vardø 3,875 .... R1
Vik 1,019 .... E6
Volda 3,511 .... E5
Voss 5,944 .... E6

OTHER FEATURES

Andøya (isl.) J2
Barentsoya (isl.) D2
Bjornøya (isl.) D3
Boknafjord (fjord) D7
Dovrefjell (hills) F5
Edgeøya (isl.) E2
Femundsjø (lake) G5
Folda (fjord) G4
Folda (fjord) J3
Frohavet (bay) F5
Frøya (isl.) F5
Glittertinden (mt.) F6
Greenland (sea) C3
Hadselfjorden (fjord) J2
Haltiatunturi (mt.) M2
Hardangerfjord (fjord) D7
Hardangervidda (plat.) E6
Hinlopenstreten (strait) C1
Hinnøya (isl.) K2
Hitra (isl.) F5
Hortensfjord (fjord) G4
Isfjorden (fjord) C2
Kjölen (mts.) K3
Kvaenangen (fjord) N2
Kvaloy (isl.) K2
Kvaløya (isl.) O1
Laksefjorden (fjord) P1
Langøya (isl.) J2
Lapland (reg.) K2
Lindesnes (cape) E8
Lofoten (isls.) H2
Lopphavet (bay) M1
Magerøya (isl.) P1
Moskenesøya (isl.) H3
Namsen (riv.) H4
Nordaustlandet (isl.) D1
Nordfjord (fjord) E6
Nordkapp (pt.) C1
North Cape (Nordkapp) (cape) P1
Norwegian (sea) F3
Ofotfjorden (fjord) K2
Oslofjord (fjord) D4
Otra (riv.) E7
Pasvikelv (riv.) Q2
Porsangen (fjord) O1
Prins Karls Forland (isl.) B2
Rana (fjord) H3
Rauma (riv.) F5
Ringvassøy (isl.) L2
Romsdalsfjorden (fjord) E5
Saltfjorden (fjord) J3
Seiland (isl.) N1
Senja (isl.) K2
Skagerrak (strait) F8
Sognafjorden (fjord) D6
Sørkapp (pt.) C2
Sorøya (isl.) N1
Spitsbergen (isl.) C2
Steinneset (cape) E2
Storfjorden (fjord) D2
Sulitjelma (mt.) J3
Svalbard (isls.) C3
Tana (riv.) P1
Tanafjord (fjord) Q1
Trondheimsfjorden (fjord) G5
Tyrifjord (lake) C3
Vannøy (isl.) L1
Varangerfjord (fjord) Q2
Varangerhalvøya (pen.) Q1
Vegafjorden (fjord) G4
Vesterålen (isls.) J2
Vestfjord (fjord) H3
Vestvågøya (isl.) H3
Vikna (isls.) G4

(continued on following page)

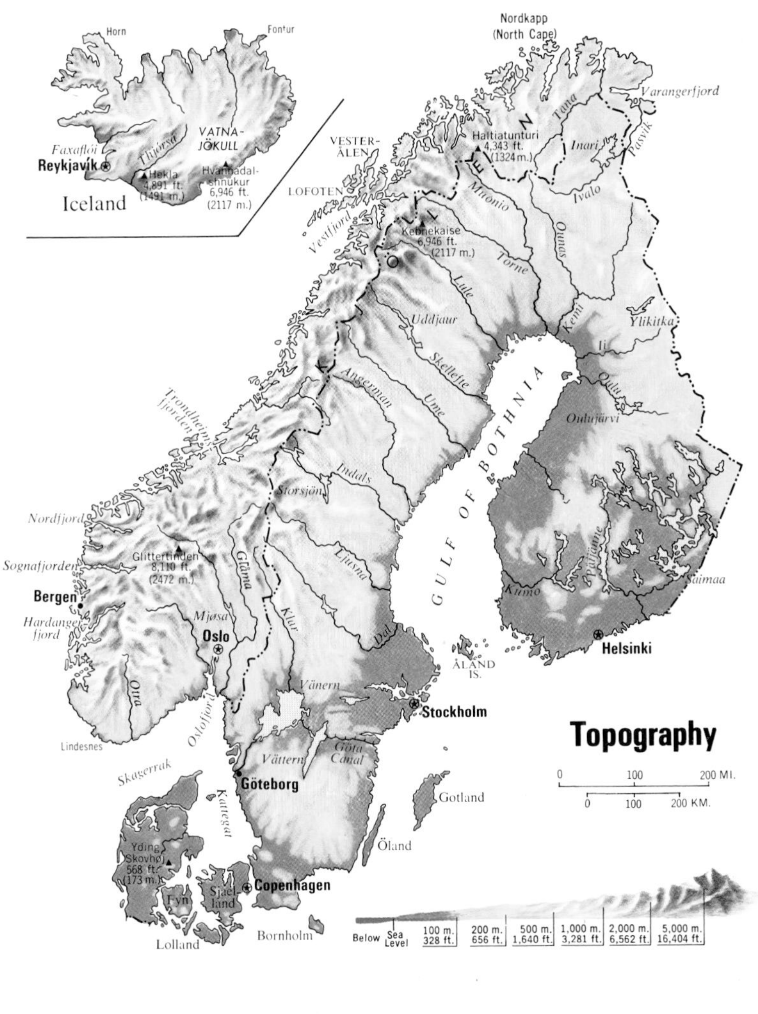
Horn
Fontur
VATNA-
JÖKULL
Faxaflói
Reykjavík
Hekla
4,891 ft.
(1491 m.)
Hvannadal-
shnukur
6,946 ft.
(2117 m.)
Iceland
Nordkapp
(North Cape)
Varangerfjord
Haltiatunturi
4,343 ft.
(1324 m.)
VESTER-
ÅLEN
LOFOTEN
Kebnekaise
6,946 ft.
(2117 m.)
GULF OF BOTHNIA
Helsinki
Bergen
Oslo
Glittertinden
8,110 ft.
(2472 m.)
ÅLAND
IS.
Stockholm
Göteborg
Gotland
Öland
Copenhagen
Bornholm
Lolland
Lindesnes
Topography
0 100 200 MI.
0 100 200 KM.
Below Sea Level
100 m. 328 ft.
200 m. 656 ft.
500 m. 1,640 ft.
1,000 m. 3,281 ft.
2,000 m. 6,562 ft.
5,000 m. 16,404 ft.

(continued)

SWEDEN

COUNTIES

Älvsborg 433,417 ..... H7
Blekinge 149,544 ..... J8
Gävleborg 287,004 ..... K6
Göteborg och Bohus 729,629 ..... G7
Gotland 56,383 ..... L8
Halland 247,417 ..... H8
Jämtland 134,116 ..... J5
Jönköping 304,021 ..... H8
Kalmar 237,781 ..... K8
Kopparberg 284,407 ..... J6
Kristianstad 283,818 ..... J8
Kronoberg 175,427 ..... J8
Malmöhus 763,349 ..... H9
Norrbotten 261,536 ..... L3
Örebro 270,031 ..... J7
Östergötland 396,919 ..... J7
Skaraborg 272,126 ..... H7
Södermanland 251,423 ..... K7
Stockholm 1,617,038 ..... L7
Uppsala 260,476 ..... K7
Värmland 280,694 ..... H7
Västerbotten 247,521 ..... K4
Västernorrland 259,964 ..... K5
Västmanland 254,847 ..... K7

CITIES and TOWNS

Åhus 6,125 ..... J9
Alingsås 32,402 ..... H7
Almhult 15,645 ..... H8
Älvkarleby 9,175 ..... K6
Alvesta 19,579 ..... J8
Älvsbyn 9,373 ..... M4
Ängelholm 32,998 ..... H8
Åmål 13,130 ..... H7
Ånge 12,653 ..... J5
Arboga 14,457 ..... J7
Åre 9,787 ..... H5
Årjäng 10,050 ..... H7
Arvika 26,668 ..... H7
Askim 17,609 ..... G8
Åtvidaberg 12,677 ..... K7
Avesta 24,671 ..... J6
Båstad 12,962 ..... H8
Bengtsfors 11,836 ..... H7
Boden 29,160 ..... M4
Bollnäs 27,724 ..... K6
Borås 100,795 ..... H8
Borgholm 11,170 ..... K8
Borlänge 46,343 ..... J6
Danderyd 28,525 ..... H1
Eksjö 17,857 ..... J8
Emmaboda 10,694 ..... J8
Enköping 33,700 ..... G1
Eskilstuna 88,850 ..... K7
Eslöv 27,097 ..... H9
Fagersta 13,744 ..... J6
Falkenberg 36,536 ..... H8
Falköping 31,532 ..... H7
Falun 52,448 ..... J6
Filipstad 13,481 ..... H7
Finspång 23,378 ..... J7
Flen 17,016 ..... K7
Forshaga 11,739 ..... H7
Frösö 10,274 ..... J5
Gällivare 22,717 ..... M3
Gävle 87,747 ..... K6
Göteborg 430,763 ..... G8
Hagfors 16,346 ..... H6
Hällefors 9,402 ..... J7
Hallsberg 16,405 ..... J7
Hallstahammar 16,637 ..... K7
Halmstad 78,607 ..... H8
Haparanda 10,159 ..... N4
Härnösand 27,248 ..... L5
Hässleholm 48,658 ..... H8
Hedemora 16,644 ..... K6
Helsingborg 107,443 ..... H8
Hjo 8,952 ..... J7
Hofors 12,204 ..... K6
Höganäs 10,866 ..... H8
Huddinge 71,921 ..... H1
Hudiksvall 37,603 ..... K6
Jönköping 109,890 ..... H8
Kalix 19,160 ..... N4
Kalmar 55,129 ..... K8
Karlshamn 31,377 ..... J8
Karlskoga 34,316 ..... J7
Karlskrona 58,634 ..... J8
Karlstad 75,412 ..... H7
Katrineholm 32,254 ..... K7
Kinna 13,676 ..... H8
Kiruna 26,312 ..... L3
Köping 26,253 ..... J7
Kramfors 24,607 ..... K5
Kristianstad 70,491 ..... J9
Kristinehamn 26,006 ..... H7
Kumla 17,884 ..... J7
Kungälv 32,549 ..... G8
Kungsbacka 52,027 ..... G8
Laholm 21,881 ..... H8
Landskrona 35,393 ..... H9
Leksand 14,115 ..... J6
Lessebo 8,769 ..... J8
Lidingö 38,819 ..... H1
Lidköping 35,168 ..... H7
Lindesberg 24,415 ..... J7
Linköping 119,167 ..... K7
Ljungby 27,176 ..... J8
Ljusdal 21,026 ..... J6
Ludvika 29,283 ..... J6
Luleå 67,443 ..... N4
Lund 85,150 ..... H9
Lycksele 14,020 ..... L4
Malmberget 10,239 ..... M3
Malmö 231,575 ..... H9
Malung 11,611 ..... H6
Mariestad 24,508 ..... H7
Markaryd 11,044 ..... H8
Märsta 17,066 ..... K7
Mellerud 10,455 ..... H7
Mjölby 25,952 ..... J7
Mölndal 47,248 ..... H8
Mönsterås 12,911 ..... K8
Mora 20,078 ..... J6
Mörbylanga 13,029 ..... K8
Motala 41,502 ..... J7
Nacka 61,931 ..... H1
Nässjö 30,623 ..... J8
Nora 10,200 ..... J7
Norrköping 119,370 ..... K7
Norrtälje 43,741 ..... L7
Nybro 20,706 ..... J8
Nyköping 64,739 ..... K7
Nynäshamn 21,395 ..... L7
Olofström 14,883 ..... J8
Örebro 119,824 ..... J7
Örnsköldsvik 58,967 ..... L5
Oskarshamn 27,217 ..... K8
Östersund 57,281 ..... J5
Östhammar 21,338 ..... L6
Oxelösund 12,923 ..... K7
Piteå 39,079 ..... M4
Rättvik 11,048 ..... J6
Ronneby 28,868 ..... J8
Säffle 17,935 ..... H7
Sala 21,381 ..... K7
Sandviken 39,740 ..... K6
Säter 11,490 ..... J6
Sävsjö 11,730 ..... J8
Sigtuna 30,182 ..... H1
Simrishamn 19,709 ..... J9
Skara 18,402 ..... H7
Skellefteå 74,127 ..... M4
Skövde 46,712 ..... H7
Smedjebacken 13,183 ..... J6
Söderhamn 29,606 ..... K6
Söderköping 12,838 ..... K7
Södertälje 80,660 ..... G1
Sollefteå 25,114 ..... K5
Sollentuna 50,242 ..... G1
Solna 50,964 ..... H1
Sölvesborg 15,782 ..... J9
Stenungsund 17,792 ..... G7
Stockholm (cap.) 669,485 ..... G1
Strängnäs 25,841 ..... F1
Strömstad 10,457 ..... G7
Strömsund 16,164 ..... J5
Sundbyberg 31,095 ..... G1
Sundsvall 92,983 ..... K5
Sunne 13,245 ..... H7
Surahammar 11,287 ..... J7
Svenljunga 11,004 ..... H8
Täby 56,339 ..... H1
Tibro 11,044 ..... J7
Tidaholm 13,048 ..... J7
Tierp 19,620 ..... K6
Timrå 18,392 ..... K5
Tomelilla 12,241 ..... J9
Torsby 15,030 ..... H6
Tranås 17,675 ..... J7
Trelleborg 34,846 ..... H9
Trollhättan 50,296 ..... H7
Uddevalla 46,489 ..... G7
Ulricehamn 22,405 ..... H8
Umeå 88,726 ..... M5
Uppsala 161,820 ..... K7
Vaggeryd 12,185 ..... J8
Vallentuna 20,823 ..... H1
Vänersborg 36,151 ..... G7
Vara 16,787 ..... H7
Varberg 47,566 ..... G8
Värnamo 31,040 ..... J8
Västeras 117,717 ..... K7
Västerhaninge 14,125 ..... H1
Västervik 39,522 ..... K8
Växjö 68,499 ..... J8
Vetlanda 27,833 ..... J8
Vimmerby 15,688 ..... J8
Visby 19,886 ..... L8
Ystad 24,484 ..... H9

OTHER FEATURES

Ångermanälven (riv.) K5
Baltic (sea) K9
Bothnia (gulf) N4
Dalälven (riv.) K6
Göta (canal) J7
Göta (riv.) H7
Gotland (isl.) L8
Hanöbukten (bay) J9
Hjälmaren (lake) J7
Hornslandet (pen.) K6
Indalsälven (riv.) H5
Kalixälv (riv.) N3
Kallsjö (lake) H5
Kalmarsund (sound) K8
Kattegat (strait) G8
Kebnekaise (mt.) L3
Klarälv (riv.) H6
Kölen (mts.) K3
Lapland (reg.) M2
Ljungan (riv.) K5
Ljusnan (riv.) H5
Luleälv (riv.) M4
Mälaren (lake) G1
Muonioälven (riv.) M2
Öland (isl.) K8
Öresund (sound) H9
Österdalälven (riv.) H6
Piteälv (riv.) M4
Siljan (lake) J6
Skagerrak (strait) F8
Skellefteälv (riv.) L4
Stora Lulevatten (lake) L3
Storsjön (lake) J5
Torneälv (riv.) M3
Torneträsk (lake) L2
Uddjaur (lake) L4
Umeälv (riv.) L4
Vänern (lake) H7
Västerdalälven (riv.) H6
Vättern (lake) J7

* City and suburbs.
† Population of commune.
‡ Population of parish.

DENMARK

COUNTIES

Århus 575,540 ..... D5
Bornholm 47,499 ..... F9
Copenhagen (commune) 493,771 ..... F6
Farøe Islands 41,969 ..... B2
Frederiksberg (commune) 88,167 ..... F6
Frederiksborg 329,992 ..... E5
Fyn 453,626 ..... D7
København (Copenhagen) (commune) 493,771 ..... F6
København 624,684 ..... F6
Nordjylland 482,501 ..... D4
Ribe 213,503 ..... B7
Ringkøbing 263,519 ..... B5
Roskilde 203,246 ..... E6
Sønderjylland 250,872 ..... C7
Storstrøm 260,160 ..... E7
Vejle 326,559 ..... C6
Vestsjaelland 278,592 ..... E6
Viborg 231,758 ..... C4

CITIES and TOWNS

Åbenrå 15,341 ..... C7
Abybro 4,229 ..... C3
Ålborg-Nørresundby 114,302 ..... C3
Ålestrup 2,288 ..... C4
Århus 181,830 ..... D5
Ars 5,972 ..... C4
Asnaes 2,361 ..... E6
Assens, Fyn 5,736 ..... D7
Augustenborg 3,114 ..... D8
Auning 2,293 ..... D5
Avlum 2,719 ..... B5
Ballerup 48,697 ..... F6
Birkerød 13,513 ..... F6
Bjerringbro 6,033 ..... C5
Bogense 3,057 ..... D6
Braedstrup 2,912 ..... C6
Bramming 5,857 ..... B7
Brande 5,693 ..... B6
Broager 2,890 ..... C8
Brønderslev 10,748 ..... C3
Brørup 3,846 ..... C7
Brovst 2,589 ..... C3
Copenhagen (cap.) 1,381,882 ..... F6
Dronninglund 2,715 ..... D3
Ebeltoft 3,763 ..... D5
Esbjerg 70,220 ..... B7
Fåborg 6,795 ..... D7
Fakse 3,350 ..... F7
Fakse Ladeplads 2,111 ..... F7
Farsø 2,954 ..... C4
Farum 16,664 ..... F6
Fjerritslev 2,780 ..... C3
Fredensborg 17,667 ..... F6
Fredericia 29,350 ..... C6
Frederiksberg 88,167 ..... F6
Frederikshavn 24,938 ..... D3
Frederikssund 13,584 ..... E6
Frederiksvaerk 11,559 ..... E6
Gentofte 66,782 ..... F6
Gilleleje 3,976 ..... F5
Give 3,522 ..... C6
Glamsbjerg 2,853 ..... D7
Glostrup 19,645 ..... F6
Gørlev 2,113 ..... E7
Graested 2,735 ..... F5
Gram 2,462 ..... C7
Gråsten 3,441 ..... C8
Grenå 13,638 ..... D5
Grindsted 8,742 ..... B6
Haderslev 19,374 ..... C7
Hadsten 5,563 ..... C5
Hadsund 4,257 ..... D4
Hammel 4,828 ..... C5
Hammerum 2,984 ..... C5
Hanstholm 2,490 ..... B3
Hårby 2,240 ..... D7
Haslev 9,146 ..... E7
Havdrup 3,374 ..... F6
Hedensted 3,397 ..... C6
Hellebaek 4,123 ..... F5
Helsinge 5,813 ..... F6
Helsingør 44,068 ..... F6
Herning 29,522 ..... B5
Hillerød 25,441 ..... F6
Hinnerup 4,517 ..... D5
Hirtshals 6,865 ..... C2
Hjallerup 2,769 ..... C3
Hjørring 23,697 ..... C3
Hobro 8,889 ..... C4
Holbaek 19,485 ..... E6
Holstebro 28,270 ..... B5
Høng 3,430 ..... E7
Hornslet 3,296 ..... D5
Horsens 46,855 ..... C6
Hørsholm 21,572 ..... F6
Hørve 2,055 ..... E6
Hundested 5,443 ..... E6
Hurup 2,747 ..... B4
Hvide Sande 3,100 ..... A6
Ikast 11,716 ..... C5
Juelsminde 2,609 ..... D6
Jyderup 3,441 ..... E6
Kalundborg 15,413 ..... D6
Karup 2,133 ..... C5
Kastrup 10,550 ..... F6
Kerteminde 4,984 ..... D7
Kjellerup 3,848 ..... C5
København (Copenhagen) (cap.) 1,381,882 ..... F6
Køge 25,683 ..... F7
Kolding 41,374 ..... C7
Korsør 15,281 ..... E7
Langå 2,498 ..... C5
Lemvig 7,303 ..... B4
Løgstør 4,160 ..... C4
Løgumkloster 2,840 ..... B7
Løsning 3,234 ..... C6
Lunderskov 2,083 ..... C7
Lyngby 51,703 ..... F6
Malling 2,451 ..... D5
Maribo 5,490 ..... E8
Marstal 2,702 ..... D8
Middelfart 12,064 ..... C7
Naestved 38,455 ..... E7
Nakskov 16,218 ..... E8
Neksø 3,783 ..... F9
Nibe 3,139 ..... C4
Nordborg 8,403 ..... C7
Nordby, Ribe 2,419 ..... B7
Nørre Aby 2,541 ..... C7
Nørre Alslev 2,024 ..... E8
Nyborg 15,466 ..... D7
Nykøbing, Storstrøm 19,038 ..... F8
Nykøbing, Vestsjaelland 5,062 ..... E6
Nykøbing, Viborg 9,503 ..... B4
Odder 8,198 ..... D6
Odense 136,646 ..... D7
Ølgod 3,470 ..... B6
Otterup 3,976 ..... D7
Padborg 4,332 ..... C8
Pandrup 2,257 ..... C3
Praestø 3,110 ..... F7
Randers 56,672 ..... C5
Ribe 7,646 ..... B7

Agriculture, Industry and Resources

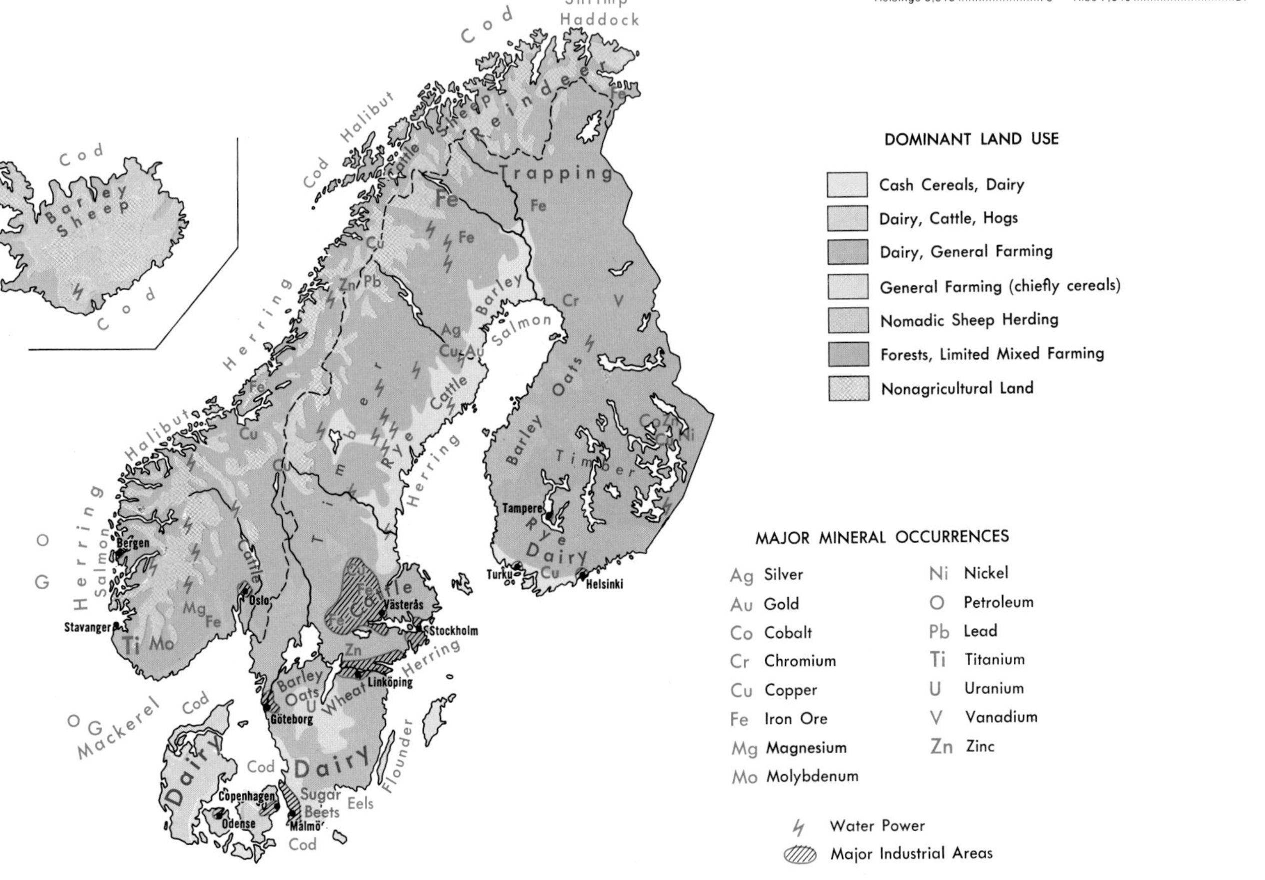

Shrimp
Haddock
Cod
Halibut
Reindeer
Trapping
Fe
Barley
Sheep
Cr
V
Salmon
Herring
Cu
Zn
Pb
Ag
Au
Cattle
Oats
Timber
Rye
Dairy
Tampere
Turku
Helsinki
Bergen
Oslo
Stavanger
Ti
Mo
Mg
Västerås
Stockholm
Linköping
Göteborg
Wheat
U
Mackerel
Flounder
Sugar Beets
Eels
Copenhagen
Odense
Malmö
DOMINANT LAND USE
Cash Cereals, Dairy
Dairy, Cattle, Hogs
Dairy, General Farming
General Farming (chiefly cereals)
Nomadic Sheep Herding
Forests, Limited Mixed Farming
Nonagricultural Land
MAJOR MINERAL OCCURRENCES
Ag Silver
Au Gold
Co Cobalt
Cr Chromium
Cu Copper
Fe Iron Ore
Mg Magnesium
Mo Molybdenum
Ni Nickel
O Petroleum
Pb Lead
Ti Titanium
U Uranium
V Vanadium
Zn Zinc
Water Power
Major Industrial Areas

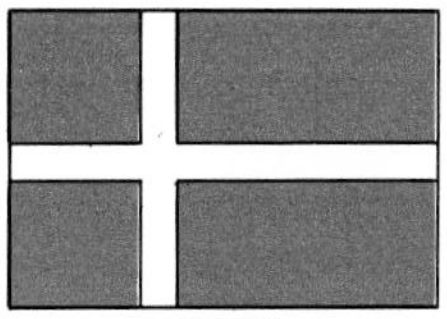

DENMARK

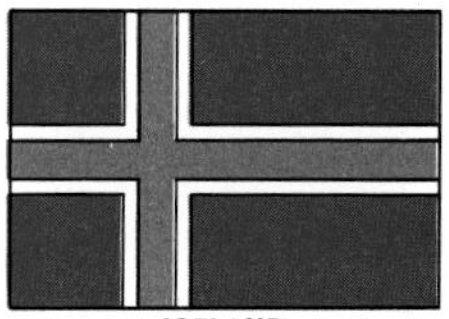

ICELAND

DENMARK

AREA 16,629 sq. mi. (43,069 sq. km.)
POPULATION 5,135,000
CAPITAL Copenhagen
LARGEST CITY Copenhagen
HIGHEST POINT Yding Skovhøj 568 ft. (173 m.)
MONETARY UNIT krone
MAJOR LANGUAGE Danish
MAJOR RELIGION Protestantism

ICELAND

AREA 39,768 sq. mi. (103,000 sq. km.)
POPULATION 250,000
CAPITAL Reykjavík
LARGEST CITY Reykjavík
HIGHEST POINT Hvannadalshnúkur 6,952 ft. (2,119 m.)
MONETARY UNIT króna
MAJOR LANGUAGE Icelandic
MAJOR RELIGION Protestantism

Ringe 4,440 ... D7
Ringkøbing 7,907 ... A5
Ringsted 16,564 ... E7
Rødby 2,572 ... E8
Rødding 2,291 ... B7
Rødekro 4,195 ... C7
Rønde 1,745 ... D5
Ronne 14,143 ... F9
Roskilde 39,659 ... E6
Rudkøbing 4,667 ... D8
Ry 3,648 ... C5
Ryomgård 1,578 ... D5
Saeby 7,464 ... D3
Sakskøbing 7,518 ... E8
Silkeborg 33,304 ... C5
Sindal 2,665 ... D3
Skaelskør 5,574 ... E7
Skaerbaek 2,946 ... B7
Skagen 11,743 ... D2
Skals 1,410 ... C4
Skanderborg 11,094 ... D5
Skibby 2,259 ... E6
Skive 19,034 ... B4
Skjern 6,351 ... B6
Skørping 2,016 ... C4
Slagelse 28,539 ... E7
Slangerup 5,218 ... E6
Søllested 1,431 ... E8
Sønderborg 25,885 ... C8
Sønder Omne 1,751 ... B6
Sondersø 2,667 ... D7
Sorø 6,067 ... E7
Stege 3,906 ... F8
Stenlille 1,370 ... E6
Stenstrup 1,501 ... D7
Stoholm 1,830 ... C5
Store Heddinge 2,881 ... F7
Støvring 4,615 ... C4
Strandby 2,264 ... D3
Struer 10,973 ... B5
Stubbekøbing 2,255 ... F8
Svendborg 23,847 ... D7
Svinninge 2,281 ... E6
Tarm 4,008 ... B6
Tårnby 41,517 ... F6
Them 1,382 ... C5
Thisted 12,469 ... B4
Thyborøn 2,766 ... A4
Tinglev 2,508 ... C8
Toftlund 3,388 ... B7
Tølløse 2,279 ... E6
Tommerup 1,890 ... D7
Tønder 7,914 ... B8
Tørring 1,922 ... C6
Ulfborg 1,781 ... B5
Vamdrup 3,960 ... C7
Varde 10,888 ... B6
Vejen 7,412 ... C7
Vejle 43,300 ... C6
Vemb 1,261 ... B5
Viborg 28,659 ... C5
Viby 2,942 ... F6
Videbaek 3,440 ... B5
Vildbjerg 2,703 ... B5
Vinderup 2,865 ... B5
Vojens 6,792 ... C7
Vordingborg 8,706 ... E7
Vrå 2,312 ... C3

OTHER FEATURES

AEro (isl.) ... D8
Alborg (bay) ... D4
Als (isl.) ... C8
Amager (isl.) ... F6
Anholt (isl.) ... E4
Baltic (sea) ... E9
Blavands Huk (pt.) ... A6
Bornholm (isl.) ... F9
Dovns Klint (cliff) ... D8
Endelave (isl.) ... D6
Fakse (bay) ... F7
Falster (isl.) ... F8
Fanø (isl.) ... B7
Fehmarn (strait) ... E8
Fejø (isl.) ... E8
Femø (isl.) ... E8
Frisian, North (isls.) ... B7
Fyn (isl.) ... D7
Fyns Hoved (pt.) ... D6
Gedser Odde (pt.) ... E8
Gelså (riv.) ... C7
Gudenå (riv.) ... C5
Isefjord (fjord) ... E6
Jammerbugt (bay) ... C3
Jutland (pen.) ... C5
Jylland (Jutland) (pen.) ... C5
Kattegat (strait) ... E4
Knosen (mt.) ... D3
Koge (bay) ... F7
Laeså (isl.) ... D3
Langeland (isl.) ... D8
Langelands Baelt (chan.) ... D8
Lille Baelt (chan.) ... C7
Lillea (riv.) ... B5
Limfjorden (fjord) ... A4
Limfjorden (fjord) ... D4
Løgstør Bredning (fjord) ... C4
Lolland (isl.) ... E8
Mariager (fjord) ... D4
Møn (isl.) ... F8
Mons Klint (cliff) ... F8
Mors (isl.) ... B4
Nissum (fjord) ... A5
North (sea) ... B9
North Frisian (isls.) ... B7
Omme (riv.) ... B6
Omø (isl.) ... E7
Öresund (sound) ... F6
Ringkobing (fjord) ... B6
Rømø (isl.) ... B7
Rosnaes (pen.) ... D6
Sams Baelt (chan.) ... D6
Samsø (isl.) ... D6
Sejerø (isl.) ... E6
Sjaelland (isl.) ... E6
Sjaellands Odde (pen.) ... E5
Skagens Odde (cape) ... D2
Skagerrak (strait) ... C2
Skaw, The (Skagens Odde) (cape) ... D2
Skive (riv.) ... C5
Stevns Klint (cliff) ... F7
Storå (riv.) ... B5
Store Baelt (chan.) ... D6
The Skaw (Skagens Odde) (cape) ... D2
Varde (riv.) ... B6
Vejle (fjord) ... C6
Vorgod (riv.) ... B6
Yding Skovhøj (mt.) ... C6

FAROE ISLANDS

CITIES and TOWNS

Klaksvík 4,536 ... B2
Tórshavn (cap.), Faroe Is. 11,618 ... A3

OTHER FEATURES

Faroe (isls.) ... B2
Sandoy (isl.) ... B3
Streymoy (isl.) ... B3
Sudhuroy (isl.) ... B3

ICELAND

CITIES and TOWNS

Akranes 5,404 ... B1
Akureyri 13,972 ... C1
Hafnarfjördhur 14,199 ... B2
Húsavík 2,499 ... C1
Ísafjördhur 3,458 ... B1
Keflavík 7,305 ... B1
Kópavogur 15,551 ... B1
Ólafsfjördhur 1,179 ... C1
Reykjavík (cap.) 95,811 ... B1
Saudhárkrókur 2,478 ... B1
Vestmannaeyjar 4,743 ... B2

OTHER FEATURES

Bjargtangar (pt.) ... A1
Breidhafjördhur (fjord) ... B1
Faxaflói (bay) ... B1
Fontur (pt.) ... D1
Gerpir (cape) ... D1
Grímsey (isl.) ... C1
Hekla (vol.) ... B1
Hofsjökull (glacier) ... C1
Horn (cape) ... B1
Húnaflói (bay) ... B1
Hvannadalshnúkur (mt.) ... C1
Jökulsá (riv.) ... C1
Lagarfljót (stream) ... C1
Langjökull (glacier) ... B1
North (Horn) (cape) ... B1
Reykjanestá (cape) ... A2
Rifstangi (cape) ... C1
Skagata (cape) ... B1
Skjálfandafljót (stream) ... C1
Surtsey (isl.) ... B2
Thjórsá (riv.) ... C1
Vatnajökull (glacier) ... C1
Vopnafjördhur (fjord) ... D1

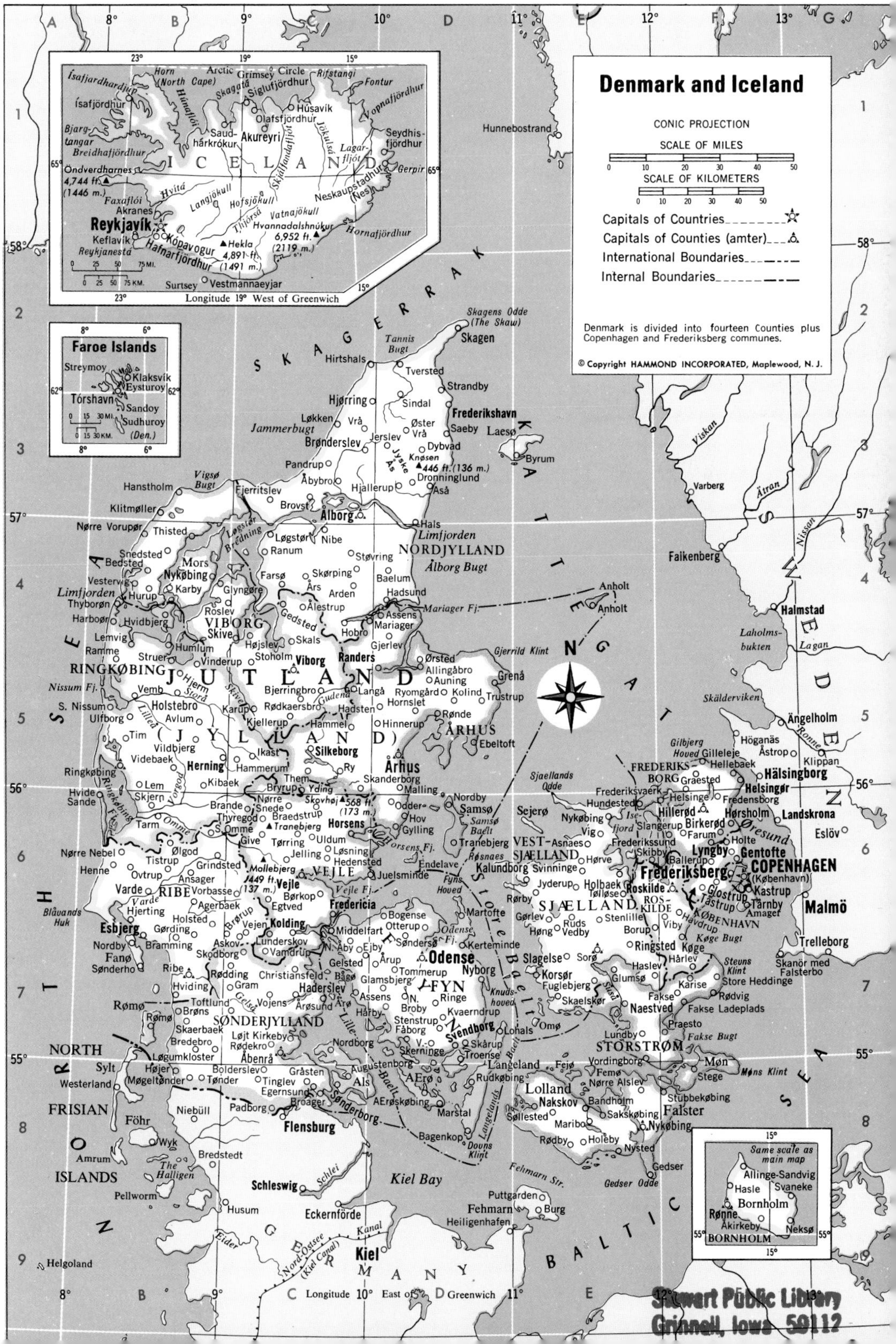
Denmark and Iceland
CONIC PROJECTION
SCALE OF MILES
SCALE OF KILOMETERS
Capitals of Countries
Capitals of Counties (amter)
International Boundaries
Internal Boundaries
Denmark is divided into fourteen Counties plus Copenhagen and Frederiksberg communes.
© Copyright HAMMOND INCORPORATED, Maplewood, N. J.
Faroe Islands
Streymoy
Klaksvík
Eysturoy
Tórshavn
Sandoy
Sudhuroy
(Den.)
ICELAND
Reykjavík
Akureyri
Vatnajökull
Hvannadalshnúkur 6,952 ft. (2119 m.)
Hekla 4,891 ft. (1491 m.)
Longitude 19° West of Greenwich
SKAGERRAK
KATTEGAT
JUTLAND (JYLLAND)
NORDJYLLAND
VIBORG
RINGKØBING
ÅRHUS
VEJLE
RIBE
SØNDERJYLLAND
FYN
VEST-SJÆLLAND
SJÆLLAND
FREDERIKSBORG
ROSKILDE
KØBENHAVN
STORSTRØM
COPENHAGEN (København)
Frederiksberg
Ålborg
Århus
Odense
Esbjerg
Skagen
Frederikshavn
Malmö
Hälsingborg
Helsingør
Lolland
Falster
Langeland
Bornholm
Rønne
SWEDEN
NORTH SEA
BALTIC SEA
NORTH FRISIAN ISLANDS
GERMANY
Flensburg
Kiel
Kiel Bay
Fehmarn
Schleswig
Helgoland
Longitude 10° East of Greenwich

Germany
CONIC PROJECTION
SCALE OF MILES
0 20 40 60 80
SCALE OF KILOMETERS
0 20 40 60 80
Capitals of Countries
State Capitals
International Boundaries
State Boundaries
Canals
Scale 1:3,040,000
Longitude East 10° of Greenwich
DENMARK
NORTH SEA
BALTIC SEA
NORTH FRISIAN ISLANDS
EAST FRISIAN ISLANDS
WEST FRISIAN ISLANDS
SCHLESWIG-HOLSTEIN
MECKLENBURG-WESTERN POMERANIA
HAMBURG
BREMEN
LOWER SAXONY
SAXONY-ANHALT
BRANDENBURG
BERLIN
NORTH RHINE-WESTPHALIA
HESSE
THURINGIA
SAXONY
RHINELAND-PALATINATE
SAARLAND
BADEN-WÜRTTEMBERG
BAVARIA
NETHERLANDS
BELGIUM
LUXEMBOURG
FRANCE
SWITZERLAND
AUSTRIA
CZECH REPUBLIC
POLAND
Kiel
Rostock
Schwerin
Lübeck
Bremen
Hannover
Magdeburg
Potsdam
Düsseldorf
Cologne
Bonn
Wiesbaden
Frankfurt
Mainz
Saarbrücken
Stuttgart
Erfurt
Leipzig
Dresden
Nürnberg
MUNICH
Berlin
© Copyright HAMMOND INCORPORATED, Maplewood, N. J.

AREA 137,753 sq. mi. (356,780 sq. km.)
POPULATION 78,890,000
CAPITAL Berlin
LARGEST CITY Berlin
HIGHEST POINT Zugspitze 9,718 ft. (2,962 m.)
MONETARY UNIT Deutsche mark
MAJOR LANGUAGE German
MAJOR RELIGIONS Protestantism, Roman Catholicism

GERMANY

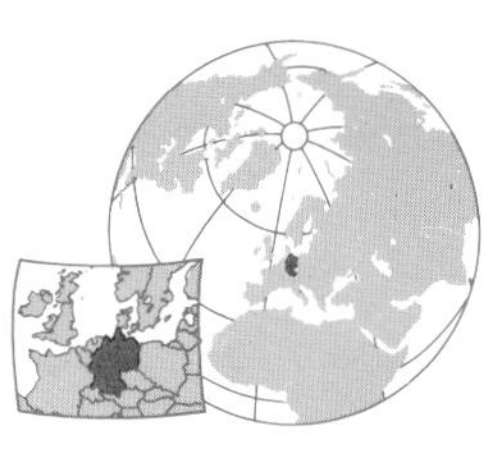

Topography

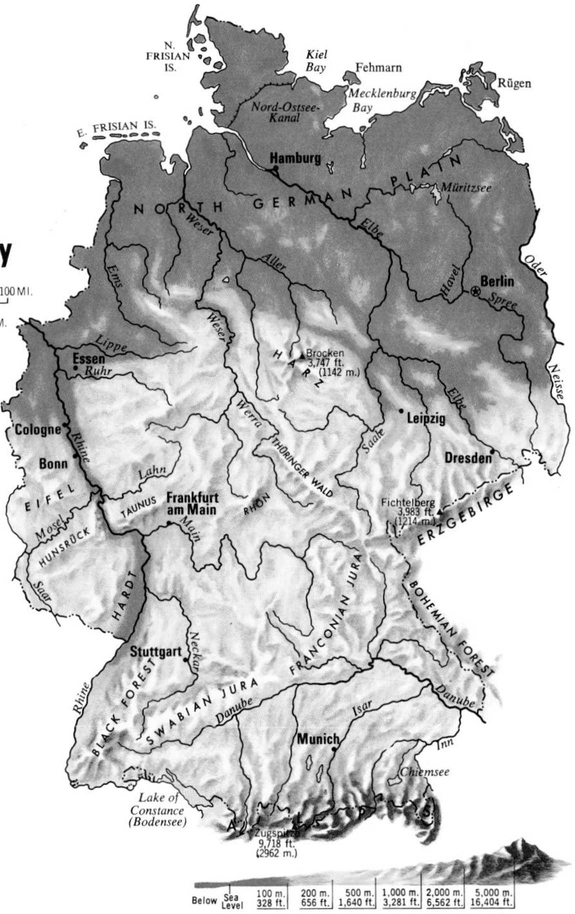
0 50 100 MI.
0 50 100 KM.
N. FRISIAN IS.
Kiel Bay
Fehmarn
Rügen
Mecklenburg Bay
Nord-Ostsee-Kanal
E. FRISIAN IS.
Hamburg
NORTH GERMAN PLAIN
Müritzsee
Weser
Elbe
Aller
Oder
Havel
Berlin
Spree
Ems
Lippe
Essen
Ruhr
HARZ
Brocken 3,747 ft. (1142 m.)
Neisse
Werra
Saale
Leipzig
Cologne
Rhine
Bonn
Lahn
THÜRINGER WALD
Dresden
EIFEL
TAUNUS
Frankfurt am Main
RHÖN
Fichtelberg 3,983 ft. (1214 m.)
ERZGEBIRGE
Mosel
HUNSRÜCK
Main
Saar
HARDT
FRANCONIAN JURA
BOHEMIAN FOREST
Stuttgart
Neckar
BLACK FOREST
SWABIAN JURA
Danube
Isar
Munich
Inn
Chiemsee
Lake of Constance (Bodensee)
Zugspitze 9,718 ft. (2962 m.)
Below Sea Level
100 m. 328 ft.
200 m. 656 ft.
500 m. 1,640 ft.
1,000 m. 3,281 ft.
2,000 m. 6,562 ft.
5,000 m. 16,404 ft.

GERMANY

STATES

Baden-Württemberg 9,432,709 .... C4
Bavaria 11,049,263 .... D4
Berlin 3,304,561 .... E4
Brandenberg* E2
Bremen 661,992 .... C2
Hamburg 1,603,070 .... D2
Hesse 5,568,892 .... C3
Lower Saxony 7,184,943 .... C2
Mecklenburg-Western Pomerania* E2
North Rhine-Westphalia 16,874,059 .... B3
Rhineland-Palatinate 3,653,155 .... B4
Saarland 1,054,142 .... B4
Saxony* E3
Saxony-Anhalt* D3
Schleswig-Holstein 2,564,565 .... C1
Thuringia* D3

*East German States 15,611,488 .... D-E 2-3

CITIES and TOWNS

Aachen 233,255 .... B3
Aalen 62,812 .... D4
Ahaus 30,180 .... B2
Ahlen 52,836 .... B3
Ahrensburg 27,174 .... D2
Alfeld 21,986 .... C2
Alsdorf 46,328 .... B3
Alsfeld 16,686 .... C3
Altena 23,301 .... B3
Altenburg 53,602 .... E3
Amberg 42,246 .... D4
Andernach 27,171 .... B3
Anklam 19,946 .... E2
Annaberg-Buchholz 26,002 .... E3
Ansbach 36,912 .... D4
Apolda 28,230 .... D3
Arnsberg 73,912 .... C3
Arnstadt 30,207 .... D3
Aschaffenburg 62,048 .... C4
Aschersleben 34,166 .... D3
Aue 27,935 .... E3
Auerbach 22,324 .... E3
Augsburg 247,731 .... D4
Aurich 36,063 .... B2
Backnang 30,583 .... C4
Bad Berleburg 20,080 .... C3
Bad Driburg 16,698 .... C3
Bad Dürkheim 16,670 .... C4
Baden-Baden 50,761 .... C4
Bad Harzburg 23,079 .... D3
Bad Hersfeld 28,214 .... C3
Bad Homburg vor der Höhe 51,035 .... C3
Bad Honnef 21,812 .... B3
Bad Kissingen 20,237 .... D3
Bad Kreuznach 39,400 .... B4
Bad Langensalza 17,027 .... D3
Bad Mergentheim 19,801 .... C4
Bad Münstereifel 15,232 .... B3
Bad Nauheim 27,561 .... C3
Bad Neuenahr-Ahrweiler 24,610 .... B3
Bad Oldesloe 20,473 .... D2
Bad Pyrmont 20,437 .... C3
Bad Reichenhall 16,365 .... E5
Bad Salzuflen 50,875 .... C2
Bad Salzungen 21,387 .... C3
Bad Schwartau 19,960 .... D2
Bad Vilbel 24,567 .... C3
Bad Zwischenahn 23,348 .... B2
Balingen 30,615 .... C4
Bamberg 69,809 .... D4
Barsinghausen 37,792 .... C2
Bautzen 52,354 .... F3
Bayreuth 70,933 .... D4
Bensheim 34,241 .... C4
Berchtesgaden 7,644 .... E5
Bergen 16,713 .... E1
Bergisch Gladbach 101,983 .... B3
Berleburg (Bad Berleburg) 20,080 .... C3
Berlin (cap.) 3,304,561 .... E4
Bernau bei Berlin 19,919 .... E2
Bernburg 40,834 .... D3
Biberach an der Riss 28,319 .... C4
Bielefeld 311,946 .... C2
Bietigheim-Bissingen 37,573 .... C4
Bingen 23,141 .... B4
Bitburg 10,758 .... B4
Bitterfeld 20,869 .... E3
Blankenburg am Harz 19,279 .... D3
Böblingen 43,400 .... C4
Bocholt 67,565 .... B3
Bochum 389,087 .... B3
Bonn 282,190 .... B3
Borghorst 17,238 .... B2
Borken 34,710 .... B3
Borna 24,397 .... E3
Bornheim 34,536 .... B3
Bottrop 116,363 .... B3
Brake 16,069 .... C2
Bramsche 24,653 .... B2
Brandenburg 94,755 .... E2
Braunschweig 253,794 .... D2
Bremen 535,058 .... C2
Bremerhaven 126,934 .... C2
Bremervörde 17,629 .... C2
Bretten 23,894 .... C4
Brilon 24,341 .... C3
Bruchsal 36,831 .... C4
Brühl 40,710 .... B3
Buchholz in der Nordheide 30,523 .... C2
Bückeburg 19,758 .... C2
Büdingen 17,013 .... C3
Bühl 23,470 .... C4
Bünde 39,103 .... C2
Büren 17,720 .... C3
Burg bei Magdeburg 28,359 .... D2
Burghausen 16,761 .... E4
Burgsteinfurt 31,367 .... B2
Butzbach 21,095 .... C3
Buxtehude 31,132 .... C2
Castrop-Rauxel 77,660 .... B3
Celle 71,050 .... D2
Cham 16,641 .... E4
Chemnitz 313,799 .... E3
Clausthal-Zellerfeld 16,069 .... D3
Cloppenburg 22,536 .... B2
Coburg 43,233 .... D3
Coesfeld 31,979 .... B3
Cologne 937,482 .... B3
Coswig 27,590 .... E3
Cottbus 126,592 .... F3
Crailsheim 26,678 .... D4
Crimmitschau 24,440 .... E3
Cuxhaven 55,249 .... C2
Dachau 34,183 .... D4
Darmstadt 136,067 .... C4
Deggendorf 28,680 .... E4
Delitzsch 27,636 .... E3
Delmenhorst 72,901 .... C2
Demmin 16,992 .... E2
Dessau 103,538 .... E3
Detmold 66,809 .... C3
Dillenburg 23,672 .... C3
Dillingen 21,358 .... B4
Döbeln 27,706 .... E3
Donaueschingen 18,296 .... C5
Donauwörth 17,420 .... D4
Dorsten 75,518 .... B3
Dortmund 587,328 .... B3
Dresden 519,810 .... E3
Duderstadt 22,265 .... D3
Duisburg 527,447 .... B3
Dülmen 39,344 .... B3
Düren 83,120 .... B3
Düsseldorf 569,641 .... B3
Eberswalde-Finow 54,566 .... E2
Eckernförde 22,197 .... C1
Ehingen 22,580 .... C4
Eilenburg 21,931 .... E3
Einbeck 25,813 .... C3
Eisenach 49,534 .... D3
Eisenhüttenstadt 51,729 .... F2
Eisleben 26,484 .... D3
Ellwangen 21,857 .... D4
Elmshorn 42,784 .... C2
Emden 49,803 .... B2
Emmendingen 22,959 .... B4
Emmerich 27,906 .... B3
Emsdetten 31,063 .... B2
Erfurt 217,134 .... D3
Erkelenz 36,525 .... B3
Erlangen 100,583 .... D4
Eschwege 21,527 .... C3
Eschweiler 53,516 .... B3
Espelkamp 23,868 .... C2
Essen 620,594 .... B3
Esslingen am Neckar 90,537 .... C4
Ettlingen 37,269 .... C4
Euskirchen 47,756 .... B3
Eutin 16,567 .... D1
Falkensee 23,024 .... E3
Fellbach 39,612 .... C4
Finsterwalde 23,857 .... E3
Flensburg 85,830 .... C1
Forchheim 28,784 .... D4
Forst 26,501 .... F3
Frankenberg-Eder 16,283 .... C3
Frankenthal 45,408 .... C4
Frankfurt am Main 625,258 .... C3
Frankfurt an der Oder 86,441 .... F2
Frechen 42,516 .... B3
Freiberg 50,415 .... E3
Freiburg im Breisgau 183,979 .... B5
Freising 35,201 .... D4
Freital 43,092 .... E3
Freudenstadt 21,355 .... C4
Friedberg 24,279 .... C3
Friedrichshafen 52,295 .... C5
Fulda 54,320 .... C3
Fürstenfeldbruck 30,313 .... D4
Fürstenwalde 35,282 .... F2
Fürth 98,832 .... D4
Füssen 13,173 .... D5
Gaggenau 28,182 .... C4
Garbsen 59,225 .... C2
Garmisch-Partenkirchen 25,908 .... D5
Geesthacht 25,054 .... D2
Geislingen an der Steige 26,176 .... C4
Geldern 28,465 .... B3
Gelnhausen 18,866 .... C3
Gelsenkirchen 287,255 .... B3
Genthin 17,347 .... E2
Georgsmarienhütte 30,880 .... B2
Gera 132,319 .... E3
Geretsried 21,081 .... D5
Gifhorn 35,697 .... D2
Glauchau 28,309 .... E3
Goch 29,592 .... B3
Göppingen 52,873 .... C4
Görlitz 78,856 .... F3
Goslar 45,614 .... D3
Gotha 57,423 .... D3
Göttingen 118,073 .... D3
Greifswald 67,298 .... E1
Greiz 34,858 .... E3
Greven 29,671 .... B2
Grevenbroich 59,204 .... B3
Griesheim 20,531 .... C4
Grimma 17,812 .... E3
Gronau 39,397 .... B2
Guben 34,665 .... F3
Gummersbach 49,017 .... B3
Günzburg 18,303 .... D4
Güstrow 38,971 .... E2
Gütersloh 83,407 .... C3
Haar 16,553 .... D4
Hagen 210,640 .... B3
Halberstadt 47,017 .... D3
Haldensleben 20,369 .... D2
Halle 236,148 .... D3
Halle-Neustadt 93,477 .... D3
Haltern 33,093 .... B3
Hamburg 1,603,070 .... D2
Hameln 57,642 .... C2
Hamm 173,611 .... B3
Hanau 84,300 .... C3
Hannover 498,495 .... C2
Hassloch 18,646 .... C4
Heide 19,909 .... C1
Heidelberg 131,429 .... C4
Heidenau 19,133 .... E3
Heidenheim an der Brenz 48,497 .... D4
Heilbronn 112,279 .... C4
Helmstedt 26,554 .... D2
Hennef 30,516 .... B3
Hennigsdorf bei Berlin 26,574 .... E3
Herborn 20,409 .... C3
Herford 61,700 .... C2
Herne 174,664 .... B3
Hettstedt 21,861 .... D3
Hildesheim 103,512 .... D2
Hof 50,938 .... D3
Holzminden 20,877 .... C3
Homburg 41,888 .... B4
Höxter 31,925 .... C3
Hoyerswerda 69,113 .... F3
Hückelhoven 33,841 .... B3
Hürth 49,094 .... B3
Husum 20,649 .... C1
Ibbenbüren 43,424 .... B2
Idar-Oberstein 33,227 .... B4
Ilmenau 29,338 .... D3
Ingolstadt 97,702 .... D4
Iserlohn 93,337 .... B3
Itzehoe 32,342 .... C2
Jena 107,610 .... D3
Jülich 30,496 .... B3
Kaiserslautern 96,990 .... B4
Kamenz 18,323 .... F3
Karlsruhe 265,100 .... C4
Kassel 189,156 .... C3
Kaufbeuren 39,192 .... D5
Kehl 28,902 .... B4
Kempten 60,052 .... D5
Kevelaer 22,633 .... B3
Kiel 240,675 .... D1
Kirchheim unter Teck 34,534 .... C4
Kitzingen 19,085 .... C4
Koblenz 107,286 .... B3
Köln (Cologne) 937,482 .... B3
Königs Wusterhausen 19,085 .... E2
Königswinter 34,136 .... B3
Konstanz 72,862 .... C5
Köpenick 118,059 .... F4
Korbach 21,406 .... C3
Kornwestheim 28,519 .... C4
Köthen 34,617 .... E3
Krefeld 235,423 .... B3
Kreuztal 29,716 .... C3
Kronach 18,246 .... D3
Kulmbach 27,116 .... D3
Lage 32,612 .... C3
Lahnstein 17,972 .... B3
Lahr 33,369 .... B4
Lampertheim 30,263 .... C4
Landau in der Pfalz 36,297 .... C4
Landsberg am Lech 19,808 .... D4
Landshut 57,194 .... E4
Langen 31,206 .... C3
Langenhagen 46,298 .... C2
Lauchhammer 24,391 .... E3
Lauenburg an der Elbe 10,786 .... D2
Lauf an der Pegnitz 22,593 .... D4
Leer 31,292 .... B2
Lehrte 39,600 .... D2
Leipzig 550,641 .... E3
Lemgo 38,351 .... C2
Lengerich 20,235 .... B2
Leverkusen 157,358 .... B3
Lichtenberg 95,426 .... F4
Lichtenfels 20,252 .... D3
Limburg an der Lahn 29,196 .... C3
Limbach-Oberfrohna 22,059 .... E3
Lindau 23,699 .... C5
Lingen 47,837 .... B2
Lippstadt 60,396 .... C3
Löbau 18,492 .... F3
Löhne 36,882 .... C2
Lörrach 41,087 .... B5
Lübbenau 20,815 .... F3
Lübeck 210,681 .... D2
Luckenwalde 26,761 .... E2
Lüdenscheid 76,118 .... B3
Ludwigsburg 79,342 .... C4
Ludwigshafen am Rhein 158,478 .... C4
Lüneburg 60,053 .... D2
Lünen 85,584 .... B3
Magdeburg 288,975 .... D2
Mainz 174,828 .... C4
Mannheim 300,468 .... C4
Marburg 70,905 .... C3
Markkleeberg 19,240 .... E3
Marktredwitz 18,605 .... E4
Marl 89,601 .... B3
Mayen 18,427 .... B3
Mechernich 21,986 .... B3
Meerane 21,879 .... E3
Meiningen 25,823 .... D3
Meissen 37,757 .... E3
Melle 40,490 .... C2
Memmingen 37,942 .... D5
Meppen 29,900 .... B2
Merseburg 46,188 .... D3
Merzig 29,312 .... B4
Meschede 30,853 .... C3
Metzingen 19,895 .... C4
Minden 75,169 .... C2
Mittenwald 7,998 .... D5
Mittweida 18,469 .... E3
Mönchengladbach 252,910 .... B3
Mosbach 23,897 .... C4
Mülhausen 43,046 .... D3
Mülheim an der Ruhr 175,454 .... B3
München (Munich) 1,211,617 .... D4
Münden 24,794 .... C3
Munich 1,211,617 .... D4
Münster 248,919 .... B3
Nagold 20,405 .... C4
Naumburg 32,100 .... D3
Neckarsulm 21,765 .... C4
Neubrandenburg 87,235 .... E2
Neuburg an der Donau 24,502 .... D4
Neu-Isenburg 34,896 .... C3
Neumarkt in der Oberpfalz 33,603 .... D4
Neumünster 79,574 .... C1
Neunkirchen 50,784 .... B4
Neuruppin 26,934 .... E2
Neuss 143,976 .... B3
Neustadt an der Weinstrasse 50,453 .... B4
Neustadt bei Coburg 16,211 .... D3
Neustrelitz 27,300 .... E2
Neu-Ulm 45,116 .... D4
Neuwied 60,665 .... B3
Nienburg 29,545 .... C2
Norden 23,655 .... B2
Nordenham 28,393 .... C2
Norderstedt 66,747 .... D2
Nordhausen 47,681 .... D3
Nordhorn 48,556 .... B2
Nördlingen 18,278 .... D4
Northeim 30,349 .... C3
Nuremberg 480,078 .... D4
Nürnberg (Nuremberg) 480,078 .... D4
Nürtingen 36,807 .... C4
Oberammergau 4,980 .... D5
Oberhausen 221,017 .... B3
Oberursel 39,105 .... C3
Offenbach am Main 112,450 .... C3
Offenburg 51,730 .... B4
Oldenburg 140,785 .... C2
Oranienburg 28,667 .... E2
Oschatz 19,100 .... E3
Oschersleben 16,976 .... D2
Osnabrück 154,594 .... C2
Osterholz-Scharmbeck 24,205 .... C2
Osterode am Harz 26,631 .... D3
Paderborn 114,148 .... C3
Pankow 62,847 .... F3
Papenburg 29,237 .... B2
Parchim 23,454 .... D2
Passau 49,137 .... E4
Peenemünde E1
Peine 45,522 .... D2
Pfaffenhofen an der Ilm 18,335 .... D4
Pforzheim 108,887 .... C4
Pinneberg 36,583 .... C2
Pirmasens 47,102 .... B4
Pirna 46,991 .... E3
Plauen 77,514 .... E3
Plettenberg 28,113 .... C3
Pössneck 17,895 .... D3
Potsdam 141,231 .... E2
Prenzlau 23,642 .... E2
Quedlinburg 29,168 .... D3
Radeberg 15,702 .... E3
Radebeul 33,757 .... E3
Radolfzell 25,712 .... C5
Rastatt 40,909 .... C4
Rastede 18,191 .... C2
Rathenow 31,302 .... E2
Ratingen 89,880 .... B3
Ravensburg 44,146 .... C5
Recklinghausen 121,666 .... B3
Regensburg 119,078 .... E4

(continued on following page)

(continued)

Germany Before World War I 1871-1914
DENMARK
SWEDEN
NETH.
Berlin
RUSSIA
BELG.
LUX.
AUSTRIA-
FRANCE
HUNGARY
SWITZ.
I T A L Y

Germany Between Wars 1919-1937
DENMARK
SWEDEN
LITH.
DANZIG
NETH.
Berlin
POLAND
BELG.
LUX.
SAAR
(To Germany 1935)
CZECHOSLOVAKIA
FRANCE
AUSTRIA
SWITZ.
ITALY
YUGO.
HUNG.

Occupied Germany 1945-1949
DENMARK
SWEDEN
U.S.S.R.
BRITISH ZONE
BERLIN
RUSSIAN ZONE
NETH.
POLAND
BELG.
LUX.
FRENCH ZONE
SAAR
AMERICAN ZONE
CZECHOSLOVAKIA
FRANCE
AUSTRIA
SWITZ.
ITALY
YUGO.
HUNG.

Reichenbach 24,749 ... E3
Remagen 14,375 ... B3
Remscheid 120,979 ... B3
Rendsburg 30,752 ... C1
Reutlingen 100,400 ... C4
Rheda-Wiedenbrück 36,990 ... C3
Rheine 69,324 ... B2
Rheinfelden 27,711 ... B5
Ribnitz-Damgarten 17,512 ... E1
Riesa 49,108 ... E3
Rietberg 23,058 ... C3
Rinteln 26,120 ... C2
Rosenheim 54,304 ... D5
Rostock 249,349 ... E1
Rotenburg 18,392 ... C2
Roth bei Nürnberg 20,288 ... D4
Rothenburg ob der Tauber 11,071 ... D4
Rottenburg am Neckar 33,907 ... C4
Rottweil 23,080 ... C4
Rudolstadt 32,264 ... D3
Rüsselsheim 58,426 ... C4
Saalfeld 33,453 ... D3
Saarbrücken 188,467 ... B4
Saarlouis 37,662 ... B4
Salzgitter 111,674 ... D2
Salzwedel 23,163 ... D2
Sangerhausen 33,604 ... D3
Sankt Ingbert 40,527 ... B4
Sankt Wendel 26,649 ... B4
Saulgau 14,864 ... C5
Schleswig 26,648 ... C1
Schmalkalden 17,409 ... D3
Schneeberg 22,105 ... E3
Schönebeck 45,155 ... D2
Schramberg 18,208 ... C4
Schwabach 34,217 ... D4
Schwäbisch Gmünd 57,861 ... C4
Schwäbisch Hall 31,375 ... C4
Schwalmstadt 17,371 ... C3
Schwandorf im Bayern 25,874 ... E4
Schwedt 51,753 ... F2
Schweinfurt 52,818 ... D3
Schwelm 29,564 ... B3
Schwerin 128,328 ... D2
Schwetzingen 18,029 ... C4
Seesen 21,604 ... D3
Selb 19,275 ... E3
Senftenberg 32,428 ... F3
Siegburg 34,402 ... B3
Siegen 106,160 ... C3
Sigmaringen 15,270 ... C4
Sindelfingen 57,524 ... C4
Singen 42,605 ... C5
Soest 40,775 ... C3
Solingen 160,824 ... B3
Soltau 19,115 ... C2
Sömmerda 23,398 ... D3
Sondershausen 24,178 ... D3
Sonneberg 28,512 ... D3
Sonthofen 20,037 ... D5
Spandau ... E3
Speyer 45,089 ... C4
Spremberg 24,815 ... F3
Springe 29,209 ... C2
Stade 41,223 ... C2
Stadthagen 22,218 ... C2
Starnberg 19,845 ... D4
Stassfurt 27,372 ... D3
Stendal 47,880 ... D2
Stolberg 56,182 ... B3
Stralsund 75,857 ... E1
Straubing 40,612 ... E4
Strausberg 27,527 ... F2
Stuttgart 562,658 ... C4
Suhl 55,295 ... D3
Sulzbach 19,753 ... B4
Sulzbach-Rosenberg 18,134 ... D4
Telgte 16,834 ... B3
Tempelhof ... F4
Thale 16,605 ... D3
Torgau 22,749 ... E3
Traunstein 17,145 ... E5
Treptow 58,938 ... F4
Treuchtlingen 12,314 ... D4
Triberg im Schwarzwald 5,697 ... C4
Trier 95,692 ... B4
Troisdorf 62,011 ... B3
Tübingen 76,046 ... C4
Tuttlingen 31,752 ... C5
Übach-Palenberg 23,005 ... B3
Überlingen 18,043 ... C5
Ueckermünde 12,304 ... F2
Uelzen 34,891 ... D2
Uetersen 17,218 ... C2
Ulm 106,508 ... C4
Varel 23,718 ... C2
Vechta 22,759 ... C2
Verden 23,770 ... C2
Viersen 76,163 ... B3
Villingen-Schwenningen 76,258 ... C4
Vöklingen 42,916 ... B4
Waldheim 10,316 ... E3
Waldkirch 18,893 ... B4
Waldkraiburg 23,177 ... E4
Waldshut-Tiengen 21,372 ... C5
Walsrode 22,232 ... C2
Waltershausen 14,127 ... D3
Wangen im Allgäu 23,822 ... C5
Warburg 21,802 ... C3
Waren 24,318 ... E2
Warendorf 33,891 ... B3
Wedel 30,158 ... C2
Weida 10,602 ... D3
Weiden in der Oberpfalz 41,539 ... D4
Weilheim im Oberbayern 17,602 ... D5
Weimar 63,910 ... D3
Weingarten 21,522 ... C5
Weinheim 41,876 ... C4
Weissenburg im Bayern 17,318 ... D4
Weissenfels 38,763 ... D3
Weissensee 31,858 ... F3
Weisswasser 36,472 ... F3
Werdau 19,451 ... E3
Wernigerode 36,499 ... D3
Wertheim 20,457 ... C4
Wesel 57,986 ... B3
Westerstede 18,184 ... B2
Wiehl 21,897 ... B3
Wiesbaden 254,209 ... B3
Wiesmoor 10,827 ... B2
Wilhelmshaven 89,892 ... B2
Winsen 26,139 ... D2
Wismar 58,066 ... D2
Witten 103,637 ... B3
Wittenberg 53,670 ... E3
Wittenberge 30,389 ... D2
Wolfen 43,606 ... E3
Wolfenbüttel 50,960 ... D2
Wolfsburg 125,831 ... D2
Worms 74,809 ... C4
Wunstorf 37,115 ... C2
Wuppertal 371,283 ... B3
Würzburg 125,589 ... C4
Wurzen 19,330 ... E3
Xanten 16,097 ... B3
Zeitz 42,985 ... E3
Zerbst 18,717 ... E3
Zeulenroda 14,409 ... D3
Zirndorf 21,608 ... D4
Zittau 39,305 ... F3
Zweibrücken 33,377 ... B4
Zwickau 120,923 ... E3

OTHER FEATURES

Aller (riv.) ... C2
Allgäu (reg.) ... D5
Altmark (reg.) ... D2
Ammersee (lake) ... D4
Amrum (isl.) ... C1
Arkona (cape) ... E1
Baltic (sea) ... E1
Bavarian (forest) ... E4
Bavarian Alps (range) ... D5
Bayerischer Wald Nat'l Park ... E4
Black (forest) ... C4
Black Elster (riv.) ... E3
Bodensee (Constance) (lake) ... C5
Bohemian (forest) ... E4
Borkum (isl.) ... B2
Breisgau (reg.) ... B5
Brocken (mt.) ... D3
Chiemsee (lake) ... E5
Constance (lake) ... C5
Danube (riv.) ... C4
Donau (Danube) (riv.) ... C4
East Friesland (reg.) ... B2
Eder (riv.) ... C3
Elbe (riv.) ... D2
Elde (riv.) ... D2
Ems (riv.) ... B2
Erzgebirge (mts.) ... E3
Fehmarn (isl.) ... D1
Feldberg (mt.) ... C5
Fichtelberg (mt.) ... E3
Fichtelgebirge (range) ... D3
Föhr (isl.) ... C1
Franconian Jura (range) ... D4
Frisian, East (isls.) ... B2
Frisian, North (isls.) ... B1
Fulda (riv.) ... C3
Grosser Arber (mt.) ... E4
Harz (mts.) ... D3
Havel (riv.) ... E2
Hegau (reg.) ... C5
Helgoland (bay) ... C1
Helgoland (isl.) ... B1
Hunsrück (mts.) ... B4
Iller (riv.) ... D4
Ilmenau (riv.) ... D2
Inn (riv.) ... E4
Isar (riv.) ... E4
Jade (bay) ... C2
Juist (isl.) ... B2
Kaiserstuhl (mt.) ... B4
Kiel (bay) ... D1
Kiel (Nord-Ostsee) (canal) ... C1
Königssee (lake) ... E5
Lahn (riv.) ... C3
Langeoog (isl.) ... B2
Lech (riv.) ... D4
Leine (riv.) ... C2
Lippe (riv.) ... C3
Lüneburger Heide (dist.) ... C2
Lusatia (reg.) ... F3
Main (riv.) ... C4
Mecklenburg (bay) ... D1
Mosel (riv.) ... B3
Mulde (riv.) ... E3
Müritzsee (lake) ... E2
Naab (riv.) ... E4
Neckar (riv.) ... C4
Neisse (riv.) ... F3
Norderney (isl.) ... B2
Nord-Ostsee (canal) ... C1
Nordstrand (isl.) ... C1
North (sea) ... B2
North Friesland (reg.) ... C1
Odenwald (forest) ... C4
Oder (riv.) ... F2
Oder-Haff (lag.) ... F2
Our (riv.) ... B3
Peene (riv.) ... E2
Pellworm (isl.) ... C1
Plauersee (lake) ... E2
Pomeranian (bay) ... F1
Regnitz (riv.) ... D4
Rhine (riv.) ... B3
Rhön (mts.) ... D3
Rügen (isl.) ... E1
Ruhr (riv.) ... B3
Saale (riv.) ... D3
Saar (riv.) ... B4
Salzach (riv.) ... E5
Sauer (riv.) ... B4
Sauerland (reg.) ... B3
Schwarzwald (Black) (forest) ... C4
Schwerinersee (lake) ... D2
Spessart (range) ... C4
Spiekeroog (isl.) ... B2
Spree (riv.) ... F3
Spreewald (forest) ... F3
Starnbergersee (lake) ... D5
Swabian Jura (range) ... C4
Sylt (isl.) ... C1
Taunus (range) ... C3
Tegernsee (lake) ... D5
Teutoburger Wald (forest) ... C2
Thüringer Wald (forest) ... D3
Unstrut (riv.) ... D3
Usedom (isl.) ... F1
Vechte (riv.) ... B2
Vogelsberg (mts.) ... C3
Walchensee (lake) ... D5
Wasserkuppe (mt.) ... C3
Watzmann (mt.) ... E5
Werra (riv.) ... D3
Weser (riv.) ... C2
Westerwald (forest) ... B3
White Elster (riv.) ... E3
Würmsee (Starnbergersee) (lake) ... D5
Zugspitze (mt.) ... D5

Agriculture, Industry and Resources

DOMINANT LAND USE

- Wheat, Sugar Beets
- Cereals (chiefly rye, oats, barley)
- Potatoes, Rye
- Dairy, Livestock
- Mixed Cereals, Dairy
- Truck Farming
- Grapes, Fruit
- Forests

MAJOR MINERAL OCCURRENCES

Ag	Silver	K	Potash
Ba	Barite	Lg	Lignite
C	Coal	Na	Salt
Cu	Copper	O	Petroleum
Fe	Iron Ore	Pb	Lead
G	Natural Gas	U	Uranium
Gr	Graphite	Zn	Zinc

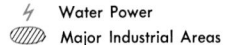

Water Power
Major Industrial Areas

Cod
Herring
Hogs
Flounder
Cattle
Sugar Beets
Potatoes
Hamburg
Bremen
Barley
Oats
Rye
Hannover
Osnabrück
Magdeburg
Berlin
Eisenhüttenstadt
Kassel
Sheep
Leipzig
Dresden
Erfurt
Chemnitz
Plauen
RUHR
Aachen
Cologne
Dairy
Frankfurt
Wine
Mannheim
Nürnberg
Wheat
Stuttgart
Munich
SAAR

AREA 15,892 sq. mi. (41,160 sq. km.)
POPULATION 14,906,000
CAPITALS The Hague, Amsterdam
LARGEST CITY Amsterdam
HIGHEST POINT Vaalserberg 1,056 ft. (322 m.)
MONETARY UNIT guilder (florin)
MAJOR LANGUAGE Dutch
MAJOR RELIGIONS Protestantism, Roman Catholicism

AREA 11,781 sq. mi. (30,513 sq. km.)
POPULATION 9,883,000
CAPITAL Brussels
LARGEST CITY Brussels (greater)
HIGHEST POINT Botrange 2,277 ft. (694 m.)
MONETARY UNIT Belgian franc
MAJOR LANGUAGES French (Walloon), Flemish
MAJOR RELIGION Roman Catholicism

AREA 999 sq. mi. (2,587 sq. km.)
POPULATION 378,000
CAPITAL Luxembourg
LARGEST CITY Luxembourg
HIGHEST POINT Ardennes Plateau 1,825 ft. (556 m.)
MONETARY UNIT Luxembourg franc
MAJOR LANGUAGES Luxembourgeois (Letzeburgisch), French, German
MAJOR RELIGION Roman Catholicism

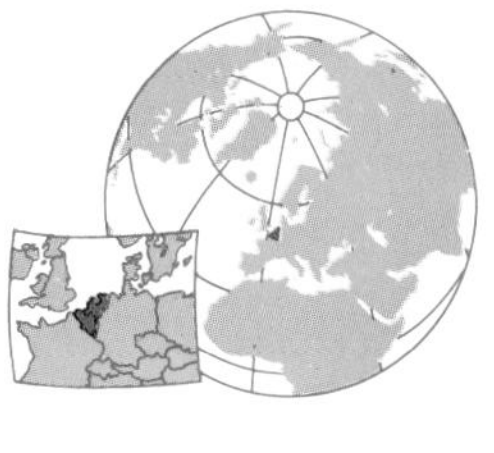

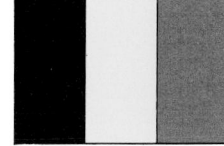

NETHERLANDS

BELGIUM

LUXEMBOURG

BELGIUM

PROVINCES

Antwerp 1,569,876 .... F6
Brabant 2,221,222 .... F7
East Flanders 1,331,192 .... D7
Hainaut 1,301,477 .... D7
Liège 999,413 .... H7
Limburg 716,888 .... G7
Luxembourg 221,926 .... G9
Namur 407,400 .... F8
West Flanders 1,079,253 .... B7

CITIES and TOWNS

Aalst 78,938 .... D7
Aalter 15,554 .... C6
Aarlen (Arlon) 22,279 .... H9
Aarschot 25,168 .... F7
Alken 9,563 .... G7
Amay 12,725 .... G7
Andenne 22,341 .... G8
Anderlecht 94,764 .... B9
Anderlues 11,700 .... E8
Ans 26,016 .... H7
Antoing 7,970 .... C7
Antwerp 185,897 .... E6
Antwerp* 918,144 .... E6
Antwerpen (Antwerp) 185,897 .... E6
Ardooie 9,458 .... C7
Arendonk 10,561 .... G6
Arlon 22,279 .... H9
Asse 26,425 .... E7
Assenede 13,353 .... D6
Aubange 14,696 .... H9
Audenarge (Oudenarde) 26,615 .... D7
Auderghem 30,435 .... C9
Aywaille 8,194 .... H8
Baerle-Hertog 2,111 .... F6
Balen 18,162 .... G6
Bastenaken (Bastogne) 11,386 .... H9
Bastogne 11,386 .... H9
Beauraing 7,641 .... F8
Beernem 13,526 .... C6
Beloeil 13,553 .... D7
Berchem 45,423 .... F6
Berchem-Sainte-Agathe 18,719 .... B9
Bergen (Mons) 94,417 .... E8
Beringen 34,254 .... G6
Bertrix 7,244 .... G9
Beveren 40,857 .... E6
Bilzen 25,683 .... G7
Binche 33,651 .... E8
Blankenberge 14,832 .... C6
Bocholt 10,142 .... H6
Boom 14,827 .... E6
Borgerhout 43,521 .... E6
Borgworm (Waremme) 11,907 .... G7
Bourg-Léopold (Leopoldsburg) 9,593 .... G6
Boussu 21,558 .... D8
Braine-l'Alleud 30,028 .... E7
Braine-le-Comte 16,475 .... D7
Brecht 16,391 .... F6
Bredene 10,538 .... B6
Bree 13,345 .... H6
Bruges 118,020 .... C6
Brugge (Bruges) 118,020 .... C6
Brussels (cap.)* 997,293 .... C9
Bruxelles (Brussels) (cap.)* 997,293 .... C9
Charleroi 222,343 .... E8
Charleroi* 443,832 .... E8
Châtelet 38,506 .... F8
Chimay 9,273 .... E8
Ciney 13,330 .... G8
Comines 18,034 .... B7
Courcelles 29,757 .... E8
Courtrai (Kortrijk) 75,917 .... C7
Couvin 12,909 .... F8
Damme 9,881 .... C6
De Haan 8,655 .... C6
Deinze 24,871 .... C7
Denderleeuw 16,497 .... E7
Dendermonde 22,119 .... E6
De Panne 9,507 .... B6
Dessel 8,074 .... G6
Destelbergen 15,741 .... D6
Deurne 77,635 .... F6
Diest 20,491 .... F7
Diksmuide 15,347 .... B6
Dilbeek 35,050 .... B9
Dilsen 15,910 .... H6
Dinant 12,105 .... G8
Dison 14,225 .... H7
Dixmude (Diksmuide) 15,347 .... B6
Doornik (Tournai) 67,906 .... C7
Dour 17,737 .... D8
Duffel 14,684 .... F6
Durbuy 7,729 .... H8
Ecaussinnes 9,739 .... E7
Edingen (Enghien) 10,095 .... D7
Eeklo 19,637 .... D6
Éghezée 10,683 .... F7
Eigenbrakel (Braine-l'Alleud) 30,028 .... E7
Ekeren 30,294 .... E6
Enghien 10,095 .... D7
Erquelinnes 10,029 .... E8
Esneux 11,559 .... H7
Essen 12,505 .... F6
Estampuis 9,601 .... C7
Etterbeek 44,218 .... B9
Eupen 16,847 .... J7
Evere 30,520 .... C9
Evergem 28,974 .... D6
Farciennes 12,205 .... E8
Flémalle 28,217 .... G7
Fleurus 22,574 .... E8
Florennes 10,537 .... F8
Forest 50,607 .... B9
Fosses-La-Ville 7,678 .... F8
Frameries 21,470 .... D8
Frasnes-lez Anvaing 10,751 .... D7
Furnes (Veurne) 11,253 .... B6
Ganshoren 21,445 .... B9
Geel 31,463 .... F6
Geldenaken (Jodoigne) 8,983 .... F7
Gembloux-sur-Orneau 17,636 .... F7
Genk 61,502 .... H7
Gent (Ghent) 239,256 .... D6
Geraardsbergen 17,533 .... D7
Gerpinnes 10,808 .... F8
Ghent 239,256 .... D6
Ghent* 485,565 .... D6
Gistel 9,531 .... B6
Grammont (Geraardsbergen) 17,533 .... D7
Grez-Doiceau 8,795 .... F7
Grimbergen 32,038 .... E7
Haacht 11,285 .... F7
Hal (Halle) 15,293 .... E7
Halen 7,865 .... G7
Halle 15,293 .... E7
Hamme 22,790 .... E6
Hamont-Achel 11,939 .... H6
Hannuit (Hannut) 11,527 .... G7
Hannut 11,527 .... G7
Harelbeke 25,214 .... C7
Hasselt 64,613 .... G7
Heist-op-den-Berg 34,617 .... F6
Hensies 6,806 .... D8
Herentals 23,797 .... F6
Herselt 11,340 .... F6
Herstal 38,592 .... H7
Herve 14,276 .... H7
Heuvelland 8,540 .... B7
Hoboken 34,563 .... E6
Hoei (Huy) 17,331 .... G8
Hoeselt 8,497 .... G7
Hoogstraten 14,368 .... F6
Huy 17,331 .... G8
Ichtegem 12,259 .... B6
Ieper 34,425 .... B7
Ingelmunster 10,434 .... C7
Ixelles 75,723 .... C9
Izegem 26,410 .... C7
Jabbeke 10,629 .... C6
Jemappes 18,632 .... D8
Jemeppe-sur-Sambre 17,120 .... F8
Jette 40,109 .... B9
Jodoigne 8,983 .... F7
Kalmthout 14,960 .... F6
Kapellen 14,536 .... E6
Kasterlee 14,612 .... F6
Kinrooi 10,138 .... H6
Knokke-Heist 28,868 .... C6
Koekelare 7,606 .... B6
Koekelberg 16,643 .... B9
Koksijde 13,679 .... B6
Kontich 17,878 .... E6
Kortemark 12,580 .... C6
Kortrijk 75,917 .... C7
Kraainem 11,780 .... C9
La Louvière 77,326 .... E8
Lanaken 20,272 .... H7
Landen 14,081 .... G7
Langemark-Poelkapelle 7,097 .... B7
Lasne 10,919 .... F7
Lede 17,249 .... D7
Lens 3,726 .... D7
Leopoldsburg 9,593 .... G6
Le Roeulx 7,754 .... E8
Lessen (Lessines) 16,553 .... D7
Lessines 16,553 .... D7
Leuven 85,076 .... F7
Leuze-en-Hainaut 12,863 .... D7
Libramont-Chevigny 7,859 .... G9
Lichtervelde 7,459 .... C6
Liedekerke 11,609 .... D7
Liège 214,119 .... H7
Liège* 605,123 .... H7
Lier 31,261 .... F6
Lierre (Lier) 31,261 .... F6
Limbourg 5,350 .... J7
Limburg (Limbourg) 5,350 .... J7
Linter 6,568 .... G7
Lochristi 16,125 .... D6
Lokeren 33,369 .... D6
Lommel 25,412 .... G6
Louvain (Leuven) 85,076 .... F7
Luik (Liège) 214,119 .... H7
Lummen 11,793 .... G7
Maaseik 20,056 .... H6
Maasmechelen 33,618 .... H7
Machelen 11,273 .... C9
Maldegem 42,694 .... C6
Malines (Mechelen) 77,269 .... F6
Malmédy 10,036 .... J8
Marche-en-Famenne 14,115 .... G8
Mechelen 77,269 .... F6
Meerhout 8,613 .... G6
Meise 15,170 .... E7
Menen 33,542 .... C7
Menin (Menen) 33,542 .... C7
Merchtem 12,972 .... E7
Merelbeke 19,773 .... D7
Merksem 41,600 .... E6
Merksplas 6,136 .... F6
Mettet 9,958 .... F8
Meulebeke 10,471 .... C7
Middelkerke 14,168 .... B6
Moeskroen (Mouscron) 54,590 .... C7
Mol 29,798 .... G6
Molenbeek-Saint-Jean 70,850 .... B9
Mons 94,417 .... E8
Montigny-le-Tilleul 9,726 .... E8
Moorslede 10,974 .... B7
Mortsel 26,746 .... E6
Mouscron 54,590 .... C7
Namen (Namur) 102,321 .... F8
Namur 102,321 .... F8
Nazareth 9,248 .... D7
Neerpelt 12,779 .... G6
Neufchâteau 6,039 .... G9
Nevele 10,471 .... D6
Nieuport (Nieuwpoort) 8,195 .... B6
Nieuwpoort 8,195 .... B6
Nijvel (Nivelles) 21,580 .... E7
Ninove 33,393 .... D7
Nivelles 21,580 .... E7
Oostende (Ostend) 68,915 .... B6
Oostkamp 19,747 .... C6
Opwijk 11,451 .... E7
Ostend 68,915 .... B6
Oudenaarde 26,615 .... D7
Oudenburg 8,138 .... B6
Oud-Turnhout 10,733 .... F6
Oupeye 22,453 .... H7
Overijse 21,428 .... F7
Overpelt 11,233 .... G6
Peer 12,099 .... G6
Péruwelz 16,664 .... D8
Philippeville 6,916 .... E8
Poelkapelle-Langemark 7,097 .... B7
Pont-à-Celles 15,444 .... E8
Poperinge 19,886 .... B7
Profondeville 8,724 .... F8
Putte 14,017 .... F6
Quaregnon 20,071 .... D8
Quévy 7,391 .... D8
Quiévrain 6,945 .... D8
Raeren 8,046 .... J7
Ravels 10,328 .... G6
Rebecq 8,891 .... E7
Renaix (Ronse) 25,056 .... D7
Retie 8,359 .... G6
Rochefort 4,357 .... G8
Roeselare 51,984 .... C7
Ronse (Renaix) 25,056 .... D7
Roulers (Roeselare) 51,984 .... C7
Saint-Gilles 46,076 .... B9
Saint-Josse-ten-Noode 20,381 .... C9
Saint-Nicolas 25,755 .... G7
Saint-Trond (Sint-Truiden) 36,374 .... G7
Saint-Vith (Sankt Vith) 8,434 .... J8

(continued on following page)

Agriculture, Industry and Resources

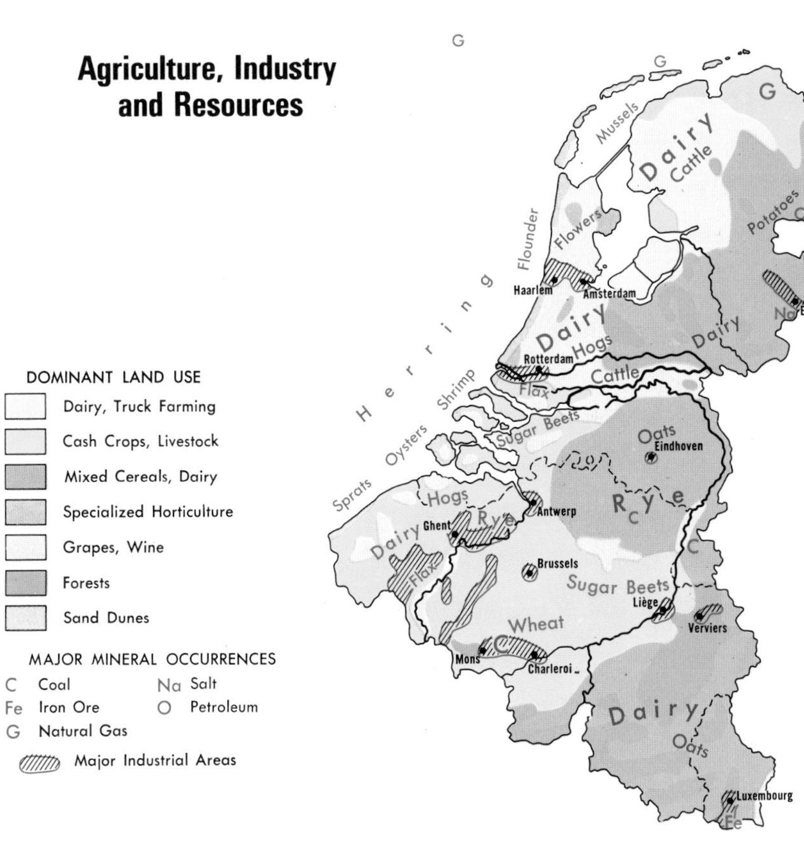
G
G
G
Mussels
Dairy
Cattle
Potatoes
Flounder
Flowers
Haarlem
Amsterdam
Herring
Dairy
Hogs
Rotterdam
Cattle
Flax
Enschede
Dairy
Shrimp
Oysters
Sugar Beets
Oats
Eindhoven
Sprats
Hogs
Antwerp
Ghent
Rye
Rye
Dairy
Flax
Brussels
Sugar Beets
Liège
Verviers
Wheat
Mons
Charleroi
Dairy
Oats
Luxembourg
Fe
DOMINANT LAND USE
Dairy, Truck Farming
Cash Crops, Livestock
Mixed Cereals, Dairy
Specialized Horticulture
Grapes, Wine
Forests
Sand Dunes
MAJOR MINERAL OCCURRENCES
C Coal
Na Salt
Fe Iron Ore
O Petroleum
G Natural Gas
Major Industrial Areas

(continued)

Sankt Vith 8,434 ... J8
Schaerbeek 106,754 ... C9
Schoten 31,128 ... F6
Seraing 64,543 ... G7
's-Gravenbrakel (Braine-le-Comte) 16,475 ... D7
Sint-Laureins 6,620 ... D6
Sint-Niklaas 67,992 ... E6
Sint-Pieters-Leeuw 27,968 ... B9
Sint-Truiden 36,374 ... G7
Soignies 23,352 ... D7
Spa 9,619 ... H8
Sprimont 9,660 ... H8
Staden 11,135 ... B7
Steenokkerzeel 9,638 ... C9
Stekene 14,125 ... E6
Tamise (Temse) 23,525 ... E6
Temse 23,525 ... E6
Termonde (Dendermonde) 22,119 ... E6
Tessenderlo 13,800 ... G6
Theux 9,167 ... H8
Thuin 13,757 ... E8
Tielt 19,103 ... C7
Tielt-Winge 8,237 ... F7
Tienen 32,620 ... F7
Tirlemont 32,620 ... F7
Tongeren 29,603 ... G7
Tongres (Tongeren) 29,603 ... G7
Torhout 17,165 ... C6
Tournai 67,906 ... C7
Tubeke (Tubize) 19,827 ... E7
Tubize 19,827 ... E7
Turnhout 37,453 ... F6
Uccle 76,004 ... B9
Ukkel (Uccle) 76,004 ... B9
Verviers 55,371 ... H7
Veurne 11,253 ... B6
Vielsalm 6,731 ... H8
Vilvoorde 33,264 ... F7
Vilvorde (Vilvoorde) 33,264 ... F7
Viroinval 5,589 ... F8
Virton 10,490 ... H9
Visé 16,469 ... H7
Vorst (Forest) 50,607 ... B9
Waarschoot 7,574 ... D6
Wachtebeke 6,951 ... D6
Waimes (Weismes) 5,713 ... J8
Walcourt 14,866 ... F8
Waregem 32,810 ... C7
Waremme 11,907 ... G7
Waterloo 24,755 ... E7
Watermael-Boitsfort 24,880 ... C9
Watermael-Bosvoorde (Watermael-Boitsfort) 24,880 ... C9
Waver (Wavre) 25,153 ... F7
Wavre 25,153 ... F7
Wemmel 13,547 ... B9
Wervik 18,086 ... B7
Westerlo 19,459 ... F6
Wetteren 23,460 ... D7
Wezembeek-Oppem 12,006 ... D9
Wezet (Visé) 16,469 ... H7
Willebroek 22,265 ... E6
Wilrijk 42,328 ... E6
Wingene 12,188 ... C6
Woluwe-Saint-Lambert 48,801 ... C9
Woluwe-Saint-Pierre 40,686 ... C9
Ypres (Ieper) 34,425 ... B7
Yvoir 6,527 ... F8
Zaventem 25,393 ... C9
Zedelgem 19,198 ... C6
Zele 19,631 ... E6
Zelzate 12,934 ... D6
Zemst 17,167 ... E7
Zinnik (Soignies) 23,352 ... D7
Zonhoven 15,965 ... G6
Zottegem 25,109 ... D7

OTHER FEATURES

Albert (canal) ... F6
Ardennes (forest) ... F9
Botrange (mt.) ... J8
Dender (riv.) ... D7
Deûle (riv.) ... B7
Dyle (riv.) ... F7
Hohe Venn (plat.) ... H8
Lys (riv.) ... B7
Mark (riv.) ... F6
Meuse (riv.) ... F8
Nethe (riv.) ... F6
North (sea) ... D4
Ourthe (riv.) ... G8
Rupel (riv.) ... F7
Sambre (riv.) ... D8
Schelde (Scheldt) (riv.) ... C7
Scheldt (riv.) ... C7
Semois (riv.) ... G9
Senne (riv.) ... E7
Vaalserberg (mt.) ... J7
Vesdre (riv.) ... H7
Yser (riv.) ... B7

LUXEMBOURG

CITIES and TOWNS

Bascharage 4,870 ... H9
Diekirch† 5,470 ... J9
Differdange 15,940 ... H9
Dudelange† 14,070 ... J1
Echternach† 4,290 ... J9
Esch-sur-Alzette† 23,800 ... H9
Ettelbruck† 6,600 ... J9
Grevenmacher† 2,940 ... J9
Hesperange 9,470 ... J9
Luxembourg (cap.) 75,540 ... J9
Mamer 6,090 ... H9
Mersch 5,560 ... J9
Mertert 3,000 ... J9
Pétange 11,800 ... H9
Remich 2,430 ... J9
Troisvierges 1,890 ... J9
Vianden† 1,510 ... J9
Wasserbillig 2,097 ... J9
Wiltz 3,850 ... H9

OTHER FEATURES

Alzette (riv.) ... J9
Clerf (riv.) ... J8
Mosel (riv.) ... J9
Our (riv.) ... J9
Sauer (riv.) ... J9

NETHERLANDS

PROVINCES

Drenthe 439,066 ... K3
Flevoland 202,678 ... G4
Friesland 599,190 ... H2
Gelderland 1,794,678 ... H4
Groningen 555,200 ... K2
Limburg 1,099,622 ... H6
North Brabant 2,172,604 ... F5
North Holland 2,365,160 ... F3
Overijssel 1,014,949 ... J4
South Holland 3,200,408 ... E5
Utrecht 1,004,632 ... G4
Zeeland 355,585 ... D6

CITIES and TOWNS

Aalsmeer 21,984 ... F4
Aalten 18,202 ... K5
Alkmaar 88,571 ... F3
Almelo 62,008 ... K4
Almere 63,785 ... G4
Alphen aan de Rijn 59,586 ... F4
Amersfoort 96,072 ... G4
Amstelveen 69,505 ... B5
Amsterdam (cap.) 694,680 ... B4
Apeldoorn 147,270 ... H4
Appingedam 12,668 ... K2
Arnhem 128,946 ... H4
Assen 49,398 ... K3
Asten 14,965 ... H6
Axel 12,219 ... D6
Baarn 24,897 ... G4
Barneveld 41,649 ... H4
Beilen 14,057 ... K3
Bemmel 15,842 ... H5
Bergen 14,075 ... F3
Bergen op Zoom 46,842 ... E5
Berkel 15,690 ... F5
Beverwijk 35,126 ... F4
Bloemendaal 8,977 ... E4
Bodegraven 17,720 ... F4
Bolsward 9,799 ... H2
Borculo 10,057 ... J4
Borger 12,730 ... K3
Borne 21,261 ... K4
Boskoop 14,524 ... F4
Boxmeer 14,363 ... H5
Boxtel 24,951 ... G5
Breda 121,362 ... F5
Brielle 14,973 ... E5
Brummen 20,802 ... J4
Brunssum 29,799 ... J7
Bussum 31,988 ... G4
Capelle 57,423 ... F5
Castricum 22,433 ... F3
Coevorden 14,344 ... K3
Culemborg 21,116 ... G5
De Bilt 31,729 ... G4
Delft 88,135 ... E4
Delfzijl 23,472 ... K2
Denekamp 12,206 ... L4
Den Helder 62,094 ... F3
Deurne 29,308 ... H6
Deventer 66,398 ... J4
Didam 16,036 ... J5
Diemen 18,083 ... C5
Dinxperlo 8,133 ... K5
Dirksland 7,341 ... E5
Doesburg 10,578 ... J4
Doetinchem 41,260 ... J5
Dongen 21,124 ... F5
Doorn 10,419 ... G4
Dordrecht 108,519 ... F5
Driebergen 18,294 ... G4
Dronten 24,281 ... H3
Druten 14,630 ... H5
Echt 16,927 ... H6
Edam-Volendam 24,572 ... G4
Ede 92,293 ... H4
Egmond aan Zee 11,163 ... E3
Eindhoven 190,736 ... G6
Elst 17,654 ... H5
Emmen 92,422 ... K3
Enkhuizen 15,939 ... G3
Enschede 145,223 ... K4
Epe 33,872 ... H4
Ermelo 25,644 ... H4
Etten-Leur 32,010 ... F5
Flushing 44,022 ... C6
Geertruidenberg 6,645 ... F5
Geldermalsen 22,017 ... G5
Geldrop 25,817 ... H6
Geleen 33,756 ... H7
Gemert 17,613 ... H5
Gendringen 20,186 ... J5
Genemuiden 7,545 ... H3
Gennep 16,264 ... H5
Giessendam 16,722 ... F5
Gilze 22,577 ... F5
Goes 31,815 ... D6
Goirle 18,852 ... G5
Goor 11,804 ... K4
Gorinchem 28,222 ... G5
Gouda 63,232 ... F4
Gramsbergen 6,080 ... K3
Grave 10,447 ... H5
Groenlo 8,895 ... K4
Groesbeek 18,221 ... H5
Groningen 167,788 ... K2
Haaksbergen 22 690 ... K4
Haarlem 149,198 ... F4
Haarlemmermeer (Hoofddorp) 93,427 ... F4
Hague, The (cap.) 443,845 ... E4
Hardenberg 32,065 ... J3
Harderwijk 34,600 ... H4
Hardinxveld-Giessendam 16,722 ... G5
Harlingen 15,727 ... G2
Hasselt 6,871 ... J3
Hattem 11,571 ... H4
Heemskerk 32,910 ... F3
Heemstede 26,308 ... F4
Heerde 18,171 ... H4
Heerenveen 37,700 ... H3
Heerhugowaard 35,522 ... F3
Heerlen 94,149 ... J7
Heesch 11,309 ... G5
Heiloo 20,467 ... F3
Hellendoorn 34,287 ... J4
Hellevoetsluis 34,276 ... E5
Helmond 66,791 ... H6
Hengelo 76,175 ... J4
's Hertogenbosch 90,584 ... G5
Heusden 5,761 ... G5
Hillegom 20,001 ... E4
Hilvarenbeek 9,975 ... G6
Hilversum 84,983 ... G4
Hoek van Holland (Hook of Holland) ... D4
Hoofddorp (Haarlemmermeer) 93,427 ... F4
Hoogeveen 45,601 ... J3
Hoogezand-Sappemeer 34,618 ... K2
Hook of Holland ... D4
Hoorn 56,474 ... G3
Horst 17,614 ... H6
Huissen 15,544 ... H5
Huizen 20,501 ... G4
Hulst 18,575 ... E6
IJsselstein 19,516 ... F4
Kampen 32,769 ... H3
Katwijk aan Zee 39,441 ... E4
Kerkrade 52,994 ... J7
Kesteren 9,389 ... G5
Krimpen aan den IJssel 27,638 ... F5
Landsmeer 9,121 ... C4
Laren 11,643 ... G4
Leek 17,743 ... J2
Leerdam 19,015 ... G5
Leeuwarden 85,296 ... H2
Leiden 109,254 ... E4
Lelystad 58,125 ... H3
Lisse 20,826 ... F4
Lith 6,115 ... G5
Lochem 18,295 ... J4
Loon op Zand 21,372 ... G5
Losser 22,526 ... L4
Maarssen 37,629 ... F4
Maasbree 11,752 ... H6
Maassluis 33,155 ... E5
Maastricht 116,380 ... H7
Margraten 13,365 ... H7
Medemblik 6,876 ... G3
Meerssen 20,462 ... H7
Meppel 23,492 ... J3
Middelburg 39,462 ... C6
Middelharnis 15,480 ... E5
Millingen aan den Rijn 5,287 ... J5
Monnickendam 9,953 ... C4
Montfoort 12,397 ... G4
Muiden 6,772 ... G4
Muntendam 5,022 ... K2
Naaldwijk 27,683 ... E4
Naarden 16,101 ... G4
Neede 10,982 ... K4
Nieuwegein 58,316 ... G4
Nieuwkoop 10,723 ... F4
Nijkerk 25,613 ... H4
Nijmegen 145,405 ... H5
Noordwijk 24,996 ... E4
Norg 6,595 ... J2
Nunspeet 24,573 ... H4
Odoorn 12,225 ... K3
Oisterwijk 18,177 ... G5
Oldenzaal 29,680 ... K4
Olst 9,039 ... J4
Ommen 17,957 ... J3
Oostburg 18,145 ... C6
Oosterhout 48,157 ... F5
Oostzaan 7,292 ... C4
Oss 50,987 ... H5
Oud-Beijerland 20,385 ... E5
Oude-Pekela 8,028 ... K2
Oudenbosch 12,576 ... E5
Oudewater 9,410 ... F4
Purmerend 56,233 ... F4
Putten 20,898 ... H4
Raalte 26,883 ... J4
Renkum 33,841 ... H5
Reusel 7,813 ... G6
Rheden 46,088 ... J4
Rhenen 16,613 ... H5
Ridderkerk 46,163 ... F5
Rijnsburg 13,412 ... F4
Rijssen 23,927 ... J4
Rijswijk 48,189 ... E4
Roden 18,331 ... J2
Roermond 38,486 ... J6
Roosendaal 59,237 ... F5
Rotterdam 576,232 ... E5
Ruurlo 7,418 ... J4
Sappemeer-Hoogezand 34,618 ... K2
Schagen 16,759 ... F3
Schiedam 69,438 ... E5
Schijndel 21,397 ... G5
Schoonebeek 7,740 ... K3
Schoonhoven 11,231 ... F5
's Gravendeel 8,424 ... E5
's Gravenhage (The Hague) (cap.) 443,845 ... E4
's Gravenzande 18,453 ... E4
Simpelveld 11,882 ... J7
Sittard 44,894 ... H6
Sliedrecht 22,833 ... F5
Slochteren 13,958 ... K2
Sloten ... H3
Sluis 2,882 ... C6
Smilde 9,212 ... K3
Sneek 29,408 ... H2
Soest 41,598 ... G4
Stadskanaal 33,047 ... L3
Staphorst 13,580 ... J3
Staveren ... G3
Steenbergen 13,826 ... E5
Steenwijk 20,907 ... J3
Stiens ... H2
Tegelen 18,991 ... J6
Ter Apel ... L3
Termunten 4,378 ... K2
Terneuzen 35,043 ... D6
The Hague (cap.) 443,845 ... E4
Tholen 19,019 ... E5
Tiel 31,394 ... G5
Tilburg 155,110 ... G5
Twello ... J4
Uden 35,057 ... H5
Uithoorn 22,205 ... F4
Uithuizen ... K2
Ulrum 3,657 ... J2
Urk 12,728 ... H3
Utrecht 230,634 ... G4
Vaals 10,639 ... H7
Valkenswaard 29,811 ... H6
Veendam 28,234 ... K2
Veenendaal 47,258 ... G4
Veere 4,836 ... D5
Veghel 25,701 ... H5
Veldhoven 38,644 ... G6
Velsen 57,608 ... F4
Venlo 63,607 ... J6
Venraij 34,172 ... H6
Vianen 18,704 ... G5
Vlaardingen 74,480 ... E5
Vlagtwedde 16,181 ... L3
Vlijmen 15,655 ... G5
Vlissingen (Flushing) 44,022 ... C6
Volendam-Edam 24,572 ... G4
Voorburg 40,455 ... E4
Voorst 23,678 ... J4
Vorden 8,282 ... J4
Vriezenveen 18,601 ... K4
Vught 23,718 ... G5
Waalre 15,126 ... G6
Waalwijk 28,674 ... F5
Wageningen 32,370 ... H5
Warmenhuizen 4,765 ... F3
Weert 40,068 ... H6
Weesp 18,362 ... C5
Westkapelle 2,666 ... C5
Wierden 22,200 ... K4
Wijhe 7,155 ... J4
Wijk bij Duurstede 15,401 ... G5
Willemstad 3,357 ... F5
Winschoten 19,680 ... L2
Winsum 6,583 ... K2
Winterswijk 28,024 ... K5
Woensdrecht 10,077 ... E6
Woerden 34,166 ... F4
Wolvega ... J3
Workum ... G3
Zaandam (Zaanstad) 129,653 ... B4
Zaltbommel 9,534 ... G5
Zandvoort 15,428 ... E4
Zeewolde 5,930 ... G4
Zeist 59,431 ... G4
Zevenaar 26,848 ... J5
Zevenbergen 15,562 ... E5
Zierikzee 9,804 ... D5
Zundert 13,385 ... F6
Zutphen 31,144 ... J4
Zwartsluis 4,465 ... H3
Zwijndrecht 41,357 ... E5
Zwolle 92,517 ... J3

OTHER FEATURES

Alkmaardermeer (lake) ... F3
Ameland (isl.) ... H2
Beulaker Wijde (lake) ... H3
Borndiep (chan.) ... H2
De Fluessen (lake) ... G3
De Honte (bay) ... D6
De Peel (reg.) ... H6
De Twente (reg.) ... K4
De Zaan (riv.) ... B4
Dollard (bay) ... L2
Dommel (riv.) ... H6
Duiveland (isl.) ... D5
Eems (riv.) ... K2
Eijerlandsche Gat (strait) ... F2
Flevoland Polders ... G4
Frisian, West (isls.) ... G2
Goeree (isl.) ... D5
Grevelingen (strait) ... E5
Griend (isl.) ... G2
Groninger Wad (sound) ... J2
Groote IJ Polder ... B4
Haarlemmermeer Polder ... B5
Haringvliet (strait) ... E5
Het IJ (est.) ... C4
Hoek van Holland (cape) ... D5
Houtrak Polder ... A4
Hunse (riv.) ... K3
IJmeer (bay) ... C4
IJssel (riv.) ... J4
IJsselmeer (lake) ... G3
Lauwers (chan.) ... J1
Lauwers Zee (bay) ... J2
Lek (riv.) ... F5
Lower Rhine (riv.) ... H5
Maas (riv.) ... G5
Marken (isl.) ... G4
Markerwaard Polder ... G3
Marsdiep (chan.) ... F3
North (sea) ... E3
North Beveland (isl.) ... D5
North East Polder ... H3
North Holland (canal) ... C4
North Sea (canal) ... F4
Old Rhine (riv.) ... E4
Oostzaan Polder ... B4
Orange (canal) ... K3
Overflakkee (isl.) ... E5
Rhine (riv.) ... J5
Roer (riv.) ... J6
Scheldt, Eastern (est.) ... D5
Scheldt, Western (De Honte) (bay) ... D6
Schiermonnikoog (isl.) ... J1
Schouwen (isl.) ... D5
Slotermeer (lake) ... H3
Sneekermeer (lake) ... H2
South Beveland (isl.) ... D6
Terschelling (isl.) ... G2
Texel (isl.) ... F2
Tjeukemeer (lake) ... H3
Vaalserberg (mt.) ... J7
Vecht (riv.) ... F4
Vechte (riv.) ... J3
Veersche Meer (lake) ... D5
Veluwe (reg.) ... H4
Vlieland (isl.) ... F2
Vliestroom (strait) ... G2
Voorne (isl.) ... D5
Waal (riv.) ... G5
Waddenzee (sound) ... G2
Walcheren (isl.) ... C5
West Frisian (isls.) ... F2
Wester Eems (chan.) ... K1
Western Scheldt (De Honte) (bay) ... D6
Wieringermeer Polder ... G3
Wilhelmina (canal) ... G6
Willems (canal) ... G5

* City and suburbs.
† Population of urban area.

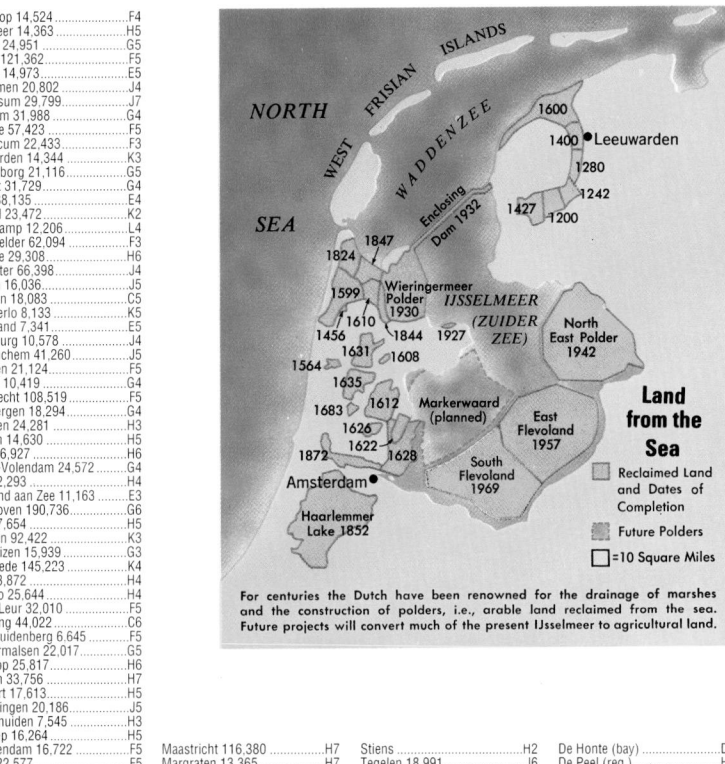

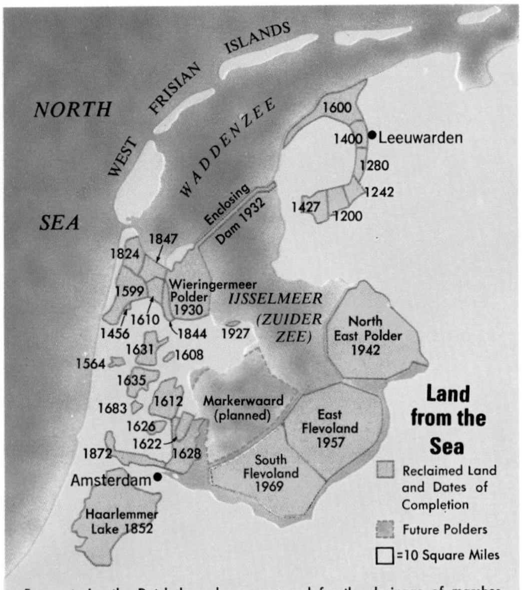
NORTH
SEA
WEST FRISIAN ISLANDS
WADDENZEE
Leeuwarden
Enclosing Dam 1932
Wieringermeer Polder 1930
IJSSELMEER (ZUIDER ZEE)
North East Polder 1942
Markerwaard (planned)
East Flevoland 1957
South Flevoland 1969
Amsterdam
Haarlemmer Lake 1852
Land from the Sea
Reclaimed Land and Dates of Completion
Future Polders
=10 Square Miles

For centuries the Dutch have been renowned for the drainage of marshes and the construction of polders, i.e., arable land reclaimed from the sea. Future projects will convert much of the present IJsselmeer to agricultural land.

Topography

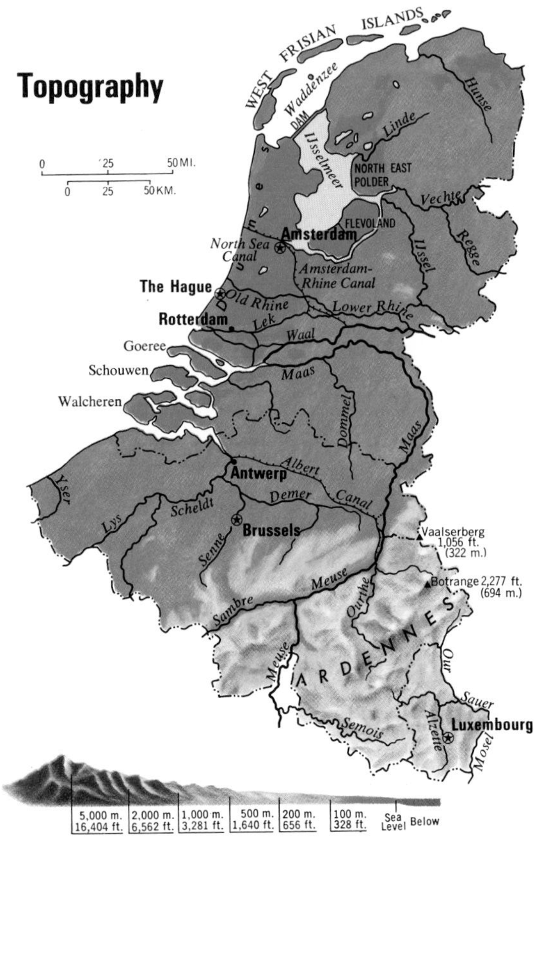
WEST FRISIAN ISLANDS
Waddenzee
IJsselmeer
NORTH EAST POLDER
FLEVOLAND
Amsterdam
North Sea Canal
Amsterdam-Rhine Canal
The Hague
Rotterdam
Old Rhine
Lek
Lower Rhine
Waal
Maas
Goeree
Schouwen
Walcheren
Dommel
Antwerp
Albert
Demer
Canal
Scheldt
Lys
Yser
Brussels
Senne
Vaalserberg 1,056 ft. (322 m.)
Botrange 2,277 ft. (694 m.)
Meuse
Sambre
Ourthe
ARDENNES
Our
Sauer
Semois
Alzette
Luxembourg
Mosel
0 25 50 MI.
0 25 50 KM.
5,000 m. 16,404 ft.
2,000 m. 6,562 ft.
1,000 m. 3,281 ft.
500 m. 1,640 ft.
200 m. 656 ft.
100 m. 328 ft.
Sea Level
Below

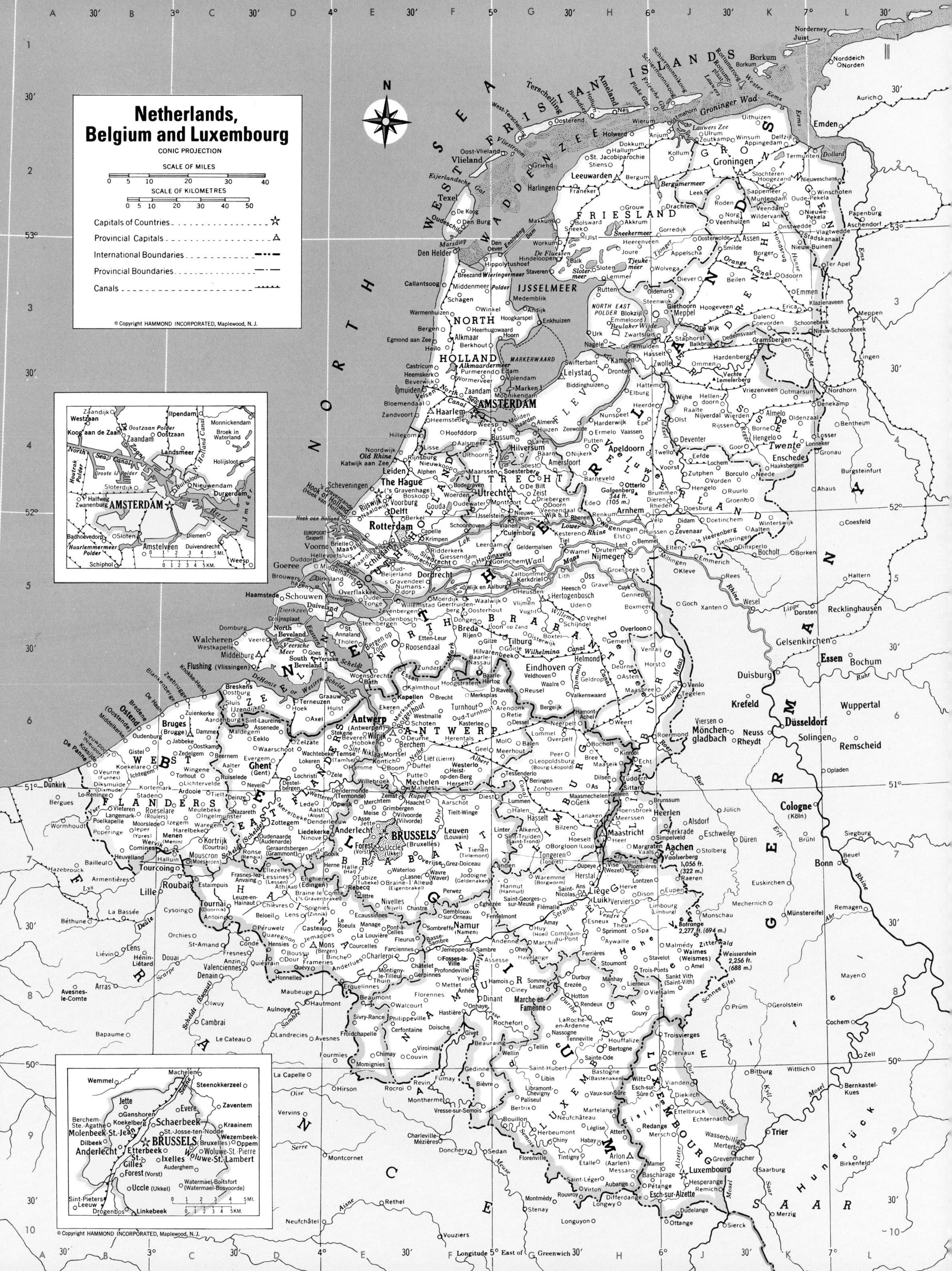
Netherlands, Belgium and Luxembourg
CONIC PROJECTION
SCALE OF MILES
0 5 10 20 30 40
SCALE OF KILOMETRES
0 5 10 20 30 40 50
Capitals of Countries
Provincial Capitals
International Boundaries
Provincial Boundaries
Canals
© Copyright HAMMOND INCORPORATED, Maplewood, N.J.
NORTH SEA
WEST FRISIAN ISLANDS
WADDEN ZEE
IJSSELMEER
MARKERWAARD
GRONINGEN
FRIESLAND
DRENTHE
OVERIJSSEL
GELDERLAND
UTRECHT
NORTH HOLLAND
SOUTH HOLLAND
ZEELAND
NORTH BRABANT
LIMBURG
WEST FLANDERS
EAST FLANDERS
ANTWERP
BRABANT
HAINAUT
NAMUR
LIÈGE
LUXEMBOURG
GERMANY
FRANCE
SAAR
AMSTERDAM
The Hague ('s Gravenhage)
Rotterdam
Utrecht
Groningen
Leeuwarden
Arnhem
Zwolle
Maastricht
Antwerp (Antwerpen)
Ghent (Gent)
Bruges (Brugge)
BRUSSELS
Liège (Luik)
Namur (Namen)
Luxembourg
Cologne (Köln)
Düsseldorf
Essen
Aachen
Longitude 5° East of Greenwich
AMSTERDAM
0 1 2 3 4 5 MI.
0 1 2 3 4 5 KM.
BRUSSELS
0 1 2 3 4 5 MI.
0 1 2 3 4 5 KM.
© Copyright HAMMOND INCORPORATED, Maplewood, N.J.

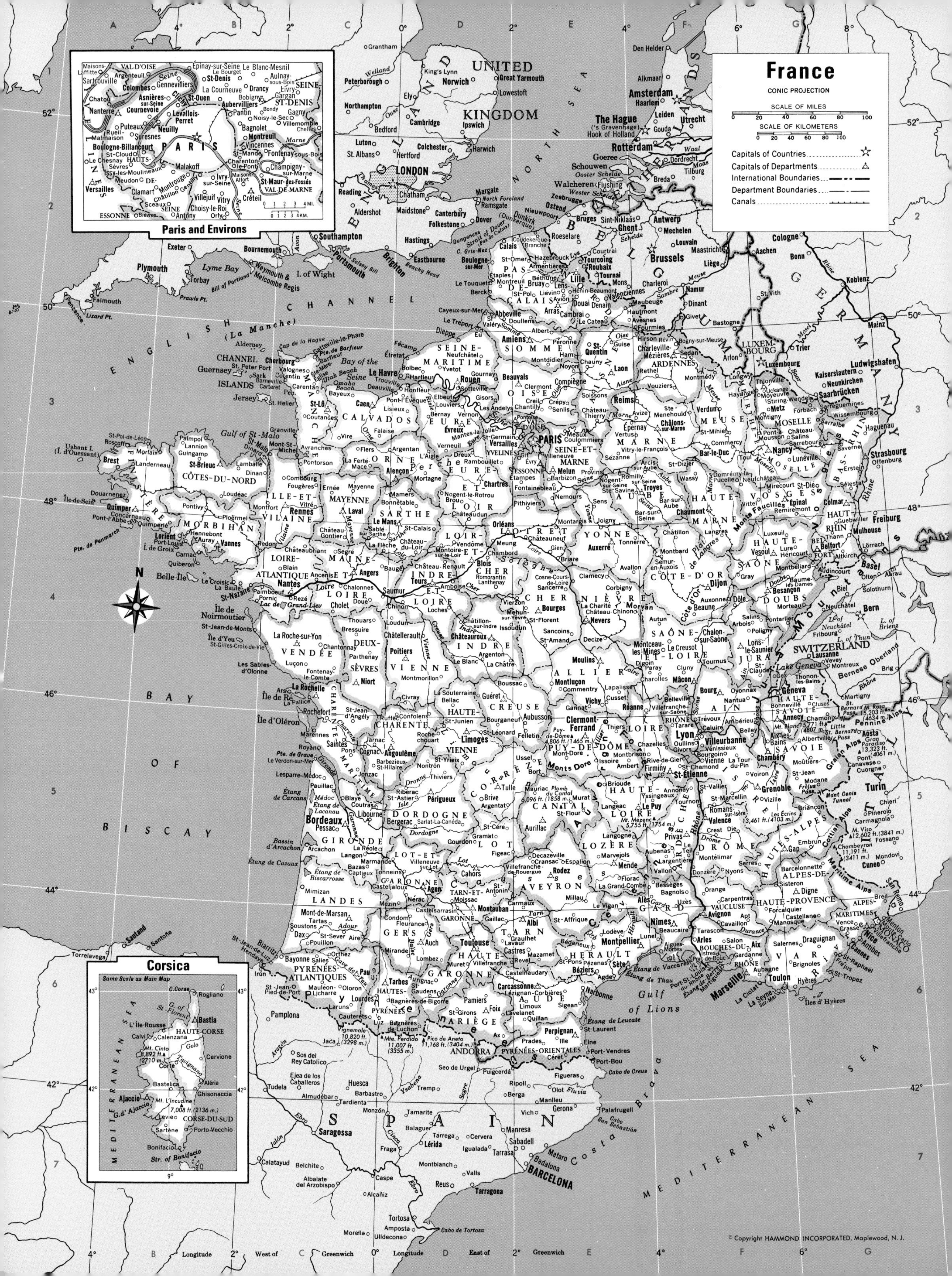

France
CONIC PROJECTION
SCALE OF MILES
0 20 40 60 80 100
SCALE OF KILOMETERS
0 20 40 60 80 100
Capitals of Countries
Capitals of Departments
International Boundaries
Department Boundaries
Canals
Paris and Environs
Corsica
Same Scale as Main Map
UNITED KINGDOM
ENGLAND
NORTH SEA
NETHERLANDS
BELGIUM
LUXEMBOURG
GERMANY
SWITZERLAND
ITALY
MONACO
ANDORRA
SPAIN
ENGLISH CHANNEL (La Manche)
CHANNEL ISLANDS
BAY OF BISCAY
Gulf of Lions
MEDITERRANEAN SEA
PARIS
London
Brussels
Amsterdam
Luxembourg
Bern
Lyon
Marseille
Bordeaux
Toulouse
Nantes
Nice
Strasbourg
Lille
Barcelona
Turin
Geneva
Ajaccio
Bastia
HAUTE-CORSE
CORSE-DU-SUD
© Copyright HAMMOND INCORPORATED, Maplewood, N. J.

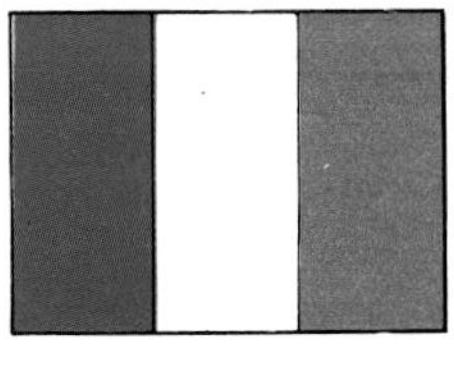

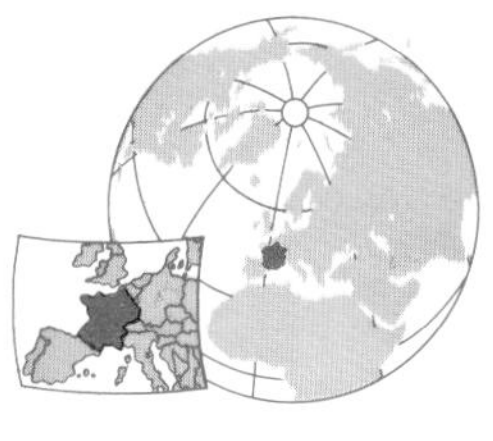

AREA 210,038 sq. mi. (543,998 sq. km.)
POPULATION 56,160,000
CAPITAL Paris
LARGEST CITY Paris
HIGHEST POINT Mont Blanc 15,771 ft. (4,807 m.)
MONETARY UNIT franc
MAJOR LANGUAGE French
MAJOR RELIGION Roman Catholicism

DEPARTMENTS

Ain 418,516. . . . F 4
Aisne 533,970. . . . E 3
Allier 369,580. . . . E 4
Alpes-de-Haute-Provence 119,068. . . . G 5
Alpes-Maritimes 881,198. . . . G 6
Ardèche 267,970. . . . F 5
Ardennes 302,338. . . . F 3
Ariège 135,725. . . . D 6
Aube 289,300. . . . E 3
Aude 280,686. . . . E 6
Aveyron 278,654. . . . E 5
Bas-Rhin 915,676. . . . G 3
Belfort 131,999. . . . G 4
Bouches-du-Rhône 1,724,199. . . . F 6
Calvados 589,559. . . . C 3
Cantal 162,838. . . . E 5
Charente 340,770. . . . D 5
Charente-Maritime 513,220. . . . C 5
Cher 320,174. . . . E 4
Corrèze 241,448. . . . D 5
Corse du Sud 108,604. . . . B 6
Côte-d'Or 473,548. . . . F 4
Côtes-du-Nord 538,869. . . . B 3
Creuse 139,968. . . . D 4
Deux-Sèvres 342,812. . . . C 4
Dordogne 377,356. . . . D 5
Doubs 477,163. . . . G 4
Drôme 389,781. . . . F 5
Essonne 988,000. . . . E 3
Eure 462,323. . . . D 3
Eure-et-Loir 362,813. . . . D 3
Finistère 828,364. . . . A 3
Gard 530,478. . . . F 6
Gers 174,154. . . . D 6
Gironde 1,127,546. . . . C 5
Haute-Corse 131,574. . . . B 6
Haute-Garonne 824,501. . . . D 6
Haute-Loire 205,895. . . . E 5
Haute-Marne 210,670. . . . F 3
Hautes-Alpes 105,070. . . . G 5
Haute-Saône 231,962. . . . G 4
Haute-Savoie 494,505. . . . G 5
Hautes-Pyrénées 227,922. . . . D 6
Haute-Vienne 355,737. . . . D 5
Haut-Rhin 650,372. . . . G 4
Hauts-de-Seine 1,387,039. . . . A 2
Hérault 706,499. . . . E 6
Ille-et-Vilaine 749,764. . . . C 3
Indre 243,191. . . . D 4
Indre-et-Loire 506,097. . . . D 4
Isère 936,771. . . . F 5
Jura 242,925. . . . F 4
Landes 297,424. . . . C 5
Loire 739,521. . . . F 5
Loire-Atlantique 995,498. . . . C 4
Loiret 535,669. . . . E 4
Loir-et-Cher 296,220. . . . D 4
Lot 154,533. . . . D 5
Lot-et-Garonne 298,522. . . . D 5
Lozère 74,294. . . . E 5
Maine-et-Loire 675,321. . . . C 4
Manche 465,948. . . . C 3
Marne 543,627. . . . F 3
Mayenne 271,784. . . . C 3
Meurthe-et-Moselle 716,846. . . . G 3
Meuse 200,101. . . . F 3
Morbihan 590,889. . . . B 4
Moselle 1,007,189. . . . G 3
Nièvre 239,635. . . . E 4
Nord 2,520,526. . . . E 2
Oise 661,781. . . . E 3
Orne 295,472. . . . C 3
Paris 2,188,918. . . . B 2
Pas-de-Calais 1,412,413. . . . E 2
Puy-de-Dôme 594,365. . . . E 5
Pyrénées-Atlantiques 555,696. . . . C 6
Pyrénées-Orientales 334,557. . . . E 6
Rhône 1,445,208. . . . F 5
Saône-et-Loire 571,852. . . . F 4
Sarthe 504,768. . . . D 3
Savoie 323,675. . . . G 5
Seine-et-Marne 887,112. . . . E 3
Seine-Maritime 1,324,301. . . . D 3
Seine-Saint-Denis 1,324,301. . . . C 1
Somme 544,570. . . . E 3
Tarn 339,345. . . . E 6
Tarn-et-Garonne 190,485. . . . D 5
Val-de-Marne 1,193,655. . . . C 1
Val-d'Oise 920,598. . . . E 3
Var 708,331. . . . G 6
Vaucluse 427,343. . . . F 6
Vendée 483,027. . . . C 4
Vienne 371,428. . . . D 4
Vosges 395,769. . . . G 3
Yonne 311,019. . . . E 4
Yvelines 1,196,111. . . . D 3

CITIES and TOWNS

Aigues-Mortes 4,106. . . . F 6
Aix-en-Provence 100,221. . . . F 6
Aix-les-Bains 22,331. . . . G 5
Ajaccio 48,324. . . . B 7
Alençon 30,952. . . . D 3
Amboise 10,823. . . . D 4
Amiens 130,302. . . . E 3
Angers 135,293. . . . C 4
Angoulême 45,495. . . . D 5
Annecy 49,753. . . . G 5
Antibes 62,427. . . . G 6
Argenteuil 94,826. . . . A 1
Arles 37,554. . . . F 6
Armentières 22,849. . . . E 2
Arras 41,376. . . . E 2
Asnières-sur-Seine 71,058. . . . A 1
Aubervilliers 67,684. . . . B 1
Aubusson 5,326. . . . E 4
Aulnay-sous-Bois 75,543. . . . B 1
Aurignac 772. . . . D 6
Avignon 75,178. . . . F 6
Ax-les-Thermes 1,283. . . . D 6
Bagnolet 32,556. . . . B 2
Barbizon 478. . . . E 3
Barcelonnette 2,674. . . . G 5
Barfleur 617. . . . C 3
Bastia 43,502. . . . B 6
Bayeux 14,568. . . . C 3
Bayonne 40,088. . . . C 6
Beaucaire 10,622. . . . F 6
Beaune 19,110. . . . F 4
Beauvais 51,542. . . . E 3
Belfort 51,034. . . . G 4
Bergerac 24,604. . . . D 5
Besançon 112,023. . . . G 4
Bessèges 4,352. . . . F 5
Béziers 74,114. . . . E 6
Biarritz 26,579. . . . C 6
Blois 46,925. . . . D 4
Bobigny 42,630. . . . B 1
Bonifacio 1,727. . . . B 7
Bordeaux 201,965. . . . C 5
Boulogne-Billancourt 102,582. . . . A 2
Boulogne-sur-Mer 47,482. . . . D 2
Bourg-en-Bresse 37,582. . . . F 4
Bourges 74,622. . . . E 4
Brest 154,110. . . . A 3
Brignoles 8,529. . . . G 6
Brive-la-Gaillarde 50,898. . . . D 5
Bruay-en-Artois 22,502. . . . E 2
Caen 112,332. . . . C 3
Calais 76,206. . . . D 2
Caluire-et-Cuire 41,864. . . . F 5
Cambrai 35,070. . . . E 2
Cannes 71,888. . . . G 6
Carcassonne 38,379. . . . E 6
Castres 39,216. . . . E 6
Chalons-sur-Marne 49,941. . . . F 3

Topography

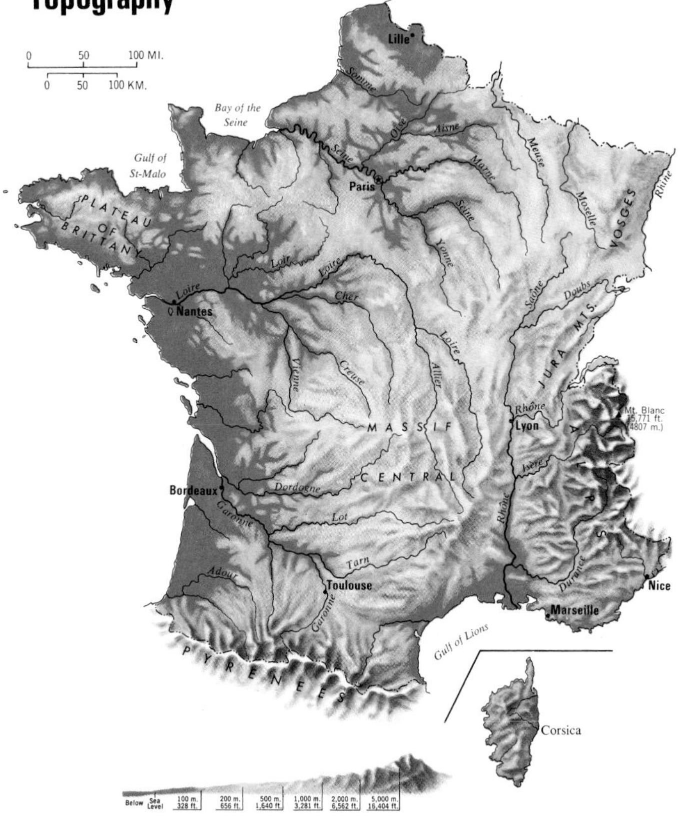
0 50 100 MI.
0 50 100 KM.
Lille
Somme
Bay of the Seine
Oise
Aisne
Gulf of St-Malo
Seine
Meuse
Marne
Paris
Moselle
Rhine
PLATEAU OF BRITTANY
VOSGES
Yonne
Loir
Loire
Saône
Doubs
Nantes
Cher
JURA MTS.
Vienne
Creuse
Allier
Rhône
Mt. Blanc 15,771 ft. (4,807 m.)
Lyon
MASSIF CENTRAL
Isère
Bordeaux
Dordogne
Garonne
Lot
Tarn
Adour
Durance
Toulouse
Nice
Marseille
Gulf of Lions
PYRENEES
Corsica
Below Sea Level
100 m. 328 ft.
200 m. 656 ft.
500 m. 1,640 ft.
1,000 m. 3,281 ft.
2,000 m. 6,562 ft.
5,000 m. 16,404 ft.

Historic Provinces

FLANDERS
ARTOIS
PICARDY
NORMANDY
ILE DE FRANCE
CHAMPAGNE
LORRAINE
ALSACE
BRITTANY
MAINE
ORLÉANAIS
ANJOU
TOURAINE
NIVERNAIS
BURGUNDY
FRANCHE COMTÉ
BERRY
POITOU
BOURBONNAIS
AUNIS
MARCHE
SAINTONGE
ANGOUMOIS
LIMOUSIN
AUVERGNE
LYONNAIS
DAUPHINÉ
GUYENNE
VENAISSIN
GASCONY
LANGUEDOC
PROVENCE
BÉARN
FOIX
ROUSSILLON

A resident of the city of Caen thinks of himself as a Norman rather than as a citizen of the modern department of Calvados. In spite of the passing of nearly two centuries, the historic provinces which existed before 1790 command the local patriotism of most Frenchmen.

Chalon-sur-Saône 53,893. . . . F 4
Chambéry 49,465. . . . F 5
Chambord 159. . . . D 4
Chamonix-Mont-Blanc 7,406. . . . G 5
Champigny-sur-Marne 76,039. . . . C 2
Chantilly 10,065. . . . E 3
Charleville-Mézières 7,814. . . . F 3
Chartres 36,706. . . . D 3
Châteaudun 15,905. . . . D 3
Châteauneuf-sur-Loire 5,630. . . . E 4
Châteauroux 51,744. . . . D 4
Château-Thierry 14,427. . . . E 3
Chatou 28,435. . . . A 1
Cherbourg 28,324. . . . C 3
Chinon 6,030. . . . D 4
Choisy-le-Roi 35,443. . . . B 2
Cholet 51,620. . . . C 4
Clamart 48,210. . . . A 2
Clermont-Ferrand 145,901. . . . E 5
Clichy 46,830. . . . B 1
Cluny 4,133. . . . F 4
Cognac 20,247. . . . C 5
Colmar 61,560. . . . G 3
Colombes 78,485. . . . A 1
Compiègne 39,909. . . . E 3
Courbevoie 59,821. . . . A 1
Creil 34,332. . . . E 3
Créteil 71,559. . . . B 2
Deauville 4,682. . . . C 3
Dieppe 35,659. . . . D 3
Digne 12,540. . . . G 5
Dijon 139,188. . . . F 4
Dinard 9,562. . . . B 3
Domrémy-la-Pucelle 162. . . . F 3
Douai 41,576. . . . E 2
Drancy 60,122. . . . B 1
Dunkirk 71,756. . . . E 2
Ernée 5,253. . . . C 3
Évreux 45,215. . . . D 3
Falaise 8,424. . . . C 3
Fécamp 21,212. . . . D 3
Foix 9,212. . . . D 6
Fontainebleau 14,687. . . . E 3
Fontenay-sous-Bois 52,397. . . . C 2
Gex 4,776. . . . G 4
Grasse 24,257. . . . G 6
Grenoble 156,437. . . . F 5
Guise 6,179. . . . E 3
Harfleur 9,470. . . . D 3
Hazebrouck 19,266. . . . E 2
Hendaye 10,492. . . . C 6
Héricourt 9,239. . . . G 4
Honfleur 8,125. . . . D 3
Issy-les-Moulineaux 45,702. . . . A 2
Istres 21,286. . . . F 6
Ivry-sur-Seine 55,682. . . . B 2
La Baule-Escoublac 13,151. . . . B 4
La Courneuve 33,525. . . . B 1
Langres 9,718. . . . F 4
Lapalisse 3,173. . . . E 4
La Rochelle 74,728. . . . C 4
La Roche-sur-Yon 42,026. . . . C 4
Laval 53,582. . . . C 3
Le Bourget 11,020. . . . B 1
Le Creusot 32,013. . . . F 4
Le Havre 198,700. . . . C 3
Le Mans 145,976. . . . C 3
Le Puy 22,806. . . . F 5
Le Tréport 6,330. . . . D 2
Levallois-Perret 53,485. . . . B 1
Lille 167,791. . . . E 2
Limoges 137,809. . . . D 5
Lisieux 24,454. . . . D 3
Lorient 62,207. . . . B 4
Lourdes 17,252. . . . C 6
Lunéville 21,200. . . . G 3
Lyon 410,455. . . . F 5
Mâcon 36,517. . . . F 4
Maisons-Alfort 51,041. . . . B 2
Maisons-Laffitte 22,565. . . . A 1
Mantes-la-Jolie 43,551. . . . D 3
Marmande 14,264. . . . C 5
Marseille 868,435. . . . F 6
Maubeuge 35,424. . . . F 2
Mayenne 12,156. . . . C 3
Meaux 44,386. . . . E 3
Melun 34,379. . . . E 3
Mende 10,520. . . . E 5
Menton 22,234. . . . G 6
Metz 113,236. . . . G 3
Meudon 29,356. . . . A 2
Montauban 36,122. . . . D 5
Montbéliard 31,174. . . . G 4
Montceau-les-Mines 26,877. . . . F 4
Mont-de-Marsan 25,896. . . . C 6
Mont-Dore 2,091. . . . E 5
Montfort 4,029. . . . C 3
Montluçon 49,737. . . . E 4
Montmédy 1,880. . . . F 3
Montpellier 190,423. . . . E 6
Montreuil 96,441. . . . B 2
Mont-Saint-Michel 65. . . . C 3
Mulhouse 111,742. . . . G 4
Nancy 95,654. . . . G 3
Nanterre 88,567. . . . A 1
Nantes 237,789. . . . C 4
Narbonne 38,222. . . . E 6
Nemours 11,624. . . . E 3
Neufchâtel-en-Bray 5,452. . . . D 3
Neuilly-sur-Seine 64,093. . . . A 1
Nice 331,165. . . . G 6
Nîmes 120,515. . . . F 6
Niort 56,256. . . . C 4
Nogent-le-Rotrou 11,963. . . . D 3
Noisy-le-Sec 36,821. . . . B 1
Nontron 3,407. . . . D 5
Noyon 13,949. . . . E 3
Nyons 5,219. . . . F 5
Orléans 81,615. . . . D 3
Orly 23,729. . . . B 2
Oyonnax 22,516. . . . F 4
Paris (cap.) 2,165,892. . . . B 2
Paris *10,073,059. . . . B 2
Pau 82,186. . . . C 6
Périgueux 32,632. . . . D 5
Perpignan 107,812. . . . E 6
Pessac 49,019. . . . C 5
Poitiers 76,793. . . . D 4
Pontoise 27,885. . . . E 3
Port-Vendres 4,871. . . . E 6
Privas 9,253. . . . F 5
Quimper 52,335. . . . A 4
Rambouillet 21,136. . . . D 3
Redon 9,071. . . . C 4
Reims 176,419. . . . E 3
Rennes 190,861. . . . C 3
Roanne 48,574. . . . E 4
Rochefort 25,392. . . . C 4
Roubaix 101,488. . . . E 2
Rouen 100,696. . . . D 3
Rueil-Malmaison 63,310. . . . A 2
Saint-Brieuc 48,259. . . . B 3
Saint-Cloud 28,561. . . . A 2
Saint-Denis 90,686. . . . B 1
Saint-Dizier 34,074. . . . F 3
Sainte-Mère-Église 1,205. . . . C 3
Saint-Étienne 193,938. . . . F 5
Saint-Germain-en-Laye 36,585. . . . D 3
Saint-Jean-d'Angély 9,268. . . . C 4

(continued on following page)

(continued)

Saint-Jean-de-Luz
12,124 . . . . . C 6
Saint-Lô 21,790 . . . . . C 3
Saint-Malo 44,030 . . . . . B 3
Saint-Maur-des-Fossés
80,686 . . . . . B 2
Saint-Nazaire 68,040 . . . . . B 4
Saint-Ouen 43,589 . . . . . B 1
Saint-Quentin
63,010 . . . . . E 3
Saint-Raphaël
22,221 . . . . . G 6
Saint-Tropez 4,956 . . . . . G 6
Salon-de-Provence
31,185 . . . . . F 6
Sarreguemines
23,699 . . . . . G 3
Sartrouville 46,018 . . . . . A 1
Saumur 30,037 . . . . . D 4
Sedan 23,357 . . . . . F 3
Senlis 14,345 . . . . . E 3
Sens 25,793 . . . . . E 3
Sète 39,258 . . . . . E 6
Sèvres 20,184 . . . . . A 2
Soissons 29,871 . . . . . E 3
Sotteville-les-Rouen
29,335 . . . . . D 3
Stiring-Wendel
13,563 . . . . . G 3
Strasbourg 247,068 . . . . . H 3
Tarascon 8,968 . . . . . F 6
Tarbes 50,306 . . . . . D 6
Thiers 13,492 . . . . . E 5
Thionville 34,758 . . . . . G 3
Thiviers 3,047 . . . . . D 5
Thonon-les-Bains
26,421 . . . . . G 4
Tonneins 7,162 . . . . . D 5
Tonnerre 5,744 . . . . . E 4
Toulon 177,443 . . . . . F 6
Toulouse 344,917 . . . . . D 6
Tourcoing 96,536 . . . . . E 2
Tours 131,265 . . . . . D 4
Trouville . . . . . D 3
Troyes 62,946 . . . . . F 3
Uckange 9,524 . . . . . G 3
Uzès 5,975 . . . . . F 5
Valence 66,143 . . . . . F 5
Valenciennes 39,979 . . . . . E 2
Vannes 39,214 . . . . . B 4
Vendôme 16,949 . . . . . D 4
Vénissieux 64,621 . . . . . F 5
Verdun-sur-Meuse
21,170 . . . . . F 3
Vernon 21,271 . . . . . D 3
Versailles 91,014 . . . . . A 2
Vesoul 18,257 . . . . . F 4
Vichy 30,522 . . . . . E 4
Vienne 25,414 . . . . . F 5
Villefranche 6,627 . . . . . G 6
Villefranche-sur-Saône
28,858 . . . . . F 4
Villejuif 50,970 . . . . . B 2
Villeneuve-Saint-
Georges 27,839 . . . . . E 3
Villeurbanne
115,378 . . . . . F 5
Vincennes 42,852 . . . . . B 2
Vitry-sur-Seine
84,956 . . . . . B 2
Voiron 16,383 . . . . . F 5
Yssingeaux 4,393 . . . . . F 5
Yvetot 10,574 . . . . . D 3

OTHER FEATURES

Adour (riv.) . . . . . C 6
Ain (riv.) . . . . . F 4
Aisne (riv.) . . . . . E 3
Ajaccio (gulf) . . . . . B 7
Allier (riv.) . . . . . E 5
Aube (riv.) . . . . . F 3
Auvergne (mt.) . . . . . E 5
Belle-Île (isl.) . . . . . B 4
Biscay (bay) . . . . . B 5
Blanc (mt.) . . . . . G 5
Bonifacio (strait) . . . . . B 7
Calais, Pas de (Dover)
(strait) . . . . . D 2
Causses (reg.) . . . . . D 5
Cévennes (mt.) . . . . . E 5
Charente (riv.) . . . . . C 5
Cher (riv.) . . . . . D 4
Corse (cape) . . . . . B 6
Corsica (isl.) 240,178 . . . . . B 6
Côte-d'Or (mt.) . . . . . F 4
Cotentin (pen.) . . . . . C 3
Cottian Alps (range) . . . . . G 5
Creuse (riv.) . . . . . D 4
Dordogne (riv.) . . . . . D 5
Dore Alps (mt.) . . . . . E 5
Doubs (riv.) . . . . . G 4
Dover (strait) . . . . . D 2
Drôme (riv.) . . . . . F 5
Dronne (riv.) . . . . . D 5
Durance (riv.) . . . . . F 6
English (chan.) . . . . . B 3
Eure (riv.) . . . . . D 3
Faucilles (mt.) . . . . . G 3
Forez (mt.) . . . . . E 5
Fréjus (pass) . . . . . G 5
Gard (riv.) . . . . . F 5
Garonne (riv.) . . . . . C 5
Gave de Pau (riv.) . . . . . C 6
Geneva (lake) . . . . . G 4
Gers (riv.) . . . . . D 6
Gironde (riv.) . . . . . C 5
Graian Alps (range) . . . . . G 5
Groix (isl.) 2,605 . . . . . B 4
Hague (cape) . . . . . C 3
Hérault (riv.) . . . . . E 6
Hyères (isl.) . . . . . G 6
Indre (riv.) . . . . . D 4
Isère (riv.) . . . . . F 5
Isle (riv.) . . . . . D 5
Jura (mt.) . . . . . F 4
Langres (plat.) . . . . . F 4
Limousin (reg.) . . . . . D 5
Lions (gulf) . . . . . F 6
Little Saint Bernard
(pass) . . . . . G 5
Loir (riv.) . . . . . D 4
Loire (riv.) . . . . . C 4
Lot (riv.) . . . . . D 5
Maritime Alps
(range) . . . . . G 5
Marne (riv.) . . . . . C 2
Mayenne (riv.) . . . . . C 4
Mediterranean (sea) . . . . . E 7
Médoc (reg.) . . . . . C 5
Meuse (riv.) . . . . . F 3
Mézenc (mt.) . . . . . E 5
Mont Cenis (tunnel) . . . . . G 5
Morvan (plat.) . . . . . E 4
Moselle (riv.) . . . . . G 3
Noirmoutier (isl.) . . . . . B 4
North (sea) . . . . . E 1
Oise (riv.) . . . . . E 3
Oléron (isl.) . . . . . C 5
Omaha (beach) . . . . . C 3
Orb (riv.) . . . . . E 6
Orne (riv.) . . . . . C 3
Penmarch (pt.) . . . . . A 4
Perche (reg.) . . . . . D 3
Puy-de-Dôme (mt.) . . . . . E 5
Pyrenees (range) . . . . . C 6
Ré (isl.) . . . . . C 4
Rhine (riv.) . . . . . G 3
Rhône (riv.) . . . . . F 5
Risle (riv.) . . . . . D 3
Riviera (reg.) . . . . . G 6
Saar (riv.) . . . . . G 3
Saint-Florent (gulf) . . . . . B 6
Saint-Malo (gulf) . . . . . B 3
Saône (riv.) . . . . . F 4
Sarthe (riv.) . . . . . D 4
Sein (isl.) 504 . . . . . A 3
Seine (bay) . . . . . C 3
Seine (riv.) . . . . . D 3
Sologne (reg.) . . . . . E 4
Somme (riv.) . . . . . D 2
Tarn (riv.) . . . . . E 6
Ushant (isl.) 1,255 . . . . . A 3
Utah (beach) . . . . . C 3
Vaccarès (lag.) . . . . . F 6
Vienne (riv.) . . . . . D 4
Vilaine (riv.) . . . . . C 4
Vosges (mt.) . . . . . G 3
Yonne (riv.) . . . . . E 3

Monaco

CITIES and TOWNS

Monte Carlo (cap.)
13,154 . . . . . G 6

* City and Suburbs.

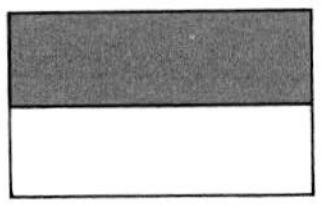

MONACO

368 acres
(149 hectares)
27,063

Wine Regions

Reims
Caen
CALVADOS
(distilled from cider)
CHAMPAGNE
ALSACE
Colmar
Chablis
BURGUNDY
Côte-d'Or
Anjou
Angers
Touraine
Tours
POUILLY
SANCERRE
QUINCY
REUILLY
LOIRE VALLEY
Beaune
Mâconnais
JURA
Mâcon
Beaujolais
COGNAC
Cognac
Médoc
BORDEAUX
Bordeaux
Bergerac
CÔTES DE DURAS
Graves
Sauternes
Valence
CÔTES DU RHÔNE
GAILLAC
ARMAGNAC
Auch
LANGUEDOC
Avignon
PROVENCE
Béziers
Toulon
Pau
JURANÇON
LIMOUX
ROUSSILLON

Climate, soil and variety of grape planted determine the quality of wine. Long, hot and fairly dry summers with cool, humid nights constitute an ideal climate. The nature of the soil is such a determining influence that identical grapes planted in Bordeaux, Burgundy and Champagne, will yield wines of widely different types.

Agriculture, Industry and Resources

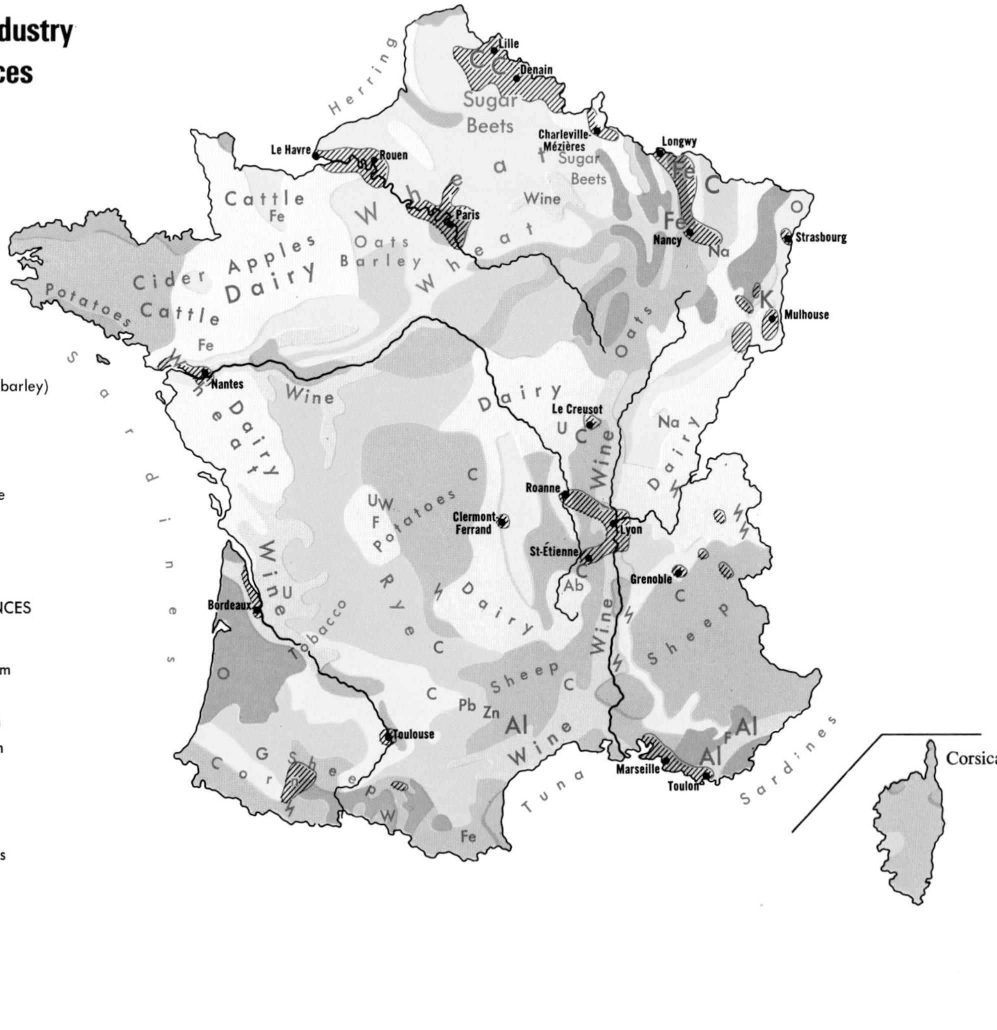
Lille
Denain
Herring
Sugar Beets
Charleville-Mézières
Longwy
Le Havre
Rouen
Cattle
Wheat
Paris
Oats Barley
Wine
Nancy
Strasbourg
Mulhouse
Cider Apples
Dairy
Potatoes
Cattle
Nantes
Dairy
Le Creusot
Roanne
Clermont-Ferrand
Lyon
St-Étienne
Grenoble
Bordeaux
Tobacco
Rye
Sheep
Toulouse
Marseille
Toulon
Tuna
Sardines
Corsica

DOMINANT LAND USE

- Cereals (chiefly wheat)
- Cereals (chiefly rye, oats, barley)
- Dairy
- Pasture Livestock
- Truck Farming, Horticulture
- Grapes, Wine
- Forests

MAJOR MINERAL OCCURRENCES

Ab	Asbestos	Na	Salt
Al	Bauxite	O	Petroleum
C	Coal	Pb	Lead
F	Fluorspar	U	Uranium
Fe	Iron Ore	W	Tungsten
G	Natural Gas	Zn	Zinc
K	Potash		

Water Power

Major Industrial Areas

ANDORRA

SPAIN

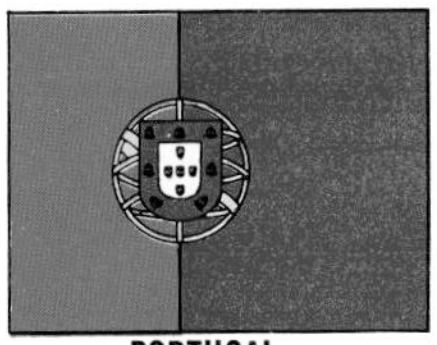
PORTUGAL

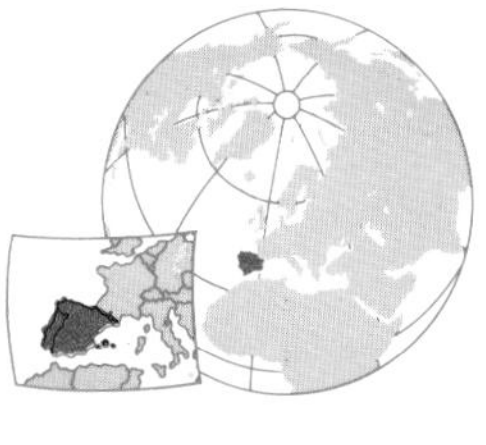

SPAIN

AREA 194,881 sq. mi. (504,742 sq. km.)
POPULATION 39,328,000
CAPITAL Madrid
LARGEST CITY Madrid
HIGHEST POINT Pico de Teide 12,172 ft. (3,710 m.) (Canary Is.); Mulhacén 11,411 ft. (3,478 m.) (mainland)
MONETARY UNIT peseta
MAJOR LANGUAGES Spanish, Catalan, Basque, Galician, Valencian
MAJOR RELIGION Roman Catholicism

PORTUGAL

AREA 35,549 sq. mi. (92,072 sq. km.)
POPULATION 10,467,000
CAPITAL Lisbon
LARGEST CITY Lisbon
HIGHEST POINT Malhão da Estrela 6,532 ft. (1,991 m.)
MONETARY UNIT escudo
MAJOR LANGUAGE Portuguese
MAJOR RELIGION Roman Catholicism

ANDORRA

AREA 188 sq. mi. (487 sq. km.)
POPULATION 50,000
CAPITAL Andorra la Vella
MONETARY UNITS French franc, Spanish peseta
MAJOR LANGUAGE Catalan
MAJOR RELIGION Roman Catholicism

GIBRALTAR

AREA 2.28 sq. mi. (5.91 sq. km.)
POPULATION 31,000
CAPITAL Gibraltar
MONETARY UNIT pound sterling
MAJOR LANGUAGES English, Spanish
MAJOR RELIGION Roman Catholicism

SPAIN

REGIONS

Andalusia 6,440,985 .... D4
Aragón 1,196,952 .... F2
Asturias 1,129,556 .... C1
Balearic Islands 655,909 .... H3
Basque Country 2,141,809 .... E1
Canary Islands 1,367,646 .... F4
Cantabria 513,115 .... D1
Castile and León 2,583,137 .... D2
Castile-La Mancha 1,648,584 .... E3
Catalonia 5,956,414 .... G2
Estremadura 1,064,968 .... C3
Galicia 2,811,912 .... B1
La Rioja 254,349 .... E1
Madrid 4,686,895 .... E2
Murcia 955,487 .... F4
Navarre 509,002 .... F1
Valencia 3,646,778 .... F3

PROVINCES

Álava 257,850 .... E1
Albacete 339,373 .... E3
Alicante 1,149,181 .... F3
Almería 410,831 .... E4
Ávila 183,586 .... D2
Badajoz 643,519 .... C3
Baleares 655,509 .... H3
Barcelona 4,623,204 .... G2
Burgos 363,523 .... E1
Cáceres 421,449 .... C3
Cádiz 988,388 .... D4
Castellón 431,893 .... G2
Ciudad Real 475,129 .... D3
Córdoba 720,823 .... D3
Cuenca 215,975 .... E2
Girona (Gerona) 467,000 .... H1
Granada 758,618 .... E4
Guadalajara 143,473 .... E2
Guipúzcoa 694,681 .... E1
Huelva 418,584 .... C4
Huesca 214,907 .... F1
Jaén 639,821 .... E4
La Coruña 1,093,121 .... B1
Las Palmas 708,762 .... C4
León 523,607 .... C1
Lleida (Lérida) 353,160 .... G2
Logroño 254,349 .... E1
Lugo 405,365 .... C1
Madrid 4,686,895 .... E2
Málaga 1,025,609 .... D4
Murcia 955,487 .... F4
Navarra 509,002 .... F1
Orense 430,159 .... C1
Oviedo 1,129,556 .... C1
Palencia 188,479 .... D1
Pontevedra 883,267 .... B1
Salamanca 364,305 .... C2
Santa Cruz de Tenerife 658,884 .... B5
Santander 513,115 .... D1
Segovia 149,361 .... D2
Sevilla 1,478,311 .... D4
Soria 100,719 .... E2
Tarragona 513,050 .... G2
Teruel 153,457 .... F2
Toledo 474,634 .... D3
Valencia 2,065,704 .... F3
Valladolid 481,786 .... D2
Vizcaya 1,189,278 .... E1
Zamora 227,771 .... D2
Zaragoza 828,588 .... F2

CITIES and TOWNS

Adra 10,851 .... E4
Aguilar 12,893 .... D4
Aguilas 15,525 .... F4
Albacete 82,607 .... F3
Alburquerque 7,530 .... C3
Alcalá de Guadaira 28,781 .... D4
Alcalá de Henares 59,783 .... E2
Alcalá de los Gazules 5,262 .... D4
Alcalá la Real 9,849 .... E4
Alcanar 5,961 .... G2
Alcañiz 10,229 .... F2
Alcantarilla 19,895 .... F4
Alcaudete 8,557 .... E4
Alcázar de San Juan 24,620 .... E3
Alcira 30,493 .... F3
Alcora 6,711 .... F2
Alcoy 61,371 .... F3
Alfaro 8,766 .... F1
Algeciras 74,754 .... D4
Algemesí 21,158 .... F3
Alhama de Granada 6,148 .... E4
Alhama de Murcia 9,274 .... F4
Alicante 177,918 .... F3
Almadén 10,713 .... D3
Almagro 9,066 .... E3
Almansa 16,965 .... F3
Almendralejo 21,929 .... C3
Almería 104,008 .... E4
Almodóvar del Campo 7,310 .... D3
Almonte del Río 9,960 .... C4
Almuñécar 7,812 .... E4
Álora 8,209 .... D4
Altea 7,262 .... G3
Amposta 11,767 .... G2
Andorra 6,485 .... F2
Andújar 25,962 .... D3
Antequera 28,039 .... D4
Aracena 5,390 .... C4
Aranda de Duero 18,183 .... E2
Aranjuez 28,559 .... E2
Archena 7,118 .... F3
Archidona 6,084 .... D4
Arcos de la Frontera 16,217 .... D4
Arenys de Mar 8,325 .... H2
Arganda 11,876 .... G4
Arnedo 9,809 .... E1
Arrecife 21,310 .... G4
Arroyo de la Luz 8,130 .... C3
Arucas 9,095 .... G4
Aspe 13,229 .... F3
Astorga 11,794 .... C1
Ávila de los Caballeros 30,958 .... D2
Avilés 67,186 .... C1
Ayamonte 9,897 .... C4
Azpeitia 7,835 .... E1
Azuaga 10,719 .... D3
Badajoz 80,793 .... C3
Badalona 162,888 .... H2
Baena 16,496 .... D4
Baeza 12,607 .... E4
Bailén 13,207 .... E3
Balaguer 11,676 .... G2
Banyoles 9,807 .... H1
Baracaldo 108,757 .... E1
Barbastro 13,243 .... F1
Barcarrota 5,012 .... C3
Barcelona 1,741,144 .... J1
Barcelona‡ 2,000,000 .... H2
Baza 14,290 .... E4
Béjar 16,804 .... D2
Benavente 11,779 .... D2
Benicarló 12,831 .... G2
Berga 11,163 .... G1
Berja 7,081 .... E4
Bermeo 16,714 .... E1
Betanzos 7,283 .... B1
Bilbao 393,179 .... E1
Bilbao‡ 450,000 .... E1
Binéfar 6,821 .... G2
Blanes 15,810 .... H2
Bujalance 8,236 .... D4
Bullas 8,131 .... F3
Burgos 118,366 .... E1
Burriana 21,298 .... F3
Cabeza del Buey 8,704 .... D3
Cabra 16,177 .... D4
Cáceres 53,108 .... C3
Cádiz 135,743 .... C4
Calahorra 16,315 .... E1
Calasparra 7,238 .... F3
Calatayud 16,524 .... F2
Calella 9,696 .... H2
Callosa de Ensarriá 5,701 .... G3
Calzada de Calatrava 5,751 .... E3
Campanario 7,722 .... D3
Campillos 7,014 .... D4
Campo de Criptana 12,604 .... E3
Candás 5,517 .... D1
Candeleda 5,153 .... D2
Cangas de Narcea 4,826 .... C1
Caniles 5,099 .... E4
Caravaca de le Cruz 10,411 .... E3
Carballo 5,542 .... B1
Carcagente 18,223 .... F3
Carmona 22,832 .... D4
Cartagena 52,312 .... F4
Caspe 8,766 .... F2
Castellón de la Plana 79,773 .... G2
Castro del Río 10,087 .... D4
Castro-Urdiales 8,369 .... E1
Castuera 8,060 .... D3
Caudete 7,332 .... F3
Cazalla de la Sierra 5,382 .... D4
Cazorla 6,938 .... E4
Cehegín 9,661 .... F3
Cervera 5,693 .... G2
Ceuta 65,264 .... D5
Chiclana de la Frontera 22,986 .... C4
Cieza 22,929 .... F3
Ciudad Real 39,931 .... D3
Ciudad-Rodrigo 11,694 .... C2
Cocentaina 8,375 .... F3
Coín 14,190 .... D4
Colmenar Viejo 12,886 .... E2
Constantina 10,227 .... D4
Consuegra 10,026 .... E3
Córdoba 216,049 .... D4
Corella 5,850 .... F1
Coria 8,083 .... C3
Coria del Río 18,085 .... C4
Corral de Almaguer 8,006 .... E3
Crevillente 15,749 .... F3
Cuéllar 6,118 .... D2
Cuenca 33,980 .... E2
Cullera 15,128 .... F3
Daimiel 17,710 .... E3
Denia 14,514 .... G3
Don Benito 21,351 .... C3
Dos Hermanas 36,921 .... D4
Durango 20,403 .... E1
Écija 27,295 .... D4
Eibar 36,729 .... E1
Ejea de los Caballeros 9,766 .... F1
El Arahal 14,703 .... D4
Elche 101,271 .... F3
Elda 41,404 .... F3
El Ferrol 75,464 .... B1
Elizondo 2,516 .... F1
El Puerto de Santa María 36,451 .... C4
El Vendrell 7,951 .... G2
Espejo 5,925 .... D4
Estella 10,371 .... E1
Estepa 9,376 .... D4
Estepona 18,560 .... D4
Felanitx 9,100 .... H3
Figueres 22,087 .... H1
Fraga 9,665 .... G2
Fregenal de la Sierra 6,826 .... C3
Fuengirola 20,597 .... D4
Fuente de Cantos 5,967 .... C3
Gandía 30,702 .... F3
Gerona (Girona) 37,095 .... H1
Getafe 68,680 .... G4
Gijón 159,806 .... D1
Girona 37,095 .... H2
Granada 185,799 .... E4
Granollers 30,066 .... H2
Guadalajara 30,924 .... E2
Guadix 15,311 .... E4
Guareña 7,706 .... C3
Guernica y Luno 12,046 .... E1
Haro 8,393 .... E1
Hellín 15,934 .... F3
Herencia 8,212 .... E3
Hinojosa del Duque 9,873 .... D3
Hospitalet 241,978 .... H1
Huelma 5,260 .... E4
Huelva 96,689 .... C4
Huercal-Overa 5,158 .... F4
Huesca 33,076 .... F1
Huéscar 6,384 .... E4
Ibiza 16,943 .... G3
Igualada 27,941 .... G2
Inca 16,930 .... H3
Irún 38,014 .... F1
Iscar 5,192 .... D2
Isla Cristina 11,402 .... C4
Jaca 9,936 .... F1
Jaén 71,145 .... E4
Jaraíz de la Vera 6,379 .... D2
Játiva 20,934 .... F3
Jávea 6,228 .... G3
Jerez de la Frontera 112,411 .... C4
Jerez de los Caballeros 8,607 .... C3
Jijona 8,117 .... F3
Jódar 11,973 .... E4
Jumilla 16,407 .... F3
La Bañeza 8,480 .... D1
La Bisbal 6,374 .... H2
La Carolina 13,138 .... E3
La Coruña 184,372 .... B1
La Línea de la Concepción 51,021 .... D4
La Orotava 8,246 .... F5
La Palma del Condado 9,256 .... C4
La Puebla 9,923 .... H3
La Puebla de Montalbán 6,629 .... D3
La Rambla 6,525 .... D4
Laredo 9,114 .... E1
La Roda 11,460 .... E3
La Seu d'Urgell 6,604 .... G1
La Solana 13,894 .... E3
Las Palmas de Gran Canaria 260,368 .... G5
Las Pedroñeras 5,846 .... E3
La Unión 9,998 .... F4
Lebrija 15,081 .... C4
Leganés 57,537 .... G4
León 99,702 .... D1
Lérida (Lleida) 73,148 .... G2
Linares 45,330 .... E3
Liria 11,323 .... F3
Lleida 73,148 .... G2
Llerena 5,728 .... C3
Llodio 15,587 .... E1
Lluchmayor 9,630 .... H3
Logroño 83,117 .... E1
Loja 11,549 .... D4
Lora del Río 15,741 .... D4
Lorca 25,208 .... F4
Los Santos de Maimona 7,899 .... C3
Los Yébenes 5,477 .... D3
Lucena 21,527 .... D4
Lugo 53,504 .... C1
Madrid (cap.) 3,146,071 .... G4
Madrid‡ 3,500,000 .... F4
Madridejos 9,948 .... E3
Madroñera 5,397 .... D3
Mahón 17,802 .... J3
Málaga 334,988 .... D4
Malpartida de Cáceres 5,054 .... C3
Manacor 20,266 .... H3
Mancha Real 7,547 .... E4
Manlleu 13,169 .... H1
Manresa 52,526 .... G2
Manzanares 15,024 .... E3
Marbella 19,648 .... D4
Marchena 16,227 .... D4
Marín 10,948 .... B1
Martos 16,395 .... E4
Mataró 73,129 .... H2
Medina del Campo 16,345 .... D2
Medina-Sidonia 7,523 .... D4
Mérida 36,916 .... C3
Miajadas 8,042 .... C3
Mieres 22,790 .... D1
Miranda de Ebro 29,355 .... E1
Moguer 7,629 .... C4
Mollerusa 6,685 .... G2
Monesterio 5,923 .... C3
Monforte 14,002 .... C1
Monóvar 9,071 .... F3
Montehermoso 5,952 .... C2
Montijo 11,931 .... C3
Montilla 18,670 .... D4
Montoro 9,295 .... D3
Monzón 14,089 .... G2
Mora 10,523 .... E3
Moratalla 5,101 .... E3
Morón de la Frontera 25,662 .... D4
Mota del Cuervo 5,130 .... E3
Motril 25,121 .... E4
Mula 9,168 .... F3
Munera 5,003 .... E3
Murcia 102,242 .... F4
Navalmoral de la Mata 9,650 .... D3
Nerja 7,413 .... E4
Nerva 10,830 .... C4
Novelda 16,867 .... F3
Nules 9,027 .... F3
Ocaña 5,603 .... E3

(continued on following page)

Agriculture, Industry and Resources

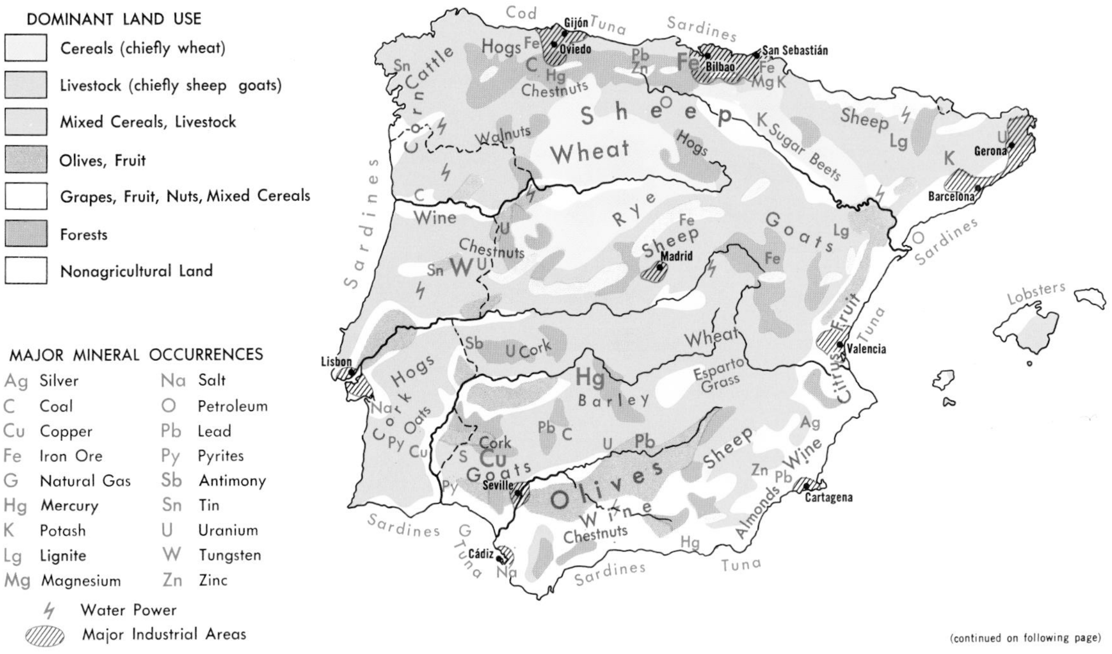
DOMINANT LAND USE
Cereals (chiefly wheat)
Livestock (chiefly sheep goats)
Mixed Cereals, Livestock
Olives, Fruit
Grapes, Fruit, Nuts, Mixed Cereals
Forests
Nonagricultural Land
MAJOR MINERAL OCCURRENCES
Ag Silver
C Coal
Cu Copper
Fe Iron Ore
G Natural Gas
Hg Mercury
K Potash
Lg Lignite
Mg Magnesium
Na Salt
O Petroleum
Pb Lead
Py Pyrites
Sb Antimony
Sn Tin
U Uranium
W Tungsten
Zn Zinc
Water Power
Major Industrial Areas
Cod
Tuna
Sardines
Gijón
Oviedo
Bilbao
San Sebastián
Hogs
Cattle
Chestnuts
Sheep
Walnuts
Wheat
Sugar Beets
Gerona
Barcelona
Corn
Wine
Rye
Goats
Madrid
Lobsters
Fruit
Valencia
Lisbon
Cork
Barley
Esparto Grass
Oats
Olives
Seville
Almonds
Cartagena
Cádiz

(continued on following page)

OTHER FEATURES

PORTUGAL

DISTRICTS

CITIES and TOWNS

Topography

0 50 100 MI.
0 50 100 KM.
Cape Finisterre
CANTABRIAN MTS.
PYRENEES
Bilbao
Miño
Sil
Esla
Pisuerga
Douro
Porto
Douro
Tormes
SA. DE GUADARRAMA
Aragón
Ebro
Cinca
Segre
Saragossa
Barcelona
IBERIAN MTS.
MESETA
Madrid
SA. DE GATA
SA. DA ESTRELA
Malhão de Estrela 6,532 ft. (1991 m.)
Tagus
Lisbon
Júcar
Valencia
Turia
Gulf of Valencia
Minorca
Majorca
Ibiza
BALEARIC ISLANDS
C. de la Nao
Guadiana
Sado
SIERRA MORENA
Segura
Córdoba
Genil
Guadalquivir
Seville
SA. NEVADA
Mulhacén
Málaga
Cape St. Vincent
Gulf of Cadiz
Europa Pt.
Below Sea Level
100 m. 328 ft.
200 m. 656 ft.
500 m. 1,640 ft.
1,000 m. 3,281 ft.
2,000 m. 6,562 ft.
5,000 m. 16,404 ft.

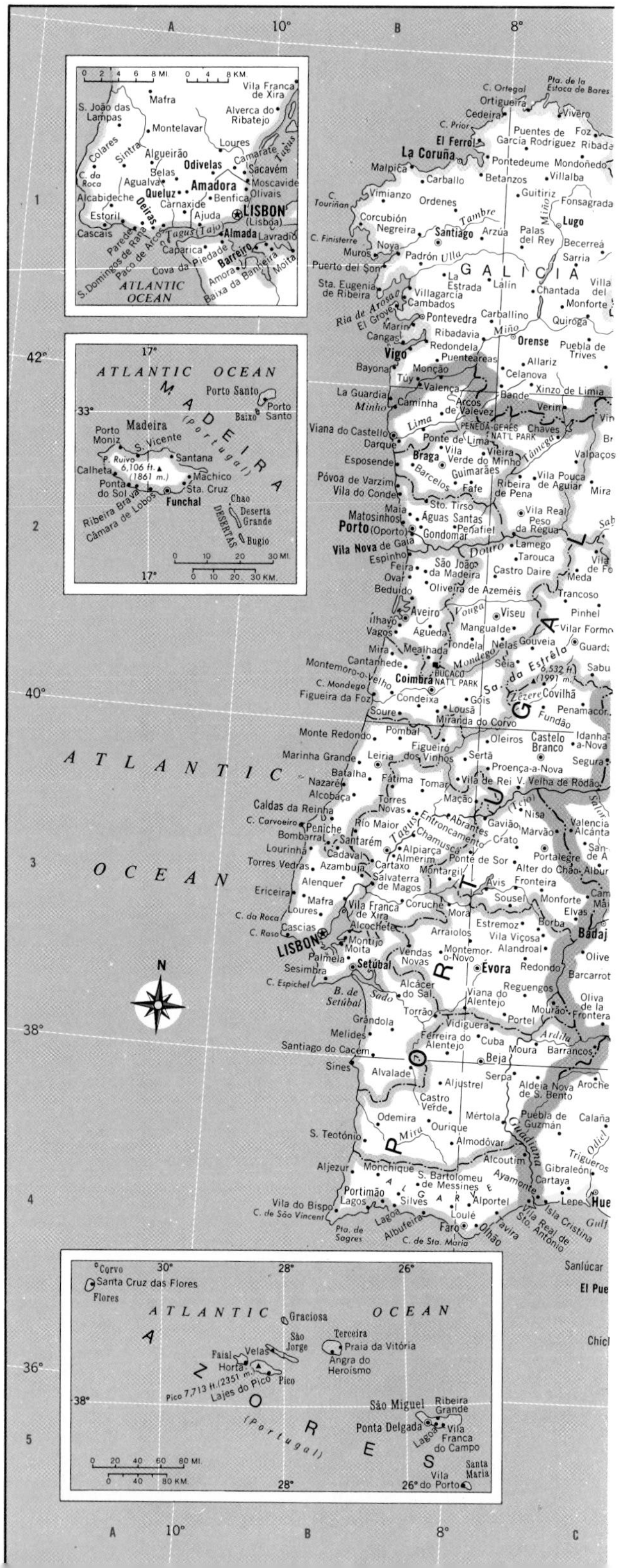
A
10°
B
8°
C
1
2
3
4
5
42°
40°
38°
36°
ATLANTIC OCEAN
N
0 2 4 6 8 MI.
0 4 8 KM.
Vila Franca de Xira
Mafra
S. João das Lampas
Alverca do Ribatejo
Montelavar
Loures
Colares
Sintra
Algueirão
Odivelas
Sacavém
Moscavide
Olivais
C. da Roca
Agualva
Queluz
Amadora
Alcabideche
Carnaxide
Benfica
Caparica
Ajuda
LISBON (Lisboa)
Estoril
Oeiras
Cascais
Almada
Lavradio
Barreiro
Amora
Cova da Piedade
ATLANTIC OCEAN
17°
33°
Porto Santo
Porto Santo
Baixo
MADEIRA (Portugal)
Porto Moniz
S. Vicente
Pico Ruivo 6,106 ft. (1861 m.)
Santana
Calheta
Machico
Ponta do Sol
Funchal
Sta. Cruz
Ribeira Brava
Câmara de Lobos
Chao
Deserta Grande
Bugio
0 10 20 30 MI.
0 10 20 30 KM.
C. Ortegal
Pta. de la Estaca de Bares
Ortigueira
Cedeira
Viveiro
C. Prior
El Ferrol
Puentes de García Rodríguez
La Coruña
Malpica
Carballo
Betanzos
Pontedeume
Mondoñedo
Villalba
C. Touriñan
Vimianzo
Ordenes
Guitiriz
Fonsagrada
Corcubión
Tambre
Lugo
C. Finisterre
Negreira
Santiago
Arzúa
Palas del Rey
Becerreá
Noya
Padrón
Ulla
Sarria
Muros
Puerto del Son
GALICIA
Sta. Eugenia de Ribeira
Villagarcía
Estrada
Lalín
Chantada
Monforte
Cambados
Ría de Arosa
Pontevedra
Carballino
Quiroga
Marín
Ribadavia
Miño
Orense
Puebla de Trives
Cangas
Redondela
Vigo
Puenteareas
Allariz
Bayona
Monção
Celanova
Tuy
Valença
Xinzo de Limia
La Guardia
Caminha
Arcos de Valdevez
Bande
Minho
Verín
Lima
Viana do Castelo
Chaves
Ponte de Lima
Braga
Vila Verde do Minho
Esposende
Guimarães
Póvoa de Varzim
Vila do Conde
Barcelos
Ribeira de Pena
Vila Pouca de Aguiar
Sto. Tirso
Matosinhos
Águas Santas
Vila Real
Peso da Regua
Porto (Oporto)
Gondomar
Penafiel
Vila Nova de Gaia
Douro
Lamego
Espinho
Tarouca
Feira
São João da Madeira
Castro Daire
Ovar
Oliveira de Azeméis
Trancoso
Ílhavo
Aveiro
Vouga
Viseu
Pinhel
Vagos
Águeda
Mangualde
Vilar Formoso
Mira
Mealhada
Tondela
Nelas
Gouveia
Guarda
Mondego
Seia
Cantanhede
Coimbra
BUÇACO NAT'L PARK
C. Mondego
Figueira da Foz
Condeixa
Soure
Lousã
Miranda do Corvo
Covilhã
Penamacor
Fundão
Monte Redondo
Pombal
Oleiros
Castelo Branco
Idanha-a-Nova
Figueiró dos Vinhos
Sertã
Marinha Grande
Leiria
Segura
Proença-a-Nova
Batalha
Nazaré
Fátima
Tomar
Vila de Rei
V. Velha de Ródão
Alcobaça
Torres Novas
Caldas da Rainha
Mação
Nisa
C. Carvoeiro
Peniche
Rio Maior
Abrantes
Gavião
Marvão
Valencia de Alcántara
Bombarral
Santarém
Chamusca
Crato
Lourinhã
Cadaval
Alpiarça
Portalegre
Torres Vedras
Azambuja
Almeirim
Ponte de Sor
Alter do Chão
Cartaxo
Montargil
Avis
Fronteira
Alenquer
Salvaterra de Magos
Ericeira
Mafra
Vila Franca de Xira
Coruche
Sousel
Monforte
Elvas
Loures
C. da Roca
Alcochete
Mora
Estremoz
Borba
Badajoz
Cascais
Arraiolos
Vila Viçosa
C. Raso
LISBON
Montijo
Moita
Vendas Novas
Montemor-o-Novo
Alandroal
Olivenza
Palmela
Sesimbra
Setúbal
Évora
Redondo
C. Espichel
Barcarrota
B. de Setúbal
Sado
Alcácer do Sal
Viana do Alentejo
Reguengos
Mourão
Oliva de la Frontera
Torrão
Portel
Grândola
Vidigueira
Ferreira do Alentejo
Cuba
Ardila
Melides
Santiago do Cacém
Beja
Moura
Barrancos
Sines
Alvalade
Serpa
Aljustrel
Aldeia Nova de S. Bento
Aroche
Castro Verde
Odemira
Ourique
Mértola
Puebla de Guzmán
Calañas
S. Teotónio
Mira
Almodôvar
Guadiana
Trigueros
Aljezur
Monchique
Alcoutim
Gibraleón
Cartaya
S. Bartolomeu de Messines
Portimão
Lagos
Silves
ALGARVE
Alportel
Lepe
Huelva
Vila do Bispo
C. de São Vincent
Loulé
Faro
Olhão
Tavira
Vila Real de Sto. António
Isla Cristina
Pta. de Sagres
Albufeira
C. de Sta. Maria
Gulf
Sanlúcar
El Puerto
Chiclana
PORTUGAL
ATLANTIC OCEAN
30°
28°
26°
Corvo
Santa Cruz das Flores
Flores
Graciosa
São Jorge
Terceira
Praia da Vitória
Angra do Heroismo
Faial
Velas
Horta
Pico 7,713 ft. (2351 m.)
Lajes do Pico
Pico
AZORES (Portugal)
38°
São Miguel
Ribeira Grande
Ponta Delgada
Vila Franca do Campo
Santa Maria
Vila do Porto
0 20 40 60 80 MI.
0 40 80 KM.

Baixa da Banheira 18,550 .... A1
Barreiro 53,690 .... A1
Beja 14,760 .... C3
Belas 12,001 .... A1
Benfica 39,459 .... A1
Braga 48,735 .... B2
Bragança 9,310 .... C2
Caldas da Rainha 13,070 .... B3
Câmara de Lobos 14,068 .... A2
Caparica 13,315 .... A1
Carnaxide 38,309 .... A1
Cascais 14,925 .... A1
Castelo Branco 18,740 .... C3
Chaves 11,465 .... C2
Coimbra 55,985 .... B2
Coruche 17,461 .... B3
Cova da Piedade 21,000 .... A1
Covilhã 26,530 .... C2
Elvas 10,305 .... C3
Espinho 11,745 .... B2
Estoril 15,740 .... A1
Évora 23,665 .... C3
Fafe 8,142 .... B2
Faro 20,470 .... B4
Figueira da Foz 10,485 .... B2
Funchal 38,340 .... A2
Gondomar 14,105 .... B2
Grândola 9,698 .... B3
Guarda 9,735 .... C2
Guimarães 24,280 .... B2
Ílhavo 11,083 .... B2
Lagos 10,359 .... B4
Lamego 10,350 .... C2
Lisbon (Lisboa) (cap.) 769,410 .... A1
Lisbon‡ 1,100,000 .... A1
Loulé 12,777 .... B4
Machico 10,905 .... A2
Marinha Grande 18,548 .... B3
Matosinhos 22,505 .... B2
Mira 12,740 .... B2
Monchique 8,155 .... B4
Montemor-o-Novo 9,284 .... B3
Montijo 26,730 .... B3
Moscavide 21,765 .... A1
Moura 9,351 .... C3
Nazaré 8,553 .... B3
Odivelas 26,020 .... A1
Oeiras 14,880 .... A1
Olhão 11,155 .... C4
Olivais 55,138 .... A1
Oporto (Porto) 300,925 .... B2
Ovar 16,004 .... B2
Paço de Arcos 11,791 .... A1
Peniche 12,555 .... B3
Pombal 12,508 .... B3
Ponta Delgada 20,195 .... B5
Ponte de Sor 9,951 .... B3
Portalegre 10,970 .... C3
Portimão 10,300 .... B4
Porto 300,925 .... B2
Póvoa de Varzim 17,415 .... B2
Queluz 25,845 .... A1
Rio Maior 10,206 .... B3
Sacavém 12,625 .... A1
Santarém 16,850 .... B3
São Brás de Alportel (Alportel) 7,632 .... C4
São João da Madeira 14,225 .... B2
Sesimbra 16,614 .... B3
Setúbal 49,670 .... B3
Silves 9,493 .... B4
Sintra 15,994 .... A1
Tavira 10,263 .... C4
Tomar 10,905 .... B3
Torres Novas 13,806 .... B3
Torres Vedras 14,833 .... B3
Vendas Novas 8,979 .... B3
Viana do Castello 12,510 .... B2
Vila do Conde 16,485 .... B2
Vila do Porto 4,149 .... B5
Vila Franca de Xira 13,070 .... B3
Vila Nova de Foz Côa 2,439 .... C2
Vila Nova de Gaia 50,805 .... B2
Vila Real 10,050 .... C2
Vila Real de Santo António 10,320 .... C4
Vila Velha de Ródão 2,658 .... C3
Viseu 16,140 .... C2

OTHER FEATURES

Algarve (reg.) B4
Atlantic Ocean A3
Azores (isls.) B4
Baixo (isl.) A2
Bugio (isl.) B2
Carvoeiro (cape) B3
Chao (isl.) A2
Corvo (isl.) A4
Deserta Grande (isl.) B2
Desertas (isls.) A2
Douro (riv.) B2
Espichel (cape) B3
Estrela, Serra da (mts.) C2
Faial (isl.) B4
Flores (isl.) A4
Graciosa (isl.) B4
Guadiana (riv.) C4
Lima (riv.) B2
Madeira (isl.) A2
Minho (riv.) B2
Mira (riv.) B4
Mondego (riv.) B2
Mondego (cape) B2
Pico (isl.) B4
Porto Santo (isl.) A2
Roca (cape) B3
Sado (riv.) B3
Santa Maria (cape) C4
Santa Maria (isl.) C5
São Jorge (isl.) B4
São Miguel (isl.) B5
São Vincent (cape) B4
Setúbal (bay) B3
Tagus (riv.) B3
Tâmega (riv.) C2
Terceira (isl.) B4

ANDORRA

CITIES and TOWNS

Andorra la Vella (cap.) 12,000 .... G1

GIBRALTAR

CITIES and TOWNS

Gibraltar 31,000 .... D4

OTHER FEATURES

Europa (pt.) D4

‡Population of metropolitan area

Spain and Portugal
CONIC PROJECTION
SCALE OF MILES
SCALE OF KILOMETERS
Capitals of Countries
District, Region, and Community Capitals
Provincial Capitals
International Boundaries
Other Boundaries
PORTUGAL is divided into 18 mainland districts bearing the same names as their respective capitals. The Azores and Madeira are offshore autonomous regions.
SPAIN is divided into 17 autonomous communities consisting of one or more provinces. The provinces bear the same names as their capitals except for Alava (capital Vitoria), Asturias (Oviedo), Balearic Islands (Palma), Cantabria (Santander), Guipúzcoa (San Sebastián), La Rioja (Logroño), Navarre (Pamplona) and Vizcaya (Bilbao).
© Copyright HAMMOND INCORPORATED, Maplewood, N. J.
BAY OF BISCAY
FRANCE
SPAIN
ANDORRA
MADRID
BARCELONA
CATALONIA
ARAGON
NAVARRE
BASQUE COUNTRY
CANTABRIA
ASTURIAS
CASTILE AND LEÓN
CASTILE - LA MANCHA
ESTREMADURA
VALENCIA
MURCIA
ANDALUSIA
LA RIOJA
MEDITERRANEAN SEA
BALEARIC ISLANDS (BALEARES)
Gulf of Valencia
Majorca (Mallorca)
Minorca (Menorca)
Ibiza
Formentera
COSTA DEL SOL
COSTA BRAVA
Strait of Gibraltar
GIBRALTAR (U.K.)
MOROCCO
AFRICA
Tangier
Ceuta (Sp.)
CANARY ISLANDS (Spain)
ATLANTIC OCEAN
Tenerife
Gran Canaria
Fuerteventura
Lanzarote
La Palma
Gomera
Hierro
Longitude West of Greenwich
Longitude East of Greenwich

Italy
CONIC PROJECTION
SCALE OF MILES
0 20 40 60 80 100
SCALE OF KILOMETERS
0 20 40 60 80 100
Capitals of Countries
Regional Capitals
Provincial Capitals
International Boundaries
Regional Boundaries
The regions are subdivided into provinces bearing the same names as their respective capitals, except:
PROVINCE
CAPITAL
MASSA-CARRARA
Massa
PESARO-URBINO
Pesaro
VATICAN CITY
ROME AND ENVIRONS
SWITZERLAND
AUSTRIA
GERMANY
LIECHTENSTEIN
FRANCE
SLOVENIA
CROATIA
BOSNIA & HERZEGOVINA
YUGO.
TUNISIA
MALTA
SAN MARINO
MONACO
CORSICA
SARDINIA
SICILY
LIGURIAN SEA
TYRRHENIAN SEA
MEDITERRANEAN SEA
ADRIATIC SEA
IONIAN SEA
TUSCAN ARCH.
Gulf of Genoa
Gulf of Venice
Gulf of Gaeta
Gulf of Salerno
Gulf of Taranto
G. of Manfredonia
Gulf of Squillace
Gulf of Sant'Eufemia
Strait of Messina
Strait of Otranto
Strait of Sicily
Str. of Bonifacio
Malta Channel
Gulf of Hammamet
G. of Tunis
LIPARI ISLANDS
EGADI ISLANDS
PONTINE ISLANDS
PELAGIE ISLANDS
Pantelleria
Lampedusa
Linosa
Ustica
Elba
Capri
Ischia
Alps
Apennines
Dolomite Alps
Lake Como
Lake Maggiore
Lake Garda
Lake Constance
Po
Adige
Arno
Tiber
MILAN
ROME
NAPLES
Turin
Genoa
Venice
Florence
Bologna
Trieste
Trento
Bolzano
Aosta
Ancona
Perugia
L'Aquila
Campobasso
Potenza
Bari
Catanzaro
Reggio di Calabria
Palermo
Messina
Catania
Cagliari
Sassari
Zürich
Bern
Innsbruck
Ljubljana
Zagreb
Tunis
Valletta
Nice
Ajaccio
Bastia
Mt. Blanc 15,771 ft. (4807 m.)
Etna 11,053 ft. (3369 m.)
Vesuvius 4,190 ft. (1277 m.)
Longitude East of Greenwich
© Copyright HAMMOND INCORPORATED, Maplewood, N. J.

VATICAN CITY

AREA 108.7 acres (44 hectares)
POPULATION 1,000

SAN MARINO

AREA 23.4 sq. mi. (60.6 sq. km.)
POPULATION 23,000

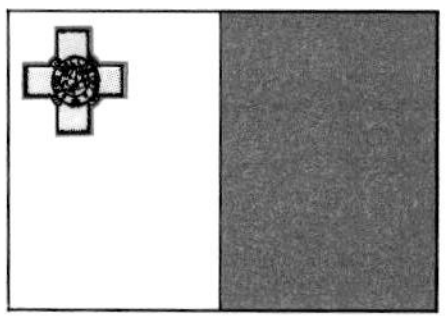

MALTA

AREA 122 sq. mi. (316 sq. km.)
POPULATION 353,000
CAPITAL Valletta
LARGEST CITY Sliema
HIGHEST POINT 787 ft. (240 m.)
MONETARY UNIT Maltese lira
MAJOR LANGUAGES Maltese, English
MAJOR RELIGION Roman Catholicism

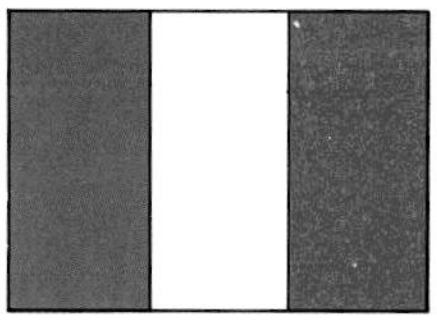

ITALY

AREA 116,303 sq. mi. (301,225 sq. km.)
POPULATION 57,574,000
CAPITAL Rome
LARGEST CITY Rome
HIGHEST POINT Dufourspitze (Mte. Rosa) 15,203 ft. (4,634 m.)
MONETARY UNIT lira
MAJOR LANGUAGE Italian
MAJOR RELIGION Roman Catholicism

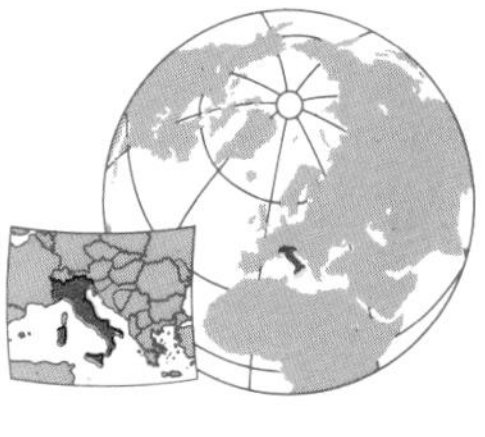

ITALY

REGIONS

Abruzzi 1,217,791 ... D3
Aosta 112,353 ... A2
Apulia (Puglia) 3,871,617 ... F4
Basilicata 610,186 ... F4
Calabria 2,061,182 ... F5
Campania 5,463,134 ... E4
Emilia-Romagna 3,957,513 ... C2
Friuli-Venezia Giulia 1,233,984 ... D1
Latium (Lazio) 5,001,684 ... D3
Liguria 1,807,893 ... B2
Lombardy 8,891,652 ... B2
Marche 1,412,404 ... D3
Molise 328,371 ... E4
Piedmont 4,479,031 ... A2
Sardinia 1,594,175 ... B4
Sicily 4,906,878 ... D6
Trentino-Alto Adige 873,413 ... C1
Tuscany 3,581,051 ... C3
Umbria 807,552 ... D3
Veneto 4,345,047 ... C2

PROVINCES

Agrigento 466,495 ... D6
Alessandria 466,102 ... B2
Ancona 433,417 ... D3
Arezzo 313,157 ... C3
Ascoli Piceno 352,567 ... D3
Asti 215,382 ... B2
Avellino 434,021 ... E4
Bari 1,464,627 ... F4
Belluno 220,335 ... D1
Benevento 289,143 ... E4
Bergamo 896,117 ... B2
Bologna 930,284 ... C2
Bolzano-Bozen 430,568 ... C1
Brescia 1,017,093 ... C2
Brindisi 391,064 ... G4
Cagliari 730,473 ... B5
Caltanissetta 285,829 ... D6
Campobasso 235,847 ... E4
Caserta 755,628 ... E4
Catania 1,005,577 ... E6
Catanzaro 744,834 ... F5
Chieti 370,534 ... E3
Como 755,979 ... B2
Cosenza 743,255 ... F5
Cremona 332,236 ... B2
Cuneo 548,452 ... A2
Enna 190,939 ... E6
Ferrara 381,118 ... C2
Florence 1,202,013 ... C3
Foggia 681,595 ... E4
Forlì 599,420 ... D2
Frosinone 460,395 ... D4
Genoa 1,045,109 ... B2
Gorizia 144,726 ... D2
Grosseto 220,905 ... C3
Imperia 223,738 ... B3
Isernia 92,524 ... E4
L'Aquila 291,742 ... D3
La Spezia 241,371 ... B2
Latina 434,086 ... D4
Lecce 762,017 ... G4
Livorno (Leghorn) 346,657 ... C3
Lucca 385,876 ... C3
Macerata 292,932 ... D3
Mantua 377,158 ... C2
Massa-Carrara 203,530 ... C2
Matera 203,570 ... F4
Messina 669,323 ... E5
Milan 4,018,108 ... B2
Modena 596,025 ... C2
Naples 2,970,563 ... E4
Novara 507,367 ... B2
Nuoro 274,817 ... B4
Padua 809,667 ... C2
Palermo 1,198,575 ... D5
Parma 400,192 ... C2
Pavia 512,895 ... B2
Perugia 580,988 ... D3
Pesaro e Urbino 333,488 ... D3
Pescara 286,240 ... E3
Piacenza 278,424 ... B2
Pisa 388,800 ... C3
Pistoia 264,995 ... C3
Pordenone 275,888 ... D2
Potenza 406,616 ... E4
Ragusa 274,583 ... E6
Ravenna 358,654 ... D2
Reggio di Calabria 573,093 ... E5
Reggio nell'Emilia 413,396 ... C2
Rieti 142,794 ... D3
Rome 3,695,961 ... F6
Rovigo 253,508 ... C2
Salerno 1,013,779 ... E4
Sassari 433,842 ... B4
Savona 297,675 ... B2
Siena 255,118 ... C3
Sondrio 174,009 ... B1
Syracuse 394,692 ... E6
Taranto 572,314 ... F4
Teramo 269,275 ... D3
Terni 807,552 ... D3
Trapani 420,865 ... D5
Trento 442,845 ... C1
Treviso 720,580 ... D2
Trieste 283,641 ... D2
Turin 2,345,771 ... A2
Udine 529,729 ... D1
Varese 788,057 ... B2
Venice 838,794 ... D2
Vercelli 395,957 ... B2
Verona 775,745 ... C2
Vicenza 726,418 ... C2
Viterbo 268,448 ... C3

CITIES and TOWNS

Acireale 46,711 ... E6
Acqui Terme 20,951 ... B2
Adrano 32,865 ... E6
Agrigento 38,681 ... D6
Alba 25,853 ... B2
Albano Laziale 27,796 ... F7
Alcamo 41,626 ... D6
Alessandria 79,552 ... B2
Alghero 32,519 ... B4
Altamura 50,539 ... F4
Amalfi 4,423 ... E4
Ancona 97,118 ... D3
Andria 84,070 ... F4
Anzio 25,932 ... D4
Aosta 36,649 ... A2
Aprilia 31,604 ... D4
Arezzo 74,477 ... C3
Ascoli Piceno 44,411 ... D3
Assisi 4,683 ... D3
Asti 65,483 ... B2
Augusta 37,162 ... E6
Avellino 50,894 ... E4
Aversa 55,788 ... E4
Avezzano 30,227 ... D3
Avola 30,360 ... E6
Bagheria 39,869 ... D5
Barcellona Pozzo di Gotto 33,404 ... E5
Bari 369,444 ... F4
Barletta 82,290 ... F4
Bassano del Grappa 33,724 ... C2
Belluno 28,468 ... D1
Benevento 51,831 ... E4
Bergamo 121,389 ... B2
Biancavilla 20,047 ... E6
Biella 52,587 ... B2
Bisceglie 46,209 ... F4
Bitonto 46,538 ... F4
Bologna 454,897 ... C2
Bolzano (Bolzen) 103,241 ... C1
Borgomanero 18,701 ... B2
Bra 21,304 ... A2
Brescia 202,539 ... C2
Brindisi 84,887 ... G4
Bronte 17,477 ... E6
Busto Arsizio 79,321 ... B2
Cagliari 219,423 ... B5
Caltagirone 32,860 ... E6
Caltanissetta 57,704 ... D6
Camaiore 24,284 ... C3
Campobasso 41,687 ... E4
Canicatti 31,726 ... D6
Canosa di Puglia 30,555 ... E4
Cantù 35,644 ... B2
Capannori 39,717 ... C3
Carbonia 25,140 ... B5
Carmagnola 19,581 ... A2
Carpi 49,370 ... C2
Carrara 61,709 ... C2
Casale Monferrato 37,157 ... B2
Cascina-Navacchio 32,570 ... C3
Caserta 59,185 ... E4
Cassino 22,406 ... D4
Castel Gandolfo 6,176 ... F7
Castelfranco Veneto 20,196 ... D2
Castellammare di Stabia 70,507 ... E4
Castelvetrano 29,503 ... D6
Castrovillari 18,648 ... F5
Catania 379,754 ... E6
Catanzaro 96,930 ... F5
Cava de'Tirreni 47,007 ... E4
Cecina 22,264 ... C3
Ceglie Messapico 17,915 ... F4
Cerignola 48,105 ... E4
Cesena 72,145 ... D2
Cesenatico 15,634 ... D2
Chiavari 29,171 ... B2
Chieri 28,296 ... A2
Chieti 49,267 ... E3
Chioggia 46,728 ... D2
Chivasso 22,230 ... A2
Ciampino 31,981 ... F7
Città di Castello 21,492 ... C3
Civitavecchia 46,465 ... C3
Comiso 25,469 ... E6
Como 94,167 ... B2
Conegliano 32,406 ... D2
Conversano 18,518 ... F4
Corato 41,078 ... F4
Cosenza 101,144 ... F5
Crema 33,901 ... B2
Cremona 74,341 ... B2
Crotone 51,204 ... F5
Cuneo 47,836 ... A2
Desenzano del Garda 17,296 ... C2
Domodossola 19,825 ... A1
Eboli 24,152 ... E4
Empoli 34,066 ... C3
Enna 26,760 ... E6
Fabriano 21,155 ... D3
Faenza 40,635 ... D2
Fano 42,440 ... D3
Fasano 22,918 ... F4
Favara 30,031 ... D6
Fermo 17,603 ... D3
Ferrara 117,590 ... C2
Fidenza 19,482 ... B2
Fiesole 3,711 ... C3
Firenze (Florence) 442,721 ... C3
Fiumicino 21,167 ... F7
Florence 442,721 ... C3
Floridia 17,790 ... E6
Foggia 150,480 ... E4
Foligno 41,696 ... D3
Fondi 19,580 ... D4
Forlì 91,366 ... D2
Formia 29,147 ... D4
Fossano 17,116 ... A2
Francavilla Fontana 31,371 ... F4
Frascati 18,356 ... F7
Frosinone 42,626 ... D4
Gaeta 23,190 ... D4
Galatina 22,611 ... G4
Gallarate 47,259 ... B2
Gela 74,077 ... E6
Genoa 755,389 ... B2
Genova (Genoa) 787,011 ... B2
Giarre 23,377 ... E6
Gioia del Colle 23,868 ... F4
Giovinazzo 18,832 ... F4
Giulianova 20,189 ... E3
Gorizia 40,679 ... D2
Gravina in Puglia 35,891 ... F4
Grosseto 55,569 ... C3
Grottaglie 27,140 ... F4
Iglesias 26,313 ... B5
Imola 47,365 ... C2
Imperia 39,151 ... B3
Isernia 16,919 ... E4
Ivrea 26,446 ... B2
Jesi 37,075 ... D3
L'Aquila 40,467 ... D3
La Spezia 110,632 ... B2
Lanciano 25,828 ... E3
Latina 64,529 ... D4
Lecce 80,127 ... G4
Lecco 51,160 ... B2
Leghorn (Livorno) 171,811 ... C3
Legnago 23,232 ... C2
Lentini 30,950 ... E6
Leonforte 15,745 ... E6
Licata 40,309 ... D6
Lido di Ostia 85,043 ... F7
Lido di Venezia 20,863 ... D2
Livorno 171,811 ... C3
Lodi 41,338 ... B2
Lucca 84,836 ... C3
Lucera 31,252 ... E4
Lugo 21,593 ... D2
Macerata 34,409 ... D3
Manduria 28,112 ... F4
Manfredonia 52,162 ... F4
Mantua 52,477 ... C2
Marino 30,261 ... F7
Marsala 76,843 ... D6
Martina Franca 34,911 ... F4
Massa 60,810 ... C2
Massafra 26,172 ... F4
Matera 48,226 ... F4
Mazara del Vallo 42,320 ... D6
Merano 31,854 ... C1
Mesagne 29,770 ... G4
Messina 240,121 ... E5
Mestre 197,952 ... D2
Milan 1,601,797 ... B2
Milazzo 29,868 ... E5
Minturno 15,795 ... D4
Mira Taglio 26,031 ... D2
Modena 164,529 ... C2
Modica 34,488 ... E6
Mola di Bari 25,744 ... F4
Molfetta 64,738 ... F4
Moncalieri 59,344 ... A2
Monfalcone 29,960 ... D2
Monopoli 33,928 ... F4
Monreale 18,168 ... D5
Monte Sant'Angelo 16,491 ... F4
Montebelluna 19,708 ... D2
Monterotondo 25,383 ... F6
Montevarchi 17,110 ... C3
Monza 122,541 ... B2
Naples 1,210,365 ... E4
Nardò 27,384 ... F4
Nettuno 27,929 ... D4
Nicastro-Sambiase 49,325 ... F5
Niscemi 25,677 ... E6
Nocera Inferiore 43,879 ... E4
Noto 20,609 ... E6
Novara 94,477 ... B2
Novi Ligure 28,756 ... B2
Nuoro 35,491 ... B4
Olbia 26,702 ... B4
Oristano 23,938 ... B5
Orvieto 7,509 ... D3
Ostia Antica 3,939 ... F7
Ostuni 27,948 ... F4
Otranto 4,334 ... G4
Pachino 20,631 ... E6
Padua 228,333 ... C2
Palermo 698,481 ... D5
Palma di Montechiaro 23,918 ... D6
Palmi 16,394 ... E5
Pantelleria 3,454 ... C6
Parma 160,374 ... C2
Partinico 27,479 ... D6
Paterno 42,916 ... E6
Pavia 82,629 ... B2
Perugia 103,542 ... D3
Pesaro 78,550 ... D3
Pescara 131,016 ... E3
Piacenza 103,584 ... B2
Piazza Armerina 20,119 ... E6
Pietrasanta 20,404 ... B3
Pinerolo 33,176 ... A2
Piombino 35,312 ... C3
Pisa 95,015 ... C3
Pistoia 78,105 ... C3
Poggibonsi 22,644 ... C3
Pomezia 19,453 ... F7
Pordenone 51,270 ... D2
Porto Empedocle 16,126 ... D6
Porto Torres 20,233 ... B4
Portocivitanova 28,155 ... D3
Portoferraio 8,108 ... C3
Portofino 615 ... B2
Potenza 55,175 ... E4
Pozzuoli 61,856 ... D4
Prato 156,894 ... C3
Putignano 22,361 ... F4
Quartu Sant'Elena 40,506 ... B5
Ragusa 60,871 ... E6
Rapallo 26,457 ... B2
Ravenna 87,582 ... D2
Reggio di Calabria 159,416 ... E5
Reggio nell'Emilia 107,484 ... C2
Rho 50,373 ... B2
Rieti 33,614 ... D3
Rimini 111,991 ... D2
Rome (cap.) 2,605,441 ... F6
Rovereto 31,286 ... C2
Rovigo 41,050 ... C2
Ruvo di Puglia 23,510 ... F4
Salerno 150,252 ... E4
Saluzzo 13,078 ... A2
San Benedetto del Tronto 43,189 ... E3
San Cataldo 20,694 ... D6
San Giovanni in Fiore 19,391 ... F5
Sannicandro Garganico 18,652 ... E4
San Remo 59,872 ... A3
San Severo 53,948 ... E4
Santa Maria Capua Vetere 32,129 ... E4
Santeramo in Colle 21,154 ... F4
San Vito dei Normanni 18,366 ... F4
Saronno 36,732 ... B2
Sassari 104,334 ... B4
Sassuolo 37,515 ... C2
Savona 65,040 ... B2
Schio 30,738 ... C2
Sciacca 35,063 ... D6
Scicli 18,419 ... E6
Senigallia 27,474 ... D3
Sesto Fiorentino 43,307 ... C3
Sestri Levante 19,672 ... B2
Siena 54,982 ... C3
Siracusa (Syracuse) 109,038 ... E6
Sondrio 19,955 ... B1
Sora 20,380 ... D4
Sorrento 15,747 ... E4
Spoleto 21,625 ... D3
Stresa 4,290 ... B2
Sulmona 21,504 ... D3
Syracuse 109,038 ... E6
Taranto 231,441 ... F4
Teramo 35,142 ... D3
Termini Imerese 24,252 ... D6

(continued on following page)

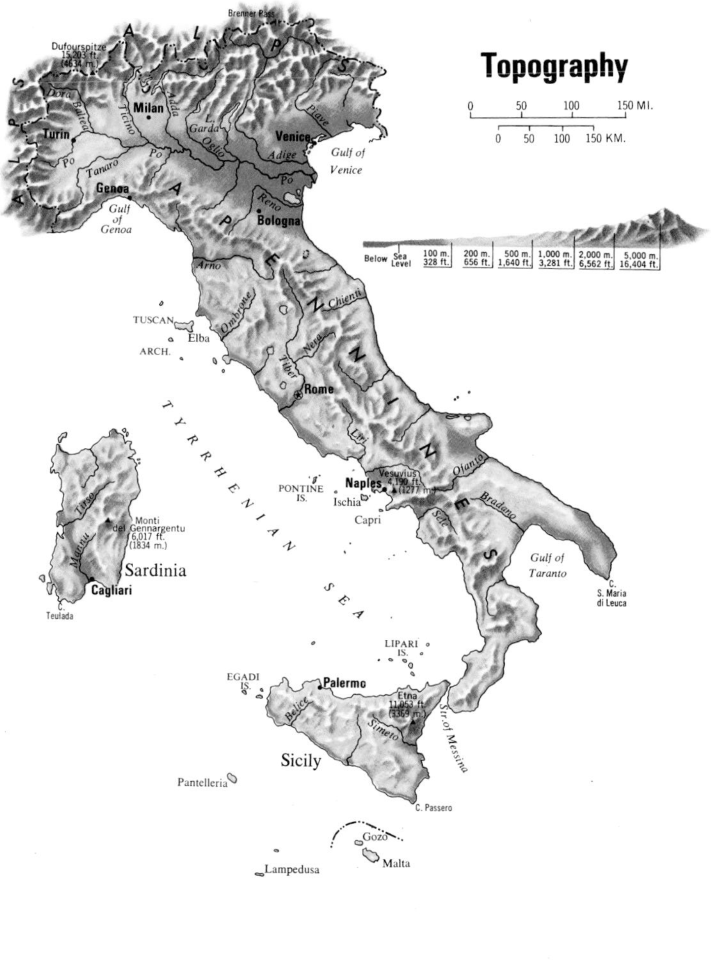
Topography
0 50 100 150 MI.
0 50 100 150 KM.
Below Sea Level
100 m. 328 ft.
200 m. 656 ft.
500 m. 1,640 ft.
1,000 m. 3,281 ft.
2,000 m. 6,562 ft.
5,000 m. 16,404 ft.
Brenner Pass
Dufourspitze 15,203 ft. (4634 m.)
A L P S
Milan
Turin
Venice
Gulf of Venice
Po
Ticino
Adda
Garda
Oglio
Adige
Piave
Tanaro
Genoa
Gulf of Genoa
Reno
Bologna
A P E N N I N E S
Arno
Ombrone
Chienti
Tiber
Nera
Rome
Liri
TUSCAN ARCH.
Elba
T Y R R H E N I A N S E A
PONTINE IS.
Ischia
Naples
Vesuvius
Capri
Ofanto
Bradano
Sele
Gulf of Taranto
C. S. Maria di Leuca
Tirso
Monti del Gennargentu 6,017 ft. (1834 m.)
Sardinia
Cagliari
C. Teulada
LIPARI IS.
EGADI IS.
Palermo
Etna
Belice
Simeto
Str. of Messina
Sicily
Pantelleria
C. Passero
Gozo
Malta
Lampedusa

(continued)

OTHER FEATURES

MALTA

CITIES and TOWNS

SAN MARINO

CITIES and TOWNS

VATICAN CITY

CITIES and TOWNS

Agriculture, Industry and Resources

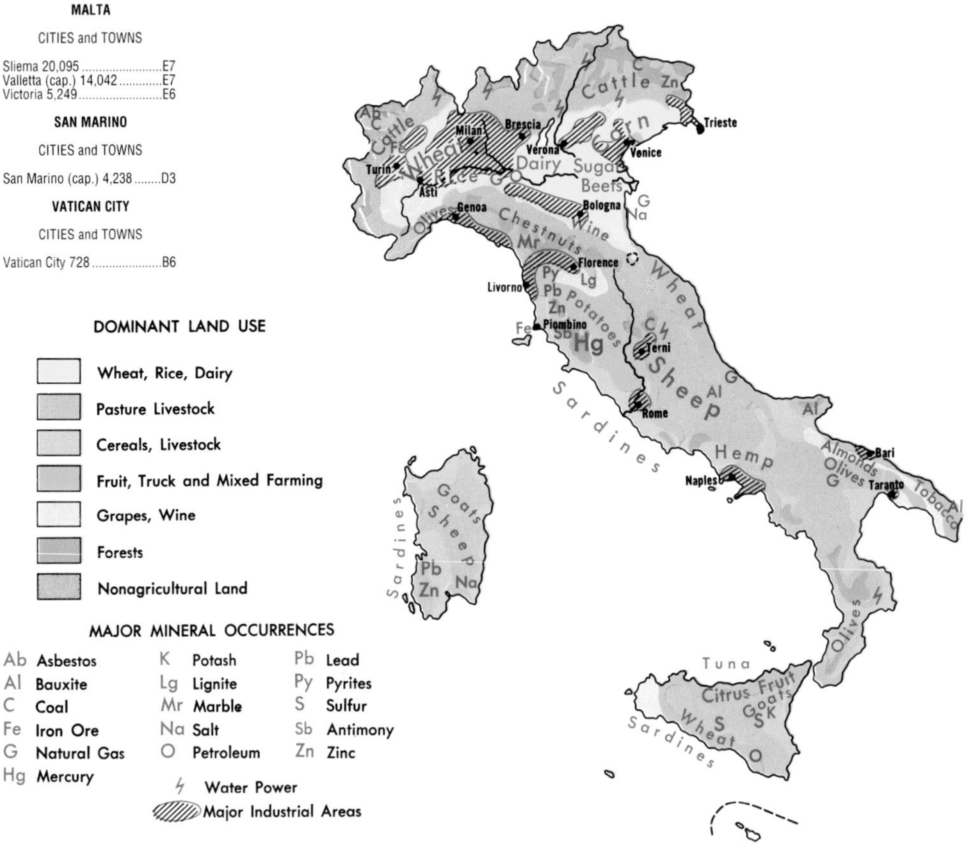
DOMINANT LAND USE
Wheat, Rice, Dairy
Pasture Livestock
Cereals, Livestock
Fruit, Truck and Mixed Farming
Grapes, Wine
Forests
Nonagricultural Land
MAJOR MINERAL OCCURRENCES
Ab Asbestos
Al Bauxite
C Coal
Fe Iron Ore
G Natural Gas
Hg Mercury
K Potash
Lg Lignite
Mr Marble
Na Salt
O Petroleum
Pb Lead
Py Pyrites
S Sulfur
Sb Antimony
Zn Zinc
Water Power
Major Industrial Areas
Milan
Brescia
Verona
Trieste
Venice
Turin
Asti
Genoa
Bologna
Florence
Livorno
Piombino
Terni
Rome
Naples
Bari
Taranto
Cattle
Wheat
Rice
Dairy
Sugar Beets
Chestnuts
Wine
Potatoes
Sheep
Hemp
Olives
Almonds
Tobacco
Goats
Sardines
Tuna
Citrus Fruit

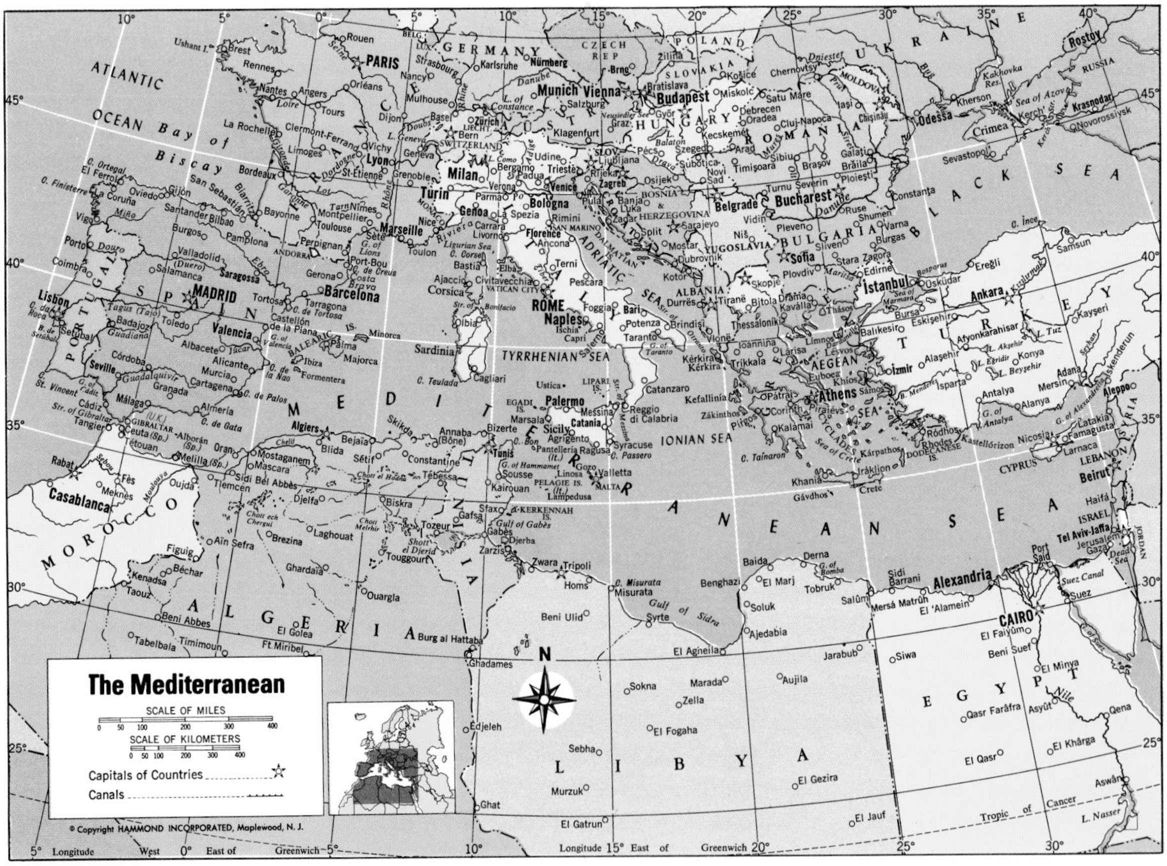
The Mediterranean
SCALE OF MILES
0 50 100 200 300 400
SCALE OF KILOMETERS
0 50 100 200 300 400
Capitals of Countries
Canals
© Copyright HAMMOND INCORPORATED, Maplewood, N. J.
ATLANTIC OCEAN
Bay of Biscay
MEDITERRANEAN SEA
TYRRHENIAN SEA
IONIAN SEA
AEGEAN SEA
BLACK SEA
SPAIN
PORTUGAL
FRANCE
ITALY
MOROCCO
ALGERIA
TUNISIA
LIBYA
EGYPT
TURKEY
GREECE
YUGOSLAVIA
BULGARIA
ROMANIA
HUNGARY
AUSTRIA
GERMANY
POLAND
UKRAINE
PARIS
MADRID
ROME
Naples
Barcelona
Marseille
Milan
Turin
Genoa
Venice
Vienna
Munich
Budapest
Belgrade
Bucharest
Sofia
Athens
Istanbul
Ankara
Algiers
Tunis
Tripoli
Alexandria
CAIRO
Casablanca
Lisbon
Palermo
Malta
Cyprus
Crete
Longitude West 0° East of Greenwich
Longitude 15° East of Greenwich 20°
Tropic of Cancer

SWITZERLAND

AREA 15,943 sq. mi. (41,292 sq. km.)
POPULATION 6,647,000
CAPITAL Bern
LARGEST CITY Zürich
HIGHEST POINT Dufourspitze (Mte. Rosa) 15,203 ft. (4,634 m.)
MONETARY UNIT Swiss franc
MAJOR LANGUAGES German, French, Italian, Romansch
MAJOR RELIGIONS Protestantism, Roman Catholicism

LIECHTENSTEIN

AREA 61 sq. mi. (158 sq. km.)
POPULATION 28,000
CAPITAL Vaduz
LARGEST CITY Vaduz
HIGHEST POINT Grauspitze 8,527 ft. (2,599 m.)
MONETARY UNIT Swiss franc
MAJOR LANGUAGE German
MAJOR RELIGION Roman Catholicism

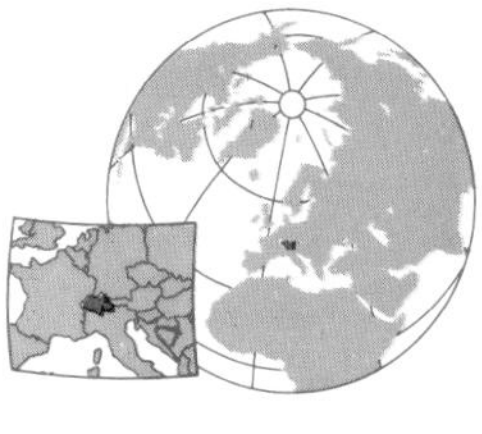

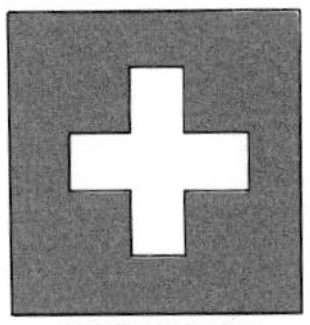

SWITZERLAND

LIECHTENSTEIN

Languages

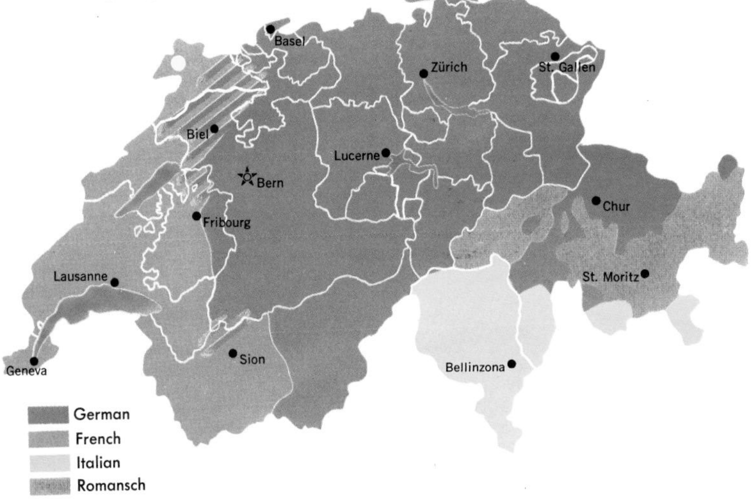
Basel
Zürich
St. Gallen
Biel
Lucerne
Bern
Chur
Fribourg
Lausanne
St. Moritz
Sion
Geneva
Bellinzona
German
French
Italian
Romansch

Switzerland is a multilingual nation with four official languages. 70% of the people speak German, 19% French, 10% Italian and 1% Romansch.

SWITZERLAND

CANTONS

Aargau 453,442 .... F2
Appenzell, Ausser Rhoden 47,611 .... H2
Appenzell, Inner Rhoden 12,844 .... H2
Baselland 219,822 .... E2
Baselstadt 203,915 .... E1
Bern 912,022 .... D2
Fribourg 185,246 .... D3
Geneva (Genève) 349,040 .... B4
Glarus 36,718 .... H3
Graubünden (Grisons) 164,641 .... H3
Jura 64,986 .... D2
Lucerne (Luzern) 296,159 .... F2
Luzern 296,159 .... F2
Neuchâtel 158,368 .... C3
Nidwalden 28,617 .... F3
Obwalden 25,865 .... F3
Sankt Gallen 391,995 .... H2
Schaffhausen 69,413 .... G1
Schwyz 97,354 .... G2
Soleure (Solothurn) 218,102 .... E2
Solothurn 218,102 .... E2
Thurgau 183,795 .... H1
Ticino 265,899 .... G4
Uri 33,883 .... G3
Valais 218,707 .... D4
Vaud 528,747 .... B3
Zug 75,930 .... G2
Zürich 1,122,839 .... G2

CITIES and TOWNS

Aadorf 3,257 .... G2
Aarau 15,788 .... F2
Aarberg 3,212 .... D2
Aarburg 5,354 .... E2
Adelboden 3,276 .... E3
Adliswil 16,418 .... F2
Affoltern am Albis 8,064 .... F2
Aigle 6,233 .... C4
Allschwil 17,952 .... D1
Alpnach 3,556 .... F3
Altdorf 8,230 .... G3
Altstätten 9,260 .... J2
Amriswil 8,790 .... H1
Appenzell 4,781 .... H2
Arbedo-Castione 3,058 .... G4
Arbon 11,333 .... H1
Arosa 2,782 .... J3
Arth 7,795 .... F2
Ascona 4,722 .... G4
Au 5,434 .... J2
Avenches 2,177 .... D3
Baar 15,196 .... F2
Bad Ragaz 3,721 .... H2
Baden 13,870 .... F2
Balerna 3,455 .... G5
Balsthal 5,090 .... E2
Bäretswil 3,145 .... G2
Basel 182,143 .... E1
Basel 364,813 .... E1
Bassecourt 2,942 .... D2
Bauma 3,010 .... G2
Bellinzona 16,743 .... H4
Belp 7,578 .... D3
Bern (cap.) 145,254 .... D3
Bettlach 3,851 .... D2
Bex 4,843 .... D4
Biasca 5,447 .... H4
Biberist 7,519 .... D2
Biel 53,793 .... D2
Binningen 14,195 .... D1
Bischofszell 3,390 .... H1
Bolligen 32,312 .... E3
Boudry 4,488 .... C3
Breitenbach 2,518 .... E2
Bremgarten 4,815 .... F2
Brienz 2,759 .... F3
Brig 9,608 .... F4
Brittnau 2,822 .... E2
Brugg 8,911 .... F2
Bubikon 3,601 .... G2
Buchs 9,066 .... H2
Bülach 12,292 .... G1
Bulle 7,595 .... D3
Buochs 3,742 .... F3
Büren an der Aare 2,761 .... D2
Burgdorf 15,379 .... E2
Bürglen 3,456 .... G3
Bussigny-près-Lausanne 4,909 .... B3
Bütschwil 3,423 .... H2
Carouge 13,100 .... B4
Castagnola 4,430 .... G4
Cham 9,275 .... F2
Château-d'Oex 2,872 .... D4
Châtel-Saint-Denis 3,141 .... C3
Chêne-Bougeries 9,068 .... B4
Chiasso 8,583 .... G5
Chur 32,037 .... J3
Collombey-Muraz 2,982 .... C4
Collonge-Bellerive 4,531 .... B4
Conthey 4,828 .... D4
Courrendlin 2,435 .... D2
Couvet 2,627 .... C3
Davos 10,468 .... J3
Degersheim 3,269 .... H2
Delémont 11,682 .... D2
Derendingen 4,675 .... E2
Dielsdorf 3,767 .... F1
Diepoldsau 3,562 .... J2
Diessenhofen 2,535 .... G1
Dietikon 21,765 .... F2
Disentis-Mustér 2,320 .... G3
Domat-Ems 6,266 .... H3
Dornach 5,442 .... E2
Döttingen 3,264 .... F1
Dübendorf 20,683 .... G2
Düdingen 5,572 .... D3
Dürnten 4,927 .... G2
Ebnat-Kappel 4,950 .... H2
Echallens 2,163 .... C3
Ecublens 7,615 .... B3
Effretikon 14,788 .... G2
Egg 6,074 .... G2
Eggiwil 2,323 .... E3
Egnach 3,397 .... H1
Einsiedeln 9,629 .... G2
Elgg 3,041 .... G2
Emmen 22,392 .... F2
Engelberg 2,963 .... F3
Ennenda 2,512 .... H2
Entlebuch 3,238 .... F3
Erstfeld 4,158 .... G3
Eschenbach 3,661 .... G2
Escholzmatt 3,033 .... E3
Estavayer-le-Lac 3,662 .... C3
Feuerthalen 2,920 .... G1
Flawil 8,575 .... H2
Fleurier 3,573 .... C3
Flims 2,136 .... H3
Flums 4,228 .... H2
Frauenfeld 18,607 .... G1
Freienbach 9,912 .... G2
Fribourg 37,400 .... D3
Frick 3,116 .... E1
Frutigen 5,779 .... E3
Fully 3,926 .... D4
Gais 2,388 .... H2
Gelterkinden 4,954 .... E2

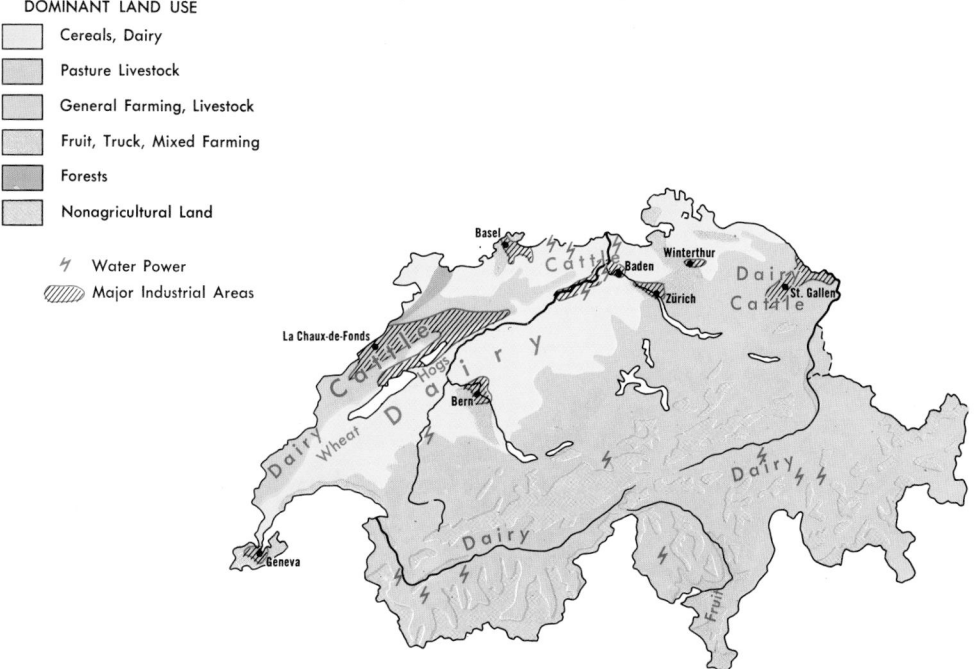

(continued on following page)

Agriculture, Industry and Resources

DOMINANT LAND USE

- Cereals, Dairy
- Pasture Livestock
- General Farming, Livestock
- Fruit, Truck, Mixed Farming
- Forests
- Nonagricultural Land

Water Power
Major Industrial Areas

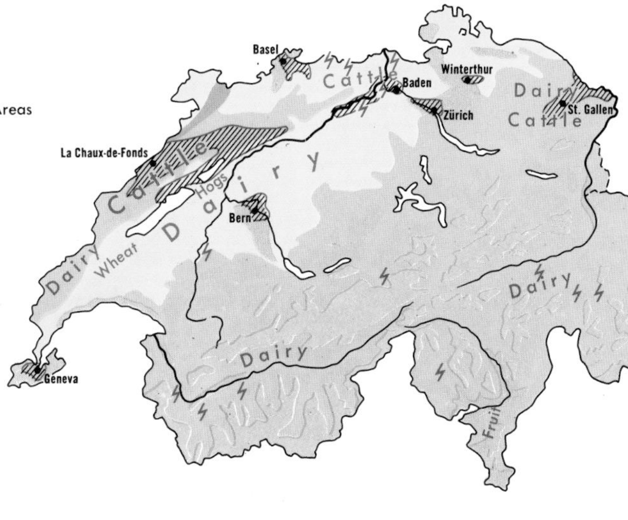
Basel
Winterthur
Baden
Zürich
St. Gallen
Cattle
Dairy
La Chaux-de-Fonds
Hogs
Bern
Wheat
Geneva
Fruit

(continued)

Topography

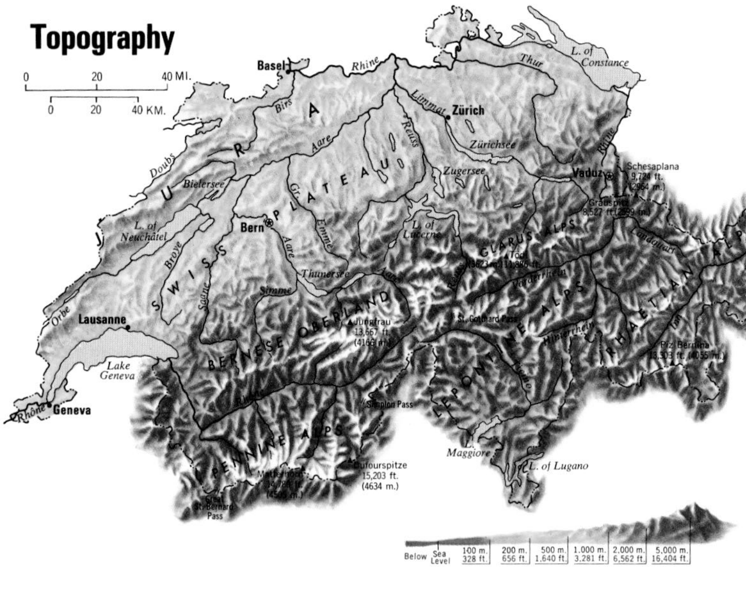
0 20 40 MI.
0 20 40 KM.
Basel
Rhine
L. of Constance
Thur
Zürich
Limmat
Zürichsee
Birs
J U R A
Doubs
Bielersee
Aare
Reuss
Zugersee
P L A T E A U
Vaduz
Schesaplana
L. of Neuchâtel
Bern
L. of Lucerne
GLARUS ALPS
S W I S S
Broye
Emme
Thunersee
Lausanne
Orbe
Jungfrau
BERNESE OBERLAND
St. Gotthard Pass
R H A E T I A N A L P S
L E P O N T I N E A L P S
Lake Geneva
Rhône
Geneva
Simplon Pass
Maggiore
L. of Lugano
PENNINE ALPS
Dufourspitze 15,203 ft. (4634 m.)
Below Sea Level 100 m. 328 ft. 200 m. 656 ft. 500 m. 1,640 ft. 1,000 m. 3,281 ft. 2,000 m. 6,562 ft. 5,000 m. 16,404 ft.

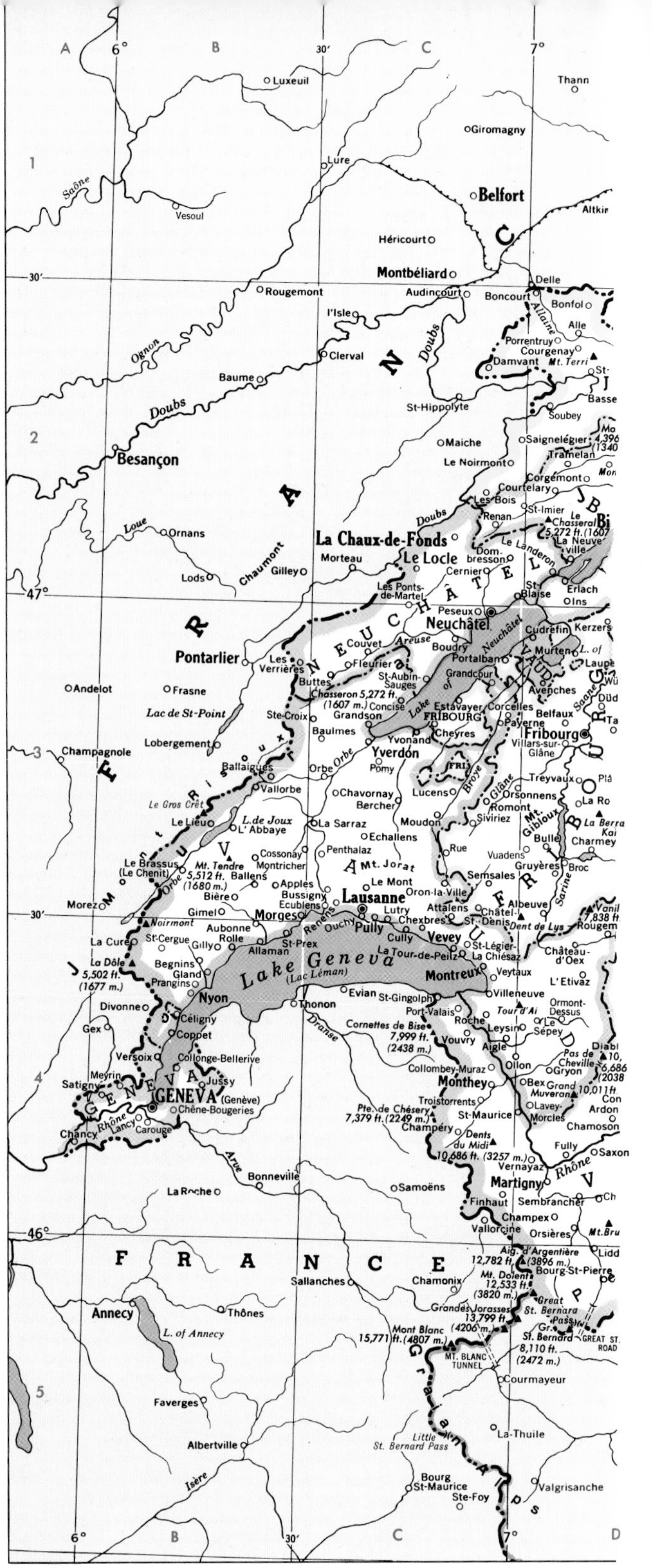
A B C D
6° 30′ 7°
Besançon
Belfort
Montbéliard
La Chaux-de-Fonds
Le Locle
Neuchâtel
Pontarlier
Fribourg
Lausanne
Lake Geneva (Lac Léman)
Montreux
GENEVA
Annecy
Chamonix
F R A N C E
Mont Blanc 15,771 ft. (4807 m.)

Geneva (Genève) 156,505 B4
Giswil 2,595 F3
Giubiasco 6,585 H4
Gland 4,906 B4
Glarus 5,969 H2
Glattfelden 2,753 F1
Glis 3,389 E4
Gordola 2,956 G4
Gossau 14,584 H2
Grabs 4,844 H2
Grenchen 16,800 D2
Grindelwald 3,555 E3
Grosswangen 2,235 F2
Gstaad D4
Heiden 3,620 H2
Heimberg 4,107 E3
Hergiswil 4,254 F3
Herisau 14,160 H2
Herzogenbuchsee 5,107 E2
Hilterfingen 3,600 E3
Hinwil 7,554 G2
Hochdorf 6,034 F2
Horgen 16,577 G2
Huttwil 4,612 E2
Igis 5,392 J3
Ingenbohl 6,232 G2
Ins 2,608 D2
Interlaken 4,852 E3
Jegenstorf 3,541 D2
Jona 12,156 G2
Kaltbrunn 2,735 H2
Kerns 4,200 F3
Kerzers 2,658 D3
Kirchberg, Bern 3,966 E2
Kirchberg, St. Gallen 6,398 G2
Klingnau 2,433 F1
Klosters-Serneus 3,487 J3
Kloten 15,845 G2
Kölliken 3,080 F2
Köniz 33,441 D3
Konolfingen 4,360 E3
Kreuzlingen 16,101 H1
Kriens 21,097 F2
Küsnacht 12,766 G2
Küssnacht am Rigi 8,091 F2
Küttigen 4,356 F2
La Chaux-de-Fonds 37,234 C2
Lachen 5,352 G2
Lancy 23,527 B4
La Neuveville 3,519 D2
Langenthal 13,408 E2
Langnau am Albis 6,694 G2
Langnau in Emmental 8,821 E3
La Tour-de-Peilz 9,411 C4
Laufen 4,444 D2
Laupen 2,261 D3
Lauperswil 2,482 E3
Lausanne 127,349 C3
Lauterbrunnen 3,077 E3
Le Brassus 4,359 B3
Le Châble 4,541 D4
Le Chenit (Le Brassus) 4,359 B3
Le Landeron 3,287 C2
Le Locle 12,039 C2
Le Mont-sur-Lausanne 3,664 C3
Lengnau 4,317 D2
Lenk 2,089 D4
Lens 2,412 D4
Lenzburg 7,585 F2
Leuk 2,983 E4
Leukerbad 1,070 E4
Liestal 12,158 E2
Liestal-Sissach 40,800 E2
Littau 14,996 F2
Locarno 14,103 G4
Lucerne 63,278 F2
Lugano 27,815 G4
Lutry 5,884 C3
Lützelflüh 3,770 E3
Luzern (Lucerne) 63,278 F2
Lyss 8,723 D2
Malters 4,900 F2
Männedorf 7,833 G2
Martigny 11,309 C4
Meilen 10,430 G2
Meiringen 4,072 F3
Mellingen 3,285 F2
Mels 6,235 H2
Mendrisio 6,590 G5
Menzingen 3,564 G2
Menznau 2,248 E2
Meyrin 18,808 B4
Minusio 5,602 G4
Möhlin 6,360 E1
Mollis 2,621 H2
Monthey 11,285 C4
Montreux 19,685 C4
Morges 13,057 B3
Moudon 3,805 C3
Moutier 7,959 D2
Mümliswil-Ramiswil 2,386 E2
Münchenbuchsee 8,395 E2
Münsingen 9,340 E3
Muotathal 2,896 G3
Muri 5,399 F2
Muri bei Bern 12,285 E3
Murten 4,558 D3
Muttenz 16,911 E1
Näfels 3,766 H2
Naters 6,662 E4
Nendaz 4,372 D4
Netstal 2,642 H2
Neuchâtel 34,428 C3
Neuenegg 3,727 D3
Neuhausen am Rheinfall 10,662 G1
Niederbipp 3,165 E2
Niederurnen 3,438 G2
Nyon 12,842 B4
Oberägeri 3,563 G2
Oberburg 2,869 E2
Oberdiessbach 2,319 E3
Oberriet 6,222 J2
Obersiggenthal 7,442 F1
Oberuzwil 4,616 H2
Oensingen 3,543 E2
Oftringen 9,006 E2
Ollon 4,429 D4
Olten 18,991 E2
Opfikon 11,444 G2
Orbe 3,985 C3
Orsières 2,357 D4
Paradiso 3,261 G5
Payerne 6,713 C3
Peseux 5,212 C3
Pfäffikon 8,306 G2
Pfaffnau 2,453 E2
Pieterlen 3,127 D2
Porrentruy 7,039 C2
Poschiavo 3,294 J4
Prangins 2,028 B4
Pratteln 15,751 E1
Pully 14,988 C4
Rafz 2,325 G1
Rapperswil 7,826 G2
Regensdorf 12,300 F2
Reichenbach im Kandertal 2,948 E3
Reiden 3,363 F2
Reinach in Aargau 5,696 F2
Reinach in Baselland 17,813 E2
Renens 16,977 C3
Rheineck 3,037 J2
Rheinfelden 9,456 E1
Richterswil 8,672 G2
Riehen 20,611 E1
Riggisberg 2,196 D3
Roggwil 3,333 E2
Rolle 3,409 B4
Romanshorn 7,893 H1
Romont 3,495 C3
Rorschach 9,878 H2
Rothrist 6,015 E2
Rüti, Zürich 9,331 G2
Rumlang 5,055 G2
Ruswil 4,870 F2
Saanen 5,522 D4
Sachseln 3,406 F3
Saint-Blaise 2,788 D2
Sainte-Croix 4,543 B3
Saint-Imier 5,430 D2
Saint-Légier-La Chiésaz 2,787 C4
Saint-Maurice 3,458 C4
Saint Moritz 5,900 J3
Saint Niklaus 2,036 E4
Saint-Prex 2,937 B4
Samedan 2,553 J3
Sankt Gallen 75,847 H2
Sankt Margrethen 4,935 J2
Sargans 4,267 H2
Sarnen 7,372 F3
Savièse 4,097 D4
Saxon 2,394 D4
Schänis 2,426 H2
Schaffhausen 34,250 G1
Schattdorf 4,516 G3
Schiers 2,253 J3
Schlieren 12,891 F2
Schönenwerd 4,746 E2
Schübelbach 4,720 G2
Schüpfheim 3,537 F3
Schwanden 2,519 H2
Schwyz 12,100 G2
Sempach 2,237 F2
Seon 3,826 F2
Seuzach 4,659 G1
Sevelen 2,839 H2
Sierre 13,050 D4
Signau 2,606 E3
Sigriswil 3,536 E3
Silenen 2,115 G3
Simplon 328 F4
Sins 2,625 F2
Sion 22,877 D4
Sirnach 4,170 G2
Sissach 4,564 E2
Solothurn (Soleure) 15,778 E2
Spiez 9,800 E3
Stäfa 10,558 G2
Stans 5,681 F3
Steckborn 3,232 G1
Steffisburg 12,539 E3
Stein am Rhein 2,507 G1
Suhr 7,366 F2
Sumiswald 5,070 E2
Sursee 7,645 F2
Tafers 2,263 D3
Tavannes 3,336 D2
Teufen 5,027 H2
Thal 4,725 J2
Thalwil 15,412 G2
Thayngen 3,751 G1
Therwil 7,311 E1
Thun 36,891 E3
Thunstetten 2,567 E2
Thusis 2,525 H3
Tramelan 4,773 D2
Turbenthal 2,975 G2
Uetendorf 4,538 E3
Unterägeri 5,371 G2
Unterkulm 2,558 F2
Unterseen 4,568 E3
Uster 23,702 G2
Utzenstorf 3,141 E2
Uznach 4,269 H2
Uzwil 9,614 H2
Vallorbe 3,375 B3
Vechigen 4,036 E3
Versoix 7,483 B4
Vevey 16,139 C4
Vevey-Montreux 60,558 C4
Villars-sur-Glâne 5,788 D3
Villeneuve 3,573 C4
Visp 6,383 E4
Wädenswil 18,485 G2
Wängi 2,909 G1
Wahlern 5,104 D3
Wald 7,447 G2
Waldkirch 2,622 H2
Walenstadt 3,605 H2
Wallisellen 10,887 G2
Wartau 3,692 H2
Wattwil 7,874 H2
Weinfelden 8,793 H1
Wettingen 18,377 F2
Wetzikon 15,859 G2
Wil 16,245 H2
Willisau 2,639 F2
Windisch 7,598 F1
Winterthur 86,758 G1
Wohlen 12,024 F2
Wohlen 15,746 F2
Wohlen bei Bern 7,666 D3
Wolhusen 3,670 F2
Worb 11,080 E3
Wünnewil 3,774 D3
Yverdon 20,802 C3
Zell 4,138 G2
Zermatt 3,548 E4
Zofingen 8,643 E2
Zollikofen 8,717 D3
Zollikon 12,134 G2
Zug 21,609 G2
Zürich 369,522 F2
Zurzach 3,068 F1
Zweisimmen 2,852 D3

OTHER FEATURES

Aa (riv.) F3
Aare (riv.) E3
Ägerisee (lake) G2
Aiguille d'Argentière (mt.) C5
Albristhorn (mt.) D4
Aletschhorn (mt.) F4
Allaine (riv.) D2
Areuse (riv.) C3
Aroser Rothorn (mt.) J3
Ault (peak) H3
Baldeggersee (lake) F2
Balmhorn (mt.) E4
Bärenhorn (mt.) H3
Basodino (peak) G4
Bernese Oberland (reg.) E3
Bernina (mts.) J4
Bernina (pass) K4
Bernina (peak) J4
Bernina (riv.) J4
Beverin (peak) H3
Bielersee (lake) D2
Bietschhorn (mt.) E4
Birs (riv.) D2
Blas (peak) G3
Blinnenhorn (mt.) F4
Blümlisalp (mt.) E3
Bodensee (Constance) (lake) H1
Borgne (riv.) D4
Breithor (mt.) E5
Breithorn (mt.) E4
Brienzer Rothorn (mt.) F3
Brienzersee (lake) F3
Broye (riv.) C3
Brule (mt.) D4
Buchegg (mts.) D4
Buin (peak) K3
Bürkelkopf (mt.) K3
Bütschelegg (mt.) D3
Calancasca (riv.) H4
Campo Tencia (peak) G4
Ceneri (mt.) G4
Chasseron (mt.) C3
Chésery, Pointe de (mt.) C4
Cheville (pass) D4
Churfirsten (mt.) H2
Clariden (mt.) G3
Collon (mt.) D5
Constance (Bodensee) (lake) H1
Cornettes de Bise (mts.) C4
Dammastock (mt.) G3
Davos (valley) J3
Dent Blanche (mt.) E4
Dent de Lys (mt.) C3
Dent de Ruth (mt.) D3
Dent d'Hérens (mt.) E5
Dents du Midi (mt.) C4
Diablerets (mt.) D4
Doldenhorn (mt.) E4
Dolent (mt.) C5
Dom (mt.) E4
Doubs (riv.) C2
Drance (riv.) D4
Dufourspitze (mt.) E5
Emmental (riv.) E3
Engadine (valley) K3
Err (peak) J3
Finsteraarhorn (mt.) F3
Finstermünz (pass) K3
Fletschhorn (mt.) F4
Fluchthorn (mt.) K3
Flüela (pass) J3
Fluhberg (mt.) G2
Fort (mt.) D4
Frienisberg (mt.) D2
Furka (pass) F3
Gelgia (riv.) J3
Generoso (mt.) H5
Geneva (lake) C4
Giacomo (pass) G4
Gibloux (mt.) D3
Glâne (riv.) C3
Glärnisch (mt.) H2
Glarus Alps (mts.) H3
Glatt (riv.) G2
Goms (valley) F4
Grand Combin (mt.) D5
Grand Muveran (mt.) D4
Grande Dixence (dam) D4
Grauehörner (mt.) H3
Great Saint Bernard (mt.) D5
Great Saint Bernard (pass) D5
Great Saint Bernard (tunnel) D5
Greifensee (lake) G2
Greina (pass) G3
Gridone (mt.) G4
Grimsel (pass) F3
Gross Emme (riv.) E2
Gross Litzner (mt.) K3
Hallwilersee (lake) F2
Hausstock (mt.) H3
Helsenhorn (mt.) F4
Hinterrhein (riv.) H3
Hochwang (mt.) J3
Hohenstollen (mt.) F3
Honegg (mt.) E3
Hörnli (mt.) G2
Ilfis (riv.) E3
Inn (riv.) K3
Joch (pass) F3
Jorat (mt.) C3
Joux (lake) B3
Jungfrau (mt.) E3
Jura (mts.) B3
Kaisteregg (mt.) D3
Kesch (peak) J3
Kisten (pass) H3
Klausen (pass) G3
Kleine Emme (riv.) F3
La Berra (mt.) D3
La Dôle (mt.) B4
Landquart (riv.) J3
Le Chasseral (mt.) D2
Le Gros Crêt (mt.) B3

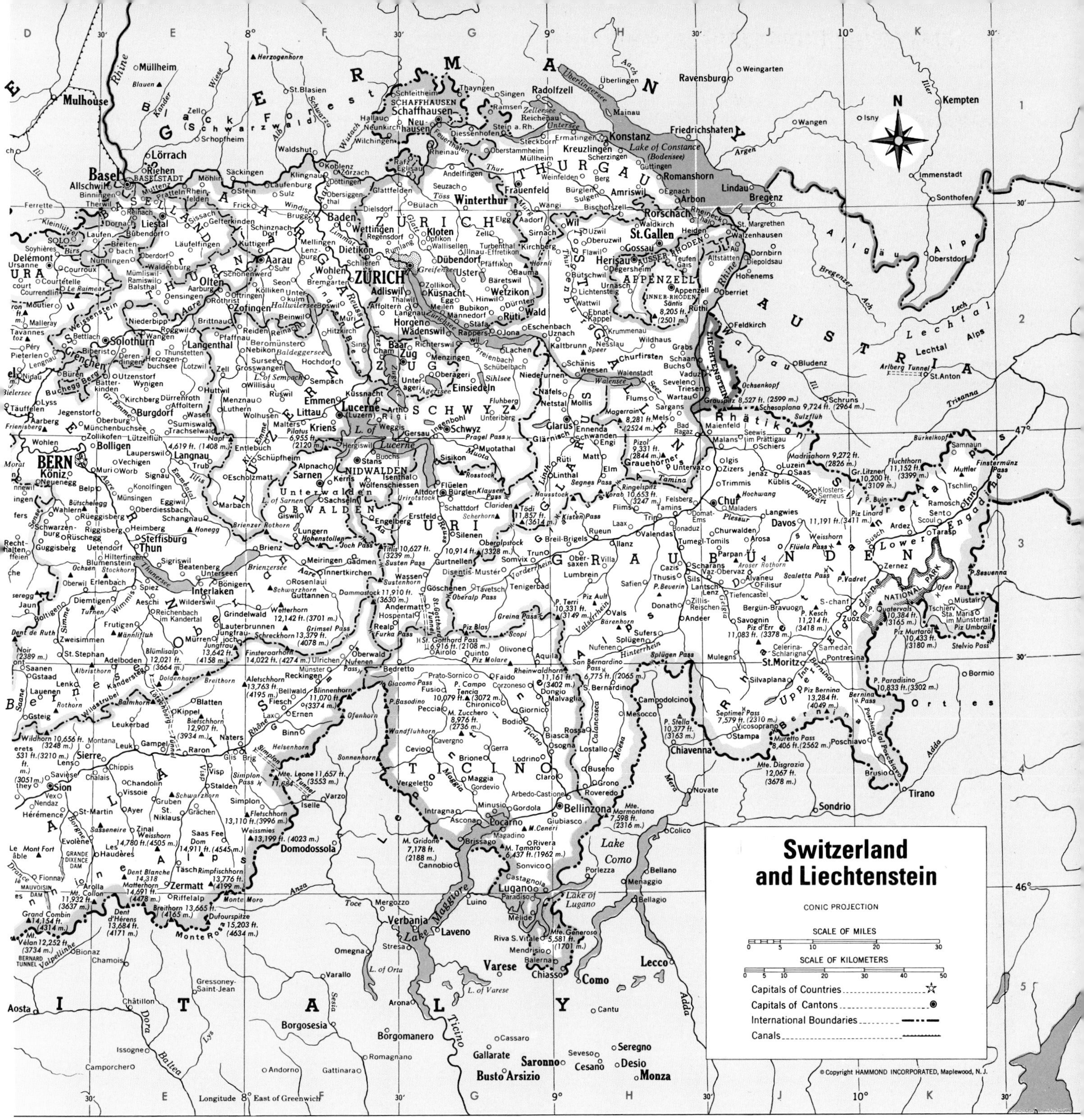
Switzerland and Liechtenstein
CONIC PROJECTION
SCALE OF MILES
SCALE OF KILOMETERS
Capitals of Countries
Capitals of Cantons
International Boundaries
Canals
© Copyright HAMMOND INCORPORATED, Maplewood, N.J.
Longitude 8° East of Greenwich

LIECHTENSTEIN

CITIES and TOWNS

OTHER FEATURES

Austria, Czech Republic, Slovakia and Hungary

AUSTRIA

PROVINCES

Burgenland 272,274 .... D3
Carinthia 536,727 .... B3
Lower Austria 1,439,137 .... C2
Salzburg 441,842 .... B3
Styria 1,187,512 .... C3
Tirol 586,139 .... A3
Upper Austria 1,270,426 .... B2
Vienna (city) 1,515,666 .... D2
Vorarlberg 305,615 .... A3

CITIES and TOWNS†

Altheim 4,702 .... B2
Althofen 4,274 .... C3
Amstetten 22,015 .... C2
Arnoldstein 6,641 .... B3
Attnang-Puchheim 8,058 .... B2
Bad Aussee 5,047 .... B3
Bad Goisern 6,500 .... B3
Bad Hofgastein 5,960 .... B3
Bad Ischl 13,027 .... B3
Bad Sankt-Leonhard im Lavanttal 5,008 .... C3
Baden 23,235 .... D2
Badgastein 5,600 .... B3
Berndorf 8,189 .... C3
Bischofshofen 9,520 .... B3
Bludenz 12,893 .... A3
Bramberg am Wildkogel 3,410 .... B3
Braunau am Inn 16,192 .... B2
Bregenz 24,683 .... A3
Bruck an der Leitha 7,170 .... D2
Bruck an der Mur 15,086 .... C3
Deutsch Feistritz 3,719 .... C3
Deutschkreutz 3,563 .... D3
Deutsch Landsberg 7,623 .... C3
Hermagor-Preseggersee 7,116 .... B3
Herzogenburg 7,313 .... C2
Hohenems 12,669 .... A3
Hollabrunn 10,254 .... D2
Hopfgarten in Nordtirol 4,956 .... B3
Horn 6,319 .... C2
Imst 6,691 .... A3
Innsbruck 116,110 .... A3
Jenbach 5,725 .... A3
Jennersdorf 4,131 .... D3
Judenburg 11,199 .... C3
Kapfenberg 25,719 .... C3
Kaprun 2,764 .... B3
Kindberg 6,269 .... C3
Kirchdorf an der Krems 3,708 .... C3
Kitzbühel 7,872 .... B3
Klagenfurt 86,303 .... C3
Klosterneuburg 23,307 .... D2
Knittelfeld 14,153 .... C3
Köflach 12,009 .... C3
Korneuburg 9,132 .... D2
Kötschach-Mauthen 3,633 ...... B3
Krems an der Donau 23,123 ... C2
Kufstein 13,125 .... B3
Laa an der Thaya 6,485 .... D2
Laakirchen 7,670 .... B3
Landeck 7,325 .... A3
Landskron 10,429 .... B3
Langenlois 6,474 .... C2
Langenwang 4,187 .... C3
Lavamünd 3,824 .... C3
Leibnitz 6,659 .... C3
Lenzing 5,079 .... B3
Leoben 32,006 .... C3
Lienz 11,699 .... B3
Liezen 7,021 .... C3
Lilienfeld 3,030 .... C3
Linz 197,962 .... C2
Salzburg 138,213 .... B3
Sankt Johann in Tirol 6,495 .... B3
Sankt Michael im Lungau 3,246 .... B3
Sankt Michael in Obersteiermark 3,604 .... C3
Sankt Paul im Lavanttal 5,770 .... C3
Sankt Pölten 51,102 .... C2
Sankt Valentin 8,759 .... C2
Sankt Veit an der Glan 12,021 C3
Schärding 5,784 .... B2
Scheibbs 4,537 .... C2
Schladming 3,930 .... B3
Schrems 6,010 .... C2
Schwarzach im Pongau 3,607 .... B3
Schwaz 10,936 .... A3
Schwechat 14,844 .... D2
Schwertberg 4,385 .... C2
Sierning 7,891 .... C2
Solbad Hall in Tirol 12,622 ...... A3
Spittal an der Drau 14,769 .... B3
Steyr 38,967 .... C2
Stockerau 12,692 .... D2
Tamsweg 5,256 .... B3
Telfs 7,749 .... A3
Ternitz 16,154 .... D3
Traiskirchen 14,102 .... D2
Traun 21,524 .... C2
Trieben 4,471 .... C3
Trofaiach 8,959 .... C3
Tulln 11,287 .... D2
Velden am Wörthersee 7,458 .. C3
Vienna (cap.) 1,515,666 .... D2
Villach 52,744 .... B3
Vöcklabruck 11,039 .... B2
Voitsberg 110,951 .... C3
Völkermarkt 10,900 .... C3
Waidhofen an der Thaya 5,401 .... C2
Waidhofen an der Ybbs 11,339 .... C3
Weitensfeld-Flattnitz 5,158 ..... C3
Weiz 8,418 .... C3
Wels 51,024 .... C2
Wien (Vienna) (cap.) 1,515,666 .... D2
Wiener Neustadt 35,050 .... D3
Wilhelmsburg 6,339 .... C2
Wolfsberg 28,182 .... C3
Wörgl 8,644 .... B3
Ybbs an der Donau 5,983 .... C2
Zell am See 7,959 .... B3
Zeltweg 8,722 .... C3
Zistersdorf 5,814 .... D2
Zwettl-Niederösterreich 11,579 .... C2

OTHER FEATURES

Allgäu Alps (mts.) A3
Atter See (lake) B3
Bavarian Alps (mts.) A3
Bodensee (Constance) (lake) .. A3
Brenner (pass) A3
Carnic Alps (mts.) B3
Coglians (mt.) B3
Constance (lake) A3
Danube (riv.) C2
Donau (Danube) (riv.) D2
Drau (riv.) C3
Enns (riv.) C3
Greiner Wald (mts.) C2
Grosser Peilstein (mt.) C2
Grossglockner (mt.) B3
Hochgolling (mt.) B3
Hohe Tauern (range) B3
Hohe Warte (Coglians) (mt.) .. B3
Inn (riv.) B2
Kamp (riv.) C2
Karawanken (range) C3
Lafnitz (riv.) D3
March (riv.) D2
Mühlviertel (reg.) C2
Mur (riv.) C3
Mürz (riv.) C3
Neusiedler See (lake) D3
Niedere Tauern (range) B3
Olsa (riv.) C3
Ötztal Alps (mts.) A3
Parseierspitze (mt.) A3
Raab (riv.) C3
Rhine (riv.) A3
Salzach (riv.) B2
Salzkammergut (reg.) B3
Semmering (pass) C3
Thaya (riv.) C2
Traun (riv.) C2
Traun See (lake) B3
Wildspitze (mt.) A3
Zugspitze (mt.) A3

CZECH REPUBLIC

REGIONS

Jihočeský 689,229 .... C2
Jihomoravský 2,040,903 .... D2
Praha (city) 1,182,186 .... C1
Severočeský 1,167,231 .... C1
Severomoravský 1,932,722 .... D2
Středočeský 1,151,265 .... C2
Východočeský 1,248,466 .... C1
Západočeský 879,925 .... B2

CITIES and TOWNS

Aš 13,551 .... B1
Austerlitz (Slavkov) 6,316 .... D2
Benešov 15,172 .... C2
Beroun 23,580 .... B2
Bílina 18,836 .... B1
Blansko 19,508 .... D2
Blatná 7,264 .... B2
Boskovice 12,025 .... D2
Brandýs nad Labem-Stará Boleslavv 15,071 .... C1
Břeclav 23,978 .... D2
Brno 371,463 .... D2
Broumov 7,834 .... D1
Bruntál 17,062 .... D2
Bystřice nad Pernštejnem 10,044 .... D2
Bystřice pod Hostýnem 10,359 .... D2
Čáslav 9,950 .... C2
Česká Kamenice 7,272 .... C1
Česká Lípa 24,924 .... C1
Česká Třebová 17,136 .... D2
České Budějovice 90,415 .... C2
Český Krumlov 13,776 .... C2
Český Těšín 23,389 .... E2
Cheb 31,039 .... B1
Chodov 14,704 .... B1
Chomutov 51,769 .... B1
Chotěboř 8,744 .... C2
Chrastava 7,022 .... C1
Chrudim 20,517 .... C2
Dačice 7,443 .... C2
Děčín 49,682 .... C1
Dobříš 7,466 .... C2
Domažlice 11,461 .... B2
Duchcov 10,554 .... B1
Dvůr Králové nad Labem 17,270 .... C1
Falknov (Sokolov) 28,523 .... B1
Frenštát pod Radhoště 10,434 .... E2
Frýdek-Místek 59,430 .... E2
Frýdlant nad Ostravicí 14,065 .... E2
Frýdlant v. Čechách 7,418 ...... C1
(continued)

Topography

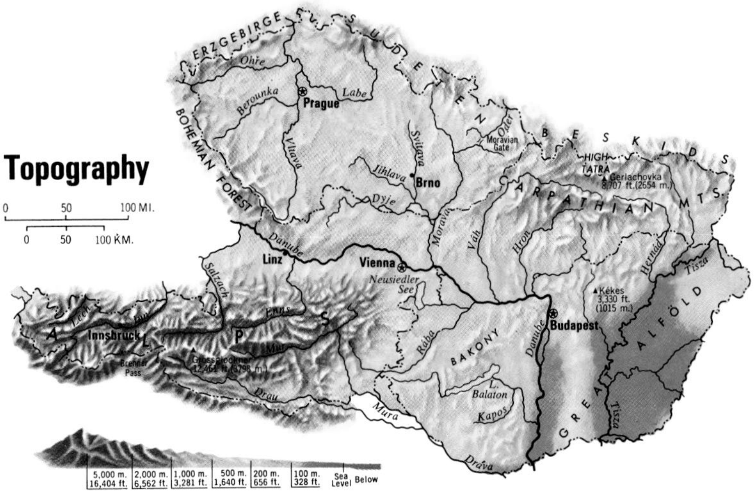

0 50 100 MI.
0 50 100 KM.
ERZGEBIRGE
SUDETEN
BOHEMIAN FOREST
Berounka
Prague
Labe
Ohře
Vltava
Svitava
Oder
Moravian Gate
BESKIDS
HIGH TATRA
Gerlachovka 8,707 ft. (2654 m.)
CARPATHIAN MTS.
Jihlava
Brno
Dyje
Morava
Váh
Hron
Hernád
Tisza
Danube
Linz
Vienna
Neusiedler See
Kékes 3,330 ft. (1015 m.)
Budapest
Enns
Innsbruck
Brenner Pass
Salzach
Raba
BAKONY
Balaton
Kapos
Drau
Mura
Dráva
ALFÖLD
GREAT
5,000 m. 16,404 ft.
2,000 m. 6,562 ft.
1,000 m. 3,281 ft.
500 m. 1,640 ft.
200 m. 656 ft.
100 m. 328 ft.
Sea Level
Below

Deutsch Wagram 5,111 .... D2
Dornbirn 38,663 .... A3
Ebensee 9,005 .... B3
Eggenburg 3,729 .... C2
Eisenerz 10,074 .... C3
Eisenkappel-Vellach 3,520 ...... C3
Eisenstadt 10,150 .... D3
Enns 9,731 .... C2
Feldbach 4,073 .... C3
Feldkirch 23,876 .... A3
Feldkirchen in Kärnten 12,181 .... B3
Ferlach 7,658 .... C3
Fieberbrunn 3,926 .... B3
Fohnsdorf 10,360 .... C3
Frankenmarkt 3,166 .... B3
Friesach 7,074 .... C3
Freistadt 6,289 .... C2
Frohnleiten 5,061 .... C3
Fürstenfeld 6,040 .... C3
Gaming 4,099 .... C3
Gänserndorf 4,948 .... D2
Gleisdorf 5,078 .... C3
Gloggnitz 6,290 .... D3
Gmünd 6,457 .... B3
Gmunden 12,720 .... B3
Golling an der Salzach 3,409 .. B3
Götzis 8,740 .... A3
Graz 243,405 .... C3
Grieskirchen 4,813 .... B2
Grosssiegharts 3,374 .... C2
Grünburg 3,630 .... C3
Güssing 3,895 .... D3
Haag 5,095 .... C2
Hainburg an der Donau 5,749 .... D2
Hainfeld 3,735 .... C2
Hallein 15,404 .... B3
Hartberg 6,048 .... C3
Heidenreichstein 5,351 .... C2
Heiligenblut 1,334 .... B3
Lustenau 17,404 .... A3
Mannersdorf am Leithagebirge 3,878 .... D3
Marchegg 2,676 .... D2
Matrei in Osttirol 4,298 .... B3
Mattersburg 5,682 .... D3
Mattighofen 4,566 .... B2
Mauthausen 4,353 .... C2
Mauthen-Kötschach 3,633 .... B3
Mayrhofen 3,274 .... A3
Melk 5,074 .... C2
Mistelbach an der Zaya 10,300 .... D2
Mittersill 5,033 .... B3
Mödling 19,333 .... D2
Mürzzuschlag 10,774 .... C3
Neumarkt am Wallersee 3,703 .... B3
Neunkirchen 10,780 .... D3
Neusiedl am See 4,154 .... D3
Ober Grafendorf 4,475 .... C2
Oberndorf bei Salzburg 3,838 . B3
Oberwart 5,973 .... D3
Oberwölz 9,510 .... C3
Paternion 5,914 .... B3
Perg 5,226 .... C2
Pinkafeld 4,802 .... D3
Pöchlarn 3,637 .... C2
Poysdorf 5,658 .... D2
Pregarten 3,823 .... C2
Raabs an der Thaya 3,839 .... C2
Radenthein 7,083 .... B3
Radstadt 3,994 .... B3
Rankweil 9,929 .... A3
Reichenau an der Rax 3,601 ... C3
Retz 4,373 .... D2
Reutte 5,145 .... A3
Ried im Innkreis 10,952 .... B2
Rottenmann 5,425 .... C3
Saalfelden am Steinernen Meer 11,436 .... B3

GERMANY
Jena
Gera
Chemnitz
Zwickau
Plauen
Hof
Aš
Cheb
Bayreuth
Amberg
Regensburg
Straubing
Ingolstadt
Landshut
Passau
MUNICH (München)
Memmingen
Kaufbeuren
Kempten
Ravensburg
Konstanz
Lake of Constance (Bodensee)
Rosenheim
Traunstein
Füssen
Garmisch-Partenkirchen
Zugspitze 9,718 ft. (2962 m.)
Erzgebirge (Krušné Hory)
Ústí nad Labem
Teplice
Most
Chomutov
Litvínov
Karlovy Vary
Žatec
Kladno
PRAGUE (Praha)
Beroun
Plzeň
ZÁPADOČESKÝ
SEVEROČESKÝ
Příbram
Klatovy
Písek
Strakonice
Domažlice
Bohemian Forest
České Budějovice
Mariánské Lázně
Danube (Donau)
Isar
Inn
UPPER AUSTRIA
Linz
Wels
Braunau am Inn
Salzburg
Bad Ischl
Bregenz
Dornbirn
Allgäu Alps
VORARLBERG
Feldkirch
Bludenz
LIECHT.
Vaduz
Innsbruck
Solbad Hall
Parseierspitze 9,967 ft. (3038 m.)
Ötztal Alps
Wildspitze 12,359 ft. (3767 m.)
Brenner Pass
Kufstein
Kitzbühel
TIROL
SALZBURG
Hohe Tauern
Grossglockner 12,457 ft. (3797 m.)
Hochgolling 8,858 ft. (2700 m.)
Lienz
CARINTHIA
Villach
Hohe Warte (Mte. Coglians) 9,121 ft. (2780 m.)
Carnic Alps
SWITZERLAND
Chur
Davos Platz
St. Moritz
Bolzano
Dolomite Alps
ITALY
Trento
Belluno
Udine
Lecco
Bergamo
Brescia
Treviso
Lake Como
Lake Iseo
Lake Garda
Ljubljana
SLOVENIA
Karawanken
Postojna
Glarus

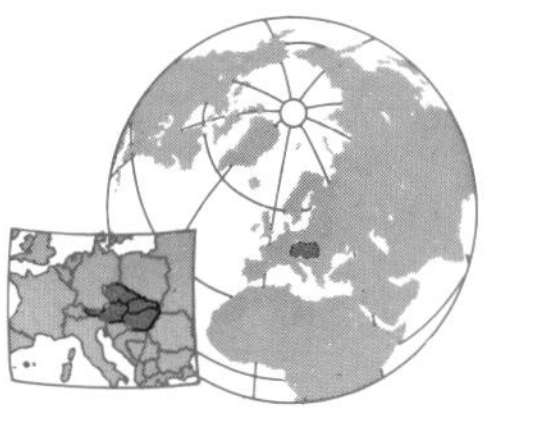

AUSTRIA

AREA 32,375 sq. mi. (83,851 sq. km.)
POPULATION 7,666,000
CAPITAL Vienna
LARGEST CITY Vienna
HIGHEST POINT Grossglockner 12,457 ft. (3,797 m.)
MONETARY UNIT schilling
MAJOR LANGUAGE German
MAJOR RELIGION Roman Catholicism

CZECH REPUBLIC

AREA 30,449 sq. mi. (78,863 sq. km.)
POPULATION 10,291,927
CAPITAL Prague
LARGEST CITY Prague
HIGHEST POINT Sněžka 5,256 ft. (1,602 m.)
MONETARY UNIT Czech koruna
MAJOR LANGUAGE Czech
MAJOR RELIGIONS Roman Catholicism, Protestantism

HUNGARY

AREA 35,919 sq. mi. (93,030 sq. km.)
POPULATION 10,558,000
CAPITAL Budapest
LARGEST CITY Budapest
HIGHEST POINT Kékes 3,330 ft. (1,015 m.)
MONETARY UNIT forint
MAJOR LANGUAGE Hungarian
MAJOR RELIGIONS Roman Catholicism, Protestantism

SLOVAKIA

AREA 18,924 sq. mi. (49,014 sq. km.)
POPULATION 4,991,168
CAPITAL Bratislava
LARGEST CITY Bratislava
HIGHEST POINT Gerlachovky Štít 8,707 ft. (2,654 m.)
MONETARY UNIT Slovak koruna
MAJOR LANGUAGE Slovak
MAJOR RELIGIONS Roman Catholicism, Protestantism

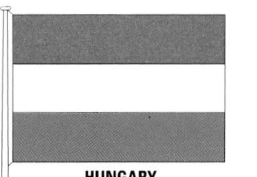
AUSTRIA

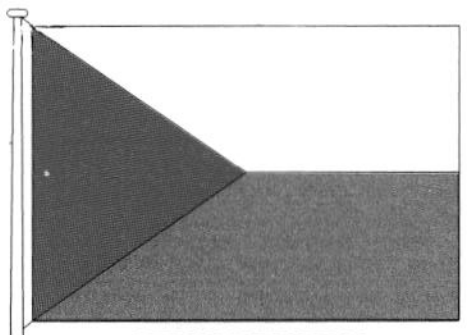
CZECH REPUBLIC

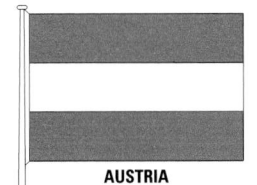

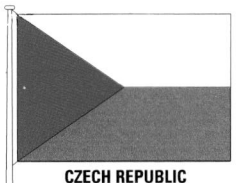

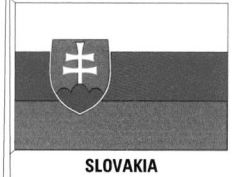
HUNGARY

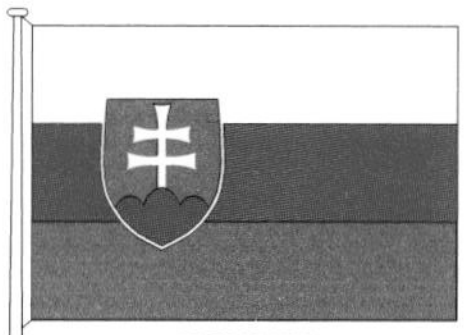
SLOVAKIA

Austria, Czech Republic
Slovakia and Hungary
CONIC PROJECTION
SCALE OF MILES
0 10 20 40 60 80
SCALE OF KILOMETERS
0 10 20 40 60 80
Capitals of Countries
Administrative Centers
International Boundaries
Internal Boundaries
Canals
POLAND
CZECH
SLOVAKIA
HUNGARY
AUSTRIA
UKRAINE
ROMANIA
YUGOSLAVIA
CROATIA
SLOVENIA
VIENNA
Bratislava
BUDAPEST
Prague
Brno
Ostrava
Košice
Debrecen
Szeged
Pécs
Győr
Graz
Linz
Zagreb
Cracow
Katowice
Gliwice
Opole
Wałbrzych
Częstochowa
Uzhgorod
Mukachevo
Satu Mare
Oradea
Arad
Timişoara
Subotica
Sombor
Maribor
Danube
Tisza
Vistula
Oder
Drava
Mur
L. Balaton
West Beskids
East Beskids
White Carpathians
High Tatra
Bohemian-Moravian Heights
Jeseníky
LOWER AUSTRIA
STYRIA
BURGENLAND
VÝCHODOČESKÝ
SEVEROMORAVSKÝ
JIHOMORAVSKÝ
ZÁPADOSLOVENSKÝ
STŘEDOSLOVENSKÝ
VÝCHODOSLOVENSKÝ
GYŐR-SOPRON
KOMÁROM
PEST
NÓGRÁD
HEVES
BORSOD-ABAÚJ-ZEMPLÉN
SZABOLCS-SZATMÁR
HAJDÚ-BIHAR
SZOLNOK
BÉKÉS
CSONGRÁD
BÁCS-KISKUN
FEJÉR
VESZPRÉM
VAS
ZALA
SOMOGY
TOLNA
BARANYA
Longitude East of Greenwich
© Copyright HAMMOND INCORPORATED, Maplewood, N.J.

Fulnek 8,214 D2
Havířov 89,920 E2
Havlíčkuv Brod 24,550 C2
Hlinsko 10,635 C2
Hlučín 22,581 E2
Hodonín 25,485 D2
Holešov 13,323 D2
Hořice v Podkrkonoší 9,251 C1
Hradec Králové 95,588 C1
Hranice 18,099 D2
Hronov 9,609 D1
Humpolec 10,042 C2
Ivančice 9,746 D2
Jablonec nad Nisou 42,179 C1
Jablunkov 15,962 E2
Jaroměř 11,562 C1
Jeseník 14,314 D1
Jičín 16,440 C1
Jihlava 51,144 C2
Jindřichuv Hradec 20,096 C2
Jiřkov 11,980 B1
Kadaň 18,420 B1
Karlovy Vary 60,950 B1
Karviná 78,334 E2
Kladno 71,141 B1
Klatovy 21,782 B2
Kojetín 8,881 D2
Kolín 30,921 C1
Kralupy nad Vltavou 17,528 C1
Kraslice 7,371 B1
Krnov 25,678 D1
Kroměříž 25,887 D2
Krupka 9,336 B1
Kutná Hora 20,927 C2
Kyjov 12,632 D2
Lanškroun 10,620 D2
Liberec 97,474 C1
Lidice C1
Lipník nad Bečvou 9,961 D2
Litoměřice 23,835 C1
Litomyšl 10,079 D2
Prague (Praha) (cap.) 1,182,186 C1
Přelouč 8,561 C1
Přerov 50,265 D2
Příbor 12,711 E2
Příbram 37,854 C2
Prostějov 49,599 D2
Rakovník 16,233 B1
Říčany u Prahy 10,703 C2
Rokycany 15,041 B2
Roudnice nad Labem 13,956 C1
Rožnov pod Radhoštěm 15,468 E2
Rumburk 10,255 C1
Rychnov nad Kněžnou 8,955 D1
Rýmařov 9,927 D2
Sedlčany 7,453 C2
Semily 8,464 C1
Slaný 14,705 C1
Slavkov 6,316 D2
Soběslav 8,406 C2
Sokolov 28,523 B1
Staré Město 6,293 D2
Šternberk 16,342 D2
Strakonice 22,611 B2
Stříbro 8,169 B2
Studénka 12,497 E2
Šumperk 31,873 D2
Sušice 11,400 B2
Svitavy 19,075 D2
Tábor 31,867 C2
Tachov 12,798 B2
Teplice 53,964 B1
Tišnov 12,179 D2
Třebíč 30,246 C2
Třeboň 8,878 C2
Třinec 44,739 E2
Trutnov 27,648 C1
Turnov 13,906 C1
Ústí nad Labem 87,909 C1
Jihlava (riv.) D2
Jizera (riv.) C1
Krušné Hory (Erzgebirge) (mts.) B1
Labe (riv.) C1
Lipno (res.) C2
Lužnice (riv.) C2
Moldau (Vltava) (riv.) C2
Morava (riv.) D2
Mže (riv.) B2
Oder (Odra) (riv.) D2
Ohře (riv.) B1
Ondava (riv.) F2
Orlice (riv.) D1
Orlická (res.) C2
Otava (riv.) B2
Radbuza (riv.) B2
Sázava (riv.) C2
Sudeten (mts.) C1
Svitava (riv.) D2
Svratka (riv.) D2
Úhlava (riv.) B2
Vltava (riv.) C2

HUNGARY

COUNTIES

Bács-Kiskun 553,000 E3
Baranya 434,000 E4
Békés 416,000 F3
Borsod-Abaúj-Zemplén 779,000 F2
Budapest (city) 2,104,000 E3
Csongrád 457,000 F3
Fejér 426,000 E3
Győr-Sopron 426,000 D3
Hajdú-Bihar 549,000 F3
Heves 338,000 F2
Komárom 320,000 E3
Nógrád 229,000 E3
Pest 988,000 E3
Csorna 13,000 D3
Dabas 13,075 E3
Debrecen 217,000 F3
Derecske 9,579 F3
Dévaványa 11,208 F3
Dombóvár 21,000 E3
Dorog 13,000 E3
Dunaföldvár 10,318 E3
Dunaharaszti 15,788 E3
Dunakeszi 29,000 E3
Dunaújváros 62,000 E3
Edelény 12,000 F2
Eger 67,000 F3
Egyek 7,956 F3
Endrőd 8,136 F3
Enying 7,518 E3
Érd 44,904 E3
Esztergom 30,476 E3
Fegyvernek 8,421 F3
Fehérgyarmat 9,000 G3
Füzesgyarmat 7,097 F3
Gödöllő 30,000 E3
Gyöngyös 36,000 E3
Gyoma 10,392 F3
Győr 131,000 D3
Gyula 36,000 F3
Hadházteglás 13,626 F3
Hajdúböszormény 31,000 F3
Hajdúdorog 10,118 F3
Hajdúnánás 18,000 F3
Hajdúsámson 7,492 F3
Hajdúszoboszló 24,000 F3
Hatvan 25,000 E3
Heves 11,000 F3
Hódmezővásárhely 54,000 F3
Izsák 7,686 E3
Jánoshalma 12,534 E3
Jászapáti 10,424 F3
Jászárokszállás 10,139 E3
Jászberény 30,000 E3
Jászladány 7,823 F3
Kalocsa 20,000 E3
Mezőtúr 21,000 F3
Mindszent 8,730 F3
Miskolc 210,000 F2
Mohács 21,000 E4
Monor 16,838 E3
Mór 12,066 E3
Mosonmagyaróvár 30,000 D3
Nádudvar 9,447 F3
Nagyatád 15,000 D3
Nagyecsed 8,225 G3
Nagykálló 11,282 F3
Nagykanizsa 55,000 D3
Nagykáta 11,922 E3
Nagykőrös 27,000 E3
Nagyszénás 7,124 F3
Nyíradony 7,146 F3
Nyírbátor 14,000 G3
Nyíregyháza 119,000 F3
Orosháza 36,000 F3
Oroszlány 22,000 E3
Ózd 45,000 F2
Paks 26,000 E3
Pápa 35,000 D3
Pásztó 12,000 E3
Pécs 182,000 E3
Pilis 9,055 E3
Pilisvörösvár 10,217 E3
Polgár 9,429 F3
Püspökladány 16,000 F3
Putnok 7,103 F2
Ráckeve 7,534 E3
Rákospalota 60,983 E3
Sajószentpéter 13,992 F2
Salgótarján 49,000 E2
Sárbogárd 13,000 E3
Sarkad 11,937 F3
Sárospatak 15,000 F2
Sárvár 16,000 D3
Sátoraljaújhely 20,000 F2
Siklós 11,000 E4
Siófok 24,000 E3
Soltvadkert 7,934 E3

OTHER FEATURES

Bakony (mts.) D3
Balaton (lake) D3
Berettyó (riv.) F3
Börzsöny (mts.) E3
Bükk (mts.) F2
Csepelsziget (isl.) E3
Danube (riv.) E3
Dráva (riv.) D3
Duna (Danube) (riv.) E3
Fertő tó (Neusiedler See) (lake) D3
Great Alföld (plain) F3
Hernád (riv.) F2
Ipoly (riv.) E2
Kapos (riv.) D3
Kékes (mt.) E3
Korishegy (mt.) D3
Körös (riv.) F3
Little Alföld (plain) D3
Maros (riv.) F3
Mátra (mts.) E3
Mecsek (mts.) D3
Mura (riv.) D3
Rába (riv.) D3
Sajó (riv.) F2
Sárviz csatorna (canal) E3
Sebes Körös (riv.) F3
Sió csatorna (canal) E3
Szentendreisziget (isl.) E3
Tarna (riv.) F3
Tisza (riv.) F3
Zagyva (riv.) E3
Zala (riv.) D3

SLOVAKIA

REGIONS

Bratislava (city) 380,259 D2
Stredoslovenský
Liptovský Mikuláš 24,520 E2
Lučenec 26,399 E2
Malacky 15,218 D2
Martin 56,208 E2
Michalovce 29,765 F2
Modra 7,679 D2
Myjava 11,668 D2
Nitra 76,663 E2
Nová Baňa 8,321 E2
Nové Mesto nad Váhom 18,170 D2
Nové Zámky 34,147 D3
Partizánske 23,266 E2
Pezinok 17,116 D2
Piešťany 30,487 D2
Poprad 38,077 F2
Považská Bystrica 30,444 E2
Prešov 71,500 F2
Prievidza 40,813 E2
Púchov 17,554 E2
Revúca 11,881 F2
Rimavská Sobota 19,699 E2
Rožňava 18,039 F2
Ružomberok 26,396 E2
Sabinov 7,008 F2
Šafárikovo 7,021 F2
Šahy 8,034 E2
Šal'a 19,167 D2
Šamorín 9,677 D2
Senec 10,772 D2
Senica 15,515 D2
Sered' 16,071 D2
Skalica 13,833 D2
Snina 13,347 G2
Spišská Nová Ves 31,917 F2
Stropkov 7,405 F2
Štúrovo 12,807 E3
Šurany 11,320 E2
Svidník 7,538 F2
Topoľčany 31,340 E2
Trebišov 14,961 F2
Trenčín 47,887 E2

Agriculture, Industry and Resources

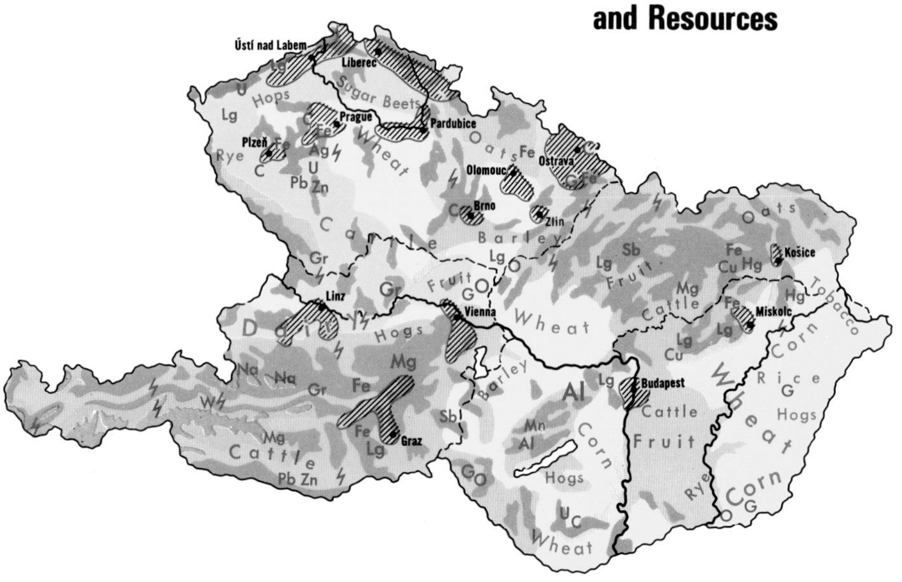
Ústí nad Labem
Liberec
Prague
Pardubice
Plzeň
Olomouc
Ostrava
Brno
Zlín
Košice
Linz
Vienna
Miskolc
Budapest
Graz
Hops
Sugar Beets
Wheat
Oats
Rye
Barley
Cattle
Fruit
Hogs
Corn
Rice
Tobacco

DOMINANT LAND USE

Cereals (chiefly wheat, corn)
Other Cereals, Livestock, Dairy
General Farming, Livestock
General Farming, Truck Farming
Pasture Livestock
Grapes, Wine
Forests
Nonagricultural Land

MAJOR MINERAL OCCURRENCES

Ag Silver
Al Bauxite
C Coal
Cu Copper
Fe Iron Ore
G Natural Gas
Gr Graphite
Hg Mercury
Lg Lignite
Mg Magnesium
Mn Manganese
Na Salt
O Petroleum
Pb Lead
Sb Antimony
U Uranium
W Tungsten
Zn Zinc

Water Power
Major Industrial Areas

Litovel 12,454 D2
Litvínov 22,624 B1
Louny 20,436 B1
Lovosice 11,456 C1
Lysá nad Labem 9,113 C1
Mariánské Lázně 17,932 B2
Mělník 18,941 C1
Mikulov 8,472 D2
Milevsko 8,852 C2
Mimoň 7,437 C1
Mladá Boleslav 45,896 C1
Mnichovo Hradiště 7,340 C1
Mohelnice 9,405 D2
Moravská Třebová 11,543 D2
Moravské Budějovice 8,943 C2
Most 60,119 B1
Náchod 19,892 D1
Nejdek 9,768 B1
Nové Město na Moravě 11,330 D2
Nový Bohumín 16,700 E2
Nový Bor 10,493 C1
Nový Bydžov 9,317 C1
Nový Jičín 31,506 D2
Nymburk 14,033 C1
Odry 10,032 D2
Olomouc 102,112 D2
Opava 59,384 D2
Orlová 31,190 E2
Ostrava 322,073 E2
Ostrov 19,618 B1
Pardubice 91,855 C1
Písek 28,104 C2
Plzeň 170,701 B2
Poděbrady 13,782 C1
Pohořelice 5,125 D2
Polička 8,972 D2
Prachatice 10,354 B2
Ústí nad Orlicí 15,945 D2
Uherské Hradiště 36,756 D2
Uherský Brod 17,459 D2
Uničov 12,507 D2
Valašské Meziříčí 26,531 D2
Varnsdorf 16,356 C1
Velké Meziříčí 14,073 D2
Veselí nad Moravou 12,464 D2
Vimperk 7,257 B2
Vítkov 7,543 D2
Vlašim 13,284 C2
Vodňany 6,989 C2
Vrbno pod Pradědem 6,912 D1
Vrchlabí 12,419 C1
Vsetín 29,927 D2
Vyškov 18,330 D2
Vysoké Mýto 10,887 D2
Zábřeh 15,184 D2
Žatec 19,529 B1
Žďár nad Sázavou 25,015 C2
Zlín 83,983 D2
Znojmo 39,271 D2

OTHER FEATURES

Bečva (riv.) E2
Berounka (riv.) C2
Bohemian (for.) B2
Bohemian-Moravian Heights (hills) C2
Chrudimka (riv.) C2
Cidlina (riv.) C1
Danube (riv.) C2
Dyje (riv.) D2
Erzgebirge (mts.) B1
Jablunka (pass) E2
Jeseniky (mts.) D1
Somogy 349,000 D3
Szabolcs-Szatmár 570,000 G3
Szolnok 428,000 F3
Tolna 263,000 E3
Vas 277,000 D3
Veszprém 387,000 D3
Zala 311,000 D3

CITIES and TOWNS

Abádszalók 6,386 F3
Abaújszántó 4,209 F2
Abony 15,624 E3
Ács 8,423 E3
Ajka 34,000 D3
Albertirsa 11,252 E3
Alsózsolca 5,045 F2
Bácsalmás 8,000 E3
Baja 41,000 E3
Balassagyarmat 20,000 E2
Balatonfüred 15,000 D3
Balkány 7,667 F3
Balmazújváros 17,371 F3
Barcs 12,000 D4
Bátaszék 7,274 E3
Battonya 9,324 F3
Békés 22,000 F3
Békéscsaba 71,000 F3
Berettyóújfalu 18,000 F3
Bicske 13,000 E3
Bonyhád 15,000 E3
Budafok 40,623 E3
Budakeszi 10,429 E3
Budaörs 22,000 E3
Budapest (cap.) 2,104,000 E3
Cegléd 40,000 E3
Celldömölk 12,000 D3
Csepel 71,693 E3
Csongrád 21,000 F3
Kaposvár 74,000 D3
Kapuvár 11,000 D3
Karcag 25,000 F3
Kazincbarcika 39,000 F2
Kecel 10,493 E3
Kecskemét 105,000 E3
Keszthely 23,000 D3
Kisbér 8,000 D3
Kiskőrös 15,000 E3
Kiskunfélegyháza 35,000 E3
Kiskunhalas 32,000 E3
Kiskunmajsa 14,439 E3
Kispest 65,106 E3
Kistelek 8,544 E3
Kisújszállás 13,000 F3
Kisvárda 17,828 G2
Komádi 8,765 F3
Komárom 19,955 E3
Komló 30,301 E3
Kondoros 7,319 F3
Körmend 12,000 D3
Kőszeg 14,000 D3
Kunhegyes 10,116 F3
Kunmadaras 7,943 F3
Kunszentmárton 12,000 F3
Kunszentmiklós 7,952 E3
Lajosmizse 12,872 E3
Leninváros 19,000 F3
Lenti 9,000 D3
Létavértes 9,106 F3
Lőrinci 10,679 E3
Makó 29,000 F3
Marcali 13,000 D3
Mátészalka 20,000 G3
Mélykút 7,640 E3
Mezőberény 12,702 F3
Mezőhegyes 8,651 F3
Mezőkovácsháza 7,000 F3
Mezőkövesd 18,000 F3
Sopron 57,000 D3
Szabadszállás 8,223 E3
Szarvas 19,000 F3
Százhalombatta 18,000 E3
Szeged 188,000 F3
Szeghalom 10,000 F3
Székesfehérvár 113,000 E3
Szekszárd 39,000 E3
Szentendre 20,000 E3
Szentes 35,000 F3
Szentgotthárd 8,000 D3
Szerencs 10,000 F2
Szigetvár 13,000 D3
Szolnok 81,000 F3
Szombathely 87,000 D3
Tamási 10,000 E3
Tapolca 18,000 D3
Tata 26,000 E3
Tatabánya 76,000 E3
Tiszaföldvár 12,560 F3
Tiszafüred 14,000 F3
Tiszakécske 12,000 E3
Tiszavasvári 14,000 F3
Tolna 8,997 E3
Törökszentmiklós 24,000 F3
Tótkomlós 8,803 F3
Tura 8,235 E3
Túrkeve 11,000 F3
Újfehértó 14,412 F3
Újpest 80,384 E3
Vác 36,000 E3
Várpalota 28,000 E3
Vásárosnamény 9,000 G2
Vecsés 19,193 E3
Veszprém 66,000 D3
Vészto 9,815 F3
Zalaegerszeg 63,000 D3
Zalaszentgrót 8,000 D3
Zirc 11,000 D3
1,524,766 E2
Východoslovenský 1,402,252 F2
Západoslovenský 1,683,891 D2

CITIES and TOWNS

Bánovce nad Bebravou 15,342 E2
Banská Bystrica 66,412 E2
Banská Štiavnica 9,180 E2
Bardejov 23,741 F2
Bratislava (capital) 380,259 D2
Brezno 17,872 E2
Bytča 11,789 E2
Čadca 19,319 E2
Čalovo 8,063 D3
Detva 14,261 E2
Dolný Kubín 13,971 E2
Dubnica nad Váhom 15,580 E2
Dunajská Streda 18,715 D3
Fil'akovo 10,497 E2
Galanta 15,477 D2
Handlová 17,777 E2
Hlohovec 21,148 D2
Holíč 8,741 D2
Hriňová 8,485 E2
Humenné 27,285 F2
Hurbanovo 7,613 E3
Kežmarok 17,570 F2
Kolárovo 11,295 D3
Komárno 32,520 D3
Košice 202,368 F2
Kremnica 7,168 E2
Krupina 7,337 E2
Kysucké Nové Mesto 14,083 E2
Levice 26,132 E2
Levoča 11,025 F2
Liptovský Hrádok 9,197 E2
Trnava 64,062 D2
Turzovka 6,962 E2
Vel'ké Kapušany 8,459 G2
Vráble 7,586 E2
Vranov nad Teplou 18,423 F2
Žiar nad Hronom 19,098 E2
Žilina 83,016 E2
Zlaté Moravce 14,119 E2
Zvolen 36,538 E2

OTHER FEATURES

Beskids, East (mts.) F2
Beskids, West (mts.) E2
Dudvá (riv.) D2
Dukla (pass) F2
Dunajec (riv.) F2
Gerlachovka (mt.) F2
Hornád (riv.) F2
Hron (riv.) E2
Ipel' (riv.) E2
Laborec (riv.) F2
Latorica (riv.) F2
Nitra (riv.) E2
Orava (riv.) E2
Poprad (riv.) F2
Slaná (riv.) F2
Slovenské Rudohorie (mts.) E2
Tatra, High (riv.) F2
Topl'a (riv.) F2
Torysa (riv.) F2
Už (riv.) G2
Váh (riv.) D2
White Carpathians (mts.) E2

†Population of Austrian cities are communes.

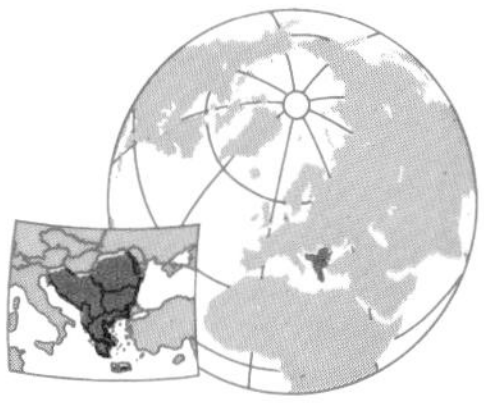

ALBANIA

AREA 11,100 sq. mi. (28,749 sq. km.)
POPULATION 3,401,126
CAPITAL Tiranë
LARGEST CITY Tiranë
HIGHEST POINT Korab 9,026 ft. (2,751 m.)
MONETARY UNIT lek
MAJOR LANGUAGE Albanian
MAJOR RELIGIONS Islam, Eastern Orthodoxy, Roman Catholicism

BOSNIA AND HERZEGOVINA

AREA 19,940 sq. mi. (51,129 sq. km.)
POPULATION 3,591,618
CAPITAL Sarajevo
LARGEST CITY Sarajevo
HIGHEST POINT Pločna 7,310 ft. (2,228 m.)
MONETARY UNIT dinar
MAJOR LANGUAGE Serbo-Croatian
MAJOR RELIGIONS Islam, Roman Catholicism, Eastern Orthodoxy,

BULGARIA

AREA 42,823 sq. mi. (110,912 sq. km.)
POPULATION 8,155,828
CAPITAL Sofia
LARGEST CITY Sofia
HIGHEST POINT Musala 9,597 ft. (2,925 m.)
MONETARY UNIT lev
MAJOR LANGUAGE Bulgarian
MAJOR RELIGION Eastern Orthodoxy

CROATIA

AREA 22,050 sq. mi. (56,538 sq. km.)
POPULATION 4,681,015
CAPITAL Zagreb
LARGEST CITY Zagreb
HIGHEST POINT Mali Rajinac 5,574 ft. (1,699 m.)
MONETARY UNIT Croatian kuna
MAJOR LANGUAGE Serbo-Croatian
MAJOR RELIGIONS Roman Catholicism, Eastern Orthodoxy

FORMER YUGOSLAV REP. OF MACEDONIA

AREA 9,889 sq. mi. (25,713 sq. km.)
POPULATION 2,035,044
CAPITAL Skopje
LARGEST CITY Skopje
HIGHEST POINT Solunska Glava 8,333 ft. (2,540 m.)
MONETARY UNIT denar
MAJOR LANGUAGES Macedonian, Serbo-Croatian, Albanian
MAJOR RELIGIONS Eastern Orthodoxy, Islam, Roman Catholicism

GREECE

AREA 50,944 sq. mi. (131,945 sq. km.)
POPULATION 10,750,705
CAPITAL Athens
LARGEST CITY Athens
HIGHEST POINT Olympus 9,570 ft. (2,917 m.)
MONETARY UNIT drachma
MAJOR LANGUAGE Greek
MAJOR RELIGION Eastern (Greek) Orthodoxy

ROMANIA

AREA 91,699 sq. mi. (237,500 sq. km.)
POPULATION 22,291,200
CAPITAL Bucharest
LARGEST CITY Bucharest
HIGHEST POINT Molodoveanul 8,343 ft. (2,543 m.)
MONETARY UNIT leu
MAJOR LANGUAGES Romanian, Hungarian
MAJOR RELIGION Eastern Orthodoxy

SLOVENIA

AREA 7,898 sq. mi. (20,251 sq. km.)
POPULATION 1,970,056
CAPITAL Ljubljana
LARGEST CITY Ljubljana
HIGHEST POINT Triglav 9,393 ft. (2,863 m.)
MONETARY UNIT tolar
MAJOR LANGUAGES Slovenian, Serbo-Croatian
MAJOR RELIGIONS Roman Catholicism, Eastern Orthodoxy

YUGOSLAVIA

AREA 38,989 sq. mi. (102,173 sq. km.)
POPULATION 11,210,243
CAPITAL Belgrade
LARGEST CITY Belgrade
HIGHEST POINT Daravica 8,714 ft. (2,656 m.)
MONETARY UNIT Yugoslav new dinar
MAJOR LANGUAGES Serbo-Croatian, Slovenian, Montenegrin, Albanian
MAJOR RELIGIONS Eastern Orthodoxy, Roman Catholicism

ALBANIA

BOSNIA AND HERZEGOVINA

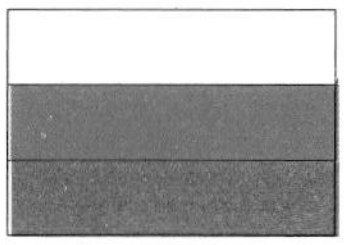
BULGARIA

CROATIA

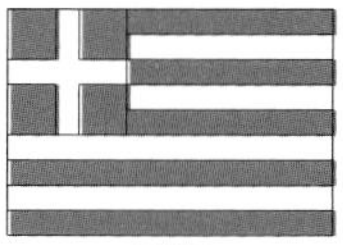
GREECE

MACEDONIA

ROMANIA

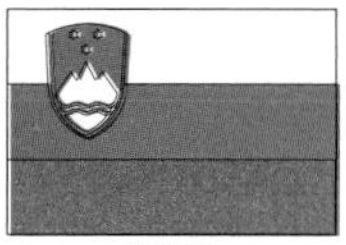
SLOVENIA

YUGOSLAVIA

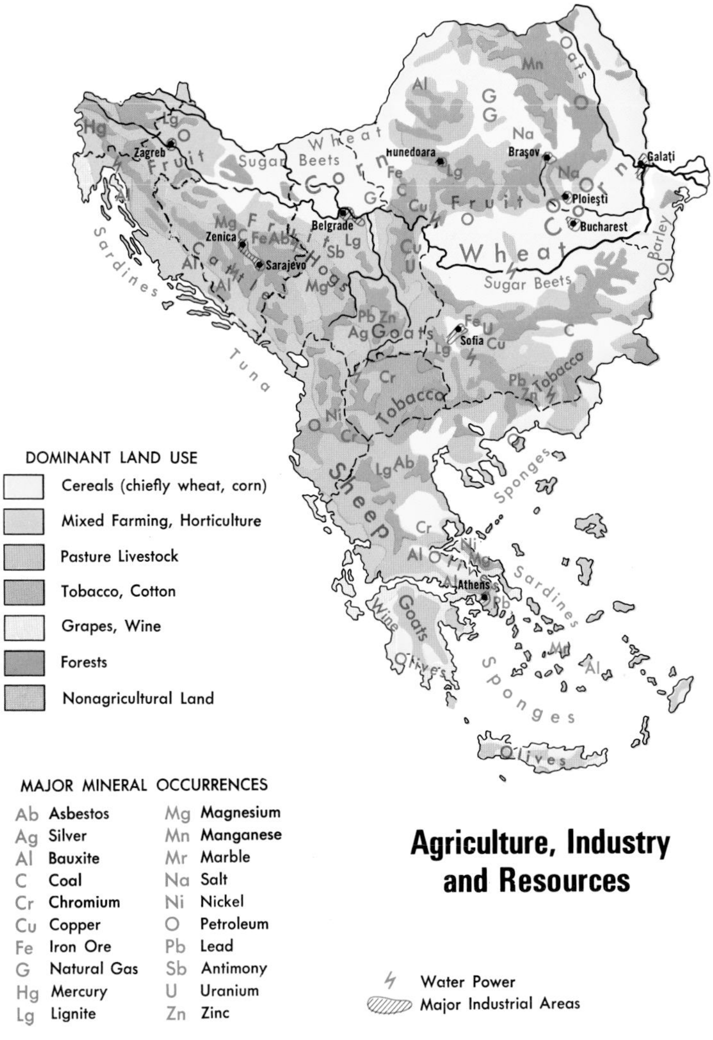
Zagreb
Belgrade
Zenica
Sarajevo
Hunedoara
Braşov
Galaţi
Ploieşti
Bucharest
Sofia
Athens
Wheat
Sugar Beets
Corn
Fruit
Hogs
Wheat
Sugar Beets
Oats
Corn
Barley
Goats
Tobacco
Tobacco
Sheep
Goats
Wine
Sponges
Sardines
Olives
Sponges
Olives
Sardines
Tuna
Sardines
DOMINANT LAND USE
Cereals (chiefly wheat, corn)
Mixed Farming, Horticulture
Pasture Livestock
Tobacco, Cotton
Grapes, Wine
Forests
Nonagricultural Land
MAJOR MINERAL OCCURRENCES
Ab Asbestos
Ag Silver
Al Bauxite
C Coal
Cr Chromium
Cu Copper
Fe Iron Ore
G Natural Gas
Hg Mercury
Lg Lignite
Mg Magnesium
Mn Manganese
Mr Marble
Na Salt
Ni Nickel
O Petroleum
Pb Lead
Sb Antimony
U Uranium
Zn Zinc
Water Power
Major Industrial Areas

Agriculture, Industry and Resources

ALBANIA

CITIES and TOWNS

Berat 40,500 ... D5
Delvinë 6,000 ... D6
Durrës (Durazzo) 78,700 ... D5
Elbasan 78,300 ... E5
Fier 40,300 ... D5
Gjirokastër 23,800 ... E5
Kavajë 24,200 ... D5
Korçë 61,500 ... E5
Krujë 9,600 ... D5
Kuçovë (Stalin) 20,600 ... D5
Kukës 9,500 ... E4
Lezhë 6,900 ... D5
Lushnjë 26,900 ... D5
Peshkopi 7,600 ... E5
Pogradec 13,100 ... E5
Sarandë 10,800 ... E6
Shijak 6,200 ... D5
Shkodër 76,300 ... D4
Stalin 20,600 ... D5
Tiranë (Tirana) (cap.) 225,700 ... E5
Vlorë 67,700 ... D5

OTHER FEATURES

Adriatic (sea) ... B4
Drin (riv.) ... E4
Korab (mt.) ... E4
Ohrid (lake) ... E5
Otranto (str.) ... D5
Prespa (lake) ... E5
Sazan (isl.) ... D5
Scutari (lake) ... D4
Vijosë (riv.) ... D5

BOSNIA and HERZEGOVINA

CITIES and TOWNS

Banja Luka 183,618 ... C3
Bihać 65,544 ... B3
Bijeljina 92,808 ... D3
Bileca 13,199 ... D4
Bosanska Dubica 30,867 ... C3
Bosanska Gradiška 58,095 ... C3
Bosanska Krupa 55,229 ... C3
Bosanski Brod 32,286 ... D3
Bosanski Novi 42,142 ... C3
Bosanski Petrovac 16,095 ... C3
Bosanski Šamac 32,320 ... D3
Brčko 82,768 ... D3
Bugojno 39,969 ... C3
Čapljina 26,032 ... C4
Cazin 57,110 ... B3
Derventa 57,010 ... C3
Doboj 99,548 ... C3
Drvar 17,983 ... C3
Donji Vakuf 22,606 ... C3
Foča 44,661 ... D4
Gacko 10,729 ... D4
Glamoč 14,120 ... C3
Gornji Vakuf 22,432 ... C4
Gračanica 54,311 ... D3
Gradačac 54,281 ... D3
Jajce 41,197 ... C3
Kladanj 15,641 ... D3
Ključ 40,008 ... C3
Konjic 43,677 ... C4
Livno 40,438 ... C4
Ljubinje 4,516 ... D4
Ljubuški 27,603 ... C4
Maglaj 42,160 ... D3
Modriča 34,541 ... D3
Mostar 110,377 ... C4
Nevesinje 16,326 ... D4
Prijedor 108,868 ... C3
Prozor 19,108 ... C4
Rogatica 23,578 ... D4
Sanski Most 62,467 ... C3
Sarajevo (cap.) 448,500 ... D4
Srebrenica 36,292 ... D3
Stolac 18,910 ... C4
Teslić 60,434 ... C3
Travnik 64,100 ... C3
Trebinje 30,372 ... D4
Tuzla 121,717 ... D3
Vareš 22,822 ... D3
Višegrad 23,201 ... D4
Visoko 40,901 ... D4
Vlasenica 30,498 ... D3
Zenica 132,733 ... C3
Žepče 19,754 ... D3
Zvornik 73,845 ... D3

OTHER FEATURES

Adriatic (sea) ... B4
Bosna (riv.) ... D3
Dinaric Alps (mts.) ... B3
Drina (riv.) ... D3
Neretva (riv.) ... D4
Tara (riv.) ... D4
Una (riv.) ... C3
Vrbas (riv.) ... C3

BULGARIA

CITIES and TOWNS

Asenovgrad 47,159 ... G5
Aytos 23,124 ... H4
Balchik 12,764 ... J4
Bansko 10,025 ... F5
Berkovitsa 16,340 ... F4
Blagoevgrad 65,481 ... F5
Botevgrad 22,659 ... F4
Burgas 182,856 ... H4
Byala 11,017 ... G4
Byala Slatina 16,034 ... F4
Chirpan 20,440 ... G4
Dimitrovgrad 54,056 ... G4
Dobrich (Tolbukhin) 109,170 ... H4
Dryanovo 10,306 ... G4
Elkhovo 13,655 ... H4
Gabrovo 81,629 ... G4
Gorna Oryakhovitsa 40,895 ... G4
Gotse Delchev 19,836 ... F5
Grudovo 10,736 ... H4
Ikhtiman 13,001 ... F4
Isperikh 11,235 ... H4
Karlovo 28,403 ... G4
Karnobat 22,536 ... H4
Kavarna 12,024 ... J4
Kazanlŭk 61,396 ... G4
Kharmanli 21,050 ... G5
Khaskovo 87,847 ... G5
Kubrat 10,758 ... H4
Kŭrdzhali 55,201 ... G5
Kyustendil 53,498 ... F4
Lom 32,307 ... F4
Lovech 48,992 ... G4
Lukovit 10,645 ... G4
Mikhaylovgrad 51,714 ... F4
Momchilgrad 10,189 ... G5
Nesebŭr 8,130 ... H4
Nova Zagora 25,327 ... H4
Novi Pazar 16,314 ... H4
Omurtag 9,505 ... H4
Oryakhovo 14,012 ... F4
Panagyurishte 22,034 ... G4
Pazardzhik 77,603 ... G4
Pernik 94,460 ... F4
Peshtera 18,763 ... G4
Petrich 26,451 ... F5
Pirdop 8,248 ... G4
Pleven 129,863 ... G4
Plovdiv 343,064 ... G4
Pomorie 13,507 ... H4
Popovo 21,236 ... H4
Provadiya 15,762 ... H4
Radomir 16,733 ... F4
Razgrad 49,582 ... H4
Razlog 14,010 ... F5
Rositsa 185,485 ... H4
Ruse 185,485 ... H4
Samokov 27,485 ... F4
Sandanski 24,629 ... F5
Sevlievo 26,560 ... G4
Shumen 100,125 ... H4
Silistra 53,537 ... H3
Sliven 9,037 ... H4
Smolyan 31,456 ... G5
Sofia (cap.) 1,121,763 ... F4
Stanke Dimitrov 41,897 ... F4
Stara Zagora 151,163 ... G4
Svilengrad 17,472 ... H5
Svishtov 30,555 ... G4
Teteven 12,784 ... G4
Tolbukhin 109,170 ... H4
Troyan 26,179 ... G4
Tŭrgovishte 46,043 ... H4
Tutrakan 12,153 ... H4
Varna 302,816 ... H4
Veliko Tŭrnovo 69,173 ... G4
Vidin 62,541 ... F4
Vratsa 75,180 ... F4
Yambol 90,019 ... H4
Zlatograd 8,780 ... G5

OTHER FEATURES

Arda (riv.) ... G5
Balkan (mts.) ... G4
Black (sea) ... J4
Danube (riv.) ... H4
Dunav (Danube) (riv.) ... H4
Emine (cape) ... J4
Iskŭr (riv.) ... G4
Kaliakra (cape) ... J4
Maritsa (riv.) ... G4
Mesta (riv.) ... F5
Midzhur (mt.) ... F4
Musala (mt.) ... F4
Osŭm (riv.) ... G4
Rhodope (mts.) ... G5
Rujen (mt.) ... F4
Struma (riv.) ... F5
Timok (riv.) ... F3
Tundzha (riv.) ... G4
Vit (riv.) ... G4

CROATIA

CITIES and TOWNS

Beli Manastir 53,409 ... D3
Biograd 15,865 ... B4
Bjelovar 66,553 ... C3
Čakovec 116,825 ... C2
Daruvar 31,424 ... C3
Djakovo 52,349 ... D3
Dubrovnik 66,131 ... D4
Fiume (Rijeka) 193,044 ... B3
Gospić 31,263 ... B3
Gračac 11,863 ... B3
Karlovac 78,363 ... B3
Knin 43,731 ... C3
Koprivnica 61,166 ... C2
Kostajnica 15,548 ... C3
Križevci 41,316 ... C2
Krk 13,334 ... B3
Kutina 38,597 ... C3
Makarska 17,819 ... C4
Našice 38,938 ... D3
Nova Gradiška 61,267 ... C3
Novska 24,530 ... C3
Ogulin 31,076 ... B3
Omiš 24,082 ... C4
Opatija 29,274 ... B3
Osijek 158,790 ... D3
Pag 7,076 ... B3
Petrinja 33,570 ... C3
Ploče (Kardeljevo) 11,328 ... C4
Pola (Pula) 77,278 ... A3

(continued on following page)

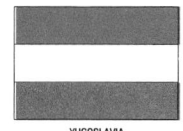

(continued)

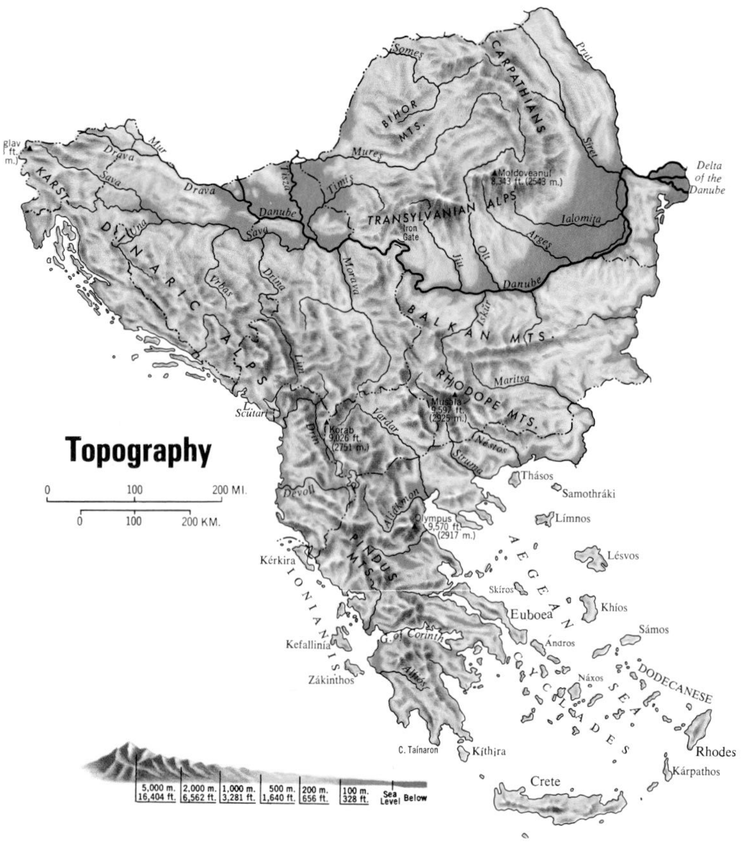
Topography
0 100 200 MI.
0 100 200 KM.
5,000 m. 16,404 ft.
2,000 m. 6,562 ft.
1,000 m. 3,281 ft.
500 m. 1,640 ft.
200 m. 656 ft.
100 m. 328 ft.
Sea Level
Below
CARPATHIANS
BIHOR MTS.
TRANSYLVANIAN ALPS
Moldoveanul 8,343 ft. (2543 m.)
Iron Gate
Delta of the Danube
Danube
Drava
Sava
Mureş
Timiş
Ialomiţa
Argeş
Olt
Jiu
Siret
Prut
Someş
Mur
KARST
DINARIC ALPS
Drina
Vrbas
Morava
Iskŭr
BALKAN MTS.
RHODOPE MTS.
Maritsa
Musala 9,596 ft. (2925 m.)
Nestos
Struma
Vardar
Korab 9,026 ft. (2751 m.)
Scutari
Devoll
Aliákmon
PINDUS MTS.
Olympus 9,570 ft. (2917 m.)
Thásos
Samothráki
Límnos
Lésvos
Khíos
Sámos
AEGEAN SEA
Skíros
Euboea
Ándros
Náxos
CYCLADES
DODECANESE
Rhodes
Kárpathos
Crete
Kíthira
C. Taínaron
Kérkira
Kefallinía
Zákinthos
IONIAN SEA
G. of Corinth

Poreč 19,946 ......A3
Pula 77,278 ......A3
Rab 8,877 ......B3
Ragusa (Dubrovnik) 66,131 ......C4
Rijeka 193,044 ......B3
Rovinj 18,277 ......A3
Samobor 43,855 ......B3
Senj 9,582 ......B3
Šibenik 80,148 ......C4
Sinj 59,298 ......C4
Sisak 84,756 ......C3
Slavonska Požega 71,286 ......C3
Slavonski Brod 106,400 ......D3
Split 235,922 ......C4
Trogir 19,856 ......C4
Varaždin 90,729 ......C2
Vinkovci 95,245 ......D3
Virovitica 47,417 ......C3
Vukovar 81,203 ......D3
Zadar 116,174 ......B3
Zagreb (cap.) 681,173 ......C3
Zara (Zadar) 116,174 ......B3

OTHER FEATURES

Adriatic (sea) B4
Brač (isl.) C4
Cazma (riv.) C3
Cres (isl.) B3
Dalmatia (reg.) C4
Danube (riv.) E3
Dinaric Alps (mts.) B3
Drava (riv.) C3
Dugi Otok (isl.) B3
Hvar (isl.) C4
Istria (pen.) A3
Kamenjak (cape) A3
Korčula (isl.) C4
Kornat (isl.) B4
Krk (isl.) B3
Kupa (riv.) B3
Kvarner (gulf) B3
Lastovo (Lagosta) (isl.) C4
Lošinj (isl.) B3
Mljet (isl.) C4
Pag (isl.) B3
Palagruža (Pelagosa) (isl.) C4
Rab (isl.) B3
Sava (riv.) D3
Slavonia (reg.) C3
Šolta (isl.) C4
Una (riv.) C3
Vis (isl.) C4
Žirje (isl.) B4

FORMER YUGOSLAV REP. OF MACEDONIA

CITIES and TOWNS

Berovo 20,226 ......F5
Bitola 137,835 ......E5
Debar 22,506 ......E5
Gevgelija 32,023 ......F5
Gostivar 101,188 ......E5
Kavadarci 39,738 ......F5
Kičevo 51,452 ......E5
Kočani 47,976 ......F5
Kumanovo 126,368 ......E4
Ohrid 64,316 ......E5
Prilep 99,941 ......E5
Radoviš 28,574 ......F5
Skopje (cap.) 506,547 ......E5
Štip 46,651 ......F5
Struga 54,489 ......E5
Strumica 87,446 ......F5
Tetovo 162,414 ......E5
Titov Veles 64,901 ......E5

OTHER FEATURES

Korab (mt.) E5
Ohrid (lake) E5
Prespa (lake) E5
Rujen (mt.) F4
Vardar (riv.) E5

GREECE

REGIONS

Aegean Islands 417,813 ......G6
Athens, Greater 3,027,331 ......F7
Áyion Óros (aut. dist.) 1,732 ......G5
Central Greece and Euboea 1,099,841 ......F6
Crete 502,165 ......G8
Epirus 324,541 ......E6
Ionian Islands 182,651 ......D6
Macedonia 2,121,953 ......F5
Pelopónnisos 1,012,528 ......F7
Thessaly 695,654 ......F6
Thrace 345,220 ......G5

CITIES and TOWNS

Agrínion 34,328 ......E6
Aíyion 20,824 ......F6
Alexandroúpolis 34,535 ......G5
Amaliás 14,698 ......E7
Árgos 20,702 ......F7
Árta 18,283 ......E6
Atalándi 5,456 ......F6
Athens (cap.) 885,737 ......F7
Áyios Nikólaos 8,130 ......G8
Candia (Iráklion) 101,634 ......G8
Canea (Khaniá) 40,564 ......G8
Corinth 22,658 ......F7
Dhidhimótikhon 8,374 ......H5
Dráma 36,109 ......G5
Édhessa 16,054 ......F5
Ermoúpolis 13,876 ......G7
Flórina 12,562 ......E5
Grevená 7,433 ......E5
Ierápetra 8,575 ......G8
Ioánnina 44,829 ......E6
Iráklion 101,634 ......G8
Itháki 2,037 ......E6
Kalámai 41,911 ......F7
Kálimnos 10,118 ......H7
Kardhítsa 27,291 ......E6
Kastoría 17,133 ......E5
Kateríni 38,016 ......F5
Kaválla 56,375 ......G5
Kérkira 33,561 ......D6
Khalkís 44,867 ......F6
Khaniá 40,564 ......G8
Khíos 24,070 ......G6
Kiáton 7,392 ......F6
Kilkís 11,148 ......F5
Komotiní 34,051 ......G5
Koropí 11,214 ......G7
Kos 11,851 ......H7
Kozáni 30,994 ......F5
Lamía 41,667 ......F6
Lárisa 102,048 ......F6
Lávrion 8,921 ......G7
Levádhia 16,864 ......F6
Marathón 2,052 ......G6
Mégara 17,719 ......F6
Mesolóngion 10,164 ......E6
Mitilíni 24,115 ......H6
Náousa 19,383 ......F5
Návpaktos 9,012 ......F6
Návplion 10,609 ......F7
Náxos 3,735 ......G7
Orestías 12,685 ......H5
Pátrai 141,529 ......E6
Piraiévs (Piraeus) 196,389 ......F7
Pírgos 21,958 ......E7
Préveza 12,662 ......E6
Psakhná 5,320 ......F6
Ptolemaís 22,109 ......E5
Réthimnon 17,736 ......G8
Rhodes (Ródhos) 40,392 ......J7
Salamís 20,437 ......F6
Salonika (Thessaloníki) 406,413 ......F5
Sámos 5,575 ......H7
Samothráki 941 ......G5
Sérrai 45,213 ......F5
Sparta 11,911 ......F7
Thásos 2,300 ......G5
Thessaloníki 406,413 ......F5
Thívai 18,712 ......F6
Tirnávos 10,965 ......F6
Trikkála 40,857 ......E6
Trípolis 21,311 ......F7
Vérria 37,087 ......F5
Vólos 71,378 ......F6
Vónitsani 3,627 ......E6
Xánthi 31,541 ......G5
Yiannitsá 21,082 ......F5
Zante (Zákinthos) 9,764 ......E7

OTHER FEATURES

Aegean (sea) G6
Akrí (cape) E7
Aktí (pen.) G5
Amorgós (isl.) G7
Anáfi (isl.) G7
Andikíthira (isl.) F8
Ándros (isl.) G7
Arda (riv.) G5
Argolís (gulf) F7
Astipálaia (isl.) H7
Áthos (mt.) G5
Áyios Evstrátios (isl.) G6
Áyios Yeóryios (cape) G5
Cephalonia (Kefalliníia) (isl.) E6
Corfu (Kérkira) (isl.) D6
Corinth (gulf) F6
Crete (isl.) G8
Crete (sea) G7
Cyclades (isls.) G7
Día (isl.) G8
Dodecanese (isls.) H8
Euboea (Évvoia) (isl.) G6
Évros (riv.) H5
Gávdhos (isl.) F8
Ídhi (mt.) G8
Ikaría (isl.) G7
Ionian (sea) D7
Íos (isl.) G7
Itháki (Ithaca) (isl.) E6
Kafirévs (cape) G6
Kálimnos (isl.) H7
Kárpathos (isl.) H8
Kásos (isl.) H8
Kassándra (pen.) F6
Kéa (isl.) G7
Kefalliníia (isl.) E6
Kérkira (isl.) D6
Khálki (isl.) H7
Khaniá (gulf) G8
Khíos (isl.) G6
Kímilos (isl.) G7
Kiparissía (gulf) E7
Kíthira (isl.) F7
Kíthnos (isl.) G7
Kos (isl.) H7
Kriós (cape) F8
Kriti (Crete) (isl.) G8
Lakonía (gulf) F7
Léros (isl.) H7
Lésvos (isl.) G6
Levítha (isl.) H7
Levkás (isl.) E6
Límnos (isl.) G6
Maléa (cape) F7
Matapan (Taínaron) (cape) F7
Merabéllou (gulf) H8
Mesará (gulf) G8
Messíni (gulf) E7
Míkinos (isl.) G7
Mílos (isl.) G7
Mirtóön (sea) F7
Náxos (isl.) G7
Néstos (riv.) G5
Nísiros (isl.) H7
Northern Sporades (isls.) F6
Olympia (isls.) E7
Olympus (mt.) F5
Parnassus (mt.) F6
Páros (isl.) G7
Pátmos (isl.) H7
Paxoí (isl.) D6
Pindus (mts.) E6
Pinió (riv.) E6
Prespa (lake) E5
Psará (isl.) G6
Psevdhókavos (cape) G6
Rhodes (isl.) H7
Rhodope (mts.) G5
Salonika (Thermaic) (gulf) F6
Sámos (isl.) H7
Samothráki (isl.) G5
Saría (isl.) H8
Saronic (gulf) F7
Sérifos (isl.) G7
Sídheros (cape) H8
Sífnos (isl.) G7
Símí (isl.) H7
Síros (isl.) G7
Sithoniá (pen.) F5
Skíros (isl.) G6
Spátha (cape) F8
Strimón (gulf) G5
Strofádhes (isls.) E7
Taínaron (cape) F7
Thásos (isls.) G5
Thermaic (gulf) F5
Thíra (isl.) G7
Tílos (isl.) H7
Tínos (isl.) G7
Toronaic (gulf) F5
Vardar (riv.) E5
Vólvi (lake) F5
Voïviis (lake) F6
Voúxa (cape) F8
Zákinthos (Zante) (isl.) E7

ROMANIA

CITIES and TOWNS

Aiud 27,600 ......F2
Alba Iulia 53,000 ......F2
Alexandria 43,700 ......G3
Anina 11,300 ......E3
Arad 182,000 ......E2
Babadag 9,000 ......J3
Bacău 156,200 ......H2
Baia Mare 123,300 ......F2
Băileşti 21,500 ......F3
Balş 17,300 ......G3
Beiuş 10,100 ......F2
Bicaz 9,300 ......G2
Bîrlad 63,800 ......H2
Bistrita 59,800 ......G2
Blaj 22,200 ......F2
Borşa 25,287 ......F2
Botoşani 84,900 ......H2
Brad 18,600 ......F2
Brăila 219,200 ......H3
Braşov 320,200 ......G3
Bucharest (Bucureşti) (cap.) 1,929,400 ......G3
Buhuşi 20,300 ......H2
Buzău 116,300 ......H3
Buziaş 8,700 ......E3
Calafat 17,100 ......F3
Călăraşi 58,000 ......H3
Caracal 33,600 ......G3
Caransebeş 28,800 ......F3
Carei 25,500 ......F2
Cernavodă 15,000 ......J3
Chişineu Criş 9,600 ......E2
Cîmpia Turzii 25,300 ......F2
Cîmpina 35,300 ......G3
Cîmpulung 37,400 ......G3
Cîmpulung Moldovenesc 20,500 ......G2
Cisnădie 21,100 ......G3
Cluj-Napoca 289,800 ......F2
Comaneşti 18,500 ......H2
Constanta 293,900 ......J3
Corabia 20,300 ......G4
Costeşti 10,900 ......G3
Craiova 239,700 ......F3
Curtea de Argeş 26,900 ......G3
Darabani 11,500 ......H1
Dej 36,500 ......F2
Deva 73,300 ......F3
Dorohoi 25,700 ......H2
Drăgăneşti Olt 11,800 ......G3
Drăgăşani 17,300 ......G3
Drobeta-Turnu Severin 86,600 ......F3
Făgăraş 37,200 ......G3
Fălticeni 24,000 ......H2
Feteşti 29,600 ......H3
Focşani 70,700 ......H3
Găeşti 14,000 ......G3
Galati 268,000 ......H3
Gheorghe Gheorghiu-Dej 46,100 ......H2
Gheorghieni 21,800 ......G2
Gherla 20,700 ......G2
Giurgiu 57,000 ......G4
Hateg 10,200 ......F3
Hîrlău 8,900 ......H2
Hîrşova 9,000 ......J3
Huedin 8,700 ......F2
Hunedoara 85,700 ......F3
Huşi 26,000 ......J2
Iaşi 279,800 ......H2
Ineu 10,800 ......E2
Jimbolia 14,600 ......E3
Lipova 12,900 ......E2
Luduş 16,000 ......G2
Lugoj 50,000 ......E3
Lupeni 29,100 ......F3
Mangalia 31,100 ......J4
Medgidia 45,300 ......J3
Mediaş 69,000 ......G2
Miercurea Ciuc 40,400 ......G2
Mizil 15,200 ......H3
Moineşti 21,200 ......H2
Moldova Nouă 17,800 ......E3
Moreni 18,900 ......G3
Ocna Mureş 16,200 ......G2
Odorheiu Secuiesc 36,200 ......G2
Oltenita 26,800 ......H3
Oradea 192,600 ......E2
Orăştie 19,900 ......F3
Oravita 114,300 ......E3
Orşova 115,800 ......F3
Panciu 77,900 ......H3
Paşcani 229,500 ......H2
Petrila 25,900 ......F3
Petroşeni 45,600 ......F3
Piatra Neamt 93,300 ......H2
Piteşti 143,600 ......G3
Ploieşti 219,900 ......H3
Pucioasa 14,100 ......G3
Rădăuti 26,000 ......G2
Reghin 33,600 ......G2
Reşita 96,800 ......E3
Rîmnicu Sărat 32,400 ......H3
Rîmnicu Vîlcea 78,900 ......G3
Roman 62,700 ......H2
Roşiori de Vede 31,700 ......G3
Săcele 33,900 ......G3
Salonta 20,400 ......E2
Satu Mare 115,600 ......F2
Sebeş 29,500 ......F3
Segarcea 8,700 ......F3
Sfîntu Gheorghe 57,900 ......G3
Sibiu 164,200 ......G3
Sighetu Marmaţiei 40,500 ......F2
Sighişoara 33,000 ......G2
Şimleul Silvaniei 15,100 ......F2
Sinaia 14,700 ......G3
Sînnicolaul Mare 13,600 ......E2
Slatina 62,800 ......G3
Slobozia 39,400 ......H3
Sovata 11,200 ......G2
Strehaia 11,800 ......F3
Suceava 76,500 ......H2
Tăşnad 10,400 ......F2
Techirghiol 11,800 ......J3
Tecuci 40,300 ......H3
Timişoara 288,200 ......E3
Tîrgovişte 77,500 ......G3
Tîrgu Jiu 75,200 ......F3
Tîrgu Mureş 141,300 ......G2
Tîrgu Neamt 16,600 ......H2
Tîrgu Ocna 12,800 ......H2
Tîrgu Secuiesc 19,800 ......H2
Tîrnăveni 27,900 ......G2
Toplita 15,200 ......G2
Tulcea 73,600 ......J3
Turda 58,700 ......F2
Turnu Măgurele 33,000 ......G4
Urlata 11,200 ......H3
Urziceni 14,300 ......H3
Vaslui 50,100 ......H2
Vatra Dornei 17,800 ......G2
Videle 11,500 ......G3
Vişeul de Sus 20,800 ......G2
Zalău 43,300 ......F2
Zărneşti 25,000 ......G3
Zimnicea 16,400 ......G4

OTHER FEATURES

Argeş (riv.) G3
Bîrlad (riv.) H2
Black (sea) J4
Brăila (marshes) H3
Buzău (riv.) H3
Carpathian (mts.) G2
Crişul Alb (riv.) F2
Crişul Repede (riv.) F2
Danube (delta) J3
Danube (riv.) H4
Ialomiţa (marshes) J3
Ialomiţa (riv.) H3
Jijia (riv.) H2
Jiu (riv.) F3
Moldoveanul (mt.) G3
Mureş (riv.) E2
Olt (riv.) G3
Peleaga (mt.) F3
Pietrosul (mt.) G2
Prut (riv.) J2
Siret (riv.) H2
Someş (riv.) F2
Timiş (riv.) E3
Tîrnava Mare (riv.) G2
Transylvanian Alps (mts.) G3

SLOVENIA

CITIES and TOWNS

Bled 4,710 ......A2
Brežice 25,238 ......C3
Celje 63,877 ......B2
Jesenice 31,094 ......A2
Kočevje 18,139 ......B3
Koper 41,843 ......A3
Kranj 66,879 ......B2
Krško 27,774 ......B3
Ljubljana (cap.) 305,211 ......B3
Maribor 185,699 ......B2
Murska Sobota 64,299 ......C2
Nova Gorizia 56,758 ......A3
Novo Mesto 55,584 ......B3
Piran 15,235 ......A3
Postojna 19,892 ......B3
Ptuj 67,754 ......B2
Ravne na Koroškem 25,907 ......B2
Škofja Loka 35,276 ......B2
Trbovlje 18,786 ......B2
Tržič 14,014 ......B2
Velenje 38,041 ......B2

OTHER FEATURES

Adriatic (sea) B4
Drava (riv.) C3
Kupa (riv.) B3
Mur (riv.) B2
Triglav (mt.) A2

YUGOSLAVIA

INTERNAL DIVISIONS

Kosovo (aut. reg.) 1,240,919 ......E4
Montenegro (rep.) 527,207 ......D4
Serbia (rep.) 8,401,673 ......E3
Vojvodina (aut. prov.) 1,953,980 ......D3

CITIES and TOWNS

Aleksinac 67,286 ......E4
Apatin 33,843 ......D3
Arendjelovac 46,803 ......E3
Bačka Topola 41,889 ......D3
Bar 32,535 ......D4
Bečej 44,243 ......E3
Bela Crkva 25,690 ......E3
Belgrade (cap.) 1,470,073 ......E3
Beograde (Belgrade) (cap.) 1,470,073 ......E3
Bijelo Polje 55,634 ......D4
Bor 56,486 ......E3
Čačak 110,676 E4
Caribrod (Dimitrovgrad) 15,158 ......F4
Cetinje 20,213 ......D4
Ćuprija 38,841 ......E4
Dimitrovgrad 15,158 ......F4
Djakovica 92,203 ......E4
Gnjilane 84,085 ......E4
Gornji Milanovac 50,651 ......E3
Herceg Novi 23,258 ......D4
Ivangrad 49,772 ......D4
Kanjiža 32,709 ......D2
Kikinda 69,854 ......E3
Knjaževac 48,789 ......F4
Kosovska Mitrovica 105,353 ......E4
Kotor 20,455 ......D4
Kragujevac 164,823 ......E3
Kraljevo 121,622 ......E4
Kruševac 132,972 ......E4
Leskovac 159,001 ......E4
Loznica 84,180 ......D3
Negotin 63,973 ......F3
Nikšíc 72,299 ......D4
Niš 230,711 ......E4
Novi Pazar 74,000 ......E4
Novi Sad 257,685 ......D3
Pančevo 123,791 ......E3
Paraćin 64,718 ......E4
Peć 111,071 ......E4
Pirot 69,653 ......F4
Plav 19,560 ......D4
Pljevlja 43,316 ......D4
Podgorica 132,290 ......D4
Požarevac 81,123 ......E3
Preševo 33,948 ......E4
Priboj 35,200 ......D4
Prijedor 108,868 ......C3
Prijepolje 46,902 ......D4
Priština 210,040 ......E4
Prizren 134,526 ......E4
Prokuplje 56,256 ......E4
Ruma 55,083 ......D3
Šabac 119,668 ......D3
Senta 30,519 ......D3
Šid 37,459 ......D3
Sjenica 35,570 ......E4
Smederevo 107,366 ......E3
Smederevska Palanka 60,945 ......E3
Sombor 99,168 ......D3
Sremska Mitrovica 85,129 ......D3
Subotica 154,611 ......D2
Surdulica 27,029 ......F4
Svetozarevo 76,460 ......E4
Svilajnac 34,888 ......E3
Titovo Užice 77,049 ......D4
Trstenik 53,695 ......E4
Ub 36,259 ......E3
Ulcinj 21,575 ......D5
Uroševac 113,680 ......E4
Valjevo 95,449 ......D3
Velika Plana 52,619 ......E3
Veliki Bečkerek (Zrenjanin) 139,000 ......E3
Vranje 82,527 ......E4
Vrbas 45,755 ......D3
Vršac 61,005 ......E3
Vučitrn 65,512 ......E4
Zaječar 76,681 ......F4
Zrenjanin 139,000 ......E3

OTHER FEATURES

Adriatic (sea) B4
Bobotov Kuk (mt.) D4
Danube (riv.) E3
Drina (riv.) D3
Ibar (riv.) E4
Lim (riv.) D4
Midzhur (mt.) F4
Morava (riv.) E3
Sava (riv.) D3
Scutari (lake) D4
Timok (riv.) F3
Tisa (riv.) E3

The Balkan States
CONIC PROJECTION
SCALE OF MILES
0 25 50 75 100 125 150 175
SCALE OF KILOMETERS
0 25 50 75 100 125 150 175
Capitals of Countries
Administrative Centers
International Boundaries
Major Internal Boundaries
Minor Internal Boundaries
Canals
* Former Yugoslav Republic of Macedonia
BULGARIA and GREECE are divided into regions and departments, respectively. Because of the scale no attempt has been made to delimit and name these subdivisions; their administrative centers have, however, been designated.
The larger divisions named in Greece are well-known geographical regions, without administrative function.
ROMANIA consists of thirty-nine counties and three cities of regional status, Bucharest, Constanţa and Petroşeni. Scale does not permit delimiting these counties.
ALBANIA is divided into twenty-seven districts. Scale does not permit the delimitation of these divisions.
CZECH REP.
SLOVAKIA
UKRAINE
MOLDOVA
AUSTRIA
HUNGARY
ROMANIA
SLOVENIA
CROATIA
BOSNIA & HERZEGOVINA
YUGOSLAVIA
MONTENEGRO
KOSOVO
ALBANIA
F.Y.R.O.M.*
BULGARIA
GREECE
TURKEY
ITALY
GERMANY
Carpathian Mts.
Transylvanian Alps
Dinaric Alps
Balkan Mts.
Rhodope Mts.
Pindus Mts.
VIENNA (Wien)
BUDAPEST
BUCHAREST (Bucureşti)
Belgrade (Beograd)
Sarajevo
Zagreb
Ljubljana
Skopje
Sofia
Tirane
Athens
İSTANBUL
ADRIATIC SEA
IONIAN SEA
AEGEAN SEA
BLACK SEA
SEA OF MARMARA
TYRRHENIAN SEA
MEDITERRANEAN SEA
SEA OF CRETE
CYCLADES ISLANDS
Crete (Kriti)
Longitude East of Greenwich
© Copyright HAMMOND INCORPORATED, Maplewood, N. J.

Topography

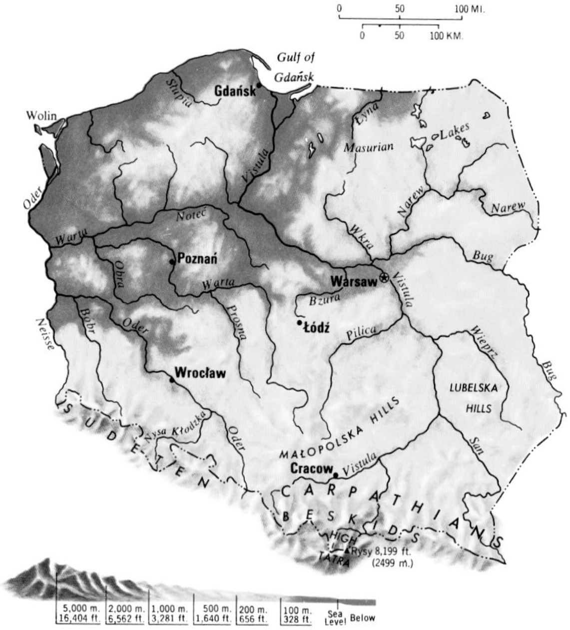
0 50 100 MI.
0 50 100 KM.
Gulf of Gdańsk
Gdańsk
Wolin
Masurian Lakes
Oder
Warta
Noteć
Poznań
Obra
Vistula
Narew
Bug
Wkra
Warsaw
Bzura
Łódź
Pilica
Prosna
Bóbr
Neisse
Wrocław
Wieprz
LUBELSKA HILLS
MAŁOPOLSKA HILLS
San
Nysa Kłodzka
SUDETEN
Cracow
CARPATHIANS
BESKIDS
HIGH TATRA
Rysy 8,199 ft. (2499 m.)
5,000 m. 16,404 ft.
2,000 m. 6,562 ft.
1,000 m. 3,281 ft.
500 m. 1,640 ft.
200 m. 656 ft.
100 m. 328 ft.
Sea Level
Below

PROVINCES	
Biała Podlaska 304,028	F3
Białystok 687,806	F2
Bielsko 895,357	D4
Bydgoszcz 1,104,048	C2
Chełm 245,484	F3
Ciechanów 425,608	E2
Cracow (Kraków) 1,223,137	E3
Cracow (city) 651,300	E3
Częstochowa 773,365	D3
Elbląg 475,862	D1
Gdańsk 1,417,801	D1
Gorzów 497,342	B2
Jelenia Góra 514,947	B3
Kalisz 706,514	D3
Katowice 3,953,769	D3
Kielce 1,123,691	E3
Konin 465,928	D2
Koszalin 502,750	C1
Krosno 491,471	E4
Legnica 510,000	C3
Leszno 383,315	C3
Łódź 777,800	D3
Łódź (city) 1,139,379	D3
Łomza 344,518	F2
Lublin 1,010,641	F3
Nowy Sącz 690,737	E4
Olsztyn 746,185	E2
Opole 1,010,416	C3
Ostrołęka 393,427	E2
Piła 475,953	C2
Piotrków 638,948	D3
Płock 512,626	D2
Poznań 1,323,368	C2
Przemyśl 404,200	F4
Radom 745,374	E3
Rzeszów 716,317	F4
Siedlce 648,111	F2
Sieradz 408,082	D3
Skierniewice 416,690	E3
Słupsk 410,049	C1
Suwałki 467,048	F1
Szczecin 964,298	B2
Tarnobrzeg 594,255	E3
Tarnów 664,953	E4
Torún 656,421	D2
Wałbrzych 738,092	C3
Warsaw 2,415,950	E2
Warsaw (city) 1,377,100	E2
Włocławek 427,418	D2
Wrocław 1,122,806	C3
Zamość 488,193	F3
Zielona Góra 655,146	B3

CITIES and TOWNS	
Aleksandrów Lódzki 19,711	D3
Allenstein (Olsztyn) 160,956	E2
Andrychów 22,387	D4
Augustów 28,307	F2
Auschwitz (Oświęcim) 45,402	D3
Bartoszyce 25,195	E1
Bedzin 76,883	B3
Belchatów 55,632	D3
Beuthen (Bytom) 229,991	A3
Biala Podlaska 52,119	F3
Bialogard 23,973	C1
Bialystok 267,670	F2
Bielawa 34,224	C3
Bielsk Podlaski 26,145	F2
Bielsko-Biala 181,072	D4
Bilgoraj 25,542	F3
Bochnia 28,846	E4
Bogatynia 18,616	B3
Boguszów-Gorce 19,452	B3
Boleslawiec 43,076	B3
Braniewo 17,594	D1
Breslau (Wrocław) 640,557	C3
Brieg (Brzeg) 38,504	C3
Brodnica 26,056	D2
Brzeg 38,504	C3
Busko Zdrój 17,675	E3
Bydgoszcz 380,426	C2
Bytom 229,991	A3
Bytów 16,720	C1
Chelm 64,683	F3
Chelmno 21,506	D2
Chodziez 19,831	C2
Chojnice 37,733	C2
Chorzów 131,850	B4
Chrzanów 42,195	B4
Ciechanów 43,068	E2
Cieszyn 36,682	D4
Cracow 745,568	E3

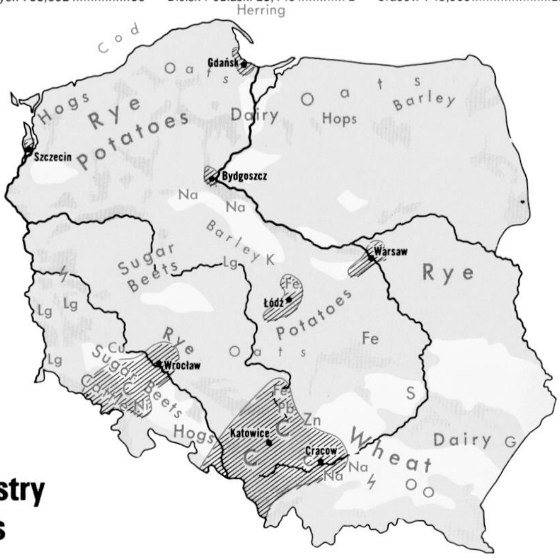
Herring
Cod
Gdańsk
Oats
Hogs
Rye
Potatoes
Dairy
Hops
Barley
Szczecin
Bydgoszcz
Na
Barley
Lg
K
Sugar Beets
Warsaw
Rye
Fe
Łódź
Potatoes
Lg
Cu
Wrocław
Oats
Sugar Beets
Hogs
Katowice
Pb
Zn
Cracow
Wheat
Dairy
S
G
O

MAJOR MINERAL OCCURRENCES

Ag	Silver	Na	Salt
C	Coal	Ni	Nickel
Cu	Copper	O	Petroleum
Fe	Iron Ore	Pb	Lead
G	Natural Gas	S	Sulfur
K	Potash	Zn	Zinc
Lg	Lignite		

ϟ Water Power

Major Industrial Areas

DOMINANT LAND USE

- Cereals (chiefly wheat)
- Rye, Oats, Barley, Potatoes
- General Farming, Livestock
- Forests

Agriculture, Industry and Resources

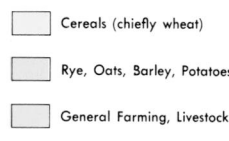

Former Republics of Yugoslavia
CONIC PROJECTION
MILES 0 25 50 75 100
KILOMETERS 0 25 50 75 100
Capitals
Boundaries
National
Federal Republics
Autonomous Provinces
Canals
© Copyright HAMMOND INCORPORATED, Maplewood, N.J.
AUSTRIA
HUNGARY
ITALY
SLOVENIA
CROATIA
BOSNIA AND HERZEGOVINA
SERBIA
VOJVODINA
KOSOVO
MONTENEGRO
ROMANIA
BULGARIA
ALBANIA
GREECE
F. Y. R. O. M.*
SAN MARINO
ADRIATIC SEA
Ljubljana
Zagreb
Sarajevo
Belgrade
Novi Sad
Priština
Podgorica
Skopje
Sofia
Tiranë (Tirana)
Budapest
Trieste
Venice
Rijeka (Fiume)
Split
Dubrovnik (Ragusa)
Danube
Sava
Drava
Tisza
Morava
Vardar
Lake Balaton
Lake Scutari
Lake Ohrid
Lake Prespa
Balkan Mts.
Triglav 9,393 ft. (2863 m.)
Korab 9,026 ft. (2751 m.)
Rujen (Ruen) 7,389 ft. (2252 m.)
Midžor 7,114 ft. (2168 m.)
Belgrade (Beograd)
Zemun
Novi Beograd
Pančevo
* Former Yugoslav Republic of Macedonia
Longitude 18° East of Greenwich 20°

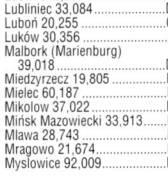

Czechowice-Dziedzice 35,194 ....D4
Czeladź 37,569 ....B4
Czestochowa 256,578 ....D3
Dabrowa Górnicza 134,934 ....B3
Danzig (Gdańsk) 462,076 ....D1
Debica 44,966 ....E3
Deblin 18,763 ....E3
Dzialdowo 19,295 ....E2
Dzierzoniów 37,908 ....C3
Elbing (Elblag) 125,778 ....D1
Elblag 125,778 ....D1
Elk 51,274 ....F2
Gdańsk 462,076 ....D1
Gdynia 251,303 ....D1
Gizycko 28,918 ....E1
Gleiwitz (Gliwice) 212,481 ....A4
Gliwice 212,481 ....A4
Głogów (Glogau) 71,854 ....C3
Gniezno 69,646 ....C2
Goleniów 21,756 ....B2
Gorlice 29,019 ....E4
Gorzów Wielkopolski 123,222 ....B2
Gostyń 19,344 ....C3
Gostynin 18,738 ....D2
Grajewo 20,635 ....F2
Grodzisk Mazowiecki 24,648 ....E2
Grudziadz 101,571 ....D2
Grünberg (Zielona Góra) 113,108 ....B3
Gryfice 17,294 ....B2
Gryfino 20,783 ....B2
Guben (Gubin) 17,779 ....B3
Hajnowka 23,390 ....F2
Hindenburg (Zabrze) 202,824 ....A4
Hirschberg (Jelenia Góra) 93,205 ....B3
Ilawa 31,312 ....D2
Inowrocław 76,497 ....D2
Jarocin 24,692 ....C3
Jaroslaw 41,267 ....F4
Jaslo 37,046 ....E4
Jastrzebie Zdroj 102,312 ....D3
Jawor 24,079 ....C3
Jaworzno 98,480 ....B4
Jedrzejów 18,109 ....E3
Jelenia Góra 93,205 ....B3
Kamienna Góra 21,000 ....B3
Katowice 366,077 ....B4
Kedzierzyn-Koźle 71,012 ....D3
Ketrzyn 29,987 ....E1
Kety 18,731 ....D4
Kielce 213,012 ....E3
Klodzko 30,261 ....C3
Kluczbork 25,988 ....D3
Knurów 44,468 ....A4
Kolberg (Kołobrzeg) 44,426 ....B1
Kolo 22,807 ....D2
Kołobrzeg 44,426 ....B1
Konin 79,315 ....D2
Końskie 21,548 ....E3
Kościan 23,554 ....C2
Kościerzyna 22,287 ....C1
Köslin (Koszalin) 107,592 ....C1
Koszalin 107,592 ....C1
Kozienice 20,557 ....E3
Kraków (Cracow) 745,568 ....E3
Krapkowice 19,452 ....D3
Kraśnik Fabryczny 36,202 ....F3
Krasnystaw 19,832 ....F3
Krosno 49,094 ....E4
Krotoszyn 27,807 ....C3
Kutno 49,753 ....D2
Kwidzin 36,409 ....D2
Landsberg (Gorzów Wielkopolski) 123,222 ....B2
Lask 19,569 ....D3
Laziska Górne 19,569 ....A4
Lebork 33,981 ....C1
Leczyca 16,491 ....D2
Legionowo 50,577 ....E2
Legnica 103,949 ....C3
Leszcyny 29,746 ....A4
Leszno 57,673 ....C3
Liegnitz (Legnica) 103,949 ....C3
Lódź 849,204 ....D3
Lomza 57,976 ....F2
Lowicz 30,322 ....D2
Lubań 23,708 ....B3
Lubartów 22,117 ....F3
Lubin 80,757 ....C3
Lublin 348,881 ....F3
Lubliniec 33,084 ....D3
Luboń 20,255 ....C2
Luków 30,356 ....F3
Malbork (Marienburg) 39,018 ....D1
Miedzyrzecz 19,805 ....B2
Mielec 60,187 ....E3
Mikolow 37,022 ....B4
Mińsk Mazowiecki 33,913 ....E2
Mlawa 28,743 ....E2
Mragowo 21,674 ....E2
Myslowice 92,009 ....B4

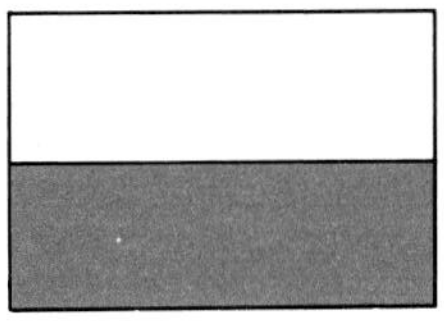

Myszków 33,084 ....D3
Naklo nad Notecia 20,056 ....C2
Neissa (Nysa) 46,686 ....C3
Nowa Ruda 27,507 ....C3
Nowa Sól 43,053 ....B3
Nowy Dwór Mazowiecki 26,842 ....E2
Nowy Sacz 76,658 ....E4
Nowy Targ 32,143 ....E4
Nysa 46,686 ....C3
Olawa 31,188 ....C3
Oleśnica 37,767 ....C3
Olkusz 40,571 ....D3
Olsztyn 160,956 ....E2
Opoczno 20,670 ....E3
Opole (Oppeln) 126,962 ....C3
Orzesze 18,100 ....A4
Ostróda 33,641 ....E2
Ostroleka 49,032 ....E2
Ostrów Mazowiecka 20,367 ....E2
Ostrów Wielkopolski 72,085 ....C3
Ostrowiec Świetokrzyski 77,466 ....E3
Oświecim 45,402 ....D3
Otwock 44,488 ....E2
Ozorków 21,676 ....D3
Pabianice 74,755 ....D3
Piaseczno 24,359 ....D2
Piekary Ślaskie 68,274 ....B4
Pila 71,109 ....C2
Pionki 20,701 ....E3
Piotrków Trybunalski 80,598 ....D3
Pisz 18,286 ....E2
Pleszew 17,712 ....C3
Plock 120,933 ....D2
Płońsk 20,956 ....E2
Police 33,478 ....B2
Polkowice 20,823 ....C3
Poznań 586,908 ....C2
Prudnik 24,598 ....C3
Pruszcz Gdanski 20,575 ....D1
Pruszków 53,889 ....E2
Przemyśl 68,121 ....F4
Pulawy 52,624 ....F3
Pultusk 17,619 ....E2
Racibórz 62,733 ....D3
Radom 226,025 ....E3
Radomsko 50,059 ....D3
Ratibor (Racibórz) 62,733 ....D3
Rawa Mazowiecka 17,428 ....E3
Rawicz 20,548 ....C3
Ruda Ślaska 169,017 ....B4
Rumia 36,762 ....D1
Rybnik 142,059 ....D3
Rzeszów 150,702 ....F4
Sandomierz 23,815 ....E3
Sanok 39,163 ....F4
Schneidemühl (Piła) 71,109 ....C2
Schweidnitz (Świdnica) 62,424 ....C3
Siedlce 70,529 ....F2
Siemianowice Ślaskie 80,412 ....B4
Sieradz 42,041 ....D3
Sierpc 18,956 ....D2
Skarzysko-Kamienna 50,455 ....E3
Skawina 23,487 ....D4
Skierniewice 43,963 ....E3
Słupsk 100,127 ....C1
Sochaczew 38,170 ....E2
Sokólka 19,059 ....F2
Sopot 46,874 ....D1
Sosnowiec 259,318 ....B4
Śrem 27,719 ....C2
Środa Wielkopolska 20,053 ....C2
Stalowa Wola 68,856 ....F3

AREA 120.725 sq. mi. (312,678 sq. km.)
POPULATION 37,931,000
CAPITAL Warsaw
LARGEST CITY Warsaw
HIGHEST POINT Rysy 8,199 ft. (2,499 m.)
MONETARY UNIT zloty
MAJOR LANGUAGE Polish
MAJOR RELIGION Roman Catholicism

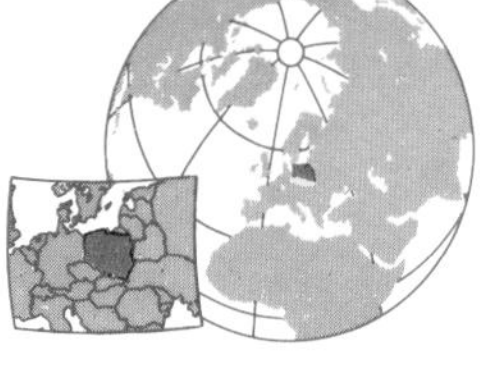

Starachowice 55,996 ....E3
Stargard Szczeciński 69,852 ....B2
Starogard Gdański 47,142 ....D2
Stettin (Szczecin) 411,275 ....B2
Stolp (Słupsk) 100,127 ....C1
Strzegom 17,185 ....C3
Strzelce Opolskie 21,238 ....D3
Suwalki 59,684 ....F1
Swarzedz 22,022 ....C2
Świdnica 62,424 ....C3
Świdnik 39,651 ....F3
Świebodzice 24,392 ....C3
Świebodzin 21,617 ....B2
Świecie 25,415 ....D2
Świetochlowice 58,770 ....A4
Świnoujście (Swinemünde) 42,932 ....B1
Szamotuly 17,970 ....C2
Szczecin 411,275 ....B2
Szczecinek 40,428 ....C2
Szczytno 26,878 ....E2
Tarnobrzeg 45,702 ....E3
Tarnów 120,639 ....E4
Tarnowskie Góry 73,460 ....A3
Tczew 58,887 ....D1
Tomaszów Lubelski 20,011 ....F3
Tomaszów Mazowiecki 69,579 ....E3
Toruń 200,860 ....D2
Trzebinia-Siersza 20,376 ....C4
Turek 28,559 ....D2
Tychy 189,816 ....B4
Wadowice 18,691 ....D4
Wagrowiec 22,736 ....C2
Wałbrzych 141,504 ....C3
Walcz 26,367 ....C2
Waldenburg (Wałbrzych) 141,504 ....C3
Warsaw (Warszawa) (cap.) 1,651,225 ....E2
Wejherowo 46,465 ....D1
Wieliczka 17,775 ....E3
Wieluń 24,061 ....D3
Włocławek 120,680 ....D2
Wodzislaw Ślaski 111,099 ....D4
Wolomin 36,762 ....E2
Wrocław 640,557 ....C3
Września 27,449 ....C2
Wyszków 23,411 ....E2
Zabrze 202,824 ....A4
Zagań 27,333 ....B3
Zakopane 28,417 ....D4
Zambrów 22,175 ....F2
Zamość 60,565 ....F3
Zary 39,172 ....B3
Zawiercie 56,017 ....D3
Zduńska Wola 44,686 ....D3
Zgierz 58,836 ....D3
Zgorzelec 36,008 ....B3
Zielona Góra 113,108 ....B3
Zlotów 17,533 ....C2
Zyrardów 33,196 ....E2
Zywiec 30,572 ....D4

OTHER FEATURES

Baltic (sea) B1
Beskids (range) D4
Biebrza (riv.) F2
Bobr (riv.) B3
Brda (riv.) C2
Brynica (riv.) B4
Bug (riv.) F2
Danzig (Gdańsk) (gulf) D1
Dukla (pass) E4
Dunajec (riv.) E4
Frisches Haff (lag.) D1
Gwda (riv.) C2
Hel (pen.) D1
High Tatra (range) D4
Jezioro Śniardwy (lake) E2
Kłodnica (riv.) A4
Łyna (riv.) E1
Mamry, Jezioro (lake) E1
Masurian (lakes) E2
Narew (riv.) E2
Neisse (riv.) B3
Noteć (riv.) B2
Nysa Łuzycka (Neisse) (riv.) B3
Nysa Kłodzka (riv.) C3
Oder (riv.) B2
Oder-Haff (lag.) B2
Orava (res.) D4
Pilica (riv.) D3
Plonia (riv.) B2
Pomeranian (bay) B1
Prosna (riv.) C3
Przemsza (riv.) B4
Rega (riv.) B2
Rysy (mt.) D4
San (riv.) F3
Słupia (riv.) C1
Sudeten (range) B3
Uznam (Usedom) (isl.) B1
Vistula (riv.) D2
Vistula (spit) D1
Warmia (reg.) D1
Warta (riv.) B2
Wieprz (riv.) F3
Wisła (Vistula) (riv.) D2
Wkra (riv.) E2
Włocławskie (lake) D2
Wolin (Wollin) (isl.) B2
Zegrzýnskie (lake) E2

Poland
CONIC PROJECTION
SCALE OF MILES
SCALE OF KILOMETERS
Capitals of Countries
Other Capitals
International Boundaries
Internal Boundaries
Canals
Poland is divided into 49 provinces (bearing the same name as their capitals) and the autonomous cities of Warsaw, Łódź and Cracow.
BALTIC SEA
Gulf of Gdańsk
Pomeranian Bay
DENMARK
RUSSIA
Kaliningrad
LITHUANIA
BELARUS
UKRAINE
GERMANY
SLOVAKIA
CZECH REP.
Berlin
Warsaw
Gdańsk
Szczecin
Poznań
Wrocław
Łódź
Kraków
Katowice
Lublin
Białystok
Dresden
Leipzig
Rostock
Brno
Ostrava
L'viv
Rysy 8,199 ft. (2499 m.)
Gerlachovka 8,707 ft. (2654 m.)
Longitude East of Greenwich
© Copyright HAMMOND INCORPORATED, Maplewood, N. J.

ARMENIA

CITIES and TOWNS

Kumayri 120,000 .... E5
Leninakan (Kumayri) 120,000 .... E5
Yerevan (cap.) 1,199,000 .... E6

OTHER FEATURES

Caucasus (mts.) E5

AZERBAIJAN

INTERNAL DIVISIONS

Nagorno-Karabakh Aut. Obl. 188,000 .... E5
Nakhichevan' Aut. Rep. 295,000 .... E6

CITIES and TOWNS

Baku (cap.) 1,150,000 .... F5
Gyandzhe 278,000 .... E5
Kirovabad (Gyandzhe) 278,000 .... E5
Lenkoran' 35,505 .... E6
Nakhichevan' 33,279 .... E6
Stepanakert 30,293 .... E6

OTHER FEATURES

Caspian (sea) F6
Caucasus (mts.) E5
Kura (riv.) E6

BELARUS

CITIES and TOWNS

Baranovichi 159,000 .... C4
Bobruysk 223,000 .... C4
Brest 258,000 .... C4
Gomel' 500,000 .... D4
Grodno 270,000 .... C4
Minsk (cap.) 1,589,000 .... C4
Mogilev 356,000 .... D4
Molodechno 73,000 .... C4
Mozyr' 101,000 .... C4
Pinsk 119,000 .... C4
Vitebsk 350,000 .... D4

OTHER FEATURES

Dnieper (riv.) D5
Dvina, Western (riv.) C4
Western Dvina (riv.) C4

GEORGIA

INTERNAL DIVISIONS

Abkhaz Aut. Rep. 537,000 .... E5
Adzhar Aut. Rep. 393,000 .... E5
South Ossetian Aut. Obl. 99,000 .... E5

CITIES and TOWNS

Batumi 136,000 .... E5
Kutaisi 235,000 .... E5
Sukhumi 121,000 .... E5
T'bilisi (cap.) 1,260,000 .... E5
Tskhinvali 30,311 .... E5

OTHER FEATURES

Black (sea) D5
Caucasus (mts.) E5

KAZAKHSTAN

CITIES and TOWNS

Abay 34,245 .... H5
Aksay 10,010 .... F4
Aktas G5
Aktyubinsk 253,000 .... F4
Alekseyevka H4
Alga 12,000 .... F5
Almaty 1,128,000 .... H5
Aqtau 12,000 .... F5
Aral'sk 37,722 .... G5
Arkalyk 15,108 .... G4
Arys' 26,414 .... G5
Astana (cap.) 277,000 .... H4
Atbasar 37,228 .... G4
Ayaguz 35,827 .... J5
Balkhash 78,000 .... H5
Balykshi 22,397 .... F5
Baykonyr G5
Charsk 10,100 .... J5
Chelkar 19,377 .... F5
Chiili G5
Chimkent 393,000 .... H5
Chu H5
Derzhavinsk G4
Dossor 10,000 .... F5
Druzhba G5
Dzhambul 307,000 .... H5
Dzhetygara 32,169 .... G4
Dzhezkazgan 109,000 .... G5
Dzhusaly 20,658 .... G5
Ekibastuz 135,000 .... H4
Emba 17,820 .... F5
Gur'yev 149,000 .... F5
Kapchagay H5
Karaganda 614,000 .... H5
Karatau 26,962 .... H5
Karazhal 17,702 .... H5
Kentau 52,000 .... G5
Khromtau 10,000 .... F4
Kirovskiy H5
Kokchetav 137,000 .... H4
Kounradskiy 10,000 .... H5
Kul'sary 16,427 .... F5
Kustanay 224,000 .... G4
Kzyl-Orda 153,000 .... G5
Leninogorsk 68,000 .... J4
Leninsk G5
Makinsk 22,850 .... H4
Nikol'skiy (Satpayev) 32,862 .... G5
Novokazalinsk 34,815 .... G5
Novyy Uzen' 18,073 .... F5
Panfilov 19,173 .... J5
Pavlodar 331,000 .... H4
Petropavlovsk 241,000 .... G4
Rudnyy 124,000 .... G4
Saksaul'skiy G5
Saran' 55,000 .... H5
Sarkand 18,296 .... J5
Saryshagan 10,000 .... H5
Satpayev 32,862 .... G5
Semipalatinsk 334,000 .... H4
Shakhtinsk 50,000 .... H5
Shchuchinsk 40,432 .... H4
Shevchenko 159,000 .... F5
Taldy-Kurgan 119,000 .... H5
Talgar 31,273 .... H5
Tekeli 29,846 .... H5
Temirtau 212,000 .... H4
Tselinograd 277,000 .... H4
Turkestan 67,000 .... G5
Ural'sk 200,000 .... F4
Ushtobe 24,484 .... H5
Ust'-Kamenogorsk 324,000 .... J5
Yermak 28,133 .... H4
Yermentau 15,276 .... H4
Yesil' 15,000 .... G4
Zaysan 10,000 .... J5
Zyryanovsk 51,000 .... J5

OTHER FEATURES

Alakol' (lake) J5
Altai (mts.) J5
Aral (sea) F5
Balkhash (lake) H5
Bet-Pak-Dala (des.) H5
Caspian (sea) F6
Chu (riv.) H5
Emba (riv.) F5
Ili (riv.) H5
Irtysh (riv.) H4
Ishim (riv.) G4
Mangyshlak (pen.) F5
Sarysu (riv.) H5
Syrdar'ya (riv.) G5
Tengiz (lake) G4
Tobol (riv.) G4
Ulutau (mts.) G5
Ural (riv.) F5
Ust'-Urt (plat.) F5
Zaysan (lake) J5

KYRGYZSTAN

CITIES and TOWNS

Dzhalal-Abad 55,000 .... H5
Bishkek (cap.) 616,000 .... H5
Issyk-Kul' H5
Naryn 21,098 .... H5
Osh 213,000 .... H5
Przheval'sk 51,000 .... H5
Rybach'ye (Issyk-Kul') H5
Tokmak H5

(continued)

Russia and Neighboring Countries
CONIC PROJECTION
SCALE OF MILES
0 100 200 300 400 500 600
SCALE OF KILOMETERS
0 100 200 300 400 500 600
Capitals
Boundaries
National
Autonomous Republic
Autonomous Oblast
Autonomous Okrug
ADMINISTRATIVE DIVISIONS NOT NAMED ON MAP
Division Ref.
1. Abkhaz Aut. Rep. E5
2. Adygey Aut. Oblast D5
3. Adzhar Aut. Rep. E5
4. Aginsk Buryat Autonomous Okrug M4
5. Checken-Ingush Aut. Rep. E5
6. Chuvash Aut. Rep. E4
7. Gorno-Altay Aut. Oblast J4
8. Gorno-Badakhshan Aut. Oblast H6
9. Jewish Aut. Oblast O5
10. Kabardin-Balkar Aut. Rep. E5
11. Karachay-Cherkess Aut. Oblast E5
12. Karakalpak Aut. Rep. G5
13. Khakass Aut. Oblast J4
14. Komi-Permyak Aut. Okrug F4
15. Mari Aut. Rep. E4
16. Mordivian Aut. Rep. E4
17. Nagorno-Karabakh Aut. Oblast E5
18. Nakhichevan' Aut. Rep. E6
19. North Ossetian Aut. Rep. E5
20. South Ossetian Aut. Oblast E5
21 Tatar Aut. Rep. F4
22. Tuvinian Aut. Rep. K4
23. Udmurt Aut. Rep. F4
24. Ust'-Ordynsk Buryat Autonomous Okrug L4
NORWEGIAN SEA
BARENTS SEA
KARA SEA
LAPTEV SEA
ARCTIC OCEAN
CASPIAN SEA
BLACK SEA
MONGOLIA
CHINA
XINJIANG
TIBET
AFGHANISTAN
PAKISTAN
INDIA
IRAN
MOSCOW
ST. PETERSBURG
100° Longitude East of Greenwich 110°

ARMENIA

AZERBAIJAN

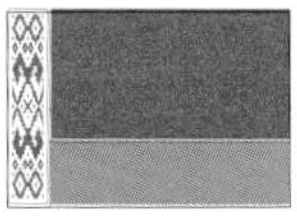
BELARUS

GEORGIA

KAZAKHSTAN

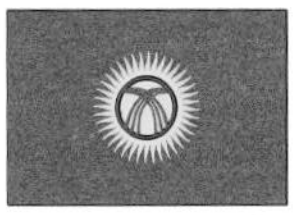
KYRGYZSTAN

MOLDOVA

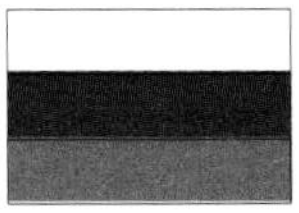
RUSSIA

TAJIKISTAN

TURKMENISTAN

UKRAINE

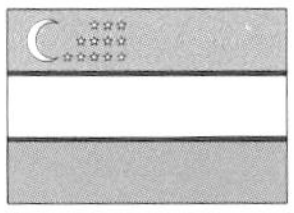
UZBEKISTAN

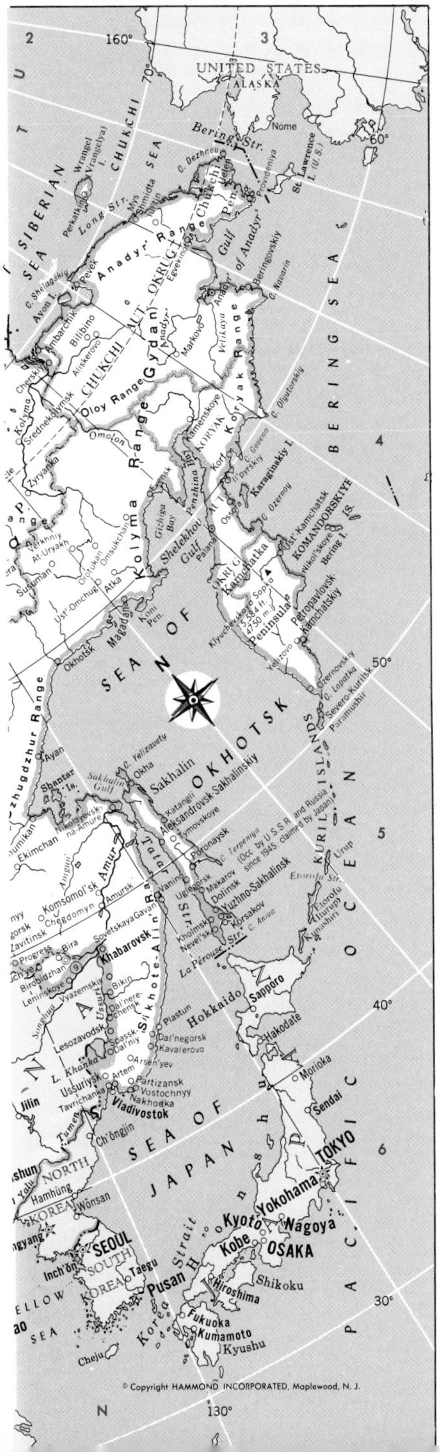
UNITED STATES
ALASKA
Nome
Bering Str.
CHUKCHI SEA
EAST SIBERIAN SEA
BERING SEA
SEA OF OKHOTSK
KURIL ISLANDS
PACIFIC OCEAN
SEA OF JAPAN
Sakhalin
Hokkaido
Sapporo
Hakodate
Sendai
TOKYO
Yokohama
Nagoya
Kyoto
Kobe
OSAKA
Hiroshima
Shikoku
Fukuoka
Kumamoto
Kyushu
SEOUL
Pusan
Taegu
Inch'ŏn
Wŏnsan
Ch'ŏngjin
Vladivostok
Nakhodka
Khabarovsk
Komsomol'sk
Okhotsk
Magadan
Petropavlovsk-Kamchatskiy
Kamchatka Peninsula
Anadyr'
Wrangel I.
St. Lawrence I. (U.S.)
© Copyright HAMMOND INCORPORATED, Maplewood, N. J.

ARMENIA

AREA 11,506 sq. mi. (29,800 sq. km.)
POPULATION 3,283,000
CAPITAL Yerevan
LARGEST CITY Yerevan
HIGHEST POINT Alagez 13,435 ft. (4,095 m.)
MAJOR LANGUAGES Armenian, Azerbaijani, Kurdish, Russian
MAJOR RELIGIONS Eastern (Armenian Apostolic) Orthodoxy, Islam

AZERBAIJAN

AREA 33,436 sq. mi. (86,600 sq. km.)
POPULATION 7,029,000
CAPITAL Baku
LARGEST CITY Baku
HIGHEST POINT Bazardyuzyu 14,653 ft. (4,466 m.)
MAJOR LANGUAGES Azerbaijani, Russian, Armenian
MAJOR RELIGIONS Islam, Eastern (Russian) Orthodoxy

BELARUS

AREA 80,154 sq. mi. (207,600 sq. km.)
POPULATION 10,200,000
CAPITAL Minsk
LARGEST CITY Minsk
HIGHEST POINT Dzerzhinskaya 1,135 ft. (346 m.)
MAJOR LANGUAGES Belorussian, Russian, Polish, Ukrainian, Yiddish
MAJOR RELIGIONS Eastern (Russian) Orthodoxy, Roman Catholicism, Judaism

GEORGIA

AREA 26,911 sq. mi. (69,700 sq. km.)
POPULATION 5,449,000
CAPITAL T'bilisi
LARGEST CITY T'bilisi
HIGHEST POINT Kazbek 16,558 ft. (5,047 m.)
MAJOR LANGUAGES Georgian, Armenian, Russian, Azerbaijani, Abkhazian, Ossetian
MAJOR RELIGIONS Eastern (Georgian) Orthodoxy, Islam

KAZAKHSTAN

AREA 1,048,300 sq. mi. (2,715,100 sq. km.)
POPULATION 16,538,000
CAPITAL Astana
LARGEST CITY Almaty
HIGHEST POINT Khan-Tengri 22,951 ft. (6,995 m.)
MAJOR LANGUAGES Kazakh, Russian, German, Ukrainian, Uzbek, Tatar
MAJOR RELIGIONS Islam, Eastern (Russian) Orthodoxy

KYRGYZSTAN

AREA 76,641 sq. mi. (198,500 sq. km.)
POPULATION 4,291,000
CAPITAL Bishkek (Frunze)
LARGEST CITY Bishkek (Frunze)
HIGHEST POINT Pobeda Peak 24,406 ft. (7,439 m.)
MAJOR LANGUAGES Kirgiz, Russian, Uzbek, Ukrainian, German, Tatar
MAJOR RELIGIONS Islam, Eastern (Russian) Orthodoxy

MOLDOVA

AREA 13,012 sq. mi. (33,700 sq. km.)
POPULATION 4,341,000
CAPITAL Chişinău
LARGEST CITY Chişinău
HIGHEST POINT 1,408 ft. (429 m.)
MAJOR LANGUAGES Moldavian (Romanian), Ukrainian, Russian, Gagauzi, Yiddish
MAJOR RELIGIONS Eastern (Romanian) Orthodoxy, Judaism

RUSSIA

AREA 6,592,812 sq. mi. (17,075,400 sq. km.)
POPULATION 147,386,000
CAPITAL Moscow
LARGEST CITY Moscow
HIGHEST POINT El'brus 18,510 ft. (5,642 m.)
MONETARY UNIT ruble
MAJOR LANGUAGES Russian, Tatar, Ukrainian, Chuvash, Bashkir, Belorussian, Mordvinian, German, Kazakh, Yiddish, Chechen, Udmurt, Ossetian, Buryat, Yakut, Ingush, Tuvan
MAJOR RELIGIONS Eastern (Russian) Orthodoxy, Roman Catholicism, Islam, Judaism, Lamaism, Buddhism, Animism

TAJIKISTAN

AREA 55,251 sq. mi. (143,100 sq. km.)
POPULATION 5,112,000
CAPITAL Dushanbe
LARGEST CITY Dushanbe
HIGHEST POINT Ismail Samani Peak 24,590 ft. (7,495 m.)
MAJOR LANGUAGES Tajik, Uzbek, Russian, Tatar, Kirgiz
MAJOR RELIGIONS Islam, Eastern (Russian) Orthodoxy

TURKMENISTAN

AREA 188,455 sq. mi. (488,100 sq. km.)
POPULATION 3,534,000
CAPITAL Ashgabat
LARGEST CITY Ashgabat
HIGHEST POINT Rize 9,653 ft. (2,942 m.)
MAJOR LANGUAGES Turkmenian, Russian, Uzbek, Kazakh, Tatar
MAJOR RELIGIONS Islam, Eastern (Russian) Orthodoxy

UKRAINE

AREA 233,089 sq. mi. (603,700 sq. km.)
POPULATION 51,704,000
CAPITAL Kiev
LARGEST CITY Kiev
HIGHEST POINT Goverla 6,762 ft. (2,061 m.)
MAJOR LANGUAGES Ukrainian, Russian, Yiddish, Belorussian, Moldavian (Romanian), Polish, Tatar
MAJOR RELIGIONS Eastern (Ukrainian) Orthodoxy, Roman (Ukrainian Uniate) Catholicism, Judaism

UZBEKISTAN

AREA 173,591 sq. mi. (449,600 sq. km.)
POPULATION 19,906,000
CAPITAL Tashkent
LARGEST CITY Tashkent
HIGHEST POINT Khodzha-Pir'yakh 14,515 ft. (4,424 m.)
MAJOR LANGUAGES Uzbek, Russian, Tajik, Kazakh, Tatar, Karakalpak, Kirgiz, Ukrainian, Turkmenian
MAJOR RELIGIONS Islam, Eastern (Russian) Orthodoxy

Topography

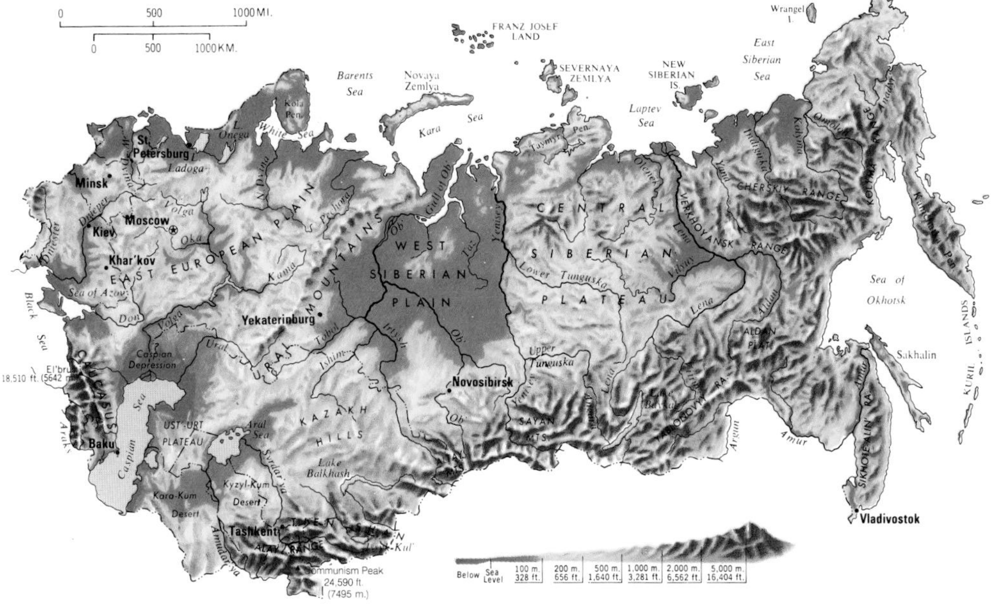
0 500 1000 MI.
0 500 1000 KM.
FRANZ JOSEF LAND
SEVERNAYA ZEMLYA
NEW SIBERIAN IS.
Wrangel I.
C. Dezhnev
East Siberian Sea
Laptev Sea
Kara Sea
Barents Sea
Novaya Zemlya
White Sea
St. Petersburg
Minsk
Kiev
Moscow
Khar'kov
EAST EUROPEAN PLAIN
URAL MOUNTAINS
Yekaterinburg
WEST SIBERIAN PLAIN
CENTRAL SIBERIAN PLATEAU
Novosibirsk
KAZAKH HILLS
Lake Balkhash
Baku
Tashkent
Caspian Depression
Caspian Sea
Black Sea
Sea of Azov
Aral Sea
El'brus 18,510 ft. (5,642 m.)
Communism Peak 24,590 ft. (7495 m.)
USTYURT PLATEAU
Kyzyl-Kum Desert
Kara-Kum Desert
CHERSKIY RANGE
VERKHOYANSK RANGE
Sea of Okhotsk
Sakhalin
KURIL ISLANDS
Vladivostok
Amur
Lena
Ob
Yenisey
Below Sea Level
100 m. 328 ft.
200 m. 656 ft.
500 m. 1,640 ft.
1,000 m. 3,281 ft.
2,000 m. 6,562 ft.
5,000 m. 16,404 ft.

(continued)

OTHER FEATURES

Chu (riv.) H5
Issyk-Kul' (lake) H5
Pobeda (peak) J5

MOLDOVA (MOLDAVIA)

CITIES and TOWNS

Chişinău (cap.) 665,000 C5

OTHER FEATURES

Black (sea) D5
Dniester (riv.) C5

RUSSIA

INTERNAL DIVISIONS

Adygey Aut. Obl. 432,000 D5
Aginsk Buryat Aut. Okr. 77,000 M4
Bashkir Aut. Rep. 3,952,000 F4
Buryat Aut. Rep. 1,042,000 M4
Chechen-Ingush Aut. Rep. 1,277,000 E5
Chukchi Aut. Okr. 158,000 R3
Chuvash Aut. Rep. 1,336,000 E4
Dagestan Aut. Rep. 1,792,000 E5
Evenki Aut. Okr. 24,000 K3
Gorno-Altay Aut. Obl. 192,000 J4
Kabardin-Balkar Aut. Rep. 760,000 E5
Kalmuck Aut. Rep. 322,000 E5
Karachay-Cherkess Aut. Obl. 418,000 E5
Karelian Aut. Rep. 792,000 D3
Khakass Aut. Obl. 569,000 J4
Khanty-Mansi Aut. Okr. 1,269,000 G3
Komi Aut. Rep. 1,263,000 F3
Komi-Permyak Aut. Okr. 159,000 F4
Koryak Aut. Okr. 39,000 R3
Mari Aut. Rep. 750,000 E4
Mordvinian Aut. Rep. 964,000 E4
Nenets Aut. Okr. 55,000 F3
North Ossetian Aut. Rep. 634,000 E5
Tatar Aut. Rep. 3,640,000 F4
Taymyr Aut. Okr. 55,000 K2
Tuvinian Aut. Rep. 309,000 K4
Udmurt Aut. Rep. 1,609,000 F4
Ust'-Ordynskiy Buryat Aut. Okr. 136,000 L4
Yakut Aut. Rep. 1,081,000 N3
Yamal-Nenets Aut. Okr. 487,000 H3
Yevrey Aut. Obl. 216,000 O5

CITIES and TOWNS

Abakan 154,000 K4
Abaza 15,202 K4
Achinsk 122,000 K4
Aginskoye 7,922 M4
Aldan 17,689 N4
Aleksandrovsk-Sakhalinskiy 20,342 P4
Aleysk 32,487 J4
Amursk 24,010 O4
Anadyr' 7,703 S3
Angarsk 266,000 L4
Anzhero-Sudzhensk 108,000 J4
Archangel (Arkhangel'sk) 416,000 E3
Armavir 161,000 E5
Arsen'yev 60,000 O5
Artem 69,000 O5
Arzamas 109,000 E4
Asbest 79,000 G4
Asino 29,395 J4
Astrakhan' 509,000 E5
Balakovo 198,000 E4
Balashov 93,000 E4
Baley 27,215 M4
Barabinsk 37,274 H4
Barnaul 602,000 J4
Belgorod 300,000 D4
Belogorsk 63,000 N4
Belomorsk 16,595 D3
Beloretsk 71,000 F4
Belovo 112,000 J4
Berdsk 67,000 J4
Berezniki 201,000 F4
Berezovo 6,000 G3
Bikin 17,473 O5
Bilibino 10,000 S3
Birobidzhan 69,000 O5
Biysk 233,000 J4
Blagoveshchensk 206,000 N4
Bodaybo 19,000 M4
Borisoglebsk 68,000 E4
Borzya 27,815 M4
Bratsk 255,000 L4
Bryansk 452,000 D4
Bugul'ma 80,000 F4
Bukachacha 10,000 M4
Buzuluk 76,000 F4
Chapayevsk 85,000 E4
Cheboksary 420,000 E4
Chegdomyn 16,499 O4
Chelyabinsk 1,143,000 G4
Cheremkhovo 77,000 L4
Cherepovets 310,000 D4
Cherkessk 113,000 E5
Chernenko (Sharypovo) 54,000 K4
Chernogorsk 71,000 K4
Chernyshevsk 10,000 M4
Chernyshevskiy 10,000 M3
Chita 366,000 M4
Dal'negorsk 33,506 O5
Dal'nerechensk 28,224 O5
Dimitrovgrad 124,000 F4
Dudinka 19,701 J3
Dzerzhinsk 285,000 E4
Elista 70,000 E5
Engel's 182,000 E4
Frolovo 33,398 E5
Gorno-Altaysk 34,413 J4
Gornyak 16,643 J4
Groznyy 401,000 E5
Gubakha 33,243 F4
Gusinoozersk 10,000 L4
Igarka 15,624 J3
Ilanskiy 22,852 K4
Inta 51,000 G3
Irkutsk 626,000 L4
Ishim 63,000 H4
Isil'kul' 25,958 H4
Ivanovo 481,000 E4
Ivdel' 15,308 G3
Izhevsk 635,000 F4
Kalachinsk 20,809 H4
Kalinin (Tver') 451,000 D4
Kaliningrad 401,000 B4
Kaluga 312,000 D4
Kamen'-na-Obi 35,604 H4
Kamenskoye R3
Kamensk-Ural'skiy 209,000 G4
Kamyshin 122,000 E4
Kandalaksha 42,656 C3
Kansk 110,000 K4
Karasuk 22,637 H4
Kartaly 42,801 G4
Kavalerovo 16,415 O5
Kazan' 1,094,000 F4
Kem' 21,025 D3
Kemerovo 520,000 J4
Khabarovsk 601,000 O5
Khanty-Mansiysk 24,754 H3
Khilok 17,000 M4
Kholmsk 37,412 P5
Kirov 441,000 E4
Kiselevsk 128,000 J4
Kizel 46,264 F4
Kolomna 162,000 D4
Kolpashevo 24,911 J4
Komsomol'sk-na-Amure 315,000 O4
Kondopoga 27,908 D3
Kopeysk 146,000 G4
Korsakov 38,210 P5
Kostroma 278,000 E4
Kotlas 61,000 E3
Kovrov 160,000 E4
Krasnodar 620,000 E5
Krasnokamensk 51,000 M4
Krasnokamsk 56,000 F4
Krasnotur'insk 61,000 G3
Krasnoural'sk 39,743 G4
Krasnoyarsk 912,000 K4
Kudymkar 26,350 F4
Kulunda 15,264 H4
Kungur 80,000 F4
Kupino 20,799 H4
Kurgan 356,000 G4
Kursk 424,000 D4
Kuybyshev 40,166 H4
Kuybyshev (Samara) 1,257,000 F4
Kyakhta 15,316 L4
Kyzyl 66,000 K4
Leningrad (St. Petersburg) 4,456,000 D4
Leninsk-Kuznetskiy 165,000 J4
Lensk 16,758 M3
Lesozavodsk 34,957 O5
Lipetsk 450,000 E4
Luga 31,905 D4
Lys'va 75,000 F4
Magadan 152,000 P4
Magdagachi 15,059 N4
Magnitogorsk 440,000 G4
Makarov 10,000 P5
Makhachkala 315,000 E5
Maykop 149,000 D5
Mednogorsk 38,024 F4
Medvezh'yegorsk 17,465 D3
Mezen' E3
Miass 168,000 G4
Michurinsk 109,000 E4
Millerovo 34,627 E5
Minusinsk 56,000 K4
Mirnyy 23,826 M3
Mogocha 17,884 M4
Monchegorsk 51,000 C3
Moscow (cap.) 8,769,000 D4
Motygino 10,000 K4
Murmansk 468,000 D3
Mys Shmidta T3
Nakhodka 165,000 O5
Nal'chik 235,000 E5
Nar'yan-Mar 16,864 F3
Nazyvayevsk 15,792 H4
Nefteyugansk 52,000 H3
Nevel'sk 20,726 P5
Nikolayevsk-na-Amure 30,082 P4
Nizhneudinsk 39,743 K4
Nizhnevartovsk 242,000 H3
Nizhniy Novgorod (Gor'kiy) 1,438,000 E4
Nizhniy Tagil 440,000 G4
Nordvik-Ugol'naya M2
Noril'sk 174,000 J3
Novgorod 229,000 D4
Novokuznetsk 600,000 J4
Novomoskovsk 146,000 E4
Novorossiysk 186,000 D5
Novosibirsk 1,436,000 J4
Novozybkov 34,433 D4
Novyy Port G3
Novyy Urengoy H3
Nyandoma 23,366 E3

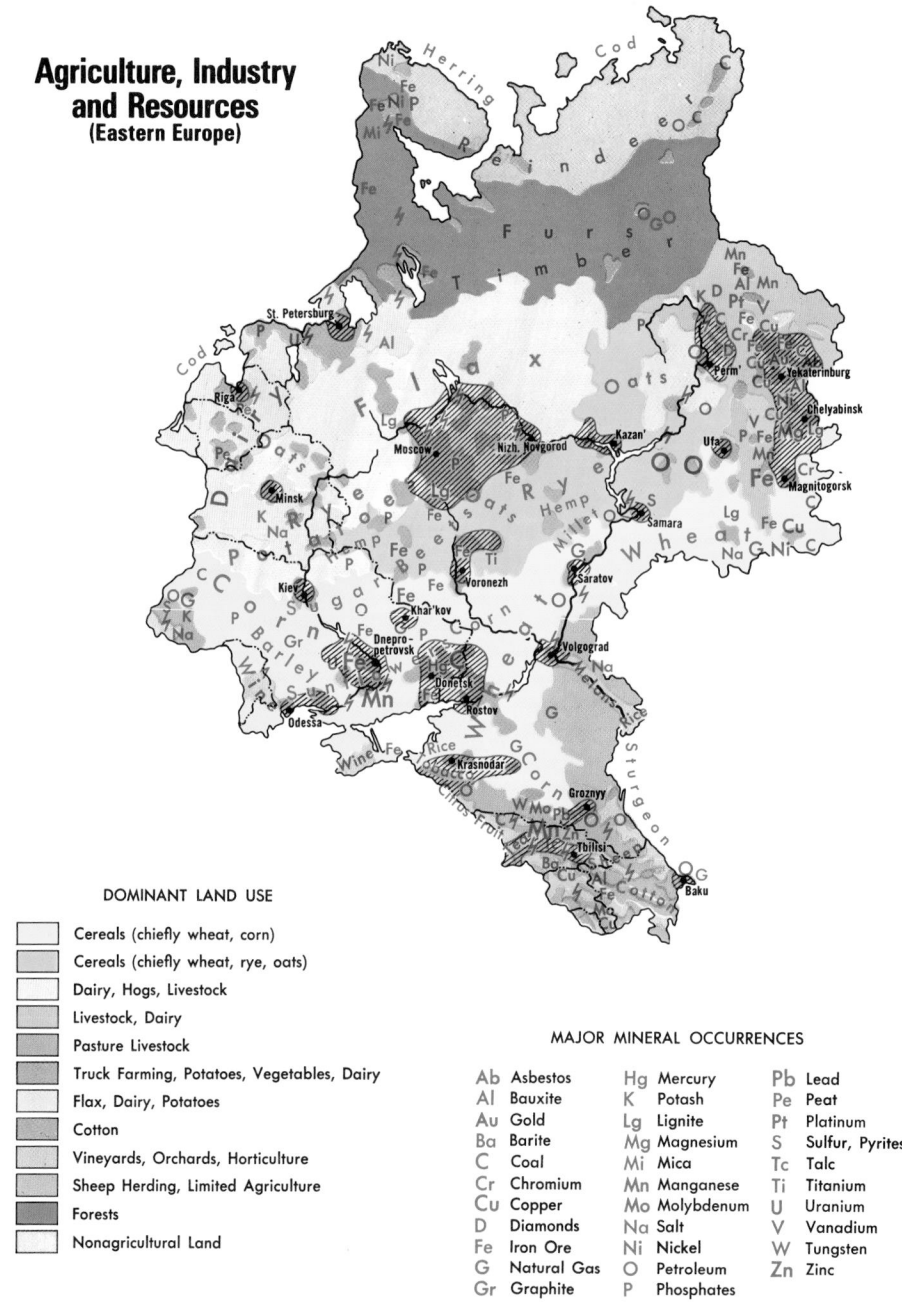

Agriculture, Industry and Resources
(Eastern Europe)

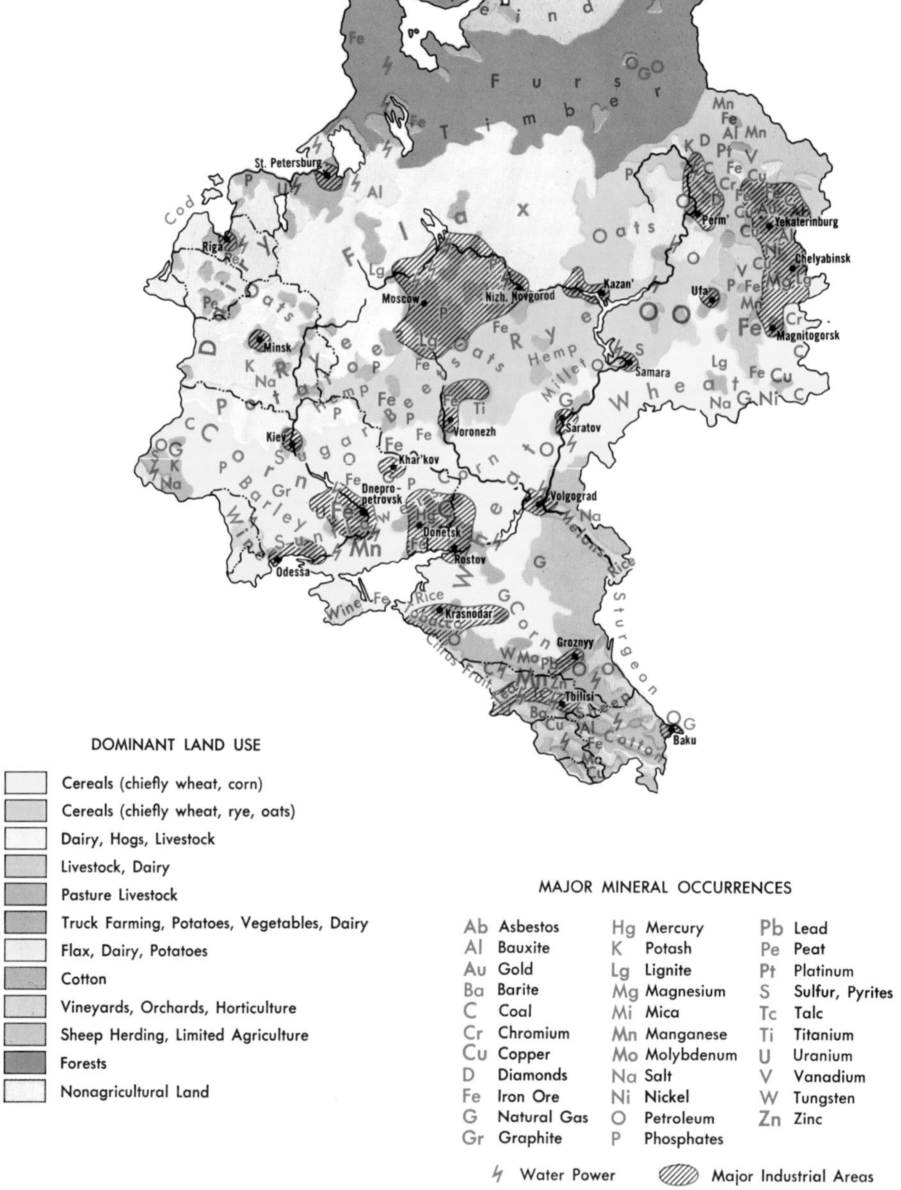
Herring
Cod
Reindeer
Furs
Timber
Flax
Oats
St. Petersburg
Riga
Minsk
Moscow
Nizh. Novgorod
Kazan'
Perm
Yekaterinburg
Chelyabinsk
Ufa
Magnitogorsk
Samara
Saratov
Voronezh
Kiev
Khar'kov
Dnepropetrovsk
Donetsk
Rostov
Odessa
Volgograd
Krasnodar
Groznyy
Tbilisi
Baku
Rye
Hemp
Millet
Wheat
Potatoes
Sugar Beets
Barley
Corn
Rice
Wine
Citrus Fruit
Cotton
Sturgeon
DOMINANT LAND USE
Cereals (chiefly wheat, corn)
Cereals (chiefly wheat, rye, oats)
Dairy, Hogs, Livestock
Livestock, Dairy
Pasture Livestock
Truck Farming, Potatoes, Vegetables, Dairy
Flax, Dairy, Potatoes
Cotton
Vineyards, Orchards, Horticulture
Sheep Herding, Limited Agriculture
Forests
Nonagricultural Land
MAJOR MINERAL OCCURRENCES
Ab Asbestos
Al Bauxite
Au Gold
Ba Barite
C Coal
Cr Chromium
Cu Copper
D Diamonds
Fe Iron Ore
G Natural Gas
Gr Graphite
Hg Mercury
K Potash
Lg Lignite
Mg Magnesium
Mi Mica
Mn Manganese
Mo Molybdenum
Na Salt
Ni Nickel
O Petroleum
P Phosphates
Pb Lead
Pe Peat
Pt Platinum
S Sulfur, Pyrites
Tc Talc
Ti Titanium
U Uranium
V Vanadium
W Tungsten
Zn Zinc
Water Power
Major Industrial Areas

Obluch'ye 17,000 O5
Okha 30,890 P4
Okhotsk P4
Omsk 1,148,000 H4
Omutninsk 28,777 F4
Onega 25,047 D3
Ordzhonikidze (Vladikavkaz) 300,000 E5
Orel 337,000 D4
Orenburg 547,000 F4
Orsk 271,000 F4
Ostrogozhsk 29,921 D4
Partizansk 48,345 O5
Pechenga D2
Pechora 56,000 F3
Penza 483,000 E4
Perm' 1,091,000 F4
Pervoural'sk 142,000 F4
Petropavlovsk-Kamchatskiy 269,000 R4
Petrovsk-Zabaykal'skiy 28,313 L4
Petrozavodsk 270,000 D3
Pionerskiy 10,000 G3
Podol'sk 210,000 D4
Polyarnyy 15,321 D3
Poronaysk 23,610 P5
Prikumsk 35,768 E5
Prokop'yevsk 274,000 J4
Pskov 204,000 C4
Pushkin 90,000 C4
Raychikhinsk 25,157 N5
Rostov 1,020,000 E5
Rubtsovsk 172,000 J4
Ryazan' 515,000 E4
Rybinsk 252,000 D4
Rzhev 69,000 D4
St. Petersburg 4,456,000 D4
Salekhard 21,929 G3
Sal'sk 61,000 E5
Samara 1,257,000 F4
Saransk 312,000 E4
Sarapul 111,000 F4
Saratov 905,000 E4
Segezha 28,810 D3
Serov 104,000 G4
Serpukhov 144,000 D4
Severodvinsk 249,000 E3
Severo-Kuril'sk 8,000 Q4
Severoural'sk 29,880 G3
Severo-Yeniseyskiy K3
Shadrinsk 82,000 G4
Shakhty 224,000 E5
Shar'ya 25,788 E4
Sharypovo 54,000 K4
Shilka 16,065 M4
Shimanovsk 16,880 N4
Shushenskoye 10,000 K4
Simbirsk 625,000 E4
Skovorodino 10,000 N4
Slavgorod 32,908 H4
Slobodskoy 34,374 E4
Slyudyanka 20,639 L4
Smolensk 341,000 D4
Sochi 337,000 D5
Sokol 48,243 E4
Solikamsk 110,000 F3
Sortavala 22,188 C3
Sosnogorsk 24,688 F3
Sovetskaya Gavan' 28,455 O5
Spassk-Dal'niy 53,000 O5
Sretensk 16,000 M4
Stalingrad (Volgograd) 999,000 E5
Stavropol' 318,000 E5
Sterlitamak 248,000 F4
Surgut 248,000 H3
Susuman 12,000 P3
Sverdlovsk (Yekaterinburg) 1,367,000 F4
Svobodnyy 75,000 N4
Syktyvkar 233,000 F3
Syzran' 174,000 E4
Taganrog 291,000 D5
Tambov 305,000 E4
Tara 22,358 H4
Tatarsk 29,589 H4
Tayshet 34,232 K4
Tobol'sk 62,000 G4
Togliatti (Tol'yatti) 630,000 F4
Tommot 8,000 N4
Tomsk 502,000 J4
Troitsk 88,000 G4
Tula 540,000 E4
Tulun 52,000 L4
Tura 3,528 L3
Tver' 451,000 D4
Tyumen' 477,000 G4
Uelen T3
Ufa 1,083,000 F4
Uglegorsk 17,921 P5
Ukhta 111,000 F3
Ulan-Ude 353,000 L4
Ul'yanovsk (Simbirsk) 625,000 E4
Uray 17,385 G3
Usol'ye-Sibirskoye 107,000 L4
Ussuriysk 162,000 O5
Ust'-Ilimsk 109,000 L4
Ust'-Kamchatsk 10,000 R4
Ust'-Kut 50,000 L4
Ust'-Olenëk M2
Ust'-Ordynskiy 10,693 L4
Vanino 15,401 P5
Velikiye Luki 114,000 D4
Velikiy Ustyug 36,737 E3
Vel'sk 21,899 E3
Verkhoyansk 2,000 N3
Vladikavkaz 300,000 E5
Vladimir 350,000 D4
Vladivostok 648,000 O5
Volgograd 999,000 E5
Vologda 283,000 E4
Vorkuta 116,000 G3
Voronezh 887,000 E4
Votkinsk 103,000 F4
Voy-Vozh 10,000 F3
Vyazemskiy 18,365 O5

Agriculture, Industry and Resources
(Northern Asia)

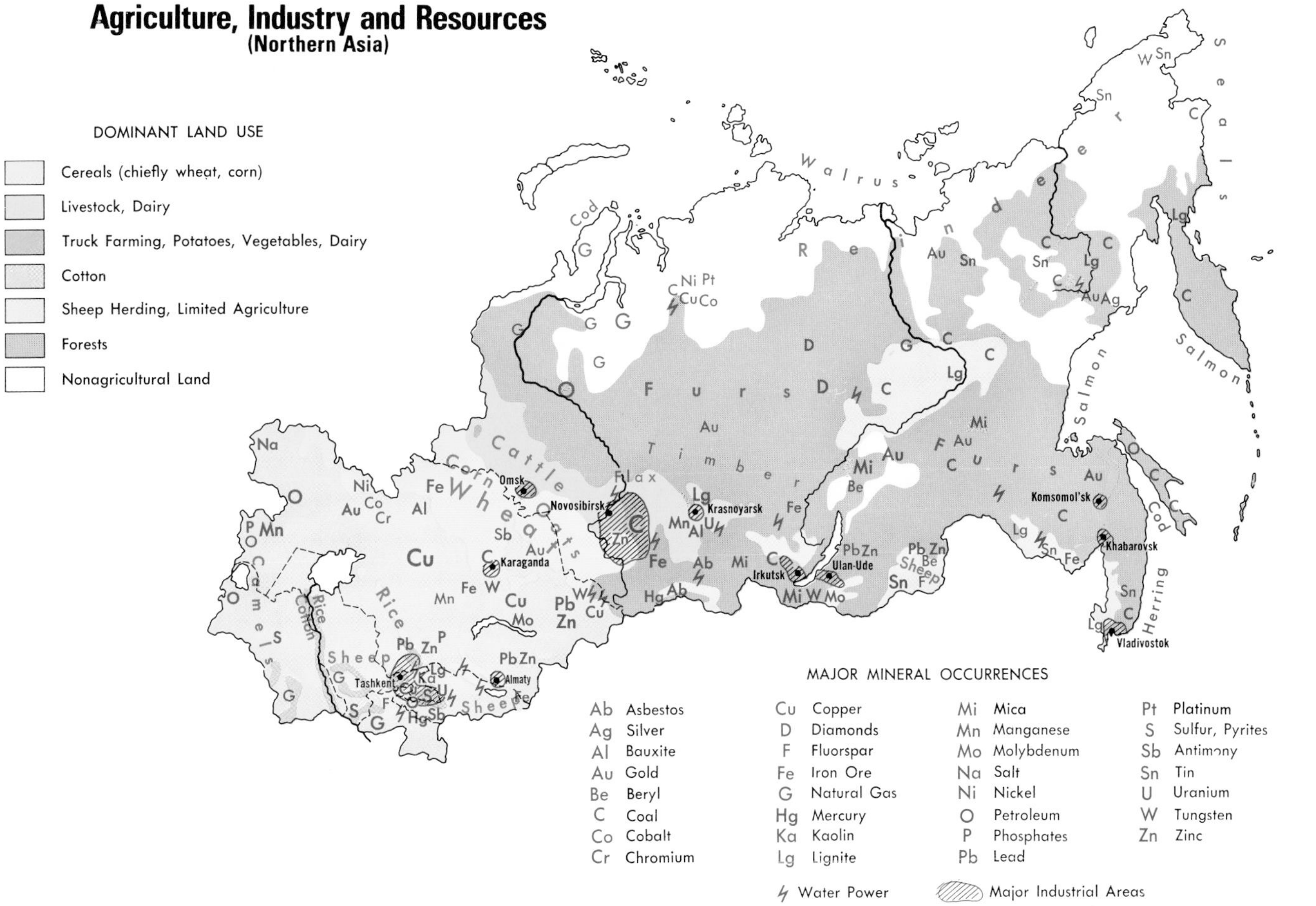
DOMINANT LAND USE
Cereals (chiefly wheat, corn)
Livestock, Dairy
Truck Farming, Potatoes, Vegetables, Dairy
Cotton
Sheep Herding, Limited Agriculture
Forests
Nonagricultural Land
Omsk
Novosibirsk
Krasnoyarsk
Karaganda
Irkutsk
Ulan-Ude
Komsomol'sk
Khabarovsk
Vladivostok
Tashkent
Almaty
Walrus
Reindeer
Furs
Timber
Cattle
Wheat
Oats
Flax
Rice
Cotton
Sheep
Camels
Cod
Salmon
Seals
Herring
MAJOR MINERAL OCCURRENCES
Ab Asbestos
Ag Silver
Al Bauxite
Au Gold
Be Beryl
C Coal
Co Cobalt
Cr Chromium
Cu Copper
D Diamonds
F Fluorspar
Fe Iron Ore
G Natural Gas
Hg Mercury
Ka Kaolin
Lg Lignite
Mi Mica
Mn Manganese
Mo Molybdenum
Na Salt
Ni Nickel
O Petroleum
P Phosphates
Pb Lead
Pt Platinum
S Sulfur, Pyrites
Sb Antimony
Sn Tin
U Uranium
W Tungsten
Zn Zinc
Water Power
Major Industrial Areas

Vyborg 76,000 C3
Vyshniy Volochek 72,000 D4
Yakutsk 187,000 N3
Yalutorovsk 25,426 G4
Yaroslavl' 633,000 D4
Yartsevo 36,662 K3
Yekaterinburg 1,367,000 F4
Yelets 120,000 D4
Yelizovo 10,000 R4
Yeniseysk 19,880 K4
Yoshkar-Ola 242,000 E4
Yurga 78,000 J4
Yuzhno-Sakhalinsk 157,000 P5
Zakamensk 10,000 L4
Zaozernyy 27,216 K4
Zavitinsk 19,009 N4
Zeya 16,684 N4
Zheleznogorsk-Ilimskiy 22,179 L4
Zhigansk N3
Zima 41,567 L4
Zlatoust 208,000 F4

OTHER FEATURES

Alazeya (riv.) Q3
Aldan (plat.) N4
Aldan (riv.) O3
Alexandra Land (isl.) E1
Altai (mts.) J5
Amga (riv.) O3
Amgun' (riv.) O4
Amur (riv.) O4
Anabar (riv.) M2
Anadyr' (gulf) T3
Anadyr' (range) S3
Anadyr' (riv.) S3
Angara (riv.) K4
Aniva (cape) P5
Arctic Ocean K1
Argun (riv.) M4
Arkticheskiy Institut (isls.) H2
Ayon (isl.) R2
Azov (sea) D5
Baltic (sea) B4
Barents (sea) D2
Baykal (lake) L4
Baykal (mts.) L4
Beloye (lake) D3
Belyy (isl.) G2
Bering (isl.) R4
Bering (sea) S4
Bering (strait) U3
Black (sea) D5
Bol'shevik (isl.) K2
Bol'shoy Lyakhovskiy (isl.) P2
Bolvanskiy Nos (cape) G2
Bratsk (res.) L4
Caspian (sea) F6
Chelyuskin (cape) L2
Cherskiy (range) P3
Chukchi (pen.) T3
Chukchi (sea) T2
Chulym (riv.) J4
Chuna (riv.) K4
Chunya (riv.) K3
Dezhnev (cape) T3
Dmitriya Lapteva (strait) O2
Dnieper (riv.) D5
Don (riv.) E5
Dulgalakh (riv.) O3
Dvina, Northern (riv.) E3
Dzhugdzhur (range) O4
East Siberian (sea) S2
Etorofu (Iturup) (isl.) P5
Etorofu (str.) P5
Faddeyevskiy (isl.) P2
Finland (gulf) C4
Franz Josef Land (isls.) F1
George Land (isl.) E1
Gizhiga (bay) Q3
Govena (cape) R4
Graham Bell (isl.) G1
Gyda (pen.) H2
Gydan (Kolyma) (range) Q3
Imandra (lake) D3
Indigirka (riv.) P3
Irtysh (riv.) H4
Ishim (riv.) G4
Japan (sea) O6
Kamchatka (pen.) Q4
Kanin (pen.) E3
Kanin Nos (cape) E3
Kara (sea) G2
Karaginskiy (isl.) R4
Karskiye Vorota (strait) F2
Khanka (lake) O5
Kharasavey (cape) G2
Kheta (riv.) K2
Klyuchevskaya Sopka (vol.) Q4
Kola (pen.) D3
Kolguyev (isl.) E3
Kolyma (range) Q3
Kolyma (riv.) Q3
Komandorskiye (isls.) R4
Komsomolets (isl.) L1
Koni (pen.) Q4
Koryak (range) S3
Kotel'nyy (isl.) O2
Kotuy (riv.) L3
Kuma (riv.) E5
Kunashiri (isl.) P5
Kuril (isls.) P5
Kuybyshev (res.) F4
Ladoga (lake) D3
La Pérouse (strait) P5
Laptev (sea) N2
Lena (riv.) N3
Little Yenisey (riv.) K4
Long (strait) S2
Lopatka (cape) Q4
Lower Tunguska (riv.) K3
Lyakhovskiye (isls.) O2
Markha (riv.) M3
Matochkin Shar (strait) F2
Maya (riv.) O4
Mezen' (riv.) E3
Nadym (riv.) H3
Narodnaya (mt.) G3
Navarin (cape) T3
New Siberian (isls.) P2
Northern Dvina (riv.) E3
Novaya Sibir' (isl.) Q2
Novaya Zemlya (isls.) F2
Ob' (gulf) H3
Ob' (riv.) G3
October Revolution (isl.) L2
Oka (riv.) L4
Okhotsk (sea) P4
Olëkma (riv.) N4
Olënek (bay) N2
Olënek (riv.) M3
Oloy (range) R3
Olyutorskiy (cape) S4
Omolon (riv.) Q3
Omoloy (riv.) O3
Onega (lake) D3
Onega (riv.) D3
Ozernoy (cape) R4
Paramushir (isl.) Q5
Pechora (riv.) F3
Peipus (lake) C4
Penzhina (bay) R3
Pioner (isl.) J2
Pur (riv.) H3
Pyasina (riv.) J2
Rybachiy (pen.) D2
Rybinsk (res.) D4
Sakhalin (gulf) P4
Sakhalin (isl.) P4
Sannikova (strait) O2
Sayan (mts.) K4
Selemdzha (riv.) O4
Sergeya Kirova (isls.) J2
Severnaya Zemlya (isls.) L1
Shantar (isls.) O4
Shelagskiy (cape) R2
Shelekhov (gulf) Q4
Siberia (reg.) M3
Sikhote-Alin' (range) O5
Stanovoy (range) N4
Stony Tunguska (riv.) K3
Tannu-Ola (range) K5
Tatar (strait) P4
Taymyr (lake) K2
Taymyr (pen.) L2
Taymyr (riv.) K2
Taz (riv.) J3
Terpeniye (cape) P5
Tsimlyansk (res.) E5
Tym (riv.) J3
Tyung (riv.) M3
Uda (riv.) O4
Ural (mts.) F4
Ural (riv.) F5
Urup (isl.) Q5
Ussuri (riv.) O5
Vakh (riv.) J3
Velikaya (riv.) S3
Verkhoyansk (range) N3
Vil'kitskogo (strait) L2
Vilyuy (range) M3
Vilyuy (res.) M3
Vilyuy (riv.) L3
Vitim (riv.) M4
Volga (riv.) E5
White (sea) D3
Wiese (isl.) H2
Wilczek Land (isl.) G1
Wrangel (isl.) T2
Yablonovyy (range) M4
Yamal (pen.) G2
Yana (riv.) O3
Yelizavety (cape) P4
Yenisey (riv.) J3
Zeya (riv.) N4

TAJIKISTAN

INTERNAL DIVISIONS

Gorno-Badakhshan Aut. Obl. 161,000 H6

CITIES and TOWNS

Dushanbe (cap.) 595,000 G6
Khorog 12,295 H6
Khudzhand 160,000 G5
Kulyab 55,000 H6
Kurgan-Tyube 34,620 G6
Leninabad (Khudzhand) 160,000 G5
Murgab G6

OTHER FEATURES

Ismail Samani (peak) H6
Pamir (mts.) H6

TURKMENISTAN

CITIES and TOWNS

Ashgabat (cap.) 398,000 F6
Bayram-Ali 31,987 G6
Chardzhou 161,000 G6
Gasan-Kuli F6
Iolotan' 10,000 G6
Kerki 10,000 G6
Kizyl-Arvat 21,671 F6
Krasnovodsk 53,000 F5
Kum-Dag 10,000 F6
Kushka G6
Mary (Merv) 74,000 G6
Nebit-Dag 71,000 F6
Serakhs G6
Takhta-Bazar G6
Tashauz 112,000 F5
Tedzhen 25,708 F6

OTHER FEATURES

Amudar'ya (riv.) G5
Atrek (riv.) F6
Caspian (sea) F6
Kara-Bogaz-Gol (gulf) F5
Kara-Kum (canal) F6
Kara-Kum (des.) F5
Murgab (riv.) G6

UKRAINE

CITIES and TOWNS

Berdichev 80,000 C5
Chernigov 296,000 D4
Chernovtsy 257,000 C5
Dnepropetrovsk 1,179,000 D5
Donetsk 1,110,000 D5
Drogobych 66,000 C5
Ivano-Frankovsk 214,000 C5
Izmail 83,000 C5
Khar'kov 1,611,000 D4
Kherson 355,000 D5
Kiev (cap.) 2,587,000 D4
Kirovograd 269,000 D5
Kovel' 33,351 C4
Kremenchug 236,000 D5
Krivoy Rog 713,000 D5
Lugansk 497,000 E5
Lutsk 198,000 C4
Lviv (L'vov) 790,000 C4
Mariupol' 517,000 D5
Nikolayev 503,000 D5
Odessa 1,115,000 D5
Poltava 315,000 D5
Rovno 228,000 C4
Sevastopol' 356,000 D5
Simferopol' 344,000 D5
Sumy 291,000 D4
Ternopol' 205,000 C5
Vinnitsa 374,000 C5
Voroshilovgrad (Lugansk) 497,000 E5
Zaporozh'ye 884,000 D5
Zhitomir 292,000 C4

OTHER FEATURES

Azov (sea) D5
Black (sea) D5
Crimea (pen.) D5
Dnieper (riv.) D5
Dniester (riv.) C5
Donets (riv.) D5
Kakhovka (res.) D5

UZBEKISTAN

INTERNAL DIVISIONS

Karakalpak Aut. Rep. 1,214,000 G5

CITIES and TOWNS

Andizhan 293,000 H5
Angren 131,000 H5
Beruni (Biruni) G5
Bukhara 224,000 G5
Chimbay 18,899 F5
Chirchik 156,000 H5
Denau G6
Fergana 200,000 H5
Gulistan 30,879 G5
Kagan 34,117 G6
Karshi 156,000 G6
Kattakurgan 53,000 G5
Khiva 24,139 F5
Khodzheyli 36,435 F5
Kokand 182,000 H5
Muynak 12,000 F5
Namangan 308,000 H5
Navoi 107,000 G6
Nukus 169,000 G5
Samarkand 366,000 G6
Takhiatash F5
Tashkent (cap.) 2,073,000 G5
Termez 57,000 G6
Urgench 128,000 G5
Zarafshan G5

OTHER FEATURES

Amudar'ya (riv.) G5
Aral (sea) F5
Kyzyl-Kum (des.) G5
Syrdar'ya (riv.) G5
Ust'-Urt (plat.) F5

Russia and Neighboring Countries
European Part
CONIC PROJECTION
SCALE OF MILES
0 50 100 200 300
SCALE OF KILOMETERS
0 50 100 200 300
National Capitals
Administrative Centers
International boundaries
Aut. Rep. Oblast, Kray boundaries
Autonomous Oblast boundaries
Autonomous Okrug boundaries
© Copyright HAMMOND INCORPORATED, Maplewood, N. J.
ARCTIC OCEAN
BARENTS SEA
KARA SEA
PECHORA SEA
WHITE SEA
BALTIC SEA
GULF OF BOTHNIA
BLACK SEA
CASPIAN SEA
Sea of Azov
NORWAY
SWEDEN
FINLAND
ESTONIA
LATVIA
LITHUANIA
BELARUS
POLAND
UKRAINE
MOLDOVA
ROMANIA
BULGARIA
TURKEY
GEORGIA
ARMENIA
AZERBAIJAN
KAZAKHSTAN
IRAN
MOSCOW (Moskva)
ST. PETERSBURG
Novaya Zemlya
Kola Pen.
Kanin Pen.
Yamal Pen.
Timan Ridge
Central Ural Mts.
Arctic Circle
Longitude East of Greenwich

Administrative Divisions bear same names as their respective Capitals or Centers, except:

Abkhaz Aut. Rep.	Sukhumi	F6
Adygey Aut. Oblast	Maykop	F6
Adzhar Aut. Rep.	Batumi	F6
Bashkir Aut. Rep.	Ufa	J4
Chechen-Ingush Aut. Rep.	Groznyy	G6
Chuvash Aut. Rep.	Cheboksary	G3
Crimean Oblast	Simferopol'	D6
Dagestan Aut. Rep.	Makhachkala	G6
Kabardin-Balkar Aut. Rep.	Nal'chik	F6
Kalmuck Aut. Rep.	Elista	F5
Karachay-Cherkess Aut. Obl.	Cherkessk	F6
Karelian Aut. Rep.	Petrozavodsk	D2
Komi Aut. Rep.	Syktyvkar	H2
Komi-Permyak Aut. Okrug	Kudymkar	H3
Mari Aut. Rep.	Yoshkar-Ola	G3
Mordvinian Aut. Rep.	Saransk	G4
Nagorno-Karabakh Aut. Obl.	Stepanakert	G7
Nenets Aut. Okrug	Nar'yan-Mar	H1
North Ossetian Aut. Rep.	Vladikavkaz	F6
South Ossetian Aut. Obl.	Tskhinvali	F6
Tatar Aut. Rep.	Kazan	G3
Trans-Carpathian Oblast	Uzhgorod	B5
Udmurt Aut. Rep.	Izhevsk	H3
Volyn Oblast	Lutsk	C4

(continued)

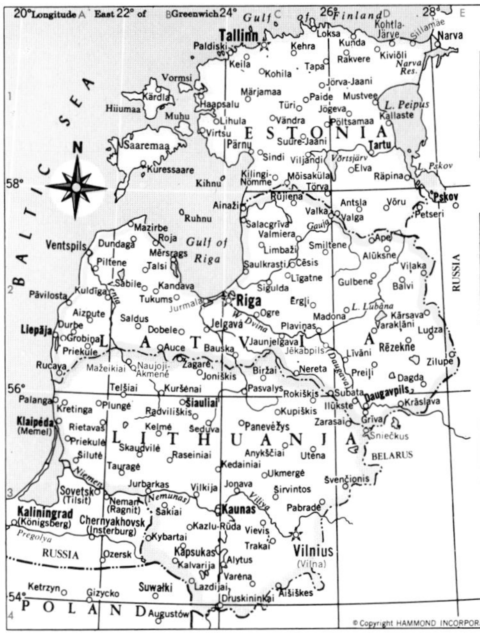

20° Longitude East 22° of Greenwich 24°
Gulf of Finland
BALTIC SEA
Tallinn
Paldiski
Keila
Kohila
Tapa
Rakvere
Kunda
Loksa
Kehra
Kohtla-Järve
Sillamäe
Narva
Kiviõli
Narva Res.
Jõhvi
Vormsi
Kärdla
Hiiumaa
Haapsalu
Märjamaa
Paide
Türi
Mustvee
Jõgeva
Põltsamaa
Kallaste
L. Peipus
Muhu
Lihula
Vändra
Virtsu
Pärnu
Suure-Jaani
Saaremaa
Kuressaare
ESTONIA
Tartu
Sindi
Viljandi
Võrtsjärv
Elva
Räpina
Kihnu
Kilingi-Nõmme
Mõisaküla
Tõrva
Valga
Võru
Pskov
Petseri
58°
Ruhnu
Ainaži
Rūjiena
Antsla
Salacgrīva
Valmiera
Valka
Mazirbe
Roja
Gulf of Riga
Limbaži
Smiltene
Ape
Ventspils
Dundaga
Mērsrags
Alūksne
Piltene
Talsi
Saulkrasti
Cēsis
Vilaka
Līgatne
Gulbene
Balvi
RUSSIA
Sabile
Kandava
Sigulda
Pāvilosta
Kuldīga
Tukums
Jurmala
Riga
Ērgli
Ogre
Madona
L. Lubāna
Aizpute
Saldus
Dobele
Jelgava
Plavinas
Kārsava
Rēzekne
Liepāja
Durbe
Grobiņa
Priekule
Ludza
LATVIA
Auce
Bauska
Jaunjelgava
Jēkabpils
Līvāni
Zilupe
Rucava
Mažeikiai
Naujoji-Akmenė
Zagarė
Joniškis
Birzai
Nereta
Preiļi
Dagda
Telšiai
Kuršenai
Pasvalys
Rokiškis
Subate
Daugavpils
Krāslava
56°
Palanga
Kretinga
Plungė
Radviliškis
Šiauliai
Kupiškis
Ilūkste
Zarasai
Griva
Klaipėda (Memel)
Rietavas
Kelmė
Šeduva
Panevėžys
Sniečkus
Priekulė
Skaudvilė
LITHUANIA
BELARUS
Šilutė
Raseiniai
Anykščiai
Utena
Taurage
Kedainiai
Ukmergė
Švenčionis
Jurbarkas
Vilkija
Jonava
Širvintos
Sovetsk (Tilsit)
Neman (Ragnit)
Sakiai
Kaunas
Pabradė
Kaliningrad (Königsberg)
Chernyakhovsk (Insterburg)
Kybartai
Kazlu-Rūda
Vievis
Trakai
Vilnius (Vilna)
Pregolya
RUSSIA
Ozersk
Kapsukas
Kalvarija
Alytus
Varėna
Ketrzyn
Gizycko
Suwałki
Lazdijai
Druskininkai
Aisiškės
54°
POLAND
Augustów
© Copyright HAMMOND INCORPORATED, Maplewood, N. J.

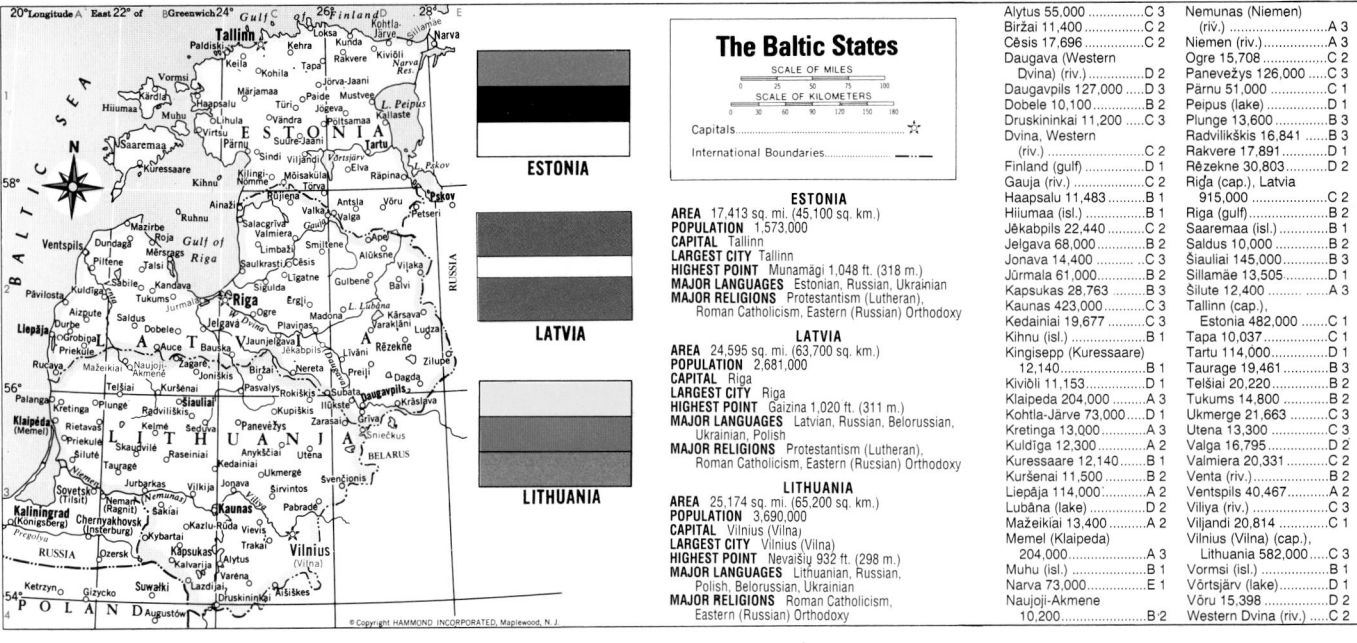

The Baltic States

SCALE OF MILES 0 25 50 75 100

SCALE OF KILOMETERS 0 30 60 90 120 150 180

Capitals ☆

International Boundaries

ESTONIA

LATVIA

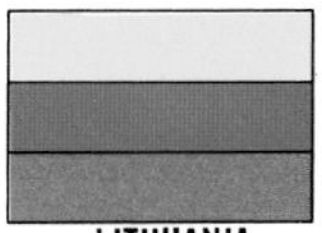

LITHUANIA

ESTONIA

AREA 17,413 sq. mi. (45,100 sq. km.)
POPULATION 1,573,000
CAPITAL Tallinn
LARGEST CITY Tallinn
HIGHEST POINT Munamägi 1,048 ft. (318 m.)
MAJOR LANGUAGES Estonian, Russian, Ukrainian
MAJOR RELIGIONS Protestantism (Lutheran), Roman Catholicism, Eastern (Russian) Orthodoxy

LATVIA

AREA 24,595 sq. mi. (63,700 sq. km.)
POPULATION 2,681,000
CAPITAL Riga
LARGEST CITY Riga
HIGHEST POINT Gaizina 1,020 ft. (311 m.)
MAJOR LANGUAGES Latvian, Russian, Belorussian, Ukrainian, Polish
MAJOR RELIGIONS Protestantism (Lutheran), Roman Catholicism, Eastern (Russian) Orthodoxy

LITHUANIA

AREA 25,174 sq. mi. (65,200 sq. km.)
POPULATION 3,690,000
CAPITAL Vilnius (Vilna)
LARGEST CITY Vilnius (Vilna)
HIGHEST POINT Nevaišiu 932 ft. (298 m.)
MAJOR LANGUAGES Lithuanian, Russian, Polish, Belorussian, Ukrainian
MAJOR RELIGIONS Roman Catholicism, Eastern (Russian) Orthodoxy

Alytus 55,000 ....C 3
Biržai 11,400 ....C 2
Cēsis 17,696 ....C 2
Daugava (Western Dvina) (riv.) ....D 2
Daugavpils 127,000 ....D 3
Dobele 10,100 ....B 2
Druskininkai 11,200 ....C 3
Dvina, Western (riv.) ....C 2
Finland (gulf) ....D 1
Gauja (riv.) ....C 2
Haapsalu 11,483 ....B 1
Hiiumaa (isl.) ....B 1
Jēkabpils 22,440 ....C 2
Jelgava 68,000 ....B 2
Jonava 14,400 ....C 3
Jūrmala 61,000 ....B 2
Kapsukas 28,763 ....B 3
Kaunas 423,000 ....C 3
Kedainiai 19,677 ....C 3
Kihnu (isl.) ....B 1
Kingisepp (Kuressaare) 12,140 ....B 1
Kiviõli 11,153 ....D 1
Klaipeda 204,000 ....A 3
Kohtla-Järve 73,000 ....D 1
Kretinga 13,000 ....A 3
Kuldīga 12,300 ....A 2
Kuressaare 12,140 ....B 1
Kuršenai 11,500 ....B 2
Liepāja 114,000 ....A 2
Lubāna (lake) ....D 2
Mažeikiai 13,400 ....A 2
Memel (Klaipeda) 204,000 ....A 3
Muhu (isl.) ....B 1
Narva 73,000 ....E 1
Naujoji-Akmene 10,200 ....B 2
Nemunas (Niemen) (riv.) ....A 3
Niemen (riv.) ....A 3
Ogre 15,708 ....C 2
Panevežys 126,000 ....C 3
Pärnu 51,000 ....C 1
Peipus (lake) ....D 1
Plunge 13,600 ....B 3
Radviliškis 16,841 ....B 3
Rakvere 17,891 ....D 1
Rēzekne 30,803 ....D 2
Rīga (cap.), Latvia 915,000 ....C 2
Riga (gulf) ....B 2
Saaremaa (isl.) ....B 1
Saldus 10,000 ....B 2
Šiauliai 145,000 ....B 3
Sillamäe 13,505 ....D 1
Šilute 12,000 ....A 3
Tallinn (cap.), Estonia 482,000 ....C 1
Tapa 10,037 ....C 1
Tartu 114,000 ....D 1
Taurage 19,461 ....B 3
Telšiai 20,220 ....B 2
Tukums 14,800 ....B 2
Ukmerge 21,663 ....C 3
Utena 13,300 ....C 3
Valga 16,795 ....D 2
Valmiera 20,331 ....C 2
Venta (riv.) ....B 2
Ventspils 40,467 ....A 2
Viliya (riv.) ....C 3
Viljandi 20,814 ....C 1
Vilnius (Vilna) (cap.), Lithuania 582,000 ....C 3
Vormsi (isl.) ....B 1
Võrtsjärv (lake) ....D 1
Võru 15,398 ....D 2
Western Dvina (riv.) ....C 2

ARMENIA

CITIES and TOWNS

Kirovakan 162,000 ....F6
Kumayri 120,000 ....F6
Leninakan (Kumayri) 120,000 ....F6
Yerevan (cap.) 1,199,000 ....F6

OTHER FEATURES

Alagez (mt.) F6
Araks (riv.) G7
Caucasus (mts.) F6
Kapydzhik (mt.) G7
Sevan (lake) G6

AZERBAIJAN

INTERNAL DIVISIONS

Nagorno-Karabakh Aut. Obl. 188,000 ....G7
Nakhichevan' Aut. Rep. 295,000 ....F7

CITIES and TOWNS

Baku (cap.) 1,150,000 ....H6
Gyandzhe 278,000 ....G6
Kirovabad (Gyandzhe) 278,000 ....G6
Mingechaur 60,000 ....G6
Nakhichevan' 33,279 ....G7
Stepanakert 30,293 ....G7
Sumgait 231,000 ....G6

OTHER FEATURES

Apsheron (pen.) H6
Araks (riv.) G7
Caspian (sea) G6
Caucasus (mts.) F6
Kura (riv.) G6

BELARUS (BELORUSSIA)

CITIES and TOWNS

Baranovichi 159,000 ....C4
Bobruysk 223,000 ....C4
Borisov 144,000 ....C4
Brest 258,000 ....B4
Gomel' 500,000 ....D4
Grodno 270,000 ....B4
Lida 73,000 ....C4
Minsk (cap.) 1,589,000 ....C4
Mogilev 356,000 ....C4
Molodechno 82,000 ....C4
Mozyr' 101,000 ....C4
Orsha 123,000 ....D4
Pinsk 119,000 ....C4
Polotsk 71,000 ....C3
Rechitsa 67,000 ....D4
Soligorsk 82,000 ....C4
Vitebsk 350,000 ....C3

OTHER FEATURES

Berezina (riv.) C4
Bug (riv.) B4
Dnieper (riv.) D5
Dvina, Western (riv.) C3
Goryn' (riv.) C4
Niemen (riv.) B4
Pripet (marshes) C4
Pripyat' (riv.) C4
Western Dvina (riv.) C3

GEORGIA

INTERNAL DIVISIONS

Abkhaz Aut. Rep. 537,000 ....F6
Adzhar Aut. Rep. 393,000 ....F6
South Ossetian Aut. Obl. 99,000 ....F6

CITIES and TOWNS

Batumi 136,000 ....F6
Gori 60,000 ....F6
Kutaisi 235,000 ....F6
Makharadze (Ozurgeti) 21,679 ....F6
Ozurgeti 21,679 ....F6
Poti 45,979 ....F6
Rustavi 159,000 ....G6
Sukhumi 121,000 ....F6
T'bilisi (cap.) 1,260,000 ....F6
Tiflis (T'bilisi) 1,260,000 ....F6
Tskhinvali 30,311 ....F6

OTHER FEATURES

Black (sea) D6
Caucasus (mts.) F6

MOLDOVA (MOLDAVIA)

CITIES and TOWNS

Bel'tsy 159,000 ....C5
Bendery 130,000 ....C5
Kishinev (cap.) 665,000 ....C5
Tighina (Bendery) 130,000 ....C5
Tiraspol' 182,000 ....D5

OTHER FEATURES

Black (sea) D6
Dniester (riv.) C5
Prut (riv.) C5

RUSSIA

INTERNAL DIVISIONS

Adygey Aut. Obl. 432,000 ....F6
Bashkir Aut. Rep. 3,952,000 ....J4
Chechen-Ingush Aut. Rep. 1,277,000 ....G6
Chuvash Aut. Rep. 1,336,000 ....G3
Dagestan Aut. Rep. 1,792,000 ....G6
Kabardin-Balkar Aut. Rep. 760,000 ....F6
Kalmuck Aut. Rep. 322,000 ....F5
Karachay-Cherkess Aut. Obl. 418,000 ....F6
Karelian Aut. Rep. 792,000 ....D2
Komi Aut. Rep. 1,263,000 ....H2
Komi-Permyak Aut. Okr. 159,000 ....H3
Mari Aut. Rep. 750,000 ....G3
Mordvinian Aut. Rep. 964,000 ....G4
Nenets Aut. Okr. 55,000 ....H1
North Ossetian Aut. Rep. 634,000 ....F6
Tatar Aut. Rep. 3,640,000 ....G3
Udmurt Aut. Rep. 1,609,000 ....H3

CITIES and TOWNS

Akhtubinsk 51,000 ....G5
Al'met'yevsk 129,000 ....H3
Archangel (Arkhangel'sk) 416,000 ....F2
Armavir 161,000 ....F5
Arzamas 109,000 ....F3
Astrakhan' 509,000 ....G5
Azov 79,000 ....E5
Balakovo 198,000 ....G4
Balashov 97,000 ....F4
Bataysk 95,000 ....E5
Belgorod 300,000 ....E4
Berezniki 201,000 ....J3
Borisoglebsk 63,000 ....F4
Borovichi 63,000 ....D3
Bryansk 452,000 ....D4
Bugul'ma 85,000 ....H4
Buzuluk 76,000 ....H4
Chapayevsk 86,000 ....G4
Chaykovskiy 76,000 ....H3
Cheboksary 420,000 ....G3
Cherepovets 310,000 ....E3
Cherkessk 113,000 ....F6
Chistopol' 65,000 ....H3
Derbent 78,000 ....G6
Dimitrovgrad 124,000 ....G4
Dzerzhinsk 285,000 ....F3
Elektrostal' 153,000 ....E3
Elista 80,000 ....F5
Engel's 182,000 ....G4
Gatchina 78,000 ....D3
Glazov 104,000 ....H3
Groznyy 401,000 ....G6
Gubkin 70,000 ....E4
Gukovo 71,000 ....F5
Gus'-Khrustal'nyy 74,000 ....F3
Ishimbay 63,000 ....J4
Ivanovo 481,000 ....F3
Izhevsk 635,000 ....H3
Kaliningrad, Kaliningrad 401,000 ....B4
Kaliningrad, Moscow Oblast 160,000 ....E3
Kaluga 312,000 ....E4
Kamensk-Shakhtinskiy 75,000 ....F5
Kamyshin 122,000 ....F4
Kazan' 1,094,000 ....G3
Khasavyurt 72,000 ....G6
Kimry 60,000 ....E3
Kineshma 105,000 ....F3
Kirov 441,000 ....G3
Kirovo-Chepetsk 83,000 ....H3
Kislovodsk 114,000 ....F6
Klintsy 71,000 ....D4
Kolomna 162,000 ....E4
Kolpino 142,000 ....D3
Königsberg (Kaliningrad) 410,000 ....B4
Kostroma 278,000 ....F3
Kotlas 66,000 ....G2
Kovrov 160,000 ....F3
Krasnodar 620,000 ....E6
Kropotkin 73,000 ....F5
Kungur 82,000 ....J3
Kursk 424,000 ....E4
Kuznetsk 97,000 ....G4
Leningrad (St. Petersburg) 4,456,000 ....C3
Lipetsk 450,000 ....E4
Lys'va 76,000 ....J3
Lyubertsy 165,000 ....E3
Makhachkala 315,000 ....G6
Maykop 149,000 ....F6
Michurinsk 109,000 ....F4
Mineral'nye Vody 72,000 ....F6
Moscow (Moskva) (cap.) 8,769,000 ....E3
Murmansk 468,000 ....D1
Murom 124,000 ....F3
Mytishchi 154,000 ....E3
Naberezhnye Chelny 501,000 ....H3
Nal'chik 235,000 ....F6
Neftekamsk 107,000 ....H3
Nevinnomyssk 121,000 ....F6
Nizhnekamsk 191,000 ....H3
Nizhniy Novgorod (Gor'kiy) 1,438,000 ....F3
Novgorod 229,000 ....D3
Novocherkassk 187,000 ....F5
Novokuybyshevsk 113,000 ....G4
Novomoskovsk 146,000 ....E4
Novorossiysk 186,000 ....E6
Novoshakhtinsk 106,000 ....E5
Novotroitsk 106,000 ....J4
Obninsk 100,000 ....E3
Oktyabr'skiy 105,000 ....H4
Ordzhonikidze (Vladikavkaz) 300,000 ....F6
Orekhovo-Zuyevo 137,000 ....D3
Orel 337,000 ....E4
Orenburg 547,000 ....J4
Orsk 271,000 ....J4
Penza 483,000 ....G4
Perm' (Molotov) 1,091,000 ....J3
Petrozavodsk 270,000 ....D2
Podol'sk 210,000 ....E3
Pskov 204,000 ....C3
Pyatigorsk 129,000 ....F6
Rostov 1,020,000 ....F5
Ryazan' 515,000 ....E4
Rybinsk 252,000 ....E3
Rzhev 70,000 ....D3
St. Petersburg 4,456,000 ....C3
Salavat 150,000 ....H4
Samara (Kuybyshev) 1,257,000 ....H4
Saransk 312,000 ....G4
Sarapul 111,000 ....H3
Saratov 905,000 ....G4
Sergiyev Posad 115,000 ....E3
Serpukhov 144,000 ....E4
Sevastopol' 356,000 ....D6
Severodvinsk 249,000 ....E2
Shakhty 224,000 ....F5
Shchekino 70,000 ....E4
Shuya 72,000 ....F3
Simbirsk 625,000 ....G4
Smolensk 341,000 ....D4
Sochi 337,000 ....E6
Solikamsk 110,000 ....J3
Stalingrad (Volgograd) 999,000 ....F5
Staryy Oskol 174,000 ....E4
Stavropol' 318,000 ....F5
Sterlitamak 248,000 ....J4
Stupino 72,000 ....E4
Syktyvkar 233,000 ....H2
Syzran' 174,000 ....G4
Taganrog 291,000 ....E5
Tambov 305,000 ....F4
Togliatti (Tol'yatti) 630,000 ....G4
Tula 540,000 ....E4
Tver' (Kalinin) 451,000 ....E3
Ufa 1,083,000 ....J4
Ukhta 111,000 ....H2
Ul'yanovsk (Simbirsk) 625,000 ....G4
Velikiye Luki 114,000 ....D3
Viipuri (Vyborg) 79,000 ....C2
Vladikavkaz 300,000 ....F6
Vladimir 350,000 ....F3
Volgodonsk 176,000 ....F5
Volgograd 999,000 ....F5
Vologda 283,000 ....F3
Volzhskiy 269,000 ....G5
Vorkuta 116,000 ....K1
Voronezh 887,000 ....E4
Voskresensk 79,000 ....E3
Votkinsk 103,000 ....H3
Vyborg 79,000 ....C2
Vyshniy Volochek 71,000 ....D3
Yaroslavl' 633,000 ....E3
Yelets 120,000 ....E4
Yessentuki 82,000 ....F6
Yeysk 75,000 ....E5
Yoshkar-Ola 242,000 ....G3
Zagorsk (Sergiyev Posad) 115,000 ....E3
Zelenodol'sk 88,000 ....G3
Zheleznodorozhnyy 76,000 ....H2
Zheleznogorsk 74,000 ....E4

OTHER FEATURES

Azov (sea) E5
Baltic (sea) B3
Barents (sea) E1
Baydarata (bay) L1
Belaya (riv.) H3
Beloye (lake) E2
Black (sea) D6
Bolvanskiy Nos (cape) K1
Caspian (sea) G6
Caucasus (mts.) F6
Central Ural (mts.) J2
Cheshskaya (bay) G1
Chir (riv.) F5
Denezhkin Kamen' (mt.) J2
Desna (riv.) D4
Dnieper (riv.) D5
Dolgiy (isl.) J1
Don (riv.) F5
Dvina (bay) E2
Dvina (riv.) F2
Dykhtau (mt.) F6
El'brus (mt.) F6
Finland (gulf) C3
Ilek (riv.) J4
Il'men' (lake) D3
Imandra (lake) D1
Izhma (riv.) H2
Kama (res.) J3
Kama (riv.) H2
Kandalaksha (gulf) D1
Kanin (pen.) G1
Kanin Nos (cape) F1
Kara (sea) K1
Karskiye Vorota (str.) J1
Kazbek (mt.) F6
Khoper (riv.) F4
Kil'din (isl.) D1
Kinel' (riv.) H4
Kola (pen.) E1
Kolguyev (isl.) G1
Kolva (riv.) J1
Kuban' (riv.) E5
Kubeno (lake) E3
Kuma (riv.) G5
Kuybyshev (res.) G4
Kuyto (lake) D2
Lacha (lake) E2
Ladoga (lake) D2
Lapland (reg.) D1
Lovat' (riv.) D3
Mansel'ka (mts.) C1
Manych-Gudilo (lake) F5
Matveyev (isl.) J1
Medveditsa (riv.) F4
Mezen' (bay) F1
Mezen' (riv.) G1
Mezhdusharskiy (isl.) H1
Moksha (riv.) F4
Moskva (riv.) E3
Msta (riv.) D3
Narodnaya (mt.) J1
Northern Dvina (riv.) F2
North Ural (mts.) K1
Novaya Zemlya (isls.) H1
Oka (riv.) F4
Onega (bay) E2
Onega (lake) E2
Onega (riv.) E2
Payyer (mt.) K1
Pechora (bay) H1
Pechora (riv.) H1
Pechora (sea) H1
Peipus (lake) C3
Pinega (riv.) G2
Ponoy (riv.) E1
Russkiy Zavorot (cape) H1
Rybachiy (pen.) D1
Rybinsk (res.) E3
Samara (riv.) H4
Seg (lake) D2
Solovetskiye (isls.) E1
South Ural (mts.) J4
Suda (riv.) E3
Sukhona (riv.) F2
Sura (riv.) G4
Svir' (riv.) D2
Sysola (riv.) H2
Tel'pos-Iz (mt.) K2
Timan (ridge) G1
Top (lake) D1
Tsil'ma (riv.) H1
Tsimlyansk (res.) F5
Tuloma (riv.) D1
Ufa (riv.) J3
Unzha (riv.) F3
Ural (mts.) J2
Ural (riv.) J4
Usa (riv.) K1
Vaga (riv.) F2
Valday (hills) D3
Vashka (riv.) G2
Vaygach (isl.) K1
Velikaya (riv.) C3
Vetluga (riv.) G3
Vishera (riv.) J2
Vodl (lake) E2
Volga (riv.) G5
Volga-Don (canal) F5
Volgograd (res.) G5
Volkhov (riv.) D3
Vorona (riv.) F4
Vorskla (riv.) E4
Vozhe (lake) F2
Vyatka (riv.) H3
Vychegda (riv.) G2
Vyg (lake) E2
Vym' (riv.) H2
Western Dvina (riv.) C3
White (sea) E1
Yamantau (mt.) J4
Yug (riv.) G2
Yugorskiy (pen.) K1

UKRAINE

INTERNAL DIVISIONS

Crimean Oblast 2,456,000 ....D6
Trans-Carpathian Obl. 1,252,000 ....B5
Volyn Oblast 1,062,000 ....C4

CITIES and TOWNS

Aleksandriya 103,000 ....D5
Balaklava D6
Belaya Tserkov' 197,000 ....D5
Belgorod-Dnestrovskiy 51,000 ....D5
Berdichev 85,000 ....C5
Berdyansk 132,000 ....E5
Cherkassy 290,000 ....D5
Chernigov 296,000 ....D4
Chernovtsy 257,000 ....C5
Dneprodzerzhinsk 282,000 ....D5
Dnepropetrovsk 1,179,000 ....D5
Donetsk 1,110,000 ....E5
Drogobych 73,000 ....B5
Feodosiya 81,000 ....D5
Gorlovka 337,000 ....E5
Ivano-Frankovsk 214,000 ....B5
Izmail 87,000 ....C5
Kadiyevka (Stakhanov) 112,000 ....E5
Kalush 64,000 ....B5
Kamenets-Podol'skiy 102,000 ....C5
Kerch' 174,000 ....E5
Khar'kov 1,611,000 ....E5
Kherson 355,000 ....D5
Khmel'nitskiy 237,000 ....C5
Kiev (cap.) 2,587,000 ....D4
Kirovograd 269,000 ....D5
Lugansk 497,000 ....E5
Lutsk 198,000 ....B4
Lviv (L'vov) (Lwów) 790,000 ....B5
Makeyevka 430,000 ....E5
Mariupol' 517,000 ....E5
Melitopol' 174,000 ....D5
Mukachevo 82,000 ....B5
Nikolayev 503,000 ....D5
Nikopol' 158,000 ....D5
Odessa 1,115,000 ....D5
Osipenko (Berdyansk) 132,000 ....E5
Pavlograd 131,000 ....E5
Pervomaysk 76,000 ....D5
Poltava 315,000 ....D5
Priluki 70,000 ....D4
Rovno 228,000 ....C4
Rubezhnoye 68,000 ....E5
Sevastopol' 356,000 ....D6
Severodonetsk 131,000 ....E5
Shostka 82,000 ....D4
Simferopol' 344,000 ....D6
Slavyansk 135,000 ....E5
Smela 70,000 ....D5
Stakhanov 112,000 ....E5
Sumy 291,000 ....E4
Ternopol' 205,000 ....C5
Uman' 85,000 ....D5
Uzhgorod 117,000 ....B5
Vinnitsa 374,000 ....C5
Voroshilovgrad (Lugansk) 497,000 ....E5
Yalta 85,000 ....D6
Yenakiyevo 121,000 ....E5
Yevpatoriya 108,000 ....D5
Zaporozh'ye 884,000 ....E5
Zhitomir 292,000 ....C4

OTHER FEATURES

Azov (sea) E5
Berezina (riv.) C4
Black (sea) D6
Bug (riv.) B4
Crimea (pen.) D5
Desna (riv.) D4
Dnieper (riv.) D5
Dniester (riv.) C5
Donets (riv.) E5
Goryn' (riv.) C4
Kakhovka (res.) D5
Kiev (res.) C4
Pripet (marshes) C4
Pripyat' (riv.) C4
Prut (riv.) C5
Psel (riv.) D4
Seym (riv.) D4
Vorskla (riv.) E4

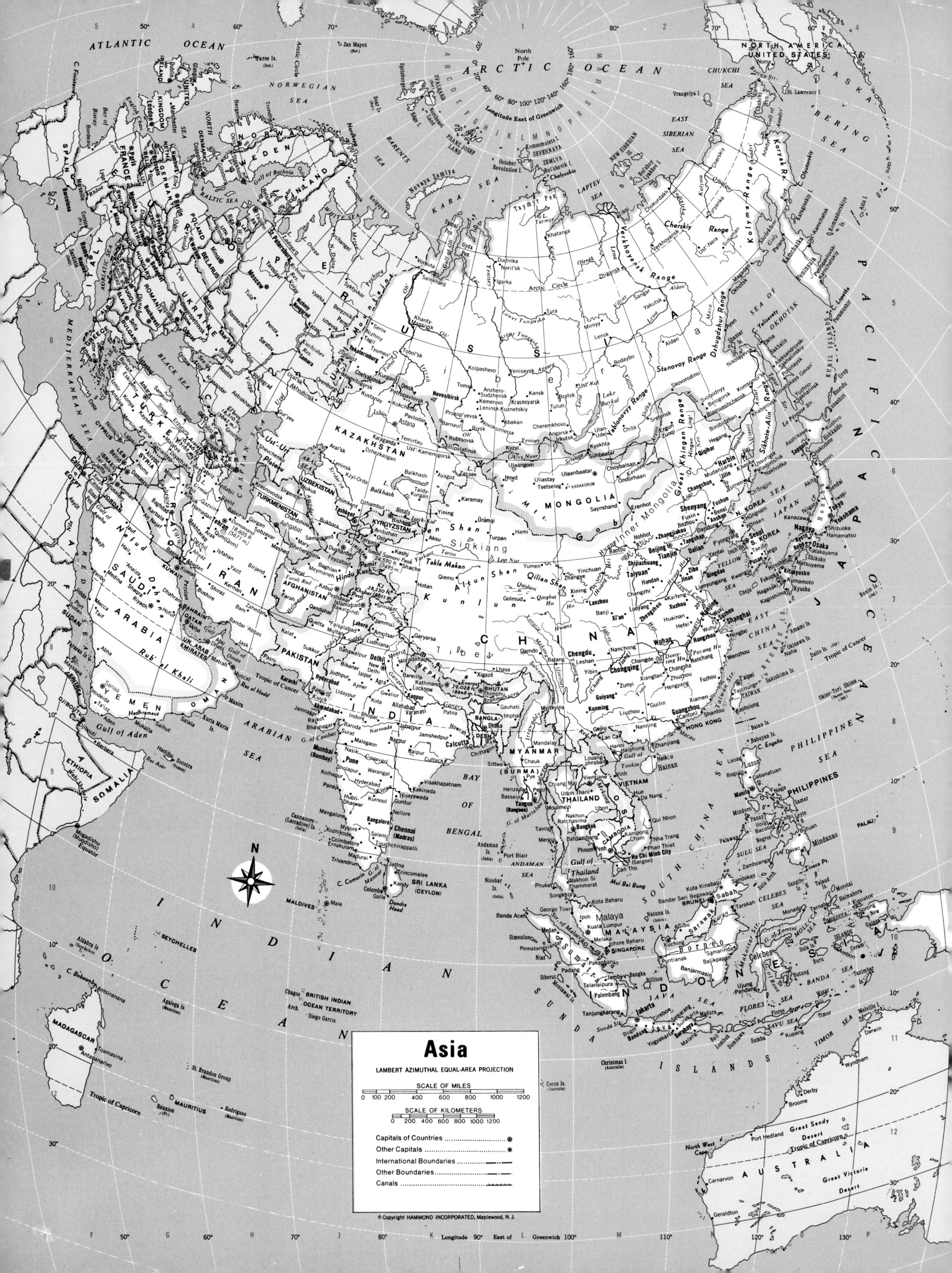
Asia
LAMBERT AZIMUTHAL EQUAL-AREA PROJECTION
SCALE OF MILES
0 100 200 400 600 800 1000 1200
SCALE OF KILOMETERS
0 200 400 600 800 1000 1200
Capitals of Countries
Other Capitals
International Boundaries
Other Boundaries
Canals
© Copyright HAMMOND INCORPORATED, Maplewood, N. J.
ARCTIC OCEAN
ATLANTIC OCEAN
NORWEGIAN SEA
BARENTS SEA
KARA SEA
LAPTEV SEA
EAST SIBERIAN SEA
CHUKCHI SEA
BERING SEA
SEA OF OKHOTSK
PACIFIC OCEAN
SEA OF JAPAN
YELLOW SEA
EAST CHINA SEA
SOUTH CHINA SEA
PHILIPPINE SEA
CELEBES SEA
SULU SEA
BANDA SEA
JAVA SEA
FLORES SEA
SAVU SEA
TIMOR SEA
ANDAMAN SEA
BAY OF BENGAL
ARABIAN SEA
INDIAN OCEAN
BLACK SEA
CASPIAN SEA
MEDITERRANEAN SEA
RED SEA
Gulf of Aden
BALTIC SEA
NORTH SEA
RUSSIA
KAZAKHSTAN
MONGOLIA
CHINA
Sinkiang
Tibet
Inner Mongolia
INDIA
PAKISTAN
AFGHANISTAN
IRAN
IRAQ
SAUDI ARABIA
YEMEN
OMAN
TURKEY
SYRIA
JORDAN
ISRAEL
LEBANON
KUWAIT
QATAR
BAHRAIN
UN. ARAB EMIRATES
UZBEKISTAN
TURKMENISTAN
KYRGYZSTAN
TAJIKISTAN
NEPAL
BHUTAN
BANGLADESH
MYANMAR (BURMA)
THAILAND
LAOS
VIETNAM
CAMBODIA
MALAYSIA
SINGAPORE
BRUNEI
INDONESIA
PHILIPPINES
TAIWAN
N. KOREA
S. KOREA
JAPAN
SRI LANKA (CEYLON)
MALDIVES
AUSTRALIA
SOMALIA
ETHIOPIA
EGYPT
SUDAN
DJIBOUTI
MADAGASCAR
NORTH AMERICA
UNITED STATES
ALASKA
Siberia
Takla Makan
Gobi
Tien Shan
Kunlun
Altun Shan
Qilian Shan
Hindu Kush
Pamir
Verkhoyansk Range
Cherskiy Range
Kolyma Range
Stanovoy Range
Yablonovyy Range
Great Khingan Range
Sikhote-Alin Range
Dzhugdzhur Range
Arctic Circle
Tropic of Cancer
Tropic of Capricorn
Equator
Longitude East of Greenwich
Moscow
Beijing
Tokyo
New Delhi
Tehran
Baghdad
Kabul
Islamabad
Ulaanbaatar
Seoul
Manila
Jakarta
Bangkok
Yangon (Rangoon)
Hanoi
Ho Chi Minh City (Saigon)
Calcutta
Mumbai (Bombay)
Chennai (Madras)
Shanghai
Hong Kong
Novosibirsk
Vladivostok
Lake Baykal
Everest 29,028 ft. (8848 m)
K2 28,250 ft. (8611 m)
Ismail Samani Peak 24,590 ft. (7495 m)
Damavand 18,605 ft. (5671 m)
BRITISH INDIAN OCEAN TERRITORY
SEYCHELLES
MAURITIUS
SUNDA ISLANDS
KURIL ISLANDS

Population Distribution

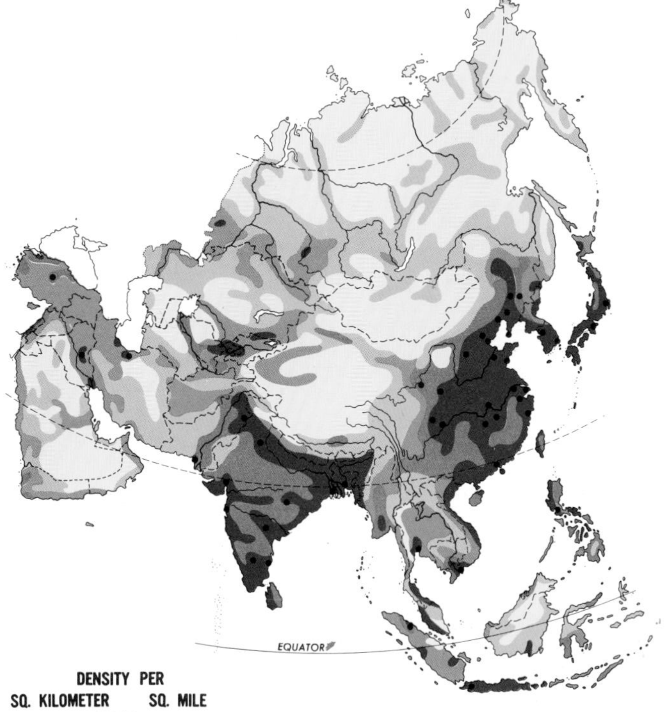
EQUATOR

DENSITY PER

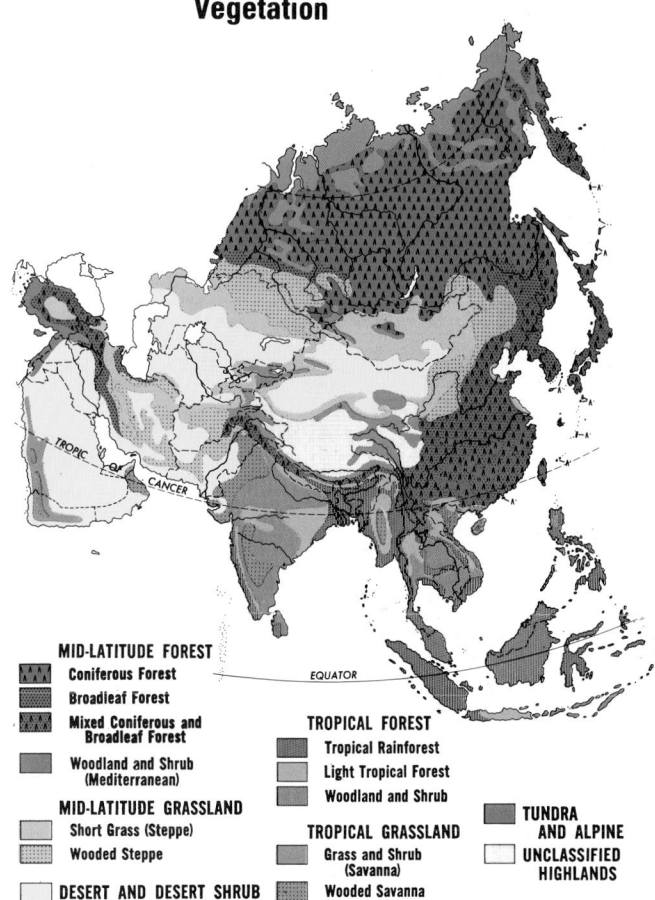

SQ. KILOMETER	SQ. MILE
Over 100	Over 260
50-100	130-260
10-50	25-130
1-10	3-25
Under 1	Under 3

• Cities with over 3,000,000 inhabitants (including suburbs)

AREA 17,128,500 sq. mi. (44,362,815 sq. km.)
POPULATION 3,176,000,000
LARGEST CITY Tokyo
HIGHEST POINT Mt. Everest 29,028 ft. (8,848 m.)
LOWEST POINT Dead Sea -1,296 ft. (-395 m.)

Vegetation

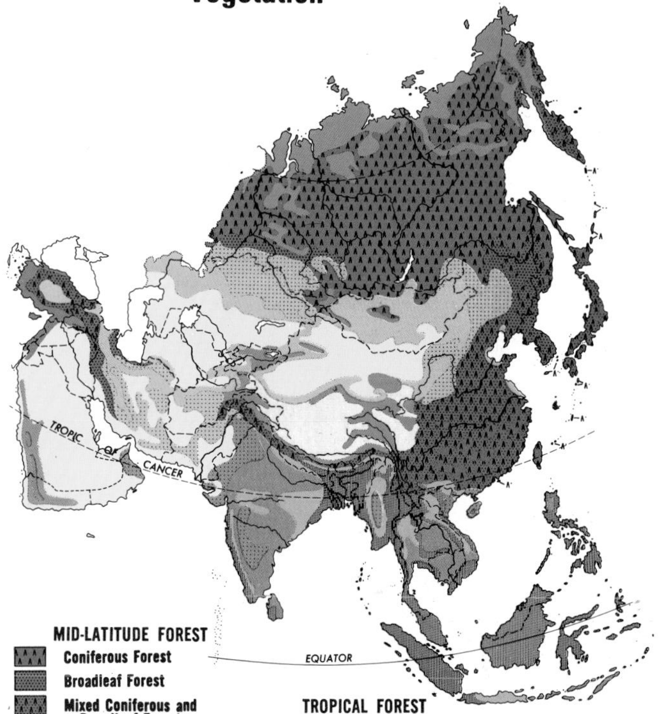
TROPIC OF CANCER
EQUATOR

MID-LATITUDE FOREST
- Coniferous Forest
- Broadleaf Forest
- Mixed Coniferous and Broadleaf Forest
- Woodland and Shrub (Mediterranean)

MID-LATITUDE GRASSLAND
- Short Grass (Steppe)
- Wooded Steppe

DESERT AND DESERT SHRUB

TROPICAL FOREST
- Tropical Rainforest
- Light Tropical Forest
- Woodland and Shrub

TROPICAL GRASSLAND
- Grass and Shrub (Savanna)
- Wooded Savanna

TUNDRA AND ALPINE

UNCLASSIFIED HIGHLANDS

Average January Temperature

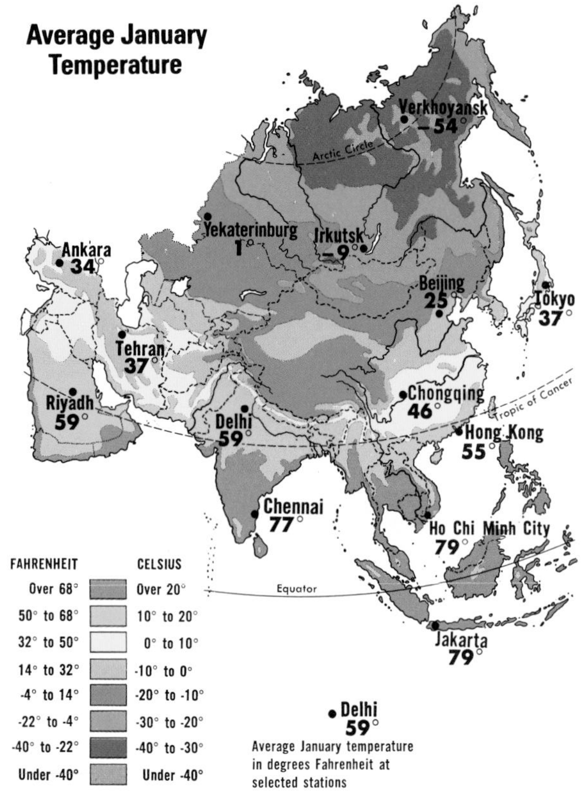
Verkhoyansk
-54°
Arctic Circle
Yekaterinburg
1°
Irkutsk
-9°
Ankara
34°
Beijing
25°
Tokyo
37°
Tehran
37°
Chongqing
46°
Tropic of Cancer
Riyadh
59°
Delhi
59°
Hong Kong
55°
Chennai
77°
Ho Chi Minh City
79°
Equator
Jakarta
79°
FAHRENHEIT
CELSIUS
Over 68° Over 20°
50° to 68° 10° to 20°
32° to 50° 0° to 10°
14° to 32° -10° to 0°
-4° to 14° -20° to -10°
-22° to -4° -30° to -20°
-40° to -22° -40° to -30°
Under -40° Under -40°
Delhi
59°
Average January temperature
in degrees Fahrenheit at
selected stations

Average July Temperature

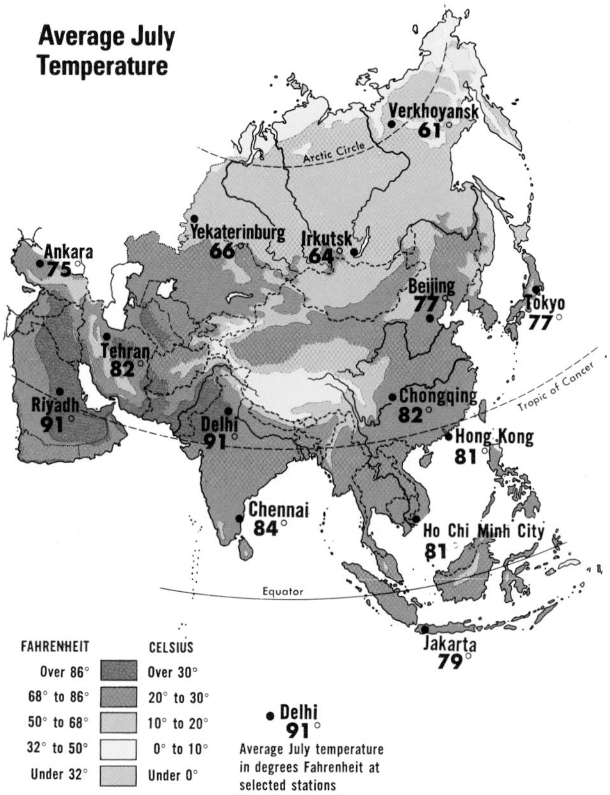
Verkhoyansk
61°
Arctic Circle
Ankara
75°
Yekaterinburg
66°
Irkutsk
64°
Beijing
77°
Tokyo
77°
Tehran
82°
Riyadh
91°
Chongqing
82°
Tropic of Cancer
Delhi
91°
Hong Kong
81°
Chennai
84°
Ho Chi Minh City
81°
Equator
Jakarta
79°
FAHRENHEIT
CELSIUS
Over 86° Over 30°
68° to 86° 20° to 30°
50° to 68° 10° to 20°
32° to 50° 0° to 10°
Under 32° Under 0°
Delhi
91°
Average July temperature
in degrees Fahrenheit at
selected stations

Rainfall

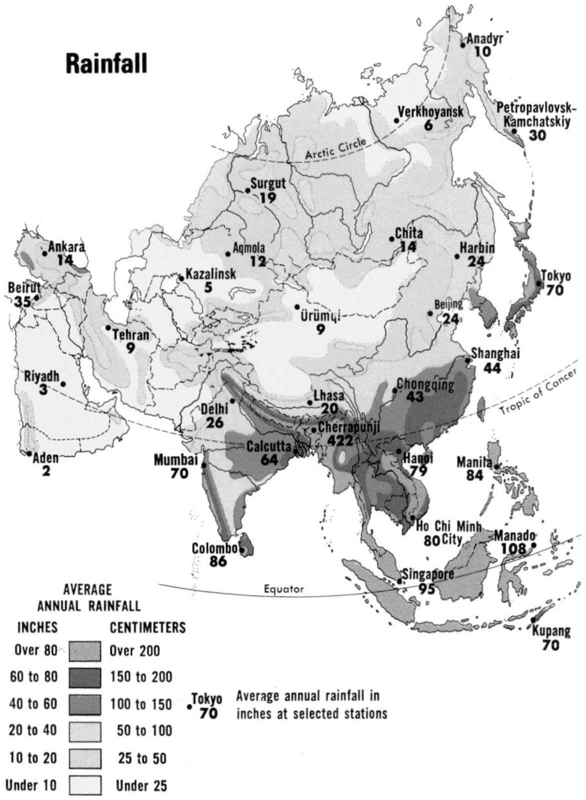
Anadyr
10
Verkhoyansk
6
Petropavlovsk-
Kamchatskiy
30
Arctic Circle
Surgut
19
Ankara
14
Aqmola
12
Chita
14
Harbin
24
Beirut
35
Kazalinsk
5
Tokyo
70
Ürümqi
9
Beijing
24
Tehran
9
Shanghai
44
Riyadh
3
Lhasa
20
Chongqing
43
Tropic of Cancer
Delhi
26
Cherrapunji
422
Aden
2
Mumbai
70
Calcutta
64
Hanoi
79
Manila
84
Ho Chi Minh
City
80
Manado
108
Colombo
86
Singapore
95
Equator
Kupang
70
AVERAGE
ANNUAL RAINFALL
INCHES
CENTIMETERS
Over 80 Over 200
60 to 80 150 to 200
40 to 60 100 to 150
20 to 40 50 to 100
10 to 20 25 to 50
Under 10 Under 25
Tokyo
70
Average annual rainfall in
inches at selected stations

Vegetation/Relief

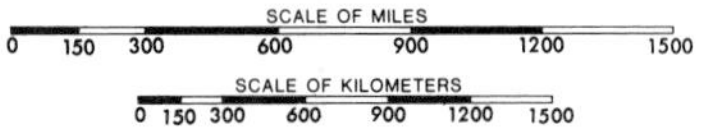
SCALE OF MILES
0 150 300 600 900 1200 1500
SCALE OF KILOMETERS
0 150 300 600 900 1200 1500

Capitals of Countries .... ⊛
International Boundaries ....
Canals ....

Elevations in Feet

Depths in Fathoms

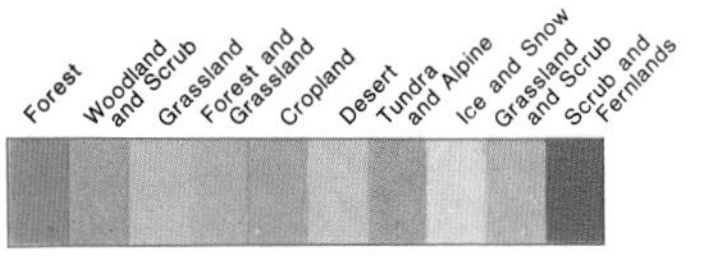
Forest
Woodland and Scrub
Grassland
Forest and Grassland
Cropland
Desert
Tundra and Alpine
Ice and Snow
Grassland and Scrub
Scrub and Fernlands

COLOR KEY

ATLANTIC OCEAN
NORWEGIAN SEA
NORTH SEA
Bay of Biscay
IRELAND
UNITED KINGDOM
London
Paris
Berlin
Rome
BALTIC SEA
POLAND
BELARUS
UKRAINE
MOSCOW
BLACK SEA
MEDITERRANEAN SEA
CYPRUS
LEBANON
ISRAEL
Cairo
SYRIA
JORDAN
IRAQ
Baghdad
KUWAIT
Tehran
IRAN
SAUDI ARABIA
Riyadh
BAHRAIN
QATAR
U.A.E.
Rub' al Khali
OMAN
Muscat
YEMEN
Aden
Gulf of Aden
Gulf of Oman
ETHIOPIA
SOMALIA
Ras Asêr
Socotra
ICELAND
GREENLAND
Arctic Circle
North Pole
Svalbard (Nor.)
Franz Josef Ld.
BARENTS SEA
Nordkapp
ARCTIC OCEAN
Novaya Zemlya
KARA SEA
Severnaya Zemlya
Chelyuskin
LAPTEV SEA
New Siberian Is.
EAST SIBERIAN SEA
C. Dezhnev
Bering Str.
BERING SEA
Aleutian Islands
Alaska
UNITED STATES
Kamchatka Peninsula
C. Lopatka
SEA OF OKHOTSK
Sakhalin
Kuril Is.
RUSSIA
Siberia
Yenisey
Ob'
Noril'sk
Vilyuy
Yakutsk
Lena
Kolyma
Angara
Krasnoyarsk
Novosibirsk
Omsk
Irtysh
Tobol
Chelyabinsk
Yekaterinburg
Ural Mountains
Volga
Ural
Astana
KAZAKHSTAN
Karaganda
L. Balkhash
ARAL SEA
CASPIAN SEA
Syrdar'ya
Amudar'ya
UZBEKISTAN
TURKMENISTAN
Tashkent
Almaty
Ürümqi
Tarim
Taklimakan
Hindu Kush
AFGHANISTAN
Kabul
K2 (Godwin Austen) 28,250 ft.
Helmand
PAKISTAN
Lahore
Indus
Karachi
Delhi
New Delhi
Kanpur
Ganges
Yamuna
INDIA
Ahmadabad
Narbada
Mumbai (Bombay)
Godavari
Hyderabad
Kistna
Chennai (Madras)
Bangalore
C. Comorin
SRI LANKA (CEYLON)
Colombo
Dondra Head
MALDIVES
ARABIAN SEA
Calcutta
BANGLADESH
Dhaka
Brahmaputra
BAY OF BENGAL
MYANMAR (BURMA)
Yangon (Rangoon)
Andaman Is.
ANDAMAN SEA
Nicobar Is.
THAILAND
Bangkok
Gulf of Siam
CAMBODIA
VIETNAM
Ho Chi Minh City
Hainan
HONG KONG
Guangzhou
Taiwan
Taipei
Tropic of Cancer
SOUTH CHINA SEA
Luzon
C. Engaño
PHILIPPINES
Manila
Palawan
SULU SEA
Mindanao
CELEBES SEA
Celebes
BRUNEI
MALAYSIA
Kuala Lumpur
SINGAPORE
Sumatra
Borneo
INDONESIA
Jakarta
Java
JAVA SEA
Surabaya
FLORES SEA
BANDA SEA
Timor
TIMOR SEA
New Guinea
Sunda Islands
Tibet
Kunlun
CHINA
Chengdu
Chongqing
Wuhan
Nanjing
Shanghai
EAST CHINA SEA
Ryukyu Is.
Lanzhou
Xi'an
Huang
Taiyuan
Beijing
Tianjin
Dalian
YELLOW SEA
Gobi
MONGOLIA
Ulaanbaatar
Lake Baikal
Yablonovyy Ra.
Harbin
Shenyang
Amur
Vladivostok
N. KOREA
Seoul
S. KOREA
SEA OF JAPAN
JAPAN
Hokkaido
Honshu
Tokyo
Nagoya
Osaka
Shikoku
Kyushu
PACIFIC OCEAN
INDIAN OCEAN
SEYCHELLES
COMOROS
Equator
BRITISH INDIAN OCEAN TERR.
MADAGASCAR
Réunion (Fr.)
MAURITIUS
Tropic of Capricorn
AUSTRALIA
Longitude 70° East of Greenwich

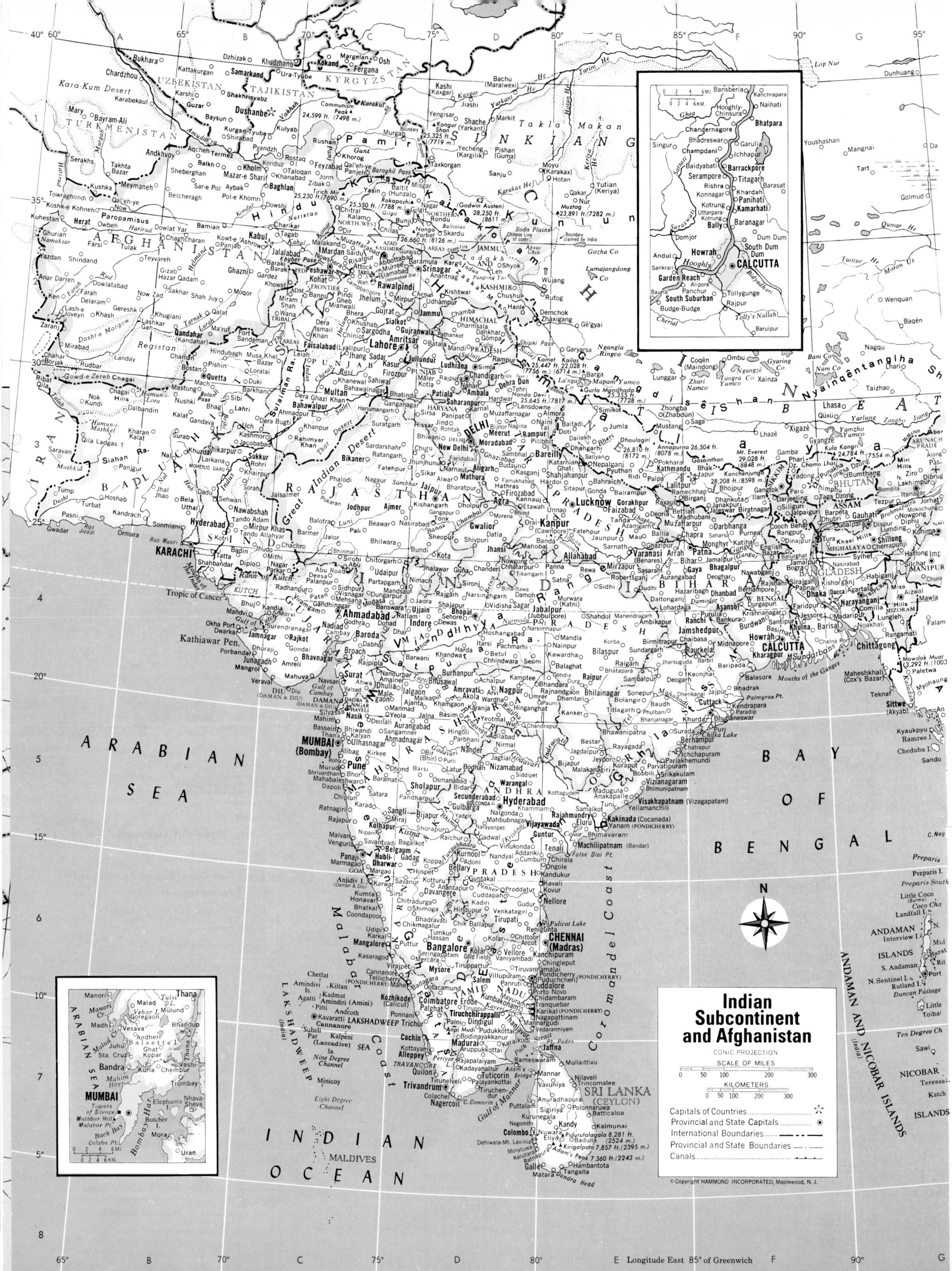
Indian Subcontinent and Afghanistan
CONIC PROJECTION
SCALE OF MILES
0 50 100 200 300
KILOMETERS
0 50 100 200 300
Capitals of Countries
Provincial and State Capitals
International Boundaries
Provincial and State Boundaries
Canals
© Copyright HAMMOND INCORPORATED, Maplewood, N.J.
Longitude East 85° of Greenwich
ARABIAN SEA
BAY OF BENGAL
INDIAN OCEAN
AFGHANISTAN
TURKMENISTAN
UZBEKISTAN
TAJIKISTAN
KYRGYZSTAN
SINKIANG
BANGLADESH
BHUTAN
SRI LANKA (CEYLON)
MALDIVES
LAKSHADWEEP (India)
ANDAMAN AND NICOBAR ISLANDS (India)
Kara-Kum Desert
Takla Makan
Great Indian Desert
Tropic of Cancer
Kathiawar Pen.
Malabar Coast
Coromandel Coast
Mouths of the Ganges
KARACHI
DELHI
New Delhi
MUMBAI (Bombay)
CALCUTTA
CHENNAI (Madras)
Bangalore
Hyderabad
Kabul
Lahore
Dhaka
Colombo
Kathmandu
Mt. Everest 29,028 ft. (8848 m.)
K2 (Godwin Austen) 28,250 ft. (8611 m.)
Calcutta inset: Bansberia, Kanchrapara, Naihati, Hooghly-Chinsura, Bhatpara, Chandernagore, Singur, Bhadreswar, Garulia, Champdani, Ichhapur, Baidyabati, Barrackpore, Serampore, Titagarh, Rishra, Konnagar, Barasat, Khardah, Panihati, Kotrung, Kamarhati, Uttarpara, Bally, Baranagar, Domjor, Dum Dum, Howrah, South Dum Dum, Andul, Sankrail, Garden Reach, CALCUTTA, Alipore, Tollygunge, Baurla, Panchur, South Suburban, Rajpur, Budge-Budge, Tolly's Nullah, Baruipur
Mumbai inset: Manori, Malad, Thana, Vehar L., Mulund, Goregaon, Madh, Bhandup, Vesava, Andheri, Salsette I., Juhu, Ghatkopar, Kurla, Sta. Cruz, Bandra, Mahim Bay, Chembur, Trombay, MUMBAI, Towers of Silence, Malabar Hill, Malabar Pt., Back Bay, Butcher I., Colaba Pt., Mora, Nhava-Sheva, Elephanta Is., Bombay Hbr., Uran

Yumen
Har Hu
Qaidam
Delingha
Ngoring Hu
Gyaring Hu
Chindu
Yushu
Qamdo
Salween
Namzha Parwa 25,445 ft. (7756 m.)
Mishmi Hills
Rima
Boundary claimed by China
Tezu
Sadiya
Tinsukia
Digboi
Sibsagar
Putao (Ft. Hertz)
Maingkwan
Singkaling Hkamti
Myitkyina
Mogaung
Thaungdut
Katha
Bhamo
Wuntho
Mogok
Ye-u
Shwebo
Maymyo
Monywa
Mandalay
Sagaing
Kyaukse
Myingyan
Pakokku
Meiktila
Yamethin
Minbu
Magwe
Pyinmana
Aulang
Thayetmyo
Pye (Prome)
Toungoo
Kyangin
Myanaung
Henzada
Tharrawaddy
Pegu
Insein
Bassein
Ma-ubin
Yangon (Rangoon)
Myaungmya
Pyapon
Mouths of the Irrawaddy
North Channel
ANDAMAN
Narcondam (India)
SEA
Car Nicobar
Batti Malv
Tillanchong
Camorta
Nancowry
Sombrero Channel
Little Nicobar
Great Nicobar
Indira Pt.
Great Channel
Banda Aceh
Sumatra
INDONESIA
100°
40°
35°
30°
25°
20°
15°
10°
5°
95°

INDIA

AREA 1,269,339 sq. mi. (3,287,588 sq. km.)
POPULATION 843,930,861
CAPITAL New Delhi
LARGEST CITY Calcutta (greater)
HIGHEST POINT Nanda Devi 25,645 ft. (7,817 m.)
MONETARY UNIT Indian rupee
MAJOR LANGUAGES Hindi, English, Bengali, Telugu, Marathi, Tamil, Urdu, Gujarati, Malayalam, Kannada, Oriya, Punjabi, Assamese, Kashmiri, Sindhi
MAJOR RELIGIONS Hinduism, Islam, Christianity, Sikhism, Buddhism, Jainism, Zoroastrianism, Animism

PAKISTAN

AREA 310,403 sq. mi. (803,944 sq. km.)
POPULATION 112,050,000
CAPITAL Islamabad
LARGEST CITY Karachi
HIGHEST POINT K2 (Godwin Austen) 28,250 ft. (8,611 m.)
MONETARY UNIT Pakistani rupee
MAJOR LANGUAGES Urdu, English, Punjabi, Pushtu, Sindhi, Baluchi, Brahui
MAJOR RELIGIONS Islam, Hinduism, Sikhism, Christianity, Buddhism

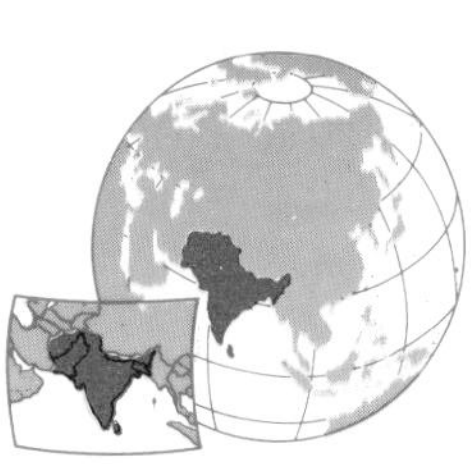

SRI LANKA (CEYLON)

AREA 25,332 sq. mi. (65,610 sq. km.)
POPULATION 16,806,000
CAPITAL Colombo
LARGEST CITY Colombo
HIGHEST POINT Pidurutalagala 8,281 ft. (2,524 m.)
MONETARY UNIT Sri Lanka rupee
MAJOR LANGUAGES Sinhala, Tamil, English
MAJOR RELIGIONS Buddhism, Hinduism, Christianity, Islam

AFGHANISTAN

AREA 250,775 sq. mi. (649,507 sq. km.)
POPULATION 15,814,000
CAPITAL Kabul
LARGEST CITY Kabul
HIGHEST POINT Nowshak 24,557 ft. (7,485 m.)
MONETARY UNIT afghani
MAJOR LANGUAGES Pushtu, Dari, Uzbek
MAJOR RELIGION Islam

NEPAL

AREA 54,663 sq. mi. (141,577 sq. km.)
POPULATION 18,442,000
CAPITAL Kathmandu
LARGEST CITY Kathmandu
HIGHEST POINT Mt. Everest 29,028 ft. (8,848 m.)
MONETARY UNIT Nepalese rupee
MAJOR LANGUAGES Nepali, Maithili, Tamang, Newari, Tharu
MAJOR RELIGIONS Hinduism, Buddhism

MALDIVES

AREA 115 sq. mi. (298 sq. km.)
POPULATION 206,000
CAPITAL Male
LARGEST CITY Male
HIGHEST POINT 20 ft. (6 m.)
MONETARY UNIT Maldivian rufiyaa
MAJOR LANGUAGE Divehi
MAJOR RELIGION Islam

BHUTAN

AREA 18,147 sq. mi. (47,000 sq. km.)
POPULATION 1,483,000
CAPITAL Thimphu
LARGEST CITY Thimphu
HIGHEST POINT Kula Kangri 24,784 ft. (7,554 m.)
MONETARY UNIT ngultrum
MAJOR LANGUAGES Dzongka, Nepali
MAJOR RELIGIONS Buddhism, Hinduism

BANGLADESH

AREA 55,126 sq. mi. (142,776 sq. km.)
POPULATION 106,507,000
CAPITAL Dhaka
LARGEST CITY Dhaka
HIGHEST POINT Keokradong 4,034 ft. (1,230 m.)
MONETARY UNIT taka
MAJOR LANGUAGES Bengali, English
MAJOR RELIGIONS Islam, Hinduism Christianity

INDIA

PAKISTAN

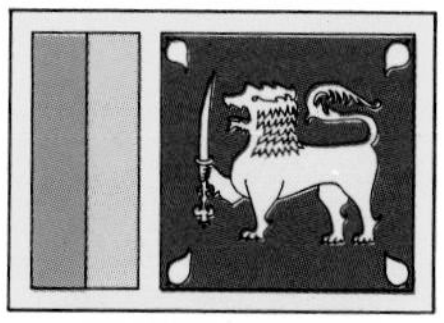
SRI LANKA (CEYLON)

BHUTAN

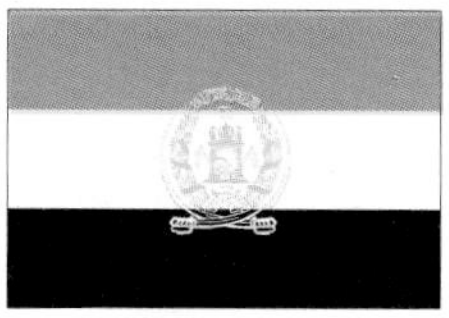
AFGHANISTAN

MALDIVES

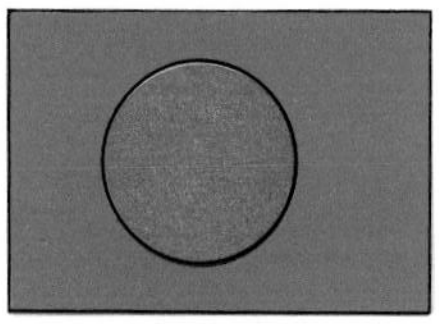
BANGLADESH

NEPAL

AFGHANISTAN

CITIES and TOWNS

Andkhvoy 13,137 .... A1
Aybak 33,016 .... B1
Baghlan 75,130 .... B1
Bamian 7,355 .... B2
Chaghcharan 2,974 .... B2
Charikar 25,093 .... B1
Farah 18,797 .... A2
Feyzabad 10,142 .... C1
Gardez 11,415 .... B2
Gereshk A2
Ghazni 30,425 .... B2
Ghurian 12,404 .... A2
Hazar Qadam B2
Herat 163,960 .... A2
Jalalabad 56,384 .... B2
Kabul (cap.) 905,108 .... B2
Kalat (Qalat) 5,946 .... B2
Kandahar (Qandahar) 178,409 .... B2
Khanabad 26,803 .... B1
Khash A2
Kholm 28,078 .... B1
Khowst B2
Konduz 107,191 .... B1
Kuhestan A2
Lashkar Gah 26,646 .... A2
Mazar-e Sharif 122,567 .... B1
Meymaneh 54,954 .... A1
Mirabad A2
Oruzgan (Hazar Qadam) B2
Panjab B2
Pol-e Khomri 31,101 .... B1
Qalat 5,946 .... B2
Qal'eh-ye Now 5,340 .... A1
Qandahar 178,409 .... B2
Qonduz (Konduz) 107,191 .... B1
Sakhar B2
Sar-e Pol 15,699 .... B1
Sheberghan 54,870 .... B1
Shindand A2
Tagab B2
Taloqan 46,202 .... B1
Zaranj 6,477 .... A2

OTHER FEATURES

Baroghil (pass) C1
Chagai (hills) A3
Margow, Dasht-e (des.) A2
Farah Rud (riv.) A2
Gowd-e Zereh (depr.) A3
Harirud (riv.) A1
Helmand (riv.) B2
Hindu Kush (mts.) B1
Kabul (riv.) C2
Konar (riv.) C1
Konduz (riv.) B1
Lurah (riv.) B2
Namaksar (salt lake) A2
Nuristan (reg.) C1
Panj (riv.) C1
Paropamisus (range) A2
Qonduz (Konduz) (riv.) B1
Registan (reg.) A2
Tarnak (riv.) B2

BANGLADESH

CITIES and TOWNS

Barisal 159,298 .... G4
Bogra 68,237 .... F4
Chalna Port 14,590 .... F4
Chittagong 1,388,476 .... G4
Comilla 126,130 .... G4
Cox's Bazar G4
Dhaka (cap.) 3,458,602 .... G4
Dinajpur 96,348 .... F3
Faridpur 66,911 .... F4
Habiganj 16,281 .... G4
Jamalpur 89,847 .... F4
Jessore 149,426 .... F4
Khulna 623,184 .... F4
Kishorganj 52,081 .... G4
Madaripur 58,645 .... G4
Maheshkhali 29,530 .... G4
Mymensingh (Nasirabad) 107,863 .... G4
Narayanganj 196,139 .... G4
Nasirabad 107,863 .... G4
Nawabganj 65,286 .... F4
Noakhali 32,490 .... G4
Pabna 101,080 .... F4
Rajshahi 171,600 .... F4
Rangamati 36,490 .... G4
Rangpur 72,829 .... F3
Sirajganj 74,457 .... F4
Sylhet 59,546 .... G4

OTHER FEATURES

Bengal, Bay of (bay) F5
Brahmaputra (riv.) G3
Ganges (riv.) F3
Ganges, Mouths of the (delta) F3
Mowdok Mual (mt.) G4
Sundarbans (reg.) F4

BHUTAN

CITIES and TOWNS

Bumthang 10,000 .... G3
Paro 35,000 .... F3
Punakha 12,000 .... G3
Taga Dzong 18,000 .... G3
Thimphu (cap.) 50,000 .... G3
Tongsa Dzong 2,500 .... G3

OTHER FEATURES

Chomo Lhari (mt.) F3
Himalaya (mts.) E2
Kula Kangri (mt.) G3

(continued on following page)

Topography

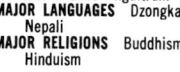

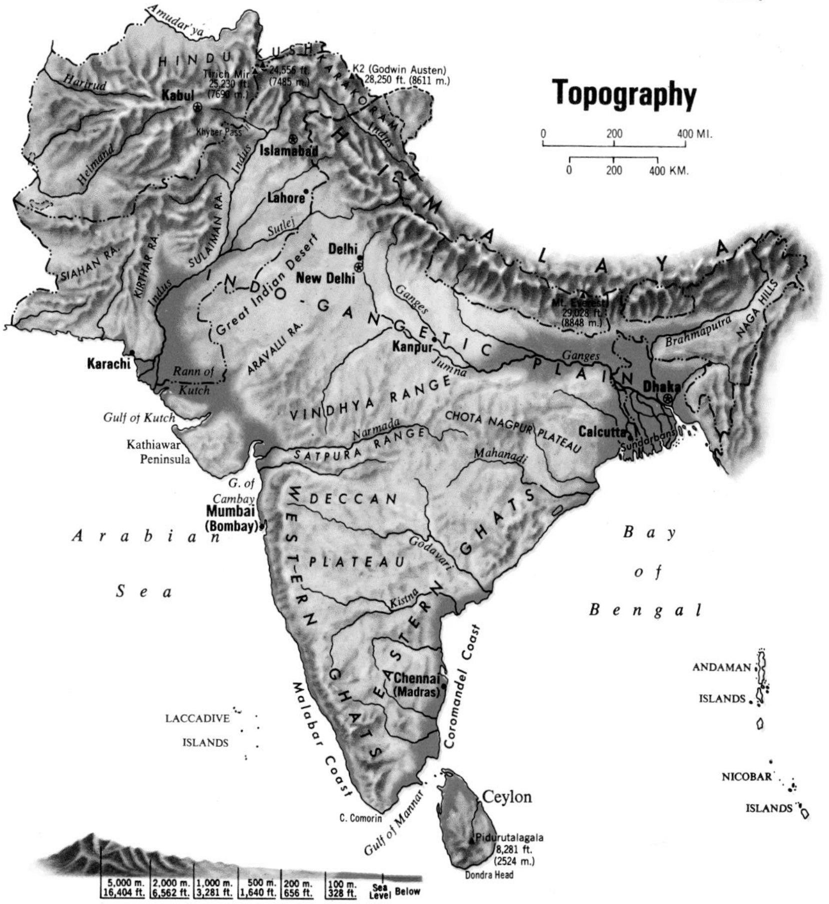
0 200 400 MI.
0 200 400 KM.
Amudar'ya
HINDU KUSH
Harirud
Kabul
Tirich Mir 25,230 ft. (7690 m.)
24,556 ft. (7485 m.)
K2 (Godwin Austen) 28,250 ft. (8611 m.)
KARAKORAM
Khyber Pass
Islamabad
Indus
Helmand
Lahore
Sutlej
SIAHAN RA.
KIRTHAR RA.
SULAIMAN RA.
Great Indian Desert
Delhi
New Delhi
HIMALAYA
INDO-GANGETIC PLAIN
Ganges
Mt. Everest 29,028 ft. (8848 m.)
Brahmaputra
NAGA HILLS
Karachi
Rann of Kutch
ARAVALLI RA.
Kanpur
Jumna
Dhaka
Gulf of Kutch
Kathiawar Peninsula
VINDHYA RANGE
Narmada
CHOTA NAGPUR PLATEAU
Calcutta
Sundarbans
SATPURA RANGE
Mahanadi
G. of Cambay
Mumbai (Bombay)
DECCAN
PLATEAU
WESTERN GHATS
EASTERN GHATS
Godavari
Kistna
Arabian Sea
Bay of Bengal
Chennai (Madras)
Coromandel Coast
Malabar Coast
LACCADIVE ISLANDS
ANDAMAN ISLANDS
NICOBAR ISLANDS
C. Comorin
Gulf of Mannar
Ceylon
Pidurutalagala 8,281 ft. (2524 m.)
Dondra Head
5,000 m. 16,404 ft.
2,000 m. 6,562 ft.
1,000 m. 3,281 ft.
500 m. 1,640 ft.
200 m. 656 ft.
100 m. 328 ft.
Sea Level
Below

(continued)

INDIA

INTERNAL DIVISIONS

Andaman and Nicobar Isls. (terr.) 188,741 G6
Andhra Pradesh (state) 53,549,673 D5
Arunachal Pradesh (state) 631,839 G3
Assam (state) 19,902,826 G3
Bihar (state) 69,914,734 F4
Chandigarh (terr.) 451,610 D2
Dādra and Nagar Haveli (terr.) 103,676 C4
Daman and Diu (state) C4
Delhi (terr.) 6,220,406 D3
Goa (state) C4
Gujarāt (state) 34,085,799 C4
Haryana (state) 12,922,618 D3
Himachal Pradesh (state) 4,280,818 D2
Jammu and Kashmir (state) 5,987,389 D2
Karnataka (state) 37,135,714 D6
Kerala (state) 25,453,680 D6
Lakshadweep (terr.) 40,249 C6
Madhya Pradesh (state) 52,178,844 D4
Mahārāshtra (state) 62,784,171 C5
Manipur (state) 1,420,953 G4
Meghalaya (state) 1,335,819 G3
Mizoram (state) 493,757 G4
Nagaland (state) 774,930 G3
Orissa (state) 26,370,271 E5
Pondicherry (terr.) 604,471 E6
Punjab (state) 16,788,915 D2
Rajasthan (state) 34,261,862 C3
Sikkim (state) 316,385 F3
Tamil Nadu (state) 48,408,077 D6
Tripura (state) 2,053,058 G4
Uttar Pradesh (state) 110,862,013 D3
West Bengal (state) 54,580,647 F4

CITIES and TOWNS

Abu 9,840 C4
Achalpur 42,326 D4
Adoni 108,905 D5
Agartala 131,513 G4
Agra 770,352 D3
Ahmadabad 2,515,195 C4
Ahmadnagar 181,239 C5
Ajmer 374,350 C3
Akola 225,402 D4
Alibag 11,913 C5
Aligarh 319,981 D3
Allahabad 642,420 E3
Alleppey-Cochin 160,166 D7
Almora 19,671 D3
Alwar 139,973 D3
Amalner 55,544 C4
Ambala 121,135 D2
Ambikapur 23,087 E4
Amravati 261,387 D4
Amreli 39,520 C4
Amritsar 589,229 C2
Anakapalle 57,273 E5
Anantapur 119,536 D6
Arrah 124,614 E3
Aruppukkottai 62,223 D7
Asansol 366,371 F4
Azamgarh 40,963 E3
Badagara 53,938 D6
Bagalkot 51,746 D5
Bahraich 102,580 E3
Baidyabati 54,130 F1
Balasore 46,239 F4
Ballia 47,101 E3
Bally 38,892 F1
Balurghat 67,088 F3
Banda 50,575 D3
Bandar (Machilipatnam) 138,525 E5
Bandra B7
Bangalore 4,100,000 D6
Bankura 79,129 F4
Bansberia 61,748 F1
Baranagar 136,842 F1
Barasat 42,642 F1
Bareilly 437,801 D3
Barmer 38,630 C3
Baroda (Vadodara) 744,043 C4
Barrackpore 96,889 F1
Barsi 62,374 D5
Barwani 22,099 D4
Basirhat 63,816 F4
Batala 100,790 D2
Beawar 66,114 C3
Belgaum 300,290 C5
Bellary 201,014 D5
Benares (Varanasi) 793,542 E3
Berhampore 100,150 F4
Berhampur 162,407 F5
Bettiah 51,018 E3
Bhadrak 40,487 F4
Bhadravati 130,459 D6
Bhadreswar 45,586 F1
Bhagalpur 221,276 F4
Bhandara 39,423 E4
Bharuch 91,589 C4
Bharatpur 105,239 D3
Bhatinda 127,450 C2
Bhatpara 204,750 F1
Bhavnagar 308,194 C4
Bhawanipatna 22,808 E5
Bhilainagar 157,173 E4
Bhilwara 122,338 C3
Bhimavaram 101,940 E5
Bhind 42,371 D3
Bhir (Bir) 49,965 D5
Bhiwandi 115,256 C5
Bhiwani 101,263 D3
Bhopal 672,329 D4
Bhubaneswar 219,419 F4
Bhuj 52,177 B4
Bhusawal 132,146 D4
Bidar 50,670 D5
Bihar 151,308 F3
Bijapur 146,808 D5
Bijnor 43,290 D3
Bikaner 280,356 C3
Bilaspur 186,885 E4
Bir 49,965 D5
Bodhan 37,589 D5
Bodinayakkanur 54,176 D6
Bolangir 35,748 E4
Broach (Bharuch) 91,589 C4
Budaun 72,204 D3
Budge-Budge 51,039 F2
Bundi 34,279 C3
Burdwan 143,318 F4
Burhanpur 141,142 D4
Calcutta 10,860,000 F2
Calicut (Kozhikode) 333,979 D6
Cambay 62,097 C4
Cannanore 157,777 C6
Cawnpore (Kanpur) 1,688,242 E3
Chaibasa 35,386 F4
Chamba 11,814 D2
Champdani 58,596 F1
Chanderi 10,294 D4
Chandernagore 75,238 F1
Chandigarh 421,256 D2
Chandrapur 115,352 D5
Chapra 111,461 F3
Chennai (Madras) 5,360,000 E6
Cherrapunji▲ 83,987 G3
Chhatarpur 32,271 D4
Chhindwara 53,492 D4
Chidambaram 48,811 E6
Chikmagalur 41,639 D6
Chinglept 38,419 E6
Chirala 54,487 E5
Chitradurga 50,254 D6
Chittoor 63,035 D6
Churachandpur 8,706 G4
Churu 52,502 D3
Cocanada (Kakinada) 226,642 E5
Cochin-Alleppey 439,066 D6
Coimbatore 917,155 D6
Colachel 18,819 D7
Cooch Behar 53,684 F3
Cuddalore 127,569 E6
Cuddapah 103,146 D6
Cuttack 326,468 F4
Dabhoi 37,892 C4
Damoh 59,489 D4
Darbhanga 175,879 F3
Darjeeling 42,873 F3
Datia 36,439 D3
Davangere 196,481 D6
Dehra Dun 293,628 D2
Delhi 8,380,000 D3
Deoghar 40,356 F4
Deolali 55,436 C5
Deoria 38,161 E3
Dewas 51,545 D4
Dhanbad 676,736 F4
Dhar 36,172 C4
Dharmsala 10,939 D2
Dharwar-Hubli 379,166 C5
Dhoraji 59,773 C4
Dhubri 36,503 G3
Dhulia 210,927 C4
Dibrugarh 80,348 G3
Dindigul 170,196 D6
Diphu 10,200 G3
Diu 6,214 C4
Dungarpur 19,773 C4
Durg 67,892 E4
Durg-Bhilainagar 490,158 E4
Durgapur 305,838 F4
Dwarka 17,801 B4
Eluru 168,148 E5
English Bazar 61,335 F3
Erode 275,103 D6
Etawah 112,426 D3
Faizabad-cum-Ayodhya 102,835 E3
Faridabad 326,968 D3
Farrukhabad-cum-Fatehgarh 160,927 D3
Firozabad 202,837 D3
Firozpur 49,545 C2
Gadag 116,596 D5
Ganganagar 121,516 C3
Gangtok 12,000 F3
Garden Reach 154,913 F2
Garulia 44,271 F1
Gauhati 123,783 G3
Gaya 246,778 F4
Ghaziabad 291,995 D3
Ghazipur 45,635 E3
Godhra 66,403 C4
Gonda 52,662 E3
Gondal 54,928 C4
Gondia 100,342 E4
Gorakhpur 306,399 E3
Gulbarga 218,621 D5
Guna 40,006 D4
Guntakal 66,320 D5
Guntur 367,219 D5
Gwalior 38,472 D3
Haflong 5,197 G3
Hanumangarh 30,017 C3
Hardoi 46,639 E3
Hardwar 146,186 D2
Hassan 51,325 D6
Hathras 74,349 D3
Hazaribagh 54,818 F4
Hindupur 42,959 D6
Hinganghat 44,349 D4
Hissar 137,254 D3
Honavar 12,444 C6
Hooghly-Chinsura 105,241 F1
Hospet 114,711 D5
Howrah 737,877 F2
Hubli-Dharwar 526,493 C5
Hyderabad 4,270,000 D5
Ichchapuram 15,850 F5
Imphal 155,639 G4
Indore 827,021 D4
Itanagar▲ 18,787 G3
Itarsi 44,191 D4
Jabalpur 757,726 D4
Jaipur 1,004,669 D3
Jaisalmer 16,578 C3
Jajpur 16,707 F4
Jalgaon 145,254 D4
Jalna 122,246 D4
Jalor 15,478 C3
Jalpaiguri 55,159 F3
Jamalpur 61,731 F3
Jammu 155,338 D2
Jamnagar 317,037 B4
Jamshedpur 669,984 F4
Jaora 37,235 D4
Jaunpur 104,994 E3
Jhansi 231,332 D3
Jind 38,161 D3
Jodhpur 493,604 C3
Jubbulpore (Jabalpur) 757,726 D4
Jullundur 296,106 D2
Junagadh 120,072 B4
Kadayanallur 50,295 D7
Kakinada 226,642 E5
Kalyan 99,547 C5
Kamarhati 169,404 F1
Kamptee 53,412 D4
Kanchipuram 145,329 E6
Kanchrapara 78,768 F1
Kandla 17,995 C4
Kanker 9,278 E4
Kanpur 1,688,242 E3
Karad 42,329 C5
Karaikudi 100,187 D7
Kargil 2,390 D2
Karnal 132,067 D3
Kasganj 46,467 D3
Katarnian Ghat E3
Katihar 121,693 F3
Katni (Murwara) 125,096 E4
Kavaratti 4,420 C6
Kendrapara 20,079 F4
Khamgaon 53,692 D4
Khamman 56,919 D5
Khandwa 114,463 D4
Kharagpur 234,931 F4
Kirkee 65,497 C5
Kishangarh 37,405 D3
Kishtwar 5,276 D2
Kohima 21,545 G3
Kolar 43,418 D6
Kolar Gold Fields 144,406 D6
Kolhapur 351,073 C5
Koraput 21,505 E5
Korba 30,963 E4
Kota 346,928 D3
Kottaguden 75,542 E5
Kottayam 59,714 D7
Kozhikode 333,979 D6
Krishnanagar 85,923 F4
Kumbakonam 141,639 D6
Kumta 19,112 C6
Kurnool 206,661 D5
Latur 111,961 D5
Leh 5,519 D2
Lucknow 1,006,538 E3
Ludhiana 606,250 D2
Machilipatnam 138,525 E5
Madugula 8,376 E5
Madurai 904,362 D7
Mahabaleshwar 7,318 C5
Mahbubnagar 51,756 D5
Mahe 8,972 D6
Mahuva 39,497 C4
Malegaon 245,769 C4
Maler Kotla 48,536 D2
Malkapur 35,476 D4
Malvan 17,579 C5
Mandi 16,849 D2
Mandla 24,406 E4
Mandsaur 52,347 C4
Mangalore 3,055,113 C6
Mannargudi 42,783 E6
Margao 41,655 C5
Marmagao 44,065 C5
Mathura 160,995 D3
Mau 64,058 E3
Mayuram 60,195 D6
Meerut 538,461 D3
Mehsana 51,598 C4
Mercara 19,357 D6
Mhow 59,037 D4
Midnapore 71,326 F4
Miraj 77,606 D5
Mirzapur-cum-Vindhyachal 128,179 E4
Monghyr 102,474 F3
Moradabad 347,983 D3
Morena 44,901 D3
Morvi 60,976 C4
Mumbai (Bombay) (Greater)* 8,227,332 B7
Murwara 125,096 E4
Muzaffarnagar 172,435 D3
Muzaffarpur 189,765 E3
Mysore 476,446 D6
Nadiad 142,279 C4
Nagapattinam 68,026 E6
Nagaur 36,448 C3
Nagercoil 171,641 D7
Nagina 37,066 D3
Nagpur 1,297,977 D4
Nahan 16,017 D2
Naihati 82,080 F1
Naini Tal 23,986 D3
Nander 190,819 D5
Nandurbar 54,070 C4
Nandyal 63,193 D5
Nasik 428,778 C5
Navsari 129,122 C4
Nellore 236,225 E6
New Delhi (cap.) 301,801 D3
Nimach 47,113 D4
Nipani 35,116 C5
Nizamabad 183,135 D5
Nova Goa (Panaji) 34,953 C5
Nowgong 56,537 G3
Okha Port 10,687 B4
Ongole 53,330 E5
Ootacamund 63,310 D6
Orai 42,513 D3
Pachmarhi 1,212 D4
Palanpur 42,114 C4
Palayankottai 70,070 D7
Palghat 117,961 D6
Pali 49,834 C3
Palni 49,575 D6
Panaji 34,953 C5
Panchur 59,021 F2
Pandharpur 53,638 D5
Panihati 148,046 F1
Panipat 137,953 D3
Panna 22,316 E4
Parbhani 109,328 D5
Pasighat 5,116 G3
Patan 105,191 C4
Pathankot 108,777 D2
Patiala 205,849 D2
Patna 916,102 F3
Pilibhit 68,273 D3
Pondicherry 251,471 E6
Ponnani 35,723 D6
Porbandar 133,545 B4
Port Blair 26,218 G6
Porto Novo 17,412 E6
Proddatur 107,068 D6
Puduchcheri (Pondicherry) 251,471 E6
Pudukkottai 66,384 D6
Pune 1,135,034 C5
Puri 101,089 F5
Purli 31,078 D5
Purnea 109,649 F3
Purulia 57,708 F4
Quilon 167,583 D7
Raichur 124,600 D5
Raigarh 46,745 E4
Raipur 338,973 E4
Rajahmundry 267,749 E5
Rajapalaiyam 101,633 D7
Rajapur 9,017 C5
Rajkot 444,156 C4
Rajnandgaon 41,183 E4
Rajpur 34,393 F2
Rameswaram 16,755 D7
Ranchi 500,593 F4
Ratlam 156,490 C4
Ratnagiri 37,551 C5
Raurkela 321,326 F4
Raxaul 12,064 E3
Rewa 100,519 E4
Rishra 63,486 F1
Rohtak 166,631 C5
Sadiya▲ 64,252 H3
Sagar 207,401 D4
Saharanpur 294,391 D3
Salem 515,021 D6
Sambalpur 162,190 E4
Sambhal 108,379 D3
Sangli 268,962 C5
Santipur 61,166 F4
Sardarshahr 37,703 C3
Sasaram 48,282 E4
Satara 66,433 C5
Satna 57,531 E4
Sehore 35,657 D4
Seoni 38,396 D4
Serampore 102,023 F1
Seringapatam 14,100 D6
Shahjahanpur 205,325 E3
Shillong 173,064 G3
Shimoga 151,562 D6
Shivpuri 42,120 D3
Sholapur 514,461 D5
Sidhi 8,341 E4
Sidhpur 40,521 C4
Sikar 102,946 C3
Silchar 52,596 G4
Siliguri 153,825 F3
Simla 55,368 D2
Sirohi 18,774 C4
Sirsa 48,808 D3
Sitapur 66,715 E3
South Dum Dum 174,538 F2
South Suburban 272,600 F2
Srikakulam 45,179 E5
Srinagar 403,413 D2
Sundargarh 17,244 E4
Surat 912,568 C4
Surendranagar 66,667 C4
Tanda 41,611 E3
Tellicherry 68,759 C6
Tenali 119,216 E5
Tezpur 39,870 G3
Thana 388,577 B6
Thanjavur 183,464 D6
Tinsukia 54,911 H3
Tiruchchirappalli 607,815 D6
Tiruchendur 18,126 D7
Tirunelveli 324,034 D7
Tirupati 115,244 D6
Tiruppattur 40,357 D6
Tiruppur 215,743 D6
Tiruvannamalai 61,370 D6
Titagarh 88,218 F1
Tonk 55,866 D3
Tranquebar 17,318 E6
Trichur 170,093 D6
Trivandrum 519,766 D7
Tumkur 109,231 D6
Tura 15,489 G3
Tuticorin 250,673 D7
Udaipur 229,762 C4
Udhampur 16,392 D2
Ujjain 231,878 D4
Ulhasnagar 648,149 C5
Unnao 38,195 E3
Uttarpara-Kotrung 67,568 F1
Vadodara 744,043 C4
Valsad 43,254 C4
Vaniyambadi 51,810 D6
Varanasi 793,542 E3
Vellore 246,937 D6
Vengurla 11,805 C5
Veraval 58,771 C4

British India

RUSSIA
AFGHANISTAN
GILGIT AGENCY
KASHMIR & JAMMU
N.W. FRONTIER PROV.
PUNJAB
PUNJAB STATES
BALUCHISTAN
Indus
BAHAWALPUR (PUNJ. ST.)
TIBET
CHINA
IRAN
DELHI
RAMPUR
UNITED PROVINCES
NEPAL
SIKKIM
BHUTAN
Brahmaputra
PUNJ. ST.
RAJPUTANA
AJMER-MERWARA
SIND
Gwadar (Oman)
GWALIOR
Ganges
E. ST.
KHASI HILLS
ASSAM
BENARES
BIHAR
MANIPUR
CENTRAL INDIA
TRIPURA (E. ST.)
WESTERN INDIA
BENGAL
EASTERN STATES
Chandernagore (Fr.)
BURMA
Arabian Sea
GUJARAT ST.
CENTRAL PROVINCES
E. ST.
BERAR
ORISSA
Diu (Port.)
Damão (Port.)
BOMBAY
EASTERN STATES
Bay of Bengal
HYDERABAD
DECCAN STATES
Yanaon (Fr.)
Gôa (Port.)
MYSORE
Bangalore (Br.)
MADRAS
COORG
Mahé (Fr.)
Pondichéry (Fr.)
Karikal (Fr.)
M. ST.
Laccadive Islands (Madras)
Cochin (Br.)
MADRAS STATES
CEYLON
Andaman Islands (Br.)
Nicobar Islands (Br.)
British India. The provinces of British India were directly administered by Britain. A few areas were leased from the Indian princes.
Indian States. The Indian States, sometimes referred to as the "Native" or "Princely States," were under the nominal control of maharajas or other hereditary princes.
Possessions of Other Countries in India
State or Provincial Boundaries
Other Internal Boundaries

- Vidisha 43,212 D4
- Vijayawada 544,958 D5
- Villupuram 60,242 D6
- Viramgam 43,790 C4
- Visakhapatnam 594,259 E5
- Visnagar 34,863 C4
- Vizagapatam (Visakhapatnam) 594,259 E5
- Vizianagaram 115,209 E5
- Warangal 336,018 D5
- Wardha 69,037 D4
- Yadgir 32,756 D5
- Yanam 8,291 E5
- Yeola 24,533 C4

OTHER FEATURES

- Abor (hills) G3
- Adam's Bridge (sound) D7
- Agatti (isl.) C6
- Amindiri (isl.) C6
- Amindivi (isls.) C6
- Amini (Amindiri) (isl.) C6
- Anai Mudi (mt.) D6
- Andaman (isls.) G6
- Andaman (sea) G6
- Androth (isl.) C6
- Anjidiv (Angedeva) (isl.) C6
- Arabian (sea) B5
- Back (bay) B7
- Banas (riv.) D3
- Baratang (isl.) G6
- Barren (isl.) G6
- Batti Malv (isl.) G7
- Bengal, Bay of (bay) F5
- Berar (reg.) D4
- Betwa (riv.) D4
- Bhima (riv.) D5
- Bidyadhari (riv.) F2
- Bombay (harbor) B7
- Brahmaputra (riv.) G3
- Butcher (isl.) B7
- Cambay (gulf) C4
- Camorta (isl.) G7
- Cannanore (isls.) C6
- Chambal (riv.) D3
- Chenab (riv.) C2
- Cherial (riv.) F2
- Chetlat (isl.) C6
- Chilka (lake) F5
- Coco (chan.) G6
- Colaba (pt.) B7
- Colair (lake) E5
- Comorin (cape) D7
- Coromandel Coast (reg.) E6
- Daman (dist.) C4
- Damodar (riv.) F4
- Deccan (plat.) D6
- Diu (dist.) C4
- Duncan (passage) G6
- Eastern Ghats (mts.) D6
- Eight Degree (chan.) C7
- Elephanta (isl.) B7
- False Divi (pt.) E5
- Ganga (Ganges) (riv.) F3
- Ganges, Mouths of the (delta) F4
- Ganges (riv.) F3
- Ghaghra (riv.) E3
- Ghea (riv.) F1
- Goa (dist.) C5
- Godavari (riv.) D5
- Golconda (ruins) D5
- Great (chan.) G7
- Great Indian (des.) C3
- Great Nicobar (isl.) G7
- Hagari (riv.) D6
- Himalaya (mts.) D2
- Hindu Kush (mts.) C1
- Hooghly (riv.) F2
- Indira (Pygmalion) (pt.) G7
- Indravati (riv.) E5
- Indus (riv.) B3
- Interview (isl.) G6
- Jhelum (riv.) C2
- Jumna (riv.) E3
- Kachchh (gulf) B4
- Kachchh (reg.) B4
- Kachchh, Rann of (salt marsh) B4
- Kadmat (isl.) C6
- Kalpeni (isl.) C7
- Kamet (mt.) D2
- Kanchenjunga (mt.) F3
- Karakoram (mts.) D1
- Katchall (isl.) G7
- Kathiawar (pen.) B4
- Kaveri (riv.) D6
- Khasi (hills) G3
- Kiltan (isl.) C6
- Kistna (Krishna) (riv.) D5
- Kunlun (range) D1
- Kutch (Kachchh) (reg.) B4
- Kutch (Kachchh), Rann of (salt marsh) B4
- Laccadive (Cannanore) (isls.) C6
- Ladakh (reg.) D2
- Lakshadweep (sea) C6
- Landfall (isl.) G6
- Little Andaman (isl.) G6
- Little Nicobar (isl.) G7
- Luni (riv.) C3
- Mahanadi (riv.) E4
- Mahim (bay) B7
- Malabar (hill) B7
- Malabar (pt.) B7
- Malabar Coast (reg.) C6
- Malad (creek) B7
- Mannar (gulf) D7
- Manori (creek) B7
- Middle Andaman (isl.) G6
- Minicoy (isl.) C7
- Miri (hills) G3
- Mishmi (hills) H3
- Mizo (hill) G4
- Nancowry (isl.) G7
- Nanda Devi (mt.) D2
- Narcondam (isl.) G6
- Narmada (riv.) D4
- Nicobar (isls.) G7
- Nine Degree (chan.) C7
- North Andaman (isl.) G6
- North Sentinel (isl.) G6
- Palk (str.) D7
- Palmyras (pt.) F4
- Pangong Tso (lake) D2
- Penganga (riv.) D5
- Penner (riv.) D6
- Periyar (lake) D7
- Pitti (isl.) C6
- Pulicat (lake) E6
- Pygmalion (pt.) G7
- Ritchies (arch.) G6
- Rutland (isl.) G6
- Salsette (isl.) B7
- Sambhar (lake) C3
- Saraswati (riv.) F1
- Sarsati (riv.) F1
- Satpura (range) D4
- Shipki (pass) D2
- Soda (plains) D1
- Sombrero (chan.) G7
- Son (riv.) E3
- South Andaman (isl.) G6
- Suheli Par (atoll) C6
- Sundarbans (reg.) F4
- Sutlej (riv.) C3
- Tapti (riv.) D4
- Tel (riv.) E4
- Ten Degree (chan.) G7
- Teressa (isl.) G7
- Thana (creek) B7
- Tillanchong (isl.) G7
- Tolly's Nullah (riv.) F2
- Towers of Silence B7
- Travancore (reg.) D7
- Tulsi (lake) B6
- Tungabhadra (riv.) D5
- Vehar (lake) B7
- Vindhya (range) D4
- Wardha (riv.) D4
- Western Ghats (mts.) C5
- Zaskar (mts.) D2

MALDIVES

- Maldives 143,046 C7

NEPAL

CITIES and TOWNS

- Baitadi 128,696 E3
- Bhaktapur 40,112 F3
- Bhaktapur▲ 110,157 F3
- Bhojpur 194,506 F3
- Biratnagar 45,100 F3
- Dailekh 156,072 E3
- Dhankuta 107,649 F3
- Doti 166,070 E3
- Janakpur 14,294 F3
- Jumla▲ 122,753 E3
- Kathmandu (cap.) 150,402 E3
- Kathmandu▲ 353,752 E3
- Lalitpur 59,049 E3
- Lalitpur▲ 154,998 E3
- Mustang▲ 26,944 E3
- Nepalganj 23,523 E3
- Palpa 212,633 E3
- Pokhara 20,611 E3
- Pyuthan▲ 137,338 E3
- Ramechhap 157,349 F3
- Sallyan▲ 141,457 E3

OTHER FEATURES

- Annapurna (mt.) E3
- Bheri (riv.) E3
- Dhaulagiri (mt.) E3
- Everest (mt.) F3
- Himalaya (mts.) D2
- Kanchenjunga (mt.) F3

PAKISTAN

PROVINCES

- Azad Kashmir C2
- Balochistan 4,332,376 B3
- Federal Administrated Tribal Areas 2,198,547 C2
- Islamabad District 340,286 C2
- Northern Areas D1
- North-West Frontier 11,061,328 C2
- Punjab 47,292,441 C2
- Sindh 19,028,666 B3

CITIES and TOWNS

- Abbottabad 66,000 C2
- Ahmadpur East 57,000 C3
- Attock 40,000 C2
- Badin 23,000 B4
- Bahawalnagar 74,000 C2
- Bahawalpur 178,000 C3
- Baltit C1
- Bannu 43,000 C2
- Bela 11,000 B3
- Bhera 29,000 C2
- Bunji C1
- Campbellpore 19,041 C2
- Chagai▲ 41,263 A3
- Chaman 30,000 B2
- Chiniot 106,000 C2
- Chitral C1
- Dadu 39,000 B3
- Dera Ghazi Khan 103,000 C3
- Dera Ismail Khan 68,000 C2
- Diplo 7,000 B4
- Faisalabad 1,092,000 C2
- Fort Sandeman 8,058 B2
- Gujranwala 654,000 C2
- Gujrat 154,000 C2
- Gwadar 17,000 A4
- Hunza (Baltit) C1
- Hyderabad 795,000 B3
- Islamabad (cap.) 201,000 C2
- Jacobabad 80,000 B3
- Jhang Sadar 195,000 C2
- Jhelum 106,000 C2
- Kalat 11,000 B3
- Karachi 4,979,000 B4
- Kasur 155,000 C2
- Khairpur 62,000 B3
- Khanewal 89,000 C2
- Khanpur 71,000 C3
- Kharan Kalat 10,000 A3
- Khushab 56,000 C2
- Kohat 78,000 C2
- Kotri 38,000 B3
- Lahore 3,922,000 C2
- Larkana 123,000 B3
- Leiah 52,000 C2
- Loralai 14,000 B2
- Lyallpur (Faisalabad) 1,092,000 C2
- Mach 8,000 B3
- Malakand C2
- Mardan 148,000 C2
- Mastung 17,000 B3
- Mianwali 59,000 C2
- Mirpur Khas 124,000 B3
- Multan 730,000 C2
- Muzaffarabad C2
- Nagar D1
- Nawabshah 102,000 B3
- Nok Kundi 861 A3
- Nowshera 75,000 C2
- Nushki 11,000 B3
- Pasni 18,000 A3
- Peshawar 555,000 C2
- Pindi Gheb 20,000 C2
- Quetta 285,000 B2
- Rahimyar Khan 119,000 C3
- Rawalpindi 806,000 C2
- Risalpur Cantonment 20,000 C2
- Rohri 32,000 B3
- Sahiwal 152,000 C2
- Saidu 15,920 C2
- Sargodha 294,000 C2
- Shikarpur 88,000 B3
- Sialkot 296,000 C2
- Sibi 23,000 B3
- Skardu D1
- Sonmiani B3
- Sukkur 193,000 B3
- Tando Adam 63,000 B3
- Tando Allahyar 31,000 B3
- Tatta 12,786 B4
- Turbat 52,000 A3
- Uch 5,483 B3
- Wah 122,000 C2
- Wana C2
- Yasin C1

OTHER FEATURES

- Aksai Chin (reg.) D2
- Arabian (sea) B5
- Baltistan (reg.) D1
- Baroghil (pass) C1
- Bejhi (riv.) B3
- Bolan (pass) B3
- Chagai (hills) A3
- Chenab (riv.) C2
- Dasht (riv.) A3
- Gilgit (dist.) C1
- Hab (riv.) B3
- Hamun-i-Lora (swamp) B3
- Hamun-i-Mashkel (swamp) A3
- Hindu Kush (mts.) B1
- Indus (riv.) B3
- Indus, Mouths of the (delta) B4
- Jaddi, Ras (pt.) A4
- Jhelum (riv.) C2
- K2 (mt.) D1
- Kabul (riv.) C2
- Kachchh, Rann of (salt marsh) B4
- Karakoram (mts.) D1
- Khyber (pass) C2
- Konar (riv.) C1
- Kutch (Kachchh), Rann of (salt marsh) B4
- Mashkid (riv.) A3
- Mohenjo Daro (ruins) B3
- Muari, Ras (cape) B4
- Nal (riv.) B3
- Nanga Parbat (mt.) D1
- Rakaposhi (mt.) C1
- Ravi (riv.) C2
- Siahan (range) A3
- Sulaiman (range) C3
- Sutlej (riv.) C3
- Talab (riv.) A3
- Taxila (ruins) C2
- Thar (des.) C3
- Tirich Mir (mt.) C1
- Zhob (riv.) B2

SRI LANKA (CEYLON)

CITIES and TOWNS

- Anuradhapura 34,836 E7
- Badulla 34,658 E7
- Batticaloa 36,761 E7
- Colombo (cap.) 618,000 D7
- Colombo* 852,098 D7
- Dehiwala-Mt. Lavinia 54,785 D7
- Galle 72,720 D7
- Hambantota 6,908 E7
- Jaffna 112,000 E7
- Kalmunai 19,176 E7
- Kalutara 28,748 D7
- Kandy 93,602 E7
- Kurunegala 25,189 E7
- Mannar 11,157 E7
- Matara 36,641 E7
- Moratuwa 96,489 D7
- Mullaittivu 4,930 E7
- Negombo 57,115 D7
- Nuwara Eliya 16,347 E7
- Polonnaruwa 9,551 E7
- Puttalam 17,982 D7
- Ratnapura 29,116 D7
- Sigiriya 1,446 E7
- Tangalla 8,748 E7
- Trincomalee 41,780 E7
- Vavuniya 15,639 E7

OTHER FEATURES

- Adam's (peak) E7
- Adam's Bridge (shoals) D7
- Dondra (head) E7
- Kirigalpota (mt.) E7
- Mannar (gulf) D7
- Palk (str.) D7
- Pedro (pt.) E6
- Pidurutalagala (mt.) E7

* City and suburbs.
▲ Population of district.

Agriculture, Industry and Resources

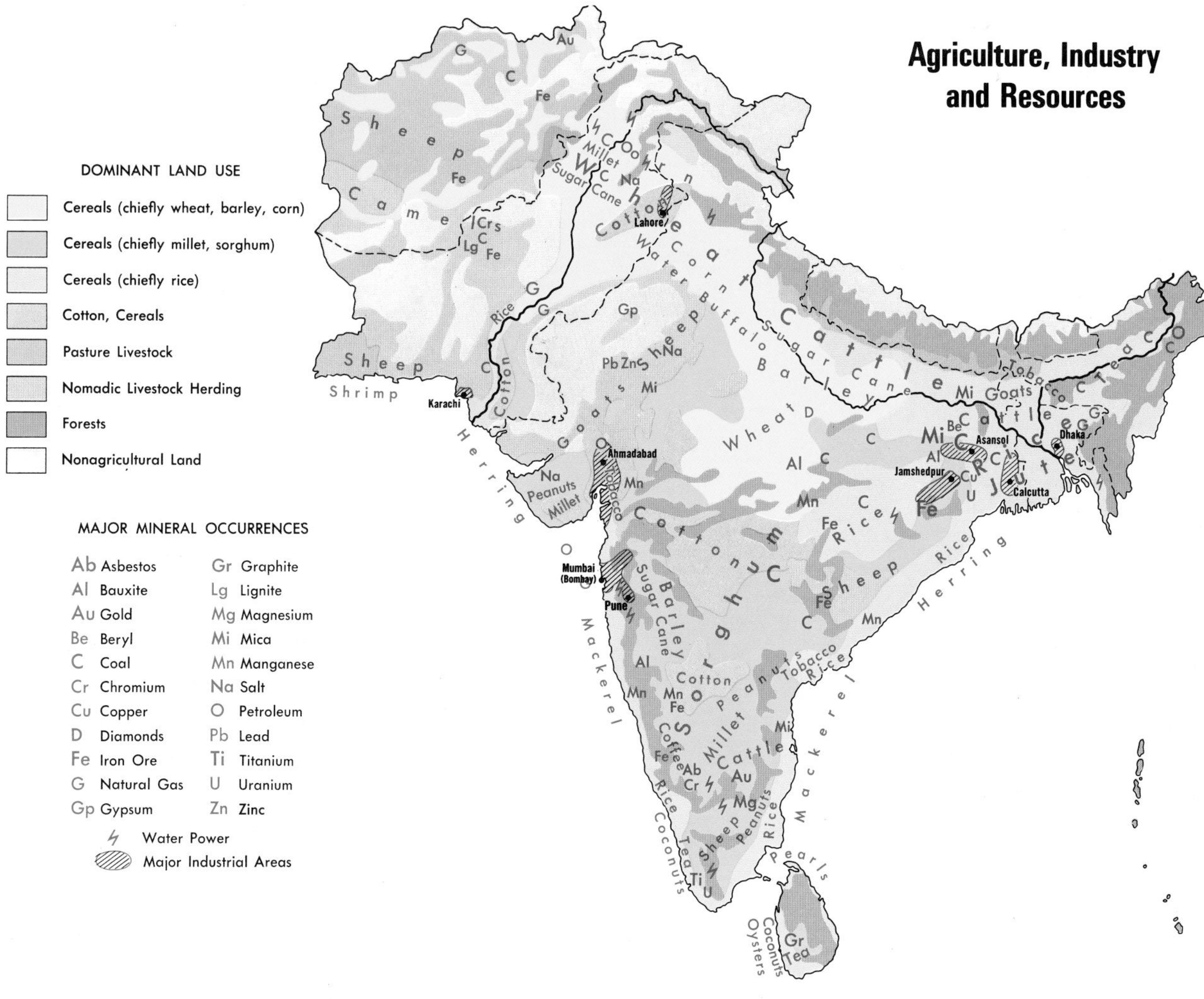
DOMINANT LAND USE
Cereals (chiefly wheat, barley, corn)
Cereals (chiefly millet, sorghum)
Cereals (chiefly rice)
Cotton, Cereals
Pasture Livestock
Nomadic Livestock Herding
Forests
Nonagricultural Land
MAJOR MINERAL OCCURRENCES
Ab Asbestos
Al Bauxite
Au Gold
Be Beryl
C Coal
Cr Chromium
Cu Copper
D Diamonds
Fe Iron Ore
G Natural Gas
Gp Gypsum
Gr Graphite
Lg Lignite
Mg Magnesium
Mi Mica
Mn Manganese
Na Salt
O Petroleum
Pb Lead
Ti Titanium
U Uranium
Zn Zinc
Water Power
Major Industrial Areas
Lahore
Karachi
Ahmadabad
Mumbai (Bombay)
Pune
Asansol
Jamshedpur
Calcutta
Dhaka
Sheep
Camel
Shrimp
Herring
Mackerel
Pearls
Oysters
Coconuts
Wheat
Cotton
Rice
Millet
Peanuts
Sugar Cane
Barley
Cattle
Goats
Tobacco
Tea
Coffee
Jute
Water Buffalo
Corn

Burma, Thailand, Indochina and Malaya
CONIC PROJECTION
SCALE OF MILES
0 50 100 150 200
SCALE OF KILOMETERS
0 50 100 200 300
International Boundaries
Division and State Boundaries
Capitals of Countries
Division and State Capitals
© Copyright HAMMOND INCORPORATED, Maplewood, N.J.
Longitude East 96° of Greenwich
MYANMAR
(BURMA)
THAILAND
CAMBODIA
LAOS
VIETNAM
CHINA
INDIA
BHUTAN
BANGLADESH
MALAYSIA
INDONESIA
SUMATRA
BAY OF BENGAL
ANDAMAN SEA
GULF OF THAILAND
GULF OF TONKIN
SOUTH CHINA SEA
HAINAN
Tropic of Cancer
JOHOR
SINGAPORE
BANGKOK
Rangoon
Hanoi
Phnom Penh
HO CHI MINH CITY
Kuala Lumpur

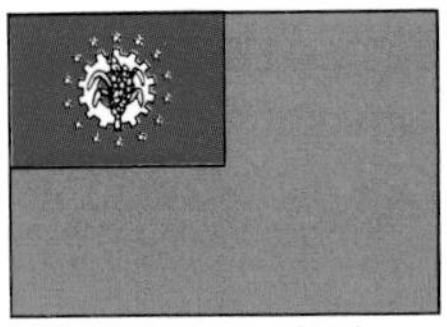

MYANMAR (BURMA)

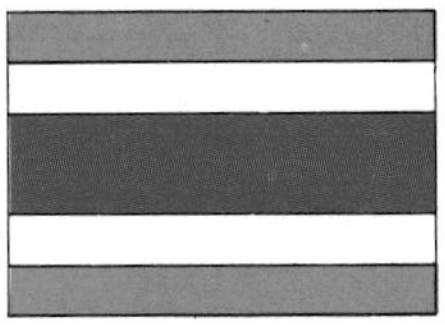

THAILAND

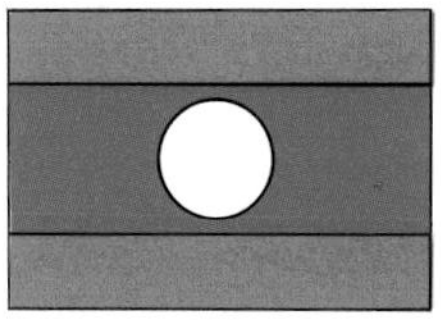

LAOS

CAMBODIA

VIETNAM

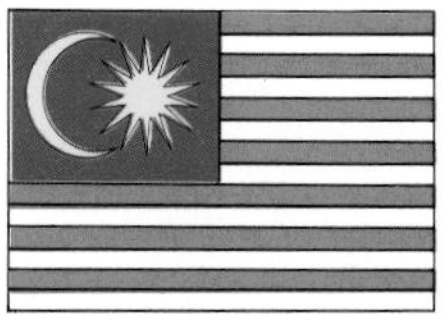

MALAYSIA

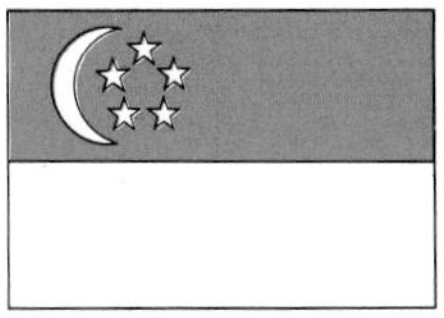

SINGAPORE

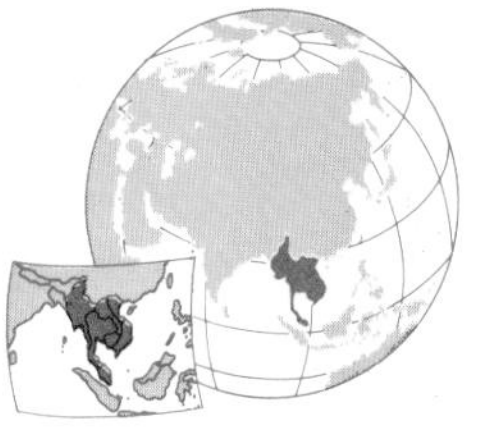

CAMBODIA

AREA 69,898 sq. mi. (181,036 sq. km.)
POPULATION 11,918,865
CAPITAL Phnom Penh
LARGEST CITY Phnom Penh
HIGHEST POINT 5,948 ft. (1,813 m.)
MONETARY UNIT new riel
MAJOR LANGUAGE Khmer (Cambodian)
MAJOR RELIGIONS Buddhism

LAOS

AREA 91,428 sq. mi. (236,800 sq. km.)
POPULATION 5,556,821
CAPITAL Vientiane
LARGEST CITY Vientiane
HIGHEST POINT Phou Bia 9,252 ft. (2,820 m.)
MONETARY UNIT new kip
MAJOR LANGUAGE Lao
MAJOR RELIGIONS Buddhism, tribal religions

MALAYSIA

AREA 128,308 sq. mi. (332,318 sq. km.)
POPULATION 21,820,143
CAPITAL Kuala Lumpur
LARGEST CITY Kuala Lumpur
HIGHEST POINT Mt. Kinabalu 13,455 ft. (4,101 m.)
MONETARY UNIT ringgit
MAJOR LANGUAGES Malay, Chinese, English, Tamil, Dayak, Kadazan
MAJOR RELIGIONS Islam, Confucianism, Buddhism, tribal religions, Hinduism, Taoism, Christianity, Sikhism

MYANMAR (BURMA)

AREA 261,789 sq. mi. (678,034 sq. km.)
POPULATION 48,852,098
CAPITAL Yangon (Rangoon)
LARGEST CITY Yangon (Rangoon)
HIGHEST POINT Hkakabo Razi 19,296 ft. (5,881 m.)
MONETARY UNIT kyat
MAJOR LANGUAGES Burmese, Karen, Shan, Kachin, Chin, Kayah, English
MAJOR RELIGIONS Buddhism, tribal religions

SINGAPORE

AREA 226 sq. mi. (585 sq. km.)
POPULATION 3,571,710
CAPITAL Singapore
LARGEST CITY Singapore
HIGHEST POINT Bukit Timah 581 ft. (177 m.)
MONETARY UNIT Singapore dollar
MAJOR LANGUAGES Chinese, Malay, Tamil, English, Hindi
MAJOR RELIGIONS Confucianism, Buddhism, Taoism, Hinduism, Islam, Christianity

THAILAND

AREA 198,455 sq. mi. (513,998 sq. km.)
POPULATION 61,163,833
CAPITAL Bangkok
LARGEST CITY Bangkok
HIGHEST POINT Doi Inthanon 8,452 ft. (2,576 m.)
MONETARY UNIT baht
MAJOR LANGUAGES Thai, Lao, Chinese, Khmer, Malay
MAJOR RELIGIONS Buddhism, tribal religions

VIETNAM

AREA 128,405 sq. mi. (332,569 sq. km.)
POPULATION 78,349,503
CAPITAL Hanoi
LARGEST CITY Ho Chi Minh City
HIGHEST POINT Fan Si Pan 10,308 ft. (3,142 m.)
MONETARY UNIT new dong
MAJOR LANGUAGES Vietnamese, Thai, Muong, Meo, Yao, Khmer, French, Chinese, Cham
MAJOR RELIGIONS Buddhism, Taoism, Confucianism, Roman Catholicism, Cao-Dai

Topography

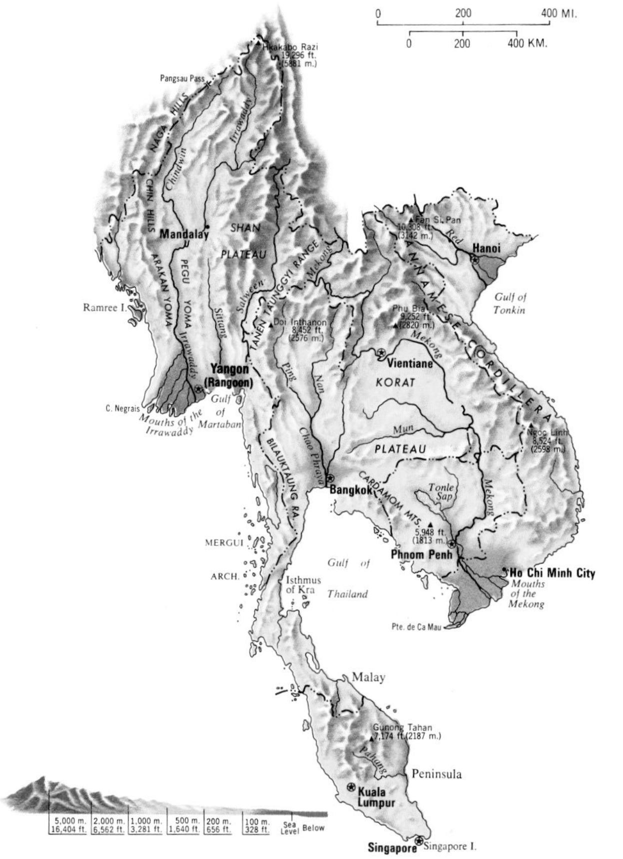
0 200 400 MI.
0 200 400 KM.
Hkakabo Razi 19,296 ft. (5,881 m.)
Pangsau Pass
Mandalay
SHAN PLATEAU
Fan Si Pan 10,308 ft. (3,142 m.)
Hanoi
Gulf of Tonkin
Ramree I.
Phou Bia 9,252 ft. (2,820 m.)
Doi Inthanon 8,452 ft. (2576 m.)
Vientiane
KORAT
PLATEAU
Yangon (Rangoon)
C. Negrais
Mouths of the Irrawaddy
Gulf of Martaban
Ngoc Linh 8,524 ft. (2598 m.)
Bangkok
Tonle Sap
5,948 ft. (1813 m.)
Phnom Penh
Ho Chi Minh City
Mouths of the Mekong
MERGUI
ARCH.
Isthmus of Kra
Gulf of Thailand
Pte. de Ca Mau
Malay
Gunong Tahan 7,174 ft. (2187 m.)
Peninsula
Kuala Lumpur
Singapore
Singapore I.
5,000 m. 16,404 ft.
2,000 m. 6,562 ft.
1,000 m. 3,281 ft.
500 m. 1,640 ft.
200 m. 656 ft.
100 m. 328 ft.
Sea Level
Below

MYANMAR (BURMA)

INTERNAL DIVISIONS

Chin (state) 368,985 B2
Irrawaddy (div.) 4,991,057 B3
Kachin (state) 903,982 C1
Karan (state) 1,057,505 C3
Kayah (state) 168,355 C3
Magwe (div.) 3,241,103 B2
Mandalay (div.) 4,580,923 B2
Mon (state) 1,682,041 C4
Pegu (div.) 3,800,240 C3
Rakhine (state) 1,710,913 B3
Rangoon (div.) 3,973,782 C3
Sagaing (div.) 3,855,991 B1
Shan (state) 3,718,706 C2
Tenasserim (div.) 917,628 C4

CITIES and TOWNS

Akyab (Sittwe) 107,607 B2
Allanmyo 15,580 B3
Amarapura 11,268 B2
Amherst 6,000 C3
Bassein 144,092 B3
Bhamo 9,821 C1
Chauk 24,466 B2
Gyobingauk 9,922 C3
Henzada 82,531 B3
Hmawbi 23,032 C3
Insein 143,625 C3
Kanbalu 3,281 B2
Katha 7,648 C1
Kawthaung 1,520 C5
Kyaikto 13,154 C3
Kyangin 6,073 B3
Kyaukpadaung 5,480 B2
Kyaukpyu 7,335 B3
Kyaukse 8,659 C2
Labutta 12,982 B3
Lashio 69,567 C2
Letpadan 15,896 C3
Madauk 4,618 C3
Magwe 13,270 B2
Mandalay 532,895 C2
Martaban 5,661 C3
Ma-ubin 23,362 B3
Maungdaw 3,772 B2
Mawlaik 2,993 B2
Maymyo 58,059 C2
Meiktila 73,210 B2
Mergui 67,351 C4
Minbu 9,096 B2
Minhla 6,470 B3
Mogaung 2,920 C1
Mogok 8,334 C2
Monywa 106,873 B2
Moulmein 219,991 C3
Mudon 20,136 C3
Myanaung 11,155 B3
Myaungmya 24,532 B3
Myingyan 70,162 B2
Myitkyina 12,382 C1
Myohaung 6,534 B2
Okkan 14,443 B3
Pakokku 58,132 B2
Palaw 5,596 C4
Paungde 17,286 B3
Pegu 150,447 C3
Prome (Pye) 36,997 B3
Pyapon 19,174 B3
Pye 36,997 B3
Pyinmana 22,025 C3
Pyu 10,443 C3
Rathedaung 2,969 B2
Sagaing 15,382 B2
Sandoway 5,172 B3
Shwebo 17,827 B2
Singu 4,027 C2
Sittwe 107,607 B2
Syriam 15,296 C3
Taungdwingyi 16,233 B2
Taunggyi 107,907 C2
Tavoy 60,435 C4
Tharrawaddy 8,977 C3
Thaton 51,025 C3
Thayetmyo 11,649 B3
Thazi 7,531 C2
Thongwa 10,829 C3
Toungoo 31,589 C3
Wakema 20,716 B3
Yamethin 11,167 C2
Yandoon 15,245 B3
Yangon (Rangoon) (cap.) 2,458,712 C3
Ye 12,852 C4
Yenangyaung 57,652 B2
Ye-u 5,307 B2
Zalun 899 B3

OTHER FEATURES

Amya (pass) C4
Andaman (sea) B4
Arakan Yoma (mts.) B3
Ataran (riv.) C4
Bengal, Bay of (bay) B3
Bentinck (isl.) C5
Bilauktaung (range) C4
Chaukan (pass) C1
Cheduba (isl.) B3
Chin (hills) B2
Chindwin (riv.) B2
Coco (chan.) B4
Combermere (bay) B3
Daung Kyun (isl.) C4
Dawna (range) C3
Great Coco (isl.) B4
Great Tenasserim (riv.) C4
Heinze Chaung (bay) C4
Heywood (chan.) B3
Hkakabo Razi (mt.) C1
Hka, Nam (riv.) C2
Indawgyi (lake) C1
Inle (lake) C2
Irrawaddy (riv.) B3
Irrawaddy, Mouths of the (delta) B4
Kadan Kyun (isl.) C4
Kaladan (riv.) B2
Kalegauk (isl.) C4
Khao Luang (mt.) C5
Lanbi Kyun (isl.) C5
Launglon Bok (isls.) C4
Letsôk-aw Kyun (isl.) C5
Little Coco (isl.) B4

(continued on following page)

(continued)

Loi Leng (mt.) C2
Mali (riv.) C1
Mali Kyun (isl.) C4
Manipur (riv.) B2
Martaban (gulf) C4
Mekong (riv.) D2
Mergui (arch.) C5
Mon (riv.) B2
Mu (riv.) B2
Myitnge (riv.) C2
Negrais (cape) B3
Nmai (riv.) C1
Pakchan (riv.) C5
Pangsau (pass) C1
Pawn, Nam (riv.) C2
Pegu Yoma (mts.) B3
Popa Hill (mt.) B2
Preparis (isl.) B4
Preparis North (chan.) B4
Preparis South (chan.) B4
Ramree (isl.) B3
Salween (riv.) C3
Shan (plat.) C2
Shweli (riv.) C2
Sittang (riv.) C3
Taping (riv.) C1
Taungthonton (mt.) B1
Tavoy (pt.) C4
Tenasserim (isl.) C4
Teng, Nam (riv.) C2
Thayawthadangyi Kyun (isl.) ... C4
Three Pagodas (pass) C4
Victoria (mt.) B2
Zadetkyi Kyun (isl.) C5

CAMBODIA (KAMPUCHEA)

CITIES and TOWNS

Batdambang (Battambang) D4
Kampong Cham E4
Kampong Chhnang D4
Kampong Saom D5
Kampong Spoe E5
Kampong Thum E4
Kampot E5
Kracheh E4
Krong Kaoh Kong D5
Krong Keb E5
Lumphat E4
Paoy Pet D4
Phnom Penh (cap.) 300,000 ... E5
Phnum Tbeng Meanchey E4
Phumi Samraong D4
Pouthisat D4
Proy Veng E5
Pursat (Pouthisat) D4
Senmonoron E4
Siemreab D4
Stoeng Treng E4
Svay Rieng E5

OTHER FEATURES

Angkor Wat (ruins) D4
Chrouy Samit (pt.) D5
Dangrek (mts.) D4
Drang, Ia (riv.) E4
Joncs (plain) E5
Kong, Kaoh (isl.) D5
Khong, Se (riv.) E4
Mekong (riv.) E4
Rung, Kaoh (isl.) D5
San, Se (riv.) E4
Sen, Stoeng (riv.) E4
Srepok (riv.) E4
Tang, Kaoh (isl.) D5
Tonle Sap (lake) D4
Wai, Poulo (isls.) D5

LAOS

CITIES and TOWNS

Attapu 2,750 .... E4
Ban Kèngkok 2,000 .... E3
Boun Nua 2,500 .... D2
Champasak 3,500 .... E4
Khamkeut▲ 31,206 .... E3
Louang Namtha 1,459 .... D2
Louangphrabang 7,596 .... D3
Mahaxai 2,000 .... E3
Muang Hinboun 1,750 .... E3
Muang Khammouan 5,500 ..... E3
Muang Không 1,750 .... E4
Muang Khôngxédôn 2,000 ..... E4
Muang Ou Tai D2
Muang Pak-Lay 2,000 .... D3
Muang Pakxan 2,500 .... D3
Muang Xaignabouri
(Sayaboury) 2,500 .... D3
Muang Xay 2,000 .... D2
Pakxé 8,000 .... E4
Phiafai▲ 17,216 .... E4
Phôngsali 2,500 .... D2
San Nua (Sam Neua) 3,000 ..... E2
Saravan 2,350 .... E4
Savannakhét 8,500 .... E3
Sayaboury (Muang Xaignabouri)
2,500 .... D3
Thakhek (Muang Khammouan)
5,500 .... E3
Viangchan (Vientiane)
132,253 .... D3
Vientiane (cap.) 132,253 .... D3
Xiangkhoang 3,500 .... D3

OTHER FEATURES

Bolovens (plat.) E4
Jars (plain) D3
Mekong (riv.) D3
Ou, Nam (riv.) D2
Phou Bia (mt.) D3
Phou Cô Pi (mt.) E3
Phou Loi (mt.) D2
Phou San (mt.) D3
Rao Co (mt.) E3
Se Khong (riv.) E4
Tha, Nam (riv.) D2
Xiangkhoang (plat.) D3

MALAYA, MALAYSIA
(See Southeast Asia, p. 85 for other part of Malaysia.)

STATES

Federal Territory 937,875 .... D7
Johor (Johore) 1,601,504 ...... D7
Kedah 1,102,200 .... D6
Kelantan 877,575 .... D6
Melaka 453,153 .... D7
Negeri Sembilan 563,955 .... D7
Pahang 770,644 .... D7
Penang (Pinang) 911,586 .... D6
Perak 1,762,288 .... D6
Perlis 147,726 .... D6
Pinang (Penang) 911,586 .... D6
Selangor 1,467,441 .... D7
Terengganu 542,280 .... D6

CITIES and TOWNS

Alor Gajah 2,222 .... D7
Alor Setar 66,260 .... D6
Bandar Maharani (Muar)
61,218 .... D7
Bandar Penggaram
(Batu Pahat) 53,291 .... D7
Batu Gajah 10,692 .... D6
Batu Pahat 53,291 .... D7
Bentong 22,683 .... D7
Butterworth 61,187 .... D6
Chukai 12,514 .... D6
Gemas 5,214 .... D7
George Town (Pinang)
269,603 .... C6
Ipoh 247,953 .... D6
Johor Baharu (Johore Bharu)
136,234 .... F5
Kampar 26,591 .... D6
Kampong Kuala Besut 3,524 .. D6
Kangar 8,758 .... D6
Kelang 113,611 .... D7
Keluang 43,272 .... D7
Kota Baharu 55,124 .... D6
Kota Tinggi 8,725 .... F5
Kuala Dungun 17,560 .... D6
Kuala Lipis 9,270 .... D6
Kuala Lumpur (cap.) 451,977 . D7
Kuala Pilah 12,508 .... D7
Kuala Rompin 1,384 .... D7
Kuala Selangor 3,132 .... D7
Kuala Terengganu 53,320 .... D6
Kuantan 43,358 .... D7
Kulai 11,841 .... F5
Lumut 3,255 .... D6
Malacca (Melaka) 87,160 .... D7
Mersing 18,246 .... E7
Muar 61,218 .... D7
Pekan 4,682 .... D7
Pinang (George Town)
269,603 .... C6
Pontian Kechil 8,349 .... E5
Port Dickson 10,300 .... D7
Port Weld 3,233 .... D6
Raub 18,433 .... D7
Segamat 17,796 .... D7
Seremban 80,921 .... D7
Sungai Petani 35,959 .... C6
Taiping 54,645 .... D6
Tanah Merah 7,012 .... D6
Teluk Intan 44,524 .... D6
Tumpat 10,673 .... D6

OTHER FEATURES

Aur, Pulau (isl.) E7
Belumut, Gunong (mt.) D7
Benom, Gunong (mt.) D7
Gelang, Tanjong (pt.) D6
Johore (str.) E6
Johor, Sungai (riv.) F5
Kelantan, Sungai (riv.) D6
Langkawi, Pulau (isl.) C6
Ledang, Gunong (mt.) D7
Lima, Pulau (isl.) F6
Malacca (str.) D7
Malay (pen.) D6
Malaya (West Malaysia)
(reg.) D6
Pahang, Sungai (riv.) D7
Pangkor, Pulau (isl.) D6
Perak, Gunong (mt.) D6
Perhentian, Kepulauan (isls.) .. D6
Piai, Tanjong (pt.) E6
Pinang, Pulau (isl.) C6
Pulai, Sungai (riv.) E5
Ramunia, Tanjong (pt.) F6
Redang, Pulau (isl.) D6
Sedili Kechil, Tanjong (pt.) F5
Singapore (str.) F6
Tahan, Gunong (mt.) D6
Temiang, Bukit (mt.) D6
Tenggol, Pulau (isl.) D6
Tinggi, Pulau (isl.) E7
Tioman, Pulau (isl.) E7

SINGAPORE

CITIES and TOWNS

Jurong 50,974 .... E6
Nee Soon 37,641 .... F6
Paya Lebar 21,636 .... F6
Serangoon 89,558 .... F6
Singapore (cap.) 2,413,945 ..... F6

OTHER FEATURES

Keppel (harb.) F6
Main (str.) F6
Singapore (str.) F6
Tekong Besar, Pulau (isl.) F6

THAILAND (SIAM)

CITIES and TOWNS

Ang Thong 7,267 .... C4
Ayutthaya (Phra Nakhon Si
Ayutthaya) 37,213 .... D4
Ban Aranyaprathet 12,276 ...... D4
Bangkok (cap.) 1,867,297 ...... D4
Ban Pak Phanang 13,590 .... D5
Buriram 16,431 .... D4
Chachoengsao 22,106 .... D4
Chainat 9,944 .... D4
Chaiyaphum 12,540 .... D4
Chanthaburi 15,479 .... D4
Chiang Mai 101,594 .... C3
Chiang Rai 13,927 .... C3
Chon Buri 115,350 .... D4
Chumphon 11,643 .... C5
Hat Yai 47,953 .... C6
Hua Hin 21,426 .... D4
Kalasin 14,960 .... D3
Kamphaeng Phet 12,378 .... C3
Kanchanaburi 16,397 .... C4
Khon Kaen 29,431 .... D3
Khorat (Nakhon Ratchasima)
66,071 .... D4
Krabi 8,764 .... C5
Krung Thep (Bangkok) (cap.)
1,867,297 .... D4
Lampang 40,100 .... C3
Lamphun 11,309 .... C3
Lang Suan 4,020 .... C5
Loei 10,137 .... D3
Lom Sak 10,597 .... D3
Lop Buri 23,112 .... D4
Mae Hong Son 3,981 .... C3
Maha Sarakham 19,707 .... D3
Nakhon Nayok 8,185 .... D4
Nakhon Pathom 34,300 .... C4
Nakhon Phanom 20,385 .... D3
Nakhon Ratchasima 66,071 .... D4
Nakhon Sawan 46,853 .... D4
Nakhon Si Thammarat
102,123 .... D5
Nan 17,738 .... D3
Narathiwat 21,256 .... D6
Nong Khai 21,150 .... D3
Pattani 21,938 .... D6
Phanat Nikhom 10,514 .... D4
Phangnga 5,738 .... C5
Phatthalung 13,336 .... D6
Phayao 20,346 .... C3
Phet Buri 27,755 .... C4
Phetchabun 6,240 .... D3
Phichit 10,814 .... D3
Phitsanulok 33,883 .... D3
Phrae 17,555 .... D3
Phra Nakhon Si Ayutthaya
37,213 .... D4
Phuket 34,362 .... C6
Prachin Buri 14,167 .... D4
Prachuap Khiri Khan 9,075 ..... D5
Rahaeng (Tak) 16,317 .... C3
Ranong 10,301 .... C5
Rat Buri 32,271 .... C4
Rayong 14,846 .... D4
Roi Et 20,242 .... D4
Sakon Nakhon 18,943 .... E3
Samut Prakan 46,632 .... D4
Samut Sakhon 33,619 .... D4
Samut Songkhram 23,574 ...... C4
Sara Buri 25,025 .... D4
Satun 7,315 .... C6
Sawankhalok 8,387 .... C3
Sing Buri 9,050 .... D4
Singora (Songkhla) 172,604 ... D6
Sisaket 13,662 .... E4
Songkhla 172,604 .... D6
Sukhothai 15,488 .... D3
Suphan Buri 18,768 .... C4
Surat Thani 24,923 .... C5
Surin 16,342 .... D4
Tak 16,317 .... C3
Takua Pa 7,825 .... C5
Thon Buri 628,015 .... D4
Trang 32,985 .... C6
Trat 7,917 .... D4
Ubon 40,650 .... E4
Udon Thani 56,218 .... D3
Uthai Thani 10,525 .... C4
Uttaradit 12,022 .... D3
Warin Chamrap 21,520 .... E4
Yala 30,051 .... D6
Yasothon 12,079 .... D4

OTHER FEATURES

Amya (pass) C4
Bilauktaung (range) C4
Chang, Ko (isl.) D4
Chan, Ko (isl.) C5
Chao Phraya, Mae Nam (riv.) .. D4
Chi, Mae Nam (riv.) D3
Dangrek (Dong Rak) (mts.) D4
Doi Inthanon (mt.) C3
Doi Pha Hom Pok (mt.) C2
Doi Pia Fai (mt.) D4
Khao Luang (mt.) C5
Kao Prawa (mt.) C3
Khwae Noi, Mae Nam (riv.) C4
Kra (isth.) C5
Kut, Ko (isl.) D5
Laem Chong Phra (cape) C5
Laem Pho (cape) D6
Laem Talumphuk (cape) D5
Lanta, Ko (isl.) C6
Libong, Ko (isl.) C6
Luang (mt.) C5
Mae Klong, Mae Nam (riv.) C4
Malay (pen.) D6
Mekong (riv.) E3
Mun, Mae Nam (riv.) D4
Nan, Mae Nam (riv.) D3
Nong Lahan (lake) D3
Pakchan (riv.) C5
Pa Sak, Mae Nam (riv.) D4
Phangan, Ko (isl.) D5
Phuket, Ko (isl.) C5
Ping, Mae Nam (riv.) C3
Rawi, Ko (isl.) C6
Salween (riv.) C3
Samui (str.) D5
Samui, Ko (isl.) D5
Tao, Ko (isl.) C5
Tapi, Mae Nam (riv.) C5
Terutao, Ko (isl.) C6
Tha Chin, Mae Nam (riv.) C4
Thale Luang (lag.) D6
Thalu, Ko (isls.) C5
Three Pagodas (pass) C4
Wang, Mae Nam (riv.) C3

VIETNAM

CITIES and TOWNS

An Loc (Binh Long) 15,276 ..... E5
An Tuc (An Khe) F4
Bac Giang E2
Bac Lieu 53,841 .... E5
Bac Ninh 22,560 .... E2
Ban Me Thuot 68,771 .... F4
Bien Hoa 87,135 .... E5
Binh Long (An Loc) 15,276 ..... E5
Cam Ranh 118,111 .... F5
Can Tho 182,424 .... E5
Cao Bang 565,967 .... E2
Cao Lanh 16,482 .... E5
Chau Phu 37,175 .... E5
Chu Lai F4
Da Lat 105,072 .... F5
Da Nang 492,194 .... E3
Dien Bien Phu D2
Dong Hoi E3
Go Cong 33,191 .... E5
Ha Giang E2
Haiphong* 1,447,614 .... E2
Hanoi (cap.) 3,056,549 .... E2
Ha Tinh E3
Ho Chi Minh City (Saigon)*
3,934,326 .... E5
Hoa Binh E2
Hoi An 45,059 .... F4
Hon Gai 100,000 .... E2
Hue 209,043 .... E3
Khanh Hung 59,015 .... E5
Khe Sanh E3
Kon Tum 33,554 .... E4
Lac Giao (Ban Me Thuot)
68,771 .... F4
Lai Chau 437,983 .... D2
Lang Son 610,501 .... E2
Lao Cai E2
Loc Ninh E5
Long Xuyen 72,658 .... E5
My Tho 119,892 .... E5
Nam Dinh 125,000 .... E2
Nha Trang 216,227 .... F4
Ninh Binh E2
Phan Rang 33,377 .... F5
Phan Thiet 80,122 .... F5
Phu Cuong 28,267 .... E5
Phu Ly E2
Phu Tho 10,888 .... E2
Phu Vinh 48,485 .... E5
Pleiku 23,720 .... E4
Quang Ngai 14,119 .... F4
Quang Tri 15,874 .... E3
Quan Long 59,331 .... E5
Qui Nhon 213,757 .... F4
Rach Gia 104,161 .... E5
Sa Dec 51,867 .... E5
Saigon (Ho Chi Minh City)*
3,934,326 .... E5
Son La 682,385 .... D2
Son Tay 19,213 .... E2
Song Cau F4
Tam Ky 38,532 .... F4
Tam Quan F4
Tan An 38,082 .... E5
Tay Ninh 791,762 .... E5
Thai Binh 1,632,525 .... E2
Thai Nguyen 110,000 .... E2
Thanh Hoa 2,991,317 .... E3
Tra Vinh (Phu Vinh) 48,485 .... E5
Truc Giang 68,629 .... E5
Tuy Hoa 63,552 .... F4
Vinh 43,954 .... E3
Vinh Long 30,667 .... E5
Vinh Yen E2
Vung Tau 136,225 .... E5
Yen Bai E2

OTHER FEATURES

Bach Long Vi, Dao (isl.) F2
Ba Den, Nui (mt.) E5
Bai Bung, Mui (Ca Mau) (pt.) .. E5
Ba Lang An, Mui (cape) F4
Ben Goi (bay) F4
Black (riv.) D2
Ca Mau (Mui Bai Bung) (pt.) ... E5
Cam Ranh, Vinh (bay) F5
Cao Nguyen Dac Lac (plat.) F4
Cat Ba, Dao (isl.) E2
Chon May, Vung (bay) F3
Con Son (isls.) E5
Cu Lao, Hon (isls.) F5
Da Nang, Mui (cape) F3
Deux Frères, Les (isls.) E5
Dinh, Mui (cape) F5
Fan Si Pan (mt.) D2
Gio, Hon (isl.) E3
Hon Tho Chau (isl.) D5
Ia Drang (riv.) E4
Indochina (reg.) D2
Joncs (plain) E5
Khoai, Hon (isl.) E5
Kontum (plat.) E4
Lang Bian, Nui (mts.) E4
Lay, Mui (cape) E3
Mekong, Mouths of the
(delta) E5
Nam Tram, Mui (cape) F4
Ngoc Linh (mt.) E4
Nightingale (Bach Long Vi)
(isl.) F2
Panjang, Hon (Hon Tho Chau)
(isl.) D5
Phu Quoc, Dao (isl.) D5
Quan Dao Nam Du (isls.) D5
Rao Co (mt.) E3
Red (riv.) E2
Ron, Mui (cape) E3
Se San (riv.) E4
Sip Song Chau Thai (mts.) D2
Song Ba (riv.) F4
Song Ca (riv.) E3
Song Cai (riv.) E4
South China (sea) F4
Tonkin (gulf) E3
Varella, Mui (cape) F4
Yang Sin, Chu (mt.) F4

*City and suburbs.
▲Population of district.

Agriculture, Industry and Resources

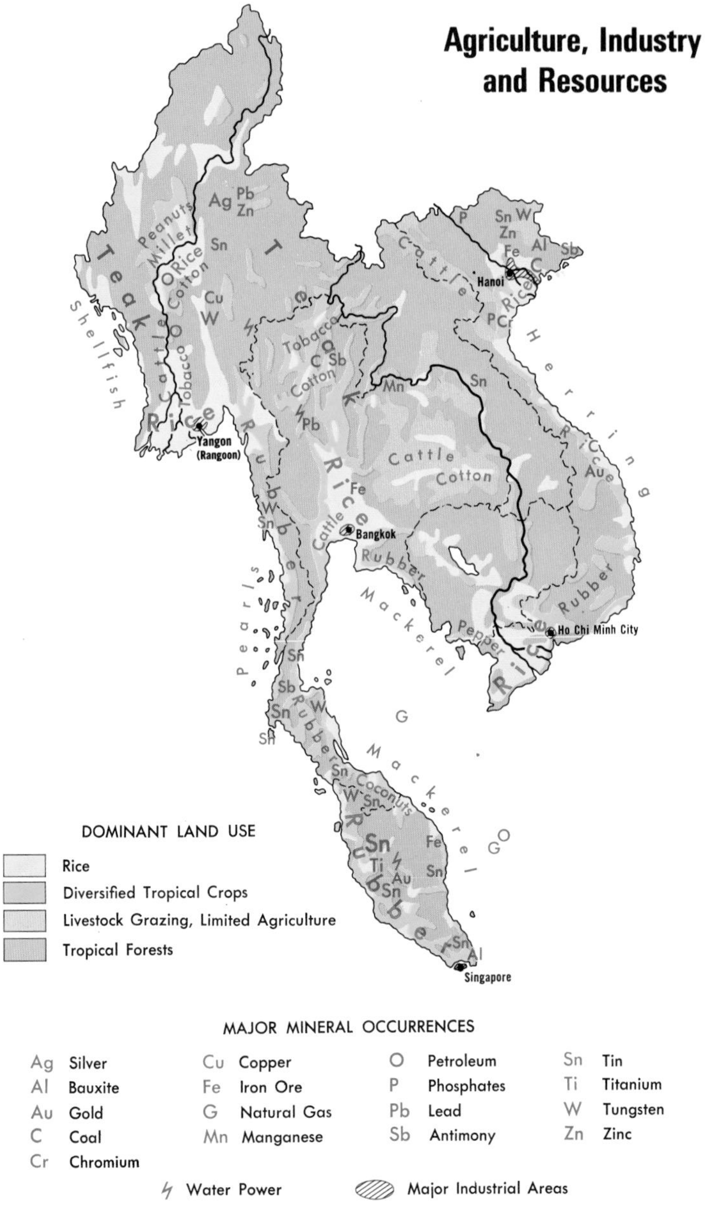

Hanoi
Ho Chi Minh City
Bangkok
Yangon
(Rangoon)
Singapore
DOMINANT LAND USE
Rice
Diversified Tropical Crops
Livestock Grazing, Limited Agriculture
Tropical Forests
MAJOR MINERAL OCCURRENCES
Ag Silver
Al Bauxite
Au Gold
C Coal
Cr Chromium
Cu Copper
Fe Iron Ore
G Natural Gas
Mn Manganese
O Petroleum
P Phosphates
Pb Lead
Sb Antimony
Sn Tin
Ti Titanium
W Tungsten
Zn Zinc
Water Power
Major Industrial Areas

CHINA (MAINLAND)

AREA 3,705,386 sq. mi. (9,596,960 sq. km.)
POPULATION 1,256,167,701
CAPITAL Beijing
LARGEST CITY Shanghai
HIGHEST POINT Mt. Everest 29,028 ft. (8,848 m.)
MONETARY UNIT yuan
MAJOR LANGUAGES Chinese, Chuang, Uiguar, Yi, Tibetan, Maio, Mongol, Kazakh
MAJOR RELIGIONS Confucianism, Buddhism, Taoism, Islam

CHINA (TAIWAN)

AREA 13,971 sq. mi. (36,185 sq. km.)
POPULATION 22,319,222
CAPITAL T'aipei
LARGEST CITY T'aipei
HIGHEST POINT Yü Shan 13,115 ft. (3,997 m.)
MONETARY UNIT new Taiwan dollar
MAJOR LANGUAGES Chinese, Formosan
MAJOR RELIGIONS Confucianism, Buddhism, Taoism, Christianity, tribal religions

MONGOLIA

AREA 606,163 sq. mi. (1,569,962 sq. km.)
POPULATION 2,538,211
CAPITAL Ulaanbaatar
LARGEST CITY Ulaanbaatar
HIGHEST POINT Tabun Bogdo 14,288 ft. (4,355 m.)
MONETARY UNIT tughrik
MAJOR LANGUAGES Khalkha Mongolian, Kazakh (Turkic)
MAJOR RELIGION Buddhism

MONGOLIA

AREA 606,163 sq. mi. (1,569,962 sq. km.)
POPULATION 2,654,572
CAPITAL Ulaanbaatar
LARGEST CITY Ulaanbaatar
HIGHEST POINT Tabun Bogdo 14,288 ft. (4,355 m.)
MONETARY UNIT tughrik
MAJOR LANGUAGES Khalkha Mongolian, Kazakh (Turkic)
MAJOR RELIGION Buddhism

MACAU

AREA 8 sq. mi. (21 sq. km.)
POPULATION 429,152
CAPITAL Macau
MONETARY UNIT pataca
MAJOR LANGUAGES Chinese, Portuguese
MAJOR RELIGIONS Confucianism, Buddhism, Taoism, Christianity

CHINA (MAINLAND)

CHINA (TAIWAN)

MONGOLIA

Scale of Miles
0
500
1000
Scale of Kilometers
0
500
1000
RUSSIA
MONGOLIA
CHINA
INDIA
PAK.
NEPAL
BHUTAN
MYANMAR (BURMA)
LAOS
THAILAND
VIETNAM
N. KOREA
S. KOREA
JAPAN
Sea of Japan
Yellow Sea
East China Sea
PACIFIC OCEAN
South China Sea
Gulf of Tonkin
Amur
Songhua
Huang He (Yellow)
Chang Jiang (Yangtze)
Xi Jiang
Mekong
Salween
Grand Canal
Ulan-Ude
Chita
Mangui
Blagoveshchensk
Khabarovsk
Aihui
Nenjiang
Hegang
Jiamusi
Hulin
Hatgal
Sühbaatar
Manzhouli
Hovd
Onon
Ulaanbaatar
Choybalsan
Qiqihar
Arxan
Harbin
Almaty
Karamay
Tsetserlig
Öndorhaan
Tamsagbulag
Osh
Ürümqi
Arvayheer
Baicheng
Mudanjiang
Kashi
Kuqa
Turpan
Hami
Saynshand
Dalandaadagad
Erenhot
Changchun
Jilin
Tumen
Vladivostok
Tongliao
Korla
Yecheng
Shenyang
Ji'an
Ruoqiang
Bayan Obo
Baotou
Jining
Jinzhou
Anshan
Dandong
Lenghu
Yumen
Jiayuguan
Datong
BEIJING
P'yŏngyang
Seoul
Da Qaidam
Shandan
Tianjin
Dalian
Yinchuan
Shijiazhuang
Yantai
Taiyuan
Dezhou
Golmud
Jinan
Qingdao
Pusan
Gar
Xining
Lanzhou
Lianyungang
Changzhou
Baoji
Xi'an
Tongchuan
Suzhou
Sa'gya
Nagqu
Xiangfan
Nanjing
SHANGHAI
Lhasa
Batang
Chengdu
Wuhan
Hangchou
Ningbo
Kanpur
Gyangzê
Darjeeling
Chongqing
Jinhua
Xichang
Ipin
Changde
Yingtan
Wenzhou
Myitkyina
Guiyang
Zhuzhou
Nanping
Fuzhou
Baoshan
Kunming
Zhanyi
Duyun
Keelung
T'aipei
Lashio
Shaoguan
Liuzhou
Xiamen
Hwalien
Taiwan
Guangzhou (Canton)
Kaohsiung
Taitung
Pingxiang
Kowloon
HONG KONG
Zhanjiang
Hanoi
Hainan
Yangon (Rangoon)
China and Mongolia Transportation
Railroads
Under Construction
Connecting Roads
Navigable Rivers
Canals
Major Seaports
© Copyright HAMMOND INCORPORATED, Maplewood, N. J.

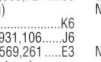

CHINA

PROVINCES

Anhui (Anhwei) 49,665,724 ....J5
Chekiang (Zhejiang) 38,884,603 ....K6
Fujian (Fukien) 25,931,106......J6
Gansu (Kansu) 19,569,261 .....E3
Guangdong (Kwangtung) 59,299,220 ....H7
Guangxi Zhuangzu (Kwangsi Chuang Aut. Reg.) 36,420,960 ....G7
Guizhou (Kweiichow) 28,552,997 ....G6
Hainan H8
Hebei (Hopei) 53,005,875 ....J4
Heilongjiang (Heilungkiang) 32,665,546 ....K2
Henan (Honan) 74,422,739 ....H5
Hubei (Hupei) 47,804,150 ......H5
Hunan 54,008,851 ....H6
Inner Mongolian Aut. Reg. (Nei Monggol) 19,274,279 .H3
Jiangsu (Kiangsu) 60,521,114 ....K5
Jiangxi (Kiangsi) 33,184,827 ..J6
Jilin (Kirin) 22,560,053 ....L3
Kansu (Gansu) 19,569,261 .....E3
Kiangsi (Jiangxi) 33,184,827 ..J6
Kiangsu (Jiangsu) 60,521,114 ....K5
Kirin (Jilin) 22,560,053 ....L3
Kwangsi Chuang Aut. Reg. (Guangxi Zhuang) 36,420,960 ....G7
Kwangtung (Guangdong) 59,299,220 ....H7
Kweiichow (Guizhou) 28,552,997 ....G6
Liaoning 35,721,693 ....K3
Nei Monggol (Inner Mongolian Aut. Reg.) 19,274,279 ....H3
Ningxia Huizu (Ningsia Hui Aut. Reg.) 3,895,578 ....F3
Qinghai (Tsinghai) 3,895,706..E4
Shaanxi (Shensi) 28,904,423 .G5
Shandong (Shantung) 74,419,054 ....J4
Shanxi (Shansi) 25,291,389 ...H4
Sichuan (Szechwan) 99,713,310 ....F5
Sinkiang-Uigur Aut. Reg. (Xinjiang Uygur) 13,081,631 ..B3
Taiwan 21,665,515 ....K7
Tibet Aut. Reg. (Xizang) 1,892,393 ....B5
Tsinghai (Qinghai) 3,895,706..E4
Xinjian Uygur (Sinkiang-Uigur Aut. Reg.) 13,081,631 ....B3
Xizang (Tibet Aut. Reg.) 1,892,393 ....B5
Yunnan 32,553,817 ....F7
Zhejiang (Chekiang) 38,884,603 ....K6

SPECIAL ADMINISTRATIVE REGIONS

Hong Kong 6,966,929 ....H7
Macau 445,427 ....H7

CITIES and TOWNS

Aihui (Aigun) (Heihe) 73,660 ..L1
Amoy (Xiamen) 507,390 ....J7
Anqing (Anking) 449,310 ....J5
Anshan 1,195,580 ....K3
Anshun 200,680 ....G6
Anyang 501,390 ....H4
Baicheng, Jilin 276,420 ....K2
Baoding (Paoting) 495,140 .....J4
Baoji (Paoki) 341,240 ....G5
Baotou (Paotow) 1,075,920....G3
Beihai (Pakhoi) 173,740 ....G7
Beijing (Peking) (cap.) 5,715,368 ....J3
Bengbu (Pengpu) 550,360 ......J5
Canton (Guangzhou, Kwangchow) 3,181,510......H7
Changchih (Changzhi) 450,320 ....H4
Changchow (Changzhou) 533,940 ....J5
Changchow (Zhangzhou) 283,490 ....J7
Changchun 1,747,410 ....K3
Changde (Changteh) 213,890.H6
Changhua 185,816 ....K7
Changsha 1,066,030 ....H6
Changteh (Changde) 213,890.H6
Changzhi (Changchih) 450,320 ....H4
Changzhou (Changchow) 533,940 ....K5
Chankiang (Zhanjiang) 853,970 ....H7
Chaotung (Zhaotung) 133,080 ....F6
Chaoyang, Liaoning 206,700...J3
Chefoo (Yantai) 385,180 ....K4
Chengchow (Zhengzhou) 1,404,050 ....H5
Chengde (Chengteh) 326,910 .J3
Chengdu (Chengtu) 2,499,000 ....F5
Chiai 251,840 ....K7
Chifeng 293,460 ....J3
Chinchow (Jinzhou) 599,490..K3
Chinkiang (Zhenjiang) 345,560 ....J5
Chinwangtao (Qinhuangdao) 374,210 ....K4
Chongqing (Chungking) 2,673,170 ....G6
Chüanchow (Quanzhou) 403,180 ....J7
Chuchow (Zhuzhou) 382,950 .H6
Chumatien (Zhumadian) 150,440 ....H5
Chungking (Chongqing) 2,673,170 ....G6
Chungshan (Zhongshan) 135,000 ....H7
Conghua 280,250 ....H7
Dafang 962,470 ....G6
Dalian 1,480,240 ....K4
Dandong (Tantung) 545,180...K3
Daqing 758,430 ....L2
Datong (Tatung), Shanxi 962,470 ....H3

(continued on following page)

China and Mongolia

(continued)

Da Xian 193,490 .... G5
Dezhou (Tehchow) 258,860 .... J4
Dukou 497,330 .... F6
Fatshan (Foshan) 273,840 ...... H7
Fengcheng 995,900 .... K3
Foochow (Fuzhou) 1,111,550 .. J6
Foshan (Fatshan) 273,840 ...... H7
Fowyang (Fuyang) 177,850 ..... J5
Fushun 1,184,940 .... K3
Fuxin (Fusin) 646,580 .... K3
Fuyang (Fowyang) 177,850 ..... J5
Fuzhou (Foochow), Fujian
1,111,550 .... J6
Fuzhou, Jiangxi 158,300 .... J6
Ganzhou (Kanchow) 362,880 . H6
Gejiu (Kokiu) 352,980 .... F7
Guangzhou (Canton)
3,181,510 .... H7
Guilin (Kweilin) 432,410 .... G6
Guiyang (Kweiyang), Guizhou
1,350,190 .... G6
Gulja (Yining) 257,280 .... B3
Haikou (Hoihow) 263,280 .... H7
Hailar 157,490 .... J2
Hanchung (Hanzhong)
374,270 .... G5
Handan (Hantan) 929,530 ...... H4
Hangzhou (Hangchow)
1,171,450 .... J5
Hanton (Handan) 929,530 ...... H4
Hanzhong (Hanchung)
374,270 .... G5
Harbin 2,519,120 .... L2
Hebi 336,430 .... H4
Hefei (Hofei) 795,420 .... J5
Hegang (Hokang) 592,470 ...... L2
Heihe (Aigun, Aihui) 73,660 .... L1
Hengshui 101,260 .... J4
Hengyang 531,730 .... H6
Hofei (Hefei) 795,420 .... J5
Hohhot (Huhehot) 754,120 .... H3
Hoihow (Haikou) 263,280 .... H7
Hokang (Hegang) 592,470 ...... L2
Horqin Youyi Qianqi
(Ulanhot) 174,050 .... K2
Houma 144,460 .... H4
Hsüchang (Xuchang)
218,960 .... H5
Huaibei 444,820 .... J5
Huainan 1,029,220 .... J5
Huangshi 375,640 .... J5
Huhehot (Hohhot) 754,120 .... H3
Huize 158,380 .... F6
Hunjiang 694,160 .... L3
Huzhou (Wuxing) 925,900 ...... K5
Hwainan (Huainan)
1,029,220 .... J5
Hwangshih (Huangshi)
375,640 .... J5
Ichang (Yichang) 365,000 ...... H5
Ichun (Yichun) 755,830 .... L2
Ipin (Yibin) 245,240 .... F6
Jiamusi (Kiamusze) 540,190 . M2
Ji'an (Kian) 167,550 .... J6
Jiangmen (Kongmoon)
212,450 .... H7
Jiaozuo (Tsiaotso) 484,370 .... H4
Jiaxing (Kashing) 656,130 ...... K5
Jilin (Kirin) 1,808,420 .... L3
Jinan (Tsinan) 1,359,130 .... J4
Jingdezhen (Kingtehchen)
611,030 .... J6
Jinhua (Kinhwa) 869,490 .... J6
Jining (Tsining), Nei Monggol
158,570 .... H3
Jining (Tsining), Shandong
190,420 .... J4
Jinzhou (Chinchow) 599,490 .. K3
Jiujiang (Kiukiang) 350,910 .... J6
Jixi (Kisi) 781,800 .... M2
Kaifeng 602,230 .... H5
Kaiyuan, Yunnan 223,420 .... F7
Kalgan (Zhangjiakou)
617,120 .... J3
Kanchow (Ganzhou) 362,880 . H6
Kaohsiung 1,227,454 .... J7
Karamay 156,970 .... B2
Kashi 256,890 .... A4
Kashing (Jiaxing) 656,130 ...... K5
Keelung 347,828 .... K6
Kiamusze (Jiamusi) 540,190 . M2
Kian (Ji'an) 167,550 .... J6
Kingtehchen (Jingdezhen)
611,030 .... J6
Kinhwa (Jinhua) 869,490 .... J6
Kirin (Jilin) 1,808,420 .... L3
Kisi (Jixi) 781,800 .... M2
Kiukiang (Jiujiang) 350,910 .... J6
Kokiu (Gejiu) 352,980 .... F7
Kongmoon (Jiangmen)
212,450 .... H7
Korla 117,690 .... C3
Kowloon 2,450,187 .... H7
Kuldja (Yining) 257,280 .... B3
Kunming 1,418,640 .... F6
Kuytun 239,870 .... C3
Kwangchow (Canton)
3,181,510 .... H7
Kweilin (Guilin) 432,410 .... G6
Kweisui (Hohhot) 754,120 ..... H3
Kweiyang (Guiyang)
1,350,190 .... G6
Lanzhou (Lanchow)
1,364,480 .... F4
Lengshuijiang 254,590 .... H6
Leshan (Loshan) 958,360 .... F6
Lhasa 83,540 .... D6
Lianyungang (Lienyünkang)
397,090 .... J5
Liaoyang 646,580 .... K3
Liaoyuan 771,510 .... K3
Linfen 208,210 .... H4
Liuzhou (Liuchow) 581,940 .... G7
Loho (Luohe) 157,670 .... H5
Longyan 346,700 .... J6
Loshan (Leshan) 958,360 .... F6
Loyang (Luoyang) 951,610 .... H5
Lu'an 145,880 .... J5
Luchow (Luzhou) 305,220 ..... G6
Lüde (Dalian) 1,480,240 .... K4
Luohe 157,670 .... H5
Luoyang (Loyang) 951,610 .... H5
Luzhou (Luchow) 305,220 ..... G6
Ma'anshan 351,880 .... J5
Macau (Macao) 238,413 .... H7
Manchouli (Manzhouli)
104,220 .... J2
Maoming (Mowming)
412,540 .... H7
Mianyang, Sichuan 768,500 ... G5
Mowming (Maoming)
412,540 .... H7
Mudanjiang (Mutankiang)
581,300 .... M3
Mukden (Shenyang)
3,944,240 .... K3
Nanchang 1,075,710 .... J6
Nanchong (Nanchung)
228,340 .... G5
Nanjing (Nanking) 2,091,400 .. J5
Nanning 889,790 .... G7
Nanping 407,810 .... J6
Nantong 402,990 .... K5
Nanyang 288,300 .... H5
Neijiang (Neikiang) 270,950 ... G6
Ningbo (Ningpo) 478,940 .... K6
Ningpo (Ningbo) 478,940 .... K6
Ningsia (Yinchuan,
Yinchwan) 354,100 .... G4
Paicheng (Baicheng)
276,420 .... K2
Pakhoi (Beihai) 173,740 .... G7
Paoki (Baoji) 341,240 .... G5
Paoting (Baoding) 495,140 ..... J4
Paotow (Baotou) 1,075,920 ... G3
Peking (Beijing) (cap.)
5,715,368 .... J3
Pengpu (Bengbu) 550,360 ...... J5
Pingtung 189,347 .... K7
Pingxiang, Guangxi
Zhuangzu 1,189,030 .... G7
Pingxiang, Jiangxi 76,260 ...... H6
Qingdao (Tsingtao)
1,172,370 .... K4
Qingjiang 234,750 .... J5
Qinhuangdao (Chinwangtao)
374,210 .... K4
Qinzhou 981,280 .... G7
Qiqihar (Tsitsihar) 1,209,180 .. K2
Qitaihe 283,420 .... M2
Quanzhou (Chüanchow)
403,180 .... J7
Sanmenxia 147,050 .... H5
Sanming 199,230 .... J6
Shanghai 7,551,236 .... K5
Shangqiu (Shangkiu))
186,760 .... J5
Shangrao (Shangjao)
135,160 .... J6
Shantou (Swatow) 717,620 ..... J7
Shaoguan (Shiukwan)
370,550 .... H7
Shaoxing (Shaohing)
1,091,170 .... K5
Shaoyang 396,600 .... H6
Shashi 238,960 .... H5
Shenyang (Mukden)
3,944,240 .... K3
Shenzhen 98,060 .... H7
Shihezi (Shihhotzu) 563,740 ... C3
Shijiazhuang (Shihkiachwang)
1,068,720 .... J4
Shiukwan (Shaoyuan)
370,550 .... H7
Shiyan 306,830 .... H5
Shuangyashan 400,050 .... M2
Siakwan (Xiaguan) 117,190 .... E6
Sian (Xi'an) 2,185,040 .... G5
Siangfan (Xiangfan) 323,000 .. H5
Siangtan (Xiangtan) 493,040 .. H6
Sienyang (Xianyang))
501,810 .... G5
Sinchu 208,038 .... K7
Singtai (Xingtai) 334,210 .... H4
Sining (Xining) 566,650 .... F4
Sinsiang (Xinxiang) 525,280 .. H4
Sinyang (Xinyang) 240,000 .... H5
Siping (Szeping) 333,850 .... K3
Soochow (Suzhou) 191,710 .... K5
Süchow (Xuzhou) 776,770 ...... J5
Suizhong 669,940 .... K3
Suzhou (Soochow) 191,710 .... K5
Swatow (Shantou) 717,620 ..... J7
Szeping (Siping) 333,850 .... K3
Tai'an 1,274,770 .... J4
Taichow (Taizhou) 161,200 .... K5
Taichung 565,255 .... K7
Tainan 541,390 .... J7
T'aipei 2,108,193 .... K7
Taiyuan 1,745,820 .... H4
Taizhou (Taichow) 161,200 .... K5
Tangshan 1,407,840 .... J4
Tantung (Dandong) 545,180 ... K3
Taoyuan 105,841 .... K6
Tatung (Datong) 962,470 .... H3
Tehchow (Dezhou) 258,860 .... J4
Tianjin (Tientsin) 4,521,266 .... J4
Tianshui 185,230 .... F5
Tieling 220,850 .... K3
Tientsin (Tianjin) 4,521,266 .... J4
Tienshui (Tianshui) 185,230 ... F5
Tongchuan (Tungchwan)
353,520 .... G5
Tongliao 213,470 .... K3
Tongling 184,060 .... J5
Tsiaotso (Jiaozuo) 484,370 .... H4
Tsinan (Jinan) 1,359,130 .... J4
Tsingkiang (Qingjiang)
234,750 .... J5
Tsingtao (Qingdao)
1,172,370 .... K4
Tsining (Jining), Nei Monggol
158,570 .... H3
Tsining (Jining), Shandong
190,420 .... J4
Tsitsihar (Qiqihar) 1,209,180 .. K2
Tsunyi (Zunyi) 250,670 .... G6
Tungchwan (Tongchuan)
353,520 .... G5
Tunghwa (Tonghua))
359,960 .... L3
Tungliao (Tongliao) 213,470 ... K3
Tunxi (Tunki) 103,560 .... J6
Tzekung (Zigong) 866,020 ...... F6
Tzepo (Zibo) 2,197,668 .... J4
Ulanhot (Horquin Youyi
Qianqi) 174,050 .... K2
Ürümqi (Urumchi)
961,240 .... C3
Victoria 1,183,621 .... H7
Wanxian (Wanhsien)
267,000 .... G5
Weifang 393,410 .... J4
Weihai (Weihaiwei) 205,010 ... K4
Wenchow (Wenzhou)
515,650 .... J6
Wenzhou 515,650 .... J6
Wuchow (Wuzhou) 245,250 ... H7
Wuchung (Wuzhong)
245,250 .... G4
Wuhan 3,287,720 .... H5
Wuhu 449,070 .... J5
Wusih (Wuxi) 798,310 .... K5
Wuxi (Wusih) 798,310 .... K5
Wuxing 925,900 .... K5
Wuzhong (Wuchung)
245,250 .... G4
Wuzhou (Wuchow) 245,250 ... H7
Xiaguan (Siakwan) 117,190 .... E6
Xiamen (Amoy) 507,390 .... J7
Xi'an (Sian) 2,185,040 .... G5
Xiangfan (Siangfan) 323,000 .. H5
Xiangtan (Siangtan) 493,040 .. H6
Xianyang (Sienyang) 501,810 . G5
Xingtai (Singtai) 334,210 .... H4
Xining (Sining) 566,650 .... F4
Xinxiang (Sinsiang) 525,280 .. H4

Topography

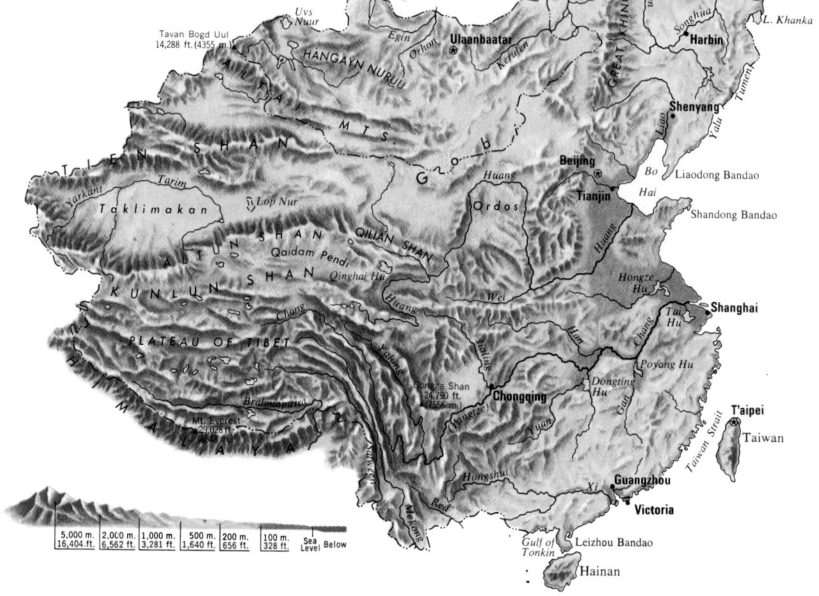

0 300 600 MI.
0 300 600 KM.
Hövsgöl Nuur
Uvs Nuur
Tavan Bogd Uul 14,288 ft. (4355 m.)
HANGAYN NURUU
ALTAY
Ulaanbaatar
Egin
Orhon
Kerulen
Argun (Ergun)
Amur (Heilong)
GREAT KHINGAN RANGE
Nen
Songhua
Ussuri (Wusuli)
L. Khanka
Harbin
Tumen
Yalu
Shenyang
Liao
Bo Hai
Liaodong Bandao
Shandong Bandao
Beijing
Tianjin
Huang
Ordos
Gobi
TIEN SHAN
Tarim
Yarkant
Taklimakan
Lop Nur
ALTUN SHAN
QILIAN SHAN
Qaidam Pendi
Qinghai Hu
KUNLUN SHAN
PLATEAU OF TIBET
HIMALAYA
Mt. Everest
Brahmaputra
Gongga Shan 24,790 ft. (7556 m.)
Chongqing
Dongting Hu
Poyang Hu
Hongze Hu
Tai Hu
Shanghai
Huai
Han
Wei
Gan
Yuan
Hongshui
Xi
Red
Mekong
Guangzhou
Victoria
T'aipei
Taiwan
Taiwan Strait
Gulf of Tonkin
Leizhou Bandao
Hainan
5,000 m. 16,404 ft.
2,000 m. 6,562 ft.
1,000 m. 3,281 ft.
500 m. 1,640 ft.
200 m. 656 ft.
100 m. 328 ft.
Sea Level
Below

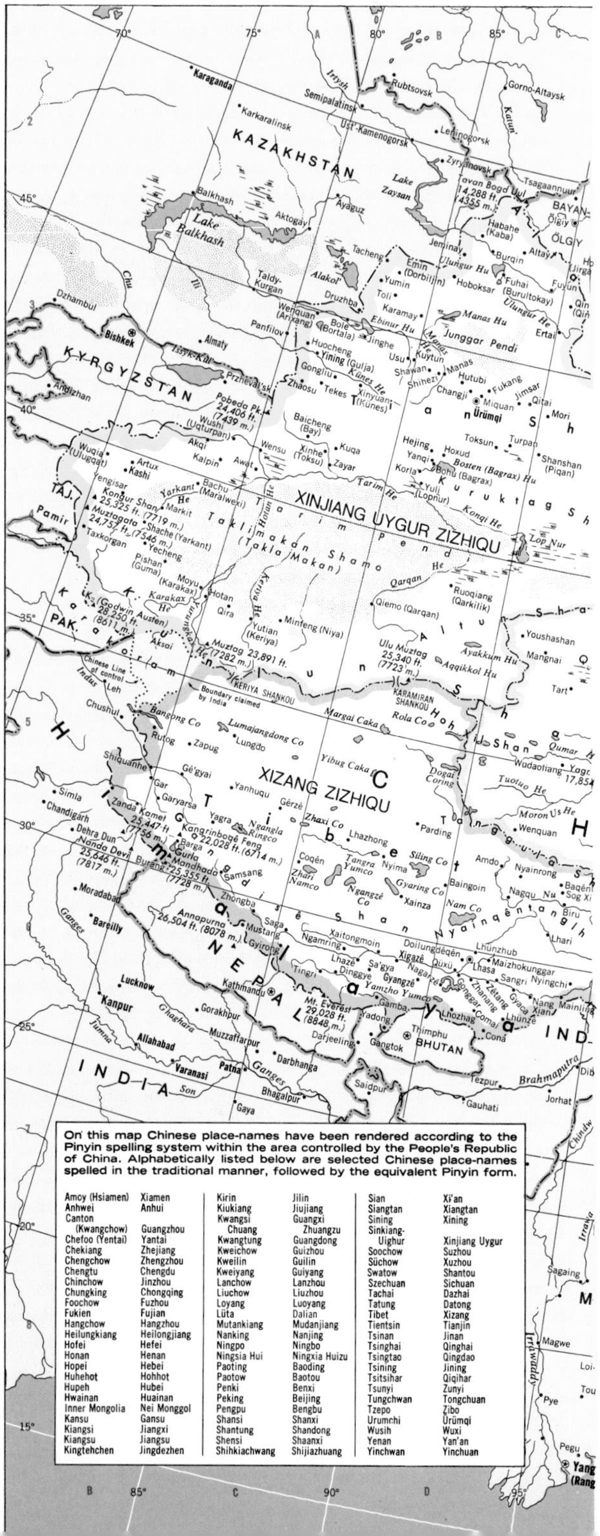

KAZAKHSTAN
Karaganda
Semipalatinsk
Rubtsovsk
Gorno-Altaysk
Karkaralinsk
Ust'-Kamenogorsk
Leninogorsk
Lake Zaysan
Balkhash
Lake Balkhash
Aktogay
Ayaguz
Tacheng
Emin (Dorbiljin)
Karamay
Taldy-Kurgan
Dzhambul
Bishkek
Almaty
KYRGYZSTAN
Issyk-Kul'
Przheval'sk
Yining (Gulja)
Kuytun
Manas
Shihezi
Ürümqi
Changji
Pobeda Pk. 24,406 ft. (7439 m.)
Aksu
Kuqa
Baicheng (Bay)
Toksun
Turpan
Korla
Hoxud
Bosten (Bagrax) Hu
Kashi
Artux
TAJ.
Pamir
Kongur Shan 25,325 ft. (7719 m.)
Muztagata 24,757 ft. (7546 m.)
Yengisar
Shache (Yarkant)
Taxkorgan
Yecheng
Pishan (Guma)
Hotan
Qira
Yutian (Keriya)
Minfeng (Niya)
K2 (Godwin Austen) 28,250 ft. (8611 m.)
Karakax
PAK.
Aksai
Muztag 23,891 ft. (7282 m.)
XINJIANG UYGUR ZIZHIQU
Taklimakan Shamo
Tarim Pendi
Tarim He
Konqi He
Lop Nur
Qarqan
Ruoqiang (Qarkilik)
Qiemo (Qarqan)
Ulu Muztag 25,340 ft. (7723 m.)
Ayakkum Hu
Aqqikkol Hu
KERIYA SHANKOU
Boundary claimed by India
Chinese Line of control
Indus
Leh
Chushul
Bangong Co
Rutog
Zapug
Lumajangdong Co
Lungdo
Margai Caka
KARAMIRAN SHANKOU
Rola Co
Hoh Xil Shan
Shiquanhe
Gê'gyai
Yibug Caka
XIZANG ZIZHIQU
Gar
Yanhuqu
Garyarsa
Zanda
Gêrzê
Kamet 25,447 ft. (7756 m.)
Simla
Chandigarh
Dehra Dun
Nanda Devi 25,646 ft. (7817 m.)
Kangrinboqê Feng 22,028 ft. (6714 m.)
Gurla Mandhada 25,355 ft. (7728 m.)
Zhaxi Co
Lhazhong
Coqên
Tangra Yumco
Nyima
Siling Co
Parding
Amdo
Nagqu
Xainza
Nam Co
Baingoin
Gyaring Co
Moradabad
Bareilly
Zhongba
Annapurna 26,504 ft. (8078 m.)
Saga
Mustang
Gyirong
Ngamring
Xaitongmoin
Lhazê
Xigazê
Lhasa
Lhünzhub
Maizhokunggar
Gyangzê
NEPAL
Kathmandu
Mt. Everest 29,028 ft. (8848 m.)
Yamzho Yumco
Gamba
Yadong
Lhozhag
Thimphu
BHUTAN
Gangtok
Darjeeling
Lucknow
Kanpur
Gorakhpur
Allahabad
Muzzaffarpur
Darbhanga
Varanasi
Patna
INDIA
Ganges
Bhagalpur
Gaya
Saidpur
Tezpur
Brahmaputra
Gauhati
Jorhat
Irrawaddy
B 85° C 90° D 95°

On this map Chinese place-names have been rendered according to the Pinyin spelling system within the area controlled by the People's Republic of China. Alphabetically listed below are selected Chinese place-names spelled in the traditional manner, followed by the equivalent Pinyin form.

Amoy (Hsiamen)	Xiamen	Kirin	Jilin	Sian	Xi'an
Anhwei	Anhui	Kiukiang	Jiujiang	Siangtan	Xiangtan
Canton (Kwangchow)	Guangzhou	Kwangsi Chuang	Guangxi Zhuangzu	Sining	Xining
Chefoo (Yentai)	Yantai	Kwangtung	Guangdong	Sinkiang-Uighur	Xinjiang Uygur
Chekiang	Zhejiang	Kweichow	Guizhou	Soochow	Suzhou
Chengchow	Zhengzhou	Kweilin	Guilin	Süchow	Xuzhou
Chengtu	Chengdu	Kweiyang	Guiyang	Swatow	Shantou
Chinchow	Jinzhou	Lanchow	Lanzhou	Szechuan	Sichuan
Chungking	Chongqing	Liuchow	Liuzhou	Tachai	Dazhai
Foochow	Fuzhou	Loyang	Luoyang	Tatung	Datong
Fukien	Fujian	Lüta	Dalian	Tibet	Xizang
Hangchow	Hangzhou	Mutankiang	Mudanjiang	Tientsin	Tianjin
Heilungkiang	Heilongjiang	Nanking	Nanjing	Tsinan	Jinan
Hofei	Hefei	Ningpo	Ningbo	Tsinghai	Qinghai
Honan	Henan	Ningsia Hui	Ningxia Huizu	Tsingtao	Qingdao
Hopei	Hebei	Paoting	Baoding	Tsining	Jining
Huhehot	Hohhot	Paotow	Baotou	Tsitsihar	Qiqihar
Hupeh	Hubei	Penki	Benxi	Tsunyi	Zunyi
Hwainan	Huainan	Peking	Beijing	Tungchwan	Tongchuan
Inner Mongolia	Nei Monggol	Pengpu	Bengbu	Tzepo	Zibo
Kansu	Gansu	Shansi	Shanxi	Urumchi	Ürümqi
Kiangsi	Jiangxi	Shantung	Shandong	Wusih	Wuxi
Kiangsu	Jiangsu	Shensi	Shaanxi	Yenan	Yan'an
Kingtehchen	Jingdezhen	Shihkiachwang	Shijiazhuang	Yinchwan	Yinchuan

Yanji (Yenki) 176,000 ....L3
Yantai (Chefoo) 385,180.........K4
Yenki (Yanji) 176,000 ....L3
Yibin (Ipin) 245,240 ....F6
Yichang (Ichang) 365,000 ......H5
Yichun, Heilongjiang 755,830 .L2
Yichun, Jiangxi 171,720 ....H6
Yinchuan Ningsia 354,100......G4
Yingkou 422,590 ....K3
Yining 257,280 ....B3
Yiyang 165,040 ....H6
Yuci (Yütze) 270,890..............H4
Yueyang 971,790.....................H6
Yumen 195,290 ....E4
Yungkia (Wenzhou) 515,650...J6
Yütze (Yuci) 270,890..............H4
Zaozhuang 1,244,020..............J5
Zhangjiakou (Kalgan)
617,120...................................J3
Zhangzhou (Changchow)
283,490...................................J7
Zhanjiang (Chankiang)
853,970...................................H7
Zhaoqing 172,080 ....H7
Zhaotong (Chaotung)
133,080...................................F6
Zhengzhou (Chengchow)
1,404,050 ....H5
Zhenjiang (Chinkiang)
345,560...................................J5
Zhongshan (Chungshan)
135,000...................................H7
Zhumadian (Chumatien)
150,440...................................H5
Zhuzhou (Chuchow) 382,950 .H6
Zibo (Tzepo) 2,197,668...........J4
Zigong (Tzekung) 866,020......F6
Zunyi (Tsunyi) 350,670 ....G6

OTHER FEATURES

Altun Shan (range)...................C4
Alxa Shamo (des.).....................F4
Amur (Heilong Jiang) (riv.) L2
A'nyêmaqên Shan (mts.).........E5
Aqqikkol Hu (lake) C4
Argun' (Ergun He) (riv.) K1
Ayakkum Hu (lake)...................C4
Bagrax (Bosten Hu) (lake).......C3
Bangong Co (lake) A5
Bashi (chan.) K7
Bayan Har Shan (range)..........E5
Bo Hai (gulf).............................J4
Bosten Hu (Bagrax) (lake).......C3
Chang Jiang (Yangtze) (riv.) ...K5
Daba Shan (range)...................G5
Da Hingan Ling (range) J3
Dian Chi (lake)..........................F7
Dogai Coring (lake) C5
Dongsha (isl.)...........................J7
Dongting Hu (lake) H6
East China (sea) L6
Ebinur Hu (lake) B2
Ergun He (Argun') (riv.) K1
Er Hai (lake) F6
Everest (mt.).............................C6
Fen He (riv.)..............................H4
Formosa (Taiwan) (isl.)............K7
Formosa (Taiwan) (str.) J7
Gangdisê Shan (range) B5
Gan He (riv.) K2
Gaoyou Hu (lake) J5
Ghenghis Khan Wall (ruin) H2
Gobi (des.)................................G3
Gongga Shan (mt.)...................F6
Grand (canal) J4
Great Wall (ruins) G4
Gurla Mandhada (mt.)..............B5
Gyaring Co (lake) C5
Gyaring Hu (lake) E4
Hailar He (riv.) K2
Hainan (isl.)..............................H8
Hangzhou Wan (bay) K5
Han Shui (riv.) H5
Har Hu (lake)............................E4
Heilong Jiang (Amur) (riv.) L2
Hengduan Shan (mts.)............E6
Himalaya (mts.)........................C6
Hoh Xil Shan (mts.)..................C4
Hongshui He (riv.) G7
Hongze Hu (lake)......................J5
Hotan He (riv.) B4
Huang He (Yellow) (riv.)..........F5
Hulun Nur (lake)........................J2
Huma He (riv.)..........................K1
Inner Mongolia (reg.) H3
Jinmen (Quemoy) (isl.) J7
Jinsha Jiang (Yangtze) (riv.) ...E5
Junggar Pendi (desert basin)..C2
Kangrinboqê Feng (mt.)...........B5
Karakax He (riv.)......................A4
Karakhoto (ruins) F3
Karamiran Shankou (pass) C4
Keriya He (riv.).........................B4
Keriya Shankou (pass).............B4
Khanka (lake)...........................M3
Kongur Shan (mt.)....................A4
Konqi He (riv.) C3
Künes He (riv.).........................B3
Kunlun Shan (range)................B4
Kuruktag Shan (range).............C3
Lancang Jiang (riv.) F7
Laoha He (riv.) J3
Leizhou Bandao (pen.).............G7
Liao He (riv.).............................K3
Liaodong Bandao (pen.) K3
Lop Nor (Lop Nur) (lake) D3
Lumajangdong Co (lake).........B5
Manas He (riv.) C3
Manas Hu (lake).......................C2
Margai Caka (lake) C4
Mazu (Matsu) (isl.) K6
Mekong (Lancang Jiang)
(riv.)...F7
Min Jiang (riv.).........................J6
Moron Us He (riv.)...................D5
Mudan Jiang (riv.)...................L3
Mu Us Shamo (des.) G4
Muztag (mt.).............................B4
Muztagata (mt.)........................A4
Nam Co (lake)..........................D5
Namzha Parwa (mt.) E6
Nan Ling (mts.)........................H6
Nanpan Jiang (riv.)..................F7
Nen Jiang (riv.)........................K2
Ngangla Ringco (lake) B5
Ngangzê Co (lake)...................C5
Ngom Qu (riv.).........................E5
Ngoring Hu (lake).....................E5
Nu Jiang (riv.)...........................E6
Nyainqêntanglha Shan
(range).....................................D5
Ordos (reg.)..............................G4
Penghu (Pescadores) (isls.)....J7
Pingtan (isl.).............................K6
Pobeda (peak)..........................A3
Poyang Hu (lake)......................J6
Pratas (Dongsha) (isl.) J7
Qaidam Pendi (basin) D4
Qarqan He (riv.) C4
Qilian Shan (range)..................E4
Qinghai Hu (lake) E4
Qumar He (riv.).........................D4
Rola Co (lake) C4
Salween (Nu Jiang) (riv.) E6
Siling Co (lake) C5
Songhua Hu (lake) L3
Songhua Jiang (Sungari)
(riv.)...M2
Tai Hu (lake).............................J5
Taiwan (Formosa) (isl.)...........K7

(continued on following page)

China and Mongolia
SCALE OF MILES
0 100 200 300 400 500
SCALE OF KILOMETERS
0 100 200 300 400 500
Capitals of Countries
Provincial Capitals
Canals
International Boundaries
Provincial Boundaries
Walls
© Copyright HAMMOND INCORPORATED, Maplewood, N. J.
RUSSIA
MONGOLIA
NORTH KOREA
SOUTH KOREA
SEA OF JAPAN
YELLOW SEA
EAST CHINA SEA
SOUTH CHINA SEA
PACIFIC OCEAN
SEA OF OKHOTSK
VIETNAM
LAOS
THAILAND
YANMAR (BURMA)
PHILIPPINES
BEIJING
SHANGHAI
Tropic of Cancer
Longitude East of Greenwich

(continued)

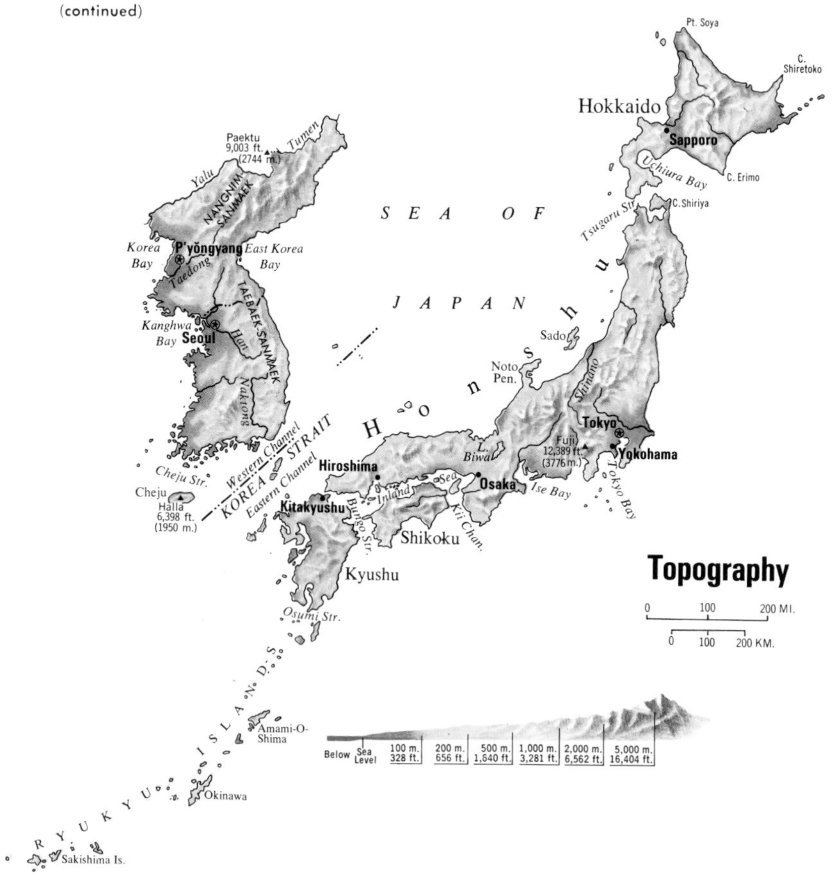
Pt. Soya
C. Shiretoko
Hokkaido
Sapporo
C. Erimo
Uchiura Bay
C. Shiriya
Tsugaru Str.
Paektu 9,003 ft. (2744 m.)
Tumen
Yalu
NANGNIM-SANMAEK
S E A O F
J A P A N
Korea Bay
P'yŏngyang
East Korea Bay
Taedong
TAEBAEK-SANMAEK
Kanghwa Bay
Seoul
Han
Naktong
Sado
Noto Pen.
Shinano
H o n s h u
Tokyo
Yokohama
Fuji 12,389 ft. (3776 m.)
L. Biwa
Osaka
Ise Bay
Tokyo Bay
Hiroshima
Inland Sea
Kii Chan.
Shikoku
Kitakyushu
Bungo Str.
Kyushu
Western Channel
KOREA STRAIT
Eastern Channel
Cheju Str.
Cheju
Halla 6,398 ft. (1950 m.)
Osumi Str.
Amami-O-Shima
Okinawa
R Y U K Y U I S L A N D S
Sakishima Is.
Topography
0 100 200 MI.
0 100 200 KM.
Below Sea Level
100 m. 328 ft.
200 m. 656 ft.
500 m. 1,640 ft.
1,000 m. 3,281 ft.
2,000 m. 6,562 ft.
5,000 m. 16,404 ft.

OTHER FEATURES

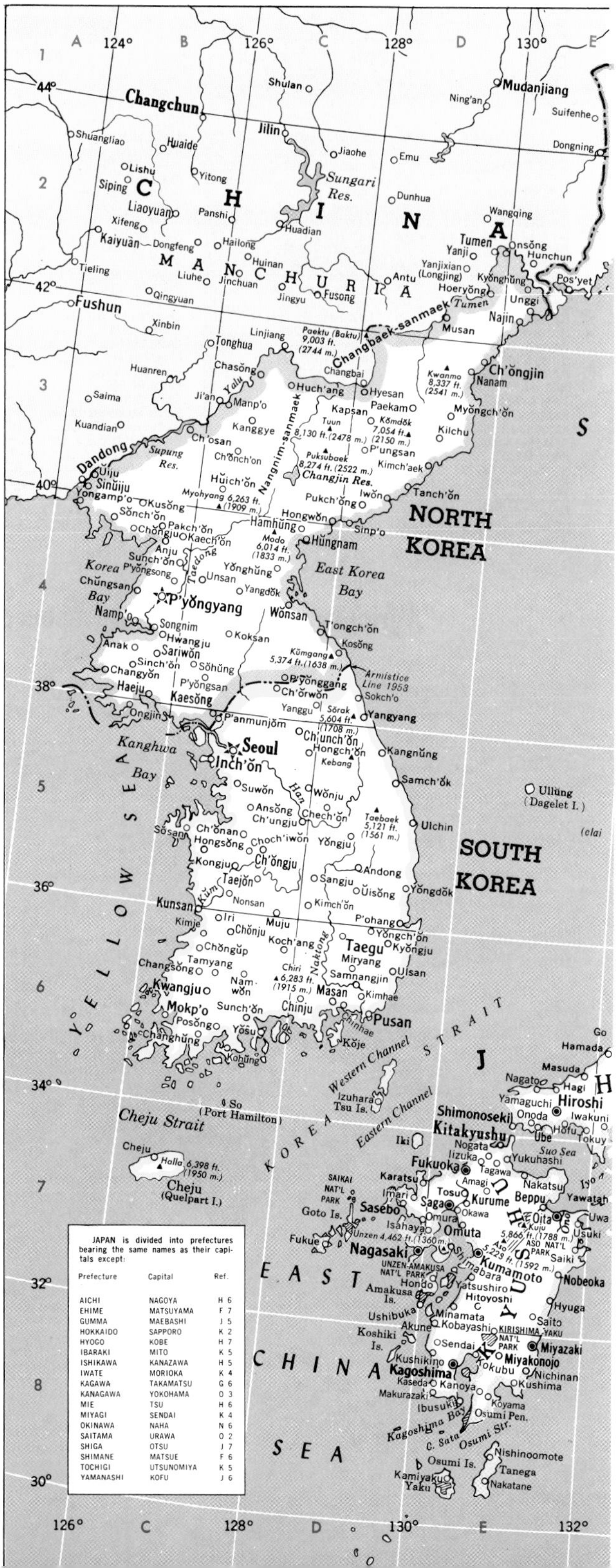
A
124°
B
126°
C
128°
D
130°
E
44°
42°
40°
38°
36°
34°
32°
30°
Changchun
Jilin
Shulan
Mudanjiang
C H I N A
M A N C H U R I A
Sungari Res.
Fushun
Tumen
Yanji
Changbaek-sanmaek
Paektu (Baektu) 9,003 ft. (2744 m.)
Ch'ŏngjin
Dandong
Sinŭiju
Yalu
Nangnim-sanmaek
NORTH KOREA
Hamhŭng
Hŭngnam
East Korea Bay
Korea Bay
P'yŏngyang
Wŏnsan
Kaesŏng
Armistice Line 1953
P'anmunjŏm
Kanghwa Bay
Seoul
Inch'ŏn
Y E L L O W S E A
SOUTH KOREA
Ullŭng (Dagelet I.)
Taejŏn
Taegu
Kwangju
Mokp'o
Pusan
K O R E A S T R A I T
Western Channel
Eastern Channel
Tsu Is.
Cheju Strait
Cheju
Halla 6,398 ft. (1950 m.)
Cheju (Quelpart I.)
So (Port Hamilton)
E A S T C H I N A S E A
Shimonoseki
Kitakyushu
Fukuoka
Nagasaki
Kumamoto
Kagoshima
Miyazaki
Oita
Osumi Is.
Tanega
Yaku

JAPAN is divided into prefectures bearing the same names as their capitals except:

Prefecture	Capital	Ref.
AICHI	NAGOYA	H 6
EHIME	MATSUYAMA	F 7
GUMMA	MAEBASHI	J 5
HOKKAIDO	SAPPORO	K 2
HYOGO	KOBE	H 7
IBARAKI	MITO	K 5
ISHIKAWA	KANAZAWA	H 5
IWATE	MORIOKA	K 4
KAGAWA	TAKAMATSU	G 6
KANAGAWA	YOKOHAMA	O 3
MIE	TSU	H 6
MIYAGI	SENDAI	K 4
OKINAWA	NAHA	N 6
SAITAMA	URAWA	O 2
SHIGA	OTSU	J 7
SHIMANE	MATSUE	F 6
TOCHIGI	UTSUNOMIYA	K 5
YAMANASHI	KOFU	J 6

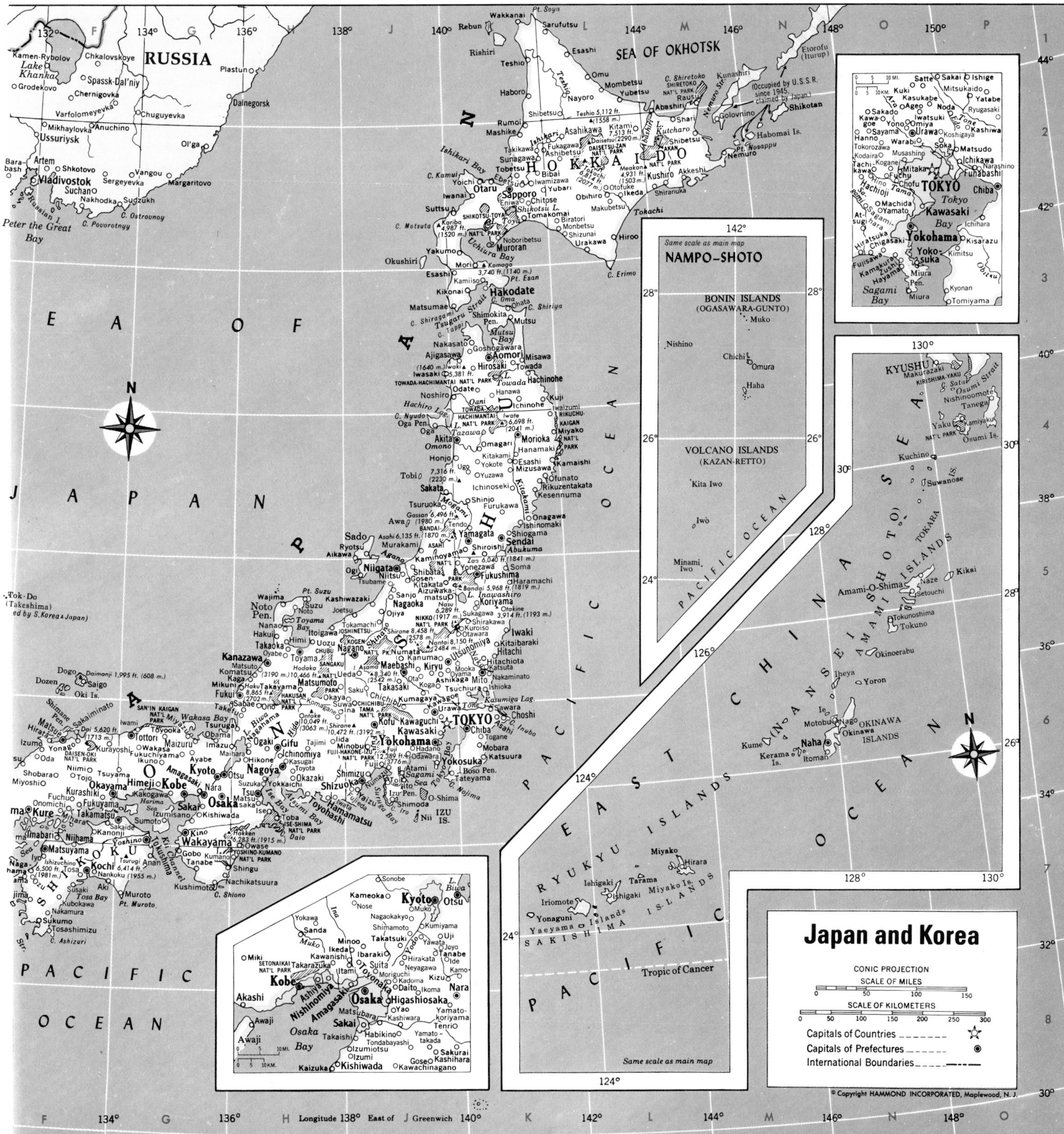

Japan and Korea
CONIC PROJECTION
SCALE OF MILES
0 50 100 150
SCALE OF KILOMETERS
0 50 100 150 200 250 300
Capitals of Countries
Capitals of Prefectures
International Boundaries
RUSSIA
SEA OF OKHOTSK
SEA OF JAPAN
PACIFIC OCEAN
EAST CHINA SEA
HOKKAIDO
HONSHU
SHIKOKU
KYUSHU
NAMPO-SHOTO
BONIN ISLANDS (OGASAWARA-GUNTO)
VOLCANO ISLANDS (KAZAN-RETTO)
RYUKYU ISLANDS
SAKISHIMA ISLANDS
AMAMI ISLANDS
OKINAWA ISLANDS
NANSEI SHOTO
TOKARA ISLANDS
TOKYO
Osaka
Kyoto
Kobe
Nagoya
Yokohama
Sapporo
Sendai
Hiroshima
Tropic of Cancer
Same scale as main map
Longitude 138° East of Greenwich

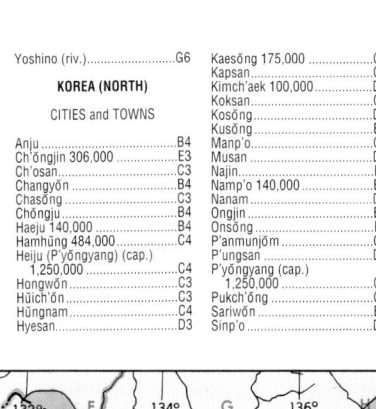

Philippines
POLYCONIC PROJECTION
SCALE OF MILES
0 10 20 40 60 80 100
SCALE OF KILOMETERS
0 25 50 75 100 150
Capitals of Countries
Provincial Capitals
Provincial Boundaries
© Copyright HAMMOND INCORPORATED, Maplewood, N. J.
Same scale as main map.
Taiwan (Formosa)
Bashi Channel
Y'Ami I.
BATANES
Itbayat I.
Diogo I.
Luzon Str.
Basco
BATAN IS.
Batan I.
Sabtang
Sabtang I.
PROV.
Balintang Is.
Balintang Channel
Babuyan I.
Calayan I.
Calayan
Dalupiri I.
BABUYAN IS.
Camiguin I.
Fuga I.
Babuyan Chan.
Claveria
Namuac
C. Engaño
Ballesteros
Aparri
Gonzaga
LUZON
BABUYAN IS.
Babuyan Chan.
Aparri
CAGAYAN
ILOCOS NORTE
Laoag
KALINGA-APAYAO
ABRA
Vigan
ILOCOS SUR
MOUNTAIN
IFUGAO
ISABELA
Tuguegarao
Palanan Bay
Palanan
LA UNION
San Fernando
BENGUET
Baguio
NUEVA VIZCAYA
QUIRINO
Lingayen Gulf
Dagupan
PANGASINAN
NUEVA ECIJA
TARLAC
ZAMBALES
PAMPANGA
BULACAN
BATAAN
Quezon City
Manila
Manila Bay
RIZAL
Cavite
CAVITE
LAGUNA
Lag. de Bay
BATANGAS
Batangas
Lucena
Lamon Bay
Polillo I.
Tayabas Bay
QUEZON
CAMARINES NORTE
CAMARINES SUR
Naga
Iriga
Mayon Vol.
Legazpi
ALBAY
CATANDUANES
SORSOGON
Sorsogon
San Bernardino Str.
Lubang Is.
Verde Island Pass.
Mindoro
OCC. MINDORO
OR. MINDORO
Calapan
MARINDUQUE
Boac
Sibuyan Sea
ROMBLON
Tablas
MASBATE
Masbate
NORTHERN SAMAR
WESTERN SAMAR
Catbalogan
Samar
EASTERN SAMAR
Borongan
Busuanga I.
CALAMIAN GROUP
Culion I.
Coron
Semirara Is.
AKLAN
Kalibo
CAPIZ
Roxas
Panay
ILOILO
Iloilo
ANTIQUE
Guimaras Str.
VISAYAN SEA
Biliran I.
LEYTE
Tacloban
Ormoc
Leyte Gulf
SOUTHERN LEYTE
CAMOTES SEA
Bacolod
NEGROS OCC.
NEGROS OR.
Negros
Dumaguete
CEBU
Cebu
BOHOL
Tagbilaran
SIQUIJOR
Siquijor I.
SURIGAO DEL NORTE
Surigao
Dinagat I.
Siargao I.
MINDANAO SEA
Butuan
AGUSAN DEL NORTE
AGUSAN DEL SUR
SURIGAO DEL SUR
CAMIGUIN
MISAMIS OR.
Cagayan de Oro
MISAMIS OCC.
Iligan
LANAO DEL NORTE
BUKIDNON
ZAMBOANGA DEL NORTE
Dipolog
MINDANAO
LANAO DEL SUR
ZAMBOANGA DEL SUR
Pagadian
Illana Bay
Cotabato
NORTH COTABATO
MAGUINDANAO
Moro Gulf
Zamboanga
Basilan Str.
Basilan I.
BASILAN
DAVAO
Davao
Davao Gulf
DAVAO ORIENTAL
Mati
SULTAN KUDARAT
SOUTH COTABATO
DAVAO DEL SUR
Gen. Santos
Sarangani Bay
Sarangani Is.
Pulau Miangas (Palmas)
KAWIO IS. (Indonesia)
Karakelong I. (Indonesia)
CELEBES SEA
SULU
Jolo I.
Jolo
Tapul Gr.
TAWI-TAWI
Sulu Archipelago
Pangutaran Group
Samales Gr.
TURTLE IS. (Tawi-Tawi Prov.)
Cagayan Sulu I. (Tawi-Tawi Prov.)
Sandakan
MALAYSIA
SABAH
Darvel Bay
Labuk Bay
Balabac I.
Balabac Str.
MANGSEE IS.
SULU SEA
Tubbataha Reefs
CAGAYAN IS.
Cagayancillo (Palawan Prov.)
Arena I.
Cavili I.
Palawan
PALAWAN
Puerto Princesa
Honda Bay
Victoria Pks. 5,666 ft. (1727 m.)
Cleopatra Needle 5,226 ft. (1593 m.)
Mt. Mantalingajan 6,739 ft. (2054 m.)
Brooke's Point
Dumaran I.
Taytay
CUYO ISLANDS
Cuyo
PALAWAN PASSAGE
SOUTH CHINA SEA
PACIFIC OCEAN
PHILIPPINE SEA
Mt. Apo 9,692 ft. (2954 m.)
Mt. Pulog
Mindoro Str.
Tablas Str.
N
Longitude 122° East of Greenwich
118°
120°
122°
124°
126°
18°
16°
14°
12°
10°
8°
6°

AREA 115,707 sq. mi. (299,681 sq. km.)
POPULATION 60,097,000
CAPITAL Manila
LARGEST CITY Manila
HIGHEST POINT Apo 9,692 ft. (2,954 m.)
MONETARY UNIT peso
MAJOR LANGUAGES Pilipino (Tagalog), English, Spanish, Bisayan, Ilocano, Bikol
MAJOR RELIGIONS Roman Catholicism, Islam, Protestantism, tribal religions

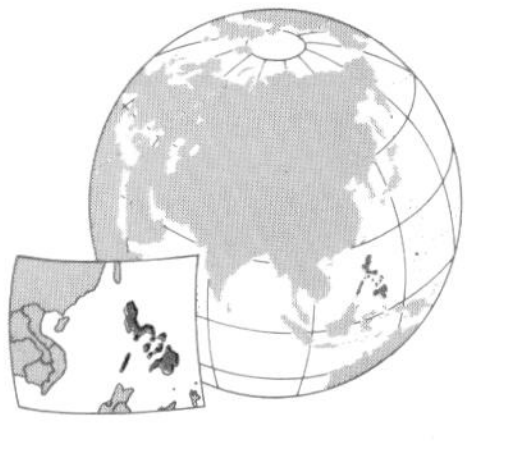

PROVINCES

Abra 160,198 . . . . . C2
Agusan del Norte 365,421 . . E6
Agusan del Sur 631,634 . . . . E6
Aklan 324,563 . . . . . D5
Albay 809,177 . . . . . D4
Antique 344,879 . . . . . D5
Aurora 107,145 . . . . . C3
Basilan 201,407 . . . . . D7
Bataan 323,254 . . . . . C3
Batanes 12,091 . . . . . A2
Batangas 1,174,201 . . . . . C4
Benguet 354,751 . . . . . C2
Bohol 806,031 . . . . . E6
Bukidnon 631,634 . . . . . E6
Bulacan 1,098,046 . . . . . C3
Cagayan 711,476 . . . . . C1
Camarines Norte 368,007 . . . D3
Camarines Sur 1,099,346 . . D4
Camiguin 57,126 . . . . . E6
Capiz 492,231 . . . . . D5
Catanduanes 175,247 . . . . . E4
Cavite 771,320 . . . . . C3
Cebu 2,091,602 . . . . . D5
Davao 725,153 . . . . . E7
Davao del Sur 1,133,599 . . . E7
Davao Oriental 339,931 . . . . . F7
Eastern Samar 320,637 . . . . E5
Ifugao 111,368 . . . . . C2
Ilocos Norte 390,666 . . . . . C1
Ilocos Sur 443,591 . . . . . C2
Iloilo 1,433,641 . . . . . D5
Isabela 870,604 . . . . . C2
Kalinga-Apayao 185,063 . . . . C1
Laguna 973,104 . . . . . C3
Lanao del Norte 461,049 . . . E6
Lanao del Sur 404,971 . . . . . E7
La Union 452,578 . . . . . C2
Leyte 1,302,648 . . . . . E5
Maguindanao 536,546 . . . . . E7
Manila 5,925,884 . . . . . C3
Marinduque 173,715 . . . . . C4
Masbate 584,526 . . . . . D4
Misamis Occidental 386,328 D6
Misamis Oriental 690,032 . . . E6
Mountain 103,052 . . . . . C2
National Capital Region (Manila) 5,925,884 . . . . . C3
Negros Occidental 1,930,301 . . . . . D6
Negros Oriental 819,399 . . . D6
North Cotabato 564,599 . . . . E7
Northern Samar 378,516 . . . E4
Nueva Ecija 1,069,409 . . . . . C3
Nueva Vizcaya 241,690 . . . . . C2
Occidental Mindoro 222,431 C4
Oriental Mindoro 448,938 . . . C4
Palawan 371,782 . . . . . B6
Pampanga 1,181,590 . . . . . C3
Pangasinan 1,636,057 . . . . . C3
Quezon 1,129,277 . . . . . C3
Quirino 83,230 . . . . . C2
Rizal 555,533 . . . . . C3
Romblon 193,174 . . . . . D4
Siquijor 70,300 . . . . . D6
Sorsogon 500,685 . . . . . E4
South Cotabato 770,473 . . . . E7
Southern Leyte 298,294 . . . . E5
Sultan Kudarat 303,784 . . . . E7
Sulu 360,588 . . . . . C7
Surigao del Norte 363,414 . . F5
Surigao del Sur 377,647 . . . . F6
Tarlac 638,457 . . . . . C3
Tawi-Tawi 194,651 . . . . . B8
Western Samar 501,439 . . . . E5
Zambales 444,037 . . . . . C3
Zamboanga del Norte 588,015 . . . . . D6
Zamboanga del Sur 1,183,845 . . . . . D7

CITIES and TOWNS

Angeles 188,834 . . . . . C3
Aparri 45,070 . . . . . C1
Bacolod 262,415 . . . . . D5
Bagac 13,109 . . . . . C3
Bago 99,631 . . . . . D5
Baguio 119,009 . . . . . C2
Balanga 39,132 . . . . . C3
Baler 18,349 . . . . . C3
Balimbing (Bato-Bato) 22,189 . . . . . C8
Bamban 26,072 . . . . . C3
Basco 4,341 . . . . . A2
Batangas 143,570 . . . . . C4
Bato-Bato 22,189 . . . . . C8
Baybay 74,640 . . . . . E5
Bislig 81,615 . . . . . F6
Boac 37,005 . . . . . C4
Bontoc 17,091 . . . . . C2
Burauen 48,058 . . . . . E5
Butuan 172,489 . . . . . E6
Cabanatuan 138,298 . . . . . C3
Cabarroquis 17,450 . . . . . C2
Cadiz 129,632 . . . . . D5
Cagayan de Oro 227,312 . . . E6
Calamba 121,175 . . . . . C3
Calbayog 106,719 . . . . . E4
Carigara 34,377 . . . . . E5
Cauayan 70,017 . . . . . D6
Cavite 87,666 . . . . . C3
Cebu 490,281 . . . . . D5
Cotabato 83,871 . . . . . D7
Dagupan 98,344 . . . . . C2
Davao 610,375 . . . . . E7
Digos 70,065 . . . . . E7
Escalante 71,293 . . . . . D5
General Santos 149,396 . . . . E7
Gingoog 79,937 . . . . . E6
Guihulngan 84,156 . . . . . D5
Guimba 58,847 . . . . . C3
Iba 22,791 . . . . . B3
Ilagan 79,336 . . . . . C2
Iligan 167,358 . . . . . E6
Iloilo 244,827 . . . . . D5
Infanta 27,914 . . . . . C3
Jaro 29,739 . . . . . E5
Jolo 52,429 . . . . . C8
Koronadal 80,566 . . . . . E7
Lagawe 15,075 . . . . . C2
Lapu-Lapu 98,723 . . . . . E5
Legazpi 99,766 . . . . . D4
Ligao 69,860 . . . . . D4
Lingayen 65,187 . . . . . C2
Lipa 121,166 . . . . . C4
Lucena 107,880 . . . . . C4
Maganoy 45,845 . . . . . E7
Mainit 18,078 . . . . . E6
Malabang 18,955 . . . . . D7
Malolos 95,699 . . . . . C3
Mandaue 110,590 . . . . . E5
Manila (cap.) 1,630,485 . . . . . C3
Mariveles 48,594 . . . . . C3
Mati 78,178 . . . . . F7
Naga 90,712 . . . . . D4
Olongapo 156,430 . . . . . C3
Ormoc 104,978 . . . . . E5
Ozamis 77,832 . . . . . D6
Pagadian 80,861 . . . . . D7
Palo 31,124 . . . . . E5
Palompon 40,242 . . . . . E5
Panabo 71,098 . . . . . E7
Prosperidad 33,824 . . . . . F6
Puerto Princesa 60,234 . . . . . B6
Quezon City 1,165,865 . . . . . C3
Romblon 24,251 . . . . . D4
Roxas 81,183 . . . . . D5
Sagay 99,118 . . . . . D5
San Antonio 42,969 . . . . . B3
San Carlos, Negros Occ. 91,627 . . . . . D5
San Carlos Pangasinan 101,243 . . . . . C3
San Fernando, La Union 68,410 . . . . . C2
San Fernando, Pampanga 110,891 . . . . . C3
San Jose 64,254 . . . . . C3
San Jose del Monte 90,732 . . C3
San Pablo ı31,655 . . . . . C3
Santa Fe 6,338 . . . . . C2
Santiago 69,877 . . . . . C2
Silay 111,131 . . . . . D5
Siquijor 17,533 . . . . . D6
Surigao 79,745 . . . . . E6
Tacloban 102,523 . . . . . E5
Tagaytay 16,322 . . . . . C3
Tagum 86,201 . . . . . E7
Tarlac 175,691 . . . . . C3
Toledo 91,668 . . . . . D5
Tuguegarao 73,507 . . . . . C2
Zamboanga 343,722 . . . . . C7

OTHER FEATURES

Agusan (riv.) E6
Alabat (isl.) D3
Apo (vol.) E7
Babuyan (isl.) B2
Balabac (isl.) A7
Balayan (bay) C4
Balintang (chan.) A2
Baloy (mt.) D5
Bantayan (isl.) D5
Banton (isl.) D4
Bashi (chan.) A1
Basilan (isl.) D7
Batan, Albay (isl.) E4
Batan, Batanes (isl.) B2
Batan (isls.) A2
Bay, Laguna de (lake) C3
Biliran (isl.) E5
Bohol (isl.) E6
Bojeador (cape) C1
Borocay (isl.) D5
Bucas Grande (isl.) F6
Bugsuk (isl.) A6
Bulilluyan (cape) A6
Bunga (pt.) E4
Burias (isl.) D4
Busuanga (isl.) B4
Cabalasan (mt.) E5
Cabulauan (isls.) C5
Cagayan (isls.) C6
Cagayan (riv.) C2
Cagayan Sulu (isl.) B7
Cagua (vol.) D1
Calagua (isls.) D3
Calamian Group (isls.) B4
Calayan (isl.) A2
Calicoan (isl.) E5
Camiguin, Cagayan (isl.) . . . B3
Camiguin, Camiguin (isl.) . . . E6
Camotes (isls.) E5
Camotes (sea) E5
Canigao (chan.) E5
Canlaon (peak) D5
Capotoan (mt.) E4
Carabao (isl.) D4
Catanduanes (isl.) E4
Cebu (isl.) D5
Celebes (sea) D8
Cleopatra Needle (mt.) B5
Coron (isl.) C5
Corregidor (isl.) C3
Culion (isl.) B5
Cuyo (isl.) C5
Cuyo (isls.) C5
Daram (isl.) E5
Davao (gulf) E7
Dinagat (isl.) E5
Diuata (mts.) E6
Dumanquilas (bay) D7
Dumaran (isl.) C5
Engaño (cape) D1
Espiritu Santo (cape) E4
Fuga (isl.) A3
Guimaras (isl.) D5
Halcon (mt.) C4
Hibuson (isl.) E5
Homonhon (isl.) E5
Honda (bay) B6
Iligan (bay) E6
Ilin (isl.) C4
Illana (bay) D7
Imuruan (bay) B5
Island (bay) B6
Itbayat (isl.) A2
Jintotolo (chan.) D5
Jolo (isl.) C7
Jomalig (isl.) D3
Lagonoy (gulf) E4
Lamon (bay) C3
Lanao (lake) E7
Laparan (isls.) B8
Lapinin (isl.) E5
Leyte (gulf) E5
Leyte (isl.) E5
Limasawa (isl.) E6
Linapacan (isl.) B5
Lingayen (gulf) C2
Lubang (isls.) B4
Luzon (isl.) C3
Luzon (str.) A2
Macajalar (bay) E6
Malindang (mt.) D6
Mangsee (isls.) A7
Manila (bay) C3
Mantalingajan (mt.) A6
Maqueda (chan.) D3
Maraira (pt.) C1
Marinduque (isl.) C4
Masbate (isl.) D4
Mayon (vol.) D4
Maytiguid (isl.) B5
Mindanao (isl.) D7
Mindanao (riv.) E7
Mindoro (isl.) C4
Mindoro (str.) C4
Mompog (passg.) D4
Moro (gulf) D7
Mount Apo National Park . . . E7
Naso (pt.) C5
Negros (isl.) D6
Olutanga (isl.) D7
Pacsan (mt.) C2
Palawan (isl.) B6
Palawan (passg.) A6
Panaon (isl.) E5
Panay (isl.) D5
Panglao (isl.) D6
Pangutaran (isl.) C7
Pangutaran Group (isls.) . . . C7
Patnanongan (isl.) D3
Philippine (sea) D3
Pilas (isl.) C7
Pinatubo (mt.) C3
Polillo (isl.) C3
Pujada (bay) F7
Pulangi (riv.) E7
Ragang (vol.) E7
Ragay (gulf) D4
Rapu-Rapu (isl.) E4
Romblon (isl.) D4
Sabtang (isl.) B2
Sacol (isl.) D7
Samal (isl.) E7
Samales Group (isls.) D7
Samar (isl.) E5
Samar (sea) E4
San Agustin (cape) F7
San Bernardino (str.) E4
San Miguel (bay) D3
San Pedro (bay) E5
Santo Tomas (mt.) C2
Semirara (isls.) C5
Siargao (isl.) F6
Sibay (isl.) C5
Sibuguey (bay) D7
Sibutu Group (isls.) B8
Sibuyan (isl.) D4
Sibuyan (sea) D4
Sierra Madre (mt.) D2
Simunul (isl.) B8
Siquijor (isl.) D6
South China (sea) B3
Subic (bay) C3
Sulu (arch.) B8
Sulu (sea) B6
Suluan (isl.) F5
Surigao (str.) E6
Taal (lake) C4
Tablas (isl.) D4
Tablas (str.) C4
Tagapula (isl.) E4
Tagolo (pt.) D6
Tanon (str.) D6
Tapul (isl.) C8
Tapul Group (isls.) C8
Tara (isl.) C4
Tawi-Tawi (isl.) B8
Tayabas (bay) C4
Ticao (isl.) D4
Tinaca (pt.) E8
Tongquil (isl.) D8
Tumindao (isl.) B8
Turtle (isls.) B7
Verde Island (passg.) C4
Victoria (peaks) B6
Visayan (sea) D5

Topography

0 100 200 MI.
0 100 200 KM.
BABUYAN IS.
C. Engaño
Luzon
C. Bolinao
Lingayen Gulf
PHILIPPINE
SEA
Manila
Bataan Pen.
Manila Bay
Lamon Bay
Catanduanes
Mindoro
Marinduque
Sibuyan Sea
Busuanga
CALAMIAN GROUP
Masbate
Samar Sea
Samar
Visayan Sea
Panay
Leyte
Leyte Gulf
Cebu
Negros
Bohol
Palawan
SULU SEA
Mindanao Sea
Mindanao
Balabac
Moro Gulf
Davao Gulf
Basilan
Jolo
SULU ARCH.
Tawi-Tawi
Tinaca Pt.
Below Sea Level
100 m. 328 ft.
200 m. 656 ft.
500 m. 1,640 ft.
1,000 m. 3,281 ft.
2,000 m. 6,562 ft.
5,000 m. 16,404 ft.

Agriculture, Industry and Resources

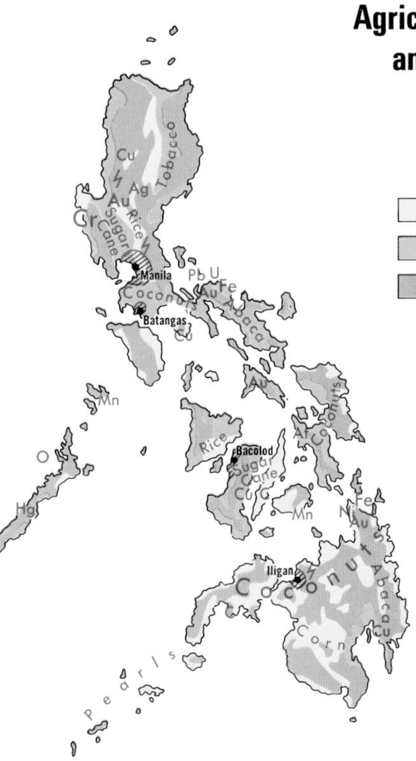

Cu
Ag
Tobacco
Au
Rice
Sugar Cane
Cr
Manila
Pb U
Fe
Coconuts
Batangas
Mn
O
Rice
Bacolod
Sugar Cane
Hg
Iligan
Coconuts
Abaca
Corn
Pearls

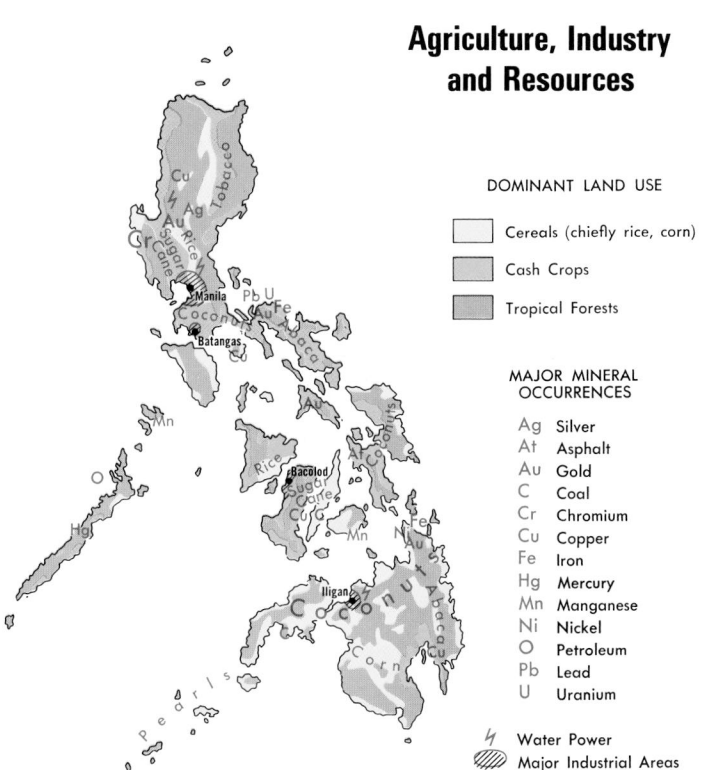

DOMINANT LAND USE

Cereals (chiefly rice, corn)
Cash Crops
Tropical Forests

MAJOR MINERAL OCCURRENCES

Ag Silver
At Asphalt
Au Gold
C Coal
Cr Chromium
Cu Copper
Fe Iron
Hg Mercury
Mn Manganese
Ni Nickel
O Petroleum
Pb Lead
U Uranium

Water Power
Major Industrial Areas

BRUNEI

CITIES and TOWNS

Bandar Seri Begawan 63,868 E4
Seria 23,511 E5

INDONESIA

CITIES and TOWNS

Adaut J7
Agats K7
Ambon (Amboina) 208,898 H6
Amuntai F6
Amurang G5
Atambua G7
Aubá H7
Baa G8
Bagansiapiapi C5
Balikpapan 280,675 F6
Banda Aceh 72,090 A4
Bandanaira H6
Bandung 1,462,637 H2
Banggai G6
Banjarmasin 381,286 E6
Banyumas J2
Batang J2
Batavia (Jakarta) (cap.) 6,503,449 H1
Baukau H7
Bekasi H2
Belawan B5
Bengkulu 64,783 C6
Beo H5
Biak K6
Binjai 76,464 B5
Bintuhan C6
Blitar 78,503 K2
Bogor 247,409 H2
Bojonegoro J2
Bukittinggi 70,771 B6
Bula J6
Bulukumba G7
Buntok F6
Cianjur H2
Cimahi H2
Cirebon 223,776 H2
Demta L6
Denpasar E7
Dili H7
Djambi (Jambi) 230,373 C6
Djokjakarta (Yogyakarta) 398,727 J2
Dobo J7
Donggala F6
Enaratoli K6
Ende G7
Fakfak J6
Garut H2
Gorontalo 97,628 G5
Hollandia (Jayapura) K6
Indramayu H2
Jailolo H5
Jakarta (cap.) 6,503,449 H1
Jambi 230,373 C6
Jayapura (Hollandia) K6
Jogjakarta (Yogyakarta) 398,727 J2
Jombang K2
Kaimana J6
Kampung Baru (Tolitoli) G5
Kediri 221,820 K2
Kendari G6
Kepi K7
Ketapang E6
Kokonau K6
Kolonodale G6
Kotabaharu E6
Kotabaru F6
Kotawaringin E6
Kragen K2
Kupang G8
Kutaraja (Banda Aceh) 72,090 A4
Labuha H6
Labuhan G2
Laiwui H6
Larantuka G7
Lekitobi G6
Longiram F5
Madiun 150,562 K2
Magelang 123,484 J2
Majalengka H2
Makassar (Ujung Pandang) 709,038 F7
Malang 511,780 K2
Malili G6
Manado 217,159 G5
Manokwari J6
Maumere G7
Medan 1,378,955 B5
Menggala D6
Merauke K7
Mindiptana L7
Mojokerto 68,849 K2
Muarasiberut B6
Nangatayap E6
Pacitan J2
Padang 480,922 B6
Padangpanjang 34,517 B6
Padangsidempuan B5
Pakanbaru 186,262 C5
Palangkaraya 60,447 E6
Palembang 787,187 D6
Pangkalanbuun E6
Pangkalpinang 90,096 D6
Parepare 86,450 F6
Pasangkayu F6
Pasuruan 95,864 K2
Payakumbuh 78,836 C6
Pekalongan 132,558 J2
Pemalang J2
Pematangsiantar 150,376 B5
Pinrang F6
Plaju D6
Pontianak 304,778 D6
Probolinggo 100,296 K2
Purbolinggo J2
Raha G6
Rantauprapat C5
Rembang K2
Sabang, Celebes F5
Sabang, Weh 23,821 B4
Salatiga 85,849 J2
Samarinda 264,718 F6
Sampit E6
Sarmi K6
Sawahlunto 13,561 C6
Seba G8
Semarang 1,026,671 J2
Semitau E5
Serui K6
Sibolga 59,897 B5
Sigli B4
Sinabang B5
Singaraja F7
Solo (Surakarta) 469,888 J2
Solok 31,724 C6
Sorong J6
Sragen J2
Subang H2
Sukabumi 109,994 H2
Sumbawa Besar F7
Sumedang H2
Surabaya 2,027,913 K2
Surakarta 469,888 J2
Tanahmerah K7
Tanjungbalai 41,894 C5
Tanjungkarang 284,275 D7
Tanjungpinang C5
Tanjungselor F5
Tarakan F5
Tebingtinggi 92,087 B5
Tegal 131,728 J2
Telukbayur C6
Tepa H7
Terempa D5
Tjilatjap (Cilicap) H2
Tjirebon (Cirebon) 223,776 H2
Tolitoli G5
Tuban K2
Ujung Pandang 709,038 F7
Vikeke H7
Wahai H6
Waigama H6
Wajabula H5
Waren K6
Weda H5
Wonreli H7
Yogyakarta 398,727 J2

OTHER FEATURES

Anambas (isls.) 29,572 D5
Arafura (sea) J8
Aru (isls.) 34,195 K7
Babar (isl.) H7
Bali (isl.) 2,074,438 F7
Banda (sea) H7
Banggai (arch.) 169,025 G6
Bangka (isl.) 298,017 D6
Banyak (isls.) 1,980 B5
Barisan (mts.) C6
Barito (riv.) E6
Batu (isls.) 16,390 B6
Bawean (isl.) 64,551 K1
Belitung (Billiton) (isl.) 128,694 D6
Berau (bay) J6
Biak (isl.) K6
Billiton (isl.) 128,694 D6
Binongko (isl.) 11,549 G7
Bone (gulf) G7
Borneo (isl.) E5
Bosch, van den (cape) J6
Bunguran (Great Natuna) (isl.) D5
Buru (isl.) 23,034 H6
Butung (isl.) 188,173 G6
Celebes (Sulawesi) (isl.) 7,732,383 G5
Celebes (sea) G5
Cenderawasih (bay) K6
Dampier (str.) J6
Digul (riv.) K7
Doberai (pen.) J6
Enggano (isl.) 1,082 C7
Ewab (Kai) (isls.) 108,328 J7
Flores (isl.) 860,328 G7
Flores (sea) F7
Frederik Hendrik (Kolepom) (isl.) K7
Geelvink (Cenderawasih) (bay) K6
Great Kai (isl.) 38,748 J7
Halmahera (isl.) 122,521 H5
Irian Jaya (reg.) 923,440 J6
Jambuair (cape) B4
Jamursba (cape) J5
Java (head) C7
Java (isl.) 73,712,411 J2
Java (sea) D6
Jaya, Puncak (mt.) K6
Jayawijaya (range) K6
Jemaja (isl.) 5,628 D5
Kabaena (isl.) G7
Kai (isls.) 108,328 J7
Kalao (isl.) G7
Kalaotoa (isl.) G7
Kalimantan (reg.) 4,956,865 E5
Kangean (isl.) F7
Kapuas (riv.) D6
Karakelong (isl.) H5
Karimata (arch.) 9,398 D6
Karimunjawa (isls.) 5,025 J1
Kerinci (mt.) C6
Kisar (isl.) H7
Komodo (isl.) 30,407 F7
Krakatau (Rakata) (isl.) C7
Laut (isl.) 55,711 F6
Leuser (mt.) B5
Lingga (arch.) 46,658 D6
Lingga (isl.) 18,027 D6
Lombok (isl.) 1,581,193 F7
Madura (isl.) 1,509,774 K2
Mahakam (riv.) F6
Makassar (str.) F6
Malacca (str.) C5
Mamberamo (riv.) K6
Maoke (mts.) K6
Mapia (isls.) J5
Mentawai (isls.) 30,107 B6
Misool (isl.) J6
Molucca (sea) H6
Moluccas (isls.) 944,240 H6
Morotai (isl.) 27,333 H5
Muli (str.) K7
Müller (mts.) E5
Muna (isl.) 156,186 G7
Musi (riv.) C6
Natuna (isls.) 23,893 D5
Ngunju (cape) F8
Nias (isl.) 356,093 B5
Numfoor (isl.) J6
Obi (isls.) 12,437 H6
Ombai (str.) H7
Pantar (isl.) 28,259 G7
Perkam (cape) K6
Puting, Borneo (cape) E6
Puting, Sumatra (cape) C7
Raja Ampat Group (isls.) H6
Rakata (isl.) C7
Rantekombola (mt.) F6
Raya (mt.) E6
Riau (arch.) 483,230 C5
Rokan (riv.) C5
Roti (isl.) 76,270 G8
Salawati (isl.) J6
Sangihe (isl.) H5
Sangihe (isls.) 183,000 G5
Sawu (isls.) 51,002 G8
Sawu (sea) G8
Schouten (isls.) 110,148 K6
Schwaner (mts.) E6
Sebuku (bay) F5
Selatan (cape) E6
Selayar (isl.) 92,342 G7
Semeru (mt.) K2
Siau (isl.) 46,801 H5
Siberut (str.) B6
Simeulue (isl.) 29,147 A5
Singkep (isl.) 28,631 D6
Sipura (isl.) 6,051 B6
Slamet (mt.) J2
Sorikmerapi (mt.) B5
South Natuna (isls.) D5
Sudirman (range) K6
Sula (isls.) 36,922 H6
Sulawesi (isl.) 7,732,383 G6
Sumatra (isl.) 19,360,400 B5
Sumba (isl.) 291,190 F7
Sumba (str.) F7
Sumbawa (isl.) 621,140 F7
Sunda (str.) C7
Tahulandang (isl.) 21,493 H5
Talaud (isls.) 46,395 H5
Taliabu (isl.) 18,303 G6
Tambelan (isls.) 4,032 D5
Tanimbar (isls.) 55,405 J7
Tariku (riv.) K6
Tidore (isl.) 28,655 H5
Timor (reg.) 1,435,527 H7
Timor (sea) H7
Toba (lake) B5
Tolo (gulf) G6
Tomini (gulf) G6
Tukangbesi (isls.) 73,106 G7
Vals (cape) K7
Vogelkop (Doberai) (pen.) J6
Waigeo (isl.) J5
Wakde (isl.) K6
Wangiwangi (isl.) 28,469 G7
We (isl.) B4
Wetar (isl.) H7
Yapen (isl.) 50,888 K6

MALAYSIA

STATES

North Borneo (Sabah) 1,002,608 F3
Sarawak 1,294,753 E5

CITIES and TOWNS

Beaufort 2,709 F4
Bintulu 4,424 E5
Kabong E5
Kampong Sibuti E5
Kapit 1,929 E5
Keningau 2,037 F4
Kota Kinabalu 40,939 F4
Kuching 63,535 E5
Kudat 5,089 F4
Labuan 7,216 E4
Lahad Datu 5,169 F5
Lamag F4
Marudi 4,700 E5
Miri 35,702 E5
Mukah 1,717 E5

Topography

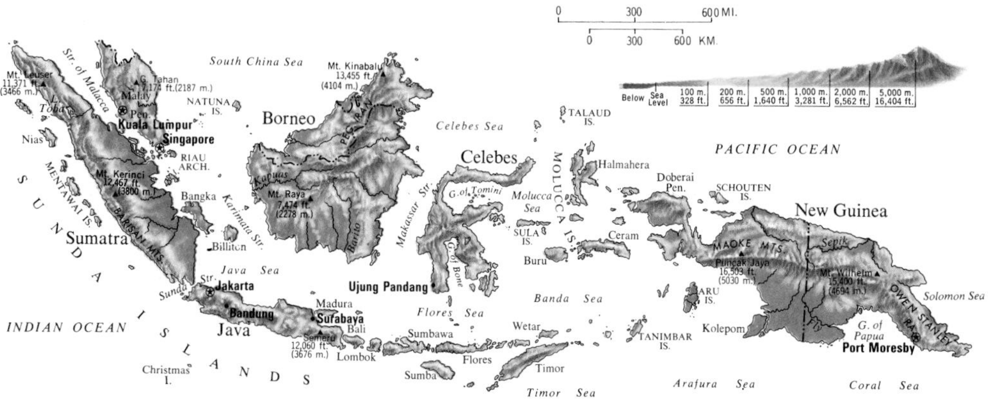
0 300 600 MI.
0 300 600 KM.
Below Sea Level
100 m. 328 ft.
200 m. 656 ft.
500 m. 1,640 ft.
1,000 m. 3,281 ft.
2,000 m. 6,562 ft.
5,000 m. 16,404 ft.
South China Sea
Mt. Kinabalu 13,455 ft. (4104 m.)
Borneo
Celebes Sea
TALAUD IS.
PACIFIC OCEAN
Celebes
Halmahera
Molucca Sea
MOLUCCA IS.
Doberai Pen.
SCHOUTEN IS.
New Guinea
Kuala Lumpur
Singapore
RIAU ARCH.
NATUNA IS.
Mt. Leuser 11,371 ft. (3466 m.)
Toba
Nias
Str. of Malacca
Mt. Kerinci 12,467 ft. (3800 m.)
Bangka
Karimata Str.
Mt. Raya 7,474 ft. (2278 m.)
Makassar Str.
G. of Tomini
Sula Is.
Buru
Ceram
MAOKE MTS.
Puncak Jaya 16,503 ft. (5030 m.)
Mt. Wilhelm 15,400 ft. (4694 m.)
OWEN STANLEY
Sumatra
Billiton
MENTAWAI IS.
BARISAN MTS.
Java Sea
Jakarta
Ujung Pandang
G. of Bone
Banda Sea
ARU IS.
Solomon Sea
Bandung
Surabaya
Madura
Bali
Java
Semeru 12,060 ft. (3676 m.)
Lombok
Flores Sea
Sumbawa
Wetar
Flores
Timor
Sumba
TANIMBAR IS.
Kolepom
G. of Papua
Port Moresby
INDIAN OCEAN
SUNDA ISLANDS
Christmas I.
Timor Sea
Arafura Sea
Coral Sea

Agriculture, Industry and Resources

Pearls
Singapore
Jakarta
Rubber
Rice
Millet
Spices
Coconuts
Coffee
Tea
Tobacco
Corn
Sugar cane
Turtles
Cu
Au
Sn
Mn
Fe
Al
Ni
G

DOMINANT LAND USE

Cereals (chiefly rice, corn)
Diversified Tropical Crops
Forests

MAJOR MINERAL OCCURRENCES

Al Bauxite	Cu Copper	Mn Manganese	O Petroleum
Au Gold	Fe Iron Ore	Ni Nickel	Sn Tin
C Coal	G Natural Gas		

Major Industrial Areas

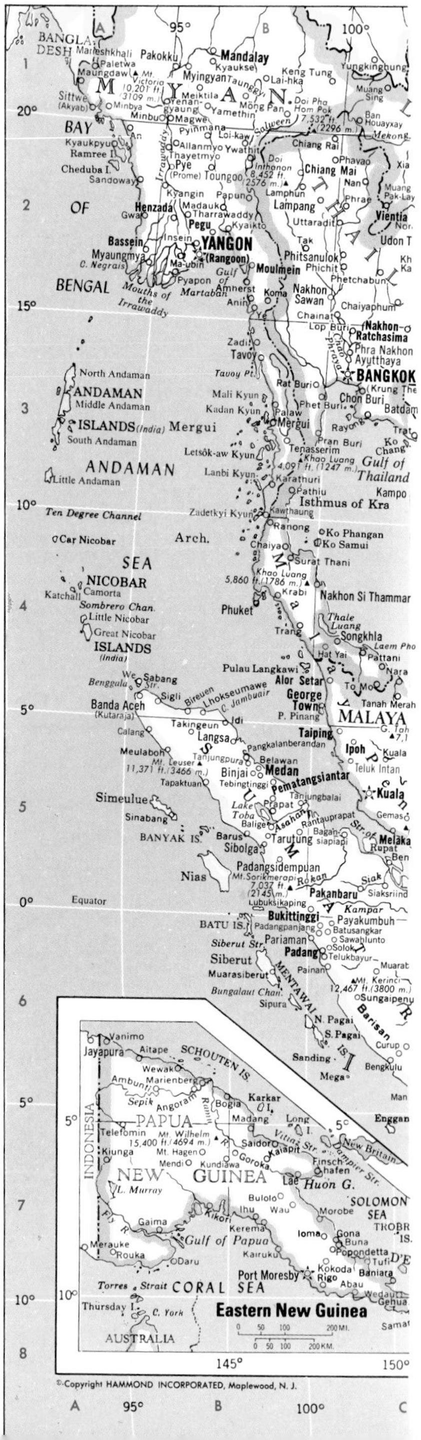
BANGLADESH
Mandalay
Myingyan
Meiktila
BAY OF BENGAL
Ramree I.
Cheduba I.
Sandoway
Henzada
Bassein
YANGON (Rangoon)
Pegu
Moulmein
Gulf of Martaban
Mouths of the Irrawaddy
North Andaman
ANDAMAN ISLANDS (India)
Middle Andaman
South Andaman
Little Andaman
ANDAMAN SEA
Ten Degree Channel
Car Nicobar
NICOBAR ISLANDS (India)
Great Nicobar
Mergui
Mergui Arch.
BANGKOK
Chiang Mai
Nakhon Ratchasima
Gulf of Thailand
Isthmus of Kra
Phuket
Songkhla
Alor Setar
George Town
MALAYA
Ipoh
Teluk Intan
Kuala
Banda Aceh
Medan
Pematangsiantar
Tebingtinggi
Tanjungbalai
Lake Toba
Simeulue
Sinabang
BANYAK IS.
Sibolga
Padangsidempuan
Nias
Pakanbaru
Equator
Bukittinggi
Payakumbuh
Padang
BATU IS.
Siberut
Muarasiberut
MENTAWAI IS.
Sipura
N. Pagai
S. Pagai
Barisan
Mt. Kerinci 12,467 ft. (3800 m.)
Eastern New Guinea
Jayapura
Aitape
SCHOUTEN IS.
Wewak
Sepik
PAPUA NEW GUINEA
Madang
Mt. Wilhelm 15,400 ft. (4694 m.)
Lae
Huon G.
New Britain
SOLOMON SEA
TROBRIAND IS.
Gulf of Papua
Port Moresby
Torres Strait
CORAL SEA
AUSTRALIA
INDONESIA
Merauke
0 50 100 200 MI.
0 50 100 200 KM.

Papar 1,855 . . . . . F4
Ranau 2,024 . . . . . F4
Sandakan 42,413 . . . . . F4
Sematan D5
Semporna 3,371 . . . . . F5
Serian 2,209 . . . . . E5
Sibu 50,635 . . . . . E5
Simanggang 8,445 . . . . . E5
Suai E5
Tawau 24,247 . . . . . F5
Weston F4

OTHER FEATURES

Balambangan (isl.) F4
Banggi (isl.) F4
Iran (mts.) E5
Kinabalu (mt.) F4
Labuan (isl.) 17,189 . . . . . E4
Labuk (bay) F4
Rajang (riv.) E5
Sirik (cape) E5

PAPUA NEW GUINEA

CITIES and TOWNS

Abau C7
Aitape 3,368 . . . . . B6
Ambunti 1,035 . . . . . B6
Angoram 1,846 . . . . . B6
Baniara C7
Bogia 755 . . . . . B6
Bulolo 6,730 . . . . . B7
Buna C7
Daru 7,127 . . . . . B7
Finschhaffen 756 . . . . . C7
Gaima B7
Gehua C8
Gona C7
Goroka 18,511 . . . . . B7
Ihu 541 . . . . . B7
Ioma C7
Kaiapit 515 . . . . . B7
Kairuku B7
Kerema 3,389 . . . . . B7
Kikori 763 . . . . . B7
Kiunga 1,407 . . . . . B7
Kokoda C7
Kundiawa 4,299 . . . . . B7
Lae 61,617 . . . . . B7
Madang 21,335 . . . . . B7
Marienberg B6
Mendi 4,130 . . . . . B7
Morobe C7
Mount Hagen 13,441 . . . . . B7
Popondetta 6,429 . . . . . C7
Port Moresby (cap.) 123,624 . . . . . B7
Rouka B7
Saidor 500 . . . . . B7
Samarai 864 . . . . . C8
Telefomin B7
Vanimo 3,071 . . . . . B6
Wau 2,349 . . . . . B7
Wedau C7
Wewak 19,890 . . . . . B6

OTHER FEATURES

Dampier (str.) C7
D'Entrecasteaux (isls.) C7
Fly (riv.) A7
Huon (gulf) C7
Karkar (isl.) B6
Kiriwina (isl.) C7
Long (isl.) B7
Louisiade (arch.) D8
Milne (bay) C8
Misima (isl.) C8
New Britain (isl.) 148,773 . . . . . C7
Ramu (riv.) B7
Rossel (isl.) D8
Schouten (isls.) B6
Sepik (riv.) B6
Solomon (sea) C7
Tagula (isl.) C8
Torres (str.) A7
Trobriand (isls.) C7
Vitiaz (str.) B7
Woodlark (isl.) C7

★See page 74 for other Malaysian entries.

INDONESIA

AREA 788,430 sq. mi. (2,042,034 sq. km.)
POPULATION 179,136,000
CAPITAL Jakarta
LARGEST CITY Jakarta
HIGHEST POINT Puncak Jaya 16,503 ft. (5,030 m.)
MONETARY UNIT rupiah
MAJOR LANGUAGES Bahasa Indonesia, Indonesian and Papuan languages, English
MAJOR RELIGIONS Islam, tribal religions, Christianity, Hinduism

PAPUA NEW GUINEA

AREA 183,540 sq. mi. (475,369 sq. km.)
POPULATION 3,593,000
CAPITAL Port Moresby
LARGEST CITY Port Moresby
HIGHEST POINT Mt. Wilhelm 15,400 ft. (4,694 m.)
MONETARY UNIT kina
MAJOR LANGUAGES pidgin English, Hiri Motu, English
MAJOR RELIGIONS Tribal religions, Christianity

BRUNEI

AREA 2,226 sq. mi. (5,765 sq. km.)
POPULATION 249,000
CAPITAL Bandar Seri Begawan
LARGEST CITY Bandar Seri Begawan
HIGHEST POINT Pagon 6,070 ft. (1,850 m.)
MONETARY UNIT Brunei Dollar
MAJOR LANGUAGES Malay, English, Chinese
MAJOR RELIGIONS Islam, Buddhism, Christianity, tribal religions

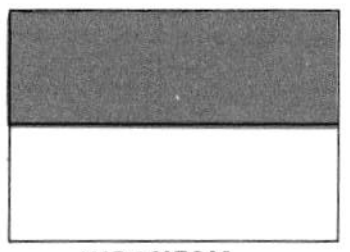
INDONESIA

PAPUA NEW GUINEA

BRUNEI

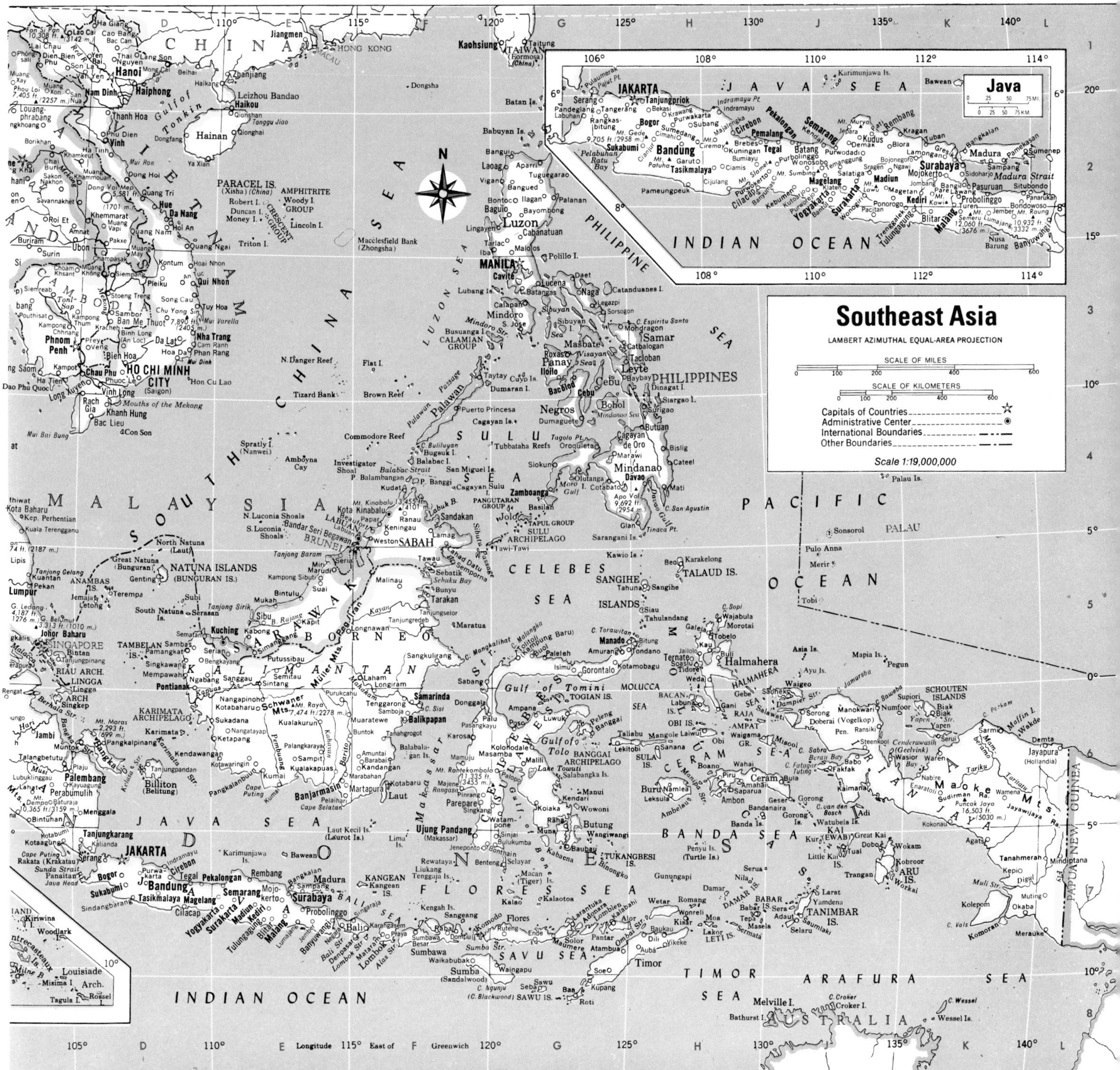
Southeast Asia
LAMBERT AZIMUTHAL EQUAL-AREA PROJECTION
SCALE OF MILES
SCALE OF KILOMETERS
Capitals of Countries
Administrative Center
International Boundaries
Other Boundaries
Scale 1:19,000,000
Java
INDIAN OCEAN
SOUTH CHINA SEA
PACIFIC OCEAN
PHILIPPINES
MALAYSIA
INDONESIA
CHINA
VIETNAM
JAVA SEA
CELEBES SEA
BANDA SEA
FLORES SEA
ARAFURA SEA
TIMOR SEA
SULU SEA
AUSTRALIA
Longitude 115° East of Greenwich

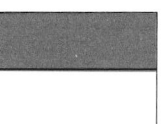

FIJI

AREA 7,055 sq. mi. (18,272 sq. km.)
POPULATION 792,441
CAPITAL Suva
LARGEST CITY Suva
HIGHEST POINT Tomaniivi 4,341 ft. (1,323 m.)
MONETARY UNIT Fijian dollar
MAJOR LANGUAGES Fijian, Hindi, English
MAJOR RELIGIONS Protestantism, Hinduism

KIRIBATI

AREA 277 sq. mi. (717 sq. km.)
POPULATION 82,449
CAPITAL Tarawa
HIGHEST POINT (on Banaba I.) 285 ft. (87 m.)
MONETARY UNIT Australian dollar
MAJOR LANGUAGES I-Kiribati, English
MAJOR RELIGIONS Protestantism, Roman Catholicism

NAURU

AREA 7.7 sq. mi. (20 sq. km.)
POPULATION 10,390
CAPITAL Yaren (district)
MONETARY UNIT Australian dollar
MAJOR LANGUAGES Nauruan, English
MAJOR RELIGION Protestantism

MARSHALL ISLANDS

AREA 70 sq. mi. (181 sq. km.)
POPULATION 60,652
CAPITAL Majuro
MONETARY UNIT U.S. dollar
MAJOR LANGUAGES English, Marshallese, Japanese
MAJOR RELIGION Protestantism

SOLOMON ISLANDS

AREA 11,500 sq. mi. (29,785 sq. km.)
POPULATION 386,000
CAPITAL Honiara
LARGEST CITY Honiara
HIGHEST POINT Mount Popomanatseu 7,647 ft. (2,331 m.)
MONETARY UNIT Solomon Islands dollar
MAJOR LANGUAGES English, pidgin English, Melanesian dialects
MAJOR RELIGIONS Tribal religions, Protestantism, Roman Catholicism

TONGA

AREA 289 sq. mi. (748 sq. km.)
POPULATION 105,000
CAPITAL Nuku'alofa
HIGHEST POINT Kao Island 3,389 ft. (1,033 m.)
MONETARY UNIT pa'anga
MAJOR LANGUAGES Tongan, English
MAJOR RELIGION Protestantism

TUVALU

AREA 9.78 sq. mi. (25.33 sq. km.)
POPULATION 10,000
CAPITAL Funafuti
MONETARY UNIT Australian dollar
MAJOR LANGUAGES English, Tuvaluan
MAJOR RELIGION Protestantism

MICRONESIA

AREA 271 sq. mi. (702 sq. km.)
POPULATION 122,950
CAPITAL Palikir
MONETARY UNIT U.S. dollar
MAJOR LANGUAGES English, Trukese, Pohnpeian, Yapese, Kosrean
MAJOR RELIGIONS Roman Catholicism, Protestantism

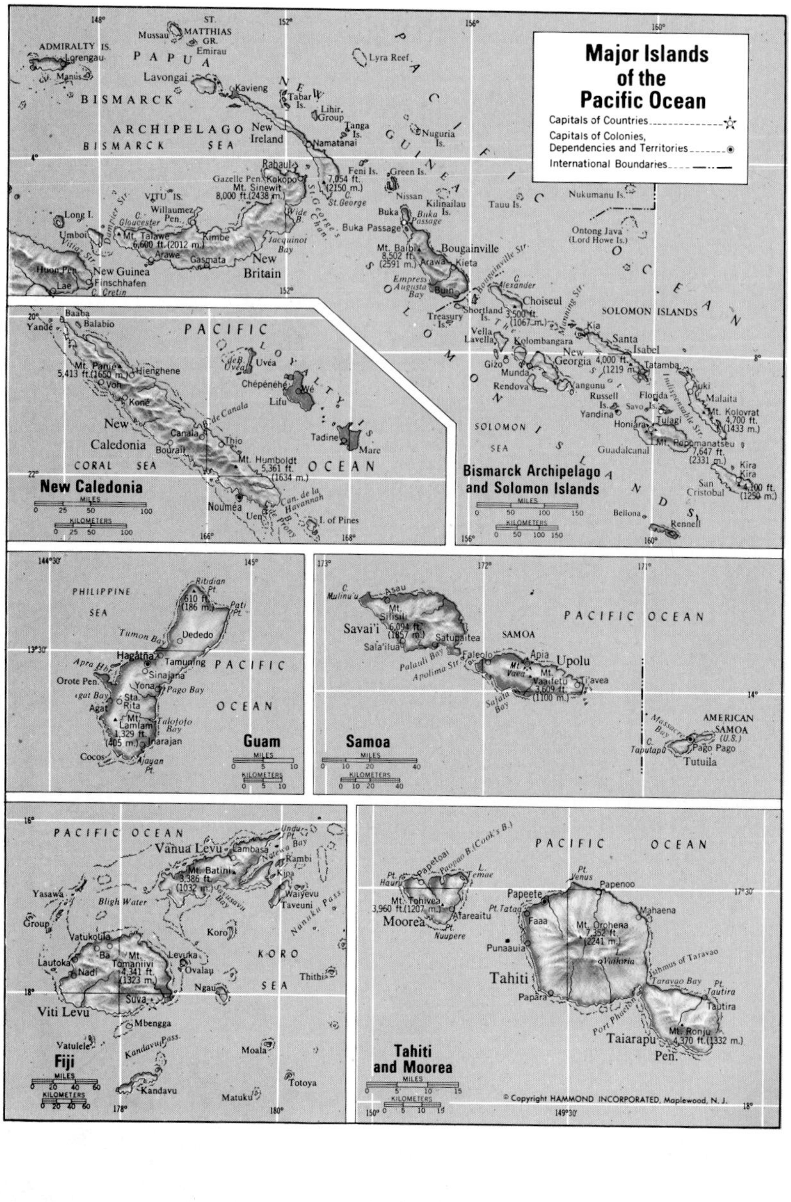
Major Islands of the Pacific Ocean
Capitals of Countries
Capitals of Colonies, Dependencies and Territories
International Boundaries
Bismarck Archipelago and Solomon Islands
New Caledonia
Guam
Samoa
Fiji
Tahiti and Moorea
© Copyright HAMMOND INCORPORATED, Maplewood, N. J.

Abaiang (atoll) 3,296 ....H 5
Abemama (atoll) 2,300 ....H 5
Adamstown (cap.), Pitcairn Is. 54 ....N 8
Admiralty (isls.) ....E 6
Agrihan (isl.) ....E 4
Ailinglapalap (atoll) 1,385 .....G 5
Ailuk (atoll) 413 ....H 4
Aitutaki (atoll) 2,348 ....K 7
Alofi (cap.), Niue 960 ....K 7
Alotau 4,310 ....E 7
Ambrym (isl.) 6,324 ....G 7
American Samoa 32,297 ......J 7
Anaa (atoll) 444 ....M 7
Angaur (isl.) 243 ....D 5
Apataki (atoll) ....M 7
Apia (cap.), Samoa 33,100 ....J 7
Arno (atoll) 1,487 ....H 5
Arorae (atoll) 1,626 ....H 6
Atafu (atoll) 577 ....J 6
Atiu (isl.) 1,225 ....L 8
Austral (isls.) 5,208 ....L 8
Avarua (cap.), Cook Is. ....L 8
Babelthuab (isl.) 10,391 ......D 5
Baker (isl.) ....J 5
Banaba (isl.) 2,314 ....G 6
Banks (isls.) 3,158 ....G 7
Belep (isls.) 624 ....G 7
Bellona (reefs) ....G 8
Beru (atoll) 2,318 ....H 6
Bikini (atoll) ....G 4
Bismarck (arch.) 218,339 .....E 6
Bonin (isls.) 1,879 ....E 3
Bora-Bora (isl.) 2,572 ....L 7
Bougainville (isl.) 71,761 ......F 6
Bounty (isls.) H10
Bourail 3,149 ....G 8
Butaritari (atoll) 2,971 ....H 5
Caroline (isl.) ....M 7
Caroline (isls.) ....E 5
Chichi (isl.) 1,879 ....E 3
Choiseul (isl.) 10,349 ....F 6
Christmas (Kiritimati) (isl.) 674 .L 5
Cook (isls.) 17,695 ....K 7
Coral (sea) ....F 7
Danger (Pukapuka) (atoll) 797 ....K 7
Daru 7,127 ....E 6
Disappointment (isls.) 373 ....N 7
Ducie (isl.) ....O 8
Easter (isl.) 1,598 ....Q 8
Ebon (atoll) 887 ....G 5
Efate (isl.) 18,038 ....G 7
Enderbury (isl.) ....J 6
Enewetak (Eniwetok) (atoll) 542 ....G 4
Erromanga (isl.) 945 ....H 7
Espiritu Santo (isl.) 16,220 ....G 7
Fais (isl.) 207 ....E 5
Fakaofo (atoll) 654 ....J 6
Fanning (Tabuaeran) (isl.), 340 .L 5
Faraulep (atoll) 132 ....E 5
Fatuhiva (isl.) 386 ....N 7
Fiji 792,441 ....H 8
Flint (isl.) ....L 7
Fly (riv.) ....E 6
Funafuti (cap.), Tuvalu ....H 6
French Polynesia 137,382 ....L 8
Funafuti (atoll) 2,120 ....H 6
Futuna (Hoom) (isls.) 3,173 ...J 7
Gambier (isls.) 556 ....N 8
Gardner (Nukumaroro) (isl.) ...J 6
Gilbert (isls.) 47,711 ....H 6
Greenwich (Kapingamarangi) (atoll) 508 ....F 5
Guadalcanal (isl.) 46,619 ......F 7
Guam (isl.) 105,979 ....E 4
Hagåtña (cap.), Guam 896 ....E 4
Hall (isls.) 647 ....F 5
Hawaiian (isls.) 964,691 ......J 3
Henderson (isl.) ....O 8
Hivaoa (isl.) 1,159 ....N 6
Honiara (cap.), Solomon Is. 14,942 ....F 6
Hoorn (isls.) 3,173 ....J 7
Howland (isl.) ....J 5
Huahine (isl.) 3,140 ....L 7
Hull (Orona) (isl.) ....J 6
Huon (Gulf) ....E 6
Ifalik (atoll) 389 ....E 5
Iwo (isl.) ....E 3
Jaluit (atoll) 1,450 ....G 5
Jarvis (isl.) ....K 6
Johnston (atoll) 327 ....K 4
Kadavu (Kandav) (isl.) 8,699 ...H 7
Kanton (isl.) ....J 6
Kapingamarangi (atoll) 508 ...F 5
Kavieng 4,633 ....E 6
Kermadec (isls.) 5 ....J 9
Kieta 3,491 ....F 6
Kimbe 4,662 ....F 6
Kingman (reef) ....K 5
Kiribati 82,449 ....J 6
Kiritimati (isl.) 674 ....L 5
Koror (cap.), Palau 6,222 .....D 5
Kosrae (isl.) 5,491 ....G 5
Kwajalein (atoll) 6,624 ....G 5
Lae 61,617 ....E 6
Lau Group (isls.) 14,452 ......J 7
Lavongal (isl.) ....F 6
Lifu (isl.) 7,585 ....G 8
Line (isls.) ....K 5
Little Makin (atoll) 1,445 ......H 5
Lord Howe (Ontong Java) (isl.) 1,082 ....G 6
Lord Howe (isl.) 287 ....G 9
Lorengau 3,986 ....E 6
Louisiade (arch.) ....F 7
Loyalty (isls.) 14,518 ....G 8
Luganville 4,935 ....G 7
Madang 21,335 ....E 6
Majuro (atoll) (cap.), Marshall Is. 8,583 ....H 5
Makin (Butaritari) (atoll) 2,971 .H 5
Malaita (isl.) 50,912 ....G 6
Malden (isl.) ....L 6
Malekula (isl.) 15,931 ....G 7
Maloelap (atoll) 763 ....H 5
Mangaia (isl.) 1,364 ....L 8
Mangareva (isl.) 556 ....N 8
Manihiki (atoll) 405 ....K 7
Manua (isls.) 1,459 ....K 7
Manus (isl.) 25,844 ....E 6
Marcus (isl.) ....F 3
Maré (isl.) 4,156 ....G 8
Marianas, Northern 16,780 ....E 4
Mariana Trench ....E 4
Marquesas (isls.) 5,419 ......N 6
Marshall Islands 60,652 ......G 4
Marutea (atoll) ....N 8
Mata Utu (cap.), Wallis and Futura 558 ....J 7
Mauke (isl.) 684 ....L 8
Melanesia (reg.) ....E 5
Micronesia (reg.) ....E 4
Micronesia Federated States, of 122,950 ....J 7
Midway (isls.) 453 ....J 3
Mili (atoll) 763 ....H 5
Moen (isl.) 10,351 ....F 5
Moorea (isl.) 5,788 ....L 7
Mururoa (isl.) ....M 8
Nadi 6,938 ....H 7
Namonuito (atool) 783 ....E 5
Namorik (atoll) 617 ....G 5
Nanumea (atoll) 844 ....H 6
Nauru 10,390 ....G 8
Ndeni (isl.) 4,854 ....G 7
New Britain (isl.) 148,773 .....F 6
New Caledonia 133,233 ......G 8
New Caledonia (isl.) 118,715 ....G 8
New Georgia (isl.) 16,472 .....F 6
New Guinea (isl.) ....E 6
New Ireland (isl.) 65,657 ......F 6
Ngatik (atoll) 560 ....F 5
Ngulu (atoll) 21 ....D 5
Niuatoputapu (isl.) 1,650 ......J 7
Niue (isl.) 3,578 ....K 7
Niutao (atoll) 866 ....H 6
Nomoi (isls.) 1,879 ....F 5
Nonouti (atoll) 2,223 ....H 6
Norfolk Island (terr.) 2,175 ....G 8
Northern Marianas 116,780 ....E 4
Nouméa (cap.), New Caled. 56,078 ....G 8
Nouméa *74,335 ....G 8
Nui (atoll) 603 ....H 6
Nuku'alofa (cap.) Tonga 18,356 ....J 8
Nukuhiva (isl.) 1,484 ....M 6

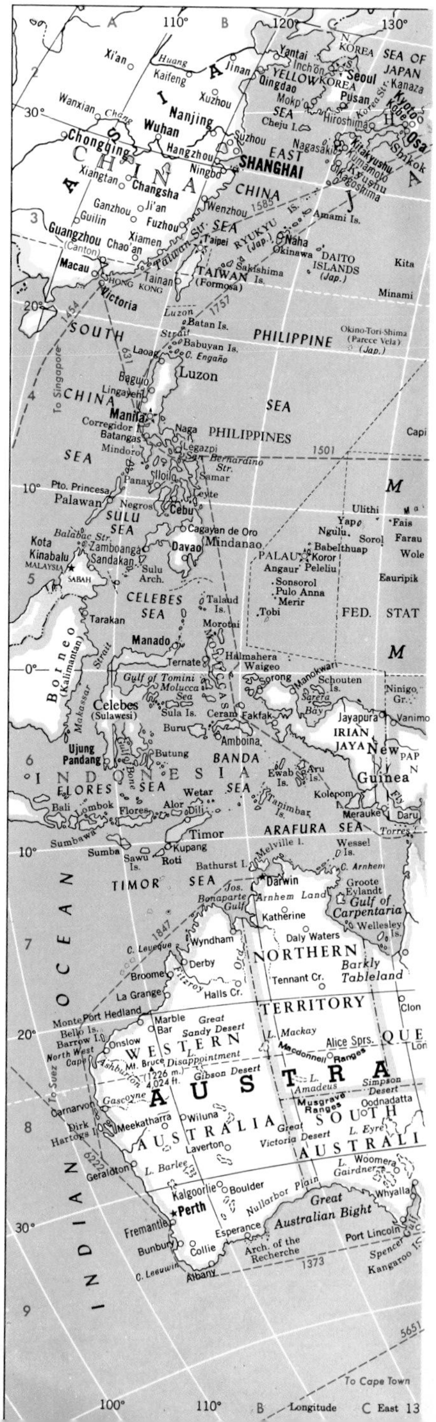
CHINA
INDONESIA
PHILIPPINES
AUSTRALIA
INDIAN OCEAN
SHANGHAI
To Cape Town
Longitude East

Ocean (Banaba) (isl.) 2,314 ...G 6
Oeno (isl.) ...O 8
Onotoa (atoll) 1,997 ...H 6
Onlong Java (isl.) 1,082 ...G 6
Pagan (isl.) ...E 4
Pago Pago (cap.), Amer. Samoa 3,075 ...J 7
Palau 12,116 ...D 5
Palikir (cap.), Micronesia 5,549 ...F 5
Palmyra (atoll) ...K 5
Papeete (cap.), Fr. Poly. 22,967 ...M 7
Papetee •51,987 ...M 7
Papua (gulf) ...E 6
Papua New Guinea 3,010,727 ...E 6
Peleliu (isl.) 609 ...D 5
Penrhyn (Tongareva) (atoll) 608 ...L 6
Phoenix (isls.) ...J 6
Pines (isl.) 1,095 ...G 8
Pitcairn (isl.) 54 ...O 8
Pohnpei (isl.) 19,935 ...F 5
Polynesia (reg.) ...K 7
Popondetta 6,429 ...E 6
Port Moresby (cap.), Papua N.G. 123,624 ...E 6
Port-Vila (cap.), Vanuatu 4,729 .G 7
Port-Vila*14,797 ...G 7
Pukapuka (atoll) 797 ...K 7
Pulap (atoll) 427 ...E 5
Puluwat (atoll) 441 ...E 5
Rabaul 14,954 ...F 6
Raiatea (isl.) 2,517 ...L 7
Raivavae (isl.) 1,023 ...M 8
Rakahanga (atoll) 269 ...K 7
Ralik Chain (isls.) ...G 5
Rangiroa (atoll) ...M 7
Rapa (isl.) 398 ...M 8
Rarotonga (isl.) 9,477 ...K 8
Ratak Chain (isls.) ...G 5
Reao (atoll) 424 ...N 7
Rennell (isl.) 1,132 ...F 7
Rikitea ...N 8
Rimatara (isl.) 813 ...L 8
Rongelap (atoll) 235 ...G 4
Rota (isl.) 1,261 ...E 4
Rotuma (isl.) 2,805 ...H 7
Rurutu (isl.) 1,555 ...L 8
Saipan (cap), No. Marianas 14,549 ...E 4
Sala y Gomez (isl.) ...P 8
Samarai 869 ...E 7
Samoa 204,000 ...J 7
Samoa (isls.) ...J 7
San Cristobal (isl.) 11,212 ...G 7
Santa Cruz (isls.) 5,421 ...G 6
Santa Isabel (isl.) 10,420 ...G 6
Savai'i (isl.) 43,150 ...J 7
Senyavin (isls.) 20,035 ...F 5
Society (isls.) 117,703 ...L 7
Solomon (isls.) ...F 6
Solomon (sea) ...F 6
Solomon Islands 221,000 ...G 6
Starbuck (isl.) ...L 6
Suva (cap.), Fiji 63,628 ...H 7
Suva *117,827 ...H 7
Swains (isl.) 27 ...K 7
Sydney (isl.) ...K 6
Tabiteuea (atoll) 3,942 ...H 6
Tabuaeran (isl.) 340 ...L 5
Tahaa (isl.) 3,513 ...L 7
Tahiti (isl.) 95,604 ...L 7
Takaroa (atoll) 337 ...M 7
Tanna (isl.) 15,715 ...H 7
Tarawa (cap.), Kiribati 17,129 ..H 5
Tasman (sea) ...G 9
Teraina (isl.) 458 ...L5
Tinian (isl.) 866 ...E 4
Tokelau (isls.) 1,575 ...J 6
Tonga 90,128 ...J 8
Tongareva (atoll) 608 ...L 6
Tongatapu (isls.) 57,130 ...J 8
Torres (isls.) 325 ...G 7
Torres (strait) ...E 7
Trobriand (isls.) ...F 6
Truk (isls.) 37,488 ...F 5
Tuamotu (arch.) 9,052 ...M 7
Tubuai (Austral) (isls.) 5,208 ..M 8
Tubuai (isl.) 1,419 ...M 8
Tutuila (isl.) 30,538 ...J 7
Tuvalu 7,349 ...H 6
Uapou (isl.) 1,563 ...M 6
Ujelang (atoll) 309 ...F 5
Ulithi (atoll) 710 ...D 4
Upolu (isl.) 114,620 ...J 7
Uturoa 2,517 ...L 7
Uvéa (isl.) 2,777 ...G 7
Vaitupu (atoll) 1,273 ...H 6
Vanikoro (isl.) 267 ...G 7
Vanimo 3,071 ...E 6
Vanua Levu (isl.) 103,122 ...H 7
Vanuatu 170,000 ...G 7
Viti Levu (isl.) 445,422 ...H 7
Volcano (isls.) ...E 3
Vostok (isl.) ...L 7
Wake (isl.) 302 ...G 4
Wallis (isls.) 8,973 ...J 7
Wallis and Futuna 13,705 ...J 7
Washington (Teraina) (isl.) 458 .L 5
Wau 2,349 ...E 6
Wewak 23,224 ...E 6
Woleai (isl.) 638 ...E 5
Wotje (atoll) 535 ...H 5
Yap (isl.) 6,670 ...D 5

*City and suburbs.
•Population of urban area.

VANUATU

AREA 5,700 sq. mi. (14,763 sq. km.)
POPULATION 170,000
CAPITAL Port-Vila
LARGEST CITY Port-Vila
HIGHEST POINT Mt. Tabwemasana 6,165 ft. (1,879 m.)
MONETARY UNIT Vatu
MAJOR LANGUAGES Bislama, English, French
MAJOR RELIGIONS Christian, animist

SAMOA

AREA 1,133 sq. mi. (2,934 sq. km.)
POPULATION 204,000
CAPITAL Apia
LARGEST CITY Apia
HIGHEST POINT Mt. Silisili 6,094 ft. (1,857 m.)
MONETARY UNIT tala
MAJOR LANGUAGES Samoan, English
MAJOR RELIGIONS Protestantism, Roman Catholicism

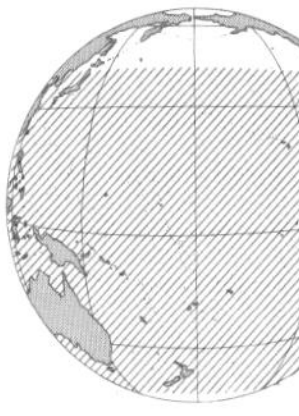

PALAU

AREA 177 sq. mi. (458 sq. km.)
POPULATION 15,122
CAPITAL Koror
HIGHEST POINT Mt. Makelulu 804 ft. (242 m.)
MONETARY UNIT U.S. dollar
MAJOR LANGUAGES English, Sonsorolese, Angaur, Japanese, Tobi, Palauan
MAJOR RELIGIONS Christian, Modekngei

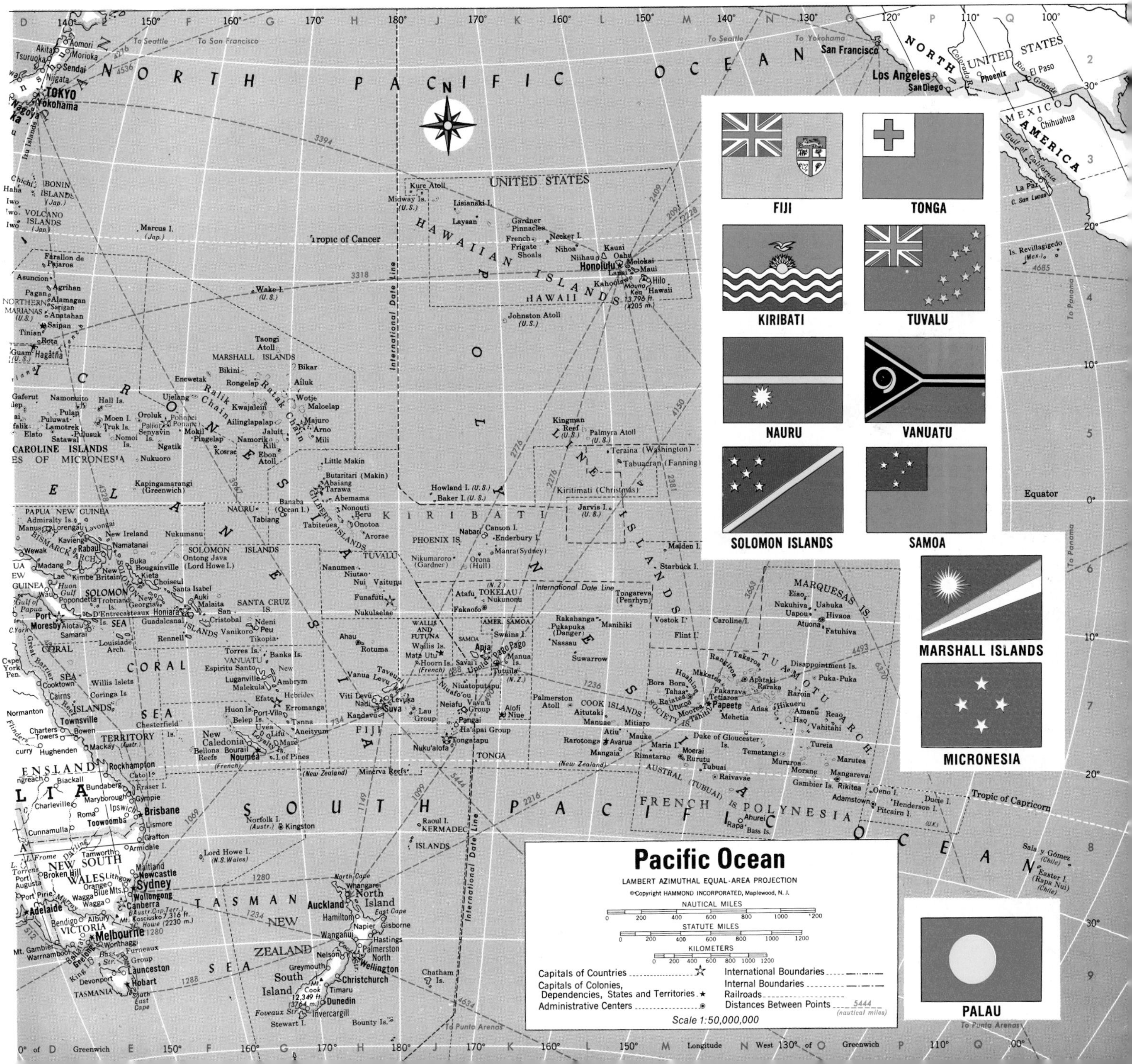

Pacific Ocean
LAMBERT AZIMUTHAL EQUAL-AREA PROJECTION
©Copyright HAMMOND INCORPORATED, Maplewood, N. J.
NAUTICAL MILES
STATUTE MILES
KILOMETERS
Capitals of Countries
Capitals of Colonies, Dependencies, States and Territories
Administrative Centers
International Boundaries
Internal Boundaries
Railroads
Distances Between Points
Scale 1:50,000,000
FIJI
TONGA
KIRIBATI
TUVALU
NAURU
VANUATU
SOLOMON ISLANDS
SAMOA
MARSHALL ISLANDS
MICRONESIA
PALAU
NORTH PACIFIC OCEAN
SOUTH PACIFIC OCEAN
HAWAIIAN ISLANDS
Honolulu
San Francisco
Los Angeles
Tokyo
Sydney
Auckland
Brisbane
Melbourne
Suva
Papeete
Nouméa
Port-Vila
Honiara
Tropic of Cancer
Tropic of Capricorn
Equator
International Date Line
TASMAN SEA
CORAL SEA
NEW ZEALAND
FRENCH POLYNESIA

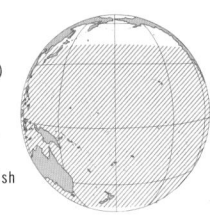

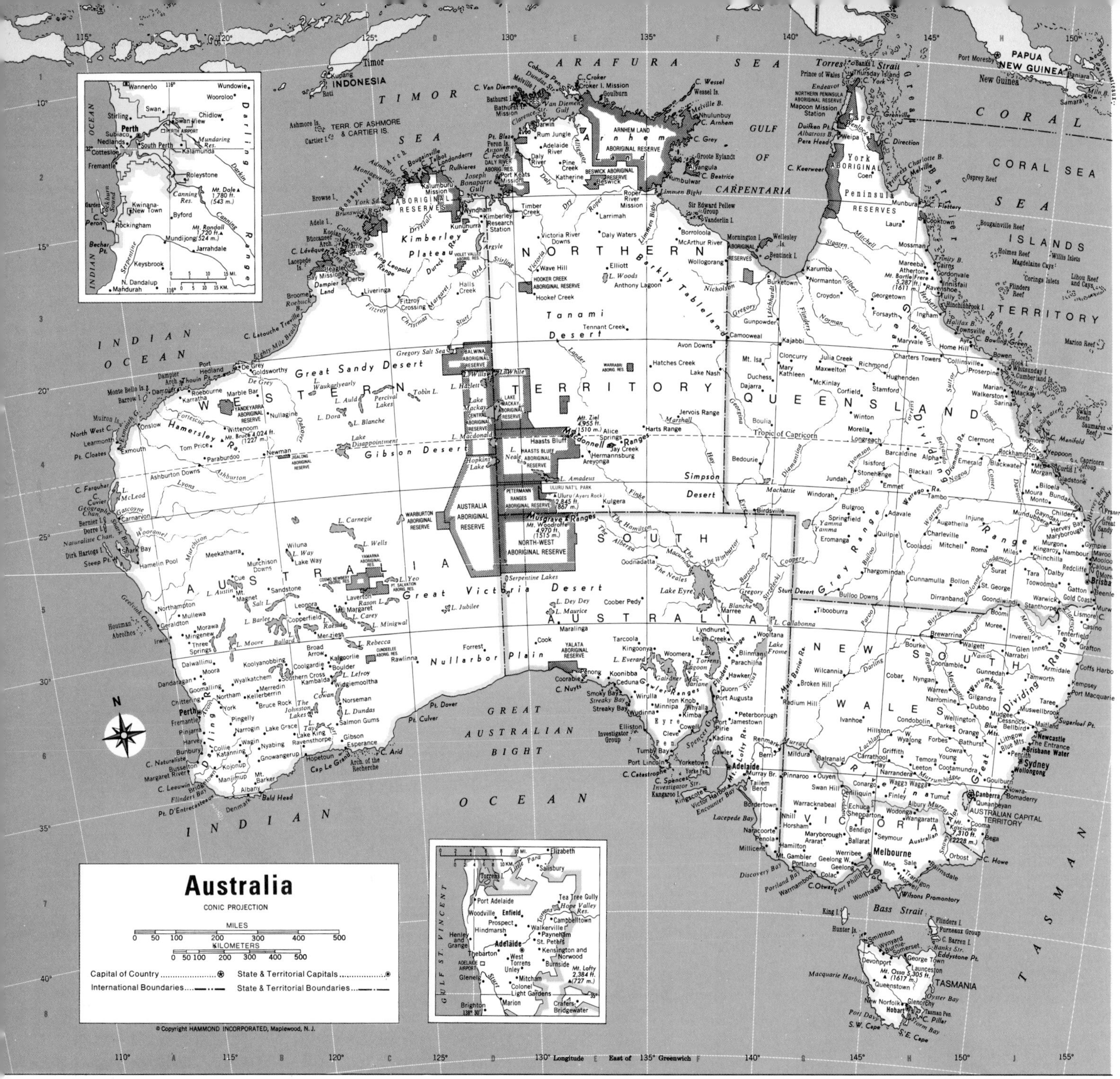

Australia
CONIC PROJECTION
MILES
0 50 100 200 300 400 500
KILOMETERS
0 50 100 200 300 400 500
Capital of Country
State & Territorial Capitals
International Boundaries
State & Territorial Boundaries
INDIAN OCEAN
ARAFURA SEA
TIMOR SEA
CORAL SEA
TASMAN SEA
GREAT AUSTRALIAN BIGHT
GULF OF CARPENTARIA
WESTERN AUSTRALIA
NORTHERN TERRITORY
QUEENSLAND
SOUTH AUSTRALIA
NEW SOUTH WALES
VICTORIA
TASMANIA
AUSTRALIAN CAPITAL TERRITORY
INDONESIA
PAPUA NEW GUINEA
Perth
Adelaide
Melbourne
Sydney
Brisbane
Hobart
Canberra
Darwin
Longitude East of Greenwich

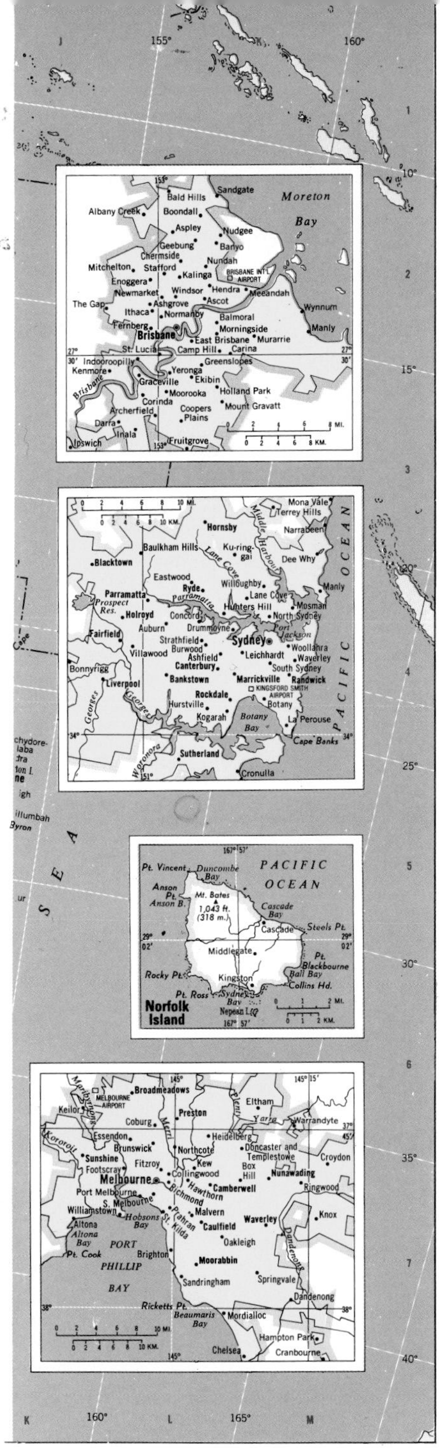
Moreton Bay
Brisbane
Sandgate
Bald Hills
Albany Creek
Boondall
Aspley
Nudgee
Geebung
Banyo
Chermside
Nundah
Mitchelton
Stafford
Kalinga
BRISBANE INT'L AIRPORT
Enoggera
Newmarket
Windsor
Hendra
Meeandah
The Gap
Ashgrove
Ascot
Wynnum
Ithaca
Normanby
Balmoral
Manly
Fernberg
Morningside
East Brisbane
Murarrie
St. Lucia
Camp Hill
Carina
Indooroopilly
Greenslopes
Kenmore
Yeronga
Graceville
Ekibin
Moorooka
Holland Park
Corinda
Archerfield
Coopers Plains
Mount Gravatt
Darra
Inala
Ipswich
Fruitgrove
Mona Vale
Terrey Hills
Narrabeen
Hornsby
Baulkham Hills
Ku-ring-gai
Dee Why
Blacktown
Eastwood
Ryde
Willoughby
Manly
Parramatta
Lane Cove
Prospect Res.
Holroyd
Hunters Hill
Mosman
Concord
North Sydney
Fairfield
Auburn
Drummoyne
Port Jackson
Strathfield
Sydney
Burwood
Woollahra
Villawood
Ashfield
Leichhardt
Waverley
Bonnyrigg
Canterbury
South Sydney
Liverpool
Bankstown
Marrickville
Randwick
KINGSFORD SMITH AIRPORT
Rockdale
Botany
Hurstville
Kogarah
Botany Bay
La Perouse
Sutherland
Cape Banks
Cronulla
PACIFIC OCEAN
Pt. Vincent
Duncombe Bay
Anson Pt.
Anson B.
Mt. Bates 1,043 ft. (318 m.)
Cascade Bay
Cascade
Steels Pt.
Middlegate
Pt. Blackbourne
Rocky Pt.
Ball Bay
Kingston
Collins Hd.
Pt. Ross
Sydney Bay
Nepean I.
Norfolk Island
Broadmeadows
MELBOURNE AIRPORT
Keilor
Preston
Eltham
Coburg
Warrandyte
Essendon
Heidelberg
Brunswick
Northcote
Doncaster and Templestowe
Croydon
Sunshine
Fitzroy
Kew
Box Hill
Nunawading
Footscray
Melbourne
Collingwood
Ringwood
Hawthorn
Camberwell
Port Melbourne
Richmond
S. Melbourne
Malvern
Knox
Williamstown
Hobsons Bay
St. Kilda
Prahran
Caulfield
Waverley
Altona
Altona Bay
Oakleigh
PORT PHILLIP BAY
Pt. Cook
Brighton
Moorabbin
Sandringham
Springvale
Dandenong
Ricketts Pt.
Beaumaris Bay
Mordialloc
Hampton Park
Chelsea
Cranbourne
SEA

*City and suburbs.
†Population of met. area.
‡Population of urban area.

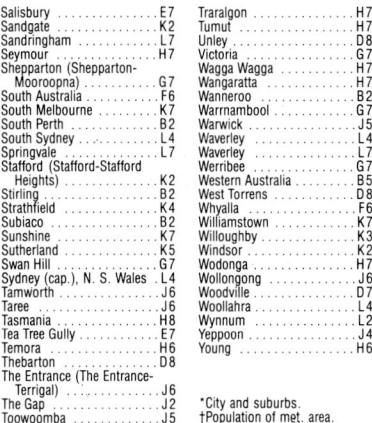

AREA 2,966,136 sq. mi. (7,682,300 sq. km.)
POPULATION 15,602,156
CAPITAL Canberra
LARGEST CITY Sydney
HIGHEST POINT Mt. Kosciusko 7,310 ft. (2,228 m.)
LOWEST POINT Lake Eyre -39 ft. (-12 m.)
MONETARY UNIT Australian dollar
MAJOR LANGUAGE English
MAJOR RELIGIONS Protestantism, Roman Catholicism

Population Distribution

Cities with over
• 500,000 inhabitants (including suburbs)

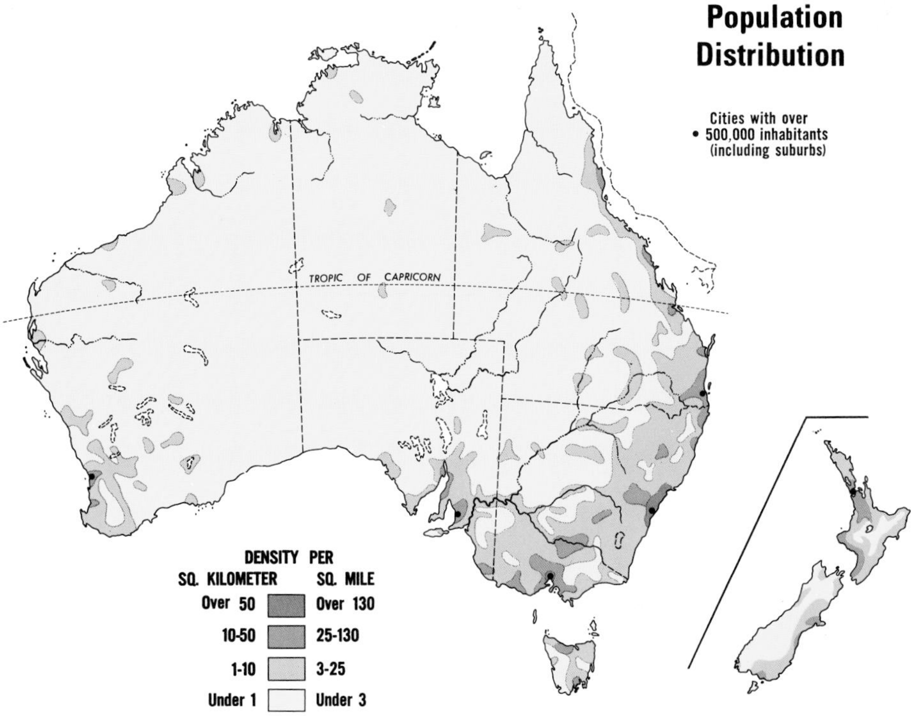
TROPIC OF CAPRICORN

DENSITY PER

SQ. KILOMETER	SQ. MILE
Over 50	Over 130
10-50	25-130
1-10	3-25
Under 1	Under 3

Vegetation

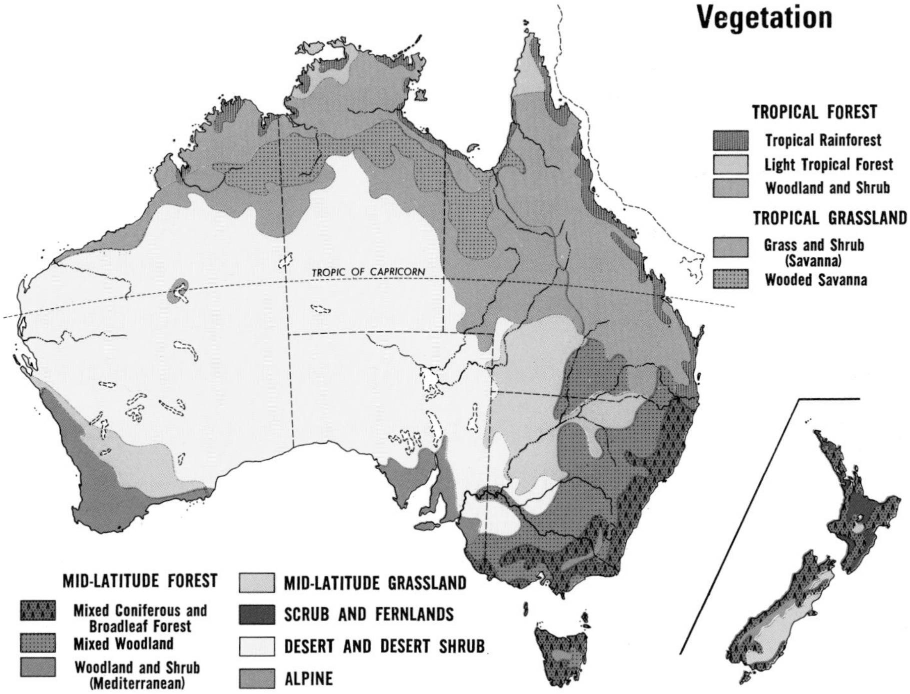
TROPIC OF CAPRICORN

TROPICAL FOREST
- Tropical Rainforest
- Light Tropical Forest
- Woodland and Shrub

TROPICAL GRASSLAND
- Grass and Shrub (Savanna)
- Wooded Savanna

MID-LATITUDE FOREST
- Mixed Coniferous and Broadleaf Forest
- Mixed Woodland
- Woodland and Shrub (Mediterranean)

MID-LATITUDE GRASSLAND

SCRUB AND FERNLANDS

DESERT AND DESERT SHRUB

ALPINE

Average January Temperature

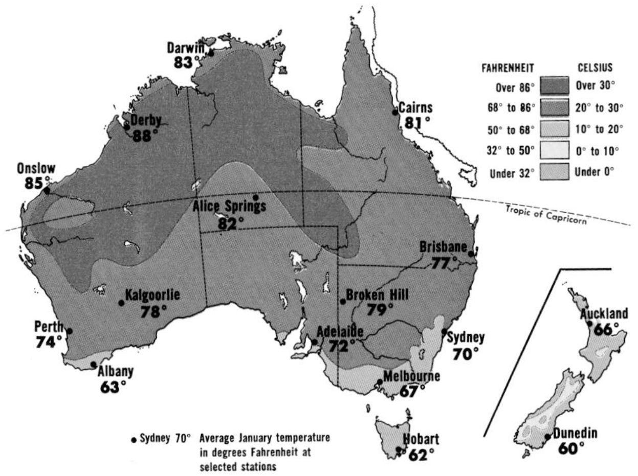
FAHRENHEIT
CELSIUS
Over 86° Over 30°
68° to 86° 20° to 30°
50° to 68° 10° to 20°
32° to 50° 0° to 10°
Under 32° Under 0°
Darwin 83°
Derby 88°
Cairns 81°
Onslow 85°
Alice Springs 82°
Tropic of Capricorn
Brisbane 77°
Kalgoorlie 78°
Broken Hill 79°
Perth 74°
Adelaide 72°
Sydney 70°
Albany 63°
Melbourne 67°
Auckland 66°
Hobart 62°
Dunedin 60°
• Sydney 70° Average January temperature in degrees Fahrenheit at selected stations

Average July Temperature

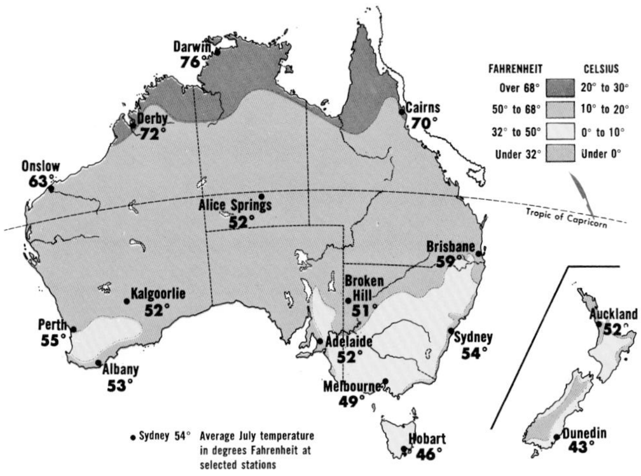
FAHRENHEIT
CELSIUS
Over 68° 20° to 30°
50° to 68° 10° to 20°
32° to 50° 0° to 10°
Under 32° Under 0°
Darwin 76°
Derby 72°
Cairns 70°
Onslow 63°
Alice Springs 52°
Tropic of Capricorn
Brisbane 59°
Kalgoorlie 52°
Broken Hill 51°
Perth 55°
Adelaide 52°
Sydney 54°
Albany 53°
Melbourne 49°
Auckland 52°
Hobart 46°
Dunedin 43°
• Sydney 54° Average July temperature in degrees Fahrenheit at selected stations

Rainfall

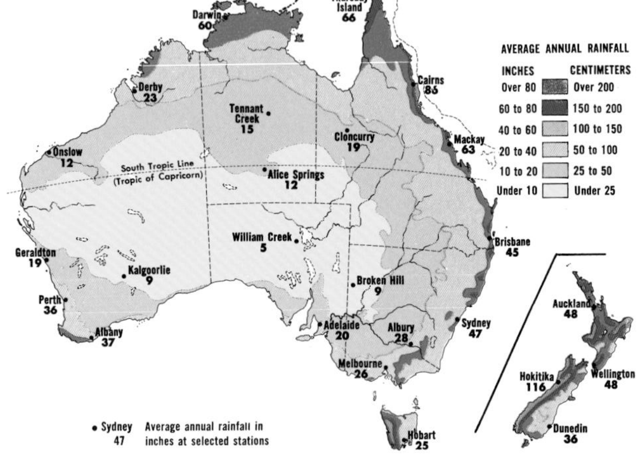
AVERAGE ANNUAL RAINFALL
INCHES
CENTIMETERS
Over 80 Over 200
60 to 80 150 to 200
40 to 60 100 to 150
20 to 40 50 to 100
10 to 20 25 to 50
Under 10 Under 25
Thursday Island 66
Darwin 60
Derby 23
Tennant Creek 15
Cairns 86
Cloncurry 19
Mackay 63
Onslow 12
South Tropic Line (Tropic of Capricorn)
Alice Springs 12
William Creek 5
Brisbane 45
Geraldton 19
Kalgoorlie 9
Broken Hill 9
Perth 36
Auckland 48
Sydney 47
Albany 37
Adelaide 20
Albury 28
Melbourne 26
Hokitika 116
Wellington 48
Dunedin 36
Hobart 25
• Sydney 47 Average annual rainfall in inches at selected stations

DOMINANT LAND USE

- Cereals (chiefly wheat), Livestock
- Dairy, Truck Farming
- Cash Crops, Horticulture, Fruit
- Pasture Livestock
- Range Livestock
- Forests
- Nonagricultural Land

MAJOR MINERAL OCCURRENCES

Ab	Asbestos	Na	Salt
Ag	Silver	Ni	Nickel
Al	Bauxite	O	Petroleum
Au	Gold	Op	Opals
C	Coal	P	Phosphates
Cu	Copper	Pb	Lead
D	Diamonds	S	Sulfur, Pyrites
Fe	Iron Ore	Sb	Antimony
G	Natural Gas	Sn	Tin
Gp	Gypsum	Ti	Titanium
Lg	Lignite	U	Uranium
Ls	Limestone	W	Tungsten
Mg	Magnesium	Zn	Zinc
Mi	Mica	Zr	Zirconium
Mn	Manganese		

- Water Power
- Major Industrial Areas

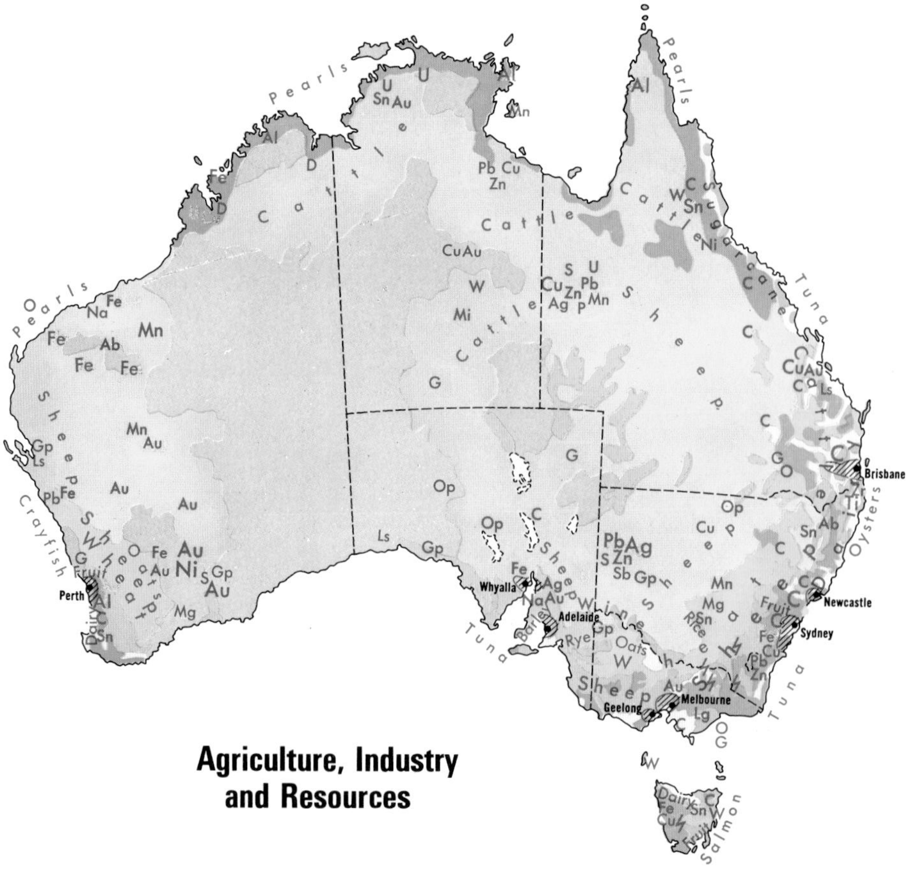
Pearls
Cattle
Sheep
Sugar cane
Tuna
Oysters
Crayfish
Fruit
Dairy
Wheat
Barley
Rye
Oats
Rice
Salmon
Perth
Whyalla
Adelaide
Geelong
Melbourne
Brisbane
Newcastle
Sydney

Agriculture, Industry and Resources

INDONESIA
Sumba
Timor
TIMOR SEA
ARAFURA SEA
New Guinea
PAPUA NEW GUINEA
Port Moresby
Torres Strait
C. York
Melville I.
Cobourg Pen.
C. Wessel
Darwin
Ashmore Is.
TERR. OF ASHMORE & CARTIER IS.
Cartier I.
Arnhem Land
Gulf of Carpentaria
Groote Eylandt
Daly
Cape York Peninsula
Great Barrier Reef
CORAL SEA
Mitchell
Cairns
Mt. Bartle Frere 5,287 ft. (1611 m.)
Townsville
Mackay
Rockhampton
Bundaberg
INDIAN OCEAN
Kimberley Plateau
Derby
Fitzroy
Ord
Victoria
NORTHERN TERRITORY
Tanami Desert
Barkly Tableland
Flinders
Great Dividing Range
Port Hedland
Great Sandy Desert
Mt. Isa
North West C.
Fortescue
WESTERN AUSTRALIA
Hamersley Ra.
Mt. Bruce 4,024 ft. (1227 m.)
Lake Disappointment
Tropic of Capricorn
Lake Mackay
Macdonnell Ranges
Alice Springs
Georgina
QUEENSLAND
Gibson Desert
Finke
Simpson Desert
Diamantina
Barcoo
Uluru (Ayers Rock) 2,845 ft. (867 m.)
Lake Carnegie
Musgrave Ranges
Grey Range
Warrego
Murchison
SOUTH AUSTRALIA
Great Victoria Desert
Lake Eyre
Sturt Desert
Brisbane
Toowoomba
Gold Coast
Geraldton
Lake Barlee
Lake Torrens
Flinders Range
Lake Frome
Nullarbor Plain
Kalgoorlie-Boulder
Darling
Broken Hill
NEW SOUTH WALES
Tamworth
Perth
Fremantle
Darling Ra.
Lake Gairdner
Whyalla
Great Australian Bight
Eyre Pen.
Spencer Gulf
Lachlan
Newcastle
Bunbury
Sydney
Wollongong
C. Leeuwin
Albany
Adelaide
Mt. Lofty Ra.
Murray
Wagga Wagga
Canberra
AUSTRALIAN CAPITAL TERRITORY
Kangaroo I.
Albury
Mt. Kosciusko 7,310 ft. (2228 m.)
Bendigo
VICTORIA
Ballarat
Mt. Gambier
Geelong
Melbourne
C. Howe
Bass Strait
King I.
TASMAN SEA
Furneaux Group
Launceston
TASMANIA
Hobart
South Cape
© Copyright HAMMOND INCORPORATED, Maplewood, N. J.
Longitude 140° East of Greenwich

Vegetation/Relief

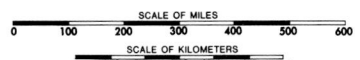

SCALE OF MILES: 0 100 200 300 400 500 600

SCALE OF KILOMETERS: 0 100 200 300 400 500 600

Capital of Country .... ⊛

State and Territorial Capitals .... ⊛

International Boundaries ....

State and Territorial Boundaries ....

Elevations in Feet

Depths in Fathoms

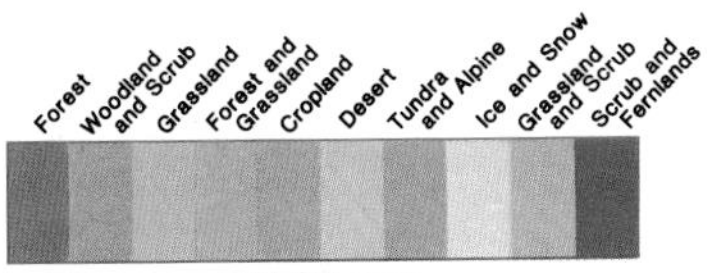
Forest
Woodland and Scrub
Grassland
Forest and Grassland
Cropland
Desert
Tundra and Alpine
Ice and Snow
Grassland and Scrub
Scrub and Fernlands

COLOR KEY

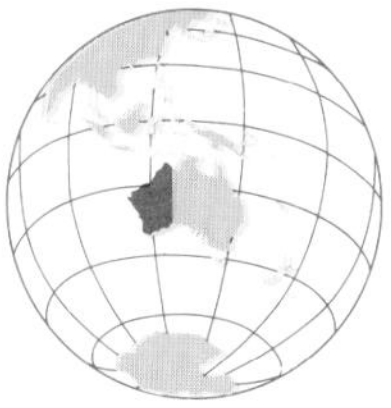

AREA 975,096 sq. mi. (2,525,500 sq. km.)
POPULATION 1,406,929
CAPITAL Perth
LARGEST CITY Perth
HIGHEST POINT Mt. Bruce 4,024 ft. (1,227 m.)

CITIES and TOWNS

Albany 15,222 .... B6
Augusta 588 .... A6
Australind 1,681 .... A2
Balladonia D6
Beverley 756 .... B1
Boddington 367 .... B2
Boulder-Kalgoorlie 19,848 .. C5
Boyanup 365 .... A2
Bridgetown 1,521 .... B6
Brookton 595 .... B2
Broome 3,666 .... C2
Bruce Rock 565 .... B5
Brunswick Junction 889 .... A2
Bunbury 21,749 .... A2
Busselton 6,463 .... A6
Canning 52,816 .... A1
Capel 680 .... A2
Carnamah 422 .... A5
Carnarvon 5,053 .... A4
Collie 7,667 .... B2
Coolgardie 891 .... C5
Coorow 226 .... B5
Corrigin 841 .... B6
Cranbrook 316 .... B6
Cuballing ○647 .... B2
Cue 320 .... B4
Cunderdin 731 .... B5
Dalwallinu 639 .... B5
Dampier 2,471 .... B3
Dandaragan ○1,748 .... A5
Darkan 242 .... B2
Denham 402 .... A4
Denmark 985 .... B6
Derby 2,933 .... C2
Dongara-Port Denison 1,155 A5
Donnybrook 1,197 .... A2
Dwellingup 453 .... B2
Esperance 6,375 .... C6
Eucla E5
Exmouth 2,583 .... A3
Fitzroy Crossing D2
Fremantle 22,484 .... A1
Geraldton 20,895 .... A5
Gingin 382 .... A1
Gnowangerup 872 .... B6
Goldsworthy 923 .... B3
Goomalling 600 .... B1
Halls Creek 966 .... D2
Harvey 2,479 .... A2
Hopetoun C6
Hyden B6
Jarrahdale 315 .... B2
Kalbarri 820 .... A4
Kalgoorlie 9,145 .... C5
Kalgoorlie-Boulder 19,848 .. C5
Kambalda 4,463 .... C5
Karratha 8,341 .... B3
Katanning 4,413 .... B6
Kellerberrin 1,091 .... B5
Kojonup 544 .... B6
Koolyanobbing 277 .... B5
Kununurra 2,081 .... E2
Kwinana New Town 12,355 .. A1
Lake Grace 575 .... B6
Laverton 872 .... C5
Learmonth A3
Leonora 524 .... C5
Madura D5
Mandurah 10,978 .... A2
Manjimup 4,150 .... B6
Marble Bar 357 .... C3
Margaret River 798 .... A6
Meekatharra 989 .... B4
Melville 61,211 .... A1
Menzies 232 .... C5
Merredin 3,520 .... B5
Mingenew 368 .... A5
Moora 1,677 .... B5
Morawa 694 .... B5
Mount Barker 1,519 .... B6
Mount Magnet 618 .... B5
Mukinbudin 370 .... B5
Mullewa 918 .... A5
Mundijong 356 .... A2
Nannup 552 .... B6
Narrogin 4,969 .... B2
Nedlands 20,257 .... A1
Newman 5,466 .... B3
New Norcia A5
Norseman 1,895 .... C6
Northam 6,791 .... B1
Northampton 750 .... A5
Northcliffe B6
Nungarin ○332 .... B5
Onslow 594 .... A3
Pannawonica 1,170 .... B3
Paraburdoo 2,357 .... B3
Pardoo B3
Pemberton 871 .... A6
Perenjori 257 .... B5
Perth (cap.) 809,035 .... A1
Perth *898,918 .... A1
Pingelly 937 .... B2
Pinjarra 1,336 .... A2
Port Denison-Dongara 1,155 A5
Port Hedland 12,948 .... B3
Quairading 741 .... B1
Ravensthorpe 327 .... B6
Rockingham 24,932 .... A2
Roebourne 1,688 .... B3
Sandstone ○133 .... B4
Shay Gap 853 .... C3
Southern Cross 798 .... B5
South Perth 31,524 .... A1
Stirling 161,858 .... A1
Three Springs 638 .... A5
Tom Price 3,540 .... B3
Toodyay 560 .... B1
Turkey Creek 212 .... E2
Wagin 1,488 .... B2
Walpole 291 .... B6
Wandering ○470 .... B2
Wanneroo 6,745 .... A1
Waroona 1,462 .... A2
Wickepin 267 .... B2
Wickham 2,387 .... B3
Williams 453 .... B2
Wiluna 221 .... C4
Wittenoom 247 .... B3
Wongan Hills 947 .... B5
Wundowie 720 .... B1
Wyalkatchem 453 .... B5
Wyndham 1,509 .... E1
Yalgoo ○315 .... B5
Yampi Sound C2
York 1,136 .... B1

OTHER FEATURES

Adele (isl.) C1
Admiralty (gulf) D1
Aloysius (mt.) E4
Argyle (lake) E2
Arid (cape) C6
Ashburton (riv.) A3
Augustus (mt.) B4
Austin (lake) B4
Australia Aboriginal Res. E4
Bald (head) B6
Balwina Aboriginal Res. E3
Barlee (lake) B5
Barrow (isl.) A3
Beaglebay Aboriginal Res. .. C2
Bluff Knoll (mt.) B6
Bonaparte (arch.) D1
Bougainville (cape) D1
Brassey (range) C4
Bruce (mt.) B3
Brunswick (bay) D1
Buccaneer (arch.) C2
Carey (lake) C5
Carnegie (lake) C4
Central Aboriginal Res. E3
Churchman (mt.) B5
Collier (bay) C1
Cosmo Newbery Aboriginal Res. C5
Cowan (lake) C5
Cundeelee Aboriginal Res. .. C5
Dale (mt.) B1
Dampier (arch.) B3
Dampier Land (reg.) C2
Darling (range) A1
De Grey (riv.) B3
D'Entrecasteaux (pt.) A6
Dirk Hartogs (isl.) A4
Disappointment (lake) C3
Drysdale (riv.) D1
Dundas (lake) C6
Egerton (mt.) B4
Eighty Mile (beach) C2
Enid (mt.) B3
Esperance (bay) C6
Exmouth (gulf) A3
Fitzroy (riv.) D2
Flinders (bay) A6
Forrest River Aboriginal Res. D1
Fortescue (riv.) B3
Garden (isl.) A1
Gascoyne (riv.) B4
Geelvink (chan.) A5
Geographe (bay) A6
Geographe (chan.) A4
Gibson (des.) D3
Great Australian (bight) E6
Great Sandy (des.) C3
Great Victoria (des.) D5
Hamersley (range) B3
Hann (mt.) D1
Hopkins (lake) E4
Houtman Abrolhos (isls.) ... A5
Indian Ocean A5
Johnston, The (lakes) C6
Joseph Bonaparte (gulf) E1
Kimberley (plat.) D2
King (sound) C2
King Leopold (range) D2
Koolan (isl.) C1
Leeuwin (cape) A6
Le Grand (cape) C6
Lévêque (cape) C2
Londonderry (cape) D1
Lyons (riv.) A4
Macdonald (lake) E3
Mackay (lake) E3
McLeod (lake) A4
Minigwal (lake) C5
Monte Bello (isls.) A3
Moore (lake) B5
Murchison (riv.) B4
Murray (riv.) A2
Naturaliste (cape) A6
Naturaliste (chan.) A4
North West (cape) A3
North-West Aboriginal Res. . E4
Nullarbor (plain) D5
Oakover (riv.) C3
Ord (mt.) D2
Ord (riv.) E2
Percival (lakes) D3
Peron (pen.) A4
Petermann (ranges) E4
Rason (lake) D5
Rebecca (lake) C5
Recherche (arch.) C6
Robinson (ranges) B4
Roebuck (bay) C2
Rottnest (isl.) A1
Saint George (ranges) D2
Shark (bay) A4
Southesk Tablelands D3
Sturt (creek) D2
Swan (riv.) A1
Timor (sea) D1
Tomkinson (ranges) E4
Wanna (lakes) E5
Warburton Aboriginal Res. .. D4
Way (lake) C4
Weld (range) B4
Wells (lake) C4
Whaleback (mt.) B3
Wooramel (riv.) A4
York (sound) D1

○ Population of district.
*Population of met. area.

Topography

0 200 400 MI.
0 200 400 KM.
KIMBERLEY PLATEAU
Lake Argyle
Fitzroy
Great Sandy Desert
L. Mackay
North West C.
Fortescue
HAMERSLEY RA.
Mt. Bruce 4,024 ft. (1226 m.)
De Grey
L. Disappointment
Gibson Desert
Ashburton
L. McLeod
Gascoyne
ROBINSON RA.
L. Carnegie
Dirk Hartogs I.
Murchison
L. Wells
Great Victoria Desert
L. Moore
Kalgoorlie
NULLARBOR PLAIN
Perth
DARLING RANGE
C. Leeuwin
Below Sea Level
100 m. 328 ft.
200 m. 656 ft.
500 m. 1,640 ft.
1,000 m. 3,281 ft.
2,000 m. 6,562 ft.
5,000 m. 16,404 ft.

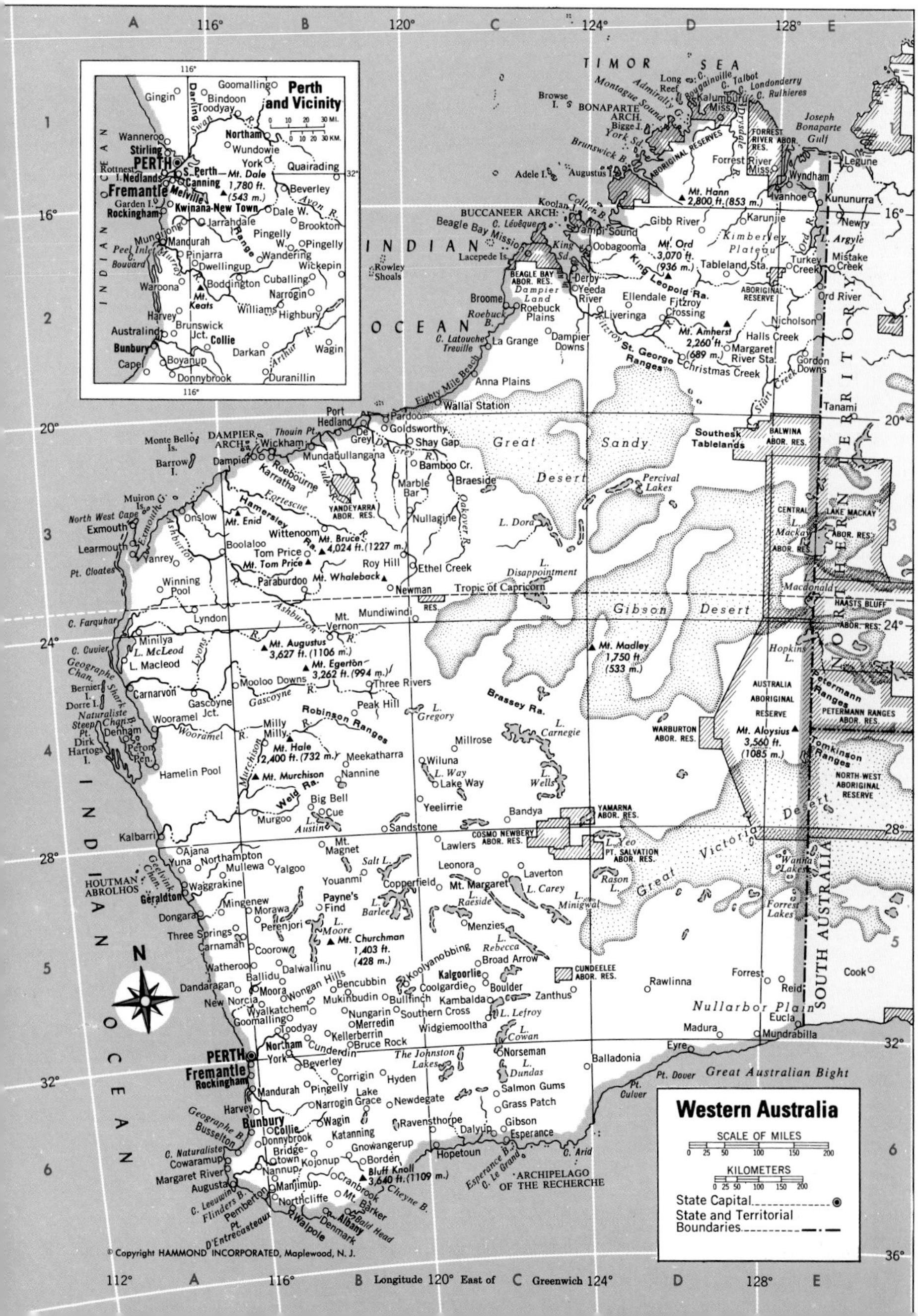

Perth and Vicinity
TIMOR SEA
INDIAN OCEAN
Great Sandy Desert
Gibson Desert
Great Victoria Desert
Nullarbor Plain
Great Australian Bight
NORTHERN TERRITORY
SOUTH AUSTRALIA
Tropic of Capricorn
Western Australia
SCALE OF MILES
KILOMETERS
State Capital
State and Territorial Boundaries
Longitude 120° East of Greenwich 124°
© Copyright HAMMOND INCORPORATED, Maplewood, N. J.

CITIES and TOWNS

Adelaide River B2
Aileron C7
Alice Springs 18,395 . . . . . D7
Alyangula 1,181 . . . . . E2
Angurugu 597 . . . . . E3
Anthony Lagoon D4
Areyonga C8
Arltunga D7
Avon Downs E5
Bamyili-Beswick 685 . . . . . C3
Banka Banka C5
Barrow Creek D6
Batchelor B2
Bathurst Island 1,032 . . . . . B1
Birdum C3
Birrimbah C3
Birrindudu A5
Borroloola 420 . . . . . E4
Bundooma D8
Burramurra E6
Charlotte Waters D8
Claravale B3
Coniston C7
Coolibah B3
Creswell Downs E4
Croker Island Mission C1
Daly River B2
Daly Waters C4
Darwin (cap.) 56,482 . . . . . B2
Docker River 217 . . . . . A8
Elliott C4
Epenarra D6
Erldunda C8
Eva Downs D5
Ewaninga D7
Goulburn Island 277 . . . . . C1
Gove (Nhulunbuy) 3,879 . . . . . E2
Harts Range D7
Hatches Creek D6
Helen Springs C5
Henbury C8
Hermannsburg 541 . . . . . C7
Hooker Creek 671 . . . . . B5
Humpty Doo B2
Katherine 3,737 . . . . . B3
Kildurk A4
Koolpinyah B2
Kulgera C8
Kurundi D6
Lake Nash E6
Larrimah C3
Legune A3
Limbunya B4
Lucy Creek E7
Mainoru C3
Maningrida 702 . . . . . C2
Mataranka C3
Milingimbi 564 . . . . . D2
Mistake Creek A4
Montejinnie C4
Mount Cavenagh C8
Mount Doreen B7
Murray Downs D6
Napperby C7
Newcastle Waters C4
Nhulunbuy 3,879 . . . . . E2
Numbulwar 422 . . . . . D3
Oenpelli 452 . . . . . C2
O. T. Downs D4
Papunya 635 . . . . . B7
Pine Creek 214 . . . . . C2
Plenty River Mine D7
Port Keats 819 . . . . . A3
Powell Creek C5
Rankine Store E5
Robinson River E4
Rockhampton Downs D5
Rodinga D8
Rum Jungle B2
Santa Teresa 479 . . . . . D8
Soudan E6
Stirling Station C6
Tanami A5
Tarlton Downs E7
Tea Tree Well C7
Tempe Downs C8
Tennant Creek 3,118 . . . . . C5
The Granites B6
Top Springs C4
Ucharonidge D4
Umbakumba 247 . . . . . E3
Umbeara C8
Urapunga D3
Utopia D7
Victoria River Downs B4
Warrabri 459 . . . . . D6
Warrego 991 . . . . . C5
Wave Hill B4
White Quartz Hill D7
Willeroo B3
Willowra C6
Wollogorang F4
Yambah C7
Yirrkala 543 . . . . . E2
Yuendumu 687 . . . . . B7

OTHER FEATURES

Amadeus (lake) B8
Arafura (sea) D1
Arnhem (cape) E2
Arnhem Land (reg.) D2
Arnhem Land Aboriginal Res. C2
Arnold (riv.) D3
Barkly Tableland D4
Bathurst (isl.) A1
Beagle (gulf) A2
Beatrice (cape) E3
Bennett (lake) B7
Beswick Aboriginal Res. C3
Bickerton (Isl.) E2
Blaze (pt.) A2
Carpentaria (gulf) E3
Central Wedge (mt.) C7
Clarence (str.) B2
Cobourg (pen.) C1
Conner (mt.) B8
Croker (cape) C1
Daly (riv.) B2
Daly River Aboriginal Res. A2
Davenport (mt.) B7
Dundas (str.) B1
East Alligator (riv.) C2
Ehrenberg (range) B7
Elcho (isl.) D1
Finke (riv.) C8
Fitzmaurice (riv.) B3
Ford (cape) A2
Georgina (riv.) E6
Goulburn (isls.) C1
Goyder (riv.) D2
Groote Eylandt (isl.) 2,230 . . . . . E3
Haasts Bluff Aboriginal Res. B7
Hale (riv.) D8

AREA 519,768 sq. mi. (1,346,200 sq. km.)
POPULATION 154,848
CAPITAL Darwin
LARGEST CITY Darwin
HIGHEST POINT Mt. Ziel 4,955 ft. (1,510 m.)

Hanson (riv.) C6
Hay (dry riv.) E7
Hogarth (mt.) E6
Hopkins (lake) A8
Joseph Bonaparte (gulf) A3
Kata Tjuta (Olga) (mt.) B8
Katherine (riv.) C3
Lake MacKay Aboriginal Res. A6
Lander (riv.) C6
Leisler (mt.) A7
Limmen Bight (riv.) D4
Macdonald (lake) B7
Macdonnell (ranges) C7
MacKay (lake) A7
Mann (riv.) D2
Marshall (riv.) D7
Melville (bay) E2
Melville (isl.) B1
Murchison (range) D6
Napier (mt.) A4
Neale (lake) A8
Newcastle (creek) C4
Nicholson (riv.) E5
Peron (isls.) A2
Petermann (ranges) A8
Petermann Ranges Aboriginal Res. A8
Port Darwin (inlet) B2
Ranken (riv.) E6
Robinson (riv.) E4
Roper (riv.) C3
Sandover (riv.) D6
Simpson (des.) E8
Singleton (mt.) B6
Sir Edward Pellew Group (isls.) E3
South Alligator (riv.) C2
Stanley (mt.) B7
Stewart (cape) D1
Stirling (creek) A4
Sturt (plain) C4
Tanami (des.) C5
Timor (sea) A2
Todd (riv.) D8
Uluru Nat'l Park B8
Vanderlin (isl.) E3
Van Diemen (cape) A1
Van Diemen (gulf) B1
Victoria (riv.) B3
Wagait Aboriginal Res B2
Warwick (chan.) E3
Wessel (cape) E1
Wessel (isls.) E1
West Baines (riv.) A4
White (lake) A6
Woods (lake) C4
Young (mt.) D3
Ziel (mt.) C7

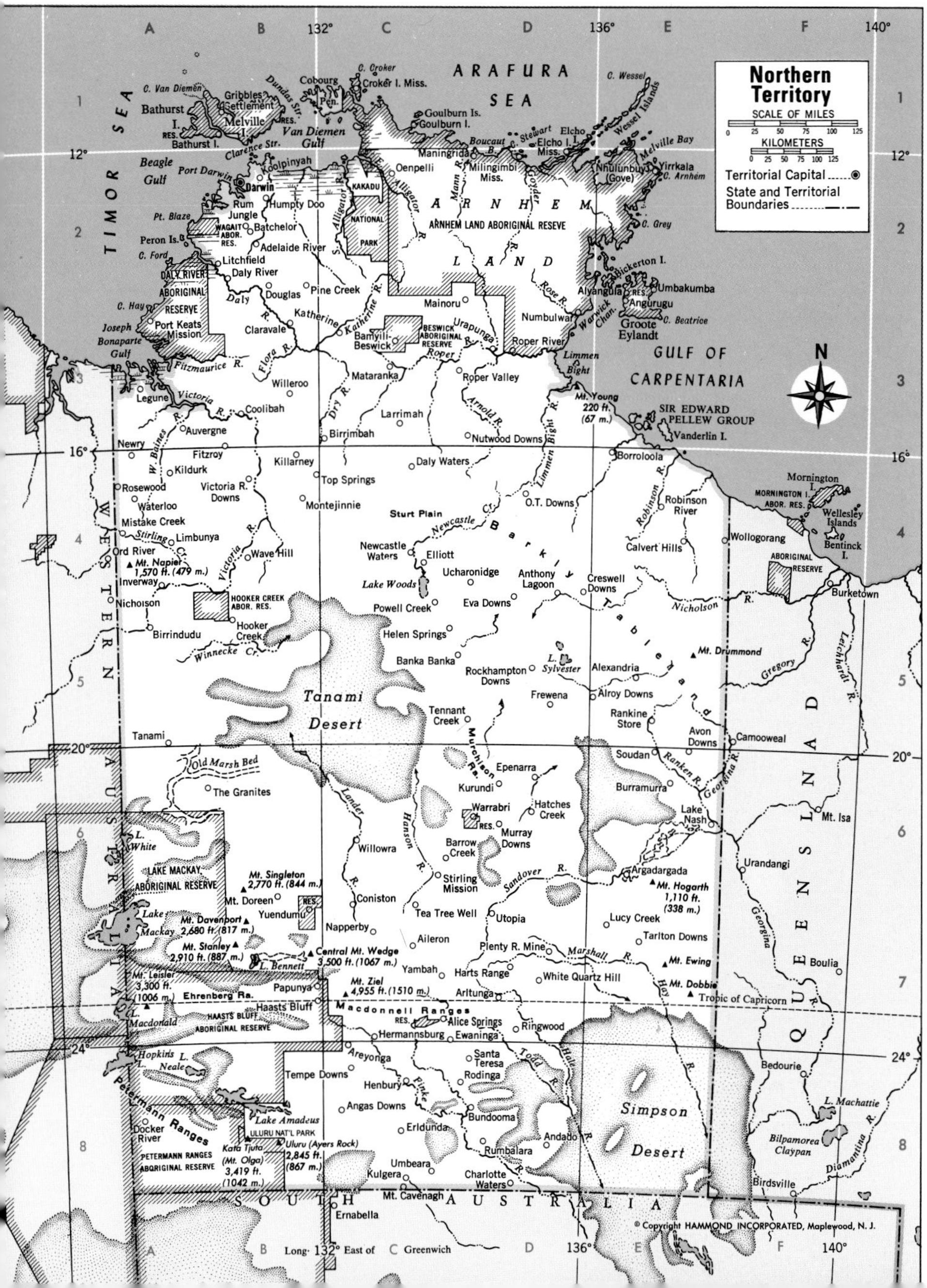
Northern Territory
SCALE OF MILES
KILOMETERS
Territorial Capital
State and Territorial Boundaries
ARAFURA SEA
TIMOR SEA
GULF OF CARPENTARIA
ARNHEM LAND ABORIGINAL RESERVE
Tanami Desert
Simpson Desert
Barkly Tableland
WESTERN AUSTRALIA
QUEENSLAND
SOUTH AUSTRALIA
Tropic of Capricorn
Macdonnell Ranges
Long. 132° East of Greenwich
© Copyright HAMMOND INCORPORATED, Maplewood, N. J.

Topography

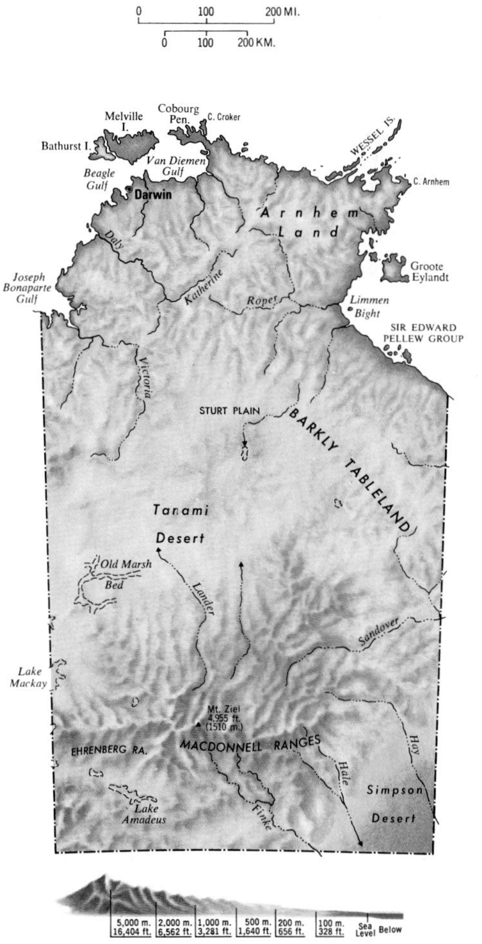
0 100 200 MI.
0 100 200 KM.
Melville I.
Cobourg Pen.
C. Croker
Bathurst I.
WESSEL IS.
Van Diemen Gulf
Beagle Gulf
Darwin
C. Arnhem
Arnhem Land
Groote Eylandt
Joseph Bonaparte Gulf
Limmen Bight
SIR EDWARD PELLEW GROUP
STURT PLAIN
BARKLY TABLELAND
Tanami Desert
Old Marsh Bed
Lake Mackay
Mt. Ziel 4,955 ft. (1510 m.)
EHRENBERG RA.
MACDONNELL RANGES
Lake Amadeus
Simpson Desert
5,000 m. 16,404 ft.
2,000 m. 6,562 ft.
1,000 m. 3,281 ft.
500 m. 1,640 ft.
200 m. 656 ft.
100 m. 328 ft.
Sea Level
Below

South Australia

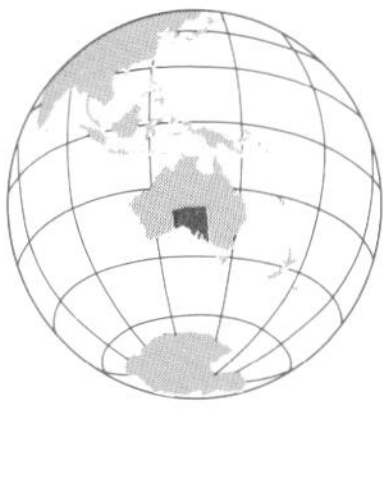

AREA 379,922 sq. mi. (984,000 sq. km.)
POPULATION 1,345,945
CAPITAL Adelaide
LARGEST CITY Adelaide
HIGHEST POINT Mt. Woodroffe 4,970 ft. (1,515 m.)

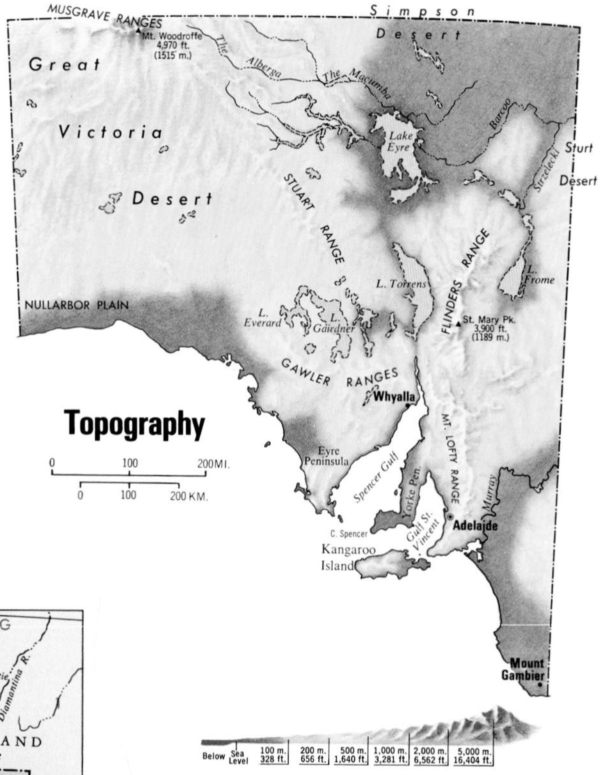

Topography
0 100 200 MI.
0 100 200 KM.
MUSGRAVE RANGES
Mt. Woodroffe 4,970 ft. (1515 m.)
Simpson Desert
Great Victoria Desert
The Alberga
The Macumba
Barcoo
Lake Eyre
Sturt Desert
Strzelecki
STUART RANGE
FLINDERS RANGE
L. Frome
L. Torrens
St. Mary Pk. 3,900 ft. (1189 m.)
NULLARBOR PLAIN
L. Everard
L. Gairdner
GAWLER RANGES
Whyalla
Eyre Peninsula
Spencer Gulf
Yorke Pen.
Gulf St. Vincent
MT. LOFTY RANGE
Murray
Adelaide
C. Spencer
Kangaroo Island
Mount Gambier
Below Sea Level
100 m. 328 ft.
200 m. 656 ft.
500 m. 1,640 ft.
1,000 m. 3,281 ft.
2,000 m. 6,562 ft.
5,000 m. 16,404 ft.

CITIES and TOWNS

Adelaide (cap.) 882,520 .... B6
Adelaide *931,886 .... B6
Andamooka 402 .... E4
Angaston 1,753 .... F6
Balaklava 1,306 .... F6
Barmera 2,014 .... G6
Beachport 357 .... F7
Berri 3,419 .... G6
Birdwood 397 .... C7
Blinman F4
Bordertown 2,138 .... G7
Brighton 19,441 .... A8
Burnside 37,593 .... B8
Burra 1,222 .... F5
Campbelltown 43,084 .... B7
Ceduna 2,794 .... D5
Clare 2,381 .... F5
Cleve 827 .... E5
Coober Pedy 2,078 .... D3
Cowell 626 .... E5
Crafters-Bridgewater 9,764 .. B8
Crystal Brook 1,240 .... E5
Cummins 767 .... D6
Edithburgh 359 .... E6
Elizabeth 32,608 .... B7
Elliston ○1,345 .... D5
Enfield 66,797 .... B7
Gawler 9,433 .... B6
Gladstone 680 .... F5
Glenelg 13,306 .... A8
Gumeracha 387 .... C7
Hahndorf 1,274 .... C8
Hawker 351 .... F4
Hindmarsh 7,593 .... A7
Iron Knob 398 .... E5
Jamestown 1,384 .... F5
Kadina 2,943 .... F5
Kapunda 1,340 .... F6
Keith 1,147 .... G7
Kensington and Norwood 8,950 .... B8
Kimba 862 .... E5
Kingscote 1,236 .... E6
Kingston 1,325 .... G7
Lameroo 599 .... G6
Laura 504 .... F5
Leigh Creek 1,635 .... F4
Lobethal 1,522 .... C7
Lock 213 .... D5
Loxton 3,100 .... G6
Lyndoch 539 .... C6
Maitland 1,085 .... E6
Mannum 1,984 .... F6
Marion 66,580 .... A8
Marree E3
Meadows 388 .... B8
Meningie 807 .... F6
Millicent 5,255 .... F7
Minlaton 865 .... E6
Mitcham 60,309 .... B8
Moonta 1,751 .... E5
Mount Barker 4,190 .... C8
Mount Gambier 18,193 .... G7
Murray Bridge 8,664 .... F6
Nairne 706 .... C8
Nangwarry 758 .... G7
Naracoorte 4,758 .... G7
Noarlunga 60,928 .... A8
Nuriootpa 2,851 .... F6
Oodnadatta D2
Orroroo 604 .... F5
Payneham 16,502 .... B7
Penola 1,205 .... G7
Peterborough 2,575 .... F5
Pinnaroo 731 .... G6
Port Adelaide 35,407 .... A7
Port Augusta 15,566 .... E5
Port Broughton 587 .... F5
Port Lincoln 9,846 .... E6
Port Pirie 14,695 .... E5
Prospect 18,591 .... B7
Quorn 1,049 .... F5
Renmark 3,475 .... G5
Robe 590 .... F7
Salisbury 86,451 .... B7
Snowtown 492 .... E5
Strathalbyn 1,756 .... F6
Streaky Bay 985 .... D5
Tailem Bend 1,677 .... F6
Tanunda 2,621 .... C6
Tea Tree Gully 67,237 .... B7
Thebarton 9,208 .... A7
Tumby Bay 933 .... E6
Unley 35,844 .... B8
Uraidla 303 .... B8
Victor Harbor 4,522 .... F6
Virginia 353 .... B7
Waikerie 1,629 .... F6
Wallaroo 2,043 .... E5
West Torrens 45,099 .... A8
Whyalla 30,518 .... E5
Williamstown 495 .... C7
Willunga 667 .... F6
Wilmington 227 .... F6
Woodside 724 .... C8
Woodville 77,634 .... A7
Woomera 1,658 .... E4
Wudinna 572 .... D5
Yorketown 713 .... E6

OTHER FEATURES

Acraman (lake) D5
Alberga, The (riv.) D2
Alexandrina (lake) F6
Anxious (bay) D5
Arckaringa (creek) D2
Barcoo (creek) F3
Birksgate (range) A2
Blanche (lake) F3
Brady (mt.) D3
Cadibarrawirracanna (lake) .. D3
Callabonna (lake) F3
Catastrophe (cape) D6
Coffin (bay) D6
Coffin Bay (pen.) D6
Coopers (Barcoo) (creek) F3
Coorong, The (lag.) F6
Dey Dey (lake) B3
Encounter (bay) F6
Everard (lake) D4
Everard (ranges) C2
Eyre (pen.) D5
Eyre North (lake) E3
Eyre South (lake) E3
Finke (riv.) C1
Flinders (range) F4
Frome (lake) G4
Gairdner (lake) D4
Gawler (ranges) E5
Gawler (riv.) B6
Gilles (lake) E5
Goyders (lag.) F2
Great Australian (bight) A5
Great Victoria (des.) B3
Gregory (lake) F3
Hack (mt.) F4
Hamilton, The (riv.) D2
Harris (lake) D4
Head of Bight (bay) B4
Indian Ocean E7
Investigator (str.) E6
Investigator Group (isls.) D5
Island (lag.) E4
Jaffa (cape) F7
Kangaroo (isl.) 3,515 .... E7
Lacepede (bay) F7
Lofty (mt.) B8
Macfarlane (lake) E5
Macumba, The (riv.) E2
Maurice (lake) B3
Meramangye (lake) C3
Morris (mt.) B2
Murray (res.) F6
Musgrave (ranges) B2
Neales, The (riv.) E3
Northumberland (cape) F8
Nukey Bluff (mt.) D5
Nullarbor (plain) A4
Nuyts (arch.) C5
Nuyts (cape) C5
Peera Peera Poolanna (lake) . F2
Saint Mary (peak) F4
Saint Vincent (gulf) F6
Serpentine (lakes) A3
Simpson (des.) E1
Sir Joseph Banks Group (isls.) E6
Spencer (cape) E6
Spencer (gulf) E6
Stevenson, The (riv.) D2
Streaky (bay) C5
Strzelecki (creek) G3
Stuart (range) D3
Sturt (des.) G3
The Alberga (riv.) D2
The Coorong (lag.) F6
The Hamilton (riv.) D2
The Macumba (riv.) E2
The Neales (riv.) E3
The Stevenson (riv.) D2
The Warburton (riv.) F2
Thistle (isl.) E6
Torrens (lake) E4
Torrens (riv.) C7
Warburton, The (riv.) F2
Wilkinson (lakes) C3
Woodroffe (mt.) B2
Yalata Aboriginal Res. B4
Yarle (lakes) B4
Yorke (pen.) E6

○ Population of district.
*Population of met. area.

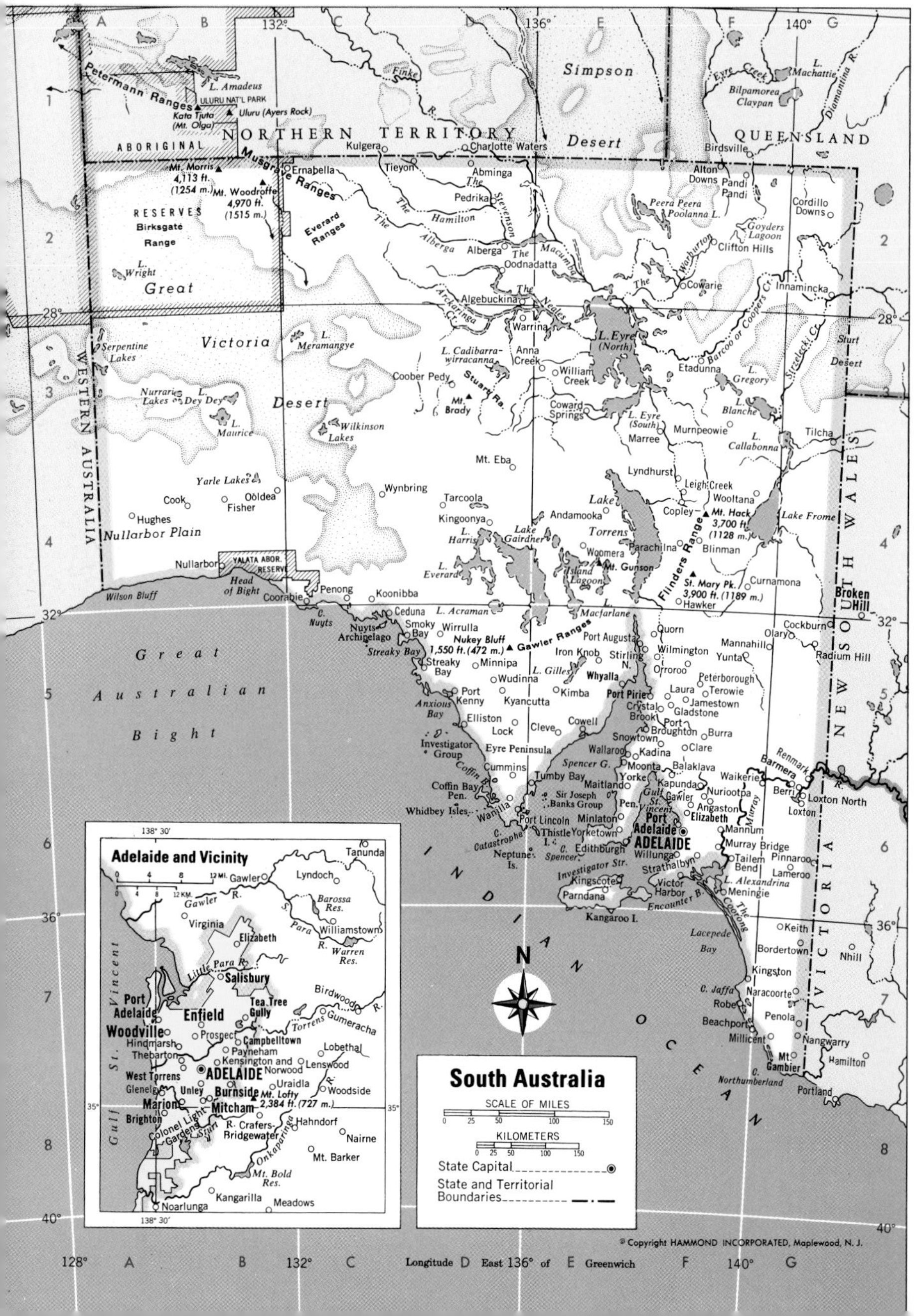

South Australia
SCALE OF MILES
0 25 50 100 150
KILOMETERS
0 25 50 100 150
State Capital
State and Territorial Boundaries
Adelaide and Vicinity
NORTHERN TERRITORY
QUEENSLAND
NEW SOUTH WALES
VICTORIA
WESTERN AUSTRALIA
Simpson Desert
Great Victoria Desert
Nullarbor Plain
Great Australian Bight
INDIAN OCEAN
ABORIGINAL RESERVES
Musgrave Ranges
Mt. Woodroffe 4,970 ft. (1515 m.)
Mt. Morris 4,113 ft. (1254 m.)
Everard Ranges
L. Eyre (North)
L. Eyre (South)
Lake Torrens
Lake Gairdner
Lake Frome
Flinders Ranges
Gawler Ranges
Mt. Hack 3,700 ft. (1128 m.)
St. Mary Pk. 3,900 ft. (1189 m.)
Nukey Bluff 1,550 ft. (472 m.)
Eyre Peninsula
Spencer G.
Gulf St. Vincent
Kangaroo I.
ADELAIDE
Mt. Lofty 2,384 ft. (727 m.)
Broken Hill
Longitude East 136° of Greenwich
© Copyright HAMMOND INCORPORATED, Maplewood, N. J.

CITIES and TOWNS

Aramac 428 . . . . C4
Archerfield 785 . . . . D3
Ascot 4,298 . . . . E2
Atherton 4,196 . . . . C3
Ayr 8,787 . . . . C3
Balmoral 2,915 . . . . E2
Barcaldine 1,432 . . . . C4
Beaudesert 3,780 . . . . E6
Biloela 4,643 . . . . D5
Birdsville A5
Blackall 1,609 . . . . C5
Blackwater 5,434 . . . . D4
Boulia 292 . . . . A4
Bowen 7,663 . . . . D3
Brisbane (cap.) 689,378 . . . . D2
Brisbane *1,028,527 . . . . . . D2
Bucasia 1,356 . . . . D4
Bundaberg 32,560 . . . . D5
Burketown 210 . . . . A3
Cairns 48,557 . . . . C3
Caloundra 16,758 . . . . E5
Camooweal 251 . . . . A3
Camp Hill 8,999 . . . . E3
Capella 660 . . . . D4
Cardwell 1,249 . . . . C3
Charleville 3,523 . . . . C5
Charters Towers 6,823 . . . . . C4
Cherbourg 963 . . . . D5
Chermside 6,892 . . . . D2
Clermont 1,659 . . . . C4
Cloncurry 1,961 . . . . B4
Collinsville 2,756 . . . . C4
Cooktown 913 . . . . C2
Coopers Plains 4,492 . . . . . . D3
Corinda 4,894 . . . . D3
Croydon ○255 . . . . B3
Cunnamulla 1,627 . . . . C5
Dalby 8,784 . . . . D5
Dirranbandi 480 . . . . D6
East Brisbane 4,853 . . . . E3
Eidsvold 613 . . . . D5
Emerald 4,628 . . . . C4
Esk 676 . . . . E5
Gatton 4,190 . . . . E5
Gayndah 1,708 . . . . D5
Geebung 4,850 . . . . E2
Georgetown 319 . . . . B3
Gladstone 22,083 . . . . D4
Gold Coast 135,437 . . . . E6
Goondiwindi 3,576 . . . . D6
Gordonvale 2,375 . . . . C3
Greenslopes 7,219 . . . . E3
Gympie 10,768 . . . . E5
Hervey Bay 13,569 . . . . E5
Holland Park 7,363 . . . . E3
Home Hill 3,138 . . . . C3
Hughenden 1,657 . . . . B4
Inala 17,383 . . . . D3
Indooroopilly 7,959 . . . . D3
Ingham 5,598 . . . . C3
Injune 407 . . . . D5
Innisfail 7,933 . . . . C3
Ipswich 68,297 . . . . E5
Isisford ○605 . . . . C5
Jandowae 781 . . . . D5
Jericho ○1,177 . . . . C4
Julia Creek 602 . . . . B4
Karumba 670 . . . . B3
Kilcoy 1,257 . . . . E5
Kingaroy 5,134 . . . . D5
Longreach 2,971 . . . . B4
Mackay 35,361 . . . . D4
Mareeba 6,309 . . . . C3
Marian 796 . . . . D4
Maroochydore-Mooloolaba 17,460 . . . . E5
Maryborough 20,111 . . . . . . E5
Mary Kathleen 830 . . . . A4
McKinlay ○1,477 . . . . B4
Millmerran 1,107 . . . . D5
Mitchell 1,171 . . . . C5
Mitchelton 5,810 . . . . D2
Monto 1,397 . . . . D5
Moorooka 8,740 . . . . D3
Moranbah 4,362 . . . . C9
Mossman 1,614 . . . . C3
Mount Isa 23,679 . . . . A4
Moura 2,871 . . . . D5
Murgon 2,327 . . . . D5
Nambour 7,965 . . . . E5
Newmarket 3,520 . . . . D2
Normanton 926 . . . . B3
Nundah 7,358 . . . . E2
Proserpine 3,058 . . . . D4
Quilpie 694 . . . . C5
Ravenshoe 915 . . . . C3
Redcliffe 42,223 . . . . E5
Richmond 784 . . . . B4
Rockhampton 50,146 . . . . . . D4
Roma 5,706 . . . . D5
Saint George 2,204 . . . . D5
Saint Lucia 6,075 . . . . D3
Sandgate 6,776 . . . . D2
Sarina 2,815 . . . . D4
Springsure 774 . . . . D5
Stafford (Stafford Heights) 13,731 . . . . D2
Stanthorpe 3,966 . . . . D6
Tara 864 . . . . D5
Taroom 688 . . . . D5
Tewantin-Noosa 9,965 . . . . . E5
Theodore 643 . . . . D5
Thursday Island 2,283 . . . . . B1
Toowoomba 63,401 . . . . D5
Townsville 86,112 . . . . C3
Tully 2,728 . . . . C3
Walkerston 1,277 . . . . D4
Warwick 8,853 . . . . D6
Weipa 2,433 . . . . B2
Windsor 6,119 . . . . D2
Winton 1,259 . . . . B4
Wynnum 10,794 . . . . E5
Yeppoon 6,447 . . . . D4
Yeronga 4,579 . . . . D3

OTHER FEATURES

Albatross (bay) B2
Archer (riv.) B2
Balonne (riv.) D6
Banks (isl.) B1
Barcoo (creek) B5
Barkly Tableland A4
Bartle Frere (mt.) C3
Beal (range) B5

AREA 666,872 sq. mi. (1,727,200 sq. km.)
POPULATION 2,587,315
CAPITAL Brisbane
LARGEST CITY Brisbane
HIGHEST POINT Mt. Bartle Frere 5,287 ft. (1,611 m.)

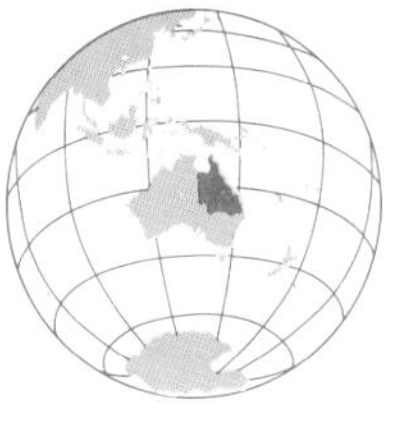

Queensland
SCALE OF MILES
KILOMETERS
Territorial Capital
State and Territorial Boundaries
Brisbane and Vicinity
PAPUA NEW GUINEA
CORAL SEA
CORAL SEA ISLS. TERR.
GULF OF CARPENTARIA
GREAT BARRIER REEF
GREAT DIVIDING RANGE
NORTHERN TERRITORY
SOUTH AUSTRALIA
NEW SOUTH WALES
Simpson Desert
Torres Strait
Thursday Island
Cairns
Townsville
Mackay
Rockhampton
Bundaberg
Maryborough
Toowoomba
Ipswich
BRISBANE
Gold Coast
Mount Isa
Longreach
Charleville
Roma
Darling Downs
Tropic of Capricorn
144° Longitude East of Greenwich 148°
© Copyright HAMMOND INCORPORATED, Maplewood, N. J.

Topography

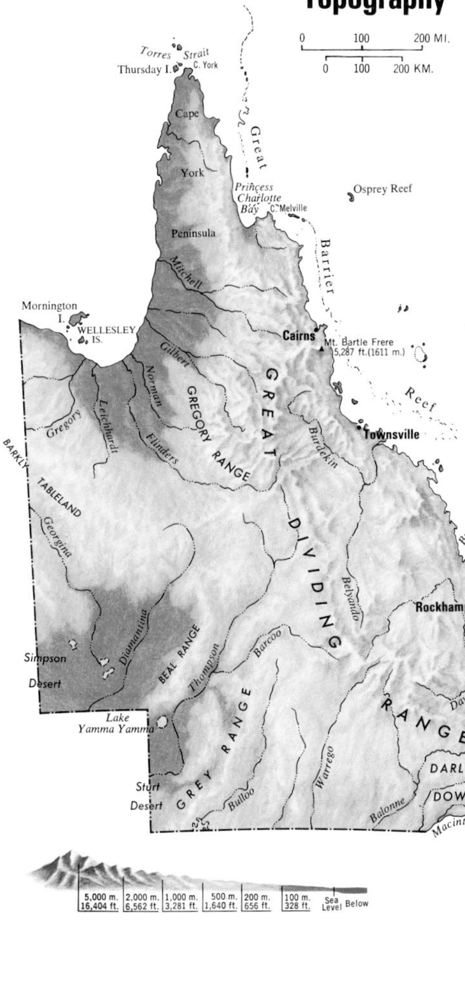
0 100 200 MI.
0 100 200 KM.
Torres Strait
Thursday I.
C. York
Cape York Peninsula
Great Barrier Reef
Osprey Reef
Princess Charlotte Bay
C. Melville
Mornington I.
WELLESLEY IS.
Cairns
Mt. Bartle Frere 5,287 ft.(1611 m.)
Townsville
GREGORY RANGE
GREAT DIVIDING RANGE
BARKLY TABLELAND
Broad Sd.
Capricorn Channel
Rockhampton
Hervey Bay
Sandy C.
Fraser or Gt. Sandy I.
Simpson Desert
BEAL RANGE
Lake Yamma Yamma
GREY RANGE
DARLING DOWNS
Brisbane
Sturt Desert
5,000 m. 16,404 ft.
2,000 m. 6,562 ft.
1,000 m. 3,281 ft.
500 m. 1,640 ft.
200 m. 656 ft.
100 m. 328 ft.
Sea Level
Below

Belyando (riv.) C4
Broad (sound) D4
Bulloo (lake) B6
Bulloo (riv.) B6
Bunker Group (isls.) E4
Burdekin (riv.) C3
Cape York (pen.) B2
Capricorn (chan.) D4
Capricorn Group (isls.) E4
Carnarvon (range) D5
Carpentaria (gulf) A2
Cloncurry (riv.) B4
Coopers (Barcoo) (creek) . . . B5
Coral (sea) C1
Culgoa (riv.) C6
Cumberland (isls.) D4
Curtis (isl.) D4
Darling Downs D5
Dawson (riv.) D5
Diamantina (riv.) B4
Drummond (range) C5
Duifken (pt.) B2
Endeavour (str.) B1
Fitzroy (riv.) D4
Flinders (riv.) B3
Fraser (isl.) E5
Georgina (riv.) A4
Gilbert (riv.) B3
Great Dividing (range) C4
Gregory (range) B3
Gregory (riv.) A3
Grey (range) B5
Hamilton (riv.) B4
Hervey (bay) E5
Hinchinbrook (isl.) C3
Hook (isl.) D4
Leichhardt (riv.) A3
Machattie (lake) B5
Macintyre (riv.) D6
Maranoa (riv.) C5
Mary (riv.) E5
Melville (cape) C2
Mitchell (riv.) B2
Moreton (bay) E5
Moreton (isl.) E5
Mornington (isl.) A3
Norman (riv.) B3
Northern Peninsula Aboriginal Res. B1
Prince of Wales (isl.) B1
Princess Charlotte (bay) C2
Sandy (cape) E5
Selwyn (range) B4
Simpson (des.) A5
Sturt (des.) B3
Suttor (riv.) C4
Swain (reefs) E4
Thompson (riv.) B5
Torres (str.) B1
Warrego (range) C5
Warrego (riv.) C5
Wellesley (isls.) A3
Whitsunday (isl.) D4
Willies (range) C6
Yamma Yamma (lake) B5
York (cape) B1

○ Population of district.
*Population of met. area.

New South Wales and Victoria

(continued)

Ryde 88,948 . . . . J3
Rylstone 651 . . . . E3
Salisbury Downs B1
Sawtell 5,970 . . . . G2
Scone 3,949 . . . . F3
Shellharbour 41,790 . . . . F4
Singleton 9,572 . . . . F3
Smithtown-Gladstone 953 . . G2
South Sydney 30,776 . . . . . . J3
South West Rocks 1,314 . . . G2
Stephen's Creek A2
Strathfield 25,882 . . . . J3
Stroud 522 . . . . G3
Sussex Inlet 1,293 . . . . F4
Sutherland 165,336 . . . . J4
Sydney (cap.) 2,876,508 . . . J3
Sydney †3,204,696 . . . . J3
Talbingo 481 . . . . E4
Tamworth 29,657 . . . . F2
Taralga 272 . . . . E4
Tarcutta 263 . . . . D4
Taree 14,697 . . . . G2
Tathra 1,077 . . . . F5
Temora 4,350 . . . . D4
Tenterfield 3,402 . . . . G1
Terrigal-The Entrance 37,891 F3
The Rock 693 . . . . D4
Thurloo Downs B1
Tibbita C4
Tibooburra B1
Tiltagara C2
Tingha 886 . . . . F1
Tocumwal 1,174 . . . . C4
Tongo B2
Torrowangee A2
Tottenham 366 . . . . D3
Trangie 977 . . . . D3
Trundle 515 . . . . D3
Tullamore 324 . . . . D3
Tumbarumba 1,536 . . . . D4
Tumut 5,816 . . . . E4
Tweed Heads G1
Ulladulla 6,018 . . . . F4
Ulmarra 395 . . . . G1
Ungarie 428 . . . . D3
Uralla 2,090 . . . . F2
Urana 419 . . . . D4
Urbenville 282 . . . . G1
Urunga 2,045 . . . . G2
Villawood H3
Wagga Wagga 36,837 . . . . . D4
Wakool 278 . . . . C4
Walcha 1,674 . . . . F2
Walgett 2,157 . . . . E2
Walla Walla 593 . . . . D4
Wallerawang 1,855 . . . . F3
Wangi-Rathmines 5,106 . . . . F3
Warialda 1,340 . . . . F1
Warragamba 1,406 . . . . F3
Warren 2,153 . . . . D2
Warringah ○172,653 . . . . . . K3
Wauchope 3,645 . . . . G2
Waverley 61,575 . . . . K3
Waverley Downs B1
Wee Waa 1,904 . . . . E2
Wellington 5,280 . . . . E3
Wentworth 1,180 . . . . B4
Werris Creek 1,924 . . . . F2
West Wyalong 3,778 . . . . . . D3
Wetuppa B4
White Cliffs B2
Whitton 344 . . . . D4
Whyjonta B1
Wilcannia 982 . . . . B2
Willoughby 52,120 . . . . J3
Willow Tree 258 . . . . F2
Wingham 3,937 . . . . G2
Wollongong 169,381 . . . . F4
Wollongong †222,539 . . . . . F4
Woodburn 647 . . . . G1
Woodenbong 409 . . . . G1
Woodstock 266 . . . . E3
Woolgoolga 2,081 . . . . G2
Wooli 457 . . . . G1
Woollahra 51,659 . . . . K3
Wyong 3,902 . . . . F3
Yallock C3
Yalpunga A1
Yamba 2,528 . . . . G1
Yancannia B2
Yanco 415 . . . . D4
Yantara B1
Yass 4,283 . . . . E4
Yenda 697 . . . . D4
Yeoval 288 . . . . E3
Young 6,906 . . . . E4

OTHER FEATURES

Ana Branch, Darling (riv.) . . . A3
Australian Alps (mts.) D5
Barrington Tops (mt.) F2
Barwon (riv.) D2
Blue (mts.) F3
Bogan (riv.) D2
Bondi (beach) K3
Botany (bay) J4
Broken (bay) F3
Burrinjuck (res.) E4
Byron (cape) G1
Caryapundy (swamp) B1
Castlereagh (riv.) E2
Cawndilla (lake) A3
Clarence (riv.) G1
Colo (riv.) F3
Cowal (lake) D3
Culgoa (riv.) D1
Cuttaburra (creek) C1
Darling (riv.) B3
Dumaresq (riv.) F1
Eucumbene (lake) E5
George (lake) E4
Georges (riv.) H4
Gower (mt.) J2
Great Dividing (range) E3
Green (cape) F5
Gunderbooka (ranges) C2
Gwydir (riv.) E1
Howe (cape) F5
Hume (res.) D4
Hunter (riv.) F3
Kosciusko (mt.) E5
Kurnell (pen.) J4
Lachlan (range) C3
Lachlan (riv.) C3
Liverpool (range) F2
Lord Howe (isl.) 287 . . . . J2
Macintyre (riv.) E1
Macquarie (lake) F3
Macquarie (riv.) D2
Main Barrier (range) A2
Manning (riv.) F2
Marthaguy (creek) D2
McPherson (range) G1
Menindee (lake) B3
Monaro (range) E5
Moonie (riv.) E1
Moulamein (creek) C4
Mount Royal (range) F2
Murray (riv.) A4
Murrumbidgee (riv.) C4
Myall (lake) G3
Namoi (riv.) E2
Narran (lake) D1
New England (range) F1
Paroo (riv.) C1
Parramatta (riv.) J3
Poopeloe (lake) C2
Port Jackson (inlet) J3
Port Stephens (inlet) G3
Richmond (range) G1
Richmond (riv.) G1
Riverina (reg.) C4
Robe (mt.) A2
Round, The (mt.) G2
Salt, The (lake) B2
Shoalhaven (riv.) E4
Smoky (cape) G2
Snowy (mts.) E5
Snowy (riv.) E5
Stony (ranges) B2
Sturt (mt.) A1
Sugarloaf (pt.) G3
Talyawalka (creek) B2
Tandou (lake) A3
Tasman (sea) F5
The Round (mts.) G2
The Salt (lake) B2
Timbarra (riv.) G1
Tuggerah (lake) F3
Victoria (lake) A3
Warrego (riv.) C1
Willandra Billabong (creek) . . C3
Wollondilly (riv.) F4

VICTORIA

CITIES and TOWNS

Alexandra 1,756 . . . . C5
Altona 30,909 . . . . H5
Apollo Bay 921 . . . . B6
Ararat 8,336 . . . . B5
Avoca 1,032 . . . . B5
Bacchus Marsh 6,224 . . . . . . C5
Bairnsdale 9,459 . . . . D5
Ballarat 35,681 . . . . C5
Ballarat †71,930 . . . . C5
Balmoral 257 . . . . A5
Beaufort 1,214 . . . . B5
Beechworth 3,154 . . . . D5
Belgrave Heights J5
Belgrave South K5
Benalla 8,151 . . . . D5
Bendigo 31,841 . . . . C5
Bendigo †58,818 . . . . C5
Berwick 36,181 . . . . K6
Beulah 290 . . . . B4
Birchip 895 . . . . B4
Birregurra 416 . . . . B6
Boort 863 . . . . B5
Box Hill 47,579 . . . . J5
Bright 1,545 . . . . D5
Brighton 33,697 . . . . J5
Broadford 1,580 . . . . C5
Broadmeadows 103,540 . . . . H4
Brunswick 44,464 . . . . H5
Bruthen 449 . . . . D5
Bundoora J4
Camberwell 85,883 . . . . J5
Camperdown 3,545 . . . . C6
Cann River 345 . . . . E5
Casterton 1,945 . . . . A5
Castlemaine 7,583 . . . . C5
Caulfield 69,922 . . . . J5
Charlton 1,377 . . . . B5
Chelsea 26,034 . . . . J6
Churchill 4,796 . . . . D6
Clunes 761 . . . . B5
Cobden 1,453 . . . . B6
Cobram 3,817 . . . . C4
Coburg 55,035 . . . . H5
Cohuna 2,178 . . . . C4
Colac 10,587 . . . . B6
Coldstream 1,395 . . . . K4
Coleraine 1,232 . . . . A5
Collingwood 15,089 . . . . J5
Corryong 1,320 . . . . D5
Craigieburn 4,296 . . . . C5
Cranbourne 9,400 . . . . C6
Creswick 2,036 . . . . B5
Croydon 36,210 . . . . K5
Dandenong 54,962 . . . . K5
Darby D6
Dartmoor 349 . . . . A5
Daylesford 2,883 . . . . C5
Derrinallum 287 . . . . B5
Dimboola 1,675 . . . . B5
Donald 1,609 . . . . B5
Doncaster and Templestowe
90,660 . . . . J5
Drouin 3,492 . . . . C6
Dunkeld 402 . . . . B5
Dunolly 621 . . . . B5
Eaglehawk 7,355 . . . . C5
Echuca 7,943 . . . . C5
Edenhope 827 . . . . A5
Eildon 737 . . . . C5
Eltham 34,648 . . . . J4
Erica 236 . . . . D5
Essendon 56,380 . . . . H5
Euroa 2,640 . . . . C5
Fitzroy 19,112 . . . . H5
Footscray 49,756 . . . . H5
Geelong 14,471 . . . . C6
Geelong †137,173 . . . . C6
Geelong West 14,823 . . . . . . C6
Goroke 370 . . . . A5
Gunbower 259 . . . . C4
Hamilton 9,751 . . . . B5
Hawthorn 30,689 . . . . J5
Healesville 4,526 . . . . C5
Heathcote 1,213 . . . . C5
Heidelberg 64,757 . . . . J5
Heyfield 1,635 . . . . D6
Heywood 1,266 . . . . A6
Hopetoun 1,832 . . . . B4
Horsham 12,034 . . . . B5
Inglewood 674 . . . . B5
Inverloch 1,523 . . . . C6
Kaniva 956 . . . . A5
Keilor 81,762 . . . . H5
Kerang 4,049 . . . . B4
Kew 28,870 . . . . J5
Kilmore 1,728 . . . . C5
Knox 88,902 . . . . K5
Koroit 1,988 . . . . B6
Korumburra 2,798 . . . . D6
Kyabram 5,414 . . . . C5
Kyneton 3,185 . . . . C5
Lake Boga 502 . . . . B4
Lake Bolac 211 . . . . B5
Lakes Entrance 3,414 . . . . . . E5
Lara 4,231 . . . . C6
Leongatha 3,736 . . . . C6
Lillydale 62,077 . . . . J4
Macarthur 322 . . . . A6
Maffra 3,822 . . . . D5
Maldon 1,009 . . . . C5
Mallacoota 726 . . . . E5
Malvern 43,211 . . . . J5
Mansfield 1,920 . . . . D5
Maryborough 7,858 . . . . B5
Melbourne (cap.)
2,578,759 . . . . H5
Melbourne †2,722,817 . . . . . H5
Melton 20,599 . . . . C5
Merbein 1,735 . . . . A4
Merino 298 . . . . A5
Mildura 15,763 . . . . A4
Minyip 567 . . . . B5
Moe 16,649 . . . . D6
Montmorency J4
Montrose K5
Moorabbin 97,810 . . . . J5
Mooroopna C5
Mordialloc 27,869 . . . . J6
Morea A5
Mornington 23,512 . . . . C6
Mortlake 1,056 . . . . B6
Morwell 16,491 . . . . D5
Mount Beauty 1,509 . . . . D5
Murrayville 313 . . . . A4
Murtoa 946 . . . . B5
Myrtleford 2,815 . . . . D5
Nagambie 1,102 . . . . C5
Narre Warren North 761 . . . . K5
Nathalia 1,222 . . . . C5
Natimuk 482 . . . . A5
Newtown 10,210 . . . . C6
Nhill 1,567 . . . . A5
Northcote 51,235 . . . . J5
Numurkah 2,713 . . . . C5
Nunawading 97,052 . . . . J5
Nyah 351 . . . . B4
Nyah West 535 . . . . B4
Oakleigh 55,612 . . . . J5
Omeo 272 . . . . D5
Orbost 2,586 . . . . E5
Ouyen 1,527 . . . . B4
Penshurst 558 . . . . B5
Porepunkah 268 . . . . D5
Port Albert 267 . . . . D6
Port Fairy 2,276 . . . . B6
Portland 9,353 . . . . A6
Port Melbourne 8,585 . . . . . . H5
Prahran 45,018 . . . . J5
Preston 84,519 . . . . J4
Quambatook 359 . . . . B4
Queenscliff 3,420 . . . . C6
Rainbow 700 . . . . A4
Red Cliffs 2,409 . . . . B4
Richmond 24,506 . . . . J5
Ringwood 38,665 . . . . K5
Robinvale 1,751 . . . . B4
Rochester 2,399 . . . . C5
Rushworth 994 . . . . C5
Rutherglen 1,454 . . . . D5
Saint Arnaud 2,721 . . . . B5
Saint Kilda 49,366 . . . . J5
Sale 12,968 . . . . D6
Sandringham 31,175 . . . . J5
Sea Lake 943 . . . . B4
Sebastopol 6,462 . . . . B5
Seymour 6,494 . . . . C5
Shepparton-Mooroopna
‡28,373 . . . . C5
South Barwon 35,307 . . . . . . C6
South Melbourne 19,955 . . . J5
Springvale 80,186 . . . . J5
Stawell 6,160 . . . . B5
Sunbury 11,085 . . . . C5
Sunshine 94,419 . . . . H5
Swan Hill 8,398 . . . . B4
Swifts Creek 288 . . . . D5
Tallangatta 950 . . . . D5
Tatura 2,697 . . . . C5
Templestowe and Doncaster
90,660 . . . . J5
Terang 2,111 . . . . B6
Tongala 994 . . . . C5
Traralgon 18,057 . . . . D6
Underbool 274 . . . . A4
Wangaratta 16,202 . . . . D5
Warburton 2,009 . . . . C5
Warracknabeal 2,735 . . . . . . B5
Warragul 7,712 . . . . D6
Warrnambool 21,414 . . . . B6
Waverley 122,471 . . . . J5
Wedderburn 868 . . . . B5
Werrimull A4
Whittlesea 65,657 . . . . C5
Willaura 377 . . . . B5
Williamstown 25,554 . . . . H5
Winchelsea 825 . . . . B6
Wodonga 19,208 . . . . D5
Wonthaggi 4,797 . . . . C6
Woodend 1,785 . . . . C5
Wycheproof 938 . . . . B5
Yallourn 26 . . . . D6
Yarram 2,085 . . . . D6
Yarrawonga 3,442 . . . . C5
Yea 996 . . . . C5

OTHER FEATURES

Australian Alps (mts.) D5
Avoca (riv.) B5
Barry (mts.) D5
Bogong (mt.) D5
Bridgewater (cape) A6
Buller (mt.) D5
Campaspe (riv.) C5
Corangamite (lake) B6
Corner (inlet) D6
Dandenong (mt.) K5
Difficult (mt.) B5
Discovery (bay) A6
Eildon (lake) C5
French (isl.) 123 . . . . C6
Gippsland (reg.) D6
Glenelg (riv.) A5
Goulburn (riv.) C5
Hindmarsh (lake) A5
Hobsons (bay) H5
Hopkins (riv.) B5
Hume (lake) D4
Indian Ocean B6
Loddon (riv.) B5
Mitchell (riv.) D5
Mitta Mitta (riv.) D5
Mornington (pen.) C6
Mount Emu (creek) B5
Murray (riv.) A4
Nelson (cape) A6
Ninety Mile (beach) D6
Otway (cape) B6
Ovens (riv.) D5
Phillip (isl.) 2,832 . . . . C6
Portland (bay) A6
Port Phillip (bay) C6
Rocklands (res.) B5
Snowy (riv.) E5
South East (pt.) D6
Tasman (sea) F5
Tyrrell (lake) B4
Waratah (bay) C6
Wellington (lake) D6
Western Port (inlet) C6
Wilsons (prom.) D6
Wimmera (riv.) A5
Yarra (riv.) C5

*City and suburbs.
○ Population of district.
†Population of met. area.
‡Population of urban area.

Irrigation Areas and Artesian Basins in Australia

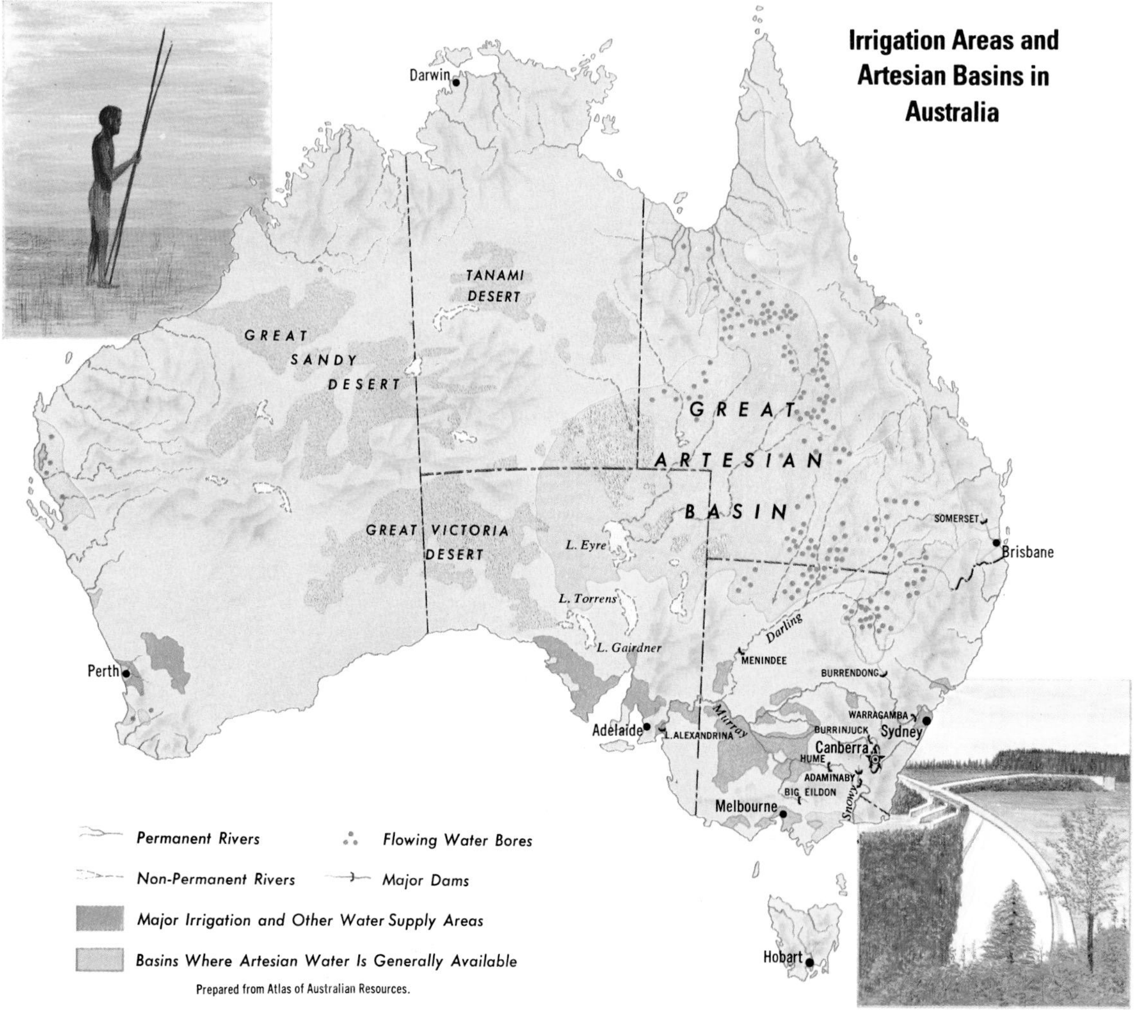

Darwin
TANAMI DESERT
GREAT SANDY DESERT
GREAT ARTESIAN BASIN
GREAT VICTORIA DESERT
L. Eyre
L. Torrens
L. Gairdner
Darling
Murray
Snowy
SOMERSET
Brisbane
MENINDEE
BURRENDONG
WARRAGAMBA
BURRINJUCK
Sydney
Canberra
HUME
ADAMINABY
EILDON
Adelaide
L. ALEXANDRINA
Perth
Melbourne
Hobart
Permanent Rivers
Non-Permanent Rivers
Flowing Water Bores
Major Dams
Major Irrigation and Other Water Supply Areas
Basins Where Artesian Water Is Generally Available

Prepared from Atlas of Australian Resources.

Topography

0 30 60 MI.
0 30 60 KM.
Flinders Island
FURNEAUX GROUP
Cape Barren I.
HUNTER ISLANDS
C. Grim
Banks Strait
Eddystone Pt.
Arthur
Mersey
Tamar
Launceston
Legges Tor 5,160 ft. (1573 m.)
South Esk
GREAT WESTERN TIERS
Mt. Ossa 5,305 ft. (1617 m.)
Great Lake
L. Sorell
Macquarie Harbour
C. Sorell
Freycinet Pen.
Oyster Bay
Derwent
Maria I.
L. Gordon
L. Pedder
Hobart
Huon
ARTHUR RA.
Storm Bay
Tasman Pen.
Port Davey
S. Bruny I.
King Island
Mt. Stanley 700 ft. (213 m.)
Stokes Pt.
South West C.
South East C.
Below Sea Level
100 m. 328 ft.
200 m. 656 ft.
500 m. 1,640 ft.
1,000 m. 3,281 ft.
2,000 m. 6,562 ft.
5,000 m. 16,404 ft.

TASMANIA

AREA 26,178 sq. mi. (67,800 sq. km.)
POPULATION 436,353
CAPITAL Hobart
LARGEST CITY Hobart
HIGHEST POINT Mt. Ossa 5,305 ft. (1,617 m.)

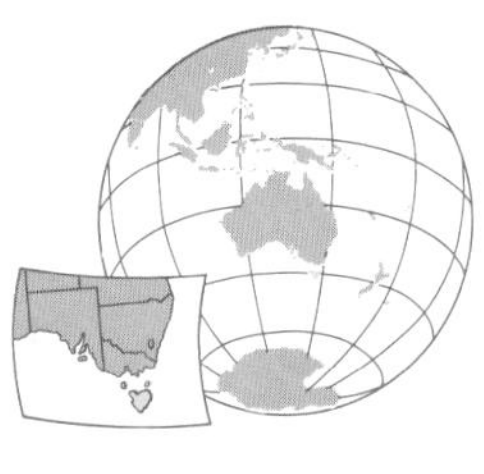

CITIES and TOWNS

Adventure Bay D5
Avoca D3
Bagdad D4
Beaconsfield 898 C3
Beauty Point 998 C3
Bell Bay C3
Bicheno 674 E3
Boat Harbour B2
Bothwell 356 C4
Bracknell 347 C3
Branxholm 273 D3
Bridgewater 6,880 D4
Bridport 885 D3
Brighton 9,441 D4
Burnie 19,994 B3
Campbell Town 879 D3
Chudleigh C3
Colebrook D4
Cressy 640 C3
Currie 859 A1
Cygnet 715 C5
Deloraine 1,923 C3
Derwent Bridge C4
Devonport 21,424 C3
Dover 570 C5
Dunalley 203 D4
Evandale 614 D3
Exeter 353 C3
Fingal 424 E3
Forth 273 C3
Franklin 479 C5
Geeveston 860 C5
George Town 5,592 C3
Glenorchy 41,019 D4
Gormanston 126 B4
Gowrie Park C3
Grassy 780 B1
Gravelly Beach 535 C3
Hadspen 908 D3
Hagley 232 C3
Hamilton 2,488 C4
Heybridge 395 C3
Hobart (cap.) 128,603 D4
Hobart *168,359 D4
Huonville-Ranelagh 1,347 C5
Kettering 288 D5
Kingston 8,556 D4
Latrobe 2,401 C3
Lauderdale 2,117 D4
Launceston 31,273 C3
Launceston *64,555 C3
Legana 964 C3
Lilydale 308 D3
Longford 2,027 C3
Luina 522 B3
Margate 476 D4
Maydena 461 C4
Meander C3
Mole Creek 303 C3
New Norfolk 6,243 C4
Nubeena 225 D5
Oatlands 545 D4
Orford 378 D4
Penguin 2,616 C3
Perth 1,229 D3
Poatina C3
Port Sorell 859 C3
Queenstown 3,714 B4
Railton 857 C3
Richmond 587 D4
Ridgley 452 B3
Ringarooma 223 D3
Rosebery 2,675 B3
Ross 289 D4
Rossarden 365 D3
Saint Helens 1,005 E3
Saint Marys 653 E3
Sassafras C3
Savage River 1,141 B3
Scottsdale 2,002 D3
Sheffield 945 C3
Smithton 3,378 A2
Snug 684 D5
Sorell-Midway Point 2,544 D4
Stanley 603 B2
Storeys Creek D3
Strahan 402 B4
Strathgordon C4
Sulphur Creek 367 C3
Swansea 428 D4
Tarraleah 498 C4
Temma A3
Triabunna 924 D4
Tullah 1,894 B3
Ulverstone 9,413 C3
Waratah 342 B3
Wesley Vale C3
Westbury 1,161 C3
Whitemark D2
Woodbridge 259 D5
Wynyard 4,582 B3
Zeehan 1,750 B3

OTHER FEATURES

Anderson (bay) D2
Anne (mt.) C4
Anser Group (isls.) C1
Arthur (lake) D4
Arthur (range) C5
Arthur (riv.) B3
Babel (isl.) E1
Banks (str.) D2
Barn Bluff (mt.) B3
Barren (cape) E2
Bass (str.) C1
Bathurst (gulf) C5
Cape Barren (isl.) E2
Chappell (isls.) D2
Circular (gulf) B2
Clarke (isl.) E2
Clyde (riv.) D4
Cox (bight) C5
Cradle (mt.) B3
Cradle Mt. Lake St. Clair Nat'l Park B3
Crescent (lake) D4
Curtis Group (isls.) C1
D'Aguilar (range) B4
Davey (riv.) B4
Deal (isl.) D1
Dee (riv.) C4
Denison (range) C4
D'Entrecasteaux (chan.) D5
Derwent (riv.) C4
East Sister (isl.) E1
Echo (lake) C4
Eddystone (pt.) E2
Elliott (bay) B5
Fires (bay) E3
Flinders (isl.) 2,150 D1
Florence (riv.) C4
Forestier (chan.) E4
Forestier (pen.) E4
Forth (riv.) C3
Frankland (cape) D1
Frankland (range) B4
Franklin (riv.) B4
Frenchmans Cap (mt.) B4
Freycinet (pen.) E4
Furneaux Group (isls.) 1,039 E1
Gordon (lake) C4
Gordon (riv.) B4
Great (lake) C3
Great Western Tiers (mts.) C3
Grim (cape) A2
Hartz (mt.) C5
Hibbs (pt.) B4
Hogan Group (isl.) D1
Hummock (isl.) D2
Hunter (isl.) A2
Hunter (isls.) B2
Huon (riv.) C5
Indian Ocean A4
Kent Group (isls.) D1
King (isl.) 2,592 A1
King (riv.) B4
King William (lake) C4
Lake (riv.) D3
Legges Tor (mt.) D3
Leven (riv.) B3
Lofty (range) B3
Low Rocky (pt.) B4
Lyell (mt.) B4
Maatsuyker (isls.) C5
Macquarie (harb.) B4
Macquarie (riv.) D3
Maria (isl.) E4
Marion (bay) E4
Mersey (riv.) C3
Munro (mt.) E2
Naturaliste (cape) E2
Nive (riv.) C4
Norfolk (bay) D4
North (pt.) E1
North Bruny (isl.) D5
North Esk (riv.) D3
Ossa (mt.) C3
Ouse (riv.) C4
Oyster (bay) E4
Pedder (riv.) B4
Phoques (bay) A1
Picton (mt.) C5
Pieman (riv.) B3
Pillar (cape) E5
Port Davey (inlet) B5
Portland (cape) D2
Ramsey (mt.) B3
Raoul (cape) D5
Reid (rapid) B1
Ringarooma (bay) D2
Robbins (isl.) B2
Saint Clair (lake) C4
Saint Helens (pt.) E3
Saint Vincent (cape) B5
Savage (riv.) B3
Schouten (isl.) E4
Sorell (cape) B4
Sorell (lake) D4
South (cape) C5
South Bruny (isl.) D5
South East (cape) C5
South Esk (riv.) D3
South West (cape) B5
Stanley (mt.) A1
Stokes (pt.) A1
Storm (bay) D5
Strzelecki (mt.) D2
Tamar (riv.) D3
Tasman (head) D5
Tasman (pen.) E5
Tasman (sea) E4
Three Hummock (isl.) B2
Vansittart (isl.) E2
West (pt.) A2
West Sister (isl.) D1
Wickham (cape) A1

○ Population of district.
*Population of met. area.

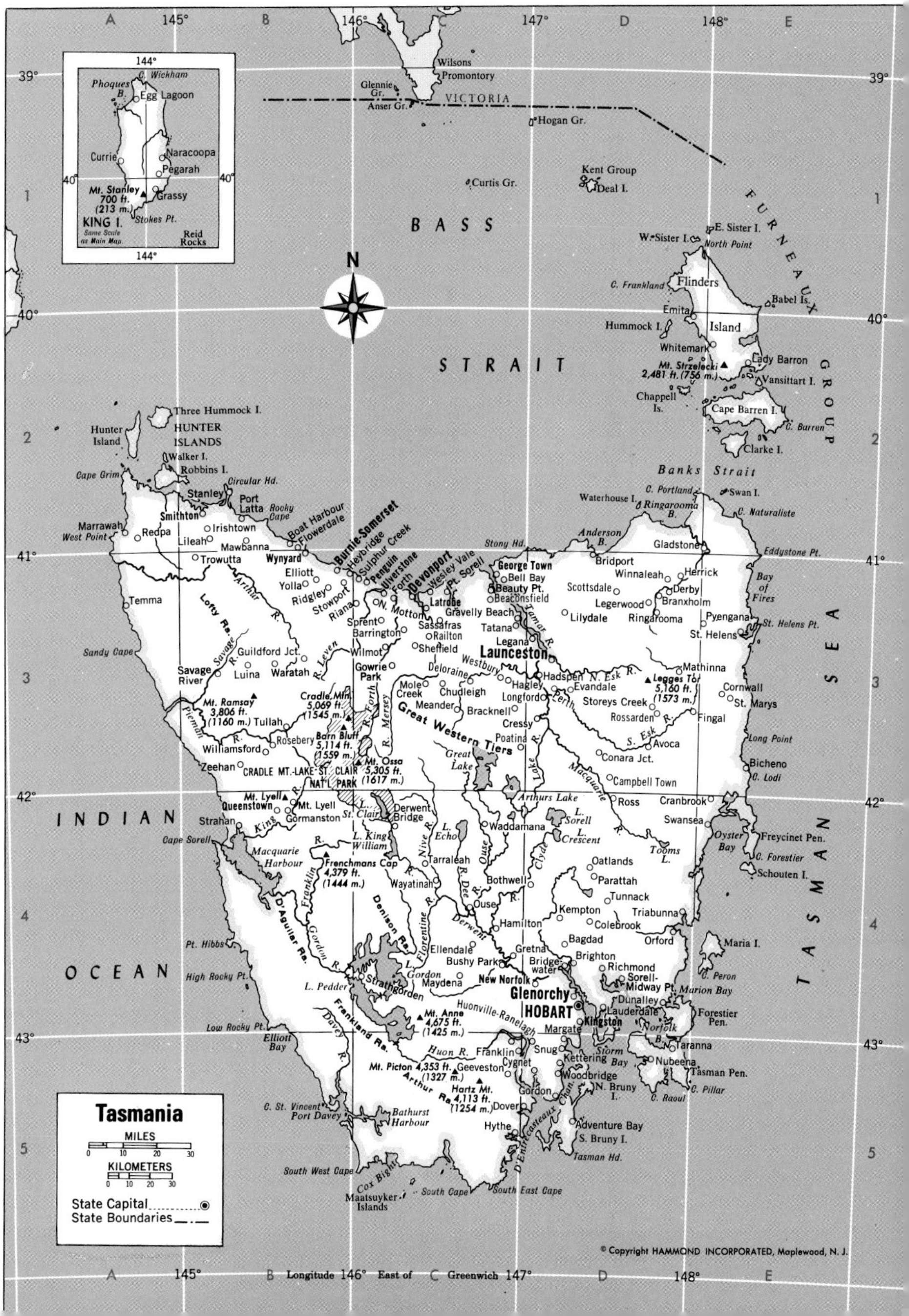
A 145° B 146° C 147° D 148° E
39° 40° 41° 42° 43°
Wilsons Promontory
VICTORIA
Glennie Gr.
Anser Gr.
Hogan Gr.
Kent Group
Deal I.
Curtis Gr.
BASS STRAIT
FURNEAUX GROUP
E. Sister I.
W. Sister I.
North Point
C. Frankland
Flinders Island
Babel Is.
Emita
Hummock I.
Whitemark
Mt. Strzelecki 2,481 ft. (756 m.)
Lady Barron
Vansittart I.
Chappell Is.
Cape Barren I.
C. Barren
Clarke I.
Banks Strait
C. Portland
Swan I.
Waterhouse I.
Ringarooma B.
C. Naturaliste
144°
C. Wickham
Phoques B.
Egg Lagoon
Currie
Naracoopa
Pegarah
Mt. Stanley 700 ft. (213 m.)
Grassy
KING I.
Same Scale as Main Map.
Stokes Pt.
Reid Rocks
N
Three Hummock I.
Hunter Island
HUNTER ISLANDS
Walker I.
Robbins I.
Cape Grim
Circular Hd.
Stanley
Smithton
Port Latta
Rocky Cape
Boat Harbour
Flowerdale
Marrawah
West Point
Redpa
Irishtown
Lileah
Mawbanna
Trowutta
Wynyard
Burnie-Somerset
Heybridge
Sulphur Creek
Penguin
Ulverstone
Devonport
Wesley Vale
Pt. Sorell
Elliott
Yolla
Ridgley
Stowport
Riana
Temma
Lofty Ra.
Arthur R.
Leven
Sprent
Barrington
Railton
Latrobe
Motton
George Town
Bell Bay
Beauty Pt.
Beaconsfield
Gravelly Beach
Sassafras
Tatana
Legana
Launceston
Stony Hd.
Anderson B.
Gladstone
Eddystone Pt.
Bridport
Winnaleah
Herrick
Scottsdale
Derby
Branxholm
Legerwood
Lilydale
Ringarooma
Pyengana
Bay of Fires
St. Helens
St. Helens Pt.
Sandy Cape
Savage R.
Guildford Jct.
Wilmot
Sheffield
Savage River
Luina
Waratah
Gowrie Park
Mole Creek
Deloraine
Westbury
Hadspen
Hagley
Evandale
N. Esk R.
Legges Tor 5,160 ft. (1573 m.)
Mathinna
Cornwall
St. Marys
Meander
Chudleigh
Longford
Bracknell
Storeys Creek
Rossarden
Fingal
Cressy
Mt. Ramsay 3,806 ft. (1160 m.)
Tullah
Cradle Mtn. 5,069 ft. (1545 m.)
Pieman R.
Forth R.
Mersey R.
Great Western Tiers
Poatina
S. Esk R.
Avoca
Long Point
Rosebery
Barn Bluff 5,114 ft. (1559 m.)
Williamsford
Conara Jct.
Bicheno
C. Lodi
Zeehan
CRADLE MT.-LAKE ST. CLAIR NAT'L PARK
Mt. Ossa 5,305 ft. (1617 m.)
Great Lake
Campbell Town
Macquarie R.
Mt. Lyell
Queenstown
Strahan
Gormanston
Arthurs Lake
Ross
Cranbrook
Swansea
Derwent Bridge
St. Clair
Waddamana
L. Sorell
L. Crescent
INDIAN OCEAN
Cape Sorell
Macquarie Harbour
L. King William
Echo
Nive R.
Ouse R.
Clyde R.
Tooms L.
Oyster Bay
Freycinet Pen.
C. Forestier
Schouten I.
Oatlands
Frenchmans Cap 4,379 ft. (1444 m.)
Tarraleah
Wayatinah
Bothwell
Parattah
Franklin R.
Dee R.
Tunnack
Kempton
Triabunna
D'Aguilar Ra.
Denison Ra.
Florentine R.
Derwent R.
Hamilton
Colebrook
Pt. Hibbs
Gordon R.
Ellendale
Gretna
Bagdad
Brighton
Orford
Maria I.
High Rocky Pt.
Bushy Park
Bridgewater
Richmond
C. Peron
L. Gordon
Maydena
New Norfolk
Sorell-Midway Pt.
Marion Bay
L. Pedder
Strathgordon
Glenorchy
HOBART
Dunalley
Forestier Pen.
Mt. Anne 4,675 ft. (1425 m.)
Huonville-Ranelagh
Lauderdale
Kingston
Margate
Norfolk B.
Low Rocky Pt.
Elliott Bay
Davey R.
Frankland Ra.
Huon R.
Franklin
Snug
Storm Bay
Taranna
Mt. Picton 4,353 ft. (1327 m.)
Geeveston
Cygnet
Kettering
Nubeena
Tasman Pen.
Arthur Ra.
Hartz Mt. 4,113 ft. (1254 m.)
Woodbridge
N. Bruny I.
C. Pillar
C. Raoul
Gordon
Dover
C. St. Vincent
Port Davey
Bathurst Harbour
D'Entrecasteaux Chan.
Hythe
Adventure Bay
S. Bruny I.
Tasman Hd.
TASMAN SEA
Tasmania
MILES 0 10 20 30
KILOMETERS 0 10 20 30
State Capital
State Boundaries
South West Cape
Cox Bight
South Cape
South East Cape
Maatsuyker Islands
Longitude 146° East of Greenwich 147°
1 2 3 4 5

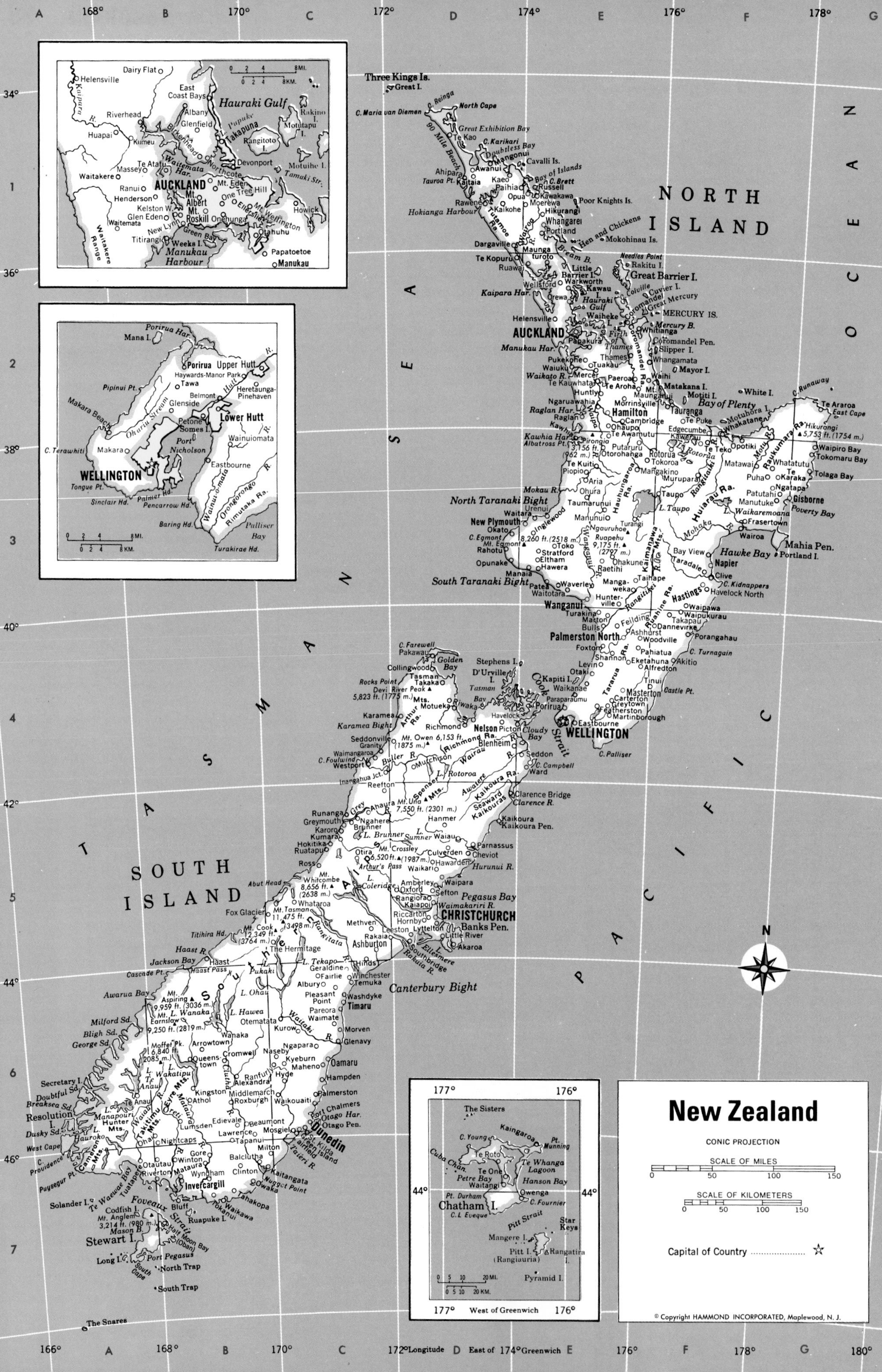

New Zealand
CONIC PROJECTION
SCALE OF MILES
0 50 100 150
SCALE OF KILOMETERS
0 50 100 150
Capital of Country
© Copyright HAMMOND INCORPORATED, Maplewood, N. J.
NORTH ISLAND
SOUTH ISLAND
TASMAN SEA
PACIFIC OCEAN
Three Kings Is.
North Cape
C. Maria van Diemen
C. Reinga
90 Mile Beach
Great Exhibition Bay
Doubtless Bay
Bay of Islands
Poor Knights Is.
Hokianga Harbour
Dargaville
Whangarei
Hen and Chickens
Mokohinau Is.
Great Barrier I.
Kaipara Har.
Hauraki Gulf
AUCKLAND
Manukau Har.
Coromandel Pen.
Mercury B.
Hamilton
Tauranga
Bay of Plenty
White I.
C. Runaway
East Cape
Hikurangi 5,753 ft. (1754 m.)
Rotorua
Whakatane
Opotiki
Gisborne
Poverty Bay
Mahia Pen.
Hawke Bay
Napier
Hastings
C. Kidnappers
L. Taupo
Taupo
Ruapehu 9,175 ft. (2797 m.)
North Taranaki Bight
New Plymouth
C. Egmont
Mt. Egmont 8,260 ft. (2518 m.)
South Taranaki Bight
Wanganui
Palmerston North
Masterton
WELLINGTON
C. Palliser
Cook Strait
C. Turnagain
Castle Pt.
C. Farewell
Golden Bay
Tasman Bay
Stephens I.
D'Urville I.
Nelson
Blenheim
Cloudy Bay
Karamea Bight
Westport
C. Foulwind
Greymouth
Hokitika
Kaikoura
Kaikoura Pen.
Pegasus Bay
CHRISTCHURCH
Banks Pen.
Canterbury Bight
Timaru
Oamaru
Dunedin
Otago Pen.
Invercargill
Foveaux Strait
Stewart I.
South Cape
The Snares
Southern Alps
Mt. Cook 12,349 ft. (3764 m.)
Mt. Tasman 11,475 ft. (3498 m.)
Mt. Aspiring 9,959 ft. (3036 m.)
L. Tekapo
L. Pukaki
L. Ohau
L. Hawea
L. Wanaka
L. Wakatipu
L. Te Anau
L. Manapouri
Milford Sd.
George Sd.
Bligh Sd.
Doubtful Sd.
Dusky Sd.
Resolution I.
West Cape
Puysegur Pt.
Solander I.
Haast
Jackson Bay
Awarua Bay
Titihira Hd.
Queenstown
Cromwell
Alexandra
Gore
Balclutha
Bluff
Hauraki Gulf
Takapuna
Devonport
Auckland
Manukau Harbour
Porirua
Upper Hutt
Lower Hutt
Port Nicholson
Wellington
Palliser Bay
Turakirae Hd.
Chatham I.
Pitt I. (Rangiauria)
Pitt Strait
The Sisters
Mangere I.
Pyramid I.
West of Greenwich
Longitude East of Greenwich

Topography

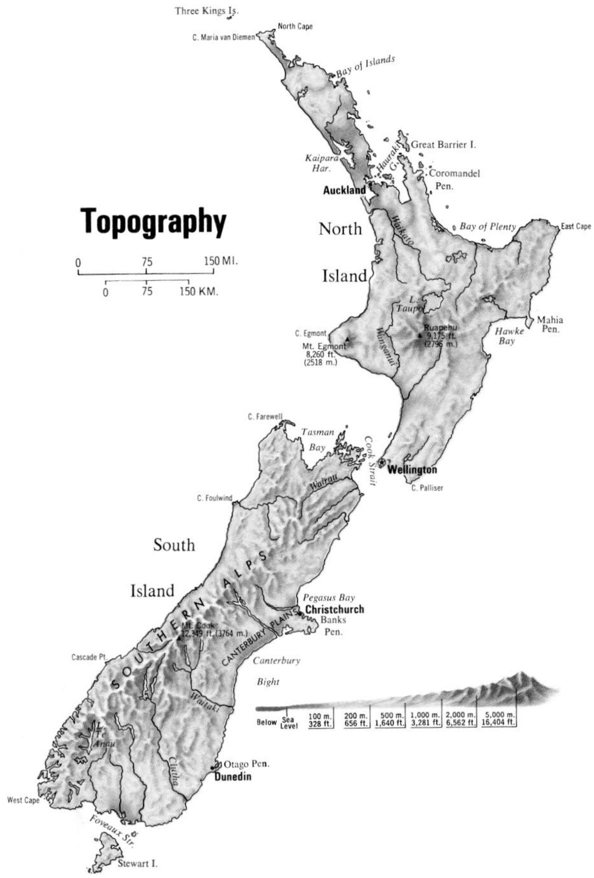
Three Kings Is.
C. Maria van Diemen
North Cape
Bay of Islands
Great Barrier I.
Kaipara Har.
Hauraki G.
Coromandel Pen.
Auckland
North
Island
Bay of Plenty
East Cape
L. Taupo
C. Egmont
Mt. Egmont 8,260 ft. (2518 m.)
Ruapehu 9,175 ft. (2796 m.)
Hawke Bay
Mahia Pen.
Wanganui
C. Farewell
Tasman Bay
Cook Strait
Wellington
C. Palliser
C. Foulwind
South
Island
Pegasus Bay
Christchurch
Banks Pen.
Mt. Cook 12,349 ft. (3764 m.)
SOUTHERN ALPS
CANTERBURY PLAINS
Canterbury Bight
Cascade Pt.
Waitaki
Clutha
Otago Pen.
Dunedin
West Cape
Foveaux Str.
Stewart I.
0 75 150 MI.
0 75 150 KM.
Below Sea Level
100 m. 328 ft.
200 m. 656 ft.
500 m. 1,640 ft.
1,000 m. 3,281 ft.
2,000 m. 6,562 ft.
5,000 m. 16,404 ft.

AREA 103,736 sq. mi. (268,676 sq. km.)
POPULATION 3,389,000
CAPITAL Wellington
LARGEST CITY Auckland
HIGHEST POINT Mt. Cook 12,349 ft. (3,764 m.)
MONETARY UNIT New Zealand dollar
MAJOR LANGUAGES English, Maori
MAJOR RELIGIONS Protestantism, Roman Catholicism

CITIES and TOWNS

Albany 2,001 . . . . . B1
Alexandra 4,348 . . . . . B6
Ashburton 14,151 . . . . . C5
Ashhurst 1,906 . . . . . E4
Auckland 144,963 . . . . . B1
Auckland †769,558 . . . . . B1
Balclutha 4,495 . . . . . B7
Belmont 2,402 . . . . . B2
Birkenhead 21,324 . . . . . B1
Blenheim 17,849 . . . . . D4
Bluff 2,720 . . . . . B7
Bulls 1,839 . . . . . E4
Cambridge 8,514 . . . . . E2
Carterton 3,971 . . . . . E4
Christchurch 164,680 . . . . . D5
Christchurch †289,959 . . . . . D5
Cromwell 2,364 . . . . . B6
Dannevirke 5,663 . . . . . F4
Dargaville 4,747 . . . . . D1
Devonport 10,410 . . . . . C1
Dunedin 77,176 . . . . . C6
Dunedin †107,445 . . . . . C6
Eastbourne 4,561 . . . . . B3
East Coast Bays 28,866 . . . . . B1
Edgecumbe 1,929 . . . . . F2
Ellerslie 5,404 . . . . . C1
Eltham 2,411 . . . . . E3
Fairfield 1,849 . . . . . C6
Featherston 2,458 . . . . . E4
Feilding 11,522 . . . . . E4
Foxton 2,719 . . . . . E4
Geraldine 2,128 . . . . . C6
Gisborne 29,986 . . . . . G3
Gisborne †32,062 . . . . . G3
Glen Eden 9,406 . . . . . B1
Glenfield 3,691 . . . . . B1
Gore 9,185 . . . . . B7
Green Bay 3,035 . . . . . B1
Green Island 6,899 . . . . . C7
Greymouth 8,103 . . . . . C5
Greytown 1,797 . . . . . E4
Half Moon Bay (Oban) 2,448 B7
Hamilton 91,109 . . . . . E2
Hamilton †97,907 . . . . . E2
Hastings 36,083 . . . . . F3
Hastings †52,563 . . . . . F3
Havelock North 8,507 . . . . . F3
Hawera 8,400 . . . . . E3
Helensville 1,360 . . . . . B1
Henderson 6,645 . . . . . B1
Heretaunga-Pinehaven 6,171 C2
Hokitika 3,414 . . . . . C5
Hornby 8,215 . . . . . D5
Howick 13,866 . . . . . C1
Huntly 6,534 . . . . . E2
Hutt (Upper and Lower) †131,257 . . . . . B2
Inglewood 2,839 . . . . . E3
Invercargill 49,446 . . . . . B7
Invercargill †53,868 . . . . . B7
Kaiapoi 4,894 . . . . . D5
Kaikohe 3,663 . . . . . D1
Kaikoura 2,180 . . . . . D5
Kaitaia 4,737 . . . . . D1
Kawerau 8,593 . . . . . F3
Kumeu 3,414 . . . . . B1
Levin 14,652 . . . . . E4
Lower Hutt 63,245 . . . . . B2
Lyttelton 3,184 . . . . . D5
Manukau 159,362 . . . . . C1
Marton 4,858 . . . . . E4
Masterton 18,785 . . . . . E4
Mataura 2,345 . . . . . B7
Milton 2,193 . . . . . B7
Morrinsville 5,080 . . . . . E2
Mosgiel 9,264 . . . . . C6
Motueka 4,693 . . . . . D4
Mount Albert 26,462 . . . . . B1
Mount Eden 18,305 . . . . . B1
Mount Maunganui 11,391 . . . E2
Mount Roskill 33,577 . . . . . B1
Mount Wellington 19,528 . . . C1
Murupara 2,964 . . . . . F3
Napier 48,314 . . . . . F3
Napier †51,330 . . . . . F3
Nelson 33,304 . . . . . D4
Nelson †43,121 . . . . . D4
New Lynn 10,445 . . . . . B1
New Plymouth 36,048 . . . . . D3
New Plymouth †44,095 . . . . D3
Ngaruawahia 4,435 . . . . . E2
Northcote 10,061 . . . . . B1
Oamaru 13,043 . . . . . C6
Oban (Half Moon Bay) 2,448 B7
Onehunga 15,386 . . . . . B1
One Tree Hill 11,078 . . . . . B1
Opotiki 3,388 . . . . . F3
Orewa 5,552 . . . . . E2
Otahuhu 10,298 . . . . . C1
Otaki 4,301 . . . . . E4
Otorohanga 2,574 . . . . . E3
Paeroa 3,702 . . . . . E2
Pahiatua 2,599 . . . . . F4
Paihia 1,740 . . . . . D1
Palmerston North 60,105 . . . E4
Palmerston North †66,691 . . E4
Papakura 22,473 . . . . . E2
Papatoetoe 21,700 . . . . . C1
Patea 1,938 . . . . . E3
Petone 8,113 . . . . . B2
Picton 3,220 . . . . . D4
Pinehaven (Heretaunga-Pinehaven) 6,171 . . . . . C2
Porirua 41,104 . . . . . B2
Port Chalmers 2,917 . . . . . C6
Pukekohe 9,070 . . . . . E2
Putaruru 4,222 . . . . . E3
Queenstown 3,367 . . . . . B6
Raetihi 1,247 . . . . . E3
Raglan 1,414 . . . . . E2
Rangiora 6,385 . . . . . D5
Reefton 1,200 . . . . . C5
Riccarton 6,709 . . . . . D5
Richmond 6,847 . . . . . D4
Riverton 1,479 . . . . . B7
Rotorua 38,157 . . . . . F3
Rotorua †48,314 . . . . . F3
Runanga 1,264 . . . . . C5
Russell 932 . . . . . E1
Saint Kilda 6,147 . . . . . C7
Shannon 1,465 . . . . . E4
Stratford 5,518 . . . . . E3
Taihape 2,586 . . . . . E3
Takapuna 64,844 . . . . . B1
Tapanui 1,042 . . . . . B6
Taradale 4,681 . . . . . F3
Taumarunui 6,541 . . . . . E3
Taupo 13,651 . . . . . F3
Tauranga 37,099 . . . . . F2
Tauranga †53,097 . . . . . F2
Tawa 12,216 . . . . . B2
Te Anau 2,610 . . . . . A6
Te Aroha 3,331 . . . . . E2
Te Atatu 14,713 . . . . . B1
Te Awamutu 7,922 . . . . . E3
Te Kauwhata 842 . . . . . E2
Te Kuiti 4,795 . . . . . E3
Temuka 3,771 . . . . . C6
Te Puke 4,577 . . . . . F2
Thames 6,456 . . . . . E2
The Hermitage C5
Timaru 28,412 . . . . . C6
Timaru †29,225 . . . . . C6
Titirangi 8,426 . . . . . B1
Tokoroa 18,713 . . . . . F3
Tuakau 1,982 . . . . . E2
Tuatapere 884 . . . . . A7
Turangi 5,517 . . . . . E3
Upper Hutt 31,405 . . . . . B2
Waihi 3,538 . . . . . E2
Waikanae 4,818 . . . . . E4
Waikouaiti 858 . . . . . C6
Waimate 3,393 . . . . . C6
Wainuiomata 19,192 . . . . . B3
Waipawa 1,732 . . . . . F3
Waipukurau 3,648 . . . . . F4
Wairoa 5,439 . . . . . F3
Waitangi D7
Waitara 6,012 . . . . . E3
Waitemata 87,452 . . . . . B1
Waiuku 3,654 . . . . . E2
Waanaka 1,155 . . . . . B6
Wanganui 37,012 . . . . . E3
Wanganui †39,595 . . . . . E3
Warkworth 1,734 . . . . . E2
Washdyke 949 . . . . . C6
Waverley 1,239 . . . . . E3
Wellington (cap.) 135,688 . . A3
Wellington †321,004 . . . . . A3
Wellsford 1,621 . . . . . E2
Westport 4,686 . . . . . C4
Whakatane 12,286 . . . . . F2
Whangamata 1,566 . . . . . F2
Whangarei 36,550 . . . . . E1
Whangarei †40,212 . . . . . E1
Whitianga 1,960 . . . . . E2
Winton 2,035 . . . . . B7
Woodville 1,647 . . . . . F4

OTHER FEATURES

Arthur's (pass) C5
Aspiring (mt.) B6
Banks (pen.) D5
Bream (bay) E1
Brett (cape) E1
Buller (riv.) D4
Campbell (cape) E4
Canterbury (bight) D6
Cascade (pt.) B6
Chatham (isls.) 751 . . . . . D7
Cloudy (bay) E4
Clutha (riv.) B6
Coleridge (lake) C5
Colville (cape) E2
Cook (mt.) C5
Cook (str.) E4
Coromandel (pen.) F2
Devil River (peak) D4
D'Urville (isl.) D4
Dusky (sound) A6
East (cape) G2
Egmont (cape) D3
Egmont (mt.) D3
Ellesmere (lake) D5
Farewell (cape) D4
Foulwind (cape) C4
Fournier (cape) E7
Foveaaux (str.) A7
Golden (bay) D4
Great Barrier (isl.) 572 . . . . . E2
Haast (pass) B6
Hauraki (gulf) C1
Hawke (bay) F3
Hikurangi (mt.) G2
Hokianga (harb.) D1
Huiarau (range) F3
Hutt (riv.) C2
Islands (bay) E1
Jackson (bay) B5
Kaikoura (range) D5
Kaimanawa (range) E3
Kaipara (harb.) D2
Karamea (bight) C4
Kawhia (harb.) E3
Kidnappers (cape) F3
Mahia (pen.) G3
Manapouri (lake) A6
Manukau (harb.) B1
Maria van Diemen (cape) . . . D1
Mataura (riv.) B6
Mercury (isls.) F2
Milford (sound) A6
Needles (pt.) E2
Nicholson, Port (inlet) B3
Ninety Mile (beach) D1
North (cape) D1
North (isl.) 2,322,989 . . . . . F1
North Taranaki (bight) D3
Otago (pen.) C6
Owen (mt.) D4
Palliser (cape) E4
Pegasus (bay) D5
Pitt (isl.) E7
Plenty (bay) F2
Port Nicholson (inlet) B3
Port Pegasus (inlet) B7
Pukaki (lake) B6
Puysegur (pt.) A7
Rakaia (riv.) C5
Rangitata (riv.) C5
Rangitikei (riv.) E3
Raukumara (range) F3
Reinga (cape) D1
Resolution (isl.) A6
Richmond (range) D4
Rocks (pt.) C4
Rotorua (lake) F3
Ruahine (range) F4
Ruapehu (mt.) E3
Ruapuke (isl.) B7
South (cape) A7
South (isl.) 852,748 . . . . . B5
Southern Alps (range) C5
South Taranaki (bight) D3
Spenser (mts.) D5
Stewart (isl.) 600 . . . . . A7
Tararua (range) E4
Tasman (bay) D4
Tasman (mt.) C5
Tasman (mts.) D4
Tasman (sea) B4
Taupo (lake) F3
Tauroa (pt.) D1
Te Anau (lake) A6
Tekapo (lake) C5
Terawhiti (cape) A3
Thames (firth) E2
Three Kings (isls.) D1
Turakirae (head) B3
Una (mt.) D5
Waiheke (isl.) 3,223 . . . . . E2
Waikato (riv.) E2
Waimakariri (riv.) D5
Waipa (riv.) E2
Wairau (riv.) D4
Waitaki (riv.) C6
Waitemata (harb.) B1
Wakatipu (lake) B6
Wanaka (lake) B6
Wanganui (riv.) E3
West (cape) A6
Whitcombe (mt.) C5

†Population of urban area.

Agriculture, Industry and Resources

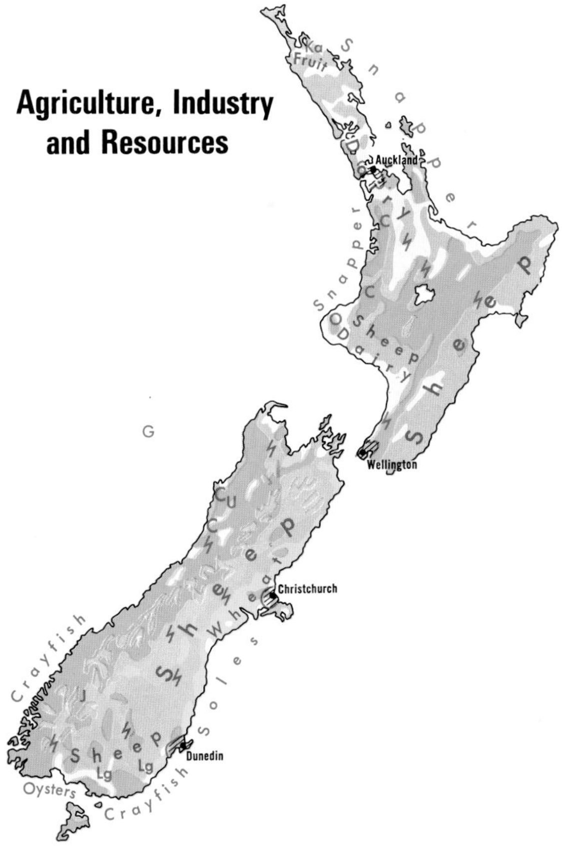
Auckland
Wellington
Christchurch
Dunedin
Fruit
Snapper
Sheep
Dairy
Wheat
Crayfish
Oysters
Soles
Ka
G
C
J
U
Lg

DOMINANT LAND USE

- Mixed Farming, Livestock
- Dairy
- Truck Farming, Horticulture
- Pasture Livestock (chiefly sheep)
- Livestock Herding
- Forests
- Nonagricultural Land

MAJOR MINERAL OCCURRENCES

- C Coal
- G Natural Gas
- J Jade
- Ka Kaolin
- Lg Lignite
- O Petroleum
- U Uranium
- Water Power
- Major Industrial Areas

Average January Temperature

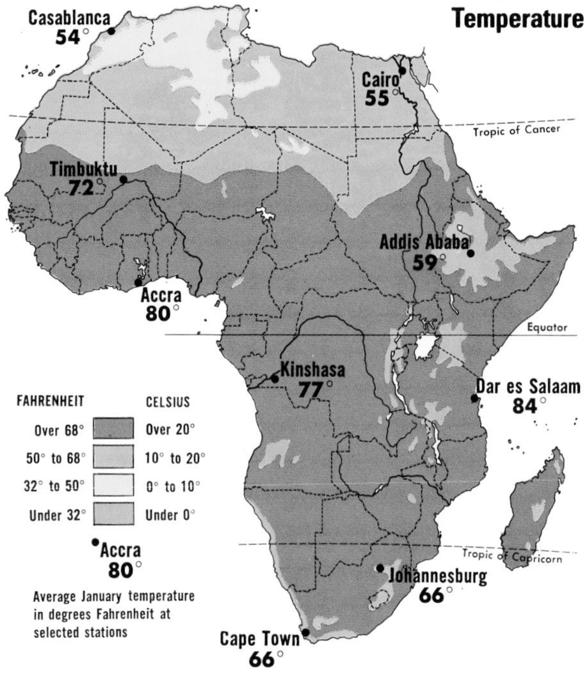
Casablanca 54°
Cairo 55°
Tropic of Cancer
Timbuktu 72°
Addis Ababa 59°
Accra 80°
Equator
Kinshasa 77°
Dar es Salaam 84°
FAHRENHEIT
CELSIUS
Over 68°
Over 20°
50° to 68°
10° to 20°
32° to 50°
0° to 10°
Under 32°
Under 0°
Accra 80°
Average January temperature in degrees Fahrenheit at selected stations
Tropic of Capricorn
Johannesburg 66°
Cape Town 66°

Average July Temperature

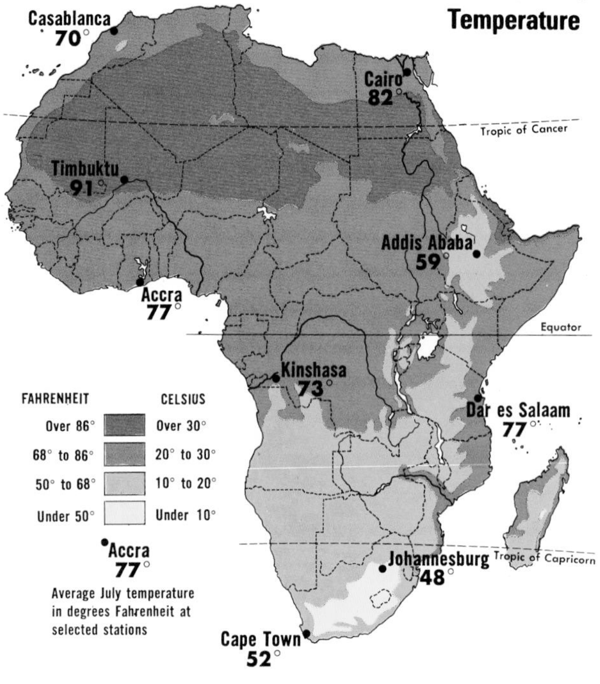
Casablanca 70°
Cairo 82°
Tropic of Cancer
Timbuktu 91°
Addis Ababa 59°
Accra 77°
Equator
Kinshasa 73°
Dar es Salaam 77°
FAHRENHEIT
CELSIUS
Over 86°
Over 30°
68° to 86°
20° to 30°
50° to 68°
10° to 20°
Under 50°
Under 10°
Accra 77°
Average July temperature in degrees Fahrenheit at selected stations
Johannesburg 48°
Tropic of Capricorn
Cape Town 52°

Rainfall

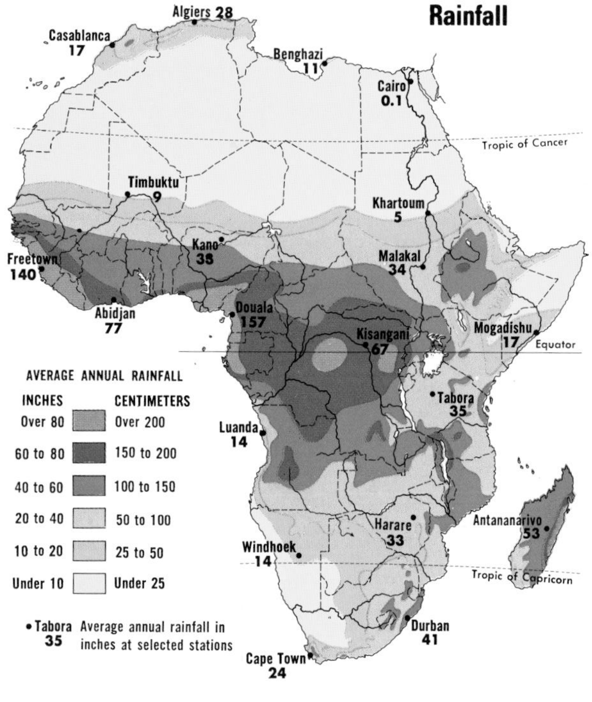
Algiers 28
Casablanca 17
Benghazi 11
Cairo 0.1
Tropic of Cancer
Timbuktu 9
Khartoum 5
Kano 35
Freetown 140
Malakal 34
Abidjan 77
Douala 157
Kisangani 67
Mogadishu 17
Equator
AVERAGE ANNUAL RAINFALL
INCHES
CENTIMETERS
Over 80
Over 200
60 to 80
150 to 200
40 to 60
100 to 150
20 to 40
50 to 100
10 to 20
25 to 50
Under 10
Under 25
Tabora 35
Luanda 14
Antananarivo 53
Harare 33
Windhoek 14
Tropic of Capricorn
Tabora 35 Average annual rainfall in inches at selected stations
Durban 41
Cape Town 24

Vegetation/Relief

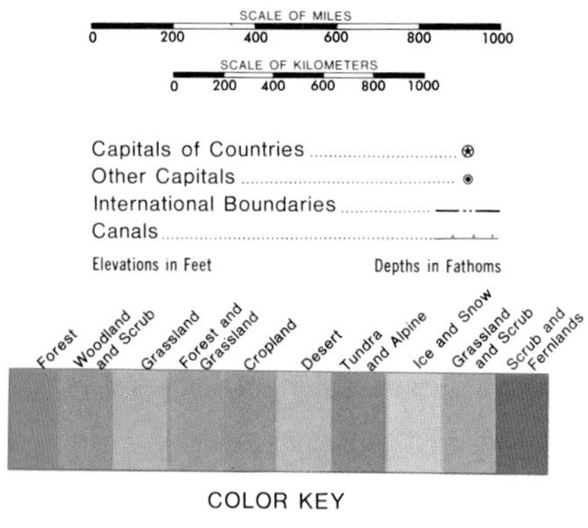
SCALE OF MILES
0 200 400 600 800 1000
SCALE OF KILOMETERS
0 200 400 600 800 1000
Capitals of Countries
Other Capitals
International Boundaries
Canals
Elevations in Feet
Depths in Fathoms
Forest
Woodland and Scrub
Grassland
Forest and Grassland
Cropland
Desert
Tundra and Alpine
Ice and Snow
Grassland and Scrub
Scrub and Fernlands
COLOR KEY

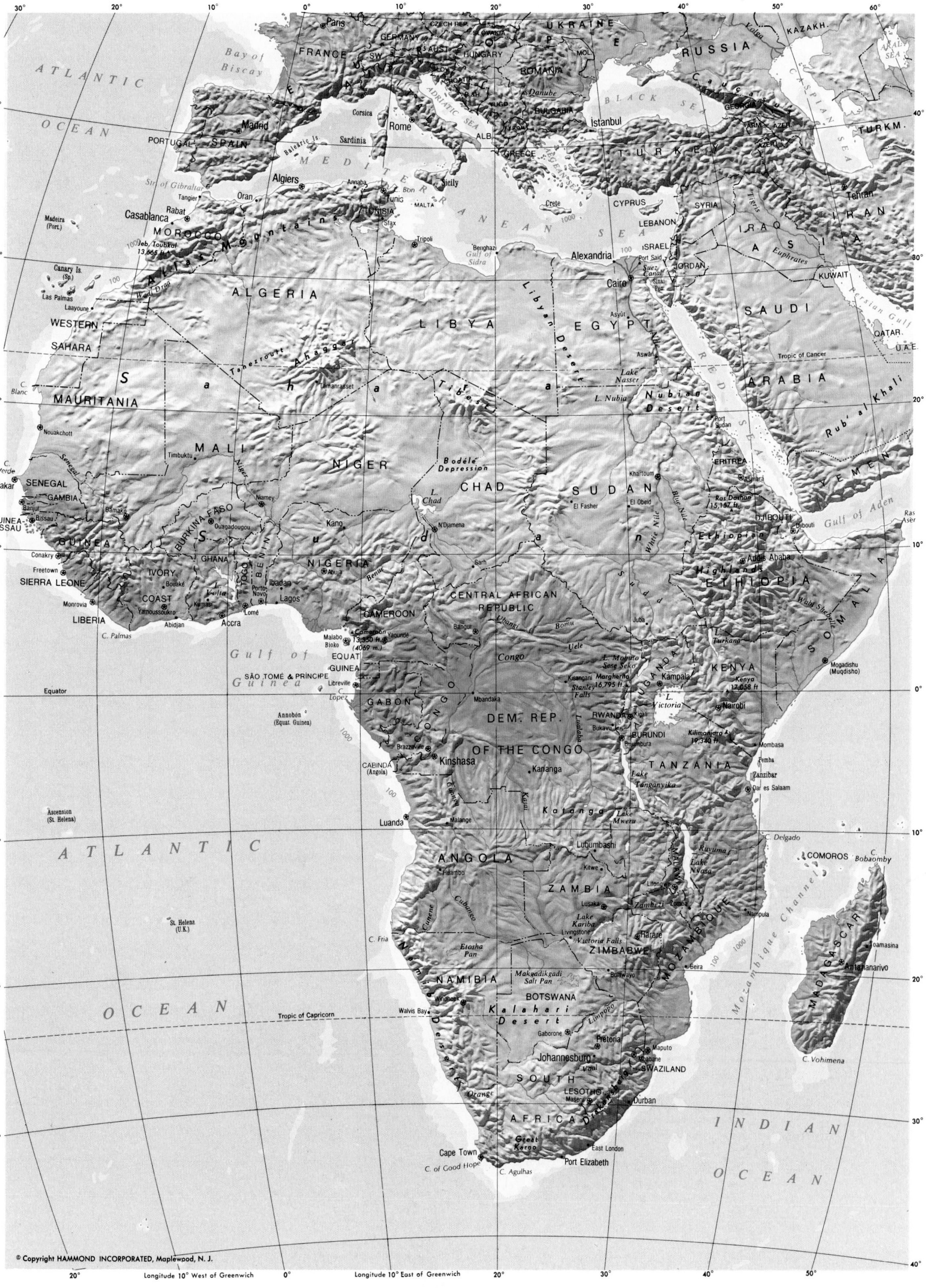

ATLANTIC OCEAN
MEDITERRANEAN SEA
BLACK SEA
CASPIAN SEA
ARAL SEA
ADRIATIC SEA
AEGEAN SEA
RED SEA
Bay of Biscay
Gulf of Guinea
Gulf of Aden
Persian Gulf
Gulf of Sidra
Mozambique Channel
INDIAN OCEAN
EUROPE
ASIA
RUSSIA
UKRAINE
KAZAKH.
FRANCE
GERMANY
CZECH REP.
SLOVAKIA
AUST.
SW.
SLOV.
CROATIA
HUNGARY
ROMANIA
MOL.
BULGARIA
YUGO.
ALB.
GREECE
ITALY
SPAIN
PORTUGAL
TURKEY
GEORGIA
ARM.
AZER.
TURKM.
CYPRUS
SYRIA
LEBANON
ISRAEL
JORDAN
IRAQ
IRAN
KUWAIT
SAUDI ARABIA
QATAR
U.A.E.
YEMEN
Paris
Madrid
Rome
İstanbul
Corsica
Sardinia
Sicily
Crete
Malta
Balearic Is.
Str. of Gibraltar
Danube
Volga
Tigris
Euphrates
Tehran
Caucasus
Rub' al Khali
Tropic of Cancer
MOROCCO
ALGERIA
TUNISIA
LIBYA
EGYPT
WESTERN SAHARA
MAURITANIA
MALI
NIGER
CHAD
SUDAN
ERITREA
DJIBOUTI
ETHIOPIA
SOMALIA
SENEGAL
GAMBIA
GUINEA-BISSAU
GUINEA
SIERRA LEONE
LIBERIA
IVORY COAST
BURKINA FASO
GHANA
TOGO
BENIN
NIGERIA
CAMEROON
CENTRAL AFRICAN REPUBLIC
EQUAT. GUINEA
SÃO TOMÉ & PRÍNCIPE
GABON
CONGO
DEM. REP. OF THE CONGO
CABINDA (Angola)
UGANDA
KENYA
RWANDA
BURUNDI
TANZANIA
ANGOLA
ZAMBIA
MALAWI
MOZAMBIQUE
ZIMBABWE
NAMIBIA
BOTSWANA
SOUTH AFRICA
LESOTHO
SWAZILAND
MADAGASCAR
COMOROS
Sahara
Sudan
Atlas Mountains
Jeb. Toubkal 13,665 ft.
Ahaggar
Tanezrouft
Tibesti
Libyan Desert
Nubian Desert
Bodélé Depression
Ethiopian Highlands
Ras Dashan 15,157 ft.
Sudd
Katanga
Kalahari Desert
Namib Desert
Great Karoo
Drakensberg
Makgadikgadi Salt Pan
Etosha Pan
Lake Nasser
L. Nubia
L. Chad
L. Turkana
L. Mobutu Sese Seko
L. Victoria
Lake Tanganyika
Lake Mweru
Lake Nyasa
Lake Kariba
Victoria Falls
Stanley Falls
Margherita 16,795 ft.
Kenya 17,058 ft.
Kilimanjaro 19,340 ft.
Cameroon 13,350 ft. (4069 m.)
Nile
Blue Nile
White Nile
Niger
Senegal
Benue
Volta
Congo
Ubangi
Uele
Bomu
Lualaba
Kasai
Cuanza
Cubango
Cunene
Zambezi
Limpopo
Orange
Vaal
Ruvuma
Webi Shebeli
Wadi Dra
Suez Canal
Sinai Pen.
Madeira (Port.)
Canary Is. (Sp.)
Las Palmas
Laayoune
Casablanca
Rabat
Tangier
Oran
Algiers
Annaba
Tunis
Sfax
Tripoli
Benghazi
Alexandria
Port Said
Cairo
Asyût
Aswân
Port Sudan
Khartoum
El Obeid
El Fasher
Asmara
Djibouti
Addis Ababa
Mogadishu (Muqdisho)
Nouakchott
Dakar
Banjul
Bissau
Conakry
Freetown
Monrovia
Timbuktu
Bamako
Niamey
Ouagadougou
Kano
Abuja
Ibadan
Lagos
Porto-Novo
Lomé
Accra
Kumasi
Bouaké
Yamoussoukro
Abidjan
N'Djamena
Sarh
Bangui
Malabo
Bioko
Yaoundé
Libreville
Mbandaka
Kisangani
Juba
Kampala
Nairobi
Kigali
Bukavu
Bujumbura
Mombasa
Pemba
Zanzibar
Dar es Salaam
Brazzaville
Kinshasa
Kananga
Luanda
Malange
Huambo
Lubumbashi
Kitwe
Lusaka
Lilongwe
Zomba
Nampula
Livingstone
Harare
Bulawayo
Beira
Windhoek
Walvis Bay
Gaborone
Pretoria
Johannesburg
Maputo
Mbabane
Maseru
Durban
East London
Port Elizabeth
Cape Town
Antananarivo
Toamasina
Annobón (Equat. Guinea)
Ascension (St. Helena)
St. Helena (U.K.)
C. Blanc
C. Verde
C. Palmas
C. Lopez
C. Fria
C. of Good Hope
C. Agulhas
C. Delgado
C. Bobaomby
C. Vohimena
Ras Aser
Equator
Tropic of Capricorn
© Copyright HAMMOND INCORPORATED, Maplewood, N. J.
Longitude 10° West of Greenwich
Longitude 10° East of Greenwich

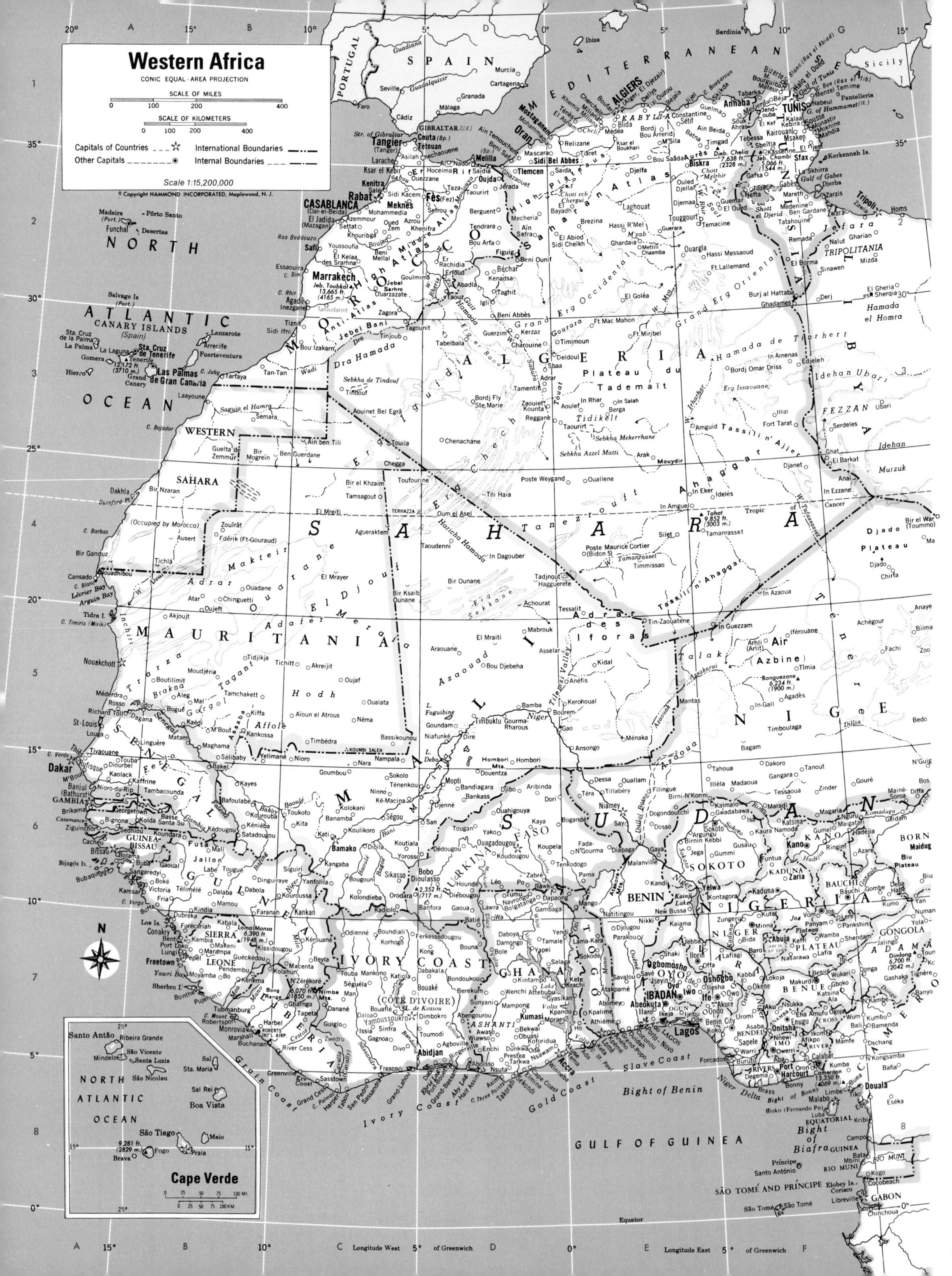

Western Africa
CONIC EQUAL-AREA PROJECTION
SCALE OF MILES
0 100 200 400
SCALE OF KILOMETERS
0 100 200 400
Capitals of Countries
Other Capitals
International Boundaries
Internal Boundaries
Scale 1:15,200,000
© Copyright HAMMOND INCORPORATED, Maplewood, N. J.
NORTH ATLANTIC OCEAN
CANARY ISLANDS (Spain)
MEDITERRANEAN SEA
SPAIN
PORTUGAL
MOROCCO
ALGERIA
LIBYA
TRIPOLITANIA
FEZZAN
TUNISIA
WESTERN SAHARA
(Occupied by Morocco)
MAURITANIA
MALI
NIGER
SAHARA
SENEGAL
GAMBIA
GUINEA-BISSAU
GUINEA
SIERRA LEONE
LIBERIA
IVORY COAST (CÔTE D'IVOIRE)
BURKINA FASO
GHANA
TOGO
BENIN
NIGERIA
CAMEROON
EQUATORIAL GUINEA
GABON
SÃO TOMÉ AND PRÍNCIPE
GULF OF GUINEA
Bight of Benin
Bight of Biafra
Slave Coast
Gold Coast
Ivory Coast
Grain Coast
Tropic of Cancer
Equator
Rabat
CASABLANCA
Marrakech
Fès
Meknès
Tangier
ALGIERS
Oran
Constantine
TUNIS
Tripoli
Dakar
Nouakchott
Banjul
Bamako
Niamey
Ouagadougou
Conakry
Freetown
Monrovia
Abidjan
Accra
Lomé
Porto-Novo
Lagos
Ibadan
Kano
Timbuktu
Ahaggar
Tamanrasset
Cape Verde
Santo Antão
São Vicente
São Nicolau
Sal
Boa Vista
Maio
São Tiago
Fogo
Brava
Praia
Longitude West 5° of Greenwich
Longitude East 5° of Greenwich

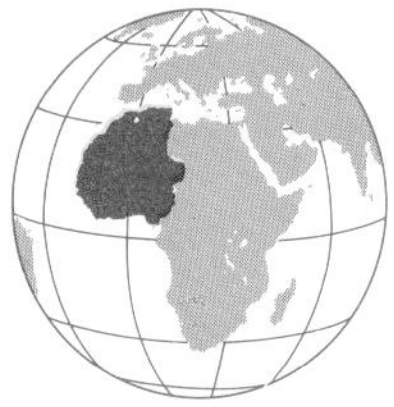

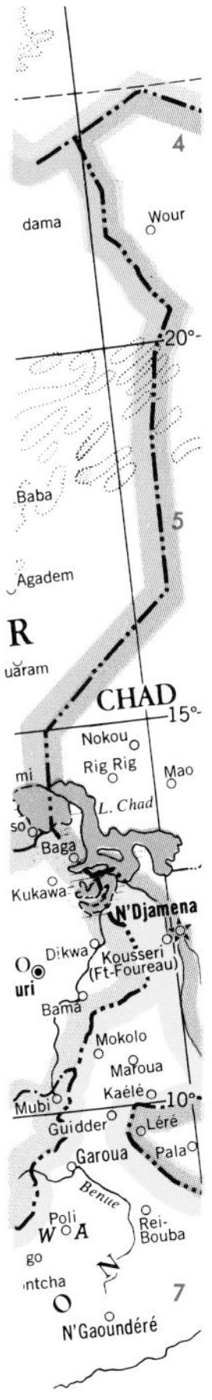
4
dama
Wour
20°
Baba
5
Agadem
R
uaram
CHAD
15°
Nokou
Rig Rig
Mao
L. Chad
Baga
Kukawa
N'Djamena
Dikwa
Kousseri (Ft-Foureau)
Bama
Mokolo
Maroua
Kaélé
10°
Mubi
Guidder
Léré
Garoua
Pala
Benue
Poli
Rei-Bouba
W A
7
N'Gaoundéré

ALGERIA

AREA 919,591 sq. mi. (2,381,740 sq. km.)
POPULATION 22,971,000
CAPITAL Algiers
LARGEST CITY Algiers
HIGHEST POINT Tahat 9,852 ft. (3,003 m.)
MONETARY UNIT Algerian dinar
MAJOR LANGUAGES Arabic, Berber, French
MAJOR RELIGION Islam

BENIN

AREA 43,483 sq. mi. (112,620 sq. km.)
POPULATION 4,591,000
CAPITAL Porto-Novo
LARGEST CITY Cotonou
HIGHEST POINT Atakora Mts. 2,083 ft. (635 m.)
MONETARY UNIT CFA franc
MAJOR LANGUAGES Fon, Somba, Yoruba, Bariba, French, Mina, Dendi
MAJOR RELIGIONS Tribal religions, Islam, Roman Catholicism

CAPE VERDE

AREA 1,557 sq. mi. (4,033 sq. km.)
POPULATION 347,000
CAPITAL Praia
LARGEST CITY Praia
HIGHEST POINT 9,281 ft. (2,829 m.)
MONETARY UNIT Cape Verde escudo
MAJOR LANGUAGE Portuguese
MAJOR RELIGION Roman Catholicism

GAMBIA

AREA 4,127 sq. mi. (10,689 sq. km.)
POPULATION 688,000
CAPITAL Banjul
LARGEST CITY Banjul
HIGHEST POINT 100 ft. (30 m.)
MONETARY UNIT dalasi
MAJOR LANGUAGES Mandingo, Fulani, Wolof, English, Malinke
MAJOR RELIGIONS Islam, tribal religions, Christianity

GHANA

AREA 92,099 sq. mi. (238,536 sq. km.)
POPULATION 13,391,000
CAPITAL Accra
LARGEST CITY Accra
HIGHEST POINT Togo Hills 2,900 ft. (884 m.)
MONETARY UNIT cedi
MAJOR LANGUAGES Twi, Fante, Dagbani, Ewe, Ga, English, Hausa, Akan
MAJOR RELIGIONS Tribal religions, Christianity, Islam

GUINEA

AREA 94,925 sq. mi. (245,856 sq. km.)
POPULATION 6,706,000
CAPITAL Conakry
LARGEST CITY Conakry
HIGHEST POINT Nimba Mts. 6,070 ft. (1,850 m.)
MONETARY UNIT syli
MAJOR LANGUAGES Fulani, Mandingo, Susu, French
MAJOR RELIGIONS Islam, tribal religions

GUINEA-BISSAU

AREA 13,948 sq. mi. (36,125 sq. km.)
POPULATION 943,000
CAPITAL Bissau
LARGEST CITY Bissau
HIGHEST POINT 689 ft. (210 m.)
MONETARY UNIT Guinea-Bissau peso
MAJOR LANGUAGES Balante, Fulani, Crioulo, Mandingo, Portuguese
MAJOR RELIGIONS Islam, tribal religions, Roman Catholicism

IVORY COAST (CÔTE-D'IVOIRE)

AREA 124,504 sq. mi. (322,465 sq. km.)
POPULATION 9,300,000
CAPITAL Yamoussoukro
LARGEST CITY Abidjan
HIGHEST POINT 5,745 ft. (1,751 m.)
MONETARY UNIT CFA franc
MAJOR LANGUAGES Bale, Bete, Senufu, French, Dioula
MAJOR RELIGIONS Tribal religions, Islam

LIBERIA

AREA 43,000 sq. mi. (111,370 sq. km.)
POPULATION 2,508,000
CAPITAL Monrovia
LARGEST CITY Monrovia
HIGHEST POINT Wutivi 5,584 ft. (1,702 m.)
MONETARY UNIT Liberian dollar
MAJOR LANGUAGES Kru, Kpelle, Bassa, Vai, English
MAJOR RELIGIONS Christianity, tribal religions, Islam

MALI

AREA 464,873 sq. mi. (1,204,021 sq. km.)
POPULATION 7,960,000
CAPITAL Bamako
LARGEST CITY Bamako
HIGHEST POINT Hombori Mts. 3,789 ft. (1,155 m.)
MONETARY UNIT CFA franc
MAJOR LANGUAGES Bambara, Senufu, Fulani, Soninke, French
MAJOR RELIGIONS Islam, tribal religions

MAURITANIA

AREA 419,229 sq. mi. (1,085,803 sq. km.)
POPULATION 1,970,000
CAPITAL Nouakchott
LARGEST CITY Nouakchott
HIGHEST POINT 2,972 ft. (906 m.)
MONETARY UNIT ouguiya
MAJOR LANGUAGES Arabic, Wolof, Tukolor, French
MAJOR RELIGION Islam

MOROCCO

AREA 172,414 sq. mi. (446,550 sq. km.)
POPULATION 24,522,000
CAPITAL Rabat
LARGEST CITY Casablanca
HIGHEST POINT Jeb. Toubkal 13,665 ft. (4,165 m.)
MONETARY UNIT dirham
MAJOR LANGUAGES Arabic, Berber, French
MAJOR RELIGIONS Islam, Judaism, Christianity

NIGER

AREA 489,189 sq. mi. (1,267,000 sq. km.)
POPULATION 7,250,000
CAPITAL Niamey
LARGEST CITY Niamey
HIGHEST POINT Banguezane 6,234 ft. (1,900 m.)
MONETARY UNIT CFA franc
MAJOR LANGUAGES Hausa, Songhai, Fulani, French, Tamashek, Djerma
MAJOR RELIGIONS Islam, tribal religions

NIGERIA

AREA 357,000 sq. mi. (924,630 sq. km.)
POPULATION 104,957,000
CAPITAL Abuja
LARGEST CITY Lagos
HIGHEST POINT Dimlang 6,700 ft. (2,042 m.)
MONETARY UNIT naira
MAJOR LANGUAGES Hausa, Yoruba, Ibo, Ijaw, Fulani, Tiv, Kanuri, Ibibio, English, Edo
MAJOR RELIGIONS Islam, Christianity, tribal religions

SÃO TOMÉ AND PRÍNCIPE

AREA 372 sq. mi. (963 sq. km.)
POPULATION 116,000
CAPITAL São Tomé
LARGEST CITY São Tomé
HIGHEST POINT Pico 6,640 ft. (2,024 m.)
MONETARY UNIT dobra
MAJOR LANGUAGES Bantu languages, Portuguese
MAJOR RELIGIONS Tribal religions, Roman Catholicism

SENEGAL

AREA 75,954 sq. mi. (196,720 sq. km.)
POPULATION 7,113,000
CAPITAL Dakar
LARGEST CITY Dakar
HIGHEST POINT Futa Jallon 1,640 ft. (500 m.)
MONETARY UNIT CFA franc
MAJOR LANGUAGES Wolof, Peul (Fulani), French, Mende, Mandingo, Dida
MAJOR RELIGIONS Islam, tribal religions, Roman Catholicism

SIERRA LEONE

AREA 27,925 sq. mi. (72,325 sq. km.)
POPULATION 4,047,000
CAPITAL Freetown
LARGEST CITY Freetown
HIGHEST POINT Loma Mts. 6,390 ft. (1,947 m.)
MONETARY UNIT leone
MAJOR LANGUAGES Mende, Temne, Vai, English, Krio (pidgin)
MAJOR RELIGIONS Tribal religions, Islam, Christianity

TOGO

AREA 21,622 sq. mi. (56,000 sq. km.)
POPULATION 3,296,000
CAPITAL Lomé
LARGEST CITY Lomé
HIGHEST POINT Agou 3,445 ft. (1,050 m.)
MONETARY UNIT CFA franc
MAJOR LANGUAGES Ewe, French, Twi, Hausa
MAJOR RELIGIONS Tribal religions, Roman Catholicism, Islam

TUNISIA

AREA 63,378 sq. mi. (164,149 sq. km.)
POPULATION 7,465,000
CAPITAL Tunis
LARGEST CITY Tunis
HIGHEST POINT Jeb. Chambi 5,066 ft. (1,544 m.)
MONETARY UNIT Tunisian dinar
MAJOR LANGUAGES Arabic, French
MAJOR RELIGION Islam

BURKINA FASO

AREA 105,869 sq. mi. (274,200 sq. km.)
POPULATION 9,001,000
CAPITAL Ouagadougou
LARGEST CITY Ouagadougou
HIGHEST POINT 2,352 ft. (717 m.)
MONETARY UNIT CFA franc
MAJOR LANGUAGES Mossi, Lobi, French, Samo, Gourounsi
MAJOR RELIGIONS Islam, tribal religions, Roman Catholicism

WESTERN SAHARA

AREA 102,703 sq. mi. (266,000 sq. km.)
POPULATION 174,000
HIGHEST POINT 2,700 ft. (823 m.)
MAJOR LANGUAGE Arabic
MAJOR RELIGION Islam

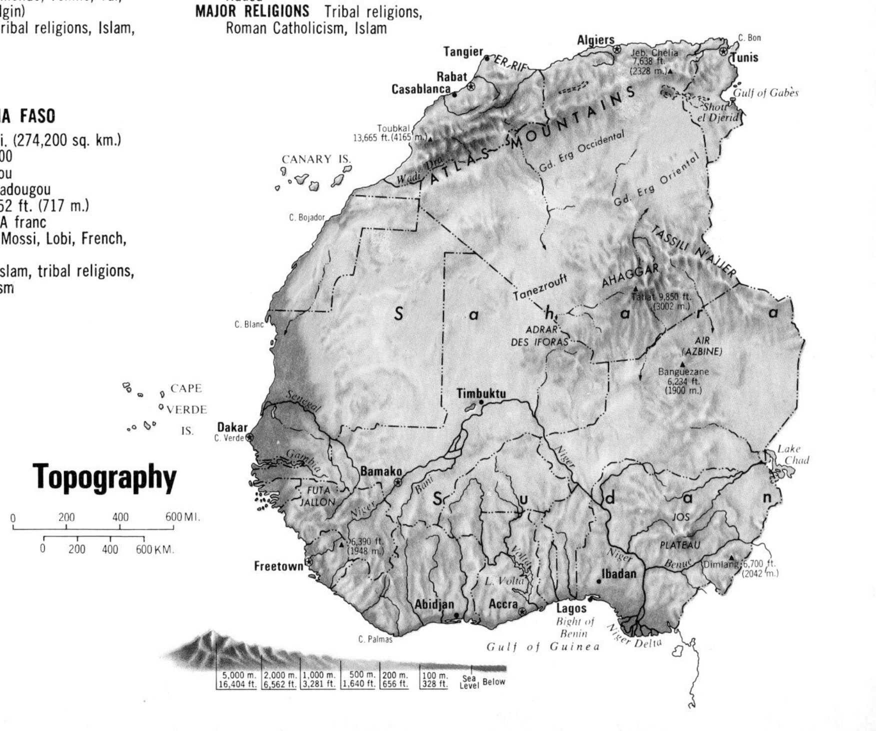
Algiers
C. Bon
Tunis
Tangier
ER-RIF
Jeb. Chélia 7,638 ft. (2328 m.)
Rabat
Casablanca
Gulf of Gabès
Shott el Djerid
Toubkal 13,665 ft. (4165 m.)
ATLAS MOUNTAINS
CANARY IS.
Gd. Erg Occidental
Gd. Erg Oriental
C. Bojador
TASSILI N'AJJER
AHAGGAR
Tanezrouft
Tahat 9,850 ft. (3002 m.)
S a h a r a
C. Blanc
ADRAR DES IFORAS
AIR (AZBINE)
Banguezane 6,234 ft. (1900 m.)
CAPE VERDE IS.
Timbuktu
Dakar
C. Verde
Senegal
Gambia
Niger
Lake Chad
Bamako
FUTA JALLON
S u d a n
JOS PLATEAU
Benue
Dimlang 6,700 ft. (2042 m.)
6,390 ft. (1948 m.)
Freetown
Volta
L. Volta
Ibadan
Abidjan
Accra
Lagos
Bight of Benin
Niger Delta
C. Palmas
Gulf of Guinea
0 200 400 600 MI.
0 200 400 600 KM.
5,000 m. 16,404 ft.
2,000 m. 6,562 ft.
1,000 m. 3,281 ft.
500 m. 1,640 ft.
200 m. 656 ft.
100 m. 328 ft.
Sea Level
Below

Topography

(continued)

ALGERIA

CITIES and TOWNS

Adrar 28,495 ... D3
Aïn Beïda 67,281 ... F1
Aïn Sefra 22,400 ... D2
Aïn Temouchent 48,935 ... D1
Algiers (cap.) 1,687,579 ... E1
Annaba 227,795 ... F1
Aoulef 10,259 ... E3
Batna 184,833 ... F1
Béchar 107,042 ... D2
Bejaïa 118,233 ... F1
Beni Abbès 7,370 ... D2
Beni Saf 30,700 ... D1
Biskra 129,611 ... F2
Blida 131,615 ... E1
Bone (Annaba) 227,795 ... F1
Bordj Bou Arreridj 86,997 ... E1
Bordj Omar Driss 1,900 ... F3
Boufarik 54,023 ... E1
Bougie (Bejaïa) 118,233 ... F1
Bou Saâda 50,000 ... E1
Brezina 10,000 ... E2
Cherchell 32,572 ... E1
Constantine 449,602 ... F1
Dellys 29,700 ... E1
Djelfa 88,929 ... E2
Djemaa 34,600 ... F2
El Abiod Sidi Cheikh 15,300 ... E2
El Asnam 103,998 ... E1
El Bayadh 44,925 ... E2
El Djezair (Algiers) (cap.) 1,687,579 ... E1
El Goléa 24,400 ... E2
El Oued 73,093 ... F2
Ghardaïa 62,518 ... E2
Ghazaouet 29,795 ... D2
Guelma 84,826 ... F1
Guerara 22,300 ... E2
Hassi Messaoud ... F2
Hassi R'Mel 10,545 ... E2
In Guezzam 10,304 ... F5
In Salah 20,733 ... E3
Jijel 69,274 ... F1
Khemis Miliana 57,101 ... E1
Ksar el Boukhari 41,200 ... E1
Laghouat 71,808 ... E2
Mascara 70,885 ... D1
Mecheria 40,251 ... D2
Médéa 84,062 ... E1
Metlili Chaamba 21,300 ... E2
Miliana 36,400 ... E1
Mohammadia 58,967 ... D1
Mostaganem 115,302 ... D1
M'Sila 82,877 ... E1
Oran 598,525 ... D1
Orléansville (El Asnam) 103,998 ... E1
Ouargla 76,270 ... F2
Ouled Djellal 33,278 ... F2
Philippeville (Skikda) 128,503 ... F1
Reggane 10,061 ... D3
Relizane 83,864 ... E1
Saïda 84,371 ... E2
Sétif 185,786 ... F1
Sidi Bel-Abbes 154,745 ... D1
Skikda 128,503 ... F1
Souk Ahras 85,873 ... F1
Tamanrasset 38,146 ... F4
Tébessa 111,688 ... F1
Ténès 26,510 ... E1
Tiaret 105,562 ... E1
Timimoun 21,556 ... E3
Tindouf 6,500 ... C3
Tizi Ouzou 93,025 ... E1
Tlemcen 108,145 ... D2
Touggourt 75,600 ... F2
Zaouiet Kounta 10,707 ... D3

OTHER FEATURES

Adrar des Iforas (plat.) ... E5
Ahaggar (range) ... F4
Anaï (well) ... G4
Aouinet Bel Egrâ (well) ... C3
Atlas (mts.) ... E2
Aurès (lag.) ... F1
Azzel Mati, Sebkha (lake) ... E3
Bougaroun (cape) ... F1
Chech, Erg (des.) ... D3
Chelia (mt.) ... F1
Chelif (riv.) ... E1
Chergui, Chott Ech (salt lake) ... E2
Dra, Wadi (dry river) ... C3
Dra Hamada (plat.) ... C3
Gourara (oasis) ... E3
Grand Erg Occidental (des.) ... E2
Grand Erg Oriental (des.) ... F2
Guir Hamada (des.) ... D2
High Plateaus (ranges) ... D2
Iguidi, Erg (des.) ... C3
In Ezzane (well) ... G4
Irharhar, Wadi (dry river) ... F3
Kabylia (reg.) ... E1
Mediterranean (sea) ... E1
Medjerda (riv.) ... F1
Mekerrhane, Sebkha (salt lake) ... E3
Melrhir, Chott (salt lake) ... F2
Mouydir (mts.) ... E3
Mya, Wadi (dry river) ... E2
M'zab (oasis) ... E2
Raoui, Erg er (des.) ... D3
Rhir, Wadi (dry river) ... F2
Sahara (des.) ... E4
Saharan Atlas (ranges) ... E2
Saoura, Wadi (dry river) ... D3
Souf (oasis) ... F2
Tademaït, Plateau du (plat.) ... E3
Tafassasset, Wadi (dry river) ... F4
Tahat (mt.) ... F4
Tamanrasset, Wadi (dry river) ... E4
Tanezrouft (des.) ... E4
Tassili N'Ahagger (plat.) ... E4
Tassili N'Ajjer (plat.) ... F3
Tidikelt (oasis) ... E3
Timmissao (well) ... E4
Tindouf, Sebkha de (salt lake) ... C3
Tinrhert, Hamada de (des.) ... F3
Tni Haïa (well) ... D4
Touat (oasis) ... E3
Touila (well) ... C3

BENIN

CITIES and TOWNS

Abomey 38,000 ... E7
Cotonou 178,000 ... E7
Grand-Popo ... E7
Kandi ... E6
Natitingou 49,000 ... E6
Ouidah ... E7
Parakou 21,000 ... E7
Porto-Novo (cap.) 104,000 ... E7

OTHER FEATURES

Atakora (mts.) ... E6
Benin (bight) ... E8
Guinea (gulf) ... E8
Mono (riv.) ... E7
Niger (riv.) ... E6
Ouémé (riv.) ... E7
Slave Coast (reg.) ... E7
Sudan (reg.) ... E6

BURKINA FASO

CITIES and TOWNS

Banfora 12,358 ... D6
Bobo Dioulasso 115,063 ... D6
Bogandé ... E6
Dédougou ... D6
Diébougou ... D6
Djibo ... D6
Dori ... D6
Fada-N'Gourma 12,000 ... E6
Gaoua ... D6
Kaya 18,000 ... D6
Koudougou 36,838 ... D6
Koupela ... D6
Léo ... D6
Ouagadougou (cap.) 172,661 ... D6
Ouahigouya 25,690 ... D6
Po ... D6
Tenkodogo ... E6
Tougan ... D6
Yako ... D6
Zabré ... D6

OTHER FEATURES

Black Volta (Mouhoun) (riv.) ... D6
Comoé (riv.) ... D7
Mouhoun (riv.) ... D6
Nakanbe (riv.) ... D6
Nazinan (riv.) ... D6
Oti (riv.) ... E7
Red Volta (Nazinan) (riv.) ... D6
Sudan (reg.) ... D6
White Volta (Nakanbe) (riv.) ... D6

CAPE VERDE

CITIES and TOWNS

Mindelo 28,797 ... A7
Praia (cap.) 21,494 ... B8
Ribeira Grande 1,892 ... B7
Sal Rei 1,296 ... B8

OTHER FEATURES

Boa Vista (isl.) ... B8
Brava (isl.) ... B8
Fogo (isl.) ... B8
Maio (isl.) ... B8
Sal (isl.) ... B7
Santa Luzia (isl.) ... B8
Santo Antão (isl.) ... A7
São Nicolau (isl.) ... B8
São Tiago (isl.) ... B8
São Vicente (isl.) ... B7

GAMBIA

CITIES and TOWNS

Banjul (cap.) 39,476 ... A6
Basse Santa Su 2,899 ... B6
Brikama 9,483 ... A6
Georgetown 2,510 ... A6

GHANA

CITIES and TOWNS

Accra (cap.) 859,600 ... D7
Attebubu 9,800 ... D7
Axim 13,100 ... D8
Bawku 33,900 ... D6
Bekwai 11,800 ... D7
Berekum 21,900 ... D7
Bolgatanga 31,500 ... D6
Cape Coast 57,700 ... D7
Damongo 12,600 ... D7
Dunkwa 16,900 ... D7
Elmina 15,600 ... D8
Ho 37,200 ... E7
Keta 12,700 ... E7
Kintampo 14,100 ... D7
Koforidua 54,400 ... D7
Kpandu 15,800 ... D7
Kumasi 348,900 ... D7
Mampong 19,800 ... D7
Nsawam 31,900 ... D7
Obuasi 60,100 ... D7
Oda 20,957 ... D7
Prestea 16,300 ... D7

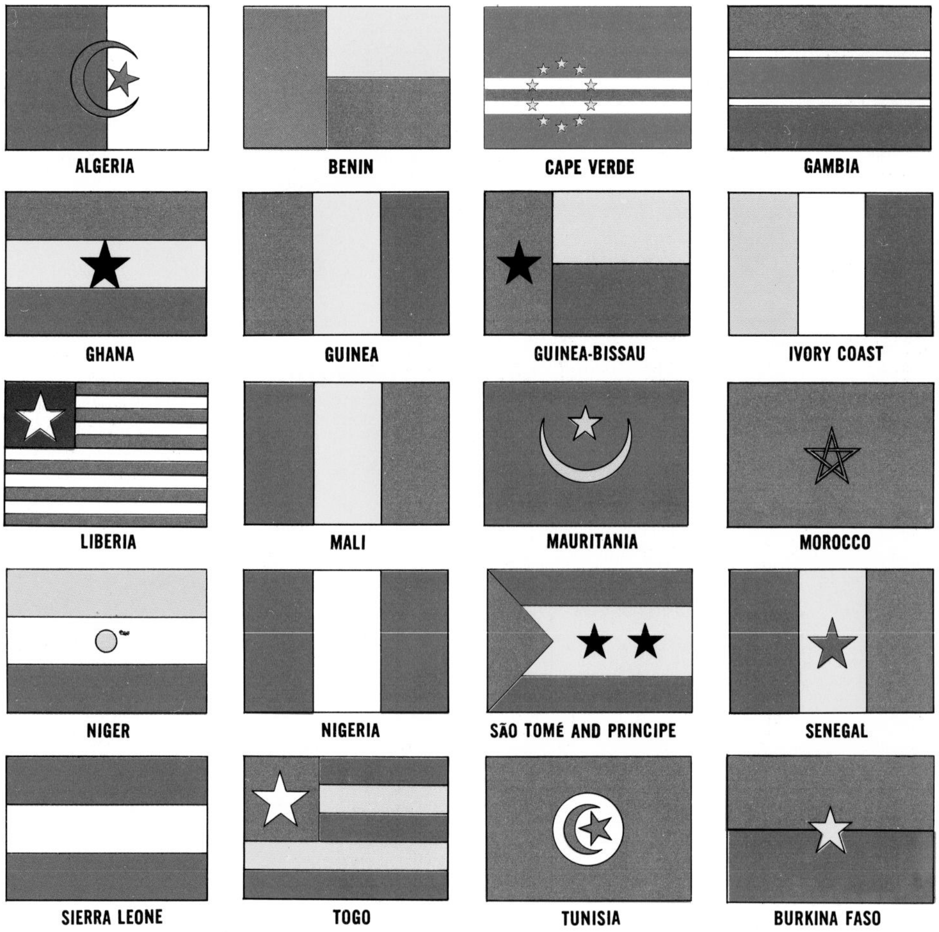
ALGERIA
BENIN
CAPE VERDE
GAMBIA
GHANA
GUINEA
GUINEA-BISSAU
IVORY COAST
LIBERIA
MALI
MAURITANIA
MOROCCO
NIGER
NIGERIA
SÃO TOMÉ AND PRINCIPE
SENEGAL
SIERRA LEONE
TOGO
TUNISIA
BURKINA FASO

Salaga 10,600 ... D7
Sekondi 32,400 ... D8
Sunyani 36,100 ... D7
Takoradi 61,500 ... D8
Tamale 136,800 ... D7
Tarkwa 22,000 ... D7
Tema 99,600 ... E7
Wa 36,000 ... D6
Wenchi 18,400 ... D7
Winneba 26,200 ... D7
Yendi 30,700 ... D7

OTHER FEATURES

Ashanti (reg.) ... D7
Benin (bight) ... E8
Black Volta (riv.) ... D7
Gold Coast (reg.) ... D8
Guinea (gulf) ... E8
Oti (riv.) ... E7
Red Volta (riv.) ... D6
Saint Paul (cape) ... E7
Three Points (cape) ... D8
Volta (lake) ... D7
Volta (riv.) ... E7
White Volta (riv.) ... D7

GUINEA

CITIES and TOWNS

Boffa ... B6
Conakry (cap.) 525,671 ... B7
Dabola ... B6
Dubréka ... B7
Fria ... B6
Kankan 85,310 ... C6
Kérouané ... C7
Kindia 79,861 ... B6
Kissidougou ... B7
Koundara 6,000 ... B6
Kouroussa ... C6
Labé 79,670 ... B6
Mali ... B6
N'Zérékoré 23,000 ... C7
Siguiri ... C6
Télimélé 12,000 ... B6
Tougué ... B6

OTHER FEATURES

Bafing (riv.) ... B6
Bakoy (riv.) ... B6
Futa Jallon (lag.) ... B6
Los (isls.) ... B7
Milo (riv.) ... C7
Moa (riv.) ... B7
Niger (riv.) ... C6
Nimba (lag.) ... C7
Verga (cape) ... B6

GUINEA-BISSAU

CITIES and TOWNS

Bissau (cap.) 109,486 ... A6
Bolama○ 9,133 ... A6
Bubaque○ 8,441 ... A6
Cacheu○ 15,194 ... A6

OTHER FEATURES

Bijagós (isls.) ... A6

IVORY COAST

CITIES and TOWNS

Abengourou 31,239 ... D7
Abidjan 6 85,828 ... D7
Aboisso 14,272 ... D7
Agboville 27,192 ... D7
Bingerville 18,218 ... D7
Bondoukou 19,111 ... D7
Bouaflé 15,917 ... C7
Bouaké 1 73,248 ... D7
Dabou 23,870 ... D7
Daloa 60,958 ... C7
Danané 19,872 ... C7
Dimbokro 30,986 ... D7
Divo 37,896 ... C7
Ferkessédougou 25,307 ... D7
Gagnoa 42,362 ... C7
Grand-Bassam 25,808 ... D7
Grand-Lahou 4,070 ... C8
Guiglo 10,441 ... C7
Issia 11,143 ... C7
Katiola 21,559 ... C7
Korhogo 47,657 ... C7
Man 50,315 ... C7
Odienné 13,864 ... C7
Port-Bouet 72,616 ... D7
San Pedro 27,616 ... C8
Séguéla 12,587 ... C7
Sinfra 16,399 ... C7
Tabou 7,255 ... C8
Toumodi 12,983 ... D7
Yamoussoukro (cap.) 35,585 ... C7

OTHER FEATURES

Aby (lag.) ... D8
Bagoé (riv.) ... C6
Bandama (riv.) ... C7
Baoulé (riv.) ... C6
Black Volta (riv.) ... D6
Cavally (riv.) ... C7
Comoé (riv.) ... D7
Ebrié (lag.) ... D8
Guinea (gulf) ... E8
Ivory Coast (reg.) ... C8
Kossou, Lac de (lake) ... C7
Nimba (lag.) ... C7
Sassandra (riv.) ... C7

LIBERIA

CITIES and TOWNS

Buchanan 23,999 ... B7
Gbarnga 6,896 ... C7
Greenville 8,462 ... C8
Harbel 11,445 ... B7
Harper 10,627 ... C8
Monrovia (cap.) 166,507 ... B7
River Cess 2,041 ... C7
Robertsport 2,562 ... B7
Tapeta 3,927 ... C7
Tubmanburg 14,089 ... B7
Zwedru 6,094 ... C7

OTHER FEATURES

Bong (range) ... B7
Cavalla (riv.) ... C7
Cestos (riv.) ... C7
Grain Coast (reg.) ... B8
Kru Coast (reg.) ... C8
Mano (riv.) ... B7
Mount (cape) ... B7
Nimba (lag.) ... C7
Palmas (cape) ... C8
Roberts Field Int'l Airport ... C7

MALI

CITIES and TOWNS

Ansongo 3,485 ... E5
Bafoulabé 2,163 ... B6
Bamako (cap.) 404,022 ... C6
Banamba 6,776 ... C6
Bandiagara 8,920 ... D6
Bankass 3,229 ... D6
Bougouni 17,246 ... C6
Bourem 4,538 ... E5
Dioila 4,953 ... C6
Dire 8,941 ... D5
Djenné 10,251 ... D6
Douentza 6,746 ... D6
Gao 30,714 ... E5
Goundam 10,262 ... D5
Gourma-Rharous 4,671 ... D5
Kéniéba 4,510 ... B6
Kadiolo 3,991 ... C6
Kangaba 3,184 ... C6
Kati 24,991 ... C6
Kayes 44,736 ... B6
Ké-Macina 5,426 ... C6
Kidal 3,308 ... E5
Kita 17,538 ... C6
Kolokani 8,923 ... C6
Kolondiéba 5,882 ... C6
Koulikoro 16,376 ... C6
Koutiala 27,497 ... C6
Ménaka 3,693 ... E5
Mopti 53,885 ... D6
Nara 6,091 ... C5
Niafunké 6,399 ... D5
Niono 12,290 ... C6
Nioro 11,617 ... C5
San 22,962 ... D6
Ségou 64,890 ... C6
Sikasso 47,030 ... C6
Ténenkou 4,708 ... C6
Timbuktu (Tombouctou) 20,483 ... D5
Yanfolila 3,809 ... C6
Yelimané 1,481 ... B5
Yorosso 2,390 ... C6

OTHER FEATURES

Achourat (well) ... D4
Adrar des Iforas (plat.) ... E5
Agueraktem (well) ... C4
Asselar (well) ... D5
Azaouad (reg.) ... D5
Azaouak (dry riv.) ... E5
Bafing (riv.) ... B6
Bagoé (riv.) ... C6
Bakoy (riv.) ... B6
Bani (riv.) ... C6
Baoulé (dry riv.) ... C6
Baoulé (riv.) ... C6
Bir Ksaib Ounane (well) ... C4
Bir Ounane (well) ... D4
Chech, Erg (des.) ... D4
Debo (lake) ... D5
El Mraiti (well) ... D5
Faguibine (lake) ... D5
Falémé (riv.) ... B6
Haricha Hamada (des.) ... D4
Hombori (mts.) ... D5
In Dagouber (well) ... D4
Macina (depr.) ... D6
Niger (riv.) ... D5
Oum el Asel (well) ... D4
Sahara (des.) ... D4
Sekkane, Erg (des.) ... D4
Senegal (riv.) ... B5
Sudan (reg.) ... D6
Tadjnout Hagguerete (well) ... D4
Terhazza (ruins) ... C4
Tilemsi (valley) ... E5
Toufourine (well) ... C4

MAURITANIA

CITIES and TOWNS

Aïoun el Atrous ... C5
Akjoujt 8,044 ... B5
Aleg 6,415 ... B5
Atar 16,326 ... B4
Bassikounou ... C5
Boutilimit 7,261 ... B5
Fdérik (Fort Gouraud) 2,160 ... B4
Káedi 20,248 ... B5
Kiffa 10,629 ... B5
M'Bout ... B5
Néma 8,232 ... C5
Nouadhibou 21,961 ... A4
Nouakchott (cap.) 134,986 ... A5
Oualata ... C5
Rosso 16,466 ... A5
Sélibaby 5,994 ... B5
Tidjikja 7,870 ... B5
Timbédra 5,317 ... C5
Zouïrât 17,474 ... B4

OTHER FEATURES

Adafer (reg.) ... B5
Adrar (reg.) ... B4
Affolé (reg.) ... B5
Agueraktem (well) ... C4
Aïn ben Tili (well) ... C3
Arguin (bay) ... A4
Assaba (reg.) ... B5
Atoui, Wadi (dry riv.) ... B4
Ben Guerdane (well) ... B3
Bir el Khzaim (well) ... C4
Blanc (cape) ... A4
Brakna (reg.) ... B5
Chegga (well) ... C3
Djouf, El (des.) ... C4
El Mrayer (well) ... C4
El Mreïti (well) ... C4
Gorgol (reg.) ... B5
Hodh (reg.) ... C5
Iguidi, Erg (des.) ... C3
Inchiri (reg.) ... A5
Koumbi Saleh (ruins) ... C5

Lévrier (bay) A4
Makteïr (des.) B4
Meraia (reg.) C5
Mirik (Timiris) (cape) A5
Ouarane (reg.) B4
Sahara (des.) C4
Senegal (riv.) B5
Tagant (reg.) B5
Tidra (isl.) A5
Timiris (cape) A5
Touila (well) C3
Trarza (reg.) A5

MOROCCO

CITIES and TOWNS

Agadir 61,192 C2
Al Hoceima 18,686 D1
Azemmour 17,182 C2
Azrou 20,756 C2
Beni Mellal 53,826 C2
Boujad 18,838 C2
Casablanca 1,506,373 C2
Dar-el-Beida (Casablanca) 1,506,373 C2
El Jadida 55,501 C2
El Kelaa des Srarhna 17,163 C2
Er Rachidia 16,775 D2
Essaouira 30,061 C2
Fès (Fez) 325,327 D2
Jerada 30,633 D2
Kenitra 139,206 C2
Khenifra 25,526 C2
Khouribga 73,667 C2
Ksar el Kebir 48,262 C2
Larache 45,710 C1
Marrakech 332,741 C2
Mazagan (El Jadida) 55,501 C2
Meknès 248,369 C2
Mogador (Essaouira) 30,061 B2
Mohammedia 70,392 C2
Nador 32,490 D1
Oued Zem 33,323 C2
Ouezzane 33,267 C2
Oujda 175,532 D2
Port-Lyautey (Kénitra) 139,206 C2
Rabat (cap.) 367,620 C2
Safi 129,113 C2
Saïdia D2
Salé 155,557 C2
Sefrou 28,607 D2
Settat 42,325 C2
Sidi Ifni 13,650 B3
Sidi Kacem 26,831 C2
Tangier (Tanger) 187,894 C1
Tarfaya 1,104 B3
Taroudannt 22,272 C2
Taza 55,157 D2
Tétouan 139,105 C1
Youssoufia 22,435 C2

OTHER FEATURES

Anti-Atlas (ranges) C3
Atlas (mts.) C2
Bani, Jebel (mts.) C3
Beddouza, Ras (cape) C2
Dra, Wadi (dry riv.) C3
Gibraltar (str.) C1
High Atlas (ranges) C2
Juby (cape) B3
Mediterranean (sea) D1
Middle Atlas (ranges) C2
Moulouya (riv.) D2
Rheris, Wadi (dry riv.) D2
Rhir (cape) B2
Rif, Er (range) D2
Sarhro, Jebel (mts.) C2
Sebou (riv.) C2
Sim (cape) B2
Toubkal, Jebel (mt.) C2
Ziz, Wadi (dry riv.) D2

NIGER

CITIES and TOWNS

Agadès 11,000 F5
Arhli (Arlit) F5
Bilma G5
Birni-N'Konni 10,000 E6
Bosso G6
Dakoro F6
Diffa G6
Dosso E6
Filingué 10,000 E6
Gaya 5,000 E6
Gouré G6
Iférouane F5
In-Gall F5
Magaria F6
Mainé-Soro G6
Maradi 45,852 F6
N'Guigmi G6
Niamey (cap.) 225,314 E6
Say E6
Tahoua 31,265 F6
Tanout F6
Tillabéry E6
Zinder 58,436 F6

OTHER FEATURES

Achégour (well) G5
Agadem (well) G5
Air (mts.) F5
Anaye (well) G5
Assakarai (dry riv.) F5
Azaoua (reg.) E5
Azbine (Air) (mts.) F5
Bagam (well) F5
Banguezane (mt.) F5
Bedouaram (well) G5
Chad (lake) G6
Dallol Bosso (dry riv.) E6
Dillia (dry riv.) G5
Djado (plat.) G4
El War (well) G4
In Azaoua (well) F4
Komadugu Yobe (riv.) G6
Mantas (well) E5
Niger (riv.) E6
Rima (riv.) F6
Sahara (des.) F4
Sudan (reg.) F6
Tafassasset, Wadi (dry riv.) F4
Talak (reg.) E5
Ténéré (des.) G5
Timboulaga (well) F5
Tummo (El War) (well) G4
Zoo Baba (well) G5

NIGERIA

STATES

Abuja Capital Territory F7
Anambra 2,300,000 F7
Bauchi 2,496,329 F6
Bendel 2,336,000 F7
Benue 2,641,496 F7
Borno 2,853,553 G6
Cross River 3,633,582 F7
Gongola 1,585,200 G7
Imo 5,000,000 F7
Kaduna 4,098,303 F6
Kano 5,775,000 F6
Kwara 5,240,600 E7
Lagos 1,100,000 E7
Niger 2,900,000 F7
Ogun 1,448,966 E7
Ondo 2,727,676 F7
Oyo 5,208,884 E7
Plateau 1,367,450 F7
Rivers 1,544,314 F8
Sokoto 1,367,450 F6

CITIES and TOWNS

Abeokuta 253,000 E7
Abuja (cap.) 1,000 F7
Ado 213,000 E7
Aku F7
Akure F7
Baga G6
Bama G6
Baro F7
Bauchi F6
Benin City 136,000 F7
Biu G6
Bonny F8
Calabar 103,000 F7
Degema F8
Dikwa G6
Ede 182,000 E7
Enugu 187,000 F7
Geidam G6
Gumel F6
Gummi F6
Gusau F6
Ibadan 847,000 E7
Ibi F7
Ife 176,000 E7
Ijebu-Ode E7
Ilesha 224,000 E7
Ilorin 282,000 E7
Iseyin 115,083 E7
Iwo 214,000 E7
Jega E6
Jos F7
Kaduna 202,000 F6
Kano 399,000 F6
Katsina 109,424 F6
Katsina Ala F7
Kontagora F6
Kumo G7
Kuta F7
Lagos 1,060,848 E7
Maiduguri 189,000 G6
Maigatari F6
Makurdi F7
Minna F7
Nnewi F7
Nsukka F7
Ogbomosho 432,000 E7
Ondo E7
Onitsha 220,000 F7
Oshogbo 282,000 F7
Owerri F7
Owo F7
Oyo 152,000 E7
Panyam F7
Port Harcourt 242,000 F8
Shaki E7
Shendam F7
Sokoto F6
Toungo G7
Wamba F7
Wukari F7
Yan G7
Yelwa F6
Yola G7
Zaria 224,000 F6

OTHER FEATURES

Adamawa (reg.) G7
Benin (bight) E8
Benue (riv.) F7
Biafra (bight) F8
Biu (plat.) G6
Bonny (bight) F8
Chad (lake) G6
Cross (riv.) F7
Dimlang (mt.) G7
Donga (riv.) G7
Gongola (riv.) G6
Guinea (gulf) E8
Hadejia (riv.) F6
Jos (plat.) F7
Kaduna (riv.) F7
Kainji (res.) E6
Komadugu Yobe (riv.) G6
Niger (delta) F8
Niger (riv.) F7
Osse (riv.) F7
Rima (riv.) F6
Slave Coast (reg.) E7
Sokoto (riv.) F6
Sudan (reg.) F6

PORTUGAL-Madeira

CITIES and TOWNS

Funchal (cap.) 38,340 A2

OTHER FEATURES

Desertas (isls.) A2
Madeira (isl.) A2
Pôrto Santo (isl.) A2

SÃO TOMÉ AND PRINCIPE

CITIES and TOWNS

São Tomé (cap.) 7,681 F8
Santo António 1,618 F8

OTHER FEATURES

Guinea (gulf) E8
Príncipe (isl.) F8
São Tomé (isl.) F8

SENEGAL

CITIES and TOWNS

Bignona 14,537 A6
Dagana 10,506 A5
Dakar (cap.) 798,792 A6
Diourbel 50,618 A6
Kaffrine 11,211 A6
Kaolack 106,899 A6
Kolda 19,302 B6
Louga 35,063 A5
Matam 10,002 B5
M'Bour 37,663 A6
Nioro-du-Rip 7,824 A6
Podor 6,914 B5
Rufisque A6
Saint-Louis 88,404 A5
Tambacounda 25,147 B6
Thiès 117,333 A5
Tivaouane 17,351 A5
Ziguinchor 72,726 A6

OTHER FEATURES

Casamance (riv.) A6
Falémé (riv.) B6
Ferlo (reg.) B6
Gambia (riv.) B6
Senegal (riv.) B5
Verde (cape) A6

SIERRA LEONE

CITIES and TOWNS

Bo 42,216 B7
Bonthe 6,230 B7
Freetown (cap.) 274,000 B7
Kabala 4,610 B7
Kenema 33,880 B7
Makeni 28,684 B7
Moyamba 4,564 B7
Pendembu 2,696 B7
Port Loko 5,809 B7
Pujehun 2,034 B7

OTHER FEATURES

Loma, Mansa (lag.) B7
Mano (riv.) B7
Moa (riv.) B7
Sherbro (isl.) B7
Yawri (bay) B7

SPAIN-Canary Islands, Ceuta and Melilla

CITIES and TOWNS

Arrecife 21,310 B3
Ceuta 60,639 C1
Las Palmas de Gran Canaria 260,368 B3
Melilla 64,942 D1
Santa Cruz de la Palma 10,393 A3
Santa Cruz de Tenerife 74,910 A3

OTHER FEATURES

Canary (isls.) A3
Fuerteventura (isl.) B3
Gomera (isl.) A3
Grand Canary (isl.) A3
Hierro (isl.) A3
Lanzarote (isl.) B3
La Palma (isl.) A3
Tenerife (isl.) A3

TOGO

CITIES and TOWNS

Aného (Anécho) 10,889 E7
Atakpamé 17,440 E7
Dapaong 10,100 E6
Kpalimé 19,801 E7
Lama-Kara 9,400 E7
Lomé (cap.) 148,443 E7
Mango 9,600 E6
Sokodé 29,623 E7

OTHER FEATURES

Benin (bight) E8
Guinea (gulf) E8
Mono (riv.) E7
Oti (riv.) E7
Slave Coast (reg.) E7

TUNISIA

CITIES and TOWNS

Béja 39,226 F1
Ben Gardane 6,593 G2
Bizerte 62,856 F1
El Djem 10,666 G1
El Kef 27,939 F1
Gabès 40,585 F2
Gafsa 42,225 F2
Halq el Oued 41,912 G1
Jendouba 18,127 F1
Kairouan 54,546 F1
Kalaa-Kebia 23,508 F1
Kasserine 22,594 F1
La Goulette (Halq el Oued) 41,912 G1
La Skhirra 4,565 G2
Mahdia 25,711 G1
Mareth 2,185 F2
Mateur 19,645 F1
Médenine 15,826 G2
Menzel Bourguiba 42,111 F1
Menzel Temime 18,857 G1
Moknine 26,035 G1
Monastir 26,759 G1
Msaken 33,559 G1
Nabeul 30,476 G1
Nefta 12,476 F2
Sfax 171,297 G2
Sousse 69,530 G1
Tatahouine 10,399 G2
Tozeur 16,772 F2
Tunis (cap.) 550,404 G1
Zarzis 14,420 G2

OTHER FEATURES

Abiad, Ras el (Blanc) (cape) G1
Blanc (cape) G1
Bon (cape) G1
Chambi, Jebel (mt.) F2
Djerba (isl.) G2
Djerid, Shott el (salt lake) F2
Gabès (gulf) G2
Grand Erg Oriental (des.) F2
Hammamet (gulf) G1
Jefara (reg.) G2
Kerkennah (isls.) G2
Mediterranean (sea) F1
Medjerda (riv.) F1
Tib, Ras el (Bon) (cape) G1
Tunis (gulf) G1

WESTERN SAHARA

CITIES and TOWNS

Dakhla 6,554 A4
El Aaiún (Laayoune) 24,519 B3
Villa Cisneros (Dakhla) 6,554 A4

OTHER FEATURES

Ausert (well) B4
Barbas (cape) A4
Bir Ganduz (well) A4
Bir Nzaran (well) B4
Blanc (cape) A4
Bojador (cape) B3
Durnford (pt.) A4
Guelta de Zemmur (well) B3
Saguia el Hamra (dry riv.) B3
Tichlá (well) B4
Atoui, Wadi (dry riv.) B4

○ Population of sub-district or division.

Agriculture, Industry and Resources

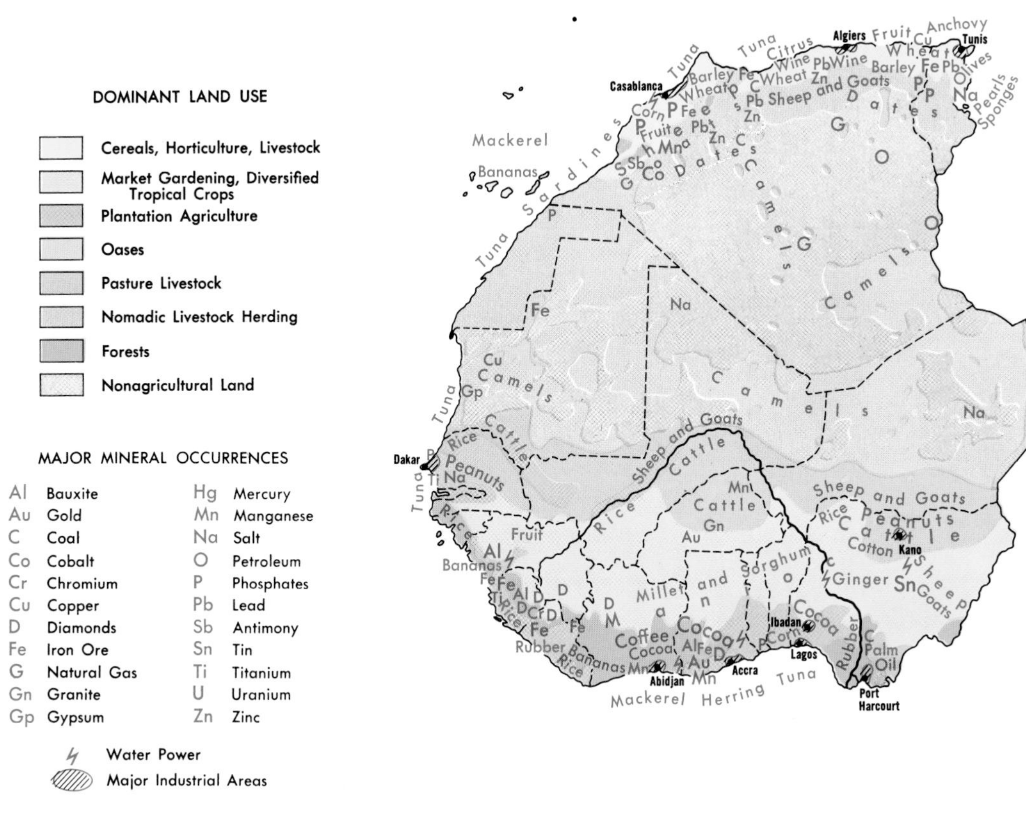
DOMINANT LAND USE
Cereals, Horticulture, Livestock
Market Gardening, Diversified Tropical Crops
Plantation Agriculture
Oases
Pasture Livestock
Nomadic Livestock Herding
Forests
Nonagricultural Land
MAJOR MINERAL OCCURRENCES
Al Bauxite
Au Gold
C Coal
Co Cobalt
Cr Chromium
Cu Copper
D Diamonds
Fe Iron Ore
G Natural Gas
Gn Granite
Gp Gypsum
Hg Mercury
Mn Manganese
Na Salt
O Petroleum
P Phosphates
Pb Lead
Sb Antimony
Sn Tin
Ti Titanium
U Uranium
Zn Zinc
Water Power
Major Industrial Areas
Algiers
Tunis
Casablanca
Dakar
Kano
Ibadan
Lagos
Abidjan
Accra
Port Harcourt
Mackerel
Tuna
Sardines
Anchovy
Pearls
Sponges
Camels
Sheep and Goats
Cattle
Rice
Peanuts
Millet and Sorghum
Cocoa
Coffee
Rubber
Bananas
Palm Oil
Ginger
Cotton
Fruit
Herring

LIBYA

EGYPT

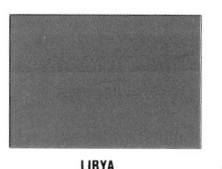

CHAD

SUDAN

ETHIOPIA

ERITREA

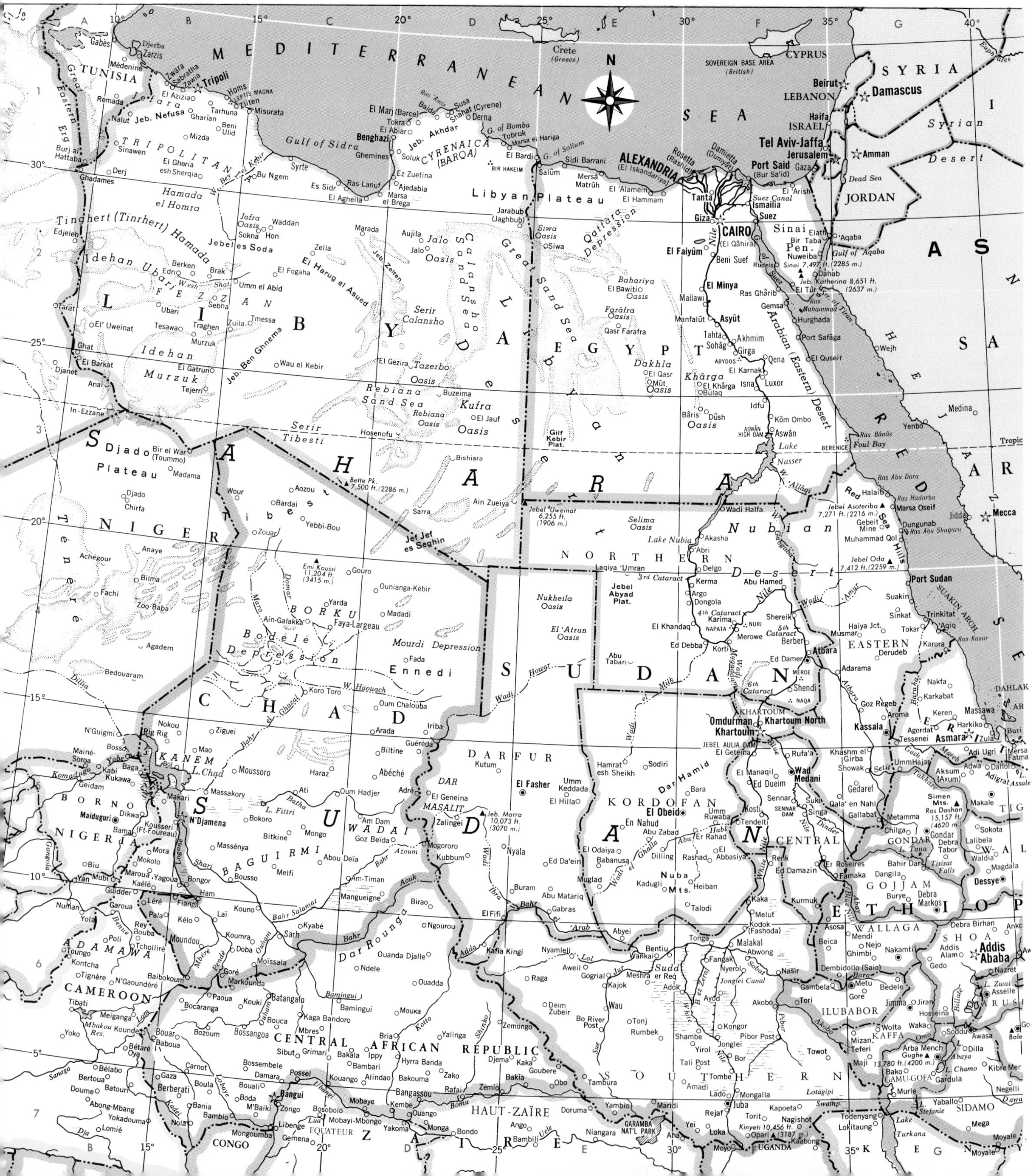
MEDITERRANEAN SEA
N
Crete
(Greece)
CYPRUS
SOVEREIGN BASE AREA
(British)
SYRIA
Damascus
Beirut
LEBANON
Haifa
ISRAEL
Tel Aviv-Jaffa
Jerusalem
Amman
JORDAN
Dead Sea
Syrian Desert
Gaza
Port Said
(Bur Sa'id)
ALEXANDRIA
(El Iskandariya)
Rosetta
(Rashid)
Damietta
(Dumyat)
Tanta
Suez Canal
Ismailia
Suez
Giza
CAIRO
(El Qâhira)
El Faiyûm
Beni Suef
El Minya
Asyût
Sohâg
Akhmim
Girga
Qena
Luxor
Isna
Idfu
Kôm Ombo
Aswân
ASWÂN HIGH DAM
Lake Nasser
Wadi Halfa
Sinai Pen.
Gulf of Aqaba
'Aqaba
Elath
Jeb. Katherina 8,651 ft. (2637 m.)
Hurghada
Port Safâga
El Quseir
Arabian (Eastern) Desert
RED SEA
Berenice
Foul Bay
Ras Bânâs
Tropic
Medina
Yenbo
Jidda
Mecca
Halaib
Marsa Oseif
Port Sudan
Suakin
Sinkat
Tokar
Trinkitat
Agordat
Asmara
Massawa
Kassala
EASTERN
Atbara
Ed Damer
Shendi
Omdurman
Khartoum
Khartoum North
KHARTOUM
Wad Medani
Sennar
Kosti
CENTRAL
Er Roseires
Ed Damazin
Kurmuk
El Obeid
KORDOFAN
Nuba Mts.
Kadugli
Babanusa
En Nahud
El Fasher
DARFUR
Jeb. Marra 10,073 ft. (3070 m.)
Nyala
El Geneina
Zalingei
Nubian Desert
NORTHERN
Dongola
Kerma
Karima
Merowe
Abu Hamed
Selima Oasis
Nukheila Oasis
El 'Atrun Oasis
Jebel Uweinat 6,255 ft. (1906 m.)
Gilf Kebir Plat.
Western Desert
Great Sand Sea
Siwa Oasis
Qattara Depression
Bahariya Oasis
Farâfra Oasis
Dakhla Oasis
Khârga Oasis
Libyan Plateau
Libyan Desert
Marsa Matrûh
El 'Alamein
Salûm
Sidi Barrani
Tobruk
Bardia
Derna
Benghazi
Cyrenaica (Barqa)
Gulf of Sidra
Ajedabia
Marsa el Brega
El Agheila
Ras Lanuf
Sirte
Misurata
Tripoli
Homs
Zuara
Sabratha
Zawia
Tripolitania
Jeb. Nefusa
Gharian
Nalut
Ghadames
Hamada el Homra
Jofra Oasis
Waddan
Hon
Sokna
Jebel es Soda
Sebha
Ubari
Murzuk
Fezzan
Ghat
El Gatrun
Tejerri
Idehan Murzuk
Jalo Oasis
Aujila
Marada
Zella
Calanscio Sand Sea
Serir Calansho
Kufra Oasis
El Jauf
Tazerbo Oasis
Rebiana Sand Sea
Rebiana Oasis
Tibesti
Bette Pk. 7,500 ft. (2286 m.)
Emi Koussi 11,204 ft. (3415 m.)
Bardai
Aozou
Zouar
Faya-Largeau
BORKU
Bodélé Depression
Ennedi
Mourdi Depression
Fada
Abéché
WADAI
Biltine
Ati
Mongo
Am Timan
N'Djamena
Massakory
Moussoro
KANEM
L. Chad
BAGUIRMI
Bousso
Sarh
Moundou
Doba
Lai
Kélo
Pala
Fianga
CHAD
SAHARA
NIGER
Djado Plateau
Bilma
Ténéré
Agadem
N'Guigmi
NIGERIA
Maiduguri
BORNO
CAMEROON
Garoua
Kousseri (Ft-Foureau)
Maroua
CENTRAL AFRICAN REPUBLIC
Bangui
Bambari
Bria
Ndélé
Berbérati
Bangassou
Mobaye
Zemio
Obo
Birao
HAUT-ZAÏRE
ZAIRE
CONGO
UGANDA
EQUATEUR
Juba
Torit
Kinyeti 10,456 ft. (3187 m.)
Wau
Malakal
Bor
Rumbek
Yei
Aweil
Bentiu
Sudd
Jonglei Canal
SOUTHERN
GARAMBA NAT'L PARK
ETHIOPIA
Addis Ababa
SHOA
WALLAGA
ILUBABOR
KAFFA
GOJJAM
GONDAR
Gondar
L. Tana
Bahir Dar
Dessye
Jimma
Gambela
Nekemte
Simen Mts.
Ras Dashen 15,157 ft. (4620 m.)
Gughe 13,780 ft. (4200 m.)
GAMU-GOFA
SIDAMO
L. Stefanie
Lake Turkana
Moyale
Mega
L. Chamo
L. Abaya
Arba Minch
Dilla
Awasa
Asela
Adigrat
Aksum
Adwa
ERITREA
DAHLAK
Tessenei
Makale
TUNISIA
Gabès
Djerba
Zarzis
Médenine
Great Eastern Erg
Tinghert (Tinrhert) Hamada
Idehan Ubari
ASIA
Euphrates

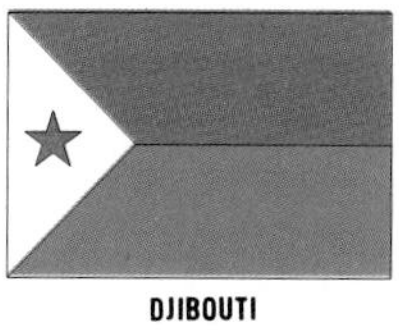
DJIBOUTI

ERITREA

AREA 45,410 sq. mi. (117,600 sq. km.)
POPULATION 2,614,700
CAPITAL Asmara
LARGEST CITY Asmara
HIGHEST POINT Mount Soira 9,885 ft. (3,013 m.)
MONETARY UNIT birr
MAJOR LANGUAGES Arabic, English, Tigre, Afar
MAJOR RELIGIONS Coptic Christianity, Islam

LIBYA

AREA 679,358 sq. mi. (1,759,537 sq. km.)
POPULATION 3,773,000
CAPITAL Tripoli
LARGEST CITY Tripoli
HIGHEST POINT Bette Pk. 7,500 ft. (2,286 m.)
MONETARY UNIT Libyan dinar
MAJOR LANGUAGES Arabic, Berber
MAJOR RELIGION Islam

EGYPT

AREA 386,659 sq. mi. (1,001,447 sq. km.)
POPULATION 53,080,000
CAPITAL Cairo
LARGEST CITY Cairo
HIGHEST POINT Jeb. Katherina 8,651 ft. (2,637 m.)
MONETARY UNIT Egyptian pound
MAJOR LANGUAGE Arabic
MAJOR RELIGIONS Islam, Coptic Christianity

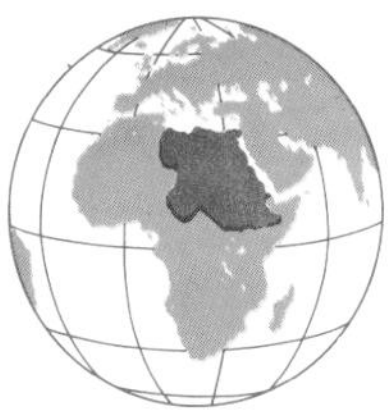

CHAD

AREA 495,752 sq. mi. (1,283,998 sq. km.)
POPULATION 5,538,000
CAPITAL N'Djamena
LARGEST CITY N'Djamena
HIGHEST POINT Emi Koussi 11,204 ft. (3,415 m.)
MONETARY UNIT CFA franc
MAJOR LANGUAGES Arabic, Bagirmi, French, Sara, Massa, Moudang
MAJOR RELIGIONS Islam, tribal religions

SUDAN

AREA 967,494 sq. mi. (2,505,809 sq. km.)
POPULATION 24,485,000
CAPITAL Khartoum
LARGEST CITY Khartoum
HIGHEST POINT Jeb. Marra 10,073 ft. (3,070 m.)
MONETARY UNIT Sudanese pound
MAJOR LANGUAGES Arabic, Dinka, Nubian, Beja, Nuer
MAJOR RELIGIONS Islam, tribal religions

ETHIOPIA

AREA 426,366 sq. mi. (1,104,300 sq. km.)
POPULATION 50,576,300
CAPITAL Addis Ababa
LARGEST CITY Addis Ababa
HIGHEST POINT Ras Dashan 15,157 ft. (4,620 m.)
MONETARY UNIT birr
MAJOR LANGUAGES Amharic, Gallinya, Tigrinya, Somali, Sidamo, Arabic, Ge'ez
MAJOR RELIGIONS Coptic Christianity, Islam

DJIBOUTI

AREA 8,880 sq. mi. (23,000 sq. km.)
POPULATION 456,000
CAPITAL Djibouti
LARGEST CITY Djibouti
HIGHEST POINT Moussa Ali 6,768 ft. (2,063 m.)
MONETARY UNIT Djibouti franc
MAJOR LANGUAGES Arabic, Somali, Afar, French
MAJOR RELIGIONS Islam, Roman Catholicism

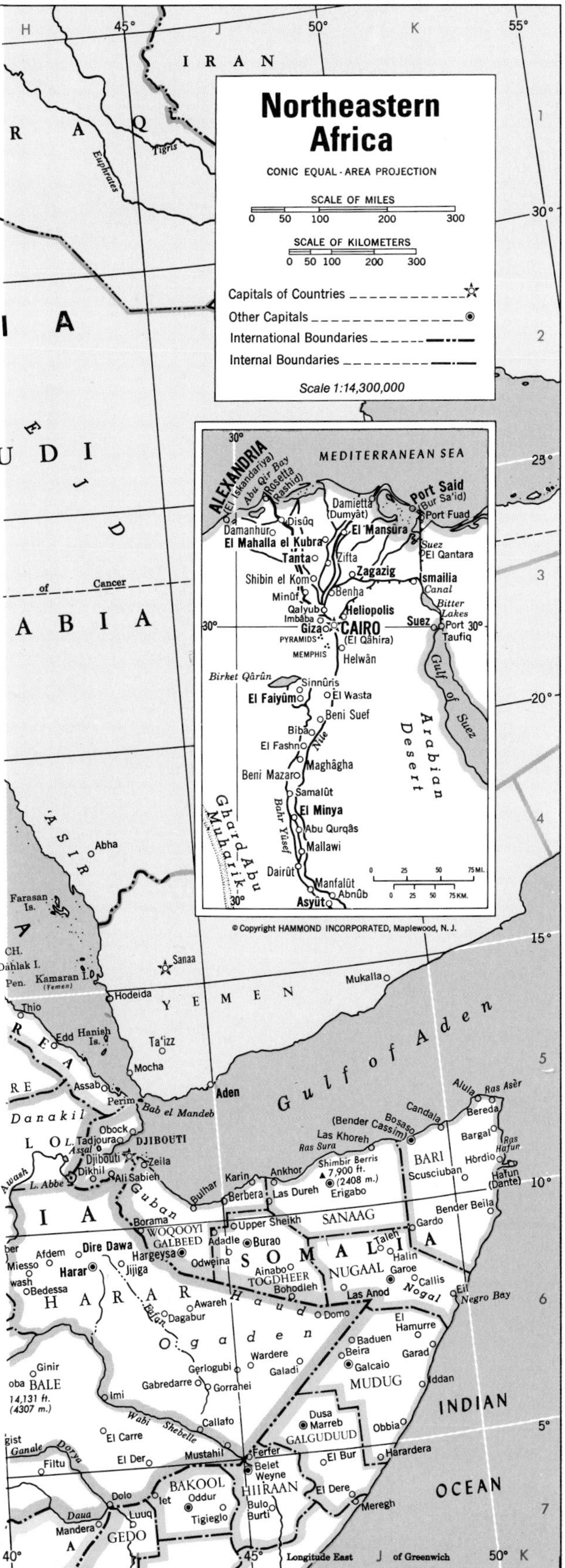
Northeastern Africa
CONIC EQUAL-AREA PROJECTION
SCALE OF MILES
0 50 100 200 300
SCALE OF KILOMETERS
0 50 100 200 300
Capitals of Countries
Other Capitals
International Boundaries
Internal Boundaries
Scale 1:14,300,000
MEDITERRANEAN SEA
ALEXANDRIA
Port Said
CAIRO
Gulf of Aden
INDIAN OCEAN
Longitude East of Greenwich
© Copyright HAMMOND INCORPORATED, Maplewood, N. J.

CHAD

CITIES and TOWNS

Abéché 28,100	D5
Abou Deïa	C5
Adré	D5
Am-Timan 4,200	D5
Arada	D4
Ati 7,500	C5
Baibokoum 5,500	C6
Biltine 3,900	D5
Bitkine 5,000	C5
Bokoro 6,500	C5
Bol 2,500	B5
Bongor 14,300	C5
Bousso 4,500	C5
Doba 13,300	C6
Fada	D4
Faya-Largeau 6,800	C4
Fianga 10,000	C6
Goré	C6
Goz Beïda	D5
Guéréda	D5
Iriba	D4
Kélo 16,800	C6
Koumra 17,000	C6
Kouno	C6
Kyabé 5,000	C6
Laï 10,400	C6
Léré	B6
Mangueigne	D5
Mao 4,900	C5
Massakory	C5
Massénya	C5
Melfi	C5
Mogororo	D5
Moïssala 5,100	C6
Mongo 8,300	C5
Moundou 39,600	C6
Moussoro 7,700	C5
N'Djamena (cap.) 179,000	C5
Oum Hadjer 5,600	C5
Ounianga-Kébir	D4
Pala 13,200	B6
Sarh 43,700	C6
Wour	C3
Zouar	C3

OTHER FEATURES

Aouk, Bahr (riv.)	D5
Azoum, Bahr (riv.)	D5
Baguirmi (reg.)	C5
Bahr el Ghazal (dry riv.)	C4
Batha (riv.)	C5
Bodélé (depr.)	C4
Borku (reg.)	C4
Chad (lake)	C5
Emi Koussi (mt.)	C4
Ennedi (plat.)	D4
Fittri (lake)	C5
Kanem (reg.)	C5
Logone (reg.)	C5
Maro (riv.)	C4
Mbéré (dry riv.)	C6
Mourdi (riv.)	D4
Ouham (depr.)	C6
Pendé (riv.)	C6
Sahara (riv.)	C3
Salamat, Bahr (des.)	C6
Shari (riv.)	C5
Sudan (riv.)	C5
Tibesti (mts.)	C3
Wadai (reg.)	D5

DJIBOUTI

CITIES and TOWNS

Ali Sabieh	H5
Dikhil	H5
Djibouti (cap.) 96,000	H5
Obock	H5
Tadjoura	H5

OTHER FEATURES

Abbe (lake)	H5
Aden (gulf)	J5
Bab el Mandeb (strait)	H5

EGYPT

CITIES and TOWNS

Abnûb 39,343	J4
Akhmim 53,234	F2
Alexandria 2,318,655	J2
Aswân 144,377	F3
Asyût 213,983	J4
Benha 88,992	J3
Beni Mazar 39,373	J4
Beni Suef 118,148	J3
Biba 33,074	J4
Bur Sa'id (Port Said) 262,620	K2
Cairo (cap.) 5,084,463	J3
Dairût 31,624	J4
Damanhur 188,927	J3
Damietta 93,546	J3
Disûq 58,650	J3

(continued on following page)

Topography

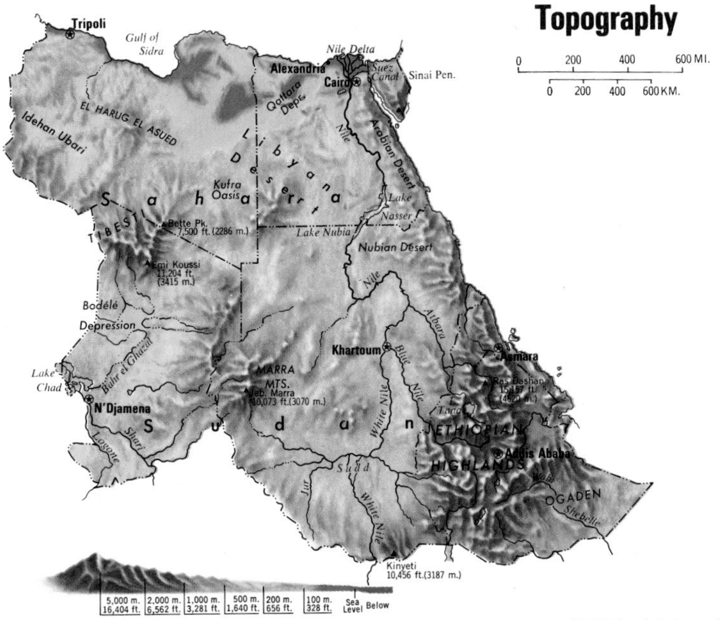
0 200 400 600 MI.
0 200 400 600 KM.
Tripoli
Gulf of Sidra
Nile Delta
Alexandria
Cairo
Suez Canal
Sinai Pen.
Libyan Desert
Sahara
Bette Pk. 7,500 ft. (2286 m.)
Emi Koussi 11,204 ft. (3415 m.)
Lake Nasser
Lake Nubia
Nubian Desert
Bodélé Depression
Lake Chad
N'Djamena
Khartoum
Marra Mts.
Sudan
Ethiopian Highlands
Addis Ababa
Ogaden
Kinyeti 10,456 ft. (3187 m.)
5,000 m. 16,404 ft.
2,000 m. 6,562 ft.
1,000 m. 3,281 ft.
500 m. 1,640 ft.
200 m. 656 ft.
100 m. 328 ft.
Sea Level
Below

(continued on following page)

(continued)

Dumyât (Damietta) 93,546 J3
El 'Alamein E1
El 'Arish F1
El Faiyûm 167,081 J3
El Fashn 33,506 J4
El Iskendariya (Alexandria) 2,318,655 J2
El Karnak F2
El Khârga 26,375 F2
El Mahalla el Kubra 292,853 J3
El Mansûra 257,866 K3
El Minya 146,423 J4
El Qahira (Cairo) (cap.) 5,084,463 J3
El Qantara 919 K3
El Quseir 12,297 F2
El Wasta 17,659 J3
Girga 51,110 F2
Giza 1,246,713 J3
Heliopolis J3
Helwân J3
Idfu 34,858 F3
Ismailia 145,978 K3
Isna 34,186 F2
Karnak (El Karnak) F2
Kôm Ombo 44,531 F3
Luxor 92,748 F2
Maghâgha 40,802 J4
Mallawi 74,256 J4
Manfalût 41,126 J4
Mersâ Matrûh 27,857 E1
Minûf 55,131 J3
Mût 8,032 E2
Port Fuad K3
Port Safâga F2
Port Said 262,620 K2
Port Taufiq K3
Qalyub 62,739 J3
Qena 94,013 F2
Rashid (Rosetta) 42,962 J2
Rudeis F2
Salûm 4,161 E1
Samalût 48,146 J4
Shibin el Kom 102,844 J3
Sidi Barrani 1,574 E1
Sinnûris 42,022 J3
Sohâg 101,758 F2
Suez 194,001 K3
Tahta 45,242 F2
Tanta 284,636 J3
Zagazig 202,637 J3
Zifta 50,410 J3

OTHER FEATURES

Abu Qir (bay) J2
Abydos (ruins) F2
Aqaba (gulf) G2
Arabian (des.) F2
Aswân (dam) F3
Aswân High (dam) F3
Bahariya (oasis) E2
Bânâs, Ras (cape) G3
Berenice (ruins) F3
Birket Qârûn (lake) J3
Bitter (lakes) K3
Dakhla (oasis) E2
Eastern (Arabian) (des.) F2
Farâfra (oasis) E2
Foul (bay) G3
Gilf Kebir (plat.) E3
Great Sand Sea (des.) D2
Katherina, Jebel (mt.) F2
Khârga (oasis) F2
Libyan (des.) E2
Libyan (plat.) E1
Mediterranean (sea) E1
Memphis (ruins) J3
Muhammad, Ras (cape) F2
Nasser (lake) F3
Nile (riv.) F2
Pyramids (ruins) J3
Qattara (depr.) E2
Sahara (des.) E3
Sinai (mt.) F2
Sinai (pen.) F2
Siwa (oasis) E2
Suez (canal) K3
Suez (gulf) F2
Tiran (strait) F2
'Uweinat, Jebel (mt.) E3

ERITREA

CITIES and TOWNS

Adi Ugri 12,800 G5
Asmara (cap.) 393,800 G4
Assab 16,000 H5
Karkabat G4
Keren G4
Massawa 19,800 G4
Mersa Fatma H5
Nakfa G4
Tessenei G4
Thio H5
Umm Hajar G5
Zula G4

OTHER FEATURES

Baraka (riv.) G4
Buri (pen.) H4
Dahlak (arch.) H4
Dahlak (isl.) H4
Kasar, Ras (cape) G4
Takkaze (riv.) G5

ETHIOPIA

PROVINCES

Arusi 852,900 G6
Bale 707,800 H6
Gamu-Gofa 698,800 G6
Gojjam 1,750,100 G5
Gondar 1,355,800 G5
Harar 3,359,200 H6
Ilubabor 688,800 F6
Kaffa 1,693,000 G6
Shoa 5,369,500 G6
Sidamo 2,479,800 G7
Tigre 1,828,900 H5
Wallaga 1,269,100 G6
Wallo 2,459,900 H5

CITIES and TOWNS

Addis Ababa (cap.) 1,196,300 G6
Addis Alam 5,500 G6
Adigrat 9,400 G5
Adwa 16,400 G5
Aksum 12,800 G5
Ankober H6
Arba Mench 7,660 G6
Asselle 19,390 G6
Awareh H6
Axum (Aksum) 12,800 G5
Bahir Dar 25,100 G5
Dagabur H6
Dangila G5
Debra Birhan 16,700 G6
Debra Markos 30,260 G5
Debra Tabor 8,700 G5
Dembidollo 7,600 F6
Dessye 49,750 G5
Dilla 13,800 G6
Dire Dawa 63,700 H6
El Carre H6
Gabredarre H6
Galadi J6
Gambela F6
Gardula 5,800 G6
Gerlogubi H6
Ghimbi 8,300 G6
Ginir H6
Goba 13,500 H6
Gondar 38,600 G5
Gore 8,500 G6
Gorrahei H6
Harar 48,440 H6
Hosseina 8,500 G6
Jijiga 8,000 H6
Jimma 47,360 G6
Jiran G6
Kibre Mengist 8,300 G6
Lalibela G5
Magdala G5
Maji G6
Makale 30,780 G5
Metamma G5
Metu 6,860 G6
Miesso H6
Mizan Teferi G6
Moyale G7
Murle G6
Mustahil H6
Nakamti 18,310 G6
Nazret 42,900 G6
Negelli 8,800 G6
Nejo G6
Saio (Dembidollo) 7,600 F6
Soddu 11,900 G6
Sokota G5
Tori F6
Waka G6
Waldia 9,600 G5
Wardere J6
Wolta G6
Yaballo G7

OTHER FEATURES

Abay (riv.) G5
Abaya (lake) G6
Abbe (lake) H5
Akobo (riv.) F6
Assal (lake) H5
Assale (lake) H5
Atbara (riv.) G4
Awash (riv.) H5
Bale (mt.) G6
Blue Nile (Abay) (riv.) G5
Chamo (lake) G6
Danakil (reg.) H5
Dawa (riv.) G7
Dinder (riv.) F5
Fafan (riv.) H6
Ganale Dorya (riv.) H6
Gughe (mt.) G6
Haud (reg.) J6
Ogaden (reg.) H6
Omo (riv.) G6
Ras Dashan (mt.) G5
Red (sea) H4
Rudolf (Turkana) (lake) G7
Simen (mts.) G5
Takkaze (riv.) G5
Tana (lake) G5
Tisisat (fall) G5
Turkana (lake) G7
Zwai (lake) G6

LIBYA

CITIES and TOWNS

Ajedabia° 53,170 D1
Aujila° 6,695 D2
Baida° 59,765 D1
Barce (El Marj)° 55,444 D1
Benghazi 286,943 C1
Beni Ulid° 19,113 B1
Brak° 16,307 B2
Cyrene (Shahat)° 17,157 D1
Derj° 2,152 B1
Derna° 44,145 D1
El Abiar° 17,685 D1
El Agheila 3 C1
El Azizia° 34,077 B1
El Bardi° 4,330 D1
El Barkat° 2,139 B3
El Gatrun B3
El Jauf° 6,481 D3
El Marj° 55,444 D1
Es Sidr° 706 C1
Ez Zuetina° 7,256 D1
Ghadames° 6,172 A2
Gharian° 65,224 B1
Ghat° 6,924 B3
Ghemines° 4,313 C1
Homs° 66,890 B1
Hon° 2,766 C2
Jaghbub (Jarabub)° 1,436 D2
Jarabub° 1,436 D2
Marada° 3,201 C2
Marsa el Brega° 2,618 D1
Marsa el Hariga° 5,043 D1
Misurata° 102,439 C1
Mizda° 11,472 B1
Murzuk° 22,185 B2
Nalut° 23,535 B1
Ras Lanuf° 1,990 C1
Sabrathaa° 30,836 B1
Sebha° 35,879 B2
Shahat° 17,157 D1
Sinawen° 1,549 B1
Sokna° 3,757 C2
Soluk° 6,501 D1
Syrte° 22,797 C1
Tarhuna° 52,657 B1
Tobruk° 58,384 D1
Tokra° 10,714 D1
Tripoli (cap.)° 550,438 B1
Ubari° 19,132 B2
Waddan° 5,347 C2
Wau el Kebir C2
Zawia° 72,092 B1
Zella° 72,092 C2
Zliten° 58,981 B1
Zwara° 15,078 B1

OTHER FEATURES

Akhdar, Jebel (mts.) D1
Barqa (Cyrenaica) (reg.) D1
Ben Ghnema, Jebel (mts.) C2
Bette (peak) C3
Bey el Kebir, Wadi (dry riv.) B1
Bir Hakeim (ruins) D1
Bomba (gulf) D1
Buzeima (well) D3
Calansho Sand Sea (des.) D2
Calansho, Serir (des.) D2
Cyrenaica (reg.) D1
Fezzan (reg.) B2
Great Sand Sea (des.) D2
Harug el Asued, El (mts.) C2
Homra, Hamada el (des.) B2
Idehan Murzuk (des.) B2
Idehan Ubari (des.) B2
Jalo (oasis) D2
Jefara (reg.) B1
Jef Jef es Seghin (plat.) D3
Jofra (oasis) C2
Kufra (oasis) D3
Leptis Magna (ruins) B1
Libyan (des.) D2
Libyan (plat.) D1
Mediterranean (sea) C1
Nefusa, Jebel (mts.) B1
Rebiana (oasis) D3
Rebiana Sand Sea (des.) D3
Sahara (des.) C3
Shati, Wadi esh (dry riv.) B2
Sidra (gulf) C1
Soda, Jebel es (mts.) C2
Tazerbo (oasis) D2
Tibesti, Serir (des.) C3
Tinghert Hamada (Tinrhert) (des.) B2
Tripolitania (reg.) B1
'Uweinat, Jebel (mt.) E3
Zelten, Jebel (mts.) D2

SUDAN

PROVINCES

Central F5
Darfur D5
Eastern G4
Khartoum F4
Kordofan E5
Northern E3
Southern E6

CITIES and TOWNS

'Abri F3
Abu Hamed F4
Adok F6
Akobo F6
Amadi F6
Argo F4
Aroma G4
Atbara 66,000 F4
Babanusa E5
Bara F5
Bentiu E6
Berber F4
Bor F6
Buram E5
Damazin (Ed Damazin) 12,000 F5
Deim Zubeir E6
Dongola 6,000 F4
Dungunab G3
Ed Damazin 12,000 F5
Ed Damer 17,000 F4
Ed Dueim 27,000 F5
El Fasher 52,000 E5
El Geneina 33,000 D5
El Obeid 90,000 E5
El Odaiya E5
En Nahud 23,000 E5
Er Roseires F5
Fashoda (Kodok) F6
Gedaref 92,000 G5
Gogrial E6
Goz Regeb G4
Haiya Junction G4
Halaib G3
Jonglei F6
Juba 57,000 F7
Kadugli 18,000 E5
Kaka F5
Karima F4
Kassala 99,000 G4
Kerma F4
Khartoum (cap.) 334,000 F4
Khartoum North 151,000 F4
Khashm el Girba G5
Kodok F6
Kosti 57,000 F5
Kurmuk F5
Kutum D5
Malakal 35,000 F6
Maridi E7
Melut F5
Merowe F4
Meshra er Req E6
Mongalla F6
Muglad E5
Muhammad Qol G3
Nagishot F7
Nasir F6
Nyala 60,000 D5
Nyamlell E6
Nyerol F6
Omdurman 299,000 F4
Opari F7
Pibor Post F6
Port Sudan 133,000 G4
Qala'en Nahl F5
Raga E6
Rashad F5
Rejaf F7
Renk F5
Rufa'a F5
Rumbek 17,000 E6
Sennar F5
Shambe F6
Shendi F4
Shereik F4
Showak G5
Singa F5
Sinkat G4
Sodiri E5
Suakin G4
Suki F5
Tali Post F6
Talodi F5
Tambura E6
Tendelti F5
Tokar G4
Tombe F6
Tonga F6
Tonj E6
Torit F7
Trinkitat G4
Umm Keddada E5
Umm Ruwaba F5
Wadi Halfa F3
Wad Medani 107,000 F5
Wankai E6
Wau 53,000 E6
Yambio 7,000 E7
Yei F7
Yirol F6
Zalingei D5

OTHER FEATURES

Abu Habl, Wadi (dry riv.) F5
Abu Shagara, Ras (cape) G3
Adda (riv.) D6
Atbara (riv.) G4
Bahr Azoum (riv.) D5
Bahr el 'Arab (riv.) E6
Bahr ez Zeraf (riv.) F6
Blue Nile (riv.) F5
Dar Hamid (reg.) F5
Dar Masalit (reg.) D5
Dinder (riv.) F5
El 'Atrun (oasis) E4
Fifth Cataract (falls) F4
Fourth Cataract (falls) F4
Gabgaba, Wadi (dry riv.) F3
Ghalla, Wadi el (dry riv.) E5
Hadarba, Ras (cape) G3
Howar, Wadi (dry riv.) E4
Ibra, Wadi (dry riv.) D5
Jebel Aulia (dam) F4
Jonglei (canal) F6
Jur (riv.) E6
Kinyeti (mt.) F7
Libyan (des.) E3
Lol (dry riv.) E6
Lotagipi Swamp (plain) F6
Marra, Jebel (mt.) D5
Meroe (ruins) F4
Milk, Wadi el (dry riv.) E4
Muqaddam, Wadi (dry riv.) F4
Napata (ruins) F4
Naqa (ruins) F4
Nile (riv.) F4
Nuba (mts.) E5
Nubia (lake) F3
Nubian (des.) F3
Nukheila (oasis) E4
Nuri (ruins) F4
Oda, Jebel (mt.) G3
Pibor (riv.) F6
Red (sea) G3
Red Sea (hills) G3
Sahara (des.) E3
Selima (oasis) E3
Sennar (dam) F5
Setit (riv.) G5
Sixth Cataract F4
Sobat (riv.) F6
Suakin (arch.) G4
Sudan (reg.) E5
Sudd (swamp) F6
Sue (riv.) E6
Third Cataract (falls) E4
'Uweinat, Jebel (mt.) E3
White Nile (riv.) F5

° Population of sub-district or division

Agriculture, Industry and Resources

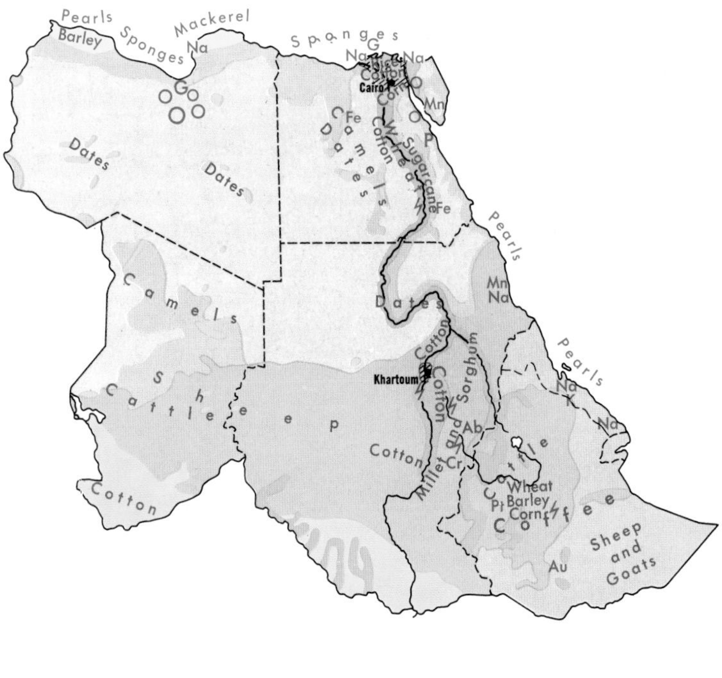

Pearls
Barley
Sponges
Mackerel
Na
Sponges
Cairo
Dates
Camels
Cotton
Sugarcane
Fe
Mn
Na
Khartoum
Sheep
Cattle
Sorghum
Millet
Wheat
Barley
Corn
Coffee
Ab
Cr
Pt
Au
Sheep and Goats

DOMINANT LAND USE

- Cereals, Horticulture, Livestock
- Cash Crops, Mixed Cereals
- Cotton, Cereals
- Market Gardening, Diversified Tropical Crops
- Plantation Agriculture
- Oases
- Pasture Livestock
- Nomadic Livestock Herding
- Forests
- Nonagricultural Land

MAJOR MINERAL OCCURRENCES

Ab	Asbestos	Mn	Manganese
Au	Gold	Na	Salt
Cr	Chromium	O	Petroleum
Fe	Iron Ore	P	Phosphates
G	Natural Gas	Pt	Platinum
K	Potash		

Water Power

Major Industrial Areas

ANGOLA

AREA 481,351 sq. mi. (1,246,700 sq. km.)
POPULATION 9,747,000
CAPITAL Luanda
LARGEST CITY Luanda
HIGHEST POINT Mt. Moco 8,593 ft. (2,620 m.)
MONETARY UNIT kwanza
MAJOR LANGUAGES Mbundu, Kongo, Lunda, Portuguese
MAJOR RELIGIONS Tribal religions, Roman Catholicism

BURUNDI

AREA 10,747 sq. mi. (27,835 sq. km.)
POPULATION 5,302,000
CAPITAL Bujumbura
LARGEST CITY Bujumbura
HIGHEST POINT 8,858 ft. (2,700 m.)
MONETARY UNIT Burundi franc
MAJOR LANGUAGES Kirundi, French, Swahili
MAJOR RELIGIONS Tribal religions, Roman Catholicism, Islam

CAMEROON

AREA 183,568 sq. mi. (475,441 sq. km.)
POPULATION 11,540,000
CAPITAL Yaoundé
LARGEST CITY Douala
HIGHEST POINT Cameroon 13,350 ft. (4,069 m.)
MONETARY UNIT CFA franc
MAJOR LANGUAGFS Fang, Bamileke, Fulani, Duala, French, English
MAJOR RELIGIONS Tribal religions, Christianity, Islam

CENTRAL AFRICAN REP.

AREA 242,000 sq. mi. (626,780 sq. km.)
POPULATION 2,740,000
CAPITAL Bangui
LARGEST CITY Bangui
HIGHEST POINT Gao 4,659 ft. (1,420 m.)
MONETARY UNIT CFA franc
MAJOR LANGUAGES Banda, Gbaya, Sangho, French
MAJOR RELIGIONS Tribal religions, Christianity, Islam

CONGO, REP. OF THE

AREA 132,046 sq. mi. (342,000 sq. km.)
PQPULATION 1,843,000
CAPITAL Brazzaville
LARGEST CITY Brazzaville
HIGHEST POINT Leketi Mts. 3,412 ft. (1,040 m.)
MONETARY UNIT CFA franc
MAJOR LANGUAGES Kikongo, Bateke, Lingala, French
MAJOR RELIGIONS Christianity, tribal religions, Islam

EQUATORIAL GUINEA

AREA 10,831 sq. mi. (28,052 sq. km.)
POPULATION 341,000
CAPITAL Malabo
LARGEST CITY Malabo
HIGHEST POINT 9,868 ft. (3,008 m.)
MONETARY UNIT CFA franc
MAJOR LANGUAGES Fang, Bubi, Spanish
MAJOR RELIGIONS Tribal religions, Christianity

GABON

AREA 103,346 sq. mi. (267,666 sq. km.)
POPULATION 1,206,000
CAPITAL Libreville
LARGEST CITY Libreville
HIGHEST POINT Ibounzi 5,165 ft. (1,574 m.)
MONETARY UNIT CFA franc
MAJOR LANGUAGES Fang and other Bantu languages, French
MAJOR RELIGIONS Tribal religions, Christianity, Islam

KENYA

AREA 224,960 sq. mi. (582,646 sq. km.)
POPULATION 24,872,000
CAPITAL Nairobi
LARGEST CITY Nairobi
HIGHEST POINT Kenya 17,058 ft. (5,199 m.)
MONETARY UNIT Kenya shilling
MAJOR LANGUAGES Kikuyu, Luo, Kavirondo, Kamba, Swahili, English
MAJOR RELIGIONS Tribal religions, Christianity, Hinduism, Islam

MALAWI

AREA 45,747 sq. mi. (118,485 sq. km.)
POPULATION 8,022,000
CAPITAL Lilongwe
LARGEST CITY Blantyre
HIGHEST POINT Mulanje 9,843 ft. (3,000 m.)
MONETARY UNIT Malawi kwacha
MAJOR LANGUAGES Chichewa, Yao, English, Nyanja, Tumbuka, Tonga, Ngoni
MAJOR RELIGIONS Tribal religions, Islam, Christianity

RWANDA

AREA 10,169 sq. mi. (26,337 sq. km.)
POPULATION 6,274,000
CAPITAL Kigali
LARGEST CITY Kigali
HIGHEST POINT Karisimbi 14,780 ft. (4,505 m.)
MONETARY UNIT Rwanda franc
MAJOR LANGUAGES Kinyarwanda, French, Swahili
MAJOR RELIGIONS Tribal religions, Roman Catholicism, Islam

SOMALIA

AREA 246,200 sq. mi. (637,658 sq. km.)
POPULATION 7,339,000
CAPITAL Mogadishu
LARGEST CITY Mogadishu
HIGHEST POINT Surud Ad 7,900 ft. (2,408 m.)
MONETARY UNIT Somali shilling
MAJOR LANGUAGES Somali, Arabic, Italian, English
MAJOR RELIGION Islam

TANZANIA

AREA 363,708 sq. mi. (942,003 sq. km.)
POPULATION 24,802,000
CAPITAL Dar es Salaam
LARGEST CITY Dar es Salaam
HIGHEST POINT Kilimanjaro 19,340 ft. (5,895 m.)
MONETARY UNIT Tanzanian shilling
MAJOR LANGUAGES Nyamwezi-Sukuma, Swahili, English
MAJOR RELIGIONS Tribal religions, Christianity, Islam

UGANDA

AREA 91,076 sq. mi. (235,887 sq. km.)
POPULATION 17,804,000
CAPITAL Kampala
LARGEST CITY Kampala
HIGHEST POINT Margherita 16,795 ft. (5,119 m.)
MONETARY UNIT Ugandan shilling
MAJOR LANGUAGES Luganda, Acholi, Teso, Nyoro, Soga, Nkole, English, Swahili
MAJOR RELIGIONS Tribal religions, Christianity, Islam

CONGO, DEM. REP. OF THE

AREA 905,063 sq. mi. (2,344,113 sq. km.)
POPULATION 34,491,000
CAPITAL Kinshasa
LARGEST CITY Kinshasa
HIGHEST POINT Margherita 16,795 ft. (5,119 m.)
MONETARY UNIT zaire
MAJOR LANGUAGES Tshiluba, Mongo, Kikongo, Kingwana, Zande, Lingala, Swahili, French
MAJOR RELIGIONS Tribal religions, Christianity

ZAMBIA

AREA 290,586 sq. mi. (752,618 sq. km.)
POPULATION 8,073,000
CAPITAL Lusaka
LARGEST CITY Lusaka
HIGHEST POINT Sunzu 6,782 ft. (2,067 m.)
MONETARY UNIT Zambian kwacha
MAJOR LANGUAGES Bemba, Tonga, Lozi, Luvale, Nyanja, English
MAJOR RELIGIONS Tribal religions

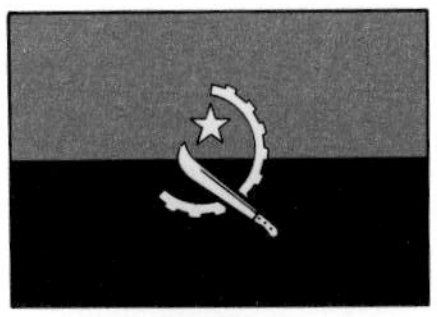
ANGOLA

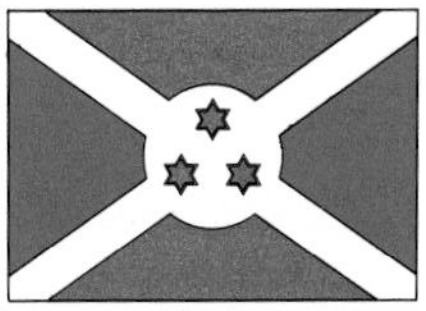
BURUNDI

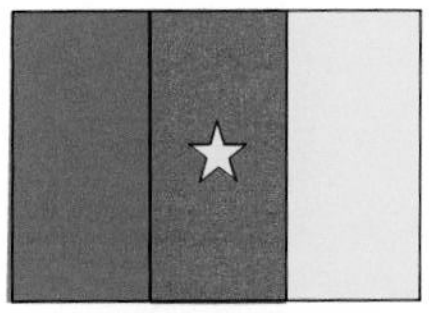
CAMEROON

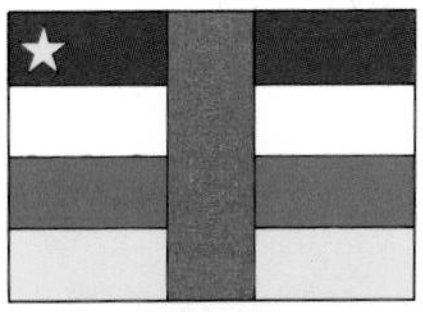
CENTRAL AFRICAN REP.

CONGO, REP. OF THE

EQUATORIAL GUINEA

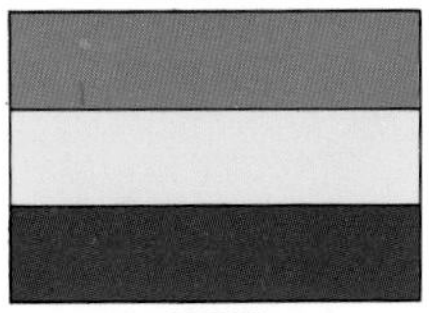
GABON

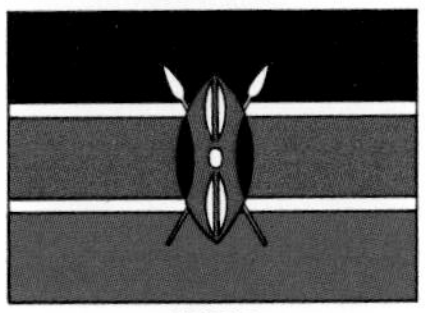
KENYA

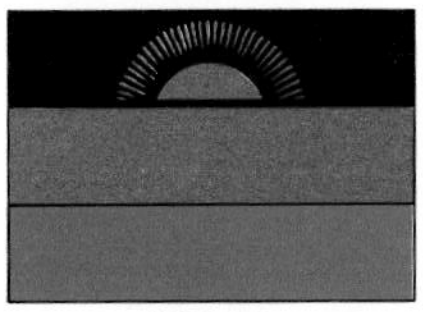
MALAWI

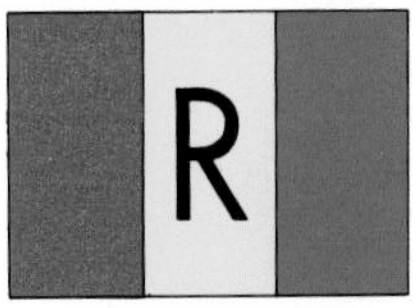
R
RWANDA

SOMALIA

TANZANIA

UGANDA

CONGO, DEM. REP. OF THE

ZAMBIA

ANGOLA

PROVINCES

Bengo 68,885 ..... B5
Benguela 474,897 ..... B6
Bié 650,337 ..... C6
Cabinda 80,857 ..... B5
Cuando Cubango 112,073 ..... C7
Cuanza-Norte 298,062 ..... B5
Cuanza-Sul 458,592 ..... C6
Cunene 147,394 ..... C7
Huambo 837,627 ..... C6
Huíla 497,470 ..... B7
Luanda 491,704 ..... B5
Lunda Norte 210,000 ..... C5
Lunda Sul 98,000 ..... D5
Malanje 558,630 ..... C6
Moxico 213,119 ..... D6
Namibe 53,058 ..... B7
Uíge 386,037 ..... B5
Zaire 41,766 ..... B5

CITIES and TOWNS

Ambriz B5
Baía dos Tigres B7
Baia Farta B6
Bembe B5
Benguela 40,996 ..... B6
Caála 8,894 ..... C6
Cabinda 21,124 ..... B5
Caconda B6
Caiundo C7
Camacupa 5,740 ..... C6
Camanongue D6
Cambundi-Catembo C5
Capelongo C6
Cassinga C7
Catumbela B6
Caxito B5
Chinguar C6
Chitato D5
Cuango C5
Cuito-Cuanavale C7
Dondo B5
Forte República C5
Foz do Cunene B7
Gabela 6,930 ..... B6
Ganda 2,538 ..... B6
Golungo Alto B5
Huambo 61,885 ..... C6
Katchiungo C6
Kuito 18,941 ..... C6
Kuvango C6
Lobito 59,528 ..... B6
Longa C6
Lóvua D5
Luacano D6
Luanda (cap.) 475,328 ..... B5
Luau D6
Lubango 31,674 ..... B6
Lucapa D5
Luena 2,539 ..... C6
Luiana D7
Malanje 31,599 ..... C5
Maquela do Zombo C5
Massango (Forte República) C5
Mbanza Congo 4,002 ..... B5
Menongue 3,023 ..... C6
Moçâmedes (Namibe) 12,076 ..... B7
Namibe 12,076 ..... B7
N'dalatando 7,342 ..... B5
N'gage 2,548 ..... C5
Ngunza (Sumbe) 7,911 ..... B6
N'zeto B5
Ondjiva C7
Porto Amboim B6
Saurimo 12,901 ..... D5
Soyo B5
Sumbe 7,911 ..... B6
Tombua 8,235 ..... B7
Uíge 11,972 ..... C5
Waku Kungo 2,784 ..... C6

OTHER FEATURES

Bero (riv.) B7
Chicapa (riv.) D5
Chiumbe (riv.) D5
Congo (riv.) C4
Coporolo (riv.) B6
Cuando (riv.) C7
Cuango (riv.) C5
Cuanza (riv.) C5
Cubango (riv.) C7
Cuito (riv.) C7
Cunene (dam) B7
Cunene (riv.) B7
Cuvo (riv.) B6
Kasai (riv.) D5
Kwilu (riv.) C5
Loange (riv.) C5
Loge (riv.) B5
Lungwebungu (riv.) D6
Matala (dam) B6
M'Bridge (riv.) B5
Moco (mt.) C6
Negro (cape) B7
Palmeirinhas (pt.) B5
Ruacana Falls (dam) B7
Santa Maria (cape) B6
Zambezi (riv.) D6

BURUNDI

CITIES and TOWNS

Bujumbura (cap.) 141,040 ..... E4
Bururi 7,800 ..... E4
Gitega 19,500 ..... F4

OTHER FEATURES

Ruzizi (riv.) E4
Tanganyika (lake) E5

CAMEROON

CITIES and TOWNS

Bafia 17,855 ..... B3
Bafoussam 62,239 ..... B2
Bamenda 48,111 ..... B2
Banyo 10,293 ..... B2
Bertoua 13,985 ..... B3
Bétaré-Oya B2
Bonabéri A3
Buea 24,584 ..... A3
Djoum B3
Douala 458,426 ..... A3
Dschang 16,629 ..... A2

(continued on following page)

Central Africa

(continued)

Ebolowa 24,000 .... B3
Fort Foureau (Kousseri) 11,627 .... B1
Foumban 33,944 .... B2
Garoua 63,900 .... B2
Guidder 16,053 .... B2
Kousseri 11,627 .... B1
Kumba 44,175 .... A3
Kumbo 11,699 .... B2
Limbe 27,016 .... A3
Lomié B3
Makari B1
Maroua 67,187 .... B1
Mbalmayo 22,106 .... B3
Meiganga 15,906 .... B2
Moloundou C3
Monatélé B3
Nanga-Eboko B3
Ngaoundéré 38,992 .... B2
Nkongsamba 71,298 .... B3
Poli B2
Sangmélima 13,776 .... B3
Tchollíré B2
Tibati B2
Tignére B2
Tiko 13,824 .... A3
Wum 15,149 .... A2
Yagoua 13,541 .... B1
Yaoundé (cap.) 313,706 .... B3
Yoko B2

OTHER FEATURES

Adamawa (reg.) B2
Benué (riv.) A2
Biafra (bight) A3
Cameroon (mt.) A3
Cross (riv.) A2
Dja (riv.) B3
Donga (riv.) B2
Ivindo (riv.) B3
Kadei (riv.) C3
Logone (riv.) C2
Lom (riv.) B2
Mbakou (res.) B2
Mbéré (riv.) B2
Sanaga (riv.) B3
Sanga (riv.) C3

CENTRAL AFRICAN REPUBLIC

CITIES and TOWNS

Alindao 12,295 .... D2
Baboua 3,999 .... C2
Bambari 31,285 .... D2
Bangassou 21,773 .... D3
Bangui (cap.) 279,792 .... C3
Bania C3
Batangáfo 12,543 .... C2
Berberati 27,285 .... C3
Birao 3,317 .... D1
Bocaranga 6,202 .... C2
Boda 8,771 .... C3
Bossangoa 25,150 .... C2
Bossembele 5,091 .... C2
Bouar 29,528 .... C2
Bouca 8,874 .... C2
Bozoum 13,573 .... C2
Bria 14,786 .... D2
Carnot 17,863 .... C3
Dekoa 7,663 .... C2
Grimari 7,308 .... C2
Ippy 10,816 .... D2
Kaga Bandoro 11,876 .... C2
Kembe 5,051 .... D3
Mbaîki 12,346 .... C3
Mobaye 4,220 .... D3
Ndele 5,858 .... D2
Nola 6,703 .... C3
Obo 3,978 .... E2
Ouadda 3,009 .... D2
Paoua 7,052 .... C2
Zemio 3,259 .... D2

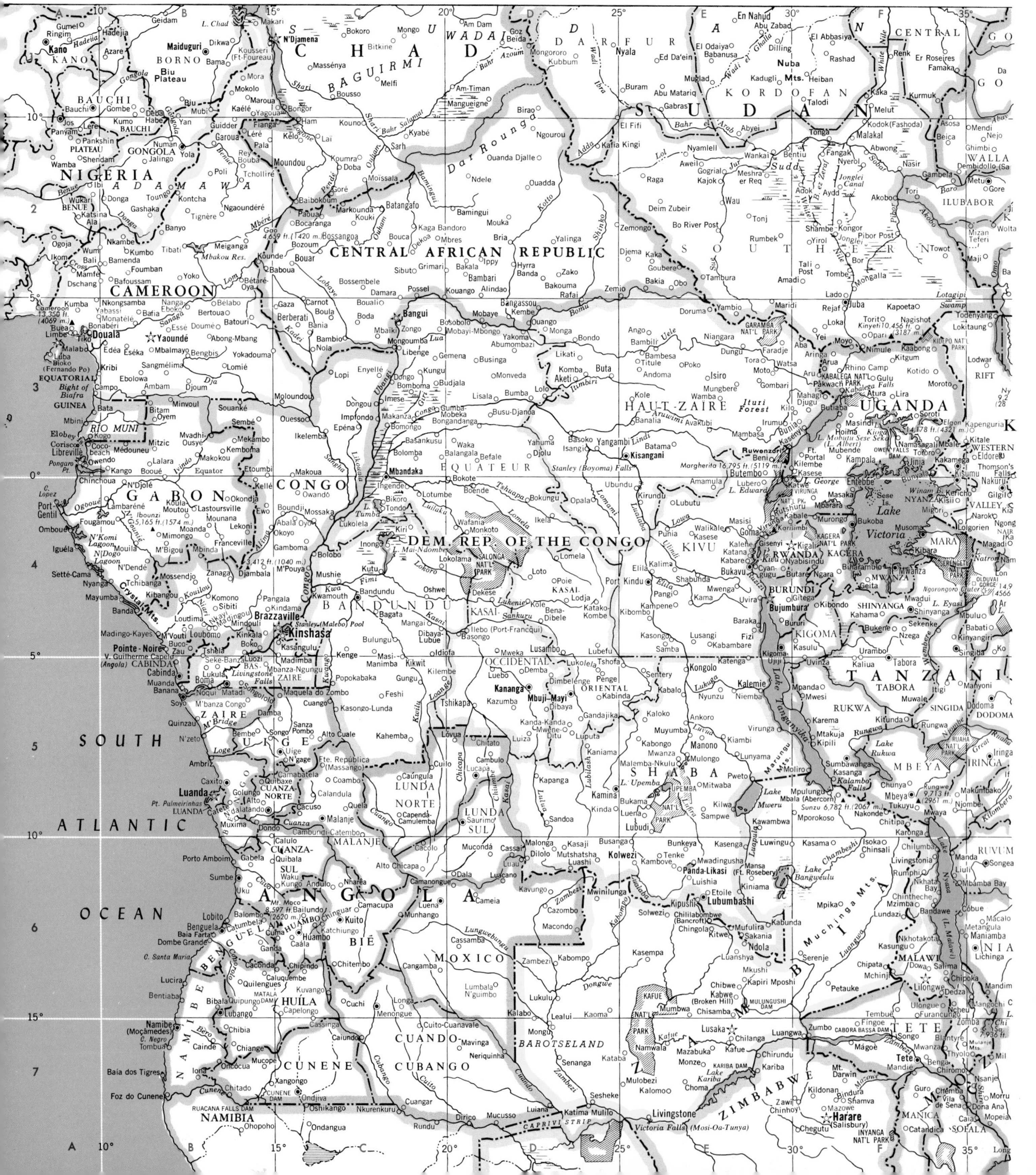

NIGERIA
CAMEROON
CHAD
SUDAN
CENTRAL AFRICAN REPUBLIC
GABON
CONGO
DEM. REP. OF THE CONGO
EQUATORIAL GUINEA
RIO MUNI
UGANDA
RWANDA
BURUNDI
TANZANIA
ANGOLA
ZAMBIA
ZIMBABWE
NAMIBIA
MALAWI
SOUTH ATLANTIC OCEAN
Bight of Biafra
L. Chad
Lake Victoria
Lake Tanganyika
N'Djamena
Bangui
Yaoundé
Douala
Libreville
Brazzaville
Kinshasa
Luanda
Kisangani
Mbandaka
Kananga
Lubumbashi
Kampala
Kigali
Bujumbura
Lusaka
Harare
Lilongwe
Kano
Maiduguri
Juba
Huambo
Malabo

OTHER FEATURES

Bamingui (riv.) C2
Bomu (riv.) D3
Dar Rounga (reg.) D2
Gao (mt.) C2
Kadei (riv.) C3
Kotto (riv.) D2
Lobaye (riv.) C2
Mbéré (riv.) B2
Ouham (riv.) C2
Pendé (riv.) C2
Sangha (riv.) C3
Shari (riv.) C2
Shinko (riv.) D2
Ubangi (riv.) C3

CONGO, REP. OF THE

CITIES and TOWNS

Abala C4
Boundji C4
Brazzaville (cap.) 298,967 C4
Djambala B4
Impfondo C3
Kinkala B4
Loubomo 29,600 B4
Makoua C3
Mbinda B4
Mossaka C4
Mossendjo B4
Nkayi 30,600 B4
Ouesso C3
Owando C4
Pointe-Noire 141,700 B4

OTHER FEATURES

Alima (riv.) B4
Congo (riv.) C4
Crystal (mts.) B4
Dja (riv.) B3
Ivindo (riv.) B3
Kadei (riv.) C3
Kouilou (riv.) B4
Likouala (riv.) C3
N'Gounié (riv.) B4
Niari (riv.) B4
Ogooué (riv.) A4
Sangha (riv.) C3
Ubangi (riv.) C3

EQUATORIAL GUINEA

TERRITORIES

Bioko 78,000 A3
Río Muni 203,000 B3

CITIES and TOWNS

Bata 270,241 A3
Luba 19,933 A3
Malabo (cap.) 37,237 A3
Mbini 14,503 A3

OTHER FEATURES

Biafra (bight) A3
Corisco (isl.) A3
Elobey (isls.) A3
Fernando Po (Bioko) (isl.) A3

GABON

CITIES and TOWNS

Bitam 5,936 B3
Cocobeach A3
Fougamou B4
Franceville 9,345 B4
Kango B3
Koula-Moutou 8,032 B4
Lambaréné 17,770 B4
Lastoursville B4
Libreville (cap.) 105,080 A3
Makokou 5,005 B3
Mayumba B4
M'Bigou B4
Médouneu B3
Mekambo B3
Mimongo B4
Minvoul B3
Moanda 10,709 B4
Mouila 15,016 B4
Mounana 4,000 B4
N'Dendé B4
N'Djolé B4
Okondja B4
Omboué A4
Owendo A3
Oyem 12,455 B3
Port-Gentil 48,190 A4
Tchibanga 14,001 B4

OTHER FEATURES

Crystal (mts.) B4
Ibounzi (mt.) B4
Ivindo (riv.) B3
Lopez (cape) A4
N'Dogo (lag.) B4
N'Gounié (riv.) B4
N'Komi (lag.) A4
Ogooué (riv.) A4
Pongara (pt.) A3

KENYA

PROVINCES

Central 1,675,647 G4
Coast 944,082 G4
Eastern 1,907,301 G4
Nairobi 509,286 G4
North-Eastern 245,757 G3
Nyanza 2,122,045 F4
Rift Valley 2,210,289 G3
Western 1,328,298 G3

CITIES and TOWNS

Baragoi 2,383 G3
Bunyala F3
Eldoret 18,196 G3
Embu 3,928 G4
Fort Hall 4,750 G4
Galole 3,609 G4
Garissa G4
Gilgil 4,178 G4
Isiolo 8,201 G3
Kajiado 1,755 G4
Kakamega 6,244 F3
Kaningo 2,450 G4
Kapenguria 1,790 G3
Kericho 10,144 F4
Kiambu 2,776 G4
Kilifi 2,662 G4
Kisii 6,080 F4
Kisumu 32,431 F3
Kitale 11,573 G3
Kitui 3,071 G4
Kwale 1,092 G4
Lamu 7,403 H4
Lokitaung 4,090 G3
Machakos 6,312 G4
Mado Gashi 1,003 G3
Malindi 10,757 H4
Maralal 3,878 G3
Marsabit 6,635 G3
Migori 2,066 F4
Mombasa 247,073 G4
Nairobi (cap.) 509,286 G4
Naivasha 6,920 G4
Nakuru 47,151 G4
Nanyuki 11,624 G3
Narok 2,608 G4
Ngong 1,583 G4
Nyeri 2,436 G4
Rumuruti 1,484 G3
Thika 18,387 G4
Thomson's Falls 7,602 G3
Vanga G4
Voi 5,313 G4
Wajir H3
Wamba 2,650 G3

OTHER FEATURES

Daua (riv.) H3
Elgon (mt.) F3
Formosa (bay) H4
Galana (riv.) G4
Gedi (ruins) G4
Kenya (mt.) G4
Lak Dera (dry riv.) H3
Lorian (swamp) G3
Natron (lake) G4
Nyiru (mt.) G3
Patta (isl.) H4
Rudolf (Turkana) (lake) G3
Tana (riv.) G4
Tsavo Nat'l Park G4
Turkana (lake) G3
Victoria (lake) F4
Winam (bay) F4

MALAWI

CITIES and TOWNS

Blantyre 222,153 F7
Chitipa 3,079 F5
Dedza 5,448 F6
Dowa 2,067 F6
Karonga 11,873 F5
Lilongwe (cap.) 102,924 F6
Mangochi 3,341 G6
Mchinji 1,962 F6
Mwanza 2,271 F7
Mzimba 4,962 F6
Ncheu 1,326 F6
Nkhata Bay 4,024 F6
Nkhotakota 10,312 F6
Nsanje 6,091 G7
Rumphi 3,998 F6
Salima 4,646 F6
Thyolo 4,186 F7
Zomba 21,000 G7

OTHER FEATURES

Chilrua (lake) G7
Malawi (Nyasa) (lake) F6
Mulanje (mts.) G7
Nyasa (lake) F6
Shire (riv.) G7

RWANDA

CITIES and TOWNS

Butare 21,691 E4
Cyangugu 7,042 E4
Gisenyi 12,436 E4
Kigali (cap.) 117,749 F4
Nyabisindu 8,587 E4

OTHER FEATURES

Kagera Nat'l Park F4
Karisimbi (mt.) E4
Kivu (lake) E4
Ruzizi (riv.) E4
Virunga (range) E4

SOMALIA

PROVINCES

Bakool 100,000 H3
Bari 155,000 J1
Bay 302,000 H3
Galguduud 182,000 J2
Gedo 202,800 H3
Hiiraan 147,000 J3
Jubbada Hoose 246,000 H3
Mogadiscio 371,000 J3
Mudug 215,000 J2
Nugaal 85,000 J2
Sanaag 369,000 J1
Shabeellaha Dhexe 237,000 J3
Shabeellaha Hoose 398,000 H3
Togdheer 258,000 J2
Woqooyi Galbeed 440,000 H1

CITIES and TOWNS

Afgoi J3
Afmadu 2,580 H3
Alula K1
Ankhor J1
Balad 1,233 J3
Barawa (Brava) 6,167 H3
Baydhabo 14,962 H3
Belet Weyne 11,426 J3
Bender Cassim J1
Berbera 12,219 J1
Borama 3,244 H1
Bosaso J1
Brava 6,167 H3
Bulo Burti 5,247 J3
Bur Acaba H3
Burao 12,617 J2
Candala J1
Chisimayu 17,872 H4
Coriole 4,341 H3
Dante (Hafun) K1
Dusa Marreb J2
Eil J2
El Athale (Itala) J3
Erigabo 4,279 J1

(continued on following page)

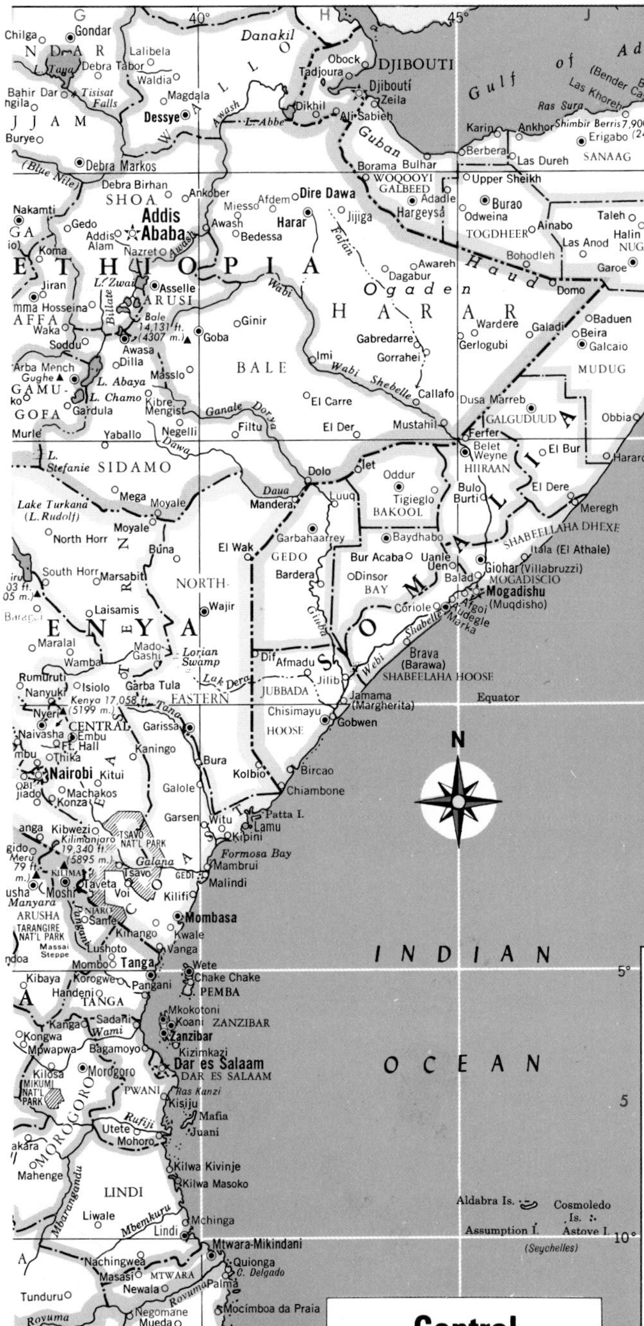

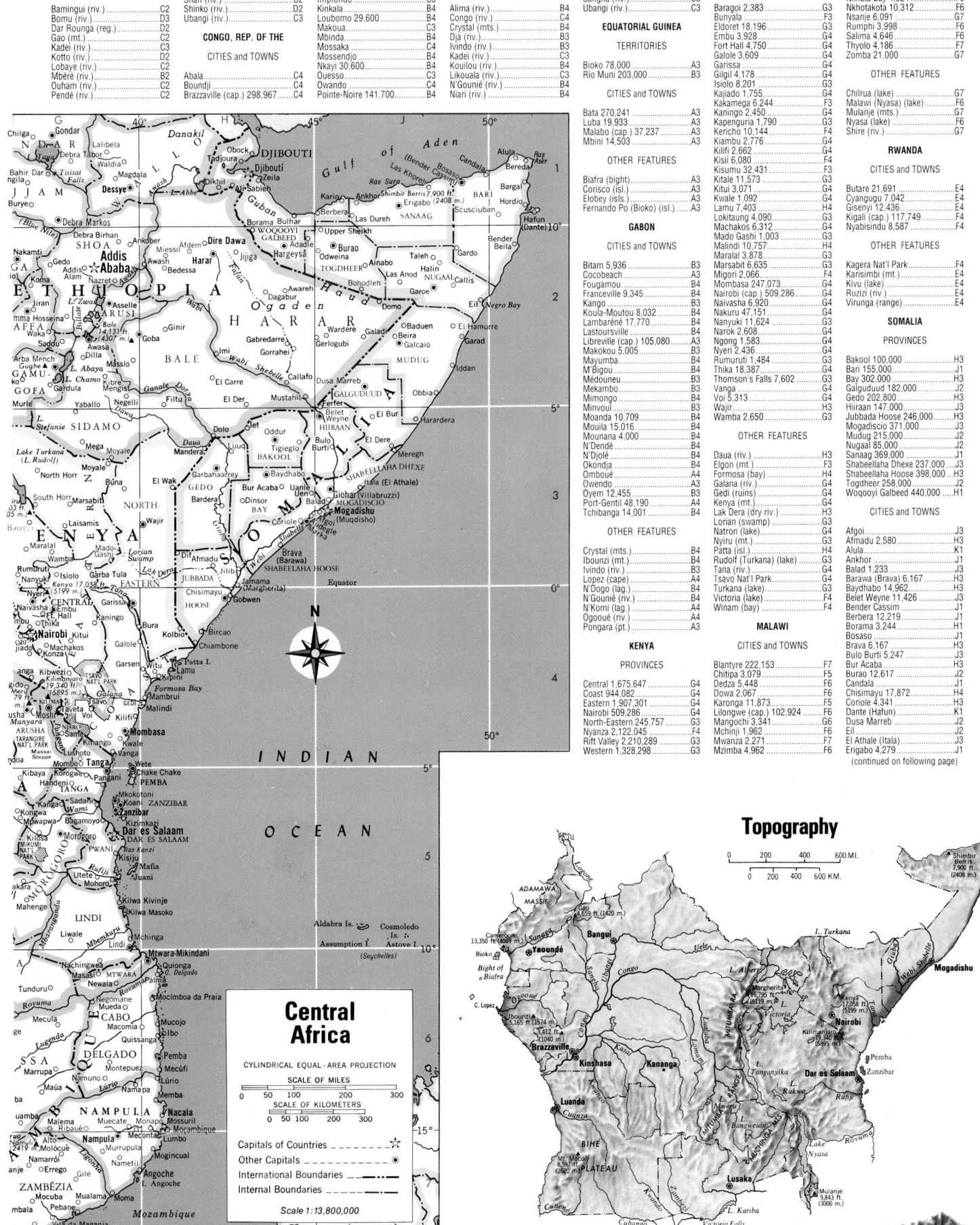

Central Africa
CYLINDRICAL EQUAL-AREA PROJECTION
SCALE OF MILES
0 50 100 200 300
SCALE OF KILOMETERS
0 50 100 200 300
Capitals of Countries
Other Capitals
International Boundaries
Internal Boundaries
Scale 1:13,800,000
INDIAN OCEAN
Gulf of Aden
Mozambique Channel

Topography

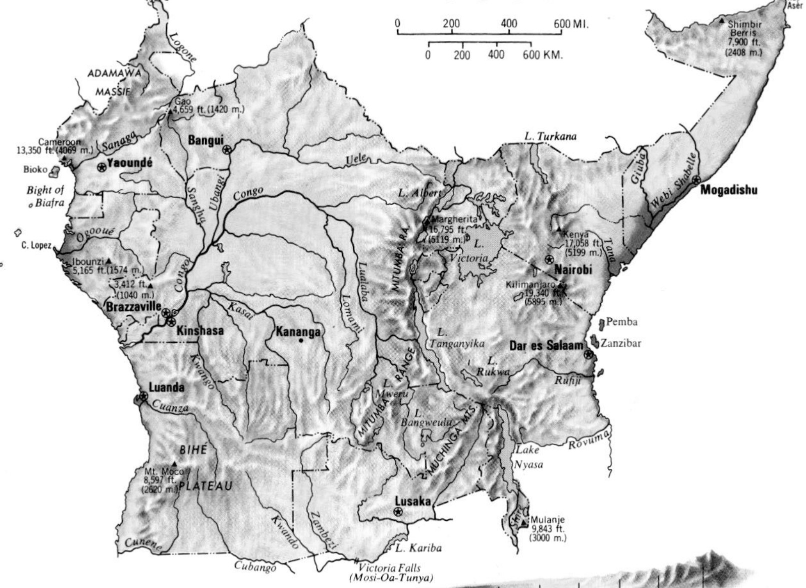

0 200 400 600 MI.
0 200 400 600 KM.
Below Sea Level
100 m. 328 ft.
200 m. 656 ft.
500 m. 1,640 ft.
1,000 m. 3,281 ft.
2,000 m. 6,562 ft.
5,000 m. 16,404 ft.

Galcaio J2
Garbahaarrey H3
Garoe J2
Giohar 13,156 .... J3
Hafun K1
Hargeysa 40,254 .... H2
Itala J3
Jamama 5,408 .... H3
Jilib 3,232 .... H3
Kismayu (Chisimayu) 17,872 .... H4
Las Anod 2,441 .... J2
Las Khoreh 2,245 .... J1
Luuq H3
Margherita (Jamama) H3
Marka (Merka) 17,708 .... H3
Mogadishu (cap.) 371,000 .... J3
Muqdisho (Mogadishu) (cap.) 371,000 .... J3
Oddur H3
Odweina 1,422 .... J2
Uanle Uen H3
Villabruzzi (Johar) J3
Zeila 1,226 .... H1

OTHER FEATURES

Aden (gulf) J1
Asèr, Ras (cape) K1
Giuba (riv.) H3
Guban (reg.) H1
Haud (plat.) J2
Lak Dera (dry riv.) H3
Negro (bay) J2
Shimbir Berris (mt.) J1
Sura, Ras (cape) J1
Webi Shabelle (riv.) H3

TANZANIA

PROVINCES

Arusha 928,478 .... G4
Dar es Salaam G5
Dodoma 971,921 .... G5
Iringa 922,801 .... G5
Kagera 1,009,379 .... F4
Kigoma 648,950 .... F4
Kilimanjaro 902,394 .... G4
Lindi 527,902 .... G5
Mara 723,295 .... F4
Mbeya 1,080,241 .... F5
Morogoro 939,190 .... G5
Mtwara 771,726 .... G5
Mwanza 1,443,418 .... F4
Pemba 205,870 .... H5
Pwani (Coast) 516,949 .... G5
Rukwa 451,897 .... F5
Ruvuma 564,113 .... G6
Shinyanga 1,323,482 .... F4
Singida 614,030 .... F5
Tabora 818,049 .... F5
Tanga 1,088,592 .... G5
Zanzibar Mjini 143,616 .... G5
Zanzibar Shambani North 77,424 .... G5
Zanzibar Shambani South 52,325 .... G5

CITIES and TOWNS

Arusha 55,281 .... G4
Bagamoyo 5,112 .... G5
Biharamulo 1,011 .... F4
Bukene 2,288 .... F4
Bukoba 20,430 .... F4
Chake Chake 4,862 .... H5
Chunya 2,398 .... F5
Dar es Salaam (cap.) 757,346 .... G5
Dodoma 45,703 .... G5
Geita 3,066 .... F4
Iringa 57,182 .... G5
Kahama 3,211 .... F4
Kasulu F4
Kibondo F4
Kigoma-Ujiji 50,044 .... E4
Kilosa 4,458 .... G5
Kilwa Kivinje 2,790 .... G5
Kilwa Masoko G5
Koani 1,102 .... G5
Kondoa 4,514 .... G4
Kongwa G5
Korogwe 6,675 .... G5
Lindi 27,308 .... G5
Lushoto 1,803 .... G4
Mahenge G5
Manyoni G5
Masasi G6
Mbeya 76,606 .... F5
Mbulu G4
Mchinga G5
Mkokotoni 2,220 .... G5
Morogoro 61,890 .... G5
Moshi 52,223 .... G4
Mpanda F5
Mpwapwa 2,429 .... G5
Mtwara-Mikindani 48,510 .... H6
Musoma 32,658 .... F4
Mwadui 7,383 .... F4
Mwanza 110,611 .... F4
Nachingwea 3,751 .... G6
Newala G6
Ngara F4
Njombe F5
Nzega 2,386 .... F4
Pangani 2,955 .... G5
Shinyanga 21,703 .... F4
Singida 29,252 .... F4
Songea 17,954 .... G6
Sumbawanga 28,586 .... F5
Tabora 67,392 .... F5
Tanga 103,409 .... G4
Tukuyu 4,089 .... F5
Tunduru G6
Utete G5
Wete 8,469 .... G4
Zanzibar 110,669 .... G5

OTHER FEATURES

Eyasi (lake) F4
Great Ruaha (riv.) G5
Juani (isl.) G5
Kagera Nat'l Park F4
Kalambo (falls) F5
Kilimanjaro (mt.) G4
Kilombero (riv.) G5
Mafia (isl.) H5
Manyara (lake) G4
Masai (steppe) G4
Mbarangandu (riv.) G5
Mbemkuru (riv.) G5
Meru (mt.) G4
Mikumi Nat'l Park G5
Natron (lake) G4
Ngorongoro (crater) F4
Njombe (riv.) F5
Nyasa (lake) F6
Olduvai Gorge (canyon) G4
Pangani (riv.) G4
Pemba (isl.) H5
Ras Kanzi (cape) G5
Rovuma (riv.) G6
Ruaha Nat'l Park F5
Rufiji (riv.) G5
Rukwa (lake) F5
Rungwa (riv.) F5
Rungwe (mt.) F5
Serengeti Nat'l Park F4
Tanganyika (lake) E5
Tarangire Nat'l Park G4
Victoria (lake) F4
Wami (riv.) G5
Wembere (riv.) F4
Zanzibar (isl.) G5

UGANDA

CITIES and TOWNS

Arua 10,837 .... F3
Butiaba 261 .... F3
Entebbe 21,096 .... F4
Fort Portal 7,947 .... F3
Gulu 18,170 .... F3
Hoima 2,339 .... F3
Jinja 52,509 .... F3
Kabale 8,234 .... E4
Kampala (cap.) 478,895 .... F3
Kasese 7,213 .... F3
Kitgum 3,242 .... F3
Lira 7,340 .... F3
Masaka 12,987 .... F4
Masindi 2,100 .... F3
Mbale 23,544 .... F3
Mbarara 16,078 .... F4
Moroto 5,488 .... F3
Moyo 266 .... F3
Mubende 6,004 .... F3
Rhino Camp 198 .... F3
Soroti 8,130 .... F3
Tororo 15,977 .... F3

OTHER FEATURES

Albert (Mobuto Sese Seko) (lake) F3
Edward (lake) E4
Elgon (mt.) F3
George (lake) F4
Kabalega (falls) F3
Kagalega Nat'l Park F3
Kidepo Nat'l Park F3
Kioga (lake) F3
Margherita (mt.) E3
Mobuto Sese Seko (lake) F3
Owen Falls (dam) F3
Ruwenzori (range) E3
Sese (isls.) F4
Victoria (lake) F4
Virunga (range) E4
Virunga Nat'l Park F4

CONGO, DEM. REP. OF THE

PROVINCES

Bandundu 2,600,556 .... C4
Bas-Zaïre 1,504,361 .... B5
Equateur 2,431,812 .... D3
Haut-Zaïre 3,356,419 .... E3
Kasai-Occidental 2,433,861 .... D4
Kasai-Oriental 1,872,231 .... D5
Kinshasa 1,323,039 .... C4
Kivu 3,361,883 .... E4
Shaba 2,753,714 .... E5

CITIES and TOWNS

Aba 7,600 .... F3
Aketi 17,200 .... D3
Bambesa E3
Banalia E3
Banana B5
Bandundu 74,467 .... C4
Basankusu C3
Basoko 9,100 .... D3
Befale D3
Beni 22,800 .... E3
Bikoro C4
Boende 12,800 .... D4
Bokungu D4
Bolobo 10,300 .... C4
Bolomba 7,200 .... C3
Boma 61,100 .... B5
Bomongo C3
Bondo 10,000 .... D3
Bongandanga 12,900 .... D3
Bosobolo 11,100 .... D3
Budjala C3
Bukama E5
Bukavu 134,861 .... E4
Bulungu 16,300 .... C4
Bumba 34,700 .... D3
Bunia 28,800 .... E3
Bunkeya 5,100 .... E6
Businga 11,000 .... D3
Busu-Djanoa D3
Buta 19,800 .... D3
Butembo 27,800 .... E3
Dekese D4
Demba 22,000 .... D5
Dibaya 11,400 .... D5
Dibaya-Lubue 7,900 .... C4
Dilolo 14,000 .... D6
Dimbelenge D5
Djolu D3
Djugu F3
Dungu 9,100 .... E3
Faradje 10,400 .... E3
Feshi C5
Fizi E4
Gandajika 60,100 .... D5
Gemena 37,300 .... D3
Goma 48,600 .... E4
Gungu C5
Idiofa C4
Ikela D4
Ilebo 32,200 .... D4
Ingende C4
Inongo 14,800 .... C4
Irumu 9,300 .... E3
Isangi D3
Isiro 49,300 .... E3
Kabalo 22,600 .... E5
Kabambare E4
Kabare 12,600 .... E4
Kabinda 60,500 .... D5
Kabongo 6,500 .... E5
Kahemba C5
Kalehe E4
Kalemie 62,300 .... E5
Kalima 27,500 .... E4
Kama 69,100 .... E4
Kambove 18,900 .... E6
Kamina 56,300 .... D5
Kampene 14,600 .... E4
Kananga 428,960 .... D5
Kaniama D5
Kapanga D5
Kasangulu 11,900 .... C4
Kasenga E6
Kasese E4
Kasongo 37,800 .... E4
Kasongo-Lunda C5
Katako-Kombe D4
Kazumba D5
Kenge 17,500 .... C4
Kibombo E4
Kikwit 111,960 .... C5
Kinshasa (cap.) 1,323,039 .... C4
Kipushi 32,900 .... E6
Kisangani 229,596 .... E3
Kolwezi 81,600 .... E6
Kongolo 14,800 .... E5
Kutu 10,000 .... C4
Libenge 13,000 .... C3
Lisala D3
Lodja 20,300 .... D4
Lomela D4
Lubefu D4
Lubudi 6,000 .... E5
Lubumbashi 318,000 .... E6
Lubutu E4
Luebo 21,800 .... D5
Lukula 9,400 .... B5
Luozi 7,000 .... B5
Lusambo 13,100 .... D4
Mambasa 7,400 .... E3
Mangai 41,200 .... C4
Manono 44,500 .... E5
Masi-Manimba 6,300 .... C4
Masisi E4
Matadi 110,436 .... B5
Mbandaka 107,910 .... C3
Mbanza-Ngungu 55,800 .... C5
Mbuji-Mayi 256,154 .... D5
Mitwaba E5
Monkoto D4
Muanda 6,400 .... B5
Mungbere E3
Mushie 13,700 .... C4
Muyumba E5
Mweka 24,900 .... D4
Mwene-Ditu 71,200 .... D5
Mwenga E4
Niangara 9,200 .... E3
Nyunzu 11,300 .... E5
Opala D4
Oshwe C4
Panda-Likasi 146,394 .... E6
Pangi E4
Poko E3
Popokabaka C5
Port Kindu 42,800 .... E4
Punia E4
Rutshuru E4
Sakania E6
Sandoa D5
Sentery 24,300 .... E5
Shabunda 6,900 .... E4
Songololo 4,600 .... B5
Tshela 10,700 .... B4
Tshikapa 38,900 .... D5
Ubundu 630 .... E4
Uvira 15,900 .... E4
Virunga 21,900 .... E5
Wamba 11,500 .... E3
Watsa 21,250 .... E3
Yangambi 22,600 .... D3

OTHER FEATURES

Albert (Mobuto Sese Seko) (lake) F3
Aruwimi (riv.) E3
Bomu (riv.) D3
Boyoma (Stanley) (falls) D3
Chicapa (riv.) D5
Congo (riv.) C4
Edward (lake) E4
Elila (riv.) E4
Fimi (riv.) C4
Garamba Nat'l Park E3
Giri (riv.) C3
Itimbiri (riv.) D3
Ituri (for.) E3
Karisimbi (mt.) E4
Kasai (riv.) C4
Kivu (lake) E4
Kwa (riv.) C4
Kwango (riv.) C5
Kwilu (riv.) C5
Lindi (riv.) E3
Livingstone (falls) B5
Loange (riv.) C5
Lokoro (riv.) C4
Lomami (riv.) D4
Lomela (riv.) D4
Lowa (riv.) E4
Lua (riv.) C3
Lualaba (riv.) E4
Luapula (riv.) E6
Lubilash (riv.) D5
Lufira (riv.) E5
Luilaka (riv.) C4
Lukenie (riv.) D4
Lukuga (riv.) E5
Lulua (riv.) D5
Luvua (riv.) E5
Mai-Ndombe (lake) C4
Malebo (Stanley Pool) (lake) C4
Margherita (mt.) E3
Marungu (mts.) E5
Mobuto Sese Seko (lake) F3
Mweru (lake) E5
Ruwenzori (range) E3
Ruzizi (riv.) E4
Salonga Nat'l Park D4
Sankuru (riv.) D4
Stanley (falls) D3
Stanley Pool (lake) C4
Tanganyika (lake) E5
Tshuapa (riv.) D4
Tumba (lake) C4
Ubangi (riv.) C3
Uele (riv.) E3
Ulindi (riv.) E4
Upemba (lake) E5
Upemba Nat'l Park E5
Virunga (range) E4
Virunga Nat'l Park E4

ZAMBIA

CITIES and TOWNS

Abercorn (Mbala) 11,179 .... F5
Bancroft (Chililabombwe) 61,928 .... E6
Broken Hill (Kabwe) 143,635 .... E6
Chilanga 12,503 .... E7
Chililabombwe 61,928 .... E6
Chingola 145,869 .... E6
Chipata 32,291 .... F6
Choma 17,943 .... E7
Fort Rosebery (Mansa) 34,801 .... E6
Isoka 6,832 .... F6
Kabompo 5,357 .... D6
Kabwe 143,635 .... E6
Kafue 29,794 .... E7
Kalabo 7,398 .... D6
Kalomo 5,878 .... E7
Kaoma 6,731 .... D6
Kapiri Mposhi 13,677 .... E6
Kasama 38,093 .... F6
Kawambwa 7,235 .... E5
Kitwe 314,794 .... E6
Livingstone 71,987 .... E7
Luanshya 132,164 .... E6
Lusaka (cap.) 538,469 .... E7
Mansa 34,801 .... E6
Mazabuka 29,602 .... E7
Mbala 11,179 .... F5
Mongu 24,919 .... D7
Monze 13,141 .... E7
Mpika 25,880 .... F6
Mporokoso 6,008 .... F5
Mpulungu 6,354 .... F5
Mufulira 149,778 .... E6
Mumbwa 7,570 .... E6
Ndola 282,439 .... E6
Petauke 7,531 .... F6
Senanga 7,204 .... D7
Serenje 6,008 .... F6
Solwezi 15,032 .... E6
Zambezi 8,166 .... D6

OTHER FEATURES

Bangweulu (lake) F6
Barotseland (reg.) D7
Chambeshi (riv.) F6
Cuando (riv.) D7
Dongwe (riv.) D6
Kabompo (riv.) D6
Kafue (riv.) E7
Kafue Nat'l Park E6
Kalambo (falls) F5
Kariba (dam) E7
Kariba (lake) E7
Luangwa (riv.) F6
Luapula (riv.) E6
Lungwebungu (riv.) D6
Mosi-Oa-Tunya (Victoria) (falls) E7
Mulungushi (dam) E6
Mweru (lake) E5
Sunzu (mt.) F5
Tanganyika (lake) E5
Victoria (falls) E7
Zambezi (riv.) D7

Agriculture, Industry and Resources

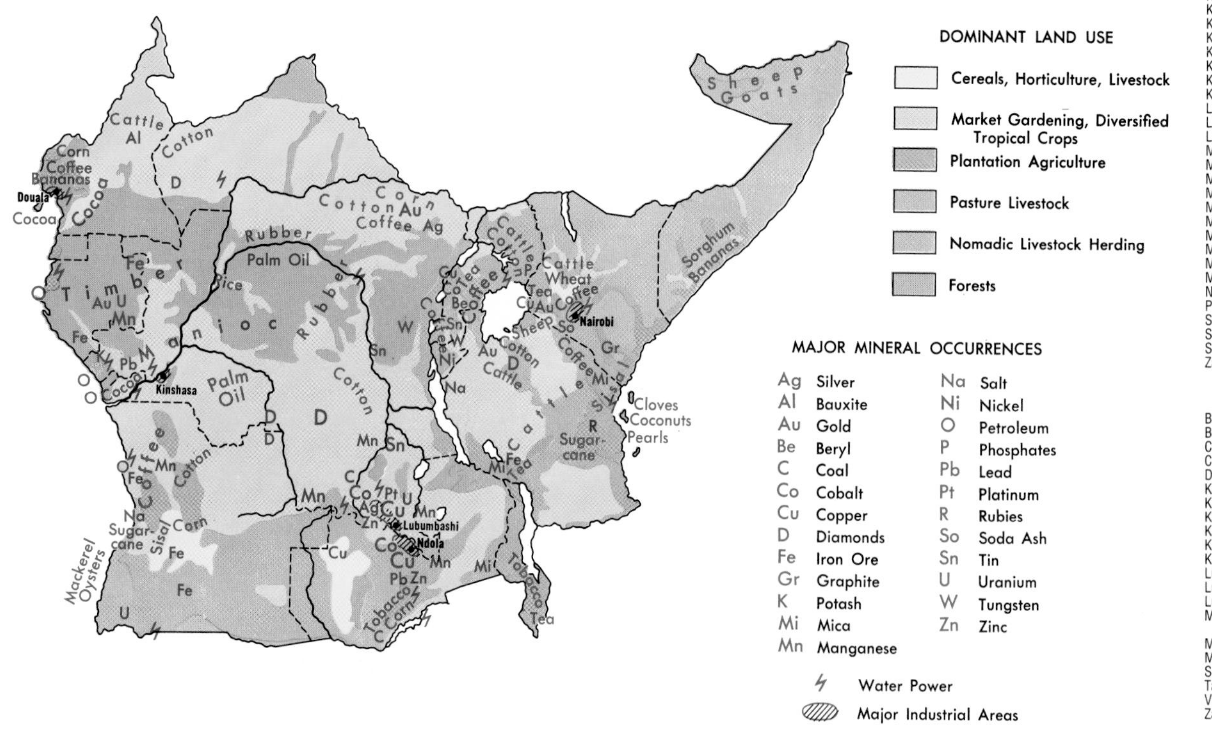
DOMINANT LAND USE
Cereals, Horticulture, Livestock
Market Gardening, Diversified Tropical Crops
Plantation Agriculture
Pasture Livestock
Nomadic Livestock Herding
Forests
MAJOR MINERAL OCCURRENCES
Ag Silver
Al Bauxite
Au Gold
Be Beryl
C Coal
Co Cobalt
Cu Copper
D Diamonds
Fe Iron Ore
Gr Graphite
K Potash
Mi Mica
Mn Manganese
Na Salt
Ni Nickel
O Petroleum
P Phosphates
Pb Lead
Pt Platinum
R Rubies
So Soda Ash
Sn Tin
U Uranium
W Tungsten
Zn Zinc
Water Power
Major Industrial Areas
Douala
Kinshasa
Lubumbashi
Ndola
Nairobi
Sheep
Goats
Cattle
Corn
Coffee
Bananas
Cocoa
Cotton
Rubber
Palm Oil
Timber
Manioc
Sorghum
Bananas
Wheat
Tea
Sisal
Sugar-cane
Cloves
Coconuts
Pearls
Tobacco
Mackerel
Oysters

NAMIBIA

AREA 317,827 sq. mi. (823,172 sq. km.)
POPULATION 1,818,000
CAPITAL Windhoek
LARGEST CITY Windhoek
HIGHEST POINT Brandberg 8,550 ft. (2,606 m.)
MONETARY UNIT rand
MAJOR LANGUAGES Ovambo, Hottentot, Herero, Afrikaans, English
MAJOR RELIGIONS Tribal religions, Protestantism

BOTSWANA

AREA 224,764 sq. mi. (582,139 sq. km.)
POPULATION 1,256,000
CAPITAL Gaborone
LARGEST CITY Francistown
HIGHEST POINT Tsodilo Hill 5,922 ft. (1,805 m.)
MONETARY UNIT pula
MAJOR LANGUAGES Setswana, Shona, Bushman, English, Afrikaans
MAJOR RELIGIONS Tribal religions, Protestantism

ZIMBABWE

AREA 150,803 sq. mi. (390,580 sq. km.)
POPULATION 9,122,000
CAPITAL Harare
LARGEST CITY Harare
HIGHEST POINT Mt. Inyangani 8,517 ft. (2,596 m.)
MONETARY UNIT Zimbabwe dollar
MAJOR LANGUAGES English, Shona, Ndebele
MAJOR RELIGIONS Tribal religions, Protestantism

SOUTH AFRICA

AREA 455,318 sq. mi. (1,179,274 sq. km.)
POPULATION 34,492,000
CAPITALS Cape Town, Pretoria
LARGEST CITY Johannesburg
HIGHEST POINT Injasuti 11,182 ft. (3,408 m.)
MONETARY UNIT rand
MAJOR LANGUAGES Afrikaans, English, Xhosa, Zulu, Sesotho
MAJOR RELIGIONS Protestantism, Roman Catholicism, Islam, Hinduism, tribal religions

MOZAMBIQUE

AREA 303,769 sq. mi. (786,762 sq. km.)
POPULATION 15,326,000
CAPITAL Maputo
LARGEST CITY Maputo
HIGHEST POINT Mt. Binga 7,992 ft. (2,436 m.)
MONETARY UNIT metical
MAJOR LANGUAGES Makua, Thonga, Shona, Portuguese
MAJOR RELIGIONS Tribal religions, Roman Catholicism, Islam

MADAGASCAR

AREA 226,657 sq. mi. (587,041 sq. km.)
POPULATION 9,985,000
CAPITAL Antananarivo
LARGEST CITY Antananarivo
HIGHEST POINT Maromokotro 9,436 ft. (2,876 m.)
MONETARY UNIT Madagascar franc
MAJOR LANGUAGES Malagasy, French
MAJOR RELIGIONS Tribal religions, Roman Catholicism, Protestantism

MAURITIUS

AREA 790 sq. mi. (2,046 sq. km.)
POPULATION 1,068,000
CAPITAL Port Louis
LARGEST CITY Port Louis
HIGHEST POINT 2,711 ft. (826 m.)
MONETARY UNIT Mauritian rupee
MAJOR LANGUAGES English, French, French Creole, Hindi, Urdu
MAJOR RELIGIONS Hinduism, Christianity, Islam

LESOTHO

AREA 11,720 sq. mi. (30,355 sq. km.)
POPULATION 1,700,000
CAPITAL Maseru
LARGEST CITY Maseru
HIGHEST POINT 11,425 ft. (3,482 m.)
MONETARY UNIT loti
MAJOR LANGUAGES Sesotho, English
MAJOR RELIGIONS Tribal religions, Christianity

SWAZILAND

AREA 6,705 sq. mi. (17,366 sq. km.)
POPULATION 681,000
CAPITAL Mbabane
LARGEST CITY Manzini
HIGHEST POINT Emlembe 6,109 ft. (1,862 m.)
MONETARY UNIT lilangeni
MAJOR LANGUAGES siSwati, English
MAJOR RELIGIONS Tribal religions, Christianity

COMOROS

AREA 719 sq. mi. (1,862 sq. km.)
POPULATION 484,000
CAPITAL Moroni
LARGEST CITY Moroni
HIGHEST POINT Karthala 7,746 ft. (2,361 m.)
MONETARY UNIT CFA franc
MAJOR LANGUAGES Arabic, French, Swahili
MAJOR RELIGION Islam

SEYCHELLES

AREA 145 sq. mi. (375 sq. km.)
POPULATION 67,000
CAPITAL Victoria
LARGEST CITY Victoria
HIGHEST POINT Morne Seychellois 2,993 ft. (912 m.)
MONETARY UNIT Seychellois rupee
MAJOR LANGUAGES English, French, Creole
MAJOR RELIGION Roman Catholicism

ZIMBABWE

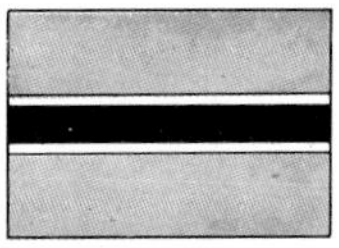
BOTSWANA

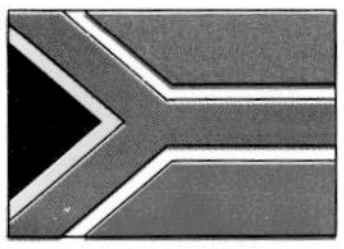
SOUTH AFRICA

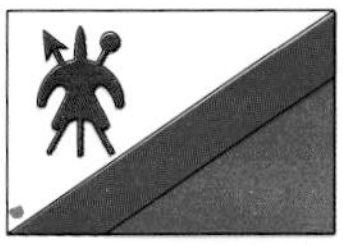
LESOTHO

SWAZILAND

REUNION

AREA 969 sq. mi. (2,510 sq. km.)
POPULATION 570,000
CAPITAL St-Denis

MAYOTTE

AREA 144 sq. mi. (373 sq. km.)
POPULATION 47,300
CAPITAL Mamoutzou

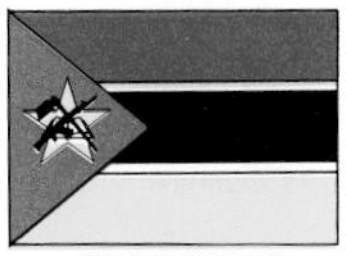
MOZAMBIQUE

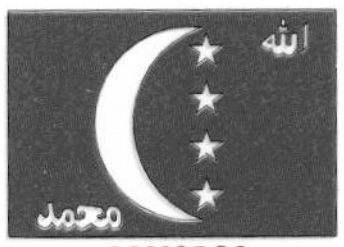
COMOROS

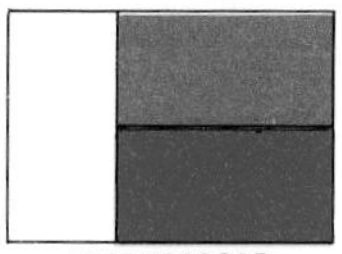
MADAGASCAR

MAURITIUS

SEYCHELLES

NAMIBIA

Agriculture, Industry and Resources

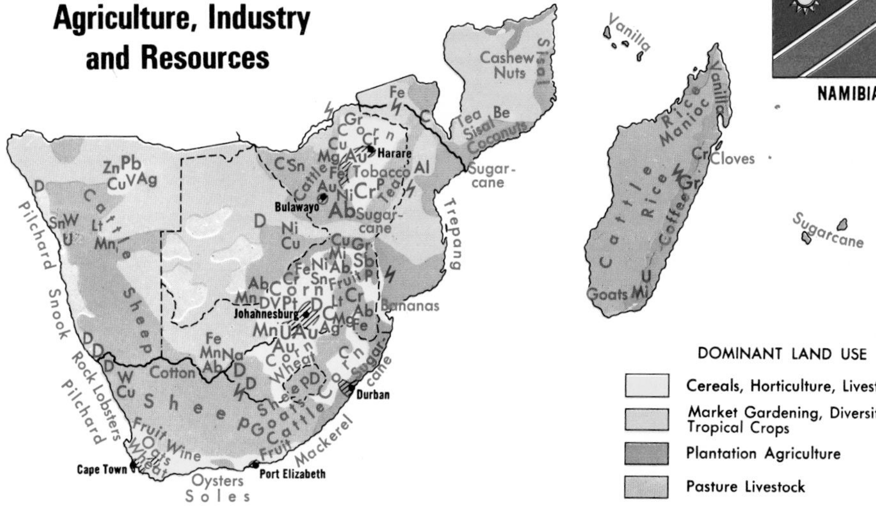
Harare
Bulawayo
Johannesburg
Durban
Cape Town
Port Elizabeth
Cashew Nuts
Sisal
Tea
Coconuts
Sugar-cane
Tobacco
Cattle
Sheep
Trepang
Pilchard
Snook
Rock Lobsters
Bananas
Cotton
Fruit
Wine
Oats
Wheat
Mackerel
Oysters
Soles
Vanilla
Rice
Manioc
Coffee
Cloves
Sugarcane
Goats

DOMINANT LAND USE

- Cereals, Horticulture, Livestock
- Market Gardening, Diversified Tropical Crops
- Plantation Agriculture
- Pasture Livestock
- Nomadic Livestock Herding
- Forests
- Nonagricultural Land

MAJOR MINERAL OCCURRENCES

Ab	Asbestos	Cu	Copper	Mn	Manganese	Sb	Antimony
Ag	Silver	D	Diamonds	Na	Salt	Sn	Tin
Al	Bauxite	Fe	Iron Ore	Ni	Nickel	U	Uranium
Au	Gold	Gr	Graphite	P	Phosphates	V	Vanadium
Be	Beryl	Lt	Lithium	Pb	Lead	W	Tungsten
C	Coal	Mg	Magnesium	Pt	Platinum	Zn	Zinc
Cr	Chromium	Mi	Mica				

ϟ Water Power

Major Industrial Areas

(continued on following page)

Topography

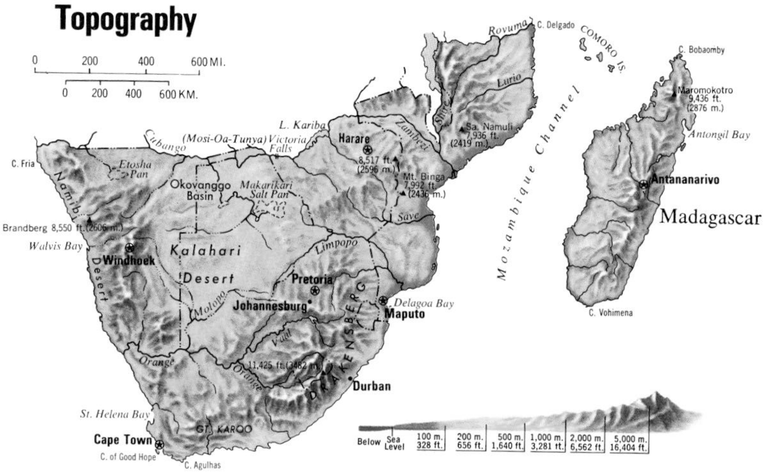
0 200 400 600 MI.
0 200 400 600 KM.
Harare
Windhoek
Kalahari
Desert
Pretoria
Johannesburg
Maputo
Delagoa Bay
Durban
Cape Town
C. of Good Hope
C. Agulhas
St. Helena Bay
Walvis Bay
Madagascar
Antananarivo
Mozambique Channel
COMORO IS.
C. Delgado
C. Bobaomby
C. Vohimena
Antongil Bay
Limpopo
Orange
Vaal
Zambezi
Lúrio
Save
L. Kariba
Victoria Falls
Etosha Pan
Okovanggo Basin
Makarikari Salt Pan
Brandberg 8,550 ft. (2606 m.)
Below Sea Level
100 m. 328 ft.
200 m. 656 ft.
500 m. 1,640 ft.
1,000 m. 3,281 ft.
2,000 m. 6,562 ft.
5,000 m. 16,404 ft.

Tananarive (Antananarivo) 451,808 H3
Tangainony 6,952 H4
Toamasina 77,395 H3
Toliara (Tuléar) 45,676 G4
Tsiroanomandidy 11,444 H3
Vangaindrano 3,249 H4
Vohibinany 1,741 H3
Vohimarina (Vohémar) 4,289 J2
Vohipeno 2,736 H4

OTHER FEATURES

Alaotra (lake) H3
Amber (Bobaomby) (cape) H2
Antongil (bay) J3
Barren (isls.) G3
Betsiboka (riv.) H3
Bobaomby (Amber) (cape) H2
Boby, Pic (mt.) H4
Chesterfield (isl.) G3
Ikopa (riv.) H3
Itasy (lake) H3
Mahajamba (bay) H2
Mananara (riv.) H4
Mananbao (riv.) G3
Mangoky (riv.) G4
Mangoro (riv.) H3
Maromokotro (mt.) H2
Masoala (pen.) J3
Menarandra (riv.) H4
Mozambique (chan.) G3
Nosy Be (isl.) H2
Nosy Boraha (isl.) J3
Onilahy (riv.) G4
Pangalanes (canal) H4
Radama (isls.) H2
Saint-André (cape) G3
Saint-Marie (Nosy Boraha) (isl.) J3
Saint-Marie (Vohimena) (cape) G5
Saint-Sébastien (cape) H2
Sofia (riv.) H3
Tsiafajavona (mt.) H3
Tsiribihina (riv.) G3
Vohimena (cape) G5

MAURITIUS

CITIES and TOWNS

Curepipe 52,709 G5
Mahébourg 15,463 G5
Port Louis (cap.) 141,022 G5
Quatre Bornes 51,638 G5
Souillac 3,361 G5

OTHER FEATURES

Mascarene (isls.) F5

MAYOTTE

CITIES and TOWNS

Mamoutzou (cap.) 196 H2

MOZAMBIQUE

PROVINCES

Cabo Delgado 940,000 F2
Gaza 999,900 E4
Inhambane 977,000 E4
Manica 541,200 E4
Maputo 491,800 E5
Maputo (city) 755,300 E5
Nampula 2,402,700 F2
Niassa 514,100 F2
Sofala 1,055,200 E3
Tete 831,000 E3
Zambézia 2,500,000 F3

CITIES and TOWNS

Angoche 1,714 G3
Bartolomeu Dias° 6,102 F4
Beira 46,293 F3
Beira* 130,398 F3
Chibuto 23,763 E4
Chicualacuala 2,050 E4
Chimoio 4,507 E3
Chinde 742 F3
Dona Ana (Mutarara) 686 F3
Dondo 2,112 F3
Funhalouro° 42,366 E4
Ibo 1,015 G2
Inhambane 4,975 F4
Inhaminga 1,607 F3
Inharrime 856 F4
Lichinga 3,011 F2
Lumbo° 11,080 G3
Lúrio° 13,417 G2
Mabalane° 13,158 E4
Mabote° 28,970 E4
Machanga° 15,754 F4
Machaze° 42,255 E4
Mandié° 24,382 E3
Mandimba° 7,634 F2
Manhiça° 1,680 E5
Maniamba° 2,045 F2
Maputo (cap.) 755,300 E5
Massangena° 3,301 E4
Massinga 517 F4
Moçambique 1,730 G3
Mocímboa da Praia 935 G2
Mocuba 2,293 F3
Montepuez 2,837 F2
Mualama° 34,992 F3
Mucojo° 15,867 G2
Mueda 1,583 F2
Mutarara (Dona Ana) 686 F3
Nacala 4,601 G2
Nampula 23,072 F3
Pafúri° 2,599 E4
Pemba 3,629 G2
Quelimane 10,522 F3
Quionga° 3,181 G2
Quissico 2,615 E4
Songo 2,230 E3
Tete 4,549 E3
Vila de Sena° 21,074 E3
Xai-Xai 5,234 E5

OTHER FEATURES

Angoche (isl.) G3
Bazaruto, Ilha do (isl.) F4
Binga (mt.) E3
Cabora Bassa (dam) E3
Changane (riv.) E4
Chirua (lake) F3
Delagoa (bay) E5
Delgado (cape) G2
Gorongosa Nat'l Park E3
Ligonha (riv.) F3
Limpopo (riv.) E4
Lugenda (riv.) F2
Lúrio (riv.) F2
Mazoe (riv.) E3
Mozambique (chan.) G3
Namuli, Serra (mt.) F3
Nyasa (lake) E2
Olifants (riv.) D4
Rovuma (riv.) F2
São Sebastião (pt.) F4
Save (riv.) E4
Shire (riv.) E3
Zambezi (riv.) E3

NAMIBIA

CITIES and TOWNS

Aroab 783 B5
Aus 767 B5
Berseba B5
Bethanie 1,207 B5
Gibeon B5
Gobabis 4,428 B4
Grootfontein 4,627 B3
Kalkfeld 587 B4
Kamanjab 713 A3
Karasburg 2,693 B5
Karibib 1,653 B4
Keetmanshoop 10,297 B5
Koes 514 B5
Lüderitz 6,642 A5
Maltahöhe 1,313 B4
Mariental 4,629 B4
Okahandja 1,688 B4
Omaruru 2,783 B4
Ondangwa B3
Opuno A3
Oranjemund 2,594 B5
Oshakati B3
Otavi 1,814 B3
Otjiwarongo 8,018 B4
Outjo 2,545 B4
Rehoboth 5,363 B4
Rundu 521 B3
Stampriet 271 B4
Swakopmund 5,681 A4
Tsumeb 12,338 B3
Usakos 2,334 B4
Walvis Bay 21,725 A4
Warmbad 810 B5
Windhoek (cap.) 61,369 B4
Witvlei 303 B4

OTHER FEATURES

Brandberg (mt.) A4
Caprivi Strip (reg.) C3
Chobe (riv.) C3
Cross (cape) A4
Cubango (riv.) B3
Cunene (riv.) A3
Damaraland (reg.) B4
Diamond Coast (reg.) A5
Elephant (riv.) B5
Etosha Pan (salt pan) B3
Fish (riv.) B5
Fria (cape) A3
Great Namaland (reg.) B4
Hollam's Bird (isl.) A4
Hottentot (bay) A5
Kalahari (des.) C4
Kaokoveld (reg.) A3
Kaukauveld (mts.) C3
Kuiseb (riv.) B4
Lüderitz (bay) A5
Namib (des.) A3
Nossob (riv.) B4
Okovango (riv.) C3
Omatako (riv.) B3
Ovamboland (reg.) B3
Ruacana Falls (falls) A3
Skeleton Coast (reg.) A3
Swakop (riv.) B4
Ugab (riv.) A4
Zambezi (riv.) C3

RÉUNION

CITIES and TOWNS

Le Port 21,564 F5
Saint-Benoît 7,778 G5
Saint-Denis (cap.) 80,075 F5
Saint-Denis* 104,603 F5
Saint-Joseph 8,928 G6
Saint-Louis 10,252 F5
Saint-Pierre 21,817 F6

OTHER FEATURES

Bassas da India (isl.) F4
Europa (isl.) G4
Glorioso (isls.) H2
Juan de Nova (isl.) G3
Mascarene (isls.) F5
Piton des Neiges (mt.) G5

SEYCHELLES

CITIES and TOWNS

Anse Boileau† 3,420 H5
Anse Royale† 3,182 H5
Cascade† 2,600 H5
Victoria (cap.) 15,559 H5
Victoria* 23,012 H5

OTHER FEATURES

Aldabra (isls.) H1
Assumption (isl.) H1
Astove (isl.) H2
Cerf (isl.) H5
Cosmoledo (isls.) H1
Curieuse (isl.) H5
Felicité (isl.) J5
Frigate (isl.) J5
La Digue (isl.) J5
Mahé (isl.) H5
Morne Seychellois (mt.) H5
North (isl.) H5
Praslin (isl.) H5
Sainte Anne (isl.) H5
Silhouette (isl.) H5

SOUTH AFRICA

PROVINCES

Eastern Cape 6,665,400 D6
Free State 2,804,600 D5
Gauteng 6,847,000 D5
KwaZulu Natal 8,549,000 E5
Mpumalanga 2,838,500 D5
Northern Cape 763,900 B5
Northern Province 5,120,600 D4
North-West 3,506,800 C5
Western Cape 3,620,200 C6

CITIES and TOWNS

Alberton 23,988 H6
Alexandra 57,040 H6
Aliwal North 12,311 D6
Barberton 12,382 E5
Beaufort West 17,862 C6
Bellville 49,026 F6
Benoni 151,294 J6
Bethlehem 29,918 D5
Bisho D6
Bloemfontein 149,836 D5
Boksburg 106,126 J6
Brakpan 73,210 J6
Brits 12,182 D5
Butterworth (Gcuwa) 2,769 D6
Cape Town (cap.) 854,616 E6
Carltonville 40,641 G7
Cradock 20,822 D6
De Aar 18,057 C6
Dundee 17,162 E5
Durban 736,852 E5
East London 119,727 D6
Edendale 41,194 D5
Edenvale 25,126 H6
Elsiesrivier 63,706 F6
Ermelo 19,036 E5
Eshowe 4,552 E5
Estcourt 10,922 D5
Fort Beaufort 11,640 D6
Gcuwa 2,769 D6
George 24,625 C6
Germiston 221,972 H6
Glencoe 10,513 E5
Goodwood 31,592 F6
Graaff-Reinet 22,392 C6
Grahamstown 41,302 D6
Grassy Park 32,709 E6
Griquatown 2,996 C5
Harrismith 16,082 D5
Heidelberg 12,521 J7
Hermanus 4,956 G7
Howick 12,429 E5
Johannesburg 654,232 H6
Kempton Park 37,205 J6
Kimberley 105,258 C5
King William's Town 15,798 D6
Klerksdorp 63,558 D5
Knysna 13,479 C6
Kokstad 10,227 D6
Kraaifontein 10,286 F6
Kroonstad 51,988 D5
Krugersdorp 92,725 H6
Ladybrand 8,757 D5
Ladysmith 28,920 D5
Lambert's Bay 3,247 B6
Mafikeng (Mafeking) 6,515 D5
Matatiele 3,853 D6
Messina 21,121 D4
Middelburg, Cape Prov. 12,121 D6
Middelburg, Transvaal 26,942 D5
Milnerton 10,893 F6
Mmabatho D5
Mossel Bay 17,574 C6
Nelspruit 25,092 E5
Newcastle 14,407 E5
Nigel 41,179 J7
Nyanga 15,655 F6
Odendaalsrus 15,603 D5
Oudtshoorn 26,907 C6
Paarl 49,244 F6
Parow 60,768 F6
Parys 17,447 D5
Pietermaritzburg 114,822 E5
Pietersburg 27,174 D4
Pinelands 11,769 F6
Pinetown 22,721 E6
Port Elizabeth 392,231 D6
Port Nolloth 2,893 B5
Port Saint Johns (Umzimbuvu) 1,817 D6
Potchefstroom 57,443 D5
Pretoria (cap.) 525,583 D5
Queenstown 39,304 D6
Randburg 43,257 H6
Randfontein 50,481 G6
Richards Bay 598 E5
Robertson 10,237 C6
Roodepoort 115,366 H6
Rustenburg 22,303 D5
Saldanha 4,994 B6
Simonstown 12,137 E7
Sishen 2,692 C5
Somerset East 10,383 D6
Somerset West 11,828 F6
Soweto 602,043 H6
Springs 142,812 J6
Standerton 21,038 D5
Stanger 11,064 E5

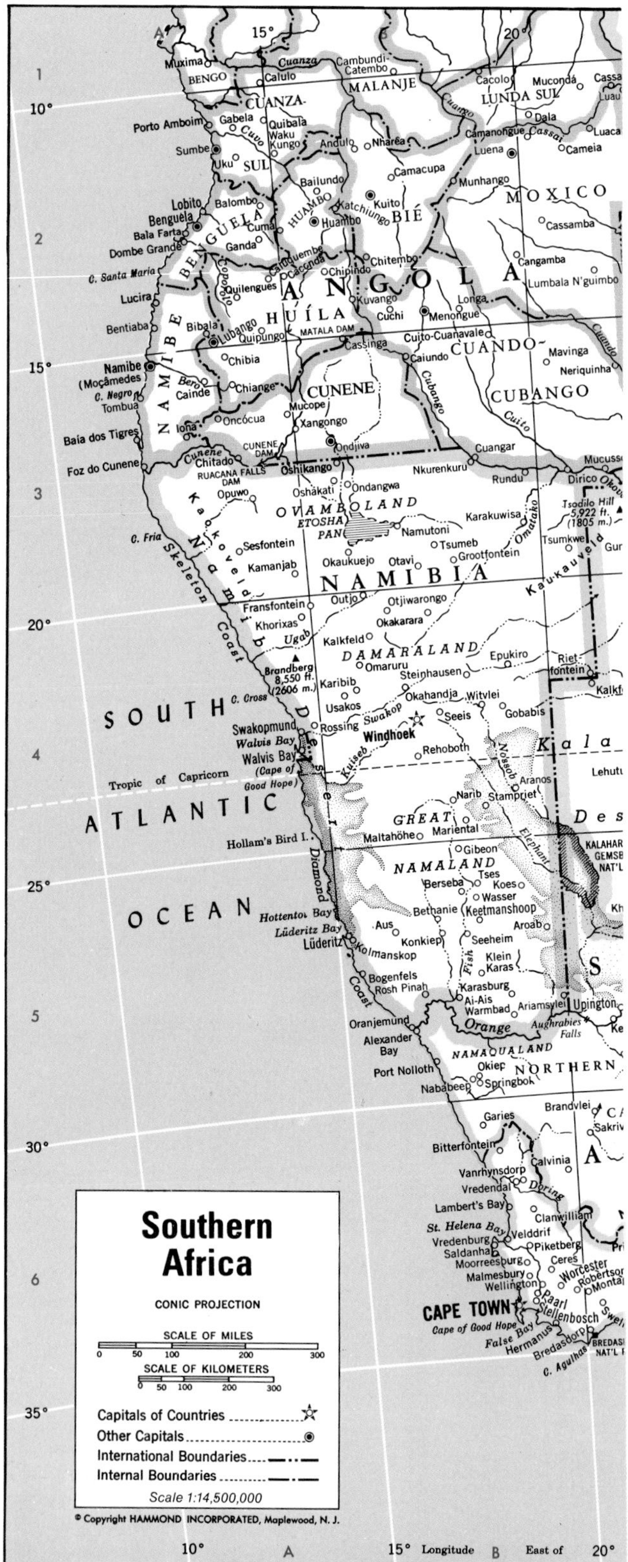
Southern Africa
CONIC PROJECTION
SCALE OF MILES
0 50 100 200 300
SCALE OF KILOMETERS
0 50 100 200 300
Capitals of Countries
Other Capitals
International Boundaries
Internal Boundaries
Scale 1:14,500,000
© Copyright HAMMOND INCORPORATED, Maplewood, N. J.
10° A 15° Longitude B East of 20°
ANGOLA
NAMIBIA
SOUTH ATLANTIC OCEAN
Tropic of Capricorn
Windhoek
Walvis Bay
Swakopmund
Lüderitz
Oranjemund
Port Nolloth
CAPE TOWN
Cape of Good Hope
Lobito
Benguela
Namibe
Skeleton Coast
ETOSHA PAN
DAMARALAND
NAMALAND
OVAMBOLAND

Stellenbosch 29,955 F6
Strand 24,503 F7
Stutterheim 12,077 D6
Taung 1,316 C5
Tembisa 81,821 H6
Thabazimbi 6,711 D4
Thohoyandou E4
Uitenhage 70,517 C6
Umtata 25,216 D6
Umzimbuvu 1,817 D6
Upington 28,632 C5
Vanderbijl Park 78,754 D5
Venterspos G6
Vereeniging 172,549 D5
Volksrust 10,238 D5
Vryburg 16,916 C5
Vryheid 16,992 E5
Warmbad 8,343 D4
Welkom 67,472 D5
Wellington 17,092 B6
Westonaria 36,253 H7
Witbank 37,456 D5
Worcester 41,198 B6
Zeerust 6,972 D5

OTHER FEATURES

Addo Nat'l Park D6
Agulhas (cape) B6
Algoa (bay) D6
Aughrabies (falls) B5
Blesbok (riv.) J7
Bot (riv.) G7
Bredasdorp Nat'l Park C6
Cape (pen.) E7
Cape (pt.) F7
Crocodile (riv.) H6
Diep (riv.) F6
Doring (riv.) B6
Drakensberg (range) D6
Duiker (pt.) E6
False (bay) F7
Good Hope (cape) E7
Great Fish (riv.) D6
Great Karoo (reg.) C6
Great Kei (riv.) D6
Griqualand West (reg.) C5
Groote (riv.) C6
Hangklip (cape) F7
Hartbees (riv.) C5
Hout (bay) E6
Jukskei (riv.) H6
Kalahari Gemsbok Nat'l Park C5
King George's (falls) B5
Klip (riv.) H6
Kruger Nat'l Park E4
Kruis (riv.) F6
Limpopo (riv.) D4
Maclear (cape) F7
Molopo (riv.) C5
Mountain Zebra Nat'l Park C6
Namaqualand (reg.) B5
Nieuwveld (range) C6
Olifants (riv.) D4
Orange (riv.) B5
Palmiet (riv.) F7
Plettenberg (bay) C6
Pondoland (reg.) D6
Robben (isl.) E6
Royal Natal Nat'l Park D5
Saint Francis (bay) D6
Saint Helena (bay) B6
Saint Lucia (cape) E5
Saint Lucia (lake) E5
Sak (riv.) C6
Sand (riv.) D4
Sandown (bay) F7
Seal (isl.) F7
Slangkop (pt.) E7
Sneeuwkop (mt.) F6
Stettyn (mt.) G6
Table (bay) E6
Table (mt.) E6
Vaal (riv.) D5
Verwoerd (dam) D6
Walvis (bay) A4
Witwatersberg (range) G6
Witwatersrand (reg.) H7
Zonderend (riv.) G6
Zululand (reg.) E5
Zwart (riv.) G7

SWAZILAND

CITIES and TOWNS

Manzini 28,837 E5
Mbabane (cap.) 23,109 E5
Siteki 1,362 E5

ZIMBABWE

CITIES and TOWNS

Bindura 17,000 E3
Bulawayo 359,000 D3
Chegutu 12,000 E3
Chinhoyi 25,000 E3
Gweru 68,000 D3
Harare (cap.) 601,000 E3
Hwange 33,000 D3
Kadoma 32,000 E3
Kwekwe 54,000 D3
Marondero 23,000 E3
Masvingo 22,000 E4
Matopos○ 11,330 D4
Mutare 61,000 E3
Mwenezi○ 7,830 E4
Rusape 5,286 E3
Salisbury (Harare) (cap.) 601,000 E3
Shurugwi 8,387 E3
Tuli○ 340 D4
Zvishavane 20,000 E4

OTHER FEATURES

Inyanga Nat'l Park E3
Kariba (dam) D3
Kariba (lake) D3
Lundi (riv.) E4
Mashonaland (reg.) E3
Matabeleland (reg.) D3
Mazowe (riv.) E3
Mushandike Nat'l Park D4
Sabi (riv.) E3
Sanyati (riv.) D3
Shangani (riv.) D3
Shashe (riv.) D4
Victoria (falls) C3
Zambezi (riv.) E3
Zimbabwe Nat'l Park E4

*City and suburbs.
†Population of parish.
○Population of subdivision.

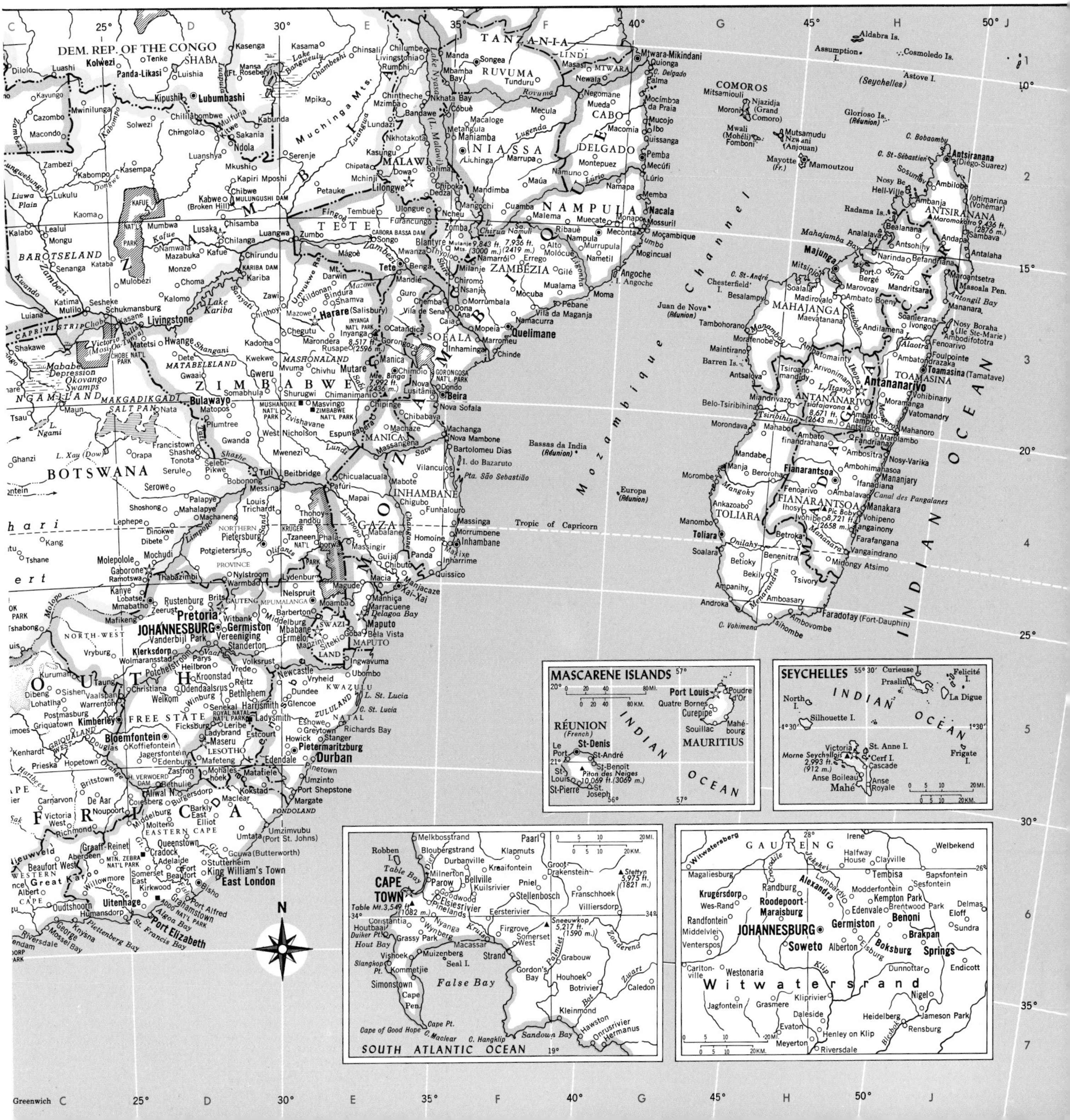

DEM. REP. OF THE CONGO
TANZANIA
ZIMBABWE
BOTSWANA
MOZAMBIQUE
Mozambique Channel
INDIAN OCEAN
Tropic of Capricorn
MASCARENE ISLANDS
RÉUNION (French)
MAURITIUS
SEYCHELLES
CAPE TOWN
SOUTH ATLANTIC OCEAN
JOHANNESBURG
Witwatersrand
Greenwich

South America
AZIMUTHAL EQUAL-AREA PROJECTION
MILES
0 100 200 400 600
KILOMETERS
0 100 200 400 600
Capitals of Countries
Other Capitals
International Boundaries
Canals
© Copyright HAMMOND INCORPORATED, Maplewood, N. J.
Longitude West 50° of Greenwich
CARIBBEAN SEA
ATLANTIC OCEAN
PACIFIC OCEAN
Equator
Tropic of Capricorn
WEST INDIES
NETHERLANDS ANTILLES
ST. VINCENT AND THE GRENADINES
BARBADOS
GRENADA
TRINIDAD & TOBAGO
PANAMA
COLOMBIA
VENEZUELA
GUYANA
SURINAME
FRENCH GUIANA
ECUADOR
PERU
BRAZIL
BOLIVIA
PARAGUAY
CHILE
ARGENTINA
URUGUAY
FALKLAND ISLANDS (U.K.)
Guiana Highlands
Planalto de Mato Grosso
Brazilian Highlands
Gran Chaco
Selvas
Caatingas
Atacama Desert
Patagonia
Pampas
Andes
Amazon
Bogotá
Caracas
Quito
Lima
La Paz
Sucre
Asunción
Santiago
Buenos Aires
Montevideo
Brasília
Rio de Janeiro
São Paulo
Georgetown
Paramaribo
Cayenne
Stanley
Cape Horn
Tierra del Fuego
Strait of Magellan

AREA 6,875,000 sq. mi. (17,806,250 sq. km.)
POPULATION 297,000,000
LARGEST CITY São Paulo
HIGHEST POINT Cerro Aconcagua 22,831 ft. (6,959 m.)
LOWEST POINT Salina Grande -131 ft. (-40 m.)

Population Distribution

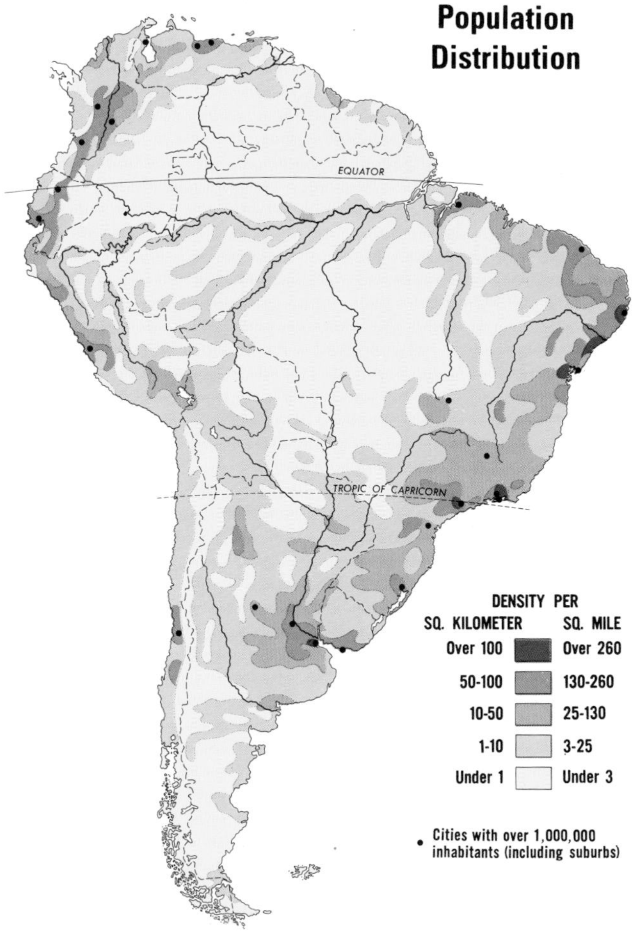
EQUATOR
TROPIC OF CAPRICORN
DENSITY PER
SQ. KILOMETER
SQ. MILE
Over 100
Over 260
50-100
130-260
10-50
25-130
1-10
3-25
Under 1
Under 3
Cities with over 1,000,000 inhabitants (including suburbs)

Vegetation

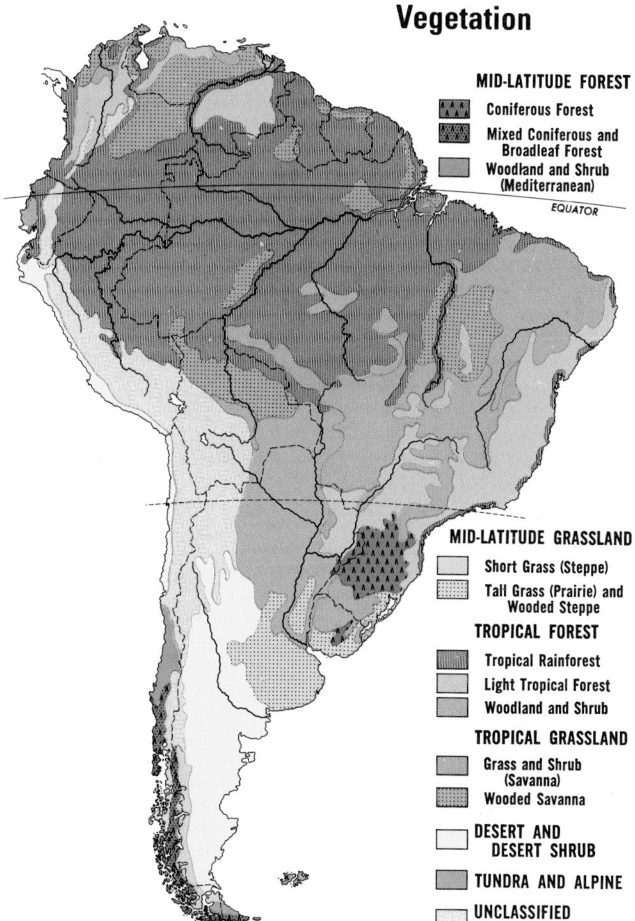
EQUATOR
MID-LATITUDE FOREST
Coniferous Forest
Mixed Coniferous and Broadleaf Forest
Woodland and Shrub (Mediterranean)
MID-LATITUDE GRASSLAND
Short Grass (Steppe)
Tall Grass (Prairie) and Wooded Steppe
TROPICAL FOREST
Tropical Rainforest
Light Tropical Forest
Woodland and Shrub
TROPICAL GRASSLAND
Grass and Shrub (Savanna)
Wooded Savanna
DESERT AND DESERT SHRUB
TUNDRA AND ALPINE
UNCLASSIFIED HIGHLANDS

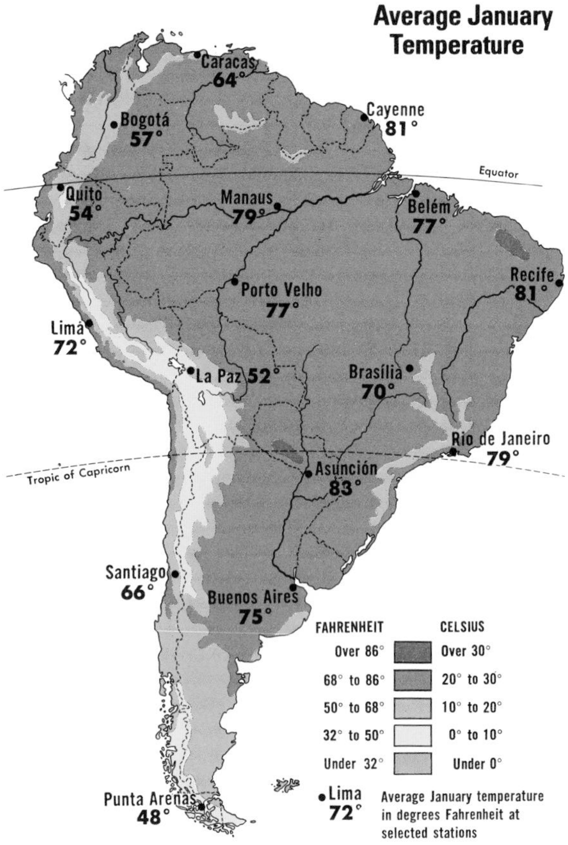
Average January Temperature
Caracas 64°
Bogotá 57°
Cayenne 81°
Equator
Quito 54°
Manaus 79°
Belém 77°
Porto Velho 77°
Recife 81°
Lima 72°
La Paz 52°
Brasília 70°
Rio de Janeiro 79°
Tropic of Capricorn
Asunción 83°
Santiago 66°
Buenos Aires 75°
FAHRENHEIT
CELSIUS
Over 86°
Over 30°
68° to 86°
20° to 30°
50° to 68°
10° to 20°
32° to 50°
0° to 10°
Under 32°
Under 0°
Punta Arenas 48°
Lima 72°
Average January temperature in degrees Fahrenheit at selected stations

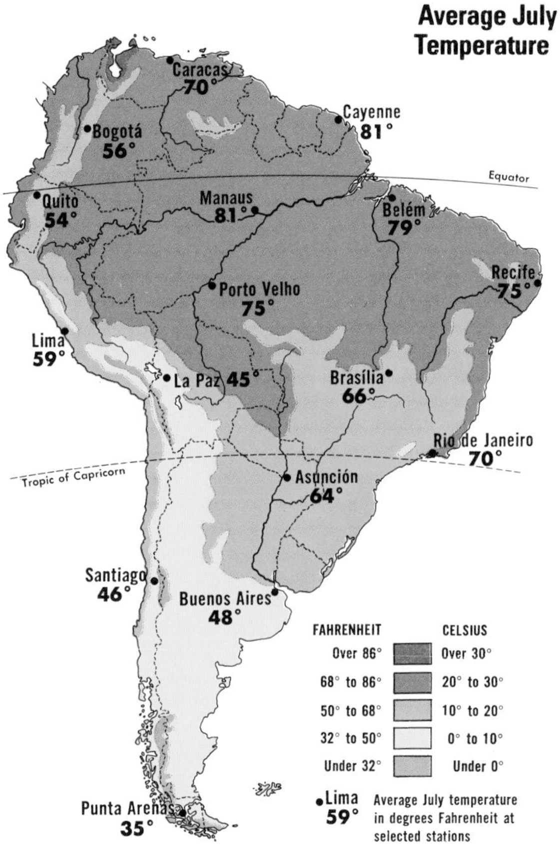
Average July Temperature
Caracas 70°
Bogotá 56°
Cayenne 81°
Equator
Quito 54°
Manaus 81°
Belém 79°
Porto Velho 75°
Recife 75°
Lima 59°
La Paz 45°
Brasília 66°
Rio de Janeiro 70°
Tropic of Capricorn
Asunción 64°
Santiago 46°
Buenos Aires 48°
FAHRENHEIT
CELSIUS
Over 86°
Over 30°
68° to 86°
20° to 30°
50° to 68°
10° to 20°
32° to 50°
0° to 10°
Under 32°
Under 0°
Punta Arenas 35°
Lima 59°
Average July temperature in degrees Fahrenheit at selected stations

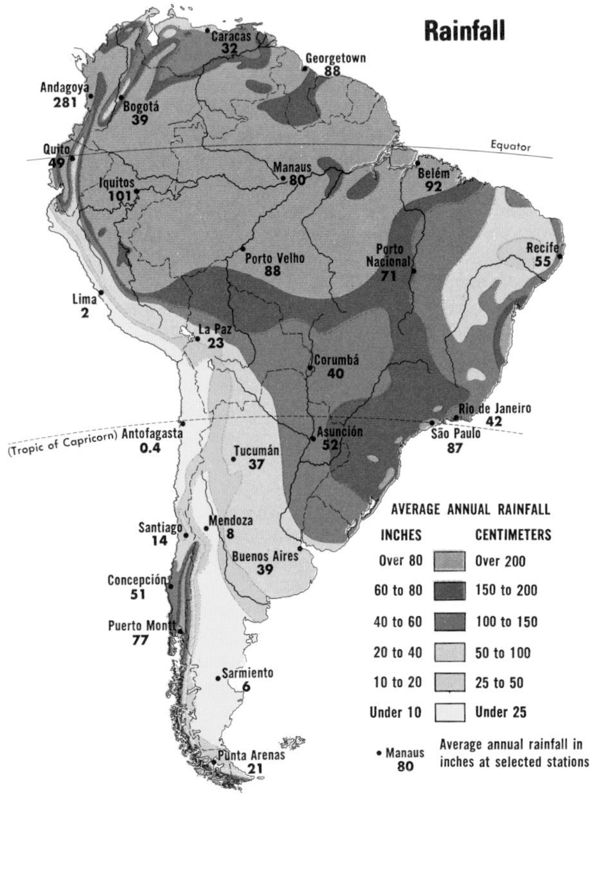
Rainfall
Caracas 32
Georgetown 88
Andagoya 281
Bogotá 39
Equator
Quito 49
Manaus 80
Belém 92
Iquitos 101
Porto Velho 88
Porto Nacional 71
Recife 55
Lima 2
La Paz 23
Corumbá 40
Rio de Janeiro 42
(Tropic of Capricorn) Antofagasta 0.4
Asunción 52
São Paulo 87
Tucumán 37
AVERAGE ANNUAL RAINFALL
Santiago 14
Mendoza 8
INCHES
CENTIMETERS
Buenos Aires 39
Over 80
Over 200
Concepción 51
60 to 80
150 to 200
Puerto Montt 77
40 to 60
100 to 150
20 to 40
50 to 100
Sarmiento 6
10 to 20
25 to 50
Under 10
Under 25
Punta Arenas 21
Manaus 80
Average annual rainfall in inches at selected stations

Vegetation/Relief

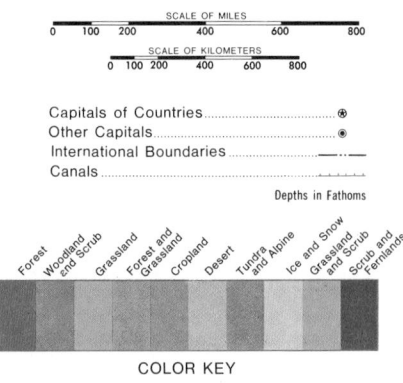

SCALE OF MILES
0 100 200 400 600 800

SCALE OF KILOMETERS
0 100 200 400 600 800

Capitals of Countries .... ⊛
Other Capitals .... ◉
International Boundaries ....
Canals ....

Depths in Fathoms

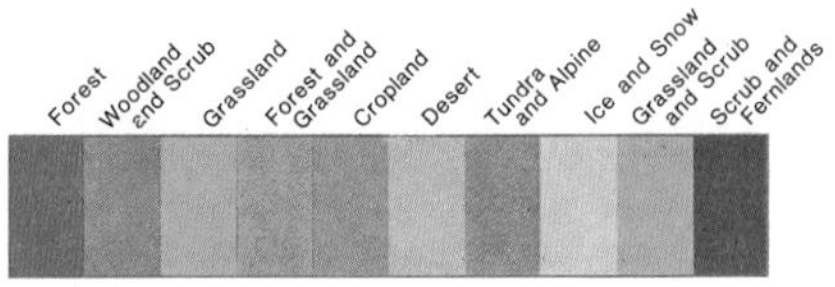
Forest
Woodland and Scrub
Grassland
Forest and Grassland
Cropland
Desert
Tundra and Alpine
Ice and Snow
Grassland and Scrub
Scrub and Fernlands

COLOR KEY

CARIBBEAN SEA
G. of Venezuela
Pta. Gallinas
ARUBA (Neth.)
NETH. ANTILLES
Curaçao
Bonaire
Willemstad
GRENADA
BARBADOS
West Indies
Tobago
TRINIDAD & TOBAGO
Port of Spain
Trinidad
Barranquilla
Maracaibo
Panamá Canal
Caracas
Ciudad Guayana
Orinoco
Guri Res.
VENEZUELA
PANAMÁ
G. of Panamá
Medellín
Magdalena
Cauca
Meta
Arauca
Bogotá
COLOMBIA
Guiana Highlands
Georgetown
GUYANA
Paramaribo
Cayenne
SURINAME
FRENCH GUIANA
Pico Phelps / Pico da Neblina 9,889 ft. (3014 m.)
Vaupés
Negro
Japurá
Putumayo
Quito
Chimborazo 20,561 ft. (6267 m.)
ECUADOR
Guayaquil
Gulf of Guayaquil
Pta. Aguja
Iquitos
Amazon
Içá
Manaus
Yavari
Juruá
Purus
Madeira
Tapajós
Xingu
Tocantins
Selvas
Equator
B. de Marajó
I. de Marajó
Belém
São Luís
Fortaleza
Teresina
Cabo de São Roque
Natal
Recife
Maceió
Caatingas
Parnaíba
Trujillo
Huascarán 22,205 ft. (6768 m.)
Ucayali
Callao
Lima
Cusco
PERU
BRAZIL
Guaporé
Mamoré
Beni
BOLIVIA
Lake Titicaca
Ancohuma 21,489 ft. (6550 m.)
La Paz
Cochabamba
Sucre
Lake Poopó
Arica
Planalto de Mato Grosso
Brasília
Goiânia
Brazilian Highlands
Araguaia
São Francisco
Jequitinhonha
Salvador
Belo Horizonte
Pico da Bandeira 9,482 ft. (2890 m.)
Campo Grande
Chaco
Paraguai
Paraná
Grande
PARAGUAY
Tietê
Paraíba
C. de São Tomé
C. Frio
Tropic of Capricorn
Antofagasta
Volcán Llullaillaco 22,057 ft. (6723 m.)
Pilcomayo
Bermejo
Asunción
ITAIPU DAM
São Paulo
Santos
Rio de Janeiro
Curitiba
Iguaçu Falls
Iguaçu
Serra do Mar
I. de Santa Catarina
I. de San Félix (Chile)
I. San Ambrosio (Chile)
CHILE
Salado del Norte
Uruguay
Córdoba
Porto Alegre
Lagoa dos Patos
Santa Fe
Rosario
Negro
URUGUAY
Lagoa Mirim
Cerro Aconcagua 22,831 ft. (6959 m.)
Valparaíso
Santiago
Mendoza
I. Robinson Crusoe
I. Alejandro Selkirk
Juan Fernandez Is. (Chile)
Salado
Buenos Aires
La Plata
Montevideo
Río de la Plata
C. San Antonio
Pampas
Concepción
Colorado
Bahía Blanca
ARGENTINA
PATAGONIA
Puerto Montt
Golfo San Matías
Pen. Valdés
Isla de Chiloé
Chubut
Archipiélago de los Chonos
Golfo San Jorge
C. Tres Puntas
Pen. Taitao
Deseado
G. de Penas
Bahía Grande
Falkland Islands (U.K.)
Stanley
Archipiélago Reina Adelaida
Str. of Magellan
Tierra del Fuego
Punta Arenas
Cape Horn
PACIFIC OCEAN
ATLANTIC OCEAN
Longitude West of Greenwich

STATES

Amazonas (terr.) 21,696 .... E5
Anzoátegui 683,717 .... F3
Apure 188,717 .... D4
Aragua 891,623 .... E3
Barinas 326,166 .... D3
Bolívar 668,340 .... F4
Carabobo 1,062,268 .... D2
Cojedes 133,991 .... D3
Delta Amacuro (terr.) 48,139 .. H3
Dependencias Federales (terr.) 463 .... E2
Distrito Federal 1,860,637 .... E2
Falcón 503,896 .... D2
Guárico 393,467 .... E3
Lara 945,064 .... C2
Mérida 459,361 .... C3
Miranda 1,421,442 .... E2
Monagas 388,536 .... G3
Nueva Esparta 197,198 .... G2
Portuguesa 424,984 .... D3
Sucre 585,698 .... G2
Táchira 660,234 .... C4
Trujillo 433,735 .... C3
Yaracuy 300,597 .... D2
Zulia 1,674,252 .... B2

CITIES and TOWNS

Acarigua 56,743 .... D3
Achaguas 4,633 .... D4
Aguada Grande 2,901 .... D2
Agua Fría D2
Agua Linda E5
Altagracia 11,116 .... C2
Altagracia de Orituco 18,717 ... E3
Amuay C2
Anaco 29,487 .... F3
Aparurén G5
Apurito 740 .... D4
Arabopó H5
Aragua de Barcelona 9,107 ..... F3
Aragua de Maturín 4,051 .... G3
Araure 22,466 .... D3
Aroa 5,418 .... D2
Bachaquero C3
Barbacoas 2,513 .... E3
Barcelona 78,201 .... F2
Barinas 56,329 .... C3
Barinitas 9,644 .... C3
Barquisimeto 330,815 .... D2
Barrancas, Barinas 4,489 .... C3
Barrancas, Monagas 5,738 ..... G3
Betijoque 5,851 .... C3
Biruaca 2,266 .... E4
Biscucuy 6,114 .... D3
Bobures 2,468 .... C3
Boca de Aroa 2,756 .... D2
Boca del Mangle D2
Boconó 15,915 .... C3
Borbón F4
Buena Vista, Anzoátegui F3
Buena Vista, Apure D4
Cabimas 118,037 .... C2
Cabruta 1,927 .... E4
Cabudare 14,593 .... D3
Cachipo G3
Cacuri F5
Cagua 29,601 .... E2
Caicara 6,092 .... G3
Caicara de Orinoco 6,867 .... E4
Calabozo 37,282 .... E3
Camaguán 4,143 .... E3
Camatagua 3,335 .... E3
Candelaria F4
Cantaura 15,839 .... F3
Capatárida 1,375 .... C2
Carabobo, Bolívar H4
Carabobo, Carabobo D3
Caracas (cap.) 1,035,499 .... E2
Carache 3,966 .... C3
Cariaco 6,549 .... G2
Caribén E4
Caripe 4,729 .... G2
Caripito 19,053 .... G2
Carirubana 15,701 .... C2
Carmelo 2,556 .... C2
Carora 36,115 .... C2
Carrasquero 2,193 .... B2
Casanay 4,985 .... G2
Casigua 3,665 .... B3
Cáua 9,953 .... E2
Caucagua 6,218 .... E2
Chaguaramas 2,748 .... E3
Chichiriviche 3,236 .... D2
Chivacoa 19,210 .... D2
Churuguara 6,636 .... D2
Ciudad Bolívar 103,728 .... G3
Ciudad Bolivia 4,864 .... C3
Ciudad Guayana 143,540 .... G3
Ciudad Ojeda 83,083 .... C2
Ciudad Piar 3,965 .... G4
Clarines 2,099 .... F3
Cojoro C2
Colón E6
Comunidad E6
Coporito H3
Coro 68,701 .... D2
Corozo Pando E3
Cuchivero F4
Cumanacoa 9,179 .... F2
Curiapo H3
Dabajuro 4,515 .... C2
Democracia E6
Ejido 11,170 .... C3
El Almacén G4
El Amparo de Apure 2,015 ...... C4
El Callao 4,270 .... G4
El Chaparro 3,768 .... F3
El Cristo G4
Elorza 3,184 .... D4
El Palmar 2,758 .... G4
El Pao 1,259 .... G3
El Perú H4
El Pilar 3,278 .... G2
El Roque E2
El Socorro F3
El Sombrero 8,373 .... E3
El Tigre 49,801 .... F3
El Tocuyo 19,351 .... C3
El Toro H3
El Vigía 20,970 .... C3
El Vínculo D1
Encontrados 5,607 .... B3
Esperanza E6
Garcitas C3
Guacara 35,111 .... D2
Guaina G5
Guana G5
Guanare 34,148 .... D3
Guanarito 3,150 .... D3
Guanoco G2
Guanta 9,017 .... F2
Guarero B2
Guarico 3,259 .... D3
Guasdualito 7,793 .... C4
Guasimal 582 .... D4
Guasipati 4,807 .... H4
Guayabal E6
Güiria 13,905 .... G2
Guri G4
Guzmán Blanco E6
Higuerote 5,008 .... F2
Icabarú H5
Independencia 4,897 .... B4
Irapa 4,470 .... G2
Juangriego 6,062 .... G2
Judibana C2
Jusepín G3
Kavanayen H5
La Aduana D3
La Canoa G3
La Ceiba C4
La Concepcíon B2
La Concepcíon 13,885 .... C2
La Esmeralda F6
La Esperanza H3
La Fría 8,134 .... B3
La Grita 9,954 .... C3
La Guaira 20,344 .... E2
Lagunetas C3
Laguniilas C2
La Horqueta G3
La Inglesa G3

Venezuela
MERCATOR PROJECTION
SCALE OF MILES
0 25 50 75 100 125
KILOMETERS
0 25 50 75 100 200
Capitals of Countries
State Capitals
International Boundaries
State Boundaries
Canals
C A R I B B E A N S E A
NETHERLANDS ANTILLES
GULF OF VENEZUELA
LAKE MARACAIBO
DEPENDENCIAS FEDERALES
NUEVA ESPARTA
CARACAS
C O L O M B I A
B R A Z I L
Longitude 68° West of Greenwich

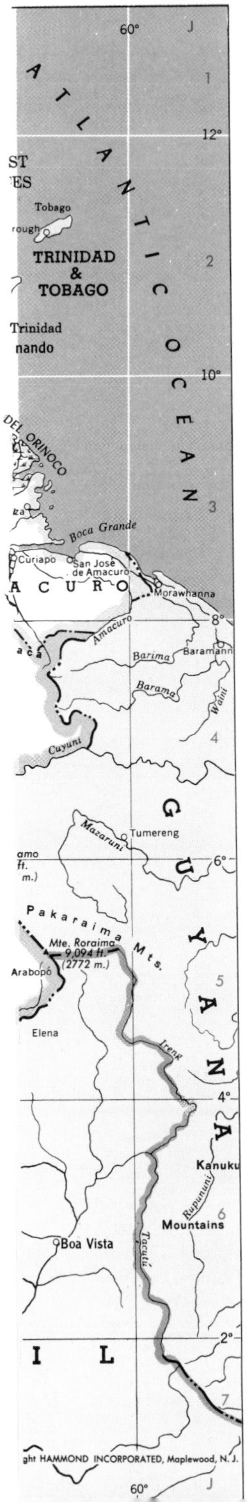

AREA 352,143 sq. mi. (912,050 sq. km.)
POPULATION 19,246,000
CAPITAL Caracas
LARGEST CITY Caracas
HIGHEST POINT Pico Bolívar 16,427 ft. (5,007 m.)
MONETARY UNIT Bolívar
MAJOR LANGUAGE Spanish
MAJOR RELIGION Roman Catholicism

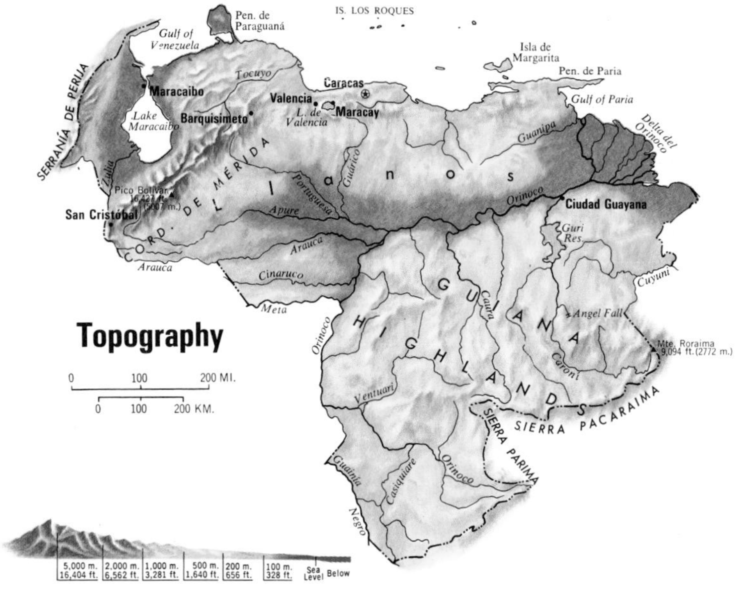

Pen. de Paraguaná
IS. LOS ROQUES
Gulf of Venezuela
Isla de Margarita
Pen. de Paria
Gulf of Paria
Delta del Orinoco
Tocuyo
Caracas
Maracaibo
Valencia
L. de Valencia
Maracay
Barquisimeto
Lake Maracaibo
SERRANÍA DE PERIJÁ
CORD. DE MÉRIDA
Pico Bolívar
San Cristóbal
Llanos
Apure
Portuguesa
Guárico
Guanipa
Orinoco
Ciudad Guayana
Guri Res.
Arauca
Cinaruco
Meta
Cuyuni
Angel Fall
Mte. Roraima 9,094 ft. (2772 m.)
GUIANA HIGHLANDS
Caroní
Caura
Ventuari
SIERRA PACARAIMA
SIERRA PARIMA
Orinoco
Casiquiare
Guainía
Negro
5,000 m. 16,404 ft.
2,000 m. 6,562 ft.
1,000 m. 3,281 ft.
500 m. 1,640 ft.
200 m. 656 ft.
100 m. 328 ft.
Sea Level
Below

Topography

0 100 200 MI.
0 100 200 KM.

OTHER FEATURES

Agriculture, Industry and Resources

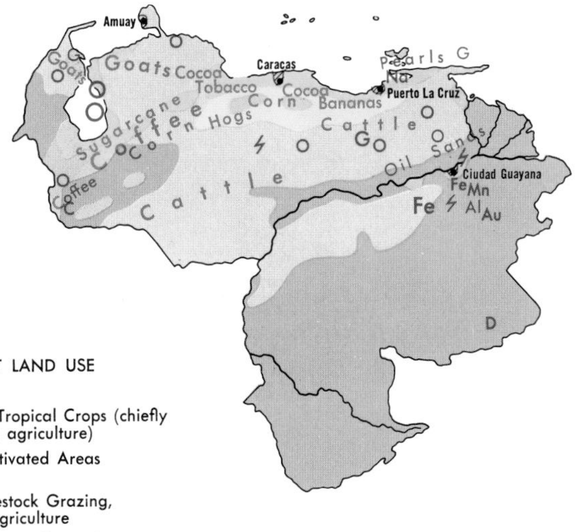

Amuay
Caracas
Pearls
Puerto La Cruz
Goats
Cocoa
Tobacco
Corn
Bananas
Sugarcane
Coffee
Hogs
Cattle
Oil Sands
Ciudad Guayana

MAJOR MINERAL OCCURRENCES

- Al Bauxite
- Au Gold
- C Coal
- D Diamonds
- Fe Iron Ore
- G Natural Gas
- Mn Manganese
- Na Salt
- O Petroleum
- Water Power
- Major Industrial Areas

DOMINANT LAND USE

- Diversified Tropical Crops (chiefly plantation agriculture)
- Upland Cultivated Areas
- Upland Livestock Grazing, Limited Agriculture
- Extensive Livestock Ranching
- Forests

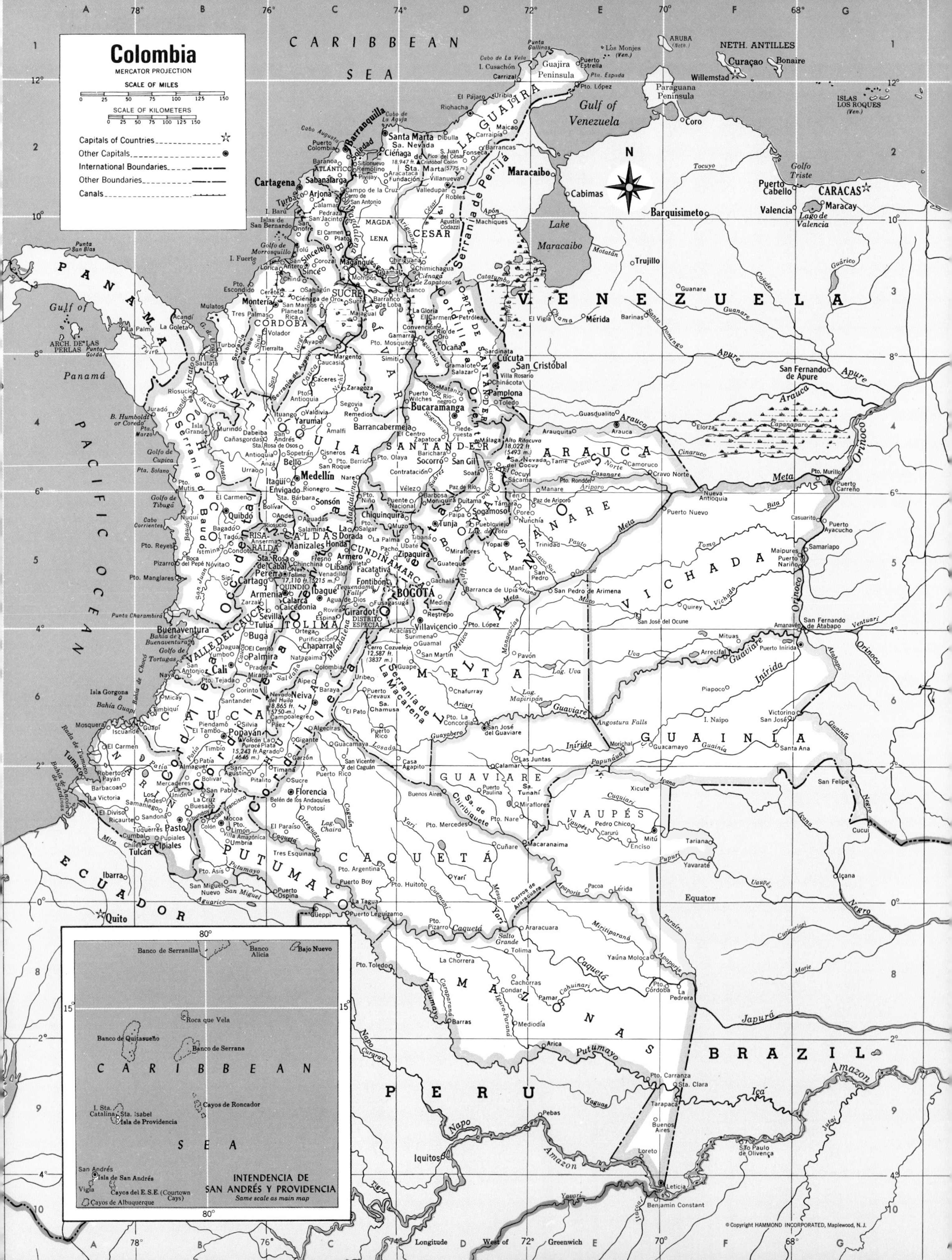
Colombia
MERCATOR PROJECTION
SCALE OF MILES
0 25 50 75 100 125 150
SCALE OF KILOMETERS
0 25 50 75 100 125 150
Capitals of Countries
Other Capitals
International Boundaries
Other Boundaries
Canals
CARIBBEAN
SEA
PACIFIC OCEAN
PANAMA
Panamá
Gulf of Panamá
ARCH. DE LAS PERLAS
VENEZUELA
ECUADOR
PERU
BRAZIL
NETH. ANTILLES
ARUBA (Neth.)
Curaçao
Bonaire
Willemstad
Los Monjes (Ven.)
ISLAS LOS ROQUES (Ven.)
Guajira Peninsula
Paraguana Peninsula
Gulf of Venezuela
Lake Maracaibo
Maracaibo
Cabimas
Coro
Barquisimeto
Valencia
Maracay
Lago de Valencia
CARACAS
Puerto Cabello
Golfo Triste
Trujillo
Mérida
Barinas
San Cristóbal
San Fernando de Apure
Puerto Ayacucho
Samariapo
San Fernando de Atabapo
Guasdualito
Elorza
Capanaparo
Arauca
Apure
Meta
Orinoco
Guaviare
Inírida
Vaupés
Caquetá
Putumayo
Amazon
Napo
Japurá
Negro
Içá
Equator
LA GUAJIRA
CESAR
MAGDALENA
ATLÁNTICO
BOLÍVAR
SUCRE
CÓRDOBA
ANTIOQUIA
CHOCÓ
CALDAS
RISARALDA
QUINDÍO
SANTANDER
NORTE DE SANTANDER
BOYACÁ
CUNDINAMARCA
DISTRITO ESPECIAL
TOLIMA
VALLE DEL CAUCA
CAUCA
HUILA
NARIÑO
PUTUMAYO
CAQUETÁ
META
ARAUCA
CASANARE
VICHADA
GUAINÍA
GUAVIARE
VAUPÉS
AMAZONAS
Cordillera Occidental
Cordillera Central
Cordillera Oriental
Serranía de Perijá
Serranía de Baudó
Serranía de la Macarena
Sa. Nevada de Santa Marta
Cristóbal Colón 18,947 ft. (5775 m.)
Alto Ritacuva 18,022 ft. (5493 m.)
Nevado del Huila 18,865 ft. (5750 m.)
Nevado del Tolima 17,110 ft. (5215 m.)
Volcán Puracé 15,243 ft. (4646 m.)
Cerro Cazuceleja 12,587 ft. (3837 m.)
Riohacha
Santa Marta
Barranquilla
Cartagena
Sincelejo
Montería
Valledupar
Cúcuta
Pamplona
Bucaramanga
Barrancabermeja
Medellín
Quibdó
Manizales
Pereira
Armenia
Ibagué
Tunja
BOGOTÁ
Villavicencio
Girardot
Neiva
Cali
Buenaventura
Palmira
Popayán
Pasto
Tumaco
Ipiales
Tulcán
Quito
Mocoa
Florencia
Yopal
Arauca
Puerto Carreño
Puerto Inírida
Mitú
San José del Guaviare
La Pedrera
Leticia
Tarapacá
Iquitos
Pebas
Benjamin Constant
São Paulo de Olivença
Puerto Leguízamo
Puerto Asís
Araracuara
La Chorrera
Longitude West of Greenwich
80°
Banco de Serranilla
Banco Alicia
Bajo Nuevo
Roca que Vela
Banco de Quitasueño
Banco de Serrana
CARIBBEAN
SEA
I. Sta. Catalina
Sta. Isabel
Isla de Providencia
Cayos de Roncador
San Andrés
Isla de San Andrés
Vigia
Cayos del E.S.E. (Courtown Cays)
Cayos de Albuquerque
INTENDENCIA DE SAN ANDRÉS Y PROVIDENCIA
Same scale as main map

INTERNAL DIVISIONS

Amazonas (comm.) 6,825......D8
Antioquia (dept.) 3,888,067...B4
Arauca (inten.) 19,884...........E4
Atlántico (dept.) 958,560.......C2
Bolívar (dept.) 802,407..........C3
Boyacá (dept.) 1,084,766.......D5
Caldas (dept.) 700,954...........C5
Caquetá (inten.) 57,103.........C7
Casanare (inten.)....................E5
Cauca (dept.) 603,894...........B6
Cesar (dept.) 339,843............D3
Chocó (dept.) 201,915...........B4
Córdoba (dept.) 645,478........C3
Cundinamarca
(dept.) 1,106,626...............C5
Distrito Especial 2,855,065....C5
Guainía (comm.) 1,792...........F6
Huila (dept.) 469,834.............C6
La Guajira (dept.) 180,520.....D2
Magdalena (dept.) 536,122....C3
Meta (dept.) 245,176.............D6
Nariño (dept.) 807,112...........B7
Norte de Santander
(dept.) 693,298..................D3
Putumayo (inten.) 22,916......C7
Quindío (dept.) 321,677.........C5
Risaralda (dept.) 452,626......B5
San Andrés y Providencia
(inten.) 22,719..................B1
Santander (dept.) 1,130,977..D4
Sucre (dept.) 354,412............C3
Tolima (dept.) 903,520..........C5
Valle del Cauca
(dept.) 2,204,722...............B6
Vaupés (comm.) 6,923...........E7
Vichada (comm.) 2,172..........F5

CITIES and TOWNS

Acacías 9,238........................D6
Acandí 2,358..........................B3
Agrado 2,771..........................C6
Aguachica 16,771...................D3
Aguadas 9,995........................C5
Agua de Dios 9,689................C5
Agustín Codazzi 28,194.........D3
Aipe 3,794.............................C6
Algeciras 5,022......................C6
Amalfi 6,494..........................C4
Andes 14,957.........................C5
Anserma 15,559.....................B5
Antioquia 6,841......................B4
Aracataca 7,511.....................D2
Arauca 7,613.........................E4
Arjona 29,465........................C2
Armenia 180,221....................B5
Armero 19,567.......................C5
Ayapel 7,475..........................C3
Baranoa 27,394......................C2
Baraya 2,581..........................C6
Barbacoas 4,653.....................A7
Barbosa 7,960........................D5
Barichara 2,548......................D4
Barrancabermeja 137,406......C4
Barrancas 2,979.....................D2
Barranco de Loba 2,215.........C3
Barranquilla 896,649..............C2
Belén de los Andaquíes 2,190 C7
Bello 206,297.........................C4
Bogotá (cap.) 3,974,813........D5
Bolívar 13,259.......................C5
Bucaramanga 341,513...........D4
Buenaventura 160,342...........B6
Buesaco 2,763.......................B7
Buga 82,992..........................B6
Cáceres 7,154........................C4
Caicedonia 21,959.................C5
Calamar 5,867.......................C2
Calarcá 29,349.......................C5
Cali 1,323,944........................B6
Campo de la Cruz 13,137.......C2
Campoalegre 11,799..............C6
Cañasgordas 3,900................B4
Cartagena 491,368.................C2
Cartago 92,524......................B5
Caucasia 24,138.....................C4
Cereté 25,890........................C3
Cerro de San Antonio 3,394...C2
Chaparral 14,546...................C6
Chimichaqua 6,382................D3
Chinácota 4,478....................D4
Chinchiná 33,441...................C5
Chinú 10,023.........................C3
Chiquinquirá 21,727...............C5
Chiriguaná 6,611...................D3
Ciénaga 56,860......................C2
Ciénaga de Oro 10,607..........C3
Cisneros 7,226......................C4
Colombia 2,903.....................C6
Condoto 4,798.......................B5
Contratación 3,057................D4
Convención 7,545..................D3
Corinto 6,933........................B6
Corozal 29,471......................C3
Cúcuta 357,026......................D4
Cumbal 2,891........................B7
Dabeiba 7,600.......................B4
Dagua 5,392..........................B6
Duitama 56,390.....................D5
El Banco 20,756....................D3
El Carmen 2,362....................D3
El Carmen de Bolívar 30,778..C3
El Cerrito 23,575...................B6
El Cocuy 2,740......................D4
El Tambo 2,179......................B6
Envigado 85,539....................C4
Espinal 37,563......................C5
Facatativá 44,331..................C5
Florencia 66,430....................C7
Fonseca 9,988.......................D2
Fontibón................................C5
Fresno 8,141.........................C5
Fundación 29,002..................C2
Fusagasugá 41,033................C5
Gamarra 5,071......................D3
Garzón 13,783.......................C6
Gigante 4,880........................C6
Girardot 66,385.....................C5
Gramalote 2,880....................D4
Guamal, Meta 2,854..............D6
Guamal, Magdalena 4,986......C3
Guapí 5,005..........................B6
Guateque 6,032.....................D5
Honda 25,040........................C5
Ibagué 269,495.....................C5
Ipiales 45,419.......................B7
Istmina 5,575........................B5
Itagüí 135,797.......................C4
Ituango 5,561........................C4
La Cruz 4,353........................B7
La Dorada 48,572..................C5
La Gloria 2,632......................D3
La Palma 5,430......................C5
La Plata 8,047.......................C6
La Unión 5,392......................B7
Líbano 23,703........................C5
Lorica 24,264........................C3
Magangué 49,160...................C3
Maicao 46,033.......................D2
Majagual 2,329......................C3
Málaga 10,645.......................D4
Manizales 275,067.................C5
Medellín 1,418,554.................C4
Mercaderes 3,877..................B7
Miraflores 3,584....................D5
Miranda 6,439.......................B6
Mitú 1,637.............................E7
Mocoa 6,221.........................B7
Mompós 14,076.....................C3
Moniquirá 5,711....................D5
Montería 157,466...................B3
Natagaima 7,772....................C6
Neiva 178,130........................C6
Ocaña 51,443........................D3
Ortega 5,150.........................C6
Pacho 6,786..........................C5
Páez 2,098............................C6
Paipa 4,260...........................D5
Palmira 175,186.....................B6
Pamplona 34,213...................D4
Pasto 197,407.......................B7
Patía 5,306............................B6
Paz de Ariporo 2,584.............E5
Paz de Río 3,464...................D4
Pereira 233,271.....................C5
Piedecuesta 34,646...............D4
Piendamó 5,046.....................B6
Pitalito 27,104.......................B7
Pivijay 10,172........................C2
Planeta Rica 24,238...............C3
Plato 24,895..........................C3
Popayán 141,964....................B6
Pradera 27,152.......................B6
Puente Nacional 4,317...........D5
Puerto Asís 6,364..................B7
Puerto Berrío 21,414..............C4
Puerto Carreño 2,172.............G4
Puerto Colombia 9,255...........C2
Puerto Escondido 1,368.........B3
Puerto Inírida 1,792...............F6
Puerto Leguízamo 3,179.........C8
Puerto López 4,948................D5
Puerto Rico 4,853...................C7
Puerto Rondón 1,010..............E4
Puerto Salgar 6,396................C5
Puerto Tejada 26,573..............B6
Puerto Wilches 5,282.............D4
Pupiales 2,723........................B7
Purificación 8,164...................C6
Quibdó 47,950........................B5
Remedios 4,681......................C4
Remolino 3,408......................C2
Restrepo 2,704.......................D5
Río de Oro 2,985....................D3
Riohacha 46,667....................D2
Rionegro, Antioquia 22,654....C4
Rionegro, Santander 3,491.....D4
Riosucio, Caldas 11,619.........C5
Riosucio, Chocó 2,184...........B4
Robles 5,422..........................D2
Rovira 5,105...........................C5
Sabanalarga 35,786................C2
Sahagún 28,686.....................C3
Salamina 12,136.....................C5
Salazar 2,791.........................D4
Samaniego 4,790....................B7
San Agustín 4,532..................B7
San Andrés, Antioquia 2,003..C4
San Andrés, San Andrés y
Providencia 23,325.............A9
San Antero 7,129....................C3
Sandoná 7,222.......................B7
San Gil 24,599........................D4
San Jacinto 13,459.................C3
San José del Guaviare 4,138..D6
San Juan del César 9,468.......D2
San Marcos 26,542.................C3
San Martín 8,281....................D6
San Onofre 7,899...................C3
San Pablo 3,662.....................B7
San Roque 4,972....................C4
San Vicente del Caguán 3,182 C6
Santa Bárbara 11,848............C5
Santa Marta 177,922..............D2
Santa Rosa de Cabal 37,112...C5
Santa Rosa de Osos 8,593.....C4
Santander 22,644...................B6
Sardinata 3,726.....................D3
Segovia 10,000......................C4
Sevilla 31,309........................C5
Sibundoy-Las Casas 2,853.....B7
Silvia 3,045............................B6
Simití 3,062...........................C4
Sincé 11,909..........................C3
Sincelejo 120,537...................C3
Sitionuevo 5,919....................C2
Soatá 4,294...........................D4
Socorro 15,596......................D4
Sogamoso 64,437..................D5
Soledad 164,494....................C2
Sonsón 15,990......................C5
Sopetrán 5,223......................C4
Tadó 3,102............................B5
Tame 4,811...........................E4
Tibaná 1,100.........................D5
Tierralta 7,950.......................C3
Timaná 4,262.........................C7
Timbío 4,755..........................B6
Timbiquí 1,048......................B6
Toledo 2,942.........................D4
Tolú 9,118.............................C3
Trinidad 729..........................E5
Tuluá 99,721..........................B5
Tumaco 45,456......................A7
Tunjá 87,851.........................D5
Túquerres 12,058...................B7
Turbaco 28,161......................C2
Turbo 25,992.........................B3
Ubaté 7,716...........................D5
Uribia 2,193...........................D2
Urrao 8,577...........................B4
Valdivia 4,318........................C4
Valledupar 142,771................D2
Vélez 8,241............................D4
Venadillo 8,383......................C5
Villa Rosario 8,668................D4
Villanueva 9,836....................D2
Villavicencio 82,869...............D5
Villeta 6,507...........................C5
Yarumal 21,333.....................C4
Yopal 5,851...........................D5
Yumbo 43,508.......................B6
Zapatoca 6,258......................D4
Zaragoza 9,660......................C4
Zarzal 22,014........................B5
Zipaquirá 45,676....................D5

OTHER FEATURES

Aguarico (riv.)......................B7
Aguja, La (cape)....................C2
Alto Ritacuva (mt.)................D4
Amazon (riv.)........................E9
Ancón de Sardinas (bay)........A7
Angostura (falls)....................E6
Apaporis (riv.).......................F8
Arauca (riv.).........................E4
Ariari (riv.)...........................D6
Ariguaní (riv.)........................D3
Ariporo (riv.).........................E4
Atabapo (riv.)........................G6
Atrato (riv.)...........................B4
Baudó, Serranía de (mts.).......B5
Caguán (riv.).........................C7
Cahuinari (riv.)......................E8
Caquetá (riv.)........................E8
Caraparaná (riv.)....................D8
Casanare (riv.).......................E4
Catatumbo (riv.).....................D3
Cauca (riv.)...........................B3
Cazueleja, Cerro (mt.)............C6
César (riv.)............................D2
Central, Cordillera (range).......C5
Charambirá (pt.)....................B5
Chicamocha (riv.)...................D4
Chocó (bay)...........................B6
Corrientes (cape)....................B5
Cristóbal Colón, Pico (peak)...D2
Cuemaní (riv.)........................D7
Cupica (gulf)..........................B4
Cusachón (isl.).......................D1
Espada (pt.)...........................E1
Gallinas (pt.)..........................E1
Grande (isl.)...........................B4
Grande, Salto (falls)................D8
Guainía (riv.)..........................F6
Guajira (pen.).........................E1
Guaviare (riv.)........................F6
Guayabero (riv.).....................D6
Huila, Nevado del (mt.)...........C6
Igara-Paraná (riv.)...................D8
Inírida (riv.)............................F6
Isana (riv.)..............................F7
La Aguja (cape).......................C2
La Macarena, Serranía de
(mts.)..................................D6
Llanos (plain).........................D5
Macarena, Serranía de La
(mts.)..................................D6
Magdalena (riv.).....................C3
Manacacías (riv.)....................D6
Meta (riv.)..............................E5
Metica (riv.)............................D6
Mira (riv.)...............................A7
Miritiparaná (riv.)....................E8
Morrosquillo (gulf)..................C3
Nechí (riv.).............................C4
Negro (riv.).............................G7
Occidental, Cordillera (range).B5
Oriental, Cordillera (range).....D5
Orinoco (riv.)..........................G5
Orteguaza (riv.).......................C7
Papurí (riv.)............................F7
Patía (riv.)..............................B6
Pauto (riv.).............................E5
Perijá, Serranía de (mts.)........D2
Providencia (isl.).....................B9
Puracé (vol.)...........................B6
Putumayo (riv.).......................E9
Quitasueño (bank)...................A8
Roncador (cays)......................B9
Saldaña (riv.)..........................C6
Salto Grande (falls)..................D8
San Andrés (isl.).....................A10
San Jorge (riv.)........................C3
San Juan (riv.).........................B5
Santa Marta, Sierra Nevada de
(range)................................D2
Serrana (bank).........................B9
Serranilla (bank)......................B8
Sinú (riv.)...............................B3
Sogamoso (riv.).......................D4
Suárez (riv.)............................D4
Taraira (riv.)............................F8
Tequendama (falls)..................C5
Tibugá (gulf)...........................B5
Tolima (vol.)...........................C5
Tomo (riv.)..............................F5
Tortugas (gulf).........................B6
Tunahí, Sierra (mts.)................E7
Urabá (gulf)............................B3
Uva (riv.)................................E6
Vaupés (riv.)...........................E7
Vela, La (cape)........................D1
Vichada (riv.)..........................F5
Yarí (riv.)................................D8
Zapatosa, Ciénaga de
(swamp)..............................D3

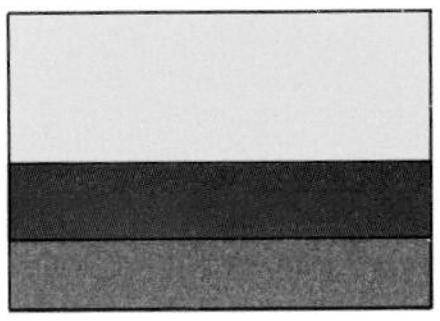

AREA 439,513 sq. mi. (1,138,339 sq. km.)
POPULATION 30,241,000
CAPITAL Bogotá
LARGEST CITY Bogotá
HIGHEST POINT Pico Cristóbal Colón 18,947 ft. (5,775 m.)
MONETARY UNIT Colombian peso
MAJOR LANGUAGE Spanish
MAJOR RELIGION Roman Catholicism

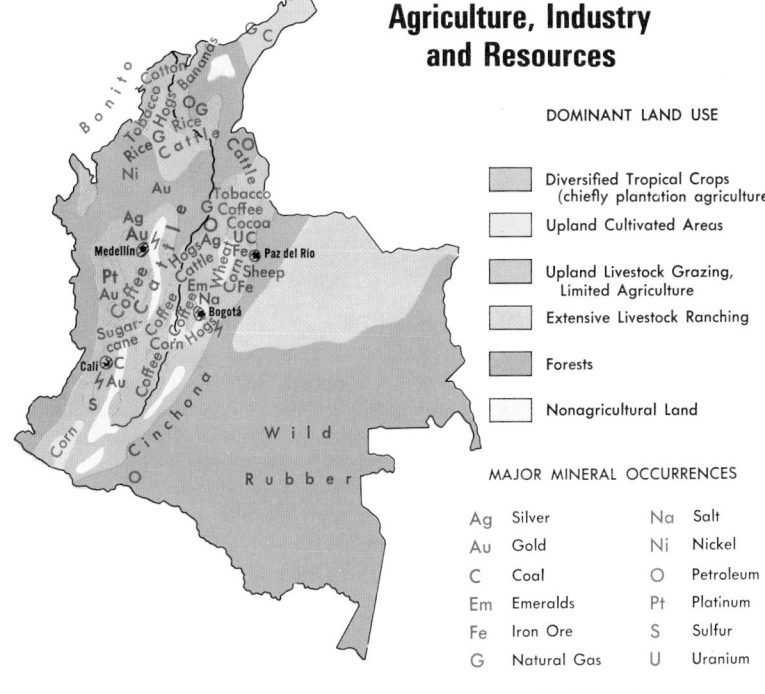

Agriculture, Industry and Resources

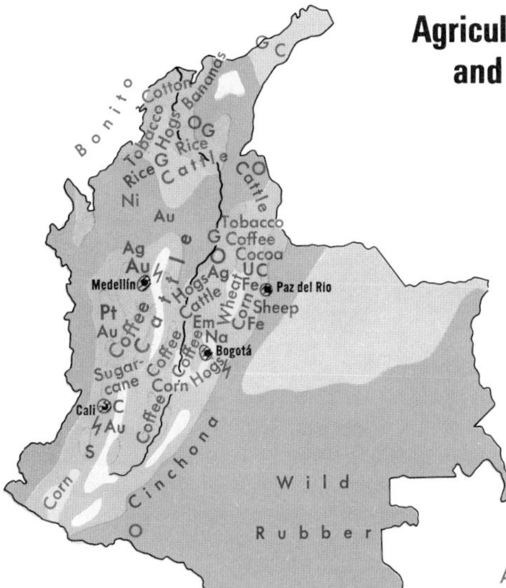
Medellín
Paz del Río
Bogotá
Cali
Wild Rubber
Cinchona

DOMINANT LAND USE

- Diversified Tropical Crops (chiefly plantation agriculture)
- Upland Cultivated Areas
- Upland Livestock Grazing, Limited Agriculture
- Extensive Livestock Ranching
- Forests
- Nonagricultural Land

MAJOR MINERAL OCCURRENCES

Ag	Silver	Na	Salt
Au	Gold	Ni	Nickel
C	Coal	O	Petroleum
Em	Emeralds	Pt	Platinum
Fe	Iron Ore	S	Sulfur
G	Natural Gas	U	Uranium

Water Power
Major Industrial Areas

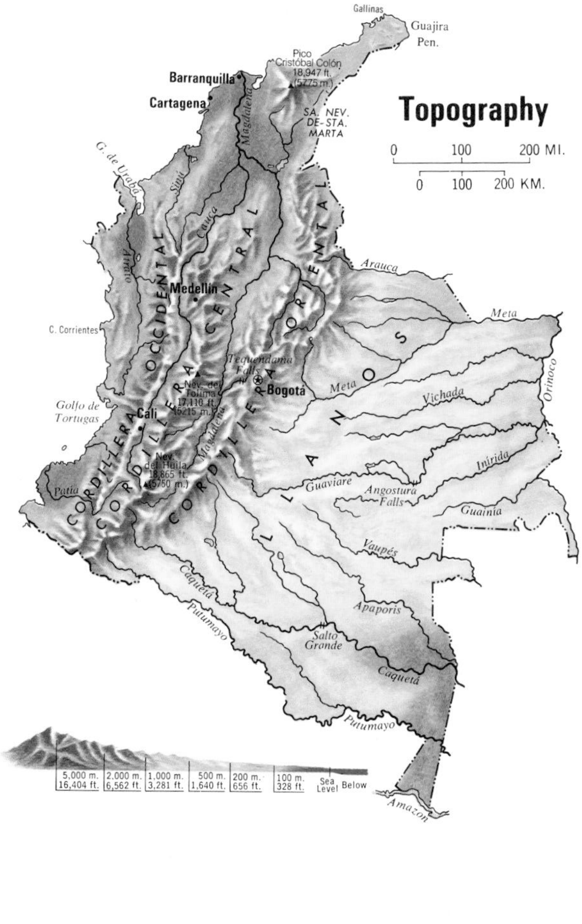
Topography
0 100 200 MI.
0 100 200 KM.
Gallinas
Guajira Pen.
Pico Cristóbal Colón 18,947 ft. (5,775 m.)
Barranquilla
Cartagena
SA. NEV. DE STA. MARTA
G. de Urabá
Medellín
C. Corrientes
Bogotá
Cali
Golfo de Tortugas
Arauca
Meta
Vichada
Orinoco
Guaviare
Angostura Falls
Guainía
Vaupés
Apaporis
Salto Grande
Caquetá
Putumayo
Amazon
5,000 m. 16,404 ft.
2,000 m. 6,562 ft.
1,000 m. 3,281 ft.
500 m. 1,640 ft.
200 m. 656 ft.
100 m. 328 ft.
Sea Level
Below

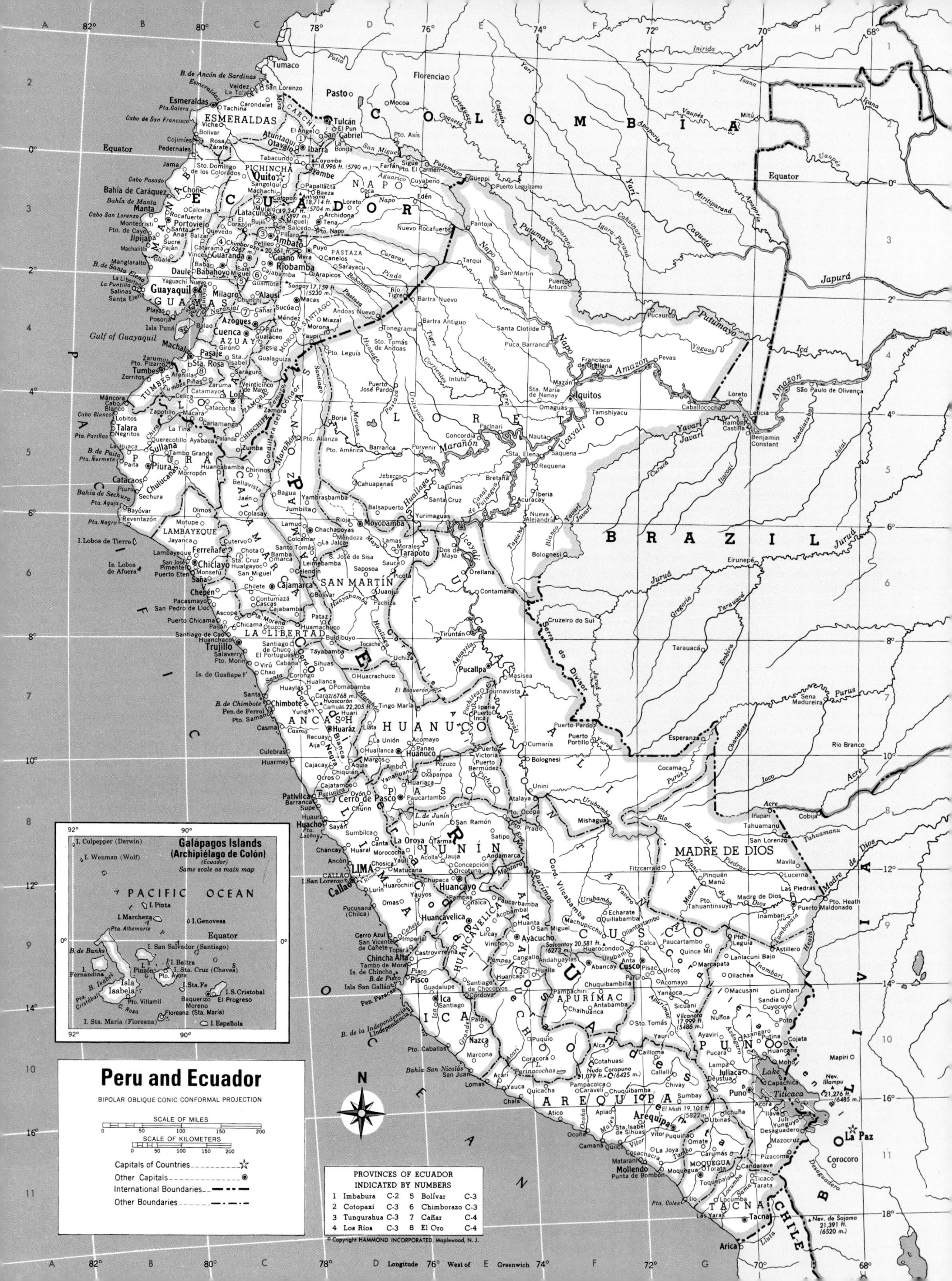
Peru and Ecuador
BIPOLAR OBLIQUE CONIC CONFORMAL PROJECTION
SCALE OF MILES
0 50 100 150 200
SCALE OF KILOMETERS
0 50 100 150 200
Capitals of Countries
Other Capitals
International Boundaries
Other Boundaries
PROVINCES OF ECUADOR INDICATED BY NUMBERS
1 Imbabura C-2
2 Cotopaxi C-3
3 Tungurahua C-3
4 Los Ríos C-3
5 Bolívar C-3
6 Chimborazo C-3
7 Cañar C-4
8 El Oro C-4
© Copyright HAMMOND INCORPORATED, Maplewood, N. J.
Galápagos Islands (Archipiélago de Colón)
(Ecuador)
Same scale as main map
PACIFIC OCEAN
COLOMBIA
ECUADOR
BRAZIL
PERU
BOLIVIA
CHILE
PACIFIC OCEAN
Equator
Longitude West of Greenwich
Quito
LIMA
La Paz
Guayaquil
Iquitos
Cusco
Arequipa
Lake Titicaca
Amazon

PERU

ECUADOR

PERU

AREA 496,222 sq. mi. (1,285,215 sq. km.)
POPULATION 22,332,000
CAPITAL Lima
LARGEST CITY Lima
HIGHEST POINT Huascarán 22,205 ft. (6,768 m.)
MONETARY UNIT inti
MAJOR LANGUAGES Spanish, Quechua, Aymara
MAJOR RELIGION Roman Catholicism

ECUADOR

AREA 109,483 sq. mi. (283,561 sq. km.)
POPULATION 10,490,000
CAPITAL Quito
LARGEST CITY Guayaquil
HIGHEST POINT Chimborazo 20,561 ft. (6,267 m.)
MONETARY UNIT sucre
MAJOR LANGUAGES Spanish, Quechua
MAJOR RELIGION Roman Catholicism

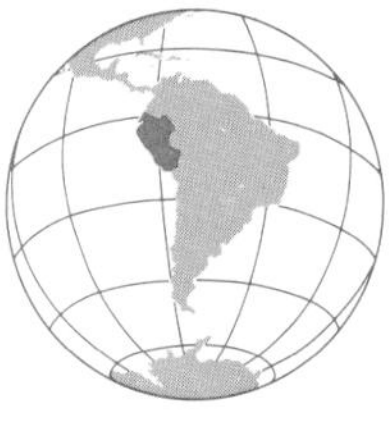

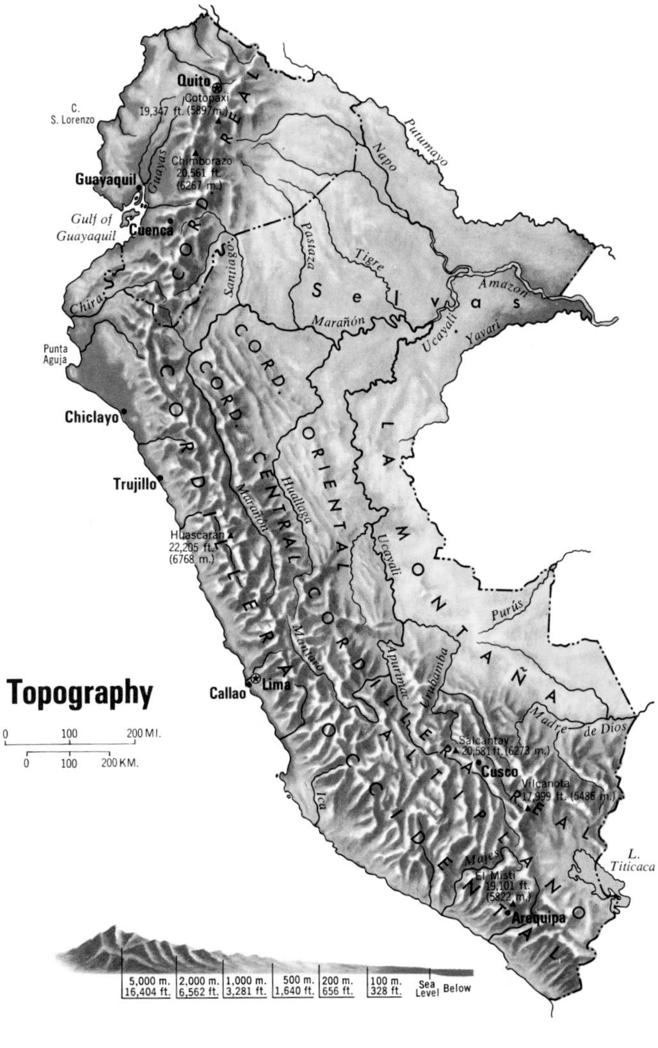
Topography
Quito
Cotopaxi 19,347 ft. (5897 m.)
C. S. Lorenzo
Chimborazo 20,561 ft. (6267 m.)
Guayaquil
Gulf of Guayaquil
Cuenca
Guayas
Putumayo
Napo
Pastaza
Tigre
Santiago
Chira
Marañón
Amazon
Ucayali
Yavarí
S e l v a s
Punta Aguja
Chiclayo
Trujillo
Huascarán 22,205 ft. (6768 m.)
CORDILLERA CENTRAL
CORDILLERA OCCIDENTAL
CORD. ORIENTAL
LA MONTAÑA
Huallaga
Purús
Madre de Dios
Apurímac
Urubamba
Mantaro
Callao
Lima
Salcantay 20,581 ft. (6273 m.)
Cusco
Vilcanota 17,999 ft. (5486 m.)
Ica
Majes
El Misti 19,101 ft. (5822 m.)
Arequipa
L. Titicaca
0 100 200 MI.
0 100 200 KM.
5,000 m. 16,404 ft.
2,000 m. 6,562 ft.
1,000 m. 3,281 ft.
500 m. 1,640 ft.
200 m. 656 ft.
100 m. 328 ft.
Sea Level
Below

PERU

DEPARTMENTS

Amazonas 256,460 C5
Ancash 815,646 D7
Apurímac 321,936 F10
Arequipa 702,308 F10
Ayacucho 500,732 E9
Cajamarca 1,044,689 C6
Callao (prov.) 446,730 D9
Cusco 829,294 F9
Huánuco 481,924 D7
Huancavelica 346,460 E9
Ica 431,442 E10
Junín 848,993 E8
La Libertad 960,537 C6
Lambayeque 683,425 B6
Lima 4,738,266 D8
Loreto 446,316 E5
Madre de Dios 36,555 G8
Moquegua 99,287 G11
Pasco 221,219 E8
Piura 1,168,442 B5
Puno 893,586 G10
San Martín 319,670 D6
Tacna 133,240 G11
Tumbes 103,979 B4
Ucayali 200,085 E6

CITIES and TOWNS

Abancay 19,807 F9
Acarí 4,907 E10
Acobamba 2,156 E9
Acolla 5,717 E8
Acomayo, Cusco 1,419 G9
Acomayo, Huánuco 2,883 E7
Acora 1,910 H11
Acuracay 1,282 F5
Aija 1,843 D7
Alca 755 F10
Ambo 3,060 D8
Ananea 668 H10
Ancón 8,610 D8
Andahuaylas 7,654 F9
Anta 3,703 F9
Antabamba 2,223 F10
Aplao 1,941 F11
Aquia 970 D8
Arequipa 107,858 G11
Arequipa* 447,431 G11
Ascope 12,070 C6
Atalaya 2,132 E8
Atico 2,316 F11
Ayabaca 4,543 C5
Ayacucho 68,535 F9
Ayaviri 11,067 G10
Azángaro 7,658 H10
Bagua 9,735 C5
Bambamarca 6,867 C6
Barranca, Lima 21,312 C8
Barranca, Loreto 1,351 D5
Bellavista 4,906 C5
Bolívar 1,106 D6
Bretaña 1,035 E5
Buldibuyo 582 D7
Cabana 1,804 C7
Cailloma 1,187 G10
Cajabamba 7,282 C6
Cajamarca 60,280 C6
Cajatambo 1,721 D8
Calca 6,112 G9
Callalli 819 G10
Callao 260,581 D9
Callao* 441,374 D9
Camaná 11,386 F11
Candarave 1,207 G11
Cangallo 1,584 E9
Canta 3,431 D8
Capachica 307 H10
Caravelí 1,827 F10
Caraz 6,376 D7
Carhuás 3,147 D7
Carumás 1,031 G11
Cascas 2,638 C6
Casma 12,725 C7
Castrovirreyna 1,749 E9
Catacaos 30,927 B5
Celendín 8,538 C6
Cerro Azul 2,314 D9
Cerro de Pasco 71,558 D8
Chachapoyas 11,919 D6
Chala 1,646 E10
Chalhuanca 3,071 F10
Chancay 18,993 D8
Chepén 29,919 C6
Chicama 11,160 C6
Chiclayo 280,244 C6
Chilca (Pucusana) 3,329 D9
Chilete 2,537 C6
Chimbote 216,406 C7
Chincha Alta 37,475 D9
Chiquián 3,521 D8
Chirinos 1,061 C5
Chivay 3,296 G10
Chota 8,299 C6
Chulucanas 34,977 B5
Chupaca 5,422 E9
Chuquibamba 2,630 F10
Chuquibambilla 2,147 F9
Churín 1,801 D8
Cocachacra 5,985 G11
Cojata 888 H10
Colasay 721 C5
Colcamar 1,216 D6
Conaica 1,154 E9
Concepción 7,129 E8
Concordia 1,372 E5
Contamana 5,718 E6
Contumazá 2,491 C6
Coracora 4,598 F10
Córdova 453 E10
Corongo 1,762 D7
Cotahuasi 1,301 F10
Cusco (Cuzco) 85,044 F9
Cusco* 171,604 F9
Cutervo 6,890 C6
Cuyocuyo 1,101 H10
Desaguadero 2,682 H11
Deustua 544 G10
Dos de Mayo 574 E6
Echarate 1,071 F9
El Portugués C7
Esperanza 375 G7
Espinar 6,381 G10
Ferreñafe 22,200 C6
Fitzcarrald G8
Francisco de Orellana 445 F4
Guadalupe 7,613 E9
Huacho 43,402 D8
Huacrachuco 1,210 D7
Hualgayoc 1,691 C6
Hualla 4,042 F9
Huallanca, Ancash 930 D7
Huallanca, Huánuco 4,806 D7
Huamachuco 8,273 D6
Huancabamba 4,393 C5
Huancané 5,227 H10
Huancapi 2,539 E9
Huancavelica 20,889 E9
Huancayo 165,132 E9
Huanchaco 6,005 C7
Huanta 11,213 E9
Huánuco 52,628 E7
Huaral 34,235 D8
Huaráz 45,116 D7
Huari 2,344 D7
Huariaca 2,671 E8
Huarmey 11,094 C8
Huarochirí 1,828 D9
Huarocondo 2,498 F9
Huaura 9,338 D8
Huaylas 1,344 C7
Iberia 2,307 F5
Ica 111,087 E10
Ichuña 277 G11
Ilave 9,891 H11
Ilo 31,549 G11
Imperial 20,894 D9
Inambari H9
Iñapari 188 H8
Intutu 746 E4
Iparia 278 E7
Iquitos 173,629 F4
Jaén 24,356 C5
Jauja 14,630 E8
Jayanca 6,401 B6
Jeberos 1,493 D5
Juanjuí 9,324 D6
Juli 5,575 H11
Juliaca 77,976 G10
Jumbilla 1,035 C5
Junín 8,988 E8
Lagunas 4,601 E5
La Huaca 5,161 B5
La Jalca 1,769 D6
La Joya 5,000 G11
Lamas 8,937 D6
Lambayeque 23,746 B6
Lampa 4,319 G10
Lamud 2,405 C6
Lanlacuni Bajo 405 G9
La Oroya 33,305 D8
Las Piedras H9
Las Yaras 759 G11
La Tina B5
La Unión 2,828 D7
Leimebamba 1,957 D6
Lima (cap.) 375,957 D8
Lima* 3,968,972 D8
Limbani 728 H10
Lircay 5,213 E9
Llata 2,922 D7
Lobitos 2,975 B5
Lurín 14,405 D9
Machupicchu 544 F9
Macusani 3,389 G10
Madre de Dios 660 G9
Manú 234 G9
Máncora 5,358 B5
Marcapata 369 G9
Marcona 25,962 E10
Margos 1,622 D8
Masisea 1,586 E7
Matarani F11
Matucana 4,196 D8
Mazocruz 1,580 H11
Mendoza 1,902 D6
Moho 2,560 H10
Mollendo 21,206 F11
Monsefú 17,186 C6
Moquegua 21,488 G11
Morales 4,370 D6
Morococha 11,234 D8
Morropón 7,611 C5
Motupe 3,411 C6
Moyobamba 14,319 D6
Nauta 4,083 F5
Nazca 22,756 E10
Negritos 12,476 B5
Nuñoa 3,613 G10
Ocoña 1,062 F11
Ocros 1,037 D8
Ollachea 1,308 G9
Ollantaytambo 1,500 F9
Olmos 7,946 C5
Omate 1,131 G11
Orcotuna 3,359 E8
Orellana 1,550 E6
Otuzco 5,765 C6
Oxapampa 5,233 E8
Oyón 6,279 D8
Pacasmayo 17,588 C6
Pachiza 889 D6
Paiján 12,699 C6
Paita 18,749 B5
Palpa 3,393 E10
Pampacolca 2,010 F10
Pampas 3,850 E9
Panao 1,363 E7
Paruro 1,727 F9
Paucarbama 534 E9
Paucartambo, Cusco 1,620 G9
Paucartambo, Pasco 3,497 E8
Pevas 1,347 G4
Picota 2,288 D6
Pimentel 9,129 B6
Pisac 1,566 G9
Pisco 53,414 D9
Piura 186,354 B5
Pomabamba 2,489 D7
Pucallpa 91,953 E7
Pucará 2,268 G10
Pucurco 628 G4
Pucusana 3,329 D9
Puerto Bermúdez 1,133 E8
Puerto Chicama 3,630 C6
Puerto Eten 2,575 B6
Puerto Inca 1,286 E7
Puerto Maldonado 12,609 H9
Puerto Ocopa 1,088 E8
Puerto Samanco 1,435 C7
Puno 66,477 G10
Punta de Bombón 4,647 F11
Puquina 1,026 G11
Putina 5,414 H10
Querecotillo 10,637 B5
Quillabamba 16,837 F9
Ramón Castilla 1,811 G5
Recuay 2,764 D7
Requena 8,270 F5
Rioja 9,876 D6
Salaverry 5,539 C7
Saña 40,144 C6
Sandia 1,682 H10
San José 4,070 B6
San José de Sisa 3,782 D6
San Miguel, Ayacucho 1,440 F9
San Miguel, Cajamarca 1,798 C6
San Pedro de Lloc 11,463 C6
San Ramón 7,145 E8
Santa 20,490 C7
Santa Clotilde 1,068 E4
Santa Cruz, Cajamarca 2,739 C6
Santa Cruz, Loreto 449 E5
Santiago 5,092 E10
Santiago de Cao 22,119 C6
Santiago de Chuco 5,189 C7
Santo Tomás, Amazonas 1,093 C6
Santo Tomás, Cusco 2,755 G10
San Vicente de Cañete 15,277 D9
Saposoa 4,541 D6
Saquena 2,755 F5
Satipo 9,208 E8
Sauce 2,263 D6
Sayán 5,129 D8
Sechura 11,724 B5
Sicuani 21,176 G10
Sihuas 2,178 D7
Sullana 80,947 B5
Sumbilca 1,155 D8
Supe 10,061 D8
Tacna 92,862 G11
Tahuamanu 2,619 H8
Talara 55,722 B5
Tambo de Mora 2,790 D9
Tambo Grande 10,087 B5
Tamshiyacu 2,040 F5
Tarapoto 33,429 D6
Tarata 2,624 H11
Tarma 34,369 E8
Tayabamba 1,649 D7
Tingo María 25,030 D7
Tocache 5,940 D7
Torata 6,320 G11
Trujillo 354,557 C7
Tumbes 48,187 B4
Uchiza 2,471 D7
Urcos 4,155 G9
Urubamba 4,686 F9
Virú 6,587 C7
Yambrasbamba 277 D5
Yanahuanca 5,109 D8
Yanaoca 1,152 G10
Yauca 1,805 E10
Yauli 1,020 D8
Yauri (Espinar) 6,381 G10
Yauyos 1,296 E9
Yunguyo 7,253 H11
Yurimaguas 22,858 E5
Zarumilla 9,713 B4
Zorritos 4,497 B4

OTHER FEATURES

Acarí (riv.) E10
Aguaytía (riv.) E7
Aguja (pt.) B5
Amazon (riv.) F4
Andes, Cordillera de los (mts.) F10
Apurímac (riv.) F9
Azángaro (riv.) G10
Azul, Cordillera (range) E7
Blanca, Cordillera (range) D7
Blanco (cape) B5
Boquerón, El (pass) E7
Cañete (riv.) D9
Chimbote (bay) C7
Chincha (isls.) C9
Chira (riv.) B5
Cóndor, Cordillera del (range) C5
Coropuna, Nudo (mt.) F10
Corrientes (riv.) E4
Ene (riv.) E8
Ferrol (pt.) C7
Grande (riv.) E10
Guañape (isls.) C7
Heath (riv.) H9
Huallaga (riv.) D5
Huasaga (riv.) D5
Huascarán (mt.) D7
Huayabamba (riv.) D6
Ica (riv.) E10
Inambari (riv.) H9
Independencia (bay) D10
Independencia (isl.) D10
Junín (lake) E8
Juruá (riv.) F7
Lobos de Afuera (isls.) B6
Lobos de Tierra (isl.) B6
Locumba (riv.) G11
Madre de Dios (riv.) G9
Majes (riv.) F1
Mantaro (riv.) E8
Manú (riv.) G8
Marañón (riv.) E5
Mayo (riv.) D6
Misti, El (mt.) G11
Montaña, La (reg.) F8
Morona (riv.) D5
Nanay (riv.) E4
Napo (riv.) F4
Negra, Cordillera (range) D7
Negra (pt.) B6
Nermete (pt.) B5
Occidental, Cordillera (range) F10
Ocoña (riv.) F11
Oriental, Cordillera (range) H10
Pachitea (riv.) E7
Paita (bay) B5
Pampas (riv.) E9
Paracas (pt.) D9
Pariñas (pt.) B5
Parinacochas (lake) F10
Pastaza (riv.) D5
Pativilca (riv.) D8
Perené (riv.) E8
Piedras, Las (riv.) G8
Pisco (bay) D9
Pisco (riv.) D9
Piura (riv.) B5
Purús (riv.) G8
Putumayo (riv.) G4
Rímac (riv.) D9
Salcantay (mt.) F9
Sama (riv.) G11
San Gallán (isl.) D9
San Lorenzo (isl.) D9
San Nicolás (bay) E10
Santa (riv.) C7
Santiago (riv.) D4
Sechura (bay) B5
Tambo (riv.) G11
Tapiche (riv.) E6
Tigre (riv.) E4
Titicaca (lake) H10
Tumbes (riv.) B4
Ucayali (riv.) F5
Urubamba (riv.) F8

(continued on following page)

ECUADOR

PROVINCES

CITIES and TOWNS

OTHER FEATURES

*City and suburbs

FRENCH GUIANA

DISTRICTS

CITIES and TOWNS

OTHER FEATURES

GUYANA

DISTRICTS

CITIES and TOWNS

OTHER FEATURES

Agriculture, Industry and Resources

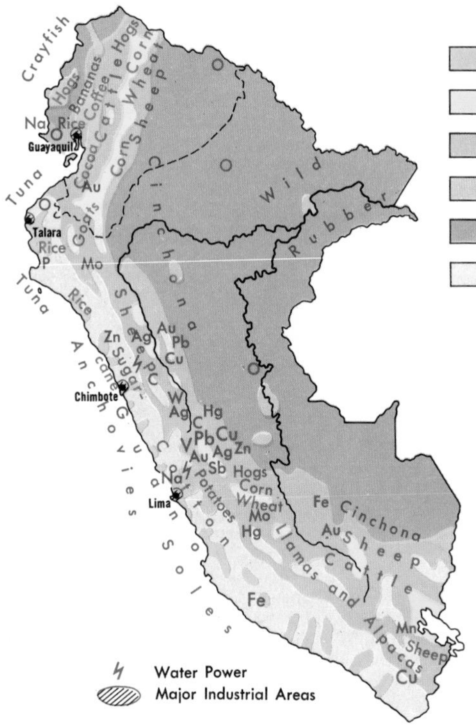
Crayfish
Tuna
Guayaquil
Talara
Chimbote
Lima
Anchovies
Soles
Rice
Cocoa
Coffee
Bananas
Hogs
Cattle
Corn
Wheat
Sheep
Goats
Wild Rubber
Cinchona
Sugar
Potatoes
Llamas and Alpacas
Water Power
Major Industrial Areas

DOMINANT LAND USE

- Diversified Tropical Crops (chiefly plantation agriculture)
- Upland Cultivated Areas
- Upland Livestock Grazing, Limited Agriculture
- Extensive Livestock Ranching
- Forests
- Nonagricultural Land

MAJOR MINERAL OCCURRENCES

Ag Silver
Au Gold
C Coal
Cu Copper
Fe Iron Ore
Hg Mercury
Mn Manganese
Mo Molybdenum
Na Salt
O Petroleum
P Phosphates
Pb Lead
Sb Antimony
V Vanadium
W Tungsten
Zn Zinc

Agriculture, Industry and Resources

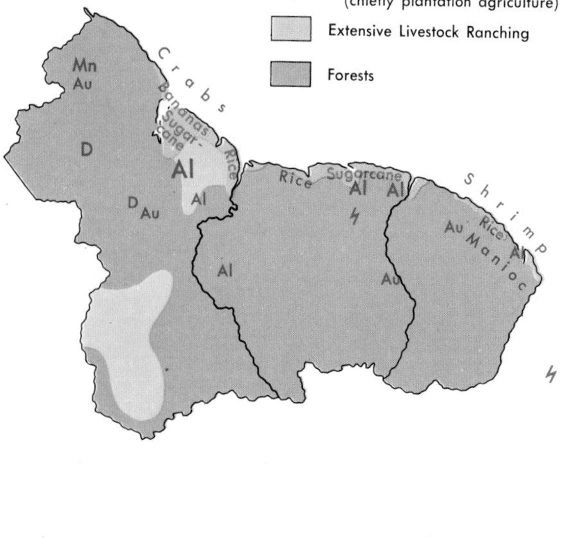
Mn
Au
Crabs
Bananas
Sugar-cane
Rice
Al
D
Sugarcane
Shrimp
Manioc

DOMINANT LAND USE

- Diversified Tropical Crops (chiefly plantation agriculture)
- Extensive Livestock Ranching
- Forests

MAJOR MINERAL OCCURRENCES

Al Bauxite
Au Gold
D Diamonds
Mn Manganese

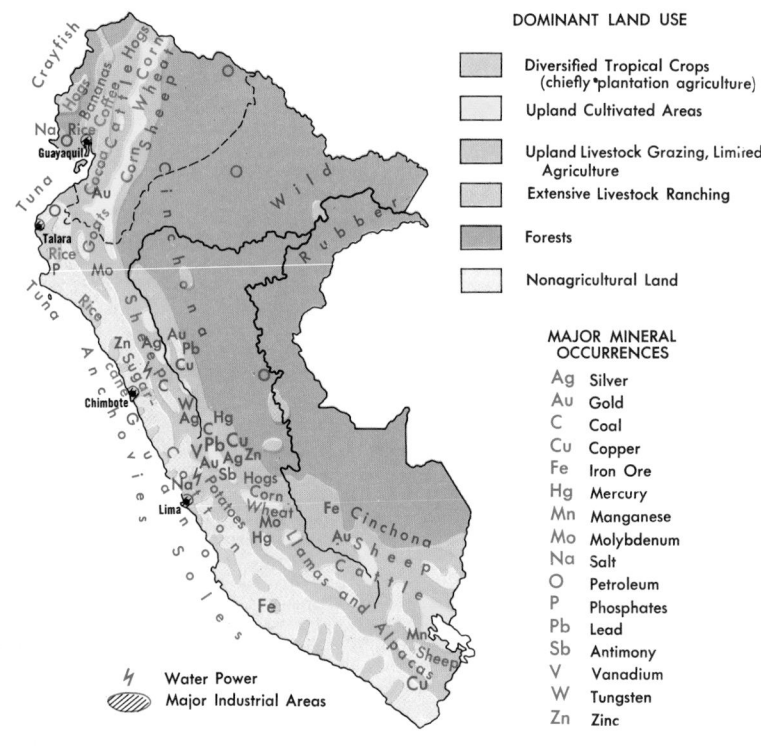

Water Power

GUYANA

AREA 83,000 sq. mi. (214,970 sq. km.)
POPULATION 1,024,000
CAPITAL Georgetown
LARGEST CITY Georgetown
HIGHEST POINT Mt. Roraima 9,094 ft. (2,772 m.)
MONETARY UNIT Guyana dollar
MAJOR LANGUAGES English, Hindi
MAJOR RELIGIONS Christianity, Hinduism, Islam

SURINAME

AREA 55,144 sq. mi. (142,823 sq. km.)
POPULATION 400,000
CAPITAL Paramaribo
LARGEST CITY Paramaribo
HIGHEST POINT Julianatop 4,200 ft. (1,280 m.)
MONETARY UNIT Suriname guilder
MAJOR LANGUAGES Dutch, Hindi, Indonesian
MAJOR RELIGIONS Christianity, Islam, Hinduism

FRENCH GUIANA

AREA 35,135 sq. mi. (91,000 sq. km.)
POPULATION 90,000
CAPITAL Cayenne
LARGEST CITY Cayenne
HIGHEST POINT 2,723 ft. (830 m.)
MONETARY UNIT French franc
MAJOR LANGUAGE French
MAJOR RELIGIONS Roman Catholicism, Protestantism

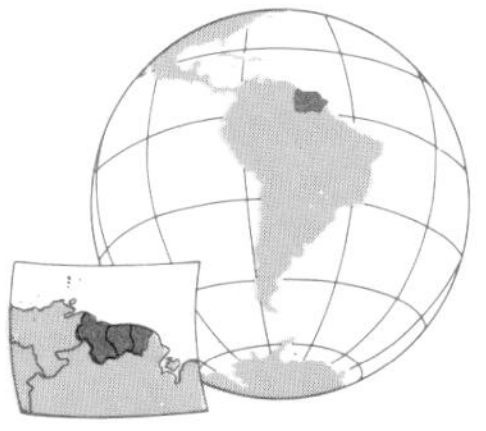

Kamaria (falls) B2
Kuyuwini (riv.) B4
Kwitaro (riv.) B4
Leguan (isl.) B2
Mazaruni (riv.) A2
Moruka (riv.) B2
New (riv.) C4
Pakaraima (mts.) A3
Pomeroon (riv.) B2
Potaro (riv.) B3
Puruni (riv.) B2
Roraima (mt.) A3
Rupununi (riv.) B4
Takutu (riv.) B4
Venamo (mt.) A3
Waini (riv.) B2
Wenamu (riv.) A2

SURINAME

DISTRICTS

Brokopondo 17,763 .... D4
Commewijne 18,740 .... D3
Coronie 3,251 .... C3
Marowijne 25,911 .... D4
Nickerie 35,178 .... C3
Para 16,635 .... D3
Paramaribo 102,297 .... D2
Saramacca 13,554 .... C3
Suriname 151,585 .... D3

CITIES and TOWNS

Albina 1,000 .... D3
Brokopondo D3
Calcutta 1,100 .... C3
Domburg 1,200 .... D3
Groningen 600 .... D2
Lelydorp 300 .... D3
Mariënburg 3,500 .... D2
Moengo 2,100 .... D3
Nieuw-Amsterdam 1,400 .... D2
Nieuw-Nickerie 34,480 .... C2
Paramaribo (cap.)⊙ 67,905 .... D2
Paranam D3
Totness 1,300 .... C3
Uitkijk D3
Wageningen 800 .... C3
Zanderij D3

OTHER FEATURES

Bakhuys (mts.) C3
Coeroeni (riv.) C4
Commewijne (riv.) D3
Coppename (riv.) C3
Corantijn (riv.) C3
Cottica (riv.) D3
Eilerts de Haan (mts.) C4
Frederik Willem IV (falls) C4
Julianatop (mt.) C4
Kutari (riv.) C4
Lely (mts.) D3
Litani (riv.) D4
Marowijne (riv.) D3
Nickerie (riv.) C3
Orange (mts.) D4
Saramacca (riv.) D3
Sipaliwini (riv.) C4
Suriname (riv.) D3
Tapanahoni (riv.) D4

*City and suburbs
○ Population of sub-district or division.
⊙ Population of district

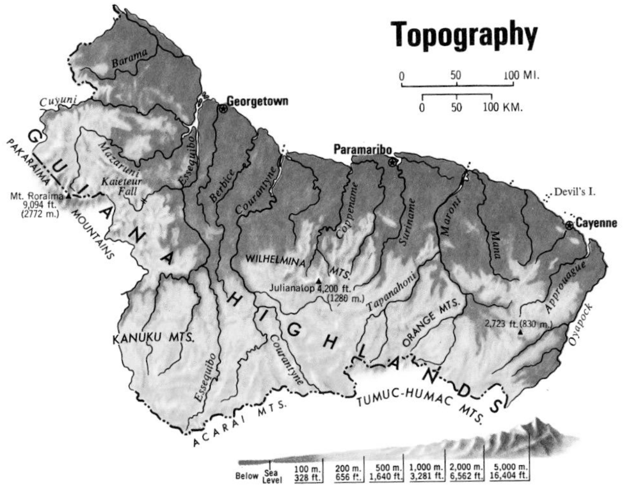

Topography
0 50 100 MI.
0 50 100 KM.
Georgetown
Paramaribo
Cayenne
Devil's I.
Mt. Roraima 9,094 ft. (2772 m.)
PAKARAIMA MOUNTAINS
GUIANA HIGHLANDS
WILHELMINA MTS.
Julianatop 4,200 ft. (1280 m.)
KANUKU MTS.
ACARAI MTS.
TUMUC-HUMAC MTS.
ORANGE MTS.
2,723 ft. (830 m.)
Below Sea Level
100 m. 328 ft.
200 m. 656 ft.
500 m. 1,640 ft.
1,000 m. 3,281 ft.
2,000 m. 6,562 ft.
5,000 m. 16,404 ft.

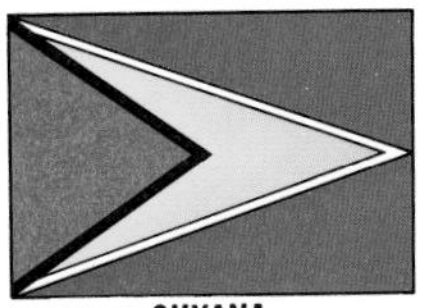

GUYANA

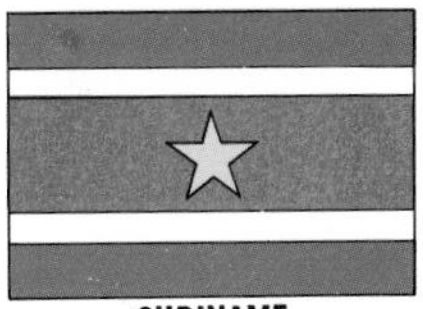

SURINAME

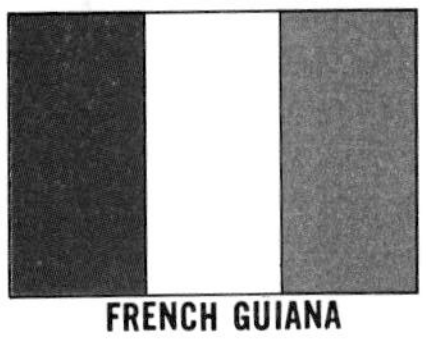

FRENCH GUIANA

The Guianas
LAMBERT CONFORMAL CONIC PROJECTION
SCALE OF MILES
0 30 60 120
KILOMETERS
0 30 60 120
Capitals of Countries
Other Capitals
International Boundaries
Other Boundaries
ADMINISTRATIVE DISTRICTS IN GUYANA INDICATED BY NUMBERS
① WEST DEMERARA-ESSEQUIBO COAST B2
② EAST DEMERARA-WEST COAST BERBICE C2
ADMINISTRATIVE DISTRICTS IN SURINAME INDICATED BY NUMBERS
① SURINAME D2
② PARA D2
ATLANTIC OCEAN
Georgetown
Paramaribo
Cayenne
New Amsterdam
Nieuw-Nickerie
GUYANA
SURINAME
FRENCH GUIANA
VENEZUELA
BRAZIL
LA GRAN SABANA
NORTH WEST
MAZARUNI-POTARO
EAST BERBICE-CORENTYNE
RUPUNUNI
NICKERIE
CORONIE
SARAMACCA
BROKOPONDO
MAROWIJNE
COMMEWIJNE
ST-LAURENT DU MARONI
CAYENNE
ÎLES DU SALUT
ÎLES RÉMIRE
ÎLES CONNÉTABLE
Tumuc-Humac Mts.
Acarai Mts.
Kanuku Mts.
Pakaraima Mts.
Mt. Roraima 9,094 ft. (2772 m.)
Julianatop 4,200 ft. (1280 m.)
Wilhelmina Mts.
Orange Mts.
Kaieteur Fall
Orinoco
Boca Grande
Boa Vista
Lethem
Bartica
Linden
Mt. Venamo 6,201 ft. (1890 m.)
Mt. Caburai 4,777 ft. (1456 m.)
Mt. St-Marcel 2,083 ft. (635 m.)
Longitude West of Greenwich
© Copyright HAMMOND INCORPORATED, Maplewood, N. J.

Brazil
BIPOLAR OBLIQUE CONIC CONFORMAL PROJECTION
SCALE OF MILES
0 50 100 200 300
KILOMETERS
0 50 100 200 300
Capitals of Countries
State Capitals
International Boundaries
State Boundaries
Scale 1:14,700,000
© Copyright HAMMOND INCORPORATED, Maplewood, N.J.
GUYANA
SURINAME
FR. GUIANA
RORAIMA
AMAPÁ
AMAZONAS
PARÁ
MARANHÃO
PIAUÍ
CEARÁ
RIO GRANDE DO NORTE
PARAÍBA
PERNAMBUCO
ALAGOAS
SERGIPE
BAHIA
TOCANTINS
GOIÁS
FEDERAL DISTRICT
Brasília
MATO GROSSO
MATO GROSSO DO SUL
RONDÔNIA
MINAS GERAIS
ESPÍRITO SANTO
RIO DE JANEIRO
SÃO PAULO
PARANÁ
SANTA CATARINA
RIO GRANDE DO SUL
BOLIVIA
PARAGUAY
ARGENTINA
URUGUAY
ATLANTIC OCEAN
Tropic of Capricorn
Equator
Amazon
Manaus
Belém
São Luís
Teresina
Fortaleza (Ceará)
Natal
João Pessoa
Recife (Pernambuco)
Maceió
Aracaju
Salvador (Bahia)
Goiânia
Cuiabá
Campo Grande
Belo Horizonte
Vitória
Niterói
RIO DE JANEIRO
SÃO PAULO
Curitiba
Florianópolis
Porto Alegre
Macapá
Boa Vista
Asunción
BRAZIL WESTERN PART
COLOMBIA
VENEZUELA
PERU
ACRE
Longitude 48° West of Greenwich 44°

Três Cora
Três Lagc
Três Pont
Três Rios
Trindade
Tubarão 6
Tucuruí 2
Tupã 44,4
Tupancire
Tutóia 4,7
Ubá 43,0
Ubaitaba
Ubatuba 2
Uberaba 1
Uberlândi
Unaí 28,1
União 9,3
União da
União dos
Uruaçu 1
Uruçuí 6,
Uruguaiar
Vacaria 3
Valença 3
Varginha
Viana 9,7
Viçosa 9,
Viçosa 29
Vigia 14,7
Vila Velha
Vilhena 12
Viscondé
17,295
Vitória 14
Vitória da
Vitória de
62,890
Volta Red
Votuporar
Xapuri 3,
Xique-Xiq

OT

Abacaxis
Abunã (riv
Acaraí, Se
Acre (riv.)
Aiama (lak
Amambaí,
Amapari (
Amazon (

1
20°
2
3
4
22°
24°

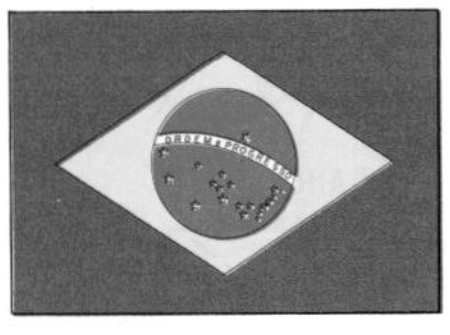

AREA 3,284,426 sq. mi. (8,506,663 sq. km.)
POPULATION 150,368,000
CAPITAL Brasília
LARGEST CITY São Paulo (greater)
HIGHEST POINT Pico da Neblina 9,889 ft. (3,014 m.)
MONETARY UNIT cruzado
MAJOR LANGUAGE Portuguese
MAJOR RELIGION Roman Catholicism

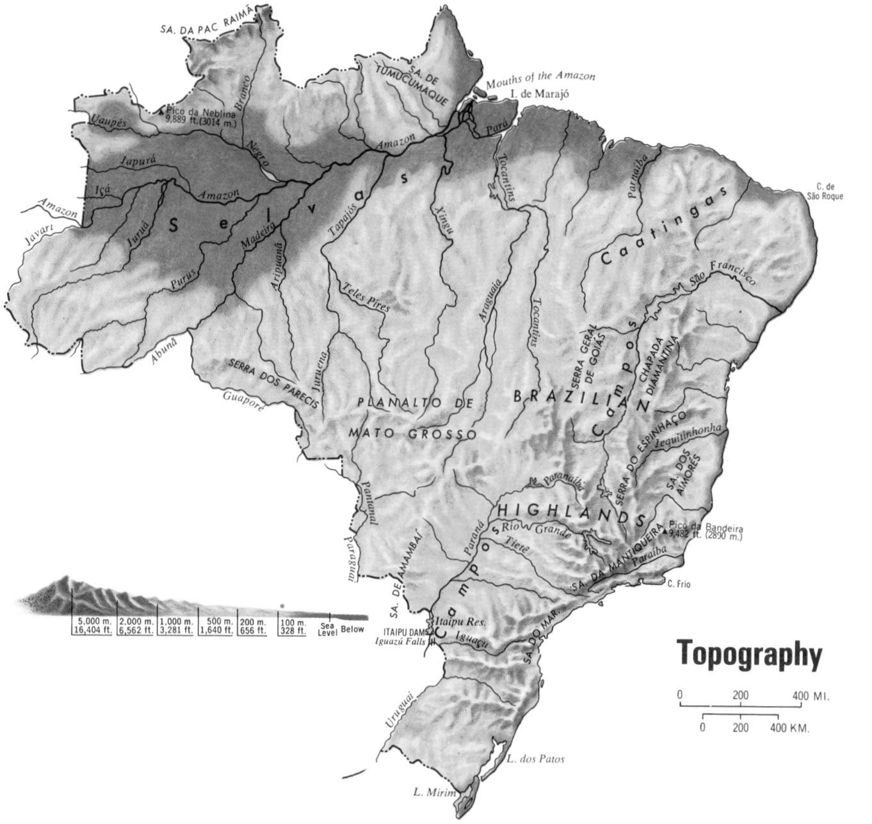
SA. DA PAC RAIMÃ
Pico da Neblina 9,889 ft. (3014 m.)
Mouths of the Amazon
I. de Marajó
Vaupés
Japurá
Negro
Branco
Amazon
Içá
Javari
Juruá
Purus
Madeira
Aripuanã
Tapajós
Xingu
Tocantins
Parnaíba
Araguaia
Teles Pires
Juruena
Guaporé
Abunã
S e l v a s
C a a t i n g a s
C. de São Roque
São Francisco
SERRA DOS PARECIS
PLANALTO DE MATO GROSSO
BRAZILIAN HIGHLANDS
SERRA GERAL DE GOIÁS
CHAPADA DIAMANTINA
SERRA DO ESPINHAÇO
Jequitinhonha
SERRA DOS AIMORÉS
Paranaíba
Rio Grande
Tietê
Paraná
Paraguai
Pantanal
SA. DE AMAMBAÍ
Pico da Bandeira 9,482 ft. (2890 m.)
SA. DA MANTIQUEIRA
Paraíba
C. Frio
SA. DO MAR
Itaipu Res.
ITAIPU DAM
Iguazú Falls
Iguaçu
Uruguai
L. dos Patos
L. Mirim
Campos
5,000 m. 16,404 ft.
2,000 m. 6,562 ft.
1,000 m. 3,281 ft.
500 m. 1,640 ft.
200 m. 656 ft.
100 m. 328 ft.
Sea Level
Below
Topography
0 200 400 MI.
0 200 400 KM.

STATES and TERRITORIES

Acre 301,605 . . . G10
Alagoas 1,987,581 . . . G5
Amapá (terr.) 175,634 . . . D2
Amazonas 1,432,066 . . . G9
Bahia 9,474,263 . . . F6
Ceará 5,294,876 . . . G4
Espirito Santo 2,023,821 . . . F7
Federal District 1,177,393 . . . E6
Goiás 3,865,482 . . . D6
Maranhão 4,002,599 . . . E4
Mato Grosso 1,141,661 . . . B6
Mato Grosso do Sul 1,370,333 . . . C7
Minas Gerais 13,390,805 . . . E7
Pará 3,411,868 . . . C4
Paraíba 2,772,600 . . . G4
Paraná 7,630,466 . . . D9
Pernambuco 6,147,102 . . . G5
Piauí 2,140,066 . . . F4
Rio de Janeiro 11,297,327 . . . F8
Rio Grande do Norte 1,899,720 . . . G4
Rio Grande do Sul 7,777,212 . . . C10
Rondônia 492,810 . . . H10
Roraima (terr.) 79,153 . . . H8
Santa Catarina 3,628,751 . . . D9
São Paulo 25,040,698 . . . D8
Sergipe 1,141,834 . . . G5
Tocantins . . . D5

CITIES and TOWNS

Abaeté 12,861 . . . E7
Abaetetuba 33,031 . . . D3
Acaraú 7,144 . . . F3
Acopiara 10,747 . . . G4
Açu 20,544 . . . G4
Agudos 18,790 . . . *B3
Alagoa Grande 14,204 . . . H4
Alagoinhas 76,377 . . . G6
Alcobaça 3,430 . . . G7
Alegre 9,441 . . . *F2
Alegrete 54,786 . . . B10
Além Paraíba 23,028 . . . *E2
Alenquer 16,477 . . . C3
Alfenas 31,815 . . . *D2
Altamira 24,846 . . . C3
Altos 13,621 . . . F4
Amambaí 12,507 . . . C8
Amapá 2,676 . . . D2
Amarante 6,848 . . . F4
Amargosa 11,118 . . . F6
Americana 121,794 . . . *C3
Amparo 26,970 . . . *C3
Anápolis 160,520 . . . D7
Anchieta 5,741 . . . F8
Andaraí 2,476 . . . F6
Andradina 42,036 . . . D8
Andrelândia 8,737 . . . *D2
Angra dos Reis 24,894 . . . *D3
Antonina 11,950 . . . *B4
Aparecida 27,265 . . . *D3
Apiai 7,809 . . . *B4
Aquidauana 21,514 . . . C8
Aracaju 288,106 . . . G5
Aracati 20,282 . . . G4
Araçatuba 113,486 . . . *A2
Araçuaí 12,292 . . . F7
Araquari 73,302 . . . D7
Araranquá 22,468 . . . D10
Araraquara 77,202 . . . *B2
Araras 54,323 . . . *C3
Araxá 51,339 . . . E7
Arcoverde 40,646 . . . G5
Areia Branca 12,979 . . . G4
Assis 57,217 . . . *A3
Avaré 40,716 . . . *B3
Bacabai 43,229 . . . E4
Bagé 66,743 . . . C10
Bahia (Salvador) 1,496,276 . . . G6
Baixo Guandu 13,714 . . . F7
Balsas 13,566 . . . E4
Bambui 14,172 . . . *C2
Barão de Cocais 11,950 . . . *E1
Barbacena 69,675 . . . *E2
Bariri 15,372 . . . *B3
Barra 10,809 . . . F5
Barra do Corda 19,280 . . . E4
Barra do Piraí 51,214 . . . *E3
Barra Mansa 123,421 . . . *D3
Barras 8,904 . . . F4
Barreiras 30,355 . . . E6
Barreiros 19,419 . . . H5
Barretos 65,294 . . . *B2
Batatais 30,478 . . . *C2
Baturité 12,388 . . . G4
Bauru 178,861 . . . *B3
Bebedouro 39,070 . . . *B2
Bela Vista 11,936 . . . C8
Belém 758,117 . . . E3
Belém †1,000,349 . . . E3
Belo Horizonte 1,442,483 . . . *D1
Belo Horizonte †2,541,788 . . . *D1
Benjamin Constant 6,563 . . . G9
Bento Gonçalves 40,323 . . . C10
Betim 71,599 . . . *D2
Bicas 8,611 . . . *E2
Birigui 45,348 . . . *A2
Blumenau 144,819 . . . D9
Boa Esperanca 17,394 . . . *D2
Boa Vista 43,131 . . . H8
Bocaiúva 16,616 . . . E7
Bom Conselho 13,196 . . . G5
Bom Despacho 22,941 . . . *D1
Bom Jesus da Lapa 19,978 . . . F6
Bom Sucesso 10,331 . . . *D2
Borba 5,366 . . . H9
Bragança Paulista 61,021 . . . *C3
Brasiléia 4,835 . . . G10
Brasília (cap.) 411,305 . . . E6
Brasilia de Minas 10,171 . . . F7
Brejo 5,859 . . . F3
Breves 31,452 . . . D3
Brumado 24,663 . . . F6
Brusque 37,898 . . . D9
Cabedolo 18,581 . . . H4
Cabo Frio 40,668 . . . *F3
Caçador 25,287 . . . D9
Caçapava 45,258 . . . *D3
Caçapava do Sul 15,180 . . . C10
Cáceres 33,472 . . . B7
Cachoeira 11,520 . . . G6
Cachoeira do Sul 59,967 . . . C10
Cachoeiro de Itapemirim 84,994 . . . G8
Caeté 23,331 . . . *E1
Caetité 8,823 . . . F6
Caiaponia 9,358 . . . C7
Caicó 30,777 . . . G4
Cajazeiras 30,834 . . . G4
Cajuru 9,670 . . . *C2
Camaquá 28,078 . . . C10
Cambará 13,218 . . . *A3
Cambui 8,552 . . . *C3
Cametá 15,539 . . . D3
Camocim 19,921 . . . F3
Campina Grande 222,229 . . . G4
Campinas 566,517 . . . *C3
Campo Belo 30,392 . . . *D2
Campo Formoso 10,324 . . . F5
Campo Grand 282,844 . . . C8
Campo Largo 34,506 . . . *B4
Campo Major 24,009 . . . F4
Campos 174,218 . . . *F2
Cananéia 5,581 . . . *C4
Canavieiras 14,076 . . . G6
Canindé 18,573 . . . G4
Canoas 214,115 . . . D10
Canoinhas 25,880 . . . D9
Capanema 28,272 . . . E3
Capão Bonito 24,081 . . . *B4
Caraguatatuba 22,932 . . . *D3
Carangola 15,621 . . . *E2
Caratinga 39,621 . . . *E1
Caravelas 3,704 . . . G7
Carazinho 41,913 . . . C10
Carolina 10,136 . . . E4
Caruaru 137,636 . . . G5
Casa Banca 13,739 . . . *C2
Cascavel 16,238 . . . G4
Cássia 10,701 . . . *C2
Castanhal 51,797 . . . E3
Castelo 9,162 . . . F8
Castro 21,079 . . . *B4
Castro Alves 11,286 . . . G6
Cataguases 40,659 . . . *E2
Catalão 30,516 . . . E7
Catanduva 64,813 . . . *B2
Catolé do Rocha 12,165 . . . G4
Caxambu 16,221 . . . *D2
Caxias 56,755 . . . F4
Caxias do Sul 198,824 . . . D10
Ceará (Fortaleza) 648,815 . . . G3
Ceará-Mirim 17,097 . . . H4
Ceres 13,671 . . . D6
Chapecó 53,198 . . . C9
Coari 14,841 . . . H9
Codajás 4,923 . . . H9
Codó 11,593 . . . E4
Colatina 61,057 . . . F7
Conceição do Araguaia 18,143 . . . D5
Concórdia 17,973 . . . D9
Conselheiro Lafaiete 66,262 E2
Corinto 17,056 . . . E7
Cornélio Procópio 31,201 . . . D8
Coroatá 16,070 . . . F3
coromandel 11,604 . . . F7
Corumbá 66,014 . . . B7
Coxim 14,876 . . . C7
Crateús 29,905 . . . F4
Crato 49,244 . . . G4
Criciúma 74,003 . . . D10
Cristalina 10,521 . . . E7
Cruz Alta 53,315 . . . C10
Cruzeiro 55,175 . . . *D3
Cruzeiro do Sul 11,189 . . . G10
Cubatão 78,327 . . . *C3
Cuiabá 167,894 . . . C6
Curitiba 843,733 . . . *B4
Curitiba †1,441,743 . . . *B4
Currais Novos 25,663 . . . G4
Cururupu 10,358 . . . E3
Curvelo 37,734 . . . E7
Diamantina 20,197 . . . F7
Divinópolis 108,344 . . . *D2
Dois Córregos 11,811 . . . *B3
Dom Pedrito 25,773 . . . C10
Dores do Indaiá 13,058 . . . E7
Dourados 76,838 . . . C8
Duque de Caxias 306,057 . . . *E3
Erexim 46,927 . . . C9
Esperanca 12,964 . . . G4
Esplanada 9,822 . . . G5
Estancia 28,250 . . . G5
Feira de Santana 225,003 . . . G5
Fernandópolis 39,737 . . . *A2
Floriano 35,761 . . . F4
Florianópolis 153,547 . . . E9
Fonte Boa 3,278 . . . G9
Formiga 36,681 . . . *D2
Formosa 29,304 . . . E6
Fortaleza 648,815 . . . G3
Fortaleza †1,581,588 . . . G3
Foz do Iguacu 93,619 . . . C9
Franca 143,630 . . . *C2
Frutal 22,955 . . . *B2
Garanhuns 64,854 . . . G5
Garca 26,527 . . . *B3
Goiana 30,108 . . . H4
Goiânia 703,263 . . . D7
Goiás 15,768 . . . D6
Governador Valadares 173,699 . . . F7
Grajaú 11,147 . . . E4
Guacul 12,715 . . . *F2
Guajará-Mirim 19,992 . . . H10
Guarapuava 17,189 . . . C9
Guarantiguetá 68,370 . . . *D3
Guarujá 67,730 . . . *C4
Guarulhos 395,117 . . . *C3
Guaxupé 23,637 . . . *C2
Guirantinga 8,981 . . . C7
Gurupi 27,39 . . . D5
Humaitá 10,004 . . . H10
Ibaiti 11,352 . . . *A3
Ibiá 11,161 . . . E7
Ibicaraí 18,202 . . . G6
Ibitinga 23,359 . . . *B2
Icó 13,007 . . . G4
Igarapava 15,342 . . . C2
Igarapé-Miri 12,172 . . . D3
Iguape 16,827 . . . *C4
Iguatu 39,611 . . . G4
Ijui 51,925 . . . C10
Ilhéus 71,240 . . . G6
Imbituba 9,998 . . . D10
Imperatiz 111,818 . . . E4
Inhumas 23,455 . . . D7
Ipameri 14,163 . . . E7
Ipu 12,787 . . . F4
Irati 21,956 . . . *A4
Itabaiana, Paraíba 17,843 . . . H4
Itabaiana, Sergipe 26,055 . . . G5
Itaberaba 27,590 . . . F6
Itabira 57,691 . . . F7
Itabirito 22,978 . . . *E2
Itabuna 129,938 . . . G6
Itacoatiara 26,737 . . . B3
Itaituba 19,644 . . . C4
Itajai 78,867 . . . D9
Itajubá 53,506 . . . *D3
Itanhaem 26,181 . . . C4
Itapecerica 10,234 . . . *D2
Itapecuru-Mirim 12,216 . . . F3
Itapemirim 16,829 . . . F8
Itaperuna 34,644 . . . *F2
Itapetinga 36,897 . . . G6
Itapetininga 61,344 . . . *B3
Itapeva 36,551 . . . *B3
Itapipoca 19,463 . . . G3
Itapira 36,308 . . . *C3
Itápolis 13,750 . . . *B2
Itaporanga 8,988 . . . G4
Itaqui 23,136 . . . B10
Itararé 24,368 . . . *B4
Itatiba 35,537 . . . *C3
Itaúna 49,372 . . . *D2
Itu 62,211 . . . *C3
Ituacu 1,749 . . . F6
Ituiutaba 65,178 . . . D7
Itumbiara 56,602 . . . D7
Iturama 12,363 . . . *A1
Ituverava 21,323 . . . *C2
Jaboatao 67,129 . . . H5
Jaboticabal 40,276 . . . *B2
Jacarel 103,652 . . . *D3
Jacarezinho 23,684 . . . *A3
Jacobina 26,723 . . . F5
Jacupiranga 7,044 . . . B4
Jaguaquara 11,336 . . . F6
Jaguarao 18,165 . . . C11
Jaguariaiva 8,566 . . . *B4
Januária 20,484 . . . E6
Jatai 40,957 . . . D7
Jaú 59,522 . . . *B3
Jequié 84,792 . . . F6
Jequitinhonha 10,900 . . . F7
Ji-Paraná 31,724 . . . H10
Joacaba 16,195 . . . D9
Joao Pessoa 290,424 . . . H4
Joao Pinheiro 17,013 . . . E7
Joinvile 217,074 . . . D9
Juazeiro 60,940 . . . G5
Juazeiro do Norte 125,248 . . . F4
Juiz de Fora 299,728 . . . *E2
Jundiai 210,015 . . . *C3
Lages 108,768 . . . D9
Laguna 27,743 . . . D10
Lambari 9,722 . . . *D2
Lapa 13,314 . . . D9
Laranjeiras do Sul 19,329 . . . C9
Lavras 35,345 . . . *D2
Leme 40,155 . . . *C3
Leopoldina 28,554 . . . *E2
Limeira 137,812 . . . *C3
Limoeiro 36,088 . . . H4
Limoeiro do Norte 13,112 . . . G4
Linhares 51,575 . . . F7
Lins 44,633 . . . *B2
Londrina 258,054 . . . D8
Lorena 51,276 . . . *D3
Luis Correia 3,576 . . . F3
Luz 10,068 . . . *D1
Luziania 67,284 . . . E7
Macaé 39,644 . . . *F3
Macalba 17,036 . . . H4
Macapá 89,081 . . . D2
Macau 17,543 . . . G4
Maceio 376,479 . . . H5
Machado 16,164 . . . *C2
Mafra 26,226 . . . D9
Magé 37,597 . . . *E3
Mamanguape 16,321 . . . H4
Manacapuru 17,016 . . . H9
Manaus 613,068 . . . H9
Manhuacu 22,678 . . . *E2
Manhumirim 11,085 . . . *E2
Manicoré 9,532 . . . H9
Marabá 41,564 . . . D4
Maracaju 9,699 . . . C8
Maragogipe 13,512 . . . G6
Maranguape 20,098 . . . G3
Marechal Deodoro 9,400 . . . H5
Mariana 11,785 . . . *E2
Marilla 103,904 . . . *A3
Maringá 158,047 . . . D8
Mata de São João 23,741 . . . G6
Mato Grosso (Vila Bela da Santissima Trindade) 1,401 . . . B6
Maués 10,846 . . . B3
Mineiros 16,844 . . . C7
Miracema 15,545 . . . *E2
Miracema do Norte . . . D5
Mirassol 25,173 . . . *B2
Mococa 33,682 . . . *C2
Mogi das Cruzes 122,265 . . . *C3
Mogi-Mirim 41,827 . . . *C3
Monte Alegre 10,646 . . . C3
Monte Aprazivel 9,767 . . . *A2
Monteiro 11,051 . . . G4
Montenegro 27,246 . . . D10
Montes Claros 151,881 . . . E7
Morrinhos 20,154 . . . D7
Mossoró 118,007 . . . G4
Muriaé 50,040 . . . *E2
Muzambinho 8,803 . . . *C2
Nanuque 34,445 . . . F7
Natal 376,552 . . . H4
Nazaré 18,068 . . . G6
Niquelandia 8,828 . . . D6
Niterói 386,185 . . . *E3
Nova Cruz 12,824 . . . H4
Nova Era 11,126 . . . *E1
Nova Friburgo 88,943 . . . *E3
Nova Iguaçu 491,802 . . . *E3
Nova Lima 35,035 . . . *E2
Nova Russas 10,021 . . . F4
Novo Hamburgo 132,066 . . . D10
Novo Horizonte 18,439 . . . *B2
Óbidos 17,143 . . . C3
Oeiras 12,406 . . . F4
Olimpia 24,376 . . . *B2
Olinda 266.392 . . . H4
Oliveira 22,642 . . . *D2
Oriximiná 12,078 . . . C3
Orlândia 22,924 . . . *C2
Osasco 376,689 . . . *C3
Ourinhos 52,698 . . . *B3
Ouro Preto 27,821 . . . *E2
Palmares 40,624 . . . H5
Palmas 15,823 . . . C9
Palmeira 11,521 . . . *B4
Palmeira das Missões 23,943 . . . C9
Pará (Belém) 758,117 . . . E3
Paracatu 29,911 . . . E7
Pará de Minas 37,127 . . . *D1
Paraguaçu Paulista 17,399 . . . D8
Paraíba do Sul 13,510 . . . *E3
Paranaíba 21,305 . . . D7
Paranaguá 68,366 . . . *B4
Parati 8,684 . . . *D3
Parintins 29,369 . . . B3
Parnaíba 78,718 . . . F3
Passo Fundo 103,121 . . . D10
Passos 56,998 . . . *C2
Patos 58,735 . . . G4
Patos de Minas 59,896 . . . E7
Patrocínio 29,520 . . . E7
Pau dos Ferros 12,985 . . . G4
Paulo Afonso 62,066 . . . G5
Pederneiras 18,864 . . . *B3
Pedra Azul 13,615 . . . F6
Pedreiras 30,843 . . . E4
Pedro Segundo 9,693 . . . F4
Pelotas 197,092 . . . C10
Penápolis 32,168 . . . *A2
Penedo 27,064 . . . G5
Pernambuco (Recife) 1,184,215 . . . H5
Petrolina 73,436 . . . G5
Petrópolis 149,427 . . . *E3
Picos 33,098 . . . F4
Piedade 13,054 . . . *C3
Pilar 14,778 . . . H5
Pindamonhangaba 51,174 . *D3

(continued on following page)

DEPARTMENTS

CITIES and TOWNS

Bolivia
BIPOLAR OBLIQUE CONIC CONFORMAL PROJECTION
SCALE OF MILES
0 25 50 100 150
SCALE OF KILOMETERS
0 25 50 100 150
Capitals of Countries
Capitals of Departments
International Boundaries
Department Boundaries
© Copyright HAMMOND INCORPORATED, Maplewood, N. J.
Longitude West of Greenwich
BRAZIL
PERU
CHILE
ARGENTINA
PARAGUAY
PANDO
EL BENI
LA PAZ
COCHABAMBA
SANTA CRUZ
ORURO
POTOSÍ
CHUQUISACA
TARIJA
Lake Titicaca
Lake Poopó
Salar de Coipasa
Salar de Uyuni
Gran Chaco
Chaco Boreal
Cord. Occidental
Serranía de Huanchaca
Serranía San Simón
Laguna Concepción
Bañados de Izozog
La Paz
Sucre
Cochabamba
Oruro
Potosí
Trinidad
Santa Cruz
Cobija
Tarija
Riberalta
Uyuni
Camiri
Villazón
Yacuiba
Tupiza
Corumbá
Puerto Suárez

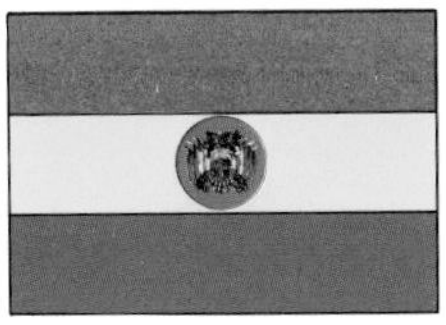

AREA 424,163 sq. mi. (1,098,582 sq. km.)
POPULATION 7,193,000
CAPITALS La Paz, Sucre
LARGEST CITY La Paz
HIGHEST POINT Nevada Ancohuma 21,489 ft. (6,550 m.)
MONETARY UNIT Bolivian peso
MAJOR LANGUAGES Spanish, Quechua, Aymara
MAJOR RELIGION Roman Catholicism

- Culpina 981 C7
- Culta‡ 4,412 B6
- Curahuara de Pacajes 510 A5
- El Palmar, Chuquisaca‡ 772 D7
- El Palmar, Tarija 832 D7
- El Puente, Santa Cruz‡ 1,185 D5
- El Puente, Tarija‡ 1,310 C7
- Entre Ríos 1,011 C7
- Esmoraca‡ 1,137 B7
- Estarca‡ 2,331 C7
- Filadelfia‡ 942 A2
- Fortaleza‡ 765 B3
- Fortín Mutum F6
- General Saavedra 1,006 D5
- Guadalupe 2,355 C6
- Guaqui 2,266 A5
- Guayaramerín 1,470 C2
- Huacaraje 673 D3
- Huachacalla 801 A6
- Huanay 574 B4
- Huanchaca B7
- Huanuni 5,696 B6
- Huari 1,070 B6
- Huarina 1,151 A5
- Ichoca 591 B5
- Independencia 1,742 B5
- Ingeniero Montero Hoyos (Tocomechi) 575 D5
- Inquisivi 530 B5
- Irupana 1,937 B5
- Ivón‡ 772 C2
- Izozog‡ 2,759 D6
- Jesús de Machaca 529 A5
- José Agustín Palacios‡ 2,273 B3
- La Capilla‡ 1,870 C8
- Lagunillas 840 D6
- La Merced‡ 688 C8
- Lanza 526 B5
- La Paz (cap.) 635,283 B5
- Limal‡ 524 C8
- Llallagua 6,719 B6
- Llanquera 613 A6
- Llica 560 A6
- Loreto 589 C4
- Macha 1,050 B6
- Machacamarca 1,746 B5
- Macharetí‡ 1,164 D7
- Magdalena 1,724 C3
- Mairana 508 D6
- Mecoya‡ 585 C8
- Mizque 870 C5
- Mocomoco 977 A4
- Mojo 469 C7
- Mojocoya 498 C6
- Monteagudo 971 D6
- Montero 2,713 D5
- Morochata 461 B5
- Moromoro 556 C6
- Motacucito‡ 585 E5
- Ocurí 1,531 C6
- Orinoca‡ 2,380 B6
- Orobayaya‡ 1,132 D3
- Oro Ingenio‡ 945 C7
- Oruro 124,213 B5
- Padcaya 324 C7
- Padilla 2,462 C6
- Palaya 300 A6
- Palca 887 A5
- Palometas‡ 3,453 D5
- Pampa Aullagas‡ 1,834 B6
- Pampa Grande 727 D5
- Panacachi 952 B6
- Paria 335 B5
- Pasorapa 1,016 C6
- Pata 122 A4
- Patacamaya 1,278 B5
- Pazña 671 B6
- Pelechuco 873 A4
- Pocoata 859 B6
- Pocona 518 C5
- Pocpo‡ 2,791 C6
- Pojo 1,047 C5
- Poopó 736 B6
- Porco 817 B6
- Poroma 171 C6
- Portachuelo 2,456 D5
- Portugalete‡ 1,590 B7
- Porvenir‡ 846 A2
- Postrervalle 750 D6
- Potosí 77,397 C6
- Presto 725 C6
- Pucara 762 C6
- Pucarani 1,041 A5
- Puerto Acosta 1,302 A4
- Puerto Almacen 358 C4
- Puerto General Ovando 658 C1
- Puerto Heath‡ 570 A3
- Puerto Rico‡ 539 B2
- Puerto Siles 357 C3
- Puerto Suárez 1,159 F6
- Pulacayo 7,984 B7
- Puna 852 C6
- Punata 5,014 C5
- Quechisla 171 C7
- Queteña 183 B8
- Quillacas 1,170 B6
- Quillacollo 9,123 B5
- Quime 1,256 B5
- Quiroga‡ 3,467 C6
- Quirusillas 433 D6
- Ravelo 907 C6
- Reyes 1,404 B4
- Riberalta 6,549 C2
- Río Grande 281 B7
- Río Mulato 381 B6
- Roboré 3,715 F6
- Rurrenabaque 1,225 B4
- Sabaya 649 A6
- Sacaba 2,752 C5
- Sacaca 1,778 B6
- Sachojere 401 C4
- Saipina 573 C6
- Sajama 231 A6
- Saladillo‡ 1,315 D7
- Salinas de Garci Mendoza 335 B6
- Samaipata 1,656 D6
- San Agustín‡ 810 B7
- Sanandita 379 D7
- San Andrés 399 C4
- San Andrés de Machaca 101 A5
- San Antonio, El Beni 436 C4
- San Antonio de Lípez‡ 177 B7
- San Antonio del Parapetí 497 D7
- San Borja 708 B4
- San Buenaventura 307 A4
- San Carlos 570 D5
- San Cristóbal‡ 1,200 B7
- San Diego‡ 773 D7
- San Francisco 185 C4
- San Ignacio, El Beni 1,757 C4
- San Ignacio, Santa Cruz 1,819 E5
- San Javier, El Beni 233 C4
- San Javier, Santa Cruz 564 D5
- San Joaquín 1,959 C3
- San José de Chiquitos 1,933 E5
- San José de Uchupiamonas 277 A4
- San Juan, Potosí 131 B7
- San Juan, Santa Cruz‡ 1,482 F5
- San Juan del Piray 541 C7
- San Juan del Potrero 263 C5
- San Lorenzo, El Beni 496 C4
- San Lorenzo, Pando‡ 317 B2
- San Lorenzo, Tarija 785 C7
- San Lucas 925 C7
- San Matías 887 F5
- San Miguel 502 E5
- San Miguel de Huachi 25 B4
- San Pablo 11 B7
- San Pedro, Chuquisaca 182 C6
- San Pedro, El Beni 262 C4
- San Pedro, Pando‡ 312 B2
- San Pedro, Santa Cruz 80 D5
- San Pedro de Buena Vista 1,094 C6
- San Pedro de Quemes‡ 290 A7
- San Rafael‡ 1,282 E5
- San Ramón, El Beni 1,161 C3
- San Ramón, Santa Cruz 379 D5
- Santa Ana, El Beni 2,225 C3
- Santa Ana, La Paz 171 B4
- Santa Ana, Santa Cruz 275 E5
- Santa Ana, Santa Cruz 2,225 F6
- Santa Cruz 254,682 D5
- Santa Cruz del Valle Ameno 442 A4
- Santa Elena‡ 4,474 C7
- Santa Isabel‡ 323 B7
- Santa Rosa, Cochabamba‡ 942 B5
- Santa Rosa, Cochabamba‡ 276 C5
- Santa Rosa, El Beni 765 B4
- Santa Rosa, Pando‡ 105 B2
- Santa Rosa, Santa Cruz 995 D5
- Santa Rosa de la Mina 99 D5
- Santa Rosa de la Roca 101 E5
- Santa Rosa del Palmar 441 E5
- Santiago, Potosí 172 A7
- Santiago, Santa Cruz 765 F6
- Santiago de Huata 948 A5
- Santiago de Machaca 218 A5
- Santo Corazón‡ 963 F5
- Sapahaqui 55 B5
- Sapse‡ 89 C6
- Sarampiuni 138 A4
- Saya 339 B5
- Sena‡ 660 B2
- Sevaruyo 475 B6
- Sicasica 1,486 B5
- Sopachuy 713 C6
- Sorata 2,087 A4
- Sotomayor 510 C6
- Suapi‡ 1,750 B4
- Suches‡ 231 A4
- Sucre (cap.) 63,625 C6
- Suipacha‡ 2,701 C7
- Tacobamba‡ 6,933 C6
- Tacopaya 795 B5
- Talina 122 B7
- Tapacarí 980 B5
- Tarabuco 2,833 C6
- Tarairi‡ 394 D7
- Tarapaya 357 B6
- Tarata 3,016 C5
- Tarija 38,916 C7
- Teduzara‡ 271 B2
- Terevinto‡ 3,790 D5
- Tiahuanacu 1,227 A5
- Tinguipaya 766 C6
- Tipuani‡ 1,216 B4
- Tiraque 1,390 C5
- Tocomechi 575 D5
- Todos Santos, Cochabamba 408 C5
- Todos Santos, Oruro 68 A6
- Toledo 3,273 B6
- Tomás Barrón 1,852 B5
- Tomave 201 B7
- Tomina 708 C6
- Toropalca‡ 199 B7
- Torotoro 1,233 C6
- Totora C5
- Trigal 749 C6
- Trinidad 14,505 C4
- Tumupasa 349 B4
- Tumusla‡ 526 C7
- Tupiza 8,248 C7
- Turco 131 A6
- Ubina‡ 462 B7
- Ucumasi‡ 1,040 B6
- Ulla Ulla 52 A4
- Ulloma 116 A5
- Umala 481 B5
- Uncía 4,507 B6
- Uriondo 860 C7
- Urubichá 1,369 D4
- Uyuni 6,968 B7
- Vallegrande 5,094 C6
- Versalles 83 D3
- Viacha 6,607 A5
- Vichacla 317 C7
- Vichaya 422 A5
- Vilacaya 200 C6
- Villa Abecia 539 C7
- Villa Bella 88 C2
- Villa E. Viscarra 658 C6
- Villa General Pérez 802 A4
- Villa Ingavi 122 D7
- Villa Martín 543 B7
- Villa Montes 3,105 D7
- Villa Orías 404 C6
- Villar 322 C6
- Villa Serrano 1,570 C6
- Villa Tunari 510 C5
- Villa Vaca Guzmán 699 D6
- Villazón 6,261 C7
- Vitichi 1,515 C7
- Warnes 1,571 D5
- Yaco 835 B5
- Yacuiba 5,027 D7
- Yamparaéz 725 C6
- Yanacachi‡ 1,964 B5
- Yatina‡ 1,850 C7
- Yocalla‡ 1,814 B6
- Yotala 1,554 C6
- Yura 136 B7
- Zongo 141 B5
- Zudáñez 1,868 C6

Topography

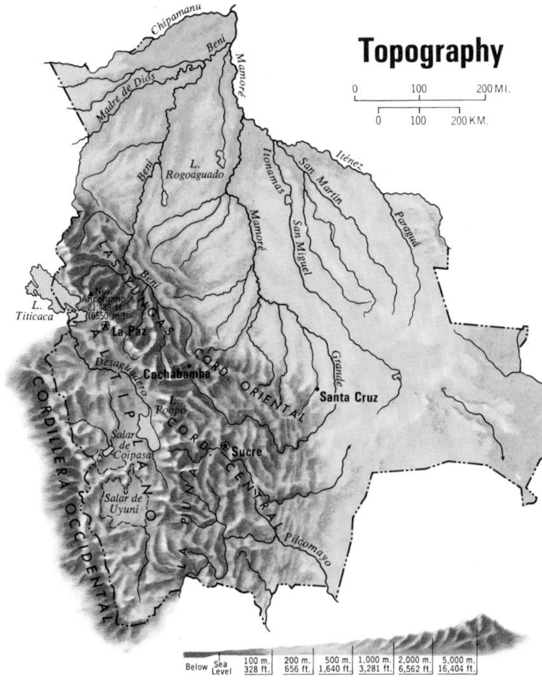

0 100 200 MI.
0 100 200 KM.
Chipamanu
Beni
Mamoré
Madre de Diós
L. Rogoaguado
Itonamas
Iténez
San Martín
San Miguel
Paraguá
L. Titicaca
La Paz
Cochabamba
Santa Cruz
Sucre
Poopó
Salar de Coipasa
Salar de Uyuni
Grande
Pilcomayo
CORDILLERA OCCIDENTAL
CORD. ORIENTAL
CORD. CENTRAL
Below Sea Level
100 m. 328 ft.
200 m. 656 ft.
500 m. 1,640 ft.
1,000 m. 3,281 ft.
2,000 m. 6,562 ft.
5,000 m. 16,404 ft.

OTHER FEATURES

- Abuná (riv.) B2
- Altamachi (riv.) B5
- Ancohuma, Nevada (mt.) A4
- Apere (riv.) C4
- Arroyas, Los (lake) C3
- Barras (riv.) B6
- Baures (riv.) D3
- Beni (riv.) B4
- Benicito (riv.) C3
- Bermejo (riv.) C8
- Blanco (riv.) D4
- Bloomfield, Sierra (mts.) D4
- Boopi (riv.) B4
- Cáceres (lag.) G6
- Candelaria (riv.) F5
- Capitán Ustarés, Cerro (mt.) E6
- Central, Cordillera (range) C6
- Challviri (salt dep.) B8
- Chaparé (riv.) C5
- Charagua, Sierra de (mts.) D6
- Chipamanu (riv.) A2
- Chovoreca, Cerro (mt.) F6
- Claro (riv.) A3
- Coipasa (lake) B6
- Coipasa (salt dep.) A6
- Colorada (lag.) A8
- Concepción (lag.) E5
- Coronel F. Gabrera E6
- Cotacajes (riv.) B5
- Desaguadero (riv.) B5
- Emero (riv.) B3
- Empexa (salt dep.) A7
- Gaiba (lag.) F5
- Grande (marsh) F5
- Grande (riv.) C4
- Grande (riv.) C6
- Grande de Lípez (riv.) B7
- Guaporé (riv.) C3
- Heath (riv.) A3
- Huanchaca, Cerro (mt.) B7
- Huanchaca, Serranía de (mts.) E4
- Huatunas (lag.) B3
- Ichilo (riv.) C5
- Ichoa (riv.) C4
- Illampu, Nevada (mt.) A4
- Illimani, Nevada (mt.) B5
- Incacamachi, Cerro (mt.) A6
- Isiboro (riv.) C5
- Iténez (Guaporé) (riv.) C3
- Itonamas (riv.) C3
- Izozog (swamp) E6
- Jara, Cerrito (mt.) F6
- Lauca (riv.) A6
- Lípez, Cordillera de (range) B8
- Liverpool (swamp) D4
- Machupo (riv.) C3
- Madidi (riv.) A3
- Madre de Diós (riv.) A3
- Mamoré (riv.) C2
- Mandioré (lag.) F6
- Manupari (riv.) B3
- Manuripi (riv.) B2
- Mapiri (riv.) A4
- Mizque (riv.) C6
- Mosetenes, Cordillera de (range) B5
- Negro (riv.) D4
- Occidental, Cordillera (range) A6
- Ollagüe (vol.) B7
- Oriental, Cordillera (range) C5
- Ortón (riv.) B2
- Otuquis (riv.) F6
- Paraguá (riv.) E4
- Paraguay (riv.) F7
- Paraiso (riv.) E4
- Parapetí (riv.) D6
- Petas, Las (riv.) F5
- Pilaya (riv.) C7
- Pilcomayo (riv.) D7
- Piray (riv.) D5
- Poopó (lake) B6
- Pupuya, Nevada (mt.) A4
- Puquintica, Nevado (mt.) A6
- Rápulo (riv.) C4
- Real, Cordillera (range) A5
- Rogagua (lake) B3
- Rogaguado (lake) C3
- Sajama, Nevada (mt.) A6
- San Fernando (riv.) F5
- San Juan (riv.) C7
- San Lorenzo, Serranía (mts.) E5
- San Luis (lake) C3
- San Martín (riv.) D3
- San Miguel (riv.) D4
- San Simón, Serranía (mts.) D4
- Santiago, Serranía de (mts.) F6
- Sécure (riv.) C4
- Sillajhuay, Cordillera (mt.) A6
- Suches (riv.) A4
- Sunsas, Serranía de (mts.) F5
- Tahuamanu (riv.) A2
- Tarija, Río Grande de (riv.) C8
- Tequeje (riv.) B3
- Tijamuchi (riv.) C4
- Titicaca (lake) A4
- Tocorpuri, Cerros de (mt.) A8
- Tucavaca (riv.) F6
- Tuichi (riv.) A4
- Uberaba (lag.) G5
- Uyuni (salt dep.) B7
- Yacuma (riv.) B3
- Yapacani (riv.) C5
- Yata (riv.) C3
- Yungas, Las (reg.) B5
- Zapaleri, Cerro (mt.) B8

‡Population of canton.

Agriculture, Industry and Resources

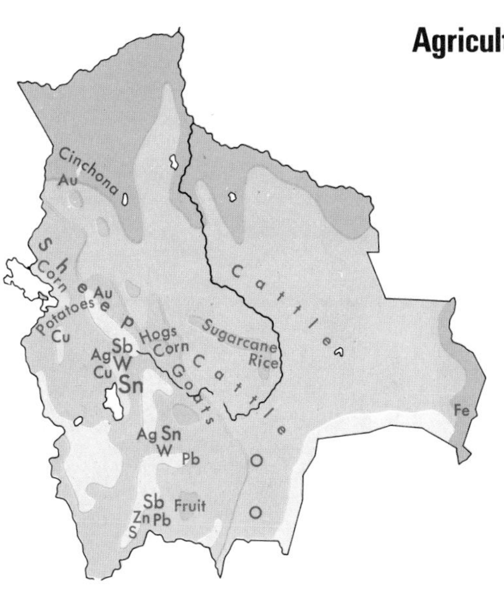

Cinchona
Au
Sheep
Corn
Potatoes
Cu
Hogs
Corn
Sugarcane
Rice
Cattle
Goats
Ag Sb W
Cu
Sn
Ag Sn W Pb
Sb Fruit
Zn Pb
S
Fe

DOMINANT LAND USE

- Diversified Tropical Crops (chiefly plantation agriculture)
- Upland Cultivated Areas
- Upland Livestock Grazing, Limited Agriculture
- Extensive Livestock Ranching
- Forests
- Nonagricultural Land

MAJOR MINERAL OCCURRENCES

Ag	Silver	G	Natural Gas	Sb	Antimony
Au	Gold	O	Petroleum	Sn	Tin
Cu	Copper	Pb	Lead	W	Tungsten
Fe	Iron Ore	S	Sulfur	Zn	Zinc

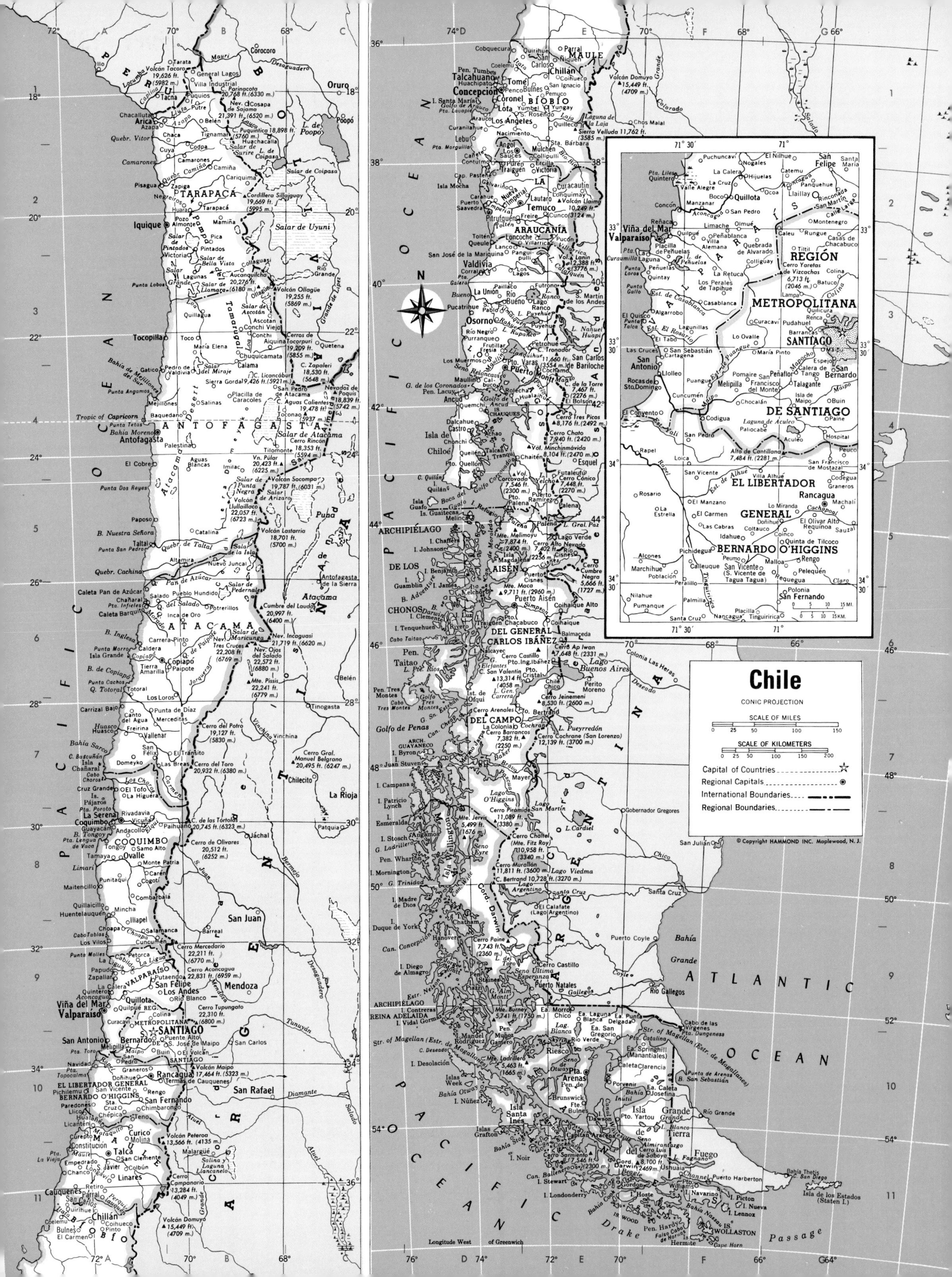
Chile
CONIC PROJECTION
SCALE OF MILES
0 25 50 150
SCALE OF KILOMETERS
0 25 50 100 150 200
Capital of Countries
Regional Capitals
International Boundaries
Regional Boundaries
© Copyright HAMMOND INC. Maplewood, N. J.
REGIÓN METROPOLITANA DE SANTIAGO
PACIFIC OCEAN
ATLANTIC OCEAN
PERU
BOLIVIA
ARGENTINA
TARAPACÁ
ANTOFAGASTA
ATACAMA
COQUIMBO
VALPARAÍSO
METROPOLITANA
EL LIBERTADOR GENERAL BERNARDO O'HIGGINS
MAULE
BÍOBÍO
LA ARAUCANÍA
LOS LAGOS
AISÉN DEL GENERAL CARLOS IBÁÑEZ DEL CAMPO
MAGALLANES
Arica
Iquique
Tocopilla
Antofagasta
Copiapó
La Serena
Coquimbo
Valparaíso
Viña del Mar
SANTIAGO
Rancagua
Talca
Concepción
Temuco
Valdivia
Osorno
Puerto Montt
Puerto Aisén
Punta Arenas
Oruro
Salar de Uyuni
Salar de Atacama
Tropic of Capricorn
Strait of Magellan (Estr. de Magallanes)
Tierra del Fuego
Isla Grande de Tierra del Fuego
Drake Passage
Cape Horn
Longitude West of Greenwich

Topography

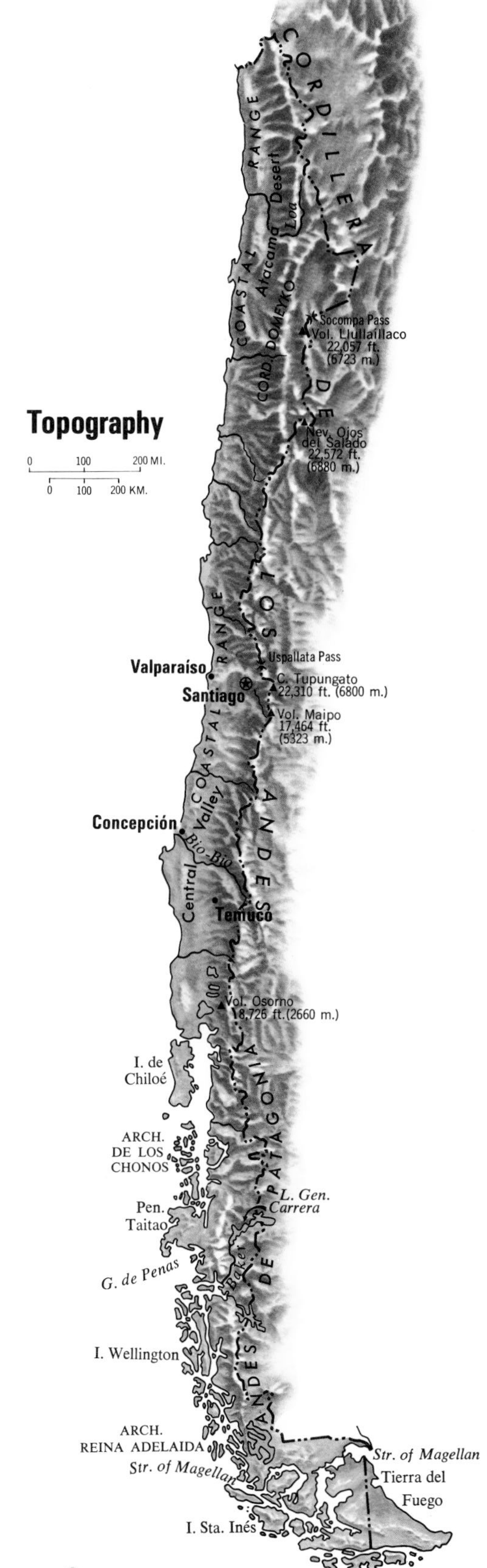
0 100 200 MI.
0 100 200 KM.
CORDILLERA DE LOS ANDES
COASTAL RANGE
Atacama Desert
Loa
CORD. DOMEYKO
Socompa Pass
Vol. Llullaillaco 22,057 ft. (6723 m.)
Nev. Ojos del Salado 22,572 ft. (6880 m.)
Uspallata Pass
Valparaíso
Santiago
C. Tupungato 22,310 ft. (6800 m.)
Vol. Maipo 17,464 ft. (5323 m.)
Central Valley
Concepción
Río Bío Bío
Temuco
Vol. Osorno 8,726 ft. (2660 m.)
I. de Chiloé
ARCH. DE LOS CHONOS
L. Gen. Carrera
Pen. Taitao
G. de Penas
Baker
ANDES DE PATAGONIA
I. Wellington
ARCH. REINA ADELAIDA
Str. of Magellan
Tierra del Fuego
I. Sta. Inés
I. Hoste
Cape Horn
5,000 m. 16,404 ft.
2,000 m. 6,562 ft.
1,000 m. 3,281 ft.
500 m. 1,640 ft.
200 m. 656 ft.
100 m. 328 ft.
Sea Level
Below

AREA 292,257 sq. mi. (756,946 sq. km.)
POPULATION 12,961,000
CAPITAL Santiago
LARGEST CITY Santiago
HIGHEST POINT Ojos del Salado 22,572 ft. (6,880 m.)
MONETARY UNIT Chilean peso
MAJOR LANGUAGE Spanish
MAJOR RELIGION Roman Catholicism

REGIONS

Aisén del General Carlos Ibáñez del Campo 65,478 . . . . E6
Antofagasta 341,203 . . . . B4
Atacama 183,071 . . . . B6
Bíobío 1,516,552 . . . . E1
Coquimbo 419,178 . . . . A8
El Libertador General Bernardo O'Higgins 584,989 . . . . A10
La Araucanía 692,924 . . . . E2
Los Lagos 843,430 . . . . D3
Magallanes 132,333 . . . . E10
Maule 723,224 . . . . A11
Santiago, Región Metropolitana de (Santiago Metropolitan Region) 4,294,938 . . . . A9
Tarapacá 273,427 . . . . B2
Valparaíso 1,204,693 . . . . A9

CITIES and TOWNS

Achao ○11,501 . . . . D4
Aguas Blancas ○203 . . . . B4
Algarrobo ○3,941 . . . . F3
Ancud 11,900 . . . . D4
Andacollo 6,000 . . . . A8
Angol 42,670 . . . . D1
Antofagasta 125,100 . . . . A4
Arauco 5,400 . . . . D1
Arica 87,700 . . . . A1
Ascotán B3
Barrancas ○184,241 . . . . G3
Belén ○925 . . . . B1
Buin 11,800 . . . . G4
Bulnes 6,900 . . . . E1
Cabildo 5,800 . . . . A9
Calama 45,900 . . . . B3
Calbuco ○21,673 . . . . D4
Caldera ○3,268 . . . . A6
Calera de Tango ○6,198 . . . G4
Calle Larga ○7,172 . . . . G2
Cañete 7,900 . . . . D2
Carahue ○12,733 . . . . D2
Cartagena ○7,124 . . . . F3
Casablanca 5,500 . . . . F3
Casas de Chacabuco G2
Castro 11,200 . . . . D4
Catalina ○1,637 . . . . B5
Catemu ○8,728 . . . . G2
Cauquenes 20,200 . . . . A11
Cerro Castillo ○537 . . . . E9
Cerro Manantiales F10
Chaitén ○4,067 . . . . E4
Chañaral ○36,949 . . . . A6
Chanco ○12,433 . . . . A11
Chépica ○11,199 . . . . A10
Chillán 128,515 . . . . A10
Chimbarongo 5,300 . . . . A10
Chonchi ○8,911 . . . . D4
Chuquicamata 22,100 . . . . B3
Cobquecura ○6,298 . . . . D1
Cochamó ○5,042 . . . . E3
Codegua ○6,757 . . . . G4
Codpa ○950 . . . . B1
Coelemu 5,400 . . . . D1
Coihaique 32,129 . . . . E6
Coihueco ○17,276 . . . . A11
Coinco ○4,942 . . . . G5
Colbún ○12,924 . . . . A11
Colina 7,400 . . . . G3
Collipulli 7,200 . . . . E2
Coltauco ○11,857 . . . . F5
Combarbalá ○17,332 . . . . A8
Concepción 206,226 . . . . D1
Constitución 11,500 . . . . A11
Contulmo ○13,987 . . . . D2
Copiapó 45,200 . . . . B6
Coquimbo 73,953 . . . . A8
Coronel 37,300 . . . . D1
Corral ○5,533 . . . . D3
Cunco ○18,836 . . . . E2
Curacautín 9,800 . . . . E2
Curacaví 5,800 . . . . G3
Curanilahue 13,200 . . . . D1
Curepto ○13,020 . . . . A10
Curicó 41,300 . . . . A10
Dalcahue ○7,084 . . . . D4
Domeiko A7
Doñihue ○8,837 . . . . G5
El Carmen ○13,226 . . . . A11
El Monte 7,000 . . . . G4
El Quisco ○2,152 . . . . E3
El Tabo ○2,180 . . . . F3
El Tofo A7
Empedrado ○7,887 . . . . A11
Ercilla ○8,061 . . . . E2
Estancia Caleta Josefina ○1,042 . . . . F10
Estancia Morro Chico ○785 . E9
Estancia San Gregorio ○1,156 . . . . E9
Estancia Springhill (Cerro Manantiales) F10
Freire ○23,313 . . . . E2
Freirina ○5,523 . . . . A7
Fresia ○15,359 . . . . D3
Frutillar ○12,721 . . . . D3
Futaleufú ○2,366 . . . . E4
Futrono ○7,109 . . . . E3
Galvarino ○9,495 . . . . D2
General Lagos ○810 . . . . B1
Graneros 8,900 . . . . G5
Guayacán A8
Hijuelas ○7,128 . . . . F2
Hualañé ○6,912 . . . . A10
Huara ○1,934 . . . . B2
Huasco ○4,971 . . . . A7
Illapel 12,200 . . . . A8
Inca de Oro 1,406 . . . . B6
Iquique 64,500 . . . . A2
Isla de Maipo ○12,903 . . . . G4
La Calera 24,600 . . . . F2
La Cruz ○8,907 . . . . F2
La Estrella ○3,707 . . . . F5
Lago Ranco ○12,767 . . . . E3
Lagunas ○5,653 . . . . B3
La Higuera ○6,991 . . . . A7
La Ligua 7,500 . . . . A9
Lampa ○10,220 . . . . G3
Lanco 5,200 . . . . D2
Las Cabras ○12,119 . . . . F5
La Serena 99,908 . . . . A8
La Unión 15,200 . . . . D3
Lautaro 11,900 . . . . E2
Lebu 12,500 . . . . D1
Licantén ○6,354 . . . . A10
Limache 15,200 . . . . F2
Linares 37,900 . . . . A11
Llay-Llay 9,700 . . . . G2
Loica F4
Loncoche ○17,539 . . . . D2
Longaví ○15,909 . . . . A11
Lonquimay ○9,524 . . . . E2
Los Andes 23,500 . . . . B9
Los Ángeles 49,500 . . . . D1
Los Lagos ○14,934 . . . . D3
Los Muermos ○9,296 . . . . D3
Los Sauces ○7,613 . . . . D2
Los Vilos ○10,453 . . . . A9
Lota 48,100 . . . . D1
Machalí 5,800 . . . . G5
Maipú ○117,872 . . . . G3
Malloa ○9,742 . . . . G5
Marchigüe ○4,451 . . . . F5
María Elena 5,900 . . . . B3
María Pinto ○5,980 . . . . G3
Maullín ○14,544 . . . . D4
Mejillones ○3,333 . . . . A4
Melipilla 23,900 . . . . F4
Mincha ○11,329 . . . . A8
Molina 9,400 . . . . A10
Monte Patria ○18,927 . . . . A8
Mulchén 13,700 . . . . E1
Nacimiento ○17,651 . . . . D1
Nancagua ○11,076 . . . . F6
Navidad ○6,618 . . . . A10
Negreiros ○1,144 . . . . B2
Niquén ○13,640 . . . . E1
Nogales ○18,529 . . . . F2
Nueva Imperial 8,000 . . . . D2
Olivar Alto ○5,414 . . . . G5
Ollagüe B3
Olmué ○8,804 . . . . F2
Osorno 68,800 . . . . D3
Ovalle 31,700 . . . . A8
Paihuano ○6,048 . . . . B8
Paillaco 5,200 . . . . D3
Paine ○21,876 . . . . G4
Palena ○2,508 . . . . E5
Palmilla ○7,965 . . . . F6
Panguipulli 5,700 . . . . E2
Panquehue ○4,230 . . . . G2
Papudo ○2,594 . . . . A9
Paredones ○7,404 . . . . A10
Parral 17,000 . . . . A11
Pedro de Valdivia 6,200 . . . . B4
Pemuco ○7,577 . . . . E1
Peñaflor 15,500 . . . . G4
Penco ○33,962 . . . . D1
Peñuelas F3
Petorca ○8,343 . . . . A9
Petrohué E3
Peumo ○11,308 . . . . F5
Pica ○1,487 . . . . B2
Pichidegua ○13,550 . . . . F5
Pichilemu ○8,042 . . . . A10
Pinto ○8,687 . . . . A11
Pisagua ○1,880 . . . . A2
Pitrufquén 7,800 . . . . D2
Placilla ○6,441 . . . . F6
Porvenir ○4,000 . . . . E10
Potrerillos 5,800 . . . . B6
Pozo Almonte ○1,798 . . . . B2
Puchuncaví ○7,542 . . . . F2
Pucón 18,000 . . . . E2
Pudahuel G3
Pueblo Hundido 6,200 . . . . B6
Puente Alto 65,100 . . . . B10
Puerto Aisén 17,848 . . . . E6
Puerto Cisnes ○2,800 . . . . E5
Puerto Ingeniero Ibáñez ○1,900 . . . . E6
Puerto Montt 119,059 . . . . E4
Puerto Natales 17,280 . . . . E9
Puerto Quellón ○7,734 . . . . D4
Puerto Varas 10,900 . . . . E3
Puerto Williams ○949 . . . . F11
Pumanque ○3,137 . . . . F6
Punitaqui ○16,167 . . . . A8
Punta Arenas 2,140 . . . . E10
Purén ○11,604 . . . . D2
Purranque 5,900 . . . . D3
Putaendo ○12,806 . . . . A9
Putre ○855 . . . . B1
Puyehue E3
Queilén ○6,055 . . . . D4
Quemchi ○6,707 . . . . D4
Quilicura 8,100 . . . . G3
Quillagua B3
Quilleco ○16,043 . . . . E1
Quillota 36,500 . . . . F2
Quilpué 40,600 . . . . F2
Quinta de Tilcoco ○6,513 . . G5
Quintero 9,900 . . . . F2
Quirihue ○11,178 . . . . E1
Rancagua 140,589 . . . . G5
Renca ○67,168 . . . . G3
Rengo 12,400 . . . . G5
Requínoa ○10,730 . . . . G5
Retiro ○15,146 . . . . A11
Rinconada San Martín ○4,118 . . . . G2
Río Blanco B9
Río Bueno 9,600 . . . . D3
Río Negro 5,100 . . . . D3
Río Verde ○554 . . . . E10
Rocas de Santo Domingo ○4,114 . . . . F4
Rosario ○3,383 . . . . F5
Salamanca ○18,741 . . . . A9
Samo Alto ○5,689 . . . . A8
San Antonio 46,700 . . . . F3
San Bernardo ○117,766 . . . G4
San Carlos 17,000 . . . . E1
San Clemente ○23,273 . . . A11
San Felipe 26,100 . . . . G2
San Fernando 23,600 . . . . G6
San Francisco de Mostazal ○11,439 . . . . G4
San Ignacio ○13,523 . . . . E1
San Javier 10,800 . . . . A11
San José de Maipo ○9,601 . . . . B10
San Pablo ○7,978 . . . . D3
San Pedro ○8,255 . . . . F4
San Pedro de Atacama C4
San Rosendo ○14,337 . . . . E1
Santa Bárbara ○14,345 . . . . E1
Santa Cruz 8,600 . . . . F6
Santa María ○8,162 . . . . G2
Santiago (cap.) 3,614,947 . . G3
Santiago *3,672,374 . . . . G3
San Vicente F4
San Vicente (San Vicente de Tagua Tagua) ○28,333 F5
Sierra Gorda ○8,805 . . . . B4
Talagante 16,500 . . . . G4
Talca 133,160 . . . . A11
Talcahuano 148,300 . . . . D1
Taltal 6,400 . . . . A5
Tamaya A8
Tarapacá B2
Temuco 197,232 . . . . E2
Teno ○17,675 . . . . A10
Termas de Cauquenes B10
Tierra Amarilla ○7,899 . . . . A6
Tiltil ○9,198 . . . . G2
Toco ○8,734 . . . . B3
Toconao C4
Tocopilla 22,000 . . . . A3
Toltén ○16,265 . . . . D2
Tomé 29,600 . . . . D1
Traiguén 11,400 . . . . D2
Valdivia 115,536 . . . . D3
Vallenar 26,800 . . . . A7
Valparaíso 271,580 . . . . E2
Victoria 16,500 . . . . D2
Vicuña 5,100 . . . . A8
Villa Alemana 29,600 . . . . F2
Villa Alhué ○5,078 . . . . G4
Villarrica 25,091 . . . . E2
Viña del Mar 281,361 . . . . F2
Yumbel ○21,858 . . . . E1
Yungay ○10,725 . . . . E1
Zapallar ○2,894 . . . . A9
Zapiga B2

OTHER FEATURES

Aconcagua (riv.) F2
Aculeo (lag.) G4
Adventure (bay) D5
Aguas Calientes, Cerro (mt.) C4
Almirantazgo (bay) F11
Almirante Montt (gulf) D9
Ancud (gulf) D4
Angamos (isl.) D8
Angamos (pt.) A4
Ap Iwan, Cerro (mt.) E6
Arauco (gulf) D1
Arenales, Cerro (mt.) D7
Atacama (des.) B4
Atacama, Salar de (salt dep.) C4
Aucanquilcha, Cerro (mt.) . . B3
Azapa, Quebrada (riv.) B1
Baker (riv.) D7
Ballenero (chan.) E11
Bascuñán (cape) A7
Beagle (chan.) E11
Bella Vista, Salar de (salt dep.) B3
Benjamín (isl.) D5
Bío-Bío (riv.) E2
Blanca (lag.) E10
Blanco (lake) F10
Bravo (riv.) D7
Brunswick (pen.) E10
Bueno (riv.) D3
Buenos Aires (lake) E6
Byron (isl.) D7
Cachapoal (riv.) G5
Cachina, Quebrada (riv.) A5
Cachos (pt.) A6
Calafquén (lake) E3
Camarones (riv.) A2
Camiña, Quebrada (riv.) B2
Campana (isl.) D7
Campanario, Cerro (mt.) . . A10
Capitán Aracena (isl.) E10
Carmen (riv.) B7
Castillo, Cerro (mt.) E6
Catalina (pt.) F10
Chaffers (isl.) D5
Chaltel, Cerro (mt.) E8
Chañaral (isl.) A7
Chatham (isl.) D9
Chauques (isls.) D4
Cheap (chan.) D7
Chiloé (isl.) 119,286 . . . . D4
Choapa (riv.) A9
Chonos (arch.) D6
Choros (cape) A7
Cisnes (riv.) E5
Clarence (isl.) E10
Clemente (isl.) D6
Cochrane (lake) E7
Cochrane, Cerro (mt.) E7
Cockburn (chan.) E11
Concepción (chan.) D9
Cónico, Cerro (mt.) E4
Contreras (isl.) D9
Cook (bay) E11
Copiapó (bay) A6
Copiapó (riv.) A6
Corcovado (gulf) D4
Corcovado (vol.) D5
Coronados (gulf) D4
Curaumilla (pt.) E2
Darwin (bay) D6
Darwin, Cordillera (mts.) . . . D8
Darwin, Cordillera (mts.) . . E11

(continued on following page)

(continued)

Dawson (isl.) E10
Deseado (cape) D10
Desolación (isl.) D10
Diego de Almagro (isl.) D9
Domeyko, Cordillera (mts.) . B4
Dos Reyes (pt.) A5
Drake (passg.) E11
Dungeness (pt.) F10
Duque de York (isl.) C9
Elefantes (gulf) D6
Elqui (riv.) A8
Esmeralda (isl.) C8
Eyre (bay) D8
Fagnano (lake) F11
Fitz Roy (Chaltel) (mt.) E8
Galera (pt.) D3
General Paz (lake) E5
Gordon (isl.) E11
Grafton (isls.) D10
Grande (isl.) A6
Grande (riv.) F10
Grande, Salar (salt dep.) . . . B3
Grande de Tierra
del Fuego (isl.) E11
Guafo (gulf) D5
Guafo (isl.) D5
Guaitecas (isls.) D5
Guamblin (isl.) D5
Guayaneco (arch.) D7
Hanover (isl.) D9
Hardy (pen.) F11
Hermite (isls.) F11
Horn (cape) F11
Hornos, Falso (cape) F11
Hoste (isl.) F11
Huasco (riv.) A7
Imperial (riv.) D2
Incaguasi, Nevada (mt.) C6
Infieles (pt.) A6
Inglesa (bay) A6
Inútil (bay) E10
James (isl.) D5
Johnson (isl.) D5
Jorge Montt (isl.) D9
Juan Stuven (isl.) D7
Lacuy (pen.) D4
Ladrillero (gulf) C8
Ladrillero (mt.) E10
Laja (riv.) E1
La Laja (lag.) E1
La Ligua (riv.) A9
Lanín (vol.) E2
Lastarria (vol.) B5
Lauca (riv.) B1
Lavapié (pt.) D1
La Vieja (pt.) A11
Lengua de Vaca (pt.) A8
Lennox (isl.) F11
Liles (pt.) F2
Limarí (riv.) A8
Llaima (vol.) E2
Llamara, Salar de (salt dep.) B3
Llanquihue (lake) E3
Llullaillaco (vol.) B5
Lluta (riv.) B1
Loa (riv.) B3
Lobos (pt.) A3
Londonderry (isl.) E11
Loros (pt.) E3
Luz (isl.) D6
Macá (mt.) D5
Madre de Dios (isl.) D8

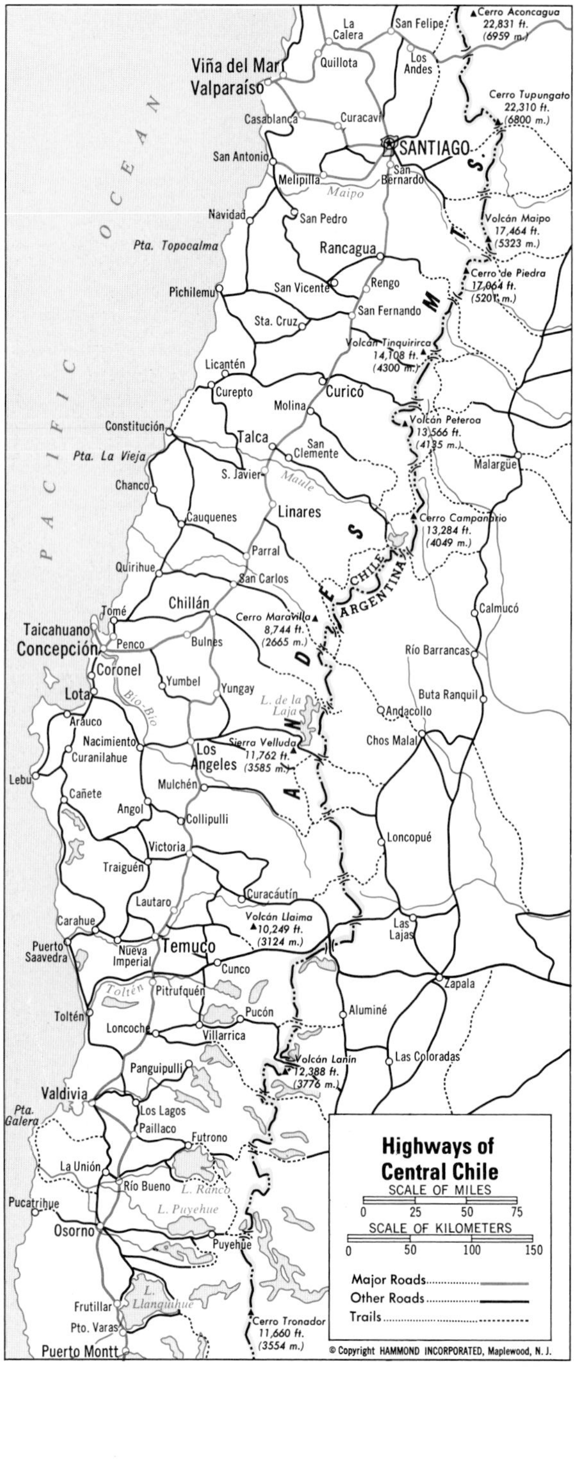
Highways of Central Chile
SCALE OF MILES
0 25 50 75
SCALE OF KILOMETERS
0 50 100 150
Major Roads
Other Roads
Trails
© Copyright HAMMOND INCORPORATED, Maplewood, N. J.
PACIFIC OCEAN
ANDES MTS.
CHILE
ARGENTINA
Cerro Aconcagua 22,831 ft. (6959 m.)
Cerro Tupungato 22,310 ft. (6800 m.)
Volcán Maipo 17,464 ft. (5323 m.)
Cerro de Piedra 17,064 ft. (5201 m.)
Volcán Tinguirirca 14,108 ft. (4300 m.)
Volcán Peteroa 13,566 ft. (4135 m.)
Cerro Campanario 13,284 ft. (4049 m.)
Cerro Maravilla 8,744 ft. (2665 m.)
Sierra Velluda 11,762 ft. (3585 m.)
Volcán Llaima 10,249 ft. (3124 m.)
Volcán Lanín 12,388 ft. (3776 m.)
Cerro Tronador 11,660 ft. (3554 m.)
Viña del Mar
Valparaíso
La Calera
Quillota
San Felipe
Los Andes
Casablanca
Curacaví
SANTIAGO
San Bernardo
San Antonio
Melipilla
Maipo
Navidad
San Pedro
Rancagua
Pta. Topocalma
Pichilemu
San Vicente
Rengo
San Fernando
Sta. Cruz
Licantén
Curepto
Curicó
Molina
Constitución
Talca
San Clemente
Pta. La Vieja
Chanco
S. Javier
Maule
Malargüe
Cauquenes
Linares
Parral
Quirihue
San Carlos
Chillán
Tomé
Taicahuano
Concepción
Penco
Bulnes
Coronel
Yumbel
Yungay
Lota
Bío-Bío
L. de la Laja
Antuco
Arauco
Nacimiento
Curanilahue
Los Angeles
Lebu
Cañete
Mulchén
Angol
Collipulli
Victoria
Traiguén
Lautaro
Curacautín
Carahue
Puerto Saavedra
Nueva Imperial
Temuco
Cunco
Toltén
Pitrufquén
Loncoche
Pucón
Villarrica
Panguipulli
Valdivia
Pta. Galera
Los Lagos
Paillaco
Futrono
La Unión
Río Bueno
L. Ranco
L. Puyehue
Pucatrihue
Osorno
Puyehue
Frutillar
L. Llanquihue
Pto. Varas
Puerto Montt
Calmucó
Río Barrancas
Buta Ranquil
Andacollo
Chos Malal
Loncopué
Las Lajas
Zapala
Aluminé
Las Coloradas

Agriculture, Industry and Resources

Valparaíso
Santiago
Concepción
Whales
Goats
Sheep
Fruit
Rice
Corn
Wheat
Cattle
Wine
Crayfish

DOMINANT LAND USE

- Cereals, Livestock
- Mediterranean Agriculture (cereals, fruit, livestock)
- Pasture Livestock
- Extensive Livestock Ranching
- Limited Seasonal Grazing
- Forests
- Nonagricultural Land

MAJOR MINERAL OCCURRENCES

Ag	Silver	Hg	Mercury
Au	Gold	Id	Iodine
C	Coal	Mn	Manganese
Cu	Copper	Mo	Molybdenum
Fe	Iron Ore	N	Nitrates
G	Natural Gas	Na	Salt
Gp	Gypsum	O	Petroleum
		S	Sulfur

Water Power — Major Industrial Areas

Magallanes (Magellan)
(str.) D10
Magdalena (isl.) D5
Magellan (str.) D10
Maipo (riv.) F4
Maipú (vol.) B10
Manso (riv.) E4
Manuel Rodríguez (isl.) . . . D10
Mapocho (riv.) G3
Mataquito (riv.) A10
Maule (riv.) A11
Maullín (riv.) D3
Mejillones del Sur (bay) A4
Melchor (isl.) D6
Melimoyu (mt.) D5
Merino Jarpa (isl.) D7
Minchinmávida (vol.) E4
Miraje, Salar del (salt dep.) . B3
Mocha (isl.) B2
Molles (pt.) A9
Morado, Quebrado (riv.) A6
Moraleda (chan.) D5
Moreno (bay) A4
Mornington (isl.) D8
Morro (pt.) A6
Muñoz Gamero (pen.) D10
Murallón, Cerro (mt.) D8
Nalcayec (isl.) D6
Nassau (bay) F11
Navarino (isl.) F11
Nelson (str.) D9
Nuestra Señora (bay) A5
Nueva (isl.) F11
Núñez (isl.) D10
O'Higgins (lake) D7
Ojos del Salado,
Nevado (mt.) B6
Otway (bay) D10
Otway (sound) E10
Oyahue (vol.) C3
Paine, Cerro (mt.) D9
Pájaros (isls.) A7
Palena (lake) E5
Palena (riv.) D5
Pan de Azúcar,
Quebrado (riv.) B5
Parinacota, Cerro (mt.) B1
Pascua (riv.) D7
Patricio Lynch (isl.) D7
Penas (gulf) D7
Perquilauquén (riv.) A11
Piazzí (isl.) D9
Picton (isl.) F11
Pilmaiquén (riv.) D3
Pintados, Salar de
(salt dep.) B2
Poroto (pt.) A7
Potro, Cerro del (mt.) B7
Prat (isl.) D7
Presidente Ríos (lake) D6
Puangue, Estero de (riv.) . . . F3
Puelo (riv.) E4
Púlar, Cerro (mt.) B4
Puquintica, Cerro (mt.) B1
Puyehue (lake) E3
Quilán (cape) D4
Ranco (lake) E3
Rapel (riv.) F4
Refugio (isl.) D5
Reina Adelaida (arch.) D9
Reloncaví (bay) D4
Riesco (isl.) E10
Rincón, Cerro (mt.) C4
Rivero (isl.) D6
Rupanco (lake) D3
San Esteban (gulf) D7
San Lorenzo, Cerro
(Cochrane) (mt.) E7
San Martín (lake) E7
San Pedro (pt.) A5
Santa Inés (isl.) D10
Santa María (isl.) D1
San Valentín, Cerro (mt.) . . . D6
Sarco (bay) A7
Sarmiento, Cerro (mt.) E11
Sillajguay, Cordillera (range) . B2
Simpson (riv.) E6
Skyring (bay) E10
Socompa (vol.) B4
Staines (pen.) D9
Stewart (isl.) E11
Stokes (bay) D10
Stosch (isl.) C8
Surire, Salar de (salt dep.) . . B2
Tablas (cape) A9
Tacora (vol.) B1
Taitao (cape) D6
Taitao (pen.) D6
Talca (pt.) E3
Taltal, Quebrada de (riv.) . . . B5
Tamarugal, Pampa del
(plain) B3
Tenquehuen (isl.) D6
Tetas (pt.) A4
Tierra del Fuego,
Grande de (isl.) E11
Tinguiririca (riv.) F5
Toltén (riv.) D2
Tongoy (bay) A8
Topocalma (pt.) A10
Toro (lake) D9
Toro, Cerro del (mt.) B7
Toro (pt.) A10
Tórtolas, Cerro de las (mt.) . B8
Totoral, Quebrada (riv.) A6
Traiguén (isl.) D6
Tranqui (isl.) D4
Tres Cruces, Nevada (mt.) . . B6
Tres Montes (cape) C7
Tres Montes (gulf) D6
Tres Montes (pen.) C6
Trinidad (gulf) D8
Tronador, Cerro (mt.) E3
Tumbes (pen.) D1
Tupungato, Cerro (mt.) B9
Última Esperanza (sound) . . . E9
Vidal Gormaz (isl.) D9
Villarrica (lake) E2
Vitor, Quebrado (riv.) A1
Week (isls.) D10
Wellington (isl.) D8
Wharton (pen.) D8
Whiteside (chan.) E10
Wollaston (isl.) F11
Wood (isls.) E11
Yelcho (lake) E4
Zapaleri, Cerro (mt.) C4

*City and suburbs.
○ Population of commune.

PROVINCES

Buenos Aires 10,796,036 . . . D4
Catamarca 206,204 . . . C2
Chaco 692,410 . . . D2
Chubut 262,196 . . . C5
Córdoba 2,407,135 . . . D3
Corrientes 657,716 . . . E2
Distrito Federal 2,908,001 . . H7
Entre Ríos 902,241 . . . E3
Formosa 292,479 . . . D1
Jujuy 408,514 . . . C1
La Pampa 207,132 . . . C4
La Rioja 163,342 . . . C2
Mendoza 1,187,305 . . . C4
Misiones 579,579 . . . F2
Neuquén 241,904 . . . C4
Rio Negro 383,896 . . . C5
Salta 662,369 . . . D1
San Juan 469,973 . . . C3
San Luis 212,837 . . . C3
Santa Cruz 114,479 . . . C6
Santa Fe 2,457,188 . . . D3
Santiago del Estero 652,318 D2
Tierra del Fuego, Antártida, e Islas del Atlántico Sur 29,451 . . . C7
Tucumán 968,066 . . . C2

CITIES and TOWNS

Abra Pampa 2,929 . . . C1
Adolfo Alsina 7,707 . . . D4
Aguaray 4,802 . . . D1
Aguilares 20,286 . . . C2
Aimogasta 4,640 . . . C2
Alberti 6,440 . . . G7
Alcorta 5,818 . . . F6
Algarrobo del Águila . . . C4
Allen 14,041 . . . C4
Alpachiri 1,657 . . . D4
Alta Gracia 30,628 . . . D3
Aluminé 1,560 . . . B4
Alvear 5,419 . . . E2
Ameghino 2,775 . . . D3
Añatuya 15,025 . . . D2
Andalgalá 6,853 . . . C2
Antofagasta de la Sierra . . . C2
Apóstoles 11,252 . . . E2
Arrecifes 17,719 . . . F7
Arroyo Seco 12,886 . . . F6
Ascensión 3,031 . . . F7
Avellaneda 330,654 . . . G7
Ayacucho 12,363 . . . E4
Azul 43,582 . . . E4
Bahía Blanca 220,765 . . . D4
Bahía Bustamante . . . C6
Bahía Thetis . . . C7
Balcarce 28,985 . . . E4
Balnearia 4,531 . . . D3
Baradero 20,103 . . . G6
Barrancas 3,602 . . . F6
Barranqueras . . . E2
Barreal 2,739 . . . C3
Basavilbaso 7,657 . . . G6
Belén 7,411 . . . C2
Bella Vista, Corrientes 14,229 . . . E2
Bella Vista, Tucuman 9,177 . D2
Bell Ville 26,559 . . . D3
Bolívar 16,382 . . . D4
Bovril 4,735 . . . G5
Bragado 27,101 . . . F7
Buenos Aires (cap.) 2,908,001 . . . H7
Buenos Aires *9,927,404 . . . H7
Cafayate 5,048 . . . C2
Calafate . . . B7
Calchaquí 5,958 . . . F5
Caleta Olivia 20,141 . . . C6
Camarones . . . C5
Campana 51,498 . . . G6
Cañada de Gómez 24,706 . . . F6
Canals 6,627 . . . D3
Cañuelas 14,831 . . . G7
Carcaraña 11,121 . . . F6
Carlos Casares 13,286 . . . F7
Carlos Tejedor 4,421 . . . D4
Carmen de Areco 7,882 . . . F7
Carmen de Patagones 13,981 . . . D5
Casilda 23,492 . . . F6
Castelli 4,507 . . . H7
Catamarca 88,432 . . . C2
Caucete 14,512 . . . C3
Ceres 10,743 . . . D2
Chabás 5,156 . . . F6
Chacabuco 26,492 . . . F7
Chajarí 15,242 . . . G5
Chamical 6,333 . . . C3
Charadai 1,078 . . . D2
Charata 13,070 . . . D2
Chascomús 21,864 . . . H7
Chepes 4,775 . . . C3
Chicoana 1,844 . . . C2
Chilecito 14,010 . . . C2
Chivilcoy 43,779 . . . F7
Choele-Choel 6,191 . . . C4
Chos-Malal 4,823 . . . C4
Cinco Saltos 15,094 . . . C4
Cipolletti 40,123 . . . C4
Clorinda 21,008 . . . E2
Colón, Buenos Aires 16,070 . F6
Colón, Entre Ríos 11,648 . . . G6
Colonia Las Heras 3,176 . . . C6
Comandante Fontana 4,468 . D2
Comandante Luis Piedrabuena 2,492 . . . C6
Comodoro Rivadavia 96,865 . C6
Concepción 29,359 . . . C2
Concepción de la Sierra 2,778 . . . E2
Concepción del Uruguay 46,065 . . . G6
Concordia 93,618 . . . G5
Constanza 1,313 . . . G6
Córdoba 982,018 . . . D3
Coronda 11,554 . . . F6
Coronel Brandsen 10,484 . . . H7
Coronel Dorrego 10,661 . . . D4
Coronel Pringles 16,592 . . . D4
Coronel Suárez 16,359 . . . D4

AREA 1,072,070 sq. mi. (2,776,661 sq. km.)
POPULATION 31,929,000
CAPITAL Buenos Aires
LARGEST CITY Buenos Aires
HIGHEST POINT Cerro Aconcagua 22,831 ft. (6,959 m.)
MONETARY UNIT austral
MAJOR LANGUAGE Spanish
MAJOR RELIGION Roman Catholicism

Agriculture, Industry and Resources

Sheep
Pb Sn Zn
Goats
Fe
Sugarcane
Llamas
Na
Tobacco
Cattle
Tucumán
Sugar-cane
Cu
Sn
Cotton
Quebracho
Yerba Maté
Tobacco
Ag Cu
Pb Zn
Be Wine
Na Mn
Sheep
Cattle
Córdoba
Santa Fe
Wine
Goats
Be
W U
Hogs
Corn
Wheat
Flax
Rice
Mendoza
Rosario
Dairy
Fruit
Buenos Aires
Sheep
Wheat
Oats
Barley
Bahía Blanca
Hake
Anchovies
Wine
Fruit
Fe
Na
Sheep
Fruit
Tuna
Sardines
Whales
Cod

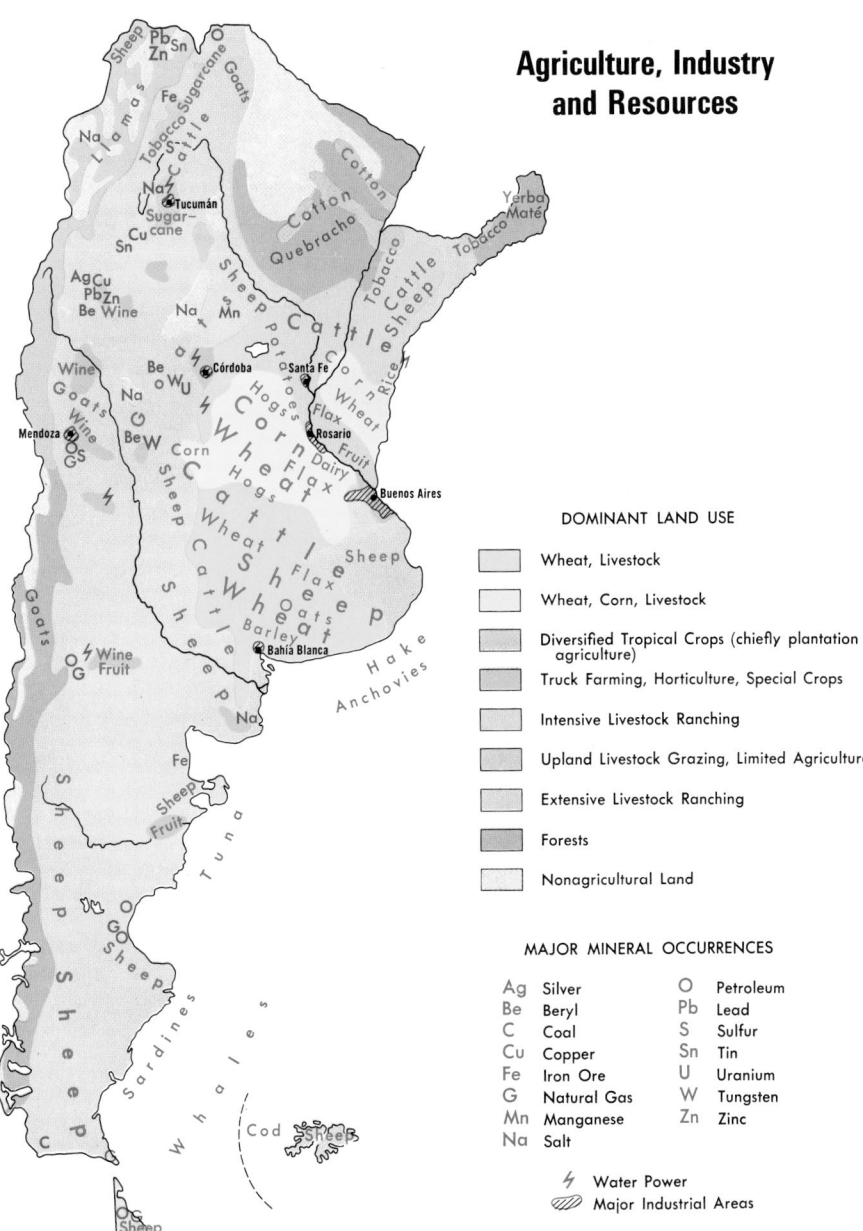

DOMINANT LAND USE

- Wheat, Livestock
- Wheat, Corn, Livestock
- Diversified Tropical Crops (chiefly plantation agriculture)
- Truck Farming, Horticulture, Special Crops
- Intensive Livestock Ranching
- Upland Livestock Grazing, Limited Agriculture
- Extensive Livestock Ranching
- Forests
- Nonagricultural Land

MAJOR MINERAL OCCURRENCES

Ag	Silver	O	Petroleum
Be	Beryl	Pb	Lead
C	Coal	S	Sulfur
Cu	Copper	Sn	Tin
Fe	Iron Ore	U	Uranium
G	Natural Gas	W	Tungsten
Mn	Manganese	Zn	Zinc
Na	Salt		

ϟ Water Power
Major Industrial Areas

Coronel Vidal 4,774 . . . E4
Corral de Bustos 8,613 . . . D3
Corrientes 179,590 . . . E2
Cosquín 13,929 . . . D3
Crespo 10,668 . . . F6
Cruz del Eje 23,473 . . . C3
Curuzú Cuatiá 24,955 . . . G5
Cutral-Có 25,870 . . . C4
Daireaux 8,150 . . . D4
Deán Funes 16,306 . . . D3
Diamante 13,464 . . . F6
Dolavon 1,778 . . . C5
Dolores 19,307 . . . E4
Eduardo Castex 5,397 . . . D4
El Bolsón 5,001 . . . B5
Eldorado 22,821 . . . F2
El Maitén 2,350 . . . B5
Elortondo 4,939 . . . F6
El Quebrachal 2,202 . . . D2
Embarcación 9,016 . . . D1
Empedrado 4,732 . . . E2
Escobar 70,829 . . . G7
Esperanza 22,838 . . . F5
Esquel 17,228 . . . B5
Esquina 10,380 . . . G5
Famatina 1,237 . . . C2
Federación 7,259 . . . G5
Felipe Yofré 1,140 . . . G4
Fernández 6,062 . . . D2
Fiambalá 1,201 . . . C2
Firmat 13,588 . . . F6
Formosa 95,067 . . . E2
Fortín Olmos 1,101 . . . F4
Frías 20,901 . . . D2
Gaiman 2,651 . . . C5
Gálvez 14,711 . . . F6
General Acha 7,647 . . . C4
General Alvear, Buenos Aires 5,481 . . . F7
General Alvear, Mendoza 21,250 . . . C3
General Arenales 3,332 . . . F7
General Belgrano 10,909 . . . G7
General Conesa 3,566 . . . C5
General Galarza 3,057 . . . C6
General Güemes 15,534 . . . D1
General José de San Martín 16,296 . . . E2
General Juan Madariaga 13,409 . . . E4
General La Madrid 5,154 . . . D4
General Las Heras 6,005 . . . G7
General Paz 5,127 . . . H7
General Pico 30,180 . . . D4
General Ramírez 5,393 . . . F6
General Roca 38,296 . . . C4
General San Martín, Buenos Aires 384,306 . . . G7
General San Martín, La Pampa 2,168 . . . D4
General Viamonte 10,112 . . . F7
General Villegas 11,307 . . . D4
Gobernador Crespo 2,972 . . . F5
Godoy Cruz 141,553 . . . C3
Goya 47,357 . . . G4
Gualeguay 24,883 . . . G6
Gualeguaychú 51,057 . . . G6
Guandacol 1,351 . . . C2
Hasenkamp 2,804 . . . F5
Helvecia 3,927 . . . F5
Hernandarias 3,002 . . . F5
Hernando 8,619 . . . D3
Huinca Renancó 7,187 . . . D3
Humahuaca 3,963 . . . C1
Humberto (Humberto Primo) 4,163 . . . F5
Ibarreta 5,262 . . . D2
Ibicuy 3,082 . . . G6
Ingeniero Huergo 3,385 . . . C4
Ingeniero Jacobacci 4,045 . . C5
Ingeniero Luiggi 3,002 . . . D4
Intendente Alvear 3,640 . . . D4
Itatí 3,269 . . . E2
Ituzaingó 8,687 . . . E2
Jáchal 8,832 . . . C3
Jesús María 17,594 . . . D3
Joaquín V. González 6,054 . . D2
Juárez 11,798 . . . E4
Jujuy 124,487 . . . C1
Junín 62,080 . . . F7
Junín de los Andes 5,638 . . . B4
La Banda 46,994 . . . D2
Laboulaye 16,883 . . . D3
La Carlota 8,614 . . . D3
La Cruz 4,132 . . . E2
La Cumbre 6,110 . . . C3
La Falda 12,502 . . . D3
Laguna Paiva 11,129 . . . F5
Lanús 465,891 . . . H7
La Paz, Entre Ríos 14,920 . . G5
La Paz, Mendoza 4,604 . . . C3
La Plata 560,341 . . . H7
Laprida 6,495 . . . D4
La Quiaca 8,289 . . . C1
La Rioja 66,826 . . . C2
Larroque 3,147 . . . F5
Las Flores 18,287 . . . E4
Las Lomitas 4,047 . . . D1
Las Palmas 5,061 . . . E2
Las Parejas 7,430 . . . F6
Las Rosas 9,725 . . . F6
Las Varillas 10,605 . . . D3
La Toma 4,325 . . . C3
Lincoln 19,009 . . . F7
Lobería 8,898 . . . E4
Lobos 20,798 . . . G7
Lomas de Zamora 508,620 . G7
Lucas González 3,015 . . . G6
Luján 38,919 . . . G7
Lules 11,391 . . . C2
Maciel 4,066 . . . F6
Magdalena 7,135 . . . H7
Maipú 7,289 . . . E4
Malabrigo 3,294 . . . F4
Malargüe 9,496 . . . C4
Maquinchao 1,299 . . . C5
Marcos Juárez 19,827 . . . D3
Mar del Plata 407,024 . . . E4
Máximo Paz 3,216 . . . F6
Mburucuya 3,044 . . . E2
Médanos 4,511 . . . D4
Mendoza 596,796 . . . C3
Mercedes, Buenos Aires 46,581 . . . G7
Mercedes, Corrientes 20,603 . . . G4
Mercedes, San Luis 50,856 . C3
Merlo 293,059 . . . G7
Metán 18,928 . . . D2
Miramar 15,473 . . . E4
Monte Caseros 18,247 . . . G5
Monte Quemado 4,707 . . . D2
Monteros 15,832 . . . C2
Morón 596,769 . . . G7
Morteros 11,456 . . . D3
Navarro 7,176 . . . G7
Necochea 50,939 . . . E4
Neuquén 90,037 . . . C4
Nogoyá 15,862 . . . F6
Ñorquincó . . . B5
Nueve de Julio 26,608 . . . F7
Oberá 27,311 . . . F2
Olavarría 63,686 . . . D4
Oliva 9,231 . . . D3
Palo Santo 3,088 . . . E2
Paraná 159,581 . . . F5
Paso de Los Libres 24,112 . . E2
Pedro Luro 3,142 . . . D4
Pehuajó 25,613 . . . D4
Pellegrini 3,940 . . . D4
Pergamino 68,989 . . . F6
Pico Truncado 9,626 . . . C6
Pigüé 10,793 . . . D4
Pilar 3,805 . . . F5
Pirané 9,039 . . . E2
Plaza Huincul 7,988 . . . B4

(continued on following page)

(continued)

Posadas 139,941 E2
Presidencia de la Plaza 4,904 D2
Presidencia Roque Sáenz Peña 49,261 D2
Puán 4,148 D4
Puerto Deseado 4,017 D6
Puerto Harberton C7
Puerto Iguazú 10,250 F2
Puerto Madryn 20,709 C5
Puerto Rico 8,195 D1
Punta Alta 54,375 D4
Quequén 11,737 E4
Quimili 8,972 D2
Quines 3,352 C3
Quitilipi 9,937 D2
Rafaela 53,132 F5
Ramallo 8,248 F6
Rauch 8,348 E4
Rawson 12,981 D5
Reconquista 32,442 F4
Recreo 3,502 C2
Resistencia 218,438 E2
Rinconada C1
Río Colorado 7,361 D4
Río Cuarto 110,148 D3
Río Gallegos 43,479 C7
Río Grande 13,271 C7
Río Segundo 12,839 D3
Río Tercero 34,735 D3
Rivadavia 10,953 C3
Rojas 14,247 F7
Romang 4,017 F4
Roque Pérez 5,434 G7
Rosario 954,606 F6
Rosario de la Frontera 13,531 D2
Rosario de Lerma 9,540 C1
Rosario del Tala 9,552 G6
Rufino 15,306 D3
Saladas 7,345 E2
Saladillo 14,806 G7
Salliqueló 5,479 D4
Salta 260,323 C1
Salto 18,462 F7
San Antonio de Areco 12,932 G7
San Antonio de los Cobres 2,357 C1
San Antonio Oeste 8,690 C5
San Carlos 7,613 F6
San Carlos de Bariloche 48,222 B5
San Cayetano 5,960 E4
San Cristóbal 13,345 F5
San Fernando 128,939 G7
San Francisco, Córdoba 58,616 D3
San Francisco, San Luis 2,448 C3
San Genaro 2,977 F6
San Ignacio 3,437 E2
San Jaime de la Frontera 2,811 G5
San Javier 7,557 F5
San José de Feliciano 4,986 G5
San Juan 290,479 C3
San Julián 4,278 C6
San Justo 14,135 F5
San Luis 70,632 C3
San Martín 29,746 C3
San Martín de los Andes 9,507 C5
San Miguel del Monte 8,414 G7
San Miguel de Tucumán 496,914 D2
San Nicolás 96,313 F6
San Pedro, Buenos Aires 27,058 F6
San Pedro, Jujuy 36,907 D1
San Rafael 70,477 C3
San Ramón de la Nva. Orán 32,955 D1
San Salvador 4,342 G5
San Sebastián C7
Santa Cruz 2,353 C7
Santa Elena 14,655 F5
Santa Fe 287,240 F5
Santa Lucía 4,452 E2
Santa María 5,380 C2
Santa Rosa, Córdoba 4,306 D3
Santa Rosa, La Pampa 51,689 C4
Santa Rosa, San Luis 2,878 C3
Santa Victoria D1
Santiago del Estero 148,357 D2
Santo Tomé, Corrientes 14,352 E2
Santo Tomé, Santa Fe 35,363 F5
Sarmiento 6,313 B6
Sauce 4,677 G5
Sierra Grande 9,585 C5
Suipacha 4,505 G7
Sunchales 12,493 F5
Suncho Corral 3,837 D2
Tafí Viejo 26,625 C2
Tandil 78,821 E4
Tapalquén 5,356 E4
Tartagal 31,367 D1
Tigre 199,366 G7
Tinogasta 7,829 C2
Toay 3,617 D4
Tornquist 4,696 D4
Tostado 10,492 D2
Trelew 52,073 C5
Trenque Lauquen 22,504 D4
Tres Arroyos 42,118 D4
Trevelín 2,935 B5
Tunuyán 14,665 C3
Urdinarrain 5,472 G6
Ushuaia 10,988 C7
Valcheta 2,994 C5
Vedia 6,273 F7
Veinticinco de Mayo 18,936 F7
Venado Tuerto 46,775 D3
Vera 13,555 F5
Verónica 5,657 H7
Viale 5,635 F5
Vicente López 289,815 G7
Victoria 18,883 F6
Victorica 3,895 C4
Vicuña Mackenna 5,665 D3
Viedma 24,338 D5
Villa Ángela 25,586 D2
Villa Atuel 2,774 C3
Villa Cañas 7,303 F6
Villa Constitución 36,157 F6
Villa del Rosario 10,133 D3
Villa Dolores 21,508 C3
Villa Elisa 4,106 G6
Villa Federal 9,222 G5
Villaguay 18,699 G5
Villa Guillermina 2,971 D2
Villa Huidobro 4,154 D3
Villa María 67,490 D3
Villa María Grande 4,517 F5
Villa Nueva 4,604 C3
Villa Ocampo 9,162 D2
Villa Regina 14,017 C4
Villa San José 6,800 G6
Villa San Martín 6,237 D2
Vinchina 1,070 C2
Zapala 18,293 B4
Zárate 65,504 G6
Zavalla 3,800 F6

OTHER FEATURES

Aconcagua, Cerro (mt.) C3
Andes, Cordillera de los (mts.) C2
Argentino (lake) B7
Arizaro, Salar de (salt dep.) C2
Arrecifes (riv.) G6
Atacama, Puna de (reg.) C2
Atuel (riv.) C4
Bermejo (riv.) E2
Blanca (bay) D4
Brazo Sur, Pilcomayo (riv.) E1
Buenos Aires (lake) B6
Campanario, Cerro (mt.) C4
Chaco Austral (reg.) D2
Chaco Central (reg.) D1
Chico (riv.) C5
Chico (riv.) C6
Chubut (riv.) C5
Colhué Huapi (lake) C6
Colorado (riv.) D4
Cónico, Cerro (mt.) B5
Corrientes (riv.) E2
Coyle (riv.) B7
Delgada (pt.) D5
Desaguadero (riv.) C3
Deseado (riv.) C6
Diamante (riv.) C3
Domuyo (vol.) B4
Dos Bahías (cape)) D5
Dulce (riv.) D2
Dungeness (pt.) C7
El Chocón (res.) C4
Estados, Los (isl.) D7
Fagnano (lake) C7
Famatina, Sierra de (mts.) C2
Feliciano (riv.) G5
Gallegos (riv.) B7
General Manuel Belgrano, Cerro (mt.) C2
Gran Chaco (reg.) D1
Grande (bay) C7
Grande (falls) E3
Grande de Tierra del Fuego (isl.) C7
Gualeguay (riv.) G5
Guayaquilaró (riv.) G5
Iguazú (falls) F2
Iguazú Nat'l Park E2
Lanín (vol.) B4
Lanín Nat'l Park B4
Lechiguanas (isls.) G6
Lennox (isl.) C8
Limay (riv.) C4
Llancanelo, Salina y Laguna (salt lake) C4
Llullaillaco (vol.) C1
Magallenes (Magellan) (str.) C7

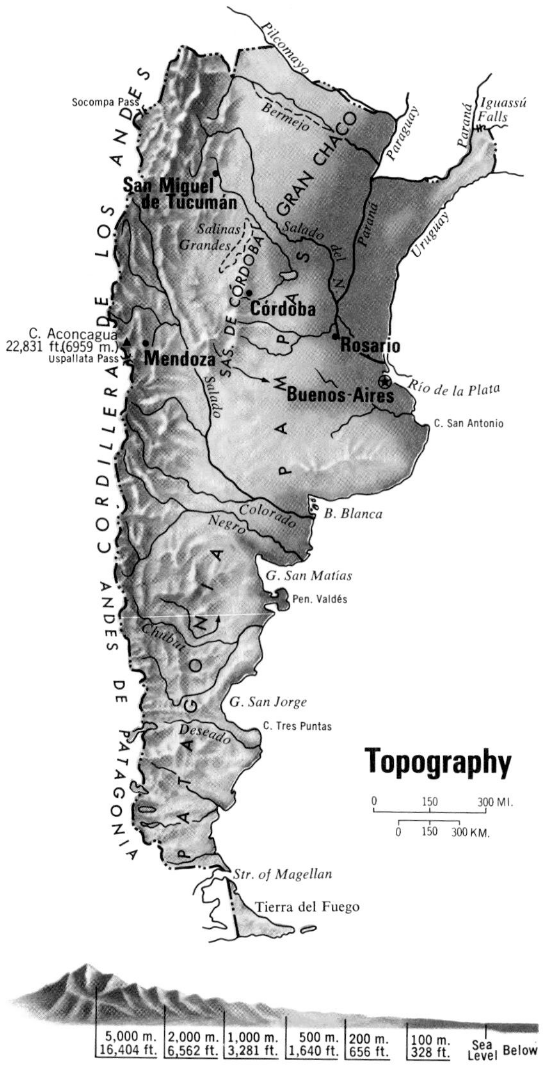
Pilcomayo
Socompa Pass
Bermejo
GRAN CHACO
Paraguay
Paraná
Iguassú Falls
San Miguel de Tucumán
Salinas Grandes
Salado
Uruguay
Córdoba
C. Aconcagua 22,831 ft.(6959 m.)
Uspallata Pass
Mendoza
Rosario
Buenos Aires
Río de la Plata
C. San Antonio
CORDILLERA DE LOS ANDES
PAMPAS
Colorado
Negro
B. Blanca
G. San Matías
Pen. Valdés
Chubut
Deseado
G. San Jorge
C. Tres Puntas
ANDES DE PATAGONIA
PATAGONIA
Str. of Magellan
Tierra del Fuego
Topography
0 150 300 MI.
0 150 300 KM.
5,000 m. 16,404 ft.
2,000 m. 6,562 ft.
1,000 m. 3,281 ft.
500 m. 1,640 ft.
200 m. 656 ft.
100 m. 328 ft.
Sea Level
Below

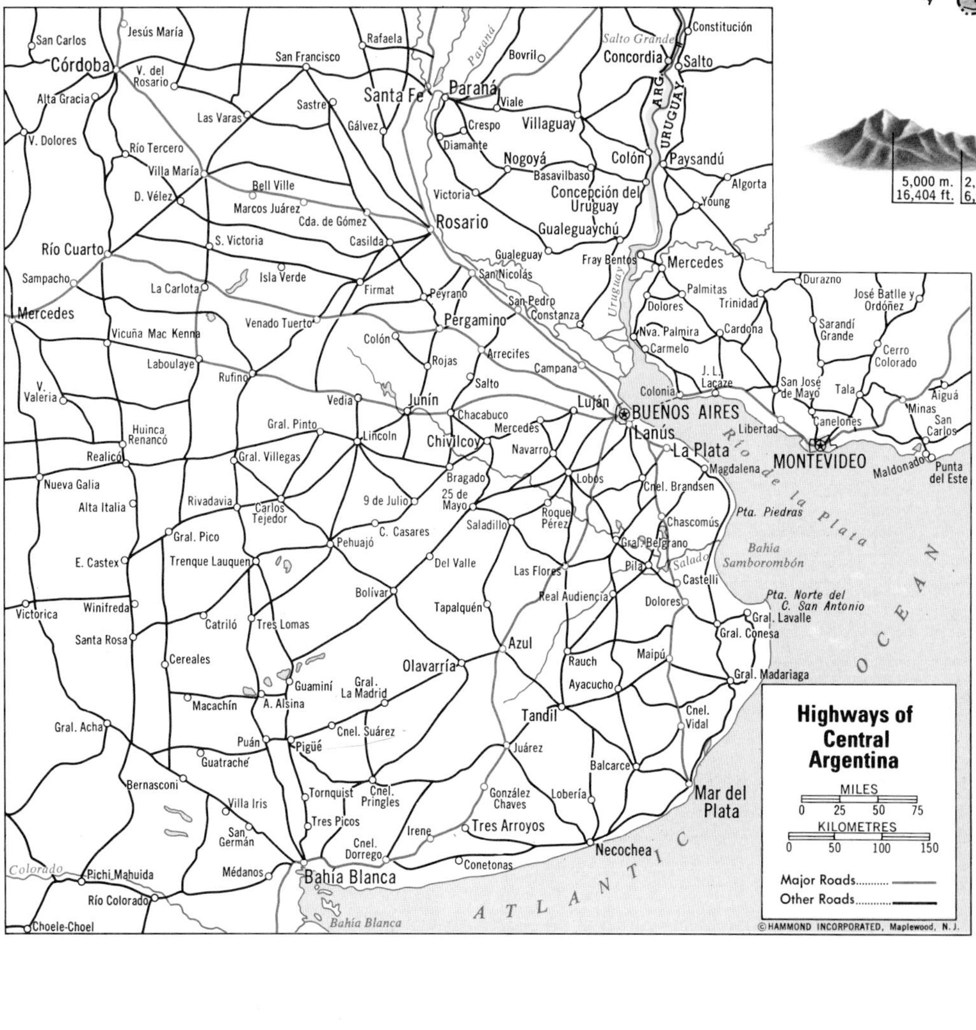
Highways of Central Argentina
MILES 0 25 50 75
KILOMETRES 0 50 100 150
Major Roads
Other Roads
San Carlos
Jesús María
Córdoba
Rafaela
Constitución
Salto Grande
San Francisco
Bovril
Concordia
Salto
Santa Fe
Paraná
Viale
Villaguay
Colón
Paysandú
Río Tercero
Villa María
Bell Ville
Rosario
Victoria
Concepción del Uruguay
Gualeguaychú
Río Cuarto
Mercedes
San Nicolás
Pergamino
Fray Bentos
Junín
Luján
BUENOS AIRES
Lanús
La Plata
MONTEVIDEO
Chivilcoy
Río de la Plata
Bahía Samborombón
Azul
Olavarría
Tandil
Mar del Plata
Necochea
Tres Arroyos
Bahía Blanca
ATLANTIC OCEAN
©HAMMOND INCORPORATED, Maplewood, N.J.

Maipo (vol.) C3
Mar Chiquita (lake) D3
Mendoza (riv.) C3
Mercedario, Cerro (mt.) B3
Mogotes (pt.) E4
Montemayor (plat.) C5
Nahuel Huapi (lake) B5
Nahuel Huapi Nat'l Park B5
Negro (riv.) D4
Neuquén (riv.) C4
Ninfas (pt.) D5
Norte (pt.) D5
Nuevo (gulf) D5
Ojos del Salado, Cerro (mt.) C2
Pampa de las Tres Hermanas (plain) C6
Pampas (plain) D4
Paraná (riv.) E2
Patagonia (reg.) C5
Peteroa (vol.) B4
Pilcomayo (riv.) E1
Pissis (mt.) C2
Plata, Río de la (est.) E4
Pueyrredón (lake) B6
Puna de Atacama (reg.) C2
Quinto (riv.) D3
Rincón, Cerro (mt.) C1
Saladillo (riv.) D2
Salado (riv.) C4
Salado (riv.) H7
Salado del Norte (riv.) D2
Salí (riv.) C2
Salto (riv.) F7
Samborombón (bay) E4
San Antonio (cape) E4
San Diego (cape) D7
San Jorge (gulf) C6
San Juan (riv.) C3
San Lorenzo, Cerro (mt.) B6
San Martín (lake) B6
San Matías (gulf) D5
Santa Cruz (riv.) B7
Senguerr (riv.) B6
Staten (Los Estados) (isl.) D7
Tarija (riv.) D1
Tercero (riv.) D3
Teuco (riv.) D1
Tierra del Fuego, Grande de (isl.) C7
Toro, Cerro del (mt.) B2
Tres Puntas (cape) D6
Trinidad (isl.) D4
Tronador (mt.) B5
Tunuyán (riv.) C3
Tupungato, Cerro (mt.) B3
Uruguay (riv.) E3
Valdés (pen.) D5
Viedma (lake) B6
Zapaleri, Cerro (mt.) C1

FALKLAND ISLANDS

CITIES and TOWNS

Stanley (cap.) 1,050 E7

OTHER FEATURES

Adventure (sound) E7
Choiseul (sound) E7
East Falkland (isl.) 1,491 E7
Falkland (isls.) D7
Falkland (sound) D7
George (isl.) E7
Jason (isls.) D7
Lively (isl.) E7
Malvinas (Falkland) (isls.) D7
Pebble (isl.) E7
Saunders (isl.) E7
Weddel (isl.) D7
West Falkland (isl.) 322 D7

*City and suburbs.

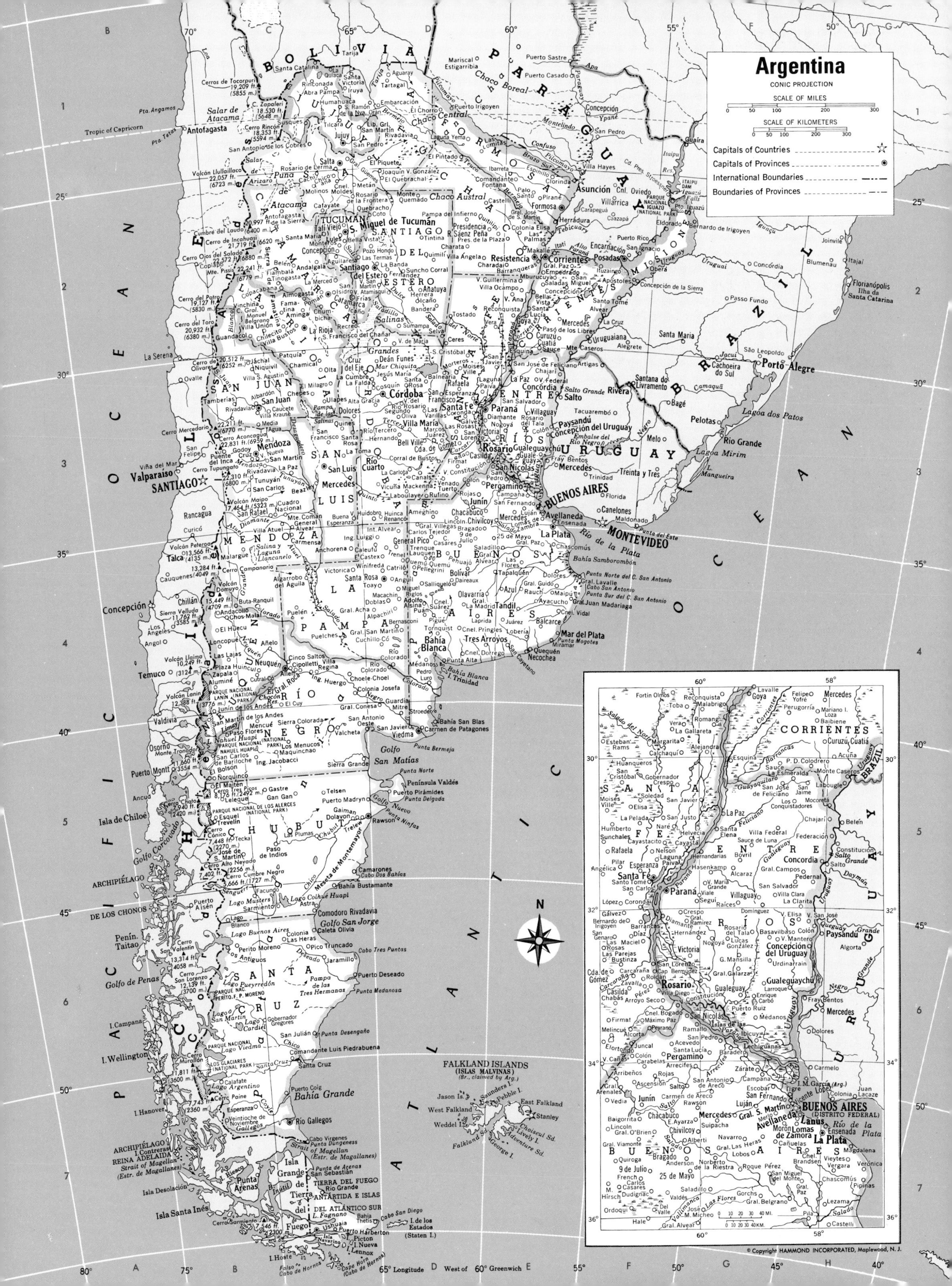

Argentina
CONIC PROJECTION
SCALE OF MILES
0 50 100 200 300
SCALE OF KILOMETERS
0 50 100 200 300
Capitals of Countries
Capitals of Provinces
International Boundaries
Boundaries of Provinces
BOLIVIA
PARAGUAY
BRAZIL
URUGUAY
PACIFIC OCEAN
ATLANTIC OCEAN
CHILE
JUJUY
SALTA
FORMOSA
CHACO
MISIONES
CORRIENTES
TUCUMÁN
SANTIAGO DEL ESTERO
CATAMARCA
LA RIOJA
SAN JUAN
CÓRDOBA
SANTA FE
ENTRE RÍOS
SAN LUIS
MENDOZA
LA PAMPA
BUENOS AIRES
NEUQUÉN
RÍO NEGRO
CHUBUT
SANTA CRUZ
TIERRA DEL FUEGO, ANTÁRTIDA E ISLAS DEL ATLÁNTICO SUR
SANTIAGO
Valparaíso
MONTEVIDEO
Asunción
Tropic of Capricorn
Antofagasta
Salar de Atacama
Puna de Atacama
Gran Chaco
Chaco Boreal
Chaco Central
Chaco Austral
Salinas Grandes
Mar Chiquita
Río de la Plata
Bahía Samborombón
Golfo San Matías
Península Valdés
Golfo San Jorge
Bahía Grande
Strait of Magellan (Estr. de Magallanes)
FALKLAND ISLANDS (ISLAS MALVINAS) (Br., claimed by Arg.)
West Falkland
East Falkland
Stanley
I. de los Estados (Staten I.)
Cabo de Hornos
Isla de Chiloé
ARCHIPIÉLAGO DE LOS CHONOS
Golfo de Penas
ARCHIPIÉLAGO REINA ADELAIDA
Isla Desolación
Isla Santa Inés
Salta
Jujuy
S. Miguel de Tucumán
Santiago del Estero
Catamarca
La Rioja
San Juan
Córdoba
Mendoza
San Luis
Santa Fe
Paraná
Resistencia
Corrientes
Posadas
Formosa
Rosario
Santa Rosa
Neuquén
Viedma
Rawson
Río Gallegos
Ushuaia
BUENOS AIRES
La Plata
Mar del Plata
Bahía Blanca
Comodoro Rivadavia
Porto Alegre
Florianópolis
Salto
Paysandú
80° 75° 70° 65° 60° 55° 50° 45° 40°
25° 30° 35° 40° 45° 50°
65° Longitude West of 60° Greenwich
CORRIENTES
SANTA FE
ENTRE RÍOS
BUENOS AIRES
URUGUAY
Concepción del Uruguay
Gualeguaychú
Pergamino
Buenos Aires (DISTRITO FEDERAL)
© Copyright HAMMOND INCORPORATED, Maplewood, N. J.

Paraguay
CONIC PROJECTION
SCALE OF MILES
0 20 40 60 80 100 120 140
SCALE OF KILOMETERS
0 20 40 60 80 100 140
Capitals of Countries
Capitals of Departments
International Boundaries
Department Boundaries
BOLIVIA
BRAZIL
ARGENTINA
CHACO
NUEVA ASUNCION
ALTO PARAGUAY
BOQUERÓN
PRESIDENTE HAYES
CONCEPCIÓN
AMAMBAY
SAN PEDRO
CANENDIYU
ALTO PARANA
CAAGUAZÚ
CORDILLERA
GUAIRÁ
PARAGUARÍ
CAAZAPÁ
ITAPÚA
MISIONES
ÑEEMBUCÚ
CENTRAL
Tropic of Capricorn
© Copyright HAMMOND INCORPORATED, Maplewood, N. J.

PARAGUAY

DEPARTMENTS

Alto Paraguay C2
Alto Paraná E4
Amambay D3
Asunción A4
Boquerón B3
Caaguazú D-E4
Caazapá D-E5
Canendiyu E4
Central D4
Chaco B-C2
Concepción D3
Cordillera D4
Guaira D4
Itapúa E5
Misiones D5
Ñeembucú C-D5
Nueva Asunción B2
Paraguarí .... D 4-5
Presidente Hayes C3
San Pedro .... D 4-5

CITIES and TOWNS

Abaí 1,507 .... E4
Acahay 1,937 .... B5
Alberdi 2,346 .... D5
Altos 1,441 .... B4
Antequera 1,281 .... D4
Areguá 3,941 .... B4
Arroyos y Esteros 1,253 .... B4
Asunción (cap.) 387,676 .... A4
Atyrá 1,427 .... B4
Belén 1,219 .... D3
Bella Vista 3,101 .... D3
Bella Vista 1,421 .... E5
Benjamín Aceval 2,877 .... C4
Buena Vista 1,353 .... D5
Caacupé 7,278 .... B5
Caaguazú 7,950 .... D4
Caapucú 1,400 .... D5
Caazapá 3,132 .... D5
Capiatá 2,827 .... B4
Carapeguá 3,416 .... B5
Carmen del Paraná 1,980 .... D5
Ciudad Presidente Stroessner 7,085 .... E4
Concepción 19,392 .... D3
Coronel Bogado 3,973 .... D5
Coronel Martínez 1,598 .... B5
Coronel Oviedo 13,786 .... C5
Doctor Cecilio Báez 1,300 .... D4
Doctor Juan L. Mallorquín 1,913 .... E4
Doctor Juan Manuel Frutos 1,494 .... E4
Encarnación 23,343 .... E5
Eusebio Ayala 4,328 .... B4
Fernando de la Mora 36,834 .... B4
Filadelfia 1,438 .... B3
Fuerte Olimpo 3,063 .... C2
General Artigas 3,542 .... D5
General Elizardo Aquino 1,304 .... D4
Guarambaré 3,640 .... B5
Hernandarias 3,898 .... E4
Horqueta 4,328 .... D3
Isla Pucú 1,766 .... B4
Itá 7,041 .... B5
Itacurubí 1,997 .... B5
Itacurubí del Rosario 2,467 .... D4
Itapé 1,376 .... C5
Itauguá 3,767 .... B5
Iturbe 3,413 .... C5
Jesús 1,495 .... E5
La Colmena 1,804 .... B5
Lambaré 31,656 .... A4
Limpio 2,219 .... B4
Loreto 1,258 .... D3
Luque 13,921 .... B4
Mariano Roque Alonso 1,492 .... A4
Mariscal Estigarribia 3,150 .... B3
Mbuyapey 1,560 .... D5
Natalicio Talavera 1,228 .... D4
Nueva Italia 1,517 .... B5
Paraguarí 5,036 .... B5
Pedro Juan Caballero 21,033 .... E3
Pilar 12,506 .... C5
Pirayú 2,698 .... B5
Piribebuy 4,497 .... B5
Primero de Marzo 696 .... B4
Puerto Casado 4,078 .... C3
Puerto Guaraní 302 .... C2
Puerto Pinasco 5,477 .... C3
Puerto Presidente Franco 4,152 .... E4
Quiindy 2,664 .... B5
Roque González de Santa Cruz 1,375 .... B5
Rosario 4,165 .... D4
San Antonio 4,906 .... A5
San Estanislao 4,753 .... D4
San Ignacio 6,116 .... D5
San José 3,102 .... B5
San Juan Bautista 6,457 .... D5
San Juan Nepomuceno 2,974 .... E5
San Lázaro 1,767 .... D3
San Lorenzo 11,616 .... B4
San Pedro 3,186 .... D3
San Pedro del Paraná 2,723 .... D5
San Salvador 1,393 .... C5
Santa Elena 1,439 .... B5
Santa Rosa 3,736 .... D5
Santiago 1,265 .... D5
Sapucaí 1,864 .... B5
Tobatí 4,983 .... B4
Unión 1,286 .... D4
Valenzuela 1,108 .... B5
Valle Mí 1,318 .... D3
Villa Florida 1,261 .... D5
Villa Hayes 4,749 .... A4
Villarrica 17,687 .... C5
Villeta 3,156 .... A5
Yaguarón 3,368 .... B5
Ybycuí 1,736 .... B5
Ypacaraí 5,195 .... B5
Ypané 1,474 .... B5
Yuty 2,392 .... D5

OTHER FEATURES

Acaray (riv.) E4
Alto Paraná (riv.) D5
Amambay, Cordillera de (mts.) D3
Ao Paray (riv.) A5
Apa (riv.) D3
Aquidabán (riv.) D3
Cabral (lake) A5
Carapa (riv.) E4
Chaco Boreal (reg.) B2
Chovoreca (mt.) C1
Confuso (riv.) C4
Coronel F. Cabrera (mt.) B1
Galván (mt.) C3
González, Riacho (riv.) C3
Gran Chaco (reg.) B2
Itaipu (dam) E4
Itaipu (res.) E4
Jara (hill) C1
Jejuí-Guazú (riv.) D4
La Bella (lag.) B4
León (mt.) B2
Mbaracayú, Cordillera de (mts.) E3
Monday (riv.) E4
Montelindo (riv.) C3
Mosquito, Riacho (riv.) C3
Negro (riv.) C4
Paraguy (riv.) D4
Pilcomayo (riv.) C4
Piribebuy (riv.) B4
Tebicuary (riv.) C5
Tebicuary Mí (riv.) C5
Tímane (riv.) B2
Vera (lag.) D5
Verde (riv.) C3
Ypané (riv.) D3
Ypoá (lake) B5

Agriculture, Industry and Resources

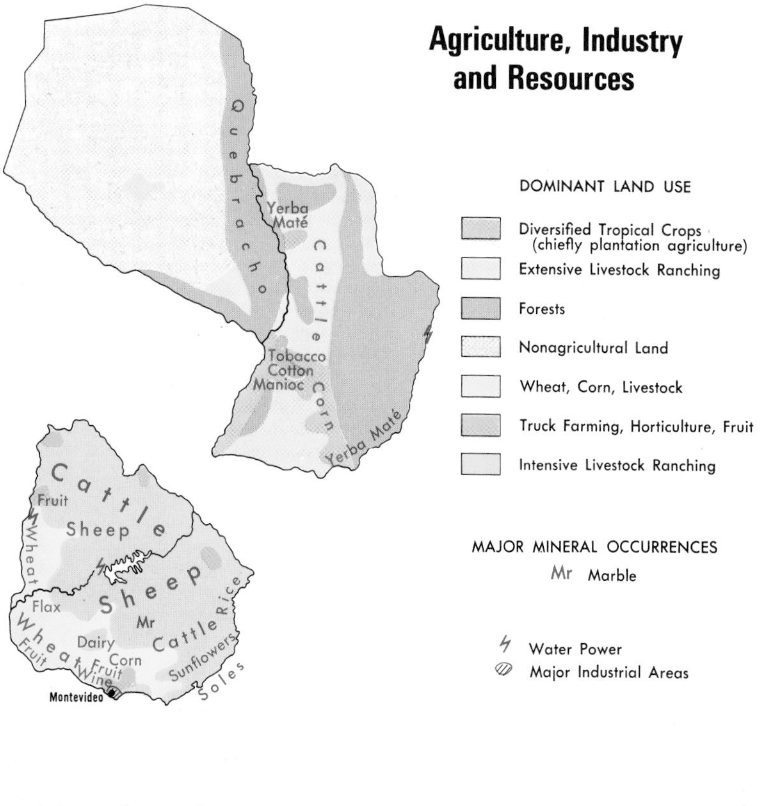

DOMINANT LAND USE
Diversified Tropical Crops (chiefly plantation agriculture)
Extensive Livestock Ranching
Forests
Nonagricultural Land
Wheat, Corn, Livestock
Truck Farming, Horticulture, Fruit
Intensive Livestock Ranching
MAJOR MINERAL OCCURRENCES
Mr Marble
Water Power
Major Industrial Areas
Quebracho
Yerba Maté
Cattle
Corn
Tobacco
Cotton
Manioc
Sheep
Fruit
Wheat
Flax
Dairy
Rice
Sunflowers
Soles
Montevideo

Topography

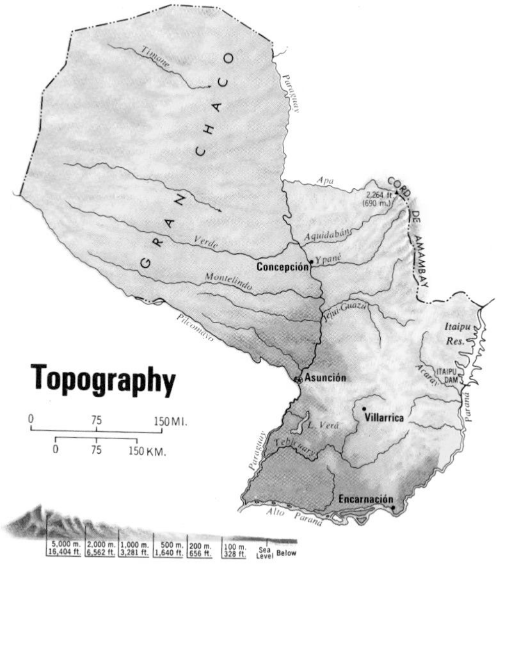

GRAN CHACO
CORD. DE AMAMBAY
Concepción
Asunción
Villarrica
Encarnación
Itaipu Res.
0 75 150 MI.
0 75 150 KM.
5,000 m. 16,404 ft.
2,000 m. 6,562 ft.
1,000 m. 3,281 ft.
500 m. 1,640 ft.
200 m. 656 ft.
100 m. 328 ft.
Sea Level
Below

URUGUAY

DEPARTMENTS

Artigas 52,843 ..... B1
Canelones 258,195 ..... D5
Cerro Largo 71,023 ..... E3
Colonia 105,350 ..... B5
Durazno 53,635 ..... C3
Flores 23,530 ..... C4
Florida 63,987 ..... D4
Lavalleja 65,823 ..... D5
Maldonado 61,259 ..... E5
Montevideo 1,202,757 ..... B7
Paysandú 88,029 ..... B3
Río Negro 46,861 ..... B3
Rivera 77,086 ..... D2
Rocha 55,097 ..... E4
Salto 92,183 ..... B2
San José 79,563 ..... C5
Soriano 77,906 ..... B4
Tacuarembó 76,964 ..... D3
Treinta y Tres 43,419 ..... E4

CITIES and TOWNS

Aceguá 930 ..... E2
Achar 606 ..... C3
Agraciada 638 ..... A4
Aguas Corrientes 992 ..... A6
Aiguá 2,470 ..... E5
Algorta 1,372 ..... B3
Artigas 29,256 ..... C1
Atlántida 2,268 ..... B6
Balneario Solís 288 ..... D5
Baltasar Brum 1,753 ..... B1
Belén 2,129 ..... B1
Bella Unión 7,778 ..... B1
Bernabé Rivera 540 ..... B1
Blanquillo 1,053 ..... D3
Cañada Nieto 503 ..... B4
Canelones 15,938 ..... B6
Cardal 847 ..... C5
Cardona 4,126 ..... B4
Carlos Reyles 961 ..... C4
Carmelo 13,631 ..... A4
Carmen 2,318 ..... D4
Casupá 2,265 ..... D5
Cebollatí 1,233 ..... F4
Cerrillos 1,690 ..... A6
Cerro Chato, Treinta y Tres 1,850 ..... D4
Chamizo 486 ..... D5
Chuy 4,472 ..... F4
Colón, Lavalleja 367 ..... E4
Colonia 16,895 ..... B5
Colonia Valdense 2,113 ..... B5
Conchillas 748 ..... B5
Constitución 3,217 ..... A2
Costa Azul 453 ..... B5
Cufré 430 ..... B5
Curtina 723 ..... C3
Diez y Nueve (19) de Abril 308 ..... E5
Diez y Ocho (18) de Julio 742 ..... F4
Dolores 12,771 ..... A4
Durazno 25,811 ..... C4
Egaña 667 ..... B4
Empalme Olmos 2,084 ..... B6
Estación Atlántida 1,845 ..... B6
Estación Migues 241 ..... C6
Florida 25,030 ..... C5
Fraile Muerto 2,468 ..... E3
Fray Bentos 19,569 ..... A4
Fray Marcos 1,573 ..... D5
Garzón 258 ..... E5
General Enrique Martínez 973 ..... F4
Goñi 278 ..... C4
Grecco 447 ..... B3
Guichón 4,720 ..... B3
Ituzaingó 717 ..... A6
Javier de Viana 286 ..... C1
Joanico 692 ..... B6
Joaquín Suárez, Canelones 3,517 ..... B6
José Batlle y Ordóñez 2,044 ..... D4
José Enrique Rodó 1,334 ..... B4
José Pedro Varela 3,541 ..... E4
Juan L. Lacaze 11,133 ..... B5
La Coronilla 571 ..... F4
La Cruz 633 ..... C4
La Paloma 1,558 ..... F5
La Paz, Canelones 14,402 ..... B6
Lascano 6,043 ..... E4
Las Flores 403 ..... D5
Las Piedras 53,983 ..... B6
Las Toscas 893 ..... E3
Libertad 6,071 ..... C5
Lorenzo Geyres 474 ..... B3
Mal Abrigo 209 ..... C5
Maldonado 22,159 ..... D6
Mariscala 1,393 ..... E5
Melo 38,260 ..... E3
Mercedes 34,667 ..... B4
Merinos 403 ..... C3
Miguelete 533 ..... B5
Migues 2,183 ..... C6
Minas 35,433 ..... D5
Minas de Corrales 2,518 ..... D2
Montes 2,217 ..... D5
Montevideo (cap.) 1,173,254 ..... B7
Nueva Helvecia 8,598 ..... B5
Nueva Palmira 6,934 ..... A4
Nuevo Berlín 1,970 ..... B3
Ombúes de Lavalle 1,689 ..... B4
Palmitas 1,332 ..... B4
Pan de Azúcar 4,862 ..... D5
Pando 16,184 ..... B6
Paso del Cerro 317 ..... C2
Paso de los Toros 13,178 ..... C3
Paysandú 62,412 ..... A3
Piedras Coloradas 487 ..... B3
Piedra Sola 233 ..... C3
Piñera 261 ..... C3
Piraraja 774 ..... E4
Piriápolis 5,221 ..... D5
Porvenir 705 ..... B3
Progreso 8,257 ..... B6
Punta del Este 6,914 ..... E6
Quebracho 1,514 ..... B2
Reboledo 373 ..... D4
Río Branco 5,697 ..... F3
Rivera 49,013 ..... D1
Rocha 21,612 ..... E5
Rodríguez 1,575 ..... C5
Rosario 8,302 ..... B5
Salto 72,948 ..... B2
San Antonio, Canelones 1,122 ..... B6
San Bautista 1,472 ..... B6
San Carlos 16,883 ..... E5
San Gregorio, Tacuarembó 2,892 ..... D3
San Jacinto 2,292 ..... C6
San Javier 1,583 ..... A3
San José de Mayo 28,427 ..... C5
San Ramón 6,570 ..... D5
Santa Catalina 885 ..... B4
Santa Clara de Olimar 2,867 ..... D3
Santa Lucía 14,101 ..... B6
Santa Rosa 2,736 ..... B6
Santiago Vázquez 1,323 ..... A7
Sarandí del Yi 6,326 ..... D4
Sarandí de Navarro 259 ..... C3
Sarandí Grande 5,598 ..... C4
Solís 356 ..... D5
Solís de Mataojo 1,763 ..... D5
Soriano 1,125 ..... A4
Tacuarembó 34,152 ..... D2
Tala 3,611 ..... D5
Tambores 1,534 ..... C2
Toledo 3,127 ..... B6
Tomás Gomensoro 2,105 ..... B1
Tranqueras 3,922 ..... D2
Treinta y Tres 25,757 ..... E4
Trinidad 17,598 ..... B4
Tupambaé 1,039 ..... E3
Valentines 153 ..... E4
Veinticinco (25) de Agosto 1,891 ..... A6
Veinticinco (25) de Mayo 1,744 ..... C5
Velázquez 1,042 ..... E5
Vergara 2,822 ..... E3
Vichadero 1,989 ..... E2
Villa Darwin 507 ..... B4
Young 11,080 ..... B3
Zapicán 764 ..... E4
Zapucay D2

OTHER FEATURES

Arapey Grande (riv.) B2
Bonete (dam) C3
Brava (pt.) B7
Cañas (range) C2
Caraguatá (riv.) D3
Castillos (lag.) F5
Cebollatí (riv.) F4
Cordobés (riv.) D3
Cuareim (riv.) B1
Cuñapirú, Arroyo (riv.) D2
Daymán (riv.) B2
Durazno, Grande del (range) D4
Este (pt.) D6
Grande (range) D4
Haedo (range) C2
India Muerta (riv.) E4
Lobos (isl.) E6
Merín (lag.) F4
Mirador Nacional (mt.) D5
Negra (lag.) F5
Negro (riv.) B4
Negro, Arroyo (riv.) B3
Olimar Grande (riv.) E4
Plata, La (riv.) B5
Polonio (cape) F5
Quequay Grande (riv.) B3
Río Negro (res.) D3
Rocha (lag.) E5
Salto Grande (falls) A2
San José (riv.) C4
San Miguel (swamp) F4
San Salvador (riv.) B4
Santa Ana (range) D2
Santa Lucía (riv.) D5
Santa María (cape) F5
Tacuarembó (riv.) D2
Tacuarí (riv.) E3
Uruguay (riv.) A3
Yaguarón (riv.) F3
Yí (riv.) B4

PARAGUAY

AREA 157,047 sq. mi. (406,752 sq. km.)
POPULATION 4,157,000
CAPITAL Asunción
LARGEST CITY Asunción
HIGHEST POINT Amambay Range 2,264 ft. (690 m.)
MONETARY UNIT guaraní
MAJOR LANGUAGES Spanish, Guaraní
MAJOR RELIGION Roman Catholicism

URUGUAY

AREA 72,172 sq. mi. (186,925 sq. km.)
POPULATION 3,077,000
CAPITAL Montevideo
LARGEST CITY Montevideo
HIGHEST POINT Mirador Nacional 1,644 ft. (501 m.)
MONETARY UNIT Uruguayan peso
MAJOR LANGUAGE Spanish
MAJOR RELIGION Roman Catholicism

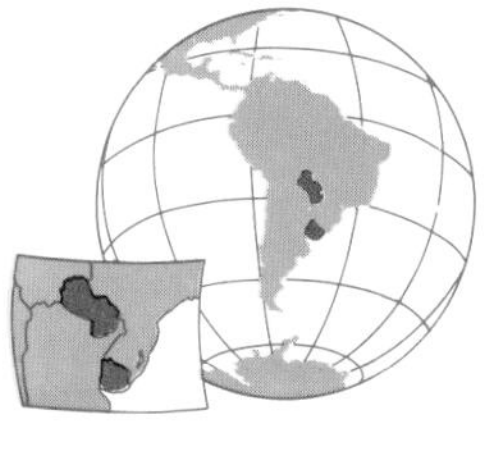

PARAGUAY

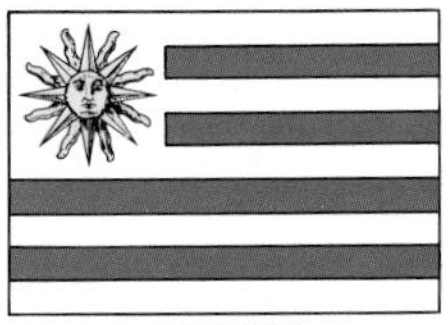

URUGUAY

Uruguay
CONIC PROJECTION
SCALE OF MILES
SCALE OF KILOMETERS
Capitals of Countries
Department Capitals
International Boundaries
Department Boundaries
ARGENTINA
BRAZIL
ATLANTIC OCEAN
MONTEVIDEO
BUENOS AIRES
Río de la Plata
C Longitude 56° West of D Greenwich 55°
© Copyright HAMMOND INCORPORATED, Maplewood, N. J.

Topography

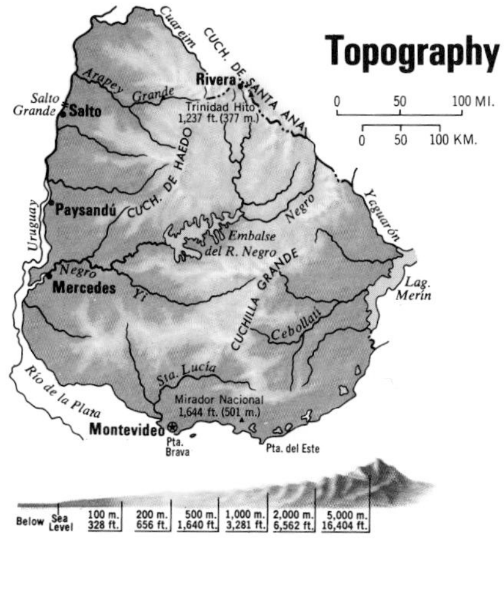

0 50 100 MI.
0 50 100 KM.
Salto
Rivera
Paysandú
Mercedes
Montevideo
Mirador Nacional 1,644 ft. (501 m.)
Trinidad Hito 1,237 ft. (377 m.)
Lag. Merín
Río de la Plata
Below Sea Level 100 m. 328 ft. 200 m. 656 ft. 500 m. 1,640 ft. 1,000 m. 3,281 ft. 2,000 m. 6,562 ft. 5,000 m. 16,404 ft.

North America
LAMBERT AZIMUTHAL EQUAL-AREA PROJECTION
MILES
0 100 200 400 600 800
KILOMETERS
0 100 200 400 600 800
Capitals of Countries
Other Capitals
International Boundaries
Other Boundaries
© Copyright HAMMOND INCORPORATED, Maplewood, N.J.
Longitude West 90° of Greenwich
NORTH POLE
ARCTIC OCEAN
PACIFIC OCEAN
ATLANTIC OCEAN
ASIA
RUSSIA
EUROPE
UNITED KINGDOM
ICELAND
GREENLAND (KALAALLIT NUNAAT) (Den.)
CANADA
UNITED STATES
MEXICO
SOUTH AMERICA
EAST SIBERIAN SEA
CHUKCHI SEA
BERING SEA
BEAUFORT SEA
LINCOLN SEA
GREENLAND SEA
NORWEGIAN SEA
LABRADOR SEA
Baffin Bay
Hudson Bay
Gulf of Alaska
Gulf of Mexico
CARIBBEAN SEA
WEST INDIES
BAHAMAS
HAITI
DOMINICAN REP.
PUERTO RICO
JAMAICA
BELIZE
GUATEMALA
HONDURAS
EL SALVADOR
NICARAGUA
COSTA RICA
PANAMA
VENEZUELA
COLOMBIA
ECUADOR
PERU
BRAZIL
BOLIVIA
YUKON TERRITORY
NORTHWEST TERRITORIES
NUNAVUT
BRITISH COLUMBIA
ALBERTA
SASKATCHEWAN
MANITOBA
ONTARIO
QUEBEC
NEWFOUNDLAND
ALASKA
Tropic of Cancer
Arctic Circle
Equator
N

AREA 9,363,000 sq. mi. (24,250,170 sq. km.)
POPULATION 443,438,000
LARGEST CITY New York
HIGHEST POINT Mt. McKinley 20,320 ft. (6,194 m.)
LOWEST POINT Death Valley -282 ft. (-86 m.)

Population Distribution

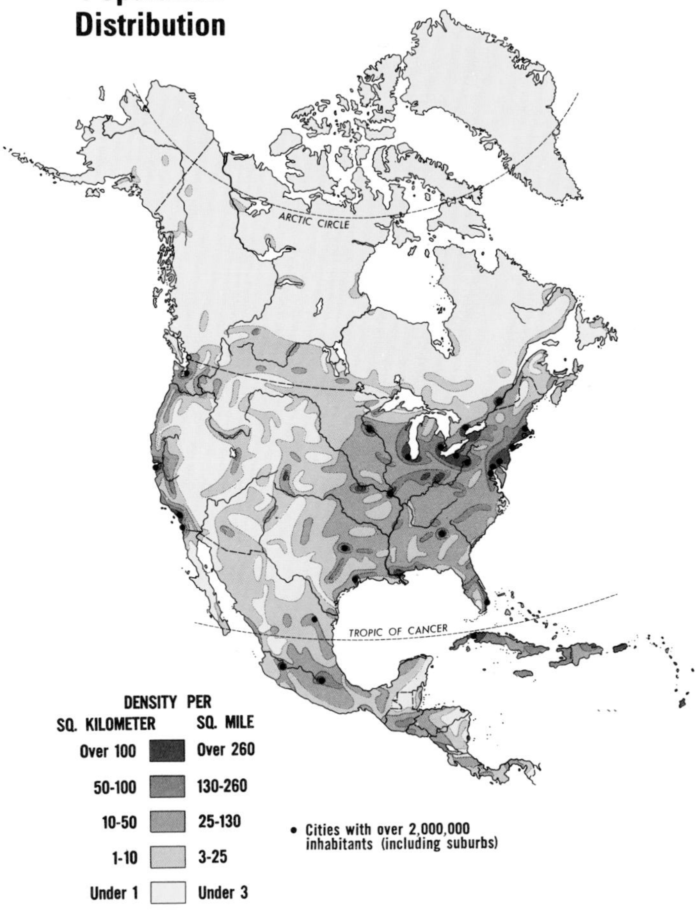
ARCTIC CIRCLE
TROPIC OF CANCER
DENSITY PER
SQ. KILOMETER
SQ. MILE
Over 100
Over 260
50-100
130-260
10-50
25-130
1-10
3-25
Under 1
Under 3
• Cities with over 2,000,000 inhabitants (including suburbs)

Vegetation

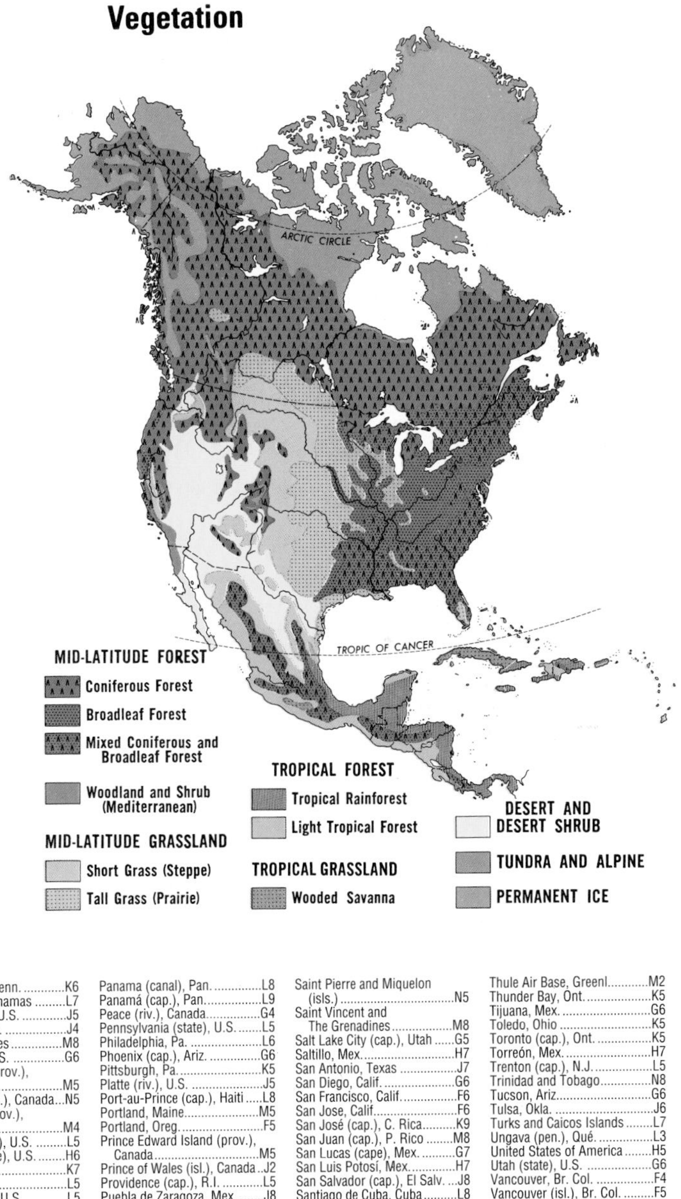
ARCTIC CIRCLE
TROPIC OF CANCER
MID-LATITUDE FOREST
Coniferous Forest
Broadleaf Forest
Mixed Coniferous and Broadleaf Forest
Woodland and Shrub (Mediterranean)
MID-LATITUDE GRASSLAND
Short Grass (Steppe)
Tall Grass (Prairie)
TROPICAL FOREST
Tropical Rainforest
Light Tropical Forest
TROPICAL GRASSLAND
Wooded Savanna
DESERT AND DESERT SHRUB
TUNDRA AND ALPINE
PERMANENT ICE

Acapulco de Juárez, Mex. H8
Akron, Ohio K5
Alabama (state), U.S. K6
Alaska (gulf) D4
Alaska (pen.), Alaska C4
Alaska (state), U.S. C3
Alberta (prov.), Canada G4
Albuquerque, N. Mex. H6
Amarillo, Texas H6
Anchorage, Alaska D3
Antigua (isl.) M8
Appalachian (mts.) K6
Arizona (state), U.S. G6
Arkansas (state), U.S. J6
Aruba (isl.) M8
Athabasca (lake), Canada H4
Atlanta (cap.), Ga. K6
Austin (cap.), Texas J6
Baffin (bay) M2
Baffin (isl.), N.W.T. L2
Bahamas L7
Baltimore, Md. L6
Barbados N8
Barrow (pt.), Alaska C2
Baton Rouge (cap.), La. J6
Beaufort (sea) D2
Belize K8
Bering (sea) A3
Bermuda (isls.) M6
Birmingham, Ala. K6
Boise (cap.), Idaho G5
Boston (cap.), Mass. L5
British Columbia (prov.), Canada F4
Buffalo, N.Y. L5
Calgary, Alta. G4
California (gulf), Mex. G7
California (state), U.S. G6
Canada G4
Canaveral (cape), Fla. L7
Caribbean (sea) K8
Cascade (range), U.S. F5
Cayman Islands K8
Charleston, S.C. L6
Charlotte, N.C. K6
Chattanooga, Tenn. K6
Chesapeake (bay), U.S. L6
Chicago, Ill. K5
Chihuahua, Mex. H7
Cincinnati, Ohio K6
Ciudad Juárez, Mex. H6
Cleveland, Ohio K5
Clipperton (isl.) H8
Coast (ranges), U.S. F5
Cod (cape), Mass. M5
Colorado (riv.), U.S. G6
Colorado (state), U.S. H6
Columbia (riv.), U.S. F5
Columbus (cap.), Ohio K6
Connecticut (state), U.S. L5
Costa Rica K8
Cuba L7
Dallas, Texas J6
Davis (strait) N3
Dayton, Ohio K6
Delaware (state), U.S. L6
Denver (cap.), Colo. H6
Des Moines (cap.), Iowa J5
Detroit, Mich. K5
Devon (isl.), N.W.T. K2
Dominica M8
Dominican Republic L8
Duluth, Minn. J5
Edmonton (cap.), Alta. G4
Ellesmere (isl.), N.W.T. K1
El Paso, Texas H6
El Salvador J8
Erie (lake) K5
Fairbanks, Alaska D3
Farewell (cape), Greenl. P4
Florida (state), U.S. K7
Fort Worth, Texas J6
Foxe (basin), N.W.T. L3
Fraser (riv.), Br. Col. F4
Fresno, Calif. G6
Georgia (state), U.S. K6
Grand Rapids, Mich. K5
Great Bear (lake), N.W.T. F3
Greater Antilles (isls.) K7
Great Salt (lake), Utah G5
Great Slave (lake), N.W.T. H3
Greenland P2
Greenland (sea) T2
Grenada M8
Guadalajara, Mex. H7
Guadeloupe (isl.) M8
Guatemala J8
Guatemala (cap.), Guat. J8
Haiti L8
Halifax (cap.), N.S. M5
Hamilton, Ont. K5
Harrisburg (cap.), Pa. L5
Hartford (cap.), Conn. L5
Hatteras (cape), N.C. L6
Havana (cap.), Cuba K7
Honduras K8
Honduras (gulf) K8
Houston, Texas J7
Hudson (bay), Canada K3
Hudson (strait), Canada L3
Huron (lake) K5
Idaho (state), U.S. G5
Illinois (state), U.S. K5
Indiana (state), U.S. K6
Indianapolis (cap.), Ind. K5
Inuvik, N.W.T. E3
Iowa (state), U.S. J5
Iqaluit (cap.), Nun. M3
Jackson (cap.), Miss. K6
Jacksonville, Fla. K6
Jamaica L8
James (bay), Canada K4
Juan de Fuca (str.) F5
Juneau (cap.), Alaska E4
Kalaallit Nunaat (Greenland) P2
Kansas (state), U.S. J6
Kansas City, Mo. J6
Kentucky (state), U.S. K6
Kingston (cap.), Jamaica L8
Knoxville, Tenn. K6
Kodiak (isl.), Alaska C4
Labrador (reg.), Newf. M4
Lansing (cap.), Mich. K5
Las Vegas, Nev. G6
León, Mex. H7
Lesser Antilles (isls.) M8
Lethbridge, Alta. G5
Lexington, Ky. K6
Lincoln (cap.), Nebr. J5
Little Rock (cap.), Ark. J6
London, Ont. K5
Los Angeles, Calif. G6
Louisiana (state), U.S. J6
Louisville, Ky. K6
Lower California (pen.), Mex. G7
Lubbock, Texas H6
Mackenzie (riv.), N.W.T. F3
Maine (state), U.S. M5
Managua (cap.), Nic. K8
Manitoba (prov.), Canada J4
Martinique (isl.) M8
Maryland (state), U.S. L6
Massachusetts (state), U.S. L5
Matanzas, Cuba K7
Mazatlán, Mex. H7
McKinley (mt.), Alaska C3
Melville (isl.), Canada G2
Memphis, Tenn. K6
Mérida, Mex. J7
Mexicali, Mex. G6
Mexico H7
Mexico (gulf) K7
Mexico City (cap.), Mex. J7
Miami, Fla. K7
Michigan (lake), U.S. K5
Michigan (state), U.S. K5
Milwaukee, Wis. K5
Minneapolis, Minn. J5
Minnesota (state), U.S. J5
Mississippi (riv.), U.S. J6
Mississippi (state), U.S. K6
Missouri (riv.), U.S. J5
Missouri (state), U.S. J6
Mobile, Ala. K6
Montana (state), U.S. H5
Monterrey, Mex. J7
Montréal, Qué. L5
Nashville (cap.), Tenn. K6
Nassau (cap.), Bahamas L7
Nebraska (state), U.S. J5
Nelson (riv.), Man. J4
Netherlands Antilles M8
Nevada (state), U.S. G6
New Brunswick (prov.), Canada M5
Newfoundland (isl.), Canada N5
Newfoundland (prov.), Canada M4
New Jersey (state), U.S. L5
New Mexico (state), U.S. H6
New Orleans, La. K7
New York, N.Y. L5
New York (state), U.S. L5
Nicaragua K8
Nicaragua (lake), Nic. K8
Nome, Alaska B3
Norfolk, Va. L6
North Carolina (state), U.S. K6
North Dakota (state), U.S. H5
Northwest Territories (terr.), Canada F3
Nova Scotia (prov.), Canada M5
Nuevo Laredo, Mex. H7
Nunavut (terr.), Canada H3
Nuuk (Godthåb) (cap.), Greenl. N3
Oakland, Calif. F6
Ohio (riv.), U.S. K6
Ohio (state), U.S. K5
Oklahoma (state), U.S. J6
Oklahoma City (cap.), Okla. J6
Omaha, Nebr. J5
Ontario (lake) O5
Ontario (prov.), Canada K4
Oregon (state), U.S. F5
Ottawa (cap.), Canada L5
Panama K9
Panama (canal), Pan. L8
Panamá (cap.), Pan. L9
Peace (riv.), Canada G4
Pennsylvania (state), U.S. L5
Philadelphia, Pa. L6
Phoenix (cap.), Ariz. G6
Pittsburgh, Pa. K5
Platte (riv.), U.S. J5
Port-au-Prince (cap.), Haiti L8
Portland, Maine M5
Portland, Oreg. F5
Prince Edward Island (prov.), Canada M5
Prince of Wales (isl.), Canada J2
Providence (cap.), R.I. L5
Puebla de Zaragoza, Mex. J8
Puerto Rico M8
Québec (cap.), Qué. L5
Québec (prov.), Canada L4
Queen Charlotte (isls.), Br. Col. E4
Race (cape), Canada N5
Raleigh (cap.), N.C. L6
Red (riv.), U.S. J6
Red River of the North (riv.), U.S. J5
Regina (cap.), Sask. H4
Rhode Island (state), U.S. M5
Richmond (cap.), Va. L6
Rochester, N.Y. L5
Rocky (mts.) F4
Sácramento (cap.), Calif. F6
Saint Kitts and Nevis M8
Saint John, N. Bruns. M5
Saint John's (cap.), Newf. N5
Saint Lawrence (gulf) M5
Saint Lawrence (riv.) L5
Saint Louis, Mo. K6
Saint Lucia M8
Saint Paul (cap.), Minn. J5
Saint Pierre and Miquelon (isls.) N5
Saint Vincent and The Grenadines M8
Salt Lake City (cap.), Utah G5
Saltillo, Mex. H7
San Antonio, Texas J7
San Diego, Calif. G6
San Francisco, Calif. F6
San Jose, Calif. F6
San José (cap.), C. Rica K9
San Juan (cap.), P. Rico M8
San Lucas (cape), Mex. G7
San Luis Potosí, Mex. H7
San Salvador (cap.), El Salv. J8
Santiago de Cuba, Cuba L8
Santo Domingo (cap.), Dom. Rep. L8
Saskatchewan (prov.), Canada H4
Saskatoon, Sask. H4
Seattle, Wash. F5
Shreveport, La. J6
Sierra Nevada (range), Calif. F6
South Carolina (state), U.S. K6
South Dakota (state), U.S. H5
Southampton (cape), Canada K3
Spokane, Wash. G5
Springfield (cap.), Ill. J6
Sudbury, Ont. K5
Superior (lake) K5
Tacoma, Wash. F5
Tallahassee (cap.), Fla. K6
Tampa, Fla. K7
Tampico, Mex. J7
Tegucigalpa (cap.), Hond. K8
Tehuantepec, Mex. J8
Tennessee (state), U.S. K6
Texas (state), U.S. J6
Thule Air Base, Greenl. M2
Thunder Bay, Ont. K5
Tijuana, Mex. G6
Toledo, Ohio K5
Toronto (cap.), Ont. K5
Torreón, Mex. H7
Trenton (cap.), N.J. L5
Trinidad and Tobago N8
Tucson, Ariz. G6
Tulsa, Okla. J6
Turks and Caicos Islands L7
Ungava (pen.), Qué. L3
United States of America H5
Utah (state), U.S. G6
Vancouver, Br. Col. F4
Vancouver (isl.), Br. Col. F5
Veracruz, Mex. J8
Vermont (state), U.S. L5
Victoria (cap.), Br. Col. F5
Victoria (isl.), N.W.T. G2
Virginia (state), U.S. L6
Virgin Islands (isls.) M8
Washington (state), U.S. F5
Washington, D.C. (cap.), U.S. L6
West Indies (isls.) M7
West Palm Beach, Fla. K7
West Virginia (state), U.S. K6
Whitehorse (cap.), Yukon E3
Wichita, Kansas J6
Wilmington, Del. L6
Winnipeg (cap.), Man. J5
Winnipeg (lake), Man. J4
Winnipegosis (lake), Man. H4
Wisconsin (state), U.S. K5
Wyoming (state), U.S. H5
Yellowknife (cap.), N.W.T. G3
Yucatán (pen.), Mex. K7
Yukon (riv.) C3
Yukon Territory (terr.), Canada E3

Average January Temperature

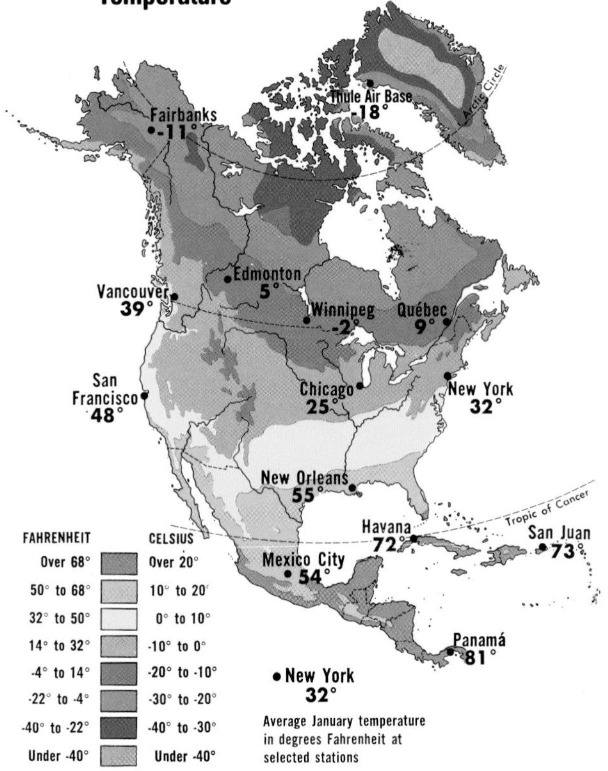
Fairbanks -11°
Thule Air Base -18°
Arctic Circle
Edmonton 5°
Vancouver 39°
Winnipeg -2°
Québec 9°
San Francisco 48°
Chicago 25°
New York 32°
New Orleans 55°
Tropic of Cancer
Havana 72°
San Juan 73°
Mexico City 54°
Panamá 81°
FAHRENHEIT
CELSIUS
Over 68° Over 20°
50° to 68° 10° to 20°
32° to 50° 0° to 10°
14° to 32° -10° to 0°
-4° to 14° -20° to -10°
-22° to -4° -30° to -20°
-40° to -22° -40° to -30°
Under -40° Under -40°
New York 32°
Average January temperature in degrees Fahrenheit at selected stations

Average July Temperature

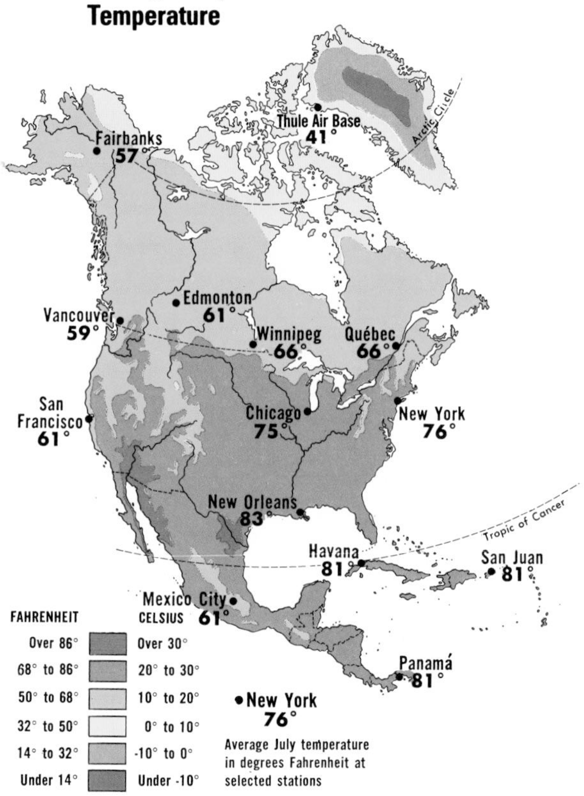
Fairbanks 57°
Thule Air Base 41°
Arctic Circle
Edmonton 61°
Vancouver 59°
Winnipeg 66°
Québec 66°
San Francisco 61°
Chicago 75°
New York 76°
New Orleans 83°
Tropic of Cancer
Havana 81°
San Juan 81°
Mexico City 61°
Panamá 81°
FAHRENHEIT
CELSIUS
Over 86° Over 30°
68° to 86° 20° to 30°
50° to 68° 10° to 20°
32° to 50° 0° to 10°
14° to 32° -10° to 0°
Under 14° Under -10°
New York 76°
Average July temperature in degrees Fahrenheit at selected stations

Rainfall

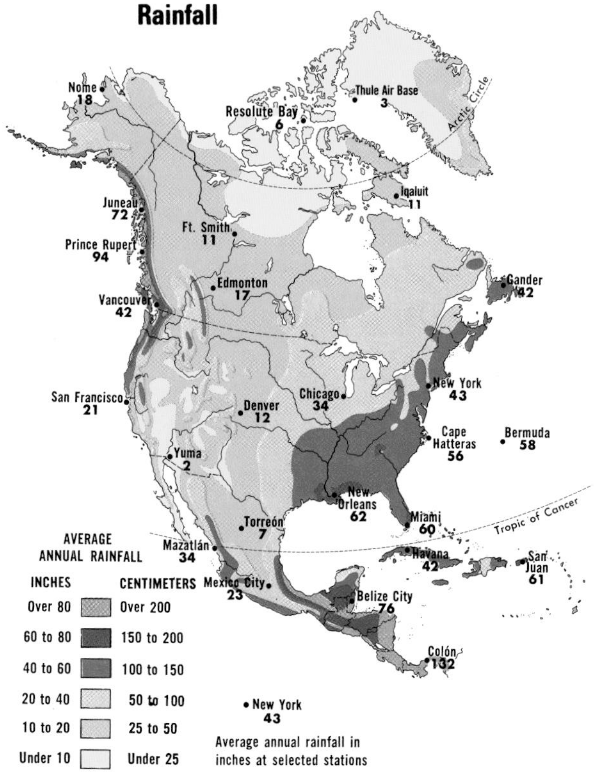
Nome 18
Thule Air Base 3
Resolute Bay 6
Arctic Circle
Iqaluit 11
Juneau 72
Ft. Smith 11
Prince Rupert 94
Edmonton 17
Gander 42
Vancouver 42
New York 43
San Francisco 21
Denver 12
Chicago 34
Cape Hatteras 56
Bermuda 58
Yuma 2
New Orleans 62
Torreón 7
Miami 60
Tropic of Cancer
Mazatlán 34
Havana 42
San Juan 61
Mexico City 23
Belize City 76
Colón 132
AVERAGE ANNUAL RAINFALL
INCHES
CENTIMETERS
Over 80 Over 200
60 to 80 150 to 200
40 to 60 100 to 150
20 to 40 50 to 100
10 to 20 25 to 50
Under 10 Under 25
New York 43
Average annual rainfall in inches at selected stations

Vegetation/Relief

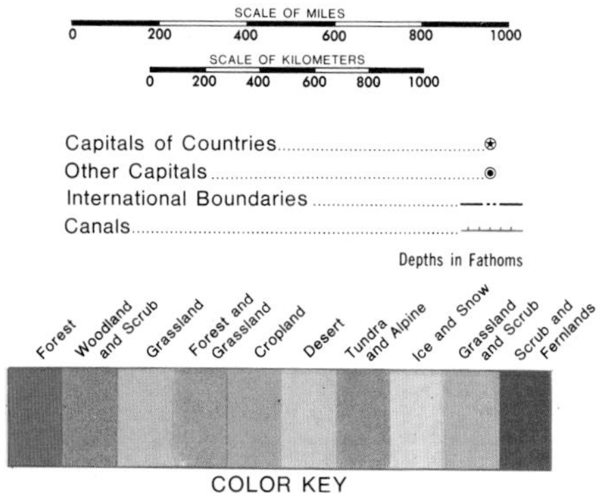
SCALE OF MILES
0 200 400 600 800 1000
SCALE OF KILOMETERS
0 200 400 600 800 1000
Capitals of Countries
Other Capitals
International Boundaries
Canals
Depths in Fathoms
Forest
Woodland and Scrub
Grassland
Forest and Grassland
Cropland
Desert
Tundra and Alpine
Ice and Snow
Grassland and Scrub
Scrub and Fernlands
COLOR KEY

North Pole
ASIA
RUSSIA
EAST SIBERIAN SEA
ARCTIC OCEAN
GREENLAND SEA
BERING SEA
Bering Strait
St. Lawrence I.
Pt. Barrow
BEAUFORT SEA
Queen Elizabeth Islands
GREENLAND (Den.)
ICELAND
Reykjavík
Denmark Strait
Arctic Circle
Baffin Bay
Devon I.
Melville I.
Banks I.
Victoria I.
Davis Strait
Nuuk
C. Farewell
Brooks Range
Alaska Range
Alaska Pen.
Kodiak I.
Gulf of Alaska
Great Bear L.
Inuvik
Yellowknife
Great Slave L.
L. Athabasca
Hudson Bay
C. Chidley
Ungava Peninsula
LABRADOR SEA
Laurentian Plateau
CANADA
Churchill
Nelson
Peace
Athabasca
North Saskatchewan
South Saskatchewan
Edmonton
Calgary
Saskatoon
Regina
Winnipeg
L. Winnipeg
Albany
James Bay
Eastmain
Newfoundland
Gander
St. John's
C. Race
Gulf of St. Lawrence
Cape Breton I.
Halifax
St. John
Québec
Montréal
Ottawa
Sudbury
Thunder Bay
Duluth
L. Superior
L. Michigan
Huron
Ontario
L. Erie
Toronto
Buffalo
Boston
C. Cod
New York
Philadelphia
Washington
Pittsburgh
Cleveland
Detroit
Columbus
Chicago
Milwaukee
Minneapolis
Mississippi
Missouri
Alexander Arch.
Prince Rupert
Queen Charlotte Is.
Vancouver I.
Vancouver
Victoria
Seattle
Mt. Rainier
Portland
Rocky Mountains
Coast Mountains
Great Plains
Great Basin
Great Salt Lake
Salt Lake City
Snake
C. Mendocino
San Francisco
Sierra Nevada
Mt. Whitney
Las Vegas
Los Angeles
San Diego
Phoenix
Tucson
Albuquerque
Colorado
Denver
Pikes Peak
Omaha
North Platte
South Platte
Kansas City
UNITED STATES
St. Louis
Indianapolis
Cincinnati
Ohio
Norfolk
C. Hatteras
Nashville
Memphis
Tennessee
Mt. Mitchell
Charlotte
Atlanta
Birmingham
Jacksonville
Appalachian Mts.
Arkansas
Wichita
Tulsa
Oklahoma City
Ozark Plateau
Red
Fort Worth
Dallas
El Paso
Ciudad Juárez
Rio Grande
San Antonio
Houston
New Orleans
Tampa
C. Canaveral
Miami
Corpus Christi
Bermuda (U.K.)
ATLANTIC OCEAN
PACIFIC OCEAN
BAHAMAS
Nassau
Tropic of Cancer
Gulf of Mexico
Gulf of California
Lower California
C. San Lucas
Chihuahua
Culiacán
Monterrey
Sierra Madre Occidental
Sierra Madre Oriental
MEXICO
Tampico
Guadalajara
Mexico City
Popocatepetl
Veracruz
Acapulco
Bay of Campeche
Mérida
Yucatán Pen.
BELIZE
GUATEMALA
Guatemala
HONDURAS
Tegucigalpa
San Salvador
EL SALVADOR
NICARAGUA
Managua
COSTA RICA
San José
PANAMA
Panamá
Panama Canal
Havana
CUBA
Santiago de Cuba
HAITI
Port-au-Prince
DOMINICAN REPUBLIC
Santo Domingo
San Juan
PUERTO RICO
JAMAICA
Kingston
Turks and Caicos Is. (U.K.)
West Indies
Greater Antilles
CARIBBEAN SEA
ARUBA (Neth.)
NETHERLANDS ANTILLES
Curaçao
Bonaire
Willemstad
Barranquilla
Caracas
VENEZUELA
Bogotá
COLOMBIA
SOUTH AMERICA
Longitude 90° West of Greenwich

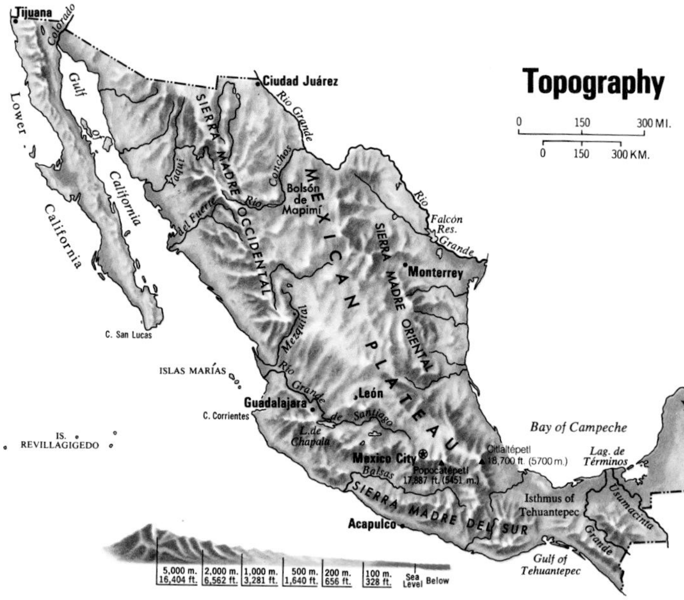
Topography
0 150 300 MI.
0 150 300 KM.
Tijuana
Ciudad Juárez
Monterrey
Guadalajara
León
Mexico City
Acapulco
Lower California
Gulf of California
SIERRA MADRE OCCIDENTAL
SIERRA MADRE ORIENTAL
MEXICAN PLATEAU
SIERRA MADRE DEL SUR
Bolsón de Mapimí
Río Grande
Bay of Campeche
Yucatán Pen.
Isthmus of Tehuantepec
Gulf of Tehuantepec
C. San Lucas
C. Corrientes
ISLAS MARÍAS
IS. REVILLAGIGEDO
L. de Chapala
Citlaltépetl 18,700 ft. (5700 m.)
Popocatépetl 17,887 ft. (5451 m.)
Lag. de Términos
Falcón Res.
5,000 m. 16,404 ft.
2,000 m. 6,562 ft.
1,000 m. 3,281 ft.
500 m. 1,640 ft.
200 m. 656 ft.
100 m. 328 ft.
Sea Level
Below

STATES

Aguascalientes 504,300..........H6
Baja California 1,227,400........B1
Baja California Sur 221,000....C3
Campeche 371,800..................O7
Chiapas 2,097,500..................N8
Chihuahua 1,935,100..............F2
Coahuila 1,561,000.................H3
Colima 339,400.......................G7
Distrito Federal 9,377,300.......L1
Durango 1,160,300..................G4
Guanajuato 3,045,600.............J6
Guerrero 2,174,200.................J8
Hidalgo 1,518,200..................K6
Jalisco 4,296,500....................H6
México 7,542,300....................K7
Michoacán 3,049,400..............H7
Morelos 931,400......................K7
Nayarit 729,500.......................G6
Nuevo León 2,463,500............K4
Oaxaca 2,517,500....................L8
Puebla 3,285,300.....................L7
Querétaro 730,900...................J6
Quintana Roo 209,900.............P7
San Luis Potosí 1,669,900......J5
Sinaloa 1,882,200....................F4
Sonora 1,498,100.....................D2
Tabasco 1,150,000...................N7
Tamaulipas 1,924,900.............K4
Tlaxcala 548,500.....................N1
Veracruz 5,263,800..................L7
Yucatán 1,034,300...................P6
Zacatecas 1,144,700................H5

CITIES and TOWNS

Acala 11,483............................N8
Acámbaro 32,257.....................J7
Acaponeta 11,844....................G5
Acapulco de Juárez 309,254...K8
Acatlán de Osorio 7,624..........K7
Acatzingo de Hidalgo 6,905....N2
Acayucan 21,173....................M8
Actopan 11,037........................K6
Agua Dulce 21,060..................M7
Agua Prieta 20,754..................E1
Aguascalientes 181,277..........H6
Aguililla 5,715..........................H7
Ahuacatitlán 6,436...................L1
Ahuacatlán 5,350.....................G6
Ahumada 6,466........................F1
Ajalpan 8,238..........................L7
Alamo 9,954............................L6
Aldama 6,047..........................G2
Allende, Coahuila 11,076.........J2
Allende, Nuevo León 9,914.....J4
Altamira 6,053........................L5
Altepexi 6,661.........................L7
Altotonga 6,754.......................P1
Alvarado 15,792......................M7
Ameca 21,018.........................H6
Amecameca de Juárez
16,276.................................L1
Amozoc de Mota 9,203...........N2
Anáhuac, Chihuahua 10,886....F2
Anáhuac, Nuevo León 8,168...J3
Apan 13,705...........................M1
Apatzingán de la Constitución
44,849.................................H7
Apizaco 21,189.......................N1
Arandas 18,934.......................H6
Arcelia 10,024.........................J7
Ario de Rosales 8,774..............J7
Armería 10,616.......................G7
Arriaga 13,193........................N8
Arteaga 5,324..........................H7
Atlixco 41,967........................M2
Atotonilco el Alto 16,271........H6
Atoyac de Álvarez 8,874..........J8
Autlán de Navarro 20,398.......G7
Axochiapan 8,283...................M2
Azcapotzalco 534,554.............L1
Bamoa 5,866...........................E4
Benjamín Hill 5,366................D1
Bernardino de Sahagún
12,327.................................M1
Cabo San Lucas 1,534............E5
Cacahoatán 5,079...................N9
Cadereyta Jiménez 13,586......K4
Calkiní 6,870..........................O6
Calpulálpan 8,659..................M1
Calvillo 6,453.........................H6
Campeche 69,506...................O7
Cananea 17,518......................D1
Canatlán 5,983.......................G4
Cancún 326............................Q6
Cañitas de Felipe Pescador
4,885...................................H5
Capulhuac de Mirafuentes
8,289...................................K1
Cárdenas, San Luis Potosí
12,020.................................K6
Cárdenas, Tabasco 15,643.....N8
Castaños 8,996.......................J3
Catemaco 11,786....................M7
Celaya 79,977.........................J6
Cerritos 10,421.......................J5
Cerro Azul 20,259...................L6
Chahuites 5,218.....................M8
Chalco de Díaz Covarrubias
12,172.................................M1
Champotón 6,606...................O7
Charcas 10,491.......................J5
Chetumal 23,685....................Q7
Chiapa de Corzo 8,571...........N8
Chiautempan 12,327...............N1
Chietla 4,602.........................M2
Chihuahua 327,313.................F2
Chilapa de Álvarez 9,204........K8
Chilpancingo de los Bravos
36,193.................................K8
China, Nuevo León 4,958........K4
Chocomán 5,114.....................P2
Cholula de Rivadavia 15,399..M1
Cihuatlán 9,451......................G7
Cintalapa de Figueroa 12,036.N8
Ciudad Acuña (Villa Acuña)
30,276..................................J2
Ciudad Altamirano 8,694.........J7
Ciudad Camargo, Chihuahua
24,030.................................G3
Ciudad Camargo, Tamaulipas
5,953...................................K3
Ciudad de Río Grande 11,651.H5
Ciudad del Carmen 34,656.....N7
Ciudad del Maíz 5,241............K5
Ciudad Delicias 52,446...........G2
Ciudad Guzmán 48,166..........H7
Ciudad Hidalgo, Chiapas
4,105...................................N9
Ciudad Hidalgo, Michoacán
24,692..................................J7
Ciudad Juárez 424,135............F1
Ciudad Lerdo 19,803..............H4
Ciudad Madero 115,302..........L5
Ciudad Mante 51,247..............K5
Ciudad Mendoza 18,696.........O2
Ciudad Miguel Alemán
11,259.................................K3
Ciudad Obregón 144,795........E3
Ciudad Río Bravo 39,018........K4
Ciudad Satélite 35,083............L1
Ciudad Serdán 9,581..............O2
Ciudad Valles 47,587..............K5
Ciudad Victoria 83,897...........K5
Coalcomán de Matamoros
4,875...................................H7
Coatepec 21,542.....................P1
Coatetelco 5,268.....................L2
Coatzacoalcos 69,753............M7
Cocorit 4,478..........................E3
Colima 58,450........................H7
Colotlán 6,135........................H5
Comala 5,592.........................H7
Comalcalco 14,963.................N7
Comitán de Domínguez
21,249.................................O8
Compostela 9,801..................G6
Concepción del Oro 8,144.......J4
Contla 7,517...........................N1
Coquimatlán 6,212.................G7
Córdoba 78,495.......................P2
Cosamaloapan de Carpio
19,766.................................M7
Coscomatepec de Bravo
6,023...................................P2
Costa Rica 11,795...................F4
Cotija de la Paz 9,178.............H7
Coyoacán 339,446..................L1
Coyotepec 8,888.....................L1
Coyuca de Benítez 6,328.........J8
Cozumel 5,858.......................Q6
Cuatrociénagas de Carranza
5,523...................................H3
Cuauhtémoc 26,598................F2
Cuautepec de Hinojosa 5,501.K6
Cuautitlán de Romero Rubio
11,439.................................L1
Cuautla Morelos 13,946..........L2
Cuernavaca 239,813...............L2
Cuitlahuac 4,813.....................P2
Culiacán 228,001....................F4
Dolores Hidalgo de la
Independencia Naci 16,849.J6
Durango 182,633....................G4
Dzidzantún 7,064...................P6
Dzitbalché 4,393.....................P6
Ebano 17,489..........................K5
Ecatepec de Morelos 11,899...L1
Ejutla de Crespo 5,263............L8
Eldorado 8,115.......................E4
El Fuerte 7,179.......................E3
El Salto 7,818.........................G5
Empalme 24,927.....................D2
Encarnación de Díaz 10,474...H6
Ensenada 77,687....................A1
Escarcega 7,248.....................O7
Escuinapa de Hidalgo 16,442.G5
Escuintla 4,111......................N9
Esperanza, Sonora 11,762......E3
Espita 5,394...........................Q6
Fortín de las Flores 9,358.......P2
Francisco I. Madero 12,613....H4
Fresnillo de González
Echeverría 44,475.................H5
Frontera 10,066......................N7
General Terán 5,354...............K4
Gómez Palacio 79,650............G4
González 6,440.......................K5
Guadalajara 1,478,383...........H6
Guadalupe, Nuevo León
51,899.................................K4
Guadalupe, Zacatecas 13,246.H5
Guadalupe Victoria, Durango
7,931...................................H4
Guamúchil 17,151...................E4
Guanajuato 36,809..................J6
Guasave 26,080......................E4
Guaymas 57,492.....................D3
Gustavo Díaz Ordaz 10,154.....K3
Gutiérrez Zamora 9,099..........L6
Halachó 4,804........................O6
Hermosillo 232,691.................D2
Heroica Caborca 20,771..........C1
Heroica Nogales 52,108..........D1
Hidalgo del Parral (Parral)
57,619.................................G3
Huachinango 16,826...............K7
Huajuapan de León 13,822.....L8
Huamantla 15,565...................N1
Huatabampo 18,506................D3
Huatusco de Chicuellar 9,501.P2
Huauchinango 16,826.............L6
Huautla de Jiménez 6,132.......L7
Huejotzingo 8,552..................M1
Huejutla 6,854........................K6
Huetamo 9,333........................J7
Huimanguillo 7,075.................N8
Huitzuco de los Figueroa
9,406...................................K7
Huixtepec 5,927......................L8
Huixtla 15,737........................N9
Hunucmá 8,020.......................O6
Iguala de la Independencia
45,355.................................K7
Irapuato 135,596.....................J6
Isla, Veracruz 8,075...............M7
Isla Mujeres 2,663..................Q6
Ixmiquilpan 6,048...................K6
Ixtapa......................................J8
Ixtapalapa 522,095..................L1
Ixtenco 5,035..........................N1
Ixtepec 14,025.......................M8
Ixtlán del Río 10,986..............G6
Izamal 9,749...........................P6
Izúcar de Matamoros 21,164.M2
Jala 4,535...............................G6
Jalapa Enríquez 161,352.........P1
Jalpa 9,904.............................H6
Jalpa de Méndez 4,785...........N7
Jáltipan de Morelos 15,170....M8
Jerez de García Salinas
20,325.................................H5
Jico 7,269...............................P1
Jiménez, Chihuahua 18,095....G3
Jojutla de Juárez 14,438.........L2
José Cardel 5,396...................Q1
Juan Aldama 9,667.................H4
Juchipila 6,328.......................H6
Juchitán de Zaragoza 30,218.M8
La Barca 18,055.....................H6
Lagos de Moreno 33,782.........J6
La Paz 46,011.........................D5
La Piedad Cavadas 34,963......H6
Las Choapas 20,166...............M7
Las Rosas 7,658.....................N8
León 468,887..........................J6
Lerdo de Tejada 11,628.........M8
Libres 4,830...........................O1
Linares 24,456........................K4
Loma Bonita 15,804...............M7
Loreto 7,132............................J5
Los Mochis 67,953..................E4
Los Reyes de Salgado
19,452.................................H7
Macuspana 12,293.................N8
Madera 9,759..........................F2
Magdalena de Kino 10,281.....D1
Maltrata 5,457........................O2
Manzanillo 20,777..................G7
Mapastepec 5,907...................N9
Martínez de la Torre 17,203....L6
Mascota 5,674........................G6
Matamoros, Coahuila 15,125..H4
Matamoros, Tamaulipas
165,124................................L4
Matehuala 28,799....................J5
Matías Romero 13,200...........M8
Maxcanú 6,505.......................O6
Mazatlán 147,010....................F5
Melchor Múzquiz 18,868........H3
Melchor Ocampo del Balsas
4,766...................................H8
Meoquí 12,308.......................G2
Mérida 233,912.......................P6
Metepec 4,625.......................M2
Mexicali 317,228.....................B1
Mexico City (cap.) 9,377,300..L1
Miahuatlán de Porfirio Díaz
5,714...................................L8
Mier 5,636..............................K3
Miguel Auza 9,303..................H4
Minatitlán 68,397...................M8
Mineral del Monte 8,887.........K6
Misantla 8,799........................P1
Monclova 78,134.....................J3
Montemorelos 18,642.............K4
Monterrey 1,006,221...............J4
Morelia 199,099.......................J7
Moroleón 25,620.....................J6
Motozintla de Mendoza 4,682.N9
Motul de Felipe Carrillo
Puerto 12,949......................P6
Muna 5,491............................P6
Naica 7,190...........................G2
Namiquipa 4,875....................F2
Nanacamilpa 6,356................M1
Naranjos 14,732......................L6
Naucalpan de Juárez 9,425.....L1
Navojoa 43,817.......................E3
Navolato 12,799......................E4
Netzahualcóyotl 580,436.........L1
Nochistlán 8,780.....................H6
Nogales 14,254.......................P2
Nueva Casas Grandes 20,023..F1
Nueva Italia de Ruiz 14,718.....J7
Nueva Rosita 34,706...............J2
Nuevo Ideal 5,252..................G4
Nuevo Laredo 184,622............J3
Oaxaca de Juárez 114,948......L8
Ocampo 4,801........................K5
Ocotlán 35,361.......................H6
Ocotlán de Morelos 5,882.......L8
Ojinaga 12,757.......................G2
Ojocaliente 7,582...................H5
Ometepec 7,342.....................K8
Oriental 6,009........................O1
Orizaba 105,150......................P2
Oxkutzcab 8,182.....................P6
Ozumba de Alzate 6,876........M1
Pachuca de Soto 83,892.........K6
Padilla 4,581..........................K5
Palenque 2,595......................O8
Pánuco 14,277........................K6
Papantla de Olarte 26,773.......L6
Paraíso 7,561.........................N7
Parral 57,619.........................G3
Parras de la Fuente 18,207.....H4
Paso de Ovejas 4,371.............Q2
Pátzcuaro 17,299....................J7
Pedro Montoya 4,563..............K6
Pénjamo 9,245........................J6
Pericos 4,445..........................F4
Perote 12,742.........................O1
Petatlán 9,419.........................J8
Peto 8,362.............................P6
Pichucalco 4,615....................N8
Piedras Negras, Coahuila
41,033..................................J2
Piedras Negras, Veracruz
4,099...................................Q2
Pijijiapan 5,053......................N9
Poza Rica de Hidalgo
152,276................................L6
Profesor Rafael Ramírez
5,338...................................O1
Progreso 17,518.....................P6

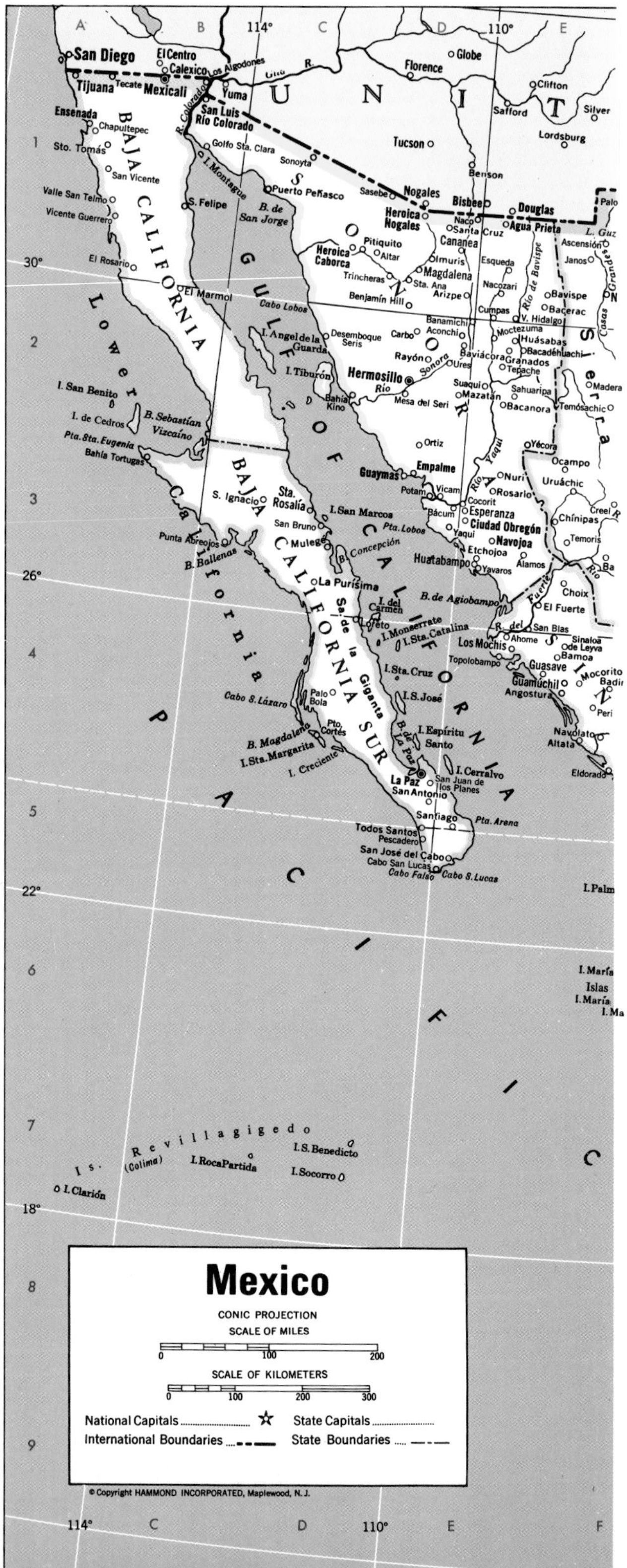
Mexico
CONIC PROJECTION
SCALE OF MILES
0 100 200
SCALE OF KILOMETERS
0 100 200 300
National Capitals
State Capitals
International Boundaries
State Boundaries
San Diego
Tijuana
Mexicali
Ensenada
Tucson
Nogales
Hermosillo
Guaymas
Ciudad Obregón
Navojoa
Los Mochis
La Paz
BAJA CALIFORNIA
BAJA CALIFORNIA SUR
SONORA
GULF OF CALIFORNIA
Lower California
PACIFIC

(continued on following page)

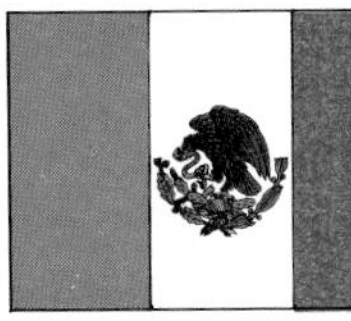

AREA 761,601 sq. mi. (1,972,546 sq. km.)
POPULATION 86,154,000
CAPITAL Mexico City
LARGEST CITY Mexico City
HIGHEST POINT Citlaltépetl 18,700 ft. (5,700 m.)
MONETARY UNIT Mexican peso
MAJOR LANGUAGE Spanish
MAJOR RELIGION Roman Catholicism

States Indicated by Numbers
1 Tlaxcala
2 Morelos
3 Distrito Federal
4 México
5 Hidalgo
6 Querétaro
7 Guanajuato
8 Aguascalientes
9 Nayarit
10 Colima
GULF OF MEXICO
BAY OF CAMPECHE
PACIFIC OCEAN
Campeche Bank
Tropic of Cancer
Gulf of Tehuantepec
Isthmus of Tehuantepec
MEXICO CITY
Guadalajara
Monterrey
Puebla
Veracruz
Mérida
Acapulco de Juárez
Longitude West of Greenwich

(continued)

San Luis de la Paz 12,654 ....J6
San Luis Potosí 271,123 ....J5
San Luis Río Colorado
49,990 ....B1
San Marcos 5,861..................K8
San Martín de las Pirámides
4,575 ....M1
San Martín Texmelucan
23,355 ....M1
San Miguel de Allende 24,286.J6
San Nicolás de los Garza
28,803...............................J3
San Pedro de las Colonias
26,882 ....H4
San Rafael 8,974...................M1
San Salvador el Seco 7,729....O1
Santa Ana 7,020 ....D1
Santa Ana Chiautempan
(Chiautempan) 12,327........N1
Santa Bárbara 16,978.............F3
Santa María del Río 4,972.......J6
Santa Rosalía 7,356................C3
Santiago Ixcuintla 17,321 ....G6
Santiago Jamiltepec 5,280......K8
Santiago Miahuatlán 4,917 .....O2
Santiago Papasquiaro 6,636 ...F4
Santiago Pinotepa Nacional
9,382 ....K8
Santiago Tuxtla 9,426 ....M7
Saucillo 8,467........................G2
Sayula 14,339........................H7
Sayula de Alemán 4,896 ....M8
Silao 31,825 ....J6
Soledad de Doblado 6,612......Q2
Soledad Díez Gutiérrez 9,622 ..J5
Sombrerete 11,077.................H5
Tacámbaro de Codallos 9,695 .J7
Tala 15,744............................H6
Tamazunchale 12,302.............K6
Tamiahua 6,264 ....L6
Tampico 212,188 ....L5
Tamuín 7,251.........................K6
Tantoyuca 11,902 ....L6
Tapachula 60,620 ....N9
Taxco de Alarcón 27,089 ....K7
Teapa 6,534...........................N8
Tecate 14,738 ....A1
Tecomán 31,625.....................H7
Tecpan de Galeana 8,095 ....J8
Tecuala 12,461 ....G5
Tehuacán 47,497 ....L7
Tehuantepec 16,179 ....M8
Tekax de Álvaro Obregón
10,326 ....P6
Teloloapan 10,335...................J7
Temax 4,915..........................P6
Tenancingo de Degollado
12,807 ....K7
Tenango de Río Blanco
12,302 ....O2
Tenosique de Pino Suárez
11,393 ....O8
Teocaltiche 13,745 ....H6
Teocelo 4,572 ....P1
Teotihuacán de Arista 2,238....L1
Tepalcingo 5,968 ....M2
Tepatitlán de Morelos 29,292 .H6
Tepatlaxco de Hidalgo 8,833 ..N1
Tepeaca 7,466 ....N2
Tepeapulco 7,027 ....M1
Tepeji del Río 10,365 ....L1
Tepic 108,924.........................G6
Tepoztlán 6,851 ....L1
Tequixquitla 4,825 ....O1
Terán 5,215 ....N8
Texcoco de Mora 18,044 ....M1
Teziutlán 23,948 ....O1
Ticul 14,341...........................P6
Tierra Blanca 22,727 ....L7
Tijuana 363,154 ....A1
Tixtla de Guerrero 10,334 ....K8
Tizayuca 6,262........................L1
Tizimín 18,343.......................Q6
Tlacolula de Matamoros
8,300...............................L8
Tlahualilo de Zaragoza 8,951 ..H3
Tlalancaneca 5,090 ....M1
Tlalmanalco de Velásquez
5,744...............................L1
Tlalnepantla de Comonfort
45,575..............................L1
Tlalpan 130,719 ....L1
Tlaltenango de Sánchez
Román 7,698.....................H6
Tlaltizapan 6,384 ....L2
Tlapacoyan 13,172..................P1
Tlapa de Comonfort 6,676 ......K8
Tlaquepaque 59,760 ....G6
Tlaquiltenango 8,625 ....L2
Tlaxcala de Xicotencatl 9,972.M1
Tlaxco 4,969..........................N1
Toluca de Lerdo 136,092........K7
Tonalá 15,611........................N8
Topolobampo 4,685................E4
Torreón 244,309.....................H4
Tula, Tamaulipas 5,407...........K5
Tula de Allende 10,720 ....K6
Tulancingo 35,799..................K7
Tultepec 8,321 ....L1
Tuxpan, Nayarit 20,322 ....G6
Tuxpan, Jalisco 14,693...........H7
Tuxpan de Rodríguez Cano
33,901..............................L6
Tuxtepec 17,701 ....L7
Tuxtla Gutiérrez 66,851 ....N8
Tzucabab 4,876 ....P7
Umán 8,371 ....P6
Unión de Tula 6,399 ....G7
Unión Hidalgo 8,658 ....M8
Uruapan del Progreso
108,124 ....H7
Valladolid 14,663...................P6
Valle de Allende 4,973 ....G3
Valle de Bravo 7,628 ....J7
Valle Hermoso 19,278............L4
Venustiano Carranza 23,624...N8

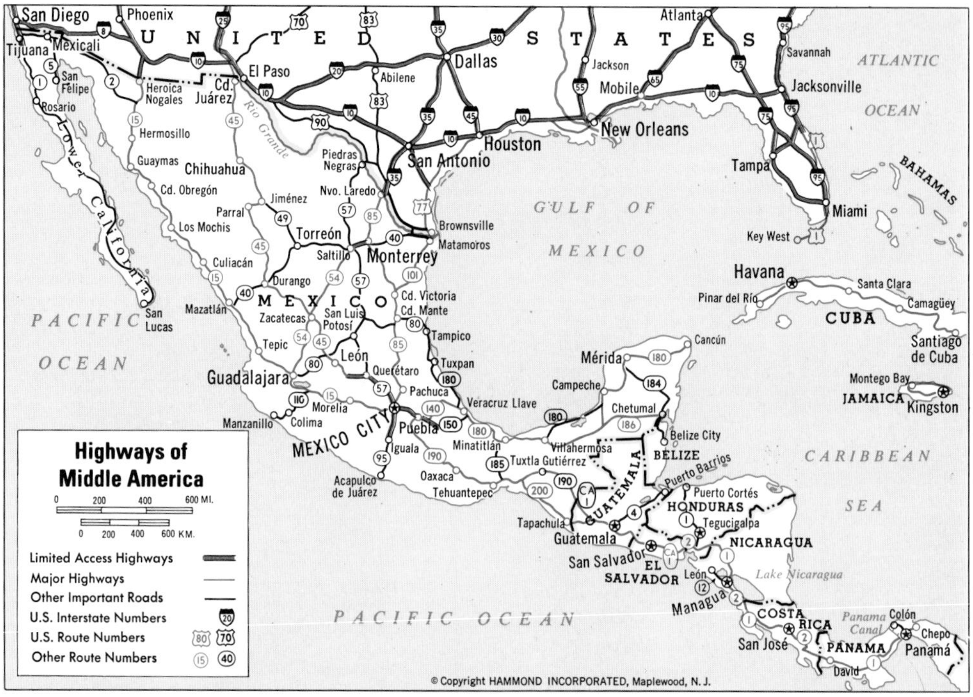
San Diego
Phoenix
Tijuana
Mexicali
U N I T E D S T A T E S
El Paso
Cd. Juárez
Heroica Nogales
San Felipe
Rosario
Hermosillo
Guaymas
Chihuahua
Cd. Obregón
Los Mochis
Parral
Jiménez
Culiacán
Durango
Torreón
Saltillo
Monterrey
Nvo. Laredo
Piedras Negras
San Antonio
Houston
Dallas
Abilene
Atlanta
Jackson
Mobile
New Orleans
Savannah
Jacksonville
Tampa
Miami
Key West
ATLANTIC OCEAN
BAHAMAS
GULF OF MEXICO
Brownsville
Matamoros
Cd. Victoria
Cd. Mante
Tampico
Tuxpan
Mazatlán
San Lucas
Zacatecas
San Luis Potosí
Tepic
León
Querétaro
Guadalajara
Pachuca
Veracruz Llave
Morelia
Colima
Manzanillo
MEXICO CITY
Puebla
Iguala
Minatitlán
Oaxaca
Tehuantepec
Acapulco de Juárez
Tuxtla Gutiérrez
Villahermosa
Campeche
Mérida
Cancún
Chetumal
Belize City
BELIZE
GUATEMALA
Guatemala
Tapachula
Puerto Barrios
Puerto Cortés
HONDURAS
Tegucigalpa
San Salvador
EL SALVADOR
León
Managua
NICARAGUA
Lake Nicaragua
COSTA RICA
San José
Panama Canal
Colón
Chepo
Panamá
PANAMA
David
Havana
Pinar del Río
Santa Clara
Camagüey
CUBA
Santiago de Cuba
Montego Bay
JAMAICA
Kingston
CARIBBEAN SEA
PACIFIC OCEAN
Highways of Middle America
0 200 400 600 MI.
0 200 400 600 KM.
Limited Access Highways
Major Highways
Other Important Roads
U.S. Interstate Numbers
U.S. Route Numbers
Other Route Numbers
© Copyright HAMMOND INCORPORATED, Maplewood, N. J.

Veracruz 255,646 ....Q1
Vicente Guerrero, Durango
8,451 ....G5
Victor Rosales 7,629 ....H5
Villa Acuña 30,276 ....J2
Villa Cuauhtémoc 6,611 ....L5
Villa de Guadelupe Hidalgo
88,537..............................L1
Villa Frontera 25,761 ....J3
Villahermosa 133,181.............N8
Villanueva 5,895 ....H5
Villa Unión, Sinaloa 6,789 ....F5
Villa Vicente Guerrero 18,280.N1
Xicoténcatl 6,374...................K5
Xicotepec de Juárez 12,656 ....L6
Xochimilco 116,493................L1
Yaqui 8,061 ....D3
Yautepec 13,952....................L2
Zaachila 7,270........................L8
Zacapoaxtla 4,527 ....O1
Zacapu 31,989 ....J7
Zacatecas 50,251...................H5
Zacatelco 14,117 ....N1
Zacatepec 16,839...................L2
Zacatlán 7,909 ....N1
Zacoalco de Torres 11,343 .....H6
Zamora de Hidalgo 5,775 ....H7
Zaragoza, Coahuila 6,797 ....J2
Zaragoza, Puebla 4,754 ....O1
Zempoala 5,064......................Q1
Zihuatanejo 4,879...................J8
Zimatlán de Álvarez 5,746.......L8
Zitácuaro 36,911 ....J7
Zumpango de Ocampo
12,923..............................L1
Zumpango del Río 8,162........J8

OTHER FEATURES

Agiobampo (bay) E3
Aguanaval (riv.) H4
Alacrán (reef)..........................P5
Amistad (res.) J2
Ángel de la Guarda (isl.) C2
Antigua (riv.) Q1
Arcas (cay) N6
Arena (pt.)..............................E5
Arenas (cay) O5
Atoyac (riv.)............................N2
Atoyac (riv.)............................Q2
Babia (riv.) J2
Bacalar (lake)..........................P7
Ballenas (bay) C3
Balsas (riv.).............................J7
Banderas (bay) G6
Bavispe, Río de (riv.)...............E1
Blanco (riv.)............................Q2
Bravo (Grande) (riv.) G2
Burro (mts.) J2
California (gulf).......................D3
Campeche (bank) O6
Campeche (bay) N7
Candelaria (riv.) O8
Carmen (isl.)...........................D3
Carranza, Venustiano (res.).....J3
Casas Grandes (riv.)................F1
Catoche (cape) Q6
Cedros (isl.) B2
Cerralvo (isl.) E4
Chamela (bay) G7
Chapala (lake).........................H6
Chetumal (bay) P8
Chichén-Itzá (ruin)..................P6
Citlaltépetl (mt.)......................O2
Clarión (isl.)............................B7
Colorado (riv.) B1
Concepción (bay) D3
Conchos (riv.).........................G2
Corrientes (cape).....................F6
Coyuca (riv.)...........................O1
Cozumel (isl.) Q6
Creciente (isl.) D5
Cuitzeo (lake) J7
Delgada (pt.) L7
Dzibichaltún (ruin) P6
El Azúcar (res.) K3
El Chichón (vol.) N8
Espíritu Santo (isl.).................D4
Falcón (res.)............................K3
Falso (cape)............................D5
Fuerte (riv.) E3
Giganta, Sierra de la (mts.).....D4
Grande (Bravo) (riv.) G2
Grande de Santiago (riv.)........G6
Grijalva (riv.)..........................N7
Guzmán (lake)........................F1
Herrero (pt.) Q7
Hondo (riv.) P7
Jesús María (reef)...................L4
La Boquilla (res.) G3
Lacantum (riv.)........................O8
La Paz (bay)............................D4
Lobos (cape)...........................C2
Lobos (pt.)..............................D3
Lower California (pen.) C3
Madre (lag.) L4
Madre del Sur, Sierra (mts.)...K8
Madre Occidental, Sierra
(mts.) F3
Madre Oriental, Sierra
(mts.) J4
Magdalena (bay).....................C4
Maldonado (pt.)......................K8
Mapimí (depr.)........................G3
María Cleófas (isl.) F6
María Madre (isl.)...................F6
María Magdalena (isl.)............F6
Marías, Islas (isls.)..................F6
Mar Muerto (lag.) N9
Mexico (gulf) N4
Mezcala (riv.) J8
Mezquital (riv.) G5
Mita (pt.) G6
Mitla (ruin)............................M8
Moctezuma (riv.) K6
Monserrate (isl.).....................D4
Montague (isl.) B1
Muerto, Mar (lag.) N9
Nauhcampatépetl (mt.)...........O1
Nayarit, Sierra (mts.).............G5
Nazas (riv.)............................G4
Nohkú (pt.)............................Q7
Nuevo, Bajo (reef)..................O6
Orizaba (Citlaltépetl) (mt.) O2
Palenque (ruin).......................O8
Palmito de la Vírgen (isl.)........F5
Palmito del Verde (isl.)...........F5
Pánuco (riv.)..........................K5
Paricutín (vol.).......................H7
Pátzcuaro (lake) J7
Pérez (isl.) P5
Petacalco (bay).......................H8
Popocatépetl (mt.) M1
Ramos (riv.) G4
Revillagigedo (isls.) C7
Roca Partida (isl.)..................C7
Rojo (cape) L6
Sabinas (riv.)..........................J3
San Antonio (reef)..................L4
San Benedicto (isl.) D7
San Benito (isl.) B2
San Jorge (bay) C1
San José (isl.).........................D4
San Lázaro (cape)...................C4
San Lucas (cape) E5
San Marcos (isl.) D3
San Rafael (reef) L4
Santa Ana (reef).....................N7
Santa Catalina (isl.)................D4
Santa Cruz (isl.) D4
Santa Eugenia (pt.) B3
Santa Margarita (isl.) C4
Santa María (lake) F1
Santa María (riv.) F1
Santiaguillo (lake)..................G4
Sebastián Vizcaíno (bay).........B2
Socorro (isl.) D7
Sonora (riv.) D2
Superior (lag.)........................M9
Teacapán (inlet)......................F5
Tehuantepec (isth.) M8
Tehuantepec (gulf).................M9
Teotihuacán (ruin) M1
Términos (lag.)........................O7
Tiburón (isl.)..........................C2
Triángulo Este (isl.) N6
Triángulo Oeste (isl.) N6
Tula (riv.) L1
Urique (riv.)...........................F3
Usumacinta (riv.)....................O8
Uxmal (ruins)..........................P6
Valsequillo (res.) N2
Venustiano Carranza (res.)......J3
Verde (riv.)............................F3
Verde (riv.)............................L8
Yaqui (riv.)............................E2
Yucatán (pen.) P7

Agriculture, Industry and Resources
Chihuahua
Piedras Negras
Monclova
Torreón
Monterrey
Saltillo
Tampico
San Luis Potosí
Salamanca
Guadalajara
Mexico City
Veracruz Llave
Orizaba
Shellfish
Tuna
Shrimp
Mackerel
Wheat
Cotton
Vegetables
Sugarcane
Tobacco
Corn
Cattle
Sheep
Coffee
Rice
Bananas
Cocoa
Henequen
DOMINANT LAND USE
Wheat, Livestock
Cereals (chiefly corn), Livestock
Diversified Tropical Cash Crops
Cotton, Mixed Cereals
Livestock, Limited Agriculture
Range Livestock
Forests
Nonagricultural Land
Water Power
Major Industrial Areas
MAJOR MINERAL OCCURRENCES
Ag Silver
Au Gold
C Coal
Cu Copper
F Fluorspar
Fe Iron Ore
G Natural Gas
Gr Graphite
Hg Mercury
Mn Manganese
Mo Molybdenum
Na Salt
O Petroleum
Pb Lead
S Sulfur
Sb Antimony
Sn Tin
W Tungsten
Zn Zinc

GUATEMALA

AREA 42,042 sq. mi. (108,889 sq. km.)
POPULATION 9,197,000
CAPITAL Guatemala
LARGEST CITY Guatemala
HIGHEST POINT Tajumulco 13,845 ft. (4,220 m.)
MONETARY UNIT quetzal
MAJOR LANGUAGES Spanish, Quiché
MAJOR RELIGION Roman Catholicism

BELIZE

AREA 8,867 sq. mi. (22,966 sq. km.)
POPULATION 180,000
CAPITAL Belmopan
LARGEST CITY Belize City
HIGHEST POINT Victoria Peak 3,681 ft. (1,122 m.)
MONETARY UNIT Belize dollar
MAJOR LANGUAGES English, Spanish, Mayan
MAJOR RELIGIONS Roman Catholicism, Protestantism

EL SALVADOR

AREA 8,260 sq. mi. (21,393 sq. km.)
POPULATION 5,207,000
CAPITAL San Salvador
LARGEST CITY San Salvador
HIGHEST POINT Santa Ana 7,825 ft. (2,385 m.)
MONETARY UNIT colón
MAJOR LANGUAGE Spanish
MAJOR RELIGION Roman Catholicism

HONDURAS

AREA 43,277 sq. mi. (112,087 sq. km.)
POPULATION 4,951,000
CAPITAL Tegucigalpa
LARGEST CITY Tegucigalpa
HIGHEST POINT Las Minas 9,347 ft. (2,849 m.)
MONETARY UNIT lempira
MAJOR LANGUAGE Spanish
MAJOR RELIGION Roman Catholicism

NICARAGUA

AREA 45,698 sq. mi. (118,358 sq. km.)
POPULATION 3,384,000
CAPITAL Managua
LARGEST CITY Managua
HIGHEST POINT Cerro Mocotón 6,913 ft. (2,107 m.)
MONETARY UNIT córdoba
MAJOR LANGUAGE Spanish
MAJOR RELIGION Roman Catholicism

COSTA RICA

AREA 19,575 sq. mi. (50,700 sq. km.)
POPULATION 2,959,000
CAPITAL San José
LARGEST CITY San José
HIGHEST POINT Chirripó Grande 12,530 ft. (3,819 m.)
MONETARY UNIT colón
MAJOR LANGUAGE Spanish
MAJOR RELIGION Roman Catholicism

PANAMA

AREA 29,761 sq. mi. (77,082 sq. km.)
POPULATION 2,418,000
CAPITAL Panamá
LARGEST CITY Panamá
HIGHEST POINT Vol. Baru 11,401 ft. (3,475 m.)
MONETARY UNIT balboa
MAJOR LANGUAGE Spanish
MAJOR RELIGION Roman Catholicism

Agriculture, Industry and Resources

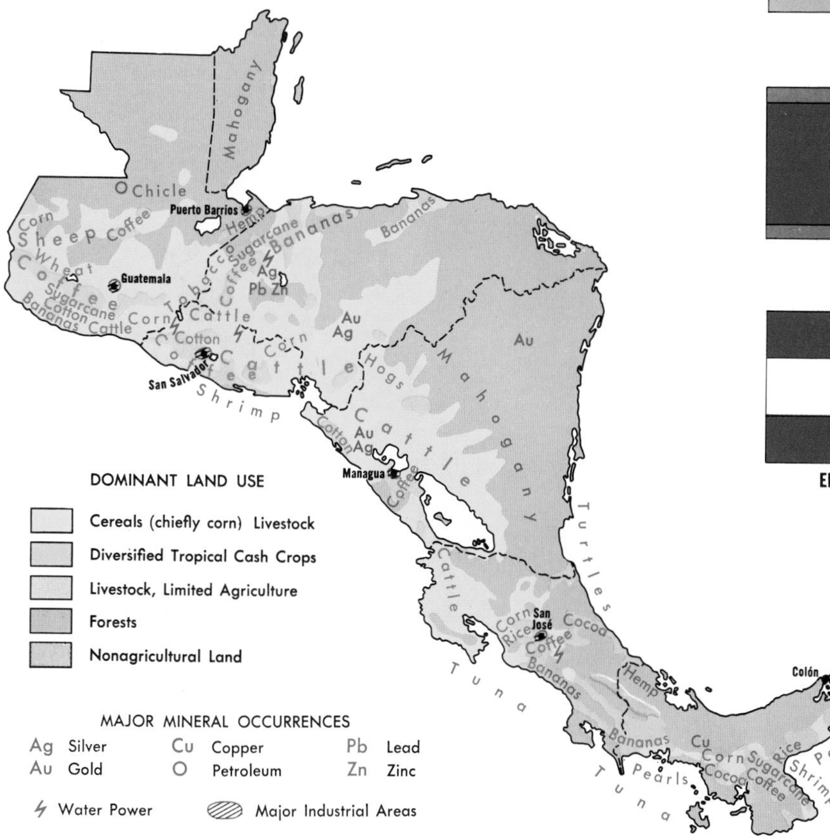
Mahogany
Chicle
Puerto Barrios
Bananas
Hemp
Sugarcane
Tobacco
Coffee
Sheep
Corn
Wheat
Guatemala
Ag
Pb Zn
Cattle
Cotton
Au
San Salvador
Shrimp
Hogs
Managua
Turtles
San José
Rice
Cocoa
Tuna
Colón
Panamá
Pearls
Cu
DOMINANT LAND USE
Cereals (chiefly corn) Livestock
Diversified Tropical Cash Crops
Livestock, Limited Agriculture
Forests
Nonagricultural Land
MAJOR MINERAL OCCURRENCES
Ag Silver
Au Gold
Cu Copper
O Petroleum
Pb Lead
Zn Zinc
Water Power
Major Industrial Areas

GUATEMALA

HONDURAS

BELIZE

NICARAGUA

EL SALVADOR

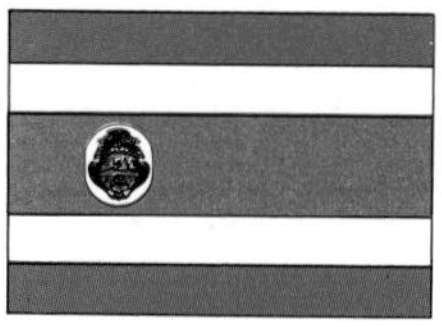
COSTA RICA

PANAMA

BELIZE

CITIES and TOWNS

Belize City 39,887 ... C2
Belmopan (cap.) 2,932 ... C2
Corozal Town 6,862 ... C1
Hattieville 904 ... C2
Independence 225 ... C2
Libertad 856 ... C1
Orange Walk Town 8,441 ... C1
Punta Gorda 2,219 ... C2
San Ignacio 5,606 ... C2
San José 420 ... C2
San Pedro 213 ... D2
Stann Creek Town 6,627 ... C2

OTHER FEATURES

Ambergris (cay) ... D1
Belize (riv.) ... C2
Glover (reef) ... D2
Half Moon (cay) ... D2
Hondo (riv.) ... C1
Honduras (gulf) ... D2
Mauger (cay) ... D2
Mya (mts.) ... C2
New (riv.) ... C2
Saint Georges (cay) ... D2
Sarstún (riv.) ... C3
Turneffe (isls.) ... D2

COSTA RICA

CITIES and TOWNS

Alajuela 33,122 ... E6
Atenas 1,728 ... E6
Bagaces 2,129 ... E5
Boruca 1,892 ... F6
Buenos Aires 302 ... F6
Cañas 6,053 ... E5
Cartago 21,753 ... F6
Ciudad Quesada 9,754 ... E5
Esparta 4,699 ... E5
Filadelfia 2,958 ... E5
Golfito 6,962 ... F6
Grecia 8,355 ... E5
Guácimo 1,168 ... F5
Guápiles 3,524 ... F5
Heredia 22,700 ... E5
Las Juntas 1,129 ... E5
Liberia 10,802 ... E5
Limón 29,621 ... F6
Miramar 1,673 ... E5
Nicoya 7,474 ... E5
Orotina 3,170 ... E6
Palmares 3,083 ... F6
Paquera ... E6
Paraíso 8,446 ... F6
Playa Bonita ... E6
Puerto Cortés 2,070 ... F6
Puntarenas 26,331 ... E6
Quepos 2,155 ... E6
San Ignacio 446 ... E6
San José (cap.) 215,441 ... F5
San Marcos 917 ... E6
San Ramón 9,245 ... E5
Santa Cruz 5,777 ... E5
Santa Rosa ... E5

(continued on following page)

(continued)

Santo Domingo 5,148 ....F6
Sibube F6
Siquirres 4,361 ....F5
Suretka F6
Turrialba 12,151 ....F6
Vesta F6

OTHER FEATURES

Blanco (cape) E6
Blanco (peak) F6
Burica (pt.) F6
Cahuita (pt.) F6
Caño (isl.) F6
Chirripó Grande (mt.) F6
Coronada (bay) F6
Cuilapa Miravalles (vol.) E5
Dulce (gulf) F6
Góngora (mt.) E5
Guardian (bank) D6
Guionos (pt.) E6
Irazú (mt.) F6
Llerena (pt.) F6
Matapalo (cape) F6
Nicoya (gulf) E6
Nicoya (pen.) E6
Papagayo (gulf) E5
Salinas (bay) D5
San Juan (riv.) E5
Santa Elena (cape) D5
Talamanca (range) F6

EL SALVADOR

CITIES and TOWNS

Acajutla 8,598 ....B4
Ahuachapán 17,242 ....B4
Atiquizaya 7,035 ....C3
Chalatenango 7,633 ....C3
Chinameca 6,303 ....C4
Cojutepeque 20,615 ....C4
Ilobasco 6,572 ....C4
Intipucá 3,469 ....D4
La Libertad C4
La Unión 17,207 ....D4
Metapán 7,704 ....C3
Nueva San Salvador 35,106 ....C4
San Francisco Gotera 4,725 ....C4
San Miguel 59,304 ....D4
San Salvador (cap.) 337,171 ....C4
Santa Ana 96,306 ....C4
Santa Rosa de Lima 5,707 ....D4
San Vicente 18,872 ....C4
Sensuntepeque 7,226 ....C4
Sonsonate 33,562 ....C4
Suchitoto 5,540 ....C4
Usulután 19,616 ....C4
Zacatecoluca 15,718 ....C4

OTHER FEATURES

Fonseca (gulf) D4
Güija (lake) C3
Lempa (riv.) C4
Remedios (pt.) B4
Santa Ana (mt.) C4

GUATEMALA

CITIES and TOWNS

Amatitlán 15,251 ....B3
Antigua 17,994 ....B3
Asunción Mita 7,477 ....C3
Chajul 4,329 ....B3
Champerico 5,722 ....A3
Chichicastenango 2,635 ....B3
Chimaltenango 12,860 ....B3
Chiquimula 16,126 ....C3
Coatepeque 15,979 ....A3
Cobán 11,418 ....B3
Comalapa 10,980 ....B3
Cubulco 2,021 ....B3
Cuilapa 4,287 ....B3
El Estor 2,324 ....C3
El Progreso 4,009 ....B3
Escuintla 33,205 ....B3
Flores 1,477 ....C2
Gualán 5,169 ....C3
Guatemala (cap.) 700,538 ....B3
Huehuetenango 12,570 ....B3
Ipala 3,386 ....C3
Iztapa 1,237 ....B4
Jacaltenango 4,517 ....B3
Jalapa 13,788 ....B3
Jutiapa 8,210 ....B3
La Gomera 2,394 ....B3
Livingston 2,898 ....C3
Los Amates 1,383 ....C3
Mazatenango 23,285 ....B3
Momostenango 5,210 ....B3
Morales 2,113 ....C3
Panzós 1,643 ....C3
Puerto Barrios 22,598 ....C3
Quezaltenango 53,021 ....B3
Quezaltepeque 2,222 ....C3
Rabinal 4,625 ....B3
Retalhuleu 19,060 ....B3
Río Hondo 1,416 ....C3
Sacapulas 1,439 ....B3
Salamá 5,529 ....B3
San Felipe 3,210 ....B3
San José 9,402 ....B4
San Luis Jilotepeque 6,055 ....C3
San Marcos 5,700 ....B3
San Martín Jilotepeque 3,770 ....B3
San Mateo Ixtatán 1,834 ....B3
San Pedro Carchá 4,465 ....B3
Santa Cruz del Quiché 7,651 ....B3
Santa Rosa de Lima 1,161 ....B3
Sololá 3,960 ....B3
Tacaná 1,280 ....A3
Tejutla 1,205 ....B3
Tikal C2
Totonicapán 8,568 ....B3
Zacapa 12,688 ....C3

OTHER FEATURES

Atitlán (lake) B3
Atitlán (vol.) B3
Azul (riv.) C2
Honduras (gulf) D2
Izabal (lake) C3
Minas (mts.) C3
Motagua (riv.) C3
Pasión (riv.) B2
Petén-Itzá (lake) B2
Salinas (riv.) B2

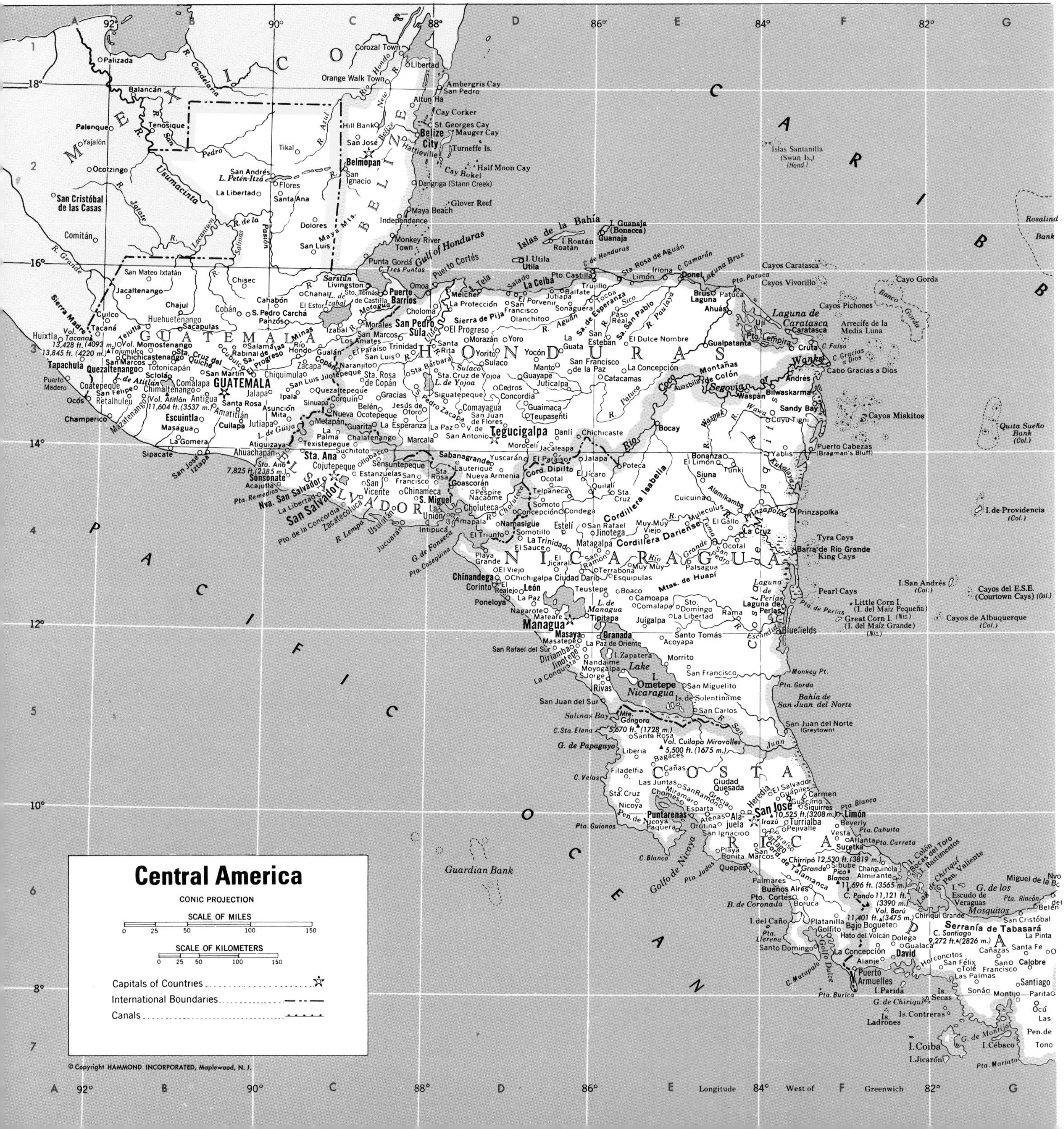

Central America
CONIC PROJECTION
SCALE OF MILES
0 25 50 100 150
SCALE OF KILOMETERS
0 25 50 100 150
Capitals of Countries
International Boundaries
Canals
© Copyright HAMMOND INCORPORATED, Maplewood, N. J.
MEXICO
BELIZE
GUATEMALA
HONDURAS
EL SALVADOR
NICARAGUA
COSTA RICA
PANAMA
CARIBBEAN
PACIFIC OCEAN
Gulf of Honduras
Belize City
Belmopan
Guatemala
Tegucigalpa
San Salvador
Managua
San José
Lake Nicaragua
Guardian Bank
Longitude West of Greenwich

San Pedro (riv.) B2
Sarstún (riv.) C3
Tacaná (vol.) A3
Tajumulco (vol.) B3
Tres Puntas (cape) C3
Usumacinta (riv.) B2

HONDURAS

CITIES and TOWNS

Amapala 2,274 .... D4
Brus Laguna 933 .... E3
Catacamas 9,134 .... E3
Cedros 917 .... D3
Choloma 961 .... C3
Choluteca 26,152 .... D4
Comayagua 15,941 .... D3
Concepción de María 579 .... D4
Concordia 646 .... D3
Corquín 2,629 .... C3
Danlí 10,825 .... D3
El Dulce Nombre 1,297 .... E3
El Paraíso 6,709 .... D4
El Paraíso 2,164 .... C3
El Porvenir 1,076 .... D3
El Progreso 28,105 .... D3
El Triunfo 2,925 .... D4
Goascorán 996 .... D4
Gracias 2,299 .... C3
Guaimaca 3,953 .... D3
Guanaja 1,947 .... E2
Guarita 419 .... C3
Guayape 804 .... D3
Jacaleapa 1,609 .... D3
Jesús de Otoro 2,976 .... C3
Jutiapa 1,126 .... D3
Juticalpa 10,075 .... D3
La Ceiba 38,788 .... D3
La Esperanza 2,146 .... C3

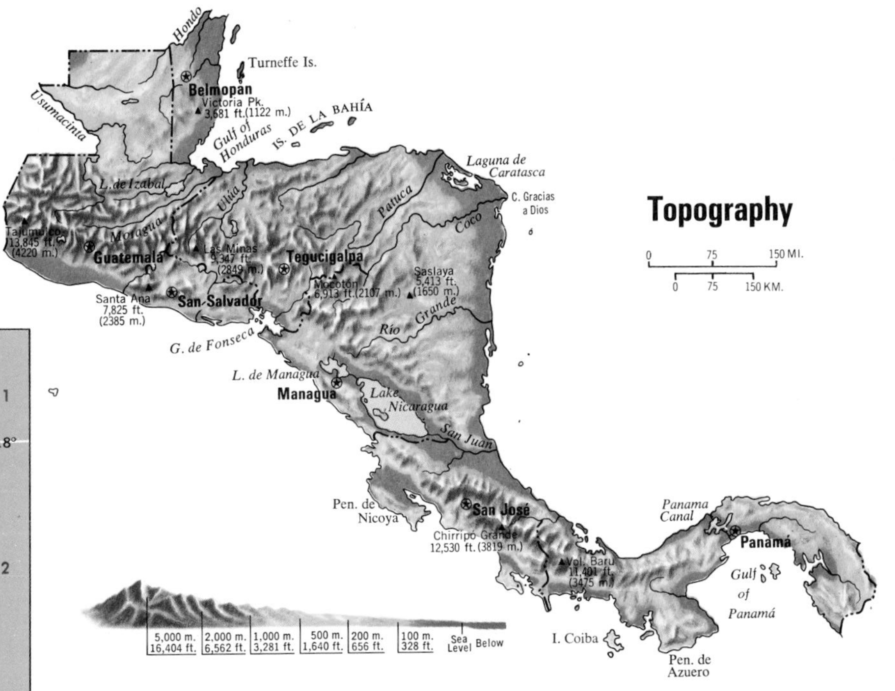
Hondo
Turneffe Is.
Belmopan
Victoria Pk. 3,681 ft. (1122 m.)
Usumacinta
Gulf of Honduras
IS. DE LA BAHÍA
Laguna de Caratasca
C. Gracias a Dios
L. de Izabal
Ulúa
Patuca
Coco
Motagua
Tajumulco 13,845 ft. (4220 m.)
Guatemala
Las Minas 9,347 ft. (2849 m.)
Tegucigalpa
Saslaya 5,413 ft. (1650 m.)
Mogotón 6,913 ft. (2107 m.)
Santa Ana 7,825 ft. (2385 m.)
San Salvador
Río Grande
G. de Fonseca
L. de Managua
Managua
Lake Nicaragua
San Juan
Pen. de Nicoya
San José
Chirripó Grande 12,530 ft. (3819 m.)
Vol. Barú 11,401 ft. (3475 m.)
Panama Canal
Panamá
Gulf of Panamá
I. Coiba
Pen. de Azuero
5,000 m. 16,404 ft.
2,000 m. 6,562 ft.
1,000 m. 3,281 ft.
500 m. 1,640 ft.
200 m. 656 ft.
100 m. 328 ft.
Sea Level
Below
Topography
0 75 150 MI.
0 75 150 KM.

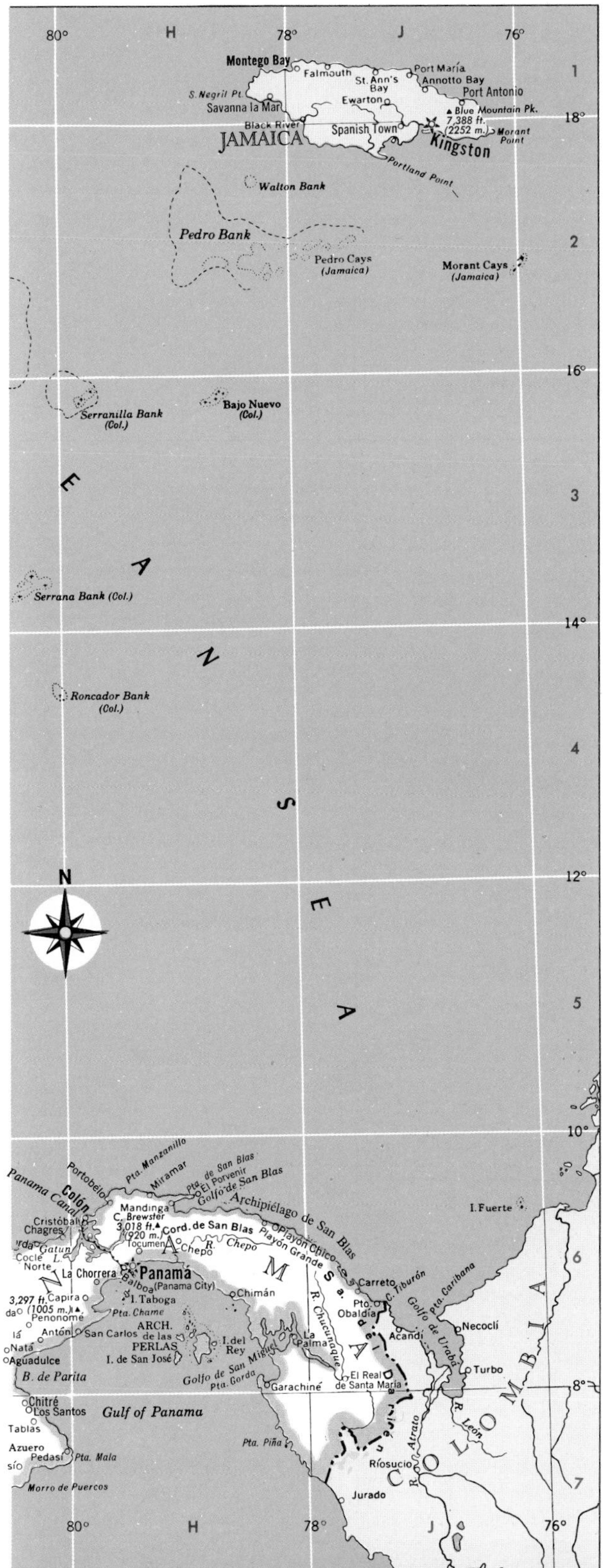
80° H 78° J 76°
Montego Bay
Falmouth
St. Ann's Bay
Port María
Annotto Bay
Port Antonio
S. Negril Pt.
Savanna la Mar
Ewarton
Blue Mountain Pk. 7,388 ft. (2252 m.)
Black River
Spanish Town
Morant Point
JAMAICA
Kingston
Portland Point
Walton Bank
Pedro Bank
Pedro Cays (Jamaica)
Morant Cays (Jamaica)
Serranilla Bank (Col.)
Bajo Nuevo (Col.)
Serrana Bank (Col.)
Roncador Bank (Col.)
C A R I B B E A N S E A
N
18° 16° 14° 12° 10° 8°
1 2 3 4 5 6 7
Portobelo
Pta. Manzanillo
Miramar
Pta. de San Blas
El Porvenir
Golfo de San Blas
Colón
Panama Canal
Mandinga
Archipiélago de San Blas
Playón Chico
C. Brewster 3,018 ft. (920 m.)
Cord. de San Blas
Cristóbal
Chagres
Gatun L.
Tocumen
Chepo
Chepo
I. Fuerte
La Chorrera
Panamá
Balboa (Panama City)
Taboga
Capira
Penonomé
Pta. Chame
Antón
San Carlos
ARCH. de las PERLAS
I. del Rey
I. de San José
Natá
Aguadulce
Chimán
Carreto
Pto. Obaldía
C. Tiburón
Golfo de Urabá
Acandí
Necoclí
Turbo
B. de Parita
Golfo de San Miguel
La Palma
El Real de Santa María
Garachiné
Chitré
Los Santos
Gulf of Panama
Tablas
Azuero
Pedasí
Pta. Mala
Pta. Piña
Ríosucio
Morro de Puercos
Jurado
COLOMBIA
80° H 78° J 76°

La Paz 6,811 .... D3
Limón 1,704 .... E3
Marcala 3,183 .... C3
Morazán 4,367 .... D3
Morocelí 1,442 .... D3
Nacaome 6,159 .... D4
Namasigüe 816 .... D4
Naranjito 2,770 .... C3
Nueva Armenia 670 .... D4
Nueva Ocotepeque 4,724 .... C3
Olanchito 7,411 .... D3
Omoa 9,161 .... C3
Pespire 1,895 .... D4
Puerto Cortés 25,817 .... D2
Puerto Lempira 727 .... F3
Roatán 1,943 .... D2
Sabanagrande 1,446 .... D4
San Esteban 610 .... D3
San Francisco 1,557 .... D3
San Francisco de la Paz 2,291 .... D3
San Juan de Flores 1,184 .... D3
San Luis 2,237 .... C3
San Marcos 2,499 .... C3
San Pedro Sula 150,991 .... C3
San Pedro Zacapa 648 .... D3
Santa Bárbara 5,883 .... C3
Santa Cruz de Yojoa 1,848 .... D3
Santa Rita 5,298 .... D3
Santa Rosa de Aguán 1,622 .... E2
Santa Rosa de Copán 12,413 .... C3
Siguatepeque 12,456 .... D3
Sinuapa 831 .... C3
Sonaguera 2,264 .... D3
Sulaco 1,121 .... D3
Tegucigalpa (cap.) 273,894 .... D3
Tela 19,055 .... D3
Teupasenti 2,003 .... D3
Tocoa 2,803 .... E3
Trinidad 1,598 .... C3
Trujillo 3,961 .... E3
Utila 1,177 .... D2
Villa de San Antonio 2,359 .... D3
Yoro 4,449 .... D3
Yuscarán 1,835 .... D4

OTHER FEATURES

Aguán (riv.) D3
Bahía (isls.) D2
Brus (lag.) E2
Camarón (cape) E2
Caratasca (lag.) F3
Choluteca (riv.) D4
Coco (riv.) E3
Colón (mts.) E3
Esperanza (mts.) E3
Fonseca (gulf) D4
Gorda (bank) F3
Guanaja (isl.) E2
Honduras (cape) E2
Honduras (gulf) D2
Patuca (pt.) E3
Patuca (riv.) E3
Paulaya (riv.) E3
Pija, Sierra de (mts.) D3
Roatán (isl.) D2
San Pablo, Sierra (mts.) E3
Santanilla (Swan) (isls.) F2
Sico (riv.) E3
Sulaco (riv.) D3
Ulúa (riv.) D3
Utila (isl.) D2
Vivorillo (cays) F3
Yojoa (lake) D3

NICARAGUA

CITIES and TOWNS

Acoyapa 2,588 .... E5
Barra de Río Grande F4
Bilwaskarma F3
Bluefields 14,252 .... F4
Boaco 6,372 .... E4
Bonanza E4
Bragmans Bluff (Puerto Cabezas) 5,457 .... F3
Cabo Gracias a Dios 3,846 .... F3
Camoapa 4,385 .... E4
Chichigalpa 14,498 .... D4
Chinandega 30,441 .... D4
Ciudad Darío 5,304 .... D4
Comalapa 508 .... E4
Condega 3,414 .... D4
Corinto 13,404 .... D4
Diriamba 10,085 .... D5
El Jícaro 1,669 .... E4
El Jicaral 428 .... D4
El Limón E4
El Realejo 2,229 .... D4
El Sauce 3,202 .... D4
El Viejo 8,507 .... D4
Esquipulas 2,232 .... E4
Estelí 20,222 .... D4
Granada 34,976 .... E5
Greytown (San Juan del Norte) 294 .... F5
Jalapa 3,633 .... E4
Jinotega 9,506 .... E4
Jinotepe 12,473 .... D5
Juigalpa 8,497 .... E4
La Conquista 458 .... D5
La Cruz 150 .... E4
La Libertad 1,286 .... E4
La Paz Central 6,175 .... D4
La Paz de Oriente 957 .... E5
La Trinidad 3,548 .... D4
León 55,625 .... D4
Managua (cap.) 398,514 .... D4
Masatepe 6,307 .... D5
Masaya 30,753 .... D5
Matagalpa 21,385 .... E4
Mateare 1,405 .... D4
Morrito 368 .... E5
Moyogalpa 1,551 .... E5
Muy Muy 1,373 .... E4
Nagarote 7,185 .... D4
Nandaime 5,631 .... E5
Ocotal 8,215 .... D4
Palsagua E4
Poneloya D4
Prinzapolka 8,979 .... F4
Puerto Cabezas 5,457 .... F3
Quilalí 1,245 .... E4
Rama 1,341 .... E4
Rivas 10,125 .... E5
San Carlos 2,022 .... E5
San Jorge 2,874 .... E5
San Juan del Norte 294 .... F5
San Juan del Sur 2,393 .... D5
San Miguelito 1,312 .... E5
San Rafael del Norte 1,938 .... E4
San Rafael del Sur 2,914 .... D5
San Ramón 477 .... E4
Santo Domingo 1,949 .... E4
Santo Tomás 2,309 .... E5
Siuna E4
Somotillo 1,864 .... D4
Somoto 5,847 .... D4
Telpaneca 991 .... D4
Terrabona 904 .... E4
Teustepe 1,060 .... E4
Tipitapa 5,758 .... E4
Waspán 1,246 .... E3
Yablis F4

OTHER FEATURES

Coco (riv.) E3
Cosegüina (pt.) D4
Dariense, Cordillera (range) E4
Dipilto, Cordillera (range) D4
Escondido (riv.) F4
Fonseca (gulf) D4
Gracias a Dios (cape) F3
Grande (riv.) E4
Great Corn (isl.) F4
Isabelia, Cordillera (range) E4
Kukalaya (riv.) F4
Little Corn (isl.) F4
Managua (lake) E4
Miskitos (cays) F3
Monkey (pt.) F5
Mosquitos, Costa de (reg.) E4
Nicaragua (lake) E5
Ometepe (isl.) E5
Perlas (lag.) F4
Perlas (pt.) F4
Prinzapolca (riv.) F4
Salinas (bay) D5
San Juan (riv.) E5
San Juan del Norte (bay) F5
Segovia (riv.) E3
Tuma (riv.) E4
Tyra (cays) F4
Waspuk (riv.) E3
Wawa (riv.) E3
Zapatera (isl.) E5

PANAMA

CITIES and TOWNS

Aguadulce 10,659 .... G6
Alanje 866 .... F6
Almirante 4,664 .... F6
Antón 4,259 .... G6
Bajo Boquete 2,831 .... F6
Balboa 1,952 .... H6
Bocas del Toro 2,515 .... F6
Calobre 609 .... G6
Cañazas 1,526 .... G6
Capira 1,749 .... G6
Changuinola 9,528 .... F6
Chepo 4,529 .... H6
Chiriquí Grande F6
Chitré 17,156 .... G7
Coclé del Norte G6
Colón 59,832 .... H6
Cristóbal⊙ 7,959 .... G6
David 50,621 .... F6
Dolega 1,019 .... F6
El Porvenir H6
El Real de Santa María 912 .... J6
Garachiné 1,116 .... H6
Gualaca 1,510 .... F6
Hato del Volcán F6
Horconcitos 1,090 .... F6
La Chorrera 36,971 .... H6
La Concepción 10,460 .... F6
La Palma 164 .... H6
La Pintada 1,100 .... G6
Las Palmas 738 .... G6
Las Tablas 5,230 .... G7
Los Santos 4,644 .... G7
Mandinga 81 .... H6
Montijo 1,152 .... G6
Natá 5,603 .... G6
Ocú 2,353 .... G7
Panamá (cap.) 388,638 .... H6
Panamá* 498,624 .... H6
Parita 1,616 .... G6
Pedasí 934 .... G7
Penonomé 7,389 .... G6
Playón Chico 1,395 .... H6
Portobelo 551 .... H6
Puerto Armuelles 12,488 .... F6
San Carlos 562 .... H6
San Félix 617 .... G6
San Francisco 990 .... G6
Santa Fe 490 .... G6
Santiago 21,809 .... G6
Soná 4,471 .... G6
Tocumen⊙ 21,745 .... H6
Tolé 1,052 .... G6
Tonosí 891 .... G7

OTHER FEATURES

Azuero (pen.) G7
Barú (vol.) F6
Bastimentos (isl.) G6
Brewster, Cerro (mt.) H6
Burica, Punta (cape) F6
Cébaco (isl.) G7
Chame (pt.) H6
Chepo (riv.) H6
Chiriquí (lag.) G6
Chiriquí (gulf) F7
Chucunaque (riv.) J6
Coiba, Isla de (isl.) F7
Colón, Isla de (isl.) G6
Contreras (isls.) F7
Darién (mts.) J6
Escudo de Veraguas (isl.) G6
Gatun (lake) G6
Gorda (pt.) H6
Jicarón (isl.) F7
Mala, Punta (cape) H7
Mariato, Punta (cape) G7
Montijo (gulf) G7
Mosquitos, Golfo de los (gulf) G6
Panama (canal) H6
Panama (gulf) H7
Pando, Cerro (mt.) F6
Parida (isl.) F6
Parita (bay) G6
Perlas (arch.) H6
Rey (isl.) H6
San Blas, Archipiélago de (arch.) J7
San Blas, Cordillera de (mts.) H6
San Blas, Golfo de (bay) H6
San Blas, Pta. de (pt.) H6
San José (isl.) H6
San Miguel, Golfo de (bay) H6
Santiago, Cerro (mt.) G6
Secas (isls.) G7
Tabasará (mts.) G6
Taboga (isl.) H6
Tiburón (pt.) J6
Valiente (pen.) G6

* City and suburbs
⊙ Population of district

CUBA

HAITI

DOMINICAN REPUBLIC

JAMAICA

TRINIDAD AND TOBAGO

BARBADOS

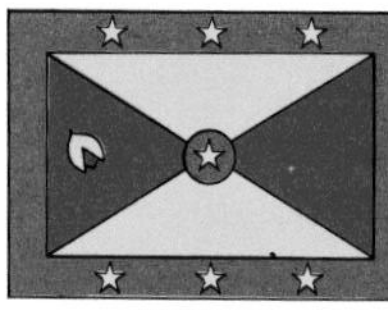

GRENADA

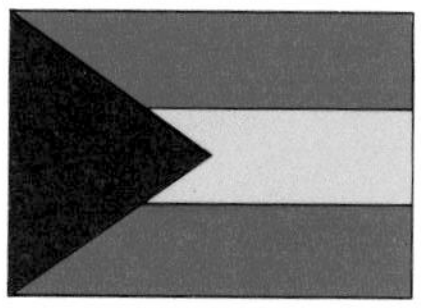

BAHAMAS

DOMINICA

ST. LUCIA

ST. VINC. & GRENS.

ANTIGUA AND BARBUDA

CUBA

AREA 44,206 sq. mi. (114,494 sq. km.)
POPULATION 10,617,000
CAPITAL Havana
LARGEST CITY Havana
HIGHEST POINT Pico Turquino 6,561 ft. (2,000 m.)
MONETARY UNIT Cuban peso
MAJOR LANGUAGE Spanish
MAJOR RELIGION Roman Catholicism

HAITI

AREA 10,694 sq. mi. (27,697 sq. km.)
POPULATION 5,609,000
CAPITAL Port-au-Prince
LARGEST CITY Port-au-Prince
HIGHEST POINT Pic La Selle 8,793 ft. (2,680 m.)
MONETARY UNIT gourde
MAJOR LANGUAGES Creole French, French
MAJOR RELIGION Roman Catholicism

DOMINICAN REPUBLIC

AREA 18,704 sq. mi. (48,443 sq. km.)
POPULATION 6,867,000
CAPITAL Santo Domingo
LARGEST CITY Santo Domingo
HIGHEST POINT Pico Duarte 10,417 ft. (3,175 m.)
MONETARY UNIT Dominican peso
MAJOR LANGUAGE Spanish
MAJOR RELIGION Roman Catholicism

JAMAICA

AREA 4,411 sq. mi. (11,424 sq. km.)
POPULATION 2,392,000
CAPITAL Kingston
LARGEST CITY Kingston
HIGHEST POINT Blue Mountain Peak 7,402 ft. (2,256 m.)
MONETARY UNIT Jamaican dollar
MAJOR LANGUAGE English
MAJOR RELIGIONS Protestantism, Roman Catholicism

PUERTO RICO

AREA 3,515 sq. mi. (9,104 sq. km.)
POPULATION 3,522,037
CAPITAL San Juan
MONETARY UNIT U.S. dollar
MAJOR LANGUAGES Spanish, English
MAJOR RELIGION Roman Catholicism

NETHERLANDS ANTILLES

AREA 390 sq. mi. (1,010 sq. km.)
POPULATION 246,000
CAPITAL Willemstad
MONETARY UNIT Antilles guilder
MAJOR LANGUAGES Dutch, Papiamento, English
MAJOR RELIGIONS Roman Catholicism, Protestantism

BERMUDA

AREA 21 sq. mi. (54 sq. km.)
POPULATION 67,761
CAPITAL Hamilton
MONETARY UNIT Bermuda dollar
MAJOR LANGUAGE English
MAJOR RELIGION Protestantism

ARUBA

AREA 75 sq. mi (193 sq. km.)
POPULATION 66,790
CAPITAL Oranjestad
MONETARY UNIT Aruba guilder
MAJOR LANGUAGES Dutch, Papiamento
MAJOR RELIGION Roman Catholic

ANGUILLA

Anguilla (isl.) 6,519 . . . . . F3

ANTIGUA and BARBUDA

Antigua (isl.) 76,213 . . . . . G3
Barbuda (isl.) 1,071 . . . . . G3
Caribbean (sea) B4
Codrington 1,071 . . . . . G3
Falmouth 1,134 . . . . . F3
Redonda (isl.) F3
Saint John's (cap.) 21,814 . . . . . G3

ARUBA

Aruba (isl.) 66,790 . . . . . E4

BAHAMAS

Acklins (isl.) 616 . . . . . C2
Andros (isl.) 8,397 . . . . . B1
Atwood (Samana) (cay) D2
Berry (isls.) 509 . . . . . B1
Biminis, The (isls.) 1,432 . . . . . B1
Caicos (passg.) D2
Cat (isl.) 2,143 . . . . . C1
Cay Sal (bank) B2
Crooked (isl.) 517 . . . . . D2
Eleuthera (isl.) 8,326 . . . . . C1
Exuma (cays) C1
Flamingo (cay) C2
Freeport 22,301 . . . . . B1
Grand Bahama (isl.) 33,102 . . . . . B1
Great Abaco (isl.) 7,324 . . . . . C1
Great Bahama (bank) B1
Great Exuma (isl.) C2
Great Inagua (isl.) 939 . . . . . D2
Great Isaac (isl.) B1
Gun (cay) B1
Harbour (isl.) C1
Little Inagua (isl.) D2
Long (cay) 33 . . . . . C2
Long (isl.) 3,353 . . . . . C2
Mayaguana (isl.) 476 . . . . . D2
Mira Por Vos (cays) C2
Nassau (cap.) 135,437 . . . . . C1
New Providence (isl.) 135,437 . . . . . C1
Old Bahama (chan.) B2
Plana (cays) D2
Ragged (isl.) 146 . . . . . C2
Rum (cay) C2
Samana (cay) D2
San Salvador (isl.) D1
Santarén (chan.) B1
Tongue of the Ocean (chan.) C1
Verde (cay) C2
Watling (San Salvador) (isl.) C1

BARBADOS

Bridgetown (cap.) 7,552 . . . . . G4
Speightstown G4

BERMUDA

Bermuda (isl.) H3
Castle (harb.) H2
Great (sound) G3
Hamilton (cap.) 1,617 . . . . . G3
Harrington (sound) G3
Ireland (isl.) G3
North (rapid) H2
Saint Davids (isl.) H2
Saint George 1,647 . . . . . H2
Saint George's (isl.) H2
Somerset (isl.) G3

CAYMAN ISLANDS

Bartlett Deep B3
Cayman Brac (isl.) 1,603 . . . . . B3
George Town (cap.) 7,617 . . . . . B3
Grand Cayman (isl.) 15,000 . . . . . B3
Little Cayman (isl.) 74 . . . . . B3
Misteriosa (bank) A3

CUBA

Bayamo 109,201 . . . . . C2
Camagüey 245,235 . . . . . B2
Cienfuegos 107,396 . . . . . B2
Florida (str.) B1
Guanabacoa 89,741 . . . . . B2
Guantánamo 178,129 . . . . . C2
Havana (cap.) 1,924,886 . . . . . A2
Holguín 190,155 . . . . . C2
Juventud (Pines) (isl.) 57,879 . . . . . A2
Manzanillo 95,420 . . . . . C2
Marianao ○127,563 . . . . . A2
Matanzas 103,302 . . . . . B2
Pinar del Río 104,598 . . . . . A2
San Felipe (cays) A2
Santa Clara 175,113 . . . . . B2
Santiago de Cuba 362,432 . . . . . C3
Windward (passg.) C3

DOMINICA

Portsmouth 2,329 . . . . . G4
Roseau (cap.) 9,968 . . . . . G4

DOMINICAN REPUBLIC

La Romana 91,571 . . . . . E3
San Francisco de Macorís 64,906 . . . . . E3
San Pedro de Macorís 78,562 . . . . . E3
Santiago 278,638 . . . . . D3
Santo Domingo (cap.) 1,313,172 . . . . . E3

GRENADA

Carriacou (isl.) 6,052 . . . . . G4
Gouyave 2,498 . . . . . F4
Grenadines (isls.) G4
Saint George's (cap.) 6,463 . . . . . F5

GUADELOUPE

Basse-Terre (cap.) 13,397 . . . . . F4
Saint-Barthélemy (isl.) 3,059 . . . . . F3
Saint Martin (isl.) 8,072 . . . . . F3

HAITI

Cap-Haïtien 64,406 . . . . . D3
Gonaïves 34,209 . . . . . D3
Port-au-Prince (cap.) 449,831 . . . . . D3
Gonâve (isl.) D3
Jamaica (chan.) C3
Tortuga (isl.) D2

JAMAICA

Blue Mountain (peak) C3
Jamaica (chan.) C3
Kingston (cap.) 106,791 . . . . . C3
Montego Bay 43,521 . . . . . B3
Pedro (cays) C3
Savanna-la-Mar 11,759 . . . . . B3

MARTINIQUE

Fort-de-France (cap.) 96,649 . . . . . G4
Saint-Pierre 4,923 . . . . . G4
Pelée (vol.) G4

MONTSERRAT

Plymouth (cap.) 1,623 . . . . . F3

NETHERLANDS ANTILLES

Bonaire (isl.) E4
Curaçao (isl.) E4
Oranjestad 10,100 . . . . . D4
Saba (isl.) F3
Saint Eustatius (isl.) F3
Saint Martin (Sint Maarten) (isl.) F3
Willemstad (cap.) 95,000 . . . . . E4

PUERTO RICO

Bayamón 185,087 . . . . . G1
Caguas 87,214 . . . . . G1
Culebra (isl.) 1,265 . . . . . G1
Mayagüez 82,968 . . . . . F1
Mona (passg.) E3
Ponce 161,739 . . . . . F1
San Juan (cap.) 424,600 . . . . . G1
Vieques (isl.) 7,662 . . . . . G1

SAINT KITTS and NEVIS

Basseterre (cap.) 14,725 . . . . . F3
Nevis (isl.) 9,300 . . . . . F3
Saint Christopher (isl.) 35,104 . . . . . F3

SAINT LUCIA

Castries (cap.) •42,770 . . . . . G4
Vieux Fort •10,675 . . . . . G4

SAINT VINCENT and THE GRENADINES

Bequia (isl.) G4
Georgetown 1,100 . . . . . G4
Grenadines (isls.) 8,371 . . . . . G4
Kingstown (cap.) 17,117 . . . . . G4

TRINIDAD and TOBAGO

Port-of-Spain (cap.) 67,978 . . . . . G5
Scarborough 6,057 . . . . . G5
Tobago (isl.) 39,695 . . . . . G5
Trinidad (isl.) 1,020,130 . . . . . G5

TURKS and CAICOS ISLANDS

Caicos (isls.) 4,008 . . . . . D2
Cockburn Harbour D2
Grand Caicos (isl.) 371 . . . . . D2
Grand Turk (isl.) 3,146 . . . . . D2
Providenciales (isl.) 979 . . . . . D2
Turks (isls.) 3,348 . . . . . D2

VIRGIN ISLANDS (British)

Anegada (isl.) 89 . . . . . H1
Jost Van Dyke (isl.) 135 . . . . . G1
Road Town (cap.) 2,200 . . . . . H1
Tortola (isl.) 9,257 . . . . . H1
Virgin Gorda (isl.) 1,443 . . . . . H1

VIRGIN ISLANDS (U.S.)

Charlotte Amalie (cap.) 11,842 . . . . . H1
Christiansted 2,914 . . . . . H2
Fredriksted 1,046 . . . . . G2
Saint Croix (isl.) 49,725 . . . . . H2
Saint John (isl.) 2,472 . . . . . H1
Saint Thomas (isl.) 44,372 . . . . . G1

WEST INDIES

Antilles, Greater (isls.) B2
Antilles, Lesser (isls.) E4
Aves (Bird) (isl.) F4
Hispaniola (isl.) D2
Leeward (isls.) F3
Navassa (isl.) C3
Windward (isls.) G4

• Population of district.
○ Population of municipality.

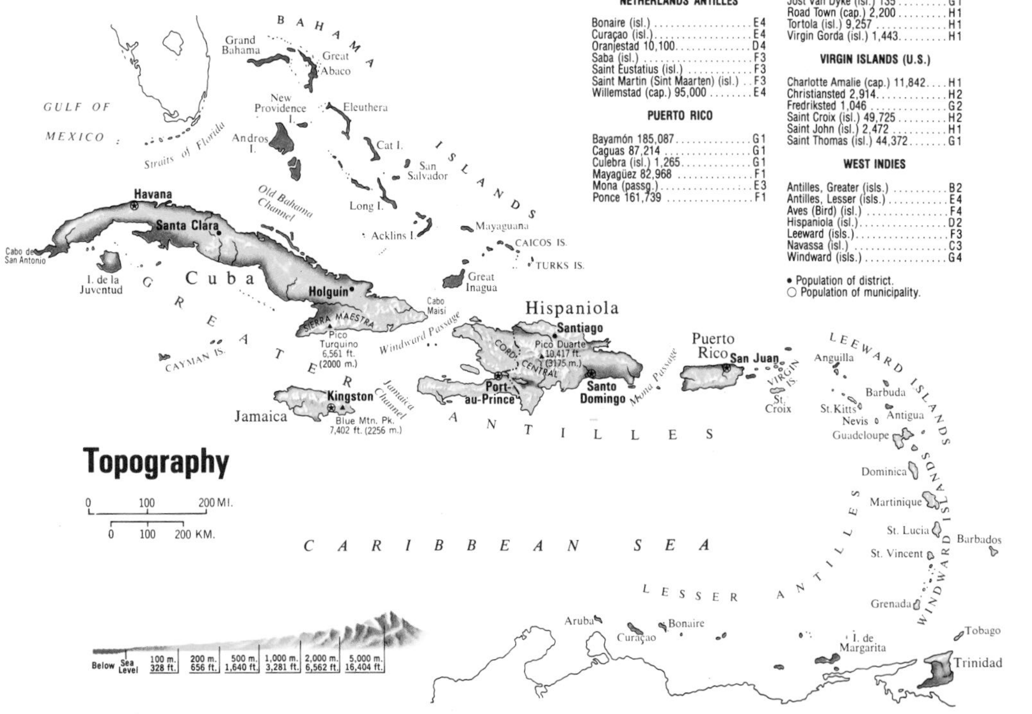
Topography
BAHAMA ISLANDS
Grand Bahama
Great Abaco
New Providence I.
Eleuthera
Andros I.
Cat I.
San Salvador
Long I.
Acklins I.
Mayaguana
CAICOS IS.
TURKS IS.
Great Inagua
GULF OF MEXICO
Straits of Florida
Old Bahama Channel
Havana
Santa Clara
Cabo de San Antonio
I. de la Juventud
Cuba
Holguin
SIERRA MAESTRA
Pico Turquino 6,561 ft. (2000 m.)
Cabo Maisi
Windward Passage
CAYMAN IS.
GREATER ANTILLES
Jamaica
Kingston
Blue Mtn. Pk. 7,402 ft. (2256 m.)
Jamaica Channel
Hispaniola
Santiago
Pico Duarte 10,417 ft. (3175 m.)
CORD. CENTRAL
Port-au-Prince
Santo Domingo
Mona Passage
Puerto Rico
San Juan
VIRGIN IS.
St. Croix
LEEWARD ISLANDS
Anguilla
Barbuda
St. Kitts
Nevis
Antigua
Guadeloupe
Dominica
Martinique
St. Lucia
St. Vincent
Barbados
Grenada
WINDWARD ISLANDS
LESSER ANTILLES
CARIBBEAN SEA
Aruba
Curaçao
Bonaire
I. de Margarita
Tobago
Trinidad
0 100 200 MI.
0 100 200 KM.
Below Sea Level
100 m. 328 ft.
200 m. 656 ft.
500 m. 1,640 ft.
1,000 m. 3,281 ft.
2,000 m. 6,562 ft.
5,000 m. 16,404 ft.

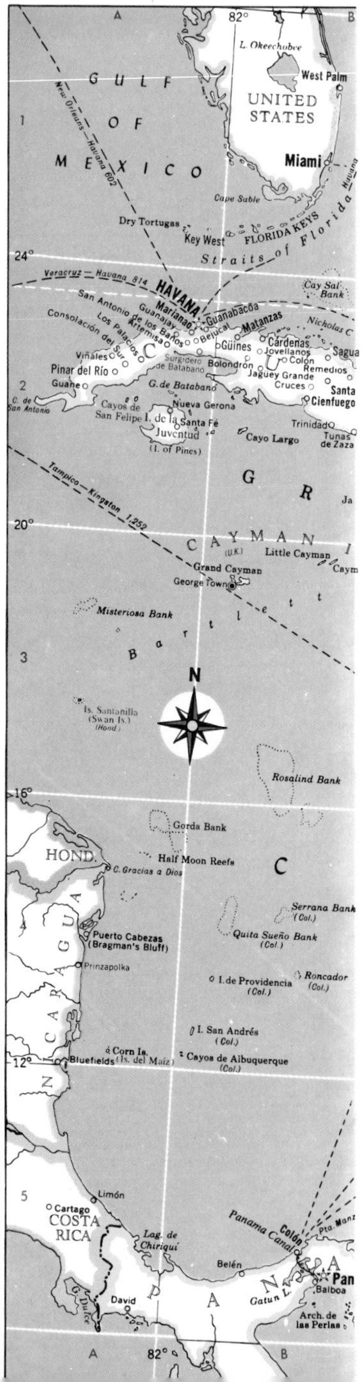
A
B
82°
L. Okeechobee
West Palm
GULF OF MEXICO
UNITED STATES
Miami
Cape Sable
Dry Tortugas
Key West
FLORIDA KEYS
Straits of Florida
24°
HAVANA
Matanzas
Cárdenas
Pinar del Río
Nueva Gerona
Cayo Largo
Trinidad
Cienfuegos
G. de Batabanó
20°
CAYMAN IS.
Grand Cayman
George Town
Little Cayman
Misteriosa Bank
Rosalind Bank
16°
Gorda Bank
HOND.
Half Moon Reefs
Serrana Bank (Col.)
Quita Sueño Bank (Col.)
Puerto Cabezas (Bragman's Bluff)
Prinzapolka
I. de Providencia (Col.)
Roncador (Col.)
I. San Andrés (Col.)
Corn Is. (Is. del Maíz)
Bluefields
Cayos de Albuquerque (Col.)
12°
NICARAGUA
Limón
Cartago
COSTA RICA
Lag. de Chiriquí
Belén
David
Colón
Balboa
Gatun L.
Arch. de las Perlas
PANAMA
Panama Canal
82°

TRINIDAD AND TOBAGO

AREA 1,980 sq. mi. (5,128 sq. km.)
POPULATION 1,212,000
CAPITAL Port of Spain
LARGEST CITY Port of Spain
HIGHEST POINT Mt. Aripo 3,084 ft. (940 m.)
MONETARY UNIT Trinidad and Tobago dollar
MAJOR LANGUAGES English, Hindi
MAJOR RELIGIONS Roman Catholicism, Protestantism, Hinduism, Islam

SAINT KITTS AND NEVIS

BARBADOS

AREA 166 sq. mi. (430 sq. km.)
POPULATION 256,000
CAPITAL Bridgetown
LARGEST CITY Bridgetown
HIGHEST POINT Mt. Hillaby 1,104 ft. (336 m.)
MONETARY UNIT Barbadian dollar
MAJOR LANGUAGE English
MAJOR RELIGION Protestantism

BAHAMAS

AREA 5,382 sq. mi. (13,939 sq. km.)
POPULATION 253,000
CAPITAL Nassau
LARGEST CITY Nassau
HIGHEST POINT Mt. Alvernia 206 ft. (63 m.)
MONETARY UNIT Bahamian dollar
MAJOR LANGUAGE English
MAJOR RELIGIONS Roman Catholicism, Protestantism

GRENADA

AREA 133 sq. mi. (344 sq. km.)
POPULATION 103,103
CAPITAL St. George's
LARGEST CITY St. George's
HIGHEST POINT Mt. St. Catherine 2,757 ft. (840 m.)
MONETARY UNIT East Caribbean dollar
MAJOR LANGUAGES English, French patois
MAJOR RELIGIONS Roman Catholicism, Protestantism

DOMINICA

AREA 290 sq. mi. (751 sq. km.)
POPULATION 81,000
CAPITAL Roseau
HIGHEST POINT Morne Diablotin 4,747 ft. (1,447 m.)
MONETARY UNIT Dominican dollar
MAJOR LANGUAGES English, French patois
MAJOR RELIGIONS Roman Catholicism, Protestantism

SAINT LUCIA

AREA 238 sq. mi. (616 sq. km.)
POPULATION 148,000
CAPITAL Castries
HIGHEST POINT Mt. Gimie 3,117 ft. (950 m.)
MONETARY UNIT East Caribbean dollar
MAJOR LANGUAGES English, French patois
MAJOR RELIGIONS Roman Catholicism, Protestantism

SAINT VINCENT AND THE GRENADINES

AREA 150 sq. mi. (388 sq. km.)
POPULATION 124,000
CAPITAL Kingstown
HIGHEST POINT Soufrière 4,000 ft. (1,219 m.)
MONETARY UNIT East Caribbean dollar
MAJOR LANGUAGE English
MAJOR RELIGIONS Protestantism, Roman Catholicism

ANTIGUA AND BARBUDA

AREA 171 sq. mi. (443 sq. km.)
POPULATION 76,000
CAPITAL St. John's
HIGHEST POINT Boggy Peak 1,319 ft. (402 m.)
MONETARY UNIT East Caribbean dollar
MAJOR LANGUAGE English
MAJOR RELIGION Protestantism

SAINT KITTS & NEVIS

AREA 104 sq. mi. (269 sq. km.)
POPULATION 44,404
CAPITAL Basseterre
HIGHEST POINT Mt. Misery 4,314 ft. (1,315 m.)
MONETARY UNIT East Caribbean dollar
MAJOR LANGUAGE English
MAJOR RELIGIONS Protestantism, Roman Catholicism

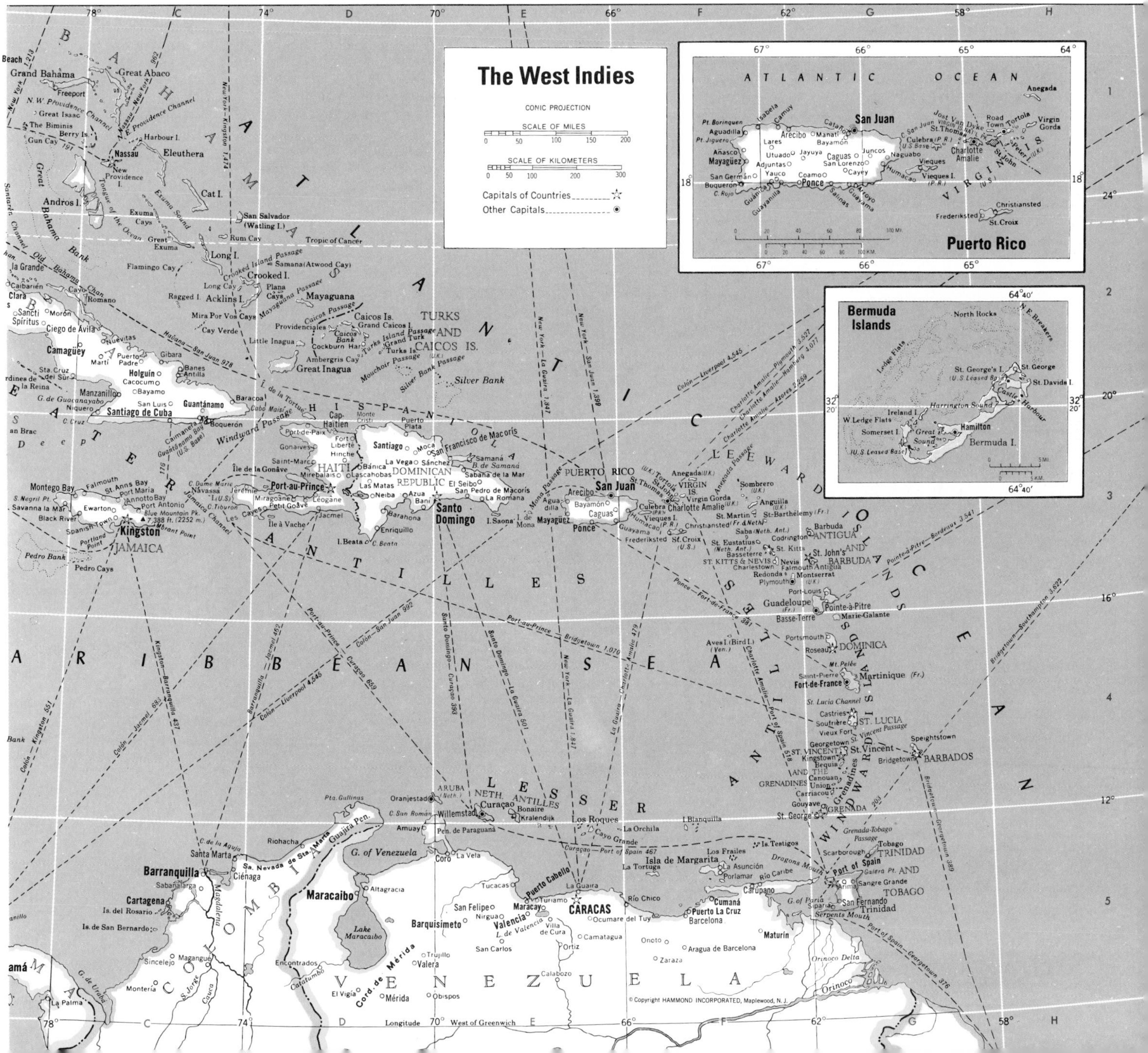
The West Indies
CONIC PROJECTION
SCALE OF MILES
SCALE OF KILOMETERS
Capitals of Countries
Other Capitals
Puerto Rico
ATLANTIC OCEAN
San Juan
Arecibo
Mayagüez
Ponce
Caguas
Bermuda Islands
Hamilton
St. George
Bermuda I.
BAHAMAS
Nassau
Grand Bahama
Great Abaco
Eleuthera
Andros I.
Cat I.
Long I.
Crooked I.
Acklins I.
Mayaguana
Great Inagua
Tropic of Cancer
TURKS AND CAICOS IS.
ATLANTIC
Santiago de Cuba
Camagüey
Holguín
Guantánamo
HAITI
Port-au-Prince
DOMINICAN REPUBLIC
Santo Domingo
JAMAICA
Kingston
HISPANIOLA
PUERTO RICO
VIRGIN IS.
Charlotte Amalie
LEEWARD ISLANDS
ANTIGUA AND BARBUDA
St. John's
ST. KITTS & NEVIS
Basseterre
Guadeloupe
DOMINICA
Roseau
Martinique
Fort-de-France
ST. LUCIA
Castries
ST. VINCENT
Kingstown
BARBADOS
Bridgetown
GRENADA
St. George's
TRINIDAD AND TOBAGO
Port of Spain
WINDWARD ISLANDS
LESSER ANTILLES
CARIBBEAN SEA
ARUBA
NETH. ANTILLES
Willemstad
Curaçao
Bonaire
COLOMBIA
Barranquilla
Cartagena
Santa Marta
VENEZUELA
CARACAS
Maracaibo
Valencia
Barquisimeto
Maracay
Cumaná
Maturín
G. of Venezuela
Lake Maracaibo
Isla de Margarita
Longitude West of Greenwich
© Copyright HAMMOND INCORPORATED, Maplewood, N.J.

(continued)

CUBA

PROVINCES

Camagüey, 664,566 .... G2
Ciego de Ávila 320,961 .... F2
Cienfuegos 326,412 .... E2
Granma 739,335 .... H4
Guantánamo 466,609 .... K4
Holguin 911,034 .... J3
Juventud (municipio especial) 57,879 .... C2
La Habana, Ciudad de Habana 1,924,886 .... C1
La Habana (Havana) 586,029 C1
Las Tunas 436,341 .... H3
Matanzas 557,628 .... D1
Pinar del Río 640,740 .... A2
Sancti Spíritus 399,700 ...... F2
Santiago de Cuba 909,506 ... H4
Villa Clara 764,743 .... E1

CITIES and TOWNS

Abreus 14,267 .... D2
Agramonte 4,603 .... D1
Aguada de Pasajeros 20,219 D2
Alacranes 4,959 .... D1
Alonso Rojas 1,427 .... B2
Alquízar 12,691 .... C1
Altagracia 1,722 .... G3
Alto Songo-La Maya 25,188 . J4
Amarillas 2,767 .... D2
Amazonas 1,066 .... F2
Antilla 10,052 .... J3
Arroyo Blanco 1,431 .... F2
Artemisa 45,689 .... B1
Báez 4,178 .... E2
Báguanos 12,678 .... J3
Bahía Honda 16,901 .... B1
Baire 4,879 .... H4
Banao 803 .... F2
Banes 38,905 .... J3
Baracoa 36,702 .... K4
Baraguá 12,633 .... F2
Bauta 26,826 .... C1
Bayamo 109,201 .... H4
Bejucal 15,649 .... C1
Bolondrón 5,840 .... D1
Buenaventura 4,711 .... H3
Buenavista 1,303 .... F2
Buey Arriba 8,017 .... H4
Cabaiguán 36,544 .... E2
Cabañas 4,897 .... B1
Cabezas 5,262 .... D1
Cacocum 14,145 .... H3
Caibarién 32,094 .... F2
Caimanera 6,664 .... J4
Calabazar de Sagua 9,023 ... E1
Calimete 19,925 .... D1
Camagüey 245,235 .... G3
Camajuaní 26,653 .... E2
Campechuela 20,743 .... G4
Canasí 1,637 .... C1
Candelaria 10,810 .... B1
Cárdenas 65,585 .... D1
Cartagena 2,166 .... D2
Cascajal 3,530 .... E1
Cauto del Embarcadero 949 . H4
Cauto el Cristo 1,626 ...... J3
Central Amancio Rodríguez 22,506 .... G3
Central Bolivia 6,301 ...... G2
Central Brasil 4,904 .... G2
Central Cándido González 3,414 .... G3
Central Colombia 16,799 ... G3
Central Frank País 9,066 .... K3
Central Guatemala 5,584 .... J3
Central Haití 3,609 .... G3
Central Los Reynaldos 3,997 J4
Central Loynaz Echevarría 3,245 .... J3
Central Manuel Tames 7,864 K4
Céspedes 6,634 .... G2
Chambas 19,877 .... F2
Chaparra 8,428 .... H3
Cidra 3,567 .... D1
Ciego de Ávila 80,010 ...... F2
Cienfuegos 107,396 .... D2
Colón 47,010 .... D1
Condado 33,115 .... E2
Consolación del Norte 4,681 B1
Consolación del Sur 34,334 . B2
Contramaestre 44,991 ...... G3
Corralillo 15,822 .... D1
Cruces 20,324 .... E2
Cueto 23,183 .... J3
Cumanayagua 25,338 ...... E2
Daiquirí J4
Delicias 10,562 .... H3
Dos Caminos 3,772 .... J4
Dos Ríos 1,786 .... J4
El Caney 3,921 .... J4
El Cobre 3,952 .... J4
El Santo 2,473 .... E1
Encrucijada 23,029 .... E1
Esmeralda 17,205 .... G1
Esperanza 9,241 .... E2
Florencia 6,979 .... F2
Florida 43,881 .... G3
Fomento 17,310 .... E2
Gaspar 2,682 .... F2
Gibara 23,137 .... J3
Guáimaro 29,712 .... G3
Guanabacoa 89,741 .... C1
Guanajay 21,042 .... B1
Guane 14,126 .... A2
Guantánamo 178,129 ...... K4
Guaro 3,086 .... J3
Guasimal 3,057 .... E2
Guayabal 3,703 .... G3
Guayos 6,753 .... F2
Güines 51,691 .... C1
Güira de Melena 19,851 .... C1
Guisa 15,182 .... H4
Havana (cap.) 1,924,886 ... C1
Herradura 3,762 .... B1
Holguín 190,155 .... J3
Ignacio Agramonte 1,487 ... G3
Imías 4,491 .... K4
Isabela de Sagua 3,721 ..... E1
Jagüey Grande 30,205 ..... D2
Jamaica 5,128 .... K4
Jaruco 16,844 .... C1
Jatibonico 17,047 .... F2
Jíbaro 1,263 .... F2
Jiguaní 25,069 .... H4
Jobabo 14.899 .... H3
Jovellanos 35,043 .... D1
La Coloma 3,462 .... B2
La Maya-Alto Songo 25,188 . J4
Las Martinas 4,511 .... A2
Limonar 9,629 .... D1
Los Arabos 10,664 .... E1
Los Palacios 21,884 .... B1
Lugareño 4,396 .... G3
Mabay 6,176 .... H4
Maceo 2,652 .... H3
Majagua 9,110 .... F2
Manacas 5,914 .... E1
Manatí 11,054 .... H3
Manguito 2,739 .... D1
Manicaragua 33,900 .... E2
Mantua 9,165 .... A2
Mapos (Amazonas) 1,066 ... F2
Manzanillo 95,420 .... H4
Marianao ○127,563 .... C1
Mariel 24,115 .... B1
Martí 11,474 .... D1
Matanzas 103,302 .... C1
Máximo Gómez, Ciego de Ávila 5,116 .... F2
Máximo Gómez, Matanzas 4,970 .... D1
Mayajigua 4,425 .... F2
Mayarí 54,699 .... J3
Mayarí Arriba 2,302 .... J4
Media Luna 13,794 .... G4
Mendoza 2,914 .... A2
Meneses 4,768 .... F2
Minas 17,675 .... G2
Minas de Matahambre 14,976 .... A1
Moa 28,696 .... K3
Morón 40,396 .... F2
Nicaro 9,506 .... J3
Niquero 15,544 .... G4
Nueva Gerona 17,175 ...... B2
Nuevitas 35,103 .... G2
Orozco 4,256 .... B1
Palma Soriano 66,222 ...... J4
Palmira 19,680 .... E2
Pedro Betancourt 22,915 ... D1
Perico 20,633 .... D1
Pilón 10,194 .... H4
Pinar del Río 104,598 ...... B2
Placetas 46,038 .... E2
Primero Enero 14,807 ...... F2
Puerto Esperanza 3,499 .... A1
Puerto Padre 46,806 ...... H3
Quemado de Güines 11,208 E1
Rancho Veloz 3,966 .... D1
Ranchuelo 34,255 .... E2
Regla 38,491 .... C1
Remedios 27,722 .... E2
Repúbliica Dominicana 2,540 .... F2
Río Cauto 19,550 .... H4
Rodas 16,350 .... E2
Sagua de Tánamo 15,327 ... K3
Sagua la Grande 52,315 .... E1
San Andrés 2,127 .... H3
San Antonio de los Baños 28,137 .... C1
San Cristóbal 30,769 ...... B1
Sancti Spíritus 79,542 ...... E2
San Diego de los Baños 1,430 .... B1
San Germán 12,362 .... J3
San José de las Lajas 37,149 .... C1
San José de los Ramos 1,726 .... D1
San Juan y Martínez 13,227 . B2
San Luis, Pinar del Río 5,677 .... B2
San Luis, Santiago de Cuba 32,826 .... J4
San Nicolás 12,368 .... C1
San Ramón 2,676 .... H4
Santa Clara 175,113 .... E2
Santa Cruz del Norte 15,239 .... C1

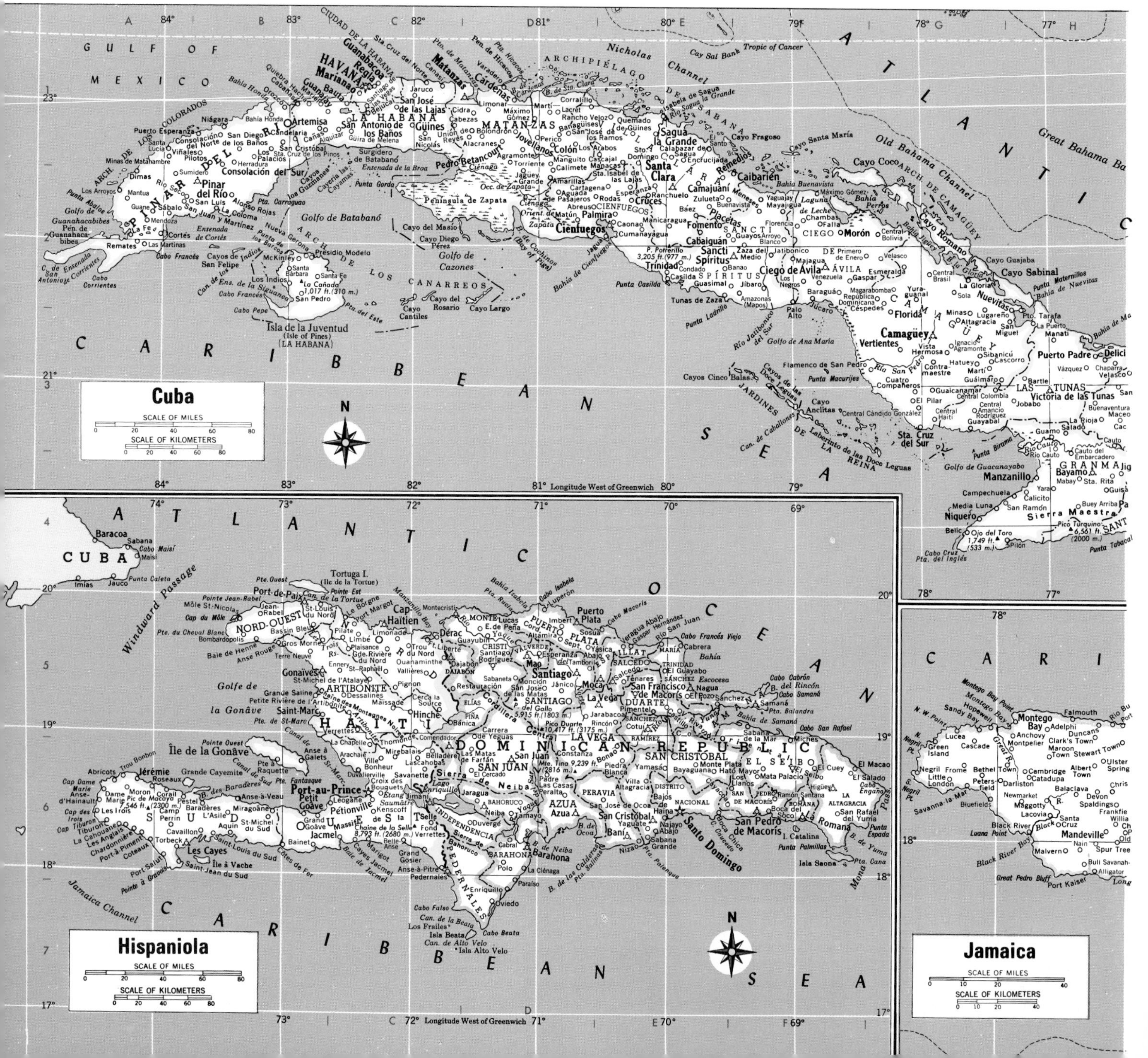
Cuba
SCALE OF MILES
SCALE OF KILOMETERS
GULF OF MEXICO
ATLANTIC
CARIBBEAN SEA
Isla de la Juventud
(Isle of Pines)
(LA HABANA)
Hispaniola
HAITI
DOMINICAN REPUBLIC
Port-au-Prince
Santo Domingo
Windward Passage
Jamaica
Montego Bay
Kingston
81° Longitude West of Greenwich 80°
C 72° Longitude West of Greenwich 71°

Santa Cruz de los Pinos 3,545 B1
Santa Cruz del Sur 27,142 G3
Santa Fe 3,925 B2
Santa Isabel de las Lajas 7,279 E2
Santa Lucía 3,734 J3
Santa Rita 6,358 H4
Santiago de Cuba 362,432 J4
Santiago de las Vegas 29,325 C1
Santo Domingo 32,950 E1
Sibanicú 14,252 G3
Sola 2,436 G2
Sumidero 980 A2
Surgidero de Batabanó 11,533 C1
Tacajó 4,469 J3
Torriente 1,759 D11
Trinidad 42,080 E2
Unión de Reyes 28,422 C1
Varadero 14,737 D1
Vázquez 3,851 H3
Velasco 5,618 H3
Venezuela 13,744 F2
Vertientes 25,178 G3
Victoria de las Tunas 87,522 H3
Viñales 2,049 A1
Yaguajay 30,720 F2
Yara 238,879 H4
Zaza del Medio 7,495 F2
Zulueta 5,425 E2

OTHER FEATURES

Abalos (pt.) A2
Ana María (gulf) F3
Anclitas (cay) F3
Batabanó (gulf) C2
Birama (pt.) G4
Broa (inlet) C1
Buenavista (bay) F2
Caballones (chan.) F3
Camagüey (arch.) G2
Cantiles (cay) C3
Cárdenas (bay) D1
Carraguao (pt.) B2
Casilda (pt.) E2
Cauto (riv.) H3
Cayamas (cays) C2
Cazones (gulf) C2
Cienfuegos (bay) D2
Cinco Balas (cays) E3
Cochinos (bay) D2
Coco (cay) G1
Corrientes (cape) A2
Corrientes (inlet) A2
Cortés (inlet) B2
Cristal, Sierra del (mts.) J3
Cruz (cape) G4
Diego Pérez (cay) C2
Doce Leguas (cays) F3
Este (pt.) C3
Fragoso (cay) F1
Francés (cape) A2
Gorda (pt.) C2
Gran Piedra (mt.) J4
Guacanayabo (gulf) G4
Guajaba (cay) G2
Guanahacabibes (gulf) A2
Guanahacabibes (pen.) A2
Guantánamo (bay) J4
Guantánamo Bay U.S. Nav. Reserve K4
Guarico (pt.) K3
Guzmanes (cays) B2
Hicacos (pen.) D1
Hicacos (pt.) D1
Honda (bay) B1
Indios (chan.) B2
Inglés (pt.) G4
Jardines de la Reina (arch.) F3
Jatibonico del Sur (riv.) F3
Jigüey (bay) G2
Juventud, Isla de la (Pines) (isl.) 57,879 B3
Laberinto de las Doce Leguas (cays) F3
Ladrillo (pt.) E3
Largo (cay) D2
Leche (lag.) F2
Los Barcos (pt.) B2
Los Canarreos (arch.) C2
Los Colorados (arch.) A1
Lucrecia (cape) J3
Macurijes (pt.) F3
Maestra, Sierra (mts.) H4
Maisí (cape) K4
Mangle (pt.) J3
Masío (cay) C2
Matanzas (bay) D1
Nicholas (chan.) E1
Nipe (bay) J3
Nuevitas (bay) H2
Ojo del Toro (mt.) G4
Old Bahama (chan.) G1
Pepe (cape) B3
Perros (bay) G2
Pigs (Cochinos) (bay) D2
Pines (Isla de la Juventud) (isl.) 7,879 B3
Potrerillo (peak) E2
Quemado (pt.) K4
Romano (cay) G2
Rosario (cay) C2
Sabana (arch.) E1
Sabinal (cay) H2
Sagua la Grande (riv.) E1
San Antonio (cape) A2
San Felipe (cays) B2
San Pedro (riv.) G3
Santa Clara (bay) D1
Santa María (cay) F1
Siguanea (bay) B2
Tabacal (pt.) H4
Toa, Cuchillas de (mts.) K4
Tortuguilla (pt.) K4
Turquino (peak) H4
Zapata (pen.) C2
Zapata Occidental (swamp) D2
Zapata Oriental (swamp) D2

DOMINICAN REPUBLIC

PROVINCES

Azua 142,770 D6
Bahoruco 78,636 D6
Barahona 137,160 D6
Dajabón 57,709 D5
Distrito Nacional 1,550,739 E6
Duarte 235,544 E5
Elías Piña 65,384 C5
El Seibo 157,866 F6
Espaillat 164,017 E5
Independencia 38,768 D6
La Altagracia 100,112 F6
La Romana 109,769 F6
La Vega 385,043 D6
María Trinidad Sánchez 112,629 E5
Monte Cristi 83,407 D5
Pedernales 17,006 D7
Peravia 168,123 E6
Puerto Plata 206,757 D5
Salcedo 99,191 E5
Samaná 65,699 E5
Sánchez Ramírez 126,567 E5
San Cristóbal 446,132 E6
San Juan 239,957 D6
San Pedro de Macorís 152,890 F6
Santiago 550,372 D5
Santiago Rodríguez 55,411 D5
Valverde 100,319 D5

CITIES and TOWNS

Altamira 2,759 D5
Azua 31,481 D6
Bajos de Haina 33,135 E6
Baní 36,705 E6
Barahona 49,334 D6
Bonao 44,486 E6
Cabrera 2,542 E5
Comendador 5,962 C6
Constanza 15,141 D6
Cotuí 16,688 E5
Dajabón 8,808 D5
El Seibo 13,511 F6
Hato Mayor 17,859 F6
Higüey 33,501 F6
Imbert 5,315 D5
Jarabacoa 13,416 E5
Jimaní 3,327 C6
La Romana 91,571 F6
La Vega 52,432 E5
Luperón 2,500 D5
Mao 33,527 D5
Moca 31,176 D5
Monción 3,344 D5
Nagua 20,912 E5
Puerto Plata 45,348 D5
Sabana de la Mar 9,983 F5
Sabaneta 9,170 D5
Samaná 5,023 F5
Sánchez 7,919 E5
San Cristóbal 58,520 E6
San Francisco de Macorís 64,906 E5
San Juan 49,764 D6
San Pedro de Macorís 78,562 F6
Santiago 278,638 D5
Santo Domingo (cap.) 1,313,172 E6
Tenares 4,065 E5
Villa Altagracia 20,890 E6

OTHER FEATURES

Alto Velo (chan.) C7
Alto Velo (isl.) D7
Balandra (pt.) F5
Beata (cape) D7
Beata (chan.) C7
Beata (isl.) C7
Cabrón (cape) F5
Calderas (bay) D6
Cana (pt.) F6
Catalina (isl.) F6
Caucedo (capee) E6
Central, Cordillera (range) D5
Duarte (peak) D5
Engaño (cape) F6
Enriquillo (lake) C6
Escocesa (bay) E5
Espada (pt.) F6
Falso (cape) C7
Francés Viejo (cape) E5
Gallo (mt.) D5
Isabela (bay) D5
Isabela (cape) D5
Los Frailes (isl.) C7
Macorís (cape) E5
Manzanillo (bay) C5
Mona (passg.) F6
Neiba (bay) D6
Neiba, Sierra de (mts.) D6
Ocoa (bay) D6
Oriental, Cordillera (range) F6
Palenque (pt.) E6
Palmillas (pt.) F6
Rincón (bay) F5
Rucia (pt.) D5
Salinas (pt.) E6
Samaná (bay) F5
Samaná (cape) F5
San Rafael (cape) F5
Saona (isl.) F6
Septentrional, Cordillera (range) D5
Tina (mt.) D6
Yaque del Norte (riv.) D5
Yaque del Sur (riv.) D6
Yuma (bay) F6
Yuna (riv.) E5

HAITI

DEPARTMENTS

Artibonite C5
Nord C5
Nord-Ouest B5
Ouest C6
Sud A6

CITIES and TOWNS

Anse-à-Galets 3,623 B6
Anse-d'Hainault 5,220 A6
Aquin 3,820 B6
Cap-Haïtien 64,406 C5
Croix des Bouquets 4,365 C6
Dame Marie 4,320 A6
Dérac 1,300 C5
Dessalines 7,984 C5
Fort Liberté 5,012 C5
Gonaïves 34,209 B5
Grande Rivière du Nord 6,007 C5
Gros Morne 4,739 B5
Hinche 10,070 C5
Jacmel 13,730 C6
Jérémie 18,493 A6
Kenscoff 2,605 C6
Lascahobas 3,805 C6
Léogâne 5,782 C6
Les Cayes 34,090 B6
Limbé 10,476 C5
Miragoâne 4,327 B6
Mirebalais 6,069 C6
Ouanaminthe 7,276 C5
Pétionville 35,333 C6
Petite Rivière de l'Artibonite 10,099 B5
Petit Goâve 7,310 B6
Pignon 4,576 C5
Port-au-Prince (cap.) 449,831 C6
Port-de-Paix 15,540 B5
Saint-Louis du Nord 7,203 B5
Saint-Marc 24,165 B5
Saint-Michel de l'Atalaye 7,559 C5
Saint-Raaphaël 3,889 C5
Trou du Nord 7,637 C5
Verrettes 3,670 C5

OTHER FEATURES

Artibonite (riv.) C5
Baradères (bay) B6
Cheval Blanc (pt.) B5
Dame Marie (cape) A6
Est (pt.) C4
Fantasque (pt.) B6
Gonâve (gulf) B5
Gonâve (isl.) B6
Grande Cayemite (isl.) B6
Gravois (pt.) A7
Irois (cape) A6
Jean-Rabel (pt.) B5
Macaya (mt.) A6
Manzanillo (bay) C5
Môle (cape) B5
Noires (mts.) C5
Ouest (pt.) B4
Ouest (pt.) B6
Saint-Marc (chan.) B6
Saint-Marc (pt.) B5
Saumâtre (lake) C6
Selle (peak) C6
Sud (chan.) B6
Tortue (chan.) C5
Tortue (Tortuga) (isl.) C4
Tortuga (isl.) C4
Trois-Rivières (riv.) B5
Vache (isl.) B6
Windward (passg.) A5

JAMAICA

CITIES and TOWNS

Alley J7
Alligator Pond H6
Anchovy 2,558 H5
Annotto Bay K6
Bamboo 2,971 J6
Bath K6
Black River 2,701 H6
Bog Walk J6
Bowden K6
Browns Town 5,479 J6
Bull Savanna-Junction 5,110 H6
Cambridge 2,449 H6
Catadupa H6
Christiana H6
Discovery Bay 1,814 J5
Falmouth 3,937 H5
Green Island G6
Hope Bay K6
Kingston (cap.) 106,791 K6
Kingston *516,865 J7
Linstead J6
Lucea 3,635 G5
Mandeville 14,421 H6
Maroon Town 2,717 H6
May Pen 26,074 J6
Montego Bay 43,521 H5
Montpelier H6
Morant Bay 7,465 K7
Negril G6
Ocho Rios 5,851 J6
Oracabessa J5
Port Antonio 10,538 K6
Port Kaiser H7
Port Maria 5,259 J6
Port Morant K6
Saint Ann's Bay 7,101 J5
Saint Margaret's Bay K6
Savanna-la-Mar 11,759 G6
Spanish Town 40,731 J6
Williamsfield H6

OTHER FEATURES

Black (riv.) H6
Black River (bay) G6
Blue (mts.) J6
Blue Mountain (peak) K6
Galina (pt.) J6
Grande (riv.) K6
Great (riv.) H6
Great Pedro Bluff (prom.) H6
Long (bay) H7
Luana (pt.) G6
Minho (riv.) J6
Montego (bay) G5
Montego Bay ((pt.) G5
North East (pt.) K6
North Negril (pt.) G6
North West (pt.) G5
Old Harbour (bay) J6
Portland (pt.) J7
Sir John's (peak) K6
South East (pt.) K6
South Negril (pt.) G6

*City and Suburbs.
○ Population of municipality.

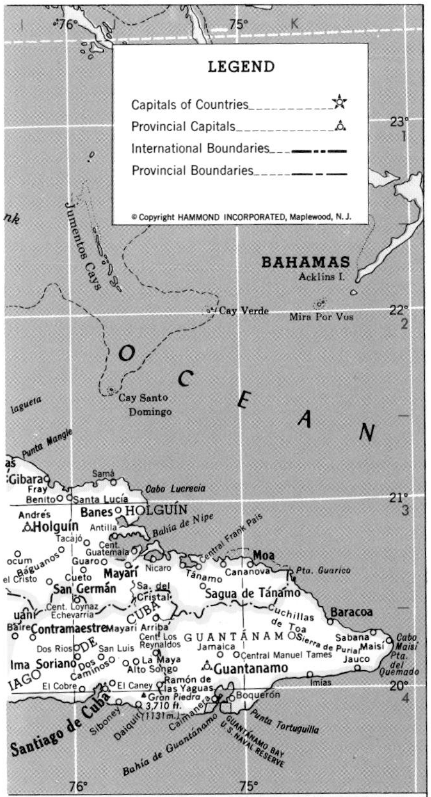
LEGEND
Capitals of Countries
Provincial Capitals
International Boundaries
Provincial Boundaries
© Copyright HAMMOND INCORPORATED, Maplewood, N. J.
BAHAMAS
Acklins I.
Cay Verde
Mira Por Vos
Cay Santo Domingo
OCEAN
Holguín
HOLGUÍN
Banes
Moa
Mayarí
Sagua de Tánamo
Baracoa
San Germán
Contramaestre
GUANTÁNAMO
Guantanamo
Santiago de Cuba
Boquerón
U.S. NAVAL RESERVE
76°
75°

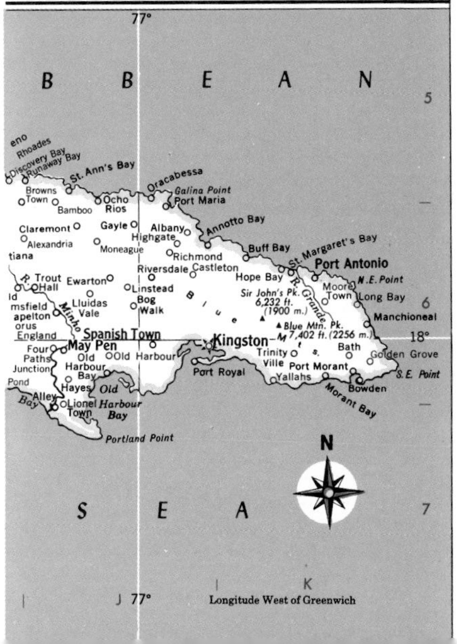
77°
CARIBBEAN
St. Ann's Bay
Oracabessa
Port Maria
Annotto Bay
Buff Bay
Port Antonio
Kingston
Spanish Town
May Pen
Old Harbour
Morant Bay
Portland Point
SEA
Longitude West of Greenwich

Agriculture, Industry and Resources

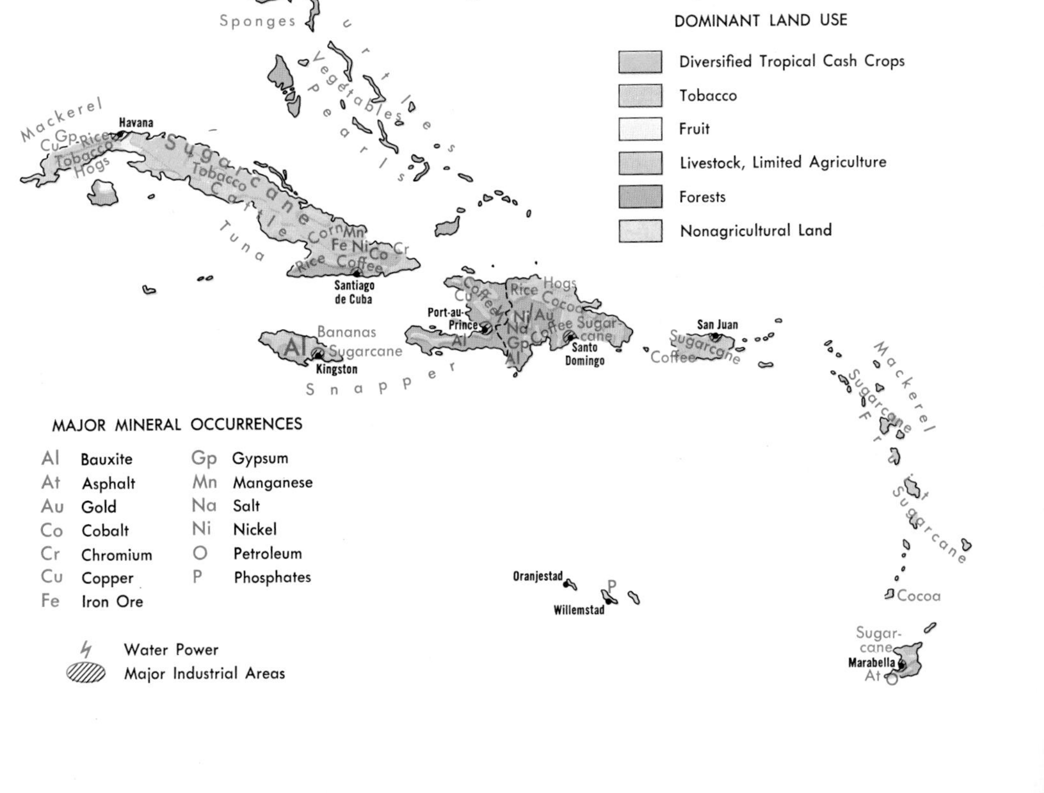
DOMINANT LAND USE
Diversified Tropical Cash Crops
Tobacco
Fruit
Livestock, Limited Agriculture
Forests
Nonagricultural Land
MAJOR MINERAL OCCURRENCES
Al Bauxite
At Asphalt
Au Gold
Co Cobalt
Cr Chromium
Cu Copper
Fe Iron Ore
Gp Gypsum
Mn Manganese
Na Salt
Ni Nickel
O Petroleum
P Phosphates
Water Power
Major Industrial Areas
Havana
Santiago de Cuba
Port-au-Prince
Santo Domingo
San Juan
Kingston
Oranjestad
Willemstad
Marabella
Sponges
Turtles
Vegetables
Pearls
Mackerel
Sugarcane
Tobacco
Cattle
Tuna
Coffee
Bananas
Snapper
Cocoa
Rice
Hogs

PUERTO RICO

DISTRICTS

Aguadilla A1
Arecibo C1
Bayamón D1
Guayama D2
Humacao E2
Mayagüez B2
Ponce C2
San Juan E1

CITIES and TOWNS

Adjuntas 5,239 B2
Aguada 5,025 A1
Aguadilla 22,039 A1
Aguas Buenas 3,766 E2
Aibonito 9,331 D2
Añasco 5,646 A1
Angeles ○2,817 B2
Arecibo 48,779 B1
Arroyo 8,435 E3
Bahomamey A1
Bajadero 3,678 C1
Barceloneta 4,502 C1
Barranquitas 3,618 D2
Bayamón 185,087 D1
Boquerón ○3,675 A3
Cabo Rojo 10,292 A2
Caguas 87,214 E2
Caguas †156,819 E2
Camuy 3,834 B1
Carolina 147,835 E1
Cataño 26,243 D1
Cayey 23,305 D2
Ceiba 4,973 F2
Central Aguirre 1,049 D3
Ciales 3,582 C1
Cidra 6,069 D2
Coamo 12,851 D2
Comerío 5,736 D2
Coquí 3,018 D3
Corozal 5,889 D1
Coto Laurel ○5,192 C2
Culebra (Dewey) 938 G1
Dorado 10,203 D1
Ensenada B3
Esperanza 1,130 G2
Fajardo 26,928 F1
Florida 3,641 C1
Guánica 9,628 B3
Guayama 21,097 E3
Guayanilla 6,163 B3
Guaynabo 65,075 D1
Gurabo 7,645 E2
Hatillo 5,019 B1
Hato Rey E1
Hormigueros 12,031 A2
Humacao 19,147 E2
Isabela 12,087 A1
Isabel Segunda 2,330 G2
Jayuya 3,588 C2
Jobos 4,194 D3
Juana Díaz 10,469 C2
Juncos 7,851 E2
Lajas 4,275 A2
Lares 5,224 B2
Las Piedras 4,857 E2
Levittown 31,613 D1
Loíza 3,932 E1
Loíza Aldea E1
Luquillo 4,531 F1
Manatí 17,347 C1
Maricao 1,390 B2
Mayagüez 82,968 A2
Mayagüez †98,155 A2
Moca 3,960 A1
Naguabo 4,135 F2
Naranjito 2,849 D1
Palmer 1,566 F1
Palo Seco 1,172 D1
Parguera A3
Patillas 3,172 E2
Peñuelas 4,235 B2
Playa de Fajardo F1
Playa de Humacao ○5,573 F2
Ponce 161,739 C3
Ponce †168,272 C3
Puerto Nuevo D1
Puerto Real 2,390 A2
Puerto Real (Playa de Fajardo) F1
Punta Santiago (Playa de Humacao) ○5,573 F2
Quebradillas 3,770 B1
Río Blanco 1,433 F2
Río Grande 12,047 E1
Río Piedras E1
Rosario A2
Sabana Grande 7,435 B2
Sabana Seca 11,431 D1
Salinas 6,220 D3
San Antonio 2,681 A1
San Germán 13,054 A2
San Juan (cap.) 424,600 E1
San Juan †1,081,193 E1
San Lorenzo 8,880 E2
San Sebastián 10,619 B1
Santa Isabel 6,948 C3
Santurce E1
Tallaboa 1,059 B3
Toa Alta 4,427 D1
Toa Baja 1,992 D1
Trujillo Alto 41,141 E1
Utuado 11,113 B2
Vega Alta 10,582 D1
Vega Baja 18,233 D1
Vieques (Isabel Segunda) 2,330 G2
Villalba 3,469 C2
Yabucoa 6,797 E2
Yauco 14,594 B2

OTHER FEATURES

Aguadilla (bay) A1
Algarrobo (pt.) A2
Añasco (bay) A1
Arenas (pt.) F2
Bauta (riv.) C2
Bayamón (riv.) D1
Boquerón (bay) A3
Borinquen (pt.) A1
Cabullones (pt.) C3
Caja de Muertos (isl.) C3
Camuy (riv.) B1
Canovanas (riv.) E1
Caonillas (lake) C2
Carite (lake) E2
Carraízo (lake) E1
Cayey, Sierra de (mts.) D2
Central, Cordillera (range) C2
Cerro Gordo (pt.) D1
Coamo (res.) D3
Coamo (riv.) D3
Culebra (isl.) 1,265 G1
Culebrinas (riv.) A1
Culebrita (isl.) G2
El Toro (mt.) F2
El Yunque (mt.) F1
Este (pt.) G2
Fajardo (riv.) F1
Figuras (pt.) E3
Fosforescente (bay) A3
Grande de Añasco (riv.) B2
Grande de Arecibo (riv.) C1
Grande de Loíza (riv.) E1
Grande de Manatí (riv.) C1
Guajataca (lake) B1
Guanajibo (pt.) A2
Guanajibo (riv.) A2
Guánica (lake) B3
Guaniquilla (pt.) A2
Guayabal (lake) C2
Guayanés (pt.) F2
Guayanés (riv.) E2
Guayanilla (bay) B3
Guayo (lake) B2
Guilarte (mt.) B2
Honda (bay) F2
Jacaguas (riv.) C2
Jaicoa, Cordillera (mts.) B1
Jiguero (pt.) A1
Jobos (bay) D3
Lima (pt.) F2
Luquillo, Sierra de (mts.) E2
Manglillo (pt.) B3
Mayagüez (bay) A2
Miquillo (pt.) F1
Molinos (pt.) G1
Mona (passg.) A2
Negra (pt.) G2
Nigua (riv.) D2
Ola Grande (pt.) D3
Palmas Altas (pt.) C1
Patillas (lake) E2
Petrona (pt.) D3
Pirata (mt.) F2
Plata (riv.) D2
Puerca (pt.) F2
Puerto Medio Mundo (bay) F2
Punta, Cerro de (mt.) C2
Ramey A.F.B. A1
Rincón (bay) D3
Rojo (cape) A3
Roosevelt Road Naval Res. F2
Salinas (pt.) D1
San José (lag.) E1
San Juan, Cabezas de (prom.) F1
San Juan Nat'l Hist. Site D1
Soldado (pt.) G2
Sucia (bay) A3
Tanamá (riv.) B1
Toro, El (mt.) F2
Torrecilla (lag.) E1
Tortuguero (lag.) D1
Tuna (pt.) E3
Vacía Talega (pt.) E1
Vieques (isl.) 7,662 G2
Vieques (passg.) F2
Vieques (sound) G2
Yagüez (riv.) A2
Yauco (lake) B2
Yeguas ((pt.) F3

ANTIGUA

CITIES and TOWNS

All Saints 1,796 E11
Cedar Grove 1,460 E11
Falmouth 1,134 E11
Freetown 1,250 E11
Jennings 1,370 D11
Liberta 2,394 E11
Old Road 1,244 D11
Parham 1,570 E11
Saint John's (cap.) 21,814 E11
Willikies 1,843 E11

OTHER FEATURES

Antigua (isl.) 76,213 E11
Boggy (peak) D11
Boon (pt.) E11
Green (isl.) E11
Guiana (isl.) E11
Long (isl.) E11
Saint John's (harb.) C11
Standfast (pt.) E11
Willoughby (bay) E11

ARUBA

CITIES and TOWNS

Aresji D9
Balashi E10
Bubali D10
Bushiribana E10
Druif D1
Oranjestad (cap.) Aruba 10,100 D10
Sint Nicolaas E10
Westpunt D10

OTHER FEATURES

Aruba (isl.) 66,790 E9
Basora (pt.) E10
Jamanota (mt.) E10
Paarden (bay) D10
Palm (beach) D10

BARBADOS

CITIES and TOWNS

Bathsheba B8
Belleplaine B8
Bridgetown (cap.) 7,552 B9
Carlton B8
Cave Hill B9
Checker Hall B8
Codrington B8
Crab Hill B8
Crane C9
Drax Hall B8
Ellerton B9
Greenland B8
Holetown B8
Kendal B8
Lodge Hill B8
Marchfield B9
Mount Standfast B8
Oistins B9
Rose Hill B8
Rouen B9
Saint Lawrence B9
Saint Martins C9
Scarboro B9
Seawell B9
Six Mens B8
Speightstown B8
Spring Hall B8
Welchman Hall B8

OTHER FEATURES

Carlisle (bay) B9
Hillaby (mt.) B8
Long (bay) B9
North (pt.) B8
Oistins (bay) B9
Pelican (isl.) B9
Ragged (pt.) C8
Sam Lord's Castle C9
South (pt.) B9

DOMINICA

CITIES and TOWNS

Barroui 1,480 E6
Castle Bruce 1,975 F6
Coulihaut 1,735 E6
Delice F7
Grand Bay 3,152 F7
Hampstead E5
La Plaine F6
Mahout 2,095 E6
Marigot 3,183 F6
Petit Soufrière F6
Portsmouth 2,329 E5
Rosalie F6
Roseau (cap.) 9,968 E7
Roseau *16,035 E7
Saint Joseph 2,643 E6
Salybia F6
Soufrière E7
Vieille Case E5
Wesley 2,002 F5

OTHER FEATURES

Capuchin (cape) E5
Carib Reserve F6
Clyde (riv.) F6
Crumpton (pt.) F5
Diablotin, Morne (mt.) E6
Dominica (passg.) E5
Douglas (bay) E5
Grand (bay) F7
Jaquet (pt.) E5
Layou (riv.) E6
Martinique (passg.) E7
Micotrin (mt.) F6
Pagoua (bay) F6
Prince Rupert (bay) E5
Scotts (head) E7
Soufrière (bay) E7
Trois Pitons, Morne (mt.) E6

GRENADA

CITIES and TOWNS

Gouyave 2,498 C8
Grand Roy C8
Grenville 1,723 D8
Hermitage D8
La Taste D8
Marquis D8
Mount Tivoli D8
Saint George's (cap.) 6,463 C9
Saint George's *34,624 C9
Sauteurs 605 D8
Victoria 1,673 D8
Woodford C8

OTHER FEATURES

Bedford (pt.) D8
David (pt.) D8
Great Bacolet (pt.) D8
Green (isl.) D8
Grenville (bay) D8
Gros (pt.) C8
Halifax (harb.) C8
Irvin's (bay) D8
Les Tantes (isls.) D7
Molinière (pt.) C8
Prickly (pt.) C9
Ronde (isl.) D7
Saint Catherine (mt.) D8
Saline (pt.) C9
Sinai (mt.) D8
Telescope (pt.) D8

GUADELOUPE

Total Population 329,017

CITIES and TOWNS

Anse-Bertrand 1,921 A5
Baie-Mahault 5,874 A6
Baillif 3,844 A7
Bananier A7
Basse-Terre (cap.) 13,397 A7
Bouillante 1,821 A6
Bourg-des-Saintes 907 A7
Capesterre 7,541 A7
Ferry A6
Gosier 13,741 B6
Gourbeyre 5,637 A7
Goyave 1,709 A6
Grand-Bourg 3,249 B7
Lamentin 2,319 A6
Les Abymes 51,837 B6
Morne-à-l'Eau 9,457 A6
Moule 9,800 B6
Petit-Bourg 5,097 A6
Petit-Canal 1,581 A6
Pigeon A6
Pointe-à-Pitre 25,151 B6
Pointe-Noire 2,180 A6
Port-Louis 4,517 B5
Saint-Claude 6,755 A7
Sainte-Anne 11,527 B6
Sainte-Marguerite B6
Sainte-Marie A6
Sainte-Rose 4,805 A6
Saint-François 3,141 B6
Trois-Rivières 7,881 A7
Vieux-Fort 1,073 B7
Vieux-Habitants 4,065 A7

OTHER FEATURES

Allègre (pt.) A6
Antigues (pt.) A5
Basse-Terre (isl.) 138,777 A6
Châteaux (pt.) B6
Constant, Morne (hill) B7
Désirade, La (isl.) 1,602 B6
Fajou (isl.) A6
Grand Cul-de-Sac Marin (bay) A6
Grande-Terre (isl.) B6
Grande Vigie (pt.) B5
Grand-Îlet (isl.) A7
Guadeloupe (isl.) 167,896 B6
Guadeloupe (passg.) A5
Guadeloupe Nat'l Park A6
Kahouanne (isl.) A6
Marie-Galante (isl.) 13,757 B7
Nord (pt.) B7
Nord-Est (bay) B6
Petit Cul-de-Sac Marin (bay) A6
Petite-Terre (isls.) B6
Saintes (chan.) A7
Saintes (isls.) 2,901 A7
Salée (riv.) A6
Sans Toucher (mt.) A6
Soufrière (mt.) A7
Terre-de-Bas (isl.) 1,427 A7
Terre-de-Haut (isl.) 1,453 A7
Vieux-Fort (pt.) A7

MARTINIQUE

Total Population 330,220

CITIES and TOWNS

Ajoupa-Bouillon 1,569 C5
Basse-Pointe 2,163 C5
Bellefontaine 818 C6
Case-Pilote 1,776 C6
Ducos 4,429 D6
Fond-Saint-Denis 962 C6
Fort-de-France (cap.) 96,649 C6
Grand' Rivière 1,053 C5
Gros-Morne 1,976 D6
La Trinité 3,380 D6
Le Carbet 2,321 C6
Le François 2,940 D6
Le Lamentin 6,872 D6
Le Lorrain 2,024 D6
Le Marin 2,651 D7
Le Morne-Rouge 2,650 C5
Le Prêcheur 1,350 C5
Le Robert 3,610 D6
Le Saint-Esprit 3,947 D6
Les Trois-Îlets 1,484 D6
Le Vauclin 3,054 D6
Macouba 1,142 C5
Marigot 1,765 D5
Rivière-Pilote 1,587 D7
Rivière-Salée 1,859 D7
Sainte-Luce 1,502 D7
Sainte-Marie 3,966 D5
Saint-Joseph 2,052 D6
Saint-Pierre 4,923 C6
Schoelcher 16,412 C6

OTHER FEATURES

Cabet, Pitons du (mt.) C6
Cabrits (isl.) D7
Caravelle (pen.) D6
Cul-de-Sac du Marin (bay) D7
Diable (pt.) D5
Ferré (cape) E7
Fort-de-France (bay) C6
Galion (bay) D6
Lézarde (riv.) D6
Long (isl.) D6
Lorrain (riv.) D5
Martinique (passg.) C5
Pelée (vol.) C5
Pilote (riv.) D7
Ramiers (isl.) C6
Ramville (isl.) D6
Robert (harb.) D6
Rose (pt.) D6
Saint-Martin (cape) C5
Saint-Pierre (bay) C6
Salines (pt.) D7
Salomon (pt.) C7
Vauclin (mt.) D6

NETHERLANDS ANTILLES

CITIES and TOWNS

Ascension F8
Bacuna E8
Boven Bolivia E8
Dokterstuin F8
Emmastad F9
Entrejo E8
Fontein E8
Groot Sint Joris G9
Hato G8
Kralendijk (cap.), Bonaire 2,500 E8
Lagoen F8
Montanja di Reij G9
New Port G9
Noord di Salinja E8
Onima E8
Otrabanda F9
Patrick F8
Rincon E8
Rooi E8
Santa Barbara G9
Santa Catharina G9
Savonet F8
Sint Kruis F8
Sint Martha F8
Sint Michiel F9
Sint Willebrordus F8
Terra Corra E8
Westpunt F8
Willemstad (cap.) 95,000 F9
Willemstad *130,000 F9

OTHER FEATURES

Bonaire (isl.) 8,087 E9
Bullen (bay) F8
Caracas (bay) G9
Curaçao (isl.) 145,430 G7
Goto (lake) D8
Kanon (pt.) G9
Klein Bonaire (isl.) E8
Kudarebe (pt.) D9
Lac (bay) D9
Lacre (pt.) E9
Malmok (mt.) D8
Noord (pt.) D8
Noord (pt.) F8
Pekelmeer (lake) E9
Piscadera (bay) F9
Schottegat (bay) G9
Sint Anna (bay) F9
Sint Christoffel (mt.) F8
Sint Joris (bay) G9
Slag (bay) D8
Vierkant (pt.) E8

SAINT KITTS and NEVIS

CITIES and TOWNS

Basseterre (cap.) 14,725 C10
Cayon C10
Charlestown 1,326 C11
Cotton Ground 471 C11
Dieppe Bay C10
Frigate Bay C10
Gingerland D11
Golden Rock C10
Newcastle D11
Old Road Town C10
Sadlers Village C10
Sandy Point 862 C10
Tabernacle C10
Zion Hill D11

OTHER FEATURES

Brimstone (hill) C10
Dogwood (pt.) D11
Fort (pt.) C11
Great Salt (pond) D10
Heldens (pt.) C11
Horse Shoe (pt.) C11
Misery (mt.) C10
Monkey (hill) C10
Narrows, The (str.) D11
Nevis (isl.) 9,300 D11
Nevis (peak) D11
North Friars (bay) D10
Pinney's (beach) D11
Saint Christopher (Saint Kitts) (isl.) 35,104 D10
South Friars (bay) C10

SAINT LUCIA

CITIES and TOWNS

Anse la Raye •5,007 F6
Canaries •2,075 G6
Castries (cap.) •42,770 G6
Choc G5
Choiseul •6,382 F7
Dauphin G5
Dennery •9,654 G6
Gros Islet •10,329 G5
Laborie •6,944 G7
Marigot G6
Marquis G6
Micoud •12,264 G6
Preslin G6
Soufrière •7,456 F6
Vieux Fort •10,675 G7

OTHER FEATURES

Beaumont (pt.) F6
Canaries, Piton (mt.) G6
Cannelles (pt.) G7
Cannelles (riv.) G6
Cap (pt.) G5
Choc (bay) G5
Fond d'Or (bay) G6
Gimie (mt.) G6
Grand Caille (pt.) F6
Grand Cul de Sac (riv.) G6
Gros Islet (bay) G5
Gros Piton (mt.) G6
La Sorcière (mt.) G6
Maria (isls.) G7
Ministre (pt.) G7
Moule-à-Chique (cape) G7
Petit Piton (mt.) G6
Pigeon (isl.) G5
Port Castries (harb.) G6
Port Praslin (bay) G6
Roseau (riv.) G6
Saint Lucia (chan.) G5
Saint Vincent (chan.) G7
Savannes (bay) G7
Sorcière, La (mt.) G6
Soufrière (bay) F6
Vierge (pt.) G6

SAINT VINCENT and THE GRENADINES

CITIES and TOWNS

Barrouallie 1,298 A9
Calliaqua 627 A9
Camden Park A9
Colonarie A9
Georgetown 1,100 A8
Kingstown (cap.) 17,117 A9
Kingstown *23,330 A9
Layou 1,147 A9
Wallibu A8

OTHER FEATURES

Colonarie (pt.) A9
Cumberland (bay) A8
Dark (head) A8
De Volet (pt.) A8
Espagnol (pt.) A8
Greathead (bay) A9
Kingstown (bay) A9
Owia (bay) A8
Porter (pt.) A8
Richmond (peak) A8
Saint Andrew (mt.) A9
Saint Vincent (passg.) A8
Soufrière (mt.) A8
Yambou (head) A9

TRINIDAD and TOBAGO

CITIES and TOWNS

Arima 11,390 B10
Arouca B10
Basse Terre B10
Biche B10
Blanchisseuse B10
California A11
Carapichaima B10
Caroni B10
Cedros A11
Chaguanas 6,122 B10
Chaguaramas A10
Couva 3,635 B10
Cunapo B10
Flanagin Town B10
Fullarton A11
Fyzabad 1,564 A11
Grande Rivière B10
Guaico B10
Guayaguayare B11
La Brea 1,487 A11
Marabella 18,158 A11
Matelot B10
Matura B10
Mayaro 2,638 B11
Moruga B11
Mucurapo A10
Palo Seco A11
Peñal 3,606 B11
Point Fortin 6,538 A11
Port-of-Spain (cap.) 67,978 A10
Princes Town 8,288 B11
Redhead B10
Rio Claro 2,423 B11
Saint Joseph 4,132 B10
Saint Joseph B11
San Fernando 33,490 A11
San Francique A11
Sangre Grande 8,948 B1
San Juan A10
Sans Souci B10
Siparia 5,773 B11
Tabaquite 2,309 B11
Talparo B10
Toco 1,287 B10
Tunapuna 10,251 B10
Upper Manzanilla B1
Valencia B10
Waterloo A10

OTHER FEATURES

Aripo, El Cerro del (mt.) B10
Boca Grande (passg.) A10
Chacachacare (isl.) A10
Chupara (pt.) B10
Cocos (bay) B10
Dragons Mouth (str.) A10
El Tucuche (mt.) B10
Erin (bay) A11
Galeota (pt.) B11
Galera (pt.) C10
Guapo (bay) A11
Guatuaro (pt.) B11
Icacos (pt.) A11
Maracas (bay) C10
Pitch (lake) A11

VIRGIN ISLANDS (Br.)

CITIES and TOWNS

Road Town (cap.) 2,200 D3
West End C4

OTHER FEATURES

Flanagan (passg.) D4
Frenchman (cay) C4
Great Thatch (isl.) C4
Great Tobago (isl.) B3
Jost Van Dyke (isl.) 135 C3
Little Tobago (isl.) B3
Narrows, The (str.) C4
Norman (isl.) D4
Peter (isl.) D4
Road (bay) D3
Sage (mt.) D4
Sir Francis Drake (chan.) D4
Tortola (isl.) 9,257 D3

VIRGIN ISLANDS (U.S.)

CITIES and TOWNS

Bethlehem E4
Canebay E3
Charlotte Amalie (cap.) 11,842 B4
Christiansted 2,914 F4
Cruz Bay 1,928 C4
Diamond F4
Eastend D4
Emmaus C4
Fredensdal F4
Frederiksted 1,046 E4
Grove Place 3,599 E4
Kingshill F4
Longford F4
Negro Bay E4

OTHER FEATURES

Altona (lag.) F4
Annaly (bay) E3
Baron Bluff (prom.) E3
Bordeaux (mt.) C4
Brass (isls.) A4
Buck (isl.) G3
Buck Island (chan.) F3
Buck Island Reef Nat'l Mon. G3
Butler (bay) E4
Caneel (bay) B4
Capella (isls.) B5
Christiansted Nat'l Hist. Site F4
Coral (bay) C4
Crown (mt.) A4
Dutch Cap (cay) A4
Eagle (mt.) E4
East (pt.) G4
Flanagan (passg.) D4
Flat (cays) A4
Grass (pt.) G4
Great (pond) F4
Great Pond (bay) F4
Green (cay) F4
Hams Bluff (prom.) E3
Hans Lollik (isls.) B4
Hassel (isl.) B4
Jersey (bay) B4
Krause Lagoon (chan.) F4
Leeward (passg.) B4
Long (pt.) B4
Long (pt.) E4
Lovango (cay) C4
Magens (bay) B4
Maho (bay) C4
Narrows, The (str.) C4
Nulliberg (mt.) B4
Perseverance (bay) A4
Picara (pt.) B4
Pillsbury (sound) B4
Privateer (pt.) D4
Pull (pt.) F3
Ram (head) C5
Red (pt.) D4
Reef (bay) C4
Saba (isl.) A4
Saint Croix (isl.) 49,725 G4
Saint James (isls.) B4
Saint John (isl.) 2,472 C4
Saint Thomas (harb.) B4
Saint Thomas (isl.) 44,372 A4
Salt (cay) A4
Salt (riv.) F4
Salt River (bay) F3
Sandy (pt.) D4
Savana (isl.) A4
Southwest (cape) E4
Tague (bay) G4
Thatch (cay) B4
Turner Hole (bay) G4
U.S. Nav. Air Sta. A4
Virgin (str.) A4
Virgin Isls. Nat'l Park C4
Water (isl.) A4
Westend Saltpond (lag.) E4

*City and suburbs.
• Population of district.
†Population of met. area.
○ Population of municipality.

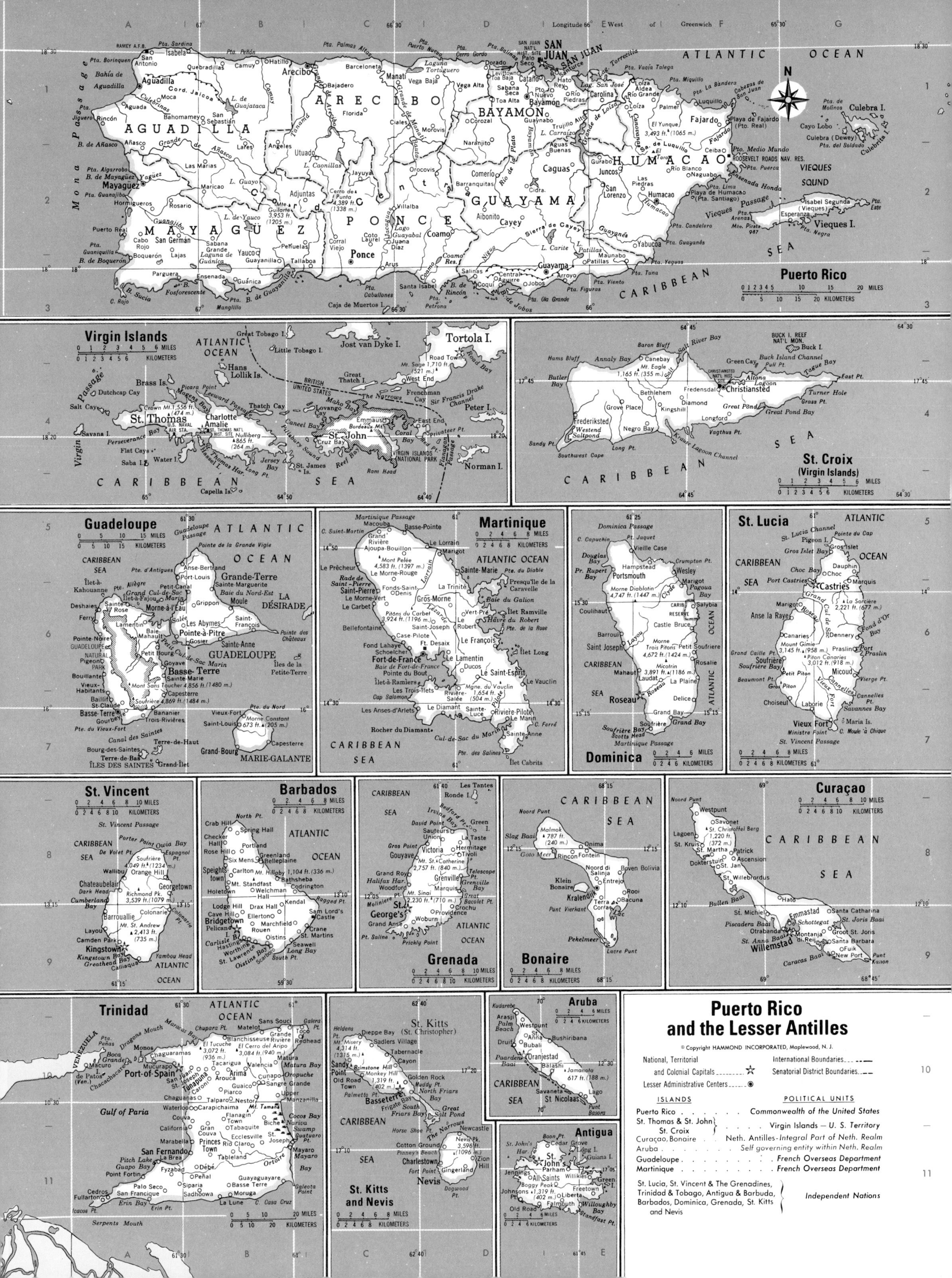

Puerto Rico
ATLANTIC OCEAN
CARIBBEAN SEA
SAN JUAN
AGUADILLA
ARECIBO
BAYAMON
HUMACAO
MAYAGÜEZ
PONCE
GUAYAMA
VIEQUES SOUND
Vieques I.
Culebra I.
Mona Passage
Virgin Islands
St. Thomas
St. John
Tortola I.
Charlotte Amalie
St. Croix (Virgin Islands)
Christiansted
Frederiksted
Guadeloupe
Grande-Terre
Basse-Terre
Pointe-à-Pitre
MARIE-GALANTE
LA DÉSIRADE
ÎLES DES SAINTES
Martinique
Fort-de-France
Dominica
Roseau
St. Lucia
Castries
St. Vincent
Kingstown
Barbados
Bridgetown
Grenada
St. George's
Bonaire
Kralendijk
Curaçao
Willemstad
Trinidad
Port-of-Spain
San Fernando
Gulf of Paria
VENEZUELA
St. Kitts (St. Christopher)
Basseterre
Nevis
Charlestown
St. Kitts and Nevis
Aruba
Oranjestad
St. Nicolaas
Antigua
St. John's
Puerto Rico and the Lesser Antilles
© Copyright HAMMOND INCORPORATED, Maplewood, N. J.
National, Territorial and Colonial Capitals
Lesser Administrative Centers
International Boundaries
Senatorial District Boundaries
ISLANDS
POLITICAL UNITS
Puerto Rico — Commonwealth of the United States
St. Thomas & St. John, St. Croix — Virgin Islands – U. S. Territory
Curaçao, Bonaire — Neth. Antilles-Integral Part of Neth. Realm
Aruba — Self governing entity within Neth. Realm
Guadeloupe — French Overseas Department
Martinique — French Overseas Department
St. Lucia, St. Vincent & The Grenadines, Trinidad & Tobago, Antigua & Barbuda, Barbados, Dominica, Grenada, St. Kitts and Nevis — Independent Nations

Canada
CONIC PROJECTION
SCALE OF MILES
0 50 100 200 300
SCALE OF KILOMETERS
0 50 100 200 300 400 500
Capitals of Countries
Provincial & Territorial Capitals
Administrative Centers
International Boundaries
Provincial Boundaries
Regional Boundaries
© Copyright HAMMOND INCORPORATED, Maplewood, N. J.
UNITED STATES
ALASKA
YUKON TERRITORY
NORTHWEST TERRITORIES
NUNAVUT
BRITISH COLUMBIA
ALBERTA
SASKATCHEWAN
MANITOBA
ONTARIO
QUÉBEC
HUDSON BAY
BAFFIN BAY
BAFFIN ISLAND
GREENLAND
DAVIS STRAIT
Hudson Str.
Ungava Peninsula
FOXE BASIN
BEAUFORT SEA
PACIFIC OCEAN
QUEEN ELIZABETH ISLANDS
Victoria Island
Banks Island
Great Bear Lake
Great Slave Lake
James Bay
ROCKY MTS.
Edmonton
Calgary
Vancouver
Victoria
Winnipeg
Regina
Saskatoon
TORONTO
Ottawa
MONTRÉAL
Québec
Seattle
Spokane
Duluth
Minneapolis
St. Paul
Milwaukee
DETROIT
Cleveland
Buffalo
NEW YORK
Longitude 90° West of Greenwich

Abitibi (lake), Ont. .... H 6
Aklavik, N.W.T. 721 .... C 2
Albany (riv.), Ont. .... H 5
Alberta (prov.) 2,365,825 ..... E 5
Amherst, N.S. 9,684 .... K 6
Amos, Que. 9,421 .... J 6
Anticosti (isl.), Que. .... K 6
Arviat, Nun. 1,022 .... G 3
Athabasca (lake) .... F 4
Athabasca (riv.), Alta. .... E 4
Axel Heiburg (isl.) Nun. .... N 3
Baffin (reg.), Nun. 8,300 ..... G 1
Baffin (bay), Nun. .... J 1
Baffin (isl.), Nun. .... J 1
Baker Lake, Nun. 954 .... G 3
Banff Nat'l Park, Alta. .... E 5
Banks (isl.), N.W.T. .... D 1
Bathurst, N. Br. 15,705 ..... K 6
Belle Isle (str.), Newf. .... L 5
Bonavista, Newf. 4,460 ..... L 6
Boothia (pen.), Nun. .... G 1
Brandon, Man. 36,242 ..... F 6
British Columbia (prov.)
2,883,367 .... D 4
Cabot (str.) .... K 6
Calgary, Alta. 592,743 .... E5
Cambridge Bay, Nun. 815 ..... F 2
Campbellton, N.Br. 9,818 ..... K 6
Camrose, Alta. 12,570 .... E 5
Cape Breton (isl.), N.S. ..... K 6
Cartwright, Newf. 658 .... L 5
Channel-Port aux Basques,
Newf. 5,988 .... L 6
Charlottetown (cap.), P.E.I.
15,282 .... K 6
Chatham, N.Br. 6,779 .... K 6
Chesterfield Inlet, Nun. 249 ... G 3
Chibougamau, Que. 10,732 ... J 6
Cnicoutimi, Que. 60,064 ..... J 6
Chidley (cape), Newf. .... K 3
Chilliwack, Br.Col. 40,642 ... D 6
Chisasibi, Que. 2,222 .... J 5
Churchill, Man. 1,186 .... G 4
Coast (mts.) .... C 4
Corner Brook, Newf. 24,339 ... K 6
Cornwall, Ont. 46,144 .... J 7
Cranbrook, Br.Col. 15,915 ..... E 6
Cree (lake), Sask. .... F 4
Dartmouth, N.S. 62,277 ..... K 7
Dauphin, Man. 8,971 .... F 5
Davis (str.), Nun. .... K 1
Dawson, Yukon 697 .... C 3
Déline, N.W.T. 521 .... D 3
Devon (isl.), Nun. .... M 3
Drumheller, Alta. 6,508 ..... E 5
Echo Bay (Port Radium),
N.W.T. 56 .... E 2
Edmonton (cap.), Alta.
532,246 .... E 5
Edmundston, N.Br. 12,044 ..... K 6
Ellesmere (isl.), Nun. .... N 3
Estevan, Sask. 9,174 .... F 6
Finlay (riv.), Br.Col. .... D 4
Flin Flon, Man.-Sask. 8,261 ... F 4
Fogo (isl.), Newf. .... L 6
Fort Frances, Ont. 8,906 ..... G 6
Fort McMurray, Alta. 31,000 ... E 4
Fort McPherson, N.W.T. 632 ... C 2
Fort Nelson, Br.Col. 3,724 ..... D 4
Fort Providence, N.W.T. 605 ... E 3
Fort Saskatchewan, Alta.
12,169 .... E 5
Fort Simpson, N.W.T. 980 ..... D 3
Fort Smith, (reg.), N.W.T.
22,384 .... E 3
Fort Smith, N.W.T. 2,298 ..... E 3
Foxe (basin), Nun. .... J 2
Fraser (riv.), Br.Col. .... D 5
Fredericton, N.Br. 43,723 ..... K 6
Fundy (bay) .... K 7
Gander, Newf. 10,404 .... L 6
Gaspé, Que. 17,261 .... K 6
Georgian (bay), Ont. .... H 6
Geraldton, Ont. 2,956 .... H 6
Glace Bay, N.S. 21,466 .... L 6
Goose Bay, Newf. 7,103 ..... K 5
Gouin (res.), Que. .... J 6
Grand Falls, Newf. 8,765 ..... L 6
Grand Prairie, Alta. 24,263 ..... E 4
Great Bear (lake), N.W.T. ..... D 2
Great Slave (lake), N.W.T. ..... E 3
Guelph, Ont. 71,207 .... H 7
Halifax (cap.), N.S. 114,594 ... K 7
Hamilton, Ont. 306,434 ..... H 7
Harbour Grace, Newf. 2,998 ... L 6
Havre-St. Pierre, Que. 3,200 ... K 5
Hay River, N.W.T. 2,863 ..... E 3
Hearst, Ont. 5,533 .... H 6
Hecate (str.) Br.Col. .... C 5
Hull, Que. 56,225 .... J 6
Inuvik, (reg.), N.W.T. 7,485 ... D 2
Inuvik, N.W.T. 3,147 .... C 2
Iqaluit (cap.), Nun. 2,333 ..... K 3
Iroquois Falls. Ont. 6,339 ..... H 6
Jasper Nat'l Park, Alta. .... E 5
Jonquière, Que. 60,354 ..... J 6
Juan de Fuca (str.), Br.Col. ..... D 6
Kamloops, Br.Col. 64,048 ..... D 5
Kane (basin), Nun. .... N 3
Kapuskasing, Ont. 12,014 ..... H 6
Keewatin (reg.), Nun. 4,327 ... G 2
Kelowna, Br.Col. 59,196 ..... E 6
Kenora, Ont. 9,817 .... G 5
Kimmirut, Nun. 252 .... J 3
Kingston, Ont. 52,616 .... J 7
Kirkland Lake, Ont. 12,219 ..... H 6
Kitikmeot (reg.), Nun. 3,245 ... F 1
Kitimat, Br.Col. 12,462 .... D 5
Kluane (lake), Yukon .... C 3
Kootenay (lake), Br.Col. ..... E 5
Kugluktuk, Nun. 809 .... E 2
Kuujjuac, Que. .... K 4
Kuujjuarapik, Que. 435 .... J 4
Labrador (reg.), Newf. .... K 4
Lacombe, Alta. 5,591 .... E 5
Lancaster (sound), Nun. ..... H 1
Leduc, Alta. 12,471 .... E 5
Lesser Slave (lake), Alta. ..... E 4
Lethbridge, Alta. 54,072 ..... E 6
Liard (riv.) .... D 3
Lloydminster, Alta.-Sask.
15,031 .... E 5
Logan (mt.), Yukon .... B 3
London, Ont. 254,280 .... H 7
Mackenzie (dist.), Nun. .... E 3
Mackenzie (riv.), N.W.T. ..... C 2
Magdalen (isls.), Que. .... K 6
Manicouagan (riv.), Que. ..... K 5
Manitoba (lake), Man. .... G 5
Manitoba (prov.), 1,063,016 ... G 5
Manitoulin (isl.), Ont. .... H 6
Maple Creek, Sask. 2,470 ..... F 6
Marathon, Ont. 2,271 .... H 6
Mayo, Yukon 398 .... C 3
M'Clintock (chan.), Nun. ..... F 1
Medicine Hat. Alta. 40,380 ..... E 5
Melville, Sask. 5,092 .... F 5
Melville, (isl.), N.W.T., Nun. ... E 1
Merritt, Br.Col. 6,110 .... D 5
Minto (lake), Que. .... J 4
Mistassibi (riv.), Que. .... J 5
Mistassini (lake), Que. .... J 5
Moncton, N.Br. 54,743 .... K 6
Mont-Joli, Que. 6,359 .... K 6
Mont-Laurier, Que. 8,405 ..... J 6
Montréal, Que. 980,354 ..... J 7
Moose Jaw, Sask. 33,941 ..... F 6
Moosonim, Sask. 2,579 ..... F 5
Moosonee, Ont. 1,433 .... H 5
Morden, Man. 4,579 .... G 6
Nain, Newf. 938 .... K 4
Nanaimo, Br.Col. 47,069 ..... D 6
Nares (str.), Nun. .... N 3
Nelson, Br.Col. 9,143 .... E 6
Nelson (riv.), Man. .... G 4
New Brunswick (prov.)
709,442 .... K 6
Newfoundland (isl.) .... L 6
Newfoundland (prov.) 568,349 . L 5
New Westminster, Br.Col.
38,550 .... D 6
Niagara Falls, Ont. 70,960 ..... J 7
Norman Wells, N.W.T. 420 ..... D 2
North Battleford, Sask.
14,030 .... F 5
North Bay, Ont. 51,268 .... J 6
North Magnetic Pole .... F 1
North Saskatchewan (riv.) ..... E 5
N. Vancouver, Br.Col. 33,952 .. D 6
Northwest Territories
39,672 .... D 3
Nove Scotia (prov.)
873,176 .... K 7
Nunavut (terr.) 24,730 .... G 3
Okanagan (lake), Br.Col. ..... D 6
Ontario (prov.) 9,101,694 ..... H 5
Ottawa (cap.), Canada
295,163 .... J 6
Ottawa (riv.) .... J 6
Owen Sound, Ont. 19,883 ..... H 7
Pangnirtung, Nun. 839 .... K 2
Parry (chan.), Nun. .... E-H 1
Parry sound, Ont. 6,124 ..... J 6
Peace (riv.), Alta. .... E 4
Peel (riv.) .... C 2
Pelly (riv.), Yukon .... C 3
Pembroke, Ont. 14,026 ..... J 6
Péribonca (riv.), Que. .... J 5
Peterborough, Ont. 60,620 ..... J 7
Pincher Creek, Alta. 3,757 ..... E 6
Pond Inlet, Nun. 705 .... J 1
Portage la Prairie, Man.
13,086 .... G 5
Povungnituk, Que. .... J 3
Prince Albert, Sask. 31,380 ... F 5
Prince Albert Nat'l Park, Sask. . F 5
Prince Edward Island (prov.)
126,646 .... K 6
Prince George, Br.Col.
67,559 .... D 5
Prince Patrick (isl.), Nun. ..... M 3
Prince Rupert, Br.Col. 16,197 .. C 5
Québec (prov.) 6,532,461 ..... J 5
Québec (cap.), Que. 166,474 .. J 6
Queen Charlotte (isls.),
Br.Col. .... C 5
Queen Elizabeth (isls.),
Nun. .... M 3
Quesnel, Br.Col. 8,240 .... D 5
Race (cape), Newf. .... L 6
Rainy (lake), Ont. .... G 5
Rainy River, Ont. 1,061 ..... G 6
Rankin Inlet, Nun. 1,109 ..... G 3
Ray (cape), Newf. .... K 6
Red Deer, Alta. 46,393 .... E 5
Regina (cap.), Sask. 162,613 .. F 5
Reindeer (lake) .... F 4
Revelstoke, Br.Col. 5,544 ..... E 5
Riding Mountain Nat'l Park,
Man. .... F 5
Rimouski, Que. 29,120 ..... K 6
Rivière-du-Loup, Que. 13,459 . K 6
Roberval, Que. 11,429 .... J 6
Robson (mt.), Br.Col. .... D 5
Rocky (mts.) .... D 4
Rocky Mountain House, Alta.
4,698 .... E 5
Rouyn, Que. 17,224 .... J 6
Sable (cape), N.S. .... K 7
Sable (isl.), N.S. .... L 7
Saint Elias (mt.), Yukon ..... B 3
Saint John, N.Br. 80,521 ..... K 6
St. John's (cap.), Newf.
83,770 .... L 6
Saint Lawrence (riv.) .... K 6

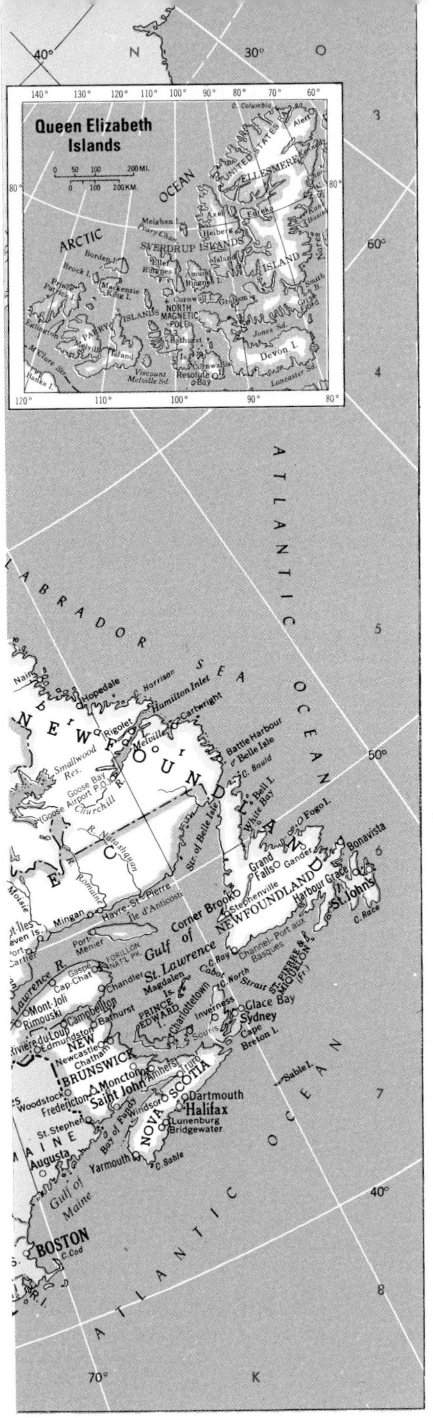
Queen Elizabeth Islands
ARCTIC
OCEAN
ELLESMERE
SVERDRUP ISLANDS
PARRY ISLANDS
NORTH MAGNETIC POLE
Devon I.
Melville Island
Banks I.
ATLANTIC
OCEAN
LABRADOR
SEA
NEWFOUNDLAND
Hopedale
Hamilton Inlet
Cartwright
Rigolet
Smallwood Res.
Goose Bay
Churchill
Battle Harbour
Belle Isle
C. Bauld
Bell I.
White Bay
Fogo I.
Bonavista
Grand Falls
Gander
Corner Brook
Stephenville
St. John's
C. Race
Harbour Grace
Channel-Port aux Basques
Mingan
Havre-St-Pierre
Île d'Anticosti
Sept-Îles
Gaspé
Gulf of St. Lawrence
Magdalen Is.
PRINCE EDWARD I.
Charlottetown
Cabot Strait
Glace Bay
Sydney
Cape Breton I.
Mont-Joli
Rimouski
Campbellton
Bathurst
Chandler
NEW BRUNSWICK
Newcastle
Chatham
Moncton
Fredericton
Saint John
Woodstock
St. Stephen
Amherst
Truro
NOVA SCOTIA
Windsor
Dartmouth
Halifax
Lunenburg
Bridgewater
Yarmouth
C. Sable
Sable I.
Augusta
Gulf of Maine
BOSTON
C. Cod
70°
K

AREA 3,851,787 sq. mi. (9,976,139 sq. km.)
POPULATION 29,123,194
CAPITAL Ottawa
LARGEST CITY Montréal
HIGHEST POINT Mt. Logan 19,524 ft. (5,951 m.)
MONETARY UNIT Canadian dollar
MAJOR LANGUAGES English, French
MAJOR RELIGIONS Protestantism, Roman Catholicism

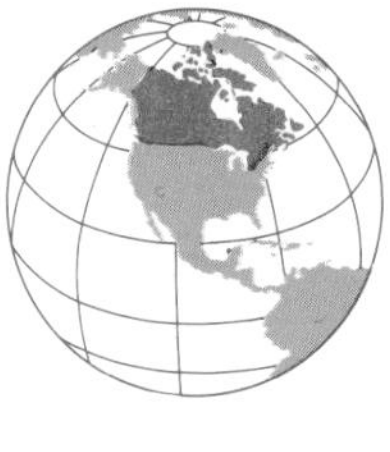

Population Distribution

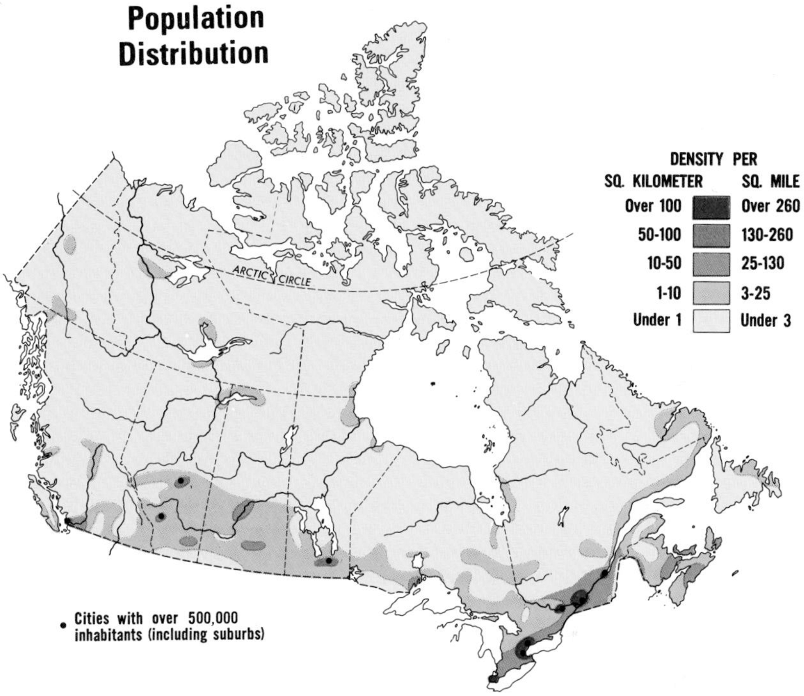
DENSITY PER
SQ. KILOMETER
SQ. MILE
Over 100
Over 260
50-100
130-260
10-50
25-130
1-10
3-25
Under 1
Under 3
ARCTIC CIRCLE
Cities with over 500,000 inhabitants (including suburbs)

Vegetation

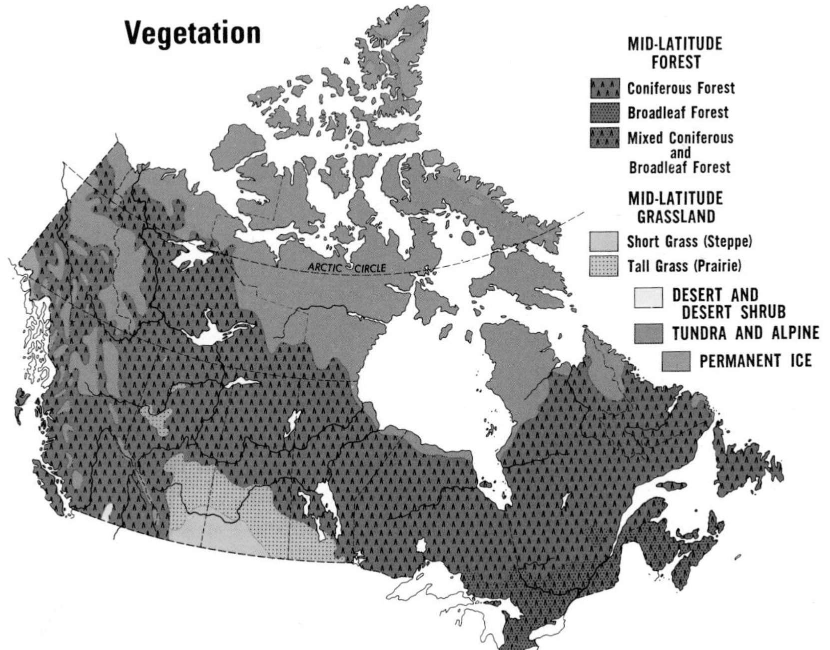
MID-LATITUDE FOREST
Coniferous Forest
Broadleaf Forest
Mixed Coniferous and Broadleaf Forest
MID-LATITUDE GRASSLAND
Short Grass (Steppe)
Tall Grass (Prairie)
DESERT AND DESERT SHRUB
TUNDRA AND ALPINE
PERMANENT ICE
ARCTIC CIRCLE

○ Population of municipality

Average January Temperature

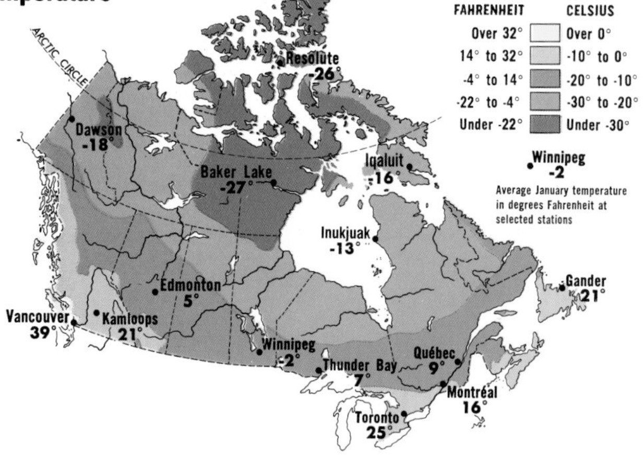
FAHRENHEIT
CELSIUS
Over 32° Over 0°
14° to 32° -10° to 0°
-4° to 14° -20° to -10°
-22° to -4° -30° to -20°
Under -22° Under -30°
Winnipeg -2
Average January temperature in degrees Fahrenheit at selected stations
ARCTIC CIRCLE
Resolute -26°
Dawson -18°
Baker Lake -27°
Iqaluit -16°
Inukjuak -13°
Gander 21°
Edmonton 5°
Vancouver 39°
Kamloops 21°
Winnipeg -2°
Thunder Bay 7°
Québec 9°
Montréal 16°
Toronto 25°

Average July Temperature

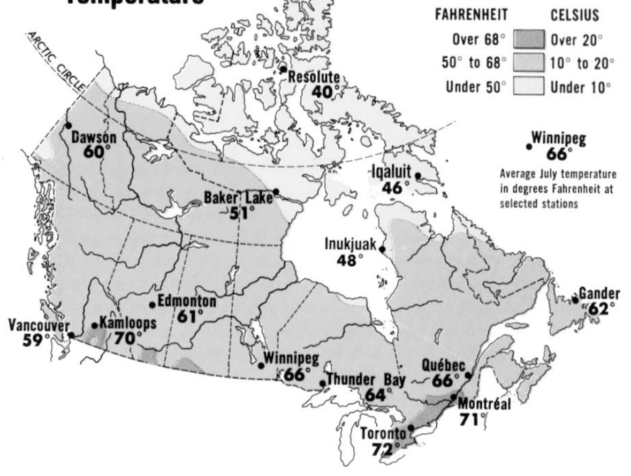
FAHRENHEIT
CELSIUS
Over 68° Over 20°
50° to 68° 10° to 20°
Under 50° Under 10°
Winnipeg 66°
Average July temperature in degrees Fahrenheit at selected stations
ARCTIC CIRCLE
Resolute 40°
Dawson 60°
Iqaluit 46°
Baker Lake 51°
Inukjuak 48°
Gander 62°
Edmonton 61°
Vancouver 59°
Kamloops 70°
Winnipeg 66°
Thunder Bay 64°
Québec 66°
Montréal 71°
Toronto 72°

Agriculture, Industry and Resources

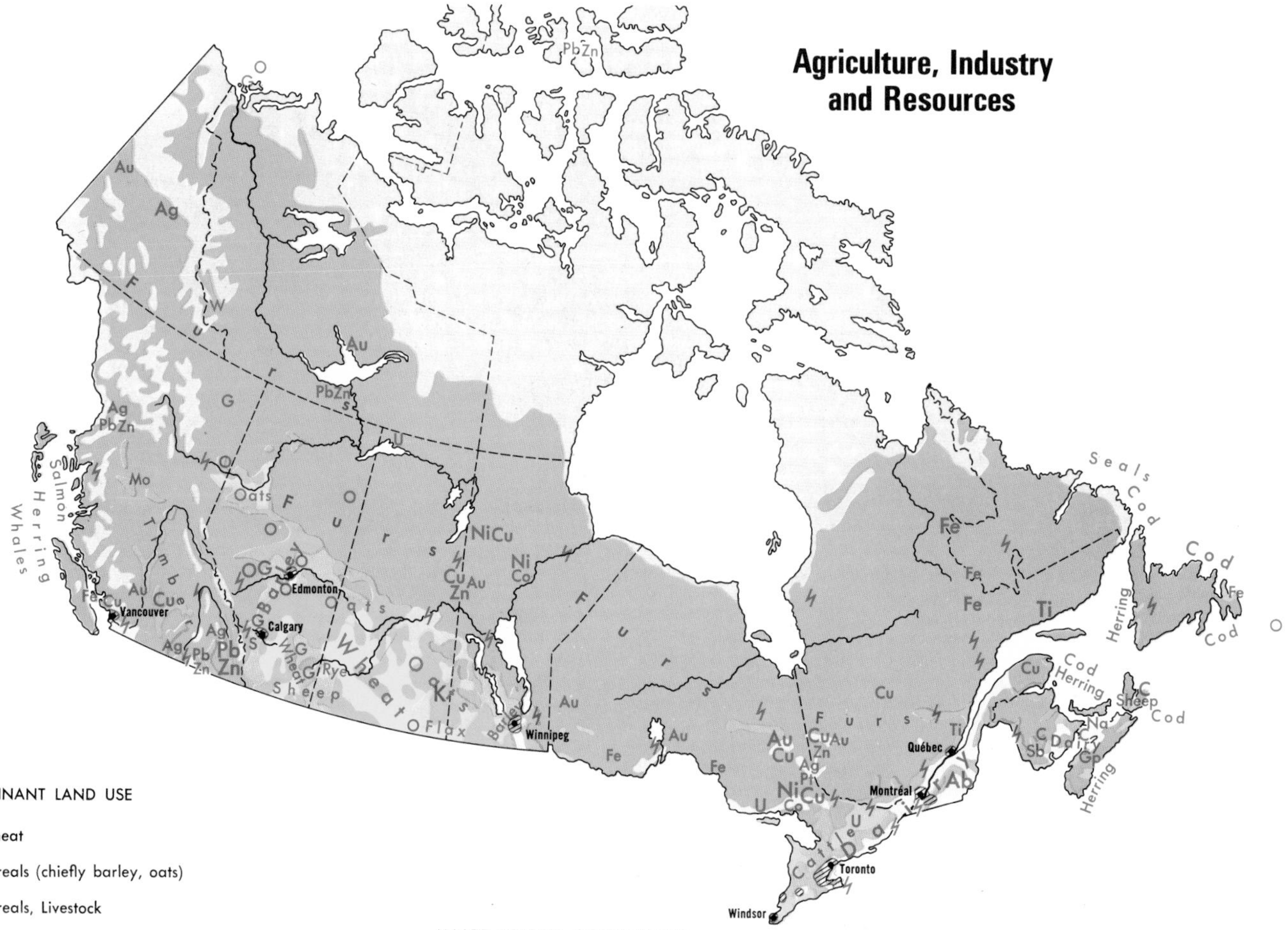
Edmonton
Calgary
Vancouver
Winnipeg
Toronto
Windsor
Québec
Montréal
Salmon
Herring
Whales
Seals
Cod
Furs
Timber
Oats
Wheat
Sheep
Flax
Barley
Rye
Dairy
Cattle

DOMINANT LAND USE

- Wheat
- Cereals (chiefly barley, oats)
- Cereals, Livestock
- General Farming, Livestock
- Dairy
- Fruit, Vegetables
- Pasture Livestock
- Range Livestock
- Forests
- Nonagricultural Land

MAJOR MINERAL OCCURRENCES

Ab	Asbestos	Fe	Iron Ore	Ni	Nickel	Sb	Antimony
Ag	Silver	G	Natural Gas	O	Petroleum	Ti	Titanium
Au	Gold	Gp	Gypsum	Pb	Lead	U	Uranium
C	Coal	K	Potash	Pt	Platinum	W	Tungsten
Co	Cobalt	Mo	Molybdenum	S	Sulfur	Zn	Zinc
Cu	Copper	Na	Salt				

- Water Power
- Major Industrial Areas

Rainfall

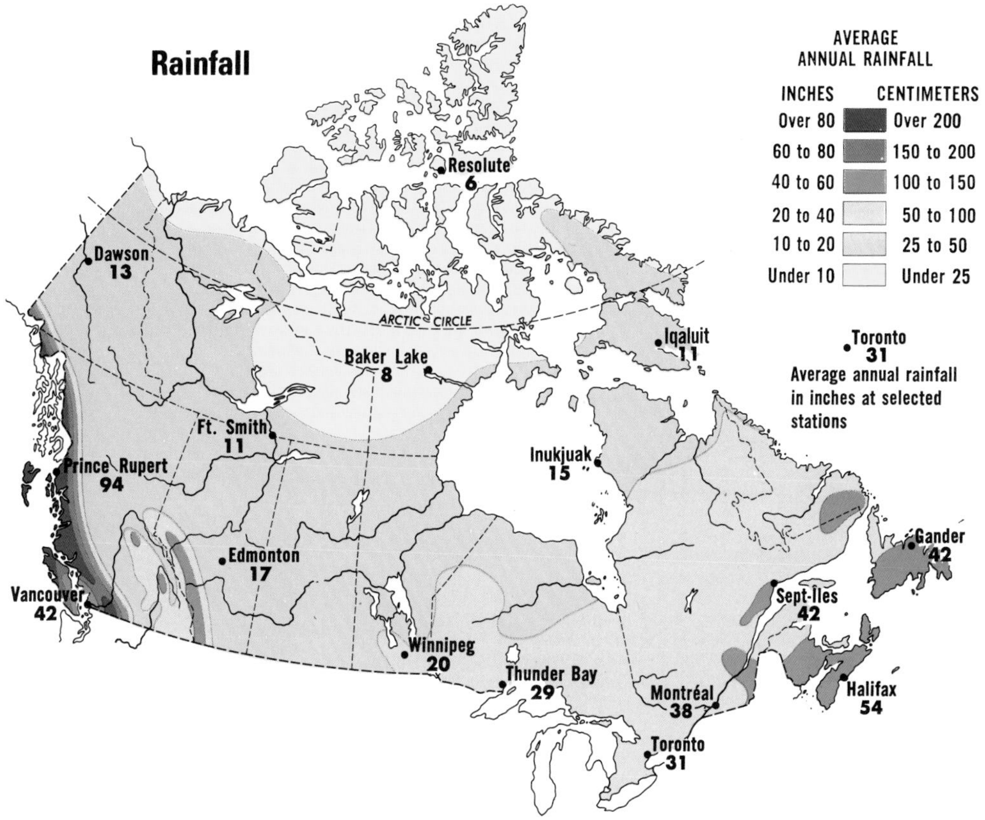
AVERAGE ANNUAL RAINFALL
INCHES
CENTIMETERS
Over 80 Over 200
60 to 80 150 to 200
40 to 60 100 to 150
20 to 40 50 to 100
10 to 20 25 to 50
Under 10 Under 25
Toronto 31
Average annual rainfall in inches at selected stations
Resolute 6
Dawson 13
ARCTIC CIRCLE
Iqaluit 11
Baker Lake 8
Ft. Smith 11
Inukjuak 15
Prince Rupert 94
Gander 42
Edmonton 17
Vancouver 42
Sept-Îles 42
Winnipeg 20
Thunder Bay 29
Montréal 38
Halifax 54
Toronto 31

Topography

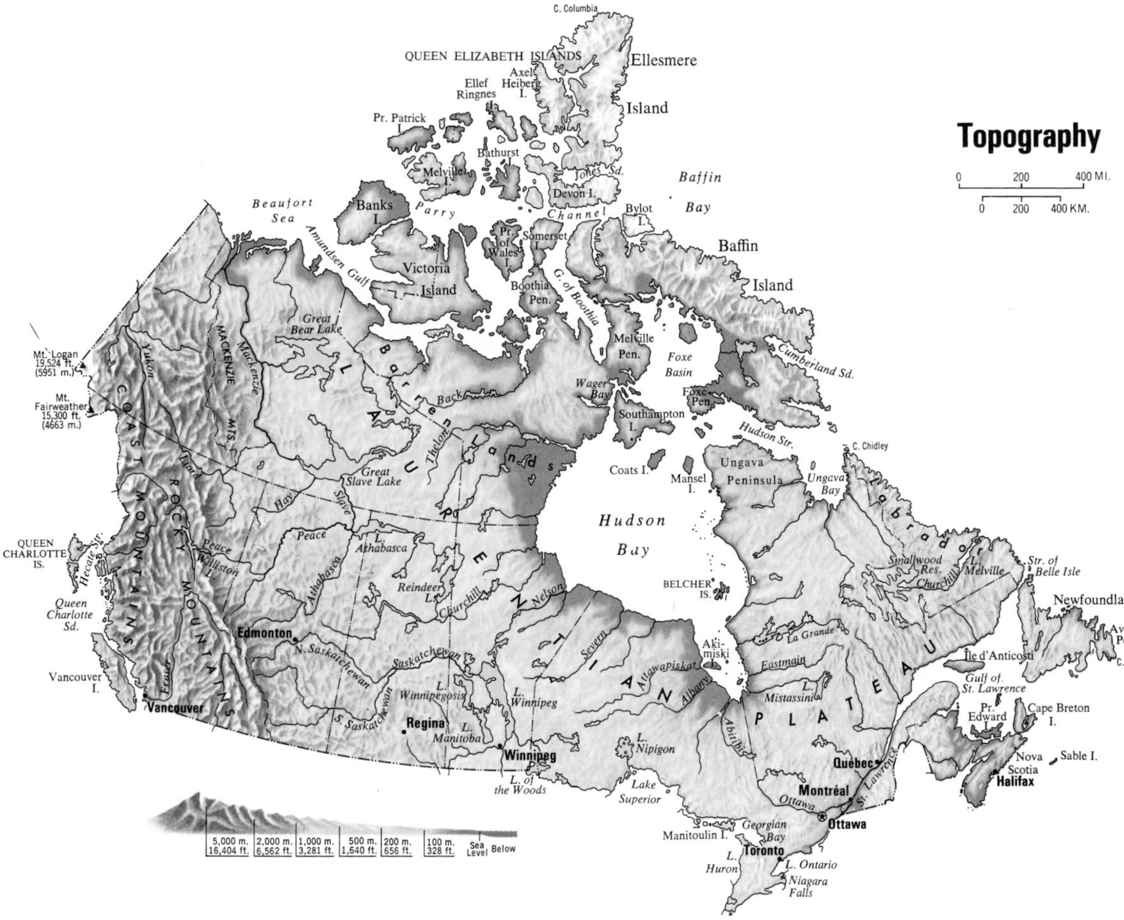
C. Columbia
QUEEN ELIZABETH ISLANDS
Ellesmere Island
Axel Heiberg I.
Ellef Ringnes I.
Pr. Patrick I.
Bathurst I.
Melville I.
Jones Sd.
Devon I.
Baffin Bay
0 200 400 MI.
0 200 400 KM.
Beaufort Sea
Banks I.
Parry Channel
Bylot I.
Baffin Island
Amundsen Gulf
Victoria Island
Pr. of Wales I.
Somerset I.
Boothia Pen.
G. of Boothia
Great Bear Lake
Mt. Logan 19,524 ft. (5951 m.)
Mt. Fairweather 15,300 ft. (4663 m.)
Yukon
MACKENZIE MTS.
Mackenzie
Barren Lands
Melville Pen.
Foxe Basin
Cumberland Sd.
Wager Bay
Back
Foxe Pen.
Southampton I.
Hudson Str.
Thelon
C. Chidley
COAST MOUNTAINS
ROCKY MOUNTAINS
Great Slave Lake
Coats I.
Mansel I.
Ungava Peninsula
Ungava Bay
Hay
Slave
LAURENTIAN PLATEAU
Labrador
Peace
Athabasca
Hudson Bay
QUEEN CHARLOTTE IS.
Hecate St.
Williston
Reindeer L.
Churchill
Smallwood Res.
L. Melville
Str. of Belle Isle
Nelson
BELCHER IS.
Newfoundland
Queen Charlotte Sd.
Edmonton
N. Saskatchewan
Saskatchewan
Severn
Akimiski I.
La Grande
Avalon Pen.
Attawapiskat
Eastmain
Île d'Anticosti
C. Race
Vancouver I.
Fraser
L. Winnipegosis
L. Winnipeg
Albany
L. Mistassini
Gulf of St. Lawrence
Vancouver
S. Saskatchewan
Regina
L. Manitoba
Abitibi
Pr. Edward I.
Cape Breton I.
Winnipeg
L. Nipigon
Québec
Sable I.
L. of the Woods
Lake Superior
St. Lawrence
Nova Scotia
Halifax
Montréal
Ottawa
Ottawa
Manitoulin I.
Georgian Bay
Toronto
L. Huron
L. Ontario
Niagara Falls
5,000 m. 16,404 ft.
2,000 m. 6,562 ft.
1,000 m. 3,281 ft.
500 m. 1,640 ft.
200 m. 656 ft.
100 m. 328 ft.
Sea Level
Below

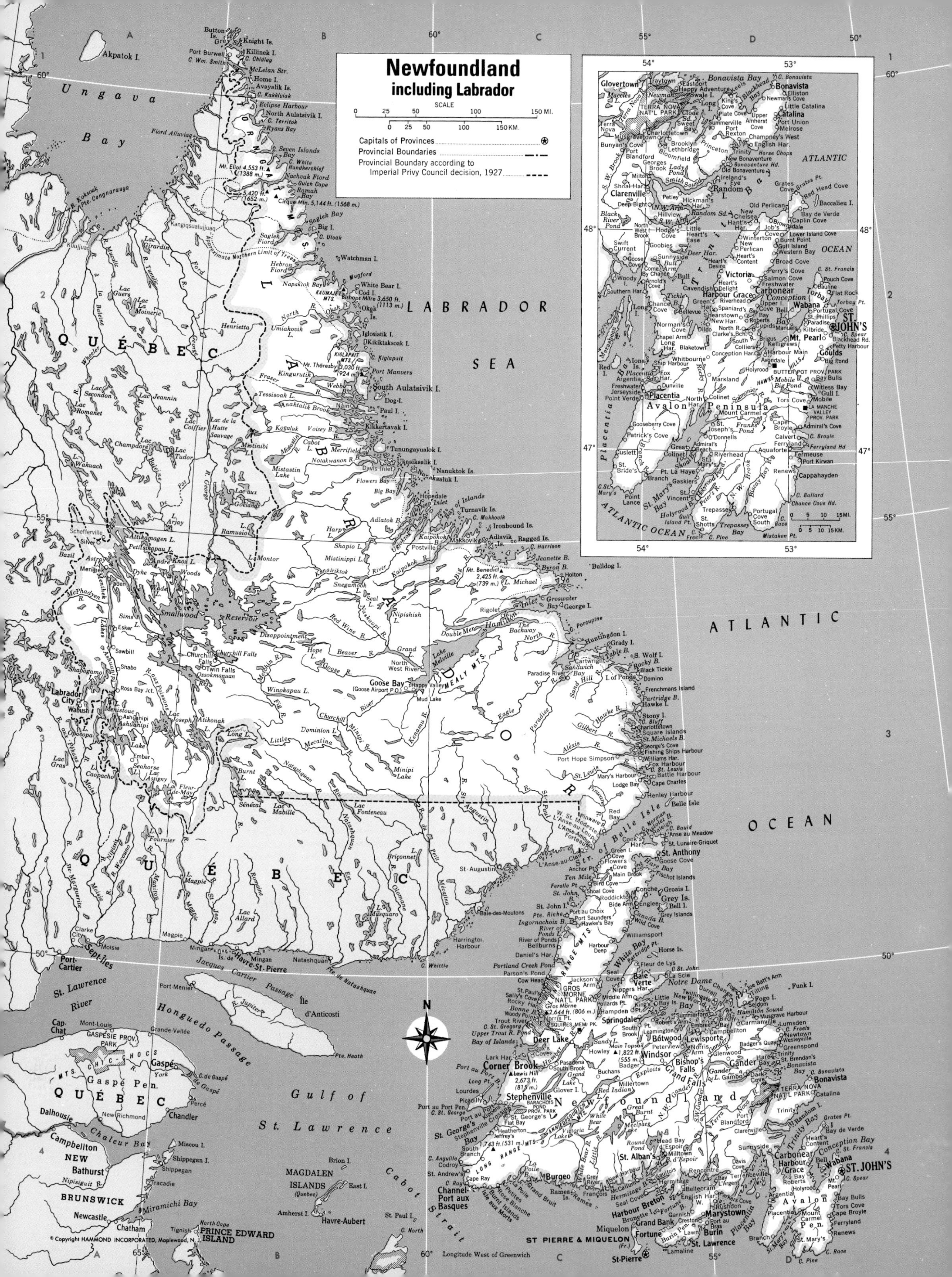

Newfoundland
including Labrador
SCALE
0 25 50 100 150 MI.
0 25 50 100 150 KM.
Capitals of Provinces
Provincial Boundaries
Provincial Boundary according to Imperial Privy Council decision, 1927
Ungava Bay
LABRADOR SEA
ATLANTIC OCEAN
QUÉBEC
LABRADOR
Smallwood Reservoir
Lake Melville
Goose Bay
Labrador City
Churchill Falls
Hamilton Inlet
Str. of Belle Isle
St. Anthony
Gulf of St. Lawrence
Cabot Strait
Honguedo Passage
Jacques Cartier Passage
Île d'Anticosti
St. Lawrence River
Gaspé Pen.
Chaleur Bay
NEW BRUNSWICK
PRINCE EDWARD ISLAND
MAGDALEN ISLANDS (Quebec)
Newfoundland
Corner Brook
Deer Lake
Stephenville
Grand Falls
Gander
Botwood
Channel-Port aux Basques
Burgeo
Harbour Breton
Marystown
Grand Bank
Burin
St. Lawrence
Carbonear
Harbour Grace
Bonavista
Wabana
ST. JOHN'S
Avalon Pen.
Trinity Bay
Conception Bay
Notre Dame Bay
White Bay
Bay of Islands
St. George's Bay
Placentia Bay
Fortune Bay
LONG RANGE MTS.
GROS MORNE NAT'L PARK
TERRA NOVA NAT'L PARK
ST PIERRE & MIQUELON (Fr.)
St-Pierre
Sept-Îles
Havre-St.-Pierre
Clarenville
Placentia
Victoria
Longitude West of Greenwich

NEWFOUNDLAND

CITIES and TOWNS

Admiral's Beach 362 D2
Admiral's Cove 99 D2
Anchor Point 368 C3
Aquaforte 200 D2
Argentia 93 C2
Arnold's Cove 1,124 C2
Avondale 890 D2
Badger 1,090 C4
Badger's Quay-Valleyfield-Pool's Island 1,566 D4
Baie Verte 2,491 C4
Battle Harbour C3
Bauline 423 D2
Bay Bulls 1,081 D2
Bay de Verde 786 D2
Bay L'Argent 483 D4
Bay Roberts 4,512 D2
Bellburns 147 C3
Belleoram 565 C4
Bellevue 286 D2
Bide Arm 339 C3
Big Pond 167 D2
Birchy Bay 707 D4
Bird Cove 400 C3
Bishop's Falls 4,395 C4
Black Tickle 194 C3
Blackhead Road 1,855 D2
Blaketown 617 D2
Bloomfield 715 D2
Bonavista 4,460 D2
Botwood 4,074 C4
Branch 462 D2
Brigus 898 D2
Broad Cove 198 D2
Brooklyn 197 D2
Brownsdale 199 D2
Buchans 1,655 C4
Bunyan's Cove 590 C2
Burgeo 2,504 C4
Burin 2,904 C4
Burnt Islands 991 C4
Burnt Point 260 D2
Calvert 482 D2
Campbellton 703 D4
Cape Broyle 698 D2
Cape Ray 484 C4
Caplin Cove 150 D2
Carbonear 5,335 D2
Carmanville 966 D4
Cartwright 658 C3
Catalina 1,162 D2
Cavendish 343 D2
Champney's West 141 D2
Chance Cove 498 D2
Change Islands 580 D4
Channel-Port aux Basques 5,988 C4
Chapel Arm 689 D2
Charlottetown 330 D2
Charlottetown 250 C3
Churchill Falls 936 B3
Clarenville 2,878 C2
Clarke's Beach 1,009 D2
Codroy 346 C4
Colinet 318 D2
Colliers 819 D2
Come By Chance 337 C2
Conception Harbour 917 D2
Conche 464 C3
Cook's Harbour 388 C3
Corner Brook 24,339 C4
Cow Head 695 C4
Cox's Cove 980 C4
Cupids 706 D2
Daniell's Harbour 614 C3
Dark Cove 1,344 D4
Davis Inlet 240 B2
Deep Bight 243 C2
Deer Lake 4,348 C4
Dildo 877 D2
Dunville 1,817 D2
Durrell 1,145 D4
Eastport 597 D1
Elliston 527 D2
Embree 846 C4
Englee 998 C3
English Harbour 118 D2
English Harbour West 327 C4
Fermeuse 584 D2
Ferryland 795 D2
Flat Bay 322 C4
Flat Rock 808 D2
Fleur de Lys 616 C3
Flowers Cove 459 C3
Fogo 1,105 D4
Forteau 520 C3
Fortune 2,473 C4
Fox Harbour 280 C3
Fox Harbour 538 D2
François 219 C4
Freshwater 1,276 C2
Freshwater 209 D2
Gambo 2,932 D4
Gander 10,404 D4
Garnish 761 C4
Gaskiers-Point la Haye 505 D2
Gaultois 558 C4
Georges Brook 356 D2
Glenwood 1,129 D4
Glovertown 2,165 C1
Goobies 185 D2
Goose Bay-Happy Valley 7,103 B3
Gooseberry Cove 195 C2
Goose Cove 134 C2
Goose Cove 368 C3
Goulds 4,242 D2
Grand Bank 3,901 C4
Grand Falls 8,765 C4
Grates Cove 275 D2
Green Island Cove 222 C3
Green's Harbour 785 D2
Greenspond 423 D4
Grey River 234 C4
Gull Island 362 D2
Hampden 838 C4
Hant's Harbour 542 D2
Happy Adventure 352 D2
Happy Valley-Goose Bay 7,103 B3
Harbour Breton 2,464 C4
Harbour Deep 278 C3
Harbour Grace 2,988 D2
Harbour Main-Chapel Cove-Lakeview 1,303 D2
Hare Bay 1,520 D4
Hawke's Bay 553 C3
Head of Bay d'Espoir 586 C4
Heart's Content 625 D2
Heart's Delight-Islington 899 D2
Heart's Desire 416 D2
Heatherton 328 C4
Hermitage 863 C4
Hickman's Harbour 479 D2
Hillview 295 D2
Hodge's Cove 438 D2
Holyrood 1,789 D2
Hopedale 425 B2
Howley 456 C4
Isle aux Morts 1,238 C4
Jackson's Arm 623 C4
Jeffrey's 276 C4
Jerseyside 641 B3
Job's Cove 201 D2
Joe Batt's Arm-Barr'd Islands 1,155 D4
Keels 129 D1
Kelligrews (Foxtrap-Greeleytown-Peachtown-Kelligrews) 2,292 D2
Kilbride 5,014 D2
King's Cove 253 D1
King's Point 825 C4
Kippens 1,219 C4
Labrador City 11,538 A3
Lamaline 548 C4
L'Anse-au-Clair 267 C3
L'Anse-au-Loup 589 C3
L'Anse au Meadow 66 C3
La Poile 186 C4
Lark Harbour 783 C4
La Scie 1,422 C4
Lawn 999 C4
Lethbridge 686 D2
Lewisporte 3,963 C4
Little Bay Islands 407 C4
Little Catalina 750 D2
Little Heart's Ease 467 D2
Lodge Bay 124 C3
Long Harbour-Mount Arlington Heights 660 D2
Lourdes 932 C4
Lower Island Cove 415 D2
Lumsden 645 D4
Main Brook 514 C3
Makkovik 347 C2
Markland 344 D2
Mary's Harbour 408 C3
Marystown 6,299 D4
McCallum 243 C4
Melrose 416 D2
Middle Arm, Green Bay 575 C4
Millertown 228 C4
Milltown-Head of Bay d'Espoir 1,376 C4
Milton 258 C2
Mobile 171 D2
Mount Carmel-Mitchell's Brook-St. Catherine's 699 D2
Mount Pearl 11,543 D2
Musgrave Harbour 1,554 D4
Musgravetown 635 C2
Nain 938 B2
New Bonaventure 106 D2
New Chelsea 144 D2
New Harbour 777 D2
Newmans Cove 231 D2
New Perlican 350 D2
Newtown 511 D4
Nippers Harbour 259 C4
Norman's Cove-Long Cove 1,152 D2
Norris Arm 1,216 C4
Norris Point 1,033 C4
North Harbour 151 D2
North River 245 D2
North West Brook 279 C2
North West River 515 B3
O'Donnells 280 D2
Old Bonaventure 111 D2
Old Perlican 709 D2
Paradise 2,861 D2
Parkers Cove 424 D4
Parson's Pond 605 C3
Pasadena 2,685 C4
Patrick's Cove 155 C2
Perry's Cove 141 D2
Peterview 1,119 C4
Petites 108 C4
Petley 147 D2
Petty Harbour-Maddox Cove 853 D2
Picadilly 524 C4
Pinware River 201 C3
Placentia 2,204 C2
Plate Cove 474 D2
Point La Haye 195 D2
Point Lance 141 C2
Point Leamington 848 C4
Point Verde 296 C2
Pollards Point 502 C4
Port au Bras 366 D4
Port au Choix 1,311 C3
Port au Port 603 C4
Port Blandford 702 C2
Port Hope Simpson 581 C3
Port Kirwan 164 D2
Port Rexton 489 D2
Port Saunders 769 C3
Portugal Cove 2,361 D2
Portugal Cove South 371 D2
Port Union 671 D2
Postville 223 B3
Pouch Cove 1,522 D2
Princeton 204 D2
Raleigh 373 C3
Ramea 1,386 C4
Red Bay 316 C3
Red Head Cove 225 D2
Rencontre East 230 C4
Renews-Cappahayden 578 D2
Rigolet 271 C3
Riverhead 431 D2
River of Ponds 304 C3
Robert's Arm 1,005 C4
Rocky Harbour 1,273 C4
Roddickton 1,142 C3
Rose Blanche-Harbour le Cou 975 C4
Rushoon 520 D4
Saint Alban's 1,968 C4
Saint Andrew's 262 C4
Saint Anthony 3,107 C3
Saint Brendan's 468 D4
Saint Bride's 599 C2
Saint George's 1,756 C4
St. John's (cap.) 83,770 D2
Saint Joseph's 262 D2
Saint Lawrence 2,012 C4
Saint Lunaire-Griquet 1,010 C3
Saint Mary's 701 D2
Saint Paul's 454 C4
Saint Phillips 1,365 D2
Saint Shotts 239 D2
Saint Vincent's-Saint Stephens-Peter's River 796 D2
Sally's Cove 100 C4
Salmon Cove 786 D2
Seal Cove 751 C3
Seal Cove-White Bay 498 C4
Seldom-Little Seldom 560 D4
Ship Harbour 265 D2
Shoal Cove 223 C3
Shoal Harbour 1,000 C2
South Branch 264 C4
South Brook, Hall's Bay Dist. 786 C4
South Brook, Humber Dist. 477 C4
Southern Harbour 772 C2
South River 645 D2
Spaniard's Bay 2,125 D2
Springdale 3,501 C4
Stephenville 8,876 C4
Stephenville Crossing 2,172 C4
Summerford 1,198 C4
Summerville 346 D2
Sunnyside 703 D2
Sweet Bay 204 D2
Swift Current 329 C2
Terrenceville 796 D4
Tilting 427 D4
Torbay 3,394 D2
Tors Cove 355 D2
Traytown 383 D1
Trepassey 1,473 D2
Trinity 522 D2
Trinity 375 D4
Trout River 759 C4
Twillingate 1,506 C4
Upper Island Cove 2,025 D2
Victoria 1,870 D2
Wabana 4,254 D2
Wabush 3,155 A3
Wesleyville 1,125 D4
Western Bay 463 D2
West Saint Modeste 273 C3
Whitbourne 1,233 D2
Wild Cove 152 C3
Windsor 5,747 C4
Winterton 753 D2
Witless Bay 907 D2

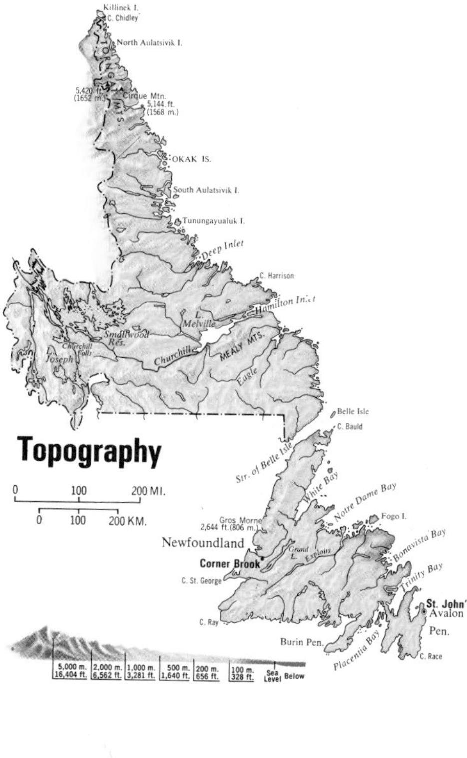

Killinek I.
C. Chidley
North Aulatsivik I.
5,420 ft. (1652 m.)
Cirque Mtn. 5,144 ft. (1568 m.)
OKAK IS.
South Aulatsivik I.
Tunungayualuk I.
Deep Inlet
C. Harrison
Hamilton Inlet
Melville
Smallwood Res.
Churchill
MEALY MTS.
Eagle
Belle Isle
C. Bauld
Str. of Belle Isle
White Bay
Notre Dame Bay
Fogo I.
Gros Morne 2,644 ft. (806 m.)
Newfoundland
Corner Brook
C. St. George
C. Ray
Burin Pen.
Placentia Bay
Trinity Bay
Bonavista Bay
St. John's
Avalon Pen.
C. Race
Topography
0 100 200 MI.
0 100 200 KM.
5,000 m. 16,404 ft.
2,000 m. 6,562 ft.
1,000 m. 3,281 ft.
500 m. 1,640 ft.
200 m. 656 ft.
100 m. 328 ft.
Sea Level
Below

OTHER FEATURES

Alexis (riv.) C3
Anguille (cape) C4
Annieopscotch (mts.) C4
Ashuanipi (lake) A3
Ashuanipi (riv.) A3
Atikonak (lake) B3
Attikamagen (lake) A3
Avalon (pen.) D2
Barachois Pond Prov. Park C4
Bauld (cape) C3
Bell (isl.) C3
Bell (isl.) D2
Belle Isle (isl.) C3
Belle Isle (str.) C3
Blackhead (bay) D2
Bonavista (bay) D1
Bonavista (cape) D1
Bonne (bay) C4
Branch (riv.) C2
Broyle (cape) D2
Bull Arm (inlet) D2
Burin (pen.) C4
Butter Pot Prov. Park D2
Cabot (str.) B4
Canada (bay) C3
Chidley (cape) B1
Churchill (falls) B3
Churchill (riv.) B3
Cirque (mt.) B2
Clode (sound) D2
Conception (bay) D2
Deep (inlet) B2
Double Mer (lake) C3
Dyke (lake) A3
Eagle (riv.) C3
Espoir (bay) C4
Exploits (riv.) C4
Fogo (isl.) D4
Fortune (bay) C4
Freels (cape) D3
Gander (lake) D4
Gander (riv.) D4
Glover (isl.) C4
Goose (riv.) B3
Grand (lake) B3
Grand (lake) C4
Grates (pt.) D2
Great Colinet (isl.) D2
Grey (isls.) C3
Groais (isl.) C3
Gros Morne (mt.) C4
Gros Morne Nat'l Park C4
Groswater (bay) C3
Hamilton (inlet) C3
Hamilton (sound) D4
Hare (bay) C3
Hawke (hills) D2
Hebron (fjord) B2
Hermitage (bay) C4
Holyrood (bay) D2
Horse (isls.) C3
Horse Chops (head) D2
Humber (riv.) C4
Ingornachoix (bay) C3
Ireland's Eye (isl.) D2
Islands (bay) C4
Kaipokok (bay) B2
Kanairiktok (riv.) B3
Kaumajet (mts.) B2
Kingurutik (mesa) B2
Labrador (reg.) B2
Labrador (sea) C2
La Manche Valley Prov. Park D2
La Poile (bay) C4
Little Mecatina (riv.) B3
Long (isl.) C2
Long (lake) A3
Long (pt.) C4
Long Range (mts.) C4
Main Topsail (mt.) C4
Makkovik (cape) C2
McLelan (str.) B1
Mealy (lake) C3
Meelpaeg (lake) C4
Melville (lake) C3
Menihek (lakes) A3
Merasheen (isl.) C2
Mistaken (pt.) D2
Mistastin (lake) B2
Nachvak (fjord) B2
Naskaupi (riv.) B3
Newfoundland (isl.) C4
Newman (sound) D2
New World (isl.) D4
Norman (cape) C3
North Aulatsivik (isl.) B2
Notre Dame (bay) C4
Okak (bay) B2
Ossokmanuan (res.) B3
Petitsikapau (lake) A3
Pine (cape) D2
Pinware (riv.) C3
Pistolet (bay) C3
Placentia (bay) C2
Ponds (isl.) C3
Port au Port (bay) C4
Port au Port (pen.) C4
Port Manvers (harb.) B2
Race (cape) D2
Ramah (bay) B2
Ramea (isls.) C4
Random (isl.) D2
Random (sound) D2
Ray (cape) C4
Red (isl.) C2
Red Indian (lake) C4
Red Wine (riv.) B3
Rocky (riv.) D2
Round (pond) C4
Saglek (bay) B2
Saint Francis (cape) D2
Saint George (cape) C4
Saint George's (bay) C4
Saint John (bay) C3
Saint John (cape) C3
Saint Lawrence (gulf) B4
Saint Lewis (cape) C3
Saint Mary's (bay) C2
Saint Mary's (cape) C2
Saint Michaels (bay) C3
Salmonier (riv.) D2
Sandwich (bay) C3
Shabogamo (lake) A3
Shoal (bay) D2
Smallwood (res.) B3
Smith (sound) D2
South Aulatsivik (isl.) B2
Spear (cape) D2
Squires Mem. Park C4
Swale (isl.) D1
Terra Nova (riv.) C2
Terra Nova Nat'l Park D2
Territok (cape) B2
Thoresby (mt.) B2
Torbay (pt.) D2
Torngat (mts.) B2
Trespassey (bay) D2
Trinity (bay) D2
Tunungayualok (isl.) B2
Ukasiksalik (isl.) B2
Victoria (lake) C4
White (bay) C3
White Bear (lake) C4
White Handkerchief (cape) B2

SAINT PIERRE and MIQUELON

CITIES and TOWNS

Saint-Pierre (cap.) 5,415 C4

OTHER FEATURES

Miquelon (isl.) 626 C4
Saint Pierre (isl.) 5,415 C4

AREA 156,184 sq. mi. (404,517 sq. km.)
POPULATION 568,349
CAPITAL St. John's
LARGEST CITY St. John's
HIGHEST POINT in Torngat Mountains 5,420 ft. (1,652 m.)
SETTLED IN 1610
ADMITTED TO CONFEDERATION 1949
PROVINCIAL FLOWER Pitcher Plant

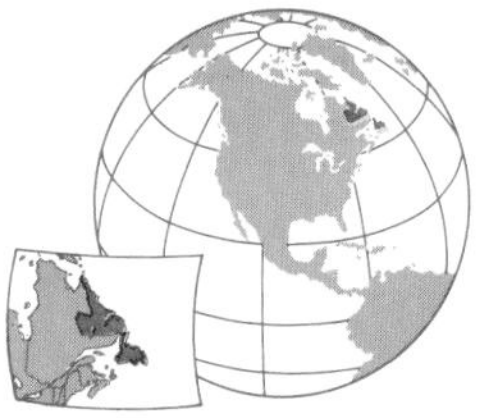

Agriculture, Industry and Resources

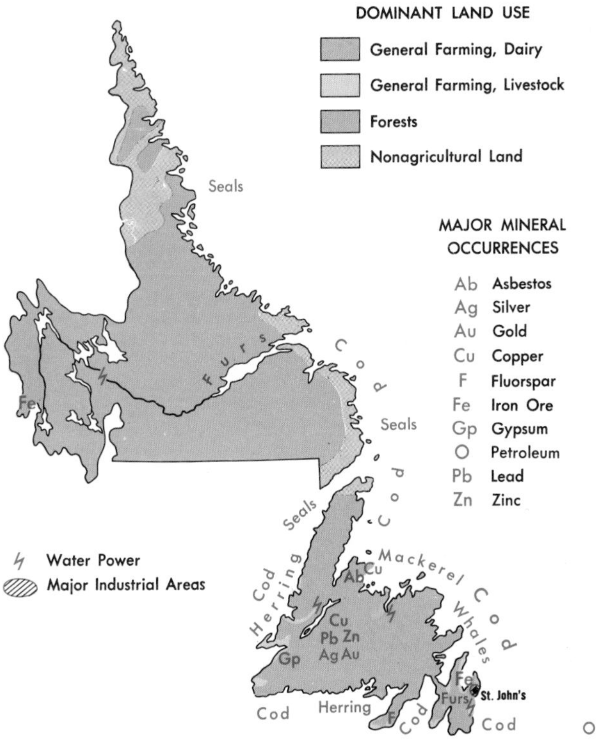

DOMINANT LAND USE
General Farming, Dairy
General Farming, Livestock
Forests
Nonagricultural Land
MAJOR MINERAL OCCURRENCES
Ab Asbestos
Ag Silver
Au Gold
Cu Copper
F Fluorspar
Fe Iron Ore
Gp Gypsum
O Petroleum
Pb Lead
Zn Zinc
Water Power
Major Industrial Areas
Seals
Furs
Cod
Herring
Mackerel
Whales
St. John's

NOVA SCOTIA

COUNTIES

Annapolis 22,522 .... C 4
Antigonish 18,110.......... F 3
Cape Breton 127,035........ H 3
Colchester 43,224 .... E 3
Cumberland 35,231 .... D 3
Digby 21,689 .... C 4
Guysborough 12,752 .... F 3
Halifax 288,126 .... E 4
Hants 33,121 .... D 4
Inverness 22,337 .... G 2
Kings 49,739 .... D 4
Lunenburg 45,746........... D 4
Pictou 50,350 .... F 3
Queens 13,126 .... C 4
Richmond 12,284 .... H 3
Shelburne 17,328 .... C 5
Victoria 8,432 .... H 2
Yarmouth 26,290............ C 5

CITIES and TOWNS

Alder Point 651 .... H 2
Aldershot .... D 3
Amherst⊙ 9,684 .... D 3
Annapolis Royal⊙ 631 .... C 4
Antigonish⊙ 5,205 .... F 3
Arichat 824................ H 3
Aylesford 744............... D 3
Baddeck⊙ 972............... H 2
Barrington Passage 722 ..... C 5
Bear River-Sissiboo 854 ..... C 4
Beaverbank 1,322........... E 4
Berwick 1,699 .... D 4
Bridgetown 1,047 .... C 4
Bridgewater 6,669........... D 4
Brookfield 619 .... E 3
Brooklyn 1,269 .... D 4
Cambridge Station 799 ...... D 3
Canning 763 .... D 3
Canso 1,255 .... H 3
Centreville 765 .... D 3
Chéticamp 1,022............ G 2
Chester 1,131 .... D 4
Chester Basin 639 .... D 4
Church Point 318 .... B 4
Clark's Harbour 1,059 .... C 5
Coldbrook Station 617 .... D 3
Cow Bay 670................ E 4
Dartmouth 62,277............ E 4
Debert 618.................. E 3
Digby⊙ 2,558................ C 4
Dominion 2,856.............. J 2
Donkin 873.................. J 2
Ellershouse-Hartville 662 .... D 4
Elmsdale 1,172.............. E 4
Enfield 1,510 .... E 4
Fall River 1,897............. E 4
Falmouth 1,110.............. D 3
Glace Bay 21,466............ J 2
Guysborough⊙ 496........... G 3
Halifax (cap.)⊙ 114,594...... E 4
Halifax *277,727 .... E 4
Hantsport 1,395 .... D 3
Herring Cove 1,323.......... E 4
Hilden 1,262 .... E 3
Ingonish 471 .... H 2
Inverness 2,013............. G 2
Judique 925................ G 3
Kentville⊙ 4,974 .... D 3
Kingston 1,612 .... D 4
Lakeside 936............... E 4
Lantz 1,172 .... E 4
Liverpool⊙ 3,304............ D 4
Lockeport 929 .... C 5
Louisbourg 1,410 .... J 3
Louisdale 979 .... G 3
Lower West Pubnico 790..... C 5
Lunenburg⊙ 3,014 .... D 4
Mahone Bay 1,228 .... D 4
Meteghan 890............... B 4
Middleton 1,834 .... C 4
Milford Station 748 .... E 3
Milton 1,678................ D 4
Mount Uniacke 1,145........ E 4
Mulgrave 1,099 .... G 3
Musquodoboit Harbour 936... E 4
New Glasgow 10,464........ F 3
New Victoria 1,374.......... H 2
New Waterford 8,808........ J 2
North Sydney 7,820 .... H 2
Oxford 1,470 .... E 3
Parrsboro 1,799............. D 3
Pictou⊙ 4,628 .... F 3
Porters Lake 893............ E 4
Port Hastings 312........... G 3
Port Hawkesbury 3,850 ...... G 3
Port Hood⊙ 701............. G 2
Port Morien 717............. J 2
Port Williams 1,227.......... D 3
Prospect 693 .... E 4
Pugwash 648............... E 3
Reserve Mines 2,472........ H 2
River Hébert 835............ D 3
Saint Peters 669 .... H 3
Sandy Point 691 .... C 5
Scotchtown 2,037........... H 2
Sheet Harbour 819.......... F 4
Shelburne⊙ 2,303........... C 5
Shubenacadie 984 .... E 3
Springhill 4,896............. E 3
Stellarton 5,435............. F 3
Stewiacke 1,174 .... E 3
Sydney⊙ 29,444 .... H 2
Sydney Mines 8,501......... H 2
Terence Bay 960 .... E 4
Thorburn 1,014 .... F 3
Three Mile Plains 1,355...... D 4
Timberlea 1,159 .... E 4
Trenton 3,154............... F 3
Truro⊙ 12,552 .... E 3
Waterville 687 .... D 3
Waverley 1,699 .... E 4
Wedgeport 827 .... C 5
Western Shore 1,712 .... D 4
Westmount 3,097 .... H 2
Westville 4,522 .... F 3
Wileville 746................ D 4
Windsor⊙ 3,646 .... D 3
Wolfville 3,235.............. D 3
Yarmouth⊙ 7,475 .... B 5

OTHER FEATURES

Advocate (bay) .... D 3
Ainslie (lake) .... G 2
Amet (sound)............... E 3
Andrew (isl.)................ H 3
Annapolis (basin) .... C 4
Annapolis (riv.)............. C 4
Antigonish (harb.)........... G 3
Argos (cape) .... G 3
Aspy (bay) .... H 2
Avon (riv.)................. D 4
Baccaro (pt.) .... C 5
Baddeck (riv.).............. H 2
Barachois (pt.)............. G 4
Barren (isl.) .... G 4
Barrington (bay) .... C 5
Bedford (basin) .... E 4
Berry (head)............... G 3
Boularderie (isl.) .... H 2
Bras d'Or (lake)............ H 3
Breton (cape).............. J 3
Brier (isl.) .... B 4
Canso (cape)............... H 3
Canso (str.) .... G 3
Cap d'Or (cape) .... D 3

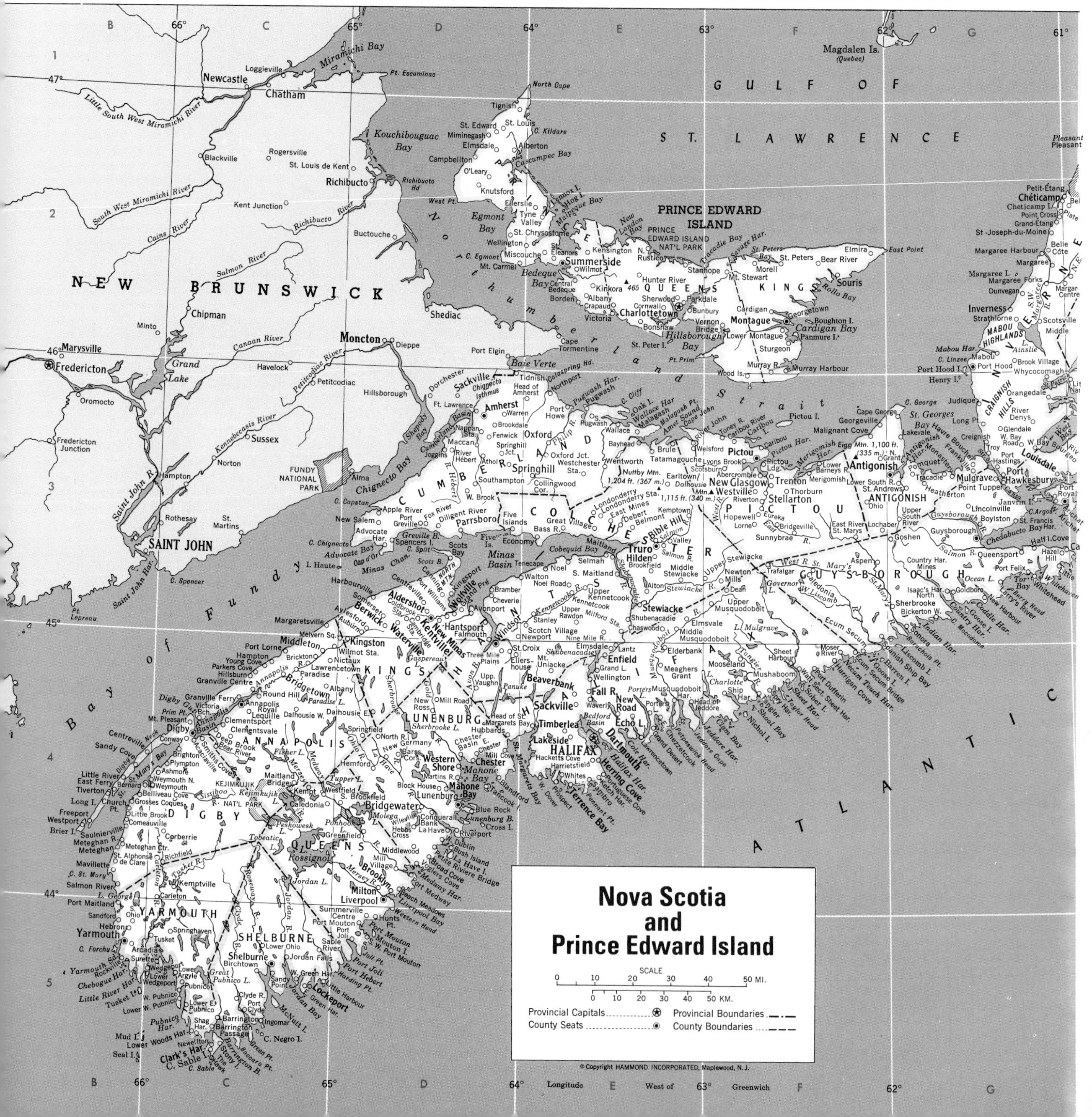

Nova Scotia and Prince Edward Island
SCALE
0 10 20 30 40 50 MI.
0 10 20 30 40 50 KM.
Provincial Capitals
County Seats
Provincial Boundaries
County Boundaries
© Copyright HAMMOND INCORPORATED, Maplewood, N. J.
Longitude West of Greenwich
GULF OF ST. LAWRENCE
PRINCE EDWARD ISLAND
NEW BRUNSWICK
Bay of Fundy
Northumberland Strait
ATLANTIC
Magdalen Is. (Quebec)

PRINCE EDWARD ISLAND

AREA 2,184 sq. mi. (5,657 sq. km.)
POPULATION 126,646
CAPITAL Charlottetown
LARGEST CITY Charlottetown
HIGHEST POINT 465 ft. (142 m.)
SETTLED IN 1720
ADMITTED TO CONFEDERATION 1873
PROVINCIAL FLOWER Lady's Slipper

NOVA SCOTIA

AREA 21,425 sq. mi. (55,491 sq. km.)
POPULATION 873,176
CAPITAL Halifax
LARGEST CITY Halifax
HIGHEST POINT Cape Breton Highlands 1,747 ft. (532 m.)
SETTLED IN 1605
ADMITTED TO CONFEDERATION **1867**
PROVINCIAL FLOWER Trailing Arbutus or Mayflower

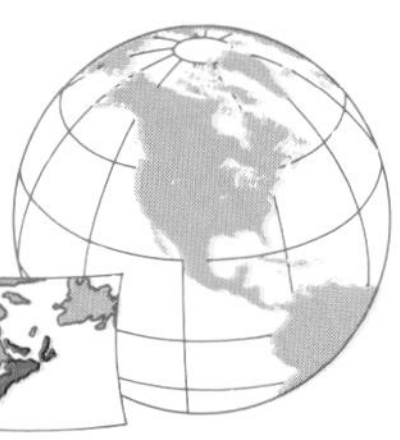

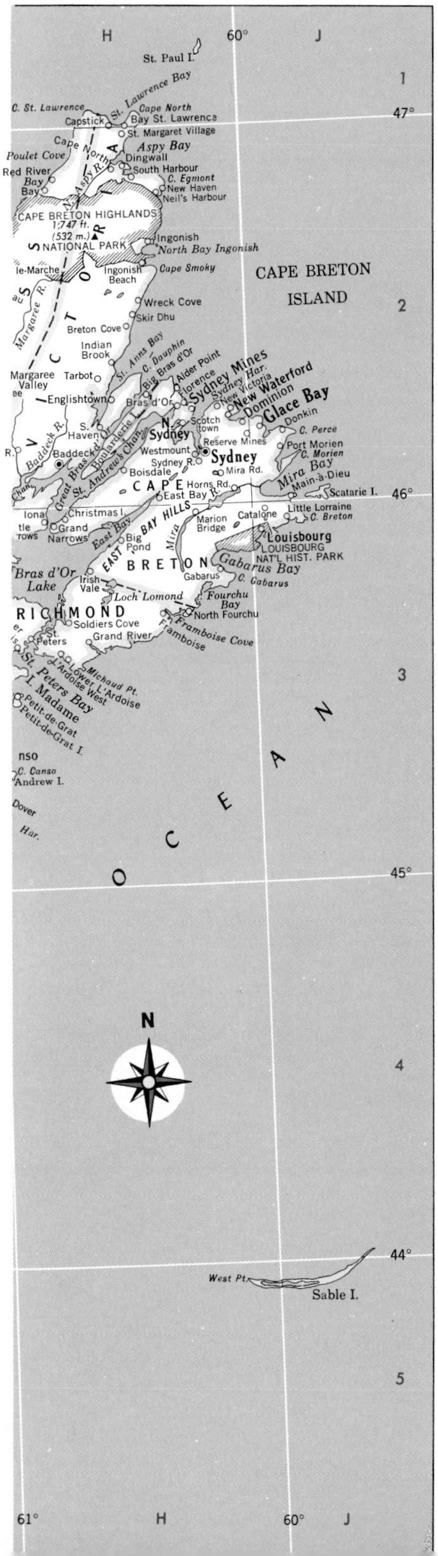
CAPE BRETON
ISLAND
CAPE BRETON HIGHLANDS NATIONAL PARK
Sydney
Glace Bay
Louisbourg
RICHMOND
Sable I.
O C E A N

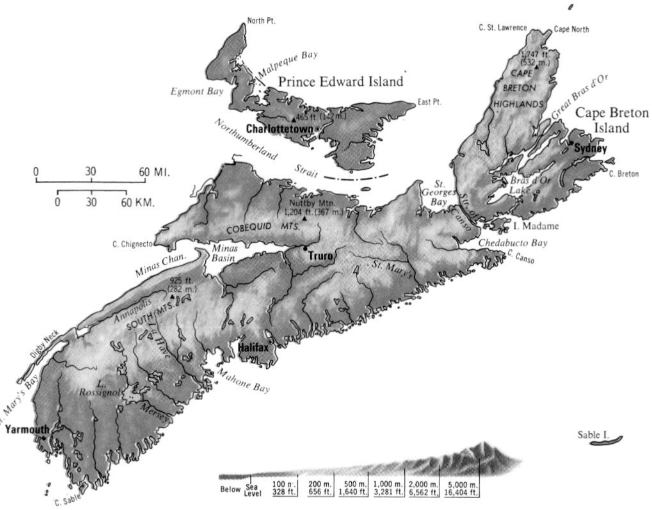
Prince Edward Island
Charlottetown
Northumberland Strait
Cape Breton Island
Sydney
Truro
Halifax
Yarmouth
Sable I.
0 30 60 MI.
0 30 60 KM.

⊙County seat.
*Population of metropolitan area.

Agriculture, Industry and Resources

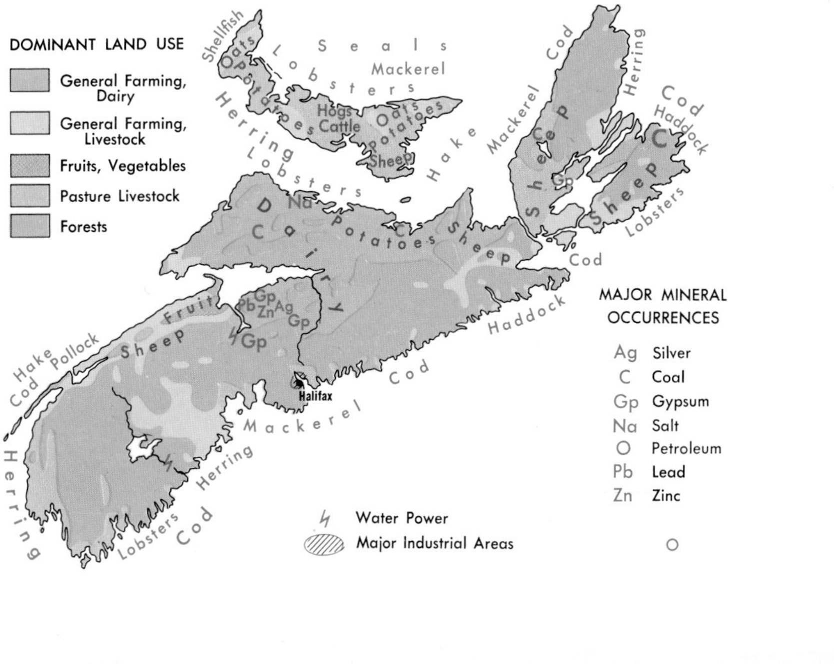
DOMINANT LAND USE
General Farming, Dairy
General Farming, Livestock
Fruits, Vegetables
Pasture Livestock
Forests
MAJOR MINERAL OCCURRENCES
Ag Silver
C Coal
Gp Gypsum
Na Salt
O Petroleum
Pb Lead
Zn Zinc
Water Power
Major Industrial Areas
Halifax

COUNTIES

Albert 23,632 .... F 3
Carleton 24,659 .... C 2
Charlotte 26,571 .... C 3
Gloucester 86,156 .... E 1
Kent 30,799 .... E 2
King's 51,114 .... E 3
Madawaska 34,892 .... B 1
Northumberland 54,134 .... D 2
Queen's 12,485 .... D 3
Restigouche 40,593 .... C 1
Saint John 86,148 .... E 3
Sunbury 21,012 .... D 3
Victoria 20,815 .... C 1
Westmorland 107,640 .... F 2
York 74,213 .... C 3

CITIES and TOWNS

Acadie Siding 64 .... E 2
Acadieville 176 .... E 2
Adamsville 94 .... E 2
Albert Mines 120 .... F 3
Alcida 174 .... E 1
Aldouane 64 .... E 2
Allardville 478 .... E 1
Alma 329 .... F 3
Anagance 114 .... E 3
Anse-Bleue 562 .... E 1
Apohaqui 341 .... E 3
Argyle 63 .... C 2
Armstrong Brook 191 .... E 1
Aroostook 403 .... C 2
Arthurette 178 .... C 2
Astle 201 .... D 2
Atholville 1,694 .... D 1
Aulac 113 .... F 3
Back Bay 455 .... D 3
Baie-Sainte-Anne 709 .... F 1
Baie-Verte 175 .... F 2
Bairdsville 81 .... C 2
Baker Brook 527 .... B 1
Balmoral 1,823 .... D 1
Barachois 686 .... F 2
Barnaby River 38 .... E 2
Barnettville 117 .... E 2
Bartibog Bridge 122 .... E 1
Bas-Caraquet 1,859 .... F 1
Bass River 112 .... E 2
Bath 794 .... C 2
Bathurst⊙ 15,705 .... E 1
Bayfield 81 .... G 2
Bayside .... C 3
Beaubois 211 .... E 1
Beaver Brook Station 95 .... E 1
Beaver Harbour 316 .... D 3
Beechwood 111 .... C 2
Beersville 52 .... E 2
Belledune 690 .... E 1
Bellefleur 83 .... C 1
Bellefond 243 .... E 1
Belleisle Creek 145 .... E 3
Benjamin River 171 .... D 1
Ben Lomond .... E 3
Benton 101 .... C 3
Beresford 3,652 .... E 1
Berry Mills 238 .... E 2
Bertrand 1,268 .... E 1
Berwick 129 .... E 3
Black Point 131 .... D 1
Black River 150 .... E 3
Blacks Harbour 1,356 .... D 3
Blackville 892 .... E 2
Blissfield 119 .... D 2
Bloomfield Ridge 153 .... D 2
Bloomfield Station 62 .... E 3
Bocabec 34 .... C 3
Boiestown 299 .... D 2
Bonny River 153 .... D 3
Bossé 193 .... B 1
Bourgeois 215 .... F 2
Brantville 1,066 .... E 1
Breau-Village 293 .... F 2
Brest 94 .... E 2
Brewers Mills 199 .... C 2
Briggs Corner 89 .... E 2
Bristol 824 .... C 2
Brockway (Lower Brockway-Brockway) 97 .... C 3
Browns Flat 295 .... D 3
Buctouche 2,476 .... F 2
Burnsville 156 .... E 1
Burton⊙ 291 .... D 3
Burtts Corner 484 .... D 2
Cambridge-Narrows 433 .... E 3
Campbellton 9,818 .... D 1
Canaan 115 .... E 2
Canaan Forks 78 .... E 2
Canaan Road 86 .... E 2
Canterbury 474 .... C 3
Cap-Bateau 417 .... F 1
Cape Tormentine 229 .... G 2
Cap Lumière 262 .... F 2
Cap-Pelé 2,199 .... F 2
Caraquet 4,315 .... E 1
Carlingford 229 .... C 2
Carlisle 75 .... C 2
Caron Brook 171 .... B 1
Carrolls Crossing 119 .... D 2
Castalia 145 .... D 4
Central Blissville 155 .... D 3
Centre-Saint-Simon (St. Simon) 991 .... E 1
Centreville 577 .... C 2
Chance Harbour 63 .... D 3
Charlo 1,603 .... D 1
Chatham 6,779 .... E 1
Chatham Head .... E 2
Chipman 1,829 .... E 2
Clair 915 .... B 1
Clarendon 80 .... D 3
Cliffordvale (Limestone-Cliffordvale) 69 .... C 2
Clifton 194 .... E 1
Coal Branch 90 .... E 2
Coal Creek 61 .... E 2
Cocagne Cape 278 .... F 2
Cocagne-Cocagne Sud 600 .... F 2
Codys 125 .... E 3
Coldstream 217 .... C 2
Coles Island 160 .... E 3
College Bridge 536 .... F 3
Collette 198 .... E 2
Connell 58 .... C 2
Connors 96 .... B 1
Cork 54 .... D 3
Cornhill 111 .... E 3
Coughlan 181 .... E 2
Cross Creek 192 .... D 2
Cumberland Bay 231 .... E 2
Dalhousie⊙ 4,958 .... D 1
Dalhousie Junction 105 .... D 1
Darlington 749 .... D 1
Daulnay 398 .... E 1
Dawsonville 278 .... C 1
Debec 200 .... C 2
Dieppe 8,511 .... F 2
Dipper Harbour 166 .... D 3
Doaktown 1,009 .... D 2
Dorchester⊙ 1,101 .... F 3
Dorchester Crossing 605 .... F 2
Douglastown 1,091 .... E 1
Drummond 849 .... C 1
Duguayville 337 .... E 1
Dumfries 150 .... C 3
Dupuis Corner 303 .... F 2
Durham Bridge 255 .... D 2
East Riverside-Kingshurst 989 .... E 3
Edmundston⊙ 12,044 .... B 1
Eel River Bridge 377 .... F 1
Eel River Crossing 1,431 .... D 1
Elgin 301 .... E 3
Enniskillen 63 .... D 3
Escuminac 194 .... F 1
Evandale 58 .... D 3
Evangeline 356 .... F 1
Everett 48 .... C 1
Fairfield 250 .... E 3
Fairhaven 142 .... C 4
Fairisle 415 .... E 1
Fairvale 3,960 .... E 3
Ferry Road 325 .... E 1
Fielding 197 .... C 2
Five Fingers 189 .... C 1
Flatlands 249 .... D 1
Florenceville 709 .... C 2
Forest City 25 .... C 3
Fosterville 58 .... C 3
Four Falls 69 .... C 2
Fredericton (cap.)⊙ 43,723 .... D 3
Fredericton Junction 711 .... D 3
Gagetown⊙ 618 .... D 3
Gardner Creek 56 .... E 3
Geary 654 .... D 3
Germantown 62 .... F 3
Gillespie 96 .... C 2
Glassville 147 .... C 2
Glencoe 147 .... D 1
Glenlivet 284 .... D 1
Gloucester Junction 36 .... E 1
Gondola Point 3,076 .... D 3
Grafton 385 .... C 2
Grand Bay 3,173 .... D 3
Grande-Anse 817 .... E 1
Grand Falls 6,203 .... C 1
Grand Falls Hill 152 .... C 1
Grand Harbour 614 .... D 4
Gray Rapids 266 .... E 2
Hammondvale 72 .... E 3
Hampstead 87 .... D 3
Hampton⊙ 3,141 .... E 3
Harcourt 127 .... E 2
Hardwicke 114 .... E 1
Hardwood Ridge 191 .... D 2
Hartland 846 .... C 2
Harvey, Albert 58 .... F 3
Harvey, York 356 .... D 3
Hatfield Point 176 .... E 3

New Brunswick
SCALE
0 5 10 20 30 40 MI.
0 5 10 20 30 40 KM.
Provincial Capitals
County Seats
International Boundaries
Provincial Boundaries
County Boundaries
RESTIGOUCHE
MADAWASKA
VICTORIA
NORTHUMBERLAND
GLOUCESTER
CARLETON
YORK
SUNBURY
QUEEN'S
KENT
WESTMORLAND
ALBERT
KINGS
ST. JOHN
CHARLOTTE
QUÉBEC
MAINE
NOVA SCOTIA
PRINCE EDWARD ISLAND
GULF OF ST. LAWRENCE
BAY OF FUNDY
CHALEUR BAY
Northumberland Strait
Fredericton
Saint John
Moncton
Campbellton
Bathurst
Edmundston
Dalhousie
Chatham
Newcastle
Woodstock
Grand Falls
St. Stephen
Sackville
Amherst
Longitude West of Greenwich
© Copyright HAMMOND INCORPORATED, Maplewood, N.J.

Havelock 439 . . . . . E 3
Hayesville 107 . . . . . D 2
Hazeldean 108 . . . . . C 2
Head of Millstream 61 . . . . . E 3
Hillman 69 . . . . . C 2
Hillsborough 1,239 . . . . . F 3
Holmesville 146 . . . . . C 2
Holtville 222 . . . . . D 2
Honeydale 77 . . . . . C 3
Hopewell Cape⊙ 144 . . . . . F 3
Hopewell Hill 172 . . . . . F 3
Howard 77 . . . . . E 2
Howland Ridge 55 . . . . . C 2
Hoyt 114 . . . . . D 3
Inkerman 396 . . . . . F 1
Irishtown 605 . . . . . F 2
Island View 240 . . . . . D 3
Jacksonville 363 . . . . . C 2
Jacquet River 778 . . . . . E 1
Janeville 204 . . . . . E 1
Jeanne Mance 89 . . . . . E 1
Jemseg 228 . . . . . D 3
Jolicure 96 . . . . . F 3
Juniper 525 . . . . . C 2
Kedgwick 1,222 . . . . . C 1
Keenan Siding 86 . . . . . E 2
Kent Junction 112 . . . . . E 2
Kent Lake 57 . . . . . E 2
Keswick 260 . . . . . D 3
Kilburn 134 . . . . . C 2
Killam 60 . . . . . E 2
Kingsclear 250 . . . . . D 3
Kingsley 145 . . . . . D 2
Kirkland 69 . . . . . C 3
Knowlesville 82 . . . . . C 2
Kouchibouguac 213 . . . . . F 2
Lac Baker 292 . . . . . B 1
Lagacéville 227 . . . . . E 1
Lake George 170 . . . . . C 3
Laketon 81 . . . . . E 2
Lakeville 201 . . . . . C 2
Lambertville 109 . . . . . C 3
Lamèque 1,571 . . . . . F 1
Landry 281 . . . . . E 1
Laplante 197 . . . . . E 1
Lavillette 576 . . . . . E 1
Lawrence Station 229 . . . . . C 3
Leech 584 . . . . . E 1
Léger Brook . . . . . F 2
Légerville 184 . . . . . F 2
Le Goulet 1,173 . . . . . F 1
Leonardville 158 . . . . . C 4
Lepreau 208 . . . . . D 3
Levesque 77 . . . . . C 1
Little Cape 513 . . . . . F 2
Little Shippegan 131 . . . . . F 1
Loggieville 781 . . . . . E 1
Lorne 937 . . . . . D 1
Lower Coverdale 616 . . . . . F 2
Lower Derby 206 . . . . . E 2
Lower Durham 52 . . . . . D 2
Lower Hainesville 66 . . . . . C 2
Lower Kars 30 . . . . . E 3
Lower Millstream 184 . . . . . E 3
Lower Sapin . . . . . F 2
Lower Southampton . . . . . C 3
Ludlow 100 . . . . . D 2
Maces Bay 182 . . . . . D 3
Madran 247 . . . . . E 1
Magaguadavic 126 . . . . . C 3
Maisonnette 757 . . . . . E 1
Malden 93 . . . . . G 2
Manners Sutton 159 . . . . . D 3
Manuels 332 . . . . . F 1
Mapleview 65 . . . . . C 2
Marcelville 61 . . . . . E 2
Martin 104 . . . . . C 1
Maugerville 249 . . . . . D 3
Maxwell 64 . . . . . C 3
McAdam 1,837 . . . . . C 3
McGivney 156 . . . . . D 2
McKendrick 608 . . . . . D 1
McNamee 147 . . . . . D 2
Meductic 234 . . . . . C 3
Melrose 121 . . . . . F 2
Memramcook 276 . . . . . F 2
Menneval 110 . . . . . C 1
Midgic Station 208 . . . . . F 3
Mill Cove 253 . . . . . D 3
Millerton 130 . . . . . E 2
Millville 309 . . . . . C 2
Minto 3,399 . . . . . D 2
Miscou Centre 554 . . . . . F 1
Miscou Harbour 106 . . . . . F 1
Mispec 180 . . . . . E 3
Moncton 54,743 . . . . . F 2
Moores Mills 117 . . . . . C 3
Morrisdale 202 . . . . . D 3
Moulin-Morneault 459 . . . . . B 1
Murray Corner 233 . . . . . G 2
Nackawic 1,357 . . . . . C 2
Napadogan 103 . . . . . D 2
Nash Creek 235 . . . . . D 1
Nashwaak Bridge 142 . . . . . D 2
Nashwaak Village 258 . . . . . D 2
Nauwigewauk 139 . . . . . E 3
Neguac 1,755 . . . . . E 1
Nelson-Miramichi 1,452 . . . . . E 2
Newcastle⊙ 6,284 . . . . . E 2
Newcastle Creek 210 . . . . . D 2
New Denmark 112 . . . . . C 1
New Jersey 65 . . . . . E 1
New Market 143 . . . . . D 3
New Maryland 485 . . . . . D 3
New River Beach 33 . . . . . D 3
Newtown 154 . . . . . E 3
New Zion 171 . . . . . D 2
Nicholas Denys 170 . . . . . D 1
Nictau 30 . . . . . C 1
Nigadoo 1,075 . . . . . E 1
Noinville 50 . . . . . E 2
Nordin 393 . . . . . E 1
North Head 661 . . . . . D 4
Norton 1,372 . . . . . E 3
Notre-Dame 344 . . . . . F 2
Oak Bay 183 . . . . . C 3
Oak Point 83 . . . . . D 3
Oromocto 9,064 . . . . . D 3
Paquetville 626 . . . . . E 1
Peel 117 . . . . . C 2
Pelletier Mills 88 . . . . . B 1
Pennfield . . . . . D 3
Penniac 179 . . . . . D 2
Penobsquis 259 . . . . . E 3
Perth-Andover⊙ 1,872 . . . . . C 2
Petitcodiac 1,401 . . . . . E 3
Petite-Rivière-de-l'Île 549 . . . . . F 1
Petit Rocher 1,860 . . . . . E 1
Petit Rocher Sud . . . . . E 1
Pigeon Hill 595 . . . . . F 1
Plaster Rock 1,222 . . . . . C 2
Pocologan 150 . . . . . D 3
Point de Bute 155 . . . . . F 3
Pointe-du-Chêne 482 . . . . . F 2
Pointe-Sapin 331 . . . . . F 2
Pointe-Verte 1,335 . . . . . E 1
Pollett River 73 . . . . . E 3
Pontgrave 229 . . . . . F 1
Pont-Lafrance 875 . . . . . E 1
Pont-Landry 444 . . . . . F 1
Port Elgin 504 . . . . . F 2
Prime 89 . . . . . B 1
Prince of Wales 138 . . . . . D 3
Prince William 225 . . . . . C 3
Quarryville 205 . . . . . E 2
Queenstown 112 . . . . . D 3
Quispamsis 6,022 . . . . . E 3
Red Bank 141 . . . . . E 2
Renforth 1,490 . . . . . E 3
Renous 192 . . . . . E 2
Rexton 928 . . . . . F 2
Richardsville . . . . . D 1
Richibucto⊙ 1,722 . . . . . E 2
Richibucto Village 442 . . . . . F 2
Richmond Corner 84 . . . . . C 2
Riley Brook 126 . . . . . C 1
Ripples 233 . . . . . D 3
River de Chute 22 . . . . . C 2
River Glade 268 . . . . . E 3
Riverside-Albert 478 . . . . . F 3
Riverview 14,907 . . . . . F 2
Rivière-du-Portage 661 . . . . . F 1
Rivière Verte 1,054 . . . . . B 1
Robertville 733 . . . . . E 1
Robichaud 485 . . . . . F 2
Robinsonville 206 . . . . . C 1
Rogersville 1,237 . . . . . E 2
Rollingdam 65 . . . . . C 3
Rosaireville 86 . . . . . E 2
Rothesay 1,764 . . . . . E 3
Rowena 73 . . . . . C 2
Roy 173 . . . . . F 2
Royal Road 41 . . . . . D 2
Rusagonis 231 . . . . . D 3
Sackville 5,654 . . . . . F 3
Saint Almo 17 . . . . . C 2
Saint-André 385 . . . . . C 1
Saint Andrews⊙ 1,760 . . . . . C 3
Saint-Antoine 1,217 . . . . . F 2
Saint Arthur 369 . . . . . D 1
Saint-Basile 3,214 . . . . . B 1
Saint-Charles 355 . . . . . F 2
Saint Croix 86 . . . . . C 3
Sainte-Anne 329 . . . . . E 1
Sainte-Anne-de-Kent 337 . . . . . F 2
Sainte-Anne-de-Madawaska 1,332 . . . . . B 1
Saint-Édouard-de-Kent 157 . . . . . F 2
Sainte-Marie-de-Kent 283 . . . . . F 2
Sainte-Marie-sur-Mer 539 . . . . . F 1
Sainte-Rose-Gloucester 410 . . . . . F 1
Saint-François-de-Madawaska 753 . . . . . B 1
Saint George 1,163 . . . . . D 3
Saint Hilaire 244 . . . . . B 1
Saint-Ignace 96 . . . . . F 2
Saint-Isidore 794 . . . . . E 1
Saint-Jacques 2,297 . . . . . B 1
Saint-Jean-Baptiste-de-Restigouche 228 . . . . . C 1
Saint John⊙ 80,521 . . . . . E 3
Saint-Joseph 630 . . . . . F 3
Saint-Joseph-de-Madawaska 173 . . . . . B 1
Saint-Léolin 799 . . . . . E 1
Saint Leonard 1,566 . . . . . C 1
Saint-Louis-de-Kent 1,166 . . . . . F 2
Saint Margarets 63 . . . . . E 2
Saint Martin de Restigouche 124 . . . . . C 1
Saint Martins 530 . . . . . E 3
Saint-Paul 365 . . . . . E 2
Saint Quentin 2,334 . . . . . C 1
Saint-Raphaël-sur-Mer 562 . . . . . F 1
Saint Sauveur 252 . . . . . E 1
Saint Stephen 5,120 . . . . . C 3
Saint Wilfred . . . . . E 1
Salisbury 1,672 . . . . . E 2
Salmon Beach 277 . . . . . E 1
Salmon Creek 38 . . . . . E 2
Saumarez 690 . . . . . E 1
Scoudouc 207 . . . . . F 2
Seal Cove 548 . . . . . D 4
Shannon 39 . . . . . E 3
Shediac 4,285 . . . . . F 2
Shediac Bridge 441 . . . . . F 2
Sheffield 112 . . . . . D 3
Sheila 1,172 . . . . . F 1
Shemogue 199 . . . . . F 2
Shepody 86 . . . . . F 3
Shippegan 2,471 . . . . . F 1
Siegas 227 . . . . . C 1
Sillikers 292 . . . . . E 2
Simonds 221 . . . . . C 2
Sisson Ridge 170 . . . . . C 2
Six Roads 239 . . . . . F 1
Smiths Creek 163 . . . . . E 3
Somerville 326 . . . . . C 2
South Branch 86 . . . . . F 2
Springfield, King's 116 . . . . . E 3
Springfield, York 130 . . . . . C 2
Stanley 432 . . . . . D 2
Stickney 232 . . . . . C 2
Storeytown 140 . . . . . D 2
Sunny Corner 405 . . . . . E 2
Sunnyside 87 . . . . . D 1
Sussex 3,972 . . . . . E 3
Sussex Corner 1,023 . . . . . E 3
Tabusintac 231 . . . . . E 1

AREA 28,354 sq. mi. (73,437 sq. km.)
POPULATION 709,442
CAPITAL Fredericton
LARGEST CITY Saint John
HIGHEST POINT Mt. Carleton 2,690 ft. (820 m.)
SETTLED IN 1611
ADMITTED TO CONFEDERATION 1867
PROVINCIAL FLOWER Purple Violet

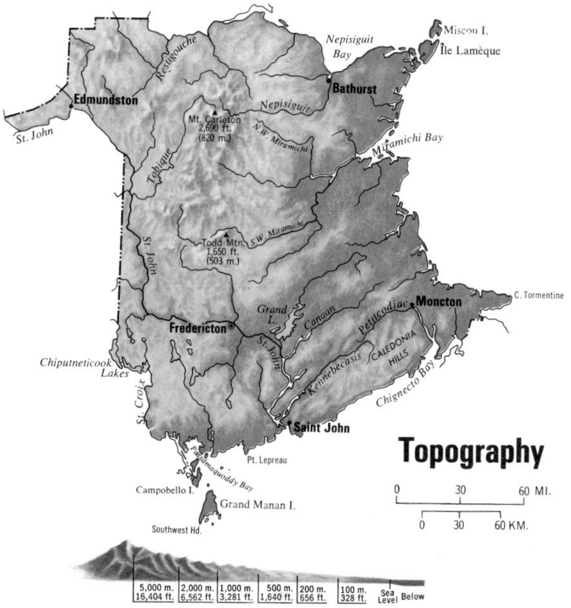

Miscou I.
Île Lamèque
Nepisiguit Bay
Restigouche
Bathurst
Edmundston
Nepisiguit
Mt. Carleton 2,690 ft. (820 m.)
N.W. Miramichi
Miramichi Bay
St. John
Tobique
St. John
Todd Mtn. 1,650 ft. (503 m.)
S.W. Miramichi
C. Tormentine
Moncton
Grand L.
Canaan
Petitcodiac
Fredericton
CALEDONIA HILLS
Chiputneticook Lakes
Kennebecasis
St. Croix
Chignecto Bay
Saint John
Pt. Lepreau
Passamaquoddy Bay
Campobello I.
Grand Manan I.
Southwest Hd.
0 30 60 MI.
0 30 60 KM.
5,000 m. 16,404 ft.
2,000 m. 6,562 ft.
1,000 m. 3,281 ft.
500 m. 1,640 ft.
200 m. 656 ft.
100 m. 328 ft.
Sea Level
Below

Topography

Agriculture, Industry and Resources

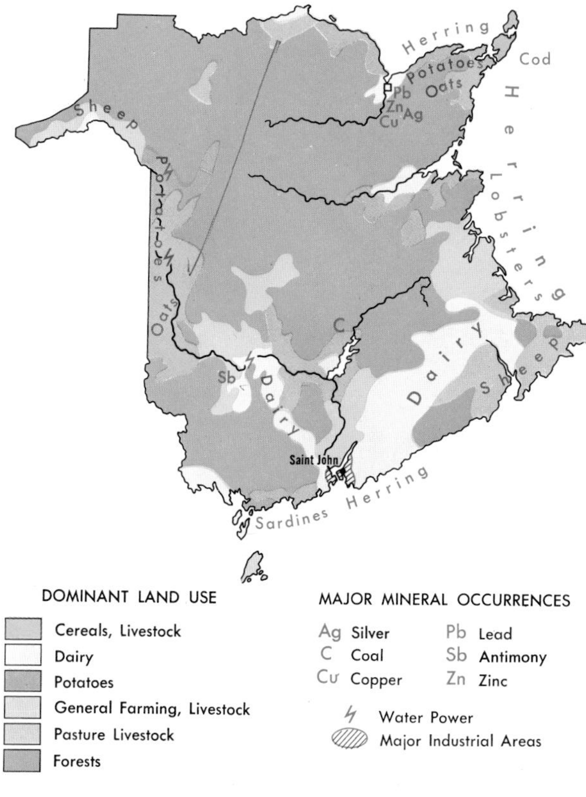

Herring
Cod
Potatoes
Oats
Pb
Zn
Ag
Cu
Sheep
Herring
Lobsters
Herring
C
Oats
Sb
Dairy
Dairy
Dairy
Sheep
Saint John
Herring
Sardines
DOMINANT LAND USE
Cereals, Livestock
Dairy
Potatoes
General Farming, Livestock
Pasture Livestock
Forests
MAJOR MINERAL OCCURRENCES
Ag Silver
C Coal
Cu Copper
Pb Lead
Sb Antimony
Zn Zinc
Water Power
Major Industrial Areas

Taxis River 118 . . . . . D 2
Tay Creek 161 . . . . . D 2
Taymouth 301 . . . . . D 2
Temperance Vale 357 . . . . . C 2
The Range 58 . . . . . E 2
Thibault 306 . . . . . C 1
Tide Head 952 . . . . . D 1
Tilley 95 . . . . . C 2
Tobique Narrows 140 . . . . . C 2
Tracadie 2,452 . . . . . F 1
Tracy 636 . . . . . D 3
Turtle Creek 81 . . . . . F 3
Tweedside 87 . . . . . C 3
Upham 107 . . . . . E 3
Upper Blackville 60 . . . . . E 2
Upper Buctouche 158 . . . . . F 2
Upper Gagetown 236 . . . . . D 3
Upper Hainesville 189 . . . . . C 2
Upper Kent 203 . . . . . C 2
Upper Maugerville 543 . . . . . D 3
Upper Mills 153 . . . . . C 3
Upper Rockport 18 . . . . . F 3
Upper Sheila 706 . . . . . E 1
Upper Woodstock 257 . . . . . C 2
Upsalquitch 112 . . . . . D 1
Val-Comeau 534 . . . . . F 1
Val d'Amour 462 . . . . . D 1
Val Doucet 505 . . . . . E 1
Verret 637 . . . . . B 1
Village-Saint-Laurent 187 . . . . . E 1
Waasis 264 . . . . . D 3
Wapske 195 . . . . . C 2
Waterford 120 . . . . . E 3
Waterville 181 . . . . . C 2
Waweig . . . . . C 3
Wayerton 188 . . . . . E 1
Weaver 86 . . . . . E 2
Weldon 227 . . . . . F 3
Welsford 230 . . . . . D 3
Welshpool 260 . . . . . D 4
Westfield 1,100 . . . . . D 3
West Quaco 48 . . . . . E 3
White Head 185 . . . . . D 4
White Rapids 238 . . . . . E 2
Whitney 216 . . . . . E 2
Wickham 72 . . . . . D 3
Wicklow 143 . . . . . C 2
Williamsburg 258 . . . . . D 2
Williamstown 156 . . . . . C 2
Willow Grove 509 . . . . . E 3
Wilmot 57 . . . . . C 3
Wilson Point 45 . . . . . F 1
Wilsons Beach 844 . . . . . D 4
Windsor 43 . . . . . C 2
Wirral 110 . . . . . D 3
Woodstock⊙ 4,649 . . . . . C 2
Woodwards Cove 146 . . . . . D 4
Youngs Cove 65 . . . . . E 3
Zealand 458 . . . . . D 2

OTHER FEATURES

Bald (mt.) . . . . . C 1
Bartibog (riv.) . . . . . E 1
Bay du Vin (riv.) . . . . . E 2
Big Tracadie (riv.) . . . . . E 1
Buctouche (harb.) . . . . . F 2
Buctouche (riv.) . . . . . F 2
Campobello (isl.) . . . . . D 4
Canaan (riv.) . . . . . E 2
Carleton (mt.) . . . . . D 1
Chaleur (bay) . . . . . E 1
Chignecto (bay) . . . . . F 3
Chiputneticook (lakes) . . . . . C 3
Cocagne (isl.) . . . . . F 2
Cumberland (basin) . . . . . F 3
Deer (isl.) . . . . . D 4
Digdeguash (riv.) . . . . . C 3
Escuminac (bay) . . . . . D 1
Escuminac (pt.) . . . . . F 1
Fundy (bay) . . . . . E 3
Fundy Nat'l Park . . . . . E 3
Gaspereau (riv.) . . . . . D 2
Grand (bay) . . . . . D 3
Grand (lake) . . . . . C 3
Grand (lake) . . . . . D 3
Grand Manan (chan.) . . . . . C 4
Grand Manan (isl.) . . . . . D 4
Grande (riv.) . . . . . C 1
Green (riv.) . . . . . B 1
Hammond (riv.) . . . . . E 3
Harvey (lake) . . . . . C 3
Heron (isl.) . . . . . D 1
Kedgwick (riv.) . . . . . C 1
Kennebecasis (riv.) . . . . . E 3
Keswick (riv.) . . . . . C 2
Kouchibouguac (bay) . . . . . F 2
Kouchibouguacis (riv.) . . . . . E 2
Kouchibouguac Nat'l Park . . . . . F 2
Lamèque (isl.) . . . . . F 1
Lepreau (riv.) . . . . . D 3
Little (riv.) . . . . . D 2
Long (isl.) . . . . . D 3
Long Reach (inlet) . . . . . D 3
Maces (bay) . . . . . D 3
Mactaquac (lake) . . . . . C 3
Madawaska (riv.) . . . . . B 1
Magaguadavic (lake) . . . . . C 3
Magaguadavic (riv.) . . . . . C 3
Miramichi (bay) . . . . . E 1
Miscou (isl.) . . . . . F 1
Miscou (pt.) . . . . . F 1
Mount Carleton Prov. Park . . . . . D 1
Musquash (harb.) . . . . . D 3
Nashwaak (riv.) . . . . . D 2
Nepisiguit (bay) . . . . . E 1
Nepisiguit (riv.) . . . . . D 1
Nerepis (riv.) . . . . . D 3
Northern (head) . . . . . D 4
North Sevogle (riv.) . . . . . D 1
Northumberland (str.) . . . . . F 2
Northwest Miramichi (riv.) . . . . . D 1
Oromocto (lake) . . . . . C 3
Oromocto (riv.) . . . . . D 3
Passamaquoddy (bay) . . . . . C 3
Patapédia (riv.) . . . . . C 1
Petitcodiac (riv.) . . . . . F 3
Pokemouche (riv.) . . . . . E 1
Pokesudie (isl.) . . . . . F 1
Pollett (riv.) . . . . . E 3
Quaco (head) . . . . . E 3
Renous (riv.) . . . . . D 2
Restigouche (riv.) . . . . . C 1
Richibucto (harb.) . . . . . F 2
Richibucto (riv.) . . . . . E 2
Roosevelt Campobello Int'l Park . . . . . D 4
Saint Croix (riv.) . . . . . C 3
Saint Francis (riv.) . . . . . A 1
Saint John (harb.) . . . . . E 3
Saint John (riv.) . . . . . C 2
Saint Lawrence (gulf) . . . . . F 1
Salisbury (bay) . . . . . F 3
Salmon (riv.) . . . . . C 1
Salmon (riv.) . . . . . E 2
Shediac (isl.) . . . . . F 2
Shepody (bay) . . . . . F 3
Shippegan (bay) . . . . . E 1
Shippegan Gully (str.) . . . . . F 1
South Sevogle (riv.) . . . . . D 1
Southwest (head) . . . . . D 4
Southwest Miramichi (riv.) . . . . . D 2
Spear (cape) . . . . . G 2
Spednik (lake) . . . . . C 3
Spencer (cape) . . . . . E 3
Tabusintac (riv.) . . . . . E 1
Tabusintac Gully (str.) . . . . . F 1
Tetagouche (riv.) . . . . . D 1
Tobique (riv.) . . . . . C 2
Upsalquitch (riv.) . . . . . D 1
Utopia (lake) . . . . . D 3
Verte (bay) . . . . . G 2
Washademoak (lake) . . . . . E 3
West (isls.) . . . . . D 4
White Head (isl.) . . . . . D 4

⊙County seat.

Topography

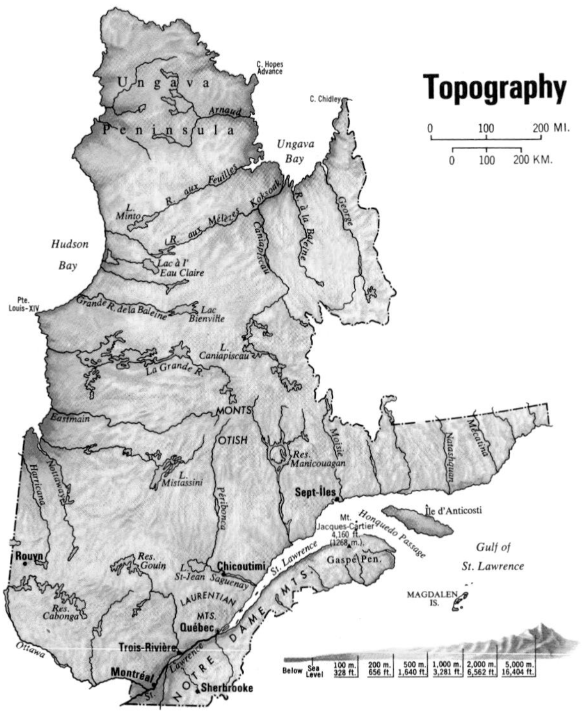
0 100 200 MI.
0 100 200 KM.
Ungava Peninsula
C. Hopes Advance
C. Chidley
Ungava Bay
Hudson Bay
Pte. Louis-XIV
L. Minto
R. aux Feuilles
R. aux Mélèzes
Kaksoak
R. à la Baleine
George
Caniapiscau
Lac à l'Eau Claire
Grande R. de la Baleine
Lac Bienville
L. Caniapiscau
La Grande R.
Eastmain
MONTS OTISH
Res. Manicouagan
L. Mistassini
Sept-Îles
Île d'Anticosti
Mt. Jacques-Cartier 4,160 ft. (1268 m.)
Honguedo Passage
Gulf of St. Lawrence
Rouyn
Res. Gouin
L. St-Jean
Chicoutimi
Saguenay
Gaspé Pen.
MAGDALEN IS.
Res. Cabonga
LAURENTIAN MTS.
Québec
Trois-Rivières
Ottawa
Montréal
Sherbrooke
NOTRE DAME MTS.
Below Sea Level
100 m. 328 ft.
200 m. 656 ft.
500 m. 1,640 ft.
1,000 m. 3,281 ft.
2,000 m. 6,562 ft.
5,000 m. 16,404 ft.

COUNTIES

Argenteuil 32,454 . . . . C 4
Arthabaska 59,277 . . . . E 4
Bagot 26,840 . . . . E 4
Beauce 73,427 . . . . G 3
Beauharnois 54,034 . . . . C 4
Bellechasse 23,559 . . . . G 3
Berthier 31,096 . . . . C 3
Bonaventure 40,487 . . . . C 2
Brome 17,436 . . . . E 4
Chambly 307,090 . . . . J 4
Champlain 119,595 . . . . E 2
Charlevoix-Est 17,448 . . . . G 2
Charlevoix-Ouest 14,172 . . . . . G 2
Châteauguay 59,968 . . . . D 4
Chicoutimi 174,441 . . . . G 1
Compton 20,536 . . . . F 4
Deux-Montagnes 71,252 . . . . . C 4
Dorchester 33,949 . . . . C 3
Drummond 69,770 . . . . E 4
Frontenac 26,814 . . . . G 4
Gaspé-Est 41,173 . . . . D 1
Gaspé-Ouest 18,943 . . . . C 1
Gatineau 54,229 . . . . B 3
Hull 131,213 . . . . B 4
Huntingdon 16,953 . . . . C 4
Iberville 23,180 . . . . D 4
Île-de-Montréal 1,760,122 . . . . H 4
Île-Jésus 268,335 . . . . H 4
Joliette 60,384 . . . . C 3
Kamouraska 28,642 . . . . H 2
Labelle 34,395 . . . . B 3
Lac-Saint-Jean-Est 47,891 . . . F 1
Lac-Saint-Jean-Ouest 62,952 . E 1
Laprairie 105,962 . . . . H 4
L'Assomption 109,705 . . . . D 4
Lévis 94,104 . . . . J 3
L'Islet 22,062 . . . . G 2
Lotbinière 29,653 . . . . F 3
Maskinongé 20,763 . . . . D 3
Matane 29,955 . . . . B 1
Matapédia 23,715 . . . . B 2
Mégantic 57,892 . . . . F 3
Missisquoi 36,161 . . . . D 4
Montcalm 27,557 . . . . C 3
Montmagny 25,622 . . . . G 3
Montmorency No. 1 23,048 . . . F 2
Montmorency No. 2 6,436 . . . . G 3
Napierville 13,562 . . . . D 4
Nicolet 33,513 . . . . E 3
Papineau 37,975 . . . . B 4
Pontiac 20,283 . . . . A 3
Portneuf 58,843 . . . . E 3
Québec 458,980 . . . . F 3
Richelieu 53,058 . . . . D 4
Richmond 40,871 . . . . E 4
Rimouski 69,099 . . . . J 1
Rivière-du-Loup 41,250 . . . . . . H 2
Rouville 42,391 . . . . D 4
Saguenay 115,881 . . . . H 1
Saint-Hyacinthe 55,888 . . . . . . D 4
Saint-Jean 55,576 . . . . D 4
Saint-Maurice 107,703 . . . . D 3
Shefford 70,733 . . . . E 4
Sherbrooke 115,983 . . . . E 4
Soulanges 15,429 . . . . C 4
Stanstead 38,186 . . . . F 4
Témiscouata 52,570 . . . . J 2
Terrebonne 193,865 . . . . H 4
Vaudreuil 50,043 . . . . C 4
Verchères 63,353 . . . . J 4
Wolfe 15,635 . . . . F 4
Yamaska 14,797 . . . . E 3

CITIES and TOWNS

Acton Vale 4,371 . . . . E 4
Albanel 992 . . . . E 1
Alma⊙ 26,322 . . . . F 1
Amqui⊙ 4,048 . . . . B 2
Ancienne-Lorette 12,935 . . . . . H 3
Angers . . . . B 4
Anjou 37,346 . . . . H 4
Annaville 712 . . . . E 3
Armagh 878 . . . . G 3
Arthabaska⊙ 6,827 . . . . F 3
Arvida . . . . F 1
Asbestos 7,967 . . . . F 4
Ascot Corner 847 . . . . F 4
Audet 760 . . . . G 4
Ayer's Cliff⊙ 810 . . . . E 4
Aylmer 26,695 . . . . B 4
Baie-Comeau 12,866 . . . . A 1
Baie-d'Urfé 3,674 . . . . G 4
Baie-Saint-Paul⊙ 3,961 . . . . . . G 2
Baie-Trinité 749 . . . . B 1
Beaconsfield 19,613 . . . . H 4
Beauceville 4,302 . . . . G 3
Beauharnois⊙ 7,025 . . . . D 4
Beaumont 791 . . . . F 3
Beauport 60,447 . . . . J 3
Beaupré 2,740 . . . . G 2
Bécancour⊙ 10,247 . . . . E 3
Bedford⊙ 2,832 . . . . E 4
Beebe Plain 1,072 . . . . E 4
Bélair (Val-Bélair) 12,695 . . . . H 3
Beloeil 17,540 . . . . D 4
Bernierville 2,120 . . . . F 3
Berthier-en-Bas 562 . . . . G 3
Berthierville⊙ 4,049 . . . . D 3
Bic 2,994 . . . . J 1
Biencourt 824 . . . . J 2
Black Lake 5,148 . . . . F 3
Blainville 14,682 . . . . H 4
Boischatel 3,345 . . . . J 3
Bois-des-Filion 4,943 . . . . H 4
Bolduc 1,565 . . . . G 4
Bonaventure 1,371 . . . . C 2
Boucherville 29,704 . . . . J 4
Bromont 2,731 . . . . E 4
Bromptonville 3,035 . . . . F 4
Brossard 52,232 . . . . H 4
Brownsburg 2,875 . . . . C 4
Buckingham 7,992 . . . . B 4
Cabano 3,291 . . . . J 2
Cacouna 1,160 . . . . H 2
Calumet 729 . . . . C 4
Candiac 8,502 . . . . J 4
Cap-à-l'Aigle 819 . . . . G 2
Cap-Chat 3,464 . . . . B 1
Cap-de-la-Madeleine 32,626 . E 3
Caplan-Rivière Caplan 1,139 . C 2
Cap-Saint-Ignace 1,485 . . . . . . G 2
Cap-Santé⊙ 671 . . . . F 3
Carignan 4,544 . . . . J 4
Carleton 2,710 . . . . C 2
Causapscal 2,501 . . . . B 2
Chambly 12,190 . . . . J 4
Chambord 961 . . . . E 1
Chandler 3,946 . . . . D 2
Charlemagne 4,827 . . . . H 4
Charlesbourg 68,326 . . . . J 3
Charny 8,240 . . . . J 3
Châteauguay 36,928 . . . . H 4
Château-Richer⊙ 3,628 . . . . . . F 3
Chénéville 633 . . . . B 4
Chicoutimi⊙ 60,064 . . . . G 1
Chicoutimi-Jonquière
*135,172 . . . . G 1
Chute-aux-Outardes 2,280 . . . A 1
Clermont 3,621 . . . . G 2
Coaticook 6,271 . . . . F 4
Coleraine 1,660 . . . . F 4
Compton 728 . . . . F 4
Contrecoeur 5,449 . . . . D 4
Cookshire⊙ 1,480 . . . . F 4
Coteau-du-Lac 1,247 . . . . C 4
Coteau-Landing⊙ 1,386 . . . . . . C 4
Côte-Saint-Luc 27,531 . . . . H 4
Courcelles 608 . . . . G 4
Courville . . . . J 3
Cowansville 12,240 . . . . E 4
Crabtree 1,950 . . . . D 4
Danville 2,200 . . . . E 4
Daveluyville 1,257 . . . . E 3
Deauville 942 . . . . E 4
Dégelis 3,477 . . . . J 2
Delisle 4,011 . . . . F 1
Delson 4,935 . . . . H 4
Desbiens 1,541 . . . . E 1
Deschaillons-sur-Saint-
Laurent 950 . . . . E 3
Deschambault 977 . . . . E 3
Deschênes . . . . B 4
Deux-Montagnes 9,944 . . . . H 4
Didyme 667 . . . . E 1
Disraëli 3,181 . . . . F 4
Dolbeau 8,766 . . . . E 1
Dollard-des-Ormeaux 39,940 . H 4
Donnacona 5,731 . . . . F 3
Dorion 5,749 . . . . C 4
Dorval 17,727 . . . . H 4
Dosquet 703 . . . . F 3
Douville . . . . D 4
Drummondville⊙ 27,347 . . . . . E 4
Drummondville-Sud 9,220 . . . . E 4
Dunham 2,887 . . . . E 4
Durham-Sud 1,045 . . . . E 4
East Angus 4,016 . . . . F 4
East Broughton 1,397 . . . . F 3
East Broughton Station 1,302 . F 3
Eastman 612 . . . . E 4
Entrelacs 1,735 . . . . C 3
Farnham 6,498 . . . . E 4
Ferme-Neuve 2,266 . . . . B 3
Forestville 4,271 . . . . H 1
Frampton 684 . . . . G 3
Francoeur 1,422 . . . . F 3
Gaspé 17,261 . . . . D 1
Gatineau 74,988 . . . . B 4
Giffard . . . . J 3
Girardville 1,128 . . . . E 1
Gracefield 869 . . . . A 3
Granby 38,069 . . . . E 4
Grand'Mère 15,442 . . . . E 3
Grande-Rivière 4,420 . . . . D 2
Grandes-Bergeronnes 748 . . . . H 1
Grande-Vallée 700 . . . . D 1
Greenfield Park 18,527 . . . . . . J 4
Grenville 1,417 . . . . C 4
Gros-Morne 672 . . . . C 1
Hampstead 7,598 . . . . H 4
Ham-Sud⊙ 62 . . . . F 4
Hauterive 13,995 . . . . A 1
Hébertville 2,515 . . . . F 1
Hébertville-Station 1,442 . . . . . F 1
Hemmingford 737 . . . . D 4
Henryville 595 . . . . D 4
Howick 639 . . . . D 4
Hudson 4,414 . . . . C 4
Hull⊙ 56,225 . . . . B 4
Huntingdon⊙ 3,018 . . . . C 4
Île-Perrot 5,945 . . . . G 4
Iberville⊙ 8,587 . . . . D 4
Inverness⊙ 329 . . . . F 3
Joliette⊙ 16,987 . . . . D 3
Jonquière 60,354 . . . . F 1
Jonquière-Chicoutimi
*135,172 . . . . F 1
Kingsey Falls 818 . . . . E 4
Kirkland 10,476 . . . . H 4
Knowlton (Lac-Brome)⊙
4,316 . . . . E 4
La Baie 20,935 . . . . G 1
Labelle 1,534 . . . . C 3
Lac-à-la-Croix 1,017 . . . . F 1
Lac-Alouette-Lac-Brière 1,356 D 4
Lac-au-Saumon 1,332 . . . . B 2
Lac-aux-Sables 838 . . . . E 3
Lac-Beaufort . . . . F 3
Lac-Bouchette 1,703 . . . . E 1
Lac-Carré 717 . . . . C 3
Lac-des-Écorces 766 . . . . B 3
Lac-Drolet 1,120 . . . . G 4
Lac-Etchemin 2,729 . . . . G 3
Lachenaie 8,631 . . . . D 4
Lachine 37,521 . . . . H 4
Lachute⊙ 11,729 . . . . C 4
Lac-Mégantic⊙ 6,119 . . . . G 4
Lacolle 1,319 . . . . D 4
Lac-Saint-Charles 5,837 . . . . . H 3
Lafontaine 4,799 . . . . C 4
La Guadeloupe 1,692 . . . . F 4
La Malbaie⊙ 4,030 . . . . G 2
Lambton 1,559 . . . . F 4
L'Annonciation 2,384 . . . . C 3
Lanoraie (Lanoraie-d'Autry)
1,613 . . . . D 4
La Pêche 4,977 . . . . B 4
La Pérade 1,039 . . . . E 3
La Pocatière 4,560 . . . . H 2
La Prairie⊙ 10,627 . . . . J 4
La Providence . . . . E 4
Larouche 662 . . . . F 1
La Salle 76,299 . . . . H 4
L'Ascension 1,287 . . . . F 1
L'Assomption⊙ 4,844 . . . . D 4
La Station-du-Coteau 892 . . . . C 4
Laterrière 788 . . . . F 1
La Tuque 11,556 . . . . E 2
Laurentides 1,947 . . . . D 4
Laurier-Station 1,123 . . . . F 3
Laurierville 939 . . . . F 3
Lauzon 13,362 . . . . J 3
Laval 268,335 . . . . H 4
Lavaltrie 2,053 . . . . D 4
L'Avenir 1,116 . . . . E 4
Lawrenceville 562 . . . . E 4
Le Moyne 6,137 . . . . J 4
L'Épiphanie 2,971 . . . . D 4
Léry 2,239 . . . . H 4
Lévis 17,895 . . . . J 3
Lennoxville 3,922 . . . . F 4
Les Méchins 803 . . . . B 1
Linière 1,168 . . . . G 3
L'Islet 1,070 . . . . G 2
L'Islet-sur-Mer 774 . . . . G 2
L'Isle-Verte 1,142 . . . . G 1
Longueuil⊙ 124,320 . . . . J 4
Loretteville⊙ 15,060 . . . . H 3
Lorraine 6,881 . . . . H 4
Louiseville⊙ 3,735 . . . . E 3
Luceville 1,524 . . . . J 1
Lyster 830 . . . . F 3
Magog 13,604 . . . . E 4
Maniwaki⊙ 5,424 . . . . B 3
Manseau 626 . . . . E 3
Maple Grove 2,009 . . . . H 4
Maria 1,178 . . . . C 2
Marieville⊙ 4,877 . . . . D 4
Mascouche 20,345 . . . . H 4
Maskinongé 1,005 . . . . E 3
Masson 4,264 . . . . B 4
Massueville 671 . . . . E 4
Matane⊙ 13,612 . . . . B 1
Matapédia 586 . . . . B 2
Melocheville 1,892 . . . . C 4
Mercier 6,352 . . . . H 4
Metabetchouan 3,406 . . . . F 1
Mirabel⊙ 14,080 . . . . H 4
Mistassini 6,682 . . . . E 1
Montauban 557 . . . . E 3
Mont-Carmel 807 . . . . H 2
Montcerf 570 . . . . A 3
Montebello 1,229 . . . . B 4
Mont-Joli 6,359 . . . . J 1
Mont-Laurier⊙ 8,405 . . . . B 3
Mont-Louis 756 . . . . C 1
Montmagny⊙ 12,405 . . . . G 3
Montréal⊙ 980,354 . . . . H 4
Montréal *2,828,349 . . . . H 4
Montréal-Est 3,778 . . . . J 4
Montréal-Nord 94,914 . . . . H 4
Mont-Rolland 1,517 . . . . C 4
Mont-Royal 19,247 . . . . H 4
Mont-Saint-Hilaire 10,066 . . . . D 4
Morin Heights 592 . . . . C 4
Murdochville 3,396 . . . . C 1
Nantes 1,167 . . . . F 4

Agriculture, Industry and Resources

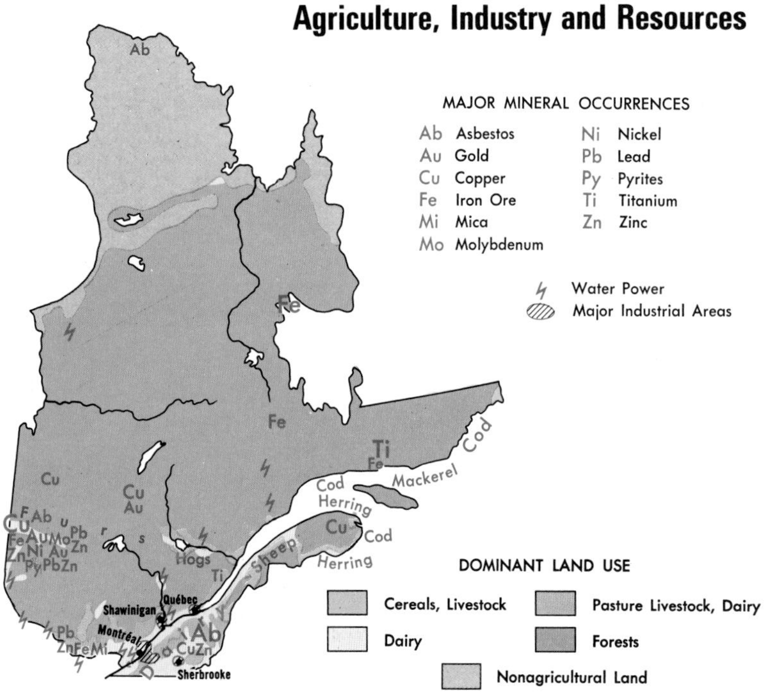
MAJOR MINERAL OCCURRENCES
Ab Asbestos
Au Gold
Cu Copper
Fe Iron Ore
Mi Mica
Mo Molybdenum
Ni Nickel
Pb Lead
Py Pyrites
Ti Titanium
Zn Zinc
Water Power
Major Industrial Areas
DOMINANT LAND USE
Cereals, Livestock
Pasture Livestock, Dairy
Dairy
Forests
Nonagricultural Land
Cod
Mackerel
Herring
Hogs
Sheep
Shawinigan
Québec
Montréal
Sherbrooke

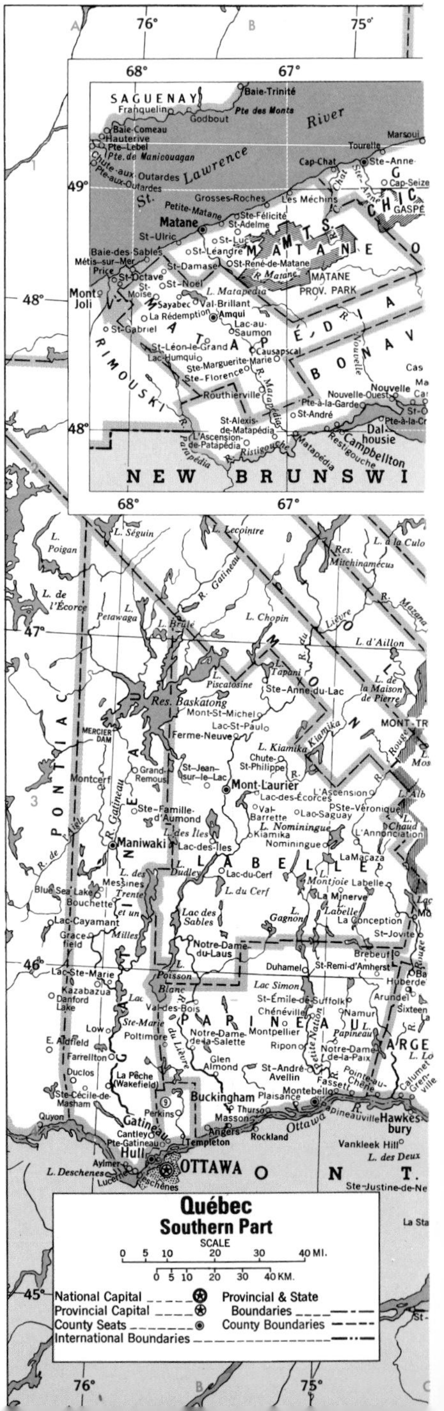
Québec
Southern Part
SCALE
0 5 10 20 30 40 MI.
0 5 10 20 30 40 KM.
National Capital
Provincial Capital
County Seats
International Boundaries
Provincial & State Boundaries
County Boundaries
SAGUENAY
Baie-Trinité
Baie-Comeau
Hauterive
Pte des Monts
Matane
MATANE PROV. PARK
Mont Joli
RIMOUSKI
Amqui
Causapscal
Matapédia
Campbellton
Dalhousie
NEW BRUNSWICK
PONTIAC
Maniwaki
Mont-Laurier
LABELLE
PAPINEAU
Buckingham
Gatineau
Hull
OTTAWA
ONT.
Hawkesbury

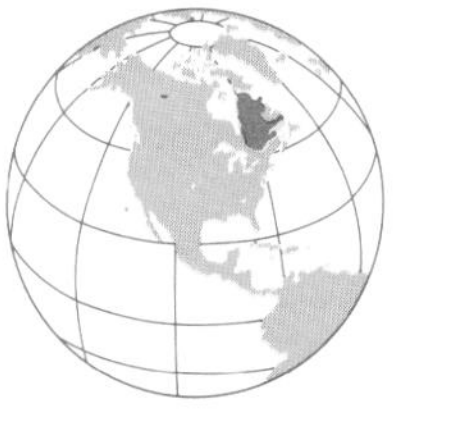

AREA 594,857 sq. mi. (1,540,680 sq. km.)
POPULATION 6,532,461
CAPITAL Québec
LARGEST CITY Montréal
HIGHEST POINT Mont D'Iberville 5,420 ft. (1,652 m.)
SETTLED IN 1608
ADMITTED TO CONFEDERATION 1867
PROVINCIAL FLOWER White Garden Lily

Napierville⊙ 2,343 D 4
Neuville 996 F 3
New Carlisle⊙ 1,292 D 2
New Richmond 4,257 C 2
Nicolet 4,880 E 4
Nominingue 881 B 3
Normandin 4,041 E 1
North Hatley 689 F 4
Notre-Dame-de-la-Doré 1,064 E 1
Notre-Dame-des-Laurentides H 3
Notre-Dame-des-Prairies 6,150 D 3
Notre-Dame-du-Bon-Conseil 1,089 E 4
Notre-Dame-du-Lac⊙ 2,258 J 2
Nouvelle 669 C 2
Oka 1,538 C 4
Omerville 1,398 E 4
Ormstown 1,659 D 4
Orsainville H 3
Otis 673 G 1
Otterburn Park 4,268 D 4
Outremont 24,338 H 4
Pabos 1,295 D 2
Pabos-Mills 1,565 D 2
Papineauville⊙ 1,481 C 4
Paspébiac 1,914 D 2
Percé⊙ 4,839 D 1
Petit-Cap 1,023 D 1
Petite-Matane 1,065 B 1
Petit-Saguenay (Saint-François-d'Assise) 804 G 1
Pierrefonds 38,390 H 4
Pierreville 1,212 E 3
Pincourt 8,750 D 4
Pintendre 1,849 J 3
Plaisance 748 B 4
Plessisville 7,249 F 3
Pohénégamook 3,702 H 2
Pointe-à-la-Croix 1,481 C 2
Pointe-au-Père 796 J 1
Pointe-au-Pic 1,054 G 2
Pointe-aux-Outardes 1,056 A 1
Pointe-aux-Trembles 36,270 J 4
Pointe-Calumet 2,935 G 4
Pointe-Claire 24,571 H 4
Pointe-du-Lac 5,359 E 3
Pointe-Gatineau B 4
Pointe-Lebel 1,573 A 1
Pont-Rouge 3,580 F 3
Port-Alfred 8,621 G 1
Portneuf 1,333 F 3
Portneuf-sur-Mer (Rivière-Portneuf-sur-Mer) 1,255 H 1
Price 2,273 A 1
Princeville 4,023 F 3
Proulxville 588 E 3
Québec (cap.) 166,474 H 3
Québec *576,075 H 3
Quyon 744 A 4
Rawdon 2,958 D 3
Repentigny 34,419 J 4
Richelieu 1,832 D 4
Richmond⊙ 3,568 E 4
Rigaud 2,268 C 4
Rimouski⊙ 29,120 J 1
Rimouski-Est 2,506 J 1
Ripon 620 B 4
Rivière-à-Pierre 615 E 3
Rivière-au-Renard 2,211 D 1
Rivière-Bleue 1,690 J 2
Rivière-Bois-Clair 604 F 3
Rivière-du-Loup⊙ 13,459 H 2
Rivière-du-Moulin G 1
Rivière-Éternité 659 G 1
Rivière-Portneuf-Portneuf-sur-Mer 1,255 H 1
Robertsonville 1,987 F 3
Roberval⊙ 11,429 E 1
Rock Island 1,179 E 4
Rosemère 7,778 H 4
Rougemont 972 D 4
Roxboro 6,292 H 4
Roxton Falls 1,245 E 4
Sacré-Coeur-de-Saguenay 1,678 H 1
Saint-Adelme 618 B 1
Saint-Adelphe 1,159 E 3
Saint-Adolphe-d'Howard 1,686 C 4
Saint-Adrien 597 F 4
Saint-Agapitville 2,954 F 3
Saint-Aimé-des-Lacs 861 G 2
Saint-Alban 673 E 3
Saint-Alexandre-de-Kamouraska 1,048 H 2
Saint-Alexis-des-Monts 1,984 D 3
Saint-Amable 2,424 J 4
Saint-Ambroise 3,606 F 1
Saint-Anaclet 1,377 J 1
Saint-André-Avellin 1,312 B 4
Saint-André-Est 1,293 C 4
Saint-Anselme 1,808 F 3
Saint-Antoine 7,012 H 4
Saint-Antonin 941 H 2
Saint-Aubert 884 G 2
Saint-Augustin-de-Québec 2,475 E 3
Saint-Basile-Sud 1,719 F 3
Saint-Basile-le-Grand 7,658 J 4
Saint-Benjamin 1,027 G 3
Saint-Bernard 585 F 3
Saint-Bernard-sur-Mer 711 G 2
Saint-Boniface-de-Shawinigan 3,164 D 3
Saint-Bruno 2,580 F 1
Saint-Bruno-de-Montarville 22,880 J 4
Saint-Camille-de-Bellechasse 1,744 G 3
Saint-Casimir 1,133 E 3
Saint-Césaire 2,935 D 4
Saint-Charles 1,019 G 3
Saint-Charles-de-Mandeville 1,392 D 3
Saint-Chrysostome 1,018 D 4
Saint-Côme 660 D 3
Saint-Constant 9,938 H 4
Saint-Cyprien 860 J 2
Saint-Cyrille 1,041 E 4
Saint-Damien-de-Buckland 1,522 G 3
Saint-David 5,380 J 3
Saint-David-de-Falardeau 1,876 F 1
Saint-Denis 861 D 4
Saint-Dominique 2,068 E 4
Saint-Donat-de-Montcalm 1,521 C 3
Sainte-Adèle 4,675 C 4
Sainte-Agathe 709 F 3
Sainte-Agathe-des-Monts 5,641 C 3
Sainte-Anne-de-Beaupré 3,292 F 2
Sainte-Anne-de-Bellevue 3,981 H 4
Sainte-Anne-des-Monts⊙ 6,062 C 1
Sainte-Anne-des-Plaines 4,258 H 4
Sainte-Anne-du-Lac 686 B 3
Sainte-Aurélie 1,045 G 3
Sainte-Blandine 849 J 1
Sainte-Catherine 1,474 F 3
Sainte-Claire 1,566 G 3
Sainte-Croix⊙ 1,814 F 3
Sainte-Félicité 711 B 1
Sainte-Foy 68,883 H 3
Sainte-Geneviève 2,573 H 4
Sainte-Geneviève-de-Batiscan⊙ 356 E 3
Sainte-Hélène-de-Bagot 1,328 E 4
Sainte-Hénédine⊙ 639 F 3
Sainte-Julie-de-Verchères 14,243 J 4
Sainte-Julienne⊙ 750 D 4
Sainte-Justine 1,080 G 3
Saint-Élie 639 E 3
Saint-Elzéar 743 F 3
Sainte-Marie 8,937 G 3
Sainte-Martine⊙ 2,196 D 4
Saint-Émile 5,216 H 3
Sainte-Monique 705 F 1
Sainte-Pétronille 982 J 3
Sainte-Perpétue-de-L'Islet 1,232 H 2
Saint-Éphrem-de-Tring 973 G 3
Saint-Épiphane 647 H 2
Sainte-Pudentienne 866 E 4
Sainte-Rosalie 2,862 E 4
Saint-Esprit 1,068 D 4
Sainte-Thérèse 18,750 H 4
Sainte-Thérèse-Ouest (Boisbriand) 13,471 H 4
Saint-Thècle 1,703 E 3
Saint-Étienne-de-Grès 845 E 3
Saint-Étienne-de-Lauzon 1,218 J 3

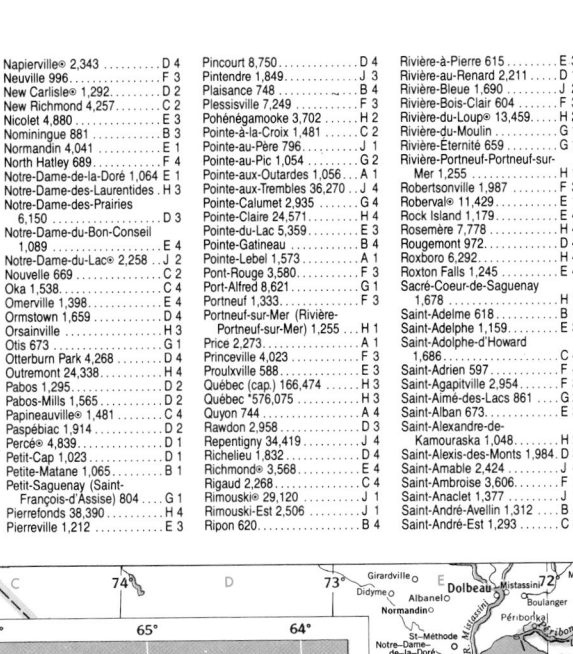

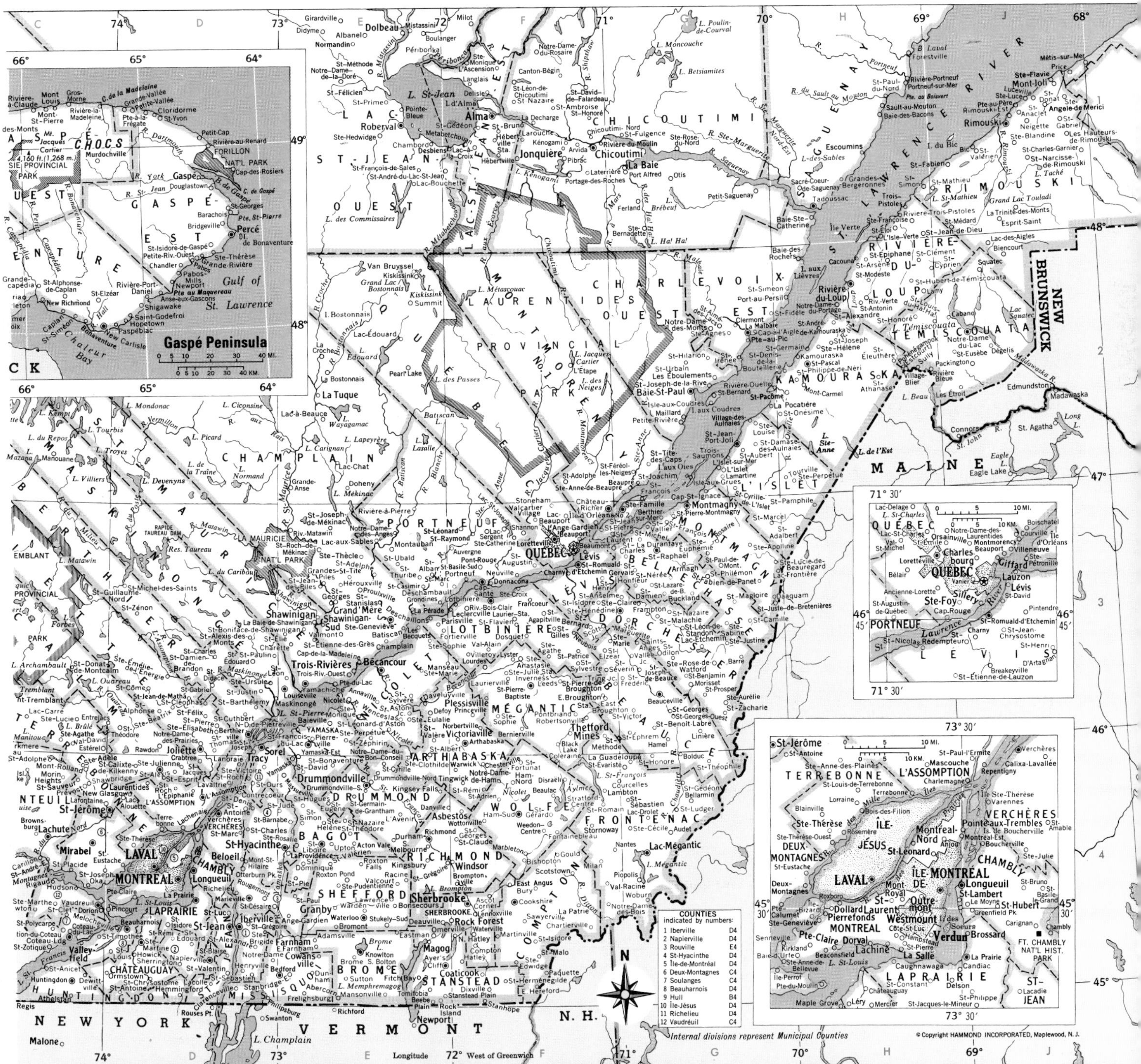
Gaspé Peninsula
Gulf of St. Lawrence
CHALEUR BAY
ST. LAWRENCE RIVER
NEW BRUNSWICK
MAINE
NEW YORK
VERMONT
N.H.
L. St-Jean
LAURENTIDES PROVINCIAL PARK
QUÉBEC
MONTRÉAL
LAVAL
SHERBROOKE
TROIS-RIVIÈRES
COUNTIES indicated by numbers:
1 Iberville D4
2 Napierville D4
3 Rouville E4
4 St-Hyacinthe D4
5 Île-de-Montréal D4
6 Deux-Montagnes C4
7 Soulanges C4
8 Beauharnois C4
9 Hull B4
10 Île-Jésus D4
11 Richelieu D4
12 Vaudreuil C4
Internal divisions represent Municipal Counties
Longitude 72° West of Greenwich

174 Quebec

(continued)

Saint-Eustache 29,716 H 4
Saint-Fabien 1,361 J 1
Saint-Félicien 9,058 E 1
Saint-Félix-de-Valois 1,462 D 3
Saint-Ferréol-les-Neiges 1,758 G 2
Saint-Flavien 734 F 3
Saint-François-de-Sales 831 E 1
Saint-François-du-Lac⊙ 942 E 3
Saint-Fulgence 950 G 1
Saint-Gabriel 3,161 D 3
Saint-Gabriel-de-Rimouski 779 J 1
Saint-Gédéon, Frontenac 1,569 G 4
Saint-Gédéon, Lac-St-Jean-E. 1,000 F 1
Saint-Georges, Beauce 10,342 G 3
Saint-Georges, Champlain 3,344 E 3
Saint-Georges-Ouest 6,378 G 3
Saint-Germain-de-Grantham 1,373 E 4
Saint-Gervais 973 G 3
Saint-Gilles 912 F 3
Saint-Grégoire (Mont-St-Grégoire) 740 D 4
Saint-Henri 1,970 J 3
Saint-Honoré, Beauce 1,116 G 4
Saint-Honoré, Chicoutimi 1,790 F 1
Saint-Hubert 60,573 J 4
Saint-Hubert-de-Témiscouata 871 J 2
Saint-Hyacinthe⊙ 38,246 D 4
Saint-Isidore 811 F 3
Saint-Isidore-de-Laprairie 769 D 4
Saint-Jacques 2,152 D 4
Saint-Jacques-le-Mineur 1,203 H 4
Saint-Jean-Chrysostome 6,930 J 3
Saint-Jean-de-Dieu 1,377 J 1
Saint-Jean-de-Matha 931 D 3
Saint-Jean-Port-Joli⊙ 1,813 G 2
Saint-Jean-sur-Richelieu⊙ 35,640 D 4
Saint-Jérôme 25,123 H 4
Saint-Joachim 1,139 G 2
Saint-Joseph-de-Beauce 3,216 G 3
Saint-Joseph-de-Sorel 2,545 D 3
Saint-Jovite 3,841 C 3
Saint-Lambert 20,557 J 4
Saint-Laurent 65,900 H 4
Saint-Lazare 731 G 3
Saint-Léonard 79,429 H 4
Saint-Léonard-d'Aston 992 E 3
Saint-Léon-de-Chicoutimi 749 F 1
Saint-Léon-de-Standon 816 G 3
Saint-Léon-le-Grand 722 B 2
Saint-Liboire⊙ 746 E 4
Saint-Louis-de-Gonzague 615 D 4
Saint-Louis-de-Terrebonne 14,172 H 4
Saint-Louis-du-Ha! Ha! 809 H 2
Saint-Luc 8,815 D 4
Saint-Luc-de-Matane 598 B 1
Saint-Marc-des-Carrières 2,822 E 3
Saint-Méthode-de-Frontenac 925 F 3
Saint-Michel-de-Bellechasse 963 G 3
Saint-Michel-des-Saints 1,584 D 3
Saint-Nazaire-de-Chicoutimi 962 F 1
Saint-Nérée 970 G 3
Saint-Nicolas 5,074 H 3
Saint-Noël 666 B 1
Saint-Odilon 580 G 3
Saint-Omer 718 C 2
Saint-Ours 625 D 4
Saint-Pacôme 1,996 G 2
Saint-Pamphile 3,428 H 3
Saint-Pascal⊙ 2,763 H 2
Saint-Paul-de-Montminy 602 G 3
Saint-Paulin 663 D 3
Saint-Paul-l'Ermite (Le Gardeur) 8,312 J 4
Saint-Philippe-de-Néri 715 H 2
Saint-Pie 1,725 E 4
Saint-Pierre 5,305 H 4
Saint-Pierre-d'Orléans 880 G 3
Saint-Polycarpe 602 C 4
Saint-Prime 2,522 E 1
Saint-Prosper-de-Dorchester 2,150 G 3
Saint-Raphaël⊙ 1,346 G 3
Saint-Raymond 3,605 F 3
Saint-Rédempteur 4,463 J 3
Saint-Régis 1,370 C 4
Saint-Rémi 5,146 D 4
Saint-Roch-de-l'Achigan 1,160 D 4
Saint-Roch-de-Richelieu 1,650 D 4
Saint-Romuald-d'Etchemin⊙ 9,849 J 3
Saint-Sauveur-des-Monts 2,348 C 4
Saint-Siméon 1,152 G 2
Saint-Simon 602 H 1
Saint-Stanislas 1,443 E 3
Saint-Sylvère 1,006 E 3
Saint-Timothée 2,113 D 4
Saint-Tite 3,031 E 3
Saint-Tite-des-Caps 626 G 2
Saint-Ubald 1,605 E 3
Saint-Ulric 792 B 1
Saint-Urbain-de-Charlevoix 1,079 G 2
Saint-Victor 1,104 G 3
Saint-Zacharie 1,284 G 3
Saint-Zotique 1,774 C 4
Sault-au-Mouton 828 H 1
Sawyerville 939 F 4
Sayabec 1,721 B 2
Scotstown 762 F 4
Senneville 1,221 G 4
Shannon 3,488 F 3
Shawbridge 942 C 4
Shawinigan 23,011 E 3
Shawinigan-Sud 11,325 E 3
Shawville 1,608 A 4
Sherbrooke⊙ 74,075 E 4
Sherrington 614 D 4
Sillery 12,825 J 3
Sorel⊙ 20,347 D 4
Squatec 1,000 J 2
Stanstead Plain 1,093 F 4
Sutton 1,599 E 4
Tadoussac⊙ 900 H 1
Templeton B 4
Terrebonne 11,769 H 4
Thetford Mines 19,965 F 3
Thurso 2,780 B 4
Tourelle (Tourelle-Grand-Tourelle) 942 C 1
Tourville 659 H 2
Tracy 12,843 D 3
Tring-Jonction 1,315 F 3
Trois-Pistoles 4,445 H 1
Trois-Rivières 50,466 E 3
Trois-Rivières *111,453 E 3
Trois-Rivières-Ouest 13,107 E 3
Upton 926 E 4
Val-Barrette 609 B 3
Val-Brillant 687 B 1
Valcourt 2,601 E 4
Val-David 2,336 C 3
Vallée-Jonction 1,200 G 3
Valleyfield (Salaberry-de-Valleyfield) 29,574 C 4
Vanier 10,725 J 3
Varennes 8,764 J 4
Vaudreuil⊙ 7,608 C 4
Verchères⊙ 4,473 J 4
Verdun 61,287 H 4
Victoriaville 21,838 F 3
Villeneuve J 3
Warwick 2,847 F 4
Waterloo⊙ 4,664 E 4
Waterville 1,397 F 4
Weedon-Centre 1,263 F 4
Westmount 20,480 H 4
Wickham 2,043 E 4
Windsor 5,233 F 4
Wottonville 673 F 4
Yamachiche⊙ 1,258 E 3

OTHER FEATURES

Alma (isl.) F 1
Aylmer (lake) F 4
Baskatong (res.) B 3
Batiscan (riv.) E 2
Bécancour (riv.) F 3
Bonaventure (isl.) D 1
Bonaventure (riv.) C 1
Brome (lake) E 4
Brompton (lake) E 4
Cascapédia (riv.) C 1
Chaleur (bay) C 2
Champlain (lake) D 4
Chaudière (riv.) G 4
Chic-Chocs (mts.) C 1
Chicoutimi (riv.) F 2
Coudres (isl.) G 2
Deschênes (lake) A 4
Deux Montagnes (lake) C 4
Ditton (riv.) F 4
Forillon Nat'l Park D 1
Fort Chambly Nat'l Hist. Park J 4
Gaspé (bay) D 1
Gaspé (cape) D 1
Gaspé (pen.) D 2
Gaspésie Prov. Park C 1
Gatineau (riv.) B 3
Îles (lake) B 3
Jacques-Cartier (mt.) C 1
Jacques-Cartier (riv.) F 2
Kénogami (lake) F 1
Kiamika (lake) B 3
La Maurice Nat'l Park D 3
Laurentides Prov. Park F 2
Lièvre (riv.) B 4
Lièvres (isl.) H 2
Maskinongé (riv.) D 3
Matane (riv.) B 1
Matane Prov. Park B 1
Matapédia (riv.) B 2
Mégantic (lake) G 4
Memphremagog (lake) E 4
Mercier (dam) A 3
Métabetchouane (riv.) F 1
Mille Îles (riv.) H 4
Montmorency (riv.) F 2
Mont-Tremblant Prov. Park C 3
Nicolet (riv.) E 3
Nominingue (lake) B 3
Nord (riv.) C 4
Orléans (isl.) F 3
Ottawa (riv.) B 4
Ouareau (riv.) D 3
Ouelle (riv.) H 2
Patapédia (riv.) B 2
Péribonca (riv.) F 1
Petite Nation (riv.) B 4
Prairies (riv.) H 4
Rimouski (riv.) J 1
Ristigouche (riv.) B 2
Saguenay (riv.) G 1
Sainte-Anne (riv.) F 3
Sainte-Anne (riv.) G 2
Saint-François (lake) F 4
Saint-François (riv.) E 4
Saint-Jean (lake) E 1
Saint Lawrence (gulf) D 2
Saint Lawrence (riv.) H 1
Saint-Louis (lake) H 4
Saint-Maurice (riv.) E 2
Saint-Pierre (lake) E 3
Shawinigan (riv.) E 3
Shipshaw (riv.) F 1
Soeurs (isl.) H 4
Témiscouata (lake) H 2
Tremblant (lake) C 3
Trente et un Milles (lake) B 3
Verte (isl.) H 1
Yamaska (riv.) E 4
York (riv.) D 1

⊙County seat.
*Population of metropolitan area.

QUÉBEC, NORTHERN

INTERNAL DIVISIONS

Abitibi (county) 93,529 B 2
Abitibi (terr.) B 3
Berthier (county) 31,096 B 3
Bonaventure (county) 40,487 D 3
Champlain (county) 119,595 C 3
Charlevoix-Est (co.) 17,448 C 3
Charlevoix-Ouest (county) 14,172 C 3
Chicoutimi (county) 174,441 C 2
Gaspé-Est (county) 41,173 E 3
Gaspé-Ouest (county) 18,943 D 3
Gatineau (county) 54,229 B 3
Joliette (county) 60,384 B 3
Lac-Saint-Jean-Est (county) 47,891 C 3
Lac-Saint-Jean-Ouest (county) 62,952 C 2
Maskinongé (county) 20,763 C 3
Matane (county) 29,955 D 3
Matapédia (county) 23,715 D 3
Mistassini (terr.) B 2
Montcalm (county) 27,557 B 3
Montmorency No. I (county) 23,048 C 3
Nouveau-Québec (terr.) E 1
Pontiac (county) 20,283 B 3
Portneuf (county) 58,843 C 3
Québec (county) 458,980 C 3
Rimouski (county) 69,099 D 3
Saguenay (county) 115,881 D 2
Saint-Maurice (co.) 107,703 C 3
Témiscamingue (co.) 52,570 B 3

CITIES and TOWNS

Alma⊙ 26,322 C 3
Amos⊙ 9,421 B 3
Baie-Comeau 12,866 D 3
Baie-du-Poste 1,690 C 2
Chicoutimi⊙ 60,064 C 3
Gaspé 17,261 E 3
Hauterive 13,995 D 3
Jonquière 60,354 C 3
Lévis 17,895 C 3
La Tuque 11,556 C 3
Manicouagan D 2
Maniwaki⊙ 5,424 B 3
Matane⊙ 13,612 D 3
Mistassini (Baie-du-Poste) 1,690 C 2
Mont-Laurier⊙ 8,405 B 3
Montmagny⊙ 12,405 C 3
New Carlisle⊙ 781 E 3
Perce⊙ 4,839 E 3
Port-Cartier-Ouest D 3
Port-Menier⊙ 275 E 3
Povungnituk 745 E 1
Québec (cap.)⊙ 166,474 C 3
Rimouski⊙ 29,120 D 3
Rivière-au-Tonnerre 480 D 2
Rivière-du-Loup 13,459 D 3
Rouyn 17,224 B 3
Sept-Îles 29,262 D 2
Shawinigan 23,011 C 3
Tadoussac 900 C 3
Val d'Or 21,371 B 3
Ville-Marie 2,651 B 3
Wemindji B 2

OTHER FEATURES

Allard (lake) E 2
Anticosti (isl.) E 3
Baleine, Grand Rivière de la (riv.) B 1
Bell (riv.) B 3
Betsiamites (riv.) C 2
Bienville (lake) C 2
Broadback (riv.) B 2
Cabonga (res.) B 3
Caniapiscau (riv.) D 1
Eastmain (riv.) B 2
Eau Claire (lake) C 1
Feuilles (riv.) C 1
Gaspésie Prov. Park D 3
George (riv.) F 2
Gouin (res.) C 3
Grande Rivière, La (riv.) B 2
Honguedo (passage) E 3
Hudson (bay) A 1
Hudson (str.) F 1
Jacques-Cartier (passage) E 3
James (bay) A 2
Koksoak (riv.) D 1
Laurentides Prov. Park C 3
Louis-XIV (pt.) B 2
Manicouagan (res.) D 2
Minto (lake) E 2
Mistassibi (riv.) C 3
Mistassini (lake) C 2
Moisie (riv.) D 2
Natashquan (riv.) E 2
Nottaway (riv.) B 2
Nouveau-Québec (crater) F 1
Otish (mts.) C 2
Ottawa (riv.) B 3
Péribonca (riv.) C 3
Plétipi (lake) C 2
Saguenay (riv.) C 3
Saint-Jean (lake) C 3
Saint Lawrence (gulf) E 3
Saint Lawrence (riv.) D 3
Ungava (pen.) E 1

⊙County seat.
*Population of metropolitan area.

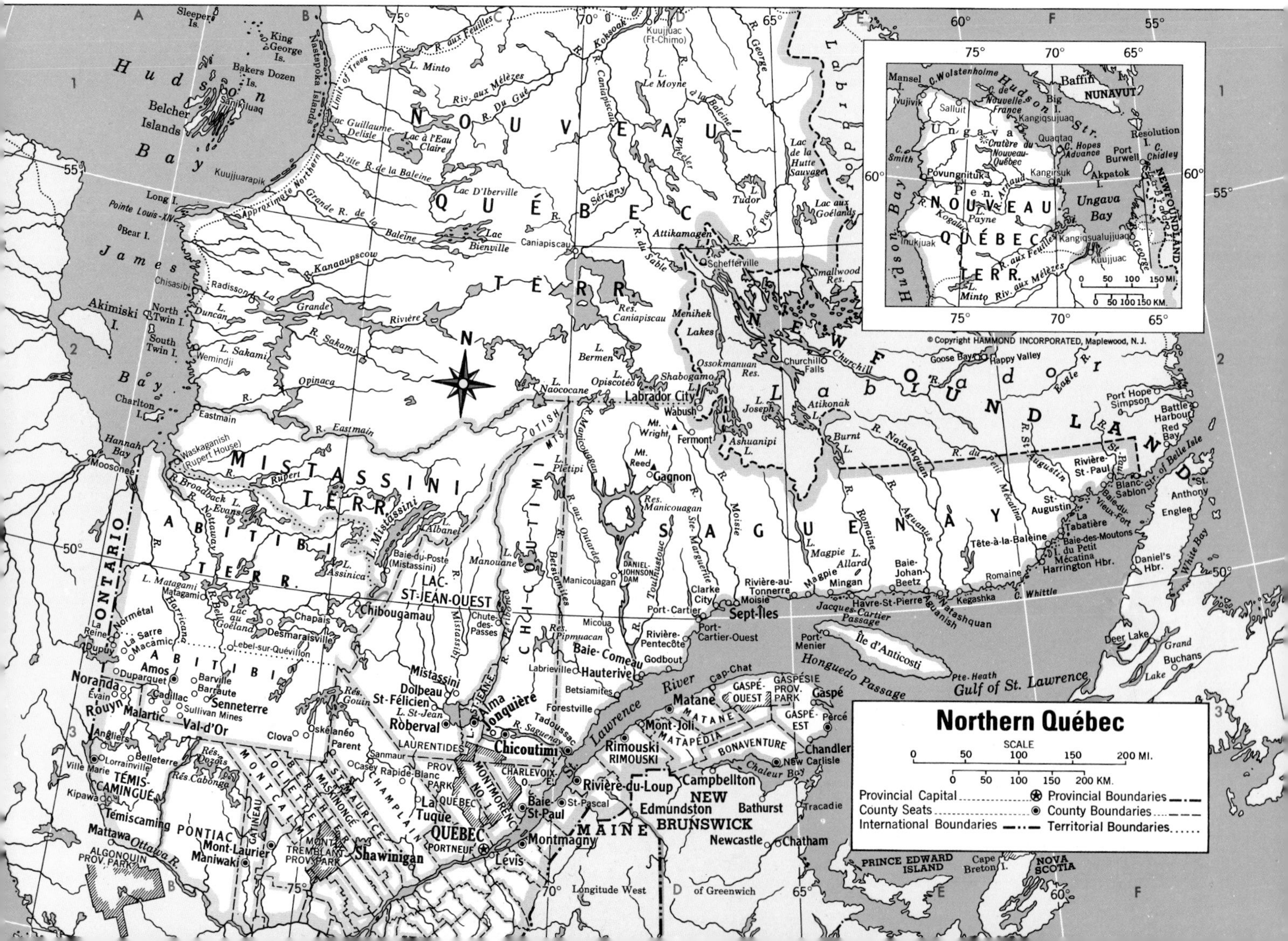
Northern Québec
SCALE
0 50 100 150 200 MI.
0 50 100 150 200 KM.
Provincial Capital
Provincial Boundaries
County Seats
County Boundaries
International Boundaries
Territorial Boundaries
© Copyright HAMMOND INCORPORATED, Maplewood, N. J.
Hudson Bay
James Bay
NOUVEAU-QUÉBEC
TERR.
MISTASSINI TERR.
ABITIBI TERR.
SAGUENAY
NEWFOUNDLAND
Labrador
ONTARIO
NEW BRUNSWICK
MAINE
Gulf of St. Lawrence
Honguedo Passage
Île d'Anticosti
Sept-Îles
Chicoutimi
Longitude West of Greenwich

ONTARIO, NORTHERN

INTERNAL DIVISIONS

Algoma (terr. dist.) 133,553 D 3
Cochrane (terr. dist.) 96,875 D 2
Kenora (terr. dist.) 59,421 C 2
Manitoulin (terr. dist.) 11,001 D 3
Nipissing (terr. dist.) 80,268 E 3
Parry Sound (terr. dist.) 33,528 E 3
Rainy River (terr. dist.) 22,798 B 3
Renfrew (county) 87,484 E 3
Sudbury (reg. munic.) 159,779 D 3
Sudbury (terr. dist.) 27,068 D 3
Thunder Bay (terr. dist.) 153,997 C 3
Timiskaming (terr. dist.) 41,288 D 3

CITIES and TOWNS

Chalk River 1,010 E 3
Elliot Lake 16,723 D 3
Fort Albany 482 D 2
Fort Frances⊙ 8,906 B 3
Kapuskasing 12,014 D 3
Kenora⊙ 9,817 B 3
Kirkland Lake 12,219 D 3
Moose Factory 1,452 D 2
Moosonee 1,433 D 2
Nickel Centre 12,318 D 3
North Bay⊙ 51,268 E 3
Pembroke⊙ 14,026 E 3
Sault Sainte Marie⊙ 82,697 D 3
Sudbury 91,829 D 3
Thunder Bay⊙ 112,486 C 3
Timmins 46,114 D 3
Valley East 20,433 D 3

OTHER FEATURES

Abitibi (lake) E 3
Abitibi (riv.) D 2
Albany (riv.) C 2
Algonquin Prov. Park E 3
Asheweig (riv.) C 2
Attawapiskat (lake) C 2
Attawapiskat (riv.) C 2
Basswood (lake) B 3
Berens (riv.) A 2
Big Trout (lake) B 2
Black Duck (riv.) C 1
Bloodvein (riv.) A 2
Caribou (isl.) C 3
Cobham (riv.) A 2
Eabamet (lake) C 2
Ekwan (riv.) C 2
English (riv.) B 2
Fawn (riv.) C 2
Finger (lake) B 2
Georgian (bay) D 3
Hannah (bay) D 2
Henrietta Maria (cape) D 1
Hudson (bay) D 1
Huron (lake) D 3
James (bay) D 2
Kapiskau (riv.) D 2
Kapuskasing (riv.) D 3
Kenogami (riv.) C 2
Kesagami (riv.) E 2
Lake of the Woods (lake) B 3
Lake Superior Prov. Park D 3
Little Current (riv.) C 2
Long (lake) C 3
Manitoulin (isl.) D 3
Mattagami (riv.) D 3
Michipicoten (isl.) C 3
Mille Lacs (lake) B 3
Missinaibi (lake) D 3
Missinaibi (riv.) D 2
Missisa (lake) D 2
Nipigon (lake) C 3
Nipissing (lake) E 3
North (chan.) D 3
North Caribou (lake) B 2
Nungesser (lake) B 2
Ogidaki (mt.) D 3
Ogoki (riv.) C 2
Opazatika (riv.) D 3
Opinnagau (riv.) D 2
Otoskwin (riv.) B 2
Ottawa (riv.) E 3
Pipestone (riv.) B 2
Polar Bear Prov. Park D 2
Pukaskwa Prov. Park C 3
Quetico Prov. Park B 3
Rainy (lake) B 3
Red (lake) B 2
Sachigo (riv.) B 2
Saganaga (lake) B 3
Saint Ignace (isl.) C 3
Saint Joseph (lake) B 2
Sandy (lake) B 2
Savant (lake) B 2
Seine (riv.) B 3
Seul (lake) B 2
Severn (lake) B 2
Severn (riv.) B 2
Shamattawa (riv.) C 2
Shibogama (lake) C 2
Sibley Prov. Park C 3
Slate (isls.) C 3
Stout (lake) B 2
Superior (lake) C 3
Sutton (lake) D 2
Sutton (riv.) D 2
Temigami (lake) D 3
Timiskaming (lake) E 3
Trout (lake) B 2
Wabuk (pt.) D 1
Winisk (lake) C 2
Winisk (riv.) C 2
Winnipeg (riv.) A 2
Woods (lake) B 3

ONTARIO

INTERNAL DIVISIONS

Algoma (terr. dist.) 133,553 J 5
Brant (county) 104,427 D 4
Bruce (county) 60,020 C 3
Cochrane (terr. dist.) 96,875 J 4
Dufferin (county) 31,145 D 3
Dundas (county) 18,946 J 2
Durham (reg. munic.) 283,639 F 3
Elgin (county) 69,707 C 5
Essex (county) 312,467 B 5
Frontenac (county) 108,133 H 3
Glengarry (county) 20,254 K 2
Grenville (county) 27,176 J 3
Grey (county) 73,824 D 3
Haldimand-Norfolk (reg. munic.) 89,456 E 5
Haliburton (county) 11,361 F 2
Halton (reg. munic.) 253,883 E 4
Hamilton-Wentworth (reg. munic.) 411,445 D 4
Hastings (county) 106,883 G 3
Huron (county) 56,127 C 4
Kenora (terr. dist.) 59,421 G 5
Kent (county) 107,022 B 5
Lambton (county) 123,445 B 5
Lanark (county) 45,676 H 3
Leeds (county) 53,765 H 3
Lennox and Addington (county) 33,040 G 3
Manitoulin (terr. dist.) 11,001 B 2
Middlesex (county) 318,184 C 4
Muskoka (dist. munic.) 38,370 E 3
Niagara (reg. munic.) 368,288 E 4
Nipissing (terr. dist.) 80,268 F 2
Northumberland (county) 64,966 G 3
Ottawa-Carleton (reg. munic.) 546,849 J 2
Oxford (county) 85,920 D 4
Parry Sound (terr. dist.) 33,528 D 2
Peel (reg. munic.) 490,731 E 4
Perth (county) 66,096 C 4
Peterborough (county) 102,452 F 3
Prescott (county) 30,365 K 2
Prince Edward (county) 22,336 G 3
Rainy River (terr. dist.) 22,798 G 5
Renfrew (county) 87,484 G 2
Russell (county) 22,412 J 2
Simcoe (county) 225,071 E 3
Stormont (county) 61,927 K 2
Sudbury (reg. munic.) 159,779 K 6
Sudbury (terr. dist.) 27,068 J 5
Thunder Bay (terr. dist.) 153,997 H 5
Timiskaming (terr. dist.) 41,288 K 5
Toronto (metro. munic.) 2,137,395 K 4
Victoria (county) 47,854 F 3
Waterloo (reg. munic.) 305,496 D 4
Wellington (county) 129,432 D 4
York (reg. munic.) 252,053 E 4

CITIES and TOWNS

Ailsa Craig 765 C 4
Ajax 25,475 E 4
Alban 342 D 1
Alexandria 3,271 K 2
Alfred 1,057 K 2
Alliston 4,712 E 3
Almonte 3,855 H 2
Alvinston 736 B 5
Amherstburg 5,685 A 5
Amherst View 6,110 H 3
Ancaster 14,428 D 4
Angus 3,085 E 3
Apsley 264 F 3
Arkona 473 C 4
Armstrong 378 H 4
Arnprior 5,828 H 2
Aroland 291 H 4
Arthur 1,700 D 4
Astorville 340 E 1
Athens 948 J 3
Atherley 366 E 3
Atikokan 4,452 G 5

AREA 412,580 sq. mi. (1,068,582 sq. km.)
POPULATION 9,101,694
CAPITAL Toronto
LARGEST CITY Toronto
HIGHEST POINT in Timiskaming Dist. 2,275 ft. (693 m.)
SETTLED IN 1749
ADMITTED TO CONFEDERATION 1867
PROVINCIAL FLOWER White Trillium

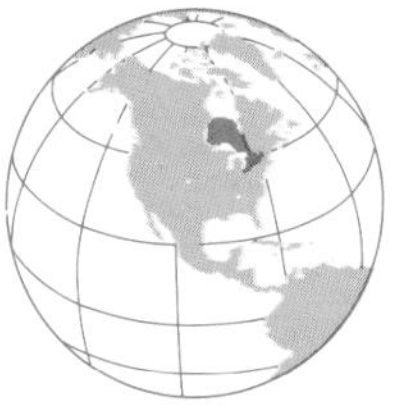

Atwood 723 D 4
Aurora 16,267 J 3
Avonmore 273 K 2
Aylmer 5,254 C 5
Ayr 1,295 D 4
Ayton 424 D 3
Baden 945 D 4
Bala 577 E 2
Bancroft 2,329 G 2
Barrie⊙ 38,423 E 3
Barry's Bay 1,216 G 2
Batawa 430 G 3
Bath 1,071 H 3
Bayfield 649 C 4
Beachburg 682 H 2
Beachville 917 D 4
Beardmore 583 H 5
Beaverton 1,952 E 3
Beeton 1,989 E 3
Belle River 3,568 B 5
Belleville⊙ 34,881 G 3
Belmont 831 C 5
Bethany 365 F 3
Bewdley 508 F 3
Binbrook 306 E 4
Blackstock 720 F 3
Blenheim 4,044 C 5
Blind River 3,444 J 5
Bloomfield 718 G 4
Blyth 926 C 4
Bobcaygeon 1,625 F 3
Bonfield 540 E 1
Bothwell 915 C 5
Bourget 1,057 J 2
Bracebridge⊙ 9,063 E 2
Bradford 7,370 E 3
Braeside 492 H 2
Brampton⊙ 149,030 J 4
Brantford⊙ 74,315 D 4
Bridgenorth 1,633 F 3
Brigden 635 B 5
Brighton 3,147 G 3
Britt 419 D 2
Brockville⊙ 19,896 J 3
Bruce Mines 635 J 5
Brussels 962 C 4
Burford 1,461 D 4
Burgessville 302 D 4
Burk's Falls 922 E 2
Burlington 114,853 E 4
Cache Bay 665 D 1
Caesarea 551 F 3
Calabogie 256 H 2
Caledon 26,645 E 4
Callander 1,158 E 1
Cambridge 77,183 D 4
Campbellford 3,409 G 3
Cannington 1,623 E 3
Capreol 3,845 K 5
Caramat 265 H 5
Cardinal 1,753 J 3
Carleton Place 5,626 H 2
Carlisle 781 D 4
Carlsbad Springs 616 J 2
Carp 707 H 2
Cartier 590 J 5
Casselman 1,675 J 2
Castleton 346 F 3
Chalk River 1,010 G 1
Chapleau 3,243 J 5
Charing Cross 443 B 5
Chatham⊙ 40,952 B 5
Chatsworth 383 D 3
Cherry Valley 289 G 4
Chesley 1,840 C 3
Chesterville 1,430 J 2
Chute-à-Blondeau 365 K 2
City View J 2
Clarence Creek 796 J 2
Clarksburg 508 D 3
Clifford 645 D 4
Clinton 3,081 C 4
Cobalt 1,759 K 5
Cobden 997 H 2
Coboconk 426 F 3
Cobourg⊙ 11,385 F 4
Cochrane⊙ 4,848 K 5
Colborne 1,796 G 4
Colchester 711 B 6
Coldwater 964 E 3
Collingwood 12,064 D 3
Comber 667 B 5
Consecon 295 G 3
Cookstown 918 E 3
Cornwall⊙ 46,144 K 2
Cottam 404 B 5
Courtland 647 D 5
Courtright 1,024 B 5
Crediton 370 C 4
Creemore 1,182 D 3
Crysler 540 J 2
Cumberland 518 J 2
Cumberland Beach-Bramshot-Buena Vista 679 E 3
Dashwood 426 C 4
Deep River 5,095 G 1
Delaware 481 C 5
Delhi 4,043 D 5
Delta 360 H 3
Deseronto 1,740 G 3
Douglas 303 H 2
Drayton 809 D 4
Dresden 2,550 B 5
Drumbo 476 D 4
Dryden 6,640 G 4
Dublin 295 C 4
Dubreuilville △988 J 5
Dundalk 1,250 D 3
Dundas 19,586 D 4
Dungannon 284 C 4
Dunnville 11,353 E 5
Durham 2,458 D 3
Dutton 1,115 C 5
Earlton 1,028 K 5
East York 101,974 J 4
Echo Bay 786 J 5
Eden Mills 318 D 4
Eganville 1,245 G 2
Egmondville 465 C 4
Elgin 327 H 3
Elk Lake 526 K 5
Elliot Lake 16,723 B 1
Elmira 7,063 D 4
Elmvale 1,183 E 3
Elmwood 364 C 3
Elora 2,666 D 4
Embro 727 C 4
Embrun 1,883 J 2
Emeryville-Puce 1,611 B 5
Emo 762 F 5
Englehart 1,689 K 5
Enterprise 357 H 3
Erieau 430 C 5
Erin 2,313 D 4
Espanola 5,836 J 5
Essex 6,295 B 5
Etobicoke 298,713 J 4
Everett 570 E 3
Exeter 3,732 C 4
Fauquier 561 J 5
Fenelon Falls 1,701 F 3
Fergus 6,064 D 4
Field 462 E 1
Finch 353 J 2
Fingal 380 C 5
Fitzroy Harbour 446 H 2
Flesherton 565 D 3
Foleyet 484 J 5
Fordwich 365 C 4
Forest 2,671 C 4
Formosa 393 C 3
Fort Erie 24,096 E 5
Fort Frances⊙ 8,906 F 5
Foxboro 597 G 3
Frankford 1,919 G 3
Fraserdale 303 J 5
Freelton 307 D 4
Gananoque 4,863 H 3
Garden Village 270 E 1
Geraldton 2,956 H 5
Glencoe 1,694 C 5
Glen Miller 639 G 3
Glen Robertson 378 K 2
Glen Walter 710 K 2
Goderich⊙ 7,322 C 4
Gogama 652 J 5
Goodwood 335 E 3
Gore Bay⊙ 777 B 2
Gorrie 468 C 4
Grafton 409 G 4
Grand Bend 680 C 4
Grand Valley 1,226 D 4
Granton 315 C 4
Gravenhurst 8,532 E 3
Greely 567 J 2
Green Valley 459 K 2
Grimsby 15,797 E 4
Guelph⊙ 71,207 D 4

(continued on following page)

All islands in Hudson Bay, James Bay, Hudson Strait and Ungava Bay lie within Nunavut.
Hudson Bay
James Bay
MANITOBA
KENORA
THUNDER BAY
COCHRANE
SUDBURY
RAINY RIVER
MINNESOTA
MICHIGAN
Lake Superior
Northern Ontario
SCALE
0 25 50 100 150 200 MI.
0 25 50 100 150 200 KM.
Provincial Capital
County Seats
International Boundaries
Provincial and State Boundaries
County Boundaries
© Copyright HAMMOND INCORPORATED, Maplewood, N. J.
Longitude West of Greenwich

Haileybury⊙ 4,925 K 5
Haldimand 16,866 E 5
Haliburton 1,443 F 2
Halton Hills 35,190 E 4
Hamilton⊙ 306,434 E 4
Hamilton *542,095 E 4
Hanover 6,316 C 3
Harriston 1,954 D 4
Harrow 2,274 B 5
Harrowsmith 599 H 3
Harwood 332 F 3
Hastings 975 G 3
Havelock 1,385 G 3
Hawkesbury 9,877 K 2
Hawkestone 275 E 3
Hawk Junction 349 J 5
Hearst 5,533 J 5
Hensall 973 C 4
Hepworth 393 C 3
Hickson 263 D 4
Highgate 435 C 5
Hillsburgh 1,065 D 4
Hillsdale 370 E 3
Holland Landing 2,771 E 3
Honey Harbour 505 E 3
Hornepayne 1,848 J 5
Hudson 515 G 4
Huntsville 11,467 E 2
Huron Park 1,104 C 4
Ignace 2,499 G 5
Ilderton 301 C 4
Ingersoll 8,494 C 4
Ingleside 1,400 J 2
Innerkip 715 D 4
Inverhuron 438 C 3
Iron Bridge 821 A 1
Iroquois 1,211 J 3
Iroquois Falls 6,339 J 5
Johnstown 789 J 3
Kakabeka Falls 300 G 5
Kanata 19,728 J 2
Kapuskasing 12,014 J 5
Kars 449 J 2
Kearney 538 E 2
Keene 353 F 3
Keewatin 1,863 F 5
Kemptville 2,362 J 2
Kenora⊙ 9,817 F 4
Killaloe Station 634 G 2
Killarney 433 C 2
Kincardine 5,778 C 3
Kingston⊙ 52,616 H 3
Kingsville 5,134 B 6
Kinmount 262 F 3
Kirkland Lake 12,219 K 5
Kitchener⊙ 139,734 D 4
Kitchener *287,801 D 4
Komoka 1,152 C 5
Lakefield 2,374 F 3
Lanark 753 H 2
Lancaster 637 K 2
Langton 348 D 5
Lansdowne 540 H 3
Larder Lake 1,084 K 5
Latchford 397 K 5
Leamington 12,528 B 5
Limoges 930 J 2
Lincoln 14,196 E 4
Linden Beach 579 B 6
Lindsay⊙ 13,596 F 3
Linwood 450 D 4
Lion's Head 467 C 2
Lisle 265 E 3
Listowel 5,026 D 4
Little Britain 265 F 3
Little Current 1,507 B 2
London⊙ 254,280 C 5
London *283,668 C 5
Longlac 2,431 H 5
Long Sault 1,227 K 2
L'Orignal⊙ 1,819 K 2
Lucan 1,616 C 4
Lucknow 1,088 C 4
Lyn 518 J 3
Lynden 451 D 4
Lynhurst 685 C 5
MacGregor's Bay 861 G 2
MacTier 647 E 2
Madawaska 264 F 2
Madoc 1,249 G 3
Maitland 667 J 3
Mallorytown 368 J 3
Manitouwadge 3,155 H 5
Manitowaning 518 C 2
Manotick-Hillside Gardens 2,694 J 2
Marathon 2,271 H 5
Markdale 1,289 D 3
Markham 77,037 K 4
Markstay 444 D 1
Marmora 1,304 G 3
Martintown 388 K 2
Massey 1,274 C 1
Matachewan 444 J 5
Matheson 966 K 5
Mattawa 2,652 F 1
Mattice 803 J 5
Maxville 836 K 2
Maynooth 277 G 2
McGregor 1,145 B 5
McKerrow 260 C 1
Meaford 4,367 D 3
Melbourne 346 C 5
Merlin 745 B 5
Merrickville 984 J 3
Metcalfe 687 J 2
Midhurst 1,457 E 3
Midland 12,132 D 3
Mildmay 929 C 3
Milford Bay 401 E 2
Millbank 337 D 4
Millbrook 927 F 3
Milton⊙ 28,067 E 4
Milverton 1,463 D 4
Minaki 319 F 4
Mindemoya 376 B 2
Minden⊙ 838 F 3
Mississauga 315,056 J 4
Mitchell 2,777 C 4
Monkton 520 C 4
Moonbeam 838 J 5
Moorefield 308 D 4
Mooretown 344 B 5
Moose Creek 393 K 2
Morewood 264 J 2
Morpeth 284 C 5
Morrisburg 2,308 J 3
Mount Albert 1,165 E 3
Mount Brydges 1,557 C 5
Mount Forest 3,474 D 4
Mount Hope 557 E 4
Munster 1,531 J 2
Nakina 936 H 4
Nanticoke⊙ 19,816 E 5
Napanee 4,803 G 3
Navan 419 J 2
Neustadt 511 D 3
Newboro 260 H 3
Newburgh 617 H 3
Newbury 441 C 5
Newcastle 32,229 F 4
New Hamburg 3,923 D 4
New Liskeard 5,551 K 5
Newmarket⊙ 29,753 E 3
Niagara Falls 70,960 E 4
Niagara-on-the-Lake 12,186 E 4
Nickel Centre 12,318 D 1
Nipigon 2,377 H 5
Nobel 386 D 2
Nobleton 1,861 J 3
Noelville 702 D 1
North Bay⊙ 51,268 E 1
North Gower 818 J 2
North York 559,521 J 4
Norwich 2,117 D 5
Norwood 1,278 F 3
Nottawa 360 D 3
Oakville 75,773 E 4
Oakwood 404 F 3
Odessa 849 H 3
Oil City 266 B 5
Oil Springs 627 B 5
Omemee 819 F 3
Onaping Falls 6,198 J 5
Opasatika 413 J 5
Orangeville⊙ 13,740 D 4
Orillia 23,955 E 3
Osgoode 1,138 J 2
Oshawa 117,519 F 4
Oshawa *154,217 F 4
Ottawa⊙ (cap.), Canada 295,163 J 2
Ottawa-Hull *717,978 J 2
Otterville 776 D 5
Owen Sound⊙ 19,883 D 3
Paincourt 414 B 5
Paisley 1,039 C 3
Pakenham 367 H 2
Palmerston 1,989 D 4
Paris 7,485 D 4
Parkhill 1,358 C 4
Parry Sound⊙ 6,124 E 2
Pefferlaw 857 E 3
Pelham 11,104 E 4
Pembroke⊙ 14,026 G 2
Penetanguishene 5,315 D 3
Perth⊙ 5,655 H 3
Petawawa 5,520 G 2
Peterborough⊙ 60,620 F 3
Petrolia 4,234 B 5
Pickering 37,754 K 4
Picton⊙ 4,361 G 3
Plantagenet 870 K 2
Plattsville 495 D 4
Point Edward 2,383 B 4
Pontypool 759 F 3
Port Burwell 655 D 5
Port Carling 629 E 2
Port Colborne 19,225 E 5
Port Elgin 6,131 C 3
Port Franks 547 C 4
Port Hope 9,992 F 4
Port Lambton 921 B 5
Portland 271 H 3
Port McNicoll 1,883 E 3
Port Perry 4,712 E 3
Port Rowan 811 D 5
Port Stanley 1,891 C 5
Pottageville 286 J 3
Powassan 1,169 E 1
Prescott⊙ 4,670 J 3
Princeton 462 D 4
Puce-Emeryville 1,611 B 5
Rainy River 1,061 F 5
Ramore 382 K 5
Rayside-Balfour 15,017 K 5
Red Rock 1,260 H 5
Renfrew 8,283 H 2
Richards Landing 405 J 5
Richmond 2,880 J 2
Richmond Hill 37,778 J 4
Ridgetown 3,062 C 5
Ripley 591 C 3
River Valley 275 D 1
Rockcliffe Park 1,869 J 2
Rockland 3,961 J 2
Rockwood 1,068 D 4
Rodney 1,007 C 5
Rosslyn Village 362 G 5
Round Lake Centre 255 G 2
Russell 1,099 J 2
Ruthven 649 B 6
Saint Albert 254 J 2
Saint Catharines⊙ 124,018 E 4
Saint Catharines-Niagara *304,353 E 4
Saint Charles 382 D 1
Saint Clair Beach 2,845 B 5
Saint Clements 890 D 4
Saint-Eugène 470 K 2
Saint George 865 D 4
Saint Isidore de Prescott 746 K 2

Ontario
Central Part
© Copyright HAMMOND INCORPORATED, Maplewood, N. J.
Longitude 80° West of Greenwich 79°
LAKE HURON
GEORGIAN BAY
LAKE ERIE
LAKE ONTARIO
MICHIGAN
NEW YORK
QUÉBEC
TORONTO
HAMILTON
LONDON
WINDSOR
DETROIT
BUFFALO
MISSISSAUGA

Saint Jacobs 1,189 .... D 4
Saint Mary's 4,883 .... C 4
Saint Thomas⊙ 28,165 .... C 5
Saint Williams 442 .... D 5
Salem 825 .... D 4
Sarnia⊙ 50,892 .... B 5
Sauble Beach 729 .... C 3
Sault Sainte Marie⊙ 82,697 .... J 5
Scarborough 443,353 .... K 4
Schomberg 923 .... J 3
Schreiber 1,968 .... H 5
Scotland 600 .... D 4
Seaforth 2,114 .... C 4
Searchmont 384 .... J 5
Sebringville 579 .... C 4
Seeleys Bay 503 .... H 3
Shakespeare 602 .... D 4
Shallow Lake 418 .... C 3
Shannonville 314 .... G 3
Shanty Bay 358 .... E 3
Sharbot Lake 495 .... H 3
Shedden 292 .... C 5
Shelburne 2,862 .... D 3
Simcoe⊙ 14,326 .... D 5
Sioux Lookout 3,074 .... G 4
Sioux Narrows 394 .... F 5
Smithfield 349 .... G 3
Smiths Falls 8,831 .... H 3
Smithville 1,936 .... E 4
Smooth Rock Falls 2,352 .... J 5
Sombra 420 .... B 5
Southampton 2,830 .... C 3
South Mountain 285 .... J 3
South River 1,109 .... E 2
Spanish 1,063 .... J 5
Sparta 283 .... C 5
Spencerville 438 .... J 3
Springfield 555 .... C 5
Springford 309 .... D 5
Stayner 2,530 .... E 3
Stirling 1,638 .... G 3
Stittsville 2,652 .... J 2
Stoney Creek 36,762 .... E 4
Stoney Point 1,090 .... B 5
Straffordville 752 .... D 5
Stratford⊙ 26,262 .... C 4
Strathroy 8,748 .... C 5
Sturgeon Falls 6,045 .... E 1
Sudbury⊙ 91,829 .... K 5
Sudbury *149,923 .... K 5
Sunderland 703 .... E 3
Sundridge 734 .... E 2
Sydenham 595 .... H 3
Tamworth 402 .... H 3
Tara 687 .... C 3
Tavistock 1,885 .... D 4
Tecumseh 6,364 .... B 5
Teeswater 1,026 .... C 3
Terrace Bay 2,639 .... H 5
Thamesford 1,920 .... C 4
Thamesville 961 .... C 5
Thedford 694 .... C 4
Thessalon 1,620 .... J 5
Thornbury 1,435 .... D 3
Thorndale 581 .... C 4
Thornton 414 .... E 3
Thorold 15,412 .... E 4
Thunder Bay⊙ 112,486 .... H 5
Thunder Bay *121,379 .... H 5
Tilbury 4,298 .... B 5
Tillsonburg 10,487 .... D 5
Timmins 46,114 .... J 5
Tiverton 806 .... C 3
Tobermory 282 .... C 2
Toronto (cap.)⊛ 599,217 .... K 4
Toronto *2,998,947 .... K 4
Tottenham 3,022 .... E 3
Trenton 15,085 .... G 3
Trout Creek 652 .... E 2
Turkey Point 407 .... D 5
Tweed 1,574 .... G 3
Udora 375 .... E 3
Union 485 .... C 5
Uxbridge 4,209 .... E 3
Valley East 20,433 .... J 5
Vanier 18,792 .... J 2
Vankleek Hill 1,774 .... K 2
Vars 527 .... J 2
Vaughan 29,674 .... J 4
Vermilion Bay 505 .... G 4
Verner 1,076 .... D 1
Vernon 303 .... J 2
Verona 754 .... H 3
Victoria Harbour 1,125 .... E 3
Vienna 369 .... D 5
Virginiatown 1,010 .... K 5
Vittoria 420 .... D 5
Wabigoon 268 .... G 5
Walden 10,139 .... J 5
Walkerton⊙ 4,682 .... C 3
Wallaceburg 11,506 .... B 5
Wardsville 450 .... C 5
Warkworth 618 .... G 3
Warren 579 .... D 1
Warsaw 314 .... F 3
Wasaga Beach 4,705 .... D 3
Washago 569 .... E 3
Waterloo 49,428 .... D 4
Watford 1,402 .... C 5
Waubaushene 878 .... E 3
Wawa 4,206 .... J 5
Webbwood 519 .... C 1
Welcome 293 .... F 4
Welland 454,448 .... E 5
Wellesley 997 .... D 4
Wellington 1,082 .... G 4
Wendover 326 .... J 2
West Lorne 1,258 .... C 5
Westmeath 262 .... H 2
Westport 621 .... H 3
Wheatley 1,638 .... B 5
Whitby⊙ 36,698 .... F 4
Whitchurch-Stouffville 13,557 .... J 3
White River △1,006 .... J 5
Whitney 766 .... F 2
Wiarton 2,074 .... C 3
Wikwemikong 1,030 .... C 2
Williamsburg 407 .... J 3
Williamsford 256 .... D 3
Williamstown 328 .... K 2
Winchester 2,001 .... J 2
Windsor⊙ 192,083 .... B 5
Windsor *246,110 .... B 5
Wingham 2,897 .... C 4
Wolfe Island 271 .... H 3
Woodstock⊙ 26,603 .... D 4
Woodville 575 .... F 3
Wroxeter 350 .... C 4
Wyoming 1,682 .... B 5
Yarker 319 .... H 3
York 134,617 .... J 4
Zephyr 330 .... E 3
Zurich 795 .... C 4

OTHER FEATURES

Abitibi (riv.) .... J 5
Algonquin Prov. Park .... F 2
Amherst (isl.) .... H 3
Balsam (lake) .... F 3
Barrie (isl.) .... B 1
Bays (lake) .... F 2
Big Rideau (lake) .... H 3
Black (riv.) .... E 3
Bruce (pen.) .... C 2
Buckhorn (lake) .... F 3
Cabot (head) .... C 2
Charleston (lake) .... J 3
Christian (isl.) .... D 3
Clear (lake) .... F 3
Cockburn (isl.) .... A 2
Couchiching (lake) .... E 3
Croker (cape) .... D 3
Don (riv.) .... J 4
Doré (lake) .... G 2
Douglas (pt.) .... C 3
Erie (lake) .... E 5
Flowerpot (isl.) .... C 2
French (riv.) .... D 1
Georgian (bay) .... D 2
Georgian Bay Is. Nat'l Park .... C 2, D 3
Georgina (isl.) .... E 3
Grand (riv.) .... D 4
Humber (riv.) .... J 3
Hurd (cape) .... C 2
Huron (lake) .... B 3
Ipperwash Prov. Park .... C 4
Joseph (lake) .... E 2
Killarney Prov. Park .... C 1
Killbear Point Prov. Park .... D 2
Lake of the Woods (lake) .... F 5
Lake Superior Prov. Park .... J 5
Lonely (isl.) .... C 2
Long (pt.) .... D 5
Long Point (bay) .... D 5
Madawaska (riv.) .... G 2
Magnetawan (riv.) .... D 2
Main (chan.) .... C 2
Manitou (lake) .... C 2
Manitoulin (isl.) .... B 2
Mattagami (riv.) .... J 5
Michipicoten (isl.) .... H 5
Missinaibi (riv.) .... J 5
Mississagi (riv.) .... A 1
Mississippi (lake) .... H 2
Muskoka (lake) .... E 2
Niagara (riv.) .... E 4
Nipigon (lake) .... H 5
Nipissing (lake) .... E 1
North (chan.) .... A 1
Nottawasaga (bay) .... D 3
Ogidaki (mt.) .... J 5
Ontario (lake) .... G 4
Opeongo (lake) .... F 2
Ottawa (riv.) .... H 2
Owen (sound) .... D 3
Panache (lake) .... C 1
Parry (isl.) .... D 2
Parry (sound) .... D 2
Pelee (pt.) .... B 6
Petre (pt.) .... G 4
Point Pelee Nat'l Park .... B 5
Presqu'ile Prov. Park .... G 4
Pukaskwa Prov. Park .... H 5
Quetico Prov. Park .... G 5
Rainy (lake) .... G 5
Rice (lake) .... F 3
Rideau (lake) .... H 3
Rondeau Prov. Park .... C 5
Rosseau (lake) .... E 2
Saint Clair (lake) .... B 5
Saint Clair (riv.) .... B 5
Saint Lawrence (lake) .... K 3
Saint Lawrence (riv.) .... J 3
Saint Lawrence Is. Nat'l Park .... J 3
Saugeen (riv.) .... C 3
Scugog (lake) .... F 3
Seul (lake) .... G 4
Severn (riv.) .... E 3
Sibley Prov. Park .... H 5
Simcoe (lake) .... E 3
South (bay) .... C 2
Spanish (riv.) .... C 1
Stony (lake) .... G 3
Superior (lake) .... H 5
Sydenham (riv.) .... B 5
Thames (riv.) .... B 5
Theano (pt.) .... J 5
Thousand (isls.) .... H 3
Timagami (lake) .... K 5
Trout (lake) .... E 1
Vernon (lake) .... E 2
Walpole (isl.) .... B 5
Welland (canal) .... E 5
Woods (lake) .... F 5

⊙County seat.
*Population of metropolitan area.
△Population of town or township.

Topography

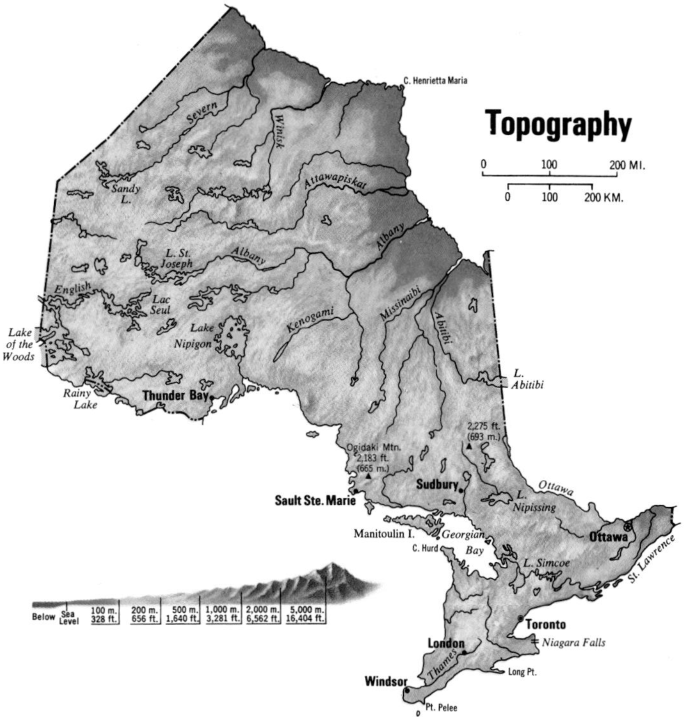

0 100 200 MI.
0 100 200 KM.
C. Henrietta Maria
Severn
Winisk
Sandy L.
Attawapiskat
L. St. Joseph
Albany
English
Lac Seul
Lake Nipigon
Kenogami
Missinaibi
Abitibi
Lake of the Woods
Rainy Lake
Thunder Bay
L. Abitibi
Ogidaki Mtn. 2,183 ft. (665 m.)
2,275 ft. (693 m.)
Sudbury
Sault Ste. Marie
Ottawa
L. Nipissing
Manitoulin I.
Georgian Bay
C. Hurd
L. Simcoe
St. Lawrence
Ottawa
Toronto
Niagara Falls
London
Thames
Long Pt.
Windsor
Pt. Pelee
Below Sea Level
100 m. 328 ft.
200 m. 656 ft.
500 m. 1,640 ft.
1,000 m. 3,281 ft.
2,000 m. 6,562 ft.
5,000 m. 16,404 ft.

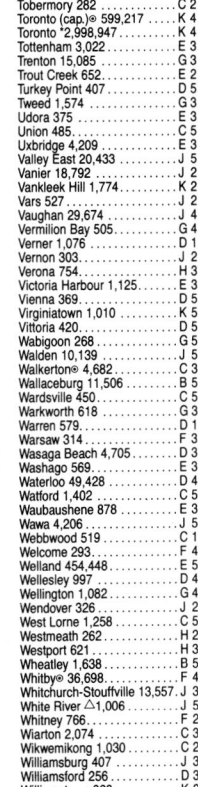

Ontario
Southern Part
SCALE
0 10 20 30 40 50 MI.
0 10 20 30 40 50 KM.
National Capital
Provincial Capital
County Seats
International Boundaries
Provincial & State Boundaries
County Boundaries
Canals
Hawkesbury
PRESCOTT
RUSSELL
CARLETON
GLENGARRY
STORMONT
DUNDAS
GRENVILLE
Cornwall
Massena
Malone
Brockville
Ogdensburg
Canton
Gouverneur
ST. LAWRENCE ISLANDS NAT'L PARK
Alexandria Bay
Aurora
Whitchurch-Stouffville
DURHAM
Richmond Hill
Markham
YORK
Vaughan
PEEL
North York
Scarborough
Pickering
Brampton
York
East York
TORONTO
Etobicoke
LAKE ONTARIO
MISSISSAUGA
COCHRANE
QUÉBEC
Hearst
Kapuskasing
Smooth Rock Falls
Iroquois Falls
Timmins
Kirkland Lake
TIMISKAMING
New Liskeard
SUDBURY
Sault Ste Marie
Sudbury
NIPISSING
Espanola

Agriculture, Industry and Resources

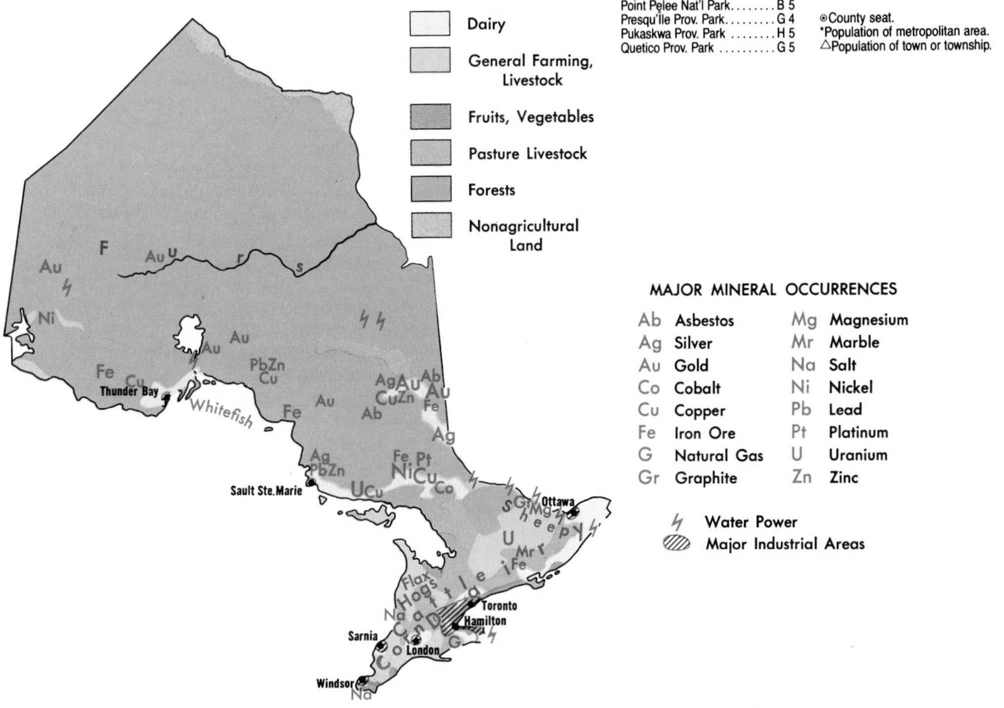

DOMINANT LAND USE
Cereals, Cash Crops, Livestock
Dairy
General Farming, Livestock
Fruits, Vegetables
Pasture Livestock
Forests
Nonagricultural Land
MAJOR MINERAL OCCURRENCES
Ab Asbestos
Ag Silver
Au Gold
Co Cobalt
Cu Copper
Fe Iron Ore
G Natural Gas
Gr Graphite
Mg Magnesium
Mr Marble
Na Salt
Ni Nickel
Pb Lead
Pt Platinum
U Uranium
Zn Zinc
Water Power
Major Industrial Areas
Thunder Bay
Whitefish
Sault Ste. Marie
Ottawa
Toronto
Hamilton
Sarnia
London
Windsor

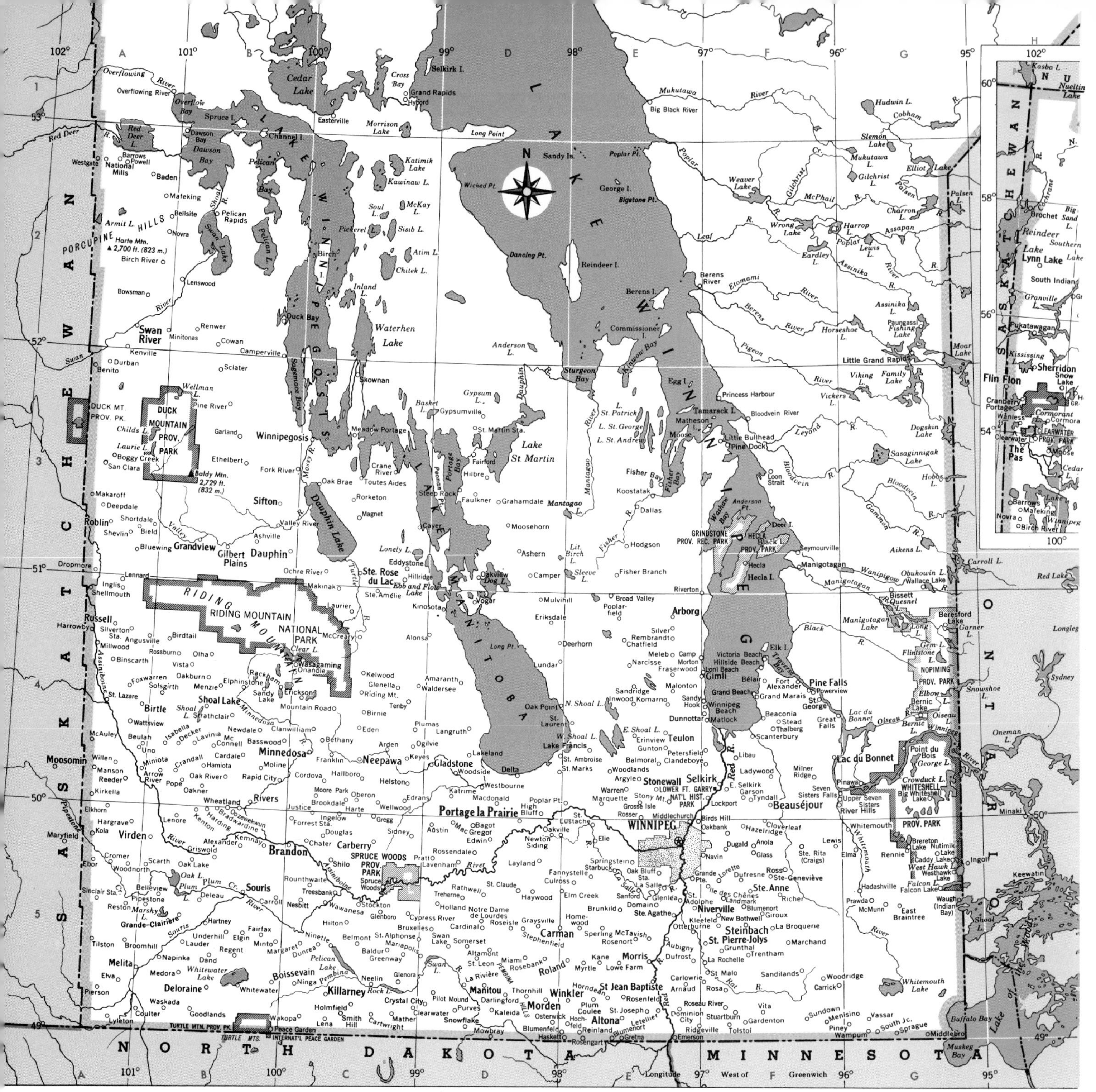

LAKE WINNIPEG
LAKE WINNIPEGOSIS
LAKE MANITOBA
Cedar Lake
Lake St. Martin
Waterhen Lake
Dauphin Lake
RIDING MOUNTAIN NATIONAL PARK
DUCK MOUNTAIN PROV. PARK
SPRUCE WOODS PROV. PARK
WHITESHELL PROV. PARK
NOPIMING PROV. PARK
HECLA PROV. PARK
GRINDSTONE PROV. REC. PARK
DUCK MT. PROV. PK.
TURTLE MTN. PROV. PK.
INTERNAT'L PEACE GARDEN
PORCUPINE HILLS
Harte Mtn. 2,700 ft. (823 m.)
Baldy Mtn. 2,729 ft. (832 m.)
SASKATCHEWAN
ONTARIO
NORTH DAKOTA
MINNESOTA
WINNIPEG
Brandon
Portage la Prairie
Selkirk
Dauphin
Swan River
Steinbach
Morden
Winkler
Flin Flon
The Pas
Longitude West of Greenwich
102°
101°
100°
99°
98°
97°
96°
95°
53°
52°
51°
50°
49°

CITIES and TOWNS

Alexander 244	B 5
Altona 2,757	E 5
Amaranth 257	D 4
Arborg 964	E 4
Arden 192	C 4
Ashern 570	D 3
Austin 416	D 5
Baldur 344	C 5
Barrows 199	A 2
Beauséjour 2,462	F 4
Belmont 314	C 5
Benito 441	A 3
Berens River 681	F 2
Binscarth 472	A 4
Birch River 597	A 2
Birds Hill 711	F 4
Birtle 887	B 4
Bloodvein River 413	F 3
Blumenort 533	F 5
Boissevain 1,660	C 5
Bowsman 454	A 2
Brandon 36,242	C 5
Brochet 215	H 2
Camperville 586	B 2
Carberry 1,510	C 5
Carman 2,408	D 5
Cartwright 384	C 5
Churchill 1,186	K 2
Cormorant 445	H 3
Cranberry Portage 948	H 3
Crane River 336	C 3
Cross Lake 510	J 3
Crystal City 489	C 5
Cypress River 260	D 5
Darlingford 170	D 5
Dauphin 8,971	B 3
Deloraine 1,136	B 5
Dominion City 437	E 5
Douglas 170	C 5
Duck Bay 594	B 2
Dugald 410	F 5
Dunnottar 287	E 4
Easterville 589	C 1
East Selkirk 985	F 4
Elgin 172	B 5
Elie 450	E 5
Elkhorn 509	A 5
Elm Creek 293	E 5
Elphinstone 201	B 4
Emerson 762	E 5
Erickson 540	C 4
Eriksdale 339	D 4
Ethelbert 474	B 3
Fairford 668	D 3
Falcon Lake 220	G 5
Fisher Branch 511	E 3
Flin Flon 7,894	H 3
Fort Alexander 1,425	F 4
Garson 318	F 4
Gilbert Plains 812	B 3
Gillam 1,427	K 2
Gimli 1,550	F 4
Gladstone 964	D 4
Glenboro 741	C 5
Grand Marais 207	F 4
Grand Rapids 567	C 1
Grandview 1,013	B 3
Great Falls 272	F 4
Gretna 545	E 5
Grosse Isle 171	E 4
Grunthal 572	F 5
Hamiota 728	B 4
Hartney 490	B 5
Haywood 240	D 5
Hillridge 201	C 3
Hochfeld 187	E 5
Holland 418	D 5
Île des Chênes 814	F 5
Inglis 209	A 4
Inwood 197	E 4
Island Lake 2,664	J 3
Kelwood 199	C 4
Killarney 2,342	C 5
Kleefeld 335	F 5
La Broquerie 429	F 5
Lac du Bonnet 985	G 4
Landmark 433	F 5
La Rivière 251	D 5
La Salle 345	E 5
Laurier 241	C 4
Letellier 178	E 5
Little Grand Rapids 559	G 2
Lockport 212	F 4
Lorette 1,092	F 5
Lowe Farm 241	E 5
Lundar 634	D 4
Lynn Lake 2,087	H 2
MacGregor 795	D 5
Mafeking 266	B 2
Manigotagan 216	F 3
Manitou 861	D 5
McCreary 618	C 4
Melita 1,156	A 5
Miami 401	D 5
Middlechurch 342	E 4
Miniota 247	B 4
Minitonas 628	B 2
Minnedosa 2,637	B 4
Moosehorn 216	D 3
Moose Lake 557	H 3
Morden 4,579	D 5
Morris 1,570	E 5
Neepawa 3,425	C 4
New Bothwell 233	F 5
Newdale 238	B 4
Ninette 287	C 5
Niverville 1,329	F 5
Norway House 441	J 3
Notre Dame de Lourdes 627	D 5
Oakbank 1,277	F 5
Oakburn 255	B 4
Oak Lake 369	B 5
Oak River 179	D 4
Oakville 383	D 5
Ochre River 284	C 3
Onanole 386	C 4
Oozewekwun 453	B 5
Paungassi 296	G 2
Pelican Rapids 178	B 2
Petersfield 170	E 4
Pierson 238	A 5
Pikwitonei 175	J 3
Pilot Mound 838	D 5
Pinawa 2,006	G 4
Pine Falls 885	F 4
Pine River 314	B 3
Pipestone 173	B 5
Plumas 269	D 4
Plum Coulee 592	E 5
Point du Bois 182	G 4
Poplar Point 264	D 4
Portage la Prairie 13,086	D 4
Powerview 691	F 4
Rapid City 431	B 4
Red Sucker Lake 312	K 3
Reinland 198	E 5
Reston 589	A 5
Richer 288	F 5
Riding Mountain 168	C 4
Rivers 1,107	B 4
Riverton 657	E 3
Roblin 1,953	A 3
Roland 301	D 5
Rorketon 229	C 3
Rosenfeld 263	E 5
Rossburn 696	B 4
Russell 1,660	A 4
Saint Adolphe 928	E 5
Saint Ambroise 263	E 4
Saint Claude 592	D 5
Sainte Agathe 326	E 5
Sainte Anne 1,338	F 5
Sainte Rose du Lac 1,090	C 3
Saint Eustache 285	E 5
Saint George 303	F 4
Saint Jean Baptiste 584	E 5
Saint Laurent 312	D 4
Saint Lazare 414	A 4
Saint Leon 197	D 5
Saint Malo 672	F 5
Saint Pierre-Jolys 919	F 5
Sandy Lake 301	B 4
Sanford 385	E 5
Selkirk 10,037	F 4
Sherridon 138	H 3
Shoal Lake 835	B 4
Sifton 210	B 3
Somerset 596	D 5
Snow Lake 1,853	H 3
Souris 1,731	B 5
South Indian Lake 770	H 2
Split Lake 985	J 2
Sprague 199	G 5
Starbuck 224	E 5
Steinbach 6,676	F 5
Stonewall 2,210	E 4
Stony Mountain 1,313	E 4
Strathclair 390	B 4
Swan Lake 367	D 5
Swan River 3,782	A 2
Teulon 925	E 4

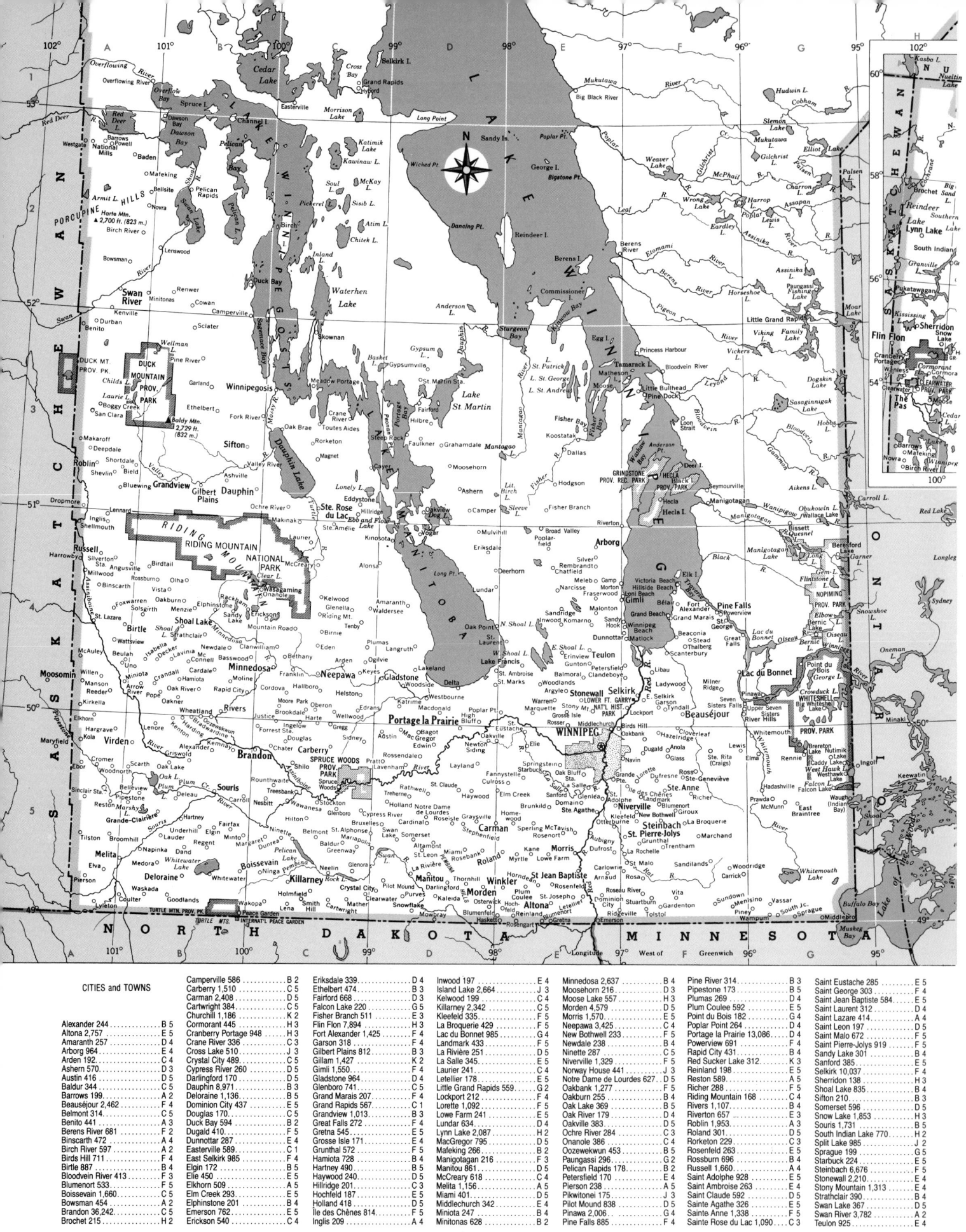

Manitoba
Northern Part
Manitoba
Southern Part
SCALE
0 5 10 20 40 60 MI.
0 5 10 20 40 60 KM.
Provincial Capital
International Boundaries
Provincial Boundaries
HUDSON BAY
Churchill
Thompson
Gillam
York Factory
Shamattawa
Chesnaye
Herchmer
Norway House
Oxford House
Gods River
Island Lake
Red Sucker Lake
Grand Rapids
Nelson House
Wabowden
Thicket Portage
Pikwitonei
Ilford
Split Lake
Brochet
Tadoule L.
Nejanilini L.
Baralzon L.
Northern Indian L.
Sipiwesk L.
Cross L.
Gods L.
Oxford L.
Knee L.
Molson L.
Sachigo L.
Sandy L.
Big Trout L.
Fry Lake
Windigo Lake
Windigo L.
Balmertown
Red Lake
© Copyright HAMMOND INCORPORATED, Maplewood, N.J.

The Pas 6,390 .... H 3
Thicket Portage 195 .... J 3
Thompson 14,288 .... J 2
Treherne 743 .... D 5
Tyndall 421 .... F 4
Virden 2,940 .... A 5
Vita 364 .... F 5
Wabowden 655 .... J 3
Wallace Lake •2,044 .... G 3
Wanless 193 .... H 3
Warren 459 .... E 4
Waskada 239 .... B 5
Wawanesa 492 .... C 5
Whitemouth 320 .... G 5
Whitewater •856 .... B 5
Winkler 5,046 .... E 5
Winnipeg (cap.) 564,473 .... E 5
Winnipeg *584,842 .... E 5
Winnipeg Beach 565 .... F 4
Winnipegosis 855 .... B 3
Woodlands 185 .... E 4
Wooodridge 170 .... G 5
York Landing 229 .... J 2

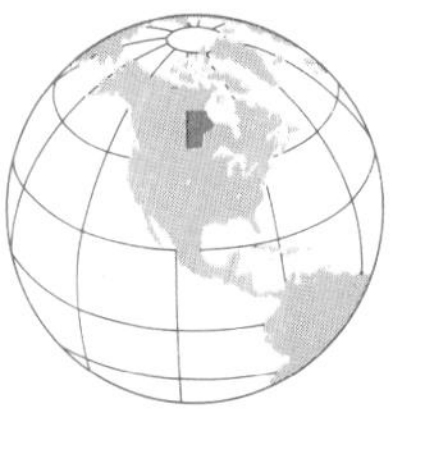

AREA 250,999 sq. mi. (650,087 sq. km.)
POPULATION 1,063,016
CAPITAL Winnipeg
LARGEST CITY Winnipeg
HIGHEST POINT Baldy Mtn. 2,729 ft. (832 m.)
SETTLED IN 1812
ADMITTED TO CONFEDERATION 1870
PROVINCIAL FLOWER Prairie Crocus

OTHER FEATURES

Aikens (lake) .... G 3
Anderson (lake) .... D 2
Anderson (pt.) .... F 3
Armit (lake) .... A 2
Assapan (riv.) .... G 2
Assiniboine (riv.) .... C 5
Assinika (lake) .... G 2
Assinika (riv.) .... G 2
Atim (lake) .... C 2
Baldy (mt.) .... B 3
Basket (lake) .... C 3
Beaverhill (lake) .... J 3
Berens (isl.) .... E 2
Berens (riv.) .... F 2
Bernic (lake) .... G 4
Big Sand (lake) .... H 2
Bigstone (lake) .... J 3
Bigstone (pt.) .... E 2
Bigstone (riv.) .... J 3
Birch (isl.) .... C 2
Black (isl.) .... F 3
Black (riv.) .... F 4
Bloodvein (riv.) .... F 3
Bonnet (lake) .... G 4
Buffalo (bay) .... G 5
Burntwood (riv.) .... J 2
Caribou (riv.) .... J 1
Carroll (lake) .... G 3
Cedar (lake) .... B 1
Channel (isl.) .... B 2
Charron (lake) .... G 2
Childs (lake) .... A 3
Chitek (lake) .... C 2
Churchill (cape) .... K 2
Churchill (riv.) .... J 2
Clear (lake) .... C 4
Clearwater Lake Prov. Park .... H 3
Cobham (riv.) .... G 1
Cochrane (riv.) .... H 2
Commissioner (isl.) .... E 2
Cormorant (lake) .... H 3
Cross (bay) .... C 1
Cross (lake) .... J 3
Crowduck (lake) .... G 4
Dancing (pt.) .... D 2
Dauphin (lake) .... C 3
Dauphin (riv.) .... D 3
Dawson (bay) .... B 2
Dog (lake) .... D 3
Dogskin (lake) .... G 3
Duck Mountain Prov. Park .... B 3
Eardley (lake) .... F 2
East Shoal (lake) .... E 4
Ebb and Flow (lake) .... C 3
Egg (isl.) .... E 3
Elbow (lake) .... G 4
Elk (isl.) .... F 4
Elliot (lake) .... G 2
Etawney (lake) .... J 2
Etomami (riv.) .... F 2
Falcon (lake) .... G 5
Family (lake) .... G 3
Fisher (bay) .... E 3
Fisher (riv.) .... E 3
Fishing (lake) .... G 2
Flintstone (lake) .... G 4
Fox (riv.) .... K 2
Gammon (riv.) .... G 3
Garner (lake) .... G 4
Gem (lake) .... G 4
George (isl.) .... E 2
George (lake) .... G 4
Gilchrist (creek) .... F 2
Gilchrist (lake) .... G 2
Gods (lake) .... K 3
Gods (riv.) .... K 3
Granville (lake) .... H 2
Grass (riv.) .... J 3
Grass River Prov. Park .... H 3
Grindstone Prov. Rec. Park .... F 3
Gunisao (lake) .... J 3
Gypsum (lake) .... D 3
Harrop (lake) .... G 2
Harte (mt.) .... A 2
Hayes (riv.) .... K 3
Hecla (isl.) .... F 3
Hecla Prov. Park .... F 3
Hobbs (lake) .... G 3
Horseshoe (lake) .... G 2
Hubbart (pt.) .... K 2
Hudson (bay) .... K 2
Hudwin (lake) .... G 1
Inland (lake) .... C 2
International Peace Garden .... B 5
Island (lake) .... K 3
Katimik (lake) .... C 2
Kawinaw (lake) .... C 2
Kinwow (bay) .... E 2
Kississing (lake) .... H 2
Knee (lake) .... J 3
Lake of the Woods (lake) .... H 5
La Salle (riv.) .... E 5
Laurie (lake) .... A 3
Leaf (riv.) .... F 2
Lewis (lake) .... G 2
Leyond (riv.) .... F 3
Little Birch (lake) .... E 3
Lonely (lake) .... C 3
Long (lake) .... G 4
Long (pt.) .... D 1
Long (pt.) .... D 4
Manigotagan (lake) .... G 4
Manigotagan (riv.) .... G 3
Manitoba (lake) .... D 4
Mantagao (riv.) .... E 3
Marshy (lake) .... B 5
McKay (lake) .... C 2
McPhail (riv.) .... F 2
Minnedosa (riv.) .... B 4
Moar (lake) .... G 2
Molson (lake) .... J 3
Moose (isl.) .... E 3
Morrison (lake) .... C 1
Mossy (riv.) .... C 3
Mukutawa (lake) .... G 2
Mukutawa (riv.) .... E 1
Muskeg (bay) .... G 6
Nejanilini (lake) .... J 1
Nelson (riv.) .... J 2
Nopiming Prov. Park .... G 4
Northern Indian (lake) .... J 2
North Knife (lake) .... J 2
North Seal (riv.) .... H 2
North Shoal (lake) .... E 4
Nueltin (lake) .... H 1
Oak (lake) .... B 5
Obukowin (lake) .... G 3
Oiseau (lake) .... G 4
Oiseau (riv.) .... G 4
Overflow (bay) .... A 1
Overflowing (riv.) .... A 1
Owl (riv.) .... K 2
Oxford (lake) .... J 3
Paint (lake) .... J 2
Palsen (riv.) .... G 2
Pelican (bay) .... B 2
Pelican (lake) .... B 2
Pelican (lake) .... C 5
Pembina (hills) .... D 5
Pembina (riv.) .... C 5
Peonan (pt.) .... D 3
Pickerel (lake) .... C 2
Pigeon (riv.) .... F 2
Pipestone (creek) .... A 5
Plum (creek) .... B 5
Plum (lake) .... B 5
Poplar (riv.) .... E 2
Porcupine (hills) .... A 2
Portage (bay) .... D 3
Punk (isl.) .... F 3
Quesnel (lake) .... G 4
Rat (riv.) .... F 5
Red (riv.) .... F 4
Red Deer (lake) .... A 2
Red Deer (riv.) .... A 2
Reindeer (isl.) .... E 2
Reindeer (lake) .... H 2
Riding (mt.) .... B 4
Riding Mountain Nat'l Park .... B 4
Rock (lake) .... C 5
Ross (isl.) .... J 3
Sagemace (bay) .... B 3
Saint Andrew (lake) .... E 3
Saint George (lake) .... E 3
Saint Martin (lake) .... D 3
Saint Patrick (lake) .... E 3
Sale (riv.) .... E 5
Sandy (isls.) .... D 2
Sasaginnigak (lake) .... G 3
Seal (riv.) .... J 2
Selkirk (isl.) .... C 1
Setting (lake) .... H 3
Shoal (lake) .... G 5
Shoal (riv.) .... B 2
Sipiwesk (lake) .... J 3
Sisib (lake) .... C 2
Sleeve (lake) .... E 3
Slemon (lake) .... G 1
Snowshoe (lake) .... G 4
Soul (lake) .... C 2
Souris (riv.) .... B 5
Southern Indian (lake) .... H 2
South Knife (riv.) .... J 2
South Seal (riv.) .... J 2
Split (lake) .... J 2
Spruce (isl.) .... B 1
Spruce Woods Prov. Park .... C 5
Stevenson (lake) .... J 3
Sturgeon (bay) .... E 3
Swan (lake) .... B 2
Swan (lake) .... D 5
Swan (riv.) .... A 3
Tadoule (lake) .... J 2
Tamarack (isl.) .... F 3
Tatnam (cape) .... K 2
Traverse (bay) .... F 4
Turtle (mts.) .... B 5
Turtle (riv.) .... C 3
Turtle Mountain Prov. Park .... B 5
Valley (riv.) .... B 3
Vickers (lake) .... F 3
Viking (lake) .... G 3
Wanipigow (riv.) .... G 3
Washow (bay) .... F 3
Waterhen (lake) .... C 2
Weaver (lake) .... F 2
Wellman (lake) .... B 3
West Hawk (lake) .... G 5
West Shoal (lake) .... E 4
Whitemouth (lake) .... G 5
Whitemouth (riv.) .... G 5
Whiteshell Prov. Park .... G 4
Whitewater (lake) .... B 5
Wicked (pt.) .... D 2
Winnipeg (lake) .... E 2
Winnipeg (riv.) .... G 4
Winnipegosis (lake) .... C 2
Woods (lake) .... H 5
Wrong (lake) .... F 2

*Population of metropolitan area.
•Population of rural municipality.

Topography

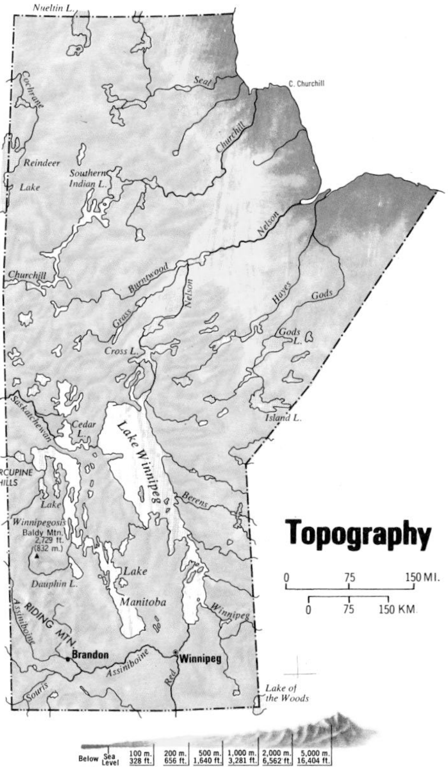
Nueltin L.
C. Churchill
Seal
Churchill
Reindeer Lake
Southern Indian L.
Nelson
Hayes
Gods
Gods L.
Burntwood
Grass
Cross L.
Island L.
Cedar L.
Lake Winnipeg
Berens
PORCUPINE HILLS
Lake Winnipegosis
Baldy Mtn. 2,729 ft. (832 m.)
Dauphin L.
Lake Manitoba
RIDING MTN.
Assiniboine
Brandon
Winnipeg
Souris
Red
Lake of the Woods
0 75 150 MI.
0 75 150 KM.
Below Sea Level
100 m. 328 ft.
200 m. 656 ft.
500 m. 1,640 ft.
1,000 m. 3,281 ft.
2,000 m. 6,562 ft.
5,000 m. 16,404 ft.

Agriculture, Industry and Resources

DOMINANT LAND USE

- Cereals (chiefly barley, oats)
- Cereals, Livestock
- Dairy
- Livestock
- Forests
- Nonagricultural Land

MAJOR MINERAL OCCURRENCES

Au	Gold	Ni	Nickel
Co	Cobalt	O	Petroleum
Cu	Copper	Pb	Lead
Na	Salt	Pt	Platinum
		Zn	Zinc

Water Power
Major Industrial Areas

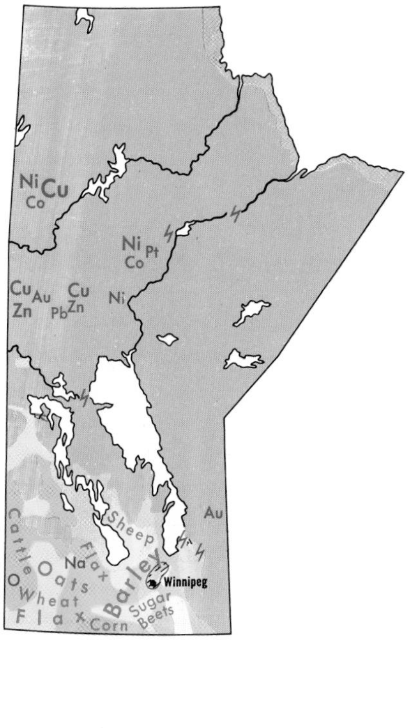
Ni Cu Co
Ni Pt Co
Cu Au Cu
Zn Pb Zn
Ni
Au
Sheep
Flax
Barley
Na
Cattle
Oats
Wheat
Flax
Corn
Sugar Beets
Winnipeg

Topography

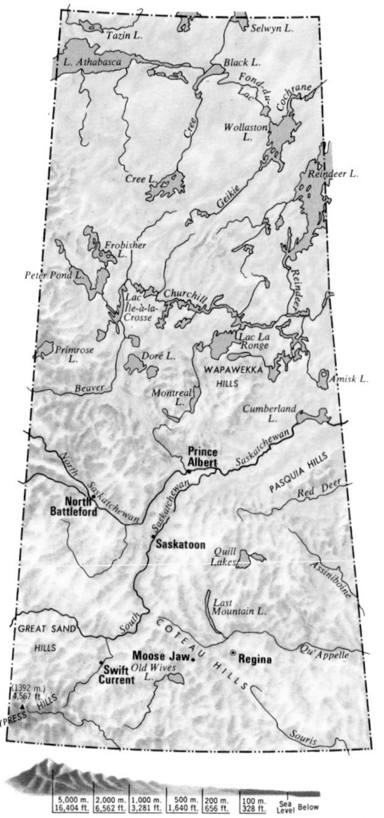
0 60 120 MI.
0 60 120 KM.
Tazin L.
Selwyn L.
L. Athabasca
Black L.
Fond du Lac
Cochrane
Wollaston L.
Cree
Reindeer L.
Cree L.
Geikie
Frobisher L.
Peter Pond L.
Churchill
Lac Île-à-la-Crosse
Reindeer
Lac La Ronge
Primrose L.
Doré L.
WAPAWEKKA HILLS
Amisk L.
Beaver
Montreal L.
Cumberland L.
Prince Albert
Saskatchewan
PASQUIA HILLS
North Battleford
Red Deer
Saskatoon
Quill Lakes
Assiniboine
Last Mountain L.
GREAT SAND HILLS
South
COTEAU HILLS
Moose Jaw
Regina
Qu'Appelle
Swift Current
Old Wives L.
Souris
CYPRESS HILLS
5,000 m. 16,404 ft.
2,000 m. 6,562 ft.
1,000 m. 3,281 ft.
500 m. 1,640 ft.
200 m. 656 ft.
100 m. 328 ft.
Sea Level
Below

CITIES and TOWNS

Abbey 218 . . . . C 5
Aberdeen 496 . . . . E 3
Abernethy 300 . . . . H 5
Air Ronge 557 . . . . M 3
Alameda 318 . . . . J 6
Alida 169 . . . . K 6
Allan 871 . . . . E 4
Alsask 652 . . . . B 4
Annaheim 209 . . . . G 3
Antelope •231 . . . . C 5
Arborfield 439 . . . . H 2
Archerwill 286 . . . . H 3
Arcola 493 . . . . J 6
Arlington Beach •432 . . . . F 4
Asquith 507 . . . . D 3
Assiniboia 2,924 . . . . E 6
Avonlea 442 . . . . G 5
Baildon •799 . . . . F 5
Balcarres 739 . . . . H 5
Balgonie 777 . . . . G 5
Batoche . . . . E 3
Battleford 3,565 . . . . C 3
Beauval 606 . . . . L 3
Beechy 279 . . . . D 5
Bengough 536 . . . . F 6
Bethune 369 . . . . F 5
Bienfait 835 . . . . J 6
Biggar 2,561 . . . . C 3
Big River 819 . . . . D 2
Birch Hills 957 . . . . F 3
Bjorkdale 269 . . . . H 3
Blaine Lake 653 . . . . D 3
Borden 197 . . . . D 3
Brabant Lake 245 . . . . M 3
Bradwell 168 . . . . E 4
Bredenbury 467 . . . . K 5
Briercrest 151 . . . . F 5
Broadview 840 . . . . J 5
Brock 184 . . . . C 4
Browning •687 . . . . J 6
Bruno 772 . . . . F 3
Buchanan 392 . . . . J 4
Buffalo Gap •598 . . . . F 6
Buffalo Narrows 1,088 . . . . L 3
Burstall 550 . . . . B 5
Cabri 632 . . . . C 5
Cadillac 173 . . . . D 6
Calder 164 . . . . K 4
Cana •1,238 . . . . J 5
Candle Lake 219 . . . . F 2
Cando 163 . . . . C 3
Canoe Lake 182 . . . . L 3
Canora 2,667 . . . . J 4
Canwood 340 . . . . E 2
Carievale 246 . . . . K 6
Carlyle 1,074 . . . . J 6
Carnduff 1,043 . . . . K 6
Carrot River 1,169 . . . . H 2
Central Butte 548 . . . . E 5
Ceylon 184 . . . . G 6
Chaplin 389 . . . . E 5
Chitek Lake 170 . . . . D 2
Choiceland 543 . . . . G 2
Christopher Lake 227 . . . . F 2
Churchbridge 972 . . . . J 5
Clavet 234 . . . . E 4
Climax 293 . . . . C 6
Cochin 221 . . . . C 2
Codette 236 . . . . H 2
Coleville 383 . . . . B 4
Colonsay 594 . . . . F 4
Connaught Heights •982 . . . . G 3
Conquest 256 . . . . D 4
Consul 153 . . . . B 6
Coronach 1,032 . . . . F 6
Craik 565 . . . . F 4
Craven 206 . . . . G 5
Creelman 184 . . . . H 6
Creighton 1,636 . . . . N 4
Cudworth 947 . . . . F 3
Cumberland House 831 . . . . J 2
Cupar 669 . . . . G 5
Cut Knife 624 . . . . B 3
Dalmeny 1,064 . . . . E 3
Davidson 1,166 . . . . E 4
Debden 403 . . . . E 2
Delisle 980 . . . . D 4
Denare Beach 592 . . . . M 4
Denzil 199 . . . . B 3
Deschambault Lake 386 . . . . M 3
Dinsmore 398 . . . . D 4
Dodsland 272 . . . . C 4
Domremy 209 . . . . F 3
Drake 211 . . . . G 4
Duck Lake 699 . . . . E 3
Dundurn 531 . . . . E 4
Dysart 275 . . . . H 5
Earl Grey 303 . . . . G 5
Eastend 723 . . . . C 6
Eatonia 528 . . . . B 4
Ebenezer 164 . . . . J 4
Edam 384 . . . . C 2
Edenwold 143 . . . . G 5
Elbow 313 . . . . E 4
Eldorado 229 . . . . L 2
Elfros 199 . . . . H 4
Elrose 624 . . . . D 4
Elstow 143 . . . . E 4
Endeavour 199 . . . . J 3
Englefeld 271 . . . . G 3
Erwood 149 . . . . J 3
Esterhazy 3,065 . . . . K 5
Estevan 9,174 . . . . J 6
Eston 1,413 . . . . C 4
Eyebrow 168 . . . . E 5
Fillmore 396 . . . . H 6
Fleming 141 . . . . K 5
Flin Flon 367 . . . . N 4
Foam Lake 1,452 . . . . H 4
Fond du Lac 494 . . . . L 2
Fort Qu'Appelle 1,827 . . . . H 5
Fox Valley 380 . . . . B 5
Francis 182 . . . . H 5
Frobisher 166 . . . . J 6
Frontier 619 . . . . C 6
Gainsborough 308 . . . . K 6
Gerald 197 . . . . K 5
Glaslyn 430 . . . . C 2
Glenavon 284 . . . . J 5
Glen Ewen 168 . . . . K 6
Goodsoil 263 . . . . L 4
Govan 394 . . . . G 4
Grand Coulee 208 . . . . G 5
Gravelbourg 1,338 . . . . E 6
Grayson 264 . . . . J 5
Green Acres 139 . . . . F 2
Green Lake 634 . . . . L 4
Grenfell 1,307 . . . . J 5
Guernsey 198 . . . . F 4
Gull Lake 1,095 . . . . C 5
Hafford 557 . . . . D 3
Hague 625 . . . . E 3
Hanley 484 . . . . E 4
Harris 259 . . . . D 4
Hawarden 137 . . . . E 4
Hearts Hill •552 . . . . B 3
Hepburn 411 . . . . E 3
Herbert 1,019 . . . . D 5
Hodgeville 329 . . . . E 5
Holdfast 297 . . . . F 5
Hudson Bay 2,361 . . . . J 3
Humboldt 4,705 . . . . F 3
Hyas 165 . . . . J 4
Île-à-la-Crosse 1,035 . . . . L 3
Imperial 501 . . . . F 4
Indian Head 1,889 . . . . H 5
Invermay 353 . . . . J 4
Ituna 870 . . . . H 4
Jansen 223 . . . . G 4
Jasmin •14 . . . . H 4
Kamsack 2,688 . . . . K 4
Kelliher 397 . . . . H 4
Kelvington 1,054 . . . . H 3
Kenaston 345 . . . . E 4
Kennedy 275 . . . . J 5
Kerrobert 1,141 . . . . C 4
Kincaid 256 . . . . D 6
Kindersley 3,969 . . . . B 4
Kinistino 783 . . . . F 3
Kipling 1,016 . . . . J 5
Kisbey 228 . . . . J 6
Kronau 154 . . . . G 5
Kyle 516 . . . . C 5
Lac Pelletier •586 . . . . C 6
Lafleche 583 . . . . E 6
Laird 233 . . . . E 3
Lake Lenore 361 . . . . G 3
La Loche 1,632 . . . . L 3
Lampman 651 . . . . J 6
Lancer 156 . . . . C 5
Landis 277 . . . . C 3
Lang 219 . . . . G 6
Langenburg 1,324 . . . . K 5
Langham 1,151 . . . . E 3
Lanigan 1,732 . . . . F 4
La Ronge 2,579 . . . . L 3
Lashburn 813 . . . . B 2
Leader 1,108 . . . . B 5
Leask 478 . . . . E 2
Lebret 274 . . . . H 5
Lemberg 414 . . . . H 5
Leoville 393 . . . . D 2
Leroy 504 . . . . G 4
Lestock 402 . . . . G 4
Limerick 164 . . . . E 6
Lintlaw 234 . . . . H 3
Lipton 364 . . . . H 5
Lloydminster 6,034 . . . . A 2
Loon Lake 369 . . . . B 1
Loreburn 201 . . . . E 4
Lucky Lake 333 . . . . D 5
Lumsden 1,303 . . . . G 5
Luseland 704 . . . . B 3
Macdowall 171 . . . . E 2
Macklin 976 . . . . A 3
Macoun 190 . . . . H 6
Maidstone 1,001 . . . . B 2
Mankota 375 . . . . D 6
Manor 368 . . . . K 6
Maple Creek 2,470 . . . . B 6
Marcelin 238 . . . . E 3
Margo 153 . . . . H 4
Marriott •627 . . . . D 4
Marsden 229 . . . . B 3
Marshall 453 . . . . B 2
Martensville 1,966 . . . . E 3
Maryfield 431 . . . . K 6
Maymont 212 . . . . D 3
McLean 189 . . . . G 5
Meacham 178 . . . . F 3
Meadow Lake 3,857 . . . . C 1
Meath Park 262 . . . . F 2
Medstead 163 . . . . C 2
Melfort 6,010 . . . . G 3
Melville 5,092 . . . . J 5
Meota 235 . . . . C 2
Mervin 155 . . . . C 2
Midale 564 . . . . H 6
Middle Lake 275 . . . . F 3
Milden 251 . . . . D 4
Milestone 602 . . . . G 5
Montmartre 544 . . . . H 5
Montreal Lake 448 . . . . F 1
Moose Jaw 33,941 . . . . F 5
Moose Range •679 . . . . H 2
Moosomin 2,579 . . . . K 5
Morse 416 . . . . D 5
Mortlach 293 . . . . E 5
Mossbank 464 . . . . E 6
Muenster 385 . . . . F 3
Naicam 886 . . . . G 3
Neilburg 354 . . . . B 3
Neuanlage 144 . . . . E 3
Neudorf 425 . . . . J 5
Neuhorst 146 . . . . E 3
Nipawin 4,376 . . . . H 2
Nokomis 524 . . . . F 4
Norquay 552 . . . . J 4
North Battleford 14,030 . . . . C 3
North Portal 164 . . . . J 6
Odessa 232 . . . . H 5
Ogema 441 . . . . G 6
Osler 527 . . . . E 3
Outlook 1,976 . . . . E 4
Oxbow 1,191 . . . . J 6
Paddockwood 211 . . . . F 2
Pangman 227 . . . . G 6
Paradise Hill 421 . . . . B 2
Patuanak 173 . . . . L 3
Paynton 210 . . . . B 2
Pelican Narrows 331 . . . . N 3
Pelly 391 . . . . K 4
Pennant 202 . . . . C 5
Pense 472 . . . . G 5
Perdue 407 . . . . D 3
Pierceland 425 . . . . K 4
Pilger 150 . . . . F 3
Pilot Butte 1,255 . . . . G 5
Pine House 612 . . . . M 3
Plenty 175 . . . . C 4
Plunkett 150 . . . . F 4
Ponteix 769 . . . . D 6
Porcupine Plain 937 . . . . H 3
Preeceville 1,243 . . . . J 4
Prelate 317 . . . . B 5
Prince Albert 31,380 . . . . F 2
Prud'homme 222 . . . . F 3
Punnichy 394 . . . . G 4
Qu'Appelle 653 . . . . H 5
Quill Lake 514 . . . . G 3
Quinton 169 . . . . G 4
Rabbit Lake 159 . . . . D 2
Radisson 439 . . . . D 3
Radville 1,012 . . . . G 6
Rama 133 . . . . H 4
Raymore 635 . . . . G 4
Redvers 859 . . . . K 6
Regina (cap.) 162,613 . . . . G 5
Regina *164,313 . . . . G 5
Regina Beach 603 . . . . F 5
Rhein 271 . . . . J 4
Richmound 188 . . . . B 5
Riverhurst 193 . . . . E 5
Rocanville 934 . . . . K 5
Roche Percé 142 . . . . J 6
Rockglen 511 . . . . F 6
Rosetown 2,664 . . . . D 4
Rose Valley 538 . . . . H 3
Rosthern 1,609 . . . . E 3
Rouleau 443 . . . . G 5
Saint Benedict 157 . . . . F 3
Saint Brieux 401 . . . . G 3
Saint Louis 448 . . . . F 3
Saint Philips •538 . . . . K 4
Saint Walburg 802 . . . . B 2
Saltcoats 549 . . . . J 4
Sandy Bay 756 . . . . N 3
Saskatoon 154,210 . . . . E 3
Saskatoon *154,210 . . . . E 3
Sceptre 169 . . . . B 5
Scott 203 . . . . C 3
Sedley 373 . . . . H 5
Semans 344 . . . . G 4
Shaunavon 2,112 . . . . C 6
Sheho 285 . . . . H 4
Shell Lake 220 . . . . D 2
Shellbrook 1,228 . . . . E 2
Simpson 231 . . . . F 4
Sintaluta 215 . . . . H 5
Smeaton 246 . . . . G 2
Southey 697 . . . . G 5
Spalding 337 . . . . G 3
Spiritwood 926 . . . . D 2
Springside 533 . . . . J 4
Spy Hill 354 . . . . K 5
Star City 527 . . . . G 3
Stenen 143 . . . . J 4
Stockholm 391 . . . . J 5
Stonehenge •701 . . . . F 6
Storthoaks 142 . . . . K 6
Stoughton 716 . . . . J 6
Strasbourg 842 . . . . G 4
Sturgis 789 . . . . J 4
Swift Current 14,747 . . . . D 5
Tantallon 196 . . . . K 5
Theodore 473 . . . . J 4
Timber Bay 152 . . . . F 1
Tisdale 3,107 . . . . H 3
Togo 181 . . . . K 4
Tompkins 275 . . . . C 5
Torch River •2,440 . . . . G 2
Torquay 311 . . . . H 6
Tramping Lake 178 . . . . B 3
Tugaske 175 . . . . E 5
Turnor Lake 166 . . . . L 3
Turtleford 505 . . . . B 2
Unity 2,408 . . . . B 3
Uranium City 2,507 . . . . L 2
Val Marie 236 . . . . D 6
Vanguard 292 . . . . D 6
Vanscoy 298 . . . . D 4
Vibank 369 . . . . H 5
Viscount 386 . . . . F 4
Vonda 313 . . . . F 3
Wadena 1,495 . . . . H 4
Wakaw 1,030 . . . . F 3
Waldeck 292 . . . . D 5
Waldheim 758 . . . . E 3
Walpole •711 . . . . K 6
Wapella 487 . . . . K 5
Warman 2,076 . . . . E 3
Waseca 169 . . . . B 2
Waskesiu Lake 176 . . . . E 2
Watrous 1,830 . . . . F 4
Watson 901 . . . . G 3
Wawota 622 . . . . J 6
Weldon 279 . . . . F 2
Welwyn 170 . . . . K 5
Weyburn 9,523 . . . . H 6
White City 602 . . . . G 5
White Fox 394 . . . . H 2
Whitewood 1,003 . . . . J 5
Wilcox 202 . . . . G 5
Wilkie 1,501 . . . . C 3
Willow Bunch 494 . . . . F 6
Willow Creek •1,218 . . . . B 6
Windthorst 254 . . . . J 5
Wiseton 195 . . . . D 4
Wishart 212 . . . . H 4
Wollaston Lake 248 . . . . N 2
Wolseley 904 . . . . H 5
Wymark 162 . . . . D 5
Wynyard 2,147 . . . . G 4
Yarbo 158 . . . . K 5
Yellow Grass 477 . . . . H 6
Yorkton 15,339 . . . . J 4
Young 456 . . . . F 4
Zenon Park 273 . . . . H 2

OTHER FEATURES

Allan (hills) . . . . E 4
Amisk (lake) . . . . M 4
Antelope (lake) . . . . C 5
Antler (riv.) . . . . K 6
Arm (riv.) . . . . F 5
Assiniboine (riv.) . . . . J 3
Athabasca (lake) . . . . L 2
Bad (lake) . . . . C 4
Bad (hills) . . . . C 4
Basin (lake) . . . . F 3
Batoche Nat'l Hist. Site . . . . E 3
Battle (creek) . . . . B 6
Battle (riv.) . . . . B 3
Bear (hills) . . . . C 4
Beaver (hills) . . . . H 4
Beaver (riv.) . . . . L 4
Beaverlodge (lake) . . . . L 2
Big Muddy (lake) . . . . G 6
Bigstick (lake) . . . . B 5
Birch (lake) . . . . C 2
Bitter (lake) . . . . B 5
Black (lake) . . . . M 2
Boundary (plat.) . . . . B 6
Brightsand (lake) . . . . B 2
Bronson (lake) . . . . B 2

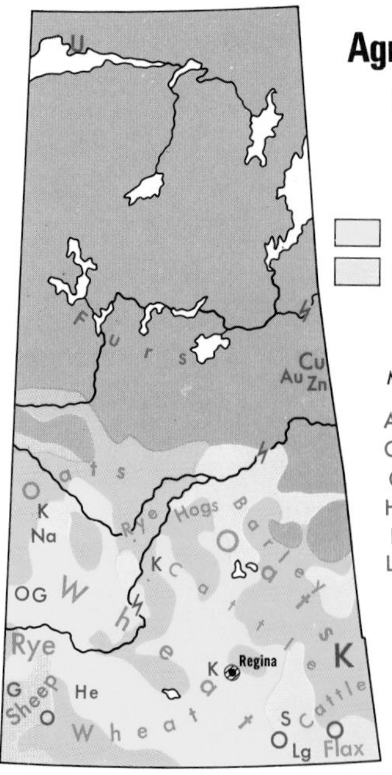
U
Furs
Au
Cu
Zn
K
Na
OG
Rye
Hogs
Oats
Barley
Cattle
Wheat
Sheep
He
Regina
Lg
Flax

Agriculture, Industry and Resources

DOMINANT LAND USE

- Wheat
- Cereals (chiefly barley, oats)
- Cereals, Livestock
- Livestock
- Forests

MAJOR MINERAL OCCURRENCES

- Au Gold
- Cu Copper
- G Natural Gas
- He Helium
- K Potash
- Lg Lignite
- Na Salt
- O Petroleum
- S Sulfur
- U Uranium
- Zn Zinc
- Water Power
- Major Industrial Areas

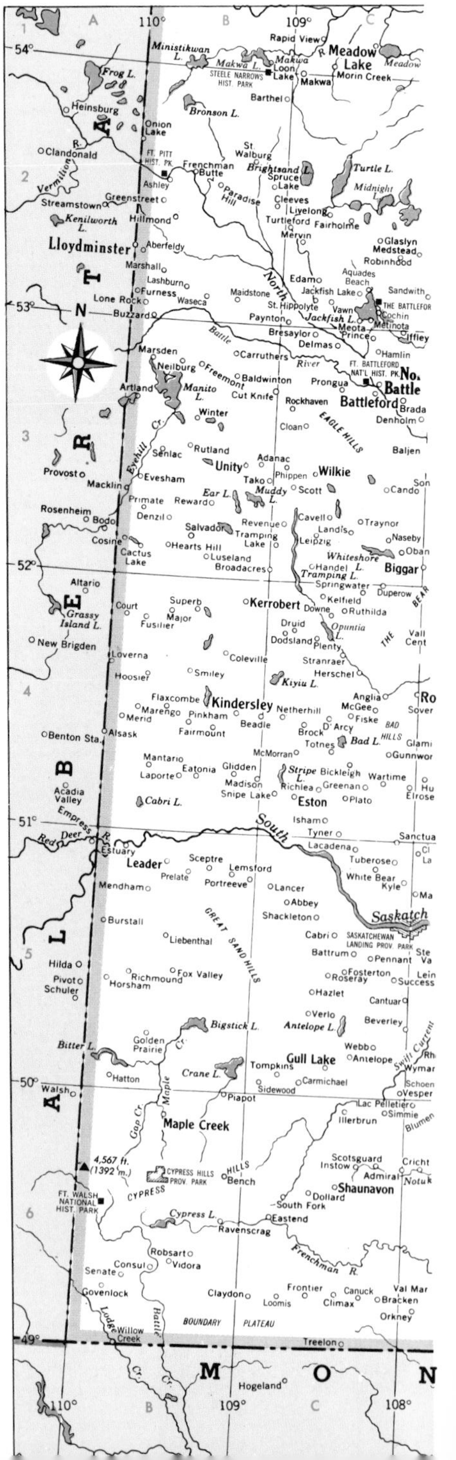
A
B
C
110°
109°
108°
54°
53°
52°
51°
50°
49°
Ministikwan L.
Makwa L.
STEELE NARROWS HIST. PARK
Loon Lake
Makwa
Rapid View
Meadow Lake
Morin Creek
Frog L.
Heinsburg
Onion Lake
Bronson L.
Barthel
Clandonald
FT. PITT HIST. PK.
Frenchman Butte
St. Walburg
Brightsand L.
Turtle L.
Ashley
Vermilion
Streamstown
Greenstreet
Hillmond
Paradise Hill
Spruce Lake
Cleeves
Lyelong
Turtleford
Fairholme
Mervin
Midnight L.
Kenilworth L.
Lloydminster
Aberfeldy
Glaslyn
Medstead
Robinhood
Marshall
Lashburn
Furness
Waseca
Maidstone
Edam
Jackfish Lake
Sandwith
Lone Rock
Buzzard
St. Hippolyte
Vawn
Paynton
Jackfish L.
Cochin
Meota
Bresaylor
Delmas
Prince
Marsden
Carruthers
Neilburg
Freemont
Baldwinton
River
FT. BATTLEFORD NAT'L HIST. PK.
Artland
Manito L.
Cut Knife
Rockhaven
Prongua
Battleford
Winter
Cloan
EAGLE HILLS
Senlac
Rutland
Unity
Adanac
Muddy L.
Phippen
Wilkie
Baljen
Provost
Macklin
Evesham
Tako
Scott
Primate
Reward
Ear L.
Rosenheim
Bodo
Denzil
Revenue
Cavell
Traynor
Salvador
Landis
Naseby
Cosine
Tramping Lake
Leipzig
Oban
Hearts Hill
Cactus Lake
Luseland
Whiteshore L.
Broadacres
Handel
Biggar
Tramping L.
Springwater
Duperow
Altario
Court
Superb
Major
Fusilier
Kerrobert
Kelfield
Downe
Ruthilda
Grassy Island L.
Druid
Opuntia L.
New Brigden
Dodsland
Plenty
Loverna
Coleville
Stranraer
Hoosier
Smiley
Herschel
Kiyiu L.
Flaxcombe
Kindersley
Anglia
Marengo
Pinkham
Netherhill
McGee
Merid
Fairmount
Beadle
Fiske
Alsask
Brock
D'Arcy
Benton Sta.
Totnes
Bad L.
BAD HILLS
McMorran
Mantario
Laporte
Eatonia
Glidden
Madison
Stripe
Richlea
Bickleigh
Greenan
Wartime
Acadia Valley
Snipe Lake
Eston
Plato
Elrose
Cabri L.
Empress
Isham
Red Deer
Estuary
Tyner
Lacadena
Sanctuary
South
Leader
Sceptre
Lemsford
Prelate
Portreeve
Tuberose
Lancer
White Bear
Kyle
Mendham
Abbey
Shackleton
GREAT SAND HILLS
Burstall
Liebenthal
Cabri
SASKATCHEWAN LANDING PROV. PARK
Saskatchewan
Battrum
Pennant
Hilda
Fox Valley
Fosterton
Pivot
Schuler
Richmound
Horsham
Roseray
Success
Hazlet
Cantuar
Verlo
Bigstick L.
Antelope L.
Beverley
Bitter L.
Golden Prairie
Gull Lake
Webb
Tompkins
Antelope
Crane L.
Hatton
Carmichael
Walsh
Piapot
Sidewood
Vesper
Lac Pelletier
Illerbrun
Simmie
Maple Creek
Scotsguard
Instow
Admiral
Crichton
Notukeu
4,567 ft. (1392 m.)
CYPRESS HILLS PROV. PARK
HILLS
Bench
Shaunavon
Dollard
FT. WALSH NATIONAL HIST. PARK
CYPRESS
South Fork
Cypress L.
Eastend
Ravenscrag
Frenchman R.
Robsart
Senate
Consul
Vidora
Govenlock
Claydon
Frontier
Loomis
Canuck
Climax
Val Marie
Bracken
Orkney
Lodge
Battle
Willow Creek
BOUNDARY PLATEAU
Treelon
Hogeland
ALBERTA
MONTANA

AREA 251,699 sq. mi. (651,900 sq. km.)
POPULATION 1,009,613
CAPITAL Regina
LARGEST CITY Regina
HIGHEST POINT Cypress Hills 4,567 ft. (1,392 m.)
SETTLED IN 1774
ADMITTED TO CONFEDERATION 1905
PROVINCIAL FLOWER Prairie Lily

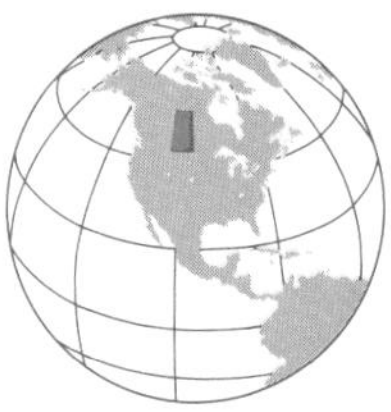

*Population of metropolitan area.
•Population of rural municipality.

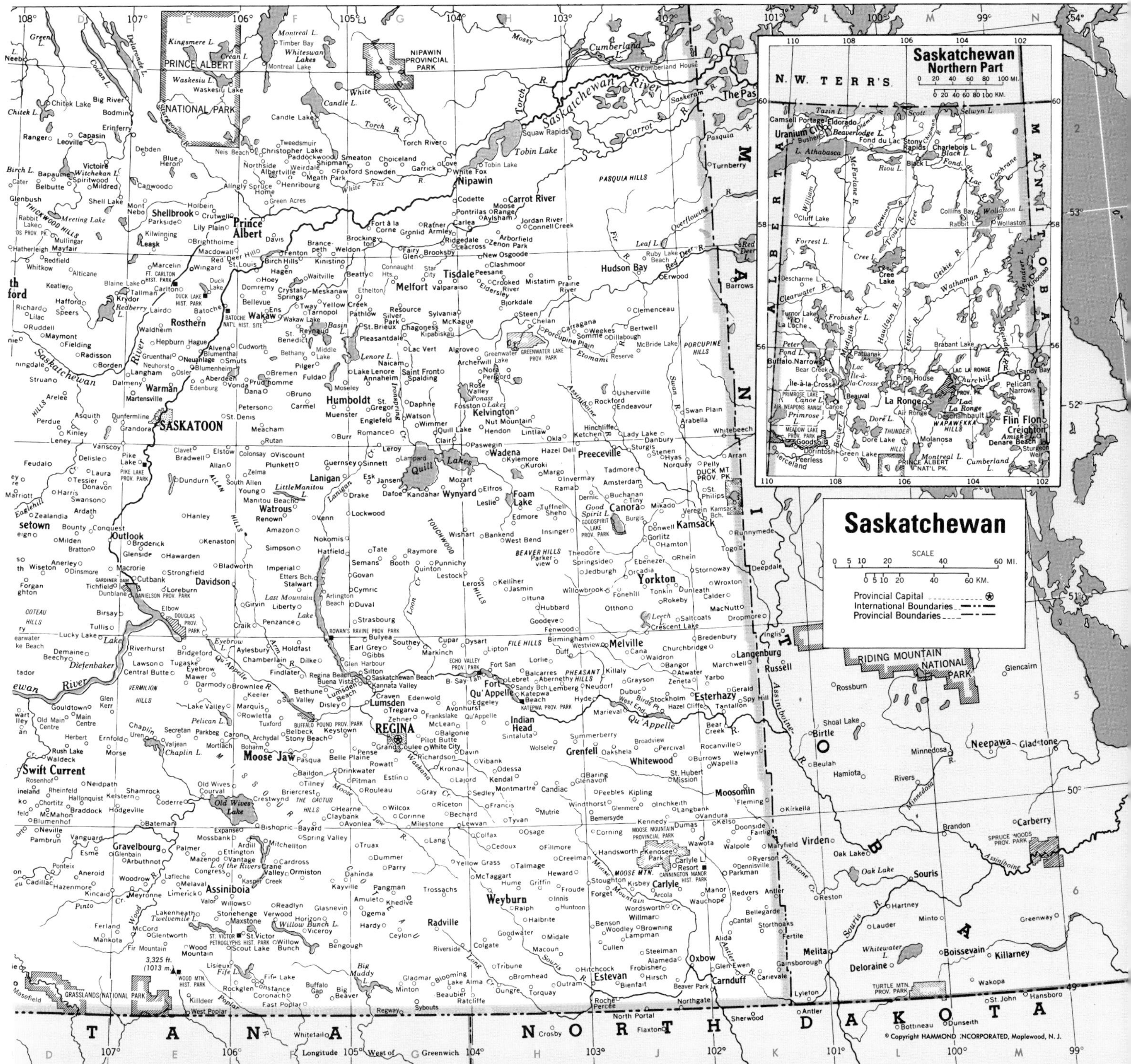
Saskatchewan
SCALE
0 5 10 20 40 60 MI.
0 5 10 20 40 60 KM.
Provincial Capital
International Boundaries
Provincial Boundaries
Saskatchewan Northern Part
Longitude 105° West of Greenwich 104°
© Copyright HAMMOND INCORPORATED, Maplewood, N. J.

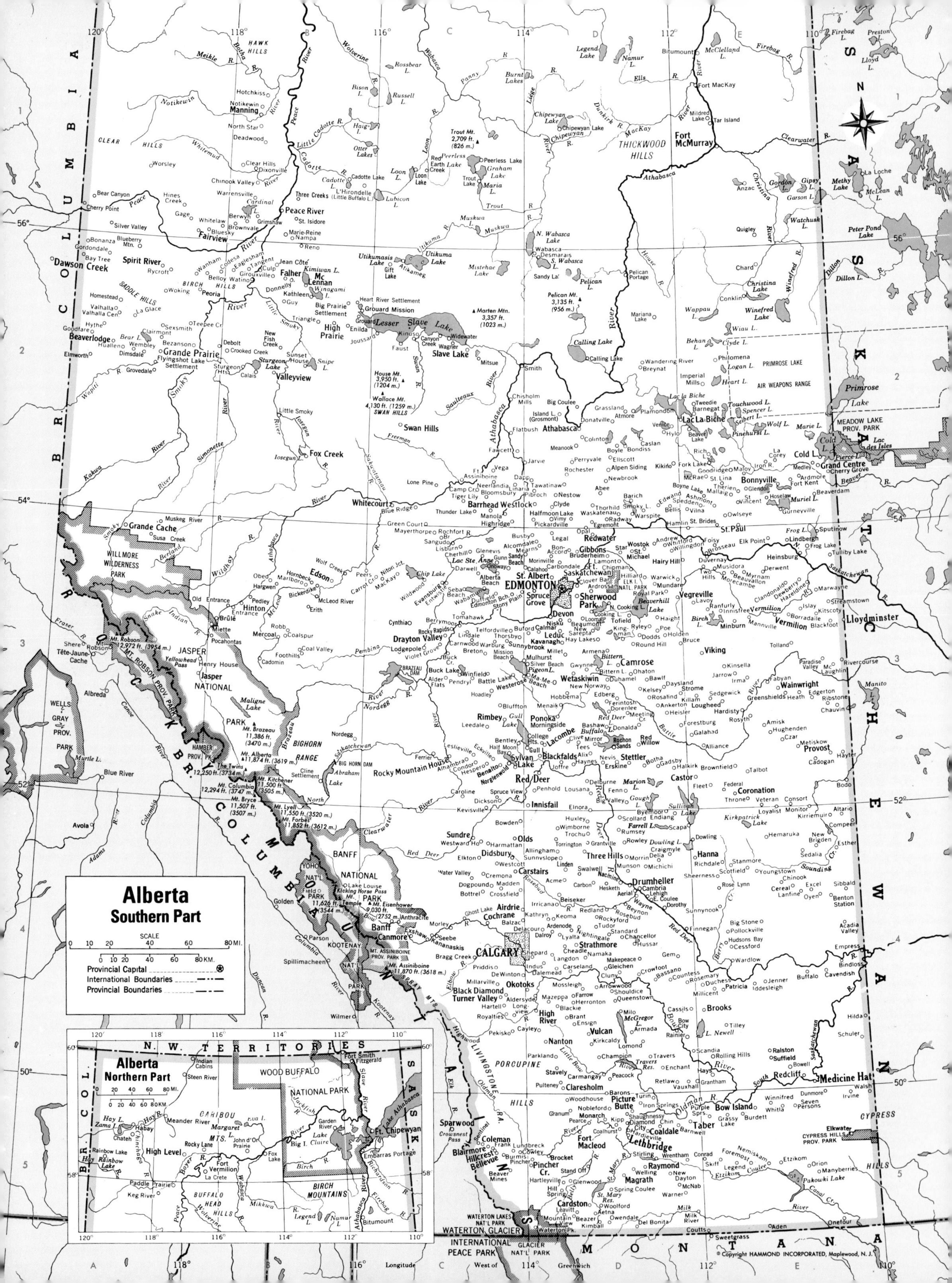

Alberta
Southern Part
SCALE
0 10 20 40 60 80 MI.
0 10 20 40 60 80 KM.
Provincial Capital
International Boundaries
Provincial Boundaries
Alberta
Northern Part
N. W. TERRITORIES
SASK.
BR. COL.
WOOD BUFFALO
NATIONAL PARK
CARIBOU MTS.
BUFFALO HEAD HILLS
BIRCH MOUNTAINS
Fort Smith
Fitzgerald
Indian Cabins
Steen River
Meander River
Hay L.
Zama L.
Habay
Chateh
Rainbow Lake
High Level
Rocky Lane
John d'Or Prairie
Fox Lake
Fort Vermilion
La Crete
Paddle Prairie
Keg River
Garden River
Lake Claire
Ft. Chipewyan
Embarras Portage
Bitumount
Legend L.
Namur L.
BRITISH COLUMBIA
SASKATCHEWAN
MONTANA
Longitude West of Greenwich
EDMONTON
CALGARY
Fort McMurray
Peace River
Grande Prairie
Lethbridge
Medicine Hat
Red Deer
Lloydminster
Jasper
Banff
Whitecourt
Athabasca
Lac La Biche
Cold L.
Grand Centre
Bonnyville
St. Paul
Vegreville
Camrose
Wetaskiwin
Ponoka
Lacombe
Drumheller
Hanna
Brooks
Taber
Cardston
Fort Macleod
Pincher Cr.
Blairmore
Coleman
Canmore
High River
Okotoks
Airdrie
Cochrane
Olds
Innisfail
Rimbey
Stettler
Castor
Coronation
Provost
Wainwright
Vermilion
Slave Lake
High Prairie
Valleyview
Fox Creek
Swan Hills
Edson
Hinton
Grande Cache
Manning
Fairview
Spirit River
Dawson Creek
Beaverlodge
WILLMORE WILDERNESS PARK
JASPER NATIONAL PARK
BANFF NATIONAL PARK
YOHO NAT'L PARK
KOOTENAY NAT'L PARK
WATERTON LAKES NAT'L PARK
WATERTON GLACIER INTERNATIONAL PEACE PARK
GLACIER NAT'L PARK
CYPRESS HILLS PROV. PARK
MEADOW LAKE PROV. PARK
PRIMROSE LAKE AIR WEAPONS RANGE
Lesser Slave Lake
THICKWOOD HILLS
CLEAR HILLS
SADDLE HILLS
BIRCH HILLS
SWAN HILLS
PORCUPINE HILLS
BIGHORN RANGE
LIVINGSTONE RA.
Mt. Robson 12,972 ft. (3954 m.)
Mt. Columbia 12,294 ft. (3747 m.)
Mt. Alberta 11,874 ft. (3619 m.)
Mt. Assiniboine 11,870 ft. (3618 m.)
© Copyright HAMMOND INCORPORATED, Maplewood, N. J.

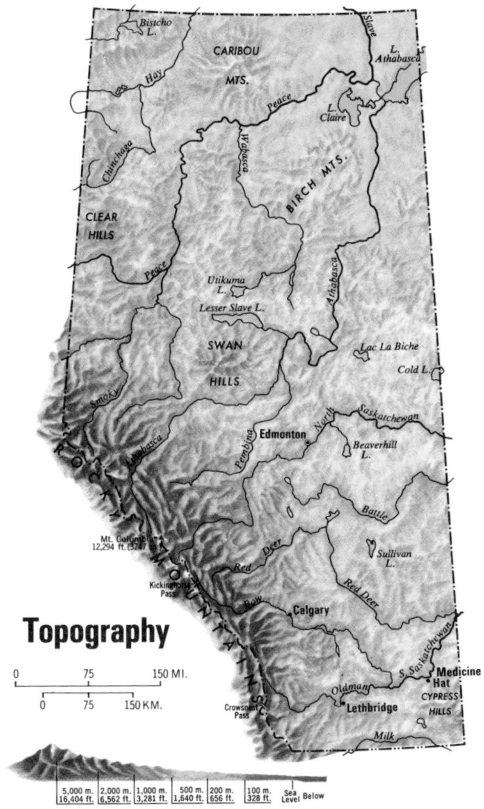
Bistcho L.
CARIBOU MTS.
Hay
L. Athabasca
Slave
Peace
L. Claire
Wabasca
BIRCH MTS.
Chinchaga
CLEAR HILLS
Peace
Utikuma L.
Lesser Slave L.
Athabasca
SWAN HILLS
Lac La Biche
Cold L.
Smoky
Saskatchewan
North
Edmonton
Pembina
Beaverhill L.
Athabasca
Battle
Mt. Columbia 12,294 ft. (3,747 m.)
Red
Deer
Sullivan L.
Kickinghorse Pass
Red Deer
Bow
Calgary
Medicine Hat
Oldman
S. Saskatchewan
Lethbridge
CYPRESS HILLS
Crowsnest Pass
Milk
0 75 150 MI.
0 75 150 KM.
5,000 m. 16,404 ft.
2,000 m. 6,562 ft.
1,000 m. 3,281 ft.
500 m. 1,640 ft.
200 m. 656 ft.
100 m. 328 ft.
Sea Level
Below

Topography

AREA 255,285 sq. mi. (661,185 sq. km.)
POPULATION 2,365,825
CAPITAL Edmonton
LARGEST CITY Edmonton
HIGHEST POINT Mt. Columbia 12,294 ft. (3,747 m.)
SETTLED IN 1861
ADMITTED TO CONFEDERATION 1905
PROVINCIAL FLOWER Wild Rose

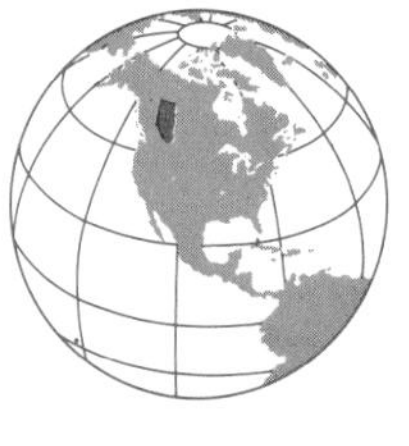

CITIES and TOWNS

Acme 457 . . . D 4
Airdrie 8,414 . . . C 4
Alberta Beach 485 . . . C 3
Alix 837 . . . D 3
Andrew 548 . . . D 3
Antler Lake 334 . . . D 3
Ardmore 224 . . . E 2
Arrowwood 156 . . . D 4
Athabasca 1,731 . . . D 2
Banff 4,208 . . . C 4
Barnwell 359 . . . D 5
Barons 315 . . . D 4
Barrhead 3,736 . . . C 2
Bashaw 875 . . . D 3
Bassano 1,200 . . . D 4
Bawlf 350 . . . D 3
Beaumont 2,638 . . . D 3
Beaverlodge 1,937 . . . A 2
Beiseker 580 . . . D 4
Bentley 823 . . . C 3
Berwyn 557 . . . B 1
Big Valley 360 . . . D 3
Black Diamond 1,444 . . . C 4
Blackfalds 1,488 . . . D 3
Blackfoot 220 . . . E 3
Blackie 298 . . . D 4
Bon Accord 1,376 . . . D 3
Bonnyville 4,454 . . . E 2
Bowden 989 . . . C 4
Bow Island 1,491 . . . E 5
Boyle 638 . . . D 2
Bragg Creek 505 . . . C 4
Breton 552 . . . C 3
Brooks 9,421 . . . E 4
Bruce 88 . . . E 3
Bruderheim 1,136 . . . D 3
Burdett 220 . . . E 5
Calgary 592,743 . . . C 4
Calgary *592,743 . . . C 4
Calmar 1,003 . . . D 3
Camrose 12,570 . . . D 3
Canmore 3,484 . . . C 4
Carbon 434 . . . D 4
Cardston 3,267 . . . D 5
Carmangay 266 . . . D 4
Caroline 436 . . . C 3
Carseland 484 . . . D 4
Carstairs 1,587 . . . D 4
Castor 1,123 . . . D 3
Cereal 249 . . . E 4
Champion 339 . . . D 4
Chauvin 298 . . . E 3
Chipman 266 . . . D 3
Clairmont 469 . . . A 2
Claresholm 3,493 . . . D 4
Clive 364 . . . D 3
Clyde 364 . . . D 2
Coaldale 4,579 . . . D 5
Coalhurst 882 . . . D 5
Cochrane 3,544 . . . C 4
Cold Lake 2,110 . . . E 2
College Heights 267 . . . D 3
Consort 632 . . . E 3
Cooking Lake 218 . . . D 3
Coronation 1,309 . . . E 3
Coutts 400 . . . D 5
Cowley 304 . . . D 5
Cremona 382 . . . C 4
Crossfield 1,217 . . . C 4
Daysland 679 . . . D 3
Delburne 574 . . . D 3
Desmarais 260 . . . D 2
Devon 3,885 . . . D 3
Didsbury 3,095 . . . C 4
Donalda 280 . . . D 3
Donnelly 336 . . . B 2
Drayton Valley 5,042 . . . C 3
Drumheller 6,508 . . . D 4
Duchess 429 . . . E 4
East Coulee 218 . . . D 4
Eckville 870 . . . C 3
Edgerton 387 . . . E 3
Edmonton (cap.) 532,246 . . . D 3
Edmonton *657,057 . . . D 3
Edmonton Beach 280 . . . C 3
Edson 5,835 . . . B 3
Elk Point 1,022 . . . E 3
Elnora 249 . . . D 3
Entwistle 462 . . . C 3
Erskine 259 . . . D 3
Evansburg 779 . . . C 3
Exshaw 353 . . . C 4
Fairview 2,869 . . . A 1
Falher 1,102 . . . B 2
Faust 399 . . . C 2
Foremost 568 . . . E 5
Forestburg 924 . . . E 3
Fort Assiniboine 207 . . . C 2
Fort Chipewyan 944 . . . C 5
Fort Macleod 3,139 . . . D 5
Fort McKay 267 . . . E 1
Fort McMurray 31,000 . . . E 1
Fort Saskatchewan 12,169 . . . D 3
Fort Vermilion 752 . . . B 5
Fox Creek 1,978 . . . B 2
Fox Lake 634 . . . B 5
Gibbons 2,276 . . . D 3
Gift Lake 428 . . . C 2
Girouxville 325 . . . B 2
Gleichen 381 . . . D 4
Glendon 430 . . . E 2
Glenwood 259 . . . D 5
Grand Centre 3,146 . . . E 2
Grande Cache 4,523 . . . A 3
Grande Prairie 24,263 . . . A 2
Granum 399 . . . D 5
Grimshaw 2,316 . . . B 1
Grouard Mission 221 . . . C 2
Hanna 2,806 . . . E 4
Hardisty 641 . . . E 3
Hay Lakes 302 . . . D 3
Heisler 212 . . . D 3
High Level 2,194 . . . A 5
High Prairie 2,506 . . . B 2
High River 4,792 . . . D 4
Hines Creek 575 . . . A 1
Hinton 8,342 . . . B 3
Holden 430 . . . D 3
Hughenden 267 . . . E 3
Hythe 639 . . . A 2
Innisfail 5,247 . . . D 3
Innisfree 255 . . . E 3
Irma 474 . . . E 3
Irricana 558 . . . D 4
Irvine 360 . . . E 5
Jasper 3,269 . . . B 3
John d'Or Prairie 437 . . . B 5
Joussard 330 . . . B 2
Killam 1,005 . . . E 3
Kinuso 285 . . . C 2
Kitscoty 497 . . . E 3
Lac La Biche 2,007 . . . E 2
Lacombe 5,591 . . . D 3
La Crete 479 . . . B 5
Lake Louise 355 . . . B 4
Lamont 1,563 . . . D 3
Leduc 12,471 . . . D 3
Legal 1,022 . . . D 3
Lethbridge 54,072 . . . D 5
Linden 407 . . . D 4
Little Buffalo Lake 253 . . . B 1
Lloydminster 8,997 . . . E 3
Longview 301 . . . C 4
Lougheed 226 . . . E 3
Lundbreck 244 . . . C 5
Magrath 1,576 . . . D 5
Manning 1,173 . . . B 1
Mannville 788 . . . E 3
Marlboro 211 . . . B 3
Marwayne 500 . . . E 3
Mayerthorpe 1,475 . . . C 3
McLennan 1,125 . . . B 2
Medicine Hat 40,380 . . . E 4
Milk River 894 . . . D 5
Millet 1,120 . . . D 3
Mirror 507 . . . D 3
Monarch 212 . . . D 5
Morinville 4,657 . . . D 3
Morrin 244 . . . D 4
Mundare 604 . . . D 3
Myrnam 397 . . . E 3
Nacmine 369 . . . D 4
Nampa 334 . . . B 1
Nanton 1,641 . . . D 4
New Norway 291 . . . D 3
New Sarepta 417 . . . D 3
Nobleford 534 . . . D 5
North Calling Lake 234 . . . D 2
Okotoks 3,847 . . . C 4
Olds 4,813 . . . D 4
Onoway 621 . . . C 3
Oyen 975 . . . E 4
Peace River 5,907 . . . B 1
Penhold 1,531 . . . D 3
Picture Butte 1,404 . . . D 5
Pincher Creek 3,757 . . . D 5
Plamondon 259 . . . D 2
Pollockville 19 . . . E 4
Ponoka 5,221 . . . D 3
Provost 1,645 . . . E 3
Rainbow Lake 504 . . . A 5
Ralston 357 . . . E 4
Raymond 2,837 . . . D 5
Redcliff 3,876 . . . E 4
Red Deer 46,393 . . . D 3
Redwater 1,932 . . . D 3
Rimbey 1,685 . . . C 3
Robb 230 . . . B 3
Rockyford 329 . . . D 4
Rocky Mountain House 4,698 . C 3
Rosemary 328 . . . E 4
Rycroft 649 . . . A 2
Ryley 483 . . . D 3
Saint Albert 31,996 . . . D 3
Saint Paul 4,884 . . . E 3
Sangudo 398 . . . C 3
Sedgewick 879 . . . E 3
Sexsmith 1,180 . . . A 2
Shaughnessy 270 . . . D 5
Sherwood Park 29,285 . . . D 3
Slave Lake 4,506 . . . C 2
Smith 216 . . . D 2
Smoky Lake 1,074 . . . D 2
Spirit River 1,104 . . . A 2
Spruce Grove 10,326 . . . D 3
Standard 379 . . . D 4
Stavely 504 . . . D 4
Stettler 5,136 . . . D 3
Stirling 688 . . . D 5
Stony Plain 4,839 . . . C 3
Strathmore 2,986 . . . D 4
Strome 281 . . . E 3
Sundre 1,742 . . . C 4
Swan Hills 2,497 . . . C 2
Sylvan Lake 3,779 . . . C 3
Taber 5,988 . . . E 5
Thorhild 576 . . . D 2
Thorsby 737 . . . C 3
Three Hills 1,787 . . . D 4
Tilley 345 . . . E 4
Tofield 1,504 . . . D 3
Trochu 880 . . . D 4
Turner Valley 1,311 . . . C 4
Two Hills 1,193 . . . E 3
Valleyview 2,061 . . . B 2
Vauxhall 1,049 . . . D 4
Vegreville 5,251 . . . E 3
Vermilion 3,766 . . . E 3
Veteran 314 . . . E 3
Viking 1,232 . . . E 3
Vilna 345 . . . E 2
Vulcan 1,489 . . . D 4
Wabamun 662 . . . C 3
Wabasca 701 . . . D 2
Wainwright 4,266 . . . E 3
Warburg 501 . . . C 3
Warner 477 . . . D 5
Waskatenau 290 . . . D 2
Wembley 1,169 . . . A 2
Westlock 4,424 . . . C 2
Wetaskiwin 9,597 . . . D 3
Whitecourt 5,585 . . . C 2
Wildwood 441 . . . C 3
Willingdon 366 . . . E 3
Youngstown 297 . . . E 4

OTHER FEATURES

Abraham (lake) . . . B 3
Alberta (mt.) . . . B 3
Assiniboine (mt.) . . . C 4
Athabasca (lake) . . . C 5
Athabasca (riv.) . . . D 1
Banff Nat'l Park . . . B 4
Battle (riv.) . . . D 3
Bear (lake) . . . A 2
Beaver (riv.) . . . E 2
Beaverhill (lake) . . . D 3
Behan (lake) . . . E 2
Belly (riv.) . . . D 5
Berland (riv.) . . . A 3
Berry (creek) . . . E 4
Biche (lake) . . . E 2
Big (isl.) . . . B 5
Big Horn (dam) . . . B 3
Bighorn (range) . . . B 3
Birch (hills) . . . A 2
Birch (lake) . . . E 3
Birch (mts.) . . . B 5
Birch (riv.) . . . B 5
Bison (lake) . . . B 1
Bittern (lake) . . . D 3
Botha (riv.) . . . B 1
Bow (riv.) . . . D 4
Boyer (riv.) . . . A 5
Brazeau (mt.) . . . B 3
Brazeau (riv.) . . . B 3
Buffalo (lake) . . . D 3
Buffalo Head (hills) . . . B 5
Burnt (lakes) . . . C 1
Cadotte (lake) . . . B 1
Cadotte (riv.) . . . B 1
Calling (lake) . . . D 2
Canal (creek) . . . E 5
Cardinal (lake) . . . B 1
Caribou (mts.) . . . B 5
Chinchaga (riv.) . . . A 5
Chip (lake) . . . C 3
Chipewyan (lake) . . . D 1
Chipewyan (riv.) . . . D 1
Christina (lake) . . . E 2
Christina (riv.) . . . E 1
Claire (lake) . . . B 5
Clear (hills) . . . A 1
Clearwater (riv.) . . . C 4
Clearwater (riv.) . . . E 1
Clyde (lake) . . . E 2
Cold (lake) . . . E 2
Columbia (mt.) . . . B 3
Crowsnest (pass) . . . C 5
Cypress (hills) . . . E 5
Cypress Hills Prov. Park . . . E 5
Dillon (riv.) . . . E 2
Dowling (lake) . . . D 4
Dunkirk (riv.) . . . D 1
Eisenhower (mt.) . . . C 4
Elbow (riv.) . . . C 4
Elk Island Nat'l Park . . . D 3
Ells (riv.) . . . D 1
Etzikom Coulee (riv.) . . . E 5
Eva (lake) . . . B 5
Farrell (lake) . . . D 4
Firebag (riv.) . . . E 1
Forbes (mt.) . . . B 4
Freeman (riv.) . . . C 2
Frog (lake) . . . E 3
Garson (lake) . . . E 1
Gipsy (lake) . . . E 1
Gordon (lake) . . . E 1
Gough (lake) . . . D 3
Graham (lake) . . . C 1
Gull (lake) . . . C 3
Haig (lake) . . . B 1
Hawk (hills) . . . B 1
Hay (lake) . . . A 5
Hay (riv.) . . . A 5
Heart (lake) . . . E 2
Highwood (riv.) . . . C 4
House (mt.) . . . C 2
House (riv.) . . . D 2
Iosegun (lake) . . . B 2
Iosegun (riv.) . . . B 2
Jackfish (riv.) . . . B 5
Jasper Nat'l Park . . . A 3
Kakwa (riv.) . . . A 2
Kickinghorse (pass) . . . B 4
Kimiwan (lake) . . . B 2
Kirkpatrick (lake) . . . E 4
Kitchener (mt.) . . . B 3
Legend (lake) . . . D 1
Lesser Slave (lake) . . . C 2
Liége (riv.) . . . D 1
Little Bow (riv.) . . . D 4
Little Cadotte (riv.) . . . B 1
Little Smoky (riv.) . . . B 2
Livingstone (range) . . . C 4
Logan (lake) . . . E 2
Loon (lake) . . . C 1
Loon (riv.) . . . C 1
Lubicon (lake) . . . C 1
Lyell (mt.) . . . B 4
MacKay (riv.) . . . D 1
Maligne (lake) . . . B 3
Margaret (lake) . . . B 5
Marie (lake) . . . E 2
Marion (lake) . . . D 3
Marten (mt.) . . . C 2
McClelland (lake) . . . E 1
McGregor (lake) . . . D 4
McLeod (riv.) . . . B 3
Meikle (riv.) . . . A 1
Mikkwa (riv.) . . . B 5
Milk (riv.) . . . D 5
Mistehae (lake) . . . C 2
Muriel (lake) . . . E 2
Muskwa (lake) . . . C 1
Muskwa (riv.) . . . C 1
Namur (lake) . . . D 1
Newell (lake) . . . E 4
Nordegg (riv.) . . . C 3
North Saskatchewan (riv.) . . . E 3
North Wabasca (lake) . . . D 1
Notikewin (riv.) . . . A 1
Oldman (riv.) . . . D 5
Otter (lakes) . . . B 1
Pakowki (lake) . . . E 5
Panny (riv.) . . . C 1
Peace (riv.) . . . B 1
Peerless (lake) . . . C 1
Pelican (lake) . . . D 2
Pelican (mts.) . . . D 2
Pembina (riv.) . . . C 3
Pigeon (lake) . . . D 3
Pinehurst (lake) . . . E 2
Porcupine (hills) . . . C 4
Primrose (lake) . . . E 2
Rainbow (lake) . . . A 5
Red Deer (lake) . . . D 3
Red Deer (riv.) . . . D 4
Richardson (riv.) . . . C 5
Rocky (mts.) . . . B-C 4
Rosebud (riv.) . . . D 4
Russell (lake) . . . C 1
Saddle (hills) . . . A 2
Sainte Anne (lake) . . . C 3
Saint Mary (res.) . . . D 5
Saint Mary (riv.) . . . D 5
Saulteaux (riv.) . . . C 2
Seibert (lake) . . . E 2
Simonette (riv.) . . . A 2
Slave (riv.) . . . C 5
Smoky (riv.) . . . A 2
Snake Indian (riv.) . . . A 3
Snipe (lake) . . . B 2
Sounding (creek) . . . E 4
South Saskatchewan (riv.) . . . E 4
South Wabasca (lake) . . . D 2
Spencer (lake) . . . E 2
Spray (mts.) . . . C 4
Sturgeon (lake) . . . B 2
Sullivan (lake) . . . D 3
Swan (hills) . . . C 2
Swan (riv.) . . . C 2
Temple (mt.) . . . B 4
The Twins (mt.) . . . B 3
Thickwood (hills) . . . D 1
Touchwood (lake) . . . E 2
Travers (res.) . . . D 4
Trout (mt.) . . . C 1
Trout (riv.) . . . C 1
Utikuma (lake) . . . C 2
Utikuma (riv.) . . . C 1
Utikumasis (lake) . . . C 2
Vermilion (riv.) . . . E 3
Wabasca (riv.) . . . C 1
Wallace (mt.) . . . C 2
Wapiti (riv.) . . . A 2
Wappau (lake) . . . E 2
Watchusk (lake) . . . E 1
Waterton-Glacier Int'l Peace Park . . . C 5
Waterton Lakes Nat'l Park . . . C 5
Whitemud (riv.) . . . A 1
Wildhay (riv.) . . . B 3
Willmore Wilderness Prov. Park . . . A 3
Winagami (lake) . . . B 2
Winefred (lake) . . . E 2
Winefred (riv.) . . . E 2
Wolf (lake) . . . E 2
Wolverine (riv.) . . . B 1
Wood Buffalo Nat'l Park . . . B 5
Yellowhead (pass) . . . A 3
Zama (lake) . . . A 5

*Population of metropolitan area.

Agriculture, Industry and Resources

DOMINANT LAND USE

- Wheat
- Cereals (chiefly barley, oats)
- Cereals, Livestock
- Dairy
- Pasture Livestock
- Range Livestock
- Forests
- Nonagricultural Land

MAJOR MINERAL OCCURRENCES

C Coal
G Natural Gas
Na Salt
O Petroleum
S Sulfur

Water Power
Major Industrial Areas

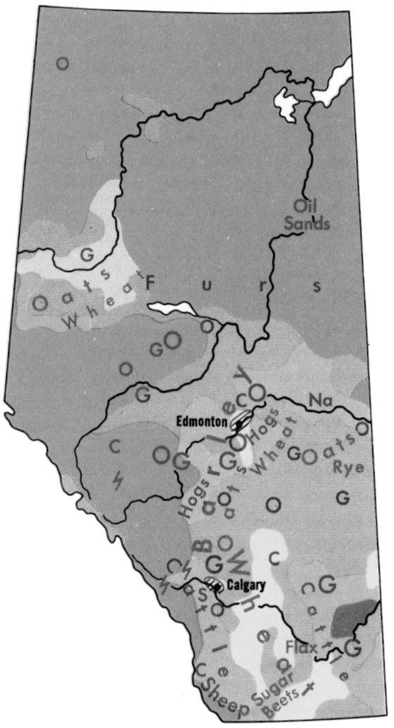
Oil Sands
Furs
Oats
Wheat
Edmonton
Hogs
Wheat
Oats
Rye
Na
Calgary
Flax
Sheep
Sugar Beets

Topography

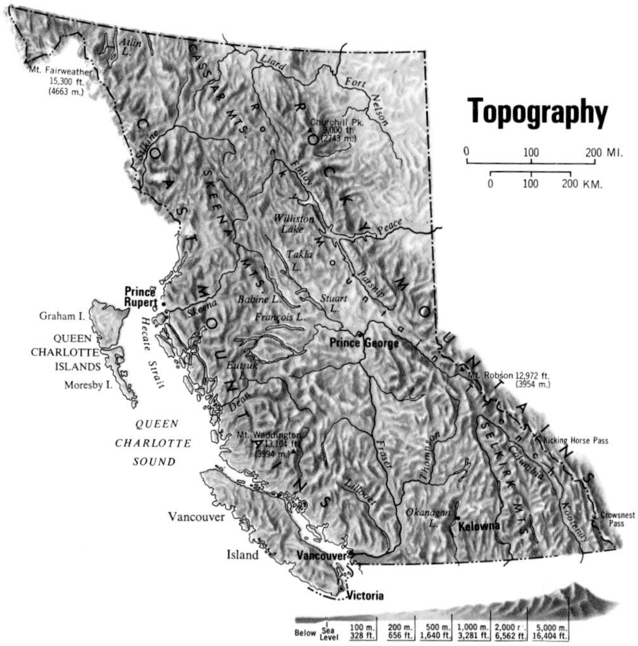
0 100 200 MI.
0 100 200 KM.
Mt. Fairweather 15,300 ft. (4663 m.)
Churchill Pk. 9,000 ft. (2743 m.)
Mt. Robson 12,972 ft. (3954 m.)
Mt. Waddington 13,104 ft. (3994 m.)
Prince Rupert
Prince George
Kelowna
Vancouver
Victoria
Graham I.
QUEEN CHARLOTTE ISLANDS
Moresby I.
QUEEN CHARLOTTE SOUND
Hecate Strait
Vancouver Island
Kicking Horse Pass
Crowsnest Pass
Williston Lake
Babine L.
Stuart L.
François L.
Okanagan L.
Below Sea Level
100 m. 328 ft.
200 m. 656 ft.
500 m. 1,640 ft.
1,000 m. 3,281 ft.
2,000 m. 6,562 ft.
5,000 m. 16,404 ft.

CITIES and TOWNS

Abbotsford 12,745 .... L 3
Alert Bay 626 .... D 5
Armstrong 2,683 .... H 5
Ashcroft 2,156 .... G 5
Ashton Creek 452 .... H 5
Balfour 472 .... J 5
Barlow 441 .... F 3
Barrière 1,370 .... H 4
Blueberry Creek 635 .... J 5
Blue River 384 .... H 4
Boston Bar 498 .... G 5
Bowen Island 1,125 .... K 3
Brackendale 1,719 .... F 5
Burnaby ○136,494 .... K 3
Burns Lake 1,777 .... D 3
Cache Creek 1,308 .... G 5
Campbell River 15,370 .... E 5
Canal Flats 919 .... K 5
Canyon 698 .... J 5
Cassiar 1,045 .... K 2
Castlegar 6,902 .... J 5
Cawston 785 .... H 5
Central Saanich ○9,890 .... K 3
Chase 1,777 .... H 5
Chemainus 2,069 .... J 3
Cherry Creek 450 .... G 5
Chetwynd 2,553 .... G 2
Chilliwack ○40,642 .... M 3
Clearwater 1,461 .... G 4
Clinton 804 .... G 4
Coldstream ○6,450 .... H 5
Comox 6,607 .... H 2
Coquitlam ○61,077 .... K 3
Courtenay 8,992 .... E 5
Cranbrook 15,915 .... K 5
Creston 4,190 .... J 5
Crofton 1,303 .... J 3
Cultus Lake 481 .... M 3
Cumberland 1,947 .... E 5
Dawson Creek 11,373 .... G 2
Delta ○74,692 .... K 3
Duncan 4,228 .... J 3
Elkford 3,126 .... K 5
Enderby 1,816 .... H 5
Erickson 972 .... J 5
Errington 609 .... J 3
Esquimalt ○15,870 .... K 4
Falkland 478 .... H 5
Fernie 5,444 .... K 5
Forest Grove 444 .... G 4
Fort Fraser 574 .... E 3
Fort Langley 2,326 .... L 3
Fort Nelson 3,724 .... M 2
Fort Saint James 2,284 .... E 3
Fort Saint John 13,891 .... G 2
Fraser Lake 1,543 .... E 3
Fruitvale 1,904 .... J 5
Gabriola 1,627 .... J 3
Galiano 669 .... K 3
Ganges 1,118 .... K 3
Gibsons 2,594 .... K 3
Gold River 2,225 .... D 5
Golden 3,476 .... J 4
Grand Forks 3,486 .... H 6
Granisle 1,430 .... D 3
Greenwood 856 .... H 5
Hagensborg 350 .... D 4
Harrison Hot Springs 569 .... M 3
Hatzic 1,055 .... L 3
Hazelton 393 .... D 2
Hedley 426 .... G 5
Holberg 444 .... C 5
Honeymoon Bay 474 .... J 3
Hope 3,205 .... M 3
Hornby Island 474 .... H 2
Horsefly 430 .... G 4
Houston 1,714 .... D 3
Hudson Hope 984 .... F 2
Invermere 1,969 .... J 5
Kaleden 998 .... H 5
Kamloops 64,048 .... G 5
Kaslo 854 .... J 5
Kelowna 59,196 .... H 5
Kent ○3,394 .... M 3
Keremeos 830 .... G 5
Kimberley 7,375 .... K 5
Kitimat 12,462 .... C 3
Kitsault 554 .... C 2
Kitwanga 369 .... D 2
Lac La Hache 647 .... G 4
Ladysmith 4,558 .... J 3
Lake Cowichan 2,391 .... J 3
Langley 15,124 .... L 3
Lantzville 969 .... J 3
Likely 425 .... G 4
Lillooet 1,725 .... G 5
Lion's Bay 1,078 .... K 3
Logan Lake 2,637 .... G 5
Lumby 1,266 .... H 5
Lytton 428 .... G 5
Mackenzie 5,797 .... F 2
Mackenzie ○5,890 .... F 2
Malakwa 392 .... H 5
Maple Bay 393 .... K 3
Maple Ridge ○32,232 .... L 3
Masset 1,569 .... B 3
Matsqui ○42,001 .... L 3
Mayne 546 .... K 3
McBride 641 .... G 3
Merritt 6,110 .... G 5
Midway 633 .... H 6
Mill Bay 583 .... K 3
Mission ○20,056 .... L 3
Mission City 9,948 .... L 3
Montrose 1,229 .... J 5
Nakusp 1,495 .... J 5
Nanaimo 47,069 .... J 3
Naramata 876 .... H 5
Nelson 9,143 .... J 5
New Denver 642 .... J 5
New Hazelton 792 .... D 2
New Westminster 38,550 .... K 3
Nicomen Island 360 .... L 3
Nootka .... D 5
North Cowichan ○18,210 .... J 3
North Pender Island 906 .... K 3
North Saanich ○6,117 .... K 3
North Vancouver 33,952 .... K 3
North Vancouver ○65,367 .... K 3
Oak Bay ○16,990 .... K 4
Okanagan Falls 1,030 .... H 5
Okanagan Landing 834 .... H 5
Okanagan Mission .... H 5
Old Barkerville 11 .... G 3
Oliver 1,893 .... H 5
One Hundred Mile House 1,925 .... G 4
Osoyoos 2,738 .... H 5
Oyama 430 .... H 5
Parksville 5,216 .... J 3
Peachland ○2,865 .... G 5
Penticton 23,181 .... H 5
Pitt Meadows ○6,209 .... L 3
Port Alberni 19,892 .... H 3
Port Alice 1,668 .... D 5
Port Clements 380 .... B 3
Port Coquitlam 27,535 .... L 3
Port Edward 989 .... B 3
Port Hardy ○3,778 .... D 5
Port McNeill 2,474 .... D 5
Port Moody 14,917 .... L 3
Pouce-Coupé 821 .... G 2
Powell River ○13,423 .... E 5
Prince George 67,559 .... F 3
Prince Rupert 16,197 .... B 3
Princeton 3,051 .... G 5
Qualicum Beach 2,844 .... J 3
Queen Charlotte 1,070 .... A 3
Quesnel 8,240 .... F 4
Radium Hot Springs 419 .... J 5
Revelstoke 5,544 .... J 5
Richmond ○96,154 .... K 3
Roberts Creek 926 .... J 3
Robson 1,008 .... J 5
Rossland 3,967 .... H 6
Royston 754 .... H 2
Saanich ○78,710 .... K 3
Salmo 1,169 .... J 5
Salmon Arm 1,946 .... H 5
Salmon Arm ○10,780 .... H 5
Saltair 1,356 .... J 3
Sandspit 794 .... B 3
Sayward 482 .... D 5
Sechelt 1,096 .... J 2
Shawnigan Lake 419 .... J 3
Shoreacres 555 .... J 5
Sicamous 1,057 .... H 5
Sidney 7,946 .... K 3
Slocan 351 .... J 5
Slocan Park 414 .... J 5
Smithers 4,570 .... D 3
Sointula 567 .... D 5
Sooke 852 .... J 4
Sorrento 659 .... H 5
South Hazelton 500 .... D 2
South Wellington 620 .... J 3
Spallumcheen 4,213 .... H 5
Sparwood 3,267 .... K 5
Sproat Lake 440 .... H 3
Squamish 1,590 .... F 5
Stewart ○1,456 .... C 2
Summerland ○7,473 .... G 5
Surrey ○147,138 .... K 3
Tahsis 1,739 .... D 5
Taylor 966 .... G 2
Telkwa 840 .... D 3
Terrace 8,893 .... C 3
Terrace ○10,914 .... C 3
Thornhill 4,281 .... C 3
Thrums 360 .... J 5
Tofino 705 .... E 5
Trail 9,599 .... J 6
Ucluelet 1,593 .... E 6
Union Bay 601 .... H 2
Valemount 1,130 .... H 4
Vancouver 414,281 .... K 3
Vancouver (Greater) *1,169,831 .... K 3
Vanderhoof 2,323 .... E 3
Vavenby 479 .... H 4
Vernon 19,987 .... H 5
Victoria (cap.) 64,379 .... K 4
Victoria *233,481 .... K 4
Warfield 1,969 .... J 5
Wasa 345 .... K 5
Wells 417 .... G 3
Westbank 1,271 .... H 5
West Vancouver ○35,728 .... K 3
Westwold 409 .... G 5
Whistler ○1,365 .... F 5
White Rock 13,550 .... K 3
Williams Lake 8,362 .... F 4
Wilson Creek 611 .... J 2
Windermere 611 .... K 5
Winlaw 435 .... J 5
Woss Lake 395 .... D 5
Wynndel 566 .... J 5
Yarrow 1,201 .... M 3
Youbou 965 .... J 3

OTHER FEATURES

Adams (lake) .... H 4
Adams (riv.) .... H 4
Alberni (inlet) .... H 3
Alsek (riv.) .... H 1
Aristazabal (isl.) .... C 4
Assiniboine (mt.) .... K 5
Atlin (lake) .... J 1
Azure (lake) .... G 4
Babine (lake) .... E 3
Babine (riv.) .... D 2
Banks (isl.) .... B 3
Barkley (sound) .... E 6
Beale (cape) .... E 6
Beatton (riv.) .... G 1
Bella Coola (riv.) .... D 4
Bennett, W.A.C. (dam) .... F 2
Birkenhead Lake Prov. Park F 5
Bowron Lake Prov. Park .... G 3
Bowser (lake) .... C 2
Brooks (pen.) .... D 5
Browning Entrance (str.) .... B 3
Bryce (mt.) .... J 4
Bugaboo Glacier Prov. Park J 5
Bulkley (riv.) .... D 2
Burke (chan.) .... D 4
Burnaby (isl.) .... B 4
Bute (inlet) .... E 5
Caamaño (sound) .... C 4
Calvert (isl.) .... C 4
Canim (lake) .... G 4
Canoe Reach (riv.) .... H 4
Cariboo (mts.) .... G 3
Carpenter (lake) .... F 5
Carp Lake Prov. Park .... F 3
Cassiar (mts.) .... K 2
Castle (mt.) .... A 2
Cathedral Prov. Park .... H 5
Charlotte (lake) .... E 4
Chatham (sound) .... B 3
Chehalis (lake) .... L 3
Chilcotin (riv.) .... E 4
Chilko (lake) .... F 4
Chilko (riv.) .... E 4
Chilkoot (pass) .... J 1
Chuchi (lake) .... E 2
Churchill (peak) .... L 2
Clayoquot (sound) .... D 5
Clearwater (lake) .... G 4
Clearwater (riv.) .... G 4
Coast (mts.) .... D 3
Columbia (lake) .... K 5
Columbia (mt.) .... J 4
Columbia (riv.) .... H 4
Columbia Reach (riv.) .... H 4
Cook (cape) .... C 5
Cowichan (lake) .... J 3
Crowsnest (pass) .... K 5
Cypress Prov. Park .... K 3
Dean (chan.) .... D 4
Dean (riv.) .... D 4
Dease (lake) .... K 2
Dease (riv.) .... K 2
Devils Thumb (mt.) .... A 1
Dixon Entrance (chan.) .... A 3
Douglas (chan.) .... C 3
Duncan (riv.) .... J 5
Dundas (isl.) .... B 3
Elk (riv.) .... K 5
Elk Lakes Prov. Park .... K 5
Eutsuk (lake) .... D 3
Fairweather (mt.) .... H 1
Finlay (riv.) .... E 1
Fitzhugh (sound) .... D 4
Flathead (riv.) .... K 6
Flores (isl.) .... D 5
Fontas (riv.) .... M 2
Forbes (mt.) .... J 4
Fort Nelson (riv.) .... M 2
François (lake) .... D 3
Fraser (lake) .... E 3
Fraser (riv.) .... F 4
Fraser Reach (chan.) .... C 3
Galiano (isl.) .... K 3
Gardner (canal) .... C 3
Garibaldi Prov. Park .... F 5
Georgia (str.) .... J 3
Germansen (lake) .... E 2
Gil (isl.) .... C 3
Glacier Nat'l Park .... J 4
Golden Ears Prov. Park .... L 2
Gordon (riv.) .... H 3
Graham (isl.) .... A 3
Graham Reach (chan.) .... C 3
Grenville (chan.) .... C 3
Halfway (riv.) .... F 2
Hamber Prov. Park .... H 4
Harrison (lake) .... M 2
Hawkesbury (isl.) .... C 3
Hazelton (mts.) .... C 2
Hecate (str.) .... B 3
Hobson (lake) .... H 4
Homathko (riv.) .... E 4
Horsefly (lake) .... G 4
Howe (sound) .... K 2
Hunter (isl.) .... C 4

Agriculture, Industry and Resources

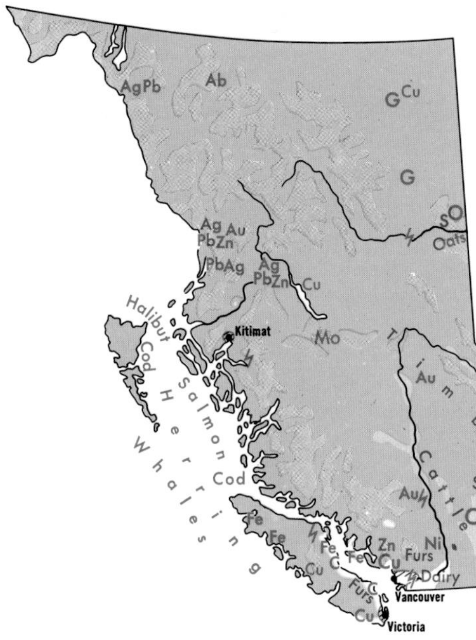
Ab
AgPb
GCu
G
SO
Oats
Ag Au PbZn
PbAg
Ag PbZn Cu
Kitimat
Mo
Halibut
Cod
Salmon
Herring
Whales
Timber
Au
Cattle
Sheep
Cu
Gp
Ag PbZnC
Sn
Fe
Zn
Ni
Furs
Dairy
AgPb ZnCu
PbZn
Vancouver
Victoria

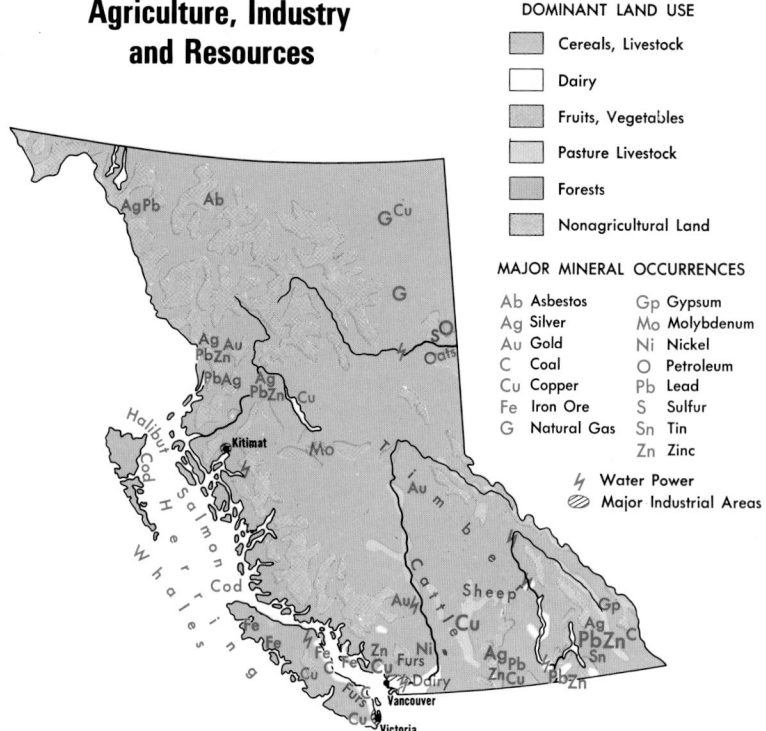

DOMINANT LAND USE

- Cereals, Livestock
- Dairy
- Fruits, Vegetables
- Pasture Livestock
- Forests
- Nonagricultural Land

MAJOR MINERAL OCCURRENCES

Ab	Asbestos	Gp	Gypsum
Ag	Silver	Mo	Molybdenum
Au	Gold	Ni	Nickel
C	Coal	O	Petroleum
Cu	Copper	Pb	Lead
Fe	Iron Ore	S	Sulfur
G	Natural Gas	Sn	Tin
		Zn	Zinc

Water Power
Major Industrial Areas

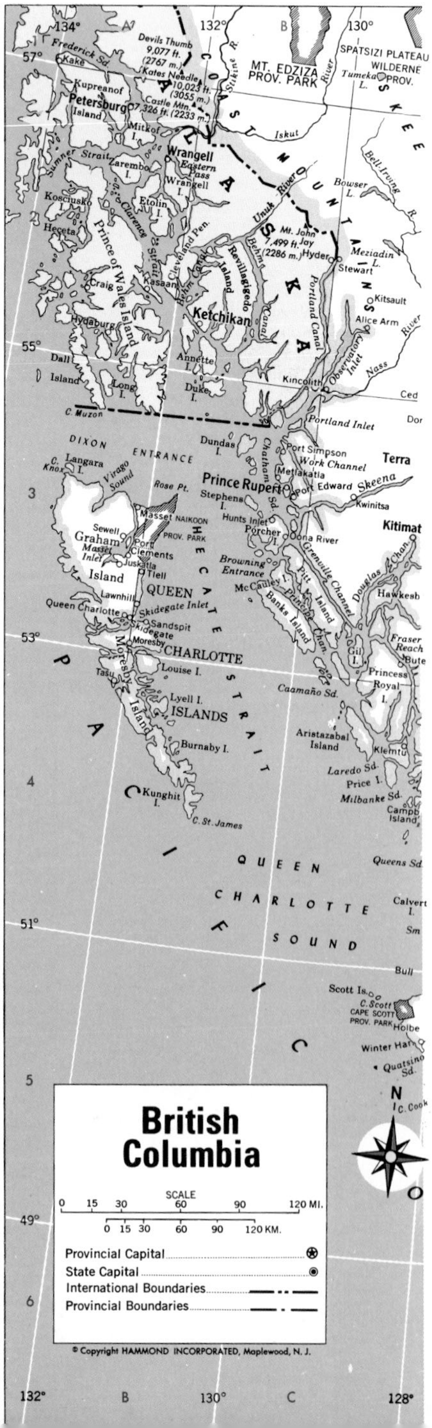
134°
132°
130°
128°
57°
55°
53°
51°
49°
Devils Thumb 9,077 ft. (2767 m.)
Kates Needle 10,023 ft. (3055 m.)
Castle Mtn. 7,326 ft. (2233 m.)
Mt. John Jay 7,499 ft. (2286 m.)
MT. EDZIZA PROV. PARK
SPATSIZI PLATEAU WILDERNESS PROV.
Petersburg
Wrangell
Ketchikan
Prince of Wales Island
Hyder
Stewart
Kitsault
Alice Arm
Kincolith
Prince Rupert
Port Edward
Kitimat
Graham Island
Masset
Port Clements
QUEEN CHARLOTTE ISLANDS
Queen Charlotte
Sandspit
Moresby Island
DIXON ENTRANCE
QUEEN CHARLOTTE SOUND
HECATE STRAIT
PACIFIC OCEAN
British Columbia
SCALE
0 15 30 60 90 120 MI.
0 15 30 60 90 120 KM.
Provincial Capital
State Capital
International Boundaries
Provincial Boundaries
© Copyright HAMMOND INCORPORATED, Maplewood, N. J.

Inzana (lake) . . . . E 3
Isaac (lake) . . . . G 3
Iskut (riv.) . . . . B 2
Jervis (inlet) . . . . E 5
John Jay (mt.) . . . . B 2
Johnstone (str.) . . . . D 5
Juan de Fuca (str.) . . . . J 4
Kates Needle (mt.) . . . . A 1
Kechika (riv.) . . . . L 2
Kenney (dam) . . . . E 3
Kettle (riv.) . . . . H 5
Kicking Horse (pass) . . . . . . J 4
Kinbasket (lake) . . . . H 4
King (isl.) . . . . D 4
Klinaklini (riv.) . . . . E 4
Kloch (lake) . . . . E 2
Knight (inlet) . . . . E 5
Knox (cape) . . . . A 3
Kokanee Glacier Prov. Park . . J 5
Koocanusa (lake) . . . . K 6
Kootenay (lake) . . . . J 5
Kootenay (riv.) . . . . K 5
Kootenay Nat'l Park . . . . . . J 4
Kotcho (lake) . . . . M 2
Kotcho (riv.) . . . . M 2
Kunghit (isl.) . . . . B 4
Kyuquot (sound) . . . . D 5
Langara (isl.) . . . . A 3
Laredo (sound) . . . . C 4
Liard (riv.) . . . . L 2
Lillooet (riv.) . . . . F 5
Louise (isl.) . . . . B 4
Lower Arrow (lake) . . . . H 5
Lyell (isl.) . . . . B 4
Lyell (mt.) . . . . J 4
Mabel (lake) . . . . H 5
Mahood (lake) . . . . G 4
Malaspina (str.) . . . . J 2
Manning Prov. Park . . . . G 5
Masset (inlet) . . . . A 3
McCauley (isl.) . . . . B 3
McGregor (riv.) . . . . G 3
Meziadin (lake) . . . . C 2
Mica (dam) . . . . H 4
Milbanke (sound) . . . . C 4
Moberly (lake) . . . . F 2
Monashee (mts.) . . . . H 4
Moresby (isl.) . . . . B 4
Morice (lake) . . . . D 3
Morice (riv.) . . . . D 3
Mount Assiniboine Prov. Park K 5
Mount Edziza Prov. Park and Rec. Area . . . . B 1
Mount Revelstoke Nat'l Park H 4
Mount Robson Prov. Park . . H 3
Muncho Lake Prov. Park . . . L 2
Murray (riv.) . . . . G 3
Murtle (lake) . . . . H 4
Muskwa (riv.) . . . . M 2
Nanika (dam) . . . . D 3
Nass (riv.) . . . . C 2
Nation (riv.) . . . . F 2
Nechako (riv.) . . . . E 3
Nitinat (lake) . . . . H 3
Nootka (isl.) . . . . D 5
Nootka (sound) . . . . D 5
Nootka (sound) . . . . D 5
North Thompson (riv.) . . . . . G 4
Observatory (inlet) . . . . C 2
Okanagan (lake) . . . . H 5
Okanagan Mtn. Prov. Park . . . G 5
Okanogan (riv.) . . . . H 6
Omineca (mts.) . . . . E 2
Omineca (riv.) . . . . E 2
Ootsa (lake) . . . . D 3
Owikeno (lake) . . . . D 4
Pacific Rim Nat'l Park . . . . . E 6
Parsnip (riv.) . . . . F 3
Peace (riv.) . . . . G 2
Pend Oreille (riv.) . . . . J 6
Petitot (riv.) . . . . M 2
Pinchi (lake) . . . . E 3
Pine (riv.) . . . . G 2
Pitt (isl.) . . . . C 3
Pitt (lake) . . . . L 2
Porcher (isl.) . . . . B 3
Portland (canal) . . . . B 2
Portland (inlet) . . . . C 2
Price (isl.) . . . . C 4
Princess Royal (isl.) . . . . . . C 3
Principe (chan.) . . . . C 3
Prophet (riv.) . . . . M 2
Purcell (mts.) . . . . J 5
Quatsino (sound) . . . . C 5
Queen Charlotte (isls.) . . . . . B 3
Queen Charlotte (sound) . . . . C 4
Queen Charlotte (str.) . . . . . D 5
Queens (sound) . . . . C 4
Quesnel (lake) . . . . G 4
Quesnel (riv.) . . . . F 4
Rivers (inlet) . . . . D 4
Robson (mt.) . . . . H 3
Rocky (mts.) . . . . F 2
Roderick (isl.) . . . . C 4
Rose (pt.) . . . . B 3
Saint James (cape) . . . . B 4
Salmon (riv.) . . . . F 3
Salmon Arm (inlet) . . . . J 2
San Juan (riv.) . . . . J 3
Schoen Lake Prov. Park . . . . E 5
Scott (cape) . . . . C 5
Scott (isls.) . . . . C 5
Seechelt (inlet) . . . . J 2
Seechelt (pen.) . . . . J 2
Selkirk (mts.) . . . . J 4
Seymour (inlet) . . . . D 4
Sheslay (riv.) . . . . J 2
Shuswap (lake) . . . . H 4
Sikanni Chief (riv.) . . . . F 1
Silver Star Prov. Park . . . . . H 5
Sir Sandford (mt.) . . . . H 4
Skagit (riv.) . . . . G 6
Skeena (mts.) . . . . C 2
Skeena (riv.) . . . . C 3
Skidegate (inlet) . . . . B 3
Slocan (lake) . . . . J 5
Smith (sound) . . . . C 4
South Bentinck Arm (inlet) . . . D 4
Stave (lake) . . . . L 3
Stephens (isl.) . . . . B 3
Stikine (riv.) . . . . B 1
Stone Mountain Prov. Park . . . L 2

AREA 366,253 sq. mi. (948,596 sq. km.)
POPULATION 2,883,367
CAPITAL Victoria
LARGEST CITY Vancouver
HIGHEST POINT Mt. Fairweather 15,300 ft. (4,663 m.)
SETTLED IN 1806
ADMITTED TO CONFEDERATION 1871
PROVINCIAL FLOWER Dogwood

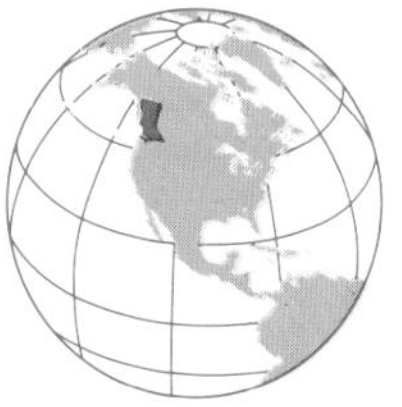

Strathcona Prov. Park . . . . . . E 5
Stuart (lake) . . . . E 3
Sustut (riv.) . . . . D 2
Tagish (lake) . . . . J 1
Tahtsa (lake) . . . . D 3
Takla (lake) . . . . D 2
Taku (riv.) . . . . J 2
Tatlatui (lake) . . . . D 2
Tatlayoko (lake) . . . . E 4
Tchentlo (lake) . . . . E 2
Teslin (lake) . . . . K 1
Tetachuck (lake) . . . . E 3
Texada (isl.) . . . . J 2
Tezzeron (lake) . . . . E 3
Thompson (riv.) . . . . G 5
Three Guardsmen (mt.) . . . . . H 1
Thutade (lake) . . . . D 2
Tiedemann (mt.) . . . . E 4
Toad (riv.) . . . . L 2
Toba (inlet) . . . . E 5
Tochcha (lake) . . . . E 3
Top Of The World Prov. Park . . K 5
Trembleur (lake) . . . . E 3
Troitsa (lake) . . . . D 3
Tumeka (lake) . . . . C 1
Turnagain (riv.) . . . . K 2
Tuya (riv.) . . . . K 2
Tweedsmuir Prov. Park . . . . . D 3
Upper Arrow (lake) . . . . H 5
Valdes (isl.) . . . . K 3
Vancouver (isl.) . . . . D 5
Virago (sound) . . . . A 3
Waddington (mt.) . . . . E 4
Wapiti (riv.) . . . . H 3
Wells Gray Prov. Park . . . . . . H 4
West Road (riv.) . . . . E 3
Whitesail (lake) . . . . D 3
Williston (lake) . . . . F 2
Work (chan.) . . . . C 3
Yellowhead (pass) . . . . H 4
Yoho Nat'l Park . . . . J 4

*Population of metropolitan area.
○Population of municipality.

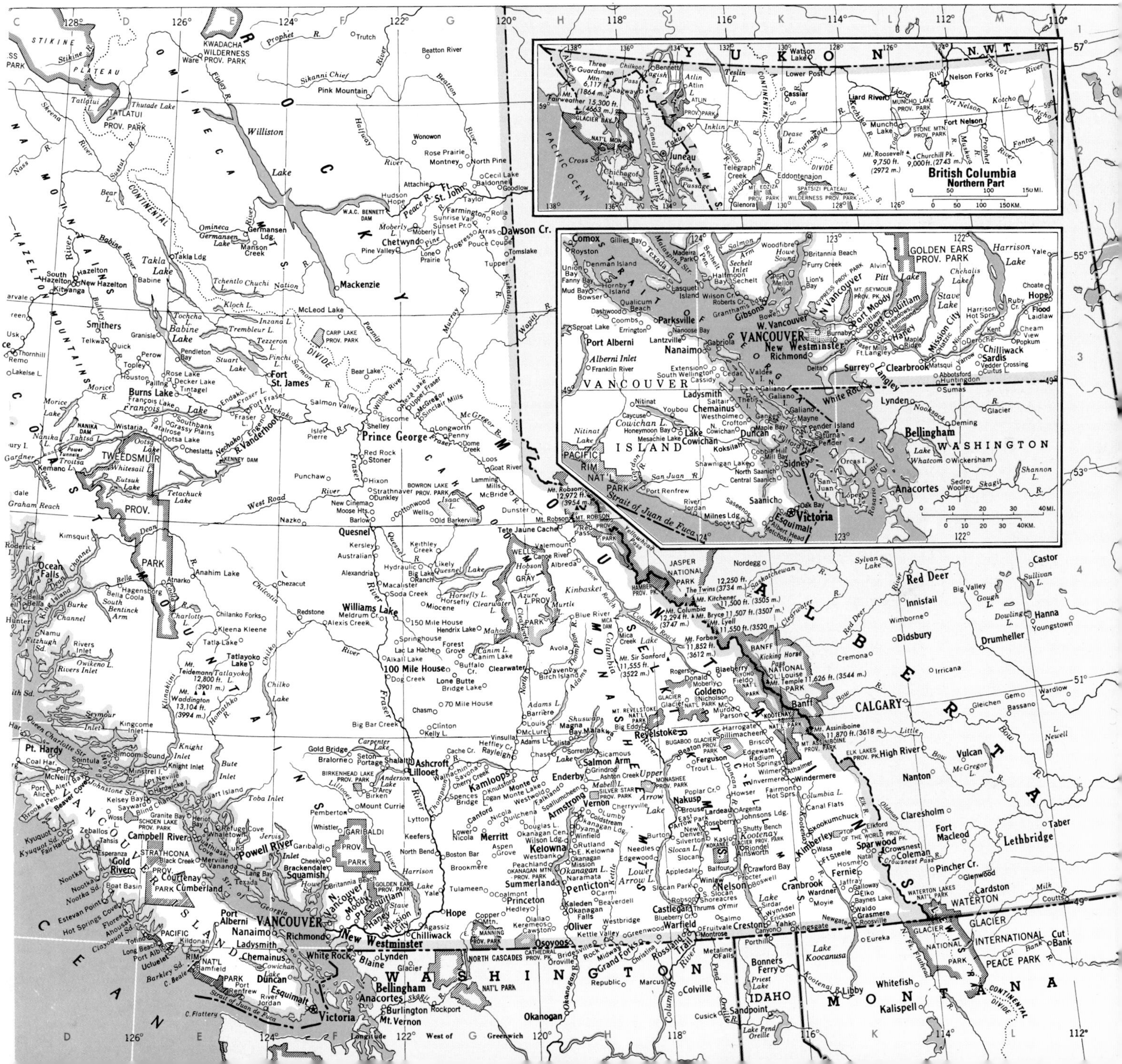

British Columbia
Northern Part
YUKON
N.W.T.
PACIFIC OCEAN
VANCOUVER ISLAND
WASHINGTON
IDAHO
MONTANA
ALBERTA
CALGARY
VANCOUVER
Victoria
Prince George
Kamloops
Kelowna
Nanaimo
New Westminster
Prince Rupert
Dawson Cr.
Red Deer
Lethbridge
Bellingham
West of Greenwich

Topography

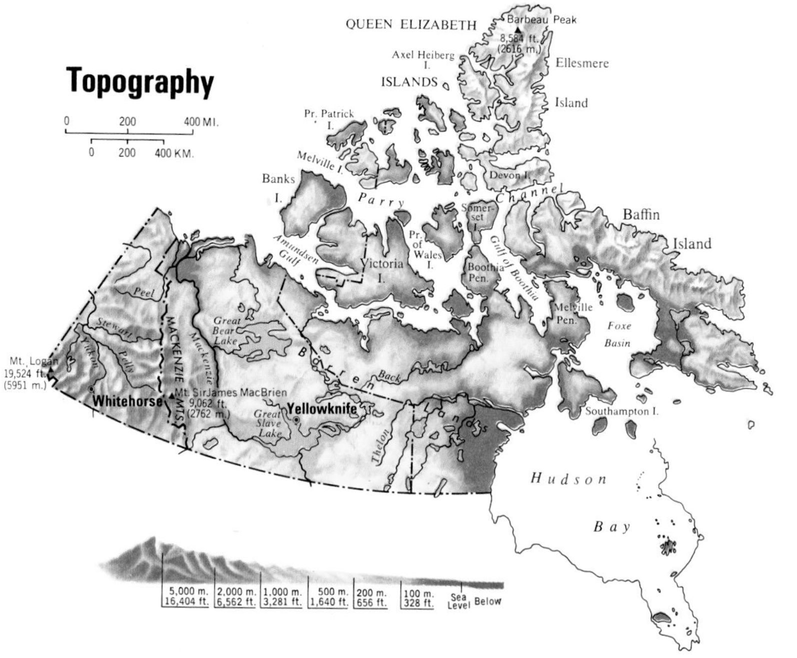

0 200 400 MI.
0 200 400 KM.
QUEEN ELIZABETH
ISLANDS
Barbeau Peak 8,584 ft. (2616 m.)
Axel Heiberg I.
Ellesmere Island
Pr. Patrick I.
Melville I.
Banks I.
Parry Channel
Devon I.
Somerset I.
Pr. of Wales I.
Victoria I.
Amundsen Gulf
Boothia Pen.
Gulf of Boothia
Baffin Island
Melville Pen.
Foxe Basin
Peel
Great Bear Lake
MACKENZIE MTS.
Mt. Logan 19,524 ft. (5951 m.)
Whitehorse
Mt. Sir James MacBrien 9,062 ft. (2762 m.)
Yellowknife
Great Slave Lake
Thelon
Back
Southampton I.
Hudson Bay
5,000 m. 16,404 ft.
2,000 m. 6,562 ft.
1,000 m. 3,281 ft.
500 m. 1,640 ft.
200 m. 656 ft.
100 m. 328 ft.
Sea Level
Below

Agriculture, Industry and Resources

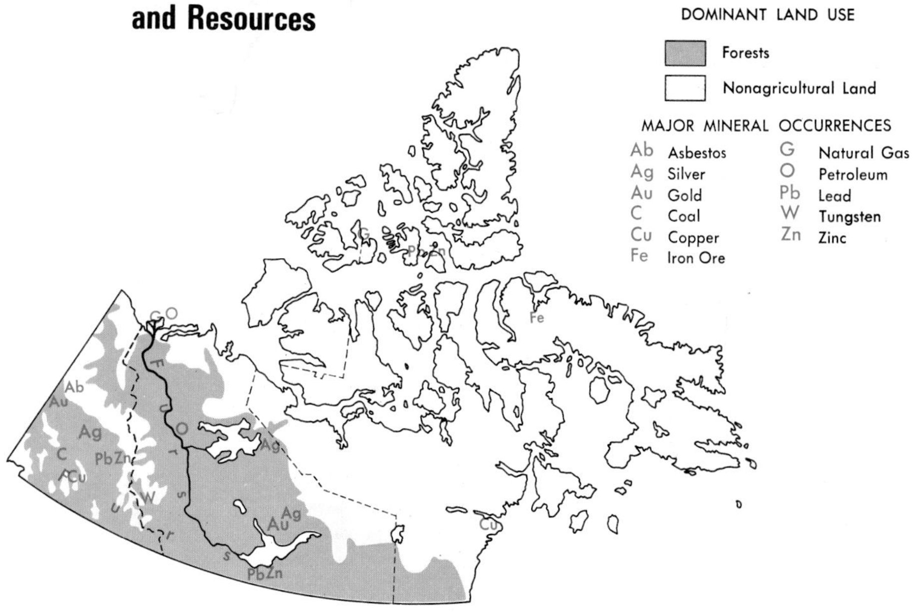

DOMINANT LAND USE
Forests
Nonagricultural Land
MAJOR MINERAL OCCURRENCES
Ab Asbestos
Ag Silver
Au Gold
C Coal
Cu Copper
Fe Iron Ore
G Natural Gas
O Petroleum
Pb Lead
W Tungsten
Zn Zinc

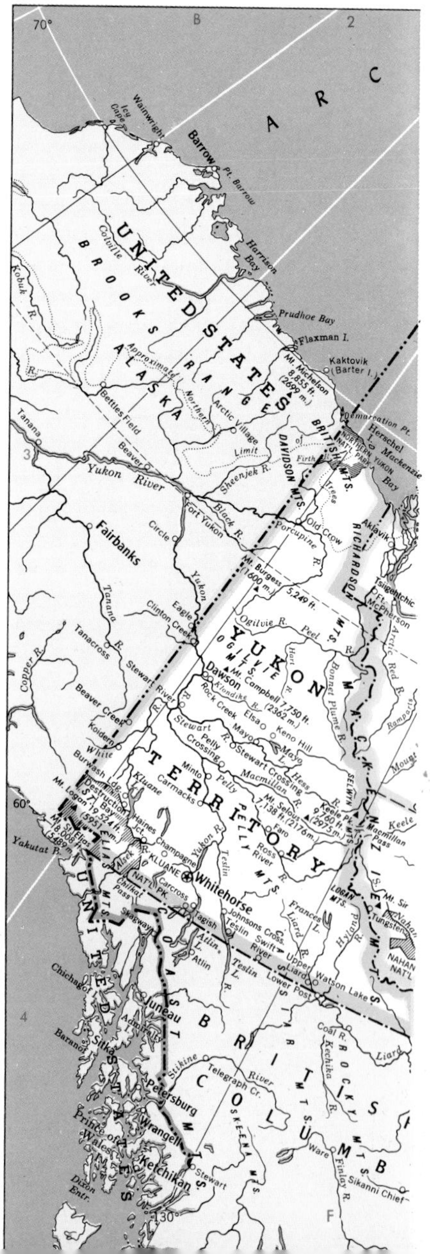

UNITED STATES
ALASKA
BROOKS RANGE
YUKON TERRITORY
BRITISH COLUMBIA
Barrow
Prudhoe Bay
Fairbanks
Yukon River
Dawson
Whitehorse
Juneau
Sitka
Petersburg
Wrangell
Ketchikan
Mt. Logan

Mistake (bay) J3
Nansen (sound) J1
Nares (str.) L2
Navy Board (inlet) K2
Nettilling (lake) L3
North Magnetic Pole H2
Norwegian (bay) J2
Nottingham (isl.) L3
Nueltin (lake) H3
Ommanney (bay) H2
Padloping (isl.) M3
Parry (bay) K3
Parry (chan.) G2
Parry (isls.) G2
Peary (chan.) H2
Peel (sound) J2
Pelly (bay) J3
Penny (str.) J2
Pond (inlet) L2
Prince Charles (isl.) L3
Prince Gustav Adolf (sea) H2
Prince of Wales (isl.) J2
Prince Regent (inlet) J2
Queen Elizabeth (isls.) H1
Queen Maud (gulf) H3
Queens (chan.) J2
Raanes (pen.) K2
Rae (isth.) K3
Rae (riv.) G3
Rae (str.) J3
Resolution (isl.) M3
Robeson (chan.) M1
Ross Welcome (sound) K3
Rowley (isl.) K3
Royal Geographic Society (isls.) J3
Russell (isl.) J2
Sabine (pen.) H2
Salisbury (isl.) L3
Seahorse (pt.) L3
Simpson (pen.) K3
Smith (bay) L2
Smith (cape) L3
Smith (sound) L2
Somerset (isl.) J2
South (bay) K3
Southampton (isl.) K3
Stallworthy (cape) J1
Steensby (inlet) L2
Stefansson (isl.) H2
Sverdrup (chan.) J1
Takijug (lake) G3
Talbot (inlet) L2
Tha'ane (riv.) J3
Thelon (riv.) H3
Thlewiasa (riv.) J3
Ungava (bay) M4
Vansittart (isl.) K3
Victoria (isl.) G2
Victoria (str.) H3
Viscount Melville (sound) G2
Wager (bay) K3
Wales (isl.) K3
Walsingham (cape) M3
Wellington (chan.) J3
Winter (harb.) H3
Wollaston (pen.) G3
Yathkyed (lake) J3

YUKON TERRITORY

AREA 186,660 sq. mi. (483,450 sq. km.)
POPULATION 27,797
CAPITAL Whitehorse
LARGEST CITY Whitehorse
HIGHEST POINT Mt. Logan 19,524 ft. (5,951 m.)
SETTLED IN 1897
ADMITTED TO CONFEDERATION 1898
PROVINCIAL FLOWER Fireweed

NORTHWEST TERRITORIES

AREA 589,315 sq. mi. (1,526,328 sq. km.)
POPULATION 39,672
CAPITAL Yellowknife
LARGEST CITY Yellowknife
HIGHEST POINT Mt. Sir James McBrien 9,062 ft. (2,762 m.)
SETTLED IN 1800
ADMITTED TO CONFEDERATION 1870
PROVINCIAL FLOWER Mountain Avens

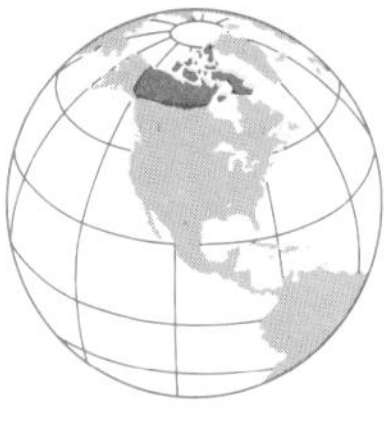

YUKON TERRITORY

CITIES and TOWNS

Beaver Creek 113 .... D3
Burwash Landing 64 .... D3
Carcross 209 .... E3
Carmacks 280 .... E3
Champagne 57 .... E3
Clinton Creek D3
Cowley E3
Dawson 1,287 .... E3
Destruction Bay 48 .... E3
Elsa 294 .... E3
Faro 1251 .... E3
Haines Junction 340 .... E3
Johnson's Crossing 18 .... E3
Keno Hill 47 .... E3
Koidern D3
Mayo 324 .... E3
Minto E3
Old Crow 232 .... E3
Pelly Crossing 177 .... E3
Rock Creek 75 .... E3
Ross River 352 .... E3
Stewart Crossing 40 .... E3
Stewart River 5 .... D3
Tagish 103 .... E3
Teslin 181 .... E3
Upper Liard 130 .... E3
Watson Lake 993 .... F3
Whitehorse (cap.) 19,157 .... E3

OTHER FEATURES

Alsek (riv.) E3
Bonnet Plume (riv.) E3
British (mts.) D3
Campbell (mt.) E3
Cassiar (mts.) E3
Frances (lake) E3
Herschel (isl.) E3
Hess (riv.) E3
Hyland (riv.) F3
Keele (peak) E3
Klondike (riv.) E3
Kluane (lake) E3
Kluane Nat'l Park E3
Liard (riv.) E3
Logan (mt.) D3
Logan (mts.) F3
Mackenzie (mts.) E3
Macmillan (riv.) E3
Mayo (lake) E3
Northern Yukon Nat'l Pk. E3
Ogilvie (mts.) E3
Ogilvie (riv.) E3
Peel (riv.) E3
Pelly (mts.) E3
Pelly (riv.) E3
Porcupine (riv.) E3
Richardson (mts.) E3
Rocky (mts.) F4
Saint Elias (mt.) D3
Saint Elias (mts.) E3
Selous (mt.) E3
Selwyn (mts.) E3
Stewart (riv.) E3
Teslin (lake) E4
Teslin (riv.) E3
White (riv.) D3
Yukon (riv.) E3

• Population of district.

Yukon and Northwest Territories
SCALE
0 50 100 200 300 MI.
0 50 100 200 300 KM.
Territorial Capitals
International Boundaries
Provincial & Territorial Boundaries
Regional Boundaries
Longitude West K of Greenwich

United States
POLYCONIC PROJECTION
SCALE OF MILES
SCALE OF KILOMETERS
Capitals of Countries
State Capitals
International Boundaries
Scale 1:17,400,000
© Copyright HAMMOND INCORPORATED, Maplewood, N. J.
GULF OF MEXICO
PACIFIC OCEAN
CANADA
MEXICO
Longitude West of Greenwich

Alabama (state) 4,040,587 ..... J4
Alaska (state) 550,043 ..... C5
Alaska (gulf), Alaska D6
Albany (cap.), N.Y. 101,082 ..... M2
Albuquerque, N. Mex. 384,736 ..... E3
Aleutian (isls.), Alaska D6
Amarillo, Texas 157,615 ..... F3
Anchorage, Alaska 226,338 ..... D6
Annapolis (cap.), Md. 33,187 ..... L3
Appalachian (mts.) K3
Arizona (state) 3,665,228 ..... D4
Arkansas (state) 2,350,725 ..... H3
Arkansas (riv.) H3
Atlanta (cap.), Ga. 394,017 ..... K4
Attu (isl.), Alaska D6
Augusta (cap.), Maine 21,325 ..... N2
Aurora Colo. 222,103 ..... F3
Austin (cap.), Texas 465,622 ..... G4
Baltimore, Md. 736,014 ..... L3
Baton Rouge (cap.), La. 219,531 ..... H4
Bering (sea), Alaska C6
Bering (str.), Alaska C5
Bighorn (riv.) E2
Bismarck (cap.), N. Dak. 49,256 ..... G1
Black Hills (mts.) F2
Boise (cap.), Idaho 125,738 ..... C2
Borah (peak), Idaho D2
Boston (cap.), Mass. 574,283 ..... M2
Brazos (riv.), Texas G4
Brooks (range), Alaska C5
Buffalo, N .Y. 328,123 ..... L2
California (state) 29,760,021 ..... B3
Canadian (riv.) F3
Canaveral (Kennedy) (cape), Fla. L5
Cape Fear (riv.), N.C. L4
Carson City (cap.), Nev. 40,443 ..... C3
Cascade (range) B1
Champlain (lake) M2
Charleston (cap.), W. Va. 57,287 ..... K3
Charlotte, N.C. 395,934 ..... L3
Chattahoochee (riv.) K4
Chesapeake (bay) L3
Cheyenne (cap.), Wyo. 50,008 ..... E2
Chicago, Ill. 2,783,726 ..... J2
Cimarron (riv.) G3
Cincinnati, Ohio 364,040 ..... K3
Cleveland, Ohio 505,616 ..... K2
Coast (ranges) B2
Cod (cape), Mass. N2
Colorado (riv.) D4
Colorado (state) 3,294,394 ..... E3
Colorado (riv.), Texas G4
Columbia (cap.), S.C. 98,052 ..... K4
Columbia (riv.) B1
Columbus (cap.), Ohio 632,910 ..... K3
Concord (cap.), N.H. 36,006 ..... M2
Connecticut (state) 3,287,116 ..... M2
Corpus Christi, Texas 257,453 ..... G5
Cumberland (riv.) J3
Dallas, Texas 1,006,877 ..... G4
Death Valley (depr.), Calif. C3
Delaware (bay) M3
Delaware (state) 666,168 ..... L3
Denver (cap.), Colo. 467,610 ..... F3
Des Moines (cap.), Iowa 193,187 ..... H2
Detroit, Mich. 1,027,974 ..... K2
District of Columbia 606,900 ..... L3
Dover (cap.), Del. 27,630 ..... L3
El Paso, Texas 515,342 ..... E4
Erie (lake) K2
Everglades, The (swamp), Fla. K5
Florida (state) 12,937,926 ..... K5
Florida (keys), Fla. K6
Fort Worth, Texas 447,619 ..... G4
Frankfort (cap.), Ky. 25,968 ..... K3
Fresno, Calif. 354,202 ..... C3
Georgia (state) 6,478,216 ..... K4
Gila (riv.) D4
Glacier Nat'l Park, Mont. D1
Golden Gate (chan.), Calif. B3
Grand Canyon Nat'l Park, Ariz. D3
Great Salt (lake), Utah D2
Harrisburg (cap.), Pa. 52,376 ..... L2
Hatteras (cape), N.C. M3
Havasu (lake) D4
Hawaii (state) 1,108,229 ..... F5
Hawaii (isl.), Hawaii F6
Helena (cap.), Mont. 24,569 ..... D1
Honolulu (cap.), Hawaii 365,272 ..... F5
Houston, Texas 1,630,553 ..... G5
Huron (lake), Mich. K2
Idaho (state) 1,006,749 ..... D2
Illinois (state) 11,430,602 ..... J3
Indiana (state) 5,544,159 ..... J3
Indianapolis (cap.), Ind. 741,952 ..... J3
Iowa (state) 2,776,755 ..... H2
Jackson (cap.), Miss. 196,637 ..... J4
Jacksonville, Fla. 672,971 ..... K4
Jefferson City (cap.), Mo. 35,481 ..... H3
Juneau (cap.), Alaska 26,751 ..... E6
Kansas (state) 2,477,574 ..... G3
Kansas City, Kans.-Mo. 435,146 ..... H3
Kentucky (state) 3,685,296 ..... J3
Lansing (cap.), Mich. 127,321 ..... K2
Las Vegas, Nev. 258,295 ..... C3
Lexington, Ky. 225,366 ..... K3
Lincoln (cap.), Nebr. 191,972 ..... G2
Little Missouri (riv.) F1
Little Rock (cap.), Ark. 175,795 ..... H4
Long (isl.), N.Y. M2
Long Beach, Calif. 429,433 ..... C4
Los Angeles, Calif. 3,485,398 ..... C4
Louisiana (state) 4,219,973 ..... H4
Madison (cap.), Wis. 191,206 ..... H2
Maine (state) 1,227,928 ..... N1
Maryland (state) 4,781,468 ..... L3
Massachusetts (state) 6,016,425 ..... M2
Maui (isl.), Hawaii F5
Mauna Kea (mt.), Hawaii G6
Mauna Loa (mt.), Hawaii G6
May (cape), N.J. M3
McKinley (mt.), Alaska D5
Memphis, Tenn. 610,337 ..... J3
Mendocino (cape), Calif. A2
Mexico (gulf) J5
Miami, Fla. 358,548 ..... K5
Michigan (state) 9,295,297 ..... J1
Michigan (lake) J2
Milwaukee, Wis. 628,088 ..... J2
Minneapolis, Minn. 368,383 ..... H1
Minnesota (state) 4,375,099 ..... H1
Mississippi (state) 2,573,216 ..... J4
Mississippi (riv.) H4
Missouri (state) 5,117,073 ..... H3
Missouri (riv.) H3
Mobile, Ala. 196,278 ..... J4
Montana (state) 799,065 ..... E1
Montgomery (cap.), Ala. 187,106 ..... J4
Montpelier (cap.), Ver. 8,247 ..... M2
Nantucket (isl.), Mass. N2
Nashville (cap.), Tenn. 510,784 ..... J3
Nebraska (state) 1,578,385 ..... F2
Nevada (state) 1,201,833 ..... C3
Newark, N.J. 275,221 ..... L2
New Hampshire (state) 1,109,252 ..... M2
New Jersey (state) 7,730,188 ..... M3
New Mexico (state) 1,515,069 ..... E4
New Orleans, La. 496,938 ..... H5
New York (state) 17,990,455 ..... L2
New York, N.Y. 7,322,564 ..... M2
Norfolk, Va. 261,229 ..... L3
North Carolina (state) 6,628,637 ..... L3
North Dakota (state) 638,800 ..... F1
Oahu (isl.), Hawaii F5
Oakland, Calif. 372,242 ..... B3
Ohio (state) 10,847,115 ..... K2
Ohio (riv.) J3
Oklahoma (state) 3,145,585 ..... G3
Oklahoma City (cap.), Okla. 444,719 ..... G3
Olympia (cap.), Wash. 33,840 ..... B1
Omaha, Nebr. 335,795 ..... G2
Ontario (lake), N.Y. L2
Oregon (state) 2,842,321 ..... B2
Ozark (mts.) H3
Pennsylvania (state) 11,881,643 ..... L2
Philadelphia, Pa. 1,585,577 ..... M2
Phoenix (cap.), Ariz. 983,403 ..... D4
Pierre (cap.), S. Dak. 12,906 ..... F2
Pikes (peak), Colo. E3
Pittsburgh, Pa. 369,879 ..... L2
Platte (riv.), Nebr. G2
Pontchartrain (lake), La. J5
Portland, Oreg. 437,319 ..... B1
Potomac (riv.) L3
Providence (cap.), R.I. 160,728 ..... M2
Rainier (mt.), Wash. B1
Raleigh (cap.), N.C. 207,951 ..... L3
Red (riv.) H4
Red River of the North (riv.) G1
Rhode Island (state) 1,003,464 ..... M2
Richmond (cap.), Va. 203,056 ..... L3
Rio Grande (riv.) F5
Rochester, N.Y. 231,636 ..... L2
Rocky (mts.) E3
Sacramento (cap.), Calif. 369,365 ..... B3

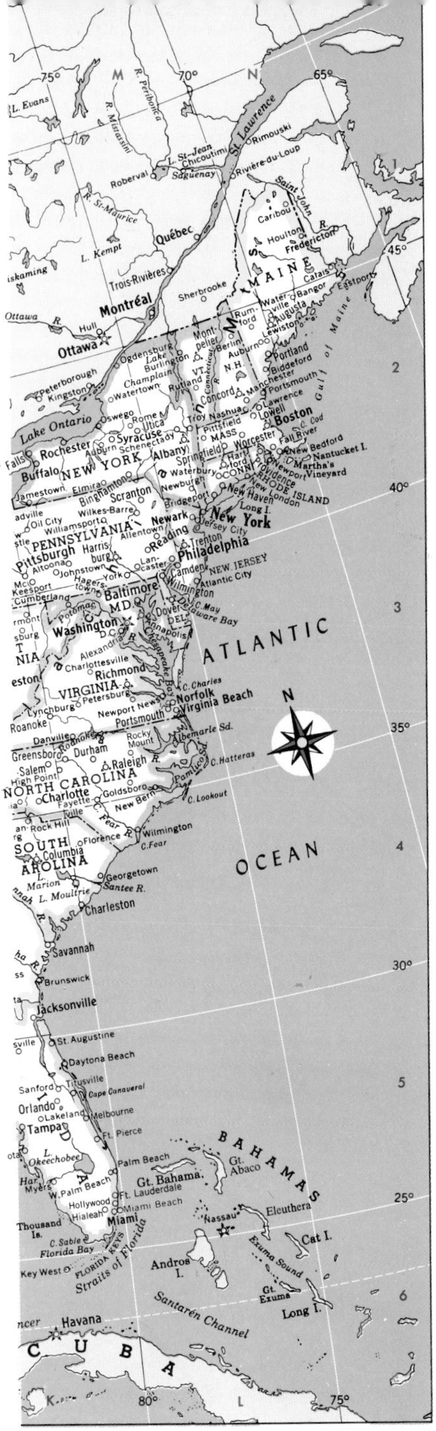
ATLANTIC
OCEAN
Québec
Montréal
Ottawa
Trois-Rivières
Sherbrooke
MAINE
Portland
Boston
Lake Ontario
Rochester
Buffalo
NEW YORK
Syracuse
Albany
New York
Philadelphia
PENNSYLVANIA
Pittsburgh
Baltimore
Washington
VIRGINIA
Richmond
Norfolk
Virginia Beach
NORTH CAROLINA
Raleigh
Charlotte
SOUTH CAROLINA
Columbia
Charleston
Savannah
Jacksonville
Daytona Beach
Orlando
Tampa
Palm Beach
Miami
Key West
BAHAMAS
Nassau
Andros I.
Havana
CUBA

AREA 3,623,420 sq. mi. (9,384,658 sq. km.)
POPULATION 249,632,692
CAPITAL Washington
LARGEST CITY New York
HIGHEST POINT Mt. McKinley 20,320 ft. (6,194 m.)
MONETARY UNIT U.S. dollar
MAJOR LANGUAGE English
MAJOR RELIGIONS Protestantism, Roman Catholicism, Judaism

Population Distribution

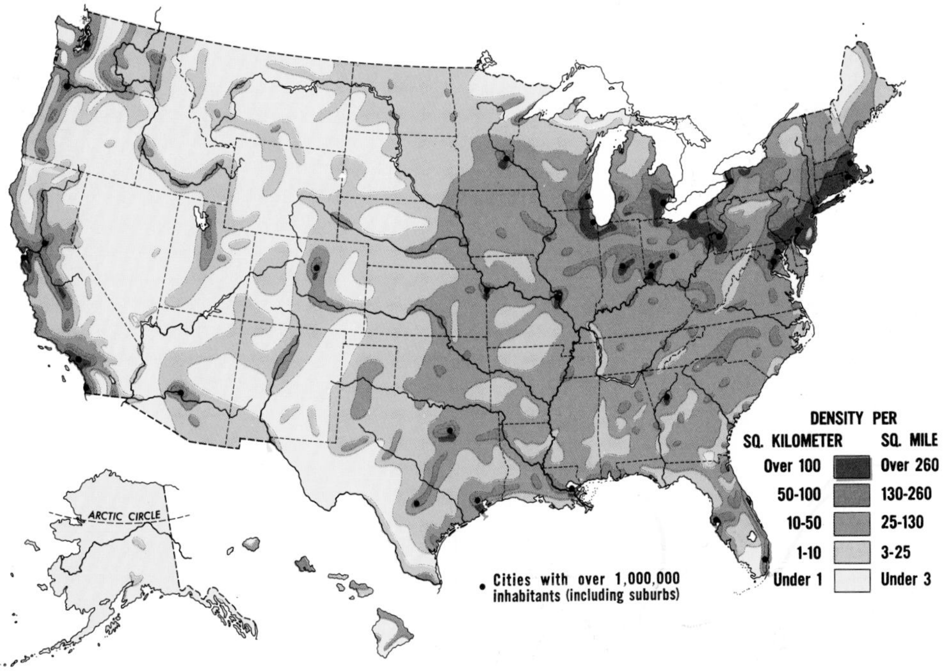
ARCTIC CIRCLE
DENSITY PER
SQ. KILOMETER SQ. MILE
Over 100 Over 260
50-100 130-260
10-50 25-130
1-10 3-25
Under 1 Under 3
• Cities with over 1,000,000 inhabitants (including suburbs)

Vegetation

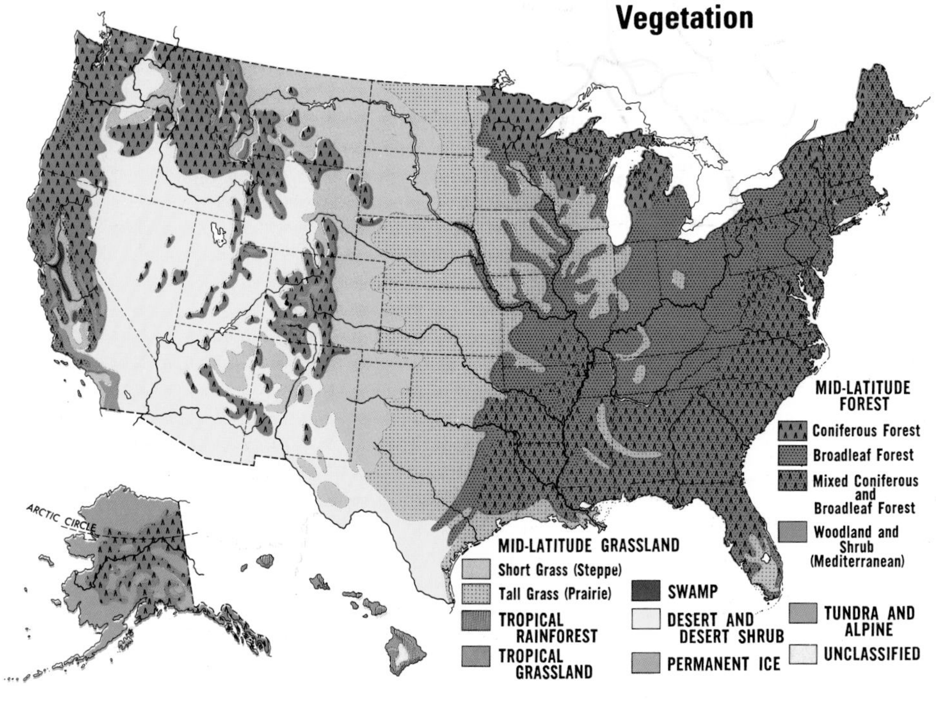
ARCTIC CIRCLE
MID-LATITUDE FOREST
Coniferous Forest
Broadleaf Forest
Mixed Coniferous and Broadleaf Forest
Woodland and Shrub (Mediterranean)
MID-LATITUDE GRASSLAND
Short Grass (Steppe)
Tall Grass (Prairie)
SWAMP
TROPICAL RAINFOREST
DESERT AND DESERT SHRUB
TUNDRA AND ALPINE
TROPICAL GRASSLAND
PERMANENT ICE
UNCLASSIFIED

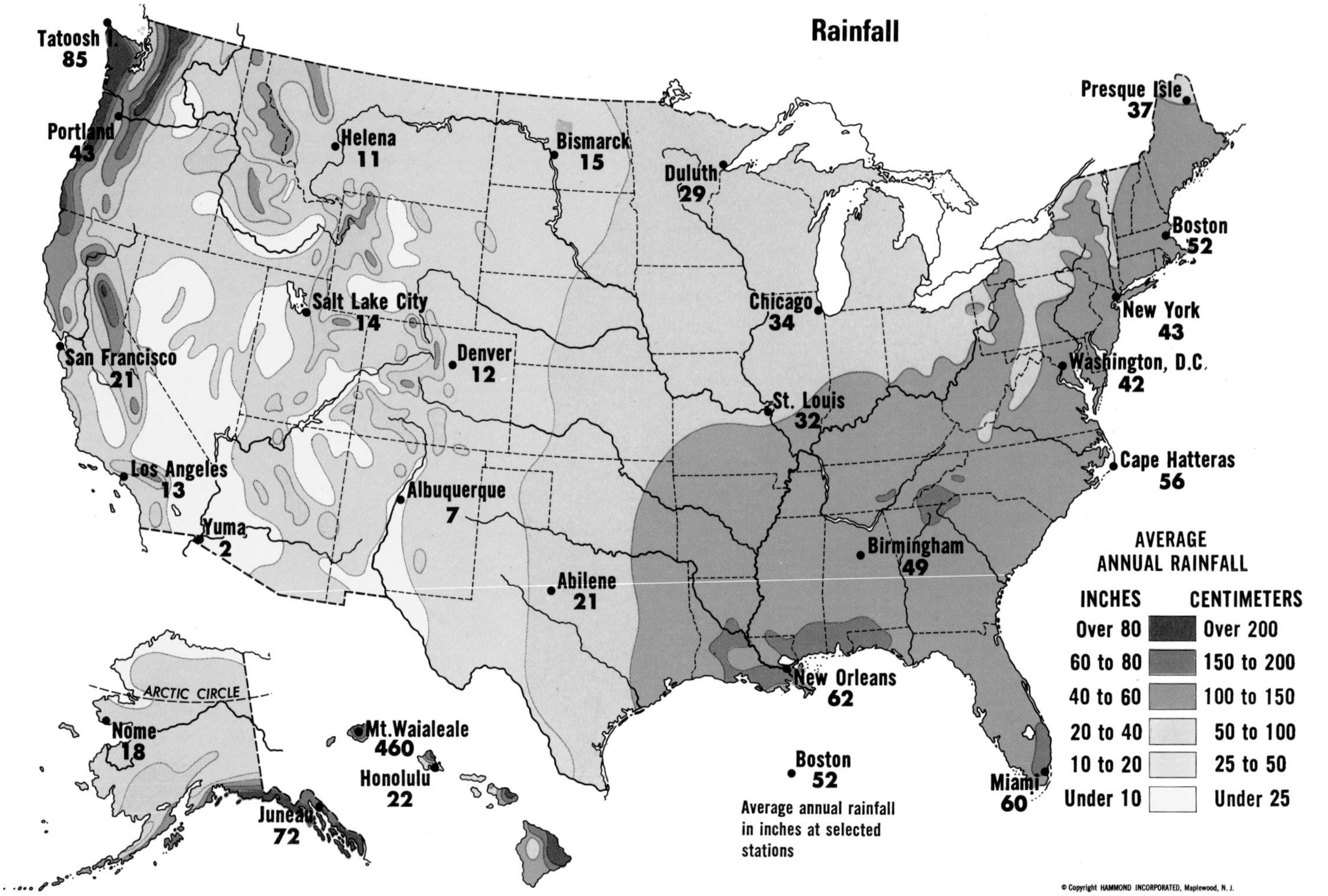
Rainfall
Tatoosh I.
85
Portland
43
Helena
11
Bismarck
15
Duluth
29
Presque Isle
37
Boston
52
New York
43
Washington, D.C.
42
Chicago
34
Salt Lake City
14
San Francisco
21
Denver
12
St. Louis
32
Cape Hatteras
56
Los Angeles
13
Albuquerque
7
Yuma
2
Birmingham
49
Abilene
21
New Orleans
62
Miami
60
ARCTIC CIRCLE
Nome
18
Mt. Waialeale
460
Honolulu
22
Juneau
72
AVERAGE
ANNUAL RAINFALL
INCHES CENTIMETERS
Over 80 Over 200
60 to 80 150 to 200
40 to 60 100 to 150
20 to 40 50 to 100
10 to 20 25 to 50
Under 10 Under 25
Boston
52
Average annual rainfall
in inches at selected
stations
© Copyright HAMMOND INCORPORATED, Maplewood, N. J.

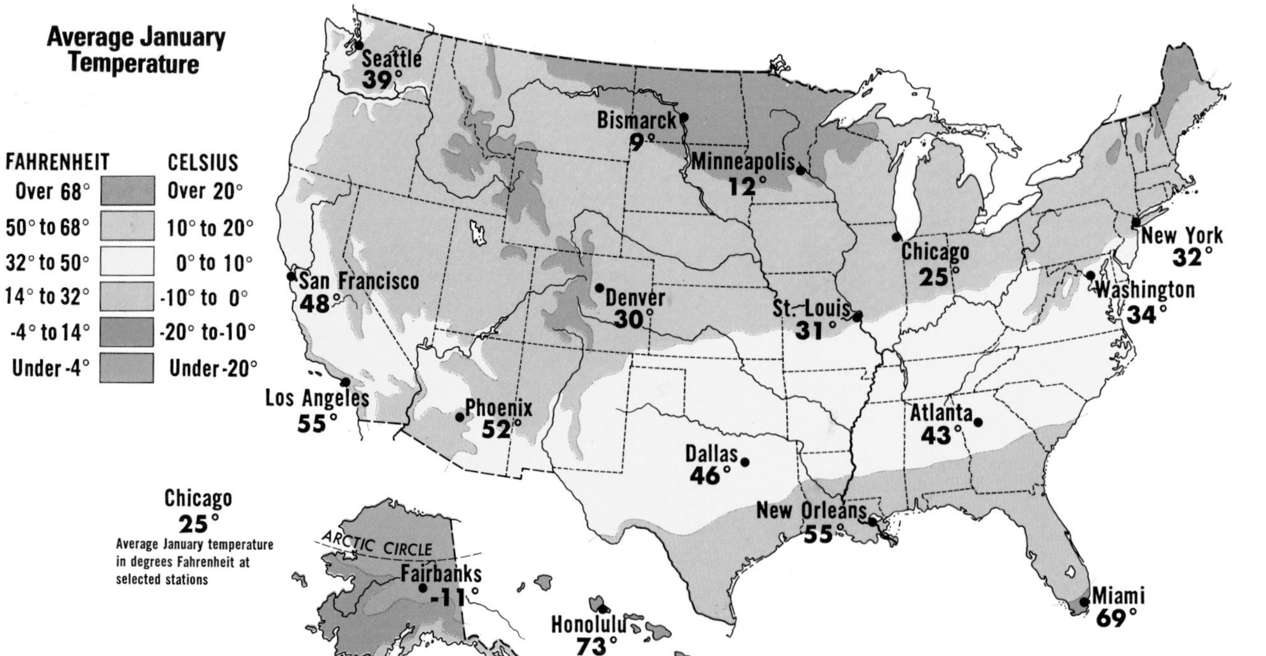
Average January
Temperature
FAHRENHEIT CELSIUS
Over 68° Over 20°
50° to 68° 10° to 20°
32° to 50° 0° to 10°
14° to 32° -10° to 0°
-4° to 14° -20° to -10°
Under -4° Under -20°
Seattle
39°
Bismarck
9°
Minneapolis
12°
New York
32°
Chicago
25°
San Francisco
48°
Denver
30°
St. Louis
31°
Washington
34°
Los Angeles
55°
Phoenix
52°
Atlanta
43°
Dallas
46°
New Orleans
55°
Chicago
25°
Average January temperature
in degrees Fahrenheit at
selected stations
ARCTIC CIRCLE
Fairbanks
-11°
Honolulu
73°
Miami
69°
© Copyright HAMMOND INCORPORATED, Maplewood, N. J.

Topography

0 200 400 MI.
0 200 400 KM.
C. Flattery
Seattle
Mt. Rainier 14,410 ft. (4392 m.)
Mt. St. Helens 8,364 ft. (2549 m.)
CASCADE RANGE
COAST RANGES
COLUMBIA PLATEAU
Columbia
Snake
BITTERROOT RANGE
ROCKY MOUNTAINS
Missouri
Yellowstone
Fort Peck Lake
Lake Sakakawea
Lake Oahe
GREAT PLAINS
PACIFIC OCEAN
Great Basin
Great Salt Lake
SIERRA NEVADA
Sacramento
Central Valley
San Francisco
Mt. Whitney 14,494 ft. (4418 m.)
L. Mead
Grand Canyon
Mojave Desert
Pt. Conception
SANTA BARBARA IS.
Los Angeles
San Diego
Phoenix
Gila
Colorado
COLORADO PLATEAU
Lake Powell
Denver
Mt. Elbert 14,431 ft. (4399 m.)
Arkansas
N. Platte
Platte
Rio Grande
LLANO ESTACADO
Pecos
EDWARDS PLATEAU
Canadian
Red
Brazos
Dallas
Houston
Kansas City
OZARK PLATEAU
St. Louis
Memphis
New Orleans
Mississippi Delta
GULF COASTAL PLAIN
Gulf of Mexico
Red
James
Rainy
Minneapolis
Mississippi
Wisconsin
Des Moines
Illinois
Lake Superior
Keweenaw Pen.
Lake Michigan
Milwaukee
Chicago
Lake Huron
Detroit
Lake Erie
Cleveland
Niagara Falls
Lake Ontario
St. Lawrence
L. Champlain
Indianapolis
Wabash
Ohio
Tennessee
Wheeler L.
ALLEGHENY MTS.
APPALACHIAN MOUNTAINS
PIEDMONT
Mt. Mitchell 6,684 ft. (2037 m.)
Atlanta
Chattahoochee
Savannah
ATLANTIC COASTAL PLAIN
Washington
Philadelphia
New York
Long Island
Boston
C. Cod
Gulf of Maine
Chesapeake Bay
C. Hatteras
C. Fear
ATLANTIC OCEAN
Jacksonville
C. Canaveral
L. Okeechobee
The Everglades
Miami
FLORIDA KEYS
ARCTIC OCEAN
0 200 400 MI.
0 200 400 KM.
BROOKS RA.
Bering Str.
Yukon
Tanana
St. Lawrence I.
Mt. McKinley 20,320 ft. (6194 m.)
Alaska Ra.
Anchorage
BERING SEA
Gulf of Alaska
Alaska Pen.
Kodiak I.
ALEXANDER ARCHIPELAGO
Aleutian Islands
Kauai
Oahu
Honolulu
Molokai
Maui
HAWAIIAN ISLANDS
PACIFIC OCEAN
Mauna Kea 13,796 ft. (4205 m.)
Hawaii
0 50 100 MI.
0 50 100 KM.
5,000 m. 16,404 ft.
2,000 m. 6,562 ft.
1,000 m. 3,281 ft.
500 m. 1,640 ft.
200 m. 656 ft.
100 m. 328 ft.
Sea Level
Below

Average July Temperature

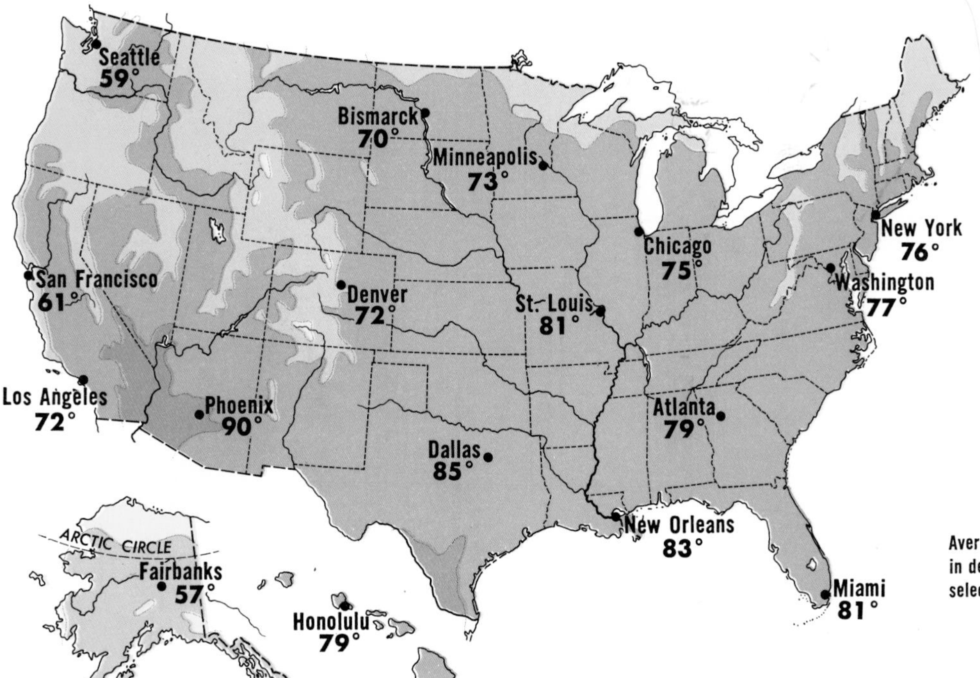
Seattle 59°
Bismarck 70°
Minneapolis 73°
Chicago 75°
New York 76°
Washington 77°
San Francisco 61°
Denver 72°
St. Louis 81°
Los Angeles 72°
Phoenix 90°
Atlanta 79°
Dallas 85°
New Orleans 83°
Miami 81°
ARCTIC CIRCLE
Fairbanks 57°
Honolulu 79°

FAHRENHEIT	CELSIUS
Over 86°	Over 30°
68° to 86°	20° to 30°
50° to 68°	10° to 20°
Under 50°	Under 10°

Chicago
75°
Average July temperature in degrees Fahrenheit at selected stations

United States Standard Time Zones

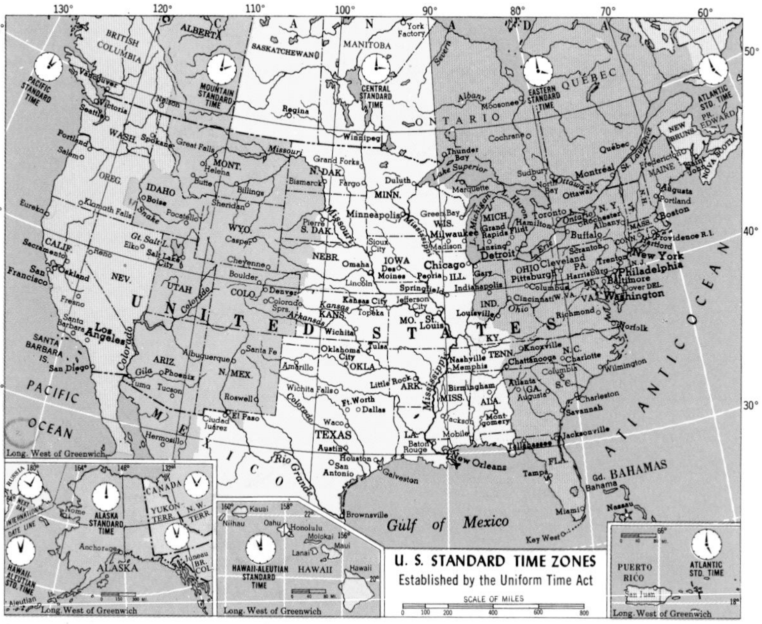
U. S. STANDARD TIME ZONES
Established by the Uniform Time Act
SCALE OF MILES
PACIFIC STANDARD TIME
MOUNTAIN STANDARD TIME
CENTRAL STANDARD TIME
EASTERN STANDARD TIME
ATLANTIC STD. TIME
ALASKA STANDARD TIME
HAWAII-ALEUTIAN STANDARD TIME
PACIFIC OCEAN
ATLANTIC OCEAN
Gulf of Mexico
UNITED STATES
PUERTO RICO
Long. West of Greenwich

Agriculture, Industry and Resources

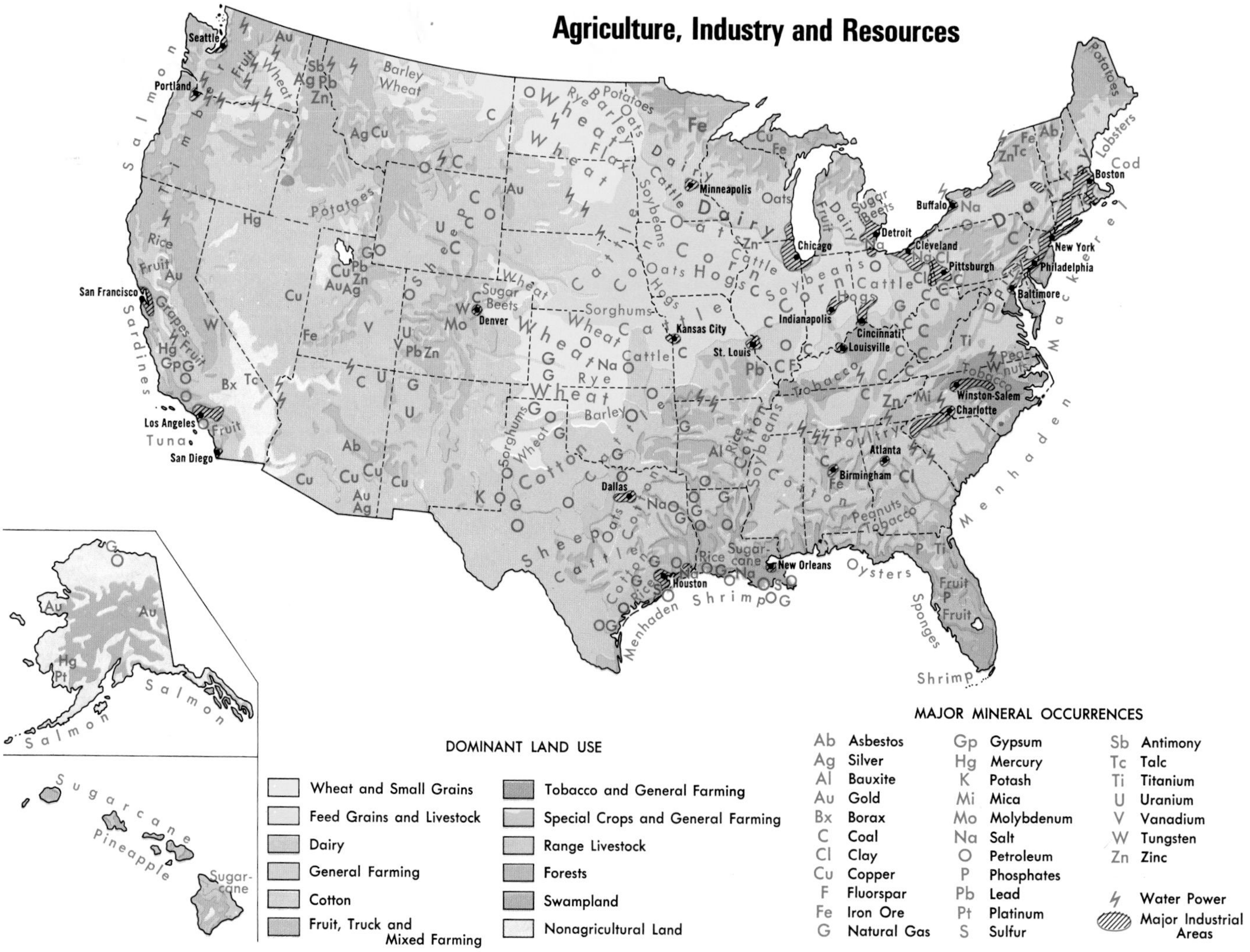
Seattle
Portland
San Francisco
Los Angeles
San Diego
Denver
Minneapolis
Chicago
Detroit
Buffalo
Cleveland
Pittsburgh
Boston
New York
Philadelphia
Baltimore
Indianapolis
Cincinnati
Louisville
Kansas City
St. Louis
Winston-Salem
Charlotte
Atlanta
Birmingham
Dallas
Houston
New Orleans
DOMINANT LAND USE
Wheat and Small Grains
Feed Grains and Livestock
Dairy
General Farming
Cotton
Fruit, Truck and Mixed Farming
Tobacco and General Farming
Special Crops and General Farming
Range Livestock
Forests
Swampland
Nonagricultural Land
MAJOR MINERAL OCCURRENCES
Ab Asbestos
Ag Silver
Al Bauxite
Au Gold
Bx Borax
C Coal
Cl Clay
Cu Copper
F Fluorspar
Fe Iron Ore
G Natural Gas
Gp Gypsum
Hg Mercury
K Potash
Mi Mica
Mo Molybdenum
Na Salt
O Petroleum
P Phosphates
Pb Lead
Pt Platinum
S Sulfur
Sb Antimony
Tc Talc
Ti Titanium
U Uranium
V Vanadium
W Tungsten
Zn Zinc
Water Power
Major Industrial Areas

AREA 51,705 sq. mi. (133,916 sq. km.)
POPULATION 4,062,608
CAPITAL Montgomery
LARGEST CITY Birmingham
HIGHEST POINT Cheaha Mtn. 2,407 ft. (734 m.)
SETTLED IN 1702
ADMITTED TO UNION December 14, 1819
POPULAR NAME Heart of Dixie; Cotton State; Yellowhammer State
STATE FLOWER Camellia
STATE BIRD Yellowhammer

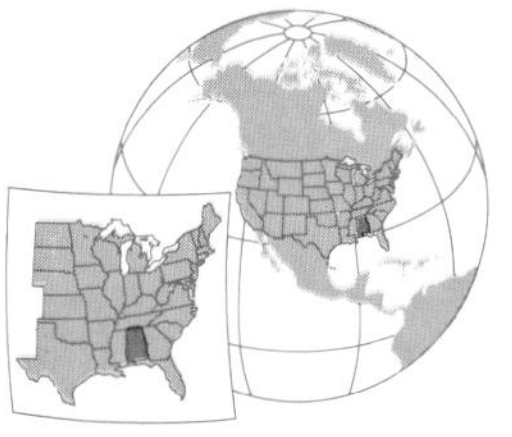

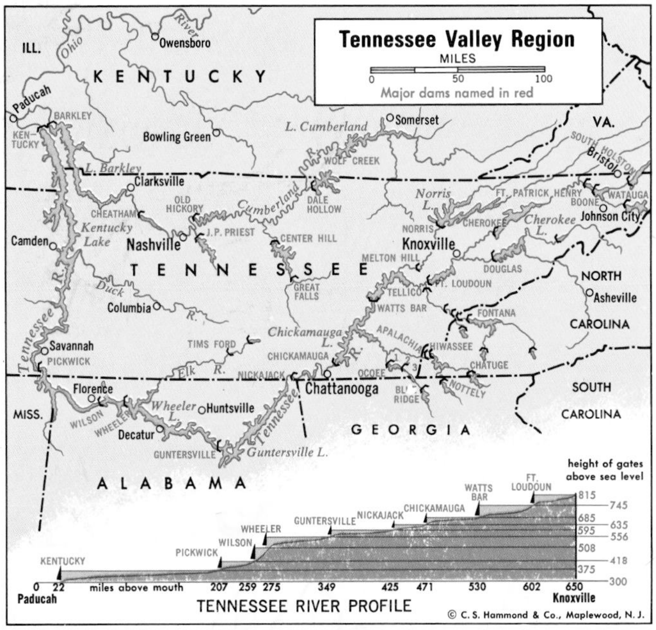
Tennessee Valley Region
MILES
0 50 100
Major dams named in red
ILL.
Owensboro
Ohio River
KENTUCKY
Paducah
BARKLEY
KEN-TUCKY
Bowling Green
L. Cumberland
Somerset
VA.
SOUTH HOLSTON
Bristol
WOLF CREEK
L. Barkley
Clarksville
OLD HICKORY
Cumberland R.
DALE HOLLOW
Norris L.
FT. PATRICK HENRY
BOONE
WATAUGA
Johnson City
CHEATHAM
Kentucky Lake
J.P. PRIEST
CENTER HILL
NORRIS
CHEROKEE
Cherokee L.
Camden
Nashville
Knoxville
MELTON HILL
DOUGLAS
TENNESSEE
NORTH
FT. LOUDOUN
Duck R.
GREAT FALLS
TELLICO
Asheville
Columbia
WATTS BAR
FONTANA
CAROLINA
Tennessee R.
Chickamauga L.
APALACHIA
HIWASSEE
Savannah
PICKWICK
TIMS FORD
CHICKAMAUGA
CHATUGE
Elk R.
NICKAJACK
OCOEE 1 2 3
Chattanooga
NOTTELY
Florence
BLUE RIDGE
SOUTH
MISS.
WILSON
WHEELER
Wheeler L.
Huntsville
CAROLINA
Decatur
GEORGIA
GUNTERSVILLE
Guntersville L.
ALABAMA
height of gates above sea level
KENTUCKY
PICKWICK
WILSON
WHEELER
GUNTERSVILLE
NICKAJACK
CHICKAMAUGA
WATTS BAR
FT. LOUDOUN
815
745
685
635
595
556
508
418
375
300
0 22 miles above mouth 207 259 275 349 425 471 530 602 650
Paducah
Knoxville
TENNESSEE RIVER PROFILE
© C. S. Hammond & Co., Maplewood, N. J.

COUNTIES

Autauga 34,222 ... E5
Baldwin 98,280 ... C9
Barbour 25,417 ... H7
Bibb 16,576 ... D5
Blount 39,248 ... E2
Bullock 11,042 ... G6
Butler 21,892 ... E7
Calhoun 116,034 ... G3
Chambers 36,876 ... H5
Cherokee 19,543 ... G2
Chilton 32,458 ... E5
Choctaw 16,018 ... B6
Clarke 27,240 ... C7
Clay 13,252 ... G4
Cleburne 12,730 ... G3
Coffee 40,240 ... G8
Colbert 51,666 ... C1
Conecuh 14,054 ... E8
Coosa 11,063 ... F5
Covington 36,478 ... F8
Crenshaw 13,635 ... F7
Cullman 67,613 ... E2
Dale 49,633 ... G8
Dallas 48,130 ... D6
De Kalb 53,658 ... G2
Elmore 49,210 ... F5
Escambia 35,518 ... D8
Etowah 99,840 ... F2
Fayette 17,962 ... C3
Franklin 27,814 ... C2
Geneva 23,647 ... G8
Greene 10,153 ... C5
Hale 15,498 ... C5
Henry 15,374 ... H7
Houston 81,331 ... H8
Jackson 47,796 ... F1
Jefferson 651,525 ... E3
Lamar 15,715 ... B3
Lauderdale 79,661 ... C1
Lawrence 31,513 ... D1
Lee 87,146 ... H5
Limestone 54,135 ... E1
Lowndes 12,658 ... E6
Macon 24,928 ... G6
Madison 238,912 ... E1
Marengo 23,084 ... C6
Marion 29,830 ... C2
Marshall 70,832 ... F2
Mobile 378,643 ... B9
Monroe 23,968 ... D7
Montgomery 209,085 ... F6
Morgan 100,043 ... E2
Perry 12,759 ... D5
Pickens 20,699 ... B4
Pike 27,595 ... G7
Randolph 19,881 ... H4
Russell 46,860 ... H6
Saint Clair 41,205 ... F3
Shelby 99,358 ... E4
Sumter 16,174 ... B5
Talladega 74,107 ... F4
Tallapoosa 38,826 ... G5
Tuscaloosa 150,522 ... C4
Walker 67,670 ... D3
Washington 16,694 ... B8
Wilcox 13,568 ... D7
Winston 22,053 ... D2

CITIES and TOWNS

Abbeville▲ 3,173 ... H7
Abernant 405 ... D4
Adamsville 4,161 ... D3
Addison 626 ... D2
Adger 400 ... D4
Akron 468 ... C5
Alabaster 14,732 ... E4
Albertville 14,507 ... F2
Aldrich 500 ... E4
Alexander City 14,917 ... G5
Alexandria 600 ... G3
Aliceville 3,009 ... B4
Allgood 464 ... F3
Allsboro 300 ... B1
Alma 500 ... C8
Altoona 960 ... F2
Andalusia▲ 9,269 ... E8
Anderson 339 ... D1
Anniston▲ 26,623 ... G3
Arab 6,321 ... E2
Ardmore 1,090 ... E1
Argo 930 ... E3
Ariton 743 ... G7
Arley 338 ... D2
Ashby 500 ... E4
Ashford 1,926 ... H8
Ashland▲ 2,034 ... G4
Ashville▲ 1,494 ... F3
Athens▲ 16,901 ... E1
Atmore 8,046 ... C8
Attalla 6,859 ... F2
Auburn 33,830 ... H5
Autaugaville 681 ... E6
Avon 462 ... H8
Axis 500 ... B9
Babbie 576 ... F8
Baileyton 352 ... E2
Baker Hill 300 ... H7
Banks 195 ... G7
Barnwell 700 ... C10
Bay Minette▲ 7,168 ... C9
Bayou La Batre 2,456 ... B10
Bear Creek 913 ... C2
Beatrice 454 ... D7
Beaverton 319 ... B3
Belgreen 500 ... C2
Belk 255 ... C3
Bellamy 700 ... B6
Belle Mina 675 ... E1
Bellwood 400 ... G8
Benton 48 ... E6
Berry 1,218 ... C3
Bessemer 33,497 ... D4
Beulah 500 ... H5
Billingsley 150 ... E5
Birmingham▲ 265,968 ... D3
Black 174 ... G8
Blountsville 1,527 ... E2
Blue Mountain 221 ... G3
Blue Springs 108 ... G7
Boaz 6,928 ... F2
Boligee 268 ... C5
Bon Air 91 ... F4
Bon Secour 850 ... C10
Branchville 370 ... F3
Brantley 1,015 ... F7
Brent 2,776 ... D5
Brewton▲ 5,885 ... D8
Bridgeport 2,936 ... G1
Brighton 4,518 ... D4
Brilliant 751 ... C2
Brookside 1,365 ... E3
Brookwood 658 ... D4
Browns 375 ... D6
Brownville 2,386 ... C4
Brundidge 2,472 ... G7
Butler▲ 1,872 ... B6
Cahaba 4,778 ... D6
Calera 2,136 ... E4
Calhoun 950 ... F6
Calvert 600 ... B8
Camden▲ 2,414 ... D7
Camp Hill 1,415 ... G5
Canoe 560 ... D8
Carbon Hill 2,115 ... D3
Cardiff 72 ... E3
Carolina 201 ... E8
Carrollton▲ 1,170 ... B4
Carrville 820 ... G5
Carson 400 ... C8
Castleberry 669 ... D8
Cedar Bluff 1,174 ... G2
Centre▲ 2,893 ... G2
Centreville▲ 2,508 ... D5
Chatom▲ 1,094 ... B8
Chelsea 1,329 ... E4
Cherokee 1,479 ... C1
Chickasaw 6,649 ... B9
Childersburg 4,579 ... F4
Choccolocco 500 ... G3
Choctaw 600 ... B6
Chrysler 400 ... C8
Chunchula 700 ... B9
Citronelle 3,671 ... B8
Clanton▲ 7,669 ... E5
Clayhatchee 411 ... G8
Clayton▲ 1,564 ... G7
Cleveland 739 ... E3
Clio 1,365 ... G7
Coaling 400 ... D4
Coden 600 ... B10
Coffee Springs 294 ... G8
Coffeeville 431 ... B7
Coker 800 ... C4
Collinsville 1,429 ... G2
Columbia 922 ... H8
Columbiana▲ 2,968 ... E4
Coosada 912 ... F5
Cordova 2,623 ... D3
Cottondale 500 ... D4
Cottonton 324 ... H6
Cottonwood 1,385 ... H8
County Line 124 ... F8
County Line 199 ... E3
Courtland 803 ... D1
Cowarts 1,400 ... H8
Coy 950 ... D7
Crane Hill 355 ... D2
Creola 1,896 ... B9
Cromwell 650 ... B6
Crossville 1,350 ... G2
Cuba 390 ... B6
Cullman▲ 13,367 ... E2
Cullomburg 325 ... B7
Cusseta 650 ... H5
Dadeville▲ 3,276 ... G5
Daleville 5,117 ... G8
Daphne 11,290 ... C9
Dauphin Island 824 ... B10
Daviston 261 ... G4
Dayton 77 ... C6
De Armanville 350 ... G3
Decatur▲ 48,761 ... D1
Demopolis 7,512 ... C6
Detroit 291 ... B2
Dolomite ... D4
Dora 2,214 ... D3
Dothan▲ 53,589 ... H8
Double Springs▲ 1,138 ... D2
Douglas 474 ... F2
Dozier 483 ... F7
Dutton 243 ... G1
East Brewton 2,579 ... E8
Eclectic 1,087 ... F5
Edwardsville 118 ... H3
Elba▲ 4,011 ... F8
Elberta 458 ... C10
Eldridge 225 ... C3
Elkmont 389 ... E1
Elmore 600 ... F5
Elrod 746 ... C4
Emelle 44 ... B5
Empire 600 ... D3
Enterprise 20,123 ... G8
Epes 267 ... B5
Ethelsville 52 ... B4
Eufaula 13,220 ... H7
Eunola 199 ... G8
Eutaw▲ 2,281 ... C5
Eva 438 ... E2
Evergreen▲ 3,911 ... E8
Excel 571 ... D8
Fairfield 12,200 ... E4
Fairhope 8,485 ... C10
Fairview 383 ... E2
Falkville 1,337 ... E2
Faunsdale 96 ... C6
Fayette▲ 4,909 ... C3
Five Points 200 ... H4
Flat Rock 750 ... G1
Flint City 1,033 ... D1
Flomaton 1,811 ... D8
Florala 2,075 ... F8
Florence▲ 36,426 ... C1
Foley 4,937 ... C10
Forestdale 10,395 ... E3
Forkland 667 ... C5
Fort Davis 500 ... G6
Fort Deposit 1,240 ... E7
Fort Mitchell 900 ... H6
Fort Payne▲ 11,838 ... G2
Fosters 400 ... C4
Franklin 133 ... G6
Franklin 152 ... D7
Frisco City 1,581 ... D8
Fruitdale 500 ... B8
Fruithurst 177 ... G3
Fulton 384 ... C7
Fultondale 6,400 ... E3
Fyffe 1,094 ... G2
Gadsden▲ 42,523 ... G2
Gainesville 449 ... B5
Gallant 475 ... F2
Gantt 265 ... E8
Gantt's Quarry ... F4
Garden City 578 ... E2
Gardendale 9,251 ... E3
Gaylesville 149 ... G2
Geiger 270 ... B5
Geneva▲ 4,681 ... G8
Georgiana 1,933 ... E7
Geraldine 801 ... G2
Gilbertown 235 ... B7
Glen Allen 350 ... C3
Glencoe 4,670 ... G3
Glenwood 208 ... F7
Goldville 61 ... G4
Good Hope 1,700 ... E2
Goodsprings 360 ... D3
Goodwater 1,840 ... F4
Gordo 1,918 ... C4
Gordon 493 ... H8
Gorgas 500 ... D3
Goshen 302 ... F7
Gosport 500 ... C7
Grand Bay 3,383 ... B10
Grant 638 ... F1
Graysville 2,241 ... D3
Green Pond 750 ... D4
Greensboro▲ 3,047 ... C5
Greenville▲ 7,492 ... E7
Grimes 443 ... H8
Grove Hill▲ 1,551 ... C7
Gu-Win 243 ... C3
Guin 2,464 ... C3
Gulf Shores 3,261 ... C10
Guntersville▲ 7,038 ... F2
Gurley 1,007 ... F1
Hackleburg 1,161 ... C2
Haleburg 97 ... H8
Haleyville 4,452 ... C2
Hamilton▲ 5,787 ... C2
Hammondville 420 ... G1
Hanceville 2,246 ... E2
Hardaway 600 ... G6
Harpersville 772 ... F4
Hartford 2,448 ... G8
Hartselle 10,795 ... E2
Harvest 1,922 ... E1
Hatchechubbee 840 ... H6
Hatton 950 ... D1
Hayden 385 ... E3
Hayneville▲ 969 ... E6
Hazel Green 2,208 ... E1
Headland 3,266 ... H8
Heath 182 ... F8
Heflin▲ 2,906 ... G3
Heiberger 310 ... D5
Helena 3,918 ... E4
Henagar 1,934 ... G1
Higdon 925 ... G1
Highland Lake 304 ... F3
Hillsboro 587 ... D1
Hobson City 794 ... G3
Hodges 272 ... C2
Hokes Bluff 3,739 ... G3
Hollins 500 ... F4
Holly Pond 602 ... E2
Hollywood 916 ... G1
Holt 4,125 ... D4
Holy Trinity 400 ... H6
Homewood 22,922 ... E4
Hoover 39,788 ... E4
Hope Hull 975 ... F6
Horn Hill 186 ... F8
Hueytown 15,280 ... D4
Huntsville▲ 159,789 ... E1
Hurtsboro 707 ... H6
Hytop 350 ... F1
Ider 671 ... G1
Inverness 2,528 ... G6
Irondale 9,454 ... E3
Jack 5,819 ... F7
Jackson 789 ... C8
Jacksons Gap 800 ... G5
Jacksonville 10,283 ... G3
Jasper▲ 13,553 ... D3
Jemison 1,898 ... E5
Kansas 230 ... C3
Kellyton 375 ... F5
Kennedy 523 ... B3
Key 400 ... G2
Killen 1,047 ... D1
Kimberly 1,096 ... E3
Kinsey 1,679 ... H8
Kinston 595 ... F8
Laceys Spring 400 ... E1
Lafayette▲ 3,151 ... H5
Lakeview 166 ... G2
Lanett 8,985 ... H5
Langdale 2,034 ... H5
Langston 207 ... G1
Larkinsville 425 ... F1
Lavaca 500 ... B6
Leeds 9,946 ... E3
Leesburg 218 ... G2
Leighton 988 ... D1
Leroy 699 ... B8
Lester 89 ... D1
Level Plains 1,473 ... G8
Lexington 821 ... D1
Libertyville 133 ... F8
Lillian 350 ... D10
Lincoln 2,941 ... F3
Linden▲ 2,548 ... C6
Lineville 2,394 ... G4
Lipscomb 2,892 ... E4
Lisman 481 ... B6
Little River 400 ... C8
Little Shawmut 2,793 ... H5
Littleville 925 ... C1
Livingston▲ 3,530 ... B5
Loachapoka 259 ... G5
Lockhart 484 ... F8
Locust Fork 342 ... E3
Longview 475 ... E4
Louisville 728 ... G7
Lower Peach Tree 926 ... C7
Lowndesboro 139 ... E6
Loxley 1,161 ... C9
Luverne▲ 2,555 ... F7
Lynn 611 ... C2
Madison 14,904 ... E1
Madrid 211 ... H8
Magnolia Springs 800 ... C10
Malvern 570 ... G8
Manchester 400 ... D3
Maplesville 725 ... E5
Margaret 616 ... F3
Marion Junction 400 ... D6
Marion▲ 4,211 ... D5
Maylene 500 ... E4
McCalla 657 ... E4
McCullough 500 ... D8
McIntosh 250 ... B8
McKenzie 464 ... E7
McWilliams 305 ... D7
Memphis 54 ... B4
Mentone 474 ... G1
Meridianville 2,852 ... F1
Midfield 5,559 ... E4
Midland City 1,819 ... H8
Midway 455 ... H6
Mignon 1,548 ... F4
Millbrook 6,050 ... F6
Millerville 345 ... G4
Millport 1,203 ... B3
Millry 781 ... B7
Minter 450 ... D6
Mobile▲ 196,278 ... B9
Monroeville▲ 6,993 ... D7
Monrovia 500 ... E1
Montevallo 4,239 ... E4
Montgomery (cap.)▲ 187,106 ... F6
Montrose 750 ... C9
Moody 4,921 ... F3
Mooresville 54 ... E1
Morris 1,136 ... E3
Morvin 355 ... C7
Moulton▲ 3,248 ... D2
Moundville 1,348 ... C5
Mount Vernon 902 ... B8
Mountain Brook 19,810 ... E4
Mountainboro 261 ... F2
Munford 700 ... F3
Muscle Shoals 9,611 ... C1
Myrtlewood 197 ... C6
Nanafalia 500 ... B6
Napier Field 462 ... H8
Nauvoo 240 ... D3
Nectar 238 ... E3
Needham 99 ... B7
New Brockton 1,184 ... G8
New Hope 2,248 ... F1
New Market 1,094 ... F1
New Site 669 ... G4
Newbern 222 ... C5
Newton 1,580 ... G8
Newville 531 ... H8
North Johns 177 ... D4
Northport 17,366 ... C4
Notasulga 979 ... G5
Oak Grove 436 ... B9
Oak Grove 638 ... F4
Oak Hill 28 ... D7
Oakman 846 ... D3
Odenville 796 ... F3
Ohatchee 1,042 ... G3
Oneonta▲ 4,844 ... E3
Onycha 150 ... F8
Opelika▲ 22,122 ... H5
Opp 6,985 ... F8
Orange Beach 2,253 ... C10
Orrville 234 ... D6
Owens Cross Roads 695 ... E1
Oxford 9,362 ... G3
Ozark▲ 12,922 ... G8
Paint Rock 214 ... F1
Parrish 1,433 ... D3
Pelham 9,765 ... E4
Pell City▲ 8,118 ... F3
Pennington 302 ... B6
Perdido 500 ... C8
Peterman 600 ... D7
Peterson ... D4
Petrey 80 ... F7
Phenix City▲ 25,312 ... H6
Phil Campbell 1,317 ... C2
Pickensville 169 ... B4
Piedmont 5,288 ... G3
Pinckard 618 ... G8
Pine Apple 365 ... E7
Pine Hill 481 ... C7
Pinson 10,987 ... E3
Pisgah 652 ... G1
Plantersville 650 ... E5
Pleasant Grove 8,458 ... D4
Point Clear 2,125 ... C10
Pollard 100 ... D8
Powell's Crossroads 636 ... G1
Prattville▲ 19,587 ... E6
Priceville 1,323 ... E1
Prichard 34,311 ... B9
Providence 307 ... C6
Ragland 1,807 ... F3
Rainbow City 7,673 ... F3
Rainsville 3,875 ... G2
Ramer 680 ... F6
Ranburne 447 ... H3
Red Bay 3,451 ... B2
Red Level 588 ... E8
Reece City 657 ... G2
Reform 2,105 ... C4
Remlap 800 ... E3
Renfroe 400 ... F4
Repton 293 ... D8
Republic 500 ... E3
River Falls 710 ... E8

(continued on following page)

Agriculture, Industry and Resources

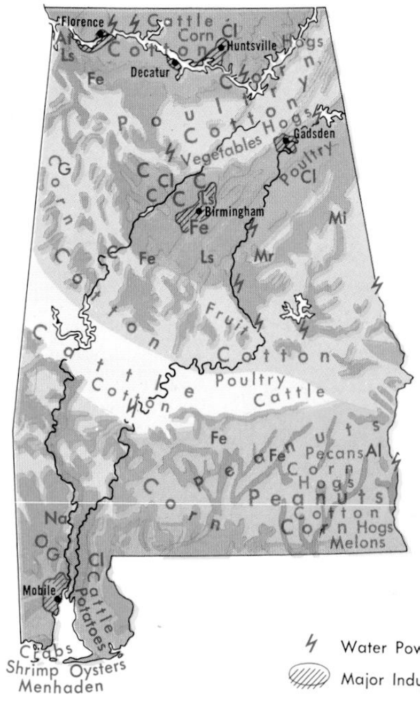
Florence
Huntsville
Decatur
Gadsden
Birmingham
Mobile
Cattle
Corn
Hogs
Cotton
Poultry
Vegetables
Fruit
Pecans
Peanuts
Melons
Potatoes
Crabs
Shrimp
Oysters
Menhaden

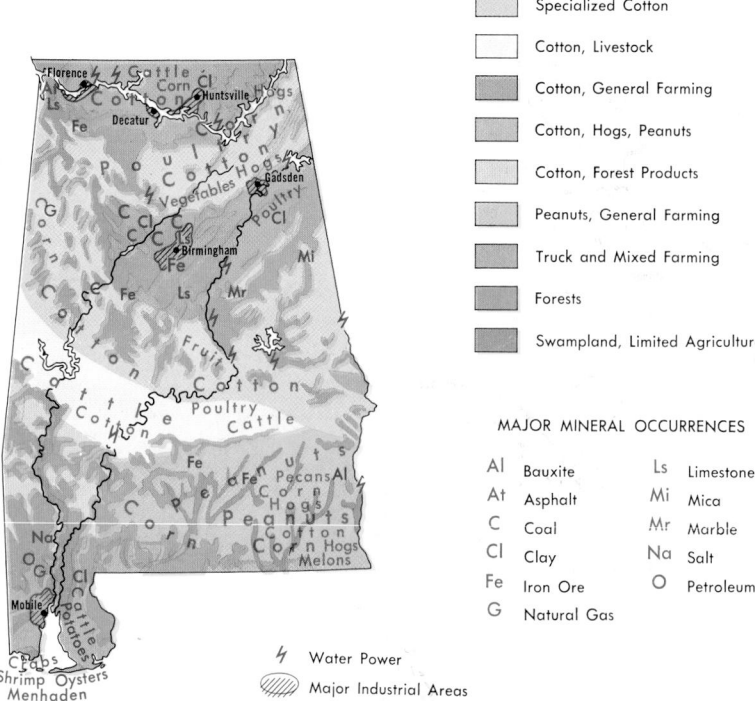

DOMINANT LAND USE

- Specialized Cotton
- Cotton, Livestock
- Cotton, General Farming
- Cotton, Hogs, Peanuts
- Cotton, Forest Products
- Peanuts, General Farming
- Truck and Mixed Farming
- Forests
- Swampland, Limited Agriculture

MAJOR MINERAL OCCURRENCES

Al	Bauxite	Ls	Limestone
At	Asphalt	Mi	Mica
C	Coal	Mr	Marble
Cl	Clay	Na	Salt
Fe	Iron Ore	O	Petroleum
G	Natural Gas		

Water Power

Major Industrial Areas

Topography

0 30 60 MI.
0 30 60 KM.

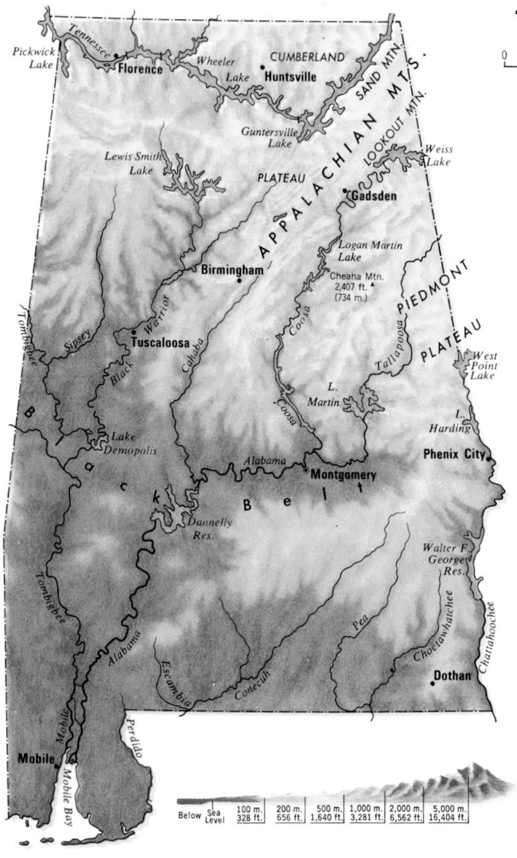
Pickwick Lake
Tennessee
Florence
Wheeler Lake
Huntsville
CUMBERLAND
PLATEAU
SAND MTN.
APPALACHIAN MTS.
LOOKOUT MTN.
Guntersville Lake
Lewis Smith Lake
Weiss Lake
Gadsden
Logan Martin Lake
Birmingham
Cheaha Mtn. 2,407 ft. (734 m.)
PIEDMONT PLATEAU
Tuscaloosa
Tombigbee
Sipsey
Black Warrior
Cahaba
Coosa
Tallapoosa
West Point Lake
L. Martin
L. Harding
Phenix City
Lake Demopolis
Alabama
Montgomery
Black Belt
Dannelly Res.
Walter F. George Res.
Chattahoochee
Choctawhatchee
Pea
Dothan
Conecuh
Escambia
Perdido
Mobile
Mobile Bay
Below Sea Level
100 m. 328 ft.
200 m. 656 ft.
500 m. 1,640 ft.
1,000 m. 3,281 ft.
2,000 m. 6,562 ft.
5,000 m. 16,404 ft.

River View 1,314 .... H5
Riverside 1,004 .... F3
Riverview 90 .... D8
Roanoke 6,362 .... H4
Robertsdale 2,401 .... C9
Rock Mills 600 .... H4
Rockford▲ 461 .... F5
Rogersville 1,125 .... D1
Roosevelt City 3,352 .... E4
Rosa 139 .... E3
Rural C7
Russellville▲ 7,812 .... C2
Rutledge 473 .... F7
Saginaw 475 .... E4
Saint Elmo 700 .... B10
Saint Florian 388 .... C1
Saint Stephens 700 .... B7
Salem 350 .... H5
Salitpa 550 .... C7
Samantha 400 .... C4
Samson 2,190 .... F8
Sanford 282 .... F8
Saraland 11,751 .... B9
Sardis 1,301 .... E6
Sardis 883 .... F2
Satsuma 5,194 .... B9
Sayre 700 .... E3
Scottsboro▲ 13,786 .... F1
Seale 350 .... H6
Section 777 .... G1
Selma▲ 23,755 .... E6
Selmont 3,823 .... E6
Shady Grove F7
Shawmut 2,284 .... H5
Sheffield 10,380 .... C1
Shelby 500 .... E4
Shiloh 252 .... C6
Shiloh 297 .... G2
Shorter 461 .... G6
Shorterville 400 .... H7
Silas 245 .... B7
Silverhill 556 .... C9
Sipsey 568 .... D3
Slocomb 1,906 .... G8
Smiths 3,456 .... H5
Snead 632 .... F2
Somerville 211 .... E2
South 543 .... E8
Southside 5,580 .... F3
Spanish Fort 3,732 .... C9
Spring Valley 600 .... C1
Springville 1,910 .... E3
Stapleton 975 .... C9
Steele 1,046 .... F3
Sterrett 350 .... F4
Stevenson 2,046 .... G1
Stewart 450 .... C5
Stockton 500 .... C9
Suggsville 400 .... C7
Sulligent 1,886 .... B3
Sumiton 2,604 .... D3
Summerdale 559 .... C10
Sunny South 350 .... C7
Sweet Water 243 .... C6
Sycamore 800 .... F4
Sylacauga 12,520 .... F4
Sylvania 932 .... G1
Talladega Springs 148 .... F4
Talladega▲ 18,175 .... F4
Tallassee 5,112 .... G5
Tanner 600 .... E1
Tarrant 8,046 .... E3
Taylor 1,352 .... H8
Theodore 6,509 .... B9
Thomaston 497 .... C6
Thomasville 4,301 .... C7
Thorsby 1,465 .... E5
Tibbie 675 .... B8
Town Creek 1,379 .... D1
Townley 500 .... D3
Toxey 211 .... B7
Trafford 739 .... E3
Triana 499 .... E1
Trinity 1,380 .... D1
Troy▲ 13,051 .... G7
Trussville 8,266 .... E3
Tuscaloosa▲ 77,759 .... C4
Tuscumbia▲ 8,413 .... C1
Tuskegee Institute G6
Tuskegee▲ 12,257 .... G6
Union 321 .... C5
Union Grove 119 .... E2
Union Springs▲ 3,975 .... G6
Uniontown 1,730 .... D6
Uriah 450 .... D8
Valhermoso Springs 500 .... E2
Valley 8,173 .... H5
Valley Head 577 .... G1
Vance 248 .... D4
Vandiver 700 .... F4
Verbena 500 .... E5
Vernon▲ 2,247 .... B3
Vestavia Hills 19,749 .... E4
Vina 356 .... B2
Vincent 1,767 .... F4
Vinemont E2
Vredenburgh 313 .... D7
Wadley 517 .... G4
Wadsworth 500 .... E5
Wagarville 550 .... B8
Waldo 309 .... F4
Walker Springs 500 .... C7
Walnut Grove 717 .... F2
Warrior 3,280 .... E3
Waterloo 250 .... B1
Wattsville 550 .... F3
Waverly 152 .... G5
Weaver 2,715 .... G3
Webb 1,039 .... H8
Wedowee▲ 796 .... H4
Wegra D3
Weogufka 500 .... F4
West Blocton 1,468 .... D4
West Jefferson 388 .... D3
West Point 257 .... D2
West Selmont 5,255 .... E6
Weston 384 .... B2
Westover 500 .... E4
Wetumpka▲ 4,670 .... F5
Whatley 800 .... C7
White Hall 814 .... E6
White Plains 350 .... G3
Whites Chapel 336 .... F3
Wicksburg 400 .... G8
Wilmer 494 .... B9
Wilsonville 1,185 .... E4
Wilton 602 .... E4
Winfield 3,689 .... C3
Woodland 189 .... H4
Woodstock 340 .... D4
Woodville 687 .... F1
Yantley 500 .... B6
Yellow Bluff 245 .... C7
Yellow Pine 350 .... B8
York 3,160 .... B6

OTHER FEATURES

Alabama (riv.) C8
Aliceville (dam) B4
Anniston Army Depot F3
Bankhead (lake) D4
Bartletts Ferry (dam) H5
Big Canoe (creek) F3
Big Creek (lake) B9
Black Warrior (riv.) C5
Bon Secour (bay) C10
Brookley Air Force Base B9
Buttahatchee (riv.) B3
Cahaba (riv.) D5
Cedar (pt.) B10
Chattahoochee (riv.) H8
Chattooga (riv.) H2
Cheaha (mt.) G4
Choctawhatchee (riv.) H8
Coffeeville (dam) B7
Conecuh (riv.) D8
Coosa (riv.) F4
Cowikee, North Fork (creek) H6
Cumberland (plat.) F1
Dannelly (res.) D6
Demopolis (dam) C5
Elk (riv.) D1
Escambia (creek) D8
Escambia (riv.) D9
Escatawpa (riv.) B9
Fort Gaines B10
Fort McClellan
Military Reservation 4,128 .... G3
Fort Morgan C10
Fort Rucker 7,593 .... G8
Gainesville (dam) B5
Goat Rock (dam) H5
Goat Rock (lake) H5
Grants Pass (chan.) B10
Gunter Air Force Base F6
Guntersville (dam) F2
Guntersville (lake) F2
Harding (lake) H5
Herbes (isl.) B10
Holt (dam) D4
Horseshoe Bend
Nat'l Mil. Park G5
Inland (lake) E3
Jordan (dam) F5
Jordan (lake) F5
Lay (dam) E5
Lewis Smith (dam) D3
Lewis Smith (lake) D2
Little (riv.) G2
Little (riv.) C8
Locust Fork (riv.) E3
Logan Martin (lake) F4
Lookout (mt.) G2
Martin (dam) G5
Martin (lake) G5
Maxwell Air Force Base F6
Mexico (gulf) E10
Mississippi (sound) B10
Mitchell (lake) F5
Mobile (bay) B10
Mobile (pt.) B10
Mobile (riv.) C9
Mulberry (creek) E5
Mulberry Fork (riv.) E3
Neely Henry (lake) F3
Oakmulgee (creek) D5
Oliver (dam) J5
Paint Rock (riv.) F1
Patsaliga (creek) F7
Pea (riv.) F8
Perdido (bay) D10
Perdido (riv.) C9
Pickwick (lake) B1
Pigeon (creek) E7
Redstone Arsenal E1
Russell Cave Nat'l Mon. G1
Sand (mt.) G1
Sandy (creek) H7
Sepulga (riv.) E7
Sipsey (riv.) B4
Sipsey Fork (riv.) D2
Tallapoosa (riv.) G4
Tennessee (riv.) C1
Tennessee-Tombigbee
Waterway B4
Tensaw (riv.) C9
Thurlow (dam) G6
Tombigbee (riv.) B7
Town (creek) C1
Tuscaloosa (lake) D4
Tuskegee Institute
Nat'l Hist. Site G6
Walter F. George (dam) H7
Walter F. George (res.) H7
Warrior (dam) C5
Weiss (lake) G2
West Point (lake) H4
Wheeler (dam) D1
Wheeler (lake) D1
Wilson (dam) C1
Yates (dam) G5

▲County seat.

Alabama
SCALE
0 5 10 20 30 40 MI.
0 5 10 20 30 40 KM.
State Capitals
County Seats
Major Limited Access Hwys.
© Copyright HAMMOND INCORPORATED, Maplewood, N. J.
TENNESSEE
GEORGIA
FLORIDA
MISSISSIPPI
GULF OF MEXICO
Longitude West of Greenwich
LAUDERDALE
LIMESTONE
MADISON
JACKSON
COLBERT
LAWRENCE
MORGAN
MARSHALL
DE KALB
FRANKLIN
MARION
WINSTON
CULLMAN
ETOWAH
CHEROKEE
BLOUNT
LAMAR
FAYETTE
WALKER
JEFFERSON
ST CLAIR
CALHOUN
CLEBURNE
PICKENS
TUSCALOOSA
SHELBY
TALLADEGA
CLAY
RANDOLPH
BIBB
COOSA
TALLAPOOSA
CHAMBERS
GREENE
HALE
CHILTON
PERRY
AUTAUGA
ELMORE
LEE
SUMTER
MARENGO
DALLAS
MACON
RUSSELL
CHOCTAW
LOWNDES
MONTGOMERY
BULLOCK
WILCOX
BARBOUR
BUTLER
CRENSHAW
PIKE
CLARKE
MONROE
CONECUH
HENRY
WASHINGTON
COFFEE
DALE
ESCAMBIA
COVINGTON
GENEVA
HOUSTON
MOBILE
BALDWIN
MONTGOMERY
BIRMINGHAM
MOBILE

Agriculture, Industry and Resources

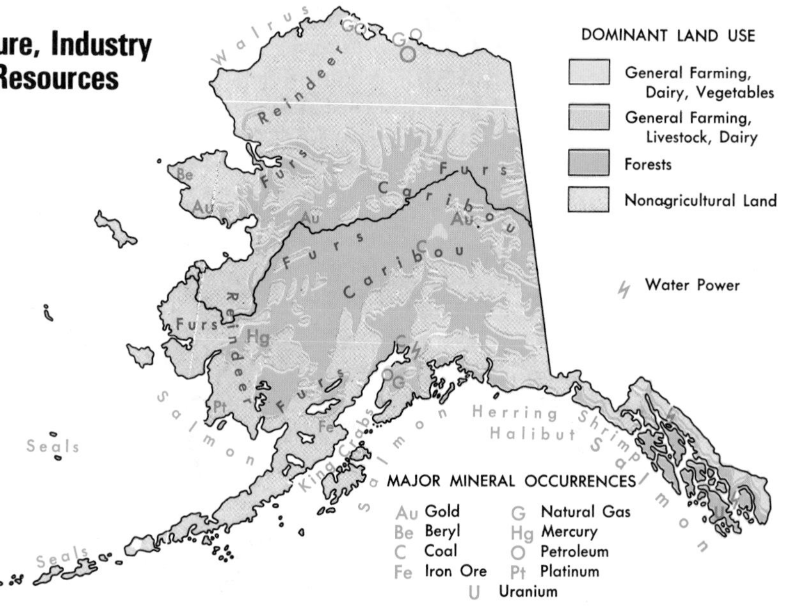

DOMINANT LAND USE
General Farming, Dairy, Vegetables
General Farming, Livestock, Dairy
Forests
Nonagricultural Land
Water Power
MAJOR MINERAL OCCURRENCES
Au Gold
Be Beryl
C Coal
Fe Iron Ore
G Natural Gas
Hg Mercury
O Petroleum
Pt Platinum
U Uranium
Walrus
Reindeer
Furs
Caribou
Seals
Salmon
Herring
Halibut
Shrimp
King Crab

Topography

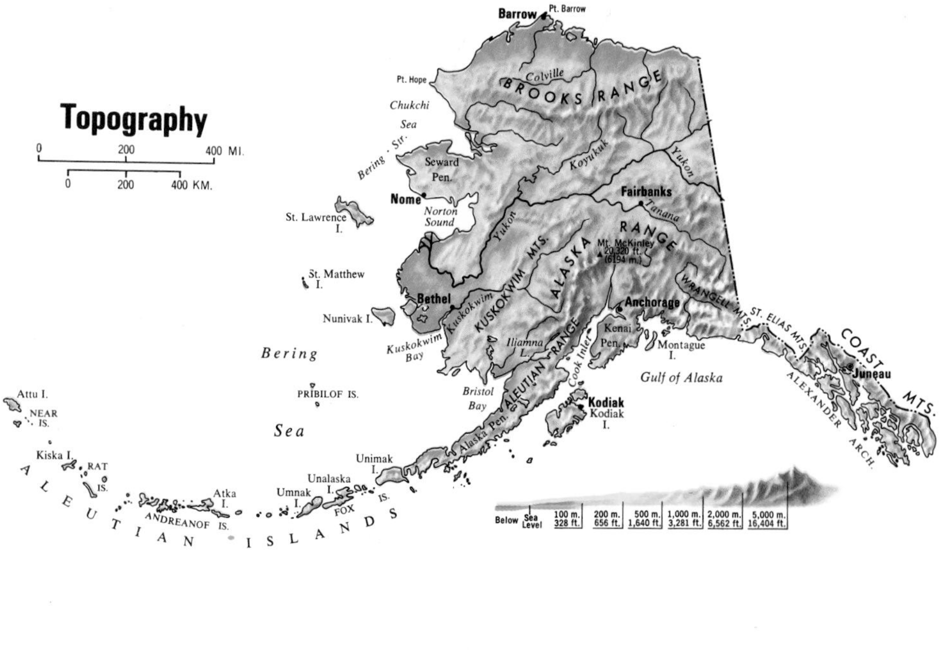

0 200 400 MI.
0 200 400 KM.
Barrow
Pt. Barrow
Pt. Hope
Chukchi Sea
BROOKS RANGE
Colville
Bering Str.
Seward Pen.
Nome
Norton Sound
Koyukuk
Yukon
Fairbanks
Tanana
St. Lawrence I.
St. Matthew I.
Nunivak I.
Bethel
KUSKOKWIM MTS.
ALASKA RANGE
Mt. McKinley 20,320 ft. (6194 m.)
WRANGELL MTS.
ST. ELIAS MTS.
COAST MTS.
Anchorage
Kenai Pen.
Montague I.
Kuskokwim Bay
Iliamna L.
ALEUTIAN RANGE
Cook Inlet
Gulf of Alaska
Juneau
ALEXANDER ARCH.
Bering Sea
PRIBILOF IS.
Bristol Bay
Kodiak
Kodiak I.
Alaska Pen.
Attu I.
NEAR IS.
Kiska I.
RAT IS.
Atka I.
ANDREANOF IS.
Umnak I.
Unalaska I.
FOX IS.
Unimak I.
ALEUTIAN ISLANDS
Below Sea Level
100 m. 328 ft.
200 m. 656 ft.
500 m. 1,640 ft.
1,000 m. 3,281 ft.
2,000 m. 6,562 ft.
5,000 m. 16,404 ft.

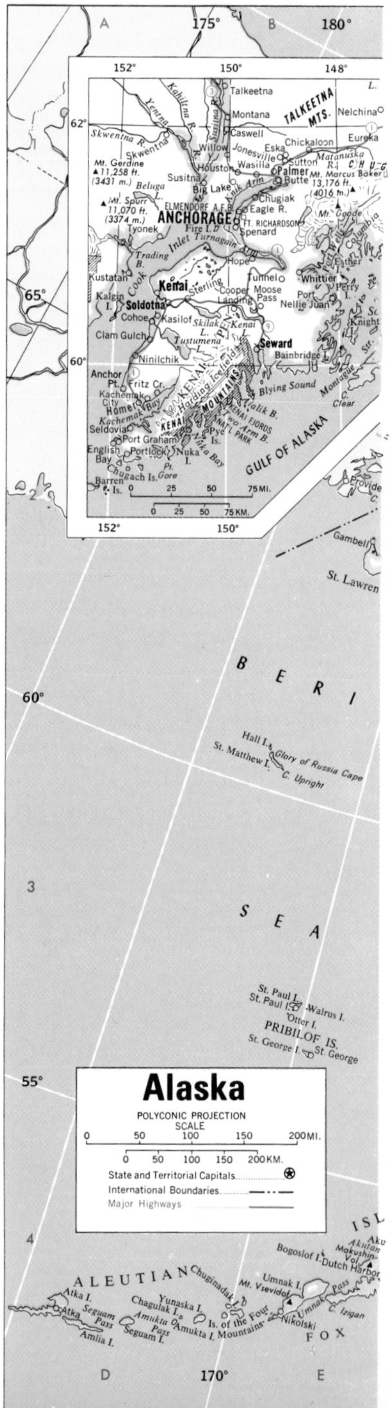

Alaska
POLYCONIC PROJECTION
SCALE
0 50 100 150 200 MI.
0 50 100 150 200 KM.
State and Territorial Capitals
International Boundaries
Major Highways
Talkeetna
TALKEETNA MTS.
Montana
Nelchina
Skwentna
Caswell
Willow
Chickaloon
Eureka
Houston
Wasilla
Palmer
Mt. Gerdine 11,258 ft. (3431 m.)
Mt. Marcus Baker 13,176 ft. (4016 m.)
Susitna
Big Lake
Mt. Spurr 11,070 ft. (3374 m.)
Chugiak
Eagle R.
ANCHORAGE
Tyonek
Fire I.
Spenard
Turnagain Arm
Hope
Kustatan
Kenai
Sterling
Cooper Landing
Moose Pass
Whittier
Soldotna
Cohoe
Kasilof
Skilak L.
Kenai L.
Tustumena L.
Clam Gulch
Ninilchik
Seward
Anchor Pt.
Fritz Cr.
Homer
Kachemak Bay
Seldovia
Port Graham
English Bay
Chugach Is.
Barren Is.
KENAI MTS.
Harding Icefield
KENAI FJORDS NAT'L PARK
Blying Sound
GULF OF ALASKA
Montague I.
Gambell
St. Lawrence
BERING SEA
Hall I.
St. Matthew I.
Glory of Russia Cape
C. Upright
St. Paul I.
Walrus I.
Otter I.
PRIBILOF IS.
St. George I.
St. George
ALEUTIAN IS.
Bogoslof I.
Dutch Harbor
Akutan
Makushin Vol.
Umnak I.
Mt. Vsevidof
Chuginadak
Yunaska I.
Chagulak I.
Amukta I.
Amukta Pass
Is. of the Four Mountains
Seguam I.
Seguam Pass
Atka I.
Amlia I.
Nikolski
FOX
Izigan

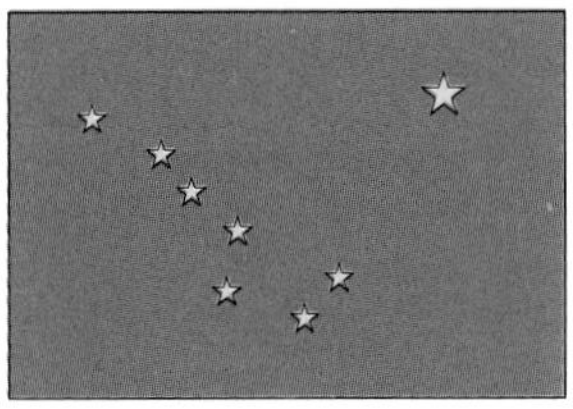

AREA 591,004 sq. mi. (1,530,700 sq. km.)
POPULATION 551,947
CAPITAL Juneau
LARGEST CITY Anchorage
HIGHEST POINT Mt. McKinley 20,320 ft. (6194 m.)
SETTLED IN 1801
ADMITTED TO UNION January 3, 1959
POPULAR NAME Great Land; Last Frontier
STATE FLOWER Forget-me-not
STATE BIRD Willow Ptarmigan

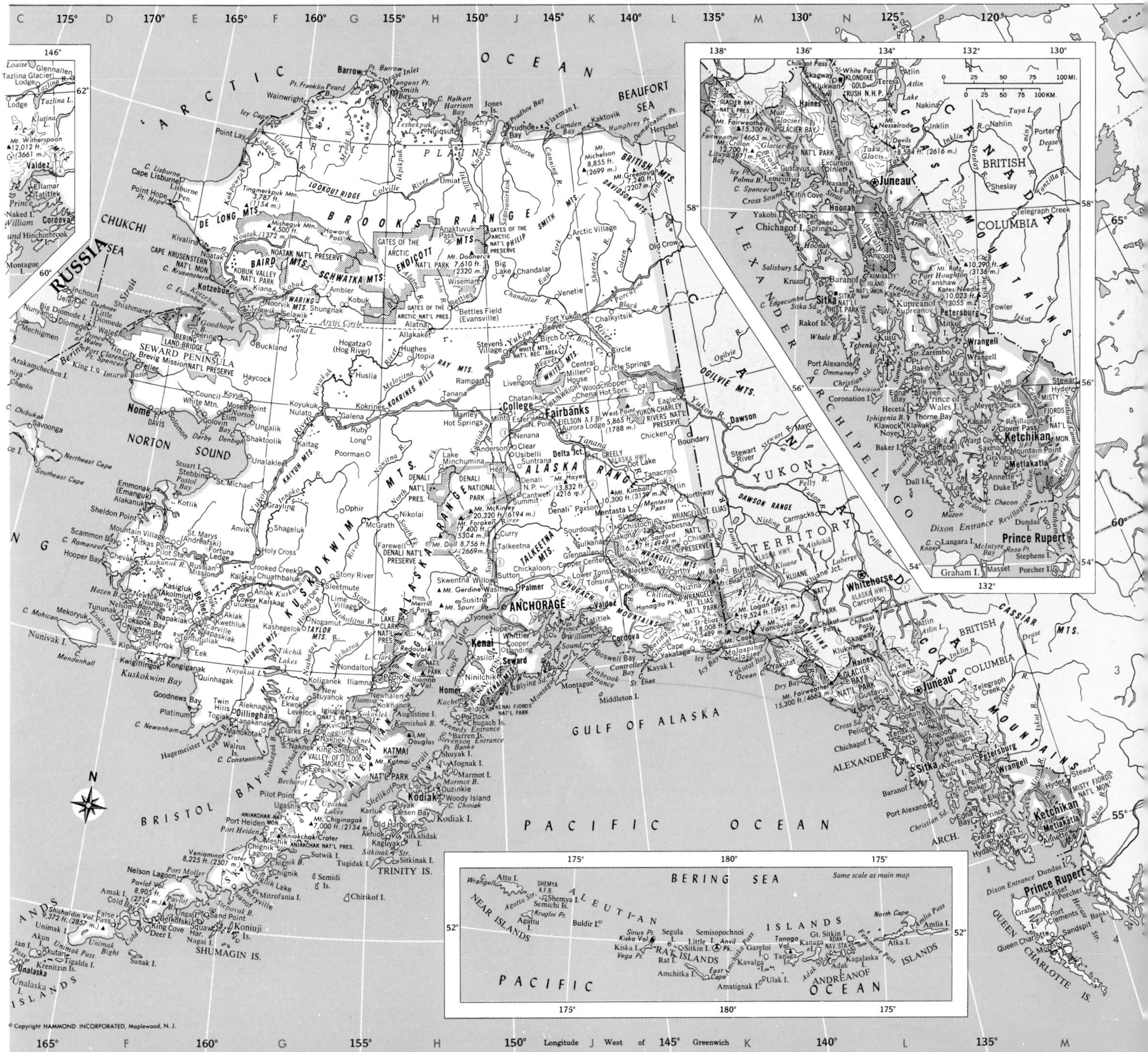

ARCTIC OCEAN
BEAUFORT SEA
CHUKCHI SEA
RUSSIA
BROOKS RANGE
ARCTIC PLAINS
ALASKA RANGE
KUSKOKWIM MTS.
NORTON SOUND
BERING SEA
BRISTOL BAY
GULF OF ALASKA
PACIFIC OCEAN
ALEXANDER ARCHIPELAGO
YUKON TERRITORY
BRITISH COLUMBIA
CANADA
ANCHORAGE
Fairbanks
Juneau
Nome
Kodiak
Sitka
Ketchikan
Prince Rupert
Whitehorse
Dawson
ALEUTIAN ISLANDS
Same scale as main map
Longitude West of Greenwich
© Copyright HAMMOND INCORPORATED, Maplewood, N. J.

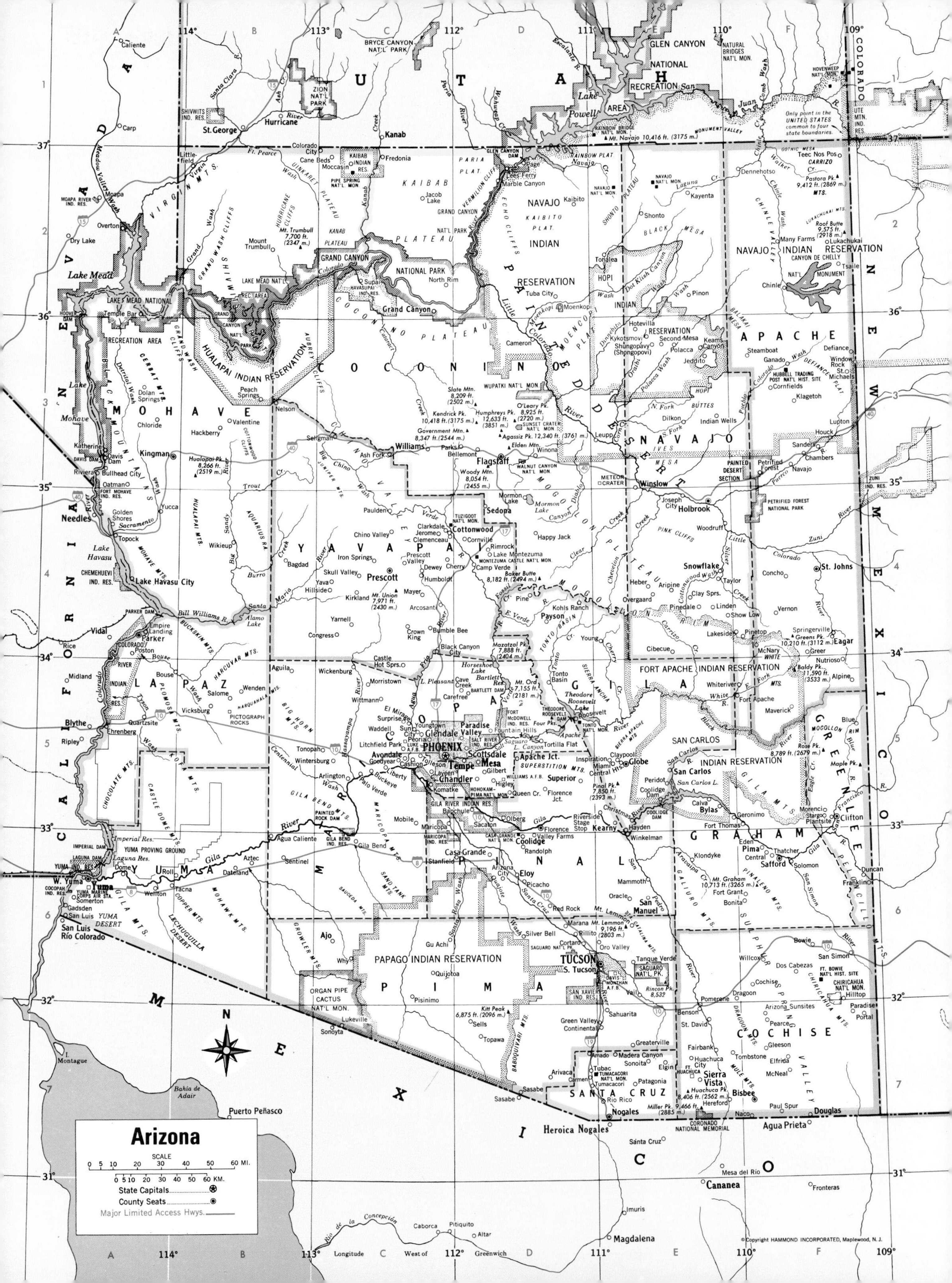

Arizona
SCALE
0 5 10 20 30 40 50 60 MI.
0 5 10 20 30 40 50 60 KM.
State Capitals
County Seats
Major Limited Access Hwys.
©Copyright HAMMOND INCORPORATED, Maplewood, N.J.
Longitude
West of
Greenwich
114°
113°
112°
111°
110°
109°
37°
36°
35°
34°
33°
32°
31°
U T A H
N E V A D A
C A L I F O R N I A
C O L O R A D O
N E W M E X I C O
M E X I C O
MOHAVE
COCONINO
YAVAPAI
LA PAZ
YUMA
MARICOPA
PINAL
PIMA
SANTA CRUZ
COCHISE
GRAHAM
GREENLEE
GILA
NAVAJO
APACHE
PHOENIX
TUCSON
Flagstaff
Prescott
Kingman
Yuma
Parker
Holbrook
St. Johns
Safford
Clifton
Globe
Florence
Nogales
Bisbee
GRAND CANYON NATIONAL PARK
GLEN CANYON NATIONAL RECREATION AREA
LAKE MEAD NATIONAL RECREATION AREA
PAINTED DESERT
PETRIFIED FOREST NATIONAL PARK
NAVAJO INDIAN RESERVATION
HOPI INDIAN RESERVATION
HUALAPAI INDIAN RESERVATION
FORT APACHE INDIAN RESERVATION
SAN CARLOS INDIAN RESERVATION
PAPAGO INDIAN RESERVATION
GILA RIVER INDIAN RES.
ORGAN PIPE CACTUS NAT'L MON.
YUMA PROVING GROUND
Only point in the UNITED STATES common to four state boundaries.
Lake Mead
Lake Powell
Lake Havasu
Colorado
Gila
Salt
Little Colorado
Humphreys Pk. 12,633 ft. (3851 m.)
Mt. Graham 10,713 ft. (3265 m.)
Baldy Pk. 11,590 ft. (3533 m.)
Mt. Lemmon 9,196 ft. (2803 m.)
Kitt Peak 6,875 ft. (2096 m.)
Mt. Navajo 10,416 ft. (3175 m.)
Heroica Nogales
Agua Prieta
Cananea
Magdalena
Caborca
Puerto Peñasco
San Luis Río Colorado
Bahía de Adair
I. Montague

AREA 114,000 sq. mi. (295,260 sq. km.)
POPULATION 3,677,985
CAPITAL Phoenix
LARGEST CITY Phoenix
HIGHEST POINT Humphreys Pk. 12,633 ft. (3851 m.)
SETTLED IN 1752
ADMITTED TO UNION February 14, 1912
POPULAR NAME Grand Canyon State
STATE FLOWER Saguaro Cactus Blossom
STATE BIRD Cactus Wren

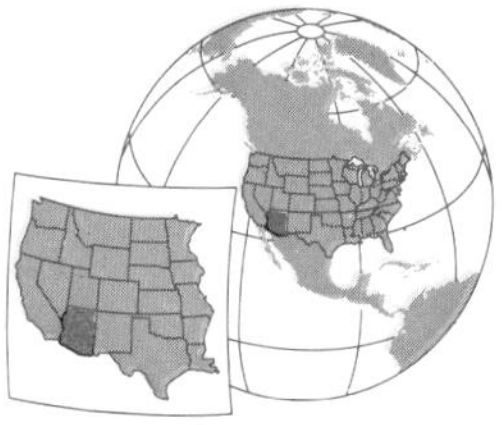

Agriculture, Industry and Resources

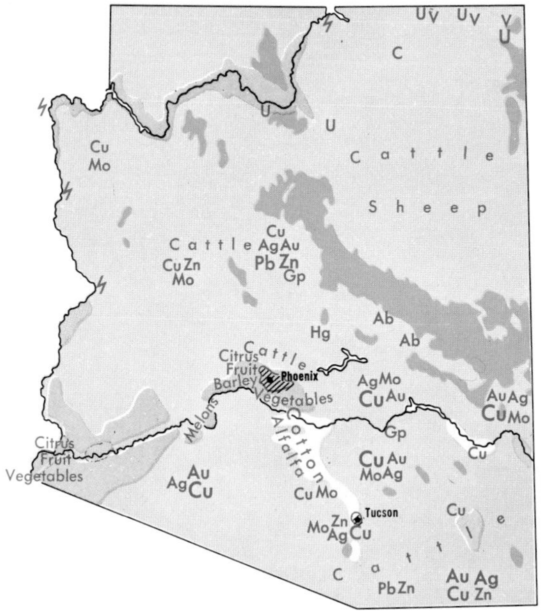

Cattle
Sheep
Cattle
Phoenix
Citrus Fruit
Barley
Vegetables
Melons
Cotton
Alfalfa
Citrus Fruit
Vegetables
Tucson

MAJOR MINERAL OCCURRENCES

Ab	Asbestos	Cu	Copper	Pb	Lead
Ag	Silver	Gp	Gypsum	U	Uranium
Au	Gold	Hg	Mercury	V	Vanadium
C	Coal	Mo	Molybdenum	Zn	Zinc

DOMINANT LAND USE

- Fruit, Truck and Mixed Farming
- Cotton and Alfalfa
- General Farming, Livestock, Special Crops
- Range Livestock
- Forests
- Nonagricultural Land

- Water Power
- Major Industrial Areas

COUNTIES

Apache 61,591	F3
Cochise 97,624	F7
Coconino 96,591	C3
Gila 40,216	E5
Graham 26,554	E6
Greenlee 8,008	F5
La Paz 13,844	A5
Maricopa 2,122,101	C5
Mohave 93,497	A3
Navajo 77,658	E3
Pima 666,880	D6
Pinal 116,379	D6
Santa Cruz 29,676	E7
Yavapai 107,714	C4
Yuma 106,895	A5

CITIES and TOWNS

Agua Caliente 60	B6
Aguila 900	B5
Ajo 2,919	C6
Alpine 450	F5
Amado 75	D7
Apache Junction 18,100	D5
Arcosanti	C4
Aripine 25	E4
Arivaca 400	D7
Arizona City 1,940	D6
Arizona Sunsites 825	F7
Arlington 950	C5
Ash Fork 800	C3
Avondale 16,169	C5
Aztec 20	B6
Bagdad 1,858	B4
Bapchule 400	D5
Bellemont 210	D3
Benson 3,824	E7
Bisbee▲ 6,288	F7
Black Canyon City 1,811	C4
Blue 50	F5
Bonita 20	E6
Bouse 500	A5
Bowie 600	F6
Buckeye 5,038	C5
Bullhead City (Bullhead City-Riviera) 21,951	A3
Bumble Bee 15	C4
Bylas 1,219	E5
Calva 10	E5
Cameron 493	D3
Camp Verde 6,243	D4
Cane Beds 30	B2
Carefree 1,666	C5
Carmen 200	D7
Casa Grande 19,082	D6
Cashion 3,014	C5
Castle Hot Springs 50	C5
Cave Creek 2,925	D5
Central 300	F6
Central Heights (Central Heights-Midland City) 2,791	E5
Chambers 500	F3
Chandler 90,533	D5
Cherry 20	C4
Chinle 5,059	F2
Chino Valley 4,837	C4
Chloride 225	A3
Christmas 201	E5
Cibecue 1,254	E4
Clarkdale 2,144	C4
Clay Springs 500	E4
Claypool 1,942	E5
Clemenceau 300	C4
Clifton▲ 2,840	F5
Cochise 150	F6
Colorado City 2,426	B2
Concho 100	F4
Congress 800	C4
Continental 250	D7
Coolidge 6,927	D6
Coolidge Dam 42	E5
Cornfields 200	F3
Cornville 2,089	D4
Cortaro 375	D6
Cottonwood 5,918	D4
Crown King 100	C4
Dateland 100	B6
Davis Dam 125	A3
Dennehotso 616	F2
Dewey 100	C4
Dilkon 90	E3
Dolan Springs 1,090	A3
Dome 48	A6
Dos Cabezas 30	F6
Douglas 12,822	F7
Dragoon 150	F6
Duncan 662	F6
Eagar 4,025	F4
Eden 89	F6
Ehrenberg 1,226	A5
El Mirage 5,001	C5
Elfrida 700	F7
Elgin 525	E7
Eloy 7,211	D6
Empire Landing	A4
Fairbank 100	E7
Flagstaff▲ 45,857	D3

(continued on following page)

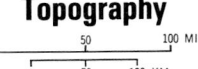

Topography

0 50 100 MI.
0 50 100 KM.

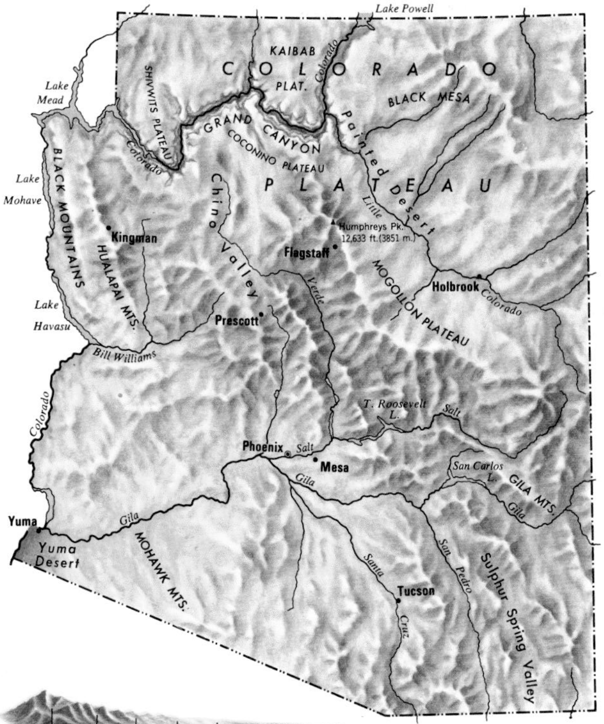

Lake Powell
KAIBAB PLAT.
COLORADO PLATEAU
BLACK MESA
Lake Mead
SHIVWITS PLATEAU
GRAND CANYON
COCONINO PLATEAU
Painted Desert
Lake Mohave
BLACK MOUNTAINS
Chino Valley
Kingman
HUALAPAI MTS.
Flagstaff
Humphreys Pk. 12,633 ft. (3851 m.)
Little Colorado
Verde
Holbrook
MOGOLLON PLATEAU
Lake Havasu
Prescott
Bill Williams
Colorado
T. Roosevelt L.
Salt
Phoenix
Mesa
San Carlos L.
GILA MTS.
Gila
Yuma
Yuma Desert
MOHAWK MTS.
Santa Cruz
San Pedro
Tucson
Sulphur Spring Valley

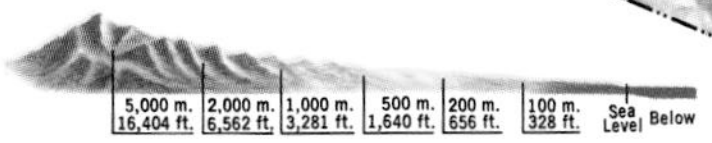

5,000 m. 16,404 ft.
2,000 m. 6,562 ft.
1,000 m. 3,281 ft.
500 m. 1,640 ft.
200 m. 656 ft.
100 m. 328 ft.
Sea Level
Below

Florence▲ 7,510 .... D5
Florence Junction 35 .... D5
Fort Apache 500 .... F5
Fort Defiance 4,489 .... F3
Fort Grant 240 .... E6
Fort Thomas 450 .... E5
Fountain Hills 10,030 .... D5
Franklin 300 .... F6
Fredonia 1,207 .... C2
Gadsden 250 .... A6
Ganado 1,257 .... F3
Geronimo 25 .... F5
Gila Bend 1,747 .... C6
Gilbert 29,188 .... D5
Gleeson 15 .... F7
Glendale 148,134 .... C5
Globe▲ 6,062 .... E5
Golden Shores A4
Goodyear 6,258 .... C5
Grand Canyon 1,348 .... C2
Greaterville 15 .... E7
Green Valley 13,231 .... D7
Greer 385 .... F4
Gu Achi 339 .... C6
Hackberry 250 .... B3
Happy Jack 50 .... D4
Hayden 909 .... E5
Heber 1,581 .... E4
Hereford 10 .... E7
Higley 500 .... D5
Hillside 100 .... B4
Hilltop 9 .... F6
Holbrook▲ 4,686 .... E4
Hotevilla 869 .... E3
Houck 900 .... F3
Huachuca City 1,782 .... E7
Humboldt 787 .... C4
Indian Wells 150 .... E3
Inspiration 500 .... D5
Iron Springs 175 .... C4
Jacob Lake 16 .... C2
Jeddito 20 .... E3
Jerome 403 .... C4
Joseph City 650 .... E4
Kaibito 641 .... D2
Katherine 102 .... A3
Kayenta 4,372 .... E2
Keams Canyon 393 .... E3
Kearny 2,262 .... E5
Kingman▲ 12,722 .... A3
Kirkland 100 .... C4
Klagetoh 200 .... F3
Klondyke 86 .... E6
Kohls Ranch 100 .... D4
Komatke 1,116 .... C5
Kykotsmovi 600 .... E3
Lake Havasu City 24,363 .... A4
Lake Montezuma 1,841 .... D4
Lakeside 1,333 .... E4
Laveen 800 .... C5
Lees Ferry 10 .... D2
Leupp 857 .... E3
Liberty 150 .... C5
Linden 50 .... E4
Litchfield Park 3,303 .... C5
Littlefield 40 .... B2
Lukachukai 113 .... F2
Lukeville 50 .... C7
Lupton 250 .... F3
Madera Canyon 75 .... E7
Mammoth 1,845 .... E6
Many Farms 1,294 .... F2
Marana 2,187 .... D6
Marble Canyon 6 .... D2
Maricopa 750 .... C5
Maverick 50 .... F5
Mayer 810 .... C4
McNary 355 .... F4
McNeal 100 .... F7
Mesa 288,091 .... D5
Miami 2,018 .... E5
Mobile 100 .... C5
Moccasin 150 .... C2
Moenkopi 924 .... D2
Morenci 1,799 .... F5
Mormon Lake 20 .... D4
Morristown 400 .... C5
Mount Lemmon 400 .... E6
Mount Trumbull 14 .... B2
Naco 750 .... E7
Navajo 100 .... F3
Nelson 39 .... B3
Nogales▲ 19,489 .... E7
North Rim 50 .... C2
Nutrioso 500 .... F5
Oatman 175 .... A3
Olberg 65 .... D5
Oracle 3,043 .... E6
Oro Valley 6,670 .... E6
Overgaard 750 .... E4
Page 6,598 .... D2
Palo Verde 500 .... C5
Paradise 15 .... F7
Paradise Valley 11,671 .... D5
Parker 2,897 .... A4
Parks 175 .... C3
Patagonia 888 .... E7
Paul Spur 34 .... F7
Paulden 350 .... C4
Payson 8,377 .... D4
Peach Springs 787 .... B3
Pearce 700 .... F7
Peoria 50,618 .... C5
Peridot 957 .... E5
Petrified Forest 80 .... F3
Phoenix (cap.)▲
983,403 .... C5
Picacho 850 .... D6
Pima 1,725 .... F6
Pine 800 .... D4
Pinedale 400 .... E4
Pinetop 1,527 .... F4
Pinon 468 .... E2
Pisinimo 187 .... C6
Plantsite F5
Polacca 1,108 .... E3
Pomerene 365 .... E6
Portal 72 .... F7
Poston 480 .... A4
Prescott▲ 26,455 .... C4
Prescott Valley 8,858 .... C4
Quartzsite 1,876 .... A5
Queen Creek 2,667 .... D5
Quijotoa 200 .... C6
Randolph 350 .... D6
Red Rock 250 .... D6
Rillito 400 .... D6
Rimrock 217 .... D4
Rio Rico 1,407 .... E7
Riverside Stage Stop 418 .... D5
Riviera (Riviera-
Bullhead City) A3
Roll 700 .... A6
Roosevelt 125 .... D5
Sacaton 1,452 .... D5
Safford▲ 7,359 .... F6
Sahuarita 200 .... E7
Saint David 1,468 .... E7
Saint Johns▲ 3,294 .... F4
Saint Michaels 1,119 .... F3
Salome 800 .... B5
San Carlos 2,918 .... E5
Sanders 900 .... F3
San Luis 4,212 .... A6
San Manuel 4,009 .... E6
San Simon 400 .... F6
Sasabe 50 .... D7
Scottsdale 130,069 .... D5
Second Mesa 929 .... E3
Sedona 7,720 .... D4
Seligman 510 .... B3
Sells 2,750 .... D7
Sentinel 40 .... B6
Shonto 710 .... E2
Show Low 5,019 .... F4
Shungopavy
(Shongopovi) 570 .... E3
Sierra Vista 32,983 .... E7
Silver Bell 900 .... D6
Skull Valley 250 .... C4
Snowflake 3,510 .... E4
Solomon 700 .... F6
Somerton 5,282 .... A6
Sonoita 220 .... E7
South Tucson 5,093 .... D6
Springerville 1,802 .... F4
Stanfield 150 .... C6
Stargo 1,038 .... F5
Steamboat 100 .... F3
Sun City 38,126 .... C5
Supai 423 .... C2
Superior 3,468 .... D5
Surprise 7,122 .... C5
Tacna 950 .... B6
Tanque Verde 850 .... E6
Taylor 2,418 .... E4
Teec Nos Pos 317 .... F2
Tempe 141,865 .... D5
Temple Bar 84 .... A2
Thatcher 3,763 .... F6
Tolleson 4,434 .... C5
Tombstone 1,220 .... F7
Tonalea 125 .... E2
Tonopah 54 .... B5
Tonto Basin 250 .... D5
Topawa 500 .... D7
Topock 325 .... A4
Tortilla Flat 37 .... D5
Tsaile 1,043 .... F2
Tubac 140 .... E7
Tuba City 7,323 .... D2
Tucson▲ 405,390 .... D6
Tumacacori 100 .... E7
Vail 175 .... E6
Valentine 120 .... B3
Valley Farms 240 .... D6
Vernon 75 .... F4
Vicksburg 16 .... B5
Waddell 100 .... C5
Wellton 1,066 .... A6
Wenden 400 .... B5
West Yuma A6
Whiteriver 3,775 .... E5
Why 65 .... C6
Wickenburg 4,515 .... C5
Wikieup 150 .... B4
Willcox 3,122 .... F6
Williams 2,532 .... C3
Window Rock 3,306 .... F3
Winkelman 676 .... E6
Winona 25 .... D3
Winslow 8,190 .... E3
Wintersburg 400 .... B5
Wittmann 600 .... C5
Woodruff 280 .... E4
Yarnell 800 .... C4
Yava 40 .... C4
Young 500 .... D4
Youngtown 2,542 .... C5
Yucca 250 .... A4
Yuma▲ 54,923 .... A6

OTHER FEATURES

Agassiz (peak) D3
Agua Fria (riv.) C5
Alamo (lake) B4
Apache (lake) D5
Aquarius (range) B4
Aravaipa (creek) E6
Aubrey (cliffs) B3
Baboquivari (mts.) D7
Baker Butte (mt.) D4
Balakai (mesa) F3
Baldy (peak) F5
Bartlett (dam) D5
Bartlett (res.) D5
Big Chino Wash (dry riv.) C4
Big Horn (mts.) B5
Big Sandy (riv.) B4
Bill Williams (riv.) B4
Black (mesa) E2
Black (mts.) A3
Black (riv.) E5
Blue (riv.) F5
Bouse Wash (dry riv.) A4
Buckskin (mts.) B4
Burro (creek) B4
Canyon (lake) D5
Canyon de Chelly Nat'l Mon. F2
Carrizo (creek) E4
Carrizo (mts.) F2
Casa Grande Ruins Nat'l Mon. D6
Castle Dome (mts.) A5
Cataract (creek) C3
Centennial Wash (dry riv.) B5
Cerbat (mts.) A3
Cherry (creek) E4
Chevelon (creek) E4
Chinle (creek) F2
Chinle (valley) F2
Chinle Wash (dry riv.) F2
Chino (valley) C3
Chiricahua (mts.) F6
Chiricahua Nat'l Mon. F6
Chocolate (mts.) A5
Clear (creek) D4
Coconino (plat.) C3
Cocopah Ind. Res. A6
Colorado (riv.) A5
Colorado River Ind. Res. A5
Coolidge (dam) E5
Copper (mts.) B6
Corn (creek) E3
Coronado Nat'l Memorial E7
Cottonwood (cliffs) B3
Cottonwood Wash (dry riv.) E4
Davis (dam) A3
Defiance (plat.) F3
Detrital Wash (dry riv.) A3
Diablo (canyon) D4
Dinnebito Wash (dry riv.) E3
Dot Klish (canyon) E2
Dragoon (mts.) F7
Eagle (creek) F5
East Verde (riv.) D4
Echo (cliffs) D2
Elden (mt.) D3
Fort Apache Ind.Res. E5
Fort Bowie Nat'l Hist. Site F6
Fort Huachuca E7
Fort McDowell Ind. Res. D5
Fort Mohave Ind. Res. A4
Fort Pearce Wash (dry riv.) B2
Fossil (creek) D4
Four Peaks (mt.) D5
Galiuro (mts.) E6
Gila (mts.) A6
Gila (mts.) F5
Gila (riv.) B6
Gila Bend (mts.) B5
Gila Bend Ind. Res. C6
Gila River Ind. Res. C5
Glen Canyon (dam) D2
Glen Canyon Nat'l Rec. Area E1
Gothic (mesa) F2
Government (mt.) C3
Graham (mt.) F6
Grand Canyon Nat'l Park C2
Grand Wash (butte) B2
Grand Wash (riv.) B2
Greens (peak) F4
Growler (mts.) B6
Harcuvar (mts.) B5
Harquahala (mts.) B5
Hassayampa (riv.) C5
Havasu (lake) A4
Havasupai Ind. Res. C2
Hohokam-Pima Nat'l Mon. D5
Hoover (dam) A2
Hopi (buttes) E3
Hopi Ind. Res. E2
Horseshoe (lake) D5
Huachuca (peak) E7
Hualapai (mts.) B4
Hualapai (peak) B3
Hualapai Ind. Res. B3
Hubbell Trading Post
Nat'l Hist. Site F3
Humphreys (peak) D3
Hurricane (cliffs) B2
Imperial (res.) A6
Ives (mesa) E3
Juniper (mts.) C3
Kaibab (plat.) C2
Kaibab Ind. Res. C2
Kaibito (plat.) D2
Kanab (creek) C2
Kanab (plat.) C2
Kendrick (peak) D3
Kitt (peak) D7
Kofa (mts.) B5
Laguna (creek) E2
Laguna (res.) A6
Lake Mead Nat'l Rec. Area A2
Lechuguilla (des.) A6
Lemmon (mt.) E6
Little Colorado (riv.) D3
Lukachukai (mts.) F2
Luke A.F.B. C5
Maple (peak) F5
Marble Canyon Nat'l Mon. D2
Maricopa (mts.) C5
Maricopa Ind. Res. C6
Mazatzal (peak) D4
Mead (lake) A2
Meteor (crater) E3
Miller (peak) E7
Moencopi (plat.) D3
Moenkopi Wash (dry riv.) D2
Mogollon (plat.) D4
Mogollon Rim (cliffs) D4
Mohave (lake) A3
Mohave (mts.) A4
Mohawk (mts.) B6
Montezuma Castle Nat'l Mon. D4
Mormon (lake) D4
Mule (mts.) E7
Navajo (creek) D2
Navajo Ind. Res. D2
Navajo Nat'l Mon. E2
Navajo Ord. Depot D3
O'Leary (peak) D3
Oraibi Wash (dry riv.) E3
Ord (mt.) D5
Organ Pipe Cactus Nat'l Mon. C6
Painted (des.) D2
Painted Desert Section
(Petrified Forest) F3
Painted Rock (dam) C5
Papago Ind. Res. C6
Paria (plat.) D2
Paria (riv.) D1
Parker (dam) A4
Pastora (peak) F2
Peloncillo (mts.) F6
Petrified Forest Nat'l Park F4
Pinal (peak) E5
Pinaleno (mts.) F6
Pink (cliffs) E4
Pipe Spring Nat'l Mon. C2
Pleasant (lake) C5
Plomosa (mts.) A5
Polacca Wash (dry riv.) E3
Powell (lake) D1
Pueblo Colorado Wash
(dry riv.) F3
Puerco (riv.) F3
Quajote Wash (dry riv.) D6
Rainbow (plat.) D2
Rincon (peak) E6
Roof Butte (mt.) F2
Rose (peak) F5
Sacramento Wash (dry riv.) A4
Saguaro (lake) D5
Saguaro Nat'l Park E6
Salt (riv.) D5
Salt River Ind. Res. D5
San Carlos (lake) E5
San Carlos (riv.) E5
San Carlos Ind. Res. E5
Sand Tank (mt.) C6
San Francisco (riv.) F5
San Pedro (riv.) E6
San Simon (riv.) F6
Santa Catalina (mts.) E6
Santa Cruz (riv.) D6
Santa Maria (riv.) B4
Santa Rosa Wash (dry riv.) D6
San Xavier Ind. Res. D6
Sauceda (mts.) C6
Shivwits (plat.) B2
Shonto (plat.) E2
Sierra Ancha (mts.) D5
Sierra Apache (mts.) E5
Silver (creek) E4
Slate (mt.) D3
Sulphur Spring (valley) F6
Sunset Crater Nat'l Mon. D3
Superstition (mts.) D5
Theodore Roosevelt (lake) D5
Tonto (creek) D4
Tonto Nat'l Mon. D5
Trout (creek) B3
Trumbull (mt.) B2
Tumacacori Nat'l Mon. E7
Tuzigoot Nat'l Mon. D4
Tyson Wash (dry riv.) A5
Uinkaret (plat.) B2
Union (mt.) C4
Verde (riv.) D5
Virgin (mts.) B2
Walker (creek) F2
Walnut Canyon Nat'l Mon. D3
White (riv.) E5
Williams A.F.B. D5
Woody (mt.) D3
Wupatki Nat'l Mon. D3
Yuma (des.) A6
Yuma Proving Ground A6
Zuni (riv.) F4

▲County seat.

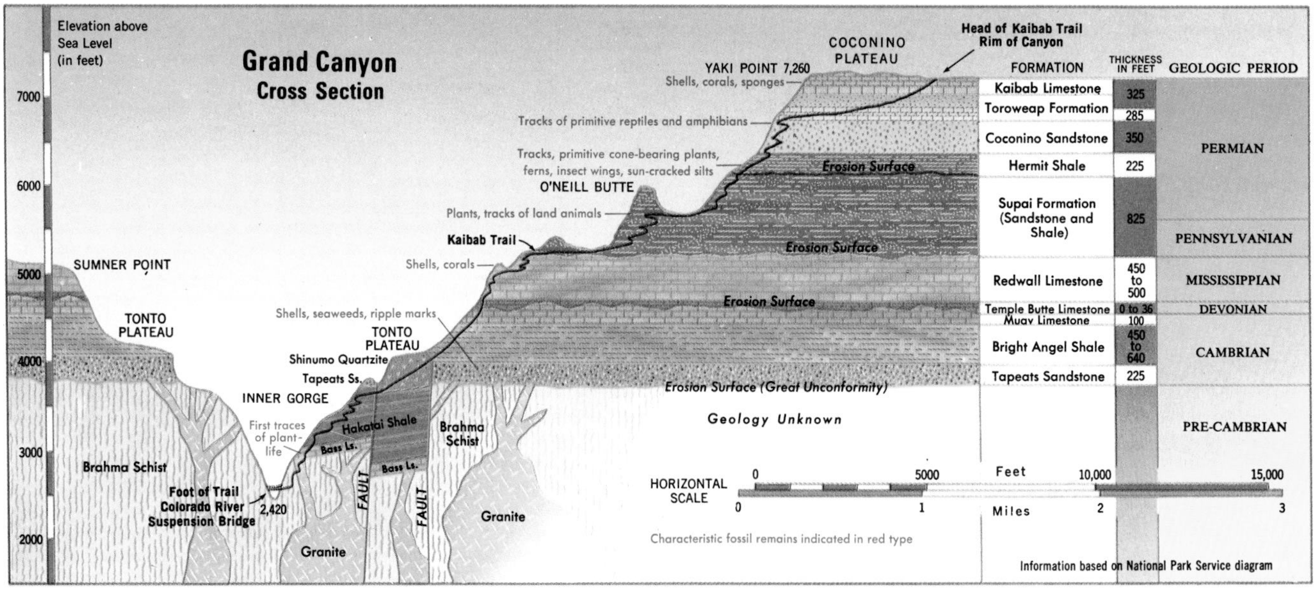
Elevation above
Sea Level
(in feet)
7000
6000
5000
4000
3000
2000
Grand Canyon
Cross Section
SUMNER POINT
TONTO
PLATEAU
YAKI POINT 7,260
Shells, corals, sponges
COCONINO
PLATEAU
Head of Kaibab Trail
Rim of Canyon
Tracks of primitive reptiles and amphibians
Tracks, primitive cone-bearing plants,
ferns, insect wings, sun-cracked silts
O'NEILL BUTTE
Plants, tracks of land animals
Kaibab Trail
Shells, corals
Erosion Surface
Erosion Surface
Erosion Surface
Shells, seaweeds, ripple marks
TONTO
PLATEAU
Shinumo Quartzite
Tapeats Ss.
INNER GORGE
First traces
of plant-
life
Hakatai Shale
Bass Ls.
Bass Ls.
Brahma Schist
Brahma
Schist
Foot of Trail
Colorado River
Suspension Bridge
2,420
FAULT
FAULT
Granite
Granite
Erosion Surface (Great Unconformity)
Geology Unknown
FORMATION
THICKNESS IN FEET
GEOLOGIC PERIOD
Kaibab Limestone
325
Toroweap Formation
285
Coconino Sandstone
350
PERMIAN
Hermit Shale
225
Supai Formation
(Sandstone and
Shale)
825
PENNSYLVANIAN
Redwall Limestone
450
to
500
MISSISSIPPIAN
Temple Butte Limestone
0 to 36
DEVONIAN
Muav Limestone
100
Bright Angel Shale
450
to
640
CAMBRIAN
Tapeats Sandstone
225
PRE-CAMBRIAN
HORIZONTAL
SCALE
0
5000
Feet
10,000
15,000
0
1
Miles
2
3
Characteristic fossil remains indicated in red type
Information based on National Park Service diagram

ARKANSAS

AREA 53,187 sq. mi. (137,754 sq. km.)
POPULATION 2,362,239
CAPITAL Little Rock
LARGEST CITY Little Rock
HIGHEST POINT Magazine Mtn. 2,753 ft. (839 m.)
SETTLED IN 1685
ADMITTED TO UNION June 15, 1836
POPULAR NAME Land of Opportunity
STATE FLOWER Apple Blossom
STATE BIRD Mockingbird

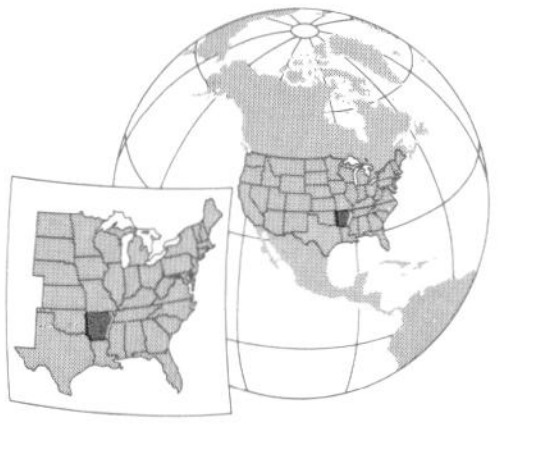

COUNTIES

Arkansas 21,653 H5
Ashley 24,319 G7
Baxter 31,186 F1
Benton 97,499 B1
Boone 28,297 D1
Bradley 11,793 F7
Calhoun 5,826 E6
Carroll 18,654 C1
Chicot 15,713 H7
Clark 21,437 D5
Clay 18,107 K1
Cleburne 19,411 F2
Cleveland 7,781 F6
Columbia 25,691 D7
Conway 19,151 E3
Craighead 68,956 J2
Crawford 42,493 B2
Crittenden 49,939 K3
Cross 19,225 J3
Dallas 9,614 E6
Desha 16,798 H6
Drew 17,369 G6
Faulkner 60,006 F3
Franklin 14,897 C2
Fulton 10,037 G1
Garland 73,397 D4
Grant 13,948 F5
Greene 31,804 J1
Hempstead 21,621 C6
Hot Spring 26,115 E5
Howard 13,569 C5
Independence 31,192 G2
Izard 11,364 G1
Jackson 18,944 H2
Jefferson 85,487 G5
Johnson 18,221 C2
Lafayette 9,643 C7
Lawrence 17,457 H1
Lee 13,053 J4
Lincoln 13,690 G6
Little River 13,966 B6
Logan 20,557 C3
Lonoke 39,268 G4
Madison 11,618 C1
Marion 12,001 E1
Miller 38,467 C7
Mississippi 57,525 K2
Monroe 11,333 H4
Montgomery 7,841 C4
Nevada 10,101 D6
Newton 7,666 D2
Ouachita 30,574 E6
Perry 7,969 E4
Phillips 28,838 J5
Pike 10,086 C5
Poinsett 24,664 J2
Polk 17,347 B5
Pope 45,883 D3
Prairie 9,518 G4
Pulaski 349,660 F4
Randolph 16,558 H1
Saint Francis 30,858 J3
Saline 64,183 E4
Scott 10,205 B4
Searcy 7,841 E2
Sebastian 99,590 B3
Sevier 13,637 B6
Sharp 14,109 G1
Stone 9,775 F2
Union 46,719 E7
Van Buren 14,008 E2
Washington 113,409 B2
White 54,676 G3
Woodruff 9,520 H3
Yell 17,759 D3

CITIES and TOWNS

Adona 146 E3
Alco 200 F2
Alexander 201 F4
Alicia 157 H2
Alix 225 C3
Alleene 200 B6
Allport 188 G4
Alma 2,959 B3
Almyra 311 H5
Alpena 319 D1
Altheimer 972 G5
Altus 433 C3
Amagon 108 H2
Amity 526 D5
Antoine 160 D5
Arkadelphia▲ 10,014 D5
Arkansas City▲ 523 H6
Armorel 500 L2
Ash Flat▲ 667 G1
Ashdown▲ 5,150 B6
Athens C5
Atkins 2,834 E3
Aubrey 204 J4
Augusta▲ 2,759 H3
Austin 235 G4
Avoca 269 B1
Bald Knob 2,653 G3
Banks 88 F6
Barling 4,078 B3
Bassett 199 K2
Bates 9,187 B4
Batesville▲ 8,263 G2
Bauxite 412 F4
Bay 1,660 J2
Bearden 1,021 E6
Beaver 57 C1
Beebe 4,455 G3
Beedville 183 H3
Bella Vista 9,083 B1
Bellefonte 361 D1
Belleville 390 D3
Ben Lomond 157 B6
Benton▲ 18,177 E4
Bentonville▲ 11,257 B1
Bergman 324 E1
Berryville▲ 3,212 C1
Bethel Heights 281 B1
Bethesda 285 G2
Big Flat 93 F1
Bigelow 340 E3
Biggers 337 J1
Birdsong 104 K3
Birta D3
Biscoe 486 H4
Black Oak 277 K2
Black Rock 736 H1
Black Springs 97 C5
Blevins 253 C6
Blue Eye 38 D1
Blue Mountain 146 C3
Bluff City 227 D6
Blytheville▲ 22,906 L2
Bodcaw 161 D6
Bonanza 520 B3
Bono 1,220 J2
Booneville▲ 3,804 C3
Bradford 874 G3
Bradley 585 C7
Branch 299 C3
Brickeys J4
Brinkley 4,234 H4
Brookland 919 J2
Bryant 5,269 F4
Buckner 325 D7
Bull Shoals 1,534 E1
Burdette 148 L2
Cabot 8,319 F4
Caddo Valley 389 D5
Caldwell 334 J3
Cale 70 D6
Calico Rock 938 F1
Calion 558 E7
Camden▲ 14,380 E6
Cammack Village 828 E4
Campbell Station 247 H2
Canfield 365 C7
Caraway 1,178 K2
Carlisle 2,253 G4
Carthage 452 E5
Casa 200 D3
Cash 214 J2
Cass 225 C2
Casscoe 297 H4
Caulksville 224 C3
Cave City 1,503 G2
Cave Springs 465 B1
Cedarville 375 B2
Center Point C5
Centerton 491 B1
Centerville 300 D3
Central City 419 B3
Charleston▲ 2,128 B3
Cherokee Village (Cherokee Village-Hidden Valley) 4,416 G1
Cherry Hill 250 B4
Cherry Valley 659 J3
Chester 125 B2
Chidester 489 D6
Clarendon▲ 2,072 H4
Clarkedale 300 K3
Clarksville▲ 5,833 D3
Cleveland E3
Clinton▲ 2,213 F2
Coal Hill 912 C3
College City 339 J1
Collins G6
Colt 334 J3
Columbus 265 C6
Concord 262 G2
Conway▲ 26,481 F3
Cord 250 H2
Corinth 63 C3
Corning▲ 3,323 J1
Cotter 867 E1
Cotton Plant 1,150 H3
Cove 346 B5
Coy 142 G4
Crawfordsville 617 K3
Crossett 6,282 G7
Crystal Springs 215 D5
Curtis 300 D6
Cushman 428 G2
Daisy 122 C5
Dalark E5
Damascus 246 F3
Danville▲ 1,585 D3
Dardanelle▲ 3,722 D3
Datto 120 J1
De Queen▲ 4,633 B5
De Valls Bluff▲ 702 H4
De Witt▲ 3,553 H5
Decatur 918 A1
Delaplaine 146 J1
Delight 311 C5
Dell 258 K2
Denning 206 C3
Dermott 4,715 H7
Des Arc▲ 2,001 G4
Diamond City 601 E1
Diaz 1,363 H2
Dierks 1,263 B5
Donaldson 300 E5
Dover 1,055 D3
Dryden J2
Dumas 5,520 H6
Dyer 502 B3
Dyess 466 K2
Earle 3,393 K3
East Camden 783 E6
Edmondson 286 K3
El Dorado▲ 23,146 E7
Elaine 846 J5
Elkins 692 C1
Elm Springs 893 B1
Emerson 317 D7
Emmet 446 D6
England 3,351 G4
Enola 179 F3
Eudora 3,155 H7
Eureka Springs▲ 1,900 C1
Evening Shade 328 G1
Everton 150 E1
Fargo 140 H4
Farmington 1,322 B1
Fayetteville▲ 42,099 B1
Felsenthal 95 F7
Fifty-Six 156 F2
Fisher 245 J2
Flippin 1,006 E1
Fordyce▲ 4,729 F6
Foreman 1,267 B6
Formosa 224 E3
Forrest City▲ 13,364 J3
Fort Smith▲ 72,798 B3
Fouke 634 C7
Fountain Hill 195 G7
Franklin 205 G1
Fredonia (Biscoe) 484 H4
Friendship 160 E5
Fulton 269 C6
Garfield 308 C1
Garland City 415 C7
Garner 191 G3
Gassville 1,167 F1
Gateway 65 C1
Genoa 350 C7
Gentry 1,726 A1
Georgetown 126 G3
Gillett 883 H5
Gillham 210 B5
Gilmore 331 K3
Glenwood 1,354 C5
Goodwin 225 J4
Goshen 589 C1
Gosnell 3,783 K2
Gould 1,470 G6
Grady 586 G5
Grannis 507 B5
Gravelly 300 C4
Gravette 1,412 B1
Green Forest 2,050 D1
Greenbrier 2,130 F3
Greenland 757 B1
Greenway 212 K1
Greenwood▲ 3,984 B3
Greers Ferry 724 F2
Griffithville 237 G3
Grubbs 528 H2
Guion 93 G2
Gum Springs 157 D5
Gurdon 2,199 D6
Guy 241 F3
Hackett 490 B3
Halley H6
Hamburg▲ 3,098 G7
Hampton▲ 1,562 F6
Hardy 538 H1
Harrell 258 F7
Harrisburg▲ 1,943 J2
Harrison▲ 9,922 D1
Hartford 721 B3
Hartman 498 C3
Haskell 1,342 E4
Hatfield 414 B5
Havana 358 D3
Haynes 268 J4
Hazen 1,668 G4
Heber Springs▲ 5,628 G2
Hector 478 E3
Helena▲ 7,491 J4
Hensley 500 F4
Hermitage 639 F7
Hickory Ridge 436 J3

Agriculture, Industry and Resources

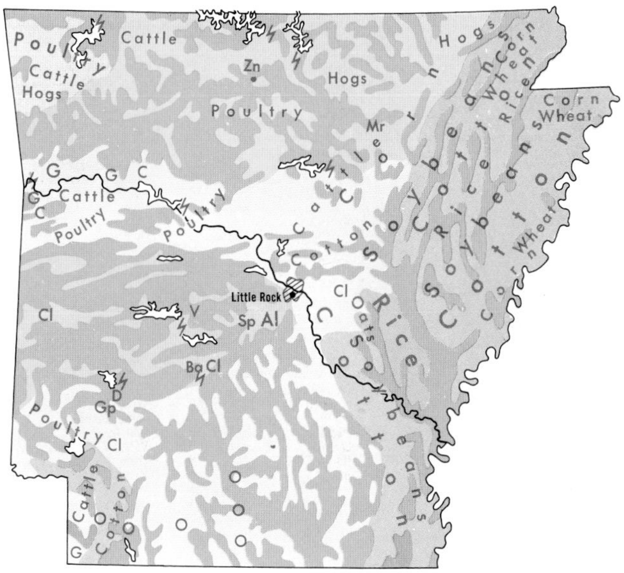
Poultry
Cattle
Hogs
Zn
Corn
Wheat
Rice
Mr
Soybeans
Cotton
G
C
Little Rock
Sp Al
Cl
V
Oats
Ba Cl
D
Gp

DOMINANT LAND USE

Fruit and Mixed Farming
Specialized Cotton
Cotton, General Farming
Rice, General Farming
General Farming, Livestock, Truck Farming, Cotton
Forests
Swampland, Limited Agriculture

MAJOR MINERAL OCCURRENCES

Al	Bauxite	Gp	Gypsum
Ba	Barite	Mr	Marble
C	Coal	O	Petroleum
Cl	Clay	Sp	Soapstone
D	Diamonds	V	Vanadium
G	Natural Gas	Zn	Zinc

Water Power
Major Industrial Areas

(continued)

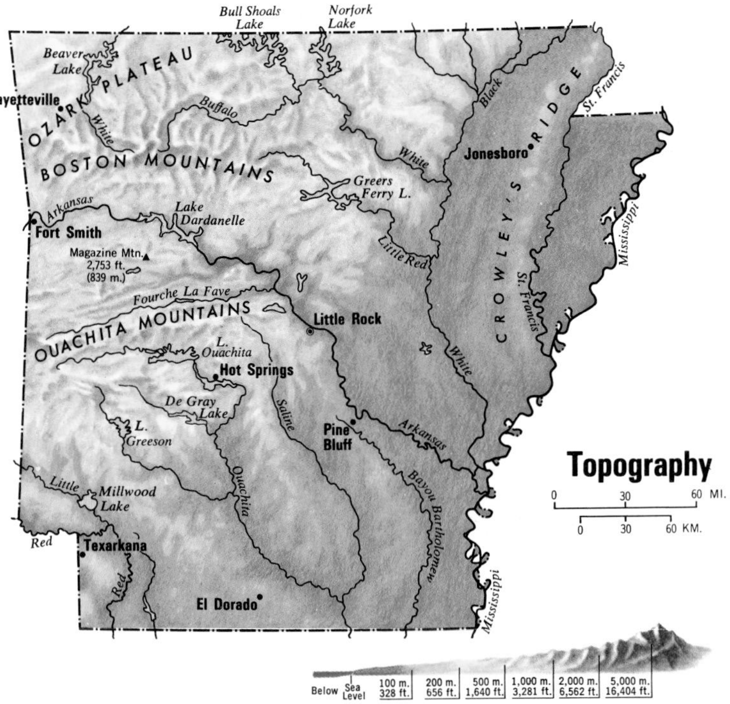
Topography
Bull Shoals Lake
Norfork Lake
Beaver Lake
Fayetteville
OZARK PLATEAU
BOSTON MOUNTAINS
Buffalo
White
Black
St. Francis
CROWLEY'S RIDGE
Jonesboro
Greers Ferry L.
Arkansas
Lake Dardanelle
Fort Smith
Magazine Mtn. 2,753 ft. (839 m.)
Little Red
Mississippi
Fourche La Fave
OUACHITA MOUNTAINS
Little Rock
L. Ouachita
Hot Springs
De Gray Lake
L. Greeson
Saline
Pine Bluff
Little
Millwood Lake
Red
Texarkana
Ouachita
Bayou Bartholomew
El Dorado
0 30 60 MI.
0 30 60 KM.
Below Sea Level
100 m. 328 ft.
200 m. 656 ft.
500 m. 1,640 ft.
1,000 m. 3,281 ft.
2,000 m. 6,562 ft.
5,000 m. 16,404 ft.

Higden 92 .... F2
Higginson 255 .... G3
Highfill 84 .... B1
Hindsville 69 .... C1
Holly Grove 675 .... H4
Hon 250 .... B4
Hope▲ 9,643 .... C6
Hopper C5
Horatio 793 .... B6
Horseshoe Bend 2,239 .... G1
Hot Springs National Park▲ 32,462 .... D4
Houston 149 .... E3
Hoxie 2,676 .... H1
Hughes 1,810 .... J4
Humnoke 311 .... G4
Humphrey 743 .... G5
Hunter 137 .... H3
Huntington 715 .... B3
Huntsville▲ 1,605 .... C1
Huttig 831 .... F7
Imboden 616 .... H1
Jacksonport 264 .... H2
Jacksonville 29,101 .... F4
Jamestown G2
Jasper▲ 332 .... D1
Jefferson 250 .... F5
Jericho 210 .... K3
Jerusalem 300 .... E3
Jessieville 350 .... D4
Johnson 599 .... B1
Joiner 645 .... K3
Jones Mills 210 .... E5
Jonesboro▲ 46,535 .... J2
Judsonia 1,915 .... G3
Junction City 674 .... E7
Keiser 805 .... K2
Kelso H6
Kensett 1,741 .... G3
Keo 154 .... G4
Kibler 931 .... B3
Kingsland 395 .... F6
Kirby 800 .... C5
Knobel 317 .... J1
Knoxville 239 .... D3
Ladelle G7
Lafe 315 .... J1
Lake City▲ 1,833 .... K2
Lake Frances B1
Lake View 526 .... J5
Lake Village▲ 2,791 .... H7
Lakeview 485 .... E1
Lamar 768 .... D3
Lavaca 1,253 .... B3
Lawson 250 .... F7
Leachville 1,743 .... K2
Lead Hill 283 .... D1
Leola 476 .... E5
Lepanto 2,033 .... K2
Leslie 446 .... E2
Letona 218 .... G3
Lewisville▲ 1,424 .... C7
Lexa 295 .... J4
Lincoln 1,460 .... B2
Little Flock 944 .... B1
Little Rock (cap.)▲ 175,795 .... F4
Lockesburg 608 .... B6
London 825 .... D3
Lonoke▲ 4,022 .... G4
Lonsdale 127 .... E4
Louann 158 .... E7
Lowell 1,224 .... B1

Lundell 250 .... H5
Luxora 1,338 .... K2
Lynn 299 .... H2
Mabelvale 350 .... F4
Madison 1,263 .... J4
Magazine 799 .... C3
Magness 158 .... H2
Magnet Cove 230 .... E5
Magnolia▲ 11,151 .... D7
Malvern▲ 9,256 .... E5
Mammoth Spring 1,097 .... G1
Manila 2,635 .... K2
Mansfield 1,018 .... B3
Marianna▲ 5,910 .... J4
Marie 129 .... K2
Marion▲ 4,391 .... K3
Marked Tree 3,100 .... K2
Marmaduke 1,164 .... K1
Marshall▲ 1,318 .... E2
Marvell 1,545 .... J4
Mayflower 1,415 .... F4
Maynard 354 .... J1
McCaskill 75 .... C6
McCrory 1,971 .... H3
McDougal 208 .... K1
McGehee 4,997 .... H6
McNab 95 .... C6
McNeil 686 .... D7
McRae 669 .... G3
Melbourne▲ 1,562 .... G1
Mellwood 250 .... H5
Mena▲ 5,475 .... B4
Menifee 355 .... E3
Midland 220 .... B3
Mineral Springs 1,004 .... C6
Minturn 124 .... H2
Mitchell 513 .... G1
Mitchellville 618 .... H6
Monette 1,115 .... K2
Monroe 250 .... H4
Monticello▲ 8,116 .... G6
Montrose 528 .... H7
Moorefield 160 .... G2
Moro 287 .... H4
Morrilton▲ 6,551 .... E3
Morrison Bluff 84 .... D3
Moscow 325 .... G5
Mount Holly 250 .... E7
Mount Ida▲ 775 .... C4
Mount Pleasant 422 .... G2
Mount Vernon 192 .... F3
Mountain Home▲ 9,027 .... F1
Mountain Pine 866 .... D4
Mountain View▲ 2,439 .... F2
Mountainburg 488 .... B2
Mulberry 1,448 .... B2
Murfreesboro▲ 1,542 .... C5
Nashville▲ 4,639 .... C6
Newark 1,159 .... H2
Newhope 300 .... C5
New Jenny Lind 250 .... B3
Newport▲ 7,459 .... H2
Nimmons 96 .... K1
Noble Lake 250 .... G5
Norfork 394 .... F1
Norman 382 .... C5
Norphlet 706 .... E7
Norristown 625 .... D3
North Crossett 3,358 .... G7
North Little Rock 61,741 .... F4
Norvell K3
O'Kean 291 .... J1

Oak Grove 231 .... C1
Oden 126 .... C4
Ogden 264 .... B6
Oil Trough 208 .... G2
Okolona 113 .... D5
Ola 1,090 .... D3
Omaha 207 .... D1
Oppelo 643 .... E3
Osceola▲ 8,930 .... K2
Oxford 562 .... G1
Ozan 69 .... C6
Ozark▲ 3,330 .... C3
Palestine 711 .... J4
Pangburn 630 .... G3
Paragould▲ 18,540 .... J1
Paraloma B6
Paris▲ 3,674 .... C3
Parkdale 393 .... H7
Parkin 1,847 .... J3
Parks 600 .... B4
Patterson 445 .... H3
Pea Ridge 1,620 .... B1
Peach Orchard 197 .... J1
Pearcy 400 .... D5
Perla 145 .... E5
Perry 228 .... E3
Perrytown 248 .... C6
Perryville▲ 1,141 .... E3
Piggott▲ 3,777 .... K1
Pindall 135 .... E1
Pine Bluff▲ 57,140 .... F5
Pineville 220 .... F1
Piney 2,500 .... D3
Plainview 685 .... D4
Pleasant Plains 256 .... G2
Plumerville 832 .... E3
Pocahontas▲ 6,151 .... H1
Pollard 229 .... K1
Poplar Grove 300 .... J4
Portia 521 .... H1
Portland 560 .... H7
Pottsville 984 .... D3
Powhatan 51 .... H1
Poyen 303 .... E5
Prairie Grove 1,761 .... B2
Prattsville 251 .... F5
Prescott▲ 3,673 .... D6
Princeton E6
Pruitt D1
Pyatt 185 .... E1
Quitman 632 .... F3
Ratcliff 180 .... C3
Ratio 250 .... J5
Ravenden 330 .... H1
Ravenden Springs 131 .... H1
Reader 56 .... D6
Readland 225 .... H7
Rector 2,268 .... K1
Redfield 1,082 .... F5
Reed 355 .... H6
Rena B3
Reyno 467 .... J1
Rison▲ 1,258 .... F6
Rivervale 225 .... K2
Rockport 388 .... E5
Roe 135 .... H4
Rogers 24,692 .... B1
Rondo 283 .... J4
Rose Bud 156 .... F3
Rosston 262 .... D6
Russell 180 .... G3
Russellville▲ 21,260 .... D3

Saint Charles 169 .... H5
Saint Francis 201 .... K1
Saint Paul 88 .... C2
Salado 250 .... G2
Salem▲ 1,474 .... G1
Salesville 374 .... F1
Saratoga C6
Scottsville 241 .... D3
Scranton 218 .... C3
Searcy▲ 15,180 .... G3
Sedgwick 86 .... J2
Shannon Hills 1,755 .... F4
Sheridan▲ 3,098 .... F5
Sherrill 55 .... F5
Sherwood 18,893 .... F4
Shirley 363 .... F2
Sidney 271 .... G1
Siloam Springs 8,151 .... B1
Smackover 2,232 .... E7

Smale H4
Smithville 86 .... H1
Snow Lake H5
Snyder 700 .... G7
South Lead Hill 96 .... D1
Sparkman 553 .... E6
Springdale 29,941 .... B1
Springtown B1
Stamps 2,478 .... D7
Star City▲ 2,138 .... G6
Stephens 1,137 .... E7
Steprock 600 .... G3
Strawberry 273 .... H2
Strong 624 .... F7
Stuttgart▲ 10,420 .... H4
Subiaco 538 .... C3
Success 170 .... J1
Sulphur Rock 356 .... H2
Sulphur Springs 523 .... B1

Summit 480 .... E1
Sunset 571 .... K3
Swan Lake G5
Sweet Home 350 .... F4
Swifton 830 .... H2
Taylor 621 .... D7
Texarkana▲ 22,631 .... C7
Thornton 502 .... F6
Tichnor 350 .... H5
Tillar 221 .... H6
Tinsman 69 .... F6
Tollette 316 .... C6
Tontitown 460 .... B1
Traskwood 488 .... E5
Trumann 6,304 .... J2
Tucker 2,020 .... G5
Tuckerman 2,078 .... H2
Tull 313 .... E5
Tupelo 208 .... H3

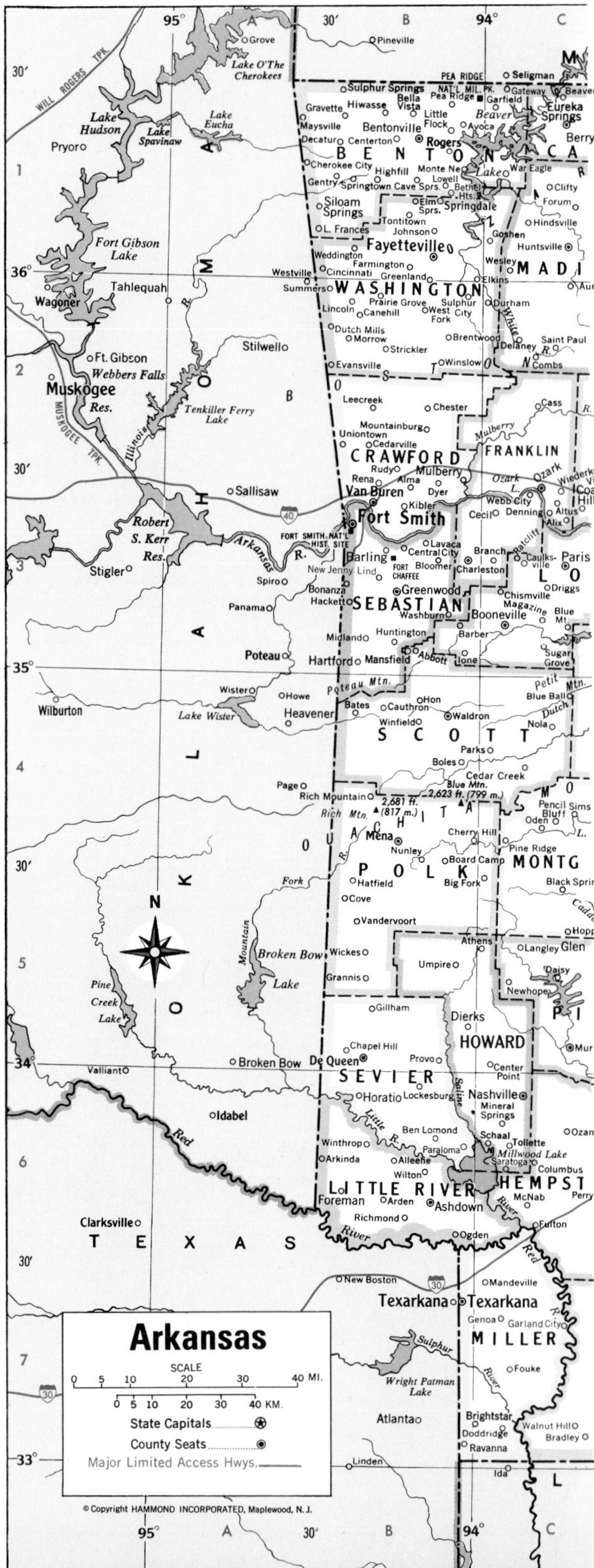
Arkansas
SCALE
0 5 10 20 30 40 MI.
0 5 10 20 30 40 KM.
State Capitals
County Seats
Major Limited Access Hwys.
95°
94°
30′
36°
35°
34°
33°
A
B
C
Grove
Pineville
Lake O'The Cherokees
WILL ROGERS TPK.
Seligman
PEA RIDGE NAT'L MIL. PK.
Sulphur Springs
Gravette
Hiwasse
Bella Vista
Pea Ridge
Garfield
Gateway
Beaver
Eureka Springs
Lake Hudson
Lake Spavinaw
Lake Eucha
Pryor
Maysville
Bentonville
Little Flock
Avoca
Decatur
Centerton
Rogers
Berry
B E N T O N
C A
Cherokee City
Highfill
Monte Ne
Lowell
Gentry
Springtown
Cave Sprs.
Bethel Hts.
War Eagle
Clifty
Siloam Springs
Elm Sprs.
Springdale
Forum
Tontitown
Johnson
Hindsville
L. Frances
Fayetteville
Goshen
Huntsville
Fort Gibson Lake
Weddington
Farmington
Wesley
MADI
Westville
Cincinnati
Greenland
Elkins
Aurora
Tahlequah
Summers
WASHINGTON
Wagoner
Prairie Grove
Sulphur City
Durham
Lincoln
Canehill
West Fork
White
Dutch Mills
Morrow
Strickler
Brentwood
Delaney
Saint Paul
Stilwell
Ft. Gibson
Webbers Falls
Evansville
Winslow
Combs
Muskogee
Res.
Tenkiller Ferry Lake
MUSKOGEE TPK.
Leecreek
Chester
Cass
Mountainburg
Uniontown
Cedarville
Mulberry
FRANKLIN
CRAWFORD
Rudy
Alma
Ozark
Wiederkehr Vill.
Coal Hill
Rena
Dyer
Van Buren
Kibler
Webb City
Sallisaw
Fort Smith
Cecil
Denning
Altus
Alix
Robert S. Kerr Res.
Arkansas
FORT SMITH NAT'L HIST. SITE
Lavaca
Central City
Branch
Caulksville
Paris
Barling
FORT CHAFFEE
Bloomer
Charleston
Stigler
New Jenny Lind
LO
Spiro
Bonanza
Greenwood
Driggs
Hackett
SEBASTIAN
Chismville
Panama
Washburn
Booneville
Magazine Mt.
Blue Mt.
Midland
Huntington
Barber
Poteau
Hartford
Mansfield
Abbott
Sugar Grove
Ione
Poteau Mtn.
Petit Jean Mtn.
Wister
Howe
Hon
Blue Ball
Wilburton
Lake Wister
Heavener
Bates
Cauthron
Waldron
Dutch
Winfield
Nola
SCOTT
Parks
Boles
Cedar Creek
Page
Rich Mountain
Blue Mtn. 2,623 ft. (799 m.)
Rich Mtn. 2,681 ft. (817 m.)
Pencil Bluff
Sims
Oden
Mena
Cherry Hill
Nunley
Board Camp
Pine Ridge
MONTG
POLK
Hatfield
Big Fork
Black Springs
Cove
Vandervoort
Caddo
Hopper
Athens
Langley
Glen
Fork
Broken Bow Lake
Wickes
Umpire
Mountain
Grannis
Daisy
Newhope
Pine Creek Lake
Gillham
Dierks
HOWARD
Mur
Chapel Hill
Broken Bow
De Queen
Provo
Center Point
Valliant
SEVIER
Horatio
Lockesburg
Nashville
Mineral Springs
Saline
Idabel
Ben Lomond
Schaal
Tollette
Ozan
Winthrop
Paraloma
Millwood Lake
Saratoga
Columbus
Arkinda
Alleene
Wilton
LITTLE RIVER
HEMPST
Foreman
Arden
Ashdown
McNab
Perry
Richmond
Clarksville
Red
Fulton
T E X A S
Ogden
New Boston
Mandeville
Texarkana
Genoa
Garland City
MILLER
Sulphur
Fouke
Wright Patman Lake
Atlanta
Brightstar
Doddridge
Walnut Hill
Bradley
Ravenna
Linden
Ida
L
© Copyright HAMMOND INCORPORATED, Maplewood, N.J.

Turrell 988 ... K3
Tyronza 858 ... K3
Ulm 193 ... H4
Umpire ... B5
Uniontown 600 ... B2
Urbana 500 ... E7
Valley Springs 200 ... D1
Van Buren▲ 14,979 ... B3
Vandervoort 111 ... B5
Vanndale 310 ... J3
Victoria 110 ... K2
Vilonia 1,133 ... F3
Vimy Ridge 600 ... F4
Viola 320 ... G1
Wabash 300 ... J5
Wabbaseka 332 ... G5
Waldenburg 103 ... J2
Waldo 1,495 ... D7
Waldron▲ 3,024 ... B4
Walnut Ridge▲ 4,388 ... J1
Ward 1,269 ... F3
Warren▲ 6,455 ... F6
Washington 148 ... C6
Watson 282 ... H6
Weiner 655 ... J2
Weldon 106 ... H3
West Crossett 2,019 ... F7
West Fork 1,607 ... B2
West Helena 9,695 ... J4
West Memphis 28,259 ... K3
West Point 146 ... G3
West Ridge 300 ... K2
Western Grove 415 ... D1
Wheatley 413 ... H4
Whelen Springs 116 ... D6
White 3,849 ... G7
White Hall 2,214 ... F5
Wickes 570 ... B5
Widener 381 ... J3
Wiederkehr Village 42 ... C3
Williford 69 ... H1
Willisville 196 ... D7
Wilmar 637 ... G6
Wilmot 1,047 ... G7
Wilson 1,068 ... K2
Wilton 449 ... B6
Winchester 239 ... G6
Winslow 342 ... B2
Winthrop 227 ... B6
Wiseman 327 ... G1
Woodberry ... E6
Woodson 450 ... F4
Wooster 414 ... F3
Wright 1,062 ... F5
Wrightsville-Tafton 1,434 ... F4
Wynne▲ 8,187 ... J3
Yellville▲ 1,181 ... E1
Zinc 91 ... E1

OTHER FEATURES

Arkansas (riv.) ... G5
Arkansas Post Nat'l Mem. ... H6
Bartholomew (bayou) ... G6
Bayou Des Arc (riv.) ... G3
Beaver (lake) ... C1
Black (riv.) ... H2
Blue Mountain (lake) ... C3
Blytheville A.F.B. ... L2
Boston (mts.) ... B2
Buffalo (riv.) ... E2
Bull Shoals (lake) ... D1
Cache (riv.) ... H3
Caddo (riv.) ... C5
Catherine (lake) ... E5
Chinkapin Knob (mt.) ... E2
Conway (mt.) ... F3
Crowley's Ridge (mt.) ... J2
Current (riv.) ... J1
Cypress (bayou) ... F3
Dardanelle (lake) ... D3
De Gray (lake) ... D5
De View (bayou) ... J3
Dutch (creek) ... C4
Erling (lake) ... C7
Fort Smith Nat'l Hist. Site ... B3
Fourche LaFave (riv.) ... D4
Greers Ferry (lake) ... G2
Greeson (lake) ... C5
Hamilton (lake) ... D5
Hot Springs Nat'l Park ... D4
Illinois (bayou) ... D3
L'Anguille (riv.) ... J3
La Grue (bayou) ... H5
Little (riv.) ... B6
Little Missouri (riv.) ... D6
Little Red (riv.) ... G3
Little Rock A.F.B. ... F4
Magazine (mt.) ... C3
Meto (bayou) ... H5
Millwood (lake) ... C6
Mississippi (riv.) ... H7
Mountain Fork (riv.) ... A5
Mulberry (riv.) ... C2
Nebo (mt.) ... D3
Nimrod (lake) ... D4
Norfork (lake) ... F1
Ouachita (lake) ... C4
Ouachita (mts.) ... B4
Ouachita (riv.) ... E7
Ozark (plat.) ... C1
Pea Ridge Nat'l Mil. Park ... B1
Peckerwood (lake) ... G4
Petit Jean (mt.) ... C3
Petit Jean (riv.) ... D3
Pine Bluff Arsenal ... F5
Poteau (mt.) ... B4
Red (riv.) ... C6
Reeves Knob (mt.) ... E2
Saint Francis (riv.) ... J4
Saline (riv.) ... B6
Saline (riv.) ... E5
Seven Devils (res.) ... G6
Spring (riv.) ... H1
Sulphur (riv.) ... B7
Table Rock (lake) ... D1
Tyronza (riv.) ... K2
Wattensaw (bayou) ... G4
White (riv.) ... H5
White Oak (lake) ... D6
Winona (lake) ... E4

▲County seat

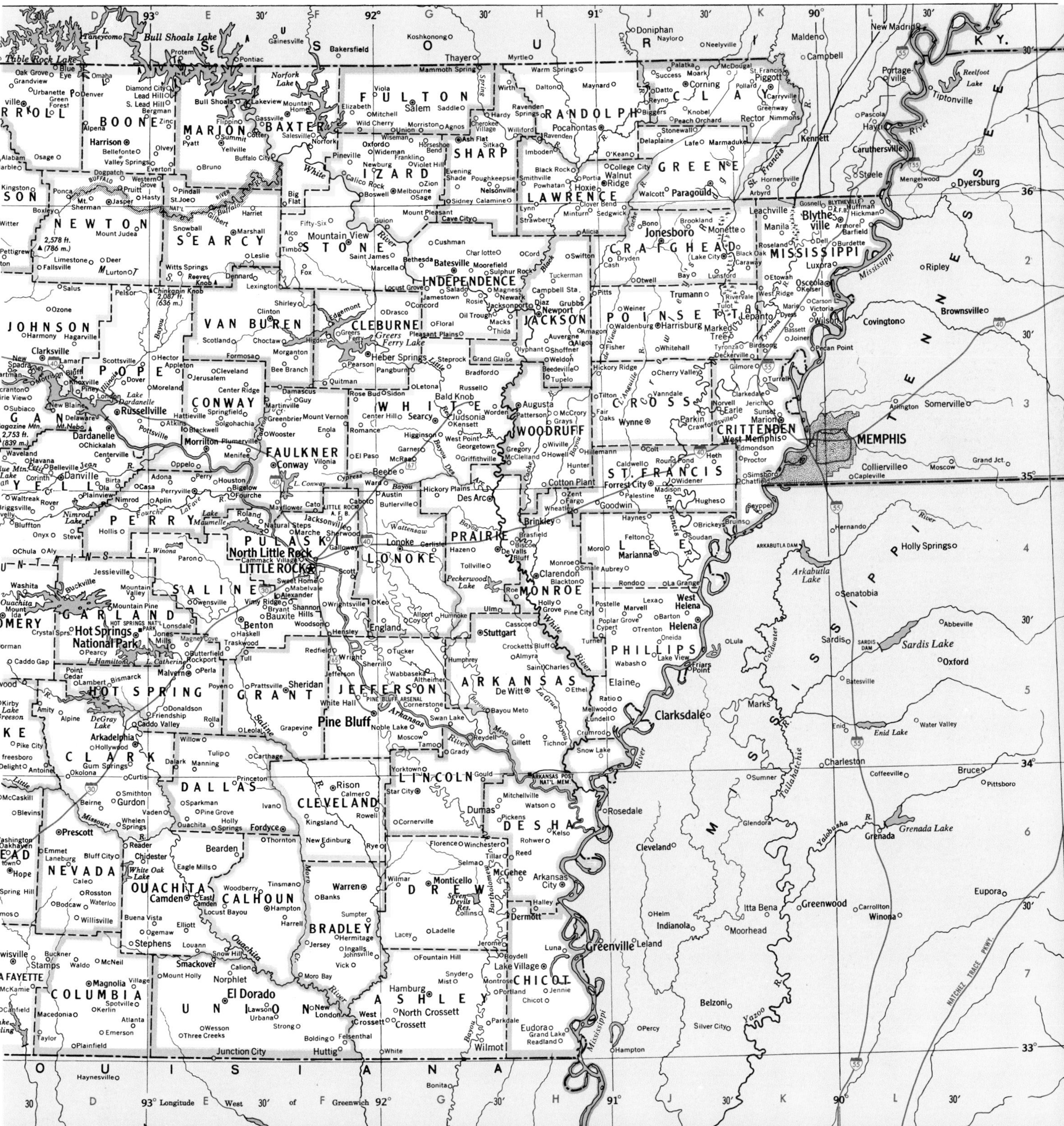
BOONE
MARION
BAXTER
FULTON
RANDOLPH
CLAY
SHARP
IZARD
LAWRENCE
GREENE
NEWTON
SEARCY
STONE
INDEPENDENCE
CRAIGHEAD
MISSISSIPPI
JOHNSON
VAN BUREN
CLEBURNE
JACKSON
POINSETT
POPE
CONWAY
WHITE
WOODRUFF
CROSS
CRITTENDEN
FAULKNER
ST. FRANCIS
PERRY
PULASKI
LONOKE
PRAIRIE
LEE
SALINE
GARLAND
MONROE
PHILLIPS
HOT SPRING
GRANT
JEFFERSON
ARKANSAS
CLARK
DALLAS
CLEVELAND
LINCOLN
DESHA
NEVADA
OUACHITA
CALHOUN
BRADLEY
DREW
COLUMBIA
UNION
ASHLEY
CHICOT
MEMPHIS
LITTLE ROCK
North Little Rock
Pine Bluff
Hot Springs National Park
El Dorado
Jonesboro
Blytheville
MISSOURI
KY.
TENNESSEE
MISSISSIPPI
LOUISIANA
93° Longitude West 30′ of Greenwich 92°
36°
35°
34°
33°

California
SCALE
0 10 20 40 60 80 MI.
0 10 20 40 60 80 KM.
State Capitals
County Seats
Canals
Major Limited Access Hwys.
San Francisco and Vicinity
Sacramento and Vicinity
Los Angeles and Vicinity
OREGON
NEVADA
ARIZONA
MEXICO
PACIFIC OCEAN
Sacramento
San Francisco
Los Angeles
San Diego
Fresno
Lake Tahoe
Mojave Desert
Death Valley National Monument
Lake Mead National Recreation Area
Longitude 119° West of Greenwich 118°
© Copyright HAMMOND INCORPORATED, Maplewood, N. J.

COUNTIES

Alameda 1,279,182 D6
Alpine 1,113 F5
Amador 30,039 E5
Butte 182,120 D4
Calaveras 31,998 E5
Colusa 16,275 C4
Contra Costa 803,732 D6
Del Norte 23,460 B2
El Dorado 125,995 E5
Fresno 667,490 E7
Glenn 24,798 C4
Humboldt 119,118 B3
Imperial 109,303 K1
Inyo 18,281 H7
Kern 543,477 G8
Kings 101,469 E8
Lake 50,631 C4
Lassen 27,598 E3
Los Angeles 8,863,164 G9
Madera 88,090 F6
Marin 230,096 C5
Mariposa 14,302 E6
Mendocino 80,345 B4
Merced 178,403 E6
Modoc 9,678 E2
Mono 9,956 F5
Monterey 355,660 D7
Napa 110,765 C5
Nevada 78,510 E4
Orange 2,410,556 H1
Placer 172,796 E4
Plumas 19,739 E4
Riverside 1,170,413 J1
Sacramento 1,041,219 D5
San Benito 36,697 D7
San Bernardino 1,418,380 J9
San Diego 2,498,016 J1
San Francisco 723,959 J2
San Joaquin 480,628 D5
San Luis Obispo 217,162 E8
San Mateo 649,623 J3
Santa Barbara 369,608 E9
Santa Clara 1,497,577 D6
Santa Cruz 229,734 C6
Shasta 147,036 C3
Sierra 3,318 E4
Siskiyou 43,531 C2
Solano 340,421 D5
Sonoma 388,222 C5
Stanislaus 370,522 D6
Sutter 64,415 D4
Tehama 49,625 C3
Trinity 13,063 B3
Tulare 311,921 G7
Tuolumne 48,456 F5
Ventura 669,016 F9
Yolo 141,092 D5
Yuba 58,228 D4

CITIES and TOWNS

Adelanto 8,517 H9
Alameda 76,459 J2
Alamo 12,277 K2
Albany 16,327 J2
Alhambra 82,106 C10
Alpine 9,695 J11
Alta Loma E10
Altadena 42,658 C10
Alturas▲ 3,231 E2
Amador City 196 C9
Anaheim 266,406 D11
Anderson 8,299 C3
Angels Camp 2,302 E5
Angwin 3,503 C5
Antioch 62,195 L1
Apple Valley 46,079 H9
Aptos 9,061 K4
Arbuckle 1,912 C4
Arcadia 48,290 C10
Arcata 15,197 A3
Arden-Arcade 92,040 B8
Armona 3,122 F7
Arnold 3,788 E5
Aromas 2,275 D7
Arroyo Grande 14,378 E8
Artesia 15,464 C11
Arvin 9,286 G8
Ashland 16,590 K2
Asti 75 C5
Atascadero 23,138 E8
Atherton 7,163 K3
Atwater 22,282 E6
Auberry 1,866 F6
Auburn▲ 10,592 C8
Avalon 2,918 G10
Avenal 9,770 E8
Azusa 41,333 D10
Baker 174,820 J8
Bakersfield▲ 105,611 G8
Baldwin Park 69,330 D10
Banning 20,570 J10
Barstow 21,472 H9
Bayview 1,318 A3
Baywood Park (Baywood Park-Los Osos) 10,933 E8
Beaumont 9,685 J10
Bell 34,365 C11
Bell Gardens 42,355 C11
Bellflower 61,815 C11
Belmont 24,127 J3
Belvedere 2,147 H2
Ben Lomond 7,884 K4
Benicia 24,437 K1
Berkeley 102,724 J2
Bethel Island 2,115 L1
Beverly Hills 31,971 B10
Big Bear City (Sugarloaf Post Office) 4,920 J9
Big Bear Lake 5,351 J9
Big Pine 1,158 G6
Biggs 1,581 D4
Bishop 3,475 G6
Bloomington 15,116 E10
Blue Lake 1,235 B3
Blythe 8,428 L10
Bodfish 1,283 G8
Bolinas 1,098 H1
Boron 2,101 H8
Borrego Springs 2,244 J10
Boulder Creek 6,725 J4
Bowman C7
Brawley 18,923 K11
Brea 32,873 D11
Brentwood 7,563 L2
Bridgeport▲ 525 F5
Brisbane 2,952 J2
Broderick (Broderick-Bryte) 10,194 B8
Bryte (Bryte-Broderick) 10,194 B8
Buellton 3,506 E9
Buena Park 68,784 D11
Burbank 93,643 C10
Burlingame 26,801 J2
Burney 3,423 D3
Buttonwillow 1,301 F8
Cabazon 1,588 J10
Calexico 18,633 K11
California City 5,955 H8
Calipatria 2,690 K10
Calistoga 4,468 C5
Calwa 6,640 F7
Camarillo 52,303 G9
Cambria 5,382 D8
Campbell 36,048 K3
Canoga Park B10
Canyon 7,938 K2
Capistrano Beach 6,168 H10
Capitola 10,171 K4
Cardiff-by-the-Sea 10,054 H10
Carlsbad 63,126 H10
Carmel 4,407 D7
Carmel Valley 4,013 D7
Carmichael 48,702 C8
Carpinteria 13,747 F9
Carson 83,995 C11
Caruthers 1,603 E7
Casitas Springs 1,038 F9
Castro Valley 48,619 K2
Castroville 5,272 D7
Cathedral City 30,085 J10
Cayucos 2,960 E8
Central Valley 4,340 C3
Ceres 26,314 D6
Cerritos 53,240 C11
Chatsworth B10
Chemeketa Park (Chemeketa Park-Redwood Estates) 1,847 K4
Cherryland 11,088 K2
Chester 2,082 D3
Chico 40,079 D4
China Lake 4,275 H8
Chinese Camp 150 E6
Chino 59,682 D10
Chowchilla 5,930 E6
Chula Vista 135,163 J11
Citrus Heights 107,439 C8
Claremont 32,503 D10
Clay 7,317 C9
Clayton 4,325 K2
Clearlake 11,804 C5
Clearlake Oaks 2,419 C4
Cloverdale 4,924 B5
Clovis 50,323 F7
Coachella 16,896 J10
Coalinga 8,212 E7
Colfax 1,306 E4
Colton 40,213 E10
Columbia 1,799 E5
Colusa▲ 4,934 C4
Commerce 12,135 C10
Compton 90,454 C11
Concord 111,348 K1
Corcoran 13,364 F7
Corning 5,870 C4
Corona 76,095 E11
Coronado 26,540 H11
Corralitos 2,513 L4
Corte Madera 8,272 J2
Costa Mesa 96,357 D11
Cotati 5,714 C5
Cottonwood 1,747 C3
Covina 43,207 D10
Crescent City▲ 4,380 A2
Crestline 8,594 H9
Crockett 3,228 J1
Crowley Lake G6
Cudahy 22,817 C11
Culver City 38,793 B10
Cupertino 40,263 K3
Cutler 4,450 F7
Cutten 1,516 A3
Cypress 42,655 D11
Daly City 92,311 H2
Dana Point 31,896 H10
Danville 31,306 K2
Davis 46,209 B8
Death Valley Junction J7
Deer Park 1,825 C5
Del Mar 4,860 H11
Del Rey Oaks 1,661 D7
Del Rosa F10
Delano 22,762 F8
Delhi 3,280 E6
Desert Hot Springs 11,668 J9
Desert View Highlands 2,154 G9
Diamond Springs 2,872 D8
Dinuba 12,743 F7
Dixon 10,401 B9
Dorris 892 D2
Dos Palos 4,196 E6
Downey 91,444 C11
Downieville▲ 500 E4
Duarte 20,688 D10
Dublin 23,229 K2
Dunsmuir 2,129 C2
Durham 4,784 D4
Earlimart 5,881 F8
East Blythe 1,511 L10
East Los Angeles 126,379 C10
Easton 1,877 F7
Edgemont E11
Edison G8
El Cajon 88,693 J11
El Centro▲ 31,384 K11
El Cerrito 4,490 J2
El Dorado 6,395 C8
El Dorado Hills 3,453 C8
El Granada 4,426 H3
El Monte 106,209 D10
El Rio 6,419 F9
El Segundo 15,223 B11
El Toro 62,685 E11
Elk 17,483 B4
Elk Grove 10,959 B9
Emeryville 5,740 J2
Empire D6
Encinitas 55,386 H10
Encino B10
Enterprise C3
Escalon 4,437 E6
Escondido 108,635 J10
Esparto 1,487 C5
Eureka▲ 27,025 A3
Exeter 7,276 F7
Fair Oaks 26,867 C8
Fairfax 6,931 H1
Fairfield▲ 77,211 K1
Fallbrook 22,095 H10
Farmersville 6,235 F7
Felton 5,350 K4
Ferndale 1,331 A3
Fillmore 11,992 G9
Firebaugh 4,429 E7
Florin 24,330 B8
Folsom 29,802 C8
Fontana 87,535 E10
Ford City 3,781 F8
Forest Knolls (Forest Knolls-Lagunitas) H1
Foresthill 1,409 E4
Fort Bragg 6,078 B4
Fortuna 8,788 A3
Foster City 28,176 J2
Fountain Valley 53,691 D11
Fowler 3,208 F7
Frazier Park 2,201 F9
Freedom 8,361 L4
Fremont 173,339 K3
Fresno▲ 354,202 F7
Fullerton 114,144 D11
Galt 8,889 C9
Garden Grove 143,050 D11
Gardena 49,847 C11
Gilroy 31,487 D6
Glen Avon Heights 8,444 E10
Glendale 180,038 C10
Glendora 47,828 D10
Goleta F9
Gonzales 4,660 D7
Goshen 1,809 F7
Granada Hills B10
Grand Terrace 10,946 E10
Grass Valley 9,048 D4
Graton 1,409 C5
Greenacres 7,379 F8
Greenfield 7,464 D7
Greenville 1,396 E3
Gridley 4,631 D4
Groveland 2,753 E6
Grover City 11,656 E8
Guadalupe 5,479 E9
Guerneville 1,966 B5
Gustine 3,931 D6
Half Moon Bay 8,886 H3
Hamilton City 1,811 C4
Hanford▲ 30,897 F7
Harbor City C11
Hawthorne 71,349 C11
Hayfork 2,605 B3
Hayward 111,498 K2
Healdsburg 9,469 B5
Heber 2,566 K11
Hemet 36,094 H10
Hercules 16,829 J1
Herlong 1,188 E3
Hermosa Beach 18,219 B11
Hesperia 50,418 H9
Hidden Hills 1,729 B10
Highgrove 3,175 E10
Highland 34,439 H9
Hillsborough 10,667 J2
Hilmar (Hilmar-Irwin) 3,392 E6
Hollister▲ 19,212 D7
Hollywood C10
Holt 4,820 D6
Holtville 4,399 K11
Home Gardens 7,780 E11
Homeland 3,312 H10
Hughson 3,259 E6
Huntington Beach 181,519 C11
Huntington Park 56,065 C11
Huron 4,766 E7
Idyllwild (Idyllwild-Pine Cove) 2,853 J10
Imperial 4,113 K11
Imperial Beach 26,512 H11
Independence▲ 748 H7
Indian Wells 2,647 J10
Indio 36,793 J10
Inglewood 109,602 B11
Inverness 1,422 B5
Ione 6,516 C9
Irvine 110,330 D11
Isla Vista 20,395 E9
Ivanhoe 3,293 F7
Jackson▲ 3,545 C9
Jamestown 2,178 E6
Joshua Tree 3,898 J9
Julian 1,284 J10
Kelseyville 2,861 C5
Kensington 4,974 J2
Kerman 5,448 E7
Kernville 1,656 G8
Kettleman City 1,411 E7
Keyes 2,878 E6
King City 7,634 D7
Kings Beach 2,796 F4
Kingsburg 7,205 F7
La Canada Flintridge 19,378 C10
La Crescenta (La Crescenta-Montrose) 16,968 C10
La Habra 51,266 D11
La Mesa 52,931 H11
La Mirada 40,452 D11
La Puente 36,955 D10
La Selva Beach 1,603 K4
La Verne 30,897 D10
Lafayette 23,501 K2
Laguna Beach 23,170 G10
Laguna Hills 46,731 D11
Laguna Niguel 44,400 H10
Lagunitas (Lagunitas-Forest Knolls) 1,821 H1
Lake Arrowhead 6,539 H9
Lake Elsinore 18,285 F11
Lake Isabella 3,323 G8
Lakeland Village 5,159 E11
Lakeport▲ 4,390 C4
Lakewood 73,557 C11
Lamont 11,517 G8
Lancaster 97,291 G9
Larkspur 11,070 H1
Lathrop 6,841 D6
Laton 1,415 F7
Lawndale 27,331 B11
Le Grand 1,205 E6
Lemon Grove 23,984 J11
Lemoore 13,622 F7
Lenwood 3,190 H9
Leucadia 9,478 H10
Lewiston 1,187 C3
Lincoln 7,248 B8
Linda 13,033 D4
Linden 1,339 D5
Lindsay 8,338 F7
Live Oak 11,482 K4
Live Oak 3,103 D4
Live Oak 4,320 K4
Livermore 56,741 L2
Livingston 7,317 E6
Locke 2,722 B9
Lockeford 1,852 C9
Lodi 51,874 C9
Loma Linda 17,400 F10
Lomita 19,382 C11
Lompoc 37,649 E9
Lone Pine 1,818 H7
Long Beach 429,433 C11
Loomis 5,705 C8
Los Alamitos 11,676 D11
Los Altos 26,303 K3
Los Altos Hills 7,514 J3
Los Angeles▲ 3,485,398 C10
Los Banos 14,519 E6
Los Gatos 27,357 K4
Los Molinos 1,709 D3
Los Osos (Los Osos-Baywood Park) 10,933 E8
Lost Hills 1,212 F8
Lower Lake 1,217 C5
Lucerne 2,011 C4
Lynwood 61,945 C11
Madera▲ 29,281 E7
Magalia 8,987 D4
Mammoth Lakes 4,785 G6
Manhattan Beach 32,063 B11
Manteca 40,773 D6
Maricopa 1,193 F8
Marina 26,436 D7
Mariposa▲ 1,152 F6
Markleeville▲ 500 F5
Martinez▲ 31,808 K1
Marysville▲ 12,324 D4
Maywood 27,850 C10
McCloud 1,555 C2
McFarland 7,005 F8
McKinleyville 10,749 A3
Mecca 1,966 K10
Meiners Oaks (Meiners Oaks-Mira Monte) 3,329 F9
Mendota 6,821 E7
Menlo Park 28,040 J3
Mentone 5,675 H9
Merced▲ 56,216 E6
Mill Valley 13,038 H2
Millbrae 20,412 J2
Milpitas 50,686 L3
Mira Loma 15,786 E10
Mission Viejo 72,820 D11
Modesto▲ 164,730 D6
Mojave 3,763 G8
Monrovia 35,761 D10
Montague 1,415 C2
Montara 2,552 H3
Montclair 28,434 D10
Monte Sereno 3,287 K4
Montebello 59,564 C10
Monterey 31,954 D7
Monterey Park 60,738 C10
Montrose (Montrose-La Crescenta) C10
Moorpark 25,494 G9
Moraga 15,852 K2
Moreno Valley 118,779 H10
Morgan Hill 23,928 L4
Morro Bay 9,664 D8
Moss Beach 3,002 H3
Mount Shasta 3,460 C2
Mountain View 67,460 K3
Mulberry 1,946 D4
Murphys 1,517 E5
Murrieta 1,628 H10
Muscoy 7,541 E10
Napa▲ 61,842 C5
National City 54,249 J11
Needles 5,191 L9
Nevada City▲ 2,855 D4
Newark 37,861 K3
Newhall 12,029 G9
Newman 4,151 D6
Newport Beach 66,643 D11
Nipomo 7,109 E8
Norco 23,302 E11
North Edwards 1,259 H8
North Highlands 42,105 B8
Norwalk 94,279 C11
Novato 47,585 H1
Oak View 3,606 F9
Oakdale 11,961 E6
Oakhurst 2,602 F6
Oakland▲ 372,242 J2
Oakley 18,374 L1
Oceano 6,169 E8
Oceanside 128,398 H10
Oildale 26,553 F8
Ojai 7,613 F9
Ontario 133,179 D10
Opal Cliffs 5,940 K4
Orange 110,658 D11
Orange Cove 5,604 F7
Orinda 16,642 J2
Orland 5,052 C4
Orosi 5,486 F7
Oroville▲ 11,960 D4
Oxnard 142,216 F9
Pacheco (Pacheco-Vine Hill) 3,325 K1
Pacific Grove 16,117 C7
Pacifica 37,670 H2
Pajaro 3,332 D7
Palermo 5,260 D4
Palm Desert 23,252 J10
Palm Springs 40,181 J10
Palmdale 68,842 G9
Palo Alto 55,900 K3
Palos Verdes Estates 13,512 B11
Paradise 25,408 D4
Paramount 47,669 C11
Parlier 7,938 F7
Pasadena 131,591 C10
Paso Robles 18,583 E8
Patterson 8,626 D6
Pebble Beach C7
Pedley 8,869 E10
Perris 21,460 F11
Petaluma 43,184 H1
Pico Rivera 59,177 C10
Piedmont 10,602 J2
Pine Valley 1,297 J11
Pinole 17,460 J1
Piru 1,157 G9
Pismo Beach 7,669 E8
Pittsburg 47,564 L1
Pixley 2,457 F8
Placentia 41,259 D11
Placerville▲ 8,355 C8
Planada 3,531 E6
Pleasant Hill 31,585 K2
Pleasanton 50,553 L2
Pollock Pines 4,291 E5
Pomona 131,723 D10
Poplar (Poplar-Cotton Center) 1,901 F7

CALIFORNIA REPUBLIC

AREA 158,706 sq. mi. (411,049 sq. km.)
POPULATION 29,839,250
CAPITAL Sacramento
LARGEST CITY Los Angeles
HIGHEST POINT Mt. Whitney 14,494 ft. (4418 m.)
SETTLED IN 1769
ADMITTED TO UNION September 9, 1850
POPULAR NAME Golden State
STATE FLOWER Golden Poppy
STATE BIRD California Valley Quail

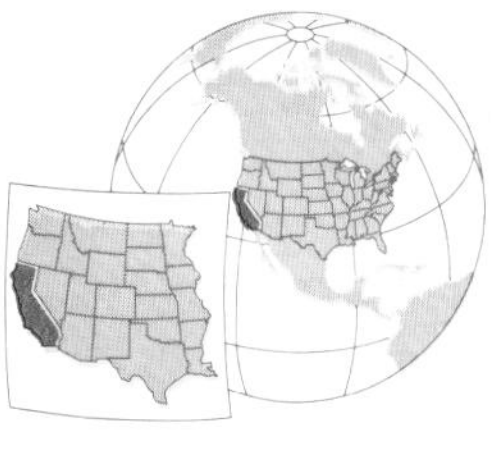

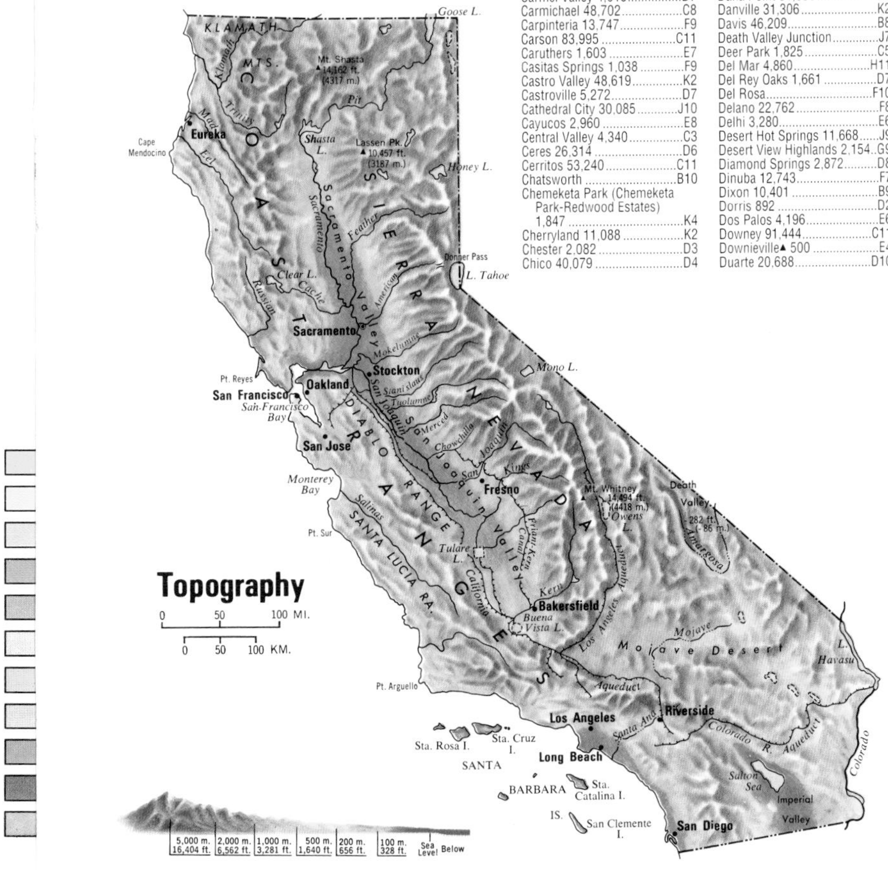

Topography
0 50 100 MI.
0 50 100 KM.
KLAMATH MTS.
Mt. Shasta 14,162 ft. (4317 m.)
Goose L.
Eureka
Cape Mendocino
Shasta L.
Lassen Pk. 10,457 ft. (3187 m.)
Honey L.
Donner Pass
L. Tahoe
Clear L.
Sacramento
Pt. Reyes
Oakland
San Francisco
San Francisco Bay
Stockton
Mono L.
San Jose
Monterey Bay
Fresno
Mt. Whitney 14,494 ft. (4418 m.)
Death Valley
Pt. Sur
Tulare L.
Bakersfield
Buena Vista L.
Mojave Desert
L. Havasu
Pt. Arguello
Los Angeles
Riverside
Sta. Rosa I.
Sta. Cruz I.
Long Beach
SANTA BARBARA IS.
Sta. Catalina I.
San Clemente I.
San Diego
Salton Sea
Imperial Valley
5,000 m. 16,404 ft.
2,000 m. 6,562 ft.
1,000 m. 3,281 ft.
500 m. 1,640 ft.
200 m. 656 ft.
100 m. 328 ft.
Sea Level
Below

(continued on following page)

Connecticut
SCALE
0 5 10 15 MI.
0 5 10 15 KM.
State Capitals
Major Limited Access Hwys.
MASSACHUSETTS
NEW YORK
LITCHFIELD
HARTFORD
TOLLAND
MIDDLESEX
NEW HAVEN
FAIRFIELD
LONG ISLAND SOUND
SPRINGFIELD
HARTFORD
WATERBURY
NEW HAVEN
BRIDGEPORT
STAMFORD
Mt. Frissell 2,380 ft. (725 m.)
Longitude West of Greenwich
73°
42°
41°

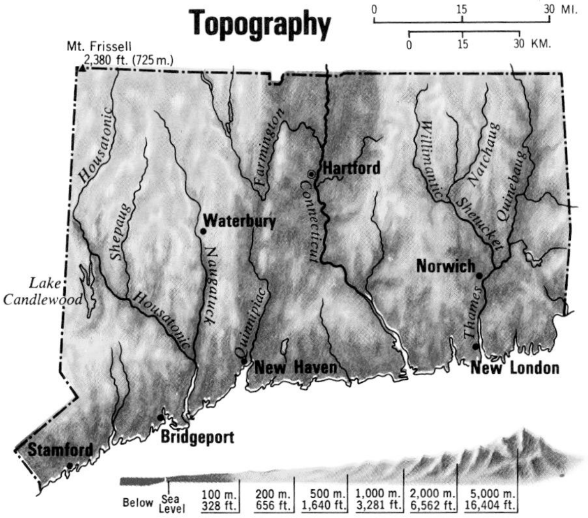

Topography
0 15 30 MI.
0 15 30 KM.
Mt. Frissell 2,380 ft. (725 m.)
Housatonic
Shepaug
Naugatuck
Farmington
Connecticut
Quinnipiac
Willimantic
Natchaug
Shetucket
Quinebaug
Thames
Lake Candlewood
Hartford
Waterbury
Norwich
New Haven
New London
Stamford
Bridgeport
Below
Sea Level
100 m. 328 ft.
200 m. 656 ft.
500 m. 1,640 ft.
1,000 m. 3,281 ft.
2,000 m. 6,562 ft.
5,000 m. 16,404 ft.

COUNTIES

Fairfield 827,645 .... B3
Hartford 851,783 .... D1
Litchfield 174,092 .... B1
Middlesex 143,196 .... E3
New Haven 804,219 .... D3
New London 254,957 .... G2
Tolland 128,699 .... F1
Windham 102,525 .... H1

CITIES and TOWNS

Abington 600 .... G1
Addison 700 .... E2
Allingtown D3
Amston 900 .... F2
Andover• 2,540 .... F2
Ansonia 18,403 .... C3
Ashford P.O. (Warrenville) 500 .... G1
Ashford• 3,765 .... G1
Avon 1,434 .... D1
Avon• 13,937 .... D1
Bakersville 750 .... C1
Ballouville 800 .... H1
Baltic G2
Bantam 757 .... B2
Barkhamsted• 3,369 .... D1
Beacon Falls• 5,083 .... C3
Berkshire 500 .... B3
Berlin• 16,787 .... E2
Bethany• 4,608 .... C3
Bethel 8,835 .... B3
Bethel• 17,541 .... B3
Bethlehem 1,762 .... C2
Bethlehem• 3,071 .... C2
Bloomfield• 19,483 .... E1
Blue Hills 3,206 .... E1
Bolton• 4,575 .... F1
Branchville 600 .... B3
Branford 5,688 .... D3
Branford• 27,603 .... D3
Bridgeport 141,686 .... C4
Bridgewater• 1,654 .... B2
Bristol 60,640 .... D2
Broad Brook 3,585 .... E1
Brookfield• 14,113 .... B3
Brookfield Center B3
Brooklyn• 6,681 .... H1
Buckingham 800 .... E2
Burlington• 7,026 .... D1
Burnside E1
Byram A4
Canaan 1,057 .... B1
Canaan• 1,194 .... B1
Canterbury• 4,467 .... H2
Canton 1,680 .... D1
Canton• 8,268 .... D1
Center Groton 600 .... G3
Centerbrook 800 .... F3
Central Village 950 .... H2
Chaplin• 2,048 .... G1
Cheshire 5,759 .... D2
Cheshire• 25,684 .... D2
Chester 1,563 .... F3
Chester• 3,417 .... F3
Clinton 3,439 .... E3
Clinton• 12,767 .... E3
Clintonville D3
Cobalt 700 .... E2
Colchester 3,212 .... F2
Colchester• 10,980 .... F2
Colebrook 1,365 .... C1
Collinsville 2,591 .... D1
Columbia• 4,510 .... F2
Cornwall• 1,414 .... B1
Cos Cob A4
Coventry 3,769 .... F1
Coventry• 10,063 .... F1
Cranbury 700 .... B4
Cromwell• 12,286 .... E2
Crystal Lake 1,175 .... F1
Danbury 65,585 .... B3
Danielson 4,441 .... H1
Darien• 18,196 .... B4
Dayville H1
Deep River 2,520 .... F3
Deep River• 4,332 .... F3
Derby 12,199 .... C3
Devon C4
Durham 2,650 .... E3
Durham• 5,732 .... E3
Durham Center 500 .... E3
East Berlin 950 .... E2
East Brooklyn 1,481 .... H1
East Canaan 800 .... B1
East Granby• 4,302 .... E1
East Haddam• 6,676 .... F3
East Hampton 2,167 .... E2
East Hampton• 10,428 .... E2
East Hartford• 50,452 .... E1
East Hartland 900 .... D1
East Haven• 26,144 .... D3
East Killingly 900 .... H1
East Lyme• 15,340 .... G3
East Morris 800 .... C2
East Norwalk B4
East Putnam 500 .... H1
East River 500 .... E3
East Windsor• 10,081 .... E1
East Windsor Hill 500 .... E1
Eastford• 1,314 .... G1
Easton• 6,303 .... B4
Ellington• 11,197 .... F1
Elmwood D2
Enfield 8,151 .... E1
Enfield• 45,532 .... E1
Essex 2,500 .... F3
Essex• 5,904 .... F3
Fabyan 600 .... H1
Fairfield• 53,418 .... B4
Falls Village 600 .... B1
Farmington• 20,608 .... D2
Fenwick 89 .... F3
Forestville D2
Foxon D3
Franklin• 1,810 .... G2

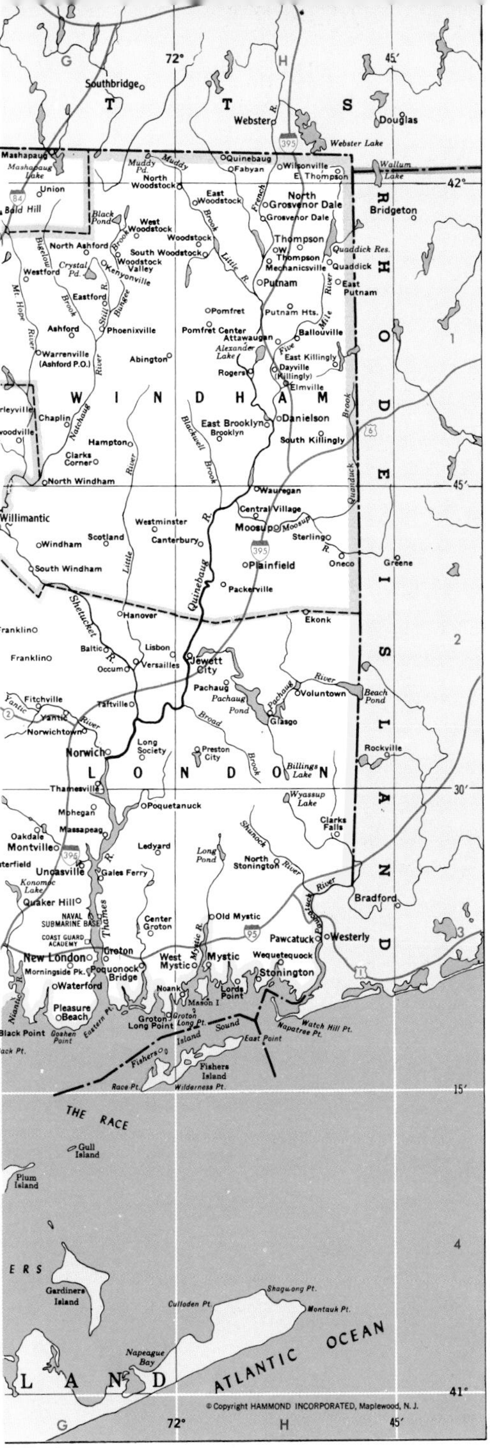

Southbridge
Webster
Douglas
Webster Lake
Mashapaug Lake
Union
Bald Hill
Quinebaug
Fabyan
Wilsonville
E. Thompson
Wallum Lake
North Woodstock
East Woodstock
North Grosvenor Dale
Grosvenor Dale
Bridgeton
West Woodstock
Woodstock
North Ashford
South Woodstock
Thompson
Quaddick Res.
Westford
Woodstock Valley
Mechanicsville
Quaddick
East Putnam
Eastford
Putnam
Pomfret
Putnam Hts.
Ashford
Phoenixville
Pomfret Center
Attawaugan
Ballouville
Warrenville (Ashford P.O.)
Abington
East Killingly
Rogers
Dayville (Killingly)
Elmville
W I N D H A M
Gurleyville
Chaplin
East Brooklyn
Danielson
Brooklyn
Atwoodville
Hampton
South Killingly
Clarks Corner
North Windham
Wauregan
Willimantic
Westminster
Central Village
Scotland
Canterbury
Moosup
Windham
Sterling
South Windham
Plainfield
Oneco
Greene
Packerville
Hanover
Ekonk
Franklin
Baltic
Lisbon
Versailles
Occum
Jewett City
Pachaug
Voluntown
Beach Pond
Fitchville
Taftville
Yantic
Norwichtown
Glasgo
Norwich
Long Society
Preston City
Rockville
L O N D O N
Billings Lake
Thamesville
Mohegan
Poquetanuck
Wyassup Lake
Massapeag
Clarks Falls
Oakdale
Montville
Ledyard
Long Pond
North Stonington
Chesterfield
Uncasville
Gales Ferry
Quaker Hill
Bradford
NAVAL SUBMARINE BASE
Center Groton
Old Mystic
COAST GUARD ACADEMY
Pawcatuck
Westerly
New London
Groton
West Mystic
Mystic
Wequetequock
Morningside Pk.
Poquonock Bridge
Stonington
Waterford
Noank
Lords Point
Mason I.
Pleasure Beach
Groton Long Pt.
Groton Long Point
Black Point
Goshen Point
Black Pt.
Watch Hill Pt.
Napatree Pt.
Fishers Island Sound
East Point
Fishers Island
Race Pt.
Wilderness Pt.
THE RACE
Gull Island
Plum Island
Gardiners Island
Culloden Pt.
Shagwong Pt.
Montauk Pt.
Napeague Bay
ATLANTIC OCEAN
© Copyright HAMMOND INCORPORATED, Maplewood, N. J.

Gales Ferry 1,191	G3
Gaylordsville 960	A2
Georgetown 1,694	B4
Glastonbury 7,082	E2
Glastonbury • 27,901	E2
Glenville	A4
Goshen • 2,329	C1
Granby 1,912	D1
Granby • 9,369	D1
Greenfield Hill	B4
Greenwich • 58,441	A4
Grosvenor Dale 700	H1
Groton 9,837	G3
Groton • 45,144	G3
Guilford 2,588	E3
Guilford • 19,848	E3
Haddam • 6,769	E3
Hamden • 52,434	D3
Hampton • 1,578	G1
Hanover 500	G2
Hartford (cap.) 139,739	E1
Hartland • 1,866	D1
Harwinton 3,293	C1
Harwinton • 5,228	C1
Hawleyville 600	B3
Hazardville 5,179	E1
Hebron • 7,079	F2
Higganum 1,692	E2
Highland Park 500	F1
Hockanum	E2
Huntington	C3
Indian Neck	D3
Ivoryton	F3
Jewett City 3,349	H2
Kensington 8,306	D2
Kent • 2,918	B2
Killingly • 15,889	H1
Killingworth • 4,814	E3
Lake Pocotopaug 3,029	F2
Lakeville	B1
Lebanon • 6,041	G2
Ledyard • 14,913	G3
Leetes Island 500	E3
Lisbon • 3,790	G2
Litchfield 1,378	C2
Litchfield • 8,365	C2
Long Hill	C3
Lords Point 500	H3
Lyons Plain 700	B4
Madison 2,139	E3
Madison • 15,485	E3
Manchester 31,058	E1
Manchester • 51,618	E1
Mansfield • 21,103	F1
Mansfield Center 1,043	G1
Marion 900	D2
Marlborough 1,039	F2
Marlborough • 5,535	F2
Meriden 59,479	D2
Middlebury • 6,145	C2
Middlefield • 3,925	E2
Middletown 42,762	E2
Milford 48,168	C4
Mill Plain 750	A3

AREA 5,018 sq. mi. (12,997 sq. km.)
POPULATION 3,295,669
CAPITAL Hartford
LARGEST CITY Bridgeport
HIGHEST POINT Mt. Frissell (S. Slope) 2,380 ft. (725 m.)
SETTLED IN 1635
ADMITTED TO UNION January 9, 1788
POPULAR NAME Constitution State; Nutmeg State
STATE FLOWER Mountain Laurel
STATE BIRD Robin

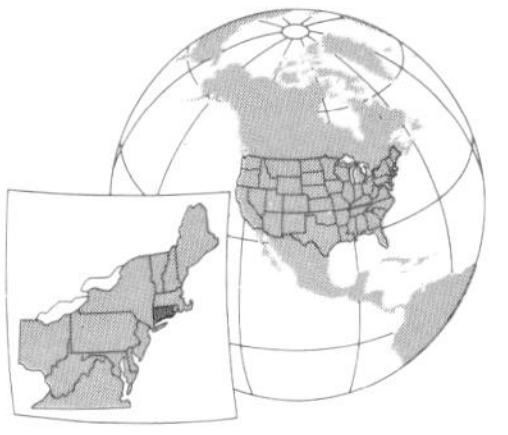

Milldale 975	D2
Milton 600	C1
Mohegan 700	G3
Monroe • 16,896	C3
Monroe P.O. (Stepney)	B3
Montowese	D3
Montville 1,711	G3
Montville • 16,673	G3
Moodus 1,170	F2
Moosup 3,289	H2
Morningside Park	G3
Morris • 2,039	C2
Mystic 2,618	H3
Naugatuck 30,625	C3
New Britain 75,491	E2
New Canaan • 17,864	B4
New Fairfield • 12,911	B3
New Hartford 1,269	C1
New Hartford • 5,769	C1
New Haven 130,474	D3
New London 28,540	G3
New Milford 5,775	B2
New Milford • 23,629	B2
New Preston 1,217	B2
Newington • 29,208	E2
Newtown 1,800	B3
Newtown • 20,779	B3
Niantic 3,048	G3
Nichols	C4
Noank 1,406	G3
Norfolk • 2,060	C1
Noroton	B4
Noroton Heights	B4
North Bloomfield 500	E1
North Branford • 12,996	E3
North Franklin 500	G2
North Granby 1,455	D1
North Grosvenor Dale 1,705	H1
North Guilford	E3
North Haven • 22,249	D3
North Lyme	F3
North Stonington • 4,884	H3
North Wilton 900	B4
North Woodbury 900	C2
Northfield 600	C2
Northford	D3
Northville 700	B2
Norwalk 78,331	B4
Norwich 37,391	G2
Norwichtown	G2
Oakdale 608	G3
Oakville 8,741	C2
Occum	G2
Old Greenwich	A4
Old Lyme • 6,535	F3
Old Mystic 600	H3
Old Saybrook 1,820	F3
Old Saybrook • 9,552	F3
Oneco 550	H2
Orange • 12,830	C3
Oxford • 8,685	C3
Pawcatuck 5,289	H3
Pequabuck 642	C2
Plainfield 2,856	H2
Plainfield • 14,363	H2
Plainville • 17,392	D2
Plantsville	D2
Pleasure Beach 1,356	G3
Plymouth • 11,822	C2
Pomfret • 3,102	H1
Poquonock	E1
Poquonock Bridge 2,770	G3
Portland 5,645	E2
Portland • 8,418	E2
Preston 5,006	H2
Prospect • 7,775	D2
Putnam 6,835	H1
Putnam • 9,031	H1
Putnam Heights 500	H1
Quaker Hill 2,052	G3
Quinebaug 1,031	H1
Quinnipiac	D3
Redding • 7,927	B3
Redding Ridge 550	B3
Ridgefield 6,363	B3
Ridgefield • 20,919	B3
Riverside	A4
Rockfall 900	E2
Rockville	F1
Rocky Hill • 16,554	E2
Rogers 650	H1
Round Hill 900	A4
Rowayton	B4
Roxbury • 1,825	B2
Salem • 3,310	F3
Salisbury • 4,090	B1
Sandy Hook	B3
Saugatuck	B4
Saybrook Point 700	F3
Scantic 500	E1
Scotland • 1,215	G2
Seymour • 14,288	C3
Sharon • 2,928	B1
Shelton 35,418	C3
Sherman • 2,809	B2
Short Beach	D3
Simsbury 5,577	D1
Simsbury • 22,023	D1
Somers 1,643	F1
Somers • 9,108	F1
Somersville 750	F1
South Coventry (Coventry) 1,257	F1
South Glastonbury	E2
South Killingly 500	H1
South Norwalk	B4
South Wilton	B4
South Windham 1,644	G2
South Windsor • 22,090	E1
South Woodstock 1,112	G1
Southbury • 15,818	C3
Southington • 38,518	D2
Southport	B4
Stafford • 11,091	F1
Stafford Springs 4,100	F1
Staffordville 500	G1
Stamford 108,056	A4
Stepney	B3
Sterling • 2,357	H2
Stonington 1,100	H3
Stonington • 16,919	H3
Stony Creek	E3
Storrs 12,198	F1
Stratford • 49,389	C4
Suffield 1,353	E1
Suffield • 11,427	E1
Taftville	G2
Talcottville 875	F1
Tariffville 1,477	D1
Terryville 5,426	C2
Thamesville	G2
Thomaston • 6,947	C2
Thompson • 8,668	H1
Thompsonville 8,458	E1
Tolland 11,001	F1
Torringford	C1
Torrington 33,687	C1
Totoket 950	D3
Trumbull • 32,016	C4
Uncasville 1,597	G3
Union • 612	G1
Union City	C2
Unionville	D1
Vernon Center	F1
Vernon • 29,841	F1
Versailles 540	G2
Voluntown • 2,113	H2
Wallingford 17,827	D3
Wallingford • 40,822	D3
Warehouse Point	E1
Warren • 1,226	B2
Washington • 3,905	B2
Washington Depot 900	B2
Waterbury 108,961	C2
Waterford 2,736	G3
Waterford • 17,930	G3
Watertown • 20,456	C2
Wauregan 1,079	H2
Weatogue 2,521	D1
West Avon	D1
West Granby 567	D1
West Hartford • 60,110	D1
West Haven 54,021	D3
West Mystic 3,595	H3
West Norwalk 950	B4
West Simsbury 2,149	D1
West Suffield	E1
Westbrook 2,060	F3
Westbrook • 5,414	F3
Westfield	E2
Weston • 8,648	B4
Westport • 24,410	B4
Wethersfield • 25,651	E2
Whitneyville	D3
Willimantic 14,746	G2
Willington • 5,979	F1
Wilton 15,989	B4
Winchester • 11,524	C1
Windham • 22,039	G2
Windsor 17,517	E1
Windsor • 27,817	E1
Windsor Locks • 12,358	E1
Winnipauk 650	B4
Winsted 8,254	C1
Winthrop 750	E3
Wolcott • 13,700	D2
Woodbridge • 7,924	D3
Woodbury 1,212	C2
Woodbury • 8,131	C2
Woodmont 1,770	D4
Woodstock • 6,008	H1
Yalesville	D3
Yantic	G2

OTHER FEATURES

Aspetuck (res.)	B4
Bantam (lake)	C2
Barkhamsted (res.)	D1
Bear (mt.)	B1
Byram (riv.)	A4
Candlewood (lake)	A2
Coast Guard Academy	G3
Colebrook River (lake)	C1
Congamond (lakes)	E1
Connecticut (riv.)	E2
Dennis (hill)	C1
Easton (res.)	B3
Eight Mile (riv.)	F3
Farmington (riv.)	D1
French (riv.)	H1
Frissell (mt.)	B1
Gaillard (lake)	D3
Gardner (lake)	G2
Hammonasset (pt.)	E3
Hammonasset (res.)	E3
Haystack (mt.)	C1
Highland (lake)	C1
Hockanum (riv.)	E1
Hop (riv.)	F1
Housatonic (riv.)	C3
Lillinonah (lake)	B3
Little (riv.)	G2
Long Island (sound)	C4
Mad (riv.)	C1
Mashapaug (lake)	G1
Mason (isl.)	H3
Mattabesset (riv.)	E2
Mianus (riv.)	A4
Mohawk (mt.)	B1
Moosup (riv.)	H2
Mount Hope (riv.)	G1
Mudge (pond)	B1
Mystic (riv.)	H3
Natchaug (riv.)	G1
Naugatuck (riv.)	C3
Nepaug (res.)	D1
Niantic (riv.)	G3
Norwalk (riv.)	B4
Pachaug (pond)	H2
Pawcatuck (riv.)	H3
Pequabuck (riv.)	D2
Pequonnock (riv.)	C3
Pocotopaug (lake)	E2
Quaddick (res.)	H1
Quinebaug (riv.)	H2
Quinnipiac (riv.)	D3
Rippowam (riv.)	A4
Sachem (head)	E4
Salmon (brook)	D1
Salmon (riv.)	F2
Saugatuck (res.)	B3
Scantic (riv.)	E1
Shenipsit (lake)	F1
Shepaug (riv.)	B2
Shetucket (riv.)	G2
Silvermine (riv.)	B4
Spectacle (lakes)	B2
Still (riv.)	B3
Still (riv.)	C1
Talcott (range)	D1
Thames (riv.)	G3
Thomaston (res.)	C2
Titicus (riv.)	A3
Trap Falls (res.)	C3
Twin (lakes)	B1
Wamgumbaug (lake)	F1
Waramaug (lake)	B2
West Rock Ridge (hills)	D3
Willimantic (riv.)	F1
Wononskopomuc (lake)	B1
Yantic (riv.)	G2

• Population of town or township

Agriculture, Industry and Resources

DOMINANT LAND USE

Specialized Dairy
Dairy, Poultry, Mixed Farming
Forests
Urban Areas

MAJOR MINERAL OCCURRENCES

Cl Clay
Mi Mica

Major Industrial Areas

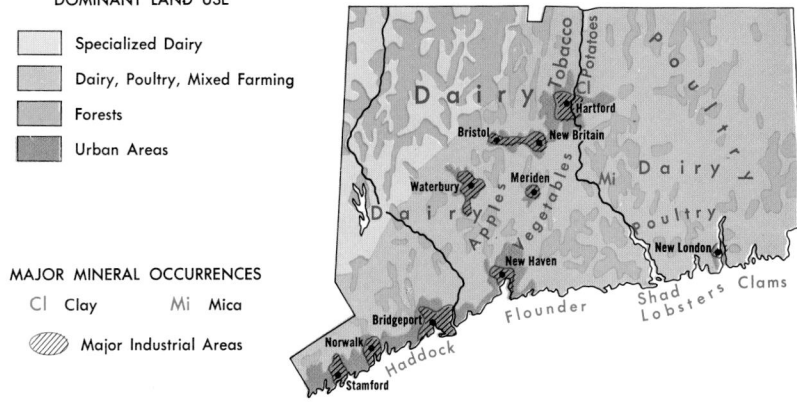

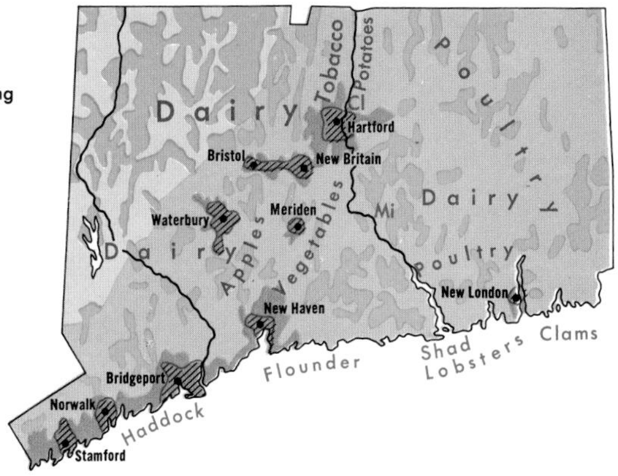

Dairy
Tobacco
Potatoes
Cl
Poultry
Hartford
Bristol
New Britain
Meriden
Waterbury
Dairy
Mi
Dairy
Apples
Vegetables
Poultry
New London
New Haven
Shad
Lobsters
Clams
Flounder
Bridgeport
Norwalk
Haddock
Stamford

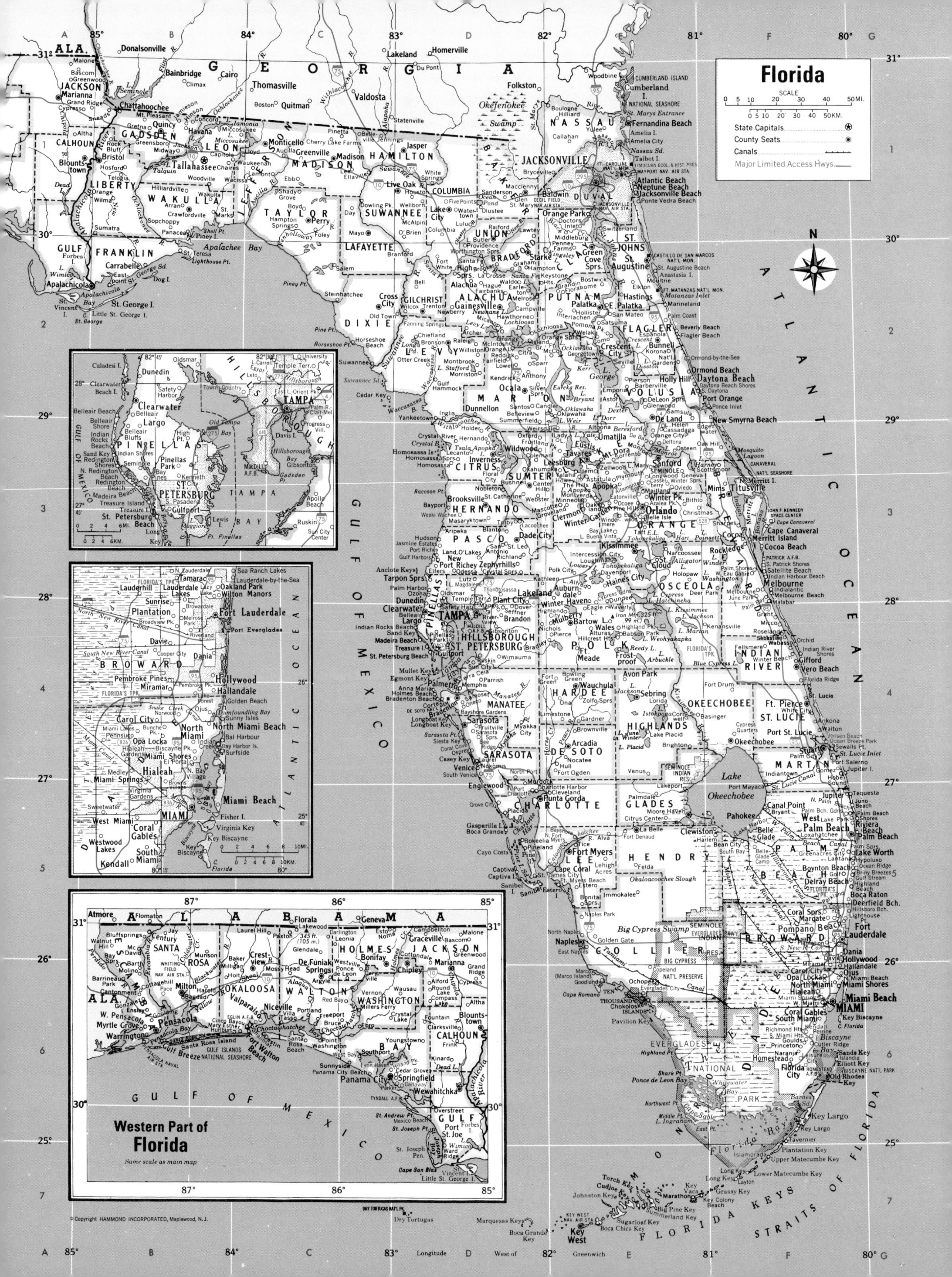
Florida
SCALE
0 5 10 20 30 40 50 MI.
0 5 10 20 30 40 50 KM.
State Capitals
County Seats
Canals
Major Limited Access Hwys.
GEORGIA
ALA.
ATLANTIC OCEAN
GULF OF MEXICO
STRAITS OF FLORIDA
FLORIDA KEYS
Okefenokee Swamp
Lake Okeechobee
Big Cypress Swamp
EVERGLADES NATIONAL PARK
Florida Bay
Tallahassee
Jacksonville
Tampa
St. Petersburg
Orlando
Miami
Fort Lauderdale
Key West
Western Part of Florida
Same scale as main map
ALABAMA
Pensacola
Longitude West of Greenwich
© Copyright HAMMOND INCORPORATED, Maplewood, N.J.

AREA 58,664 sq. mi. (151,940 sq. km.)
POPULATION 13,003,362
CAPITAL Tallahassee
LARGEST CITY Jacksonville
HIGHEST POINT (Walton County) 345 ft. (105 m.)
SETTLED IN 1565
ADMITTED TO UNION March 3, 1845
POPULAR NAME Sunshine State; Peninsula State
STATE FLOWER Orange Blossom
STATE BIRD Mockingbird

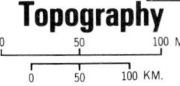

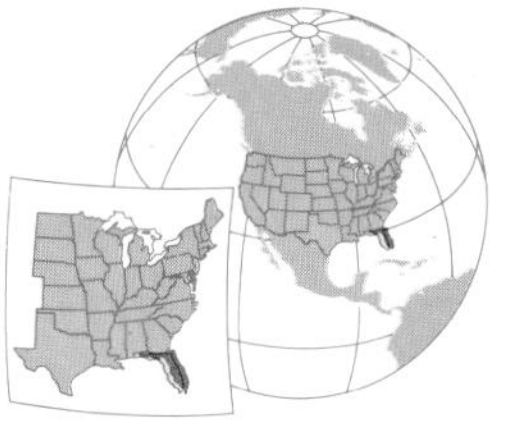

Topography

0 50 100 MI.
0 50 100 KM.

Perdido
Escambia
345 ft. (105 m.)
Choctawhatchee
L. Seminole
Pensacola
Pensacola Bay
Santa Rosa I.
Apalachicola
Tallahassee
Ochlockonee
Apalachee Bay
C. San Blas
C. St. George
Okefenokee Swamp
St. Marys
Suwannee
Jacksonville
St. Johns
L. George
Daytona Beach
Tsala Apopka L.
Withlacoochee
L. Apopka
Orlando
Merritt I.
C. Canaveral
Indian
Iron Mtn. 325 ft. (99 m.)
L. Kissimmee
Tampa
St. Petersburg
Tampa Bay
Peace
Kissimmee
Lake Okeechobee
West Palm Beach
Charlotte Har.
Caloosahatchee
Fort Myers
Fort Lauderdale
Big Cypress Swamp
The Everglades
Tamiami Canal
TEN THOUSAND IS.
Miami
Biscayne Bay
Whitewater Bay
C. Sable
Key Largo
Florida Bay
FLORIDA KEYS
Dry Tortugas
Marquesas Keys
Key West
0 50 100 MI.
0 50 100 KM.
5,000 m. 16,404 ft.
2,000 m. 6,562 ft.
1,000 m. 3,281 ft.
500 m. 1,640 ft.
200 m. 656 ft.
100 m. 328 ft.
Sea Level
Below

COUNTIES

Alachua 181,596 ..... D2
Baker 18,486 ..... D1
Bay 126,994 ..... C6
Bradford 22,515 ..... D2
Brevard 398,978 ..... F3
Broward 1,255,488 ..... F5
Calhoun 11,011 ..... D6
Charlotte 110,975 ..... E5
Citrus 93,515 ..... D3
Clay 105,986 ..... E2
Collier 152,099 ..... E5
Columbia 42,613 ..... D1
Dade 1,937,094 ..... F6
De Soto 19,039 ..... E4
Dixie 10,585 ..... C2
Duval 672,971 ..... E1
Escambia 262,798 ..... B6
Flagler 28,701 ..... E2
Franklin 8,967 ..... B2
Gadsden 41,105 ..... B1
Gilchrist 9,667 ..... D2
Glades 7,591 ..... E5
Gulf 11,504 ..... D7
Hamilton 10,930 ..... D1
Hardee 19,499 ..... E4
Hendry 25,773 ..... E5
Hernando 101,115 ..... D3
Highlands 68,432 ..... E4
Hillsborough 834,054 ..... D4
Holmes 15,778 ..... C5
Indian River 90,208 ..... F4
Jackson 41,375 ..... D5
Jefferson 11,296 ..... C1
Lafayette 5,578 ..... C2
Lake 152,104 ..... E3
Lee 335,113 ..... E5
Leon 192,493 ..... B1
Levy 25,923 ..... D2
Liberty 5,569 ..... B1
Madison 16,569 ..... C1
Manatee 211,707 ..... D4
Marion 194,833 ..... D2
Martin 100,900 ..... F4
Monroe 78,024 ..... E7
Nassau 43,941 ..... E1
Okaloosa 143,776 ..... C6
Okeechobee 29,627 ..... F4
Orange 677,491 ..... E3
Osceola 107,728 ..... E3
Palm Beach 863,518 ..... F5
Pasco 281,131 ..... D3
Pinellas 851,659 ..... D4
Polk 405,382 ..... E4
Putnam 65,070 ..... E2
Saint Johns 51,303 ..... E2
Saint Lucie 87,182 ..... F4
Santa Rosa 81,608 ..... B6
Sarasota 277,776 ..... D4
Seminole 287,529 ..... E3
Sumter 31,577 ..... D3
Suwannee 26,780 ..... C1
Taylor 17,111 ..... C1
Union 10,252 ..... D1
Volusia 370,712 ..... E2
Wakulla 14,202 ..... B1
Walton 27,760 ..... C6
Washington 16,919 ..... C6

CITIES and TOWNS

Alachua 4,529 ..... D2
Alford 472 ..... D6
Altamonte Springs 34,879 ..... E3
Altha 497 ..... A1
Altoona 800 ..... E3
Alturas 900 ..... E4
Alva 1,036 ..... E5
Anna Maria 1,744 ..... D4
Anthony 500 ..... D2
Apalachicola▲ 2,602 ..... A2
Apollo Beach 6,025 ..... C3
Apopka 13,512 ..... E3
Arcadia▲ 6,488 ..... E4
Archer 1,372 ..... D2
Aripeka 450 ..... D3
Astatula 981 ..... E3
Astor 1,273 ..... E2
Atlantic Beach 11,636 ..... E1
Auburndale 8,858 ..... E3
Avon Park 8,042 ..... E4
Azalea Park 8,926 ..... E3
Babson Park 1,125 ..... E4
Bagdad 1,457 ..... B6
Baker 500 ..... C5
Bal Harbour 3,045 ..... C4
Baldwin 1,450 ..... E1
Barberville 500 ..... E2
Bartow▲ 14,716 ..... E4
Bascom 90 ..... A1
Basinger 300 ..... F4
Bay Harbor Islands 4,703 ..... B4
Bay Lake E3
Bay Pines 4,171 ..... B3
Bayshore 17,062 ..... E5
Bayshore Gardens 14,945 ..... D4
Bee Ridge 6,406 ..... D4
Bell 267 ..... D2
Belle Glade 16,177 ..... F5
Belle Glade Camp 1,616 ..... F5
Belle Isle 5,272 ..... E3
Belleair 3,968 ..... B2
Belleair Beach 2,070 ..... B2
Belleair Bluffs 2,128 ..... B3
Belleair Shore 80 ..... B3
Belleview 2,666 ..... D2
Beverly Beach 312 ..... E2
Biscayne Park 3,068 ..... B4
Bithlo 4,834 ..... E3
Blountstown▲ 2,404 ..... A1
Boca Grande 900 ..... D5
Boca Raton 61,492 ..... F5
Bokeelia 750 ..... D5
Bonifay▲ 2,612 ..... C5
Bonita Sings 5,435 ..... E5
Bostwick 500 ..... E2
Boulogne E1
Bowling Green 1,836 ..... E4
Boynton Beach 46,194 ..... F5
Bradenton Beach 1,657 ..... D4
Bradenton▲ 43,779 ..... D4
Bradley 1,108 ..... D4
Brandon 57,985 ..... D4
Branford 670 ..... D2
Briny Breezes 400 ..... G5
Bristol▲ 937 ..... B1
Broadview Park-Rock Hill 6,022 ..... B4
Bronson▲ 875 ..... D2
Brooker 312 ..... D2
Brooksville▲ 7,440 ..... D3
Browardale 6,257 ..... B4
Browns Village B5
Bruce 221 ..... C6
Bunche Park 4,388 ..... B4
Bunnell▲ 1,873 ..... E2
Bushnell▲ 1,998 ..... D3
Callahan 946 ..... E1
Callaway 12,253 ..... D6
Campbellton 202 ..... D5
Canal Point 900 ..... F5
Candler 275 ..... E2
Cantonment B6
Cape Canaveral 8,014 ..... F3
Cape Coral 74,991 ..... E5
Carol City 53,331 ..... B4
Carrabelle 1,200 ..... B2
Caryville 631 ..... C6
Cassadaga 325 ..... E3
Casselberry 18,911 ..... E3
Cedar Grove 1,479 ..... D6
Cedar Key 668 ..... C2
Center Hill 735 ..... D3
Century 1,989 ..... B5
Charlotte Harbor 3,327 ..... E5
Chattahoochee 4,382 ..... B1
Cherry Lake Farms 400 ..... C1
Chiefland 1,917 ..... D2
Chipley▲ 3,866 ..... D6
Chokoloskee 600 ..... E6
Christmas 800 ..... E3
Cinco Bayou 322 ..... B6
Citra 500 ..... D2
Clarksville 350 ..... D6
Clearwater▲ 98,784 ..... B2
Clermont 6,910 ..... E3
Cleveland 2,896 ..... E5
Clewiston 6,085 ..... E5
Cocoa 17,722 ..... F3
Cocoa Beach 12,123 ..... F3
Coconut Creek 27,485 ..... F5
Coleman 857 ..... D3
Compass Lake 296 ..... D6
Concord 300 ..... B1
Cooper City 20,791 ..... B4
Copeland 350 ..... E6
Coral Cove 2,042 ..... D4
Coral Gables 40,091 ..... B5
Coral Springs 79,443 ..... F5
Cornwell 700 ..... E4
Cortez 4,509 ..... D4
Cottagehill 500 ..... B6
Cottondale 900 ..... D6
Crawfordville▲ 1,110 ..... B1
Crescent City 1,859 ..... E2
Crestview▲ 9,886 ..... C6
Cross City▲ 2,041 ..... C2
Crystal Lake 5,300 ..... D6
Crystal River 4,044 ..... D3
Crystal Springs 800 ..... D3
Cutler Ridge 21,268 ..... F6
Cypress 9,188 ..... A1
Cypress Gardens 8,043 ..... E3
Cypress Quarters 1,343 ..... F4
Dade City▲ 5,633 ..... D3
Dania 13,024 ..... B4
Davenport 1,529 ..... E3
Davie 47,217 ..... B4
Day 61,921 ..... C1
Daytona Beach 2,335 ..... F2
Daytona Beach Shores 1,324 ..... F2
De Bary 7,176 ..... E3
De Funiak Springs▲ 5,120 ..... C6
De Land▲ 16,491 ..... E2
De Leon Springs 1,481 ..... E2
Deer Park 250 ..... F3
Deerfield Beach 46,325 ..... F5
Delray Beach 47,181 ..... F5
Deltona 50,828 ..... E3
Destin 8,080 ..... C6
Doctors Inlet 800 ..... E1
Dover 2,606 ..... D4
Dowling Park 250 ..... C1
Dundee 2,335 ..... E3
Dunedin 34,012 ..... B2
Dunnellon 1,624 ..... D2
Eagle Lake 1,758 ..... E4
Earleton 350 ..... D2
East Lake-Orient Park 6,171 ..... C2
East Naples 22,951 ..... E5
East Palatka 1,989 ..... E2
Eastpoint 1,577 ..... B2
Eatonville 2,170 ..... E3
Ebro 255 ..... C6
Edgewater 15,337 ..... F3
Edgewood 1,062 ..... E3
Egypt Lake 14,580 ..... C2
El Portal 2,457 ..... B4
Elfers 12,356 ..... D3
Elkton 240 ..... E2
Englewood 15,025 ..... D5
Ensley 16,362 ..... B6
Espanola 300 ..... E2
Estero 3,177 ..... E5
Esto 253 ..... C5
Eustis 12,967 ..... E3
Everglades City 524 ..... E6
Fairbanks 300 ..... D2
Fairfield 450 ..... D2
Fanning Springs 493 ..... C2
Felda 500 ..... E5
Fellsmere 2,179 ..... F4
Fernandina Beach▲ 8,765 ..... E1
Five Points 1,136 ..... D1
Flagler Beach 3,820 ..... E2
Florahome 400 ..... E2
Floral City 2,609 ..... D3
Florida City 5,806 ..... F6
Florida Ridge 12,218 ..... F4
Foley 525 ..... C1
Fort Denaud 600 ..... E5
Fort Green 300 ..... E4
Fort Lauderdale▲ 149,377 ..... C4
Fort McCoy 600 ..... E2
Fort Meade 4,976 ..... E4
Fort Myers Beach 9,284 ..... E5
Fort Myers▲ 45,206 ..... E5
Fort Ogden 900 ..... E4
Fort Pierce▲ 36,830 ..... F4
Fort Walton Beach 21,471 ..... C6
Fort White 268 ..... D2
Fountain 900 ..... D6
Freeport 843 ..... C6
Frink 275 ..... D6
Frostproof 2,808 ..... E4
Fruitland Park 2,754 ..... D3
Fruitville 9,808 ..... D4
Gainesville▲ 84,770 ..... D2
Geneva 1,120 ..... E3
Georgetown 687 ..... E2
Gibsonton 7,706 ..... C3
Gifford 6,278 ..... F4
Glen Saint Mary 462 ..... D1
Glenwood 400 ..... E2
Golden Beach 774 ..... C4
Golden Gate 14,148 ..... E5
Golf 234 ..... F5
Gomez 400 ..... F4
Gonzalez 7,669 ..... B6
Goodland 600 ..... E6
Goulding 4,159 ..... B6
Goulds 7,284 ..... F6
Graceville 2,675 ..... D5
Graham 225 ..... D2
Grand Ridge 536 ..... A1
Grandin 250 ..... E2
Grant 500 ..... F4
Green Cove Springs▲ 4,497 ..... E2
Greenacres City 18,683 ..... F5
Greensboro 586 ..... B1
Greenville 950 ..... C1
Greenwood 474 ..... A1
Gretna 1,981 ..... B1
Grove City 2,374 ..... D5
Groveland 2,300 ..... E3
Gulf Breeze 5,530 ..... B6
Gulf Hammock 325 ..... D2
Gulf Harbors D3
Gulf Stream 690 ..... F5
Gulfport 11,727 ..... B3
Haines City 11,683 ..... E3
Hallandale 30,996 ..... B4
Hampton 296 ..... D2
Harlem 2,826 ..... F5
Harold 500 ..... B6
Hastings 595 ..... E2
Havana 1,654 ..... B1
Hawthorne 1,305 ..... D2
Hernando 2,103 ..... D3
Hialeah 188,004 ..... B4
Hialeah Gardens 7,713 ..... B4
High Point 2,288 ..... B3
High Springs 3,144 ..... D2
Highland Beach 3,209 ..... F5
Highland City 1,919 ..... E4
Highland Park 155 ..... E4
Hiland Park 3,865 ..... C6
Hillcrest Heights 221 ..... E4
Hilliard 1,751 ..... E1
Hillsboro Beach 1,748 ..... F5
Hinson 250 ..... B1
Hobe Sound 11,507 ..... F4
Holder 350 ..... D3
Hollister 980 ..... E2
Holly Hill 11,141 ..... E2
Hollywood 121,697 ..... B4
Holmes Beach 4,810 ..... D4
Holt 850 ..... C6
Homestead 26,866 ..... F6
Homosassa 2,113 ..... D3
Homosassa Springs 6,271 ..... D3
Horseshoe Beach 252 ..... C2
Hosford 750 ..... B1
Howey In The Hills 724 ..... E3
Hudson 7,344 ..... D3
Hurlburt B6
Hypoluxo 830 ..... F5
Immokalee 14,120 ..... E5
Indialantic 2,844 ..... F3
Indian Creek 44 ..... B4
Indian Harbour Beach 6,933 ..... F3
Indian River Shores 2,278 ..... F4
Indian Rocks Beach 3,963 ..... B3
Indian Shores 1,405 ..... B3
Indiantown 4,794 ..... F4
Inglis 1,241 ..... D2
Intercession City 600 ..... E3
Interlachen 1,160 ..... E2
Inverness▲ 5,797 ..... D3
Islamorada 1,220 ..... F7
Islandia 13 ..... F6
Jacksonville Beach 17,839 ..... E1
Jacksonville▲ 672,971 ..... E1
Jasmine Estates 17,136 ..... D3
Jasper▲ 2,099 ..... D1
Jay 666 ..... B5
Jennings 712 ..... C1
Jensen Beach 9,884 ..... F4
June Park 4,080 ..... F3
Juno Beach 2,121 ..... F5
Jupiter 24,986 ..... F5
Jupiter Island 549 ..... F4
Kathleen 2,743 ..... D3
Kenansville 650 ..... F4
Kendall 87,271 ..... B5
Kenneth City 4,462 ..... B3
Key Biscayne 8,854 ..... B5
Key Colony Beach 977 ..... F7
Key Largo 11,336 ..... F6
Key West▲ 24,832 ..... E7
Keystone Heights 1,315 ..... E2
Kinard 295 ..... D6
Kissimmee▲ 30,050 ..... E3
La Belle▲ 2,703 ..... E5
La Crosse 122 ..... D2
Lacoochee 2,072 ..... D3
Lady Lake 8,071 ..... E3
Lake Alfred 3,622 ..... E3
Lake Buena Vista 1,776 ..... E3
Lake Butler▲ 2,116 ..... D1
Lake Carroll 13,012 ..... C2
Lake City▲ 10,005 ..... D1
Lake Como 340 ..... E2
Lake Forest B4
Lake Harbor 600 ..... F5
Lake Helen 2,344 ..... E3
Lake Jem 314 ..... E3
Lake Magdalene 15,973 ..... D3
Lake Mary 5,929 ..... E3
Lake Monroe 500 ..... E3
Lake Park 6,704 ..... F5
Lake Placid 1,158 ..... E4
Lake Wales 9,670 ..... E4
Lake Worth 28,564 ..... G5
Lakeland 70,576 ..... D3
Lakeport 375 ..... E5
Lakewood 7,211 ..... C5
Land O'Lakes 7,892 ..... D3
Lantana 8,392 ..... F5
Largo 65,674 ..... B3
Lauderdale Lakes 27,341 ..... B3
Lauderdale-by-the-Sea 2,990 ..... C3
Lauderhill 49,708 ..... B3
Laurel 8,245 ..... D4
Laurel Hill 543 ..... C5
Lawtey 676 ..... D1
Layton 183 ..... F7
Lazy Lake 33 ..... B3
Lecanto 1,243 ..... D3
Lee 306 ..... C1
Leesburg 14,903 ..... E3

(continued on following page)

(continued)

Lehigh Acres 13,611 ... E5
Leisure City 19,379 ... F6
Leonia 350 ... C5
Leto ... C2
Lighthouse Point 10,378 ... F5
Live Oak▲ 6,332 ... D1
Lloyd 500 ... C1
Lochloosa 400 ... E2
Longboat Key 5,937 ... D4
Longwood 13,316 ... E3
Lorida 950 ... E4
Loughman 1,214 ... E3
Lowell 250 ... D2
Loxahatchee 950 ... F5
Lutz 10,552 ... D3
Lynn Haven 9,298 ... C6
Macclenny▲ 3,966 ... D1
Madeira Beach 4,225 ... B3
Madison▲ 3,345 ... C1
Maitland 9,110 ... E3
Malabar 1,977 ... F3
Malone 765 ... A1
Mango 8,700 ... D4
Marathon 8,857 ... E7
Marco (Marco Island) 9,493 ... E6
Margate 42,985 ... F5
Marianna▲ 6,292 ... A1
Marineland 21 ... E2
Mary Esther 4,139 ... B6
Masaryktown 389 ... D3
Mascotte 1,761 ... E3
Mayo▲ 917 ... C1
McDavid 500 ... B5
McIntosh 411 ... D2
Medley 663 ... B4
Melbourne 59,646 ... F3
Melbourne Beach 3,021 ... F3
Melrose 6,477 ... D2
Melrose Park 5,672 ... B4
Memphis 6,760 ... D4
Merritt Island 32,886 ... F3
Mexico Beach 992 ... D6
Miami▲ 358,548 ... B5
Miami Beach 92,639 ... C5
Miami Lakes 12,750 ... B4
Miami Shores 10,084 ... B4
Miami Springs 13,268 ... B5
Micanopy 612 ... D2
Micco 8,757 ... F4
Miccosukee 300 ... B1
Middleburg 6,223 ... E1
Midway 852 ... B1
Milligan 950 ... C6
Milton▲ 7,216 ... B6
Mims 9,412 ... F3
Minneola 1,515 ... E3
Miramar 40,663 ... B4
Molino 1,207 ... B6
Montbrook 250 ... D2
Monticello▲ 2,573 ... C1
Montverde 890 ... E3
Moore Haven▲ 1,432 ... E5
Mossy Head 280 ... C6
Mount Dora 7,196 ... E3
Mulberry 2,988 ... E4
Murdock 272 ... D4
Myakka City 672 ... D4
Myrtle Grove 17,402 ... B6
Naples▲ 19,505 ... E5
Naples Park 8,002 ... E5
Naranja 5,790 ... F6
Neptune Beach 6,816 ... E1
Newberry 1,644 ... D2
New Port Richey 14,044 ... D3
New Smyrna Beach 16,543 ... F2
Niceville 10,507 ... C6
Nichols 300 ... E4
Nocatee 950 ... E4
Nokomis 3,448 ... D4
Noma 207 ... C5
Norland 22,109 ... B4
North Bay Village 5,383 ... B4
North Fort Myers 30,027 ... E5
North Lauderdale 26,506 ... B3
North Miami 49,998 ... B4
North Miami Beach 35,359 ... C4
North Naples 13,422 ... E5
North Palm Beach 11,343 ... F5
North Port 11,973 ... D4
North Redington Beach 1,135 ... B3
Oak Hill 917 ... F3
Oakland 700 ... E3
Oakland Park 26,326 ... B3
Ocala▲ 42,045 ... D2
Ocean Breeze Park 519 ... F4
Ocean Ridge 1,570 ... F5
Ochopee 750 ... E6
Ocoee 12,778 ... E3
Odessa 500 ... D3
Ojus 15,519 ... B4
Okahumpka 900 ... D3
Okeechobee▲ 4,943 ... F4
Oklawaha 700 ... E2
Old Town 850 ... C2
Oldsmar 8,361 ... B2
Olustee 400 ... D1
Ona ... E4
Oneco ... D4
Opa Locka 15,283 ... B4
Orange ... B1
Orange City 5,347 ... E3
Orange Lake 900 ... D2
Orange Park 9,488 ... E1
Orange Springs 500 ... E2
Orchid 10 ... F4
Orlando▲ 164,693 ... E3
Ormond Beach 29,721 ... E2
Ormond-by-the-Sea 8,157 ... E2
Osprey 2,597 ... D4
Osteen 875 ... E3
Otter Creek 136 ... D2
Oviedo 11,114 ... E3
Oxford ... D3
Ozona 900 ... D3
Pace 6,277 ... B6
Pahokee 6,822 ... F5
Palatka▲ 10,201 ... E2
Palm Bay 62,632 ... F3
Palm Beach 9,814 ... G5
Palm Beach Gardens 22,965 ... F5
Palm Beach Shores 1,040 ... G5
Palm City 3,925 ... F4
Palm Coast 14,287 ... E2
Palmetto 9,268 ... D4
Palm Harbor 50,256 ... D3
Palm River-Clair Mel 13,691 ... C3
Palm Shores 210 ... F3
Palm Springs 9,763 ... F5
Panacea 950 ... B1
Panama City▲ 34,378 ... C6
Panama City Beach 4,051 ... C6
Parker 4,598 ... C6
Parkland 3,558 ... F5
Parrish 950 ... D4
Paxton 600 ... C5
Pembroke Park 4,933 ... B4
Pembroke Pines 65,452 ... B4
Penney Farms 609 ... E2
Pennsuco 15 ... B4
Pensacola▲ 58,165 ... B6
Perrine 15,576 ... F6
Perry▲ 7,151 ... C1
Pierce 500 ... E4
Pierson 2,988 ... E2
Pine Hills 35,322 ... E3
Pineland 700 ... D5
Pinellas Park 43,426 ... B3
Placida 250 ... D5
Plantation 1,885 ... B4
Plant City 22,754 ... D3
Plymouth 950 ... E3
Polk City 1,439 ... E3
Pomona Park 663 ... E2
Pompano Beach 72,411 ... F5
Ponce de Leon 406 ... C6
Ponce Inlet 1,704 ... F2
Ponte Vedra Beach ... E1
Port Charlotte 41,535 ... D5
Portland 300 ... C6
Port Mayaca 400 ... F5
Port Orange 35,317 ... F2
Port Richey 2,523 ... D3
Port Saint Joe 4,044 ... D6
Port Saint Lucie 55,866 ... F4
Port Salerno 7,786 ... F4
Princeton 7,073 ... F6
Progress Village ... C3
Punta Gorda▲ 10,747 ... E5
Quincy▲ 7,444 ... B1
Raiford 198 ... D1
Raleigh 275 ... D2
Red Bay 300 ... C6
Reddick 554 ... D2
Redington Beach 1,626 ... B3
Redington Shores 2,366 ... B3
Richland 250 ... D3
Richmond Heights 8,583 ... F6
Riverland 5,376 ... B4
Riverview 6,478 ... D4
Riviera Beach 27,639 ... G5
Rockledge 16,023 ... F3
Roseland 1,379 ... F4
Round Lake 275 ... D6
Ruskin 6,046 ... C3
Safety Harbor 15,124 ... B2
Saint Augustine▲ 11,692 ... E2
Saint Augustine Beach 3,657 ... E2
Saint Catherine 486 ... D3
Saint Cloud 12,453 ... E3
Saint James City 1,904 ... D5
Saint Leo 1,009 ... D3
Saint Lucie 584 ... F4
Saint Marks 307 ... B1
Saint Petersburg 238,629 ... B3
Saint Petersburg Beach 9,200 B3
Samoset 3,119 ... D4
Samsula (Samsula-Spruce Creek) 3,404 ... E2
San Antonio 776 ... D3
Sanderson 800 ... D1
Sanford▲ 32,387 ... E3
Sanibel 5,468 ... D5
San Mateo 975 ... E2
Sarasota▲ 50,961 ... D4
Sarasota Springs 16,088 ... D4
Satellite Beach 9,889 ... F3
Satsuma 610 ... E2
Scottsmoor 900 ... F3
Sea Ranch Lakes 619 ... C3
Sebastian 10,205 ... F4
Sebring▲ 8,900 ... E4
Seffner 5,371 ... D4
Seminole 9,251 ... B3
Seville 500 ... E2
Sewall's Point 1,588 ... F4
Shalimar 341 ... C6
Sharpes 3,348 ... F3
Siesta Key 7,772 ... D4
Silver Springs ... D2
Sneads 1,746 ... B1
Sopchoppy 367 ... B1
Sorrento 500 ... E3
South Bay 3,558 ... F5
South Daytona 12,482 ... F2
South Miami 10,404 ... B5
South Miami Heights 30,030 ... F6
South Pasadena 5,644 ... B3
South Patrick Shores 10,249 ... F3
Southport 1,992 ... C6
South Venice 11,951 ... D4
Sparr 902 ... D2
Springfield 8,715 ... D6
Starke▲ 5,226 ... D2
Steinhatchee 800 ... C2
Stuart▲ 11,936 ... F4
Summerfield 780 ... D2
Summerland Key 350 ... E7
Sun City ... D4
Sun City Center 8,326 ... C3
Sunny Isles 11,772 ... C4
Sunnyside 1,008 ... C6
Sunrise 64,407 ... B4
Surfside 4,108 ... B4
Suwannee 365 ... C2
Sweetwater 13,909 ... B5
Switzerland ... E1
Taft 900 ... E3
Tallahassee (cap.)▲ 124,773 ... B1
Tamarac 44,822 ... B3
Tampa▲ 280,015 ... C2
Tarpon Springs 17,906 ... D3
Tavares▲ 7,383 ... E3
Tavernier 2,433 ... F6
Telogia 400 ... B1
Temple Terrace 16,444 ... C2
Tequesta 4,499 ... F5
Terra Ceia 450 ... D4
Thonotosassa 900 ... D3
Tice 3,971 ... E5
Titusville▲ 39,394 ... F3
Town'n Country 60,946 ... B2
Treasure Island 7,266 ... B3
Trenton▲ 1,287 ... D2
Trilby 930 ... D3
Umatilla 2,350 ... E3
University 23,760 ... C2
Valparaiso 4,672 ... C6
Venice 16,922 ... D4
Venus 500 ... E4
Vernon 778 ... C6
Vero Beach▲ 17,350 ... F4
Villa Tasso 365 ... C6
Virginia Gardens 2,212 ... B5
Wabasso 1,145 ... F4
Wacissa 350 ... B1
Wakulla 225 ... B1
Waldo 1,017 ... D2
Walnut Hill 500 ... B5
Ward Ridge 104 ... D7
Warrington 16,040 ... B6
Watertown 3,340 ... D1
Wauchula▲ 3,253 ... E4
Wausau 313 ... D6
Waverly 2,071 ... E4
Webster 746 ... D3
Weeki Wachee 53 ... D3
Weirsdale 995 ... D3
Welaka 533 ... E2
Wellborn 500 ... D1
West Bay 500 ... C6
West Eau Gallie ... F3
West Melbourne 8,399 ... F3
West Miami 5,727 ... B5
West Palm Beach▲ 67,643 ... F5
West Pensacola 22,107 ... B6
Westville 257 ... C6
Westwood Lakes 11,522 ... B5
Wewahitchka▲ 1,779 ... D6
White City 4,645 ... F4
White Springs 704 ... D1
Wildwood 3,421 ... D3
Williston 2,179 ... D2
Wilton Manors 11,804 ... B3
Wimauma 2,932 ... D4
Windermere 1,371 ... E3
Winter Beach 350 ... F4
Winter Garden 9,745 ... E3
Winter Haven 24,725 ... E3
Winter Park 22,242 ... E3
Winter Springs 22,151 ... E3
Woodville 2,760 ... B1
Worthington Springs 178 ... D2
Yalaha 1,168 ... E3
Yankeetown 635 ... D2
Youngstown 900 ... D6
Yulee 6,915 ... E1
Zellwood 1,760 ... E3
Zephyrhills 8,220 ... D3
Zolfo Springs 1,219 ... E4

OTHER FEATURES

Alapaha (riv.) ... C1
Alligator (lake) ... E3
Amelia (isl.) ... E1
Anastasia (isl.) ... E2
Anclote (keys) ... D3
Apalachee (bay) ... B2
Apalachicola (bay) ... B2
Apalachicola (riv.) ... A1
Apopka (lake) ... E3
Arbuckle (lake) ... E4
Aucilla (riv.) ... C1
Banana (riv.) ... F3
Beresford (lake) ... E3
Big Cypress (swamp) ... E5
Big Cypress Nat'l Preserve ... E5
Biscayne (bay) ... F6
Biscayne (key) ... B5
Biscayne Nat'l Park ... F6
Blackwater (riv.) ... B6
Blue Cypress (lake) ... F4
Boca Chica (key) ... E7
Boca Ciega (key) ... B3
Boca Grande (key) ... D7
Bryant (lake) ... E2
Caloosahatchee (riv.) ... E5
Canaveral (cape) ... F3
Captiva (isl.) ... D5
Casey (key) ... D4
Castillo de San Marcos Nat'l Mon. ... E2
Cecil Field Naval Air Sta. ... E1
Charlotte (harb.) ... D5
Chattahoochee (riv.) ... B1
Chipola (riv.) ... D6
Choctawhatchee (riv.) ... C6
Crescent (lake) ... E2
Cumberland Island Nat'l Seashore ... E1
Cypress (lake) ... E3
De Soto Nat'l Mem. ... D4
Dead (lake) ... D6
Dexter (lake) ... E2
Dog (isl.) ... B2
Dorr (lake) ... E2
Dry Tortugas (keys) ... D7
Dry Tortugas Nat'l Park ... C7
Dumfoundling (bay) ... C4
East (pt.) ... E6
Eglin A.F.B 8,347. ... C6
Egmont (key) ... D4
Elliott (key) ... F6
Escambia (riv.) ... B6
Estero (isl.) ... E5
Eureka (res.) ... E2
Everglades, The (swamp) ... F6
Everglades Nat'l Park ... E6
Fenholloway (riv.) ... C1
Florida (bay) ... F6
Florida (cape) ... F6
Florida (keys) ... E7
Florida (strs.) ... F7
Fort Caroline Nat'l Mem. ... E1
Fort Matanzas Nat'l Mon. ... E2
Gasparilla (isl.) ... D5
George (lake) ... E2
Grassy (key) ... F7
Gulf Islands Nat'l Seashore ... B6
Harney (lake) ... F3
Hart (lake) ... E3
Hillsborough (bay) ... C3
Hillsborough (canal) ... F5
Hillsborough (riv.) ... C2
Homestead A.F.B 5,153. ... F6
Homosassa (isls.) ... D3
Iamonia (lake) ... B1
Indian (riv.) ... F3
Iron (mt.) ... E4
Istokpoga (lake) ... E4
Jackson (lake) ... B1
Jackson (lake) ... E4
Jacksonville Naval Air Sta. ... E1
John F. Kennedy Space Center ... F3
June in Winter (lake) ... E4
Kerr (lake) ... E2
Key Largo (key) ... F6
Key Vaca (key) ... E7
Key West Naval Air Sta. ... E7
Kissimmee (lake) ... E4
Kissimmee (riv.) ... E4
Largo (key) ... F6
Levy (lake) ... D2
Lochloosa (lake) ... D2
Long (key) ... B3
Long (key) ... F7
Longboat (key) ... D4
Lower Matecumbe (key) ... F7
Lowery (lake) ... E3
MacDill A.F.B. ... C3
Manatee (riv.) ... D4
Marco (isl.) ... E6
Marian (lake) ... E4
Marquesas (keys) ... D7
Matanzas (inlet) ... E2
Mayport Naval Air Sta. ... E1
McCoy A.F.B. ... E3
Merritt (isl.) ... F3
Mexico (gulf) ... C4
Miami (canal) ... F5
Miami (riv.) ... B5
Miccosukee (lake) ... B1
Monroe (lake) ... E3
Mosquito (lag.) ... F3
Mullet (key) ... D4
Myakka (riv.) ... D4
Nassau (riv.) ... E1
Nassau (sound) ... E1
New (riv.) ... B1
New (riv.) ... D1
Newnans (lake) ... D2
North Merritt (isl.) ... F3
North New River (canal) ... F5
Ochlockonee (riv.) ... B1
Okaloacoochee Slough (swamp) ... E5
Okeechobee (lake) ... F5
Okefenokee (swamp) ... D1
Oklawaha (riv.) ... E2
Old Rhodes (key) ... F6
Old Tampa (bay) ... B3
Olustee (riv.) ... D1
Orange (lake) ... D2
Patrick A.F.B. ... F3
Peace (riv.) ... E4
Pensacola (bay) ... B6
Pensacola Naval Air Sta. ... B6
Perdido (riv.) ... B6
Pine (isl.) ... D5
Pine Island (sound) ... D5
Pinellas (pt.) ... B3
Piney (isl.) ... B1
Piney (pt.) ... C2
Placid (lake) ... E4
Plantation (key) ... F7
Poinsett (lake) ... F3
Ponce de Leon (bay) ... E6
Port Everglades (harb.) ... C4
Poet Tampa (harb.) ... B3
Raccoon (pt.) ... D3
Reedy (lake) ... E4
Romano (cape) ... E6
Sable (cape) ... E6
Saint Andrew (pt.) ... D6
Saint George (cape) ... A2
Saint George (isl.) ... B2
Saint George (sound) ... B2
Saint Johns (riv.) ... E2
Saint Joseph (bay) ... D6
Saint Joseph (pt.) ... D6
Saint Lucie (canal) ... F4
Saint Lucie (inlet) ... F4
Saint Marys (riv.) ... D1
Saint Marys Entrance (inlet) ... E1
Saint Vincent (isl.) ... D7
San Blas (cape) ... D7
Sand (key) ... B3
Sands (key) ... F6
Sanibel (isl.) ... D5
Santa Fe (lake) ... D2
Santa Fe (riv.) ... D2
Santa Rosa (isl.) ... B6
Santa Rosa (sound) ... B6
Sarasota (pt.) ... D4
Seminole (lake) ... B1
Seminole Ind. Res. ... E4
Seminole Ind. Res. ... E5
Shark (pt.) ... E6
Shoal (riv.) ... C6
Snake Creek (canal) ... B4
South New River (canal) ... F5
Stafford (lake) ... D2
Sugarloaf (key) ... E7
Suwannee (riv.) ... C2
Suwannee (sound) ... C2
Talbot (isl.) ... E1
Talquin (lake) ... B1
Tamiami (canal) ... E5
Tampa (bay) ... D4
Ten Thousand (isls.) ... E6
Timucuan Ecological and Historical Preserve ... E1
Torch (key) ... E7
Treasure (isl.) ... B3
Tsala Apopka (lake) ... D3
Tyndall A.F.B. ... C6
Upper Matecumbe (key) ... F7
Vaca (key) ... E7
Virginia (key) ... B5
Waccasassa (bay) ... D2
Waccasassa (riv.) ... D2
Washington (lake) ... F3
Weir (lake) ... E2
Weohyakapka (lake) ... E4
West Palm Beach (canal) ... F5
Whitewater (bay) ... F6
Whiting Field Naval Air Sta. ... B6
Wimico (lake) ... A2
Winder (lake) ... F3
Withlacoochee (riv.) ... C1
Withlacoochee (riv.) ... D2
Yale (lake) ... E3
Yellow (riv.) ... B6

▲County seat

Agriculture, Industry and Resources

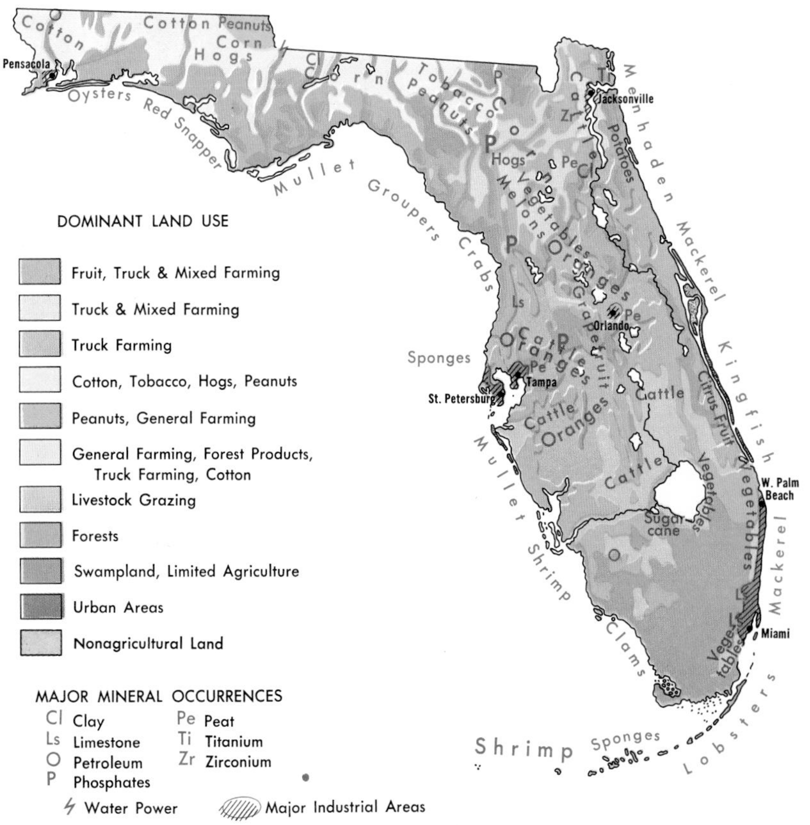

Cotton
Cotton Peanuts
Corn
Hogs
Pensacola
Oysters
Red Snapper
Mullet
Groupers
Crabs
Tobacco
Peanuts
Jacksonville
Menhaden
Potatoes
Mackerel
Vegetables
Melons
Oranges
Orlando
Grapefruit
Sponges
Tampa
St. Petersburg
Cattle
Kingfish
Citrus Fruit
W. Palm Beach
Sugar cane
Shrimp
Miami
Clams
Lobsters
DOMINANT LAND USE
Fruit, Truck & Mixed Farming
Truck & Mixed Farming
Truck Farming
Cotton, Tobacco, Hogs, Peanuts
Peanuts, General Farming
General Farming, Forest Products, Truck Farming, Cotton
Livestock Grazing
Forests
Swampland, Limited Agriculture
Urban Areas
Nonagricultural Land
MAJOR MINERAL OCCURRENCES
Cl Clay
Ls Limestone
O Petroleum
P Phosphates
Pe Peat
Ti Titanium
Zr Zirconium
Water Power
Major Industrial Areas

STATE OF GEORGIA
1776

AREA 58,910 sq. mi. (152,577 sq. km.)
POPULATION 6,508,419
CAPITAL Atlanta
LARGEST CITY Atlanta
HIGHEST POINT Brasstown Bald 4,784 ft. (1458 m.)
SETTLED IN 1733
ADMITTED TO UNION January 2, 1788
POPULAR NAME Empire State of the South; Peach State
STATE FLOWER Cherokee Rose
STATE BIRD Brown Thrasher

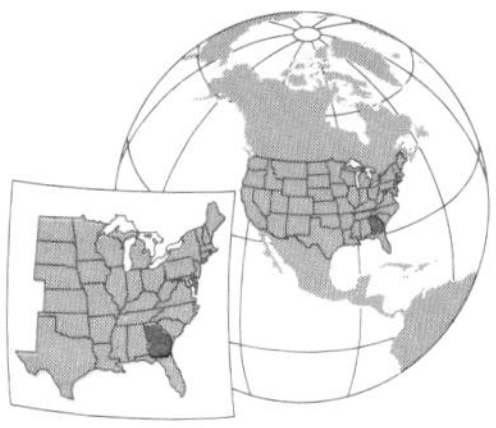

COUNTIES

Appling 15,744 .... H7
Atkinson 6,213 .... G8
Bacon 9,566 .... G7
Baker 3,615 .... D8
Baldwin 39,530 .... F4
Banks 10,308 .... E2
Barrow 29,721 .... E2
Bartow 55,911 .... C2
Ben Hill 16,245 .... F7
Berrien 14,153 .... F8
Bibb 149,967 .... E5
Bleckley 10,430 .... F6
Brantley 11,077 .... J8
Brooks 15,398 .... E9
Bryan 15,438 .... K6
Bulloch 43,125 .... J6
Burke 20,579 .... J4
Butts 15,326 .... E4
Calhoun 5,013 .... C7
Camden 30,167 .... J9
Candler 7,744 .... H6
Carroll 71,422 .... B3
Catoosa 42,464 .... B1
Charlton 8,496 .... H9
Chatham 216,935 .... K6
Chattahoochee 16,934 .... C6
Chattooga 22,242 .... B1
Cherokee 90,204 .... D2
Clarke 87,594 .... F3
Clay 3;364 .... B7
Clayton 182,052 .... D3
Clinch 6,160 .... G9
Cobb 447,745 .... C3
Coffee 29,592 .... G8
Colquitt 36,645 .... E8
Columbia 66,031 .... H3
Cook 13,456 .... F8
Coweta 53,853 .... C4
Crawford 8,991 .... E5
Crisp 20,011 .... E7
Dade 13,147 .... A1
Dawson 9,429 .... D2
De Kalb 483,024 .... D3
Decatur 25,511 .... C9
Dodge 17,607 .... F6
Dooly 9,901 .... E6
Dougherty 96,311 .... D7
Douglas 71,120 .... C3
Early 11,854 .... C8
Echols 2,334 .... G9
Effingham 25,687 .... K6
Elbert 18,949 .... G2
Emanuel 20,546 .... H5
Evans 8,724 .... J6
Fannin 15,992 .... D1
Fayette 62,415 .... C4
Floyd 81,251 .... B2
Forsyth 44,083 .... D2
Franklin 16,650 .... F2
Fulton 648,951 .... D3
Gilmer 13,368 .... D1
Glascock 2,357 .... G4
Glynn 62,496 .... J8
Gordon 35,072 .... C2
Grady 20,279 .... D9
Greene 11,793 .... F3
Gwinnett 352,910 .... D2
Habersham 27,621 .... E1
Hall 95,428 .... E2
Hancock 8,908 .... G4
Haralson 21,966 .... B3
Harris 17,788 .... C5
Hart 19,712 .... G2
Heard 8,628 .... B4
Henry 58,741 .... D4
Houston 89,208 .... E6
Irwin 8,649 .... F7
Jackson 30,005 .... E2
Jasper 8,453 .... E4
Jeff Davis 12,032 .... G7
Jefferson 17,408 .... H4
Jenkins 8,247 .... J5
Johnson 8,329 .... G5
Jones 20,739 .... E5
Lamar 13,038 .... D4
Lanier 5,531 .... F8
Laurens 39,988 .... G6
Lee 16,250 .... D7
Liberty 52,745 .... J7
Lincoln 7,442 .... H3
Long 6,202 .... J7
Lowndes 75,981 .... F9
Lumpkin 14,573 .... D1
Macon 13,114 .... D6
Madison 21,050 .... F2
Marion 5,590 .... C6
McDuffie 20,119 .... H4
McIntosh 8,634 .... K7
Meriwether 22,411 .... C4
Miller 6,280 .... C8
Mitchell 20,275 .... D8
Monroe 17,113 .... E4
Montgomery 7,163 .... G6
Morgan 12,883 .... F3
Murray 26,147 .... C1
Muscogee 179,278 .... C6
Newton 41,808 .... E3
Oconee 17,618 .... F3
Oglethore 8,929 .... F3
Paulding 41,611 .... C3
Peach 21,189 .... E5
Pickens 14,432 .... D2
Pierce 13,328 .... H8
Pike 10,224 .... D4
Polk 33,815 .... B3
Pulaski 8,108 .... E6
Putnam 14,137 .... F4
Quitman 2,209 .... B7
Rabun 11,648 .... F1
Randolph 8,023 .... C7
Richmond 189,719 .... H4
Rockdale 54,091 .... D3
Schley 3,588 .... D6
Screven 13,842 .... J5
Semincle 9,010 .... C9
Spalding 54,457 .... D4
Stephens 23,257 .... F1
Stewart 5,654 .... C6
Sumter 30,228 .... D6
Talbot 6,524 .... C5
Taliaferro 1,915 .... G3
Tattnall 17,722 .... H6
Taylor 7,642 .... D5
Telfair 11,000 .... G7
Terrell 10,653 .... D7
Thomas 38,986 .... E9
Tift 34,998 .... E7
Toombs 24,072 .... H6
Towns 6,754 .... E1
Treutlen 5,994 .... G6
Troup 55,536 .... B4
Turner 8,703 .... E7
Twiggs 9,806 .... F5
Union 11,993 .... E1
Upson 26,300 .... D5
Walker 58,340 .... B1
Walton 38,586 .... E3
Ware 35,471 .... H8
Warren 6,078 .... G4
Washington 19,112 .... G4
Wayne 22,356 .... J7
Webster 2,263 .... C6
Wheeler 4,903 .... G6
White 13,006 .... E1
Whitfield 72,462 .... B1
Wilcox 7,008 .... F7
Wilkes 10,597 .... G3
Wilkinson 10,228 .... F5
Worth 19,745 .... E8

CITIES and TOWNS

Abbeville▲ 907 .... F7
Acworth 4,519 .... C2
Adairsville 2,131 .... C2
Adel▲ 5,093 .... F8
Adrian 615 .... G5
Ailey 579 .... G6
Alamo▲ 855 .... G6
Alapaha 812 .... F8
Albany▲ 78,122 .... D7
Aldora 127 .... D4
Allenhurst 594 .... J7
Allentown 273 .... F5
Alma▲ 3,663 .... G7
Alpharetta 13,002 .... D2
Alston 160 .... H6
Alto 651 .... E2
Alvaton 91 .... C4
Ambrose 288 .... G7
Americus▲ 16,512 .... D6
Andersonville 277 .... D6
Appling▲ 150 .... H3
Arabi 433 .... E7
Aragon 902 .... B2
Arcade 697 .... E2
Arco 6,189 .... J8
Argyle 206 .... G8
Arlington 1,513 .... C8
Armuchee 600 .... B2
Arnoldsville 275 .... F3
Ashburn▲ 4,827 .... E7
Athens▲ 45,734 .... F3
Atlanta (cap.)▲ 394,017 .... K1
Attapulgus 380 .... D9
Auburn 3,139 .... E2
Augusta▲ 44,639 .... J4
Austell 4,173 .... J1
Avalon 159 .... F1
Avera 215 .... G4
Avondale Estates 2,209 .... L1
Baconton 623 .... D8
Bainbridge▲ 10,712 .... C9
Baldwin 1,439 .... E2
Ball Ground 905 .... D2
Barnesville▲ 4,747 .... D4
Barney 146 .... E8
Bartow 292 .... G5
Barwick 385 .... E9
Baxley▲ 3,841 .... H7
Bellville 192 .... H6
Belvedere 18,089 .... L1
Benevolence 138 .... C7
Berkeley Lake 791 .... D3
Berlin 480 .... E8
Bethlehem 348 .... E3
Between 82 .... E3
Bibb City 597 .... B5
Bishop 158 .... F3
Blackshear▲ 3,263 .... H8
Blairsville▲ 564 .... E1
Blakely▲ 5,595 .... C8
Bloomingdale 2,271 .... K6
Blue Ridge▲ 1,336 .... D1
Bluffton 138 .... C7
Blythe 300 .... H4
Bogart 1,018 .... E3
Boston 1,395 .... E9
Bostwick 307 .... E3
Bowdon 1,981 .... B3
Bowersville 311 .... F2
Bowman 791 .... G2
Box Springs 518 .... C5
Braselton 418 .... E2
Braswell 247 .... C3
Bremen 4,356 .... B3
Brinson 238 .... C9
Bronwood 513 .... D7
Brookfield 600 .... F8
Brookhaven K1
Brooklet 1,013 .... J6
Brooks 328 .... D4
Broxton 1,211 .... G7
Brunswick▲ 16,433 .... K8
Buchanan▲ 1,009 .... B3
Buckhead 176 .... F3
Buena Vista▲ 1,472 .... D6
Buford 8,771 .... D2
Butler▲ 1,673 .... D5
Byromville 452 .... E6
Byron 2,276 .... E5
Cadwell 458 .... G6
Cairo▲ 9,035 .... D9
Calhoun▲ 7,135 .... C1
Calvary 500 .... D9
Camak 220 .... G4
Camilla▲ 5,008 .... D8
Campton E3
Canon 737 .... F2
Canton▲ 4,817 .... C2
Carl 263 .... E3
Carlton 282 .... F2
Carnesville▲ 514 .... F2
Carrollton▲ 16,029 .... C3
Carters 12,035 .... C1
Cartersville▲ 9,247 .... C2
Cataula 500 .... C5
Cave Spring 950 .... B2
Cecil 376 .... F8
Cedar Grove A1
Cedartown▲ 7,978 .... B2
Center 3,251 .... F2
Centerville 2,622 .... E5
Centralhatchee 301 .... B4
Chalybeate Springs 265 .... C5
Chamblee 7,668 .... K1
Charles H6
Chatsworth▲ 2,865 .... C1
Chauncey 312 .... F6
Chester 1,072 .... F6
Chickamauga 2,149 .... B1
Chula 500 .... E7
Clarkesville▲ 1,151 .... F1
Clarkston 5,385 .... L1
Claxton▲ 2,464 .... J6
Clayton▲ 1,613 .... F1
Clermont 402 .... E2
Cleveland▲ 1,653 .... E1
Climax 226 .... D9
Clyattville 500 .... F9
Cobb 338 .... E7
Cobbtown 494 .... H6
Cochran▲ 4,390 .... F6
Cohutta 529 .... C1
Colbert 443 .... F2
Coleman 137 .... C7
Colemans Lake H5
College Park 20,457 .... K2
Collins 528 .... H6
Colquitt▲ 1,991 .... C8
Columbus▲ 179,278 .... C6
Comer 939 .... F2
Commerce 4,108 .... E2
Concord 211 .... D4
Conley 5,528 .... K2
Constitution K2
Conyers▲ 7,380 .... D3
Coolidge 610 .... E8
Coosa 600 .... B2
Cordele▲ 10,321 .... E7
Corinth 136 .... B4
Cornelia 3,219 .... E1
Cotton 122 .... D8
Covington▲ 10,026 .... E3
Crandall C1
Crawford 694 .... F3
Crawfordville▲ 577 .... G3
Crosland E8
Crystal Springs 500 .... B2
Culloden 242 .... D5
Cumming▲ 2,828 .... D2
Cusseta▲ 1,107 .... C6
Cuthbert▲ 3,730 .... C7
Dacula 2,217 .... E3
Dahlonega▲ 3,086 .... D1
Daisy 138 .... J6
Dallas▲ 2,810 .... C3
Dalton▲ 21,761 .... C1
Damascus 290 .... C8
Danielsville▲ 318 .... F2
Danville 480 .... F5
Darien▲ 1,783 .... K8
Dasher 659 .... F9
Davisboro 407 .... G5
Dawson▲ 5,295 .... D7
Dawsonville▲ 467 .... D2
De Soto 258 .... D7
Dearing 547 .... H4
Decatur▲ 17,336 .... K1
Deenwood 2,055 .... H8
Deepstep 111 .... G4
Demorest 1,088 .... F1
Denton 335 .... G7
Dexter 475 .... G6
Dickey C7
Dillard 199 .... F1
Dixie 259 .... E9
Dock Junction (Arco) J8
Doerun 899 .... E8
Donalsonville▲ 2,761 .... C8
Dooling 28 .... E6
Doraville 7,626 .... K1
Douglas▲ 10,464 .... G7
Douglasville▲ 11,635 .... C3
Dry Branch 700 .... F5
Du Pont 177 .... G9
Dublin▲ 16,312 .... G5
Ducktown D2
Dudley 430 .... F5
Duluth 9,029 .... D2
Dunwoody 26,302 .... K1
Durand 206 .... C5
East Dublin 2,524 .... G5
East Ellijay 303 .... C1
East Juliette E4
East Newnan 1,173 .... C4
East Point 34,402 .... K2
Eastman▲ 5,153 .... F6
Eastville E3
Eatonton▲ 4,737 .... F4
Eden 990 .... K6
Edge Hill 22 .... G4
Edison 1,182 .... C7
Elberta 1,559 .... E5
Elberton▲ 5,682 .... G2
Elizabeth 950 .... J1
Ellabell 500 .... K6
Ellaville▲ 1,724 .... D6
Ellenton 227 .... E8
Ellenwood L2
Ellerslie 700 .... C5
Ellijay▲ 1,178 .... C1
Emerson 1,201 .... C2
Enigma 611 .... F8
Ephesus 324 .... B4

(continued on following page)

Agriculture, Industry and Resources

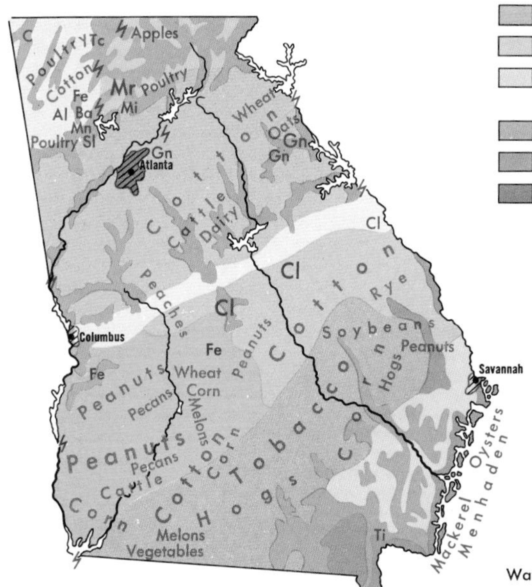
Apples
Poultry
Cotton
Mr
Fe
Al
Ba
Mi
Mn
Sl
Gn
Atlanta
Wheat
Oats
Cattle
Dairy
Cl
Rye
Peaches
Columbus
Peanuts
Soybeans
Savannah
Corn
Pecans
Melons
Tobacco
Hogs
Oysters
Menhaden
Mackerel
Vegetables
Ti

DOMINANT LAND USE

- Specialized Cotton
- Cotton, General Farming
- Cotton, Tobacco, Hogs, Peanuts
- Peanuts, General Farming
- General Farming, Livestock, Fruit, Tobacco
- General Farming, Forest Products, Cotton, Truck Farming
- Forests
- Swampland, Limited Agriculture
- Urban Areas

MAJOR MINERAL OCCURRENCES

- Al Bauxite
- Ba Barite
- C Coal
- Cl Clay
- Fe Iron Ore
- Gn Granite
- Mi Mica
- Mn Manganese
- Mr Marble
- Sl Slate
- Tc Talc
- Ti Titanium

Water Power

Major Industrial Areas

(continued)

Eton 315 ....C1
Euharlee 850 ....C2
Evans 13,713 ....H3
Experiment 3,762 ....D4
Fair Oaks 6,996 ....J1
Fairburn 4,013 ....J2
Fairmount 657 ....C2
Fargo 800 ....G9
Farmington F3
Farrar E4
Fayetteville▲ 5,827 ....C4
Felton 500 ....B3
Finleyson 101 ....F6
Fitzgerald▲ 8,612 ....F7
Fleming 279 ....K7
Flemington 440 ....K7
Flippen 600 ....D3
Flovilla 602 ....E4
Flowery Branch 1,251 ....E2
Floyd J1
Folkston▲ 2,285 ....H9
Forest Park 16,925 ....K2
Forsyth▲ 4,268 ....E4
Fort Gaines▲ 1,248 ....C7
Fort Oglethorpe 5,880 ....B1
Fort Valley▲ 8,198 ....E5
Franklin Springs 475 ....F2
Franklin▲ 876 ....B4
Funston 248 ....E8
Gainesville▲ 17,885 ....E2
Garden City 7,410 ....K6
Garfield 255 ....H5
Gay 133 ....C4
Geneva 182 ....C5
Georgetown▲ 913 ....B7
Gibson▲ 679 ....G4
Gillsville 113 ....E2
Gilmore J1
Girard 195 ....J4
Glenn 3,676 ....B4
Glennville 4,144 ....J7
Glenwood 824 ....G6
Glenwood 881 ....L1
Glynco J8
Good Hope 181 ....E3
Gordon 2,468 ....F5
Grantville 1,180 ....C4
Gray▲ 2,189 ....F4
Grayson 529 ....E3
Graysville 193 ....B1
Greensboro▲ 2,860 ....F3
Greenville▲ 1,167 ....C4
Griffin▲ 21,347 ....D4
Grovetown 3,596 ....H4
Gumbranch 291 ....J7
Guyton 740 ....K6
Haddock 800 ....F4
Hagan 787 ....J6
Hahira 1,353 ....F9
Hamilton▲ 454 ....C5
Hampton 2,694 ....D4
Hapeville 5,483 ....K2
Haralson 139 ....C4
Hardwick (Midway-Hardwick) 8,977 ....F4
Harlem 2,199 ....H4
Harrison 414 ....G5
Hartwell▲ 4,555 ....G2
Hawkinsville▲ 3,527 ....E6
Hazlehurst▲ 4,202 ....G7
Helen 300 ....E1
Helena 1,256 ....G6
Hephzibah 2,466 ....H4
Hiawassee▲ 547 ....E1
Higgston 274 ....G6
Hilltonia 402 ....J5
Hinesville▲ 21,603 ....J7
Hiram 1,389 ....C3
Hoboken 440 ....H8
Hogansville 2,976 ....C4
Holly Springs 2,406 ....D2
Homeland 981 ....H9
Homer▲ 742 ....F2
Homerville▲ 2,560 ....G8
Hoschton 642 ....E2
Howell F9
Hull 156 ....F2
Ideal 554 ....D6
Ila 297 ....F2
Indian Springs 1,273 ....E4
Industrial City 1,054 ....C1
Inman 500 ....D4
Iron City 503 ....C8
Irwinton▲ 641 ....F5
Isle of Hope 975 ....K7
Ivey 1,053 ....F5
Jackson▲ 4,076 ....E4
Jacksonville 128 ....G7
Jakin 137 ....C8
Jasper▲ 1,772 ....D2
Jefferson▲ 2,763 ....F2
Jeffersonville▲ 1,545 ....F5
Jenkinsburg 213 ....E4
Jersey 149 ....E3
Jesup▲ 8,958 ....J7
Jonesboro▲ 3,635 ....D4
Juliette 600 ....E4
Junction City 182 ....C5
Juno 522 ....D2
Kennesaw 8,936 ....C2
Keysville 284 ....H4
Kingsland 4,699 ....J9
Kingston 616 ....C2
Kite 297 ....G5
Knoxville▲ 75 ....E5
La Fayette▲ 6,313 ....B1
La Grange▲ 25,597 ....B4
Lake City 2,733 ....K2
Lake Park 500 ....F9
Lakeland▲ 2,467 ....F8
Lavonia 1,840 ....F2
Lawrenceville▲ 16,848 ....D3
Leary 701 ....C8
Lebanon 800 ....D2
Leesburg▲ 1,452 ....D7
Leland J1
Lenox 783 ....F8
Leslie 445 ....D7
Lexington▲ 230 ....F3
Lilburn 9,301 ....D3
Lilly 138 ....E6
Lincoln Park 1,755 ....D5
Lincolnton▲ 1,476 ....G3
Lindale 4,187 ....B2
Linwood 342 ....B1
Lithia Springs 11,403 ....C3
Lithonia 2,448 ....D3
Lizella 975 ....E5
Locust Grove 1,681 ....D4
Loganville 3,180 ....E3
Lollie G6
Lone Oak 161 ....C4
Lookout Mountain 1,636 ....B1
Louisville▲ 2,429 ....H4
Lovejoy 754 ....D4
Lovett G5
Ludowici▲ 1,291 ....J7
Lula 1,018 ....E2
Lumber City 1,429 ....G7
Lumpkin▲ 1,250 ....C6
Luthersville 741 ....C4
Lyerly 493 ....B2
Lyons▲ 4,502 ....H6
Mableton 25,725 ....J1
Macon▲ 106,612 ....E5
Madison▲ 3,483 ....F3
Manassas 123 ....H6
Manchester 4,104 ....C5
Mansfield 341 ....E4
Marietta▲ 44,129 ....J1
Marlow 500 ....K6
Marshallville 1,457 ....D6
Martin 243 ....F2
Martinez 33,731 ....H3
Matthews H4
Maxeys 180 ....F3
Maysville 728 ....E2
McCaysville 1,065 ....D1
McDonough▲ 2,929 ....D4
McIntosh 500 ....K7
McIntyre 552 ....F5
McRae▲ 3,007 ....G6
Meansville 250 ....D4
Mechanicsville L1
Meigs 1,120 ....D8
Meldrim 510 ....K6
Menlo 538 ....B2
Merrillville E9
Metcalf E9
Metter▲ 3,707 ....H6
Middleton G2
Midville 620 ....H5
Midway 863 ....K7
Milan 1,056 ....G6
Milledgeville▲ 17,727 ....F4
Millen▲ 3,808 ....J5
Milner 321 ....D4
Milstead D3
Mineral Bluff 153 ....D1
Mitchell 181 ....G4
Modoc H5
Molena 439 ....D4
Monroe▲ 9,759 ....E3
Montezuma 4,506 ....E6
Monticello▲ 2,289 ....E4
Montrose 117 ....F5
Moreland 366 ....C4
Morgan▲ 252 ....C7
Morganton 295 ....D1
Morrow 5,168 ....K2
Morven 536 ....E9
Moultrie▲ 14,865 ....E8
Mount Airy 543 ....F1
Mount Berry B2
Mount Bethel K1
Mount Vernon▲ 1,914 ....G6
Mount Zion 511 ....B3
Mountain City 784 ....F1
Mountain Park 554 ....D2
Mountain View K2
Mountville 168 ....C4
Murrayville 550 ....E2
Nahunta▲ 1,049 ....H8
Nashville▲ 4,782 ....F8
Naylor 111 ....F9
Nelson 486 ....D2
New Holland 950 ....E2
Newborn 404 ....E3
Newington 319 ....J5
Newnan▲ 12,497 ....C4
Newton▲ 703 ....D8
Nicholls 1,003 ....G7
Nicholson 535 ....F2
Norcross 5,947 ....D3
Norman Park 711 ....E8
Normantown H6
North Canton 950 ....C2
North High Shoals 268 ....F3
Norwood 238 ....G4
Nunez 135 ....H5
Oak Park 269 ....H6
Oakfield 113 ....E7
Oakman 150 ....C1
Oakwood 1,464 ....E2
Ochlocknee 588 ....E9
Ocilla▲ 3,182 ....F7
Oconee 234 ....G5
Odessadale 142 ....C5
Odum 388 ....H7
Oglethorpe▲ 1,302 ....D6
Ohoopee H6
Oliver 242 ....J5
Omaha 116 ....C6
Omega 912 ....E8
Orchard Hill 239 ....D4
Oxford 1,945 ....E3
Palmetto 2,612 ....C3
Panthersville 9,874 ....L1
Parrott 140 ....D7
Patterson 626 ....H8
Pavo 774 ....E9
Payne 192 ....E5
Peachtree City 19,027 ....C4
Pearson▲ 1,714 ....G8
Pelham 3,869 ....D8
Pembroke▲ 1,503 ....J6
Pendergrass 298 ....E2
Penfield F3
Perry▲ 9,452 ....E6
Phillipsburg 1,044 ....E8
Piedmont D4
Pine Lake 810 ....D3
Pine Mountain 875 ....C5
Pine Park D9
Pinehurst 388 ....E6
Pineora 387 ....K6
Pineview 594 ....F6
Pitts 214 ....E7
Pittsburg L1
Plainfield 128 ....F6
Plains 716 ....D6
Plainville 231 ....C2
Pocotalago F2
Pooler 4,453 ....K6
Port Wentworth 4,012 ....K6
Portal 522 ....J5
Porterdale 1,278 ....E3
Poulan 962 ....E8
Powder Springs 6,893 ....C3
Preston▲ 388 ....C6
Primrose 30 ....C4
Pulaski 264 ....J6
Putney 3,108 ....D8
Quitman▲ 5,292 ....E9
Raleigh C5
Ranger 153 ....C2
Ray City 603 ....F8
Rayle 107 ....G3
Rebecca 148 ....E7
Red Oak 950 ....J2
Register 195 ....J6
Reidsville▲ 2,469 ....H6
Remerton 463 ....F9
Reno D9
Rentz 364 ....G6
Resaca 410 ....C1
Rest Haven 176 ....E2
Reynolds 1,166 ....D5
Rhine 466 ....F7
Riceboro 745 ....K7
Richland 1,668 ....C6
Richmond Hill 2,934 ....K7
Riddleville 79 ....G5
Rincon 2,697 ....K6
Ringgold▲ 1,675 ....B1
Riverdale 9,359 ....K2
Riverside 74 ....B2
Riverside 99 ....E8
Roberta 939 ....D5
Rochelle 1,510 ....F7
Rockmart 3,356 ....B2
Rocky Face 500 ....C1
Rocky Ford 197 ....J5
Rocky Mount 56 ....C4
Rome▲ 30,326 ....B2
Roopville 248 ....B4
Rossville 3,601 ....B1
Roswell 47,923 ....D2
Royston 2,758 ....F2
Ruckersville G2
Russell 871 ....E3
Rutledge 659 ....E3
Saint George 600 ....H9
Saint Marks 36 ....C4
Saint Marys 8,187 ....J9
Saint Simons Island 12,026 ....K8
Sale City 324 ....D8
Sandersville▲ 6,290 ....G5
Sandy Springs 67,842 ....K1
Santa Claus 154 ....H6
Sardis 1,116 ....J5
Sargent 800 ....C4
Sasser 335 ....D7
Savannah▲ 137,560 ....L6
Scotland 244 ....G6
Scott 8,636 ....G5
Scottdale 8,770 ....L1
Screven 819 ....H7
Sea Island 600 ....K8
Senoia 956 ....C4
Seville 209 ....E7
Shady Dale 180 ....E4
Shannon 1,703 ....B2
Sharon 94 ....G3
Sharpsburg 224 ....C4
Shellman 1,162 ....C7
Shiloh 329 ....C5
Siloam 329 ....F3
Silver Creek 500 ....B2
Six Flags Over Georgia J1
Sky Valley 187 ....F1
Smithonia F2
Smithville 804 ....D7
Smyrna 30,981 ....K1
Snellville 12,084 ....D3
Social Circle 2,755 ....E3
Soperton▲ 2,797 ....G6
Sparks 1,205 ....F8
Sparta▲ 1,710 ....F4
Spring Place 246 ....C1
Springfield▲ 1,415 ....K6
Stapleton 330 ....H4
Statenville▲ 700 ....G9
Statesboro▲ 15,854 ....J6
Statham 1,360 ....E3
Stillmore 615 ....H6
Stockbridge 3,359 ....D3
Stockton 532 ....G9
Stone Mountain 6,494 ....D3
Stonewall 950 ....J2
Sugar Hill 4,557 ....E2
Sugar Valley C1
Summertown 153 ....H5
Summerville▲ 5,025 ....B2
Sumner 209 ....E7
Sunny Side 215 ....D4
Surrency 253 ....H7
Suwanee 2,412 ....D2
Swainsboro▲ 7,361 ....H5
Sycamore 417 ....E7
Sylvania▲ 2,871 ....J5
Sylvester▲ 5,702 ....E7
Talbotton▲ 1,046 ....C5
Talking Rock 62 ....D1
Tallapoosa 2,805 ....B3
Tallulah Falls 147 ....F1
Talmo 189 ....E2
Tarrytown 130 ....H6
Tate 950 ....D2
Taylorsville 269 ....C2
Tazewell D6
Tell J2
Temple 1,870 ....B3
Tennille 1,552 ....G5
The Rock 88 ....D5
Thomaston▲ 9,127 ....D5
Thomasville▲ 17,457 ....E9
Thomson▲ 6,862 ....H4
Thunderbolt 2,786 ....K6
Tifton▲ 14,215 ....F8
Tiger 301 ....F1
Tignall 711 ....G3
Toccoa▲ 8,266 ....F1
Toco Hills K1
Toomsboro 617 ....F5
Towns G7
Trenton▲ 1,994 ....A1
Trion 1,661 ....B1
Tunnel Hill 970 ....C1
Turin 189 ....C4
Twin City 1,466 ....H5
Ty Ty 579 ....E8
Tybee Island 2,842 ....L6
Tyrone 2,724 ....C4
Unadilla 1,620 ....E6
Union City 8,375 ....J2
Union Point 1,753 ....F3
Unionville 2,710 ....F8
Uvalda 561 ....H6
Valdosta▲ 39,806 ....F9
Van Wert 303 ....B3
Vanna F2
Varnell 358 ....C1
Vernonburg 74 ....K7
Vidalia 11,078 ....H6
Vidette H4
Vienna▲ 2,708 ....E6
Villa Rica 6,542 ....C3
Vinings 7,417 ....K1
Waco 461 ....B3
Wadley 2,473 ....H5
Waleska 700 ....D2
Walnut Grove 458 ....E3
Walthourville 2,024 ....J7
Waresboro 582 ....H8
Warm Springs 407 ....C5
Warner Robins 43,726 ....E5
Warrenton▲ 2,056 ....G4
Warwick 501 ....E7
Watkinsville▲ 1,600 ....E3
Waverly 769 ....J8
Waverly Hall 913 ....C5
Waycross▲ 16,410 ....H8
Waynesboro▲ 5,701 ....J4
Welcome All J2
Wesley H6
West Point 3,571 ....B5
Weston 42 ....C7
Whigham 605 ....D9
White 542 ....C2
White Plains 286 ....F4
White Sulphur Springs 118 ....C5
Whitesburg 643 ....B4
Willacoochee 1,205 ....G8
Williamson 295 ....D4
Wilmington Island 11,230 ....L7
Winder▲ 7,373 ....E3
Winterville 876 ....F3
Woodbine▲ 1,212 ....J9
Woodbury 1,429 ....C5
Woodland 552 ....D5
Woodstock 4,361 ....D2
Woodville 415 ....F3
Woolsey 120 ....D4
Wrens 2,414 ....H4
Wrightsville▲ 2,331 ....G5
Yatesville 409 ....D5
Young Harris 604 ....E1
Zebulon▲ 1,035 ....D4

OTHER FEATURES

Alapaha (riv.) F7
Allatoona (lake) C2
Altamaha (riv.) H7
Andersonville Nat'l Hist. Site D6
Atlanta Naval Air Sta. J1
Banks (lake) F9
Bartletts Ferry (dam) B5
Blackshear (lake) E7
Blue Ridge (mts.) D1
Brasstown Bald (mt.) E1
Burton (lake) E1
Carters (lake) C1
Chattahoochee (riv.) B8
Chattahoochee River Nat'l Rec. Area K1
Chattooga (riv.) A2
Chattooga (riv.) F1
Chatuge (lake) E1
Chickamauga and Chattanooga Nat'l Mil. Park B1
Coosa (riv.) A2
Coosawattee (riv.) C1
Cumberland (isl.) K9
Cumberland Island Nat'l Seashore K9
Dobbins A.F.B. J1
Doboy (sound) K8
Etowah (riv.) C2
Flint (riv.) D8
Fort Benning B6
Fort Frederica Nat'l Mon. K8
Fort Gordon 9,140 ....H4
Fort McPherson K1
Fort Pulaski Nat'l Mon. L6
Fort Stewart 13,774 ....J7
Goat Rock (lake) B5
Harding (lake) B5
Hartwell (lake) G2
Jekyll (isl.) K8
Jimmy Carter Nat'l Hist. Site D6
Kennesaw Mtn. Nat'l Battlefield Park J1
Martin Luther King, Jr., Nat'l Hist. Site K1
Moody A.F.B.1,288 ....F9
Morgan Falls (dam) K1
Nottely (lake) D1
Ochlockonee (riv.) 10
Ocmulgee (riv.) E5
Ocmulgee Nat'l Mon. F5
Oconee (riv.) F5
Ogeechee (riv.) J5
Okefenokee (swamp) H9
Oliver (lake) B5
Oostanaula (riv.) B2
Ossabaw (sound) K7
Rabun (lake) E1
Robins A.F.B. 3,092 ....F5
Saint Andrew (sound) K9
Saint Catherines (isl.) K7
Saint Mary's (riv.) J9
Saint Simons (isl.) K8
Sapelo (isl.) K8
Satilla (riv.) G8
Savannah (riv.) K5
Sea (isls.) K9
Seminole (lake) B9
Sidney Lanier (lake) D2
Sinclair (lake) F4
Skidaway (isl.) L7
Springer (mt.) D1
Strom Thurmond (lakes) H3
Suwannee (riv.) G 10
Walter F. George (res.) B7
Wassaw (sound) L7
Weiss (lake) A2
West Point (lake) B4

▲County seat

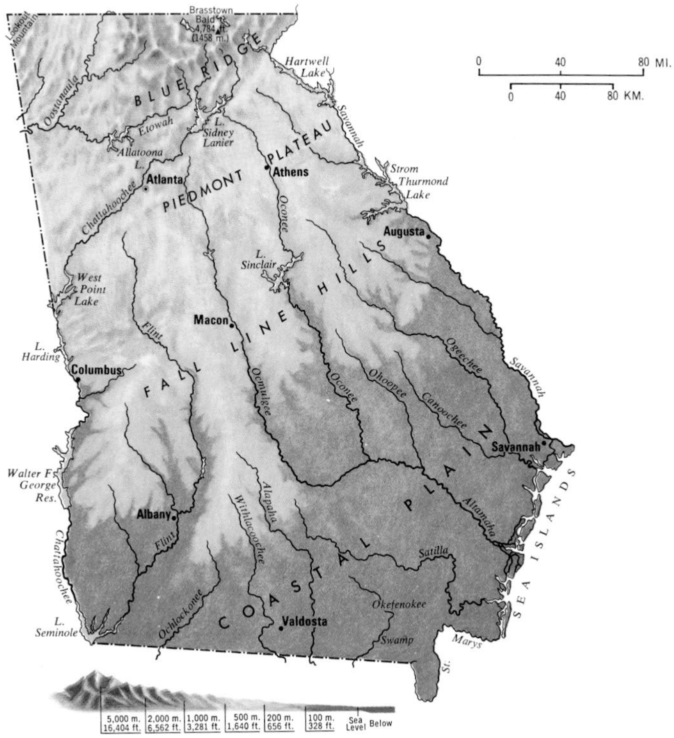

Brasstown Bald 4,784 ft. (1458 m.)
Lookout Mountain
BLUE RIDGE
Hartwell Lake
Oostanaula
Etowah
Allatoona L.
L. Sidney Lanier
Savannah
PLATEAU
Atlanta
Athens
PIEDMONT
Strom Thurmond Lake
Chattahoochee
Oconee
Augusta
L. Sinclair
West Point Lake
Macon
Flint
FALL LINE HILLS
L. Harding
Columbus
Ocmulgee
Oconee
Ohoopee
Ogeechee
Canoochee
Savannah
Savannah
Walter F. George Res.
Albany
Alapaha
Withlacoochee
COASTAL PLAIN
Altamaha
SEA ISLANDS
Satilla
Chattahoochee
Flint
Ochlockonee
Okefenokee Swamp
Valdosta
L. Seminole
St. Marys
0 40 80 MI.
0 40 80 KM.
5,000 m. 16,404 ft.
2,000 m. 6,562 ft.
1,000 m. 3,281 ft.
500 m. 1,640 ft.
200 m. 656 ft.
100 m. 328 ft.
Sea Level
Below

Georgia
SCALE
0 5 10 20 30 40 MI.
0 5 10 20 30 40 KM.
State Capitals
County Seats
Major Limited Access Hwys.
© Copyright HAMMOND INCORPORATED, Maplewood, N. J.
Longitude West of 83° Greenwich
TENNESSEE
NORTH CAROLINA
SOUTH CAROLINA
ALABAMA
FLORIDA
GULF OF MEXICO
ATLANTIC OCEAN
SEA ISLANDS
ATLANTA
CHATTANOOGA
Augusta
Macon
Columbus
Savannah
Albany
Athens
Tallahassee
JACKSONVILLE
COLUMBIA
GREENVILLE
SPARTANBURG
COBB
FULTON
DEKALB
CLAYTON
Marietta
Decatur
East Point
College Park
Hapeville
OKEFENOKEE SWAMP

COUNTIES

Hawaii 120,317 ..... K7
Honolulu 836,231 ..... D3
Kalawao 130 ..... G1
Kauai 51,177 ..... A1
Maui 100,374 ..... J1

CITIES and TOWNS

Aiea 8,906 ..... B3
Aina Haina F2
Ala Moana C4
Anahola 1,181 ..... C1
Barbers Point 2,218 ..... E2
Captain Cook 2,595 ..... G5
Eleele 1,489 ..... C2
Ewa 14,315 ..... A4
Ewa Beach 14,369 ..... A4
Haena 200 ..... C1
Haiku 4,509 ..... J2
Haina 333 ..... H3
Hakalau J4
Halawa Heights B3
Halawa, Hawaii 50 ..... G3
Haleiwa 2,442 ..... E1
Halfway House 150 ..... H6
Haliimaile 841 ..... J2
Hana 683 ..... K2
Hanalei 461 ..... C1
Hanamaulu 3,611 ..... C1
Hanapepe 1,395 ..... C2
Hauula 3,479 ..... E1
Hawaii Kai F2
Hawaii National Park 250 ..... J6
Hawi 924 ..... G3
Hickam Housing 6,553 ..... B4
Hilo▲ 37,808 ..... J5
Holualoa 3,834 ..... G5
Honaunau 2,373 ..... G6
Honohina 125 ..... J4
Honokaa 2,186 ..... H4
Honokahua 309 ..... H1
Honokohau 200 ..... G5
Honokohau 309 ..... J1
Honolulu (cap.)▲ 365,272 ..... C4
Honomu 532 ..... J4
Honouliuli 600 ..... A3
Hoolehua G1
Huehue 100 ..... G5
Hulopoe Bay H2
Huumula 50 ..... H5
Iroquois Point 4,188 ..... A4
Iwilei C4
Kaaawa 1,138 ..... F1
Kaanapali 579 ..... H2
Kahakuloa 75 ..... J1
Kahala D5
Kahaluu 3,068 ..... E2
Kahuku 2,063 ..... E1
Kahului 16,889 ..... J2
Kailua (Kailua Kona), Hawaii 9,126 ..... F5
Kailua Kona F5
Kailua, Oahu 36,818 ..... F2
Kaimuki D4
Kainaliu 512 ..... G5
Kalae 150 ..... G1
Kalaheo 3,592 ..... C2
Kalaoa 4,490 ..... G5
Kalapana 75 ..... J6
Kalaupapa▲ 170 ..... G1
Kalihi 435 ..... C4
Kamalo 60 ..... H1
Kamuela 1,179 ..... G4
Kaneohe 35,448 ..... F2
Kapaa 8,149 ..... D1
Kapaahu 850 ..... J6
Kapaau 1,083 ..... G3
Kapalama C4
Kapoho 300 ..... K5
Kapulena 125 ..... H4
Kaumakani 803 ..... C2
Kaumalapau Harbor G2
Kaunakakai 2,658 ..... G1
Kaupakulua 600 ..... K2
Kaupo 65 ..... K2
Kawaihae 50 ..... G4
Kawailoa 200 ..... E1
Keaau 1,584 ..... J5
Kealakekua 1,453 ..... G5
Kealia 550 ..... G6
Kealia, Kauai 300 ..... D1
Keanae 280 ..... K2
Keauhou F5
Kekaha 3,506 ..... C2
Keokea 500 ..... G6
Keokea 750 ..... J2
Kihei 11,107 ..... J2
Kilauea 1,685 ..... C1
Kipahulu 75 ..... K2
Koali 60 ..... K2
Kohala (Kapaau) G3
Kokomo 500 ..... K2
Koloa 1,791 ..... C2
Koloa Landing C2
Kualapuu 1,661 ..... G1
Kukaiau 75 ..... H4
Kukuihaele 316 ..... H3
Kula 800 ..... J2
Kunia 550 ..... E2
Kurtistown 910 ..... J5
Lahaina 9,073 ..... H2
Laie 5,577 ..... E1
Lanai City 2,400 ..... H2
Laupahoehoe 508 ..... J4
Lawai 1,787 ..... C2
Lihue▲ 5,536 ..... C2
Lower Paia 1,500 ..... J1
Maalaea 443 ..... J2
Maili 6,059 ..... D2
Makaha 7,990 ..... D2
Makaiwa H2
Makakilo 9,828 ..... E2
Makapala G3
Makawao 5,405 ..... K2
Makaweli 500 ..... B2
Makena 100 ..... J2
Makiki C4
Mana B2
Manele Bay H2
Maunaloa 405 ..... G1
Maunawili 4,847 ..... F2
Mililani Town 29,359 ..... E2
Milolii 120 ..... G6
Moiliili C4
Mokapu 11,615 ..... F2
Mokuleia 1,776 ..... D1
Mountain View 3,075 ..... J5
Naalehu 1,027 ..... H7
Nanakuli 9,575 ..... D2
Napili-Honokowai 4,332 ..... H1
Ninole 75 ..... J4
Olowalu 750 ..... H2
Ookala 401 ..... J4
Opihikao 125 ..... K6
Paauhau 350 ..... H4
Paauilo 620 ..... H4
Pacific Heights 5,305 ..... C4
Pacific Palisades E2
Pahala 1,520 ..... H6
Pahoa 1,027 ..... J5
Paia 2,091 ..... J2
Papa 1,634 ..... G6
Papaaloa J4
Papaikou 1,567 ..... J5
Paukaa 495 ..... J5
Pauwela 468 ..... K2
Peahi 308 ..... K2
Pearl City 30,993 ..... B3
Pepeekeo 1,813 ..... J4
Poipu 975 ..... C2
Princeville 1,244 ..... C1
Puako 397 ..... G4
Puhi 1,210 ..... C2
Pukalani 5,879 ..... J2
Punaluu 672 ..... H7
Puuanahulu 56 ..... G4
Puuiki 75 ..... K2
Puunene 572 ..... J2
Puunui C4
Puuwai 200 ..... A2
Schofield Barracks 19,597 ..... E2
Spreckelsville 350 ..... J1
Sunset Beach E1
Ulumalu 201 ..... K2
Ulupalakua 75 ..... J2
Volcano 1,516 ..... J6
Wahiawa 17,386 ..... E2
Waiakoa J2
Waialae D4
Waialua, Oahu 3,943 ..... E1
Waianae 8,758 ..... D2
Waihee 4,004 ..... J2
Waikane 717 ..... E2
Waikapu 729 ..... J2
Waikii 50 ..... H4
Waikiki C4
Wailea, Hawaii 150 ..... J4
Wailea-Makena, Maui 3,799 ..... J2
Wailua 2,018 ..... D2
Wailuku▲ 10,688 ..... J2
Waimalu 29,967 ..... B3
Waimanalo 3,508 ..... F2
Waimanalo Beach 4,185 ..... F2
Waimea (Kamuela), Hawaii 1,840 ..... G3
Waimea 200 ..... E1
Waimea, Kauai 5,972 ..... B2
Wainaku 1,243 ..... J5
Wainiha 175 ..... C1
Waiohinu 200 ..... G7
Waipahu 31,435 ..... A3
Waipio 11,812 ..... H3
Waipio Acres 5,304 ..... E2
Whitmore Village 3,373 ..... E1

OTHER FEATURES

Alalakeiki (chan.) J3

Topography

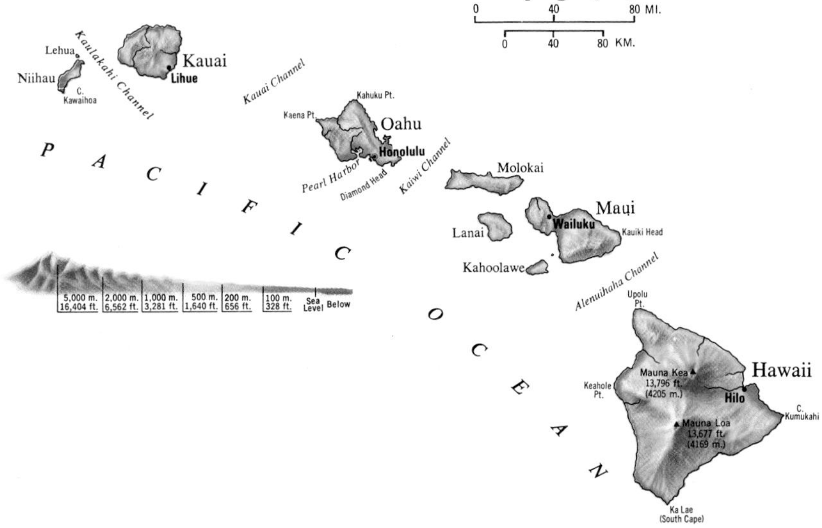

0 40 80 MI.
0 40 80 KM.
Kauai
Lihue
Lehua
Niihau
Kaulakahi Channel
Kauai Channel
Oahu
Honolulu
Kahuku Pt.
Kaena Pt.
Pearl Harbor
Diamond Head
Kaiwi Channel
Molokai
Maui
Wailuku
Kauiki Head
Lanai
Kahoolawe
Alenuihaha Channel
Upolu Pt.
Hawaii
Hilo
Keahole Pt.
Mauna Kea 13,796 ft. (4205 m.)
Mauna Loa 13,677 ft. (4169 m.)
C. Kumukahi
Ka Lae (South Cape)
PACIFIC OCEAN
5,000 m. 16,404 ft.
2,000 m. 6,562 ft.
1,000 m. 3,281 ft.
500 m. 1,640 ft.
200 m. 656 ft.
100 m. 328 ft.
Sea Level
Below

Agriculture, Industry and Resources

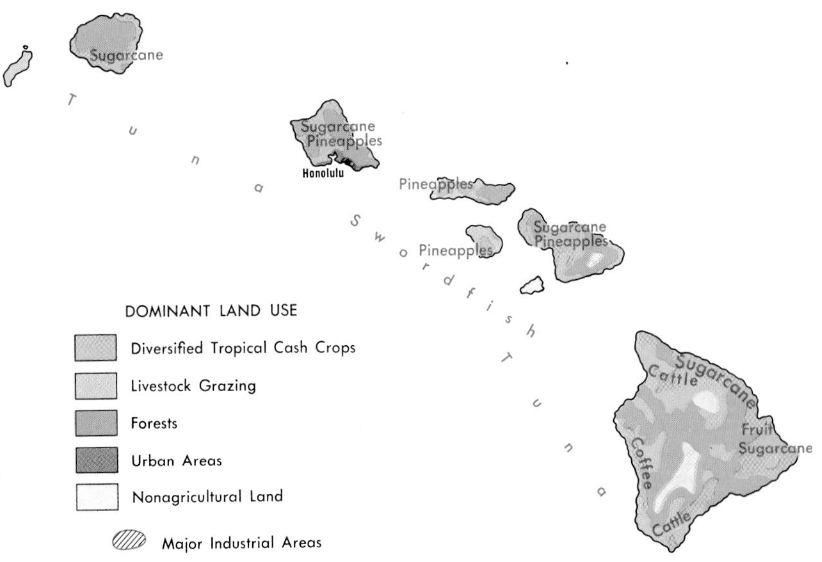

Sugarcane
Sugarcane
Pineapples
Honolulu
Pineapples
Sugarcane
Pineapples
Pineapples
Sugarcane
Cattle
Fruit
Sugarcane
Coffee
Cattle
Tuna
Swordfish
Tuna
DOMINANT LAND USE
Diversified Tropical Cash Crops
Livestock Grazing
Forests
Urban Areas
Nonagricultural Land
Major Industrial Areas

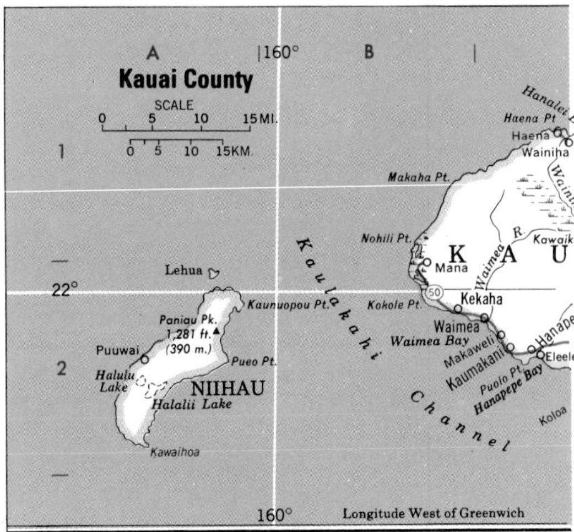

Kauai County
SCALE
0 5 10 15 MI.
0 5 10 15 KM.
A
160°
B
Hanalei Bay
Haena Pt.
Haena
Wainiha
Makaha Pt.
Nohili Pt.
Mana
Waimea R.
Kawaikini
KAU
Lehua
Kaunuopou Pt.
Paniau Pk. 1,281 ft. (390 m.)
Puuwai
Halulu Lake
Pueo Pt.
NIIHAU
Halalii Lake
Kawaihoa
Kaulakahi Channel
Kokole Pt.
Kekaha
Waimea
Waimea Bay
Makaweli
Kaumakani
Hanapepe
Eleele
Puolo Pt.
Hanapepe Bay
Koloa
22°
160°
Longitude West of Greenwich

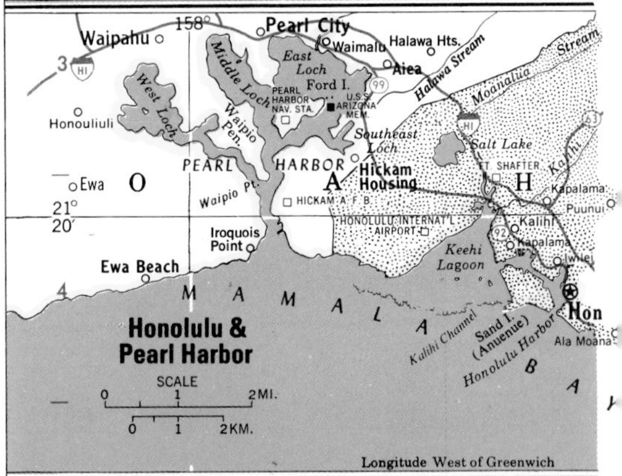

Waipahu
158°
Pearl City
Waimalu
Halawa Hts.
Aiea
Halawa Stream
Moanalua Stream
East Loch
Ford I.
Middle Loch
West Loch
Waipio Pen.
PEARL HARBOR NAV. STA.
U.S.S. ARIZONA MEM.
Southeast Loch
Honouliuli
Ewa
OAHU
PEARL HARBOR
Hickam Housing
HICKAM A.F.B.
Salt Lake
FT. SHAFTER
Kapalama
Puunui
Kalihi
HONOLULU INTERNAT'L AIRPORT
Keehi Lagoon
Iwilei
Hon
Ala Moana
Waipio Pt.
Iroquois Point
Ewa Beach
MAMALA BAY
Kalihi Channel
Sand I. (Anuenue)
Honolulu Harbor
21° 20′
Honolulu & Pearl Harbor
SCALE
0 1 2 MI.
0 1 2 KM.
Longitude West of Greenwich

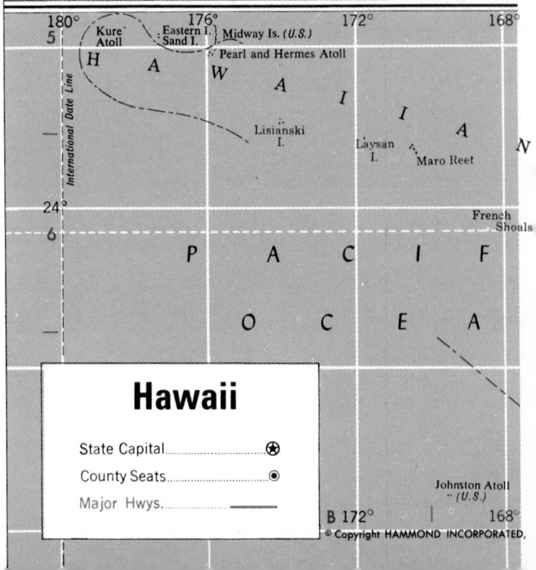

180°
176°
172°
168°
Kure Atoll
Eastern I.
Sand I.
Midway Is. (U.S.)
Pearl and Hermes Atoll
HAWAIIAN
Lisianski I.
Laysan I.
Maro Reef
International Date Line
24°
French Frigate Shoals
PACIFIC OCEAN
Hawaii
State Capital
County Seats
Major Hwys.
Johnston Atoll (U.S.)
B 172°
168°

Alenuihaha (chan.) E7
Anuenue (Sand) (isl.) C4
Auau (chan.) H2
Barbers Point Naval Air Sta. E2
Diamond (head) C5
East Loch (inlet) B3
Ford (isl.) B3
Fort Shafter 2,952 C3
French Frigate (shoals) C6
Gardner Pinnacles (isls.) C6
Halalii (lake) A2
Halawa (bay) H1
Haleakala (crater) K2
Haleakala Nat'l Park K2
Hawaii (isl.) H5
Hawaii Volcanoes Nat'l Park H6
Hickam A.F.B. B4
Hilo (bay) J5
Honolulu (harb.) C4
Honolulu Int'l Airport B4
Ilio (pt.) G1
Kaala (mt.) D1
Kahala (pt.) D1
Kahana (bay) F1
Kaiwi (chan.) E6
Ka Lae (cape) G7
Kalaupapa Nat'l Hist. Park H1
Kalohi (chan.) G1
Kaloko-Honokohau Nat'l Hist. Park F5
Kamakou (peak) H1
Kanapou (bay) J3
Kaneohe Bay U.S.M.C. Air Station F2
Kau (des.) J6
Kauai (chan.) E6
Kauai (isl.) C1
Kauiki (head) K2
Kaula (isl.) D6
Kaulakahi (chan.) B2
Kawaihae (bay) G4
Kawaihoa (cape) A2
Kawaikini (peak) C1
Keahi (pt.) A4
Kealaikahiki (chan.) H3
Kealakekua (bay) F6
Keanapapa (pt.) G2
Keehi (lag.) B4
Kiholo (bay) F4
Kilauea (crater) H6
Kohala (mts.) G4
Koko (head) F2
Konahuanui (peak) D3
Koolau (range) E2
Kumukahi (cape) K5
Kure (atoll) A5
Laau (pt.) G1
Lanai (isl.) H2
Lanaihale (mt.) H2
Laysan (isl.) B6
Lisianski (isl.) B5
Lua Makika (mt.) J3
Maalaea (bay) J2
Makaha (pt.) B1
Makahuena (pt.) C2
Makapuu (pt.) F2
Mamala (bay) B4
Manana (isl.) F2
Maro (reef) C6
Maui (isl.) J2
Mauna Kea (mt.) H4
Mauna Loa (mt.) G6
Middle Loch (inlet) A3
Moanalua (stream) B3
Mokapu (pen.) F2
Mokuaweoweo (crater) H6
Molokai (isl.) G1
Molokini (isl.) J2
Nawiliwili (bay) D2
Necker (isl.) D6
Nihoa (isl.) D6
Niihau (isl.) A2
Oahu (isl.) E1
Pailolo (chan.) H1
Palolo (stream) D4
Paniau (peak) A2
Pearl (harb.) A3
Pearl and Hermes (atoll) B5
Pearl Harbor Naval Sta. B3
Punchbowl (hill) C4
Puolo (pt.) C2
Puuhonua O Honaunau Nat'l Hist. Park F6
Puu Keahiakahoe (mt.) D3
Puukohola Heiau Nat'l Hist. Park G4
Puu Kukui (mt.) J2
Red Hill (mt.) K2
Roundtop (mt.) C4
Salt (lake) B3
Sand (isl.) B4
South (Ka Lae) (cape) G7
Southeast Loch (inlet) B3
Sugarloaf (hill) C4
Tantalus (mt.) D4
Upolu (pt.) G3
U.S.S. Arizona Memorial B3
Waialeale (mt.) C1
Waikiki (beach) C4
Wailuku (riv.) J5
Waimea (bay) B2
Waimea (riv.) C2
Wainiha (riv.) C1
Waipio (bay) H3
Waipio (pen.) A3
Waipio (pt.) A4
West Loch (inlet) A3
Wheeler A.F.B. 2,600 E1

▲County seat

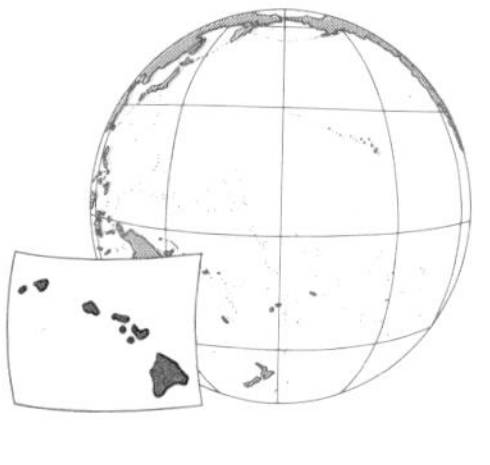

HAWAII

AREA 6,471 sq. mi. (16,760 sq. km.)
POPULATION 1,115,274
CAPITAL Honolulu
LARGEST CITY Honolulu
HIGHEST POINT Mauna Kea 13,796 ft. (4205 m.)
SETTLED IN —
ADMITTED TO UNION August 21, 1959
POPULAR NAME Aloha State
STATE FLOWER Hibiscus
STATE BIRD Nene (Hawaiian Goose)

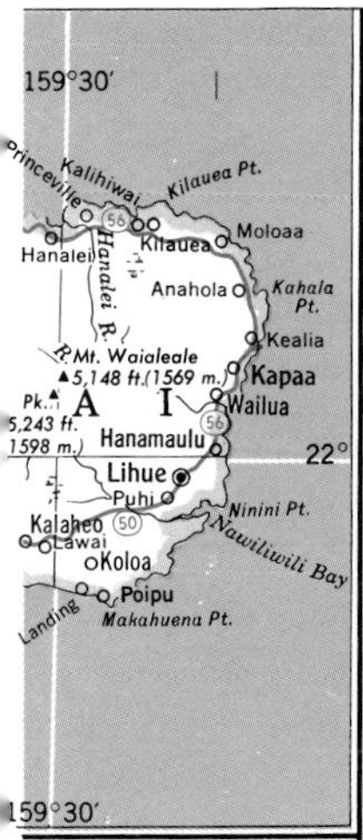
159°30'
Kilauea Pt.
Hanalei
Moloaa
Anahola
Kealia
Mt. Waialeale 5,148 ft. (1569 m.)
Kapaa
Wailua
Hanamaulu
Lihue
Puhi
Kalaheo
Lawai
Koloa
Poipu
Makahuena Pt.
Ninini Pt.
Nawiliwili Bay
159°30'

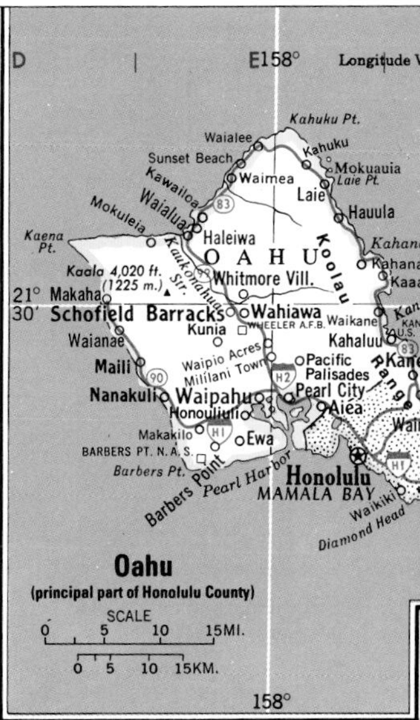
158°
Longitude West of Greenwich
Kahuku Pt.
Waialee
Sunset Beach
Kahuku
Waimea
Laie
Hauula
Kahana Bay
Kaena Pt.
Haleiwa
OAHU
Kaala 4,020 ft. (1225 m.)
Makaha
Whitmore Vill.
Schofield Barracks
Wahiawa
Waianae
Kunia
Maili
Nanakuli
Waipahu
Pearl City
Aiea
Kaneohe
Mokapu
Kailua
Waimanalo
Waimanalo Beach
Ewa
Barbers Point
Pearl Harbor
Honolulu
MAMALA BAY
Waikiki
Diamond Head
Hawaii Kai
Koko Head
Makapuu Point
Oahu
(principal part of Honolulu County)
SCALE
0 5 10 15MI.
0 5 10 15KM.
158°

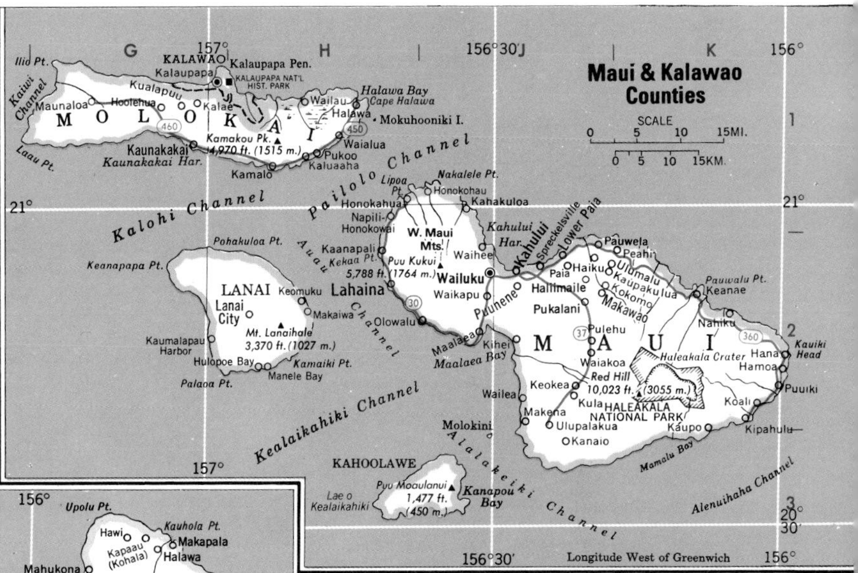
157°
156°30'
156°
Maui & Kalawao Counties
SCALE
0 5 10 15MI.
0 5 10 15KM.
KALAWAO
Kalaupapa
Kalaupapa Pen.
KALAUPAPA NAT'L HIST. PARK
Ilio Pt.
Maunaloa
Hoolehua
MOLOKAI
Halawa Bay
Mokuhooniki I.
Kaunakakai
Kamakou Pk. 4,970 ft. (1515 m.)
Waialua
Pukoo
Kamalo
Laau Pt.
Kalohi Channel
Pailolo Channel
Nakalele Pt.
Honokahua
Kahakuloa
Kahului
Wailuku
W. Maui Mts.
Puu Kukui 5,788 ft. (1764 m.)
Lahaina
LANAI
Lanai City
Mt. Lanaihale 3,370 ft. (1027 m.)
Manele Bay
Palaoa Pt.
Keanapapa Pt.
Paia
Haiku
Makawao
Pukalani
Pulehu
MAUI
Kihei
Maalaea Bay
Haleakala Crater
Hana
Hamoa
Red Hill 10,023 ft. (3055 m.)
HALEAKALA NATIONAL PARK
Kula
Keokea
Makena
Ulupalakua
Kanaio
Kaupo
Kipahulu
Kealaikahiki Channel
Molokini
KAHOOLAWE
Puu Moaulanui 1,477 ft. (450 m.)
Kanapou Bay
Alalakeiki Channel
Alenuihaha Channel
Longitude West of Greenwich

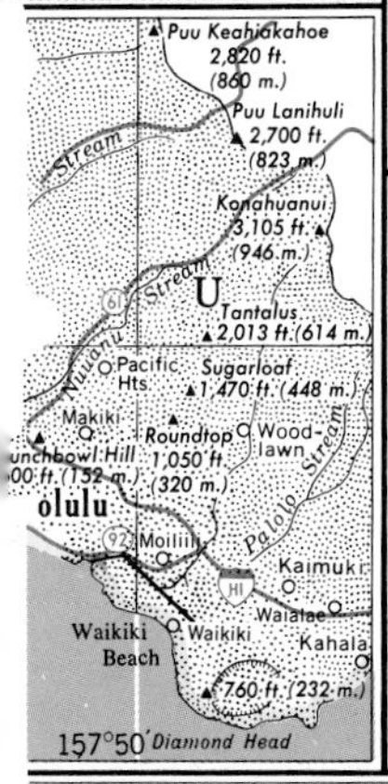
Puu Keahiakahoe 2,820 ft. (860 m.)
Puu Lanihuli 2,700 ft. (823 m.)
Konahuanui 3,105 ft. (946 m.)
Tantalus 2,013 ft. (614 m.)
Sugarloaf 1,470 ft. (448 m.)
Roundtop 1,050 ft. (320 m.)
Makiki
Moiliili
Kaimuki
Waikiki
Waikiki Beach
Kahala
760 ft. (232 m.)
157°50' Diamond Head

Map below shows relative position of the islands comprising the State of Hawaii. The other maps show the more important island counties in detail.

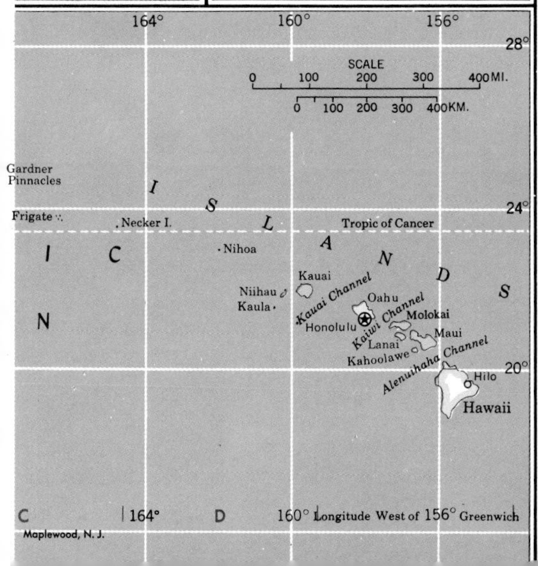
164°
160°
156°
28°
24°
20°
SCALE
0 100 200 300 400MI.
0 100 200 300 400KM.
Gardner Pinnacles
Frigate
Necker I.
Tropic of Cancer
Nihoa
Kauai
Niihau
Kaula
Oahu
Honolulu
Molokai
Lanai
Maui
Kahoolawe
Hilo
Hawaii
Kauai Channel
Kaiwi Channel
Alenuihaha Channel
HAWAIIAN ISLANDS
Longitude West of Greenwich

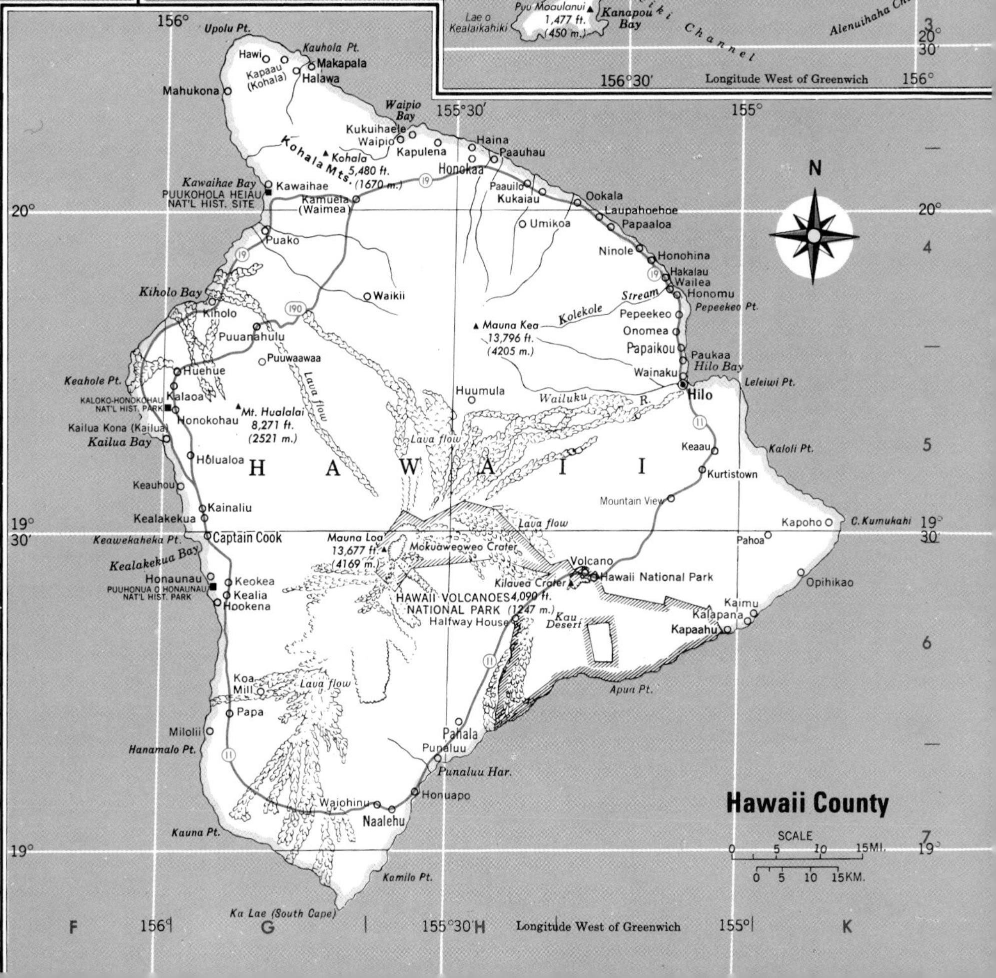
156°
155°30'
155°
Upolu Pt.
Hawi
Kohala Pt.
Makapala
Halawa
Mahukona
Waipio Bay
Waipio
Haina
Honokaa
Kohala Mts.
Kohala 5,480 ft. (1670 m.)
Kawaihae Bay
Kawaihae
PUUKOHOLA HEIAU NAT'L HIST. SITE
Kamuela (Waimea)
Puako
Laupahoehoe
Papaaloa
Honohina
Kiholo Bay
Waikii
Mauna Kea 13,796 ft. (4205 m.)
Pepeekeo
Honomu
Papaikou
Hilo Bay
Hilo
Keahole Pt.
Kailua Kona (Kailua)
Kailua Bay
Mt. Hualalai 8,271 ft. (2521 m.)
Holualoa
HAWAII
Keaau
Kurtistown
Mountain View
Kealakekua
Captain Cook
Kealakekua Bay
Honaunau
Mauna Loa 13,677 ft. (4169 m.)
Mokuaweoweo Crater
Kilauea Crater
Volcano
Hawaii National Park
HAWAII VOLCANOES NATIONAL PARK
Kau Desert
Kapoho
C. Kumukahi
Pahoa
Kalapana
Kaimu
Apua Pt.
Milolii
Hanamalo Pt.
Pahala
Punaluu
Honuapo
Waiohinu
Naalehu
Kauna Pt.
Kamilo Pt.
Ka Lae (South Cape)
Hawaii County
SCALE
0 5 10 15MI.
0 5 10 15KM.
Longitude West of Greenwich

Maplewood, N.J.

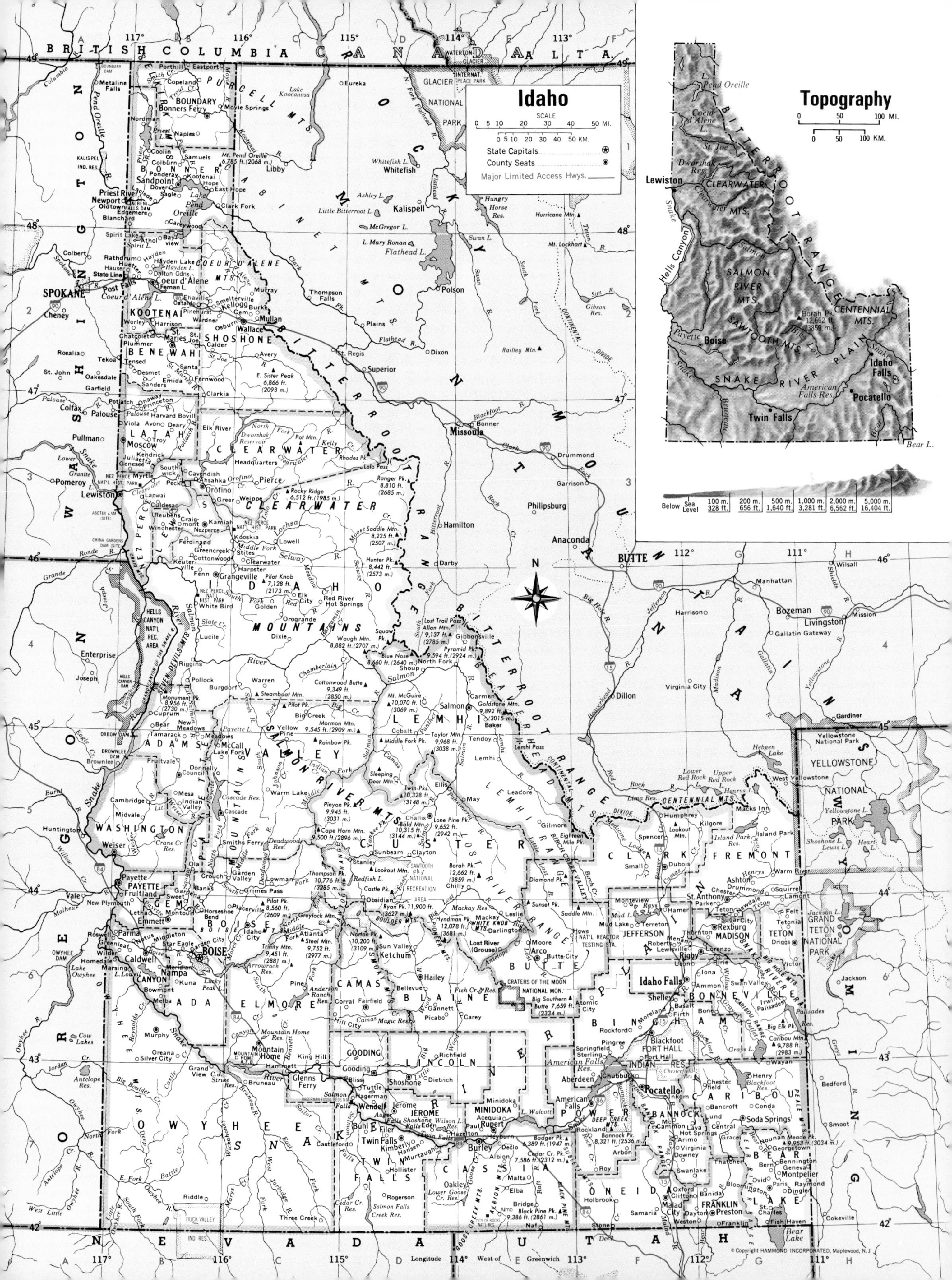
Idaho
SCALE
0 5 10 20 30 40 50 MI.
0 5 10 20 30 40 50 KM.
State Capitals
County Seats
Major Limited Access Hwys.
Topography
0 50 100 MI.
0 50 100 KM.
Below Sea Level
100 m. 328 ft.
200 m. 656 ft.
500 m. 1,640 ft.
1,000 m. 3,281 ft.
2,000 m. 6,562 ft.
5,000 m. 16,404 ft.
BRITISH COLUMBIA
CANADA
ALTA.
WASHINGTON
OREGON
NEVADA
UTAH
WYOMING
MONTANA
IDAHO
BOUNDARY
BONNER
KOOTENAI
SHOSHONE
BENEWAH
LATAH
CLEARWATER
NEZ PERCE
LEWIS
IDAHO
ADAMS
VALLEY
WASHINGTON
PAYETTE
GEM
BOISE
CANYON
ADA
ELMORE
OWYHEE
CAMAS
BLAINE
CUSTER
LEMHI
CLARK
FREMONT
JEFFERSON
MADISON
TETON
BUTTE
BINGHAM
BONNEVILLE
POWER
BANNOCK
CARIBOU
BEAR LAKE
FRANKLIN
ONEIDA
CASSIA
MINIDOKA
JEROME
GOODING
LINCOLN
TWIN FALLS
BOISE
Lewiston
Coeur d'Alene
Pocatello
Idaho Falls
Twin Falls
SPOKANE
Missoula
BUTTE
BITTERROOT RANGE
SALMON RIVER MTS.
SAWTOOTH MTS.
SNAKE RIVER PLAIN
CENTENNIAL MTS.
CLEARWATER MTS.
Borah Pk. 12,662 ft. (3859 m.)
Hells Canyon
Longitude 114° West of Greenwich 113°
117° 116° 115° 114° 113° 112° 111°
49° 48° 47° 46° 45° 44° 43° 42°
© Copyright HAMMOND INCORPORATED, Maplewood, N.J.

GREAT SEAL OF THE STATE OF IDAHO
STATE OF IDAHO

AREA 83,564 sq. mi. (216,431 sq. km.)
POPULATION 1,011,986
CAPITAL Boise
LARGEST CITY Boise
HIGHEST POINT Borah Pk. 12,662 ft. (3859 m.)
SETTLED IN 1842
ADMITTED TO UNION July 3, 1890
POPULAR NAME Gem State
STATE FLOWER Syringa
STATE BIRD Mountain Bluebird

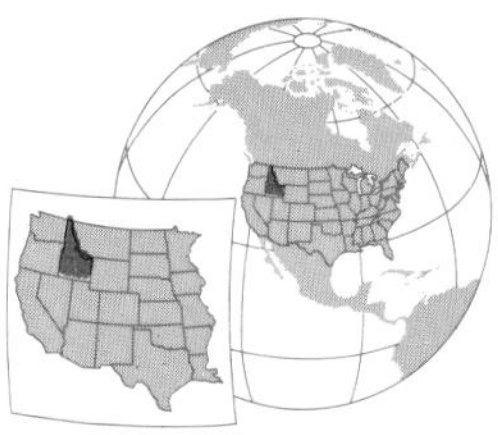

COUNTIES

Ada 205,775 ... B6
Adams 3,254 ... B5
Bannock 66,026 ... F7
Bear Lake 6,084 ... G7
Benewah 7,937 ... B2
Bingham 37,583 ... F6
Blaine 13,552 ... D6
Boise 3,509 ... C6
Bonner 26,622 ... B1
Bonneville 72,207 ... G6
Boundary 8,332 ... B1
Butte 2,918 ... E6
Camas 727 ... D6
Canyon 90,076 ... B6
Caribou 6,963 ... G7
Cassia 19,532 ... E7
Clark 762 ... F5
Clearwater 8,505 ... C3
Custer 4,133 ... D5
Elmore 21,205 ... C6
Franklin 9,232 ... G7
Fremont 10,937 ... G5
Gem 11,844 ... B6
Gooding 11,633 ... D6
Idaho 13,783 ... C4
Jefferson 16,543 ... F6
Jerome 15,138 ... D7
Kootenai 69,795 ... B2
Latah 30,617 ... B3
Lemhi 6,899 ... D4
Lewis 3,516 ... B3
Lincoln 3,308 ... D6
Madison 23,674 ... G6
Minidoka 19,361 ... E7
Nez Perce 33,754 ... B3
Oneida 3,492 ... F7
Owyhee 8,392 ... B7
Payette 16,434 ... B5
Power 7,086 ... F7
Shoshone 13,931 ... B2
Teton 3,439 ... G6
Twin Falls 53,580 ... D7
Valley 6,109 ... C5
Washington 8,550 ... B5

CITIES and TOWNS

Aberdeen 1,406 ... F7
Acequia 106 ... E7
Ahsahka 160 ... B3
Albion 305 ... E7
American Falls▲ 3,757 ... E7
Ammon 5,002 ... G6
Arco▲ 1,016 ... E6
Arimo 311 ... F7
Ashton 1,114 ... G5
Athol 346 ... B2
Atomic City 25 ... F6
Bancroft 393 ... G7
Basalt 407 ... F6
Bayview 350 ... B2
Bellevue 1,275 ... D6
Bern 154 ... G7
Blackfoot▲ 9,646 ... F6
Bliss 185 ... D7
Bloomington 197 ... G7
Boise (cap.)▲ 102,160 ... B6
Bonners Ferry▲ 2,193 ... B1
Bovill 256 ... B3
Bruneau 160 ... C7
Buhl 3,516 ... D7
Burgdorf ... B4
Burke 150 ... C2
Burley▲ 8,702 ... E7
Butte City 59 ... E6
Calder 200 ... B2
Caldwell▲ 18,400 ... B6
Cambridge 374 ... B5
Carey 800 ... E6
Cascade▲ 877 ... C5
Castleford 179 ... C7
Cataldo 150 ... B2
Challis▲ 1,073 ... D5
Chatcolet 72 ... B2
Chester 300 ... G5
Chilly ... E5
Chubbuck 7,791 ... F7
Clark Fork 448 ... B1
Clarkia 175 ... B2
Clayton 26 ... D5
Clifton 228 ... F7
Coeur d'Alene▲ 24,563 ... B2
Colburn 250 ... B1
Conda 200 ... G7
Coolin 150 ... B1
Cottonwood 822 ... B3
Council▲ 831 ... B5
Craigmont 542 ... B3
Crouch 75 ... B5
Culdesac 280 ... B3
Dalton Gardens 1,951 ... B2
Dayton 357 ... F7
Deary 529 ... B3
Declo 279 ... E7
Dietrich 127 ... D7
Dingle 300 ... G7
Donnelly 135 ... B5
Dover 294 ... B1
Downey 626 ... F7
Driggs▲ 846 ... G6
Drummond 37 ... G5
Dubois▲ 420 ... F5
Eagle 3,327 ... B6
East Hope 215 ... B1
Eden 314 ... D7
Elk City 500 ... C4
Elk River 149 ... B3
Emida 175 ... B2
Emmett▲ 4,601 ... B6
Fairfield▲ 371 ... D6
Ferdinand 135 ... B3
Fernan Lake 178 ... B2
Fernwood 608 ... B2
Filer 1,511 ... D7
Firth 429 ... F6
Fort Hall 2,681 ... F6
Franklin 478 ... G7
Fruitland 2,400 ... B6
Fruitvale 200 ... B5
Garden City 6,369 ... B6
Garden Valley 250 ... C5
Genesee 725 ... B3
Geneva 220 ... G7
Georgetown 558 ... G7
Gilmore ... E5
Glenns Ferry 1,304 ... C7
Gooding▲ 2,820 ... D7
Grace 973 ... G7
Grand View 330 ... B7
Grangeville▲ 3,226 ... B4
Greenleaf 648 ... B6
Grimes Pass ... C5
Hagerman 600 ... D7
Hailey▲ 3,687 ... D6
Hamer 79 ... F6
Hammett 180 ... C7
Hansen 848 ... D7
Harrison 226 ... B2
Hauser 380 ... A2
Hayden 3,744 ... B2
Hayden Lake 338 ... B2
Hazelton 394 ... E7
Headquarters 165 ... C3
Heise 84 ... G6
Heyburn 2,714 ... E7
Hollister 144 ... D7
Homedale 1,963 ... A6
Hope 99 ... B1
Horseshoe Bend 643 ... B6
Huetter 82 ... B2
Idaho City▲ 322 ... C6
Idaho Falls▲ 43,929 ... F6
Inkom 769 ... F7
Iona 1,049 ... G6
Irwin 108 ... G6
Island Park 159 ... G5
Jerome▲ 6,529 ... D7
Juliaetta 488 ... B3
Kamiah 1,157 ... B3
Kellogg 2,591 ... B2
Kendrick 325 ... B3
Ketchum 2,523 ... D6
Kimberly 2,367 ... D7
Kooskia 692 ... C3
Kootenai 327 ... B1
Kuna 1,955 ... B6
Laclede 400 ... B1
Lake Fork 250 ... B5
Lapwai 932 ... B3
Lava Hot Springs 420 ... F7
Leadore 74 ... E5
Lewiston▲ 28,082 ... A3
Lewisville 471 ... F6
Lost River (Grouse) 29 ... E6
Lowman 180 ... C5
Mackay 574 ... E6
Macks Inn 200 ... G5
Malad City▲ 1,946 ... F7
Malta 171 ... E7
Marsing 798 ... B6
McCall 2,005 ... C5
McCammon 722 ... F7
Meadows 250 ... B5
Melba 252 ... B6
Menan 601 ... F6
Meridian 9,596 ... B6
Middleton 1,851 ... B6
Midvale 110 ... B5
Minidoka 67 ... E7
Monteview 200 ... F6
Montpelier 2,656 ... G7
Moore 190 ... E6
Moreland 600 ... F6
Moscow▲ 18,519 ... B3
Mountain Home▲ 7,913 ... C6
Moyie Springs 415 ... B1
Mud Lake 179 ... F6
Mullan 821 ... C2
Murphy▲ 200 ... B6
Murtaugh 114 ... D7
Nampa 28,365 ... B6
Naples 250 ... B1
New Meadows 534 ... B4
New Plymouth 1,313 ... B6
Newdale 377 ... G6
Nezperce▲ 453 ... B3
Nordman 300 ... B1
North Fork 250 ... D4
Notus 380 ... B6
Oakley 635 ... D7
Ola 175 ... B5
Oldtown 151 ... A1
Onaway 203 ... B3
Orofino▲ 2,868 ... B3
Osburn 1,579 ... B2
Oxford 44 ... F7
Paris▲ 581 ... G7
Parker 288 ... G6
Parma 1,597 ... B6
Patterson 4 ... E5
Paul 901 ... E7
Payette▲ 5,592 ... B5
Pearl 8 ... B6
Peck 160 ... B3
Pierce 746 ... C3
Pinehurst 1,722 ... B2
Placerville 14 ... C6
Plummer 804 ... B2
Pocatello▲ 46,080 ... F7
Ponderay 449 ... B1
Post Falls 7,349 ... A2
Potlatch 790 ... A3
Preston▲ 3,710 ... G7
Priest River 1,560 ... A1
Rathdrum 2,000 ... A2
Reubens 46 ... B3
Rexburg▲ 14,302 ... G6
Richfield 383 ... D6
Rigby▲ 2,681 ... F6
Riggins 443 ... B4
Ririe 596 ... G6
Roberts 557 ... F6
Rockland 264 ... F7
Rupert▲ 5,455 ... E7
Sagle 600 ... B1
Saint Anthony▲ 3,010 ... G6
Saint Charles 211 ... G7
Saint Maries▲ 2,442 ... B2
Salmon▲ 2,941 ... D4
Samuels 467 ... B1
Sandpoint▲ 5,203 ... B1
Shelley 3,536 ... F6
Shoshone▲ 1,249 ... D7
Silver City 1 ... B6
Smelterville 464 ... B2
Soda Springs▲ 3,111 ... G7
Spencer 11 ... F5
Spirit Lake 790 ... A2
Stanley 71 ... D5
Star 500 ... B6
State Line 26 ... A2
Stites 204 ... C3
Sugar City 1,275 ... G6
Sun Valley 938 ... D6
Swan Valley 141 ... G6
Sweet 290 ... B6
Tendoy 155 ... E5
Tensed 90 ... B2
Terreton 400 ... F6
Teton 570 ... G6
Tetonia 132 ... G6
Thatcher 300 ... G7
Thornton 177 ... G6
Troy 699 ... B3
Twin Falls▲ 27,591 ... D7
Ucon 895 ... F6
Victor 292 ... G6
Wallace▲ 1,010 ... C2
Wardner 246 ... B2
Warm Lake 200 ... C5
Warm River 9 ... G5
Wayan 175 ... G7
Weippe 532 ... C3
Weiser▲ 4,571 ... B5
Wendell 1,963 ... D7
Weston 390 ... F7
White Bird 108 ... B4
Wilder 1,232 ... A6
Winchester 262 ... B3
Worley 182 ... B2

OTHER FEATURES

Albeni Falls (dam) ... B1
Albion (mts.) ... E7
Allan (mt.) ... D4
American Falls (res.) ... F6
Anderson Ranch (res.) ... C6
Antelope (creek) ... E6
Arrowrock (res.) ... C6
Auger (falls) ... D7
Badger (peak) ... E7
Bald (mt.) ... D5
Bannock (creek) ... F7
Bannock (peak) ... F7
Bannock (range) ... F7
Bargamin (creek) ... C4
Battle (creek) ... B7
Bear (lake) ... G7
Bear (riv.) ... G7
Bear River (range) ... G7
Beaver (creek) ... F5
Beaverhead (mts.) ... E4
Big (creek) ... C4
Big Boulder (creek) ... B7
Big Elk (peak) ... G6
Big Hole (mts.) ... G6
Big Lost (riv.) ... E6
Big Southern (butte) ... E6
Big Wood (riv.) ... D6
Birch (creek) ... F5
Birch Creek (valley) ... E5
Bitterroot (range) ... D3
Blackfoot (res.) ... G7
Black Pine (mts.) ... E7
Blue Nose (mt.) ... D4
Boise (mts.) ... B6
Boise (riv.) ... B6
Borah (peak) ... E5
Boulder (mts.) ... D6
Brownlee (dam) ... B5
Bruneau (riv.) ... C7
Camas (creek) ... D5
Camas (creek) ... D6
Camas (creek) ... F5
Canyon (creek) ... C6
Cape Horn (mt.) ... C5
Caribou (mt.) ... G6
Caribou (range) ... G6
Cascade (res.) ... C5
Castle (creek) ... B7
Castle (peak) ... D5
Cedar Creek (peak) ... E7
Cedar Creek (res.) ... D7
Centennial (mts.) ... F5
Chesterfield (res) ... F7
Clearwater (mts.) ... C3
Clearwater (riv.) ... B3
Coeur d'Alene (lake) ... B2
Coeur d'Alene (mts.) ... C2
Coeur d'Alene (riv.) ... B2
Cottonwood (butte) ... C4
Craig (mts.) ... B4
Crane Creek (res.) ... B5
Craters of the Moon Nat'l Mon. ... E6
Deadwood (res.) ... C5
Deep (creek) ... B7
Deep (creek) ... F7
Deep Creek (mts.) ... F7
Diamond (peak) ... E5
Duck Valley Ind. Res. ... B7
Dworshak (res.) ... C3
East Sister (peak) ... C2
Eighteen Mile (peak) ... E5
Fish Creek (res.) ... E6
Fort Hall Ind. Res. ... F6
Goldstone (mt.) ... E4
Goose (creek) ... E7
Goose Creek (mts.) ... E7
Grand Canyon of the Snake River (canyon) ... B4
Grays (lake) ... G6
Grays Lake Outlet (creek) ... G6
Greylock (mt.) ... C6
Hayden (lake) ... B2
Hells (canyon) ... B4
Hells Canyon Nat'l Rec. Area ... B4
Henrys (lake) ... G5
Henrys Fork, Snake (riv.) ... G5
Hunter (peak) ... D3
Hyndman (peak) ... D6
Indian (creek) ... C5
Island Park (res.) ... G5
Jarbidge (riv.) ... C7
Johnson (creek) ... C5
Jordan (creek) ... A7
Kootenai (riv.) ... C1
Lemhi (pass) ... E5
Lemhi (range) ... E5
Lemhi (riv.) ... E5
Little Lost (riv.) ... E5
Little Owyhee (riv.) ... B7
Little Salmon (riv.) ... B4
Little Weiser (riv.) ... B5
Little Wood (riv.) ... D6
Lochsa (riv.) ... C3
Lolo (creek) ... C3
Lolo (pass) ... D3
Lone Pine (peak) ... D5
Lookout (mt.) ... D5
Lookout (mt.) ... F5
Lost River (range) ... E5
Lost Trail (pass) ... D4
Lowell (lake) ... B6
Lower Goose Creek (res.) ... D7
Lower Granite (lake) ... A3
Lucky Peak (lake) ... B6
Mackay (res.) ... E6
Magic (res.) ... D6
Malad (riv.) ... F7
Marsh (creek) ... F7
McGuire (mt.) ... D4
Meade (peak) ... G7
Meadow (creek) ... C4
Medicine Lodge (creek) ... F5
Middle Fork (peak) ... D5
Monument (peak) ... B4
Moose (creek) ... D3
Mores (creek) ... C6
Mormon (mt.) ... C4
Mountain Home (res.) ... C6
Mountain Home A.F.B. 5,936 ... C6
Moyie (riv.) ... B1
Mud (lake) ... F6
National Reactor Testing Sta. ... F6
Nez Perce Nat'l Hist. Park ... C3
Norton (peak) ... D6
Orofino (creek) ... C3
Owyhee (mts.) ... B6
Owyhee, East Fork (riv.) ... B7
Oxbow (dam) ... B5
Pack (riv.) ... B1
Pahsimeroi (riv.) ... E5
Palisades (res.) ... G6
Palouse (riv.) ... B3
Panther (creek) ... D4
Payette (lake) ... C4
Payette (mts.) ... B5
Payette (riv.) ... B6
Peale (mts.) ... G7
Pend Oreille (lake) ... B1
Pend Oreille (mt.) ... B1
Pend Oreille (riv.) ... A1
Pilot (peak) ... C4
Pilot (peak) ... C6
Pilot Knob (mt.) ... C4
Pinyon (peak) ... C5
Pioneer (mts.) ... D6
Pot (mt.) ... C3
Potlatch (riv.) ... B3
Priest (lake) ... B1
Priest (riv.) ... B1
Purcell (mts.) ... B1
Pyramid (peak) ... E4
Raft (riv.) ... E7
Rainbow (mt.) ... C5
Ranger (peak) ... D3
Rays (lake) ... F6
Red (riv.) ... C4
Redfish (lake) ... D5
Reynolds (creek) ... B6
Rhodes (peak) ... D3
Rock (creek) ... F7
Rocky (mts.) ... D1
Rocky Ridge (mt.) ... C3
Ryan (peak) ... D6
Saddle (mt.) ... D3
Saddle (mt.) ... F6
Sailor (creek) ... C7
Saint Joe (riv.) ... B2
Saint Maries (riv.) ... B2
Salmon (falls) ... C7
Salmon (riv.) ... B4
Salmon Falls (creek) ... D7
Salmon Falls Creek (res.) ... D7
Salmon River (mts.) ... C5
Sawtooth (range) ... C6
Sawtooth Nat'l Rec. Area ... D5
Secesh (riv.) ... C4
Selkirk (mts.) ... B1
Selway (riv.) ... C3
Seven Devils (mts.) ... B4
Shoshone (falls) ... D7
Sleeping Deer (mt.) ... D5
Smith (creek) ... B1
Smoky (mts.) ... D6
Snake (riv.) ... A3
Snake River (plain) ... D7
Snake River (range) ... G6
Spirit (lake) ... B2
Squaw (creek) ... B5
Squaw (peak) ... D4
Steamboat (mt.) ... C4
Steel (mt.) ... C6
Strike, C.J. (res.) ... C7
Sublett (mts.) ... E7
Sunset (peak) ... E6
Taylor (mt.) ... D5
Teton (riv.) ... G6
Thompson (peak) ... C5
Trinity (mt.) ... C6
Trout (creek) ... B1
Twin (falls) ... D7
Twin Peaks (mt.) ... D5
Walcott (lake) ... E7
Waugh (mt.) ... D4
Weiser (riv.) ... B5
White Knob (mts.) ... E6
Wickahoney (creek) ... C7
Willow (creek) ... G6
Wilson Lake (res.) ... D7
Yankee Fork, Salmon (riv.) ... D5
Yellowstone Nat'l Park ... H5

▲County seat

Agriculture, Industry and Resources

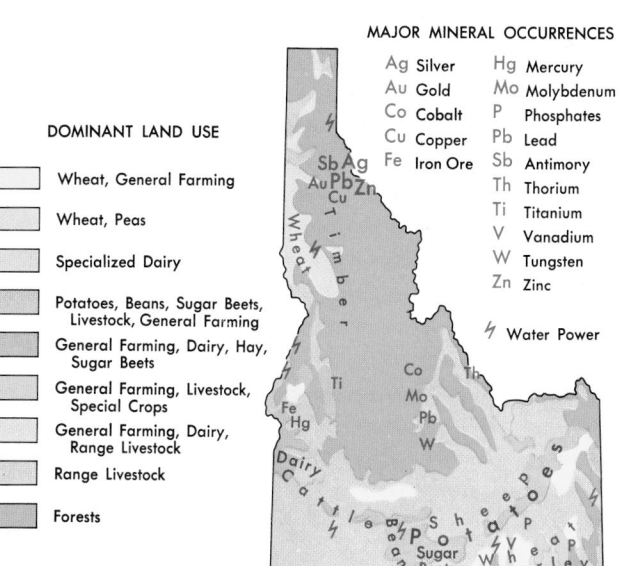

DOMINANT LAND USE

- Wheat, General Farming
- Wheat, Peas
- Specialized Dairy
- Potatoes, Beans, Sugar Beets, Livestock, General Farming
- General Farming, Dairy, Hay, Sugar Beets
- General Farming, Livestock, Special Crops
- General Farming, Dairy, Range Livestock
- Range Livestock
- Forests

MAJOR MINERAL OCCURRENCES

Ag	Silver	Hg	Mercury
Au	Gold	Mo	Molybdenum
Co	Cobalt	P	Phosphates
Cu	Copper	Pb	Lead
Fe	Iron Ore	Sb	Antimony
		Th	Thorium
		Ti	Titanium
		V	Vanadium
		W	Tungsten
		Zn	Zinc

ϟ Water Power

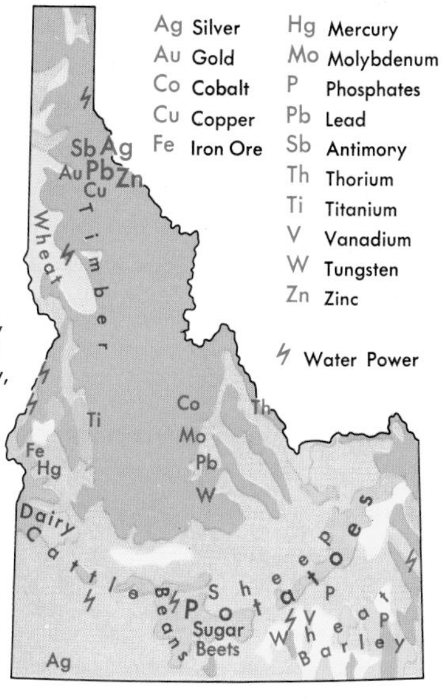

Sb Ag
Au Pb Zn
Cu
Timber
Wheat
Ti
Co
Mo
Pb
W
Th
Fe
Hg
Dairy
Cattle
Sheep
Potatoes
Beans
Sugar Beets
Wheat
Barley
Ag
P
V

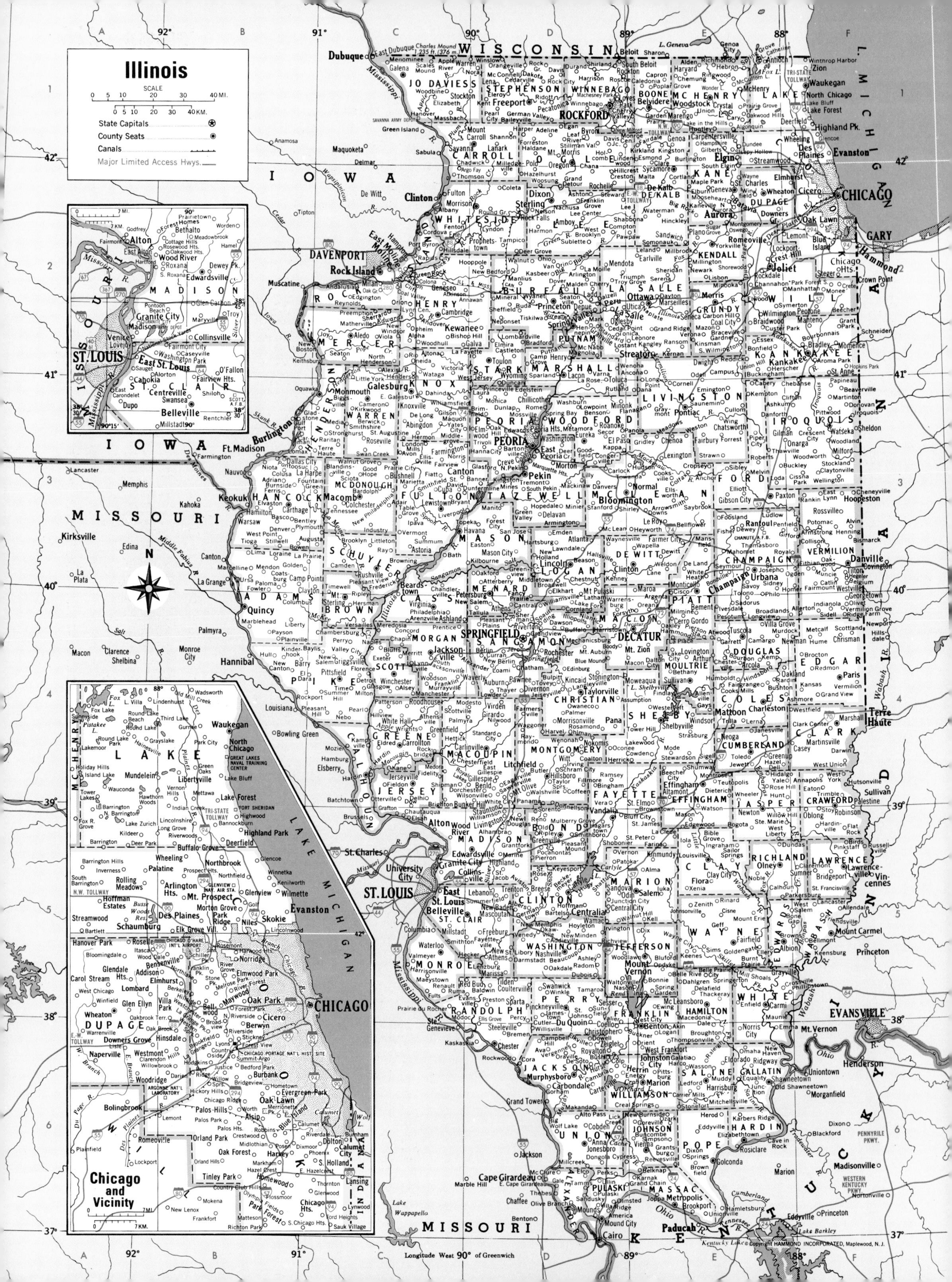

Illinois
SCALE
0 5 10 20 30 40 MI.
0 5 10 20 30 40 KM.
State Capitals
County Seats
Canals
Major Limited Access Hwys.
WISCONSIN
IOWA
MISSOURI
KENTUCKY
INDIANA
LAKE MICHIGAN
CHICAGO
ROCKFORD
PEORIA
SPRINGFIELD
DECATUR
DAVENPORT
Rock Island
Moline
ST. LOUIS
EVANSVILLE
GARY
Hammond
Joliet
Aurora
Elgin
Waukegan
Evanston
Bloomington
Normal
Champaign
Urbana
Danville
Kankakee
Galesburg
Quincy
Jacksonville
Alton
East St. Louis
Belleville
Cairo
Paducah
Terre Haute
Vincennes
Dubuque
Burlington
Keokuk
Hannibal
Cape Girardeau
Carbondale
Mt. Vernon
Centralia
Mattoon
Charleston
Kewanee
Ottawa
La Salle
Streator
Freeport
Sterling
Dixon
Clinton
Pekin
Lincoln
Effingham
Vandalia
Marion
Harrisburg
Metropolis
St. Louis and Vicinity inset: MADISON, ST. CLAIR, Granite City, Alton, East St. Louis, Belleville, ST. LOUIS
Chicago and Vicinity
Longitude West 90° of Greenwich
© Copyright HAMMOND INCORPORATED, Maplewood, N.J.

ILLINOIS

AREA 56,345 sq. mi. (145,934 sq. km.)
POPULATION 11,466,682
CAPITAL Springfield
LARGEST CITY Chicago
HIGHEST POINT Charles Mound 1,235 ft. (376 m.)
SETTLED IN 1720
ADMITTED TO UNION December 3, 1818
POPULAR NAME Prairie State; Land of Lincoln
STATE FLOWER Native Violet
STATE BIRD Cardinal

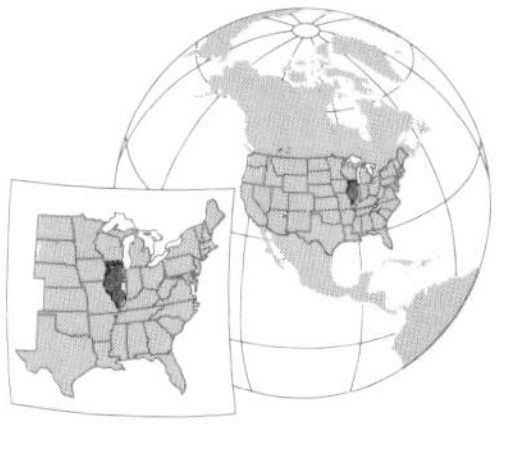

COUNTIES

Adams 66,090 B4
Alexander 10,626 D6
Bond 14,991 D5
Boone 30,806 E1
Brown 5,836 C4
Bureau 35,688 D2
Calhoun 5,322 C4
Carroll 16,805 D1
Cass 13,437 C4
Champaign 173,025 E3
Christian 34,418 D4
Clark 15,921 F4
Clay 14,460 E5
Clinton 33,944 D5
Coles 51,644 E4
Cook 5,105,067 F2
Crawford 19,464 F4
Cumberland 10,670 E4
De Kalb 74,624 E2
De Witt 16,516 E3
Douglas 19,464 E4
Du Page 658,858 E2
Edgar 19,595 F4
Edwards 7,440 E5
Effingham 31,704 E4
Fayette 20,893 D4
Ford 14,275 E3
Franklin 40,319 E5
Fulton 38,080 C3
Gallatin 6,909 E6
Greene 15,317 C4
Grundy 32,337 E2
Hamilton 8,499 E5
Hancock 21,373 B3
Hardin 5,189 E6
Henderson 8,096 C3
Henry 51,159 C2
Iroquois 30,787 F3
Jackson 61,067 D6
Jasper 10,609 E4
Jefferson 37,020 E5
Jersey 20,539 C4
Jo Daviess 21,821 C1
Johnson 11,347 E6
Kane 317,471 E2
Kankakee 96,255 F2
Kendall 39,413 E2
Knox 56,393 C3
La Salle 106,913 E2
Lake 516,418 E1
Lawrence 15,972 F5
Lee 34,392 D2
Livingston 39,301 E3
Logan 30,798 D3
Macon 117,206 E4
Macoupin 47,679 D4
Madison 249,238 D5
Marion 41,561 E5
Marshall 12,846 D2
Mason 16,269 D3
Massac 14,752 E6
McDonough 35,244 C3
McHenry 183,241 E1
McLean 129,180 E3
Menard 11,164 D3
Mercer 17,290 C2
Monroe 22,422 C5
Montgomery 30,728 D4
Morgan 36,397 C4
Moultrie 13,930 E4
Ogle 45,957 D1
Peoria 182,827 D3
Perry 21,412 D5
Piatt 15,548 E4
Pike 17,577 C4
Pope 4,373 E6
Pulaski 7,523 D6
Putnam 5,730 D2
Randolph 34,583 D5
Richland 16,545 E5
Rock Island 148,723 C2
Saint Clair 267,531 D5
Saline 26,551 E6
Sangamon 178,386 D4
Schuyler 7,498 C3
Scott 5,644 C4
Shelby 22,261 E4
Stark 6,534 D2
Stephenson 48,052 D1
Tazewell 123,692 D3
Union 17,619 D6
Vermilion 88,257 F3
Wabash 13,111 F5
Warren 19,181 C3
Washington 14,965 D5
Wayne 17,241 E5
White 16,522 E5
Whiteside 60,186 D2
Will 357,313 F2
Williamson 57,733 E6
Winnebago 252,913 D1
Woodford 32,653 D3

CITIES and TOWNS

Abingdon 3,597 C3
Addison 32,058 B5
Albany 835 C2
Albers 700 D5
Albion▲ 2,116 E5
Aledo▲ 3,681 C2
Alexis 908 C2
Algonquin 11,663 E1
Alhambra 709 D5
Allendale 476 F5
Alorton 2,960 B2
Alpha 753 C2
Alsip 18,227 B6
Altamont 2,296 E4
Alton 32,905 A2
Altona 559 C2
Amboy 2,377 D2
Andalusia 1,052 C2
Andover 579 C2
Anna 4,805 D6
Annawan 802 C2
Antioch 6,105 E1
Arcola 2,678 E4
Arenzville 432 C4
Argenta 940 E4
Arlington Heights 75,460 B5
Aroma Park 690 F2
Arthur 2,112 E4
Ashkum 650 E3
Ashland 1,257 C4
Ashley 583 D5
Ashmore 800 F4
Ashton 1,042 D2
Assumption 1,244 E4
Astoria 1,205 C3
Athens 1,404 D4
Atkinson 950 C2
Atlanta 1,616 D3
Atwood 1,253 E4
Auburn 3,724 D4
Augusta 614 C3
Aurora 99,581 E2
Ava 674 D6
Aviston 924 D5
Avon 957 C3
Baldwin 426 D5
Bannockburn 1,388 B5
Barrington 9,504 A5
Barrington Hills 4,202 A5
Barry 1,391 B4
Bartlett 19,373 A5
Bartonville 5,643 D3
Batavia 17,076 E2
Beardstown 5,270 C3
Beckemeyer 1,070 D5
Bedford Park 566 B6
Beecher 2,032 F2
Beecher City 437 E4
Belgium 511 F3
Belleville▲ 42,785 B3
Bellwood 20,241 B5
Belvidere▲ 15,958 E1
Bement 1,668 E4
Benld 1,604 D4
Bensenville 17,767 B5
Benton▲ 7,216 E6
Berkeley 5,137 B5
Berwyn 45,426 B6
Bethalto 9,507 B2
Bethany 1,369 E4
Blandinsville 762 C3
Bloomingdale 16,614 A5
Bloomington▲ 51,972 D3
Blue Island 21,203 B6
Blue Mound 1,161 D4
Bluffs 774 C4
Bluford 747 E5
Bolingbrook 40,843 A6
Bourbon 13,934 E4
Bourbonnais 13,280 F2
Bowen 462 B3
Braceville 587 E2
Bradford 678 D2
Bradley 10,792 F2
Braidwood 3,584 E2
Breese 3,567 D5
Bridgeport 2,118 F5
Bridgeview 14,402 B6
Brighton 2,270 C4
Brimfield 797 D3
Broadview 8,713 B6
Brookfield 18,876 B6
Brooklyn (Lovejoy) 1,144 A2
Brookport 1,070 E6
Brownstown 668 E5
Buckley 557 F3
Buckner 478 E6
Buda 563 D2
Buffalo 503 D4
Buffalo Grove 36,427 B5
Bunker Hill 1,722 D4
Burbank 27,600 B6
Burnham 3,916 C6
Burr Ridge 7,669 B6
Bushnell 3,288 C3
Byron 2,284 D1
Cahokia 17,550 A3
Cairo▲ 4,846 D6
Calumet City 37,840 C6
Calumet Park 8,418 C6
Cambria 1,230 D6
Cambridge▲ 2,124 C2
Camp Point 1,230 B3
Canton 13,922 C3
Capron 682 E1
Carbon Cliff 1,492 C2
Carbondale 27,033 D6
Carlinville▲ 5,416 D4
Carlyle▲ 3,474 D5
Carmi▲ 5,564 E5
Carol Stream 31,716 A5
Carpentersville 23,049 E1
Carrier Mills 2,268 E6
Carrollton▲ 2,507 C4
Carterville 3,630 D6
Carthage▲ 2,657 B3
Cary 10,043 E1
Casey 2,914 F4
Caseyville 4,419 B2
Catlin 2,173 F3
Cave in Rock 381 E6
Cedarville 751 D1
Central City 1,390 D5
Centralia 14,274 D5
Centreville 7,489 B3
Cerro Gordo 1,436 E4
Chadwick 557 D1
Champaign 63,502 E3
Chandlerville 689 C3
Channahon 4,266 E2
Chapin 632 C4
Charleston▲ 20,398 E4
Chatham 6,074 D4
Chatsworth 1,186 E3
Chebanse 1,082 F3
Chenoa 1,732 E3
Cherry 487 D2
Cherry Valley 1,615 D1
Chester▲ 8,194 D6
Chicago Heights 33,072 C6
Chicago Ridge 13,643 B6
Chicago▲ 2,783,726 C5
Chillicothe 5,959 D3
Chrisman 1,136 F4
Christopher 2,774 D6
Cicero 67,436 B5
Cisne 645 E5
Cissna Park 805 F3
Clarendon Hills 6,994 B6
Clay City 929 E5
Clayton 726 B3
Clifton 1,347 F3
Clinton▲ 7,437 E3
Coal City 3,907 E2
Coal Valley 2,683 C2
Cobden 1,090 D6
Coffeen 736 D4
Colchester 1,645 C3
Colfax 854 E3
Collinsville 22,446 B2
Colona 2,237 C2
Columbia 5,524 C5
Cordova 638 C2
Cornell 556 E3
Cortland 963 E2
Coulterville 984 D5
Country Club Hills 15,431 B6
Countryside 5,716 B6
Cowden 599 E4
Creal Springs 791 E6
Crescent City 541 F3
Crest Hill 10,643 E2
Creston 535 D2
Crestwood 10,823 B6
Crete 6,773 F2
Creve Coeur 5,938 D3
Crossville 805 F5
Crystal Lake 24,512 E1
Cuba 1,440 C3
Cullom 568 E3
Cutler 523 D5
Dahlgren 512 E5
Dakota 549 D1
Dallas City 1,037 B3
Dalton City 573 E4
Dalzell 587 D2
Danforth 457 E3
Danvers 981 D3
Danville▲ 33,828 F3
Darien 18,341 B6
Davis 541 D1
Dawson 536 D4
De Kalb 34,925 E2
De Land 458 E3
De Soto 1,500 D6
Decatur▲ 83,885 E4
Deer Creek 630 D3
Deer Park 2,887 A5
Deerfield 17,327 B5
Delavan 1,642 D3
Depue 1,729 D2
Des Plaines 53,223 B5
Dieterich 568 E4
Divernon 1,178 D4
Dix 456 E5
Dixmoor 3,647 C6
Dixon▲ 15,144 D2
Dolton 23,930 C6
Dongola 728 D6
Dow 465 C4
Dowell 480 D6
Downers Grove 46,858 A6
Downs 620 E3
Du Quoin 6,697 D5
Dundee (East and West Dundee) 6,169 E1
Dunlap 851 D3
Dupo 3,164 A3
Durand 1,100 D1
Dwight 4,230 E2
Earlville 1,435 E2
East Alton 7,063 A2
East Cape Girardeau 451 D6
East Carondelet 630 A3
East Dubuque 1,914 C1
East Dundee (Dundee) 2,721 E1
East Galesburg 813 C3
East Hazelcrest 1,570 C6
East Moline 20,147 C2
East Peoria 21,378 D3
East Saint Louis 40,944 A2
Edgewood 502 E5
Edinburg 982 D4
Edwards 14,579 D3
Edwardsville▲ 12,480 B2
Effingham▲ 11,851 E4
El Paso 2,499 D3
Elburn 1,275 E2
Eldorado 4,536 E6
Elgin 77,010 E1
Elizabeth 641 C1
Elizabethtown▲ 427 E6
Elk Grove Village 33,429 B5
Elkhart 475 D3
Elkville 958 D6
Elmhurst 42,029 B5
Elmwood 1,841 D3
Elmwood Park 23,206 B5
Elsah 851 C5
Elwood 951 E2
Emden 459 D3
Energy 1,106 E6
Enfield 683 E5
Equality 748 E6
Erie 1,572 C2
Essex 482 E2
Eureka▲ 4,435 D3
Evanston 73,233 B5
Evansville 844 D5
Evergreen Park 20,874 B6
Fairbury 3,643 E3
Fairfield▲ 5,439 E5
Fairmont 2,894 A2
Fairmont City 2,140 B2
Fairmount 678 F3
Fairview 510 C3
Fairview Heights 14,351 B3
Farina 575 E5
Farmer City 2,114 E3
Farmersville 698 D4
Farmington 2,535 C3
Findlay 787 E4
Fisher 1,526 E3
Fithian 512 F3
Flanagan 987 E3
Flat Rock 421 F5
Flora 5,054 E5
Flossmoor 8,651 B6
Ford Heights 4,259 C6
Forest Homes 1,701 B2
Forest Park 14,918 B5
Forest View 743 B6
Forrest 1,124 E3
Forreston 1,361 D1
Forsyth 1,275 D4
Fox Lake 7,478 A4
Fox River Grove 3,551 A5
Frankfort 7,180 B6
Franklin 634 C4
Franklin Grove 968 D2
Franklin Park 18,485 B5
Freeburg 3,115 D5
Freeport▲ 25,840 D1
Fulton 3,698 C2
Galatia 983 E6
Gale 3,647 D6
Galena▲ 3,876 C1
Galesburg▲ 33,530 C3
Galva 2,742 D2
Gardner 1,237 E2
Geneseo 5,990 C2
Geneva▲ 12,617 E2
Genoa 3,083 E1
Georgetown 3,678 F4
German Valley 480 D1
Germantown 1,167 D5
Gibson City 3,498 E3
Gifford 845 E3
Gilberts 987 E1
Gillespie 3,645 D4
Gilman 1,816 E3
Glasford 1,115 D3
Glen Carbon 7,731 B2
Glen Ellyn 24,944 A5
Glencoe 8,499 B5
Glendale Heights 27,973 A5
Glenview 37,093 B5
Glenwood 9,289 C6
Godfrey 5,436 A2
Golconda▲ 823 E6
Golden 565 B3
Golf 454 B5
Goodfield 454 D3
Goreville 872 E6
Grafton 918 C5
Grand Ridge 560 E2
Grand Tower 775 D6
Grandview 1,647 D4
Granite City 32,862 A2
Grant Park 1,024 F2
Granville 1,407 D2
Grayslake 7,388 B4
Grayville 2,043 E5
Green Oaks 2,101 B4
Green Rock 2,615 C2
Green Valley 745 D3
Greenfield 1,162 C4
Greenup 1,616 E4
Greenview 848 D3
Greenville▲ 4,806 D5
Gridley 1,304 E3
Griggsville 1,218 C4
Gurnee 13,701 B4
Hamel 530 B2
Hamilton 3,281 B3
Hammond 527 E4
Hampshire 1,843 E1
Hampton 1,601 C2
Hanna City 1,205 D3
Hanover 908 C1
Hanover Park 32,895 A5
Hardin▲ 1,071 C4
Harrisburg▲ 9,289 E6
Harristown 1,319 D4
Hartford 1,676 A2
Harvard 5,975 E1
Harvey 29,771 B6
Harwood Heights 7,680 B5
Havana▲ 3,610 D3
Hawthorn Woods 4,423 B5
Hazel Crest 13,334 B6
Hebron 809 E1
Hecker 534 D5
Hegeler 1,853 F3
Hennepin▲ 669 D2
Henry 2,591 D2
Herrick 466 D4
Herrin 10,857 E6
Herscher 1,278 E2
Heyworth 1,627 E3
Hickory Hills 13,021 B6
Highland 7,525 D5
Highland Park 30,575 B5
Highwood 5,331 B5
Hillcrest 828 D2
Hillsboro▲ 4,400 D4
Hillsdale 489 C2
Hillside 7,672 B5
Hinckley 1,682 E2
Hinsdale 16,029 B6
Hodgkins 1,963 B6
Hoffman 492 D5
Hoffman Estates 46,561 A5
Holiday Hills 807 A4
Homer 1,264 F3
Hometown 4,769 B6
Homewood 19,278 B6
Hoopeston 5,871 F3
Hopedale 805 D3
Hopkins Park 601 F2
Hoyleton 508 D5
Hudson 1,006 E3
Hull 514 B4
Humboldt 470 E4
Hunt 2,453 E4
Huntley 1,646 E1
Hurst 842 D6
Hutsonville 622 F4
Illiopolis 934 D4
Ina 489 E5
Industry 571 C3
Inverness 6,503 A5
Ipava 483 C3
Irving 516 D4
Irvington 827 D5
Island Lake 4,449 A4
Itasca 6,947 B5
Jacksonville▲ 19,324 C4
Jerome 1,206 D4
Jerseyville▲ 7,382 C4
Johnston City 3,706 E6
Joliet▲ 76,836 E2
Jonesboro▲ 1,728 D6
Joppa 492 E6
Joy 452 C2
Junction City 539 D5
Justice 11,137 B6

(continued on following page)

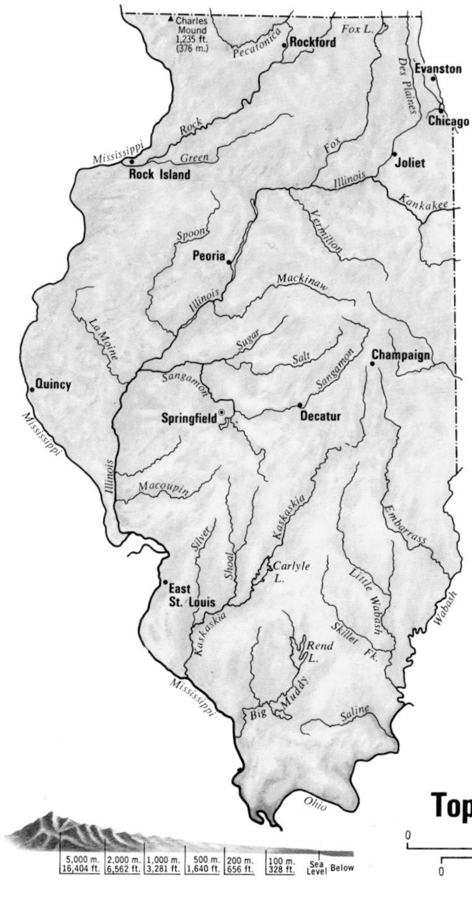
Charles Mound 1,235 ft. (376 m.)
Pecatonica
Rockford
Fox L.
Evanston
Des Plaines
Chicago
Rock
Mississippi
Green
Rock Island
Fox
Joliet
Illinois
Kankakee
Spoon
Vermilion
Peoria
Mackinaw
Illinois
La Moine
Sugar
Salt
Champaign
Quincy
Sangamon
Sangamon
Springfield
Decatur
Mississippi
Illinois
Macoupin
Kaskaskia
Embarrass
Silver
Shoal
Carlyle L.
Little Wabash
Wabash
East St. Louis
Kaskaskia
Skillet Fk.
Rend L.
Mississippi
Big Muddy
Saline
Ohio
5,000 m. 16,404 ft.
2,000 m. 6,562 ft.
1,000 m. 3,281 ft.
500 m. 1,640 ft.
200 m. 656 ft.
100 m. 328 ft.
Sea Level
Below

Topography

0 40 80 MI.
0 40 80 KM.

Agriculture, Industry and Resources

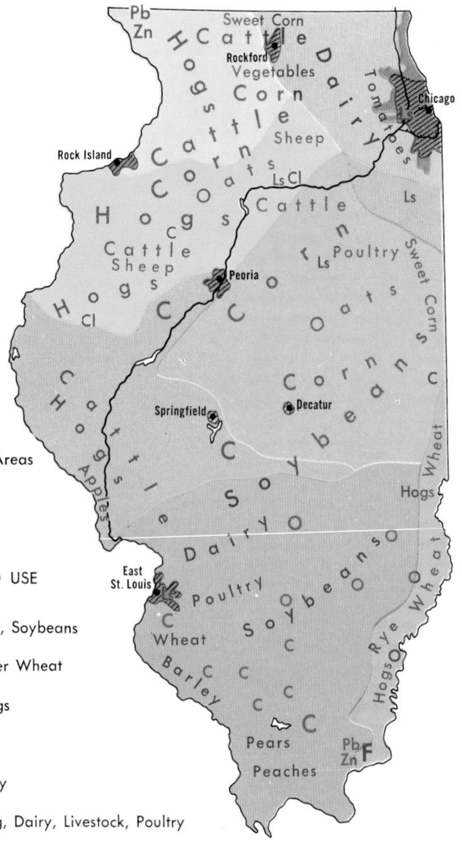
Sweet Corn
Cattle
Rockford
Vegetables
Dairy
Tomatoes
Chicago
Hogs
Corn
Sheep
Oats
Rock Island
Ls Cl
Ls
Poultry
Peoria
Springfield
Decatur
Soybeans
Wheat
Apples
East St. Louis
Barley
Pears
Peaches
Rye
Pb
Zn
F

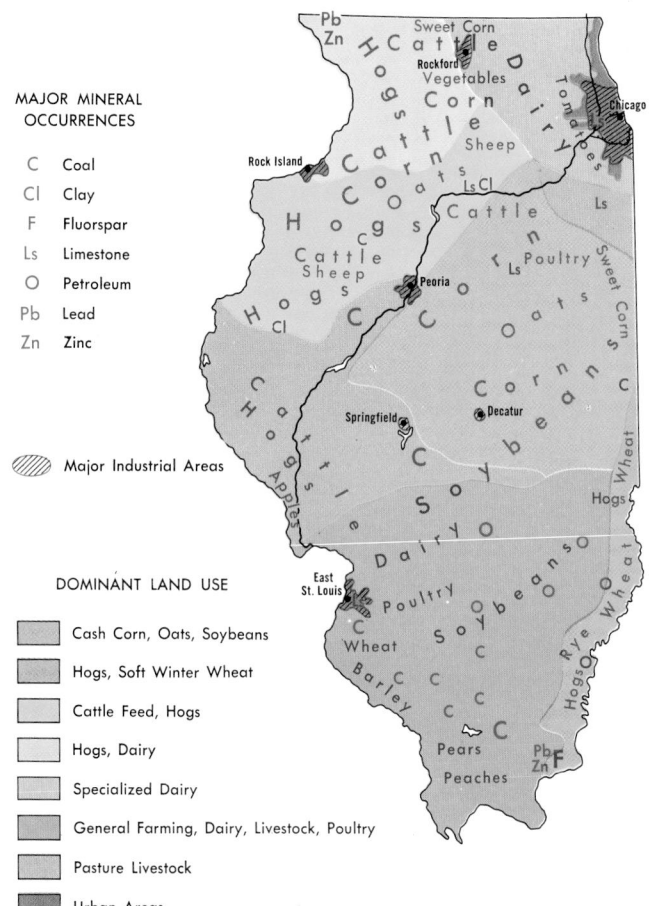

MAJOR MINERAL OCCURRENCES

- C Coal
- Cl Clay
- F Fluorspar
- Ls Limestone
- O Petroleum
- Pb Lead
- Zn Zinc

Major Industrial Areas

DOMINANT LAND USE

- Cash Corn, Oats, Soybeans
- Hogs, Soft Winter Wheat
- Cattle Feed, Hogs
- Hogs, Dairy
- Specialized Dairy
- General Farming, Dairy, Livestock, Poultry
- Pasture Livestock
- Urban Areas

OTHER FEATURES

▲County seat

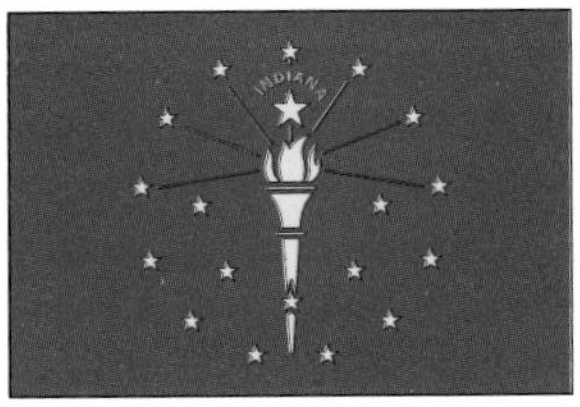
INDIANA

AREA 36,185 sq. mi. (93,719 sq. km.)
POPULATION 5,564,228
CAPITAL Indianapolis
LARGEST CITY Indianapolis
HIGHEST POINT 1,257 ft. (383 m.) (Wayne County)
SETTLED IN 1730
ADMITTED TO UNION December 11, 1816
POPULAR NAME Hoosier State
STATE FLOWER Peony
STATE BIRD Cardinal

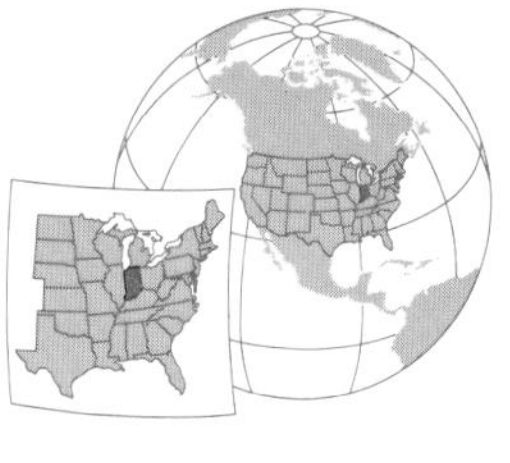

COUNTIES

Adams 31,095 .... H3
Allen 300,836 .... G2
Bartholomew 63,657 .... F6
Benton 9,441 .... C3
Blackford 14,067 .... G4
Boone 38,147 .... E4
Brown 14,080 .... E6
Carroll 18,809 .... D3
Cass 38,413 .... E3
Clark 87,777 .... F8
Clay 24,705 .... C6
Clinton 30,974 .... E4
Crawford 9,914 .... E8
Daviess 27,533 .... C7
De Kalb 35,324 .... H2
Dearborn 38,835 .... H6
Decatur 23,645 .... G6
Delaware 119,659 .... G4
Dubois 36,616 .... D8
Elkhart 156,198 .... F1
Fayette 26,015 .... G5
Floyd 64,404 .... F8
Fountain 17,808 .... C4
Franklin 19,580 .... G6
Fulton 18,840 .... E2
Gibson 31,913 .... B8
Grant 74,169 .... F3
Greene 30,410 .... D6
Hamilton 108,936 .... E4
Hancock 45,527 .... F5
Harrison 29,890 .... E8
Hendricks 75,717 .... D5
Henry 48,139 .... G5
Howard 80,827 .... E4
Huntington 35,427 .... G3
Jackson 37,730 .... E7
Jasper 24,960 .... C2
Jay 21,512 .... G4
Jefferson 29,797 .... G7
Jennings 23,661 .... F7
Johnson 88,109 .... E6
Knox 39,884 .... C7
Kosciusko 65,294 .... F2
LaPorte 108,632 .... D1
Lagrange 29,477 .... G1
Lake 475,594 .... C2
Lawrence 42,836 .... E7
Madison 130,669 .... F4
Marion 797,159 .... E5
Marshall 42,182 .... E2
Martin 10,369 .... D7
Miami 36,897 .... E3
Monroe 108,978 .... D6
Montgomery 34,436 .... D4
Morgan 55,920 .... E6
Newton 13,551 .... C3
Noble 37,877 .... G2
Ohio 5,315 .... H7
Orange 18,409 .... E7
Owen 17,281 .... D6
Parke 15,410 .... C5
Perry 19,107 .... D8
Pike 12,509 .... C8
Porter 128,932 .... C2
Posey 25,968 .... B8
Pulaski 12,643 .... D2
Putnam 30,315 .... D5
Randolph 27,148 .... G4
Ripley 24,616 .... G6
Rush 18,129 .... G5
Saint Joseph 241,617 .... E1
Scott 20,991 .... F7
Shelby 40,307 .... F5
Spencer 19,490 .... C9
Starke 22,747 .... D2
Steuben 27,446 .... G1
Sullivan 18,993 .... C6
Switzerland 7,738 .... G7
Tippecanoe 130,598 .... D4
Tipton 16,119 .... E4
Union 6,976 .... H5
Vanderburgh 165,058 .... B8
Vermillion 16,773 .... C5
Vigo 106,107 .... C6
Wabash 35,069 .... F3
Warren 8,176 .... C4
Warrick 44,920 .... C8
Washington 23,717 .... E7
Wayne 71,951 .... G5
Wells 25,948 .... G3
White 23,265 .... D3
Whitley 27,651 .... F2

CITIES and TOWNS

Abington 200 .... H5
Adams 250 .... F6
Adamsboro 325 .... E3
Advance 520 .... D5
Akron 1,001 .... E2
Alamo 112 .... C5
Albany 2,357 .... G4
Albion▲ 1,823 .... G2
Alexandria 5,709 .... F4
Altona 156 .... G2
Ambia 249 .... C4
Amboy 370 .... F3
Americus 150 .... D3
Amity 200 .... E6
Amo 380 .... D5
Anderson▲ 59,459 .... F4
Andersonville 225 .... G5
Andrews 1,118 .... F3
Angola▲ 5,824 .... G1
Anthony 130 .... G4
Arcadia 1,468 .... E4
Arcola 300 .... G2
Ardmore 800 .... E1
Argos 1,642 .... E2
Arlington 500 .... F5
Ashley 767 .... G1
Athens 145 .... E2
Atlanta 703 .... E4
Attica 3,457 .... C4
Atwood 300 .... F2
Auburn▲ 9,379 .... G2
Aurora 3,825 .... H6
Austin 4,310 .... F7
Avilla 1,366 .... G2
Avoca 400 .... D7
Azalia 194 .... F6
Bainbridge 682 .... D5
Bargersville 1,681 .... E5
Batesville 4,720 .... G6
Battle Ground 806 .... D3
Bear Branch 150 .... G7
Bedford▲ 13,817 .... E7
Beech Grove 13,383 .... E5
Bellmore 160 .... C5
Bennetts Switch 138 .... E3
Benton 220 .... F2
Berne 3,559 .... H3
Bethany 90 .... E5
Beverly Shores 622 .... D1
Bicknell 3,357 .... C7
Bippus 300 .... F3
Birdseye 472 .... D8
Black Oak C1
Blanford 500 .... B5
Blocher 400 .... F7
Bloomfield▲ 2,592 .... D6
Blooming Grove 300 .... G5
Bloomingdale 341 .... C5
Bloomington▲ 60,633 .... D6
Blountsville 155 .... G4
Blue Ridge 219 .... F5
Bluffton▲ 9,020 .... G3
Boggstown 200 .... F5
Boone Grove 220 .... C2
Boonville▲ 6,724 .... C8
Borden F8
Boston 159 .... H5
Boswell 767 .... C3
Bourbon 1,672 .... E2
Bowling Green 200 .... D6
Bradford 350 .... E8
Brazil▲ 7,640 .... C5
Bremen 4,725 .... E2
Bridgeton 250 .... C5
Bright 3,945 .... H6
Brimfield 292 .... G2
Bringhurst 275 .... E3
Bristol 1,133 .... F1
Brook 899 .... C3
Brooklyn 1,162 .... E5
Brooksburg 79 .... G7
Brookston 1,804 .... D3
Brookville▲ 2,529 .... G6
Brownsburg 7,628 .... E5
Brownstown▲ 2,872 .... F7
Brownsville 250 .... H5
Bruceville 471 .... C7
Bryant 273 .... G3
Buck Creek 225 .... D4
Buckskin 200 .... C8
Buffalo 500 .... D3
Bunker Hill 1,010 .... E3
Burket 200 .... F2
Burlington 568 .... E4
Burnettsville 401 .... D3
Burney 300 .... F6
Burns City 140 .... D7
Burns Harbor 788 .... C1
Burrows 250 .... E3
Butler 2,601 .... H2
Butlerville 300 .... F6
Byron 200 .... C5
Cadiz 202 .... G5
Cambridge City 2,091 .... G5
Camden 607 .... D3
Cammack 250 .... G4
Campbellsburg 606 .... E7
Cannelburg 97 .... C7
Cannelton▲ 1,786 .... D9
Carbon 350 .... C5
Carefree 26 .... E8
Carlisle 613 .... C7
Carmel 25,380 .... E5
Cartersburg 300 .... E5
Carthage 887 .... F5
Cassville 159 .... E3
Cates 125 .... C4
Cayuga 1,083 .... C5
Cedar Grove 246 .... H6
Cedar Lake 8,885 .... C2
Celestine 150 .... D8
Centenary 150 .... B5
Center 278 .... E4
Centerpoint 242 .... C6
Centerton 250 .... E5
Centerville 2,398 .... H5
Chalmers 525 .... D3
Chandler 3,099 .... C8
Chapel Hill 175 .... E6
Charlestown 5,889 .... F8
Charlottesville 300 .... F5
Chelsea 200 .... F7
Chester 2,730 .... H5
Chesterfield 2,701 .... F4
Chesterton 9,124 .... D1
Chili 280 .... F3
Chrisney 511 .... C8
Churubusco 1,781 .... G2
Cicero 3,268 .... E4
Clarks Hill 716 .... D4
Clarksburg 300 .... G6
Clarksville 19,833 .... F8
Clay City 929 .... C6
Claypool 411 .... F2
Clayton 610 .... D5
Clear Creek 200 .... E6
Clear Lake 272 .... H1
Clifford 308 .... F6
Clinton 5,040 .... C5
Cloverdale 1,681 .... D5
Cloverland 175 .... C6
Clymers 150 .... E3
Coal City 225 .... D6
Coalmont 450 .... C6
Coatesville 469 .... D5
Coesse 150 .... G2
Colburn 300 .... D3
Colfax 727 .... D4
Collegeville 993 .... C3
Columbia City▲ 5,706 .... G2
Columbus▲ 31,802 .... E6
Commiskey 150 .... F7
Connersville▲ 15,550 .... G5
Converse 1,144 .... F3
Correct 131 .... G7
Cortland 175 .... F7
Corunna 241 .... G2
Cory 2,661 .... C6
Corydon▲ 2,724 .... E8
Covington▲ 2,747 .... C4
Cowan 428 .... G4
Craigville 130 .... G3
Crandall 147 .... E8
Crane 216 .... D7
Crawfordsville▲ 13,584 .... D4
Cromwell 520 .... F2
Cross Plains 254 .... G7
Crothersville 1,687 .... F7
Crown Point▲ 17,728 .... C2
Crumstown 175 .... E1
Culver 1,404 .... E2
Cumberland 1,624 .... F5
Cutler 140 .... D4
Cynthiana 669 .... B8
Dale 1,553 .... D8
Daleville 1,681 .... F4
Dana 612 .... C5
Danville▲ 4,345 .... D5
Darlington 740 .... D4
Darmstadt 1,346 .... B8
Dayton 996 .... D4
Decatur▲ 8,644 .... H3
Decker 281 .... B7
Deer Creek 250 .... E3
Deerfield 300 .... H4
Delaware 135 .... G6
Delong 156 .... E2
Delphi▲ 2,531 .... D3
Demotte 2,482 .... C2
Denham 140 .... D2
Denver 504 .... E3
Depauw 150 .... E8
Deputy 200 .... F7
Desoto 385 .... G4
Dillsboro 1,200 .... G6
Donaldson 320 .... E2
Doolittle Mills 200 .... D8
Dublin 805 .... G5
Dubois 550 .... D8
Dugger 936 .... C6
Dundee 160 .... F4
Dune Acres 263 .... C1
Dunkirk 2,739 .... G4
Dunlap 5,705 .... F1
Dunreith 205 .... F5
Dupont 391 .... G7
Dyer 10,923 .... C1
Eagletown 306 .... E4
Earl Park 443 .... C3
East Chicago 33,892 .... C1
East Enterprise 250 .... H7
East Germantown (Pershing) 372 .... G5
Eaton 1,614 .... G4
Economy 151 .... G5
Edgewood 2,057 .... F4
Edinburgh 4,536 .... E6
Edwardsport 380 .... C7
Edwardsville 700 .... F8
Elberfeld 635 .... C8
Elizabeth 153 .... F8
Elizabethtown 495 .... F6
Elkhart 43,627 .... F1
Ellettsville 3,275 .... D6
Elnora 679 .... C7
Elrod 200 .... G6
Elston 500 .... D4
Elwood 9,494 .... F4
Eminence 200 .... D5
English▲ 614 .... E8
Etna 578 .... F2
Etna Green 522 .... E2
Eugene 400 .... B5
Evansville▲ 126,272 .... C9
Everton 500 .... G5
Fair Oaks 175 .... C2
Fairbanks 165 .... B6
Fairland 1,348 .... F5
Fairmount 3,130 .... F4
Fairview 1,446 .... G7
Fairview Park 1,545 .... C5
Farmersburg 1,159 .... C6
Farmland 1,412 .... G4
Fayetteville 180 .... D7
Ferdinand 2,318 .... D8
Fillmore 497 .... D5
Finly 400 .... F5
Fishers 7,508 .... E5
Flat Rock 323 .... F6
Flora 2,179 .... E3
Florence 155 .... H7
Floyds Knobs 500 .... F8
Fontanet 325 .... C5
Forest 400 .... E4
Fort Branch 2,447 .... B8
Fort Wayne▲ 173,072 .... G2
Fortville 2,690 .... F5
Fountain 766 .... C4
Fountain City 839 .... H5
Fountaintown 225 .... F5
Fowler▲ 2,333 .... C3
Fowlerton 306 .... F4
Francesville 969 .... D3
Francisco 560 .... B8
Frankfort▲ 14,754 .... E4
Franklin▲ 12,907 .... E6
Frankton 1,736 .... F4
Fredericksburg 155 .... E8
Freelandville 600 .... C7
Freetown 600 .... E7
Fremont 1,407 .... H1
French Lick 2,087 .... D7
Fulton 371 .... E3
Galena 1,231 .... F8
Galveston 1,609 .... E3
Garrett 5,349 .... G2
Gary 116,646 .... C1
Gas City 6,296 .... F4
Gaston 979 .... G4
Geneva 1,280 .... H3
Gentryville 277 .... C8
Georgetown 2,092 .... F8
Gessie 144 .... C4
Glenwood 285 .... G5
Glezen 300 .... C8
Goldsmith 235 .... E4
Goodland 1,033 .... C3
Goshen▲ 23,797 .... F1
Gosport 764 .... D6
Grabill 751 .... H2
Grandview 761 .... C9
Granger 20,241 .... E1
Grantsburg 189 .... E8
Gravelton 150 .... F2
Greencastle▲ 8,984 .... D5
Greendale 3,881 .... H6
Greenfield▲ 11,657 .... F5

(continued on following page)

Agriculture, Industry and Resources

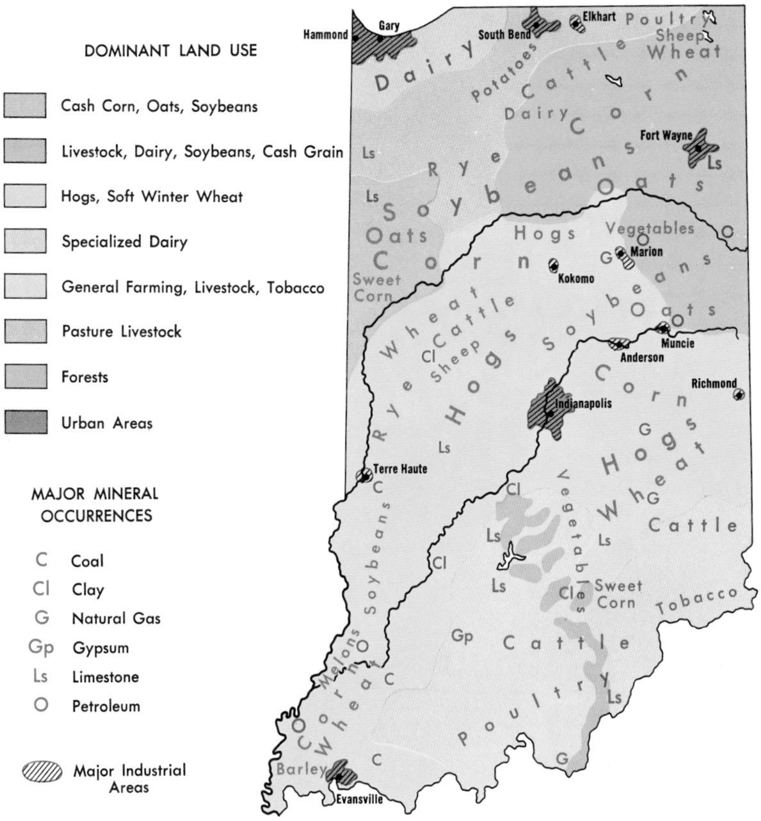
DOMINANT LAND USE
Cash Corn, Oats, Soybeans
Livestock, Dairy, Soybeans, Cash Grain
Hogs, Soft Winter Wheat
Specialized Dairy
General Farming, Livestock, Tobacco
Pasture Livestock
Forests
Urban Areas
MAJOR MINERAL OCCURRENCES
C Coal
Cl Clay
G Natural Gas
Gp Gypsum
Ls Limestone
O Petroleum
Major Industrial Areas
Hammond
Gary
South Bend
Elkhart
Fort Wayne
Marion
Kokomo
Muncie
Anderson
Richmond
Indianapolis
Terre Haute
Evansville
Dairy
Potatoes
Cattle
Poultry
Sheep
Wheat
Corn
Rye
Soybeans
Oats
Hogs
Vegetables
Sweet Corn
Tobacco
Melons
Barley

Greens Fork 416 H5
Greensboro 204 G5
Greensburg▲ 9,286 G6
Greentown 2,172 E4
Greenville 508 F8
Greenwood 26,265 E5
Griffin 171 B8
Griffith 17,916 C1
Grovertown 150 D2
Gwynneville 250 F5
Hagerstown 1,835 G5
Hamilton 684 H1
Hamlet 789 D2
Hammond 84,236 B1
Hanna 550 D2
Hanover 3,610 F7
Hardinsburg 322 E8
Harlan 840 H2
Harmony 645 C5
Harrodsburg 400 D6
Hartford City▲ 6,960 G4
Hartsville 391 F6
Hatfield 800 C9
Haubstadt 1,455 B8
Hayden 300 F7
Haysville 600 D8
Hazelwood 650 D5
Hazleton 357 B8
Hebron 3,183 C2
Helmsburg 150 E6
Heltonville 400 E7
Hemlock 300 F4
Henryville 1,132 F7
Hibbard 150 E2
Highland 23,696 B1
Hillisburg 180 E4
Hillsboro 499 C4
Hillsdale 500 C5
Hoagland 600 H3
Hobart 21,822 C1
Hobbs 200 F4
Holland 675 C8
Hollandsburg 150 C5
Holton 451 G6
Homer 235 F5
Hope 2,171 F6
Hortonville 240 E4
Houston 200 E6
Howe 800 G1
Hudson 438 G1
Hudson Lake 1,347 D1
Huntertown 1,330 G2
Huntingburg 5,242 D8
Huntington▲ 16,389 G3
Huntsville 1,200 G4
Huron 250 D7
Hymera 771 C6
Idaville 655 D3
Independence 150 C4
Indian Village 142 E1
Indianapolis (cap.)▲ 741,952 E5
Ingalls 889 F5
Inglefield 378 B8
Inwood 150 E2
Ireland 600 C8
Jamestown 764 D5
Jasonville 2,200 C6
Jasper▲ 10,030 D8
Jefferson 21,841 D4
Jeffersonville▲ 21,220 F8
Jolietville 300 E4
Jonesboro 2,073 F4
Jonesville 221 F6
Kempton 362 E4
Kendallville 7,773 G2
Kennard 382 G5
Kent 1,798 F7
Kentland▲ 1,936 C3
Kewanna 542 E2
Keystone 204 G3
Kimmell 250 F2
Kingman 561 C5
Kingsbury 258 D1
Kingsford Heights 1,486 D2
Kirklin 707 E4
Knightstown 2,048 F5
Knightsville 740 C5
Knox▲ 3,705 D2
Kokomo▲ 44,962 E4
Koontz Lake 1,615 D2
Kouts 1,603 C2
La Crosse 677 D2
La Fontaine 909 F3
Ladoga 1,124 D5
Lafayette▲ 43,764 D4
Lagrange▲ 2,382 F1
Lagro 496 F3
Lake Bruce 160 E2
Lake James 400 H1
Lake Station 13,899 C1
Lake Village 900 C2
Laketon 500 F3
Lakeville 655 E1
Lancaster 275 F7
Landess 150 F3
Lanesville 512 E8
Laotto 361 G2
Lapaz 562 E2
Lapel 1,742 F4
LaPorte▲ 21,507 D1
Laconia 75 E8
Larwill 219 F2
Laurel 544 G6
Lawrence 26,763 E5
Lawrenceburg▲ 4,375 H6
Leavenworth 320 E8
Lebanon▲ 12,059 D4
Lee 584 D3
Leesburg 629 F2
Leesville 164 E7
Leiters Ford 280 E2
Leo 500 G2
Leopold 175 D8
Leroy 400 C2
Letts 247 F6
Lewis 437 C6
Lewisville 577 G5
Lexington F7
Liberty Center 275 G3
Liberty Mills 200 F2
Liberty▲ 2,051 H5
Ligonier 3,443 F2
Lincoln City 160 C8
Lincolnville 150 F3
Linden 718 D4
Linn Grove 175 H3
Linton 5,814 C6
Linwood 157 F4
Lisbon 200 G2
Little York 155 F7
Livonia 136 E7
Lizton 410 D5
Logan 16,812 H6
Logansport▲ 17,731 E3
Long Beach 2,044 D1
Loogootee 2,884 D7
Losantville 253 G4
Lowell 6,430 C2
Lucerne 135 E3
Lydick E1
Lyford 400 C5
Lynn 1,183 H4
Lynnville 640 C8
Lyons 753 C7
Mackey 89 C8
Macy 218 E3
Madison▲ 12,006 G7
Majenica 150 G3
Manchester 250 H6
Manilla 350 F5
Mansfield 200 C5
Marco 150 C7
Marengo 856 E8
Mariah Hill 300 D8
Marietta 234 F6
Marion▲ 32,618 F3
Markle 1,208 G3
Markleville 412 F5
Marshall 379 C5
Martinsburg 200 E8
Martinsville▲ 11,677 D6
Matthews 571 F4
Mauckport 95 E8
Maxinkuckee 150 E2
Maxwell 300 F5
Mays 156 G5
McCordsville 684 F5
Mecca 331 C5
Mechanicsburg 150 G5
Medaryville 689 D2
Medora 805 E7
Mellott 222 C4
Memphis 300 F8
Mentone 912 E2
Merom 257 B6
Merrillville 27,257 C2
Metamora 350 G6
Metz 200 H1
Mexico 1,003 E3
Miami 350 E3
Michiana Shores 378 D1
Michigan City 33,822 C1
Michigantown 472 E4
Middlebury 2,004 F1
Middletown 2,333 F4
Midland 250 C6
Milan 1,529 G6
Milford 126 F2
Milford 177 F6
Mill Creek 208 D1
Millersburg 854 F1
Millhousen 151 G6
Milltown 917 E8
Millville 275 G5
Milroy 750 G6
Milton 634 G5
Mishawaka 42,608 E1
Mitchell 4,669 E7
Modoc 218 G4
Mongo 225 G1
Monon 1,585 D3
Monroe 788 H3
Monroe City 538 C7
Monroeville 1,232 H3
Monrovia 800 E5
Monterey 230 D2
Montezuma 1,134 C5
Montgomery 351 C7
Monticello▲ 5,237 D3
Montmorenci 300 D4
Montpelier 1,880 G3
Mooreland 465 G5
Moores Hill 649 G6
Mooresville 5,541 E5
Morgantown 978 E6
Morocco 1,044 C3
Morris 980 G6
Morristown 989 F5
Mount Auburn 138 G5
Mount Ayr 151 C3
Mount Carmel 108 H6
Mount Etna 111 F3
Mount Summit 238 G4
Mount Vernon▲ 7,217 B9
Mulberry 1,262 D4
Muncie▲ 71,035 G4
Munster 19,949 B1
Murray 136 G3
Nabb 150 F7
Napoleon 238 G6
Nappanee 5,510 F2
Nashville▲ 873 E6
Needmore 200 E7
New Albany▲ 36,322 F8
New Amsterdam 30 E8
New Carlisle 1,446 E1
New Castle▲ 17,753 G5
New Chicago 2,066 C1
New Goshen 500 B5
New Harmony 846 B8
New Haven 9,320 H2
New Lebanon 150 C6
New Lisbon 300 G5
New London 200 E4
New Marion 200 G6
New Market 614 D5
New Middletown 82 E8
New Palestine 671 F5
New Paris 1,007 F2
New Pekin 1,095 F7
New Point 296 G6
New Providence (Borden) 270 F8
New Richmond 312 D4
New Ross 331 D5
New Salem 200 G5
New Salisbury 350 E8
New Trenton 200 H6
New Washington 800 F7
New Waverly 162 E3
New Whiteland 4,097 E5
New Winchester 180 D5
Newbern 150 F6
Newberry 207 C7
Newburgh 2,880 C9
Newport▲ 627 C5
Newtonville 136 D8
Newtown 243 C4
Newville 150 H2
Noblesville▲ 17,655 F4
North Grove 91 F3
North Judson 1,582 D2
North Liberty 1,366 E1
North Manchester 6,383 F3
North Salem 499 D5
North Terre Haute 4,331 C5
North Vernon 5,311 F6
North Webster 881 F2
Norway 300 D3
Notre Dame E1
Nulltown 235 G5
Oakford 325 E4
Oakland City 2,810 C8
Oaktown 655 C7
Oakville 220 G4
Odon 1,475 C7
Ogden Dunes 1,499 C1
Oldenburg 715 G6
Onward 63 E3
Oolitic 1,424 E7
Ora 200 D2
Orange 200 G5
Orestes 458 F4
Orland 361 G1
Orleans 2,083 D7
Osceola 1,999 E1
Osgood 1,688 G6
Ossian 2,428 G3
Oswego 150 F2
Otis 250 D1
Otisco 425 F7
Otterbein 1,291 C4
Otwell 600 C8
Owensburg 785 D7
Owensville 1,053 B8
Oxford 1,273 C3
Packertown 150 F2
Palestine 800 F2
Palmyra 621 E8
Paoli▲ 3,542 E7
Paragon 515 D6
Parker City 1,323 G4
Patoka 704 B8
Patricksburg 250 D6
Patriot 190 H7
Paxton 200 C6
Pekin 950 E7
Pendleton 2,309 F5
Pennville 637 G4
Perkinsville 175 F4
Perrysville 443 C4
Pershing 425 E2
Pershing G5
Peru▲ 12,843 E3
Petersburg▲ 2,449 C7
Petroleum 212 G3
Pierceton 1,030 F2
Pilot Knob 150 E8
Pimento 150 C6
Pine Lake 1,676 D1
Pine Village 134 C4
Pittsboro 815 D5
Pittsburg 175 D3
Plainfield 10,433 E5
Plainville 444 C7
Pleasant Lake 800 H1
Pleasant Mills 175 H3
Plymouth▲ 8,303 E2
Poe 162 G3
Poland 230 C6
Poneto 236 G3
Portage 29,060 C1
Porter 3,118 C1
Portland▲ 6,483 H4
Poseyville 1,089 B8
Pottawattomie Park 281 C1
Prairie Creek 275 C6
Prairieton 200 B6
Preble 150 H3
Princes Lakes 1,055 E6
Princeton▲ 8,127 B8
Providence 250 E6
Putnamville 250 D5
Quincy 250 D6
Ragsdale 135 C7
Ramsey 550 E8
Ray 200 H1
Rays Crossing 157 F5
Reddington 400 F6
Redkey 1,383 G4
Reelsville 210 D5
Remington 1,247 C3
Rensselaer▲ 5,045 C3
Reynolds 528 D3
Richland 500 C9
Richmond▲ 38,705 H5
Ridgeville 808 G4
Rigdon 150 F4
Riley 232 C6
Rising Sun▲ 2,311 H7
Roachdale 902 D5
Roann 447 F3
Roanoke 1,018 G3
Rochester▲ 5,969 E2
Rockfield 300 D3
Rockport▲ 2,315 C9
Rockville▲ 2,706 C5
Rolling Prairie 550 D1
Rome 1,138 D9
Rome City 1,319 G1
Romney 250 D4
Rosedale 783 C5
Roseland 706 E1
Roselawn 200 C2
Rossville 1,175 D4
Royal Center 859 E3
Royerton 300 G4
Rushville▲ 5,533 G5
Russellville 336 D5
Russiaville 988 E4
Saint Anthony 470 D8
Saint Bernice 500 C5
Saint Henry 560 D8
Saint Joe 452 H2
Saint John 4,921 C2
Saint Leon 493 H6
Saint Louis Crossing 150 F6
Saint Mary-of-the-Woods 920 B6
Saint Marys E1
Saint Meinrad 910 D8
Saint Paul 1,032 F6
Saint Peter 175 H6
Saint Philip 400 B9
Saint Wendel 250 B8
Salamonia 138 H4
Salem 5,619 H3
Salem▲ 5,290 E7
Saltillo 117 E7
San Pierre 325 D2
Sandborn 455 C7
Santa Claus 927 D8
Saratoga 266 H4
Sardinia 133 F6
Schererville 19,926 C2
Schneider 310 C2
Schnellville 250 D8
Scipio 200 F6
Scott 5,334 F1
Scottsburg▲ 5,068 F7
Sedalia 160 E4
Seelyville 1,090 C6
Sellersburg 5,745 F8
Selma 800 G4
Servia 212 F3
Seymour 15,576 F7
Shadeland 1,674 C4
Shamrock Lakes 207 G4
Sharpsville 769 E4
Shelburn 1,147 C6
Shelby 15,336 C2
Shelbyville▲ 14,989 F6
Shepardsville 325 B5
Sheridan 2,046 E4
Shideler 275 G4
Shipshewana 524 F1
Shirley 817 F5
Shirley City (Woodburn) H2
Shoals▲ 853 D7
Sidney 167 F2
Silver Lake 528 F2
Sims 250 F3
Smith Valley E5
Smithville 500 D6
Solsberry 200 D6
Somerset 350 F3
Somerville 223 C8
South Bend▲ 105,511 E1
South Milford 270 G1
South Whitley 1,482 F2
Southport 1,969 E5
Spartanburg 201 H4
Speed 13,092 F8
Speedway 12,641 E5
Spelterville 200 C5
Spencer▲ 2,609 D6
Spencerville 400 G2
Spiceland 757 F5
Spring Grove 420 H5
Spring Lake 216 E5
Springport 194 G4
Springville 279 D7
Spurgeon 149 C8
Stanford 200 D6
Star City 351 D3
State Line 182 C4
Staunton 592 C6
Stendal 175 C8
Stewartsville 225 B8
Stilesville 298 D5
Stillwell 225 D1
Stinesville 204 D6
Stockwell 310 D4
Straughn 318 G5
Stroh 350 G1
Sullivan▲ 4,663 C6
Sulphur 257 E8
Sulphur Springs 345 G4
Sumava Resorts 300 C2
Summitville 1,010 F4
Sunman 623 G6
Swayzee 1,059 F4
Sweetser 924 F3
Switz City 257 C6
Syracuse 2,729 F2
Talma 170 E2
Taylorsville 1,044 F6
Tell City 8,088 D9
Tennyson 267 C8
Terhune 150 E4
Terre Haute▲ 57,483 C6
Thayer 350 C2
Thorntown 1,506 D4
Tippecanoe 320 E2
Tipton▲ 4,751 E4
Tocsin 160 G3
Topeka 912 F1

Topography

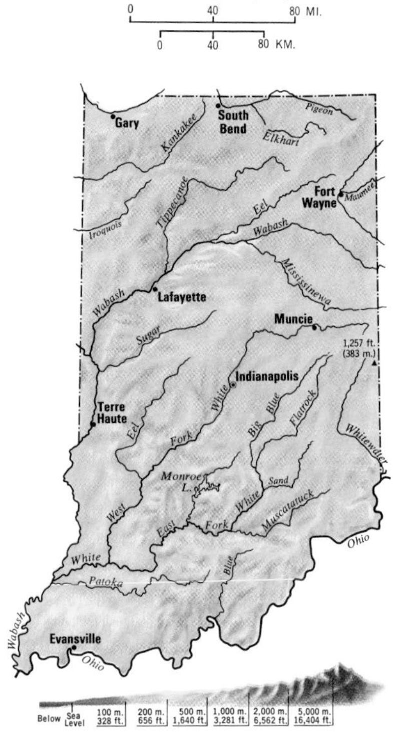

0 40 80 MI.
0 40 80 KM.
Gary
South Bend
Pigeon
Kankakee
Elkhart
Fort Wayne
Maumee
Eel
Tippecanoe
Iroquois
Wabash
Mississinewa
Lafayette
Wabash
Sugar
Muncie
1,257 ft. (383 m.)
Indianapolis
Terre Haute
Eel
White
Big Blue
Flatrock
Whitewater
Fork
Monroe L.
Sand
West
East
Fork
White
Muscatatuck
Ohio
White
Patoka
Blue
Wabash
Evansville
Ohio
Below Sea Level
100 m. 328 ft.
200 m. 656 ft.
500 m. 1,640 ft.
1,000 m. 3,281 ft.
2,000 m. 6,562 ft.
5,000 m. 16,404 ft.

Town of Pines 789 D1
Trafalgar 531 E6
Trail Creek 2,463 D1
Tri Lakes 3,299 G2
Troy 465 D9
Tunnelton 150 E7
Twelve Mile 240 E3
Tyner 245 E2
Underwood 550 F7
Union 3,612 C8
Union City 3,908 H4
Union Mills 650 D2
Uniondale 289 G3
Unionville 225 E6
Universal 392 C5
Upland 3,295 F4
Urbana 400 F3
Utica 411 F8
Valeene 150 E8
Vallonia 550 E7
Valparaiso▲ 24,414 C2
Van Buren 934 F3
Veedersburg 2,192 C4
Velpen 375 C8
Vera Cruz 83 G3
Vernon▲ 370 F7
Versailles▲ 1,791 G6
Vevay▲ 1,393 G7
Vicksburg 175 C6
Vienna 175 F7
Vincennes▲ 19,859 C7
Wabash▲ 12,127 F3
Wadesville 450 B8
Wakarusa 1,667 F1
Waldron 850 F6
Walesboro 214 F6
Walkerton 2,061 E2
Wallace 89 C5
Wallen 945 G2
Walton 1,053 E3
Wanatah 852 D2
Warren 1,185 G3
Warrington 200 F5
Warsaw▲ 10,968 F2
Washington▲ 10,838 C7
Waterloo 2,040 G2
Watson 200 F8
Waveland 474 D5
Wawaka 320 F2
Wawasee 600 F2
Wawpecong 175 F3
Waynetown 911 C4
Webster 350 H5
West Baden Springs 675 D7
West College Corner 686 H5
West Harrison 318 H6
West Lafayette 25,907 D4
West Lebanon 760 C4
West Middleton 327 E4
West Terre Haute 2,495 B6
Westfield 3,304 E4
Westphalia 300 C7
Westpoint 375 C4
Westport 1,478 F6
Westville 5,255 D1
Wheatfield 621 C2
Wheatland 439 C7
Wheeler 540 C1
Wheeling 180 G4
Wheeling 500 C8
Whiteland 2,446 E5
Whitestown 476 E5
Whitewater 111 H5
Whiting 5,155 C1
Wilkinson 446 F5
Williams 425 D7
Williamsport▲ 1,798 C4
Willow Branch 145 F5
Wilmington 600 H6
Winamac▲ 2,262 D2
Winchester▲ 5,095 G4
Windfall 779 F4
Windsor 150 G4
Wingate 275 C4
Winona Lake 4,053 F2
Winslow 875 C8
Wirt 150 G7
Wolcott 886 C3
Wolcottville 879 G1
Wolflake 230 F2
Woodburn 1,321 H2
Woodland 400 E1
Woodlawn Heights 109 F4
Worthington 1,473 C6
Wyandotte 26 E8
Wyatt 250 E1
Yankeetown 250 C9
Yeoman 131 D3
Yoder 250 G3
Yorktown 4,106 G4
Young America 259 E3
Youngstown 350 C6
Zanesville 575 G3
Zenas 225 G6
Zionsville 5,281 E5

OTHER FEATURES

Anderson (riv.) D8
Bass (lake) D2
Beanblossom (creek) D6
Big (creek) B8
Big Blue (riv.) F5
Big Pine (creek) C3
Big Raccoon (creek) C5
Big Walnut (creek) D5
Blue (riv.) E8
Brookville (lake) G6
Buck (creek) E8
Busseron (creek) C7
Camp (creek) E6
Cedar (creek) G2
Clifty (creek) F6
Coal (coal) C4
Crooked (creek) D2
Cypress (pond) B8
Deer (creek) E3
Deer (creek) D5
Eagle (creek) E4
Eel (riv.) C6
Eel (riv.) F3
Elkhart (riv.) F1
Fawn (riv.) G1
Flatrock (creek) F5
Fort Benjamin Harrison E5
Freeman (lake) D3
Geist (res.) F5
George Rogers Clark Nat'l Hist. Park B7
Graham (creek) F7
Grissom A.F.B. 4,271 E3
Huntington (lake) F3
Indian (riv.) D6
Indian (creek) E8
Indiana Dunes Nat'l Lakeshore C1
Iroquois (riv.) B3
Jefferson Proving Ground G7
Kankakee (riv.) C2
Lemon (lake) E6
Lincoln Boyhood Nat'l Mem. C8
Little (riv.) G3
Little Elkhart (riv.) F1
Little Pigeon (creek) C9
Little Vermilion (riv.) B5
Lost (riv.) D7
Maria (creek) C7
Maumee (riv.) H2
Maxinkuckee (lake) E2
Michigan (lake) C1
Mill (creek) D5
Mississinewa (lake) F3
Mississinewa (riv.) F3
Monroe (lake) E6
Morse (res.) E4
Muscatatuck (riv.) E7
Ohio (riv.) B9
Patoka (riv.) C8
Pigeon (creek) C8
Pigeon (riv.) F1
Pipe (creek) F4
Prairie (creek) C7
Richland (creek) D6
Saint Joseph (riv.) E1
Saint Joseph (riv.) H2
Saint Marys (lake) H3
Saint Marys (riv.) H3
Salamonie (lake) F3
Salamonie (riv.) G4
Salt (creek) E6
Sand (creek) F6
Shafer (lake) D3
Silver (creek) F8
Sugar (creek) B3
Sugar (creek) C5
Sugar (creek) F5
Tippecanoe (riv.) E2
Vermilion (riv.) B4
Vernon Fork (creek) F7
Wabash (riv.) B7
Wawasee (lake) F2
White (riv.) B8
White, East Fork (riv.) C7
White, West Fork (riv.) C7
Whitewater (riv.) H6
Wildcat (creek) E4

▲County seat

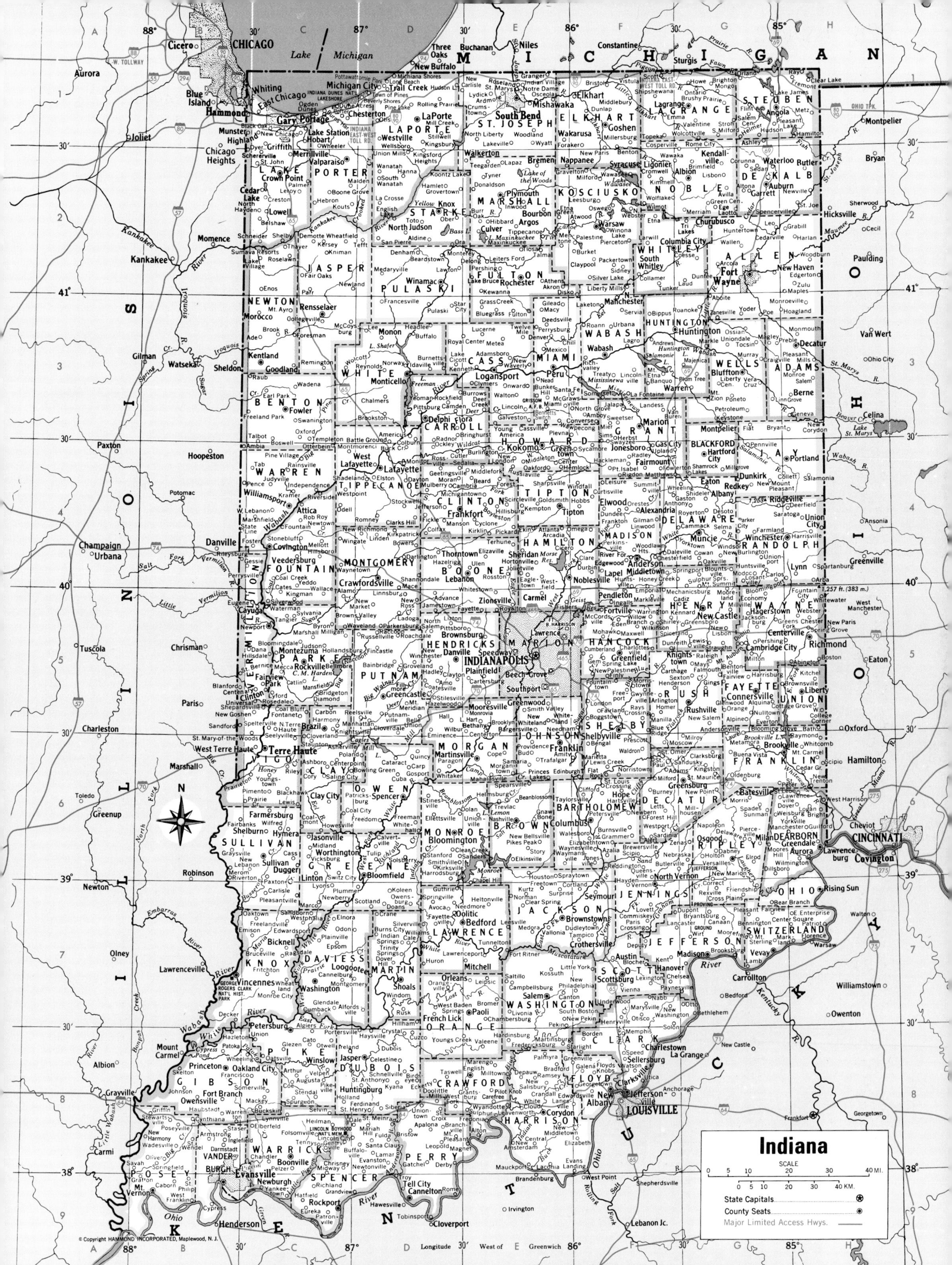

Indiana
SCALE
0 5 10 20 30 40 MI.
0 5 10 20 30 40 KM.
State Capitals
County Seats
Major Limited Access Hwys.
© Copyright HAMMOND INCORPORATED, Maplewood, N. J.
Longitude 30′ West of Greenwich 86°
MICHIGAN
ILLINOIS
OHIO
KENTUCKY
Lake Michigan
CHICAGO
INDIANAPOLIS
CINCINNATI
LOUISVILLE
LAKE
PORTER
LAPORTE
ST. JOSEPH
ELKHART
LAGRANGE
STEUBEN
NOBLE
DE KALB
KOSCIUSKO
MARSHALL
STARKE
JASPER
NEWTON
PULASKI
FULTON
WHITLEY
ALLEN
BENTON
WHITE
CASS
MIAMI
WABASH
HUNTINGTON
WELLS
ADAMS
CARROLL
HOWARD
GRANT
BLACKFORD
JAY
WARREN
TIPPECANOE
CLINTON
TIPTON
MADISON
DELAWARE
RANDOLPH
FOUNTAIN
MONTGOMERY
BOONE
HAMILTON
HENRY
WAYNE
VERMILLION
PARKE
PUTNAM
HENDRICKS
MARION
HANCOCK
RUSH
FAYETTE
UNION
VIGO
CLAY
OWEN
MORGAN
JOHNSON
SHELBY
DECATUR
FRANKLIN
SULLIVAN
GREENE
MONROE
BROWN
BARTHOLOMEW
JENNINGS
RIPLEY
DEARBORN
OHIO
SWITZERLAND
KNOX
DAVIESS
MARTIN
LAWRENCE
JACKSON
SCOTT
JEFFERSON
ORANGE
WASHINGTON
CLARK
GIBSON
PIKE
DUBOIS
CRAWFORD
HARRISON
FLOYD
POSEY
VANDERBURGH
WARRICK
SPENCER
PERRY

COUNTIES

Adair 8,409 ... E6
Adams 4,866 ... D6
Allamakee 13,855 ... L2
Appanoose 13,743 ... H7
Audubon 7,334 ... D5
Benton 22,429 ... J4
Black Hawk 123,798 ... J4
Boone 25,186 ... F5
Bremer 22,813 ... J3
Buchanan 20,844 ... K4
Buena Vista 19,965 ... C3
Butler 15,731 ... H3
Calhoun 11,508 ... D4
Carroll 21,423 ... D4
Cass 15,128 ... D6
Cedar 17,381 ... L5
Cerro Gordo 46,733 ... G2
Cherokee 14,098 ... B3
Chickasaw 13,295 ... J2
Clarke 8,287 ... F6
Clay 17,585 ... C2
Clayton 19,054 ... L3
Clinton 51,040 ... M5
Crawford 16,775 ... C4
Dallas 29,755 ... E5
Davis 8,312 ... J7
Decatur 8,338 ... F7
Delaware 18,035 ... L4
Des Moines 42,614 ... L7
Dickinson 14,909 ... C2
Dubuque 86,403 ... M4
Emmet 11,569 ... D2
Fayette 21,843 ... K3
Floyd 17,058 ... H2
Franklin 11,364 ... G3
Fremont 8,226 ... B7
Greene 10,045 ... E5
Grundy 12,029 ... H4
Guthrie 10,935 ... D5
Hamilton 16,071 ... F4
Hardin 19,094 ... G4
Harrison 14,730 ... B5
Henry 19,226 ... K6
Howard 9,809 ... J2
Humboldt 10,756 ... E3
Ida 8,365 ... C4
Iowa 14,630 ... J5
Iowa 2,913,808 ... J5
Jackson 19,950 ... M4
Jasper 34,795 ... G5
Jefferson 16,310 ... K6
Johnson 96,119 ... K5
Jones 19,444 ... L4
Keokuk 11,624 ... J6
Kossuth 18,591 ... E2
Lee 38,687 ... L7
Linn 168,767 ... K4
Louisa 11,592 ... L6
Lucas 9,070 ... G6
Lyon 11,952 ... A2
Madison 12,483 ... E6
Mahaska 21,522 ... H6
Marion 30,001 ... G6
Marshall 38,276 ... G4
Mills 13,202 ... B6
Mitchell 10,928 ... H2
Monona 10,034 ... B4
Monroe 8,114 ... H7
Montgomery 12,076 ... C6
Muscatine 39,907 ... L5
O'Brien 16,972 ... B2
Osceola 7,267 ... B2
Page 16,870 ... C7
Palo Alto 10,669 ... D2
Plymouth 23,388 ... A3
Pocahontas 9,525 ... D3
Polk 327,140 ... F5
Pottawattamie 82,628 ... B6
Poweshiek 19,033 ... H5
Ringgold 5,420 ... E7
Sac 12,324 ... C4
Scott 150,979 ... M5
Shelby 13,230 ... C5
Sioux 29,903 ... A2
Story 74,252 ... G4
Tama 17,419 ... H4
Taylor 7,114 ... D7
Union 12,750 ... E6
Van Buren 7,676 ... K7
Wapello 35,687 ... J6
Warren 36,033 ... F6
Washington 19,612 ... K6
Wayne 7,067 ... G7
Webster 40,342 ... E4
Winnebago 12,122 ... F2
Winneshiek 20,847 ... K2
Woodbury 98,276 ... B4
Worth 7,991 ... G2
Wright 14,269 ... F3

CITIES and TOWNS

Ackley 1,696 ... G3
Adair 894 ... D6
Adel▲ 3,304 ... E5
Afton 953 ... E6
Agency 616 ... J7
Ainsworth 506 ... K6
Akron 1,450 ... A3
Albert City 779 ... C3
Albia▲ 3,870 ... H6
Albion 585 ... H4
Alburnett 456 ... K4
Alden 855 ... G4
Alexander 170 ... G3
Algona▲ 6,015 ... E2
Alleman 340 ... F5
Allerton 599 ... G7
Allison▲ 1,000 ... H3
Alta 1,820 ... C3
Alta Vista 246 ... J2
Alton 1,063 ... A3
Altoona 7,191 ... G5
Alvord 204 ... A2
Amana 300 ... K5
Ames 47,198 ... F4
Anamosa▲ 5,100 ... L4
Andrew 319 ... M4
Anita 1,068 ... D6
Ankeny 18,482 ... F5
Anthon 638 ... B4
Aplington 1,034 ... H3
Arcadia 485 ... C4
Arion 148 ... B5
Arlington 465 ... K3
Armstrong 1,025 ... D2
Arnolds Park 953 ... C2
Arthur 272 ... C4
Asbury 2,013 ... M4
Ashton 462 ... B2
Atalissa 357 ... L5
Atkins 637 ... K4
Atlantic▲ 7,432 ... D6
Auburn 283 ... D4
Audubon▲ 2,524 ... D5
Aurelia 1,034 ... C3
Aurora 196 ... K3
Avoca 1,497 ... C6
Ayrshire 195 ... D2
Badger 569 ... E3
Bagley 303 ... E5
Baldwin 137 ... M4
Bancroft 857 ... E2
Barnes City 221 ... H6
Barnum 174 ... E3
Batavia 520 ... J7
Battle Creek 818 ... B4
Baxter 938 ... G5
Bayard 511 ... D5
Beacon 509 ... H6
Beaman 183 ... H4
Bedford▲ 1,528 ... D7
Belle Plaine 2,834 ... J5
Bellevue 2,239 ... M4
Belmond 2,500 ... F3
Bennett 395 ... L5

MINNESOTA
SOUTH DAKOTA
NEBRASKA
MISSOURI
WINNEBAGO IND. R.
OMAHA IND. RES.
LYON
OSCEOLA
DICKINSON
EMMET
KOSSUTH
WINNEBAGO
WORTH
MITCHELL
HOWARD
SIOUX
O'BRIEN
CLAY
PALO ALTO
HANCOCK
CERRO GORDO
FLOYD
CHICKASAW
PLYMOUTH
CHEROKEE
BUENA VISTA
POCAHONTAS
HUMBOLDT
WRIGHT
FRANKLIN
BUTLER
BREMER
WOODBURY
IDA
SAC
CALHOUN
WEBSTER
HAMILTON
HARDIN
GRUNDY
BLACK HAWK
MONONA
CRAWFORD
CARROLL
GREENE
BOONE
STORY
MARSHALL
TAMA
BENTON
HARRISON
SHELBY
AUDUBON
GUTHRIE
DALLAS
POLK
JASPER
POWESHIEK
IOWA
POTTAWATTAMIE
CASS
ADAIR
MADISON
WARREN
MARION
MAHASKA
KEOKUK
MILLS
MONTGOMERY
ADAMS
UNION
CLARKE
LUCAS
MONROE
WAPELLO
FREMONT
PAGE
TAYLOR
RINGGOLD
DECATUR
WAYNE
APPANOOSE
DAVIS
SIOUX CITY
OMAHA
Council Bluffs
DES MOINES
Fort Dodge
Waterloo
Cedar Falls
Mason City
Ames
Marshalltown
Ottumwa
Longitude West of 30' Greenwich

Bertram 201 K5
Bettendorf 28,132 N5
Birmingham 386 K7
Blairsburg 269 F4
Blairstown 672 J5
Blakburg 404 H7
Blencoe 250 A5
Blockton 213 D7
Bloomfield▲ 2,580 J7
Blue Grass 1,214 M5
Bode 335 E3
Bonaparte 465 K7
Bondurant 1,584 G5
Boone▲ 12,392 F4
Bouton 149 E5
Boxholm 214 E4
Boyden 651 B2
Braddyville 219 D7
Bradgate 124 E3
Brandon 320 K4
Brayton 148 D5
Breda 467 C4
Bridgewater 209 D6
Brighton 684 K6
Bristow 197 H3
Britt 2,133 F2
Bronson 209 A4
Brooklyn 1,439 J5
Brunsville 137 A3
Buffalo 1,260 M6
Buffalo Center 1,081 F2
Burlington▲ 27,208 L7
Burt 575 E2
Bussey 494 H6
Calamus 379 M5
Callender 384 E4
Calmar 1,026 K2
Calumet 160 B3
Camanche 4,436 N5
Cambridge 714 G5
Cantril 262 J7
Carlisle 3,241 G6
Carroll▲ 9,579 D4
Carson 705 C6
Carter Lake 3,200 B6
Cascade 1,812 L4
Casey 441 D5
Castalia 177 K2

OUR LIBERTIES WE PRIZE AND OUR RIGHTS WE WILL MAINTAIN
IOWA

AREA 56,275 sq. mi. (145,752 sq. km.)
POPULATION 2,787,424
CAPITAL Des Moines
LARGEST CITY Des Moines
HIGHEST POINT (Osceola Co.) 1670 ft. (509 m.)
SETTLED IN 1788
ADMITTED TO UNION December 28, 1846
POPULAR NAME Hawkeye State
STATE FLOWER Wild Rose
STATE BIRD Eastern Goldfinch

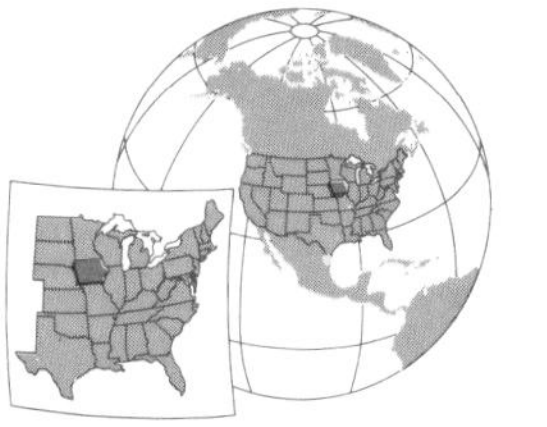

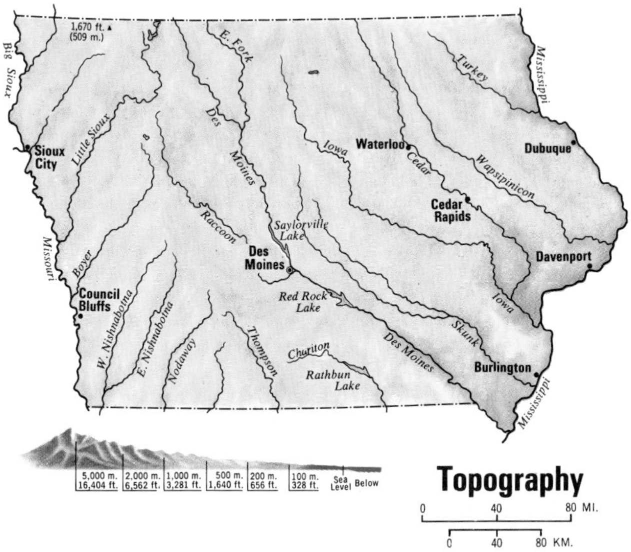

1,670 ft. (509 m.)
Big Sioux
Sioux City
Little Sioux
E. Fork
Des Moines
Turkey
Mississippi
Iowa
Waterloo
Cedar
Wapsipinicon
Dubuque
Cedar Rapids
Saylorville Lake
Raccoon
Des Moines
Boyer
Missouri
Council Bluffs
Red Rock Lake
Davenport
Iowa
Skunk
W. Nishnabotna
E. Nishnabotna
Nodaway
Thompson
Chariton
Rathbun Lake
Des Moines
Burlington
Mississippi
5,000 m. 16,404 ft.
2,000 m. 6,562 ft.
1,000 m. 3,281 ft.
500 m. 1,640 ft.
200 m. 656 ft.
100 m. 328 ft.
Sea Level
Below
0 40 80 MI.
0 40 80 KM.

Topography

Castana 159 B4
Cedar 34,298 H6
Cedar Falls 36,322 H3
Cedar Rapids▲ 108,751 K5
Center Junction 166 L4
Center Point 1,693 K4
Centerville▲ 5,936 H7
Central City 1,063 K4
Chariton▲ 4,616 G6
Charles City▲ 7,878 H2
Charlotte 359 M5
Charter Oak 497 C4
Chelsea 336 J5
Cherokee▲ 6,026 B3
Chester 158 J2
Churdan 423 D4
Cincinnati 363 G7
Clare 161 E3
Clarence 936 M5
Clarinda▲ 5,104 C7
Clarion▲ 2,703 F3
Clarksville 1,382 H3
Clear Lake 8,183 G2
Clearfield 417 D7
Cleghorn 275 B3
Clemons 173 G4
Clermont 523 K3
Clinton▲ 29,201 N5
Clive 7,462 F5
Clutier 219 J4
Coggon 645 L4
Coin 278 C7
Colesburg 439 L3
Colfax 2,462 G5
College Springs 230 C7
Collins 455 G5
Colo 771 G4
Columbus City 328 L6
Columbus Junction 1,616 L6
Conesville 334 L6
Conrad 964 H4
Coon Rapids 1,266 D5
Coralville 10,347 K5
Corning▲ 1,806 D7
Correctionville 897 B4
Corwith 354 F3
Corydon▲ 1,675 G7
Coulter 252 G3
Council Bluffs▲ 54,315 B6
Crawfordsville 265 K6
Cresco▲ 3,669 J2
Creston▲ 7,911 E6
Crystal Lake 266 F2
Cumberland 295 D6
Cumming 132 F6
Cushing 220 B4
Dakota City▲ 1,024 E3
Dallas 1,454 G6
Dallas Center 1,360 E5
Danbury 430 B4
Danville 926 L7
Davenport▲ 95,333 M5
Davis City 257 F7
Dawson 174 E5
Dayton 818 E4
De Soto 1,033 E5
De Witt 4,514 N5
Decatur 177 F7
Decorah▲ 8,063 K2
Dedham 264 D5
Deep River 345 J5
Defiance 312 C5
Delaware 176 L4
Delhi 485 L4
Delmar 517 M4
Deloit 296 C4
Delta 409 J6
Denison▲ 6,604 C4
Denver 1,600 J3
Derby 135 G7
Des Moines (cap.)▲ 193,187 F5
Dexter 628 E5
Diagonal 298 E7
Dickens 214 C2
Dike 875 H4
Dixon 202 M5
Donahue 316 M5
Donnellson 940 K7
Doon 476 A2
Dow City 439 B5
Dows 660 F3
Drakesville 172 J7
Dubuque▲ 57,546 M3
Dumont 705 H3
Duncombe 488 E4
Dundee 174 L3
Dunkerton 746 J3
Dunlap 1,251 B5
Durant 1,549 M5
Dyersville 3,703 L3
Dysart 1,230 J4
Eagle Grove 3,671 F3
Earlham 1,157 E6
Earling 466 C5
Earlville 822 L4
Early 649 C4
Eddyville 1,010 H6
Edgewood 776 K3
Elberon 203 J4
Eldon 1,070 J7
Eldora▲ 3,038 G4
Eldridge 3,378 M5
Elgin 637 K3
Elk Horn 672 C5
Elk Run Heights 1,088 J4
Elkader▲ 1,510 L3
Elkhart 388 F5
Elliott 399 C6
Ellsworth 451 F4
Elma 653 J2
Ely 517 K5
Emerson 476 C6
Emmetsburg▲ 3,940 D2
Epworth 1,297 M4
Essex 916 C7
Estherville▲ 6,720 D2
Evansdale 4,638 J4
Everly 706 C2
Exira 955 D5
Exline 187 H7
Fairbank 1,018 K3
Fairfax 780 K5
Fairfield▲ 9,768 J6
Farley 1,354 L4
Farmersburg 291 L3
Farmington 655 K7
Farnhamville 414 D4
Farragut 498 C7
Fayette 1,317 K3
Fenton 346 E2
Ferguson 166 H5
Fertile 382 G2
Floris 172 J7
Floyd 359 H2
Fonda 731 D3
Fontanelle 712 E6
Forest City▲ 4,430 F2
Fort Atkinson 367 J2
Fort Dodge▲ 25,894 E3
Fort Madison▲ 11,618 L7
Fostoria 205 C2
Franklin 152 L7
Fredericksburg 1,011 J3
Frederika 188 J3
Fredonia 201 L6
Fremont 701 H6
Fruitland 511 L6
Galva 398 C3
Garden Grove 229 F7
Garnavillo 727 L3
Garner▲ 2,916 F2
Garrison 320 J4
Garwin 533 H4
Geneva 169 G3
George 1,066 B2
Gilbert 796 F4
Gilbertville 748 J4
Gilman 586 H5
Gilmore City 560 D3
Gladbrook 881 H4
Glenwood▲ 4,571 B6
Glidden 1,099 D4
Goldfield 710 F3
Goodell 201 F3
Goose Lake 221 N5
Gowrie 1,028 E4
Graettinger 813 D2
Grafton 282 G2
Grand Junction 808 E4
Grand Mound 619 M5
Grand River 171 F7
Grandview 514 L6
Granger 624 F5
Granville 298 B3
Gravity 218 D7
Greeley 263 L3
Greene 1,142 H3
Greenfield▲ 2,074 D6
Grimes 2,653 F5
Grinnell 8,902 H5
Griswold 1,049 C6
Grundy Center▲ 2,491 H4

(continued on following page)

Iowa
SCALE
0 5 10 20 30 40 MI.
0 5 10 20 30 40 KM.
State Capitals
County Seats
Major Limited Access Hwys.
WISCONSIN
ILLINOIS
ALLAMAKEE
CLAYTON
DELAWARE
DUBUQUE
JACKSON
JONES
LINN
CLINTON
CEDAR
JOHNSON
MUSCATINE
SCOTT
WASHINGTON
LOUISA
HENRY
DES MOINES
LEE
CEDAR RAPIDS
DAVENPORT
Dubuque
Rock Island
Burlington
Iowa City
Muscatine
Keokuk
Fort Madison
Clinton
Galesburg
Mississippi
© Copyright HAMMOND INCORPORATED, Maplewood, N. J.

Agriculture, Industry and Resources

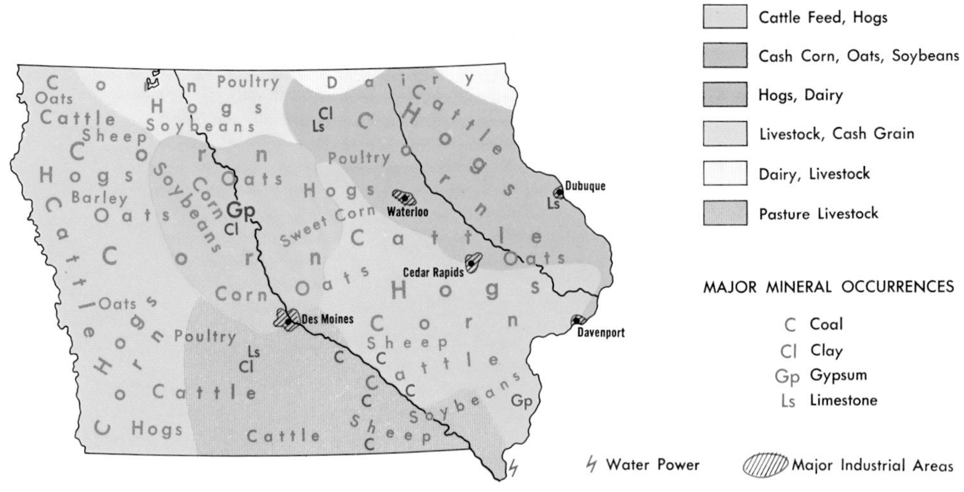

DOMINANT LAND USE
Cattle Feed, Hogs
Cash Corn, Oats, Soybeans
Hogs, Dairy
Livestock, Cash Grain
Dairy, Livestock
Pasture Livestock
MAJOR MINERAL OCCURRENCES
C Coal
Cl Clay
Gp Gypsum
Ls Limestone
Water Power
Major Industrial Areas
Dubuque
Waterloo
Cedar Rapids
Des Moines
Davenport
Poultry
Dairy
Oats
Cattle
Sheep
Hogs
Soybeans
Barley
Sweet Corn
Corn

Guthrie Center▲ 1,614 .... D5
Guttenberg 2,257 .... L3
Halbur 215 .... D4
Hamburg 1,248 .... B7
Hampton▲ 4,133 .... G3
Hancock 201 .... C6
Hanlontown 193 .... G2
Harcourt 306 .... E4
Harlan▲ 5,148 .... C5
Harper 147 .... J6
Harpers Ferry 284 .... L2
Harris 170 .... C2
Hartford 768 .... G6
Hartley 1,632 .... C2
Harvey 235 .... H6
Hastings 187 .... C6
Havelock 217 .... D3
Haverhill 144 .... H5
Hawarden 2,439 .... A2
Hawkeye 460 .... J3
Hazleton 733 .... K3
Hedrick 810 .... J6
Henderson 206 .... B6
Hiawatha 4,986 .... K4
Hills 662 .... K5
Hillsboro 151 .... K7
Hinton 697 .... A3
Holland 215 .... H4
Holstein 1,449 .... B4
Holy Cross 304 .... L3
Hopkinton 695 .... L4
Hornick 222 .... A4
Hospers 643 .... B2
Hubbard 814 .... G4
Hudson 2,037 .... H4
Hull 1,724 .... A2
Humboldt 4,438 .... E3
Humeston 553 .... G7
Huxley 2,047 .... F5
Ida Grove▲ 2,357 .... B4
Independence▲ 5,972 .... K4
Indianola▲ 11,340 .... F6
Inwood 824 .... A2
Ionia 304 .... J2
Iowa City▲ 59,738 .... L5
Iowa Falls 5,424 .... G3
Ireton 597 .... A3
Irwin 394 .... C5
Jamaica 232 .... E5
Janesville 822 .... J3
Jefferson▲ 4,292 .... E4
Jesup 2,121 .... J4
Jewell 1,106 .... F4
Johnston 4,702 .... F5
Joice 245 .... G2
Kalo 1,942 .... E4
Kalona 1,862 .... K6
Kamrar 203 .... F4
Kanawha 763 .... F3
Kellerton 314 .... E7
Kelley 246 .... F5
Kellogg 626 .... H5
Kensett 298 .... G2
Keokuk▲ 12,451 .... L8
Keosauqua▲ 1,020 .... J7
Keota 1,000 .... K6
Keswick 284 .... J6
Keystone 568 .... J5
Kimballton 289 .... D5
Kingsley 1,129 .... A3
Kirkville 177 .... H6
Kiron 301 .... C4
Klemme 587 .... F3
Knoxville▲ 8,232 .... G6
La Motte 219 .... M4
La Porte City 2,128 .... J4
Lacona 357 .... G6
Ladora 308 .... J5
Lake City 1,841 .... D4
Lake Mills 2,143 .... F2
Lake Park 996 .... C2
Lake View 1,303 .... C4
Lakeside 522 .... C3
Lakota 281 .... E2
Lambs Grove 212 .... G5
Lamoni 2,319 .... E7
Lamont 471 .... K3
Lanesboro 182 .... D4
Lansing 1,007 .... L2
Larchwood 739 .... A2
Larrabee 175 .... B3
Latimer 430 .... G3
Laurel 271 .... H5
Laurens 1,550 .... D3
Lawler 517 .... J2
Lawton 482 .... A4
Le Claire 2,734 .... N5
Le Grand 854 .... H5
Le Mars▲ 8,454 .... A3
Ledyard 164 .... E2
Lehigh 536 .... E4
Leighton 142 .... H6
Leland 311 .... F2
Lenox 1,303 .... D7
Leon▲ 2,047 .... F7
Lester 257 .... A2
Letts 390 .... L6
Lewis 433 .... C6
Libertyville 264 .... K7
Lidderdale 202 .... D4
Lime Springs 438 .... J2
Lincoln 173 .... H4
Linden 201 .... E5
Lineville 289 .... G7
Linn Grove 194 .... C3
Lisbon 1,452 .... L5
Liscomb 258 .... H4
Little Rock 493 .... B2
Little Sioux 205 .... B5
Livermore 436 .... E3
Lockridge 270 .... K7
Logan▲ 1,401 .... B5
Lohrville 453 .... D4
Lone Rock 185 .... E2
Lone Tree 979 .... L6
Long Grove 605 .... M5
Lorimor 377 .... E6
Lost Nation 467 .... M5
Lovilia 551 .... H6
Low Moor 280 .... N5
Lowden 726 .... L5
Lu Verne 328 .... E3
Luana 190 .... K2
Lucas 224 .... G6
Luther 154 .... F5
Luxemburg 257 .... L3
Lynnville 393 .... H5
Lytton 320 .... D4
Macedonia 262 .... C6
Madrid 2,395 .... F5
Magnolia 204 .... B5
Malcom 447 .... H5
Mallard 360 .... D3
Malvern 1,210 .... B7
Manchester▲ 5,137 .... L3
Manilla 898 .... C5
Manly 1,349 .... G2
Manning 1,484 .... C5
Manson 1,844 .... D3
Mapleton 1,294 .... B4
Maquoketa▲ 6,111 .... M4
Marathon 320 .... C3
Marble Rock 361 .... H3
Marcus 1,171 .... B3
Marengo▲ 2,270 .... J5
Marion 20,403 .... K4
Marne 149 .... C6
Marquette 479 .... L2
Marshalltown▲ 25,178 .... G4
Martelle 290 .... L4
Martensdale 491 .... F6
Martinsburg 157 .... J6
Mason City▲ 29,040 .... G2
Masonville 129 .... K4
Massena 372 .... D6
Maurice 243 .... A3
Maxwell 788 .... G5
Maynard 513 .... K3
Maysville 170 .... M5
McCallsburg 292 .... G4
McCausland 308 .... M5
McClelland 139 .... B6
McGregor 797 .... L2
McIntire 147 .... H2
Mechanicsville 1,012 .... L5
Mediapolis 1,637 .... L6
Melbourne 669 .... G5
Melcher 1,302 .... G6
Melrose 150 .... G7
Melvin 250 .... B2
Menlo 356 .... E5
Meriden 193 .... B3
Merrill 729 .... A3
Meservey 292 .... G3
Middle 386 .... K5
Middletown 487 .... L7
Miles 409 .... N4
Milford 2,170 .... C2
Miller 188 .... F2
Millersburg 184 .... J5
Milo 864 .... G6
Milton 506 .... J7
Minburn 346 .... E5
Minden 498 .... C6
Mingo 252 .... G5
Missouri Valley 2,888 .... B5
Mitchell 170 .... H2
Mitchellville 1,670 .... G5
Modale 289 .... B5
Mondamin 403 .... B5
Monmouth 169 .... M4
Monona 1,520 .... L2
Monroe 1,739 .... G5
Montezuma▲ 1,651 .... H5
Monticello 3,522 .... L4
Montour 312 .... H5
Montrose 957 .... L7
Moorhead 259 .... B5
Moorland 209 .... E4
Moravia 679 .... H7
Morning Sun 841 .... L6
Moulton 613 .... H7
Mount Auburn 134 .... J4
Mount Ayr▲ 1,796 .... E7
Mount Pleasant▲ 8,027 .... L7
Mount Union 140 .... L6
Mount Vernon 3,657 .... K5
Moville 1,306 .... A4
Murray 731 .... F6
Muscatine▲ 22,881 .... L6
Mystic 545 .... H7
Nashua 1,476 .... J3
Neola 894 .... B6
Nevada▲ 6,009 .... G5
New Albin 534 .... L2
New Hampton▲ 3,660 .... J2
New Hartford 683 .... H3
New Liberty 139 .... M5
New London 1,922 .... L7
New Market 454 .... D7
New Providence 240 .... G4
New Sharon 1,136 .... H6
New Vienna 376 .... L3
New Virginia 433 .... F6
Newell 1,089 .... D3
Newhall 854 .... K5
Newton▲ 14,789 .... H5
Nichols 366 .... L6
Nodaway 153 .... D7
Nora Springs 1,505 .... H2
North Buena Vista 145 .... L3
North English 944 .... J5
North Liberty 2,926 .... K5
Northwood▲ 1,940 .... G2
Norwalk 5,726 .... F6
Norway 583 .... K5
Numa 151 .... G7
Oakland 1,496 .... C6
Oakland Acres 152 .... H5
Oakville 442 .... L6
Ocheyedan 539 .... B2
Odebolt 1,158 .... C4
Oelwein 6,493 .... K3
Ogden 1,909 .... E4
Okoboji 775 .... C2
Olds 205 .... K6
Olin 663 .... L5
Ollie 207 .... J6
Onawa▲ 2,936 .... A4
Onslow 216 .... M4
Oran 4,940 .... J3
Orange City▲ 4,588 .... A2
Orient 376 .... E6
Orleans 560 .... C2
Osage▲ 3,439 .... H2
Osceola▲ 4,164 .... F6
Oskaloosa▲ 10,632 .... H6
Ossian 810 .... K2
Otho 529 .... E4
Ottumwa▲ 24,488 .... J6
Oxford 663 .... K5
Oxford Junction 581 .... M4
Pacific Junction 548 .... B6
Packwood 208 .... J6
Palmer 230 .... D3
Palo 514 .... K4
Panama 201 .... B5
Panora 1,100 .... E5
Parkersburg 1,804 .... H3
Parnell 209 .... J5
Paton 255 .... E4
Patterson 128 .... F6
Paullina 1,134 .... B3
Pella 9,270 .... H6
Peosta 128 .... M4
Perry 6,652 .... E5
Persia 312 .... B5
Peterson 390 .... C3
Pierson 341 .... B3
Pilot Mound 199 .... F4
Pisgah 268 .... B5
Plainfield 455 .... J3
Pleasant Hill 3,671 .... G5
Pleasant Plain 128 .... K6
Pleasantville 1,536 .... G6
Plymouth 453 .... G2
Pocahontas▲ 2,085 .... D3
Polk City 1,908 .... F5
Pomeroy 762 .... D3
Portsmouth 209 .... C5
Postville 1,472 .... K2
Prairie City 1,360 .... G5
Prairieburg 213 .... L4
Prescott 287 .... D6
Preston 1,025 .... N4
Primghar▲ 950 .... B2
Princeton 806 .... N5
Protivin 305 .... J2
Pulaski 221 .... J7
Quasqueton 579 .... K4
Quimby 334 .... B3
Radcliffe 574 .... G4
Rake 238 .... F2
Randall 161 .... F4
Randolph 243 .... B7
Raymond 619 .... J4
Readlyn 773 .... J3
Reasnor 191 .... G5
Red Oak▲ 6,264 .... C6
Redfield 883 .... E5
Reinbeck 1,605 .... H4
Rembrandt 229 .... C3
Remsen 1,513 .... B3
Renwick 287 .... E3
Rhodes 272 .... G5
Riceville 827 .... H2
Richland 522 .... K6
Rickardsville 171 .... M3
Ridgeway 295 .... K2
Ringsted 481 .... D2
Rippey 275 .... E5
Riverdale 433 .... N5
Riverside 824 .... K6
Riverton 333 .... B7
Robins 875 .... K4
Rock Falls 130 .... G2
Rock Rapids▲ 2,601 .... A2
Rock Valley 2,540 .... A2
Rockford 863 .... H2
Rockwell 1,008 .... G3
Rockwell City▲ 1,981 .... D4
Roland 1,035 .... F4
Rolfe 721 .... D3
Rose Hill 171 .... J6
Rowan 189 .... F3
Rowley 272 .... K4
Royal 466 .... C2
Rudd 429 .... H2
Runnells 306 .... G5
Russell 531 .... G7
Ruthven 707 .... D2
Rutland 149 .... E3
Ryan 382 .... K4
Sabula 710 .... N4
Sac City▲ 2,492 .... C4
Sageville 288 .... M3
Saint Ansgar 1,063 .... H2
Saint Anthony 112 .... G4
Saint Charles 537 .... F6
Saint Donatus 145 .... M4
Saint Lucas 174 .... K2
Saint Olaf 111 .... L3
Saint Paul 120 .... L7
Salem 453 .... K7
Salix 367 .... A4
Sanborn 1,345 .... B2
Schaller 768 .... C4
Schleswig 851 .... B4
Scranton 583 .... D4
Searsboro 164 .... H5
Sergeant Bluff 2,772 .... A4
Seymour 869 .... G7
Shambaugh 190 .... D7
Sheffield 1,174 .... G3
Shelby 637 .... C5
Sheldahl 315 .... F5
Sheldon 4,937 .... B2
Shell Rock 1,385 .... H3
Shellsburg 765 .... K4
Shenandoah 5,572 .... C7
Sherrill 148 .... M3
Shueyville 223 .... K5
Sibley▲ 2,815 .... B2
Sidney▲ 1,253 .... B7
Sigourney▲ 2,111 .... J6
Silver City 252 .... B6
Sioux Center 5,074 .... A2
Sioux City▲ 80,505 .... A3
Sioux Rapids 761 .... C3
Slater 1,268 .... F5
Sloan 938 .... A4
Smithland 235 .... B4
Soldier 205 .... B5
Solon 1,050 .... L5
Somers 161 .... E4
South English 224 .... J6
Spencer▲ 11,066 .... C2
Spillville 387 .... J2
Spirit Lake▲ 3,871 .... C2
Springville 1,068 .... L4
Stacyville 481 .... H2
Stanhope 447 .... F4
Stanton 692 .... C7
Stanwood 646 .... L5
State Center 1,248 .... G5
Steamboat Rock 335 .... G4
Stockport 260 .... K7
Stockton 187 .... M5
Storm Lake▲ 8,769 .... C3
Story City 2,959 .... F4
Stout 192 .... H3
Stratford 715 .... F4
Strawberry Point 1,357 .... K3
Stuart 1,522 .... E6
Sully 841 .... H5
Sumner 2,078 .... J3
Superior 128 .... D2
Sutherland 714 .... B3
Swaledale 190 .... G3
Swea City 634 .... E2
Swisher 645 .... K5
Tabor 957 .... B7
Tama 2,697 .... H5
Templeton 321 .... D5
Terril 383 .... C2
Thompson 498 .... F2
Thor 205 .... E3
Thornton 431 .... G3
Thurman 239 .... B7
Tiffin 460 .... K5
Tingley 179 .... E7
Tipton▲ 2,998 .... L5
Titonka 612 .... E2
Toledo▲ 2,380 .... H4
Traer 1,552 .... J4
Treynor 897 .... B6
Tripoli 1,188 .... J3
Truesdale 132 .... C3
Truro 391 .... F6
Underwood 515 .... B6
Union 448 .... G4
Unionville 133 .... H7
University Heights 1,042 .... K5
University Park 604 .... H6
Urbana 595 .... K4
Urbandale 23,500 .... F5
Ute 395 .... B4
Vail 388 .... C4
Van Horne 695 .... J4
Van Meter 751 .... E5
Van Wert 249 .... F7
Ventura 590 .... F2
Victor 966 .... J5
Villisca 1,332 .... C7
Vincent 185 .... E3
Vinton▲ 5,103 .... J4
Volga 306 .... L3
Wadena 236 .... K3
Wahpeton 484 .... C2
Walcott 1,356 .... M5
Walford 303 .... K5
Walker 673 .... K4
Wall Lake 875 .... C4
Wallingford 196 .... D2
Walnut 857 .... C6
Wapello▲ 2,013 .... L6
Washington▲ 7,074 .... K6
Washta 284 .... B3
Waterloo▲ 66,467 .... J4
Waterville 140 .... L2
Waucoma 277 .... J2
Waukee 2,512 .... F5
Waukon▲ 4,019 .... L2
Waverly▲ 8,539 .... J3
Wayland 838 .... K6
Webb 167 .... D3
Webster City▲ 7,894 .... F4
Weldon 151 .... F7
Wellman 1,085 .... K6
Wellsburg 682 .... H4
Welton 177 .... M5
Wesley 444 .... E2
West 862 .... J5
West Bend 941 .... D3
West Branch 1,908 .... L5
West Burlington 3,083 .... L7
West Chester 178 .... K6
West Des Moines 31,702 .... F5
West Liberty 2,935 .... L5
West Okoboji 263 .... C2
West Point 1,079 .... K7
West Union▲ 2,490 .... K3
Westfield 160 .... A3
Westgate 207 .... K3
Westphalia 144 .... C5
Westside 348 .... C4
What Cheer 762 .... J6
Wheatland 723 .... M5
Whiting 683 .... A4
Whittemore 535 .... E2
Whitten 137 .... H4
Williams 368 .... F3
Williamsburg 2,174 .... J5
Williamson 166 .... G6
Wilton 2,577 .... M5
Windsor Heights 5,190 .... F5
Winfield 1,051 .... L6
Winterset▲ 4,196 .... E6
Winthrop 742 .... K4
Wiota 160 .... D6
Woden 259 .... F2
Woodbine 1,500 .... B5
Woodburn 240 .... F7
Woodward 1,197 .... E5
Woolstock 212 .... F3
Worthington 439 .... L4
Wyoming 659 .... L4
Yale 220 .... E5
Zearing 614 .... G4

OTHER FEATURES

Big Sioux (riv.) A3
Boyer (riv.) B5
Cedar (riv.) K4
Chariton (riv.) G7
Clear (lake) G2
Des Moines (riv.) J7
Eagle (lake) F2
East Nishnabotna (riv.) C6
Effigy Mounds Nat'l Mon. L2
Five Island (lake) D2
Floyd (riv.) A3
Herbert Hoover Nat'l Hist. Site L5
Iowa (riv.) H4
Little Sioux (riv.) B3
Lost Island (lake) D2
Mississippi (riv.) L7
Missouri (riv.) A5
Nodaway (riv.) D7
Palo Alto (lake) D2
Platte (riv.) D8
Raccoon (riv.) D4
Rathbun (lake) G7
Red Rock (lake) G6
Rock (riv.) A2
Sac and Fox Ind. Res. H5
Skunk (riv.) K6
Spirit (lake) C2
Storm (lake) C3
Summit (lake) E6
Thompson (riv.) E7
Trumbull (lake) C2
Turkey (riv.) K2
Upper Iowa (riv.) K2
Wapsipinicon (riv.) J3
West Nishnabotna (riv.) C6

▲County seat

KANSAS

AREA 82,277 sq. mi. (213,097 sq. km.)
POPULATION 2,485,600
CAPITAL Topeka
LARGEST CITY Wichita
HIGHEST POINT Mt. Sunflower 4,039 ft. (1231 m.)
SETTLED IN 1831
ADMITTED TO UNION January 29, 1861
POPULAR NAME Sunflower State
STATE FLOWER Sunflower
STATE BIRD Western Meadowlark

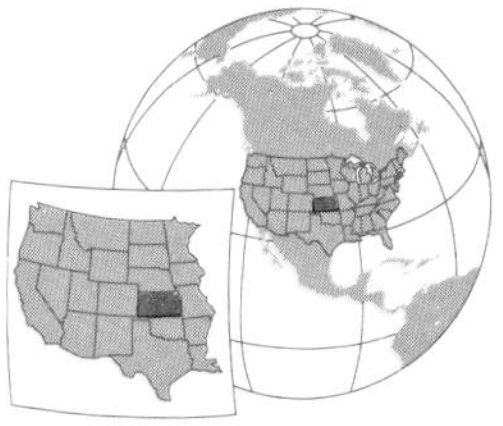

Agriculture, Industry and Resources

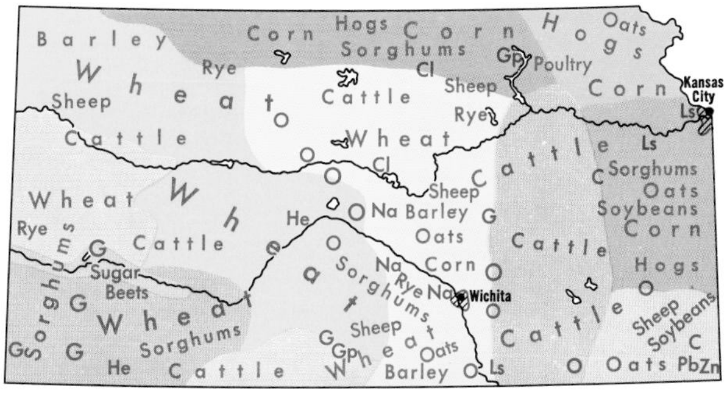
Barley
Corn
Hogs
Oats
Wheat
Rye
Sorghums
Cattle
Sheep
Poultry
Kansas City
Soybeans
Sugar Beets
Wichita
Pb Zn

DOMINANT LAND USE

- Specialized Wheat
- Wheat, General Farming
- Wheat, Range Livestock
- Wheat, Grain Sorghums, Range Livestock
- Cattle Feed, Hogs
- Livestock, Cash Grain
- Livestock, Cash Grain, Dairy
- General Farming, Livestock, Cash Grain
- General Farming, Livestock, Special Crops
- Range Livestock

MAJOR MINERAL OCCURRENCES

C	Coal	Ls	Limestone
Cl	Clay	Na	Salt
G	Natural Gas	O	Petroleum
Gp	Gypsum	Pb	Lead
He	Helium	Zn	Zinc

Major Industrial Areas

COUNTIES

Allen 15,654 .... G4
Anderson 7,803 .... G3
Atchison 16,932 .... G2
Barber 5,874 .... D4
Barton 29,382 .... D3
Bourbon 14,966 .... H4
Brown 11,128 .... G2
Butler 50,580 .... F4
Chase 3,021 .... F3
Chautauqua 4,407 .... F4
Cherokee 21,374 .... H4
Cheyenne 3,243 .... A2
Clark 2,418 .... C4
Clay 9,158 .... E2
Cloud 11,023 .... E2
Coffey 8,404 .... G3
Comanche 2,313 .... C4
Cowley 36,915 .... F4
Crawford 35,568 .... H4
Decatur 4,021 .... B2
Dickinson 18,958 .... E3
Doniphan 8,134 .... G2
Douglas 81,798 .... G3
Edwards 3,787 .... C4
Elk 3,327 .... F4
Ellis 26,004 .... C3
Ellsworth 6,586 .... D3
Finney 33,070 .... B3
Ford 27,463 .... C4
Franklin 21,994 .... G3
Geary 30,453 .... F3
Gove 3,231 .... B3
Graham 3,543 .... C2
Grant 7,159 .... A4
Gray 5,396 .... B4
Greeley 1,774 .... A3
Greenwood 7,847 .... F4
Hamilton 2,388 .... A3
Harper 7,124 .... D4
Harvey 31,028 .... E3
Haskell 3,886 .... B4
Hodgeman 2,177 .... C3
Jackson 11,525 .... G2
Jefferson 15,905 .... G2
Jewell 4,251 .... D2
Johnson 355,054 .... H3
Kearny 4,027 .... A3
Kingman 8,292 .... D4
Kiowa 3,660 .... C4
Labette 23,693 .... G4
Lane 2,375 .... B3
Leavenworth 64,371 .... G2
Lincoln 3,653 .... D2
Linn 8,254 .... H3
Logan 3,081 .... A3
Lyon 34,732 .... F3
Marion 12,888 .... E3
Marshall 11,705 .... F2
McPherson 27,268 .... E3
Meade 4,247 .... B4
Miami 23,466 .... H3
Mitchell 7,203 .... D2
Montgomery 38,816 .... G4
Morris 6,198 .... F3
Morton 3,480 .... A4
Nemaha 10,446 .... F2
Neosho 17,035 .... G4
Ness 4,033 .... C3
Norton 5,947 .... C2
Osage 15,248 .... G3
Osborne 4,867 .... D2
Ottawa 5,634 .... E2
Pawnee 7,555 .... C3
Phillips 6,590 .... C2
Pottawatomie 16,128 .... F2
Pratt 9,702 .... D4
Rawlins 3,404 .... A2
Reno 62,389 .... D4
Republic 6,482 .... E2
Rice 10,610 .... D3
Riley 67,139 .... F2
Rooks 6,039 .... C2
Rush 3,842 .... C3
Russell 7,835 .... D3
Saline 49,301 .... E3
Scott 5,289 .... B3
Sedgwick 403,662 .... E4
Seward 18,743 .... B4
Shawnee 160,976 .... G2
Sheridan 3,043 .... B2
Sherman 6,926 .... A2
Smith 5,078 .... D2
Stafford 5,365 .... D3
Stanton 2,333 .... A4
Stevens 5,048 .... A4
Sumner 25,841 .... E4
Thomas 8,258 .... A2
Trego 3,694 .... C3
Wabaunsee 6,603 .... F3
Wallace 1,821 .... A3
Washington 7,073 .... E2
Wichita 2,758 .... A3
Wilson 10,289 .... G4
Woodson 4,116 .... G4
Wyandotte 161,993 .... H2

CITIES and TOWNS

Abbyville 123 .... D4
Abilene▲ 6,242 .... E3
Ada 120 .... E2
Admire 147 .... F3
Agenda 81 .... E2
Agra 322 .... C2
Alamota 50 .... B3
Albert 229 .... C3
Alden 182 .... D3
Alexander 85 .... C3
Aliceville 60 .... G3
Allen 191 .... F3
Alma▲ 871 .... F2
Almena 423 .... C2
Alta Vista 477 .... F3
Altamont 1,048 .... G4
Alton 115 .... D2
Altoona 456 .... G4
Americus 891 .... F3
Ames 65 .... E2
Andale 566 .... E4
Andover 4,047 .... E4
Angola 55 .... G4
Anthony▲ 2,516 .... D4
Arcadia 338 .... H4
Argonia 529 .... E4
Arkansas City 12,762 .... E4
Arlington 457 .... D4
Arma 1,542 .... H4
Ash Valley 50 .... C3
Ashland▲ 1,032 .... C4
Assaria 387 .... E3
Atchison▲ 10,656 .... G2
Athol 86 .... D2
Atlanta 232 .... F4
Attica 716 .... D4
Atwood▲ 1,388 .... B2
Auburn 908 .... G3
Augusta 7,876 .... F4
Aurora 101 .... E2
Axtell 432 .... F2
Baileyville 130 .... F2
Baldwin City 2,961 .... G3
Barnard 129 .... D2
Barnes 167 .... F2
Bartlett 107 .... G4
Basehor 1,591 .... G2
Bassett 20 .... G4
Bavaria 100 .... E3
Baxter Springs 4,351 .... H4
Bazine 373 .... C3
Beagle 88 .... G3
Beattie 221 .... F2
Beaumont 112 .... F4
Beaver 57 .... D3
Beeler 80 .... B3
Belle Plaine 1,649 .... E4
Belleville▲ 2,517 .... E2
Beloit▲ 4,066 .... D2
Belpre 116 .... C4
Belvue 207 .... F2
Bendena 125 .... G2
Benedict 16 .... G4
Bennington 568 .... E2
Bentley 360 .... E4
Benton 669 .... E4
Bern 190 .... F2
Berryton 150 .... G3
Beverly 131 .... E2
Big Bow 55 .... A4
Bird City 467 .... A2
Bison 252 .... C3
Blaine 50 .... F2
Bloom 65 .... C4
Blue Mound 251 .... H3
Blue Rapids 1,131 .... F2
Bluff City 69 .... E4
Bogue 150 .... C2
Bonner Springs 6,413 .... H2
Brazilton 91 .... H4
Bremen 60 .... F2
Brewster 296 .... A2
Bridgeport 95 .... E3
Bronson 343 .... H4
Brookville 226 .... E3
Brownell 44 .... C3
Bucklin 710 .... C4
Bucyrus 135 .... H3
Buffalo 293 .... G4
Buhler 1,277 .... E3
Bunker Hill 111 .... D3
Burden 518 .... F4
Burdett 248 .... C3
Burdick 100 .... F3
Burlingame 1,074 .... G3
Burlington▲ 2,735 .... G3
Burns 226 .... F3
Burr Oak 278 .... D2
Burrton 866 .... E3
Bushong 57 .... F3
Bushton 341 .... D3
Byers 46 .... D4
Caldwell 1,351 .... E4
Cambridge 74 .... F4
Caney 2,062 .... G4
Canton 794 .... E3
Carbondale 1,526 .... G3
Carlton 39 .... E3
Carlyle 75 .... G4
Cassoday 95 .... F3
Catharine 121 .... C3
Cawker City 588 .... D2
Cedar 25 .... D2
Cedar Point 39 .... F3
Cedar Vale 760 .... F4
Centerville 104 .... H3
Centralia 452 .... F2
Chanute 9,488 .... G4
Chapman 1,264 .... E3
Chase 577 .... D3
Chautauqua 132 .... F4
Cheney 1,560 .... E4
Cherokee 651 .... H4
Cherryvale 2,464 .... G4
Chetopa 1,357 .... G4
Chicopee 300 .... H4
Cimarron▲ 1,626 .... B4
Circleville 153 .... G2
Claflin 678 .... D3
Clay Center▲ 4,613 .... E2
Clayton 91 .... B2
Clearview City G3
Clearwater 1,875 .... E4
Clifton 561 .... E2
Climax 57 .... F4
Clyde 793 .... E2
Coats 127 .... D4
Codell 90 .... C2
Coffeyville 12,917 .... G4
Colby▲ 5,396 .... A2
Coldwater▲ 939 .... C4
Collyer 144 .... B2
Colony 447 .... G3
Columbus▲ 3,268 .... H4
Colwich 1,091 .... E4
Concordia▲ 6,167 .... E2
Conway 1,384 .... E3
Conway Springs 1,313 .... E4
Coolidge 90 .... A3
Copeland 290 .... B4
Corning 142 .... F2
Cottonwood Falls▲ 889 .... F3
Council Grove▲ 2,228 .... F3
Courtland 343 .... E2
Coyville 78 .... G4
Crestline 85 .... H4
Cuba 242 .... E2
Cullison 120 .... D4
Culver 162 .... E3
Cummings 150 .... G2
Cunningham 535 .... D4
Damar 112 .... C2
Danville 56 .... E4
De Soto 2,291 .... H3
Dearing 428 .... G4
Deerfield 677 .... A4
Delia 172 .... G2
Delphos 494 .... E2
Denison 225 .... G2
Dennis 96 .... G4
Denton 166 .... G2
Derby 14,699 .... E4
Detroit 90 .... E3
Devon 108 .... H4
Dexter 320 .... F4
Dighton▲ 1,361 .... B3
Dodge City▲ 21,129 .... B4
Dorrance 195 .... D3
Douglass 1,722 .... F4
Dover 192 .... G3
Downs 1,119 .... D2
Dresden 73 .... B2
Dunlap 65 .... F3
Durham 119 .... E3
Dwight 365 .... F3
Earlton 69 .... G4
Eastborough 896 .... E4
Easton 405 .... G2
Edgerton 1,244 .... H3
Edmond 37 .... C2
Edna 438 .... G4
Edson 55 .... A2
Edwardsville 3,979 .... H2
Effingham 540 .... G2
El Dorado▲ 11,504 .... F4
Elbing 184 .... E3
Elgin 118 .... F4
Elk City 334 .... G4
Elk Falls 122 .... F4
Elkhart▲ 2,318 .... A4
Ellinwood 2,329 .... D3
Ellis 1,814 .... C3
Ellsworth▲ 2,294 .... D3
Elmdale 83 .... F3
Elmont 112 .... G2
Elsmore 91 .... G4
Elwood 1,079 .... H2
Elyria 100 .... E3
Emmett 165 .... F2
Emporia▲ 25,512 .... F3
Englewood 96 .... C4
Ensign 192 .... B4
Enterprise 865 .... E3
Erie▲ 1,276 .... G4
Esbon 167 .... D2
Eskridge 518 .... F3
Eudora 3,006 .... G3
Eureka▲ 2,974 .... F4
Everest 310 .... G2
Fairview 306 .... G2
Fairway 4,173 .... H2
Fall River 113 .... G4
Falun 89 .... E3
Farlington 80 .... H4
Florence 636 .... E3
Fontana 131 .... H3
Ford 247 .... C4
Formoso 128 .... D2
Fort Dodge 400 .... C4
Fort Leavenworth H2
Fort Scott▲ 8,362 .... H4
Fowler 571 .... B4
Frankfort 927 .... F2
Franklin 400 .... H4
Frederick 18 .... D3
Fredonia▲ 2,599 .... G4
Freeport 8 .... E4
Frontenac 2,588 .... H4
Fulton 191 .... H4
Galatia 47 .... D3
Galena 3,308 .... H4
Galesburg 160 .... G4
Galva 651 .... E3
Garden City▲ 24,097 .... B4
Garden Plain 731 .... E4
Gardner 3,191 .... H3
Garfield 236 .... C3
Garland 112 .... H4
Garnett▲ 3,210 .... G3
Gas 505 .... G4
Gaylord 173 .... D2
Gem 104 .... B2
Geneseo 382 .... D3
Geuda Springs 219 .... E4
Girard▲ 2,794 .... H4
Glade 101 .... C2
Glasco 556 .... E2
Glen Elder 448 .... D2
Goddard 1,804 .... E4
Goessel 506 .... E3
Goff 156 .... G2
Goodland▲ 4,983 .... A2
Gorham 284 .... D3
Gove▲ 103 .... B3
Grainfield 357 .... B2
Grandview Plaza 1,233 .... F2
Grantville 220 .... G2
Great Bend▲ 15,427 .... D3
Greeley 339 .... G3
Green 150 .... E2
Greenleaf 353 .... E2
Greensburg▲ 1,792 .... C4
Grenola 256 .... F4
Gridley 356 .... G3

(continued on following page)

(continued)

Grinnell 348 .... B2
Gypsum 365 .... E3
Haddam 195 .... E2
Hallowell 100 .... H4
Halstead 2,015 .... E4
Hamilton 301 .... F4
Hamlin 50 .... G2
Hanover 696 .... F2
Hanston 326 .... C3
Hardtner 198 .... D4
Harlan 62 .... D2
Harper 1,735 .... D4
Harris 39 .... G3
Hartford 541 .... F3
Harveyville 267 .... F3
Havana 121 .... G4
Haven 1,198 .... E4
Havensville 135 .... F2
Haviland 624 .... C4
Hays▲ 17,767 .... C3
Haysville 8,364 .... E4
Hazelton 128 .... D4
Healy 275 .... B3
Hepler 150 .... H4
Herington 2,685 .... E3
Herkimer 80 .... F2
Herndon 170 .... B2
Hesston 3,012 .... E3
Hiattville 60 .... H4
Hiawatha▲ 3,603 .... G2
Hickok 68 .... A4
Highland 942 .... G2
Hill City▲ 1,835 .... C2
Hillsboro 2,704 .... E3
Hillsdale 210 .... H3
Hoisington 3,182 .... D3
Holcomb 1,400 .... B3
Hollenberg 28 .... F2
Holton▲ 3,196 .... G2
Holyrood 492 .... D3
Home 145 .... F2
Homewood 75 .... G3
Hope 404 .... E3
Horace 168 .... A3
Horton 1,885 .... G2
Howard▲ 815 .... F4
Hoxie▲ 1,342 .... B2
Hoy 489 .... G2
Hudson 159 .... D3
Hugoton▲ 3,179 .... A4
Humboldt 2,178 .... G4
Hunnewell 87 .... E4
Hunter 116 .... D2
Huron 75 .... G2
Hutchinson▲ 39,308 .... D3
Idana 96 .... E2
Independence▲ 9,942 .... G4
Industry 60 .... E2
Ingalls 301 .... B4
Inman 1,035 .... E3
Iola▲ 6,351 .... G4
Ionia 90 .... D2
Isabel 104 .... D4
Iuka 197 .... D4
Jamestown 325 .... E2
Jarbalo 73 .... G2
Jennings 188 .... B2
Jetmore▲ 850 .... B3
Jewell 529 .... D2
Johnson▲ 1,348 .... A4
Junction City▲ 20,604 .... E2
Kanopolis 605 .... D3
Kanorado 276 .... A2
Kansas City▲ 149,767 .... H2
Keats 150 .... F2
Kechi 517 .... E4
Kendall 50 .... A4
Kensington 553 .... C2
Kincaid 170 .... G3
Kingman▲ 3,196 .... D4
Kingsdown 130 .... C4
Kinsley▲ 1,875 .... C4
Kiowa 1,160 .... D4
Kipp 77 .... E3
Kirwin 269 .... C2
Kismet 421 .... B4
La Crosse▲ 1,427 .... C3
La Cygne 1,066 .... H3
La Harpe 650 .... G4
Labette 74 .... G4
Lafontaine 115 .... G4
Lake City 76 .... D4
Lakin▲ 2,060 .... A4
Lancaster 299 .... G2
Lane 247 .... G3
Langdon 62 .... D4
Lansing 7,120 .... H2
Larned▲ 4,490 .... C3
Latham 160 .... F4
Latimer 20 .... F3
Lawrence▲ 65,608 .... G3
Lawton 65 .... H4
Le Loup 61 .... G3
Le Roy 568 .... G3
Leavenworth▲ 38,495 .... H2
Leawood 19,693 .... H3
Lebanon 364 .... D2
Lebo 835 .... G3
Lecompton 619 .... G2
Lehigh 180 .... E3
Lenexa 34,034 .... H2
Lenora 329 .... C2
Leon 707 .... F4
Leona 39 .... G2
Leonardville 374 .... F2
Leoti▲ 1,738 .... A3
Leoville 57 .... B2
Levant 85 .... A2
Lewis 451 .... C4
Liberal▲ 16,573 .... B4
Liberty 140 .... G4
Liebenthal 112 .... C3
Lincoln▲ 1,381 .... D2
Lincolnville 197 .... F3
Lindsborg 3,076 .... E3
Linn 472 .... E2
Linwood 409 .... G2
Little River 496 .... E3
Logan 633 .... C2
Lone Elm 32 .... G3
Long Island 170 .... C2
Longford 68 .... E2
Longton 389 .... F4
Lorraine 147 .... D3
Lost Springs 106 .... E3
Louisburg 1,964 .... H3
Louisille 207 .... F2
Lucas 452 .... D2
Ludell 90 .... B2
Luray 261 .... D2
Lyndon▲ 964 .... G3
Lyons▲ 3,688 .... D3
Macksville 488 .... D4
Madison 845 .... F3
Mahaska 98 .... E2
Maize 1,520 .... E4
Manchester 80 .... E2
Manhattan▲ 37,712 .... F2
Mankato▲ 1,037 .... D2
Manter 186 .... A4
Maple Hill 406 .... F2
Mapleton 96 .... H3
Marienthal 100 .... A3
Marion▲ 1,906 .... F3
Marquette 593 .... E3
Marysville▲ 3,359 .... F2
Matfield Green 33 .... F3
Mayetta 267 .... G2
Mayfield 110 .... E4
McCracken 231 .... C3
McCune 462 .... G4
McDonald 184 .... A2
McFarland 224 .... F2
McLouth 719 .... G2
McPherson▲ 12,422 .... E3
Meade▲ 1,526 .... B4
Medicine Lodge▲ 2,453 .... D4
Medora 62 .... E3

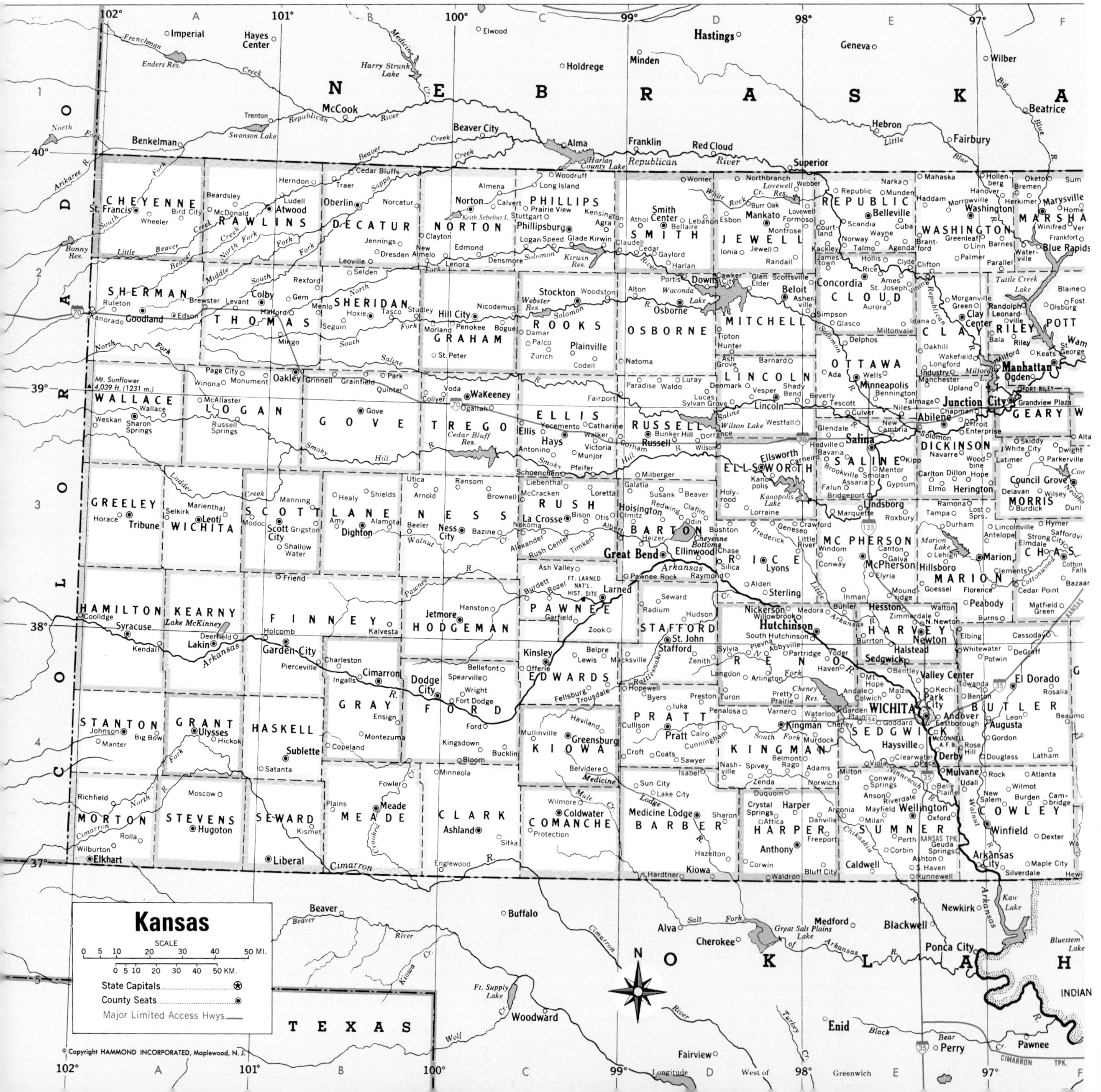

N E B R A S K A
O K L A H
T E X A S
C O L O R A D O
CHEYENNE
RAWLINS
DECATUR
NORTON
PHILLIPS
SMITH
JEWELL
REPUBLIC
WASHINGTON
SHERMAN
THOMAS
SHERIDAN
GRAHAM
ROOKS
OSBORNE
MITCHELL
CLOUD
WALLACE
LOGAN
GOVE
TREGO
ELLIS
RUSSELL
LINCOLN
OTTAWA
SALINE
DICKINSON
GEARY
RILEY
ELLSWORTH
GREELEY
WICHITA
SCOTT
LANE
NESS
RUSH
BARTON
RICE
MC PHERSON
MARION
MORRIS
HAMILTON
KEARNY
FINNEY
HODGEMAN
PAWNEE
STAFFORD
RENO
HARVEY
BUTLER
GRAY
FORD
EDWARDS
PRATT
KINGMAN
SEDGWICK
STANTON
GRANT
HASKELL
KIOWA
MORTON
STEVENS
SEWARD
MEADE
CLARK
COMANCHE
BARBER
HARPER
SUMNER
COWLEY
Kansas
SCALE
0 5 10 20 30 40 50 MI.
0 5 10 20 30 40 50 KM.
State Capitals
County Seats
Major Limited Access Hwys.
© Copyright HAMMOND INCORPORATED, Maplewood, N. J.
Longitude West of Greenwich

Melvern 423 G3
Menlo 50 B2
Mentor 100 E3
Mercier 85 G2
Meriden 622 G2
Merriam 11,821 H3
Michigan Valley 65 G3
Milan 109 E4
Mildred 46 G3
Milford 384 F2
Milton 484 E4
Miltonvale 588 E2
Minneapolis▲ 1,983 E2
Minneola 705 C4
Mission 9,504 H2
Moline 473 F4
Montezuma 838 B4
Monument 85 A2
Moran 551 G4
Morehead 65 G4
Morganville 181 E2
Morland 234 B2
Morrill 299 G2
Morrowville 173 E2
Moscow 252 A4
Mound City▲ 789 H3
Mound Valley 405 G4
Moundridge 1,531 E3
Mount Hope 805 E4
Mulberry 555 H4
Mullinville 289 C4
Mulvane 4,674 E4
Munden 143 E2
Munjor 200 C3
Murdock 75 E4
Muscotah 194 G2
Narka 113 E2
Nashville 118 D4
Natoma 392 D2
Navarre 66 E3
Neal 72 F4
Neodesha 2,837 G4
Neosho Falls 157 G3
Neosho Rapids 235 F3
Ness City▲ 1,724 C3
Netawaka 167 G2
New Albany 60 G4
New Almelo 80 B2

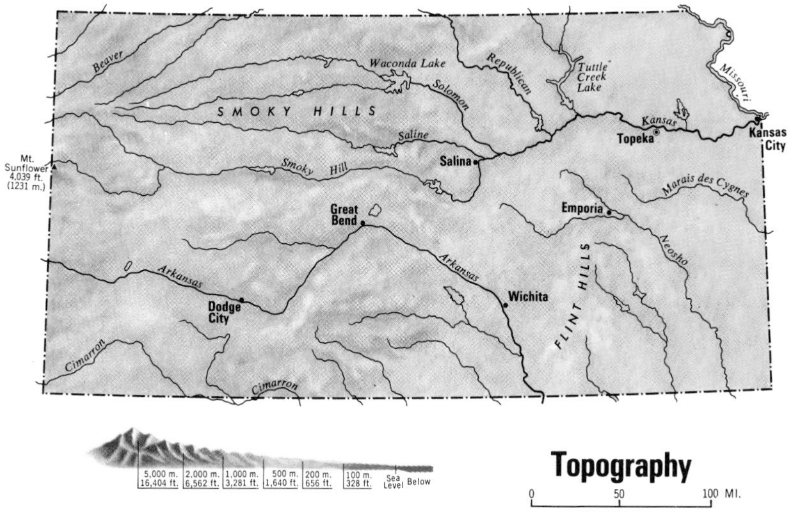
Beaver
Waconda Lake
Republican
Tuttle Creek Lake
Missouri
SMOKY HILLS
Solomon
Kansas
Topeka
Kansas City
Saline
Salina
Mt. Sunflower 4,039 ft. (1231 m.)
Smoky Hill
Marais des Cygnes
Great Bend
Emporia
Neosho
Arkansas
FLINT HILLS
Wichita
Dodge City
Cimarron
5,000 m. 16,404 ft.
2,000 m. 6,562 ft.
1,000 m. 3,281 ft.
500 m. 1,640 ft.
200 m. 656 ft.
100 m. 328 ft.
Sea Level
Below
0 50 100 MI.
0 50 100 KM.

Topography

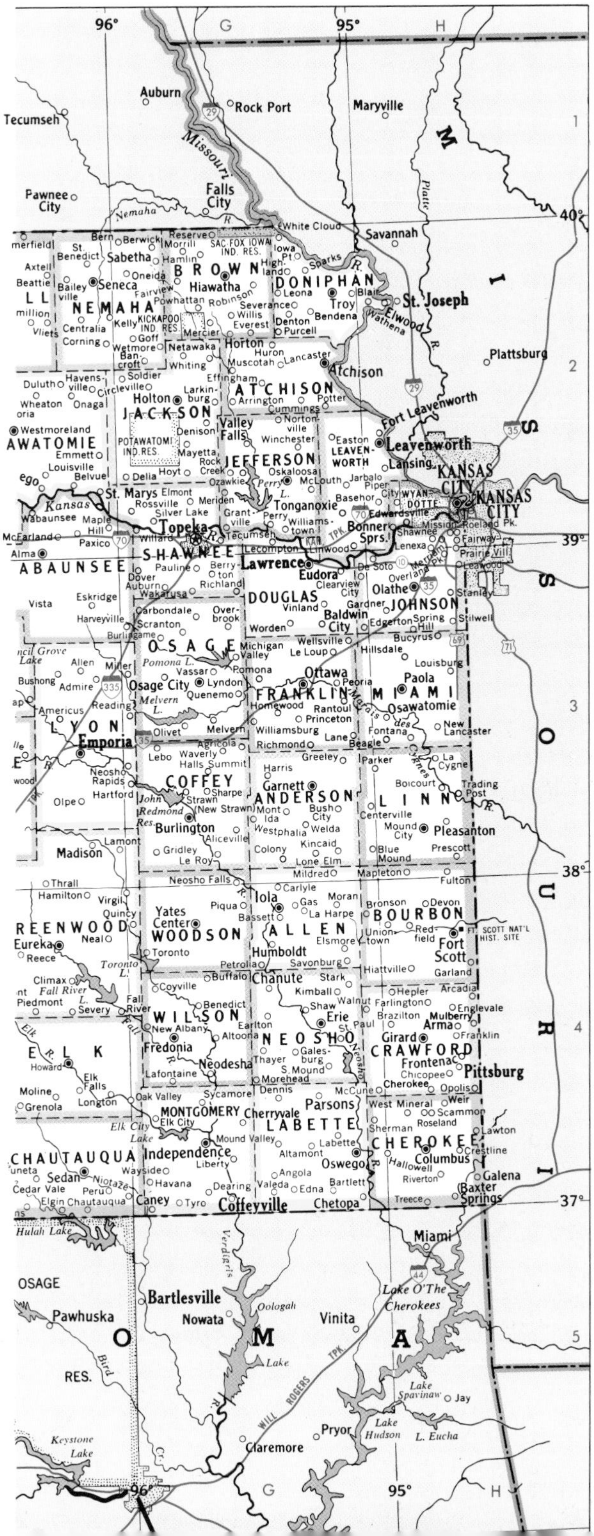

New Cambria 152 E3
New Lancaster 52 H3
New Salem 100 F4
New Strawn (Strawn) 428 G3
Newton▲ 16,700 E3
Nickerson 1,137 D3
Niles 75 E2
Niotaze 99 F4
Norcatur 198 B2
North Newton 1,262 E3
Norton▲ 3,017 C2
Nortonville 643 G2
Norway 60 E2
Norwich 455 E4
Oakhill 13 E2
Oakley▲ 2,045 B2
Oberlin▲ 2,197 B2
Odin 105 D3
Offerle 228 C4
Ogallah 75 C3
Ogden 1,494 F2
Oketo 116 F2
Olathe▲ 63,352 H3
Olivet 59 G3
Olmitz 130 D3
Olpe 431 F3
Olsburg 192 F2
Onaga 761 F2
Oneida 79 G2
Opolis 165 H4
Osage City 2,689 G3
Osawatomie 4,590 H3
Osborne▲ 1,778 D2
Oskaloosa▲ 1,074 G2
Oswego▲ 1,870 G4
Otis 385 C3
Ottawa▲ 10,667 G3
Overbrook 920 G3
Overland Park 111,790 H3
Oxford 1,143 E4
Ozawkie 403 G2
Page City 60 A2
Palco 295 C2
Palmer 121 E2
Paola▲ 4,698 H3
Paradise 66 D2
Park 150 B2
Park City 5,050 E4
Parker 256 H3
Parkerville 28 F3
Parsons 11,924 G4
Partridge 213 D4
Pauline 200 G3
Pawnee Rock 367 D3
Paxico 174 F2
Peabody 1,349 E3
Peck 250 E4
Penalosa 21 D4
Penokee 73 C2
Perry 881 G2
Peru 206 F4
Petrolia 69 G4
Pfeifer 80 C3
Phillipsburg▲ 2,828 C2
Piedmont 96 F4
Pierceville 135 B4
Piper City H2
Piqua 103 G4
Pittsburg 17,775 H4
Plains 957 B4
Plainville 2,173 C2
Pleasanton 1,231 H3
Plevna 117 D4
Pomona 835 G3
Portis 129 D2
Potter 175 G2
Potwin 448 F4
Powhattan 111 G2
Prairie View 111 C2
Prairie Village 23,186 H3
Pratt▲ 6,687 D4
Prescott 301 H3
Preston 177 D4
Pretty Prairie 601 D4
Princeton 275 G3
Protection 625 C4
Quenemo 369 G3
Quinter 945 B2
Radium 47 D3
Ramona 106 E3
Randall 96 D2
Randolph 129 F2
Ransom 386 C3
Rantoul 200 G3
Raymond 125 D3
Reading 264 F3
Redfield 143 H4
Reece 60 F4
Republic 177 E2
Reserve 108 G2
Rexford 171 B2
Richfield 50 A4
Richland 100 G3
Richmond 528 G3
Riley 804 F2
Riverton 650 H4
Robinson 268 G2
Rock 250 F4
Rock Creek 93 G2
Roeland Park 7,706 H2
Rolla 387 A4
Rosalia 125 F4
Rose Hill 2,399 E4
Roseland 98 H4
Rossville 1,052 G2
Roxbury 115 E3
Rozel 187 C3
Rush Center 177 C3
Russell Springs 29 A3
Russell▲ 4,781 D3
Sabetha 2,341 G2
Saint Benedict 55 F2
Saint Francis▲ 1,495 A2
Saint George 397 F2
Saint John▲ 1,357 D3
Saint Marys 1,791 G2
Saint Paul 687 G4
Salina▲ 42,303 E3
Satanta 1,073 B4
Savonburg 93 G4
Sawyer 183 D4
Scammon 466 H4
Scandia 421 E2
Schoenchen 128 C3
Scott City▲ 3,785 B3
Scottsville 26 D2
Scranton 674 G3
Sedan▲ 1,306 F4
Sedgwick 1,438 E4
Selden 248 B2
Seneca▲ 2,027 F2
Severance 98 G2
Severy 357 F4
Seward 71 D3
Shallow Water 100 B3
Sharon 256 D4
Sharon Springs▲ 872 A3
Shaw 37,993 G4
Shawnee 29,653 H2
Shields 110 B3
Silver Lake 1,390 G2
Simpson 107 E2
Skiddy 55 F3
Smith Center▲ 2,016 D2
Smolan 195 E3
Soldier 135 G2
Solomon 939 E3
South Haven 420 E4
South Hutchinson 2,444 D3
Sparks 71 G2
Spearville 716 C4
Speed 64 C2
Spivey 88 D4
Spring Hill 2,191 H3
Stafford 1,344 D4
Stanley 450 H3
Stark 79 G4
Sterling 2,115 D3
Stilwell 350 H3
Stockton▲ 1,507 C2
Strawn G3
Strong City 617 F3
Studley 60 B2
Stuttgart 70 C2
Sublette▲ 1,378 B4
Summerfield 169 F2
Sun City 88 D4
Sycamore 150 G4
Sylvan Grove 321 D2
Sylvia 308 D4
Syracuse▲ 1,606 A3
Talmage 130 E2
Tampa 113 E3
Tecumseh 300 G2
Tescott 317 E2
Thayer 435 G4
Timken 87 C3
Tipton 267 D2
Tonganoxie 2,347 G2
Topeka (cap.)▲ 119,883 G2
Toronto 317 G4
Towanda 1,289 E4
Treece 172 H4
Tribune▲ 918 A3
Trousdale 54 C4
Troy▲ 1,073 G2
Turon 393 D4
Tyro 243 G4
Udall 824 E4
Ulysses▲ 5,474 A4
Uniontown 290 G4
Utica 208 B3
Valley Center 3,624 E4
Valley Falls 1,253 G2
Vassar 90 G3
Vermillion 113 F2
Victoria 1,157 C3
Vining 55 E2
Vinland 102 G3
Viola 185 E4
Virgil 91 F4
Vliets 56 F2
WaKeeney▲ 2,161 C2
Wabaunsee 75 F2
Wakarusa 171 G3
Wakefield 900 E2
Waldo 57 D2
Waldron 19 D4
Walker 104 C3
Wallace 75 A3
Walnut 214 G4
Walton 226 E3
Wamego 3,706 F2
Washington▲ 1,304 E2
Waterville 601 F2
Wathena 1,160 H2
Waverly 618 G3
Wayside 85 G4
Webber 39 E2
Weir 730 H4
Welda 150 G3
Wellington▲ 8,411 E4
Wells 1,563 E2
Wellsville 1,612 G3
Weskan 200 A3
West Mineral 226 H4
West Plains (Plains) B4
Westmoreland▲ 541 F2
Westphalia 152 G3
Wetmore 284 G2
Wheaton 106 F2
White City 533 F3
White Cloud 255 G2
Whitewater 683 E4
Whiting 213 G2
Wichita▲ 304,011 E4
Willard 110 G2
Williamsburg 261 G3
Williamstown 89 G2
Willis 86 G2
Willowbrook 95 D3
Wilmore 78 C4
Wilsey 149 F3
Wilson 834 D3
Winchester 613 G2
Windom 136 E3
Winfield▲ 11,931 F4
Winifred 80 F2
Winona 194 A2
Woodbine 186 E3
Woodston 121 C2
Wright 300 C4
Yates Center▲ 1,815 G4
Yoder 160 E4
Zenda 96 D4
Zurich 151 C2

OTHER FEATURES

Arkansas (riv.) D3
Beaver (creek) A2
Big Blue (riv.) F1
Cedar Bluff (res.) C3
Cheney (res.) E4
Cheyenne Bottoms (lake) D3
Chikaskia (riv.) E4
Cimarron (riv.) B4
Cottonwood (riv.) F3
Council Grove (lake) F3
Crooked (creek) B4
Elk (riv.) F4
Fall (riv.) G4
Fall River (lake) F4
Fort Larned Nat'l Hist. Site C3
Fort Riley-Camp Whiteside F2
Fort Scott Nat'l Hist. Site H4
Hulah (lake) F5
John Redmond (res.) G3
Kanopolis (lake) D3
Kansas (riv.) F2
Keith Sebelius (lake) C2
Kickapoo Ind. Res. G2
Kirwin (res.) C2
Little Arkansas (riv.) E3
Little Blue (riv.) E1
Lovewell (res.) D2
Marion (lake) E3
McConnell A.F.B. E4
McKinney (lake) A3
Medicine Lodge (riv.) D4
Milford (lake) E2
Missouri (riv.) G1
Nemaha (riv.) G1
Neosho (riv.) G4
Ninnescah (riv.) E4
Pawnee (riv.) B3
Perry (lake) G2
Pomona (lake) G3
Potawatomi Ind. Res. G2
Rattlesnake (creek) D4
Republican (riv.) E2
Sac-Fox-Iowa Ind. Res. G2
Saline (riv.) D3
Sappa (creek) B2
Smoky Hill (riv.) C3
Solomon (riv.) E2
Sunflower (mt.) A2
Toronto (lake) F4
Tuttle Creek (lake) F2
Verdigris (riv.) G5
Walnut (riv.) E4
Webster (res.) C2
White Rock (creek) D2
Wilson (lake) D3

▲County seat

KENTUCKY

COUNTIES

Adair 15,360 L6
Allen 14,628 J7
Anderson 14,571 M5
Ballard 7,902 C6
Barren 34,001 K7
Bath 9,692 O4
Bell 31,506 O7
Boone 57,589 M3
Bourbon 19,236 N4
Boyd 51,150 R4
Boyle 25,641 M5
Bracken 7,766 N3
Breathitt 15,703 P5
Breckinridge 16,312 J5
Bullitt 47,567 K5
Butler 11,245 H6
Caldwell 13,232 F6
Calloway 30,735 E7
Campbell 83,866 N3
Carlisle 5,238 C7
Carroll 9,292 L3
Carter 24,340 P4
Casey 14,211 M6
Christian 68,941 F7
Clark 29,496 N4
Clay 21,746 O6
Clinton 9,135 L7
Crittenden 9,196 E6
Cumberland 6,784 L7
Daviess 87,189 G5
Edmonson 10,357 J6
Elliott 6,455 P4
Estill 14,614 O5
Fayette 225,366 M5
Fleming 12,292 O4
Floyd 43,586 R5
Franklin 43,781 M4
Fulton 8,271 C7
Gallatin 5,393 M3
Garrard 11,579 M5
Grant 15,737 M3
Graves 33,550 D7
Grayson 21,050 J5
Green 10,371 K6
Greenup 36,742 R3
Hancock 7,864 H5
Hardin 89,240 K5
Harlan 36,574 P7
Harrison 16,248 N4
Hart 14,890 K6
Henderson 43,044 F5
Henry 12,823 L4
Hickman 5,566 C7
Jackson 11,955 N6
Jefferson 664,937 K4
Jessamine 30,508 M5
Johnson 23,248 R5
Kenton 142,031 M3
Knott 17,906 R6
Knox 29,676 O7
Larue 11,679 K5
Laurel 43,438 N6
Lawrence 13,998 R4
Lee 7,422 O5
Leslie 13,642 P6
Letcher 27,000 R6
Lewis 13,029 P3
Lincoln 20,045 M6
Livingston 9,062 E6
Logan 24,416 H7
Lyon 6,624 E7
Madison 57,508 N5
Magoffin 13,077 P5
Marion 16,499 L5
Marshall 27,205 E7
Martin 12,526 R5
Mason 16,666 O3
McCracken 62,879 D6
McCreary 15,603 N7
McLean 9,628 G5
Meade 24,170 J5
Menifee 5,092 O5
Mercer 19,148 M5
Metcalfe 8,963 K7
Monroe 11,401 K7
Montgomery 19,561 O4
Morgan 11,648 P5
Muhlenberg 31,318 G6
Nelson 29,710 K5
Nicholas 6,725 N4
Ohio 21,105 H6
Oldham 33,263 L4
Owen 9,035 M3
Owsley 5,036 O6
Pendleton 12,036 N3
Perry 30,283 P6
Pike 72,583 S6
Powell 11,686 O5
Pulaski 49,489 M6
Robertson 2,124 N3
Rockcastle 14,803 N6
Rowan 20,353 P4
Russell 14,716 L6
Scott 23,867 M4
Shelby 24,824 L4
Simpson 15,145 H7
Spencer 6,801 L4
Taylor 21,146 L6
Todd 10,940 G7
Trigg 10,361 F7
Trimble 6,090 L3
Union 16,557 F5
Warren 76,673 H6
Washington 10,441 L5
Wayne 17,468 M7
Webster 13,955 F5
Whitley 33,326 N7
Wolfe 6,503 O5
Woodford 19,955 M4

CITIES and TOWNS

Adairville 906 H7
Ages 500 P7
Albany▲ 2,062 L7
Alexandria▲ 5,592 N3
Allen 229 R5
Allensville 218 G7
Amburgey 500 R6
Anchorage 2,082 L2
Annville 470 O6
Arjay 975 O7
Arlington 449 D7
Ashland 23,622 R4
Auburn 1,273 H7
Audubon Park 1,520 J2
Augusta 1,336 N3
Austin 500 K7
Auxier 900 R5
Bancroft 582 K1
Banner 950 R5
Barbourmeade 1,402 K1
Barbourville▲ 3,658 O7
Bardstown▲ 6,801 L5
Bardwell▲ 819 D7
Barlow 706 D6
Baskett 550 F5
Beattyville▲ 1,131 O5
Beauty 800 S5
Beaver Dam 2,904 H6
Bedford▲ 761 L3
Bee Spring 500 J6
Beechwood Village 1,263 K2
Belcher 500 S6
Belfry 800 S5
Bellemeade 927 L2
Bellevue 6,997 S1
Benham 717 R7
Benton▲ 3,899 E7
Berea 9,126 N5
Berry 240 N3
Betsy Layne 975 R5
Big Creek 700 O6
Blaine 271 R4
Blandville 95 D7
Bloomfield 845 L5
Blue Ridge Manor 565 L2
Boldman 510 R5
Bonnieville 300 K6
Bonnyman 800 P6
Boone 232 N5
Booneville▲ 191 O6
Bowling Green▲ 40,641 H7
Bradford 199 N3
Bradfordsville 331 L6
Brandenburg▲ 1,857 J4
Bremen 267 G6
Briensburg E7
Broadfields 273 K2
Brodhead 1,140 N6
Bromley 1,137 S2
Brooks 2,464 K4
Brooksville▲ 670 N3
Brownsboro Farm 670 L1
Brownsville 897 J6
Buechel 7,081 K2
Buffalo K6
Bulan 800 P6
Burgin 1,009 M5
Burkesville▲ 1,815 L7
Burlington▲ 6,070 R2
Burnside 695 M6
Butler 625 N3
Cadiz▲ 2,148 F7
Calhoun▲ 854 G5
California 130 N3
Calvert City 2,531 E6
Camargo 1,022 O4
Campbellsburg 604 L3
Campbellsville▲ 9,577 L6
Campton▲ 484 O5
Caney 549 P5
Caneyville 642 J6
Cannel City 600 P5
Carlisle▲ 1,639 N4
Carrollton▲ 3,715 L3
Carter P4
Catlettsburg▲ 2,231 R4
Cave City 1,953 K6
Cawood 800 P7
Center 383 K6
Centertown 462 G6
Centerville S6
Central City 4,979 G6
Cerulean F7
Clarkson 611 J6
Clay 1,173 F6
Clay City 1,258 O5
Clearfield 1,250 P4
Clinton▲ 1,547 D7
Clover Bottom 600 N5
Cloverport 1,207 H5
Coal Run 262 R5
Cold Spring 2,880 T2
Columbia▲ 3,845 L6
Columbus 252 C7
Combs 900 P6
Corbin 7,419 N7
Corinth 137 M3
Corydon 790 F5
Covington 43,264 S2
Crab Orchard 825 M6
Crescent Springs 2,179 R2
Crestview 356 S2
Crestview Hills 2,546 R2
Crestwood 1,435 L4
Crittenden 731 M3
Crofton 699 G6
Cumberland 3,112 R6
Cynthiana▲ 6,497 N4
Danville▲ 12,420 M5
Dawson Springs 3,129 F6
Dayton 6,576 T1
Devondale 1,164 K2
Dexter E7
Dixon▲ 552 F5
Dorton 750 R6
Douglass Hills 5,549 L2
Dover 297 O3
Drakesboro 565 H6
Dry Ridge 1,601 M3
Earlington 1,833 F6
East Bernstadt 550 N6
Echols 576 H6
Eddyville▲ 1,889 E6
Edgewood 8,143 S2
Edmonton▲ 1,477 K7
Elizabethtown▲ 18,167 K5
Elkhorn City 813 S6
Elkton▲ 1,789 G7
Elsmere 6,847 R2
Eminence 2,055 L4
Eolia 875 R6
Erlanger 15,979 R2
Essie 650 P6
Eubank 354 M6
Evarts 1,063 P7
Ewing 268 O4
Fairdale 6,563 K4
Fairfield 142 L5
Fairview 119 G7
Fairview 198 S2
Fallsburg R4
Falmouth▲ 2,378 N3
Fancy Farm 800 D7
Farmington 600 D7
Fedscreek 950 S6
Ferguson 934 M6
Fincastle 838 L1
Flat 7,799 O5
Flat Lick 600 O7
Flatwoods 8,354 R4
Fleming (Fleming-Neon) 759 R6
Flemingsburg▲ 3,071 O4
Florence 18,624 R2
Ford 522 N5
Fordsville 561 H5
Forest Hills 454 L2
Fort Knox 21,495 K5
Fort Mitchell 7,438 S2
Fort Thomas 16,032 S2
Fort Wright 6,570 S2
Fountain Run 259 K7
Frankfort (cap.)▲ 25,968 M4
Franklin▲ 7,607 J7
Fredonia 490 E6
Frenchburg▲ 625 O5
Fullerton 950 P3
Fulton 3,078 D7
Gamaliel 462 K7
Garrison 700 P3
Georgetown▲ 11,414 M4
Germantown 213 O3
Ghent 365 L3
Gilbertsville E7
Glasgow▲ 12,351 J7
Glencoe 257 M3
Glenview 653 K1
Goose Creek 321 L1
Goshen 2,447 K4
Gramoor 1,167 K1
Grand Rivers 351 E7
Gray 2,911 O7
Grayson▲ 3,510 R4
Greensburg▲ 1,990 K6
Greenup▲ 1,158 R3
Greenville▲ 4,689 G6
Guthrie 1,504 G7
Hammond 510 O7
Hanson 450 G6
Hardin 595 E7
Hardinsburg▲ 1,906 H5
Hardy 900 S5
Harlan▲ 2,686 P7
Harold 520 R5
Harrodsburg▲ 7,335 M5
Hartford▲ 2,532 H6
Hatfield 700 S5
Hawesville▲ 998 H5
Hazard▲ 5,416 P6
Hazel 460 E7
Hebron 930 R2
Helton 600 P7
Henderson▲ 25,945 F5
Hickman▲ 2,689 C7
Hickory 152 D7
Highland Heights 4,223 T2
Hima 600 O6
Himyar 545 O7
Hindman▲ 798 R6
Hiseville 220 K6
Hitchins 750 R4
Hodgenville▲ 2,721 K5
Hollow Creek 991 K4
Hopkinsville▲ 29,809 F7
Horse Cave 2,284 K6
Houston Acres 496 K2
Hustonville 313 M6
Hyden▲ 375 P6
Independence▲ 10,444 M3
Indian Hills 1,074 K1
Inez▲ 511 S5
Irvine▲ 2,836 O5
Irvington 1,180 J5
Island 446 G6
Ivel 850 R5
Jackson▲ 2,466 P5
Jamestown▲ 1,641 L7
Jeff 23,221 P6
Jeffersontown 15,795 L2
Jeffersonville 1,854 O5
Jenkins 2,751 R6
Junction City 1,983 M5
Keavy 900 N6
Keene 393 M5
Kenton 358 N3
Kenton Vale 145 S2
Kenvir 800 P7
Kevil 337 D6
King 399 O7
Kingsley 464 K2
Kitts 800 P7
Kuttawa 535 E6
La Center 1,040 C6
La Fayette 106 F7
La Grange▲ 3,853 L4
Lackey R6
Lake 3,131 O6
Lakeside Park 3,062 R2
Lancaster▲ 3,421 M5
Lawrenceburg▲ 5,911 M4
Leatherwood 800 P6
Lebanon Junction 1,741 K5
Lebanon▲ 5,695 L5
Leitchfield▲ 4,965 J6
Lejunior 597 P7
Lewisburg 772 G6
Lewisport 1,778 H5
Lexington▲ 204,165 N4
Liberty▲ 1,937 M6
Littcarr 645 R6
Livermore 1,534 G5
Livingston 241 N6
Lockport 84 M4
London▲ 5,757 N6
Lone Oak 465 D6
Lookout 600 S6
Lookout Heights S2
Loretto 820 L5
Lothair 600 P6
Louisa▲ 1,990 R4
Louisville▲ 269,063 J2
Loyall 1,100 P7
Ludlow 4,736 S2
Lynch 1,166 R7
Mackville 200 L5
Madisonville▲ 16,200 F6
Majestic 600 S5
Manchester▲ 1,634 O6
Marion▲ 3,320 E6
Marshes Siding 800 M7
Martha 650 R4
Martin 694 R5
Mary 177 O5
Mason 1,119 M3
Mayfield▲ 9,935 D7
Maysville▲ 7,169 O3
McAndrews 975 S5
McCarr 592 S5
McHenry 414 H6
McKee▲ 870 O6
McRoberts 1,101 R6
McVeigh 650 S5
Meadow Vale 798 L1
Meally 550 R5
Melbourne 660 T2
Mentor 169 N3
Meta 600 S5
Middlesboro 11,328 O7
Middletown 5,016 L2
Midway 1,290 M4
Millersburg 937 N4
Millstone 550 R6
Milton 563 L3
Minor Lane Heights 1,675 K4
Monterey 164 M4
Monticello▲ 5,357 M7
Moorland 467 L2
Morehead▲ 8,357 P4
Morgan 3,776 N3
Morganfield▲ 3,781 E5
Morgantown▲ 2,284 H6
Mortons Gap 987 F6
Mount Olivet▲ 384 N3
Mount Sterling▲ 5,362 N4
Mount Vernon▲ 2,654 N6
Mount Washington 5,226 K4
Mouthcard 900 S6
Muldraugh 1,376 J5
Munfordville▲ 1,556 J6
Murray▲ 14,439 E7
Nebo 227 F6
Neon (Neon-Fleming) R6
New Castle▲ 893 L4
New Concord 800 E7
New Haven 796 K5
New Hope L5
Newport 18,871 S2
Nicholasville▲ 13,603 N5
North Middletown 602 N4
Northfield 898 K1
Nortonville 1,209 G6
Oak Grove 2,863 G7
Oakland 202 J6
Oil Springs 900 P5
Okolona 18,902 K4
Oldtown 570 R4
Olive Hill 1,809 P4
Owensboro▲ 53,549 G5
Owenton▲ 1,306 M3
Owingsville▲ 1,491 O4
Paducah▲ 27,256 D6
Paintsville▲ 4,354 R5
Paris▲ 8,730 N4
Park City 549 J6
Park Hills 3,321 S2
Parksville 560 M5
Parkway Village 707 J2
Pembroke 640 G7
Perryville 815 M5
Petersburg M2
Pewee Valley 1,283 L4
Phelps 1,298 S6
Philpot 700 H5
Pikeville▲ 6,324 S6
Pine Knot 1,549 M7
Pineville▲ 2,198 O7
Pittsburg N6
Plantation 830 K1
Pleasure Ridge Park 25,131 J4
Pleasureville 761 L4
Plum Springs 361 J7
Powderly 748 G6
Premium 729 R6
Preston 3,558 O4
Prestonsburg▲ 4,011 R5
Prestonville 205 L3
Princeton▲ 6,940 F6
Prospect 2,788 K4
Providence 4,123 F6
Raceland 2,256 R3
Radcliff 19,772 K5
Ravenna 804 O5
Raywick 157 L5
Richmond▲ 21,155 N5
Riverwood 506 K1
Robards 701 F5
Rochester 191 H6
Rockholds 775 N7
Rockport 385 H6
Rolling Fields 593 K2
Rolling Hills 1,135 L1
Russell 4,014 R3
Russell Springs 2,363 L6
Russellville▲ 7,454 H7
Ryland Heights 279 M3
Sacramento 563 G6
Sadieville 255 M4
Saint Charles 316 F6
Saint Matthews 15,800 K2

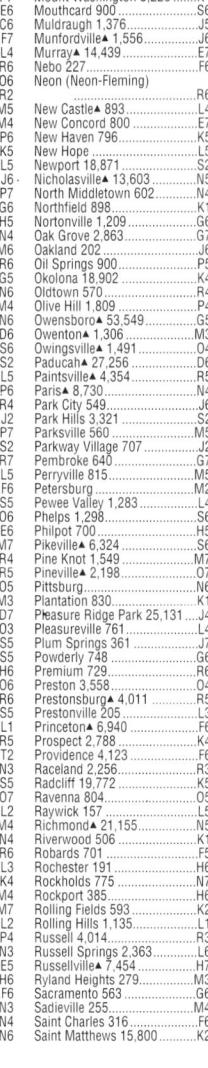

Agriculture, Industry and Resources

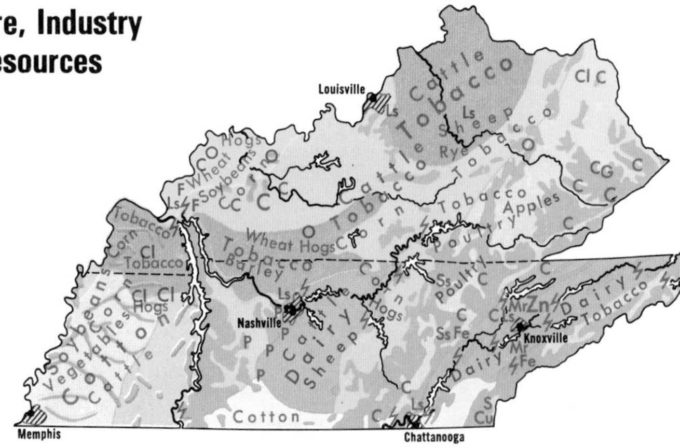

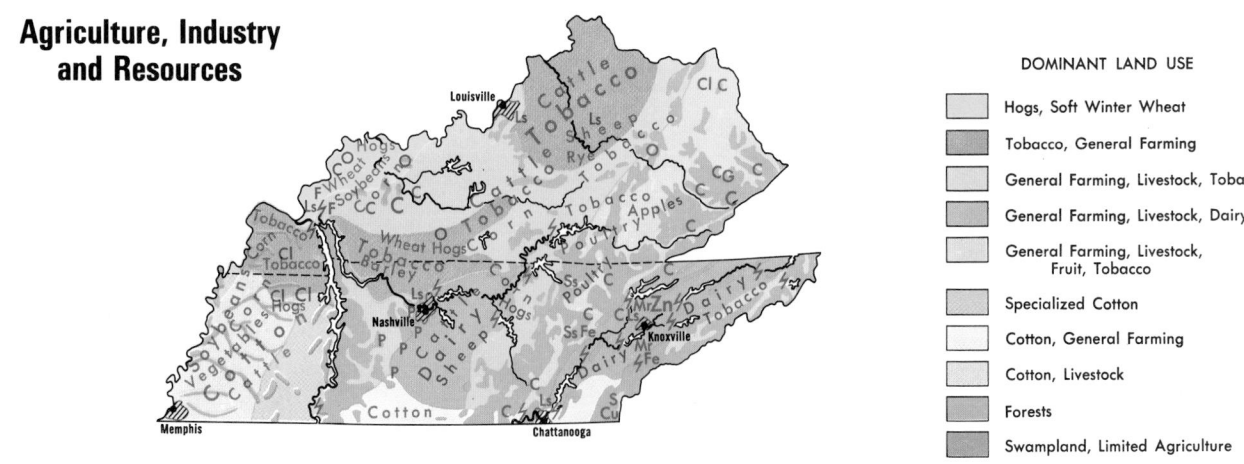

Louisville
Nashville
Knoxville
Memphis
Chattanooga
Cattle
Tobacco
Sheep
Hogs
Wheat
Soybeans
Corn
Apples
Poultry
Dairy
Cotton
Barley

DOMINANT LAND USE

- Hogs, Soft Winter Wheat
- Tobacco, General Farming
- General Farming, Livestock, Tobacco
- General Farming, Livestock, Dairy
- General Farming, Livestock, Fruit, Tobacco
- Specialized Cotton
- Cotton, General Farming
- Cotton, Livestock
- Forests
- Swampland, Limited Agriculture

MAJOR MINERAL OCCURRENCES

C	Coal	G	Natural Gas	P	Phosphates
Cl	Clay	Ls	Limestone	S	Pyrites
Cu	Copper	Mr	Marble	Ss	Sandstone
F	Fluorspar	O	Petroleum	Zn	Zinc
Fe	Iron Ore				

Water Power

Major Industrial Areas

Saint Regis Park 1,756 K2
Salem 770 E6
Salt Lick 342 O4
Salyersville▲ 1,917 P5
Sanders 231 M3
Sandy Hook▲ 548 P4
Sardis 171 O3
Science Hill 628 M6
Scottsville▲ 4,278 J7
Sebree 1,510 F5
Seco R6
Sedalia D7
Seneca Gardens 684 K2
Sextons Creek 975 O6
Sharpsburg 315 O4
Shelbyville▲ 6,238 L4
Shepherdsville▲ 4,805 K4
Shively 15,535 K4
Silver Grove 1,102 T2
Simpson 907 P5
Simpsonville 642 L4
Slaughters 235 F6
Smilax 987 P6
Smithfield 115 L4
Smithland▲ 384 E6
Smiths Grove 703 J6
Somerset▲ 10,733 M6
Sonora 295 K5
South 202 J6
South Carrollton 262 G6
South Portsmouth 900 P3
South Shore 1,318 R3
South Williamson 1,016 S5
Southgate 3,266 T2
Sparta 133 M3
Spottsville 914 G5
Springfield▲ 2,875 L5
Springlee 451 K2
Staffordsville 700 R5
Stamping Ground 698 M4
Stanford▲ 2,686 M5
Stanton▲ 2,795 O5
Stearns 1,550 N7
Stone 900 S5
Strathmoor Village 361 K2
Sturgis 2,184 F5
Tateville 680 M7
Taylor Mill 5,530 S2
Taylorsville▲ 774 L4
Thealka 600 R5
Thornhill 146 K1
Tollesboro 808 O3
Tompkinsville▲ 2,861 K7
Trenton 378 G7
Tyner 590 O6
Union 1,001 M3
Uniontown 1,008 F5
Upton 719 K6
Valley Station 22,840 K4
Van 1,050 R6
Van Lear 2,035 R5
Vanceburg▲ 1,713 P3
Verda 1,133 P7
Versailles▲ 7,269 M4
Vicco 244 P6
Villa Hills 7,739 R2
Vine Grove 3,586 K5
Virgie 600 R6
Visalia 190 N3
Wallins Creek 261 O7
Walton 2,034 M3
Warfield 364 S5
Warsaw▲ 1,202 M3
Washington 795 O3
Water Valley 321 D7
Waverly 345 F5
Wayland 359 R6
Weeksbury 850 R6
Wellington 593 O5
Wellington 653 K2
West Buechel 1,587 K2
West Liberty▲ 1,887 P5
West Point 1,216 J4
West Somerset 850 M6
Westwood 734 R4
Westwood 826 L1
Wheatcroft 206 F5
Wheelwright 721 R6
White Plains 598 G6
Whitesburg▲ 1,636 R6
Whitesville 682 H5
Whitley City▲ 1,133 N7
Wickliffe▲ 851 C7
Wilders 633 S2
Willard R4
Williamsburg▲ 5,493 N7
Williamstown▲ 3,023 M3
Willisburg 223 L5
Wilmore 4,215 M5
Winchester▲ 15,799 N5
Windy Hills 2,452 K1
Wingo 568 D7
Winston Park S2
Wolf Creek 600 J4
Woodbine 900 N7
Woodburn 343 J7
Woodbury 117 H6
Woodland Hills 714 L2
Woodlawn (Oakdale) 308 D6
Woodlawn 331 T2
Woodlawn Park 1,099 K2
Wooton 750 P6
Worthington 1,751 R3
Worthville 191 L3
Wurtland 1,221 R3
Zebulon 750 S5

OTHER FEATURES

Abraham Lincoln Birthplace Nat'l Hist. Site K5
Barkley (dam) E6
Barkley (lake) F7
Barren (riv.) H6
Barren River (lake) J7
Beech Fork (riv.) L5
Big Sandy (riv.) R4
Black (mt.) R7
Buckhorn (lake) O6
Chaplin (riv.) L5
Clarks, East Fork (riv.) E7
Cove Run (lake) P4
Cumberland (lake) M7
Cumberland (mt.) P7
Cumberland (riv.) K8
Cumberland Gap Nat'l Hist. P7
Dale Hollow (lake) L7
Dewey (lake) R5
Dix (riv.) M5
Drakes (creek) J7
Dry (creek) R2
Eagle (creek) M3
Fishtrap (lake) S6
Fort Campbell G7
Grayson (lake) P4
Green (riv.) G6
Green River (lake) L6
Herrington (lake) M5
Hinkston (creek) N4
Kentucky (dam) E7
Kentucky (lake) E8
Kentucky (riv.) M3
Land Between The Lakes Rec. Area E7
Laurel River (lake) N6
Lexington Blue Grass Army Depot N4
Licking (riv.) N3
Mammoth Cave Nat'l Park J6
Mayfield (creek) C7
Mississippi (riv.) 10
Mud (riv.) H7
Nolin (lake) K6
Nolin (riv.) J6
Obion (creek) C7
Ohio (riv.) F5
Paint Lick (riv.) M5
Panther (creek) G5
Pine (mt.) O7
Pond (riv.) G6
Red (riv.) G7
Red (riv.) O5
Rockcastle (riv.) N6
Rolling Fork (riv.) K5
Rough (riv.) H5
Rough River (lake) J5
Salt (riv.) K5
Tennessee (riv.) D6
Tradewater (riv.) F6
Tug Fork (riv.) S5

KENTUCKY

KENTUCKY

AREA 40,409 sq. mi. (104,659 sq. km.)
POPULATION 3,698,969
CAPITAL Frankfort
LARGEST CITY Louisville
HIGHEST POINT Black Mtn. 4,145 ft. (1263 m.)
SETTLED IN 1774
ADMITTED TO UNION June 1, 1792
POPULAR NAME Bluegrass State
STATE FLOWER Goldenrod
STATE BIRD Cardinal

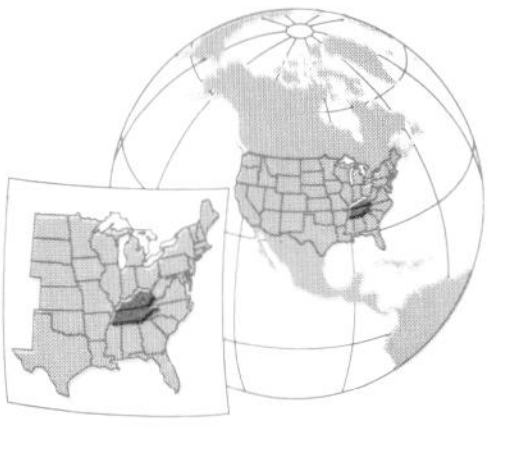

TENNESSEE

TENNESSEE

AREA 42,144 sq. mi. (109,153 sq. km.)
POPULATION 4,896,641
CAPITAL Nashville
LARGEST CITY Memphis
HIGHEST POINT Clingmans Dome 6,643 ft. (2025 m.)
SETTLED IN 1757
ADMITTED TO UNION June 1, 1796
POPULAR NAME Volunteer State
STATE FLOWER Iris
STATE BIRD Mockingbird

TENNESSEE

COUNTIES

Anderson 68,250 N8
Bedford 30,411 J9
Benton 14,524 E8
Bledsoe 9,669 L9
Blount 85,969 O9
Bradley 73,712 M1
Campbell 35,079 N8
Cannon 10,467 J9
Carroll 27,514 E9
Carter 51,505 S8
Cheatham 27,140 G8
Chester 12,819 D1
Claiborne 26,137 O8
Clay 7,238 K7
Cocke 29,141 P9
Coffee 40,339 J9
Crockett 13,378 C9
Cumberland 34,736 L9
Davidson 510,784 H8
De Kalb 13,589 K9
Decatur 10,472 E9
Dickson 35,061 G8
Dyer 34,854 C8
Fayette 25,559 C1
Fentress 14,669 M8
Franklin 34,725 J1
Gibson 46,315 D9
Giles 25,741 G1
Grainger 17,095 O8
Greene 55,853 R8
Grundy 13,362 K1
Hamblen 50,480 P8
Hamilton 285,536 L1
Hancock 6,739 P7
Hardeman 23,377 C1
Hardin 22,633 E1
Hawkins 44,565 P8
Haywood 19,437 C9
Henderson 21,844 E9
Henry 27,888 E8
Hickman 16,754 G9
Houston 7,018 F8
Humphreys 15,795 F8
Jackson 9,297 K8
Jefferson 33,016 P8
Johnson 13,766 T7
Knox 335,749 O9
Lake 7,129 B8
Lauderdale 23,491 B9
Lawrence 35,303 G1
Lewis 9,247 F9
Lincoln 28,157 H1
Loudon 31,255 N9
Macon 15,906 J7
Madison 77,982 D9
Marion 24,860 K1
Marshall 21,539 H1
Maury 54,812 G9
McMinn 42,383 M1
McNairy 22,422 D1
Meigs 8,033 M9
Monroe 30,541 N1
Montgomery 100,498 G8
Moore 4,721 J1
Morgan 17,300 M8
Obion 31,717 C8
Overton 17,636 L8
Perry 6,612 F9
Pickett 4,548 M7
Polk 13,643 N1
Putnam 51,373 K8
Rhea 24,344 M9
Roane 47,227 M9
Robertson 41,494 H7
Rutherford 118,570 J9
Scott 18,358 M8
Sequatchie 8,863 L1
Sevier 51,043 O9
Shelby 826,330 B1
Smith 14,143 J8
Stewart 9,479 F7
Sullivan 143,596 S7
Sumner 103,281 J8
Tipton 37,568 B9
Trousdale 5,920 J8
Unicoi 16,549 S8
Union 13,694 O8
Van Buren 4,846 L9
Warren 32,992 K9
Washington 92,315 R8
Wayne 13,935 F1
Weakley 31,972 D8
White 20,090 L9
Williamson 81,021 H9
Wilson 67,675 J8

CITIES and TOWNS

Adams 587 G7
Adamsville 1,745 E10
Afton 800 R8
Alamo▲ 2,426 C9
Alcoa 6,400 N9
Alexandria 730 J8
Algood 2,399 K8
Allardt 609 M8
Allons 600 L8
Altamont▲ 679 K10
Apison 750 L10
Ardmore 866 H10
Arlington 1,541 B10
Armathwaite 700 M8
Arthur 500 O7
Ashland City▲ 2,552 G8
Athens▲ 12,054 M10
Atoka 659 B10
Atwood 1,066 D9
Auburntown 240 J9
Baileyton 309 R8
Banner Hill 1,717 R8
Bartlett 26,989 B10
Bath Springs 800 E10
Baxter 1,289 K8
Bean Station 500 P8
Beechgrove 550 J9
Beersheba Springs 596 K10
Bell Buckle 326 J9
Belle Meade 2,839 H8
Bells 1,643 C9
Benton▲ 992 M10
Berry Hill 802 H8
Berry's Chapel 2,703 H9
Bethel Springs 755 D10
Big Sandy 505 E8
Birchwood 550 M10
Blaine 1,326 O8
Bloomingdale 10,953 R7
Bloomington Springs 800 K8
Blountville▲ 2,605 S7
Bluff City 1,390 S8
Bolivar▲ 5,969 C10
Braden 354 B10
Bradford 1,154 D8
Braemar S8
Brentwood 16,392 H8
Briceville 850 N8
Brighton 717 B10
Bristol 23,421 S7
Brownsville▲ 10,019 C9
Bruceton 1,586 E8
Buena Vista 500 E9
Bulls Gap 659 P8
Burlison 394 B9
Burns 1,127 G8
Butler 500 T8
Byrdstown▲ 998 L7
Calhoun 552 M10
Camden▲ 3,643 E8
Carthage▲ 2,386 K8
Caryville 1,751 N8
Castalian Springs 650 J8
Cedar Hill 347 H7
Celina▲ 1,493 K7
Centertown 332 K9
Centerville▲ 3,616 G9
Chapel Hill 833 H9
Charleston 653 M10
Charlotte▲ 854 G8
Chattanooga▲ 152,466 K10
Chuckey 500 R8
Church Hill 4,834 R7
Clairfield 650 O7
Clarksburg 321 E9
Clarksville▲ 75,494 G7
Cleveland▲ 30,354 M10
Clifton 620 F10
Clinton▲ 8,972 N8
Coalfield 712 N8
Coalmont 813 K10
Cokercreek 500 N10
College Grove 580 H9
Collegedale 5,048 M10
Collierville 14,427 B10
Collinwood 1,014 F10
Colonial Heights 6,716 R8
Columbia▲ 28,583 G9
Concord 8,569 N9
Cookeville▲ 21,744 L8
Copperhill 362 N10
Cordova 600 B10
Cornersville 683 H10
Corryton 500 O8
Counce 975 E10
Covington▲ 7,487 B9
Cowan 1,738 K10
Crab Orchard 876 M9
Crockett Mills 500 C9
Cross Plains 1,025 H7
Crossville▲ 6,930 L9
Crump 2,028 E10
Cumberland City 319 F8
Cumberland Gap 210 O8
Cypress Inn 500 F10
Dandridge▲ 1,540 O8
Dayton▲ 5,671 L9
Decatur▲ 1,361 M9
Decaturville▲ 879 E9
Decherd 2,196 J10
Dickson 8,791 G8
Dover▲ 1,341 F8
Dowelltown 308 K9
Doyle 345 K9
Dresden▲ 2,488 D8
Drummonds 800 A10
Duck River 750 G9
Ducktown 421 N10
Dunlap▲ 3,731 L10
Dyer 2,204 D8
Dyersburg▲ 16,317 C8
Eads 550 B10
Eagleton Village 5,169 O9
Eagleville 462 H9
East Ridge 21,101 L11
Eastview 563 D10
Elgin 700 M8
Elizabethton▲ 11,931 S8
Elk Valley 750 N7
Elkton 448 H10
Ellendale 850 B10
Embreeville Junction R8
Emory Gap 500 M9
Englewood 1,611 M10
Enville 211 E10
Erin▲ 1,586 F8
Erwin▲ 5,015 S8
Estill Springs 1,408 J10
Ethridge 565 G10
Etowah 3,815 M10
Eva 500 E8
Fairfield 2,209 J9
Fairview 4,210 G9
Fall Branch 1,203 R8
Farner 750 N10
Fayetteville▲ 6,921 H10
Finger 279 D10
Finley 1,014 B8
Flintville 500 H10
Forest Hills 4,231 H8
Fort Pillow 700 B9
Fowlkes 700 C9
Franklin▲ 20,098 H9
Friendship 467 C9
Friendsville 792 N9
Gadsden 561 D9
Gainesboro▲ 1,002 K8
Gallatin▲ 18,794 H8
Gallaway 762 B10
Garland 194 B9
Gates 608 C9
Gatlinburg 3,417 O9
Germantown 32,893 B10
Gibson 281 D9
Gilt Edge 447 B9
Gleason 1,402 D8
Goodlettsville 8,177 H8
Gordonsville 891 K8
Grand Junction 365 C10
Grandview M9
Graysville 1,301 L10
Greenback 611 N9
Greenbrier 2,873 H8
Greeneville▲ 13,532 R8
Greenfield 2,105 D8
Grimsley 650 L8
Gruetli 1,810 K10
Guys 497 D10
Habersham 750 N8
Halls 2,431 C9
Halls Crossroads O8
Hampshire 788 G9
Hampton 2,236 S8
Harriman 7,119 M9
Harris 7,191 C8
Harrison 6,206 L10
Harrogate (Shawanee) 2,657 O8
Hartsville▲ 2,188 J8
Helenwood 675 M8
Henderson▲ 4,760 D10
Hendersonville 32,188 H8
Henning 802 B9
Henry 317 E8
Hickory Valley 159 C10
Hixson L10
Hohenwald▲ 3,760 F9
Hollow Rock 902 E8
Hornbeak 445 C8
Hornsby 313 D10
Humboldt 9,651 D9
Huntingdon▲ 4,180 E8
Huntland 885 J10
Huntsville▲ 660 N8
Hurricane Mills 850 F9
Iron City 402 F10
Jacksboro▲ 1,568 N8
Jackson▲ 48,949 D9
Jamestown▲ 1,862 M8
Jasper▲ 2,780 K10
Jefferson City 5,494 P8
Jellico 2,447 N7
Johnson City 49,381 S8
Jones 3,091 C9
Jonesborough▲ 2,829 R8
Karns 1,458 N9
Kenton 1,366 C8
Kimball 1,243 K10
Kimberlin Heights 500 O9
Kingsport 36,365 R7
Kingston Springs 1,529 G8
Kingston▲ 4,552 N9
Knoxville▲ 165,121 O9
Kodak 700 O9
La Follette 7,192 N8
La Grange 167 C10
La Vergne 7,499 H9
Laager 675 K10
Lafayette▲ 3,641 J7
Lake City 2,166 N8
Lakeland 1,204 B10
Lakesite 732 L10
Lakewood 2,009 H8
Lawrenceburg▲ 10,412 G10
Lebanon▲ 15,208 J8
Lenoir City 6,147 N9
Leoma 600 G10
Lewisburg▲ 9,879 H10
Lexington▲ 5,810 E9
Liberty 391 K8
Linden▲ 1,099 F9
Livingston▲ 3,809 L8
Lobelville 830 F9
Long Island S7
Lookout Mountain 1,901 L11
Loretto 1,515 G10
Loudon▲ 4,026 N9
Louisville 500 N9
Luttrell 812 O8
Lutts 740 F10
Lyles 500 G9
Lynchburg▲ 668 J10
Lynnville 344 G10
Madisonville▲ 3,033 N9
Malesus 600 D9
Manchester▲ 7,709 J10
Martel 500 N9
Martin 8,600 D8
Maryville▲ 19,208 O9
Mascot 2,138 O8
Mason 337 B10
Maury City 782 C9
Maynardville▲ 1,298 O8
McDonald 500 M10
McEwen 1,442 F8
McKenzie 5,168 E8
McLemoresville 280 D9
McMinnville▲ 11,194 K9
Medina 658 D9
Medon 137 D10
Memphis▲ 610,337 B10
Michie 677 E10
Middleton 536 D10
Midway 2,953 P8
Milan 7,512 D9
Milledgeville 279 E10
Milligan College 600 S8
Millington 17,866 B10
Minor Hill 372 G10
Mitchellville 193 J7
Monteagle 1,138 K10
Monterey 2,559 L8
Morley 600 N7
Morrison 570 K9
Morrison City 2,032 R7
Morristown▲ 21,385 P8
Moscow 384 C10
Mosheim 1,451 R8
Mount Carmel 4,082 R8
Mount Juliet 5,389 H8
Mount Pleasant 4,278 G9
Mountain City▲ 2,169 T8
Munford 2,326 B10
Murfreesboro▲ 44,922 J9
Murray Lake Hills L10
Nashville (cap.)▲ 488,374 H8
Neubert 800 O9
New Hope 854 K11
New Johnsonville 1,643 E8
New Market 1,086 O8
New Tazewell 1,864 O8
Newbern 2,515 C8
Newport▲ 7,123 P9
Niota 745 M9
Norma 118 N8
Normandy 118 J10
Norris 1,303 N8
Oak Hill 4,301 H8
Oak Ridge 27,310 N8
Oakdale 268 M9
Oakland 392 B10
Obion 1,241 C8
Oliver Springs 3,433 N8
Oneida 3,502 N7
Ooltewah 4,903 M10
Orebank 1,284 R7
Orlinda 469 H7
Orme 150 K10
Pall Mall 750 M7
Palmer 769 K10
Paris▲ 9,332 E8
Parrotsville 121 P8
Parsons 2,033 E9
Pegram 1,371 H8
Petersburg 514 H10
Petros 1,286 M8
Philadelphia 463 M9
Pickwick Dam 650 E10
Pigeon Forge 3,027 O9
Pikeville▲ 1,771 L9
Piperton 612 B10
Pittman Center 478 P9
Pleasant Hill 494 L9
Pleasant View 625 G8
Portland 5,165 H7
Powder Springs 600 O8
Powell 7,534 N8
Powells Crossroads 1,098 L10
Primm Springs 750 G9
Pulaski▲ 7,895 G10
Puryear 592 E8
Ramer 337 D10
Red Bank 12,322 L10
Red Boiling Springs 905 K7
Rheatown R8
Ridgely 1,775 B8
Ridgeside 400 L10
Ripley▲ 6,188 B9
Rives 344 C8
Roan Mountain 1,220 S8
Rockford 646 O9
Rockwood 5,348 M9
Rogersville▲ 4,149 P8
Rosemark 950 B10
Rossville 291 B10
Russellville 1,069 P8
Rutherford 1,303 C8
Rutledge▲ 903 P8
Saint Joseph 789 G10
Sale Creek 900 L10
Saltillo 383 E10
Samburg 374 C8
Sardis 305 E10
Saulsbury 106 C10
Saundersville H8
Savannah▲ 6,547 E10
Scotts Hill 594 E10
Selmer▲ 3,838 D10
Sequatchie 800 K10
Sevierville▲ 7,178 P9
Sewanee 2,128 K10
Seymour 7,026 O9
Sharon 1,047 D8
Shelbyville▲ 14,049 H10
Sherwood 900 K10
Signal Mountain 7,034 L10
Smithville▲ 3,791 K9
Smyrna 13,647 H9
Sneedville▲ 1,446 P7
Soddy-Daisy (Daisy-Soddy) 8,240 L10
Somerville▲ 2,047 C10
South Carthage 851 K8
South Cleveland 5,372 M10
South Clinton 1,671 N8
South Fulton 2,688 D8
South Pittsburg 3,295 K10
Southside 800 G8
Sparta▲ 4,681 K9
Spencer▲ 1,125 L9
Spring City 2,199 M9
Spring Hill 1,464 H9
Springfield▲ 11,227 H8
Stanton 487 C10
Stantonville 264 E10
Strawberry Plains 680 O8
Sullivan Gardens 2,513 R8
Summertown 850 G10
Surgoinsville 1,499 R8
Sweetwater 5,066 N9
Talbott 975 P8
Tazewell▲ 2,150 O8
Tellico Plains 657 N10
Ten Mile 700 M9
Tennessee Ridge 1,271 F8
Tiftona L11
Tipton 2,149 B10
Tiptonville▲ 2,438 B8
Toone 279 D10
Townsend 329 O9
Tracy City 1,556 K10
Treadway 712 P8
Trenton▲ 4,836 D9
Trezevant 874 D8
Trimble 694 C8
Troy 1,047 C8
Tullahoma 16,761 J10
Tusculum 1,918 R8
Union City▲ 10,513 C8
Vanleer 369 G8
Victoria 800 K10
Viola 123 K9
Vonore 605 N9
Walden 1,523 L10
Walterhill 1,043 J9
Wartburg▲ 932 M8
Wartrace 494 J9

(continued on following page)

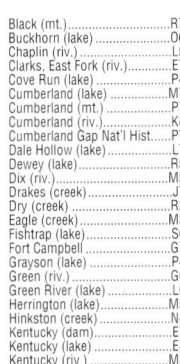

OTHER FEATURES

▲ County seat.

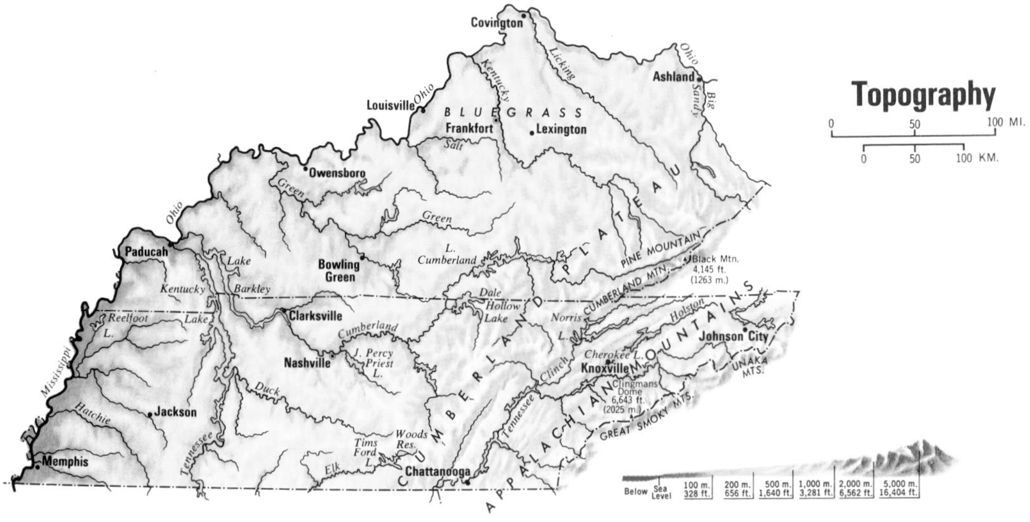
Topography
0 50 100 MI.
0 50 100 KM.
Covington
Ashland
Louisville
BLUEGRASS
Frankfort
Lexington
Owensboro
Paducah
Bowling Green
L. Cumberland
PINE MOUNTAIN
CUMBERLAND MTN.
Black Mtn. 4,145 ft. (1263 m.)
CUMBERLAND PLATEAU
Clarksville
Dale Hollow Lake
Norris L.
Johnson City
Nashville
J. Percy Priest L.
Cherokee L.
Knoxville
UNAKA MTS.
Clingmans Dome 6,643 ft. (2025 m.)
GREAT SMOKY MTS.
APPALACHIAN MOUNTAINS
Jackson
Memphis
Tims Ford L.
Woods Res.
Chattanooga
Reelfoot L.
Kentucky Lake
Barkley
Below Sea Level 100 m. 328 ft. 200 m. 656 ft. 500 m. 1,640 ft. 1,000 m. 3,281 ft. 2,000 m. 6,562 ft. 5,000 m. 16,404 ft.

MISSOURI
ILLINOIS
ARKANSAS
MISSISSIPPI
ALABAMA
Evansville
Paducah
Memphis
Jackson
Clarksville
NASHVILLE
Owensboro
Cape Girardeau

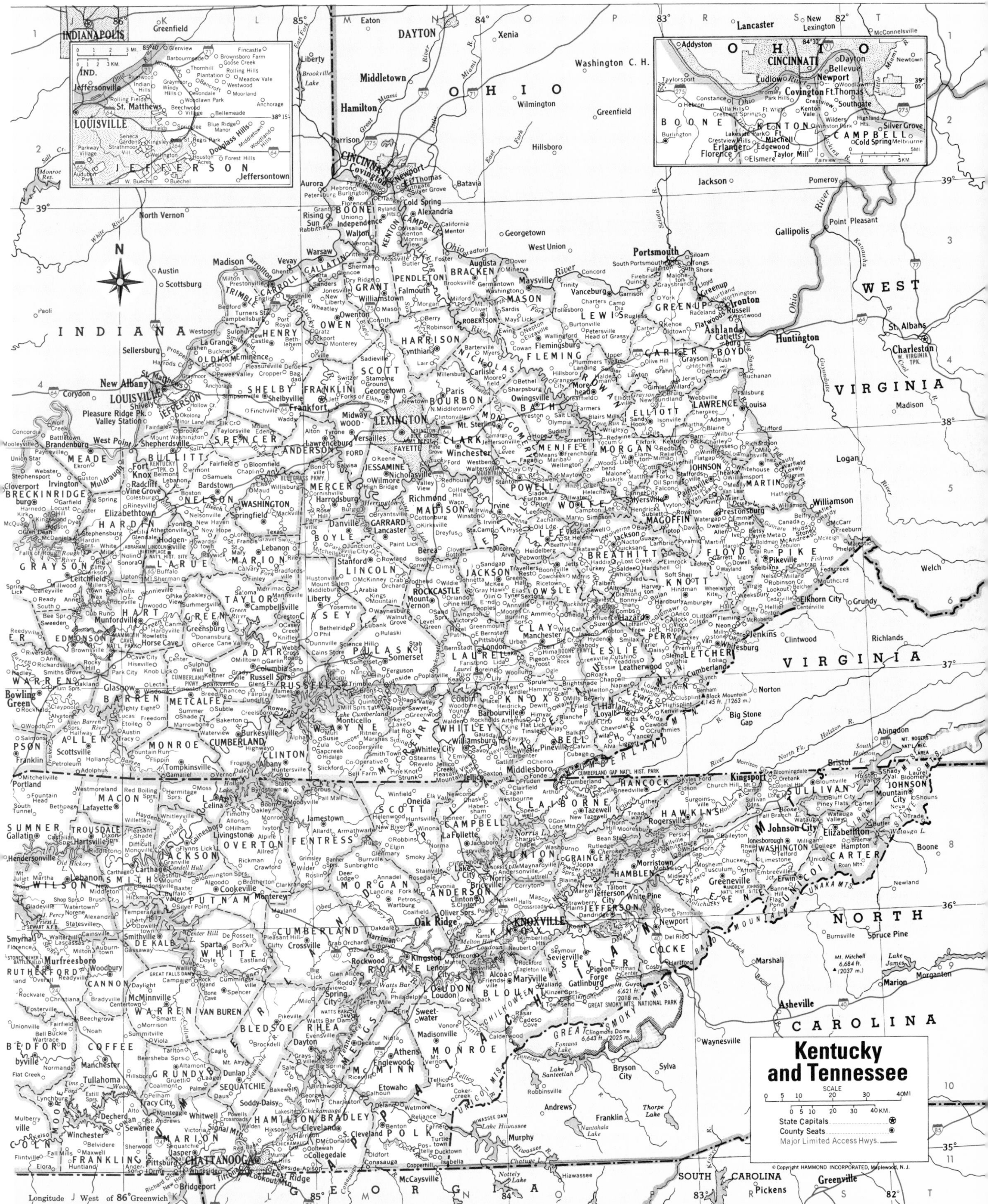

Kentucky
and Tennessee
SCALE
0 5 10 20 30 40 MI.
0 5 10 20 30 40 KM.
State Capitals
County Seats
Major Limited Access Hwys.
© Copyright HAMMOND INCORPORATED, Maplewood, N. J.
Longitude J West of 86° Greenwich
INDIANA
OHIO
WEST VIRGINIA
VIRGINIA
NORTH CAROLINA
SOUTH CAROLINA
GEORGIA
LOUISVILLE
JEFFERSON
CINCINNATI
KENTON
CAMPBELL
BOONE
LEXINGTON
Frankfort
Nashville
KNOXVILLE
CHATTANOOGA
Charleston
INDIANAPOLIS
DAYTON
CUMBERLAND GAP NAT'L HIST. PARK
GREAT SMOKY MTS. NATIONAL PARK
Mt. Mitchell 6,684 ft. (2037 m.)
Black Mountain 4,145 ft. (1263 m.)
Mt. Guyot 6,621 ft. (2018 m.)
Clingmans Dome 6,643 ft. (2025 m.)

Topography

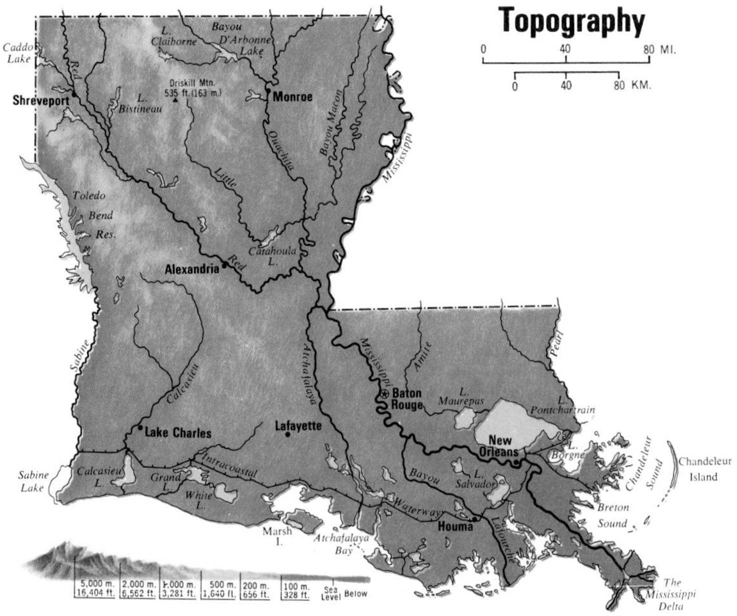
Topography
0 40 80 MI.
0 40 80 KM.
Caddo Lake
L. Claiborne
Bayou D'Arbonne Lake
Driskill Mtn. 535 ft. (163 m.)
Shreveport
L. Bistineau
Monroe
Ouachita
Bayou Macon
Mississippi
Little
Toledo Bend Res.
Catahoula L.
Alexandria
Red
Sabine
Calcasieu
Atchafalaya
Amite
Pearl
Baton Rouge
L. Maurepas
L. Pontchartrain
Lake Charles
Lafayette
New Orleans
L. Borgne
Chandeleur Sound
Chandeleur Island
Sabine Lake
Calcasieu L.
Grand L.
White L.
Intracoastal Waterway
Bayou
L. Salvador
Breton Sound
Houma
Lafourche
Marsh I.
Atchafalaya Bay
The Mississippi Delta
5,000 m. 16,404 ft.
2,000 m. 6,562 ft.
1,000 m. 3,281 ft.
500 m. 1,640 ft.
200 m. 656 ft.
100 m. 328 ft.
Sea Level
Below

Louisiana
SCALE
0 5 10 20 30 40 MI.
0 5 10 20 30 40 KM.
State Capitals
Parish Seats
Canals
Major Limited Access Hwys.
A R K A N S A S
T E X A S
G U L F O F
SHREVEPORT
Bossier City
Minden
Natchitoches
Alexandria
Leesville
De Ridder
LAKE CHARLES
Sulphur
Jennings
Toledo Bend Res.
Sam Rayburn Reservoir
Beaumont
Port Arthur
Orange
Sabine Lake
C A D D O
B O S S I E R
W E B S T E R
C L A I B O R N E
L I N C O L N
B I E N V I L L E
D E S O T O
R E D R I V E R
N A T C H I T O C H E S
S A B I N E
W I N N
G R A N T
R A P I D E S
V E R N O N
B E A U R E G A R D
A L L E N
C A L C A S I E U
J E F F E R S O N D A V I S
C A M E R O N

PARISHES

Acadia 56,427 .... F6
Allen 21,390 .... E5
Ascension 50,068 .... L3
Assumption 22,084 .... H7
Avoyelles 41,393 .... G4
Beauregard 29,692 .... D5
Bienville 16,387 .... D2
Bossier 80,721 .... C1
Caddo 252,437 .... C1
Calcasieu 167,223 .... D6
Caldwell 10,761 .... F2
Cameron 9,336 .... D7
Catahoula 12,287 .... G3
Claiborne 17,095 .... D1
Concordia 22,981 .... G4
De Soto 25,727 .... C2
East Baton Rouge 366,191 .... K1
East Carroll 11,772 .... H1
East Feliciana 19,015 .... H5
Evangeline 33,343 .... F5
Franklin 24,141 .... G2
Grant 16,703 .... E3
Iberia 63,752 .... G7
Iberville 32,159 .... H6
Jackson 17,321 .... E2
Jefferson 454,592 .... K7
Jefferson Davis 32,168 .... E6
La Salle 17,004 .... F3
Lafayette 150,017 .... F6
Lafourche 82,483 .... K7
Lincoln 39,763 .... E1
Livingston 58,806 .... L2
Madison 15,682 .... H2
Morehouse 34,803 .... G1
Natchitoches 39,863 .... D3
Orleans 557,927 .... L6
Ouachita 139,241 .... F2
Plaquemines 26,049 .... L8
Pointe Coupee 24,045 .... G5
Rapides 135,282 .... E4
Red River 10,433 .... D2
Richland 22,187 .... G2
Sabine 25,280 .... C3
Saint Bernard 64,097 .... L7
Saint Charles 37,259 .... K7
Saint Helena 9,827 .... J5
Saint James 21,495 .... L3
Saint John the Baptist 31,924 .... M3
Saint Landry 84,128 .... F5
Saint Martin 40,214 .... G6
Saint Mary 64,253 .... H7
Saint Tammany 110,869 .... L6
Tangipahoa 80,698 .... K5
Tensas 8,525 .... H2
Terrebonne 94,393 .... J8
Union 21,167 .... F1
Vermilion 48,458 .... F7
Vernon 53,475 .... D4
Washington 44,207 .... K5
Webster 43,631 .... D1
West Baton Rouge 19,086 .... H6
West Carroll 12,922 .... H1
West Feliciana 12,186 .... H5
Winn 17,253 .... E3

CITIES and TOWNS

Abbeville▲ 11,187 .... F7
Abita Springs 1,296 .... L6
Acme 235 .... G4
Acy 570 .... L3
Addis 1,222 .... J2
Adeline 200 .... G7
Akers 150 .... N2
Albany 645 .... M1
Alberta 150 .... D2
Alexandria▲ 49,188 .... E4
Allen 175 .... D3
Alto 132 .... G2
Alton 500 .... L6
Amelia 2,447 .... H7
Amite▲ 4,301 .... K5
Anacoco 823 .... D4
Anandale F4
Andrew 100 .... F6
Angie 235 .... L5
Angola 600 .... G5
Ansley 100 .... E2
Arabi 8,787 .... P4
Arbroth 250 .... H5
Arcadia▲ 3,079 .... E1
Archibald 425 .... G2
Archie 280 .... G3
Arcola 200 .... K5
Arnaudville 1,444 .... G6
Ashland 289 .... D2
Athens 278 .... E1
Atlanta 118 .... E3
Avery Island 500 .... G7
Bains 400 .... H5
Baker 13,233 .... K1
Baldwin 2,379 .... G7
Ball 3,305 .... F4
Bancroft 114 .... C5
Baptist 150 .... M1
Barataria 1,160 .... K7
Basile 1,808 .... E5
Baskin 243 .... G2
Bastrop▲ 13,916 .... G1
Batchelor 500 .... G5
Baton Rouge (cap.)▲ 219,531 .... K2
Bayou Barbary 200 .... M2
Bayou Cane 15,876 .... J7
Bayou Goula 850 .... J3
Bayou Vista 4,733 .... H7
Baywood 100 .... K1
Beaver 350 .... E5
Beekman 150 .... G1
Bel 150 .... D6
Belcher 249 .... C1
Bell City 400 .... D6
Belle Alliance H6
Belle Chasse 8,512 .... O4
Belle D'Eau 120 .... F4
Belle Rose 900 .... K3
Bellwood 150 .... D3
Belmont 350 .... C3
Benson 200 .... C3
Bentley 120 .... E3
Benton▲ 2,047 .... C1
Bernice 1,543 .... E1
Bertrandville 175 .... L7
Berwick 4,375 .... H7
Bethany 300 .... B2
Bienville 316 .... D2
Blanchard 1,175 .... C1
Bogalusa 14,280 .... L5
Bolinger 200 .... C1
Bonita 265 .... G1
Boothville 300 .... M8
Bordelonville 350 .... G4
Bosco 480 .... F2
Bossier City 52,721 .... C1
Boudreaux 275 .... J8
Bourg 2,073 .... J7
Boutte 2,702 .... N4
Boyce 1,361 .... E4
Braithwaite 350 .... P4
Branch 200 .... F6
Breaux Bridge 6,515 .... G6
Brittany 475 .... L3
Broussard 3,213 .... G6
Brusly 1,824 .... J2
Bryceland 103 .... E2
Buckeye 280 .... F4
Bunkie 5,044 .... F5
Buras (Buras-Triumph) 4,137 .... L8
Burnside 500 .... L3
Bush 275 .... L5
Cade 175 .... G6
Calcasieu 400 .... E4
Calhoun 350 .... F2
Calumet 100 .... H7
Calvin 207 .... E3
Cameron▲ 2,041 .... D7
Campti 929 .... D3
Cankton 323 .... F6
Carencro 5,429 .... G6
Carlisle 975 .... L7
Carville 1,108 .... K3
Castor 196 .... D2
Cecelia 550 .... G6
Center Point 850 .... F4
Centerville 600 .... H7
Central 546 .... L3
Chacahoula 150 .... J7
Chalmette▲ 31,860 .... P4
Charenton 1,584 .... H7
Chase 200 .... G2
Chataignier 281 .... F5
Chatham 617 .... F2
Chauvin 3,375 .... J8
Cheneyville 1,005 .... F4
Chopin 175 .... E4
Choudrant 557 .... F1
Church Point 4,677 .... F6
Clarence 577 .... E3
Clarks 650 .... F2
Clay 400 .... E2
Clayton 917 .... H3
Clear Lake 100 .... E3
Clinton▲ 1,904 .... J5
Clio 125 .... M2
Cloutierville 100 .... E3
Colfax▲ 1,696 .... E3
Collinston 375 .... G1
Columbia▲ 386 .... F2
Convent▲ 400 .... L3
Converse 436 .... C3
Corey 110 .... F2
Cotton Valley 1,130 .... D1
Cottonport 2,600 .... F5
Couchwood 150 .... D1
Coushatta▲ 1,845 .... D2
Covington▲ 7,691 .... K5
Cow Island 200 .... F7
Cravens 200 .... E5
Creole 175 .... D7
Crescent 300 .... J2
Creston 135 .... E3
Crowley▲ 13,983 .... F6
Crowville 400 .... G2
Cullen 1,642 .... D1
Curtis 110 .... C2
Cut Off 5,325 .... K7
Dalcour 275 .... P4
Danville 100 .... E2
Darrow 500 .... K3
Davant 600 .... L7
De Quincy 3,474 .... D6
De Ridder▲ 9,868 .... D5
Deerford 100 .... K1
Delcambre 1,978 .... G7
Delhi 3,169 .... H2
Delta 234 .... J2
Denham Springs 8,381 .... L2
Des Allemands 2,504 .... N4
Destrehan 8,031 .... N4
Deville 1,113 .... F4
Diamond 370 .... L7
Dixie 330 .... C1
Dixie Inn 347 .... D1
Dodson 350 .... E2
Donaldsonville▲ 7,949 .... K3
Donner 500 .... J7
Downsville 101 .... F1
Doyline 884 .... D1
Dry Creek 300 .... D5
Dry Prong 380 .... E3
Dubach 843 .... E1
Dubberly 253 .... D1
Dulac 3,273 .... J8
Dunn 225 .... G2
Duplessis 500 .... K2
Duson 1,465 .... F6
East Hodge 421 .... E2
East Point 100 .... D2
Easton 365 .... F5
Echo 525 .... F4
Edgard▲ 2,753 .... M3
Edgefield 207 .... D2
Edgerly 250 .... C6
Effie 300 .... F4
Elizabeth 414 .... E5
Elm Grove 100 .... C2
Elm Park 200 .... H5
Elmer 200 .... E4
Elton 1,277 .... E6
Empire 2,654 .... L8
Enterprise 375 .... G3
Epps 541 .... G1
Erath 2,428 .... F7
Eros 177 .... F2
Erwinville 790 .... H5
Esther 745 .... F7
Estherwood 745 .... F6
Ethel 250 .... H5
Eunice 11,162 .... F6
Eva 100 .... G4
Evangeline 400 .... F6
Evans 500 .... D5
Evergreen 283 .... F5
Extension 950 .... G3
Fairbanks 300 .... F1
Farmerville▲ 3,334 .... F1
Fenton 265 .... E6
Ferriday 4,111 .... G3
Fields 125 .... C5
Fisher 277 .... D4
Flatwoods 360 .... E4
Flora 300 .... D3
Florien 626 .... D4
Fluker 400 .... K5
Folsom 469 .... K5
Forbing 100 .... C2
Fordoche 869 .... G5
Forest 263 .... H1
Forest Hill 408 .... E4
Fort Jesup 100 .... C3
Fort Necessity 150 .... G2
Franklin▲ 9,004 .... G7
Franklinton▲ 4,007 .... K5
French Settlement 829 .... L2
Frierson 700 .... C2
Frost 500 .... L2
Fryeburg 150 .... D2
Fullerton 120 .... D4
Galliano 4,294 .... K8
Galvez 200 .... L2
Garden City 225 .... H7
Garyville 3,181 .... M3

(continued)

UNION, JUSTICE & CONFIDENCE

AREA 47,752 sq. mi. (123,678 sq. km.)
POPULATION 4,238,216
CAPITAL Baton Rouge
LARGEST CITY New Orleans
HIGHEST POINT Driskill Mtn. 535 ft. (163 m.)
SETTLED IN 1699
ADMITTED TO UNION April 30, 1812
POPULAR NAME Pelican State
STATE FLOWER Magnolia
STATE BIRD Eastern Brown Pelican

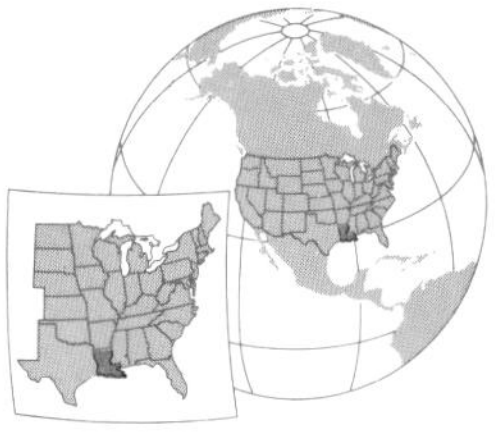

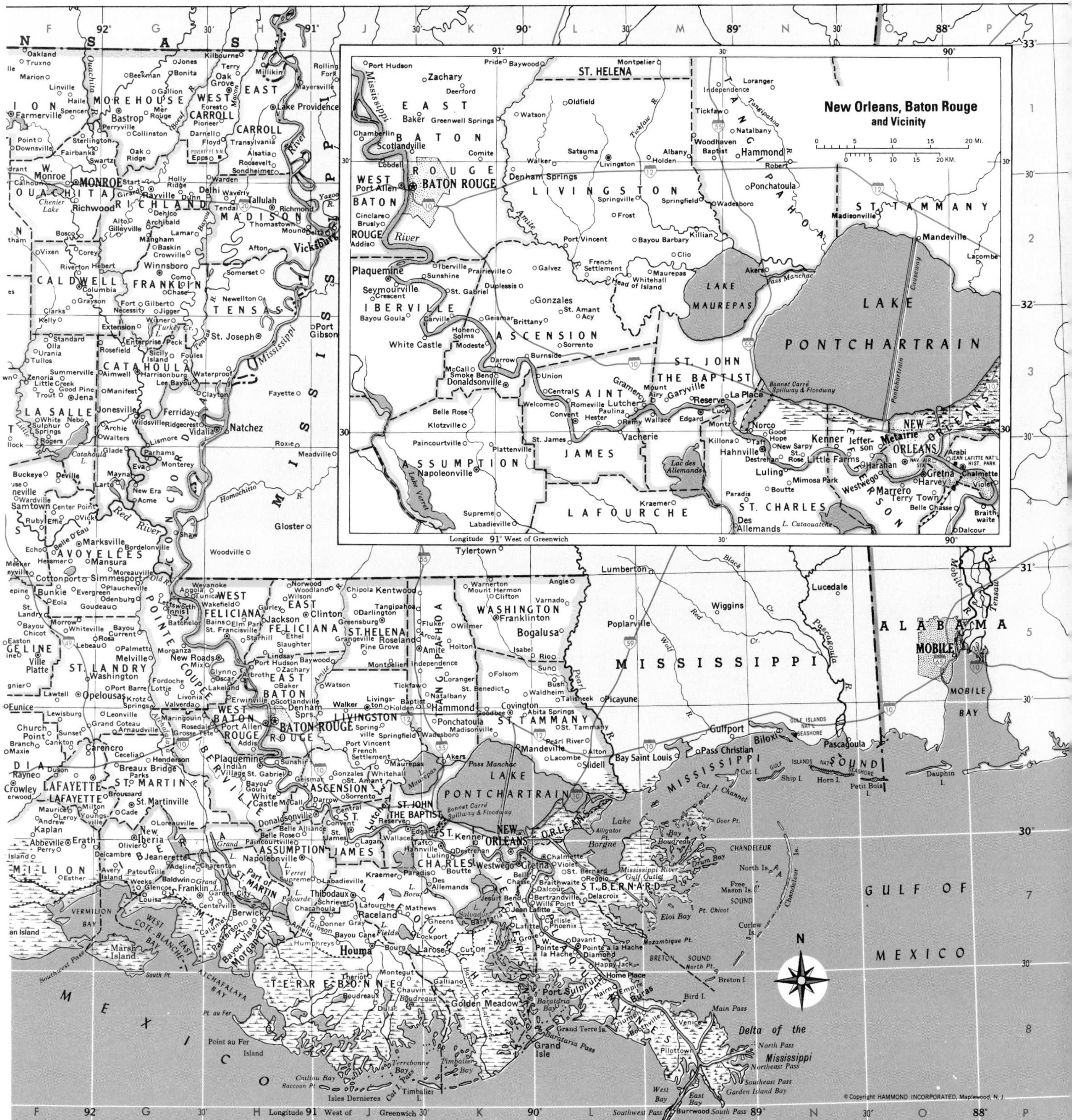
New Orleans, Baton Rouge
and Vicinity
EAST BATON ROUGE
WEST BATON ROUGE
ST. HELENA
LIVINGSTON
TANGIPAHOA
ST. TAMMANY
IBERVILLE
ASCENSION
ST. JOHN THE BAPTIST
SAINT JAMES
ASSUMPTION
LAFOURCHE
ST. CHARLES
JEFFERSON
ORLEANS
LAKE MAUREPAS
LAKE PONTCHARTRAIN
BATON ROUGE
NEW ORLEANS
Longitude 91° West of Greenwich
MOREHOUSE
WEST CARROLL
EAST CARROLL
OUACHITA
RICHLAND
MADISON
CALDWELL
FRANKLIN
TENSAS
CATAHOULA
LA SALLE
CONCORDIA
AVOYELLES
ST. LANDRY
POINTE COUPEE
WEST FELICIANA
EAST FELICIANA
LAFAYETTE
ST. MARTIN
IBERIA
ST. MARY
TERREBONNE
PLAQUEMINES
ST. BERNARD
MISSISSIPPI
ALABAMA
MOBILE
GULF OF MEXICO
MISSISSIPPI SOUND
CHANDELEUR SOUND
BRETON SOUND
Delta of the Mississippi
Longitude 91° West of Greenwich
© Copyright HAMMOND INCORPORATED, Maplewood, N.J.

Geismar 300 ..... K3
Georgetown 273 ..... F3
Gheens 350 ..... K7
Gibsland 1,354 ..... E1
Gibson 950 ..... J7
Gilbert 704 ..... G2
Gilleyville G2
Gilliam 202 ..... C1
Girard 150 ..... G2
Glencoe 200 ..... G7
Glenmora 1,686 ..... E5
Gloster 780 ..... C2
Glynn 700 ..... H5
Golden Meadow 2,049 ..... K8
Goldonna 417 ..... D2
Gonzales 7,003 ..... L2
Good Hope 500 ..... N4
Good Pine (Good Pine-Trout) 1,033 ..... F3
Gorum 150 ..... E4
Grambling 5,484 ..... E1
Gramercy 2,412 ..... M3
Grand Cane 233 ..... C2
Grand Chenier 710 ..... E7
Grand Coteau 1,118 ..... G6
Grand Isle 1,455 ..... L8
Grand Lake 400 ..... D6
Grant 225 ..... E5
Gray 4,260 ..... J7
Grayson 529 ..... F2
Greensburg▲ 583 ..... J5
Greenwell Springs 350 ..... K1
Greenwood 2,092 ..... B2
Gretna▲ 17,208 ..... O4
Grosse Tete 541 ..... G6
Gueydan 1,611 ..... E6
Gurley 150 ..... H5
Hackberry 1,664 ..... D7
Hahnville▲ 2,599 ..... N4
Haile 300 ..... F1
Hall Summit 227 ..... D2
Hammond 15,871 ..... N1
Hanna 138 ..... D3
Happy Jack 800 ..... L7
Harahan 9,927 ..... O4
Harrisonburg▲ 453 ..... G3
Harvey 21,222 ..... O4
Haughton 1,664 ..... C1
Hawthorn 400 ..... D4
Hayes 600 ..... E6
Haynesville 2,854 ..... D1
Head of Island 420 ..... L2
Hebert 150 ..... G2
Heflin 253 ..... D2
Henderson 1,543 ..... G6
Hessmer 578 ..... F4
Hester 250 ..... L3
Hicks 379 ..... E4
Hico 120 ..... E1
Hineston 400 ..... E4
Hodge 562 ..... E2
Hohen Solms 125 ..... K3
Holden 600 ..... M1
Holly Ridge 100 ..... G2
Hollywood D6
Home Place 600 ..... L8
Homer▲ 4,152 ..... D1
Hornbeck 427 ..... D4
Hosston 417 ..... C1
Houma▲ 30,495 ..... J7
Humphreys 900 ..... J7
Iberville 367 ..... K2
Ida 250 ..... C1
Independence 1,632 ..... M1
Indian Village 100 ..... H6
Innis 3,474 ..... G5
Iota 1,256 ..... E6
Iowa 2,588 ..... D6
Isabel 550 ..... K5
Ivan 125 ..... C1
Jackson 3,891 ..... H5
Jamestown 148 ..... D2
Jean Lafitte 1,469 ..... K7
Jeanerette 6,205 ..... G7
Jefferson 14,521 ..... O4
Jena▲ 2,626 ..... F3
Jennings▲ 11,305 ..... E6
Jesuit Bend 100 ..... K7
Jigger 300 ..... G2
Johnsons Bayou 300 ..... C7
Jones 4,305 ..... G1
Jonesboro▲ 4,305 ..... E2
Jonesville 2,720 ..... G3
Joyce 700 ..... E3
Junction City 749 ..... E1
Kaplan 4,535 ..... F6
Keatchie 342 ..... C2
Keithville 500 ..... C2
Kelly 325 ..... F3
Kenner 72,033 ..... N4
Kentwood 2,468 ..... J5
Kilbourne 409 ..... H1
Killian 721 ..... M2
Killona 950 ..... M4
Kinder 2,246 ..... E6
Kisatchie 150 ..... D4
Klotzville 248 ..... K3
Kraemer 350 ..... M4
Krotz Springs 1,285 ..... G5
La Place 24,194 ..... N3
Labadieville 1,821 ..... K4
Lacamp 150 ..... E4
Lacassine 400 ..... E6
Lacombe 6,523 ..... L6
Lafayette▲ 94,440 ..... F6
Lafitte 1,507 ..... K7
Lafourche 200 ..... J7
Lagan L7
Lake Arthur 3,194 ..... E6
Lake Charles▲ 70,580 ..... D6
Lake Providence▲ 5,380 ..... H1
Lakeland 800 ..... H5
Larose 5,772 ..... K7
Larto 500 ..... G4
Lawtell 1,014 ..... F5
Le Blanc 400 ..... E5
Leander 145 ..... E4

DOMINANT LAND USE

- Specialized Cotton
- Cotton, General Farming
- Cotton, Livestock
- Cotton, Sugarcane
- Cotton, Forest Products
- Truck and Mixed Farming
- General Farming, Forest Products, Truck Farming, Cotton
- Sugarcane, General Farming
- Rice, General Farming
- Forests
- Swampland, Limited Agriculture

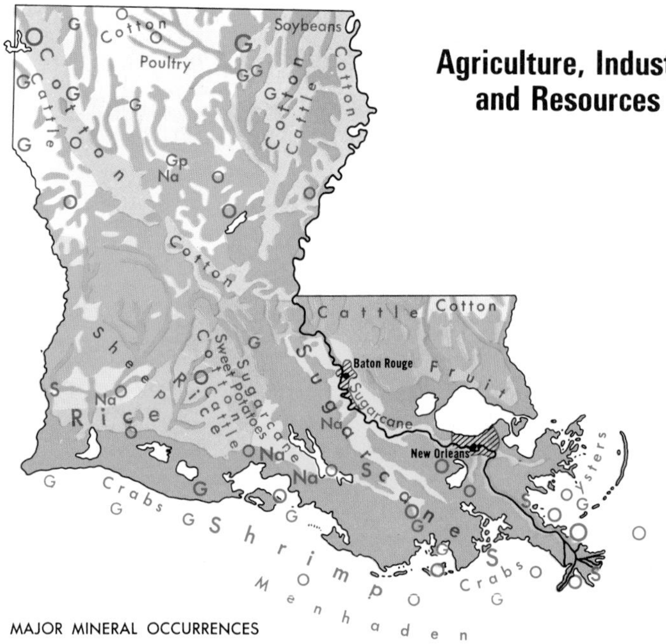
Cotton
Poultry
Soybeans
Cattle
Cotton
Cattle
Cotton
Gp
Na
Cotton
Cattle
Cotton
Sheep
Rice
Sweet Potatoes
Sugarcane
Sugarcane
Fruit
Baton Rouge
New Orleans
Oysters
Crabs
Shrimp
Menhaden

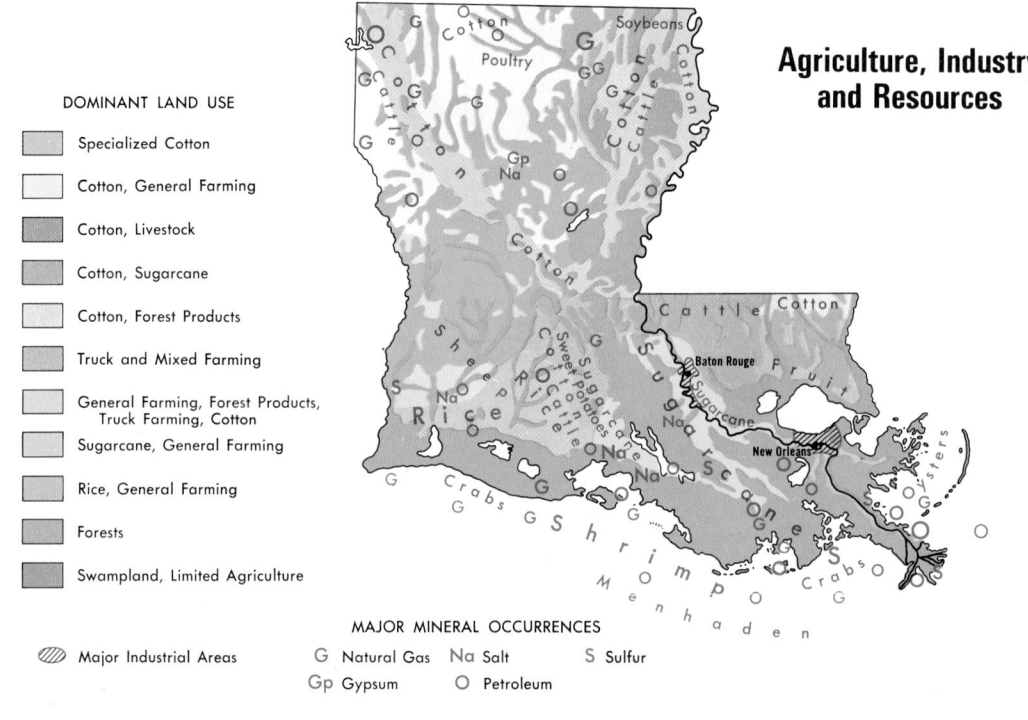

Agriculture, Industry and Resources

MAJOR MINERAL OCCURRENCES

- Major Industrial Areas
- G Natural Gas
- Na Salt
- S Sulfur
- Gp Gypsum
- O Petroleum

Lebeau 200 ..... F5
Lecompte 1,661 ..... F4
Leesville▲ 7,638 ..... D4
Lena 300 ..... E4
Leonville 825 ..... G6
Leton 125 ..... D1
Lettsworth 200 ..... G5
Lewisburg 265 ..... F6
Libuse 500 ..... F4
Lillie 145 ..... E1
Linville 150 ..... F1
Lisbon 160 ..... E1
Lismore 380 ..... G3
Little Farms N4
Livingston▲ 999 ..... L1
Livonia 970 ..... G5
Lobdell 200 ..... J1
Lockport 2,503 ..... K7
Logansport 1,390 ..... C3
Lonepine 850 ..... F5
Longstreet 189 ..... B2
Longville 300 ..... D5
Loranger 250 ..... N1
Loreauville 860 ..... G6
Lottie 400 ..... G5
Lucky 342 ..... E2
Lucy 825 ..... M3
Luling 2,803 ..... N4
Lunita 100 ..... C6
Lutcher 3,907 ..... L3
Madisonville 659 ..... K6
Mamou 3,483 ..... F5
Mandeville 7,083 ..... L6
Mangham 598 ..... G2
Mansfield▲ 5,389 ..... C2
Mansura 1,601 ..... G4
Many▲ 3,112 ..... C3
Maplewood D6
Maringouin 1,149 ..... G6
Marion 775 ..... F1
Marksville▲ 5,526 ..... G4
Marrero 36,671 ..... O4
Marthaville 150 ..... D3
Martin 545 ..... D2
Mathews 3,009 ..... J7
Maurepas 200 ..... M2
Maurice 432 ..... F6
Mayna 122 ..... G4
McCall 150 ..... K3
McNary 248 ..... E5
Melder 150 ..... E4
Melrose 500 ..... E3
Melville 1,562 ..... G5
Mer Rouge 586 ..... G1
Mermentau 760 ..... E6
Merryville 1,235 ..... D5
Metairie 149,428 ..... O4
Midland 560 ..... F6
Milton 450 ..... F6
Mimosa Park 4,516 ..... N4
Minden▲ 13,661 ..... D1
Mira 354 ..... C1
Mitchell 155 ..... C3
Mix 150 ..... G5
Modeste 225 ..... K3
Monroe▲ 54,909 ..... F1
Montegut 1,784 ..... J8
Monterey 800 ..... G4
Montgomery 645 ..... E3
Montpelier 247 ..... M1
Montz 200 ..... M3
Mooringsport 873 ..... B1
Mora 427 ..... E4
Moreauville 919 ..... G4
Morgan City 14,531 ..... H7
Morganza 759 ..... G5
Morrow 600 ..... F5
Morse 782 ..... F6
Mound 16 ..... H2
Mount Airy 700 ..... M3
Mount Hermon 170 ..... K5
Mount Lebanon 102 ..... D2
Myrtle Grove 100 ..... K7
Nairn 500 ..... L8
Napoleonville▲ 802 ..... K4
Natalbany 1,289 ..... N1
Natchez 434 ..... D3
Natchitoches▲ 16,609 ..... D3
Nebo 200 ..... F3
Negreet 400 ..... C4
New Era 200 ..... G4
New Iberia▲ 31,828 ..... G6
New Orleans▲ 496,938 ..... O4
New Roads▲ 5,303 ..... G5
New Sarpy 2,946 ..... N4
Newellton 1,576 ..... H2
Newllano 2,660 ..... D4
Noble 225 ..... C3
Norco 3,385 ..... N3
North Hodge 477 ..... E2
Norwood 317 ..... H5
Oak Grove▲ 2,126 ..... H1
Oak Ridge 174 ..... G1
Oakdale 6,832 ..... E5
Oberlin▲ 1,808 ..... E5
Odenburg 175 ..... G5
Oil City 1,282 ..... C1
Olivier 300 ..... G7
Olla 1,410 ..... F3
Opelousas▲ 18,151 ..... G5
Oretta 110 ..... D5
Oscar 650 ..... H5
Otis 400 ..... E4
Oxford 125 ..... C3
Paincourtville 1,550 ..... K3
Palmetto 229 ..... G5
Paradis 750 ..... M4
Parhams 100 ..... G4
Parks 400 ..... G6
Patoutville 230 ..... G7
Patterson 4,736 ..... H7
Paulina 500 ..... L3
Pearl River 1,507 ..... L6
Peason 120 ..... D4
Pecan Island 480 ..... F7
Pelican 250 ..... C3
Perry 230 ..... F7
Perryville 100 ..... G1
Phoenix 525 ..... L7
Pilottown 175 ..... M8
Pine Grove 570 ..... J5
Pine Prairie 713 ..... E5
Pineville 12,251 ..... F4
Pioneer 116 ..... H1
Pitkin 600 ..... E5
Plain Dealing 1,074 ..... C1
Plaquemine▲ 7,186 ..... J2
Plattenville 205 ..... K4
Plaucheville 187 ..... G5
Pleasant Hill 824 ..... C3
Pointe a la Hache▲ 750 ..... L7
Pollock 330 ..... F3
Ponchatoula 5,425 ..... N2
Port Allen▲ 6,277 ..... J2
Port Barre 2,144 ..... G5
Port Hudson 200 ..... J1
Port Sulphur 3,523 ..... L8
Port Vincent 446 ..... L2
Powhatan 147 ..... D3
Prairieville 500 ..... K2
Pride 100 ..... K1
Princeton 350 ..... C1
Provencal 538 ..... D3
Quitman 162 ..... E2
Raceland 5,564 ..... J7
Rayne 8,502 ..... F6
Rayville▲ 4,411 ..... G2
Reddell 500 ..... F5
Reeves 188 ..... D5
Reggio 400 ..... L7
Remy 850 ..... L3
Reserve 8,847 ..... M3
Richmond 447 ..... H2
Richwood 1,253 ..... F2
Ridgecrest 804 ..... G3
Ringgold 1,655 ..... D2
Rio 400 ..... L5
Roanoke 800 ..... E6
Robeline 149 ..... D3
Robert 600 ..... N1
Rocky Mount 150 ..... C1
Rodessa 294 ..... B1
Rogers 150 ..... F3
Romeville 133 ..... L3
Rosa 300 ..... G5
Rosedale 807 ..... G6
Roseland 1,093 ..... J5
Rosepine 1,135 ..... D5
Ruby 400 ..... F4
Ruston▲ 20,027 ..... E1
Saint Amant 900 ..... L2
Saint Benedict 190 ..... K5
Saint Bernard 750 ..... L7
Saint Francisville▲ 1,700 ..... H5
Saint Gabriel 975 ..... K2
Saint James 600 ..... L3
Saint Joseph▲ 1,517 ..... H3
Saint Landry 550 ..... F5
Saint Martinville▲ 7,137 ..... G6
Saint Maurice 560 ..... E3
Saint Rose 6,259 ..... N4
Saint Tammany 150 ..... L6
Saline 272 ..... E2
Samtown F4
Sarepta 886 ..... D1
Schriever 4,958 ..... J7
Scotlandville 15,113 ..... J1
Scott 4,912 ..... F6
Seymourville 2,891 ..... J2
Shongaloo 161 ..... D1
Shreveport▲ 198,525 ..... C2
Sibley 997 ..... D1
Sicily Island 421 ..... G3
Sieper 226 ..... E4
Sikes 120 ..... F2
Simmesport 2,092 ..... G5
Simpson 536 ..... D4
Simsboro 634 ..... E1
Singer 250 ..... D5
Slagle 650 ..... D4
Slaughter 827 ..... H5
Slidell 24,124 ..... L6
Smoke Bend 300 ..... K3
Sondheimer 225 ..... H1
Sorrento 1,119 ..... L3
South Mansfield 407 ..... C3
Spearsville 132 ..... E1
Springfield 439 ..... M2
Springhill 5,668 ..... D1
Standard 190 ..... F3
Stanley 131 ..... C3
Starks 750 ..... C6
Start 200 ..... G2
Sterlington 1,140 ..... F1
Stonewall 1,266 ..... C2
Sugartown 375 ..... D5
Sulphur 20,125 ..... D6
Summerfield 170 ..... E1
Sun 429 ..... L5
Sunset 2,201 ..... F6
Sunshine 900 ..... K2
Supreme 1,020 ..... K4
Swartz 3,698 ..... G1
Sweet Lake 300 ..... D7
Talisheek 315 ..... L5
Tallulah▲ 8,526 ..... H2
Tangipahoa 569 ..... J5
Taylor 500 ..... D1
Taylortown 150 ..... C2
Temple 250 ..... E4
Tendal 200 ..... H2
Terry Town 23,548 ..... O4
Theriot 450 ..... J8
Thibodaux▲ 14,035 ..... J7
Tickfaw 565 ..... M1
Tioga 457 ..... F4
Toro 100 ..... C4
Transylvania 400 ..... H1
Trees 327 ..... B1
Triumph (Triumph-Buras) 4,137 ..... L8
Trout (Trout-Good Pine) 1,033 ..... F3
Tullos 427 ..... F3
Tunica 500 ..... G5
Turkey Creek 283 ..... F5
Union 665 ..... L3
Urania 782 ..... F3
Vacherie 2,169 ..... L3
Valverda 200 ..... G5
Varnado 236 ..... L5
Venice 900 ..... M8
Vernon 150 ..... E2
Vick 500 ..... F4
Vidalia▲ 4,953 ..... G3
Vienna 404 ..... E1
Ville Platte▲ 9,037 ..... F5
Vinton 3,154 ..... C6
Violet 8,574 ..... P4
Vivian 4,156 ..... B1
Wadesboro 125 ..... M2
Wakefield 400 ..... H5
Walker 3,727 ..... L1
Wallace 200 ..... M3
Walters 500 ..... G3
Warden 130 ..... H1
Wardville F4
Washington 1,253 ..... G5
Waterproof 1,080 ..... H3
Watson 800 ..... L1
Waverly 350 ..... H2
Weeks 400 ..... G7
Welcome 450 ..... L3
Welsh 3,299 ..... E6
West Monroe 14,096 ..... F1
West Pointe a la Hache 250 ..... L7
Westlake 5,007 ..... D6
Westwego 11,218 ..... O4
Weyanoke 500 ..... H5
White Castle 2,102 ..... J3
Whitehall 380 ..... M2
Whiteville 150 ..... F5
Wildsville 800 ..... G3
Wills Point 150 ..... L7
Wilson 707 ..... H5
Winnfield▲ 6,138 ..... E3
Winnsboro▲ 5,755 ..... G2
Wisner 1,153 ..... G3
Woodhaven M1
Woodlawn 150 ..... E6
Woodworth 754 ..... E4
Youngsville 1,195 ..... G6
Zachary 9,036 ..... K1
Zwolle 1,779 ..... C3

OTHER FEATURES

Allemands (lake) M4
Alligator (pt.) L6
Amite (riv.) L2
Anacoco (lake) D4
Atchafalaya (bay) H8
Atchafalaya (riv.) G6
Barataria (bay) L8
Barataria (passage) L8
Barksdale A.F.B. C2
Bayou D'Arbonne (lake) E1
Bird (isl.) M8
Bistineau (lake) D2
Black (lake) D3
Black Lake (bayou) D1
Boeuf (lake) J7
Boeuf (riv.) G1
Bonnet Carré Spillway and Floodway N3
Borgne (lake) L7
Boudreau (bay) M7
Boudreaux (lake) J8
Breton (isl.) M8
Breton (sound) M7
Bundick (lake) D5
Caddo (lake) B1
Caillou (bay) J8
Calcasieu (lake) D7
Calcasieu (passage) D7
Calcasieu (riv.) E5
Catahoula (lake) F4
Cataouatche (lake) N4
Cat Island (chan.) M6
Cat Island (passage) J8
Chandeleur (isls.) N7
Chandeleur (sound) M7
Chenier (lake) F2
Chicot (pt.) M7
Claiborne (lake) E1
Clear (lake) D3
Cocodrie (lake) E5
Cotile (lake) E4
Cross (lake) C2
Curlew (isls.) M7
Dernieres (isls.) J8
Door (pt.) M6
Driskill (mt.) E2
Drum (bay) M7
East (bay) M8
East Cote Blanche (bay) G7
Edwards (lake) C2
Eloi (bay) M7
England A.F.B. E4
Fields (lake) J7
Fort Polk 14,730 ..... D4
Free Mason (isls.) M7
Garden Island (bay) M8
Grand (lake) E7
Grand (lake) H7
Grand Terre (isls.) L8
Iatt (lake) E3
Jean Lafitte Nat'l Hist. Park P4
Lafourche (bayou) K8
Little (riv.) F3
Louisiana (pt.) C7
Macon (bayou) H1
Main (passage) M8
Manchac (passage) N2
Marsh (isl.) G7
Maurepas (lake) M2
Mermentau (riv.) E7
Mexico (gulf) F8
Mississippi (delta) M8
Mississippi (riv.) H3
Mississippi (sound) M6
Mississippi River Gulf Outlet (canal) L7
Mozambique (pt.) M7
Mud (lake) D7
Naval Air Sta. O4
North (isls.) M7
North (pass) N8
North (pt.) M7
Northeast (pass) M8
Ouachita (riv.) F1
Palourde (lake) H7
Pearl (riv.) L5
Point au Fer (isl.) H8
Point au Fer (pt.) H8
Pontchartrain (lake) O3
Pontchartrain Causeway O3
Poverty Pt. Nat'l Mon H1
Raccoon (pt.) H8
Red (riv.) G4
Sabine (lake) C7
Sabine (passage) C7
Sabine (riv.) C5
Saline (lake) E3
Salvador (lake) K7
Smithport (lake) C2
South (pass) M8
South (pt.) G8
Southeast (pass) M8
Southwest (pass) L8
Tangipahoa (riv.) N1
Tensas (riv.) G3
Terrebonne (bay) J8
Tickfaw (riv.) M1
Timbalier (bay) K8
Timbalier (isl.) K8
Toledo Bend (res.) C3
Turkey Creek (lake) G3
Vermilion (bay) F7
Vernon (lake) D4
Verret (lake) H7
Wallace (lake) C2
West (bay) M8
West Cote Blanche (bay) G7
White (lake) E7

▲ Parish seat

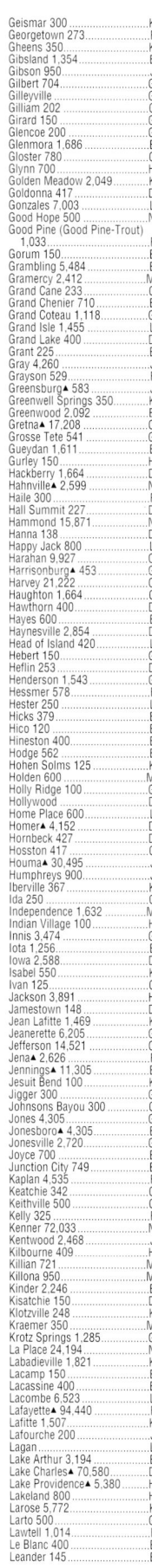

AREA 33,265 sq. mi. (86,156 sq. km.)
POPULATION 1,233,223
CAPITAL Augusta
LARGEST CITY Portland
HIGHEST POINT Katahdin 5,268 ft. (1606 m.)
SETTLED IN 1624
ADMITTED TO UNION March 15, 1820
POPULAR NAME Pine Tree State
STATE FLOWER White Pine Cone & Tassel
STATE BIRD Chickadee

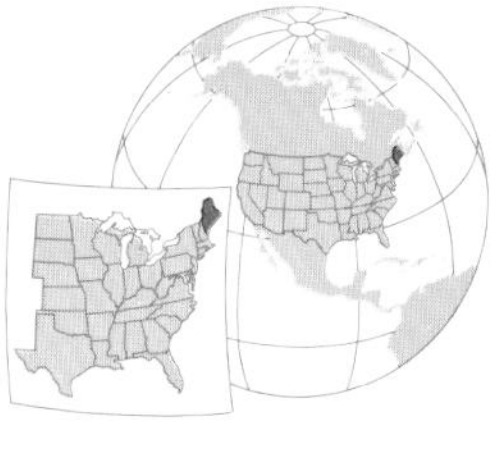

COUNTIES

Androscoggin 105,259 .... C7
Aroostook 86,936 .... F2
Cumberland 243,135 .... C8
Franklin 29,008 .... B5
Hancock 46,948 .... G6
Kennebec 115,904 .... D7
Knox 36,310 .... E7
Lincoln 30,357 .... D7
Oxford 52,602 .... B7
Penobscot 146,601 .... F5
Piscataquis 18,653 .... E4
Sagadahoc 33,535 .... D7
Somerset 49,767 .... C4
Waldo 33,018 .... E6
Washington 35,308 .... H6
York 164,587 .... B9

CITIES and TOWNS

Abbot Village • 576 .... D5
Acton 850 .... B8
Acton • 1,727 .... B8
Addison 350 .... H6
Addison • 1,114 .... H6
Albion • 1,736 .... E6
Alexander • 478 .... H5
Alfred 1,890 .... B9
Alfred • 2,238 .... B9
Allagash • 359 .... F1
Alna • 571 .... D7
Alton • 771 .... F5
Amherst • 226 .... G6
Andover 350 .... B6
Andover • 953 .... B6
Anson 950 .... D6
Anson • 2,382 .... D6
Appleton • 1,069 .... E7
Argyle 202 .... F5
Ashland 750 .... G2
Ashland • 1,542 .... G2
Athens 300 .... D6
Athens • 897 .... D6
Atkinson • 332 .... E5
Auburn▲ 24,309 .... C7
Augusta (cap.)▲ 21,325 .... D7
Aurora • 82 .... G6
Bailey Island 500 .... D8
Bancroft H4
Bancroft • 66 .... H4
Bangor▲ 33,181 .... F6
Bar Harbor 2,685 .... G7
Bar Harbor • 2,768 .... G7
Bar Mills 800 .... C8
Baring 235 .... J5
Baring • 275 .... J5
Bass Harbor 450 .... G7
Bath▲ 9,799 .... D8
Bayside F7
Beals • 667 .... H7
Beddington • 43 .... H6
Belfast▲ 6,355 .... F7
Belgrade 950 .... D7
Belgrade • 2,375 .... D7
Belgrade Lakes 700 .... D6
Beimont • 652 .... E7
Benedicta • 225 .... G4
Benton • 2,312 .... D6
Berwick 2,378 .... B9
Berwick • 5,995 .... B9
Bethel 750 .... B7
Bethel • 2,329 .... B7
Biddeford 20,710 .... B9
Biddeford Pool 500 .... C9
Bingham 1,074 .... D5
Bingham • 1,071 .... D5
Birch Harbor 300 .... H7
Blaine-Mars Hill 1,921 .... H2
Blaine • 784 .... H2
Blanchard 78 .... D5
Blue Hill 850 .... F7
Blue Hill • 1,941 .... F7
Bolsters Mills 150 .... B7
Boothbay 200 .... D8
Boothbay • 2,648 .... D8
Boothbay Harbor 1,267 .... D8
Bowdoinham • 2,192 .... D7
Bowerbank • 72 .... E5
Bradford 150 .... F5
Bradford • 1,103 .... F5
Bradley • 1,136 .... F6
Brewer 9,021 .... F6
Bridgewater • 647 .... H3
Bridgton 1,639 .... B7
Bridgton • 2,195 .... B7
Brighton • 94 .... D5
Bristol 450 .... D8
Bristol • 2,326 .... D8
Brooklin • 785 .... F7
Brooks 900 .... E6
Brooksville • 760 .... F7
Brookton 175 .... H4
Brownfield 300 .... B8
Brownfield • 1,034 .... B8
Brownville 600 .... E5
Brownville • 1,506 .... E5
Brownville Junction 950 .... E5
Brunswick 10,990 .... C8
Brunswick • 14,683 .... C8
Bryant Pond 600 .... B7
Buckfield • 1,566 .... C7
Bucks Harbor 300 .... J6
Bucksport 2,853 .... F6
Bucksport • 2,989 .... F6
Burlington • 360 .... G5
Burnham • 961 .... E6
Buxton • 6,494 .... C8
Byron • 111 .... B6
Calais 3,963 .... J5
Cambridge • 490 .... E5
Camden 3,743 .... F7
Camden • 4,022 .... F7
Canaan • 1,636 .... D6
Canton • 951 .... C7
Cape Neddick 2,193 .... B9
Cape Porpoise 500 .... C9
Caratunk 98 .... C5
Cardville 223 .... F5
Caribou 9,415 .... G2
Carmel • 1,906 .... E6
Carrabassett Valley • 325 .... C5
Carroll • 185 .... G5
Carthage • 458 .... C6
Cary • 235 .... H4
Casco 400 .... B7
Casco • 3,018 .... B7
Castine • 1,161 .... F7
Centerville • 30 .... H6
Chapman • 422 .... G2
Charleston • 1,187 .... F5
Charlotte • 271 .... J5
Chebeague Island 900 .... C8
Chelsea • 2,497 .... D7
Cherryfield • 1,183 .... H6
Chester • 442 .... F5
Chesterville • 1,012 .... C6
China 2,918 .... E7
China • 3,713 .... E7
Chisholm 1,653 .... C7
Clifton • 607 .... G6
Clinton 1,305 .... D6
Clinton • 1,485 .... D6
Columbia • 437 .... H6
Columbia Falls • 552 .... H6
Cooper • 124 .... H6
Coopers Mills 200 .... E7
Corea 375 .... H7
Corinna • 2,196 .... E6
Cornish • 1,178 .... B8
Cornville • 1,008 .... D6
Costigan 200 .... F5
Cranberry Isles • 189 .... G7
Crawford • 89 .... H5
Crescent Lake 325 .... C7
Criehaven F8
Crouseville 450 .... G2
Crystal • 303 .... G4
Cumberland Center 2,015 .... C8
Cumberland Center • 1,890 .... C8
Cundys Harbor 150 .... D8
Cushing • 988 .... E7
Cutler 400 .... J6
Cutler • 779 .... J6
Damariscotta • 1,811 .... E7
Damariscotta-Newcastle
1,567 .... E7
Danforth 650 .... H4
Danforth • 710 .... H4
Deblois • 73 .... H6
Dedham • 1,229 .... F6
Deer Isle 600 .... F7
Deer Isle • 1,829 .... F7
Denmark • 855 .... B8
Dennysville • 355 .... J6
Derby 300 .... E5
Detroit • 751 .... E6
Dexter 3,118 .... E5
Dexter • 2,650 .... E5
Dixfield 1,725 .... C6
Dixfield • 1,300 .... C6
Dixmont • 1,007 .... E6
Dover-Foxcroft▲ 2,974 .... E5
Dover-Foxcroft • 3,077 .... E5
Dresden • 1,332 .... D7
Dry Mills 700 .... C8
Dryden 675 .... C6
Dyer Brook • 243 .... G3
Eagle Lake 675 .... F1
Eagle Lake • 942 .... F1
East Andover 250 .... B6
East Baldwin 175 .... B8
East Blue Hill 150 .... G7
East Boothbay 800 .... D8
East Corinth 525 .... F5
East Dixfield 250 .... C6
East Eddington 200 .... F6
East Hiram 198 .... B8
East Holden 600 .... F6
East Lebanon 950 .... B9
East Limington 200 .... B8
East Livermore 500 .... C7
East Machias 850 .... J6
East Machias • 1,218 .... J6
East Madison 400 .... D6
East Millinocket 2,361 .... F4
East Millinocket • 2,075 .... F4
East Parsonfield 400 .... B8
East Peru 200 .... C7
East Poland 200 .... C7
East Stoneham 300 .... B7
East Sullivan 496 .... G6
East Vassalboro 300 .... D7
East Waterboro 365 .... B8
East Wilton 650 .... C6
Easton • 1,291 .... H2
Eastport 1,965 .... K6
Eddington 250 .... F6
Eddington • 1,947 .... F6
Edgecomb • 993 .... D8
Edmunds 430 .... J6
Eliot • 5,329 .... B9
Ellsworth▲ 5,975 .... F6
Enfield 150 .... F5
Enfield • 1,476 .... F5
Etna • 977 .... E6
Eustis • 616 .... B5
Exeter • 937 .... E6
Fairbanks 400 .... C6
Fairfield 3,169 .... D6
Fairfield Center 975 .... D6
Fairfield • 2,794 .... D6
Falmouth 1,655 .... C8
Falmouth • 7,610 .... C8
Farmingdale 2,014 .... D7
Farmingdale • 2,070 .... D7
Farmington▲ 3,583 .... C6
Farmington • 4,197 .... C6
Farmington Falls 500 .... C6
Fayette • 855 .... C7
Five Islands 225 .... D8
Fort Fairfield 2,282 .... H2
Fort Fairfield • 1,729 .... H2
Fort Kent 2,375 .... F1
Fort Kent • 2,123 .... F1
Fort Kent Mills 200 .... F1
Foxcroft 2,974 .... E5
Frankfort • 1,020 .... F6
Franklin 350 .... G6
Franklin • 1,141 .... G6
Freedom • 593 .... E7
Freeport 1,906 .... C8
Freeport • 1,829 .... C8
Frenchboro • 44 .... G7
Frenchville 980 .... G1
Frenchville • 1,338 .... G1
Friendship 700 .... E7
Friendship • 1,099 .... E7
Fryeburg 1,644 .... A7
Fryeburg • 1,580 .... A7
Gardiner • 6,746 .... D7
Garland 300 .... E5
Garland • 1,064 .... E5
Georgetown 190 .... D8
Georgetown • 914 .... D8
Gilead • 204 .... B7
Glen Cove 250 .... E7
Glenburn • 3,198 .... F6
Goodwins Mills 340 .... B8
Goose Rocks Beach 200 .... C9
Gorham 4,052 .... C8
Gorham • 3,618 .... C8
Gouldsboro 498 .... H7
Gouldsboro • 1,986 .... H7
Grand Isle 600 .... G1
Grand Isle • 558 .... G1
Grand Lake Stream • 174 .... H5
Gray 525 .... C8
Gray • 5,904 .... C8
Great Pond • 59 .... G6
Greene • 3,661 .... C7
Greenville • 1,839 .... D5
Greenville 1,601 .... D5
Greenville Junction 650 .... D5
Guilford 1,235 .... E5
Guilford • 1,082 .... E5
Hallowell 2,534 .... D7
Hamlin • 204 .... H1
Hampden 3,538 .... F6
Hampden • 3,895 .... F6
Hampden Highlands 950 .... F6
Hancock • 1,757 .... G6
Hanover • 272 .... B7
Harmony 450 .... D6
Harmony • 838 .... D6
Harpswell • 5,012 .... D8
Harrington • 893 .... H6
Harrison • 1,951 .... B7
Hartford • 722 .... C7
Hartland 1,041 .... D6
Hartland • 1,038 .... D6
Haynesville • 243 .... G4
Hebron • 878 .... C7
Hermon • 3,755 .... F6
Highland Lake 600 .... C8
Hiram 175 .... B8
Hiram • 1,260 .... B8
Hodgdon • 1,257 .... H3
Hollis Center • 2,892 .... B8
Hope 175 .... E7
Hope • 1,017 .... E7
Houlton▲ 5,730 .... H3
Houlton • 5,627 .... H3
Howland 1,502 .... F5
Howland • 1,304 .... F5
Hudson • 1,048 .... F5
Hulls Cove 200 .... G7
Island Falls • 897 .... G3
Isle Au Haut • 57 .... F7
Islesboro 200 .... F7
Islesboro • 579 .... F7
Jackman 700 .... C4
Jackman • 920 .... C4
Jacksonville 200 .... J6
Jay 850 .... C7
Jay • 5,080 .... C7
Jefferson • 2,111 .... D7
Jonesboro • 585 .... J6
Jonesport 1,050 .... H6
Jonesport • 1,525 .... H6
Keegan 450 .... G1
Kenduskeag • 1,234 .... E6
Kennebunk 3,294 .... B9
Kennebunk • 4,206 .... B9
Kennebunk Beach 200 .... C9
Kennebunkport 1,685 .... C9
Kennebunkport • 1,100 .... C9
Kents Hill 300 .... D7
Kezar Falls 680 .... B8
Kingfield • 1,114 .... C6
Kingman 246 .... G4
Kingsbury • 13 .... D5
Kittery 5,465 .... B9
Kittery • 5,151 .... B9
Kittery Point 1,093 .... B9
Knox • 681 .... E6
Lagrange 250 .... F5
Lagrange • 509 .... F5
Lake View • 23 .... F5
Lamoine • 1,311 .... G7
Lee • 832 .... G5
Leeds • 1,669 .... C7
Levant • 1,627 .... F6
Lewiston 39,757 .... C7
Liberty 200 .... E7
Liberty • 790 .... E7
Lille 300 .... G1
Limerick • 1,688 .... B8
Limestone 1,334 .... H2
Limestone • 1,245 .... H2
Limington • 2,796 .... B8
Lincoln 3,524 .... G5
Lincoln • 3,399 .... G5
Lincoln Center 325 .... G5
Lincolnville 800 .... E7
Lincolnville • 1,809 .... E7
Lincolnville Center 200 .... E7
Linneus • 810 .... H3
Lisbon • 9,457 .... C7
Lisbon Falls 4,674 .... D7
Lisbon-Lisbon Center 1,865 .... C7
Litchfield • 2,650 .... D7
Little Deer Isle 475 .... F7
Little Falls-South Windham
1,715 .... C8
Littleton • 956 .... H3
Livermore 280 .... C7
Livermore • 1,950 .... C7
Livermore Falls 2,441 .... C7
Livermore Falls • 1,935 .... C7
Locke Mills 600 .... B7
Lovell 180 .... B7
Lovell • 888 .... B7
Lowell • 267 .... F5
Lubec 900 .... K6
Lubec • 1,853 .... K6
Ludlow • 430 .... G3
Machias▲ 1,277 .... J6
Machias • 1,773 .... J6
Machiasport 374 .... H6
Machiasport • 1,166 .... H6
Macwahoc • 114 .... G4
Madawaska 4,165 .... G1
Madawaska • 3,653 .... G1
Madison 2,788 .... D6
Madison • 2,956 .... D6
Madrid • 178 .... B6
Manchester • 2,099 .... D7
Mapleton • 1,853 .... G2
Mars Hill • 1,760 .... H2
Mars Hill-Blaine 1,717 .... H2
Masardis • 305 .... G3

(continued on following page)

Agriculture, Industry and Resources

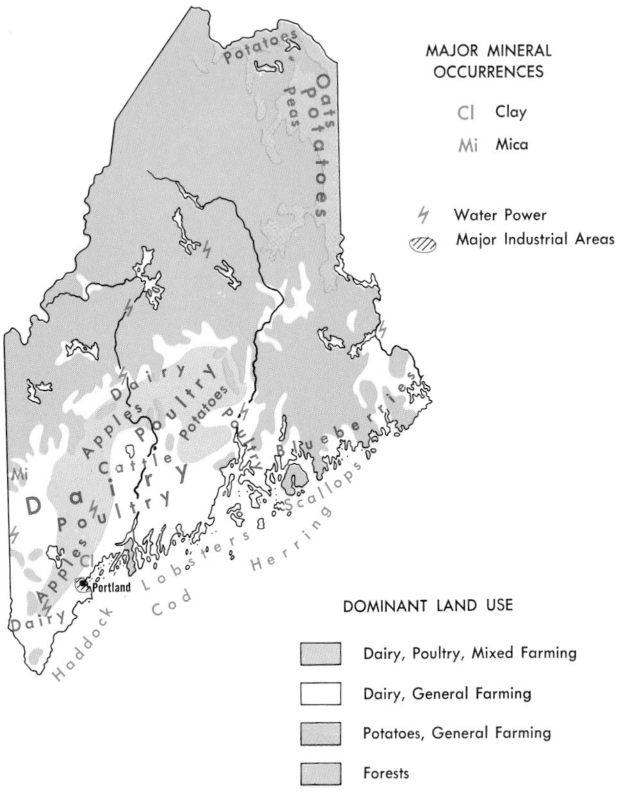
Potatoes
Oats
Peas
Potatoes
Dairy
Poultry
Apples
Cattle
Potatoes
Poultry
Blueberries
Scallops
Herring
Lobsters
Cod
Haddock
Dairy
Apples
Portland
Cl
Mi
MAJOR MINERAL OCCURRENCES
Cl Clay
Mi Mica
Water Power
Major Industrial Areas
DOMINANT LAND USE
Dairy, Poultry, Mixed Farming
Dairy, General Farming
Potatoes, General Farming
Forests

(continued)

Matinicus 66 ..... F8
Mattawamkeag• 830 ..... G5
Mechanic Falls 2,198 ..... C7
Mechanic Falls• 2,388 ..... C7
Meddybemps• 133 ..... J5
Medford 194 ..... F5
Medway• 1,922 ..... G4
Mercer• 593 ..... D6
Mexico 3,207 ..... B6
Mexico• 2,302 ..... B6
Milbridge• 1,305 ..... H6
Milford 1,688 ..... F6
Milford• 2,228 ..... F6
Millinocket• 6,922 ..... F4
Milo 2,255 ..... F5
Milo• 2,129 ..... F5
Minot 250 ..... C7
Minot• 1,664 ..... C7
Minturn 150 ..... G7
Monhegan• 88 ..... E8
Monmouth 500 ..... D7
Monmouth• 3,353 ..... C7
Monroe• 802 ..... E6
Monson• 744 ..... E5
Monticello• 872 ..... H3
Montville• 877 ..... E7
Moody 500 ..... B9
Moose River• 233 ..... C4
Morrill• 644 ..... E7
Mount Desert 150 ..... G7
Mount Desert• 1,899 ..... G7
Mount Vernon• 1,362 ..... D7
Naples• 2,860 ..... B8
New Gloucester 400 ..... C8
New Gloucester• 3,916 ..... C8
New Harbor 850 ..... E8
New Limerick• 524 ..... G3
New Portland 300 ..... C6
New Portland• 789 ..... C6
New Sharon• 1,175 ..... C6
New Sweden 175 ..... G2
New Sweden• 715 ..... G2
New Vineyard• 661 ..... C6
Newburgh• 1,317 ..... F6
Newcastle• 1,538 ..... D7
Newcastle-Damariscotta 1,411 ..... E7
Newfield 200 ..... B8
Newfield• 1,042 ..... B8
Newport 1,748 ..... E6
Newport• 1,843 ..... E6
Newry• 316 ..... B6
Nobleboro• 1,455 ..... D7
Norridgewock 1,318 ..... D6
Norridgewock• 1,496 ..... D6
North Anson 950 ..... D6
North Belgrade 300 ..... D7
North Berwick 1,436 ..... B9
North Berwick• 1,568 ..... B9
North Bridgton 300 ..... B7
North Cutler 153 ..... J6
North Fryeburg 250 ..... B7
North Haven 400 ..... F7
North Haven• 332 ..... F7
North Jay 800 ..... C6
North Limington 400 ..... B8
North Livermore 250 ..... C7
North Lubec 250 ..... J6
North New Portland 500 ..... C6
North Penobscot 403 ..... F7
North Raymond 225 ..... C8
North Turner 350 ..... C7
North Vassalboro 950 ..... D7
North Waldoboro 250 ..... E7
North Waterboro 200 ..... B8
North Waterford 390 ..... B7
North Wayne 175 ..... C7
North Whitefield 300 ..... D7
North Windham 4,077 ..... C8
North Yarmouth 500 ..... C8
North Yarmouth• 2,429 ..... C8
Northeast Harbor 800 ..... G7
Northfield• 99 ..... H6
Northport• 1,201 ..... E7
Norway 2,653 ..... B7
Norway• 3,023 ..... B7
Oakfield• 846 ..... G3
Oakland 3,387 ..... D6
Oakland• 3,510 ..... D6
Ocean Park 200 ..... C9
Ogunquit 974 ..... B9
Olamon 150 ..... F5
Old Orchard Beach 6,023 ..... C9
Old Orchard Beach• 7,789 ..... C9
Old Town 8,317 ..... F6
Oquossoc 150 ..... B6
Orient• 157 ..... H4
Orland 200 ..... F6
Orland• 1,805 ..... F6
Orono 9,891 ..... F6
Orono• 9,789 ..... F6
Orrington 250 ..... F6
Orrington• 3,309 ..... F6
Orrs Island 600 ..... D8
Otisfield• 1,136 ..... B7
Otter Creek 260 ..... G7
Owls Head• 1,574 ..... F7
Oxbow• 69 ..... G3
Oxford 550 ..... B7
Oxford• 1,284 ..... B7
Palermo• 1,021 ..... E7
Palmyra• 1,867 ..... E6
Paris• 4,492 ..... B7
Parkman• 790 ..... D5
Passadumkeag• 428 ..... F5
Patten 1,057 ..... F4
Patten• 1,256 ..... F4
Pejepscot 200 ..... D8
Pemaquid 200 ..... E8
Pembroke 300 ..... J6
Pembroke• 852 ..... J6
Penobscot 150 ..... F7
Penobscot• 1,131 ..... F7
Perham• 395 ..... G2
Perry• 758 ..... J6
Peru• 1,541 ..... C6
Phillips• 1,148 ..... C6
Phippsburg 1,527 ..... D8
Phippsburg• 1,815 ..... D8
Pine Point 650 ..... C8
Pittsfield 3,117 ..... E6
Pittsfield• 3,222 ..... E6
Pittston• 2,444 ..... D7
Plymouth• 1,152 ..... E6
Poland 500 ..... C7
Poland• 4,342 ..... C7
Port Clyde 400 ..... E8
Portage• 562 ..... G2
Porter 225 ..... B8
Porter• 1,301 ..... B8
Portland▲ 64,358 ..... C8
Pownal• 1,262 ..... C8
Prentiss• 245 ..... G5
Presque Isle 10,550 ..... H2
Princeton• 973 ..... H5
Prospect• 542 ..... F6
Prospect Harbor 445 ..... H7
Randolph• 1,949 ..... D7
Rangeley 900 ..... B6
Rangeley• 103 ..... B6
Raymond 550 ..... B8
Raymond• 3,311 ..... B8
Readfield 300 ..... D7
Readfield• 2,033 ..... D7
Red Beach 210 ..... J5
Richmond 1,578 ..... D7
Richmond• 1,775 ..... D7
Richmond Corner 200 ..... D7
Ripley• 445 ..... E5
Robbinston 200 ..... J5
Robbinston• 495 ..... J5
Robinsons 160 ..... H3
Rockland▲ 7,972 ..... E7
Rockport 875 ..... E7
Rockport• 2,854 ..... E7
Rockville 250 ..... E7
Rockwood 265 ..... D4
Rome• 758 ..... D6
Roque Bluffs• 234 ..... H6
Round Pond 400 ..... E8
Roxbury• 437 ..... B6
Rumford 6,256 ..... B6
Rumford• 5,419 ..... B6
Rumford Center 325 ..... B7
Rumford Point 320 ..... B6
Sabattus 1,234 ..... C7
Sabattus• 3,696 ..... C7
Saco 15,181 ..... C8
Saint Agatha• 1,035 ..... G1
Saint Albans• 1,400 ..... E6
Saint David 915 ..... G1
Saint Francis• 839 ..... E1
Saint George 700 ..... E7
Saint George• 1,948 ..... E7
Saint John• 322 ..... F1
Sandy Point 350 ..... F7
Sanford 10,268 ..... B9
Sanford• 10,296 ..... B9
Sangerville• 1,398 ..... E5
Scarborough 2,280 ..... C8
Scarborough• 2,586 ..... C8
Seal Cove 215 ..... G7
Seal Harbor 500 ..... G7
Searsmont 400 ..... E7
Searsmont• 938 ..... E7
Searsport 1,348 ..... F7
Searsport• 1,151 ..... F7
Sebago Lake 800 ..... B8
Sebec• 554 ..... E5
Seboeis• 40 ..... F5
Sedgwick• 905 ..... F7
Shapleigh• 1,911 ..... B8
Shawmut 500 ..... D6
Sheepscott 150 ..... D7
Sheridan 300 ..... F2
Sherman 1,021 ..... G4
Sherman• 1,027 ..... G4
Sherman Mills 600 ..... G4
Sherman Station 650 ..... F4
Shirley Mills 242 ..... D5
Shirley Mills• 208 ..... D5
Sidney• 2,593 ..... D7
Sinclair• 264 ..... G1
Skowhegan▲ 6,517 ..... D6
Skowhegan• 6,990 ..... D6
Smithfield• 865 ..... D6
Smyrna Mills• 354 ..... G3
Soldier Pond 500 ..... F1
Solon• 916 ..... D6
Somerville• 458 ..... D7
Somesville (Mount Desert) 150 ..... D7
Sorrento• 295 ..... G7
South Berwick 2,120 ..... B9
South Berwick• 5,877 ..... B9
South Bridgton 373 ..... B8
South Bristol• 825 ..... D8
South Casco 750 ..... B8
South China 225 ..... D7
South Eliot 3,112 ..... B9
South Harpswell 650 ..... C8
South Hiram 350 ..... B8
South Hope 200 ..... E7
South La Grange 150 ..... F5
South Lebanon 200 ..... A9
South Lincoln 150 ..... F5
South Monmouth 400 ..... D7
South Orrington 400 ..... F6
South Paris▲ 2,320 ..... C7
South Penobscot 150 ..... F7
South Portland 23,163 ..... C8
South Sanford 3,929 ..... B9
South Thomaston• 1,227 ..... E7
South Waldoboro 300 ..... E7
South Waterford 300 ..... B7
South Windham (Little Falls-South Windham) C8
Southport 400 ..... D8
Southport• 645 ..... D8
Southwest Harbor 1,052 ..... G7
Southwest Harbor• 1,952 ..... G7
Springfield• 406 ..... G5
Springvale 3,542 ..... B9
Stacyville 155 ..... F4
Stacyville• 480 ..... F4
Standish 700 ..... B8
Standish• 7,678 ..... B8
Starks• 508 ..... D6
Steep Falls 500 ..... B8
Stetson• 847 ..... E6
Steuben 190 ..... H6
Steuben• 1,084 ..... H6
Stillwater 700 ..... F6
Stockholm• 286 ..... G1
Stockton Springs 500 ..... F7
Stockton Springs• 1,383 ..... F7
Stonington• 1,252 ..... F7
Stow• 283 ..... A7
Stratton 600 ..... B5
Strong• 1,217 ..... C6
Sullivan• 1,118 ..... G6
Sumner• 761 ..... C7
Sunset 165 ..... F7
Surry• 1,004 ..... F7
Swans Island• 348 ..... G7
Swanville• 1,130 ..... E6
Sweden• 222 ..... B7
Temple• 560 ..... C6
Tenants Harbor 900 ..... E8
Thomaston 2,348 ..... E7
Thomaston• 2,445 ..... E7
Thorndike• 702 ..... E6
Topsfield• 235 ..... H5
Topsham 4,657 ..... D8
Topsham• 6,147 ..... D8
Tremont 175 ..... G7
Tremont• 1,324 ..... G7
Trenton• 1,060 ..... G7
Trevett 400 ..... D8
Troy• 802 ..... E6
Turner 400 ..... C7
Turner• 4,315 ..... C7
Union 300 ..... E7
Union• 1,989 ..... E7
Unity• 36 ..... E6
Upper Frenchville 405 ..... G1
Upton• 70 ..... B6
Van Buren 3,282 ..... G1
Van Buren• 2,759 ..... G1
Vanceboro• 201 ..... J4
Vassalboro• 3,679 ..... D7
Veazie• 1,633 ..... F6
Vienna• 417 ..... D6
Vinalhaven• 1,072 ..... F7
Waite• 119 ..... H5
Waldo• 626 ..... E6
Waldoboro 1,195 ..... E7
Waldoboro• 1,420 ..... E7
Walnut Hill 400 ..... C8
Waltham• 276 ..... G6
Warren 770 ..... E7
Warren• 3,192 ..... E7
Washburn 1,221 ..... G2
Washburn• 1,880 ..... G2
Washington• 1,185 ..... E7
Waterboro 700 ..... B8
Waterboro• 4,510 ..... B8
Waterford• 1,299 ..... B7
Waterville 17,173 ..... D6
Wayne 175 ..... D7
Wayne• 1,029 ..... D7
Weeks Mills 235 ..... E7
Weld• 430 ..... C6
Wellington• 270 ..... D5
Wells 950 ..... B9
Wells• 7,778 ..... B9
Wells Beach 600 ..... B9
Wesley• 146 ..... H6
West Baldwin 198 ..... B8
West Bath• 1,716 ..... D8
West Bethel 160 ..... B7
West Brooksville 156 ..... F7
West Buxton 185 ..... B8
West Enfield 609 ..... F5
West Farmington 700 ..... C6
West Forks• 63 ..... D5
West Franklin 350 ..... G6
West Gouldsboro 225 ..... G7
West Jonesport 400 ..... H6
West Kennebunk 750 ..... B9
West Lubec 275 ..... J6
West Minot 400 ..... C7
West Newfield 300 ..... B8
West Paris• 1,514 ..... B7
West Peru 700 ..... C7
West Poland 250 ..... C7
West Rockport 350 ..... E7
West Scarborough 500 ..... C8
West Tremont 250 ..... G7
Westbrook 16,121 ..... C8
Westfield• 589 ..... G2
Weston• 207 ..... H4
Whitefield 550 ..... D7
Whitefield• 1,931 ..... D7
Whiting• 407 ..... J6
Whitneyville• 241 ..... H6
Willimantic• 170 ..... E5
Wilton 4,382 ..... C6
Wilton• 2,453 ..... C6
Windsor• 1,895 ..... D7
Winn 250 ..... G5
Winn• 479 ..... G5
Winslow 5,903 ..... D6
Winslow• 5,436 ..... D6
Winter Harbor• 1,157 ..... G7
Winterport 1,126 ..... F6
Winterport• 1,274 ..... F6
Winterville• 217 ..... F2
Winthrop 3,264 ..... C7
Winthrop• 2,819 ..... C7
Wiscasset 975 ..... D7
Wiscasset• 1,233 ..... D7
Woodland• 1,287 ..... H5
Woolwich• 2,570 ..... D8
Wyman Dam 300 ..... D5
Yarmouth 2,981 ..... C8
Yarmouth• 3,338 ..... C8
York 4,530 ..... B9
York Beach 900 ..... B9
York Harbor 2,555 ..... B9
York• 9,818 ..... B9

OTHER FEATURES

Abraham (mt.) C5
Acadia Nat'l Park G7
Allagash (lake) D3
Allagash (riv.) E2
Androscoggin (riv.) C7
Aroostook (riv.) G2
Attean (pond) C4
Baker (lake) D3
Baskahegan (lake) H5
Bear (riv.) B6
Big (brook) E2
Big (lake) H5
Big Black (riv.) D2
Bigelow (bight) C9
Big Spencer (mt.) E4
Black (pond) D3
Blue (mt.) C6
Blue Hill (bay) G7
Bog (lake) H6
Brassua (lake) D4
Casco (bay) C8
Cathance (lake) J6
Caucomgomoc (lake) D3
Center (pond) E5
Chamberlain (lake) E3
Chemquasabamticook (lake) D3
Chesuncook (lake) E3
Chiputneticook (lakes) H4
Clayton (lake) D2
Clifford (lake) H5
Cold Stream (pond) G5
Crawford (lake) H5
Cross (isl.) J6
Cross (lake) G1
Cupsuptic (riv.) B5
Dead (riv.) C5
Deer (isl.) F7
Duck (isls.) G7
Eagle (lake) E3
Eagle (lake) F1
East Machias (riv.) H6
East Musquash (lake) H5
Elizabeth (cape) C8
Ellis (pond) B6
Ellis (riv.) B6
Embden (pond) D6
Endless (lake) F5
Englishman (bay) J6
Eskutassis (pond) G5
Fifth (lake) H5
Fish (riv.) F2
Fish River (lake) F2
Flagstaff (lake) C5
Fourth (lake) H5
Frenchman (bay) G7
Gardner (lake) J6
Georges (isls.) E8
Graham (lake) G6
Grand (lake) H4
Grand Falls (lake) H5
Grand Lake Seboeis (lake) F3
Grand Manan (chan.) K6
Great Moose (lake) D6
Great Wass (isl.) J7
Green (isl.) F8
Harrington (lake) E4
Haut (isl.) G7
Indian (pond) D4
Islesboro (isl.) F7
Jo-Mary (lakes) E4
Katahdin (mt.) F4
Kennebec (riv.) D7
Kezar (lake) B7
Kezar (pond) B7
Kingsbury (pond) D5
Little Black (riv.) E1
Little Madawaska (riv.) G2
Lobster (lake) E4
Long (lake) B7
Long (lake) E2
Long (lake) G1
Long (pond) C4
Long (pond) D6
Long (pond) E5
Long Falls (dam) C5
Longfellow (mts.) B6
Loon (lake) D3
Loring A.F.B. 7,829 ..... H2
Lower Roach (pond) E4
Lower Sysladobsis (lake) G5
Machias (bay) J6
Machias (riv.) F2
Machias (riv.) H6
Machias Seal (isl.) J7
Madagascal (pond) G5
Marshall (isl.) G7
Matinicus Rock (isl.) F8
Mattamiscontis (lake) F4
Mattawamkeag (lake) G4
Mattawamkeag (riv.) G4
Meddybemps (lake) J5
Metinic (isl.) E8
Millinocket (lake) F3
Millinocket (lake) F4
Molunkus (lake) G4
Monhegan (isl.) E8
Moose (pond) B7
Moose (riv.) D4
Moosehead (lake) D4
Mooseleuk (stream) F2
Mooselookmeguntic (lake) B6
Mopang (lake) H6
Mount Desert (isl.) G7
Mount Desert Rock (isl.) G8
Moxie (lake) D5
Munsungan (lake) E3
Muscongus (bay) E8
Musquacook (lakes) E2
Nahmakanta (lake) E4
Nicatous (lake) G5
Nollesemic (lake) F4
Old (stream) H6
Onawa (lake) E5
Parlin (pond) C4
Parmachenee (lake) B5
Passamaquoddy (bay) J5
Passamaquoddy Ind. Res. J6
Pemadumcook (lake) E4
Penobscot (bay) F7
Penobscot (lake) C4
Penobscot (riv.) F5
Penobscot Ind. Res. F6
Pierce (pond) C5
Piscataqua (riv.) B9
Piscataquis (riv.) E5
Pleasant (lake) E3
Pleasant (lake) G3
Pleasant (lake) H5
Pleasant (riv.) H6
Pocomoonshine (lake) H5
Portage (lake) F2
Presque Isle A.F.B. G2
Priestly (lake) E2
Pushaw (lake) F6
Ragged (isl.) F8
Ragged (lake) E4
Rainbow (lake) E4
Rangeley (lake) B6
Richardson (lakes) B6
Rocky (lake) J6
Round (pond) E2
Rowe (lake) F2
Saco (riv.) B8
Saint Croix (riv.) J5
Saint Croix Island Nat'l Mon. J5
Saint Francis (riv.) E1
Saint Froid (lake) F2
Saint John (pond) D3
Saint John (riv.) G1
Salmon Falls (riv.) B9
Sandy (riv.) C6
Schoodic (lake) F5
Scraggly (lake) F3
Scraggly (lake) H5
Seal (isl.) F8
Sebago (lake) B8
Sebasticook (lake) E6
Seboeis (lake) F5
Seboeis (riv.) F3
Seboomook (lake) D4
Shallow (lake) E3
Small (cape) D8
Sourdnahunk (lake) F3
Spencer (pond) D4
Spencer (stream) C5
Spider (lake) E3
Squa Pan (lake) G2
Square (lake) G1
Sunday (riv.) B6
Swift (riv.) B6
Sysladobsis, Lower (lake) G5
Third (lake) H5
Twin (lakes) F4
Umbagog (lake) A6
Umcalcus (lake) G3
Umsaskis (lake) E2
Union, West Branch (riv.) G6
Vinalhaven (isl.) F7
Wassataquoik (stream) F4
Webb (lake) C6
Webster (brook) E3
West Grand (lake) H5
West Musquash (lake) H5
West Quoddy (head) K6
Wilson (ponds) E5
Winnecook (lake) E6
Wooden Ball (isl.) F8
Wyman (lake) C5
Wytopitlock (lake) G4

▲County seat.
•Population of town or township.

Topography

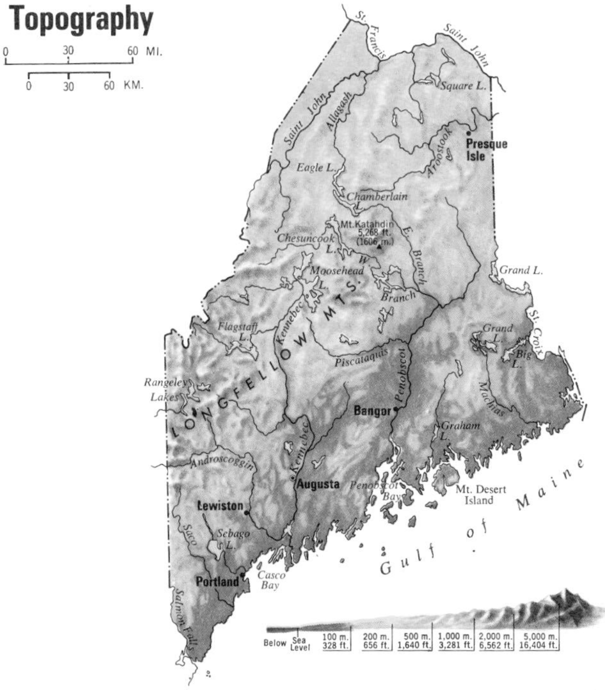
0 30 60 MI.
0 30 60 KM.
St. Francis
Saint John
Square L.
Allagash
Saint John
Aroostook
Presque Isle
Eagle L.
Chamberlain
Mt. Katahdin 5,268 ft. (1606 m.)
Chesuncook L.
E. Branch
Grand L.
Moosehead L.
W. Branch
Flagstaff L.
Kennebec
LONGFELLOW MTS.
Piscataquis
Penobscot
Grand L.
St. Croix
Big L.
Rangeley Lakes
Machias
Bangor
Graham L.
Kennebec
Androscoggin
Augusta
Penobscot Bay
Mt. Desert Island
Lewiston
Saco
Sebago L.
Gulf of Maine
Portland
Casco Bay
Salmon Falls
Below Sea Level
100 m. 328 ft.
200 m. 656 ft.
500 m. 1,640 ft.
1,000 m. 3,281 ft.
2,000 m. 6,562 ft.
5,000 m. 16,404 ft.

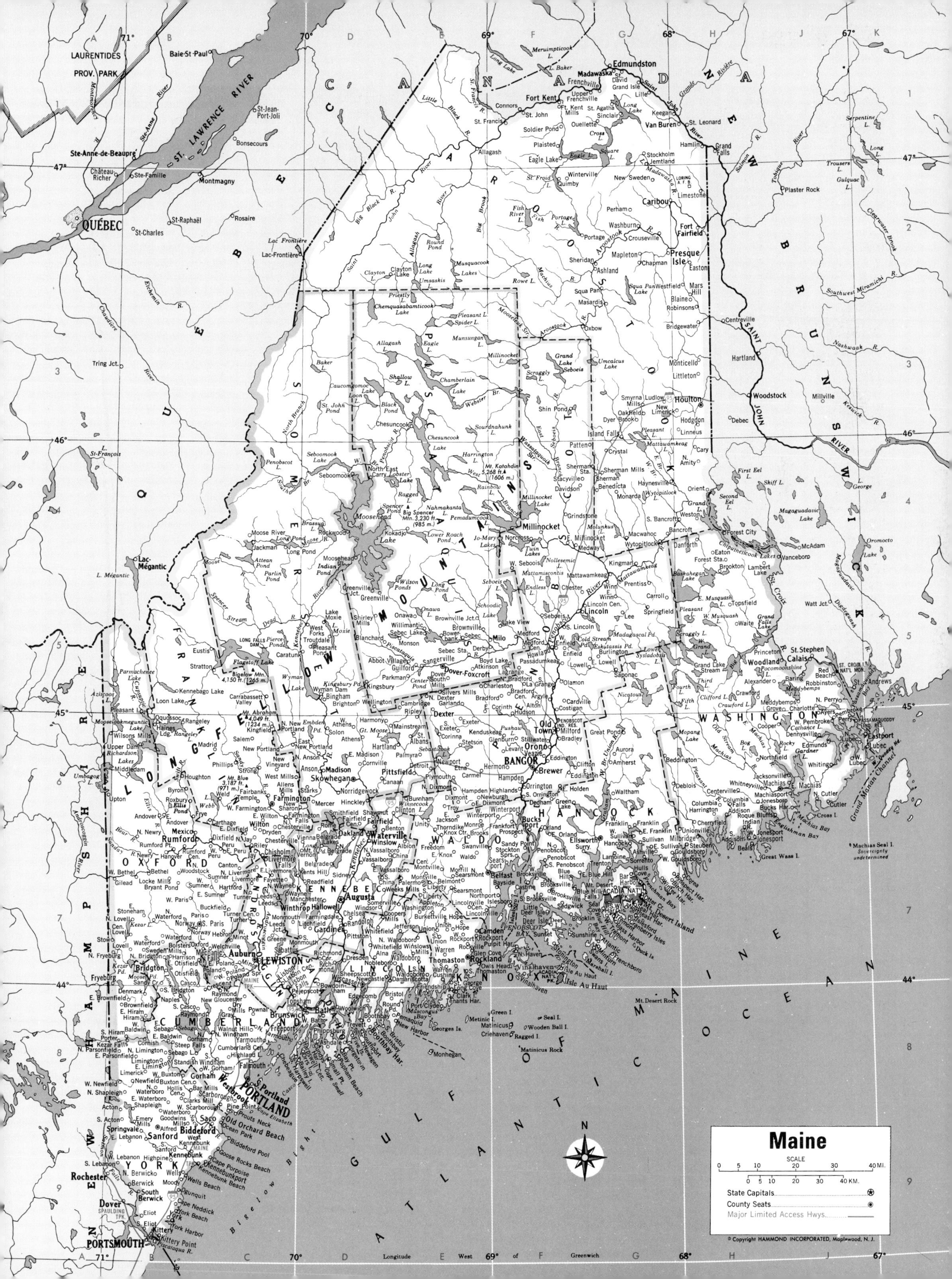

Maine
SCALE
0 5 10 20 30 40 MI.
0 5 10 20 30 40 KM.
State Capitals
County Seats
Major Limited Access Hwys.
© Copyright HAMMOND INCORPORATED, Maplewood, N. J.
Longitude West of Greenwich
GULF OF MAINE
ATLANTIC OCEAN
CANADA
NEW BRUNSWICK
QUEBEC
NEW HAMPSHIRE

MARYLAND

COUNTIES

Allegany 74,946 .... C2
Anne Arundel 427,239 .... M4
Baltimore 692,134 .... M3
Baltimore (city county) 736,775 .... M3
Calvert 51,372 .... M6
Caroline 27,035 .... P5
Carroll 123,372 .... K2
Cecil 71,347 .... P2
Charles 101,154 .... K6
Dorchester 30,236 .... O7
Fredrick 114,792 .... J3
Garrett 28,138 .... A2
Harford 182,132 .... N2
Howard 187,328 .... L4
Kent 17,842 .... O3
Montgomery 757,027 .... J4
Prince Georges 665,071 .... L5
Queen Annes 25,508 .... P4
Saint Marys 59,895 .... M7
Somerset 23,440 .... R8
Talbot 30,549 .... O5
Washington 121,393 .... G2
Wicomico 74,339 .... R7
Worcester 35,028 .... S8

CITIES and TOWNS

Aberdeen 13,087 .... O2
Abingdon 500 .... N3
Accident 349 .... A2
Accokeek 4,477 .... L6
Adamstown 300 .... H3
Allen 250 .... R7
Annapolis (cap.)▲ 33,187 .... M5
Annapolis Junction 775 .... M4
Aquasco 950 .... L6
Arbutus 19,750 .... M3
Ardmore 500 .... G4
Aspen Hill 45,494 .... K4
Baltimore 736,014 .... M3
Barclay 170 .... P4
Barnesville 170 .... J4
Barstow 500 .... M6
Barton 530 .... B2
Bayview 200 .... P2
Beaver Creek 290 .... H2
Bel Air▲ 8,860 .... N2
Bel Alton 800 .... L7
Bellevue 300 .... O6
Beltsville 14,476 .... G3
Benedict 850 .... M6
Berlin 2,616 .... T7
Berwyn Heights 2,952 .... G4
Bethesda 62,936 .... E4
Bethlehem 500 .... P6
Betterton 360 .... O3
Bishops Head 250 .... O7
Bishopville 300 .... T7
Bivalve 175 .... P7
Bladensburg 8,064 .... G4
Bloomington 486 .... B3
Boonsboro 2,445 .... H2
Borden Shaft 200 .... B2
Boring 290 .... L2
Boulevard Heights 500 .... F5
Bowens 250 .... M6
Bowie 37,589 .... L4
Boyds 300 .... J4
Bozman 700 .... N5
Brandywine 1,406 .... L6
Brentwood 3,005 .... F4
Brooklyn Park 10,987 .... M4
Brownsville 190 .... H3
Brunswick 5,117 .... H3
Buckeystown 400 .... J3
Burkittsville 194 .... H3
Bushwood 750 .... L7
Butler 200 .... M2
Cabin John (Cabin John-Brookmont) 5,341 .... D4
California 7,626 .... M7
Calvert 1,728 .... O2
Calverton 12,046 .... L4
Cambridge▲ 11,514 .... O6
Camp Springs 16,392 .... G6
Cape Saint Claire 7,878 .... N4
Capitol Heights 3,633 .... G5
Cardiff 475 .... N2
Carmody Hills (Carmody Hills-Pepper Mill Village) 4,815 .... G5
Cascade (Cascade-Highfield) 1,096 .... J2
Castleton 750 .... N2
Catoctin Furnace 516 .... J2
Catonsville 35,233 .... M3
Cavetown 1,533 .... H2
Cecilton 489 .... P3
Cedar Grove 300 .... K4
Cedar Heights G5
Cedarville 200 .... L6
Centreville▲ 2,097 .... O4
Chance 600 .... P8
Chaptico 300 .... M7
Charlestown 578 .... P2
Charlotte Hall 1,992 .... M7
Chase 900 .... N3
Cheltenham 950 .... L6
Cherry Hill 250 .... P2
Chesapeake Beach 2,403 .... N6
Chesapeake City 735 .... P2
Chester 4,005 .... N5
Chestertown▲ 3,300 .... O4
Cheverly 6,023 .... G4
Chevy Chase 2,675 .... E4
Chevy Chase Section Four 2,903 .... E4
Chewsville 300 .... H2
Chillum 31,309 .... F4
Church Hill 481 .... O4
Churchville 500 .... N2
Claiborne 225 .... N5
Clarksburg 400 .... J4
Clarksville 500 .... L4
Clear Spring 415 .... G2
Clements 800 .... L7
Clinton 19,987 .... G6
Cockeysville 18,668 .... M3
Colesville 18,819 .... K4
College Park 21,927 .... G4
Colmar Manor 1,249 .... F4
Coltons Point 600 .... M8
Columbia 75,883 .... L4
Compton 500 .... M7
Cooksville 497 .... K3
Coral Hills 11,032 .... G5
Cordova 365 .... O5
Corriganville 1,020 .... C2
Cottage City 1,236 .... F4
Cox Station (Bel Alton) 800 .... L7
Creagerstown 240 .... J2
Crellin 275 .... A3
Cresaptown 4,586 .... C2
Crisfield 2,880 .... P9
Crofton 12,781 .... M4
Crownsville 1,514 .... M4
Crumpton 350 .... P4
Cumberland▲ 23,706 .... D2
Damascus 9,817 .... K3
Dameron 759 .... N8
Dames Quarter 250 .... P8
Dargan 352 .... H3
Darlington 850 .... N2
Darnestown 950 .... J4
Davidsonville 250 .... M5
Deal Island 800 .... P8
Deale 4,151 .... M5
Deer Park 419 .... A3
Defense Heights G4
Delmar 1,430 .... R7
Denton▲ 2,977 .... P5
Derwood 413 .... K4
Dickerson 530 .... J4
District Heights 6,704 .... G5
Doubs 200 .... J3
Downsville 255 .... G2
Drayden 400 .... N8
Dublin 366 .... N2
Dundalk 65,800 .... N3
Eagle Harbor 38 .... M6
East New Market 153 .... P6
Easton▲ 9,372 .... O5
Eckhart Mines 1,333 .... C2
Eden 800 .... R7
Edgemere 9,226 .... N4
Edgewood 23,903 .... N3
Edmonston 851 .... F4
Eldersburg 9,720 .... L3
Elk Mills 550 .... P2
Elk Neck 700 .... P2
Elkridge 12,953 .... M4
Elkton▲ 9,073 .... P2
Ellerslie 950 .... C2
Ellicott City▲ 41,396 .... L3
Emmitsburg 1,688 .... J2
Essex 40,872 .... N3
Ewell 595 .... O9
Fair Hill 250 .... P2
Fairlee 300 .... O4
Fairmount 1,238 .... P8
Fairmount Heights 1,616 .... G5
Fallston 5,730 .... N2
Federalsburg 2,365 .... P6
Ferndale 16,355 .... M4
Finksburg 950 .... L3
Fishing Creek 595 .... N7
Flintstone 400 .... D2
Forest Heights 2,859 .... F5
Forest Hill 450 .... N2
Forestville 16,731 .... G5
Fort Foote 700 .... F6
Fort Howard N4
Fountain Head 1,745 .... G2
Foxville 175 .... H2
Frederick▲ 40,148 .... J3
Freeland 500 .... M2
Friendship 600 .... M6
Friendsville 577 .... A2
Frizzellburg 300 .... K2
Frostburg 8,075 .... C2
Fruitland 3,511 .... R7
Funkstown 1.136 .... H2
Gaithersburg 39,542 .... K4
Galena 324 .... P3
Galestown 123 .... P6
Galesville 600 .... M5
Gamber 500 .... L3
Gambrills 460 .... M4
Garrett Park 884 .... E3
Garrison 5,045 .... L3
Germantown 41,145 .... J4
Girdletree 350 .... S8
Glen Arm 350 .... N3
Glen Burnie 37,305 .... M4
Glen Echo 234 .... E4
Glenarden 5,025 .... G4
Glenelg 400 .... L3
Glyndon L3
Goldsboro 185 .... P4
Good Luck G4
Graceham 300 .... J2
Granite 950 .... L3
Grantsville 505 .... B2
Grasonville 2,439 .... O5
Green Haven 14,416 .... M4
Greenbelt 21,096 .... G4
Greenmount 325 .... L2
Greensboro 1,441 .... P5
Hagerstown▲ 35,445 .... G2
Halfway 8,873 .... G2
Hampstead 2,608 .... L2
Hancock 1,926 .... F2
Hanover 500 .... M4
Harmans 400 .... M4
Harney 270 .... K2
Havre de Grace 8,952 .... O2
Hebron 665 .... R7
Helen 300 .... M7
Henryton 300 .... L3
Hereford 680 .... M2
Hillandale 10,318 .... F4
Hillcrest Heights 17,136 .... F5
Hillsboro 164 .... P5
Hollywood 500 .... M7
Hoopersville 180 .... O7
Hughesville 1,319 .... L6
Huntingtown 450 .... M6
Hurlock 1,706 .... P6
Hyattsville 13,864 .... F4
Indian Head 3,531 .... K6
Island Creek 400 .... M7
Issue 250 .... L7
Jacksonville 172 .... M2
Jarrettsville 2,148 .... M2
Jefferson 300 .... J3
Jennings 172 .... B2
Johnsville 200 .... K2

(continued)

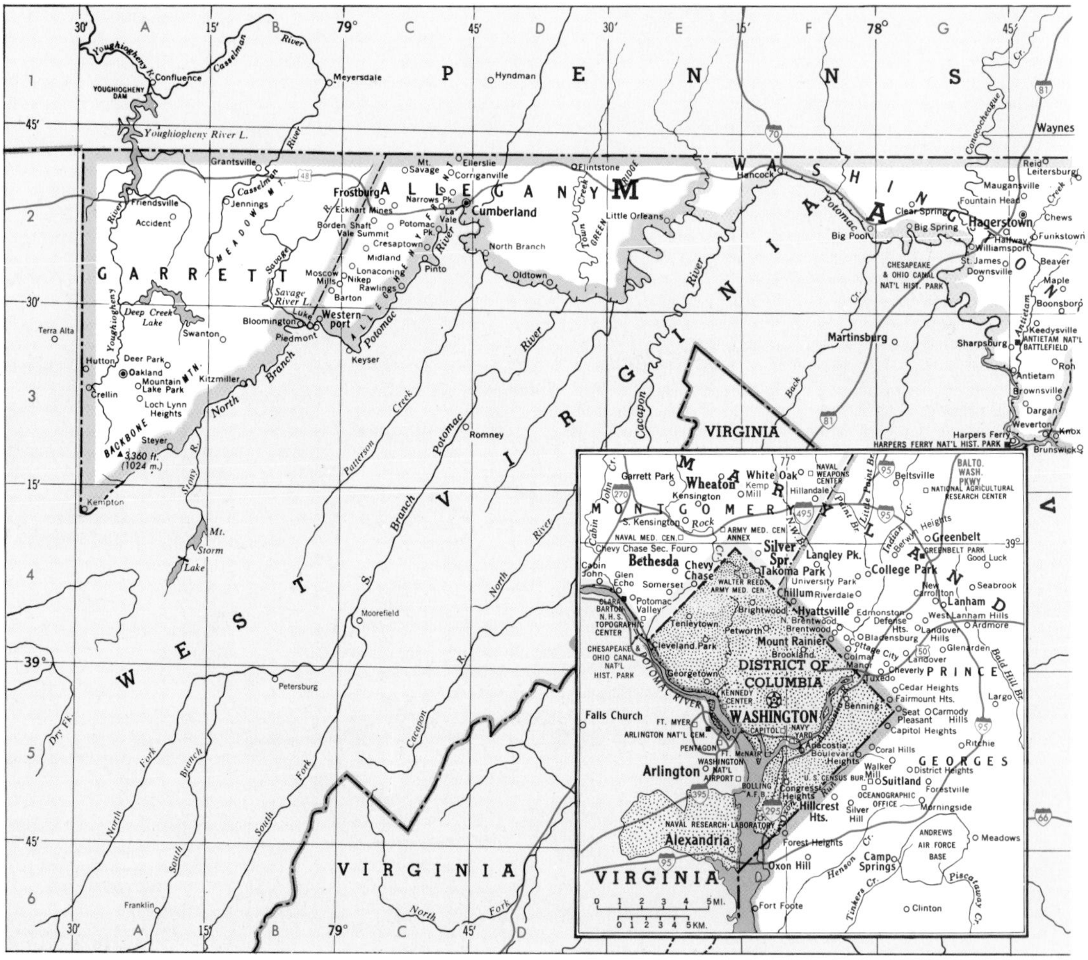
PENNSYLVANIA
WEST VIRGINIA
VIRGINIA
MARYLAND
GARRETT
ALLEGANY
WASHINGTON
Cumberland
Frostburg
Hagerstown
Hancock
Grantsville
Oakland
Westernport
Martinsburg
Meyersdale
Hyndman
Romney
Keyser
Petersburg
Moorefield
Franklin
Confluence
Deep Creek Lake
Savage River L.
Youghiogheny River L.
BACKBONE MTN.
3,360 ft. (1024 m.)
Mt. Storm Lake
Potomac
North Branch
South Branch
DISTRICT OF COLUMBIA
WASHINGTON
Alexandria
Arlington
Falls Church
Bethesda
Wheaton
Silver Spr.
Takoma Park
College Park
Greenbelt
Hyattsville
Mount Rainier
Georgetown
MONTGOMERY
PRINCE GEORGES
ANDREWS AIR FORCE BASE
Camp Springs
Oxon Hill
Fort Foote
Forest Heights
Suitland
Clinton

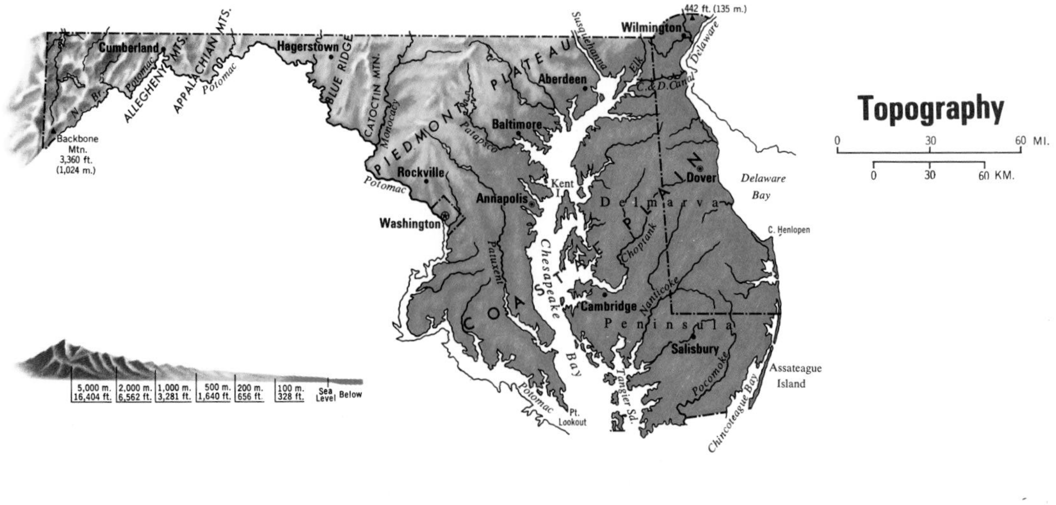
Cumberland
Hagerstown
Wilmington
442 ft. (135 m.)
Aberdeen
Baltimore
Rockville
Annapolis
Washington
Kent
Dover
Cambridge
Salisbury
ALLEGHENY MTS.
APPALACHIAN MTS.
BLUE RIDGE
CATOCTIN MTN.
PIEDMONT
PLATEAU
COASTAL PLAIN
Delmarva Peninsula
Backbone Mtn. 3,360 ft. (1,024 m.)
Chesapeake Bay
Delaware Bay
C. Henlopen
Assateague Island
Pt. Lookout
Potomac
Susquehanna
C.&D. Canal
Choptank
Nanticoke
Pocomoke
Tangier Sd.
Chincoteague Bay
5,000 m. 16,404 ft.
2,000 m. 6,562 ft.
1,000 m. 3,281 ft.
500 m. 1,640 ft.
200 m. 656 ft.
100 m. 328 ft.
Sea Level
Below
0 30 60 MI.
0 30 60 KM.

Topography

MARYLAND

AREA 10,460 sq. mi. (27,091 sq. km.)
POPULATION 4,798,622
CAPITAL Annapolis
LARGEST CITY Baltimore
HIGHEST POINT Backbone Mtn. 3,360 ft. (1024 m.)
SETTLED IN 1634
ADMITTED TO UNION April 28, 1788
POPULAR NAME Old Line State; Free State
STATE FLOWER Black-eyed Susan
STATE BIRD Baltimore Oriole

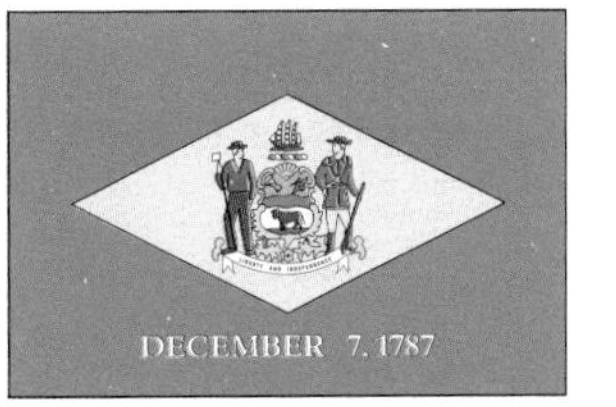
DECEMBER 7, 1787

DELAWARE

AREA 2,044 sq. mi. (5,294 sq. km.)
POPULATION 668,696
CAPITAL Dover
LARGEST CITY Wilmington
HIGHEST POINT Ebright Road 442 ft. (135 m.)
SETTLED IN 1627
ADMITTED TO UNION December 7, 1787
POPULAR NAME First State; Diamond State
STATE FLOWER Peach Blossom
STATE BIRD Blue Hen Chicken

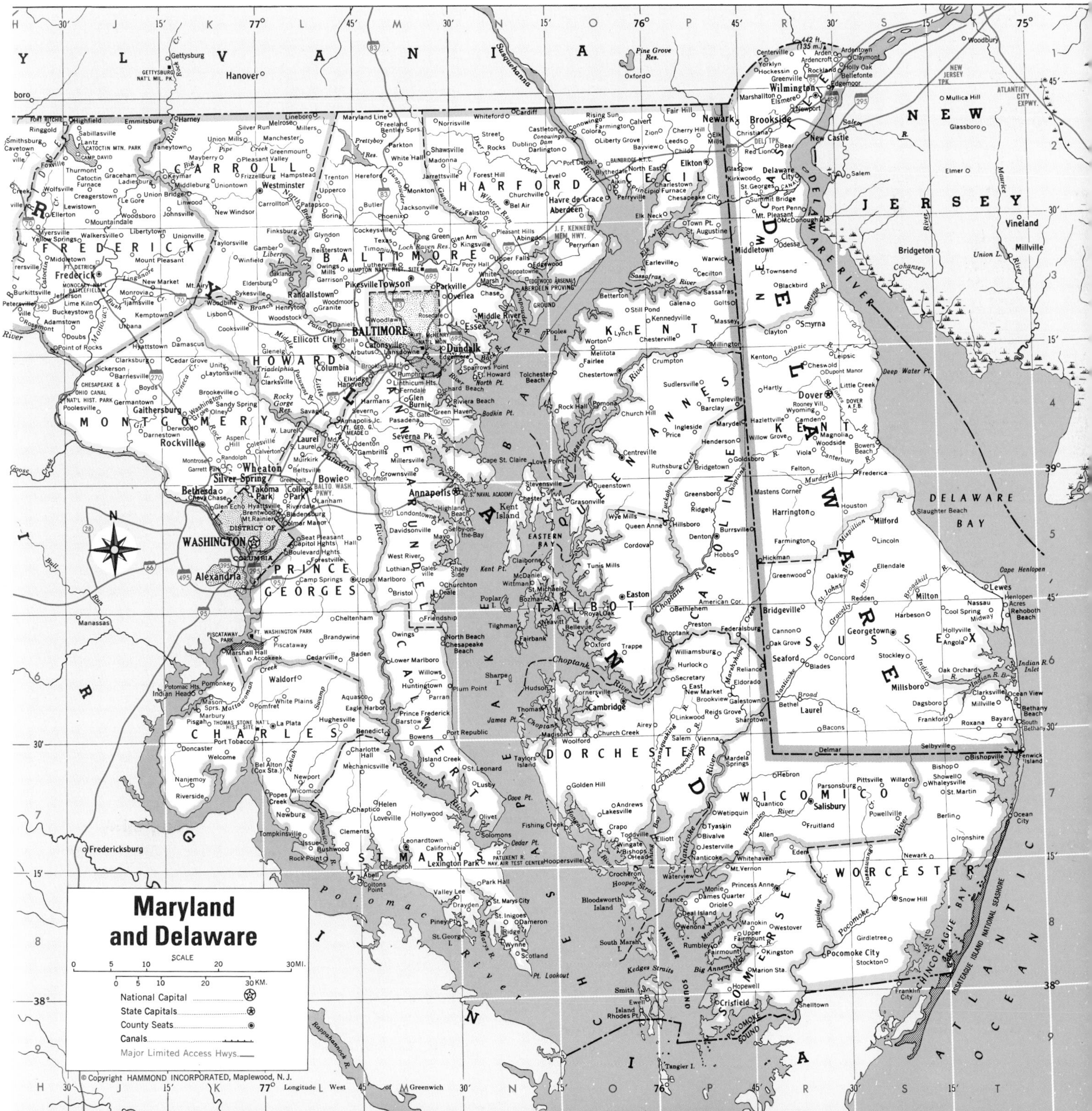
Maryland and Delaware
SCALE
0 5 10 20 30 MI.
0 5 10 20 30 KM.
National Capital
State Capitals
County Seats
Canals
Major Limited Access Hwys.
© Copyright HAMMOND INCORPORATED, Maplewood, N.J.
Longitude West of Greenwich
WASHINGTON
BALTIMORE
Annapolis
Dover
Wilmington
CARROLL
FREDERICK
BALTIMORE
HARFORD
CECIL
KENT
HOWARD
MONTGOMERY
PRINCE GEORGES
ANNE ARUNDEL
QUEEN ANNES
CAROLINE
TALBOT
CALVERT
CHARLES
ST. MARYS
DORCHESTER
WICOMICO
SOMERSET
WORCESTER
NEW CASTLE
SUSSEX
NEW JERSEY
DELAWARE BAY
CHESAPEAKE BAY
Potomac River
DELAWARE RIVER
ATLANTIC OCEAN
TANGIER SOUND
POCOMOKE SOUND
CHINCOTEAGUE BAY
ASSATEAGUE ISLAND NATIONAL SEASHORE

OTHER FEATURES

DELAWARE

COUNTIES

CITIES and TOWNS

OTHER FEATURES

DISTRICT OF COLUMBIA

CITIES and TOWNS

OTHER FEATURES

▲County seat.

Agriculture, Industry and Resources

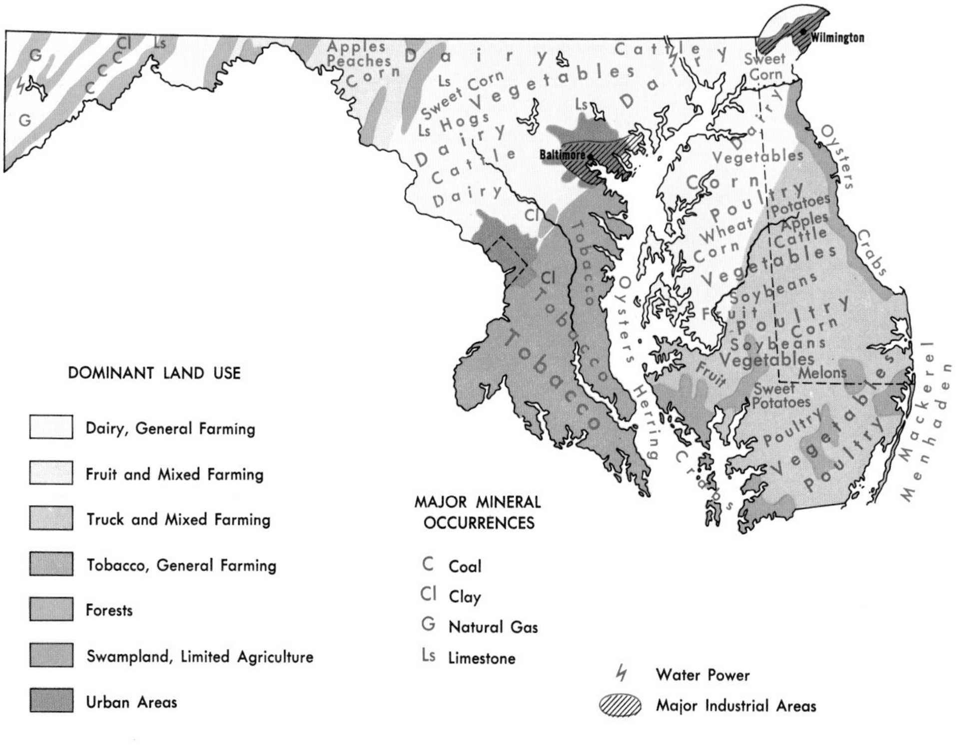
Apples
Peaches
Dairy
Cattle
Corn
Sweet Corn
Vegetables
Hogs
Ls
Cl
G
C
Baltimore
Wilmington
Tobacco
Oysters
Crabs
Poultry
Potatoes
Wheat
Soybeans
Fruit
Melons
Sweet Potatoes
Herring
Mackerel
Menhaden
DOMINANT LAND USE
Dairy, General Farming
Fruit and Mixed Farming
Truck and Mixed Farming
Tobacco, General Farming
Forests
Swampland, Limited Agriculture
Urban Areas
MAJOR MINERAL OCCURRENCES
C Coal
Cl Clay
G Natural Gas
Ls Limestone
Water Power
Major Industrial Areas

MASSACHUSETTS

AREA 8,284 sq. mi. (21,456 sq. km.)
POPULATION 6,029,051
CAPITAL Boston
LARGEST CITY Boston
HIGHEST POINT Mt. Greylock 3,491 ft. (1064 m.)
SETTLED IN 1620
ADMITTED TO UNION February 6, 1788
POPULAR NAME Bay State; Old Colony
STATE FLOWER Mayflower
STATE BIRD Chickadee

HOPE

RHODE ISLAND

AREA 1,212 sq. mi. (3,139 sq. km.)
POPULATION 1,005,984
CAPITAL Providence
LARGEST CITY Providence
HIGHEST POINT Jerimoth Hill 812 ft. (247 m.)
SETTLED IN 1636
ADMITTED TO UNION May 29, 1790
POPULAR NAME Little Rhody; Ocean State
STATE FLOWER Violet
STATE BIRD Rhode Island Red

Agriculture, Industry and Resources

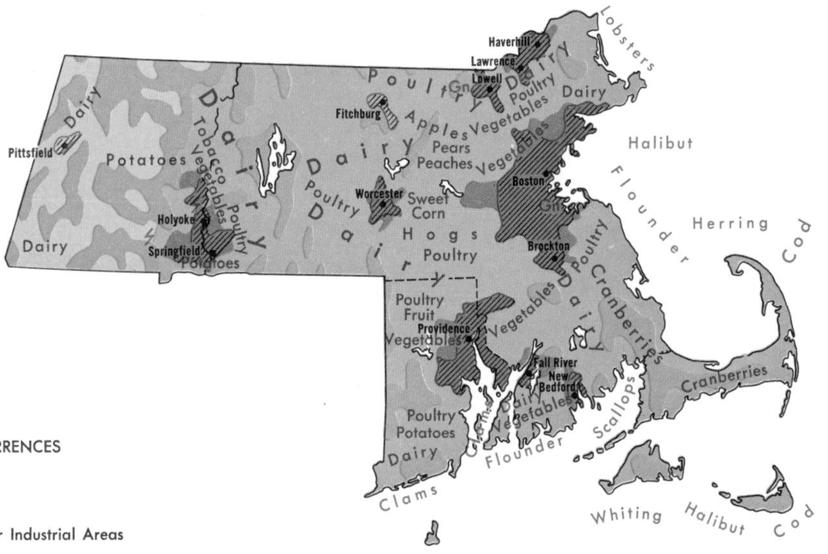

Haverhill
Lawrence
Lowell
Fitchburg
Pittsfield
Worcester
Boston
Holyoke
Springfield
Brockton
Providence
Fall River
New Bedford
Lobsters
Halibut
Flounder
Herring
Cod
Poultry
Dairy
Potatoes
Tobacco
Vegetables
Apples
Pears
Peaches
Sweet Corn
Hogs
Fruit
Cranberries
Scallops
Clams
Whiting
Gn

DOMINANT LAND USE

- Specialized Dairy
- Dairy, Poultry, Mixed Farming
- Forests
- Urban Areas

MAJOR MINERAL OCCURRENCES

Gn Granite

Water Power

Major Industrial Areas

MASSACHUSETTS

COUNTIES

Barnstable 186,605 N6
Berkshire 139,352 B3
Bristol 506,325 K5
Dukes 11,639 M7
Essex 670,080 L2
Franklin 70,092 D2
Hampden 456,310 D4
Hampshire 146,568 D3
Middlesex 1,398,468 J3
Nantucket 6,012 O7
Norfolk 616,087 K4
Plymouth 435,276 L5
Suffolk 663,906 K3
Worcester 709,705 G3

CITIES and TOWNS

Abington• 13,817 L4
Acton• 17,872 J3
Acushnet• 9,554 L6
Adams 6,356 B2
Adams• 9,445 B2
Agawam• 27,323 D4
Alford• 418 A4
Allerton 900 E7
Amesbury 12,109 L1
Amesbury• 14,997 L1
Amherst 17,824 E3
Amherst• 35,228 E3
Andover 8,242 K2
Andover• 29,151 K2
Arlington• 44,630 C6
Ashburnham 900 G2
Ashburnham• 5,433 G2
Ashby• 2,717 G2
Ashfield• 1,715 C2
Ashland• 12,066 J3
Ashley Falls 600 A4
Assinippi 950 E8
Assonet 950 K5
Athol 8,732 F2
Athol• 11,451 F2
Attleboro 38,383 J5
Attleboro Falls J5
Auburn• 15,005 G4
Auburndale B7
Avon• 4,558 K4
Ayer 2,889 H2
Ayer• 6,871 H2
Baldwinville 1,795 F2
Ballardvale K2
Barnstable▲ 2,790 N6
Barnstable• 30,898 N6
Barre 1,094 F3
Barre• 4,546 F3
Barrowsville 500 K5
Becket• 1,481 B3
Bedford• 12,996 B6
Belchertown 2,339 E3
Belchertown• 10,579 E3
Bellingham 4,535 J4
Bellingham• 14,877 J4
Belmont• 24,720 C6
Berkley• 4,237 K5
Berlin• 2,293 H3
Bernardston• 2,048 D2
Beverly 38,195 E5
Billerica• 37,609 J2
Blackstone• 8,023 H4
Blandford• 1,187 C4
Bolton• 3,134 H3
Bondsville 1,992 E4
Boston (cap.)▲ 574,283 D7
Bourne 1,284 M6
Bourne• 16,064 M6
Boxborough• 3,343 H3
Boxford 2,072 L2
Boxford• 6,266 L2
Boylston• 3,517 H3
Braintree• 33,836 D8
Brant Rock-Ocean Bluff M4
Brewster 1,818 O5
Brewster• 8,440 O5
Bridgewater 7,242 K5
Bridgewater• 21,249 K5
Brimfield• 3,001 F4
Brockton 92,788 K4
Brookfield 2,968 F4
Brookfield• 2,397 F4
Brookline• 54,718 C7
Brookville K4
Buckland• 1,928 C2
Burlington• 23,302 C5
Buzzards Bay 3,250 M5
Byfield 950 L1
Cambridge▲ 95,802 C7
Canton• 18,530 C8
Carlisle• 4,333 J2
Carver• 10,590 M5
Cataumet 650 M6
Centerville 9,190 N6
Central Village 800 K6
Charlemont• 1,249 C2
Charlton• 9,576 F4
Charlton City 950 F4
Chartley 950 K5
Chatham 1,916 P6
Chatham• 6,579 P6
Chelmsford• 32,388 J2
Chelsea 28,710 D6
Cherry Valley G3
Cheshire• 3,479 B2
Chester• 1,280 C3
Chesterfield• 1,048 C3
Chicopee 56,632 D4
Chilmark• 650 M7
Chiltonville 600 M5
City Mills 500 J4
Clicquot-Millis A8
Clinton• 7,943 H3
Cochituate 6,046 A7
Cohasset• 7,075 F7
Collinsville J2
Colrain• 1,757 D2
Concord• 17,076 B6
Conway• 1,529 D2
Cordaville 1,530 H3
Cotuit 2,364 N6
Cummington• 785 C3
Dalton• 7,155 B3
Danvers• 24,174 D5
Danversport E5
Dartmouth• 27,244 K6
Dedham▲ 23,782 C7
Deerfield• 5,018 D2
Dennis• 2,633 O5
Dennis Port 2,775 O6
Dighton• 5,631 K5
Dorchester D7
Douglas• 5,438 H4
Dover 2,163 B7
Dover• 4,915 B7
Dracut• 25,594 J2
Dudley• 9,540 G4
Dunstable• 2,236 J2
Duxbury 1,637 M4
Duxbury• 13,895 M4
East Braintree D8
East Brewster 900 O5
East Bridgewater• 11,104 L4
East Brookfield 1,396 G4
East Brookfield• 2,033 G4
East Dedham C8
East Dennis 2,584 O5
East Douglas 1,945 G4
East Falmouth (Teaticket) 5,577 M6
East Foxboro 750 K4
East Freetown 600 L5
East Harwich 3,828 O6
East Longmeadow• 13,367 E4
East Milton D7
East Norton 750 K5
East Orleans 600 P5
East Otis 600 B4
East Pembroke 582 M4
East Pepperell 2,296 H2
East Sandwich 3,171 N6
East Templeton 950 G2
East Walpole C8
East Wareham 950 M5
East Weymouth E8
East Whately 650 D3
Eastham• 4,462 O5
Easthampton• 15,537 D3
Easton 19,807 K4
Eastondale 600 K4
Edgartown▲ 3,062 M7
Edgartown• 2,204 M7
Erving• 1,372 E2
Essex 1,507 L2
Essex• 3,260 L2
Everett 35,701 D6
Fairhaven• 16,132 L6
Fall River 92,703 K6
Falmouth 4,047 M6
Falmouth• 27,960 M6
Fayville 975 H3
Feeding Hills D4
Fisherville H4
Fiskdale 2,189 F4
Fitchburg▲ 41,194 G2
Florida• 742 B2
Forge Village 925 H2
Foxboro 5,706 J4
Foxboro• 14,148 J4
Framingham• 64,994 A7
Framingham Center 16,000 J3
Franklin 9,965 J4
Franklin• 22,095 J4
Gardner 20,125 G2
Gay Head• 201 L7
Georgetown• 6,384 L2
Gilbertville 1,029 F3
Gill• 1,583 D2
Gloucester 28,716 M2
Goshen• 830 C3
Grafton• 13,035 H4
Granby 1,327 E3
Granby• 5,565 E3
Graniteville 970 J2
Granville• 1,403 C4
Great Barrington 2,810 A4
Great Barrington• 7,725 A4
Green Harbor 2,002 M4
Greenbush 950 F8
Greenfield▲ 14,016 D2
Greenfield• 18,666 D2
Greenwood D6
Groton 1,044 H2
Groton• 7,511 H2
Groveland• 5,214 L1
Hadley• 4,231 D3
Halifax• 6,526 L5
Hamilton• 7,280 L2
Hampden• 4,709 E4
Hancock• 628 A2
Hanover• 11,912 L4
Hanson 2,188 L4
Hanson• 9,028 L4
Hardwick• 2,385 F3
Harvard• 12,329 H2
Harwich 10,275 O6
Harwich• 1,668 O6
Harwich Port 1,742 O6
Hatfield 1,234 D3
Hatfield• 3,184 D3
Haverhill 51,418 K1
Haydenville 900 C3
Heath• 716 C2
Hingham 5,454 E8
Hingham• 19,821 E8
Hinsdale• 1,959 B3
Holbrook• 11,041 D8
Holden• 14,628 G3
Holland• 1,331 F4
Holliston• 12,926 A8
Holyoke 43,704 D4
Hopedale 3,961 H4
Hopedale• 5,666 H4
Hopkinton 2,305 J4
Hopkinton• 9,191 J4
Housatonic 1,184 A3
Hubbardston• 2,797 F3
Hudson 14,267 H3
Hudson• 17,233 H3
Hull• 10,466 E7
Huntington• 1,987 C4
Hyannis 14,120 N6
Hyannis Port 750 N6
Hyde Park C7
Interlaken 700 A3
Ipswich 4,132 L2
Ipswich• 11,873 L2
Islington C8
Jamaica Plain C7
Jefferson G3
Kingston 4,774 M5
Kingston• 9,045 M5
Lakeville 7,785 L5
Lakeville• 5,931 L5
Lancaster• 6,661 H3
Lanesboro• 3,131 A2
Lawrence▲ 70,207 K2
Lee 2,020 B3
Lee• 5,849 B3
Leicester• 10,191 G4
Lenox 1,687 A3
Lenox• 5,069 A3
Lenox Dale 600 B3
Leominster 38,145 G2
Leverett• 1,785 E3
Lexington• 28,974 B6
Leyden• 662 D2
Lincoln• 7,666 B6
Lincoln Center 945 B6
Linwood 995 H4
Littleton Common 2,867 J2
Littleton• 7,051 H2
Longmeadow• 15,467 D4
Lowell▲ 103,439 J2
Ludlow• 18,820 E4
Ludlow Center 750 E4
Lunds Corner L6
Lunenburg 1,694 H2
Lunenburg• 9,117 H2
Lynn 81,245 D6
Lynnfield• 11,274 C5
Malden 53,884 D6
Manchaug 975 G4
Manchester-by-the-Sea• 5,286 F5
Manomet 950 M5
Mansfield 7,170 J4
Mansfield• 13,453 J4
Marblehead• 19,971 E7
Marion 1,426 L6
Marion• 3,932 L6
Marlborough 31,813 H3
Marshfield 4,002 M4
Marshfield• 21,531 M4
Marshfield Hills 2,201 M4
Marstons Mills 8,017 N6
Mashpee• 7,884 M6
Mattapan C7
Mattapoisett 2,949 L6
Mattapoisett• 5,597 L6
Maynard• 10,325 J3
Medfield 5,985 B8
Medfield• 10,531 B8
Medford 57,407 C6
Medway• 9,931 J4
Melrose 28,150 D6
Mendon• 4,010 H4
Merino Village G4
Merrimac• 5,166 L1
Methuen• 39,990 K2
Middleboro 6,837 L5
Middleboro• 16,404 L5
Middlefield• 392 B3
Middleton• 4,921 K2
Milford 23,339 H4
Milford• 25,355 H4
Millbury• 12,228 H4
Millers Falls 1,084 E2
Millis-Clicquot 4,081 A8
Millis• 7,613 A8
Millville• 2,236 H4
Milton• 25,725 D7
Monson 2,101 E4
Monson• 7,315 E4
Montague• 8,316 E2
Monterey• 805 B4
Monument Beach 1,842 M6
Moores Corner E2
Mount Washington• 135 A4
Nabnasset 975 J2
Nahant• 3,828 E6
Nantasket Beach E7
Nantucket▲ 3,069 O7
Nantucket• 6,012 O7
Natick• 30,510 A7
Needham Heights B7
Needham• 27,557 B7
Neponset D7
New Bedford▲ 99,922 K6
New Braintree• 881 F3
New Marlborough• 1,240 B4
New Salem• 802 E2
Newbury• 5,623 L1
Newburyport▲ 16,317 L1
Newton 82,585 C7
Newton Center C7
Newton Highlands C7
Newton Lower Falls 950 B7
Newton Upper Falls C7
Newtonville C7
Norfolk• 9,270 J4
North Abington L4
North Adams 16,797 B2
North Amherst 6,239 E3
North Andover• 22,792 K2
North Attleboro• 16,178 J5
North Billerica J2
North Brookfield 2,635 F3
North Brookfield• 4,708 F3
North Chelmsford J2
North Dartmouth K6
North Dighton 1,174 K5
North Eastham 1,570 O5
North Easton K4
North Falmouth 2,625 M6
North Grafton H4
North Hadley 600 D3
North Hanover 950 L4
North Oxford G4
North Pembroke 2,485 M4
North Plymouth 3,450 L5
North Reading• 12,002 C5
North Scituate 4,891 F8
North Truro 675 O4
North Uxbridge H4
North Waltham B6
North Weymouth D8
North Wilbraham E4
Northampton▲ 29,289 D3
Northborough 5,761 H3
Northborough• 11,929 H3
Northbridge• 13,371 H4
Northfield 1,322 E2
Northfield• 2,838 E2
Norton 1,899 K5
Norton• 12,690 K5
Norwell• 9,279 F8
Norwood• 28,700 B8
Nutting Lake B5
Oak Bluffs 2,804 M7
Oak Bluffs• 1,984 M7
Oakdale 850 G3
Oakham• 1,503 F3
Ocean Bluff-Brant Rock 4,541 M4
Ocean Grove 3,169 K6
Old Sturbridge Village 500 F4
Onset 1,461 M6
Orange 3,791 E2
Orange• 7,312 E2
Orleans 1,699 O5
Orleans• 5,838 O5
Osterville 2,911 N6
Otis• 1,073 B4
Otter River 700 F2
Oxford 5,969 G4
Oxford• 12,588 G4
Palmer 4,069 E4
Palmer• 12,054 E4
Paxton• 4,047 G3
Peabody 47,039 E5
Pelham• 1,373 E3

(continued on following page)

(continued)

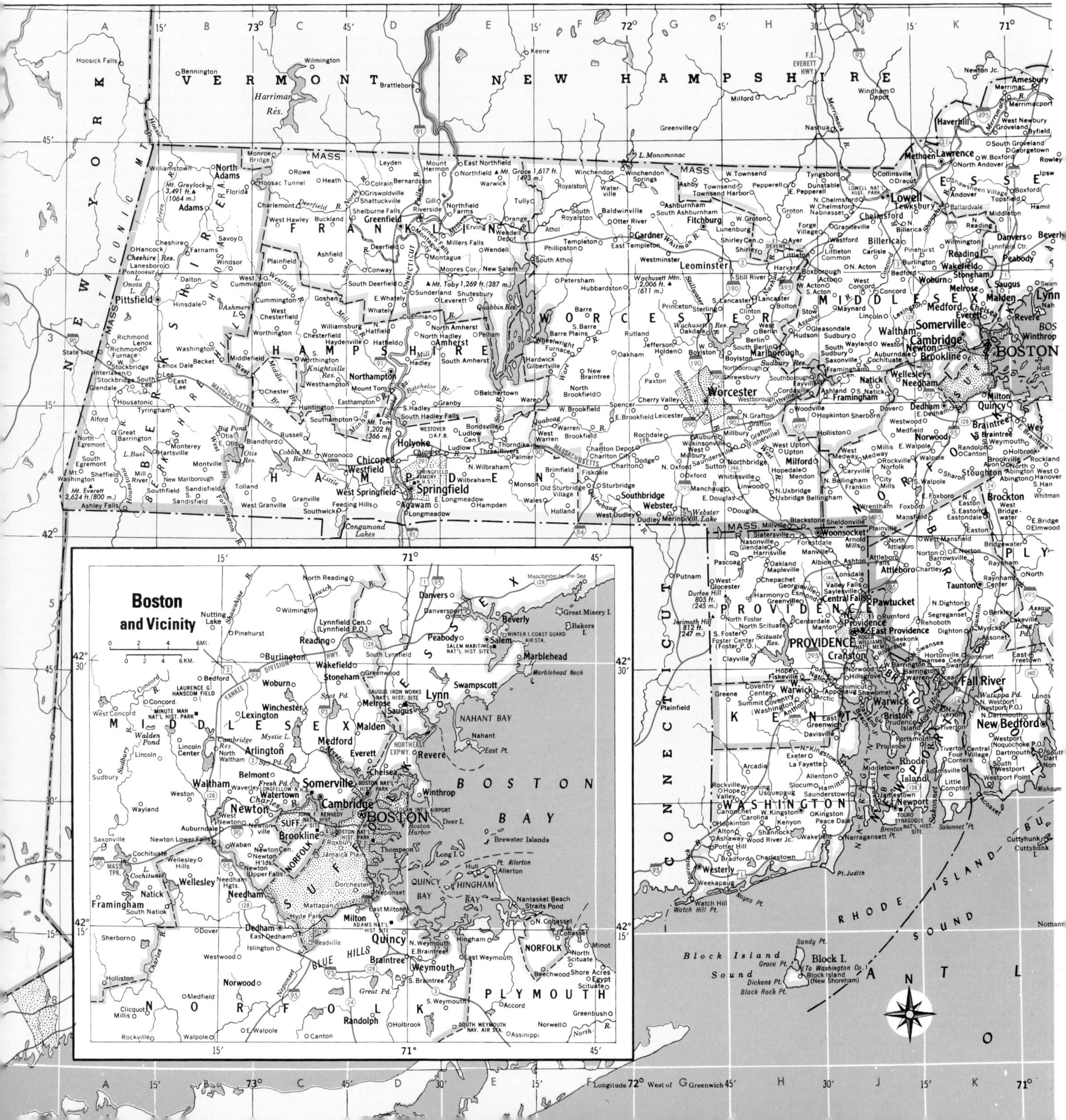

VERMONT
NEW HAMPSHIRE
NEW YORK
MASS.
FRANKLIN
BERKSHIRE
HAMPSHIRE
HAMPDEN
WORCESTER
MIDDLESEX
ESSEX
NORFOLK
PROVIDENCE
KENT
WASHINGTON
BRISTOL
NEWPORT
CONNECTICUT
Pittsfield
Springfield
Worcester
Fitchburg
Leominster
Lowell
Lawrence
Haverhill
Boston
Cambridge
Quincy
Brockton
Taunton
Fall River
New Bedford
Woonsocket
Pawtucket
PROVIDENCE
Cranston
Warwick
Newport
Westerly
Block Island Sound
RHODE ISLAND SOUND
Block I.
Boston and Vicinity
BOSTON BAY
Longitude 72° West of Greenwich

Vineyard Haven 1,762 ....M7
Waban B7
Wakefield• 24,825 ....C5
Wales• 1,566 ....F4
Walpole 5,495 ....B8
Walpole• 20,212 ....B8
Waltham 57,878 ....B6
Ware 6,533 ....E3
Ware• 9,808 ....E3
Wareham 19,232 ....L5
Wareham• 18,457 ....L5
Wareham Center 2,607 ....L5
Warren 1,516 ....F4
Warren• 4,437 ....F4
Warwick• 740 ....E2
Washington• 615 ....B3
Watertown• 33,284 ....C6
Waverley B6
Wayland• 11,874 ....A7
Webster 11,849 ....G4
Webster• 16,196 ....G4
Wellesley• 26,615 ....B7
Wellesley Hills B7
Wellfleet• 2,493 ....O5
Wendell• 899 ....E2
Wenham• 4,212 ....L2
West Acton 975 ....H3
West Barnstable 1,508 ....N6
West Boxford 950 ....K2
West Boylston• 6,611 ....G3
West Bridgewater• 6,389 ....K4
West Brookfield 1,419 ....F4
West Brookfield• 3,532 ....F4
West Chatham 1,504 ....O6
West Chelmsford J2
West Concord 5,761 ....A6
West Dennis 2,307 ....O6
West Falmouth 1,752 ....M6
West Groton 950 ....H2
West Hanover L4
West Harwich 883 ....O6
West Mansfield 950 ....K5
West Medway J4
West Newbury• 3,421 ....L1
West Newton B7
West Springfield• 27,537 ....D4
West Stockbridge• 1,483 ....A3
West Tisbury• 1,704 ....M7
West Townsend 950 ....H2
West Upton-Upton H4
West Wareham 2,059 ....L5
West Warren F4
West Yarmouth 5,409 ....N6
Westborough 3,917 ....H3
Westborough• 14,133 ....H3
Westfield• 38,372 ....D4
Westford• 16,392 ....J2
Westhampton• 1,327 ....C3
Westminster• 6,191 ....G2
Weston• 10,200 ....B6
Westport 13,852 ....K6
Westport• 13,763 ....K6
Westwood• 12,557 ....B8
Weymouth 54,063 ....D8
Whately• 1,375 ....D3
Whitinsville 5,639 ....H4
Whitman• 13,240 ....L4
Wilbraham 3,352 ....E4
Wilbraham• 12,635 ....E4
Williamsburg• 2,515 ....C3
Williamstown 4,791 ....B2
Williamstown• 8,220 ....B2
Wilmington• 17,654 ....C5
Winchendon 4,316 ....F2
Winchendon• 8,805 ....F2
Winchester• 20,267 ....C6
Windsor• 770 ....B2
Winthrop• 18,127 ....D6
Woburn 35,943 ....C6
Woods Hole 1,080 ....M6
Worcester▲ 169,759 ....H3
Worthington• 1,156 ....C3
Wrentham• 9,006 ....J4
Yarmouth Port 4,271 ....N6
Yarmouth• 21,174 ....O6

OTHER FEATURES

Adams Nat'l Hist. Site D7
Agawam (riv.) M5
Allerton (pt.) E7
Ann (cape) M2
Ashmere (lake) B3
Assabet (riv.) H3
Assawompset (pond) L5
Batchelor (brook) D3
Berkshire (hills) B4
Big (pond) B4
Bigelow (bight) M1
Blackstone (riv.) G3
Blue (hills) C8
Boston (bay) E6
Boston (harb.) D7
Boston Nat'l Hist. Park D6
Brewster (isls.) E7
Buel (lake) A4
Buzzards (bay) L7
Cambridge (res.) B6
Cape Cod (bay) N5
Cape Cod (canal) N5
Cape Cod Nat'l Seashore P5
Chappaquiddick (isl.) N7
Charles (riv.) C7
Chicopee (riv.) D4
Cobble Mountain (res.) C4
Cochituate (lake) A7
Cod (cape) O4
Concord (riv.) J2
Congamond (lakes) D4
Connecticut (riv.) D2
Cuttyhunk (isl.) L7
Deer (isl.) E7
Deerfield (riv.) C2
East (pt.) E6
East Chop (pt.) M7
Eastern (pt.) M2
Elizabeth (isls.) L7
Everett (mt.) A4
Falls (riv.) D2
Fort Devens 8,973 ....H2
Fresh (pond) C6
Gammon (pt.) N6
Gay Head (prom.) L7
Grace (mt.) E2
Great (pt.) O7
Green (riv.) B2
Greylock (mt.) B2
Gurnet (pt.) M4
Hingham (bay) E7
Holyoke (range) D3
Hoosac (mts.) B2
Hoosic (riv.) A1
Housatonic (riv.) A4
Ipswich (riv.) L2
John F. Kennedy
Nat'l Hist. Site C7
Knightville (res.) C3
Laurence G. Hanscom Field B6
Little (riv.) C4
Logan Int'l Airport D7
Long (isl.) E7
Long (pt.) O4
Long (pond) L5
Longfellow Nat'l Hist. Site C6
Lowell Nat'l Hist. Park J2
Maine (gulf) M2
Manhan (riv.) D4
Manomet (pt.) N5
Marblehead (neck) F6
Martha's Vineyard (isl.) M7
Massachusetts (bay) M4
Merrimack (riv.) K1
Mill (riv.) C3
Mill (riv.) D3
Millers (riv.) E2
Minute Man Nat'l Hist. Park B6
Mishaum (pt.) L6
Monomonac (lake) G2
Monomoy (isl.) O6
Monomoy (pt.) O6
Mount Hope (bay) K6
Muskeget (chan.) N7
Muskeget (isl.) N7
Mystic (lake) C6
Mystic (riv.) C6
Nahant (bay) E6
Nantucket (isl.) O8
Nantucket (sound) N6
Nashawena (isl.) L7
Nashua (riv.) H3
Naushon (isl.) L7
Neponset (riv.) C8
Nomans Land (isl.) L7
Nonamesset (isl.) M6
North (riv.) D2
North (riv.) L4
Onota (lake) A3
Otis (res.) B4
Otis A.F.B. M6
Pasque (isl.) L7
Plum (isl.) L2
Plymouth (bay) M5
Poge (cape) N7
Pontoosuc (lake) A3
Quabbin (res.) E3
Quaboag (riv.) F4
Quincy (bay) D7
Quinebaug (riv.) F4
Race (pt.) N4
Salem Maritime
Nat'l Hist. Site E5
Saugus Iron Works
Nat'l Hist. Site D6
Shawshine (riv.) K2
Silver (lake) L4
South (riv.) D2
South Weymouth
Nav. Air Sta. E8
Springfield Armory
Nat'l Hist. Site D4
Squibnocket (pt.) M7
Stillwater (riv.) G3
Sudbury (res.) H3
Sudbury (riv.) A6
Swift (riv.) E4
Taconic (mts.) A2
Taunton (riv.) K5
Thompson (isl.) D7
Toby (mt.) E3
Tom (mt.) D4
Tuckernuck (isl.) N7
Vineyard (sound) L7
Wachusett (mt.) G3
Wachusett (res.) G3
Walden (pond) A6
Ware (riv.) F3
Watuppa (pond) K6
Webster (lake) G4
Wellfleet (harb.) O5
West (riv.) H4
West Chop (pt.) M7
Westfield (riv.) C3
Westover A.F.B. D4
Weweantic (riv.) L5
Whitman (riv.) G2
Winter I. Coast Guard Air Sta. E5

RHODE ISLAND

COUNTIES

Bristol 48,859 ....J6
Kent 161,135 ....H6
Newport 87,194 ....K6
Providence 596,270 ....H5
Washington 110,006 ....H7

CITIES and TOWNS

Anthony H6
Apponaug J6
Arctic J6
Arnold Mills J5
Ashaway 1,584 ....G7
Ashton J5
Barrington• 15,849 ....J6
Block Island• H8
Bradford 1,604 ....H7
Bristol▲• 21,625 ....J6
Centerdale H5
Central Falls 17,637 ....J5
Charlestown 6,478 ....H7
Conimicut J6
Coventry (Washington)
31,083 ....H6
Coventry Center H6
Cranston 76,060 ....J5
East Greenwich▲• 11,865 ....H6
East Providence 50,380 ....J5
Esmond H5
Exeter• 5,461 ....H6
Georgiaville H5
Greenville 8,303 ....H5
Harrisville 1,654 ....H5
Hillsgrove J6
Hope Valley 1,446 ....H6
Hopkinton• 6,873 ....H7
Island Park J6
Jamestown 4,999 ....J6
Jamestown• 4,040 ....J6
Kingston 6,504 ....J7
La Fayette H6
Little Compton• 3,339 ....K6
Lonsdale J5
Manville H5
Middletown• 19,460 ....J6
Narragansett 14,985 ....J7
Narragansett• 12,088 ....J7
Natick H6
New Shoreham
(Block Island)• 836 ....H8
Newport▲ 28,227 ....J7
North Kingstown• 23,786 ....J6
North Providence• 32,090 ....J5
North Tiverton K6
Norwood J6
Oakland Beach J6
Pascoag 5,011 ....H5
Pawtucket 72,644 ....J5
Peace Dale-Wakefield 7,134 ....J7
Pontiac J6
Portsmouth• 16,857 ....J6
Providence (cap.)▲ 160,728 ....H5
Riverside J5
Rumford J5
Tiverton 7,259 ....K6
Tiverton• 14,312 ....K6
Valley Falls 11,175 ....J5
Wakefield-Peace Dale 7,134 ....J7
Warren• 11,385 ....J6
Warwick 85,427 ....J6
Watch Hill 300 ....G7
West Kingston 950 ....H7
West Warwick 29,268 ....H6
Westerly▲ 16,477 ....G7
Westerly• 21,605 ....G7
Woonsocket▲ 43,877 ....J4

OTHER FEATURES

Black Rock (pt.) H8
Block (isl.) H8
Block Island (sound) H8
Brenton (pt.) J7
Conanicut (isl.) J6
Dickens (pt.) H8
Durfee (hill) G5
Grace (pt.) H8
Jerimoth (hill) G5
Judith (pt.) J7
Mount Hope (bay) K6
Narragansett (bay) J6
Noyes (pt.) H7
Pawcatuck (riv.) G7
Prudence (isl.) J6
Rhode Island (isl.) J6
Rhode (sound) J7
Roger Williams Nat'l Mem. J5
Sakonnet (pt.) K7
Sakonnet (riv.) K7
Sandy (pt.) H8
Scituate (res.) H5
Touro Synagogue
Nat'l Hist. Site J7
Watch Hill (pt.) G7

▲County seat or Shire town
•Population of town or township

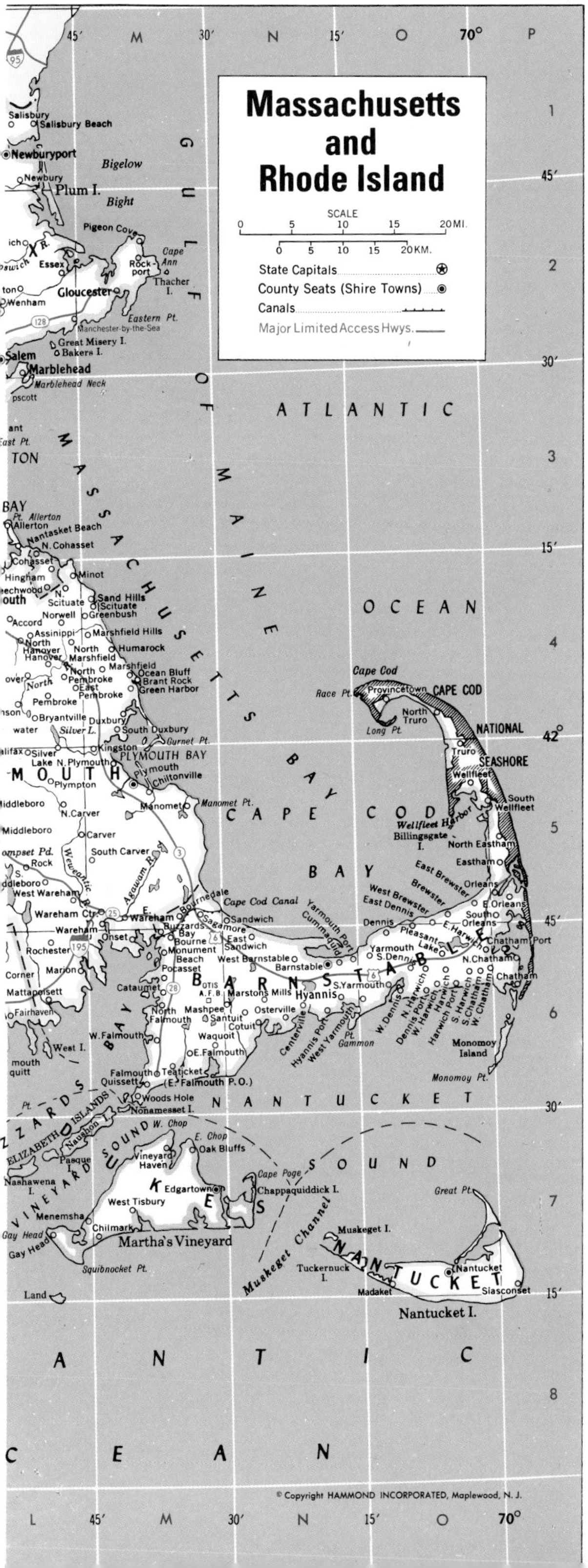
Massachusetts and Rhode Island
SCALE
0 5 10 15 20 MI.
0 5 10 15 20 KM.
State Capitals
County Seats (Shire Towns)
Canals
Major Limited Access Hwys.
ATLANTIC
OCEAN
GULF OF MAINE
MASSACHUSETTS BAY
CAPE COD BAY
NANTUCKET SOUND
CAPE COD NATIONAL SEASHORE
Bigelow Bight
Plum I.
Newburyport
Gloucester
Salem
Marblehead
Provincetown
Cape Cod Canal
Hyannis
Falmouth
Martha's Vineyard
Edgartown
Nantucket I.
Monomoy Island
Muskeget Channel
© Copyright HAMMOND INCORPORATED, Maplewood, N. J.

Topography

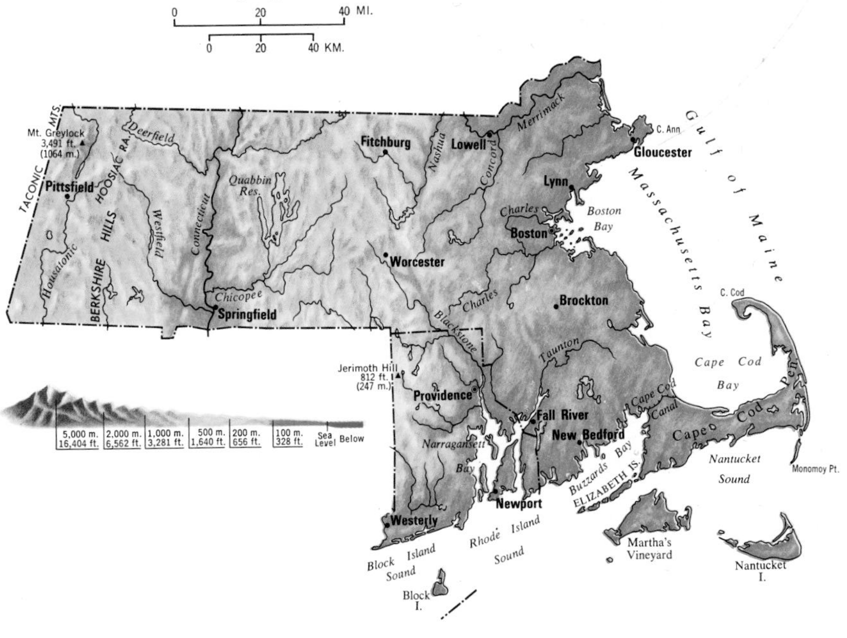
0 20 40 MI.
0 20 40 KM.
Mt. Greylock 3,491 ft. (1064 m.)
Jerimoth Hill 812 ft. (247 m.)
5,000 m. 16,404 ft.
2,000 m. 6,562 ft.
1,000 m. 3,281 ft.
500 m. 1,640 ft.
200 m. 656 ft.
100 m. 328 ft.
Sea Level
Below
Pittsfield
Fitchburg
Lowell
Gloucester
Lynn
Boston
Boston Bay
Worcester
Springfield
Brockton
Providence
Fall River
New Bedford
Newport
Westerly
Gulf of Maine
Massachusetts Bay
Cape Cod Bay
Nantucket Sound
Martha's Vineyard
Nantucket I.
Block Island Sound
Rhode Island Sound
Block I.
Quabbin Res.
BERKSHIRE HILLS
TACONIC MTS.
HOOSAC RA.

Michigan
SCALE
0 5 10 20 30 40 50 MI.
0 5 10 20 30 40 50 KM
State Capitals
County Seats
Canals
Major Limited Access Hwys.
Same scale as main map
Same scale as main map.
© Copyright HAMMOND INCORPORATED, Maplewood, N. J.

AREA 58,527 sq. mi. (151,585 sq. km.)
POPULATION 9,328,784
CAPITAL Lansing
LARGEST CITY Detroit
HIGHEST POINT Mt. Curwood 1,980 ft. (604 m.)
SETTLED IN 1650
ADMITTED TO UNION January 26, 1837
POPULAR NAME Wolverine State
STATE FLOWER Apple Blossom
STATE BIRD Robin

COUNTIES

Alcona 10,145 F4
Alger 8,972 C2
Allegan 90,509 D6
Alpena 30,605 F4
Antrim 18,185 D3
Arenac 14,931 F4
Baraga 7,954 A2
Barry 50,057 D6
Bay 111,723 E5
Benzie 12,200 C4
Berrien 161,378 C7
Branch 41,502 D7
Calhoun 135,982 D6
Cass 49,477 C7
Charlevoix 21,468 D3
Cheboygan 21,398 E3
Chippewa 34,604 E2
Clare 24,952 E5
Clinton 57,883 E6
Crawford 12,260 E4
Delta 37,780 C2
Dickinson 26,831 B2
Eaton 92,879 E6
Emmet 25,040 E3
Genesee 430,459 F5
Gladwin 21,896 E4
Gogebic 18,052 F2
Grand Traverse 64,273 D4
Gratiot 38,982 E5
Hillsdale 43,431 E7
Houghton 35,446 G1
Huron 34,951 F5
Ingham 281,912 E6
Ionia 57,024 D6
Iosco 30,209 F4
Iron 13,175 G2
Isabella 54,624 E5
Jackson 149,756 E6
Kalamazoo 223,411 D6
Kalkaska 13,497 D4
Kent 500,631 D5
Keweenaw 1,701 A1
Lake 8,583 D5
Lapeer 74,768 F5
Leelanau 16,527 D4
Lenawee 91,476 E7
Livingston 115,645 F6
Luce 5,763 D2
Mackinac 10,674 D2
Macomb 717,400 G6
Manistee 21,265 C4
Marquette 70,887 B2
Mason 25,537 C4
Mecosta 37,308 D5
Menominee 24,920 B3
Midland 75,651 E5
Missaukee 12,147 D4
Monroe 133,600 F7
Montcalm 53,059 D5
Montmorency 8,936 E3
Muskegon 158,983 C5
Newaygo 38,202 D5
Oakland 1,083,592 F6
Oceana 22,454 C5
Ogemaw 18,681 E4
Ontonagon 8,854 F1
Osceola 20,146 D5
Oscoda 7,842 E4
Otsego 17,957 E3
Ottawa 187,768 C6
Presque Isle 13,743 F3
Roscommon 19,776 E4
Saginaw 211,946 E5
Saint Clair 138,802 G6
Saint Joseph 56,083 D7
Sanilac 39,928 G5
Schoolcraft 8,302 C2
Shiawassee 69,770 E6
Tuscola 55,498 F5
Van Buren 66,814 C6
Washtenaw 282,937 F6
Wayne 2,111,687 F6
Wexford 26,360 D4

CITIES and TOWNS

Addison 632 E7
Adrian▲ 22,097 F7
Akron 421 F5
Alabaster 46 F4
Alanson 677 E3
Albion 10,066 E6
Algonac 4,551 G6
Allegan▲ 4,547 D6
Allen 201 E7
Allen Park 31,092 B7
Alma 9,034 E5
Almont 2,354 F6
Alpena▲ 11,354 F3
Alpha 219 A2
Anchorville 3,202 G6
Ann Arbor▲ 109,592 F6
Applegate 297 G5
Arcadia 780 C4
Armada 1,548 G6
Ashley 518 E5
Athens 990 D6
Atlanta▲ 475 E3
Atlantic Mine 809 G1
Au Gres 838 F4
Au Sable 1,542 F4
Auburn 1,855 F5
Auburn Heights 7,500 F6
Augusta 927 D6
Averill 800 E5
Bad Axe▲ 3,484 G5
Baldwin▲ 821 D5
Bancroft 599 E6
Bangor 1,922 C6
Baraga 1,231 G1
Bark River 800 B3
Baroda 657 C7
Barryton 393 D5
Barton Hills 320 F6
Battle Creek 53,540 D6
Bay City▲ 38,936 F5
Bay Port 750 F5
Beal City 345 D5
Bear Lake 339 C4
Beaverton 1,150 E5
Beechwood 2,676 C6
Belding 5,969 D5
Bellaire▲ 1,104 D4
Belleville 3,270 F6
Bellevue 1,401 E6
Benton Harbor 12,818 C6
Benton Heights 5,465 C6
Benzonia 449 D4
Berkley 16,960 B6
Berrien Springs 1,927 C7
Bessemer▲ 2,272 F2
Beulah▲ 421 C4
Beverly Hills 10,610 B6
Big Rapids▲ 12,603 D5
Birch Run 992 F5
Birmingham 19,997 B6
Bitely 750 D5
Blissfield 3,172 F7
Bloomfield Hills 4,288 B6
Bloomingdale 503 C6
Boyne City 3,478 E3
Boyne Falls 369 E3
Breckenridge 1,301 E5
Breedsville 213 C6
Bridgeport 8,569 F5
Bridgman 2,140 C7
Brighton 5,686 F6
Britton 694 F6
Bronson 2,342 D7
Brooklyn 1,027 E6
Brown City 1,244 G5
Buchanan 4,992 C7
Buckley 402 D4
Burlington 294 D6
Burr Oak 882 D7
Burt 1,169 F5
Burton 27,617 F6
Byron 573 E6
Byron Center 900 D6
Cadillac▲ 10,104 D4
Caledonia 885 D6
Calumet 818 A1
Camden 482 E7
Capac 1,583 G5
Carleton 2,770 F6
Carney 197 B3
Caro▲ 4,054 F5
Carrollton 6,521 E5
Carson City 1,158 E5
Carsonville 583 G5
Caseville 857 F5
Casnovia 376 D5
Caspian 1,031 G2
Cass City 2,276 F5
Cassopolis▲ 1,822 C7
Cedar Springs 2,600 D5
Cement City 493 E6
Center Line 9,026 B6
Central Lake 954 D3
Centreville▲ 1,516 D7
Charlevoix▲ 3,116 D3
Charlotte▲ 8,083 E6
Chatham 268 B2
Cheboygan▲ 4,999 E3
Chelsea 3,772 E6
Chesaning 2,567 E5
Clare 3,021 E5
Clarkston 1,005 F6
Clarksville 360 D6
Clawson 13,874 B6
Clayton 384 E7
Clifford 354 F5
Climax 677 D6
Clinton 2,475 F6
Clio 2,629 F5
Coldwater▲ 9,607 D7
Coleman 1,237 E5
Coloma 1,679 C6
Colon 1,224 D7
Columbiaville 934 F5
Comstock• 11,162 D6
Concord 944 E6
Constantine 2,032 D7
Coopersville 3,421 C5
Copemish 222 D4
Copper City 198 A1
Corunna▲ 3,091 E6
Croswell 2,174 G5
Crystal 800 E5
Crystal Falls▲ 1,922 A2
Curtis 800 D2
Custer 312 C5
Cutierville 11,228 D6
Daggett 260 B3
Dansville 437 E6
Davison 5,693 F5
De Tour Village 407 E3
De Witt 3,964 E6
Dearborn 89,286 B7
Dearborn Heights 60,838 B7
Decatur 1,760 C6
Deckerville 1,015 G5
Deerfield 922 F7
Detroit Beach 2,113 F7
Detroit▲ 1,027,974 B7
Dexter 1,497 F6
Dimondale 1,247 E6
Dollar Bay 950 G1
Douglas 1,040 C6
Dowagiac 6,409 D6
Drayton Plains F6
Drummond Island• 746 F3
Dryden 628 F6
Dundee 2,664 F7
Durand 4,283 E6
Eagle River▲ 20 A1
East Detroit 35,283 B6
East Grand Rapids 10,807 D6
East Jordan 2,240 D3
East Kingsford A3
East Lansing 50,677 E6
East Tawas 2,887 F4
Eastlake 473 C4
Eastwood 6,340 D6
Eaton Rapids 4,695 E6
Eau Claire 494 C6
Ecorse 12,180 B7
Edmore 1,126 E5
Edwardsburg 1,142 C7
Elberta 478 C4
Elk Rapids 1,626 D4
Elkton 958 F5
Ellsworth 418 D3
Elsie 957 E5
Emmett 297 G6
Empire 355 C4
Erie 750 F7
Escanaba▲ 13,659 C3
Essexville 4,088 F5
Estral Beach 430 F7
Evart 1,744 D5
Ewen 821 F2
Fair Haven 1,505 G6
Fair Plain 8,051 C6
Fairgrove 592 F5
Farmington 10,132 F6
Farmington Hills 74,652 F6
Farwell 851 E5
Fennville 1,023 C6
Fenton 8,444 F6
Ferndale 25,084 B6
Ferrysburg 2,919 C5
Fife Lake 394 D4
Flat Rock 7,290 F6
Flint▲ 140,761 F5
Flushing 8,542 F5
Fountain 165 C4
Fowler 912 E5
Fowlerville 2,648 F6
Frankenmuth 4,408 F5
Frankfort 1,546 C4
Franklin 2,626 B6
Fraser 13,899 B6
Freeland 1,421 E5
Freeport 458 D6
Fremont 3,875 D5
Fruitport 1,090 C5
Gaastra 376 G2
Gagetown 337 F5
Gaines 427 F6
Galesburg 1,863 D6
Galien 596 C7
Garden 268 C3
Garden City 31,846 F6
Gaylord▲ 3,256 E3
Gibraltar 4,297 F6
Gladstone 4,565 C3
Gladwin▲ 2,682 E5
Gobles 769 D6
Goodrich 916 F6
Grand Blanc 7,760 F6
Grand Haven▲ 11,951 C5
Grand Ledge 7,579 E6
Grand Rapids▲ 189,126 D5
Grandville 15,624 D6
Grant 764 D5
Grass Lake 903 E6
Grayling▲ 1,944 E4
Greenville 8,101 D5
Grosse Ile 9,781 B7
Grosse Pointe 5,681 B7
Grosse Pointe Farms 10,092 B6
Grosse Pointe Park 12,857 B7
Grosse Pointe Shores 2,955 B6
Grosse Pointe Woods 17,715 B6
Gulliver 962 D2
Gwinn 2,370 B2
Hamilton 950 C6
Hamtramck 18,372 B6
Hancock 4,547 G1
Hanover 481 E6
Harbor Beach 2,089 G5
Harbor Springs 1,540 D3
Harper Woods 14,903 B6
Harrison▲ 1,835 E4
Harrisville▲ 470 F4
Hart▲ 1,942 C5
Hartford 2,341 C6
Haslett 10,230 E6
Hastings▲ 6,549 D6
Hazel Park 20,051 B6
Hemlock 1,601 E5
Hermansville 950 B3
Hersey 354 D5
Hesperia 846 D5
Highland Park 20,121 B6
Hillman 643 F3
Hillsdale▲ 8,170 E7
Holland 30,745 C6
Holly 5,595 F6
Holt 11,744 E6
Homer 1,758 E6
Honor 292 D4
Hopkins 546 D6
Houghton Lake 3,353 E4
Houghton Lake Heights E4
Houghton▲ 7,498 G1
Howard City 1,351 D5
Howell▲ 8,184 E6
Hubbardston 404 E5
Hubbell 1,174 A1
Hudson 2,580 E7
Hudsonville 6,170 D6
Huntington Woods 6,419 B6
Ida 970 F7
Imlay City 2,921 F5
Indian River 950 E3
Inkster 30,772 B7
Interlochen 600 D4
Ionia▲ 5,935 D6
Iron Mountain▲ 8,525 B3
Iron River 2,095 G2
Ironwood 6,849 F2
Ishpeming 7,200 B2
Isle Royale National Park E1
Ithaca▲ 3,009 E5
Jackson▲ 37,446 E6
Jenison 17,882 D6
Jonesville 2,283 E6
Kalamazoo▲ 80,277 D6
Kaleva 484 C4
Kalkaska▲ 1,952 D4
Keego Harbor 2,932 F6
Kent City 899 D5
Kentwood 37,826 D6
Kinde 473 G5
Kingsford 5,480 A3
Kingsley 738 D4
Kingston 439 F5
L'Anse▲ 2,151 G1
Laingsburg 1,148 E6
Lake Ann 217 D4
Lake City▲ 858 D4
Lake George 950 E5
Lake Linden 1,203 A1
Lake Michigan Beach 1,694 C6
Lake Odessa 2,256 D6
Lake Orion 3,057 F6
Lakeview 1,108 D5
Lakewood Club 659 C5

(continued on following page)

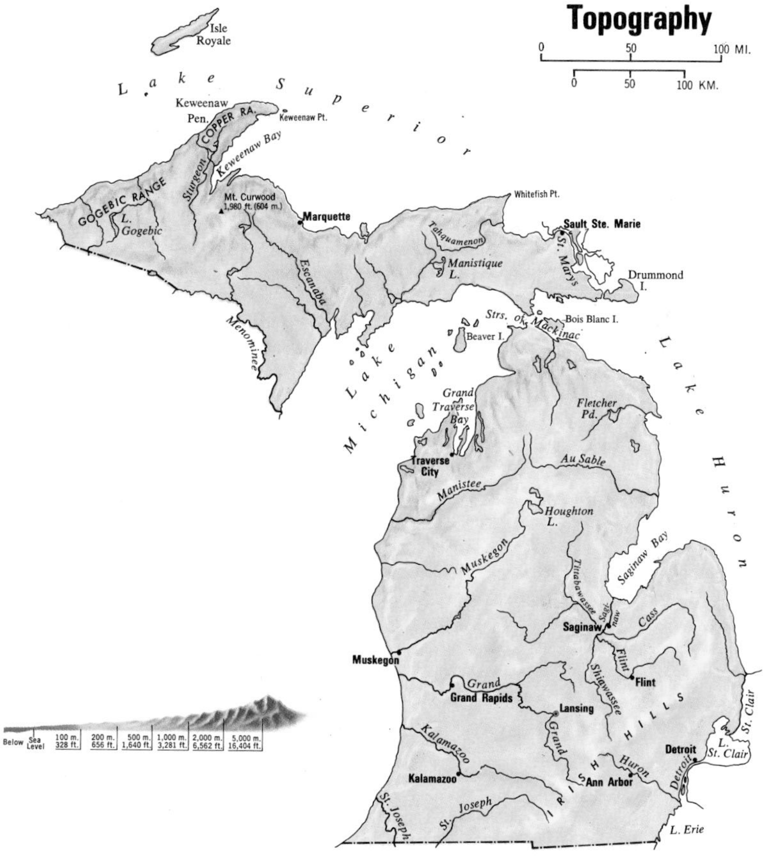
Topography
0 50 100 MI.
0 50 100 KM.
Isle Royale
Lake Superior
Keweenaw Pen.
Keweenaw Pt.
COPPER RA.
Keweenaw Bay
Sturgeon
GOGEBIC RANGE
L. Gogebic
Mt. Curwood 1,980 ft. (604 m.)
Marquette
Whitefish Pt.
Sault Ste. Marie
Tahquamenon
St. Marys
Manistique L.
Drummond I.
Escanaba
Menominee
Strs. of Mackinac
Bois Blanc I.
Beaver I.
Lake Michigan
Lake Huron
Grand Traverse Bay
Fletcher Pd.
Traverse City
Au Sable
Manistee
Houghton L.
Muskegon
Tittabawassee
Saginaw Bay
Saginaw
Cass
Flint
Muskegon
Grand
Grand Rapids
Shiawassee
Lansing
Flint
IRISH HILLS
St. Clair
L. St. Clair
Kalamazoo
Detroit
Huron
Ann Arbor
Kalamazoo
St. Joseph
L. Erie
Below Sea Level
100 m. 328 ft.
200 m. 656 ft.
500 m. 1,640 ft.
1,000 m. 3,281 ft.
2,000 m. 6,562 ft.
5,000 m. 16,404 ft.

Lambertville 7,860 F7
Lansing (cap.) 127,321 E6
Lapeer▲ 7,759 F5
Laurium 2,268 A1
Lawrence 915 C6
Lawton 1,685 D6
Le Roy 251 D4
Leland▲ 776 D3
Lennon 534 E5
Leonard 357 F6
Leslie 1,872 E6
Levering 967 E3
Lexington 779 G5
Lincoln 337 F4
Lincoln Park 41,832 B7
Linden 2,415 F6
Litchfield 1,317 E6
Little Lake 975 B2
Livonia 100,850 F6
Lowell 3,983 D6
Ludington▲ 8,507 C5
Luna Pier 1,507 F7
Luther 343 D4
Lyons 824 E6
Mackinac Island 469 E3
Mackinaw City 875 E3
Madison Heights 32,196 B6
Mancelona 1,370 E4
Manchester 1,753 E6
Manistee▲ 6,734 C4
Manistique▲ 3,456 C3
Manton 1,161 D4
Maple Rapids 680 E5
Marcellus 1,193 D6
Marine City 4,556 G6
Marion 807 D4
Marlette 1,924 G5
Marquette▲ 21,977 B2
Marshall▲ 6,891 E6
Martin 462 D6
Marysville 8,515 G6
Mason▲ 6,768 E6
Mass City 850 G1
Mattawan 2,456 D6
Maybee 500 F6
Mayville 1,010 F5
McBain 692 D4
McBrides 252 D5
Mecosta 393 D5
Melvindale 11,216 B7
Memphis 1,221 G6
Mendon 920 D7
Menominee▲ 9,398 B3
Merrill 755 E5
Mesick 406 D4
Metamora 447 F6
Michiana 164 C7
Michigan Center 4,863 E6
Middleville 1,966 D6
Midland▲ 38,053 E5
Milan 4,040 F6
Milford 5,511 F6
Millersburg 250 F3
Millington 1,114 F5
Minden City 233 G5
Mineral Hills 200 G2
Mio▲ 1,886 E4
Mohawk 800 A1
Monroe▲ 22,902 F7
Montague 2,276 C5
Montgomery 388 E7
Montrose 1,811 F5
Morenci 2,342 E7
Morley 528 D5
Morrice 630 E6
Mount Clemens▲ 18,405 G6
Mount Morris 3,292 F5
Mount Pleasant▲ 23,285 E5
Muir 667 D5
Mulliken 590 E6
Munising▲ 2,783 C2
Muskegon▲ 40,283 C5
Muskegon Heights 13,176 C5
Napoleon 1,332 E6
Nashville 1,654 D6
Naubinway 850 D2
Negaunee 4,741 B2
New Baltimore 5,798 G6
New Boston 1,200 F6
New Buffalo 2,317 C7
New Era 520 C5
New Haven 2,331 G6
New Lothrop 596 F5
Newaygo 1,336 D5
Newberry▲ 1,873 D2
Niles 12,458 C7
North Adams 512 E7
North Branch 1,023 F5
North Muskegon 3,919 C5
Northport 605 D3
Northville 6,226 F6
Norton Shores 21,755 C5
Norway 2,910 B3
Novi 32,998 F6
Oak Park 30,462 B6
Oakley 362 E5
Okemos 20,216 E6
Olivet 1,604 E6
Omer 385 F4
Onaway 1,039 E3
Onekama 515 C4
Onsted 801 E6
Ontonagon▲ 2,040 F1
Orchard Lake 1,798 F6
Ortonville 1,252 F6
Oscoda 1,061 F4
Ossineke 1,091 F4
Otisville 724 F5
Otsego 3,937 D6
Otter Lake 474 F5
Ovid 1,442 E5
Owendale 285 F5
Owosso 16,322 E5
Oxford 2,929 F6
Parchment 1,958 D6
Parma 809 E6
Paw Paw Lake 3,782 C6
Paw Paw▲ 3,169 D6
Pearl Beach 3,394 G6
Peck 558 G5
Pellston 583 E3
Pentwater 1,050 C5
Perrinton 393 E5
Perry 2,163 E6
Petersburg 1,201 F7
Petoskey▲ 6,056 E3
Pewamo 520 E5
Pierson 207 D5
Pigeon 1,207 F5
Pinckney 1,603 F6
Pinconning 1,291 F5
Plainwell 4,057 D6
Pleasant Ridge 2,775 B6
Plymouth 9,560 F6
Pontiac▲ 71,166 F6
Port Austin 815 F4
Port Hope 313 G5
Port Huron▲ 33,694 G6
Port Sanilac 656 G5
Portage 41,042 D6
Portland 3,889 E6
Posen 263 F3
Potterville 1,523 E6
Powers 271 B3
Prescott 314 F4
Prudenville 1,513 E4
Quincy 1,680 E7
Quinnesec 1,254 A3
Ramsay F2
Rapid River 950 C3
Ravenna 919 D5
Reading 1,127 E7
Reed City▲ 2,379 D5
Reese 1,414 F5
Republic 900 B2
Richland 465 D6
Richmond 4,141 G6
River Rouge 11,314 B7
Riverview 13,894 B7
Rochester 7,130 F6
Rockford 3,750 D5
Rockwood 3,141 F6
Rogers City▲ 3,642 F3
Romeo 3,520 F6
Romulus 22,897 F6
Roosevelt Park 3,885 C5
Roscommon▲ 858 E4
Rose City 686 E4
Rosebush 333 E5
Roseville 51,412 B6
Rothbury 407 C5
Royal Oak 65,410 B6
Rudyard 950 E2
Saginaw▲ 69,512 F5
Saint Charles 2,144 E5
Saint Clair 5,116 G6
Saint Clair Shores 68,107 B6
Saint Ignace▲ 2,568 E3
Saint James• 240 D3
Saint Johns▲ 7,284 E6
Saint Joseph▲ 9,214 C6
Saint Louis 3,828 E5
Saline 6,660 F6
Sand Lake 456 D5
Sandusky▲ 2,403 G5
Sanford 889 E5
Saranac 1,461 D6
Saugatuck 954 C6
Sault Sainte Marie▲ 14,689 E2
Schoolcraft 1,517 D6
Scottville 1,287 C5
Sebewaing 1,923 F5
Shelby 1,871 C5
Shepherd 1,413 E5
Sheridan 730 D5
Sherwood 320 D6
Shoreham 737 C6
Shorewood 1,735 C7
South Haven 5,563 C6
South Lyon 5,857 F6
South Monroe 5,266 F7
South Range 745 G1
South Rockwood 1,221 F7
Southfield 75,728 F6
Southgate 30,771 F6
Sparlingville 1,974 G6
Sparta 3,968 D5
Spring Arbor 2,010 E6
Spring Lake 2,537 C5
Springfield 5,582 D6
Springport 707 E6
Stambaugh 1,281 G2
Standish▲ 1,377 F5
Stanton▲ 1,504 D5
Stanwood 174 D5
Stephenson 904 B3
Sterling 520 E4
Sterling Heights 117,810 B6
Stevensville 1,230 C6
Stockbridge 1,202 E6
Sturgis 10,130 D7
Sunfield 610 D6
Suttons Bay 561 D3
Swartz Creek 4,851 F6
Sylvan Lake 1,884 F6
Tawas City▲ 2,009 F4
Taylor 70,811 B7
Tecumseh 7,462 E7
Tekonsha 722 E6
Temperance 6,542 F7
Thompsonville 416 C4
Three Oaks 1,786 C7
Three Rivers 7,413 D7
Traverse City▲ 15,155 D4
Trenton 20,586 B7
Troy 72,884 B6
Tustin 236 D4
Twin Lake 1,328 C5
Twining 169 F4
Ubly 821 G5
Union City 1,767 D6
Union Pier 1,039 C7
Unionville 590 F5
Utica 5,081 F6
Vandalia 357 D7
Vanderbilt 605 E3
Vassar 2,559 F5
Vermontville 776 E6
Vernon 913 F6
Vicksburg 2,216 D6
Wakefield 2,318 F2
Waldron 581 E7
Walker 17,279 D6
Walkerville 262 C5
Walled Lake 6,278 F6
Warren 144,864 B6
Watersmeet 850 G2
Watervliet 1,867 C6
Wayland 2,751 D6
Wayne 19,899 F6
Webberville 1,698 E6
Weidman 696 D5
Wells B3
West Branch▲ 1,914 E4
Westland 84,724 F6
Westphalia 780 E6
White Cloud▲ 1,147 D5
White Pigeon 1,458 D7
White Pine 1,142 F1
Whitehall 3,027 C5
Whitmore Lake 3,251 F6
Whittemore 463 F4
Williamston 2,922 E6
Wixom 8,550 F6
Wolf Lake 4,110 D5
Wolverine 364 E3
Wolverine Lake 4,727 F6
Woodhaven 11,631 F6
Woodland 466 D6
Wyandotte 30,938 B7
Wyoming 63,891 D6
Yale 1,977 G5
Ypsilanti 24,846 F6
Zeeland 5,417 D6
Zilwaukee 1,850 F5

OTHER FEATURES

Abbaye (pt.) B2
Au Sable (pt.) C2
Au Sable (pt.) F4
Au Sable (riv.) E4
Au Train (bay) C2
Bad (riv.) E5
Barques (pt.) C3
Beaver (lake) D3
Beaver (isl.) F4
Belle (riv.) G6
Bete Grise (bay) B1
Big Bay (pt.) B2
Big Bay de Noc (bay) C3
Big Iron (riv.) F1
Big Sable (pt.) C4
Big Sable (riv.) C4
Big Star (lake) C5
Black (lake) E3
Black (riv.) E3
Black (riv.) G5
Blake (pt.) E1
Boardman (riv.) D4
Bois Blanc (isl.) E3
Bond Falls (res.) G2
Brevoort (lake) D3
Brule (riv.) A3
Burt (lake) E3
Cass (riv.) F5
Cedar (lake) F4
Charlevoix (lake) D3
Chippewa (riv.) E5
Crisp (pt.) D2
Crystal (lake) C4
Curwood (mt.) A2
Dead (riv.) B2
Deer (riv.) A2
De Tour (passage) E3
Detour (pt.) C3
Detroit (riv.) B7
Drummond (isl.) F2
Duck (lake) F4
Elk (lake) D4
Erie (lake) G7
Escanaba (riv.) B2
False Detour (chan.) F3
Father Marquette Nat'l Mem. E3
Fawn (riv.) D7
Fence (riv.) A2
Firesteel (riv.) G1
Fletcher (pond) F4
Flint (riv.) F5
Ford (riv.) B2
Forty Mile (pt.) F3
Fourteen Mile (pt.) F1
Garden (isl.) D3
Garden (pen.) C3
Glen (lake) C4
Gogebic (lake) F2
Good Harbor (bay) D3
Government (peak) F1
Grand (isl.) C2
Grand (lake) F3
Grand (riv.) D6
Grand Traverse (bay) D3
Granite (pt.) B2
Green (bay) B4
Gun (lake) D6
Hamlin (lake) C4
Higgins (lake) E4
High (isl.) D3
Hog (isl.) D3
Houghton (lake) E4
Hubbard (lake) F4
Huron (bay) A2
Huron (lake) G4
Huron (riv.) F6
Huron River (pt.) B2
Independence (lake) B2
Indian (lake) C2
Isle Royale (isl.) D1
Isle Royale Nat'l Park E1
Kalamazoo (riv.) C6
Keweenaw (bay) A1
Keweenaw (pt.) B1
K.I. Sawyer A.F.B. 6,577 B2
L'Anse Ind. Res. A2
Laughing Fish (pt.) B2
Leelanau (lake) D4
Light House (pt.) D3
Little Bay de Noc (bay) B3
Little Girl (pt.) E1
Little Sable (pt.) C5
Little Summer (isl.) C3
Little Traverse (bay) D3
Long (lake) F3
Lookingglass (riv.) E6
Mackinac (isl.) E3
Mackinac (str.) E3
Manistee (riv.) C4
Manistique (lake) D2
Manistique (riv.) C2
Manitou (isl.) B1
Maple (riv.) E5
Margrethe (lake) E4
Marquette (isl.) E3
Maumee (bay) F7
Menominee (riv.) B3
Michigamme (lake) A2
Michigamme (res.) B2
Michigamme (riv.) A2
Michigan (lake) B5
Mill (creek) G5
Millecoquins (lake) D2
Misery (bay) G1
Misery (riv.) G1
Montreal (riv.) F1
Mullett (lake) E3
Munuscong (lake) E2
Muskegon (riv.) C5
Neebish (isl.) E2
Net (riv.) G2
Ninemile (pt.) E3
North (chan.) F2
North (pt.) F3
North Fox (isl.) D3
North Manitou (isl.) C3
Oak (pt.) F5
Ontonagon (riv.) G1
Ontonagon Ind. Res. F1
Otsego (lake) E4
Paint (riv.) A2
Paradise (lake) E3
Passage (isl.) E1
Patterson (pt.) D3
Paw Paw (riv.) C6
Peninsula (pt.) C3
Perch (lake) G2
Perch (riv.) G2
Pere Marquette (riv.) D5
Pictured Rocks (cliff) C2
Pictured Rocks Nat'l Lakeshore C2
Pigeon (riv.) D7
Pigeon (riv.) E3
Pine (riv.) D4
Pine (riv.) E5
Platte (lake) C4
Porcupine (mts.) F1
Potagannissing (bay) F2
Poverty (isl.) C3
Prairie (riv.) D7
Presque Isle (riv.) F1
Rabbit (riv.) D6
Raisin (riv.) F7
Rapid (riv.) B2
Reedsburg (res.) E4
Rifle (riv.) E4
Royale (isl.) E1
Saginaw (bay) F5
Saginaw (riv.) F5
Saint Clair (lake) G6
Saint Clair (riv.) G6
Saint Joseph (riv.) C7
Saint Martin (bay) E3
Saint Martin (isl.) C3
Saint Marys (riv.) E2
Salt (pt.) E2
Sand (pt.) F5
Seul Choi (pt.) D3
Shelldrake (riv.) D2
Shiawassee (riv.) E5
Siskiwit (bay) E1
Sleeping Bear Dunes Nat'l Lakeshore C4
South (bay) C2
South (pt.) F4
South (chan.) E3
South Fox (isl.) D3
South Manitou (isl.) C3
Sturgeon (riv.) C2
Sugar (isl.) E2
Summer (isl.) C3
Superior (lake) C2
Tahquamenon (falls) D2
Tahquamenon (riv.) D2
Tawas (lake) F4
Tawas (pt.) F4
Thunder (bay) F4
Thunder Bay (riv.) F3
Tittabawassee (riv.) E5
Torch (lake) D3
Traverse (isl.) A1
Traverse (pt.) A1
Turtle (lake) F4
Two Hearted (riv.) D2
Vieux Desert (lake) G2
Walloon (lake) E3
White (riv.) C5
Whitefish (bay) E2
Whitefish (pt.) E2
Whitefish (riv.) C2
Wood (isl.) C2
Wurtsmith A.F.B. 5,080 F4
Yellow Dog (riv.) B2

▲County Seat
•Population of town or township

Agriculture, Industry and Resources

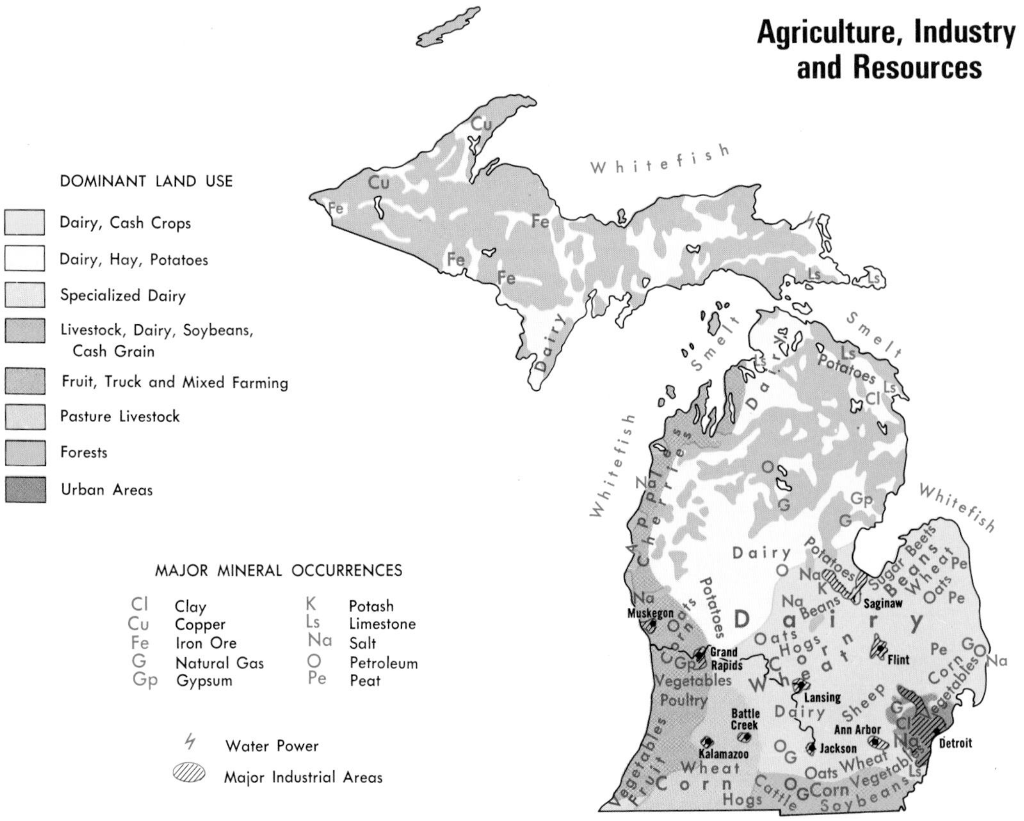
DOMINANT LAND USE
Dairy, Cash Crops
Dairy, Hay, Potatoes
Specialized Dairy
Livestock, Dairy, Soybeans, Cash Grain
Fruit, Truck and Mixed Farming
Pasture Livestock
Forests
Urban Areas
MAJOR MINERAL OCCURRENCES
Cl Clay
Cu Copper
Fe Iron Ore
G Natural Gas
Gp Gypsum
K Potash
Ls Limestone
Na Salt
O Petroleum
Pe Peat
Water Power
Major Industrial Areas
Whitefish
Smelt
Dairy
Potatoes
Cherries
Oats
Sugar Beets
Beans
Wheat
Corn
Hogs
Sheep
Vegetables
Poultry
Fruit
Cattle
Soybeans
Muskegon
Grand Rapids
Saginaw
Flint
Lansing
Battle Creek
Ann Arbor
Kalamazoo
Jackson
Detroit

MINNESOTA

AREA 84,402 sq. mi. (218,601 sq. km.)
POPULATION 4,387,029
CAPITAL St. Paul
LARGEST CITY Minneapolis
HIGHEST POINT Eagle Mtn. 2,301 ft. (701 m.)
SETTLED IN 1805
ADMITTED TO UNION May 11, 1858
POPULAR NAME North Star State; Gopher State
STATE FLOWER Pink & White Lady's-Slipper
STATE BIRD Common Loon

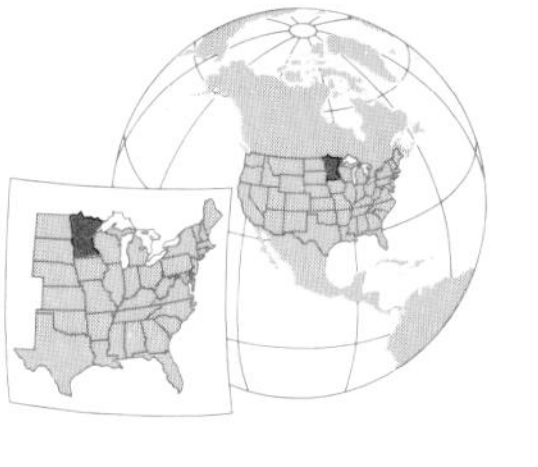

COUNTIES

Aitkin 12,425 .... E4
Anoka 243,641 .... E5
Becker 27,881 .... C4
Beltrami 34,384 .... C2
Benton 30,185 .... D5
Big Stone 6,285 .... B5
Blue Earth 54,044 .... D6
Brown 26,984 .... D6
Carlton 29,259 .... F4
Carver 47,915 .... E6
Cass 21,791 .... D4
Chippewa 13,228 .... C5
Chisago 30,521 .... F5
Clay 50,422 .... B4
Clearwater 8,309 .... C3
Cook 3,868 .... H3
Cottonwood 12,694 .... C6
Crow Wing 44,249 .... D4
Dakota 275,227 .... E6
Dodge 15,731 .... F7
Douglas 28,674 .... C5
Faribault 16,937 .... D7
Fillmore 20,777 .... F7
Freeborn 33,060 .... E7
Goodhue 40,690 .... F6
Grant 6,246 .... B5
Hennepin 1,032,431 .... E5
Houston 18,497 .... G7
Hubbard 14,939 .... D3
Isanti 25,921 .... E5
Itasca 40,863 .... E3
Jackson 11,677 .... C7
Kanabec 12,802 .... E5
Kandiyohi 38,761 .... C5
Kittson 5,767 .... B2
Koochiching 16,299 .... E2
Lac qui Parle 8,924 .... B6
Lake 10,415 .... G3
Lake of the Woods 4,076 .... D2
Le Sueur 23,239 .... E6
Lincoln 6,890 .... B6
Lyon 24,789 .... C6
Mahnomen 5,044 .... C3
Marshall 10,993 .... B2
Martin 22,914 .... D7
McLeod 32,030 .... D6
Meeker 20,846 .... D5
Mille Lacs 18,670 .... E5
Morrison 29,604 .... D4
Mower 37,385 .... F7
Murray 9,660 .... C6
Nicollet 28,076 .... D6
Nobles 20,098 .... C7
Norman 7,975 .... B3
Olmsted 106,470 .... F7
Otter Tail 50,714 .... C4
Pennington 13,306 .... B2
Pine 21,264 .... F4
Pipestone 10,491 .... B6
Polk 32,498 .... B3
Pope 10,745 .... C5
Ramsey 485,765 .... E5
Red Lake 4,525 .... B3
Redwood 17,254 .... C6
Renville 17,673 .... C6
Rice 49,183 .... E6
Rock 9,806 .... B7
Roseau 15,026 .... C2
Saint Louis 222,229 .... F3
Scott 57,846 .... E6
Sherburne 41,945 .... E5
Sibley 14,366 .... D6
Stearns 118,791 .... D5
Steele 30,729 .... E7
Stevens 10,634 .... B5
Swift 10,724 .... C5
Todd 23,363 .... D4
Traverse 4,463 .... B5
Wabasha 19,744 .... F6
Wadena 13,154 .... D4
Waseca 18,079 .... E6
Washington 145,896 .... F5
Watonwan 11,682 .... D7
Wilkin 7,516 .... B4
Winona 47,828 .... G6
Wright 68,710 .... D5
Yellow Medicine 11,684 .... B6

CITIES and TOWNS

Ada▲ 1,708 .... B3
Adams 756 .... F7
Adrian 1,141 .... C7
Afton 2,645 .... F6
Aitkin▲ 1,698 .... E4
Akeley 393 .... D3
Albany 1,548 .... D5
Albert Lea▲ 18,310 .... E7
Alberta 136 .... B5
Albertville 1,251 .... E5
Alborn 500 .... F4
Alden 623 .... E7
Aldrich 70 .... C4
Alexandria▲ 7,838 .... C5
Alpha 105 .... D7
Altura 349 .... G6
Alvarado 356 .... B2
Amboy 517 .... D7
Andover 15,216 .... E5
Annandale 2,054 .... D5
Anoka▲ 17,192 .... E5
Apple Valley 34,598 .... G6
Appleton 1,552 .... C5
Arco 104 .... B6
Argyle 636 .... B2
Arlington 1,886 .... D6
Arnold 2,891 .... F4
Ashby 469 .... C4
Askov 343 .... F4
Atwater 1,053 .... D5
Audubon 411 .... C4
Aurora 1,965 .... F3
Austin▲ 21,907 .... E7
Avoca 150 .... C7
Avon 970 .... D5
Babbitt 1,562 .... G3
Backus 240 .... D4
Badger 381 .... B2
Bagley▲ 1,388 .... C3
Balaton 737 .... C6
Barnesville 2,066 .... B4
Barnum 482 .... F4
Barrett 350 .... B5
Barry 40 .... B5
Battle Lake 698 .... C4
Baudette▲ 1,146 .... D2
Baxter 3,695 .... D4
Bayport 3,200 .... F5
Beardsley 297 .... B5
Beaver Bay 147 .... G3
Beaver Creek 249 .... B7
Becker 902 .... E5
Bejou 110 .... B3
Belgrade 700 .... C5
Belle Plaine 3,149 .... E6
Bellechester 110 .... F6
Bellingham 247 .... B5
Beltrami 137 .... B3
Belview 383 .... C6
Bemidji▲ 11,245 .... D3
Bena 147 .... D3
Benson▲ 3,235 .... C5
Bertha 507 .... C4
Bethel 394 .... E5
Big Falls 341 .... E2
Big Lake 3,113 .... E5
Bigelow 232 .... C7
Bigfork 384 .... E3
Bingham Lake 155 .... C7
Bird Island 1,326 .... D6
Biscay 113 .... D6
Biwabik 1,097 .... F3
Blackduck 718 .... D3
Blaine 38,975 .... G5
Blomkest 183 .... D6
Blooming Prairie 2,043 .... E7
Bloomington 86,335 .... G6
Blue Earth▲ 3,745 .... D7
Bluffton 187 .... C4
Bock 115 .... E5
Borup 119 .... B3
Bovey 662 .... E3
Bowlus 260 .... D5
Boy River 43 .... D3
Boyd 251 .... C6
Braham 1,139 .... E5
Brainerd▲ 12,353 .... D4
Branch 2,400 .... F5
Brandon 441 .... C5
Breckenridge▲ 3,708 .... B4
Breezy Point 432 .... D4
Brewster 532 .... C7
Bricelyn 426 .... E7
Brook Park 125 .... F5
Brooklyn Center 28,887 .... G5
Brooklyn Park 56,381 .... G5
Brooks 158 .... B3
Brookston 107 .... F4
Brooten 589 .... C5
Browerville 782 .... D4
Browns Valley 804 .... B5
Brownsdale 695 .... F7
Brownsville 415 .... G7
Brownton 781 .... D6
Bruno 89 .... F4
Buckman 201 .... D5
Buffalo Lake 734 .... D6
Buffalo▲ 6,856 .... E5
Buhl 915 .... F3
Burnsville 51,288 .... E6
Burtrum 172 .... D5
Butterfield 509 .... D7
Byron 2,441 .... F6
Caledonia▲ 2,846 .... G7
Callaway 212 .... C3
Calumet 382 .... E3
Cambridge▲ 5,094 .... E5
Campbell 233 .... B4
Canby 1,826 .... B6
Cannon Falls 3,232 .... F6
Canton 362 .... F7
Carlos 361 .... C5
Carlton▲ 923 .... F4
Carver 744 .... E6
Cass Lake 923 .... D3
Cedar Mills 80 .... D6
Center City▲ 451 .... F5
Centerville 1,633 .... E5
Ceylon 461 .... D7
Champlin 16,849 .... G5
Chandler 316 .... C7
Chanhassen 11,732 .... F6
Chaska▲ 11,339 .... F6
Chatfield 2,226 .... F7
Chickamaw Beach 132 .... D4
Chisago City 2,009 .... E5
Chisholm 5,290 .... E3
Chokio 521 .... B5
Circle Pines 4,704 .... G5
Clara City 1,307 .... C6
Claremont 530 .... E6
Clarissa 637 .... C4
Clarkfield 924 .... C6
Clarks Grove 675 .... E7
Clear Lake 315 .... E5
Clearbrook 560 .... C3
Clearwater 597 .... D5
Clements 191 .... D6
Cleveland 699 .... E6
Climax 264 .... B3
Clinton 574 .... B5
Clitherall 109 .... C4
Clontarf 172 .... C5
Cloquet 10,885 .... F4
Coates 186 .... E6
Cobden 62 .... D6
Cohasset E3
Cokato 2,180 .... D5
Cold Spring 2,459 .... D5
Coleraine 1,041 .... E3
Cologne 563 .... E6
Columbia Heights 18,910 .... G5
Comfrey 433 .... D6
Comstock 123 .... B4
Conger 143 .... E7
Cook 680 .... F3
Coon Rapids 52,978 .... G5
Corcoran 5,199 .... F5
Correll 60 .... B5
Cosmos 610 .... D6
Cottage Grove 22,935 .... F6
Cotton 982 .... F3
Cottonwood 924 .... C6
Courtland 412 .... D6
Cromwell 221 .... F4
Crookston▲ 8,119 .... B3
Crosby 2,073 .... D4
Crosslake 1,132 .... E4
Crystal 23,788 .... G5
Currie 303 .... C6
Cuyuna 172 .... E4
Cyrus 328 .... C5
Dakota 360 .... G7
Dalton 234 .... C4
Danube 562 .... C6
Danvers 98 .... C5
Darfur 128 .... D6
Darwin 252 .... D5
Dassel 1,082 .... D5
Dawson 1,626 .... B6
Day 4,443 .... E5
Dayton 4,070 .... E5
De Graff 149 .... C5
Deephaven 3,653 .... G5
Deer Creek 303 .... C4
Deer River 838 .... E3
Deerwood 524 .... E4
Delano 2,709 .... E5
Delavan 245 .... D7
Delhi 69 .... C6
Dellwood 887 .... F5
Denham 36 .... F4
Dennison 152 .... E6
Dent 177 .... C4
Detroit Lakes▲ 6,635 .... C4
Dexter 303 .... F7
Dilworth 2,562 .... B4
Dodge Center 1,954 .... F6
Donaldson 57 .... B2
Donnelly 221 .... B5
Doran 78 .... B4
Dover 416 .... F7
Dovray 60 .... C6
Duluth▲ 85,493 .... F4
Dumont 126 .... B5
Dundas 473 .... E6
Dundee 107 .... C7
Dunnell 187 .... D7
Eagan 47,409 .... G6
Eagle Bend 524 .... D4
Eagle Lake 1,703 .... E6
East Bethel 8,050 .... E5
East Grand Forks 8,658 .... B3
East Gull Lake 687 .... D4
Easton 229 .... E7
Echo 304 .... C6
Eden Prairie 39,311 .... G6
Eden Valley 732 .... D5
Edgerton 1,106 .... B7
Edina 46,070 .... G5
Effie 130 .... E3
Eitzen 221 .... G7
Elba 220 .... F6
Elbow Lake▲ 1,186 .... B5
Elgin 733 .... F6
Elizabeth 152 .... B4
Elk River▲ 11,143 .... E5
Elko 223 .... E6
Elkton 142 .... F7
Ellendale 549 .... E7
Ellsworth 580 .... C7
Elmdale 130 .... D5
Elmore 709 .... D7
Elrosa 205 .... C5
Ely 3,968 .... G3
Elysian 445 .... E6
Emily 613 .... E4
Emmons 439 .... E7
Erhard 181 .... B4
Erskine 422 .... B3
Esko 500 .... F4
Evan 83 .... D6
Evansville 566 .... C4
Eveleth 4,064 .... F3
Excelsior 2,367 .... E6
Eyota 1,448 .... F7
Fairfax 1,276 .... D6
Fairmont▲ 11,265 .... D7
Falcon Heights 5,380 .... G5
Faribault▲ 17,085 .... E6
Farmington 5,940 .... E6
Farwell 74 .... C5
Federal Dam 118 .... D3
Felton 211 .... B3
Fergus Falls▲ 12,362 .... B4
Fertile 853 .... B3
Fifty Lakes 299 .... D4
Finlayson 242 .... F4
Fisher 413 .... B3
Flensburg 213 .... D5
Floodwood 574 .... E4
Florence 53 .... B6
Florenton 635 .... F3
Foley▲ 1,854 .... D5
Forada 171 .... C5
Forest Lake 5,833 .... F5
Foreston 354 .... E5
Fort Ripley 92 .... D4
Fosston 1,529 .... C3
Fountain 327 .... F7
Foxhome 160 .... B4
Franklin 512 .... D6
Frazee 1,176 .... C4
Freeborn 301 .... E7
Freeport 556 .... D5
Fridley 28,335 .... G5
Frost 236 .... D7
Fulda 1,212 .... C7
Garfield 203 .... C5
Garrison 138 .... E4
Garvin 149 .... C6
Gary 200 .... B3
Gaylord▲ 1,935 .... D6
Geneva 444 .... E7
Genola 85 .... D5
Georgetown 107 .... B3
Ghent 316 .... C6
Gibbon 712 .... D6
Gilbert 1,934 .... F3
Gilman 192 .... E5
Glen 4,648 .... E4
Glencoe▲ 4,396 .... D6
Glenville 778 .... E7
Glenwood▲ 2,573 .... C5
Glyndon 862 .... B4
Golden Valley 20,971 .... G5
Gonvick 302 .... C3
Good Thunder 561 .... D6
Goodhue 533 .... F6
Goodridge 115 .... C2
Goodview 2,878 .... G6
Graceville 671 .... B5
Granada 374 .... D7
Grand Marais▲ 1,171 .... G2
Grand Meadow 967 .... F7
Grand Rapids▲ 7,976 .... E3
Granite Falls▲ 3,083 .... C6
Grasston 119 .... E5
Green Isle 239 .... E6
Greenbush 800 .... B2
Greenfield 1,450 .... F5
Greenwald 209 .... D5
Grey Eagle 353 .... D5
Grove City 547 .... D5
Grygla 220 .... C2
Gully 128 .... C3
Hackensack 245 .... D4
Hadley 94 .... C7
Hallock▲ 1,304 .... A2
Halma 73 .... B2
Halstad 611 .... B3
Ham Lake 8,924 .... E5
Hamburg 492 .... D6
Hamel F5
Hammond 205 .... F6
Hampton 363 .... E6
Hancock 723 .... C5
Hanley Falls 246 .... C6
Hanover 787 .... E5
Hanska 443 .... D6
Harding 76 .... E4
Hardwick 234 .... B7
Harmony 1,081 .... F7
Harris 843 .... F5
Hartland 270 .... E7
Hastings▲ 15,445 .... F6
Hatfield 66 .... B7
Hawley 1,655 .... B4
Hayfield 1,283 .... F7
Hayward 246 .... E7
Hazel Run 81 .... C6
Hector 1,145 .... D6
Heidelberg 73 .... E6
Henderson 746 .... E6
Hendricks 684 .... B6
Hendrum 309 .... B3
Henning 738 .... C4
Henriette 78 .... E5
Herman 485 .... B5
Hermantown 6,761 .... F4
Heron Lake 730 .... C7
Hewitt 269 .... C4
Hibbing 18,046 .... F3

(continued on following page)

Agriculture, Industry and Resources

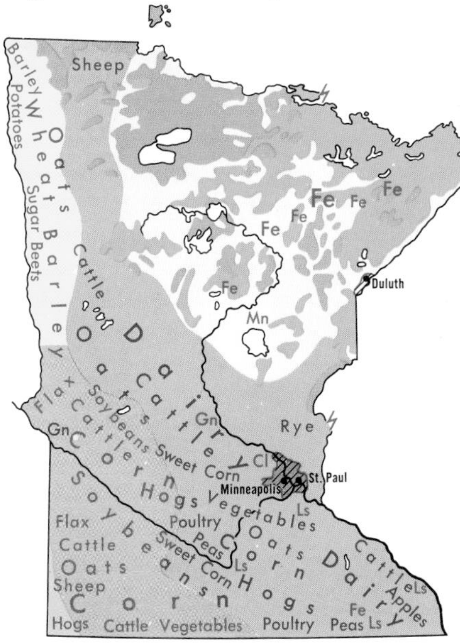
Sheep
Barley
Wheat
Potatoes
Oats
Sugar Beets
Cattle
Dairy
Fe
Mn
Duluth
Rye
Gn
Cl
Minneapolis
St. Paul
Flax
Soybeans
Sweet Corn
Hogs
Vegetables
Poultry
Peas
Ls
Apples
Corn

MAJOR MINERAL OCCURRENCES

Cl Clay
Fe Iron Ore
Gn Granite
Ls Limestone
Mn Manganese

Water Power
Major Industrial Areas

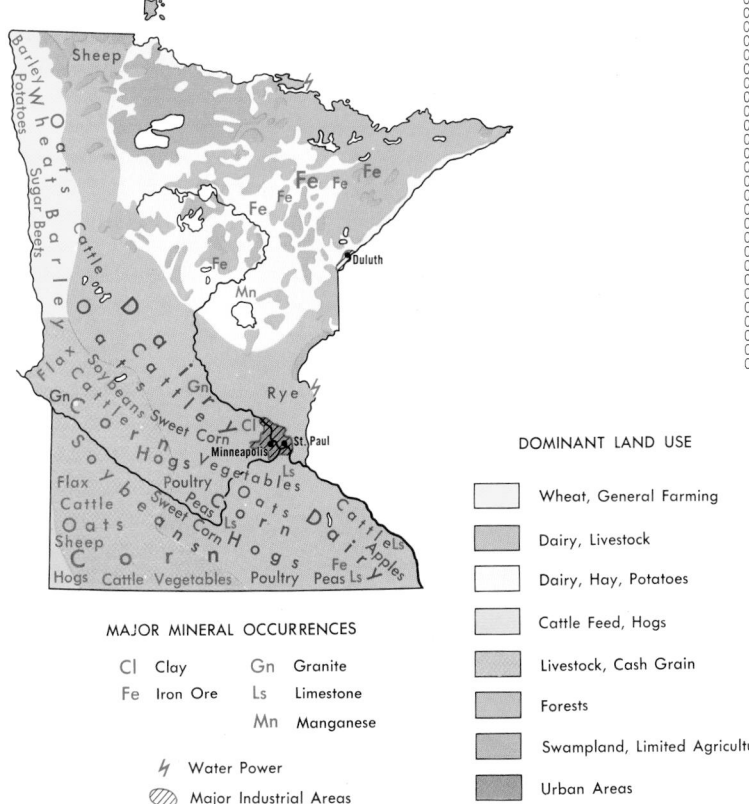

DOMINANT LAND USE

Wheat, General Farming
Dairy, Livestock
Dairy, Hay, Potatoes
Cattle Feed, Hogs
Livestock, Cash Grain
Forests
Swampland, Limited Agriculture
Urban Areas

Hill City 469 E4
Hillman 45 E4
Hills 607 B7
Hinckley 946 E4
Hitterdal 242 B4
Hoffman 576 C5
Hokah 687 G7
Holdingford 561 D5
Holland 216 B6
Hollandale 289 E7
Holloway 123 C5
Holt 88 B2
Hopkins 16,534 G5
Houston 1,013 G7
Howard Lake 1,343 D5
Hoyt Lakes 2,348 F3
Hugo 4,417 E5
Humboldt 74 A2
Hutchinson 11,523 D6
Ihlen 101 B7
Independence 2,822 F5
Indus E2
International Falls▲ 8,325 E2
Inver Grove Heights 22,477 E6
Iona 158 C7
Iron 133 F3
Ironton 553 D4
Isanti 1,228 E5
Island View 150 E2
Isle 566 E4
Ivanhoe▲ 751 B6
Jackson▲ 3,559 C7
Janesville 1,969 E6
Jasper 599 B7
Jeffers 443 C6
Jenkins 262 D4
Johnson 46 B5
Jordan 2,909 E6
Kandiyohi 506 D5
Karlstad 881 B2
Kasota 655 D6
Kasson 3,514 F6
Keewatin 1,118 E3
Kelliher 348 D3
Kellogg 423 G6
Kelly Lake 900 F3
Kennedy 337 B2
Kenneth 81 B7
Kensington 295 C5
Kent 131 B4
Kenyon 1,552 E6
Kerkhoven 732 C5
Kerrick 56 F4
Kettle River 190 E4
Kiester 606 E7
Kilkenny 167 E6
Kimball 690 D5
Kingston 131 D5
Kinney 257 F3
La Crescent 4,311 G7
La Prairie 438 E3
La Salle 98 D6
Lafayette 462 D6
Lake Benton 693 B6
Lake Bronson 272 B2
Lake City 4,391 F6
Lake Crystal 2,084 D6
Lake Elmo 5,903 F6
Lake Henry 90 D5
Lake Lillian 229 C6
Lake Park 638 B4
Lake Saint Croix Beach 1,078 F6
Lake Shore 693 D4
Lake Wilson 319 B7
Lakefield 1,679 C7
Lakeland 2,000 F6
Lakeville 24,854 E6
Lamberton 972 C6
Lancaster 342 B2
Lanesboro 858 G7
Laporte 101 D3
Lastrup 112 D4
Lauderdale 2,700 G5
Le Center▲ 2,006 E6
Le Roy 904 F7
Le Sueur 3,714 E6
Lengby 112 C3
Leonard 26 C3
Leonidas 70 F3
Lester Prairie 1,180 D6
Lewiston 1,298 G7
Lewisville 255 D7
Lexington 2,279 G5
Lilydale 506 G5
Lindstrom 2,461 F5
Lino Lakes 8,807 G5
Lismore 248 B7
Litchfield▲ 6,041 D5
Little Falls▲ 7,232 D5
Little Rock 714 D5
Littlefork 838 E2
Long Beach 204 C5
Long Lake 1,984 F5
Long Prairie▲ 2,786 D5
Longville 224 D4
Lonsdale 1,252 E6
Loretto 404 F5
Louisburg 42 B5
Lowry 233 C5
Lucan 235 C6
Luverne▲ 4,382 B7
Lyle 504 F7
Lynd 287 C6
Mabel 745 G7
Madelia 2,237 D6
Madison Lake 643 E6
Madison▲ 1,951 B5
Magnolia 155 B7
Mahnomen▲ 1,154 C3
Mahtomedi 5,569 F5
Manchester 69 E7
Manhattan Beach 61 E4
Mankato▲ 31,477 E6
Mantorville▲ 874 F6
Maple Grove 38,736 G5
Maple Lake 1,394 D5
Maple Plain 2,005 F5
Mapleton 1,526 E7
Mapleview 206 E7
Maplewood 30,954 G5
Marble 618 E3
Marietta 211 B5
Marine on Saint Croix 602 F5
Marshall▲ 12,023 C6
Mayer 471 E6
Maynard 419 C6
Mazeppa 722 F6
McGrath 62 E4
McGregor 376 E4
McIntosh 665 C3
McKinley 116 F3
Meadowlands 92 F3
Medford 733 E6
Medicine Lake 385 G5
Medina (Hamel) 3,096 F5
Meire Grove 124 C5
Melrose 2,561 D5
Menahga 1,076 C4
Mendota 164 G5
Mendota Heights 9,431 G6
Mentor 94 B3
Middle River 285 B2
Miesville 135 F6
Milaca▲ 2,182 E5
Milan 353 C5
Millerville 104 C4
Millville 163 F6
Milroy 297 C6
Miltona 181 C4
Minneapolis▲ 368,383 G5
Minneiska 127 G6
Minneota 1,417 C6
Minnesota City 258 G6
Minnesota Lake 681 E7
Minnetonka 48,370 G5
Minnetrista 3,439 F5
Mizpah 100 D3
Montevideo▲ 5,499 C6
Montgomery 2,399 E6
Monticello 4,941 E5
Montrose 1,008 E5
Moorhead▲ 32,295 B4
Moose Lake 1,206 F4
Mora▲ 2,905 E5
Morgan 965 D6
Morris▲ 5,613 C5
Morristown 784 E6
Morton 448 C6
Motley 441 D4
Mound 9,634 E6
Mounds View 12,541 G5
Mountain Iron 3,362 F3
Mountain Lake 1,906 D7
Murdock 282 C5
Myrtle 72 E7
Nashua 63 B4
Nashwauk 1,026 E3
Nassau 83 B5
Naytahwaush 378 C3
Nelson 177 C5
Nerstrand 210 E6
Nevis 375 D4
New Auburn 363 D6
New Brighton 22,207 G5
New Germany 353 E6
New Hope 21,853 G5
New London 971 C5
New Market 227 E6
New Munich 314 D5
New Prague 3,569 E6
New Richland 1,237 E7
New Trier 96 F6
New Ulm▲ 13,132 D6
New York Mills 940 C4
Newfolden 345 B2
Newport 3,720 F6
Nicollet 795 D6
Nielsville 100 B3
Nimrod 65 D4
Nisswa 1,391 D4
Norcross 86 B5
North Branch 1,867 F5
North Mankato 10,164 D6
North Oaks 3,386 G5
North Redwood 203 D6
North Saint Paul 12,376 G5
Northfield 14,684 E6
Northome 283 D3
Northrop 276 D7
Norwood 1,351 E6
Oak Park 3,486 E5
Oakdale 18,374 E5
Odessa 155 B5
Odin 102 D7
Ogema 164 C3
Ogilvie 510 E5
Okabena 223 C7
Oklee 441 C3
Olivia▲ 2,623 C6
Onamia 676 E4
Ormsby 159 D7
Oronoco 727 F6
Orr 265 F2
Ortonville▲ 2,205 B5
Osakis 1,256 C5
Oslo 362 A2
Osseo 2,704 G5
Ostrander 276 F7
Ottertail 313 C4
Owatonna▲ 19,386 E6
Palisade 144 E4
Park Rapids▲ 2,863 D4
Parkers Prairie 956 C4
Payne 2,275 F3
Paynesville 2,140 D5
Pease 178 E5
Pelican Lakes (Breezy Point) D4
Pelican Rapids 1,886 B4
Pemberton 228 E7
Pengilly 625 E3
Pennock 476 C5
Pequot Lakes 843 D4
Perham 2,075 C4
Perley 132 B3
Peterson 259 G7
Pierz 1,014 D5
Pillager 306 D4
Pine City▲ 2,613 F5
Pine Island 2,125 F6
Pine River 871 D4
Pipestone▲ 4,554 B7
Plainview 2,768 F6
Plato 355 D6
Pleasant Lake 79 D5
Plummer 277 B3
Plymouth 50,889 G5
Ponemah 704 D2
Porter 210 B6
Preston▲ 1,530 F7
Princeton 3,719 E5
Prinsburg 502 C6
Prior Lake 11,482 E6
Proctor 2,974 F4
Quamba 124 E5
Racine 288 F7
Ramsey 12,408 E5
Randall 571 D4
Randolph 331 E6
Ranier 199 E2
Ray 668 E2
Raymond 723 C5
Red Lake Falls▲ 1,481 B3
Red Wing▲ 15,134 F6
Redby 787 D3
Redwood Falls▲ 4,859 C6
Regal 51 D5
Remer 342 E3
Renville 1,315 C6
Revere 117 C6
Rice 610 D5
Richfield 35,710 G6
Richmond 965 D5
Richville 121 C4
Riverton 122 D4
Robbinsdale 14,396 G5
Rochester▲ 70,745 F6
Rock Creek 1,040 F5
Rockford 2,665 F5
Rockville 579 D5
Rogers 698 E5
Rollingstone 697 G6
Ronneby 58 E5
Roosevelt 180 C2
Roscoe 141 D5
Rose Creek 363 F7
Roseau▲ 2,396 C2
Rosemount 8,622 E6
Roseville 33,485 G5
Rothsay 443 B4
Round Lake 463 C7
Royalton 802 D5
Rush City 1,497 F5
Rushford 1,485 G7
Rushmore 381 C7
Russell 394 C6
Ruthton 328 B6
Rutledge 152 F4
Sabin 495 B4
Sacred Heart 603 C6
Saint Anthony 7,727 G5
Saint Anthony 81 D5
Saint Bonifacius 1,180 F5
Saint Charles 2,642 F7
Saint Clair 633 E6
Saint Cloud▲ 48,812 D5
Saint Francis 2,538 E5
Saint Hilaire 298 B2
Saint James▲ 4,364 D7
Saint Joseph 3,294 D5
Saint Leo 111 C6
Saint Louis Park 43,787 G5
Saint Martin 274 D5
Saint Michael 2,506 E5
Saint Paul (cap.)▲ 272,235 G6
Saint Paul Park 4,965 G6
Saint Peter▲ 9,421 E6
Saint Rosa 75 D5
Saint Stephen 607 D5
Saint Vincent 116 A2
Sanborn 459 C6
Sandstone 2,057 F4
Sargeant 78 F7
Sartell 5,393 D5
Sauk Centre 3,581 C5
Sauk Rapids 7,825 D5
Savage 9,906 G6
Scanlon 878 F4
Seaforth 87 C6
Sebeka 662 C4
Sedan 63 C5
Shafer 368 F5
Shakopee▲ 11,739 F6
Shelly 225 B3
Sherburn 1,105 D7
Shevlin 157 C3
Shoreview 24,587 G5
Shorewood 5,917 F5
Silver Bay 1,894 G3
Silver Lake 764 D6
Skyline 272 D6
Slayton▲ 2,147 C7
Sleepy Eye 3,694 D6
Sobieski 199 D5
Solway 74 C3
Soudan 900 F3
South Haven 193 D5
South International Falls 2,806 E2
South Saint Paul 20,197 G6
Spicer 1,020 C5
Spring Grove 1,153 G7
Spring Hill 77 D5
Spring Lake 6,532 E5
Spring Lake Park 6,477 E5
Spring Park 1,571 F5
Spring Valley 2,461 F7
Springfield 2,173 C6
Squaw Lake 139 D3
Stacy 1,081 E5
Staples 2,754 D4
Starbuck 1,143 C5
Steen 176 B7
Stephen 707 A2
Stewart 566 D6
Stewartville 4,520 F7
Stillwater▲ 13,882 F5
Stockton 529 G6
Storden 283 C6
Strandquist 98 B2
Strathcona 40 B2
Sturgeon Lake 230 F4
Sunburg 117 C5
Sunfish Lake 413 E6
Swanville 324 D5
Taconite 310 E3
Tamarack 53 E4
Taopi 83 F7
Taunton 175 B6
Taylors Falls 694 F5
Tenstrike 184 D3
Thief River Falls▲ 8,010 B2
Thomson 132 F4
Tintah 74 B5
Tonka Bay 1,472 F5
Tower 502 F3
Tracy 2,059 C6
Trail 67 C3
Trimont 745 D7
Trommald 80 D4
Trosky 120 B7
Truman 1,292 D7
Turtle River 62 D3
Twin Lakes 154 E7
Twin Valley 821 B3
Two Harbors▲ 3,651 G3
Tyler 1,257 B6
Ulen 547 B3
Underwood 284 C4
Upsala 371 D5
Urbank 73 C4
Utica 220 G7
Vadnais Heights 11,041 G5
Vergas 287 C4
Vermillion 510 F6
Verndale 560 C4
Vernon Center 339 D7
Vesta 302 C6
Victoria 2,354 F6
Viking 103 B2
Villard 247 C5
Vining 84 C4
Virginia 9,410 F3
Wabasha▲ 2,384 G6
Wabasso 684 C6
Waconia 3,498 E6
Wadena▲ 4,131 C4
Wahkon 197 E4
Waite Park 5,020 D5
Waldorf 243 E7
Walker▲ 950 D3
Walnut Grove 625 C6
Walters 86 E7
Waltham 170 F7
Wanamingo 847 F6
Wanda 103 C6
Warba 137 E3
Warren▲ 1,813 B2
Warroad 1,679 C2
Waseca▲ 8,385 E6
Watertown 2,408 E6
Waterville 1,771 E6
Watkins 849 D5
Watson 211 C5
Waubun 330 C3
Waverly 600 E5
Wayzata 3,806 G5
Welcome 790 D7
Wells 2,465 E7
Wendell 159 B4
West Concord 871 F6
West Saint Paul 19,248 G5
West Union 54 C5
Westbrook 853 C6
Westport 47 C5
Whalan 94 G7
Wheaton▲ 1,615 B5
White Bear Lake 24,704 G5
White Earth 319 C3
Wilder 83 C7
Willernie 584 G5
Williams 212 D2
Willmar▲ 17,531 C5
Willow River 284 F4
Wilmont 351 C7
Wilton 171 C3
Windom▲ 4,283 C7
Winger 167 B3
Winnebago 1,565 D7
Winona▲ 25,399 G6
Winsted 1,581 D6
Winthrop 1,279 D6
Winton 169 G3
Wolf Lake 35 C4
Wolverton 158 B4
Wood Lake 406 C6
Woodbury 20,075 F6
Woodstock 159 B7
Worthington▲ 9,977 C7
Wrenshall 296 F4
Wright 144 E4
Wykoff 493 F7
Wyoming 2,142 F5
Young America 1,354 E6
Zemple 63 E3
Zim 1,350 F3
Zumbro Falls 237 F6
Zumbrota 2,312 F6

OTHER FEATURES

Ash (riv.) F2
Bald Eagle (lake) G3
Basswood (lake) G2
Battle (riv.) D3
Baudette (riv.) D2
Bear (riv.) E3
Bemidji (lake) D3
Benton (lake) B6
Big Fork (riv.) E2
Big Sandy (lake) E4
Big Stone (lake) B5
Birch (lake) G3
Black (riv.) D2
Blue Earth (riv.) D7
Bois de Sioux (riv.) B4
Bowstring (lake) E3
Buffalo (riv.) B4
Burntside (lake) F3
Cass (lake) D3
Cedar (riv.) F7
Chippewa (riv.) C5
Christina (lake) C4
Clearwater (riv.) C3
Cloquet (riv.) F4
Cobb (riv.) E7
Cottonwood (riv.) C6
Crooked (creek) F4
Crooked (lake) G2
Crow (riv.) F5
Crow Wing (riv.) D4
Cuyuna (range) D4
Dead (lake) C4
Deer (lake) E3
Des Moines (riv.) C7
Eagle (mt.) G2
East Swan (riv.) F3
Elbow (lake) C3
Emily (lake) C5
Fond du Lac Ind. Res. F4
Grand Portage Ind. Res. G2
Grand Portage Nat'l Mon. G2
Green (lake) D5
Greenwood (lake) G3
Gull (lake) D4
Heron (lake) C7
Hill (riv.) C3
Independence (lake) F5
Isabella (lake) G3
Itasca (lake) C3
Kabetogama (lake) E2
Kanaranzi (creek) C7
Kettle (riv.) F4
Knife (lake) G2
La Croix (lake) F2
Lac qui Parle (lake) C5
Lac qui Parle (riv.) B6
Lake of the Woods (lake) D1
Leaf (riv.) C4
Leech (lake) D3
Leech Lake Ind. Res. D3
Lida (lake) C4
Little Fork (riv.) E2
Little Rock (creek) C7
Long (lake) D4
Long (lake) F3
Long Prairie (riv.) D4
Lost (riv.) C3
Lower Red (lake) C3
Maple (lake) B3
Maple (riv.) E7
Marsh (lake) B5
Mary (lake) C5
Mesabi (range) E3
Middle (riv.) B2
Mille Lacs Ind. Res. E4
Mille Lacs (lake) E4
Miltona (lake) C4
Minneapolis-Saint Paul Airport G5
Minnesota (riv.) E6
Minnetonka (lake) F5
Minnewaska (lake) C5
Misquah (hills) F2
Mississippi (riv.) D4
Moose (riv.) C2
Mud (lake) C2
Mud (riv.) C2
Muskeg (bay) C2
Mustinka (riv.) B5
Nemadji (riv.) F4
Nett (lake) E2
Nett Lake Ind. Res. E2
North (lake) F1
Otter Tail (lake) C4
Otter Tail (riv.) B4
Partridge (riv.) G3
Pelican (lake) C4
Pelican (lake) D4
Pelican (riv.) F2
Pelican (riv.) B4
Pelican (riv.) F2
Pepin (lake) F6
Pigeon (riv.) G2
Pike (riv.) F3
Pipestone Nat'l Mon. B6
Pokegama (lake) E3
Pomme de Terre (riv.) C5
Poplar (riv.) C3
Prairie (riv.) E3
Rainy (lake) E2
Rainy (riv.) D2
Rapid (riv.) D2
Redeye (riv.) D4
Red Lake (riv.) B2
Red Lake Ind. Res. C2
Red River of the North (riv.) A2
Redeye (riv.) D4
Redwood (riv.) C6
Reno (lake) C5
Rice (lake) E4
Rock (riv.) B7
Root (riv.) G7
Roseau (riv.) B2
Rum (riv.) E5
Saganaga (lake) H2
Saint Croix (riv.) F5
Saint Louis (riv.) F4
Sand (creek) F5
Sand Hill (riv.) B3
Sarah (lake) F5
Schoolcraft C3
Shakopee (creek) C5
Shell (riv.) C4
Shetek (lake) C6
Sleepy Eye (creek) C6
Snake (riv.) A2
Snake (riv.) E4
South Fowl (lake) G1
Star (lake) C4
Sturgeon (riv.) F3
Superior (lake) G3
Swan (lake) D6
Tamarac (riv.) A2
Tamarack (riv.) D2
Thief (lake) C2
Thief (riv.) B2
Traverse (lake) B5
Trout (lake) F2
Two Rivers (riv.) A1
Upper Red (lake) D2
Vermilion (lake) F3
Vermilion (range) F3
Vermilion (riv.) F2
Voyageurs Nat'l Park F2
Wabatawangang (lake) D3
West Swan (riv.) F3
White Earth Ind. Res. C3
Whiteface (riv.) F3
Whitefish (lake) D4
White Iron (lake) G3
Wild Rice (lake) F4
Wild Rice (riv.) B3
Willow (riv.) E4
Winnibigoshish (lake) D3
Woods (lake) D1
Zumbro (riv.) F6

▲County seat

Topography

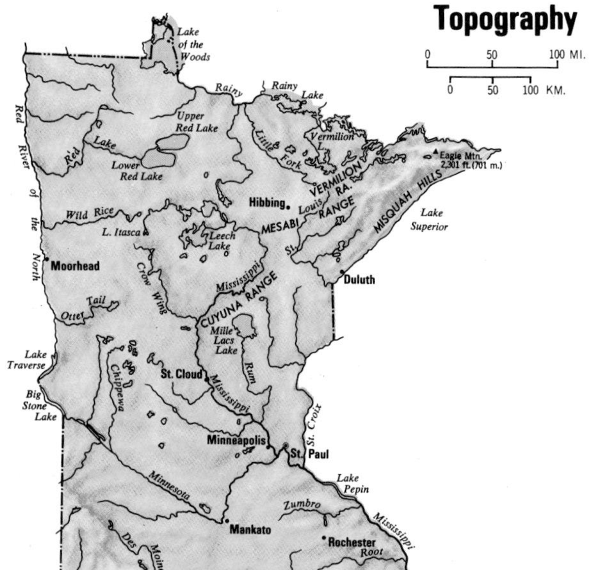
0 50 100 MI.
0 50 100 KM.
Lake of the Woods
Rainy
Rainy Lake
Upper Red Lake
Lower Red Lake
Red Lake
Red River of the North
Vermilion
Little Fork
Eagle Mtn. 2,301 ft. (701 m.)
VERMILION RA.
MISQUAH HILLS
Hibbing
MESABI RANGE
Wild Rice
L. Itasca
Leech Lake
Lake Superior
Moorhead
Crow Wing
Mississippi
Duluth
Otter Tail
CUYUNA RANGE
Mille Lacs Lake
Lake Traverse
Big Stone Lake
Chippewa
St. Cloud
Rum
St. Croix
Minneapolis
St. Paul
Minnesota
Lake Pepin
Zumbro
Mankato
Rochester
Root
Des Moines
Below Sea Level
100 m. 328 ft.
200 m. 656 ft.
500 m. 1,640 ft.
1,000 m. 3,281 ft.
2,000 m. 6,562 ft.
5,000 m. 16,404 ft.

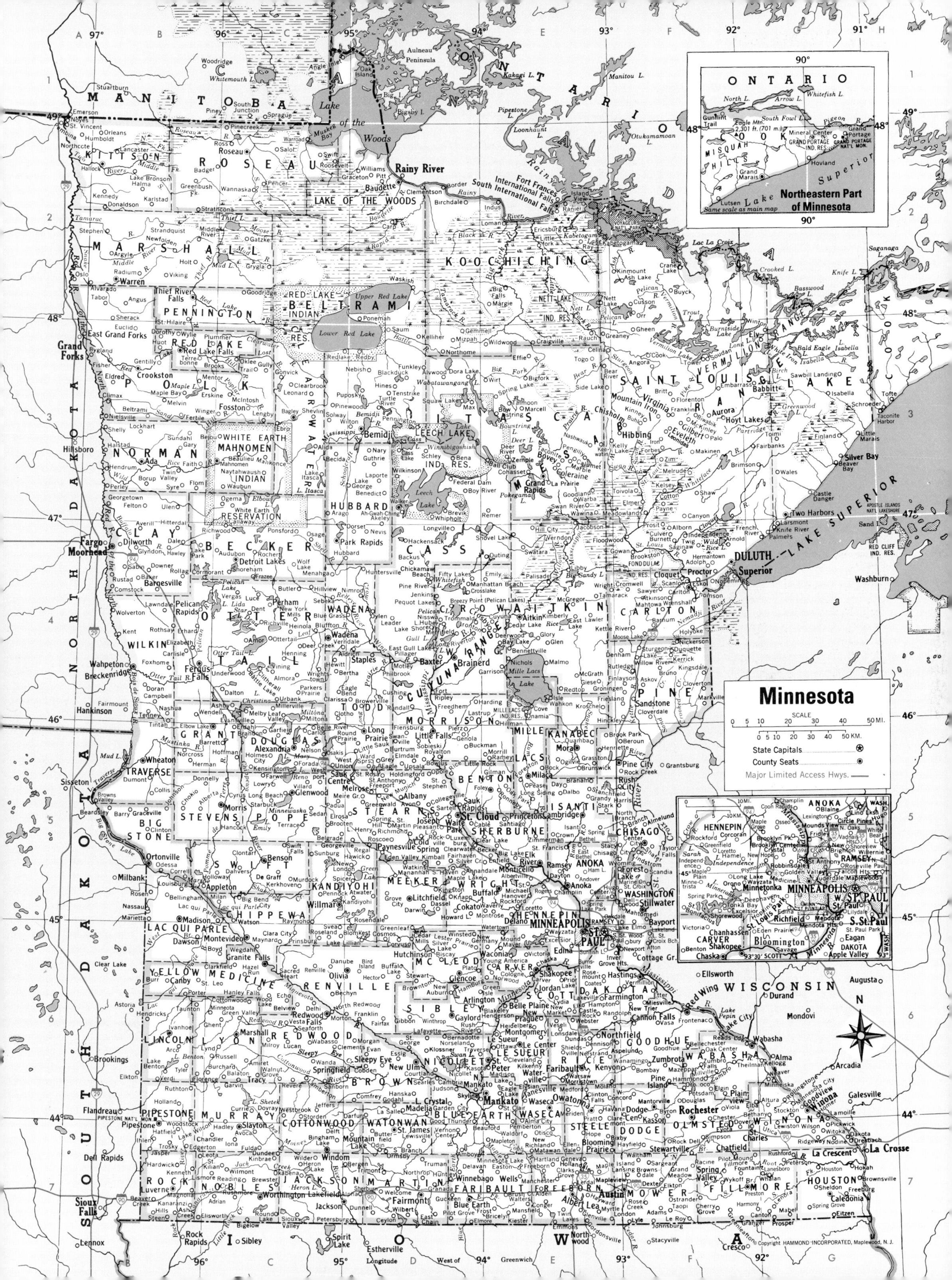
Minnesota
SCALE
0 5 10 20 30 40 50 MI.
0 5 10 20 30 40 50 KM.
State Capitals
County Seats
Major Limited Access Hwys.
Northeastern Part of Minnesota
Same scale as main map
ONTARIO
MANITOBA
NORTH DAKOTA
SOUTH DAKOTA
IOWA
WISCONSIN
Lake Superior
Lake of the Woods
KITTSON
ROSEAU
LAKE OF THE WOODS
MARSHALL
KOOCHICHING
PENNINGTON
BELTRAMI
RED LAKE
POLK
CLEARWATER
ITASCA
SAINT LOUIS
LAKE
COOK
NORMAN
MAHNOMEN
HUBBARD
CASS
CLAY
BECKER
WADENA
CROW WING
AITKIN
CARLTON
WILKIN
OTTER TAIL
TODD
MORRISON
MILLE LACS
KANABEC
PINE
GRANT
DOUGLAS
TRAVERSE
STEVENS
POPE
STEARNS
BENTON
SHERBURNE
ISANTI
CHISAGO
BIG STONE
SWIFT
KANDIYOHI
MEEKER
WRIGHT
ANOKA
HENNEPIN
RAMSEY
WASHINGTON
CHIPPEWA
LAC QUI PARLE
YELLOW MEDICINE
RENVILLE
MC LEOD
CARVER
SCOTT
DAKOTA
SIBLEY
LINCOLN
LYON
REDWOOD
NICOLLET
LE SUEUR
RICE
GOODHUE
WABASHA
BROWN
PIPESTONE
MURRAY
COTTONWOOD
WATONWAN
BLUE EARTH
WASECA
STEELE
DODGE
OLMSTED
WINONA
ROCK
NOBLES
JACKSON
MARTIN
FARIBAULT
FREEBORN
MOWER
FILLMORE
HOUSTON
DULUTH
ST. PAUL
MINNEAPOLIS
Rochester
Longitude West of Greenwich
© Copyright HAMMOND INCORPORATED, Maplewood, N. J.

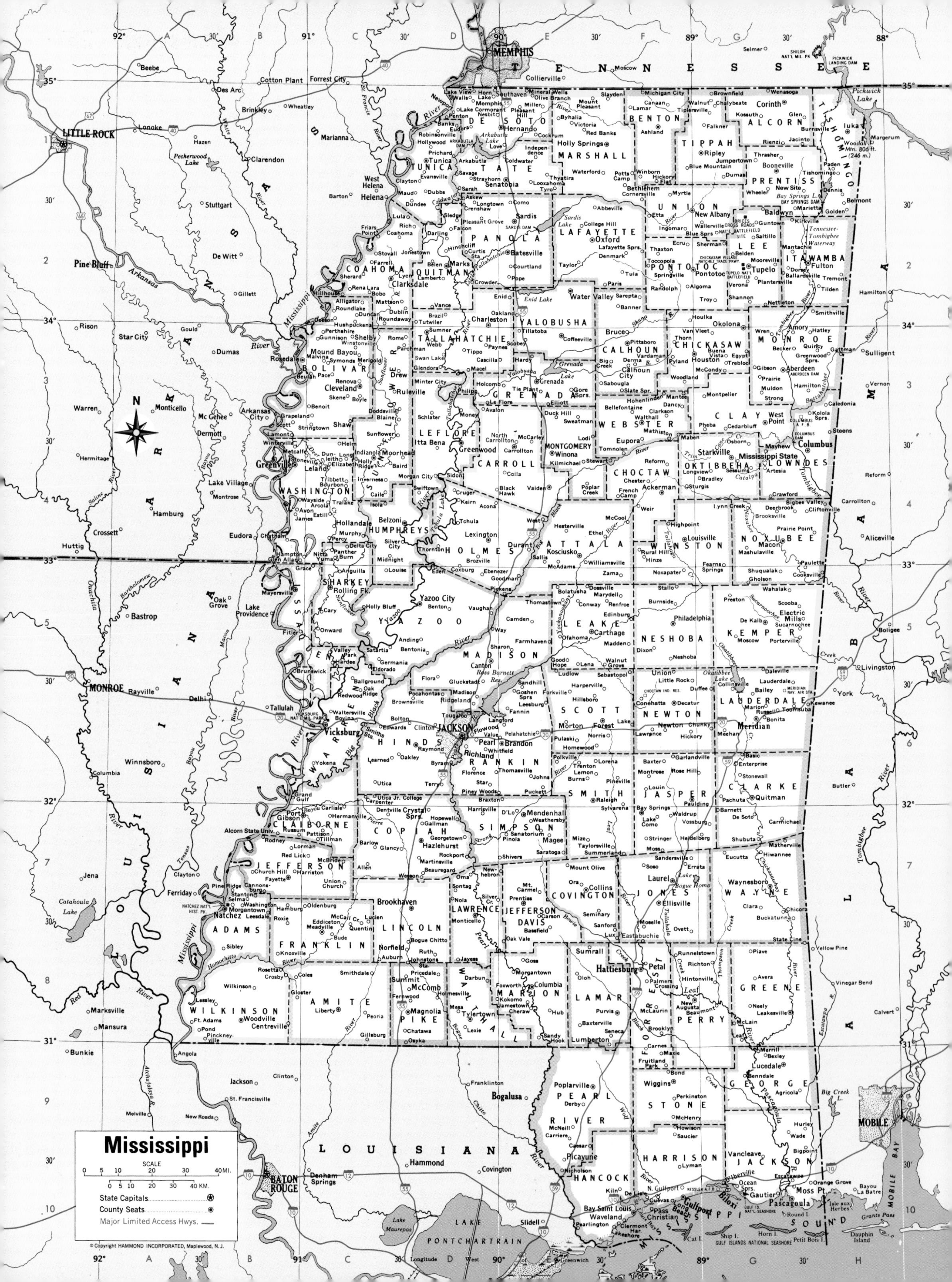
Mississippi
SCALE
0 5 10 20 30 40 MI.
0 5 10 20 30 40 KM.
State Capitals
County Seats
Major Limited Access Hwys.
© Copyright HAMMOND INCORPORATED, Maplewood, N.J.
TENNESSEE
ARKANSAS
LOUISIANA
ALABAMA
MISSISSIPPI SOUND
LAKE PONTCHARTRAIN
MOBILE BAY
MEMPHIS
LITTLE ROCK
JACKSON
MONROE
BATON ROUGE
MOBILE
DE SOTO
MARSHALL
BENTON
TIPPAH
ALCORN
TISHOMINGO
TUNICA
TATE
PRENTISS
UNION
PANOLA
LAFAYETTE
LEE
ITAWAMBA
PONTOTOC
COAHOMA
QUITMAN
YALOBUSHA
CALHOUN
CHICKASAW
MONROE
TALLAHATCHIE
BOLIVAR
SUNFLOWER
GRENADA
WEBSTER
CLAY
LEFLORE
CARROLL
MONTGOMERY
CHOCTAW
OKTIBBEHA
LOWNDES
WASHINGTON
HUMPHREYS
HOLMES
ATTALA
WINSTON
NOXUBEE
SHARKEY
ISSAQUENA
YAZOO
LEAKE
NESHOBA
KEMPER
MADISON
SCOTT
NEWTON
LAUDERDALE
WARREN
HINDS
RANKIN
SMITH
JASPER
CLARKE
CLAIBORNE
COPIAH
SIMPSON
JEFFERSON
COVINGTON
JONES
WAYNE
ADAMS
FRANKLIN
LINCOLN
LAWRENCE
JEFFERSON DAVIS
WILKINSON
AMITE
PIKE
WALTHALL
MARION
LAMAR
FORREST
PERRY
GREENE
PEARL RIVER
STONE
GEORGE
HANCOCK
HARRISON
JACKSON
Gulfport
Biloxi
Pascagoula
Hattiesburg
Meridian
Vicksburg
Natchez
Greenville
Tupelo
Columbus
Oxford
Clarksdale
Greenwood
Laurel

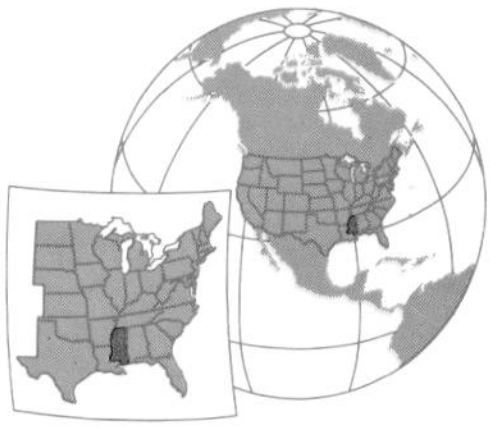

AREA 47,689 sq. mi. (123,515 sq. km.)
POPULATION 2,586,443
CAPITAL Jackson
LARGEST CITY Jackson
HIGHEST POINT Woodall Mtn. 806 ft. (246 m.)
SETTLED IN 1716
ADMITTED TO UNION December 10, 1817
POPULAR NAME Magnolia State
STATE FLOWER Magnolia
STATE BIRD Mockingbird

Topography

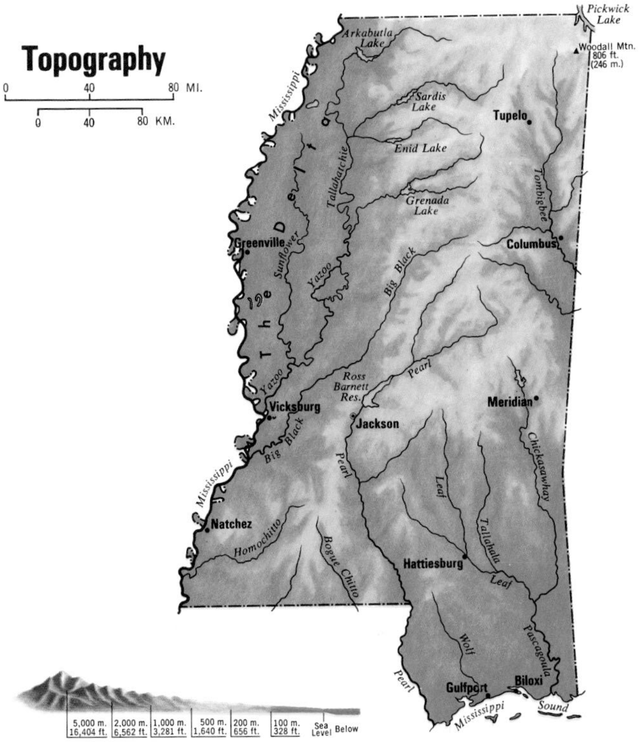

0 40 80 MI.
0 40 80 KM.
Pickwick Lake
Woodall Mtn. 806 ft. (246 m.)
Arkabutla Lake
Sardis Lake
Enid Lake
Grenada Lake
Tupelo
Mississippi
Tallahatchie
Tombigbee
Columbus
Greenville
The Delta
Sunflower
Yazoo
Big Black
Ross Barnett Res.
Pearl
Vicksburg
Jackson
Meridian
Chickasawhay
Leaf
Natchez
Homochitto
Bogue Chitto
Tallahala
Hattiesburg
Wolf
Pascagoula
Gulfport
Biloxi
Mississippi Sound
5,000 m. 16,404 ft.
2,000 m. 6,562 ft.
1,000 m. 3,281 ft.
500 m. 1,640 ft.
200 m. 656 ft.
100 m. 328 ft.
Sea Level
Below

COUNTIES

Adams 35,356 B8
Alcorn 31,722 G1
Amite 13,328 C8
Attala 18,481 E4
Benton 8,046 F1
Bolivar 41,875 C3
Calhoun 14,908 F3
Carroll 9,237 E4
Chickasaw 18,085 G3
Choctaw 9,071 F4
Claiborne 11,370 C7
Clarke 17,313 G6
Clay 21,120 G3
Coahoma 31,665 C2
Copiah 27,592 D7
Covington 16,527 E7
De Soto 53,930 E1
Forrest 68,314 F8
Franklin 8,377 C8
George 16,673 G9
Greene 10,220 G8
Grenada 21,555 E3
Hancock 31,760 E10
Harrison 165,365 F10
Hinds 254,441 D6
Holmes 21,604 D4
Humphreys 12,134 C4
Issaquena 1,909 B5
Itawamba 20,017 H2
Jackson 115,243 G9
Jasper 17,114 F6
Jefferson 8,653 B7
Jefferson Davis 14,051 E7
Jones 62,031 F7
Kemper 10,356 G5
Lafayette 31,826 E2
Lamar 30,424 E8
Lauderdale 75,555 G6
Lawrence 12,458 D7
Leake 18,436 E5
Lee 65,581 G2
Leflore 37,341 D3
Lincoln 30,278 D8
Lowndes 59,308 H4
Madison 53,794 D5
Marion 25,544 E8
Marshall 30,361 E1
Monroe 36,582 H3
Montgomery 12,388 E4
Neshoba 24,800 F5
Newton 20,291 F6
Noxubee 12,604 G4
Oktibbeha 38,375 G4
Panola 29,996 E2
Pearl River 38,714 E9
Perry 10,865 G8
Pike 36,882 D8
Pontotoc 22,237 F2
Prentiss 23,278 G1
Quitman 10,490 D2
Rankin 87,161 E6
Scott 24,137 E6
Sharkey 7,066 C5
Simpson 23,953 E7
Smith 14,798 E6
Stone 10,750 F9
Sunflower 32,867 C3
Tallahatchie 15,210 D3
Tate 21,432 E1
Tippah 19,523 G1
Tishomingo 17,683 H1
Tunica 8,164 D1
Union 22,085 F2
Walthall 14,352 D8
Warren 47,880 C6
Washington 67,935 C4
Wayne 19,517 G7
Webster 10,222 F3
Wilkinson 9,678 B8
Winston 19,433 F4
Yalobusha 12,033 E2
Yazoo 25,506 D5

CITIES and TOWNS

Abbeville 399 F2
Aberdeen▲ 6,837 H3
Ackerman▲ 1,573 F4
Acona 200 D4
Agricola 200 G9
Alcorn State University B7
Algoma 420 G2
Alligator 187 C2
Amory 7,093 H3
Anguilla 883 C5
Arcola 564 C4
Arkabutla 400 D1
Artesia 484 G4
Ashland▲ 490 F1
Askew 300 D1
Auburn 500 C8
Avalon 100 D3
Avera 150 G8
Avon 400 B4
Bailey 320 G6
Baird 150 C4
Baldwyn 3,204 G2
Ballardsville 105 H2
Banks 100 D1
Banner 120 F2
Bassfield 249 E8
Batesville▲ 6,403 E2
Baxterville 100 E8
Bay Saint Louis▲ 8,063 F10
Bay Springs▲ 1,729 F7
Beaumont 1,054 G8
Beauregard 206 D7
Becker 350 G3
Belden 241 G2
Belen 400 D2
Bellefontaine 400 F3
Belmont 1,554 H1
Belzoni▲ 2,536 C4
Benndale 500 G9
Benoit 641 C3
Benton 390 D5
Bentonia 518 D5
Bethlehem 210 F1
Beulah 460 B3
Bexley 130 G9
Big Creek 123 F3
Bigbee Valley 370 H4
Bigpoint 350 H9
Biloxi 46,319 G10
Blue Mountain 667 G1
Blue Springs 140 G2
Bobo 200 C2
Bogue Chitto 689 D8
Bolatusha 87 E5
Bolton 637 D6
Bond 350 F9
Bonita 300 G6
Booneville▲ 7,955 G1
Bourbon 200 C4
Boyle 651 C3
Brandon▲ 11,077 E6
Braxton 141 D6
Brazil 229 D2
Brookhaven▲ 10,243 C7
Brooklyn 450 F8
Brooksville 1,098 G4
Brownfield 125 G1
Brownsville 200 D6
Brozville 150 D4
Bruce 2,127 F3
Brunswick 90 C5
Buckatunna 500 G7
Bude 969 C8
Burns 949 E6
Burnsville 889 H1
Byhalia 955 E1
Byram 250 D6
Caesar 80 E9
Caledonia 821 H3
Calhoun City 1,838 F3
Camden 150 E5
Canaan 200 F1
Cannonsburg 240 B7
Canton▲ 10,062 D5
Carlisle 425 C7
Carpenter 200 C6
Carriere 900 E9
Carrollton▲ 221 E4
Carson 400 E7
Carthage▲ 3,819 E5
Cary 392 C5
Cascilla 230 D3
Cedarbluff 175 G3
Centreville 1,771 B8
Chalybeate 350 G1
Charleston▲ 2,328 D2
Chatawa 300 D8
Chatham 150 B4
Cheraw 100 E8
Chunky 292 G6
Church Hill 350 B7
Clara 275 G7
Clarksdale▲ 19,717 D2
Clarkson 100 F3
Clermont Harbor 550 F10
Cleveland▲ 15,384 C3
Cliftonville 280 H4
Clinton 21,847 D6
Coahoma 254 C2
Cockrum 150 E1
Coffeeville▲ 825 E3
Coldwater 1,502 E1
Coles 150 C8
College Hill 150 E2
Collins▲ 2,541 E7
Collinsville 1,364 G6
Columbia▲ 6,815 E8
Columbus▲ 23,799 H3
Como 1,387 E1
Conehatta 925 F6
Corinth▲ 11,820 G1
Courtland 329 E2
Coxburg 300 D5
Crawford 668 G4
Crenshaw 978 D2
Crosby 465 B8
Crowder 758 D2
Cruger 548 D4
Crystal Springs 5,643 D7
Cuevas 200 F10
Curtis Station 350 D2
D'Iberville 6,566 G10
D'Lo 421 E7
Daleville 210 G5
Dancy 116 F3
Darbun 100 D8
Darling 275 D2
De Kalb▲ 1,073 G5
De Lisle 450 F10
De Soto 150 G7
Decatur▲ 1,248 F6
Delta City 310 C4
Dennis 150 H1
Dentville 175 C7
Derby 298 E9
Derma 959 F3
Dixon 125 F5
Doddsville 149 C3
Dorsey 100 H2
Drew 2,349 C3
Dublin 100 C2
Duck Hill 586 E3
Duffee 175 G6
Dumas 407 G1
Duncan 416 C2
Dundee 600 D1
Dunleith 140 C4
Durant 2,838 E4
Eastabuchie 200 F8
Ebenezer 200 D5
Ecru 696 F2
Eden 88 D5
Edinburg 200 F5
Edwards 1,279 C6
Egypt 100 G3
Electric Mills 100 G5
Elizabeth 500 C4
Elliott 200 E3
Ellisville▲ 3,634 F7
Enid E2
Enterprise 477 G6
Errata 85 F7
Escatawpa 3,902 G10
Estill 100 C4
Ethel 454 F4
Eudora 200 D1
Eupora 2,145 F3
Falcon 167 D2
Falkner 232 G1
Fannin 250 E6
Farrell 300 C2
Fayette▲ 1,853 B7
Fernwood 500 D8
Fitler 175 B5
Flora 1,482 D5
Florence 1,831 D6
Flowood 2,860 D6
Forest▲ 5,060 F6
Forkville 185 E6
Foxworth 800 E8
French Camp 320 F4
Friars Point 1,334 C2
Fulton▲ 3,387 H2
Gallman D7
Garlandville 150 F6
Gattman 120 H3
Gautier 10,088 G10
Georgetown 332 D7
Glen 165 H1
Glen Allan 650 B4
Glendora 220 D3
Gloster 1,323 B8
Gluckstadt 150 D5
Golden 202 H2
Good Hope 125 E5
Goodman 1,256 E5
Gore Springs 125 E3
Goshen Springs 100 E6
Goss 100 E8
Grace 325 C5
Grapeland 200 B3
Greenville▲ 45,226 B4
Greenwood Springs 170 H3
Greenwood▲ 18,906 D4
Grenada▲ 10,864 E3
Gulfport▲ 40,775 F10
Gunnison 611 C3
Guntown 692 G2
Hamburg 150 B7
Hamilton 500 H3
Hampton 200 B4
Hardee 100 C5
Harperville 200 E6
Harriston 500 C7
Harrisville 500 D7
Hatley 529 H3
Hattiesburg▲ 41,882 F8
Hazlehurst▲ 4,221 D7
Heidelberg 981 F7
Helm 80 C4
Hermanville 750 C7
Hernando▲ 3,125 E1
Hickory 493 F6
Hickory Flat 535 F1
Hillsboro 800 E6
Hintonville 300 F8
Hiwannee 250 G7
Hohenlinden 96 F3
Hollandale 3,576 C4
Holly Bluff 700 C5
Holly Ridge 350 C4
Holly Springs▲ 7,261 E1
Hollywood 80 D1
Hopewell 250 D7
Horn Lake 9,069 D1
Houlka G2
Houston▲ 3,903 G3
Howison 300 F9
Hub 80 E8
Hurley 500 H9
Independence 150 E1
Indianola▲ 11,809 C4
Ingomar 150 F2
Inverness 1,174 C4
Isola 732 C4
Itta Bena 2,377 D4
Iuka▲ 3,122 H1
Jackson (cap.)▲ 196,637 D6
James 100 B4
Jayess 200 D8
Johns 90 E6
Jonestown 1,467 D2
Jumpertown 438 G1
Kewanee 250 H6
Kilmichael 826 E4
Kiln 1,262 F10
Kirkville 200 H2
Kokomo 250 D8
Kolola Springs 100 H3
Kosciusko▲ 6,986 E4
Kossuth 245 G1
Lafayette Springs 80 F2
Lake 369 F6
Lake Como 150 F7
Lake Cormorant 300 D1
Lake View 125 D1
Lakeshore 550 F10
Lamar 200 F1
Lambert 1,131 D2
Lamont 400 B3
Langford 100 E6
Lauderdale 600 G5
Laurel▲ 18,827 F7
Lawrence 250 F6
Le Flore 99 D3
Leaf 250 G8
Leakesville▲ 1,129 G8
Learned 111 C6
Leland 6,366 C4
Lemon 90 E6
Lena 175 E5
Lessley 100 B8
Lexington▲ 2,227 D4
Liberty▲ 624 C8
Long 15,804 C4
Long Beach 7,967 F10
Longtown 150 D1
Longview 800 G4
Looxahoma 200 E1
Lorena 90 F6
Lorman 350 B7
Louin 289 F6
Louise 343 C5
Louisville▲ 7,169 G4
Lucedale▲ 2,592 G9
Ludlow 350 E5
Lula 224 C2
Lumberton 2,121 E8
Lyman 1,117 F10
Lyon 446 D2
Maben 752 F3
Macon▲ 2,256 G4
Madden 450 F5
Madison 7,471 D6
Magee 3,607 E7
Magnolia▲ 2,245 D8
Malvina 100 C3
Mantachie 651 H2
Mantee 134 F3
Marietta 287 H2
Marion 1,359 G6
Marks▲ 1,758 D2
Marydell 99 F5
Mashulaville 227 G4
Matherville 150 G7
Mathiston 818 F3
Mattson 200 C2
Maxie 233 F9
Mayersville▲ 329 B5
Mayhew 150 G4
McAdams 350 E4
McCall Creek 250 C7
McCarley 250 E3
McComb 11,591 D8
McCondy 150 G3
McCool 169 F4
McHenry 660 F9
McLain 536 G8
McLaurin 100 F8
McNeill 800 E9
Meadville▲ 453 C8
Meehan 100 G6
Mendenhall▲ 2,463 E7
Meridian▲ 41,036 G6
Merigold 572 C3
Merrill 100 G9
Metcalfe 1,092 B4
Michigan City 350 F1
Midnight 500 C4
Mineral Wells 250 E1
Minter City 150 D3
Mississippi State G4
Mize 312 E7
Money 350 D3
Monticello▲ 1,755 D7
Montpelier 175 G3
Montrose 106 F6
Mooreville 200 G2
Moorhead 2,417 C4
Morgan City 139 D4
Morgantown 32,880 B7
Morgantown 325 E8
Morton 3,212 E6
Moselle 525 F8
Moss 17,837 F7
Moss Point 18,998 G10
Mound Bayou 2,222 C3
Mount Olive 914 E7
Mount Pleasant 250 E1
Murphy 100 C4
Myrtle 358 F1
Natchez▲ 19,460 B7
Neely 270 G8
Nesbit 366 D1
Neshoba 250 F5
Nettleton 2,462 G2
New Albany▲ 6,775 G2
New Augusta▲ 668 F8
New Houlka (Houlka) 558 G2
New Site 100 H1
Newhebron 470 D7
Newton 3,701 F6
Nicholson 400 E10
Nitta Yuma 150 C4
Nola 120 D7
North Carrollton 578 E3
North Gulfport 4,966 F10
Noxapater 441 F5
Oak Ridge 350 C6
Oak Vale E8
Oakland 553 E2
Oakley 133 D6
Ocean Springs 14,658 G10
Ofahoma 350 E5
Okolona▲ 3,267 G2
Olive Branch 3,567 E1
Oloh 93 E8
Oma 200 D7
Ora 15,676 E7
Orange Grove H10
Osyka 483 D8
Ovett 600 F8
Oxford▲ 9,984 F2
Pace 354 C3
Pachuta 268 G6
Paden 123 H1
Palmers Crossing 2,765 F8
Panther Burn 300 C4
Parchman 200 D3
Paris 253 F2
Pascagoula▲ 25,899 G10
Pass Christian 5,557 F10
Pattison 540 C7
Paulding▲ 630 F6
Paulette 230 H4
Paynes 100 D3
Pearl 19,588 D6
Pearlington 1,603 E10
Pelahatchie 1,553 E6
Penton 175 D1
Peoria 100 C8
Perkinston 950 F9
Petal 7,883 F8
Pheba 280 G3
Philadelphia▲ 6,758 F5
Philipp 975 D3
Piave 150 G8
Picayune 10,633 E9
Pickens 1,285 E5
Pine Ridge 175 B7
Pineville 80 F6
Piney Woods 450 D6
Pinola E7
Pittsboro▲ 277 F3
Plantersville 1,046 G2
Pleasant Grove 100 D2
Pleasant Hill 400 E1
Polkville 129 E6

(continued on following page)

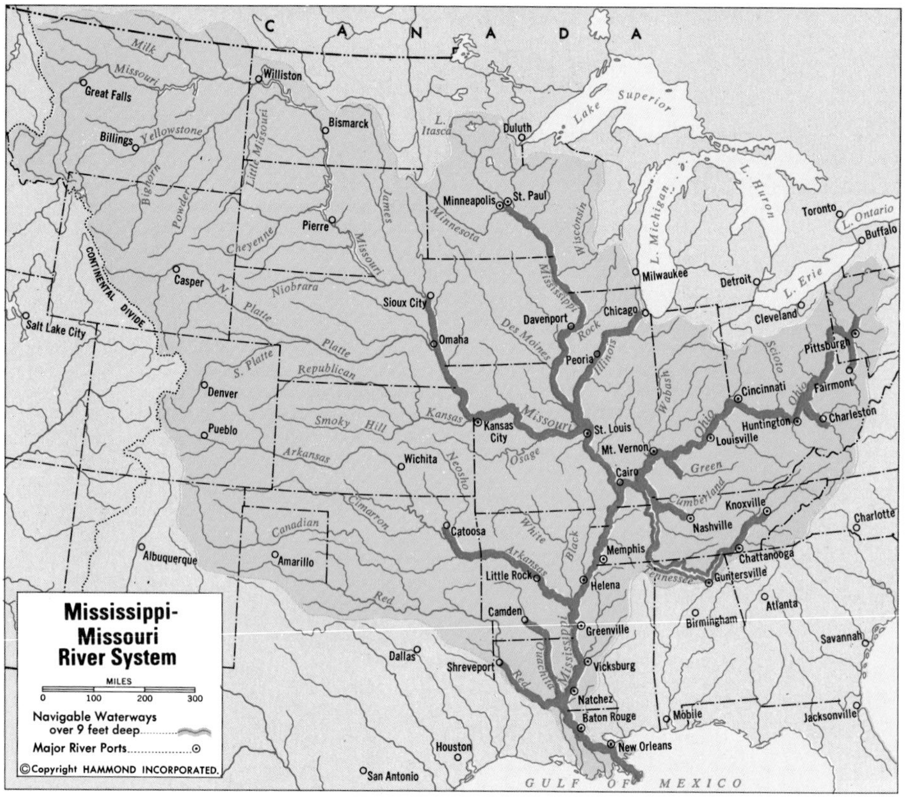
Mississippi-
Missouri
River System
MILES
0 100 200 300
Navigable Waterways over 9 feet deep
Major River Ports
©Copyright HAMMOND INCORPORATED.
CANADA
GULF OF MEXICO
CONTINENTAL DIVIDE
Great Falls
Billings
Williston
Bismarck
Duluth
Minneapolis
St. Paul
Pierre
Casper
Salt Lake City
Sioux City
Omaha
Davenport
Chicago
Milwaukee
Detroit
Toronto
Buffalo
Cleveland
Pittsburgh
Peoria
Denver
Pueblo
Kansas City
St. Louis
Mt. Vernon
Cincinnati
Huntington
Charleston
Fairmont
Louisville
Wichita
Cairo
Nashville
Knoxville
Charlotte
Catoosa
Memphis
Chattanooga
Guntersville
Little Rock
Helena
Atlanta
Albuquerque
Amarillo
Camden
Greenville
Birmingham
Savannah
Dallas
Shreveport
Vicksburg
Natchez
Baton Rouge
Mobile
Jacksonville
Houston
New Orleans
San Antonio
Milk
Missouri
Yellowstone
Bighorn
Powder
Little Missouri
James
Cheyenne
Niobrara
Platte
S. Platte
Republican
Smoky Hill
Arkansas
Kansas
Cimarron
Canadian
Red
Osage
Neosho
White
Black
Ouachita
Mississippi
Des Moines
Rock
Illinois
Wabash
Ohio
Scioto
Green
Cumberland
Tennessee
Wisconsin
Minnesota
L. Itasca
Lake Superior
L. Michigan
L. Huron
L. Erie
L. Ontario

Agriculture, Industry and Resources

DOMINANT LAND USE

- Specialized Cotton
- Cotton, Livestock
- Cotton, General Farming
- Cotton, Forest Products
- Truck and Mixed Farming
- Forests
- Swampland, Limited Agriculture

MAJOR MINERAL OCCURRENCES

- Cl Clay
- Fe Iron Ore
- G Natural Gas
- O Petroleum
- Major Industrial Areas

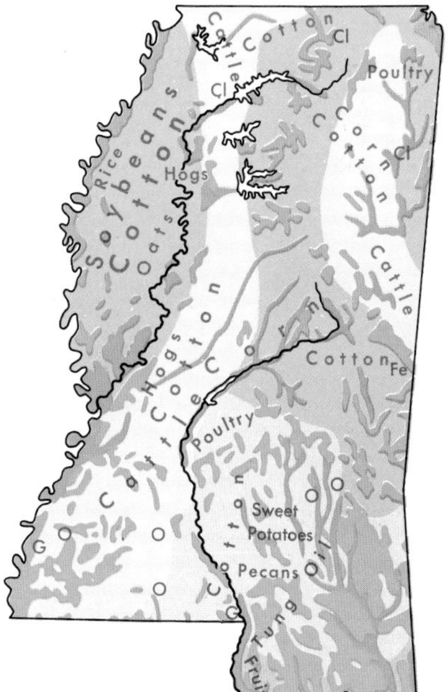
Cotton
Cl
Poultry
Cattle
Rice
Soybeans
Cotton
Oats
Hogs
Corn
Cotton
Cattle
Cotton
Fe
Poultry
Hogs
Cattle
Corn
Sweet Potatoes
Pecans
Tung Oil
Fruit
Pascagoula
Oysters
Shrimp
Menhaden
G

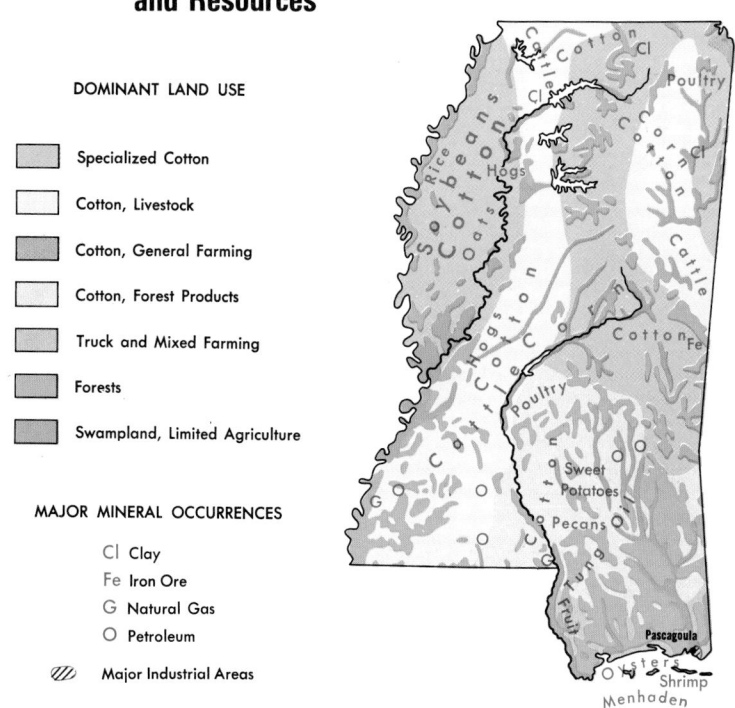

Pontotoc▲ 4,570 G2
Pope 171 E2
Poplar Creek 100 E4
Poplarville▲ 2,561 E9
Port Gibson▲ 1,810 B7
Porterville 150 G5
Potts Camp 483 F1
Prairie G3
Prairie Point 150 H4
Prentiss▲ 1,487 E7
Preston 500 G5
Pricedale 400 D8
Puckett 294 E6
Pulaski 108 E6
Purvis▲ 2,140 F8
Pyland 120 F3
Quitman▲ 2,736 G6
Raleigh▲ 1,291 F6
Randolph F2
Raymond▲ 2,275 D6
Red Banks 350 F1
Red Lick 100 B7
Reform 100 F4
Rena Lara 350 C2
Renova 636 C3
Rich 4,014 D2
Richland 3,955 D6
Richton 1,034 G8
Ridgeland 11,714 D6
Rienzi 339 G1
Ripley▲ 5,371 G1
Robinsonville 285 D1
Rodney 100 B7
Rolling Fork▲ 2,444 C5
Rome C3
Rose Hill 500 F6
Rosedale▲ 2,595 B3
Rosetta 120 B8
Roundaway 175 C2
Roundlake 105 C2
Roxie 568 B8
Ruleville 3,245 D3
Runnelstown 200 F8
Russell 300 G6
Russum 200 B7
Ruth 400 D8
Sabougla 100 F3
Sallis 139 E4
Saltillo 1,782 G2
Sanatorium 400 E7
Sandersville 853 F7
Sandhill 100 E5
Sanford 150 F8
Sarah 150 D1
Sardis▲ 2,128 E2
Sarepta 120 F2
Saucier 100 F9
Savage 100 D1
Schlater 404 D3
Scobey 100 E3
Scooba 541 G5
Scott 400 B3
Sebastopol 281 F5
Seminary 231 E7
Senatobia▲ 4,772 E1
Sessums 150 G4
Shannon 1,419 G2
Sharon 200 E5
Shaw 2,349 C3
Shelby 2,806 C3
Sherard 150 C2
Sherman 528 G2
Shivers 100 E7
Shubuta 577 G7
Shuqualak 570 G5
Sibley 350 B8
Sidon 596 D4
Silver City 348 C4
Silver Creek 190 D7
Skene 250 C3
Slate Spring 118 F3
Slayden 310 F1
Sledge 577 D2
Smithdale 200 C8
Smithville 871 H2
Sontag 200 D7
Soso 366 F7
Southaven 17,949 E1
Springville 100 F2
Stallo 100 F5
Stanton 90 B7
Star 18,458 D6
Starkville▲ 15,169 G4
State Line 395 G8
Steens 125 H3
Stewart 350 F4
Stoneville 250 C4
Stonewall 1,148 G6
Strayhorn 275 D1
Stringer 350 F7
Stringtown 300 C3
Sturgis 198 G4
Summerland 150 F7
Summit 1,566 D8
Sumner▲ 368 D3
Sumrall 903 E8
Sunflower 729 C3
Swan Lake 325 D3
Swiftown 320 D4
Sylvarena 110 F6
Symonds 200 C3
Taylor 288 E2
Taylorsville 1,412 F7
Tchula 2,186 D4
Terry 613 D6
Thaxton 431 F2
Thomastown 400 E5
Thon 125 F3
Thornton 135 D4
Thrasher 100 G1
Thyatira 100 E1
Tie Plant 500 E3
Tilden 250 H2
Tillatoba 124 E3
Tiplersville 100 G1
Tippo 200 D3
Tishomingo 332 H1
Toccopola 154 F2
Tomnolen 200 F4
Toomsuba 500 G6
Tougaloo 800 D6
Tralake 200 C4
Trebloc 100 G3
Tremont 342 H2
Tribbett 100 C4
Troy 150 G2
Tula 140 F2
Tunica▲ 1,175 D1
Tupelo▲ 30,685 G2
Tutwiler 1,391 D2
Tylertown▲ 1,938 D8
Union 1,875 F5
Utica 1,033 C6
Vaiden▲ 789 E4
Valley Park 400 C5
Value 327 D6
Van Vleet 400 G3
Vance 200 D2
Vancleave 3,214 G9
Vardaman 920 F3
Vaughan 210 D5
Verona 2,893 G2
Vicksburg▲ 20,908 C6
Victoria 800 E1
Vossburg 300 F7
Wade 800 G9
Wahalak 92 G5
Waldrup 125 F7
Walnut 523 G1
Walnut Grove 389 F5
Waltersville 150 C6
Walthall▲ 167 F3
Washington 250 B7
Water Valley▲ 3,610 E2
Waterford 400 E1
Waveland 5,369 F10
Way 5,143 E5
Waynesboro▲ 5,349 G7
Wayside 500 C4
Weathersby E7
Webb 605 D3
Weir 525 F4
Wenasoga 175 G1
Wesson 1,510 D7
West 184 E4
West Point▲ 8,489 G3
Wheeler 600 G1
Whitfield 900 E6
Wiggins▲ 3,185 F9
Williamsville 250 F4
Winona▲ 5,705 E4
Winstonville 277 C3
Winterville 200 B4
Woodland 182 F3
Woodville▲ 1,393 B8
Wren 150 G3
Yazoo City▲ 12,427 D5
Zama 100 F5

OTHER FEATURES

Amite (riv.) C9
Arkabutla (lake) D1
Big Black (riv.) C6
Black (creek) F8
Bogue Chitto (riv.) D8
Bogue Homo (lake) F7
Bowie (creek) E7
Brices Cross Roads Nat'l Battlefield Site G2
Buttahatchee (riv.) H3
Cat (isl.) F10
Catalpa (creek) G4
Chickasaw Village, Natchez Trace Parkway G2
Chickasawhay (riv.) G7
Coldwater (riv.) D1
Columbus A.F.B. 2,890 H3
Deer (creek) C4
Enid (lake) E2
Grenada (lake) E3
Gulf Islands Nat'l Seashore G10
Homochitto (riv.) B8
Horn (isl.) G10
Keesler A.F.B. G10
Leaf (riv.) F8
Little Tallahatchie (riv.) D2
Meridian Naval Air Sta. G5
Mississippi (riv.) A8
Mississippi (sound) G10
Natchez Nat'l Hist. Park A7
Noxubee (riv.) G4
Okatibbee (lake) G5
Pascagoula (riv.) G9
Pearl (riv.) D8
Petit Bois (isl.) H10
Pickwick (lake) H1
Pierre (bayou) C7
Ross Barnett (res.) D6
Round (isl.) G10
Saint Louis (bay) F10
Sardis (lake) E2
Ship (isl.) G10
Skuna (riv.) F2
Strong (riv.) D7
Sunflower (riv.) C5
Tallahaga (creek) F4
Tallahala (creek) F7
Tallahatchie (riv.) D3
Tchula (lake) D4
Tennessee-Tombigbee Waterway H2
Thompson (creek) G8
Tombigbee (riv.) H4
Trim Cane (creek) G4
Tupelo Nat'l Battlefield G2
Vicksburg Nat'l Mil. Park C6
Wolf (riv.) F9
Woodall (mt.) H1
Yalobusha (riv.) E3
Yazoo (riv.) C5
Yockanookany (riv.) E5

▲County seat

AREA 69,697 sq. mi. (180,515 sq. km.)
POPULATION 5,137,804
CAPITAL Jefferson City
LARGEST CITY St. Louis
HIGHEST POINT Taum Sauk Mtn. 1,772 ft. (540 m.)
SETTLED IN 1764
ADMITTED TO UNION August 10, 1821
POPULAR NAME Show Me State
STATE FLOWER Hawthorn
STATE BIRD Bluebird

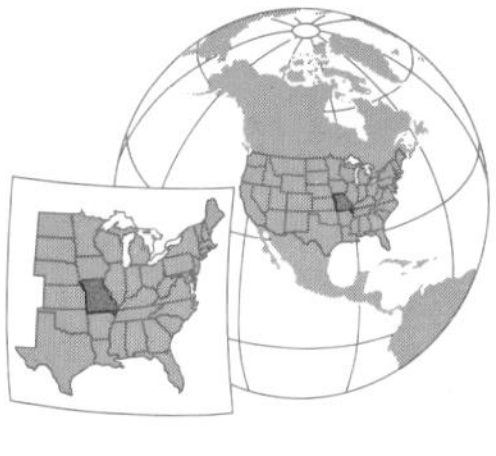

COUNTIES

Adair 24,577 ..... G2
Andrew 14,632 ..... C3
Atchison 7,457 ..... B2
Audrain 23,599 ..... J4
Barry 27,547 ..... E9
Barton 11,312 ..... D7
Bates 15,025 ..... D6
Benton 13,859 ..... F6
Bollinger 10,619 ..... M8
Boone 112,379 ..... H4
Buchanan 83,083 ..... C3
Butler 38,765 ..... M9
Caldwell 8,380 ..... E3
Callaway 32,809 ..... J5
Camden 27,495 ..... G6
Cape Girardeau 61,633 ..... N8
Carroll 10,748 ..... F4
Carter 5,515 ..... L9
Cass 63,808 ..... D5
Cedar 12,093 ..... E7
Chariton 9,202 ..... F3
Christian 32,644 ..... F9
Clark 7,547 ..... J2
Clay 153,411 ..... D4
Clinton 16,595 ..... D3
Cole 63,579 ..... H6
Cooper 14,835 ..... G5
Crawford 19,173 ..... K7
Dade 7,449 ..... E8
Dallas 12,646 ..... F7
Daviess 7,865 ..... E3
De Kalb 8,222 ..... D3
Dent 13,702 ..... J7
Douglas 11,876 ..... G9
Dunklin 33,112 ..... M1
Franklin 80,603 ..... K6
Gasconade 14,006 ..... J6
Gentry 6,848 ..... D2
Greene 207,949 ..... F8
Grundy 10,536 ..... E2
Harrison 8,469 ..... E2
Henry 20,044 ..... E6
Hickory 7,335 ..... F7
Holt 6,034 ..... B2
Howard 9,631 ..... G4
Howell 31,447 ..... J9
Iron 10,726 ..... L7
Jackson 633,232 ..... R5
Jasper 90,465 ..... D8
Jefferson 171,380 ..... L6
Johnson 42,514 ..... E5
Knox 4,482 ..... H2
Laclede 27,158 ..... G7
Lafayette 31,107 ..... E4
Lawrence 30,236 ..... E8
Lewis 10,233 ..... J2
Lincoln 28,892 ..... L4
Linn 13,885 ..... F3
Livingston 14,592 ..... E3
Macon 15,345 ..... G3
Madison 11,127 ..... M8
Maries 7,976 ..... J6
Marion 27,682 ..... J3
McDonald 16,938 ..... D9
Mercer 3,723 ..... E2
Miller 20,700 ..... H6
Mississippi 14,442 ..... O9
Moniteau 12,298 ..... G5
Monroe 9,104 ..... H3
Montgomery 11,355 ..... K5
Morgan 15,574 ..... G6
New Madrid 20,928 ..... N9
Newton 44,445 ..... D9
Nodaway 21,709 ..... C2
Oregon 9,470 ..... K9
Osage 12,018 ..... J6
Ozark 8,598 ..... H9
Pemiscot 21,921 ..... N1
Perry 16,648 ..... N7
Pettis 35,437 ..... F5
Phelps 35,248 ..... J7
Pike 15,969 ..... K4
Platte 57,867 ..... C4
Polk 21,826 ..... F7
Pulaski 41,307 ..... H7
Putnam 5,079 ..... F2
Ralls 8,476 ..... J3
Randolph 24,370 ..... G3
Ray 21,971 ..... E4
Reynolds 6,661 ..... L8
Ripley 12,303 ..... L9
Saint Charles 144,107 ..... M2
Saint Clair 8,622 ..... E6
Saint Francois 42,600 ..... M7
Saint Louis 974,180 ..... O3
Saint Louis (city county) 452,801 ..... P3
Sainte Genevieve 15,180 ..... M7
Saline 23,523 ..... F4
Schuyler 4,236 ..... G2
Scotland 4,822 ..... H2
Scott 39,376 ..... N8
Shannon 7,613 ..... K8
Shelby 6,942 ..... H3
Stoddard 28,895 ..... N9
Stone 19,078 ..... F9
Sullivan 6,326 ..... F2
Taney 25,561 ..... F9
Texas 21,476 ..... J8
Vernon 19,041 ..... D7
Warren 19,534 ..... K5
Washington 20,380 ..... L7
Wayne 11,543 ..... L8
Webster 23,753 ..... G8
Worth 2,440 ..... D2
Wright 16,758 ..... H8

CITIES and TOWNS

Adrian 1,582 ..... D6
Advance 1,139 ..... N8
Affton 21,106 ..... P4
Agency 642 ..... C3
Alba 465 ..... D8
Albany▲ 1,958 ..... D2
Alexandria 341 ..... K2
Alma 446 ..... E4
Altamont 188 ..... D3
Altenburg 307 ..... O7
Alton▲ 692 ..... K9
Amazonia 257 ..... C3
Amoret 212 ..... C6
Amsterdam 237 ..... D6
Anderson 1,432 ..... D9
Annapolis 363 ..... L8
Anniston 288 ..... O9
Appleton City 1,280 ..... D6
Arbyrd 597 ..... M10
Arcadia 609 ..... L7
Archie 799 ..... D5
Argyle 178 ..... J6
Armstrong 310 ..... G4
Arnold 18,828 ..... M6
Asbury 220 ..... C8
Ash Grove 1,128 ..... E8
Ashland 1,252 ..... H5
Atlanta 411 ..... H3
Augusta 263 ..... L5
Aurora 6,459 ..... E9
Auxvasse 821 ..... J4
Ava▲ 2,938 ..... G9
Avondale 550 ..... P5
Bakersfield 292 ..... H9
Ballwin 21,816 ..... N3
Baring 182 ..... H2
Barnard 234 ..... C2
Barnett 215 ..... G6
Bates City 197 ..... E5
Battlefield 1,526 ..... F8
Bel-Nor 2,935 ..... P2
Bel-Ridge 3,199 ..... P2
Bell City 469 ..... N8
Bella Villa 708 ..... R4
Belle 1,218 ..... J6
Bellefontaine 10,922 ..... N2
Bellefontaine Neighbors 12,082 ..... R2
Bellflower 413 ..... K4
Belton 18,150 ..... C5
Benton City 139 ..... J4
Benton▲ 575 ..... O8
Berger 247 ..... K5
Berkeley 12,450 ..... P2
Bernie 1,847 ..... M9
Bertrand 692 ..... O9
Bethany▲ 3,005 ..... E2
Beverly 660 ..... O4
Bevier 643 ..... G3
Billings 989 ..... F8
Birch Tree 599 ..... K9
Birmingham 222 ..... R5
Bismarck 1,579 ..... L7
Black 6,128 ..... L7
Black Jack 5,293 ..... R1
Blackburn 308 ..... F4
Blackwater 221 ..... G5
Blairstown 185 ..... E5
Bland 651 ..... J6
Blodgett 202 ..... O8
Bloomfield▲ 1,800 ..... M9
Bloomsdale 353 ..... M6
Blue Springs 40,153 ..... R6
Bogard 228 ..... E4
Bolckow 253 ..... C2
Bolivar▲ 6,845 ..... F7
Bonne Terre 3,871 ..... L7
Boonville▲ 7,095 ..... G5
Bosworth 334 ..... F4
Bourbon 1,188 ..... K6
Bowling Green▲ 2,976 ..... K4
Brandsville 167 ..... J9
Branson 3,706 ..... F9
Brashear 318 ..... H2
Braymer 886 ..... E3
Breckenridge 418 ..... E3
Breckenridge Hills 5,404 ..... O2
Brentwood 8,150 ..... P3
Bridgeton 17,779 ..... O2
Bridgeton Terrace 334 ..... O2
Bronaugh 211 ..... C7
Brookfield 4,888 ..... F3
Browning 331 ..... F2
Brunswick 1,074 ..... F4
Bucklin 616 ..... G3
Buckner 2,873 ..... R5
Buffalo▲ 2,414 ..... F7
Bunceton 341 ..... G5
Bunker 390 ..... K8
Burlington Junction 634 ..... B2
Butler▲ 4,099 ..... D6
Butterfield 248 ..... E9
Cabool 2,006 ..... H8
Cainsville 387 ..... E2
Cairo 282 ..... H4
Caledonia 142 ..... L7
Calhoun 450 ..... E6
California▲ 3,465 ..... H5
Callao 332 ..... G3
Calverton Park 1,404 ..... P2
Camden 238 ..... D4
Camden Point 373 ..... C4
Camdenton▲ 2,561 ..... G6
Cameron 4,831 ..... D3
Campbell 2,165 ..... M9
Canalou 319 ..... N9
Canton 2,623 ..... J2
Cape Girardeau 34,438 ..... O8
Cardwell 792 ..... M10
Carl Junction 4,123 ..... C8
Carrollton▲ 4,406 ..... E4
Carterville 2,013 ..... D8
Carthage▲ 10,747 ..... D8
Caruth 7,389 ..... N10
Caruthersville▲ 7,958 ..... N10
Carytown 149 ..... D8
Cassville▲ 2,371 ..... E9
Cedar City 427 ..... H5
Cedar Hill Lakes 227 ..... L6
Center 552 ..... J3
Centertown 356 ..... H5
Centerview 214 ..... E5
Centerville▲ 89 ..... L8
Centralia 3,414 ..... H4
Chaffee 3,059 ..... N8
Chamois 449 ..... J5
Charlack 1,388 ..... P2
Charleston▲ 5,085 ..... O9
Chesterfield 37,991 ..... N2
Chilhowee 335 ..... E5
Chillicothe▲ 8,804 ..... E3
Chula 183 ..... F3
Circle City 154 ..... N9
Clarence 1,026 ..... H3
Clark 257 ..... H4
Clarksburg 358 ..... G5
Clarksdale 287 ..... D3
Clarkson Valley 2,508 ..... N3
Clarksville 480 ..... K4
Clarkton 1,113 ..... M10
Claycomo 1,668 ..... P5
Clayton▲ 13,874 ..... P3
Clearmont 175 ..... C1
Cleveland 506 ..... C5
Clever 580 ..... F8
Clinton▲ 8,703 ..... E6
Cobalt City 254 ..... M7
Cole Camp 1,054 ..... F6
Collins 144 ..... E7
Columbia▲ 69,101 ..... H5
Commerce 173 ..... O8
Conception Junction 236 ..... C2
Concord 19,859 ..... P4
Concordia 2,160 ..... E5
Conway 629 ..... G7
Cool Valley 1,407 ..... P2
Cooter 451 ..... N10
Corder 485 ..... E4
Cottleville 2,936 ..... M2
Country Club Village 1,234 ..... C3
Cowgill 257 ..... E3
Craig 346 ..... B2
Crane 1,218 ..... E9
Creighton 289 ..... D6
Crestwood 11,234 ..... O3
Creve Coeur 12,304 ..... O2
Crocker 1,077 ..... H7
Cross Timbers 168 ..... F6
Crystal City 4,088 ..... M6
Crystal Lake Park 506 ..... O3
Cuba 2,537 ..... K6
Curryville 261 ..... K4
Dadeville 220 ..... E8
De Kalb 222 ..... C3
De Soto 5,993 ..... L6
Dearborn 480 ..... C3
Deepwater 441 ..... E6
Dellwood 5,245 ..... R2
Delta 450 ..... N8
Des Arc 173 ..... L8
Des Peres 8,395 ..... O3
Desloge 4,150 ..... M7
Dexter 7,559 ..... N9
Diamond 775 ..... D9
Diehlstadt 145 ..... N9
Diggins 258 ..... G8
Dixon 1,585 ..... H6
Doniphan▲ 1,713 ..... L9
Doolittle 599 ..... J7
Downing 359 ..... H2
Drexel 936 ..... C6
Dudley 271 ..... M9
Duenweg 940 ..... D8
Duquesne 1,229 ..... D8
Eagleville 275 ..... D2
East Lynne 289 ..... D5
East Prairie 3,416 ..... O9
Easton 232 ..... C3
Edgar Springs 215 ..... J7
Edgerton 565 ..... C3
Edina▲ 1,283 ..... H2
Edmundson 1,111 ..... O2
El Dorado Springs 3,830 ..... E7
Eldon 4,419 ..... G6
Ellington 994 ..... L8
Ellisville 7,545 ..... M3
Ellsinore 405 ..... L9
Elmo 179 ..... B1
Elsberry 1,898 ..... L4
Elvins 1,391 ..... L7
Eminence▲ 582 ..... K8
Emma 194 ..... F5
Eolia 389 ..... L4
Essex 531 ..... N9
Esther 1,071 ..... M7
Eugene 141 ..... H6
Eureka 4,683 ..... M4
Everton 325 ..... E8
Ewing 463 ..... J2
Excelsior Springs 10,354 ..... R4
Exeter 597 ..... D9
Fair Grove 919 ..... F8
Fair Play 442 ..... E7
Fairfax 699 ..... B2
Fairview 298 ..... D9
Farber 418 ..... J4
Farley 217 ..... O4
Farmington▲ 11,598 ..... M7
Fayette▲ 2,888 ..... G4
Fenton 3,346 ..... O4
Ferguson 22,286 ..... P2
Ferrelview 338 ..... O4
Festus 8,105 ..... M6
Fillmore 256 ..... C2
Fisk 422 ..... M9
Flat 4,823 ..... J7
Flat River 4,443 ..... M7
Fleming 130 ..... D4
Flemington 141 ..... F7
Flinthill 219 ..... L5
Florissant 51,206 ..... P1
Foley 209 ..... L4
Fordland 523 ..... G8
Forest City 380 ..... B3
Foristell 144 ..... L5
Forsyth▲ 1,175 ..... F9
Foster 161 ..... D6
Frankford 396 ..... K4
Franklin 181 ..... G4
Fredericktown▲ 3,950 ..... M7
Freeburg 446 ..... J6
Freeman 480 ..... C5
Freistatt 166 ..... E8
Fremont 201 ..... K9
Frohna 162 ..... N7
Frontenac 3,374 ..... O3
Fulton▲ 10,033 ..... J5
Gainesville▲ 659 ..... G9
Galena▲ 401 ..... F9
Gallatin▲ 1,864 ..... E3
Galt 296 ..... F2
Garden City 1,225 ..... D5
Gasconade 253 ..... J5
Gerald 888 ..... K6
Gideon 1,104 ..... N10
Gilliam 212 ..... F4
Gilman City 393 ..... D2
Gladstone 26,243 ..... P5
Glasgow 1,295 ..... G4
Glenaire 597 ..... R5
Glendale 5,945 ..... P3
Glenwood 195 ..... G1
Golden 794 ..... E9
Golden City 900 ..... D8
Goodman 1,094 ..... C9
Gordonville 345 ..... N8
Gower 1,249 ..... C3
Graham 204 ..... C2
Grain Valley 1,898 ..... S6
Granby 1,945 ..... D9
Grandin 233 ..... L9
Grandview 24,967 ..... P6
Grant City▲ 998 ..... D2
Grantwood 904 ..... O4
Gray Summit 2,505 ..... L6
Green Castle 285 ..... G2
Green City 671 ..... F2
Green Ridge 452 ..... F5
Greenfield▲ 1,416 ..... E8
Greentop 425 ..... H2
Greenville▲ 437 ..... M8
Greenwood 1,505 ..... R6
Hale 480 ..... F3
Half Way 157 ..... F7
Hallsville 917 ..... H4
Halltown 161 ..... E8
Hamilton 1,737 ..... E3
Hanley Hills 2,325 ..... P2
Hannibal 18,004 ..... K3
Hardin 598 ..... E4
Harrisburg 169 ..... H4
Harrisonville▲ 7,683 ..... D5
Hartville▲ 495 ..... G8
Hawk Point 472 ..... K5
Hayti 3,280 ..... N10
Hayti Heights 893 ..... N10
Haywood City 263 ..... N9
Hazelwood 15,324 ..... P2
Henrietta 412 ..... E4
Herculaneum 2,263 ..... M6
Hermann▲ 2,754 ..... K5
Hermitage▲ 512 ..... F7
Higbee 639 ..... H4
Higginsville 4,693 ..... E4
High Hill 204 ..... K5

(continued on following page)

Agriculture, Industry and Resources

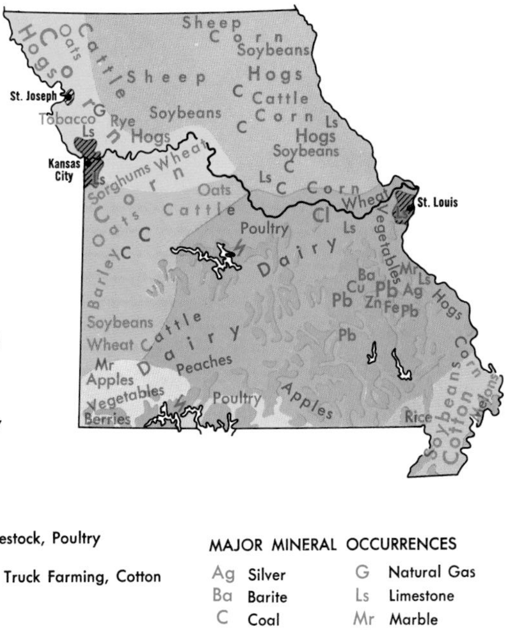
St. Joseph
Kansas City
St. Louis
Sheep
Corn
Soybeans
Hogs
Cattle
Oats
Tobacco
Rye
Wheat
Sorghums
Poultry
Dairy
Vegetables
Barley
Peaches
Apples
Berries
Rice
Cotton
Melons

DOMINANT LAND USE

- Cattle Feed, Hogs
- Livestock, Cash Grain, Dairy
- Pasture Livestock
- Specialized Cotton
- General Farming, Dairy, Livestock, Poultry
- General Farming, Livestock, Truck Farming, Cotton
- Fruit and Mixed Farming
- Forests
- Urban Areas

MAJOR MINERAL OCCURRENCES

Ag	Silver	G	Natural Gas
Ba	Barite	Ls	Limestone
C	Coal	Mr	Marble
Cl	Clay	Pb	Lead
Cu	Copper	Zn	Zinc
Fe	Iron Ore		

Water Power — Major Industrial Areas

High Ridge 4,423 .... M6
Hillsboro▲ 1,625 .... L6
Hillsdale 1,948 .... R2
Holcomb 531 .... N10
Holden 2,389 .... E5
Holland 237 .... N10
Holliday 139 .... H3
Hollister 2,628 .... F9
Holt 311 .... D4
Holts Summit 2,292 .... H5
Homestown 230 .... N10
Hopkins 575 .... C1
Horine 1,043 .... M6
Hornersville 629 .... M10
Houston Lake 303 .... O5
Houston▲ 2,118 .... J8
Houstonia 283 .... F5
Howardville 440 .... N9
Hughesville 174 .... F5
Humansville 1,084 .... E7
Hume 287 .... C6
Hunnewell 219 .... J3
Huntleigh 392 .... O3
Huntsville▲ 1,567 .... H4
Hurdland 212 .... H2
Hurricane Deck 210 .... G6
Iberia 650 .... H6
Illmo 1,368 .... O8
Imperial 4,156 .... M6
Independence▲ 112,301 .... R5
Iron Gates 309 .... C8
Irondale 474 .... L7
Ironton▲ 1,539 .... L7
Jackson▲ 9,256 .... N8
Jameson 149 .... E2
Jamesport 570 .... E3
Jamestown 298 .... G5
Jasper 994 .... D8
Jefferson City (cap.)▲ 35,481 .... H5
Jennings 15,905 .... R2
Jerico Springs 247 .... E7
Jonesburg 630 .... K5
Joplin 40,961 .... C8
Junction City 326 .... M7
Kahoka▲ 2,195 .... J2
Kansas City 435,146 .... P5
Kearney 1,790 .... D4
Kelso 526 .... O8
Kennett▲ 10,941 .... M10
Keytesville▲ 564 .... G4
Kidder 241 .... D3
Kimberling City 1,590 .... F9
Kimmswick 135 .... M6
King City 986 .... D2
Kingston▲ 279 .... E3
Kingsville 279 .... D5
Kinloch 2,702 .... P2
Kirksville▲ 17,152 .... H2
Kirkwood 27,291 .... O3
Knob Noster 2,261 .... E5
Knox City 262 .... H2
Koshkonong 198 .... J9
La Belle 655 .... J2
La Grange 1,102 .... K2
La Monte 995 .... F5
La Plata 1,401 .... H2
Laclede 410 .... F3
Laddonia 581 .... J4
Ladue 8,847 .... P3
Lake Lotawana 2,141 .... R6
Lake Ozark 681 .... G6
Lake Saint Louis 7,400 .... L5
Lake Tapawingo 761 .... R6
Lake Waukomis 1,027 .... P5
Lake Winnebago 748 .... R6
Lakeshire 1,467 .... P4
Lamar Heights 176 .... D8
Lamar▲ 4,168 .... D8
Lanagan 501 .... C9
Lancaster▲ 785 .... H1
Laredo 205 .... E2
Lathrop 1,794 .... D3
Laurie 507 .... G6
Lawson 1,876 .... D4
Leadington 201 .... M7
Leadwood 1,247 .... L7
Leasburg 289 .... K6
Lebanon▲ 9,983 .... G7
Lee's Summit 46,418 .... R6
Leeton 632 .... E5
Lemay 18,005 .... R4
Levasy 279 .... S5
Lewis 142 .... E6
Lewis and Clark Village 131 .... C3
Lewistown 453 .... J2
Lexington▲ 4,860 .... E4
Liberal 684 .... D7
Liberty▲ 20,459 .... R5
Licking 1,328 .... J8
Lilbourn 1,378 .... N9
Lincoln 874 .... F6
Linn Creek 232 .... G6
Linn▲ 1,148 .... J5
Linneus▲ 364 .... F3
Lockwood 1,041 .... E8
Lohman 154 .... H5
Lone Jack 392 .... S6
Louisiana 3,967 .... K4
Lowry City 723 .... E6
Ludlow 147 .... E3
Lutesville 865 .... M8
Mackenzie 148 .... P3
Macks Creek 272 .... G7
Macon▲ 5,571 .... H3
Madison 518 .... H4
Maitland 338 .... B2
Malden 5,123 .... M9
Malta Bend 289 .... F4
Manchester 6,542 .... O3
Mansfield 1,429 .... G8
Maplewood 9,962 .... P3
Marble Hill▲ 1,447 .... N8
Marceline 2,645 .... F3
Marionville 1,920 .... E8
Marlborough 1,949 .... P3
Marquand 278 .... M8
Marshall▲ 12,711 .... F4
Marshfield▲ 4,374 .... G8
Marston 691 .... N9
Marthasville 674 .... L5
Martinsburg 337 .... J4
Maryland Heights 25,407 .... O2
Maryville▲ 10,663 .... C2
Matthews 614 .... N9
Maysville▲ 1,176 .... D3
Mayview 279 .... E4
McFall 142 .... D2
Meadville 360 .... F3
Mehlville 27,557 .... P4
Memphis▲ 2,094 .... H2
Mendon 207 .... F3
Mercer 297 .... F2
Meta 249 .... H6
Mexico▲ 11,290 .... J4
Miami 142 .... F4
Middletown 217 .... J4
Milan▲ 1,767 .... F2
Mill Spring 252 .... L8
Miller 753 .... E8
Mindenmines 346 .... C8
Mine La Motte 125 .... M7
Miner 1,218 .... N9
Mineral Point 384 .... L7
Missouri City 348 .... R5
Moberly 12,839 .... G4
Mokane 186 .... J5
Moline Acres 2,710 .... R2
Monett 6,529 .... E9
Monroe City 2,701 .... J3
Montgomery City▲ 2,281 .... K5
Monticello▲ 106 .... J2
Montrose 440 .... E6
Morehouse 1,068 .... N9
Morley 683 .... N8
Morrison 160 .... J5
Morrisville 293 .... F8
Mosby 194 .... R4
Moscow Mills 924 .... K5
Mound City 1,273 .... B2
Moundville 140 .... C7
Mount Vernon▲ 3,726 .... E8
Mountain Grove 4,182 .... H8
Mountain View 2,036 .... J8
Murphy 9,342 .... O4
Napoleon 233 .... E4
Naylor 642 .... L9
Neelyville 381 .... M9
Nelson 181 .... F4
Neosho▲ 9,254 .... D9
Nevada▲ 8,597 .... D7
New Bloomfield 480 .... J5
New Cambria 225 .... G3
New Florence 801 .... K5
New Franklin 1,107 .... G4
New Hampton 320 .... D2
New Haven 1,757 .... K5
New London▲ 988 .... K3
New Madrid▲ 3,350 .... O9
New Melle 486 .... L5
Newburg 589 .... J7
Newtonia 204 .... D9
Niangua 459 .... G8
Nixa 4,707 .... F8
Noel 1,169 .... D9
Norborne 856 .... E4
Normandy 4,480 .... R2
North Kansas City 4,130 .... P5
Northmoor 441 .... P5
Northwoods 5,106 .... R2
Norwood 449 .... H8
Novelty 143 .... H2
Novinger 542 .... G2
O'Fallon 18,698 .... L5
Oak Grove 4,067 .... S6
Oak Grove 402 .... K6
Oak Ridge 202 .... N7
Oakland 1,593 .... P3
Oaks 130 .... P5
Oakview 351 .... P5
Oakwood 212 .... P5
Oakwood Manor 137 .... P5
Oakwood Park 213 .... P5
Odessa 3,695 .... E5
Old Monroe 242 .... L5
Olivette 7,573 .... O2
Olympian Village 752 .... M6
Oran 1,164 .... N8
Oregon▲ 935 .... B2
Oronogo 595 .... D8
Orrick 935 .... D4
Osage Beach 2,599 .... G6
Osborn 400 .... D3
Osceola▲ 755 .... E6
Otterville 507 .... G5
Overland 17,987 .... O2
Owensville 2,325 .... K6
Ozark▲ 4,243 .... F8
Pacific 4,350 .... L5
Pagedale 3,771 .... P2
Palmyra▲ 3,371 .... J3
Paris▲ 1,486 .... J4
Parksdale 270 .... F6
Parkville 2,402 .... O5
Parkway 277 .... L6
Parma 995 .... N9
Parnell 157 .... C2
Patton 414 .... M8
Pattonsburg 502 .... D2
Peculiar 1,777 .... D5
Perry 711 .... J4
Perryville▲ 6,933 .... N7
Pevely 2,831 .... M6
Phillipsburg 170 .... G7
Pickering 171 .... C2
Piedmont 2,166 .... L8
Pierce City 1,382 .... E8
Pilot Grove 714 .... G5
Pilot Knob 783 .... L7
Pine 5,092 .... K9
Pine Lawn 6,600 .... R2
Pineville▲ 580 .... D9
Platte City▲ 2,947 .... C4
Platte Woods 427 .... O5
Plattsburg▲ 2,248 .... D3
Pleasant Hill 3,827 .... D5
Pleasant Hope 360 .... F8
Pleasant Valley 2,731 .... R5
Polo 539 .... D3
Poplar Bluff▲ 16,996 .... L9
Portage Des Sioux 503 .... M5
Portageville 3,401 .... N10
Potosi▲ 2,683 .... L7
Prairie Home 215 .... G5
Princeton▲ 1,021 .... E2
Purcell 359 .... D8
Purdin 217 .... F3
Purdy 977 .... E9
Puxico 819 .... M9
Queen City 704 .... H2
Qulin 384 .... M9
Ravenwood 409 .... C2
Raymondville 425 .... J8
Raymore 5,592 .... D5
Raytown 30,601 .... P6
Rayville 170 .... E4
Reeds Spring 411 .... F9
Renick 195 .... H4
Republic 6,292 .... E8
Rhineland 157 .... J5
Rich Hill 1,317 .... D6
Richland 2,029 .... H7
Richmond Heights 10,448 .... P3
Richmond▲ 5,738 .... D4
Ridgeway 379 .... D2
Risco 434 .... N9
Rivermines 459 .... L7
Riverside 3,010 .... O5
Riverview 3,242 .... R2
Rocheport 255 .... H5
Rock Hill 5,217 .... P3
Rock Port▲ 1,438 .... B2
Rockaway Beach 275 .... F9
Rockville 193 .... D6
Rogersville 995 .... G8
Rolla▲ 14,090 .... J7
Rosebud 380 .... K6
Rosendale 186 .... C2
Rushville 306 .... B3
Russellville 869 .... H6
Saginaw 384 .... C8
Saint Ann 14,489 .... O2
Saint Charles▲ 54,555 .... N1
Saint Clair 3,917 .... K6
Saint Elizabeth 257 .... H6
Saint George 1,270 .... P4
Saint James 3,256 .... J6
Saint John 7,466 .... P2
Saint Joseph▲ 71,852 .... C3
Saint Louis▲ 396,685 .... R3
Saint Martins 717 .... H5
Saint Marys 461 .... M7
Saint Paul 1,192 .... L5
Saint Peters 45,779 .... M1
Saint Robert 1,730 .... H7
Saint Thomas 263 .... H6
Sainte Genevieve▲ 4,411 .... M6
Salem▲ 4,486 .... J7
Salisbury 1,881 .... G4
Sappington 10,917 .... O4
Sarcoxie 1,330 .... D8
Savannah▲ 4,352 .... C3
Schell City 292 .... D6
Scott City 4,292 .... O8
Sedalia▲ 19,800 .... F5
Sedgewickville 138 .... N7
Seligman 593 .... D9
Senath 1,622 .... M10
Seneca 1,885 .... C9
Seymour 1,636 .... G8
Shelbina 2,172 .... H3
Shelbyville▲ 582 .... H3
Sheldon 464 .... D7
Sheridan 174 .... C1
Shrewsbury 6,416 .... P3
Sibley 367 .... S5
Sikeston 17,641 .... N9
Silex 197 .... K4
Skidmore 404 .... B2
Slater 2,186 .... G4
Smithton 532 .... F5
Smithville 2,525 .... D4
South West City 600 .... D9
Spanish Lake 20,322 .... R1
Sparta 751 .... F9
Spickard 326 .... F2
Springfield▲ 140,494 .... F8
Stanberry 1,310 .... C2
Steele 2,395 .... N10
Steelville▲ 1,465 .... K7
Stewartsville 732 .... C3
Stockton▲ 1,579 .... E7
Stotts City 235 .... E8
Stoutland 207 .... G7
Stover 964 .... G6
Strafford 1,166 .... F8
Sturgeon 838 .... H4

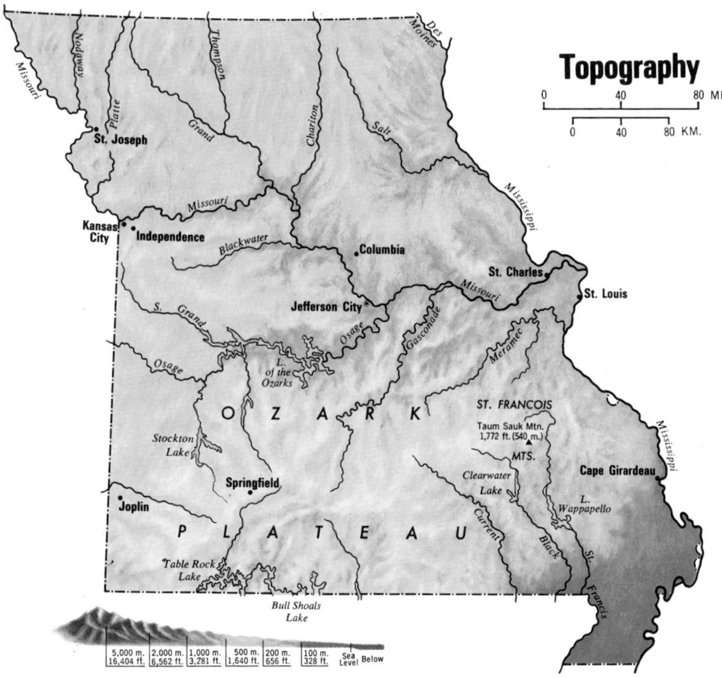
Topography
0 40 80 MI.
0 40 80 KM.
Missouri
Nodaway
Platte
St. Joseph
Grand
Thompson
Chariton
Salt
Des Moines
Mississippi
Missouri
Kansas City
Independence
Blackwater
Columbia
St. Charles
St. Louis
Jefferson City
Osage
Gasconade
Meramec
L. of the Ozarks
O Z A R K
ST. FRANCOIS
Taum Sauk Mtn. 1,772 ft. (540 m.)
MTS.
Stockton Lake
Springfield
Clearwater Lake
L. Wappapello
Cape Girardeau
Joplin
P L A T E A U
Current
Black
St. Francis
Table Rock Lake
Bull Shoals Lake
5,000 m. 16,404 ft.
2,000 m. 6,562 ft.
1,000 m. 3,281 ft.
500 m. 1,640 ft.
200 m. 656 ft.
100 m. 328 ft.
Sea Level
Below

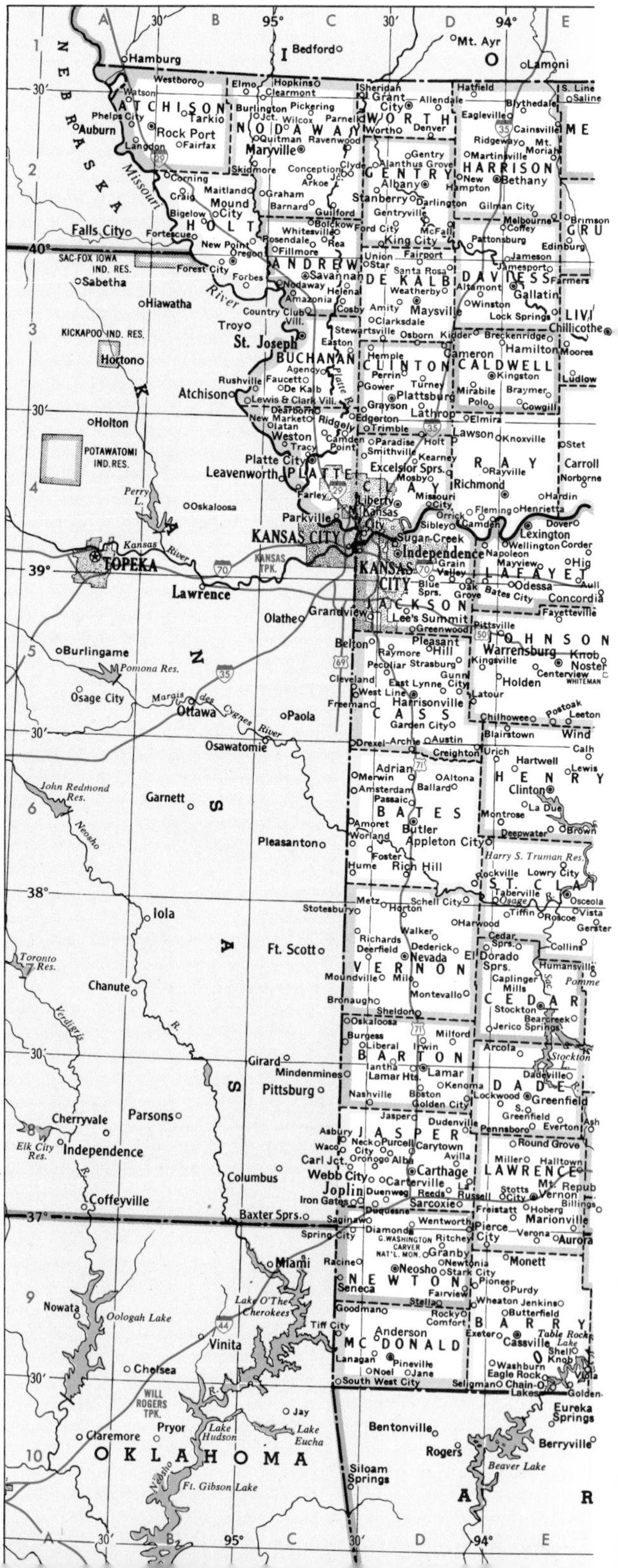

Sugar Creek 3,982 R5
Sullivan 5,661 K6
Summersville 571 J8
Sunrise Beach 181 G6
Sunset Hills 4,915 O4
Sweet Springs 1,595 F5
Sycamore 667 H9
Syracuse 185 G5
Tallapoosa 174 N9
Taneyville 279 F9
Taos 802 H5
Tarkio 2,243 B2
Tarsney Lakes 329 R6
Thayer 1,996 J9
Theodosia 235 G9
Tina 199 F3
Tipton 2,026 G5
Town and Country 9,519 O3
Tracy 287 C4
Trenton▲ 6,129 E2
Trimble 405 D4
Troy▲ 3,811 L5
Truesdale 285 K5
Tuscumbia▲ 148 H6
Twin Oaks 506 N3
Union Star 432 C2
Union▲ 5,909 L6
Unionville▲ 1,989 G2
Unity Village 138 R6
University City 40,087 P3
Urbana 350 F7
Urich 498 E6
Utica 299 E3
Valley Park 4,165 O3
Van Buren▲ 893 L8
Vandalia 2,683 J4
Vanduser 187 N9
Velda 1,597 P2
Verona 546 E9
Versailles▲ 2,365 G6
Viburnum 743 K7
Vienna▲ 611 H6
Vinita Park 2,001 P2
Walker 283 D7
Walnut Grove 549 F8
Wardell 325 N10
Wardsville 513 H6
Warren 15,244 J3
Warrensburg▲ 13,807 E5
Warrenton▲ 3,564 K5
Warsaw▲ 1,696 F6
Warson Woods 2,049 O3
Washburn 362 E9
Washington 10,704 K5
Waverly 837 E4
Wayland 391 J2
Waynesville▲ 3,207 H7
Weatherby Lake 1,613 O5
Weaubleau 436 F7
Webb City 7,449 C8
Webster Groves 22,987 P3
Wellington 779 E4
Wellston 3,612 R2
Wellsville 1,430 K4
Wentworth 138 D8
Wentzville 5,088 L5
West Plains▲ 8,913 J9
Westboro 182 B1
Weston 1,528 C4
Westphalia 287 J6
Westwood 309 O3
Wheatland 363 F7
Wheaton 637 E9
Wheeling 284 F3
Wilbur Park 522 P3
Willard 2,177 F8
Williamsville 391 L9
Willow Springs 2,038 H9
Wilson City 210 O9
Winchester 1,678 N3
Windsor 3,044 E5
Winfield 672 L5
Winona 1,081 K8
Winston 251 D3
Woods Heights 708 S4
Woodson Terrace 4,362 P2
Wright City 1,250 K5
Wyaconda 347 J2
Wyatt 376 O9

OTHER FEATURES

Bagnell (dam) G6
Big (riv.) L6
Black (riv.) L10
Bull Shoals (lake) G10
Chariton (riv.) G1
Clearwater (lake) L8
Cuivre (riv.) N2
Current (riv.) K8
Des Moines (riv.) J1
Fort Leonard Wood 15,863 H7
Gasconade (riv.) H7
George Washington Carver Nat'l Mon. D9
Grand (riv.) F3
Harry S Truman (res.) E6
Harry S Truman Nat'l Hist. Site R5
Jefferson Nat'l Expansion Mem. R3
Lake City Arsenal R5
Meramec (riv.) N3
Mississippi (riv.) L4
Missouri (riv.) H5
Norfork (lake) H10
Osage (riv.) E6
Ozark (plat.) F9
Ozark National Scenic Riverways K8
Ozarks, Lake of the (lake) F6
Platte (riv.) C3
Pomme de Terre (lake) E7
Richards Gebaur A.F.B. P6
Sac (riv.) E7
Saint Francis (riv.) M9
Saint Francis (mts.) L7
Salt (riv.) J3
Stockton (lake) E7
Table Rock Lake (res.) E9
Taneycomo (lake) F9
Taum Sauk (mt.) L7
Wappapello (lake) L8
White (riv.) G10
Whiteman A.F.B. 4,174 E5
Wilson's Creek Nat'l Battlefield F8

▲County seat

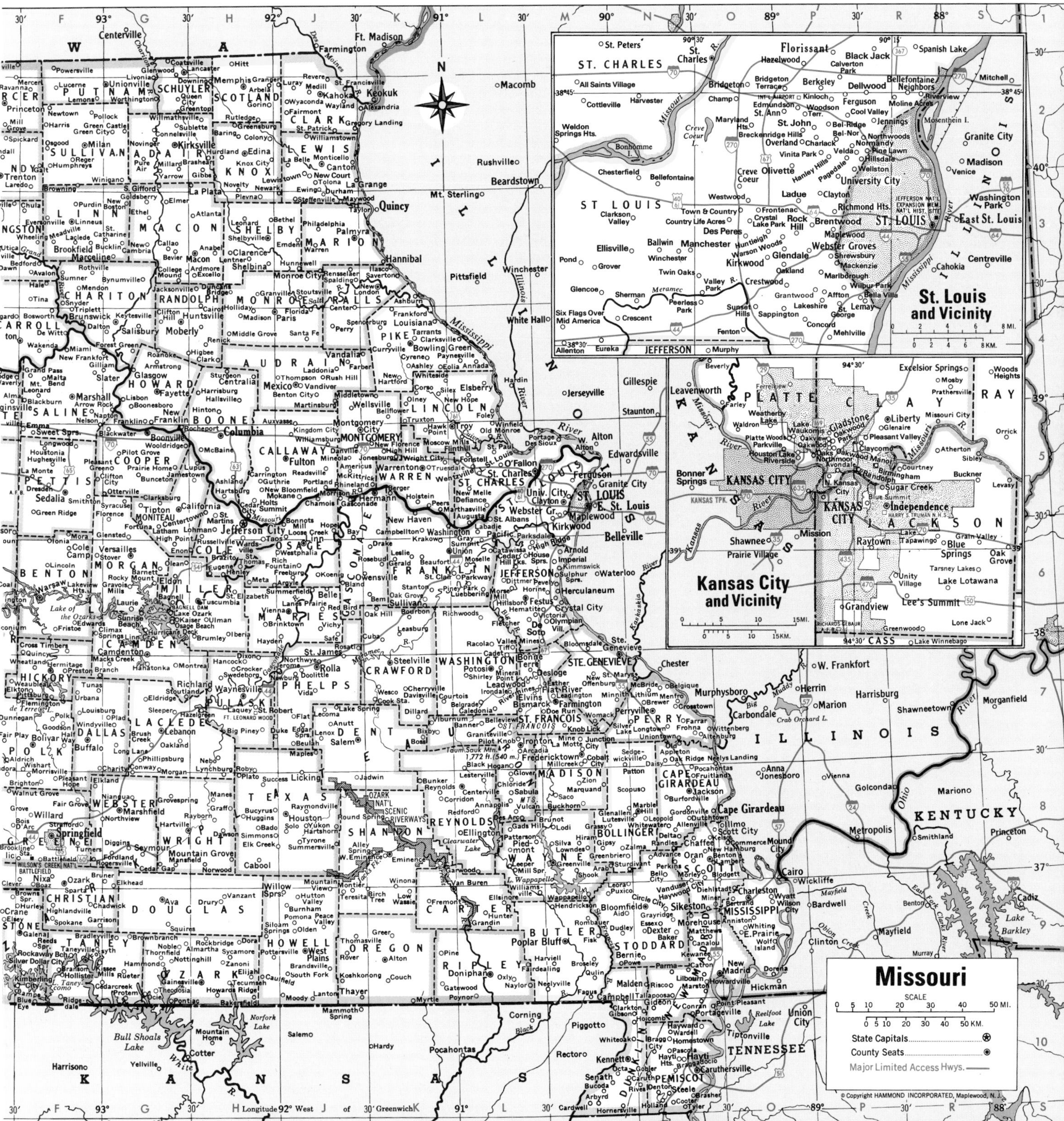

St. Louis and Vicinity
Kansas City and Vicinity
Missouri
SCALE
State Capitals
County Seats
Major Limited Access Hwys.
KENTUCKY
ILLINOIS
TENNESSEE
Longitude 92° West of 30′ Greenwich

Agriculture, Industry and Resources

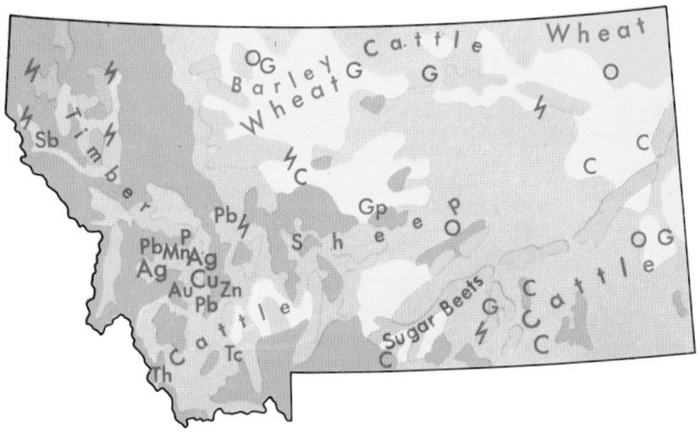
Barley
Wheat
Cattle
Timber
Sheep
Sugar Beets

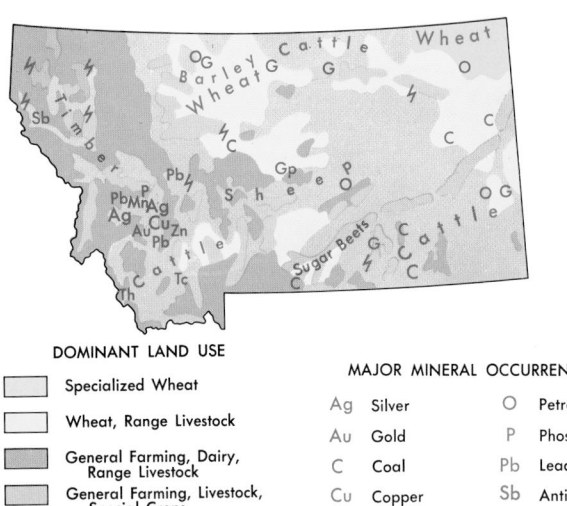

DOMINANT LAND USE

- Specialized Wheat
- Wheat, Range Livestock
- General Farming, Dairy, Range Livestock
- General Farming, Livestock, Special Crops
- Range Livestock
- Sugar Beets, Beans, Livestock, General Farming
- Forests

MAJOR MINERAL OCCURRENCES

Ag	Silver	O	Petroleum
Au	Gold	P	Phosphates
C	Coal	Pb	Lead
Cu	Copper	Sb	Antimony
G	Natural Gas	Tc	Talc
Gp	Gypsum	Th	Thorium
Mn	Manganese	Zn	Zinc

Water Power

COUNTIES

Beaverhead 8,424 .... C5
Big Horn 11,337 .... J5
Blaine 6,728 .... G2
Broadwater 3,318 .... E4
Carbon 8,080 .... G5
Carter 1,503 .... M5
Cascade 77,691 .... E3
Chouteau 5,452 .... F3
Custer 11,697 .... L4
Daniels 2,266 .... L2
Dawson 9,505 .... M3
Deer Lodge 10,278 .... C5
Fallon 3,103 .... M4
Fergus 12,083 .... G3
Flathead 59,218 .... B2
Gallatin 50,463 .... E5
Garfield 1,589 .... J3
Glacier 12,121 .... C2
Golden Valley 912 .... G4
Granite 2,548 .... C4
Hill 17,654 .... F2
Jefferson 7,939 .... D4
Judith Basin 2,282 .... F4
Lake 21,041 .... B3
Lewis and Clark 47,495 .... D3
Liberty 2,295 .... E2
Lincoln 17,481 .... A2
Madison 5,989 .... D5
McCone 2,276 .... L3
Meagher 1,819 .... F4
Mineral 3,315 .... B3
Missoula 78,687 .... C3
Musselshell 4,106 .... H4
Park 14,562 .... F5
Petroleum 519 .... H3
Phillips 5,163 .... J2
Pondera 6,433 .... D2
Powder River 2,090 .... L5
Powell 6,620 .... D4
Prairie 1,383 .... L4
Ravalli 25,010 .... B4
Richland 10,716 .... M3
Roosevelt 10,999 .... L2
Rosebud 10,505 .... K4
Sanders 8,669 .... A3
Sheridan 4,732 .... M2
Silver Bow 33,941 .... D5
Stillwater 6,536 .... G5
Sweet Grass 3,154 .... G5
Teton 6,271 .... D3
Toole 5,046 .... E2
Treasure 874 .... J4
Valley 8,239 .... K2
Wheatland 2,246 .... G4
Wibaux 1,191 .... M4
Yellowstone 113,419 .... H4

CITIES and TOWNS

Absarokee 1,067 .... G5
Acton 50 .... H5
Alberton 354 .... B3
Alder 120 .... D5
Alzada 52 .... M5
Amsterdam 130 .... E5
Anaconda-Deer Lodge County▲ C4
Angela 50 .... K4
Antelope 83 .... M2
Apgar 25 .... B2
Arlee 489 .... B3
Armington 75 .... F3
Ashland 484 .... K5
Augusta 497 .... D3
Avon 125 .... D4
Babb 150 .... C2
Bainville 165 .... M2
Baker▲ 1,818 .... M4
Ballantine 380 .... J5
Bannack 2 .... C5
Basin 350 .... D4
Bearcreek 37 .... G5
Becket 35 .... G4
Belfry 300 .... H5
Belgrade 3,411 .... E5
Belt 571 .... E3
Biddle 28 .... L5
Big Arm 250 .... B3
Big Sandy 740 .... G2
Big Sky 50 .... E5
Big Timber▲ 1,557 .... G5
Bigfork 1,080 .... C2
Billings▲ 81,151 .... H5
Birney 100 .... K5
Black Eagle 1,500 .... E3
Blackfoot 100 .... D2
Bloomfield 28 .... M3
Bonner-West Riverside 1,669 .... C4
Boulder▲ 1,316 .... E4
Box Elder 300 .... F2
Boyd 32 .... G5
Bozeman▲ 22,660 .... E5
Brady 450 .... E2
Bridger 692 .... H5
Broadus▲ 572 .... L5
Broadview 133 .... H4
Brockton 365 .... M2
Brockway 55 .... L3
Browning 1,170 .... C2
Busby 409 .... J5
Butte-Silver Bow County▲ 33,336 .... D5
Bynum 49 .... D3
Camas Prairie 160 .... B3
Cameron 150 .... E5
Canyon Creek 100 .... D4
Canyon Ferry 100 .... E4
Cardwell 34 .... E5
Carter 70 .... E3
Cartersville 115 .... K4
Cascade 729 .... E3
Charlo 358 .... B3
Chester▲ 942 .... E2
Chinook▲ 1,512 .... G2
Choteau▲ 1,741 .... D3
Christina 60 .... G3
Circle▲ 805 .... L3
Clancy 550 .... E4
Clinton 250 .... C4
Clyde Park 282 .... F5
Coffee Creek 62 .... F3
Colstrip 3,035 .... K5
Columbia Falls 2,942 .... B2
Columbus▲ 1,573 .... G5
Condon 300 .... C3
Conner 420 .... B5
Conrad▲ 2,891 .... D2
Cooke City 120 .... G5
Coram 450 .... C2
Corvallis 500 .... C4
Craig 100 .... D3
Crane 163 .... M3
Creston 60 .... C2
Crow Agency 1,446 .... J5
Culbertson 796 .... M2
Custer 300 .... J4
Cut Bank▲ 3,329 .... D2
Dagmar 35 .... M2

Montana
SCALE
0 5 10 20 40 60 MI.
0 5 10 20 40 60 KM.
State Capitals
County Seats
Major Limited Access Hwys.
ALBERTA
SASKATCHEWAN
BR. COL.
IDAHO
WYOMING
YELLOWSTONE NATIONAL PARK
110° Longitude West of 109° Greenwich

Topography

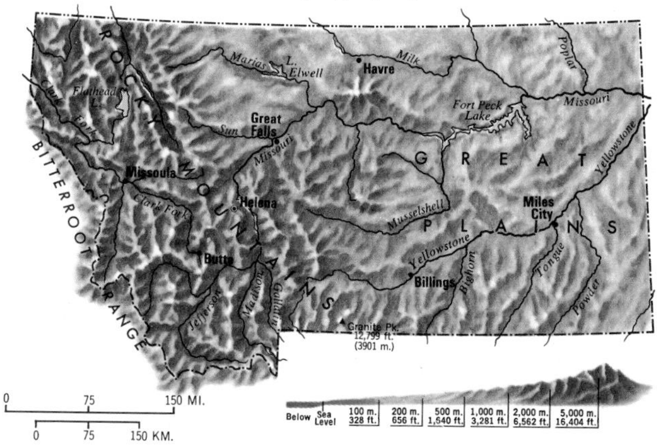
Havre
Milk
Marias
L. Elwell
Great Falls
Sun
Fort Peck Lake
Missouri
Poplar
Missoula
Helena
Butte
Billings
Miles City
Yellowstone
Musselshell
Bighorn
Tongue
Powder
Flathead
Clark Fork
Jefferson
Madison
Gallatin
BITTERROOT RANGE
ROCKY MOUNTAINS
GREAT PLAINS
Granite Pk. 12,799 ft. (3901 m.)
0 75 150 MI.
0 75 150 KM.
Below Sea Level
100 m. 328 ft.
200 m. 656 ft.
500 m. 1,640 ft.
1,000 m. 3,281 ft.
2,000 m. 6,562 ft.
5,000 m. 16,404 ft.

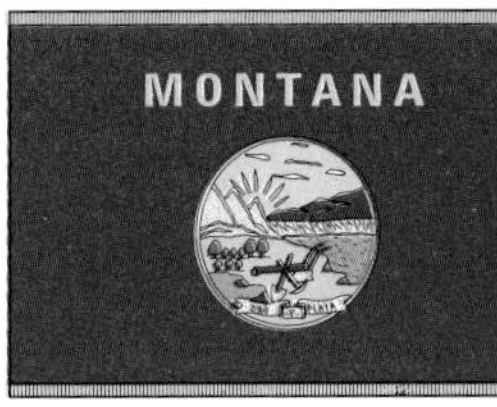
MONTANA

AREA 147,046 sq. mi. (380,849 sq. km.)
POPULATION 803,655
CAPITAL Helena
LARGEST CITY Billings
HIGHEST POINT Granite Pk. 12,799 ft. (3901 m.)
SETTLED IN 1809
ADMITTED TO UNION November 8, 1889
POPULAR NAME Treasure State; Big Sky Country
STATE FLOWER Bitterroot
STATE BIRD Western Meadowlark

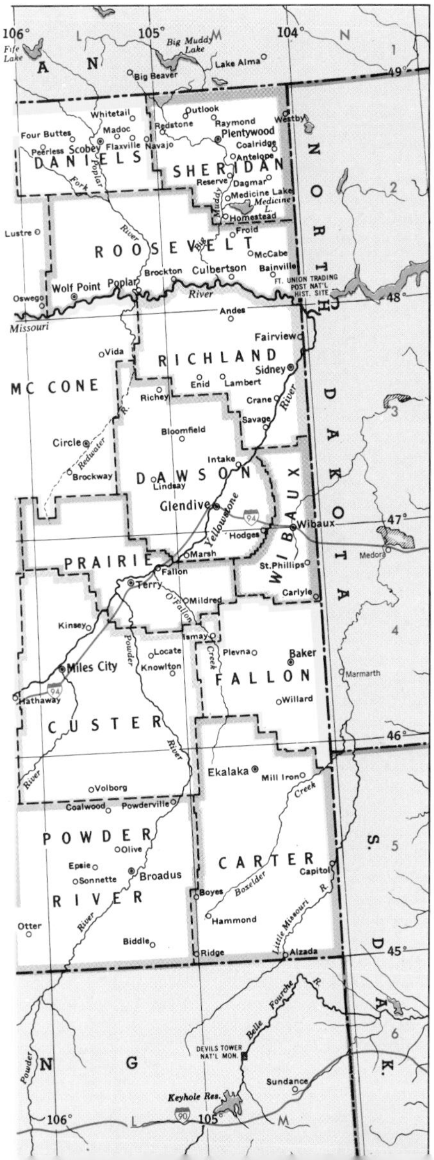
DANIELS
SHERIDAN
ROOSEVELT
RICHLAND
MC CONE
DAWSON
WIBAUX
PRAIRIE
FALLON
CUSTER
POWDER RIVER
CARTER
NORTH DAKOTA
S. DAK.
Wolf Point
Poplar
Scobey
Plentywood
Sidney
Glendive
Miles City
Baker
Ekalaka
Broadus
Terry
Wibaux
Missouri
Yellowstone
Powder
Big Muddy
106°
105°
104°
49°
48°
47°
46°
45°

Darby 625 ... B4
Dayton 140 ... B3
De Borgia 300 ... A3
Decker 150 ... K5
Deer Lodge▲ 3,378 ... D4
Dell 29 ... D6
Delpine 33 ... F4
Denton 350 ... G3
Dillon▲ 3,991 ... D5
Divide 275 ... D5
Dixon 550 ... B3
Dodson 137 ... H2
Drummond 264 ... D4
Dupuyer 105 ... D2
Dutton 392 ... E3
East Glacier Park 326 ... C2
East Helena 1,538 ... E4
Edgar 220 ... H5
Ekalaka▲ 439 ... M5
Elliston 250 ... D4
Elmo 250 ... B3
Emigrant 80 ... F5
Ennis 773 ... E5
Epsie 60 ... L5
Essex 48 ... C2
Eureka 1,043 ... B2
Fairfield 660 ... D3
Fairview 869 ... M3
Fallon 225 ... L4
Fishtail 46 ... G5
Flaxville 88 ... L2
Florence 700 ... B4
Floweree 48 ... E3
Forestgrove 100 ... H3
Forsyth▲ 2,178 ... K4
Fort Belknap 422 ... H2
Fort Benton▲ 1,660 ... F3
Fort Peck 325 ... K2
Fort Shaw 200 ... E3
Fort Smith 300 ... J5
Fortine 250 ... A2
Four Buttes 50 ... L2
Frazer 403 ... K2
Frenchtown 300 ... B3
Froid 195 ... M2
Fromberg 370 ... H5
Galata 100 ... E2
Galen 210 ... D4
Gallatin Gateway 600 ... E5
Gardiner 600 ... F5
Garneill 61 ... G4
Garrison 300 ... D4
Garryowen 200 ... J5
Geraldine 299 ... F3
Geyser 125 ... F3
Gildford 250 ... F2
Glasgow▲ 3,572 ... K2
Glen 4,802 ... D5
Glendive▲ 5,978 ... M3
Goldcreek 100 ... D4
Grant 25 ... C5
Grantsdale 500 ... B4
Grass Range 159 ... H3
Great Falls▲ 55,097 ... E3
Greenough 120 ... C4
Greycliff 37 ... G5
Hall 130 ... C4
Hamilton▲ 2,737 ... B4
Hardin▲ 2,940 ... J5
Harlem 882 ... H2
Harlowton▲ 1,049 ... F4
Harrison 94 ... E5
Hathaway 55 ... K4
Haugan 90 ... A3
Havre▲ 10,201 ... G2
Hays 333 ... H2
Heart Butte 499 ... C2
Helena (cap.)▲ 24,569 ... E4
Helmville 250 ... C4
Heron 79 ... A2
Highwood 150 ... F3
Hilger 38 ... G3
Hingham 181 ... F2
Hinsdale 260 ... K2
Hobson 226 ... G4
Hodges 50 ... M4
Hogeland 35 ... H2
Homestead 50 ... M2
Hot Springs 411 ... B3
Hungry Horse 700 ... C2
Huntley 250 ... H5
Huson 97 ... B3
Hysham▲ 361 ... J4
Ingomar 48 ... J4
Intake 60 ... M3
Inverness 150 ... F2
Jackson 210 ... C5
Jardine 30 ... F5
Jeffers 70 ... E5
Jefferson City 162 ... E4
Jefferson Island 25 ... E5
Joliet 522 ... G5
Joplin 300 ... F2
Jordan▲ 494 ... J3
Judith Gap 133 ... G4
Kalispell▲ 11,917 ... B2
Kevin 185 ... D2
Kila 350 ... B2
Kinsey 100 ... L4
Kirby 30 ... J5
Klein 250 ... H4
Kremlin 304 ... F2
Lakeside 663 ... B2
Lakeview 28 ... E6
Lambert 203 ... M3
Lame Deer 1,918 ... K5
Landusky 40 ... H3
Laurel 5,686 ... H5
Laurin 60 ... D5
Lavina 151 ... H4
Lewistown▲ 6,051 ... G3
Libby▲ 2,532 ... A2
Lima 265 ... D6
Lincoln 473 ... D4
Lindsay 50 ... L3
Livingston▲ 6,701 ... F5
Locate 55 ... L4
Lodge Grass 517 ... J5
Lodge Pole 292 ... H2
Logan 53 ... E5
Lohman 25 ... G2
Lolo 2,746 ... B4
Lolo Hot Springs 25 ... B4
Loma 200 ... F3
Lonepine 50 ... B3
Lothair 29 ... E2
Malta▲ 2,340 ... J2
Manhattan 1,034 ... E5
Marion 450 ... B2
Martinsdale 75 ... F4
Marysville 76 ... D4
Maxville 44 ... C4
McAllister 55 ... E5
McLeod 150 ... G5
Medicine Lake 357 ... M2
Melrose 350 ... D5
Melstone 166 ... H4
Melville 100 ... F4
Miles City▲ 8,461 ... L4
Mill Iron 66 ... M5
Milltown 300 ... C4
Missoula▲ 42,918 ... C4
Moccasin 57 ... F3
Molt 31 ... H5
Monarch 120 ... F3
Moore 211 ... G4
Musselshell 117 ... H4
Myers 120 ... J4
Nashua 375 ... K2
Neihart 53 ... F4
Nibbe 30 ... H4
Norris 55 ... E5
North Havre 1,230 ... G2
Noxon 800 ... A3
Nye 50 ... G5
Oilmont 50 ... E2
Olney 200 ... B2
Opheim 145 ... K2
Oswego 75 ... L2
Outlook 109 ... M2
Ovando 300 ... C3
Pablo 1,298 ... B3
Paradise 400 ... B3
Park City 800 ... H5
Peerless 110 ... L2
Pendroy 100 ... D2
Perma 50 ... B3
Philipsburg▲ 925 ... C4
Plains 992 ... B3
Plentywood▲ 2,136 ... M2
Plevna 140 ... M4
Polaris 53 ... C5
Polson▲ 3,283 ... B3
Pompeys Pillar 300 ... J5
Pony 130 ... E5
Poplar 881 ... L2
Potomac 80 ... C4
Power 159 ... E3
Pray 40 ... F5
Proctor 150 ... B3
Pryor 654 ... H5
Radersburg 104 ... E4
Ramsay 95 ... D4
Rapelje 50 ... G5
Ravalli 150 ... B3
Raymond 26 ... M2
Raynesford 35 ... F3
Red Lodge▲ 1,958 ... G5
Redstone 40 ... M2
Reedpoint 160 ... G5
Regina 83 ... J3
Reserve 80 ... M2
Rexford 132 ... A2
Richey 259 ... L3
Richland 48 ... K2
Ringling 102 ... F4
Roberts 312 ... G5
Rocky Boy 150 ... G2
Rollins 200 ... B3
Ronan 1,547 ... C3
Roscoe 40 ... G5
Rosebud 259 ... K4
Roundup▲ 1,808 ... H4
Roy 200 ... H3
Rudyard 450 ... F2
Ryegate▲ 260 ... G4
Saco 261 ... J2
Saint Ignatius 778 ... C3
Saint Regis 500 ... A3
Saint Xavier 200 ... J5
Saltese 90 ... A3
Sand Coulee 600 ... E3
Sanders 50 ... J4
Santa Rita 120 ... D2
Savage 300 ... M3
Scobey▲ 1,154 ... L2
Seeley Lake 900 ... C3
Shawmut 66 ... G4
Sheffield 49 ... K4
Shelby▲ 2,763 ... E2
Shepherd 200 ... H5
Sheridan 652 ... D5
Sidney▲ 5,217 ... M3
Silesia 90 ... H5
Silver Star 125 ... D5
Simms 200 ... E3
Simpson 70 ... F2
Somers 700 ... B2
Sonnette 42 ... L5
Springdale 45 ... F5
Square Butte 48 ... F3
Stanford▲ 529 ... F3
Stark 51 ... B3
Stevensville 1,221 ... C4
Stockett 500 ... E3
Stryker 96 ... B2
Suffolk 45 ... G3
Sula 200 ... B5
Sun River 300 ... E3
Sunburst 437 ... E2
Superior▲ 881 ... B3
Swan Lake 100 ... C3
Sweetgrass 250 ... E2
Terry▲ 659 ... L4
Thompson Falls▲ 1,319 ... A3
Three Forks 1,203 ... E5
Thurlow 84 ... K4
Toston 70 ... E4
Townsend▲ 1,635 ... E4
Trego 50 ... B2
Trident 50 ... E5
Trout Creek 300 ... A3
Troy 953 ... A2
Turner 150 ... H2
Twin Bridges 374 ... D5
Twodot 285 ... F4
Ulm 450 ... E3
Utica 30 ... F4
Valier 519 ... D2
Vananda 50 ... K4
Vandalia 35 ... J2
Vaughn 2,270 ... E3
Victor 700 ... B4
Vida 50 ... L3
Virgelle 28 ... F2
Virginia City▲ 142 ... E5
Volborg 125 ... L5
Wagner 32 ... H2
Walkerville 605 ... D4
Warmsprings 500 ... D4
Waterloo 102 ... D5
West Glacier 150 ... C2
West Yellowstone 913 ... E6
Westby 253 ... M2
White Sulphur Springs▲ 963 ... E4
Whitefish 4,368 ... B2
Whitehall 1,067 ... D5
Whitetail 150 ... L2
Whitewater 100 ... J2
Whitlash 50 ... E2
Wibaux▲ 628 ... M3
Wickes 60 ... D4
Willow Creek 150 ... E5
Wilsall 250 ... F5
Windham 63 ... F3
Winifred 150 ... G3
Winnett▲ 188 ... H4
Winston 120 ... E4
Wisdom 140 ... C5
Wise River 150 ... C5
Wolf Creek 500 ... D3
Wolf Point▲ 2,880 ... L2
Woodside 75 ... B4
Worden 600 ... H5
Wyola 350 ... J5
Zurich 60 ... G2

OTHER FEATURES

Absaroka (range) ... F5
Allen (mt.) ... C2
Arrow (creek) ... F3
Ashley (lake) ... B2
Battle (creek) ... G1
Bearhat (mt.) ... C2
Bears Paw (mts.) ... G2
Beartooth (mts.) ... G5
Beaver (creek) ... J2
Beaverhead (riv.) ... D5
Benton (lake) ... E3
Big (lake) ... G5
Big Belt (mts.) ... E4
Big Dry (creek) ... K3
Big Hole (riv.) ... C5
Big Hole Nat'l Battlefield ... C5
Bighorn (lake) ... H5
Bighorn (riv.) ... J5
Bighorn Canyon Nat'l Rec. Area ... H5
Big Muddy (riv.) ... M2
Big Porcupine (creek) ... J4
Birch (creek) ... D2
Birch Creek (res.) ... D2
Bitterroot (range) ... B4
Bitterroot (riv.) ... B4
Blackfeet Ind. Res. ... D2
Blackfoot (riv.) ... C4
Blackmore (mt.) ... F5
Bowdoin (lake) ... J2
Boxelder (creek) ... H3
Boxelder (creek) ... M5
Bynum (res.) ... D2
Cabinet (mts.) ... A2
Canyon Ferry (lake) ... E4
Clark Canyon (res.) ... D6
Clark Fork (riv.) ... A3
Clarks Fork, Yellowstone (riv.) ... G6
Cottonwood (creek) ... E2
Cow (creek) ... G2
Crazy peak) ... F4
Crow Ind. Res. ... H5
Cut Bank (creek) ... D2
Douglas (mt.) ... F5
Earthquake (lake) ... E6
Electric (peak) ... F6
Elwell (lake) ... E2
Emigrant (peak) ... F5
Ennis (lake) ... E5
Flathead (lake) ... C3
Flathead (riv.) ... B2
Flathead, North Fork (riv.) ... B2
Flathead, South Fork (riv.) ... C3
Flathead Ind. Res. ... B3
Flatwillow (creek) ... H4
Fort Belknap Ind. Res. ... H2
Fort Peck (lake) ... K3
Fort Union Trading Post Nat'l Hist. Site ... N2
Frances (lake) ... D2
Freezeout (lake) ... D3
Frenchman (riv.) ... J1
Fresno (res.) ... F2
Gallatin (peak) ... E5
Gallatin (riv.) ... E5
Georgetown (lake) ... C4
Gibson (res.) ... D3
Glacier Nat'l Park ... C2
Granite (peak) ... F5
Grant-Kohrs Ranch Nat'l Hist. Site ... D4
Hauser (lake) ... E4
Haystack (peak) ... A3
Hebgen (lake) ... E6
Helena (lake) ... E4
Holter (lake) ... D4
Hungry Horse (res.) ... C2
Hurricane (mt.) ... D2
Hyalite (peak) ... E5
Jackson (mt.) ... C2
Jefferson (riv.) ... D5
Judith (riv.) ... G3
Koocanusa (lake) ... A2
Kootenai (riv.) ... A2
Lemhi (pass) ... C6
Lewis and Clark (range) ... C3
Lima (res.) ... D6
Little Bighorn (riv.) ... J5
Little Bitterroot (lake) ... B2
Little Dry (creek) ... K3
Little Missouri (riv.) ... M5
Lockhart (mt.) ... D3
Lodge (creek) ... G1
Lolo (pass) ... B4
Lone (mt.) ... E5
Lost Trail (pass) ... B5
Lower Red Rock (lake) ... E6
Lower Saint Mary (lake) ... C2
Madison (riv.) ... E5
Malmstrom A.F.B. 5,938 ... E3
Marias (riv.) ... D2
Martinsdale (res.) ... F4
Mary Ronan (lake) ... B3
McDonald (lake) ... B2
McGloughlin (peak) ... C4
McGregor (lake) ... B3
Medicine (lake) ... M2
Milk (riv.) ... J2
Mission (range) ... C3
Missouri (riv.) ... L3
Musselshell (riv.) ... J3
Nelson (res.) ... J2
Ninepipe (res.) ... C3
Northern Cheyenne Indian Reservation ... K5
O'Fallon (creek) ... L4
Pishkun (res.) ... D3
Poplar (riv.) ... L2
Porcupine (creek) ... K2
Powder (riv.) ... L4
Purcell (mts.) ... A2
Railley (mt.) ... C3
Red Rock (lakes) ... E6
Red Rock (riv.) ... D6
Redwater (riv.) ... L3
Rock (creek) ... C4
Rocky (mts.) ... D4
Rocky Boy's Ind. Res. ... G2
Rosebud (creek) ... K4
Ruby (riv.) ... D5
Ruby River (res.) ... D5
Sage (creek) ... F2
Saint Mary (lake) ... C2
Saint Mary (riv.) ... C1
Sandy (creek) ... F2
Sheep (mt.) ... C2
Shields (riv.) ... F4
Siyeh (mt.) ... C2
Smith (riv.) ... E3
Sphinx (mt.) ... E5
Stillwater (riv.) ... G5
Stimson (mt.) ... C2
Sun (riv.) ... D3
Swan (lake) ... C3
Teton (riv.) ... E3
Tongue (riv.) ... K5
Upper Red Rock (lake) ... E6
Ward (peak) ... A3
Waterton-Glacier Int'l Peace Park ... C2
Whitefish (lake) ... B2
Willow (creek) ... E2
Willow Creek (res.) ... D3
Yellowstone (riv.) ... M3
Yellowstone National Park ... F6

▲County seat

COUNTIES

Adams 29,625 F4
Antelope 7,965 F2
Arthur 462 C3
Banner 852 A3
Blaine 675 E3
Boone 6,667 F3
Box Butte 13,130 A2
Boyd 2,835 F2
Brown 3,657 E2
Buffalo 37,447 E4
Burt 7,868 H3
Butler 8,601 G3
Cass 21,318 H4
Cedar 10,131 G2
Chase 4,381 C4
Cherry 6,307 C2
Cheyenne 9,494 A3
Clay 7,123 F4
Colfax 9,139 G3
Cuming 10,117 H3
Custer 12,270 E3
Dakota 16,742 H2
Dawes 9,021 A2
Dawson 19,940 E4
Deuel 2,237 B3
Dixon 6,143 H2
Dodge 34,500 H3
Douglas 416,444 H3
Dundy 2,582 C4
Fillmore 7,103 G4
Franklin 3,938 F4
Frontier 3,101 D4
Furnas 5,553 E4
Gage 22,794 H4
Garden 2,460 B3
Garfield 2,141 F3
Gosper 1,928 E4
Grant 769 C3
Greeley 3,006 F3
Hall 48,925 F4
Hamilton 8,862 F4
Harlan 3,810 E4
Hayes 1,222 C4
Hitchcock 3,750 C4
Holt 12,599 F2
Hooker 793 C3
Howard 6,055 F3
Jefferson 8,759 G4
Johnson 4,673 H4
Kearney 6,629 F4
Keith 8,584 C3
Keya Paha 1,029 E2
Kimball 4,108 A3
Knox 9,534 G2
Lancaster 213,641 H4
Lincoln 32,508 D4
Logan 878 D3
Loup 683 E3
Madison 32,655 G3
McPherson 546 C3
Merrick 8,042 F3
Morrill 5,423 A3
Nance 4,275 F3
Nemaha 7,980 J4
Nuckolls 5,786 F4
Otoe 14,252 H4
Pawnee 3,317 H4
Perkins 3,367 C4
Phelps 9,715 E4
Pierce 7,827 G2
Platte 29,820 G3
Polk 5,675 G3
Red Willow 11,705 D4
Richardson 9,937 J4
Rock 2,019 E2
Saline 12,715 G4
Sarpy 102,583 H3
Saunders 18,285 H3
Scotts Bluff 36,025 A3
Seward 15,450 G4
Sheridan 6,750 B2
Sherman 3,718 F3
Sioux 1,549 A2
Stanton 6,244 G3
Thayer 6,635 G4
Thomas 851 D3
Thurston 6,936 H2
Valley 5,169 E3
Washington 16,607 H3
Wayne 9,364 G2
Webster 4,279 F4
Wheeler 948 F3
York 14,428 G4

CITIES and TOWNS

Adams 472 H4
Ainsworth▲ 1,870 D2
Albion▲ 1,916 F3
Alda 540 F4
Alexandria 224 G4
Allen 331 H2
Alliance▲ 9,765 A2
Alma▲ 1,226 E4
Alvo 164 H4
Amherst 231 E4
Anselmo 189 E3
Ansley 555 E3
Arapahoe 1,001 E4
Arcadia 385 F3
Arlington 1,178 H3
Arnold 679 D3
Arthur▲ 128 C3
Ashland 2,136 H3
Ashton 251 F3
Atkinson 1,380 E2
Auburn▲ 3,443 J4
Aurora▲ 3,810 F4
Avoca 254 H4
Axtell 707 E4
Bancroft 494 H2
Bartlett▲ 131 F3
Bartley 339 D4
Bassett▲ 739 E2
Battle Creek 997 G3
Bayard 1,196 A3
Beatrice▲ 12,354 H4
Beaver City▲ 707 E4
Beaver Crossing 448 G4
Bee 209 H3
Beemer 672 H3
Belden 149 G2
Belgrade 157 G3
Bellevue 30,982 J3
Bellwood 395 G3
Benedict 230 G3
Benkelman▲ 1,193 C4
Bennet 544 H4
Bennington 866 H3
Bertrand 708 E4
Big Springs 495 B3
Bladen 280 F4
Blair▲ 6,860 H3
Bloomfield 1,181 G2
Blue Hill 810 F4
Blue Springs 431 H4
Boys Town 794 H3
Bradshaw 330 G4
Brady 331 D3
Brainard 326 G3
Brewster▲ 22 D3
Bridgeport▲ 1,581 A3
Broadwater 160 B3
Brock 143 H4
Broken Bow▲ 3,778 E3
Brownville 148 J4
Brule 411 C3
Bruning 332 G4
Bruno 141 G3
Brunswick 182 G2
Burwell▲ 1,278 E3
Butte▲ 452 F2
Cairo 733 F3
Callaway 539 D3
Cambridge 1,107 D4
Campbell 432 F4
Carleton 144 G4
Carroll 237 G2
Cedar Bluffs 591 H3
Cedar Creek 334 H3
Cedar Rapids 396 F3
Center▲ 112 G2
Central City▲ 2,868 F3
Ceresco 825 H3
Chadron▲ 5,588 B2
Chambers 341 F2
Chapman 292 F3
Chappell▲ 979 B3
Chester 351 G4
Clarks 379 G3
Clarkson 699 G3
Clatonia 296 H4
Clay Center▲ 825 F4
Clearwater 401 F2
Cody 177 C2
Coleridge 596 G2
Columbus▲ 19,480 G3
Concord 156 H2
Cook 333 H4
Cordova 147 G4
Cortland 393 H4
Cozad 3,823 E4
Craig 228 H3
Crawford 1,115 A2
Creighton 1,223 G2
Creston 220 G3
Crete 4,841 G4
Crofton 820 G2
Culbertson 795 C4
Curtis 791 D4
Dakota City▲ 1,470 H2
Dalton 282 B3
Dannebrog 324 F3
Davenport 383 G4
Davey 160 H4
David City▲ 2,522 G3
Dawson 157 J4
Daykin 188 G4
De Witt 598 G4
Decatur 641 H2
Denton 161 H4
Deshler 892 G4
Diller 298 H4
Dix 229 A3
Dodge 693 H3
Doniphan 736 F4
Dorchester 614 G4
Douglas 199 H4
Dunbar 171 J4
Duncan 387 G3
Dwight 227 G3
Eagle 1,047 H4
Edgar 600 F4
Edison 148 E4
Elba 196 F3
Elgin 731 F3
Elkhorn 1,398 H3
Elm Creek 852 E4
Elmwood 584 H4
Elsie 153 C4
Elwood▲ 679 E4
Emerson 791 H2
Endicott 163 G4
Eustis 452 D4
Ewing 449 F2
Exeter 661 G4
Fairbury▲ 4,335 G4
Fairfield 458 G4
Fairmont 708 G4
Falls City▲ 4,769 J4
Farnam 188 D4
Farwell 152 F3
Filley 157 H4
Firth 471 H4
Fordyce 190 G2
Fort Calhoun 648 J3
Franklin▲ 1,112 E4
Fremont▲ 23,680 H3
Friend 1,111 G4
Fullerton▲ 1,452 F3
Funk 198 E4
Garland 247 G4
Geneva▲ 2,310 G4
Genoa 1,082 G3
Gering▲ 7,946 A3
Gibbon 1,525 F4
Giltner 367 F4
Glenvil 304 F4
Goehner 192 G4
Gordon 1,803 B2
Gothenburg 3,232 D4
Grafton 167 G4
Grand Island▲ 39,386 F4
Grant▲ 1,239 C4
Greeley▲ 562 F3
Greenwood 531 H3
Gresham 253 G3
Gretna 2,249 H3
Guide Rock 290 F4
Gurley 198 B3
Hadar 291 G2
Haigler 225 C4
Hallam 309 H4
Hampton 432 G4
Hardy 206 G4
Harrisburg▲ 75 A3
Harrison▲ 291 A2
Hartington▲ 1,583 G2
Harvard 976 F4
Hastings 22,837 F4
Hay Springs 693 B2
Hayes Center▲ 259 C4
Hebron▲ 1,765 G4
Hemingford 953 A2
Henderson 999 G4
Henry 145 A2
Herman 186 H3
Hershey 579 D3
Hickman 1,081 H4
Hildreth 364 E4
Holbrook 233 D4
Holdrege▲ 5,671 E4
Holstein 207 F4
Homer 553 H2
Hooper 850 H3
Hordville 164 G3
Hoskins 307 G2
Howells 615 H3
Hubbard 199 H2
Humboldt 1,003 J4
Humphrey 741 G3
Hyannis▲ 210 C3
Imperial▲ 2,007 C4
Indianola 672 D4
Inglewood 286 H3
Inman 159 F2
Jackson 230 H2
Johnson 323 J4
Juniata 811 F4
Kearney▲ 24,396 E4
Kenesaw 818 F4
Kennard 371 H3
Kimball▲ 2,574 A3
La Vista 9,840 J3
Laurel 981 G2
Lawrence 323 F4
Leigh 447 G3
Lewellen 307 B3
Lexington▲ 6,601 E4
Lincoln (cap.)▲ 191,972 H4
Lindsay 321 G3
Litchfield 314 E3
Lodgepole 368 B3
Long Pine 396 E2
Loomis 376 E4
Louisville 998 H3
Loup City▲ 1,104 E3
Lyman 452 A3
Lynch 296 F2
Lyons 1,144 H3
Macy 836 H2
Madison▲ 2,135 G3
Madrid 288 C4
Malcolm 181 H4
Manley 170 H4
Marquette 211 G4
Mason City 160 E3
Max 285 C4
Maxwell 410 D3
Maywood 313 D4
McCook▲ 8,112 D4
McCool Junction 372 G4
Mead 513 H3
Meadow Grove 332 G2
Merna 377 E3
Merriman 151 C2
Milford 1,886 H4
Milligan 328 G4
Minatare 807 A3
Minden▲ 2,749 F4
Mitchell 1,743 A3
Monroe 309 G3
Morrill 974 A3
Mullen▲ 554 C2
Murdock 267 H4
Murray 418 J4
Nebraska City▲ 6,547 J4
Nehawka 260 H4
Neligh▲ 1,742 G2
Nelson▲ 627 F4
Nemaha 188 J4
Newcastle 271 H2
Newman Grove 787 G3
Newport 136 E2
Nickerson 291 H3
Niobrara 376 G2
Norfolk 21,476 G2
North Bend 1,249 H3
North Loup 361 F3
North Platte▲ 22,605 D3
O'Neill▲ 4,049 F2
Oakdale 362 F2
Oakland 1,279 H3
Oconto 147 E3
Odell 291 H4
Ogallala▲ 5,095 C3
Ohiowa 146 G4
Omaha▲ 335,795 J3
Orchard 439 F2
Ord▲ 2,481 F3
Orleans 490 E4
Osceola▲ 879 G3
Oshkosh▲ 986 B3
Osmond 774 G2
Otoe 196 H4
Overton 547 E4
Oxford 949 E4
Page 191 F2
Palisade 381 C4
Palmer 753 F3
Palmyra 545 H4
Panama 207 H4
Papillion▲ 10,372 J3
Pawnee City▲ 1,008 H4
Paxton 536 C3
Pender▲ 1,208 H2
Peru 1,110 J4
Petersburg 388 G3
Phillips 316 F4
Pickrell 201 H4
Pierce▲ 1,615 G2
Pilger 361 G2
Plainview 1,333 G2
Platte Center 387 G3
Plattsmouth▲ 6,412 J3
Pleasant Dale 253 G4
Pleasanton 372 E4
Plymouth 455 G4
Polk 345 G3
Ponca▲ 877 H2
Potter 388 A3
Prague 282 H3
Ralston 6,236 J3
Randolph 983 G2
Ravenna 1,317 F4
Raymond 167 H4
Red Cloud▲ 1,204 F4
Republican City 199 E4
Rising City 341 G3
Riverdale 208 E4
Riverton 162 F4
Rosalie 178 H2
Rose 247 E2
Roseland 254 F4
Rulo 191 J4
Rushville▲ 1,127 B2
Ruskin 187 G4
Saint Edward 822 G3
Saint Paul▲ 2,009 F3
Salem 160 J4
Santee 365 G2
Sargent 710 E3
Schuyler▲ 4,052 G3
Scotia 318 F3
Scottsbluff 13,711 A3
Scribner 950 H3
Seward▲ 5,634 H4
Shelby 690 G3
Shelton 954 F4
Shickley 360 G4
Shubert 237 J4
Sidney▲ 5,959 B3
Silver Creek 625 G3
Snyder 280 H3
South Sioux City 9,677 H2
Spalding 592 F3
Spencer 536 F2
Sprague 157 H4
Springfield 1,426 H3
Springview▲ 304 E2
Stamford 188 E4
Stanton▲ 1,549 G3
Staplehurst 281 G4
Stapleton▲ 299 D3
Stella 248 J4
Sterling 451 H4
Stockville▲ 32 D4
Stratton 427 C4
Stromsburg 1,241 G3
Stuart 650 E2
Sumner 210 E4
Superior 2,397 F4
Sutherland 1,032 C3
Sutton 1,353 G4
Swanton 145 H4
Syracuse 1,646 H4
Table Rock 308 H4
Talmage 246 H4
Taylor▲ 186 E3
Tecumseh▲ 1,702 H4
Tekamah▲ 1,852 H3
Terrytown 656 A3
Thedford▲ 243 D3
Tilden 895 G2

Agriculture, Industry and Resources

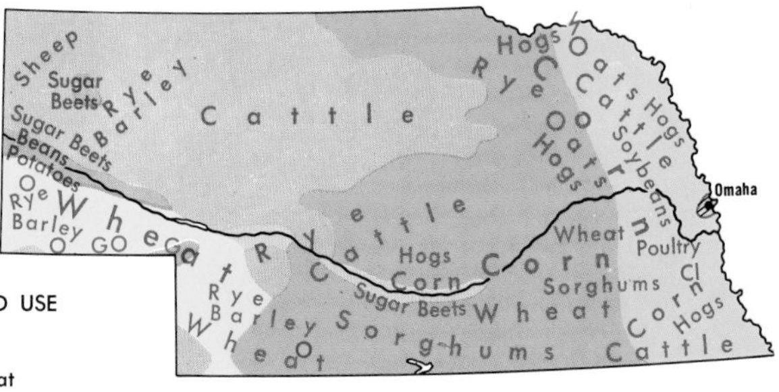
Sheep
Sugar Beets
Rye
Barley
Cattle
Hogs
Oats
Corn
Soybeans
Sugar Beets
Beans
Potatoes
Wheat
Omaha
Poultry
Sorghums
Cattle

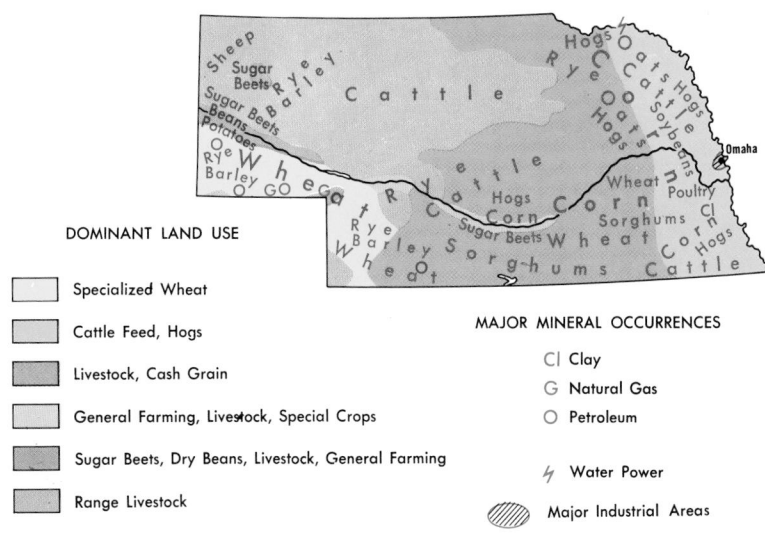

DOMINANT LAND USE

Specialized Wheat
Cattle Feed, Hogs
Livestock, Cash Grain
General Farming, Livestock, Special Crops
Sugar Beets, Dry Beans, Livestock, General Farming
Range Livestock

MAJOR MINERAL OCCURRENCES

Cl Clay
G Natural Gas
O Petroleum
Water Power
Major Industrial Areas

PINE RIDGE IND. RES.
S O U
Pine Ridge
Martin
Whiteclay
Merriman
Chadron
Whitney
Crawford
DAWES
Fort Robinson
Harrison
Rushville
Gordon
Clinton
Hay Springs
SIOUX
Marsland
Box Butte Res.
Niobrara
Agate
AGATE FOSSIL BEDS NAT'L MON.
SHERIDAN
Hemingford
BOX BUTTE
Berea
Alliance
Antioch
Ellsworth
Lakeside
Bingham
Ashby
Henry
Lake Alice
Morrill
Lyman
Mitchell
Lake Minatare
SCOTTS BLUFF
Terrytown
Scottsbluff
SCOTTS BLUFF NAT'L MON.
Gering
Angora
Melbeta
Minatare
MORRILL
McGrew
Bayard
CHIMNEY ROCK NAT'L HIST. SITE
North
Northport
Pumpkin
Bridgeport
Harrisburg
Redington
Broadwater
BANNER
Swan Lake
Crescent Lake
GARDEN
Arthur
Lisco
Oshkosh
Dalton
Gurley
Bushnell
Kimball
Dix
CHEYENNE
Potter
Lewellen
KIMBALL
Sidney
Sunol
Lodgepole
Lake C. W. McConaughy
DEUEL
Chappell
Big Springs
Brule
5,426 ft. (1,654 m.)
Julesburg
Sterling Res.
COLORADO
PERK
Grant
Brandon
Venango
Sterling
Holyoke
Lamar
CHA
Champion
Enders Res.
Frenchman
Wray
Haigler
Benkelman
Parks
DUN
Nebraska
SCALE
0 5 10 20 30 40 50 60 MI.
0 5 10 20 30 40 50 60 KM.
State Capitals
County Seats
Major Limited Access Hwys.
© Copyright HAMMOND

▲County seat

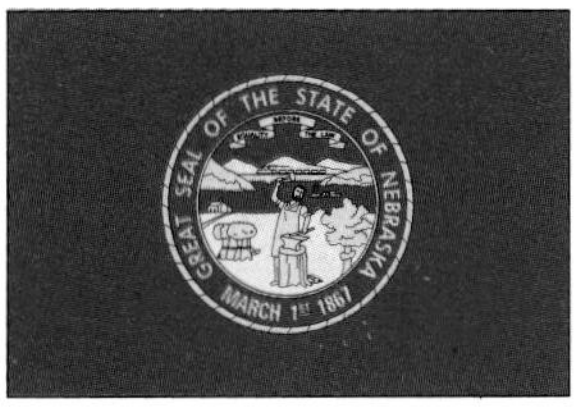

AREA 77,355 sq. mi. (200,349 sq. km.)
POPULATION 1,584,617
CAPITAL Lincoln
LARGEST CITY Omaha
HIGHEST POINT (Kimball Co.) 5,246 ft. (1654 m.)
SETTLED IN 1847
ADMITTED TO UNION March 1, 1867
POPULAR NAME Cornhusker State
STATE FLOWER Goldenrod
STATE BIRD Western Meadowlark

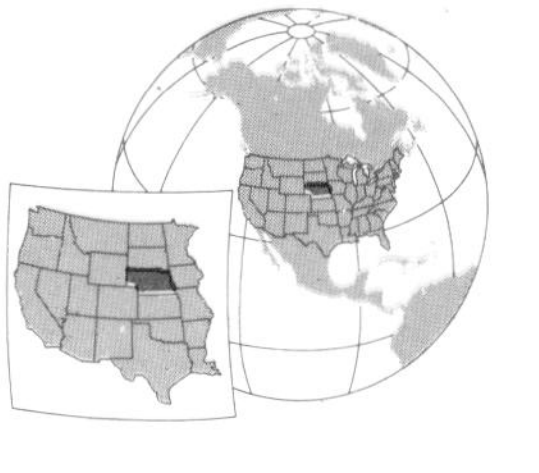

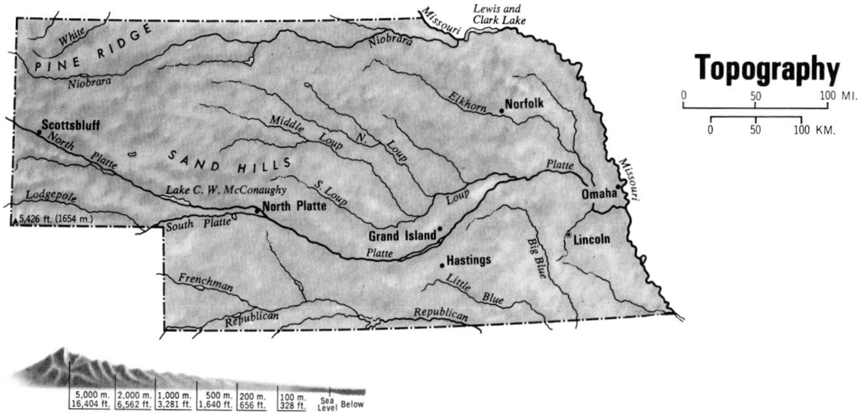
Topography
0 50 100 MI.
0 50 100 KM.
Lewis and Clark Lake
Missouri
White
PINE RIDGE
Niobrara
Elkhorn
Norfolk
Scottsbluff
North Platte
SAND HILLS
Middle Loup
N. Loup
S. Loup
Loup
Platte
Omaha
Lake C. W. McConaughy
North Platte
Lodgepole
5,426 ft. (1654 m.)
South Platte
Grand Island
Platte
Lincoln
Big Blue
Hastings
Frenchman
Little Blue
Republican
5,000 m. 16,404 ft.
2,000 m. 6,562 ft.
1,000 m. 3,281 ft.
500 m. 1,640 ft.
200 m. 656 ft.
100 m. 328 ft.
Sea Level
Below

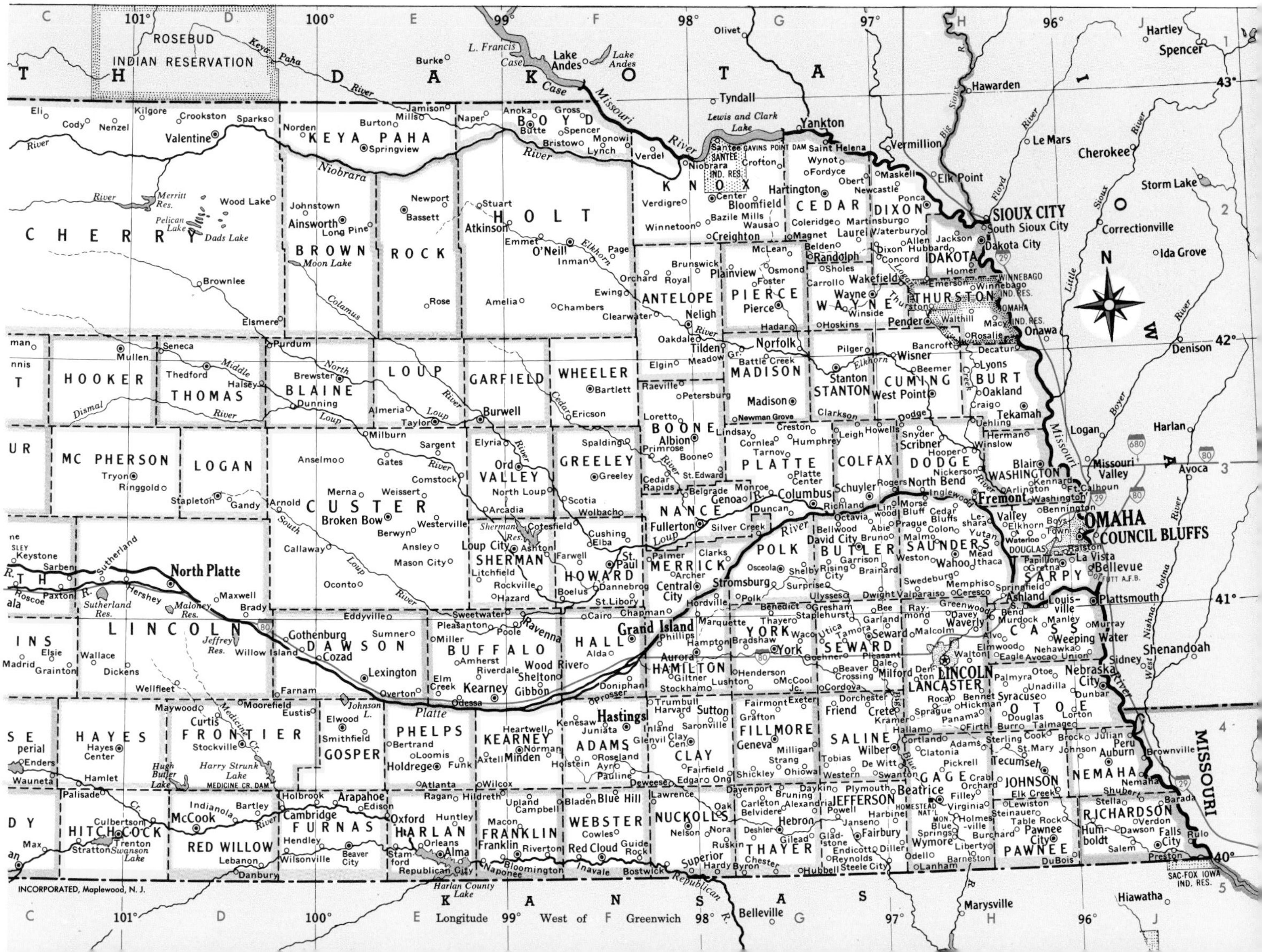
ROSEBUD INDIAN RESERVATION
SOUTH DAKOTA
IOWA
MISSOURI
KANSAS
CHERRY
KEYA PAHA
BOYD
HOLT
BROWN
ROCK
KNOX
CEDAR
DIXON
DAKOTA
ANTELOPE
PIERCE
WAYNE
THURSTON
HOOKER
THOMAS
BLAINE
LOUP
GARFIELD
WHEELER
MADISON
STANTON
CUMING
BURT
MC PHERSON
LOGAN
CUSTER
VALLEY
GREELEY
BOONE
PLATTE
COLFAX
DODGE
WASHINGTON
NANCE
SHERMAN
HOWARD
MERRICK
POLK
BUTLER
SAUNDERS
SARPY
LINCOLN
DAWSON
BUFFALO
HALL
HAMILTON
YORK
SEWARD
LANCASTER
CASS
OTOE
HAYES
FRONTIER
GOSPER
PHELPS
KEARNEY
ADAMS
CLAY
FILLMORE
SALINE
GAGE
JOHNSON
NEMAHA
HITCHCOCK
RED WILLOW
FURNAS
HARLAN
FRANKLIN
WEBSTER
NUCKOLLS
THAYER
JEFFERSON
PAWNEE
RICHARDSON
OMAHA
COUNCIL BLUFFS
LINCOLN
SIOUX CITY
North Platte
Grand Island
Hastings
Kearney
Norfolk
Longitude 99° West of F Greenwich 98°
INCORPORATED, Maplewood, N. J.

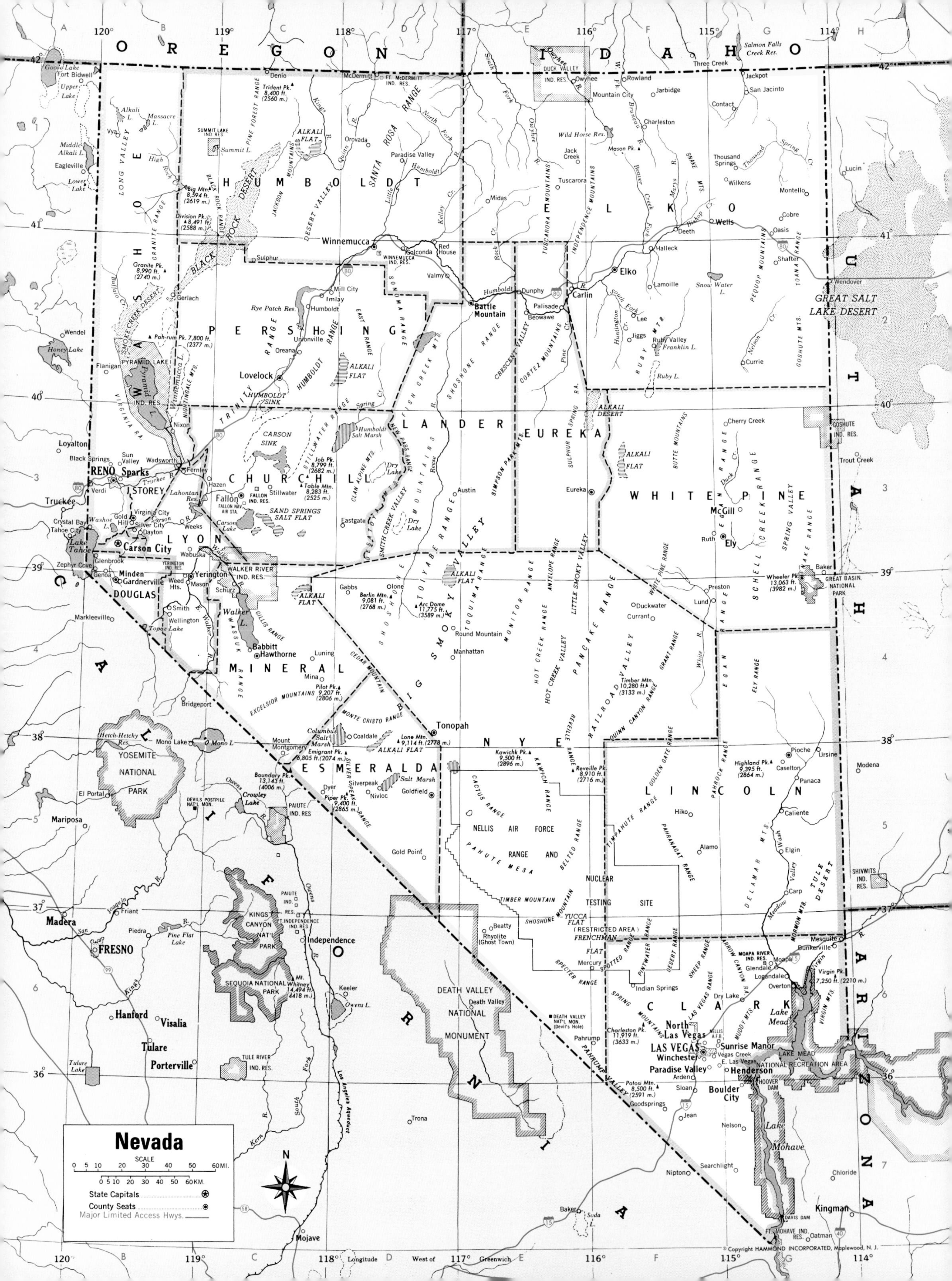

Nevada
SCALE
0 5 10 20 30 40 50 60 MI.
0 5 10 20 30 40 50 60 KM.
State Capitals
County Seats
Major Limited Access Hwys.
N
OREGON
IDAHO
UTAH
ARIZONA
CALIFORNIA
WASHOE
HUMBOLDT
ELKO
PERSHING
LANDER
EUREKA
CHURCHILL
STOREY
LYON
DOUGLAS
WHITE PINE
MINERAL
NYE
ESMERALDA
LINCOLN
CLARK
Carson City
RENO
Sparks
LAS VEGAS
North Las Vegas
Henderson
Boulder City
Winnemucca
Elko
Ely
Tonopah
Hawthorne
Lovelock
Fallon
Yerington
Minden
Gardnerville
Virginia City
Eureka
Austin
Battle Mountain
Goldfield
Pioche
Carlin
Wells
McGill
Caliente
Mesquite
Denio
McDermitt
Jackpot
Owyhee
Mountain City
Gerlach
Empire
Sulphur
Golconda
Imlay
Mill City
Humboldt
Unionville
Oreana
Nixon
Wadsworth
Fernley
Hazen
Stillwater
Dayton
Silver City
Gold Hill
Weeks
Wabuska
Mason
Smith
Wellington
Schurz
Babbitt
Luning
Mina
Gabbs
Ione
Round Mountain
Manhattan
Coaldale
Silverpeak
Dyer
Nivloc
Gold Point
Beatty
Rhyolite (Ghost Town)
Mercury
Indian Springs
Pahrump
Goodsprings
Sloan
Jean
Nelson
Searchlight
Nipton
Arden
Paradise Valley
Winchester
Sunrise Manor
Overton
Logandale
Glendale
Moapa
Bunkerville
Alamo
Hiko
Panaca
Caselton
Ursine
Elgin
Carp
Lund
Preston
Duckwater
Currant
Baker
Ruth
Cherry Creek
Shafter
Oasis
Cobre
Montello
Wilkens
Thousand Springs
Contact
San Jacinto
Rowland
Jarbidge
Charleston
Tuscarora
Midas
Jack Creek
Deeth
Halleck
Lamoille
Lee
Jiggs
Ruby Valley
Currie
Palisade
Beowawe
Dunphy
Valmy
Red House
Paradise Valley
Orovada
Vya
Eagleville
Fort Bidwell
Glenbrook
Zephyr Cove
Genoa
Verdi
Truckee
Crystal Bay
Tahoe City
Lake Tahoe
Pyramid Lake
Walker L.
Humboldt Sink
Carson Sink
Black Rock Desert
Smoke Creek Desert
Great Salt Lake Desert
Lake Mead
Lake Mohave
Hoover Dam
Davis Dam
Lake Mead National Recreation Area
Great Basin National Park
Death Valley National Monument
Nellis Air Force Range and Nuclear Testing Site
Yucca Flat (Restricted Area)
Frenchman Flat
Yosemite National Park
Kings Canyon Nat'l Park
Sequoia National Park
Devils Postpile Nat'l Mon.
Boundary Pk. 13,143 ft. (4006 m.)
Wheeler Pk. 13,063 ft. (3982 m.)
Charleston Pk. 11,919 ft. (3633 m.)
Mt. Whitney 14,494 ft. (4418 m.)
Arc Dome 11,775 ft. (3589 m.)
Toiyabe Range
Toquima Range
Monitor Range
Shoshone Range
Ruby Mts.
Snake Range
Schell Creek Range
Spring Mountains
Fresno
Madera
Hanford
Visalia
Tulare
Porterville
Bishop
Independence
Mojave
Trona
Baker
Kingman
Chloride
Oatman
Bridgeport
Markleeville
Loyalton
Mono Lake
Longitude West of Greenwich
120°
119°
118°
117°
116°
115°
114°
42°
41°
40°
39°
38°
37°
36°
© Copyright HAMMOND INCORPORATED, Maplewood, N. J.

BATTLE BORN

AREA 110,561 sq. mi. (286,353 sq. km.)
POPULATION 1,206,152
CAPITAL Carson City
LARGEST CITY Las Vegas
HIGHEST POINT Boundary Pk. 13,143 ft. (4006 m.)
SETTLED IN 1850
ADMITTED TO UNION October 31, 1864
POPULAR NAME Silver State; Sagebrush State
STATE FLOWER Sagebrush
STATE BIRD Mountain Bluebird

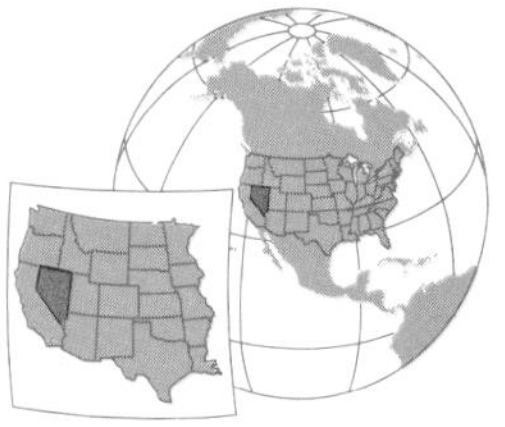

Agriculture, Industry and Resources

MAJOR MINERAL OCCURRENCES

- Ag Silver
- Au Gold
- Ba Barite
- Cu Copper
- Gp Gypsum
- Hg Mercury
- Lt Lithium
- Mg Magnesium
- Mo Molybdenum
- Na Salt
- O Petroleum
- Pb Lead
- S Sulfur
- W Tungsten
- Zn Zinc
- ϟ Water Power

DOMINANT LAND USE

- General Farming, Dairy, Livestock
- General Farming, Livestock, Special Crops
- Range Livestock
- Forests
- Nonagricultural Land

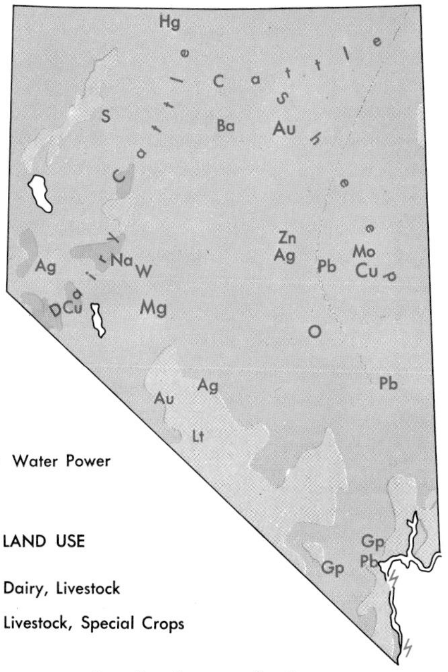
Hg
Cattle
Sheep
Dairy
S
Ba
Au
Zn
Ag
Pb
Mo
Cu
Na
W
Mg
Ag
Cu
D
O
Au
Lt
Pb
Gp
Gp
Pb

Topography

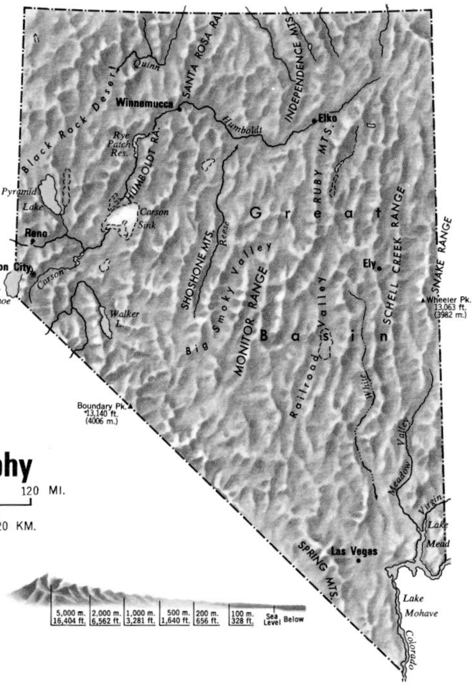
Quinn
SANTA ROSA RA.
INDEPENDENCE MTS.
Black Rock Desert
Winnemucca
Humboldt
Elko
Rye Patch Res.
HUMBOLDT RA.
RUBY MTS.
Pyramid Lake
Carson Sink
Reno
Carson City
L. Tahoe
Carson
Walker L.
Great Basin
SHOSHONE MTS.
Big Smoky Valley
MONITOR RANGE
Railroad Valley
SCHELL CREEK RANGE
SNAKE RANGE
Ely
Wheeler Pk. 13,063 ft. (3982 m.)
Boundary Pk. 13,140 ft. (4006 m.)
White
Meadow Valley
Virgin
Lake Mead
SPRING MTS.
Las Vegas
Lake Mohave
Colorado
0 60 120 MI.
0 60 120 KM.
5,000 m. 16,404 ft.
2,000 m. 6,562 ft.
1,000 m. 3,281 ft.
500 m. 1,640 ft.
200 m. 656 ft.
100 m. 328 ft.
Sea Level
Below

COUNTIES

Carson City (city) 40,443 .... B3
Churchill 17,938 .... C3
Clark 741,459 .... F6
Douglas 27,637 .... B4
Elko 33,530 .... F1
Esmeralda 1,344 .... D5
Eureka 1,547 .... E3
Humboldt 12,844 .... C1
Lander 6,266 .... D3
Lincoln 3,775 .... F5
Lyon 20,001 .... B3
Mineral 6,475 .... C4
Nye 17,781 .... E4
Pershing 4,336 .... C2
Storey 2,526 .... B3
Washoe 254,667 .... B2
White Pine 9,264 .... F3

CITIES and TOWNS

Alamo 300 .... F5
Austin 300 .... E3
Babbitt C4
Baker 140 .... G3
Battle Mountain▲ 3,542 .... E2
Beatty 1,623 .... E6
Beowawe 77 .... E2
Black Springs 180 .... B3
Boulder City 12,567 .... G7
Bunkerville 300 .... G6
Caliente 1,111 .... G5
Carlin 2,220 .... E2
Carp 30 .... G5
Carson City (cap.) 40,443 .... B3
Caselton G5
Cherry Creek 80 .... G3
Coaldale 31 .... D4
Crystal Bay 6,225 .... A3
Currant 30 .... F4
Dayton 2,217 .... B3
Deeth 125 .... F1
Denio 35 .... C1
Duckwater 80 .... F4
Dunphy 25 .... E2
Dyer 56 .... C5
East Las Vegas 11,087 .... F6
Elko▲ 14,736 .... F2
Ely▲ 4,756 .... G3
Eureka▲ 300 .... E3
Fallon▲ 6,438 .... C3
Fernley 5,164 .... B3
Gabbs 667 .... D4
Gardnerville 2,177 .... B4
Genoa 254 .... B4
Gerlach 400 .... B2
Glenbrook 800 .... B3
Glendale 25 .... G6
Golconda 275 .... D2
Gold Hill 80 .... B3
Goldfield▲ 500 .... D5
Goodsprings 80 .... F7
Halleck 68 .... F2
Hawthorne▲ 4,162 .... C4
Hazen 76 .... C3
Henderson 64,942 .... G6
Hiko 210 .... F5
Imlay 250 .... C2
Indian Springs 1,164 .... F6
Jack Creek E1
Jackpot 400 .... G1
Jean 125 .... F7
Lamoille 100 .... F2
Las Vegas▲ 258,295 .... F6
Lee 125 .... F2
Logandale 410 .... G6
Lovelock▲ 2,069 .... C2
Lund 380 .... F4
Luning 90 .... C4
Manhattan 93 .... E4
Mason 200 .... B4
McDermitt 373 .... D1
McGill 1,258 .... G3
Mercury 900 .... E6
Mesquite 1,871 .... G6
Mina 450 .... C4
Minden▲ 1,441 .... B4
Moapa 3,444 .... G6
Montello 100 .... G1
Mountain City 100 .... F1
Nelson 75 .... G7
Nixon 400 .... B3
North Las Vegas 47,707 .... F6
Oreana 45 .... C2
Orovada 200 .... D1
Overton 1,111 .... G6
Owyhee 908 .... F1
Pahrump 7,424 .... E6
Panaca 650 .... G5
Paradise Valley 115 .... D1
Paradise Valley 84,818 .... F6
Pioche▲ 850 .... G5
Preston 50 .... G4
Reno▲ 133,850 .... B3
Round Mountain 400 .... E4
Ruby Valley 150 .... F2
Ruth 455 .... F3
Schurz 617 .... C4
Searchlight 500 .... F7
Silver City 150 .... B3
Silverpeak 100 .... D5
Sloan 30 .... F7
Smith 1,033 .... B4
Sparks 53,367 .... B3
Stillwater 150 .... C3
Sulphur C2
Sun Valley 11,391 .... B3
Sunrise Manor 95,362 .... F6
Thousand Springs G1
Tonopah▲ 3,616 .... D4
Ursine 45 .... G5
Valmy 200 .... D2
Vegas Creek G6
Verdi 100 .... B3
Virginia City▲ 750 .... B3
Wabuska 150 .... B3
Wadsworth 640 .... B3
Wellington 505 .... B4
Wells 1,256 .... G1
Winchester 23,365 .... F6
Winnemucca▲ 6,134 .... D2
Yerington▲ 2,367 .... B4
Zephyr Cove 1,434 .... A3

OTHER FEATURES

Alkali (lake) B1
Antelope (range) E3
Arc Dome (mt.) D4
Arrow Canyon (range) G6
Beaver Creek Fork, Humboldt (riv.) F1
Belted (range) E5
Berlin (mt.) D4
Big (mt.) B1
Big Smoky (valley) D4
Bishop (creek) F1
Black Rock (des.) B2
Black Rock (range) B1
Boundary (peak) C5
Buffalo (creek) B2
Butte (mts.) F3
Cactus (range) E5
Carson (lake) C3
Carson (riv.) B3
Carson (sink) C3
Cedar (mt.) D4
Charleston (peak) F6
Clan Alpine (mts.) D3
Columbus (salt marsh) C4
Cortez (mts.) E2
Crescent (valley) E2
Davis (dam) G7
Death Valley Nat'l Mon. E6
Delamar (mts.) G5
Desatoya (mts.) D3
Desert (range) F6
Desert (valley) C1
Devil's Hole (Death Valley Nat'l Mon.) E6
Division (peak) B1
Duck (creek) G3
Duck Valley Ind. Res. E1
East (range) D2
East Walker (riv.) B4
Egan (range) G4
Ely (range) G4
Emigrant (peak) C5
Excelsior (mts.) C4
Fallon Ind. Res. C3
Fallon Nav. Air Sta. C3
Fish Creek (mts.) D2
Fort McDermitt Ind. Res. D1
Fort Mohave Ind. Res. G7
Franklin (lake) F2
Frenchman Flat (basin) F6
Gillis (range) C4
Golden Gate (range) F5
Goshute (mts.) G2
Goshute Ind. Res. G3
Granite (peak) B2
Granite (range) B2
Grant (range) F4
Great Basin Nat'l Park G4
Great Salt Lake (des.) H2
High Rock (creek) B1
Highland (peak) G5
Hoover (dam) G7
Hot Creek (range) E4
Hot Creek (valley) E4
Humboldt (range) C2
Humboldt (riv.) E2
Humboldt (salt marsh) D3
Humboldt (sink) C2
Huntington (creek) F2
Independence (mts.) E1
Jackson (mts.) C1
Job (peak) C3
Kawich (range) E5
Kelley (creek) D1
Kings (riv.) C1
Lahontan (res.) B3
Lake Mead National Rec. Area G6
Las Vegas (range) F6
Little Humboldt (riv.) D1
Little Smoky (valley) E4
Lone (mt.) D4
Long (valley) B1
Marys (riv.) F1
Mason (peak) F1
Massacre (lake) B1
Mead (lake) G6
Meadow Valley Wash (riv.) G5
Moapa River Ind. Res. G6
Mohave (lake) G7
Monitor (range) E4
Monte Cristo (range) D4
Mormon (mts.) G5
Muddy (mts.) G6
Nellis A.F.B. 8,377 .... F6
Nellis Air Force Range and Nuclear Test Site E5
Nelson (creek) G2
New Pass (range) D3
Nightingale (mts.) B2
Owyhee (riv.) E1
Pahranagat (range) F5
Pahrock (range) F5
Pah-rum (peak) B2
Pahrump (valley) F6
Pahute (mesa) E5
Pancake (range) F4
Pequop (mts.) G2
Pilot (peak) C4
Pine (creek) E2
Pine Forest (range) C1
Pintwater (range) F6
Piper (peak) D5
Potosi (mt.) F7
Pyramid (lake) B2
Pyramid Lake Ind. Res. B2
Quinn (riv.) D1
Quinn Canyon (range) F4
Railroad (valley) F4
Reese (riv.) D3
Reveille (peak) E5
Reveille (range) E4
Ruby (lake) F2
Ruby (mts.) F2
Rye Patch (res.) C2
Sand Springs (salt flat) C3
Santa Rosa (range) D1
Schell Creek (range) G3
Sheep (range) F6
Shoshone (mt.) E6
Shoshone (mts.) D3
Shoshone (range) E2
Silver Peak (range) D5
Simpson Park (mts.) E3
Smith Creek (valley) D3
Smoke Creek (des.) B2
Snake (mts.) F1
Snake (range) G3
Snow Water (lake) G2
Sonoma (range) D2
Specter (range) E6
Spotted (range) F6
Spring (creek) D2
Spring (mts.) F6
Spring (valley) G3
Stillwater (range) C3
Sulphur Spring (range) E3
Summit (lake) C1
Summit Lake Ind. Res. B1
Table (mt.) C3
Tahoe (lake) B3
Thousand Spring (creek) G1
Timber (mt.) E5
Timber (mt.) F4
Timpahute (range) F5
Toana (range) G2
Toiyabe (range) D3
Topaz (lake) B4
Toquima (range) E4
Trident (peak) C1
Trinity (range) C2
Truckee (riv.) B3
Tule (des.) G5
Tuscarora (mts.) E1
Virgin (mts.) G6
Virgin (peak) G6
Virgin (riv.) G6
Virginia (range) B3
Walker (lake) C4
Walker (riv.) C3
Walker River Ind. Res. C3
Washoe (lake) B3
Wassuk (range) C4
Wheeler (peak) G4
White (riv.) F4
White Pine (range) F3
Wild Horse (res.) E1
Winnemucca (lake) B2
Winnemucca Ind. Res. D2
Yerington Ind. Res. B3
Yucca Flat (basin) E6

▲County seat

New Hampshire and Vermont
SCALE
0 5 10 15 20 25 MI.
0 5 10 15 20 25 KM.
State Capitals
County Seats
Major Limited Access Hwys.
C A N A D A
Q U É B E C
M A I N E
N E W Y O R K
M A S S A C H U S E T T S
V E R M O N T
N E W H A M P S H I R E
ATLANTIC OCEAN
GRAND ISLE
FRANKLIN
ORLEANS
ESSEX
COOS
LAMOILLE
CALEDONIA
CHITTENDEN
WASHINGTON
ADDISON
ORANGE
GRAFTON
CARROLL
RUTLAND
WINDSOR
BELKNAP
SULLIVAN
MERRIMACK
STRAFFORD
BENNINGTON
WINDHAM
CHESHIRE
HILLSBOROUGH
ROCKINGHAM
Sherbrooke
Waterloo
Magog
Knowlton
Coaticook
Burlington
South Burlington
Montpelier
Barre
Saint Albans
Rutland
Bennington
Brattleboro
Concord
Manchester
Nashua
Portsmouth
Dover
Keene
Laconia
Lawrence
Lowell
Plattsburgh
Rumford
Sanford
Mt. Washington 6,288 ft. (1917 m.)
L. Memphremagog
Lake Winnipesaukee
Lake Champlain
Connecticut R.
© Copyright HAMMOND INCORPORATED, Maplewood, N. J.
Longitude 72° West of Greenwich
73°
72°
71°
45°
44°
43°

NEW HAMPSHIRE
AREA 9,279 sq. mi. (24,033 sq. km.)
POPULATION 1,113,915
CAPITAL Concord
LARGEST CITY Manchester
HIGHEST POINT Mt. Washington 6,288 ft. (1917 m.)
SETTLED IN 1623
ADMITTED TO UNION June 21, 1788
POPULAR NAME Granite State
STATE FLOWER Purple Lilac
STATE BIRD Purple Finch

VERMONT
AREA 9,614 sq. mi. (24,900 sq. km.)
POPULATION 564,964
CAPITAL Montpelier
LARGEST CITY Burlington
HIGHEST POINT Mt. Mansfield 4,393 ft. (1339 m.)
SETTLED IN 1764
ADMITTED TO UNION March 4, 1791
POPULAR NAME Green Mountain State
STATE FLOWER Red Clover
STATE BIRD Hermit Thrush

Topography

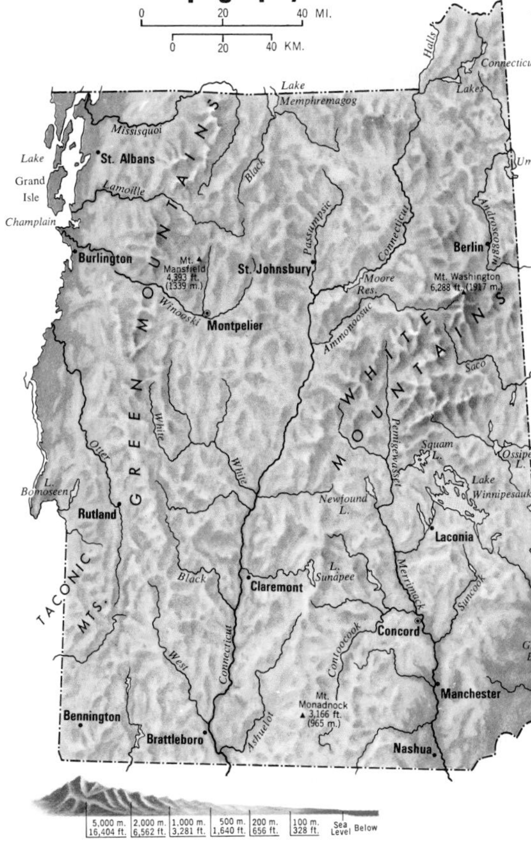
0 20 40 MI.
0 20 40 KM.
Lake Memphremagog
Missisquoi
St. Albans
Lake
Grand Isle
Lamoille
Champlain
Burlington
Mt. Mansfield 4,393 ft. (1339 m.)
Winooski
Montpelier
St. Johnsbury
Passumpsic
Black
Connecticut
Halls
Connecticut Lakes
Umbagog L.
Androscoggin
Berlin
Mt. Washington 6,288 ft. (1917 m.)
Moore Res.
Ammonoosuc
WHITE MOUNTAINS
GREEN MOUNTAINS
Saco
White
Otter
L. Bomoseen
Rutland
Pemigewasset
Squam L.
Ossipee L.
Lake Winnipesaukee
Newfound L.
Laconia
Salmon Falls
Black
Claremont
L. Sunapee
Merrimack
Suncook
TACONIC MTS.
Concord
Contoocook
Great Bay
Portsmouth
West
Connecticut
Manchester
Bennington
Ashuelot
Mt. Monadnock 3,166 ft. (965 m.)
Brattleboro
Nashua
5,000 m. 16,404 ft.
2,000 m. 6,562 ft.
1,000 m. 3,281 ft.
500 m. 1,640 ft.
200 m. 656 ft.
100 m. 328 ft.
Sea Level
Below

NEW HAMPSHIRE

COUNTIES

Belknap 49,216 .... D4
Carroll 35,410 .... E4
Cheshire 70,121 .... C6
Coos 34,828 .... E2
Grafton 74,929 .... D4
Hillsborough 336,073 .... D6
Merrimack 120,005 .... D5
Rockingham 245,845 .... E5
Strafford 104,233 .... E5
Sullivan 38,592 .... C5

CITIES and TOWNS

Acworth• 776 .... C5
Albany• 536 .... E4
Alexandria• 1,190 .... D4
Allenstown• 4,649 .... E5
Alstead• 1,721 .... C5
Alton Bay 500 .... E5
Alton• 3,286 .... E5
Amherst• 9,068 .... D6
Andover• 1,883 .... D5
Antrim 1,325 .... D5
Antrim• 2,360 .... D5
Ashland 1,915 .... D4
Ashland• 1,807 .... D4
Ashuelot 810 .... C6
Atkinson• 5,188 .... E6
Auburn• 4,085 .... E5
Barnstead• 3,100 .... E5
Barrington• 6,164 .... F5
Bartlett• 2,290 .... E3
Bath• 784 .... D3
Bedford• 12,563 .... D6
Beebe River 355 .... D4
Belmont• 5,796 .... E5
Bennington• 1,236 .... D5
Benton• 330 .... D3
Berlin 11,824 .... E3
Bethlehem• 2,033 .... D3
Boscawen• 3,586 .... D5
Bow Mills 802 .... D5
Bradford• 1,405 .... D5
Brentwood• 2,590 .... E6
Bretton Woods E3
Bridgewater• 796 .... D4
Bristol 1,483 .... D4
Bristol• 2,537 .... D4
Brookfield• 518 .... E4
Brookline• 2,410 .... D6
Campton• 2,377 .... D4
Canaan• 3,045 .... C4
Candia• 3,557 .... E5
Canobie Lake 500 .... E6
Canterbury• 1,687 .... D5
Carroll• 528 .... D3
Cascade 350 .... E3
Center Barnstead 400 .... E5
Center Conway 558 .... E4
Center Harbor• 996 .... E4
Center Ossipee• 800 .... E4
Center Tuftonboro 300 .... E4
Charlestown 1,173 .... C5
Charlestown• 4,630 .... C5
Chatham• 268 .... E3
Chester• 2,691 .... E6
Chesterfield• 3,112 .... C6
Chichester• 1,942 .... E5
Chocorua 575 .... E4
Claremont 13,902 .... C5
Clarksville• 232 .... E1
Colebrook 2,444 .... E2
Colebrook• 2,459 .... E2
Concord• (cap.) 36,006 .... D5
Contoocook 1,334 .... D5
Conway 1,604 .... E4
Conway• 7,940 .... E4
Cornish Flat 450 .... C4
Croydon• 627 .... C5
Dalton• 827 .... D3
Danbury• 881 .... D4
Danville• 2,534 .... E6
Deerfield• 3,124 .... E5
Deering• 1,707 .... D5
Derry 20,446 .... E6
Derry• 29,603 .... E6
Dorchester• 392 .... D4
Dover▲ 25,042 .... F5
Dublin• 1,474 .... C6
Dummer• 327 .... E2
Durham 9,236 .... F5
Durham• 11,818 .... F5
East Andover 500 .... D5
East Hampstead 900 .... E6
East Kingston• 1,352 .... F6
East Lempster 300 .... C5
East Sullivan 300 .... C6
East Swanzey 500 .... C6
East Wolfeboro 400 .... E4
Easton• 223 .... D3
Eaton (Eaton Center) 362 .... E4
Ellsworth• 74 .... D4
Enfield 1,560 .... C4
Enfield• 3,979 .... C4
Epping 1,384 .... E5
Epping• 5,162 .... E5
Epsom• 3,591 .... E5
Errol• 292 .... E2
Etna 550 .... C4
Exeter▲ 9,556 .... F6
Exeter• 12,481 .... F6
Farmington 3,567 .... E5
Farmington• 5,739 .... E5
Fitzwilliam• 2,011 .... C6
Fitzwilliam Depot 350 .... C6
Francestown• 1,217 .... D6
Franconia• 811 .... D3
Franklin 8,304 .... D5
Freedom• 935 .... E4
Fremont• 2,576 .... E6
Georges Mills 375 .... C5
Gerrish 500 .... D5
Gilford• 5,867 .... E4
Gilmanton• 2,609 .... E5
Gilmanton Iron Works 300 .... E5
Gilsum• 745 .... C5
Glen 600 .... E3
Goffstown• 14,621 .... D5
Gorham 1,910 .... E3
Gorham• 3,173 .... E3
Goshen• 742 .... C5
Grafton• 923 .... D4
Grantham• 1,247 .... C5
Grasmere 400 .... D5
Greenfield• 1,519 .... D6
Greenland• 2,768 .... F5
Greenville 1,135 .... D6
Greenville• 2,231 .... D6
Groton• 318 .... D4
Groveton 1,255 .... D2
Guild 500 .... C5
Hampstead• 6,732 .... E6
Hampton 7,989 .... F6
Hampton• 12,278 .... F6
Hampton Beach 975 .... F6
Hampton Falls• 1,503 .... F6
Hancock• 1,604 .... C6
Hanover 6,538 .... C4
Hanover• 9,212 .... C4
Harrisville• 981 .... C6
Haverhill• 4,164 .... C3
Hebron• 386 .... D4
Henniker 1,693 .... D5
Henniker• 4,151 .... D5
Hill• 814 .... D4
Hillsboro 1,826 .... D5
Hillsboro• 4,498 .... D5
Hinsdale 1,718 .... C6
Hinsdale• 3,936 .... C6
Holderness• 1,694 .... D4
Hollis• 5,705 .... D6
Hooksett 2,573 .... E5
Hooksett• 8,767 .... E5
Hopkinton• 4,806 .... D5
Hudson 7,626 .... E6
Hudson• 19,530 .... E6
Intervale 725 .... E3
Jackson• 678 .... E3
Jaffrey 2,558 .... C6
Jaffrey• 5,361 .... C6
Jaffrey Center 340 .... C6
Jefferson• 965 .... D3
Kearsarge 350 .... E3
Keene▲ 22,430 .... C6
Kingston• 5,591 .... E6
Laconia▲ 15,743 .... E4
Lancaster▲ 1,859 .... D3
Lancaster• 3,522 .... D3
Landaff• 350 .... D3
Langdon• 580 .... C5
Lebanon 12,183 .... C4
Lee• 3,729 .... F5
Lempster• 947 .... C5
Lincoln• 1,229 .... D3
Lisbon 1,246 .... D3
Lisbon• 1,664 .... D3
Litchfield• 5,516 .... E6
Littleton 4,633 .... D3
Littleton• 5,827 .... D3
Lochmere 300 .... D5
Londonderry• 19,781 .... E6
Loudon• 4,114 .... E5
Lyman• 388 .... D3
Lyme• 1,496 .... C4
Lyndeborough• 1,294 .... D6
Madbury• 1,404 .... F5
Madison• 1,704 .... E4
Manchester 99,567 .... E6
Marlborough 1,211 .... C6
Marlborough• 1,927 .... C6
Marlow• 650 .... C5
Melvin Village 450 .... E4
Meredith 1,654 .... D4
Meredith• 4,837 .... D4
Meriden 800 .... C4
Merrimack• 22,156 .... D6
Middleton• 1,183 .... E5
Milan• 1,295 .... E2
Milford 8,015 .... D6
Milford• 11,795 .... D6
Milton• 3,691 .... F5
Milton Mills 450 .... F4
Mirror Lake 350 .... E4
Monroe• 746 .... C3
Mont Vernon• 1,812 .... D6
Moultonboro• 2,956 .... E4
Nashua▲ 79,662 .... D6
Nelson• 535 .... C5
New Boston• 3,214 .... D6
New Castle• 840 .... F5
New Durham• 1,974 .... E5
New Hampton• 1,606 .... D4
New Ipswich• 4,014 .... D6
New London 3,180 .... D5
New London• 2,935 .... D5
Newbury• 1,347 .... C5
Newfields• 888 .... F5
Newington• 990 .... F5
Newmarket 4,917 .... F5
Newmarket• 7,157 .... F5
Newport▲ 3,772 .... C5
Newport• 6,110 .... C5
Newton Junction 450 .... E6
Newton• 3,473 .... E6
North Chichester 450 .... E5
North Conway 2,032 .... E3
North Hampton• 3,637 .... F6
North Haverhill 400 .... D3
North Stratford 600 .... D2
North Walpole 950 .... C5
North Weare 400 .... D5
North Woodstock 750 .... D3
Northfield-Tilton D5
Northfield• 4,263 .... D5
Northumberland• 2,492 .... D2
Northwood• 3,124 .... E5
Northwood Narrows 325 .... E5
Nottingham• 2,939 .... E5
Orange• 237 .... D4
Orford• 1,008 .... C4
Ossipee 3,309 .... E4
Pelham• 9,408 .... E6
Pembroke• 6,561 .... E5
Peterborough 2,685 .... D6
Peterborough• 5,239 .... D6
Piermont• 624 .... C4
Pike 433 .... C3
Pittsburg• 901 .... E1
Pittsfield 1,717 .... E5
Pittsfield• 3,701 .... E5
Plainfield• 2,056 .... C4
Plaistow• 7,316 .... E6
Plymouth 3,967 .... D4
Plymouth• 5,811 .... D4
Portsmouth 25,925 .... F5
Randolph• 371 .... E3
Raymond 2,516 .... E5
Raymond• 8,713 .... E5
Redstone 300 .... E3
Richmond• 877 .... C6
Rindge• 4,941 .... C6
Rochester 26,630 .... E5
Roxbury• 248 .... C6
Rumney• 1,446 .... D4
Rye• 4,612 .... F5
Rye Beach 600 .... F6
Rye North Beach 700 .... F5
Salem• 25,746 .... E6
Salem Depot 975 .... E6
Salisbury• 1,061 .... D5
Salmon Falls 950 .... F5
Sanbornton• 2,136 .... D5
Sanbornville 750 .... F4
Sandown• 4,060 .... E6
Sandwich• 1,066 .... E4
Seabrook• 6,503 .... F6
Sharon• 299 .... D6
Shelburne 437 .... E3
Shelburne• 318 .... E3
Silver Lake 350 .... E4
Somersworth 11,249 .... F5
South Deerfield 500 .... E5
South Hampton• 740 .... F6
South Lyndeboro 300 .... D6
South Merrimack 650 .... D6
South Seabrook 500 .... F6
South Weare 400 .... D5
Spofford 750 .... C6
Springfield• 788 .... C4
Stark• 518 .... E2
Stewartstown• 1,048 .... E2
Stoddard• 622 .... C5
Strafford• 2,965 .... E5
Stratford• 927 .... D2
Stratham• 4,955 .... F5
Sugar Hill• 464 .... D3
Sullivan• 706 .... C5
Sunapee• 2,559 .... C5
Suncook 5,214 .... C5
Surry• 667 .... C5
Sutton• 1,457 .... D5
Swanzey• 6,236 .... C6
Tamworth• 2,165 .... E4
Temple• 1,194 .... D6
Thornton• 1,505 .... D4
Tilton-Northfield 3,081 .... D5
Tilton• 3,240 .... D5
Troy 2,097 .... C6
Troy• 2,131 .... C6
Tuftonboro• 1,842 .... E4
Twin Mountain 500 .... D3
Unity• 1,341 .... C5
Wakefield• 3,057 .... F4
Walpole• 3,210 .... C5
Warner• 2,250 .... D5
Warren• 820 .... D4
Washington• 628 .... C5
Waterville Valley• 151 .... D4
Weare• 6,193 .... D5
Webster• 1,405 .... D5
Wentworth• 630 .... D4
Wentworths Location 53 .... E2
West Campton 400 .... D4
West Epping 400 .... E5
West Henniker 500 .... D5
West Lebanon C4
West Milan 350 .... E2
West Rye 350 .... F6
West Stewartstown 700 .... E2
West Swanzey 1,055 .... C6
Westmoreland• 1,596 .... C6
Westville 750 .... E6
Whitefield 1,041 .... D3
Whitefield• 1,909 .... D3
Wilmot Flat 450 .... D5
Wilmot• 935 .... D5
Wilton 1,165 .... D6
Wilton• 3,122 .... D6
Winchester• 1,735 .... C6
Windham• 9,000 .... E6
Winnisquam 500 .... E5
Wolfeboro 2,783 .... E4
Wolfeboro• 4,807 .... E4
Wolfeboro Falls 600 .... E4
Woodstock• 1,167 .... D4
Woodsville▲ 1,122 .... C3

OTHER FEATURES

Adams (mt.) E3
Ammonoosuc (riv.) D3
Androscoggin (riv.) E2
Ashuelot (riv.) C6
Back (lake) E1
Baker (riv.) D4
Bearcamp (riv.) E4
Beaver (brook) E6
Belknap (mt.) E5
Blackwater (res.) D5
Blue (mt.) E2
Bond (mt.) E3
Bow (lake) E5
Cabot (mt.) E2
Cannon (mt.) D3
Cardigan (mt.) D4
Carrigain (mt.) E3
Carter Dome (mt.) E3
Chocorua (mt.) E4
Cocheco (riv.) E5
Cold (riv.) C5
Comerford (dam) D3
Connecticut (riv.) B6
Contoocook (riv.) D6
Conway (lake) E4
Crawford Notch (pass) E3
Croydon (peak) C5
Croydon Branch, Sugar (riv.) C5
Crystal (lake) E5
Cube (mt.) D4
Dixville (peak) E2
Dixville Notch (pass) E2
Edward MacDowell (res.) D6
Ellis (riv.) E3
Everett (dam) D5
Exeter (riv.) E6
First Connecticut (lake) E1
Francis (lake) E1
Franconia Notch (pass) D3
Franklin Falls (res.) D4
Gale (riv.) D3
Great (bay) F5
Halls (stream) E1
Hancock (mt.) D3
Highland (lake) C5
Hutchins (mt.) E2
Indian (stream) E1
Jefferson (mt.) E3
Kearsarge (mt.) D5
Kinsman (mt.) D3
Kinsman Notch (pass) D3
Lafayette (mt.) D3
Lamprey (riv.) E5
Liberty (mt.) D3
Lincoln (mt.) D3
Long (mt.) E2
Mad (riv.) D4
Madison (mt.) E3
Mascoma (lake) C4
Massabesic (lake) E6
Merrimack (riv.) D5
Merrymeeting (lake) E5
Mohawk (riv.) E2
Monadnock (mt.) C6
Monroe (mt.) E3
Moore (dam) D3
Moore (res.) D3
Moosilauke (mt.) D3
Nash (stream) E2
Newfound (lake) D4
North Carter (mt.) E3
North Twin (mt.) D3
Nubanusit (lake) C5
Osceola (mt.) E3
Ossipee (lake) E4
Ossipee (mts.) E4
Ossipee (riv.) F4
Passaconaway (mt.) E4
Pawtuckaway (pond) E5
Pease A.F.B. F5
Pemigewasset (riv.) D4
Perry (stream) E1
Pine (riv.) E4
Pinkham Notch (pass) E3
Piscataqua (riv.) F5
Piscataquog (riv.) D5
Presidential (range) E3
Rice (mt.) E2
Saco (riv.) E3

Agriculture, Industry and Resources

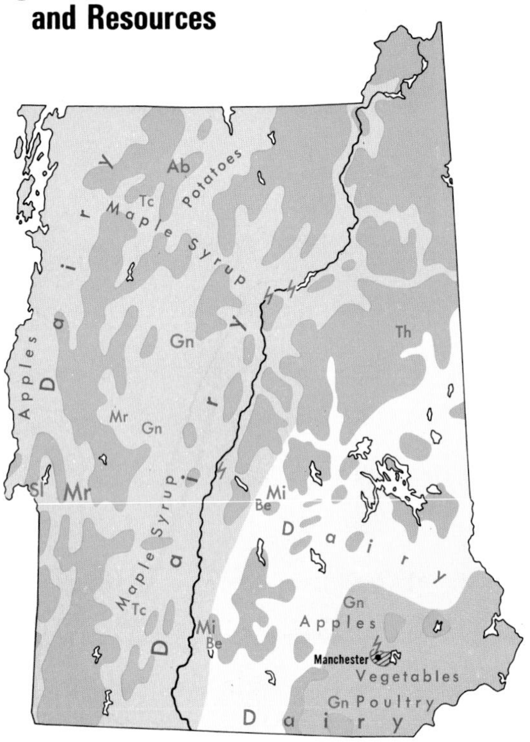
Ab
Tc
Potatoes
Maple Syrup
Dairy
Apples
Gn
Mr
Sl
Th
Mi
Be
Manchester
Vegetables
Gn Poultry
Dairy

DOMINANT LAND USE

Specialized Dairy
Dairy, General Farming
Dairy, Poultry, Mixed Farming
Forests

Water Power
Major Industrial Areas

MAJOR MINERAL OCCURRENCES

Ab Asbestos
Be Beryl
Gn Granite
Mi Mica
Mr Marble
Sl Slate
Tc Talc
Th Thorium

Saint-Gaudens Nat'l Hist. Site ... B4
Salmon Falls (riv.) ... F5
Sandwich (mt.) ... E4
Sandwich (range) ... E4
Second (lake) ... E1
Shaw (mt.) ... E4
Shoals (isls.) ... F6
Smarts (mt.) ... C4
Souhegan (riv.) ... D6
South Twin (mt.) ... D3
Squam (lake) ... E4
Starr King (mt.) ... E3
Stub Hill (mt.) ... E1
Sugar (riv.) ... C5
Sunapee (lake) ... C5
Suncook (lakes) ... E5
Suncook (riv.) ... E5
Surry Mountain (lake) ... C5
Tarleton (lake) ... D4
Tecumseh (mt.) ... D4
Third (lake) ... E1
Tom (mt.) ... E3
Umbagog (lake) ... E2
Upper Ammonoosuc (riv.) ... E2
Warner (riv.) ... D5
Washington (mt.) ... E3
Waumbek (mt.) ... E3
Wentworth (lake) ... E4
White (isl.) ... F6
White (mts.) ... E3
Whiteface (mt.) ... D4
Wild Ammonoosuc (riv.) ... D3
Wilder (dam) ... C4
Winnipesaukee (lake) ... E4
Winnipesaukee (riv.) ... D5
Winnisquam (lake) ... D4

VERMONT

COUNTIES

Addison 32,953 ... A3
Bennington 35,845 ... A6
Caledonia 27,846 ... C2
Chittenden 131,761 ... A3
Essex 6,405 ... D2
Franklin 39,980 ... B2
Grand Isle 5,318 ... A2
Lamoille 19,735 ... B2
Orange 26,149 ... C3
Orleans 24,053 ... C2
Rutland 62,142 ... A4
Washington 54,928 ... B3
Windham 41,588 ... B5
Windsor 54,055 ... B4

CITIES and TOWNS

Addison 1,023 ... A2
Albany 180 ... C2
Albany• 782 ... C2
Alburg 436 ... A1
Alburg• 1,362 ... A2
Andover• 373 ... B5
Arlington 1,311 ... A4
Arlington• 2,299 ... A5
Ascutney 274 ... C5
Averill• 7 ... D2
Bakersfield• 977 ... B1
Barnard• 872 ... B4
Barnet• 1,415 ... C2
Barre 9,482 ... C2
Barre• 7,411 ... C3
Barton 908 ... C1
Barton• 2,967 ... C2
Bartonsville 300 ... B5
Beebe Plain 500 ... C2
Beecher Falls 950 ... D1
Bellows Falls 3,313 ... C4
Belvidere• 228 ... B2
Bennington▲ 9,532 ... A5
Bennington• 16,451 ... A6
Benson• 847 ... A4
Berkshire• 1,190 ... B2
Bethel 1,866 ... B3
Bethel• 1,715 ... B4
Bloomfield• 253 ... D1
Bolton• 971 ... B3
Bomoseen 700 ... A4
Bondville 500 ... B5
Bradford 672 ... C2
Bradford• 2,522 ... C3
Braintree• 1,174 ... B4
Brandon 1,902 ... A4
Brandon• 4,223 ... A3
Brattleboro 8,612 ... B5
Brattleboro• 12,241 ... B6
Bridgewater• 895 ... B3
Bridport• 1,137 ... A4
Bristol 1,801 ... A2
Bristol• 3,762 ... A3
Brookfield• 1,089 ... B3
Brookline• 403 ... B5
Brownington• 705 ... C2
Burke• 1,406 ... D2
Burlington▲ 39,127 ... A3
Cabot 220 ... C2
Cabot• 1,043 ... C3
Calais• 1,521 ... B3
Cambridge 292 ... B2
Cambridge• 2,667 ... B2
Canaan• 1,121 ... D1
Castleton• 4,278 ... A3
Cavendish• 1,323 ... B5
Center Rutland 465 ... A4
Charlotte• 3,148 ... A3
Chelsea• 1,166 ... C3
Chester-Chester Depot 1,057 ... B4
Chester• 2,832 ... B5
Chittenden• 1,102 ... B4
Clarendon• 2,835 ... A4
Colchester• 14,731 ... A1
Concord• 1,093 ... D2
Corinth• 1,244 ... C3
Cornwall• 1,101 ... A4
Coventry• 806 ... C2
Craftsbury• 994 ... C2
Cuttingsville 200 ... B4
Danby• 1,193 ... B4
Danville• 1,917 ... C2
Derby• 4,479 ... C2
Derby (Derby Center) 684 ... C1
Derby Line 855 ... C1
Dorset• 1,918 ... A4
Duxbury• 976 ... B3
East Albany 250 ... C2
East Arlington 600 ... A5
East Barre-Graniteville ... C3
East Berkshire 200 ... B2
East Charleston 300 ... D2
East Dorset• 550 ... A5
East Dover 275 ... B6
East Hardwick 200 ... C2
East Haven• 269 ... D2
East Jamaica 200 ... B5
East Middlebury 550 ... A3
East Montpelier• 2,239 ... B2
East Poultney 450 ... A4
East Ryegate 210 ... C3
East Wallingford 500 ... B5
Eden Mills 200 ... C2
Eden• 840 ... B1
Enosburg Falls 1,350 ... B1
Essex Junction 8,396 ... A2
Essex• 16,498 ... A1
Fair Haven 2,432 ... A3
Fair Haven• 2,887 ... A4
Fairfax• 2,486 ... B1
Fairfield• 1,680 ... B2
Fairlee• 883 ... C4
Ferrisburg• 2,317 ... A3
Fletcher• 941 ... B2
Florence 250 ... A4
Forest Dale 500 ... A3
Franklin• 1,068 ... B2
Georgia• 3,753 ... A2
Georgia Center 225 ... A2
Gilman 600 ... D2
Glover• 820 ... C2
Grafton• 602 ... B5
Granby• 85 ... D2
Grand Isle• 1,642 ... A1
Graniteville-East Barre 2,189 ... B2
Granville• 309 ... B3
Greensboro• 717 ... C1
Groton• 862 ... C2
Guildhall 270 ... D1
Guilford• 1,941 ... B6
Halifax• 588 ... B6
Hancock• 340 ... B4
Hardwick 2,964 ... C2
Hardwick• 2,613 ... C2
Hartford• 9,404 ... C3
Hartland• 2,988 ... C4
Hartland Four Corners 400 ... C4
Highgate• 3,020 ... B2
Highgate Center 350 ... B2
Highgate Falls 400 ... A2
Hinesburg• 3,780 ... A3
Holland• 423 ... D2
Hubbardton• 576 ... A4
Huntington• 1,609 ... B3
Hyde Park▲ 457 ... B2
Hyde Park• 2,344 ... B2
Hydeville 500 ... A4
Ira• 426 ... A4
Irasburg• 907 ... C2
Island Pond 1,222 ... D2
Isle La Motte• 408 ... A2
Jacksonville 244 ... B6
Jamaica• 754 ... B5
Jay• 381 ... C2
Jeffersonville 462 ... B2
Jericho 1,405 ... A2
Jericho• 4,302 ... A2
Johnson 1,470 ... B2
Johnson• 3,156 ... B2
Jonesville 300 ... B3
Killington 700 ... B4
Lake Elmore 250 ... B2
Leicester• 871 ... A4
Lemington• 102 ... D2
Lincoln• 974 ... B3
Londonderry• 1,506 ... B5
Lowell• 594 ... C2
Ludlow 1,123 ... B5
Ludlow• 2,302 ... B5
Lunenburg• 1,176 ... D3
Lyndon• 5,371 ... C2
Lyndon Center ... C2
Lyndonville 1,255 ... D2
Maidstone• 131 ... D2
Manchester▲ 561 ... A5
Manchester• 3,622 ... A5
Manchester Center 1,574 ... A5
Marlboro• 924 ... B6
Marshfield 257 ... C3
Marshfield• 1,331 ... C3
Mendon• 1,049 ... B4
Middlebury▲ 6,007 ... A3
Middlebury• 8,034 ... A3
Middlesex• 1,514 ... B3
Middletown Springs• 686 ... A5
Milton 1,578 ... A2
Milton• 8,404 ... A2
Monkton 1,482 ... A3
Montgomery• 823 ... B2
Montgomery Center 400 ... B2
Montpelier▲ (cap.) 8,247 ... B3
Moretown• 1,415 ... B3
Morgan• 497 ... D2
Morristown• 4,733 ... B2
Morrisville 1,984 ... B2
Morses Line 200 ... A2
Moscow 250 ... B3
Mount Holly• 1,093 ... B5
Mount Tabor• 214 ... B5
New Haven• 1,375 ... A3
Newark• 354 ... D2
Newbury 412 ... C3
Newbury• 1,985 ... C3
Newfane▲ 164 ... B6
Newfane• 1,555 ... B6
Newport▲ 4,434 ... C2
Newport Center 250 ... C2
North Bennington 1,520 ... A6
North Clarendon 750 ... B4
North Concord 263 ... D3
North Hartland 500 ... C4
North Hero• 502 ... A2
North Hyde Park 450 ... B2
North Pomfret 400 ... B4
North Pownal 700 ... A6
North Springfield 1,200 ... B5
North Thetford 350 ... C4
North Troy 723 ... C2
North Westminster 268 ... B5
North Williston 300 ... A3
Northfield 1,889 ... B3
Northfield• 5,610 ... B3
Northfield Falls 600 ... B3
Norton• 169 ... D2
Norwich• 3,093 ... C4
Old Bennington 279 ... A6
Orange• 915 ... C3
Orleans 806 ... C2
Orwell• 1,114 ... A4
Panton• 606 ... A3
Pawlet• 1,314 ... A5
Peacham• 627 ... C3
Perkinsville 148 ... B5
Peru• 324 ... B5
Pittsfield• 389 ... B4
Pittsford• 2,919 ... A4
Plainfield 1,302 ... C3
Plainfield• 1,249 ... C3
Plymouth• 440 ... B4
Pomfret• 874 ... B4
Post Mills 500 ... C4
Poultney 1,731 ... A4
Poultney• 3,498 ... A4
Pownal• 3,485 ... A6
Pownal Center 250 ... A6
Proctor• 1,979 ... A4
Proctorsville 481 ... B5
Putney• 2,352 ... B6
Quechee 900 ... C4
Randolph 4,764 ... B4
Randolph• 4,689 ... B4
Reading• 647 ... B5
Reading (Felchville) 614 ... B5
Readsboro• 762 ... B6
Richford 1,425 ... B2
Richford• 2,178 ... B2
Richmond• 3,729 ... A3
Ripton• 444 ... A4
Riverton 250 ... B3
Rochester• 1,181 ... B4
Rockingham• 5,484 ... B5
Roxbury• 575 ... B3
Royalton• 2,389 ... B4
Rupert• 654 ... A5
Rutland▲ 18,230 ... B4
Rutland• 3,781 ... B4
Ryegate• 1,058 ... C3
Saint Albans▲ 7,339 ... A2
Saint Albans• 4,606 ... A2
Saint Albans Bay 350 ... A2
Saint George• 705 ... A2
Saint Johnsbury▲ 6,424 ... D3
Saint Johnsbury• 7,608 ... D3
Saint Johnsbury Center 400 ... D3
Salisbury• 1,024 ... A4
Sandgate• 278 ... A5
Saxtons River 541 ... B5
Searsburg• 85 ... A6
Shaftsbury• 3,368 ... A6
Sharon• 1,211 ... C4
Sheffield• 541 ... C2
Shelburne• 5,871 ... A3
Sheldon• 1,748 ... B2
Sheldon Springs 300 ... A2
Shoreham• 1,115 ... A4
Shrewsbury• 1,107 ... B4
South Barre 1,314 ... B3
South Burlington 12,809 ... A3
South Hero• 1,404 ... A2
South Londonderry 500 ... B5
South Pomfret 250 ... B4
South Royalton 700 ... C4
South Ryegate 400 ... C3
South Shaftsbury 650 ... A6
South Strafford 260 ... C4
South Woodstock 360 ... B4
Springfield 4,207 ... B5
Springfield• 9,579 ... B5
Stamford• 773 ... A6
Starksboro• 1,511 ... A3
Stockbridge• 618 ... B4
Stowe 450 ... B3
Stowe• 3,433 ... B3
Strafford• 902 ... C4
Stratton• 121 ... B5
Sudbury• 516 ... A4
Sunderland• 872 ... A5
Sutton• 854 ... C2
Swanton 2,360 ... A2
Swanton• 5,636 ... A2
Taftsville 260 ... C4
Thetford• 2,438 ... C4
Tinmouth• 455 ... A5
Topsham• 944 ... C3
Townshend• 1,019 ... B5
Troy• 1,609 ... C2
Tunbridge• 1,154 ... C4
Underhill• 2,799 ... B2
Underhill Center 575 ... B2
Vergennes 2,578 ... A3
Vernon• 1,850 ... B6
Vershire• 560 ... C4
Waitsfield• 1,422 ... B3
Walden• 703 ... C3
Wallingford 1,148 ... B5
Wallingford• 2,184 ... B5
Waltham• 454 ... A3
Wardsboro• 654 ... B5
Warren• 1,172 ... B3
Washington• 937 ... C3
Waterbury 1,702 ... B3
Waterbury• 4,589 ... B3
Waterbury Center 900 ... B3
Waterville• 532 ... B2
Websterville 700 ... B3
Wells• 902 ... A5
Wells River 424 ... C3
West Brattleboro 3,135 ... B6
West Burke 353 ... C2
West Cornwall 350 ... A4
West Danville 225 ... C3
West Dover 550 ... B6
West Fairlee• 633 ... C4
West Glover ... C2
West Hartford 300 ... C4
West Haven• 273 ... A4
West Pawlet 300 ... A5
West Rupert 300 ... A5
West Rutland 2,246 ... A4
West Rutland• 2,448 ... A4
West Townshend 500 ... B5
West Woodstock 250 ... B4
Westfield• 422 ... C2
Westford• 1,740 ... A2
Westminster 399 ... C5
Westminster• 3,026 ... C5
Westminster West 400 ... B5
Westmore• 305 ... C2
Weston• 488 ... B5
Weybridge• 749 ... A3
Wheelock• 481 ... C2
White River Junction 2,521 ... C4
Whiting• 407 ... A4
Whitingham• 1,177 ... B6
Wilder 1,576 ... C4
Williamstown• 2,839 ... B3
Williston• 4,887 ... A3
Wilmington• 1,968 ... B6
Windham• 251 ... B5
Windsor 3,714 ... C5
Windsor• 4,084 ... C5
Winooski 6,649 ... A2
Wolcott• 1,229 ... C2
Woodbury• 766 ... C3
Woodford• 331 ... A6
Woodstock▲ 1,037 ... B4
Woodstock• 3,212 ... B4
Worcester• 906 ... B3

OTHER FEATURES

Abraham (mt.) ... B3
Arrowhead Mountain (lake) ... A2
Ascutney (mt.) ... C5
Bald (mt.) ... D2
Barton (riv.) ... C2
Batten Kill (riv.) ... A5
Belvidere (mt.) ... B2
Black (riv.) ... B5
Black (riv.) ... C2
Bloodroot (mt.) ... B4
Bolton (mt.) ... B3
Bomoseen (lake) ... A4
Brandon Gap (pass) ... B4
Bread Loaf (mt.) ... A3
Bromley (mt.) ... B5
Brown's (riv.) ... A2
Burke (mt.) ... D2
Camels Hump (mt.) ... B3
Carmi (lake) ... B2
Caspian (lake) ... C2
Champlain (lake) ... A2
Chittenden (res.) ... B4
Clyde (riv.) ... C2
Comerford (dam) ... D3
Connecticut (riv.) ... C4
Crystal (lake) ... C2
Dorset (peak) ... A5
Dunmore (lake) ... A4
Echo (lake) ... D2
Ellen (mt.) ... B3
Equinox (mt.) ... A5
Fairfield (pond) ... A2
Glastenbury (mt.) ... A6
Gore (mt.) ... D2
Green (mts.) ... B4
Green River (res.) ... B2
Groton (lake) ... C3
Hardwick (lake) ... C2
Harriman (res.) ... B6
Harveys (lake) ... C3
Haystack (mt.) ... B6
Hoosic (riv.) ... A6
Hortonia (lake) ... A4
Hunger (mt.) ... B3
Iroquois (lake) ... A3
Island (pond) ... D2
Jay (peak) ... B2
Joes (brook) ... C3
Killington (peak) ... B4
Lamoille (riv.) ... A2
Lewis (creek) ... A3
Lincoln Gap (pass) ... B3
Little (riv.) ... B3
Mad (riv.) ... B3
Maidstone (lake) ... D2
Mansfield (mt.) ... B2
Memphremagog (lake) ... C1
Mettawee (riv.) ... A5
Middlebury Gap (pass) ... B4
Mill (riv.) ... B4
Missisquoi (riv.) ... B2
Mollys Falls (pond) ... C3
Moore (dam) ... D3
Moore (res.) ... D3
Moose (riv.) ... D2
Norton (pond) ... D2
Nulhegan (riv.) ... D2
Ottauquechee (riv.) ... B4
Otter (creek) ... A3
Passumpsic (riv.) ... D2
Pico (peak) ... B4
Poultney (riv.) ... A4
Saint Catherine (lake) ... A5
Salem (lake) ... C2
Seymour (lake) ... D2
Shelburne (pond) ... A3
Smugglers Notch (pass) ... B2
Snow (mt.) ... B6
Somerset (res.) ... A5
Spruce (mt.) ... C3
Stratton (mt.) ... B5
Tabor (mt.) ... B5
Trout (riv.) ... B2
Waits (riv.) ... C3
Waterbury (res.) ... B3
Wells (riv.) ... C3
West (riv.) ... B5
White (riv.) ... C4
White Face (mt.) ... B2
Wilder (dam) ... C4
Willoughby (lake) ... D2
Winooski (riv.) ... B3

▲County seat.
•Population of town or township.

AREA 7,787 sq. mi. (20,168 sq. km.)
POPULATION 7,748,634
CAPITAL Trenton
LARGEST CITY Newark
HIGHEST POINT High Point 1,803 ft. (550 m.)
SETTLED IN 1617
ADMITTED TO UNION December 18, 1787
POPULAR NAME Garden State
STATE FLOWER Purple Violet
STATE BIRD Eastern Goldfinch

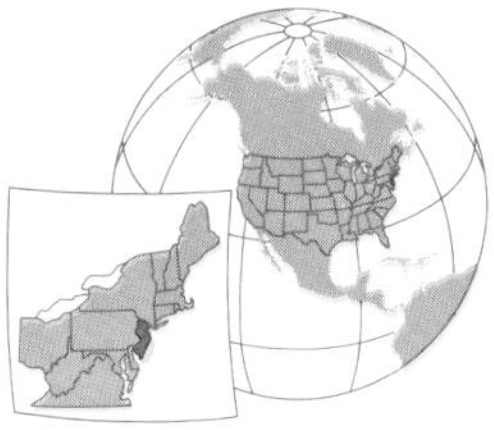

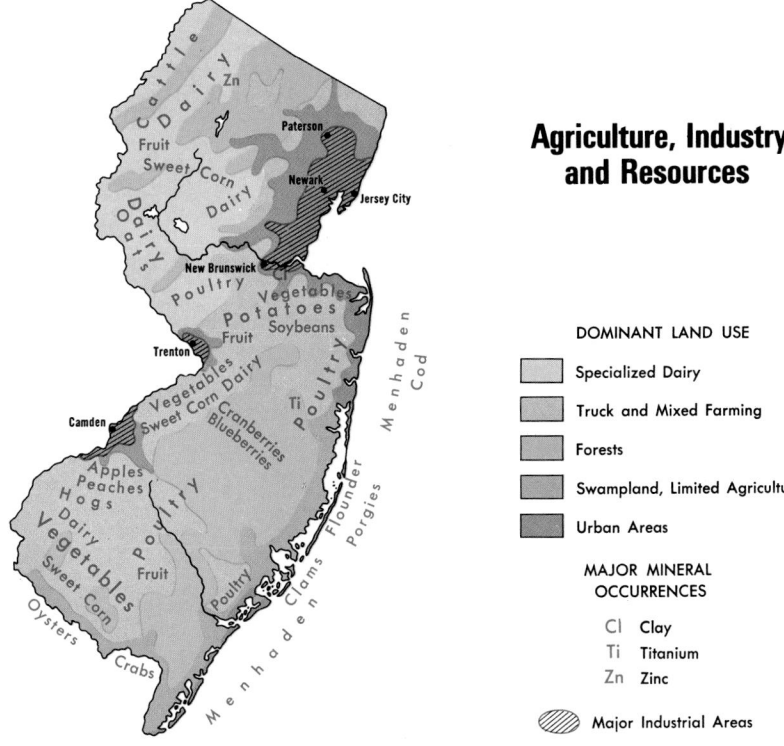

Agriculture, Industry and Resources

Cattle
Dairy
Zn
Fruit
Sweet Corn
Dairy
Oats
Paterson
Newark
Jersey City
New Brunswick
Poultry
Vegetables
Potatoes
Soybeans
Fruit
Trenton
Cl
Vegetables
Sweet Corn
Dairy
Cranberries
Blueberries
Ti
Poultry
Camden
Apples
Peaches
Hogs
Dairy
Vegetables
Sweet Corn
Fruit
Poultry
Oysters
Crabs
Menhaden
Clams
Flounder
Porgies
Menhaden
Cod

DOMINANT LAND USE

- Specialized Dairy
- Truck and Mixed Farming
- Forests
- Swampland, Limited Agriculture
- Urban Areas

MAJOR MINERAL OCCURRENCES

- Cl Clay
- Ti Titanium
- Zn Zinc

Major Industrial Areas

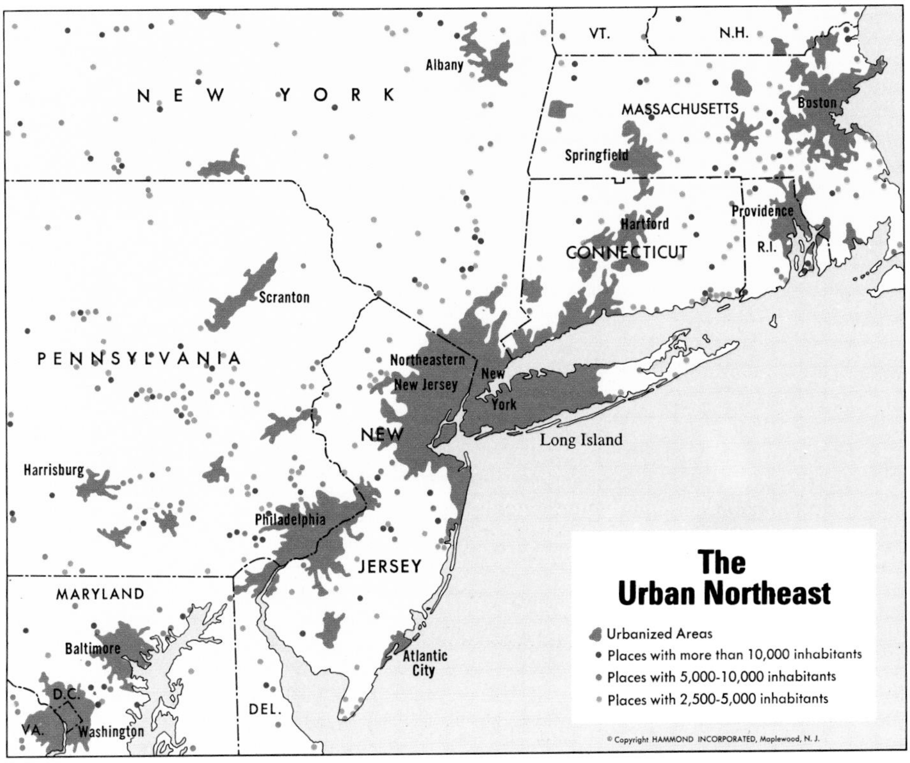

VT.
N.H.
Albany
NEW YORK
MASSACHUSETTS
Boston
Springfield
Providence
Hartford
CONNECTICUT
R.I.
Scranton
PENNSYLVANIA
Northeastern New Jersey
New York
NEW JERSEY
Long Island
Harrisburg
Philadelphia
MARYLAND
Baltimore
D.C.
VA.
Washington
DEL.
Atlantic City
The Urban Northeast
Urbanized Areas
Places with more than 10,000 inhabitants
Places with 5,000-10,000 inhabitants
Places with 2,500-5,000 inhabitants
© Copyright HAMMOND INCORPORATED, Maplewood, N. J.

COUNTIES

Atlantic 224,327 ..... D5
Bergen 825,380 ..... E2
Burlington 395,066 ..... D4
Camden 502,824 ..... D4
Cape May 95,089 ..... D5
Cumberland 138,053 ..... C5
Essex 778,206 ..... E2
Gloucester 230,082 ..... C4
Hudson 553,099 ..... E2
Hunterdon 107,776 ..... D2
Mercer 325,824 ..... D3
Middlesex 671,780 ..... E3
Monmouth 553,124 ..... E3
Morris 421,353 ..... D2
Ocean 433,203 ..... E4
Passaic 453,060 ..... E1
Salem 65,294 ..... C4
Somerset 240,279 ..... D2
Sussex 130,943 ..... D1
Union 493,819 ..... E2
Warren 91,607 ..... C2

CITIES and TOWNS

Aberdeen 17,235 ..... E3
Absecon 7,298 ..... D5
Allamuchy 600 ..... D2
Allendale 5,900 ..... B1
Allenhurst 759 ..... F3
Allentown 1,828 ..... D3
Allenwood E3
Alloway 1,371 ..... C4
Alpha 2,530 ..... C2
Alpine 1,716 ..... C1
Andover 700 ..... D2
Annandale 1,074 ..... D2
Asbury Park 16,799 ..... F3
Ashland B3
Atlantic City 37,986 ..... E5
Atlantic Highlands 4,629 ..... F3
Audubon 9,205 ..... B3
Audubon Park 1,150 ..... B3
Augusta 500 ..... D1
Aura 500 ..... C4
Avalon 1,809 ..... D5
Avenel 15,504 ..... E2
Avon By The Sea 2,165 ..... E3
Barnegat 1,160 ..... E4
Barnegat Light 675 ..... E4
Barrington 6,774 ..... B3
Basking Ridge D2
Bay Head 1,226 ..... E3
Bayonne 61,444 ..... B2
Beach Haven 1,475 ..... E4
Beach Haven Crest 500 ..... E4
Beach Haven Terrace 500 ..... E4
Beachwood 9,324 ..... E4
Bedminster• 2,469 ..... D2
Belford E3
Belle Mead D3
Belleplain 500 ..... D5
Belleville 34,213 ..... B2
Bellmawr 12,603 ..... B3
Belmar 5,877 ..... E3
Belvidere▲ 2,669 ..... C2
Bergenfield 24,458 ..... C1
Berkeley Heights• 11,980 ..... E2
Berlin 5,672 ..... D4
Bernardsville 6,597 ..... D2
Beverly 2,973 ..... D3
Blackwood 5,120 ..... C4
Blackwood Terrace C4
Blairstown• 4,360 ..... C2
Bloomfield 45,061 ..... B2
Bloomingdale 7,530 ..... E1
Bloomsbury 890 ..... C2
Bogota 7,824 ..... B2
Boonton 8,343 ..... E2
Bordentown 4,341 ..... D3
Bound Brook 9,487 ..... D2
Bradley Beach 4,475 ..... F3
Branchville 851 ..... D1
Brant Beach 500 ..... E4
Breton Woods E3
Brick• 66,473 ..... E3
Bridgeport 750 ..... C4
Bridgeton▲ 18,942 ..... C5
Bridgewater• 29,175 ..... D2
Brielle 4,406 ..... E3
Brigantine 11,354 ..... E5
Brooklawn 1,805 ..... B3
Brookside D2
Browns Mills 11,429 ..... D4
Budd Lake 7,272 ..... D2
Buena 4,441 ..... D4
Burlington 9,835 ..... D3
Butler 7,392 ..... E2
Caldwell 7,549 ..... B2
Califon 1,073 ..... D2
Camden▲ 87,492 ..... B3
Candlewood 6,750 ..... E3
Cape May 4,668 ..... D6
Cape May Court House▲ 4,426 ..... D5
Cape May Point 248 ..... D6
Carlstadt 5,510 ..... B2
Carneys Point 7,686 ..... C4
Carteret 19,025 ..... E2
Cedar Brook 600 ..... D4
Cedar Grove▲ 12,053 ..... B2
Cedar Knolls E2
Cedarville 900 ..... C5
Cedarwood Park E3
Chatham 8,007 ..... E2
Chatsworth 700 ..... D4
Cheesequake E3
Cherry Hill• 69,319 ..... B3
Chesilhurst 1,526 ..... D4
Chester 1,214 ..... D2
Chesterfield• 3,867 ..... D3
Cinnaminson• 14,583 ..... B3
Clark• 14,629 ..... A3
Clarksboro C4
Clarksburg 800 ..... E3
Clayton 6,155 ..... C4
Clementon 5,601 ..... D4
Cliffside Park 20,393 ..... C2
Cliffwood E3
Clifton 71,742 ..... B2
Clinton 2,054 ..... D2
Closter 8,094 ..... C1
Cold Spring 500 ..... D6
Collingswood 15,289 ..... B3
Cologne 800 ..... D4
Colonia 18,238 ..... E2
Colts Neck 950 ..... E3
Columbia 600 ..... C2
Columbus 800 ..... D3
Convent Station E2
Corbin City 412 ..... D5
Cranberry Lake 500 ..... D2
Cranbury 1,255 ..... E3
Cranford• 22,624 ..... E2
Cresskill 7,558 ..... C1
Dayton 4,321 ..... D3
Deal 1,179 ..... F3
Deepwater 800 ..... C4
Delanco• 3,316 ..... D3
Delran• 14,811 ..... B3
Demarest 4,800 ..... C1
Dennisville 890 ..... D5
Denville• 14,380 ..... E2
Deptford• 23,473 ..... B4
Dividing Creek 500 ..... C5
Dorchester 500 ..... D5
Dorothy 900 ..... D5
Dover 15,115 ..... D2
Dumont 17,187 ..... C1
Dunellen 6,528 ..... D2
East Brunswick• 43,548 ..... E3
East Hanover• 9,926 ..... E2
East Keansburg E3
East Millstone 950 ..... D3
East Newark 2,157 ..... B2
East Orange 73,552 ..... B2
East Rutherford 7,902 ..... B2
Eatontown 13,800 ..... E3
Edgewater 5,001 ..... C2
Edgewater Park• 8,388 ..... D3
Edison• 88,680 ..... E2
Egg Harbor City 4,583 ..... D4
Elberon F3
Elizabeth▲ 110,002 ..... B2
Elmer 1,571 ..... C4
Elmwood Park 17,623 ..... B2
Elwood 1,538 ..... D4
Emerson 6,930 ..... B1
Englewood 24,850 ..... C2
Englewood Cliffs 5,634 ..... C2
English Creek 500 ..... D5
Englishtown 1,268 ..... E3
Essex Fells 2,363 ..... B2
Estell Manor 1,404 ..... D5
Ewan 610 ..... C4
Ewing 34,185 ..... D3
Fair Haven 5,270 ..... E3
Fair Lawn 30,548 ..... B1
Fairfield• 7,615 ..... A2
Fairton 1,359 ..... C5
Fairview 10,733 ..... C2
Fanwood 7,115 ..... E2
Far Hills 657 ..... D2
Farmingdale 1,462 ..... E3
Fieldsboro 579 ..... D3
Flagtown 800 ..... D2
Flanders D2
Flemington▲ 4,047 ..... D2
Florence-Roebling 8,564 ..... D3
Florham Park 8,521 ..... E2
Folsom 2,181 ..... D4
Fords 14,392 ..... E2
Forked River 4,243 ..... E4
Fort Lee 31,997 ..... C2
Franklin 4,977 ..... D1
Franklin Lakes 9,873 ..... B1
Franklin Park• 31,358 ..... D3
Franklinville C4
Freehold▲ 10,742 ..... E3
Frenchtown 1,528 ..... C2
Garfield 26,727 ..... B2

(continued on following page)

(continued)

Garwood 4,227 ....E2
Gibbsboro 2,383 ....B4
Gibbstown 3,902 ....C4
Gilford Park 8,668 ....E4
Gillette E2
Glassboro 15,614 ....C4
Glasser D2
Glen Gardner 1,665 ....D2
Glen Ridge 7,076 ....B2
Glen Rock 10,883 ....B1
Glendora 5,201 ....B4
Glenwood 500 ....D1
Gloucester City 12,649 ....B3
Green Brook D2
Green Creek 600 ....D5
Green Pond 800 ....E1
Green Village 800 ....D2
Greenwich• 973 ....C5
Grenloch 700 ....C4
Greystone Park D2
Groveville D3
Guttenberg 8,268 ....C2
Hackensack▲ 37,049 ....B2
Hackettstown 8,120 ....D2
Haddon Heights 7,860 ....B3
Haddonfield 11,628 ....B3
Hainesport• 3,236 ....D4
Haledon 6,951 ....B1
Hamburg 2,566 ....D1
Hamilton Square-Mercerville D3
Hammonton 12,208 ....D4
Hampton 1,515 ....D2
Harrington Park 4,623 ....C1
Harrison 13,425 ....B2
Hartford 650 ....D4
Harvey Cedars 362 ....E4
Hasbrouck Heights 11,488 ....B2
Haskell A1
Haworth 3,384 ....C1
Hawthorne 17,084 ....B2
Hazlet 23,013 ....E3
Helmetta 1,211 ....E3
Hewitt 950 ....E1
Hi-Nella 1,045 ....B4
High Bridge 3,886 ....D2
Highland Lakes 4,550 ....E1
Highland Park 13,279 ....D2
Highlands 4,849 ....F3
Hightstown 5,126 ....D3
Hillsdale 9,750 ....B1
Hillside• 21,044 ....B2
Ho Ho Kus 3,935 ....B1
Hoboken 33,397 ....C2
Holmdel• 8,447 ....E3
Hopatcong 15,586 ....D2
Hopewell 1,968 ....D3
Howell• 25,065 ....E3
Huntington C2
Interlaken 910 ....E3
Ironia D2
Irvington 59,774 ....B2
Iselin 16,141 ....E2
Island Heights 1,470 ....E4
Jackson• 25,644 ....E3
Jamesburg 5,294 ....E3
Jersey City▲ 228,537 ....B2
Johnsonburg 600 ....D2
Juliustown 500 ....D3
Keansburg 11,069 ....E3
Kearny 34,874 ....B2
Keasbey E2
Kendall Park 7,127 ....D3
Kenilworth 7,574 ....E2
Keyport 7,586 ....E3
Kingston 1,047 ....D3
Kinnelon 8,470 ....E2
Kirkwood 800 ....B4
Lafayette 900 ....D1
Lake Hiawatha E2
Lake Hopatcong D2
Lake Mohawk 8,930 ....D1
Lakehurst 3,078 ....E3
Lakewood 26,095 ....E3
Lambertville 3,927 ....D3
Landisville D4
Lanoka Harbor E4
Laurel Springs 2,341 ....B4
Laurence Harbor 6,361 ....E3
Lavallette 2,299 ....E4
Lawnside 2,841 ....B3
Lawrenceville 6,446 ....D3
Layton 700 ....D1
Lebanon 1,036 ....D2
Ledgewood D2
Leeds Point 500 ....E4
Leesburg 700 ....D5
Leonardo 3,788 ....E3
Leonia 8,365 ....C2
Liberty Corner D2
Lincoln Park 10,978 ....A1
Lincroft 6,193 ....E3
Linden 36,701 ....A3
Lindenwold 18,734 ....B4
Linwood 6,866 ....D5
Little Falls• 11,294 ....B2
Little Ferry 9,989 ....B2
Little Silver 5,721 ....F3
Livingston• 26,609 ....E2
Lodi 22,355 ....B2
Long Branch 28,658 ....F3
Long Valley 1,744 ....D2
Longport 1,224 ....D5
Lumberton 600 ....D4
Lyndhurst• 18,262 ....B2
Lyons D2
Madison 15,850 ....E2
Magnolia 4,861 ....B3
Mahwah• 12,127 ....E1
Malaga 950 ....C4
Manahawkin 1,594 ....E4
Manasquan 5,369 ....E3
Mantoloking 334 ....E3
Mantua• 9,193 ....C4
Manville 10,567 ....D2
Maple Shade• 19,211 ....B3
Maplewood• 21,756 ....E2
Marcella 540 ....E2
Margate City 8,431 ....E5
Marlboro• 17,560 ....E3
Marlton 10,228 ....D4
Marmora 650 ....D5
Martinsville D2
Matawan 9,270 ....E3
Mays Landing▲ 2,090 ....D5
Maywood 9,473 ....B2
McAfee 800 ....D1
McKee City 950 ....D5
Medford D4
Medford Lakes 4,462 ....D4
Mendham 4,890 ....D2
Menlo Park E2
Mercerville-Hamilton Square 26,873 ....D3
Merchantville 4,095 ....B3
Metuchen 12,804 ....E2
Mickleton 950 ....C4
Middlesex 13,055 ....E2
Middletown• 62,298 ....E3
Midland Park 7,047 ....B1
Milford 1,273 ....C2
Millburn• 18,630 ....E2
Millington 975 ....D2
Millstone 450 ....D2
Milltown 6,968 ....E3
Millville 25,992 ....C5
Milmay 798 ....D5
Milton D1
Mine Hill• 3,325 ....D2
Minotola D4
Mizpah 900 ....D5
Monmouth Beach 3,303 ....F3
Monmouth Junction 1,570 ....D3
Monroe• 15,858 ....D1
Montague 750 ....D1
Montclair 37,729 ....B2
Montvale 6,946 ....B1
Montville• 14,290 ....E2
Moonachie 2,817 ....B2
Moorestown 13,695 ....B3
Morganville E3
Morris Plains 5,219 ....D2
Morristown▲ 16,189 ....D2
Mount Arlington 3,630 ....D2
Mount Ephraim 4,517 ....B3
Mount Freedom D2
Mount Holly 10,639 ....D4
Mount Hope D2
Mount Laurel• 17,614 ....D4
Mount Olive• 18,748 ....D2
Mount Royal 900 ....C4
Mountain Lakes 3,847 ....E2
Mountain View B2
Mountainside 6,657 ....E2
Mullica Hill 1,117 ....C4
Mystic Islands 7,400 ....E4
National Park 3,413 ....B3
Navesink E3
Neptune City 4,997 ....E3
Neshanic Station D3
Netcong 3,311 ....D2
New Brunswick▲ 41,711 ....E3
New Egypt 2,327 ....E3
New Gretna 800 ....E4
New Milford 15,990 ....B1
New Providence 11,439 ....E2
New Vernon D2
Newark▲ 275,221 ....B2
Newfield 1,592 ....D4
Newfoundland 900 ....D1
Newport 700 ....C5
Newton▲ 7,521 ....D1
Newtonville 950 ....D4
Nixon E2
North Arlington 13,790 ....B2
North Bergen• 48,414 ....B2
North Branch 610 ....D2
North Brunswick• 31,287 ....D3
North Caldwell 6,706 ....B2
North Cape May 3,574 ....C6
North Haledon 7,987 ....B1
North Plainfield 18,820 ....E2
North Wildwood 5,017 ....D6
Northfield 7,305 ....D5
Northvale 4,563 ....F1
Norwood 4,858 ....C1
Nutley 27,099 ....B2
Oak Ridge 750 ....E1
Oakhurst 4,130 ....E3
Oakland 11,997 ....B1
Oaklyn 4,430 ....B3
Ocean City 15,512 ....D5
Ocean Gate 2,078 ....E4
Ocean Grove 4,818 ....F3
Ocean View 950 ....D5
Oceanport 6,146 ....F3
Oceanville 600 ....D5
Ogdensburg 2,722 ....D1
Old Bridge 22,151 ....E3
Old Tappan 4,254 ....C1
Oradell 8,024 ....B1
Orange 29,925 ....B2
Osbornsville E3
Oxford 1,767 ....C2
Packanack Lake B1
Palermo 600 ....D5
Palisades Park 14,536 ....C2
Palmyra 7,056 ....B3
Paramus 25,067 ....B1
Park Ridge 8,102 ....B1
Parsippany-Troy Hills• 48,478 ....E2
Passaic 58,041 ....E2
Paterson▲ 140,891 ....B2
Paulsboro 6,577 ....C4
Peapack-Gladstone 2,111 ....D2
Pedricktown C4
Pemberton 1,367 ....D4
Pennington 2,537 ....D3
Penns Grove 5,228 ....C4
Pennsauken• 34,733 ....B3
Pennsville 12,218 ....C4
Pequannock• 12,844 ....B1
Perth Amboy 41,967 ....E2
Petersburg 750 ....D5
Phillipsburg 15,757 ....C2
Pine Beach 1,954 ....E4
Pine Brook E2
Pine Hill 9,854 ....D4
Piscataway• 42,223 ....D2
Pitman 9,365 ....C4
Plainfield 46,567 ....E2
Plainsboro D3
Pleasantville 16,027 ....D5
Point Pleasant 18,177 ....E3
Point Pleasant Beach 5,112 ....E3
Pomona 2,624 ....D5
Pompton Lakes 10,539 ....A1
Pompton Plains B1
Port Monmouth 3,558 ....E3
Port Morris 616 ....D2
Port Norris 1,701 ....C5
Port Reading 3,977 ....E2
Port Republic 992 ....D4
Princeton 12,016 ....D3
Princeton Junction 2,362 ....D3
Prospect Park 5,053 ....B1
Quinton 750 ....C4
Rahway 25,325 ....E2
Ralston 650 ....D2
Ramblewood 6,181 ....D4
Ramsey 13,228 ....B1
Randolph• 17,828 ....D2
Raritan 5,798 ....D2
Red Bank 10,636 ....E3
Richland 950 ....D5
Ridgefield 9,996 ....B2
Ridgefield Park 12,454 ....B2
Ridgewood 24,152 ....B1
Ringoes 682 ....D3
Ringwood 12,623 ....E1
Rio Grande 2,505 ....D5
River Edge 10,603 ....B1
River Vale• 9,410 ....B1
Riverdale 2,370 ....A1
Riverside• 7,974 ....B3
Riverton 2,775 ....B3
Robbinsville 650 ....D3
Rochelle Park• 5,587 ....B2
Rockaway 6,243 ....D2
Rockleigh 270 ....C1
Rocky Hill 693 ....D3
Roebling-Florence D3
Roosevelt 884 ....E3
Roseland 4,847 ....A2
Roselle 20,314 ....B2
Roselle Park 12,805 ....A2
Rosenhayn 1,053 ....C5
Roxbury• 18,878 ....D2
Rumson 6,701 ....F3
Runnemede 9,042 ....B3
Rutherford 17,790 ....B2
Saddle Brook• 13,296 ....B1
Saddle River 2,950 ....B1
Salem▲ 6,883 ....C4
Sayreville 34,986 ....E3
Scotch Plains• 21,160 ....E2
Sea Bright 1,693 ....F3
Sea Girt 2,099 ....E3
Sea Isle City 2,692 ....D5
Seabrook 1,457 ....C5
Seaside Heights 2,366 ....E4
Seaside Park 1,871 ....E4
Secaucus 14,061 ....B2
Sewaren 2,569 ....E2
Sewell C4
Shiloh 408 ....C5
Ship Bottom 1,352 ....E4
Shore Acres E3
Short Hills E2
Shrewsbury 3,096 ....E3
Sicklerville D4
Singac B2
Skillman D3
Smithburg 750 ....E3
Somerdale 5,440 ....B4
Somers Point 11,216 ....D5
Somerville▲ 11,632 ....D2
South Amboy 7,863 ....E3
South Belmar 1,482 ....E3
South Bound Brook 4,185 ....E2
South Brunswick• 17,127 ....E3
South Orange• 16,390 ....A2
South Plainfield 20,489 ....E2
South River 13,692 ....E3
South Seaville 600 ....D5
South Toms River 3,869 ....E4
Sparta• 13,333 ....D1
Spotswood 7,983 ....E3
Spring Lake 3,499 ....F3
Spring Lake Heights 5,341 ....E3
Springfield• 13,420 ....E2
Stanhope 3,393 ....D2
Stanton 700 ....D2
Stewartsville 950 ....C2
Stirling E2
Stockholm D1
Stockton 629 ....D3
Stone Harbor 1,025 ....D5
Stratford 7,614 ....B4
Strathmore 7,060 ....E3
Succasunna 10,931 ....D2
Summit 19,757 ....E2
Surf City 1,375 ....E4
Sussex 2,201 ....D1
Swedesboro 2,024 ....C4
Teaneck• 37,825 ....B2
Tenafly 13,326 ....C1
Teterboro 22 ....B2
Thorofare B4
Three Bridges 750 ....D2
Tinton Falls 12,361 ....E3
Titusville 900 ....D3
Toms River▲ 7,524 ....E4
Totowa 10,177 ....B1
Towaco E2
Townsends Inlet D5
Trenton (cap.)▲ 88,675 ....D3
Tuckerton 3,048 ....E4
Turnersville 3,843 ....C4
Union Beach 6,156 ....E3

Topography

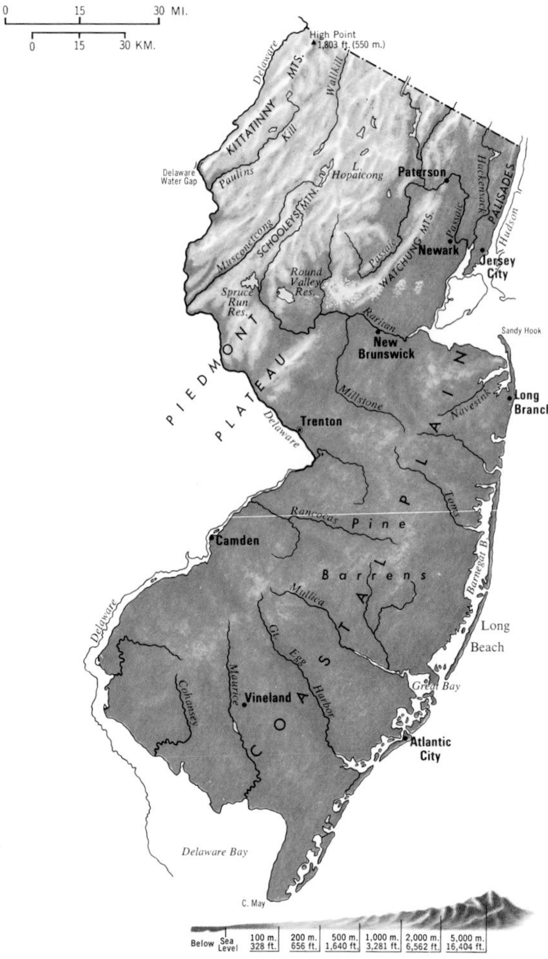

0 15 30 MI.
0 15 30 KM.
High Point 1,803 ft. (550 m.)
Delaware
KITTATINNY MTS.
Wallkill
Kill
Delaware Water Gap
Paulins
L. Hopatcong
Paterson
Hackensack
PALISADES
Hudson
Musconetcong
SCHOOLEYS MTN.
WATCHUNG MTS.
Passaic
Newark
Jersey City
Round Valley Res.
Spruce Run Res.
Raritan
Sandy Hook
New Brunswick
PIEDMONT PLATEAU
Millstone
Navesink
Long Branch
Trenton
Delaware
COASTAL PLAIN
Toms
Rancocas
Pine
Camden
Barrens
Barnegat B.
Mullica
Long Beach
Gt. Egg Harbor
Maurice
Cohansey
Vineland
Great Bay
Atlantic City
Delaware Bay
C. May
Below Sea Level
100 m. 328 ft.
200 m. 656 ft.
500 m. 1,640 ft.
1,000 m. 3,281 ft.
2,000 m. 6,562 ft.
5,000 m. 16,404 ft.

Union City 58,012 ....C2
Union• 50,024 ....A2
Upper Greenwood Lake 2,734 ....E1
Upper Saddle River 7,198 ....B1
Vauxhall A2
Ventnor City 11,005 ....E5
Vernon 800 ....E1
Verona 13,597 ....B2
Villas 8,136 ....D5
Vincentown 900 ....D4
Vineland 54,780 ....C5
Voorhees• 12,919 ....B3
Waldwick 9,757 ....B1
Wall• 18,952 ....E3
Wallington 10,828 ....B2
Wanamassa 4,530 ....E3
Wanaque 9,711 ....B1
Waretown 1,283 ....E4
Warren• 9,805 ....D2
Washington 6,474 ....D2
Watchung 5,110 ....E2
Waterford Works 950 ....D4
Wayne• 47,025 ....A1
Weehawken• 12,385 ....C2
Wenonah 2,331 ....C4
West Berlin D4
West Caldwell 10,422 ....A2
West Cape May 1,026 ....D6
West Creek 827 ....E4
West Deptford• 18,002 ....B3
West Long Branch 7,690 ....F3
West Milford 25,430 ....E1
West New York 38,125 ....C2
West Orange 39,103 ....A2
West Paterson 10,982 ....B2
West Trenton D3
West Wildwood 453 ....D6
Westfield 28,870 ....E2
Westmont 15,875 ....B3
Westville 4,573 ....B3
Westwood 10,446 ....B1
Wharton 5,405 ....D2
Whippany E2
White House Station 1,287 ....D2
White Meadow Lake 8,002 ....D2
Whitehouse 852 ....D2
Whitesboro 1,583 ....D5
Whitesville 600 ....E3
Whiting 750 ....E4
Wickatunk 950 ....E3
Wildwood 4,484 ....D6
Wildwood Crest 3,631 ....D6
Williamstown 10,891 ....D4
Willingboro• 36,291 ....D3
Winfield• 1,785 ....B2
Winslow 950 ....D4
Wood-Lynne 2,578 ....B3
Wood-Ridge 7,506 ....B2
Woodbine 2,678 ....D5
Woodbridge• 90,074 ....E2
Woodbury Heights 3,392 ....B4
Woodbury▲ 10,904 ....B4
Woodcliff Lake 5,303 ....B1
Woodport D2
Woodstown 3,154 ....C4
Wrightstown 3,843 ....D3
Wyckoff• 15,372 ....B1
Yardville 9,414 ....D3

OTHER FEATURES

Absecon (inlet) E5
Alloways (creek) C4
Arthur Kill (str.) B3
Atlantic Highlands (ridge) E3
Barnegat (bay) E4
Batsto (riv.) D4
Bayonne Military Ocean Terminal B2
Beach Haven (inlet) E4
Beaver (brook) C2
Ben Davis (pt.) C5
Big Flat (brook) D1
Big Timber (creek) C4
Boonton (res.) E2
Brigantine (inlet) E5
Budd (lake) D2
Canistear (res.) E1
Cedar (creek) E4
Clinton (res.) E1
Cohansey (riv.) C5
Cooper (riv.) B3
Corson (inlet) D5
Crosswicks (creek) D3
Culvers (lake) D1
Delaware (bay) C5
Delaware (riv.) D3
Delaware Water Gap Nat'l Rec. Area C1
Earle Naval Weapons Sta. E3
Echo (lake) E1
Edison Nat'l Hist. Site A2
Egg Island (pt.) C5
Fort Dix 10,205 ....D3
Fort Hancock F3
Fort Monmouth E3
Gateway Nat'l Rec. Area E2
Great (bay) E4
Great Egg Harbor (inlet) E5
Greenwood (lake) E1
Hackensack (riv.) C1
Hereford (inlet) D5
High Point (mt.) D1
Hopatcong (lake) D2
Hudson (riv.) C1
Island (beach) E4
Kill Van Kull (str.) B2
Kittatinny (mts.) D1
Lakehurst Naval Air-Engineering Center E3
Lamington (riv.) D2
Landing (creek) D4
Little Egg (harb.) E4
Lockatong (creek) C3
Long (beach) E4
Long Beach (isl.) E4
Lower New York (bay) E2
Manasquan (riv.) E3
Manumuskin (riv.) D5
Maurice (riv.) C4
May (cape) C6
McGuire A.F.B. 7,580 ....D3
Metedeconk (riv.) E3
Mill (creek) E4
Millstone (riv.) D3
Mohawk (lake) D1
Morristown Nat'l Hist. Park D2
Mullica (riv.) D4
Musconetcong (riv.) C2
Navesink (riv.) E3
Newark (bay) B2
Oak Ridge (res.) D1
Oldmans (creek) C4
Oradell (res.) B1
Oswego (riv.) E4
Owassa (lake) D1
Palisades (cliffs) C1
Passaic (riv.) E2
Paulins Kill (riv.) D1
Pennsauken (creek) B3
Pequest (riv.) D2
Picatinny Arsenal D2
Pohatcong (creek) C2
Pompton (lake) B1
Raccoon (creek) C4
Ramapo (riv.) E1
Rancocas (creek) D3
Raritan (bay) E3
Raritan (riv.) D2
Ridgeway Branch, Toms (riv.) E3
Round Valley (res.) D2
Saddle (riv.) B1
Salem (riv.) C4
Sandy Hook (split) F3
Shoal Branch, Wading (riv.) D4
Spruce Run (res.) D2
Statue of Liberty Nat'l Mon. B2
Stony (brook) D3
Stow (creek) C5
Swartswood (lake) D1
Tappan (lake) C1
The Narrows (str.) E2
Toms (riv.) E3
Townsend (inlet) D5
Tuckahoe (riv.) D5
Union (lake) C5
Upper New York (bay) B2
Wading (riv.) D4
Wallkill (riv.) D1
Wanaque (res.) E1
Wawayanda (lake) E1

▲County Seat
•Population of town or township

New Jersey
SCALE
0 5 10 15 20 MI.
0 5 10 15 20 KM.
State Capitals
County Seats
Canals
Major Limited Access Hwys.
Copyright HAMMOND INCORPORATED, Maplewood, N. J.
Longitude 75° West of Greenwich
PENNSYLVANIA
NEW YORK
DELAWARE
MARYLAND
ATLANTIC OCEAN
DELAWARE BAY
SUSSEX
WARREN
MORRIS
PASSAIC
BERGEN
ESSEX
HUDSON
UNION
HUNTERDON
SOMERSET
MIDDLESEX
MERCER
MONMOUTH
OCEAN
BURLINGTON
CAMDEN
GLOUCESTER
SALEM
CUMBERLAND
ATLANTIC
CAPE MAY
TRENTON
Newark
Jersey City
Paterson
Elizabeth
Camden
Atlantic City
New Brunswick
Perth Amboy
Philadelphia
Wilmington
New York
Port Jervis
High Point 1,803 ft. (550 m.)
DELAWARE WATER GAP NATIONAL RECREATION AREA
Long Island
Sandy Hook
Cape May
Cape May Inlet
Barnegat Bay
Great Egg Harbor Inlet
Little Egg Inlet
Brigantine Inlet
Absecon Inlet
Hereford Inlet
Townsends Inlet
Corson Inlet
Barnegat Inlet
Beach Haven Inlet
PALISADES INTERSTATE PKWY.
GARDEN STATE PKWY.
N.J. TPK.
ATLANTIC CITY EXPWY.
N.E. EXT. PA. TPK.
PENNSYLVANIA TPK.
STATUE OF LIBERTY NAT'L MON.
GATEWAY NAT'L REC. AREA
LAKEHURST NAV. AIR ENG. CTR.
FT. DIX
McGUIRE A.F.B.
PICATINNY ARSENAL
MORRISTOWN NAT'L HIST. PARK
EDISON NAT'L HIST. SITE
EARLE NAV. WEAPONS STA.
FT. MONMOUTH
FT. HANCOCK
CAPE MAY COAST GUARD CENT.

COUNTIES

Bernalillo 480,577 ... C4
Catron 2,563 ... A4
Chaves 57,849 ... E5
Cibola 23,794 ... A4
Colfax 12,925 ... E2
Curry 42,207 ... F4
De Baca 2,454 ... E4
Dona Ana 135,510 ... C6
Eddy 48,605 ... E6
Grant 27,676 ... A5
Guadalupe 4,156 ... E4
Harding 987 ... F3
Hidalgo 5,958 ... A7
Lea 55,765 ... F6
Lincoln 12,219 ... D5
Los Alamos 18,115 ... C3
Luna 18,110 ... B6
McKinley 60,686 ... A3
Mora 4,264 ... E3
Otero 51,928 ... D6
Quay 10,823 ... F3
Rio Arriba 34,365 ... B2
Roosevelt 16,702 ... F4
San Juan 91,605 ... A2
San Miguel 25,743 ... D3
Sandoval 34,799 ... C3
Santa Fe 98,928 ... C3
Sierra 9,912 ... B5
Socorro 14,764 ... C5
Taos 23,118 ... D2
Torrance 10,285 ... D4
Union 4,124 ... F2
Valencia 45,235 ... A4

CITIES and TOWNS

Abiquiu 500 ... C2
Acoma 150 ... B4
Acomita (Pueblo of Acoma) 975 ... B3
Alameda ... C3
Alamogordo▲ 27,596 ... C6
Albuquerque▲ 384,736 ... C3
Alcalde 308 ... C2
Algodones 195 ... C3
Allison ... A3
Alma 120 ... A5
Alto 285 ... D5
Amalia 200 ... D2
Animas 75 ... A7
Anthony 5,160 ... C6
Anton Chico 400 ... D3
Arrey 367 ... B6
Arroyo Hondo 400 ... D2
Arroyo Seco 500 ... D2
Artesia 10,610 ... E6
Aztec▲ 5,479 ... B2
Bayard 2,598 ... A6
Belen 6,547 ... C4
Bent 294 ... D5
Berino 600 ... C6
Bernalillo▲ 5,960 ... C3
Blanco 200 ... B2
Bloomfield 5,214 ... A2
Bluewater 300 ... A3
Bosque 3,791 ... C4
Bosque Farms ... C4
Buckhorn 85 ... A5
Buena Vista 178 ... D3
Caballo 225 ... B6
Canjilon 380 ... C2
Canones 300 ... C2
Capitan 842 ... D5
Capulin 100 ... F2
Carlsbad▲ 24,952 ... E6
Carrizozo▲ 1,075 ... D5
Casa Blanca 560 ... B4
Cebolla 100 ... C2
Cedar Crest 600 ... C3
Cedar Hill 145 ... B2
Central 1,835 ... A6
Cerrillos 500 ... D3
Cerro 400 ... D2
Chacon 310 ... D2
Chama 1,048 ... C2
Chamberino 700 ... C6
Chamisal 272 ... D2
Chilili 80 ... C4
Chimayo 2,789 ... D3
Cimarron 774 ... E2
Clayton▲ 2,484 ... F2
Cleveland 450 ... D2
Cliff 600 ... A6
Cloudcroft 636 ... D6
Clovis▲ 30,954 ... F4
Cochiti 434 ... C3
Columbus 641 ... B7
Conchas Dam 240 ... E3
Cordova 750 ... D2
Corona 215 ... D4
Corrales 5,453 ... C3
Costilla 400 ... D2
Coyote 125 ... C2
Crownpoint 2,108 ... A3
Crystal 200 ... A2
Cuba 760 ... B2
Cubero 300 ... B3
Cuervo 80 ... E3
Cundiyo 200 ... D3
Datil 150 ... B4
Deming▲ 10,970 ... B6
Derry 175 ... B6
Des Moines 168 ... F2
Dexter 898 ... E5
Dilia 100 ... D3
Dixon 800 ... D2
Dona Ana 1,202 ... C6
Dora 167 ... F5
Dulce 2,438 ... B2
Duran 90 ... D4
Eagle Nest 189 ... D2
Edgewood 3,324 ... C3
El Porvenir 150 ... D3
El Prado 200 ... D2
El Rito 475 ... C2
Elephant Butte 500 ... B5
Elida 201 ... F5
Embudo 400 ... C2
Encino 131 ... D4

New Mexico
SCALE
0 5 10 20 30 40 50 60 MI.
0 5 10 20 30 40 50 60 KM.
State Capitals
County Seats
Major Limited Access Hwys.
© Copyright HAMMOND INCORPORATED, Maplewood, N. J.

Espanola 8,389 C3
Estancia▲ 792 D4
Eunice 2,676 F6
Fairacres 700 C6
Farmington 33,997 A2
Faywood 100 B6
Fence Lake 150 A4
Fierro 200 A6
Flora Vista 1,021 A2
Floyd 117 F4
Folsom 71 F2
Fort Bayard 400 A6
Fort Stanton 80 D5
Fort Sumner▲ 1,269 E4
Fort Wingate 800 A3
Fruitland 800 A2
Galisteo 125 D3
Gallina 420 C2
Gallup▲ 19,154 A3
Gamerco 800 A3
Garfield 600 B6
Garita 66 E3
Gila 350 A6
Glencoe 125 D5
Glenwood 220 A5
Glorieta 300 D3
Golden 100 C3
Grady 110 F4
Grants▲ 8,626 B3
Guadalupita 300 D2
Hachita 75 A7
Hagerman 961 E5
Hanover 300 A6
Hatch 1,136 B6
Hernandez 500 C2
High Rolls-Mountain Park 555 D5
Hillsboro 175 B6
Hobbs 29,115 F6
Holman 400 D2
Hondo 425 D5
Hope 101 E6
Hot Springs▲ (Truth or Consequences) 6,221 B5
House 85 F4
Humble City 65 F6
Hurley 1,534 A6
Ilfeld 68 D3
Isleta 1,703 C4
Jal 2,156 F6
Jarales 700 C4
Jemez Pueblo 1,301 C3
Jemez Springs 413 C3
Kenna 100 F5
Kirtland 3,552 A2
La Cueva 200 D3
La Jara 210 B2
La Luz 1,625 C6
La Madera 200 C2
La Mesa 900 C6
La Plata 150 A2
La Union 200 C7
Laguna 434 B3
Lajoya 97 C4
Lake Arthur 336 E5
Lamy 66 D3
Las Cruces▲ 62,126 C6
Las Vegas▲ 14,753 D3
Ledoux 300 D3
Lemitar 800 B4
Lincoln 100 D5
Lindrith 349 C2
Llano 325 D2
Loco Hills 375 F6
Logan 870 F3
Lordsburg▲ 2,951 A6
Los Alamos▲ 11,455 C3
Los Lunas▲ 6,013 C4
Los Ojos C2
Los Ranchos de Albuquerque 3,955 C3
Loving 1,243 E6
Lovington▲ 9,322 F6
Lumberton 175 C2
Luna 200 A5
Magdalena 861 B4
Malaga 300 E6
Manuelito 200 A3
Manzano 65 C4
Maxwell 247 E2
Mayhill 300 D6
McAlister 320 F4
McDonald 65 F5
McIntosh 325 D4
Meadow Vista 3,377 C7
Melrose 662 F4
Mentmore 315 A3
Mescalero 1,159 D5
Mesilla 1,975 C6
Mesilla Park C6
Mesquite 500 C6
Mexican Springs 242 A3
Miami 112 E2
Milan 1,911 B3
Mimbres 300 B6
Montezuma 250 D3
Monticello 125 B5
Monument 300 F6
Mora▲ D3
Moriarty 1,399 D4
Mosquero▲ 164 F3
Mountainair 926 C4
Mule Creek 62 A5
Nambe 1,246 D3
Nara Visa 250 F3
Navajo 1,985 A3
New Laguna 250 B4
Newcomb 388 A2
Newkirk 54 E3
Nogal 150 D5
Ocate 75 E2
Oil Center 236 F6
Ojo Caliente 600 D2
Ojo Feliz 133 E2
Ojo Sarco 380 D2
Organ 300 C6
Orogrande 80 D6
Otis 200 E6
Paguate 492 B3
Pecos 1,012 D3
Pena Blanca 300 C3
Penasco 648 D2
Peralta 3,182 C4
Petaca 84 C2
Picacho 100 D5
Pie Town 90 A4
Pinos Altos 250 A6
Placitas 1,611 C3
Pleasanton 70 A5
Pojoaque 1,037 C3
Ponderosa 300 C3
Portales▲ 10,690 F4
Prewitt 300 B3
Puerto de Luna 175 E4
Questa 1,707 D2
Radium Springs 150 B6
Rainsville 350 D2
Ramah 574 A3
Ranchos de Taos 1,779 D2
Raton▲ 7,372 E2

AREA 121,593 sq. mi. (314,926 sq. km.)
POPULATION 1,521,779
CAPITAL Santa Fe
LARGEST CITY Albuquerque
HIGHEST POINT Wheeler Pk. 13,161 ft. (4011 m.)
SETTLED IN 1605
ADMITTED TO UNION January 6, 1912
POPULAR NAME Land of Enchantment
STATE FLOWER Yucca
STATE BIRD Road Runner

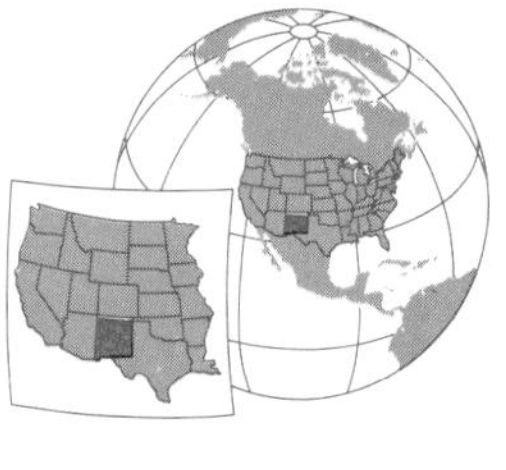

Red River 387 D2
Regina 80 B2
Rehoboth 200 A3
Reserve▲ 319 A5
Ribera 84 D3
Rincon 300 C6
Rio Rancho 32,505 C3
Rociada 140 D3
Rodarte 650 D2
Rodeo 200 A7
Roswell▲ 44,654 E5
Rowe 290 D3
Roy 362 E3
Ruidoso 4,600 D5
Ruidoso Downs 920 D5
Rutheron 95 C2
Salem 400 B6
San Acacia 286 B4
San Antonio 359 B5
San Cristobal 350 D2
San Felipe Pueblo 1,557 C3
San Fidel 150 B3
San Ildefonso 447 C3
San Jon 277 F3
San Jose 150 D3
San Juan Pueblo 4,107 C2
San Lorenzo 200 B6
San Mateo 200 B3
San Miguel 400 C6
San Patricio 300 D5
San Rafael 300 A3
San Ysidro 233 C3
Sandia Park 450 C3
Santa Cruz 2,504 D2
Santa Fe (cap.)▲ 55,859 C3
Santa Rita 600 B6
Santa Rosa▲ 2,263 E4
Santo Domingo Pueblo 2,866 C3
Sapello 600 D3
Seboyeta 125 B3
Sedan 60 F2
Sena 150 D3
Serafina 225 D3
Sherman 100 B6
Shiprock 7,687 A2
Silver City▲ 10,683 A6
Socorro▲ 8,159 C4
Soham 104 D3
Solano 114 E3
Springer 1,262 E2
Sunspot 78 D6
Taiban 120 F4
Tajique 145 C4
Taos Pueblo 1,187 D2
Taos▲ 4,065 D2
Tatum 768 F5
Tesuque 1,490 C3
Texico 966 F4
Thoreau 1,099 A3
Tierra Amarilla▲ 850 C2
Tijeras 340 C3
Tinnie 100 D5
Toadlena 200 A2
Tohatchi 661 A3
Tome 500 C4
Torreon 200 C4
Trampas 76 D2
Trementina 80 E3
Tres Piedras 200 D2
Truchas 275 D2
Trujillo 148 E3
Truth or Consequences▲ 6,221 B5
Tucumcari▲ 6,831 F3
Tularosa 2,615 C5
Tyrone 100 A6
University Park 4,520 C6
Ute Park 67 D2
Vadito 283 D2
Vado 325 C6
Valdez 300 D2
Valencia 3,917 C4
Vallecitos 450 C2
Vanadium 150 A6
Vaughn 633 D4
Velarde 950 D2
Vermejo Park 85 D2
Villanueva 500 D3
Virden 108 A6
Wagon Mound 319 E2
Waterflow 475 A2
Watrous 175 D3
White Horse Lake B3
White Rock 6,192 C3
White Sands Missile Range 2,616 C6
Willard 183 D4
Williamsburg 456 B5
Yeso 200 E4
Youngsville 125 C2
Zia Pueblo 637 C3
Zuni 5,551 A3

OTHER FEATURES

Abiquiu (res.) C2
Alamosa (riv.) B5
Animas (riv.) B1
Avalon (res.) E6
Aztec Ruins Nat'l Mon. A2
Baldy (peak) D3
Bandelier Nat'l Mon. C3
Big Burro (mts.) A6
Black (mt.) A6
Black (range) B5
Blanco (creek) F4
Bluewater (creek) B4
Bluewater (creek) D6
Bluewater (lake) A3
Boulder (lake) C2
Brazos (peak) C2
Burford (lake) C2
Caballo (res.) B6
Canadian (riv.) F3
Cannon A.F.B. 3,312 F4
Canyon Blanco (creek) B2
Capitan (mts.) D5
Capitan (peak) D5
Capulin Volcano Nat'l Mon. E2
Carlsbad Caverns Nat'l Park E6
Carrizo (creek) F2
Chaco (mesa) B3
Chaco (riv.) A2
Chaco Culture Nat'l Hist. Park B2
Chico Arroyo (creek) B3
Chivato (mesa) B3
Chupadera (mesa) C5
Chuska (mts.) A2
Cimarron (riv.) E2
Colorado, Arroyo (riv.) B4
Compañero, Arroyo (creek) B2
Conchas (lake) E3
Conchas (riv.) E3
Cookes (range) B6
Corrumpa (creek) F2
Costilla (peak) D2
Cuchillo Negro (creek) B5
Cuervo (creek) E3
Dark Canyon (creek) E6
Datil (mts.) B4
Dry Cimarron (riv.) F2
Eagle Nest (lake) D2
Elephant Butte (res.) B5
El Morro Nat'l Mon. A3
El Rito (riv.) C2
Fifteenmile Arroyo (creek) D4
Florida (mts.) B7
Fort Bliss Mil. Res. C6
Fort Union Nat'l Mon. E3
Gallinas (mts.) B4
Gallinas (riv.) E3
Gila (riv.) A6
Gila Cliff Dwellings Nat'l Mon. A5
Grouse (mt.) A5
Guadalupe (mts.) D6
Hatchet (mts.) A7
Holloman A.F.B. 5,891 C6
Hueco (mts.) D6
Jemez (riv.) C3
Jemez Canyon (res.) C3
Jicarilla Ind. Res. B2
Jornada del Muerto (valley) C5
Kirtland A.F.B. C3
Ladron (mts.) B4
La Plata (riv.) A1
Lake Avalon (res.) E6
Largo, Cañon (creek) B2
Las Animas (creek) B5
Llano Estacado (Staked) (plain) F5
Lucero (lake) C6
Macho, Arroyo del (creek) D5
Magdalena (mts.) B4
Manzano (mts.) C4
Manzano (peak) C4
McMillan (lake) E6
Mescalero (ridge) F6
Mescalero (valley) F5
Mescalero Apache Ind. Res. D5
Mimbres (mts.) B6
Mimbres (riv.) B6
Mogollon (mts.) A5
Mogollon Baldy (peak) A5
Montosa (mesa) E3
Mora (riv.) E3
Nacimiento (mts.) C3
Nacimiento (peak) C2
Navajo (res.) B2
Navajo Ind. Res. A2
North Truchas (peak) D3
Ocate (creek) E2
O'Keeffe Nat'l Hist. Site C2
Oscura (mts.) C5
Osha (peak) C4
Padilla (creek) D5
Pajarito (creek) A2
Pecos (riv.) E5
Pecos Nat'l Mon. D3
Peloncillo (mts.) A6
Perro (lake) D4
Pinos, Rio de los (riv.) B2
Pintada Arroyo (creek) E4
Playas (lake) A7
Potrillo (mts.) B7
Pueblo Ind. Res. B4
Pueblo Ind. Res. C4
Pueblo Ind. Res. C2
Pueblo Ind. Res. D3
Puerco (riv.) A3
Red Bluff (lake) E7
Revuelto (creek) F3
Rio Brazos (riv.) C2
Rio Chama (riv.) C2
Rio Felix (riv.) E5
Rio Grande (riv.) C5
Rio Hondo (riv.) E5
Rio Penasco (riv.) E6
Rio Puerco (riv.) C4
Rio Salado (riv.) B4
Rocky (mts.) C1
Sacramento (mts.) D6
Salinas Pueblo Missions Nat'l Mon. C4
Salt (creek) E5
Salt (lake) F4
San Agustin (plains) B5
San Andres (mts.) C6
San Antonio (peak) C2
Sandia (peak) C3
San Francisco (riv.) A5
Sangre de Cristo (mts.) D3
San Jose (riv.) B3
San Juan (riv.) B2
San Mateo (mts.) B5
Seven Rivers (riv.) E6
Ship Rock (peak) A2
Sierra Blanca (peak) C5
Staked (Llano Estacado) (plain) F5
Sumner (lake) E4
Taylor (mt.) B3
Tecolote (creek) D3
Tequesquite (creek) E2
Thompson (peak) D3
Tierra Blanca (creek) B6
Tramperos (creek) F2
Tularosa (valley) C6
Ute (creek) F3
Ute (peak) D2
Ute (res.) F3
Ute Mountain Ind. Res. A1
Vermejo (riv.) E2
Wheeler (peak) D2
White Sands (des.) C5
White Sands Missile Range C5
White Sands Nat'l Mon. C6
Whitewater Baldy (mt.) A5
Wingate Army Depot A3
Yeso (creek) E4
Zuni (mts.) A3
Zuni (riv.) A3
Zuni-Cibola Nat'l Hist. Park A3
Zuni Ind. Res. A3

▲County seat

Topography

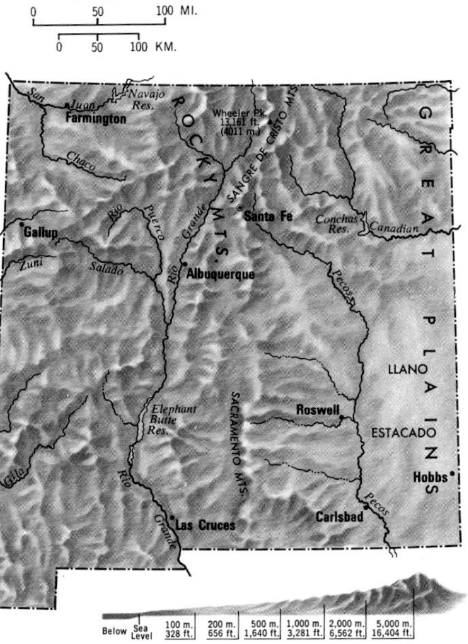
0 50 100 MI.
0 50 100 KM.
Navajo Res.
San Juan
Farmington
Wheeler Pk. 13,161 ft. (4011 m.)
ROCKY MTS.
SANGRE DE CRISTO MTS.
GREAT PLAINS
Chaco
Gallup
Rio Puerco
Rio Grande
Santa Fe
Conchas Res.
Canadian
Zuni
Salado
Albuquerque
Pecos
LLANO
ESTACADO
Elephant Butte Res.
SACRAMENTO MTS.
Roswell
Hobbs
Gila
Las Cruces
Carlsbad
Below Sea Level
100 m. 328 ft.
200 m. 656 ft.
500 m. 1,640 ft.
1,000 m. 3,281 ft.
2,000 m. 6,562 ft.
5,000 m. 16,404 ft.

Agriculture, Industry and Resources

DOMINANT LAND USE

- Wheat, Grain Sorghums, Range Livestock
- General Farming, Livestock, Special Crops
- General Farming, Livestock, Cash Grain
- Dry Beans, General Farming
- Cotton, Forest Products
- Range Livestock
- Forests
- Nonagricultural Land

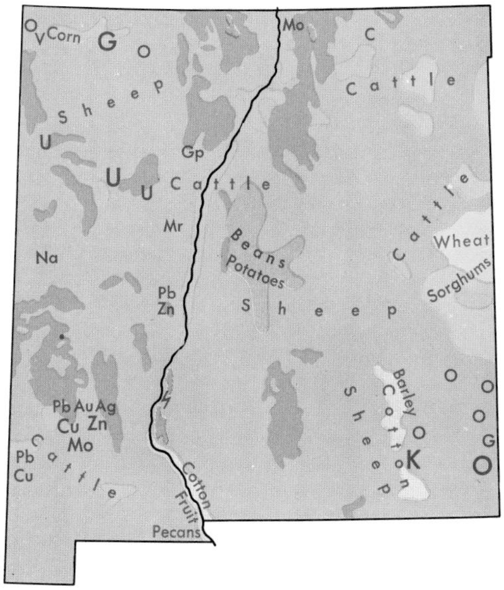
Corn
Sheep
Cattle
Wheat
Sorghums
Beans
Potatoes
Barley
Cotton
Fruit
Pecans

MAJOR MINERAL OCCURRENCES

Ag Silver
Au Gold
C Coal
Cu Copper
G Natural Gas
Gp Gypsum
K Potash
Mo Molybdenum
Mr Marble
Na Salt
O Petroleum
Pb Lead
U Uranium
V Vanadium
Zn Zinc
Water Power

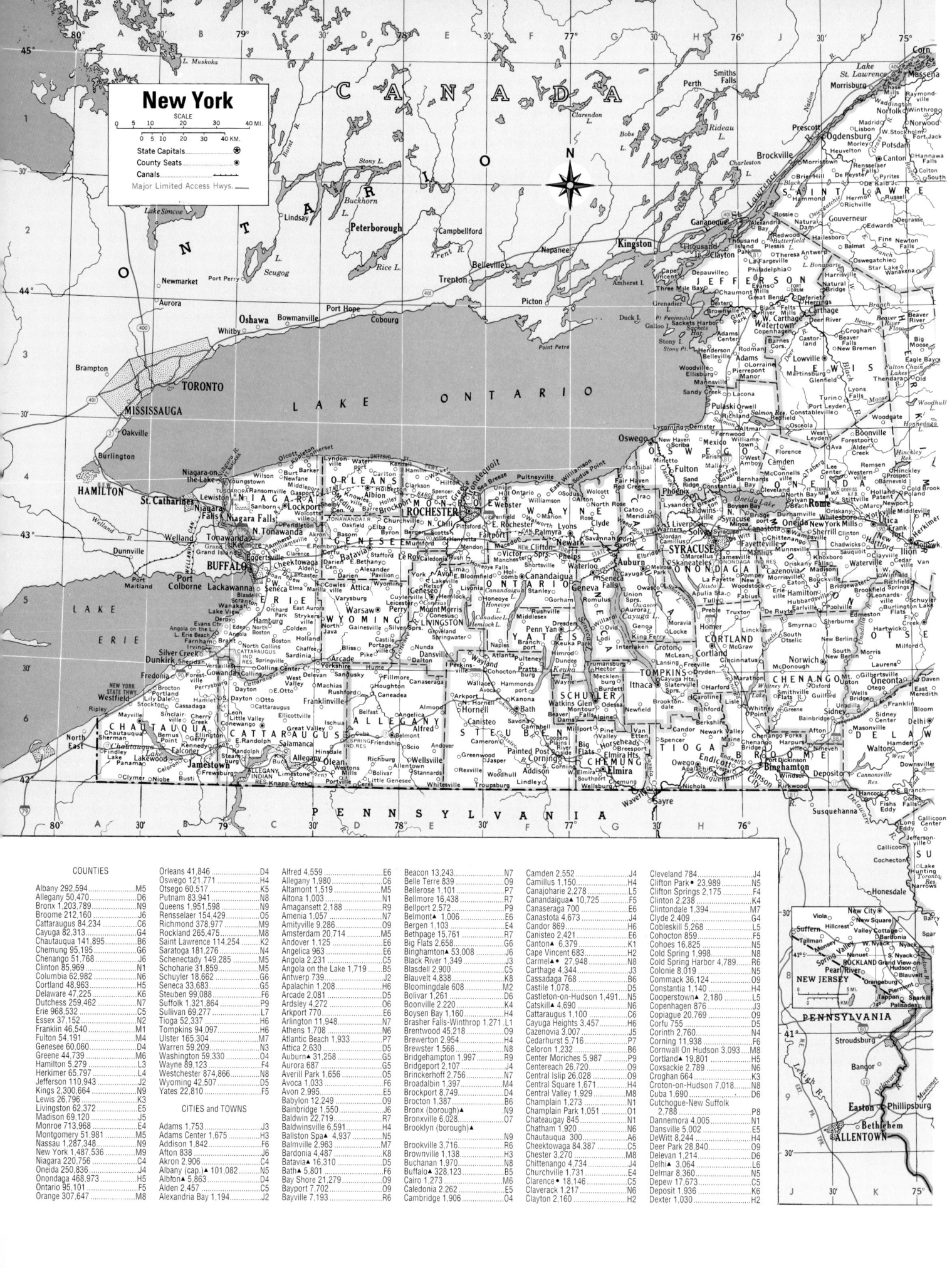

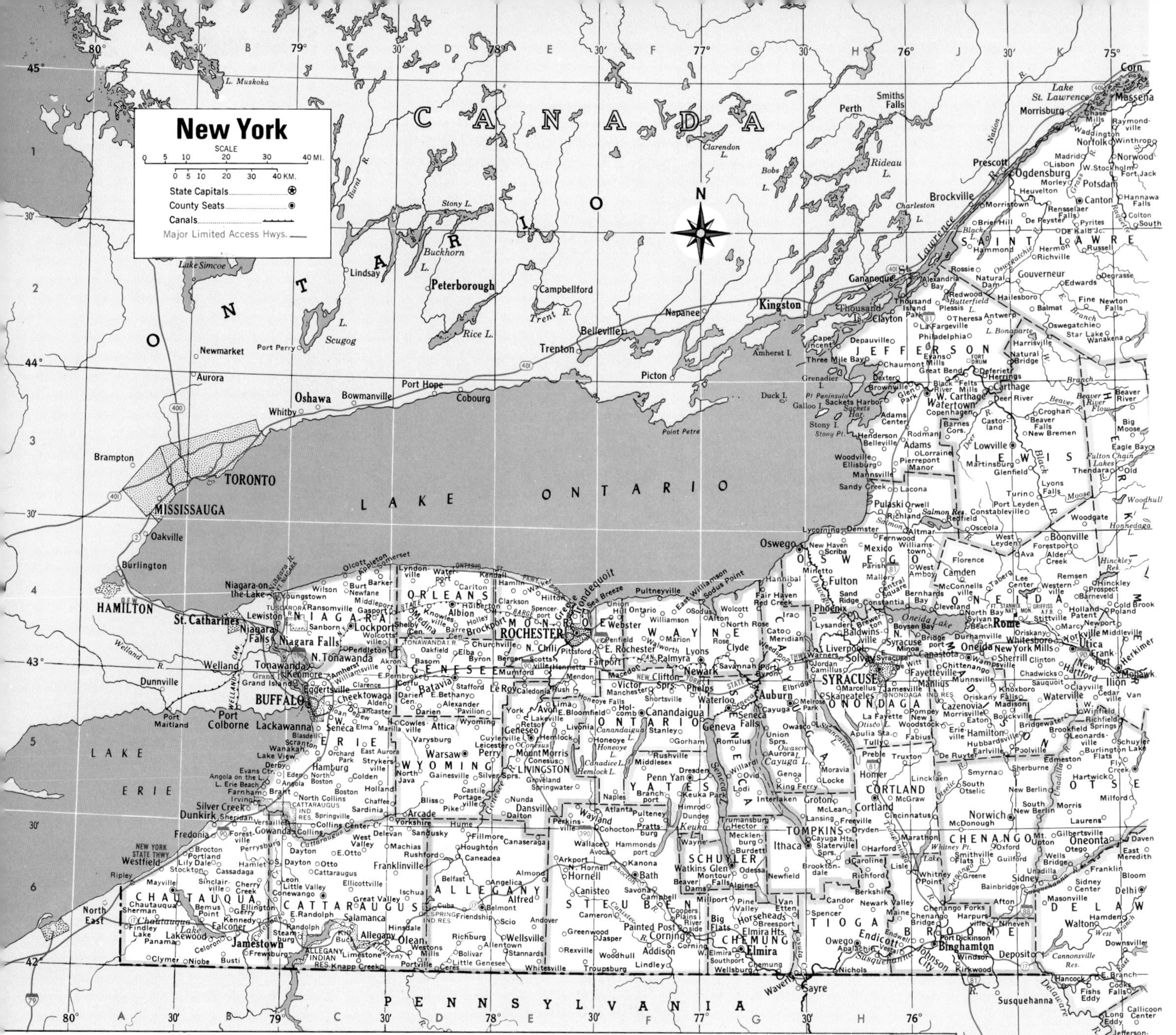
New York
SCALE
0 5 10 20 30 40 MI.
0 5 10 20 30 40 KM.
State Capitals
County Seats
Canals
Major Limited Access Hwys.
C A N A D A
O N T A R I O
L A K E O N T A R I O
L A K E E R I E
P E N N S Y L V A N I A
TORONTO
MISSISSAUGA
HAMILTON
BUFFALO
ROCHESTER
SYRACUSE
Utica
Albany
Binghamton
Elmira
Kingston
Ogdensburg
Watertown
Oswego
Niagara Falls
Jamestown
Ithaca
Rome
Massena

NEW JERSEY
PENNSYLVANIA
ROCKLAND
Easton
Phillipsburg
Bethlehem
ALLENTOWN
Stroudsburg
Bangor

COUNTIES

Albany 292,594 ... M5
Allegany 50,470 ... D6
Bronx 1,203,789 ... N9
Broome 212,160 ... J6
Cattaraugus 84,234 ... C6
Cayuga 82,313 ... G4
Chautauqua 141,895 ... B6
Chemung 95,195 ... G6
Chenango 51,768 ... J6
Clinton 85,969 ... N1
Columbia 62,982 ... N6
Cortland 48,963 ... H5
Delaware 47,225 ... K6
Dutchess 259,462 ... N7
Erie 968,532 ... C5
Essex 37,152 ... N2
Franklin 46,540 ... M1
Fulton 54,191 ... M4
Genesee 60,060 ... D4
Greene 44,739 ... M6
Hamilton 5,279 ... L3
Herkimer 65,797 ... L4
Jefferson 110,943 ... J2
Kings 2,300,664 ... N9
Lewis 26,796 ... K3
Livingston 62,372 ... E5
Madison 69,120 ... J5
Monroe 713,968 ... E4
Montgomery 51,981 ... M5
Nassau 1,287,348 ... N9
New York 1,487,536 ... M9
Niagara 220,756 ... C4
Oneida 250,836 ... J4
Onondaga 468,973 ... H5
Ontario 95,101 ... F5
Orange 307,647 ... M8
Orleans 41,846 ... D4
Oswego 121,771 ... H4
Otsego 60,517 ... K5
Putnam 83,941 ... N8
Queens 1,951,598 ... N9
Rensselaer 154,429 ... O5
Richmond 378,977 ... M9
Rockland 265,475 ... M8
Saint Lawrence 114,254 ... K2
Saratoga 181,276 ... N4
Schenectady 149,285 ... M5
Schoharie 31,859 ... M5
Schuyler 18,662 ... G6
Seneca 33,683 ... G5
Steuben 99,088 ... F6
Suffolk 1,321,864 ... P9
Sullivan 69,277 ... L7
Tioga 52,337 ... H6
Tompkins 94,097 ... H6
Ulster 165,304 ... M7
Warren 59,209 ... N3
Washington 59,330 ... O4
Wayne 89,123 ... F4
Westchester 874,866 ... N8
Wyoming 42,507 ... D5
Yates 22,810 ... F5

CITIES and TOWNS

Adams 1,753 ... J3
Adams Center 1,675 ... H3
Addison 1,842 ... F6
Afton 838 ... J6
Akron 2,906 ... C4
Albany (cap.)▲ 101,082 ... N5
Albion▲ 5,863 ... D4
Alden 2,457 ... C5
Alexandria Bay 1,194 ... J2
Alfred 4,559 ... E6
Allegany 1,980 ... C6
Altamont 1,519 ... M5
Altona 1,003 ... N1
Amagansett 2,188 ... R9
Amenia 1,057 ... N7
Amityville 9,286 ... O9
Amsterdam 20,714 ... M5
Andover 1,125 ... E6
Angelica 963 ... E6
Angola 2,231 ... C5
Angola on the Lake 1,719 ... B5
Antwerp 739 ... J2
Apalachin 1,208 ... H6
Arcade 2,081 ... D5
Ardsley 4,272 ... O6
Arkport 770 ... E6
Arlington 11,948 ... N7
Athens 1,708 ... N6
Atlantic Beach 1,933 ... P7
Attica 2,630 ... D5
Auburn▲ 31,258 ... G5
Aurora 687 ... G5
Averill Park 1,656 ... O5
Avoca 1,033 ... F6
Avon 2,995 ... E5
Babylon 12,249 ... O9
Bainbridge 1,550 ... J6
Baldwin 22,719 ... R7
Baldwinsville 6,591 ... H4
Ballston Spa▲ 4,937 ... N5
Balmville 2,963 ... M7
Bardonia 4,487 ... K8
Batavia▲ 16,310 ... D5
Bath▲ 5,801 ... F6
Bay Shore 21,279 ... O9
Bayport 7,702 ... O9
Bayville 7,193 ... R6
Beacon 13,243 ... N7
Belle Terre 839 ... O9
Bellerose 1,101 ... P7
Bellmore 16,438 ... R7
Bellport 2,572 ... P9
Belmont▲ 1,006 ... E6
Bergen 1,103 ... E4
Bethpage 15,761 ... R7
Big Flats 2,658 ... G6
Binghamton▲ 53,008 ... J6
Black River 1,349 ... J3
Blasdell 2,900 ... C5
Blauvelt 4,838 ... K8
Bloomingdale 608 ... M2
Bolivar 1,261 ... D6
Boonville 2,220 ... K4
Boysen Bay 1,160 ... H4
Brasher Falls-Winthrop 1,271 ... L1
Brentwood 45,218 ... O9
Brewerton 2,954 ... H4
Brewster 1,566 ... N8
Bridgehampton 1,997 ... R9
Bridgeport 2,107 ... J4
Brinckerhoff 2,756 ... N7
Broadalbin 1,397 ... M4
Brockport 8,749 ... D4
Brocton 1,387 ... B6
Bronx (borough)▲ ... N9
Bronxville 6,028 ... O7
Brooklyn (borough)▲ ... N9
Brookville 3,716 ... R6
Brownville 1,138 ... H3
Buchanan 1,970 ... N8
Buffalo▲ 328,123 ... B5
Cairo 1,273 ... M6
Caledonia 2,262 ... E5
Cambridge 1,906 ... O4
Camden 2,552 ... J4
Camillus 1,150 ... H4
Canajoharie 2,278 ... L5
Canandaigua▲ 10,725 ... F5
Canaseraga 700 ... E6
Canastota 4,673 ... J4
Candor 869 ... H6
Canisteo 2,421 ... E6
Canton▲ 6,379 ... K1
Cape Vincent 683 ... H2
Carmel▲• 27,948 ... N8
Carthage 4,344 ... J3
Cassadaga 768 ... B6
Castile 1,078 ... D5
Castleton-on-Hudson 1,491 ... N5
Catskill▲ 4,690 ... N6
Cattaraugus 1,100 ... C6
Cayuga Heights 3,457 ... H6
Cazenovia 3,007 ... J5
Cedarhurst 5,716 ... P7
Celoron 1,232 ... B6
Center Moriches 5,987 ... P9
Centereach 26,720 ... O9
Central Islip 26,028 ... O9
Central Square 1,671 ... H4
Central Valley 1,929 ... M8
Champlain 1,273 ... N1
Champlain Park 1,051 ... O1
Chateaugay 845 ... N1
Chatham 1,920 ... N6
Chautauqua 300 ... A6
Cheektowaga 84,387 ... C5
Chester 3,270 ... M8
Chittenango 4,734 ... J4
Churchville 1,731 ... E4
Clarence• 18,146 ... C5
Claverack 1,217 ... N6
Clayton 2,160 ... H2
Cleveland 784 ... J4
Clifton Park• 23,989 ... N5
Clifton Springs 2,175 ... F4
Clinton 2,238 ... K4
Clintondale 1,394 ... M7
Clyde 2,409 ... G4
Cobleskill 5,268 ... L5
Cohocton 859 ... F5
Cohoes 16,825 ... N5
Cold Spring 1,998 ... N8
Cold Spring Harbor 4,789 ... R6
Colonie 8,019 ... N5
Commack 36,124 ... O9
Constantia 1,140 ... H4
Cooperstown▲ 2,180 ... L5
Copenhagen 876 ... J3
Copiague 20,769 ... O9
Corfu 755 ... D5
Corinth 2,760 ... N4
Corning 11,938 ... F6
Cornwall On Hudson 3,093 ... M8
Cortland▲ 19,801 ... H5
Coxsackie 2,789 ... N6
Croghan 664 ... K3
Croton-on-Hudson 7,018 ... N8
Cuba 1,690 ... D6
Cutchogue-New Suffolk 2,788 ... P8
Dannemora 4,005 ... N1
Dansville 5,002 ... E5
DeWitt 8,244 ... H4
Deer Park 28,840 ... O9
Delevan 1,214 ... D6
Delhi▲ 3,064 ... L6
Delmar 8,360 ... N5
Depew 17,673 ... C5
Deposit 1,936 ... K6
Dexter 1,030 ... H2

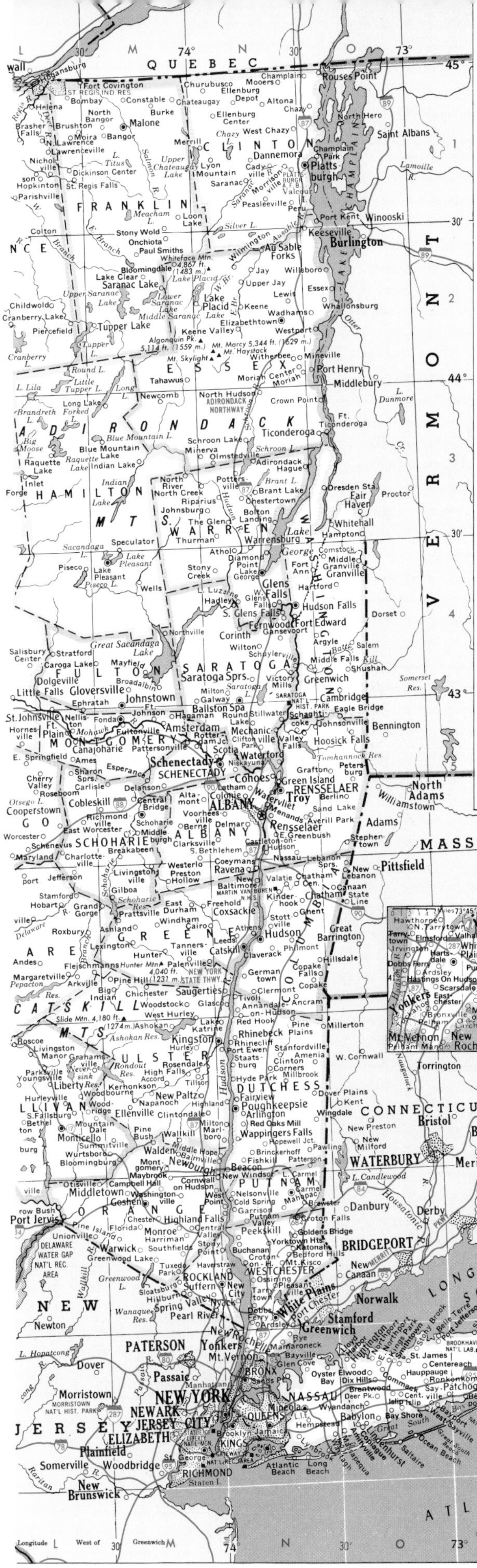

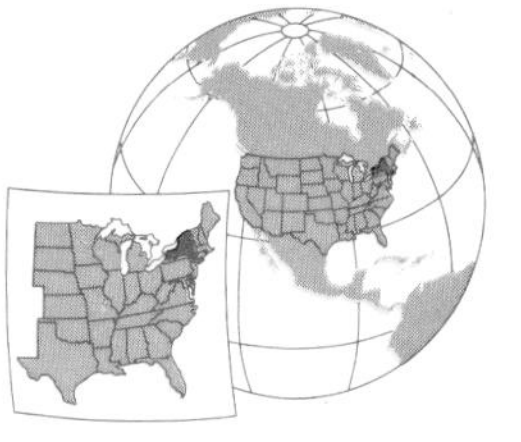

AREA 49,108 sq. mi. (127,190 sq. km.)
POPULATION 18,044,505
CAPITAL Albany
LARGEST CITY New York
HIGHEST POINT Mt. Marcy 5,344 ft. (1629 m.)
SETTLED IN 1614
ADMITTED TO UNION July 26, 1788
POPULAR NAME Empire State
STATE FLOWER Rose
STATE BIRD Bluebird

Topography

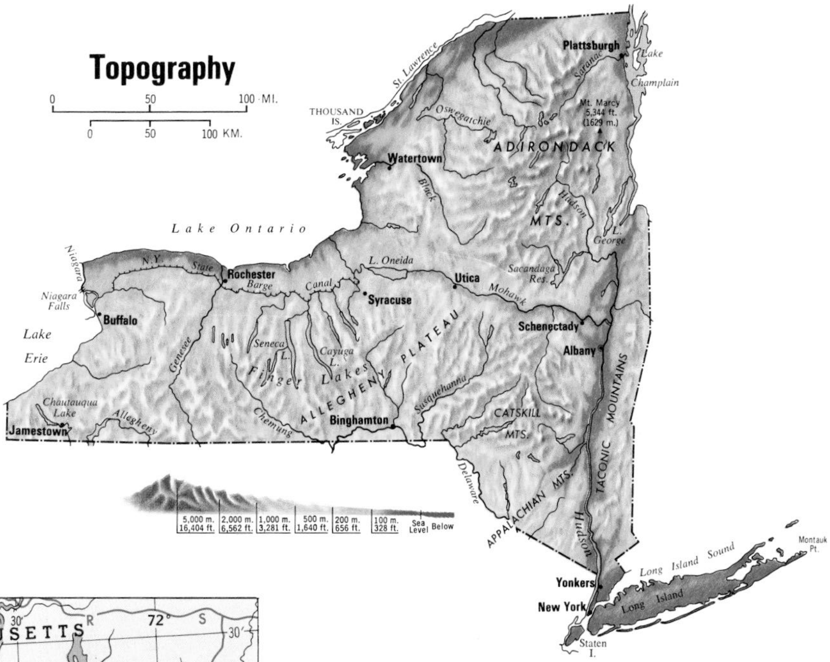
0 50 100 MI.
0 50 100 KM.
THOUSAND IS.
St. Lawrence
Oswegatchie
Plattsburgh
Lake Champlain
Saranac
Mt. Marcy 5,344 ft. (1629 m.)
ADIRONDACK
MTS.
Watertown
Black
Hudson
Lake Ontario
Niagara
Niagara Falls
N.Y. State Barge Canal
Rochester
L. Oneida
Syracuse
Utica
Mohawk
Sacandaga Res.
L. George
Buffalo
Lake Erie
Genesee
Seneca L.
Cayuga L.
Finger Lakes
ALLEGHENY PLATEAU
Schenectady
Albany
Chautauqua Lake
Allegheny
Chemung
Susquehanna
Binghamton
Jamestown
CATSKILL MTS.
TACONIC MOUNTAINS
Delaware
APPALACHIAN MTS.
Hudson
5,000 m. 16,404 ft.
2,000 m. 6,562 ft.
1,000 m. 3,281 ft.
500 m. 1,640 ft.
200 m. 656 ft.
100 m. 328 ft.
Sea Level
Below
Long Island Sound
Montauk Pt.
Yonkers
New York
Long Island
Staten I.

Dix Hills 25,849 ..... O9
Dobbs Ferry 9,940 ..... O6
Dolgeville 2,452 ..... L4
Dover Plains 1,847 ..... O7
Dryden 1,908 ..... H6
Dundee 1,588 ..... F5
Dunkirk 13,989 ..... B5
Earlville 883 ..... J5
East Aurora 6,647 ..... C5
East Greenbush 3,784 ..... N5
East Hampton 1,402 ..... R9
East Hills 6,746 ..... R7
East Meadow 36,909 ..... R7
East Moriches 4,021 ..... P9
East Northport 20,411 ..... O9
East Rochester 6,932 ..... F4
East Rockaway 10,152 ..... R7
East Syracuse 3,343 ..... H4
Eastchester 18,537 ..... P6
Eden 3,088 ..... C5
Elba 703 ..... D4
Elbridge 1,099 ..... G5
Elizabethtown▲ 659 ..... N2
Ellenville 4,243 ..... M7
Elma 2,354 ..... C5
Elmira Heights 4,359 ..... G6
Elmira▲ 33,724 ..... G6
Elmont 28,612 ..... P7
Elmsford 3,938 ..... O6
Elwood 10,916 ..... O9
Endicott 13,531 ..... H6
Endwell 12,602 ..... H6
Evans Mills 661 ..... J2
Fair Haven 895 ..... G4
Fairport 5,943 ..... F4
Fairview 4,811 ..... N7
Falconer 2,653 ..... B6
Farmingdale 8,022 ..... R7
Fayetteville 4,248 ..... J4
Fernwood 3,640 ..... N4
Fishkill 1,957 ..... N7
Flanders-Riverside 5,400 ..... P9
Floral Park 15,947 ..... P7
Florida 2,497 ..... M8
Fonda▲ 1,007 ..... M5
Forestville 738 ..... B6
Fort Covington• 1,804 ..... M1
Fort Edward 3,561 ..... O4
Fort Johnson 615 ..... M5
Fort Plain 2,416 ..... L5
Frankfort 2,693 ..... K4
Franklin Square 28,205 ..... R7
Franklinville 1,739 ..... D6
Fredonia 10,436 ..... B6
Freeport 39,894 ..... R7
Frewsburg 1,817 ..... B6
Friendship 1,423 ..... D6
Fulton 12,929 ..... H4
Fultonville 748 ..... M5
Garden City 21,686 ..... R7
Gasport 1,336 ..... C4
Geneseo▲ 7,187 ..... E5
Geneva 14,143 ..... G5
Glasco 1,538 ..... M6
Glen Cove 24,149 ..... R6
Glens Falls 15,023 ..... N4
Gloversville 16,656 ..... M4
Golden's Bridge 1,589 ..... N8
Goshen▲ 5,255 ..... M8
Gouverneur 4,604 ..... K2
Gowanda 2,901 ..... B6
Granville 2,646 ..... O4
Great Neck 8,745 ..... P6
Greece 15,632 ..... E4
Green Island 2,490 ..... N5
Greene 1,812 ..... J6
Greenport 2,070 ..... P8
Greenwich 1,961 ..... O4
Greenwood Lake 3,208 ..... M8
Groton 2,398 ..... H5
Hadley-Lake Luzerne 1,988 ..... N4
Hagaman 1,377 ..... M5
Hamburg 10,442 ..... C5
Hamilton 3,790 ..... J5
Hammondsport 929 ..... F6
Hampton Bays 7,893 ..... R9
Hancock 1,330 ..... K7
Hannibal 680 ..... G4
Harriman 2,288 ..... M8
Harrison 23,308 ..... P6
Harrisville 703 ..... K2
Hartsdale 9,587 ..... P6
Hastings On Hudson 8,000 ..... O6
Hauppauge 19,750 ..... O9
Haverstraw 9,438 ..... M8
Hawthorne 4,764 ..... O6
Hempstead 49,453 ..... R7
Herkimer▲ 7,945 ..... L4
Heuvelton 771 ..... K1
Hewlett 6,620 ..... P7
Hewlett Harbor 1,193 ..... P7
Hicksville 40,174 ..... R7
Highland 4,492 ..... M7
Highland Falls 3,937 ..... M8
Hillburn 892 ..... M8
Hillcrest 6,447 ..... K8
Hilton 5,216 ..... E4
Holcomb 790 ..... F5
Holland 1,288 ..... C5
Holley 1,890 ..... D4
Homer 3,476 ..... H5
Honeoye Falls 2,340 ..... F5
Hoosick Falls 3,490 ..... O5
Hopewell Junction 1,786 ..... N7
Hornell 9,877 ..... E6
Horseheads 6,802 ..... G6
Houghton 1,740 ..... D6
Hudson Falls▲ 7,651 ..... O4
Hudson▲ 8,034 ..... N6
Huntington 18,243 ..... R6

(continued on following page)

(continued)

Huntington Station 28,247 .....R6
Hurley 4,644 ....M7
Hyde Park 2,550 ....N6
Ilion 8,888 ....K5
Interlaken 680....G5
Inwood 7,767 ....P7
Irondequoit 52,322 ....E4
Irvington 6,348....O6
Island Park 4,860 ....R7
Islip 18,924 ....O9
Ithaca▲ 29,541 ....G6
Jamestown 34,681 ....B6
Jericho 13,141....R6
Johnson City 16,890 ....J6
Johnstown▲ 9,058....M4
Jordan 1,325 ....H4
Keeseville 1,854....O2
Kenmore 17,180 ....C5
Kerhonkson 1,629....M7
Keuka Park 1,153 ....F5
Kinderhook 1,293 ....N6
Kings Park 17,773....O9
Kings Point 4,843 ....P6
Kingston▲ 23,095 ....M7
Lackawanna 20,585....B5
Lake Carmel 8,489....N8
Lake Erie Beach 4,509 ....B5
Lake George▲ 933 ....N4
Lake Katrine 1,998....M7
Lake Luzerne-Hadley 2,042 ....N4
Lake Placid 2,485 ....N2
Lake Pleasant▲ 700 ....M4
Lake Success 2,484....P7
Lakewood 3,564 ....B6
Lancaster 11,940....C5
Lansing 3,281....H5
Larchmont 6,181 ....P7
Latham 10,131 ....N5
Lattingtown 1,859 ....R6
Lawrence 6,513 ....P7
Le Roy 4,974....E5
Levittown 53,286....R7
Lewiston 3,048....B4
Liberty 4,128....L7
Lima 2,165....E5
Lindenhurst 26,879 ....O9
Little Falls 5,829....L4
Little Valley▲ 1,188....C6
Liverpool 2,624 ....H4
Livingston Manor 1,482....L7
Livonia 1,434 ....E5
Lloyd Harbor 3,343....R6
Lockport▲ 24,426....C4
Locust Grove 9,670....R6
Long Beach 33,510....R7
Lowville▲ 3,632....J3
Lynbrook 19,208 ....P7
Lyndonville 953....D4
Lyons Falls 698....K3
Lyons▲ 4,280....F4
Macedon 1,400 ....F4
Machias 1,191 ....D6
Mahopac 7,755....N8
Malone▲ 6,777....M1
Malverne 9,054....R7
Mamaroneck 17,325....P7
Manchester 1,598 ....F5
Manhasset 7,718 ....P7
Manhattan (borough) M9
Manlius 4,764 ....J5
Manorville 6,198....P9
Marathon 1,107....J6
Marcellus 1,840....H5
Margaretville 639 ....L6
Marion 1,080....F4
Marlboro 2,200 ....M7
Massapequa 22,018 ....R7
Massapequa Park 18,044 ....R7
Massena 11,719....L1
Mastic Beach 10,293 ....P9
Mattituck 3,902....P9
Maybrook 2,802....M8
Mayfield 817 ....M4
Mayville▲ 1,636 ....A6
McGraw 1,074 ....H5
Mechanicville 5,249....N5
Medina 6,686....D4
Melrose Park 2,091 ....G5
Melville 12,586 ....S7
Menands 4,333....N5
Merrick 23,042 ....R7
Mexico 1,555....H4
Middle Hope 3,229....M7
Middleburgh 1,436 ....M5
Middleport 1,876 ....C4
Middletown 24,160 ....L8
Middleville 624 ....K4
Mill Neck 977....R6
Millbrook 1,339 ....N7
Millerton 884 ....O7
Milton 1,140 ....M7
Milton 2,063 ....N4
Mineola▲ 18,994 ....R7
Minetto 1,252 ....H4
Mineville-Witherbee 1,740....O2
Minoa 3,745 ....H4
Mohawk 2,986 ....L4
Monroe 6,672 ....M8
Monsey 13,986 ....J8
Montauk 3,001....S8
Montgomery 2,696 ....M7
Monticello▲ 6,597....L7
Montour Falls 1,845 ....G6
Moravia 1,559 ....H5
Morris 642....K5
Morrisonville 1,742 ....N1
Morrisville 2,732 ....J5
Mount Kisco 9,108 ....N8
Mount Morris 3,102....E5
Mount Vernon 67,153....O7
Nanuet 14,065 ....K8
Napanoch 1,068....M7
Naples 1,237 ....F5
Nassau 1,254....N5
New Berlin 1,220 ....K5
New City▲ 33,673 ....K8
New Hartford 2,111 ....K4
New Hyde Park 9,728 ....P7
New Paltz 5,463....M7
New Rochelle 67,265....P7
New Square 2,605 ....K8
New Windsor 8,898....N8
New York Mills 3,534....K4
New York▲ 7,322,564....M9
Newark 9,849 ....G4
Newark Valley 1,082....H6
Newburgh 26,454 ....M7
Newfane 3,001....C4
Newport 676....K4
Niagara Falls 61,840 ....C4
Nichols 573 ....H6
Niskayuna 4,942....N5
Norfolk 1,412....K1
North Boston 2,581 ....C5
North Collins 1,335....C5
North Hornell 822 ....E6
North Syracuse 7,363....H4
North Tarrytown 8,152 ....O6
North Tonawanda 34,989 ....C4
Northport 7,572....O9
Northville 1,180 ....M4
Norwich▲ 7,613 ....J5
Norwood 1,841 ....L1
Nunda 1,347 ....E5
Nyack 6,558....K8
Oakfield 1,818 ....D4
Oceanside 32,423....R7
Odessa 986....G6
Ogdensburg 13,521 ....K1
Olcott 1,432....C4
Old Forge 1,061 ....L3
Olean 16,946 ....D6
Oneida 10,850....J4
Oneonta 13,954 ....K6
Orangeburg 3,583....K8
Orchard Park 3,280....C5
Oriskany 1,450....K4
Oriskany Falls 795 ....J5
Ossining 22,582 ....N8
Oswego▲ 19,195 ....G4
Otego 1,068....K6
Otisville 1,078 ....L8
Ovid 660....G5
Owego▲ 4,442....H6
Oxford 1,738 ....J6
Oyster Bay 6,687 ....R6
Painted Post 1,950....F6
Palmyra 3,566....F4
Patchogue 11,060....P9
Pawling 1,974....N7
Pearl River 15,314 ....K8
Peconic 1,100....P8
Peekskill 19,536 ....N8
Pelham 6,413 ....O7
Pelham Manor 5,443 ....O7
Penn Yan▲ 5,248 ....F5
Perry 4,219....D5
Peru 1,565....N1
Phelps 1,978 ....F5
Philadelphia 1,478....J2
Philmont 1,623....N6
Phoenix 2,435 ....H4
Piermont 2,163....K8
Pine Bush 1,445....M7
Pine Plains 1,312....N7
Pine Valley 1,486....G6
Pittsford 1,488....E4
Plainview 26,207 ....R7
Plattsburgh▲ 21,255....O1
Pleasantville 6,592....N8
Port Byron 1,359 ....G4
Port Chester 24,728....P7
Port Dickinson 1,785....J6
Port Ewen 3,444....N7
Port Henry 1,263 ....O2
Port Jefferson 7,455....P9
Port Jervis 9,060....L8
Port Leyden 723 ....K3
Port Washington 15,387....R6
Portville 1,040 ....D6
Potsdam 10,251 ....K1
Poughkeepsie▲ 28,844....N7
Prattsburg• 1,657 ....F5
Pulaski 2,525....H3
Putnam Valley• 8,994....N8
Queens (borough) N9
Quogue 898....P9
Randolph 1,298 ....C6
Ransomville 1,542....C4
Ravena 3,547....N6
Red Hook 1,794....N7
Red Oaks Mill 4,906 ....N7
Rensselaer 8,255....N5
Rhinebeck 2,725....N7
Richfield Springs 1,565 ....K5
Richmond (borough) (Staten Island) M9
Richmondville 843....M5
Ripley 1,189....A6
Riverhead▲ 8,814 ....P9
Rochester▲ 231,636 ....E4
Rockville Centre 24,727....R7
Rome 44,350 ....J4
Ronkonkoma 20,391 ....O9
Roosevelt 15,030....R7
Rosendale 1,134....M7
Roslyn 1,965 ....R6
Rotterdam Junction 1,010....N5
Round Lake 765 ....N5
Rouses Point 2,377 ....O1
Rye 14,936 ....P6
Sackets Harbor 1,313....H3
Sag Harbor 2,134 ....R8
Saint James 12,703....O9
Saint Johnsville 1,825....L5
Salamanca 6,566 ....C6
Salem 958 ....O4
Sand Ridge 1,312 ....H4
Sands Point 2,477 ....P6
Sandy Creek 793 ....H3
Saranac Lake 5,377 ....M2
Saratoga Springs 25,001....N4
Saugerties 3,915....M6
Savannah• 1,905....G4
Savona 974 ....F6
Sayville 16,550....O9
Scarsdale 16,987....P6
Schaghticoke 794....N5
Schenectady▲ 65,566 ....M5
Schoharie▲ 1,045 ....M5
Schuylerville 1,364 ....N4
Scotia 7,359 ....N5
Scottsville 1,912 ....E4
Sea Cliff 5,054....R6
Seaford 15,597....R7
Seneca Falls 7,370....G5
Sherburne 1,531 ....K5
Sherman 694 ....A6
Sherrill 2,864 ....J4
Shortsville 1,485 ....F5
Sidney 4,720....K6
Silver Creek 2,927....B5
Silver Springs 852 ....E5
Sinclairville 708 ....B6
Skaneateles 2,724 ....H5
Sloan 3,830 ....C5
Sloatsburg 3,035 ....M8
Smithtown 25,638....O9
Sodus 1,904 ....G4
Sodus Point 1,190....G4
Solvay 6,717....H4
South Corning 1,025....F6
South Fallsburg 2,115....L7
South Glens Falls 3,506....N4
South Nyack 3,352 ....K8
Southampton 1,302....R9
Southold 5,192....P8
Southport 7,753 ....G6
Sparrow Bush 1,049 ....L8
Spencer 815 ....H6
Spencerport 3,606 ....E4
Spring Valley 21,802....K8
Springville 4,310....C5
Stamford 1,211....L6
Stannards 1,028....E6
Star Lake 1,092....K2
Staten Island (borough) M9
Stillwater 1,531 ....N5
Stony Brook 13,726....O9
Stony Point 10,587 ....M8
Stottville 1,369 ....N6
Suffern 11,055 ....J8
Sylvan Beach 1,119....J4
Syosset 18,967....R6
Syracuse▲ 163,860 ....H4
Tappan 6,867....K8
Tarrytown 10,739....O6
Theresa 889 ....J2
Thomaston 2,612....P7
Ticonderoga 2,770....N3
Tillson 1,688....M7
Tivoli 1,035....N6
Tonawanda 17,284 ....B4
Troy▲ 54,269....N5
Trumansburg 1,611....G5
Tuckahoe 6,302....O7
Tully 911....H5
Tupper Lake 4,087 ....M2
Tuxedo Park 706....M8
Unadilla 1,265....K6
Union Springs 1,142....G5
Uniondale 20,328 ....R7
Utica▲ 68,637 ....K4
Valatie 1,487....N6
Valley Cottage 9,007 ....K8
Valley Stream 33,946....P7
Vestal• 27,238....H6
Victor 2,308 ....F5
Victory Mills 571 ....N4
Viola 4,504 ....J8
Voorheesville 3,225 ....M5
Waddington 944 ....K1
Wading River 5,317 ....P9
Walden 5,836....M7
Wallkill 2,125 ....M7
Walton 3,326 ....K6
Wampsville▲ 501 ....J4
Wantagh 18,567 ....R7
Wappingers Falls 4,605 ....N7
Warrensburg 3,204 ....N3
Warsaw▲ 3,830 ....D5
Warwick 5,984....M8
Washingtonville 4,906 ....M8
Waterford 2,370 ....N5
Waterloo▲ 5,116....G5
Watertown▲ 29,429 ....J3
Waterville 1,664....K5
Watervliet 11,061 ....N5
Watkins Glen▲ 2,207 ....G6
Waverly 4,787 ....G7
Wayland 1,976....E5
Webster 5,464....F4
Weedsport 1,996....G4
Wellsburg 617 ....G6
Wellsville 5,241....E6
West Carthage 2,166....J3
West Elmira 5,218....G6
West Glens Falls 5,964....N4
West Hurley 2,252 ....M6
West Nyack 3,437....K8
West Point 8,024 ....M8
West Sayville 4,680....O9
West Seneca 47,866....C5
West Winfield 871 ....K5
Westbury 13,060....R7
Westfield 3,451....A6
Westhampton 2,129 ....P9
Westhampton Beach 1,571....P9
Westons Mills 1,837....D6
White Plains▲ 48,718 ....P6
Whitehall 3,071 ....O3
Whitesboro 4,195 ....K4
Whitney Point 1,054....J6
Willard 1,339....G5
Williamson 1,768 ....F4
Williamsville 5,583....C5
Williston Park 7,516 ....R7
Wilson 1,307 ....C4
Windsor 1,051 ....J6
Witherbee-Mineville 1,925....N2
Wolcott 1,544....G4
Woodmere 15,578....P7
Woodridge 783 ....L7
Woodstock 1,870....M6
Wurtsboro 1,048....L7
Wyandanch 8,950....N9
Yonkers 188,082 ....O6
Yorkshire 1,340....D5
Yorktown Heights 7,690....N8
Yorkville 2,972....K4
Youngstown 2,075 ....C4

OTHER FEATURES

Adirondack (mts.)....M3
Algonquin (peak) M2
Allegany Ind. Res.....C6
Allegheny (res.) C7
Allegheny (riv.) C6
Ashokan (res.) M7
Ausable (riv.)....N2
Batten Kill (riv.)....O4
Beaver (riv.)....K3
Big Moose (lake)....L3
Black (lake) J1
Black (riv.) K3
Block Island (sound)....S8
Blue Mountain (lake)....M3
Bonaparte (lake) K2
Brandreth (lake) L3
Brant (lake)....N3
Brookhaven Nat'l Lab.....P9
Butterfield (lakes)....J2
Canandaigua (lake)....F5
Canisteo (riv.)....F6
Cannonsville (res.)....K6
Catskill (lake) L6
Cattaraugus (creek) C6
Cattaraugus Ind. Res. C5
Cayuga (lake)....G5
Champlain (lake)....O1
Chateaugay, Upper (lake)....M1
Chautauqua (lake)....A6
Chazy (lake)....N1
Chenango (riv.) J6
Cohocton (riv.) F6
Conesus (lake) E5
Conewango (creek)....B6
Cranberry (lake) L2
Deer (riv.)....J3
Deer (riv.)....L1
Delaware (riv.) K7
East (riv.)....N9
Erie (lake) A5
Fire Island Nat'l Seashore P9
Fishers (isl.)....S8
Forked (lake) L3
Fort Drum 11,578....J2
Fort Niagara C4
Fort Stanwix Nat'l Mon.....J4
Fulton Chain (lakes) K3
Galloo (isl.)....H3
Gardiners (bay)....R8
Gardiners (isl.)....R8
Gateway Nat'l Rec. Area....M9
Genesee (riv.)....E5
George (lake)....N4
Grand (isl.)....B5
Grass (riv.)....K1
Great Sacandaga (lake) M4
Great South (bay) O9
Great South (beach) O9
Greenwood (lake)....M8
Grenadier (isl.)....H2
Griffiss A.F.B.....K4
Haystack (mt.)....N2
Hemlock (lake)....E5
Hinckley (res.) K4
Honeoye (lake) F5
Honnedaga (lake)....L3
Hudson (riv.) N7
Hunter (mt.)....M6
Indian (lake)....M3
Jones (beach)....R7
Keuka (lake) F5
Lila (lake) L2
Little Tupper (lake)....L2
Long (isl.) P9
Long (lake)....M2
Long Island (sound) P9
Lower Saranac (lake) M2
Manhattan (isl.)....M9
Marcy (mt.) N2
Martin Van Buren Nat'l Hist. Site....N6
Meacham (lake) M1
Mohawk (riv.)....L5
Montauk (pt.)....S8
Moose (riv.)....K3
Neversink (res.) L7
New York State Barge (canal) .C4
Niagara (riv.)....B4
Oil Spring Ind. Res. D6
Oneida (lake) J4
Onondaga Ind. Res.....H5
Ontario (lake) F3
Orient (pt.)....R8
Oswegatchie (riv.)....K2
Oswego (riv.)....H4
Otisco (lake) H5
Otsego (lake)....L5
Otselic (riv.) J5
Owasco (lake)....G5
Peconic (bay) R9
Peninsula (pt.)....H3
Pepacton (res.) L6
Piseco (lake)....M4
Placid (lake)....N2
Plattsburgh A.F.B. 5,483....N1
Pleasant (lake) M4
Plum (isl.)....R8
Poosepatuck Ind. Res.....P9
Raquette (lake)....L3
Rondout (pt.) M7
Round (lake) L2
Sacandaga (lake)....L3
Sackets (harb.) H3
Sagamore Hill Nat'l Hist. Site..R6
Saint Lawrence (lake) K1
Saint Lawrence (riv.)....J2
Saint Regis (riv.) L1
Saint Regis Ind. Res. M1
Salmon (res.) J3
Salmon (riv.) H3
Salmon (riv.)....M1
Saranac (lakes) M2
Saranac (riv.)....N1
Saratoga (lake) N4
Saratoga Nat'l Hist. Park....N4
Schoharie (res.) M6
Schroon (lake)....N3
Seneca (lake)....G5
Seneca (riv.) G5
Shelter (isl.)....R8
Shinnecock Ind. Res.....R9
Silver (lake) N1
Skaneateles (lake)....H5
Skylight (mt.)....M2
Slide (mt.)....L6
Staten (isl.) M9
Statue of Liberty Nat'l Mon. ...M9
Stony (isl.)....H3
Stony (pt.) H3
Susquehanna (riv.) H6
Thousand (isls.)....H2
Tioughnioga (riv.)....H6
Titus (lake)....M1
Tomhannock (res.) O5
Tonawanda Ind. Res.....D4
Toronto (res.)....L7
Tupper (lake) M2
Tuscarora Ind. Res. B4
Unadilla (riv.) K5
Upper Chateaugay (lake)....M1
Valcour (isl.)....N1
Wallkill (riv.)....L8
Whiteface (mt.)....N2
Whitney Point (lake)....J6
Woodhull (lake)....L3

▲County seat
•Population of town or township

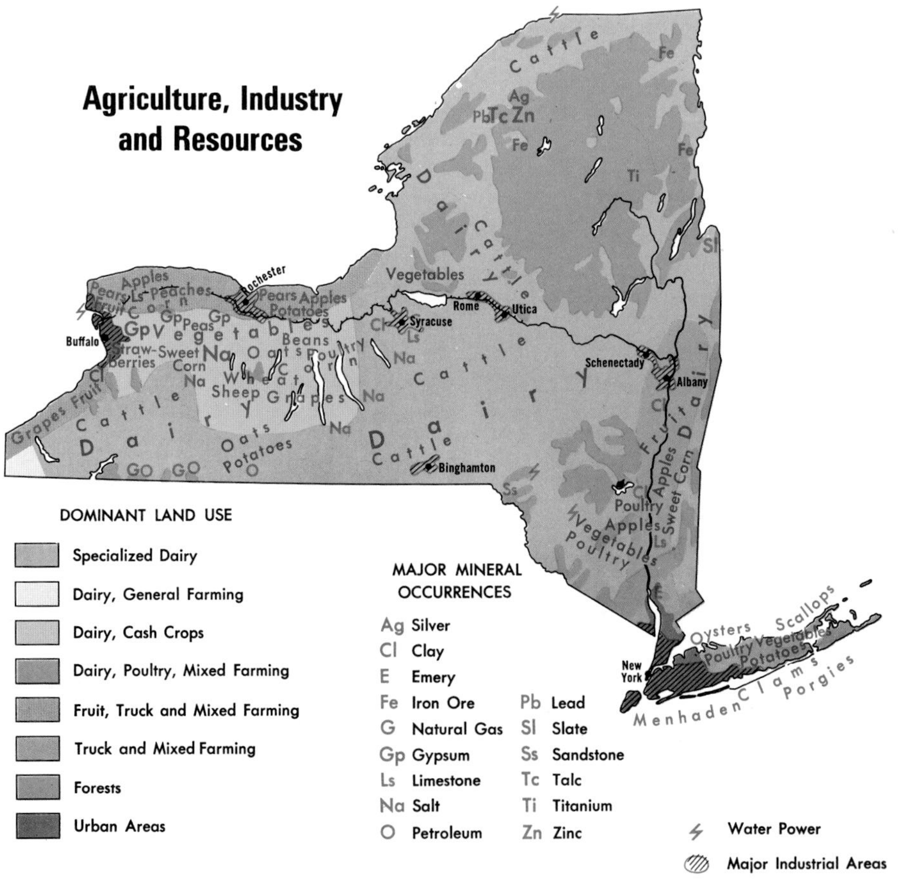

Agriculture, Industry and Resources
DOMINANT LAND USE
Specialized Dairy
Dairy, General Farming
Dairy, Cash Crops
Dairy, Poultry, Mixed Farming
Fruit, Truck and Mixed Farming
Truck and Mixed Farming
Forests
Urban Areas
MAJOR MINERAL OCCURRENCES
Ag Silver
Cl Clay
E Emery
Fe Iron Ore
G Natural Gas
Gp Gypsum
Ls Limestone
Na Salt
O Petroleum
Pb Lead
Sl Slate
Ss Sandstone
Tc Talc
Ti Titanium
Zn Zinc
Water Power
Major Industrial Areas
Buffalo
Rochester
Syracuse
Rome
Utica
Schenectady
Albany
Binghamton
New York
Cattle
Dairy
Vegetables
Apples
Pears
Peaches
Potatoes
Grapes
Fruit
Straw-Sweet Berries
Corn
Wheat
Sheep
Oats
Beans
Poultry
Sweet Corn
Oysters
Scallops
Clams
Porgies
Menhaden

MAY 20th 1775
N ★ C
APRIL 12th 1776

AREA 52,669 sq. mi. (136,413 sq. km.)
POPULATION 6,657,630
CAPITAL Raleigh
LARGEST CITY Charlotte
HIGHEST POINT Mt. Mitchell 6,684 ft. (2037 m.)
SETTLED IN 1650
ADMITTED TO UNION November 21, 1789
POPULAR NAME Tarheel State
STATE FLOWER Flowering Dogwood
STATE BIRD Cardinal

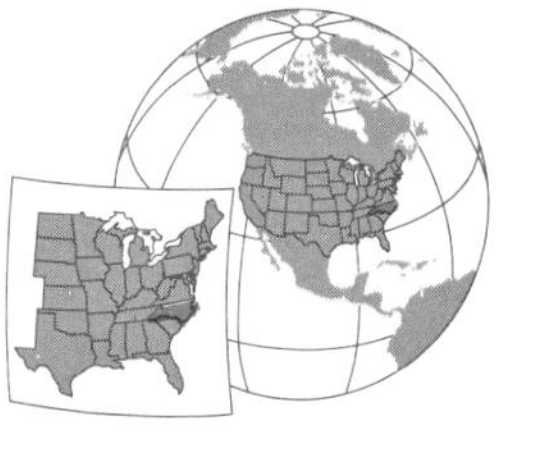

COUNTIES

Alamance 108,213 L3
Alexander 27,544 G3
Alleghany 9,590 G1
Anson 23,474 J4
Ashe 22,209 F2
Avery 14,867 F2
Beaufort 42,283 R4
Bertie 20,388 P2
Bladen 28,663 M5
Brunswick 50,985 N6
Buncombe 174,821 D3
Burke 75,744 F3
Cabarrus 98,935 H4
Caldwell 70,709 F3
Camden 5,904 S2
Carteret 52,556 R5
Caswell 20,693 L2
Catawba 118,412 G3
Chatham 38,759 L3
Cherokee 20,170 A4
Chowan 13,506 R2
Clay 7,155 B4
Cleveland 84,714 F4
Columbus 49,587 M6
Craven 81,613 P4
Cumberland 274,566 M4
Currituck 13,736 S2
Dare 22,746 T3
Davidson 126,677 J3
Davie 27,859 H3
Duplin 39,995 O5
Durham 181,835 M3
Edgecombe 56,558 O3
Forsyth 265,878 J2
Franklin 36,414 N2
Gaston 175,093 G4
Gates 9,305 R2
Graham 7,196 B4
Granville 38,345 M2
Greene 15,384 O3
Guilford 347,420 K3
Halifax 55,516 O2
Harnett 67,822 M4
Haywood 46,942 C3
Henderson 69,285 D4
Hertford 22,523 P2
Hoke 22,856 L4
Hyde 5,411 S3
Iredell 92,931 H3
Jackson 26,846 C4
Johnston 81,306 N4
Jones 9,414 P4
Lee 41,374 L4
Lenoir 57,274 O4
Lincoln 50,319 G3
Macon 23,499 B4
Madison 16,953 D3
Martin 25,078 P3
McDowell 35,681 E3
Mecklenburg 511,433 H4
Mitchell 14,433 E2
Montgomery 23,346 K4
Moore 59,013 L4
Nash 76,677 O2
New Hanover 120,284 O6
Northampton 20,798 P2
Onslow 149,838 P5
Orange 93,851 L2
Pamlico 11,372 R4
Pasquotank 31,298 S2
Pender 28,855 O5
Perquimans 10,447 S2
Person 30,180 M2
Pitt 107,924 P3
Polk 14,416 E4
Randolph 106,546 K3
Richmond 44,518 K4
Robeson 105,179 L5
Rockingham 86,064 K2
Rowan 110,605 H3
Rutherford 56,918 E4
Sampson 47,297 N4
Scotland 33,754 L5
Stanly 51,765 J4
Stokes 37,223 J2
Surry 61,704 H2
Swain 11,268 B3
Transylvania 25,520 D4
Tyrrell 3,856 S3
Union 84,211 H4
Vance 38,892 N2
Wake 423,380 M3
Warren 17,265 N2
Washington 13,997 R3
Watauga 36,952 F2
Wayne 104,666 N4
Wilkes 59,393 G2
Wilson 66,061 O3
Yadkin 30,488 H2
Yancey 15,419 E3

CITIES and TOWNS

Abbottsburg 425 M5
Aberdeen 2,700 L4
Acme N6
Advance J3
Ahoskie 4,391 P2
Alamance 258 K2
Alarka 900 C4
Albemarle▲ 14,939 J4
Alexander Mills 662 F4
Alliance 583 R4
Altamahaw 1,076 L2
Andrews 2,551 B4
Angier 2,235 M4
Ansonville 614 J4
Apex 4,968 M3
Arapahoe 430 R4
Archdale 6,913 K3
Arlington 795 H2
Ash 16,362 N6
Asheboro▲ 15,252 K3
Asheville▲ 61,607 D3
Askewville 201 R2
Atkinson 275 N5
Atlantic 1,938 S5
Atlantic Beach 941 R5
Aulander 1,209 P2
Aurora 654 R4
Autryville 166 M4
Avon 500 U4
Avondale F4
Ayden 4,740 P4
Badin 1,481 J4
Bahama 280 M2
Bailey 553 N3
Bakersville▲ 332 E2
Balfour 1,118 E4
Banner Elk 933 F2
Bannertown 1,028 H1
Barco 325 T2
Barker Heights 1,137 D4
Bat Cave 450 E4
Bath 154 R4
Battleboro 447 O2
Bayboro▲ 733 R4
Bear Creek 500 L3
Beargrass 77 P3
Beaufort▲ 3,808 R5
Belhaven 2,269 R3
Bellarthur 350 O3
Belmont 8,434 H4
Belvidere 275 S2
Belville 66 N6
Belwood 631 F4
Benham 400 G2
Bennett 254 K3
Benson 2,810 N4
Bessemer City 4,698 G4
Beta 500 C4
Bethel 1,842 P3
Beulaville 933 O5
Biltmore Forest 1,327 E3
Biscoe 1,484 K4
Black Creek 615 O3
Black Mountain 5,418 E3
Bladenboro 1,821 M5
Blowing Rock 1,257 F2
Boardman 250 M6
Boger City 1,373 G4
Boiling Spring Lakes 1,650 N7
Boiling Springs 2,445 F4
Bolivia▲ 228 N6
Bolton 531 N6
Bonlee 300 L3
Boomer 250 G2
Boone▲ 12,915 F2
Boonville 1,009 H2
Brevard▲ 5,388 D4
Bridgeton 453 R4
Broadway 973 L4
Brookford 451 G3
Browns Summit 500 K2
Brunswick 302 M6
Bryson City▲ 1,145 C4
Buies 2,085 L5
Buies Creek 1,939 M4
Bullock 525 M2
Bunn 364 N3
Bunnlevel M4
Burgaw▲ 1,807 N5
Burlington 39,498 K2
Burnsville▲ 1,482 E3
Butner 4,679 M2
Buxton 700 U4
Bynum 312 L3
Calabash 1,210 M7
Calypso 481 N4
Camden▲ 300 S2
Cameron 215 L4
Candler 950 D3
Candor 748 K4
Canton 3,790 D3
Cape Carteret 1,008 P5
Carolina Beach 3,630 O6
Carrboro 11,553 L3
Carthage▲ 976 K4
Cary 43,858 M3
Casar 328 F3
Cashiers 553 C4
Castalia 261 O2
Castle Hayne 1,182 O6
Caswell Beach 175 N7
Catawba 467 G3
Catharine Lake 500 O5
Cedar Falls 400 K3
Cedar Grove 250 L2
Cedar Island 310 S5
Cedar Mountain 250 D4
Centerville 115 N2
Cerro Gordo 227 M6
Chadbourn 2,005 M6
Chadwick Acres 15 P6
Chapel Hill 38,719 L3
Charlotte▲ 395,934 H4
Cherokee 975 C4
Cherry 4,756 R3
Cherryville 4,844 G4
China Grove 2,732 H3
Chinquapin 280 O5
Chocowinity 624 P4
Claremont 980 G3
Clarendon 300 M6
Clark 739 P4
Clarkton 664 M6
Clayton 4,756 N3
Clemmons 6,020 J2
Cleveland 696 H3
Cliffside 950 F4
Climax 475 K3
Clinton▲ 8,204 N5
Clyde 1,041 D3
Coats 1,493 M4
Cofield 407 R2
Coinjock 650 S2
Colerain 139 R2
Collettsille 275 F3
Columbia▲ 836 S3
Columbus▲ 812 E4
Comfort 325 O5
Como 71 P1
Concord▲ 27,347 H4
Conetoe 292 O3
Connellys Springs 500 F3
Conover 5,465 G3
Conway 759 P2
Cooleemee 971 H3
Cornelius 2,581 H4
Council M6
Cove City 497 P4
Cramerton 2,371 G4
Creedmoor 1,504 M2
Creswell 361 S3
Crisp 435 O3
Crossnore 271 F2
Cruso 800 D4
Culberson A4
Cullowhee 4,029 C4
Cumberland 400 M5
Currie 294 N6
Currituck▲ 700 T2
Dallas 3,012 G4
Dalton 400 J2
Danbury▲ 119 J2
Davidson 4,046 H4
Davis 612 R5
Delco 450 N6
Denton 1,292 J3
Dillsboro 95 C4
Dobson▲ 1,195 H2
Dortches 840 O2
Dover 451 P4
Drexel 1,746 F3
Dublin 246 M5
Dudley N4
Dulah 350 M6
Dundarrach L5
Dunn 8,336 M4
Durham▲ 136,611 M2
Dysartsville 950 F3
Eagle Springs 280 K4
Earl 230 F4
East Arcadia 468 N6
East Bend 619 H2
East Flat Rock 3,218 E4
East Laurinburg 302 L5
East Marion 1,851 F3
East Spencer 2,055 J3
Eden 15,238 K1
Edenton▲ 5,268 R2
Edward R4
Efland 600 L2
Elizabeth City▲ 14,292 S2
Elizabethtown▲ 3,704 M5
Elk Park 486 E2
Elkin 3,790 H2
Ellenboro 514 F4
Ellerbe 1,132 K4
Elm City 1,624 O3
Elon College 4,394 L2
Emerald Isle 2,434 P5
Enfield 3,082 O2
Engelhard 500 T3
Enka 5,567 D3
Ernul 350 P4
Erwin 4,061 M4
Ether 425 K4
Etowah 1,997 D4
Eure 282 R2

(continued on following page)

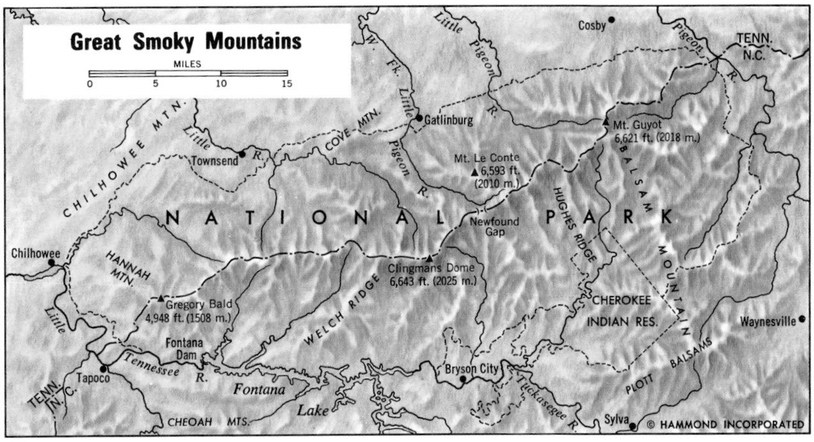
Great Smoky Mountains
MILES
0 5 10 15
NATIONAL PARK
Cosby
TENN.
N.C.
Gatlinburg
Mt. Guyot 6,621 ft. (2018 m.)
Mt. Le Conte 6,593 ft. (2010 m.)
Townsend
CHILHOWEE MTN.
COVE MTN.
BALSAM MOUNTAIN
Newfound Gap
HUGHES RIDGE
Chilhowee
HANNAH MTN.
Clingmans Dome 6,643 ft. (2025 m.)
Gregory Bald 4,948 ft. (1508 m.)
WELCH RIDGE
CHEROKEE INDIAN RES.
Waynesville
Fontana Dam
Tapoco
Tennessee R.
Fontana Lake
Bryson City
Tuckasegee R.
PLOTT BALSAMS
CHEOAH MTS.
Sylva
© HAMMOND INCORPORATED

Agriculture, Industry and Resources

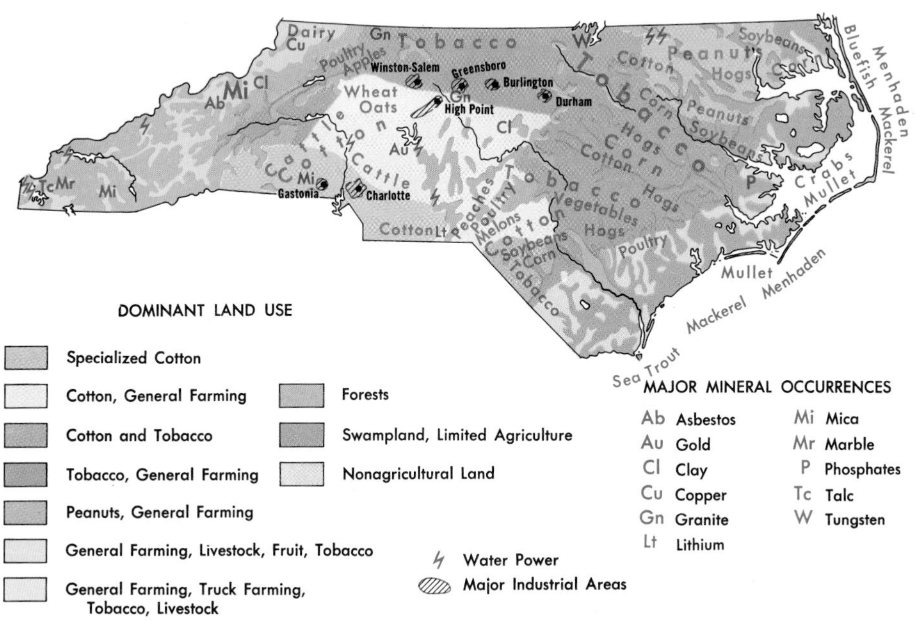
Dairy
Tobacco
Winston-Salem
Greensboro
Burlington
Durham
High Point
Wheat
Oats
Cotton
Peanuts
Soybeans
Hogs
Corn
Cattle
Poultry
Apples
Gastonia
Charlotte
Peaches
Melons
Vegetables
Bluefish
Menhaden
Mackerel
Crabs
Mullet
Sea Trout
DOMINANT LAND USE
Specialized Cotton
Cotton, General Farming
Cotton and Tobacco
Tobacco, General Farming
Peanuts, General Farming
General Farming, Livestock, Fruit, Tobacco
General Farming, Truck Farming, Tobacco, Livestock
Forests
Swampland, Limited Agriculture
Nonagricultural Land
Water Power
Major Industrial Areas
MAJOR MINERAL OCCURRENCES
Ab Asbestos
Au Gold
Cl Clay
Cu Copper
Gn Granite
Lt Lithium
Mi Mica
Mr Marble
P Phosphates
Tc Talc
W Tungsten

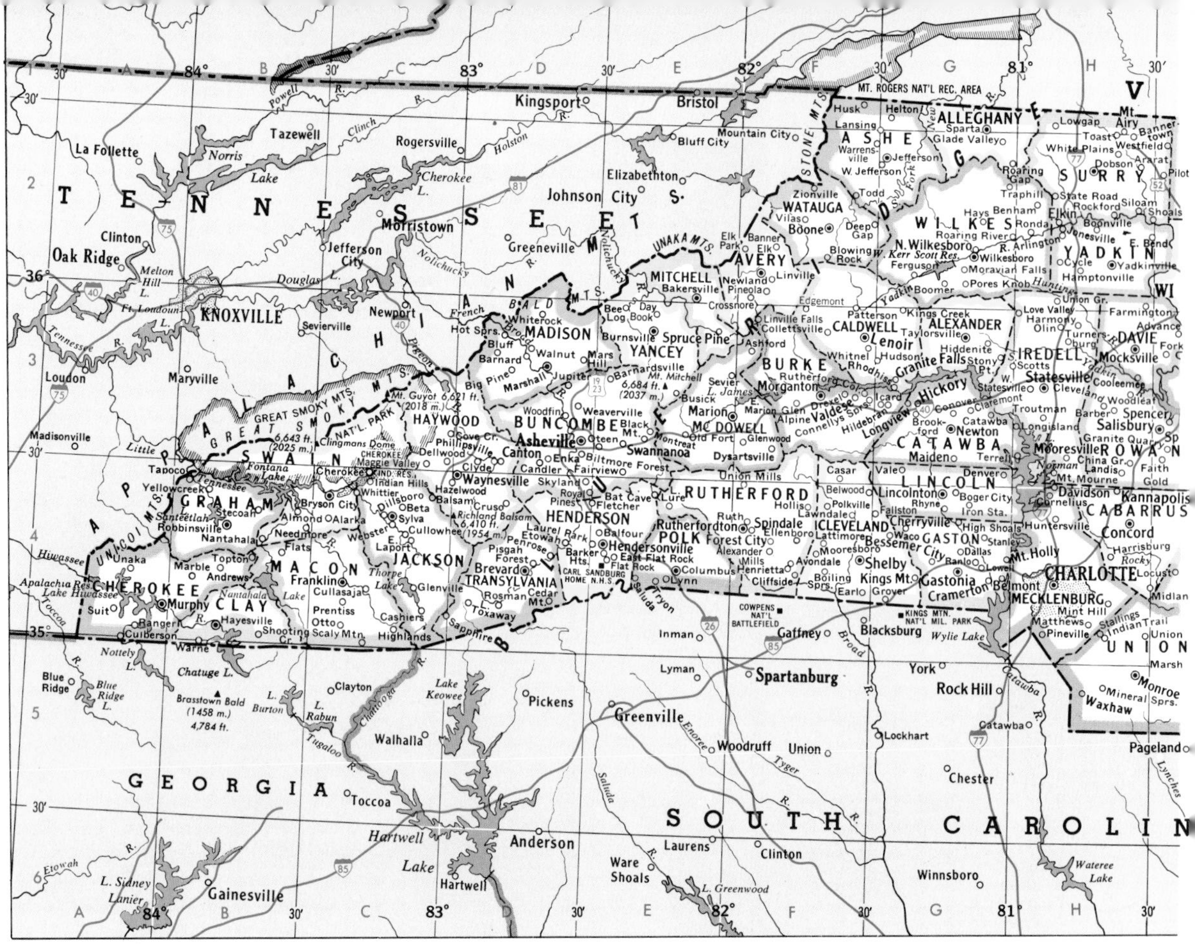
T E N N E S S E E
G E O R G I A
S O U T H C A R O L I N
A P P A L A C H I A N
KNOXVILLE
CHARLOTTE
Asheville
Spartanburg
Greenville
Kingsport
Bristol
Johnson City
Morristown
Oak Ridge
Rock Hill
Anderson
Gainesville
ALLEGHANY
ASHE
WATAUGA
WILKES
SURRY
YADKIN
AVERY
MITCHELL
MADISON
YANCEY
CALDWELL
ALEXANDER
BURKE
MC DOWELL
BUNCOMBE
HAYWOOD
SWAIN
GRAHAM
CHEROKEE
CLAY
MACON
JACKSON
TRANSYLVANIA
HENDERSON
POLK
RUTHERFORD
CLEVELAND
GASTON
LINCOLN
CATAWBA
IREDELL
DAVIE
ROWAN
CABARRUS
MECKLENBURG
UNION

Topography

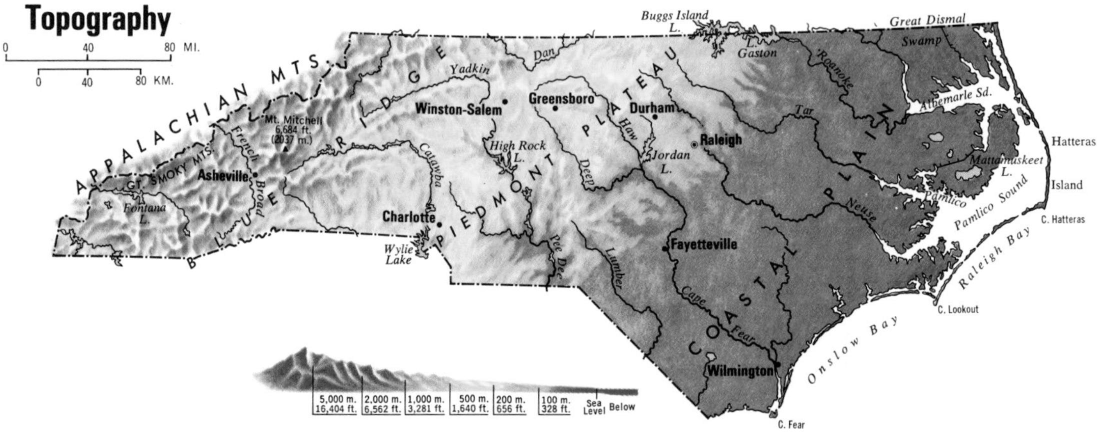
0 40 80 MI.
0 40 80 KM.
APPALACHIAN MTS.
GT. SMOKY MTS.
Mt. Mitchell 6,684 ft. (2037 m.)
Asheville
Fontana L.
Winston-Salem
Greensboro
Durham
Raleigh
High Rock L.
Jordan L.
Charlotte
Wylie Lake
PIEDMONT PLATEAU
COASTAL PLAIN
Fayetteville
Wilmington
Buggs Island L.
Gaston
Great Dismal Swamp
Albemarle Sd.
Mattamuskeet L.
Hatteras Island
C. Hatteras
Pamlico Sound
Raleigh Bay
C. Lookout
Onslow Bay
C. Fear
Yadkin
Dan
Roanoke
Tar
Neuse
Haw
Deep
Catawba
French Broad
Pee Dee
Lumber
Cape Fear
5,000 m. 16,404 ft.
2,000 m. 6,562 ft.
1,000 m. 3,281 ft.
500 m. 1,640 ft.
200 m. 656 ft.
100 m. 328 ft.
Sea Level
Below

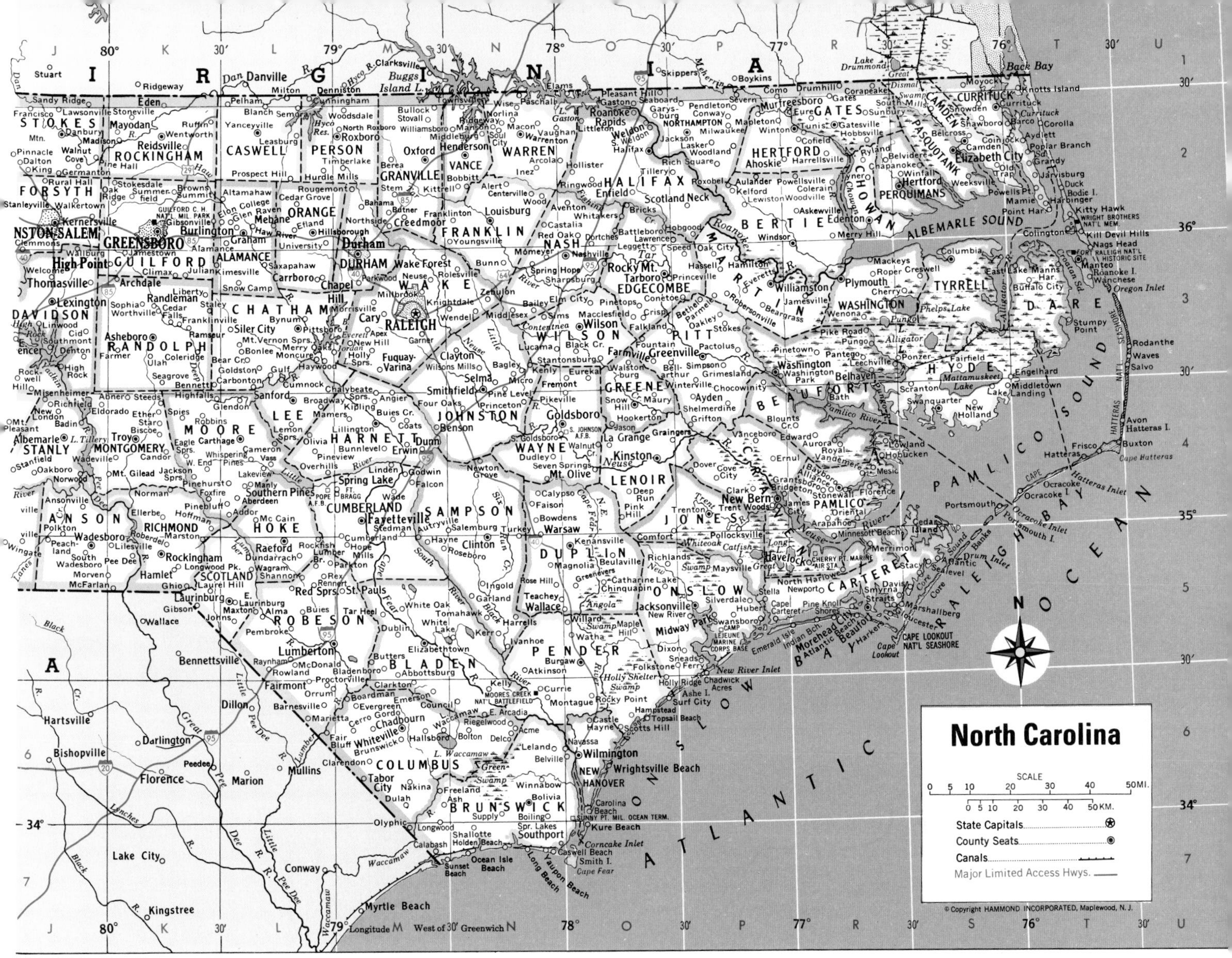
North Carolina
SCALE
0 5 10 20 30 40 50 MI.
0 5 10 20 30 40 50 KM.
State Capitals
County Seats
Canals
Major Limited Access Hwys.
© Copyright HAMMOND INCORPORATED, Maplewood, N. J.
ATLANTIC OCEAN
PAMLICO SOUND
ALBEMARLE SOUND
ONSLOW BAY
RALEIGH BAY
Longitude West of Greenwich

Rhodhiss 638 .... F3
Rich Square 1,058 .... P2
Richfield 535 .... J4
Richlands 996 .... O5
Ridgeway 500 .... N2
Riegelwood 459 .... N6
Roanoke Rapids 15,722 .... O2
Roaring Gap 450 .... H2
Roaring River 287 .... G2
Robbins 970 .... K4
Robbinsville▲ 709 .... B4
Robersonville 1,940 .... P3
Rockingham▲ 9,399 .... K5
Rockwell 1,598 .... J3
Rocky Mount 48,997 .... O3
Rocky Point 975 .... O6
Rolesville 572 .... N3
Ronda 367 .... H2
Roper 669 .... R3
Rose Hill 1,287 .... N5
Roseboro 1,441 .... N5
Rosman 385 .... D4
Rougemont 400 .... L2
Rowland 1,139 .... L5
Roxboro▲ 7,332 .... M2
Roxobel 244 .... P2
Royal 4,418 .... R4
Royal Pines D4
Ruffin 680 .... K2
Rural Hall 1,652 .... J2
Ruth 366 .... E4
Rutherford College 1,126 .... F3
Rutherfordton▲ 3,617 .... E4
Saint Pauls 1,992 .... M5
Salemburg 409 .... N4
Salisbury▲ 23,087 .... H3
Saluda 488 .... E4
Sandy Ridge 500 .... J1
Sanford▲ 14,475 .... L4
Sapphire 350 .... D4
Saxapahaw 1,178 .... L3
Scaly Mountain 250 .... C4
Scotland Neck 2,575 .... P2
Scotts 500 .... H3
Scranton 250 .... S4
Seaboard 791 .... O1
Seagrove 244 .... K3
Sealevel 600 .... S5
Selma 4,600 .... N3
Semora 500 .... L2
Seven Springs 163 .... O4
Severn 260 .... P2
Sevier 302 .... E3
Shallotte 965 .... N7
Sharpsburg 1,536 .... O3
Shawboro 300 .... S2
Shelby▲ 14,669 .... G4
Shoals 350 .... J2
Shooting Creek 250 .... B4
Siler City 4,808 .... L3
Silverdale 250 .... P5
Simpson 410 .... P3
Sims 124 .... N3
Skyland D4
Smithfield▲ 7,540 .... N3
Smyrna 291 .... R5
Sneads Ferry 2,031 .... P5
Snow Hill▲ 1,378 .... O4
Sophia 350 .... K3
South Goldsboro 2,531 .... N4
South Mills 950 .... S2
South Wadesboro J5
South Weldon 1,640 .... O2
Southern Pines 9,129 .... L4
Southmont 950 .... J3
Southport 2,369 .... N7
Sparta▲ 1,957 .... G1
Speed 88 .... P3
Spencer 3,219 .... H3
Spindale 4,040 .... F4
Spring Hope 1,221 .... N3
Spring Lake 7,524 .... M4
Spruce Pine 2,010 .... E3
Stacy 410 .... S5
Staley 204 .... K3
Stallings 2,132 .... H4
Stanfield 517 .... J4
Stanley 2,823 .... G4
Stanleyville 4,779 .... J2
Stantonsburg 782 .... O3
Star 775 .... K4
Statesville▲ 17,567 .... H3
Stecoah 250 .... B4
Stedman 577 .... M4
Stella 700 .... P5
Stem 249 .... M2
Stokes 2,134 .... P3
Stokesdale 1,070 .... K2
Stoneville 1,109 .... K2
Stonewall 279 .... R4
Stony Point 1,286 .... G3
Stovall 409 .... M2
Stumpy Point 250 .... T3
Suit 350 .... A4
Summerfield 2,051 .... K2
Sunbury 400 .... R2
Sunset Beach 311 .... N7
Supply 300 .... N6
Surf City 970 .... O6
Swannanoa 3,538 .... E3
Swanquarter▲ 550 .... S4
Swansboro 1,165 .... P5
Sylva▲ 1,809 .... C4
Tabor City 2,330 .... M6
Tar Heel 115 .... M5
Tarboro▲ 11,037 .... O3
Taylorsville▲ 1,566 .... G3
Teachey 244 .... N5
Terrell 319 .... G3
Thomasville 15,915 .... J3
Tillery 400 .... O2
Timberlake 500 .... M2
Toast 2,125 .... H2
Todd F2
Topsail Beach 346 .... O6
Traphill 550 .... H2
Trent Woods 2,366 .... P4
Trenton▲ 248 .... P4
Troutman 1,493 .... H3
Troy▲ 3,404 .... K4
Tryon 1,680 .... E4
Turkey 234 .... N4
Tyner 264 .... R2
Ulah 546 .... K3
Union Grove 614 .... H2
Union Mills 500 .... F3
Valdese 3,914 .... F3
Vanceboro 946 .... P4
Vandemere 299 .... R4
Vass 670 .... L4
Waco 320 .... G4
Wade 238 .... M4
Wadesboro▲ 3,645 .... J5
Wagram 480 .... L5
Wake Forest 5,769 .... M3
Walkertown 1,200 .... J2
Wallace 2,939 .... N5
Wallburg 300 .... J3
Walnut 1,088 .... D3
Walnut Cove 1,147 .... J2
Walnut Creek 623 .... O4
Walstonburg 188 .... O3
Wanchese 1,380 .... T3
Warrensville F2
Warrenton▲ 949 .... N2
Warsaw 2,859 .... N4
Washington Park 403 .... R3
Washington▲ 9,075 .... R3
Watha 99 .... O5
Waxhaw 1,294 .... H5
Waynesville▲ 6,758 .... D4
Weaverville 2,107 .... D3
Webster 410 .... C4
Weeksville 500 .... S2
Welcome 3,377 .... J3
Weldon 1,392 .... O2
Wendell 2,822 .... N3
Wentworth▲ 150 .... K2
West End 950 .... K4
West Jefferson 1,002 .... F2
West Statesville G3
Westfield 450 .... H2
Whispering Pines 1,243 .... L4
Whitakers 860 .... O2
White Lake 390 .... M5
White Plains 1,027 .... H2
Whiteville▲ 5,078 .... M6
Whitnel 975 .... F3
Wilkesboro▲ 2,573 .... G2
Willard 300 .... O5
Williamsboro 59 .... M2
Williamston▲ 5,503 .... R3
Wilmington▲ 55,530 .... N6
Wilson▲ 36,930 .... O3
Wilsons Mills M3
Windsor▲ 2,056 .... P2
Winfall 501 .... S2
Wingate 2,821 .... J5
Winston-Salem▲ 143,485 .... J2
Winterville 2,816 .... P3
Winton▲ 796 .... P2
Wise 550 .... N2
Wood 2,736 .... N2
Woodfin 3,260 .... D3
Woodland 760 .... P2
Woodleaf 550 .... H3
Worthville 350 .... K3
Wrightsville Beach 2,937 .... O6
Yadkinville▲ 2,525 .... H2
Yanceyville▲ 1,973 .... L2
Yaupon Beach 734 .... N7
Youngsville 424 .... N2
Zebulon 3,173 .... N3

OTHER FEATURES

Albemarle (sound) S2
Alligator (lake) S3
Alligator (riv.) S3
Angola (swamp) O5
Apalachia (res.) A4
Appalachian (mts.) D2
Ashe (isl.) P6
Bald (mts.) D3
Black (riv.) N5
Blue Ridge (mts.) E3
Bodie (isl.) T2
Broad (riv.) E4
Buggs Island (lake) M1
Camp Lejeune
Marine Corps Base P5
Cape Fear (riv.) M5
Cape Hatteras Nat'l Seashore T4
Carl Sandburg Home
Nat'l Hist. Site D4
Catawba (lake) G4
Catawba (riv.) H5
Catfish (lake) P5
Chatuge (lake) B5
Cherokee Ind. Res. C3
Cherry Point Marine Air Sta. R5
Chowan (riv.) R2
Clingmans Dome (mt.) C3
Contentnea (creek) N3
Core (banks) S5
Core (sound) S5
Corncake (inlet) O7
Croatan (sound) T3
Currituck (sound) T2
Dan (riv.) L1
Deep (riv.) K3
Drum (inlet) S5
Fear (cape) O7
Fishing (creek) O2
Fontana (lake) B4
Fort Bragg 34,744 .... M4
Fort Raleigh Nat'l Hist. Site T3
French Broad (riv.) D3
Gaston (res.) O2
Great (lake) P5
Great Dismal (swamp) S1
Great Smoky (mts.) B3
Great Smoky Mts. Nat'l Park B3
Green (swamp) N6
Guyot (mt.) C3
Hatteras (cape) U4
Hatteras (inlet) T4
Hatteras (isl.) U4
Haw (riv.) K2
High Rock (lake) J3
Hiwassee (lake) A4
Hiwassee (riv.) A4
Holly Shelter (swamp) O6
Hunting (riv.) H2
Hyco (riv.) L2
James (lake) E3
Jordan, B. Everett (lake) M3
Lanes (creek) J5
Little (riv.) N3
Little (riv.) L4
Little Pee Dee (riv.) L6
Little Tennessee (riv.) B4
Long (lake) P5
Lookout (cape) S5
Lumber (riv.) L6
Mattamuskeet (lake) S3
Meherrin (riv.) P1
Mitchell (mt.) E3
Moores Creek
Nat'l Battlefield N6
Nantahala (lake) B4
Neuse (riv.) R5
New (riv.) O5
New, South Fork (riv.) G2
New River (inlet) P6
Nolichucky (riv.) E2
Norman (lake) H3
North East Cape Fear (riv.) O4
Ocracoke (inlet) T5
Ocracoke (isl.) T4
Onslow (bay) P6
Oregon (inlet) U3
Pamlico (riv.) R4
Pamlico (sound) S4
Pee Dee (riv.) J4
Phelps (lake) S3
Pigeon (riv.) C3
Pope A.F.B. 2,857 .... L4
Portsmouth (isl.) T5
Pungo (lake) S3
Pungo (riv.) R4
Raleigh (bay) S5
Richland Balsam (mt.) D4
Roanoke (isl.) T3
Roanoke (riv.) P2
Rocky (riv.) H4
Santeetlah (lake) B4
Seymour Johnson A.F.B. O4
Six Run (creek) N4
Smith (isl.) O7
South (riv.) M5
South Yadkin (riv.) H3
Stone (mts.) F2
Sunny Point
Mil. Ocean Term. O6
Tar (riv.) O3
Thorpe (lake) C4
Tillery (lake) J4
Trent (riv.) P4
Unaka (mts.) E2
Unicoi (mts.) A4
Waccamaw (lake) N6
Waccamaw (riv.) M7
Whiteoak (swamp) P5
W. Scott Kerr (res.) G2
Wright Brothers Nat'l Mem. T2
Yadkin (riv.) J3

▲County seat.

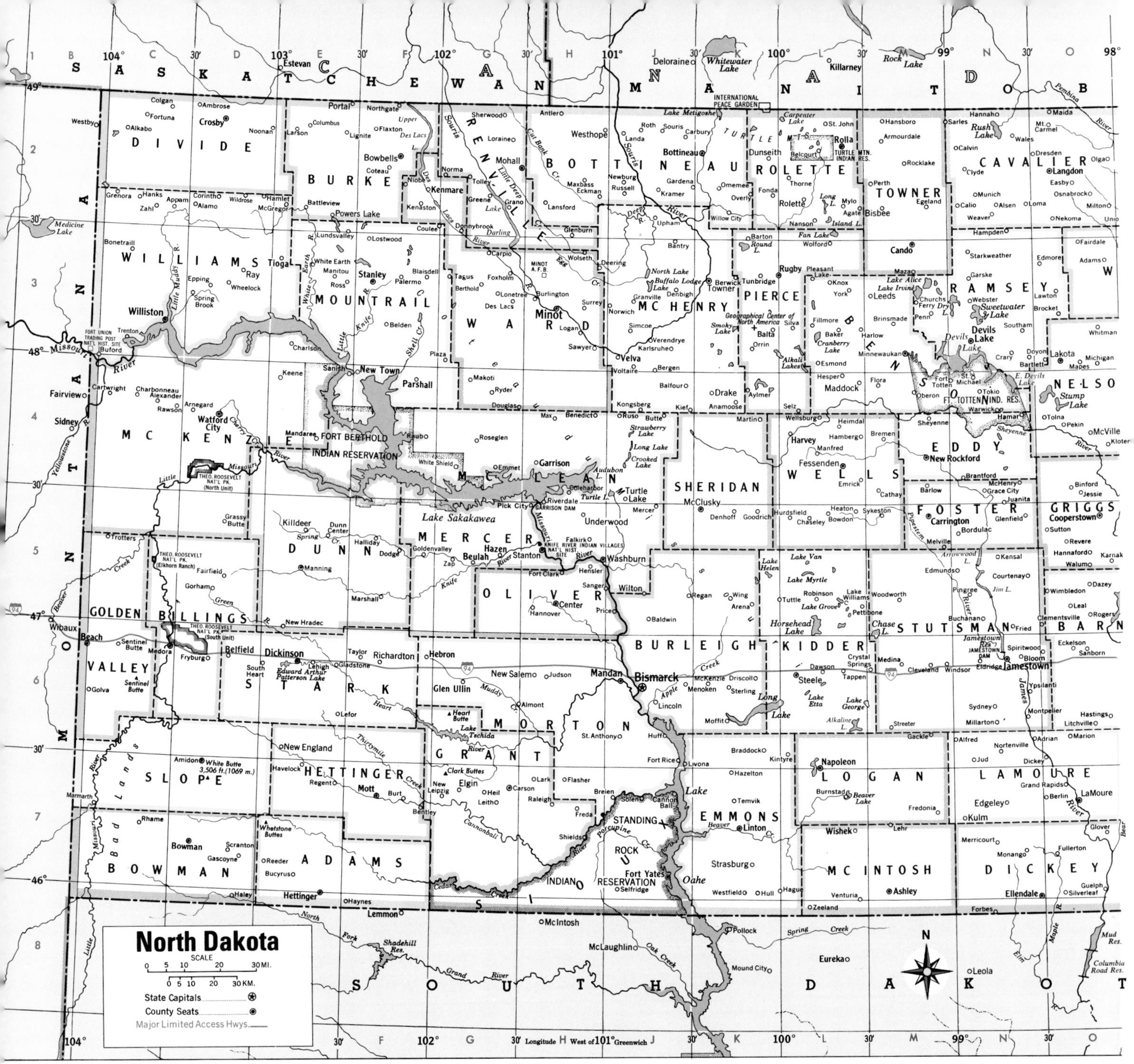
North Dakota
SCALE
0 5 10 20 30 MI.
0 5 10 20 30 KM.
State Capitals
County Seats
Major Limited Access Hwys.
S A S K A T C H E W A N
M A N I T O B A
S O U T H D A K O T A
M O N T A N A
Longitude West of 101° Greenwich

COUNTIES

Adams 3,174	F7
Barnes 12,545	O5
Benson 7,198	M3
Billings 1,108	D5
Bottineau 8,011	J2
Bowman 3,596	C7
Burke 3,002	E2
Burleigh 60,131	J6
Cass 102,874	R5
Cavalier 6,064	N2
Dickey 6,107	N7
Divide 2,899	C2
Dunn 4,005	E5
Eddy 2,951	N4
Emmons 4,830	K7
Foster 3,983	N5
Golden Valley 2,108	C5
Grand Forks 70,683	P3
Grant 3,549	G6
Griggs 3,303	O5
Hettinger 3,445	E7
Kidder 3,332	L6
LaMoure 5,383	N7
Logan 2,847	L7
McHenry 6,528	J3
McIntosh 4,021	L7
McKenzie 6,383	D4
McLean 10,457	G4
Mercer 9,808	G5
Morton 23,700	H6
Mountrail 7,021	E3
Nelson 4,410	O4
Oliver 2,381	H5
Pembina 9,238	P2
Pierce 5,052	K3
Ramsey 12,681	N3
Ransom 5,921	P7
Renville 3,160	G2
Richland 18,148	R7
Rolette 12,772	L2
Sargent 4,549	P7
Sheridan 2,148	K4
Sioux 3,761	H7
Slope 907	C7
Stark 22,832	E6
Steele 2,420	P4
Stutsman 22,241	M5
Towner 3,627	M2
Traill 8,752	R5
Walsh 13,840	P3
Ward 57,921	G3
Wells 5,864	L4
Williams 21,129	C3

CITIES and TOWNS

Abercrombie 252	S7
Adams 248	O3
Alexander 216	C4
Almont 117	H6
Alsen 113	N2
Amidon▲ 24	D7
Anamoose 277	K4
Aneta 314	P4
Argusville 161	R5
Arnegard 122	D4
Arthur 400	R5
Ashley▲ 1,052	M7
Beach▲ 1,205	C6
Belcourt 2,458	L2
Belfield 887	D6
Berthold 409	G3
Beulah 3,363	G5
Binford 233	O4
Bisbee 227	M2
Bismarck (cap.)▲ 49,256	J6
Bottineau▲ 2,598	J2
Bowbells▲ 498	F2
Bowdon 196	L5
Bowman▲ 1,741	D7
Buffalo 204	R6
Burlington 995	H3
Butte 129	J4
Buxton 343	R4
Cando▲ 1,564	M3
Cannon Ball 702	J7
Carpio 178	G3
Carrington▲ 2,267	M5
Carson▲ 383	H7
Casselton 1,601	R6
Cavalier▲ 1,508	P2
Center▲ 826	H5
Christine 140	S6
Church's Ferry 118	M3
Cleveland 121	M6
Cogswell 184	P7
Coleharbor 88	H4
Columbus 223	E2
Cooperstown▲ 1,247	O5
Crary 145	N3
Crosby▲ 1,312	D2
Crystal 199	P2
Davenport 218	R6
Dazey 129	O5
Deering 99	J3
Des Lacs 216	G3
Devils Lake▲ 7,782	N3
Dickinson▲ 16,097	E6
Dodge 135	F5
Donnybrook 106	G2
Drake 361	K4
Drayton 961	R2
Dunn Center 128	E5
Dunseith 723	K2
Edgeley 680	N7
Edinburg 284	P3
Edmore 329	O3
Egeland 103	M2
Elgin 765	G7
Ellendale▲ 1,798	N7
Emerado 483	R4
Enderlin 997	P6
Esmond 196	L3
Fairmount 427	S7
Fargo▲ 74,111	S6
Fessenden▲ 655	L4
Fingal 138	P6
Finley▲ 543	P4
Flasher 317	H7
Flaxton 121	F2
Fordville 299	P3
Forest River 148	P3
Forman▲ 586	P7
Fort Ransom 111	P6
Fort Totten 867	M4
Fort Yates▲ 183	J7
Frontier 218	S6
Fullerton 94	O7
Gackle 450	M6
Galesburg 161	R5
Garrison 1,530	H4
Gilby 262	R3
Gladstone 224	F6
Glen Ullin 927	G6
Glenburn 439	H2
Glenfield 118	N5
Goldenvalley 287	F5
Golva 101	C6
Goodrich 192	K5
Grace City 108	N4
Grafton▲ 4,840	R3
Grand Forks▲ 49,425	R4
Grandin 213	R5
Granville 236	J3
Great Bend 108	S7
Grenora 261	C2
Gwinner 585	P7
Hague 109	L7
Halliday 288	F5
Hankinson 1,038	S7
Hannaford 204	O5
Harvey 2,263	L4
Harwood 590	S6
Hatton 800	R4
Havana 124	P8
Hazelton 240	K7
Hazen 2,818	G5
Hebron 888	G6
Hettinger▲ 1,574	E8
Hillsboro▲ 1,488	S5
Hoople 310	P2
Hope 281	P5
Horace 662	S6
Hunter 341	R5
Inkster 95	P3
Jamestown▲ 15,571	N6
Karlsruhe 143	J3
Kenmare 1,214	G2
Kensal 191	N5
Killdeer 722	E5
Kindred 569	R6
Kulm 514	N7
LaMoure▲ 970	O7
Lakota▲ 898	O3
Langdon▲ 2,241	O2
Lankin 152	P3
Lansford 249	H2
Larimore 1,464	P4
Leeds 542	M3
Lehr 191	M7
Leonard 310	R6
Lidgerwood 799	R7
Lignite 242	F2
Lincoln 1,132	J6
Linton▲ 1,410	K7
Lisbon▲ 2,177	P7
Litchville 205	O6
Maddock 559	L4
Makoti 145	G4
Mandan▲ 15,177	J6
Mandaree 367	E4
Manning▲ 75	E5
Manvel 333	R3
Mapleton 682	R6
Marion 169	O6
Marmarth 144	B7
Martin 117	K4
Max 301	H4
Maxbass 123	H2
Mayville 2,092	R4
McClusky▲ 492	K4
McVille 559	O4
Medina 387	M6
Medora▲ 101	C6
Mercer 104	J5
Michigan 413	O3
Milnor 651	R7
Milton 133	O2
Minnewaukan▲ 401	M3
Minot▲ 34,544	H3
Minto 560	R3
Mohall▲ 931	G2
Mooreton 193	S7
Mott▲ 1,019	F7
Mountain 134	P2
Munich 310	N2
Napoleon▲ 930	L6
Neche 434	P2
New England 663	E6

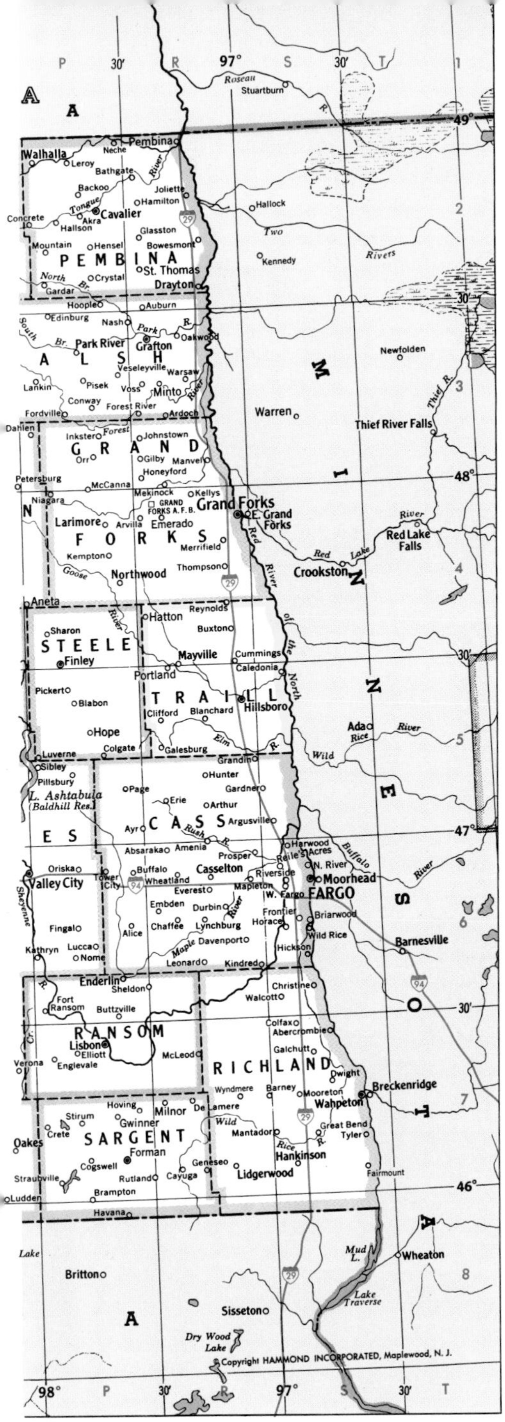
Roseau
Stuartburn
49°
97°
Walhalla
Neche
Pembina
Leroy
Bathgate
Backoo
Joliette
Tongue
Hamilton
Concrete
Akra
Cavalier
Hallson
Glasston
Mountain
Hensel
Bowesmont
P E M B I N A
St. Thomas
North Br.
Crystal
Drayton
Gardar
Hallock
Two
Rivers
Kennedy
Hoople
Auburn
Edinburg
Nash
Park
Grafton
Oakwood
South Br.
Park River
A L S H
Veseleyville
Warsaw
Lankin
Pisek
Voss
Minto
Conway
Forest River
Fordville
Ardoch
Newfolden
Warren
Thief River Falls
Thief R.
Dahlen
Inkster
Johnstown
G R A N D
Orr
Gilby
Manvel
Honeyford
Petersburg
McCanna
Mekinock
Kellys
Niagara
Grand Forks
E. Grand Forks
Larimore
Arvilla
Emerado
F O R K S
Merrifield
Kempton
Goose
Northwood
Thompson
Red Lake Falls
Red Lake River
Crookston
Aneta
Reynolds
Hatton
Buxton
Sharon
S T E E L E
Finley
Mayville
Cummings
Caledonia
Portland
Pickert
Blabon
T R A I L L
Hillsboro
Clifford
Blanchard
Hope
Colgate
Galesburg
Luverne
Sibley
Pillsbury
L. Ashtabula (Baldhill Res.)
Page
Erie
Gardner
Hunter
Arthur
Ayr
C A S S
Argusville
Absaraka
Amenia
Prosper
Harwood
Reile's Acres
Oriska
Buffalo
Casselton
N. River
Moorhead
Valley City
Tower City
Wheatland
Mapleton
Everest
W. Fargo
FARGO
Embden
Durbin
Fingal
Chaffee
Lynchburg
Horace
Briarwood
Alice
Davenport
Frontier
Wild Rice
Kathryn
Lucca
Nome
Leonard
Kindred
Hickson
Barnesville
Enderlin
Sheldon
Fort Ransom
Buttzville
Christine
Walcott
R A N S O M
Colfax
Abercrombie
Lisbon
Elliott
McLeod
Verona
Englevale
Galchutt
R I C H L A N D
Wyndmere
Barney
Mooreton
Dwight
Breckenridge
Wahpeton
Hoving
Milnor
De Lamere
Stirum
Gwinner
Oakes
Crete
S A R G E N T
Mantador
Great Bend
Tyler
Forman
Hankinson
Cogswell
Geneseo
Rutland
Cayuga
Lidgerwood
Fairmount
Straubville
Brampton
Ludden
Havana
46°
Lake
Britton
Wheaton
Mud L.
Lake Traverse
Sisseton
Dry Wood Lake
Copyright HAMMOND INCORPORATED, Maplewood, N. J.
98°
P
30′
R
97°
S
T

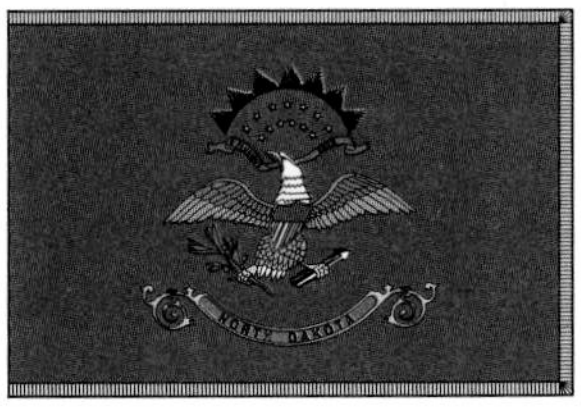
NORTH DAKOTA

AREA 70,702 sq. mi. (183,118 sq. km.)
POPULATION 641,364
CAPITAL Bismarck
LARGEST CITY Fargo
HIGHEST POINT White Butte 3,506 ft. (1069 m.)
SETTLED IN 1780
ADMITTED TO UNION November 2, 1889
POPULAR NAME Flickertail State; Sioux State
STATE FLOWER Wild Prairie Rose
STATE BIRD Western Meadowlark

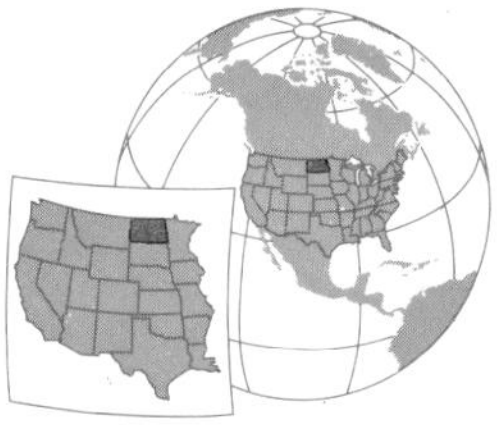

New Leipzig 326 .... G7
New Rockford▲ 1,604 .... N4
New Salem 909 .... G6
New Town 1,388 .... F4
Newburg 104 .... J2
Noonan 231 .... D2
Northwood 1,166 .... P4
Oakes 1,775 .... O7
Oberon 103 .... M4
Oriska 103 .... P6
Osnabrock 214 .... O2
Page 266 .... P5
Palermo 95 .... F3
Park River 1,725 .... P3
Parshall 943 .... F4
Pekin 101 .... O4
Pembina 642 .... R2
Petersburg 219 .... P3
Pick City 203 .... G5
Pisek 130 .... P3
Plaza 193 .... G3
Portal 192 .... E2
Portland 602 .... R5
Powers Lake 408 .... E2
Ray 603 .... D3
Reeder 252 .... E7
Regent 268 .... E7
Reile's Acres 210 .... S6
Reynolds 299 .... R4
Rhame 186 .... C7
Richardton 625 .... F6
Riverdale 283 .... H4
Riverside 465 .... S6
Rocklake 221 .... M2
Rolette 623 .... L2
Rolla▲ 1,286 .... L2
Rugby▲ 2,909 .... L3
Rutland 212 .... P7
Ryder 121 .... G4
Saint John 368 .... L2
Saint Thomas 444 .... R2
Sanborn 164 .... O6
Sanish E4
Sawyer 319 .... H3
Scranton 294 .... D7
Selfridge 242 .... J7
Sharon 119 .... P4
Sheldon 149 .... P6
Sherwood 286 .... G2
Sheyenne 272 .... M4
Souris 97 .... J2
South Heart 322 .... D6
Stanley▲ 1,371 .... F3
Stanton▲ 517 .... H5
Starkweather 197 .... N3
Steele▲ 762 .... L6
Strasburg 553 .... K7
Streeter 161 .... M6
Surrey 856 .... H3
Sykeston 167 .... M5
Tappen 239 .... L6
Taylor 163 .... F6
Thompson 930 .... R4
Tioga 1,278 .... E3
Tolna 230 .... O4
Tower City 233 .... P6
Towner▲ 669 .... K3
Turtle Lake 681 .... J4
Tuttle 160 .... L5
Underwood 976 .... H5
Upham 205 .... J2
Valley City▲ 7,163 .... P6
Velva 968 .... J3
Verona 103 .... O7
Wahpeton▲ 8,751 .... S7
Walcott 178 .... R6
Walhalla 1,131 .... P2
Washburn▲ 1,506 .... J5
Watford City▲ 1,784 .... D4
West Fargo 12,287 .... S6
Westhope 578 .... H2
White Shield 274 .... G4
Wildrose 193 .... D2
Williston▲ 13,131 .... C3
Willow City 281 .... K2
Wilton 728 .... J5
Wimbledon 275 .... O5
Wing 208 .... K5
Wishek 1,171 .... L7
Woodworth 102 .... M5
Wyndmere 501 .... R7
Zap 287 .... G5
Zeeland 197 .... L8

OTHER FEATURES

Alkali (lakes) L3
Alkaline (lake) L6
Apple (creek) J6
Arrowwood (lake) N5
Ashtabula (Baldhill Res.) (lake) P5
Audubon (lake) H4
Bad Lands (reg.) C7
Baldhill (Ashtabula Lake) (res.) P5
Bear (creek) O7
Beaver (creek) K7
Beaver (creek) B5
Beaver (lake) L7
Buffalo Lodge (lake) J3
Cannonball (riv.) G7
Carpenter (lake) L2
Cedar (creek) G7
Chase (lake) M5
Cherry (creek) D4
Clark (buttes) G7
Coteau du Missouri (plain) G3
Cranberry (lake) L3
Crooked (lake) J4
Cut Bank (creek) H2
Darling (lake) G2
Deep (riv.) J1
Des Lacs (riv.) G3
Devils (lake) N3
Dry (lake) M3
East Devils (lake) N4
Egg (creek) H3
Elm (riv.) N8
Elm (riv.) R5
Etta (lake) L6
Fan (lake) L2
Forest (riv.) P3
Fort Berthold Ind. Res. E4
Fort Totten Ind. Res. N4
Fort Union Trading Post Nat'l Hist. Site B3
Garrison (dam) H5
George (lake) L6
Goose (riv.) P4
Grand, North Fork (riv.) E8
Grand Forks A.F.B. 9,343 .... R4
Green (riv.) D5
Grove (lake) L5
Heart (butte) G6
Heart (riv.) F6
Helen (lake) K5
Horsehead (lake) L5
International Peace Garden K1
Irvine (lake) M3
Island (lake) L2
James (riv.) N6
Jamestown (res.) N6
Jim (lake) N5
Knife (riv.) G5
Knife R. Indian Villages Nat'l Hist. Site H5
Little Deep (creek) G2
Little Knife (riv.) F3
Little Missouri (riv.) D4
Little Muddy (riv.) C3
Long (lake) J4
Long (lake) K6
Long (lake) L2
Maple (riv.) O8
Maple (riv.) R6
Metigoshe (lake) K2
Minot A.F.B. 9,095 .... H3
Missouri (riv.) H5
Muddy (creek) G6
Myrtle (lake) L5
North (lake) J3
Oahe (lake) J7
Oak (creek) J8
Park (riv.) R3
Patterson, Edward A. (lake) E6
Pembina (riv.) O1
Pipestem (riv.) M5
Porcupine (creek) J7
Red River of the North (riv.) S4
Round (lake) K3
Rush (lake) N2
Rush (riv.) R5
Sakakawea (lake) G5
Sentinel (butte) C6
Shell (creek) F3
Sheyenne (riv.) O6
Smoky (lake) K3
Souris (riv.) J2
Spring (creek) E5
Standing Rock Ind. Res. J7
Strawberry (lake) J4
Stump (lake) O4
Sweetwater (lake) N3
Theodore Roosevelt Nat'l Park C5
Theodore Roosevelt Nat'l Park D4
Theodore Roosevelt Nat'l Park D6
Thirty Mile (creek) F6
Tongue (riv.) P2
Tschida (lake) G6
Turtle (lake) H4
Turtle (mts.) K2
Turtle Mountain Ind. Res. L2
Upper Des Lacs (lake) F2
Van (lake) L5
Whetstone (buttes) E7
White Butte (buttes) D7
White Earth (riv.) E3
Wild Rice (riv.) R7
Yellowstone (riv.) B4

▲County seat

Topography

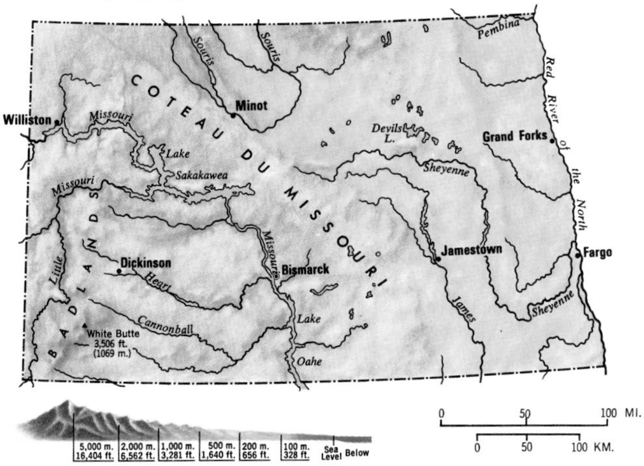
Souris
Pembina
Minot
Williston
Missouri
COTEAU DU MISSOURI
Lake Sakakawea
Devils L.
Grand Forks
Sheyenne
Red River of the North
Little Missouri
BADLANDS
Dickinson
Heart
Bismarck
Jamestown
Fargo
James
Cannonball
Lake Oahe
White Butte 3,506 ft. (1069 m.)
5,000 m. 16,404 ft.
2,000 m. 6,562 ft.
1,000 m. 3,281 ft.
500 m. 1,640 ft.
200 m. 656 ft.
100 m. 328 ft.
Sea Level
Below
0
50
100 MI.
0
50
100 KM.

Agriculture, Industry and Resources

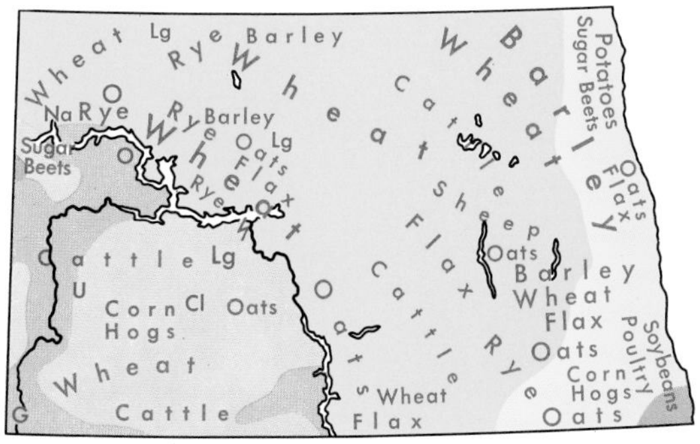
Wheat
Lg
Rye
Barley
Wheat
Barley
Potatoes
Sugar Beets
Na
Rye
Sugar Beets
Oats
Flax
Cattle
Sheep
Oats
Wheat
Lg
Corn
Cl
Oats
Hogs
Flax
Soybeans
Poultry
Hogs
Wheat
Cattle
U
G

DOMINANT LAND USE

- Specialized Wheat
- Wheat, General Farming
- Wheat, Range Livestock
- Livestock, Cash Grain
- Sugar Beets, Dry Beans, Livestock, General Farming
- Range Livestock
- Water Power

MAJOR MINERAL OCCURRENCES

- Cl Clay
- G Natural Gas
- Lg Lignite
- Na Salt
- O Petroleum
- U Uranium

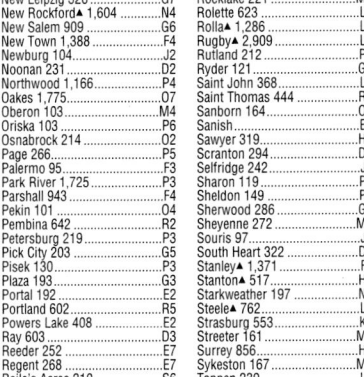

Ohio
SCALE
0 5 10 20 30 40 MI.
0 5 10 20 30 40 KM.
State Capitals
County Seats
Major Limited Access Hwys.
MICHIGAN
INDIANA
PENNSYLVANIA
KENTUCKY
WEST VIRGINIA
ONTARIO CANADA
LAKE ERIE
Lake St. Clair
DETROIT
Windsor
Toledo
CLEVELAND
Akron
Canton
Youngstown
Columbus
Dayton
Springfield
CINCINNATI
Huntington
Parkersburg
Wheeling
Steubenville
Lima
Mansfield
Zanesville
Portsmouth
Marietta
Sandusky
Lorain
Elyria
Ohio R.
Longitude West of Greenwich

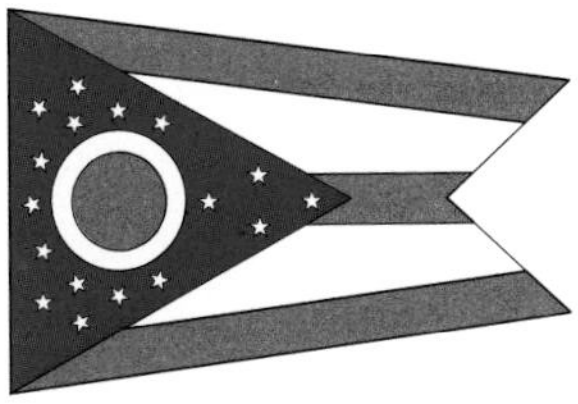

AREA 41,330 sq. mi. (107,045 sq. km.)
POPULATION 10,887,325
CAPITAL Columbus
LARGEST CITY Cleveland
HIGHEST POINT Campbell Hill 1,550 ft. (472 m.)
SETTLED IN 1788
ADMITTED TO UNION March 1, 1803
POPULAR NAME Buckeye State
STATE FLOWER Scarlet Carnation
STATE BIRD Cardinal

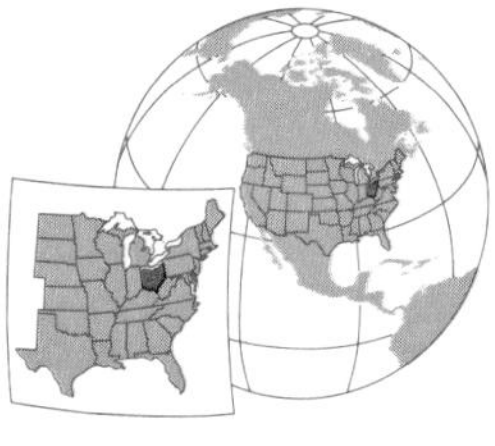

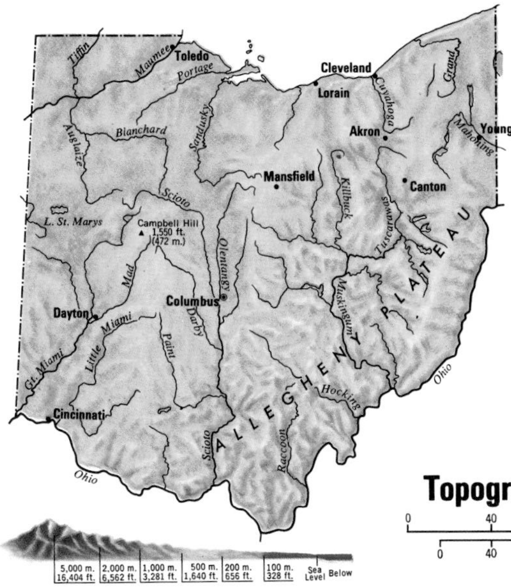
Toledo
Cleveland
Lorain
Akron
Youngstown
Canton
Mansfield
Columbus
Dayton
Cincinnati
Campbell Hill
1,550 ft.
(472 m.)
L. St. Marys
Tiffin
Maumee
Portage
Blanchard
Sandusky
Auglaize
Cuyahoga
Grand
Mahoning
Scioto
Killbuck
Tuscarawas
Olentangy
Mad
Miami
Little Miami
Gt. Miami
Darby
Paint
Muskingum
Hocking
Raccoon
Ohio
ALLEGHENY PLATEAU
5,000 m. 16,404 ft.
2,000 m. 6,562 ft.
1,000 m. 3,281 ft.
500 m. 1,640 ft.
200 m. 656 ft.
100 m. 328 ft.
Sea Level
Below

Topography

0 40 80 MI.
0 40 80 KM.

COUNTIES

Adams 25,371 D8
Allen 109,755 B4
Ashland 47,507 F4
Ashtabula 99,821 J2
Athens 59,549 F7
Auglaize 44,585 B4
Belmont 71,074 J5
Brown 34,966 C8
Butler 291,479 A7
Carroll 26,521 H4
Champaign 36,019 C5
Clark 147,548 C6
Clermont 150,187 B7
Clinton 35,415 C7
Columbiana 108,276 J4
Coshocton 35,427 G5
Crawford 47,870 E4
Cuyahoga 1,412,140 G3
Darke 53,619 A5
Defiance 39,350 A3
Delaware 66,929 D5
Erie 76,779 E3
Fairfield 103,461 E6
Fayette 27,466 D6
Franklin 961,437 E5
Fulton 38,498 B2
Gallia 30,954 F8
Geauga 81,129 H3
Greene 136,731 C6
Guernsey 39,024 H5
Hamilton 866,228 A7
Hancock 65,536 C3
Hardin 31,111 C4
Harrison 16,085 H5
Henry 29,108 B3
Highland 35,728 C7
Hocking 25,533 F6
Holmes 32,849 G4
Huron 56,240 E3
Jackson 30,230 E7
Jefferson 80,298 J5
Knox 47,473 F5
Lake 215,499 H2
Lawrence 61,834 E8
Licking 128,300 F5
Logan 42,310 C5
Lorain 271,126 F3
Lucas 462,361 C2
Madison 37,068 D6
Mahoning 264,806 J4
Marion 64,274 D4
Medina 122,354 G3
Meigs 22,987 F7
Mercer 39,443 A4
Miami 93,182 B5
Monroe 15,497 H6
Montgomery 573,809 B6
Morgan 14,194 G6
Morrow 27,749 E4
Muskingum 82,068 G5
Noble 11,336 G6
Ottawa 40,029 D2
Paulding 20,488 A3
Perry 31,557 F6
Pickaway 48,255 D6
Pike 24,249 D7
Portage 142,585 H3
Preble 40,113 A6
Putnam 33,819 B3
Richland 126,137 E4
Ross 69,330 D7
Sandusky 61,963 D3
Scioto 80,327 D8
Seneca 59,733 D3
Shelby 44,915 B5
Stark 367,585 H4
Summit 514,990 G3
Trumbull 227,813 J3
Tuscarawas 84,090 H5
Union 31,969 D5
Van Wert 30,464 A4
Vinton 11,098 E7
Warren 113,909 B7
Washington 62,254 H7
Wayne 101,461 G4
Williams 36,956 A2
Wood 113,269 C3
Wyandot 22,254 D4

CITIES and TOWNS

Aberdeen 1,329 C8
Ada 5,413 C4
Adamsville 151 G5
Addyston 1,198 B9
Adelphi 398 E7
Adena 842 J5
Akron▲ 223,019 G3
Albany 795 F7
Alexandria 468 E5
Alger 864 C4
Alliance 23,376 H4
Alvordton 298 A2
Amanda 729 E6
Amberley 3,108 C9
Amelia 1,837 D10
Amesville 250 F7
Amherst 10,332 F3
Amsterdam 669 J5
Andover 1,216 J2
Anna 1,164 B5
Ansonia 1,279 A5
Antioch 68 H6
Antwerp 1,677 A3
Apple Creek 860 G4
Aquilla 360 H2
Arcadia 546 D3
Arcanum 1,953 A6
Archbold 3,440 B2
Arlington 1,267 C4
Arlington Heights 1,084 C9
Ashland▲ 20,079 F4
Ashley 1,059 E5
Ashtabula 21,633 J2
Ashville 2,254 E6
Athalia 346 F8
Athens▲ 21,265 F7
Attica 944 E3
Aurora 9,192 H3
Austintown 32,371 J3
Avon 7,337 F3
Avon Lake 15,066 F2
Bailey Lakes 367 F4
Bainbridge 968 D7
Bairdstown 130 C3
Ballville 3,083 D3
Baltic 659 G5
Baltimore 2,971 E6
Barberton 27,623 G4
Barnesville 4,326 H6
Barnhill 313 H5
Barton 1,039 J5
Batavia▲ 1,700 B7
Batesville 95 H6
Bay View 739 E3
Bay Village 17,000 G9
Beach City 1,051 G4
Beachwood 10,677 J9
Beallsville 464 J6
Beaver 336 E7
Beavercreek 33,626 C6
Beaverdam 467 C4
Bedford 14,822 H9
Bedford Heights 12,131 J9
Bellaire 6,028 J5
Bellbrook 6,511 C6
Belle Center 796 C4
Belle Valley 267 G6
Bellefontaine▲ 12,142 C5
Bellevue 8,146 E3
Bellville 1,568 E4
Belmont 471 J5
Belmore 161 B3
Beloit 1,037 J4
Belpre 6,796 G7
Bentleyville 674 J9
Benton 351 G4
Benton Ridge 343 C4
Berea 19,051 G10
Bergholz 713 J4
Berkey 264 C2
Berlin 691 G4
Berlin Heights 756 E3
Bethel 2,407 B8
Bethesda 1,161 H5
Bettsville 752 D3
Beverly 1,444 G6
Bexley 13,088 E6
Blakeslee 128 A2
Blanchester 4,206 B7
Bloomdale 632 D3
Bloomingburg 769 D6
Bloomingdale 227 J5
Bloomville 949 D3
Blue Ash 11,860 C9
Bluffton 3,367 C4
Boardman 38,596 J3
Bolivar 914 G4
Boston Heights 733 J10
Botkins 1,340 B5
Bowerston 343 H5
Bowersville 225 C6
Bowling Green▲ 28,176 C3
Bradford 2,005 B5
Bradner 1,093 C3
Brady Lake 490 H3
Brecksville 11,818 H10
Bremen 1,386 F6
Brewster 2,307 G4
Brice 109 E6
Bridgeport 2,318 J5
Bridgetown 11,748 B9
Brilliant 1,672 J5
Brimfield 3,223 H3
Broadview Heights 12,219 H10
Brook Park 22,865 G9
Brookfield 1,396 J3
Brooklyn 11,706 H9
Brooklyn Heights 1,450 H9
Brookside 703 J5
Brookville 4,621 B6
Broughton 151 B3
Brunswick 28,230 G3
Bryan▲ 8,348 A3
Buchtel 640 F7
Buckeye Lake 2,986 F6
Buckland 239 B4
Bucyrus▲ 13,496 E4
Burbank 289 F4
Burgoon 224 D3
Burkettsville 268 A5
Burlington 3,003 F9
Burton 1,349 H3
Butler 968 F4
Butlerville 188 B7
Byesville 2,435 G6
Cadiz▲ 3,439 J5
Cairo 473 B4
Calcutta 1,212 J4
Caldwell▲ 1,786 G6
Caledonia 644 D4
Cambridge▲ 11,748 G5
Camden 2,210 A6
Campbell 10,038 J3
Canal Fulton 4,157 H4
Canal Winchester 2,617 E6
Canfield 5,409 J3
Canton▲ 84,161 H4
Cardington 1,770 E5
Carey 3,684 D4
Carlisle 4,872 B6
Carroll 558 E6
Carrollton▲ 3,042 J4
Casstown 246 B5
Castalia 915 E3
Castine 163 A6
Catawba 268 C6
Cecil 249 A3
Cedarville 3,210 C6
Celina▲ 9,650 A4
Centerburg 1,323 E5
Centerville 128 B6
Chagrin Falls 4,146 J9
Chardon▲ 4,446 H2
Chatfield 206 E4
Chauncey 980 F7
Cherry Fork 178 C8
Cherry Grove 4,972 C10
Chesapeake 1,073 E9
Cheshire 250 F8
Chester 309 G7
Chesterhill 395 G6
Chesterland 2,078 H2
Chesterville 286 E5
Cheviot 9,616 B9
Chickasaw 378 A5
Chillicothe▲ 21,923 E7
Chilo 130 B8
Christiansburg 599 C5
Cincinnati▲ 364,040 B9
Circleville▲ 11,666 D6
Clarington 406 J6
Clark 523 G5
Clarksburg 483 D7
Clarksville 485 C7
Clay Center 289 D2
Clayton 713 B6
Cleveland Heights 54,052 H9
Cleveland▲ 505,616 H9
Cleves 2,208 B9
Clinton 1,175 G4
Cloverdale 270 B3
Clyde 5,776 E3
Coal Grove 2,251 E9
Coalton 553 E7
Coldwater 4,335 A5
College Corner 379 A6
Columbiana 4,961 J4
Columbus (cap.)▲ 632,910 E6
Columbus Grove 2,231 B4
Commercial Point 405 D6
Conesville 420 G5
Congress 162 F4
Conneaut 13,241 J2
Continental 1,214 B3
Convoy 1,200 A4
Coolville 663 G7
Corning 703 F6
Cortland 5,666 J3
Corwin 225 B6
Coshocton▲ 12,193 G5
Cove 6,669 E8
Covedale 5,830 B10
Covington 2,603 B5
Craig Beach 1,402 H3
Crestline 4,934 E4
Creston 1,848 G3
Cridersville 1,885 B4
Crooksville 2,601 F6
Crown City 445 F8
Cumberland 318 G6
Custar 209 C3
Cuyahoga Falls 48,950 G3
Cuyahoga Heights 682 H9
Cygnet 560 C3
Dalton 1,377 G4
Danville 1,001 F5
Darbydale 825 D6
Darbyville 272 D6
Dayton▲ 182,044 B6
Deer Park 6,181 C9
Deersville 86 H5
Defiance▲ 16,768 B3
Degraff 1,331 C5
Delaware▲ 20,030 E5
Dellroy 314 H4
Delphos 7,093 B4
Delta 2,849 B2
Dennison 3,282 H5
Dent 6,416 B9
Deshler 1,876 C3
Devola 2,736 H7
Dexter City 161 G6
Dillonvale 857 J5
Dover 11,329 G4
Doylestown 2,668 G4
Dresden 1,581 G5
Dublin 16,366 D5
Dunkirk 869 C4
Dupont 279 B3
East Canton 1,742 H4
East Cleveland 33,096 H9
East Liverpool 13,654 J4
East Palestine 5,168 J4
East Sparta 771 H4
Eastlake 21,161 J8
Eaton Estates 1,586 G3
Eaton▲ 7,396 A6
Edgerton 1,896 A3
Edgewood 5,189 J2
Edison 488 E4
Edon 880 A2
Eldorado 549 A6
Elgin 71 A4
Elida 1,486 B4
Elmore 1,334 D3
Elmwood Place 2,937 B9
Elyria▲ 56,746 F3
Empire 364 J5
Englewood 11,432 B6
Euclid 54,875 J9
Evendale 3,175 C9
Fairborn 31,300 B6
Fairfax 2,029 C9
Fairfield 39,729 A7
Fairlawn 5,779 G3
Fairport Harbor 2,978 H2
Fairview Park 18,028 G9
Farmer 932 A3
Farmersville 950 A6
Fayette 1,248 B2
Fayetteville 393 C7
Felicity 856 B8
Findlay▲ 35,703 C3
Fletcher 545 B5
Florida 304 B3
Flushing 1,042 J5
Forest 1,594 C4
Forest Park 18,609 B9
Forestville 9,185 C10
Fort Jennings 436 B4
Fort Loramie 1,042 B5
Fort McKinley 9,740 B6
Fort Recovery 1,313 A5
Fort Shawnee 4,128 B4
Fostoria 14,983 D3
Frankfort 1,065 D7
Franklin 11,026 B6
Franklin Furnace 1,212 E8
Frazeysburg 1,165 F5
Fredericksburg 502 G4
Fredericktown 2,443 F5
Freeport 475 H5
Fremont▲ 17,648 D3
Fulton 325 E5
Fultonham 178 F6
Gahanna 27,791 E5
Galena 361 E5
Galion 11,859 E4
Gallipolis▲ 4,831 F8
Gambier 2,073 F5
Garfield Heights 31,739 J9
Garrettsville 2,014 H3
Gates Mills 2,508 J9
Geneva 6,597 J2
Geneva-on-the-Lake 1,626 H2
Genoa 2,262 D2
Georgetown▲ 3,627 C8
Germantown 4,916 B6
Gettysburg 539 A5
Gibsonburg 2,579 D3
Gilboa 208 C3
Girard 11,304 J3
Glandorf 829 B3
Glendale 2,445 C9
Glenford 208 F6
Glenmont 233 F4
Glenwillow 455 J10
Glouster 2,001 F6
Gnadenhutten 1,226 G5
Golf Manor 4,154 C9
Gordon 206 B6
Grafton 3,344 F3
Grand Rapids 955 C3
Grand River H2
Grandview 1,301 H7
Grandview Heights 7,010 D6
Granville 4,353 E5
Gratiot 195 F6
Gratis 998 A6
Green Camp 393 D4
Green Springs 1,446 E3
Greenfield 5,172 D7
Greenhills 4,393 B9
Greensburg 3,306 G4
Greentown 1,856 H4
Greenville▲ 12,863 A5
Greenwich 1,442 E3
Groesbeck 6,684 B9
Grove City 19,661 D6
Groveport 2,948 E6
Grover Hill 518 B3
Hamden 877 F7
Hamersville 586 C8
Hamilton▲ 61,368 A7
Hamler 623 B3
Hanging Rock 306 E8
Hanover 803 F5
Hanoverton 434 J4
Harbor View 122 C2
Harpster 233 D4
Harrisburg 340 D6
Harrison 7,518 A9
Harrisville 308 J5
Harrod 537 C4
Hartford 418 J3
Hartford 444 E5
Hartville 2,031 H4
Harveysburg 437 C7
Haskins 549 C3
Haviland 210 A3
Hayesville 457 F4
Heath 7,231 F5
Hebron 2,076 E6
Helena 267 D3
Hemlock 203 F6
Hicksville 3,664 A3
Higginsport 298 C8
Highland 275 C7
Highland Heights 6,249 J9
Hilliard 11,796 D5
Hillsboro▲ 6,235 C7
Hiram 1,330 H3
Holgate 1,290 B3
Holland 1,210 C2
Hollansburg 300 A5
Holloway 354 H5
Holmesville 419 G4
Hopedale 685 J5
Hoytville 301 C3
Hubbard 8,248 J3
Huber Heights 38,696 B6
Hudson 5,159 H3
Hunting Valley 799 J9
Huntsville 343 C5
Huron 7,030 E3
Independence 6,500 H9
Indian Hill 5,383 C9
Irondale 382 J4
Ironton▲ 12,751 E8
Ithaca 119 A6
Jackson Center 1,398 B5
Jackson▲ 6,144 E7
Jacksonville 544 F7
Jamestown 1,794 C6
Jefferson (West Jefferson) 3,331 D6
Jefferson▲ 2,952 J2
Jeffersonville 1,281 C6
Jenera 285 C4
Jeromesville 582 F4
Jerry City 517 C3
Jerusalem 144 H6
Jewett 778 H5
Johnstown 3,237 E5
Junction City 770 F6
Kalida 947 B4
Kelleys Island 172 E2
Kent 28,835 H3
Kenton▲ 8,356 C4
Kettering 60,569 B6
Kettlersville 194 B5
Killbuck 809 G5
Kimbolton 134 G5
Kingston 1,153 E7
Kingsville 1,243 J2
Kipton 283 F3
Kirby 155 D4
Kirkersville 563 E6
Kirtland 5,881 H2
Kirtland Hills 628 H2
La Rue 802 D4
Lafayette 449 C4
Lagrange 1,199 F3
Lakeline 210 J8
Lakemore 2,684 H3
Lakeview 1,056 C4
Lakewood 59,718 G9
Lancaster▲ 34,507 E6
Latty 205 A3
Laura 483 B6
Laurelville 605 E7
Lawrenceville 304 C6
Lebanon▲ 10,453 B7
Leesburg 1,063 D7
Leesville 156 H5
Leetonia 2,070 J4
Leipsic 2,203 C3
Lewisburg 1,584 A6
Lewisville 261 H6
Lexington 4,124 E4
Liberty Center 1,084 B3
Lima▲ 45,549 B4
Limaville 152 H4
Lincoln Heights 4,805 C9
Lindsey 529 D3
Linndale 159 G9
Lisbon▲ 3,037 J4
Lithopolis 563 E6
Lockbourne 173 E6
Lockington 214 B5
Lockland 4,357 C9
Lodi 3,042 F3
Logan▲ 6,725 F6
London▲ 7,807 C6
Lorain 71,245 F3
Lordstown 3,404 J3
Lore City 384 H6
Loudonville 2,915 F4
Louisville 8,087 H4
Loveland 9,990 D9
Lowell 617 H6
Lowellville 1,349 J3
Lower Salem 103 H6
Lucas 730 F4
Lucasville 1,575 E8
Luckey 848 D3
Ludlow Falls 300 B6
Lynchburg 1,212 C7
Lyndhurst 15,982 J9
Lyons 579 B2
Macedonia 7,509 J10
Mack 2,816 B9
Macksburg 218 G6
Madeira 9,141 C9
Madison 2,477 H2
Magnetic Springs 373 D5
Magnolia 937 H4
Maineville 359 C9
Malinta 294 B3

(continued on following page)

Agriculture, Industry and Resources

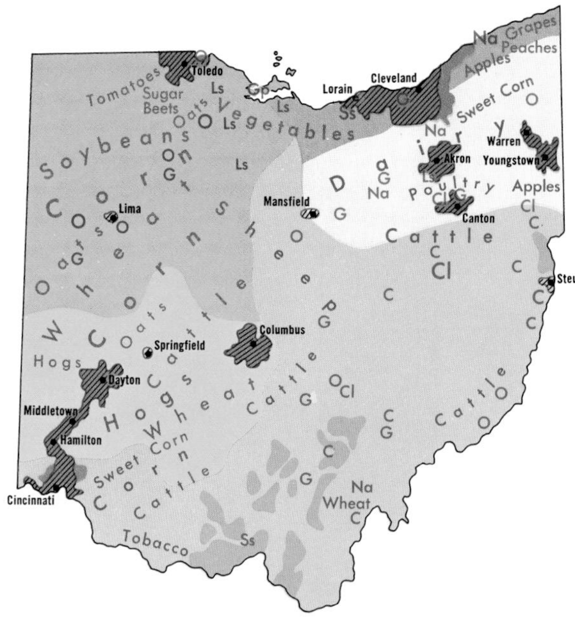

Toledo
Lorain
Cleveland
Akron
Warren
Youngstown
Lima
Mansfield
Canton
Steubenville
Columbus
Springfield
Dayton
Middletown
Hamilton
Cincinnati
Tomatoes
Sugar Beets
Oats
Vegetables
Soybeans
Corn
Hogs
Wheat
Cattle
Dairy
Poultry
Sweet Corn
Grapes
Peaches
Apples
Tobacco

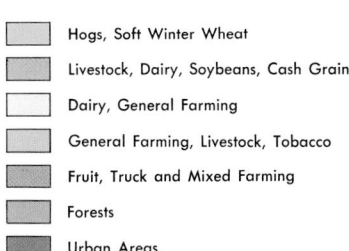

DOMINANT LAND USE

- Hogs, Soft Winter Wheat
- Livestock, Dairy, Soybeans, Cash Grain
- Dairy, General Farming
- General Farming, Livestock, Tobacco
- Fruit, Truck and Mixed Farming
- Forests
- Urban Areas

MAJOR MINERAL OCCURRENCES

C	Coal
Cl	Clay
G	Natural Gas
Gp	Gypsum
Ls	Limestone
Na	Salt
O	Petroleum
Ss	Sandstone

Major Industrial Areas

Malta 802 ... G6
Malvern 1,112 ... H4
Manchester 2,223 ... C8
Mansfield▲ 50,627 ... F4
Mantua 1,178 ... H3
Maple Heights 27,089 ... H9
Marblehead 745 ... E2
Marengo 393 ... E5
Mariemont 3,118 ... C9
Marietta▲ 15,026 ... G7
Marion▲ 34,075 ... D4
Marseilles 130 ... D4
Marshall 758 ... C7
Marshallville 788 ... G4
Martin 7,990 ... D2
Martins Ferry 9,331 ... J5
Martinsburg 213 ... F5
Martinsville 476 ... C7
Marysville▲ 9,656 ... D5
Mason 11,452 ... B7
Massillon 31,007 ... H4
Masury 1,836 ... J3
Maumee 15,561 ... C2
Mayfield 3,462 ... J9
Mayfield Heights 19,847 ... J9
McArthur▲ 1,541 ... F7
McClure 781 ... C3
McComb 1,544 ... C3
McConnelsville▲ 1,804 ... G6
McDonald 3,526 ... J3
McGuffey 550 ... C4
Mechanicsburg 1,803 ... D5
Medina▲ 19,231 ... G3
Melrose 307 ... B3
Mendon 717 ... A4
Mentor 47,358 ... H2
Mentor-on-the-Lake 8,271 ... G2
Metamora 543 ... C2
Meyers Lake 493 ... H4
Miamisburg 17,834 ... B6
Middle Point 639 ... B4
Middleburg 14,702 ... C5
Middleburg Heights 16,218 .. G10
Middlefield 1,898 ... H3
Middleport 2,725 ... F7
Middletown 46,022 ... A6
Midland 319 ... C7
Midvale 575 ... H5
Mifflin 162 ... F4
Milan 1,464 ... E3
Milford 5,660 ... D9
Milford Center 651 ... D5
Millbury 1,081 ... D2
Milledgeville 120 ... C6
Miller 173 ... F8
Miller City 168 ... B3
Millersburg▲ 3,051 ... F4
Millersport 1,010 ... E6
Millville 755 ... A7
Milton Center 200 ... C3
Mineral 725 ... F7
Mineral City 884 ... H4
Minerva 4,318 ... H4
Minerva Park 1,463 ... E5
Mingo 4,297 ... C5
Mingo Junction 4,834 ... J5
Minster 2,650 ... B5
Mogadore 4,008 ... H3
Monroe 4,490 ... B7
Monroeville 1,381 ... E3
Montezuma 199 ... A4
Montgomery 9,753 ... C9
Montpelier 4,299 ... A2
Moraine 5,989 ... B6
Moreland Hills 3,354 ... J9
Morral 373 ... D4
Morristown 296 ... H5
Morrow 1,206 ... B7
Moscow 279 ... B8
Mount Blanchard 491 ... D4
Mount Carmel 4,462 ... C10
Mount Cory 245 ... C4
Mount Eaton 236 ... G4
Mount Gilead▲ 2,846 ... E4
Mount Healthy 7,580 ... B9
Mount Orab 1,929 ... C7
Mount Pleasant 498 ... J5
Mount Sterling 1,647 ... D6
Mount Vernon▲ 14,550 ... E5
Mount Victory 551 ... D4
Mowrystown 460 ... C7
Mulberry 2,856 ... B7
Munroe Falls 5,359 ... H3
Murray City 499 ... F6
Mutual 126 ... C5
Napoleon▲ 8,884 ... B3
Nashville 181 ... F4
Navarre 1,635 ... H4
Neffs 1,213 ... J5
Nellie 130 ... F5
Nelsonville 4,563 ... F7
Nevada 849 ... D4
Neville 226 ... B8
New Albany 1,621 ... E5
New Alexandria 257 ... J5
New Athens 370 ... H5
New Bloomington 282 ... D4
New Boston 2,717 ... E8
New Bremen 2,558 ... B5
New Carlisle 6,049 ... C6
New Concord 2,086 ... G6
New Holland 841 ... D6
New Knoxville 838 ... B5
New Lebanon 4,323 ... B6
New Lexington▲ 5,117 ... F6
New London 2,642 ... F3
New Madison 928 ... A6
New Miami 2,555 ... A7
New Middletown 1,912 ... J4
New Paris 1,801 ... A6
New Philadelphia▲ 15,698 ... G5
New Richmond 2,408 ... B8
New Riegel 298 ... D3
New Straitsville 865 ... F6
New Vienna 932 ... C7
New Washington 1,057 ... E4
New Waterford 1,278 ... J4
New Weston 148 ... A5
Newark▲ 44,389 ... F5
Newburgh Heights 2,310 ... H9
Newcomerstown 4,012 ... G5
Newton Falls 4,866 ... J3
Newtonsville 427 ... B7
Newtown 1,589 ... C10
Ney 331 ... B3
Niles 21,128 ... J3
North Baltimore 3,139 ... C3
North Bend 541 ... B9
North Canton 14,748 ... H4
North College Hill 11,002 ... B9
North Fairfield 504 ... E3
North Hampton 417 ... C5
North Kingsville 2,672 ... J2
North Lewisburg 1,160 ... C5
North Madison 8,699 ... H2
North Olmsted 34,204 ... G9
North Perry 824 ... H2
North Randall 977 ... H9
North Ridgeville 21,564 ... F3
North Robinson 216 ... E4
North Royalton 23,197 ... H10
North Star 246 ... A5
North Zanesville 2,121 ... G6
Northfield 3,624 ... J10
Northridge 5,939 ... B6
Northwood 5.506 ... D2
Norton 11,477 ... G3
Norwalk▲ 14,731 ... E3
Norwich 133 ... G6
Norwood 23,674 ... C9
Oak Harbor 2,637 ... D2
Oak Hill 1,831 ... E8
Oakwood 709 ... H9
Oakwood 886 ... B3
Oakwood 9,372 ... B6
Oberlin 8,191 ... F3
Obetz 3,167 ... E6
Ohio City 899 ... A4
Olmsted Falls 6,741 ... G9
Ontario 4,026 ... E4
Orange 2,810 ... J9
Orangeville 253 ... J3
Oregon 18,334 ... D2
Orient 273 ... D6
Orrville 7,712 ... G4
Orwell 1,258 ... J2
Osgood 255 ... A5
Ostrander 431 ... D5
Ottawa Hills 4,543 ... C2
Ottawa▲ 3,999 ... B3
Ottoville 842 ... B4
Otway 105 ... D8
Owensville 1,019 ... B7
Oxford 18,937 ... A6
Painesville▲ 15,699 ... H2
Palestine 197 ... A5
Pandora 1,009 ... C4
Parma 87,876 ... H9
Parma Heights 21,448 ... G9
Parral 255 ... G4
Pataskala 3,046 ... E5
Patterson 145 ... C4
Paulding▲ 2,605 ... A3
Payne 1,244 ... A3
Peebles 1,782 ... D8
Pemberville 1,279 ... C3
Peninsula 562 ... G3
Pepper Pike 6,185 ... J9
Perry 1,012 ... H2
Perrysburg 12,551 ... C2
Perrysville 691 ... F4
Phillipsburg 644 ... B6
Philo 810 ... G6
Pickerington 5,668 ... E6
Piketon 1,717 ... E7
Pioneer 1,287 ... A2
Piqua 20,612 ... B5
Pitsburg 425 ... A6
Plain City 2,278 ... D5
Plainfield 178 ... G5
Pleasant City 419 ... G6
Pleasant Hill 1,066 ... B5
Pleasant Plain 138 ... B7
Pleasantville 926 ... F6
Plymouth 1,942 ... E4
Poland 2,992 ... J3
Polk 355 ... F4
Pomeroy▲ 2,259 ... G7
Port Clinton▲ 7,106 ... E2
Port Jefferson 381 ... C5
Port Washington 513 ... G5
Port Wiliam 242 ... C6
Portage 469 ... C3
Portsmouth▲ 22,676 ... D8
Potsdam 250 ... B6
Powell 2 154 ... D5
Powhatan Point 1,807 ... J6
Proctorville 765 ... F9
Prospect 1,148 ... D5
Put-in-Bay 141 ... E2
Quaker City 560 ... H6
Quincy 697 ... C5
Racine 729 ... G8
Rarden 184 ... D8
Ravenna▲ 12,069 ... H3
Rawson 482 ... C4
Ray 490 ... E7
Rayland 566 ... J5
Reading 12,038 ... C9
Reminderville 2,163 ... J10
Republic 611 ... D3
Reynoldsburg 25,748 ... E6
Richfield 3,117 ... G3
Richmond (Grand River) ... H2
Richmond 624 ... J5
Richmond Heights 9,611 ... H9
Richwood 2,186 ... D5
Ridgeway 378 ... C4
Rio Grande 995 ... F8
Ripley 1,816 ... C8
Risingsun 659 ... C3
Rittman 6,147 ... G4
Riverlea 503 ... D5
Rochester 206 ... F3
Rock Creek 553 ... J2
Rockford 1,119 ... A4
Rocky Ridge 425 ... D2
Rocky River 20,410 ... G9
Rogers 247 ... J4
Rome 99 ... J2
Rosemount 1,926 ... D8
Roseville 1,847 ... F6
Ross 2,124 ... B9
Rossburg 250 ... A5
Rossford 5,861 ... C2
Roswell 257 ... H5
Rushsylvania 573 ... C5
Rushville 229 ... F6
Russells Point 1,504 ... C5
Russellville 459 ... C8
Russia 442 ... B5
Rutland 469 ... F7
Sabina 2,662 ... C7
Saint Bernard 5,344 ... B9
Saint Clairsville▲ 5,162 ... J5
Saint Henry 1,907 ... A5
Saint Louisville 372 ... F5
Saint Martin 141 ... C7
Saint Marys 8,441 ... B4
Saint Paris 1,842 ... C5
Salem 12,233 ... J4
Salineville 1,474 ... J4
Sandusky▲ 29,764 ... E3
Sarahsville 162 ... H6
Sardinia 792 ... C7
Savannah 363 ... F4
Scio 856 ... H5
Sciotodale 1,128 ... E8
Scott 339 ... A4
Seaman 1,013 ... C8
Sebring 4,848 ... H4
Senecaville 434 ... H6
Seven Hills 12,339 ... H9
Seven Mile 804 ... A7
Seville 1,810 ... G3
Shadyside 3,934 ... J6
Shaker Heights 30,831 ... H9
Sharon 13,153 ... G6
Sharonville 10,108 ... C9
Shawnee 742 ... F6
Shawnee Hills 423 ... D5
Sheffield 1,943 ... F3
Sheffield Lake 9,825 ... F3
Shelby 9,564 ... E4
Sherrodsville 284 ... H4
Sherwood 828 ... A3
Shiloh 778 ... E4
Shreve 1,584 ... F4
Sidney▲ 18,710 ... B5
Silver Lake 3,052 ... G3
Silverton 5,859 ... C9
Sinking Spring 189 ... D7
Smithfield 722 ... J5
Smithville 1,354 ... G4
Solon 18,548 ... J9
Somerset 1,390 ... F6
Somerville 279 ... A6
South Amherst 1,765 ... F3
South Bloomfield 900 ... D6
South Charleston 1,626 ... C6
South Euclid 23,866 ... H9
South Lebanon 2,696 ... B7
South Point 3,823 ... E9
South Russell 3,402 ... H3
South Salem 227 ... D7
South Solon 379 ... C6
South Vienna 550 ... C6
South Webster 806 ... E8
South Zanesville 1,969 ... F6
Sparta 201 ... E5
Spencer 726 ... F3
Spencerville 2,288 ... B4
Spring Valley 507 ... C6
Springboro 6,590 ... B6
Springdale 10,621 ... B9
Springfield▲ 70,487 ... C6
Steubenville▲ 22,125 ... J5
Stockport 462 ... G6
Stone Creek 181 ... G5
Stout 518 ... D8
Stoutsville 537 ... E6
Stow 27,702 ... H3
Strasburg 1,995 ... G4
Stratton 278 ... J4
Streetsboro 9,932 ... H3
Strongsville 35,308 ... G10
Struthers 12,284 ... J3
Stryker 1,468 ... B3
Sugar Grove 465 ... E6
Sugarcreek 2,062 ... G5
Summerfield 295 ... H6
Summitville 125 ... J4
Sunbury 2,046 ... E5
Swanton 3,557 ... C2
Sycamore 919 ... D4
Sylvania 17,301 ... C2
Syracuse 827 ... G7
Tallmadge 14,870 ... H3
Tarlton 315 ... E6
Taylorsville (Philo) ... G6
Terrace Park 2,133 ... D9
The Plains 2,644 ... F7
Thornville 758 ... F6
Thurston 539 ... E6
Tiffin▲ 18,604 ... D3
Tiltonsville 1,517 ... J5
Timberlake 833 ... J8
Tipp City 6,027 ... B6
Tiro 246 ... E4
Toledo▲ 332,943 ... D2
Tontogany 364 ... C3
Toronto 6,127 ... J5
Tremont City 493 ... C5
Trenton 6,189 ... B7
Trimble 441 ... F7
Trotwood 8,816 ... B6
Troy▲ 19,478 ... B5
Tuscarawas 826 ... H5
Twinsburg 9,606 ... J10
Uhrichsville 5,604 ... H5
Union 5,501 ... B6
Union City 1,984 ... A5
Uniontown 3,074 ... H4
Unionville 238 ... J2
Unionville Center 272 ... D5
Uniopolis 261 ... B4
University Heights 14,790 ... H9
Upper Arlington 34,128 ... D6
Upper Sandusky▲ 5,906 ... D4
Urbana▲ 11,353 ... C5
Urbancrest 862 ... D6
Utica 1,997 ... F5
Valley Hi 217 ... C5
Valley View 2,137 ... H9
Valley View 730 ... D6
Van Buren 337 ... C3
Van Wert▲ 10,891 ... A4
Vandalia 13,882 ... B6
Vanlue 373 ... C4
Venedocia 158 ... B4
Vermilion 11,127 ... F3
Verona 472 ... A6
Versailles 2,351 ... A5
Vienna 1,067 ... J3
Vinton 293 ... F8
Wadsworth 15,718 ... G3
Waite Hill 454 ... H2
Wakeman 948 ... F3
Walbridge 2,736 ... C2
Waldo 340 ... D5
Walton Hills 2,371 ... J10
Wapakoneta▲ 9,214 ... B4
Warren▲ 50,793 ... J3
Warrensville Heights 15,745 ... H9
Warsaw 699 ... G5
Washington Court House▲ 12,682 ... D6
Washingtonville 894 ... J4
Waterville 4,517 ... C3
Wauseon▲ 6,322 ... B2
Waverly▲ 4,477 ... D7
Wayne 803 ... C3
Waynesburg 1,068 ... H4
Waynesfield 831 ... C4
Waynesville 1,949 ... B6
Wellington 4,140 ... F3
Wellston 6,049 ... F7
Wellsville 4,532 ... J4
West Alexandria 1,460 ... A6
West Carrollton 14,403 ... B6
West Elkton 208 ... A6
West Farmington 542 ... J3
West Jefferson ... D6
West Lafayette 2,129 ... G5
West Leipsic 244 ... B3
West Liberty 1,613 ... C5
West Manchester 464 ... A6
West Mansfield 830 ... C5
West Millgrove 171 ... C3
West Milton 4,348 ... B6
West Portsmouth 3,551 ... D8
West Rushville 134 ... E6
West Salem 1,534 ... F4
West Union▲ 3,096 ... C8
West Unity 1,677 ... B2
Westerville 30,269 ... D5
Westfield Center 784 ... G3
Westlake 27,018 ... G9
Weston 1,716 ... C3
Wharton 378 ... D4
Wheelersburg 5,113 ... E8
Whitehall 20,572 ... E6
Whitehouse 2,528 ... C2
Wickliffe 14,558 ... J9
Wilberforce 2,639 ... C6
Wilkesville 151 ... F7
Willard 6,210 ... E3
Williamsburg 2,322 ... B7
Williamsport 851 ... D6
Willoughby 20,510 ... J8
Willoughby Hills 8,427 ... J9
Willowick 15,269 ... J8
Willshire 541 ... A4
Wilmington▲ 11,199 ... C7
Wilmot 261 ... G4
Wilson 136 ... H6
Winchester 978 ... C8
Windham 2,943 ... H3
Wintersville 4,102 ... J5
Withamsville 2,834 ... B7
Woodlawn 2,674 ... C9
Woodmere 834 ... J9
Woodsfield▲ 2,832 ... H6
Woodstock 296 ... C5
Woodville 1,953 ... D3
Wooster▲ 22,191 ... G4
Worthington 14,869 ... E5
Wren 190 ... A4
Wyoming 8,128 ... C9
Xenia▲ 24,664 ... C6
Yankee Lake 88 ... J3
Yellow Springs 3,973 ... C6
Yorkshire 126 ... B5
Yorkville 1,246 ... J5
Youngstown▲ 95,732 ... J3
Zaleski 294 ... F7
Zanesfield 183 ... C5
Zanesville▲ 26,778 ... G6
Zoar 177 ... H4

OTHER FEATURES

Atwood (lake) ... H4
Auglaize (riv.) ... B4
Berlin (lake) ... H4
Big Walnut (creek) ... E5
Black (riv.) ... F3
Black Fork, Mohican (riv.) ... F4
Blanchard (riv.) ... C4
Blennerhassett (isl.) ... G7
Buckeye (lake) ... F6
Campbell (hill) ... C5
Captina (creek) ... J6
Cedar (pt.) ... D2
Chagrin (riv.) ... J8
Clear Fork (res.) ... E4
Clear Fork, Mohican (riv.) ... F4
Clendening (lake) ... H5
Cuyahoga (riv.) ... H10
Cuyahoga Valley Nat'l Rec. Area ... H10
Darby (creek) ... D5
Deer (creek) ... D6
Deer Creek (lake) ... D6
Delaware (lake) ... E5
Dillon (lake) ... F5
Dover (lake) ... H4
Duck (creek) ... H6
Erie (lake) ... H1
Grand (riv.) ... H2
Great Miami (riv.) ... A7
Hocking (riv.) ... F7
Hoover (res.) ... E5
Huron (riv.) ... E3
Indian (lake) ... C5
James A. Garfield Nat'l Hist. Site ... G2
Kelleys (isl.) ... E2
Killbuck (creek) ... G4
Kokosing (riv.) ... E5
Leesville (lake) ... H5
Licking (riv.) ... F5
Little Beaver (creek) ... J4
Little Miami (riv.) ... B6
Little Miami, East Fork (riv.) ... C7
Little Muskingum (riv.) ... H6
Loramie (lake) ... B5
Mad (riv.) ... C6
Maumee (bay) ... D2
Maumee (riv.) ... A3
Middle Bass (isl.) ... E2
Mohican (riv.) ... F4
Mosquito Creek (lake) ... J3
Mound City Group Nat'l Mon. ... E7
Muskingum (riv.) ... G6
North Bass (isl.) ... E2
Ohio (riv.) ... B8
Ohio Brush (creek) ... D8
Olentangy (riv.) ... D4
Paint (creek) ... D7
Perry's Victory and Int'l Peace Mem. ... E2
Piedmont (lake) ... H5
Portage (riv.) ... D3
Pymatuning (res.) ... J2
Raccoon (creek) ... F8
Rattlesnake (creek) ... C7
Rickenbacker A.F.B. ... E6
Rocky (riv.) ... G9
Rocky Fork (lake) ... D7
Saint Joseph (riv.) ... A3
Saint Marys (lake) ... A4
Saint Marys (riv.) ... A4
Salt Fork (creek) ... H5
Sandusky (bay) ... E3
Sandusky (riv.) ... D3
Scioto (riv.) ... D8
Senecaville (lake) ... H6
Sevenmile (creek) ... A6
South Bass (isl.) ... E2
Stillwater (riv.) ... B5
Symmes (creek) ... F8
Tappan (lake) ... H5
Tiffin (riv.) ... B3
Tuscarawas (riv.) ... H5
Vermilion (riv.) ... F3
Wabash (riv.) ... A5
West Sister (isl.) ... D2
Whiteoak (creek) ... C7
William H. Taft Nat'l Hist. Site ... C10
Wills (creek) ... G5
Wills Creek (lake) ... G5
Wright-Patterson A.F.B. 8,579 ... B6
Yellow (creek) ... J4

▲County seat

OKLAHOMA

AREA 69,956 sq. mi. (181,186 sq. km.)
POPULATION 3,157,604
CAPITAL Oklahoma City
LARGEST CITY Oklahoma City
HIGHEST POINT Black Mesa 4,973 ft. (1516 m.)
SETTLED IN 1889
ADMITTED TO UNION November 16, 1907
POPULAR NAME Sooner State
STATE FLOWER Mistletoe
STATE BIRD Scissor-tailed Flycatcher

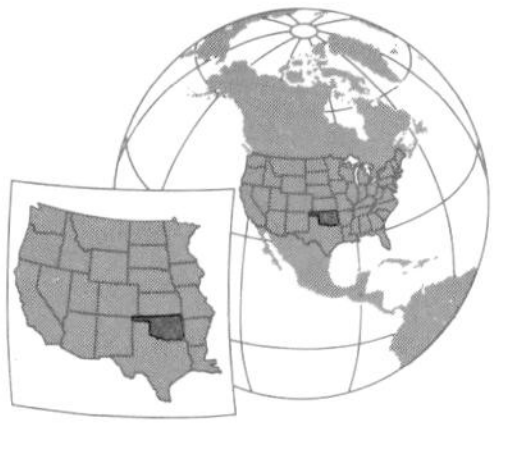

COUNTIES

Adair 18,421 S3
Alfalfa 6,416 K1
Atoka 12,778 O6
Beaver 6,023 E1
Beckham 18,812 G4
Blaine 11,470 K3
Bryan 32,089 O7
Caddo 29,550 K4
Canadian 74,409 K3
Carter 42,919 M6
Cherokee 34,049 R3
Choctaw 15,302 P6
Cimarron 3,301 A1
Cleveland 174,253 M4
Coal 5,780 O5
Comanche 111,486 K5
Cotton 6,651 K6
Craig 14,104 R1
Creek 60,915 O3
Custer 26,897 H3
Delaware 28,070 S2
Dewey 5,551 H2
Ellis 4,497 G2
Garfield 56,735 L2
Garvin 26,605 M5
Grady 41,747 L5
Grant 5,689 L1
Greer 6,559 G5
Harmon 3,793 G5
Harper 4,063 G1
Haskell 10,940 R4
Hughes 13,023 O4
Jackson 28,764 H5
Jefferson 7,010 L6
Johnston 10,032 N6
Kay 48,056 M1
Kingfisher 13,212 L3
Kiowa 11,347 J5
Latimer 10,333 R5
Le Flore 43,270 S5
Lincoln 29,216 N3
Logan 29,011 M3
Love 8,157 M7
Major 8,055 K2
Marshall 10,829 N6
Mayes 33,366 R2
McClain 22,795 L5
McCurtain 33,433 S6
McIntosh 16,779 P4
Murray 12,042 M6
Muskogee 68,078 R3
Noble 11,045 M2
Nowata 9,992 P1
Okfuskee 11,551 O3
Oklahoma 599,611 M3
Okmulgee 36,490 P3
Osage 41,645 O1
Ottawa 30,561 S1
Pawnee 15,575 N2
Payne 61,507 N2
Pittsburg 40,581 P5
Pontotoc 34,119 N5
Pottawatomie 58,760 N4
Pushmataha 10,997 R6
Roger Mills 4,147 G3
Rogers 55,170 P2
Seminole 25,412 N4
Sequoyah 33,828 S3
Stephens 42,299 L6
Texas 16,419 C1
Tillman 10,384 J6
Tulsa 503,341 P2
Wagoner 47,883 P3
Washington 48,066 P1
Washita 11,441 J4
Woods 9,103 J1
Woodward 18,976 H2

CITIES and TOWNS

Achille 491 O7
Ada▲ 15,820 N5
Adair 685 R2
Adams 150 D1
Adamson 150 P5
Addington 100 L6
Afton 915 S1
Agra 334 N3
Akins 250 S3
Albany 65 O7
Albert 100 K4
Albion 88 R5
Alderson 395 P5
Alex 639 L5
Alfalfa 70 J4
Aline 295 K1
Allen 972 O5
Altus▲ 21,910 H5
Alva▲ 5,495 J1
Amber 418 L4
Ames 268 K2
Amorita 56 K1
Anadarko▲ 6,586 K4
Antlers▲ 2,524 P6
Apache 1,591 K5
Apperson 30 N1
Aqua Park R3
Arapaho▲ 802 H3
Arcadia 320 M3
Ardmore▲ 23,079 M6
Arkoma 2,393 T4
Arnett▲ 547 G2
Asher 449 N5
Ashland 56 O5
Atoka▲ 3,298 O6
Atwood 225 O5
Avant 369 O2
Avard 37 J1
Avery 35 N3
Bache 100 P5
Bacone 786 R3
Baker 70 D1
Balko 100 E1
Barnsdall 1,316 O1
Baron 300 S3
Bartlesville▲ 34,256 O1
Battiest 250 S6
Bearden 142 O4
Beaver▲ 1,584 F1
Beggs 1,150 P3
Belzoni 50 R6
Bengal 300 R5
Bennington 251 P7
Bentley 75 O6
Berlin 50 G4
Bernice 330 S1
Bessie 248 H4
Bethany 20,075 L3
Bethel 2,505 S6
Bethel Acres 2,314 M4
Big Cabin 271 R1
Billings 555 M1
Binger 724 K4
Bison 103 L2
Bixby 9,502 P3
Blackburn 110 N2
Blackgum 150 S3
Blackwell 7,538 M1
Blair 922 H5
Blanchard 1,922 L4
Blanco 215 P5
Blocker 135 P4
Blue 175 O7
Bluejacket 247 R1
Boggy Depot 100 O6
Boise City▲ 1,509 B1
Bokchito 576 O6
Bokhoma 35 S7
Bokoshe 403 S4
Boley 908 O4
Boswell 643 P6
Bowlegs 398 N4
Bowring 115 O1
Boyd 10 E1
Boynton 391 P3
Braden 15 S4
Bradley 166 L5
Braggs 308 R3
Braman 251 M1
Bray 925 L5
Breckinridge 261 L2
Briartown 55 R4
Bridgeport 137 K3
Brinkman G4
Bristow 4,062 O3
Broken Arrow 58,043 P2
Broken Bow 3,961 S7
Bromide 162 N6
Brooksville 69 M4
Bryant 74 P4
Buffalo▲ 1,312 G1
Bunch 64 S3
Burbank 165 N1
Burlington 169 K1
Burneyville 150 M7
Burns Flat 1,027 H4
Butler 341 H3
Byars 263 N5
Byng 755 N5
Byron 57 K1
Cache 2,251 J5
Caddo 918 O6
Cairo 50 O5
Calera 1,536 O7
Calumet 560 K3
Calvin 251 O5
Camargo 185 H2
Cameron 327 T4
Canadian 261 P4
Canadian City L4
Caney 184 O6
Canton 632 J2
Canute 538 H4
Capron 38 J1
Cardin 165 S1
Carmen 459 J1
Carnegie 1,593 J4
Carney 558 N3
Carrier 171 K2
Carter 286 H4
Cartersville 79 S4
Cashion 430 L3
Castle 94 O4
Catoosa 2,954 P2
Cement 642 K5
Center 100 N5
Centrahoma 106 O5
Centralia R1
Chandler▲ 2,596 N3
Chattanooga 437 J6
Checotah 3,290 R4
Chelsea 1,620 P1
Cherokee▲ 1,787 K1
Chester 104 J2
Cheyenne▲ 948 G3
Chickasha▲ 14,988 L4
Chilocco 400 M1
Choctaw 8,545 M3
Chouteau 1,771 R2
Christie 375 S3
Cimarron 71 L3
Claremore▲ 13,280 R2
Clarita 72 O6
Clayton 636 R5
Clearview 47 O4
Clemscot 52 L6
Cleo Springs 359 K2
Cleora 45 S1
Cleveland 3,156 O2
Clinton 9,298 H3
Cloud Chief 12 J4
Cloudy 175 R6
Coalgate▲ 1,895 O5
Cogar 40 K4
Colbert 1,043 O7
Colcord 628 S2
Cold Springs 24 J5
Cole 355 L4
Coleman 200 O6
Collinsville 3,612 P2
Colony 163 J4
Comanche 1,695 L6
Commerce 2,426 R1
Concho 300 L3
Connerville 150 N6
Cooperton 15 J5
Copan 809 P1
Cordell▲ H4
Corinne 100 R6
Corn 548 J4
Cornish 164 L6
Council Hill 139 P3
Countyline 550 L6
Courtney 12 L7
Covington 590 L2
Coweta 6,159 P3
Cowlington 756 S4
Cox City 285 L5
Coyle 289 M3
Crawford 53 G3
Crescent 1,236 L3
Cromwell 268 N4
Crowder 339 P4
Cumberland 100 N6
Curtis 30 H2
Cushing 7,218 N3
Custer City 443 J3
Cyril 1,072 K5
Dacoma 182 J1
Daisy 250 P5
Dale 160 M4
Darwin 50 P6
Davenport 979 N3
Davidson 473 J6
Davis 2,543 M5
Deer Creek 124 L1
Del City 23,928 L4
Dela 434 P6
Delaware 544 P1
Delhi 41 G4
Depew 502 O3
Devol 165 J6
Dewar 921 P4
Dewey 3,326 P1
Dibble 181 L4
Dickson 942 M6
Dill City 622 H4
Disney 257 S2
Dougherty 138 M6
Douglas 55 L2
Douthat 30 S1
Dover 376 L3
Dow 300 P5
Driftwood K1
Drummond 408 L2
Drumright 2,799 N3
Duke (E. Duke) 360 G5
Duncan▲ 21,732 L5
Durant▲ 12,823 O6
Durham 30 G3
Dustin 429 O4
Eagle City 56 J3
Eagletown 650 S6
Eakly 277 K4
Earlsboro 535 N4
Edmond 52,315 M3
El Reno▲ 15,414 K3
Eldorado 573 G6
Elgin 975 K5
Elk City 10,428 G4
Elmer 132 H6
Elmore City 493 M5
Elmwood 300 F1
Empire City 219 L6
Enid▲ 45,309 L2
Enterprise 130 R4
Erick 1,083 G4
Eucha 210 S2
Eufaula▲ 2,652 P4
Fair Oaks 1,133 P2
Fairfax 1,749 N1
Fairland 916 S1
Fairmont 129 L2
Fairview▲ 2,936 J2
Fallis 49 M3
Fanshawe 331 S5
Fargo 299 G2
Farris 100 P6
Faxon 127 J6
Fay 140 J3
Featherston 75 P4
Felt 120 A1
Fillmore 60 N6
Finley 350 R6
Fittstown 500 N5
Fitzhugh 196 N5
Fleetwood 12 L7
Fletcher 1,002 K5
Foraker 25 O1
Forest Park 1,249 M3
Forgan 489 E1
Fort Cobb 663 K4
Fort Gibson 3,359 R3
Fort Supply 369 G1
Fort Towson 568 R7
Foss 148 H4
Foster 100 M5
Fox 400 M6
Foyil 86 R2
Francis 346 N5
Frederick▲ 5,221 H6
Freedom 264 H1
Gage 473 G2
Gans 218 S4
Garber 959 M2
Garvin 128 S7
Gate 159 F1
Geary 1,347 K3
Gene Autry 97 N6
Geronimo 990 K6
Gerty 95 O5
Glencoe 473 M2
Glenpool 6,688 P3
Glover 244 S6
Golden 300 S6
Goldsby 816 L4
Goltry 297 K1
Goodwater 240 S7
Goodwell 1,065 C1
Gore 690 R3
Gotebo 370 J4
Gould 237 G5
Gowen 75 R5
Gracemont 339 K4
Grady 85 L6
Graham 200 M6
Grainola 58 N1
Grand Lake Towne 58 S1
Grandfield 1,224 J6
Granite 1,844 H5
Grant R7
Gray Horse 60 N1
Grayson 66 P3
Greenfield 200 K3
Griggs 15 B1
Grove 4,020 S1
Guthrie▲ 10,518 M3
Guymon▲ 7,803 D1
Haileyville 918 P5
Hall Park 1,090 M4
Hallett 159 N2
Hammon 611 H3
Hanna 99 P4
Hanson 250 S4
Harden City 250 N5
Hardesty 228 D1
Hardy N1
Harjo 35 N4
Harmon 27 G2
Harrah 4,206 M4
Harris 192 S7
Hartshorne 2,120 R5
Haskell 2,143 P3
Hastings 164 K6
Haworth 293 S7
Haywood 175 P5
Headrick 183 H5
Healdton 2,872 M6
Heavener 2,601 S5
Helena 1,043 K1
Hendrix 108 O7
Hennepin 300 M5
Hennessey 1,902 L2
Henryetta 5,872 O4
Herd 18 O1
Hess 29 H6
Hester 25 H5
Hickory 77 N5
Hillsdale 96 K1
Hinton 1,233 K4
Hitchcock 139 K3
Hitchita 118 P3
Hobart▲ 4,305 J5
Hockerville 125 S1
Hodgen 150 S5
Hoffman 175 P4
Holdenville▲ 4,792 O4
Hollis▲ 2,584 G5
Hollister 59 J6
Homestead 35 K2
Hominy 2,342 O2
Honobia 80 R5
Hooker 1,551 D1
Hoot Owl 5 R2
Hopeton 42 J1
Howe 510 S5
Hoyt 160 R4
Hugo▲ 5,978 P7
Hulah 50 O1
Hulbert 499 R3
Humphreys 68 H5
Hunter 218 L1
Hydro 977 J3
Idabel▲ 6,957 S7
Indiahoma 337 J5

(continued on following page)

Agriculture, Industry and Resources

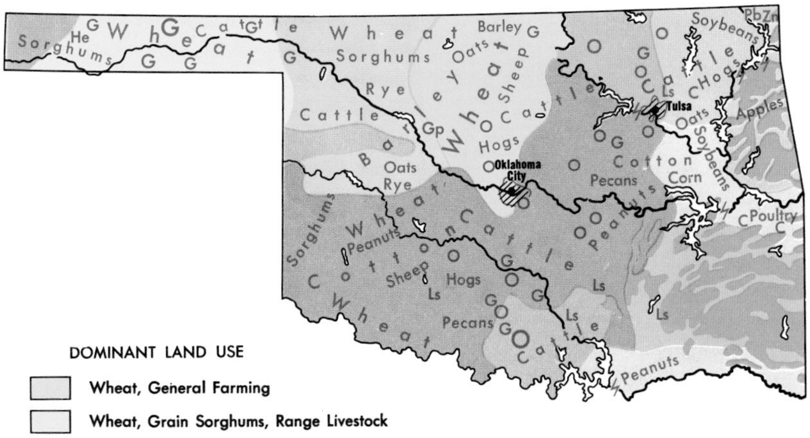
Wheat
Sorghums
Cattle
Barley
Soybeans
Oats
Sheep
Rye
Hogs
Tulsa
Oklahoma City
Apples
Cotton
Pecans
Corn
Poultry
Peanuts

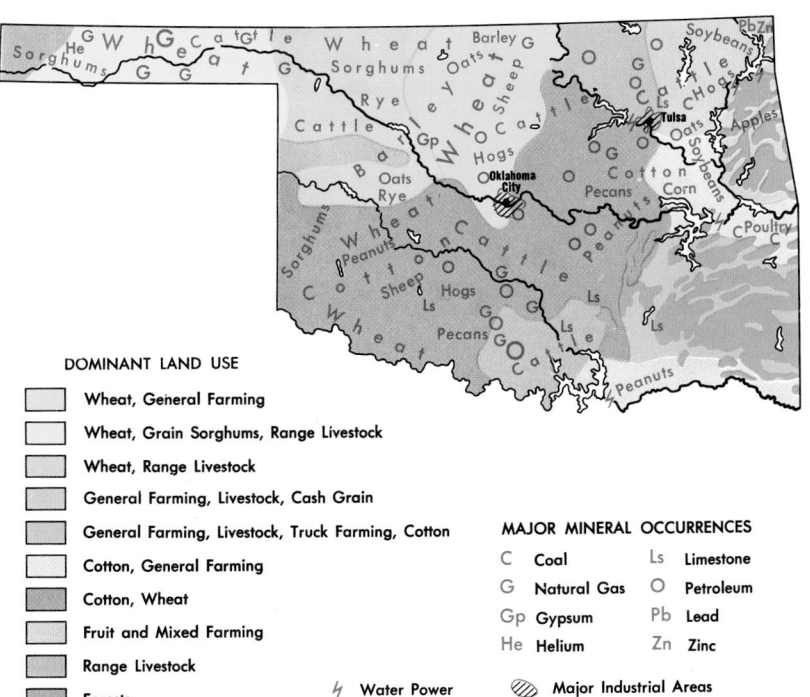

DOMINANT LAND USE

- Wheat, General Farming
- Wheat, Grain Sorghums, Range Livestock
- Wheat, Range Livestock
- General Farming, Livestock, Cash Grain
- General Farming, Livestock, Truck Farming, Cotton
- Cotton, General Farming
- Cotton, Wheat
- Fruit and Mixed Farming
- Range Livestock
- Forests

MAJOR MINERAL OCCURRENCES

C Coal
G Natural Gas
Gp Gypsum
He Helium
Ls Limestone
O Petroleum
Pb Lead
Zn Zinc

Water Power
Major Industrial Areas

(continued)

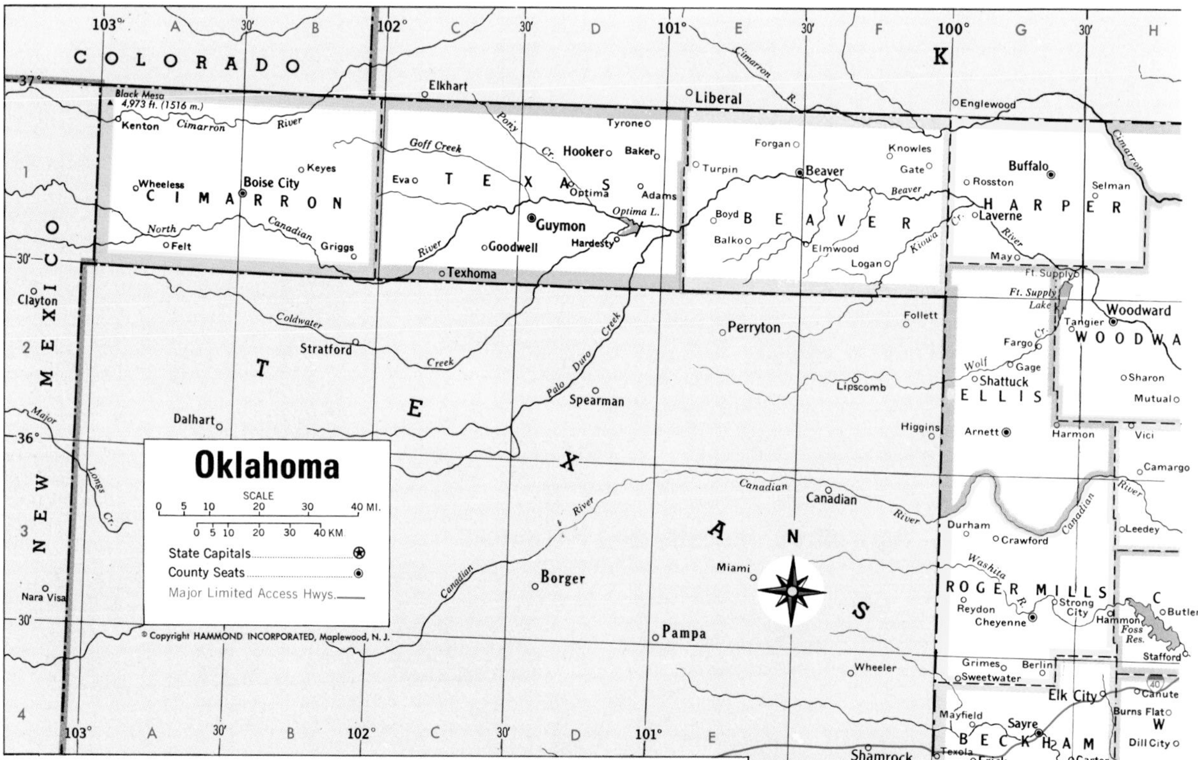
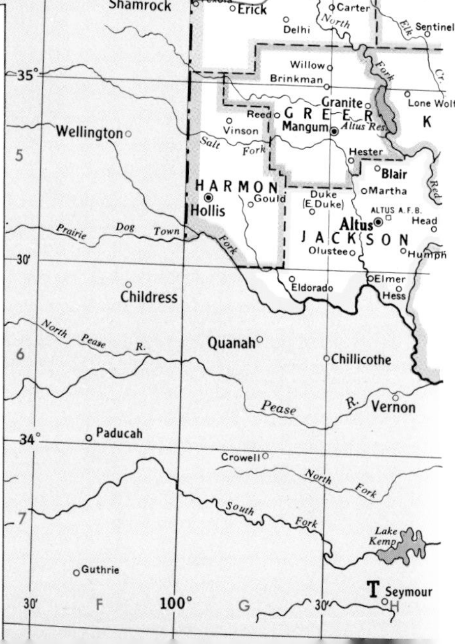

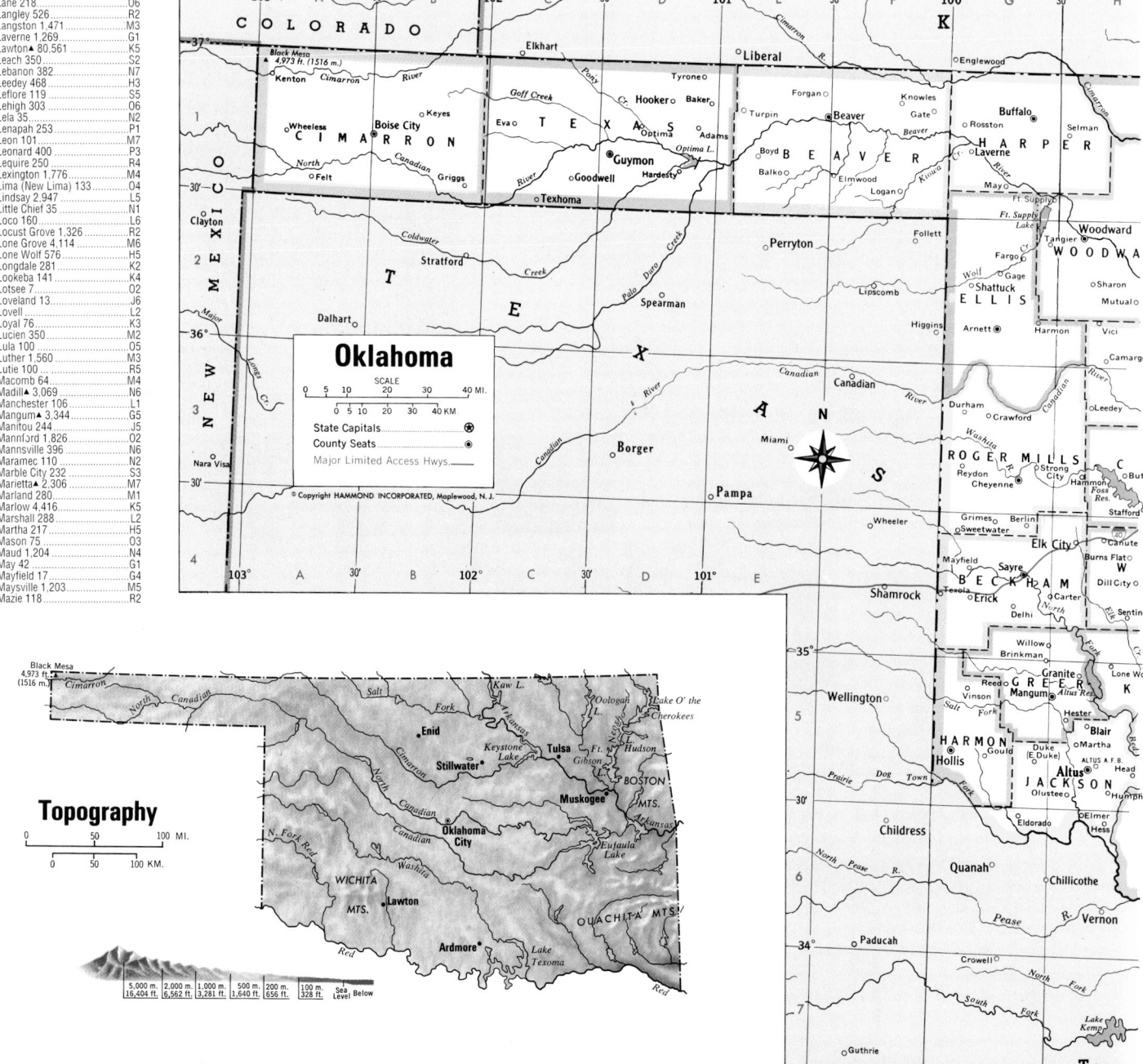

Oklahoma
SCALE
0 5 10 20 30 40 MI.
0 5 10 20 30 40 KM.
State Capitals
County Seats
Major Limited Access Hwys.
© Copyright HAMMOND INCORPORATED, Maplewood, N. J.

Topography

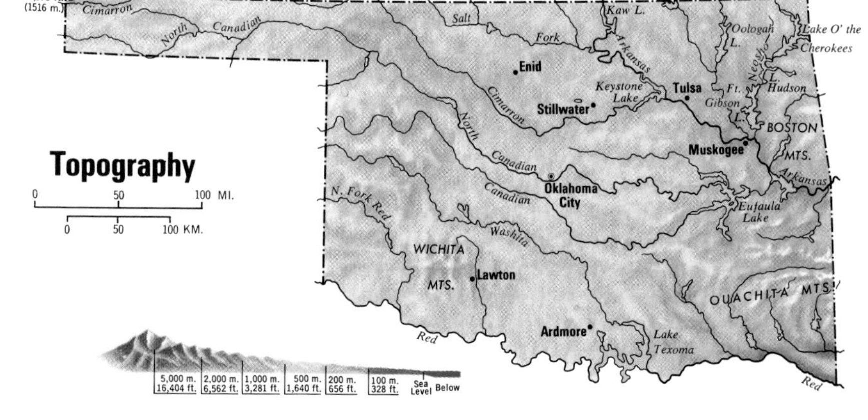

0 50 100 MI.
0 50 100 KM.
Black Mesa 4,973 ft. (1516 m.)
Enid
Stillwater
Tulsa
Muskogee
Oklahoma City
Lawton
Ardmore
WICHITA MTS.
OUACHITA MTS.
BOSTON MTS.
5,000 m. 16,404 ft.
2,000 m. 6,562 ft.
1,000 m. 3,281 ft.
500 m. 1,640 ft.
200 m. 656 ft.
100 m. 328 ft.
Sea Level
Below

Slick 124 ..... O3
Smithville 111 ..... S6
Snow 200 ..... R6
Snyder 1,619 ..... J5
Soper 305 ..... P6
South Coffeyville 791 ..... P1
Southard 130 ..... K2
Sparks 202 ..... N3
Spavinaw 432 ..... R2
Spencer 3,972 ..... M3
Spencerville 275 ..... R6
Sperry 937 ..... P2
Spiro 2,146 ..... S4
Springer 485 ..... M6
Stafford 18 ..... H3
Stanley 30 ..... R5
Sterling 684 ..... K5
Stidham 48 ..... P4
Stigler▲ 2,574 ..... R4
Stillwater▲ 36,676 ..... N2
Stilwell▲ 2,663 ..... S3
Stonebluff 50 ..... P3
Stonewall 519 ..... O5
Strang 141 ..... R2
Stratford 1,404 ..... M5
Stringtown 366 ..... P6
Strong City 49 ..... G3
Stroud 2,666 ..... N3
Stuart 228 ..... O5
Sugden 65 ..... L6
Sulphur▲ 4,824 ..... N5
Summerfield 150 ..... S5
Sweetwater 85 ..... G4
Swink R6
Tabler 28 ..... L4
Taft 400 ..... R3
Tahlequah▲ 10,398 ..... R3
Talala 206 ..... P1
Talihina 1,297 ..... S5
Tallant 14 ..... O1
Taloga▲ 415 ..... J2
Tamaha 188 ..... S4
Tatums 176 ..... M6
Tecumseh 5,750 ..... N4
Temple 1,223 ..... K6
Terlton 121 ..... O2
Terral 469 ..... L7
Texhoma 746 ..... C1
Texola 45 ..... G4
Thackerville 290 ..... M7
The Village 10,353 ..... L3
Thomas 1,246 ..... J3
Tiawah 125 ..... P2
Tipton 1,043 ..... H6
Tishomingo▲ 3,116 ..... N6
Tom 600 ..... S7
Tonkawa 3,127 ..... M1
Tribbey 288 ..... M4
Trousdale 38 ..... M4
Troy 92 ..... N6
Trpin 450 ..... E1
Tryon 514 ..... N3
Tullahassee 92 ..... P3
Tulsa▲ 367,302 ..... O2
Tupelo 323 ..... O5
Tushka 256 ..... O6
Tuskahoma 168 ..... R5
Tussy 150 ..... L6
Tuttle 2,807 ..... L4
Tyrone 880 ..... D1
Union City 1,000 ..... L4
Utica 38 ..... O7
Valley Brook 744 ..... M4
Valliant 873 ..... R6
Vanoss 130 ..... N5
Velma 661 ..... L6
Vera 167 ..... P2
Verden 546 ..... K4
Verdigris 150 ..... P2
Vernon 100 ..... P4
Vian 1,414 ..... S4
Vici 751 ..... H2
Vinita▲ 5,804 ..... R1
Vinson 42 ..... G5
Wade 50 ..... O7
Wagoner▲ 6,894 ..... R3
Wainwright 223 ..... R3
Wakita 453 ..... L1
Walters▲ 2,519 ..... K6
Wanette 346 ..... M5
Wann 126 ..... P1
Wapanucka 402 ..... N6
Wardville 52 ..... P5
Warner 1,479 ..... R4
Warr Acres 9,288 ..... L3
Warwick 160 ..... M3
Washington 279 ..... L4
Washita 180 ..... K4
Watonga▲ 3,408 ..... K3
Watova 35 ..... P1
Watson 48 ..... S6
Watts 303 ..... S2
Waukomis 1,322 ..... K2
Waurika▲ 2,088 ..... L6
Wayne 519 ..... M5
Waynoka 947 ..... J1
Weatherford 10,124 ..... J4
Weathers 100 ..... P5
Webb City 99 ..... N1
Webbers Falls 722 ..... R3
Welch 499 ..... R1
Weleetka 1,112 ..... O4
Welling 115 ..... S3
Wellston 912 ..... M3
Welty 80 ..... O3
West Siloam Springs 539 ..... S2
Westport 326 ..... O2
Westville 1,374 ..... S2
Wetumka 1,427 ..... O4
Wewoka▲ 4,050 ..... O4
White Oak 200 ..... R1
Whitefield 253 ..... R4
Whitesboro 450 ..... S5
Wilburton▲ 3,092 ..... R5
Williams 110 ..... T4
Willis 250 ..... N7
Willow 142 ..... G4
Wilson 1,639 ..... M6
Wirt 350 ..... L6
Wister 956 ..... S5
Wolco 14 ..... O1
Wolf 200 ..... N4
Woodford 30 ..... M6
Woodville 31 ..... N7
Woodward▲ 12,340 ..... H2
Wright City 836 ..... R6
Wyandotte 366 ..... S1
Wynnewood 2,451 ..... M5
Wynona 531 ..... O1
Yale 1,392 ..... N2
Yanush 123 ..... R5
Yeager 40 ..... O4
Yuba 63 ..... O7
Yukon 20,935 ..... L3

OTHER FEATURES

Altus (res.) H5
Altus A.F.B. H5
Arbuckles, Lake of the (lake) M6
Arbuckle Nat'l Rec. Area N6
Arkansas (riv.) S4
Atoka (res.) P5
Beaver (creek) K6
Beaver (riv.) F1
Bird (creek) O1
Black Bear (creek) M2
Black Mesa (mt.) A1
Blue (riv.) O6
Bluestem (lake) O1
Boston (mts.) S3
Broken Bow (lake) S6
Cache (creek) K6
Canadian (riv.) O4
Caney (riv.) O1
Canton (lake) J2
Carl Blackwell (lake) M2
Cherokees, Lake O'The (lake) S1
Chickasaw Nat'l Rec. Area N6
Chickasha (lake) K4
Cimarron (riv.) N2
Clear Boggy (creek) O6
Deep Fork, North Canadian (riv.) N3
Denison (dam) O7
Elk (creek) H4
Ellsworth (lake) K5
Eucha (lake) S2
Eufaula (lake) P4
Fort Cobb (res.) J4
Fort Gibson (lake) R2
Fort Sill 12,107 ..... K5
Fort Supply (lake) G1
Foss (res.) H3
Great Salt Plains (lake) K1
Heyburn (res.) O3
Hudson (lake) R2
Hugo (lake) R6
Hulah (lake) O1
Illinois (riv.) S3
Jackfork (mt.) P5
Kaw (lake) N1
Kerr, Robert S. (res.) S4
Keystone (lake) O2
Kiamichi (mts.) R5
Kiamichi (riv.) R6
Kiowa (creek) F1
Lawtonka (lake) K5
Little (riv.) R6
McAlester (lake) P4
Mountain Fork (riv.) S6
Mud (creek) L6
Muddy Boggy (creek) O5
Murray (lake) M6
Neosho (riv.) R1
North Canadian (riv.) K3
North Carrizo (riv.) A1
Oologah (lake) P1
Optima (lake) D1
Osage Ind. Res. O1
Ouachita (mts.) R5
Pine Creek (lake) R6
Poteau (riv.) S5
Prairie Dog Town Fork Red (riv.) F5
Red (riv.) R7
Red, North Fork (riv.) H4
Salt Fork, Arkansas (riv.) J1
Salt Fork, Red (riv.) G5
Sans Bois (mts.) R4
Scott (mt.) K5
Spavinaw (lake) S2
Tenkiller Ferry (lake) S3
Texoma (lake) N7
Thunderbird (lake) M4
Tinker A.F.B. M4
Tom Steed (res.) J5
Vance A.F.B. K2
Verdigris (riv.) P2
Washita (riv.) M5
Waurika (lake) K6
Webbers Falls (res.) R3
Wichita (mts.) J5
Wildhorse (creek) L5
Wister (lake) S5
Wolf (creek) G2

▲County seat.

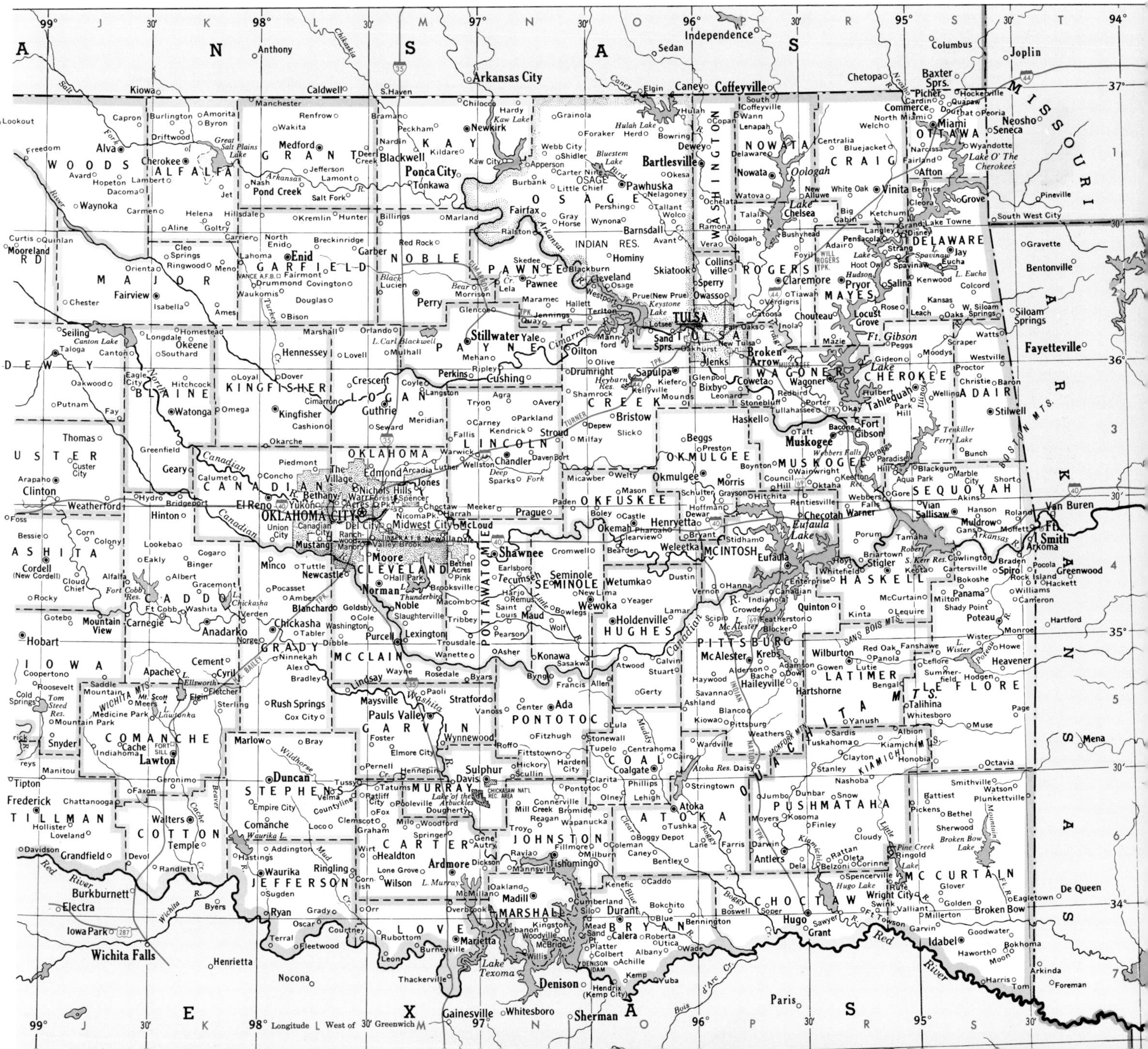

99°
J
K
98°
L
M
97°
N
O
96°
P
R
95°
S
T
94°
37°
36°
35°
34°
Longitude West of Greenwich
KANSAS
MISSOURI
ARKANSAS
TEXAS
WOODS
ALFALFA
GRANT
KAY
OSAGE
WASHINGTON
NOWATA
CRAIG
OTTAWA
DELAWARE
MAJOR
GARFIELD
NOBLE
PAWNEE
ROGERS
MAYES
BLAINE
KINGFISHER
LOGAN
PAYNE
CREEK
TULSA
WAGONER
CHEROKEE
ADAIR
CANADIAN
OKLAHOMA
LINCOLN
OKMULGEE
MUSKOGEE
SEQUOYAH
CADDO
GRADY
CLEVELAND
POTTAWATOMIE
SEMINOLE
OKFUSKEE
McINTOSH
HASKELL
LE FLORE
COMANCHE
STEPHENS
GARVIN
McCLAIN
PONTOTOC
HUGHES
PITTSBURG
LATIMER
COTTON
JEFFERSON
CARTER
MURRAY
JOHNSTON
COAL
ATOKA
PUSHMATAHA
McCURTAIN
LOVE
MARSHALL
BRYAN
CHOCTAW
TILLMAN
OKLAHOMA CITY
TULSA
Enid
Lawton
Norman
Muskogee
Bartlesville
Ponca City
Shawnee
Stillwater
Ardmore
Duncan
McAlester
Ada
Wichita Falls
Arkansas City
Coffeyville
Fayetteville
Ft. Smith
Sherman
Denison
Independence
Joplin

COUNTIES

Baker 15,317 .... K3
Benton 70,811 .... D3
Clackamas 278,850 .... E2
Clatsop 33,301 .... D1
Columbia 37,557 .... D2
Coos 60,273 .... C4
Crook 14,111 .... G3
Curry 19,327 .... C5
Deschutes 74,958 .... F4
Douglas 94,649 .... D4
Gilliam 1,717 .... G2
Grant 7,853 .... J3
Harney 7,060 .... H4
Hood River 16,903 .... F2
Jackson 146,389 .... E5
Jefferson 13,676 .... F3
Josephine 62,649 .... D5
Klamath 57,702 .... F5
Lake 7,186 .... G5
Lane 282,912 .... E4
Lincoln 38,889 .... D3
Linn 91,227 .... E3
Malheur 26,038 .... K4
Marion 228,483 .... E3
Morrow 7,625 .... H2
Multnomah 583,887 .... E2
Polk 49,541 .... D3
Sherman 1,918 .... G2
Tillamook 21,570 .... D2
Umatilla 59,249 .... J2
Union 23,598 .... K2
Wallowa 6,911 .... K2
Wasco 21,683 .... F2
Washington 311,554 .... D2
Wheeler 1,396 .... G3
Yamhill 65,551 .... D2

CITIES and TOWNS

Adair Village 554 .... D3
Adams 223 .... J2
Adel 24 .... H5
Adrian 131 .... K4
Agate Beach 975 .... C3
Agness 150 .... C5
Airlie 40 .... D3
Albany▲ 29,462 .... D3
Algoma 77 .... F5
Alicel 30 .... J2
Allegany 300 .... D4
Aloha 34,284 .... A2
Alpine 80 .... D3
Alsea 125 .... D3
Altamont 18,591 .... F5
Alvadore 800 .... D3
Amity 1,175 .... D2
Andrews 10 .... J5
Antelope 34 .... G3
Antone 40 .... H3
Applegate 150 .... D5
Arago 200 .... C4
Arch Cape 100 .... D2
Arlington 425 .... G2
Arock 31 .... K5
Ash 80 .... D4
Ashland 16,234 .... E5
Ashwood 98 .... G3
Astoria▲ 10,069 .... D1
Athena 997 .... J2
Aumsville 1,650 .... E3
Aurora 567 .... B2
Austin 19 .... J3
Azalea 900 .... D5
Baker▲ 9,140 .... K3
Ballston 120 .... D2
Bancroft 40 .... D5
Bandon 2,215 .... C4
Banks 563 .... A1
Bar View 170 .... C2
Barlow 118 .... B2
Barton 100 .... B2
Barview 1,402 .... C4
Bates 56 .... J3
Bay City 1,027 .... D2
Beatty 350 .... F5
Beaver 350 .... D2
Beavercreek 708 .... B2
Beaverton 53,310 .... A2
Bellfountain 50 .... D3
Bend▲ 20,469 .... F3
Beulah 4 .... J4
Biggs 50 .... G2
Birkenfeld 38 .... D1
Blachly 80 .... D3
Blaine 38 .... D2
Blodgett 250 .... D3
Blue River 318 .... E3
Bly 800 .... F5
Boardman 1,387 .... H2
Bonanza 323 .... F5
Bonneville 80 .... F2
Boring 150 .... E2
Boyd 20 .... F2
Breitenbush 50 .... F3
Bridal Veil 20 .... E2
Bridge 200 .... D4
Bridgeport 60 .... K3
Brighton 150 .... C2
Brightwood 200 .... E2
Broadacres 80 .... A3
Broadbent 400 .... C4
Brogan 130 .... K3
Brookings 4,400 .... C5
Brooks 490 .... A3
Brothers 11 .... G4
Brownlee 50 .... L3
Brownsboro 150 .... E5
Brownsville 1,281 .... E3
Buena Vista 130 .... D3
Bunker Hill 1,242 .... C4
Burns Junction 14 .... K5
Burns▲ 2,913 .... H4
Butte Falls 252 .... E5
Butteville 20 .... A2
Buxton 450 .... D2
Camas Valley 750 .... D4
Camp Sherman 350 .... F3
Canary 23 .... D4
Canby 8,983 .... B2
Cannon Beach 1,221 .... D2
Canyon City▲ 648 .... J3
Canyonville 1,219 .... D5
Carlton 1,289 .... D2
Carpenterville 30 .... C5
Cascade Locks 930 .... E2
Cascade Summit 10 .... F4
Cascadia 250 .... E3
Cave Junction 1,126 .... D5
Cayuse 200 .... J2
Cecil 75 .... H2
Cedar Hills 9,294 .... A2
Cedar Mill 9,697 .... A2
Celilo 50 .... G2
Central Point 7,509 .... D5
Charleston 500 .... C4
Chemawa 400 .... A3
Chemult 800 .... F4
Chenoweth 3,246 .... F2
Cherry Grove 350 .... D2
Cherryville 75 .... E2
Cheshire 300 .... D3
Chiloquin 673 .... F5
Clackamas 2,578 .... B2
Clatskanie 1,629 .... D1
Cloverdale 260 .... D2
Coburg 763 .... E3
Colton 305 .... B3
Columbia City 1,003 .... E2
Condon▲ 635 .... G2
Coos Bay 15,076 .... C4
Coquille▲ 4,121 .... C4
Cornelius 6,148 .... A2
Corvallis▲ 44,757 .... D3
Cottage Grove 7,402 .... D4
Cove 507 .... K2
Cove Orchard 50 .... D2

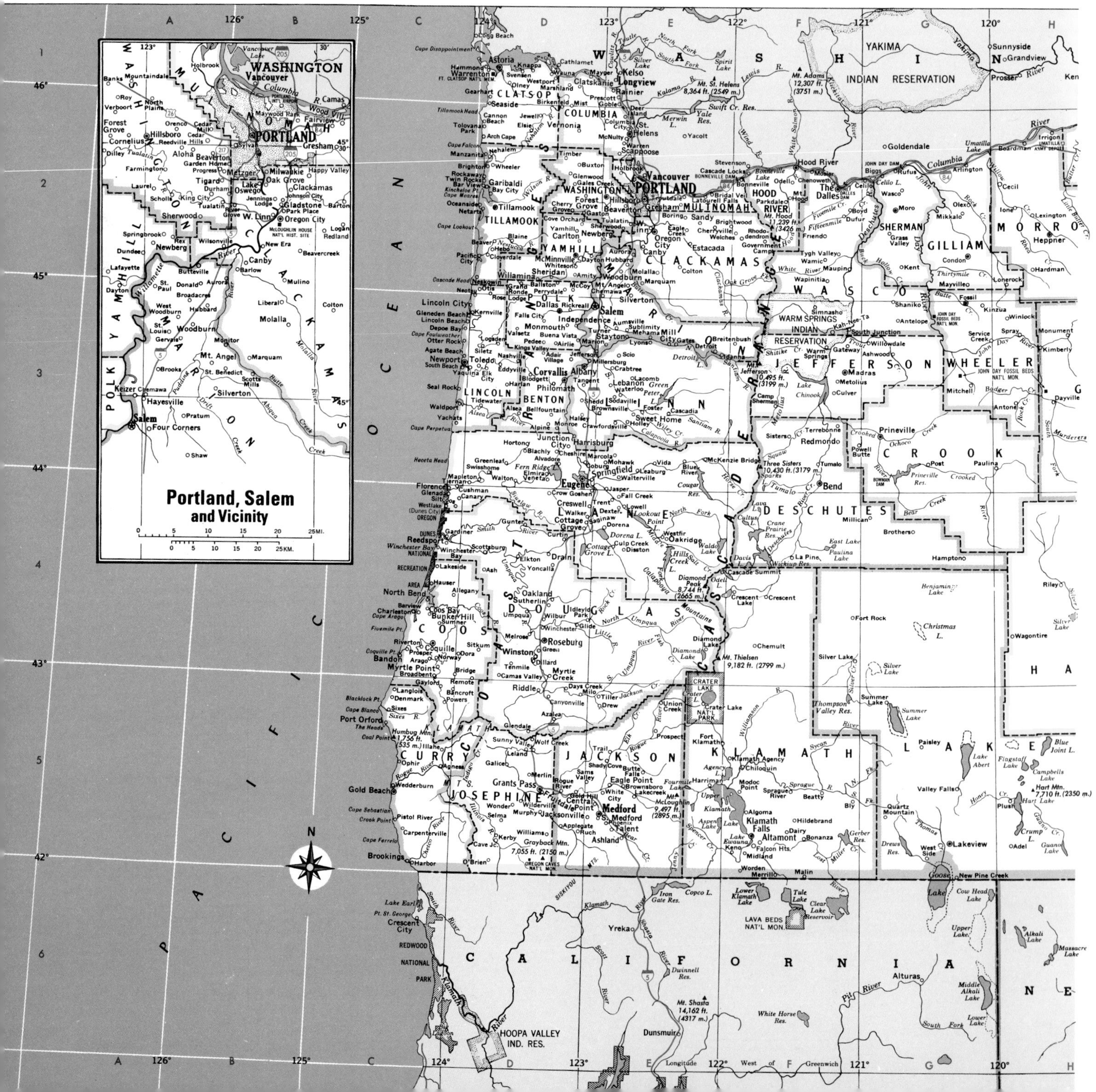

WASHINGTON
PORTLAND
Salem
Eugene
Medford
PACIFIC OCEAN
CALIFORNIA
Portland, Salem and Vicinity
Longitude West of Greenwich

Crabtree 200 ... E3
Crane 84 ... J4
Crater Lake 36 ... E5
Crawfordsville 350 ... E3
Crescent 750 ... F4
Crescent Lake 120 ... F4
Creswell 2,431 ... D4
Crow 200 ... D4
Culp Creek 600 ... E4
Culver 570 ... F3
Curtin 350 ... D4
Cushman 175 ... D4
Dairy 80 ... F5
Dale 85 ... J3
Dallas▲ 9,422 ... D3
Dalles, The▲ 11,060 ... F2
Danner 12 ... K5
Days Creek 550 ... D5
Dayton 1,526 ... A3
Dayville 144 ... H3
Deer Island 225 ... E2
Denmark 15 ... C5
Depoe Bay 870 ... C3
Detroit 331 ... E3
Dexter 500 ... E4
Diamond 6 ... J4
Diamond Lake 56 ... E4
Dillard 602 ... D4
Dilley 250 ... A2
Disston 123 ... E4
Donald 316 ... A3
Dora 100 ... D4
Dorena 200 ... E4
Drain 1,011 ... D4
Drew 60 ... E5
Drewsey ... J4
Dufur 527 ... F2
Dundee 1,663 ... A2
Dunes City (Westlake) ... C4
Durham 748 ... A2
Durkee 158 ... K3
Eagle Creek 250 ... E2
Eagle Point 3,008 ... E5
Echo 499 ... H2
Eddyville 564 ... D3
Elgin 1,586 ... K2
Elk City 30 ... D3
Elkton 172 ... D4

STATE OF OREGON
1859

AREA 97,073 sq. mi. (251,419 sq. km.)
POPULATION 2,853,733
CAPITAL Salem
LARGEST CITY Portland
HIGHEST POINT Mt. Hood 11,239 ft. (3426 m.)
SETTLED IN 1810
ADMITTED TO UNION February 14, 1859
POPULAR NAME Beaver State
STATE FLOWER Oregon Grape
STATE BIRD Western Meadowlark

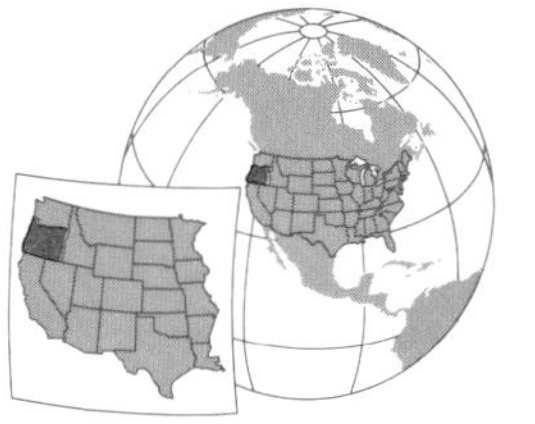

Topography

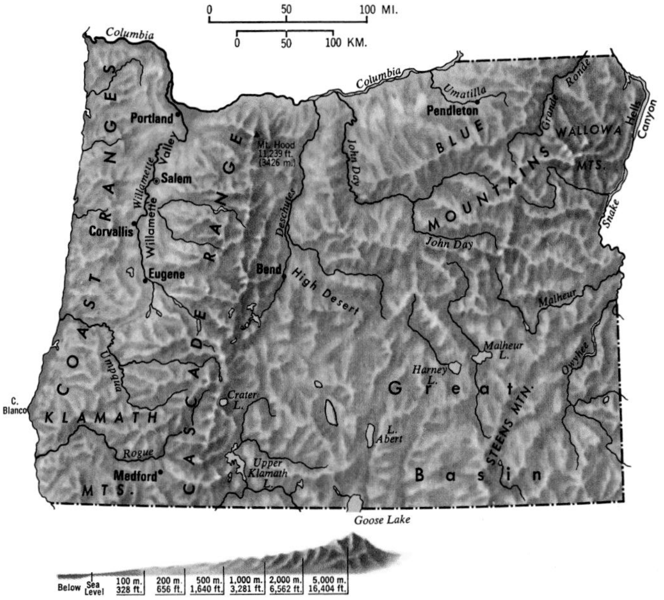
0 50 100 MI.
0 50 100 KM.
Columbia
Portland
Salem
Corvallis
Eugene
Bend
Pendleton
Medford
Mt. Hood 11,239 ft. (3426 m.)
COAST RANGES
CASCADE RANGE
KLAMATH MTS.
BLUE MOUNTAINS
WALLOWA MTS.
STEENS MTN.
Great Basin
High Desert
Willamette Valley
Willamette
Deschutes
John Day
Umatilla
Grande Ronde
Snake
Hells Canyon
Malheur
Owyhee
Umpqua
Rogue
Crater L.
Upper Klamath
Harney L.
Malheur L.
L. Abert
Goose Lake
C. Blanco
Below Sea Level
100 m. 328 ft.
200 m. 656 ft.
500 m. 1,640 ft.
1,000 m. 3,281 ft.
2,000 m. 6,562 ft.
5,000 m. 16,404 ft.

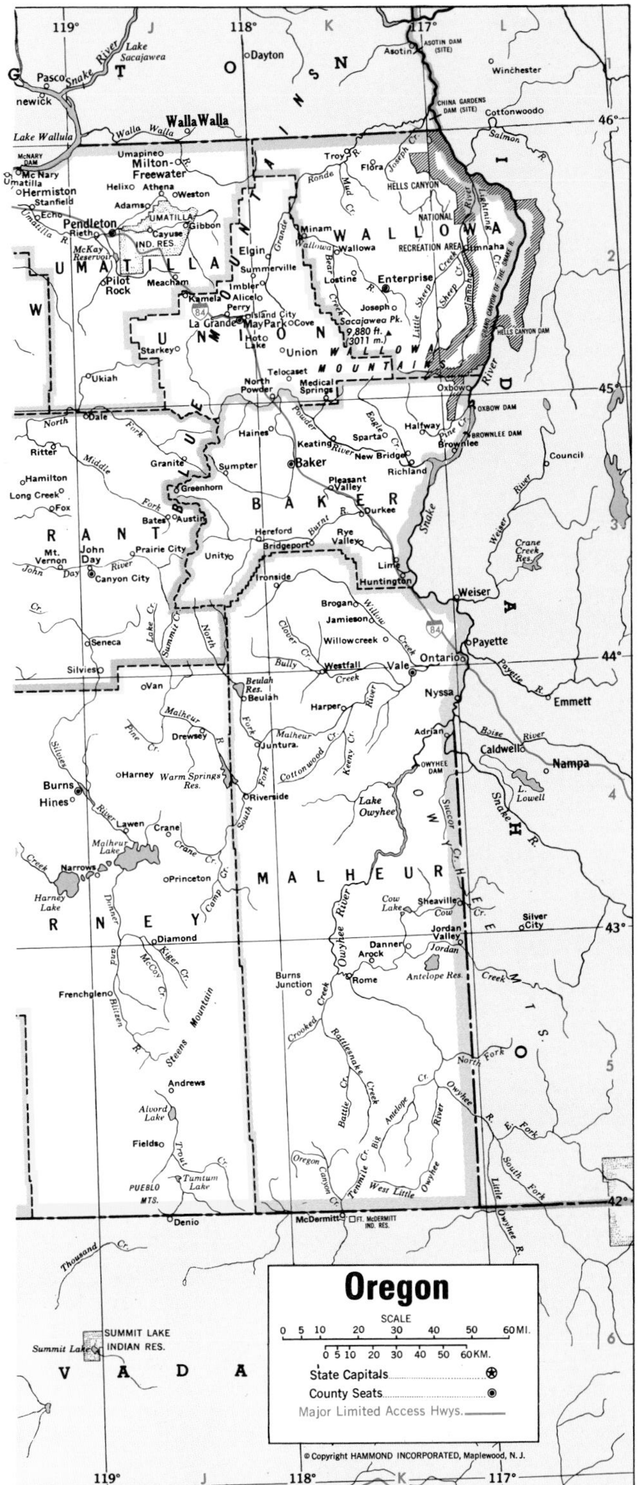
119°
118°
117°
Walla Walla
Pendleton
Hermiston
Milton-Freewater
Enterprise
La Grande
Baker
Ontario
Burns
Hines
Vale
Nyssa
Joseph
Elgin
Union
Halfway
Huntington
John Day
Canyon City
Prairie City
Jordan Valley
McDermitt
Denio
Weiser
Payette
Caldwell
Nampa
Emmett
Council
UMATILLA
WALLOWA
UNION
BAKER
MALHEUR
WALLOWA MOUNTAINS
HELLS CANYON NATIONAL RECREATION AREA
UMATILLA IND. RES.
Snake River
Malheur Lake
Harney Lake
Sacajawea Pk. 9,880 ft. (3011 m.)
Oregon
SCALE
0 5 10 20 30 40 50 60 MI.
0 5 10 20 30 40 50 60 KM.
State Capitals
County Seats
Major Limited Access Hwys.
© Copyright HAMMOND INCORPORATED, Maplewood, N. J.

Elmira 900 ... D3
Elsie 30 ... D2
Enterprise▲ 1,905 ... K2
Estacada 1,419 ... E2
Eugene▲ 112,669 ... D3
Fairview 2,391 ... B2
Falcon Heights ... F5
Fall Creek 58 ... E4
Falls City 818 ... D3
Farmington 100 ... A2
Fields 150 ... J5
Flora 45 ... K2
Florence 5,162 ... C4
Forest Grove 13,559 ... A2
Fort Klamath 200 ... E5
Fort Rock 150 ... G4
Fossil▲ 399 ... G2
Foster 850 ... E3
Four Corners 12,156 ... A3
Fox 30 ... H3
Frenchglen 45 ... H5
Fruitdale-Harbeck 4,733 ... D5
Gales Creek 150 ... D2
Galice 30 ... D5
Garden Home-Whitford 6,652 ... A2
Gardiner 750 ... C4
Garibaldi 877 ... D2
Gaston 563 ... D2
Gates 499 ... E3
Gateway 108 ... F3
Gaylord 80 ... C5
Gearhart 1,027 ... C1
Gervais 992 ... A3
Gibbon 100 ... J2
Gladstone 10,152 ... B2
Glenada 300 ... C4
Glendale 707 ... D5
Gleneden Beach 400 ... C3
Glenwood 225 ... D2
Glide 470 ... D4
Goble 108 ... E1
Gold Beach▲ 1,546 ... C5
Gold Hill 964 ... D5
Goshen 200 ... D4
Government Camp 230 ... F2
Grand Ronde 289 ... D2
Granite 8 ... J3
Grants Pass▲ 17,488 ... D5
Grass Valley 160 ... G2
Green 5,076 ... D4
Greenhorn 0 ... J3
Greenleaf 60 ... D3
Gresham 68,235 ... B2
Gunter 8 ... D4
Haines 405 ... J3
Halfway 311 ... K3
Halsey 667 ... D3
Hamilton 12 ... H3
Hammond 589 ... C1
Hampton 24 ... G4
Happy Valley 1,519 ... B2
Harbor 2,143 ... C5
Hardman ... H2
Harlan 200 ... D3
Harney 15 ... J4
Harper 400 ... K4
Harriman 250 ... E5
Harrisburg 1,939 ... D3
Hauser 400 ... C4
Hayesville 14,318 ... A3
Hebo 400 ... D2
Helix 150 ... J2
Heppner▲ 1,412 ... H2
Hereford 128 ... K3
Hermiston 10,040 ... H2
Hildebrand 50 ... F5
Hillsboro▲ 37,520 ... A2
Hines 1,452 ... H4
Holbrook 494 ... A1
Holley 75 ... E3
Hood River▲ 4,632 ... F2
Horton 175 ... D3
Hubbard 1,881 ... A3
Huntington 522 ... K3
Idanha 289 ... E3
Idleyld Park 300 ... D4
Illahe 30 ... C5
Imbler 299 ... J2
Imnaha 150 ... L2
Independence 4,425 ... D3
Ione 255 ... H2
Ironside 50 ... K3
Irrigon 737 ... H2
Island City 696 ... K2
Jacksonville 1,896 ... D5
Jamieson 120 ... K3
Jasper 231 ... E3
Jefferson 1,805 ... D3
Jennings Lodge 6,530 ... B2
Jewell 10 ... D2
John Day 2,012 ... J3
Johnson City 586 ... B2
Jordan Valley 364 ... K5
Joseph 1,073 ... K2
Junction City 3,670 ... D3
Juntura ... K4
Kah-Nee-Ta 100 ... F3
Kamela 11 ... J2
Keizer 21,884 ... A3
Keno 500 ... F5
Kent 200 ... G2
Kerby 650 ... D5
Kernville 450 ... D3
Kimberly 14 ... H3
King City 2,060 ... A2
Kings Valley 50 ... D3
Klamath Agency 10 ... F5
Klamath Falls▲ 17,737 ... F5
Knappa 950 ... D1
La Grande▲ 11,766 ... J2
La Pine 850 ... F4
Lacomb 425 ... E3
Lafayette 1,292 ... A2
Lake Oswego 30,576 ... B2
Lakecreek 160 ... E5
Lakeside 1,437 ... C4
Lakeview▲ 2,526 ... G5
Langlois 150 ... C5
Latourell Falls 40 ... E2
Lawen 95 ... J4
Leaburg 150 ... E3
Lebanon 10,950 ... E3
Leland 70 ... D5
Lexington 286 ... H2
Liberal 300 ... B3
Lime 25 ... K3
Lincoln Beach 1,507 ... C3
Lincoln City 5,892 ... C3
Logan 450 ... B2
Logsden 55 ... D3
Lonerock 11 ... H2
Long Creek 249 ... H3
Lostine 231 ... K2
Lowell 785 ... E4
Lyons 938 ... E3
Madras▲ 3,443 ... F3
Malin 725 ... F5
Manzanita 513 ... C2
Mapleton 950 ... C3
Marcola 900 ... E3
Marion 300 ... D3
Marquam 40 ... B3
Marshland 30 ... D1
Maupin 456 ... F2
May Park ... J2
Mayger 35 ... D1
Mayville 25 ... G2
Maywood Park 781 ... B2
McCoy 40 ... D2
McKenzie Bridge 500 ... E3
McMinnville▲ 17,894 ... D2
McNary 330 ... H2
McNulty 1,805 ... E2
Meacham 150 ... J2
Medford▲ 46,951 ... E5
Mehama 250 ... E3
Melrose 30 ... D4
Merlin 500 ... D5
Merrill 837 ... F5
Metolius 450 ... F3
Metzger 3,149 ... A2
Midland 520 ... F5
Mikkalo 40 ... G2
Mill City 1,555 ... E3
Millersburg 715 ... E3
Milo 600 ... E5
Milton-Freewater 5,533 ... J2
Milwaukie 18,692 ... B2
Mist 40 ... D1
Mitchell 163 ... G3
Modoc Point 65 ... F5
Mohawk 50 ... E3
Molalla 3,651 ... B3
Monitor 82 ... B3
Monmouth 6,288 ... D3
Monroe 448 ... D3
Monument 162 ... H3
Moro▲ 292 ... G2
Mosier 244 ... F2
Mount Angel 2,778 ... B3
Mount Hood 2,234 ... F2
Mount Vernon 538 ... H3
Mountaindale 25 ... A1
Mulino 720 ... B2
Murphy 500 ... D5
Myrtle Creek 3,063 ... D4
Myrtle Point 2,712 ... C4
Nashville 23 ... D3
Nehalem 232 ... D2
Neotsu 300 ... C2
Neskowin 250 ... D2
Netarts 975 ... C2
New Bridge 28 ... K3
New Era 27 ... B2
New Pine Creek 400 ... G5
Newberg 13,086 ... A2
Newport▲ 8,437 ... C3
North Bend 9,614 ... C4
North Plains 972 ... A2
North Powder 448 ... K2
Norway 150 ... C4
Nyssa 2,629 ... K4
O\'Brien 850 ... D5
Oak Grove 12,576 ... B2
Oakland 844 ... D4
Oakridge 3,063 ... E4
Oceanside 300 ... C2
Odell 450 ... F2
Olex 40 ... G2
Olney 75 ... D1
Ontario 9,392 ... K3
Ophir 275 ... C5
Oregon City▲ 14,698 ... B2
Orenco 220 ... A2
Otis 200 ... D2
Otter Rock 450 ... C3
Oxbow 100 ... L2
Pacific City 500 ... C2
Paisley 350 ... G5
Park Place 500 ... B2
Parkdale 350 ... F2
Paulina 80 ... G3
Pedee 45 ... D3
Pendleton▲ 15,126 ... J2
Perry 50 ... J2
Perrydale 200 ... D2

(continued on following page)

Agriculture, Industry and Resources

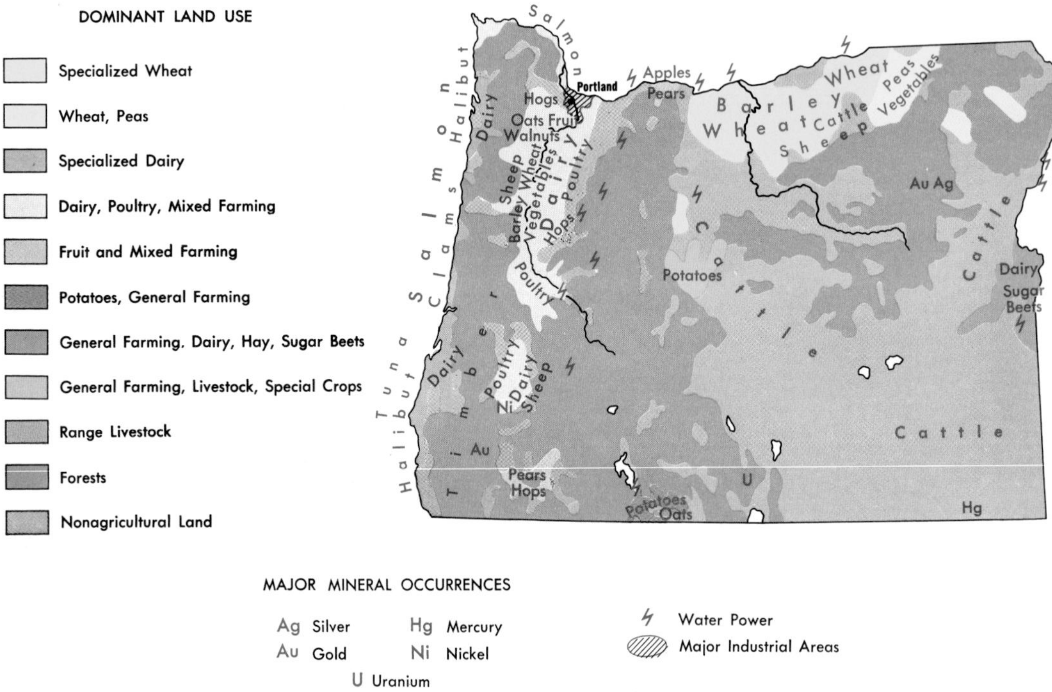
DOMINANT LAND USE
Specialized Wheat
Wheat, Peas
Specialized Dairy
Dairy, Poultry, Mixed Farming
Fruit and Mixed Farming
Potatoes, General Farming
General Farming, Dairy, Hay, Sugar Beets
General Farming, Livestock, Special Crops
Range Livestock
Forests
Nonagricultural Land
Salmon
Halibut
Salmon
Clams
Tuna
Halibut
Portland
Hogs
Oats Fruit
Walnuts
Dairy
Sheep
Barley Wheat
Vegetables
Dairy
Poultry
Hops
Poultry
Apples
Pears
Wheat
Peas
Vegetables
Barley
Wheat
Cattle
Sheep
Au Ag
Cattle
Dairy
Sugar Beets
Potatoes
Cattle
Timber
Dairy
Poultry
Dairy
Sheep
Ni
Au
Pears
Hops
Potatoes
Oats
U
Cattle
Hg
MAJOR MINERAL OCCURRENCES
Ag Silver
Au Gold
Hg Mercury
Ni Nickel
U Uranium
Water Power
Major Industrial Areas

Philomath 2,983 ..... D3
Phoenix 3,239 ..... E5
Pilot Rock 1,478 ..... J2
Pistol River 70 ..... C5
Pleasant Valley 23 ..... K3
Plush 150 ..... H5
Port Orford 1,025 ..... C5
Portland▲ 437,319 ..... B2
Powell Butte 350 ..... G3
Powers 682 ..... D5
Prairie City 1,117 ..... J3
Pratum 40 ..... A3
Prescott 63 ..... D1
Prineville▲ 5,355 ..... G3
Progress 100 ..... A2
Prospect 200 ..... E5
Prosper 110 ..... C4
Rainier 1,674 ..... E1
Redland 700 ..... B2
Redmond 7,163 ..... F3
Reedsport 4,796 ..... C4
Reedville 850 ..... A2
Remote 84 ..... D5
Rex 150 ..... A2
Rhododendron F2
Richland 161 ..... K3
Rickreall 700 ..... D3
Riddle 1,143 ..... D5
Rieth 300 ..... J2
Riley 100 ..... H4
Ritter 70 ..... H3
River Grove 314 ..... B2
Riverside 25 ..... J4
Riverton 150 ..... C4
Rockaway 906 ..... C2
Rogue River 1,759 ..... D5
Rome 8 ..... K5
Rose Lodge 1,257 ..... D3
Roseburg▲ 17,032 ..... D4
Roy 200 ..... A2
Ruch 25 ..... E5
Rufus 295 ..... G2
Rye Valley 15 ..... K3
Saginaw 150 ..... E4
Saint Benedict 70 ..... B3
Saint Helens▲ 7,535 ..... E2
Saint Louis 102 ..... A3
Saint Paul 322 ..... A3
Salem (cap.)▲ 107,786 ..... A3
Sams Valley 100 ..... E5
Sandy 4,152 ..... E2
Scappoose 3,529 ..... E2
Scholls 150 ..... A2
Scio 623 ..... E3
Scotts Mills 283 ..... B3
Scottsburg 300 ..... D4
Seal Rock 430 ..... C3
Seaside 5,359 ..... D2
Selma 150 ..... D5
Seneca 191 ..... J3
Service Creek 5 ..... G3
Shady Cove 1,351 ..... E5
Shaniko 26 ..... G3
Shaw 800 ..... A3
Sheaville 8 ..... K4
Shedd 850 ..... D3
Sheridan 3,979 ..... D2
Sherwood 3,093 ..... A2
Siletz 926 ..... D3
Siltcoos 25 ..... C4
Silver Lake 200 ..... F4
Silverton 5,635 ..... B3
Silvies 11 ..... H3
Simnasho 25 ..... F3
Sisters 679 ..... F3
Sitkum 45 ..... D4
Sixes 300 ..... C5
Sodaville 192 ..... E3
South Junction 20 ..... F3
South Medford 2,898 ..... E5
South Beach 300 ..... C3
Sparta 30 ..... K3
Sprague River 200 ..... F5
Spray 149 ..... H3
Springbrook 500 ..... A2
Springfield 44,683 ..... E3
Stanfield 1,568 ..... H2
Starkey 60 ..... J2
Stayton 5,011 ..... E3
Sublimity 1,491 ..... E3
Summer Lake 97 ..... G5
Summerville 111 ..... K2
Sumner 100 ..... C4
Sumpter 119 ..... J3
Sunny Valley 159 ..... D5
Sutherlin 5,020 ..... D4
Svensen 950 ..... D1
Sweet Home 6,850 ..... E3
Swisshome 350 ..... D3
Sylvan B2
Talent 3,274 ..... E5
Tangent 556 ..... D3
Telocaset 50 ..... K2
Tenmile 500 ..... D4
Terrebonne 1,143 ..... F3
The Dalles▲ 10,820 ..... F2
Tidewater 100 ..... D3
Tiernan 75 ..... C3
Tigard 29,344 ..... A2
Tillamook▲ 4,001 ..... D2
Tiller 300 ..... E5
Timber 175 ..... D2
Toledo 3,174 ..... D3
Tolovana Park 165 ..... C2
Trail 350 ..... E5
Trent 100 ..... E4
Troutdale 7,852 ..... E2
Troy 65 ..... K2
Tualatin 15,013 ..... A2
Tumalo 500 ..... F3
Turner 1,281 ..... E3
Twin Rocks 450 ..... C2
Tygh Valley 663 ..... F2
Ukiah 250 ..... J2
Umapine 100 ..... J2
Umatilla 3,046 ..... H2
Umpqua 705 ..... D4
Union 1,847 ..... K2
Union Creek 35 ..... E5
Unity 87 ..... J3
Vale▲ 1,491 ..... K4
Valley Falls 18 ..... G5
Valsetz 320 ..... D3
Veneta 2,519 ..... D3
Verboort 280 ..... A2
Vernonia 1,808 ..... D2
Vida 300 ..... E3
Wagontire 3 ..... H4
Waldport 1,595 ..... C3
Walker 50 ..... D4
Wallowa 748 ..... K2
Walterville 250 ..... E3
Walton 300 ..... D3
Wamic 255 ..... F2
Wapinitia 10 ..... F2
Warm Springs 2,287 ..... F3
Warren 2,493 ..... E2
Warrenton 2,681 ..... C1
Wasco 374 ..... G2
Waterloo 191 ..... E3
Wauna 10 ..... D1
Wedderburn 700 ..... C5
Welches 100 ..... E2
West Linn 16,367 ..... B2
West Side 16 ..... G5
West Woodburn 600 ..... A3
Westfall 105 ..... K3
Westfir 278 ..... E4
Westlake 1,081 ..... C4
Weston 606 ..... J2
Westport 400 ..... D1
Wheeler 335 ..... D2
White City 5,891 ..... E5
Whiteson 100 ..... D2
Wilbur 476 ..... D4
Wilderville 600 ..... D5
Willamina 1,717 ..... D2
Williams 750 ..... D5
Willowcreek 20 ..... K3
Willowdale 67 ..... G3
Wilsonville 7,106 ..... A2
Winchester 900 ..... D4
Winchester Bay 535 ..... C4
Winlock 25 ..... H3
Winston 3,773 ..... D4
Wolf Creek 500 ..... D5
Wonder 200 ..... D5
Wood Village 2,814 ..... B2
Woodburn 13,404 ..... A3
Worden 32 ..... F5
Yachats 533 ..... C3
Yamhill 867 ..... D2
Yaquina 175 ..... C3
Yoncalla 919 ..... D4

OTHER FEATURES

Abert (lake) G5
Abiqua (creek) B3
Agency (lake) E5
Alsea (riv.) D3
Alvord (lake) J5
Arago (cape) C4
Aspen (lake) E5
Badger (creek) H3
Battle (creek) K5
Bear (creek) E5
Bear (creek) G4
Bear (creek) K2
Benjamin (lake) G4
Beulah (res.) J4
Big Antelope (creek) K5
Blacklock (pt.) C5
Blanco (cape) C5
Blue (mts.) J3
Bonneville (dam) E2
Brownlee (dam) L3
Buck Hollow (creek) G2
Bully (creek) K3
Burnt (riv.) K3
Butte (creek) B3
Butte (creek) G2
Butter (creek) H2
Calapooia (riv.) E3
Calapooya (mts.) E4
Camp (creek) J4
Campbells (lake) H5
Cascade (head) C2
Cascade (range) E4
Celilo (lake) G2
Chetco (riv.) C5
Clackamas (riv.) E2
Clover (creek) K3
Coal (pt.) C5
Coast (ranges) D5
Columbia (riv.) G2
Coos (riv.) D4
Coquille (pt.) C4
Cottage Grove (lake) E4
Cottonwood (creek) K4
Cougar (res.) E3
Cow (creek) K4
Crane (creek) J4
Crane Prairie (res.) F4
Crater (lake) E5
Crater Lake Nat'l Park E5
Crook (pt.) C5
Crooked (creek) K5
Crooked (riv.) G3
Cultus (lake) F4
Dalles, The (dam) F2
Davis (lake) F4
Deschutes (riv.) G2
Detroit (lake) E3
Diamond (lake) E4
Donner and Blitzen (riv.) J4
Dorena (lake) E4
Drews (res.) G5
Drift (creek) B3
Eagle (creek) K3
East (lake) F4
Elk (creek) E5
Ewauna (lake) F5
Falcon (cape) C2
Fern Ridge (lake) D3
Ferrelo (cape) C5
Fifteenmile (creek) F2
Fish (creek) E4
Fivemile (creek) F2
Fivemile (pt.) C4
Flagstaff (lake) H5
Fort Clatsop Nat'l Mem. C1
Foulweather (cape) C3
Fourmile (lake) E5
Gerber (res.) F5
Goose (lake) G5
Grand Canyon of the Snake River L2
Grande Ronde (riv.) K2
Green Peter (lake) E3
Guano (creek) H5
Guano (lake) H5
Harney (lake) H4
Hart (lake) H5
Hart (mt.) H5
Heads, The (prom.) C5
Heceta (head) C3
Hells Canyon (dam) L2
Hells Canyon Nat'l Rec. Area K2
Hills Creek (lake) E4
Honey (creek) G5
Hood (mt.) F2
Hood (riv.) F2
Horse (creek) F3
Illinois (riv.) D5
Imnaha (riv.) L2
Indigo (creek) D5
Jackson (creek) E5
Jefferson (mt.) F3
Jenny (creek) E5
John Day (dam) G2
John Day (riv.) G2
John Day Fossil Beds Nat'l Mon. G3
Jordan (creek) K5
Joseph (creek) K2
Keeny (creek) K4
Kiger (creek) J5
Kincheloe (pt.) C2
Klamath (mts.) C5
Lake (creek) J3
Lava (lake) F4
Lightning (creek) L2
Little (riv.) E4
Little Butter (creek) H2
Little Sheep (creek) K2
Lookout (cape) C2
Lookout Point (lake) E4
Lost (riv.) F5
Malheur (lake) J4
Malheur (riv.) J4
McCoy (creek) J5
McKay (res.) J2
McKenzie, South Fork (riv.) E3
McLoughlin (mt.) E5
McLoughlin House Nat'l Hist. Site B2
McNary (dam) H2
Meares (cape) C2
Metolius (riv.) F3
Miller (creek) F5
Molalla (riv.) B3
Mud (creek) K2
Murderers (creek) H3
Nehalem (riv.) D2
Nestucca (riv.) D2
North Santiam (riv.) E3
North Umpqua (riv.) E4
Oak Grove Fork, Clackamas (riv.) F2
Ochoco (creek) G3
Odell (lake) E4
Oregon Canyon (creek) K5
Oregon Caves Nat'l Mon. D5
Oregon Dunes Nat'l Rec. Area C4
Owyhee (dam) K4
Owyhee (lake) K4
Owyhee (mts.) K4
Owyhee (riv.) K5
Owyhee, North Fork (riv.) K5
Oxbow (dam) L3
Paulina (lake) F4
Perpetua (cape) C3
Pine (creek) J4
Pine (creek) L3
Portland Int'l Airport B2
Powder (riv.) K3
Prineville (res.) G3
Pudding (riv.) A3
Pueblo (mts.) J5
Rattlesnake (creek) K5
Rhea (creek) H2
Rock (creek) E4
Rock (creek) G2
Rock (creek) H3
Rogue (riv.) C5
Salt (creek) E4
Sebastian (cape) C5
Sheep (creek) L2
Shitike (creek) F3
Silver (creek) F4
Silver (creek) H4
Silver (lake) G4
Silver (lake) H4
Silvies (riv.) H4
Siskiyou (mts.) D6
Siuslaw (riv.) D4
Sixes (riv.) C5
Smith (riv.) D4
Snake (riv.) K3
South Santiam (riv.) E3
South Umpqua (riv.) E4
Sparks (lake) F3
Spencer (creek) E5
Sprague (riv.) F5
Squaw (creek) F3
Steens (mt.) J5
Succor (creek) K4
Summer (lake) G5
Summit (creek) J3
Sycan (riv.) F5
Tenmile (creek) K5
The Dalles (dam) F2
Thielsen (mt.) F4
Thirtymile (creek) G2
Thomas (creek) G5
Three Sisters (mt.) F3
Tillamook (head) C2
Trout (creek) F3
Trout (creek) J5
Tualatin (riv.) A2
Tumalo (creek) F3
Tumtum (lake) J5
Umatilla (lake) G2
Umatilla (riv.) H2
Umatilla Army Depot H2
Umatilla Ind. Res. J2
Umpqua (riv.) D4
Upper Klamath (lake) E5
Waldo (lake) E4
Walla Walla (riv.) J1
Wallowa (mts.) K2
Wallowa (riv.) K2
Wallula (lake) H1
Warm Springs (res.) J4
Warm Springs Ind. Res. F3
White (riv.) F2
Wickiup (res.) F4
Wiley (creek) E3
Willamette (riv.) A3
Willamette, Middle Fork (riv.) E4
Williamson (riv.) F5
Willow (creek) H2
Willow (creek) K3
Wilson (riv.) D2
Winchester (bay) C4

▲County seat

AREA 45,308 sq. mi. (117,348 sq. km.)
POPULATION 11,924,710
CAPITAL Harrisburg
LARGEST CITY Philadelphia
HIGHEST POINT Mt. Davis 3,213 ft. (979 m.)
SETTLED IN 1682
ADMITTED TO UNION December 12, 1787
POPULAR NAME Keystone State
STATE FLOWER Mountain Laurel
STATE BIRD Ruffed Grouse

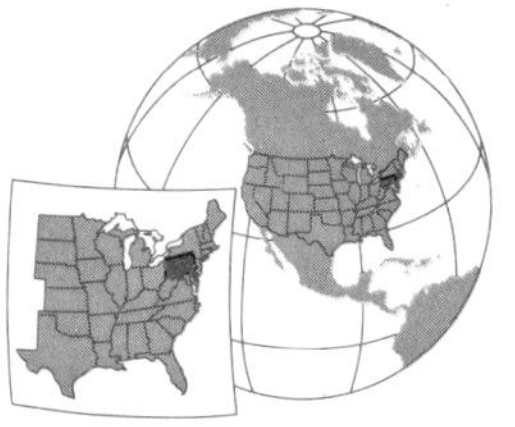

Agriculture, Industry and Resources

DOMINANT LAND USE

- Specialized Dairy
- Dairy, General Farming
- Fruit and Mixed Farming
- Fruit, Truck and Mixed Farming
- General Farming, Livestock, Tobacco
- General Farming, Livestock, Fruit, Tobacco
- Forests
- Urban Areas

MAJOR MINERAL OCCURRENCES

C	Coal	G	Natural Gas	Sl	Slate
Cl	Clay	Ls	Limestone	Ss	Sandstone
Co	Cobalt	O	Petroleum	Zn	Zinc
Fe	Iron Ore				

Water Power
Major Industrial Areas

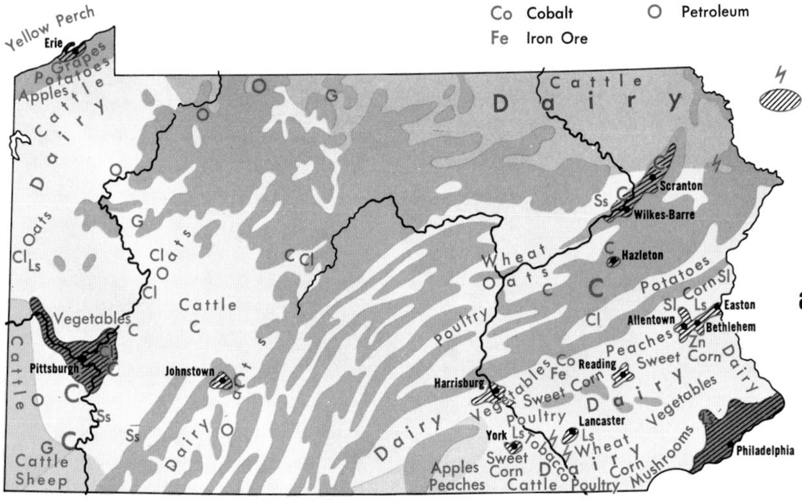
Yellow Perch
Erie
Grapes
Potatoes
Apples
Cattle
Dairy
Oats
Clats
Cattle
Vegetables
Pittsburgh
Johnstown
Cattle
Sheep
Dairy
Scranton
Wilkes-Barre
Hazleton
Wheat
Oats
Potatoes
Corn
Allentown
Easton
Bethlehem
Poultry
Peaches
Sweet Corn
Reading
Harrisburg
Vegetables
Sweet Corn
Lancaster
York
Tobacco
Mushrooms
Philadelphia
Apples
Peaches
Sweet Corn
Poultry

COUNTIES

Adams 78,274 .... H6
Allegheny 1,336,449 .... B5
Armstrong 73,478 .... D4
Beaver 186,093 .... B4
Bedford 47,919 .... E6
Berks 336,523 .... K5
Blair 130,542 .... F4
Bradford 60,967 .... J2
Bucks 541,174 .... M5
Butler 152,013 .... C4
Cambria 163,029 .... E4
Cameron 5,913 .... F3
Carbon 56,846 .... L4
Centre 123,786 .... G4
Chester 376,396 .... L6
Clarion 41,699 .... D3
Clearfield 78,097 .... F3
Clinton 37,182 .... G3
Columbia 63,202 .... K3
Crawford 86,169 .... B2
Cumberland 195,257 .... H5
Dauphin 237,813 .... J5
Delaware 547,651 .... M6
Elk 34,878 .... E3
Erie 275,572 .... B2
Fayette 145,351 .... C6
Forest 4,802 .... D2
Franklin 121,082 .... G6
Fulton 13,837 .... F6
Greene 39,550 .... B6
Huntingdon 44,164 .... F5
Indiana 89,994 .... D4
Jefferson 46,083 .... D3
Juniata 20,625 .... H4
Lackawanna 219,039 .... L3
Lancaster 422,822 .... K5
Lawrence 96,246 .... B4
Lebanon 113,744 .... K5
Lehigh 291,130 .... L4
Luzerne 328,149 .... L3
Lycoming 118,710 .... H3
McKean 50,635 .... E2
Mercer 121,003 .... B3
Mifflin 46,197 .... G4
Monroe 95,709 .... M3
Montgomery 678,111 .... M5
Montour 17,735 .... J3
Northampton 247,105 .... M4
Northumberland 96,771 .... J4
Perry 41,172 .... H5
Philadelphia (city county) 1,688,210 .... M6
Pike 27,966 .... M3
Potter 16,717 .... G2
Schuylkill 152,585 .... K4
Snyder 36,680 .... H4
Somerset 78,218 .... D6
Sullivan 6,104 .... J3
Susquehanna 40,380 .... L2
Tioga 41,126 .... H2
Union 36,176 .... H4
Venango 59,381 .... C3
Warren 45,050 .... D2
Washington 204,584 .... B5
Wayne 39,944 .... M2
Westmoreland 370,321 .... D5
Wyoming 28,076 .... K2
York 339,574 .... J6

CITIES and TOWNS

Abbottstown 539 .... J6
Abington• 58,836 .... M5
Adamstown 1,108 .... K5
Akron 3,869 .... K5
Albion 1,575 .... B2
Alburtis 1,415 .... L5
Aldan 4,549 .... M7
Alexandria 411 .... F4
Aliquippa 13,374 .... B4
Allentown▲ 105,090 .... L4
Allison Park 10,000 .... C4
Altoona 51,881 .... F4
Ambler 6,609 .... M5
Ambridge 8,133 .... B4
Annville 4,294 .... J5
Apollo 1,895 .... C4
Archbald 6,291 .... F6
Ardmore 12,646 .... M6
Arendtsville 693 .... H6
Arnold 6,113 .... C4
Ashland 3,859 .... K4
Ashley 3,291 .... E7
Aspinwall 2,880 .... C6
Atglen 825 .... K6
Athens 3,468 .... K2
Atlas 1,162 .... K4
Auburn 913 .... K4
Austin 569 .... F2
Avalon 5,784 .... B6
Avella 900 .... B5
Avis 1,506 .... H3
Avoca 2,897 .... F7
Avondale 954 .... L6
Avonmore 1,089 .... C4
Baden 5,074 .... B4
Bala-Cynwyd N6
Baldwin 21,923 .... B7
Bally 973 .... L5
Bangor 5,383 .... M4
Barnesboro 2,530 .... E4
Bath 2,358 .... M4
Beallsville 530 .... C5
Beaver Falls 10,687 .... B4
Beaver Meadows 985 .... L4
Beaver▲ 5,028 .... B4
Beaverdale 1,187 .... E5
Beavertown 853 .... H4
Bedford▲ 3,137 .... F5
Beech Creek 716 .... G3
Belle Vernon 1,213 .... C5
Bellefonte▲ 6,358 .... G4
Belleville 1,589 .... G4
Bellevue 9,126 .... B6
Bellwood 1,976 .... F4
Ben Avon 2,096 .... B6
Bendersville 560 .... H6
Bentleyville 2,673 .... B5
Benton 958 .... K3
Berlin 2,064 .... E6
Bernville 789 .... K5
Berrysburg 376 .... J4
Berwick 10,976 .... K3
Berwyn Devon 5,019 .... L5
Bessemer 1,196 .... B4
Bethel Park 33,823 .... B7
Bethlehem 71,428 .... M4
Big Run 699 .... E4
Biglerville 993 .... H6
Birdsboro 4,222 .... L5
Black Lick 1,100 .... D4
Blairsville 3,595 .... D5
Blakely 7,222 .... F6
Blawnox 1,626 .... C6
Bloomfield (New Bloomfield)▲ 1,092 .... H5
Blooming Valley 391 .... B2
Bloomsburg▲ 12,439 .... J3
Blossburg 1,571 .... H2
Boalsburg 2,206 .... G4
Bobtown 1,008 .... B6
Boiling Springs 1,978 .... H5
Bolivar 544 .... D5
Boothwyn 5,069 .... L7
Boswell 1,485 .... E5
Bowmanstown 888 .... L4
Boyertown 3,759 .... L5
Brackenridge 3,784 .... C4
Braddock 4,682 .... C7
Bradford 9,625 .... E2
Brentwood 10,823 .... B7
Briar Creek 616 .... K3
Brickerville 1,268 .... K5
Bridgeport 4,292 .... M5
Bridgeville 5,445 .... B5
Bridgewater 751 .... B4
Brisbin 369 .... F4
Bristol 10,405 .... N5
Bristol• 587,330 .... N5
Broad Top 331 .... F5
Brockway 2,207 .... E3
Brodheadsville 1,389 .... M4
Brookhaven 8,567 .... M7
Brookville▲ 4,184 .... D3
Broomall 10,930 .... M6
Brownstown 937 .... K5
Brownsville 3,164 .... C5
Bruin 646 .... C3
Bryn Athyn 1,081 .... M5
Bryn Mawr 3,271 .... M5
Burgettstown 1,634 .... A5
Burlington 479 .... J2
Burnham 2,197 .... H4
Burnside 350 .... E4
Butler▲ 15,714 .... C4
Cadogan• 459 .... C4
Cairnbrook 1,081 .... E5
California 5,748 .... C5
Callery 420 .... C4
Cambridge Springs 1,837 .... C2
Camp Hill 7,831 .... H5
Canonsburg 9,200 .... B5
Canton 1,966 .... J2
Carbondale 10,664 .... L2
Carlisle▲ 18,419 .... H5
Carmichaels 532 .... B6
Carnegie 9,278 .... B7
Carroll Valley 1,457 .... H6
Carrolltown 1,286 .... E4
Castle Shannon 9,135 .... B7
Catasauqua 6,662 .... M4
Catawissa 1,683 .... K4
Centerville 4,207 .... B6
Central City 1,246 .... E5
Centre Hall 1,203 .... G4
Chalfont 3,069 .... M5
Chambersburg▲ 16,647 .... G6
Charleroi 5,014 .... C5
Cheltenham• 35,509 .... M5
Cherry Tree 431 .... E4
Chester 41,856 .... L7
Chester Heights 2,273 .... L7
Chester Hill 945 .... F4
Cheswick 1,971 .... C6
Chicora 1,058 .... C4
Christiana 1,045 .... K6
Churchill 3,883 .... C7
Clairton 9,656 .... C7
Clarendon 650 .... D2
Clarion▲ 6,457 .... D3
Clark (Clarksville) 610 .... B3
Clarks Green 1,603 .... F6
Clarks Summit 5,433 .... F6
Claysburg 1,399 .... F5
Claysville 962 .... B5
Clearfield▲ 6,633 .... F3
Clifton Heights 7,111 .... M7
Clintonville 520 .... C3
Clymer 1,499 .... E4
Coalport 578 .... E4
Coatesville 11,038 .... L5
Cochranton 1,174 .... B2
Codorus (Jefferson) 685 .... J6
Cokeburg 724 .... B5
Collegeville 4,227 .... M5
Collingdale 9,175 .... N7
Columbia 10,701 .... K5
Colver 1,024 .... E4
Colwyn 2,613 .... N7
Confluence 873 .... D6
Conneaut Lake 699 .... B2
Conneautville 822 .... A2
Connellsville 9,229 .... C5
Connoquenessing 507 .... B4
Conshohocken 8,064 .... M5
Conway 2,424 .... B4
Conyngham 2,060 .... K3
Coopersburg 2,599 .... M5
Cooperstown 506 .... C2
Coplay 3,267 .... L4
Coraopolis 6,747 .... B4
Cornwall 3,231 .... K5
Corry 7,216 .... C2
Coudersport▲ 2,854 .... G2
Crabtree 900 .... D5
Crafton 7,188 .... B7
Cranesville 598 .... B2
Cresson 1,784 .... E5
Cressona 1,694 .... K4
Cross Roads 322 .... J6
Curwensville 2,924 .... E4
Dale 1,642 .... E5
Dallas 2,567 .... E7
Dallastown 3,974 .... J6
Dalton 1,369 .... L2
Danville▲ 5,165 .... J4
Darby 10,955 .... M7
Dauphin 845 .... J5
Dayton 572 .... D4
Delaware Water Gap 733 .... M4
Delmont 2,041 .... D5
Delta 761 .... K6
Denver 2,861 .... K5
Derry 2,950 .... D5
Dickson City 6,276 .... F7
Dillsburg 1,925 .... J5
Donora 5,928 .... C5
Dormont 9,772 .... B7
Dover 1,884 .... J6
Downingtown 7,749 .... L5
Doylestown▲ 8,575 .... M5
Dravosburg 2,377 .... C7
Drexel Hill 29,744 .... M6
Drifton 1,786 .... L3
DuBois 8,286 .... E3
Dublin 1,985 .... M5
Duboistown 1,201 .... H3
Dunbar 1,213 .... C6
Duncannon 1,450 .... H5
Duncansville 1,309 .... F5
Dunmore 15,403 .... F7
Dupont 2,984 .... F7
Duquesne 8,525 .... C7
Duryea 4,869 .... F7
Dushore 738 .... K2
East Bangor 1,006 .... M4
East Berlin 1,175 .... J6
East Berwick 2,128 .... K3
East Brady 1,047 .... C3
East Butler 725 .... C4
East Conemaugh 1,470 .... E5
East Faxon 3,951 .... J3
East Greenville 3,117 .... L5
East Lansdowne 2,691 .... M7
East Petersburg 4,197 .... K5
East Pittsburgh 2,160 .... C7
East Prospect 558 .... J6
East Stroudsburg 8,781 .... M4
East Washington 2,126 .... B5
Easton▲ 26,276 .... M4
Eau Claire 371 .... C3
Ebensburg▲ 3,872 .... E5
Economy 9,519 .... B4
Eddystone 2,446 .... M7
Edgewood 2,719 .... B7
Edgeworth 1,670 .... B4
Edinboro 7,736 .... B2
Edwardsville 5,399 .... E7
Elderton 371 .... D4
Eldred 869 .... F2
Elizabeth 1,610 .... C5
Elizabethtown 9,952 .... J5
Elizabethville 1,467 .... J4
Elkland 1,849 .... H1
Ellsworth 1,048 .... B5
Ellwood City 8,894 .... B4
Elverson 470 .... L5
Elysburg 1,890 .... K4
Emigsville 2,580 .... J5
Emlenton 834 .... C3
Emmaus 11,157 .... M4
Emporium▲ 2,513 .... F2
Emsworth 2,892 .... B6
Enola 5,961 .... J5
Enon Valley 355 .... B4
Ephrata 12,133 .... K5
Erie▲ 108,718 .... B1
Ernest 492 .... D4
Espy 1,430 .... K4
Etna 4,200 .... B6
Etters (Goldsboro) 477 .... J5
Evans City 2,054 .... B4
Everett 1,777 .... F5
Everson 939 .... C5
Exeter 5,691 .... F7
Export 981 .... C5
Factoryville 1,310 .... L2
Fairchance 1,918 .... C6
Fairfield 524 .... H6
Fairless Hills 9,026 .... N5
Falls Creek 1,087 .... E3
Farrell 6,841 .... A3
Fawn Grove 489 .... J6
Fayette City 713 .... C5
Fayetteville 3,033 .... G6
Felton 438 .... J6
Ferndale 2,020 .... E5
Finleyville 446 .... B5
Fleetwood 3,478 .... L5
Fleming (Unionville) 361 .... G4
Flemington 1,321 .... G3
Folcroft 7,506 .... M7
Folsom 8,173 .... M7
Ford City 3,413 .... D4
Ford Cliff 450 .... D4
Forest City 1,846 .... L2
Forest Hills 7,335 .... C7
Forty Fort 5,049 .... F7
Fountain Hill 4,637 .... L4
Fox Chapel 5,319 .... C6
Frackville 4,700 .... K4
Franklin▲ 7,329 .... C3
Franklintown 373 .... H5
Fredericksburg 1,269 .... B2
Fredericktown 1,052 .... C6
Fredonia 683 .... B3
Freeburg 640 .... H4
Freedom 1,897 .... B4
Freeland 3,909 .... L3
Freemansburg 1,946 .... M4
Freeport 1,983 .... C4
Galeton 1,370 .... G2
Gallitzin 2,003 .... E4
Gap 1,226 .... L6
Garden View 2,687 .... H3
Garrett 520 .... D6
Geistown 2,749 .... E5
Gettysburg▲ 7,025 .... H6
Gilberton 953 .... K4
Girard 2,879 .... B2
Girardville 1,889 .... K4
Glassport 5,582 .... C7
Glen Lyon 2,082 .... E7
Glen Rock 1,688 .... J6
Glenolden 7,260 .... M7
Glenside 8,704 .... M5
Grampian 395 .... E4
Gratz 696 .... J4
Great Bend 704 .... L2
Greencastle 3,600 .... G6
Greensburg▲ 16,318 .... D5
Greentree 4,905 .... B7
Greenville 6,734 .... B3
Grove City 8,240 .... B3
Halifax 911 .... J5
Hallstead 1,274 .... L2
Hamburg 3,987 .... L4
Hanover 14,399 .... J6
Harmony 1,054 .... B4
Harrisburg (cap.)▲ 52,376 .... H5
Harrisville 862 .... B3
Harveys Lake 2,746 .... E7
Hastings 1,431 .... E4
Hatboro 7,382 .... M5
Hatfield 2,650 .... M5
Haverford• 52,371 .... M6
Havertown M6
Hawley 1,244 .... M3
Hawthorn 528 .... D3
Hazleton 24,730 .... L4
Heidelberg 1,238 .... B7
Hellam (Hallam) 1,428 .... J6
Hellertown 5,662 .... M4
Herndon 422 .... J4
Hershey 11,860 .... J5
Highland Park 1,583 .... H4
Highspire 2,668 .... J5
Hollidaysburg▲ 5,624 .... F5
Homer City 1,809 .... D4
Homestead 4,179 .... B7
Honesdale▲ 4,972 .... M2
Honey Brook 1,184 .... L5
Hooversville 731 .... E5
Hop Bottom 345 .... L2
Hopwood 2,021 .... C6
Houston 1,445 .... B5
Houtzdale 1,204 .... F4
Howard 749 .... G3
Hughestown 1,734 .... F7
Hughesville 2,049 .... J3
Hummelstown 3,981 .... J5
Huntingdon▲ 6,843 .... G5
Hyde 1,643 .... F4
Hyde Park 542 .... D4
Hydetown 681 .... C2
Hyndman 1,019 .... E6
Imperial-Enlow 3,449 .... B5
Indian Lake 388 .... E5
Indiana▲ 15,174 .... D4
Industry 2,124 .... B4
Ingram 3,901 .... B7
Irvona 666 .... E4
Irwin 4,604 .... C5
Jacobus 1,370 .... J6
Jamestown 761 .... A3
Jeannette 11,221 .... C5
Jenkintown 4,574 .... M5
Jennerstown 635 .... D5
Jermyn 2,263 .... L2
Jerome 1,074 .... D5
Jersey Shore 4,353 .... H3
Jessup 4,605 .... F6
Jim Thorpe (Mauch Chunk)▲ 5,048 .... L4

(continued on following page)

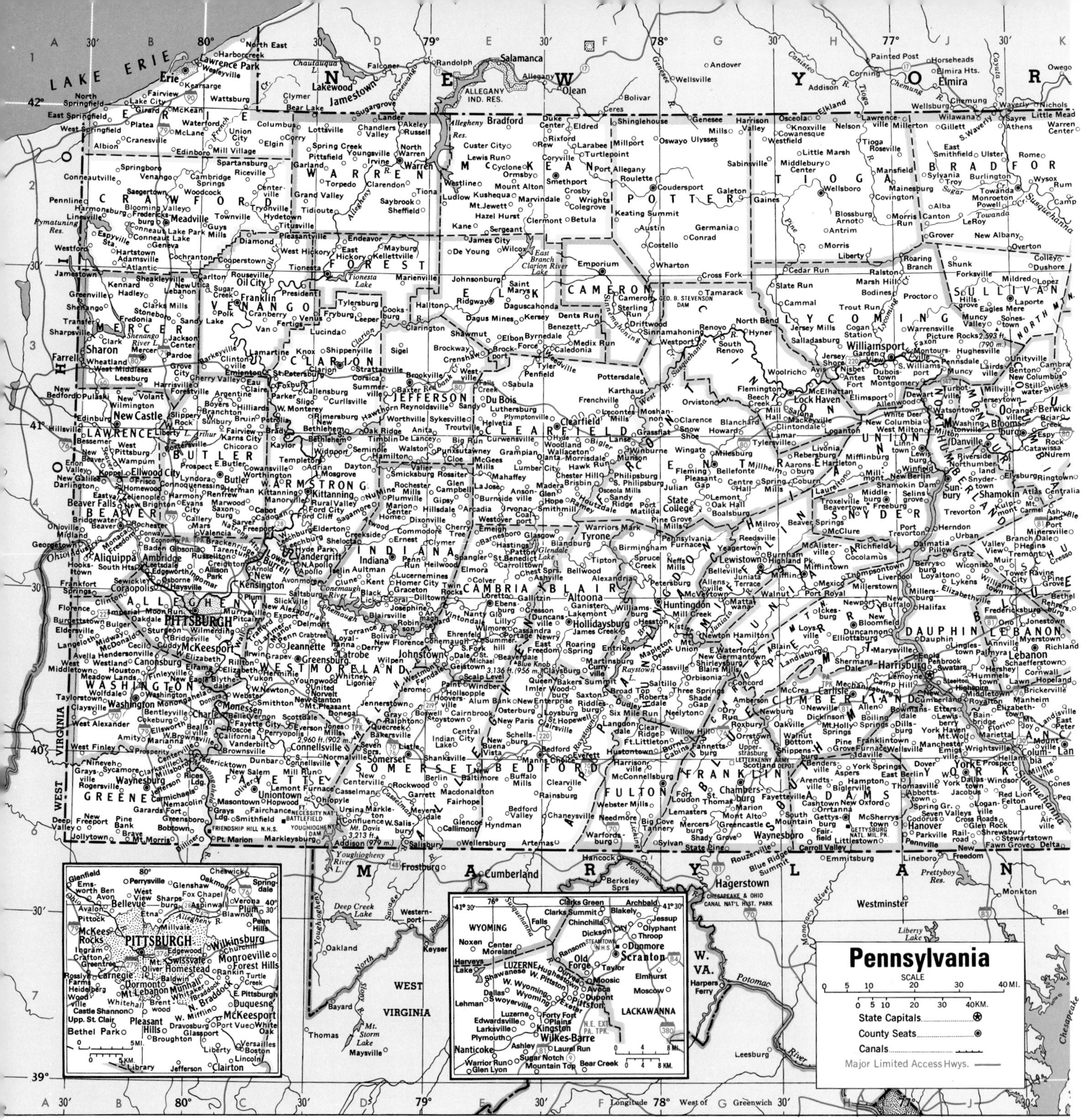
Pennsylvania
SCALE
0 5 10 20 30 40 MI.
0 5 10 20 30 40 KM.
State Capitals
County Seats
Canals
Major Limited Access Hwys.
LAKE ERIE
NEW YORK
MARYLAND
WEST VIRGINIA
PITTSBURGH
Longitude 78° West of Greenwich

Johnsonburg 3,350 .... E3
Johnstown 28,134 .... D5
Jonestown 931 .... K5
Juniata Terrace 556 .... G4
Kane 4,590 .... E2
Kenhorst 2,918 .... L5
Kennett Square 5,218 .... L6
Kingston 14,507 .... F7
Kittanning▲ 5,120 .... D4
Knox 1,182 .... C3
Knoxville 589 .... H2
Koppel 1,024 .... B4
Kulpmont 3,233 .... J4
Kulpsville 5,183 .... M5
Kutztown 4,704 .... L4
Laceyville 436 .... K2
Lake City 2,519 .... B1
Lancaster▲ 55,551 .... K5
Lanesboro 659 .... L2
Langeloth 1,112 .... A5
Langhorne 1,361 .... N5
Lansdale 16,362 .... M5
Lansdowne 11,712 .... M7
Lansford 4,583 .... L4
Laporte▲ 328 .... K3
Larksville 4,700 .... E7
Latrobe 9,265 .... D5
Laurel Run 708 .... F7
Laureldale 3,726 .... L5
Lawrence Park 4,310 .... C1
Lawrenceille 481 .... H2
Lebanon▲ 24,800 .... K5
Leechburg 2,504 .... C4
Leesport 1,270 .... K5
Leetsdale 1,387 .... B4
Lehighton 5,914 .... L4
Lemont 2,613 .... G4
Lemoyne 3,959 .... J5
Levittown 55,362 .... N5
Lewis Run 578 .... E2
Lewisburg▲ 5,785 .... J4
Lewistown▲ 9,341 .... G4
Liberty 2,744 .... H2
Ligonier 1,638 .... D5
Lilly 1,162 .... E5
Lima 2,670 .... L7
Lincoln 1,187 .... C7
Linesville 1,166 .... A2
Linglestown 5,862 .... J5
Linntown 1,640 .... J4
Linwood 3,425 .... L7
Lititz 8,280 .... K5
Littlestown 2,974 .... H6
Liverpool 934 .... H4
Lock Haven▲ 9,230 .... H3
Loganton 443 .... H3
Loganville 954 .... J6
Loretto 1,072 .... E4
Lower Burrell 12,251 .... C4
Loyalhanna 4,108 .... D5
Lucernemines 1,074 .... D4
Luzerne 3,206 .... E7
Lykens 1,986 .... J4
Lyndora 8,333 .... B4
Lyon Station (Lyons) 499 .... L5
Macungie 2,597 .... L4
Mahaffey 341 .... E4
Mahanoy City 5,209 .... K4
Malvern 2,944 .... L5
Manchester 1,830 .... J5
Manheim 5,011 .... K5
Manor 2,627 .... C5
Manorville 418 .... C4
Mansfield 3,538 .... H2
Mapleton Depot (Mapleton) 529 .... F5
Marcus Hook 2,546 .... L7
Marianna 616 .... B5
Marietta 2,778 .... J5
Marion Center 476 .... D4
Markleysburg 320 .... C6
Mars 1,713 .... C4
Martinsburg 2,119 .... F5
Marysville 2,425 .... H5
Masontown 3,759 .... C6
Matamoras 1,934 .... N3
Mauch Chunk (Jim Thorpe)▲ L4
Mayfield 1,890 .... L2
McAdoo 2,459 .... L4
McClure 1,070 .... H4
McConnellsburg▲ 1,106 .... F6
McDonald 2,252 .... B5
McKean (Middleboro) 418 .... B2
McKees Rocks 7,691 .... B7
McKeesport 26,016 .... C7
McSherrystown 2,769 .... H6
McVeytown 408 .... G4
Meadville▲ 14,318 .... B2
Mechanicsburg 9,452 .... H5
Media▲ 5,957 .... L7
Mercer▲ 2,444 .... B3
Mercersburg 1,640 .... G6
Merion Station M6
Meshoppen 439 .... L2
Meyersdale 2,518 .... E6
Middleburg▲ 1,422 .... H4
Middleport 520 .... K4
Middletown 9,254 .... J5
Midland 3,321 .... A4
Midway 1,043 .... B5
Mifflin 660 .... H4
Mifflinburg 3,480 .... H4
Mifflintown▲ 866 .... H4
Milesburg 1,144 .... G4
Milford▲ 1,064 .... N3
Mill Creek 392 .... G5
Mill Hall 1,702 .... G3
Mill Village 429 .... C2
Millbourne 831 .... M6
Millersburg 2,729 .... J4
Millerstown 646 .... H4
Millersville 8,099 .... K6
Millheim 847 .... G4
Millvale 4,341 .... B7
Millville 969 .... J3
Milroy 1,456 .... G4
Milton 6,746 .... J3
Minersville 4,877 .... K4
Mohnton 2,484 .... L5
Monaca 6,739 .... B4
Monessen 9,901 .... C5
Monongahela 4,928 .... B5
Monroeton (Monroe) 627 .... J2
Monroeville 29,169 .... C7
Mont Alto 1,395 .... G6
Montgomery 1,631 .... H3
Montoursville 4,983 .... J3
Montrose 1,982 .... L2
Moosic 5,339 .... F7
Morrisville 9,765 .... N5
Morton 2,851 .... M7
Moscow 1,527 .... F7
Mount Carmel 7,196 .... K4
Mount Holly Springs 1,925 .... H5
Mount Jewett 1,029 .... E2
Mount Joy 6,398 .... K5
Mount Lebanon 33,362 .... B7
Mount Oliver 4,160 .... B7
Mount Penn 2,883 .... L5
Mount Pleasant 4,787 .... D5
Mount Pocono 1,795 .... M3
Mount Union 2,878 .... G5
Mount Wolf 1,365 .... J5
Mountainhome 1,042 .... M3
Mountville 1,977 .... K5
Muncy 2,702 .... J3
Munhall 13,158 .... C7
Murrysville 17,240 .... C5
Myerstown 3,236 .... K5
Nanticoke 12,267 .... E7
Nanty Glo 3,190 .... E5
Narberth 4,278 .... M6
Nazareth 5,713 .... M4
Nemacolin 1,097 .... B6
Nescopeck 1,651 .... K3
Nesquehoning 3,364 .... L4
New Alexandria 571 .... C5

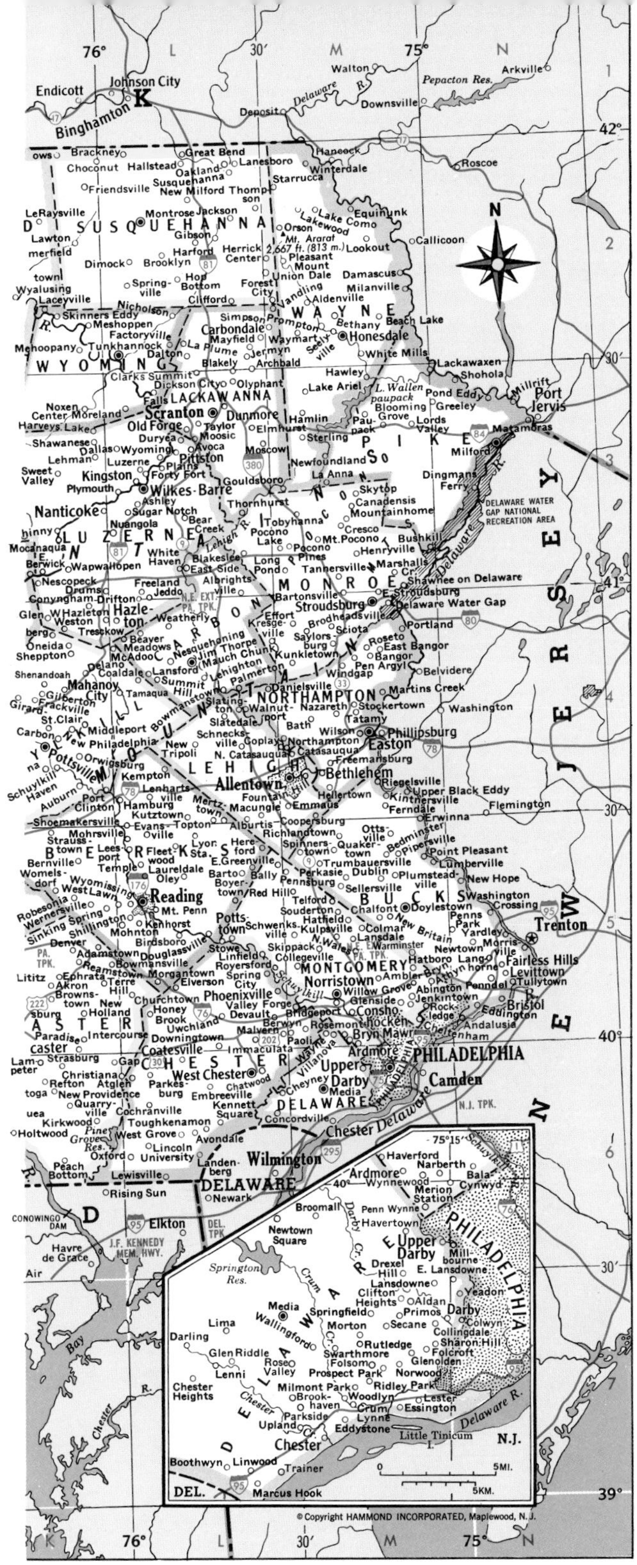

PHILADELPHIA
Camden
Trenton
Wilmington
Allentown
Bethlehem
Reading
Scranton
Wilkes-Barre
Norristown
Stroudsburg
Easton
Phillipsburg
Chester
Binghamton
Johnson City
Endicott
Elkton
LUZERNE
MONROE
NORTHAMPTON
LEHIGH
BUCKS
MONTGOMERY
CHESTER
DELAWARE
WAYNE
PIKE
WYOMING
LACKAWANNA
SUSQUEHANNA
CARBON
NEW JERSEY
DELAWARE WATER GAP NATIONAL RECREATION AREA

Petersburg 469 G4
Philadelphia▲ 1,585,577 N6
Philipsburg 3,048 F4
Phoenixville 15,066 L5
Picture Rocks 660 J3
Pillow 341 J4
Pine Grove 2,118 K4
Pine Grove Mills 1,129 G4
Pitcairn 4,087 C5
Pittsburgh▲ 369,879 B7
Pittston 9,389 F7
Plains 4,694 F7
Platea 467 B2
Pleasant Gap 1,699 G4
Pleasant Hills 8,884 B7
Plum 25,609 C5
Plumville 390 D4
Plymouth 7,134 E7
Plymptonville 1,074 E3
Pocono Pines 824 M3
Point Marion 1,344 C6
Polk 1,267 C3
Port Allegany 2,391 F2
Port Carbon 2,134 K4
Port Matilda 669 F4
Port Royal 836 H4
Port Vue 4,641 C7
Portage 3,105 E5
Portland 516 M4
Pottstown 21,831 L5
Pottsville▲ 16,603 K4
Prospect 1,122 B4
Prospect Park 6,764 M7
Punxsutawney 6,782 E4
Quakertown 8,982 M5
Quarryville 1,642 K6
Ramey 536 F4
Rankin 2,503 C7
Reading▲ 78,380 L5
Reamstown 2,649 K5
Red Hill 1,794 L5
Red Lion 6,130 J6
Reedsville 1,023 G4
Renovo 1,526 G3
Reynoldsville 2,818 D3
Rices Landing 457 C6
Richland 1,457 K5
Richlandtown 1,195 M5
Ridgway▲ 4,793 E3
Ridley Park 7,592 M7
Riegelsville 912 M4
Rimersburg 1,053 D3
Ringtown 853 K4
Riverside 1,991 J4
Roaring Spring 2,615 F5
Robesonia 1,944 K5
Rochester 4,156 B4
Rockledge 2,679 M5
Rockwood 1,014 D6
Rome 475 K2
Roscoe 872 C5
Rose Valley 982 L7
Roseto 1,555 M4
Rosslyn Farms 483 B7
Rouseville 583 C3
Rouzerville 1,188 G6
Royalton 1,120 J5
Royersford 4,458 L5
Rural Valley 957 D4
Russellton 1,691 C4
Rutledge 843 M7
Saegertown 1,066 B2
Saint Clair 3,524 K4
Saint Marys 5,511 E3
Saint Michael-Sidman 1,189 E5
Saint Petersburg 349 C3
Salisbury 716 D6
Saltillo 347 G5
Saltsburg 990 C4
Sandy 1,795 E3
Sandy Lake 722 B3
Saxonburg 1,345 C4
Saxton 838 F5
Sayre 5,791 K2
Scalp Level 1,158 E5
Schnecksville 1,780 L4
Schuylkill Haven 5,610 K4
Schwenksville 1,326 L5
Scottdale 5,184 C5
Scranton▲ 81,805 F7
Selinsgrove 5,384 J4
Sellersville 4,479 M5
Seven Valleys 483 J6
Seward 522 E5
Sewickley 4,134 B4
Shamokin 9,184 J4
Shamokin Dam 1,690 J4
Sharon 17,493 B3
Sharon Hill 5,771 N7
Sharpsburg 3,781 B6
Sharpsville 4,729 A3
Sheffield 1,294 D2
Shenandoah 6,221 K4
Shickshinny 1,108 K3
Shillington 5,062 K5
Shinglehouse 1,243 F2
Shippensburg 5,331 H5
Shippenville 474 D3
Shoemakersville 1,443 K4
Shrewsbury 2,672 J6
Sinking Spring 2,467 K5
Skippack 2,042 M5
Slatington 4,678 L4
Slickville 1,178 C5
Sligo 706 C3
Slippery Rock 3,008 B3
Smethport▲ 1,734 F2
Smithfield 1,000 C6
Smithton 388 C5
Snow Shoe 800 G3
Snydertown 416 J4
Somerset▲ 6,454 D6
Souderton 5,957 M5
South Bethlehem 479 D4
South Connellsville 2,204 C6
South Fork 1,197 E5
South Heights 647 B4
South Philipsburg 438 F4
South Renovo 579 G3
South Waverly 1,049 J2
South Williamsport 6,496 J3
Spangler 2,068 E4
Spartansburg 403 C2
Spring City 3,433 L5
Spring Grove 1,863 J6
Springboro 557 B2
Springdale 3,992 C6
Springfield 24,160 M7
State College 38,923 G4
State Line 1,253 G6
Steelton 5,152 J5
Stewartstown 1,308 K6
Stockertown 641 M4
Stoneboro 1,091 B3
Stowe 3,598 L5
Stoystown 389 E5
Strasburg 2,568 K6
Strattanville 490 D3
Strausstown 353 K5
Stroudsburg▲ 5,312 M4
Sturgeon 1,312 B5
Sugar Creek 5,532 C3
Sugar Notch 1,044 E7
Sugargrove 630 D1
Summerhill 614 E5
Summerville 675 D3
Summit Hill 3,332 L4
Sunbury▲ 11,591 J4
Susquehanna 1,994 L2
Swarthmore 6,157 M7
Swatara• 18,796 J5
Swissvale 10,637 C7
Swoyerville 5,630 E7
Sykesville 1,387 E3
Tamaqua 7,943 L4
Tarentum 5,674 C4
Tatamy 873 M4
Taylor 6,941 F7
Telford 4,238 M5
Temple 1,491 L5
Terre Hill 1,282 L5
Thompsontown 582 H4
Three Springs 422 G5
Throop 4,070 F7
Tidioute 791 D2
Tioga 638 H2
Tionesta▲ 634 C2
Tipton 1,194 F4
Titusville 6,434 C2
Topton 1,987 L5
Toughkenamon 1,273 L6
Towanda▲ 3,242 J2
Tower City 1,518 J4
Townville 358 C2
Trafford 3,345 C5
Trainer 2,271 L7
Tremont 1,814 K4
Tresckow 1,033 K4
Trevorton 2,058 J4
Troy 1,262 J2
Trumbauersville 894 M5
Tullytown 2,339 N5
Tunkhannock▲ 2,251 L2
Turbotville 675 J3
Turtle Creek 6,556 C7
Tyrone 5,743 F4
Ulysses (Lewisville) 653 G2
Union City 3,537 C2
Uniontown▲ 12,034 C6
Upland 3,334 L7
Upper Darby• 84,054 M6
Upper Saint Claire• 19,023 B7
Valencia 364 C4
Valley Forge 400 L5
Valley View 1,749 J4
Vanderbilt 545 C5
Vandergrift 5,904 D4
Vandling 660 M2
Verona 3,260 C6
Versailles 2,150 C7
Villanova M6
Vintondale 582 E5
Wall 853 C5
Walnutport 2,055 L4
Wampum 666 B4
Warren▲ 11,122 D2
Warrior Run 656 E7
Washington▲ 15,864 B5
Waterford 1,492 B2
Watsontown 2,310 J3
Waymart 1,337 M2
Wayne M6
Waynesboro 9,578 G6
Waynesburg▲ 4,270 B6
Weatherly 2,640 L4
Wellsboro▲ 3,430 H2
Wernersville 1,934 K5
Wesleyville 3,655 C1
West Brownsville 1,170 C5
West Chester▲ 18,041 L6
West Elizabeth 634 C5
West Grove 2,128 L6
West Hazleton 4,136 K4
West Kittanning 1,253 C4
West Lawn 1,606 K5
West Leechburg 1,359 C4
West Middlesex 982 B3
West Mifflin 23,644 C7
West Newton 3,152 C5
West Pittsburg 1,133 B4
West Pittston 5,590 F7
West View 7,734 B6
West Wyoming 3,117 E7
West York 4,283 J6
Westfield 1,119 H2
Westmont 5,789 D5
Westover 446 E4
Wheatland 760 B3
Whitaker 1,416 C7
White Haven 1,132 L3
White Oak 8,761 C7
Whitehall 14,451 B7
Wiconisco 1,321 J4
Wilkes-Barre▲ 47,523 F7
Wilkinsburg 21,080 C7
Williamsburg 1,456 F5
Williamsport▲ 31,933 H3
Williamstown 1,509 J4
Willow Grove 16,325 M5
Wilmerding 2,421 C5
Wilson 7,830 M4
Windber 4,756 E5
Windgap 2,651 M4
Windsor 1,355 J6
Wolfdale 2,906 B5
Womelsdorf 2,270 K5
Woodlyn 10,151 M7
Worthington 713 C4
Wrightsville 2,396 J5
Wyalusing 686 K2
Wyoming 3,255 E7
Wyomissing 7,332 K5
Yardley 2,288 N5
Yeadon 11,980 N7
Yeagertown 1,150 G4
York Haven 758 J5
York Springs 547 H6
York▲ 42,192 J6
Youngsville 1,775 D2
Youngwood 3,372 D5
Zelienople 4,158 B4

OTHER FEATURES

Allegheny (res.) E2
Allegheny (riv.) D2
Allegheny Front (mts.) E5
Appalachian (mts.) H4
Ararat (mt.) M2
Arthur (lake) C4
Beaver (riv.) B4
Blue (mt.) G5
Blue Knob (mt.) E5
Casselman (riv.) D6
Clarion (riv.) D3
Conemaugh (riv.) D5
Conemaugh River (lake) D4
Conewango (creek) D1
Davis (mt.) D6
Delaware (riv.) N3
Delaware Water Gap Nat'l Rec. N3
Erie (lake) B1
Fort Necessity Nat'l Battlefield C6
George B. Stevenson (dam) G3
Gettysburg Nat'l Mil. Park H6
Glendale (lake) F4
Juniata (riv.) G5
Laurel Hill (mt.) D5
Lehigh (riv.) L3
Letterkenny Army Depot G6
Licking (creek) F6
Little Tinicum (isl.) M7
Lycoming (creek) H3
Monongahela (riv.) C6
North (mt.) K3
Ohio (riv.) A4
Oil (creek) C2
Pine (creek) H2
Pine Grove (res.) K6
Pocono (mts.) M3
Pymatuning (res.) A2
Redbank (creek) E3
Schuylkill (riv.) M5
Shenango River (lake) B3
Sinnemahoning (creek) F3
South (mt.) H6
Steamtown Nat'l Hist. Site F7
Susquehanna (riv.) K6
Tioga (riv.) H1
Tionesta Creek (lake) D3
Towanda (creek) J2
Tuscarora (mt.) G5
Wallenpaupack (lake) M3
Youghiogheny River (lake) D6

▲County seat
•Population of town or township

New Beaver 1,736 B4
New Berlin 892 J4
New Bethlehem 1,151 D3
New Bloomfield▲ H5
New Brighton 6,854 B4
New Britain 2,174 M5
New Castle▲ 28,334 B3
New Cumberland 7,665 J5
New Eagle 2,172 B5
New Florence 854 D5
New Freedom 2,920 J6
New Galilee 500 A4
New Holland 4,484 K5
New Hope 1,400 N5
New Kensington 15,894 C4
New Milford 953 L2
New Oxford 1,617 H6
New Philadelphia 1,283 K4
New Salem (Delmont) 669 D5
New Stanton 2,081 C5
New Wilmington 2,706 B3
Newport 1,568 H5
Newtown 2,565 N5
Newtown Square• 11,775 L6
Newville 1,349 H5
Nicholson 857 L2
Norristown▲ 30,749 M5
North Apollo 1,391 D4
North Braddock 7,036 C7
North Catasauqua 2,867 L4
North East 4,617 C1
North Wales 3,802 M5
North Warren 1,232 D2
Northampton 8,717 M4
Northumberland 3,860 J4
Norvelt 2,541 D5
Norwood 6,162 M7
Nuangola 701 L3
Oakdale 1,752 B5
Oakland 641 L2
Oakmont 6,961 C6
Ohioville 3,865 B4
Oil City 11,949 C3
Old Forge 8,834 F7
Oliver 3,271 C6
Olyphant 5,222 F7
Orangeville 504 K3
Orbisonia 447 G5
Orwigsburg 2,780 K4
Osborne 565 B4
Osceola Mills 1,310 F4
Oxford 3,769 K6
Paint 1,091 E5
Palmerton 5,394 L4
Palmyra 6,910 J5
Paoli 5,603 M5
Paradise 1,107 K5
Parker 853 C3
Parkesburg 2,981 L6
Parkside 2,369 M7
Parkville 6,014 J6
Patton 2,206 E4
Pen Argyl 3,492 M4
Penbrook 2,791 J5
Penn 511 C5
Penn Hills 51,430 C7
Penn Wynne 5,807 M6
Pennsburg 2,460 M5
Penndel 2,703 N5
Pennville 1,559 J6
Perkasie 7,878 M5
Perryopolis 1,833 C5

Topography

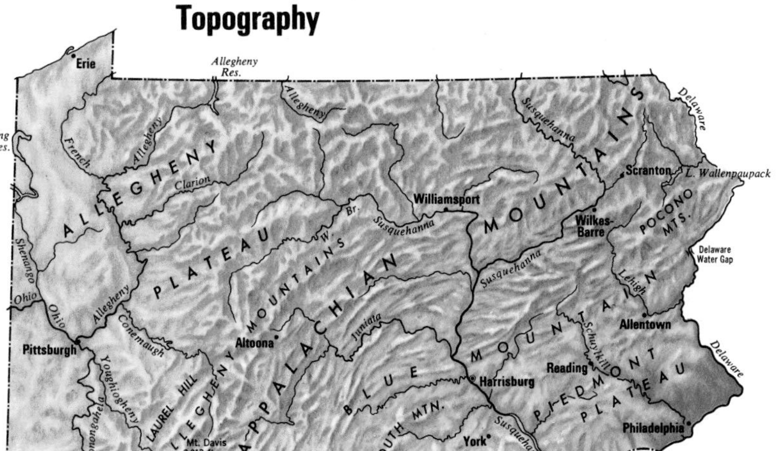

Erie
Allegheny Res.
Pymatuning Res.
ALLEGHENY
PLATEAU
APPALACHIAN
MOUNTAINS
ALLEGHENY MOUNTAINS
BLUE MOUNTAIN
PIEDMONT
PLATEAU
POCONO MTS.
LAUREL HILL
SOUTH MTN.
Williamsport
Scranton
L. Wallenpaupack
Wilkes-Barre
Delaware Water Gap
Allentown
Reading
Harrisburg
Philadelphia
York
Altoona
Pittsburgh
Mt. Davis 3,213 ft. (979 m.)
Susquehanna
Juniata
Clarion
Allegheny
Ohio
Shenango
Conemaugh
Youghiogheny
Monongahela
Lehigh
Schuylkill
Delaware
French
0 30 60 MI.
0 30 60 KM.
5,000 m. 16,404 ft.
2,000 m. 6,562 ft.
1,000 m. 3,281 ft.
500 m. 1,640 ft.
200 m. 656 ft.
100 m. 328 ft.
Sea Level
Below

South Carolina
SCALE
0 5 10 20 30 40 MI.
0 5 10 20 30 40 KM.
State Capitals
County Seats
Canals
Major Limited Access Hwys.
© Copyright HAMMOND
Longitude West of 81° Greenwich
NORTH CAROLINA
GEORGIA
ATLANTIC OCEAN
SEA ISLANDS
COLUMBIA
CHARLESTON
AUGUSTA
SAVANNAH
CHARLOTTE

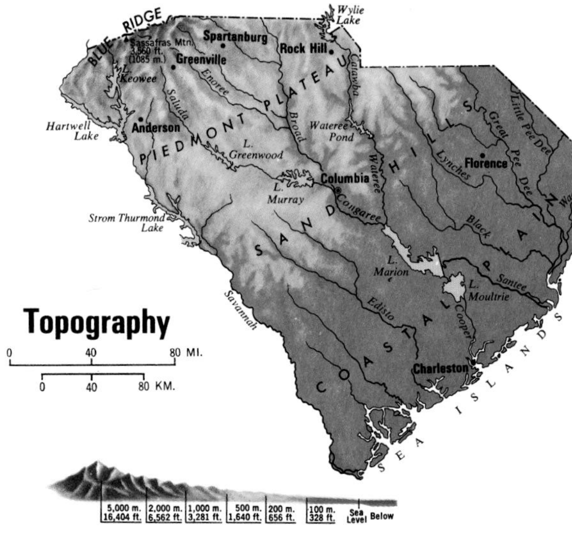
Topography
0 40 80 MI.
0 40 80 KM.
BLUE RIDGE
PIEDMONT PLATEAU
SAND HILLS
COASTAL PLAIN
SEA ISLANDS
Spartanburg
Greenville
Rock Hill
Anderson
Columbia
Florence
Charleston
Myrtle Beach
Hartwell Lake
Strom Thurmond Lake
L. Marion
L. Moultrie
L. Murray
L. Greenwood
Wateree Pond
Wylie Lake
Keowee
Sassafras Mtn. 3,560 ft. (1085 m.)
5,000 m. 16,404 ft.
2,000 m. 6,562 ft.
1,000 m. 3,281 ft.
500 m. 1,640 ft.
200 m. 656 ft.
100 m. 328 ft.
Sea Level
Below

COUNTIES

Abbeville 23,862 ..... B3
Aiken 120,940 ..... D4
Allendale 11,722 ..... E6
Anderson 145,196 ..... B2
Bamberg 16,902 ..... E5
Barnwell 20,293 ..... E5
Beaufort 86,425 ..... F7
Berkeley 128,776 ..... G5
Calhoun 12,753 ..... F4
Charleston 295,039 ..... H6
Cherokee 44,506 ..... D1
Chester 32,170 ..... E2
Chesterfield 38,577 ..... G2
Clarendon 28,450 ..... G4
Colleton 34,377 ..... F6
Darlington 61,851 ..... H3
Dillon 29,114 ..... J3
Dorchester 83,060 ..... G5
Edgefield 18,375 ..... D4
Fairfield 22,295 ..... E3
Florence 114,344 ..... H3
Georgetown 46,302 ..... J5
Greenville 320,167 ..... C2
Greenwood 59,567 ..... C3
Hampton 18,191 ..... E6
Horry 144,053 ..... J4
Jasper 15,487 ..... E6
Kershaw 43,599 ..... F3
Lancaster 54,516 ..... F2
Laurens 58,092 ..... D2
Lee 18,437 ..... G3
Lexington 167,611 ..... E4
Marion 33,899 ..... J3
Marlboro 29,361 ..... H2
McCormick 8,868 ..... C4
Newberry 33,172 ..... D3
Oconee 57,494 ..... A2
Orangeburg 84,803 ..... F5
Pickens 93,894 ..... B2
Richland 285,720 ..... F4
Saluda 16,357 ..... D3
Spartanburg 226,800 ..... D2
Sumter 102,637 ..... G4
Union 30,337 ..... D2
Williamsburg 36,815 ..... H4
York 131,497 ..... E2

CITIES and TOWNS

Abbeville▲ 5,778 ..... C3
Adams Run 500 ..... G6
Adamsburg 300 ..... D2
Aiken West 3,083 ..... D4
Aiken▲ 19,872 ..... D4
Alcolu 600 ..... G4
Allendale▲ 4,410 ..... E5
Allsbrook 100 ..... K3
Anderson 26,184 ..... B2
Andrews 3,050 ..... H5
Antioch 500 ..... F3
Antreville 500 ..... B3
Appleton 200 ..... E5
Arcadia 899 ..... C2
Arcadia Lakes 611 ..... F3
Ariail 2,419 ..... B2
Arkwright 2,623 ..... C2
Atlantic Beach 446 ..... K4
Awendaw 200 ..... H5
Aynor 470 ..... J3
Ballentine 550 ..... E3
Bamberg▲ 3,843 ..... E5
Barnwell▲ 5,255 ..... E5
Batesburg 4,082 ..... D4
Bath 2,242 ..... D5
Beaufort▲ 9,576 ..... F7
Beech Island 400 ..... D5
Belton 4,646 ..... C2
Bennettsville 9,345 ..... H2
Berea 13,535 ..... C2
Bethera 265 ..... H5
Bethune 405 ..... G3
Bingham 200 ..... H3
Bishopville▲ 3,560 ..... G3
Blacksburg 1,907 ..... D1
Blackville 2,688 ..... E5
Blenheim 191 ..... H2
Bluffton 738 ..... F7
Blythewood 164 ..... E3
Bonneau 374 ..... H5
Bowman 1,063 ..... F5
Boykin 350 ..... F3
Branchville 1,107 ..... F5
Brunson 587 ..... E6
Bucksport 1,022 ..... J4
Buffalo 1,569 ..... D2
Burgess 250 ..... J4
Burnettown 493 ..... D5
Burton 6,917 ..... F7
Calhoun Falls 2,328 ..... B3
Camden▲ 6,696 ..... F3
Cameron 504 ..... F4
Campobello 465 ..... C1
Canadys 130 ..... F5
Carlisle 470 ..... D2
Cashville 200 ..... C2
Catawba 607 ..... F2
Cateechee 225 ..... B2
Cayce 11,163 ..... E4
Centenary 700 ..... J3
Central 2,438 ..... B2
Central Pacolet 257 ..... D2
Chapin 282 ..... D3
Chappells 45 ..... D3
Charleston▲ 80,414 ..... G6
Cheraw 5,505 ..... H2
Cherokee Falls 250 ..... D1
Chesnee 1,280 ..... D1
Chester▲ 7,158 ..... E2
Chesterfield▲ 1,373 ..... G2
City View 1,490 ..... C2
Clarks Hill 200 ..... C4
Claussen 500 ..... H3
Clearwater 4,731 ..... D4
Clemson 11,096 ..... B2
Cleveland 800 ..... C1
Clifton 950 ..... D2
Clinton 7,987 ..... D3
Clio 882 ..... H2
Clover 3,422 ..... E1
Columbia (cap.)▲ 98,052 ..... F4

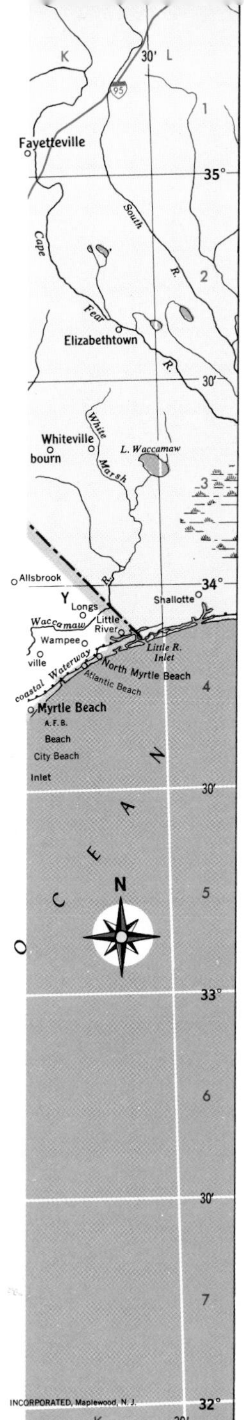

Fayetteville
35°
Cape Fear R.
South R.
Elizabethtown
Whiteville
L. Waccamaw
White Marsh
Allsbrook
34°
Shallotte
Longs
Little River
Wampee
Little R. Inlet
North Myrtle Beach
Atlantic Beach
Myrtle Beach
A.F.B.
33°
32°
INCORPORATED, Maplewood, N. J.

AREA 31,113 sq. mi. (80,583 sq. km.)
POPULATION 3,505,707
CAPITAL Columbia
LARGEST CITY Columbia
HIGHEST POINT Sassafras Mtn. 3,560 ft. (1085 m.)
SETTLED IN 1670
ADMITTED TO UNION May 23, 1788
POPULAR NAME Palmetto State
STATE FLOWER Carolina (Yellow) Jessamine
STATE BIRD Carolina Wren

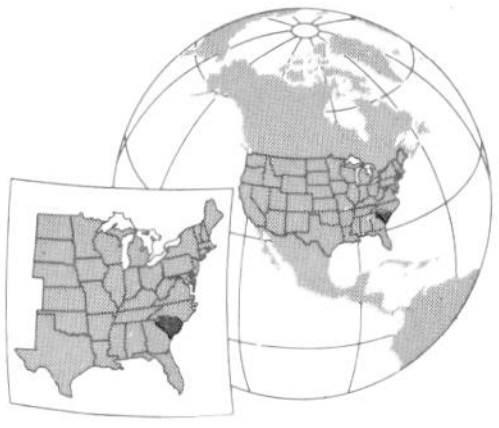

Conestee 500 ..... C2
Converse 1,173 ..... D2
Conway▲ 9,819 ..... J4
Coosawhatchie 250 ..... F6
Cope 124 ..... E5
Cordesville 300 ..... H5
Cordova 135 ..... F5
Coronaca 200 ..... C3
Cottageville 572 ..... G6
Coward 532 ..... H4
Cowpens 2,176 ..... D1
Cross 469 ..... G5
Cross Anchor 350 ..... D2
Cross Hill 604 ..... D3
Cross Keys 250 ..... D2
Cummings 275 ..... E6
Dacusville 350 ..... B2
Dale 500 ..... F6
Dalzell 625 ..... G3
Darlington▲ 7,311 ..... H3
Davis Station 300 ..... G4
Denmark 3,762 ..... E5
Dillon▲ 6,829 ..... J3
Donalds 326 ..... C3
Doneraile 1,276 ..... H3
Dorchester 400 ..... G5
Due West 1,220 ..... C3
Duncan 2,152 ..... C2
Easley 15,195 ..... B2
East Gaffney 3,278 ..... D1
Eastover 1,044 ..... F4
Edgefield 2,563▲ C4
Edgemoor 500 ..... E2
Edisto Beach 340 ..... G7
Edisto Island 900 ..... G6
Effingham 300 ..... H3
Ehrhardt 442 ..... E5
Elgin 622 ..... F3
Elko 214 ..... E5
Elliott 500 ..... G3
Elloree 939 ..... F4
Enoree 1,107 ..... D2
Estill 2,387 ..... E6
Eureka 1,738 ..... E2
Eutawville 350 ..... G5
Fair Play 500 ..... A2
Fairfax 2,317 ..... E6
Filbert 203 ..... E1
Fingerville 320 ..... D1
Florence▲ 29,813 ..... H3
Floyd Dale 450 ..... J3
Folly Beach 1,398 ..... H6
Forest Acres 7,197 ..... E3
Forest Beach 500 ..... F7
Foreston 300 ..... G4
Fort Lawn 718 ..... F2
Fort Mill 4,930 ..... F1
Fort Motte 700 ..... F4
Fountain Inn 4,388 ..... C2
Furman 260 ..... E6
Gable 230 ..... G4
Gadsden 500 ..... F4
Gaffney▲ 13,145 ..... D1
Gantt 13,891 ..... C2
Garden City Beach 300 ..... K4
Garnett 500 ..... E6
Gaston 984 ..... E4
Georgetown▲ 9,517 ..... J5
Gifford 313 ..... E6
Gilbert 324 ..... E4
Gillisonville 350 ..... E6
Givhans 400 ..... G5
Glendale 1,049 ..... D2
Glenn Springs 350 ..... D2
Gloverville 2,753 ..... D4
Goose Creek 24,692 ..... H6
Govan 84 ..... E5
Gowensville 200 ..... C1
Gramling 400 ..... C1
Graniteville 1,158 ..... D4
Gray Court 914 ..... C2
Great Falls 2,307 ..... F2
Greeleyville 464 ..... H4
Greenville▲ 58,282 ..... C2
Greenwood▲ 20,807 ..... C3
Greer 10,322 ..... C2
Gresham 350 ..... J4
Gurley 425 ..... J3
Hamer 588 ..... J3
Hampton 2,997▲ E6
Hanahan 13,176 ..... H6
Hardeeville 1,583 ..... E7
Harleyville 633 ..... G5
Hartsville 8,372 ..... G3
Heath Springs 907 ..... F2
Helena 500 ..... D3
Hemingway 829 ..... J4
Hemlock (Eureka) E2
Hickory Grove 287 ..... E2
Hilda 342 ..... E5
Hilton Head Island 23,694 ..... F7
Hodges 125 ..... C3
Holly Hill 1,478 ..... G5
Hollywood 2,094 ..... G6
Honea Path 3,841 ..... C3
Hopkins 300 ..... F4
Horatio 500 ..... F3
Huger 500 ..... H5
Inman 1,742 ..... C1
Irmo 11,280 ..... D3
Irwin 1,296 ..... F2
Isle of Palms 3,680 ..... H6
Iva 1,174 ..... B3
Jackson 1,681 ..... D5
Jacksonboro 475 ..... G6
Jamestown 84 ..... H5
Jedburg 900 ..... G5
Jefferson 745 ..... G2
Joanna 1,735 ..... D3
Johns Island 200 ..... G6
Johnsonville 1,415 ..... J4
Johnston 2,688 ..... D4
Jonesville 1,205 ..... D2
Kershaw 1,814 ..... G2
Kinards 300 ..... D3
Kingsburg 300 ..... H4
Kingstree▲ 3,858 ..... H4
Kingville 500 ..... F4
Kline 285 ..... E5
La France 875 ..... B2
Ladson 13,540 ..... G6
Lake City 7,153 ..... H4
Lake View 872 ..... J3
Lamar 1,125 ..... G3
Lancaster Mills 2,096 ..... F2
Lancaster▲ 8,914 ..... F2
Lando 250 ..... E2
Landrum 2,347 ..... C1
Lane 523 ..... H5
Langley 1,714 ..... D4
Latta 1,565 ..... J3
Laurel Bay 4,972 ..... F7
Laurens▲ 9,694 ..... C3
Leesville 2,025 ..... E4
Lena 275 ..... E6
Lesslie 1,102 ..... E2
Level Land 100 ..... C3
Lexington▲ 3,289 ..... E4
Liberty 3,228 ..... B2
Lincolnville 716 ..... G6
Little Mountain 235 ..... E3
Little River 3,470 ..... K4
Little Rock 500 ..... J3
Livingston 171 ..... E4
Lobeco 345 ..... F6
Lockhart 58 ..... E2
Lodge 147 ..... F5
Longcreek 200 ..... A2
Longtown 400 ..... F3
Loris 2,067 ..... K3
Lowndesville 162 ..... B3
Lowrys 200 ..... E2
Lugoff 3,211 ..... F3
Luray 102 ..... E6
Lydia 500 ..... G3
Lydia Mills 925 ..... D3
Lyman 2,271 ..... C2
Lynchburg 475 ..... G3
Madison A2
Madison 1,150 ..... D4
Manning▲ 4,428 ..... G4
Marietta-Slater C1
Marion▲ 7,658 ..... J3
Mars Bluff 500 ..... H3
Mauldin 11,587 ..... C2
Mayesville 694 ..... G4
Mayo 1,569 ..... D1
McBee 715 ..... G3
McClellanville 333 ..... H5
McColl 2,685 ..... H2
McConnells 157 ..... E2
McCormick▲ 1,659 ..... C4
Meggett 787 ..... G6
Modoc 300 ..... C4
Monarch Mills 2,353 ..... D2
Moncks Corner▲ 5,607 ..... G5
Monetta 285 ..... D4
Montmorenci 500 ..... D4
Moore 500 ..... D2
Mount Carmel 117 ..... C3
Mount Croghan 131 ..... G2
Mount Holly 200 ..... H5
Mount Pleasant 30,108 ..... H6
Mountain Rest 500 ..... A2
Mullins 5,910 ..... J3
Murrells Inlet 3,334 ..... K4
Myrtle Beach 24,848 ..... K4
Neeses 410 ..... E4
Nesmith 350 ..... H4
New Ellenton 2,515 ..... D5
New Town 950 ..... J3
New Zion 200 ..... H4
Newberry▲ 10,542 ..... D3
Newry 400 ..... B2
Nichols 528 ..... J3
Ninety Six 2,099 ..... C3
Norris 884 ..... B2
North 809 ..... E4
North Augusta 15,351 ..... C5
North Charleston 70,218 ..... G6
North Hartsville 2,906 ..... G3
North Myrtle Beach 8,636 ..... K4
Norway 401 ..... E5
Oakley 250 ..... G5
Olanta 687 ..... H4
Olar 391 ..... E5
Ora 13,739 ..... D2
Orangeburg▲ 14,933 ..... F4
Oswego 500 ..... G3
Pacolet 1,736 ..... D2
Pacolet Mills 696 ..... D2
Pageland 2,666 ..... G2
Pamplico 1,314 ..... H4
Parksville 193 ..... C4
Parr 7,172 ..... E3
Patrick 368 ..... G2
Pauline 750 ..... D2
Pawleys Island 176 ..... J5
Paxville 218 ..... G4
Peak 78 ..... E3
Peedee 350 ..... H3
Pelion 336 ..... E4
Pelzer 81 ..... B2
Pendleton 3,314 ..... B2
Perry 241 ..... E4
Pickens▲ 3,042 ..... B2
Piedmont 4,143 ..... C2
Pineland 800 ..... E6
Pineridge 1,731 ..... E4
Pineville 900 ..... H5
Pinewood 600 ..... G4
Pinopolis 788 ..... G5
Plantersville 231 ..... J4
Plum Branch 101 ..... C4
Pomaria 267 ..... E3
Port Royal 2,985 ..... F7
Poston 250 ..... J4
Princeton 300 ..... C2
Prosperity 1,116 ..... D3
Quinby 865 ..... H3
Rains 450 ..... J3
Ravenel 2,165 ..... G6
Red River F2
Reevesville 244 ..... F5
Reidville C2
Rembert 350 ..... G3
Richburg 405 ..... E2
Ridge Spring 861 ..... D4
Ridgeland▲ 1,071 ..... E7
Ridgeville 1,625 ..... G5
Ridgeway 407 ..... F3
Rimini 525 ..... G4
Rion 300 ..... E3
Ritter 300 ..... F6
Rock Hill 41,643 ..... E2
Rodman 500 ..... E2
Rowesville 316 ..... F5
Ruby 300 ..... G2
Ruffin 400 ..... F6
Saint Andrews 26,692 ..... G6
Saint George▲ 2,077 ..... F5
Saint Matthews▲ 2,345 ..... F4
Saint Paul 725 ..... G4
Saint Stephen 1,697 ..... H5
Salem 192 ..... A2
Salley 451 ..... E4
Salters 300 ..... H4
Saluda▲ 2,798 ..... D4
Santee 638 ..... F5
Sardinia 225 ..... G4
Saxon 4,002 ..... D2
Scotia 182 ..... E6
Scranton 802 ..... H4
Sea Pines 500 ..... F7
Seabrook 948 ..... F6
Sellers 358 ..... H3
Seneca 7,726 ..... A2
Shannontown G4
Sharon 270 ..... E2
Sheldon 225 ..... F6
Shulerville 375 ..... H5
Silverstreet 156 ..... D3
Simpsonville 11,708 ..... C2
Six Mile 562 ..... B2
Slater-Marietta 2,245 ..... C1
Smoaks 142 ..... F5
Smyrna 57 ..... E1
Snelling 125 ..... E5
Society Hill 686 ..... H2
South Bennettsville 1,065 ..... H2
South Congaree 2,406 ..... E4
Spartanburg▲ 43,467 ..... C1
Spring Mills 1,419 ..... F2
Springdale 2,643 ..... F2
Springdale 2,985 ..... E4
Springfield 523 ..... E4
Starr 164 ..... B3
Startex 1,162 ..... C2
Stuckey 311 ..... H4
Sullivans Island 1,623 ..... H6
Summerton 975 ..... G4
Summerville 22,519 ..... G5
Summit 242 ..... E4
Sumter▲ 41,943 ..... G4
Surfside Beach 3,845 ..... K4
Swansea 527 ..... E4
Sycamore 208 ..... E5
Tamassee 320 ..... A2
Tatum 49 ..... H2
Taylors 19,619 ..... C2
Tigerville 975 ..... C1
Tillman 225 ..... E7
Timmonsville 2,182 ..... H3
Toddville 200 ..... J4
Townville 300 ..... B2
Tradesville 500 ..... F2
Travelers Rest 3,069 ..... C2
Trenton 303 ..... D4
Trio 400 ..... H5
Troy 140 ..... C4
Turbeville 698 ..... G4
Ulmer 90 ..... E5
Union▲ 9,836 ..... D2
Utica 1,478 ..... B2
Van Wyck 500 ..... F2
Vance 214 ..... G5
Varnville 1,970 ..... E6
Vaucluse 606 ..... D7
Wade-Hampton 20,014 ..... C2
Wagener 731 ..... E4
Walhalla▲ 3,755 ..... A2
Wallace 500 ..... H2
Walterboro▲ 5,492 ..... F6
Wampee 200 ..... K4
Wando 500 ..... H6
Ward 132 ..... D4
Ware Shoals 2,497 ..... C3
Warrenville 1,029 ..... D4
Waterloo 122 ..... C3
Watts Mill 1,535 ..... D2
Wedgefield 550 ..... F4
Wellford 2,511 ..... C2
West Columbia 10,588 ..... E4
West Pelzer 989 ..... B2
West Springs 500 ..... D2
West Union 260 ..... B2
Westminster 3,120 ..... A2
Westview 1,999 ..... C2
Westville 440 ..... F3
White Pond 200 ..... D5
White Rock 600 ..... E3
Whitmire 1,702 ..... D3
Whitney 4,052 ..... D1
Williams 188 ..... F5
Williamston 3,876 ..... B2
Williston 3,099 ..... E5
Windsor 124 ..... E5
Windy Hill 1,622 ..... H3
Winnsboro Mills 2,275 ..... E3
Winnsboro▲ 3,475 ..... E3
Wisacky 250 ..... G3
Woodford 200 ..... E4
Woodruff 4,365 ..... D2
Woodville C2
Yemassee 728 ..... F6
Yonges Island 500 ..... G6
York▲ 6,709 ..... E1

OTHER FEATURES

Ashepoo (riv.) F6
Ashley (riv.) G6
Bay Point (isl.) F7
Beaufort Marine Air Sta. F7
Big Black (creek) G2
Black (riv.) H4
Blue Ridge (mts.) B1
Broad (riv.) E2
Broad (riv.) F7
Buck (creek) J3
Bull (isl.) H6
Bullock (creek) E2
Bulls (bay) H6
Bush (riv.) D3
Buzzard Roost (dam) D3
Cape (isl.) J5
Capers (isl.) H6
Catawba (riv.) F2
Catfish (creek) J3
Chattooga (riv.) A2
Combahee (riv.) F6
Congaree (riv.) F4
Congaree Nat'l Mon. F4
Cooper (riv.) H6
Coosaw (riv.) G7
Coosawhatchie (riv.) E6
Cowpens Nat'l Battlefield D1
Crooked (creek) H2
Deep (creek) B2
Dewees (isl.) H6
Donaldson A.F.B. C2
Edisto (isl.) G6
Edisto (riv.) G7
Enoree (riv.) C2
Fort Jackson F4
Fort Sumter Nat'l Mon. H6
Four Hole Swamp (creek) F5
Fripp (isl.) G7
Great Pee Dee (riv.) J4
Greenwood (lake) D3
Hartwell (dam) B3
Hartwell (lake) A3
Hilton Head (isl.) F7
Hunting (isl.) G7
Intracoastal Waterway H5
James (isl.) H6
Johns (isl.) G6
Juniper (creek) H2
Keowee (lake) B2
Keowee (riv.) B2
Kiawah (isl.) G6
Kings Mountain Nat'l Mil. Park E1
Little (riv.) C3
Little (riv.) D3
Little Lynches (riv.) G3
Little Pee Dee (riv.) J4
Little River (inlet) L4
Lumber (riv.) J3
Lynches (riv.) H3
Marion (lake) G5
Morris (isl.) H6
Moultrie (lake) G5
Murphy (isl.) J5
Murray (lake) D4
Myrtle Beach A.F.B. K4
Naval Base H6
New (riv.) E6
Ninety Six Nat'l Hist. Site C3
North (inlet) J5
North (isl.) J5
North Edisto (riv.) G6
Pacolet (riv.) D1
Palms, Isle of (isl.) H6
Parris Island Marine Base F7
Pee Dee (riv.) J4
Pocotaligo (riv.) G4
Port Royal (sound) F7
Pritchards (isl.) G7
Reedy (riv.) C2
Robinson (lake) G3
Romain (cape) J6
Saint Helena (isl.) F7
Saint Helena (sound) G7
Salkehatchie (riv.) E5
Saluda (riv.) D3
Sandy (pt.) H6
Sandy (riv.) E2
Santee (dam) G4
Santee (riv.) H5
Sassafras (mt.) B1
Savannah (riv.) E6
Savannah River Plant D5
Sea (isls.) G7
Seabrook (isl.) G6
Seneca (riv.) B2
Shaw A.F.B. F4
South (isl.) J5
Stevens (creek) C4
Stono (inlet) H6
Strom Thurmond (dam) C4
Strom Thurmond (lake) C4
Thompsons (creek) G2
Tugaloo (riv.) A2
Turkey (creek) E2
Tybee Roads (chan.) F7
Tyger (riv.) D2
Waccamaw (riv.) J5
Wadmalaw (isl.) G6
Wando (riv.) H6
Wateree (lake) F3
Winyah (bay) J5
Wylie (lake) E1

▲County seat

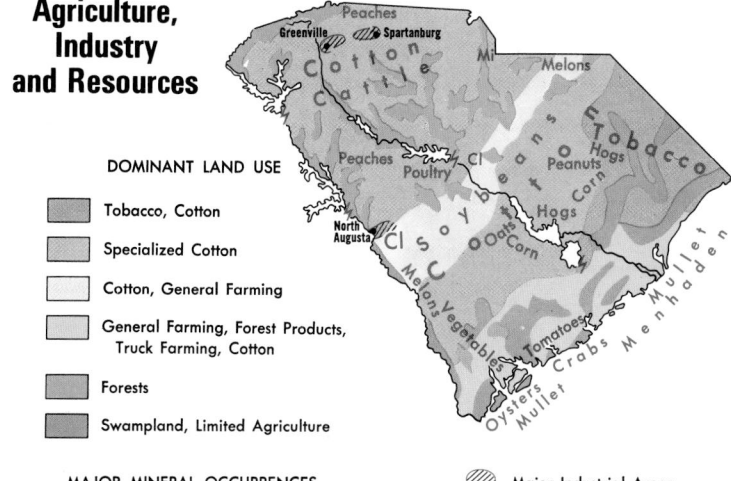

Agriculture, Industry and Resources

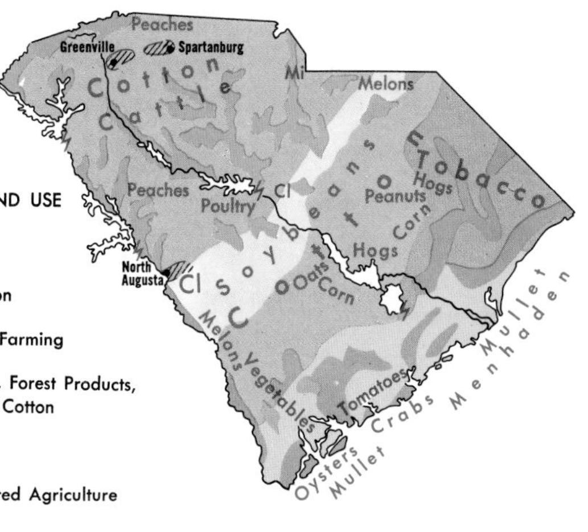

Peaches
Greenville
Spartanburg
Cotton
Cattle
Mi
Melons
Tobacco
Hogs
Peanuts
Corn
Peaches
Poultry
Cl
Soybeans
Hogs
North Augusta
Cl
Oats
Corn
Melons
Vegetables
Tomatoes
Crabs
Menhaden
Mullet
Oysters
Mullet

DOMINANT LAND USE

- Tobacco, Cotton
- Specialized Cotton
- Cotton, General Farming
- General Farming, Forest Products, Truck Farming, Cotton
- Forests
- Swampland, Limited Agriculture

MAJOR MINERAL OCCURRENCES

Cl Clay
Mi Mica

Major Industrial Areas
Water Power

COUNTIES

Aurora 3,135 .... M6
Beadle 18,253 .... N5
Bennett 3,206 .... F7
Bon Homme 7,089 .... O7
Brookings 25,207 .... R5
Brown 35,580 .... N2
Brule 5,485 .... L6
Buffalo 1,759 .... L5
Butte 7,914 .... B4
Campbell 1,965 .... J2
Charles Mix 9,131 .... M7
Clark 4,403 .... O4
Clay 13,186 .... P8
Codington 22,698 .... P4
Corson 4,195 .... G2
Custer 6,179 .... B6
Davison 17,503 .... N6
Day 6,978 .... O3
Deuel 4,522 .... R4
Dewey 5,523 .... G3
Douglas 3,746 .... N7
Edmunds 4,356 .... L3
Fall River 7,353 .... B7
Faulk 2,744 .... L3
Grant 8,372 .... R3
Gregory 5,359 .... L7
Haakon 2,624 .... F5
Hamlin 4,974 .... P4
Hand 4,272 .... L4
Hanson 2,994 .... O6
Harding 1,669 .... B2
Hughes 14,817 .... J5
Hutchinson 8,262 .... O7
Hyde 1,696 .... K4
Jackson 2,811 .... F6
Jerauld 2,425 .... M5
Jones 1,324 .... H6
Kingsbury 5,925 .... O5
Lake 10,550 .... P5
Lawrence 20,655 .... B5
Lincoln 15,427 .... R7
Lyman 3,638 .... J6
Marshall 4,844 .... O2
McCook 5,688 .... P6
McPherson 3,228 .... L2
Mellette 2,137 .... H6
Meade 21,878 .... D5
Miner 3,272 .... O5
Minnehaha 123,809 .... R6
Moody 6,507 .... R5
Pennington 81,343 .... C6
Perkins 3,932 .... D3
Potter 3,190 .... J3
Roberts 9,914 .... P2
Sanborn 2,833 .... N5
Shannon 9,902 .... D7
Spink 7,981 .... N4
Stanley 2,453 .... H5
Sully 1,589 .... J4
Todd 8,352 .... H7
Tripp 6,924 .... K7
Turner 8,576 .... P7
Union 10,189 .... R8
Walworth 6,087 .... J3
Yankton 19,252 .... P7
Ziebach 2,220 .... F4

CITIES and TOWNS

Aberdeen▲ 24,927 .... M3
Agar 82 .... J4
Akaska 52 .... J3
Albee 15 .... S3
Alcester 843 .... R7
Alexandria▲ 518 .... O6
Allen 300 .... F7
Alpena 251 .... N5
Altamont 48 .... R4
Amherst 75 .... O2
Andover 106 .... O3
Ardmore 16 .... B7
Arlington 908 .... P5
Armour▲ 854 .... N7
Artas 28 .... K2
Artesian 217 .... O6
Ashton 148 .... N3
Astoria 155 .... S4
Aurora 619 .... R5
Avon 576 .... N8
Badger 114 .... P5
Baltic 666 .... R6
Bancroft 30 .... O4
Barnard 65 .... N2
Batesland 124 .... E7
Bath 175 .... N3
Belle Fourche▲ 4,335 .... B4
Belvidere 63 .... G6
Beresford 1,849 .... R7
Big Stone City 669 .... S3
Bison▲ 451 .... E2
Black Hawk 1,995 .... C5
Blunt 342 .... J4
Bonesteel 297 .... M7
Bowdle 589 .... K3
Box Elder 2,680 .... D5
Bradley 117 .... O3
Brandon 3,543 .... R6
Brandt 123 .... R4
Brentford 69 .... N3
Bridgewater 533 .... P6
Bristol 419 .... O3
Britton▲ 1,394 .... O2
Broadland 40 .... N4
Brookings▲ 16,270 .... R5
Bruce 235 .... R5
Bryant 374 .... P4
Buffalo Gap 173 .... C6
Buffalo▲ 488 .... B2
Bullhead 179 .... G2
Burbank 90 .... R8
Burke▲ 756 .... L7
Bushnell 81 .... R5
Butler 17 .... O3
Camp Crook 146 .... B2
Canistota 608 .... P6
Canning 40 .... L5
Canova 172 .... O6
Canton▲ 2,787 .... R7
Caputa 50 .... D5
Carter 7 .... J7
Carthage 221 .... O5
Castlewood 549 .... R4
Cavour 166 .... N5
Center 887 .... P6
Centerville 892 .... R7
Central City 185 .... B5
Chamberlain▲ 2,347 .... L6
Chancellor 276 .... R7
Chelsea 33 .... M3
Cherry Creek 500 .... F4
Chester 375 .... R6
Claire City 85 .... P2
Claremont 135 .... N2
Clark▲ 1,292 .... O4
Clear Lake▲ 1,247 .... R4
Colman 482 .... R6
Colome 309 .... K7
Colton 657 .... P6
Columbia 133 .... N2
Conde 203 .... N3
Corona 118 .... R3
Corsica 619 .... N7

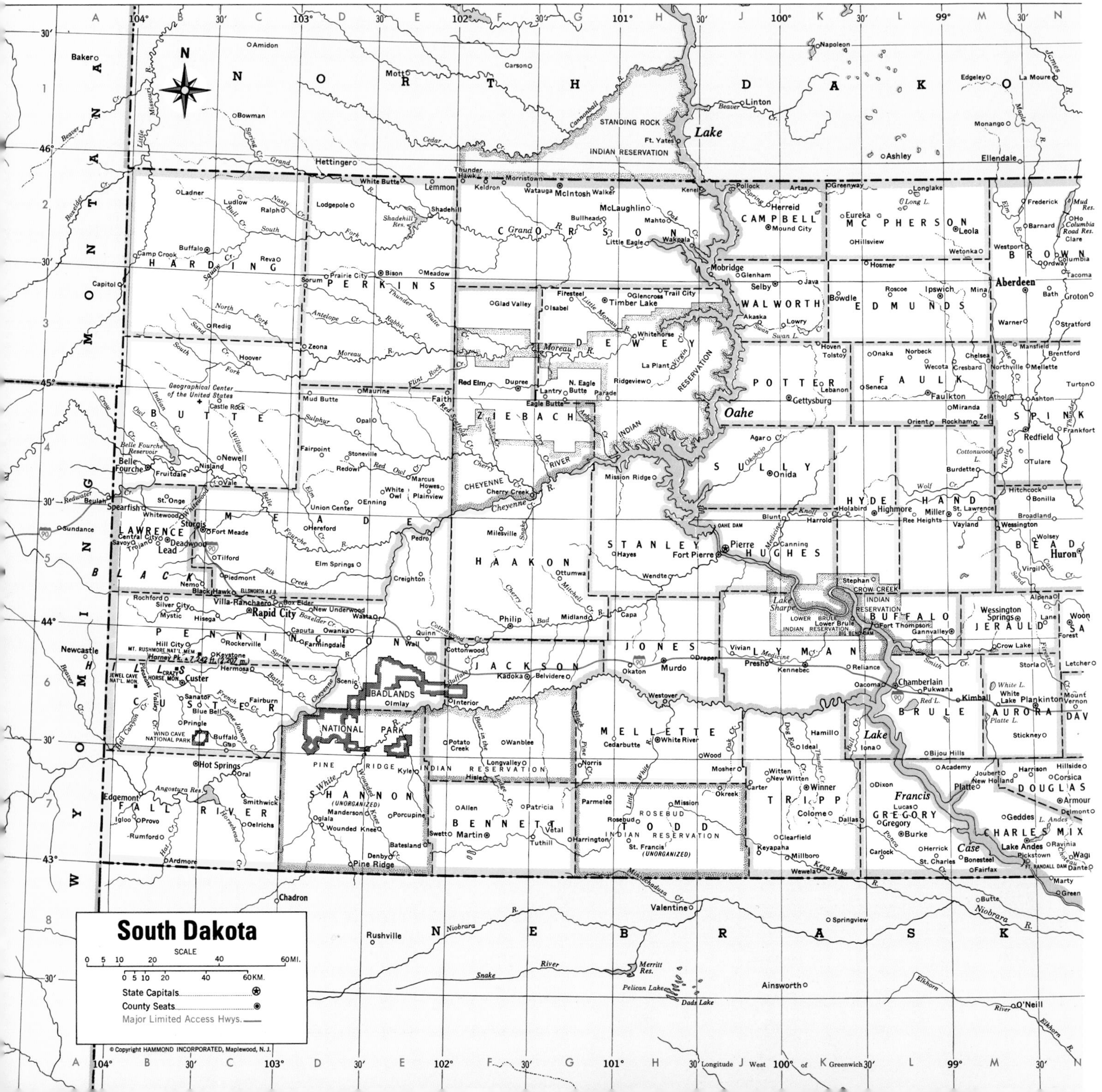

South Dakota
SCALE
0 5 10 20 40 60 MI.
0 5 10 20 40 60 KM.
State Capitals
County Seats
Major Limited Access Hwys.
© Copyright HAMMOND INCORPORATED, Maplewood, N. J.
NORTH DAKOTA
NEBRASKA
MONTANA
WYOMING
Longitude West of Greenwich

(continued on following page)

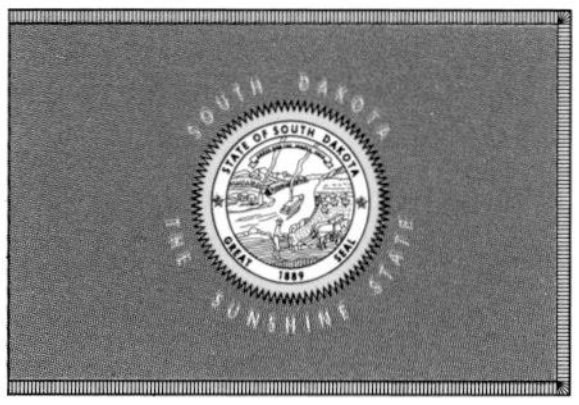

SOUTH DAKOTA
THE SUNSHINE STATE

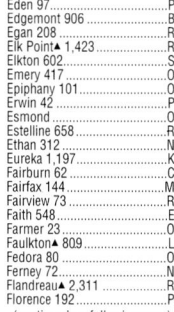

AREA 77,116 sq. mi. (199,730 sq. km.)
POPULATION 699,999
CAPITAL Pierre
LARGEST CITY Sioux Falls
HIGHEST POINT Harney Pk. 7,242 ft. (2207 m.)
SETTLED IN 1856
ADMITTED TO UNION November 2, 1889
POPULAR NAME Coyote State; Sunshine State
STATE FLOWER Pasqueflower
STATE BIRD Ring-necked Pheasant

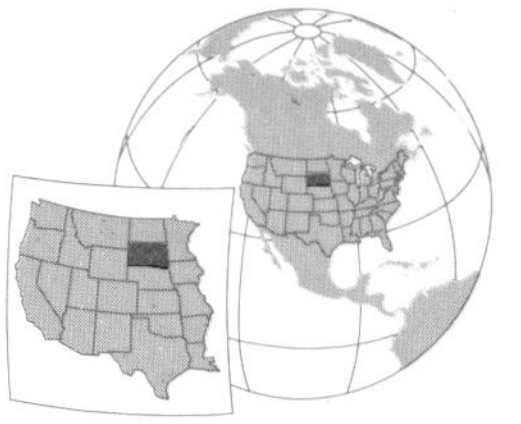

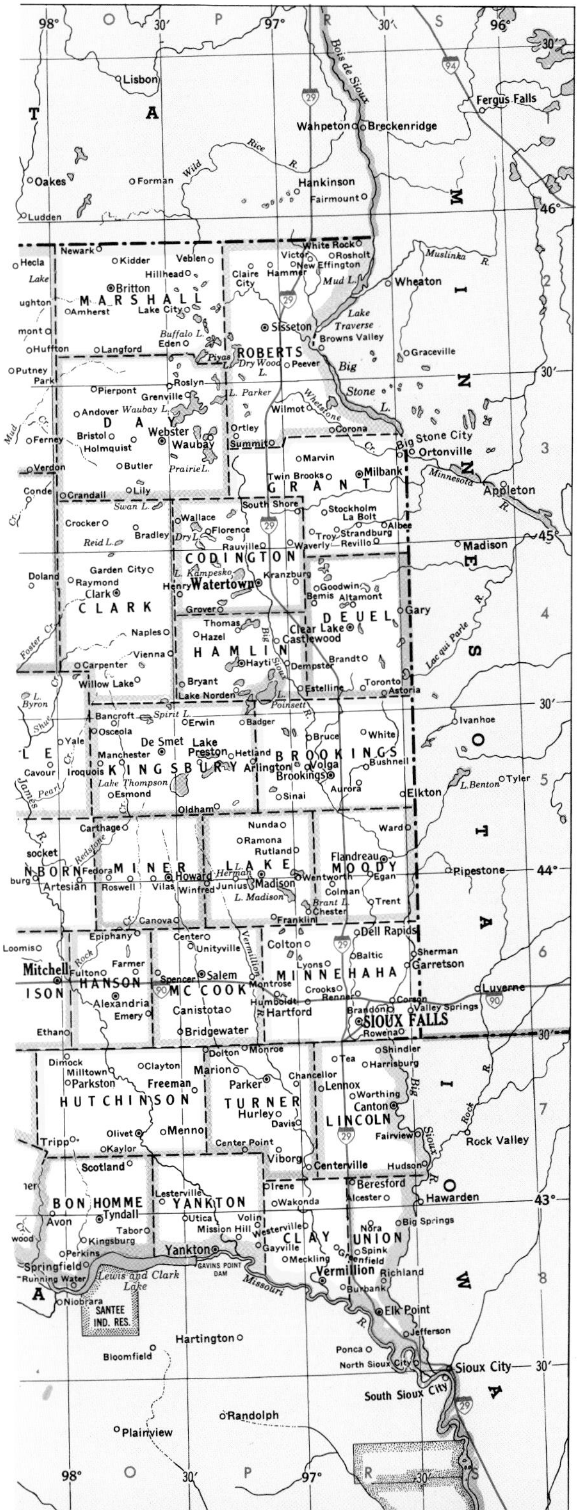

MARSHALL
ROBERTS
DAY
GRANT
CODINGTON
CLARK
DEUEL
HAMLIN
KINGSBURY
BROOKINGS
MINER
LAKE
MOODY
HANSON
MC COOK
MINNEHAHA
HUTCHINSON
TURNER
LINCOLN
BON HOMME
YANKTON
CLAY
UNION
Sioux Falls
Watertown
Brookings
Mitchell
Yankton
Vermillion
Sioux City
MINNESOTA
IOWA
Lewis and Clark Lake
Big Stone L.
Lake Traverse
SANTEE IND. RES.
GAVINS POINT DAM

Topography

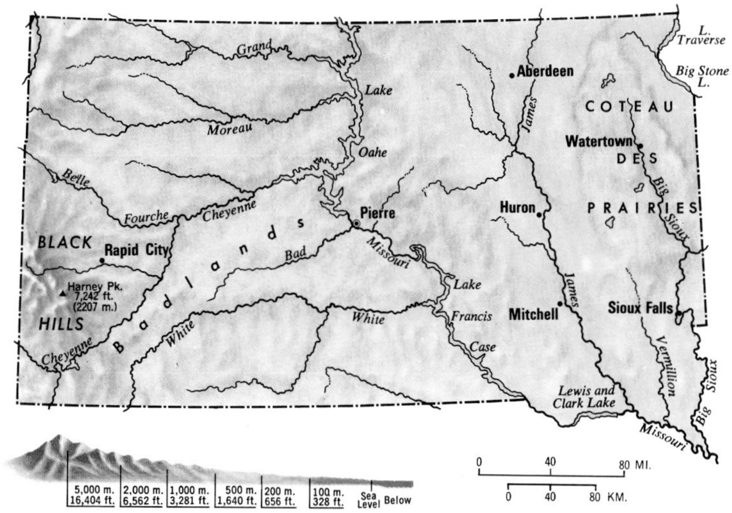

L. Traverse
Big Stone L.
Grand
Lake
Aberdeen
Moreau
Oahe
COTEAU
Watertown
DES
PRAIRIES
Belle
Fourche
Cheyenne
Pierre
Huron
BLACK
Rapid City
Badlands
Bad
Missouri
Lake
Francis
Case
Harney Pk. 7,242 ft. (2207 m.)
HILLS
White
Mitchell
Sioux Falls
James
Big Sioux
Vermillion
Lewis and Clark Lake
0 40 80 MI.
0 40 80 KM.
5,000 m. 16,404 ft.
2,000 m. 6,562 ft.
1,000 m. 3,281 ft.
500 m. 1,640 ft.
200 m. 656 ft.
100 m. 328 ft.
Sea Level
Below

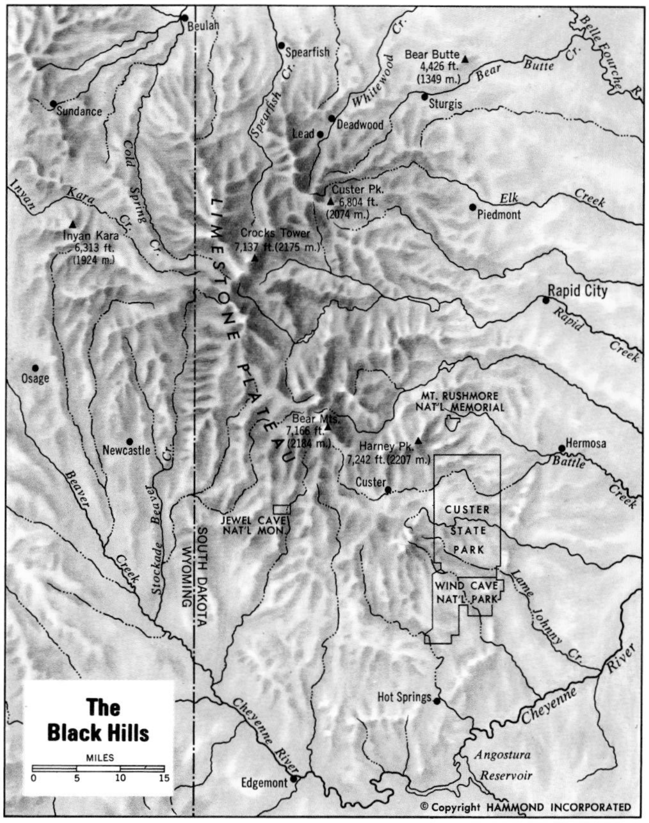

Beulah
Spearfish
Bear Butte 4,426 ft. (1349 m.)
Belle Fourche R.
Sundance
Lead
Deadwood
Sturgis
Custer Pk. 6,804 ft. (2074 m.)
Inyan Kara 6,313 ft. (1924 m.)
Crocks Tower 7,137 ft. (2175 m.)
LIMESTONE PLATEAU
Piedmont
Elk Creek
Rapid City
Rapid Creek
Osage
MT. RUSHMORE NAT'L MEMORIAL
Bear Mtn. 7,166 ft. (2184 m.)
Harney Pk. 7,242 ft. (2207 m.)
Newcastle
Hermosa
Battle Creek
Custer
JEWEL CAVE NAT'L MON.
CUSTER STATE PARK
WIND CAVE NAT'L PARK
SOUTH DAKOTA
WYOMING
Beaver Creek
Stockade Beaver Cr.
Lame Johnny Cr.
Hot Springs
Cheyenne River
Angostura Reservoir
Edgemont
The Black Hills
MILES
0 5 10 15

Agriculture, Industry and Resources

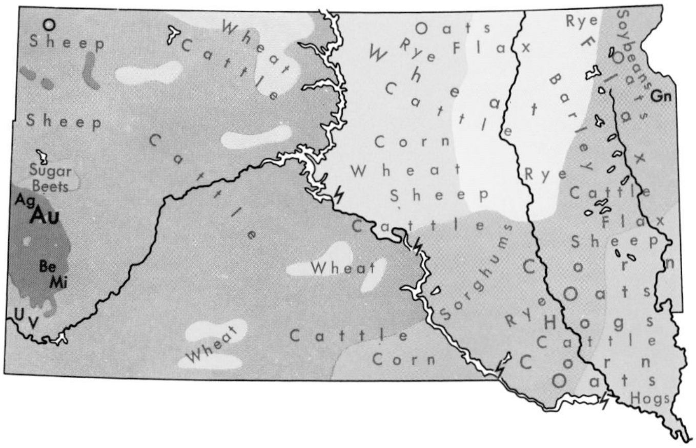
Sheep
Sheep
Wheat
Cattle
Cattle
Sugar Beets
Ag
Au
Be
Mi
U
V
O
Oats
Rye
Flax
Wheat
Cattle
Corn
Wheat
Sheep
Cattle
Wheat
Wheat
Cattle
Corn
Sorghums
Rye
Barley
Soybeans
Oats
Flax
Gn
Rye
Cattle
Flax
Sheep
Corn
Oats
Hogs
Cattle
Corn
Oats
Hogs

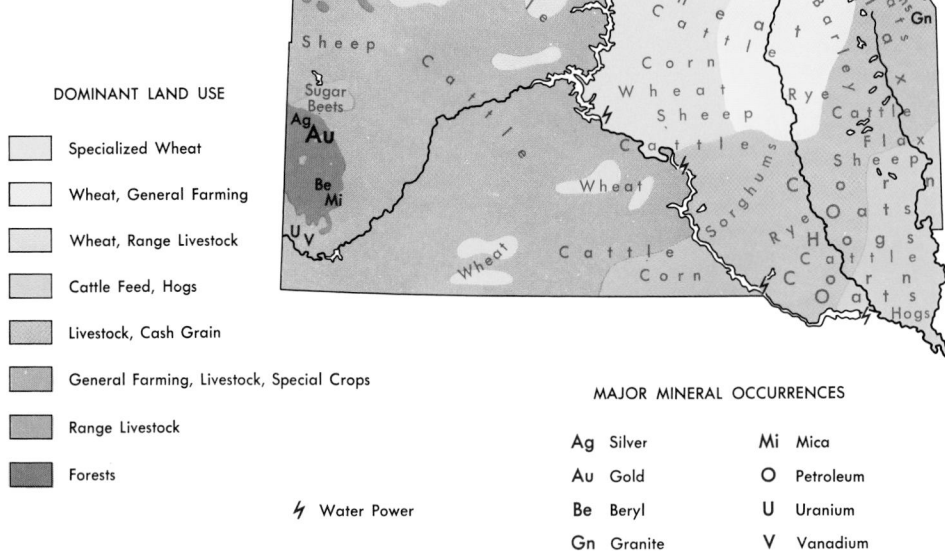

DOMINANT LAND USE

- Specialized Wheat
- Wheat, General Farming
- Wheat, Range Livestock
- Cattle Feed, Hogs
- Livestock, Cash Grain
- General Farming, Livestock, Special Crops
- Range Livestock
- Forests

ϟ Water Power

MAJOR MINERAL OCCURRENCES

Ag	Silver	Mi	Mica
Au	Gold	O	Petroleum
Be	Beryl	U	Uranium
Gn	Granite	V	Vanadium

OTHER FEATURES

▲County seat

COUNTIES

- Anderson 48,024 J6
- Andrews 14,338 B5
- Angelina 69,884 K6
- Aransas 17,892 H10
- Archer 7,973 F4
- Armstrong 2,021 C3
- Atascosa 30,533 F9
- Austin 19,832 H8
- Bailey 7,064 B3
- Bandera 10,562 E8
- Bastrop 38,263 G7
- Baylor 4,385 E4
- Bee 25,135 G9
- Bell 191,088 G6
- Bexar 1,185,394 F8
- Blanco 5,972 F8
- Borden 799 C5
- Bosque 15,125 G6
- Bowie 81,665 K4
- Brazoria 191,707 J8
- Brazos 121,862 H7
- Brewster 8,681 A8
- Briscoe 1,971 C3
- Brooks 8,204 F11
- Brown 34,371 F6
- Burleson 13,625 H7
- Burnet 22,677 F7
- Caldwell 26,392 G8
- Calhoun 19,053 H9
- Callahan 11,859 E5
- Cameron 260,120 G11
- Camp 9,904 K5
- Carson 6,576 C2
- Cass 29,982 K4
- Castro 9,070 B3
- Chambers 20,088 K8
- Cherokee 41,049 J6
- Childress 5,953 D3
- Clay 10,024 F4
- Cochran 4,377 B4
- Coke 3,424 D6
- Coleman 9,710 E6
- Collin 264,036 H4
- Collingsworth 3,573 D3
- Colorado 18,383 H8
- Comal 51,832 F8
- Comanche 13,381 F5
- Concho 3,044 E6
- Cooke 30,777 G4
- Coryell 64,213 G6
- Cottle 2,247 D3
- Crane 4,652 B6
- Crockett 4,078 C7
- Crosby 7,304 C4
- Culberson 3,407 C11
- Dallam 5,461 B1
- Dallas 1,852,810 H5
- Dawson 14,349 C5
- De Witt 18,903 G9
- Deaf Smith 19,153 B3
- Delta 4,857 J4
- Denton 273,525 G4
- Dickens 2,571 D4
- Dimmit 10,433 E9
- Donley 3,696 D2
- Duval 12,918 F10
- Eastland 18,488 F5
- Ector 118,934 B6
- Edwards 2,266 D7
- El Paso 591,610 A10
- Ellis 85,167 H5
- Erath 27,991 F5
- Falls 17,712 H6
- Fannin 24,804 H4
- Fayette 20,095 H8
- Fisher 4,842 D5
- Floyd 8,497 C3
- Foard 1,794 E3
- Fort Bend 225,421 J8
- Franklin 7,802 J4
- Freestone 15,818 H6
- Frio 13,472 E9
- Gaines 14,123 B5
- Galveston 217,399 K8
- Garza 5,143 C4
- Gillespie 17,204 F7
- Glasscock 1,447 C6
- Goliad 5,980 G9
- Gonzales 17,205 G8
- Gray 23,967 D2
- Grayson 95,021 H4
- Gregg 104,948 K5
- Grimes 18,828 J7
- Guadalupe 64,873 G8
- Hale 34,671 C3
- Hall 3,905 D3
- Hamilton 7,733 F6
- Hansford 5,848 C1
- Hardeman 5,283 E3
- Hardin 41,320 K7
- Harris 2,818,199 J8
- Harrison 57,483 K5
- Hartley 3,634 B2
- Haskell 6,820 E4
- Hays 65,614 F7
- Hemphill 3,720 D2
- Henderson 58,543 J5
- Hidalgo 383,545 F11
- Hill 27,146 G5
- Hockley 24,199 B4
- Hood 28,981 G5
- Hopkins 28,833 J4
- Houston 21,375 J6
- Howard 32,343 C5
- Hudspeth 2,915 B10
- Hunt 64,343 H4
- Hutchinson 25,689 C2
- Irion 1,629 C6
- Jack 6,981 F4
- Jackson 13,039 H9
- Jasper 31,102 K7
- Jeff Davis 1,946 C11
- Jefferson 239,397 K8
- Jim Hogg 5,109 F11
- Jim Wells 37,679 F10
- Johnson 97,165 G5
- Jones 16,490 E5
- Karnes 12,455 G9
- Kaufman 52,220 H5
- Kendall 14,589 F8
- Kenedy 460 G11
- Kent 1,010 D4
- Kerr 36,304 E7
- Kimble 4,122 E7
- King 354 D4
- Kinney 3,119 D8
- Kleberg 30,274 G10
- Knox 4,837 E4
- La Salle 5,254 E9
- Lamar 43,949 J4
- Lamb 15,072 B3
- Lampasas 13,521 F6
- Lavaca 18,690 H8
- Lee 12,854 H7
- Leon 12,665 J6
- Liberty 52,726 K7
- Limestone 20,946 H6
- Lipscomb 3,143 D1
- Live Oak 9,556 F9
- Llano 11,631 F7
- Loving 107 A6
- Lubbock 222,636 C4
- Lynn 6,758 C4
- Madison 10,931 J6
- Marion 9,984 K5
- Martin 4,956 C5
- Mason 3,423 E7
- Matagorda 36,928 H9
- Maverick 36,378 D9
- McCulloch 8,778 E6
- McLennan 189,123 G6
- McMullen 817 F9
- Medina 27,312 E8
- Menard 2,252 E7
- Midland 106,611 B6
- Milam 22,946 H7
- Mills 4,531 F6
- Mitchell 8,016 D5
- Montague 17,274 G4
- Montgomery 182,201 J7
- Moore 17,865 C2
- Morris 13,200 K4
- Motley 1,532 D3
- Nacogdoches 54,753 K6
- Navarro 39,926 H5
- Newton 13,569 L7
- Nolan 16,594 D5
- Nueces 291,145 G10
- Ochiltree 9,128 D1
- Oldham 2,278 B2
- Orange 80,509 L7
- Palo Pinto 25,055 F5
- Panola 22,035 K5
- Parker 64,785 G5
- Parmer 9,863 B3
- Pecos 14,675 B7
- Polk 30,687 K7
- Potter 97,874 C2
- Presidio 6,637 C12
- Rains 6,715 J5
- Randall 89,673 C2
- Reagan 4,514 C6
- Real 2,412 E8
- Red River 14,317 J4
- Reeves 15,852 D11
- Refugio 7,976 G9
- Roberts 1,025 D2
- Robertson 15,511 H6
- Rockwall 25,604 H5
- Runnels 11,294 E6
- Rusk 43,735 K5
- Sabine 9,586 L6
- San Augustine 7,999 K6
- San Jacinto 16,372 J7
- San Patricio 58,749 G10
- San Saba 5,401 F6
- Schleicher 2,990 D7
- Scurry 18,634 D5
- Shackleford 3,915 E5
- Shelby 22,034 K6
- Sherman 2,858 C1
- Smith 151,309 J5
- Somervell 5,360 G5
- Starr 40,518 F11
- Stephens 9,010 F5
- Sterling 1,438 C6
- Stonewall 2,013 D4
- Sutton 4,135 D7
- Swisher 8,133 C3
- Tarrant 1,170,103 G5
- Taylor 119,655 E5
- Terrell 1,410 B7
- Terry 13,218 B4
- Throckmorton 1,880 E4
- Titus 24,009 K4
- Tom Green 98,458 D6
- Travis 576,407 G7
- Trinity 11,445 J6
- Tyler 16,646 K7
- Upshur 31,370 K5
- Upton 4,447 B6
- Uvalde 23,340 E8
- Val Verde 38,721 C8
- Van Zandt 37,944 J5
- Victoria 74,361 H9
- Walker 50,917 J7
- Waller 23,390 J8
- Ward 13,115 A6
- Washington 26,154 H7
- Webb 133,239 E10
- Wharton 39,955 H8
- Wheeler 5,879 D2
- Wichita 122,378 F3
- Wilbarger 15,121 E3
- Willacy 17,705 G11
- Williamson 139,551 G7
- Wilson 22,650 F8
- Winkler 8,626 A6
- Wise 34,679 G4
- Wood 29,380 J5
- Yoakum 8,786 B4
- Young 18,126 F4
- Zapata 9,279 E11
- Zavala 12,162 E9

AREA 266,807 sq. mi. (691,030 sq. km.)
POPULATION 17,059,805
CAPITAL Austin
LARGEST CITY Houston
HIGHEST POINT Guadalupe Pk. 8,749 ft. (2667 m.)
SETTLED IN 1686
ADMITTED TO UNION December 29, 1845
POPULAR NAME Lone Star State
STATE FLOWER Bluebonnet
STATE BIRD Mockingbird

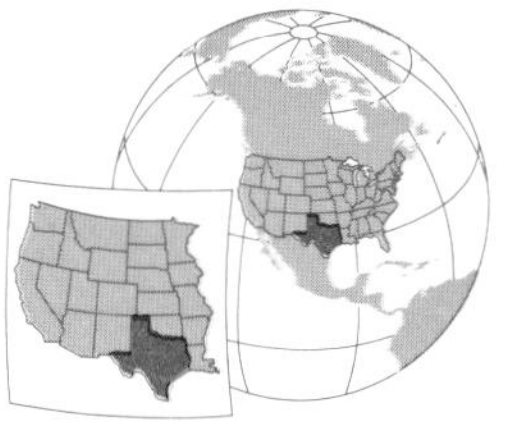

CITIES and TOWNS

- Abernathy 2,720 B4
- Abilene▲ 106,654 E5
- Addison 8,783 G2
- Alamo 8,210 F11
- Alamo Heights 6,502 K10
- Albany▲ 1,962 E5
- Alice▲ 19,788 F10
- Allen 18,309 H1
- Alpine▲ 5,637 D12
- Alvarado 2,918 G5
- Alvin 19,220 J3
- Amarillo▲ 157,615 C2
- Anahuac▲ 1,993 K8
- Anderson▲ 500 J7
- Andrews▲ 10,678 B5
- Angleton▲ 17,140 J8
- Anson▲ 2,644 E5
- Anthony 3,328 A10
- Aransas Pass 7,180 G10
- Archer City▲ 1,748 F4
- Arlington 261,721 F2
- Aspermont▲ 1,214 D4
- Athens▲ 10,967 J5
- Atlanta 6,118 K4
- Austin (cap.)▲ 465,622 G7
- Azle 8,868 E2
- Bacliff 5,549 K2
- Baird▲ 1,658 E5
- Balch Springs 17,406 H2
- Balcones Heights 3,022 J10
- Ballinger▲ 3,975 E6
- Bandera▲ 877 F8
- Barrett 3,052 K1
- Bastrop▲ 4,044 G7
- Bay City▲ 18,170 H9
- Baytown 63,850 L2
- Beaumont▲ 114,323 K7
- Bedford 43,762 F2
- Beeville▲ 13,547 G9
- Bellaire 13,842 J2
- Bellmead 8,336 H6
- Bellville▲ 3,378 H8
- Belton▲ 12,476 G7
- Benavides 1,788 F10
- Benbrook 19,564 E2
- Benjamin▲ 225 E4
- Big Lake▲ 3,672 C6
- Big Spring▲ 23,093 C5
- Bishop 3,337 G10
- Bloomington 1,888 H9
- Blue Mound 2,133 E2
- Boerne▲ 4,274 J10
- Bonham▲ 6,686 H4
- Borger 15,675 C2
- Boston▲ 400 K4
- Bowie 4,990 G4
- Brackettville▲ 1,740 D8
- Brady▲ 5,946 E6
- Brazoria 2,717 J9
- Breckinridge▲ 5,665 F5
- Brenham▲ 11,952 H7
- Briar 3,899 E1
- Bridge City 8,034 L7
- Bridgeport 3,581 G4
- Brookshire 2,922 J8
- Brownfield▲ 9,560 B4
- Brownsville▲ 98,962 G12
- Brownwood▲ 18,387 F6
- Bryan▲ 55,002 H7
- Buda 1,795 G7
- Buna 2,127 L7
- Bunker Hill Village 3,391 J1
- Burkburnett 10,145 F3
- Burleson 16,113 F3
- Burnet▲ 3,423 F7
- Caldwell▲ 3,181 H7
- Cameron▲ 5,580 H7
- Canadian▲ 2,417 D2
- Canton▲ 2,949 J5
- Canutillo 4,442 A10
- Canyon▲ 11,365 C3
- Carrizo Springs▲ 5,745 E9
- Carrollton 82,169 G2
- Carthage▲ 6,496 K5
- Castle Hills 4,198 J10
- Castroville 2,159 J11
- Cedar Hill 19,976 G3
- Cedar Park 5,161 G7
- Center▲ 4,950 K6
- Centerville▲ 812 H6
- Channelview 25,564 K1
- Channing▲ 277 B2
- Childress▲ 5,055 D3
- Cisco 3,813 E5
- Clarendon▲ 2,067 C3
- Clarksville▲ 4,311 K4
- Claude▲ 1,199 C2
- Clear Lake Shores 1,096 K2
- Cleburne▲ 22,205 G5
- Cleveland 7,124 K7
- Clifton 3,195 G6
- Clute 8,910 J9
- Clyde 3,002 E5
- Cockrell Hill 3,746 G2
- Coldspring▲ 538 J7
- Coleman▲ 5,410 E6
- College Station▲ 52,456 H7
- Colleyville 12,724 F2
- Colorado City▲ 4,749 C5
- Columbus▲ 3,367 H8
- Comanche▲ 4,087 F6
- Commerce 6,825 J4
- Conroe▲ 27,610 J7
- Converse 8,887 K11
- Cooper▲ 2,153 J4
- Coppell 16,881 G2
- Copperas Cove 24,079 G6
- Corpus Christi▲ 257,453 G10
- Corsicana▲ 22,911 H5
- Cotulla▲ 3,694 E9
- Crane▲ 3,533 B6
- Crockett▲ 7,024 J6
- Crosby 1,811 J8
- Crosbyton▲ 2,026 C4
- Crowell▲ 1,230 E4
- Crowley 6,974 E3
- Crystal City▲ 8,263 E9
- Cuero▲ 6,700 G8
- Daingerfield▲ 2,572 K4
- Dalhart▲ 6,246 B1
- Dallas▲ 1,006,877 G2
- Dalworthington Gardens 1,758 F2
- Dayton 5,151 J7
- De Kalb 1,976 K4
- De Leon 2,190 F5
- De Soto 30,544 G3
- Decatur▲ 4,252 G4
- Deer Park 27,652 K2
- Del Rio▲ 30,705 D8
- Denison 21,505 H4
- Denton▲ 66,270 G4
- Denver City 5,145 B4
- Devine 3,928 E8
- Diboll 4,341 K6
- Dickens▲ 322 D4
- Dickinson 9,497 K3
- Dilley 2,632 E9
- Dimmitt▲ 4,408 B3
- Donna 12,652 F11
- Double Oak 1,664 F1

(continued on following page)

Agriculture, Industry and Resources

DOMINANT LAND USE

- Wheat, Grain Sorghums, Range Livestock
- Cotton, Wheat
- Specialized Cotton
- Cotton, General Farming
- Cotton, Forest Products
- Cotton, Range Livestock
- Rice, General Farming
- Peanuts, General Farming
- General Farming, Livestock, Cash Grain
- General Farming, Forest Products, Truck Farming, Cotton
- Fruit, Truck and Mixed Farming
- Range Livestock
- Forests
- Swampland, Limited Agriculture
- Nonagricultural Land
- Urban Areas

MAJOR MINERAL OCCURRENCES

- At Asphalt
- Cl Clay
- Fe Iron Ore
- G Natural Gas
- Gn Granite
- Gp Gypsum
- Gr Graphite
- He Helium
- Ls Limestone
- Na Salt
- O Petroleum
- S Sulfur
- Tc Talc
- U Uranium

- Water Power
- Major Industrial Areas

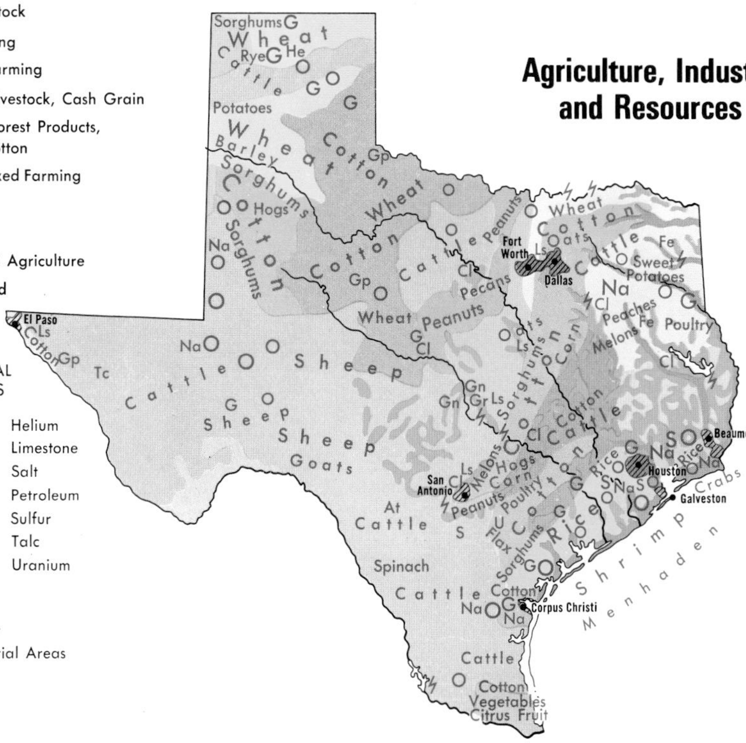

Sorghums
Wheat
Rye
Cattle
Potatoes
Barley
Cotton
Hogs
Sorghums
Peanuts
Fort Worth
Dallas
Pecans
Oats
Sweet Potatoes
Peaches
Poultry
Melons
Corn
El Paso
Sheep
Goats
San Antonio
Houston
Beaumont
Galveston
Rice
Flax
Crabs
Shrimp
Menhaden
Spinach
Corpus Christi
Vegetables
Citrus Fruit

Dublin 3,190 F5
Dumas▲ 12,871 C2
Duncanville 35,748 G3
Eagle Lake 3,551 H8
Eagle Pass▲ 20,651 D9
Eastland▲ 3,690 F5
Edcouch 2,878 G11
Edgecliff 2,715 E2
Edinburg▲ 29,885 F11
Edna▲ 5,343 H9
El Campo 10,511 H8
El Lago 3,269 K2
El Paso▲ 515,342 A10
Eldorado▲ 2,019 D7
Electra 3,113 F4
Elgin 4,846 G7
Elsa 5,242 G11
Emory▲ 963 J5
Ennis 13,883 H5
Euless 38,149 F2
Everman 5,672 F3
Fabens 5,599 B10
Fairfield▲ 3,234 H6
Falfurrias▲ 5,788 F10
Farmers Branch 24,250 G2
Farmersville 2,640 H4
Farwell▲ 1,373 A3
Ferris 2,212 H3
Floresville▲ 5,247 K11
Flower Mound 15,527 F1
Floydada▲ 3,896 C3
Forest Hill 11,482 F2
Forney 4,070 H5
Fort Davis▲ 900 D11
Fort Stockton▲ 8,524 A7
Fort Worth▲ 447,619 F2
Franklin▲ 1,336 H7
Fredericksburg▲ 6,934 E7
Fredonia 50 E7
Freeport 11,389 J9
Freer 3,271 F10
Fresno 3,182 J2
Friendswood 22,814 J2
Friona 3,688 B3
Frisco 6,141 H4
Fritch 2,335 C2
Gail▲ 171 C5
Gainesville▲ 14,256 G4
Galena Park 10,033 J1
Galveston▲ 59,070 L3
Ganado 1,701 H8
Garden City▲ 350 C6
Garland 180,650 H2
Gatesville▲ 11,492 G6
George West▲ 2,586 F9
Georgetown▲ 14,842 G7
Giddings▲ 4,093 H7
Gilmer▲ 4,822 J5
Gladewater 6,027 K5
Glen Rose▲ 1,949 G5
Glenn Heights 4,564 G2
Goldthwaite▲ 1,658 F6
Goliad▲ 1,946 G9
Gonzales▲ 6,527 G8
Graham▲ 8,986 F4
Granbury▲ 4,045 G5
Grand Prairie 99,616 G2
Grand Saline 2,630 J5
Grapevine 29,202 F2
Greenville▲ 23,071 H4
Groesbeck▲ 3,185 H6
Groves 16,513 L8
Groveton▲ 1,071 J7
Guthrie▲ 170 D4
Hale Center 2,067 C3
Hallettsville▲ 2,718 G8
Hallsville 2,288 K5
Haltom City 32,856 F2
Hamilton▲ 2,937 G6
Hamlin 2,791 E5
Harlingen 48,735 G11
Haskell▲ 3,362 E4
Hearne 5,132 H7
Hebbronville▲ 4,465 F10
Hedwig Village 2,616 H1
Hemphill▲ 1,182 L6
Hempstead▲ 3,551 J7
Henderson▲ 11,139 K5
Henrietta▲ 2,896 F4
Hereford▲ 14,745 B3
Hickory Creek 1,893 F1
Hidalgo 3,292 F11
Highland Park 8,739 G2
Highland Village 7,027 F1
Highlands 6,632 K1
Hillsboro▲ 7,072 G5
Hitchcock 5,868 K3
Hollywood 3,231 K10
Hondo▲ 6,018 E8
Honey Grove 1,681 J4
Hooks 2,684 K4
Houston▲ 1,630,553 J2
Howe 2,173 H4
Hughes Springs 1,938 K5
Humble 12,060 J7
Hunters Creek Village 3,954 J1
Huntington 1,794 K6
Huntsville▲ 27,925 J7
Hurst 33,574 F2
Hutchins 2,719 G3
Idalou 2,074 C4
Iowa Park 6,072 F4
Irving 155,037 G2
Italy 1,699 H5
Jacinto City 9,343 J1
Jacksboro▲ 3,350 F4
Jacksonville 12,765 J5
Jasper▲ 6,959 L7
Jayton▲ 608 D4
Jefferson▲ 2,199 K5
Jersey Village 4,826 J1
Johnson City▲ 932 F7
Jones Creek 2,160 J9
Jourdanton▲ 3,220 F9
Junction▲ 2,654 E7
Karnes City▲ 2,916 G9
Katy 8,005 J8
Kaufman▲ 5,238 H5
Keene 3,944 G5
Keller 13,683 F2
Kenedy 3,763 G9
Kennedale 4,096 F3
Kerens 1,702 H5
Kermit▲ 6,875 B6
Kerrville▲ 17,384 E7
Kilgore 11,066 K5
Killeen 63,535 G6
Kingsland 2,725 F7
Kingsville▲ 25,276 G10
Kirby 8,326 K11
Kirbyville 1,871 K7
Kountze▲ 2,056 K7
Kyle 2,225 G8
La Feria 3,495 G11
La Grange▲ 3,951 G8
La Joya 2,604 F11
La Marque 14,120 K3
La Porte 27,910 K2
Lake Dallas 3,656 G1
Lake Jackson 22,776 J8
Lake Worth 4,591 E2
Lamesa▲ 10,809 C5
Lampasas▲ 6,382 F6
Lancaster 22,117 G3
Laredo▲ 122,899 E10
League City 30,159 K2
Leakey▲ 399 E8
Leon Valley 9,581 J10
Leonard 1,744 H4
Levelland▲ 13,986 B4
Lewisville 46,521 G1
Liberty▲ 7,733 K7
Lindale 2,428 J5
Linden▲ 2,375 K4
Lipscomb▲ 52 D1
Littlefield▲ 6,489 B4
Live Oak 10,023 K10
Livingston▲ 5,019 K7
Llano▲ 2,962 F7
Lockhart▲ 9,205 G8
Lockney 2,207 C3
Lomax 2,991 K2
Longview▲ 70,311 K5
Los Fresnos 2,473 G11
Lubbock▲ 186,206 C4
Lucas 2,205 H1
Lufkin▲ 30,206 K6
Luling 4,661 G8
Lumberton 6,640 K7
Lyford 1,674 G11
Lytle 2,255 J11
Mabank 1,739 H5
Madisonville▲ 3,569 J7
Malakoff 2,038 H5
Mansfield 15,607 F3
Manvel 3,733 J3
Marble Falls 4,007 F7
Marfa▲ 2,424 C12
Marlin▲ 6,386 H6
Marshall▲ 23,682 K5
Mart 2,004 H6
Mason▲ 2,041 E7
Matador▲ 790 D3
Mathis 5,423 G9
McAllen 84,021 F11
McCamey 2,493 B6
McGregor 4,683 G6
McKinney▲ 21,283 H4
Memphis▲ 2,465 D3
Menard▲ 1,606 E7
Mentone▲ 50 D10
Mercedes 12,694 F12
Meridian▲ 1,390 G6
Merkel 2,469 E5
Mertzon▲ 778 C6
Mesquite 101,484 H2
Mexia 6,933 H6
Miami▲ 675 D2
Midland▲ 89,443 C6
Midlothian 5,141 G5
Mineola 4,321 J5
Mineral Wells 14,870 F5
Mission 28,653 F11
Missouri City 36,176 J2
Monahans▲ 8,101 B6
Montague▲ 1,253 G4
Morton▲ 2,597 B4
Mount Pleasant▲ 12,291 K4
Mount Vernon▲ 2,219 J4
Muleshoe▲ 4,571 B3
Nacogdoches▲ 30,872 J6
Nash 2,162 K4
Nassau Bay 4,320 K2
Navasota 6,296 J7
Nederland 16,192 K8
Needville 2,199 J8
New Boston 5,057 K4
New Braunfels▲ 27,334 K10
Newton▲ 1,885 L7
Nixon 1,995 G8
Nocona 2,870 G4
North Richland Hills 45,895 F2
Odessa▲ 89,699 B6
Olmos Park 2,161 K11
Olney 3,519 F4
Olton 2,116 B3
Orange▲ 19,381 L7
Overton 2,105 K5
Ovilla 2,027 G3
Ozona▲ 3,181 C7
Paducah▲ 1,788 D4
Paint Rock▲ 227 E6
Palacios 4,418 H9
Palestine▲ 18,042 J6
Palo Pinto▲ 350 F5
Pampa▲ 19,959 D2
Panhandle▲ 2,353 C2
Pantego 2,371 F2
Paris▲ 24,699 J4
Pasadena 119,363 J2
Pearland 18,697 J2
Pearsall▲ 6,924 E9
Pecos▲ 12,069 D10
Perryton▲ 7,607 D1

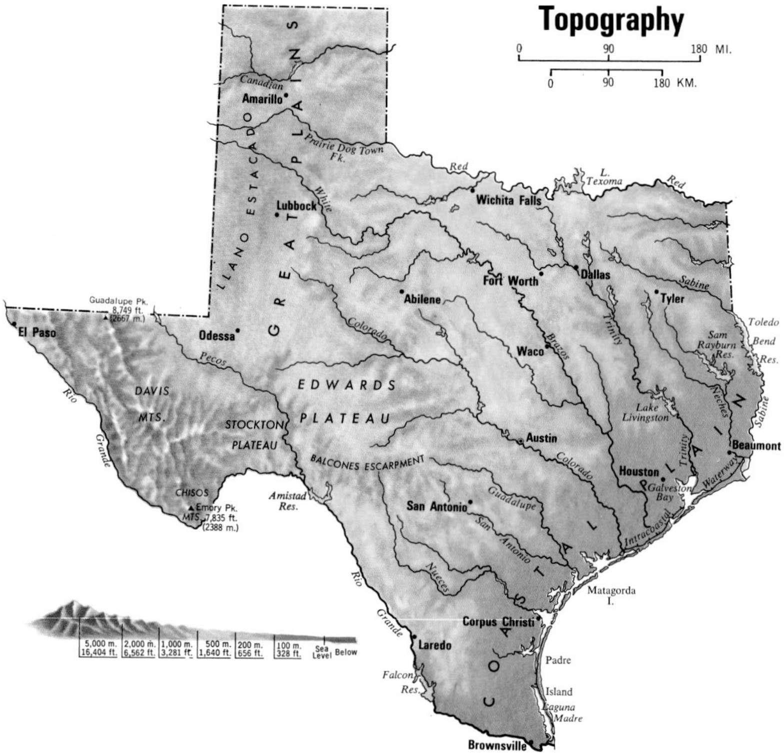
Topography
0 90 180 MI.
0 90 180 KM.
Amarillo
Lubbock
Wichita Falls
Fort Worth
Dallas
Tyler
Abilene
Waco
El Paso
Odessa
Austin
Houston
Beaumont
San Antonio
Corpus Christi
Laredo
Brownsville
Guadalupe Pk. 8,749 ft. (2667 m.)
Emory Pk. 7,835 ft. (2388 m.)
CHISOS MTS.
DAVIS MTS.
STOCKTON PLATEAU
EDWARDS PLATEAU
BALCONES ESCARPMENT
LLANO ESTACADO
GREAT PLAINS
COASTAL PLAIN
Canadian
Prairie Dog Town Fk.
Red
L. Texoma
White
Colorado
Brazos
Trinity
Sabine
Neches
Pecos
Rio Grande
Nueces
Guadalupe
San Antonio
Toledo Bend
Sam Rayburn Res.
Lake Livingston
Amistad Res.
Falcon Res.
Galveston Bay
Intracoastal Waterway
Matagorda I.
Padre Island
Laguna Madre
5,000 m. 16,404 ft.
2,000 m. 6,562 ft.
1,000 m. 3,281 ft.
500 m. 1,640 ft.
200 m. 656 ft.
100 m. 328 ft.
Sea Level
Below

Pflugerville 4,444 G7
Pharr 32,921 F11
Pickton 1,729 C2
Pilot Point 2,538 H4
Piney Point Village 3,197 J1
Pittsburg▲ 4,007 J4
Plains▲ 1,422 B4
Plainview▲ 21,700 C3
Plano 128,713 G1
Pleasanton 7,678 F9
Port Aransas 2,233 H10
Port Arthur 58,724 K8
Port Isabel 4,467 G11
Port Lavaca▲ 10,886 H9
Port Neches 12,974 K7
Portland 12,224 G10
Post▲ 3,768 C4
Poteet 3,206 F8
Prairie View 4,004 J7
Premont 2,914 F10
Presidio 3,072 C12
Quanah▲ 3,413 E3
Queen City 1,748 L4
Quitman▲ 1,684 J5
Ralls 2,172 C4
Ranger 2,803 F5
Rankin▲ 1,011 B6
Raymondville▲ 8,880 G11
Red Oak 3,124 H5
Refugio▲ 3,158 G9
Reno 1,784 E2
Richardson 74,840 G2
Richland Hills 7,978 F2
Richmond▲ 9,801 J8
Rio Grande City▲ 9,891 F11
Rio Hondo 1,793 G11
River Oaks 6,580 E2
Robert Lee▲ 1,276 D6
Robstown 12,849 G10
Roby▲ 616 D5
Rockdale 5,235 G7
Rockport▲ 4,753 H9
Rocksprings▲ 1,339 D8
Rockwall▲ 10,486 H5
Roma-Los Saenz 3,384 E11
Rosenberg 20,183 J8
Rotan 1,913 D5
Round Rock 30,923 G7
Rowlett 23,260 H2
Royse City 2,206 H4
Rusk▲ 4,366 J6
Sachse 5,346 H2
Saginaw 8,551 E2
San Angelo▲ 84,474 D6
San Antonio▲ 935,933 J11
San Augustine▲ 2,337 K6
San Benito 20,125 G12
San Diego▲ 4,983 F10
San Elizario 4,385 A10
San Juan 10,815 F11
San Leon 3,328 L2
San Marcos▲ 28,743 F8
San Saba▲ 2,626 F6
Sanderson▲ 1,128 B7
Sanger▲ 3,508 G4
Sansom Park Village 3,921 E2
Santa Fe 8,429 K3
Sarita▲ 200 G10
Schertz 10,555 K10
Schulenburg 2,455 H8
Seabrook 6,685 K2
Seagoville 8,969 H3
Seagraves 2,398 B5
Sealy 4,541 H8
Seguin▲ 18,853 G8
Seminole▲ 6,342 K10
Seymour▲ 3,185 E4
Shamrock 2,286 D2
Shepherd 1,812 K7
Sherman▲ 31,601 H4
Shiner 2,074 G8
Sierra Blanca▲ 800 B11
Silsbee 6,368 K7
Silverton▲ 779 C3
Sinton▲ 5,549 G9
Slaton 6,078 C4
Smithville 3,196 G7
Snyder▲ 12,195 D5
Sonora▲ 2,751 D7
South Houston 14,207 J2
South Padre Island 1,677 F11
Spearman▲ 3,197 C1
Spring 33,111 J7
Spring Valley 3,392 J1
Stafford 8,397 J2
Stamford 3,817 E5
Stanton▲ 2,576 C5
Stephenville▲ 13,502 F5
Sterling City▲ 1,096 D6
Stinnett▲ 2,166 C2
Stratford▲ 1,781 C1
Sugar Land 24,529 J8
Sulphur Springs▲ 14,062 J4
Sundown 1,759 B4
Sunnyvale 2,228 H2
Sweeny 3,297 J8
Sweetwater▲ 11,967 D5
Taft 3,222 G9
Tahoka▲ 2,868 C4
Taylor 11,472 G7
Taylor Lake Village 3,394 K2
Teague 3,268 H6
Temple 46,109 G6
Terlingua 100 D12
Terrell 12,490 H5
Terrell Hills 4,592 K11
Texarkana 31,656 L4
Texas City 40,822 K3
Texhoma 291 C1
The Colony 22,113 G1
Three Rivers 1,889 F9
Throckmorton▲ 1,036 F4
Tilden▲ 450 F9
Tomball 6,370 J7
Trinity 2,648 J7
Tulia▲ 4,699 C3
Tyler▲ 75,450 J5
Universal City 13,057 K10
University Park 22,259 F2
Uvalde▲ 14,729 E8
Van 1,854 J5
Van Alstyne 2,090 H4
Van Horn▲ 2,930 C11
Vega▲ 840 B2
Vernon▲ 12,001 E3
Victoria▲ 55,076 H9
Vidor 10,935 L7
Waco▲ 103,590 G6
Wake Village 4,757 K4
Waskom 1,812 L5
Watauga 20,009 F2
Waxahachie▲ 18,168 H5
Weatherford▲ 14,804 G5
Webster 4,678 K2
Weimar 2,052 H8
Wellington▲ 2,456 D3
Weslaco 21,877 F11
West 2,515 G6
West Columbia 4,372 J8
West Orange 4,187 L7
West University Place 12,920 J2
Westworth 2,350 E2
Wharton▲ 9,011 J8
Wheeler▲ 1,393 D2
White Oak 5,136 K5
White Settlement 15,472 E2
Whitesboro 3,209 H4
Whitewright 1,713 H4
Wichita Falls▲ 96,259 F4
Willis 2,764 J7
Wills Point 2,986 J5
Wilmer 2,479 H3
Windcrest 5,331 K11
Winnie 2,238 K8
Winnsboro 2,904 J5
Winters 2,905 E6
Wolfforth 1,941 C4
Woodsboro 1,731 G9
Woodville▲ 2,636 K7
Wylie 8,716 H1
Yoakum 5,611 G8
Yorktown 2,207 G9
Zapata▲ 7,119 E11

OTHER FEATURES

Alibates Flint Quarries Nat'l Mon. C2
Amistad (res.) C8
Amistad Nat'l Rec. Area D8
Angelina (riv.) K6
Apache (mts.) C11
Aransas (passage) H10
Arlington (lake) F2
Baffin (bay) G10
Balcones Escarpment (plat.) E8
Benbrook (lake) E3
Bergstrom A.F.B. G7
Big Bend Nat'l Park A8
Big Thicket Nat'l Preserve K7
Bolivar (pen.) K8
Brazos (riv.) H7
Brooks A.F.B. K11
Brownwood (lake) E6
Buchanan (lake) F7
Caddo (lake) L5
Calaveras (lake) K11
Canadian (riv.) D1
Carrizo (creek) A1
Carswell A.F.B. E2
Cathedral (mt.) D12
Cavallo (passage) H9
Cedar (lake) B5
Cerro Alto (mt.) B10
Chamizal Nat'l Mon. A10
Chinati (mts.) C12
Chinati (peak) C12
Chisos (mts.) A8
Cibolo (creek) K11
Clear Fork, Brazos (riv.) D5
Coldwater (creek) B1
Colorado (riv.) F7
Copano (bay) G9
Corpus Christi (lake) F9
Corpus Christi N.A.S. G10
Cottonwood Draw (dry riv.) C10
Davis (mts.) C11
Deep (creek) C5
Delaware (creek) C10
Delaware (mts.) C10
Denison (dam) H4
Devils (riv.) D7
Double Mountain Fork, Brazos (riv.) C4
Dyess A.F.B. D5
Eagle (peak) C11
Eagle Mountain (lake) E2
Edwards (plat.) C7
Elephant (mt.) D12
Elm Fork, Trinity (riv.) G2
Emory (peak) A8
Falcon (res.) E11
Finlay (mts.) B10
Fort Bliss 13,915 A10
Fort Davis Nat'l Hist. Site D11
Fort Hood 35,580 G6
Fort Sam Houston K11
Frio (riv.) E8
Galveston (bay) L2
Galveston (isl.) K8
Glass (mts.) A7
Goodfellow A.F.B. D6
Grapevine (lake) F2
Guadalupe (mts.) C10
Guadalupe (peak) B10
Guadalupe (riv.) G8
Guadalupe Mountains Nat'l Park C10
Houston (lake) J8
Houston Ship (chan.) K2
Howard (creek) C7
Hubbard Creek (lake) F5
Hueco (mts.) B10
Intracoastal Waterway J9
Johnson Draw (dry riv.) C7
Kelly A.F.B. J11
Kemp (lake) E4
Kingsville N.A.S. G10
Kiowa (creek) D1
Lackland A.F.B. 9,352 J11
Lake Meredith Nat'l Rec. Area C2
Lampasas (riv.) G6
Laughlin A.F.B. 2,556 D8
Lavon (lake) H1
Leon (riv.) F6
Livermore (mt.) C11
Livingston (lake) K7
Llano (riv.) D7
Llano Estacado (plain) B4
Locke (mt.) D11
Los Olmos (creek) F10
Los Olmos (creek) F11
Lyndon B. Johnson Nat'l Hist. Site F7
Lyndon B. Johnson Space Ctr. K2
Madre (lag.) G11
Maravillas (creek) A7
Matagorda (bay) H9
Matagorda (isl.) H9
Matagorda (pen.) J9
Medina (lake) E8
Medina (riv.) J11
Mexico (gulf) K9
Middle Concho (riv.) C6
Mountain Creek (lake) G2
Mustang (creek) A1
Mustang (isl.) G10
Mustang Draw (dry riv.) B5
Navasota (riv.) H7
Navidad (riv.) H8
Neches (riv.) K6
North Concho (riv.) C6
North Pease (riv.) D3
Nueces (riv.) F9
Padre (isl.) G10
Padre Island Nat'l Seashore G11
Palo Duro (creek) B2
Palo Duro (creek) C1
Pease (riv.) D3
Pecos (riv.) C7
Pedernales (riv.) F7
Possum Kingdom (lake) F5
Prairie Dog Town Fork, Red (riv.) C3
Quitman (mts.) B11
Randolph A.F.B. K10
Ray Hubbard (lake) H2
Red (riv.) F3
Red Bluff (lake) D10
Reese A.F.B. B4
Rio Grande (riv.) D9
Rita Blanca (creek) B2
Sabine (riv.) L7
Salt Fork, Red (riv.) D3
Sam Rayburn (res.) K6
San Antonio (bay) H9
San Antonio (mt.) B10
San Antonio Missions Nat'l Hist. Park J11
San Francisco (creek) B8
San Luis (passage) K8
San Martine Draw (dry riv.) C11
San Saba (riv.) D7
Santa Isabel (creek) E10
Santiago (mts.) A8
Santiago (peak) D12
Sheppard A.F.B. F3
Sierra Diablo (mts.) C10
Sierra Vieja (mts.) C11
Staked (Llano Estacado) (plain) B4
Stamford (lake) E4
Stockton (plat.) B7
Sulphur (riv.) J4
Sulphur Draw (dry riv.) B4
Sulphur Springs (creek) B4
Tenmile (creek) G3
Terlingua (creek) D12
Texoma (lake) H3
Thomas (lake) C5
Tierra Blanca (creek) B3
Toledo Bend (res.) L6
Toyah (creek) D11
Toyah (lake) A6
Travis (lake) G7
Trinity (bay) L2
Trinity (riv.) H5
Trinity, West Fork (riv.) G2
Trujillo (creek) A2
Washita (riv.) D2
West (bay) K3
White (riv.) C3
White River (lake) C4
White Rock (creek) G2
Wichita (riv.) F4
Wolf (creek) D1
Worth (lake) E2
Wright Patman (lake) K4

▲County seat

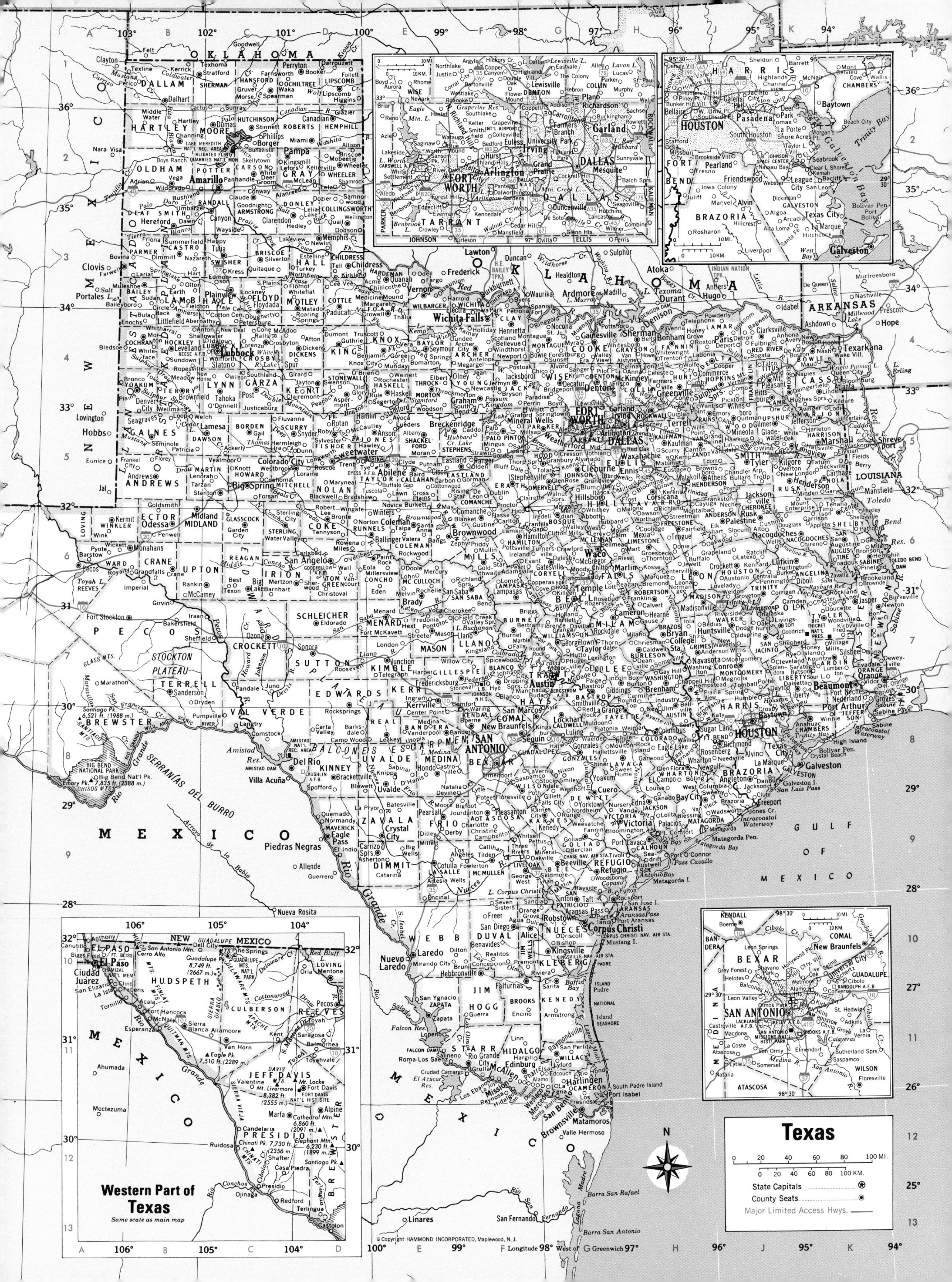
Texas
0 20 40 60 80 100 MI.
0 20 40 60 80 100 KM.
State Capitals
County Seats
Major Limited Access Hwys.
Western Part of Texas
Same scale as main map
OKLAHOMA
NEW MEXICO
ARKANSAS
LOUISIANA
MEXICO
GULF OF MEXICO
HOUSTON
DALLAS
FORT WORTH
SAN ANTONIO
Austin
El Paso
Amarillo
Lubbock
Corpus Christi
Galveston
Longitude 98° West of Greenwich 97°
© Copyright HAMMOND INCORPORATED, Maplewood, N. J.

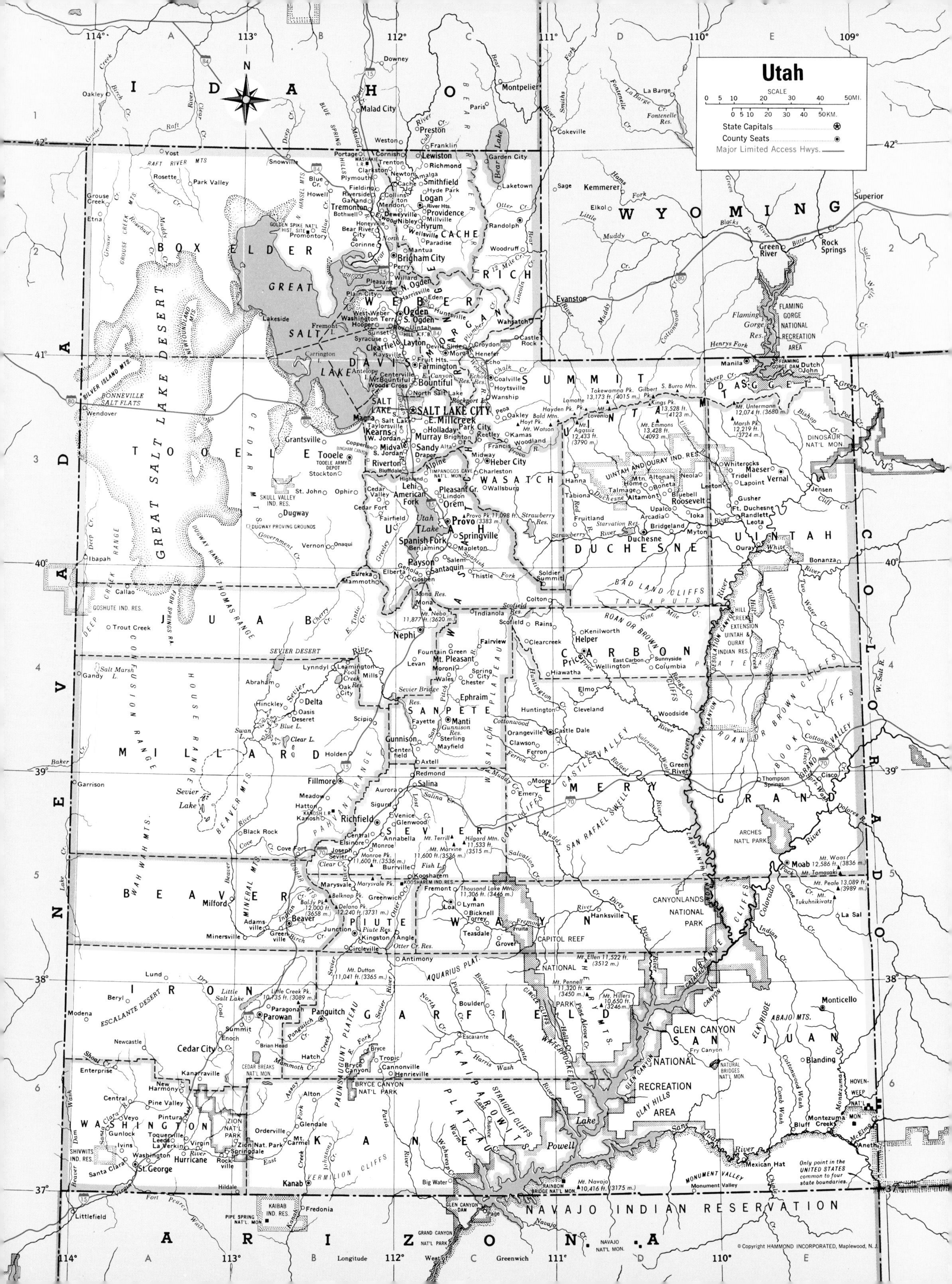

Utah
SCALE
0 5 10 20 30 40 50 MI.
0 5 10 20 30 40 50 KM.
State Capitals
County Seats
Major Limited Access Hwys.
IDAHO
WYOMING
NEVADA
COLORADO
ARIZONA
BOX ELDER
CACHE
RICH
WEBER
MORGAN
DAVIS
SUMMIT
DAGGETT
SALT LAKE
TOOELE
UTAH
WASATCH
DUCHESNE
UINTAH
JUAB
SANPETE
CARBON
MILLARD
SEVIER
EMERY
GRAND
BEAVER
PIUTE
WAYNE
IRON
GARFIELD
SAN JUAN
WASHINGTON
KANE
GREAT SALT LAKE
GREAT SALT LAKE DESERT
BONNEVILLE SALT FLATS
SEVIER DESERT
ESCALANTE DESERT
Utah Lake
Sevier Lake
Bear Lake
Lake Powell
Flaming Gorge Res.
FLAMING GORGE NATIONAL RECREATION AREA
GLEN CANYON NATIONAL RECREATION AREA
CANYONLANDS NATIONAL PARK
CAPITOL REEF NATIONAL PARK
ARCHES NAT'L PARK
ZION NAT'L PARK
BRYCE CANYON NAT'L PARK
CEDAR BREAKS NAT'L MON.
NATURAL BRIDGES NAT'L MON.
DINOSAUR NAT'L MON.
TIMPANOGOS CAVE NAT'L MON.
GOLDEN SPIKE NAT'L HIST. SITE
HOVENWEEP NAT'L MON.
RAINBOW BRIDGE NAT'L MON.
PIPE SPRING NAT'L MON.
NAVAJO NAT'L MON.
GRAND CANYON NAT'L PARK
NAVAJO INDIAN RESERVATION
UINTAH AND OURAY IND. RES.
SKULL VALLEY IND. RES.
GOSHUTE IND. RES.
SHIVWITS IND. RES.
KAIBAB IND. RES.
KOOSHAREM IND. RES.
KANOSH I.R.
DUGWAY PROVING GROUNDS
TOOELE ARMY DEPOT
HILL A.F.B.
GLEN CANYON DAM
FLAMING GORGE DAM
SALT LAKE CITY
Ogden
Provo
Logan
Brigham City
Orem
Bountiful
Layton
Murray
Sandy
Tooele
Heber City
Coalville
Morgan
Farmington
Nephi
Manti
Price
Castle Dale
Fillmore
Richfield
Junction
Loa
Beaver
Parowan
Cedar City
St. George
Kanab
Panguitch
Duchesne
Vernal
Manila
Randolph
Moab
Monticello
Green River
Wendover
Delta
Mt. Pleasant
Spanish Fork
Springville
Payson
American Fork
Lehi
Helper
Blanding
Bluff
Mexican Hat
Hurricane
Tremonton
Kemmerer
Evanston
Rock Springs
Malad City
Preston
Montpelier
Uinta Mountains
Kings Pk. 13,528 ft. (4123 m.)
Mt. Peale 13,089 ft. (3989 m.)
Mt. Nebo 11,877 ft. (3620 m.)
Delano Pk. 12,240 ft. (3731 m.)
Mt. Ellen 11,522 ft. (3512 m.)
Navajo Mtn. 10,416 ft. (3175 m.)
Only point in the UNITED STATES common to four state boundaries.
Longitude West of Greenwich
© Copyright HAMMOND INCORPORATED, Maplewood, N.J.

AREA 84,899 sq. mi. (219,888 sq. km.)
POPULATION 1,727,784
CAPITAL Salt Lake City
LARGEST CITY Salt Lake City
HIGHEST POINT Kings Pk. 13,528 ft. (4123 m.)
SETTLED IN 1847
ADMITTED TO UNION January 4, 1896
POPULAR NAME Beehive State
STATE FLOWER Sego Lily
STATE BIRD Sea Gull

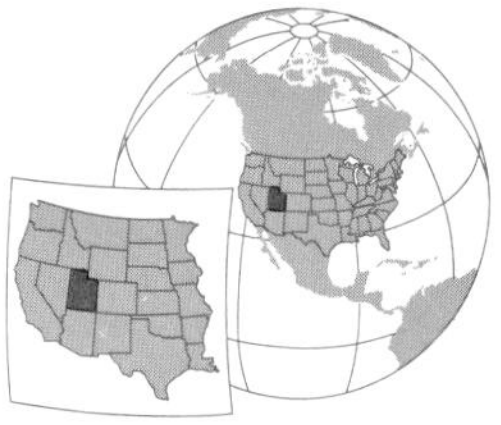

COUNTIES

Beaver 4,765 A5
Box Elder 36,485 A2
Cache 70,183 C2
Carbon 20,228 D4
Daggett 690 E3
Davis 187,941 B3
Duchesne 12,645 D3
Emery 10,332 D4
Garfield 3,980 C6
Grand 6,620 E5
Iron 20,789 A6
Juab 5,817 A4
Kane 5,169 B6
Millard 11,333 A4
Morgan 5,528 C2
Piute 1,277 B5
Rich 1,725 C2
Salt Lake 725,956 B3
San Juan 12,621 E6
Sanpete 16,259 C4
Sevier 15,431 C5
Summit 15,518 C5
Tooele 26,601 A3
Uintah 22,211 E3
Utah 263,590 C3
Wasatch 10,089 C3
Washington 48,560 A6
Wayne 2,177 C5
Weber 158,330 B2

CITIES and TOWNS

Alpine 3,492 C3
Alta 397 C3
Amalga 366 C2
American Fork 15,696 C3
Annabella 487 B5
Aurora 911 B5
Bear River City 700 B2
Beaver▲ 1,998 B5
Bicknell 327 C5
Big Water 326 C6
Blanding 3,162 E6
Bluffdale 2,152 B3
Bountiful 36,659 C3
Brigham City▲ 15,644 C2
Brighton 150 C3
Castle Dale▲ 1,704 D4
Castle Rock C2
Cedar City 13,443 A6
Cedar Fort 284 B3
Centerfield 766 C4
Centerville 11,500 C3
Charleston 336 C3
Circleville 417 B5
Clarkston 645 B2
Clearfield 21,435 B2
Cleveland 522 D4
Coalville▲ 1,065 C3
Corinne 639 B2
Delta 2,998 B4
Deweyville 318 B2
Draper 7,257 C3
Duchesne▲ 1,308 D3
Dugway 1,761 B3
East Carbon 1,270 D4
East Millcreek 21,184 C3
Elmo 267 D4
Elsinore 608 B5
Elwood 575 B2
Emery 300 C5
Enoch 1,947 A6
Enterprise 936 A6
Ephraim 3,363 C4
Escalante 818 C6
Eureka 562 B4
Fairview 960 C4
Farmington▲ 9,028 C4
Ferron 1,606 C4
Fielding 422 B2
Fillmore▲ 1,956 B5
Fort Duchesne 655 E3
Fountain Green 578 C4
Francis 381 C3
Fruit Heights 3,900 C2
Garden City 193 C2
Garland 1,637 B2
Genola 803 C4
Glendale 282 B6
Glenwood 437 C5
Goshen 578 C4
Grantsville 4,500 B3
Green River 866 D4
Gunnison 1,298 C4
Harrisville 3,004 C2
Heber City▲ 4,782 C3
Helper 2,148 D4
Henefer 554 C2
Highland 5,002 C3
Hildale 1,325 A6
Hinckley 658 B4
Holden 402 B4
Holladay 22,189 C3
Honeyville 1,112 B2
Hooper 3,468 B2
Howell 237 B2
Huntington 1,875 C4
Huntsville 561 C2
Hurricane 3,915 A6
Hyde Park 2,190 C2
Hyrum 4,829 C2
Ivins 1,630 A6
Joseph 198 B5
Junction▲ 132 B5
Kamas 1,061 C3
Kanab▲ 3,289 B6
Kanarraville 228 A6
Kanosh 386 B5
Kaysville 13,961 B2
Kearns 28,374 B3
Koosharem 266 C5
La Verkin 1,771 A6
Laketown 261 C2
Layton 41,784 C2
Leamington 253 B4
Leeds 254 A6
Lehi 8,475 C3
Levan 416 C4
Lewiston 1,532 C2
Lindon 3,818 C3
Loa▲ 444 C5
Logan▲ 32,762 C2
Lyman 198 C5
Maeser 2,598 E3
Magna 17,829 B3
Manila▲ 207 E3
Manti▲ 2,268 C4
Mantua 665 C2
Mapleton 3,572 C3
Marysvale 364 B5
Mayfield 438 C4
Meadow 250 B5
Mendon 684 B2
Mexican Hat 259 E6
Midvale 11,886 B3
Midway 1,554 A5
Milford 1,107 A5
Millville 1,202 C2
Minersville 608 A5
Moab▲ 3,971 E5
Mona 584 C4
Monroe 1,472 B5
Montezuma Creek 345 E6
Monticello▲ 1,806 E6
Morgan▲ 2,023 C2
Moroni 1,115 C4
Mount Pleasant 2,092 C4
Murray 31,282 C3
Myton 468 D3
Neola 511 D3
Nephi▲ 3,515 C4
Newton 659 C2
Nibley 1,167 C2
North Ogden 11,668 C2
North Salt Lake 6,474 C3
Oak City 587 B4
Oakley 522 C3
Ogden▲ 63,909 C2
Orangeville 1,459 C4
Orderville 422 B6
Orem 67,561 C3
Panguitch▲ 1,444 B6
Paradise 561 C2
Paragonah 307 B6
Park City 4,468 C3
Parowan▲ 1,873 B6
Payson 9,510 C3
Perry 1,211 C2
Plain City 2,722 B2
Pleasant Grove 13,476 C3
Pleasant View 3,603 B2
Plymouth 267 B2
Price▲ 8,712 D4
Providence 3,344 C2
Provo▲ 86,835 C3
Randlett 283 E3
Randolph▲ 488 C2
Redmond 648 C4
Richfield▲ 5,593 B5
Richmond 1,955 C2
River Heights 1,274 C2
Riverton 11,261 B3
Roosevelt 3,915 D3
Roy 24,603 C2
Saint George▲ 28,502 A6
Salem 2,284 C3
Salina 1,943 C5
Salt Lake City (cap.)▲ 159,936 C3
Sandy 75,058 C3
Santa Clara 2,322 A6
Santaquin 2,386 C4
Scipio 291 B4
Sigurd 385 B5
Smithfield 5,566 C2
South Jordan 12,220 B3
South Ogden 12,105 C2
South Salt Lake 10,129 C3
Spanish Fork 11,272 C3
Spring City 715 C4
Springdale 275 B6
Springville 13,950 C3
Stockton 426 B3
Sunnyside 339 D4
Sunset 5,128 B2
Syracuse 4,658 B2
Taylorsville-Bennion 52,351 B3
Tooele▲ 13,887 B3
Toquerville 488 A6
Tremonton 4,264 B2
Trenton 464 B2
Tropic 374 B6
Uintah 760 C2
Vernal▲ 6,644 E3
Wallsburg 252 C3
Washington 4,198 A6
Washington Terrace 8,189 B2
Wellington 1,632 D4
Wellsville 2,206 C2
Wendover 1,127 A3
West Bountiful 4,477 B3
West Jordan 42,892 B3
Whiterocks 312 E3
Willard 1,298 C2
Woods Cross 5,384 B3

OTHER FEATURES

Abajo (mts.) E6
Agassiz (mt.) D3
Antelope (isl.) B3
Aquarius (plat.) C5
Arches Nat'l Park E5
Assay (creek) B6
Bad Land (cliffs) D4
Baldy (peak) B5
Bear (lake) C2
Bear (riv.) B2
Beaver (mts.) A5
Beaver (riv.) A5
Beaver Dam Wash (creek) A6
Birch (creek) B5
Blue (creek) B2
Bonneville (salt flats) A3
Book (cliffs) E4
Bryce Canyon Nat'l Park B6
Canyonlands Nat'l Park D5
Capitol Reef Nat'l Park C5
Castle (valley) D4
Cedar (mts.) B3
Cedar Breaks Nat'l Mon. B6
Chalk (creek) C3
Chinle (creek) E6
Clear (lake) B4
Cliff (creek) E3
Coal (cliffs) C5
Colorado (riv.) E5
Confusion (range) A4
Cottonwood (creek) C4
Cub (creek) C1
Deep (creek) B1
Deep Creek (range) A4
Delano (peak) B5
Desolation (canyon) E4
Dinosaur Nat'l Mon. E3
Dirty Devil (riv.) D5
Dolores (riv.) E5
Dry Coal (creek) A6
Duchesne (riv.) D3
Dugway (range) A3
Dugway Proving Grounds B3
Dutton (mt.) B5
East Canyon (res.) C3
Echo (res.) C3
Elk (ridge) E6
Ellen (mt.) D5
Emmons (mt.) D3
Escalante (des.) A6
Escalante (riv.) C6
Fish (lake) C5
Fish Springs (range) A4
Flaming Gorge (res.) E3
Flaming Gorge Nat'l Rec. Area E2
Fool Creek (res.) B4
Fremont (isl.) B2
Fremont (riv.) C5
Glen Canyon Nat'l Rec. Area D6
Golden Spike Nat'l Hist. Site B2
Goshute Ind. Res. A4
Government (creek) B3
Gray (canyon) D4
Great Salt (lake) B2
Great Salt Lake (des.) A3
Greeley (creek) B3
Green (riv.) D4
Grouse (creek) A2
Grouse Creek (mts.) A2
Gunnison (res.) C4
Henry (mts.) D6
Hilgard (mt.) C5
Hill (creek) E4
Hill A.F.B. C2
Hill Creek Extension, Uintah and Ouray Ind. Res. E4
Hillers (mt.) D6
House (range) A4
Hovenweep Nat'l Mon. E6
Hoyt (peak) C3
Huntington (creek) C4
Indian (creek) B5
Jordan (riv.) C3
Kaiparowits (plat.) C6
Kanab (creek) B7
Kanosh Ind. Res. B5
Kings (peak) D3
Koosharem Ind. Res. C5
Little Creek (peak) B6
Little Salt (lake) A6
Malad (riv.) B1
Marsh (peak) E3
Marvine (mt.) C5
Mineral (mts.) B5
Mona (res.) C4
Monroe (peak) B5
Montezuma (creek) E6
Monument (valley) D6
Muddy (creek) C4
Natural Bridges Nat'l Mon. E6
Navajo (mt.) D6
Navajo Ind. Res. D7
Nebo (mt.) C4
Newfoundland (mts.) A2
Nine Mile (creek) D4
North (lake) B2
Orange (cliffs) D5
Otter (creek) C5
Otter Creek (res.) C5
Paria (riv.) B6
Paunsaugunt (plat.) B6
Pahvant (range) B5
Peale (mt.) E5
Pennell (mt.) D6
Piute (res.) B5
Plumber (creek) C2
Powell (lake) D6
Price (riv.) D4
Provo (peak) C3
Provo (riv.) C3
Raft River (mts.) A2
Rainbow Bridge Nat'l Mon. C6
Roan (cliffs) E4
Rockport (lake) C3
Salvation (creek) C5
San Juan (riv.) D6
San Pitch (riv.) C4
San Rafael (riv.) D4
San Rafael Swell (mts.) D5
Santa Clara (riv.) A6
Sevier (des.) B4
Sevier (lake) A5
Sevier (riv.) B4
Sevier Bridge (res.) C4
Shivwits Ind. Res. A6
Silver Island (mts.) A3
Skull Valley Ind. Res. B3
Spanish Fork (riv.) C3
Strait (cliffs) C6
Strawberry (res.) C3
Strawberry (riv.) D3
Swan (lake) B4
Tavaputs (plat.) D4
Thomas (range) A4
Thousand Lake (mt.) C5
Timpanogos Cave Nat'l Mon. C3
Tokewamna (peak) D3
Tooele Army Depot B3
Two Water (creek) E4
Uinta (mts.) D3
Uinta (riv.) D3
Uintah and Ouray Ind. Res. D3
Utah (lake) C3
Virgin (riv.) A6
Waas (mt.) E5
Wah Wah (mts.) A5
Wasatch (range) C3
Washakie Ind. Res. B2
Waterpocket Fold (cliffs) D6
Weber (riv.) C3
White (riv.) E3
Willow (creek) E4
Zion Nat'l Park A6

▲County seat

Agriculture, Industry and Resources

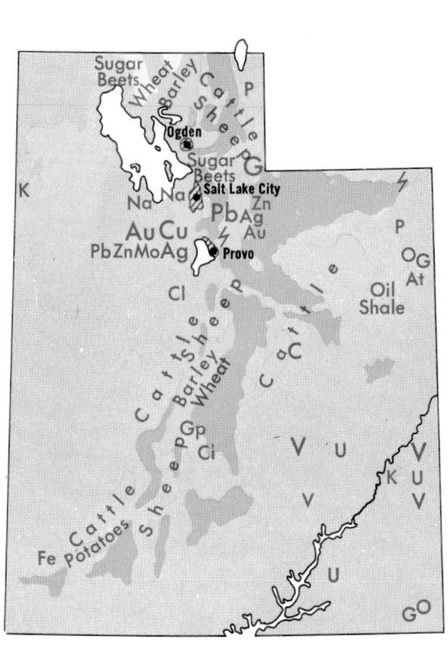
Sugar Beets
Wheat
Barley
Cattle
Sheep
Ogden
Sugar Beets
Salt Lake City
Provo
K
Na
Na
Pb Ag
Zn
Au
Au Cu
PbZnMoAg
P
O G
At
Oil Shale
Cl
Cattle
Sheep
Barley
Wheat
Gp
Cl
V
U
V
K
U
V
Cattle
Sheep
Potatoes
Fe
U
G O

DOMINANT LAND USE

- Wheat, General Farming
- General Farming, Livestock, Special Crops
- Range Livestock
- Forests
- Nonagricultural Land

MAJOR MINERAL OCCURRENCES

Ag	Silver	Fe	Iron Ore	O	Petroleum
At	Asphalt	G	Natural Gas	P	Phosphates
Au	Gold	Gp	Gypsum	Pb	Lead
C	Coal	K	Potash	U	Uranium
Cl	Clay	Mo	Molybdenum	V	Vanadium
Cu	Copper	Na	Salt	Zn	Zinc

Water Power

Major Industrial Areas

Topography

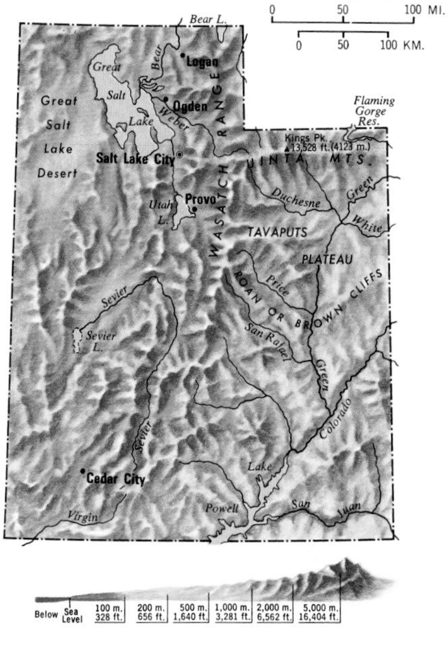
0 50 100 MI.
0 50 100 KM.
Bear L.
Great Salt Lake
Bear
Logan
Ogden
Weber
Great Salt Lake Desert
Salt Lake City
WASATCH RANGE
Flaming Gorge Res.
Kings Pk. 13,528 ft. (4123 m.)
UINTA MTS.
Utah L.
Provo
Duchesne
Green
White
TAVAPUTS
PLATEAU
Price
ROAN OR BROWN CLIFFS
Sevier
Sevier L.
San Rafael
Green
Colorado
Sevier
Cedar City
Lake
Powell
San Juan
Virgin
Below Sea Level
100 m. 328 ft.
200 m. 656 ft.
500 m. 1,640 ft.
1,000 m. 3,281 ft.
2,000 m. 6,562 ft.
5,000 m. 16,404 ft.

Topography

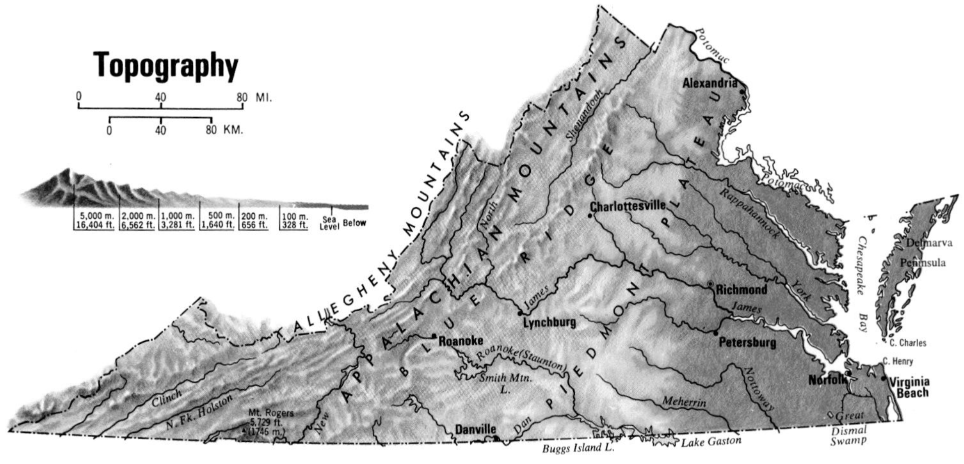
0 40 80 MI.
0 40 80 KM.
5,000 m. 16,404 ft.
2,000 m. 6,562 ft.
1,000 m. 3,281 ft.
500 m. 1,640 ft.
200 m. 656 ft.
100 m. 328 ft.
Sea Level
Below
ALLEGHENY MOUNTAINS
APPALACHIAN MOUNTAINS
BLUE RIDGE
PIEDMONT
PLATEAU
Potomac
Shenandoah
North
Alexandria
Charlottesville
Rappahannock
Richmond
York
James
Lynchburg
Roanoke
Roanoke (Staunton)
Smith Mtn. L.
Petersburg
Nottoway
Meherrin
Norfolk
Virginia Beach
Chesapeake Bay
Delmarva Peninsula
C. Charles
C. Henry
Clinch
N. Fk. Holston
Mt. Rogers 5,729 ft. (1746 m.)
New
Danville
Dan
Buggs Island L.
Lake Gaston
Great Dismal Swamp

COUNTIES

- Accomack 31,703 ... S5
- Albemarle 68,040 ... L5
- Alleghany 13,176 ... H5
- Amelia 8,787 ... M6
- Amherst 28,578 ... K5
- Appomattox 12,298 ... L6
- Arlington 170,936 ... S2
- Augusta 54,677 ... K4
- Bath 4,799 ... J4
- Bedford 45,656 ... J6
- Bland 6,514 ... F6
- Botetourt 24,992 ... J5
- Brunswick 15,987 ... N7
- Buchanan 31,333 ... D6
- Buckingham 12,873 ... L5
- Campbell 47,572 ... K6
- Caroline 19,217 ... O4
- Carroll 26,594 ... G7
- Charles City 6,282 ... O6
- Charlotte 11,688 ... L6
- Chesterfield 209,274 ... N6
- Clarke 12,101 ... M2
- Craig 4,372 ... H6
- Culpeper 27,791 ... M3
- Cumberland 7,825 ... M6
- Dickenson 17,620 ... D6
- Dinwiddie 20,960 ... N6
- Essex 8,689 ... P5
- Fairfax 818,584 ... O3
- Fauqier 35,889 ... N3
- Floyd 12,005 ... H7
- Fluvanna 12,429 ... M5
- Franklin 39,549 ... J6
- Frederick 45,723 ... M2
- Giles 16,366 ... G6
- Gloucester 30,131 ... P6
- Goochland 14,163 ... N5
- Grayson 16,278 ... F7
- Greene 10,297 ... M4
- Greensville 8,853 ... N7
- Halifax 29,033 ... L7
- Hanover 63,306 ... N5
- Henrico 217,881 ... O6
- Henry 56,942 ... J7
- Highland 2,635 ... J4
- Isle of Wight 25,053 ... P7
- James City 34,859 ... P6
- King George 13,527 ... O4
- King William 10,913 ... O5
- King and Queen 6,289 ... P5
- Lancaster 10,896 ... R5
- Lee 24,496 ... B7
- Loudoun 86,129 ... N2
- Louisa 20,325 ... N5
- Lunenburg 11,419 ... M7
- Madison 11,949 ... M4
- Mathews 8,348 ... R6
- Mecklenburg 29,241 ... M7
- Middlesex 8,653 ... R5
- Montgomery 73,913 ... H6
- Nelson 12,778 ... L5
- New Kent 10,445 ... P5
- Northampton 13,061 ... S6
- Northumberland 10,524 ... R5
- Nottoway 14,993 ... M6
- Orange 21,421 ... M4
- Page 21,690 ... M3
- Patrick 17,473 ... H7
- Pittsylvania 55,655 ... K7
- Powhatan 15,328 ... N5
- Prince Edward 17,320 ... M6
- Prince George 27,394 ... O6
- Prince William 215,686 ... O3
- Pulaski 34,496 ... G6
- Rappahannock 6,622 ... M3
- Richmond 7,273 ... P5
- Roanoke 79,332 ... H6
- Rockbridge 18,350 ... K5
- Rockingham 57,482 ... L4
- Russell 28,667 ... D7
- Scott 23,204 ... C7
- Shenandoah 31,636 ... L3
- Smyth 32,370 ... E7
- Southampton 17,550 ... O7
- Spotsylvania 57,403 ... N4
- Stafford 61,236 ... O4
- Surry 6,145 ... P6
- Sussex 10,248 ... O7
- Tazewell 45,960 ... E6
- Warren 26,142 ... M3
- Washington 45,887 ... D7
- Westmoreland 15,480 ... P4
- Wise 39,573 ... C6
- Wythe 25,466 ... F7
- York 42,422 ... P6

CITIES and TOWNS

- Abingdon▲ 7,003 ... D7
- Accomac▲ 466 ... S5
- Achilles 525 ... R6
- Afton 350 ... L4
- Alberene 200 ... L5
- Alberta 337 ... N7
- Alexandria (I.C.) 111,183 ... S3
- Allisonia 325 ... G7
- Altavista 3,686 ... K6
- Alton 500 ... K7
- Amelia Court House▲ 500 ... N6
- Amherst▲ 1,060 ... K5
- Ammissville 150 ... M3
- Amonate 350 ... E6
- Andover 180 ... C7
- Annandale 50,975 ... S3
- Appalachia 1,994 ... C7
- Appomattox▲ 1,707 ... L6
- Ararat 500 ... G7
- Arlington▲ 170,936 ... T3
- Arrington 500 ... L5
- Arvonia 500 ... M5
- Ashburn 3,393 ... O2
- Ashland 5,864 ... N5
- Atkins 1,130 ... F7
- Augusta Springs 600 ... K4
- Austinville 750 ... F7
- Axton 540 ... J7
- Bailey's Crossroads 19,507 ... S3
- Ballsville 150 ... M6
- Bandy 200 ... E6
- Banner 327 ... D7
- Barboursville 600 ... M4
- Barren Springs 125 ... G7
- Bassett 1,579 ... J7
- Bastian 600 ... F6
- Batesville 575 ... L5
- Bealeton 200 ... N3
- Beaverdam 500 ... N5
- Beaverlett 200 ... R6
- Bedford (I.C.)▲ 6,073 ... J6
- Belle Haven 526 ... S5
- Belle View ... T3
- Ben Hur 400 ... B7
- Bent Mountain 140 ... H6
- Bentonville 500 ... M3
- Bergton 150 ... L3
- Berryville▲ 3,097 ... M2
- Big Island 500 ... K5
- Big Rock 900 ... D6
- Big Stone Gap 4,748 ... C7
- Birchleaf 650 ... D6
- Birdsnest 736 ... S6
- Bishop 600 ... E6
- Blacksburg 34,590 ... H6
- Blackstone 3,497 ... N6
- Blackwater 130 ... B7
- Blairs 500 ... K7
- Bland▲ 950 ... F6
- Bloxom 357 ... S5
- Blue Grass 200 ... J3
- Blue Ridge 2,840 ... J6
- Bluefield 5,363 ... F6
- Bluemont 200 ... N2
- Boissevain 975 ... F6
- Bolar 135 ... J4
- Bon Air 16,413 ... N5
- Boones Mill 239 ... J6
- Boston 400 ... M3
- Bowling Green▲ 727 ... O4
- Boyce 520 ... M2
- Boydton▲ 453 ... M7
- Boykins 658 ... O7
- Brandy Station 400 ... N4
- Breaks 550 ... D6
- Bremo Bluff 200 ... M5
- Bridgewater 3,918 ... K4
- Bristol (I.C.) 18,426 ... D7
- Broadford 500 ... E7
- Broadway 1,209 ... L3
- Brodnax 388 ... N7
- Brooke 245 ... O4
- Brookneal 1,344 ... L6
- Brownsburg 300 ... K5
- Browntown 300 ... M3
- Brucetown 250 ... M2
- Buchanan 1,222 ... J5
- Buckingham▲ 200 ... L5
- Buena Vista (I.C.) 6,406 ... K5
- Buffalo Junction 300 ... L7
- Burgess 200 ... R5
- Burke 57,734 ... R3
- Burkes Garden 2,687 ... F6
- Burkeville 535 ... M6
- Burnsville 140 ... J4
- Callao 500 ... P5
- Callaway 225 ... H7
- Calverton 500 ... N3
- Cana 168 ... G7
- Cape Charles 1,398 ... R6
- Capeville 325 ... R6
- Capron 144 ... O7
- Cardwell 200 ... N5
- Carrsville 300 ... P7
- Carson 500 ... O6
- Casanova 370 ... N3
- Cascade 835 ... J7
- Castlewood 2,110 ... D7
- Catawba 350 ... H6
- Catlett 500 ... N3
- Cedar Bluff 1,290 ... E6
- Cedar Springs 200 ... F7
- Cedarville 200 ... M3
- Center Cross 360 ... P5
- Ceres 200 ... F6
- Champlain 160 ... O4
- Chancellorsville 40 ... N4
- Chantilly 29,337 ... O3
- Charles City▲ 5 ... O6
- Charlotte Court House▲ 531 ... L6
- Charlottesville (I.C.)▲ 40,341 ... M4
- Chase City 2,442 ... M7
- Chatham▲ 1,354 ... K7
- Cheriton 515 ... R6
- Chesapeake 151,976 ... R7
- Chester 14,986 ... O6
- Chester Gap 400 ... M3
- Chesterfield▲ 950 ... N6
- Chilhowie 1,971 ... E7
- Chincoteague 3,572 ... T5
- Christiansburg▲ 15,004 ... H6
- Chula 150 ... N6
- Church View 200 ... P5
- Churchville 250 ... K4
- Claremont 380 ... P6
- Clarksville 1,243 ... L7
- Claudville 180 ... H7
- Clay Bank 200 ... P6
- Clayville 200 ... N6
- Clear Brook 300 ... M2
- Cleveland 214 ... D7
- Clifford 150 ... K5
- Clifton Forge (I.C.) 4,679 ... J5
- Clinchburg 250 ... E7
- Clinchco 900 ... D6
- Clintwood▲ 1,542 ... D6
- Clover 198 ... L7
- Cloverdale 1,689 ... J6
- Cluster Springs 350 ... L7
- Cobbs Creek 700 ... R6
- Coeburn 2,165 ... D7
- Coleman Falls 250 ... K6
- Collierstown 300 ... J5
- Collinsville 7,280 ... J7
- Colonial Beach 3,132 ... P4
- Colonial Heights (I.C.) 16,064 ... O6
- Concord 500 ... K6
- Copper Valley 425 ... G7
- Courtland▲ 819 ... O7
- Covesville 475 ... L5
- Covington (I.C.)▲ 6,991 ... H5
- Craigsville 812 ... J4
- Crandon 250 ... G6
- Crewe 2,276 ... M6
- Crimora 1,752 ... L4
- Cripple Creek 200 ... F7
- Critz 125 ... H7
- Crockett 200 ... F7
- Cross Junction 125 ... M2
- Crozet 2,256 ... L4
- Crozier 300 ... N5
- Crystal Hill 475 ... L7
- Cullen 725 ... L6
- Culpeper▲ 8,581 ... M4
- Cumberland▲ 300 ... M6
- Dahlgren 950 ... O4
- Dale City 47,170 ... O3
- Daleville 1,163 ... J6
- Damascus 918 ... E7
- Dante 1,083 ... D7
- Danville (I.C.) 53,056 ... J7
- Davenport 230 ... D6

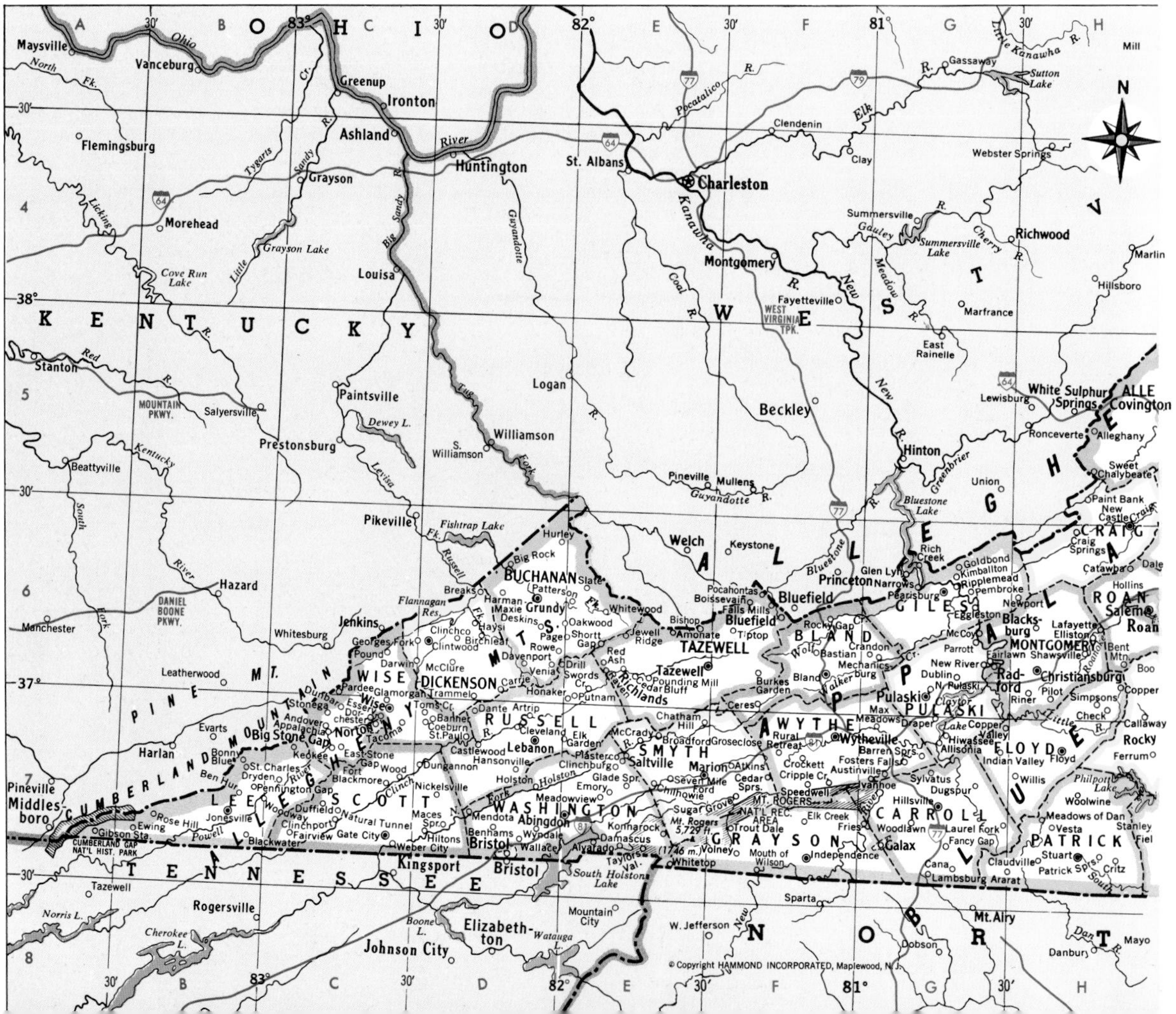
OHIO
KENTUCKY
WEST VIRGINIA
TENNESSEE
NORTH CAROLINA
Maysville
Vanceburg
Greenup
Ironton
Ashland
Huntington
Grayson
Flemingsburg
Morehead
Louisa
Paintsville
Prestonsburg
Pikeville
Williamson
Charleston
St. Albans
Montgomery
Beckley
Bluefield
Princeton
Welch
Hazard
Whitesburg
Jenkins
Grundy
Tazewell
Richlands
Lebanon
Abingdon
Bristol
Kingsport
Johnson City
Elizabethton
Big Stone Gap
Norton
Wise
Marion
Wytheville
Pulaski
Radford
Christiansburg
Blacksburg
Salem
Galax
Hillsville
Floyd
Stuart
Mt. Airy
Middlesboro
Cumberland Gap Nat'l. Hist. Park
Mt. Rogers Nat'l. Rec. Area
BUCHANAN
DICKENSON
WISE
RUSSELL
SCOTT
LEE
WASHINGTON
SMYTH
TAZEWELL
BLAND
WYTHE
GRAYSON
CARROLL
PULASKI
MONTGOMERY
FLOYD
PATRICK
GILES
CRAIG
ROANOKE
ALLEGHANY
© Copyright HAMMOND INCORPORATED, Maplewood, N.J.

Dayton 921 L4
Deerfield 500 K4
Deltaville 1,082 R5
Dendron 305 P6
Denniston 200 L7
Dewitt 140 N6
Dillwyn 458 M5
Dinwiddie▲ 500 N6
Disputanta 800 O6
Drakes Branch 565 L7
Drewryville 200 O7
Drill 192 E6
Dry Fork 200 K7
Dryden 400 B7
Dublin 2,012 G6
Duffield 54 C7
Dumfries 4,282 O3
Dundas 200 M7
Dungannon 250 D7
Dunn Loring 6,509 S2
Dunnsville 800 P5
Eagle Rock 750 J5
Earlysville 210 M4
East Stone Gap 240 C7
Eastville▲ 185 R6
Ebony 400 N7
Edinburg 860 M3
Eggleston 350 G6
Elkton 1,935 L4
Elliston-Lafayette 1,243 H6
Emory-Meadowview 2,292 E7
Emporia (I.C.)▲ 5,306 N7
Esmont 950 L5
Esserville 750 C2
Ettrick 5,290 O6
Evergreen 300 L6
Evington 175 K6
Ewing 800 B7
Exmore 1,115 S5
Faber 125 L5
Fairfax (I.C.)▲ 19,622 R3
Fairfax Station R3
Fairfield 465 K5
Fairlawn 2,399 G6
Fairport 175 R5
Falls Church (I.C.) 9,578 S2
Falls Mills 800 F6
Falmouth 3,541 O4
Fancy Gap 200 G7
Farmville▲ 6,046 M6
Farnham 150 P5
Ferrum 1,514 H7
Fieldale 1,018 H7
Fincastle▲ 236 J6
Fishersville 3,230 K4
Flint Hill 750 M3
Floyd▲ 396 H7
Forest 5,624 K6
Fork Union 350 M5
Fort Blackmore 150 C7
Fort Defiance 600 L4
Fort Mitchell 125 M7

AREA 40,767 sq. mi. (105,587 sq. km.)
POPULATION 6,216,568
CAPITAL Richmond
LARGEST CITY Norfolk
HIGHEST POINT Mt. Rogers 5,729 ft. (1746 m.)
SETTLED IN 1607
ADMITTED TO UNION June 26, 1788
POPULAR NAME Old Dominion
STATE FLOWER Dogwood
STATE BIRD Cardinal

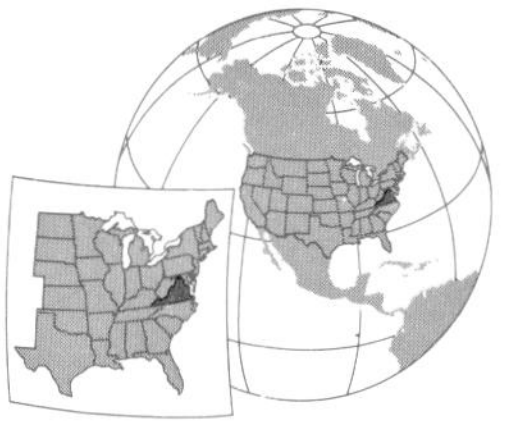

Foxwells 400 R5
Franconia 19,882 S3
Franklin (I.C.) 7,864 P7
Franktown 500 S6
Fredericksburg (I.C.) 19,027 N4
Free Union 121 L4
Fries 690 F7
Front Royal▲ 11,880 M3
Fulks Run 130 L3
Gainesville 600 N3
Galax (I.C.) 6,617 G7
Garrisonville 200 N4
Gasburg 150 N7
Gate City▲ 2,214 C7
Georges Fork 200 C6
Gibson Station 150 A7
Glade Spring 1,435 E7
Gladehill 150 J7
Gladys 500 K6
Glasgow 1,140 K5
Glen Allen 9,010 N5
Glen Lyn 170 G6
Glen Wilton 190 J5
Glenwood 2,276 K7
Gloucester▲ 1,545 P6
Gloucester Point 8,509 R6
Goldbond 250 G6
Goldvein 500 N4
Goochland▲ 800 N5
Goode 200 K6
Gordonsville 1,351 M4
Gore 500 M2
Goshen 366 K5
Grafton 500 P6
Green Bay 500 M6
Greenbackville 300 T5
Greenbush 200 S5
Greenville 400 K5
Greenwood 800 L4
Gretna 1,339 K7
Grottoes 1,455 L4
Groveton 19,997 T3
Grundy▲ 1,305 D6
Gum Spring 125 N5
Gwynn 205 R5
Hague 425 P4
Halifax▲ 772 L7
Hallwood 228 S5
Hamilton 700 N2
Hampden-Sydney 1,240 L6
Hampton (I.C.) 133,793 R6
Hanover▲ 500 O5
Hansonville 150 D7
Harborton 200 S5
Hardy 325 J6
Harman-Maxie 650 D6
Harrisonburg (I.C.)▲ 30,707 K4
Hartfield 700 R5
Haymarket 483 N3
Haynesville 500 P5

(continued on following page)

Virginia
SCALE
0 5 10 20 30 40 MI.
0 5 10 20 30 40 KM.
National Capital
State Capitals
County Seats
Canals
Major Limited Access Hwys.
Longitude 30′ West of Greenwich 78°
ATLANTIC OCEAN
CHESAPEAKE BAY
DELAWARE

Agriculture, Industry and Resources

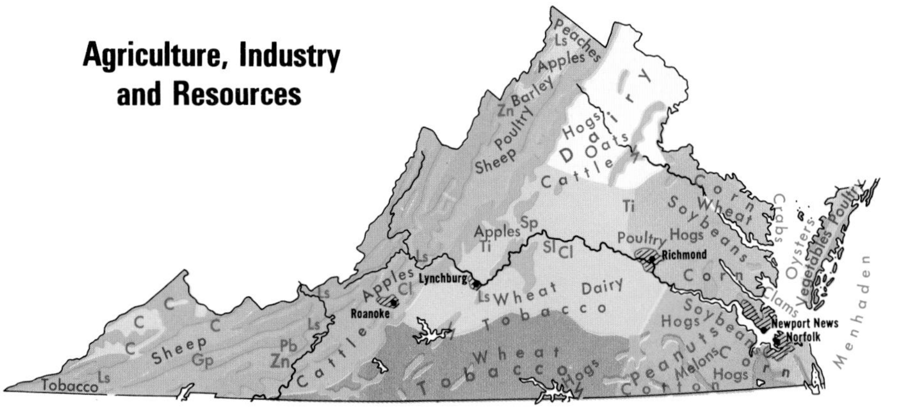
Peaches
Apples
Barley
Zn
Ls
Poultry
Sheep
Hogs
Dairy
Oats
Cattle
Corn
Wheat
Soybeans
Ti
Sp
Sl
Cl
C
Pb
Gp
Apples
Poultry
Hogs
Richmond
Lynchburg
Roanoke
Wheat
Dairy
Tobacco
Sheep
Cattle
Hogs
Peanuts
Melons
Cotton
Newport News
Norfolk
Crabs
Oysters
Vegetables
Clams
Menhaden

MAJOR MINERAL OCCURRENCES

C	Coal	Sl	Slate		Water Power
Cl	Clay	Sp	Soapstone		Major Industrial Areas
Gp	Gypsum	Ti	Titanium		
Ls	Limestone	Zn	Zinc		
Pb	Lead				

DOMINANT LAND USE

- Dairy, General Farming
- General Farming, Livestock, Dairy
- General Farming, Livestock, Tobacco
- General Farming, Livestock, Fruit, Tobacco
- General Farming, Truck Farming, Tobacco, Livestock
- Tobacco, General Farming
- Peanuts, General Farming
- Fruit and Mixed Farming
- Truck and Mixed Farming
- Forests
- Swampland, Limited Agriculture

Haysi 222 D6
Healing Springs 175 J5
Heathsville▲ 300 P5
Henry 300 J7
Herndon 16,139 O3
Highland Springs 13,823 O5
Hillsville▲ 2,008 G7
Hiltons 300 D7
Hiwassee 250 G7
Hoadly 400 O3
Hollins College 12,295 H6
Honaker 950 D6
Hopewell (I.C.) 23,101 O6
Horntown 400 T5
Hot Springs 300 J4
Huddleston 200 K6
Hume 350 N3
Huntington 7,489 S3
Hurley 850 D6
Hurt 1,294 K6
Independence▲ 988 F7
Indian Valley 300 G7
Iron Gate 417 J5
Irvington 496 R5
Isle of Wight▲ 185 P7
Ivanhoe 900 G7
Ivor 324 P7
Ivy 900 L4
Jamestown 12 P6
Jamesville 500 S5
Jarratt 556 O7
Jefferson 25,782 N5
Jefferson Manor S3
Jeffersonton 300 N3
Jewell Ridge 600 E6
Jonesville▲ 927 B7
Keeling 680 K7
Keezletown 975 L4
Keller 235 S5
Kenbridge 1,264 M7
Kents Store 130 M5
Keokee 300 C7
Keswick 300 M4
Keysville 606 M6
Kilmarnock 1,109 R5
King George▲ 575 O4
King William▲ 100 O5
King and Queen Court House▲ 500 P5
Kinsale 250 P4
La Crosse 549 M7
Lacey Spring 140 L3
Ladysmith 360 N4
Lafayette-Elliston H6
Lake Barcroft 8,686 S3
Lakeside 12,081 N5
Lambsburg 800 G7
Lancaster▲ 110 R5
Laurel Fork 300 G7
Lawrenceville▲ 1,486 N7
Lebanon Church 300 L2
Lebanon▲ 3,206 D7
Leesburg▲ 16,202 N2
Lewisetta 125 R4
Lexington (I.C.)▲ 6,959 J5
Lincolnia 13,041 S3
Linden 320 M3
Linville 500 L3
Little Plymouth 195 P5
Lively 400 P5
Loretto 150 O4
Lorton 15,385 O3
Louisa▲ 1,088 M4
Lovettsville 749 N2
Lovingston▲ 600 L5
Lowesville 500 K5
Lowmoor 700 J5
Lucketts 500 N2
Lunenburg▲ 13 M7
Luray▲ 4,587 M3
Lynch Station 500 K6
Lynchburg (I.C.) 66,049 K6
Machipongo 400 S6
Madison Heights 11,700 K6
Madison▲ 267 M4
Manakin-Sabot 200 N5
Manassas (I.C.)▲ 27,957 O3
Manassas Park (I.C.) 6,734 O3
Mannboro 175 N6
Manquin 576 O5
Mantua 6,804 S3
Mappsville 700 T5
Marion▲ 6,630 E7
Markham 300 N3
Marshall 800 N3
Martinsville (I.C.)▲ 16,162 J7
Massies Mill 225 K5
Mathews▲ 500 R6
Matoaca 1,967 N6
Mattaponi 300 P5
Maurertown 158 L3
Max Meadows 782 G6
McClure 300 D6
McCoy 600 G6
McGaheysville 600 L4
McKenney 386 N7
McLean 38,168 S2
Meadows of Dan 150 H7
Meadowview-Emory 2,292 D7
Mechanicsburg 350 G6
Mechanicsville 22,027 O5
Meherrin 400 M6
Melfa 428 S5
Mendota 375 D7
Merrifield 8,399 S3
Middlebrook 125 K4
Middleburg 549 B3
Middletown 841 M2
Midland 600 N3
Midlothian 950 N6
Milford 650 O4
Millboro 400 J5
Millboro Springs 200 J4
Millwood 400 N2
Mine Run 450 N4
Mineral 471 N4
Mobjack 210 R6
Modest Town 225 T5
Mollusk 800 P5
Moneta 300 J6
Monroe 500 K6
Monterey▲ 222 K4
Montross▲ 359 P4
Montvale 900 J6
Morattico 225 (5
Moseley 210 N6
Mount Crawford 228 L4
Mount Holly 200 P4
Mount Jackson 1,583 L3
Mount Sidney 500 K4
Mount Solon 124 K4
Mount Vernon 27,485 O3
Mouth of Wilson 400 F7
Mustoe 150 K4
Narrows 2,082 G6
Naruna 175 L6
Nassawadox 564 S6
Nathalie 200 L7
Natural Bridge 200 J5
Natural Bridge Sta. 450 K5
Naxera 300 R6
Nellysford 290 L5
New Baltimore 125 N3
New Castle▲ 152 H5
New Church 427 S5
New Hope 200 L4
New Kent▲ 25 P5
New Market 1,435 L3
New River 500 G6
Newington 17,965 S3
Newport 600 H6
Newport News (I.C.) 170,045 P6
Newsoms 337 O7
Nickelsville 411 D7
Nokesville 520 N3
Nora 550 D6
Norfolk (I.C.) 261,229 R7
Norge 750 P6
North Garden 300 L5
North Pulaski 1,405 G6
North Springfield 8,996 S3
Norton (I.C.) 4,247 C7
Nottoway▲ 170 M6
Oak Hall 221 S5
Oakpark 150 M4
Oakton 24,610 R3
Oakwood 715 E6
Occoquan 361 O3
Onancock 1,434 S5
Onley 532 S5
Orange▲ 2,582 M4
Owenton 400 O5
Oyster 200 S6
Paint Bank 235 H5
Painter 259 S5
Palmyra▲ 250 M5
Pamplin 273 L6
Pardee 190 C6
Parksley 779 S5
Parrott 750 G6
Patrick Springs 800 H7
Peaks 500 D6
Pearisburg▲ 2,064 G6
Pembroke 1,064 G6
Penhook 500 J7
Pennington Gap 1,922 C7
Petersburg (I.C.) 38,386 N6
Phenix 260 L6
Philomont 265 N2
Pilot 360 H6
Pimmit 6,658 S2
Piney River 778 L5
Pittsville 600 K7
Pleasant Valley 150 L4
Pocahontas 513 F6
Poquoson 11,005 R6
Port Royal 204 O4
Portsmouth (I.C.) 103,907 R7
Potomac Beach 200 P4
Pound 995 C6
Pounding Mill 399 E6
Powhatan▲ 600 N5
Prince George▲ 150 O6
Prospect 275 L6
Providence Forge 500 P6
Pulaski▲ 9,985 G6
Pungoteague 500 S5
Purcellville 1,744 N2
Purdy 350 N7
Quantico 670 O3
Quicksburg 160 L3
Quinby 350 S5
Radford (I.C.) 15,940 G6
Radiant 250 M4
Randolph 150 L7
Raphine 500 K5
Rapiden 176 M4
Raven 2,640 E6
Rawlings 200 N7
Rectortown 225 N3
Red Ash 300 E6
Red House 150 L6
Red Oak 250 L7
Reedville 400 R5
Reliance 150 M3
Remington 460 N3
Republican Grove 125 K7
Reston 48,556 R2
Rice 194 M6
Rich Creek 746 G6
Richlands 4,456 E6
Richmond (cap.) (I.C.)▲ 203,056 O5
Ridgeway 752 J7
Riner 360 H6
Ringgold 150 K7
Ripplemead 600 G6
Riverton 500 M3
Rixeyville 150 M3
Roanoke (I.C.) 96,397 H6
Rockville 290 N5
Rocky Gap 200 F6
Rocky Mount▲ 4,098 J7
Rose Hill 12,675 B7
Rosedale 760 E7
Roseland 300 K5
Round Hill 514 N2
Rowe 150 D6
Ruby 188 N3
Rural Retreat 972 F7
Rushmere 1,064 P6
Rustburg▲ 650 K6
Ruther Glen 200 O5
Ruthville 300 P6
Saint Charles 206 B7
Saint Paul 1,007 D7
Saint Stephens Church 500 O5
Salem (I.C.)▲ 23,756 H6
Saltville 2,376 E7
Saluda▲ 150 P5
Sandy Hook 700 M5
Saxis 367 S5
Schuyler 250 L5
Scottsburg 152 L7
Scottsville 239 L5
Sealston 200 O4
Sebrell 160 O7
Sedley 523 P7
Selma 500 J5
Seven Corners 7,280 S3
Seven Mile Ford 425 E7
Shanghai 150 P5
Shawsville 1,260 H6
Shenandoah 2,213 L4
Shiloh 150 O4
Shipman 350 L5
Simpsons 150 H6
Singers Glen 155 K3
Skippers 150 O7
Skipwith 128 L7
Smithfield 4,686 P7
Snell 300 N4
Somerset 200 M4
South Boston (I.C.) 6,997 L7
South Hill 4,217 M7
Sparta 485 o4
Speedwell 650 F8
Spencer 500 J7
Sperryville 500 M3
Spotsylvania▲ 350 N4
Springfield 23,706 S3
Stafford▲ 750 O4
Stanardsville▲ 257 L4
Stanley 1,186 L3
Stanleytown 1,563 H7
Star Tannery 500 L2
Staunton (I.C.)▲ 24,461 K4
Steeles Tavern 200 K5
Stephens City 1,186 M2
Sterling 20,512 O2
Stevensburg 125 N4
Stonega 275 C7
Stony Creek 271 N7
Strasburg 3,762 M3
Stuart▲ 965 H7
Stuarts Draft 5,087 L4
Studley 500 O5
Suffolk (I.C.) 52,141 P7
Sugar Grove 1,027 E7
Surry▲ 192 P6
Susan 500 R6
Sussex▲ 75 O7
Sutherlin 180 K7
Sweet Briar 900 K5
Swords Creek 315 E6
Sylvatus 200 G7
Tacoma 150 C7
Tangier 659 R5
Tappahannock▲ 1,550 O5
Tazewell▲ 4,176 E6
Temperanceville 400 T5
Thaxton 450 J6
The Plains 219 N3
Thornburg 135 N4
Timberville 1,596 L3
Tiptop 175 F6
Toano 950 P6
Toms Brook 227 L3
Townsend 525 R6
Trammel 450 D6
Triangle 4,740 O3
Triplet 300 N7
Trout Dale 248 F7
Troutville 455 J6
Tyro 125 K5
Union Hall 125 J6
Unionville 500 N4
Upperville 250 N2
Urbanna 529 P5
Valentines 400 N7
Vansant 1,187 D6
Vera 150 L6
Vernon Hill 250 K7
Verona 3,479 K4
Vesta 350 H7
Vesuvius 500 K5
Victoria 1,830 M6
Vienna 14,852 R2
Vinton 7,665 J6
Virgilina 161 L7
Virginia Beach (I.C.) 393,069 S7
Wachapreague 291 S5
Wakefield 1,070 O7
Walkerton 985 O5
Warm Springs▲ 325 J4
Warrenton▲ 4,830 N3
Warsaw▲ 961 P5
Washington▲ 198 M3
Water View 265 P5
Waterford 350 N2
Waverly 2,223 O6
Waynesboro (I.C.) 18,549 K4
Weber City 1,377 C7
Weems 500 P5
Weirwood 300 S6
West Augusta 325 K4
West Point 2,938 P5
West Springfield 28,126 S3
Weyers Cave 300 L4
White Hall 250 L4
White Stone 372 R5
Whitetop 860 E7
Whitewood 350 E6
Wicomico Church 500 R5
Wilderness 200 N4
Williamsburg (I.C.)▲ 11,530 P6
Williamsville 145 J4
Willis 170 H7
Willis Wharf 360 S5
Winchester (I.C.)▲ 21,947 M2
Windsor 1,025 P7
Wirtz 500 J6
Wise▲ 3,193 C7
Wolftown 350 M4
Woodberry Forest 450 M4
Woodbridge 26,401 O3
Woodlawn 1,689 G7
Woodstock▲ 3,182 L3
Woodville 200 M3
Woodway 400 C7
Woolwine 150 H7
Wylliesburg 213 L7
Wytheville▲ 8,038 G7
Zuni 300 P7

OTHER FEATURES

Aarons (creek) L7
Allegheny (mts.) H5
Anna (lake) N4
Appalachian (mts.) J5
Appomattox (riv.) M6
Appomattox Court House Nat'l Hist. Park K6
Arlington Nat'l Cemetery T3
Assateague Island Nat'l Seashore T4
Back (bay) S7
Back (creek) J4
Banister (riv.) K7
Big Otter (riv.) K6
Blackwater (riv.) J6
Blackwater (riv.) O6
Blue Ridge (mts.) J6
Bluestone (lake) G5
Booker T. Washington Nat'l Mon. J6
Buggs Island (lake) L8
Bull Run (creek) N3
Cedar (isl.) S5
Central Intelligence Agency (C.I.A.) S2
Charles (cape) R6
Chesapeake (bay) R5
Chesapeake and Ohio Canal Nat'l Hist. Park O2
Chincoteague (bay) T4
Chincoteague (inlet) T5
Claytor (lake) G6
Clinch (riv.) C7
Cobb (isl.) S6
Colonial Nat'l Hist. Park P6
Cowpasture (riv.) J4
Craig (creek) H5
Cub (creek) L6
Cumberland (mt.) B7
Cumberland Gap Nat'l Hist. Park A7
Dan (riv.) K7
Drummond (lake) P7
Fishermans (isl.) S6
Flannagan (res.) C6
Flat (creek) M6
Fort A.P. Hill O4
Fort Belvoir 8,590 O3
Fort Eustis P6
Fort Lee 6,595 O6
Fort Monroe R6
Fort Myer T2
Fort Pickett N6
Fort Story S7
Gaston (lake) M8
George Washington Birthplace Nat'l Mon. P4
Goose (creek) J6
Goose (creek) N3
Great Machipongo (inlet) S6
Great North (mt.) L2
Hampton Roads (est.) R7
Henry (cape) R7
Hog (isl.) S6
Hog Island (bay) S6
Holston, North Fork (riv.) D7
Hyco (riv.) K8
Jackson (riv.) J4
James (riv.) O6
Jamestown Nat'l Hist. Site P6
John H. Kerr (dam) M7
Langley A.F.B. R6
Leesville (lake) K6
Levisa Fork (riv.) C5
Little (inlet) S6
Little (riv.) H7
Little (riv.) N5
Manassas Nat'l Battlefield Pk. N3
Massanutten (mt.) L3
Mattaponi (riv.) O5
Mattaponi Ind. Res. P5
Maury (riv.) K3
Meherrin (riv.) M7
Metompkin (inlet) T5
Metompkin (isl.) T5
Mobjack (bay) R6
Mount Rogers Nat'l Rec. Area F7
New (inlet) S6
New (riv.) F8
Ni (riv.) N4
North Anna (riv.) M4
Nottoway (riv.) O7
Oceana N.A.S. S7
Pamunkey (riv.) O5
Pamunkey Ind. Res. P5
Parramore (isl.) S5
Pentagon T3
Petersburg Nat'l Battlefield O6
Philpott (lake) H7
Piankatank (riv.) R5
Pigg (riv.) J7
Po (riv.) N4
Pocomoke (sound) S5
Potomac (riv.) O4
Powell (riv.) B7
Quantico Marine Corps Air Sta. O4
Quinby (inlet) S6
Rapidan (riv.) M4
Rappahannock (riv.) P4
Red Hill Patrick Henry Nat'l Mem. L6
Richmond Nat'l Battlefield Pk. O6
Rivanna (riv.) M5
Roanoke (riv.) N8
Rogers (mt.) E7
Russell Fork (riv.) C5
Sand Shoal (inlet) S6
Shenandoah (mt.) K3
Shenandoah (riv.) N2
Shenandoan Nat'l Park L3
Ship Shoal (isl.) S6
Slate (riv.) L5
Smith (isl.) S6
Smith (riv.) J7
Smith Mountain (lake) J6
South Anna (riv.) N5
South Holston (lake) E7
South Mayo (riv.) H7
Stony (creek) N6
Swift (creek) O6
Tangier (isl.) R5
Tangier (sound) S5
Tug Fork (riv.) D5
U.S. Naval Base R7
Vint Hill Farms Mil. Res. N3
Wachapreague (inlet) T6
Walker (creek) F6
Wallops (isl.) T5
Willis (riv.) M5
Wolf (creek) F6
Wolf Trap Farm Park S2
York (riv.) P6

I.C. Independent City
▲County seat

AREA 68,139 sq. mi. (176,480 sq. km.)
POPULATION 4,887,941
CAPITAL Olympia
LARGEST CITY Seattle
HIGHEST POINT Mt. Rainier 14,410 ft. (4392 m.)
SETTLED IN 1811
ADMITTED TO UNION November 11, 1889
POPULAR NAME Evergreen State
STATE FLOWER Western Rhododendron
STATE BIRD Willow Goldfinch

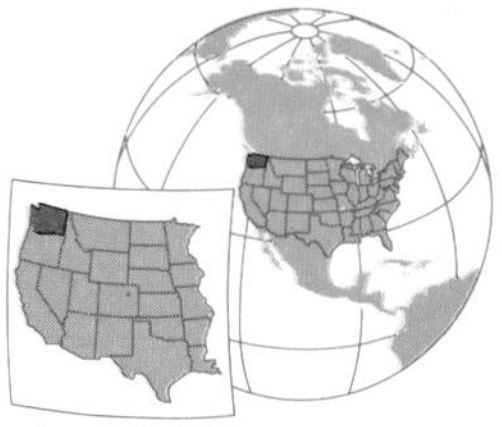

COUNTIES

Adams 13,603 G3
Asotin 17,605 H4
Benton 112,560 F4
Chelan 52,250 E3
Clallam 56,464 B2
Clark 238,053 C5
Columbia 4,024 H4
Cowlitz 82,119 C4
Douglas 26,205 F3
Ferry 6,295 G2
Franklin 37,473 G4
Garfield 2,248 H4
Grant 54,758 F3
Grays Harbor 64,175 B3
Island 60,195 C2
Jefferson 20,146 B3
King 1,507,319 D3
Kitsap 189,731 C3
Kittitas 26,725 E3
Klickitat 16,616 E5
Lewis 59,358 C4
Lincoln 8,864 G3
Mason 38,341 B3
Okanogan 33,350 F2
Pacific 18,882 B4
Pend Oreille 8,915 H2
Pierce 586,203 C3
San Juan 10,035 C2
Skagit 79,555 D2
Skamania 8,289 D5
Snohomish 465,642 D2
Spokane 361,364 H3
Stevens 30,948 H2
Thurston 161,238 C4
Wahkiakum 3,832 B4
Walla Walla 48,439 G4
Whatcom 127,780 D2
Whitman 38,775 H4
Yakima 188,823 E4

CITIES and TOWNS

Aberdeen 16,565 B3
Acme 500 C2
Addy 180 H2
Airway Heights 1,971 H3
Albion 632 H4
Alder 300 C4
Algona 1,694 C3
Allyn 850 C3
Almira 310 G3
Aloha 140 A3
Amanda Park 495 A3
Amboy 480 C5
Anacortes 11,451 C2
Appleton 120 D5
Ardenvoir 150 E3
Ariel 386 C5
Arlington 4,037 C2
Ashford 300 C4
Asotin▲ 981 H4
Auburn 33,102 C3
Azwell 152 F3
Bainbridge Island-Winslow (Winslow) A2
Baring 200 D3
Battle Ground 3,758 C5
Bay Center 187 A4
Bay City 187 B4
Beaux Arts Village 303 B2
Beaver 450 A2
Belfair 500 C3
Bellevue 86,874 B2
Bellingham▲ 52,179 C2
Benton City 1,806 F4
Beverly 200 F4
Biglake 105 C2
Bingen 645 D5
Black Diamond 1,422 D3
Blaine 2,489 C2
Blanchard 125 C2
Bonney Lake 7,494 C3
Bothell 12,345 B1
Bow 200 C2
Boyds 125 G2
Bremerton 38,142 A2
Brewster 1,633 F2
Bridgeport 1,498 F3
Brier 5,633 C3
Brinnon 500 B3
Brownstown 200 E4
Brush Prairie 2,650 C5
Bryn Mawr-Skyway 12,514 B2
Buckley 3,516 C3
Bucoda 536 C4
Buena 590 E4
Burbank 1,745 G4
Burien 25,089 A2
Burley 300 C3
Burlington 4,349 C2
Burton 650 C3
Camas 6,442 C5
Carbonado 495 D3
Carlsborg 500 B2
Carlton 410 F2
Carnation 1,243 D3
Carson 500 D5
Cashmere 2,544 E3
Castle Rock 2,067 B4
Cathlamet▲ 508 B4
Cedar Falls 200 D3
Central Park 2,669 B3
Centralia 12,101 C4
Chattaroy 250 H3
Chehalis▲ 6,527 C4
Chelan 2,969 E3
Chelan Falls 250 E3
Cheney 7,723 H3
Chewelah 1,945 H2
Chimacum 275 C3
Chinook 928 B4
Cinebar 200 C4
Clallam Bay 600 A2
Clarkston 6,753 H4
Clayton 175 H3
Cle Elum 1,778 E3
Clearlake 750 C2
Clearwater 194 A3
Clinton 1,564 C3
Clyde F4
Clyde Hill 2,972 B2
Coalfield 500 B2
Colbert 225 H3
Colby 150 A2
Colfax▲ 2,713 H4
College Place 6,308 G4
Colton 325 H4
Columbia Heights 2,515 C4
Colville▲ 4,360 H2
Conconully 153 F2
Concrete 735 D2
Connell 2,005 G4
Conway 150 C2
Copalis Beach 600 A3
Copalis Crossing 500 B3
Cosmopolis 1,372 B4
Coulee City 568 F3
Coulee Dam 1,087 G3
Coupeville▲ 1,377 C2
Cowiche 150 E4
Creston 230 G3
Cumberland 250 D3
Curlew 168 G2
Cusick 195 H2
Custer 300 C2
Dallesport 600 D5
Danville 215 G2
Darrington 1,042 D2
Davenport▲ 1,502 G3
Dayton▲ 2,468 H4
Deer Harbor 400 B2
Deer Park 2,278 H3
Deming 200 C2
Des Moines 17,283 B2
Dishman 9,671 H3
Dixie 210 G4
Doe Bay 150 C2
Doty 245 B4
Dryad 125 B4
Dryden 500 E3
Du Pont 592 C3
Dungeness 675 B2
Duvall 2,770 D3
East Olympia 300 B4
East Wenatchee 2,701 E3
Easton 250 D3
Eastsound 800 B2
Eatonville 1,374 C4
Edison 250 C2
Edmonds 30,744 C3
Edwall 150 H3
Electric City 910 F3
Ellensburg▲ 12,361 E3
Elma 3,011 B4
Elmer City 290 G2
Eltopia 200 G4
Endicott 320 H4
Enetai 2,638 A2
Entiat 449 E3
Enumclaw 7,227 D3
Ephrata▲ 5,349 F3
Erlands Point 1,254 A2
Ethel 180 C4
Everett▲ 69,961 C3
Everson 1,490 C2
Fairfield 446 H3
Fairview-Sumach 2,749 E4
Fall City 1,582 D3
Farmington 126 H3
Ferndale 5,398 C2
Fife 3,864 C3
Finley 4,897 F4
Fircrest 5,258 C3
Fords Prairie 2,480 B4
Forks 2,862 A3
Four Lakes 500 H3
Frances 144 B4
Freeland 1,278 C2
Freeman 150 H3
Friday Harbor▲ 1,492 B2
Fruitland 150 G2
Fruitvale 4,125 E4
Galvin 250 B4
Garfield 544 H3
Garrett 1,004 G4
Geiger Heights H3
George 253 F3
Gig Harbor 3,236 C3
Glacier 150 D2
Glenoma 500 C4
Glenwood 626 D4
Gold Bar 1,078 D3
Goldendale▲ 3,319 E5
Gorst 750 C3
Grand Coulee 984 G3
Grand Mound 1,394 C4
Grandview 7,169 F4
Granger 2,053 E4
Granite Falls 1,060 D2
Grapeview 250 C3
Grayland 750 A4
Grays River 350 B4
Greenacres 4,626 J3
Greenbank 600 C2
Hadlock-Irondale 2,742 C2
Hamilton 228 D2
Hansville 250 C3
Harper 300 A2
Harrah 341 E4
Harrington 449 G3
Hartline 176 F3
Hatton 71 F4
Heisson 200 C5
Hobart 500 D3
Hoodsport 500 B3
Hoquiam 8,972 A3
Humptulips 275 A3
Hunters 200 G2
Hunts Point 513 B2
Husum 200 D5
Ilwaco 815 A4
Inchelium 393 G2
Index 139 D3
Indianola 1,729 A1
Ione 507 H2
Issaquah 7,786 C3
Joyce 375 B2
Juanita 17,232 B1
Kahlotus 167 B4
Kalama 1,210 C4
Kapowsin 500 C4
Keller 195 G2
Kelso▲ 11,820 C4
Kenmore 8,917 B1
Kennewick 42,155 F4
Kent 37,960 C3
Kettle Falls 1,272 H2
Keyport 900 A2
Kingston 1,270 C3
Kiona 230 F4
Kirkland 40,052 B2
Kittitas 843 E4
Klickitat 750 D5
Krupp (Marlin) 53 F3
La Center 451 C5
La Conner 656 C2
La Push 500 A3
Lacey 19,279 C3
Lacrosse 336 H4
Lake Forest Park 4,031 B1
Lake Stevens 3,380 D3
Lakewood 58,412 C2
Lamont 91 H3
Langley 845 C2
Latah 175 H3
Laurel 972 D5
Leavenworth 1,692 E3
Lebam 275 B4
Liberty Lake 2,015 J3
Lind 472 G4
Littlerock 850 B4
Long Beach 1,236 A4
Longbranch 640 C3
Longview 31,499 B4
Loomis 150 F2
Loon Lake 500 H2
Lummi Island 675 C2
Lyle 580 D5
Lyman 275 D2
Lynden 5,709 C2
Lynnwood 28,695 C3
Mabton 1,482 E4
Malaga 125 E3
Malden 189 H3
Malo 240 G2
Malone 175 B4
Malott 350 F2
Manchester 4,031 A2
Mansfield 311 F3
Manson 220 E3
Maple Falls 300 D2
Maple Valley 1,211 C3
Marblemount 300 D2
Marcus 135 H2
Marietta-Alderwood 2,766 C2
Markham 117 B4
Marlin F3
Marysville 10,328 C2
Matlock 255 B3
Mattawa 941 F4
McCleary 1,235 B3
McKenna 300 C4
Mead H3
Medical Lake 3,664 H3
Medina 2,981 B2
Menlo 237 B4
Mercer Island (city) 20,816 B2
Mesa 252 G4
Metaline 198 H2
Metaline Falls 210 H2
Mica 105 H3
Milan 150 H3
Millwood 1,559 H3
Milton 4,995 C3
Mineral 550 C4
Moclips 500 A3
Monitor 650 E3
Monroe 4,278 D3
Montesano▲ 3,064 B4
Moses Lake 11,235 F3
Mossyrock 452 C4
Mount Vernon▲ 17,647 C2
Mountlake Terrace 19,320 B1
Moxee City 814 E4
Mukilteo 7,007 C3
Naches 596 E4
Nahcotta 200 A4
Napavine 745 C4
Naselle 500 B4
Navy Yard City 2,905 A2
Neah Bay 916 A2
Neilton 250 B3
Nespelem 291 G2
Newhalem 350 D2
Newman Lake 102 J3
Newport▲ 1,691 H2
Nine Mile Falls 150 H3
Nisqually 558 C3
Nooksack 584 C2
Nordland 706 C2
Normandy Park 6,709 A2
North Bend 2,578 D3
North Bonneville 411 C5
Northport 308 H2
Oak Harbor 17,176 C2
Oakesdale 346 H3
Oakville 493 B4

(continued on following page)

Agriculture, Industry and Resources

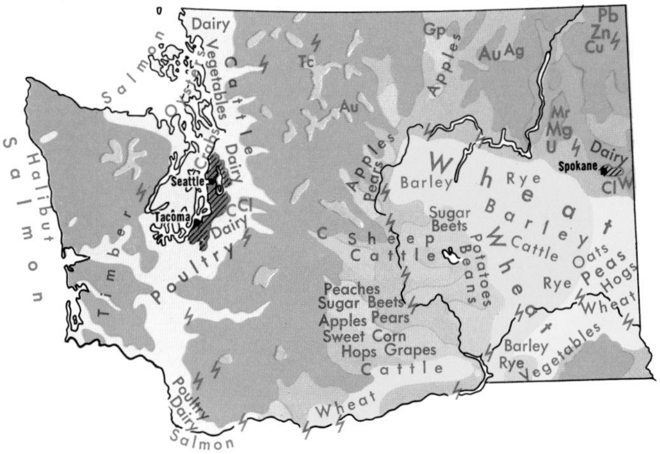
Dairy
Vegetables
Cattle
Salmon
Halibut
Salmon
Timber
Poultry
Dairy
Seattle
Tacoma
Cl
Gp
Tc
Au Ag
Apples
Au
Pb
Zn
Cu
Mr
Mg
U
Dairy
Spokane
Cl
W
Apples
Pears
Barley
Wheat
Rye
Barley
Sugar Beets
Sheep
Cattle
Potatoes
Beans
Oats
Peas
Hogs
Wheat
Rye
Peaches
Sugar Beets
Apples Pears
Sweet Corn
Hops Grapes
Cattle
Barley
Rye
Vegetables
Wheat
Poultry
Dairy
Salmon

DOMINANT LAND USE

- Specialized Wheat
- Wheat, Peas
- Dairy, Poultry, Mixed Farming
- Fruit and Mixed Farming
- General Farming, Dairy, Range Livestock
- General Farming, Livestock, Special Crops
- Range Livestock
- Forests
- Urban Areas
- Nonagricultural Land

MAJOR MINERAL OCCURRENCES

- Ag Silver
- Au Gold
- C Coal
- Cl Clay
- Cu Copper
- Gp Gypsum
- Mg Magnesium
- Mr Marble
- Pb Lead
- Tc Talc
- U Uranium
- W Tungsten
- Zn Zinc

Water Power
Major Industrial Areas

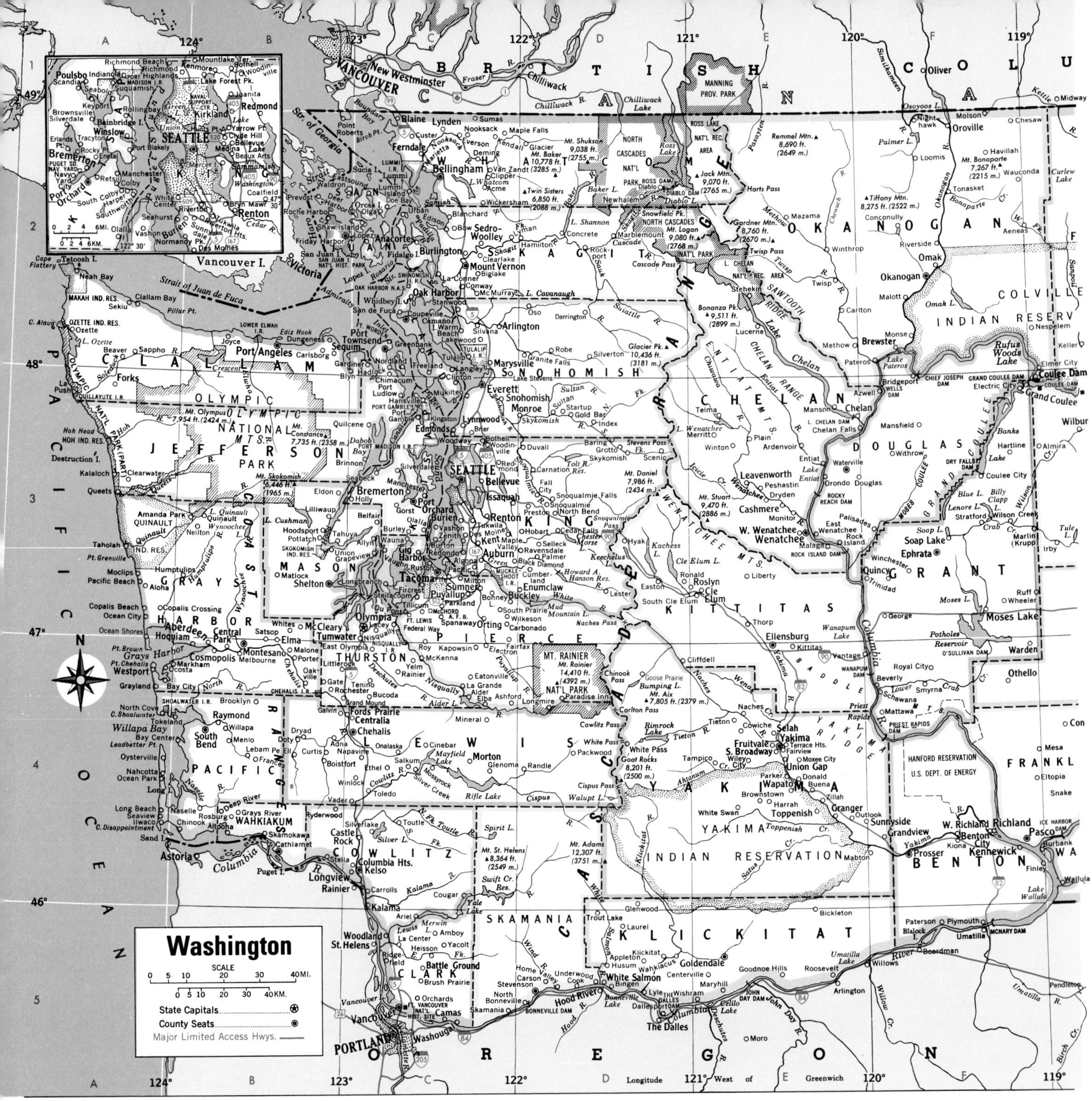
Washington
SCALE
0 5 10 20 30 40 MI.
0 5 10 20 30 40 KM.
State Capitals
County Seats
Major Limited Access Hwys.
BRITISH COLUMBIA
OREGON
PACIFIC OCEAN
Longitude West of Greenwich
SEATTLE
Olympia
Spokane
Tacoma
Vancouver I.
Strait of Juan de Fuca
OLYMPIC NATIONAL PARK
MT. RAINIER NAT'L PARK
NORTH CASCADES NAT'L PARK
CASCADE RANGE
COLVILLE INDIAN RESERV.
YAKIMA INDIAN RESERVATION
HANFORD RESERVATION U.S. DEPT. OF ENERGY
MANNING PROV. PARK
CLALLAM
JEFFERSON
GRAYS HARBOR
PACIFIC
WAHKIAKUM
COWLITZ
CLARK
SKAMANIA
KLICKITAT
LEWIS
THURSTON
MASON
KITSAP
PIERCE
KING
SNOHOMISH
SKAGIT
WHATCOM
SAN JUAN
ISLAND
OKANOGAN
CHELAN
DOUGLAS
KITTITAS
YAKIMA
BENTON
GRANT

Ocean City 350 .... A3
Ocean Park 1,409 .... A4
Ocean Shores 2,301 .... A3
Ocosta 369 .... B4
Odessa 935 .... G3
Okanogan▲ 2,370 .... F2
Olalla 500 .... A2
Olympia (cap.)▲ 33,840 .... C3
Omak 4,117 .... F2
Onalaska 600 .... C4
Opportunity 22,326 .... H3
Orchards 8,828 .... C5
Orondo 130 .... E3
Oroville 1,505 .... F2
Orting 2,106 .... C3
Oso 150 .... D2
Othello 4,638 .... F4
Otis Orchards-East Farms 5,811 .... H3
Outlook 300 .... E4
Oysterville 150 .... A4
Ozette 50 .... A2
Pacific 4,622 .... C3
Pacific Beach 900 .... A3
Packwood 800 .... D4
Palisades 150 .... E3
Palmer 200 .... D3
Palouse 915 .... H4
Parker 500 .... E4
Parkland 20,882 .... C3
Pasco▲ 20,337 .... F4
Pateros 570 .... E2
Paterson 250 .... F5
Pe Ell 547 .... B4
Peshastin 500 .... E3
Plymouth 220 .... F5
Point Roberts 500 .... B2
Pomeroy▲ 1,393 .... H4
Port Angeles▲ 17,710 .... B2
Port Blakely 600 .... A2
Port Gamble 122 .... C3
Port Ludlow 200 .... C3
Port Orchard▲ 4,984 .... A2
Port Townsend▲ 7,001 .... C2
Porter 200 .... B4
Poulsbo 4,848 .... A1
Prescott 267 .... G4
Preston 500 .... D3
Prosser▲ 4,476 .... F4
Pullman 23,478 .... H4
Puyallup 23,875 .... C3
Queets 180 .... A3
Quilcene 900 .... B3
Quinault 450 .... B3
Quincy 3,738 .... F3
Rainier 991 .... C4
Randle 950 .... D4
Ravensdale 400 .... D3
Raymond 2,901 .... B4
Reardan 482 .... H3
Redmond 35,800 .... B1
Redondo 950 .... C3
Renton 41,688 .... B2
Republic▲ 940 .... G2
Retsil 1,524 .... A2
Richland 32,315 .... F4
Richmond Beach-Innis Arden 7,242 .... A1
Richmond Highlands 26,037 .... A1
Ridgefield 1,297 .... C5
Riparia 210 .... G4
Ritzville▲ 1,725 .... G3
Riverside 223 .... F2
Riverton 14,182 .... B2
Riverton Heights B2
Roche Harbor 200 .... B2
Rochester 1,250 .... C4
Rock Island 524 .... E3
Rockford 481 .... H3
Rockport 200 .... D2
Rocky Point 1,495 .... A2
Rollingbay 950 .... A2
Ronald 200 .... E3
Rosalia 552 .... H3
Rosburg 419 .... B4
Roslyn 869 .... E3
Roy 258 .... C4
Royal City 1,104 .... F4
Ruston 693 .... C3
Ryderwood 367 .... B4
Saint John 499 .... H3
Salkum 390 .... C4
San de Fuca 150 .... C2
Satsop 300 .... B3
Schawana 150 .... F4
Seabeck 200 .... C3
Seabold 250 .... A1
Seahurst A2
Seattle▲ 516,259 .... A2
Seaview 500 .... A4
Sedro-Woolley 6,031 .... C2
Sekiu 328 .... A2
Selah 5,113 .... E4
Selleck 150 .... D3
Sequim 3,616 .... B2
Shaw Island 125 .... B2
Shelton▲ 7,241 .... B3
Silver Creek 175 .... C4
Silverdale 7,660 .... A2
Skamania 200 .... C5
Skamokawa 450 .... B4
Skykomish 273 .... D3
Snohomish 6,499 .... D3
Snoqualmie 1,546 .... D3
Snoqualmie Falls 250 .... D3
Soap Lake 1,149 .... F3
South Bend▲ 1,551 .... B4
South Broadway 2,735 .... E4
South Cle Elum 457 .... D3
South Colby 500 .... A2
South Prairie 180 .... D3
Southworth 175 .... A2
Spanaway 15,001 .... C3
Spangle 229 .... H3
Spokane▲ 177,196 .... H3
Sprague 410 .... G3
Springdale 260 .... H2
Stanwood 1,961 .... C2
Starbuck 170 .... G4
Startup 350 .... D3
Steilacoom 5,728 .... C3
Steptoe 215 .... H3
Stevenson▲ 1,147 .... C5
Sultan 2,236 .... D3
Sumas 744 .... C2
Sumner 6,281 .... C3
Sunnydale B2
Sunnyside 11,238 .... F4
Suquamish 3,105 .... A1
Tacoma▲ 176,664 .... C3
Taholah 788 .... A3
Tahuya 150 .... B3
Tekoa 750 .... H3
Tenino 1,292 .... C4
Terrace Heights 4,223 .... E4
Thorp 500 .... E3
Tieton 693 .... E4
Tillicum C3
Tokeland 500 .... A4
Toledo 586 .... C4
Tonasket 847 .... F2
Toppenish 7,419 .... E4
Touchet 450 .... G4
Toutle 825 .... C4
Town and Country 4,921 .... H3
Tracyton 2,621 .... A2
Trout Lake 900 .... D5
Tukwila 11,874 .... B2
Tulalip 250 .... C2
Tumtum 250 .... H3
Tumwater 9,976 .... B3

118°
117°
49°
48°
47°
46°
Grand Forks
Rossland
Trail
Fruitvale
Danville
Laurier
Curlew
Malo
Republic
Orient
Northport
Leadpoint
Metaline
Metaline Falls
Boundary Dam
Mt. Abercrombie 7,308 ft. (2227 m.)
Box Canyon Dam
Sullivan L.
Bossburg
Evans
Marcus
Kettle Falls
Colville
Boyds
Snow Pk. 7,109 ft. (2167 m.)
Coulee Dam Nat'l Rec. Area
Ione
Tiger
Lost Creek
Ruby
PEND OREILLE
Priest L.
Orin
Park Rapids
Rice
Arden
Daisy
Addy
Gifford
Bluecreek
Chewelah
STEVENS
Kalispel Ind. Res.
Cusick
Usk
Franklin
Inchelium
Impach
Twin Lakes
Kewa
Valley
Dalkena
Newport
Priest River
Albeni Falls Dam
Cedonia
Hunters
Roosevelt
Fruitland
Springdale
Deer L.
Loon Lake
Sacheen L.
Diamond L.
Elk
Deer Park
Milan
Clayton
Tumtum
Mt. Spokane 5,878 ft. (1792 m.)
Chattaroy
Spokane Ind. Res.
Wellpinit
Ford
Denison
Colbert
Long Lake
Newman L.
Newman Lake
Coeur d'Alene
Lincoln
Creston
Nine Mile Falls
Mead
Otis Orchards
Spokane
Millwood
Greenacres
Liberty Lake
Veradale
Opportunity
Dishman
Town & Country
Reardan
Deepcreek
Fairchild A.F.B.
Airway Hts.
Davenport
Espanola
Medical Lake
Four Lakes
Waukon
Edwall
Cheney
Valleyford
Freeman
Mica
Rockford
LINCOLN
Harrington
Tyler
Spangle
Fairfield
Mohler
Amber
Plummer
Waverly
Lamona
Sylvan L.
Plaza
Odessa
Crab
Sprague
Sprague L.
Latah
Rock L.
Rosalia
Tekoa
Malden
Lamont
Pine City
Oakesdale
Ritzville
Thornton
Belmont
Farmington
Ewan
Saint John
Marengo
Steptoe
Garfield
ADAMS
Elberton
Lind
Ralston
Winona
Endicott
Diamond
Colfax
Palouse
Benge
WHITMAN
Albion
Moscow
Cunningham
Lacrosse
Dusty
Hatton
Washtucna
Hooper
Pullman
L. Bryan
Almota
Lower Granite Dam
Kahlotus
Lower Monumental Lake
Little Goose Dam
Hay
Riparia
Colton
Lower Monumental Dam
Ayer
Starbuck
GARFIELD
Uniontown
Pataha
Pomeroy
Clyde
Turner
Clarkston
Lewiston
Asotin
Asotin Dam (Site)
COLUMBIA
Sacajawea
Eureka
Prescott
Huntsville
Dayton
Waitsburg
ASOTIN
Cloverland
WALLA WALLA
Dixie
Anatone
Walla Walla
China Gardens Dam (Site)
Whitman Mission Nat'l Hist. Site
College Place
Touchet
Milton-Freewater
Hells Canyon Nat'l Rec. Area
Wallowa
Elgin
Pilot Rock
Enterprise
© Copyright HAMMOND INCORPORATED, Maplewood, N. J.

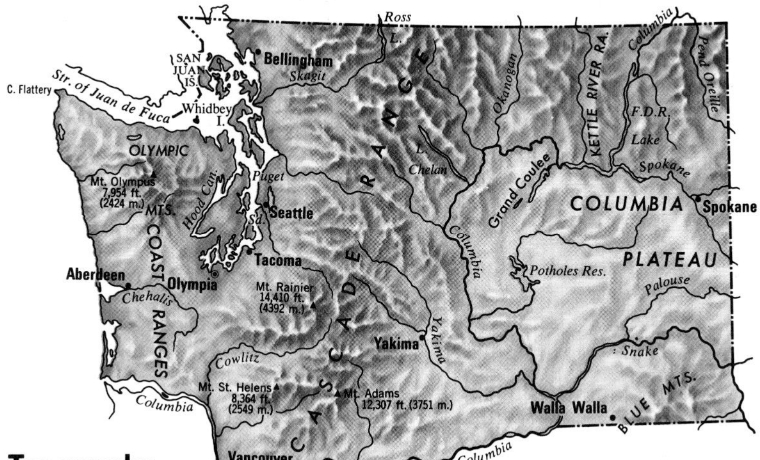
Ross L.
San Juan Is.
Bellingham
Skagit
C. Flattery
Str. of Juan de Fuca
Whidbey I.
Okanogan
Columbia
Kettle River Ra.
Pend Oreille
F.D.R. Lake
Spokane
Chelan
Olympic
Mt. Olympus 7,954 ft. (2424 m.)
Puget
Seattle
Grand Coulee
COLUMBIA
Spokane
Cascade Range
Coast Ranges
Tacoma
Potholes Res.
PLATEAU
Aberdeen
Olympia
Mt. Rainier 14,410 ft. (4392 m.)
Palouse
Chehalis
Yakima
Cowlitz
Snake
Mt. St. Helens 8,364 ft. (2549 m.)
Mt. Adams 12,307 ft. (3751 m.)
Walla Walla
Blue Mts.
Vancouver

Topography

0 40 80 MI.
0 40 80 KM.

Below Sea Level | 100 m. 328 ft. | 200 m. 656 ft. | 500 m. 1,640 ft. | 1,000 m. 3,281 ft. | 2,000 m. 6,562 ft. | 5,000 m. 16,404 ft.

Twisp 872 ....E2
Underwood 640 ....D5
Union 380 ....B3
Union Gap 3,120 ....E4
Uniontown 277 ....H4
Usk 180 ....H2
Vader 414 ....B4
Valley 156 ....H2
Valleyford 175 ....H3
Vancouver▲ 46,380 ....C5
Vantage 300 ....E4
Vashon 350 ....A2
Vaughn 600 ....C3
Veradale 7,836 ....H3
Waitsburg 990 ....G4
Walla Walla▲ 26,478 ....G4
Wallula 148 ....G4
Wapato 3,795 ....E4
Warden 1,639 ....F4
Washougal 4,764 ....C5
Washtucna 231 ....G4
Waterville▲ 995 ....E3
Wauna 300 ....C3
Waverly 37 ....H3
Wellpinit 250 ....G3
Wenatchee▲ 21,756 ....E3
West Richland 3,962 ....F4
West Wenatchee 2,220 ....E3
Westport 1,892 ....A4
White Center-Shorewood 20,531 ....A2
White Salmon 1,861 ....D5
White Swan 2,669 ....E4
Wickersham 200 ....C2
Wilbur 863 ....G3
Wiley City 250 ....E4
Wilkeson 366 ....D3
Willapa 300 ....B4
Wilson Creek 148 ....F3
Winlock 1,027 ....C4
Winslow (Bainbridge Island-Winslow) 3,081 ....A2
Winthrop 302 ....E2
Wishram 575 ....D5
Woodinville 23,654 ....B1
Woodland 2,500 ....C5
Woodway 914 ....C3
Yacolt 600 ....C5
Yakima▲ 54,827 ....E4
Yarrow Point 962 ....B2
Yelm 1,337 ....C4
Zenith-Saltwater 8,982 ....C3
Zillah 1,911 ....E4

OTHER FEATURES

Abercrombie (mt.) H2
Adams (mt.) D4
Admiralty (inlet) B2
Ahtanum (creek) D4
Aix (mt.) D4
Alava (cape) A2
Alder (lake) C4
Asotin (creek) H4
Asotin (dam) J4
Bainbridge (isl.) A2
Baker (lake) D2
Baker (mt.) D2
Baker (riv.) D2
Banks (lake) F3
Birch (pt.) C2
Blalock (isl.) F5
Blue (lake) F3
Blue (mts.) H4
Bonanza (peak) E2
Bonaparte (creek) F2
Bonaparte (mt.) F2
Bonneville (dam) D5
Bonneville (lake) D5
Boundary (bay) C1
Boundary (dam) H2
Boundary (lake) H2
Box Canyon (dam) H2
Brown (pt.) A4
Bumping (lake) D4
Camano (isl.) C2
Carlton (pass) D4
Cascade (pass) D2
Cascade (range) D4
Cascade (riv.) D2
Cavanaugh (lake) D2
Cedar (riv.) B2
Celilo (lake) E5
Chehalis (pt.) A4
Chehalis (riv.) B4
Chehalis Ind. Res. B4
Chelan (dam) E3
Chelan (lake) E2
Chelan (range) E2
Chester Morse (lake) D3
Chewuch (riv.) E2
Chief Joseph (dam) F3
China Gardens (dam) J4
Chinook (pass) D4
Chiwawa (riv.) E2
Cispus (pass) D4
Cispus (riv.) D4
Cle Elum (lake) E3
Coal (creek) G3
Coast (ranges) B3
Columbia (riv.) B4
Colville (riv.) H2
Colville Ind. Res. G2
Constance (mt.) B3
Coulee Dam Nat'l Rec. Area G2
Cow (creek) G3
Cowlitz (pass) D4
Cowlitz (riv.) C4
Crab (creek) F3
Crescent (lake) B2
Curlew (lake) G2
Cushman (lake) B3
Dabob (bay) C3
Dalles, The (dam) D5
Daniel (mt.) D3
Deadman (creek) H4
Deer (lake) H2
Deschutes (riv.) C4
Destruction (isl.) A3
Diablo (lake) D2
Diamond (lake) H2
Disappointment (cape) A4
Dry Falls (dam) F3
Ediz Hook (pen.) B2
Elwha (riv.) B3
Entiat (lake) E3
Entiat (mts.) E2
Entiat (riv.) E3
Fairchild A.F.B. 4,854 ....H3
Fidalgo (isl.) C2
Flattery (cape) A2
Fort Lewis 22,224 ....C3
Fort Vancouver Nat'l Hist. Site C5
Fort Worden C2
Franklin D. Roosevelt (lake) G2
Gardner (mt.) E2
Georgia (str.) B2
Glacier (peak) D2
Goat Rocks (mt.) D4
Grand Coulee (canyon) F3
Grand Coulee (dam) F3
Grande Ronde (riv.) H5
Grays (harb.) A4
Green (lake) A2
Green (riv.) C3
Grenville (pt.) A3
Hanford Reservation-U.S. Dept. of Energy F4
Hangman (creek) H3
Haro (str.) B2
Harts (pass) E2
Hells Canyon Nat'l Rec. Area H5
Hoh (head) A3
Hoh (riv.) A3
Hoh Ind. Res. A3
Hood Canal (inlet) B3
Howard A. Hanson (res.) D3
Humptulips (riv.) B3
Ice Harbor (dam) G4
Icicle (creek) E3
Jack (mt.) E2
John Day (dam) E5
Juan de Fuca (str.) A2
Kachness (lake) D3
Kalama (riv.) C4
Kalispel Ind. Res. H2
Keechelus (lake) D3
Kettle (riv.) G2
Kettle River (range) G2
Klickitat (riv.) D4
Lake (creek) G3
Lake Chelan Nat'l Rec. Area E2
Leadbetter (pt.) A4
Lenore (lake) F3
Lewis (riv.) C5
Little Goose (dam) G4
Little Spokane (riv.) H3
Logan (mt.) E2
Long (isl.) A4
Long (lake) H3
Loon (lake) H2
Lopez (isl.) C2
Lower Crab (creek) F4
Lower Elwah Ind. Res. B2
Lower Granite (lake) H4
Lower Monumental (lake) G4
Lummi (isl.) C2
Lummi Ind. Res. C2
Makah Ind. Res. A2
Mayfield (lake) C4
McChord A.F.B. 4,538 ....C3
McNary F5
Merwin (lake) C5
Methow (riv.) E2
Moses (lake) F3
Moses Coulee (canyon) F3
Mount Rainier Nat'l Park D4
Muckleshoot Ind. Res. C3
Mud Mountain (lake) D3
Naches (pass) D3
Naches (riv.) E4
Naselle (riv.) B4
Naval Support Ctr. B1
Newman (lake) H3
Nisqually (riv.) C4
Nisqually Ind. Res. C4
Nooksack (riv.) C2
North (riv.) B4
North Cascades Nat'l Park D2
Oak Harobr Naval Air Sta. C2
Okanogan (riv.) F2
Olympic (mts.) B3
Olympic Nat'l Park B3
Olympus (mt.) B3
Omak (lake) F2
Orcas (isl.) C2
Osoyoos (lake) F1
O'Sullivan (dam) F4
Ozette (lake) A2
Ozette Ind. Res. A2
Padilla (bay) C2
Palmer (lake) F2
Pasayten (riv.) E2
Pataha (creek) H4
Pateros (lake) F2
Pend Oreille (riv.) H2
Pillar (pt.) A2
Pine (creek) H3
Port Angeles Ind. Res. B2
Port Gamble Ind. Res. C3
Port Madison Ind. Res. A1
Potholes (res.) F3
Priest Rapids (lake) E4
Puget (isl.) B4
Puget (sound) C3
Puget Sound Navy Yard A2
Puyallup (riv.) C4
Queets (riv.) A3
Quillayute Ind. Res. A3
Quinault (lake) B3
Quinault (riv.) A3
Quinault Ind. Res. A3
Rainier (mt.) D4
Remmel (mt.) E2
Rifle (lake) C4
Rimrock (lake) D4
Rock (creek) H3
Rock (lake) H3
Rock Island (dam) E3
Rocky (mts.) H2
Rocky Reach (dam) E3
Rosario (str.) C2
Ross (dam) D2
Ross (lake) D2
Ross Lake Nat'l Rec. Area E2
Rufus Woods (lake) F2
Sacajawea (lake) G4
Sacheen (lake) H2
Saddle (mts.) E4
Saint Helens (mt.) C4
Samish (lake) C2
Sammamish (lake) B2
Sand (isl.) A4
San Juan (isl.) B2
San Juan Island Nat'l Hist. Park B2
Sanpoil (riv.) G2
Satus (creek) E4
Sauk (riv.) D2
Sawtooth (ridge) E2
Shannon (lake) D2
Shoalwater (cape) A4
Shoalwater Ind. Res. B4
Shuksan (mt.) D2
Silver (lake) C4
Similkameen (riv.) F1
Skagit (riv.) C2
Skokomish (mt.) B3
Skokomish Ind. Res. B3
Skykomish (riv.) D3
Snake (riv.) G4
Snohomish (riv.) C3
Snoqualmie (pass) D3
Snoqualmie (riv.) D3
Snow (peak) G2
Snowfield (peak) D2
Soap (lake) F3
Soleduck (riv.) A3
Spirit (lake) C4
Spokane (mt.) H3
Spokane (riv.) H3
Spokane Ind. Res. G3
Sprague (lake) G3
Stevens (pass) D3
Stuart (mt.) E3
Sucia (isl.) C2
Suiattle (riv.) D2
Sullivan (lake) H2
Sultan (riv.) D3
Swift Creek (res.) C4
Swinomish Ind. Res. C2
Sylvan (lake) G3
Tatoosh (isl.) A2
The Dalles (dam) D5
Tieton (riv.) D4
Tiffany (mt.) F2
Tolt River (res.) D3
Toppenish (creek) E4
Touchet (riv.) G4
Toutle, North Fork (riv.) C4
Toutle, South Fork (riv.) C4
Tucannon (riv.) G4
Tulalip Ind. Res. C2
Tule (lake) G3
Twin (lakes) G2
Twin Sisters (mt.) D2
Twisp (pass) E2
Twisp (riv.) E2
Umatilla (lake) E5
Union (lake) B2
Vancouver (lake) C5
Walla Walla (riv.) G4
Wallula (lake) F4
Walupt (lake) D4
Wanapum (lake) E3
Washington (lake) B2
Wells (dam) F3
Wenas (creek) E4
Wenatchee (lake) E3
Wenatchee (mts.) E3
Wenatchee (riv.) E3
Whatcom (lake) C2
Whidbey (isl.) C2
White (pass) D4
White (riv.) D3
White Salmon (riv.) D4
Whitman Mission Nat'l Hist. Site G4
Willapa (bay) A4
Wilson (creek) F3
Wind (riv.) D5
Wynoochee (lake) B3
Wynoochee (riv.) B3
Yakima (ridge) E4
Yakima (riv.) F4
Yakima Ind. Res. E4
Yale (lake) C4

▲County seat

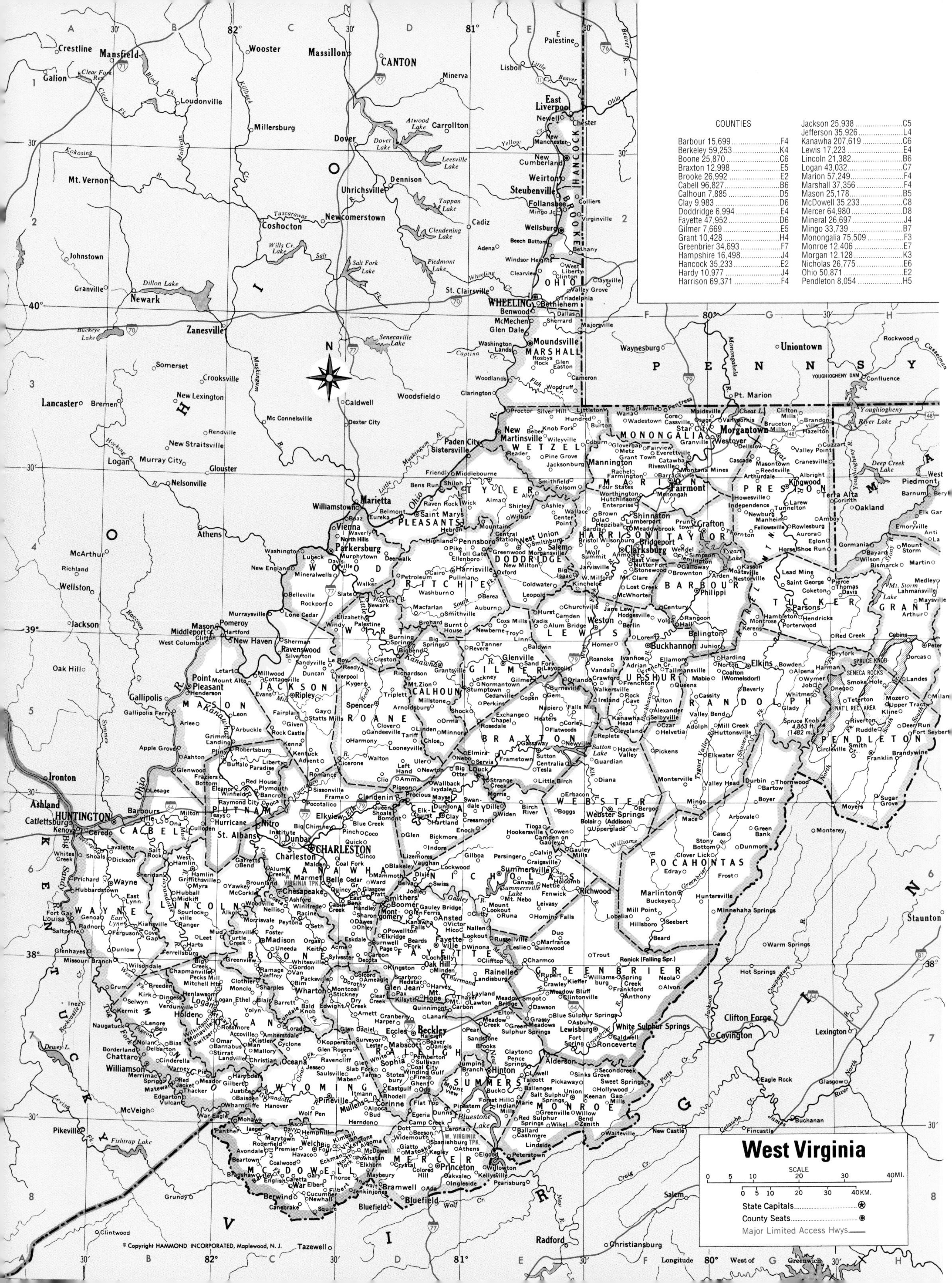

OHIO
PENNSYLVANIA
MARYLAND
VIRGINIA
KENTUCKY
CHARLESTON
HUNTINGTON
WHEELING
Parkersburg
Morgantown
Clarksburg
Fairmont
Beckley
Bluefield
Martinsburg
HANCOCK
BROOKE
OHIO
MARSHALL
WETZEL
MONONGALIA
MARION
PRESTON
TYLER
PLEASANTS
DODDRIDGE
HARRISON
TAYLOR
WOOD
RITCHIE
BARBOUR
TUCKER
GRANT
LEWIS
UPSHUR
RANDOLPH
PENDLETON
JACKSON
CALHOUN
GILMER
ROANE
BRAXTON
MASON
PUTNAM
KANAWHA
CLAY
WEBSTER
POCAHONTAS
NICHOLAS
CABELL
WAYNE
LINCOLN
BOONE
FAYETTE
GREENBRIER
LOGAN
MINGO
RALEIGH
SUMMERS
MONROE
WYOMING
MERCER
McDOWELL

COUNTIES

Barbour 15,699	F4	Jackson 25,938	C5
Berkeley 59,253	K4	Jefferson 35,926	L4
Boone 25,870	C6	Kanawha 207,619	C6
Braxton 12,998	E5	Lewis 17,223	E4
Brooke 26,992	E2	Lincoln 21,382	B6
Cabell 96,827	B6	Logan 43,032	C7
Calhoun 7,885	D5	Marion 57,249	F4
Clay 9,983	D6	Marshall 37,356	E4
Doddridge 6,994	E4	Mason 25,178	B5
Fayette 47,952	D6	McDowell 35,233	C8
Gilmer 7,669	E5	Mercer 64,980	D8
Grant 10,428	H4	Mineral 26,697	J4
Greenbrier 34,693	F7	Mingo 33,739	B7
Hampshire 16,498	J4	Monongalia 75,509	F3
Hancock 35,233	E2	Monroe 12,406	E7
Hardy 10,977	J4	Morgan 12,128	K3
Harrison 69,371	F4	Nicholas 26,775	E6
		Ohio 50,871	E2
		Pendleton 8,054	H5

West Virginia

SCALE
0 5 10 20 30 40 MI.
0 5 10 20 30 40 KM.

State Capitals
County Seats
Major Limited Access Hwys.

Pleasants 7,546 ... D4
Pocahontas 9,008 ... F6
Preston 29,037 ... G4
Putnam 42,835 ... C6
Raleigh 76,819 ... D7
Randolph 27,803 ... G5
Ritchie 10,233 ... D4
Roane 15,120 ... D5
Summers 14,204 ... E7
Taylor 15,144 ... F4
Tucker 7,728 ... F4
Tyler 9,796 ... E4
Upshur 22,867 ... F5
Wayne 41,636 ... B6
Webster 10,729 ... F6
Wetzel 19,258 ... E3
Wirt 5,192 ... D4
Wood 86,915 ... D4
Wyoming 28,990 ... C7

STATE OF WEST VIRGINIA

AREA 24,231 sq. mi. (62,758 sq. km.)
POPULATION 1,801,625
CAPITAL Charleston
LARGEST CITY Charleston
HIGHEST POINT Spruce Knob 4,863 ft. (1482 m.)
SETTLED IN 1774
ADMITTED TO UNION June 20, 1863
POPULAR NAME Mountain State
STATE FLOWER Big Rhododendron
STATE BIRD Cardinal

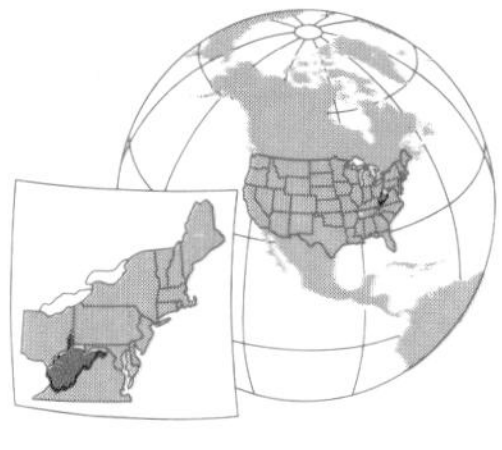

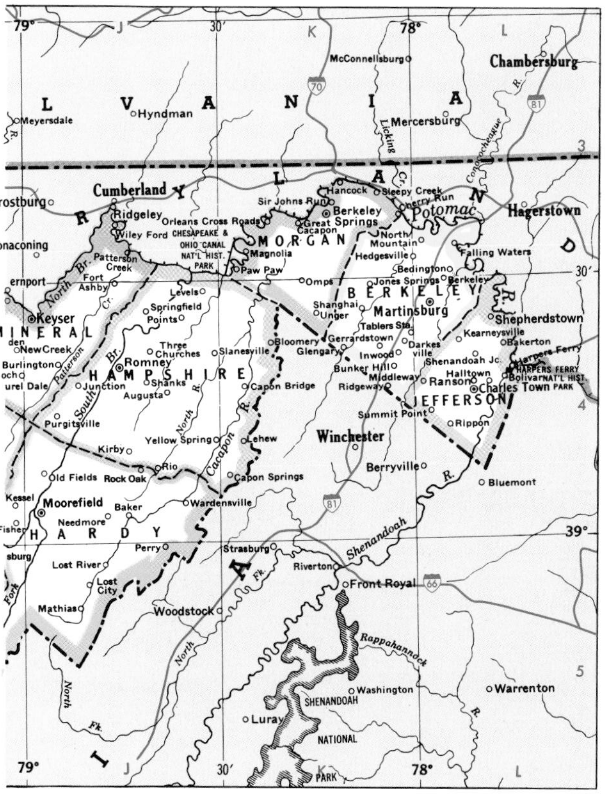
Chambersburg
McConnellsburg
Hyndman
Meyersdale
Mercersburg
Cumberland
Hancock
Hagerstown
Frostburg
Berkeley Springs
Potomac
Lonaconing
Keyser
Romney
Martinsburg
Shepherdstown
Harpers Ferry
Charles Town
Winchester
Berryville
Bluemont
Moorefield
Strasburg
Front Royal
Woodstock
Washington
Warrenton
Luray
SHENANDOAH NATIONAL PARK
MORGAN
BERKELEY
HAMPSHIRE
JEFFERSON
MINERAL
HARDY

Topography

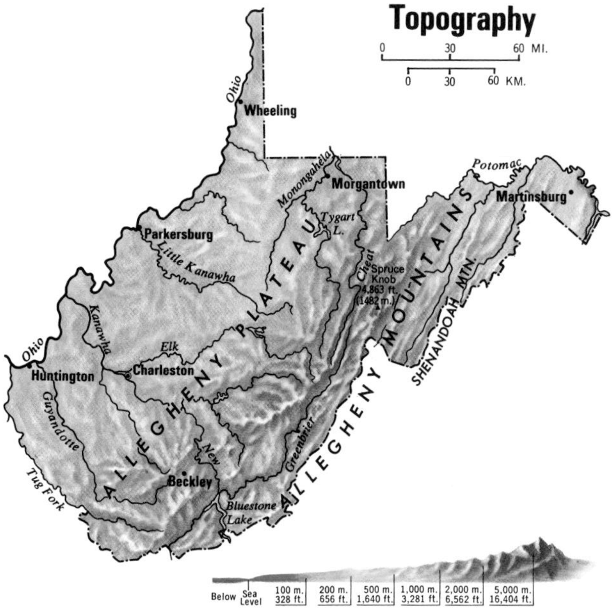
0 30 60 MI.
0 30 60 KM.
Ohio
Wheeling
Morgantown
Potomac
Martinsburg
Parkersburg
Little Kanawha
Tygart L.
Spruce Knob 4,863 ft. (1482 m.)
Cheat
ALLEGHENY PLATEAU
ALLEGHENY MOUNTAINS
SHENANDOAH MTN.
Kanawha
Elk
Charleston
Huntington
Guyandotte
New
Greenbrier
Beckley
Tug Fork
Bluestone Lake
Below Sea Level
100 m. 328 ft.
200 m. 656 ft.
500 m. 1,640 ft.
1,000 m. 3,281 ft.
2,000 m. 6,562 ft.
5,000 m. 16,404 ft.

CITIES and TOWNS

Accoville 975 ... C7
Acme 165 ... D6
Ada 250 ... D8
Addison▲ (Webster Springs) 674 ... F6
Adrian 510 ... F5
Albright 195 ... G3
Alderson 1,152 ... E7
Algoma 200 ... D8
Alkol 500 ... C6
Alma 197 ... E4
Alpoca 200 ... D7
Alum Bridge 150 ... F5
Alum Creek 1,602 ... C6
Alvy 150 ... E4
Ameagle 230 ... D7
Amherstdale 1,057 ... C7
Amma 200 ... D5
Anawalt 329 ... D8
Anmoore 686 ... F4
Ansted 1,643 ... D6
Apple Grove 900 ... B5
Arbovale 610 ... G6
Arden 130 ... G4
Arnett 300 ... D7
Arnoldsburg 175 ... D5
Arthur 350 ... H4
Arthurdale 1,063 ... G3
Asbury 280 ... E7
Asco 175 ... C8
Ashford 400 ... C6
Ashton 259 ... B5
Athens 741 ... E8
Auburn 89 ... E4
Augusta 750 ... J4
Aurora 250 ... G4
Avondale 250 ... C8
Baisden 500 ... C7
Baker 200 ... J4
Bakerton 125 ... L4
Bald Knob 356 ... C7
Ballard 220 ... E8
Ballengee 170 ... E7
Bancroft 381 ... C5
Barboursville 2,774 ... B6
Barnabus 750 ... C7
Barrackville 1,443 ... F3
Barrett 950 ... C7
Bartley 900 ... C8
Bartow 500 ... G5
Bayard 414 ... H4
Beards Fork 400 ... D6
Beartown 500 ... C8
Beaver (Glen Hedrick) 1,244 ... D7
Bebee 125 ... E3
Beckley▲ 18,296 ... D7
Bedington 150 ... L3
Beech Bottom 415 ... E2
Beeson 300 ... D8
Belington 1,850 ... F4
Belle 1,421 ... C6
Belmont 912 ... D4
Belva 275 ... D6
Benwood 1,669 ... E2
Bergoo 220 ... F6
Berkeley 600 ... L4
Berkeley Springs▲ 789 ... K3
Berwind 615 ... C8
Bethany 1,139 ... E2
Bethlehem 2,694 ... E2
Beverly 696 ... G5
Bickmore 300 ... D6
Big Chimney 450 ... C6
Big Creek 500 ... B7
Big Four 150 ... C8
Big Otter 150 ... D5
Big Springs 485 ... D5
Bim 500 ... C7
Birch River 650 ... E6
Blacksville 168 ... F3
Blair 800 ... C7
Bloomery 200 ... K4
Blue Creek 650 ... D6
Bluefield 12,756 ... D8
Boaz 1,137 ... D4
Boggs 131 ... E6
Bolair 450 ... F6
Bolivar 1,013 ... L4
Bomont 170 ... D6
Boomer 1,051 ... D6
Borderland 250 ... B7
Bowden 135 ... G5
Bradshaw 394 ... C8
Bramwell 620 ... D8
Brandonville 73 ... G3
Brandywine 300 ... H5
Breeden 600 ... B7
Bridgeport 6,739 ... F4
Brooks 196 ... E7
Brounland 900 ... C6
Brownton 400 ... F4
Bruceton Mills 132 ... G3
Buck 150 ... E7
Buckhannon▲ 5,909 ... F5
Bud 400 ... D7
Buffalo 969 ... C5
Bunker Hill 600 ... K4
Burlington 300 ... J4
Burning Springs 137 ... D5
Burnsville 495 ... E5
Burnt House 175 ... D4
Burnwell 140 ... D6
Burton 200 ... F3
Cabin Creek 900 ... C6
Cabins 300 ... H4
Cairo 290 ... D4
Caldwell 795 ... F7
Calvin 400 ... E6
Camden on Gauley 171 ... E6
Cameron 1,177 ... E3
Camp Creek 200 ... D7
Canebrake 300 ... C8
Canvas 300 ... E6
Capon Bridge 192 ... K4
Capon Springs 580 ... K4
Carbon 300 ... D6
Caretta 650 ... C8
Cass 148 ... G6
Cassity 150 ... F5
Cassville 1,458 ... F3
Catawba 186 ... F3
Cedar Grove 1,213 ... D6
Center Point 250 ... E4
Central Station 200 ... E4
Ceredo 1,916 ... F4
Chapmanville 1,110 ... B7
Charles Town▲ 3,122 ... L4
Charleston (cap.)▲ 57,287 ... C6
Charmco 800 ... E6
Chattaroy 1,182 ... B7
Chesapeake 1,896 ... C6
Chester 2,905 ... E1
Christian 200 ... C7
Cinco 500 ... D6
Circleville 180 ... H5
Clarksburg▲ 18,059 ... F4
Clay▲ 592 ... D6
Clear Creek 300 ... D7
Clearview 622 ... E2
Clendenin 1,203 ... D5
Clifton 325 ... B5
Clifton Mills 136 ... G3
Clifty 250 ... E6
Clinton 350 ... E2
Clintonville 250 ... E7
Clio 300 ... D5
Clothier 900 ... C7
Clover 350 ... D5
Clover Lick 250 ... F6
Coal City 1,876 ... D7
Coal Fork 2,100 ... D6
Coalton 277 ... G5
Coalwood 650 ... C8
Coburn 230 ... F3
Colcord 600 ... D7
Colliers 864 ... E2
Colored Hill 900 ... D8
Core 250 ... F3
Corinne 900 ... D7
Corinth 195 ... H4
Costa 250 ... C6
Cottageville 300 ... C5
Cove Gap 650 ... B6
Cowen 549 ... E6
Coxs Mills 275 ... E4
Craigsville 1,955 ... E6
Cranberry 315 ... D7
Crawley 395 ... E7
Crum 500 ... B7
Crystal 150 ... D8
Cucumber 274 ... C8
Culloden 2,907 ... B6
Cyclone 500 ... C7
Dallas 450 ... E2
Daniels 1,714 ... D7
Danville 595 ... C6
Darkesville 150 ... L4
Davis 799 ... H4
Davisville 200 ... C4
Davy 403 ... C8
Dawes 800 ... D6
Dawson 300 ... E7
Decota 800 ... D6
Deerwalk 150 ... D4
Delbarton 705 ... B7
Dellslow 300 ... G3
Diana 300 ... F5
Dickson 200 ... B6
Dille 300 ... E6
Dingess 600 ... B7
Dixie 985 ... D6
Dola 200 ... F4
Dorothy 400 ... D7
Dry Creek 441 ... D7
Dryfork 425 ... H5
Dunbar 8,697 ... C6
Dunlow 169 ... B6
Dunmore 280 ... G6
Durbin 278 ... G5
East Bank 892 ... D6
East Lynn 150 ... B6
East View 1,222 ... F4
Eastgulf 300 ... D7
Eccles 1,162 ... D7
Eckman 750 ... C8
Edgarton 415 ... B7
Edray 175 ... F6
Egeria 150 ... D7
Elbert 400 ... C8
Eleanor 1,256 ... C5
Elizabeth▲ 900 ... D4
Elk Garden 261 ... H4
Elkhorn 150 ... D8
Elkins▲ 7,420 ... G5
Elkridge 500 ... D6
Elkview 1,047 ... C6
Ellenboro 453 ... F5
Elton 200 ... E7
English 500 ... C8
Enterprise 1,058 ... F4
Erbacon 350 ... E6
Eskdale 400 ... D6
Ethel 450 ... C7
Evans 400 ... C5
Everettville 175 ... F3
Fairmont 20,210 ... F4
Fairplain 200 ... C5
Fairview 513 ... F3
Falling Spring (Renick) 191 ... F6
Falling Waters 130 ... L3
Farmington 414 ... F3
Fayetteville▲ 2,182 ... D6
Fenwick 500 ... E6
Ferguson 150 ... B6
Ferrellsburg 300 ... B6
Filbert 130 ... D8
Fireco 200 ... D7
Fisher 500 ... H4
Flat Top 550 ... D7
Flatwoods 324 ... E5
Flemington 352 ... F4
Follansbee 3,339 ... E2
Folsom 360 ... E4
Forest Hill 314 ... E7
Fort Ashby 1,288 ... J4
Fort Gay 852 ... A6
Fort Seybert 200 ... H5
Fort Spring 250 ... E7
Foster 500 ... C6
Four States 500 ... F4
Frametown 150 ... E5
Frankford 200 ... F7
Franklin▲ 914 ... H5
Fraziers Bottom 250 ... B5
French Creek 200 ... F5
Friendly 146 ... D3
Gallipolis Ferry 325 ... B5
Galloway 500 ... F4
Gandeeville 150 ... D5
Gap Mills 300 ... F7
Gary 1,355 ... C8
Gassaway 946 ... E5
Gauley Bridge 691 ... D6
Gauley Mills 165 ... E6
Gay 300 ... C5
Gerrardstown 240 ... K4
Ghent 500 ... D7
Giatto 400 ... D8
Gilbert 456 ... C7
Gilboa 500 ... E6
Glady 175 ... G5
Glasgow 906 ... D6
Glen 175 ... D6
Glen Dale 1,612 ... E3
Glen Daniel 300 ... D7
Glen Ferris 200 ... D6
Glen Hedrick (Beaver) ... B7
Glen Jean ... D7
Glen Rogers 500 ... D7
Glen White 300 ... D7
Glengary 250 ... K4
Glenhayes 175 ... A6
Glenville▲ 1,923 ... E5
Glenwood 400 ... B5
Gordon 300 ... C7
Grafton▲ 5,524 ... G4
Grant Town 694 ... F3
Grantsville▲ 671 ... D5
Granville 798 ... F3
Great Cacapon 750 ... K3
Green Bank 115 ... G6
Green Sulphur Springs 225 ... E7
Greenview 250 ... C6
Greenwood 750 ... E4
Griffithsville 300 ... B6
Grimms Landing 350 ... B5
Guardian 175 ... F5
Hacker Valley 440 ... F5
Halltown 375 ... L4
Hambleton 265 ... G4
Hamlin▲ 1,030 ... B6
Hampden 300 ... C7
Hancock 175 ... K3
Handley 334 ... D6
Hanover 300 ... C7
Harman 128 ... G5

(continued on following page)

Agriculture, Industry and Resources

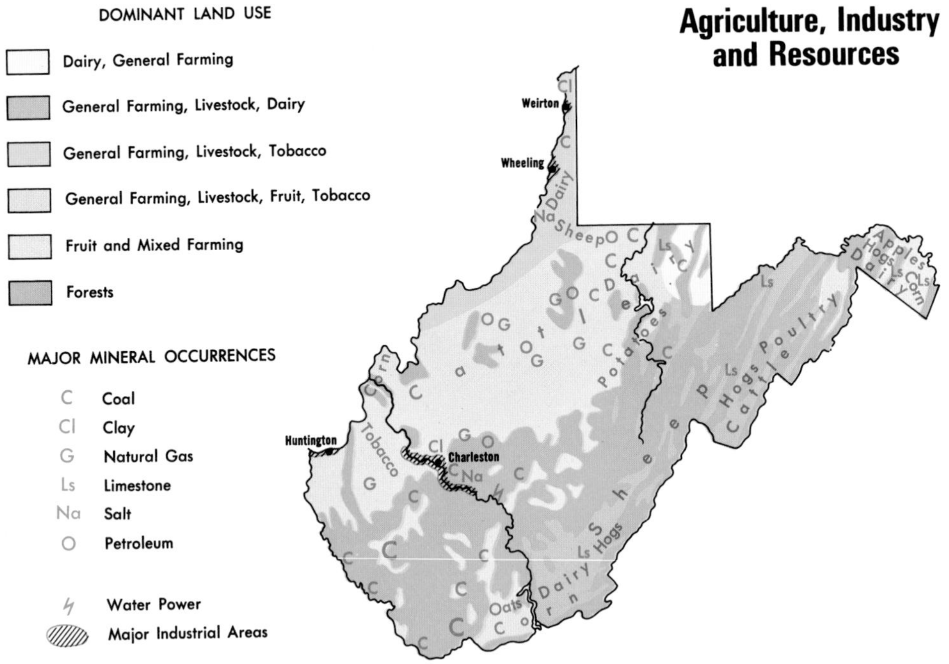
DOMINANT LAND USE
Dairy, General Farming
General Farming, Livestock, Dairy
General Farming, Livestock, Tobacco
General Farming, Livestock, Fruit, Tobacco
Fruit and Mixed Farming
Forests
MAJOR MINERAL OCCURRENCES
C Coal
Cl Clay
G Natural Gas
Ls Limestone
Na Salt
O Petroleum
Water Power
Major Industrial Areas
Weirton
Wheeling
Huntington
Charleston
Dairy
Sheep
Tobacco
Corn
Potatoes
Apples
Hogs
Poultry
Cattle
Oats

Harmony 600 ... D5
Harper 400 ... D7
Harpers Ferry 308 ... L4
Harrisville▲ 1,839 ... E4
Hartford 487 ... C4
Harts 2,332 ... B6
Harvey 300 ... D7
Havaco 350 ... C8
Heaters 440 ... E5
Hedgesville 227 ... K3
Helvetia 130 ... F5
Hemphill 700 ... C8
Henderson 549 ... B5
Hendricks 303 ... G4
Henlawson 900 ... B7
Hepzibah 600 ... F4
Herndon 500 ... D7
Hico 750 ... D6
Hillsboro 188 ... F6
Hinton▲ 3,433 ... E7
Hodgesville 200 ... F4
Holcomb 200 ... E6
Holden 1,246 ... B7
Hollywood 150 ... F7
Hominy Falls 175 ... E6
Hookersville 250 ... E6
Horse Shoe Run 500 ... G4
Howesville 600 ... G4
Hubball 145 ... B6
Hundred 386 ... E3
Huntington▲ 54,844 ... A6
Hurricane 4,461 ... C6
Hutchinson 285 ... F4
Huttonsville 211 ... G5
Iaeger 551 ... C8
Independence 200 ... G4
Indian Mills 150 ... E7
Indore 300 ... D6
Inwood 1,360 ... K4
Itmann 600 ... D7
Ivanhoe 200 ... F5
Ivydale 800 ... D5
Jacksonburg 400 ... E3
Jane Lew 439 ... F4
Jarvisville 250 ... F4
Jeffrey 900 ... C7
Jenkinjones 750 ... D8
Jesse 400 ... C7
Jodie 440 ... D6
Jumping Branch 700 ... E7
Junior 542 ... G5
Justice 600 ... C7
Kearneysville 250 ... L4
Kegley 900 ... D8
Keith 175 ... C6
Kellysville 165 ... E8
Kenna 150 ... C5
Kenova 3,748 ... A6
Kentuck 200 ... C5
Kermit 342 ... B7
Keyser▲ 5,870 ... J4
Keystone 627 ... D8
Kieffer 135 ... E7
Kilsyth 200 ... D7
Kimball 550 ... C8
Kingston 189 ... D7
Kingwood▲ 3,243 ... G4
Kirk 400 ... B7
Kistler 200 ... C7
Kopperston 700 ... C7
Lahmansville 200 ... H4
Lanark 559 ... D7
Landisburg 250 ... E7
Landville 400 ... C7
Lavalette 600 ... B6
Layland 500 ... E7
Layopolis (Sand Fork) ... E5
Leet 175 ... B6
Left Hand 700 ... D5
Leivasy 200 ... E6
Lenore 800 ... B7
Leon 145 ... C5
Lerona 550 ... D8
Lesage 600 ... B5
Leslie 350 ... E6
Lester 420 ... D7
Letart 350 ... C5
Levels 180 ... J4
Lewisburg▲ 3,598 ... E7
Liberty 150 ... C5
Lindside 225 ... E8
Linn 165 ... E4
Little Birch 400 ... E5
Littleton 198 ... F3
Lizemores 400 ... D6
Lochgelly 250 ... D6
Lockney 190 ... E5
Lockwood 300 ... D6
Logan▲ 2,206 ... B7
Lookout 200 ... E6
Lorado 400 ... C7
Lorentz 200 ... F4
Lost City 130 ... J5
Lost Creek 413 ... F4
Lost River 500 ... J5
Lowell 140 ... E7
Lubeck 1,579 ... C4
Lumberport 1,014 ... F4
Lundale 525 ... C7
Maben 450 ... D7
Mabie 550 ... F5
Mabscott 1,543 ... D7
Macfarlan 436 ... D4
Madison▲ 3,051 ... C6
Maidsville 500 ... F3
Malden 900 ... C6
Mallory 1,126 ... C7
Mammoth 563 ... D6
Man 914 ... C7
Mannington 2,184 ... F3
Marfrance 225 ... E6
Marlinton▲ 1,148 ... F6
Marmet 1,879 ... C6
Martinsburg▲ 14,073 ... K4
Mason 1,053 ... B4
Masontown 737 ... G3
Matewan 619 ... B7
Matoaka 366 ... D8
Maybeury 300 ... D8
Maysel 350 ... D5
Maysville 150 ... H4
McCorkle 300 ... C6
McDowell 500 ... D8
McMechen 2,130 ... E3
McWhorter 150 ... F4
Meador 225 ... B7
Meadow Bridge 325 ... E7
Meadow Creek 300 ... E7
Meadowbrook 500 ... F4
Merrimac 140 ... B7
Metz 150 ... F3
Middlebourne▲ 922 ... E3
Middleway 350 ... K4
Midkiff 650 ... B6
Mill Creek 685 ... G5
Mill Point 148 ... F6
Millstone 850 ... D5
Millwood 800 ... C5
Milton 2,242 ... B6
Minden 800 ... D7
Mineralwells 1,698 ... C4
Mingo 350 ... F5
Minnora 500 ... D5
Missouri Branch 250 ... A7
Mitchell Heights 265 ... B7
Moatsville 150 ... G4
Monaville 950 ... B7
Monclo 242 ... C7
Monomgah 1,132 ... F4
Montana Mines 200 ... F3
Montcoal 150 ... D7
Monterville 250 ... F5
Montgomery 2,449 ... D6
Montrose 140 ... G4
Moorefield▲ 2,148 ... J4
Morgansville 164 ... E4
Morgantown▲ 25,879 ... F3
Morrisvale 450 ... C6
Moundsville▲ 10,753 ... E3
Mount Alto 200 ... C5
Mount Carbon 450 ... D7
Mount Clare 950 ... F4
Mount Gay 4,366 ... C7
Mount Hope 1,573 ... D7
Mount Lookout 500 ... E6
Mount Nebo 535 ... E6
Mount Storm 500 ... H4
Mount Zion 350 ... D5
Mountain 200 ... E4
Mud 143 ... C6
Mullens 2,006 ... D7
Murphytown 600 ... D4
Nallen 250 ... E6
Napier 158 ... E5
Naugatuck 500 ... B7
Nebo 200 ... D5
Nellis 600 ... C6
Neola 300 ... F7
Nettie 500 ... E6
New Cumberland▲ 1,363 ... E2
New England 335 ... C4
New Haven 1,632 ... C5
New Manchester 800 ... E1
New Martinsville▲ 6,705 ... E3
Newburg 378 ... G4
Newell 1,724 ... E1
Newhall 400 ... C8
Newton 390 ... D5
Newville 160 ... E5
Nitro 6,851 ... C6
Nolan 250 ... B7
North Hills 849 ... D4
Northfork 656 ... D8
Norton 400 ... G5
Nutter Fort 1,819 ... F4
Oak Hill 6,812 ... D6
Oakvale 165 ... D8
Oceana 1,791 ... C7
Odd 500 ... D7
Ohley 450 ... D6
Omar 900 ... C7
Ona 200 ... B6
Onego 400 ... H5
Orgas 500 ... C6
Orlando 700 ... E5
Orleans Cross Roads 150 ... K3
Orma ... D5
Osage 183 ... F3
Packsville 225 ... C7
Paden City 2,862 ... D3
Page 600 ... D6
Panther 450 ... C8
Parkersburg▲ 33,862 ... D4
Parsons▲ 1,453 ... G4
Patterson Creek 157 ... J3
Paw Paw 538 ... K3
Pax 167 ... D7
Pecks Mill 350 ... B7
Pemberton 300 ... D7
Pence Springs 300 ... E7
Pennsboro 1,282 ... E4
Pentress 250 ... F3
Petersburg▲ 2,360 ... H5
Peterstown 550 ... E8
Peytona 175 ... C6
Philippi▲ 3,132 ... G4
Pickaway 225 ... E7
Pickens 240 ... F5
Pie 250 ... B7
Piedmont 1,094 ... H4
Pinch 2,695 ... D6
Pine Grove 701 ... E3
Pineville▲ 865 ... C7
Pliny 900 ... B5
Poca 1,124 ... C6
Pocotalico 2,420 ... C6
Point Pleasant▲ 4,996 ... B5
Points 250 ... J4
Powellton 1,905 ... D6
Powhatan 400 ... D8
Pratt 640 ... D6
Premier 400 ... C8
Prichard 500 ... A6
Princeton▲ 7,043 ... D8
Procious 600 ... D5
Proctor 350 ... E3
Pruntytown 145 ... F4
Pullman 109 ... D4
Purgitsville 450 ... J4
Quick 400 ... D6
Quincy 150 ... C6
Quinwood 559 ... E6
Rachel 550 ... F3
Racine 725 ... C6
Radnor 300 ... A6
Rainelle 1,681 ... E7
Raleigh 900 ... D7
Ramage 350 ... C7
Ranger 300 ... B6
Ranson 2,890 ... L4
Ravencliff 350 ... C7
Ravenswood 4,189 ... C5
Raymond City 400 ... C6
Reader 950 ... E3
Red House 600 ... C5
Red Jacket 760 ... B7
Redstar 200 ... D7
Reedsville 482 ... G3
Reedy 271 ... D5
Renick ... F6
Replete 200 ... F5
Rhodell 221 ... D7
Richwood 2,808 ... F6
Ridgeley 779 ... J3
Ridgeway 200 ... K4
Rio 140 ... J4
Ripley▲ 3,023 ... C5
Rippon 500 ... L4
Rivesville 1,064 ... F3
Robertsburg 140 ... C5
Rock Cave 400 ... F5
Roderfield 900 ... C8
Romney▲ 1,966 ... J4
Ronceverte 1,754 ... F7
Rosedale 400 ... E5
Rossmore 200 ... C7
Rowlesburg 648 ... G4
Runa 150 ... E6
Rupert 1,104 ... E7
Russellville 280 ... E6
Saint Albans 11,194 ... C6
Saint George 150 ... F4
Saint Marys▲ 2,148 ... D4
Salem 2,063 ... E4
Salt Rock 350 ... B6
Sand Fork 196 ... E5
Sandstone 300 ... E7
Sandyville 500 ... C5
Saulsville 250 ... C7
Scarbo 800 ... D7
Selwyn 500 ... B7
Seth 950 ... C6
Shanghai 200 ... K4
Shanks 500 ... J4
Sharon 450 ... D6
Sharples 250 ... C7
Shenandoah Junction 600 ... L4
Shepherdstown 1,287 ... L4
Sheridan 160 ... B6
Sherrard 400 ... E3
Shinnston 2,543 ... F4
Shirley 275 ... E4
Shoals 150 ... B6
Shock 200 ... D5
Silverton 250 ... C5
Simpson 250 ... F4
Sinks Grove 156 ... F7
Sissonville 4,290 ... C5
Sistersville 1,797 ... D3
Slab Fork 210 ... D7
Slaneville 250 ... K4
Smithburg 130 ... E4
Smithers 1,162 ... D6
Smithfield 205 ... E4
Smithville 200 ... D4
Smoot 300 ... E7
Sophia 1,182 ... D7
South Charleston 13,645 ... C6
Spanishburg 550 ... D8
Spencer▲ 2,279 ... D5
Sprigg 225 ... B7
Springfield 250 ... J4
Spurlockville 250 ... B6
Squire 900 ... C8
Star City 1,251 ... F3
Statts Mills 400 ... C5
Stickney 150 ... D7
Stirrat 250 ... C7
Stonewood 1,996 ... F4
Stotesbury 199 ... D7
Strange Creek 175 ... E5
Sullivan 700 ... D7
Summersville▲ 2,906 ... E6
Summit Point 455 ... K4
Surveyor 300 ... D7
Sutton▲ 939 ... E5
Swiss 500 ... D6
Switzer 1,004 ... B7
Sylvester 191 ... C6
Talcott 800 ... E7
Tallmansville 140 ... F5
Tanner 375 ... E5
Teays 200 ... B6
Terra Alta 1,713 ... H4
Tesla 300 ... E5
Thacker 525 ... B7
Thomas 573 ... H4
Thornton 200 ... G4
Thorpe 600 ... D8
Three Churches 350 ... J4
Thurmond 39 ... D7
Tioga 825 ... E6
Triadelphia 835 ... E2
Troy 110 ... E4
Tunnelton 331 ... G4
Turtle Creek 566 ... C6
Uneeda 700 ... C6
Unger 300 ... K4
Union▲ 566 ... E7
Upper Tract 155 ... H5
Upperglade 750 ... F6
Vadis 130 ... E4
Valley Bend 950 ... F5
Valley Grove 569 ... E2
Valley Head 900 ... G5
Van 800 ... C7
Varney 750 ... B7
Vaughan 375 ... D6
Verdunville 950 ... B7
Victor 500 ... D6
Vienna 10,862 ... D4
Vivian 500 ... D8
Vulcan 130 ... B7
Wadestown 300 ... F3
Waiteville 230 ... F8
Walkersville 135 ... F5
Wallace 325 ... E4
Wallback 150 ... D5
Walton 550 ... D5
Wana 150 ... F3
War 1,081 ... C8
Ward 850 ... D6
Wardensville 140 ... J4
Washington 1,030 ... C4
Washington Lands 400 ... E3
Waverly 500 ... D4
Wayne▲ 1,128 ... B6
Webster Springs▲ 674 ... F6
Weirton 22,124 ... E2
Welch▲ 3,028 ... C8
Wellsburg▲ 3,385 ... E2
West Columbia 245 ... B5
West Hamlin 423 ... B6
West Liberty 1,434 ... E2
West Logan 524 ... C7
West Milford 519 ... F4
West Union▲ 830 ... E4
Weston▲ 4,994 ... F4
Westover 4,201 ... G3
Wharncliffe 900 ... C7
Wharton 450 ... C7
Wheeling▲ 34,882 ... E2
White Sulphur Springs 2,779 ... F7
Whites Creek 500 ... A6
Whitesville 486 ... C6
Whitmer 400 ... G5
Widen 230 ... E6
Wiley Ford 1,224 ... J3
Wileyville 175 ... E3
Wilkinson 975 ... B7
Williamsburg 350 ... F7
Williamson▲ 4,154 ... B7
Williamstown 2,774 ... C4
Wilsonburg 350 ... F4
Wilsondale 250 ... B7
Windsor Heights 800 ... E2
Winfield▲ 1,164 ... C5
Winifrede 750 ... C6
Winona 250 ... E6
Wolf Pen 175 ... C7
Wolf Summit 750 ... F4
Womelsdorf (Coalton) 277 ... G5
Woodlands 200 ... E3
Woodville 300 ... C6
Worthington 233 ... F4
Yawkey 985 ... C6
Yellow Spring 280 ... J4
Yolyn 400 ... C7

OTHER FEATURES

Big Sandy (riv.) ... A6
Bluestone (lake) ... E7
Buckhannon (riv.) ... F5
Cacapon (riv.) ... J4
Cheat (riv.) ... G3
Cherry (riv.) ... E6
Chesapeake and Ohio Canal Nat'l Hist. Park ... J3
Clear Fork, Guyandotte (riv.) ... C7
Coal (riv.) ... C6
Dry Fork (riv.) ... C8
Dry Fork (riv.) ... G5
East Lynn (lake) ... B6
Elk (riv.) ... D6
Fish (creek) ... E3
Gauley (riv.) ... D6
Greenbrier (riv.) ... F6
Guyandotte (riv.) ... B6
Harpers Ferry Nat'l Hist. Park ... L4
Hughes (riv.) ... D4
Kanawha (riv.) ... C5
Little Kanawha (riv.) ... D5
Meadow (riv.) ... E6
Mill (creek) ... C5
Monongahela (riv.) ... G3
Mount Storm (lake) ... H4
Mud (riv.) ... B6
New (riv.) ... E7
North (riv.) ... J4
Ohio (riv.) ... B5
Patterson (creek) ... J4
Pigeon (creek) ... B7
Pocatalico (riv.) ... C5
Pond Fork (riv.) ... C6
Potomac (riv.) ... L3
Potts (creek) ... F7
Reedy (creek) ... D5
Shavers Fork (riv.) ... G5
Shenandoah (riv.) ... K4
Spruce Knob (mt.) ... G5
Spruce Knob-Seneca Rocks Nat'l Rec. Area ... H5
Stony (riv.) ... H4
Summersville (lake) ... E6
Sutton (lake) ... F5
Tug Fork (riv.) ... B7
Twelvepole (creek) ... A6
Tygart (lake) ... G4
Tygart Valley (riv.) ... F5
West Fork (riv.) ... E5
Williams (riv.) ... F6

▲County seat

WISCONSIN
1848

AREA 56.153 sq. mi. (145,436 sq. km.)
POPULATION 4,906,745
CAPITAL Madison
LARGEST CITY Milwaukee
HIGHEST POINT Timms Hill 1,951 ft. (595 m.)
SETTLED IN 1670
ADMITTED TO UNION May 29, 1848
POPULAR NAME Badger State
STATE FLOWER Wood Violet
STATE BIRD Robin

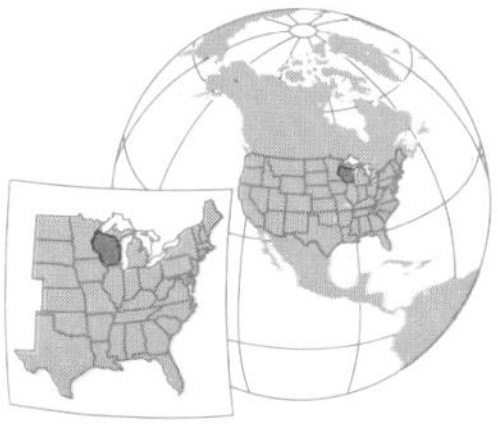

COUNTIES

Adams 15,682 G7
Ashland 16,307 E3
Barron 40,750 C5
Bayfield 14,008 D3
Brown 194,594 L7
Buffalo 13,584 C7
Burnett 13,084 B4
Calumet 34,291 K7
Chippewa 52,360 D5
Clark 31,647 E6
Columbia 45,088 H9
Crawford 15,940 E9
Dane 367,085 H9
Dodge 76,559 J9
Door 25,690 M6
Douglas 41,758 C3
Dunn 35,909 C6
Eau Claire 85,183 D6
Florence 4,590 K4
Fond du Lac 90,083 K8
Forest 8,776 J4
Grant 49,264 E10
Green 30,339 G10
Green Lake 18,651 H8
Iowa 20,150 F9
Iron 6,153 F9
Jackson 16,588 F3
Jefferson 67,783 J9
Juneau 21,650 F8
Kenosha 128,181 K10
Kewaunee 18,878 L6
La Crosse 97,904 D8
Lafayette 16,076 F10
Langlade 19,505 H5
Lincoln 26,993 G5
Manitowoc 80,421 L7
Marathon 115,400 G6
Marinette 40,548 K5
Marquette 12,321 H8
Menominee 3,890 J5
Milwaukee 959,275 L9
Monroe 36,633 E8
Oconto 30,226 K6
Oneida 31,679 G4
Outagamie 140,510 K7
Ozaukee 72,831 L9
Pepin 7,107 C6
Pierce 32,765 B6
Polk 34,773 B5
Portage 61,405 G6
Price 15,600 F4
Racine 175,034 K10
Richland 17,521 F9
Rock 139,510 H10
Rusk 15,079 D5
Saint Croix 43,262 B5
Sauk 46,975 G9
Sawyer 14,181 D4
Shawano 37,157 J6
Sheboygan 103,877 L8
Taylor 18,901 E5
Trempealeau 25,263 D7
Vernon 25,617 E8
Vilas 17,707 G3
Walworth 75,000 J10
Washburn 13,772 C4
Washington 95,328 K9
Waukesha 304,715 K9
Waupaca 46,104 J6
Waushara 19,385 H7
Winnebago 140,320 J8
Wood 73,605 F7

CITIES and TOWNS

Abbotsford 1,916 F6
Abrams 300 L6
Adams 1,715 G8
Adell 510 L8
Afton 225 H10
Albany 1,140 G10
Albion 300 H10
Algoma 3,353 M6
Allenton 915 K9
Allouez 14,431 L7
Alma Center 416 E7
Alma▲ 790 C7
Almena 625 B5
Almond 455 G7
Alto 235 J8
Altoona 5,889 C6
Alvin 160 J4
Amberg 875 K5
Amery 2,657 B5
Amherst 792 H7
Amherst Junction 269 H7
Angelica 200 K6
Angelo 100 E3
Aniwa 249 H6
Antigo▲ 8,276 H5
Appleton▲ 65,695 J7
Arbor Vitae 900 G4
Arcadia 2,166 D7
Arena 525 G9
Argonne 600 G9
Argyle 798 G10
Arkansaw 400 B6
Arlington 440 H9
Armstrong Creek 615 K4
Arpin 312 G6
Ashippun 750 H1
Ashland▲ 8,695 E2
Ashwaubenon 16,376 K7
Athens 951 G5
Auburndale 665 F6
Augusta 1,510 D6
Auroraville 250 H7
Avoca 474 F9
Avon 120 H10
Babcock 250 F7
Bagley 306 D10
Baileys Harbor 250 M5
Baldwin 2,022 B6
Balsam Lake▲ 792 B5
Bancroft 355 G7
Bangor 1,076 E8
Baraboo▲ 9,203 G9
Barnes 225 D3
Barneveld 660 F10
Barron▲ 2,986 C5
Barronett 575 B4
Batavia 125 K8
Bay City 578 B6
Bayfield 686 E2
Bayside 4,789 M1
Bear Creek 418 J6
Beaver 100 K5
Beaver Dam 14,196 J9
Beetown 150 E10
Beldenville 175 A6
Belgium 928 L8
Bell Center 127 E9
Belleville 1,456 G10
Belmont 823 F10
Beloit 35,573 H10
Bennett 350 C3
Benton 898 F10
Berlin 5,371 H8
Bethel 210 F6
Bevent 200 H6
Big Bend 1,299 K2
Birchwood 443 C4
Birnamwood 693 H6
Biron 794 G7
Black Creek 1,152 K7
Black Earth 1,248 G9
Black River Falls▲ 3,490 E7
Blackwell 550 K4
Blair 1,126 D7
Blanchardville 802 G10
Bloom City 167 E8
Bloomer 3,085 D5
Bloomington 776 E10
Blue Mounds 446 G9
Blue River 438 E9
Boardman 100 A5
Boaz 131 E9
Bohners Lake 1,553 K10
Bonduel 1,210 K6
Boscobel 2,706 E9
Boulder Junction 780 G3
Bowler 279 J6
Boyceville 913 C5
Boyd 683 E6
Brackett 150 D6
Bradley 100 G4
Branch 300 L7
Brandon 872 J8
Brantwood 500 F4
Bridgeport 250 D9
Briggsville 250 H8
Brighton 100 K3
Brill 200 C4
Brillion 2,840 L7
Brodhead 3,165 G10
Brokaw 224 G5
Brookfield 35,184 K1
Brooklyn 789 H10
Brooks 103 G8
Brothertown 100 K7
Brown Deer 12,236 L1
Brown's Lake 1,725 K3
Brownsville 415 J8
Browntown 256 G10
Bruce 844 D5
Brule 335 C2
Brussels 500 L6
Buffalo 915 C7
Burlington 8,855 K10
Burnett 260 J9
Butler 2,079 K1
Butte Des Morts J7
Butternut 416 E3
Cable 227 D3
Cadott 1,328 D6
Caldwell 101 J2
Caledonia 100 L2
Cambria 768 H8
Cambridge 963 H9
Cameron 1,273 C5
Camp Douglas 512 F8
Camp Lake 2,291 K10
Campbellsport 1,732 K8
Canton 100 C5
Caroline 450 J6
Carter 100 J5
Cascade 620 K8
Casco 544 L6
Cashton 780 E8
Cassville 1,144 E10
Cataract 200 E7
Catawba 178 E4
Cazenovia 288 F8
Cecil 373 K6
Cedar Grove 1,521 L8
Cedarburg 9,895 L9
Centuria 790 A5
Chaseburg 365 D8
Chelsea 120 F5
Chenequa 601 J1
Chetek 1,953 C5
Chili 185 F6
Chilton▲ 3,240 K7
Chippewa Falls▲ 12,727 D6
City Point 110 F7
Clam Lake 140 E3
Clayton 450 B5
Clear Lake 932 B5
Clearwater Lake 200 H4
Cleveland 1,398 L8
Clinton 1,849 J10
Clintonville 4,351 J6
Clyman 370 J9
Cobb 440 F10
Cochrane 475 C7
Colby 1,532 F6
Coleman 839 L5
Colfax 1,110 C6
Coloma 383 H7
Columbus 4,093 H9
Combined Locks 2,190 K7
Commonwealth 240 K4
Como 1,353 K10
Comstock 160 C5
Concord 200 H1
Conover 480 H3
Conrath 92 E5
Coon Valley 817 E8
Cornell 1,541 D5
Cornucopia 250 D2
Couderay 92 D4
Crandon▲ 1,958 H4
Cream 120 C7
Crivitz 996 L5
Cross Plains 2,098 G9
Cuba City 2,024 F10
Cudahy 18,659 M2
Cumberland 2,163 C4
Curtiss 173 F6
Cushing 150 A4
Cylon 100 B5
Dale 410 J7
Dallas 452 C5
Dalton 300 H8
Danbury 350 B3
Dane 621 G9
Darien 1,158 J10
Darlington▲ 2,235 F10
De Forest 4,882 H9
De Pere 16,569 K7
De Soto 326 D9
Deer Park 237 B5
Deerfield 1,617 H9
Delafield 5,347 J1
Delavan 6,073 J10
Delavan Lake 2,177 J10
Dellwood 120 G7
Denmark 1,612 L7
Dexterville 100 F7
Diamond Bluff 100 A6
Dickeyville 862 E10
Dodge 185 D7
Dodgeville▲ 3,882 F10
Dorchester 697 F5
Dousman 1,277 J1
Downing 250 B5
Downsville 200 C6
Doylestown 316 H9
Draper 125 E4
Dresser 614 A5
Drummond 200 D3
Dunbar 106 K4
Durand▲ 2,003 C6
Dyckesville 300 L6
Eagle 1,182 H2
Eagle River▲ 1,374 H4
East Troy 2,664 J2
Eastman 369 D9
Easton 130 G8
Eau Claire▲ 56,856 D6
Eden 610 K8
Edgar 1,318 G6
Edgerton 4,254 H10
Egg Harbor 183 M5
Eland 247 H6
Elcho 500 H5
Elderon 175 H6
Eldorado 200 J8
Eleva 491 D6
Elk Mound 765 C6
Elkhart Lake 1,019 L8
Elkhorn▲ 5,337 J10
Ellison Bay 112 M5
Ellsworth▲ 2,706 A6
Elm Grove 6,261 K1
Elmwood 775 B6
Elmwood Park 534 M3
Elroy 1,533 F8
Elton 150 J5
Embarrass 461 J6
Emerald 128 B5
Endeavor 316 G8
Ephraim 261 M5
Ettrick 461 D7
Evansville 3,174 H10
Exeland 180 D4
Fair Water 310 J8
Fairchild 504 D6
Fall Creek 1,034 D6
Fall River 842 H9
Fence 200 K4
Fennimore 2,378 E9
Fenwood 214 F6
Ferryville 154 D9
Fifield 310 F4
Fish Creek 119 M5
Florence▲ 780 K4
Fond du Lac▲ 37,757 K8
Fontana 1,635 J10
Footville 764 H10
Forest Junction 140 K7
Forestville 470 L6
Fort Atkinson 10,227 J10
Fountain City 938 C7
Fox Lake 1,269 J8
Fox Point 7,238 M1
Foxboro 360 B2
Francis Creek 562 L7
Franklin 21,855 L2
Franksville 375 M3
Frederic 1,124 B4
Fredonia 1,558 L8
Fremont 632 J7
Friendship▲ 728 G8
Friesland 271 H8
Galesville 1,278 D7
Galloway 200 H6
Gays Mills 578 E9
Genesee 375 J2
Genesee Depot 350 J2
Genoa 266 D8
Genoa City 1,277 K11
Germantown 13,658 K1
Gibbsville 408 L8
Gillett 1,303 K6
Gilman 412 E5
Gilmanton 300 C7
Gleason 200 G5
Glen Flora 108 E4
Glen Haven 160 E10
Glenbeulah 386 L8
Glendale 14,088 M1
Glenwood City 1,026 B5
Glidden 940 E3
Goodman 875 K4
Gordon 600 C3
Gotham 250 F9
Grafton 9,340 L9
Grand Marsh 725 G8
Grand View 447 D3
Granton 379 E6
Grantsburg▲ 1,144 A4
Gratiot 207 F10
Green Bay▲ 96,466 K6
Green Lake▲ 1,064 H8
Green Valley 104 K6
Greendale 15,128 L2
Greenfield 33,403 L2
Greenleaf 300 L7
Greenville 900 J7
Greenwood 969 E6
Gresham 515 J6
Gurney 145 F3
Hager City 110 A6
Hales Corners 7,623 K2
Hallie D6
Hamburg 170 G5
Hammond 1,097 A6
Hancock 382 G7
Hartford 8,188 K9
Hartland 6,906 J1
Hatfield 500 E7

(continued on following page)

Agriculture, Industry and Resources

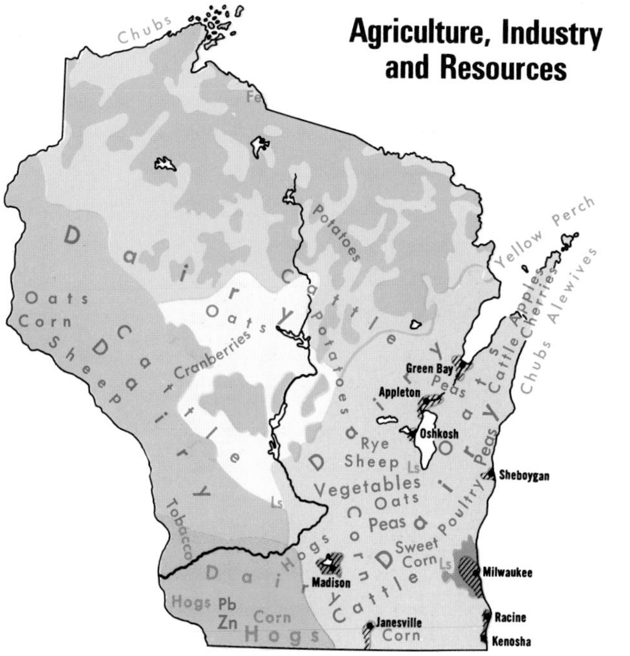
Chubs
Fe
Potatoes
Yellow Perch
Alewives
Apples
Cherries
Chubs
Cattle
Oats
Corn
Sheep
Cranberries
Potatoes
Green Bay
Appleton
Peas
Oshkosh
Rye
Sheep
Ls
Sheboygan
Vegetables
Oats
Peas
Poultry
Tobacco
Hogs
Sweet Corn
Milwaukee
Madison
Hogs Pb
Zn
Corn
Hogs
Janesville
Corn
Racine
Kenosha

DOMINANT LAND USE

Specialized Dairy
Dairy, Hay, Potatoes
Dairy, General Farming
Hogs, Dairy
Dairy, Livestock
Forests
Urban Areas

MAJOR MINERAL OCCURRENCES

Fe Iron Ore
Pb Lead
Ls Limestone
Zn Zinc

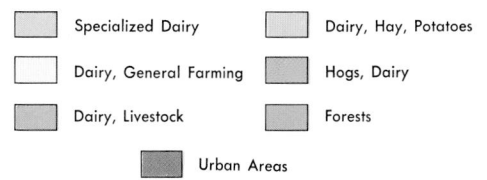

Major Industrial Areas

Hatley 295 ..... H6
Haugen 305 ..... C4
Hawkins 375 ..... E4
Hawthorne 200 ..... C3
Hayward▲ 1,897 ..... D3
Hazel Green 1,171 ..... F11
Hazelhurst 630 ..... G4
Heafford Junction 110 ..... G4
Hebron 450 ..... J10
Helenville 300 ..... J10
Hersey 125 ..... B6
Hewitt 595 ..... F6
High Bridge 525 ..... E3
Highland 799 ..... F9
Hilbert 1,211 ..... K7
Hiles 350 ..... J4
Hillsboro 1,288 ..... F8
Hillsdale 160 ..... C5
Hingham 250 ..... K8
Hixton 345 ..... E7
Holcombe 200 ..... D5
Hollandale 256 ..... G10
Holmen 3,220 ..... D8
Holy Cross 150 ..... L9
Honey Creek 300 ..... J3
Horicon 3,873 ..... J9
Hortonville 2,029 ..... J7
Houlton 915 ..... A5
Howard 9,874 ..... K6
Howards Grove-Millersville 1,838 ..... L8
Hubertus 600 ..... K1
Hudson▲ 6,378 ..... A6
Humbird 190 ..... E6
Hurley▲ 1,782 ..... F3
Hustisford 979 ..... J9
Hustler 156 ..... F8
Independence 1,041 ..... D7
Ingram 91 ..... E5
Iola 1,125 ..... H6
Iron Belt 300 ..... F3
Iron Ridge 887 ..... K9
Iron River 878 ..... D2
Ironton 200 ..... F8
Ithaca 160 ..... F9
Ixonia 525 ..... H1
Jackson 2,486 ..... K9
Jacksonport 150 ..... M6
Janesville▲ 52,133 ..... H10
Jefferson▲ 6,078 ..... J10
Johnson Creek 1,259 ..... J9
Juda 500 ..... H10
Junction City 502 ..... G6
Juneau▲ 2,157 ..... J9
Kansasville 150 ..... L3
Kaukauna 11,982 ..... K7
Kekoskee 188 ..... J8
Kellnersville 350 ..... L7
Kempster 121 ..... H5
Kendall 453 ..... F8
Kennan 169 ..... F5
Kenosha▲ 80,352 ..... M3
Keshena▲ 685 ..... J6
Kewaskum 2,515 ..... K8
Kewaunee▲ 2,750 ..... M7
Kiel 2,910 ..... L8
Kieler 800 ..... E10
Kimberly 5,406 ..... K7
King H7
Kingston 346 ..... H8
Knapp 419 ..... B6
Knowlton 127 ..... G6
Kohler 1,817 ..... L8
Krakow 345 ..... K6
La Crosse▲ 51,003 ..... D8
La Farge 766 ..... E8
La Pointe 300 ..... E2
La Valle 446 ..... F8
Lac La Belle 258 ..... H1
Lac du Flambeau 1,423 ..... G4
Ladysmith▲ 3,938 ..... D5
Lake Church 175 ..... L9
Lake Delton 1,470 ..... G8
Lake Geneva 5,979 ..... K10
Lake Mills 4,143 ..... H9
Lake Nebagamon 900 ..... C3
Lake Tomahawk 600 ..... H4
Lake Wazeecha 2,278 ..... G7
Lake Wissota 2,175 ..... D6
Lakewood 425 ..... K5
Lamartine 190 ..... J8
Lancaster▲ 4,192 ..... E10
Land O'Lakes 786 ..... H3
Lannon 924 ..... K1
Lebanon 250 ..... H1
Lena 590 ..... K6
Leopolis 200 ..... J6
Lewis 200 ..... B4
Lily 125 ..... J5
Lima Center 175 ..... J10
Limeridge 152 ..... F9
Linden 429 ..... F10
Little Chute 9,207 ..... K7
Little Suamico 190 ..... L6
Livingston 576 ..... E10
Lodi 2,093 ..... G9
Loganville 228 ..... F9
Lohrville 368 ..... H7
Lomira 1,542 ..... J8
London 317 ..... H9
Lone Rock 641 ..... F9
Long Lake 150 ..... J4
Loretta 200 ..... E4
Lowell 300 ..... J9
Loyal 1,244 ..... E6
Lublin 129 ..... E5
Luck 1,022 ..... B4
Luxemburg 1,151 ..... L6
Lyndon Station 474 ..... F8
Lynn 117 ..... F6
Lynxville 153 ..... D9
Lyons 550 ..... K10
Madison (cap.)▲ 191,262 ..... H9
Maiden Rock 146 ..... B6
Manawa 1,169 ..... J7
Manchester 160 ..... J8
Manitowoc▲ 32,520 ..... L7

Maple 596 ..... C2
Maplewood 200 ..... M6
Marathon 1,606 ..... G6
Marengo 130 ..... E3
Maribel 372 ..... L7
Marinette▲ 11,843 ..... L5
Marion 1,242 ..... J6
Markesan 1,496 ..... J8
Marquette 182 ..... H8
Marshall 2,329 ..... H9
Marshfield 19,291 ..... F6
Martell 200 ..... B6
Mason 102 ..... D3
Mattoon 431 ..... J5
Mauston▲ 3,439 ..... F8
Mayville 4,374 ..... K9
Mazomanie 1,377 ..... G9
McFarland 5,232 ..... H10
McNaughton 450 ..... H4
Medford▲ 4,283 ..... F5
Mellen 935 ..... E3
Melrose 551 ..... E7
Melvina 115 ..... E8
Menasha 14,711 ..... J7
Menomonee Falls 26,840 ..... K1
Menomonie▲ 13,547 ..... C6
Mequon 18,885 ..... L1
Mercer V3
Merrill▲ 9,860 ..... G5
Merrillan 553 ..... E7
Merrimac 392 ..... G9
Merton 1,199 ..... K1
Middle Inlet 200 ..... K5
Middleton 13,289 ..... G9
Mikana 200 ..... C4
Milan 153 ..... F6
Milladore 314 ..... G6
Millston 110 ..... E7
Milltown 786 ..... J10
Milton 4,434 ..... J10
Milwaukee▲ 628,088 ..... M1
Mindoro 200 ..... D7
Mineral Point 2,428 ..... F10
Minocqua 950 ..... G4
Minong 521 ..... C3
Mishicot 1,296 ..... L7
Mondovi 2,491 ..... C6
Monico 250 ..... H4
Monona 8,637 ..... G10
Monroe▲ 10,241 ..... G10
Montello▲ 1,329 ..... H8
Monterey 150 ..... J1
Montfort 676 ..... E10
Monticello 1,140 ..... G10
Montreal 838 ..... F3
Morrisonville 375 ..... G9
Mosinee 3,820 ..... G6
Mount Calvary 558 ..... K8
Mount Hope 173 ..... D10
Mount Horeb 4,182 ..... G10
Mount Sterling 217 ..... D9
Mount Vernon 138 ..... G10
Mountain 250 ..... K5
Mukwonago 4,457 ..... J2
Muscoda 1,287 ..... F9
Muskego 16,813 ..... K2
Nashotah 567 ..... J1
Navarino 140 ..... J6
Necedah 743 ..... F7
Neenah 23,219 ..... J7
Neillsville▲ 2,680 ..... E6
Nekoosa 2,557 ..... G7
Nelson 388 ..... C7
Nelsonville 171 ..... H7
Neopit 615 ..... J6
Neosho 658 ..... J9
Neshkoro 384 ..... H8
New Amsterdam 120 ..... C8
New Auburn 485 ..... D5
New Berlin 33,592 ..... K2
New Franken 150 ..... L6
New Glarus 1,899 ..... G10
New Holstein 3,342 ..... K8
New Libson 1,491 ..... F8
New London 6,658 ..... J7
New Richmond 5,106 ..... A5
Newald 375 ..... J4
Newburg 875 ..... K9
Niagara 1,999 ..... K4
Nichols 254 ..... K6
North Bay 246 ..... M3
North Bend 200 ..... D7
North Fond du Lac 4,292 ..... J8
North Freedom 591 ..... G9
North Hudson 3,101 ..... A5
North Lake 400 ..... J1
North Prairie 1,322 ..... J2
North Shore 14,272 ..... M1
Norwalk 564 ..... E8
Oak Creek 19,513 ..... M2
Oakdale 162 ..... F8
Oakfield 1,003 ..... J8
Oconomowoc 10,993 ..... H1
Oconomowoc Lake 493 ..... H1
Oconto Falls 2,584 ..... K6
Oconto▲ 4,474 ..... L6
Odanah 190 ..... E2
Ogdensburg 220 ..... J7
Ogema 238 ..... F5
Okauchee 3,958 ..... J1
Okee 250 ..... H9
Oliver 265 ..... B2
Omro 2,836 ..... J7
Onalaska 11,284 ..... D8
Oneida 808 ..... K7
Ontario 407 ..... E8
Oostburg 1,931 ..... L8
Oregon 4,519 ..... H10
Orfordville 1,219 ..... H10
Osceola 2,075 ..... A5
Oshkosh▲ 55,006 ..... J8
Osseo 1,551 ..... D6
Owen 895 ..... F6
Oxford 499 ..... H8
Packwaukee 271 ..... G8
Paddock Lake 2,662 ..... K10
Palmyra 1,539 ..... H2

Pardeeville 1,630 ..... H8
Park Falls 3,104 ..... F4
Park Ridge 546 ..... H6
Patch Grove 202 ..... D10
Pearson 102 ..... H5
Peeksville 250 ..... E3
Pell Lake 2,018 ..... K10
Pembine 500 ..... L4
Pence 234 ..... F3
Pensaukee 225 ..... L6
Pepin 873 ..... B7
Perrygo Place J10
Peshtigo 3,154 ..... L5
Pewaukee 4,941 ..... K1
Phelps 950 ..... H3
Phillips▲ 1,592 ..... E4
Phlox 150 ..... J5
Pickerel 107 ..... J5
Pickett 120 ..... J8
Pigeon Falls 289 ..... D7
Pine River 110 ..... H7
Pittsville 838 ..... F7
Plain 691 ..... F9
Plainfield 839 ..... G7
Plat 120 ..... K1
Platteville 9,708 ..... F10
Pleasant Prairie 11,961 ..... L10
Plover 8,176 ..... G7
Plum City 534 ..... B6
Plymouth 6,769 ..... L8
Polonia 200 ..... H6
Poplar 516 ..... C2
Port Edwards 1,848 ..... G7
Port Washington▲ 9,338 ..... L9
Port Wing 290 ..... D2
Portage▲ 8,640 ..... G8
Potosi 654 ..... E10
Potter 252 ..... K7
Pound 434 ..... L5
Poy Sippi 425 ..... J7
Poynette 1,662 ..... G9
Prairie Farm 494 ..... C5
Prairie du Chien▲ 5,659 ..... D9
Prairie du Sac 2,380 ..... G9
Prentice 571 ..... F4
Prescott 3,243 ..... A6
Presque Isle 251 ..... G3
Princeton 1,458 ..... H8
Pulaski 2,200 ..... K6
Racine▲ 84,298 ..... M3
Radisson 237 ..... D4
Randolph 1,729 ..... H8
Random Lake 1,439 ..... K8
Raymond 300 ..... L2
Readfield 200 ..... J7
Readstown 420 ..... E9
Red Cliff 250 ..... E2
Redgranite 1,009 ..... H7
Reedsburg 5,834 ..... G8
Reedsville 1,182 ..... L7
Reeseville 673 ..... J9
Reserve 371 ..... D4
Rewey 220 ..... F10
Rhinelander▲ 7,427 ..... H4
Rib Falls 145 ..... G6
Rice Lake 7,998 ..... F5
Richfield 247 ..... K1
Richland Center▲ 5,018 ..... F9
Ridgeland 246 ..... B5
Ridgeway 577 ..... F10
Rio 768 ..... H9
Rio Creek 200 ..... L6
Ripon 7,241 ..... J8
River Falls 10,610 ..... A6
River Hills 1,612 ..... M1
Roberts 1,043 ..... A6
Rochester 978 ..... K3
Rock Falls 200 ..... C6
Rock Springs 432 ..... F8
Rockdale 235 ..... J10
Rockfield 200 ..... L1
Rockland 509 ..... D8
Rome 200 ..... H1
Rosendale 777 ..... J8
Rosholt 512 ..... H6
Rothschild 3,310 ..... G6
Roxbury 260 ..... G9
Royalton 200 ..... J7
Rozellville 150 ..... G6
Rubicon 261 ..... K9
Rudolph 451 ..... G7
Saint Cloud 494 ..... K8
Saint Croix Falls 1,640 ..... A5
Saint Francis 9,245 ..... M2
Saint Joseph Ridge 450 ..... D8
Saint Nazianz 693 ..... L7
Sand Creek 225 ..... C5
Sauk City 3,019 ..... G9
Saukville 3,695 ..... L9
Saxon 375 ..... F3
Sayner 300 ..... H4
Scandinavia 298 ..... H7
Schofield 2,415 ..... H6
School Hill 228 ..... L8
Seneca 235 ..... E9
Sextonville 225 ..... F9
Seymour 1,557 ..... K6
Sharon 1,250 ..... J11
Shawano▲ 7,598 ..... J6
Sheboygan▲ 49,676 ..... L8
Sheboygan Falls 5,823 ..... L8
Sheldon 268 ..... D5
Shell Lake▲ 1,161 ..... C4
Sherry 115 ..... G6
Sherwood 837 ..... K7
Shiocton 805 ..... K7
Shopiere 350 ..... H10
Shorewood 14,116 ..... M1
Shorewood Hills 1,680 ..... G9
Shullsburg 1,236 ..... F10
Silver Lake 1,801 ..... K10
Siren 863 ..... B4
Sister Bay 675 ..... M5
Slinger 2,340 ..... K9
Soldiers Grove 564 ..... E9
Solon Springs 575 ..... C3
Somers 400 ..... M3

Topography

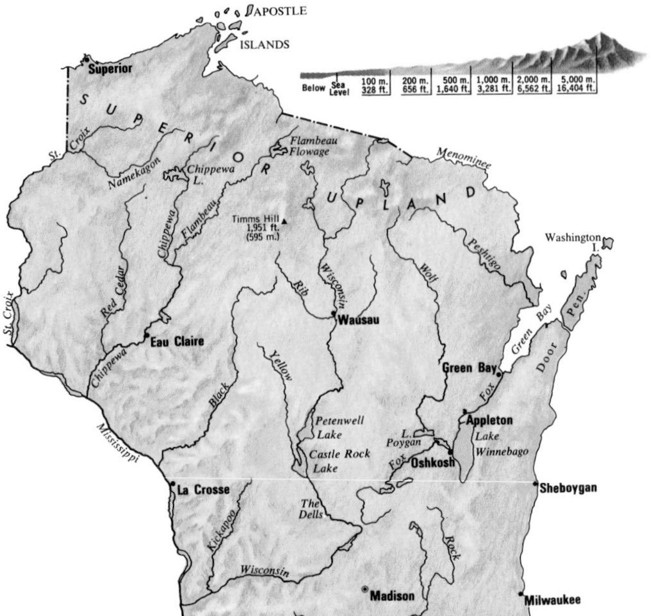

0 40 80 MI.
0 40 80 KM.
Below Sea Level
100 m. 328 ft.
200 m. 656 ft.
500 m. 1,640 ft.
1,000 m. 3,281 ft.
2,000 m. 6,562 ft.
5,000 m. 16,404 ft.
APOSTLE ISLANDS
Superior
SUPERIOR UPLAND
St. Croix
Namekagon
Chippewa L.
Flambeau Flowage
Menominee
Timms Hill 1,951 ft. (595 m.)
Chippewa
Flambeau
Red Cedar
St. Croix
Rib
Wisconsin
Wolf
Peshtigo
Washington I.
Wausau
Eau Claire
Green Bay
Green Bay
Door Pen.
Yellow
Black
Fox
Mississippi
Petenwell Lake
Castle Rock Lake
L. Poygan
Appleton
Lake Winnebago
Fox
Oshkosh
La Crosse
Sheboygan
The Dells
Kickapoo
Rock
Wisconsin
Madison
Milwaukee
Rock
Janesville
Racine
Kenosha

Somerset 1,065 ..... A5
South Milwaukee 20,958 ..... M2
South Range 149 ..... B2
South Wayne 478 ..... G10
Sparta▲ 7,788 ..... E8
Spencer 1,757 ..... F6
Spirit 400 ..... F5
Spooner 2,464 ..... B4
Spring Green 1,283 ..... G9
Spring Valley 1,051 ..... B6
Springbrook 150 ..... C4
Stangelville 150 ..... L7
Stanley 2,011 ..... E6
Star Prairie 507 ..... A5
Stetsonville 511 ..... F5
Steuben 161 ..... E9
Stevens Point▲ 23,006 ..... G7
Stiles 300 ..... L6
Stitzer 190 ..... E10
Stockbridge 579 ..... K7
Stoddard 775 ..... D8
Stone Bank 390 ..... J1
Stone Lake 210 ..... C4
Stoughton 8,786 ..... H10
Stratford 1,515 ..... F6
Strum 949 ..... D6
Sturgeon Bay▲ 9,176 ..... M6
Sturtevant 3,803 ..... M3
Suamico 900 ..... K6
Sullivan 432 ..... H1
Summit Lake 250 ..... H5
Sun Prairie 15,333 ..... H9
Superior▲ 27,134 ..... C2
Superior Village 481 ..... B2
Suring 626 ..... K5
Sussex 5,039 ..... K1
Symco 102 ..... J6
Taycheedah 350 ..... K8
Taylor 419 ..... E7
Tennyson 378 ..... E10
Theresa 771 ..... K8
Thiensville 3,301 ..... L1
Thorp 1,657 ..... E6
Three Lakes 950 ..... H4
Tichigan Lake 500 ..... K2
Tigerton 815 ..... H6
Tilleda 102 ..... J6
Tisch Mills 315 ..... L7
Tomah 7,570 ..... F8
Tomahawk 3,328 ..... G5
Tony 114 ..... E5
Townsend 450 ..... K5
Trego 280 ..... C4
Trempealeau 1,039 ..... C8
Troy Center 250 ..... J2
Tunnel City 200 ..... E7
Turtle Lake 817 ..... B5
Tustin 101 ..... J7
Twin Lakes 3,989 ..... K11
Two Rivers 13,030 ..... M7
Union Center 197 ..... F8
Union Grove 3,669 ..... L3
Unity 452 ..... F6

Upson 115 ..... F3
Valders 905 ..... L7
Verona 5,374 ..... G9
Vesper 598 ..... F7
Viola 644 ..... E8
Viroqua▲ 3,922 ..... D8
Wabeno 800 ..... J5
Waldo 442 ..... L8
Wales 2,471 ..... J1
Walworth 1,614 ..... J10
Warrens 343 ..... E7
Washburn▲ 2,285 ..... D2
Washington Island 550 ..... M5
Waterford 2,431 ..... K3
Waterloo 2,712 ..... J9
Watertown 19,142 ..... J9
Waubeka 450 ..... L9
Waukesha▲ 56,958 ..... K1
Waumandee 115 ..... C7
Waunakee 5,897 ..... G9
Waupaca▲ 4,957 ..... H7
Waupun 8,207 ..... J8
Wausau▲ 37,060 ..... G6
Wausaukee 656 ..... K5
Wautoma▲ 1,784 ..... H7
Wauwatosa 49,366 ..... L1
Wauzeka 595 ..... E9
Wayside 140 ..... L7
Webster 623 ..... B4
West Allis 63,221 ..... L1
West Baraboo 1,021 ..... G9
West Bend▲ 23,916 ..... K9
West Milwaukee 3,973 ..... L1
West Salem 3,611 ..... D8
Westboro 750 ..... F5
Westby 1,866 ..... E8
Westfield 1,125 ..... H8
Weston 8,775 ..... G6
Weston 9,714 ..... C6
Weyauwega 1,665 ..... H7
Weyerhaeuser 283 ..... D5
Wheeler 348 ..... C5
White Lake 304 ..... J5
Whitefish Bay 14,272 ..... M1
Whitehall▲ 1,494 ..... D7
Whitelaw 700 ..... L7
Whitewater 12,636 ..... J10
Whiting 1,838 ..... H7
Wild Rose 676 ..... H7
Williams Bay 2,108 ..... J10
Wilson 163 ..... B6
Wilton 478 ..... F8
Winchester 300 ..... G3
Wind Lake 3,748 ..... K2
Wind Point 1,941 ..... M2
Windsor 2,182 ..... H9
Winnebago 1,433 ..... J7
Winneconne 2,059 ..... J7
Winter 383 ..... E4
Wiota 125 ..... G10
Wisconsin Dells 2,393 ..... G8
Wisconsin Rapids▲ 18,245 ..... G7
Withee 503 ..... E6

Wittenberg 1,145 ..... H6
Wonewoc 793 ..... F8
Woodford 107 ..... G10
Woodman 120 ..... E9
Woodruff 850 ..... G4
Woodville 942 ..... B6
Wrightstown 1,262 ..... K7
Wyeville 154 ..... F7
Wyocena 620 ..... H9
Yuba 77 ..... F8

OTHER FEATURES

Apostle (isls.) F2
Apostle Islands Nat'l Lakeshore E1
Apple (riv.) A5
Bad River Ind. Res. E2
Bardon (lake) E2
Bear (isl.) E1
Beaver Dam (lake) J9
Beulah (lake) J2
Big Eau Pleine (res.) G6
Big Muskego (lake) L2
Big Rib (riv.) G5
Black (riv.) E7
Butternut (lake) J4
Castle Rock (lake) G8
Cat (isl.) E1
Chambers (isl.) M5
Chequamegon (bay) E2
Chetac (lake) D4
Chippewa (lake) D4
Chippewa (riv.) B7
Clam (lake) B4
Clam (riv.) A4
Dells, The (valley) G8
Denoon (lake) K2
Door (pen.) M6
Du Bay (lake) G6
Eagle (lake) H2
Eagle (lake) K3
Eau Claire (riv.) D6
Flambeau (riv.) E4
Flambeau Flowage (res.) F3
Fox (riv.) K2
Fox (riv.) K7
General Mitchell Field M2
Geneva (lake) K10
Golden (lake) H1
Green (bay) L6
Grindstone (lake) C4
Holcombe Flowage (res.) D5
Jump (riv.) E5
Kegonsa (lake) H10
Kickapoo (riv.) E9
Koshkonong (lake) H10
La Belle (lake) H1
Lac Court Oreilles Ind. Res. D4
Lac du Flambeau Ind. Res. G3
Long (lake) C4
Madeline (isl.) E2
Mendota (lake) H9

Menominee (riv.) L5
Menominee Ind. Res. J5
Metonga (lake) J4
Michigan (isl.) F2
Michigan (lake) M9
Mississippi (riv.) D10
Montreal (riv.) F2
Moose (lake) E3
Moose (lake) F3
Nagawicka (lake) J1
Namekagon (lake) D3
Namekagon (riv.) C3
North (lake) J1
Oak (isl.) E2
Oconomowoc (lake) H1
Oconto (riv.) K5
Okauchee (lake) J1
Outer (isl.) F1
Owen (lake) D3
Pecatonica (riv.) H11
Pelican (lake) H4
Pepin (lake) B7
Peshtigo (riv.) K5
Petenwell (lake) G7
Pewaukee (lake) K1
Phantom (lake) J2
Pine (lake) J1
Porte des Morts (str.) N5
Poygan (lake) J7
Puckaway (lake) H8
Red Cedar (riv.) C5
Red Cliff Ind. Res. E2
Rock (riv.) J9
Round (lake) F4
Round (lake) D3
Saint Croix (lake) A6
Saint Croix (riv.) A4
Saint Croix Flowage (res.) C3
Saint Louis (riv.) A2
Sand (isl.) D2
Shawano (lake) K6
Shell (lake) C4
Spider (lake) D3
Stockbridge Ind. Res. J6
Stockton (isl.) F2
Sugar (riv.) H10
Sugarbush Hill (mt.) J4
Superior (lake) F1
Thunder (lake) H4
Tichigan (lake) K2
Timms Hill (mt.) F5
Trempealeau (riv.) C7
Trout (lake) G3
Washington (isl.) M5
Willow (res.) F4
Wind (lake) K2
Winnebago (lake) K7
Wisconsin (riv.) E9
Wolf (riv.) J5
Yellow (lake) B4
Yellow (riv.) F7

▲County seat

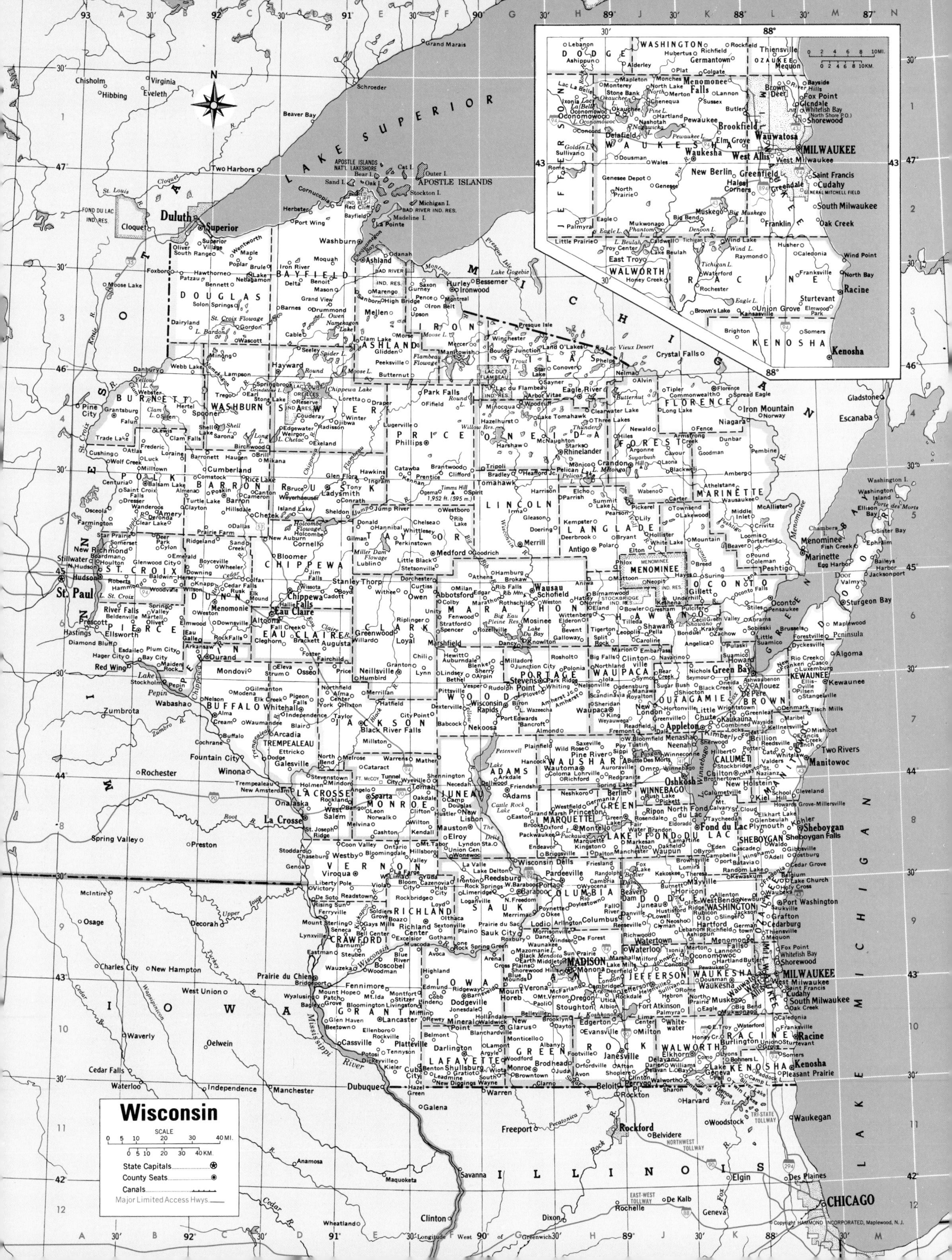
Wisconsin
SCALE
0 5 10 20 30 40 MI.
0 5 10 20 30 40 KM.
State Capitals
County Seats
Canals
Major Limited Access Hwys.
LAKE SUPERIOR
LAKE MICHIGAN
MICHIGAN
MINNESOTA
IOWA
ILLINOIS
APOSTLE ISLANDS
APOSTLE ISLANDS NAT'L LAKESHORE
MILWAUKEE
MADISON
CHICAGO
Duluth
Superior
St. Paul
Green Bay
Oshkosh
Appleton
Eau Claire
La Crosse
Racine
Kenosha
Sheboygan
Janesville
Wausau
Rockford
Dubuque
DOUGLAS
BAYFIELD
ASHLAND
IRON
VILAS
FLORENCE
FOREST
MARINETTE
BURNETT
WASHBURN
SAWYER
PRICE
ONEIDA
LINCOLN
LANGLADE
MENOMINEE
OCONTO
POLK
BARRON
RUSK
TAYLOR
ST. CROIX
DUNN
CHIPPEWA
MARATHON
SHAWANO
PIERCE
PEPIN
EAU CLAIRE
CLARK
PORTAGE
WAUPACA
OUTAGAMIE
BROWN
KEWAUNEE
DOOR
BUFFALO
TREMPEALEAU
JACKSON
WOOD
ADAMS
WAUSHARA
WINNEBAGO
CALUMET
MANITOWOC
LA CROSSE
MONROE
JUNEAU
MARQUETTE
GREEN LAKE
FOND DU LAC
SHEBOYGAN
VERNON
RICHLAND
SAUK
COLUMBIA
DODGE
WASHINGTON
OZAUKEE
CRAWFORD
IOWA
DANE
JEFFERSON
WAUKESHA
GRANT
LAFAYETTE
GREEN
ROCK
WALWORTH
RACINE
KENOSHA
WASHINGTON
DODGE
OZAUKEE
WAUKESHA
JEFFERSON
WALWORTH
RACINE
KENOSHA
Longitude West 90° of Greenwich
© Copyright HAMMOND INCORPORATED, Maplewood, N. J.

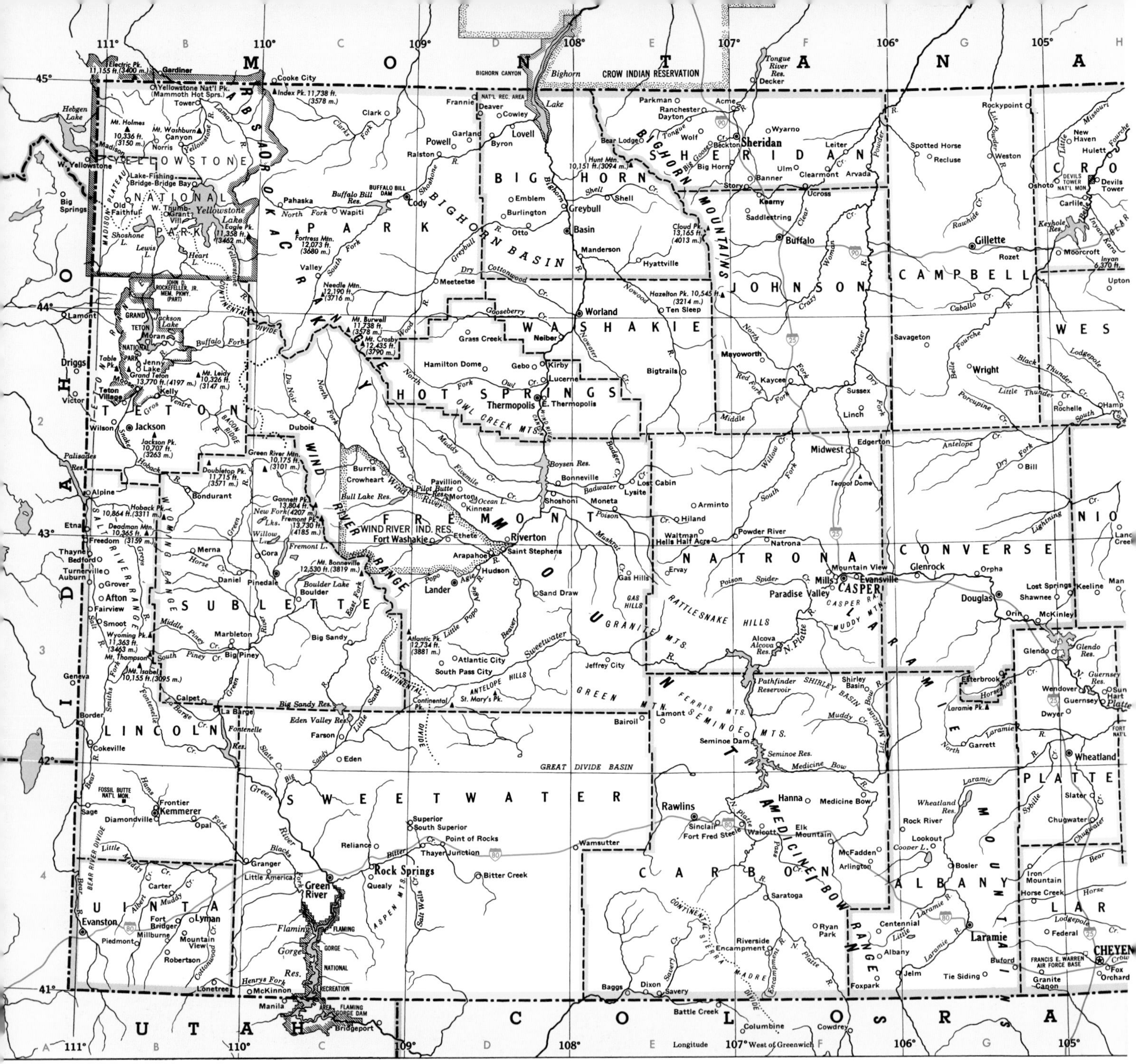
MONTANA
IDAHO
UTAH
COLORADO
YELLOWSTONE NATIONAL PARK
PARK
BIG HORN
SHERIDAN
CAMPBELL
CROOK
JOHNSON
WASHAKIE
HOT SPRINGS
TETON
SUBLETTE
FREMONT
NATRONA
CONVERSE
NIOBRARA
WESTON
LINCOLN
SWEETWATER
CARBON
ALBANY
PLATTE
GOSHEN
LARAMIE
UINTA
ABSAROKA RANGE
BIGHORN MOUNTAINS
BIGHORN BASIN
WIND RIVER RANGE
WIND RIVER IND. RES.
OWL CREEK MTS.
RATTLESNAKE HILLS
GRANITE MTS.
GREAT DIVIDE BASIN
MEDICINE BOW RANGE
LARAMIE MOUNTAINS
CROW INDIAN RESERVATION
Cheyenne
Casper
Laramie
Rock Springs
Sheridan
Rawlins
Gillette
Riverton
Lander
Cody
Evanston
Green River
Jackson
Worland
Douglas
Buffalo
Thermopolis
Kemmerer
Wheatland
Longitude 107° West of Greenwich

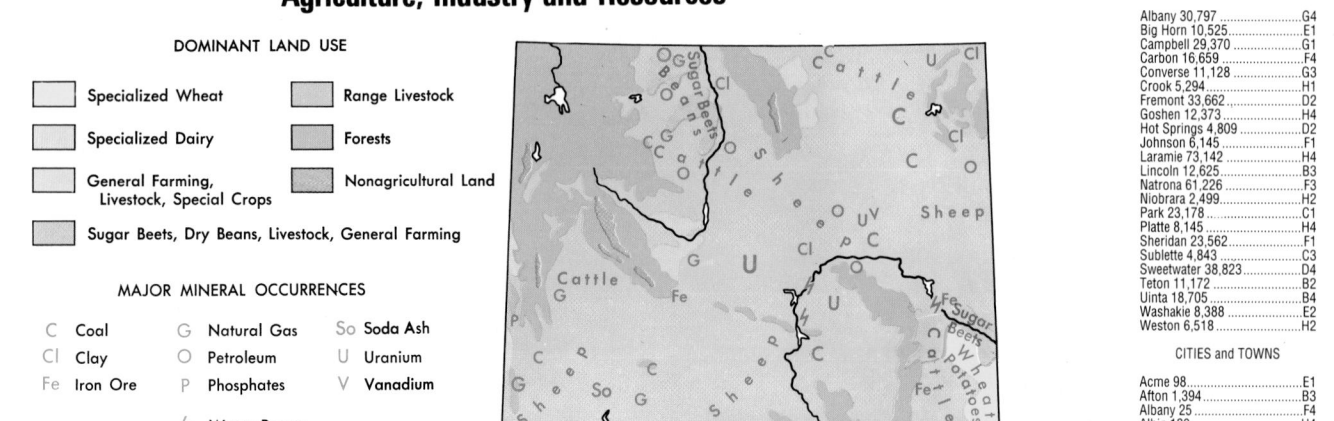

Agriculture, Industry and Resources

DOMINANT LAND USE

- Specialized Wheat
- Range Livestock
- Specialized Dairy
- Forests
- General Farming, Livestock, Special Crops
- Nonagricultural Land
- Sugar Beets, Dry Beans, Livestock, General Farming

MAJOR MINERAL OCCURRENCES

C	Coal	G	Natural Gas	So	Soda Ash
Cl	Clay	O	Petroleum	U	Uranium
Fe	Iron Ore	P	Phosphates	V	Vanadium
ϟ	Water Power				

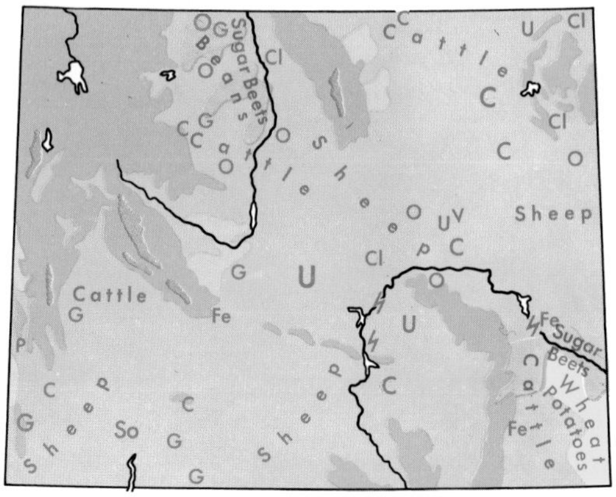
Sugar Beets
Beans
Cattle
Sheep
Wheat
Potatoes

COUNTIES

Albany 30,797 .... G4
Big Horn 10,525 .... E1
Campbell 29,370 .... G1
Carbon 16,659 .... F4
Converse 11,128 .... G3
Crook 5,294 .... H1
Fremont 33,662 .... D2
Goshen 12,373 .... H4
Hot Springs 4,809 .... D2
Johnson 6,145 .... F1
Laramie 73,142 .... H4
Lincoln 12,625 .... B3
Natrona 61,226 .... F3
Niobrara 2,499 .... H2
Park 23,178 .... C1
Platte 8,145 .... H4
Sheridan 23,562 .... F1
Sublette 4,843 .... C3
Sweetwater 38,823 .... D4
Teton 11,172 .... B2
Uinta 18,705 .... B4
Washakie 8,388 .... E2
Weston 6,518 .... H2

CITIES and TOWNS

Acme 98 .... E1
Afton 1,394 .... B3
Albany 25 .... F4
Albin 120 .... H4

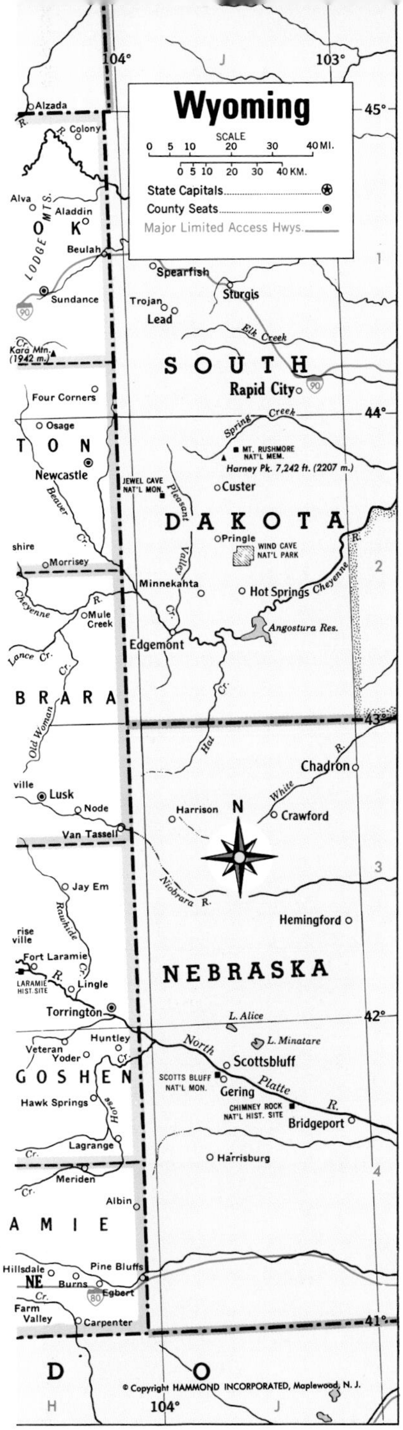
Wyoming
SCALE
0 5 10 20 30 40 MI.
0 5 10 20 30 40 KM.
State Capitals
County Seats
Major Limited Access Hwys.
SOUTH
DAKOTA
NEBRASKA
Rapid City
Sturgis
Spearfish
Lead
Custer
Newcastle
Edgemont
Hot Springs
Chadron
Crawford
Harrison
Lusk
Torrington
Scottsbluff
Gering
Bridgeport
Lagrange
Pine Bluffs
Egbert
Carpenter
Hemingford
Angostura Res.
WIND CAVE NAT'L PARK
JEWEL CAVE NAT'L MON.
MT. RUSHMORE NAT'L MEM.
Harney Pk. 7,242 ft. (2207 m.)
SCOTTS BLUFF NAT'L MON.
CHIMNEY ROCK NAT'L HIST. SITE
© Copyright HAMMOND INCORPORATED, Maplewood, N. J.

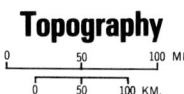

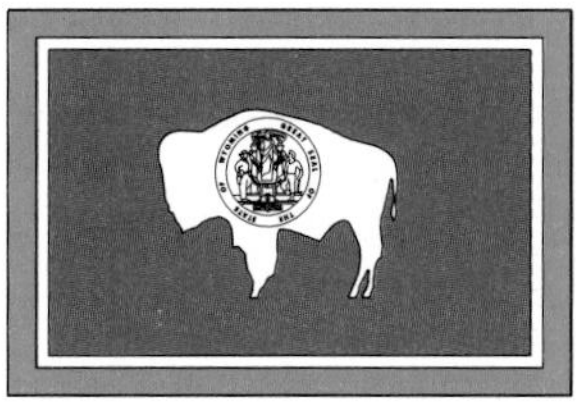

AREA 97,809 sq. mi. (253,325 sq. km.)
POPULATION 455,975
CAPITAL Cheyenne
LARGEST CITY Casper
HIGHEST POINT Gannett Pk. 13,804 ft. (4207 m.)
SETTLED IN 1834
ADMITTED TO UNION July 10, 1890
POPULAR NAME Equality State
STATE FLOWER Indian Paintbrush
STATE BIRD Meadowlark

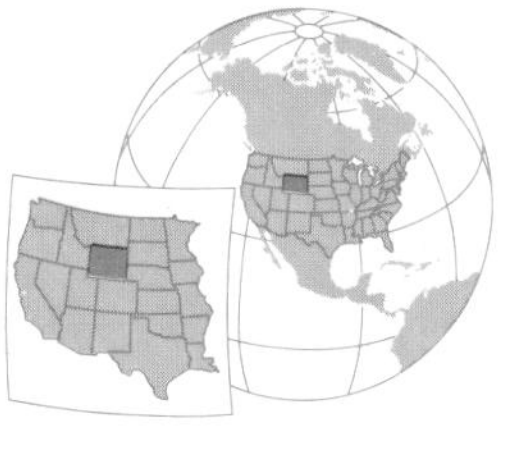

Topography

0 50 100 MI.
0 50 100 KM.

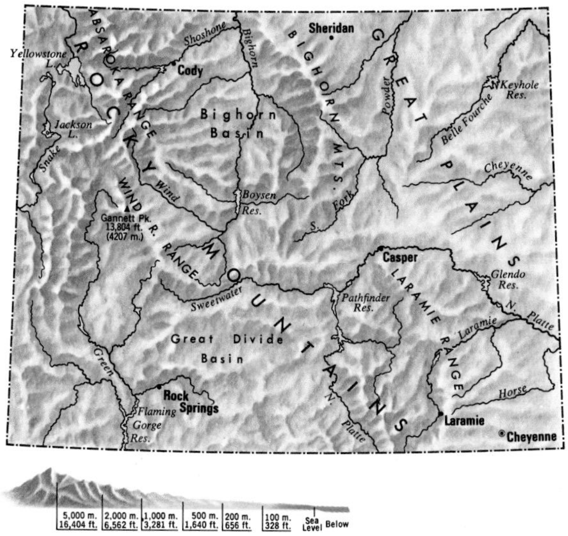
Sheridan
Cody
Yellowstone L.
Jackson L.
Bighorn Basin
BIGHORN MTS.
GREAT PLAINS
ROCKY MOUNTAINS
WIND R. RANGE
ABSAROKA RANGE
Gannett Pk. 13,804 ft. (4207 m.)
Boysen Res.
Keyhole Res.
Casper
Glendo Res.
Pathfinder Res.
LARAMIE RANGE
Great Divide Basin
Rock Springs
Flaming Gorge Res.
Laramie
Cheyenne
5,000 m. 16,404 ft.
2,000 m. 6,562 ft.
1,000 m. 3,281 ft.
500 m. 1,640 ft.
200 m. 656 ft.
100 m. 328 ft.
Sea Level
Below

Alcova 275 .... F3
Alpine 200 .... B2
Alva 50 .... H1
Arapahoe 393 .... D3
Arvada 30 .... F1
Atlantic City 25 .... D3
Auburn 360 .... A3
Baggs 272 .... E4
Bairoil 228 .... E3
Banner 40 .... F1
Basin▲ 1,180 .... E1
Beckton 110 .... E1
Bedford 350 .... A3
Beulah 184 .... H1
Big Horn 350 .... E1
Big Piney 454 .... B3
Bondurant 90 .... B2
Border 25 .... B3
Bosler 195 .... G4
Boulder 50 .... C3
Buffalo▲ 3,302 .... F1
Buford 36 .... G4
Burlington 184 .... D1
Burns 254 .... H4
Burris 30 .... C2
Byron 470 .... D1
Carpenter 75 .... H4
Carter 33 .... B4
Casper▲ 46,742 .... F3
Centennial 140 .... F4
Cheyenne (cap.)▲ 50,008 .... H4
Chugwater 192 .... H4
Clearmont 119 .... F1
Cody▲ 7,897 .... D1
Cokeville 493 .... B3
Colony 50 .... H1
Cowley 477 .... D1
Crowheart 200 .... C2
Daniel 130 .... B3
Dayton 565 .... E1
Deaver 199 .... D1
Devils Tower 28 .... H1
Diamondville 864 .... B4
Dixon 70 .... E4
Douglas▲ 5,076 .... G3
Dubois 895 .... C2
East Thermopolis 221 .... D2
Eden 198 .... C3
Edgerton 247 .... F2
Egbert 75 .... H4
Elk Mountain 174 .... F4
Encampment 611 .... F4
Ethete 1,059 .... D2
Etna 200 .... A2
Evanston▲ 10,903 .... B4
Evansville 1,403 .... F3
Fairview 150 .... B3
Farson 350 .... C3
Fort Bridger 300 .... B4
Fort Laramie 243 .... H3
Fort Washakie 1,334 .... C2
Fox Farm 2,850 .... H4
Foxpark 78 .... F4
Frannie 148 .... D1
Freedom 400 .... B3
Frontier 150 .... B4
Garland 57 .... D1
Gas Hills 150 .... E3
Gillette▲ 17,635 .... G1
Glendo 195 .... G3
Glenrock 2,153 .... G3
Granger 126 .... C4
Granite Canon 80 .... G4
Grass Creek 152 .... D2
Green River▲ 12,711 .... C4
Greybull 1,789 .... E1
Grover 425 .... B3
Guernsey 1,155 .... H3
Hamilton Dome 80 .... D2
Hanna 1,076 .... F4
Hartville 78 .... H3
Hawk Springs 84 .... H4
Hillsdale 160 .... H4
Horse Creek 225 .... G4
Hudson 392 .... D3
Hulett 429 .... H1
Huntley 50 .... H4
Hyattville 110 .... E1
Iron Mountain 45 .... G4
Jackson▲ 4,472 .... B2
Jeffrey City 1,882 .... E3
Jelm 29 .... G4
Kaycee 256 .... F2
Kearny 49 .... F1
Kelly 100 .... B2
Kemmerer▲ 3,020 .... B4
Kinnear 145 .... D2
Kirby 59 .... D2
La Barge 493 .... B3
Lagrange 224 .... H4
Lamont 30 .... E3
Lance Creek 100 .... H2
Lander▲ 7,023 .... D3
Laramie▲ 26,687 .... G4
Leiter 46 .... F1
Linch 187 .... F2
Lingle 473 .... H3
Little America 175 .... C4
Lost Cabin 25 .... E2
Lovell 2,131 .... D1
Lucerne 240 .... D2
Lusk▲ 1,504 .... H3
Lyman 1,896 .... B4
Lysite 175 .... E2
Mammoth Hot Springs (Yellowstone Nat'l Park) 350 .... B1
Manderson 83 .... E1
Manville 97 .... H3
Marbleton 634 .... B3
Mayoworth F2
McFadden 47 .... F4
McKinnon 135 .... C4
Medicine Bow 389 .... F4
Meeteetse 368 .... D1
Meriden 55 .... H4
Midwest 495 .... F2
Millburne 54 .... B4
Mills 1,574 .... F3
Moorcroft 768 .... H1
Moose 150 .... B2
Moran 200 .... B2
Morrisey 28 .... H2
Morton 35 .... D2
Mountain View 1,345 .... B4
Mountain View 76 .... F3
Neiber D2
New Haven 35 .... H1
Newcastle▲ 3,003 .... H2
Old Faithful 75 .... B1
Opal 95 .... B4
Orchard Valley 3,327 .... H4
Osage 500 .... H2
Otto 50 .... D1
Pahaska 75 .... C1
Paradise Valley F3
Parkman 30 .... E1
Pavillion 126 .... D2
Piedmont 25 .... B4
Pine Bluffs 1,054 .... H4
Pinedale▲ 1,181 .... C3
Point of Rocks 425 .... D4
Powder River 70 .... F2
Powell 5,292 .... D1
Ralston 109 .... D1
Ranchester 676 .... E1
Rawlins▲ 9,380 .... E4
Recluse 225 .... G1
Reliance 325 .... C4
Riverside 85 .... F4
Riverton 9,202 .... D2
Robertson 142 .... B4
Rock River 190 .... G4
Rock Springs 19,050 .... C4
Rozet 30 .... G1
Saddlestring 100 .... F1
Sage 45 .... B4
Saint Stephens 80 .... D3
Sand Draw 40 .... D3
Saratoga 1,969 .... F4
Savageton 30 .... G2
Savery 29 .... E4
Shell 80 .... E1
Sheridan▲ 13,900 .... F1
Shirley Basin 400 .... F3
Shoshoni 497 .... D2
Sinclair 500 .... E4
Smoot 310 .... B3
South Superior 586 .... D4
Story 637 .... F1
Sundance▲ 1,139 .... H1
Sunrise 29 .... H3
Superior 273 .... D4
Sussex 25 .... F2
Ten Sleep 311 .... E1
Teton Village B2
Thayne 267 .... A3
Thermopolis▲ 3,247 .... D2
Torrington▲ 5,651 .... H3
Turnerville 65 .... A3
Ulm 25 .... F1
Upton 980 .... H1
Veteran 60 .... H4
Walcott 200 .... F4
Wamsutter 240 .... E4
Wapiti 130 .... C1
Wheatland▲ 3,271 .... H3
Wilson 480 .... B2
Worland▲ 5,742 .... E1
Wright 1,236 .... G2
Wyarno 101 .... F1
Yellowstone National Park 350 .... B1
Yoder 136 .... H4

OTHER FEATURES

Absaroka (range) C1
Antelope (creek) G2
Antelope (hills) D3
Aspen (mts.) C4
Atlantic (peak) D3
Bear (creek) H4
Bear (riv.) B4
Bear Lodge (mts.) H1
Bear River Divide (mts.) B4
Beaver (creek) D3
Beaver (creek) H2
Belle Fourche (riv.) H1
Big Goose (creek) E1
Bighorn (basin) D1
Bighorn (lake) D1
Bighorn (mts.) E1
Bighorn (riv.) D1
Bighorn Canyon Nat'l Rec. Area D1
Big Sandy (riv.) C3
Bitter (creek) C4
Blacks Fork, Green (riv.) C4
Black Thunder (creek) G2
Bonneville (mt.) C3
Boysen (res.) D2
Buffalo Bill (dam) C1
Buffalo Bill (res.) C1
Buffalo Fork, Snake (riv.) B2
Burwell (mt.) C2
Caballo (creek) G1
Casper (range) F3
Cheyenne (riv.) H2
Chugwater (creek) H4
Clarks Fork (riv.) C1
Clear (creek) F1
Cloud (peak) E1
Cottonwood (creek) B4
Crazy Woman (creek) F1
Crosby (mt.) C2
Crow (creek) H4
Deadman (mt.) B2
Devils Tower Nat'l Mon. H1
Doubletop (peak) B2
Dry (creek) C2
Dry Cottonwood (creek) D1
Eagle (peak) B1
Fivemile (creek) D2
Flaming Gorge (res.) C4
Flaming Gorge Nat'l Rec. Area C4
Fontenelle (creek) B3
Fontenelle (res.) B3
Fort Laramie Nat'l Hist. Site H3
Fortress (mt.) C1
Fossil Butte Nat'l Mon. B4
Francis E. Warren A.F.B. 3,832 .... G4
Fremont (lake) C3
Fremont (peak) C2
Gannett (peak) C2
Gas (hills) E3
Glendo (res.) H3
Gooseberry (creek) D1
Grand Teton (mt.) B2
Grand Teton Nat'l Park B2
Granite (mts.) E3
Great Divide (basin) E3
Green (mt.) E3
Green (riv.) C4
Green, East Fork (riv.) C3
Green River (mt.) C2
Greybull (riv.) D1
Greys (riv.) B3
Gros Ventre (riv.) B2
Guernsey (res.) H3
Hams Fork (riv.) B4
Hazelton (peak) E1
Henrys Fork, Green (riv.) C4
Hoback (peak) B2
Hoback (riv.) B2
Holmes (mt.) B1
Horse (creek) H4
Horseshoe (creek) G3
Hunt (mt.) E1
Index (peak) C1
Inyan Kara (creek) H1
Inyan Kara (mt.) H1
Isabel (mt.) B3
Jackson (lake) B2
Jackson (peak) B2
John D. Rockefeller, Jr., Mem. Pkwy. B1
Keyhole (res.) H1
Lamar (riv.) B1
Lance (creek) H2
Laramie (mts.) G3
Laramie (peak) G3
Laramie (riv.) G4
Leidy (mt.) B2
Lewis (lake) B1
Lightning (creek) G2
Little Missouri (riv.) H1
Little Muddy (creek) B4
Little Powder (riv.) G1
Little Sandy (creek) C3
Little Thunder (creek) G2
Lodgepole (creek) H2
Lodgepole (creek) H4
Madison (plat.) B1
Medicine Bow (range) F4
Medicine Bow (riv.) F3
Middle Piney (creek) B3
Muddy (creek) D2
Muskrat (creek) E2
Needle (mt.) C1
Niobrara (riv.) J3
North Laramie (riv.) G3
North Platte (riv.) H3
Nowater (creek) E2
Nowood (riv.) E1
Owl, North Fork (creek) D2
Owl Creek (mts.) D2
Palisades (res.) A2
Pass (creek) F4
Pathfinder (res.) F3
Poison (creek) E2
Poison Spider (creek) F3
Popo Agie (riv.) D3
Powder (riv.) F2
Rattlesnake (hills) E3
Rawhide (creek) G1
Rocky (mts.) C1
Salt (riv.) B3
Salt River (range) B3
Salt Wells (creek) D4
Seminoe (mts.) E3
Seminoe (res.) F3
Shell (creek) E1
Shirley (basin) F3
Shoshone (lake) B1
Shoshone (riv.) D1
Sierra Madre (mts.) E4
Slate (creek) C3
Smiths Fork (riv.) B3
Snake (riv.) B2
South Cheyenne (riv.) H2
South Piney (creek) B3
Sweetwater (riv.) D3
Sybille (creek) G4
Teapot Dome (mt.) F2
Teton (range) B2
Tongue (riv.) E1
Washburn (mt.) B1
Wheatland (res.) G4
Willow (creek) F2
Wind (riv.) C2
Wind River (canyon) D2
Wind River (range) C2
Wind River Ind. Res. C2
Wood (riv.) C2
Wyoming (peak) B3
Wyoming (range) B2
Yellowstone (lake) B1
Yellowstone (riv.) B1
Yellowstone Nat'l Park B1

▲County seat

Acquisitions of Territory

OREGON COUNTRY
OREGON 1846
Treaty with Great Britain
LOUISIANA
1803
Purchased from France
RED RIVER
Title Established 1818
MEXICAN CESSION
1848
TEXAS
Annexed in 1845
GADSDEN PURCHASE
1853
UNITED STATES
1783
FLORIDA
1819
Treaty with Spain
ALASKA
1867
Purchased from Russia
HAWAII
Annexed in 1898
WASHINGTON
IDAHO
MONTANA
NORTH DAKOTA
SOUTH DAKOTA
WYOMING
NEBRASKA
IOWA
MINNESOTA
WISCONSIN
MICHIGAN
NEW YORK
MAINE
VT.
N.H.
MASS.
CONN.
R.I.
NEW JERSEY
PENNSYLVANIA
DEL.
MD.
OHIO
INDIANA
ILLINOIS
WEST VIRGINIA
VIRGINIA
KENTUCKY
MISSOURI
KANSAS
COLORADO
UTAH
NEVADA
CALIFORNIA
ARIZONA
NEW MEXICO
OKLAHOMA
ARKANSAS
TENNESSEE
NORTH CAROLINA
SOUTH CAROLINA
GEORGIA
ALABAMA
MISSISSIPPI
LOUISIANA
TEXAS

The United States in 1783 comprised the thirteen original states and included lands acquired by conquest during the Revolution and by the Treaty of 1783.

Rank by Area

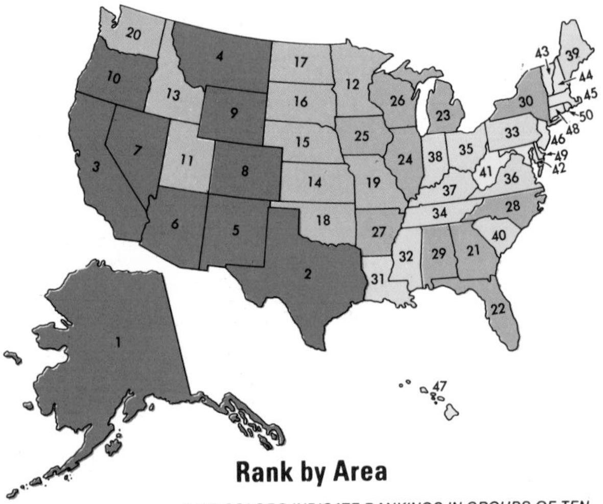

Rank by Area

MAP COLORS INDICATE RANKINGS IN GROUPS OF TEN

Rank by Population
1990

Rank by Population

YEAR OF ADMISSION TO THE UNION

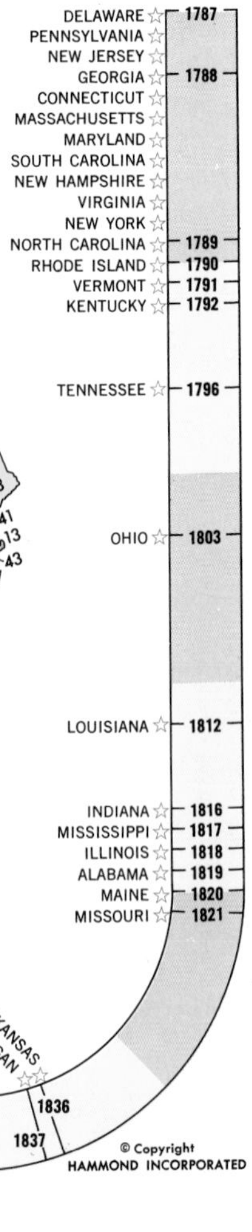
DELAWARE 1787
PENNSYLVANIA
NEW JERSEY
GEORGIA 1788
CONNECTICUT
MASSACHUSETTS
MARYLAND
SOUTH CAROLINA
NEW HAMPSHIRE
VIRGINIA
NEW YORK
NORTH CAROLINA 1789
RHODE ISLAND 1790
VERMONT 1791
KENTUCKY 1792
TENNESSEE 1796
OHIO 1803
LOUISIANA 1812
INDIANA 1816
MISSISSIPPI 1817
ILLINOIS 1818
ALABAMA 1819
MAINE 1820
MISSOURI 1821
ARKANSAS 1836
MICHIGAN 1837
FLORIDA 1845
TEXAS
IOWA 1846
WISCONSIN 1848
CALIFORNIA 1850
MINNESOTA 1858
OREGON 1859
KANSAS 1861
WEST VIRGINIA 1863
NEVADA 1864
NEBRASKA 1867
COLORADO 1876
NORTH DAKOTA 1889
SOUTH DAKOTA
MONTANA
WASHINGTON
IDAHO 1890
WYOMING
UTAH 1896
OKLAHOMA 1907
ARIZONA 1912
NEW MEXICO
HAWAII 1959
ALASKA

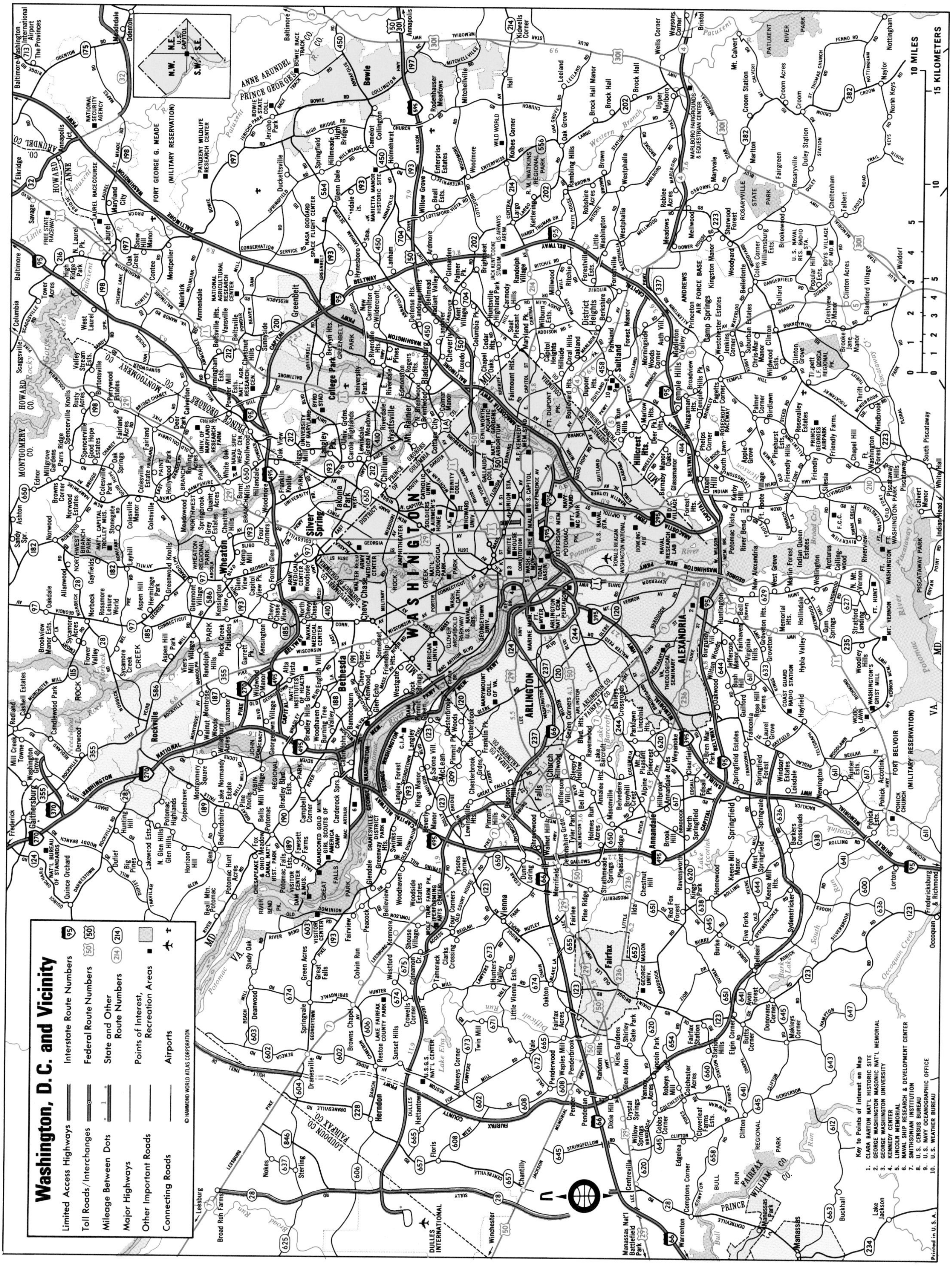
Washington, D.C. and Vicinity
Limited Access Highways
Interstate Route Numbers
Toll Roads/Interchanges
Federal Route Numbers
Mileage Between Dots
State and Other Route Numbers
Major Highways
Points of Interest, Recreation Areas
Other Important Roads
Airports
Connecting Roads
© HAMMOND WORLD ATLAS CORPORATION
Key to Points of Interest on Map
1. CLARA BARTON NAT'L HISTORIC SITE
2. GEORGE WASHINGTON MASONIC NAT'L MEMORIAL
3. GEORGE WASHINGTON UNIVERSITY
4. KENNEDY CENTER
5. LINCOLN MEMORIAL
6. NAVAL SHIP RESEARCH & DEVELOPMENT CENTER
7. SMITHSONIAN INSTITUTION
8. U.S. CENSUS BUREAU
9. U.S. NAVY OCEANOGRAPHIC OFFICE
10. U.S. WEATHER BUREAU
10 MILES
15 KILOMETERS
WASHINGTON
ALEXANDRIA
ARLINGTON
Printed in U.S.A.

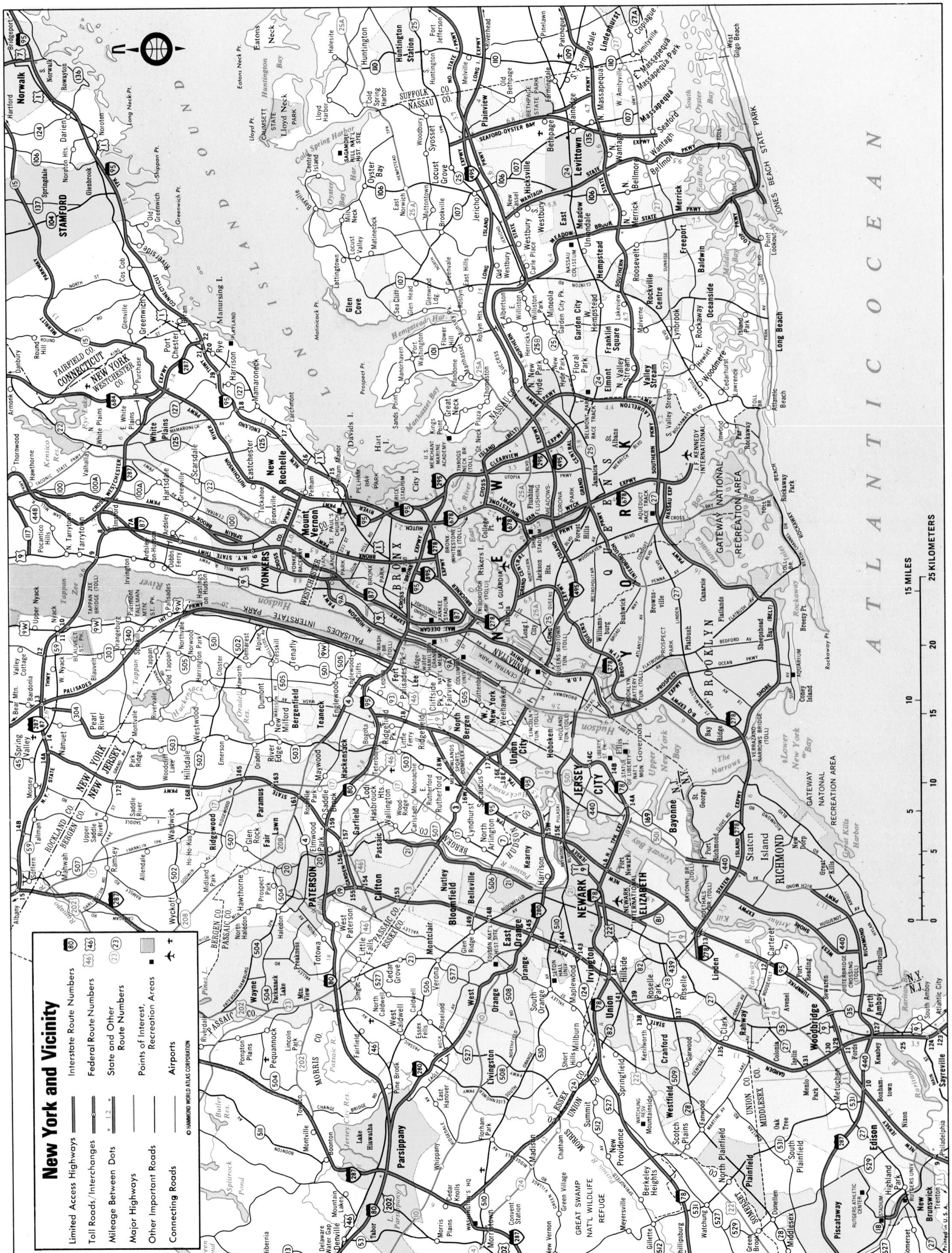
New York and Vicinity
Limited Access Highways
Toll Roads/Interchanges
Mileage Between Dots
Major Highways
Other Important Roads
Connecting Roads
Interstate Route Numbers
Federal Route Numbers
State and Other Route Numbers
Points of Interest, Recreation Areas
Airports
© HAMMOND WORLD ATLAS CORPORATION
ATLANTIC OCEAN
LONG ISLAND SOUND
15 MILES
25 KILOMETERS
Printed in U.S.A.

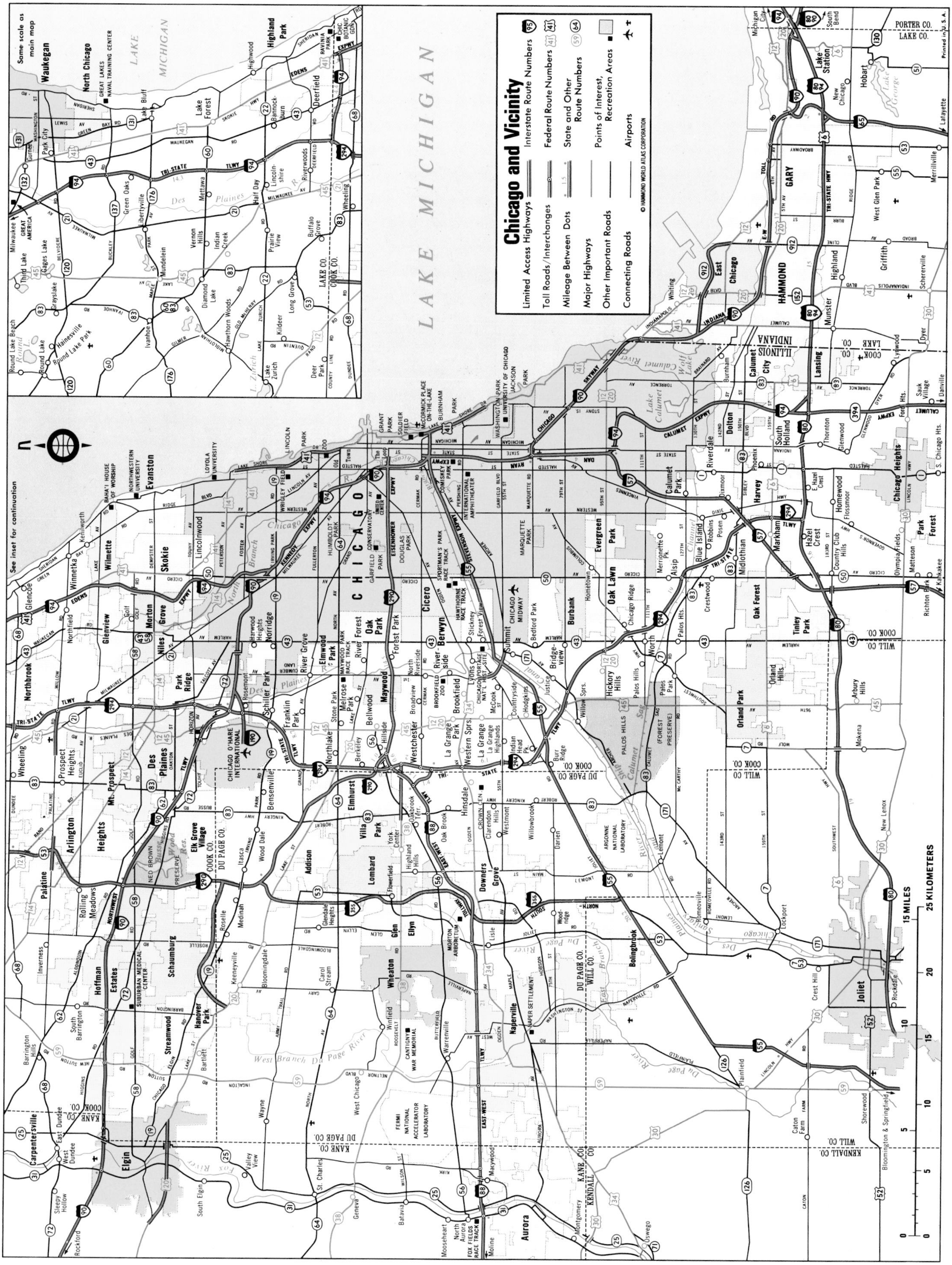

Chicago and Vicinity
Limited Access Highways
Toll Roads/Interchanges
Mileage Between Dots
Major Highways
Other Important Roads
Connecting Roads
Interstate Route Numbers
Federal Route Numbers
State and Other Route Numbers
Points of Interest, Recreation Areas
Airports
© HAMMOND WORLD ATLAS CORPORATION
See inset for continuation
Same scale as main map
LAKE MICHIGAN
CHICAGO
Waukegan
North Chicago
Highland Park
Evanston
Skokie
Wilmette
Des Plaines
Arlington Heights
Schaumburg
Elgin
Naperville
Aurora
Joliet
Wheaton
Oak Park
Cicero
Gary
Hammond
East Chicago
CHICAGO O'HARE INTERNATIONAL
CHICAGO MIDWAY
COOK CO.
DU PAGE CO.
KANE CO.
WILL CO.
LAKE CO.
KENDALL CO.
PORTER CO.
ILLINOIS
INDIANA
15 MILES
25 KILOMETERS
Printed in U.S.A.

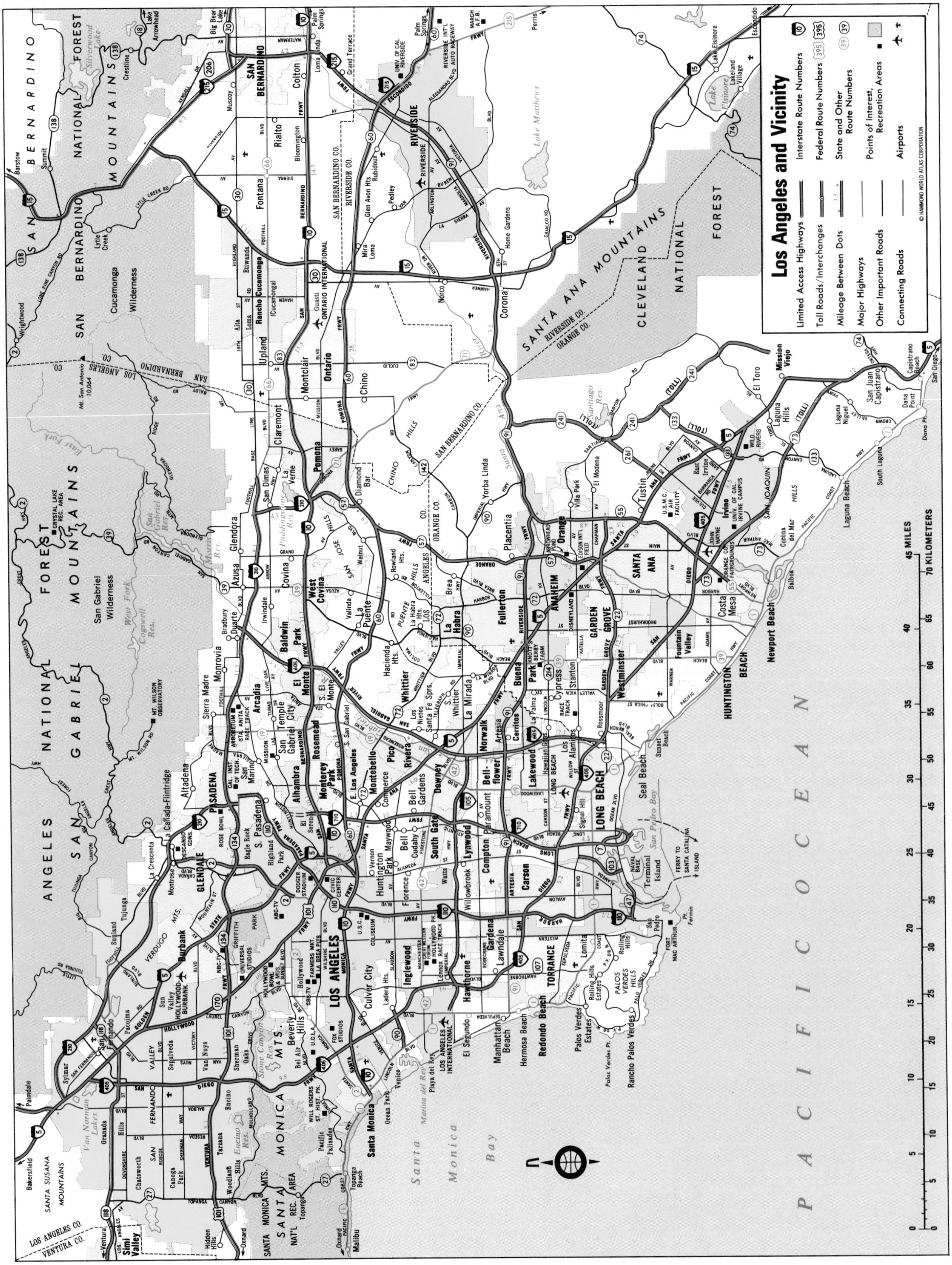
Los Angeles and Vicinity
Limited Access Highways
Toll Roads/Interchanges
Mileage Between Dots
Major Highways
Other Important Roads
Connecting Roads
Interstate Route Numbers
Federal Route Numbers
State and Other Route Numbers
Points of Interest, Recreation Areas
Airports
© HAMMOND WORLD ATLAS CORPORATION
PACIFIC OCEAN
Santa Monica Bay
ANGELES NATIONAL FOREST
SAN GABRIEL MOUNTAINS
SAN BERNARDINO NATIONAL FOREST
SAN BERNARDINO MOUNTAINS
SANTA ANA MOUNTAINS
CLEVELAND NATIONAL FOREST
SANTA MONICA MTS.
SANTA SUSANA MOUNTAINS
SAN FERNANDO VALLEY
LOS ANGELES
LONG BEACH
PASADENA
SAN BERNARDINO
RIVERSIDE
ANAHEIM
SANTA ANA
HUNTINGTON BEACH
Newport Beach
Santa Monica
Glendale
Burbank
Pomona
Ontario
Fontana
Corona
Fullerton
Torrance
Inglewood
Irvine
Mission Viejo
LOS ANGELES INTERNATIONAL
ONTARIO INTERNATIONAL
LOS ANGELES CO.
ORANGE CO.
RIVERSIDE CO.
SAN BERNARDINO CO.
VENTURA CO.
45 MILES
70 KILOMETERS

GEOGRAPHICAL TERMS

A. = Arabic Burm. = Burmese Camb. = Cambodian Ch. = Chinese Czech. = Czechoslovakian Dan. = Danish Du. = Dutch Finn. = Finnish Fr. = French Ger. = German Ice. = Icelandic It. = Italian Jap. = Japanese Mong. = Mongol Nor. = Norwegian Per. = Persian Port. = Portuguese Russ. = Russian Sp. = Spanish Sw. = Swedish Turk. = Turkish

Å	Nor., Sw.	Stream
Aas	Dan., Nor.	Hills
Abajo	Sp	Lower
Ada, Adasi	Turk	Island
Altipiano	It	Plateau
Altiplano	Sp	Plateau
Alv, Alf, Elf	Sw	River
Arrecife	Sp	Reef
Asa	Nor., Sw	Hill
Asaga	Turk	Lower
Austral	Sp	Southern
Baai	Du	Bay
Bab	Arabic	Gate or Strait
Bahia	Sp	Bay
Bahr	Arabic	Marsh, Lake, Sea, River
Baia	Port	Bay
Baie	Fr	Bay, Gulf
Baizo	Port	Low
Bakke	Dan	Hill
Bana	Jap	Cape
Bañados	Sp	Marshes
Band	Per	Mt. Range
Bandao	Ch	Peninsula
Bandar	Per	Harbor
Barra	Sp	Reef
Bel	Turk	Pass
Belt	Ger	Strait
Ben	Gaelic	Mountain
Bera	Du	Mountain
Berg	Ger., Du	Mountain
Bir	Arabic	Well
Boca	Sp	Gulf, Inlet
Boğhaz	Turk	Strait
Bolshoi, Bolshaya	Russ	Big
Bolson	Sp	Depression
Bong	Korean	Mountain
Boreal	Sp	Northern
Breen	Nor	Glacier
Bro	Dan., Nor., Sw.	Bridge
Bucht	Ger	Bay
Bugt	Dan	Bay
Bukhta	Russ	Bay
Bukit	Malay	Hill, Mountain
Bukt	Nor., Sw	Bay, Gulf
Burnu, Burun	Turk	Cape, Point
By	Dan., Nor., Sw	Town
Cabo	Port., Sp	Cape
Campos	Port	Plains
Canal	Port., Sp	Channel
Cap, Capo	Fr., It	Cape
Cataratas	Sp	Falls
Catena	It	Mt. Range
Catingas	Port	Open Woodlands
Cayos	Sp	Islands
Central, Centrale	Fr., It	Middle
Cerrito, Cerro	Sp	Hill
Cerros	Sp	Hills, Mountains
Chai	Turk	River
Chott	Arabic	Salt Lake
Ciénaga	Sp	Swamp
Ciudad	Sp	City
Col	Fr	Pass
Cordillera	Sp	Mt. Range, Mts.
Côte	Fr	Coast
Csatoria	Magyar	Canal
Cuchilla	Sp	Mt. Range
Curiche	Sp	Swamp
Dağ, Dağı	Turk	Mountain, Peak
Dağlari	Turk	Mt. Range
Dal	Nor., Sw	Valley
Dar	Arabic	Land
Dar'ya	Russ	River
Daryacheh	Per	Marshy Lake
Dasht	Per	Desert, Plain
Deniz, Denizi	Turk	Sea, Lake
Desierto	Sp	Desert
Détroit	Fr	Strait
Djeziret	Arabic, Turk	Island
Do	Korean	Island
Doi	Thai	Mountain
Eiland	Du	Island
Elv	Dan., Nor	River
Embalse	Sp	Reservoir
Emi	Berber	Mountain
Erg	Arabic	Dune, Desert
Eski	Turk	Old
Est, Este	Fr., Port., Sp	East
Estero	Sp	Estuary, Creek
Estrecho, Estreito	Sp., Port	Strait
Etang	Fr	Pond, Lagoon, Lake
Feng	Ch	Mountain
Fiume	It	River
Fjäll	Sw	Mountain
Fjeld, Fjell	Nor	Hills, Mountain
Fjord	Dan., Nor., Sw	Fiord
Fleuve	Fr	River
Fljót	Ice	Stream
Fluss	Ger	River
Fors	Sw	Waterfall
Fos, Foss	Dan., Nor	Waterfall
Gamla	Nor	Old
Gamle	Dan	Old
Gata	Jap	Lake
Gawa	Jap	River
Gebel	Arabic	Mountain
Gebergte	Du	Mt. Range
Gebirge	Ger	Mt. Range
Gobi	Mongol	Desert
Goe	Jap	Pass
Gol	Mongol, Turk	Lake, Stream
Golf	Ger., Du	Gulf
Golfe	Fr	Gulf
Golfo	Sp., It., Port	Gulf
Gölü	Turk	Lake
Gora	Russ	Mountain
Grand, Grande	Fr., Sp	Big
Groot	Du	Big
Gross	Ger	Big
Grosso	It., Port	Big
Guba	Russ	Bay, Gulf
Gunto	Jap	Archipelago
Gunung	Malay	Mountain
Hai	Ch	Sea
Haixia	Ch	Strait
Halbinsel	Ger	Peninsula
Hamáda, Hammada	Arabic	Rocky Plateau
Hamn	Sw	Harbor
Hamún	Per	Marsh
Hanto	Jap	Peninsula
Has, Hassi	Arabic	Well
Hav	Dan., Nor., Sw	Sea, Ocean
Havet	Nor	Bay
Havn	Dan., Nor	Harbor
Havre	Fr	Harbor
He	Ch	River, Stream
Higashi, Higasi	Jap	East
Hochebene	Ger	Plateau
Hoek	Du	Cape
Hoku	Jap	North
Holm	Dan., Nor., Sw	Island
Hory	Czech	Mountains
Hoved	Dan., Nor	Cape, Promontory
Hu	Ch	Lake
Huang	Ch	Yellow
Huk	Dan., Nor., Sw	Point
Hus, Huus	Dan., Nor., Sw	House
Idehan	Arabic	Desert
Ile	Fr	Island
Ilet	Fr	Islet
Ilot	Fr	Islet
Indre	Dan., Nor	Inner
Inferieur, Inferiore	Fr., It	Lower
Inner, Inre	Sw	Inner
Insel	Ger	Island
Irmak	Turk	River
Isla	Sp	Island
Isola	It	Island
Jabal, Jebel	Arabic	Mountains
Järvi	Finn	Lake
Jaure	Sw	Lake
Jiang	Ch	River, Stream
Jima	Jap	Island
Joki	Finn	River
Kaap	Du	Cape
Kabir, Kebir	Arabic	Big
Kai	Jap	Sea
Kaikyo	Jap	Strait
Kami	Turk	Upper
Kanaal	Du	Canal
Kanal	Russ., Ger	Canal, Channel
Kao	Thai	Mountain
Kap, Kapp	Nor., Sw., Ice	Cape
Kaupunki	Finn	Town
Kawa	Jap	River
Khao	Thai	Mountain
Khrebet	Russ	Mt. Range
Kita	Jap	North
Klein	Du., Ger	Small
Klint	Dan	Promontory
Kô	Jap	Lake
Ko	Thai	Island
Koh	Camb., Khmer	Island
Kop	Du	Peak, Head
Köping	Sw	Market, Borough
Körfez, Körfezi	Turk	Gulf
Kosa	Russ	Spit
Kosui	Jap	Lake
Kraal	Du	Native Village
Kuchuk	Turk	Small
Kuh, Kuhha	Per	Mt. Range, Mts.
Kul	Sinkiang Turki	Lake
Kum	Turk	Desert
Kuro	Jap	Black
Laag	Du	Low
Lac	Fr	Lake
Lago	Port., Sp., It	Lake
Lagoa	Port	Lagoon
Laguna	Sp	Lagoon
Lagune	Fr	Lagoon
Lahti	Finn	Bay, Bight
Län	Sw	County
Liedao	Ch	Islands, Archipelago
Lilla	Sw	Small
Lille	Dan., Nor	Small
Ling	Ch	Mountain
Llanos	Sp	Plains
Mae Nam	Thai	River
Mali, Malaya	Russ	Small
Man	Korean	Bay
Mar	Sp., Port	Sea
Mare	It	Sea
Medio	Sp	Middle
Meer	Du	Lake
Meer	Ger	Sea
Mer	Fr	Sea
Meridionale	It	Southern
Meseta	Sp	Plateau
Middelst, Midden	Du	Middle
Minami	Jap	Southern
Mis	Russ	Cape
Misaki	Jap	Cape
Mittel	Ger	Middle
Mont	Fr	Mountain
Montagne	Fr	Mountain
Montaña	Sp	Mountains
Monte	Sp., It., Port.	Mountain
More	Russ	Sea
Mörön	Mong	Stream
Morro	Port., Sp	Mountain, Promontory
Morue	Fr	Hill
Moyen	Fr	Middle
Muang	Siamese	Town
Mui	Vietnamese	Cape, Point
Mys	Russ	Cape
Nada	Jap	Sea
Naka	Jap	Middle
Nam	Burm., Lao	River
Namakzar	Per	Salt Waste
Nan	Jap	South
Nes	Nor	Cape, Point
Nevado	Sp	Snow-covered Peak
Nieder	Ger	Lower
Nishi, Nisi	Jap	West
Nizhni, Nizhnyaya	Russ	Lower
Njarga	Finn	Peninsula, Promontory
Nong	Thai	Lake
Noord	Du	North
Nord	Fr., Ger	North
Norte	Sp., It., Port	North
Nos	Russ	Cape
Novi, Novaya	Russ	New
Nur, Nuur	Ch., Mong	Lake
Nuruu	Mong	Mountains
Nusa	Malay	Island
Ny, Nya	Nor., Sw	New
O	Jap	Big
Ö	Nor., Sw	Island
Ober	Ger	Upper
Occidental, Occidentale	Sp., It	Western
Odde	Dan	Point
Oeste	Port	West
Ooster	Du	Eastern
Opper, Over	Du	Upper
Oriental	Sp., Fr	Eastern
Orientale	It	Eastern
Orta	Turk	Middle
Ost	Ger	East
Ostrov	Russ	Island
Ouest	Fr	West
öy	Nor	Island
Ozero	Russ	Lake
Pampa	Sp	Plain
Pas	Fr	Channel, Strait
Paso	Sp	Pass
Passo	It., Port	Pass
Peña	Sp	Rock, Mountain
Pendi	Ch	Basin
Penisola	It	Peninsula
Pequeño	Sp	Small
Pereval	Russ	Pass
Peski	Russ	Desert
Petit, Petite	Fr	Small
Phu	Lao, Annamese	Mtn.
Pic	Fr	Mountain
Piccolo	It	Small
Pico	Port., Sp	Mountain, Peak
Pik	Russ	Mountain, Peak
Piton	Fr	Mountain, Peak
Planalto	Port	Plateau
Plato	Russ	Plateau
Pointe	Fr	Point
Poluostrov	Russ	Peninsula
Ponta	Port	Point
Presa	Sp	Reservoir
Presqu'île	Fr	Peninsula
Proliv	Russ	Strait
Pulou, Pulo	Malay	Island
Punt	Du	Point
Punta	Sp., It., Port	Point
Qiryat	Hebrew	City, Settlement
Qum	Turk	Desert
Qundao	Ch	Islands
Rada	Sp	Inlet
Rade	Fr	Bay, Inlet
Ras	Arabic	Cape
Reka	Russ	River
Retto	Jap	Archipelago
Ria	Sp	Estuary
Río	Sp	River
Rivier, Rivière	Du., Fr	River
Rud	Per	River
Sai	Jap	West
Saki	Jap	Cape
Salar, Salina	Sp	Salt Deposit
Salto	Sp., Port	Falls
San	Jap., Korean	Hill
Sanmaek	Korean	Mt. Range
Schiereiland	Du	Peninsula
Se	Camb., Khmer	River
See	Ger	Sea, Lake
Selvas	Sp., Port	Woods, Forest
Seno	Sp	Bay, Gulf
Serra	Port	Mts.
Serranía	Sp	Mts.
Seto	Jap	Strait
Settentrionale	It	Northern
Severni, Severnaya	Russ	North
Shamo	Ch	Desert
Shan	Ch., Jap	Hill, Mts.
Shankou	Ch	Pass
Shatt	Arabic	River
Shima	Jap	Island
Shimo	Jap	Lower
Shin	Jap	Land
Shiro	Jap	White
Shoto	Jap	Islands
Si	Ch	West
Sierra	Sp	Mt. Range, Mts.
Sjö	Nor., Sw	Lake, Sea
Sok, Suk, Souk	Arabic	Market
Song	Annamese	River
Sopka	Russ	Volcano
Spitze	Ger	Mt. Peak
Sredni, Srednyaya	Russ	Middle
Stad	Dan., Nor., Sw	City
Stari, Staraya	Russ	Old
Step	Russ	Treeless Plain
Straat	Du	Strait
Strasse	Ger	Strait
Stretto	It	Strait
Ström	Dan., Nor., Sw	Sound
Stung	Camb., Khmer	River
Su	Turk	River
Sud, Süd	Sp., Fr., Ger	South
Suido	Jap	Strait, Channel
Sul	Port	South
Sund	Dan., Nor., Sw.	Sound
Sungei	Malay	River
Supérieur	Fr	Upper
Superior, Superiore	Sp., It	Upper
Sur	Sp	South
Suyu	Turk	River
Ta	Ch	Big
Tafelland	Du	Plateau
Tagh	Turk	Mt. Range
Take	Jap	Peak, Ridge
Takht	Arabic	Lower
Tal	Ger	Valley
Tanjung	Malay	Cape, Point
Tell	Arabic	Hill
Thale	Thai	Sea, Lake
Tind	Nor	Peak
Tō	Jap	East
To	Jap	Island
Toge	Jap	Pass
Trask	Finn	Lake
Tugh	Somali	Dry River
Ujung	Malay	Point
Umi	Jap	Bay
Unter	Ger	Lower
Ura	Jap	Inlet
Uul	Mong	Mountain
Val	Fr	Valley
Vatn	Nor	Lake
Vecchio	It	Old
Veld	Du	Plain, Field
Velho	Port	Old
Verkhni	Russ	Upper
Vesi	Finn	Lake
Viejo	Sp	Old
Vik	Nor., Sw	Bay
Vishni, Vishnyaya	Russ	High
Vodokhranilishche	Russ	Reservoir
Volcán	Sp	Volcano
Vostochni, Vostochnaya	Russ	East, Eastern
Wadi	Arabic	Dry River
Wald	Ger	Forest
Wan	Jap	Bay
Westersch	Du	Western
Wüste	Ger	Desert
Yama	Jap	Mountain
Yug, Yuzhni, Yuzhnaya	Russ	South, Southern
Zaki	Jap	Cape
Zaliv	Russ	Bay, Gulf
Zangbo	Tibetan	River, Stream
Zapadni, Zapadnaya	Russ	Western
Zee	Du	Sea
Zemlya	Russ	Land
Zizhiqu	Ch	Autonomous Region
Zuid	Du	South

WORLD STATISTICS

Elements of the Solar System

	Mean Distance from Sun: in Miles	in Kilometers	Period of Revolution around Sun	Period of Rotation on Axis	Equatorial Diameter in Miles	in Kilometers	Surface Gravity (Earth = 1)	Mass (Earth = 1)	Mean Density (Water = 1)	Number of Satellites
Mercury	35,990,000	57,900,000	87.97 days	58.7 days	3,032	4,880	0.38	0.055	5.4	0
Venus	67,240,000	108,200,000	224.70 days	243.7 days†	7,521	12,104	0.91	0.815	5.2	0
Earth	93,000,000	149,700,000	365.26 days	23h 56m	7,926	12,755	1.00	1.00	5.5	1
Mars	141,610,000	227,900,000	686.98 days	24h 37m	4,221	6,794	0.38	0.107	3.9	2
Jupiter	483,675,000	778,400,000	11.86 years	9h 55m	88,846	142,984	2.36	317.8	1.3	16
Saturn	886,572,000	1,426,800,000	29.46 years	10h 30m	74,898	120,536	0.92	95.2	0.7	18
Uranus	1,783,957,000	2,871,000,000	84.01 years	17h 14m†	31,763	51,118	0.89	14.5	1.3	15
Neptune	2,795,114,000	4,498,300,000	164.79 years	16h 6m	30,778	49,532	1.13	17.1	1.6	8
Pluto	3,670,000,000	5,906,400,000	247.70 years	6.4 days†	1,413	2,274	0.07	0.002	2.1	1

† Retrograde motion

Source: NASA, National Space Science Data Center

Dimensions of the Earth

	Area in: Sq. Miles	Sq. Kilometers
Superficial area	196,939,000	510,072,000
Land surface	57,506,000	148,940,000
Water surface	139,433,000	361,132,000
	Distance in: Miles	**Kilometers**
Equatorial circumference	24,902	40,075
Polar circumference	24,860	40,007
Equatorial diameter	7,926.4	12,756.4
Polar diameter	7,899.8	12,713.6
Equatorial radius	3,963.2	6,378.2
Polar radius	3,949.9	6,356.8
Volume of the Earth	2.6×10^{11} cubic miles	10.84×10^{11} cubic kilometers
Mass or weight	6.6×10^{21} short tons	6.0×10^{21} metric tons
Maximum distance from Sun	94,600,000 miles	152,000,000 kilometers
Minimum distance from Sun	91,300,000 miles	147,000,000 kilometers

Oceans and Major Seas

	Area in: Sq. Miles	Sq. Kms.	Greatest Depth in: Feet	Meters
Pacific Ocean	63,855,000	166,241,000	36,198	11,033
Atlantic Ocean	31,744,000	82,217,000	28,374	8,648
Indian Ocean	28,417,000	73,600,000	25,344	7,725
Arctic Ocean	5,427,000	14,056,000	17,880	5,450
Caribbean Sea	970,000	2,512,300	24,720	7,535
Mediterranean Sea	969,000	2,509,700	16,896	5,150
South China Sea	895,000	2,318,000	15,000	4,600
Bering Sea	875,000	2,266,250	15,800	4,800
Gulf of Mexico	600,000	1,554,000	12,300	3,750
Sea of Okhotsk	590,000	1,528,100	11,070	3,370
East China Sea	482,000	1,248,400	9,500	2,900
Yellow Sea	480,000	1,243,200	350	107
Sea of Japan	389,000	1,007,500	12,280	3,740
Hudson Bay	317,500	822,300	846	258
North Sea	222,000	575,000	2,200	670
Black Sea	185,000	479,150	7,365	2,245
Red Sea	169,000	437,700	7,200	2,195
Baltic Sea	163,000	422,170	1,506	459

The Continents

	Area in: Sq. Miles	Sq. Kms.	Percent of World's Land
Asia	17,128,500	44,362,815	29.5
Africa	11,707,000	30,321,130	20.2
North America	9,363,000	24,250,170	16.2
South America	6,879,725	17,818,505	11.9
Antarctica	5,405,000	14,000,000	9.4
Europe	4,057,000	10,507,630	7.0
Australia	2,967,893	7,686,850	5.1

Major Ship Canals

	Length in: Miles	Kms.	Minimum Depth in: Feet	Meters
Volga-Baltic, Russia	225	362	–	–
Baltic-White Sea, Russia	140	225	16	5
Suez, Egypt	100.76	162	42	13
Albert, Belgium	80	129	16.5	5
Moscow-Volga, Russia	80	129	18	6
Volga-Don, Russia	62	100	–	–
Göta, Sweden	54	87	10	3
Kiel (Nord-Ostsee), Germany	53.2	86	38	12
Panama Canal, Panama	50.72	82	41.6	13
Houston Ship, U.S.A.	50	81	36	11

Largest Islands

	Area in: Sq. Miles	Sq. Kms.
Greenland	840,000	2,175,600
New Guinea	305,000	789,950
Borneo	286,000	740,740
Madagascar	226,656	587,040
Baffin, Canada	195,928	507,454
Sumatra, Indonesia	164,000	424,760
Honshu, Japan	88,000	227,920
Great Britain	84,400	218,896
Victoria, Canada	83,896	217,290
Ellesmere, Canada	75,767	196,236
Celebes, Indonesia	72,986	189,034
South I., New Zealand	58,393	151,238
Java, Indonesia	48,842	126,501
North I., New Zealand	44,187	114,444
Cuba	42,803	110,860
Newfoundland, Canada	42,031	108,860
Luzon, Philippines	40,420	104,688
Iceland	39,768	103,000
Mindanao, Philippines	36,537	94,631
Ireland	32,589	84,406
Hokkaido, Japan	30,436	75,066
Sakhalin, Russia	29,500	76,405

	Area in: Sq. Miles	Sq. Kms.
Hispaniola, Haiti & Dom. Rep.	29,399	76,143
Banks, Canada	27,038	70,028
Ceylon,Sri Lanka	25,332	65,610
Tasmania, Australia	24,600	63,710
Svalbard, Norway	23,957	62,049
Devon, Canada	21,331	55,247
Novaya Zemlya (north isl.), Russia	18,600	48,200
Marajó, Brazil	17,991	46,597
Tierra del Fuego, Chile & Argentina	17,900	46,360
Alexander, Antarctica	16,700	43,250
Axel Heiberg, Canada	16,671	43,178
Melville, Canada	16,274	42,150
Southhampton, Canada	15,913	41,215
New Britain, Papua New Guinea	14,100	36,519
Taiwan, China	13,836	35,835
Kyushu, Japan	13,770	35,664
Hainan, China	13,127	33,999
Prince of Wales, Canada	12,872	33,338
Spitsbergen, Norway	12,355	31,999
Vancouver, Canada	12,079	31,285
Timor, Indonesia	11,527	29,855
Sicily, Italy	9,926	25,708

	Area in: Sq. Miles	Sq. Kms.
Somerset, Canada	9,570	24,786
Sardinia, Italy	9,301	24,090
Shikoku, Japan	6,860	17,767
New Caledonia, France	6,530	16,913
Nordaustlandet, Norway	6,409	16,599
Samar, Philippines	5,050	13,080
Negros, Philippines	4,906	12,707
Palawan, Philippines	4,550	11,785
Panay, Philippines	4,446	11,515
Jamaica	4,232	10,961
Hawaii, United States	4,038	10,458
Viti Levu, Fiji	4,010	10,386
Cape Breton, Canada	3,981	10,311
Mindoro, Philippines	3,759	9,736
Kodiak, Alaska, U.S.A.	3,670	9,505
Cyprus	3,572	9,251
Puerto Rico, U.S.A.	3,435	8,897
Corsica, France	3,352	8,682
New Ireland, Papua New Guinea	3,340	8,651
Crete, Greece	3,218	8,335
Anticosti, Canada	3,066	7,941
Wrangel, Russia	2,819	7,301

Principal Mountains

	Height in: Feet	Meters
Everest, Nepal-China	29,028	8,848
K2 (Godwin Austen), Pakistan-China	28,250	8,611
Kanchenjunga, Nepal-India	28,208	8,598
Lhotse, Nepal-China	27,923	8,511
Makalu, Nepal-China	27,789	8,470
Dhaulagiri, Nepal	26,810	8,172
Nanga Parbat, Pakistan	26,660	8,126
Annapurna, Nepal	26,504	8,078
Nanda Devi, India	25,645	7,817
Rakaposhi, Pakistan	25,550	7,788
Kongur Shan, China	25,325	7,719
Tirich Mir, Pakistan	25,230	7,690
Gongga Shan, China	24,790	7,556
Ismail Samani Peak, Tajikistan	24,590	7,495
Pobeda Peak, Kyrgyzstan	24,406	7,439
Chomo Lhari, Bhutan-China	23,997	7,314
Muztag, China	23,891	7,282
Cerro Aconcagua, Argentina	22,831	6,959
Ojos del Salado, Chile-Argentina	22,572	6,880
Bonete, Chile-Argentina	22,546	6,872
Tupungato, Chile-Argentina	22,310	6,800

	Height in: Feet	Meters
Pissis, Argentina	22,241	6,779
Mercedario, Argentina	22,211	6,770
Huascarán, Peru	22,205	6,768
Llullaillaco, Chile-Argentina	22,057	6,723
Nevada Ancohuma, Bolivia	21,489	6,550
Chimborazo, Ecuador	20,561	6,267
McKinley, Alaska	20,320	6,194
Logan, Yukon, Canada	19,524	5,951
Cotopaxi, Ecuador	19,347	5,897
Kilimanjaro, Tanzania	19,340	5,895
El Misti, Peru	19,101	5,822
Pico Cristóbal Colón, Colombia	18,947	5,775
Huila, Colombia	18,865	5,750
Citlaltépetl (Orizaba), Mexico	18,700	5,700
Damavand, Iran	18,605	5,671
El'brus, Russia	18,510	5,642
St. Elias, Alaska, U.S.A.-Yukon, Canada	18,008	5,489
Dykhtau, Russia	17,070	5,203
Kenya, Kenya	17,058	5,199
Ararat, Turkey	16,946	5,165
Vinson Massif, Antarctica	16,864	5,140

	Height in: Feet	Meters
Margherita, D.R. Congo-Uganda	16,795	5,119
Kazbek, Georgia-Russia	16,558	5,047
Puncak Jaya, Indonesia	16,503	5,030
Blanc, France	15,771	4,807
Klyuchevskaya Sopka, Russia	15,584	4,750
Fairweather, Br. Col., Canada	15,300	4,663
Dufourspitze, Italy-Switzerland	15,203	4,634
Ras Dashen, Ethiopia	15,157	4,620
Matterhorn, Switzerland	14,691	4,478
Whitney, California, U.S.A.	14,494	4,418
Elbert, Colorado, U.S.A.	14,433	4,399
Rainier, Washington, U.S.A.	14,410	4,392
Shasta, California, U.S.A.	14,162	4,317
Pikes Peak, Colorado, U.S.A.	14,110	4,301
Finsteraarhorn, Switzerland	14,022	4,274
Mauna Kea, Hawaii, U.S.A.	13,796	4,205
Mauna Loa, Hawaii, U.S.A.	13,677	4,169
Jungfrau, Switzerland	13,642	4,158
Grossglockner, Austria	12,457	3,797
Fuji, Japan	12,389	3,776
Cook, New Zealand	12,349	3,764

Longest Rivers

	Length in: Miles	Kms.
Nile, Africa	4,145	6,671
Amazon, S. America	4,007	6,448
Mississippi-Missouri-Red Rock, U.S.A.	3,710	5,971
Chang Jiang (Yangtze), China	3,500	5,633
Ob'-Irtysh, Russia-Kazakhstan	3,362	5,411
Yenisey-Angara, Russia	3,100	4,989
Huang He (Yellow), China	2,950	4,747
Congo, Africa	2,780	4,474
Amur-Shilka-Onon, Asia	2,744	4,416
Lena, Russia	2,734	4,400
Mackenzie-Peace-Finlay,Canada	2,635	4,241
Paraná-La Plata, S. America	2,630	4,232
Mekong, Asia	2,610	4,200
Niger, Africa	2,580	4,152
Missouri-Red Rock, U.S.A.	2,564	4,125
Yenisey, Russia	2,500	4,028
Mississippi, U.S.A.	2,348	3,778
Murray-Darling, Australia	2,310	3,718
Volga, Russia	2,290	3,685
Madeira, S. America	2,013	3,240
Purus, S. America	1,995	3,211
Yukon, Alaska-Canada	1,979	3,185
Zambezi, Africa	1,950	3,138
São Francisco, Brazil	1,930	3,106
St. Lawrence, Canada-U.S.A.	1,900	3,058

	Length in: Miles	Kms.
Rio Grande, Mexico-U.S.A.	1,885	3,034
Syrdar'ya-Naryn, Asia	1,859	2,992
Indus, Asia	1,800	2,897
Danube, Europe	1,775	2,857
Brahmaputra, Asia	1,700	2,736
Tocantins, Brazil	1,677	2,699
Salween, Asia	1,675	2,696
Euphrates, Asia	1,650	2,655
Xi Jiang, China	1,650	2,655
Amudar'ya, Asia	1,616	2,601
Nelson-Saskatchewan, Canada	1,600	2,575
Orinoco, S. America	1,600	2,575
Paraguay, S. America	1,584	2,549
Kolyma, Russia	1,562	2,514
Ganges, Asia	1,550	2,494
Ural, Russia-Kazakhstan	1,509	2,428
Japurá, S. America	1,500	2,414
Arkansas, U.S.A.	1,450	2,334
Colorado, U.S.A.-Mexico	1.450	2,334
Negro, S. America	1,400	2,253
Dnieper, Russia-Belarus-Ukraine	1,368	2,202
Orange, Africa	1,350	2,173
Irrawaddy, Burma	1,325	2,132
Brazos, U.S.A.	1,309	2,107
Ohio-Allegheny, U.S.A.	1,306	2,102

	Length in: Miles	Kms.
Kama, Russia	1,252	2,031
Don, Russia	1,222	1,967
Red, U.S.A.	1,222	1,966
Columbia, U.S.A.-Canada	1,214	1,953
Tigris, Asia	1,181	1,901
Darling, Australia	1,160	1,867
Angara, Russia	1,135	1,827
Songhua Jiang (Sungari), Asia	1,130	1,819
Pechora, Russia	1,124	1,809
Snake, U.S.A.	1,038	1,670
Churchill, Canada	1,000	1,609
Pilcomayo, S. America	1,000	1,609
Uruguay, S. America	994	1.600
Platte-N. Platte, U.S.A.	990	1,593
Ohio, U.S.A.	981	1,578
Magdalena, Colombia	956	1,538
Pecos, U.S.A.	926	1,490
Oka, Russia	918	1,477
Canadian, U.S.A.	906	1,458
Colorado, Texas, U.S.A.	894	1,439
Dniester, Ukraine-Moldova	876	1,410
Fraser, Canada	850	1,369
Rhine, Europe	820	1,319
Northern Dvina, Russia	809	1,302
Ottawa, Canada	790	1,271

Principal Natural Lakes

	Area in:		Max. Depth in:	
	Sq. Miles	Sq. Kms.	Feet	Meters
Caspian Sea, Asia	143,243	370,999	3,264	995
Lake Superior, U.S.A.-Canada	31,820	82,414	1,329	405
Lake Victoria, Africa	26,628	69,215	270	82
Lake Huron, U.S.A.-Canada	23,010	59,596	748	228
Lake Michigan, U.S.A.	22,400	58,016	923	281
Aral Sea, Kazakhstan-Uzbekistan	15,830	41,000	213	65
Lake Tanganyika, Africa	12,650	32,764	4,700	1,433
Lake Baykal, Russia	12,162	31,500	5,316	1,620
Great Bear Lake, Canada	12,096	31,328	1,356	413
Lake Nyasa (Malawi), Africa	11,555	29,928	2,320	707
Great Slave Lake, Canada	11,031	28,570	2,015	614
Lake Erie, U.S.A.-Canada	9,940	25,745	210	64
Lake Winnipeg, Canada	9,417	24,390	60	18
Lake Ontario, U.S.A.-Canada	7,540	19,529	775	244
Lake Balkhash, Kazakhstan	7,081	18,340	87	27
Lake Ladoga, Russia	6,900	17,871	738	225
Lake Maracaibo, Venezuela	5,120	13,261	100	31
Lake Chad, Africa*	10,000 –	25,900 –		
	4,000	10,360	25	8
Lake Onega, Russia	3,761	9,741	377	115

	Area in:		Max. Depth in:	
	Sq. Miles	Sq. Kms.	Feet	Meters
Lake Eyre, Australia*	3,500-0	9,065-0	–	–
Lake Titicaca, Peru-Bolivia	3,200	8,288	1, 000	305
Lake Nicaragua, Nicaragua	3,100	8,029	230	70
Lake Athabasca, Canada	3,064	7,936	400	122
Reindeer Lake, Canada*	2,568	6,651	–	–
Lake Turkana (Rudolf), Africa	2,463	6,379	240	73
Issyk-Kul', Kyrgyzstan	2,425	6,281	2,303	702
Lake Torrens, Australia*	2,230	5,776	–	–
Vänern, Sweden	2,156	5,584	328	100
Nettilling Lake, Canada*	2,140	5,543	–	–
Lake Winnipegosis, Canada	2,075	5,374	38	12
Lake Mobutu Sese Seko (Albert), Africa	2,075	5,374	160	49
Lake Kariba, Zambia-Zimbabwe	2,050	5,310	295	90
Lake Nipigon, Canada	1,872	4,848	540	165
Lake Mweru, Dem. Rep. of the Congo-Zambia	1,800	4,662	60	18
Lake Manitoba, Canada	1,799	4,659	12	4
Lake Taymyr, Russia	1,737	4,499	85	26
Lake Khanka, China-Russia	1,700	4,403	33	10
Lake Kioga, Uganda	1,700	4,403	25	8
Lake of the Woods, U.S.A.-Canada	1,679	4,349	70	21

* Figures subject to great seasonal variations.

TABLES OF AIRLINE DISTANCES

ALL DISTANCES IN STATUTE MILES

BETWEEN PRINCIPAL CITIES OF THE WORLD

FROM/TO	Azores	Baghdad	Berlin	Bombay	Buenos Aires	Callao	Cairo	Cape Town	Chicago	Istanbul	Guam	Honolulu	Juneau	London	Los Angeles	Melbourne	Mexico City	Montreal	New Orleans	New York	Panama	Paris	Rio de Janeiro	San Francisco	Santiago	Seattle	Shanghai	Singapore	Tokyo	Wellington
Azores	....	3906	2118	5930	5385	4825	3325	5670	3305	2880	8985	7421	4715	1562	5034	12190	4584	2548	3718	2604	3918	1617	4312	5114	5718	4720	7324	8338	7370	11475
Baghdad	3906	....	2040	2022	8215	8618	785	4923	6490	1085	6380	8445	6180	2568	7695	8150	8155	5814	7212	6066	7807	2385	7012	7521	8876	6848	4468	4443	5242	9782
Berlin	2148	2040	....	3947	7411	6937	1823	5949	4458	1068	7158	7384	4638	575	5849	9992	6119	3776	5182	4026	5902	540	6246	5744	7842	5121	5323	6226	5623	11384
Bombay	5930	2022	3947	....	9380	10530	2698	5133	8144	3043	4831	8172	6992	4526	8810	6140	9818	7582	8952	7875	9832	4391	8438	8523	10127	7830	3219	2425	4247	7752
Buenos Aires	5385	8215	7411	9380	....	1982	7428	4332	5598	7638	10516	7653	7964	6919	6148	7336	4609	5619	4902	5295	3319	6891	1230	6487	731	6956	12295	9940	11601	6341
Callao	4825	8618	6937	10530	1982	....	7870	6195	3765	7666	9760	5993	5806	6376	4155	8196	2619	3954	2990	3633	1450	6455	2490	4500	1548	4964	10760	11700	9740	6696
Cairo	3325	785	1823	2698	7428	7870	....	4476	6231	780	7175	8925	6352	2218	7675	8720	7807	5502	6862	5701	7230	2020	6242	7554	8100	6915	5290	5152	6005	10360
Cape Town	5670	4923	5949	5133	4332	6195	4476	....	8551	5210	8918	11655	10382	5975	10165	6510	8620	7975	8390	7845	7090	5732	3850	10340	5080	10305	8179	6025	9234	7149
Chicago	3305	6490	4458	8144	5598	3765	6231	8551	....	5530	7510	4315	2310	4015	1741	9837	1690	750	827	727	2320	4219	5320	1875	5325	1753	7155	9475	6410	8465
Istanbul	2880	1085	1068	3043	7638	7666	780	5210	5530	....	7015	8200	5665	1540	6895	9189	7160	4825	6220	5060	6797	1390	6420	6770	8230	6124	5084	5440	5649	10790
Guam	8985	6380	7158	4831	10516	9760	7175	8918	7510	7015	....	3896	5225	7605	6255	3497	7690	7840	7895	8115	9220	7675	11710	5952	9946	5785	1945	2990	1596	4206
Honolulu	7421	8445	7384	8172	7653	5993	8925	11655	4315	8200	3896	....	2825	7320	2620	5581	3846	4992	4305	5051	5347	7525	8400	2407	6935	2707	5009	6874	3940	4676
Juneau	4715	6180	4638	6992	7964	5806	6352	10382	2310	5665	5225	2825	....	4496	1835	8162	3210	2647	2860	2874	4456	4700	7611	1530	7320	870	4968	7375	4117	7501
London	1562	2568	575	4526	6919	6376	2218	5975	4015	1540	7605	7320	4496	....	5496	10590	5605	3370	4656	3500	5310	210	5747	5440	7275	4850	5841	6818	6050	11790
Los Angeles	5034	7695	5849	8810	6148	4155	7675	10165	1741	6895	6255	2620	1835	5496	....	8098	1445	2468	1695	2466	3025	5711	6330	345	5595	961	6598	8955	5600	6806
Melbourne	12190	8150	9992	6140	7336	8196	8720	6510	9837	9189	3497	5581	8162	10590	8098	....	8599	10553	9455	10541	9211	10500	8340	7970	7130	8330	4967	3768	5172	1655
Mexico City	4584	8155	6119	9818	4609	2619	7807	8620	1690	7160	7690	3846	3210	5605	1445	8599	....	2247	940	2110	1532	5800	4810	1870	4122	2339	8120	10495	7190	7003
Montreal	2548	5814	3776	7582	5619	3954	5502	7975	750	4825	7840	4992	2647	3370	2468	10553	2247	....	1390	340	2545	3490	5110	2557	5461	2309	7141	9280	6546	9206
New Orleans	3718	7212	5182	8952	4902	2990	6862	8390	827	6220	7895	4305	2860	4656	1695	9455	940	1390	....	1161	1600	4846	4798	1960	4553	2137	7830	10255	6993	7950
New York	2604	6066	4026	7875	5295	3633	5101	7845	727	5060	8115	5051	2874	3500	2466	10541	2110	340	1161	....	2211	3600	4810	2606	5134	2440	7460	9617	6846	9067
Panama	3918	7807	5902	9832	3319	1450	7230	7090	2320	6797	9220	5347	4456	5310	3025	9211	1532	2545	1600	2211	....	5440	3311	3349	3000	3680	9430	11800	8560	7580
Paris	1617	2385	540	4391	6891	6455	2020	5762	4219	1390	7675	7525	4700	210	5711	10500	5800	3490	4846	3600	5440	....	5710	5680	7300	5080	5855	6730	6132	11865
Rio de Janeiro	4312	7012	6246	8438	1230	2400	6242	3850	5320	6420	11710	8400	7611	5747	6330	8340	4810	5110	4798	4810	3311	5710	....	6655	1852	6945	11510	9875	11600	7510
San Francisco	5114	7521	5744	8523	6487	4500	7554	10340	1875	6770	5952	2407	1530	5440	345	7970	1870	2557	1960	2606	3349	5680	6655	....	5960	692	6245	8440	5250	6800
Santiago	5718	8876	7842	10127	731	1548	8100	5080	5325	8230	9946	6935	7320	7275	5595	7130	4122	5461	4553	5134	3000	7300	1852	5960	....	6466	11850	10270	10850	5925
Seattle	4720	6848	5121	7830	6956	4964	6915	10305	1753	6124	5785	2707	870	4850	961	8330	2339	2309	2137	2440	3680	5080	6945	692	6466	....	5780	8200	4863	7310
Shanghai	7324	4468	5323	3219	12295	10760	5290	8179	7155	5084	1945	5009	4968	5841	6598	4967	8120	7141	7830	7460	9430	5855	11510	6245	11850	5780	....	2395	1095	6080
Singapore	8338	4443	6226	2425	9940	11700	5152	6025	9475	5440	2990	6874	7375	6818	8955	3768	10495	9280	10255	9617	11800	6730	9875	8440	10270	8200	2395	....	3350	5360
Tokyo	7370	5242	5623	4247	11601	9740	6005	9234	6410	5649	1596	3940	4117	6050	5600	5762	7190	6546	6993	6846	8560	6132	11600	5250	10850	4863	1095	3350	....	5730
Wellington	11475	9782	11384	7752	6341	6696	10360	7149	8465	10790	4206	4676	7501	11790	6806	1655	7003	9206	7950	9067	7580	11865	7510	6800	5925	7310	6080	5360	5730	....

BETWEEN PRINCIPAL CITIES OF EUROPE

FROM/TO	Amsterdam	Athens	Baku	Barcelona	Belgrade	Berlin	Brussels	Bucharest	Budapest	Cologne	Copenhagen	Istanbul	Dresden	Dublin	Frankfurt	Hamburg	St. Petersburg	Lisbon	London	Lyon	Madrid	Marseilles	Milan	Moscow	Munich	Oslo	Paris	Riga	Rome	Sofia	Stockholm	Toulouse	Warsaw	Vienna	Zurich
Amsterdam	....	1340	2218	770	875	365	105	1100	710	128	381	1360	385	468	228	232	1090	1140	220	458	912	627	517	1325	415	568	257	820	808	1073	695	625	673	580	375
Athens	1340	....	1395	1160	500	1112	1292	460	698	1200	1320	350	1022	1765	1113	1250	1535	1770	1476	1100	1463	1025	900	1388	925	1610	1300	1310	650	335	1495	1215	990	795	1000
Baku	2218	1395	....	2427	1487	1867	2240	1220	1562	2127	1980	1070	1837	2490	2055	2020	1570	3050	2435	2238	2742	2238	2028	1175	1912	2118	2335	1590	1900	1360	1862	2425	1555	1700	2050
Barcelona	770	1160	2427	....	998	925	658	1210	924	692	1085	1380	860	919	665	910	1740	610	707	327	316	211	450	1852	648	1330	518	1440	530	1072	1410	156	1150	830	513
Belgrade	875	500	1487	998	....	618	850	295	205	750	840	502	530	1327	652	760	1165	1555	1040	752	1235	750	540	1160	475	1112	890	855	440	231	1005	930	510	300	590
Berlin	365	1112	1867	925	618	....	401	798	425	300	225	1068	95	815	268	165	815	1410	575	601	1149	730	570	995	310	520	540	520	730	810	503	815	320	322	410
Brussels	105	1292	2240	658	850	401	....	1110	700	110	475	1345	407	480	198	301	1175	998	202	352	807	521	435	1392	372	672	170	900	730	945	793	515	720	568	312
Bucharest	1100	460	1220	1210	295	798	1110	....	295	982	970	272	725	1560	890	950	1080	1842	1285	1025	1518	1020	819	920	725	1245	1152	870	700	194	1080	1210	580	520	855
Budapest	710	698	1562	924	205	425	700	295	....	590	629	650	345	1176	504	572	965	1515	900	680	1214	718	476	965	350	920	770	685	500	395	820	883	342	128	498
Cologne	128	1200	2127	692	750	300	110	982	590	....	400	1240	292	585	93	228	1090	1126	308	370	875	528	390	1285	282	635	250	805	675	945	722	875	602	460	259
Copenhagen	381	1320	1960	1085	840	225	475	970	629	400	....	1240	315	768	412	180	708	1520	590	760	1272	906	720	970	520	303	634	453	948	1010	330	962	415	538	595
Istanbul	1360	350	1070	1380	502	1068	1345	272	650	1240	1240	....	995	1830	1150	1222	1292	2005	1540	1238	1690	1205	1030	1180	975	1505	1390	1115	840	315	1340	1400	852	790	1090
Dresden	385	1022	1837	860	530	95	407	725	345	292	315	995	....	852	236	238	885	1380	592	540	1100	655	435	1200	227	620	523	585	630	730	598	762	325	235	342
Dublin	468	1765	2490	919	1327	815	480	1560	1176	585	768	1830	852	....	671	668	1440	1015	300	720	902	875	880	1728	855	786	480	1210	1175	1525	1010	761	1130	1040	768
Frankfurt	228	1113	2055	665	652	268	198	890	504	93	412	1150	236	671	....	250	1075	1160	392	350	888	492	323	1240	193	675	295	780	698	860	730	560	550	370	193
Hamburg	232	1250	2020	910	760	165	301	950	572	228	180	1222	238	668	250	....	880	1301	448	580	1098	730	570	1100	378	445	459	600	810	954	502	780	462	460	432
St. Petersburg	1090	1535	1570	1740	1165	815	1175	1080	965	1090	708	1292	885	1440	1075	880	....	2235	1300	1420	1980	1540	1315	391	1100	670	1335	300	1440	1218	435	1635	640	975	1225
Lisbon	1140	1770	3050	610	1555	1410	998	1842	1515	1126	1520	2005	1380	1015	1160	1301	2235	....	975	850	313	810	1350	430	1208	1690	890	1940	1150	1685	1848	640	1700	1415	1058
London	220	1476	2435	707	1040	575	202	1285	900	308	590	1540	592	300	392	448	1300	975	....	455	777	620	595	1540	526	720	210	1035	890	1235	885	550	890	762	480
Lyon	458	1100	2238	327	752	601	352	1025	680	370	760	1238	540	720	350	580	1420	850	455	....	577	170	210	1560	352	1005	248	1122	462	928	1080	228	850	562	206
Madrid	912	1463	2742	316	1235	1149	807	1518	1214	875	1272	1690	1100	902	888	1098	1980	313	777	557	....	394	728	2120	910	1474	645	1670	840	1385	1598	344	1410	1110	765
Marseilles	627	1025	2238	211	750	730	521	1020	718	528	906	1205	655	875	492	730	1540	810	620	170	394	....	238	1642	445	1165	410	1238	372	895	1225	196	950	620	318
Milan	517	900	2028	450	540	570	435	819	476	390	720	1030	435	880	323	570	1315	1350	595	210	728	238	....	1408	215	1000	400	1010	295	715	1020	400	705	385	137
Moscow	1325	1388	1175	1852	1160	995	1392	920	965	1285	970	1180	1200	1728	1240	1100	391	430	1540	1560	2120	1642	1408	....	1220	1030	1538	520	1462	1100	770	1770	710	1028	1350
Munich	415	925	1912	648	475	310	372	725	350	282	520	975	227	855	193	378	1100	1208	526	352	910	445	215	1220	....	810	425	800	430	672	811	570	500	222	158
Oslo	568	1610	2118	1330	1112	520	672	1245	920	635	303	1505	620	786	675	445	670	1690	720	1005	1474	1165	1000	1030	810	....	830	531	1242	1295	267	1140	653	835	869
Paris	257	1300	2335	518	890	540	170	1152	770	250	634	1390	523	480	295	459	1335	890	210	248	645	410	400	1538	425	830	....	1050	690	1080	950	431	845	770	295
Riga	820	1310	1590	1440	855	520	900	870	685	805	453	1115	585	1210	780	600	300	1940	1035	1122	1670	1238	1010	520	800	531	1050	....	1155	985	276	1335	350	685	930
Rome	808	650	1900	530	440	730	730	700	500	675	948	840	630	1175	698	810	1440	1150	890	462	840	372	295	1462	430	1242	690	1155	....	545	1220	569	810	470	421
Sofia	1073	335	1360	1072	231	810	945	194	395	945	1010	315	730	1525	860	954	1218	1685	1235	928	1385	895	715	1100	672	1295	1080	985	545	....	1170	1080	662	500	780
Stockholm	695	1495	1862	1410	1005	503	793	1080	820	722	330	1340	598	1010	730	502	435	1848	885	1080	1598	1225	1020	770	811	267	950	276	1220	1170	....	1281	500	770	908
Toulouse	625	1215	2425	156	930	815	515	1210	883	875	962	1400	762	761	560	780	1635	640	550	228	344	196	400	1770	570	1140	431	1335	569	1080	1281	....	1062	725	425
Warsaw	673	990	1555	1150	510	320	720	580	342	602	415	852	325	1130	550	462	640	1700	890	850	1410	950	705	710	500	653	845	350	810	662	500	1062	....	345	640
Vienna	580	795	1700	830	300	322	568	520	128	460	538	790	235	1040	370	460	975	1415	762	562	1110	620	385	1028	222	835	770	685	470	500	770	725	345	....	365
Zurich	375	1000	2050	513	590	410	312	855	498	259	595	1090	342	768	193	432	1225	1058	480	206	765	318	137	1350	158	869	295	930	421	780	908	425	640	365	....